ANTHONY MILTON is currently Lecturer in History at the University of Sheffield. He has published numerous articles on religion in early Stuart England, and further projects include a text-book on this theme.

Catholic and Reformed transcends the current boundaries of the historical debate concerning the role of religious conflict in the politics of the early Stuart period. While earlier studies have focused more narrowly on the doctrine of predestination, Dr Milton analyses the broader attitudes which underlay notions of religious orthodoxy in this period. He achieves this through the first comprehensive analysis of how contemporaries viewed the Roman and foreign Reformed Churches in the early Stuart period. Milton's account demonstrates the way in which an author's choice of a particular *style* of religious discourse could be used either to mediate or to provoke religious conflict. This study challenges many current historical orthodoxies. It identifies the theological novelty of Laudianism, but also exposes significant areas of ideological tension within the Jacobean Church. Its wide-ranging conclusions will be of vital concern to all students of early Stuart religion and the origins of the English civil war.

Cambridge Studies in Early Modern British History

CATHOLIC AND REFORMED

Cambridge Studies in Early Modern British History

Series editors

This is a series of monographs and studies covering many aspects of the history of the British Isles between the late fifteenth century and the early eighteenth century. It includes the work of established scholars and pioneering work by a new generation of scholars. It includes both reviews and revisions of major topics and books which open up new historical terrain or which reveal startling new perspectives on familiar subjects. All the volumes set detailed research into broader perspectives and the books are intended for the use of students as well as of their teachers.

For a list of titles in the series, see end of book

CATHOLIC AND REFORMED

The Roman and Protestant Churches in English Protestant Thought 1600–1640

ANTHONY MILTON
University of Sheffield

Published by the Press Syndicate of the University of Cambridge
The Pitt Building, Trumpington Street, Cambridge CB2 1RP
40 West 20th Street, New York, NY 10011–4211, USA
10 Stamford Road, Oakleigh, Melbourne 3166, Australia

First published 1995

Printed in Great Britain at the University Press, Cambridge

A catalogue record for this book is available from the British Library

Library of Congress cataloguing in publication data

Milton, Anthony.
Catholic and Reformed: the Roman and Protestant Churches in
English Protestant thought, 1600–1640 / Anthony Milton.
p. cm. – (Cambridge studies in early modern British history)
Includes bibliographical references.
ISBN 0 521 40141 0
1. England – Church history – 17th century.
2. Church of England – Relations – Catholic Church – History – 17th century.
3. Anglican Communion – Relations – Catholic Church – History – 17th century.
4. Church of England – Relations – Reformed Church – History – 17th century.
5. Anglican Communion – Relations – Reformed Church – History – 17th century.
I. Title. II. Series.
BR756.M55 1994
274.2′06 – dc20 93–46984 CIP

ISBN 0 521 40141 0 hardback

CE

For Julia, with much love

CONTENTS

ACKNOWLEDGEMENTS

A first author carries many different kinds of debts – intellectual, personal – and I am particularly grateful to those institutions that have helped to ensure that I have avoided financial ones. The British Academy and the trustees of the Dr Lightfoot Scholarship jointly helped to see me through my PhD years in reasonable comfort, and I am also delighted to have the opportunity to thank the Bank Clerks' Orphans' Fund for their very kind support and interest in my welfare over many years. A great deal of further research and writing was necessary to complete this book after my initial PhD dissertation, and I was fortunate to be blessed with a perfect environment for post-doctoral study. I am very grateful to the President and Fellows of Clare Hall, Cambridge, for electing me into a research fellowship there – surely one of the most welcoming and civilized academic communities that one could hope to find. I will always look back on my years at Clare Hall with gratitude and great affection. The final teething problems of the book were ironed out with the indulgence of my new and sympathetic employers at the University of Sheffield, who also assisted me in covering the costs of preparing my typescript.

Intellectual debts inevitably reach back to early university days. My undergraduate supervisors at Clare College showed a spontaneous warmth and kindness that a northerner with a comprehensive school education had not dared to hope for. Brendan Bradshaw first fired my interest in religious history as an undergraduate, and has always cast a benign eye over my halting steps in the historical profession. I owe a very special debt to John Morrill, who as a caring and inspiring supervisor of my PhD dissertation, and then as an attentive editor, has shown limitless reserves of encouragement and patience.

Peter Lake has had a tremendous influence on this book. I owe him an incalculable debt for the unique stimulus which he has provided me in countless hundreds of conversations in tea-rooms, pubs and living rooms. Conrad Russell has been unfailingly kind and generous in advice, references and above all encouragement since the early days of my research. John Adamson has also provided constant inspiration and advice, and has displayed a gift for asking awkward and illuminating questions. My PhD examiners Patrick Collinson and Willie Lamont guided me through an enlightening and stimulating *viva*, and have offered very beneficial help and advice thereafter. Julia Merritt has been a unique and invaluable source of priceless advice and searching questions.

Many other historians have been kind and generous in their assistance. For reading and commenting on earlier drafts of these chapters, for permitting me to read unpublished work, or for generously donating illuminating references and advice (and in many cases all three) I am very grateful to Professor Peter Lake, Professor the Earl Russell, Professor John Morgan, Dr Julia Merritt, Dr John Morrill, Ms Alexandra Walsham, Professor Brown Patterson, Dr Mark Dever, Dr John Adamson, Dr Michael Questier, Mr Peter Salt, Dr Ole Grell, Dr Nicholas Tyacke, Mr Peter White, Dr Fred Trott, Rev. Dr John Platt, Professor Karl Bottigheimer, Professor Conal Condren, Dr Richard Cust, Rev. Dr David Lunn, Rev. Dr Judith Maltby, Rev. Dr David Hoyle, Professor Caroline Hibbard, Dr Ian Atherton, Dr Julian Davies, Dr Kenneth Fincham, Dr Andrew Foster, Dr Ronald Asch, Dr Peter Borschberg and Dr David Smith. Any errors that remain in the final text are, of course, entirely my own work. Primordial thoughts relating to some of the material in these chapters were delivered at early modern history seminars in the Universities of Cambridge, Oxford and Sheffield, at the Institute of Historical Research in London and at the Reformation Studies Colloquium at the University of Kent at Canterbury. I am grateful to those present at each of these performances for their patience in listening, and their generosity in the advice that they offered.

Books of this sort cannot be written without imposing hugely upon the goodwill of the staff of libraries and archives, and I am very grateful to all those who bore with fortitude my constant requests for books and manuscripts. Those manning the desk in the Rare Books Room in Cambridge University Library were unfailingly courteous and helpful when they could have been forgiven for fleeing at my approach. I am especially grateful to Mr A.I. Doyle at Durham for sharing with me his unrivalled knowledge of John Cosin and his library, and for a richly illuminating correspondence thereafter. The members of the Hartlib Papers Project at the University of Sheffield also deserve special thanks for having provided a uniquely warm and friendly welcome on my visits up from Cambridge, little imagining that they would have to put up with my being based in Sheffield for a good deal longer.

The completion of a book is impossible without the help of non-historians too, who can offer a gentle (and sometimes not so gentle) reminder that there is life beyond the seventeenth century. I am grateful to many friends – historians and non-historians alike – who have helped to keep me going through my years of research and writing, especially Amanda Whitmore, Peter Lillington, Helen Evans, Nancy Kontou, Lisa Nevitt, Katharine Hodgson and a host of British gamelan players. I especially thank my mother, who has suffered the seventeenth century to interfere far more than it should have done with the family obligations of the twentieth century, and my siblings, for refraining from asking the forbidden question 'when will you finish?'.

My final debt is frankly overwhelming. As a fellow-historian she has constantly stimulated my work, encouraged me to think from new and more penetrating perspectives and provided a constant and generous stream of advice and references; as a phenomenally dedicated and careful reader of the text of this book she has wielded a merciless editorial pen and has performed miracles in transforming it into a readable text; as a friend she has provided constant help, support and diversion; and as a wife she has helped to make my life worthwhile. Julia Merritt has transformed this book and its author, and a grateful dedication seems (and is) a paltry acknowledgement. My old Roman Catholic schoolteachers may take heart from the reflection of this most unrepentant of lapsed Catholics that the salvation of this book and of its author has been achieved by Merritt of Good Works.

Feast Day of St Helidorus of Altino
1993

In the text of the book dates are Old Style but the year is taken to begin on 1 January. Of printed works cited below, the place of publication is London unless otherwise stated. Where more than one edition of a work is entered in the Bibliography, it is the earlier edition that is cited in the footnotes except where the date of the later edition is explicitly given.

ABBREVIATIONS

AfR	*Archiv für Reformationsgeschichte*
BCO	Balliol College, Oxford
BL	British Library
Bodl.	Bodleian Library, Oxford
CSPD	*Calendar of State Papers, Domestic*
CSPVen	*Calendar of State Papers, Venetian*
CUL	Cambridge University Library
DNB	*Dictionary of National Biography* (63 vols., 1885–1900)
DUL	Durham University Library
EHR	*English Historical Review*
HJ	*Historical Journal*
HMC	*Historical Manuscripts Commission*
JEH	*Journal of Ecclesiastical History*
LPL	Lambeth Palace Library
NAvK	*Nederlands Archief voor Kerkgeschiedenis*
P&P	*Past and Present*
Panzani, *Diary*	Transcript of Archivio Segreto Vaticano Nunziatura Inghilterra, tom.3a, in Archives of the English Province of the Society of Jesus (Mount Street, London)
PRO	Public Record Office, London
QCO	Queen's College, Oxford
SSC	Sidney Sussex College, Cambridge
STC	*A Short Title Catalogue of Books Printed in England, Scotland and Ireland 1475–1640* (2nd edn, 3 vols., 1976–91)
SUL	Sheffield University Library
TCBS	*Transactions of the Cambridge Bibliographical Society*
TRHS	*Transactions of the Royal Historical Society*

* Denotes my translation from Latin
† Denotes my translation from Italian

Prologue

Every book that is published on early modern religious thought serves to deplete the range of titles available to later historians, and it is with little surprise that I find myself duplicating the title of Florence Higham's 1962 study of the same period. The motives behind our two books, however, are somewhat different. Ms Higham's study of the period was written, she explained, in order to describe the Anglican Church's struggles to retain its 'via media', and 'the emergence of Anglicanism as a living way'.[1] In the years since Ms Higham's work, historians have questioned the existence of an ideologically coherent, unitary and stable 'Anglicanism', distinctive of the English Church and dedicated to a self-consciously achieved golden mean between Rome and Geneva, which could be read back into the Tudor and early Stuart Church. Notions of a definitively Anglican 'via media' have proved hard to find in the Tudor Church, whose orientation towards the Protestantism of the continent was more pronounced than later Anglicans might have wished.

In addition to their aversion to the anachronistic use of the term 'Anglican', with the allied assumption of the existence of a stable Anglican 'essence', Tudor historians have emphasized that Anglicanism's obverse – 'puritanism' – cannot be used to explain the religious divisions of the period as straightforwardly as past historians have tended to employ it. The Elizabethan and Jacobean Church has instead been depicted as an arena in which puritans, far from being at odds with the establishment, in fact played a leading and creative role and were in a sense a part of the 'mainstream'. The church was populated by 'puritan bishops' of Calvinist beliefs and evangelical principles, which they actively pursued in co-operation with those self-appointedly 'godly' puritan preachers and lay magistrates.[2]

Historians' increasing insistence on the ease with which advanced Prot-

1 F.M.G. Higham, *Catholic and Reformed. A Study of the Anglican Church, 1559–1662* (1962), pp.vii, 1, 34.

2 See especially the pioneering research of Patrick Collinson in his *The Elizabethan Puritan Movement* (1967) and *The Religion of Protestants* (Oxford, 1982).

estant views and their adherents could be absorbed into the English Church and State has had profound implications for the way in which the political history of the period is understood. Whereas earlier depictions of an 'Anglican/puritan' division made the upheavals of the civil war easy to fathom, the interrogation of these terms has necessarily reshaped our understanding of the forces at work in the undermining of the early Stuart regime. Although historians are no longer preoccupied with tracing the origins of the 'Puritan Rebellion', this shift of priorities has not banished religion from explanations of the civil war and its origins. On the contrary, religion has recaptured the centre stage in an even more vivid form. Instead of Whiggish models of a political conflict between a reactionary king and freedom-loving parliament, many revisionist historians have emphasized the role of religious conflict in generating wider political upheaval in an otherwise peaceful and consensually minded nation that had hitherto been blessed with a unified political culture free of notions of party or opposition. Whereas Whig historiography depicted this religious conflict in terms of the clash between conservative 'Anglicans' and rebellious 'puritans', this model has been inverted by revisionist historians. In fact, they have followed trends set by religious historians of the period, and have suggested that puritan values, and the 'godly' MPs who upheld them, were not inherently oppositionist, but rather could be conservative, and supportive of the social hierarchy. According to this argument, the radicals were in fact a small group of anti-Calvinist or 'Arminian' divines grouped around Archbishop Laud, whose doctrines dissolved the 'common and ameliorating bond' of Calvinist theology which had united puritans with the religious establishment. The rise to power of Laud and his associates in the late 1620s, it is argued, forced quiescent puritans into a renewed, but essentially defensive, political activism. It was thus the new Arminian leadership which initiated a liturgical and doctrinal revolution, and it was the moderate episcopalian, Calvinist majority, together with the puritans, who staged a counter-revolution in 1640.[3]

In the ensuing crisis of 1640–2, historians have again emphasized the significant impact of religion on events. It has been maintained that it was religion – most especially perceptions of religious deviance – which played a crucial role in driving men to arms, whether they be parliamentarians fearing a popish plot, or royalists fearing a puritan conspiracy. These competing religious conspiracy theories, based upon perceptions of a religio-political 'other', helped contemporaries to explain and understand

[3] N. Tyacke, 'Puritanism, Arminianism, and Counter-Revolution', in C. Russell (ed.), *The Origins of the English Civil War* (1973); *idem*, *Anti-Calvinists. The Rise of English Arminianism c.1590–1640* (Oxford, 1987); C. Russell, *Parliaments and English Politics 1621–1629* (Oxford, 1979).

the drift into civil war, while providing a radical agenda for religious activists.[4]

While all historians consider religious issues to have exercised a crucial role in the political events of the early Stuart period, certain aspects of the picture painted above have prompted disagreement. Historians are still divided over the best way to represent and understand pre-1640 religious politics, and particularly over the question of how far these earlier conflicts can explain the tensions of 1640–2, which ended in civil war. Some scholars have continued to query the extent to which puritanism was integrated within the national church, or have disputed the originality of Laudian policies or 'Arminian' ideas, while others have questioned the sole determinative role of religion in the outbreak of civil war.[5] Although some of these counter-arguments have been more convincing than others, it is still clear that the religious identity of the Church of England in this period appears to be as open to dispute as it has ever been.

It may well be that the single issue of doctrines of grace is unable to bear the weight of historiographical argument that has come to rest upon it. Indeed, the link between the 'Arminian' scares of the 1620s, and the religious disturbances of the later 1630s, when opposition to the Caroline government was more exercised by fears of popery, has seemed obscure to some historians. Similarly, the outbreak of civil war in 1642 clearly requires an explanation of why Calvinists themselves divided: while the issue of predestination may have increased tensions, it cannot in itself explain the later divisions. Moreover, it has been argued in some circles that lines of division over predestinarian doctrines were not clear-cut, and that it was the doctrinal ties which bound Laud and his associates to their Calvinist episcopalian colleagues which were more significant than those which united moderate puritans to the same evangelical bishops.[6]

Nevertheless, conformists clearly *believed* that they were divided on

[4] A.J. Fletcher, *The Outbreak of the English Civil War* (1981), pp.407–19 and *passim*; M.G. Finlayson, *Historians, Puritanism and the English Revolution* (Toronto, 1983), *passim*; J.S. Morrill, 'The religious context of the English civil war', *TRHS* 5th ser. 34 (1984); *idem*, 'The attack on the Church of England in the Long Parliament, 1640–42', in D. Beales and G. Best (eds.), *History, Society and the Churches* (1985); C. Russell, *The Causes of the English Civil War* (Oxford, 1990), pp.109–30, 220–6; *idem*, *The Fall of the British Monarchies* (Oxford, 1991), pp.525–32.

[5] K. Sharpe, *The Personal Rule of Charles I* (Yale, 1992); P. White, *Predestination, Policy and Polemic* (Cambridge, 1992). For different perspectives, equally critical of *some* aspects of the revisionist reading of religious issues, but also in conflict with aspects of Sharpe's and White's accounts, see J.P. Sommerville, *Politics and Ideology in England, 1603–1640* (1986), pp.221–4; I.M. Green, '"England's wars of religion"? Religious conflict and the English civil wars', in J. van den Berg and P.G. Hoftijzer (eds.), *Church, Change and Revolution* (Leiden, 1991); J. Davies, *The Caroline Captivity of the Church* (Oxford, 1992).

[6] See especially White, *Predestination*; Davies, *Caroline Captivity*, ch.3.

these issues, and conforming Calvinist bishops certainly perceived men such as Richard Montagu to be their doctrinal opponents, however close their theological positions might appear from a detached twentieth-century perspective. Contemporaries, at least, were convinced that they upheld starkly contrary positions even if, when it came to illustrating this polarization, many of the religious controversies of the period relied, as Peter Lake has observed, on the manipulation and assimilation of the opponent's position into an anti-type of either 'popery' or 'puritanism'.[7] This work suggests that we need to turn our attention to the actual mechanics of religious controversy, especially people's perceptions of the polarities within which religious debate was conducted, and around which opponents' positions were interpreted. Before we can analyse religious controversies, we must first understand how contemporaries understood 'orthodoxy' in the first place, and under what circumstances they were likely to believe it to be threatened.

Clearly, if the religious divisions of this period are to be elucidated, it will be necessary to look beyond single-issue doctrinal divisions. Recent historiography which has pursued single doctrinal issues has often fallen into the trap of presenting divisions within the church in the starkly dualistic terms which were employed by early modern controversialists, thereby dividing the church along either simple Anglican/puritan or Calvinist/Arminian lines.[8]

It may well be that divisions over the application of these polarizing labels, rather than doctrines of grace, lie at the heart of the religious disputes that disturbed the early Stuart Church. Some historians have already hinted that conflict both in pre- and post-1640 England can be partly understood with reference to different perceptions of the nature of the Church of Rome and of Reformed Protestantism. Indeed, one scholar has declared that 'two different conceptions of Protestant orthodoxy' were in conflict in the later 1620s which 'related essentially to perceptions of Rome', and has emphasized that 'Rome' was 'the real issue'. Another anti-revisionist author, however, has insisted on 'the amount of doctrinal

[7] P. Lake, 'Calvinism and the English Church, 1570–1635', *P&P* 114 (1987), pp.61–9.

[8] It could be argued that in its more extreme forms the revisionist case has tended at times to produce a simplistic Arminian/Calvinist divide to replace the traditional Anglican/puritan paradigm, although their focus has been on what divided conformists among themselves, rather than what divided conformists from puritans. Writings which have challenged the 'rise of Arminianism' hypothesis have often tended to retreat in their turn into the old Anglican/puritan framework once more, focusing their attention on what divided conformists from puritans (see e.g. Sharpe, *Personal Rule*, ch.12). Peter White has insisted that he is happy to avoid using the *terms* 'Anglican' and 'puritan' but his analytical framework presupposes precisely this division, built upon the conviction that 'there were from the early Elizabethan period doctrinal tensions between moderate and radical Protestants': *Predestination*, p.xii (cf. p.125).

common ground among English Protestants, especially against the teachings of Rome'.[9]

A study of the parameters within which contemporaries viewed the orthodoxy of their own church, and the heterodoxy of their opponents, should also assist assessments of the significance of the ubiquity of religious labels in the period leading up to the outbreak of civil war. How far can the fears of popish plots, for example, be read off from prevailing understandings of the nature of the Roman Church? Was the conventional dialectic of the Protestant Cause opposing the papal Antichrist as uncomplicated as it might appear? How far did the view that the pope was Antichrist colour and determine an individual's view of his Roman Catholic neighbours, and his government's foreign policy, for example?

This book seeks to illuminate controversies over the nature of the English Church and the political implications of the conflicts within her by an examination of the assumptions which underlay much religious controversial writing – namely, how divines identified the nature of their church itself, *vis-à-vis* the alternatives abroad. Unlike Ms Higham, therefore, my attention is not focused on an Anglican 'via media' – both 'Catholic and Reformed' – and its puritan critics. Rather, I am concerned to examine the divisions within a Church of England whose ultimate doctrinal and ideological identity was still unclear, as different groups within the church contended over just how the English Church was to be understood as both 'Catholic and Reformed'. To what extent had the English Church truly separated from Rome, and what was her precise relationship with the Reformed Churches of the continent? The title of this volume thus has a deliberate ambiguity: it explores conflicting ideas of the Church of England's identity as 'Catholic and Reformed', but it does so by analysing the ways in which the Roman Catholic (in Part I) and the Reformed Churches (in Part II) were understood during the early Stuart period.

It is the intention of this study to avoid the by now traditional Arminian/Calvinist divide, and to look behind the polemical categories through which modes of controversial discourse operated during this period. Instead, it will seek to present a broad spectrum of views running from crypto-popish 'Arminian' zealots on the one hand, through to die-hard puritan nonconformists on the other. Polarizations of opinion will often be seen to have been a *function* of polemical debate, rather than its trigger.

[9] Russell, *Causes*, ch.3; White, *Predestination*, pp.255, 231, 308, 310; *idem*, 'The rise of Arminianism reconsidered', *P&P* 101 (1983), p.54; *idem*, 'A rejoinder', *P&P* 115 (1987), p.218; W. Lamont, *Godly Rule: Politics and Religion 1603–1660* (1969), pp.65–6; Collinson, *Religion of Protestants*, p.19; Green, 'England's wars', p.107; Sharpe, *Personal Rule*, pp.285–6 .

While clear conceptual divisions and innovations do emerge, they were often misunderstood or misrepresented at the time, and require a more careful analysis than that offered by the contemporary polemical exchanges themselves. There may often have been a significant distance between what divided people, and what people directly disagreed about (and with whom they disagreed). Such an analysis may therefore help to assuage the doubts of some recent historians who, having found a dualistic model unconvincing, are prone to adopt an agnostic approach which abandons attempts to explain the religious divisions of the period, allowing them to vanish in the hazy mist of a creative diversity which is taken to exemplify the true spirit of 'Anglican' moderation.[10]

It might be argued that an analysis of religious thought in this period demands the juxtaposition, collation and comparison of rounded evocations of the overall positions occupied by individual divines. This sort of detailed analysis of individual positions, and of the personal and polemical situations which shaped them, will be essayed elsewhere.[11] The present work, however, is intended to provide a guide to the broad contours of early seventeenth-century religious literature and debate. It is only when this context has been established that the relative significance of individual positions can be properly assessed.

It should be emphasized that the following study generally limits itself to the religious thought of the clergy of the Church of England. There will be no examination of the religious thought of the English population at large. With a few exceptions, the religious thought of the laity does not lend itself to the same detailed doctrinal analysis that is possible with the body of clerics who had received a professional training in theology, and what lay theology there is often does not survive in sufficient quantities to permit any clear judgement of the individual's doctrinal position. Nevertheless, if the centre of attention is therefore the culture of educated, literate Protestants, it must be emphasized that the university-educated clergy constituted an influential section of the educated elite of early Stuart England, who expounded their views to congregations throughout the length and breadth of the land.

This book has also chosen to focus on educated religious literature because, contrary to widely held assumptions, the greater proportion of printed religious literature of the period 1600–40 remains almost wholly unstudied, and much historiographical debate has focused on a tiny sample

[10] E.g. S. Lambert, 'Committees, religion, and parliamentary encroachment on royal authority in early Stuart England', *EHR* 105 (1990), p.87; G.W. Bernard, 'The Church of England, c.1559–1642', *History* 75 (1990).

[11] See P. Lake and A. Milton, *The Struggle for Anglicanism. Studies in the Disintegration of the English Protestant Tradition* (forthcoming).

of surviving material. The writings of Richard Montagu are a case in point. Although his two popular controversial pamphlets – the *New Gagg* and *Appello Caesarem* – have been endlessly studied, they constitute less than 10 per cent of his controversial output, while the great bulk of his Latin controversial works remains almost wholly unread. More generally, the vast majority of anti-papal controversial works composed during this period have been almost entirely neglected by historians.[12] The current work makes no claims to provide a comprehensive or definitive account of this rich and underexploited resource, but hopes to demonstrate the subtlety and complexity of a body of writing which is too often assumed to be homogeneous and repetitive, and therefore unrewarding to the scholar. It is also intended to demonstrate the polemical constraints under which English Protestants were required to work. Anti-papal religious controversy, it will be demonstrated, did not simply serve as an escape valve for puritan energies. Instead, it could impose significant restraints upon these energies, and in the process could generate important inconsistencies between the different polemical writings and perspectives of either a single individual, or of the English Church itself. It could also prompt the more systematic formulation of differences in feeling and assumption which were already beginning to cause friction, not just between Laudians and their opponents, but also between English Calvinists themselves.

A NOTE ON TERMINOLOGY

Writing in 1616, the Venetian ambassador Foscarini reported the existence of twelve different religious parties in England – three of Catholics, three of the merely indifferent, 'four of the religion of his Majesty, and two Puritan parties'.[13] The rigidly dualistic cast of much recent scholarship on early Stuart religion, revolving around either an Anglican/puritan or Arminian/Calvinist paradigm, has served to obscure the extent to which a broad spectrum of different religious views did exist before the civil war. The problem for the historian of the period is of how to do justice to this range of opinion without losing sight of the dualistic terminology with which contemporaries portrayed and understood (and therefore ultimately shaped) their situation, and the polarizations of opinion which social and political upheavals could so effortlessly provoke. While the present work does not intend to reproduce Foscarini's twelve-fold division of English religious thought, it does seek to recapture a spectrum of opinion running

12 One remarkable exception is the splendid unpublished study by Graham Windsor: 'The controversy between Roman Catholics and Anglicans from Elizabeth to the Revolution' (Cambridge University PhD, 1967).

13 *CSPVen 1617–19*, p.387; Higham, *Catholic and Reformed*, pp.56–7.

from the moderate puritanism of a man like Andrew Willet, through the different styles of 'Calvinist conformity' of authors such as Robert Abbot and John Davenant, to the extreme ceremonialism of divines such as William Laud and Richard Montagu, taking sufficient cognizance of the many shifting and transitional colours in between.

The use of certain terms to denominate the different peaks on this spectrum of thought is unavoidable. All the following, however, are employed without any desire to denote stable and sterile identities. Instead, they are used to delineate particular positions between which divines might adapt their own views in reaction to the political and polemical circumstances of the time.

The term 'Calvinist' is used, in common with current historiography, to denote a general sympathy with the continental Reformed tradition in all its purely doctrinal aspects, and a sense of identification with the West European Calvinist Churches and their fortunes.[14] My use of the term 'puritan' follows the principles laid down by Patrick Collinson and Peter Lake, being applied to those Protestants who were distinctive in their enthusiasm and zeal for the cause of true religion in a way in which both they themselves (regarding themselves as a 'godly' elite) and their hostile opponents (seeing them as overprecise hypocrites) could and did recognize.[15]

The choice of terms to describe non-puritans presents greater difficulties. The term 'conformist' is employed here to describe a divine who not only conformed to the ceremonies of the English Church, but did so with alacrity, and was prepared both to make an issue of ceremonial conformity and points of church government, and to use the epithet of 'puritan' against his opponents.[16] There is no entirely satisfactory term to describe the new patterns of ceremonialist and sacerdotal conformist thought which began to find expression later in the Elizabethan period, and which Professor Lake has recently identified in the persons of Richard Hooker and Lancelot Andrewes.[17] The term 'avant-garde conformity' has been

[14] While some recent historians have been unhappy with the term 'Calvinist', they have generally used allied terms to refer to the same basic phenomenon: see e.g. Julian Davies' use of the term 'reformed' in *idem*, *Caroline Captivity*, p.298. Peter White's reference to 'those who theologically respected Calvin' (and yet might in practice differ from him theologically) or those who 'liked to see their faith as homogeneous with that of the continental Reformed churches' (*Predestination*, pp.153, 222) are the group that I intend here.

[15] P. Collinson, 'A comment: concerning the name puritan', *JEH* 31 (1980), pp.483–8; P. Lake, 'Puritan identities', *JEH* 35 (1984), pp.112–23.

[16] See also P. Lake, *Anglicans and Puritans?* (1988), p.7.

[17] *Ibid.*, ch.4; *idem*, 'Lancelot Andrewes, John Buckeridge and avant-garde conformity at the court of James I', in L. Levy Peck (ed.), *The Mental World of the Jacobean Court*, (Cambridge, 1991).

employed by Professor Lake to describe this trend, a term which serves a useful purpose in distinguishing their style of piety from that of other conformists who had not granted the same edifying value to these ceremonies, while avoiding the anachronistic label of 'Anglican'. I have therefore employed the term where necessary, especially as it helps to capture the dynamic and evolving nature of this style of piety in the early Stuart period, and does not simply collapse it into the ideas and policies of Archbishop Laud.

The term 'Laudian' is applied to all those clerics who were closely associated with Laud and who were unequivocal in their support for his ecclesiastical policies in the 1630s. This agenda included anti-Sabbatarianism; the placing of the communion table at the east end of the church; the freeing of the clergy, their courts and their maintenance from lay control; and a general de-emphasis on preaching and forms of voluntary religion in favour of the 'beauty of holiness', greater ceremonial and more lavish church adornment. As with the 'puritans', this was a group perceptible both to themselves and to outsiders, most noticeably in the form of the 'Durham House Group'.[18] The term is applied to the friends, clients and chaplains of members of the Durham House faction, and to any other clerics who seem to have offered *unambiguous* support to Laud's ecclesiastical programme, in treatises, visitation sermons or practical enforcement.[19] The term is not applied, however, to mere conformists. It is important to make the distinction which Lord Falkland urged on parliament in 1641 'betweene those who have beene carried away with the streame, and those that have been the stream that carry'd them': that is, between the divines who were unequivocal in their support, and those who merely acquiesced in the policies adopted, or offered conditional support at a time when it was simply imprudent to express open dissent from Laudian practices.[20]

18 See Davies, *Caroline Captivity*, *passim*; Tyacke, *Anti-Calvinists*, ch.5; A. Foster, 'The function of a bishop: the career of Richard Neile, 1562–1640', in R. O'Day and F. Heal (eds.), *Continuity and Change* (Leicester, 1976), pp.44–6; V.E. Raymer, 'Durham House and the emergence of Laudian piety' (Harvard University PhD, 1981), *passim*.

19 On definitions of Laudians, see especially A. Milton, 'The Laudians and the Church of Rome, c.1625–1640' (Cambridge University PhD, 1989), pp.6–13.

20 Lord Falkland, *A Speech to the House of Commons concerning Episcopacy* (1641), p.11. See the examples of Walter Balcanquahall, Joseph Mede and Abraham Wheelock in Milton, 'Laudians', pp.9–11.

Introduction: English Protestantism at the dawn of the seventeenth century

The Church of England presents innumerable problems of definition for the historian. The first century of its existence, when it still aspired to be the inclusive church of the English people, witnessed the conflicts of a variety of different visions of what its identity should be. That such a range of different doctrinal and ecclesiological predilections were able to lay claim to the national church was a reflection of the flexible character of the reformation settlement itself. The First Edwardian Prayer Book has been described as 'a masterpiece of compromise, even of studied ambiguity', and the same phrase could justly be taken to describe the later Elizabethan settlement *in toto*.[1] While her doctrinal formulations were clearly of a Reformed character (although more reflective of mid-century Protestant thought rather than its later Calvinist elaborations) the English Church still retained a structure of worship and administration which had not broken as decisively with the Romanist past as had been the case in other Protestant countries. The question of where the Church of England stood *vis-à-vis* the Roman Church and the Reformed Churches of the continent was therefore an issue which remained unsettled and was subject to constant reinterpretation and sometimes bitter recrimination in the ensuing years.

It is in English Protestant divines' perceptions of these foreign churches – Roman and Reformed – that their different images of the nature of the English Church come into clearer perspective, and it is these perceptions which will be the concern of this book. Before these views can be thoroughly analysed, however, it will be necessary to provide a picture of the state of English Protestantism around the year 1600, when our survey begins. The protean character of the Church of England at this time renders the application of the term 'Anglican' to any single group within it essentially meaningless, if not positively misleading. Nevertheless, it is still possible to chart some of the currents of religious thought prominent in the

[1] A.G. Dickens, *The English Reformation* (1964), p.302.

church at this time. To sharpen our focus, we will concentrate on a single minister who presented in the early years of the seventeenth century his own impressions of the nature of the changes taking place within his church, and attempted to play his own part in shaping its future.

The 1590s had been (*par excellence*) the period of crisis in the history of Tudor England, when old hands left the rudder of the ship of state, and old certainties and orthodoxies seemed to be shaken. The Elizabethan establishment waxed old, and was transformed as the decade began with the deaths following closely upon one another of Robert Dudley, earl of Leicester, Sir Walter Mildmay, Sir Francis Walsingham and Sir Christopher Hatton – a removal of the old guard which was symbolized by the final demise in 1598 of the venerable William Cecil, Lord Burghley, after a lifetime's service to the crown dating back to the time of Elizabeth's accession to the throne. An unmistakable air of *fin de siècle* hung over court and country as the war with Spain dragged on inconclusively and the country was afflicted by a series of harvest failures, combined with plague, inflation, unemployment, depression in overseas trade and increasing crime and vagrancy.[2]

The 1590s were also marked by the same sense of change, decay and ferment in religious affairs. The decade opened with the final crushing of the presbyterian movement. The activist political movement which had sought to bring into England a presbyterian form of church government in line with the Calvinist Churches of Western Europe, and whose efforts had dominated the religious politics of the previous two decades, finally met its end. In part the movement itself was falling apart as moderates and radicals moved nearer to a complete rift, hastened by the publication of the inflammatory Marprelate tracts against the bishops. At the same time, the cause of further reformation suffered with the deaths of the old guard of Elizabethan government, which removed some of its most faithful protectors from the court. The examinations of puritan ministers in the winter of 1589–90 brought the whole underground 'classis' organization out into the open, and puritan leaders such as Thomas Cartwright were hauled before the courts of Star Chamber and High Commission. The deranged antics of the would-be regicides Edmund Copinger and William Hacket led to a further surge of repression against sectaries in 1593, and the executions of the leading separatists Henry Barrow, John Greenwood and John Penry.[3]

2 I.W. Archer, *The Pursuit of Stability. Social Relations in Elizabethan London* (Cambridge, 1991), pp.8–9, 14; see also the remarks of George Abbot in 1595–6, published in his *An Exposition upon the Prophet Jonah* (1613), p.104 – quoted in John Strype, *The Life and Acts of John Whitgift* (3 vols., Oxford, 1822), II: 337.

3 Collinson, *Puritan Movement*, pp.317–29, 385–431.

Radical puritanism was forced into hiding or fled abroad although, as events were to prove, it had far from disappeared.[4]

With its radical wing under pressure, what happened to puritanism? Recent historians have emphasized the extent to which beliefs and attitudes that have conventionally been regarded as puritan had in fact penetrated into the very centre of establishment thought during the Elizabethan period. Calvinist predestinarianism, Sabbatarianism, the belief that the pope was Antichrist, and many other doctrines that have been thought of in the past as typifying puritan piety, were held by Elizabethan bishops as intensely as puritan nonconformists. Presbyterianism, it has been argued, was merely a temporary programme, a passing expression of the reforming ideals of a group who constituted merely a zealous subset within the Church of England. Puritans were not inevitably committed to an oppositionist stance towards authority; rather, they sought to sanctify the existing social and political order by co-opting secular and spiritual leaders into the moral reform of community and nation. It was the internal religious experience which shaped puritan behaviour; external forms of government and ceremony could be accepted or discarded depending on whether they served to promote godly ideals. Puritanism has thus been defined as being founded essentially upon a sense of a common core of religious experience and values, which could transcend the formal outward issues of conformity and church government.[5] On this reading, the 1590s came as a blessing to the puritan movement in general. Forced to abandon their active political programme to remould the external structures of the national church, puritans were now free to accommodate themselves to political realities and to follow moderate puritan paths. Indeed, as issues of church government were removed from the agenda, many puritan writers may be seen to be moving away from a preoccupation with directly political issues towards an attempt to transform the church from within through works of practical divinity.[6]

The stage was thus apparently set for the reintegration of puritan values into English Protestantism, for puritans to take their place merely as an especially zealous subset within a Church of England of an unambiguously Reformed character. But it was not quite that simple. The dynamic essence of puritanism could not simply be whittled down to a pietistic tendency, and the reigns of James and Charles would demonstrate the lengths to

[4] *Ibid.*, pp.439–43; N. Tyacke, *The Fortunes of English Puritanism, 1603–1640* (1990).

[5] P. Collinson, *English Puritanism* (1983); Lake, *Moderate Puritans, passim*; *idem*, 'Puritan identities'; *idem*, *Anglicans and Puritans*, pp.1–6.

[6] Collinson, *Puritan Movement*, pp.432–7; C.M. Dent, *Protestant Reformers in Elizabethan Oxford* (Oxford, 1983), pp.150–1, and chs.8 and 9. For important qualifications, see Lake, *Anglicans and Puritans*, pp.240–4.

which the reforming zeal of puritanism could lead, even when not accompanied by a radical presbyterian or anti-ceremonial thrust. But the problem did not simply lie in the inherently dynamic and politically assertive nature of puritanism. The structure of English Protestantism was itself changing in the 1590s, and the Church of England to which the more moderate strain of puritanism sought to accommodate itself was nourishing new patterns of thought which were less than keen to welcome a rehabilitated puritanism back into the fold.

A clear illustration of the different forces at work in the Church of England in 1600 may be derived from a study of how they appeared to a single member of that church – the prolific anti-papal divine Dr Andrew Willet. Willet appears as a classic product of the Cambridge 'moderate puritan tradition' which has been so vividly delineated in the work of Dr Lake. He gained his MA at Cambridge in 1584, and a year before was made a fellow of Christ's College – the home of the archetypal puritan William Perkins – where he operated within a network of godly-minded puritans which included the later bishop George Downame, as well as the conforming puritan lecturer Robert Hill, and the later separatist Francis Johnson. From 1599 until his death Willet was rector of Barley in Hertfordshire, fourteen miles from Cambridge, whence he produced a torrent of theological works throughout the Jacobean period. Willet was Calvinist in his theology, strongly anti-Roman Catholic, and was also to reveal himself as a strong advocate of further reformation in the English Church. Nevertheless, he continued a loyal member of the Church of England, and was therefore a classic moderate puritan.[7]

In 1600 Willet published the third edition of his celebrated *Synopsis Papismi*. This was a voluminous work which surveyed all the controversies between the Protestants and the Church of Rome. It had already expanded considerably from its modestly sized quarto first edition of 1592, and by its fifth edition in 1634 it had become a considerable folio volume of over 1,300 pages. The *Synopsis* was a famous and much-read guide to religious controversies: clearly laid out and easy to read, it yet commanded a scholarly reputation of sufficient importance to be cited in university determinations in England, and read in Latin translation abroad by respectful Calvinist and Lutheran divines alike. The royal patent issued for

[7] On Willet's career, see the life in Andrew Willet, *Synopsis Papismi*, ed. J. Cumming (10 vols., 1852), I: 41–79, and *DNB*, s.n. 'Andrew Willet'. The suggestion in *The Folger Library Edition of the Works of Richard Hooker*, ed. W.S. Hill (5 vols., Cambridge, Mass., 1977–91), IV: xxi, that Willet could not be a puritan *because* he conformed is arguably based on a misformulation of the categories of definition. For Willet's 'moderate puritan' links, see his *Sacrorum Emblematum Centuria Una* (Cambridge, 1588), which includes verses addressed to (among others) Laurence Chaderton and his father-in-law Roger Goad (sigs.D4, D2).

its fifth edition noted that the *Synopsis* 'hath been seen and allowed by the Lords, the Reverend Bishops, and hath also ever since been in great esteem in both of our Universities, and also much desired by all the learned both of our clergy and laity throughout our Dominions'.[8]

The third edition of Willet's *Synopsis* is of particular interest, not merely because it was printed in the year that our survey begins, but also because in a new preface its author offered a review of developments within the Church of England over the previous decade, and suggested the means of rectifying the tensions that had grown up within the English Church. It is these tensions which will provide the essential framework for an analysis of the ways in which English Protestants understood the nature of their church and its relationship with the Roman and Reformed Churches of the continent.

Willet's new dedication in 1600 was addressed to the archbishop of Canterbury, John Whitgift, and to Richard Bancroft, bishop of London – the two men who had led the suppression of the presbyterian movement in England over the previous decade. Willet himself was a man who had close links, both personal and theological, with those godly ministers who had pushed for the further reform of the outward discipline of the English Church along presbyterian lines. But in his new dedication Willet, along with the more moderate wing of the puritan movement, accepted defeat. He applauded the fact that the bitter contentions and strife that had so afflicted the English Church were now at an end, and that the fires of dissension had now been smothered, and even praised the bishops' own actions in securing this happy conclusion. The puritan radicals 'were once troublesome, but have now become quiet, either won over by your humanity, or becalmed by your prudence, or confirmed by your sounder judgement'.* It was now the duty of all the Church of England, Willet urged, to unite against the common enemy – the Church of Rome.

If the bishops would give the lead, then, the puritans would happily follow them in the anti-papal crusade. But this was no mere anti-papal rant. Willet was appealing to professional religious scholars to engage with the foremost Roman controversialists of the day, and the particular area in which he urged further academic research was patristics – a field which is

[8] John Prideaux, *Viginti-duae Lectiones de Totidem Religionis Capitibus* (3rd edn, Oxford, 1648), i. p.9; Johann Gerhard, *Locorum Theologicorum* (9 vols. in 4, Geneva, 1639), II: 359; BL, Add. MS 22961 fol.75: Festus Hommius to Sibrandus Lubbertus, 7 April 1609; W. Goode, *The Doctrine of the Church of England as to the Effects of Baptism in the Case of Infants* (1850), pp.372–3 n. +. The stationer who held the copyright was not prepared to reprint the work, and therefore the royal patent gave the licence for reprinting to Willet's son Paul, given that 'few or none at all of the said Books are to be had and gotten; and that also, by reason of the great price and value of the said Book, many of the clergy of this our kingdom are not able to purchase or procure the same'.

too often assumed to have been the sole property of more 'high church' divines such as Lancelot Andrewes. A full exposition of patristic bible commentaries, Willet opined, would be highly efficacious in ensuring the ultimate downfall of popery, as well as serving towards a more general Protestant edification.[9]

Willet's own *Synopsis* exemplified this exhortation to scholarly controversy with Rome. If his general opponent in this work was the Church of Rome, Willet's particular adversary was Cardinal Bellarmine, Rome's most impressive champion, who had published his voluminous *Disputationes* during the 1590s. These continued to represent the most important single defence of Roman Catholic doctrine throughout the early Stuart period, and all subsequent controversies were indebted to Bellarmine's works for laying out the structure of their argument. It was a frequent jibe of later Protestant polemicists that their Romanist opponents were merely copying Bellarmine's arguments.[10] Willet's *Synopsis* was just the most widely circulated of a whole series of treatises that were published by Protestant scholars in England and abroad and which were dedicated to the task of refuting Bellarmine's works. Throughout Europe, attacks on Bellarmine were regarded by Protestants as a way of demonstrating their confessional orthodoxy, or as a means of reasserting Protestant unity against the threat of inter-Protestant tensions.[11] In England, active scholars included esteemed university professors such as William Whitaker and John Rainolds (the latter as holder of the anti-papal lectureship in Oxford, founded by Sir Francis Walsingham), as well as dedicated anti-puritan pamphleteers such as Matthew Sutcliffe.[12]

In appealing for English Protestants to concentrate on opposing Rome, Willet emphasized the disproportionate threats levelled by the radical puritans on the one side, and the Jesuits on the other. Radical Protestants 'bark somewhat ... like complaining dogs for a time, but these [Romanists] bite and tear like devouring wolves, and still do not rest; these [puritans] break off tiny branches and twigs, but these [Romanists] strive to tear out the very root'.* Nevertheless, Willet here explicitly directed his words against some members of the Church of England who, he claimed, felt that domestic enemies (whom they called 'puritans') were more to be

9 Willet, *Synopsis* (1600), sig.B3r–v.

10 E.g. Robert Abbot, *The Second Part of the Defence of the Reformed Catholicke* (1611), sig.A2v, pp.4–5, 980, 1241.

11 Both Arminius and Vorstius wrote against Bellarmine when they felt their Protestant orthodoxy to be in question. On the many refutations of Bellarmine published by continental Calvinist theologians, see F.G.M. Broeyer, *William Whitaker: leven en werk van een Anglocalvinistisch theoloog* (Utrecht, 1982), pp.88, 155, 319 n.531.

12 Dent, *Reformers*, pp.148–9; P. Milward, *Religious Controversies of the Elizabethan Age* (1977), pp.152–6.

feared than the Romanists.[13] This was no imaginary opponent. English anti-puritanism was not a static entity. As a recent historian has noted, by the early 1590s a far more polemically aggressive position was being adopted by some conformist divines. Partly in response to the more vitriolic tone of the Marprelate tracts of the late 1580s, authors such as Matthew Sutcliffe, and especially Richard Bancroft and Adrianus Saravia, were prepared to parallel the threat from Rome and from presbyterianism, and (in Bancroft's case) to insist that the threat was equally grave from both sides. Bancroft had imputed the ideas of the more extreme puritan tracts to the activities of the native presbyterian movement, and had included sideswipes at Calvin's Geneva. Willet's epistle, dedicated to Bancroft himself as well as Whitgift, was clearly hoping to dissuade him, and other more recent defenders of the ecclesiastical establishment, from this unwelcome set of priorities.[14] Willet's concern at what he saw as an unbalanced approach towards the relative threat posed by radical puritans here echoed the sentiments expressed by the Calvinist Heads of Colleges in Cambridge in a letter sent to Lord Burghley in 1591, in which they had sought to remind the chancellor of the greater threat posed to the Church of England by the Romanists, and had complained that lovers of the gospel were being treated more severely than Roman opponents.[15]

Willet also directed his energies, in more oblique fashion, against a theory that was beginning to infiltrate the conformist position – namely, that government by bishops was not merely desirable and apostolic, but was also *iure divino*, by divine right. As he was trying to make his peace with Bancroft and Whitgift, Willet was keen to emphasize that he did not wish to attack the institution of episcopacy, and included within his *Synopsis* of 1600 a new section which argued, with citations from Bishop Bilson's *Perpetual Government*, 'that the calling of Bishops as it is received in the Church of England is not Antichristian'.[16] Nevertheless, in another new section, which was ostensibly aimed at Bellarmine, Willet argued against all claims that episcopacy was *iure divino*, and warned ominously that this doctrine could as a consequence unchurch the foreign non-episcopal Reformed Churches (which was not, of course, a consequence that would have worried the cardinal!).[17]

13 Willet, *Synopsis* (1600), sig.B2v.

14 Lake, *Anglicans and Puritans*, pp.111–13.

15 J. Heywood and T. Wright (eds.), *Cambridge University Transactions during the Puritan Controversies* (2 vols., 1854), II: 30–2. The letter was signed by William Whitaker, Laurence Chaderton, Edmund Barwell and Roger Goad. Cf. Thomas Digges, *Humble Motives* (1601), p.25.

16 Willet, *Synopsis* (1600), pp.726–9. Note also the careful removal of the reference to William Fulke (1594, p.298; 1600, p.230), who had initially been a supporter of presbyterianism.

17 Willet, *Synopsis* (1600), pp.235–7, 240.

These were not the only new developments in conformist thought that threatened to undermine the integration of puritanism within the Church of England. Towards the end of his dedicatory epistle, Willet made it plain that his support for Whitgift and Bancroft was conditional upon their acting to curb new domestic controversies which threatened to undermine the integrity of English Protestantism itself. These revolved around what Willet saw as dangerous new crypto-popish doctrines which were beginning to spread within the church, and which he specified as being concerned with the doctrines of free will, hypothetical election and universal grace. Willet instructed the bishops directly: 'Suppress by your authority whosoever would propose dogmas which either savour of superstition, deviate from the common faith, or degenerate however slightly towards popery.'* Willet clearly had in mind the anti-Calvinist doctrines of grace propounded by William Barrett, Peter Baro and John Overall during his own residence in Cambridge. These had excited considerable controversy, leading to the initially neutral intervention of Archbishop Whitgift and the drawing up of the uncompromisingly Calvinist Lambeth Articles of 1595.[18] Willet also doubtless had his eye on the new developments in English Protestant thought that had found expression in Richard Hooker's *Laws of Ecclesiastical Polity*, whose allegedly new perspective on doctrines of predestination, justification, salvation, the efficacy of the sacraments and the nature of the Church of Rome Willet would attack more clearly three years later. Hooker's doctrines had already drawn a concerned response in the form of the brief tract *A Christian Letter of Certaine English Protestants*. The anonymous authors of this tract had claimed the personae of moderate ministers reconciled to the polity and ceremonies of the Church of England, who were appreciative of the works of Whitgift, but alarmed by the infusion of new and crypto-popish ideas in the works of Hooker, and also in the anonymous tract *Querimonia Ecclesiae* and Bancroft's anonymously published *Dangerous Positions*. The authors of *A Christian Letter* (who may well have included Willet himself) claimed that Hooker's works were frustrating their attempts to defend the integrity of the Church of England against 'foolish carpers'.[19] Many of the accusations of novelty made against Hooker by these authors were repeated by Willet in a series of tracts which he published in the years 1603–5.

[18] On the background to the Lambeth Articles, see Lake, *Moderate Puritans*, pp.218–26; H.C. Porter, *Reformation and Reaction in Tudor Cambridge* (Cambridge, 1958), ch.16. See also Dent, *Protestant Reformers*, pp.103–25.

[19] Hooker, *Works*, IV: 9, 69, 72, 231 (for the circumstantial argument that Willet was involved in the authorship of *A Christian Letter*, see *ibid.*, pp.xix–xxv). On the novelty of Hooker's doctrines, see Lake, *Anglicans and Puritans*, ch.4. The *Querimonia* is an important tract which has been strangely neglected by historians. I hope to discuss it in more detail elsewhere.

Willet's epistle helps to illustrate the problems that moderate puritanism faced in reconciling itself to an English Protestantism which in some quarters was already beginning to change its doctrinal complexion. Willet could applaud the anti-papal polemics of an anti-presbyterian activist like Matthew Sutcliffe, who also shared the puritans' distaste for the new breed of anti-Calvinist divinity, and was prepared to recognize the overwhelming priority that the papal threat demanded. Yet Sutcliffe was at the same time an exponent of the more vigorous form of anti-puritan rhetoric, and was also a firm defender of the new orthodoxy that episcopacy was *iure divino*.[20] There would therefore be no simple doctrinal overlap between Calvinist conformist divines and moderate puritans.

Moreover, Willet was destined to find problems when he sought to eject the ideas of Hooker and his followers from the church. Although in a minority, Hooker's disciples resided at the centre of the church hierarchy, profiting from the more fixedly anti-puritan preoccupations of conformists in the 1590s. Crucially, too, these divines – whom Dr Lake has dubbed 'avant-garde conformists' – were precisely those churchmen who were most determined to prevent the attempts of Willet and other puritans to reintegrate themselves into the established church.

But Willet's compromise with the Church of England was even more problematical than this. He was not merely out of step with developments in Calvinist conformist thought, and hostile to the new breed of 'semi-popish' errors. For all his display of conforming credentials, Willet would still seem to have retained a latent dissatisfaction with the English liturgy. The second edition of his *Synopsis*, published in 1594, had contained a short treatise urging separatists to remain within the Church of England. This had included a decidedly unenthusiastic defence of the Book of Common Prayer which, as Willet admitted, contained some 'defects and imperfections', but which he excused as being the best order of worship that was realistically available for the time being. In 1600, seeking to build bridges with Bancroft, Willet obviously had to do something about this passage, but rather than insert a more committed defence of the Prayer Book he chose to remove the short treatise from the *Synopsis* altogether. Moreover, with considerable audacity, Willet pretended that he had never written this part of the *Synopsis*, and claimed that the brief treatise had still been only in a draft stage when the printer of the 1600 edition had demanded the final proofs. Willet suggested to the readers of this third edition that he might complete the brief treatise and publish it later elsewhere, but confessed that he felt little impulse to do so, as the separatists were less dangerous than the Roman Catholics, since they did not

[20] See Willet's praise of Sutcliffe in *Synopsis* (1600), sig.B3r.

dissent from the Church of England 'in the fundamentall poynts of faith'.[21] In fact, the promised treatise never appeared, as Willet was of course merely suppressing his earlier composition, and there was no half-drafted treatise to complete. This subterfuge was merely an attempt to disguise Willet's dissatisfaction with the status quo in the English Church – a fact which emerged most clearly three years later, when he and other puritan divines recognized a new opportunity to effect more wide-ranging ecclesiastical reform.

The apparent puritan quietism of the 1590s had been pre-eminently tactical in nature. The accession of King James VI of Scotland to the English throne in 1603 was greeted by a revival of the puritan political lobbying that had characterized the 1580s in England, as temporary reconciliations with the establishment were abandoned by puritan divines who hoped once more to effect some change in the Church of England's structure of worship. A new flood of petitions made the familiar criticisms of aspects of the liturgy and of the ecclesiastical establishment but (with a few exceptions) deliberately avoided raising the issue of episcopacy directly.[22] The complaints of doctrinal innovations emergent during the 1590s were repeated. They focused on anti-Calvinism in Cambridge, but also complained of anti-Sabbatarianism and crypto-popish doctrines of absolution and auricular confession, apparently referring (among others) to the sermons of the new breed of avant-garde conformists, such as John Howson and Lancelot Andrewes.[23] Conformists rallied in the face of this threat, with divines from Oxford University drawing up a reply to the Millenary Petition, and writers such as William Covell complaining that the argument over church government had been needlessly reopened, after it had already been 'appeased with discretion'. There was thereby renewed 'an unnaturall contention, that was almost buried, & especially at that time, when all proceedings in the Church wer without rigor'.[24]

21 Willet, *Synopsis* (1594), pp.697–704 (esp. pp.702–3); *ibid.* (1600), p.621.

22 Collinson, *Puritan Movement*, pp.448–54; Tyacke, *Fortunes*, pp.3–4; S.B. Babbage, *Puritanism and Richard Bancroft* (1962), pp.44–57, 62–4.

23 Doctrinal innovations are only briefly alluded to in the Millenary Petition, but are discussed at greater length in the reply to Oxford University's *Answere*: Bodl., Bodley MS 124 pp.58–63. See also *An Abridgment of that Booke which the Ministers of Lincoln Diocess Delivered to his Maiestie* (1605), pp.25–6. On the scandal caused by Lancelot Andrewes' court sermon of 1600 on confession, see Andrewes, *Two Answers to Cardinal Perron and Other Miscellaneous Works* (Oxford, 1854), p.lxii. Another target may have been John Buckeridge's 1602 sermon at the Temple Church on the same subject: *The Diary of John Manningham*, ed. R.P. Sorlien (Hanover, N.H., 1976), p.73. For Howson's inflammatory sermons on feast-days and preaching, see Dent, *Protestant Reformers*, pp.208–18. On 'avant-garde conformity', see Lake, 'Lancelot Andrewes'.

24 William Covell, *A Modest and Reasonable Examination* (1604), p.27.

Andrew Willet's response to James' accession was swift. He immediately dispatched a copy of the 1600 edition of his *Synopsis* to James, pointedly removing his conciliatory epistle to Whitgift and Bancroft, and inserting instead a new dedicatory epistle to the king, in which he declared that 'God hath a greate worke to be perfected by your hands: what David begun, Solomon must finish.'[25] Willet elaborated on his intentions in a series of tracts published in the next two years in which he exhorted James towards a further reformation of certain features of England's ecclesiastical discipline. In *An Antilogie* (1603), Willet suggested to the king that some things still remained to be amended, and applauded James' resolution to restore church revenues, to promote preaching and to oppose non-residence, pluralism and non-preaching ministers. But Willet also suggested that in the case of the indifferent ceremonies which had provoked controversy, the king might remove 'the iust occasions of offence; or so indifferently moderate them, that they breede no strife'. In his *Ecclesia Triumphans*, written to celebrate the king's coronation, Willet again emphasized God's ordinance to kings to reform religion and ecclesiastical abuses. Appealing to the separatists to return to the church, Willet suggested that James might now be in a position to remove some of the abuses in outward discipline, although he himself emphasized that he believed discipline to pertain merely to the well being (*bene esse*) of a church, rather than to its very existence (*esse*). The Church of England's discipline was sufficient to make it a church, he explained, although it could be much improved. She was a famous and beautiful sister of the Reformed Churches abroad, although she did have some blemishes in external matters.[26] Willet thus constructed a 'via media' for himself, by which he condemned not only those conformists who saw no need for any reform, but also distanced himself from the die-hard presbyterians who 'would have all purged, not the superfluous humours onely, but some profitable parts; as the very calling itselfe of reverend Pastors and Bishops: who while they attend the sincere preaching of the word, and the uncorrupt administration of discipline, may (no doubt) do the Church much good'.[27]

At the same time, Willet also delivered more detailed and pointed warnings regarding the spread of crypto-popish doctrines, in which he clearly alluded at length to the work of Richard Hooker as well as the Cambridge anti-Calvinists, and implored the king to impose doctrinal orthodoxy and thus unify his kingdom. These dangerous new books 'maintaining offensive doctrine, too much declining to poperie' should be

[25] Willet, *Synopsis* (1600/1603: BL shelfmark C.46.k.4 – STC 25698.3), sig.A4v.
[26] Willet, *An Antilogie* (1603), preface to King James (unfoliated); *idem*, *Ecclesia Triumphans* (1603), pp.60–6.
[27] Willet, *Antilogie*, preface to King James (unfoliated).

suppressed by the king, Willet urged. He also insisted that James should ensure 'that they receive some answer by publike allowance, or sufficient satisfaction from the authors, lest the infection spread further'.[28] The next year (1604) saw Willet make a similar address to parliament. Praising its endeavours to establish and improve both church and religion, Willet urged that 'whereas men have of late daies taken unto themselves great libertie, in Sermons, Lectures, writings, to set abroach [*sic*] strange & uncouth doctrines, exorbitant from the current doctrine among Protestants', parliament should take this problem in hand and enforce a uniformity of doctrine, either by authorizing an augmentation to the Thirty-Nine Articles in order to counter the new 'unsound doctrines', or by suppressing such doctrines altogether.[29]

Puritan hopes for major structural reform were dashed once more at the Hampton Court Conference, followed by the suspension and subsequent deprivation of between seventy-three and eighty-three beneficed nonconformist ministers.[30] A number of moderate puritan divines, and even bishops sympathetic to puritanism such as Anthony Rudd of St David's, made appeals for clemency. Willet was especially active, and with this aim inserted a dedicatory epistle to his *Hexapla in Genesin* of 1605 addressed to the newly enthroned Archbishop Bancroft and Bishop Vaughan of London. Recognizing the failure of his appeals for further reform, Willet's epistle was reminiscent in tone of the more conciliatory one which he had addressed to Bancroft and Whitgift in his *Synopsis* of 1600, although this time he was more urgent in his appeals for clemency and tolerance of puritan dissenters. Moreover, Willet no longer considered it wise to appeal for the expulsion of 'unsound doctrines' from the church.[31]

Despite the pleas of Willet and others, the expulsion of non-subscribing ministers was not reversed. Radical puritanism survived among unbeneficed ministers, or in the backwaters of the Netherlands or the New World, a weakened force though still lingering on.[32] Moderate puritans returned once again to the political quietism of the 1590s, and concentrated their attention on the spiritual transformation of the English Church from

28 Willet, *Ecclesia Triumphans*, sig.¶¶1r, 35–6, 90–3; cf. *idem*, *Antilogie*, preface to King James (unfoliated), 'Preface to the Christian Reader', sig.A3r–v, p.57.

29 Andrew Willet, *Limbo-Mastix* (1604), sig.A4r. This section is clumsily expressed in the original, or perhaps wrongly transcribed at the press, as it seems to contradict itself.

30 K. Fincham, *Prelate as Pastor* (Oxford, 1990), pp.323–6; on Hampton Court, see P. Collinson, 'The Jacobean religious settlement: the Hampton Court Conference', in H. Tomlinson (ed.), *Before the Civil War* (1983), pp.27–51; F. Shriver, 'Hampton Court revisited: James I and the puritans', *JEH* 33 (1982); K. Fincham and P. Lake, 'The ecclesiastical policy of King James I', *Journal of British Studies* 24 (1985), pp.171–6.

31 Willet, *Hexapla in Genesin* (Cambridge, 1605), 'Ad Reverendiss. Archiepis. Cantuariens.' (unfoliated).

32 Tyacke, *Fortunes*, *passim*.

within. Under an evangelically minded episcopate and sovereign, this was to prove a remarkable success. By the fourth edition of Willet's *Synopsis* in 1613 its author was able to praise his new dedicatees, Archbishop Abbot and Bishop King of London, for their efforts in this regard. In his dedicatory epistle, and in the body of the work, Willet especially praised the preaching record and pastoral diligence of the English bishops 'which', he affirmed, 'is the most weightie part, and giveth greatest grace to their pastoral office'.[33] Willet also expressed satisfaction in his 1613 epistle with Abbot and King's successful efforts to defend true doctrine against the 'semi-popish errors'* that had been beginning to grow in the English Church – a clear reference to the errors of Hooker and other 'avant-garde conformists' which had concerned Willet so much at the turn of the century.[34] However, Willet's confidence was here misplaced. The 'semi-popish errors' which he identified had never received the explicit condemnation for which he had earlier petitioned King James, and the following year saw Abbot fail to rout one of their protagonists, John Howson, in a full-scale confrontation before the king.[35] King James was clearly aiming at a broader vision of the English Church than that envisaged by Willet (or, indeed, by Archbishop Abbot).

For all their claims to be loyal members of the Church of England, prepared to make their peace with Whitgift and Bancroft and to work in harmony with Abbot and other evangelically inclined bishops, the early years of James' reign had revealed among men such as Willet a tactical readiness to urge more thoroughgoing ecclesiastical reform whenever the political opportunity presented itself, and this could only serve to confirm the suspicions of anti-puritans within the English Church. Their fears were heightened rather than diminished by the extent to which moderate puritans were prepared to yield occasional outward conformity to the Church of England, and the result was increasing calls among some conformists for a more severe execution of ecclesiastical discipline against them. When he took up his pen to defend Richard Hooker against their criticisms, the conformist William Covell showed no disposition to believe the claims made by the authors of *A Christian Letter* that they were loyal members of the church. Instead, Covell declared that the puritans' claim that they accepted the doctrines of Whitgift, but rejected Hooker's works as depart-

33 Willet, *Synopsis* (1613), p.827 – also cited in Fincham, *Prelate as Pastor*, p.300; Willet *Synopsis* (1852), I: 37, 39–40. See also Willet's dedicatory epistle to Archbishop Abbot and Bishop Andrewes of book 2 of his *Hexapla ... upon the ... Epistle ... to the Romans* (Cambridge, 1611), sig.Yy3v.

34 Willet, *Synopsis* (1852), I: 39.

35 See N. Cranfield and K. Fincham (eds.), 'John Howson's answers to Archbishop Abbot's accusations at his "trial" before James I at Greenwich, 10 June 1615', *Camden Miscellany XXIX* (Camden Society 4th ser. 34, 1987).

ing from them, was merely 'an uncivill Ironie . . . to make themselves sport, & in the end proudly and maliciously to contemne both'. In the wake of further puritan petitioning after James' accession to the throne, Covell displayed even less readiness to tolerate puritan claims. Initially, it is true, Covell adopted an irenical posture in his *Modest and Reasonable Examination* of 1604, where he complained that radical puritans such as Josias Nichols had unnecessarily destroyed the church's unity by stirring up long-buried contentions. Nevertheless, Covell also took the opportunity in the same work to regret the moderation that Elizabethan bishops had displayed towards puritans. A greater severity in the execution of just laws, Covell averred, would have given the puritans more occasion for complaint, 'but surely the Unitie of the Church had beene much more. There is nothing so dangerous as lenitie in that case.' Throwing his moderate rhetoric to the winds, Covell ended his tract with a lengthy and intemperate appeal to King James for severe justice to be enacted against the puritans. Just as Willet had done, Covell appealed to the authorities to prevent the printing of his opponent's writings.[36]

Covell was doubtless unusual among early Jacobean government apologists in the vehemence of his anti-puritanism, but he was expressive of a more widespread reaction against creeping puritanism that was catching up with Andrew Willet himself. Willet's determination to root out 'semi-popish errors' soon landed him in hot water. The rector of Barley received a stinging attack from the dean of Chester, William Barlow, in the preface to the latter's semi-official account of the Hampton Court Conference, published in 1604. Barlow was one of the new breed of avant-garde conformists, and had been incensed by the charges of 'popery' that had been levelled against the Cambridge anti-Calvinists in the 1590s. In the preface to his account of the Conference, Barlow accused Willet, the 'Synopticall Theolog', of stirring up divisions within the church, specifically in his recent tract *Limbo-Mastix*. In this work, Willet had taken the opportunity to attack a tract composed by a minor conformist divine Richard Parkes, which had criticized the interpretation that had been advanced by a number of puritan authors (including Willet himself) of the article of the Creed concerning Christ's descent into hell. It is important to appreciate that this was no mere 'puritan versus Anglican' controversy. On the specific doctrine of Christ's descent into hell, Willet was prepared to tolerate the different, more literalist interpretation advanced by *some* conformist authors (including Bishop Bilson), while the position which Willet himself upheld had enjoyed the support of that hammer of puritans

36 William Covell, *A Iust and Temperate Defence of the Five Books of Ecclesiastical Policy by R. Hooker* (1603), p.6; *idem*, *Modest Examination*, pp.47–8, 53–4, 206–15.

Bishop Aylmer of London, among others. Willet's reply to Parkes had also won the prior approval of the conformist pamphleteer Matthew Sutcliffe. Indeed, Willet was so anxious to protect his own self-image as a defender of the Reformed establishment that he refused to tackle the issue of Christ's descent directly for fear of having publicly to disagree with the opinion of Bilson and other conformists.[37] Willet's concern in *Limbo-Mastix* was thus not to oppose the literalist position held by Bilson and other conformists, but rather to condemn what he saw as Parkes' failure to avoid the Roman doctrine of 'limbus patrum', and therefore of purgatory: yet another example of the creeping semi-popish errors which Willet detected in the church.[38]

However, Parkes wrote a spirited reply in which he sought to overturn the foundations of Willet's *modus vivendi* with the Church of England establishment. Not only did Parkes accuse Willet of blasphemy and atheism on this particular point of doctrine, but he also conducted a careful trawl through Willet's appeal for further reform in his *Ecclesia Triumphans*, *Antilogie* and *Hexapla*, and sought to use these passages to equate Willet's position with that of the doctrinaire presbyterians.[39] More generally, Parkes strove to isolate and marginalize puritans, insisting that they deserved the name to designate their new opinions as different in kind from those of the Protestants, thereby 'to discerne and separate them from others, who by their owne pravity, have wilfully deprived themselves of that name'. But Parkes was aiming wider than radical presbyterians. He warned also of those 'of that Sect' who 'would beare the world in hand, that they dissent not from others in matters of substance, but in ceremonies only: & this to cloake their schisme withal against the Church, & to countenance their errors (if not heresies rather) in oppuging the Doctrine therof'. The solution, as Parkes urged Archbishop Bancroft, was that more severity should be used towards the puritans who, he insisted, would not be won over by persuasion.[40]

37 William Barlow, *The Summe and Substance of the Conference* (1604), sig.A3v; *idem*, *A Defence of the Articles of the Protestants Religion* (1601), sigs.A2v–A4r; Willet, *Limbo-Mastix*, pp.4–7; *idem*, *Loidoromastix* (1607), sigs.¶¶2r–3r; John Strype, *The Life and Acts of John Aylmer* (Oxford, 1821), p.162. For the initial attack on Willet, see Richard Parkes, *A Briefe Answere unto Certaine Objections* (Oxford, 1604), pp.33, 57 (and note Willet's complaints in his *Hexapla in Genesin*, 'Certaine Directions to the Reader' (unfoliated)). For the different views on Christ's descent into hell during this period, see D.D. Wallace, 'Puritan and Anglican: the interpretation of Christ's descent into hell in Elizabethan theology', *AfR* 69 (1978).

38 Willet, *Limbo-Mastix*, pp.1–3 and *passim*; *idem*, *Loidoromastix*, sig.¶¶¶2r–¶¶¶¶2r and *passim*.

39 Richard Parkes, *An Apologie of Three Testimonies* (1607), ii. pp.10, 19–20. For suggestions that Willet was a presbyterian see *ibid.*, i. sig.¶6v, ii. pp.8, 9, 10, 18, 19, 23, 29, 31, 33, 68, 110.

40 *Ibid.*, ii. pp.30–1, i. sigs.¶4v–¶5r.

Willet wrote a desperate reply, dedicated to Bancroft, in which he sought to exculpate himself from Parkes' charges. He strongly complained of the charge that he was anti-episcopalian, and cited his defence of bishops in his *Synopsis* and *Antilogie*, claiming also that he had dedicated more books to bishops and prelates than had any other contemporary member of the English Church. Rather, Willet protested that he had been active in reconciling nonconformists to the Church of England, and intimated that Bancroft was already well acquainted with Willet and with this aspect of his career. Nevertheless, he stood by his earlier protest that some books had recently been printed which expounded doctrines declining to popery 'which', he added, 'can not be denied by any of sound iudgement'.[41]

Parkes did not succeed in his attempt to brand Willet as a die-hard presbyterian, and he disappeared into the obscurity from whence he came, while Willet (possibly with Bancroft's encouragement) vowed to abandon religious controversy altogether and to concentrate instead on scriptural commentary, which he continued to publish at a phenomenal rate throughout James' reign.[42] Nevertheless, Parkes was voicing a distrust of the accommodation of moderate puritanism within the English Church which would become increasingly voluble in the ensuing years. Moreover, it must be emphasized that Willet's defence of the establishment, and of English episcopacy in particular, was strictly conditional upon its defence of doctrinal orthodoxy and active promotion of godly values. If English bishops were to shift towards a preoccupation with issues of order and uniformity, then Willet's loyalty might yet prove to be as fleeting as Parkes had claimed it to be. Indeed, the defence of episcopacy in the *Synopsis* would later provide the Dutch polemicist Gerson Bucerus with all the material necessary for an assault on the doctrine of *iure divino* episcopacy.[43] Moreover, passages can be found in Willet's works which opposed the services in cathedral churches, and condemned the use of all images in churches, including those erected merely for ornament.[44] As we shall see, Willet would later find himself imprisoned when he sought to intervene to dissuade the king from the Spanish Match and thereby to ensure a more vigorously confessional foreign policy.[45]

41 Willet, *Loidoromastix*, pp.13–15.

42 See *ibid.*, 'Further Advertisements to the Reader', sig.¶¶¶¶3v; *idem*, *Hexapla in Danielem* (Cambridge, 1610), sig.R4v. Willet's first forays into scriptural commentary would seem to have been encouraged by Bancroft: Willet, *Hexapla in Exodum* (1608), sig.A6v.

43 Gerson Bucerus, *Dissertatio de Gubernatione Ecclesiae* (Middelburg, 1618), pp.47, 286–8, 294–5, 319, 337, 340, 397, and especially p. 594. For a more detailed discussion of this treatise, see below, ch.9.

44 Andrew Willet, *Thesaurus Ecclesiae* (Cambridge, 1604), p.132; *Hexapla in Danielem*, ii. p.170.

45 *The Letters of John Chamberlain*, ed. N.E. McClure (2 vols., Philadelphia, 1939), II: 140; *Acts of the Privy Council 1618–19*, pp.37–40; BL, Add. MS 24275 fols.9–10. Note also the

Willet's career thus serves to illustrate some of the complexities in the shifting mass of doctrines and attitudes that was the early Stuart Church. The story of English Protestantism in the period before the civil war is that of the struggles and pitfalls encountered by this moderate puritan tradition as it sought to gain a secure foothold in the respectable mainstream of the English Church, and of its increasing conflict with the new trends of conformist thought which Willet had identified in 1600, and which were themselves anxious to lay claim to this golden circle of orthodoxy and to exclude Willet and his allies from it. But it is also the story of those in the middle – those evangelical Calvinist bishops and conformist divines such as George and Robert Abbot, Matthew Sutcliffe, John Davenant and Thomas Morton – in whom Willet felt able to place his trust. Much recent scholarship has focused on these men, and on the extent to which their theology and aspirations overlapped with those of both conforming and nonconforming puritans. Indeed, it has even been suggested that Whitgift's friend Matthew Hutton, Elizabeth's last archbishop of York, might in a sense be described as a 'puritan bishop'. However, Dr Fincham, while anxious to emphasize the personal ties linking evangelical Calvinist bishops and conforming puritans, has also noted the slight changes in emphasis which might distinguish the views of an evangelical Calvinist bishop such as Arthur Lake from those of his puritan chaplain, William Sclater.[46] As we shall see, the Jacobean and Caroline periods were also to witness the gradual drifting apart of these two groups, as Calvinist conformists found the logic of their own position, the polemical demands of the debate with Rome and their own increasing fears of the radicalization of puritan thinking impelling them towards positions on certain issues which seemed increasingly incompatible with the world-view of conforming puritans. If the early Stuart period saw the increasing conflict of the worlds of Richard Hooker and Andrew Willet, it also witnessed increasing fault-lines developing between even the evangelical conformist and puritan positions – positions which the excesses of the Laudian period would help to prise further apart.

The early Stuart period was above all a time of change and development in the theology of the Church of England. None of the positions which Willet had delineated in 1600 were static. Avant-garde conformists, Calvinist conformists, moderate and radical puritans alike were developing and modifying their ideas over this period, moving closer or further from the establishment as events dictated, or as new fears arose, and within this

comments in his sermon on the marriage of Princess Elizabeth and the Elector Frederick: Andrew Willet, *A Treatise of Salomons Mariage* (1612/13), especially sig.A1r, p.56.

46 P. Lake, 'Matthew Hutton – a puritan bishop?', *History* 64 (1979); Fincham, *Prelate as Pastor*, pp.260–1.

constantly evolving spectrum of views many individuals evolved and modified their own theological stance. It was in this dynamic mass of shifting positions that English ministers trod their wary way during the reigns of James and his son Charles. The tensions involved in absorbing both the evangelical impulse of moderate puritanism and new styles of avant-garde conformity within the Jacobean Church took a considerable time to manifest themselves openly, but they helped to create an atmosphere in which divines warily studied the limits of acceptable behaviour and thought, as represented in the ways in which ministers perceived and wrote about the different foreign churches which they faced, Rome and Geneva, Catholic and Reformed.

Part I

THE CHURCH OF ROME

1

'This immortal fewde': anti-popery, 'negative popery' and the changing climate of religious controversy

THE ATTRACTIONS OF ANTI-POPERY

In 1600 Andrew Willet had urged anti-popery as the main vocation of the Church of England. He argued that it would unite puritans and bishops, enabling them to put the presbyterian upheavals behind them, and would stimulate an awareness of a common identity which conformists and precisians shared. In practice, things were rarely that simple. Estimations of the relative importance of the papal threat, and therefore of the value of opposition to it, were changing during the early Stuart period. Later chapters will study the structure of anti-papal thought in England and will investigate some of the doctrinal changes which possibly underlay these different assessments. However, it will be necessary to devote this first chapter to exploring the rationale of Elizabethan and Jacobean anti-popery, and the purposes which it served. After an initial examination of the evaluations built into this ideology, the changes within it will then be placed within the context of the political chronology of the period, and the rapid developments during the 1630s, when the value of anti-popery was fundamentally challenged.

Recent scholarship has already demonstrated how anti-papal polemic acted during the Elizabethan period as the established means whereby moderate puritans such as Willet could both display their loyalty to the Church of England, and at the same time affirm their commitment to further reformation.[1] In Jacobean times anti-papal writings, at least in the first half of the reign, were the most distinctive feature of English Protestant theology and occupied the energies of all the principal members of the Jacobean episcopate. It has been calculated that contributions to the

[1] Lake, *Moderate Puritans*, pp.55–76. On popular anti-popery in this period, see P. Lake, 'Anti-popery: the structure of a prejudice', in R. Cust and A. Hughes (eds.), *Conflict in Early Stuart England* (1989); C.Z. Weiner, 'The beleaguered isle. A study of Elizabethan and early Jacobean anticatholicism', *P&P* 51 (1971); R. Clifton, 'The popular fear of Catholics during the English Revolution', *P&P* 52 (1971); *idem*, 'Fear of popery', in Russell, *Origins*.

pamphlet controversies between the Church of England and Rome amounted to over 500 works in the period 1605–25, published by some 150 different Romanist and Protestant authors. It was controversies with Rome, rather than inter-Protestant disputes, that were the principal concern of divinity disputations in both Universities throughout this period.[2] Willet's aspirations, it would seem, were being fully realized.

The debate over the Oath of Allegiance led to the king's own participation in anti-papal pamphlet controversy, and the conscription of the Church of England's clerical elite into the subsequent plethora of related controversies helped to provide a sure-fire route for preferment in the Jacobean Church. The king certainly retained an academic interest in anti-papal controversy throughout his life, as is evident in his own collected *Workes*, his constant commissioning of anti-popish material beyond the political necessities of the Oath of Allegiance controversy, and in his enthusiastic participation in the open debate with the Jesuit John Percy (alias Fisher) in 1622, when he took over the defence of the Protestant position from its appointed advocate Francis White with considerable relish. He was also prepared to tolerate the presence of violently anti-papal preachers at court.[3]

Moreover, James gave his direct support to the most ambitious scheme for corporate polemical activity among English Protestant divines that was ever devised: the founding of Chelsea College as an institution for the systematic production of anti-papal polemic.[4] King James himself laid the

[2] T.H. Wadkins, 'Theological polemic and religious culture in early Stuart England' (Graduate Theological Union, Berkeley, Calif., PhD, 1988), p.71; W.T. Costello, *The Scholastic Curriculum at Early Seventeenth Century Cambridge* (Cambridge, Mass., 1958), p.113. On styles of polemic, see G.R. Cragg, *Freedom and Authority* (Philadelphia, 1975), ch.6; J.C.H. Aveling, 'The English clergy, Catholic and Protestant, in the 16th and 17th centuries', in J.C.H. Aveling, D.M. Loades and H.R. McAdoo, *Rome and the Anglicans* (Berlin, 1982), p.131.

[3] On the composition of King James' *Triplici nodo, triplex cuneus*, see *HMC Salisbury* XIX: 343–4; *CSPVen 1609–10*, p.74; D.H. Willson, 'James I and his literary assistants', *Huntington Library Quarterly* 8 (1944–5). On his prompting of Andrewes to reply to Bellarmine, see Chamberlain, *Letters*, I: 264–5, 270; *HMC Salisbury* XX: 260; Andrewes, *Two Answers*, pp.ix, xlii–xliv. On his debate with Percy: LPL, Lambeth MS 1372 fols.58v–61v – published in T.H. Wadkins, 'King James I meets John Percy, S.J. (26 May, 1622)', *Recusant History* 19 (1988–9), pp.147–53. For examples of King James' commissions, see Joseph Hall, *The Honour of the Married Clergy* in *The Works of ... Joseph Hall*, ed. P. Wynter (10 vols., Oxford, 1863), VIII: 481; Bodl., Tanner MS 290 fol.65.

[4] On Chelsea College, see D.E. Kennedy, 'King James I's College of Controversial Divinity at Chelsea' in *idem* (ed.), *Grounds of Controversy. Three Studies of Late 16th and Early 17th Century English Polemics* (Melbourne, 1989), pp.97–119; A.C.F. Beales, *Education under Penalty* (1963), pp.191–2; *HMC Downshire* II: 221, III: 194, IV: 308–9; *HMC Salisbury* XXII: 57–8; T. Faulkner, *An Historical and Topographical Description of Chelsea and its Environs* (2 vols., 1829), II: 219–29. For an earlier proposal for such a collegiate scheme, see Strype, *Aylmer*, pp.32–3.

foundation-stone in May 1609, and gave the project his full blessing.[5] He wrote to Archbishop Abbot in 1616 instructing him to solicit charitable donations for the College, which had been established 'for learned divines to be employed to write, as occasion shall require, for maintaining the religion professed in our kingdoms, and confuting the impugners thereof'. This had been necessary because 'the enemies of the gospel have ever been forward to write and publish books for confirming their erroneous doctrine, and impugning the truth, and now of late seem more carefull than before, to send dayly into our realms such their writings, whereby our loving subjects, though otherwise disposed, might be seduced, unless some remedy thereof should be provided'.[6]

The College was the brainchild of Matthew Sutcliffe, the scourge of presbyterians in the 1590s, and its early fellows included mainstream Calvinist conformists such as Thomas Morton and Robert Abbot. By Sutcliffe's death in 1629, its list of fellows included similar figures in John Prideaux (who acted as one of Sutcliffe's executors) and John Young, dean of Winchester. The project eventually foundered for many reasons, not the least of which was the fact that, however much they might approve of the College in principle, Englishmen were far from enthusiastic when it came to providing the necessary financial support out of their own pockets.[7]

A related project grew up around the concern that Willet had expressed regarding popish corruptions of the Fathers of the early church and later writers. The study and correction of these corruptions became the life's work of Thomas James, Bodley's first librarian, who lobbied the project constantly and worked in close collusion with a nexus of Calvinist divines in Oxford who were dedicated to anti-papal causes – men such as Robert Abbot, George Hakewill, Richard Crakanthorp and John Prideaux. It was divines such as these, along with more recognizably puritan figures such as William Twisse, whom Archbishop Bancroft recommended to Thomas James as a panel to assist his schemes. These men also kept in close contact with Lambeth after Abbot's brother George had succeeded as archbishop of Canterbury, where Abbot's chaplains Richard Mocket, Daniel Featley and Thomas Goad kept up close links with other prominent anti-papal pamphleteers such as Richard Sheldon, William Crashaw and Alexander

5 James gave as his personal contribution to the project 'all the timber thereunto, which was to be fetched out of Windsor forest'. He also revived the ancient 'King's Silver' tax to be imposed on those taking the Oaths of Allegiance and Supremacy, and directed that the tax's profits should go to Chelsea College 'for the better handling of religious controversy': R. Blunt, *The Wonderful Village* (1918), pp.127–8.

6 Faulkner, *Description*, p.223; Thomas Fuller, *The Church History of Britain*, ed. J.S. Brewer (6 vols., Oxford, 1845), V: 391–2.

7 Faulkner, *Description*, pp.225, 226. For possible economic reasons for the College's failure, see *ibid*., p.224. See also Fuller's assessment in *Church History*, V: 393–6.

Cooke.[8] Thomas James' own schemes were in time to hit the same sort of financial problems that afflicted Chelsea College, but his surviving correspondence helps to demonstrate the co-operation and interaction of a closely knit network of Calvinist conformist and moderate puritan anti-papal authors during the Jacobean period.[9]

Not the least of the many influences which helped to give to Jacobean religious thought its anti-papal complexion was the attitude of the successive incumbents at Lambeth Palace. Richard Bancroft supported Sutcliffe's Chelsea College as well as the plans of Thomas James, and also commissioned anti-papal works by the moderate Calvinist episcopalians Thomas Morton and Robert Abbot. His successor George Abbot was a dedicated anti-papal activist whose theology, it has been suggested, was built around 'an intense, even pathological, fear of popery', and who took a prominent part in attempting to convert such convictions into confessionally based foreign and domestic policies under James.[10] Moreover, an abiding concern with the cosmic struggle against the Romish Antichrist was not merely the pre-eminent orientation of the Jacobean clergy, but was also a prominent mode of thought in parliament and among JPs in the provinces. The famous debates with the Jesuit Fisher in James' reign, for example, were sponsored by prominent members of the laity.[11]

This bustling hive of official anti-papal activity and publications

[8] For the personal links between these anti-papal polemicists, see *Letters Addressed to Thomas James*, ed. G.W. Wheeler (1933), pp.25, 26–7, 35, 45, 53, 55; James Ussher, *The Whole Works ... of James Ussher*, ed. C.R. Elrington (17 vols., Dublin, 1847–64), XV: 116 and *passim*. A typical example of the anti-papal interaction of moderate puritan and establishment divines is one of the conferences with the Jesuit Fisher in the early 1620s, which was attended by Francis White, Abbot's chaplains Featley and Goad, and the puritan Thomas Gataker, as well as the earls of Lincoln and Warwick: Daniel Featley, *The Romish Fisher Caught and Held in His Owne Net* (1624), p.46.

[9] On James' schemes for a volume correcting corruptions of the Fathers, see James, *Letters*, pp.9–11, 14, 16–17, 46–7, 55, 56, 57–8, 62–4; *idem*, *The Humble Supplication of Thomas James* (n.d.); *idem*, *The Humble and Earnest Request of Thomas James* (n.d.); *idem*, *An Explanation or Enlarging of the Ten Articles* (Oxford, 1625). Bancroft's recommendations are in James, *Letters*, p.39. Several published works resulted – e.g. William Crashaw, *Falsificationum Romanorum* (1606); Thomas James, *Bellum Gregorianum* (Oxford, 1610); *idem*, *A Treatise of the Corruption of Scripture, Councils and Holy Fathers* (1611). By 1624, Thomas James was hoping that his own projected 'college' for printing medieval manuscripts and books censored by Rome would supersede the struggling Chelsea College: Ussher, *Works*, XV: 214–16.

[10] Faulkner, *Description*, II: 219–20; Babbage, *Puritanism*, p.388; James, *Letters*, p.39; Thomas Morton, *Apologia Catholica* (1605), ep. ded. (cf. H. Foley (ed.), *Records of the English Province of the Society of Jesus* (7 vols., 1877–83), VII: 1006–7, 1015); Robert Abbot, *A Defence of the Reformed Catholicke* (1611), sigs.*2v, A1v, A2v. Bancroft also accepted the dedication of Book 2 of Gabriel Powel's *Disputationum ... de Antichristo* (1605). On Abbot, see K. Fincham, 'Prelacy and politics: Archbishop Abbot's defence of Protestant orthodoxy', *Historical Research* 61 (1988).

[11] Wadkins, 'Theological polemic', pp.116–17.

undoubtedly helped to fulfil Willet's hopes that puritan activists might thereby be assured of the Protestant credentials of the ecclesiastical hierarchy. For example, Lancelot Andrewes was clearly a proponent of a different style of churchmanship from that represented by evangelical Calvinists such as the Abbots, and reports of his court sermon in defence of auricular confession may have led to some of the puritan complaints in 1603. Yet Willet himself was prepared to applaud the bishop for his contributions to the Oath of Allegiance controversy, and these same anti-papal works of Andrewes were also cited with approval by puritan writers such as Henry Burton who would have found little that appealed to them in Andrewes' sermons.[12] It was only among radical congregationalists and separatists, such as Robert Parker and Henry Jacob, that the anti-papal controversy embarked upon by the bishops was interpreted as mere hypocrisy. These sectarians repeatedly made the accusation that the bishops played at being puritans when they wrote against papists, but were then papists when they wrote against puritans.[13]

THE RATIONALE OF JACOBEAN ANTI-POPERY

Anti-popery was not simply intended to endear puritans to the establishment or vice versa. While it undoubtedly held these (usually unspoken) strategic merits, strong and public opposition to Rome was also seen as serving several other important purposes. First of all, a hatred of popery was seen as a positive manifestation of true religion, a testimony of the individual's commitment to God. This was not just the view of extreme puritans, but was also strongly maintained by establishment divines. The Regius Professor of Divinity at Oxford, John Prideaux, declared that it was the implacable hostility of the Marian Martyrs to Rome's religion which most required revival: 'Our first love to Gods Word was a great deale more fervent when so many burned in defiance of Romish mixtures.'[14] Any slackening by Protestants of this hatred was a sign of the Church of Ephesus' forsaking of its first love (Revelation 2.4). As Prideaux explained, 'to hate the abominations of Popery . . . is an evidence of a soule prepared,

12 Willet, *Hexapla on Romans*, sig.Yy3r; Henry Burton, *The Baiting of the Popes Bull* (1627), sigs.¶3v, **2r, pp.4, 7, 10, 61–2. Cf. John Downame, *A Guide to Godlynesse* (1622), sig.A4 – cited in Fincham and Lake, 'Ecclesiastical policy', p.201. On Andrewes' sermons, see Lake, 'Lancelot Andrewes'.

13 Robert Parker, *A Scholasticall Discourse against Symbolizing with Antichrist* (?Amsterdam, 1607), cited in Dent, *Protestant Reformers*, p.70; Kennedy, 'King James I's College', p.106. This was an accusation which was also levelled by Roman controversialists: Gabriel Powel, *A Consideration of the Papists Reasons of State and Religion* (1604), pp.73–4.

14 John Prideaux, *Ephesus Backsliding* (1614), p.37.

for the entertaining and relishing of this first love'.[15] In a sense, it was impossible to have too much anti-popery. When the Roman priest William Bishop complained of the slanderous and vehement attacks being made against popery in sermons in the wake of the Gunpowder Plot, Robert Abbot, soon to be bishop of Salisbury, professed himself dissatisfied even with the extreme attacks already delivered. Indeed, he declared that 'there is not one Minister amongst us, who in his sermons doth so th[o]roughly lay foorth the villanie and wickednesse of your profession as in trueth the cause and matter thereof doth require'. Abbot was happy to repeat the common saying that 'the neerer the [Roman] church, the farther from God'.[16]

For puritans, anti-popery had a particular significance – a heightened sense of the threat from the papal Antichrist was held to be one of the signs of election. As Thomas Beard observed, 'the more wee know and detest Antichrist, the more are we enamored with Christ, and long for his comming, and desire the full revelation of his glory'. As recent scholars have demonstrated, at the heart of puritanism lay a polarized vision of the world, and a greater readiness to read prophetic import into temporal conflicts. Opposition to popery was thus *ipso facto* godly; the puritan commitment to further reformation implied a constant state of conflict with the forces represented by the papal enemy. This opposition was also important for more extreme puritans in providing them with evidence of how the established church was itself bearing witness to the truth.[17]

Moreover, whatever else was gained by anti-papal conflict, it was deemed by many divines to be inevitable. Their insistence that it was the destiny of the true church on earth to be in perpetual warfare with the forces of darkness seemed to entail that conflict with Rome was therefore unavoidable and to be encouraged. Thus the puritan William Gouge stressed that, if there were Israelites (Protestants) in the world, then there must also be Amalekites (Romanists): this was part of 'this immortal fewde against worshippers of the true God, and professours of the true Religion'. Indeed, Gouge argued that Romanist opposition was important in validating the Protestant religion: 'this their malice against us is an evidence that our Religion is true'. Puritans argued that the church should be at perpetual war while on earth, that there could be no peace without truth and that unlimited peace was against grace and truth. It was the wordly

15 *Ibid.*, p.38.

16 Abbot, *Defence*, p.208; *idem*, *The Third Part of the Defence of the Reformed Catholicke* (1609), p.99.

17 P. Lake, 'William Bradshaw, Antichrist and the community of the godly', *JEH* 36 (1985), p.576; Thomas Beard, *Antichrist the Pope of Rome* (1625), sig.*2r. Note Joseph Hall's attempt to use this point when appealing to separatists: Hall, *Works*, IX: 113.

prosperity and peace of the church that had sent it into the spiritual wilderness. If these emphases were more clear and consistent in puritan works, they were not alien to more mainstream writers. At times of crisis the duty to make holy war rather than peace could be argued by moderates such as Joseph Hall with just as much venom as the more radical puritans.[18] Calls for Protestant peace were often made the better to be able to make war on the Roman Church, not just in the works of a man like Willet, but also in the sermons of Joseph Hall and Isaac Bargrave.[19]

Conflict with Rome was seen as being of the essence of Protestantism. Every Protestant act could thus be interpreted as effectively a rejection of popery, and vice versa. John Donne told his congregation that 'as often as you meet here, you renew your band to God, that you will never be reconciled to the superstitions of Rome'. The puritan Richard Sibbes argued in similar fashion that 'the more we justify Christ, the more we will be against anti-christ and his religion. We may know the owning of the one truth by the vilifying of the other.'[20]

One of the most public manifestations of anti-popery was the publication of anti-papal controversial literature. Whatever their other ends, the composition of these works was seen as serving a positive spiritual function for the individual engaged in it, as a demonstration of his commitment to the true faith. Polemical controversy was also believed to serve a good purpose inasmuch as it helped to confirm Protestant readers more deeply in their faith. Similarly, books of remembrance of God's past blessings in saving the Church of England from Roman iniquity were seen as profitable texts for godly meditation.[21] These formed only one part of a whole system of popular remembrances, feast-days and festivals which commemorated previous conflicts with the forces of Rome – the Armada, the accession of Elizabeth and (under James) the discovery of the Gunpowder Plot.[22]

[18] William Gouge, *Gods Three Arrows* (1631), pp.187, 188; Thomas Taylor, *Christs Victorie over the Dragon* (1633), pp.132–3, 293–4, 332–42, 740–1; Hall, *Works*, V: 228–9, 261–73.

[19] See below ch.9.

[20] *The Sermons of John Donne*, ed. G.R. Potter and E.M. Simpson (10 vols., Berkeley, Calif. 1953–62), IV: 370 – quoted in Cragg, *Freedom and Authority*, p.160; Richard Sibbes, *Bowels Opened*, in *The Works of Richard Sibbes*, ed. A.B. Grosart (7 vols., 1862–4), II: 164.

[21] Daniel Featley admitted to finding delight in religious controversy: Featley, *The Practice of Extraordinary Devotion* (1630), ep. ded. (quoted in Cragg, *Freedom and Authority*, p.163 n.25). Note also John White's lengthy defence of his career as an anti-papal controversialist in the preamble to his will: PRO, PROB 11/135/17. On books of remembrance, see Thomas Taylor, *Two Sermons* (1624), ii. p.6; George Carleton, *A Thankfull Remembrance of God's Mercy* (1624); Thomas Gataker, *An Anniversarie Memoriall of Englands Delivery from the Spanish Invasion* (1626); Isaac Bargrave, *A Sermon Preached before the Honorable Assembly* (1624), p.34.

[22] D. Cressy, *Bonfires and Bells* (1989), pp.124–52.

Violent attacks on popery, and the systematic production of anti-papal polemic, were also seen as important because of their direct effect in preventing what was believed to be the constant threat of conversion to Rome. It was argued that this justified the most vitriolic attacks upon Roman faith and practices. It was important, maintained 'T.B.' in 1629, 'to shew unto the people aforehand the filthy, black, infernal stuff which lies at the bottom of the whore's cup, which they must one day drink off assuredly if they will become her disciples and followers'. Robert Abbot explained that the readers of his anti-papal works would 'learne the more deeply to detest the mystery of iniquitie'.[23] The confutation of popish errors was therefore believed to be necessary whenever the opportunity presented itself. Catechizing was inspired to some extent by the fear of popery. A recent scholar has noted how peaks in the publication of new catechisms during this period coincided with times of increasing anti-papal sentiment. Joseph Hall in *The Old Religion* noted that King James had remarked that a lack of familiarity with 'the points of catechism' was the cause of many people falling into popery. Many of the resulting catechisms were explicitly anti-papist in their aim, and included sections advising the reader on what to say when confronted by Romanist arguments.[24] A variety of other handbooks were produced to protect the vulnerable laity from Romanist proselytizers. One example is James Warre's *The Touch-stone of Truth*, which provided tables of scriptural citations in support of the principal points of Protestant doctrine, so that (as its title-page declared) 'one of meane capacity, by helpe of this Booke, may be able to argue with any Papist, and confute them by Scripture'.[25]

At a higher level, such anti-popery was manifested in the systematic production of works of anti-papal controversial divinity. Even some of the larger works of anti-papal controversy were intended to inform the public at large.[26] In part, these tracts merely aimed to present Rome's errors to the reader in the worst possible light. Robert Abbot argued that it was important to demonstrate the Roman Church's profession so that people would understand its wickedness and abominations. Roman errors were so bad

[23] T.B., *A Preservative to Keep a Protestant from Becoming a Papist* (Oxford, 1629), p.44 – quoted in Cragg, *Freedom and Authority*, p.161; Abbot, *Second Part*, sig.A3r; see also Ussher's remarks on Mariolatry, below p.67.

[24] Cragg, *Freedom and Authority*, pp.163–4; I. Green, '"For children in yeeres and children in understanding": the emergence of the English catechism under Elizabeth and the early Stuarts', *JEH* 37 (1986), p.401. Cf. *The Diary of Sir Simonds d'Ewes 1622–1624*, ed. E. Bourcier (Paris, 1974), pp.94–5.

[25] James Warre, *The Touch-stone of Truth* (1634).

[26] E.g. Beard, *Antichrist*, sig.A3r (contrast Covell, *Just and Temperate Defence*, p.140). It was often assumed, however, that committed Romanists would never read Protestant works: James, *Letters*, p.57; Richard Sheldon, *A Sermon Preached at Paules Crosse* (1625), p.43; John Dove, *A Perswasion to the English Recusants* (1603), p.7.

that 'to discover them, is sufficient to confute them'.[27] Nevertheless, great importance was attached to the systematic scholarly refutation of individual Roman Catholic polemical works, not simply for symbolic reasons, but also because this was believed to work in informing and protecting the wider public against the threat of Roman Catholic proselytizing activity. This period is marked by a heightened anxiety that English Protestants might defect if major works of Romanist opponents were left unanswered. Tobie Matthew, bishop of Durham, proposed in his 'Memoriall of some things to be considered of in the Parlament and Convocation' of 1597 an ambitious solution to the problem. He recommended to Whitgift

> that Popish Auctores of Controversies in Religion, as Bellarmyne, Stapleton, Gregorius de Valentia, with such like, should no sooner come forth, but the Universities, Cathedrall Sees, and Churches (with some other learned men at large) should be enioyned to aunswere them by a certayne reasonable tyme, upon l[ette]res dyrected unto them from your Grace, And the said popish bookes to be utterly forbidden to be vendible, untill they shalbe published with the aunswere.

Matthew added sombrely that 'It is incredible what decaie the Contrarie Custome hath bredd in Religion, and what increase of superstition in these parts especially.'[28]

Such fears were to some extent justified. Scattered evidence seems to indicate that from the 1590s onwards Romanists were increasingly relying on polemical works as a serious proselytizing agent, with dramatic increases in the number of titles in circulation, and in their proportionate share of the output of the Romanist presses.[29] Certainly, too, there is evidence of conversions prompted by the reading of Roman controversial works during this period.[30] This anxiety to refute papal polemic inspired various schemes for corporate polemical activity among English Protestant divines, which were finally realized, as we have seen, in the founding of Chelsea College.

Nevertheless, a concern to engage with Roman polemicists might also

27 Abbot, *Defence*, p.208; *idem*, *Second Part*, pp.762–3. The same thinking lay behind William Crashaw's *Mittimus to the Iubile at Rome* (1625).

28 LPL, Lambeth MS 3470 fol.196r. Note also William Bedell's anxiety in 1605 at the fact that 'none of us represses their [the Catholic writers'] insolency save Mr. Sutcliffe' (*Two Biographies of William Bedell Bishop of Kilmore*, ed. E.S. Shuckburgh (Cambridge, 1902), p.221), though for a more optimistic view (for Roman digestion), see Sir Edward Hoby, *A Letter to T.H.* (1609), pp.102–3. For further examples of concern at the effect of Roman polemical works, see Taylor, *Christs Victorie*, pp.685–6; John Gee, *The Foot out of the Snare* (1624), p.21 and appendices 1 and 2. This need not have been an alarm at the availability of Roman works in themselves, so much as their possible readership. Most puritan divines kept many such books in their own libraries. See below, ch.5 n.32.

29 M.C. Questier, 'The phenomenon of conversion: change of religion to and from Catholicism in England, 1580–1625' (University of Sussex DPhil, 1991), pp.35–8.

30 E.g. Francis Walsingham, *A Search Made into Matters of Religion* (St Omer, 1609); LPL, Lambeth MS 943 pp.383–8 (Wat Montague); Questier, 'Phenomenon', pp.100–1.

direct writers towards a tactical moderation in their argument. Some, admittedly, held that the poisonous abuse of papal controversialists meant that Protestants should respond in kind, and that the concession of any points which might appear favourable to Rome (however true they might be) should be avoided.[31] But even puritans such as William Perkins acknowledged that there was a tactical advantage to be gained at times by appearing more moderate and irenical than the Romanist opponent, and English Protestant pamphleteers in general showed an eagerness to deny all Roman Catholic accusations that the English government was guilty of persecuting papists for their religion.[32] It is notable that even thick-skinned Romanists were sensitive when anti-papal preachers occasionally seemed to go too far in their attacks and exceeded the norms of what was already an acrimonious debate.[33] As we shall see, it became commonplace under James to find high Calvinist divines paying lip-service to an ardent desire to come to a reconciliation with Rome in order to claim the high ground of moderation on particular points of controversy.[34] More pacific justifications of the separation from the Church of Rome proved increasingly profitable during James' reign as they were congenial to the king's own sensibilities and were increasingly necessary as Roman Catholic writers shifted the terms of the debate and concentrated on issues which required the defence of the continuity of the Church of England's institutional foundations and episcopal succession.

Certain polemical contexts inevitably required a more irenical approach, especially when recusants were being appealed to directly. Edmund Bunny, John Dove and William Bedell produced strikingly moderate accounts of the issues separating the Church of England and Rome in treatises aimed at enticing recusants to attend Church of England services. Yet all three also argued in print that the pope was Antichrist and were noticeably less

[31] E.g. Joseph Hall's remarks at the beginning of his *The Honour of the Married Clergy* (1621) that the insolence of his Romanist opponent meant that Hall would have been 'cruel to my cause' if he did not respond in kind: *Works*, VIII: 481. Also William Barlow, *An Answer to a Catholicke English-man* (1609), sigs.A1v–A3r and 'Admonition to the Reader'. On avoiding true points favourable to Rome, see Bodl., Rawlinson MS D.47 fol.15v (Daniel Featley to John Prideaux, n.d.); Henry Burton, *The Seven Vials* (1628), p.28; Hall, *Works*, VIII: 746.

[32] William Perkins, *A Reformed Catholike* (1634 edn), sigs.A3v–A4r; Willet, *Synopsis* (1600), sig.A4r–v. Cf. Barlow, *Summe*, p.51; George Downame, *A Treatise concerning Antichrist* (1603), ii. pp.67–9; John Prideaux, *Castigatio cuiusdam circulatoris, qui R.P. Andream Eudaemon-Johannem Cydonium seipsum nuncupat* (Oxford, 1614), p.166; Robert Abbot, *Antilogia adversus Apologiam Andreae Eudaemon-Ioannis* (1613), ch.6.

[33] John Brereley, *The Protestants Apologie for the Roman Church* (St Omer, 1608), sig.Hr–v, pp.2, 10; PRO, SP 14/81 fol.82r; Richard Sheldon, *The First Sermon . . . after his Conversion from the Romish Church* (1612), sig.A2r; Abbot, *Defence*, pp.204–5 (quoting William Bishop).

[34] See below p.345.

moderate in their other writings.[35] Whenever recusants were not being appealed to directly, they were generally required to attend English Protestant services, not because their own doctrines of the church required such attendance, but because they risked eternal damnation by adhering to their idolatrous and antichristian Roman Church.[36]

Clearly, some anti-papists were more flexible in their response to polemical challenges than others, but this did not necessarily imply any disagreements among them at this stage, and there seems to have been a general recognition that the varying tone of anti-papal pamphlets was appropriate to their differing contexts.[37] When Archbishop Bancroft was confronted by the wavering deacon Francis Walsingham, he recommended that he read pamphlets by the notoriously intemperate anti-papal polemicist Thomas Bell, but also advised that Walsingham should discuss his problems with the moderate-minded avant-garde conformists William Covell and John Overall.[38]

At certain times, however, tactical moderation in anti-papal controversy could generate alarm. Whenever the government sought to impose more rigid standards of ceremonial conformity or showed a readiness to tolerate recusancy, they thereby created among puritan divines the fear that individual Church of England ministers were being tempted into betraying their Protestant principles. In these circumstances there was more likely to be resentment and hostility if individuals employed tactically moderate language towards the Church of Rome. Thus William Bedell, an apologist

35 For explanations of these tactics, see Dove, *A Perswasion*, 'To the Protestant Reader'; Edmund Bunny, *A Briefe Answer* (1589), preface. Cf. D. Gaffney, 'The practice of religious controversy in Dublin, 1600–1641', in W.J. Sheils and D. Wood (eds.), *The Churches, Ireland and the Irish* (Studies in Church History 25, Oxford, 1989), pp.157–8. For their references to the papal Antichrist, see Bunny, *Briefe Answer*, pp.49–50, 116–17; William Bedell, *An Examination of Certaine Motives to Recusansie* (Cambridge, 1628), pp.13–14; Dove, *A Perswasion*, 'To the Protestant Reader'. The issue of Romanists' attendance became prominent in the first decade of the seventeenth century, not just as part of the aftermath of the Gunpowder Plot and Oath of Allegiance, but also partly due to the impact of the works of the Romanist writers Thomas Wright and Azorius, which seemed to condone attendance by Romanists at Church of England services: see J.P. Sommerville, 'Jacobean political thought and the controversy over the Oath of Allegiance' (Cambridge University PhD, 1981), pp.28, 28a; J.V. Gifford, 'The controversy over the Oath of Allegiance' (Oxford University DPhil, 1971), pp.61, 85.

36 John Davenant, *Determinationes Quaestionum Quarundam Theologicarum* (2nd edn, Cambridge, 1639), pp.124–7 (this was presumably delivered at the 1613 Cambridge Commencement, when Thomas Paske was respondent for this thesis: BL, Harleian MS 7038 p.89); Abbot, *Antilogia*, ch.5 (esp. fols.67v–68r); Willet, *Synopsis* (1600), pp.615–21. Puritans such as John Field felt happier adopting this tone even when addressing recusants directly: John Field, *A Caveat for Parsons Howlet* (1581); cf. Perceval Wiburn, *A Checke or Reproofe of M. Howlets Untimely Shreeching* (1581).

37 William Bedell, however, may be found in 1605 voicing his concern that Matthew Sutcliffe's 'too much bitternesse marres all': Bedell, *Two Biographies*, p.221.

38 Walsingham, *A Search*, pp.39, 49, 50.

for those puritans petitioning parliament for toleration of occasional conformity under James, complained that his tactical moderation towards the Church of Rome had been alienating his puritan friends, and he was to find himself constantly misinterpreted by his more radically minded colleagues.[39] For those divines more dedicated to a positive re-evaluation of the Roman Church, the jibe of 'papist' would never be far away.

THE PAPAL THREAT – HOME AND ABROAD

The contemporary regard for anti-popery was expressive of, and exacerbated by, the magnitude of the perceived political and military threat from the foreign Roman Catholic powers, and the fact that it was generally held to exceed the danger posed by dissenting puritans within the English Church. Concern for the international threat from Rome, and appeals for intervention in the confessional conflicts abroad, galvanized not just extreme puritans, but also Bancroft's successor as archbishop – George Abbot – and future bishops and royal chaplains such as Joseph Hall and Isaac Bargrave. The language of *ideological* conflict between the Protestant and Roman Catholic confessions employed vivid military images which easily lent themselves to literal applications to the confessional warfare abroad.[40]

There had been constant fears of a papal invasion from the continent during Elizabeth's reign, and such anxieties still sometimes flickered into life in the early seventeenth century – especially in the 1620s when England found herself at war with Spain and France.[41] The continental conflict with the forces of Roman Catholicism exercised a powerful grip on the imaginations of many Englishmen, especially as the Thirty Years War erupted. Even when England did not seem directly threatened, the palpable danger to the forces of Protestantism on the continent meant that many English minds continued to be preoccupied with the military confrontations. The

39 LPL, Lambeth MS 772 pp.42–3, and see below ch.4. For Bedell's appeals for toleration and forbearance in the aftermath of the Hampton Court Conference, see Babbage, *Puritanism*, pp.80–1.

40 Polemicists set the intellectual issues into a nationalistic, embattled context: see e.g. Richard Bernard, *Looke beyond Luther* (1623), ep. ded.; John White, *The Way to the True Church* (1608) – cited in Wadkins, 'Theological polemic', p.136. In the wake of the Thirty Years War and the threat of the Spanish Match, martial sermons became *de rigueur*, with preachers such as Samuel Bachiler reminding their listeners that 'Christ was not to send peace, but a sword'. English military intervention on the continent would thus simply be part of 'the mysticall warre ... against the Papacie': Thomas Cogswell, *The Blessed Revolution* (Cambridge, 1989), pp.296–7. Cf. Hall, *Works*, V: 228–9, 261–73; Richard Bernard, *The Bible-battells. Or the Sacred Art Military* (1629). See also Collinson, *Birthpangs*, pp.127–32.

41 E.g. Russell, *Parliaments*, pp.8, 73, 326.

English crown's personal link with the suffering Protestants of the Palatinate through the marriage of James' daughter Elizabeth to the Elector Palatine brought the conflicts of the Thirty Years War into every English parish church, where prayers for the Elector and his family were regularly read.

However, anti-popery in England was more generally preoccupied with fears of plots and conspiracies engineered by Romish priests and Jesuits at home, aimed at the deposition or assassination of the king as the only means of regaining the island for Roman Catholicism. In this respect, the Gunpowder Plot served merely to confirm and intensify long-established fears. It was this political threat from Rome which caused King James himself most anxiety, and which was the engine behind the Oath of Allegiance and the subsequent pamphlet controversy.

But if this apparent threat prompted a fear of subversion by imported priests, and especially Jesuits, at the service of the pope, it also provoked commensurate fears of the political threat from lay Romanists within England, who might provide a ready audience for the subversive doctrines of the Jesuits. When they were refuting papal authors anxious to stress the vitality of underground Romanism in England, it was not uncommon for English Protestants to downplay the internal papist threat and to talk scornfully of the tiny and inconsequential band of country papists who remained.[42] Outside this particular polemical context, however, fears of subversion by English papists were voiced unremittingly. Almost all anti-papal tracts appealed for the more stringent implementation of the laws against Romanists, complaining of the rise in the number of recusants.[43] Some made calls for the execution of all Jesuits and seminary priests, and the removal of all Catholic recusants from England.[44] This could lead to appeals for a ban on all forms of civil relations with Roman Catholics. These were aggressive positions, and were not shared by a number of moderate Calvinist episcopalians, but they were occasionally voiced by men such as Archbishop Abbot and John Prideaux, and so cannot be written off merely as puritan extremism.[45]

[42] Abbot, *Defence*, p.234; Matthew Sutcliffe, *A Briefe Examination of a ... Petition* (1606), p.91, argued that there were very few papists left in England 'except certaine stage plaiers, old women addicted to superstition, sely husbands overruled by theire wives and certaine Malcontentes ... that despaire to obtaine preferment'.

[43] E.g. Thomas Jackson (of Canterbury), *Judah Must into Captivitie* (1622), pp.41, 96 – cited in Cogswell, *Blessed Revolution*, p.30.

[44] Richard Bernard, *A Key of Knowledge for the Opening of the Secret Mysteries of St Iohns Mysticall Revelation* (1617), sigs.B2v–B8r; Taylor, *Two Sermons*, i. p.14; Henry Burton, *Israels Fast* (1628), sigs.A3, B1.

[45] Prideaux, *Ephesus Backsliding*, pp.24–5; Hall, *Works*, V: 11; Taylor, *Christs Victorie*, pp.332–42; Daniel Featley, *Clavis Mystica* (1636), p.175. On fears of Romanist subversion, see more generally Weiner, 'Beleaguered isle', esp. pp.36–44.

Nevertheless, such writings were rarely converted into direct and overt violence against local recusants, even after the Gunpowder Plot and the discovery of the Clerkenwell Jesuits. While fears of Romanist plots did occasionally arise, they were not severe outside times of general political crisis, and popular fears of popery did not necessarily translate themselves into distrust of known Romanist neighbours. The practical accommodations which people made on the ground found effective expression in those tracts which embraced a more tactically irenical line towards Roman Catholic recusants such as William Bedell's *Certaine Motives to Recusansie*, which defended certain forms of civil correspondency with those of differing religions according to a set of careful definitions.[46]

To many minds, however, Roman Catholic recusants were a manageable, easily recognized threat. The greater danger was held to lie among 'church papists' – those Romanists who occasionally conformed to the established church while yet harbouring a devotion to Rome. Andrew Willet remarked in frustration

> I could wish with all my heart, that all the Papists at this present day in England, were Recusants, that we might the better take heede of them. But it is to be feared, that there be many close Papists in England, that are content for a while to temporize, watching for an houre, which I trust they shall never see ... I would we had no such Romanists now in England, which faine themselves to be true Catholike Protestants.

Current research on Roman Catholicism in Elizabethan and Jacobean England is helping to vindicate Willet's fears, suggesting that a sizeable 'church papist' group did indeed exist in the population, its compromises with the Protestant establishment justified by a sophisticated body of casuistical divinity which permitted laypeople to conceal their Roman Catholicism as long as they still worked underhand for the long-term interests of their religion.[47]

The phenomenon of church papists generated fears of subversion of the Church of England from within by insincere Protestants. While English Protestants might have experienced sustained anxieties over the military threat posed to the forces of continental Protestantism, at home there were recurrent fears that a national conversion to Roman Catholicism might be achieved, less by military force than by the religious conversion of a national political hierarchy that was notoriously faction-ridden and fickle

[46] A. Dures, *English Catholicism 1558–1642* (1983), pp.83–4; Clifton, 'Fear of popery'; *idem*, 'Popular fear of Catholics'; Bedell, *Examination of Motives*, pp.2–7.

[47] Willet, *Synopsis* (1600), p.619; Dures, *English Catholicism*, p.33; A. Walsham, *Church Papists: Catholicism, Casuistry and Confessional Polemic in Early Modern England* (forthcoming); Questier, 'Phenomenon', *passim*. I am very grateful to Alexandra Walsham and Michael Questier for many illuminating discussions of this issue.

in religious matters. Persistent fears were entertained that a royal dynastic marriage alliance with a Roman Catholic nation might work a national conversion by relaxing anti-Romanist legislation and increasing the political advantages to be gained by conversion to Roman Catholicism. Concern that a political faction might work for the conversion of the country also dovetailed with fears that a 'popish' marriage could generate a royal heir who professed the Roman faith.[48]

This evaluation of the threat from Roman Catholicism both abroad and at home, and the consequent imperative of anti-papal activity, was generally accompanied by a parallel conviction that the problem posed by nonconforming puritans was relatively minimal. There was, of course, a certain amount of special pleading by the puritans themselves here. If anti-popery was already prominent in puritan theology, it did the puritans' cause no harm to emphasize this fact, whether they be presbyterians urging that a reform of church discipline would strengthen the Protestant position against Rome, or moderate puritans such as Willet attempting to find a home for evangelical Calvinism within the existing Church of England. This relative indulgence towards puritans in the face of the universal threat from Rome also found regular expression among conformist divines, who had less of a personal axe to grind. Most English Protestant divines writing against Rome during this period emphasized that the puritans shared all the same articles of faith as the Church of England and did not constitute a political threat. Apart from differing on a few minor issues relating to church government, it was maintained that puritans and the Church of England establishment were in fundamental agreement. Examples of divines maintaining this position are legion in the early years of James' reign, and include not only puritans such as Willet and Anthony Wotton, but also establishment divines such as George Abbot, Thomas Morton and Lancelot Andrewes, and anti-puritan pamphleteers such as Matthew Sutcliffe and Gabriel Powel.[49] Powel, writing on the instructions of 'some in auctoritie', assured his puritan opponents in 1606 that he regarded them as devoted to the king, although he implied that some more hardline conformists thought otherwise, commenting 'I cannot allow the opinion of such as give out, that these our factious Brethren, are as dangerous enemies unto the State, as the Papistes.' Nevertheless, Powel did stress that, while free of suspicion of treason and rebellion, nonconforming puritans were

[48] Questier, 'Phenomenon', pp.3–33; S. Doran, 'Religion and politics at the court of Elizabeth I: the Habsburg marriage negotiations of 1559–1567', *EHR* 413 (1989).

[49] See the passages cited in Richard Broughton, *Protestants Demonstrations, for Catholiks Recusance* (Douai, 1615), sigs.B1r, B2r, pp.64, 78, 97; Gabriel Powel, *A Consideration of the Deprived and Silenced Ministers Arguments* (1606), pp.10–11, 20, 21. Willet confessed in his *Synopsis* that he felt no need to publish arguments even against the Brownists, as the papal threat was comparatively far more important: see above, pp.18–19.

disobedient to the magistrate, and were guilty of impugning the king's authority and making a schism.[50]

'DISSENTING VOICES': HOOKER AND HIS DISCIPLES

As we have seen, Powel was right to note that some conformist divines saw the puritan and papal threat as an equivalent one. Many of the declarations which affirmed that the puritans were in agreement with conformist divines were made for Roman Catholic digestion. This was partly necessary in order to overturn Roman accusations that the Protestants were chronically divided and hence were no true church. Such declarations were also important in the early years of James' reign in order to refute Roman appeals for toleration, which insisted that the puritan threat was greater than that emitting from Rome. In fact, Roman Catholic pamphleteers claimed that puritanism differed from Protestantism in no less than thirty-two doctrinal articles. In Romanist eyes, puritan singularity not only demonstrated how divided the English Church was, but it also supported the argument that, if toleration was already extended to puritan heretics, then the toleration of another religion (that of Rome) would not represent a change of policy. The contingent necessity of opposing such Roman arguments is evident in the differing stance of Lancelot Andrewes, whose sermons display a decidedly less irenical approach to puritanism than that which he was forced to adopt in controversy with Cardinal Bellarmine.[51]

Other hardline conformist divines, less involved in anti-papal polemic, provided a more critical reading of puritanism. As we have seen, the rigours of the Admonition controversy had led some anti-puritan writers by the 1590s to claim that the threats from the two sides of popery and puritanism were equivalent, although men such as Bancroft and Sutcliffe were dedicated and broad-minded in their promotion of anti-papal works, and were concerned by the rise of apparently crypto-popish heterodoxies within the English Church. Nevertheless, the direct comparison of the puritan and papist threats became axiomatic of the new conformist orthodoxy under James. It was a point which the king himself regularly made, although he was generally speaking only of the purely *political* threat that puritans posed, and usually referred to doctrinaire presbyterians such as he

[50] Powel, *Consideration of the Deprived Ministers*, pp.10, 11.

[51] Powel, *Consideration of the Papists*, pp.8–9, 19, 123; Lancelot Andrewes, *Responsio ad Apologiam Cardinalis Bellarmini* (Oxford, 1851), pp.38–9, 161, 162, 291, 473–4, 486; Lake, 'Lancelot Andrewes'; Tyacke, 'Puritanism, Arminianism, and Counter-Revolution', pp.124–5. Cf. also Richard Hooker, *Of the Laws of Ecclesiastical Polity*, V, ep.ded., 3.

had encountered in Scotland, whom he equated with the Jesuits in their anti-monarchical clericalism.[52]

Moreover, the puritan campaigns for toleration in the early years of James' reign raised acute fears among a clutch of minor anti-puritan writers – men such as Oliver Ormerod, Richard Parkes and David Owen – who claimed not only that the puritans represented a *political* threat equivalent to that of Rome, but also declared that puritans were guilty of *doctrinal* errors.[53] Most of these stridently anti-puritan divines made it clear that popery still ultimately represented a greater collective threat. Oliver Ormerod followed his highly critical *Picture of a Puritane* of 1605 with the even more virulent *Picture of a Papist* of 1606, which included as an appendix a brief treatise entitled 'Pagano-Papismus', which undertook to prove 'that Papisme is flat Paganisme; and that the Papists doe resemble the very Pagans, in above sevenscore severall things'. Nevertheless, it is possible to detect new currents of thought developing, prepared to push further the anti-puritan polemic of the 1590s, and to question more fundamentally the relative importance attached to anti-papal activity. It was 1615 before this re-evaluation found clear public expression, when John Howson argued before King James that the puritans actually represented a *greater* threat to the status quo. While Howson yielded to King James' advice that he deliver more sermons against popery in order to display his allegiance to the English Church, he justified his relative neglect of anti-papal preaching 'because in my tyme there were never above 3 or 4 att once, that were suspected of popery, and there were 33 preachers who opposed them by sermons and disputacons: contrary wise there were ever 300 supporters of puritanizinge, and but 3 or 4 to oppose'. At the conclusion of his enforced sermons attacking the pope's claims to universal jurisdiction, Howson still managed to make clear where he thought the real threat to lie. Popery in Oxford, he declared, was 'eviscerated, unbowelled, and the heart of it broken', whereas the puritan error spread fast 'among the younger sort', who held positions as destructive of episcopacy as the papists' monarchical claims.[54]

But this was no mere reaffirmation of the importance of anti-puritanism.

[52] Fincham and Lake, 'Ecclesiastical policy', pp.170–1; King James I, *The Political Works of James I*, ed. C.H. McIlwain (Cambridge, Mass., 1918), p.126.

[53] Oliver Ormerod, *The Picture of a Puritane* (1605), ii. pp.23–5; Parkes, *A Briefe Answere*, sig.A2r–v; *idem*, *An Apologie*, i. sigs.¶3v, ¶4v; Broughton, *Protestants Demonstrations*, pp.69–70, 71–8, 98–100; David Owen, *Herod and Pilate Reconciled: Or the Concord of Papist and Puritan ... for the Coercion, Deposition, and Killing of Kings* (Cambridge, 1610), *passim*.

[54] PRO, SP 14/80 fol.175r; John Howson, *Certaine Sermons Made in Oxford* (1622), p.162; cf. p.159.

It is also possible to trace (among a minority of avant-garde conformist divines) the emergence of a more sceptical assessment of the innate value of opposition to Rome in securing conversions and retaining the allegiance of English Protestants. This diminishing preoccupation with the threat from Rome led these divines naturally towards a reassessment of the relative dangers posed to the Church of England by the forces of Rome and of puritanism. These were divines who were happier than most to go along with a non-confessional foreign policy, being more worried that the system of values at work in Jacobean anti-popery might be undermining the Church of England itself. This sort of questioning of the value traditionally attached to anti-popery, and omission of anti-papal caveats in the formulation of doctrinal statements, may be seen emerging in the latter stages of the Admonition controversy. Where some anti-presbyterian writers such as Sutcliffe had rushed into the fray against Rome as soon as their presbyterian foes were vanquished, men such as Richard Hooker lingered, and re-evaluated the emphases in English Protestant polemical writing.

Hooker had complained in his *Laws* of how 'they which measure religion by dislike of the church of Rome think every man so much the more sound, by how much he can make the corruptions thereof to seem more large'. He suggested that a constant preoccupation with the evils of popery and 'being in a fretting mood at the church of Rome' served no useful purpose, but rather created an 'angry disposition' which, having 'always one eye fixed upon the countenances of our enemies', created a fundamental imbalance in religious perceptions.[55] Among later followers of Hooker, we may detect an increasing wariness towards the dangers posed by anti-popery, and an unwillingness to recommend anti-papal polemical writing either to the pens of puritan authors or to the eyes of the larger public.

A concern with the effects of obsessive anti-popery was not in itself new. In its most extreme forms, anti-popery had always posed a threat to the Church of England. Radical puritans had focused their attack upon the popish remnants which they claimed were still at work within the ceremonies of the English Church.[56] Even when presbyterian divines chose to direct their hostility towards the Church of Rome rather than their native church, conformist divines in Elizabethan times had shown a willingness to pick and choose which forms of puritan anti-papal controversy they preferred. While Whitgift had been a dedicated patron of the anti-papal works of the moderate puritan William Whitaker, he was not prepared to allow the publication of anti-papal polemic by the more clearly presbyterian

[55] Hooker, *Laws*, IV, ch.viii, 2.
[56] Lake, *Anglicans and Puritans*, pp.17–21, 42–9.

Thomas Cartwright.[57] But while Whitgift reserved his distrust for his presbyterian opponents, under James some conformists expressed opposition to the anti-papal activity even of conforming members of the Church of England, not because it was directed against the Church of England, but because it supposedly undermined the established church's self-defence against Rome.

Hints of this new attitude can already be discerned in the way in which the divines of Oxford University responded to the puritan Millenary Petition's complaints of 'popish opinions' in the Church of England. The Oxford authors stingingly complained of those 'who are ready to make everything Popery which they do not fancy', and thereby (it was claimed) provided Bellarmine and others with weapons with which to reproach the Church of England. The flood of anti-papal polemic and satire which followed upon the discovery of the Gunpowder Plot also raised some concerns over the style of argument being employed. Oliver Ormerod complained that 'divers bookes printed against the papists are . . . fit for the fyer . . . and the publishers of such phantasticall bookes should bee hanged. Bookes are written by Protestants, and suffered to bee published, which bee a greate disgrace to protestant Religion'. Ormerod's own book was hardly less extreme and satirical than the rumbustious tract of the dramatist Thomas Dekker which he attacked,[58] but Hooker's heirs were providing a more sustained critique of puritan anti-popery, even when puritans wrote directly against Rome rather than the 'popish remnants' within the Church of England.

John Overall warned Convocation of the dangers of some forms of anti-popery in 1606. He made a point of encouraging divines to examine and refute individual Romanist arguments; this could be most profitable work for the church. It was important, however, that they should not produce refutations of Romanists 'ex privato cerebro atque ingenio', but instead, like the Romanists themselves, 'conjunctis consiliis et collatis operis in communi rem gererent'.[59] It was partly in order to ensure such collaboration and consistency in argument that Chelsea College was founded. Yet it was increasingly suggested by divines such as Overall that the analysis of the points at issue between Rome and the Church of England, like the disputes over predestination, was an area of theological complexity which could lead unsophisticated ministers astray, and should be left to experienced divines. As we shall see, this was due in part to the

57 Lake, *Moderate Puritans*, pp.59, 74–5.

58 Oxford University, *The Answere of the Vicechancelour* (Oxford, 1603), p.13; Oliver Ormerod, *The Picture of a Papist* (1606), sig.A4v. Ormerod was particularly aiming at Thomas Dekker's prose and verse tract *The Double PP* (1606).

59 CUL, MS Gg/1/29 fol.85r; Windsor, 'The controversy', pp.237–8.

increasing recognition that anti-popery could be expressed in ways which threatened to overturn the polity of the English Church, as well as the Roman. It was no longer an area into which radical Protestants' zeal could safely be channelled. Such radicals were more likely to impute to the Church of England doctrines which overthrew the reforms which the new breed of divines associated with the Durham House Group were attempting to implement.[60]

By the early 1620s, some hardline conformist divines were beginning to question whether the private composition of controversial works against Rome could still be considered to be a positive form of religious expression, rather than a potential front for seditious activity. This was certainly the case at the height of the unrest over the Spanish Match in 1622, when Walter Curll (later Laudian bishop of Winchester) stressed that it was neither necessary nor fit 'for every man in defence, or pretence of the trueth, to answer every dog that barkes with barking againe . . . it is but the distempered passion of some, to thinke the truth betrayed, except they write and fight for it'. While it was expedient in some cases to write in matters of controversy to justify the truth, this was only the case 'so it bee done in Season, with learning, gravity, moderation, and judgement'. There was no room for independent anti-papal writings: 'For he that enters upon the publike defence and maintenance of any cause, without necessity compelling, or authoritie calling him thereunto, is either contentious, or in danger to be contentious.'[61] By the 1630s, divines such as William Laud and Robert Shelford were emphasizing the need for extreme care and sophistication when venturing into the arena of Protestant/Romanist debate, and warning of the effect on the general public of the immoderate consumption of knowledge on such issues. Where Willet and others hoped to inform the people at large so that they would be able to refute papal doctrine, Shelford was struck by the fear that the people might 'wax proud . . . and will be moderatours between Papists and Protestants'.[62]

The emergence of more sceptical attitudes towards anti-popery was duly noted by puritan writers. William Sclater complained in 1610 at Paul's

[60] The works of William Ames against the ceremonies of the Church of England demonstrate that these conformist fears might in some cases have been well grounded. Ames makes frequent use of the anti-papal writings of moderate puritans and Calvinist bishops such as William Whitaker, John Davenant, Robert Abbot and Matthew Sutcliffe in order to oppose the new emphasis on signifying ceremonies: *A Fresh Suit against Human Ceremonies in Gods Worship* (Amsterdam, 1633), i. p.79; ii. pp.43–4, 176, 398, 434, 474.

[61] Walter Curll, *A Sermon Preached at White-Hall on the 28. of April* (1622), p.16.

[62] William Laud, *The Works of William Laud*, ed. W. Scott and J. Bliss (7 vols., Oxford, 1847–60), III: 325; Robert Shelford, *Five Pious and Learned Discourses* (Cambridge, 1635), pp.85–6.

Cross: 'what is become of that ancient detestation of Antichrist, and his corruptions? while we begin to thinke, we may separate too farre from Antichrist, as Antichrist; and to study . . . compounding of the two Religions: when as soone shall we compound light with darknes, Christ with Belial, as Christ with Antichrist'. Thomas Taylor noted in 1624 that 'Many are afraid to offend the Babylonians by departing too far from them', and in a work posthumously published in 1633 he observed that some people now complained of anti-papal preaching, and charged the ministers with ignorance or falsification of Romanist doctrines. He also remarked how some people conspicuously failed to join in those festivals of public anti-popery at which the nation's deliverance from the scourge of the pope was celebrated.[63]

Many of the reservations voiced against extreme anti-popery were emerging from the group of divines which would later form the basis of the Durham House Group, and typified their rejection of the importance of the evangelical Calvinism which underwrote the pre-eminence granted to anti-popery in the Elizabethan and Jacobean Church. It was this same stream of thought that had excited Willet's concerns at the turn of the century, and which he had labelled as 'semi-popish'. In Willet's accusation of 'semi-popery', however, we may see how far the anti-popery with which Willet hoped to unite the Church of England could also serve to divide it.[64] Jacobean forms of anti-popery could only encourage people to uncover crypto-popery within the English Church: a mere lack of dedication to anti-popery could be seen to imply it. As Dr Lake has demonstrated, the anti-popery which was so prominent a feature of moderate puritanism was also dedicated to carrying its anxieties into the battle over the intrusion of less rigorously Reformed doctrines into the English Church in the later years of Elizabeth's reign. In this way the moderate puritan anti-papal divine William Whitaker was anxious to hound out the singular Everard Digby from St John's. It was in his desire to label the views of Digby, and later of Barrett and Baro, as 'popery' that Whitaker found himself coming into conflict with Archbishop Whitgift, who granted 'popery' a far less elastic definition. As opposed to the puritan Whitaker, Whitgift required more concrete evidence of doctrinal heterodoxy rather than a mere unwillingness to endorse Whitaker's particular brand of hardline Calvinism and

63 William Sclater, *A Threefold Preservative* (1610), sig.C1v; Taylor, *Two Sermons*, i. p.14; *idem*, *Christs Victorie*, p.491.

64 This is not to suggest that men such as Willet could not see the value of occasionally refraining from such accusations. When anxious to prove his moderation and irenical intent against Parkes' accusations, Willet was forced to (quite falsely) deny having called any Church of England writers popish: Willet, *Loidoromastix*, pp.14–15.

anti-popery. The archbishop more generally limited the label of 'popish' to those who held communion with the Church of Rome.[65]

A preparedness to extend the label 'popery' to cover all non-Calvinist patterns of behaviour and belief may thus provide a useful yardstick for distinguishing puritans like Whitaker from conformists such as Whitgift in the Elizabethan Church. In the Jacobean period, however, this extended use of the term 'popery' can no longer simply be taken to be the puritan's calling card. Under James, prominent members of the establishment such as Archbishop Abbot and Joseph Hall used the term to brand the ideas and actions of the new breed of 'Arminians' such as John Howson and William Laud. Fears of indifferent and wary Protestants were not the preserve of puritan extremists. Dean Matthew Sutcliffe, the first provost of Chelsea College, directed his foundation towards opposition, not just to popery, but to those who might seem to be inclining towards it, whom Sutcliffe clearly understood to include the new 'Arminian' divines in the church. Sutcliffe declared the College's purpose to be 'for the practice of sound learning against the pedantry, sophistries, and novelties of the jesuits and other the pope's factors and followers; and against the treachery of pelagians and arminians and others that draw towards popery and Babylonian slavery'.[66]

England's 'Arminians' were certainly not involved in a disengagement from *all* the aspects of the anti-papal system of values outlined earlier in this chapter. Nevertheless, it is noteworthy that practically all those churchmen later prominent in the Laudian movement endured accusations of crypto-popery at one time or another in their careers, sometimes in the courts and even before parliament and the king. The accusations made against John Howson, William Laud, Lancelot Andrewes and Richard Neile are well known. Samuel Harsnett was condemned by parliament in 1624, but had also been accused of popery by his college of Pembroke in Cambridge. Harsnett's deputies at Pembroke, Thomas Muriell and John Pocklington (the latter a notorious Laudian pamphleteer in the 1630s), were both examined on charges of popery early in their careers. Muriell was examined in 1599 before the University, and before Archbishop Whitgift at Lambeth, on the charge of defending points of popery relating to justification and auricular confession, while Pocklington appeared before

[65] Lake, *Moderate Puritans*, pp.171–80; P. Lake, 'The significance of the Elizabethan identification of the pope as Antichrist', *JEH* 31 (1980), pp.171–5; Russell, *Causes*, p.75. Cf. Samuel Ward's remarks in *Two Elizabethan Puritan Diaries*, ed. M.M. Knappen (Chicago, 1933), p.126.

[66] Hall, *Works*, VI: 201–3; Cranfield and Fincham, 'John Howson's answers', pp.330–1, 335–8; Blunt, *Village*, p.131.

the University court on a number of similar charges in 1616.[67] It need hardly be emphasized that the levelling of such charges against them merely served to confirm the scepticism which these divines already felt towards the value and wisdom of contemporary anti-popery.

There was an obvious temptation for Sutcliffe and others to conflate their opponents' position with that of Rome. Yet the fear that even among Protestant ministers there were some who harboured popish notions, or whose doctrines were drifting towards the Church of Rome, cannot be dismissed as mere scaremongering, still less as merely the typical puritan response when faced with conformist piety. The first years of James' reign witnessed a number of well-publicized conversions to Rome among the more enthusiastically conformist members of the Church of England, including Humfrey Leech and, most notoriously, Benjamin Carier. Leech, who had been attacked by the later Calvinist bishop John King for 'playing with Popery', claimed those prominent 'Arminians' John Buckeridge and John Howson among his supporters at Oxford.[68] Carier, an ex-chaplain of Whitgift and friend of Isaac Casaubon, was a member of Bishop Neile's circle and had been a regular Lent preacher at court right up to the time of his defection to Rome. At his confrontation with Howson in 1615, Abbot claimed that Howson had been on good terms with Carier. In response, his opponent defended Carier's reputation and accused Abbot of having forced Carier out of the church. William Covell confessed to the wavering deacon Francis Walsingham his concern over the number of his own friends and relatives who were tending towards popery.[69] Moreover, Roman Catholics were often among the most influential supporters of the new breed of avant-garde conformists. Some anti-puritan ministers owed their livings to the patronage of crypto-Catholic laity, while Richard Montagu's cause was supported by the church papist Sir Thomas Riddell in parliament, and at court by the notorious crypto-Catholic Endymion

[67] For Howson and Laud, see above n.66. For Andrewes and Neile, see *DNB*; Tyacke, *Anti-Calvinists*, p.164 (Harsnett); LPL, Lambeth MS 3470 fols.209–12 (Muriell); CUL, MS VC Ct I.8 fols.255–8 (Pocklington).

[68] Foley, *Records*, I: 643; A. Davidson, 'The conversion of Bishop King: a question of evidence', *Recusant History* 9 (1967–8), p.250; Dent, *Protestant Reformers*, pp.234–7. Foley misread Howson as 'Houseman' – I am grateful to Dr Tyacke for advice on this point.

[69] Fincham, *Prelate as Pastor*, pp.46–7; Westminster Abbey, Muniment Book 15 fols.6, 34–9; Cranfield and Fincham, 'John Howson's answers', pp.335–6; Walsingham, *A Search*, p.41. On Carier's links with members of the Durham House circle, see also Fincham, 'Prelacy and politics', p.54 and n.97; M. Pattison, *Isaac Casaubon 1559–1614* (2nd edn, Oxford, 1892), p.277.

Porter and the Roman Catholic peers Lord Savage, the earl of Rutland, and the earl of Worcester.[70]

The accusation of favouring popery is thus a problematical one, and is certainly not sufficient to brand the accuser a puritan and the accused as either a traditional or 'avant-garde' conformist. When Archbishop Bancroft warned Oxford University in 1609 against broaching 'any opinions contrary to the receaved doctrine of the Church of England coming verie neare unto Poperie, albeit a little they seeme to mince and qualifie it', it would be unwise to assume that he was merely stretching definitions in the same manner as Willet and Whitaker. What is clear, however, is that he resembled them in being more concerned at divines 'playing with Popery' than were the future members of the Durham House circle.[71]

A further problem for the historian in assessing the significance of such attacks on 'crypto-popery' (for both accuser and accused) lies in the fact that, as we have emphasized, there *was* a significant crypto-popish element among lay members of the English Church. Recusants and so-called 'church papists' could not always be clearly distinguished: the phenomenon of occasional conformity often meant that the two categories overlapped. Alarm at the threat posed by concealed Roman Catholicism could be expressed in attacks on crypto-popish councillors such as the earl of Northampton, but also took the form of more general warnings of the threat from 'neuters' within the Church of England. These could be either those who were popish at heart but had conformed for mere political reasons, or 'swarmes of Atheists' of no particular religion but 'ready to take the strongest side', who were therefore only fairweather friends of the Protestant Church.[72] The regular complaints made by preachers such as Sclater, Richard Sheldon and Thomas Taylor that some members of the Church of England were overly irenical or moderate towards the Roman Church might as easily refer to the conduct and views of such genuine 'church papists', just as much as to the more low-key treatment of Roman Catholicism by anti-Calvinist Protestants within the Church of England.[73]

70 D. MacCulloch, *Suffolk and the Tudors* (Oxford, 1986), pp.210–11; Tyacke, *Anti-Calvinists*, p.147; J.S. Macauley, 'Richard Montague, Caroline Bishop, 1575–1641' (Cambridge University PhD, 1965), pp. 429–30; *The Correspondence of John Cosin*, ed. G. Ornsby (Surtees Society 52, 55, 1868–1872), I: 101, 103.

71 Tyacke, *Anti-Calvinists*, pp.63–4. While their testimony must always be used with caution, it is notable that Roman authorities also identified some 'crypto-popish' Church of England ministers at this time: Foley, *Records*, VII: 980, 982–3.

72 Taylor, *Two Sermons*, sig.A3v.

73 E.g. the passage in Taylor, *Two Sermons*, i. pp.29–30. For attacks on 'Neutralizers', see Sheldon, *Sermon at Paules Crosse*, pp.30, 49; Burton, *Israels Fast*, sig.B2v. See also two Paul's Cross sermons delivered in 1613 and 1615: Sampson Price, *Londons Warning by Laodiceas Luke-Warmnesse* (1613), p.24; Thomas Sutton, *Englands First and Second*

This was, of course, an ambiguity which made for an effective polemical weapon for dedicated anti-papal activists against the 'Arminian' faction.

It is therefore not possible simply to associate all complaints of crypto-popery with the emergence of a more moderate 'Hookerian' attitude among certain Protestant divines towards Rome, and a consequent devaluation of anti-popery. Nevertheless, the Jacobean period witnessed the emergence of increasingly distinct theological factions in the church, as Willet had feared at the turn of the century. Just as these factions became identified with different styles of churchmanship, as Dr Fincham has demonstrated, so too did differences increasingly emerge in the importance that the different parties attached to anti-popery.[74] These were personal and factional rivalries too, not always theological in origin, and the attempts to label some anti-popery as puritan (or lacklustre anti-popery as dissembling popery) were in part merely a polemical tactic aimed at undermining the position of a rival faction in the struggle for power and influence. Under James, this was a power struggle from which the victor had yet to emerge. Criticism of anti-papal writings would become more prominent and articulate under Charles, but for the moment the fortunes of both parties were at the mercy of political developments, and the shifting role that anti-popery had to play in them.

THE POLITICAL FORTUNES OF JACOBEAN ANTI-POPERY

Government favour and endorsement of anti-papal activity was not sustained during the early Stuart period. Whatever his sympathy for individual Romanists, James, as we have seen, retained an academic interest in anti-papal controversy throughout his reign. Nevertheless, however congenial James might have found such intellectual debates, he was not prepared to allow them to dictate his conduct of foreign or domestic policy, in which he was chiefly preoccupied with the purely political threat posed by popery in the form of the doctrine of the papal deposition of kings.[75] His fear of popery thus shifted continually throughout his reign in accordance with the varying political threat that it posed. As a result, anti-papal writing continued to flourish, but James was also tempted to patronize those anti-papal writings which were less likely to dictate direct political action, and hence did not threaten to stifle his freedom of

Summons (1616), pp.216–42. I owe these last references to the kindness of Alexandra Walsham.

74 Fincham, *Prelate*, ch.8.

75 This is not to say that his doctrinal objections to Rome revolved around this point: see below chs.2 and 5. The reluctance to let anti-papal excesses impinge upon diplomatic niceties was equally visible under Elizabeth – see, for example, the outrage caused by a pamphlet mocking Philip II in 1589: Strype, *Aylmer*, p.103.

manoeuvre. He hoped to achieve the safety of his person and crown in part by offering *de facto* tolerance (rather than *de jure* toleration) to moderate Roman Catholics who were prepared to swear the Oath of Allegiance. James was therefore keen to promote those tactically moderate writings which might persuade his Romanist subjects to accept the Oath in good faith. As a result, his court was peopled by both crypto-papists, and by the type of evangelical Calvinists who held strongly anti-papal ideas.[76]

Moreover, James had an even-handed view of the relative threats posed by Romanists and puritans, and frequently tended to equate the political (as opposed to the doctrinal) threat posed by the two in Bancroftian style. This led him to work in both cases to detach the moderates from the radical minority who alone were held to represent a political threat.[77] The early years of his reign were marked by rumours of possible toleration for either papists or puritans, and both groups presented petitions to the king to this end. Romanist appeals for toleration provoked a strong brand of anti-popery from many churchmen. These Protestant divines depicted the differences between the two churches in starkly polarized terms, and warned of the dangerous political and religious consequences of any form of toleration of what they claimed was a separate religion. In the vanguard of these pamphleteers was the redoubtable Andrew Willet, but he was also joined in the polemical attack by men more at the centre of the ecclesiastical establishment, such as Matthew Sutcliffe and Gabriel Powel. These pamphlets also strongly refuted Romanist claims that puritans differed from other Protestants in any substantial way compared with the absolute dichotomy between Protestants and Romanists, although only Willet's work accompanied this with an appeal for toleration for the authors of the puritan Millenary Petition.[78]

The Gunpowder Plot generated a new wave of anti-popery in tracts and verses which demanded the savage treatment of priests and recusants, but James struggled to dampen down the vehemence of this reaction.[79] While the parliament which passed the Oath of Allegiance in a package of anti-recusant measures probably intended it merely as another means of rooting out Romanist disaffection, the king seems to have hoped to use the Oath as a way of detaching moderate from hardline Romanists and of accommodating the former to the regime. The opposition to the Oath initially served as an incentive to further anti-papal controversy, and

[76] Fincham and Lake, 'Ecclesiastical policy', p.186. [77] *Ibid.*, pp.182–5.

[78] Willet, *An Antilogie*; Gabriel Powel, *The Catholikes Supplication unto the Kings Maiestie* (1603); *idem*, *Consideration of the Papists*; *idem*, *A Refutation of an Epistle Apologeticall* (1605); Matthew Sutcliffe, *The Supplication of Certaine Masse-Priests* (1604); *idem*, *A Briefe Examination*.

[79] Gifford, 'The controversy', pp.21–38.

James' determination to attack papal policies towards kings on the theoretical level meant that his reign marked a golden age for anti-papal polemic. Nevertheless, the defence of the Oath imposed on its apologists a tactically moderate line of argument, especially if the Oath were to serve the purpose which the king intended, and as a result increasingly moderate writers and styles of argument were employed. Here again there was conflict beneath the apparent unity of Jacobean anti-popery. On the one hand there were those churchmen who attempted to follow the king's path in making their defence of the Oath plausible to moderate Romanists. On the other hand were those divines who were keener to use the Oath as a way of attacking recusants, or were even more preoccupied by the fear that Romanists might actually take the Oath, and then form a fifth column within the church, immune from prosecution or further investigation.[80] The years following the Plot also saw the first examples of an increasingly critical assessment by English Calvinists of James' policy of practical toleration towards moderate Romanists – a policy which came under implicit attack even in Bishop James Mountague's preface to the collected edition of the king's *Workes*. By 1610 William Sclater was complaining at Paul's Cross: 'where is that ancient severity and strict hand over Papists? ... And who ever saw the fruite of lenity this way, that the number hath bin any more abated, and not rather increased by forbearance?'[81]

The style of anti-popery to which James lent his support thus varied over the years. He supported Chelsea College, but insisted on making his own appointments to the fellowship. He thereby ensured that a range of views would be represented there, as the appointees included avant-garde conformists such as John Howson, John Overall and even the imminent Roman convert Benjamin Carier.[82] The imperatives of anti-popery might occasionally be yielded to when political events dictated: James thus agreed to proceedings against recusants in 1604 in order to keep parliament happy and thereby increase the chances of its passing the Union treaty and the necessary subsidies.[83] Moreover, the assassination of Henry IV of France in 1610 greatly accentuated James' fears of papal assassination, thereby increasing the value to him of a dedicated anti-papist such as George Abbot and doubtless aiding the latter's promotion to the see of

[80] *Ibid.*, ch.4; Bernard, *A Key*, sig.B2v. See also below, ch.5.

[81] *The Workes of the Most High and Mighty Prince Iames* (1616), 'Preface', sig.e2r; Sclater, *Threefold Preservative*, sig.E1r; Gifford, 'The controversy', p.36. Cf. G. Lewis, *A Life of Joseph Hall* (1886), p.155.

[82] Faulkner, *Description*, p.225 (also included was Dr Peter Lilly, whom the convert Humphrey Leech had claimed as a supporter); Fincham and Lake, 'Ecclesiastical policy', pp.187, 189.

[83] Dures, *English Catholicism*, pp.40–2.

Canterbury.[84] After 1613, James' fears waned to some extent as he increasingly came under the influence of the Spanish ambassador Gondomar and of other crypto-papists at court. The Oath of Allegiance controversy also began to have more practical consequences, as the emphasis on defending the king's catholicity became the nub of the debate. It now became necessary to defend the Church of England according to a standard increasingly being dictated by Rome, thus making a more irenical line of anti-popery essential. This was a shift of policy which Abbot was careful to humour when necessary, warning William Trumbull to moderate his anti-papal language when writing directly to James. James' policy could still fluctuate according to parliamentary pressure and fiscal necessity, but by 1617 serious negotiations were underway for a Spanish marriage for Prince Charles, and the proponents of a less than full-blooded form of anti-popery began to gain the upper hand.[85] Here, traditional forms of court anti-popery were confronted with something that they could not simply bend and accept – namely the spectacle of the marriage of the future king to a heretic and formal idolater. This was a policy which James himself had counselled his first son Henry against in his *Basilicon Doron*, and against which conformist writers such as Gabriel Powel had offered dire warnings as early as 1604.[86] The particular problem was that this pacific, irenical policy towards the Roman Church was being pursued in the years after 1618 and the outbreak of the Thirty Years War, when the Bohemian crisis seemed to threaten the forces of continental Protestantism. In these circumstances, Andrew Willet rediscovered his political activism, and found himself imprisoned for his outspoken opposition to the Match and the king's related foreign policy. He was joined in prison, not merely by moderate puritans like himself who had previously made their peace with the regime, but also by conformist writers and royal chaplains such as George Hakewill and Thomas Winniffe, and even the provost of Chelsea College himself, Matthew Sutcliffe.[87]

In the wake of this agitation, and a potentially treasonous exposition of the political doctrines of the Palatine divine Paraeus made by John Knight in Oxford in 1622,[88] James issued a set of 'Directions concerning Preachers' in the same year. These attempted to curb the excesses of anti-popery by directing

[84] Fincham, 'Prelacy and politics', pp.40–1, 44–6. [85] *Ibid.*, pp.46–9.

[86] King James, *Political Works*, p.35 (although James does not mention idolatry); Powel, *Consideration of the Papists*, pp.21, 31–2. Even William Covell had implied that marriage to an idolater might be forbidden: Covell, *Modest Examination*, pp.200–1. Opposition to royal matches with Roman Catholic countries had been voiced throughout James' reign: e.g. *CSPD 1611–18*, pp.22, 149, 151, 465.

[87] Fincham and Lake, 'Ecclesiastical policy', p.200; BL, Add. MS 24275 fols.9v–10v.

[88] On this incident, see below ch.9.

that no preacher of what title or denomination soever, shall consciously and without invitation from the text, fall into bitter invectives, and indecent railing speeches against the person of either papists or puritans; but modestly and gravely (when they are occasioned thereunto by the text of scripture) free both the doctrine and the discipline of the Church of England from the aspersions of either auditory.[89]

While the message was clear, it is important to note that James was still careful to qualify his warnings against extreme anti-popery with a similar warning against anti-puritanism.[90]

As the handicaps of certain forms of anti-popery became clear to James, the king, as recent historians have demonstrated, was naturally driven towards 'those divines whose theology allowed them to endorse his foreign policy' and also the concessions to English Romanists which treaty obligations would inevitably demand.[91] Nevertheless, this argument should not be overstated. Although Calvinist divines were clearly less flexible, it should not be thought that they were simply incapable of countenancing the conduct of non-confessional policies. They were certainly aware of the political dangers of giving such an impression. A telling example of this point is the sermon given at Paul's Cross in 1623, at the height of the unrest over the Spanish Match, by Richard Sheldon – the hardline anti-papist and friend of Archbishop Abbot's chaplains. Sheldon, as we might expect, emphasized the duty of magistrates – especially if they had written against the Whore of Babylon (a clear reference to James) – to make war on her or else receive God's fearful judgement. Yet Sheldon was careful at the same time not to make it appear as if his brand of anti-popery would exercise a stranglehold on the king's policies. Indeed, he covered himself by explicitly leaving room for *raison d'état*, pointing out that the Christian magistrate might even offer toleration towards peaceable Romanists within his dominions 'for some high respects', if thereby he might ensure the better treatment of Protestants in other countries (which was precisely King James' own justification for such a policy).

But this should not lead us to equate Sheldon's position with that of the avant-garde conformist clerics who were happy to connive at the Match.

89 E. Cardwell (ed.), *Documentary Annals of the Reformed Church of England* (2 vols., 1844), II: 202.

90 Fincham and Lake have plausibly suggested that James' concern with the excesses of anti-popery may also have been prompted by the embarrassment caused him by the departure of de Dominis in the same year, as the archbishop of Spalato's main complaint was that anti-popery undermined any claim which the Church of England might have to moderation in its separation from Rome: Fincham and Lake, 'Ecclesiastical policy', p.203; [Richard Neile], *M. Ant. de Dominis . . . his Shiftings in Religion* (1624), p.72; *The Second Manifesto of Marcus Antonius de Dominis* (Liège, 1623), sigs.F1v–F2r.

91 Fincham and Lake, 'Ecclesiastical policy', pp.198–201; Dures, *English Catholicism*, pp.50–1.

Indeed, one of Sheldon's main targets in his sermon was those 'Neutralizers' who were adopting a more moderate and accommodating line towards Rome's errors. In Sheldon's eyes, if reason of state demanded toleration of Roman Catholics' persons, it was all the more important that the condemnation of Rome's religion should remain as clear and firm as possible, and indeed should be made all the more implacable in the face of such a pragmatic toleration. Yet it was precisely the upholding of the traditions of vituperative anti-papal polemic which was proving increasingly difficult in the last years of James' reign. Sheldon's sermon, like many other works, had to wait for the 'blessed revolution' of 1624–5, when war with Spain was again on the political agenda, before it could be published. So hostile was the official climate for anti-papal works in the early 1620s that Sheldon felt the need to preface another tract in 1622 with a lengthy apologia for any sections which might seem 'some what tart and pregnant against the errours of Poperie', emphasizing that charges such as Antichrist, false prophets, blasphemy and idolatry were not prompted by any spleen against particular persons, and 'will not seeme harsh, nor ill-sounding to the intelligent reader'.[92]

The Durham House prelates and their allies thus began to become more prominent at the centre of politics, as their own concern over the *religious* harm caused by anti-popery dovetailed with the king's reservations over its *political* disadvantages. In addition, their preoccupation with the puritan threat mirrored James' reawakened anti-puritan paranoia. At the time of James' death, royal patronage was certainly tending to favour this avant-garde conformist perspective on anti-popery, although anti-papists in the traditional mould continued to dominate the lists of royal chaplains and Lent preachers at court. Nevertheless, whatever his anxieties over the political consequences of extreme anti-popery, James clearly did not lose his purely intellectual appetite for anti-papal disputation in his final years, as his debate with the Jesuit Fisher in 1622 makes clear.

ANTI-POPERY UNDER CHARLES I

Traditional anti-popery continued to lose its currency under James' son. This did not necessarily always work to the advantage of individual

[92] Sheldon, *Sermon at Paules Crosse*, pp.41–3, 45, 31 ('30'); *idem*, *Christ on His Throne* (1622), sig.a3v. Examples of less tactful condemnations of the government's political expediency on religious issues are not, of course, hard to find: e.g. John Preston, *Sermons Preached before his Maiestie* (1630), i. p.16. Also, contrast Sheldon's remarks with those of Lord Saye in the 1621 parliament: *Notes of the Debates in the House of Lords ... 1621–28*, ed. F.H. Relf (Camden Society 3rd ser. 42, 1929), pp.6, 7. On anti-papal publications 1623–5, see Cogswell, *Blessed Revolution*, pp.40–6, 281–94. Robert Abbot's enormous manuscript commentary on Romans was later reported as having been a

English Roman Catholics. Charles shared with his father a readiness at times to allow political or fiscal needs to dictate his practical policies towards Romanists. He might therefore occasionally pander to those who argued for more confessionally based policies, especially in the early years of his reign when he was anxious to secure parliamentary support for war against France and Spain. Charles' reign thus saw a full return to (and indeed an intensification of) the fiscal persecution of Roman Catholics. Nevertheless, there was less confessionally motivated harassment, the Oath of Allegiance was rarely imposed, and there was an unprecedented toleration of Roman Catholicism at court.[93]

Charles was aware of the political danger of offering *de jure* toleration to Roman Catholicism, however. The early years of his reign witnessed in Ireland a storm of controversy comparable to that raised by the Spanish Match. The prosecution of war with both France and Spain required that Charles mobilize his Irish Roman Catholic subjects in order to defend their country. To secure their financial support Charles agreed to a series of concessions, known as the Graces, which offered security of land tenure to Irish Roman Catholics. During negotiations towards the Graces, Charles offered a limited *de facto* toleration to the Roman Catholics – a policy that was strongly condemned by the Irish bishops. They drew up a fiercely worded Protestation in 1626 in which they deplored the toleration of an 'apostatical' religion, and condemned the government for selling religion 'and with it, the souls of the people' for financial gain. The toleration of idolatry, it was claimed, would inevitably lead to divine punishment. The most outspoken advocate of the Protestation was George Downame, bishop of Derry, who had formerly been a prominent conformist author in the early days of James' reign, when similar arguments had been marshalled against fears of Roman Catholic toleration. Downame read out the Protestation in a sermon on 11 April 1626 before the lord deputy and 'the whole State', and declared that he feared no one and was willing to justify his actions before King Charles himself.[94] With the coming of peace the Graces lapsed, and a formal toleration was no longer likely. Charles displayed no anxiety to offer toleration for its own sake: it was the changing political situation that would dictate the fortunes of Roman Catholics under his rule.

While his policies towards Roman Catholics might fluctuate, however,

casualty of printing controls at this time 'because it was too sharp against the Papists', although purely commercial considerations would have been a powerful motive against publication: SUL, Hartlib MS 30/4 fol.82v.

[93] Dures, *English Catholicism*, pp.70–4; K.J. Lindley, 'The lay Catholics in England in the reign of Charles I', *JEH* 22 (1971).

[94] Russell, *Causes*, pp.56–7; A. Ford, *The Protestant Reformation in Ireland, 1590–1641* (Frankfurt am Main, 1985), pp.262–6; Bodl., Sancroft MS 18 pp.18–19.

Charles had none of his father's taste for theological controversy itself, and anti-papal controversy was certainly not popular at court after 1625. The ailing Chelsea College, now with Daniel Featley as its provost, received no support from the king. Charles refused to restore the College to its original purpose, and complained that 'too much time is spent on controversies which displease me. I would rather study were devoted to reunion'.[95] One Dr Moore testified in the Commons in 1629 that Richard Neile had reprimanded him over an anti-papal sermon that he had preached at court, the bishop allegedly remarking that 'You have pleased King James with some pretty passages agaynst Papists but you must not preach soe now.'[96] Thomas Morton clearly felt the pressure: in 1628 he was careful to explain, when dedicating a conventionally anti-papal work to King Charles, that he was in no way attempting to make the breach between Rome and the Protestants any greater, but was rather seeking to reveal and remove 'the onely Bar and Partition-wall' between them. In the same year, Charles' ex-chaplain Henry Burton complained that it was becoming impossible to have a work licensed against Rome 'but with some qualification'.[97]

This is not to suggest that Charles himself was wavering in his commitment to Protestantism.[98] Nevertheless, Charles clearly enjoyed the Roman Catholic cultural ambience and this, combined with his increasing devotion to his Roman Catholic wife, helped to create an atmosphere conducive to more moderate accounts of the differences with Rome. In 1635 Laud's ally, Richard Montagu, commented to the papal agent Panzani that, if he had known England ten years before, he would have witnessed such an alteration in the people's language and inclinations that he would not only have been led to hope for reunion, but would conclude that it was now near at hand. Sir Francis Cottington, in conversation with Panzani, similarly stressed the remarkable change which had taken place in England in recent times, commenting how previously people would turn away at the mention of Rome, but that now men were less bitter and spoke honourably

[95] G. Albion's translation (*Charles I and the Court of Rome* (Louvain, 1935), p.187) of 'Il Re all' hora replico queste parole. Questo non furo io, perche si e' studiato tanto interno alle controversie che mi dispiace; voglio piu' presto. che si studii per l'unione, intendendo S. Mta. dell' unione con la Chiesa Romana' (PRO, MS 31/9/17B: Panzani to Barberini, 20/30 September 1636). Father Philip confirmed this remark as being said in his presence, and exclaimed 'Non e questo assai ? non dimostra questo il buon' animo del Re ?'

[96] *Commons Debates for 1629*, ed. W. Notestein and F.H. Relf (Minneapolis, 1921), pp.50–2, 203. See also Neile's role in the case of Thomas Beard and William Alabaster: *ibid*., pp.59, 139, 192–3, 249.

[97] Thomas Morton, *The Grand Imposture of the (now) Church of Rome* (2nd edn, 1628), ep. ded.; Burton, *Israels Fast*, sig.B3r.

[98] For discussions of Charles' own religious beliefs, and his perception of Rome, see A.O. Meyer, 'Charles I and Rome', *American Historical Review* 19 (1913); M.J. Havran, 'The character and principles of an English king: the case of Charles I', *Catholic Historical Review* (1983), pp.199–208.

of her. The change in atmosphere was also noted by Father Cyprien de Gamache, one of the Queen's Capuchins, and the Jesuit polemicist Edward Knott.[99] All these individuals clearly found it in their interests to identify and emphasize such a change in attitudes, but the fact remains that, at least in court circles and among most of the Laudian clergy, anti-popery was on the retreat. The newly emerging priorities of Laud and his associates were now given full rein.

LAUDIANISM AND 'NEGATIVE POPERY'

More outspoken attacks on anti-papal extremism had already begun to appear in the 1620s. For the first time, some writers expressed a general distaste for religious controversy *per se*, in terms which included the Roman Church. Richard Montagu contrasted the mildness and brotherly love exhibited by the Fathers of the early church, despite their differences of opinion, with the temper of 'these our dayes of gall and wormwood', in which all was perverted by private interests and opinions. 'It is mens delight', he observed, 'to engarboyle the Church upon high termes of Heresie, Recusancie, Separation, most commonly for points of that nature and assise, which no way or advance or impeach salvation.' The needless controversies of 'our contentious times' led to a more general 'neglect and contempt of the Truth'.[100] While noting that 'the Roman Confessionists' hated Protestants more than Turks and Jews, Montagu also noted, as the apostate Archbishop Marc'Antonio de Dominis had done, that the Protestants did no better: 'the Protestant, to bee quit with him, doth in his charity and affection preferre a Mahometan before him, and will tolerate any, the most blasphemous heretick, rather then him. It is an ordinary Apothegme, in some mens mouthes ... "Better a Turk then a Papist", though the Papist beleeves all the Articles of the Creed.'[101]

Walter Curll, later a Laudian bishop, had expressed a general wish in 1622 'that there might not be so many bookes of controversies written as there are. For while men thus wrangle and print one against another, there

99 PRO, MS 31/9/17B: Panzani to Barberini, 11/21 May 1636, 21/31 October 1635; *The Court and Times of Charles I*, ed. R.F. Williams (2 vols., 1848), II: 332–3; [Edward Knott], *A Direction to be Observed by N.N.* (1636), pp.21–5.

100 Richard Montagu, *The Acts and Monuments of the Church before Christ Incarnate* (1642), pp.67, 383.

101 *Ibid.*, p.471; *idem*, *Apparatus ad Origines Ecclesiasticarum* (Oxford, 1635), p.282; *idem*, *Appello Caesarem* (1625), p.113. Cf. Shelford, *Discourses*, p.237; Meric Casaubon, *The Vindication or Defence of Isaac Casaubon* (1624), pp.29, 42. De Dominis also complained that an English divine had said in his hearing that it would be better to unite with the Turk than the pope: Neile, *Shiftings*, p.72. Thomas Goad claimed that de Dominis must have made this up, but the argument is made in Matthew Sutcliffe, *De Turcopapismo* (1599).

can be no peace in the Church.' He lamented that 'even Religion it selfe is in a maner lost in the quarrels and questions of Religion' and concluded that 'it were better for the Church, to want some trueth, then to have no peace'.[102] Curll's chaplain William Page maintained the brotherhood of all churches, and emphasized that men should set aside partiality and the names of faction and division, and rejoice in what they agreed in a general Christian concord. He deplored in general terms 'the manifold distractions of Christians about Religion, and the great fiercenes and violence used on all sides, every one thinking his own opinion truest, and consequently damning all others that differ from him'.[103] 'Are we not yet full with more then fourescore yeares bloud?' demanded the Laudian Robert Shelford. He saw no reason to quarrel with Romanists, given that they believed in the same Baptism and Trinity as the Protestants; it were better that 'Christians cover one anothers infirmities, and help each other, till Christ mend us all.'[104]

The same minority of writers began to display a more critical rejection of traditional forms of anti-papal polemic. James' Directions of 1622 had been principally motivated by fears of the *political* subversion which anti-popery might provoke in the wake of the unrest over the Spanish Match and the Thirty Years War. Under Archbishop Laud, restrictions on anti-popery represented a greater fear of the *religious* damage which careless writings against Rome might inflict upon the doctrines and discipline of the Church of England. Laud himself stressed the need for extreme care and sophistication when venturing into the arena of Protestant/Romanist debate, and one of the purposes of Richard Montagu's controversial pamphlet *A New Gagg* was to reject many of the traditional arguments used against Rome by English Protestant polemicists, and to focus solely on the official doctrinal formulations of the Church of England.[105]

In fact, Laudians even came to blame the excesses of anti-popery for an increase in recusancy. They maintained that extreme anti-popery discouraged conversions from Rome. Speaking in the 1640 Convocation, Laud partly attributed the increase in popery in England to the behaviour of ignorant preachers whose sermons charged Roman Catholics with tenets which they never held. Meric Casaubon, a dedicated member of the

102 Curll, *Sermon*, pp.11–12.

103 William Page (tr. and ed.), *The Imitation of Christ* (Oxford, 1639), 'To the Christian Reader' (unpaginated).

104 Shelford, *Discourses*, pp.239, 238, 240.

105 Richard Montagu, *A Gagg for the New Gospel? No. A New Gagg for an Old Goose* (1624), *passim*; Laud, *Works*, III: 325. Laud emphasized here that conversion was a difficult work, and that the church should not set every cleric to attempt it 'lest their weak and indifferent performance hurt the cause, and blemish the Church'.

Durham House circle and author of the prefatory epistle to the 1629 edition of Andrewes' *Opuscula*, complained vigorously of puritan anti-papists who put calumnies upon the Roman adversary and thereby betrayed a good cause and alienated Romanists' minds.[106] Indeed, in the decade before the civil war there is evidence among Laudian divines of an increasing unease with anti-popery. In their eyes anti-popery no longer seemed a positive form of religious expression, but rather was increasingly seen as a front for potentially seditious activity.

There was nothing new in criticizing extreme forms of anti-popery when their venom seemed to undermine and discredit the Church of England's polemical position against Rome, and even Calvinist conformists such as John Davenant may be observed making such complaints under puritan provocation.[107] From Whitgift onwards, the defence of the established polity and liturgy of the Church of England against Protestant nonconformity had set itself to counter extreme forms of anti-popery which led puritans and separatists to oppose elements of the Church of England's structure and worship which had in the past been abused to popish superstition. Laudian writers, however, took this trend several stages further. They more regularly invoked an anti-Romanist opposition against which they defined themselves, and which they saw as being directed against the Church of England's ceremonies.[108]

To Montagu, 'Puritans' and extreme anti-Romanists were effectively the same thing. The main task of his *New Gagg* and *Appello Caesarem* was the systematic rooting out of 'doctrinal Puritanism', which had intruded itself into the arena of Protestant/Romanist polemics. Humphrey Sydenham warned in a sermon *ad clerum* at Bishop Piers's primary visitation of Bath and Wells diocese in 1633 that violent forms of anti-popery in the Church of England could be a cloak for presbyterianism: 'There are some ... turbulent spirits in our Church, which are at such a defiance with the Romish See, that they are impatient of any other; and whilst they endeavour to dis-pope her, they would un-bishop all Christendome.'[109] Peter Heylyn, in his later biography of Laud, described how anti-popery was used as a cloak by the puritan faction for their nefarious designs: they invoked the threat from Rome in order to make the king anxious and to

106 PRO, SP 16/456/44: Edward Rossingham to Viscount Conway, 8 June 1640; Casaubon, *Vindication*, pp.21–2; DUL Shelfmark K.IV.34. I owe this last reference to Mr A.I. Doyle.

107 See Davenant's remarks in Hall, *Works*, VIII: 742.

108 Montagu, *Appello*, pp.112–13; Christopher Dow, *Innovations Unjustly Charged upon the Present Church and State* (1637), p.45; Christopher Potter, *Want of Charitie* (Oxford, 1633), i. p.75; Casaubon, *Vindication*, pp.10–12, 42–3.

109 Humphrey Sydenham, *Sermons upon Solemne Occasions* (1637), p.298. This collection of sermons is dedicated to Laud. Cf. Casaubon, *Vindication*, p.44.

distract attention from their gradual encroaching upon his authority.[110] It was this anti-papal smokescreen, rather than popery, which Heylyn dubbed 'the mystery of iniquity'.[111]

It was not just contemporary anti-popery which came under attack. Increasingly, Laud's supporters came to identify with the medieval Roman Church, especially when their seventeenth-century opponents seemed to adopt the policies of medieval heretics or of the iconoclasts of the early Reformation.[112] Early anti-popery in the Church of England's own reformation was criticized as overzealous and uncharitable by Richard Montagu, and by the Laudian pamphleteers Peter Heylyn and Christopher Dow. Dow depicted the early Reformation as the time of greatest heat and immoderation among English Protestant writers who unwisely asserted the pope to be Antichrist.[113]

In the 1630s, vigorously anti-papal language and arguments were not simply censured, but were also censored. Laud's chaplains William Heywood and William Bray, and Bishop Juxon's chaplains Samuel Baker and Thomas Weekes, were responsible as licensers in the 1630s for systematically purging large numbers of anti-papal passages from several books, most notably the sermon collections of Daniel Featley and Richard Clerke, William Jones' Commentaries on the Epistles to Philemon and the Hebrews, Richard Ward's Commentary on Matthew, and Sir Anthony Hungerford's *The Advice of a Sonne*.[114] Some deletions were clearly made because passages seemed directly to undermine aspects of the Church of England's established government and patterns of worship.[115] But there also seems to have been a more general aversion to the use of harsh and irreverent language towards Rome, even though such language had been the staple fare of English Protestantism since the Reformation. This distaste is clear in Bray's removal of a long quote from Guicciardini which attacked the lifestyle of Pope Alexander V. In addition, all four licensers purged passages which claimed that Rome's religion was almost all lies, along with peremptory references to Rome's idolatry, to the Romish Baal

[110] Peter Heylyn, *Cyprianus Anglicus* (1668), pp.50, 51, 93, 129, 178. [111] *Ibid.*, p.93.

[112] See below, pp.312–14.

[113] Dow, *Innovations*, p.53; Heylyn, *Cyprianus*, p.28; Montagu, *Appello*, pp.263–4. Contrast Robert Abbot's defence of the bishop of Hereford's burning of Roman crosses and pictures: Abbot, *Second Part*, pp.1125–6.

[114] William Prynne, *Canterburies Doome* (1646), pp.252–6. Prynne reports 210 alterations and purgations made in Clerke's sermons, while the alterations made to Ward's work were sufficiently numerous to fill two small written volumes.

[115] E.g. *ibid.*, pp.260 (the passage promoting a non-episcopal succession), 299 (against the necessity of building churches facing east and west), 301–3 (passages against the behaviour of courtiers), 314 (against holy days dedicated to saints).

and the Temple of Rimmon, the 'Romish Pox', the pope as Antichrist and the papacy as 'that drunken woman'.[116]

The licensers also removed lengthy critiques of the mass, and allusions to the Romanists' practice of 'bread-worship'.[117] These last examples reflect these divines' more general fear of the dangerous extremes to which anti-papal overreaction had driven Protestantism. This negative anti-papal reaction now threatened to frustrate Laudians' attempts to revive old ceremonies, to promote the beautification of churches and to re-establish a doctrinal balance in the church. In the short term, at least, it was necessary to place more emphasis on criticism of Protestant overreaction than on the Romanist errors that had provoked it. Thus Montagu was anxious not to condemn Roman Catholics' invocation of saints as impious, fearing instead the dishonouring of the saints which had become all too frequent in Protestantism.[118]

Further examples of the Laudians' reversal of polemical priorities are plentiful. When discussing the honouring of Christ's mother James Ussher, the Calvinist archbishop of Armagh, had felt it important to compile a detailed list of all the errors which medieval writers had committed in their worship of the Virgin in order to dissuade possible converts to popery. Ussher did this despite the fact that this undermined his immediate polemical objective of demonstrating Protestant continuity with the medieval past.[119] By contrast, however, Anthony Stafford's priorities were precisely the opposite when he published his life of the Blessed Virgin, *The Female Glory*, in 1635. While briefly taking care to avoid the profanity committed by those who offered idolatrous worship to the Virgin, thereby giving her the honour due only to the Deity,[120] Stafford's main concern was to counteract 'the Puritans'' neglect of the Virgin's honour, which undermined the worship of Christ.[121] 'Till they are good Marians', he claimed, 'they shall never be good Christians, while they derogate from the dignity of the Mother, thay cannot truly honour the Sonne.'[122] Given her importance, the threat of dishonour to the Blessed Virgin was actually greater

116 *Ibid.*, pp.252–3, 257, 258, 259, 260, 261–2, 264, 266, 271–2. Cf. Henry Burton, *A Replie to a Relation of the Conference between William Laude and Mr. Fisher the Jesuite* (1640), p.123. See also Wedderburn's claim that 'we' do not commend 'those, who fill their bookes with the narrations of the wicked lives of some popes and their followers, thereby to prove the pope to be Antichrist, and the Church of Rome Antichristian' (BL, Harleian MS 750 fol.71r).

117 Prynne, *Canterburies Doome*, pp.322–3.

118 Richard Montagu, *Immediate Addresse unto God Alone* (1624), p.66.

119 James Ussher, 'Answer to a Challenge made by a Jesuit', in *Works*, III: 496.

120 Anthony Stafford, *The Life of the Blessed Virgin; Together with the Apology of the Author* (1860), pp.lxviii, xxvi–xxviii, 9–10. On Stafford's background, see *DNB*, s.n. 'Anthony Stafford'. His 'Apology' is directed to Bishops Laud and Juxon.

121 Stafford, *Life of the Blessed Virgin*, pp.168–70.

122 *Ibid.*, p.170.

than that of idolatry. Stafford declared unequivocally that the profanity uttered against the Virgin by his opponent Henry Burton was actually worse than giving her 'that Worship I onely owe to God'.[123] Richard Montagu was more careful to refute some of the legends and qualities which Romanists attributed to the Virgin[124] but he also emphasized that 'much more doubtlesse doth belong unto her, the Mother of God, then some lewd, profane, and impious tongues and pens can afford her'.[125] Rather than wholly combating Rome's errors on this point, Montagu was more eager to establish that ideas such as the Virgin's impeccability were points for debate rather than *de fide* doctrines, and he stressed that the Council of Trent had not defined such ideas in formal doctrinal terms.[126]

Similar concerns may be seen in the treatment of the doctrine of purgatory and prayers for the dead. William Forbes, the Caroline bishop of Edinburgh, feared that English Protestants' opposition to the Roman error of purgatory had led them 'on account of the errors and abuses which little by little crept in afterwards' to abolish entirely the 'most ancient and universal custom' of prayers for the dead, 'to the great scandal of almost all other Christians'.[127] Forbes also claimed that many Protestants, including the moderate Calvinist Bishop Davenant, were too rigid in their opposition to the necessity of good works, while the arguments of some of them on the issue of merits ran directly contrary to Scripture.[128] On the matter of invocation, Forbes maintained that Protestants' rigid opposition to private addresses to saints ran a perilous course in despising and condemning the universal consent of the whole church.[129] He also claimed that Protestants had perilously over-reacted against transubstantiation in a way that threatened the doctrine of Christ's true presence in the sacrament.[130]

This repugnance towards the damage caused by anti-popery was simply one manifestation of a more general reluctance among Laudians to construct doctrines and forms of piety in simple opposition to Rome. Richard Montagu complained in his *Appello* that his opponents had charged him with 'negative popery' for not explicitly condemning some of Rome's errors in the points at issue. The term 'negative popery' thus coined by Montagu provides a useful shorthand to describe the phenomenon whereby Laudians deliberately refrained from attacking Roman errors when discussing matters of doctrine or ceremony. They thereby sought to

123 *Ibid.*, p.xxx.

124 Montagu, *Acts and Monuments*, pp.529–30, 535–6, 540–2; *idem*, *Apparatus*, pp.297–8, 301–11.

125 Montagu, *Acts and Monuments*, p.527. Cf. *ibid.*, p.530; *idem*, *Apparatus*, p.329.

126 Montagu, *Acts and Monuments*, p.533; *idem*, *Apparatus*, p.340.

127 William Forbes, *Considerationes Modestae et Pacificae*, ed. and tr. G. Forbes (2 vols., Oxford, 1850–6), II: 97.

128 *Ibid.*, I: 377, 387, 395, 445–7.

129 *Ibid.*, II: 265, 149, 225.

130 *Ibid.*, II: 425.

ensure that their ceremonialist message was not blunted by anti-papal qualifications. Montagu claimed that his 'Puritan' opponents, who had levelled the charge of 'negative popery' against him, built their whole religion upon such negative objections. '"Not to take exception"', he complained, was 'no Peccadillo, but a capitall crime with Puritanicall quick-silver Spirits, whose service unto God is performed by "taking exception" against all things that sute not with their fancy.'[131] Thomas Taylor may have been one of the 'Puritanicall Spirits' whom Montagu had in mind. Taylor had complained volubly in a sermon of 1624 of 'our indifferent and wary Protestants' who partook of Rome's sins 'by silence, and not professing against the Idolatry of Popery in doctrine or practise; when a man hath a calling in publike or private, and in not hindering it, so far as a man hath power or place; for qui non prohibet malum cum potest, facit'.[132]

We have already observed this tendency to avoid anti-papal discussions in the work of Richard Hooker. Part of the bewilderment suffered by the authors of the *Christian Letter* seems to have been caused by Hooker's failure to discuss issues such as justification, the eucharist and the like in the traditional way, by using the conventional terms with which papal errors were specifically rebutted. It was this failure to engage with Roman errors (even if they were not necessarily germane to his argument) which prompted his puritan readers' fears of 'semi-popery'. Even Hooker's friends George Cranmer and Edwin Sandys had urged him to make more specific rebuttals of the Roman position in Book 6 of the *Laws*, and it is not surprising to read Cranmer's report that the dedicated Calvinist conformist Robert Some complained more generally of Hooker's lack of perspicuity in his book. William Covell's defence of Hooker's work showed the same reluctance explicitly to deal with and refute specific Romish errors, preferring instead to leave Rome to be reproved by 'those, whom that businesse doth concerne, and to bee iudged by the searcher of all hearts'. Much of the controversy surrounding Andrewes' court sermon of 1600 on auricular confession may also have derived, less from any easily identifiable doctrinal novelty, but rather from the fact that a practice so notable

[131] Montagu, *Appello*, p.304. John Pocklington was similarly accused of arguing for 'Pontificial Doctrines' without any contrary conclusion to inform otherwise: CUL, VC Ct I.8 fols.256v, 257v; *The Petition and Articles or Severall Charge Exhibited in Parliament against John Pocklington* (1641), p.29. For an extreme example of such 'negative popery' in action, see the purging of Richard Ward's *Commentary on Matthew*, where at one point the licenser (Thomas Weekes) printed a quotation from a Jesuit, and then wholly expunged what Ward said against it, so that Ward appeared to subscribe to what the Jesuit affirmed: Prynne, *Canterburies Doome*, p.256. For earlier examples of 'positive anti-popery' in action in sermons, see Cragg, *Freedom and Authority*, p.170.

[132] Taylor, *Two Sermons*, i. pp.29–30.

for its associated Roman errors was expounded and encouraged without a single caveat or even allusion to any papal corruption.[133]

Complaints of burgeoning 'negative popery' continued under James, intensifying during the time of the Spanish Match when a readiness to forgo anti-papal caveats was more in line with government policies. In 1621 the stoutly anti-papist Daniel Featley, in his capacity as licenser, struggled in vain to insert more categorically anti-papal language into Edward Maie's discussion of the eucharist in the latter's controversial and possibly crypto-papist sermon, *The Communion of Saints*.[134] During the 1630s there was an even more marked tendency among some writers to omit the normal caveats against superstitious popish excesses when promoting 'the beauty of holiness' in church ceremony and reverence which had lain so close to Hooker's and Andrewes' hearts.[135] This was in acute contrast to preachers such as Joseph Hall, Jeremiah Dyke and John Brinsley, who in their consecration sermons had been careful to place exhortations (the 'spurre') to the repair of churches in the context of a severe warning of the dangers of popish abuses (the 'bridle'), and an overwhelming emphasis on the importance of the Word preached, and of God's spiritual presence in the Word and sacraments.[136] Even the anti-puritan pamphleteers of the early years of James' reign had been careful to place their defence of ceremonies within an anti-papal framework, and John Howson in sermons delivered in 1597 and 1602 had offered severe

133 Hooker, *Works*, III: 108, 112; Covell, *Just and Temperate Defence*, p.77; Lancelot Andrewes, *Sermons* (5 vols., Oxford, 1841–53), V: 82–103.

134 Sheldon, *Christ, On His Throne*, sigs.A3v–A4r, a2r. Maie had been chaplain at Lincoln's Inn for five years, but the Council of the Inn voted unanimously to dismiss him because of the 'scandalles and indiscreet passages' in his *Communion of Saints*: *The Records of the Honourable Society of Lincoln's Inn. The Black Books*, ed. W.P. Blaidon and R.F. Roxburgh (3 vols., 1897–1969), II: 179, 188, 224–5. For further discussion of this remarkable sermon, see below pp.199 and 351–2; see also my 'Means and motives in the licensing and censorship of religious literature in England, 1620–1640' (forthcoming).

135 See below, pp.72–7.

136 Hall, *Works*, V: 186–99; Jeremiah Dyke, *A Sermon Dedicatory* (1623). When the puritan John Brinsley preached the sermon at the consecration of the parish church of Flixton, Suffolk, he praised 'the decent beautifying of the places of Gods publique worship' and exhorted his hearers to repair the national scandal of the ruined fabric of English churches, admitting that 'in this case I should rather make use of a spurre then a bridle', yet at the same time was careful to maintain his 'bridle' by placing this appeal in an anti-papal context: John Brinsley, *The Glorie of the Latter Temple* (1631), pp.15–21, and *passim*. Also note Brinsley's explicit approval of the consecration of churches, and his attack on those who called it Judaism (*ibid.*, p.22) – evidence of just how far a puritan could go down the 'ceremonialist' track while still preserving the all-important anti-papal 'bridle'. Brinsley's sermon was clearly intended to display his orthodox credentials to the dedicatee, Bishop Francis White, in the hope that he would be able to gain White's support in his bid for the town lectureship in Great Yarmouth. For the background to this, see R. Cust, 'Anti-puritanism and urban politics: Charles I and Great Yarmouth', *HJ* 35 (1992), pp.19–20.

criticism of papists' excessive honouring of churches and observance of feast-days.[137] By contrast, when preachers such as Robert Skinner and Gyles Fleming exhorted their hearers to the repair of St Paul's Cathedral (Laud's pet project), no reference was made to Romanist abuses.[138] The 1630s might be typified as a time when it was all 'spurre' and precious little, if any, 'bridle', such that the nature of the bridle itself was becoming increasingly problematical. It was the danger of profanity and sacrilege which loomed largest in Laudian eyes. These priorities were summed up in an alteration made to William Jones' *Commentary* by the licenser Samuel Baker. Where Jones had written 'Let us not end in Popery, in Atheisme, in Brownisme, in Anabaptisme', Baker blotted out the word 'Popery' and instead inserted the word 'prophanenesse'.[139]

Not merely was profanity now seen as giving greater cause for concern than popery; increasingly, those who discussed church ceremonies but retained a traditional anti-papal framework found their motives questioned, and their works censored. Attempts in the 1630s to follow the spiritual emphases and anti-papal caveats of Hall's, Dyke's, and Brinsley's sermons soon ran into trouble. One Richard Spinkes found himself summoned and forced to recant a sermon delivered in Cambridge in 1632 which (among other things) emphasized the *spiritual* 'beauty of holiness' to the detriment of the *physical*.[140] Similarly, Daniel Featley found expunged at the press a whole section of one of his sermons which contained a typical Jacobean attack on Romanists' priorities, contrasting their superfluity in ceremonial worship with their lack of attention to spiritual purity. 'What meane our adversaries', he had exclaimed, 'to spend so much in embellishing their churches, and so little in beautifying their soules? to lay out so much cost upon the materiall, and so little upon the spirituall Temple of God?'[141] These sentences, along with many others, were removed by Laud's chaplain William Bray – an action which Laud himself fully

137 John Howson, *A Sermon Preached at S. Maries in Oxford ... 1602* (Oxford, 1603), pp.14, 15–16; *idem, A Second Sermon, Preached at Paules Crosse* (1598), p.30. See also the Lenten sermon preached by Daniel Featley before the king which maintained a similarly careful balance between attacking 'our Disciplinarians' who opposed the cross in baptism, and the Romanists who made an idol of the cross: Featley, *Clavis Mystica*, pp.156–9.

138 Gyles Fleming, *Magnificence Exemplified: And The Repaire of Saint Pauls Exhorted unto* (1634); Robert Skinner, *A Sermon Preached before the King at White-Hall* (1634).

139 Prynne, *Canterburies Doome*, p.259.

140 Bodl., Rawlinson MS E.148 fols.33r, 46v.

141 Prynne, *Canterburies Doome*, p.299. For a clear example of how literal interpretations of the 'Temple of God' were usurping purely spiritual ones in this period, see the example of Edmund Boldero, a fellow of Pembroke, Cambridge, who blotted out the last clause of I Corinthians 3.17 inscribed on a wall of his church (i.e. omitting the phrase 'which temple ye are' from the sentence 'If any man defile the temple of God, him shall God destroy; for the temple of God is holy'): A.G. Matthews, *Walker Revised* (Oxford, 1948), p.328.

defended at his trial.[142] Similarly, the 1635 edition of the Fast Book omitted a passage which had warned against the popish error of regarding fasting as a meritorious work. Laud defended this omission in the same way as he did the purging of Featley's sermon, arguing that there was little need for such caveats when there was rank contempt and scorn of all fasting in the Church of England. Besides, he added complacently, 'in this age and kingdom there is little opinion of meriting by fasting'.[143]

CRYPTO-POPERY AND LAUDIAN CAMBRIDGE

These priorities made the Laudian establishment more prepared to tolerate extreme crypto-popish utterances within the Church of England's communion. Laud and his colleagues were preoccupied more with what they saw as the covert threat to the Church of England from those who opposed these more exalted forms of ceremonialism, however doctrinally suspect they might appear. We have already observed how future converts such as Carier and Leech were able to find a home in the circles of Durham House figures such as Howson and Neile. In the ceremonialist drive of the 1630s, the dividing line became even more blurred between the doctrinal writings of moderate Romanists and those of English crypto-papists whom the Laudians defended. In their eagerness to promote neglected forms of worship the Laudians were prepared to make the Church of England's doctrinal boundaries increasingly flexible. This allowed them to incorporate more and more outspoken and crypto-popish defences of church ceremonies, on the grounds that the Church of England's official formularies did not explicitly renounce such views.

Cambridge in the 1630s witnessed the confusion and controversy which Laudian doctrinal indulgence could generate. The treatment of one Sylvester Adams, tutor to Richard Montagu's eldest son, is a case in point which deserves detailed discussion.[144] Preaching in Great St Mary's in June 1637, Adams argued from John 20.23 that confession of sins to a priest was implicitly required by Scripture as an act necessary to absolution. According to the account written by the Laudian master of Peterhouse, Adams maintained that 'without Confession then there can be no Remission of

142 Laud, *Works*, IV: 282. For the avoidance of caveats against the abuse of images in churches, see the example of Christopher Newsted, who as the rector at Abingdon blotted out texts of Scripture on the wall which showed religious pictures to be unlawful and had other texts put up: Matthews, *Walker Revised*, p.160.

143 Henry Burton, *For God and the King* (1636), p.142; Laud, *Works*, VI: 49.

144 For Adams' links with Montagu, see Macauley, 'Richard Montague', pp.405–6, 461. Macauley notes that Montagu appointed Adams vicar of Rudgwick in 1637, in the middle of the controversy described below. It is certainly possible that Montagu corresponded with his friend Cosin over the case, although no evidence of this survives.

sins, & without Remission of sins no Salvation, therefore in the iudgement of the Schoolemen & almost all antiquitie Confession was reputed necessarie both necessitate medii & necessitate praecepti'.[145] The non-Laudian College Heads – Samuel Ward, Ralph Brownrigg, Richard Holdsworth and Richard Love – attempted to prosecute Adams for this sermon (which clearly edged dangerously close to Romanist ideas of the necessity of auricular confession). The Heads deemed that Adams' sermon was 'scandalous and popish', and maintained in fact 'that many Papists said lesse, but none more'.[146]

Cosin strongly objected to the idea that Adams should make a public recantation of his views on confession, unless they could be shown to be 'directly contrary and repugnant to the publick and autorized doctrine of the Church of England'. The recantation drawn up by the vice-chancellor, Dr Brownrigg, did not attack the principle of confession to a minister as such, and it is hard to see where it differed from previous accounts of this issue delivered by Jacobean writers. It simply called upon Adams to reject the doctrine 'that speciall Confession of sins to a Priest was a necessary meanes (necessitate medii & praecepti) to remission of sins, absolution, and salvation', as being contrary to the doctrine of the Church of England.[147] Rejecting Brownrigg's proposed form of recantation, Cosin objected that the Church of England had nowhere *explicitly* denounced Adams' opinion. He maintained:

> that the Church of England in the 39. Articles where it condemned all the opinions & points of poperie, that he thought Mr. Adams or others are bound also to condemne, did not yet condemne the opinion that some men had of the necessitie of speciall Confession, & that the Book of Common Prayer seemed rather to give a man libertie to be of that opinion, then to condemne him for it . . . That this point had bin along while disputed in the Church, and was likely to be so still. That it was . . . the wisdome of the Church of England not to determine it; & therefore that it might be dangerous for us to doe otherwise, or at least to determine it under the name of the publick autorized doctrine of the Church of England.[148]

Cosin, and indeed Benjamin Laney (master of Pembroke) and William Beale (master of St John's), his friends and allies, did not necessarily share all of Adams' views, although in private Cosin seems to have come very close to them, as did some other divines at this time.[149] They were anxious,

145 PRO, SP 16/385 fol.137r. On Adams' case, see also Samuel Ward's account in Bodl., Cherry MS 23 pp.181–3; BL, Harleian MS 7019 fols.57–9; Prynne, *Canterburies Doome*, pp.192–3; CUL, MS VC Ct I.57 fols.60r, 64r, 70r, 82r, 86v, 87r, 88v, 90v.

146 PRO, SP 16/385 fol.137v.

147 *Ibid.*, fol.138r. See also the original recantation, CUL, MS VC Ct I.57 fol.104B, F–G. There is a copy of the recantation in BL, Harleian MS 7019 fol.58.

148 PRO, SP 16/385 fol.138v.

149 Cosin himself admitted that 'he wished many things in Mr. Adams and his Sermon amended' (*ibid.*, fols.138r, 140r). However, his views on the necessity of priestly absol-

however, that the drive to encourage private confession to a priest should not be hindered by any public recantation of errors on this point. Adams' liberty to believe that priestly absolution was necessary should not be impugned. Cosin's suggested alterations to the recantation would have rendered it scarcely a recantation at all, requiring that Adams merely deny that his opinion had a *certain* warrant from Scripture. He was merely to admit that he had expressed his private opinion on an issue which the Church of England had not previously determined. Adams would thus not have been called upon to declare his views to be erroneous.[150]

Ironically, this case illustrates the reverse side of Montagu's argument in the 1620s that Calvinist doctrines should remain merely as debating points in the universities, and should not be imputed directly to the Church of England. In the 1630s Cosin was applying the same principle with rigour to opinions which came perilously close to popery, freeing them to become points for general discussion rather than outlawing them in the name of the Church of England. Taken to its logical extreme, Cosin's argument would have denied that any point of popery could be rejected if the Thirty-Nine Articles did not explicitly renounce it – all such doctrines could now be considered to be matters indifferent.

In the case of Adams, however, some Laudians went beyond a mere toleration of such views. Some Laudian Heads were even less equivocal than Cosin in their support for Adams. Richard Sterne, the master of Jesus, said simply that the Church of England 'spake very much for Confession both publike and private, but he saw not where it had any where condemned it'. Edward Martin, the president of Queens' and always the extremist, saw no reason why Adams should be required to make any recantation at all. Both Martin and Sterne (both ex-chaplains of Arch-

ution would, in private at least, seem to have gone almost as far as Adams: see John Cosin, *The Works of ... John Cosin*, ed. J. Sansom (5 vols., Oxford, 1843–55), V: 163–4, where he seems to impose it as necessary, although elsewhere he recommends it rather than insisting upon it (*ibid.*, I: 97, V: 484–6; Cosin, *Correspondence*, I: 117, 131, 134; Cosin, *A Collection of Private Devotions*, ed. P.G. Stanwood (Oxford, 1967), pp.54, 235, 236, 240). The papal agent Panzani reported to Cardinal Barberini in early March 1635 that one of the English bishops, in a sermon before the king, had preached the necessity of sacramental confession: PRO, MS 31/9/17B: Panzani to Barberini, 6/16 March 1635. Jeremy Taylor was accused of teaching 'that a man cannot be saved without confession to a preist': BL, Harleian MS 541 fol.110v (I am grateful to Professor Russell for drawing these articles to my attention). See also the charges against Seth Chapman, rector of Hasketon, Suffolk: Matthews, *Walker Revised*, p.326. See also below, n.151.

150 PRO, SP 16/385 fol.140v. Cosin reports that he and Samuel Collins attempted to dissuade Adams from the questions which he chose for his BD Act in 1638, which were to be still on the subject of confession and absolution, whereat Adams took offence and decided not to keep the Act for his Degree (*ibid.*, fol.141r). Cosin's action need not be interpreted as an attempt to stifle Adams' views, but was more likely an attempt to avoid a further public controversy over confession, and possibly a forced recantation of Adams' views on the subject.

bishop Laud) urged Adams' release, rather than any more moderate form of recantation.[151] In this context, it is interesting to note that Laudian licensers also removed passages condemning popish auricular confession from a number of books, despite the fact that these extracts (like Brownrigg's proposed recantation) still allowed some forms of confession to a minister.[152]

Other traditional points of difference and controversy with the Church of Rome also came to be redefined in the Laudian Cambridge of the 1630s. On no point was this redefinition more striking than on the issues of justification and good works. John Tournay, a fellow of Pembroke, gave a sermon in Cambridge in 1634 in which he argued that works co-operated with faith in the increase of justification. He maintained that the Protestants did not separate faith from good works; rather, 'it is a Meere Scandall that lyeth upon our Church, we are noe such enemyes to good workes as the Papists make us'. The vice-chancellor Richard Love drew up a recantation, to which Tournay initially subscribed. This provided a careful qualification of Tournay's position in order to align it with more traditional Protestant expositions of this doctrine, denying that good works were a necessary *cause* of either justification, or of the increase of justification. The recantation also emphasized that, according to its treatment in the Thirty-Nine Articles, justification was by faith alone, although it carefully sought to balance this position by affirming that good works were required in the regenerate and were necessary to be done after formal justification. This moderate and orthodox recantation merely sought to distinguish more carefully Tournay's use of the term 'justification' in his sermon (as meaning the making more just of the inherent righteousness of the regenerate) from initial formal 'justification', which was by faith alone. But this was not enough for Tournay. He seems to have infringed upon this point again by arguing in his sermon *ad clerum* for his BD 'that we are justified in part by workes & by inherent righteousness'. When Tournay refused to provide Love with a copy of this sermon he was denied his BD, although this ruling was opposed by the Laudian Heads Laney and Sterne. Through the agency of 'good friends' at court, however, Tournay was able to secure a letter from the king ordering that he be given his degree.[153]

Other Cambridge preachers similarly flouted traditional distinctions on the issue of faith and works. John Normanton of Caius traduced the

151 *Ibid.*, fol.139r–v. Sterne was later accused of having tried to corrupt Jesus College and the University with 'the popish doctrine of the necessity of auricular confession to a Priest': BL, Loan MS 29/50/Bundle 74 (unpaginated). I am grateful to Ian Atherton for this reference. See also BL, Harleian MS 7019 fol.63.

152 Prynne, *Canterburies Doome*, pp.288–9.

153 BL, Harleian MS 7019 fol.53.

doctrine of justification by faith alone, but was pardoned by the Laudian Heads. William Norwich of Peterhouse was accused of preaching in 1640 'that not meere faith but workes doe also Justify us', but was acquitted by Doctors Cosin, Laney, Martin and Sterne, while one Mr Nowell, also of Pembroke, proposed as a Commencement thesis that justifying faith includes hope and charity.[154] The most striking example, however, was that of Eleazar Duncon, a chaplain of Bishop Neile and close friend of Laud and Cosin, who defended at the 1633 Commencement the thesis 'Bona opera sunt efficaciter necessaria ad salutem'. This was printed as an appendix in Shelford's *Discourses*, and was seized upon with enthusiasm by the Jesuit Petrasanta, and also by the irenicist Franciscan Sancta Clara for use in his ecumenical work *Deus, Natura, Gratia* as evidence of the proximity of English Protestants and Romanists on this point.[155] At the same time, Laud's and Juxon's licensers were busy removing passages from books which argued that works could not be in any sense meritorious.[156] Important shifts were also occurring in related doctrinal points. Anthony Sparrow of Queens', John Tournay of Pembroke and a Mr Howorth of Magdalene were all accused of teaching that concupiscence was no sin.[157]

The net result of 'negative popery', however, was not to redefine confessional boundaries, but to make them more fluid. As a result, it became increasingly difficult to identify potential converts to Rome. For example, one John Normanton of Caius delivered a rather eccentric sermon in January 1636 in which he praised the diligent fasting and penance of the Carthusians, and applauded the learning, humility and admirable lives of Baronius and Bellarmine, 'those two grave men of the Church of Rome', who had been exalted by God from their lowly beginnings as humble scholars. He went on to quote from Montagu's *Apparatus* in praise of Baronius, and affirmed (contrary to the whole tradition of Protestant polemical writings) the internal consistency of Bellarmine's works, citing the evidence marshalled by the Jesuit Edward Knott in praise of Bellarmine's devotional writings.[158] Just for good measure, he also traduced the

154 CUL, MS Comm Ct I.18 fol.130v; BL, Harleian MS 7019 fols.62, 61, 65.

155 BL, Harleian MS 7019 fol.65; Shelford, *Discourses*, p.120; Franciscus a Sancta Clara, *Deus, Natura, Gratia* (Lyons, 1634), p.159. Cf. Heylyn, *Cyprianus*, p.29.

156 Prynne, *Canterburies Doome*, pp.314–18, 328, 346–7. For an example of 'negative popery' on this issue, see John Gore, *The Way to Well-Doing* (1635) – a sermon which exhorts its hearers to good works without once warning against the abuse of popish ideas of merit.

157 BL, Harleian MS 7019 fols.60, 66.

158 CUL, MS Comm Ct I.18 fol.130; SSC, Ward MS F fols.23v–35r [from back]. Normanton declared in his reply to the charges that he thought that Bellarmine's controversies 'were as uniforme as yf they had beine written in one hower' (*ibid.*, fol.131r). Note also John Pocklington's praise of the 'virtuous and pious' Cardinal Borromeo: John Pocklington, *Altare Christianum* (2nd edn, 1637), pp.34–5. For more typical abuse of Bellarmine, see

doctrine of justification by faith alone, and ridiculed the tale of Pope Joan (which had been accepted by such scholars as Thomas James and Lancelot Andrewes) as a fable devised by the wives of the first Protestant ministers.[159] The Laudian Heads Martin, Laney, Cosin and Beale impeded Normanton's censure by the College Heads for this sermon, the last making him a university preacher. Cosin publicly declared that 'for any popery or propension thereto he discovered none'. Yet Normanton appears to have converted to Rome soon afterwards.[160]

LAUDIANS AND THE PROBLEM OF RECUSANCY

The treatment of John Normanton should not lead us to suppose that men like Laud were indifferent to the problem of conversions to Rome, or indeed to the need to proselytize. Laud and his colleagues did not simply feel a heightened concern for the damage which unrestrained anti-popery was doing to the Church of England. Rather, many of these divines were also sceptical of the value of traditional forms of anti-popery in dissuading potential converts to popery or in persuading Romanists to attend Church of England services. They also displayed a greater sensitivity towards Romanist criticisms of irreverence, and a more acute awareness of the need to meet such criticisms in a positive and practical way.

John Cosin laid out the plans for such a policy publicly in 1626, when preaching at the consecration of Francis White as bishop of Carlisle in 1626 by Bishops Neile, Buckeridge, Theophilus Field and William Murray. In

Abbot, *Second Part*, pp.5, 502, 980, 981, 1023, 1241. Even the saintly Isaac Casaubon was abusive towards the cardinal in his manuscript annotations: T.A. Birrell, 'The reconstruction of the library of Isaac Casaubon', in *Hellinga: Festschrift* (Amsterdam, 1980), p.64.

159 CUL, MS Comm Ct I.18 fol.130v. The Jesuit controversialist Robert Parsons had earlier claimed that the 'learneder sort of Protestants' thought the tale a mere fable: C.A. Patrides, *Premises and Motifs in Renaissance Thought and Literature* (Princeton, 1982), pp.171–2. For Thomas James' endorsement of the tale of Pope Joan, see QCO, MS 249 pp.511–20 (also *A Manuduction* (1625), pp.51–2). The story of Pope Joan was fully accepted by Lancelot Andrewes (Lancelot Andrewes, *Tortura Torti* (Oxford, 1851), p.261) and by Peter Heylyn in his *ΜΙΚΡΟΚΟΣΜΟΣ* (Oxford, 1621, p.105; Oxford, 1625 (2nd edn), pp.181–2; Oxford, 1636 (7th edn), p.183). See also Francis Mason, *Vindiciae Ecclesiae Anglicanae* (1625), p.469; Alexander Cooke, *Pope Joane* (1610); Powel, *Disputationum*, pp.274–6; SSC, Ward MS F fol.25v [from back]. On the fable of Pope Joan, see also Patrides, *Premises*, pp.152–81; S. Lawson, 'From Latin pun . . . ', *Sixteenth-Century Journal* 9 (1978).

160 BL, Harleian MS 7019 fol.56, reports that Normanton had since renounced Church of England orders and confessed himself a papist. Venn records that Normanton was deprived of his fellowship in 1639 after being cited to return from abroad, where he presumably converted: J.Venn *et al.*, *Biographical History of Gonville and Caius College* (7 vols., Cambridge, 1897–1978), I: 248. There is no evidence that Normanton became a Roman priest, or became involved in any way with English Roman Catholic communities abroad.

the presence of Endymion Porter, the countess of Denbigh, and 'many Deans and Prelates, with five hundred persons beside', Cosin lamented that

> We suffer scandal from them of the Church of Rome in many things, ... that we have a service, but no servants at it; that we have churches, but keep them not like houses of God; that we have the sacraments, but few to frequent them; confession, but few to practise it; finally, that we have all religious duties (for they cannot deny it), but seldom observed; all good laws and canons of the Church, but few or none kept; the people are made to do nothing; the old discipline is neglected, and men do what they list. It should be otherwise, and our Church intends it otherwise.[161]

The need to refute Roman criticisms of the decay of the 'beauty of holiness' also featured prominently in exhortations to support the repair of St Paul's Cathedral in the 1630s. Laud stressed that the Cathedral's decay was 'a reproach to religion, a shame to our nation', and beseeched the clergy, by their donations, to stop the mouths of 'them that say "Pater Noster" built Churches and "Our Father" pulls them downe or lets them fall down'. Gyles Fleming argued that the Church of England must build churches in order to confute Romanist charges of solifidianism. John Jones and Edmund Reeve similarly complained that Romanists constantly charged the Church of England with irreverence. Unless these objections could be met there would be little hope of converting recusants.[162] Part of the Laudian drive towards greater ceremonialism therefore justified itself as an attempt to entice recusants back into the church by a more reverent style of worship. Seen in these terms, the anti-popery of Chelsea College was clearly not the answer to the problem of recusancy.

Most pre-Laudian conformist writers had accepted the general point that puritan divisions and their spurning of Church of England ceremonies gave the Church of Rome an advantage by dissuading converts to Protestantism. Thus Thomas Morton, in his *Defence of the Innocencie of Three Ceremonies* of 1618, complained to semi-separatists in the Church of England that their 'divisions and oppositions against our Church' were frustrating attempts to win Romanists to Protestantism, 'being utterly unpersuaded to enter into a Church, where all ancient Rites are professedly rejected'.[163] Conformist writers of the 1630s, however, made more frequent and systematic use of this charge. They often recounted the story (reported in William Barlow's account of the Hampton Court Conference) of a

161 Cosin, *Works*, V: 96–7.

162 *Diary of John Young*, ed. F.R. Goodman (1928), p.98 n.4; Gyles Fleming, *Magnificence Exemplified*, p.39; John Jones, *Londons Looking Backe to Jerusalem* (1630), p.24; Edmund Reeve, *The Communion Booke Catechisme* (1636), p.132. For a typical Romanist attack on English church fabric and interiors, see the passages from William Bishop quoted in Abbot, *Third Part*, pp.169–70.

163 Thomas Morton, *Defence of the Innocencie of Three Ceremonies* (1618), p.168. For the background to this treatise, see Fincham and Lake, 'Ecclesiastical policy', pp.188–9 n.85.

French ambassador to the new Stuart king who, witnessing the ceremonial at Canterbury and at James' court, averred that if French Protestants had kept such orders there would be many more Protestants in France.[164] John Swan observed that, if the same ambassador could have seen the present state of English parish churches, he would have said the same thing with regard to English Protestants. There was no greater bar to the conversion of recusants, it was maintained, than puritan irreverence in worship.[165]

It was, of course, a handy polemical weapon for those defending the Laudian innovations in worship to claim that they aided the conversion of recusants. However, there is evidence to suggest that this may indeed have been a coherent policy. Laud certainly gave his personal backing to a work which offered this perspective as a major rationale of his ceremonialist policies. In his *Religion of Protestants*, William Chillingworth rejected the Jesuit Edward Knott's claim that the Laudians were preparing the way for a reintroduction of popery, and asserted instead that 'the governors of our church, more of late then formerly, have set themselves to adorn and beautify the places where God's honour dwells' partly 'out of a persuasion and desire that Papists may be won over to us the sooner, by the removing of this scandal [of irreverence] out of their way'.[166]

The campaign against anti-popery was aimed in part at effecting the easier conversion of recusants. The need to avoid offending potential converts was also cited by Laud and others to justify the omission of certain anti-papal sections from the prayer for 5 November in the Prayer Book. The removal of the anti-papal clause from Edward VI's litany in the Elizabethan liturgy (an act which even a conformist such as Hakewill regretted) was now cited as a precedent for the removal of further clauses likely to cause offence to those in England of a Romanist inclination, despite the substantial erosion of Roman Catholic forces in England since the early years of Elizabeth's reign.[167]

The policy of downplaying anti-popery in order to secure recusants' conversion was also consistently invoked by Laud's and Juxon's licensers in order to justify their removal of anti-papal passages from books. Thus Samuel Baker, in refusing to give a license to John Vicars' *History of the*

164 Barlow, *Summe*, p.38 – quoted in Samuel Hoard, *The Churches Authority Asserted* (1637), p.39; John Swan, *Profanomastix* (1639), p.7; Peter Heylyn, *A Briefe and Moderate Answer* (1637), p.175; *idem*, *ΜΙΚΡΟΚΟΣΜΟΣ* (Oxford, 1636), p.470.

165 Swan, *Profanomastix*, pp.6, 7; Matthew Wren, *A Sermon Preached before the Kings Maiestie* (Cambridge, 1627), p.18.

166 C. Hibbard, *Charles I and the Popish Plot* (Chapel Hill, 1983), p.57; William Chillingworth, *The Religion of Protestants* (1845 edn), p.23.

167 Laud, *Works*, VI: 53; Heylyn, *Briefe Answer*, p.158; Cosin, *Works*, V: 67; Heylyn, *Cyprianus*, p.18; George Hakewill, *An Answere to a Treatise Written by Dr. Carier* (1616), ii. p.9.

Gunpowder Treason, allegedly said 'that we were not so angry with the Papists now as we were about 20 yeares since, and that there was no need of any such bookes as these to exasperate them, there being now an endeavour to winne them to us by fairnesse and mildnesse'.[168] It was similarly alleged that Baker had refused to allow the publication of the recantation sermon of a former Roman priest, one Richard Carpenter, explaining that the Roman and English Churches were now in a peaceable way, and that it was therefore not fit to augment their controversies. In addition, Baker advised Carpenter to 'be patient, the time may come that you may be heartily glad that your sermon is not printed', and further instructed him to refashion his recantation sermon by emphasizing 'as a speciall motive for his conversion, the outward sight of order and decency in this church' and 'to say as little as might be against the church of Rome'.[169] William Bray, Laud's chaplain, was similarly accused of having justified his deletion of anti-papal passages from another book on the grounds that 'we were now in a faire way to win the Papists, and therefore we must not use any harsh phrases against them'.[170] Laud himself, it was claimed, had remonstrated with a Mistress Griffin, who was trying (at Prynne's instigation) to reprint Thomas Becon's *Display of the Popish Masse* and *Reliques of Rome* (printed 'cum privilegio' in 1560) 'why she did reprint this book against the Masse now, above all other times, and whether she could find no other time but this to print it?'[171] A desire to curb the excesses of anti-popery in this period also reflected the king's growing concern to secure the Roman Catholics' subscription to the Oath of Allegiance. In fact, the king was so anxious to promote subscription that he was prepared to negotiate with Rome for the alteration of certain passages in the Oath.[172] But the remarks of Baker and others seem strongly to imply that the Laudians were looking beyond this limited political goal.

A Laudian tract which addressed recusants directly also implied that more was afoot. As we have seen, some earlier writers such as William Bedell and John Dove had appealed directly to English recusants in order

[168] Prynne, *Canterburies Doome*, p.184.

[169] L.B. Larking (ed.), *Proceedings in Kent* (Camden Society 80, 1862) p.85. Baker's words to Carpenter may have been prompted by Laud. While Laud treated Carpenter with 'all fatherly courtesie' and secured a benefice for him, he 'advised him to carrie himself discreetly & prudently & words to that purpose': LPL, Lambeth MS 943 p.729. On Carpenter's case, see also BL, Stowe MS 743 fols.163–4; Kent Archives Office, MS U.350, C.2/53; U.350, Q.5. I am grateful to Peter Salt for the last two references.

[170] Prynne, *Canterburies Doome*, pp.252–3. The book in question was the late Sir Anthony Hungerford's *The Advice of a Sonne*, which was later printed at Oxford in 1639 without Laud's privity – an interesting reflection on the lack of co-ordination in Laudian book censorship.

[171] Prynne, *Canterburies Doome*, p.184.

[172] G. Albion, *Charles I and the Court of Rome* (Louvain, 1935), pp.245–87.

to persuade them that they might legitimately attend Church of England services. It is therefore not surprising that in the 1630s Richard Montagu devoted a manuscript tract to this issue.[173] While this was a sphere of argument which was always liable to prompt more tactically moderate assessments of Rome's errors, Montagu's tract is particularly noteworthy for the way in which it qualifies and diminishes the extent of the Church of England's separation from Rome. The master of Emmanuel College, Cambridge, William Sancroft the elder, complained in his annotated copy of Montagu's tract that the author had urged Romanists to communion in terms which would permit intercommunion by English Protestants in papal countries.[174] We know from the correspondence of the papal agent Panzani that Sancroft's concern was quite justified, as Montagu was indeed prepared to promote intercommunion with the Roman Church.[175]

However, the Laudian attitude towards recusancy was not simply one of a self-confident proselytization conducted in an untraditionally tactful way. They were also deeply concerned to prevent conversions to Rome, which were visibly increasing among the aristocracy and gentry. Laudians were preoccupied with Romanist accusations of irreverence precisely because they believed that such attacks struck home, and were responsible for securing conversions to Rome. Laudian writings reveal a deep-seated conviction that irreverence within the Church of England was driving Protestants into the arms of Roman Catholic priests.

The real dilemma for Laudianism was that those people most likely to convert to Rome on aesthetic grounds were precisely those who most strongly championed the 'beauty of holiness' within the Church of

173 CUL, MS Gg/1/29 contains two drafts of this work: 'Certaine Considerations touching Recusancy' (fols.97v–98v (from back)) and 'Concerning Recusancie of Communion with the Church of England' (fols.99v–102r (from back)). Another partial copy of this tract is in a commonplace book of William Sancroft the elder (Master of Emmanuel College, Cambridge 1628–37): Bodl., Rawlinson MS D.1331 fols.151r–153r. The Cambridge MS refers to Montagu as bishop of Chichester, so the tract must have been written some time between 1628 and 1637. Robert Baillie listed 'a little writing for the recusants, going from hand to hand in Cambridge' by Montagu among those works whose Protestant orthodoxy he doubted, and from which he composed his *Ladensium ΑΥΤΟΚΑΤΑΚΡΙΣΙΣ*: New College Library, Edinburgh, MS X15b 3/1 vol.2 fol.66v. I am grateful to Peter Donald for this reference.

174 'It is the same way from Rome to London, which is from London to Rome, why then may not a Protestant goe to the Popish Masse? or how will our common tenet hold, Non licet interesse Missae papisticae?': Bodl., Rawlinson MS D.1331 fol.153r. For a defence of this 'common tenet', see Davenant, *Determinationes*, pp.39–41. The same appeal to Romanist ideals, and many of the same arguments in defence of the Church of England's service which appear in Montagu's tract, are evident in Richard Corbet's arguments assembled around the early 1620s for the same purpose in Bodl., Rawlinson MS D.853 fols.172r–175v. Note also Corbet's specific appeal to the arguments of Azorius: *ibid.*, fol.175v.

175 PRO, MS 31/9/17B: Panzani to Barberini, 23 March/2 April 1636.

England. It was this section of the laity who, theoretically, should have formed the bedrock of support for the Laudian programme. Not surprisingly, then, Laudian writers increasingly maintained that those converting to Rome were not simply misguided, or traitors whom the Church of England could well do without, but were in fact those worthy appreciators of antiquity who were most needed in the English Church. It was generally argued that puritan irreverence was giving justifiable scandal to the 'godly and learned reverencing antiquity', who were then converting to Rome, and it was therefore urged that church affairs should be so ordered as not to give offence to 'good professors'. The use of the term is striking when it is remembered that these 'good professors' were yet prepared to waver in their allegiance to the Church of England and to Protestantism itself. William Quelch, in a sermon delivered at Bishop Neile's primary visitation of Winchester diocese in 1628, claimed that puritan contentions had caused 'good professors' to convert to popery. John Pocklington feared that irreverence might drive the 'godly' (a striking appropriation of the puritans' own self-appellation) to recusancy, and expressed his surprise that there were not yet more recusants. Laud himself complained that the decay of reverence in the Church of England was causing many conscientious people to waver towards popery, and told a later New England minister that their ignorance and railing made many papists.[176]

The flood of court conversions in the 1630s might have given Laudian divines, and especially Laud himself, justifiable cause for alarm.[177] However, the Laudians' heightened awareness of the Church of England's vulnerability in losing the allegiance of godly respecters of antiquity to the Church of Rome might be taken to reflect a more general anxiety that a regard for true antiquity might indeed draw 'the godly and learned' towards the Church of Rome rather than traditional Protestantism. This loss of confidence in the persuasive powers of traditional Protestantism hints at an attitudinal reorientation of the Church of England away from the Protestant bloc. The emphasis was now not on the liberating force of 'sola scriptura' to convert papists to the true religion, but rather on the need to sustain an elaborate liturgy and ceremonial sufficient to *rival* the drawing power of the Counter-Reformation in order to prevent members of the Church of England defecting to Rome.[178]

176 William Quelch, *Church-Customes Vindicated: In Two Sermons Preached at Kingstone upon Thames* (1636), p.14; John Pocklington, *Sunday no Sabbath* (1636), p.39; Laud, *Works*, III: 408; IV: 41, II: xvi.

177 See Hibbard, *Popish Plot*, pp.50, 55, 56, 61; Albion, *Court of Rome*, pp.193–215.

178 This is not to say that the Laudians did not operate their own forms of censorship on Counter-Reformation material. For example, while they were prepared to use bible illustrations derived from imported, fashionable Counter-Reformation models, representations of God the Father were altered – see G. Henderson, 'Bible illustrations in the age

Laudians never contemplated the possibility that their more elaborate forms of ceremonial, and their willingness to discuss Romanist ideas without the distortions of traditional anti-popery, might in fact tempt people into popish errors. Men such as Laud and Montagu attributed the increase of popery in England to the want of due reverence in churches, and to the excesses of ignorant anti-popery. Unpalatable Reformed doctrines were also held to blame: the Arminian Thomas Jackson suggested that the Calvinist doctrine of irrespective reprobation was a prominent cause of defections to popery.[179] By contrast, when ministers had noted a similar increase in recusancy half a century earlier, Secretary Walsingham had connected this rise with the insufficient provision of learned ministers to preach against popery, and the persuasive activities of Romanist priests. Under James, Joseph Hall focused on the same points as Walsingham when accounting for the increase of popery. He, and even John Overall, were deeply anxious regarding the dangerous availability of popish books and their role in conversions to Rome.[180] Yet the preoccupation of Laud and his supporters with the effects of irreverence and anti-popery came at a time when the reading of Romanist authors was clearly playing an important role in conversions. As we have seen, John Normanton, before his presumed conversion abroad, had read Bellarmine and found no contradictions in his works.[181] One Thomas Normington, a fellow at Pembroke, declared in his *responsa* at the English College that he had been converted around 1637 by his reading of Bellarmine, among other writers.[182] In fact, many Counter-Reformation literary, devotional and controversial works were commonly available in Cambridge in the 1630s.[183]

of Laud', *TCBS* 8 (1982), pp.173–216. Compare also Cosin's treatment of his material: Cosin, *Collection of Private Devotions*, pp.xxx, 353. The crucial point is that this censorship of Romanist material was not conducted in a public manner to serve as an edifying caveat.

179 PRO, SP 16/456/44; Thomas Jackson, *The Works of Thomas Jackson* (12 vols., Oxford, 1844), IX: 383. Bishop Montagu's 1638 visitation articles warn that the bread and wine should not be 'musty or unsavoury ... which beside the profanation, of my knowledge hath been occasion to some of turning Papists; who could not swallow it in disrelishment, and abhorred such negligence and contempt of Christ's institution in their minister': *Articles of Inquiry Put Forth at the Primary Visitation of R. Montague ... Bishop of Norwich* (Cambridge, 1841), p.83 (tit.VII n.11).

180 C. Read, *Mr Secretary Walsingham and the Policy of Queen Elizabeth* (3 vols., Oxford, 1925), II: 291; Hall, *Works*, VI: 245–51, V: 11–12, 401; Overall's preface in John Jewel, *Works*, ed. J. Ayre (4 vols., Cambridge, 1845–50), IV: 1311. See also above, pp.38–9.

181 CUL, MS Comm Ct I.18 fol.131.

182 *The Responsa Scholarum of the English College, Rome. Part Two: 1622–1685*, ed. A. Kenny (Catholic Record Society 55, 1963), p.46. Normington left England in the company of George Con, the papal agent, in September 1639. On his career, see E. Chaney, *The Grand Tour and the Great Rebellion* (Geneva, 1985), pp.236–43, 367–8.

183 T.F. Healy, *Richard Crashaw* (Leiden, 1986), pp.47, 59–63, 65. Contrast Ussher's advice to his students that they 'read no Jesuits at all, for they are nothing but ostentation and

Laudian sensitivity to the conscientious scruples of Romanist converts may be contrasted with the reaction of Calvinist conformists such as Bishop Davenant, who saw only secular motives in those fleeing to Rome, especially among those who took up the Romish ministry, thereby becoming Baalitish priests.[184] To Robert Abbot, such converts were 'but chaffe of light beleefe, [they] have but wanted winde to blow them out of the floore'. Laud's concern with this issue, and his gentle treatment of his friend Sir Kenelm Digby on the latter's conversion, stands in stark contrast to the letter which Joseph Hall sent to his erstwhile friend James Wadsworth in similar circumstances, and to Archbishop Abbot's cold contempt for the convert Benjamin Carier.[185]

Laudian writers seem generally to have been more conscious of the need to accommodate potential or confirmed Roman Catholics, rather than puritans or separatists, within the Church of England. Their determination to appease those at the popish margins of Church of England conformity may be compared with the readiness of Jacobean evangelical Calvinist bishops to bend the rules of ceremonial conformity in order to retain more radical puritan ministers within the Church of England's communion.[186] Both Laudians and Calvinists used the term 'the godly' to define those elements whom they feared might be alienated from the English Church, but they had very different groups in mind. To bishops such as Thomas Morton it was important that the godly zeal of evangelical puritan preachers should be retained and directed to serve the church. Laud and his allies seem to have been more ready to condemn the evils inherent in such occasional conformity. In their eyes, people who were not fully committed to the Church of England's structures of worship were a cancerous growth bent on undermining the church's polity.[187] If their obedience needed to be

never understood the scriptures': H. Kearney, *Scholars and Gentlemen: Universities and Society in Pre-Industrial Britain, 1500–1700* (1970), p.69. Laud seems to have been more concerned at the availability of the works of radical Protestant writers such as William Ames and Festus Hommius: Laud, *Works*, V: 254–5.

184 John Davenant, *Expositio Epistolae D. Pauli ad Colossenses* (3rd edn, Cambridge, 1639), p.409; Abbot, *Second Part*, sig.A3r. See also John Prideaux, 'A plot for preferment', p.20 in *Certaine Sermons* (Oxford, 1637).

185 Laud, *Works*, VI: 447–55; Hall, *Works*, VI: 128–31; *HMC Downshire* IV: 194, 331–2. Abbot was, however, alive to the propaganda value of regaining Carier for the Protestant camp: see M. Questier, 'Anti-Calvinism, crypto-Catholicism and careerism at the Jacobean court: the enigma of Benjamin Carier' (forthcoming).

186 See K.C. Fincham, 'Pastoral roles of the Jacobean episcopate in Canterbury province' (London University PhD, 1985), pp.230–41, 279–312; Fincham and Lake, 'Ecclesiastical policy', p.179.

187 For Laudian perceptions of an underground presbyterian plot based on occasional conformity, which would allow the Church of England to be undermined from within, see Montagu, *Appello*, pp.43–4; William Nicholls, *A Supplement to the Commentary on the Book of Common Prayer . . . To which is Added an Introduction to the Liturgy of the*

bought by a moderation in ceremonial, Laudians were more prepared to sacrifice them in order to retain within the church those 'godly' respecters of antiquity whose allegiance would be lost by such compromises in the splendour of the church's formal worship. Prynne's accusation that Laud 'will far sooner hug a Popish priest in his bosom, than take a Puritan by the little finger' was undoubtedly unfair, but there may be some truth in its general assessment of certain Laudians' priorities.[188]

This is not to deny that even the most hardline conformist writers of the 1630s could, on occasion, employ severely anti-Romanist language or, as administrators, preside over the rigorous enforcement of legislation against Roman priests and recusants. The reason for these occasional outbursts may be located in a fundamental Laudian problem of self-presentation. They wanted to remove the excesses of anti-popery which inhibited their positive emphasis on ceremonial worship, while at the same time they needed to protect themselves against accusations that their reforms were simply a plot to reintroduce popery. The charge of popery was one which was constantly raised against Laudian innovations, and it was one which threatened to undermine their whole programme.

In this context, nothing could be more fatal to the Laudian cause than the conversion to Rome of figures closely associated with their faction. It is thus not surprising to read of the vehement anti-Romanist remarks that Richard Montagu and John Cosin reportedly made when they failed to prevent Lady Falkland's conversion to Rome. Montagu was alleged to have told her 'that dying an English papist, she died in the state of damnation', while Cosin had added 'that she had sinned damnably in departing from that Church wherein she was born and baptized, before she had consulted with the governors thereof'.[189] The reporter of this incident, however, offered a cogent explanation of the rationale behind these words. He commented that 'Mr. Mountague, Mr. Coosens, and the college, as it is called, at Durham-house, are sensible of the disgrace which they sustain by reason of her [Lady Falkland's] fall.'[190] It was this sensitivity which accounted for the vehemence of their language, although their general argument was consistent with Laudians' emphasis on the importance of

Church of England (1711), p.20. This brief tract (bound in LPL, Lambeth MS 731) may have been composed by Heylyn: see Milton, 'Laudians', p.148 n.121.

188 Laud, *Works*, IV: 496. Note also the Laudians' refusal to accept the good faith of those who opposed their innovations. Eleazar Duncon argued that those who accused him of sacrilege and idolatry for bowing towards the altar did so 'I verily believe against the sense of their own conscience': Eleazar Duncon, *Of Worshipping God towards the Altar*, ed. and tr. 'J.D.' (1660), p.7. See also Howson, *Certaine Sermons*, pp.162–3.

189 Ussher, *Works*, XV: 356–7. 190 *Ibid.*

obedience to the national church and the heinousness of separation from it.[191]

The need to defend themselves against charges of popery could provoke Laudians into launching strong attacks on Roman Catholic errors. When Bishop Neile needed to vindicate himself from charges of popery in the 1620s, he prepared a speech for the 1629 parliament which was implacable in its condemnation of the Church of Rome, and its rejection of the mass, transubstantiation, idolatry, purgatory, 'merit of Workes' and the abuse of confession. Neile also drew attention to his earlier condemnation of the apostate Archbishop de Dominis, his activities in bringing recusants before the courts and especially his actions at Durham House in stopping the attendance of recusants at mass with the French ambassador in the 1620s.[192] A similar concern presumably inspired Francis White and Laud in their sermons at court on Christmas Day 1632, when it was reported that they 'made sharp invectives against some points of popery'.[193]

Archbishop Laud himself could be particularly sensitive to the need to defend himself against charges of crypto-popery. Amid a crushing administrative burden in the later 1630s, Laud still found time to edit for publication a revised version of his *Relation of a Conference* with Fisher the Jesuit as a way of demonstrating his Protestant zeal (he stressed that he himself had no appetite for religious controversy), although this was too late to save him from suffering the indignity of having his anti-papal tract refuted from the Protestant side, by Henry Burton. As chancellor of Oxford University in the 1630s, Laud was especially anxious that all copies of an English translation of a book of devotion written by the Jesuit Francis de Sales should be seized and publicly burnt, and that the few dispersed copies should be swiftly traced and destroyed. The intensity of Laud's reaction was doutless due to the fact that the book had been licensed by his chaplain, William Heywood, who had marked various passages for omission – omissions which had subsequently been inserted in the printed copy. Laud's primary fear was not that readers of de Sales' unexpurgated work would be converted to popery, but that he himself might in some way be associated with the printing of it, as indeed happened at his trial.[194] Laud

[191] See also Montagu, *Articles*, tit.IV n.15, which states that both Protestant and papist recusants are in schism and 'in that state be in hazard of salvation' (p.58).

[192] Durham Dean and Chapter Library, Hunter MS 67/14.

[193] *Court and Times of Charles I*, II: 213–14.

[194] Laud, *Works*, V: 166–7, cf. IV: 286–8. Laud's instructions to the chancellor of Oxford were written ten days before he secured an official proclamation recalling the de Sales volume. The official proclamation is printed in *A Bibliography of Royal Proclamations 1485–1714*, ed. R. Steele (2 vols., Oxford, 1910), I: 210. On Heywood's licensing of the work see also *The Petition and Articles Exhibited in Parliament against Doctor Heywood* (1641), pp.1, 3–5; and Heywood's account in R.M., *An Answer to a Lawless*

was similarly anxious in 1637 and 1639 to urge his vice-chancellor to respond swiftly to reports that the Jesuits were active in the University, seducing youths to popery.[195] Self-defence was again an important motive. As Laud explained, 'This falls out very unhappily, not only for the thing itself, which ought by all means to be prevented; but also for the clamours which the late libellers have made that there are great endeavours for re-introducing popery.'[196]

As opposition to Laudianism grew in the later 1630s, and with the unrest in Scotland, it became imperative for Laud to curb the increasing number of conversions to Rome at court and to clear himself from accusations of Romanist sympathies.[197] He was deeply aware of the unpopularity of his church programme, and diligently collected the growing number of libels circulating which accused him of crypto-popery.[198] After Lord Newport complained directly to him of his wife's conversion, Laud raised the problem of court conversions at a Privy Council meeting in October 1637, and secured the passage of a Royal Proclamation against conversions in December of the same year.[199]

Other of Laud's associates showed themselves to be resolute opponents of recusancy. Bishop Warner joined Laud in signing a very severe warrant against papists and popery from the High Commission Court to all Justices of the Peace, mayors and sheriffs in July 1640. Bishop Juxon similarly sent a letter to JPs in Cornwall requiring the indictment and conviction of all popish recusants in the county who had not already been prosecuted. In March 1637, just before the storm broke over de Sales' *Introduction to the Devout Life*, Laud's chaplain William Heywood, with others of his London parish, petitioned the Privy Council for action against the increase

Pamphlet (1641), pp.12–14, 15–17. See also Bodl., Rawlinson MS D.831 fol.113r; CUL, VC Ct I.57 fols.43–4.

195 Laud, *Works*, V: 180–1, 215.

196 *Ibid.*, V: 181.

197 Hibbard, *Popish Plot*, pp.60–4; Albion, *Court of Rome*, pp.217–31. This is not to argue that all manifestations of Laudian anti-popery were purely attempts to defuse puritan criticism, as Father Philip and Richard Montagu claimed: PRO, MS 31/9/17B: Panzani to Barberini, 10/20 June 1635, 11/21 May 1636.

198 E.g. PRO, SP 16/267/89; 453/96; 454/42; 456/36; 459/69. See also Laud, *Works*, VII: 269; BL, Add. MS 35331 fol.73v.

199 For the text of the Proclamation, see Albion, *Court of Rome*, Appendix VI pp.415–16. For Laud's sponsoring of other proclamations and proposals against Romanist proselytizing, see Hibbard, *Popish Plot*, pp.58, 61–2. By early 1640 even John Cosin was moving against crypto-popery in his own college. See his very swift moves to examine the crypto-papist (and later convert) fellow of Peterhouse Richard Nicholls in the Vice-Chancellor's Court, and his close personal interest in the examination and subsequent recantation: CUL, VC Ct. I.57 fols.206–12. In August of the same year Bishop Wren moved swiftly to warn Laud that the printed version of the Oath attached to the 1640 canons omitted the word 'popish' from the phrase 'any Popish doctrine contrary to that which is so established': PRO, SP 16/464/13.

of Romanists in the parish, listing many of his parishioners as having been 'perverted' into adhering to the Roman Church.[200]

However, such strong opposition to recusancy and to Jesuit proselytizing on the part of some Laudians should not simply be understood as an attempt to deflect accusations of crypto-popery. On a more fundamental level, Roman Catholic recusants represented a denial of the legitimacy and integrity of the Laudian church. However moderate their position might be towards the Roman Church, the Laudians would therefore still have had little sympathy for recusants who were ultimately just another type of native separatist, rejecting the authority and communion of their native established church. Nevertheless, some Laudians undoubtedly endorsed the attempts of men such as Secretary Windebank to limit the activities of the pursuivants. Richard Montagu, indeed, felt insulted by the suggestion that he had acted against recusants, complaining to Windebank 'you never knew me such a zealot against Roman Catholics'.[201] Moreover, even the more zealous anti-recusant views expressed by some Laudians were hardly comparable to the opinions of men such as John Prideaux, who warned against any mere civility to papists, and exhorted his audiences 'if . . . thou bee on our side, tumble out the Romane Jezebel at the window, howsoever shee be painted. Babylons Brats must not be dandled, but dasht against the stones.'[202]

A few Laudians, however, were ready to vary not just the intensity, but even the very nature of their attack upon the Church of Rome's doctrines according to the need to defend themselves against charges of popery. The most striking examples of this phenomenon are to be found in the court sermons delivered in the later 1630s by the Laudian polemicist Peter Heylyn. The anti-papal content of these sermons (as we shall see) runs strongly counter to writings which Heylyn produced for other occasions. According to Heylyn's own account, by 1636 he had noted that the English presses were swarming with seditious pamphlets, 'in most of which the Bishops generally were accused of having a design to bring in Popery, [and] the regular Clergie of this Church (my self more frequently then any of my ranck and quality) traduced and defamed for subservient instruments'.[203] Hardly a libel was published 'in which I was not openly accused of Popery, or at the least at being an under-factor unto those who had the chief managing of that design'. Lacking any major patron outside the court,

200 PRO, SP 16/459/15; 406/121; 349/116.

201 PRO, SP 16/422/120. See also Montagu's comments to Panzani, reported in PRO, MS 31/9/17B: Panzani to Barberini, 27 April/7 May 1636.

202 Prideaux, *Ephesus Backsliding*, pp.24–5. Prideaux depicted religious toleration as the mixing of two separate religions, and cited all the scriptural injunctions against dealing with heretics or Babylon (*ibid.*, pp.21–5).

203 Peter Heylyn, *The Parable of the Tares Expounded & Applyed* (1659), sig.A3v.

Heylyn felt threatened, and resorted to a propaganda campaign on his own behalf:

For the decrying of wch scandal so unjustly raised ... I fell upon a resolution of preaching ... Sermons before the king ... upon the Parable of the Tares, and giving in them such an assurance of my Orthodoxie in Religion and aversenesse from Popery, as might declare me for a true son of the Church of England. And this I did at such a time when the inclinations unto popery were thought (but falsely thought) to be most predominant both in Court and Clergy.[204]

If we accept the sermons which Heylyn later printed to be authentic in contents and dates, he would seem to have attempted to disarm his enemies by offering them a traditional brand of Elizabethan or Jacobean anti-popery, with its emphasis on Antichrist and the descent of the 'true church' in the Middle Ages through a sequence of heretical sects. In his sermons delivered in his capacity as royal chaplain in January 1638 and January 1639, Heylyn mounted a devastating attack upon the Church of Rome. He lambasted Rome's heresies, and launched scathing attacks on her errors of hyperdulia, the invocation of saints and idolatry.[205] He described the Middle Ages as a blighted time of darkness and ignorance, and championed as proto-Protestants the Waldensians, Jan Hus, Jerome of Prague and John Wyclif, citing with approval the list of Protestant witnesses in the *Catalogus testium veritatis*.[206] He depicted Antichrist at work even in the time of the Apostles, and stressed that Antichrist had now been revealed in the papacy, even repeating Scaliger's report that the word 'mystery' had been engraved in capital letters on the front of the Triple Crown.[207] That these were all points selected merely to serve Heylyn's immediate situation seems clear from the fact that he had actually opposed most of them in his *Briefe and Moderate Answer* to Henry Burton, published the previous year.[208] Moreover, Heylyn's *volte-face* on issues of anti-popery was rather less audacious than he tries to suggest. He commenced his sermons *after* the publication of the king's Declaration against Romanist proselytizing at court, and it was doubtless this which inspired his assault in one of his sermons upon those who were busy 'taking up provision of the choicest wits, and persons of most power and quality for the Church of Rome'.[209] The Laudian bishop William Piers left his own anti-papist self-defence until it was too late. It was only when he was imprisoned in the Tower that

[204] *Ibid.*, sig.A4r. [205] *Ibid.*, pp.65–7, 75, 105–12.
[206] For the context of this discussion, see below ch.6.
[207] Heylyn, *Parable of the Tares*, pp.70–1. Even William Crashaw had his doubts about Scaliger's report (Ussher, *Works*, XV: 115), though see also Beard, *Antichrist*, p.152; Hakewill, *Answere*, ii. p.4.
[208] See below, pp.117, 304. [209] Heylyn, *Parable of the Tares*, pp.83–4.

he thought to preach and subsequently print two sermons attacking Rome's doctrines of election, justification and satisfaction.[210]

However much they might yield to their opponents' demands for anti-papal polemic, the Laudians remained consistent in echoing the complaints of Hooker, Howson and the rest that there had in the past been an overemphasis upon the popish threat which had led Englishmen gravely to neglect the equal, if not greater, threat that puritanism posed within the English Church. Heylyn's court sermons on the parable of the tares, while full-blooded in their anti-popery, made constant complaint of people's unbalanced perception of the relative threat from Rome and from the puritans. The two dangers were alike, Heylyn maintained, but 'we perhaps are not alike or equally affected in apprehension of those dangers'. As regards the papist threat, people were prone to think that 'there never can be watch enough; that all those Laws and Proclamations which are out against them are not sufficient to secure us, and dispossess us of our feares'. By contrast, when it came to evaluating the puritan threat, people tended to 'think there needs no watch at all, that those few Lawes and Canons which are now in force for preservation of the Churches peace and safety, may very well be spared, and layed by for ever'. It was this 'misapprehension of the Churches danger' that was Heylyn's principal complaint. He chastised those prone to think that puritans who resisted the unity and uniformity of the English Church were harmless, 'and that their wheat is pure and clean, not any dangerous tare amongst it'. On the contrary, Heylyn warned the court, 'they have introduced into the Church the ancient Heresies of the Novatians, Donatists, Aerians, Priscillianists, and of the Apostolici ... not to say anything of those dangerous principles which they are known to hold among them against peace and government'. Compared with the Romanists, who opposed the Church of England openly, the puritans were 'a more close and secret enemy', 'a bosom Traytor, which grindeth our very entrails like Prometheus vulture'. It was 'High time assuredly both for Prince and Prelate to have an eye upon them, and to watch their doings'.[211]

Laud and his allies felt a strong sense of the need to restore an impartial balance to arguments against sedition and nonconformity. Anti-popery had tended to limit concern on this issue purely to the popish threat, thereby neglecting the growth of similar errors among radical Protestants. Instead, Laudians favoured the view that anti-popery was itself the Trojan Horse of presbyterian sectaries. This distinction emerged most clearly in

210 William Piers, *Two Sermons Preached in the Tower* (1642), pp.9, 29–30, 34–5. The sermons include most vehement and unqualified attacks upon the papists' invocation of saints and abuse of relics (*ibid.*, pp.23–4, 54).

211 Heylyn, *Parable of the Tares*, pp.55–7.

the controversies over the alterations made to the 1635 edition of the Prayer Book. In the highly emotive prayer for 5 November, the anti-papal phrase 'that Babilonish and Antichristian Sect which say' had been subtly altered to read 'that Babilonish and Antichristian Sect *of them* which say', an alteration which Henry Burton noted by implication generalized the accusation of sedition to include puritans too.[212] The manner in which Christopher Dow and Peter Heylyn defended this alteration suggests that Burton's fears were amply justified. Dow remarked that when 'such curious cryers downe of Popery, as Master B. hath shewed himselfe' chose to oppose the Church of England, he could not see why they 'may not bee accounted of a Babylonish and Antichristian sect, as well as any Jesuit in the world'.[213] Heylyn similarly argued that puritans who espoused Burton's views now came within the compass of the prayer. The prayer had first been aimed against the Jesuits, but if the puritans shared similar aims then it was quite appropriate that they should be condemned too.[214] The same thinking prompted Laud to remove passages which attacked papists and popery by name from the proposed Scottish Canons. When this action was brought against Laud at his trial, the archbishop argued that the canon in question expressly forbade and abolished all foreign power repugnant to the king's jurisdiction in the church. 'And sure', Laud commented, 'I think 'tis no great matter whether Papists or Popery be named, so long as the Canons go directly against them.'[215] Similarly, the Gunpowder Plot sermons of Laud's protégés such as Jeremy Taylor were more likely to attack traitors in general rather than Romanists in particular. Finally, there is evidence that several minor divines not only avoided dwelling upon the Plot itself, but were even prepared to explain it away.[216]

Thus, by the 1630s, Andrew Willet's aspirations for English Protestant unity in opposing Rome had been wholly defeated. In contrast to the flood of anti-papal literature produced under James, only Morton and Featley

212 Burton, *For God and the King*, pp.130–1. While this alteration was itself the work of King Charles, Laud nevertheless gave it his full support and justified in public the assumptions behind it: Laud, *Works*, VI: 52, 53–4.

213 Dow, *Innovations*, p.137.

214 Heylyn, *Briefe Answer*, pp.151–3. Heylyn compared this development with the history of the Act of Uniformity and of the Court of High Commission, which had originally been established in order to deal with popish recusants, but whose penalties now were justly laid upon puritans for the same offences. Cf. Pocklington's remark that 'when treason and rebellion is with like zeal detested and declaimed against in Puritans, as in Papists, I shall believe there is some religion and pi[e]ty in that generation': PRO, SP 16/414/25: Pocklington to Sir John Lambe, 4 March 1639.

215 Laud, *Works*, III: 324–5.

216 Cressy, *Bonfires*, pp.152–5. A petition against the vicar of Banbury, addressed to the Long Parliament, complained that 'hee would not read the words "faith is faction and religion is rebellion" etc. Nor would read that Act of Parlt. [on] Nov. 5, 1639, which is

among conforming Calvinist divines continued to churn out controversial works against Rome. The internecine conflicts within the English Church over the sabbath and the altar so monopolized the attention of religious authors that in 1636, for the first time since the accession of Elizabeth, no work of anti-papal polemic appears to have been printed in England. As establishment divines downgraded the value of anti-papal controversy, some puritan divines seem in response to have questioned the efficacy of anti-papal controversy in uniting the English Church. By the 1630s, the occasional anti-papal gesture by the bishops could no longer be relied upon to deflect puritan criticism. Indeed, it often seemed to enshrine 'semi-popish' doctrinal errors. In 1640, Henry Burton remarked cynically that 'this Art of writing against Jesuits is now grown so stale, and triviall, as in these dayes it begets new Suspicions of a Popish Spirit'.[217] Richard Montagu's *New Gagg* would seem to have been one of the first conformist tracts against Rome to have encountered accusations, not merely of hypocrisy, but of crypto-popery. After him, William Laud found his own anti-papal tract actually refuted by Henry Burton, and Joseph Hall's *Old Religion*, although directed against Roman errors, was condemned by the same author. Christopher Potter's *Want of Charitie* and William Chillingworth's *Religion of Protestants* both found their Protestant, as well as Romanist, opponents.[218] But if this marked a new intensification of the conflict between English Protestants, it was not a new departure: Meric Casaubon had already seen fit to publish a scornful refutation of a puritan anti-papal tract published under his father's name. Anti-popery, which had previously served as a means to unite English Protestants, had now become a channel through which the church's own internal conflicts found expression.

appointed to bee read though the church wardens brought him the statute booke': Sir Simonds D'Ewes, *The Journal of Sir Simonds D'Ewes* (New Haven, 1923), p.77. One Kemp, a fellow of St John's, Cambridge, was accused that in a sermon on 5 November 1637 'he extenuated the fact of the powder traitors': BL, Harleian MS 7019 fol.78.

[217] Burton, *A Replie*, p.17. Cf. SUL, Hartlib MS 29/3 fol.33r. Cf. Burton's earlier complaint in his *A Tryall of Private Devotions* (1628) (sig.D1v) of books recently published which 'doe in part maintaine our Church, and in part comply and symbolize with Poperie, and by seeming to slight Poperie, slily to bring it into credite'.

[218] P. Milward, *Religious Controversies of the Jacobean Age* (1978), pp.40–4; Francis Cheynell, *Chillingworthi novissima* (1644); on Hall's *Old Religion* see below ch.3. Francis Rous composed a manuscript refutation of Potter's *Charitie Mistaken* in the 1630s: SUL, Hartlib MS 29/2 fol.21r, 29/3 fol.19r.

2

The rejection of Antichrist

THE APOCALYPTIC TRADITION

Among the many themes prominent in anti-papal writings of the early modern period, few strike a more jarring note to modern ears than the claim that the pope was Antichrist. Nevertheless, as recent historians have demonstrated, the identification of the pope as Antichrist commanded an unchallenged orthodoxy and substantial doctrinal importance in the Elizabethan Church.[1] Indeed, it has been suggested that it was 'the most important component of the "ideological filter" through which British reformers and reformed viewed the church of Rome and its supporters'. A whole genre of sermons, treatises and popular manuals written to prove the pope to be the Antichrist prophesied by Scripture developed during this period, and extended well into early Stuart times. It has been estimated that between 1588 and 1628 over 100 systematic expositions of the Romish Antichrist were published in England, or by British authors, while the doctrine's appearance in the marginal notes to the Geneva Bible and in Foxe's *Acts and Monuments* spread such apocalyptic ideas still further.[2] As historians have emphasized, this doctrine was not the preserve of an extreme millenarian minority, but rather cut across theological boundaries, and embraced all the Protestant archbishops of Canterbury from Thomas Cranmer through to George Abbot. The doctrine was also regularly defended in the Universities.[3] Even the collapse of the military threat

[1] See Lamont, *Godly Rule*, pp.23–5, 31–5, 41–2, 66–7; R. Bauckham, *Tudor Apocalypse* (Abingdon, 1978); K. Firth, *The Apocalyptic Tradition in Reformation Britain 1530–1645* (Oxford, 1979); P. Christianson, *Reformers and Babylon* (Toronto, 1978); C. Hill, *Antichrist in Seventeenth-Century England* (Oxford, 1971); Lake, 'Significance', pp.161–78; B. Capp, 'The political dimension of apocalyptic thought', in C.A. Patrides and J. Wittreich (eds.), *The Apocalypse in English Renaissance Thought and Literature* (Manchester, 1984). See also D. Brady, *The Contribution of British Writers between 1560 and 1830 to the Interpretation of Revelation 13.16–18* (Tübingen, 1983).

[2] Christianson, *Reformers*, pp.5, 93–4; Bauckham, *Tudor Apocalypse*, pp.101, 136–40; Firth, *Apocalyptic Tradition*, pp.228–9.

[3] Hill, *Antichrist*, ch.1; Christianson, *Reformers*, p.10; Nicholas Bernard, *The Judgement of the Late Arch-Bishop of Armagh* (1659), ii. pp.139–42; Neile, *Shiftings*, p.27; A Clark (ed.),

to England from Spain after 1588 and the drive against presbyterianism did not lead to the marginalization of this tenet. Rather, the doctrine reached its zenith, as an important article of belief upon which puritans and establishment divines could unite. The years immediately following the Armada saw the composition of substantial tracts on this subject by a range of scholars including puritans and anti-puritan activists, such as Arthur Dent, George Gifford, Thomas Rogers and Matthew Sutcliffe.[4] Far from being a marginal puritan preoccupation, the doctrine played a prominent role in the international theological controversy between Protestants and the Church of Rome. Several of the English treatises mentioned above, and many subsequent ones, were directed against Cardinal Bellarmine's detailed treatment of this issue in volume I of his *Disputationes*. The works of Bellarmine, and of other Jesuit apocalyptic scholars such as Francisco Ribera, continued to provide work for English scholars well into James' reign.[5]

With the accession of King James, the promotion of this doctrine reached a high-point in the Church of England – indeed, the years after 1600 witnessed a flood of writing on this topic. The first years of the new reign were marked by the publication of several major treatises concerning the papal Antichrist composed by important conformist divines, who included the future bishops Robert Abbot and George Downame.[6] Moreover, for the first time in English history, the reigning monarch had himself written on this issue, and the doctrine thus gained an enhanced significance and became still more fashionable. King James identified the pope as Antichrist in a meditation on the Book of Revelation which he wrote in 1588, and in a further paraphrase of the same piece of Scripture first published in his collected *Workes* of 1616 – a volume whose official editor singled out James' treatment of the papal Antichrist for special applause in his preface. By 1610, this same identification carried a semi-official status in the Church of England when James, in painstaking detail, applied the scriptural prophecies of the Antichrist to the papacy in the *Monitory Preface* to his Apology for the Oath of Allegiance. The king's

The Register of the University of Oxford (Oxford Hist. Society 10, 1887–9), pt.i. pp.195, 199, 200, 204, 213; CUL, Add. MS 3320 fols.222–5; Thomas Barlow, *Genuine Remains* (1693), p.192.

[4] Arthur Dent, *The Ruine of Rome* (1603); George Gifford, *Sermons upon the Whole Booke of Revelation* (1596); Thomas Rogers, *An Historical Dialogue Touching Antichrist and Poperie* (1589); Matthew Sutcliffe, *De Pontifico Romano* (1599); Francis Dillingham, *A Disswasive from Popery* (1599).

[5] Firth, *Apocalyptic Tradition*, pp.100, 163, 165, 171–2, 176, 228; Bauckham, *Tudor Apocalypse*, p.140. The Protestant works also received Jesuit replies: Milward, *Jacobean Controversies*, pp.132–6.

[6] Robert Abbot, *Antichristi Demonstratio* (1603); Downame, *Treatise*; Powel, *Disputationum*.

approval of contemporary writings on the issue was recognized by Cardinal Bellarmine, who complained that James had borrowed his arguments from the treatises of Robert Abbot and Thomas Brightman. Indeed, the second edition of Abbot's work in 1608 printed James' commentary on chapter 20 of the Apocalypse as an appendix (doubtless with the king's permission). While James argued that this definition was not to be urged 'as a matter of Faith to be necessarily beleeved of all Christians', nevertheless all subsequent English Protestant contributors to the Oath of Allegiance controversy, including Lancelot Andrewes, were called upon to defend the king's arguments on this point against Bellarmine's criticisms.[7]

Although varying in their interpretation of a number of passages of scriptural prophecy, by the late Elizabethan and early Jacobean period English apocalyptic writers espoused an essentially standardized interpretation of the pope's identity as Antichrist. Some early Tudor writers had occasionally spoken of Antichrist more in terms of a spiritual principle in opposition to Christ manifested in different guises throughout history, with the papacy embodying the worst form of it, while Islam could be regarded as another manifestation. By the end of the sixteenth century, however, Antichrist had come to be identified exclusively with the papacy. This was prompted in part by the polemical need to refute the earlier 'spiritual' identification of Antichrist with the general body of the wicked, since this was a point which had been taken up by Romanist writers in order to deny the identification of Antichrist with the papacy. While the term might still have a certain general reference to opponents of the Gospel, by the late Elizabethan period the papacy had thus come to be identified as *the* Antichrist – the single, specific historical entity to which the apocalyptic prophecies were held to refer.[8]

It was argued that the pope was 'that Antichrist' foretold by a number of passages of Scripture: chiefly the Little Horn of Daniel 7 and 8, the 'Man of Sin' of 2 Thessalonians 2.3–12 and especially the Second Beast and the Whore of Babylon of Revelation 13 and 17. Against Romanist arguments that Antichrist would be one particular man and would reign merely three and a half years (the so-called 'Antichrist legend'), it was maintained that

[7] King James, *Workes*, sigs.d3v–d4r, pp.1–80; *idem*, *Political Works*, pp.129–50; Christianson, *Reformers*, pp.85–7; Andrewes, *Responsio*, pp.304–5. King James' arguments were employed by Andrew Willet in the fourth edition of his *Synopsis Papismi* as representative of the position of the Church of England: *Synopsis* (1613), pp.224–5, 229, 242, 244, 246, 255. King James may well have pressurized John Selden into avowing clearer support for the king's arguments: see Firth, *Apocalyptic Tradition*, p.178. George Downame was later reported to have complained of the problems involved in defending the specific arguments which James used: SUL, Hartlib MS 29/3 fol.36v. James' act of identifying the pope as Antichrist was allotted a significant place in the apocalyptic schema of several puritans: e.g. Burton, *Seven Vials*, pp.77–9; Bernard, *A Key*, sig.C4v.

[8] Bauckham, *Tudor Apocalypse*, pp.91–108; Firth, *Apocalyptic Tradition*, pp.6–7, 23–6.

Antichrist had already come, and was a whole company and succession of heretics. The mark of Antichrist was not to be understood as any visible sign or badge (as Romanist authors claimed), but was rather the profession of fealty and obedience to the pope, and agreement with him in his corruptions of faith and doctrine. Where Roman Catholic writers claimed that Antichrist would be an open and manifest opponent of Christ, abolishing all religion, Protestant writers argued that Antichrist was a secret adversary, who would take away all religion 'under pretence of religion' – he could not therefore be Mohammed, who opposed Christianity directly. Protestant writers held the seat of Antichrist to be the present Christian Rome, against Roman Catholic claims that it had been pagan Rome, or would be Jerusalem or Babylon. Finally, writers concluded that the pope was Antichrist because all the qualities and properties attributed to him in Daniel, Thessalonians and Revelation were fulfilled in the papacy: that he would magnify himself against God, sit in the Temple of God, bring strong delusions and false miracles and would be an adversary to Christ.[9]

The theme of deception and dissimulation provided one of the most crucial features of this interpretation, and was especially important when answering specific Romanist objections. It was maintained that Antichrist did not openly declare himself, but worked through a *pretence* of religion, a counterfeit Christianity. This was, in Whitaker's words, 'a certain mystery of iniquity, which in words establishes Christ, but in fact destroys him'. The greatest subversion of religion was thus understood to come from within Christianity itself. This meant that the fact that Rome did not deny Christ, and indeed retained the sacraments and many doctrines of orthodox Christianity, could be dismissed as beside the point, or (as we shall see) could even be invoked as proof of her antichristian identity.[10]

While this position was generally held, this is not to say that the Book of Revelation (or indeed other prophetic texts) was therefore believed to be all resolved and understood in other points. It was not simply sceptics such as John Selden who expressed doubts concerning overenthusiastic and schematic interpretations of the Book which sought too exact a prediction of the end of the world and the destruction of Antichrist. Even puritan apocalyptic enthusiasts such as Richard Bernard and Thomas Taylor

[9] For a useful summary of these points, see Willet, *Synopsis* (1600), pp.188–220 (esp. pp.212–20).

[10] William Whitaker, *A Disputation of Holy Scripture*, tr. and ed. W. Fitzgerald (Cambridge, 1849), p.21 – quoted in Bauckham, *Tudor Apocalypse*, p.104. For this point see also Willet, *Synopsis* (1600), pp.205–6, 217; Abbot, *Demonstratio*, pp.14–18; Beard, *Antichrist*, pp.22, 138–9; Downame, *Treatise*, i. pp.18, 21–2, 127–8, 228–30; Sheldon, *Sermon at Paules Crosse*, pp.36–8.

emphasized the obscurity of some passages, and warned against too exact renderings of the date of the end of the world.[11]

Moreover, whatever use they might make of King James' endorsement of the doctrine, most Jacobean writers would have accepted that the Church of England did not formally accept the identification of the pope as Antichrist as explicit doctrine, and that this tenet was not a fundamental point of faith necessary to salvation. The puritan Thomas Beard noted that it was 'a point undecided in our Church', and professed that if he saw a contrary determination of the church he would always be ready to subscribe to it. Nevertheless, on the next page Beard maintained that 'next unto the knowledge of our Lord and Savior Jesus Christ, there is nothing so necessarie, as the true and solide knowledge of Antichrist'.[12] Even moderate episcopalian authors made similar claims, admitting on the one hand that the point was not fundamental to the faith, while simultaneously maintaining that the identification itself was blindingly obvious and easily proven to anyone who was not wilfully obtuse. Robert Abbot wrote in wonder of the blindness of men, like owls at noon-day, who could not see the pope to be Antichrist. Thomas Morton argued that there was 'plaine and direct evidence' and 'direct proofe shewing the pope to be Antichrist', while John Prideaux believed himself to have demonstrated in his lecture at the 1626 Oxford Divinity Act that the pope was Antichrist, 'non ex conjecturis, vel obscuris, vel dubiis oraculis, sed ex certissimis Prophetiis, rerum eventu comprobatis'.[13]

This attitude was not even limited to strong Calvinists. To the Arminian Thomas Jackson, Rome's doctrine of infallibility was the very essence of antichristianism, and put the question of the identity of Antichrist beyond dispute. Even the moderate Arminian Dr Walter Raleigh, who commanded the admiration of William Chillingworth and was an enthusiastic defender of ceremonies in his sermons as royal chaplain during the 1630s, remarked of the Book of Revelation that

11 Bernard, *A Key*, sigs.C7r–v, pp.90–1; Taylor, *Christs Victorie*, p.790; *idem*, *The Principles of Christian Practice* (1635), p.250 – quoted in B.W. Ball, *A Great Expectation. Eschatological Thought in English Protestantism to 1660* (Leiden, 1975), p.194; Willet, *Synopsis* (1600), p.193. For similar warnings from William Perkins, and even the great exegetes Brightman and Mede, see Bauckham, *Tudor Apocalypse*, pp.171–3; Ball, *Expectation*, pp.63–4; Christianson, *Reformers*, p.105.

12 Beard, *Antichrist*, sigs.A2v, A3r, A4r.

13 Abbot, *Antichristi demonstratio*, p.92 (cited in Bernard, *Judgement*, ii. pp.127–8); Thomas Morton, *A Catholike Appeale for Protestants* (1610), pp.162, 152; Prideaux, *Viginti-duae Lectiones*, i. pp.165, 175. Cf. Bernard, *A Key*, sig.A3v; L. Rimbault, *Pierre du Moulin* (Paris, 1966), p.69. This attitude might usefully be compared with that of the same 'credal' Calvinists towards the doctrine of predestination: see J.M. Atkins, 'Calvinist bishops, church unity, and the rise of Arminianism', *Albion* 18 (1986), p.416.

though in other Points it be dark and mysterious, yet in that, which is principally intended, the discovery of gorgeous Rome, and her false Prophet ... is so evident, and unto rational and unprejudicated Minds, I take it so demonstrative, as it may well justify the Name of a Revelation ... I am sure, if not in this, it will trouble any Man to make good the Title in much, if in any thing besides.

Gabriel Powel's notorious remark that he was as sure that the pope was Antichrist as that Jesus was the Son of God was only the most outspoken example of the ready acceptance of this doctrine as a self-evident truth, although it was only among more puritan authors that the knowledge of Antichrist was claimed, not just to be straightforward, but also to form a necessary part of godly life.[14]

This combination of theoretical agnosticism and practical dogmatic assumption stemmed partly from the polemical value that the identification held. All groups in the Jacobean Church found it of value in justifying the break with Rome. It provided a powerful, self-evident condemnation of the pope and Church of Rome which could serve as a short-cut through the wearisome and hazardous labyrinth of Romanist/Protestant doctrinal controversies. Puritans such as Thomas Brightman were not alone in attaching fundamental significance to the doctrine. George Downame, Robert Abbot and John Prideaux – all future bishops – made similar claims of its polemical importance. In his lecture at the Oxford Divinity Act of 1626, the Regius Professor John Prideaux insisted that all the points in dispute between Rome and the Protestants could be resolved by the simple question of the identity of the pope as Antichrist. George Downame identified it in his 1603 tract as the issue on which all popery depended, 'the cheefe of all controversies betwixt us and the Papists, and of the greatest consequence. For if all this were once throughly cleared, all others would easily be decided.'[15]

Thomas Beard emphasized the value of the doctrine in keeping Protestants out of the clutches of the sophistical Jesuit missionaries: 'truth may [not] be sufficiently taught, and error confuted, without making any mention of Antichrist', given 'how great imbecility is in man, and how easie hee is to be transported into error ... and therefore how needfull it is

[14] Jackson, *Works*, XII: 183; *Certain Queries Proposed by Roman Catholicks, and Answered by Dr. Walter Raleigh*, ed. Laurence Howel (1719), pp.12–13; Powel, *Disputationum*, 'Christiano Lectori' (unfol.). Wood reports that Raleigh was said to have written a 'Tract of Millenianism', 'he having for some time been much addicted to that opinion' (Anthony Wood, *Athenae Oxonienses*, ed. P. Bliss (4 vols., 1813–20), III: 198).

[15] Thomas Brightman, *Works* (1644), p.611; Prideaux, *Viginti-duae Lectiones*, i. p.161; Downame, *Treatise*, sig.A2v, p.2, cf. ii. p.189; Abbot, *Demonstratio*, sig.[*4]r. See also George Downame, *Papa Antichristus* (1620), pp.1–3, 651–3; Willet, *Synopsis* (1600), p.211; Bernard, *A Key*, pp.33–4; Burton, *Baiting*, p.94; William Fulke, *A Sermon Preached at Hampton Court* (1570), sig.Biir; Rimbault, *Pierre du Moulin*, p.69.

to be pressed to the quicke.'[16] Even when it came to the subtle business of trying to persuade Roman Catholics that they might legitimately attend Church of England services, Robert Abbot and even William Bedell were happy to invoke the pope's identity as Antichrist as one of their arguments. The moderate Bedell, otherwise so keen to stress the need for a positive, constructive approach to the evangelization of Roman Catholics, still affirmed the importance of the identification of the pope as Antichrist and Rome as Babylon in the process of conversion. It had a central role to play in the Gospel message which must be brought to all Romanists, who must be told that it was acknowledged by their own papal divines that Rome is Babylon, 'and it is averred that this is the present Papall Monarchie, that out of this they must depart by the Commands of our Lord Jesus Christs owne Voyce, under paine of being an accessary to all her sinnes, and lyable to all her punishments'.[17] Not only was the argument clearer than on many other issues, but the words of Revelation stressed that all those living in Babylon were damned unless they could recognize that the pope was Antichrist and depart from him accordingly.

The doctrine's value did not rest solely in its role as an Occam's razor applied to burgeoning religious controversies. A number of other aspects of the Elizabethan and early Jacobean Protestant theological position against Rome were also dependent upon it, so that it could not be questioned without doing violence to wider aspects of English Protestantism. For example, the identification played a central role in the English Protestant understanding of church history. Against Rome's claims of institutional continuity through the medieval centuries, Protestants developed an historical exegesis of biblical prophecy which answered the problem of the disappearance of the true church during this period by asserting that this apostasy had been prophesied in the Book of Revelation. It was argued that the persecution and resultant seclusion of true believers during this period in fact confirmed their status as a true church fighting against the antichristian oppressions of Rome. This developing apocalyptic tradition of Protestant historiography was widely disseminated through Foxe's popular *Acts and Monuments*, which systematically applied prophecy to the organization and presentation of history. Foxe's work also reinforced an increasing trend towards applying the prophecies exclusively to the Church of Rome as the specific historical embodiment of the false church.[18]

16 Beard, *Antichrist*, sig.*2r. Beard and others therefore deliberately wrote 'ad captum vulgi' (*ibid.*, sig.A3r). Cf. the comments of Richard Baxter, cited in W. Lamont, 'Richard Baxter, the Apocalypse and the mad major', *P&P* 55 (1972).

17 Bernard, *Judgement*, ii. pp.95–6; Bedell, *Examination of Motives*, pp.13–14; Abbot, *Antilogia*, pp.67v–68v; Bernard, *A Key*, pp.18–31. Cf. Sir Edwin Sandys, *Europae Speculum* (The Hague, 1629) p.115; Downame, *Treatise*, i. pp.1–2; Burton, *Baiting*, pp.93–5.

18 Firth, *Apocalyptic Tradition*, chs. 1–4; Bauckham, *Tudor Apocalypse*, pp. 54–5, 98–103.

Moreover, the more absolute the separation from Rome was understood to be, the more desirable it became to be able to urge the text of Revelation 18.4 – the divine command to desert Babylon or be damned for sharing in her sins – in order to justify the Reformation against Roman accusations that it was an act of schism. If the pope were not Antichrist, Thomas Beard demanded, 'what colour can we have for our so peremptory and exact a separation?' Thus English divines across the doctrinal spectrum, from Richard Bernard and Anthony Wotton, through George Abbot and Francis Mason, to Thomas Jackson, identified this upheaval in terms of the departure of God's people from the Romish Babylon.[19]

The notion that the pope was Antichrist, then, commanded the intellectual assent of the Elizabethan and Jacobean Church, and the chronological, apocalyptic interpretation of church history which it spawned was widely accepted and was (in Christianson's words) 'embodied at presupposition level' in works on other issues.[20] This is not to suggest, however, that this consensus amounted to a uniformity of belief regarding the details and importance of the doctrine, or concerning its implications for secular politics or for the formulation of other doctrines.

One of the most important points about the doctrine of the papal Antichrist was that it could be taken to imply that the religions of Rome and of Protestantism were absolute opposites. It was therefore a tempting weapon for any divines who wished to promote strongly anti-papal policies. The establishment divines Gabriel Powel and Robert Abbot, for example, deliberately wrote their expositions of the Apocalypse in 1603–5 in order to ensure that the new Jacobean regime would not yield to Romanists' appeals for religious toleration. George Downame tried to push its implications still further: if the pope was Antichrist, he insisted, 'it followeth necessarily, that Christian princes are not to tolerate either the religion of papists or their persons within their dominions'.[21] The doctrine was also employed, in England as well as in France, by men such as Downame who were anxious to attack the perceived spread of 'crypto-popish' *politique* ideas which maintained that the differences between Rome and the Protestants might easily be compounded. Its use could thus

[19] Beard, *Antichrist*, sig.A3r; Mason, *Vindiciae*, p.167; Jackson, *Works*, I: 296; Anthony Wotton, *A Dangerous Plot Discovered* (1626), pp.34–6, 47; Bernard, *Looke beyond Luther*, p.45; Christianson, *Reformers*, p.132. In Mason's tract, the Romanist disputant 'Philodox' retorts to this apocalyptic reference in Laudian fashion: 'Haec est haereticorum perpetua vox.'

[20] Christianson, *Reformers*, p.93.

[21] Powel, *Disputationum*, ep. ded. sigs.A4v–A5v (cf. Powel, *The Catholikes Supplication*, pp.37, 38); Abbot, *Demonstratio*, ep. ded.; Downame, *Treatise*, sig.A3r; cf. Ford, *Protestant Reformation*, p.239 n.120. Downame had become increasingly concerned at the growing insolence of papists 'within these few yeares', and the fear that many English Protestants had been drifting back towards Rome (Downame, *Treatise*, i. sig.A2, p.2).

reflect Protestant fears of internal betrayal, and the need to shore up an increasingly compromised position, just as much as it might imply a confessional triumphalism.[22] Accordingly, conformist divines did not limit themselves to invoking the doctrine in paper controversies with Rome, but at least some of them were also quite capable on occasion of employing it as an active political agenda. Archbishop Abbot was committed to a confessional foreign policy and interpreted international events such as the Elector Frederick's acceptance of the Bohemian crown in 1619 with direct reference to the Book of Revelation.[23]

Such perspectives on foreign affairs were themselves representative of what has been identified as an increasingly aggressive and military style entering apocalyptic works after 1588. This tended to place a new emphasis in exegeses of Revelation 19.14 on the role of temporal, military power rather than mere spiritual forces in the overthrow of Antichrist. Arthur Dent's popular and regularly reprinted *Ruine of Rome* has a clear emphasis on the use of military force, and the armed struggle of godly princes against papal forces.[24] A form of 'apocalyptic nationalism' developed which highlighted England's special eschatological role in the final conquest of the Roman Antichrist, and placed especial emphasis on the role of the godly prince, although the lassitude of early Stuart foreign policy drew attention away from King James himself and towards foreign Protestant princes such as Gustavus Adolphus or the Elector Palatine.[25] The doctrine was employed directly to exhort Protestant princes to wage war upon the Roman Catholic powers. Thus William Bradshaw objected that those who denied that the pope was Antichrist 'hinder . . . the zeal of Christian Princes from executing that against him in general and against his members in particular which the word partly foretelleth and partly commandeth to be done'.[26]

22 Downame, *Treatise*, ii. p.192; Perkins, *Reformed Catholike*, sigs.A2r, A3v; Windsor, 'The controversy', p.169; Sheldon, *Sermon at Paules Crosse*, p.31 ('30'). For this argument, see below ch.3. See also F. Laplanche, *L'Ecriture, le sacre et l'histoire. Erudits et politiques protestants devant la bible en France au XVIIe siècle* (Amsterdam and Maarssen, 1986), pp.172–3. This also accounts for the commentaries on Revelation produced during the time of the Spanish Match, such as Thomas Beard's, *Antichrist the Pope of Rome*, the titlepage of which bears the text of Judges 5.23, the curse of Meroz.

23 S. Adams, 'Foreign policy and the parliaments of 1621 and 1624', in K. Sharpe (ed.), *Faction and Parliament* (1978), pp.146–7.

24 Capp, 'Political dimension' p.98; Bauckham, *Tudor Apocalypse*, pp.174–8; Christianson, *Reformers*, pp.113–19.

25 Capp, 'Political dimension', pp.96, 102, 106, 108; Bauckham, *Tudor Apocalypse*, pp.174–80.

26 William Bradshaw, *A Myld and Iust Defence of Certeyne Arguments* (n.p., 1606), pp.44–5 – cited in Lake, *Moderate Puritans*, p.266; Gifford, *Sermons*, sigs.A3v–A5r; Bernard, *A Key*, sigs.C3r–C6v; Bauckham, *Tudor Apocalypse*, p.176. The puritan Walter Welles intended to dedicate his notes on the Apocalypse to Gustavus Adolphus of Sweden so that the king

While this agitation for an apocalyptic crusade was certainly not absent from conformist works, its most consistent and conspicuous advocates were overwhelmingly puritan writers. It was among puritans, too, that the Book of Revelation consistently acquired an activist imperative in the life of every individual believer. As Richard Bernard explained, to keep the words of the prophecy of Revelation required Protestants 'in our places, to seeke the fulfilling thereof, and to bring that to passe which is prophesied of us, so shall wee be blessed'.[27] For many puritans, then, the absolute language of the Apocalypse was not merely an invaluable polemical ploy against Romanist or tolerationist arguments: they also routinely converted the rhetoric of Antichrist more directly into a mediating guide to social and political behaviour *vis-à-vis* the Church of Rome and her members. Treatises on Antichrist could invoke the doctrine in order to warn against any form of civil contact with papists, and to demand the severest execution of the laws against Jesuits, priests and recusants. In these cases, the absolute rhetoric of Revelation allowed puritans to ride rough-shod over any supposed distinctions between moderate and radical papists, or fears of the charge of religious persecution. The apocalyptic framework confirmed the argument that relations with Rome could only ever be those of inevitable and perpetual conflict.

The moderate puritan Richard Bernard's *A Key of Knowledge* of 1617 is a clear example of the treatment of the Apocalypse as a blueprint for anti-papal activity.[28] His commentary is preceded by no less than five lengthy dedicatory epistles. These include appeals to the judges and the Inns of Court, which emphasize that the Book of Revelation can show them how to justify the equity of the laws against papists, and explain why these laws should be carried out with all possible force (and no qualms of conscience) against all recusants who wandered after the Beast of the Apocalypse. His epistle to the Justices of the Peace similarly urged them to search out popish priests and Jesuits. Bernard especially warned of the great and insidious danger posed by recusants, and most of all by those church papists who took the Oath of Allegiance. He urged the verses of Revelation 18.6 and 17.16 as direct commandments to the magistrates to root out antichristianism, an act which 'is so farre from being persecution, that it is a very glorious service unto the Majesty of the God of heaven'. Another dedicatory epistle was directed to 'martiall men and lovers of Armes', steeling them for the forthcoming conflict with the military forces

and those about him might take the more notice of the prophecy, thereby encouraging them in their military action against the Romanist forces: SUL, Hartlib MS 33/3 fol.9r.

27 Bernard, *A Key*, p.14.

28 For Bernard's career, see Fincham, *Prelate*, pp.193–4, 229, 230; Collinson, *Religion of Protestants*, pp.85–6.

of Rome, warning against 'fleshly and foolish pitie', and emphasizing the especial eschatological role of Protestant England in the forthcoming battle with Antichrist.[29]

Why did the apocalyptic tradition have this special attraction for puritan writers? The answer lies in part in the way that the absolute, polarized vision of the churches engendered by the apocalyptic schema complemented and encouraged the more general dualistic world-view typical of puritan spirituality. Puritan practical divinity sought to make dynamic use of the division of the world into the elect and the reprobate. Puritan devotional writers called upon the individual believer to make his election sure, and to join the purified ranks of the community of the fellow-godly, in opposition to the wickedness of the ungodly mass outside. This activist form of predestinarian doctrine has been dubbed 'experimental predestinarianism'. Puritan commentators found that the dualistic vision of the Book of Revelation dovetailed effectively with the divisions between the godly and profane promoted in this style of spirituality, and as such, it was seen as a valuable aid to puritan practical divinity. Richard Bernard enthusiastically observed that the Book of Revelation 'so cleerely setteth out in flat opposition the true and false Church', separating out all issues and people clearly into two sides, the good and the evil, that the reader could easily find out which side he was on.[30]

It was in the division between the true and false churches, expressed by the doctrine of the Two Churches, that puritan doctrines of the Antichrist overlapped with the prerogatives of puritan spirituality. The doctrine of the Two Churches was partly derived from Augustine and elaborated by John Bale and his successors. In it, the companies of the elect and the reprobate were conceived as belonging to two separate camps or 'churches', the true church and the false, running parallel throughout history, to one of which every man was held to belong. Each 'church' represented both the sum of all those people in history who would be found on that side, and also could refer more explicitly to 'specific historical embodiments in social and organisational forms' (in Bauckham's words). The more that this dualistic doctrine of the Two Churches featured in apocalyptic thought, the more tempting it was to translate its stark antithesis of good and evil, true and false churches, directly into the division between the two earthly churches of Rome and Protestantism. Dr Bauckham has noted how difficult it is in Tudor Protestant thought to pin

[29] Bernard, *A Key*, sigs.A4r–B1v, B2r–v, B8v, C1r–v, C3r–C6v.

[30] *Ibid*., pp.32–3, 34, 35–42. Dr Lake also notes the parallel of the 'unending oscillation between anxiety and confidence' in both the puritan doctrine of assurance, and in the balance of fear of the Roman Antichrist with confidence in his ultimate fall: Lake, 'Significance', pp.168–9.

down the precise relationship between the false 'church of the wicked' and the Church of Rome. By the Jacobean period, however, there was clearly a tendency among puritan interpreters of the Apocalypse directly to associate Rome with the false Church of Cain, thereby interpreting the cosmic battle between the true and false churches in a directly political way. On the other hand, conformists such as Robert Abbot were more careful to distinguish the false church of the wicked from its historical embodiment in Rome.[31]

Thus, just as experimental predestinarians worked on the active assumption that the true church of the elect was coterminous with the community of the godly (while formally accepting that the identities of the elect and reprobate are known only to God), so in the apocalyptic tradition the false church came increasingly to be identified more exclusively with the power of Rome. Both themes, by relating theoretical divisions to daily life, demanded an active role in personal and national political terms. The perception of Rome as the false church increased the pressure for a confessional foreign policy, and for a radical breach with the forces of Roman Catholicism. On the doctrinal plane, Rome's identity as Babylon was held to unchurch the Roman communion, leaving no possibility of salvation for those still within her. In social terms, it led to demands that Protestants refrain from all conversation and friendship with recusants, and even to avoid living in the same neighbourhood.[32]

TENSIONS AND AMBIGUITIES

Recent work has demonstrated how the attack on Antichrist could be a means of mobilizing the national community to oppose the power of Spain, thereby helping to integrate godly aspirations within the national church. The opposition of the established church to the military powers of Antichrist could be used to vindicate the same church against the cavils of separatists. Yet puritans were also prone to direct the same rhetoric of Antichrist inward, and to argue in similar absolute terms regarding the remnants of popery which supposedly remained within the Church of England. The arguments of the nonconforming puritan Thomas Brightman and others drew upon a strain of radical puritan apocalypticism whose crusading fervour was still directed towards the reformation of the Church of England itself, and especially towards the removal of episcopacy.[33]

31 Bauckham, *Tudor Apocalypse*, ch.3; G.J.R. Parry, *A Protestant Vision* (Cambridge, 1987), pp.188–98 and *passim*; Abbot, *Second Part*, pp.42–4.

32 E.g. Taylor, *Two Sermons*, i. pp.12–14.

33 Christianson, *Reformers*, pp.47–92, 104; Hill, *Antichrist*, pp.41–69; S. Brachlow, *The Communion of Saints* (Oxford, 1988), pp.77–113; Lake, *Moderate Puritans*, pp.253–4, 266–7.

Moderate puritan writers such as Richard Bernard opposed Brightman's application of the prophecies to the Church of England itself, but the seeds of Bernard's own apocalypticism, and that of other moderate puritans, could actually threaten the status quo of the English Church. Like experimental predestinarianism itself, apocalyptic rhetoric in puritan hands was constantly straining against the confines of the national church and the forced cohabitation of the godly and profane. Richard Bernard had noted ominously that the Book of Revelation distinguished between true Christians in name and deed, and those in name only. While Thomas Taylor spoke of the national church opposing Antichrist, he could also speak of there being only a small, persecuted number of the truly godly in England who really opposed Antichrist.[34] One would not need to be William Laud to perceive in such language a potential threat to the integrity of the all-inclusive national church.

Indeed, not all divines accepted the radically polarizing and politically activist forms of apocalypticism which flourished among puritans. Peter Lake has noted important 'half-formulated divergences of feeling and assumption' within this apocalyptic consensus in the later Elizabethan period. On the one hand men such as Archbishop Whitgift accepted the doctrine as a central element in the formal Protestant polemical case against Rome, but would not allow it in practice to dictate their conduct of foreign policy above other considerations. On the other hand stood 'moderate puritans' such as William Whitaker, for whom the antichristian principle of popery was the basis of their whole world-view, requiring a more direct conflict with popery as a principle of evil that was active throughout society.[35] In the Jacobean Church these divergences were still visible, but less clearly represented a division between church hierarchy and puritan opinion. As we have seen, episcopalian Calvinists such as Archbishop Abbot, Gabriel Powel and George Downame could on occasion use the imperatives of the Book of Revelation to press for changes in government policy. The division was not a simple one between 'theorists' and 'activists'; but rather between theorists prepared on occasion to embrace activist emphases, and activists for whom apocalyptic doctrines provided both a framework for the consideration of all other doctrinal issues and a programme which they were prepared more regularly to invoke and to stand by.

Many conformist divines in the Jacobean Church found it possible to adhere to the doctrine of the papal Antichrist while still adopting a more moderate and pragmatic attitude towards the Roman Church. 'To be

[34] Lake, 'William Bradshaw'; Bernard, *A Key*, p.42; Taylor, *Christs Victorie*, pp.831–4.
[35] Lake, 'Significance', pp.161–78.

nearer or further from the man of sin', wrote the apocalyptic theorist and ceremonial conformist Joseph Mede, 'is not (I think) the measure of Truth and Falsehood.' While prepared to accept the doctrine, these moderate Calvinist conformists were also prepared to de-emphasize the absolute nature of the judgements and demands prompted by the identification of the pope as Antichrist, and would not let apocalyptic arguments exert a stranglehold over ecclesiology and sacramental theology. As Dr Bauckham has carefully noted, 'the doctrine of the two churches was not so much a doctrine of formal ecclesiology as an aspect of the Tudor apocalyptic outlook. The status of the church of Rome was . . . generally recognised to be a less simple question than the use of the terminology of apocalyptic dualism often implied.'[36] Certainly, Jacobean conformist divines did not necessarily accept that the doctrine that the pope was Antichrist implied an absolute difference between the two churches. In fact, they were prepared to argue that, despite her identity as Babylon, Rome might notwithstanding still preserve some aspects of a true church. There was, of course, a sense in which the apocalyptic identification itself implied this. As the pope was maintained to be Antichrist precisely *because* he sat in the Church of God (2 Thessalonians 2.4), so controversialists such as George Downame, Thomas Beard, Robert Some and even Richard Hooker allowed that Rome must therefore be considered to be in some sense a church of God.[37] John Prideaux, ironically, was forced to emphasize the importance of the Church of Rome's Christianity in her identification as the Temple in which Antichrist sat, in order to repulse the claims made by Richard Montagu and Jesuit controversialists that the Turk might more rightly be called Antichrist.[38]

Nevertheless, there were divisions of opinion over the precise ecclesiological significance of identifying the pope as Antichrist and Rome as Babylon. At the end of the 1620s, these different lines of argument briefly came into open conflict in the course of the controversy over Joseph Hall's tract *The Old Religion*. The moderate Calvinist contributors to the controversy – Joseph Hall, Thomas Morton, John Prideaux and John Davenant – while all identifying the pope as Antichrist and the Church of Rome as Babylon, allowed that the Church of Rome might still be a true church at the same time. Indeed, they averred that her members might even owe her some obedience, and might yet attain salvation (according to certain carefully defined conditions) within her communion. Rome, as Hall suggested and the other writers accepted, might simultaneously possess a

[36] Joseph Mede, *The Works of ... Joseph Mede*, ed. J. Worthington (1664), p.1082; Bauckham, *Tudor Apocalypse*, p.65 n.28.

[37] Hooker, *Works*, V: 118, 126–7, 146–7. Cf. Jackson, *Works*, XII: 145, 152; Beard, *Antichrist*, pp.22, 138–9; see below ch.3.

[38] Prideaux, *Viginti-duae Lectiones*, i. pp.171–9.

Christian face and an antichristian heart. In response, puritans such as Henry Burton and Thomas Spencer cited the Book of Revelation, and its absolute lines of division, in order to deny Hall's argument that Rome could simultaneously be both Babylon and a true church.[39]

Such conflicts were fleeting, but they demonstrate that at least some more moderate establishment divines were happy to employ an apocalyptic rhetoric, and indeed to invoke it on occasion as a guide to conduct whenever specific policy objectives might require it, but did not share the puritans' all-consuming interest in the Apocalypse or their readiness to recognize it as a general guide to other doctrinal controversies. Their reservations concerning the overuse of apocalyptic schema appear to have increased over the course of James' and Charles' reigns as the radicalization of the Protestant apocalyptic tradition, and the growth of millenarianism, became objects of more general concern, prompting warnings from Patrick Forbes, Thomas Adams, John Prideaux and George Hakewill, among others.[40] Chiliasm, and outspoken attacks on the Church of England as a lukewarm Laodicea or decadent Babylon, were a source of concern for moderate puritan writers too, but those more tied to the establishment might be prompted to even greater reservations in response.[41] Moderate Calvinist episcopalians became increasingly uneasy with the apocalyptic tradition. Archbishop Abbot was complaining in 1632 that sectaries were saying 'that we carry the marks of the beast'.[42] Despite

[39] Hall, *Works*, VIII: 639, 720–6, 741–2, 744–5; Burton, *Seven Vials*, pp.44–5 and *Babel no Bethel* (1629), p.74; Thomas Spencer, *Maschil Unmasked* (1629), pp.29–31; Wotton, *Dangerous Plot*, pp.41–3. See below ch.3.

[40] Bauckham, *Tudor Apocalypse*, p.236; Firth, *Apocalyptic Tradition*, pp.177–8; Ball, *Expectation*, p.43; Willet, *Hexapla on Romans*, pp.227–8; Patrick Forbes, *An Exquisite Commentarie* (1613), p.225; John Prideaux, 'The Great Prophets Advent', p.27, and 'The Christians Expectation', pp.21–6, in *Certaine Sermons*; *idem*, *Viginti-duae Lectiones*, i. pp.199–214; George Hakewill, *An Apologie of the Power and Providence of God* (Oxford, 1627), p.452; John Mayer, *Ecclesiastica interpretatio* (1627), pp.311, 401, 419, 503–4. On the new wave of millenarian influence from the continent after 1620, and increasing examples of popular prophecy, see Firth, *Apocalyptic Tradition*, pp.204–29; P. Toon (ed.), *Puritans, the Millennium and the Future of Israel* (1970), pp.32, 42–65; B.S. Capp, *The Fifth Monarchy Men* (1972), pp.30–3.

[41] Thomas Taylor firmly denied separatists' attempts to identify the Church of England with Babylon, and Richard Bernard refuted Thomas Brightman's identification of the same church with the Church of Laodicea: Taylor, *Two Sermons*, i. pp.16–19; Bernard, *A Key*, sig. D4r. Nevertheless, Bernard complained of those who carped too much at Brightman's errors and used them in order to vilify the whole work (*ibid.*, sig. D4v). The new millenarianism initially prompted opposition even from congregationalists such as William Ames and John Cotton: Brachlow, *Communion*, p.91. Also note William Twisse's initially sceptical response to Joseph Mede's millennial ideas: Joseph Mede, *The Apostasy of the Latter Times* (1641), preface, sig.A2v.

[42] S.R. Gardiner (ed.), *Reports of Cases in the Courts of Star Chamber and High Commission* (Camden Society n.s. 39, 1886), p.309. The mark of the beast was applied to the sign

the confirmation of the pope's identity as Antichrist in the Irish Articles of 1615, the British delegates at the Synod of Dort in 1618–19 expressed reservations over whether the Synod should explicitly refer to the pope as Antichrist without any previous determining of the point, although they emphasized that they themselves allowed that the pope was the great Antichrist.[43] By 1621 King James himself was trying to qualify his own earlier arguments that the pope was Antichrist when he attempted to secure a Spanish bride for his son.[44]

In point of fact, not all Jacobean divines manifested enthusiasm for the question of the pope's identity as Antichrist, or for apocalypticism in general. As Dr Bauckham has noted of the later Tudor period, while apocalyptic ideas were certainly widely prevalent among the educated clergy, they were not equally popular with everyone. Some puritans, such as Richard Greenham, were more preoccupied with pastoral concerns, and made minimal use of them.[45] Although most writers were ready to interpret the appropriate passages in Daniel, Thessalonians and the Gospels, some important early Reformers such as Peter Martyr, Bucer, Calvin and Tyndale had been noticeably silent on the subject of the Book of Revelation.[46] That this tendency persisted into the late Elizabethan period is attested by Arthur Dent. In the introduction to his *The Ruine of Rome* (1603) Dent admitted that there were still in England some divines 'both learned and godly . . . rare and reverend men for learning, & great variety of gifts' who preferred out of 'modesty and humility' not to 'meddle with this booke of the Revelations'. Dent, it must be emphasized, did not identify a coherent body of divines opposed to the Revelation, and did not consider them to be in any way his opponents, or open to any charge of crypto-Catholicism. It was not therefore the new band of avant-garde conformists whom he had in mind. Dent merely begged leave to persuade

of the cross by Napier, Simonds, Parker, Beard and especially Burton and Hughes, though Willet expressed reservations: Brady, *Contribution*, pp.47–52.

43 John Hales, *Golden Remains* (1688), p.540. The delegates suggested using the phrase 'antichristian tyranny' rather than 'the tyranny of Antichrist'. Compromise was reached with the phrase 'the tyranny of the roman Antichrist' (*ibid.*, p.543). See also Exeter College, Oxford, MS 48 fol.27v.

44 During the Spanish Marriage negotiations, James seems to have sought to reinterpret his own arguments in a conversation with Gondomar in which he implied that the identification of the pope as Antichrist was dependent (but not necessarily exclusively) on the pope's deposing of kings (C.H. Carter, *The Secret Diplomacy of the Habsburgs* (New York, 1964), pp.243–4). Nevertheless, his own works imply that it was this issue which determined his readiness openly to argue the case of the pope's being Antichrist, rather than that his doctrinal case for the identification relied solely upon it: King James, *Political Works*, pp.129–50; Milton, 'Laudians', p. 38 n.103.

45 Bauckham, *Tudor Apocalypse*, p.136.

46 *Ibid.*, p.42. On Calvin's restraint in dealing with the Apocalypse, see also Firth, *Apocalyptic Tradition*, pp.33–7; Parry, *Protestant Vision*, pp.38–9.

those superior to him in godliness that they change their minds, and attempt to overcome any problems in the prophecy with study and prayer. The crucial point about varying degrees of interest in the Apocalypse in this period, as one scholar has pointed out, is that 'no distinguishable class of the clergy was unenthusiastic'.[47] Furthermore, the reticence of some divines on such issues need not necessarily imply that they did not accept that the pope was Antichrist, or that the prophecies of the Apocalypse might not be applied in detail to church history. It is true that Lancelot Andrewes managed to deliver ten Gunpowder Plot sermons without ever giving the event an apocalyptic interpretation.[48] However, it is equally significant that, when he was required to defend the king's interpretation of Revelation in the Oath of Allegiance controversy, Andrewes showed in his *Tortura Torti* and *Responsio ad Apologiam Cardinalis Bellarmini* that he was quite prepared to argue in considerable detail from the Book of Revelation to prove the pope to be Antichrist and papal Rome to be Babylon, and to refute all arguments to the contrary.[49] Indeed, Joseph Hall would later appeal to Andrewes as an authority for his identification of the pope as Antichrist when Archbishop Laud urged him not to assert this 'positively and determinately' in the draft of his *Episcopacy by Divine Right Asserted*.[50]

Nevertheless, it is instructive to compare Arthur Dent's remarks with those of Richard Bernard, writing fourteen years later. Bernard was clearly more provoked by some contemporaries' scepticism regarding the value of the Book of Revelation, and he was decidedly less convinced of the good faith of those who avoided it. Almost a third of Bernard's commentary is an apologia for the study of the Book of Revelation against various objections. He complains of the 'too generally received ... opinion' that the book is too obscure to be of value, and typifies these sceptics as either papists, as 'carnall gospellers' who have never actually read the book, or as learned men overcome by pride, sloth and lack of commitment, who by trying to dishearten others from studying the work are acting as the instruments of Satan.[51]

Bernard's remarks bear witness to the waning of the popularity of apocalyptic study among the more theologically informed ministers during the Jacobean period. In part this was due to the increasingly rarefied,

47 Dent, *Ruine of Rome*, Epistle to Reader, sig.aa2r; Bauckham, *Tudor Apocalypse*, p.136.

48 Christianson, *Reformers*, p.107 n.21. See also the account of Andrewes in Hall, *Works*, VIII: 295.

49 Andrewes, *Tortura Torti*, pp.217–23, 304–11; *idem*, *Responsio*, pp.21–3, 304–411. See also his remark in a 1613 sermon before King James: Lancelot Andrewes, *Opuscula Quaedam Posthuma* (Oxford, 1852), p.88.

50 Laud, *Works*, VI: 577–8; Hall, *Works*, X: 543.

51 Bernard, *A Key*, pp.85, 96–8; cf. pp.100–3. Cf. Beard, *Antichrist*, sig.*2r–v.

academically demanding and stiflingly complex nature of apocalyptic study under the early Stuarts, as the discipline increasingly became the preserve of a minority of skilled linguists, historians and mathematicians.[52] It would therefore be unwise to assume too great a homogeneity of apocalyptic belief in Jacobean England, or to imply that each new development in the intellectual tradition was necessarily reflected in the beliefs of the clergy as a whole. Even so, diminishing numbers of researchers did not necessarily imply in the clergy at large a simple indifference, or a rejection of the orthodoxy that the pope was Antichrist. While some divines such as Prideaux or Adams might express concern over the potentially seditious use of apocalyptic material by extreme millenarians, or academic scruples at the lack of philological accuracy displayed by apocalyptic interpreters, they did not deny the relevance of the Apocalypse, or the importance of its application to church history.[53] The belief that the pope was Antichrist, and that this identification provided the key to the prophetic interpretation of church history, enjoyed almost universal intellectual assent in the Jacobean Church. No radically alternative exegesis was advanced against this orthodoxy, at least in print, although degrees of enthusiasm undoubtedly varied, and commentators might differ on some details of interpretation.[54]

If Bernard's remarks (and the conflicts over Joseph Hall's *The Old Religion*) illustrate a certain tension among English Protestants over the relative importance of apocalyptic studies and conclusions, what may have helped to keep together the different streams of apocalyptic thought, and the different degrees of enthusiasm for the issue, was the need to close ranks. For there was a minority of divines beginning to emerge who were prepared to undermine the apocalyptic tradition at its roots, and to deny that the pope was alone the Antichrist foretold in Scripture.

THE REJECTION OF THE TRADITION

Even in the 1590s there is evidence that, under the surface, some individuals in the Universities were beginning to question aspects of this

52 Brachlow, *Communion*, p.102; Firth, *Apocalyptic Tradition*, pp.179, 202.

53 See above, n.40.

54 Firth, *Apocalyptic Tradition*, pp.201–2; Bauckham, *Tudor Apocalypse*, p.236. P. White (*Predestination*, p.225 n.59) notes a possible exception in E. Arber (ed.), *A Transcript of the Registers of the Company of Stationers, 1554–1640* (5 vols., 1875–94), II: 191r, where the registers of the Stationers' Company record that on 2 October 1582 an anonymous work, 'Prima demonstratio quod Papa non sit Antechristus ille insignis', was licensed under the hand of Bishop Aylmer 'and divers others'. However, the tract with this title is the work of the Romanist polemicist Nicholas Sander, and the entry in the Stationers' Register must in fact refer to the refutation of this work by William Whitaker – *Ad Nicolai Sanderi Demonstrationes Quadraginta ... responsio* (1583). This was an official work, dedicated to Sir William Cecil, and was published together with the full text of

orthodoxy. John Overall, the Regius Professor of Divinity at Cambridge, provoked the opposition of other College Heads in 1599 when he opposed as too extreme the thesis that the pope alone was the Antichrist. Instead, he demonstrated that all the notes of Antichrist might as easily pertain to Mohammed and the Turks, and suggested that it was most likely that the pope and the Turk together constituted 'that Antichrist' foretold in Scripture. It was presumably reports of Overall's opinions which led to the complaints made in 1603–4 by a variety of puritan writers (including William Bradshaw) that the point of the pope's identity as Antichrist was being rejected by English writers – an accusation which was strongly denied by the government apologist Gabriel Powel.[55] By 1609 the puritan William Sclater was making similar complaints in a sermon at Paul's Cross. At Oxford, too, there were hints of dissent. Archbishop Abbot claimed before the king in 1615 that John Williams, the recently deceased Lady Margaret Professor of Divinity who was a friend of John Howson, had 'defended that the pope was not Anti-Christ'.[56] It was possibly Williams, and those who might have been influenced by him, whom Prideaux had in mind a year earlier when he demanded in a sermon at the Oxford Act: 'Is this a time to make a doubt, whether the pope be Antichrist or no, seeing his hornes and markes are so apparently discovered?'[57] By 1617, Richard Bernard was complaining directly of 'Some particular men, (out of curiosity and conceit of their owne wit, affectation of singularity, doting addiction to popish writers, want of further illumination in the point, partiall inclinations towards the divinity of Rome, or the like)' who denied that the pope was Antichrist.[58]

Nevertheless, Overall's views were not initially representative of the attitude held on this issue by the new breed of anti-Calvinist divines. Andrewes, as we have seen, endorsed the identification of the pope as

Sander's original tract (complete with Sander's titlepage, which has prompted the subsequent error).

55 CUL, MS Gg/1/29 fols.39–42r, 67v, 102–5. For a holograph of the arguments put to Overall by Laurence Chaderton and others as to why neither the Turk, nor the Turk and pope together, were the Antichrist, and Overall's comments in reply, see LPL, Lambeth MS 2550 fol.105. Overall's more detailed replies are in CUL, MS Gg/1/29 fols.40r–41r. For the complaints, see Bradshaw, *Myld and lust Defence*, pp.44–5; Gabriel Powel, *A Reioynder unto the Mild Defence* (1607), pp.118–19. This point was taken up by Roman polemicists, who maintained that the more learned in the Church of England denied that the pope was Antichrist: e.g. Walsingham, *A Search*, p.184.

56 Sclater, *Threefold Preservative*, sig.D4v; PRO, SP 14/80 fol.177v. I owe the first reference to Ken Fincham.

57 Prideaux, *Ephesus Backsliding*, p.36. Any nascent tradition stemming from Williams' views would presumably have been sustained by the residence at Balliol of the Greek Christopher Angelos, who had received a vision that Mohammed was the Antichrist: Hill, *Antichrist*, pp.181–2.

58 Bernard, *A Key*, 'Epistle to the Justices of Peace', sig.[B8]v.

Antichrist when pushed, and so did Overall's friend Richard Thomson.[59] The first clear assault in print on this consensus was not mounted until the publication of Richard Montagu's *New Gagg* of 1624.[60] When dealing with this issue, Montagu was mainly concerned to reject the claim of his Romanist opponent that all Protestants believed that Antichrist would not be a particular man (the 'Antichrist legend'), and that the pope was Antichrist. Montagu's chosen tactic (and one which he employed throughout the work when discussing numerous different doctrinal points) was to stress the obscurity of the issue, and to emphasize that the Church of England in her official formularies did not bind him to any one view. Few moderate writers would have denied this. Before Montagu, however, they did not feel this to be an obstacle to the recognition that the pope's identity as Antichrist was self-evidently true and an important doctrine which was vital to the Protestants' polemical position against Rome. Thus William Bedell, writing like Montagu against a Romanist opponent foisting extreme opinions on the Church of England, had freely acknowledged that the identification of the pope as Antichrist 'is no part of the doctrine of our Church', but had still insisted that it was 'yet a commonly received opinion', and emphasized that conscience and truth demanded its assertion, as well as its being an important force for unity among Protestants.[61]

Richard Montagu chose instead to stress the obscurity of the matter, and appealed to the uncertainty of the early church Fathers on this point. He also referred to the Fathers' interpretation of the Antichrist as a single individual several times without making adverse comment.[62] Montagu's

[59] Richard Thomson, *Elenchus Refutationis Torturae Torti* (1611), pp.61–6. The doctrine was also endorsed by anti-Calvinist figures such as Thomas Jackson and Nicholas Ferrar (Hill, *Antichrist*, p.25). Note also its use by the violently anti-puritan absolutist David Owen in BL, Royal MS 10.B.xiii fol.53v.

[60] Montagu had dealt with this issue in print three years earlier in his *Diatribae upon the First Part of the Late History of Tithes* (1621). Here, however, his main purpose had been to reprimand the anti-clerical tone of his opponent Selden in condemning clerics' ignorant speculations on the issue, which Montagu complained was 'unrespectfull, undutifull, and sawcy' (*ibid.*, p.284). Montagu's polemical position thus forced him towards accepting the clergy's apocalyptic speculations: indeed, he was prepared to demonstrate that the present pope's name made 666, and to defend the importance of the Book of Revelation (pp.289, 292). Even here, however, he followed the tenor of his later *New Gagg* and *Appello Caesarem* by emphasizing the uncertainty of the whole issue, and advised that the wisest men should 'professe their owne Ignorance in things of that nature' and should not dare to determine positively or conclude anything 'untill we see all things fully completed and fulfilled' (pp.290–1). Montagu also suggested, as he did in his later works, that Mohammed might just as easily be identified as the Antichrist, and that Rome and the Turk 'may make one spirituall State ad oppositum to Christ, and be sedes Antichristi' (pp.289–90).

[61] William Bedell, *The Copies of Certaine Letters which have Passed betweene Spaine and England in Matter of Religion* (1624), pp.81–2.

[62] Montagu, *New Gagg*, p.73, and *Appello*, p.147.

treatment of patristic authors here flew in the face of the established position of Jacobean writers on this point. No less a patristic scholar than Lancelot Andrewes, after applying the prophecies of Revelation chapters 17 and 18 to the See of Rome, had explained away the Fathers' uncertain interpretation of these points by arguing that in the days of the early church this was an obscured 'mystery of iniquity', whereas to contemporaries these things were now clear, 'qui consummatum jam prophetiam illam quotidie oculis usurpamus'.[63]

Montagu chose to distance himself and the Church of England from the 'private imaginations' and 'severall fancies of men' who peremptorily affirmed the pope to be Antichrist. He also contradicted the claims of authors such as Bedell that Protestant writers were united in denying that Antichrist would be a particular man, or on the issue of whether the Turk or the pope were 'the State Antichristian'.[64] By identifying a supposed division among Protestant writers, Montagu was able to claim the support of some orthodox divines for his own assertion that 'that Antichrist' would be a future individual, 'some varlet above the rest', and that 'for the State Antichristian, the Turke and Pope together may seeme to make it'.[65] The list of 'many Protestant divines' to whom Montagu appealed for this view was taken (unacknowledged) from Overall, and the divines in question were all foreign sixteenth-century authors.[66]

The lack of any earlier English Protestant divines to whom Montagu could appeal (despite his general concern in these works to focus on English Protestantism alone) is striking. It is especially noteworthy given the prodigious output of printed material on this subject in Elizabethan and Jacobean England. This in itself bears testimony to the unity of English apocalyptic thought before Montagu, and the unprecedented nature of his break with it.[67] Indeed, Montagu's opponent John Yates

63 Andrewes, *Tortura Torturi*, pp.220–1. Cf. Andrewes, *Responsio*, pp.338–9. See also Jackson, *Works*, I: 314; Abbot, *Demonstratio*, pp.11–12; Downame, *Treatise*, i. p.5; Willet, *Synopsis* (1613), p.224; Bernard, *A Key*, p.93; Beard, *Antichrist*, sig.A4v. Montagu quoted Thomas Morton making the same point only so that he could extend the veiled nature of the prophecies into the contemporary age and assert it as a general principle, against those who had been 'too violently forward' on the issue, thereby dodging the whole point of Morton's (and Andrewes') argument (Montagu, *Appello*, pp.143, 146).

64 Montagu, *New Gagg*, pp.73–5; *idem*, *Appello*, p.146.

65 Montagu, *New Gagg*, p.75.

66 Montagu cites mostly Reformed writers – Zanchius, Hyperius, Lambert, Grynaeus, Draconites and Oecolampadius, as well as Melanchthon – see *New Gagg*, p.75; CUL, MS Gg/1/29 fol.39r. See also *Appello*, p.159. For Prideaux's refutation of Montagu's citations from these authors, see his *Viginti-duae Lectiones*, i. p.178.

67 The only British writer whom Montagu cites in this discussion is Jewel, based on a passage in which Jewel refuses to say that the pope is Antichrist (*Appello*, p.159). But for a more convincing interpretation of this passage see Firth, *Apocalyptic Tradition*, p.86. For

noted with some delight that even Montagu's licenser and defender at York House, Francis White, had strongly affirmed the pope to be Antichrist, 'and', Yates commented, 'I am content they joyne battell to fight it out.'[68]

By arguing that the papacy and Turk jointly represented the political 'state' of Antichrist, and in making the suggestion that 'that Antichrist' might in fact be a future individual composed of the two, Montagu had essentially duplicated the arguments made by Overall in his 1599 disputation. In fact, Montagu slavishly followed Overall's order of points and collections of references in a way that suggests that he must have had Overall's manuscript to hand.[69] He also followed Overall in his *Appello Caesarem*, published in the following year, in which Montagu focused in greater detail on the argument that both the Turk and pope were Antichrist as 'the more moderate and temperate Tenent'. At the same time, he rejected the 'too violently forward' opinion which would not extend the application of *the* Antichrist beyond the papacy as being held mostly by Calvinists.[70] Like Overall, Montagu then went on to argue in detail that, not just a few, but *all* the scriptural prophecies might be applied to the Turkish State and Tyranny in 'every way', thereby ignoring all the well-worn Protestant arguments for preferring the papacy on particular points.[71]

Mohammed and the Turks had always had a significant part to play in the interpretation of scriptural prophecies in Protestant thought. They were important in preventing the prophecies of Antichrist from being applied exclusively to Rome and played a significant role in early Protestant exegesis. If greater stress was placed on Rome in later years, Islam still remained important in prophecy. The idea of a close association

Jewel's clear acceptance of the apocalyptic tradition elsewhere, see Christianson, *Reformers*, pp.32–3; Bauckham, *Tudor Apocalypse*, p.136.

[68] John Yates, *Ibis ad Caesarem* (1626), iii. p.12. See Francis White, *The Orthodox Faith and Way to the Church* (1617), pp. 279–80. In White's defence of Montagu (Bodl., Rawlinson MS C.573 fols.66r–67v) he stresses that Montagu still admitted the pope to be *an* Antichrist and popery antichristian, and that Montagu only presented his argument as a personal opinion, and with humble submission to any demonstrative argument of learned divines which could make the controversy seem clearer to him. White was clearly not yet prepared to renounce his own view.

[69] Compare CUL, MS Gg/1/29 fols.39r–40r, 41r; Montagu, *New Gagg*, p.75; *idem*, *Appello*, pp.148–9, 159. It is possible that Montagu's friend John Cosin, who had been the late bishop's secretary, may have passed Overall's notes on to Montagu. For a further indication that Montagu had access to Overall's notes, see Cosin, *Correspondence*, I: 87.

[70] Montagu, *Appello*, pp.143, 148–9.

[71] *Ibid*., pp.151–9; CUL, MS Gg/1/29 fols.39r–40r; cf. Montagu, *Diatribae*, pp.289–90. For a useful summary of the traditional arguments for preferring the application to the papacy of most of the major scriptural prophecies, marshalled specifically to rebut Montagu's arguments, see Prideaux, *Viginti-duae Lectiones*, i. pp.171–9. Brady notes that Montagu was practically alone among seventeenth-century Protestant writers in associating Mohammed with the number 666 (Brady, *Contribution*, pp.89–95).

between Islam and popery remained widespread, and generally one or two apocalyptic images (such as Magog, or sometimes the Little Horn) were specifically applied to the Turks, although the most important prophecies of Antichrist (such as the Second Beast of the Apocalypse and the Whore of Babylon) were now treated as referring to the papacy alone, as *the* final Antichrist, while the Turk was merely *an* Antichrist.[72] If the Turk occasionally seemed to rise to equal prominence with the pope, this generally occurred in the Central European Protestant tradition, at times when the military threat from the East was most acute. In such circumstances, the threat of invasion worked against the general desire to preserve Antichrist for exclusive application to the papacy.[73]

Montagu diverged from this tradition in that, like Overall before him, he chose to emphasize continental writers' use of the Turks essentially in order to diminish the prophetic importance attached to the pope, and he distorted these Protestants' arguments and intentions accordingly. But here Montagu did not merely invoke Luther's and other early Reformers' distinction between the open and secret nature of Antichrist to suggest that the papacy and Islam jointly constituted the Antichrist.[74] Rather, he went beyond even Overall's position by maintaining that, comparing the Turkish and Popish States, the scriptural prophecies of Antichrist fitted 'rather the Turk by much, than the pope; rather the Mahometan iniquity, than the Hildebrandinian impiety ... because ... the Marks and Cognisances of that eminent and great Antichrist ... do all as much accrue unto, and fit the Turk, or rather, and indeed more, Him and Them, than they doe the popes, in their State and Government ad oppositum'.[75] While refusing to commit himself to any single view at the end of his discourse, Montagu had equipped his reader with all the evidence for an exclusive identification of Antichrist with the Turk.

Moreover, at other points in his discussion, Montagu seemed prepared to apply the term 'Antichrist' to the papacy only according to the generalized sense of the term as it occurs in St John's Epistles. He explained that the papacy was Antichrist only 'in as much as there were of old, are now, and alway will bee, many Antichrists: and hee that any way opposeth

[72] E.g. Downame, *Treatise*, i. p.6; Willet, *Synopsis* (1852), II: 350; Firth, *Apocalyptic Tradition*, pp.18–19, 34, 54–5, 82–3, 95–100; Bauckham, *Tudor Apocalypse*, pp.96–9, 235; Ball, *Expectation*, pp.78–80; Christianson, *Reformers*, pp.17, 38–9, 64. Also note that Sutcliffe's *De Turcopapismo* actually argued, not just for the similarity of popery and Islam, but that papists were actually worse than the Turks (pp.91–133, 600–1). Cf. Willet, *Antilogie*, p.61; Ormerod, *Picture of a Papist*, i. pp.182–265. See also above, p.63.

[73] Firth, *Apocalyptic Tradition*, p.18.

[74] Montagu, *Appello*, p.148; Firth, *Apocalyptic Tradition*, p.19.

[75] Montagu, *Appello*, p.149.

Christ in his Kingdom, his Word, his Church, is an Antichrist'.[76] Writers such as Prideaux, Downame, Richard Sheldon and Dove had accepted that there were many different kinds of 'Antichrists', each of which could be understood as applicable to different groups, but had been equally firm in maintaining that the pope was 'that Antichrist', to be distinguished from other 'petty Antichrists' such as the Turk, and other bands of heretics.[77] By contrast, when Montagu called the pope 'Antichrist', he meant merely that the papacy dissented from Scripture, 'or proposeth any thing as Credendum against that Rule', which could in effect make Rome simply one among a host of unsound and heretical churches, and the pope merely one among many 'petty Antichrists'.[78]

Montagu's arguments were attacked by a series of divines – not merely by puritans such as Anthony Wotton, John Yates and Henry Burton, but also by episcopalian Calvinists such as Abbot's chaplain Daniel Featley, and at the York House Conference by the Calvinist bishop Thomas Morton.[79] His arguments were also refuted the following year at the Oxford Divinity Act by the Regius Professor, John Prideaux, while lecturing on the question 'Papa potius quam Turca habendus sit pro Antichristo'.[80] Prideaux hinted that Montagu was not alone in his heterodoxy on this issue, remarking of the opinion that Mohammed rather than the pope was the Antichrist that 'nonnulli ex nostris (nescio quo consilio, aut

[76] *Ibid.*, p.145. Cf. *idem*, *New Gagg*, p.75. While Overall believed it to be important to emphasize the other generalized sense of the term Antichrist, he was clearer than Montagu in applying 'that Antichrist' to the papacy, as well as to the Turk: CUL, MS Gg/1/29 fols.40r, 41r, 42r.

[77] Prideaux, *Viginti-duae Lectiones*, i. p.166; Downame, *Treatise*, i. pp.3, 6. Cf. Sheldon, *First Sermon*, p.33; Taylor, *Christs Victorie*, p.717; William Whitaker, *Praelectiones ... de Ecclesia* (Cambridge, 1599), pp.70–1; John Dove, *A Sermon Preached at Pauls Crosse ... Intreating of the Second Comming of Christ* (1594), sigs.D2r–D3v.

[78] Montagu, *Appello*, pp.160–1.

[79] Cosin, *Works*, II: 21–3, 80–1; Yates, *Ibis*, iii. pp.12–14; Burton, *Baiting*, p.55; Daniel Featley, *A Second Parallel* (1626), ii. pp.37–9.

[80] Prideaux, *Viginti-duae Lectiones*, i. pp.161–79. Although Prideaux nowhere mentions Montagu by name, there can be no doubt that his lecture is intended as a detailed refutation of the arguments presented on this subject in *Appello Caesarem*. In his lecture, Prideaux treats one by one all of Montagu's arguments for Antichrist being the Turk (pp.175–9). The list of Protestant writers referred in Objection No. 12 (pp.178–9) is identical to that compiled by Montagu in *Appello*, p.149 (and in the *New Gagg*, p.75). While Prideaux talks of several 'ex nostris' who seemed to favour the opinion of Mohammed being the Antichrist, he refers especially to a particular individual (p.166). Prideaux had rebuked George Palmer of Lincoln College in the Schools the year before for allying himself with Montagu's views on Arminianism: Anthony Wood, *The History and Antiquities of the University of Oxford*, ed. J. Gutch (2 vols., Oxford, 1792–6), II: 354–5; Prynne, *Canterburies Doome*, pp.157–8. Given the furore following his open attack on Montagu the previous year it was obviously in Prideaux's best interests not to name his opponent directly. His audience, however, can have had little doubt as to who was intended.

supercilio) videnter huic commento favere'.[81] The rejection of the pope's identity as Antichrist was to become the hallmark of the Laudian era although its roots, as we have seen, may be traceable back to early Jacobean times.

While Laud and Montagu wisely restricted themselves to the condemnation of those who 'peremptorily' asserted the pope to be Antichrist, and declared the issue to be an area of impenetrable obscurity,[82] there were others who addressed the question more directly. Gilbert Sheldon, probably at his DD disputation in 1628, was the first person in Oxford whom Thomas Barlow heard deny publicly that the pope was Antichrist. This drew a typically acerbic response from Prideaux.[83] The tradition that the pope was Antichrist was also firmly rejected by the pro-government polemicists Christopher Dow and Peter Heylyn. Heylyn ignored a century of Protestant reasoning on the matter by arguing that the pope could not be Antichrist because he did not deny Christ's incarnation directly.[84] Since the volume in which Heylyn advanced this argument had been specifically commissioned 'by authority' to defend it against the charges levelled by Henry Burton, this might be taken to express the Caroline government's official 'line' on this point. Christopher Dow received promotion at court specifically on the strength of his own tract.[85] On the point of the papal Antichrist, Dow admitted that some 'immoderate' writers had been licensed by authority in the past, and that many learned in the Church of England had made the identification, but saw this as being the result of overzealousness in the early years of the Reformation, since 'to them that calmely and seriously consider it, it may not without good reason bee disputed as doubtfull: whether the pope, or any of them, in his person, or the Papall Hierarchy bee that great Antichrist, which is so much spoken of'.[86]

The most detailed rejection of the traditional identification of the pope

[81] Prideaux, *Viginti-duae Lectiones*, i. p.166; cf. p.161. It is possible, of course, that Prideaux claimed these opinions to be held by several people in order to disguise the fact that it was the arguments of Montagu's *Appello Caesarem* which he was directly opposing.

[82] Laud, *Works*, IV: 308–9, 313. Montagu did not tackle the issue of Antichrist in print again after 1625, although in his posthumously published *Acts and Monuments*, p.423, he refers to Mohammed in passing as 'that Antichrist'.

[83] Barlow, *Genuine Remains*, p.192. Barlow reports having heard the Question 'An Papa sit Antichristus?' constantly held 'Affirmative' between 1624 and 1633. See also the thesis proposed by one Howorth of Magdalene College for the Cambridge Act of 1631 that 'Nondum constat, Quid sit insignis ille Antichristus': PRO, SP 16/193 fol.158. On Sheldon's links with Laud, see Laud, *Works*, V: 186; R. Orr, *Reason and Authority. The Thought of William Chillingworth* (Oxford, 1967), pp.31, 39–41.

[84] Heylyn, *Briefe Answer*, pp.127–9. Cf. *idem*, *Cyprianus*, p.18. However, Heylyn's true position (if he had one) on this issue is deeply problematical: see above, p.89. I hope to deal with Heylyn's early career in more detail elsewhere.

[85] Laud, *Works*, IV: 86–7.

[86] Dow, *Innovations*, p.53.

as Antichrist to be published during the years of Laudian ascendancy was made by Robert Shelford in his 'Treatise Shewing the Antichrist not to be yet come'. This formed one of his *Five Pious and Learned Discourses* which were published in Cambridge in 1635 when the Laudian William Beale was vice-chancellor. Shelford identified the Turk as the Second Beast, resurrected the ancient 'Antichrist legend' that Antichrist must be a single man and reign for only three and a half years and, like Heylyn (who possibly borrowed his argument from him), overturned the whole tradition of Protestant exegesis on this point by arguing that Rome's Christianity proved that she was not the Antichrist, who must deny Christ absolutely.[87] All of Shelford's arguments, in the mouths of Jesuit controversialists, had been refuted in detail by Lancelot Andrewes in his *Responsio ad Apologiam Cardinalis Bellarmini* over twenty years earlier.[88]

Detailed alternative expositions of the Book of Revelation were rare during the 1630s, however; possibly because they could only be derived from arguments already developed by Roman polemicists. Thus it was not until the 1650s that Henry Hammond not only rejected the pope's identity as Antichrist, but also rationalized this into a refusal to accept the Book of Revelation as an account of the church's entire history, developing instead a full-scale praeterist interpretation.[89] Nevertheless, apocalyptic rhetoric was not entirely abandoned under Laud. Instead, Antichrist was occasionally applied to the Turks, or to the puritans and separatists. There was certainly nothing new in identifying separatists as a part of the Antichrist; Richard Cox and John Whitgift had been happy to do so in Elizabethan times. But these men had all clearly affirmed that the pope was the first and greatest Antichrist,[90] and Whitgift's main grievance had been that the separatists were dividing the army of Christ, which 'should unanimiter fight against that Antichrist'.[91] Laudian divines, however, were prepared to give a more prominent antichristian role to puritans. Preaching in Cambridge on Christmas Eve 1639, John Cosin, having ignored the papal Antichrist, seemed to offer 'the Puritane Antichrist' more as an alternative, allegedly denouncing the puritans as 'Hydra, Locusts ascending out of the

87 Shelford, *Discourses*, pp.282, 284, 235, 293–6.

88 Andrewes, *Responsio*, pp.304–411. For responses to Shelford's arguments on this point, see CUL, CUR 18/6/9.

89 Firth, *Apocalyptic Tradition*, p.246; Ball, *Expectation*, pp.72–4; Brady, *Contribution*, pp.157–64. The praeterist interpretation limits the major prophecies to the pre-Constantinian church.

90 Bauckham, *Tudor Apocalypse*, pp.135, 130; Parry, *Protestant Vision*, pp.193–5.

91 *The Works of John Whitgift*, ed. J. Ayre (3 vols., Cambridge, 1851–3), II: 182; cf. Richard Curteys, *Two Sermons* (1576), sig.B1v – both cited in Bauckham, *Tudor Apocalypse*, pp.135, 142.

bottomlesse pitt, the very forme of the beast, hellhounds'.[92] Prophecies from Revelation were applied to the practices of the Laudians' opponents within the Church of England rather than to the Romanists abroad. Francis White's dedication to Laud of his *Treatise of the Sabbath-Day* compared 'the Rising up of some schismaticall spirits among us' with the New Testament prophecies of the appearence of false prophets. John Pocklington saw Sabbatarian doctrines in a similar light, claiming that 'this name Sabbath ... is a mysterie of iniquitie, intended against the Church'. Jeremy Taylor also attacked presbyterianism as antichristian.[93]

Few writers had any doubts in the 1630s that the traditional identification of Antichrist was frowned upon by Laud's ecclesiastical establishment. Writing from Cambridge to his puritan friend William Twisse in May 1635, Joseph Mede clearly perceived a current trend against calling the pope Antichrist, which had now become a bar to preferment. Rejecting the accusation that he was falling in with the Laudians, Mede averred that 'if I did so, I should quickly renounce my Tenet of the Apocalyptical Beast, which I know few men now hold, yea or would fain do'.[94] Indeed it was this tenet, Mede claimed, that had prevented him from gaining the support of an ecclesiastical establishment which might otherwise have rewarded his regard for ceremonialism: 'it may be that I have had so many Notions that way as would have made another man a Dean or a Prebend or something else ere this. But the point of the pope's being Antichrist as a dead fly, marred the savour of that ointment.'[95] In January of the same year Mede explained to Twisse his reluctance to publish his apocalyptical specu-

92 BL, Harleian MS 7019 p.63. Cosin's language might conceivably have been intended as a parody of puritan rhetoric.

93 Francis White, *A Treatise of the Sabbath-Day* (3rd edn, 1636), Epistle Dedicatorie; Pocklington, *Sunday no Sabbath*, pp.6–7; Jeremy Taylor, *Works*, ed. R.G. Heber and C.P. Eden (10 vols., 1847–54), V: 14. Cf. William Page, *A Treatise or Justification of Bowing at the Name of Jesus* (Oxford, 1631), Epistle Dedicatory. See also Lamont, *Godly Rule*, pp.67–8. John Barwick and Griffith Williams later applied the number 666 to the Solemn League and Covenant, while Williams' *The Great Antichrist Revealed* (1660) applies all the apocalyptic passages to puritanism which had earlier been used against the established church (Brady, *Contribution*, pp.125–6, 152–4). On royalist apocalyptic thought in the 1640s, see also Capp, *Fifth Monarchy*, p.41; Matthews, *Walker Revised*, pp.158, 263.

94 Mede, *Works*, p.1003. The thesis 'Verisimile est Romanum Pontificem esse insignem Antichristum' was maintained in Cambridge as late as 8 June, 1632 – CUL, Add. MS. 3320 fol.221v (cf. fols.222–5). This may have been a response to Howorth's proposed thesis of the previous year – see above n.83.

95 Mede, *Works*, p.1003. Mede was, however, clearly concerned to reassure Twisse that he was not a lackey of the Laudian establishment, and he probably exaggerated the extent of his disaffection. In fact, Mede, on the strength of his written defences of altars and church ritual, was soon to become closer to Laud's circle than he suggests would be possible. On the complexities of Mede's position, see Milton, 'Laudians', p.29 n.59.

lations 'for fear of incurring ... a dangerous prejudice by an overpotent opposition'.[96] In fact, it appears that no treatises specifically dealing with Antichrist were licensed for the press between 1633 and 1640, while Laud was archbishop of Canterbury. Mede clearly identified within the Church of England 'a party ... [which] loves not the pope should be Antichrist' – a party which was also noted by the Jesuit Edward Knott and the Scottish presbyterian Alexander Henderson.[97]

There is only sparse evidence, however, to suggest that the papal Antichrist was publicly denied in sermons at a parish level. Among the articles prepared against John Cosin, Augustine Lindsell, Francis Burgoyne and other prebendaries of Durham Cathedral was the charge 'that you, contrary to the tenour of the Church of England, and the learned and reverend divines therof, bewraying therby your affection to the Church of Roome, of which you Arminians are rotten members, doe teach and maintayne that the Bishopp of Rome is not ille Antichristus, that great Antichrist, which exalteth himselfe above all that is called God'.[98] However, few such specific charges were made against individual Laudians by their parishioners in the 1640s. Immanuel Uty, a royal chaplain who was accused in a petition read against him in parliament in January 1641 that he had said 'that the pope was not Antichrist and hee loved him', seems to be a rare example.[99]

Efforts were directed more towards removing references to the papal Antichrist from Protestant polemical writings, and discouraging speculation on such issues altogether.[100] This may usefully be compared with the outlawing of Calvinist predestinarian views in the 1630s.[101] On the issue of Antichrist Laudian censorship was understandably less effective, as they had no Royal Declaration to invoke. The Laudian position, argued by Bishop Buckeridge at the York House Conference, and insisted upon by Montagu, Laud, Heylyn and others in their own defence, was simply that

96 Mede, *Works*, p.957.

97 *Ibid.*, p.1017; Knott, *A Direction*, pp.22–3; *Records of the Kirk of Scotland*, ed. A. Peterkin (Edinburgh, 1838), p.178. See also the Kent Petition against episcopacy in Larking, *Proceedings in Kent*, p.33.

98 Cosin, *Correspondence*, I: 196.

99 D'Ewes, *Journal*, p.232; PRO, LC 3/1 fol.38. Another example from Scotland is John Creighton, the minister of Paisley who was accused by his parishioners of having taught 'that the Turk is the very and only Anti-Christ, and no other': J.C. Lees, *The Abbey of Paisley* (Paisley, 1878), p.288. See also the reports in early January 1640 that Richard Nicholls of Peterhouse denied the pope to be Antichrist in conversation with fellow-commoners: CUL, VC Ct I.57 fols.208r, 210v.

100 Thus James Wedderburn, the Laudian bishop of Dunblane, stressed that 'we' do not commend 'those, who fill their bookes with the narrations of the wicked lives of some popes & their followers, thereby to prove the pope to be Antichrist, and the Church of Rome Antichristian': BL, Harleian MS 750 fol.71r.

101 See Tyacke, *Anti-Calvinists*, pp.49–50, 181–8, 248–65.

the Church of England had not determined the controversy either way in her official doctrinal formulations (regardless of the unanimous opinion of her own divines since the Reformation). The issue was therefore an obscure, non-fundamental point, upon which firm conclusions should be strongly discouraged.[102] Thus Articles 78 and 80, which unequivocally asserted the pope's antichristian nature, were among the Irish Articles revoked in 1634. Passages in books by Dr Richard Clerke and Richard Ward which affirmed the pope to be Antichrist were altered or removed by Laud's chaplain William Heywood and Juxon's chaplain Thomas Weekes respectively.[103]

The whole significance of the doctrine was under attack. Its value was denied in the conversion of Roman Catholics. Its employment in defences of the Church of England and the Reformation was avoided, and previous examples of such use were discounted as unstatesmanlike language, or as the unfortunate consequence of overzealousness in the heat of the early Reformation. It was not just systematic expositions of the papal Antichrist which were now suppressed; even casual allusions, or the use of apocalyptic language as such, were opposed. Vague references to the pope as Antichrist abound in the Book of Homilies and Jacobean statutes,[104] but in Laud's view even such passing allusions were dangerous and misleading, and should be avoided. Thus he excepted against the use of the term 'the Antichristian yoke' to describe the papal tyranny in a brief for a charitable collection for the Palatinate, partly for its unstatesmanlike language, but also partly 'because it could move nothing but scorn in the common adversary, that we should offer to determine such a controversy by a broad seal'.[105]

Laud himself did not make a point of rejecting the identification of the pope as Antichrist in his public works, but simply avoided the subject altogether. He followed Montagu (and, incidentally, the Roman convert Benjamin Carier) in emphasizing that it was a disputed point among learned Protestants, citing King James' remark that it was only a probable opinion.[106] But this was not the only possible reading of James' position. King James' reserve had not prevented him from identifying the pope as

102 Cosin, *Works*, II: 23, 41–2, 68; Montagu, *New Gagg*, pp.73–4; *idem*, *Appello*, p.143; Heylyn, *Briefe Answer*, pp.127–8; Laud, *Works*, IV: 308–9.

103 Prynne, *Canterburies Doome*, pp.271–2. Thus Clerke's remark 'But the pope is Antichrist' was altered by Heywood to read 'But one is Antichrist.'

104 See the list of the relevant passages in the Homilies in Bernard, *Judgement*, ii. pp.146–50, and the quotation from the Act for Confirmation of Subsidies of 3.Jac. in Prynne, *Canterburies Doome*, p.390.

105 Laud, *Works*, IV: 313.

106 *Ibid.*, IV: 309, 308; cf. VI: 577–8; Cosin, *Works*, II: 80–1. Cf. Benjamin Carier, *A Treatise* (Liège, 1614), p.42.

Antichrist and justifying the same in authoritative terms in his *Monitory Preface*, or from peremptorily talking of the pope and Rome as Antichrist and Babylon elsewhere.[107] Though not a matter of faith, it was not an indifferent matter to James: it was the course of political events that determined whether or not he chose to air his views in public, but there was no doubting the certainty with which he held them. James' treatment of doctrinal issues was always conditioned by his ultimately political concerns.[108] In the case of Whitgift, such concerns had directed that foreign policy should not be dictated by the apocalyptic doctrine. To Laud, such concerns demanded that the doctrine itself should be avoided, and reduced to the level of obscure debates not worth settling. In the archbishop's eyes, the doctrine boiled down to little more than another example of the use of 'foul language in controversies' (a regular complaint made by Roman polemicists).[109] In fact, as we have seen, alleging that the pope was Antichrist was not necessarily an incitement to bloodshed. The millenarian Joseph Mede, while predicting the fall of Rome, hoped that its end would occur without bloodshed. Anticipating possible Romanist offence at his calling the pope Antichrist, William Bedell had stressed that in making the accusation 'I write according to my perswasion & as an accuser must of necessity, without any tooth to any person, without any gall to those, that are otherwise minded.'[110]

Under Laud, the doctrine was systematically deprived of any positive value. Where Bedell, Downame and others had seen it as the most potent single issue to convert Romanists, Laud simply denied 'that the calling of Pope "Antichrist" did ever yet convert an understanding Papist'.[111] When Venice had seemed on the point of embracing Protestantism, Gabriel Powel's *Disputationum de Antichristo* (much admired by Matthew Sutcliffe) had been included among the Protestant works passed on to Sarpi and Fulgenzio in order to secure their conversion. Yet Laud singled out the same book as an illustration of the 'peremptoriness ... in this point, [which] did the Church of England no good, no honour in foreign parts'.[112]

107 King James, *Political Works*, pp.129–49, 155, 158, 159, 322.

108 *Ibid.*, pp.129, 80, 128; Fincham and Lake, 'Ecclesiastical policy', pp. 169–207.

109 Lake, 'Significance', pp. 161–78; Laud, *Works*, IV: 309. Cf. Richard Crashaw's remark that the doctrine was 'no point of Charitie': *The Complete Poetry of Richard Crashaw*, ed. G.W. Williams (New York, 1974), p.70. For Romanist complaints of the ill-mannered nature of the term, see e.g. William Bishop (quoted in Abbot, *Defence*, pp.204–5).

110 Capp, 'Political dimension', p.108; LPL, Lambeth MS 772 p.3 (cf. pp.189–91, 203). Cf. Abbot, *Defence*, pp.204–5, 210.

111 Laud, *Works*, IV: 309.

112 Bedell, *Two Biographies*, p.245; Matthew Sutcliffe, *A Briefe Examination* (1606), p.40; Laud, *Works*, IV: 309. Laud, as in most of his discussion of Antichrist, here follows Montagu, who explicitly attacked Powel's work in his *Appello*, p.144 (see also Cosin, *Works*, II: 80). See also the allusion in the last lines of the verses which Richard Crashaw

The Book of Revelation and the figure of Antichrist clearly held little positive value to men such as Laud. Their determination to proscribe the use of the historical apocalyptic tradition, however, doubtless owed much to the threat which they perceived it to pose – a threat which seemed to endanger far more than diplomatic niceties. Apocalyptic language was the staple diet of the Laudians' opponents, and had been used to challenge the ecclesiastical hierarchy and church ceremonies.[113] It also intruded potentially dangerous complications into the historical defence of the English ecclesiastical polity, which had in the Jacobean period come to lay increasing emphasis on the Church of England's episcopal succession through the medieval Latin Church. The Roman polemicists Richard Broughton, Anthony Champney and Matthew Kellison had recognized and attempted to exploit the problem encountered by English Protestant controversialists such as Francis Mason in maintaining an episcopal succession through the Church of Rome's ordination while at the same time holding the pope to be Antichrist. The Romanists argued that, in claiming ordination from papists, English ministers had proved themselves by their own arguments to be ministers of Antichrist – and could quote Matthew Sutcliffe's assertion that the pope as Antichrist was incapable of consecrating bishops.[114] The anti-Laudian pamphleteer Nicholas Bernard, writing in 1659, saw this in retrospect as a major concern prompting the Laudian rejection of the papal Antichrist model. He attacked 'those of ours, who in defence of our Ordination from the scandal of Antichristian, by its passing through the See of Rome, have endeavoured to take off that See, from being such', and added the baleful but telling comment that 'as it was a needlesse refuge, so the cure is worse than the disease'.[115] Other Laudians seem to have been concerned that those who traced the anti-christian 'mystery of iniquity' back to the earliest days of the primitive church thereby threatened to undermine the authority of the early Fathers and of antiquity.[116] More committed adherents to this apocalyptic belief

prefaced to Robert Shelford's *Five Pious Discourses* of 1635: Crashaw, *Complete Poetry*, p.70.

113 Christianson, *Reformers*, ch.4.

114 Broughton, *Protestants Demonstrations*, pp.25–6, 27, 36–7; Anthony Champney, *A Treatise of the Vocation of Bishops* (1616), p.123; Matthew Kellison, *Examen Reformationis Novae Praesertim Calvinianae* (1616), p.156; Sutcliffe, *An Abridgement*, pp.251–2. For Francis Mason's rather uncomfortable reply to this charge, see his *Vindiciae*, pp.189–90, 398–9.

115 Bernard, *Judgement*, ii. p.168.

116 John Cosin, Augustine Lindsell, Francis Burgoyne and other Durham prebendaries were accused in the articles exhibited against them in 1630 that, as well as denying the pope to be Antichrist, 'under praetense of defending the fathers and reverend antiquity, you feare not to contradict the Holy Scripture it selfe, unadvisedly and unlearnedly denying that the mystery of iniquity began betymes to worke, by small beginnings': Cosin, *Correspondence*, I: 196.

had also been dangerously vocal and (in King James' eyes) potentially seditious in their denunciation of the Spanish Match, and their demands for a more actively Protestant foreign policy in defence of the Palatinate.[117]

Moreover, apocalyptic expositions of the history of the Reformation attached great importance to Revelation 12.6 as the key to the medieval centuries. Its accompanying theme of persecution and of the 'invisibility' of God's elect during the reign of Antichrist tended to throw a greater emphasis on to the medieval proto-Protestant sects, rather than the ecclesiastical hierarchy, as representing best the Protestants' ancestry, and could thus pose a threat in Laudian eyes to the integrity of the episcopal church. Similarly, the use of Revelation 18.4 to justify the Reformation itself tended to emphasize doctrinal motives and absolute scriptural injunctions which might be taken to encourage separatism, and accorded ill with the Laudians' increasingly legalistic view of the break with Rome.[118]

Jacobean divines had demonstrated how such potentially subversive ideas might be accommodated and made powerful elements in a defence of the Church of England which protected her episcopal succession and ceremonial demands. Nevertheless, as we have seen, the increasing radicalization of the apocalyptic tradition, and its intrusion into ecclesiological debates, was beginning to prompt concern among conformist divines. For many divines associated with Laud, these ecclesiological issues were at the centre of their concerns. They were primarily aware of the threat to a settled ecclesiastical polity that apocalyptic ideas might pose in the hands of extremists, and this was enough to discredit the doctrine in their eyes and to render its continued public use undesirable.

As we shall see, the rejection of the model of the papal Antichrist had important implications for many of the ways in which both Roman and Protestant Churches were understood.[119] Nevertheless, more general conformist anxieties over the radicalization of apocalyptic doctrine meant that the downplaying of apocalypticism under Laud did not offend everyone to the same extent. After all, the apocalyptic tradition could assume a different role and importance in the divinity of the various groups which endorsed it.[120] While Laudian restraints on apocalypticism undermined an important plank of the puritan world-view, they also served to proscribe apocalyptical speculation of a kind which (as we have seen) was worrying

117 Fincham and Lake, 'Ecclesiastical policy', pp.198–201; S.L. Adams, 'The Protestant cause: religious alliance with the West European Calvinist communities as a political issue in England, 1585–1630' (Oxford University DPhil, 1973), pp.255–344.

118 See below, pp.336–40.

119 See below, pp.347–8, 446.

120 Moreover, Laud and his associates' preference for a more spiritual interpretation of Revelation, like their doctrine of grace, meant that they shared an unlikely common ground with some of the more radical sectaries such as Familists and Quakers: Hill, *Antichrist*, pp.12, 95–6, 142–5.

a far larger proportion of English Protestants. Richard Farmer doubtless voiced the feelings of many in his Paul's Cross sermon of 1629 in which he criticized those who searched too much in the Scriptures and Book of Revelation to know the time of Christ's coming and other future events.[121] Thomas Beard had noted with frustration in 1625 that many upright Calvinist divines who could defend true religion still preferred not to refer to Antichrist. Joseph Hall held the pope to be Antichrist, but was prepared to fall in with the new tone of the 1630s. He thus refrained from such direct identifications in his *Plaine and Familiar Explication of All the Hard Texts of the Old and New Testament* of 1633, where he applied many apocalyptic texts to the Turks or the early Roman Empire which had previously been reserved for the medieval papacy.[122]

Nevertheless, the crucial point is that Hall attempted to refer to the pope as Antichrist again in 1640, as he tried to construct a defence of *iure divino* episcopacy in the face of the Scottish troubles.[123] Hall's intention was presumably to appeal to moderate puritan opinion – and this in itself reflects what may have been one of the most important roles fulfilled by the doctrine of the papal Antichrist in the Church of England. This was its capacity to act as a bulwark against popery in the perceptions of moderate puritans, and thereby to assure them of the goodwill and Protestant credentials of an increasingly compromised episcopalian Calvinist position. The puritans Richard Bernard, Thomas Taylor and the author of the *Sacrae heptades* had thus in the past been able to cite approvingly the published commentaries of two bishops – Robert Abbot and George Downame – in their discussions of apocalyptic issues.[124] Both bishops were defenders of *iure divino* episcopacy, but their apocalyptical studies made such opinions on church polity more palatable (or at least, less objectionable) to puritan tastes. Similarly, Francis Mason and William Bedell included denunciations of the papal Antichrist within treatises promoting the Church of England's episcopal succession.[125]

John Dove's irenical *Perswasion to the English Recusants* demonstrates clearly the value of the doctrine of the papal Antichrist as a bulwark to reassure stronger puritans of the good intent of those who embraced tactically moderate postures towards Rome. At the end of a remarkably

121 Richard Farmer, *A Sermon Preached at Pauls Crosse* (1629), pp.12–14. Cf. John Swan, *Speculum Mundi* (Cambridge, 1635).

122 Hall, *Works*, IV: 568–633 (see also especially pp.481–2, 488 and 562). Hall regularly refers to the spiritual tyranny exercised by the successors of the heathen Roman Empire, but deliberately (and sometimes tortuously) avoids naming the pope or the Roman Church directly (e.g. *ibid.*, pp.591, 605–6, 610, 612 and 617).

123 Hall, *Works*, X: 543. For Laud's letter to Hall, see Laud, *Works*, VI: 577–8.

124 Bernard, *A Key*, p.44; Taylor, *Christs Victorie*, p.790; Christianson, *Reformers*, p.112.

125 Mason, *Vindiciae*, p.186; LPL, Lambeth MS 772 p.3.

moderately expressed treatise, Dove was evidently anxious that his moderation might be misinterpreted, and therefore appended a brief explanatory epistle 'To the Protestant Reader'. In this section he referred any potential critic, as earnest of his good faith, to his Paul's Cross sermon of eight years earlier in which he had proved the pope to be Antichrist and maintained it to be 'sound and currant divinitie'. A similar case is that of Joseph Mede, who prompted puritan suspicions by his support for Laudian ceremonialism, but tried to assuage them by emphasizing the Laudian establishment's antipathy towards his apocalyptic ideas. This tactic was not an option for those Laudian divines who rejected the apocalyptic tradition, and thus their puritan readers were left to draw the inevitable conclusions from their more moderate expositions of Rome's errors and their defence of episcopacy. Thus it was that when Joseph Hall attempted to place references to the papal Antichrist into his defence of *iure divino* episcopacy as a sop to puritan fears, Archbishop Laud insisted that such passages be removed.[126]

Writing in 1623, the puritan firebrand Thomas Scot had drawn comfort from the fact that, although the Reformed Churches differed widely in their opinions of how far they should separate from the Roman Church, they all at least agreed that the pope was Antichrist, and that the separation was necessary.[127] In removing Antichrist and scriptural prophecies from perceptions of church history, the Reformation and the Church of Rome, Laudian divines inevitably questioned received ideas about the history, purpose, nature and permanence of the divisions within Christendom. They thus crucially altered the context in which they developed the more conservative notions of episcopacy and the institutional church which they had inherited from more moderate Jacobean divines. Just as crucially, they changed the context in which these earlier developments were regarded by their puritan opponents.

Writing just two decades after Scot, and attempting to trace the origins of the doctrinal novelties which he believed the Laudians to have introduced, the Scots Covenanter Robert Baillie attached great importance to the removal of 'the popes Antichristianisme', which was the Protestant

126 Dove, *Perswasion*, 'To the Protestant Reader'; Dove, *A Sermon ... of the Second Coming of Christ*, sig.D5v; Laud, *Works*, VI: 577–8. For Mede, see above pp.119–20. One Laudian polemicist who did attempt to do this was Peter Heylyn: contrast his remarks in a court sermon of January 1639 defending himself against charges of popery (Heylyn, *Parable*, pp.70–1) with his ridicule of the doctrine just two years earlier (Heylyn, *Briefe Answer*, pp.127–9). Heylyn had, however, dissociated himself too plainly and publicly from the doctrine, and bound himself too closely to the establishment, for his *volte-face* to be successful.

127 Thomas Scot, *A Tongue-Combate* (1623), p.88, in *The Workes of ... Mr Thomas Scot* (Utrecht, 1624).

Churches' 'chiefe bulwark to keepe all their people from looking back towards that Babilonish Whore'. 'This scarre-crow being set aside', he noted, 'at once the pope, the Cardinals, and all their Religion began to looke with a new face.'[128]

[128] Robert Baillie, *Ladensium ΑΥΤΟΚΑΤΑΚΡΙΣΙΣ* (Edinburgh, 1640), pp.33, 35–6. John Dury similarly identified this point as being the first stage of the Laudians' move towards popery: BL, Sloane MS 654 fols.218r–23r (Dury to Andrew Ramsay, 21 March 1642). See also Beard's comments on the beginnings of de Dominis' apostasy: *Antichrist*, sig.A3r. Note also the significance attached to this point by Dean John Young during the cross-examination of de Dominis: Neile, *Shiftings*, p.27.

3

Rome as a true church

THE 'TRUE CHURCH' IN PROTESTANT ECCLESIOLOGY AND THE PROBLEM OF ROME

The precise nature of the Church of Rome was a problem which exercised and perplexed the minds of English Protestant divines throughout the early Stuart period, provoking recurrent confusion and occasionally violent conflict. In his *Ecclesia Triumphans* and *Antilogie* of 1603, Andrew Willet had joined the authors of *A Christian Letter* in condemning the assertion made in Hooker's *Laws* that the Roman Church was a member of the family of Christ.[1] Unrest on this issue continued in the 1610s, and it figured among the accusations made against Richard Montagu in parliament and pamphlets during the 1620s, and complaints against Laudian writers in the 1630s. Yet this was not merely a reaction against the innovations of Hooker and Laud: open pamphlet controversies broke out on this very issue between puritans and episcopalian Calvinists in the late 1620s. Much of the reason for these conflicts, it will be argued, rested in the confusion caused by the inconsistent use of polemical categories, but (as we shall see) these disputes were also rooted in profound inconsistencies within the Protestant doctrine of the church.

From the Reformation onwards, Protestant ecclesiology in England, as elsewhere, was preoccupied with the need to combat the claims of the visible Church of Rome to be the universal Catholic Church, the one true church of God, in which alone salvation was to be found. Against these claims, it was argued that the Holy Catholic Church of the Creed was fundamentally distinct from the national, institutional churches on earth. It was comprised solely of the predestinate, of God's elect. Only the elect were truly members of the body of Christ and it was to the elect alone that the scriptural promises of infallibility and indefectibility truly applied, rather than to the visible Church of Rome. This Catholic Church was 'invisible' in a number of respects. Its head, Christ, was now invisible,

[1] Willet, *Ecclesia Triumphans*, p.91; *idem*, *Antilogie*, sig.A3v; Hooker, *Works*, IV: 28–31.

while some of its members were already in heaven, and others were still unborn. Moreover, those members who were alive on earth, while visible *as men*, could not be outwardly perceived to be true members of Christ's church, because the kingdom of God lay within men's souls, and God alone truly knew who were his elect. This argument was not the preserve of dangerous puritan radicals, but was a commonplace of Protestant ecclesiology, argued with similar force and conviction by moderate puritans such as William Perkins, Andrew Willet and William Whitaker, and by the future Calvinist bishops Robert Abbot and John Davenant.[2]

The essential argument of these divines was that institutional churches should not be confused with this invisible 'church of the elect'. Members of the church of the elect could include the unbaptized and the excommunicate, who had no contact with any visible institutional church.[3] Roman writers (it was claimed) were in error in alleging that mere outward profession of the faith and communion of the sacraments were sufficient for a man to belong to the Catholic Church. They thereby allowed that the wicked and ungodly might be members of Christ's body.[4]

The 'visible church' thus consisted of the entire number of people who outwardly professed Christianity on earth, and was therefore a 'mixed church' including both elect and reprobate, with apparently no common spiritual bonds. When English Protestant divines discussed this 'visible church' they theoretically fragmented it into the various particular national churches. However, the unity of the visible church continued to be implied. As historians have noted, the Reformed Confessions tend to switch from talking of the universal church of the elect to discussions of the nature of the visible, particular church without any clear transition, so that the visible church might occasionally be described in terms identical to those used when describing the invisible church of the elect.[5] This ambiguity was in part deliberate, and helped to infuse the discussion of the visible church with the absolute spiritual values of the invisible. Also it helped to deflect Roman charges that Protestants set up two separate churches, allowing Protestant writers to claim that they were merely referring to two different aspects of the same church, in the same manner as the distinction that all

2 Abbot, *Third Part*, p.138; cf. p.225; Davenant, *Determinationes*, pp.156–7, 214–18; Jackson, *Works*, XII: 41–5; I. Breward (ed.), *The Work of William Perkins* (Appleford, 1970), pp.263–5 (from Perkins' *An Exposition of the Symbol or Creed of the Apostles*); Whitaker, *Praelectiones*, pp.4, 6–8, 10, 24–52; Willet, *Synopsis* (1613), pp.62–5 (a lengthier treatment than in the earlier editions).

3 Whitaker, *Praelectiones*, pp.12–13, 19–24, 116.

4 *Ibid.*, pp.7–8, 33–7, 82, 87; Matthew Sutcliffe, *De Vera Christi Ecclesia* (1600), sig.A2v, p.4v; *idem*, *A Briefe Examination*, p.21.

5 Brachlow, *Communion*, pp.115–16; J.F.H. New, *Anglican and Puritan* (Stanford, 1964), p.33; J.T. McNeill, *Unitive Protestantism* (1964), pp.44, 68–9. See also Windsor, 'The controversy', pp.145–7.

divines (including Roman ones) made between the church militant and the church triumphant. On this point it is possible to detect a subtle difference between the writings of divines such as Whitaker and Sutcliffe, who implied that they were merely referring to the company of the elect in two different states, and to those of Jacobean conformists such as Prideaux and Field, who seemed to imply that the church on earth and in heaven had effectively a separate membership.[6] While theologians such as Whitaker entered the caveat that we should charitably assume that all those in a visible church are elect, other Jacobean Calvinist conformist divines such as Field circumvented the need for such caveats by simply implying a more inclusive membership of the visible church *tout court*.[7] Nevertheless, it was the church of the elect which continued to be the principal concern of these divines, and a dualistic style of exposition inevitably resulted.

There thus emerged a tendency to discuss the differences between the various particular churches on earth in the language of the division between the reprobate and the saved. Where the invisible church model treated of 'true believers' and 'the faithful' in the sense of the truly elect, the same terms would be used in the visible church model to describe those particular *Protestant* churches which retained the profession of *pure* doctrine. 'The faithful' in the visible church model would thus refer to those Christians who belonged to a church which externally professed the true, Reformed faith. The unity of the Protestant churches in opposition to Rome was thus often spoken of in terms of the unity of the true church against men of merely formal belief. These elisions between the visible and invisible churches are made directly only in presbyterian and separatist writings, where links between church polity and salvation were more directly expressed.[8] Nevertheless, this dimension was often implied in the rhetoric of conformist divines, where the contrast between the 'true Churches' of Protestantism and Rome which is a church 'onely in title and profession' mirrored the distinctions made elsewhere between the true internal faith of elect believers and the mere outward 'historicall faith' of the non-elect.[9] These distinctions occurred most clearly in apocalyptic

6 Whitaker, *Praelectiones*, pp.21–3, 57; Sutcliffe, *De Ecclesia*, sigs.4v–5r; Prideaux, *Viginti-duae Lectiones*, i. pp.129–30; Richard Field, *Of the Church* (4 vols., Cambridge, 1847–52), I: 31. See also Windsor's comment on the 'insouciance' of Whitaker's reply: 'The controversy', p.142.

7 Whitaker, *Praelectiones*, p.37.

8 On radical puritan ecclesiology, see especially Brachlow, *Communion*, although Brachlow may underestimate the extent to which separatists made a practical *assumption* of an elision between the godly and the elect, however much they might repeat the conventional caveat that it is impossible to have infallible knowledge of the identity of God's elect in this life.

9 E.g. Downame, *Treatise*, ii. p.128.

exegesis, where the doctrine of the Two Churches was always more prominent than in strictly ecclesiological works.[10]

The church on earth was thus not allowed merely to disintegrate into a number of particular institutional churches all outwardly professing Christianity. Rather, it was the 'true church' of orthodox believers which was at the centre of ecclesiological interest. Protestant divines became preoccupied with identifying the marks of the 'true church', in opposition to those promoted by Romanist divines such as Bellarmine. These Protestant marks were generally understood to be the Word truly preached and the sacraments rightly administered, to which discipline was occasionally added, although categorizations varied. Prime emphasis, however, was always placed on purity of doctrine, and divines such as William Perkins and William Whitaker were happy to maintain that the true church could survive without the sacraments if required.[11] The 'true church' which emerged from these definitions was restricted to people of orthodox belief, and excluded heretics and schismatics, even though these groups might still formally profess Christianity. These marks of the 'true church' were marshalled against Roman claims for the marks of antiquity, universality, succession, unity and so on. The Protestants' marks were not necessarily seen as constitutive of the true church *in themselves*, however, and the problem remained of what was to be said of the status of a congregation where these means of grace still existed, but in a corrupt form. The minor conformist divine Robert Butterfield was entirely correct when he argued in the later 1620s that, while the Church of England's Article 19 concluded affirmatively that the true church was where God's Word was purely preached and the sacraments duly administered, it did not conclude negatively that there was no church where God's Word was only corruptly taught. 'We know', Butterfield maintained, 'that these markes are not so essentiall to the true Church, that so soone as unsound Doctrine is mingled with the truth of God's Word, and the Sacraments unduely administered; that which was a Church should cease to bee one.'[12] Calvinist divines had generally sought to avoid this problem of definition by using gratifyingly imprecise corporeal analogies. They might thus suggest that Rome was an infected body *about to* die, without having to state precisely what this signified in terms of the efficacy or otherwise of Rome's sacraments.[13]

[10] See above, pp.103–4. For exceptions, see Whitaker, *Praelectiones*, p.5; Carleton, *Thankfull Remembrance*, pp.182, 224 (see also frontispiece).

[11] P.D.L. Avis, *The Church in the Theology of the Reformers* (1981), ch.3; Lake, *Moderate Puritans*, pp.105–7; Breward, *Perkins*, p.269.

[12] Robert Butterfield, *Maschil. Or a Treatise to Give Instruction, Touching the State of the Church of Rome since the Councell of Trent* (1629), pp.86, 84–5.

[13] E.g. John Rainolds, *The Summe of the Conference betweene John Rainoldes and John Hart* (1609), p.651.

The precise status of the Church of Rome thus remained unclear. This was not necessarily an immediate problem, as the main concern of anti-papal polemic was to demonstrate that Rome was not a true particular church. Emphasis therefore came to be placed overwhelmingly on the importance of the Protestants' preservation of true doctrine, and on Rome's doctrinal errors, which separated her from 'the true church'. The principal concern of the evangelical English Protestant was to find the one true church on earth, and not to be misled when Rome claimed to hold this status herself. None could deny that Rome outwardly professed the principal points of Christianity, and that the ordained means of God's grace remained within her (though in corrupted form). Nevertheless, the weight of argument was directed towards emphasizing the depths of antichristian heresy into which Rome had fallen, and the overwhelming corruption of these same means of divine grace. It was Rome's unsoundness and heterodoxy that were to be proved, and the utter separation of her religion from that of the true church of orthodox Christian believers. The extent to which this apostasy undermined the means of grace for those who remained within Rome was not a major concern of these Calvinist divines.

This meant that in the writings of a host of English Protestant writers in this period – not just moderate puritans, but Calvinist conformists like Sutcliffe, Morton, Hall, Carleton, Crakanthorp, the Abbots and Powel – the difference between the Church of Rome and the Protestant Churches was expressed in terms of an absolute division, corresponding to the distinction between the elect and the reprobate, which often dovetailed with the distinction between the true church and the false. The tendency here was to read the doctrinal divisions between the churches in the same absolute light as the physical separation of the Roman and Protestant Churches, and thus into the division between the true and the false church. This sort of absolute partition was expressed at least partly in reaction to that expounded by Romanist writers, who argued in precisely these terms and would not admit any more qualified distinction between merely sound and unsound churches.[14]

This was not simply a relic of earlier radical puritanism. Well into the Jacobean period, certain types of polemical argument against Rome treated her as no church at all. George Carleton, soon to be made bishop of Landaff, argued in a series of treatises that since Rome's *definition* of the church included heretics, schismatics and the damned – groups which could not be included in the Protestant definition of the Catholic Church – it therefore followed that Rome herself should not be accounted a church at all. Instead, Rome was merely on a par with any mere congregation of

[14] Windsor, 'The controversy', p.145.

individuals.[15] As Henry Burton would later summarize this argument, 'things of different definitions have different denominations'. Since Rome and the Church of England propounded different definitions of the true church, it therefore followed that one of them must be the true church and the other the false. The sheer illogicalness of this argument may in part account for the fact that it did not gain a general currency in this period, although the puritans Wotton and Burton were to make effective polemical use of it in the 1620s.[16] Apocalyptic argument, too, by branding Rome as Babylon, encouraged the assumption that she should not be considered to be a church at all, and led William Perkins to argue that the Roman Church had indeed received the final bill of divorce from Christ.[17]

Nevertheless, it is comparatively rare to find among these authors direct denials that Rome was in any sense a church, although she might be excluded from the true church. While writers often presented the division from Rome in absolute terms, it is important to note that this perspective was not as inflexible as some historians have tended to suggest. The 'true church' argument did not represent the limits of ecclesiological discussion or presupposition. In particular polemical contexts, it was necessary for the very same writers to acknowledge Rome's claims to be a church, and indeed most divines worked on the practical assumption that Rome was a church, though unsound. This was as true for Luther and Calvin as for Elizabethan and Jacobean Protestants.[18]

The need to defend Rome's status as a church arose from a variety of polemical imperatives. First, there was the need to ensure the salvation of the Protestants' natural forefathers who had dwelt in communion with the Church of Rome before the Reformation. Both Richard Hooker and Robert Some, the fiercely Calvinist opponent of John Overall in Cambridge in the 1590s, defended Rome's status as a church on these grounds.[19] Also, as Edmund Bunny noted in the 1580s, if Protestants wished to claim the high ground of moderation in their separation from Rome, and to avoid the charge of schism, then it was essential that they resist the temptation to follow Romanist writers' claims that Protestants had departed absolutely from Rome. Instead, Bunny urged, they should

[15] George Carleton, *Consensus Ecclesiae Catholicae contra Tridentinos* (1613), pp.166–84, 234–42; *idem*, *Directions to Know the True Church* (1615), pp.8–9.

[16] Wotton, *Dangerous Plot*, i. pp.40–6; Burton, *Babel*, p.129.

[17] Perkins, *Reformed Catholike*, p.295. Contrast Hall, *Works*, VIII: 639.

[18] Avis, *Church*, pp.36–43; B.C. Milner, *Calvin's Doctrine of the Church* (Leiden, 1970), pp.153–4. Note also the apposite quotations from Calvin in Robert Some, *A Godly Treatise ... Touching the Ministerie, Sacraments, and the Church* (1588), pp.147–51, 163, 182 and Bunny, *Briefe Answer*, pp.115–16.

[19] R. Bauckham, 'Hooker, Travers and the Church of Rome in the 1580s', *JEH* 29 (1978), pp.44–7; Some, *Godly Treatise*, pp.152–3.

maintain that Rome was a church and that Protestants had departed merely from her *errors*, and not from her self. The need for this line of argument, and its value in confirming the continuity of the Church of England, was recognized by puritan pamphleteers such as Richard Bernard, as well as establishment figures such as Bishops Hall and Davenant.[20]

Another impulse – no less pressing – arose from the problem of separatists from the Church of England's own communion. These individuals were keen to argue that doctrinal error in the English Church could invalidate the power of sacraments and unchurch her. Robert Some's defence of Rome's status as a church in his *Godly Treatise* occurred in disputation with the separatist John Penry, when Some sought to defend the argument that popish and unpreaching ministers in the Church of England still had a calling, and could still administer true and efficacious sacraments.[21] As a greater emphasis was placed on the general efficacy of the Word and sacraments, even in churches which were not fully reformed, it became more important (for the sake of consistency) to maintain them to be efficacious in Rome, and Rome to be a church of Christ.

ROME AS A CHURCH 'SECUNDUM QUID'

Most mainstream Jacobean divines accepted the principle that Rome was still a church of Christ, but carefully qualified this point in ways which all but overthrew it. Rome was never simply a church of God, but always *secundum quid*, 'in some sense', according to some aspects of her nature.[22]

It was Rome's retention of the means of regeneration through God's Word and sacraments that merited her status as a church. However, Protestant writers seldom focused on the Christian features that Rome chose to retain, but dwelt instead on the irresistible action of God through the antichristian church, regardless of all Rome's attempts to corrupt the means by which He operated. As Davenant explained in a letter to Hall, the essence of a church

> does principally stand upon the gracious action of God, calling them out of darkness and death unto the participation of light and life in Christ Jesus. So long as God continues this calling unto any people, though they, as much as in them

[20] Edmund Bunny, *A Treatise Tending to Pacification* (1586), pp.79–81, 83, 93; Bernard, *Looke beyond Luther*, p.44; Hall, *Works*, VIII: 733–4 (Hall), 742 (Davenant).

[21] On Some's career and thought, see P. Lake, 'Robert Some and the ambiguities of moderation', *AfR* 71 (1980), pp. 254–78. George Gifford's defence of the Church of Rome in his *Short Treatise against the Donatists of England* (1589) was similarly born out of separatists' arguments that any who professed Christ with some weakness and infirmities were infidels.

[22] Richard Crakanthorp, *Defensio Ecclesiae Anglicanae* (Oxford, 1847), p.78; Some, *Godly Treatise*, pp.148–9 (quoting Daneau); Bunny, *Briefe Answer*, p.114.

lies, darken this light, and corrupt the means which should bring them to life and salvation in Christ; yet where God calls men unto participation of life in Christ by the word and by the sacraments, there is the true being of a Christian church, let men be never so false in their expositions of God's word, or never so untrusty in mingling their own traditions with God's ordinances.[23]

Among writers of a more puritanical disposition this distinction between what Rome intended, and the fact that the means of regeneration still remained within her, was rendered even more starkly. Thus Perkins claimed that the Scriptures and sacraments remained within the Church of Rome, not for the use of that church, but in order to provide the means of salvation for the true church of God which existed as a tiny, suffering congregation of pure worshippers within the Roman Church. The Roman institutional church therefore acted like a lantern which held a candle, not for itself, but for the benefit of others.[24]

That baptism within the Roman Church was still effectual was clear. All divines accepted that there was no true baptism outside the church and, since rebaptism was not practised towards popish converts, the Church of Rome must therefore still retain true baptism.[25] She thus met the crucial requirement for any church – that by baptism she brought forth children unto God.[26] Once brought forth, however, it was admitted that these children were unlikely to survive in true religion. Richard Field followed Augustine in admitting that, in possessing effectual baptism, heretics such as Roman Catholics were in a sense a part of the visible church of God. Nevertheless, Field carefully qualified this admission. Rome was only part of the church of God, he declared, because 'it ministereth the true sacrament of baptism to the salvation of the souls of many thousand infants *that die after they are baptized, before she have poisoned them with her errors*'.[27] The only hope for salvation in the Church of Rome was thus to die immediately after baptism. Field seems to moderate this position somewhat elsewhere,[28] but the basic attitude which underlay it was com-

23 Hall, *Works*, VIII: 742. Cf. Some, *Godly Treatise*, pp.163, 182; Downame, *Treatise*, ii. p.230. Downame follows Calvin in accepting that Rome is still a church in its preservation of the sacraments and the outward profession of Christianity, and also by the existence within it of 'some secret reliques of the invisible church' (the elect).

24 Perkins, *Reformed Catholike*, pp.292, 294. Downame's position (n.23) thus stands between the two tendencies outlined here.

25 E.g. Some, *Godly Treatise*, pp.149–51, 156–7; William Fulke, *Two Treatises Written against the Papistes* (1577), i. pp.50–1; Dove, *Perswasion*, p.28. But contrast Burton, *Babel*, pp.105–8; Spencer, *Maschil Unmasked*, pp.77, 85, 91.

26 Field, *Of the Church*, IV: 527.

27 *Ibid.*, IV: 527 (my italics). This important italicized passage was omitted by Joseph Hall when he quoted Field in 'The Reconciler' – see Hall, *Works*, VIII: 722. For a more reliable exposition of Field's position, see John Downe, *Certaine Treatises* (Oxford, 1633), xii. p.42.

28 E.g. Field, *Of the Church*, I: 359.

monplace among Jacobean divines: Rome's retention of baptism was seen as almost an accident which bore little relation to the way that the Church of Rome actually operated. Whatever Rome did thereafter was bound to impede any hope of salvation.

It is true that most mainstream writers accepted that salvation was still possible for some who survived their baptism and lived within the Roman Church. King James argued this very point in parliament in 1605.[29] Salvation, however, was only deemed possible on the grounds of invincible or compelled ignorance of Roman errors, and of points 'necessitate praecepti' either commanded by God or deduced from His Word. Simple ignorance was not sufficient. Invincible ignorance must be accompanied by holding the true faith of Christ, by a true repentance for sins both known and unknown and by a final reliance on God's mercy in Christ.[30] This last point was especially significant, as it was maintained by most divines, including Hooker, that Rome's formal teaching overthrew the nature of justification by Christ's merits. Roman Catholics were thus only saved by their ignorance of the most important formal doctrines of their particular church, and by their belief in an article of faith which their church rejected. The only hope for the salvation of a member of the Church of Rome was thus for him to be no true member of it.[31]

These somewhat contradictory arguments must be borne in mind when considering Protestant attitudes towards Rome's retention of the sacraments and the ministry. It was important to the Church of England's case against the separatists to defend the proposition that the sacraments might be effectually dispensed even by an heretical minister. Even so, divines fiercely condemned Romanist notions of the priesthood as a sacrificing order. While Robert Some strongly defended the efficacy of the sacraments administered by a popish priest, he insisted that 'the Popish Priesthoode is Sacriledge', and that popish priests 'have no lawfull calling'. The administration of the eucharist had been horrifically abused by the intrusion of transubstantiation and the idolatry that it promoted, and by the fact that the sacrament was only administered in one kind. By abusing the administration of the sacrament, Davenant declared, the Church of Rome publicly overthrew the Scriptures, while the Roman ministry had become one of

[29] King James, *Political Works*, p.285.

[30] See John Overall's Dedication of the Collected Works of Jewel in the 1609 and 1611 folios – Jewel, *Works*, IV: 1308; Morton, *Catholike Appeale*, pp.443–5.

[31] Cf. Carleton's claim that no members of the Roman Church could partake of the communion of saints with the Head of the Catholic Church (since they thought that it was the pope) and that therefore none of them could be members of the Holy Catholic Church. He did not deny that there were saints within the Roman communion, but only according to their external profession, and not as far as they had any communion with 'membris Satanae': Carleton, *Consensus*, pp.229–33.

'Baalitish priests'. Francis Mason maintained that Rome's sacrificing priests were the 'servants of Antichrist'.[32] While in practical terms Rome's ordination was accepted (there was no reordination for converted priests) the arguments used to condemn the Roman ministry can often sound very strongly as if Rome's orders were being denied altogether. In one particular passage, Matthew Sutcliffe, that doughty defender of *iure divino* episcopacy, seemed to imply that Rome's orders were entirely void, and that she was hence no church at all.[33]

Rome possessed not only the sacraments and ministry, but also the Scriptures, and through them those few essential doctrines by which a Christian church could be identified, namely those of the Trinity and the Incarnation. By acknowledging such doctrines, Rome showed herself to be distinct from Jews and Turks in her religion. But even this was an argument that was highly qualified by English Protestant divines. While admitting Rome to be a true visible church in her outward profession of Christianity, Joseph Hall emphasized that she was still, at the same time, 'a heretical, apostatical, antichristian Synagogue, in respect of doctrine and practice'.[34] Rome, in fact, 'by necessary inferences' overturned the foundation which she openly professed.[35] Davenant agreed with Hall in dubbing Rome 'apostatical'. This did not mean a full and plain defection from Christianity such as clearly occurred in Islam, but this was the only positive remark that could be made about Rome's faith.[36] Rome was as

[32] Some, *Godly Treatise*, pp.85, 84; cf. p.192; Davenant, *Determinationes*, pp.103–4; *idem*, *Expositio*, p.409; Mason, *Vindiciae*, p.663.

[33] Sutcliffe argued that the Roman Church has 'no true bishops, nor priests'. It has no true bishops because the pope is no bishop and Rome's bishops are ordained by Antichrist rather than by the successors of the Apostles. Sutcliffe mustered several further arguments in support of this contention. He maintained that heretics and schismatics cannot ordain; that women cannot ordain, and thus that Pope Joan has destroyed the Roman succession (Sutcliffe, *An Abridgement*, pp.251–2); also that the Roman doctrine of the necessity of intent (which cannot be outwardly determined) for the internal efficacy of the sacrament means that the Roman succession could have been broken at any stage (p.252); and that Roman priests are not ordered to preach the Word and duly administer the sacraments (pp.252–3). Quoting Jerome and Cyprian that there can be no church without priests and bishops, Sutcliffe concluded 'if then that cannot be the church, that wanteth priests and bishops: then are we not to looke for the true church among the papists' (p.253). For a similar confutation of Rome's ministerial succession from a fervently episcopalian writer, see Thomas Bilson, *The True Difference between Christian Subjection and Unchristian Rebellion* (1585), pp.120–1. For other strong passages against Rome's orders, see Fulke, *Two Treatises*, i. p.50; Andrew Willet, *A Retection* (1603), p.67; Powel, *Consideration of the Papists*, p.71; and those collected in Silvester Norris, *An Antidote or Soveraigne Remedie* (1615), pp.194–5.

[34] Hall, *Works*, VIII: 719.

[35] *Ibid.*, VIII: 729. Cf. *ibid.*, VI: 288–90, where Hall argued that popery overthrows the foundation as a direct consequence of her erroneous beliefs.

[36] Davenant, *Determinationes*, p.102. Cf. Hall, *Works*, VIII: 733. On Rome's 'apostasy', see also Bedell, *Certaine Letters*, pp.40–1 and below, ch.4.

bad as the Galatians and the Corinthians had been in their departure from the truth and purity of Christian religion, and Davenant equated this apostasy with the sense used by Paul in 1. Tim. 4.1, which refers to a prophesied time to come when some men would abandon the faith and follow the doctrines of devils. Moreover, divines such as George Carleton and Richard Crakanthorp argued that the true doctrines which remained in the Roman Church were nullified by the fact that they were now held on the foundation of the authority of the pope, rather than of God.[37] Again, there is a strong tendency to regard the Scriptures and the foundations of true doctrine found within the Roman Church as accidental survivals, which Rome's religion was bent on subverting. Although Edmund Bunny was among the first English Protestant authors to make a polemical fuss about the value of granting Rome to be a church of Christ, he too made the sour remark that Rome retained the Scriptures, not out of any regard for the Word of God, but merely to avoid the outcry and shame that would result if she were to reject them altogether.[38]

Indeed, it was the Romanists' outward recognition of Christ which made their sins against Him all the more deplorable. As the Arminian Thomas Jackson explained, 'the idolatry of the Romish church is so much worse than the idolatry of the heathens, by how much that church's general belief in one God, of the glorious Trinity, and of the redemption of mankind, is better than the heathen's belief or knowledge of the same point'.[39] Joseph Hall insisted that, as far as Rome was concerned, 'trueness of being and outward visibility are no praise to her: yea, these are aggravations to her falsehood'.[40] Addressing Romanists directly, he warned that 'your errors may be, and are, no less damnable, for that ye are by outward profession Christians, *yea, so much the more*'.[41] It was Rome's status as a church which made her crimes all the greater.[42]

In fact, one of the most regularly used arguments in support of Rome's status as a church of Christ stemmed from the identification of the pope as Antichrist.[43] Robert Some advanced as his first argument to show that 'the Popish Church is a Church, though not a sound Church' the point that 'the

[37] Davenant, *Determinationes*, p.102; Richard Crakanthorp, *Vigilius Dormitans* (1631), pp.186, 189, 190–1, 193; Jackson, *Works*, II: 95, 125, 160; Carleton, *Directions*, p.64; Perkins, *Reformed Catholike*, p.299. See also below, ch.4.

[38] Bunny, *Briefe Answere*, p.51.

[39] Jackson, *Works*, XII: 152.

[40] Hall, *Works*, VIII: 729.

[41] *Ibid.*, VIII: 726 (my italics).

[42] Hall explained this point as follows: 'were the Church of Rome and ours laid upon several foundations, these errors should not be altogether so detestable; since the symbolizing in many truths makes gross errors more intolerable, as the Samaritan idolatry was more odious to the Jews than merely paganish. If the dearest daughter of God upon earth should commit spiritual whoredom, her uncleanliness is so much more to be hated, as her obligations were greater': *ibid.*, VIII: 717.

[43] See above, p.106.

pope is Antichrist, therefore the Church of Rome is a Church'. He was able in 1588 to remark complacently that 'no Protestant doubteth of the antecedent'.[44] If there were no marks of God's church in the popish church, so the argument ran, then Daniel and Paul would not have foretold that Antichrist would sit in it. To deny Rome to be a church was to give Romanists a great advantage, since it implied that the pope could not be Antichrist.[45] Even such renowned moderates as Edmund Bunny, Joseph Hall and Francis Mason did not scruple to use the same argument.[46]

It need hardly be pointed out that an argument based on the identity of the pope as Antichrist was far from being a mitigating point in Rome's favour. If Rome's Christianity was used to demonstrate her antichristianity, then this was to emphasize an essential deceit and guile in her outward profession of the fundamental divine truths, which made her worse than the heathens. The point was, as Jackson explained, that unless Antichrist sat in the Temple of God, 'his contrariety unto Christ would not be so essential, so immediate or direct, as by the rules of sacred philosophy we are taught it must be'.[47] Antichrist depended on deceit and guile, and therefore must be opposite to Christ, not by way of mere negation or contradiction, like the Jew or Turk, 'but by a positive contrariety or hostility; Christian religion and Antichristianism must, as all other contrarieties, agree in some kind or matter'.[48] As Jackson saw it, Rome had just enough true doctrine to allow the label of Antichrist to be unambiguously pinned upon her: 'there is so much of the true church in the present Roman visible church, as a man cannot say it is no church at all; so much true doctrine in it as sufficeth to support the title of Antichrist, and to make it the very seat of all abominations, or impieties more than natural'.[49]

The admission that Rome was in a sense a church was thus highly qualified. Nevertheless, treated in isolation, it could engender surprisingly positive implications, and leave the potential for a vision of particular churches as definable merely by their shared profession of the fundamentals of Christianity. This was especially true of a particular line of argument developed against Rome's claims to be *the* Catholic Church,

[44] Some, *Godly Treatise*, p.147. [45] *Ibid.*, pp.148–9, 166.

[46] Hall, *Works*, VIII: 731–2 (quoting Zanchius); Mason, *Vindiciae*, p.198; Bunny, *Briefe Answer*, p.116; Jackson, *Works*, XII: 145, 152. Bellarmine and other Roman controversialists attempted to use this very point to suggest that Protestants thereby granted Rome to be the true church: Perkins, *Reformed Catholike*, p.294; Sandys, *Europae Speculum*, p.180; Abbot, *Demonstratio*, p.41; Beard, *Antichrist*, pp.138–9; Downame, *Treatise*, i. pp.21–2, ii. pp.127–8, 229.

[47] Jackson, *Works*, II: 162.

[48] *Ibid.*, II: 267. Jackson compared the recognition of Christ in the Roman religion to that made by the Gadarene swine: *ibid.*, II: 266. Cf. Whitaker, *Disputation*, p.21.

[49] Jackson, *Works*, XII: 152.

which effectively allowed her to be a *member* of the Catholic Church. John Rainolds employed this argument in public disputations in Oxford in 1579, and thereafter it was urged by a number of episcopalian Calvinists, including James Ussher, Arthur Lake and, most regularly, Robert Abbot. In order to repulse Rome's claims to be *the* Catholic Church on earth, they maintained that Rome was only a particular member of this universal church on earth, who erroneously claimed exclusive authority, as a part laying claim to the rights of the whole. The term 'Catholic Church' might thus at times be used to signify the aggregation of all churches which professed Christianity, of which Rome was held to be a member, albeit an over-reaching one. She was, in Ussher's words, a branch of the Catholic Church which 'would fain be acknowledged to be the root of it'.[50] This point gradually became more prominent as a means of deflecting Roman controversialists' increasing emphasis on the charge of schism against Protestants, and was of particular use to writers such as Bedell who were attempting to persuade English recusants to attend the Church of England's services.[51]

As we shall see below, this was a line of argument which theoretically embodied significant modifications of understandings of the nature of the divisions between visible churches on earth. Nevertheless, at this stage it was merely an isolated argument among many anti-papal positions of a more traditional ecclesiological nature, and was generally used in a purely negative sense as a way of imputing to Rome the early Christian heresy of the Donatists, who had similarly tried to aggregate to themselves the title and qualities of the Catholic Church. As such, this style of argument did not immediately excite concern among puritan divines, and indeed was happily embraced by many of them, such as Andrew Willet, Thomas Taylor and Richard Bernard.[52]

These puritan examples are important. Undoubtedly, puritans did not feel the same impulse as their Calvinist conformist brethren to embrace a more tactically positive assessment of Rome, and were always more comfortable paying attention to Rome's shortcomings rather than to her

50 Ussher, *Works*, II: 476, 477–8; Arthur Lake, *Ten Sermons* (1640), p.165; Abbot, *Defence*, pp.14–15; *idem*, *The True Ancient Roman Catholike* (1611), 41–2 and *passim*; Rainolds, *Summe of the Conference*, 649–50.

51 See also more generally for the distinction of healthy and unhealthy churches: Bedell, *Examination of Motives*, pp.29–30.

52 Abbot, *Defence*, 15–16; *idem*, *True Ancient*, 52–7, 59–62, 63–5, 65–8, 69–78, 87–90; Bernard, *A Key*, ep. ded. (citing Abbot directly); Taylor, *Christs Victorie*, p.99; Willet, *Antilogie*, p.42. It was George Downame who treated this issue with greater care than even these puritan writers by his emphasis that this was only a hypothetical point. Downame argued that *even if* Rome were a true visible church, she would only be a particular church, but since she was now the Whore of Babylon the question did not even arise: *Treatise*, ii. pp.228–9.

positive nature as a church. Recognitions of Rome as a church *secundum quid* are far more frequent in conformist works. Nevertheless, this was not necessarily a line of argument developed in opposition to the puritan position. Puritans might make similar points themselves when writing against the separatists, and the issue also arose when they were identifying the pope as Antichrist, as we have seen. It is in these passages, when writers were most keen to stress that Rome was a church so that the pope could be Antichrist, that puritans made their clearest assertions of Rome's status as a church.

That being said, however, puritan writers tended to argue either that the qualifications expressed by Crakanthorp and others regarding Rome's antichristian nature essentially meant that she was no church at all, or felt that the over-riding need to oppose Rome and all her works meant that it was best to avoid this point.[53] Certainly, any attempt to present Rome's status as a church in a positive light would excite strong suspicions. This was especially so if it seemed in any way to undermine the traditional division of the Christian congregations on earth between the unified 'true church' of Protestants and the 'false church' of false believers. The division between these different ways of talking about Rome in different polemical contexts was undoubtedly becoming more awkward under James – perhaps exemplified by the problems incurred by English Protestant writers as they attempted to explain away the king's repeated admission that Rome was 'the mother church'.[54] This discomfort increased as popish doctrines and sympathies seemed to begin to intrude into the English church and polity.

THE *OLD RELIGION* CONTROVERSY

Arguments that Rome was or was not a church could both be derived from the tradition of anti-papal polemic, which by its very nature was seldom wholly specific on this point. Both Calvinist episcopalians and radical puritans could thus claim with some justice to be the descendants of this ambiguous tradition. There were potential conflicts of interpretation which occasionally flickered into life. William Bedell and Samuel Ward found themselves disagreeing amicably in 1619 about whether Rome was a church of Christ.[55] But it was the controversy between puritans and conforming Calvinists in the late 1620s over Joseph Hall's treatise *The Old*

[53] For examples of the latter approach, see Burton, *Seven Vials*, p.28; Bodl., Rawlinson MS D.47 fol.15v (Daniel Featley); Hall, *Works*, VIII: 746 (Gilbert Primerose).

[54] E.g. Willet, *Loidoromastix*, pp.17–18; Sutcliffe, *Briefe Examination*, p.100. See also below, ch.6.

[55] Bedell, *Two Biographies*, p.257.

Religion that pushed these potential differences to the forefront of debate. A detailed analysis of this hitherto neglected controversy serves to reveal just how great the divisions of opinion among Calvinists actually were on this issue.

Hall's *The Old Religion*, published in 1628, was a conventional and unremarkable piece of anti-papal writing, except for two passages which defended in stronger terms than usual Rome's nature as a church, and spoke of it rather carelessly as 'a True Visible Church'.[56] The tenor of Hall's arguments still implied that this was only true in a certain sense, *secundum quid*. Nevertheless, Hall's use of the term 'true' – by which he meant merely that Rome was true in her being and definition as a congregation professing faith in Christ, though false in her belief[57] – seemed to threaten that the admission that Rome was *in a sense* a church might override and supersede the insistence that she was *not* part of the '*true church*'.

As his tract began to come under criticism, Hall swiftly added an 'Apologetical Advertisement' to a second edition of the work, in which he spelt out more clearly his meaning concerning the word 'true'. Nevertheless, Henry Burton, formerly clerk of the closet to Prince Charles, chose to take up his pen against Hall in his apocalyptical commentary *The Seven Vials*, also published in 1628. Burton complained that he saw no difference between the terms 'true church' and 'truly visible Church', and invited 'an humble and ingenuous recantation' from 'our divine Seneca'.[58] Hall's chaplain Hugh Cholmley and another minor divine Robert Butterfield leapt to Hall's defence, but their tracts written in support of Hall were themselves opposed in Henry Burton's *Babel no Bethel. That is, the Church of Rome no True Visible Church of Christ* and Thomas Spencer's *Maschil Unmasked*. The failure of these latter tracts to gain a licence from Laud's chaplain Thomas Turner was remarked upon in parliament, and Hall was forced to appeal to his friend Sir John Eliot to block possible moves against his chaplain Cholmley. Eliot obliged, and Hall ended the debate by issuing a further edition of his work with a brief appendix entitled *The Reconciler*, in which he printed letters supporting his position, solicited from those paragons of establishment English Calvinism and staunch anti-Arminians John Davenant, Thomas Morton and John Prideaux, along with the pastor of the French Church in London, Gilbert Primerose. While these writers endorsed Hall's position, Prideaux for one had come under pressure from Daniel Featley to offer a far more guarded and admonitory comment on Hall's work.[59]

[56] Hall, *Works*, VIII: 639 – cf. 716. [57] *Ibid.*, VIII: 729, 730–2, 742.

[58] Burton, *Seven Vials*, pp.34, 52.

[59] *Commons' Debates*, ed. Notestein and Relf, pp.39, 125; *De Jure Majestatis ... and the Letter-Book of Sir John Eliot*, ed. A.B. Grosart (2 vols., 1882), II: 40–4; Hall, *Works*, VIII:

The position defended by Hall, Morton, Davenant and Prideaux could stand as a definitive exposition of the moderate Calvinist *secundum quid* position. Rome is a church in a certain sense, has a Christian face but an antichristian heart, is at the same time Babel and Bethel, is a church of Christ but is also the synagogue of Satan.[60] It is notable that, while he defended Hall's position, Davenant gently chided Hall for his failure to explain more clearly in his original tract what he meant by Rome's being a 'true' visible church, and for having thereby allowed the reader to conclude that Rome might be orthodox in her faith. Most importantly, Davenant and the other Calvinist divines did not wish in their statements to suggest any fundamental division of opinion from Burton and other puritans on this issue. Primerose was tempted to follow the opinion of those like Burton who wrote, Primerose averred, 'out of a most fervent zeal to God and perfect hatred to idolatry', while Prideaux voiced his conviction that 'if it were to be discussed . . . after our scholastical manner, it might well be defended either pro or con without prejudice to the truth'.[61]

Nevertheless, the exigencies of the controversy revealed clearer divisions of opinion. In the adversarial atmosphere of the debate, the two aspects of the Jacobean view of Rome (the senses in which Rome was and was not a church) essentially underwent an artificial polarization, in which both sides gave only a one-sided interpretation of previous writers. Hall's opponent Henry Burton attacked him with the arguments of Carleton and Crakanthorp, claiming that they denied Rome to be a church at all, and marshalled to this end the qualifications usually made to affirmations of Rome's status as a church. In response, Hall was forced to distort references from Crakanthorp, Field and others to remove suggestions that the foundation of the faith had been destroyed in Rome, or that baptized infants would be swiftly perverted. In his search for unequivocal English Protestant affirmations of Rome's claims to be a church, Hall, and also his chaplain Cholmley, were forced to resort to the collections of such opinions made by the Roman polemicist John Brereley, who had disregarded any qualifications that these authors might make in order to make them speak directly in favour of the Church of Rome.[62] Nevertheless, Hall's argument was still a reasonably balanced one, although a revelation of just

727–55; Bodl., Rawlinson MS D.47 fol.15v: Featley to Prideaux (draft, n.d.). See also Hall's later summary and self-defence, written in 1654 and published in *Works*, VIII: 289–92. See also Robert Sanderson's brief account – quoted in Lewis, *Joseph Hall*, p.253.

60 Hall, *Works*, VIII: 720–55.

61 *Ibid.*, VIII: 742, 746, 745; cf. 734 (Hall). The Smectymnuans later tried to set Davenant's position against Hall's on this issue: see Hall, *Works*, IX: 420.

62 Burton, *Seven Vials*, p.52; Hall, *Works*, VIII: 722, 724; Hugh Cholmley, *The State of the Now-Romane Church* (1629), p.38; Burton, *Babel*, pp.5–6, 51–3; Spencer, *Maschil Unmasked*, p.14.

how far the admission that Rome was in a sense a church could be used to assault more absolute visions of the break with Rome.

However, Hall's defenders Cholmley and Butterfield, in their eagerness to defend Hall, were forced by the polemical context to combat directly many of the traditional qualifications made to the admission that Rome was a church, and to reject explicitly many of the absolute emphases of the 'true church' position. Thus Cholmley defended the soundness of the Tridentine catechism, and of Trent's conclusions regarding justification, and he and Butterfield several times implied that Rome's unsoundness, and the fact that her heresies undermined the faith by implication, placed her merely in the same position as the Greek and Lutheran Churches.[63] Traditional arguments that Rome still preserved the sacraments, and that popery merely constituted a body of additions to a secure foundation of truth, were for the first time presented in a wholly positive light, rather than as grudging admissions or polemical tools.[64]

On the other side, Burton and Spencer gave a similarly distorted account of previous writings, implying that the absolute definitions of 'true church' arguments necessarily overthrew any practical suppositions that Rome was still in a sense a church of Christ. They were essentially unable to accept a view of the modern Church of Rome which attempted to describe it as concurrently both a true church (in her visible profession of Christianity) and Babylon (with relation to her errors). While they did not seriously differ from Hall on the question of salvation within the Roman Church, Burton and Spencer rejected the notion that an heretical assembly might still be considered a church in a certain sense. Instead, they saw purity of doctrine as an essential and constitutive mark of the church. Their persistent attempts to cite authors denying Rome to be *the* true church in order to deny it to be *a* true church display, not a basic confusion on their part, but rather the fact that for them the two terms meant essentially the same thing. If Rome was not a part of *the* true church, then it was not a church at all.[65] Burton and Spencer's arguments owed something to the arguments of Carleton and Perkins, but also were one among a number of possible readings of more familiar parts of the English Protestant tradition. Thus they repeated the arguments of staunch episcopalians such as Francis Mason that, although Roman converts were not reordained or rebaptized, the addition of true faith completed internally what was lacking in the original ceremonies. However, these arguments were now taken by the puritan pamphleteers to imply, not that the origi-

[63] Cholmley, *The State*, pp.8–9, 16–19, 107–11; Butterfield, *Maschil*, pp.25–6.
[64] Butterfield, *Maschil*, pp.37–57.
[65] E.g. Burton, *Babel*, pp.50–3.

nal ceremony was imperfect, but that it was essentially null until true doctrine was added.[66]

But why did Burton choose to make the original attack upon Hall? If it is true, as Hall claimed, that the basic argument that Rome was 'in a certain sense' a true church had been regularly advanced by previous writers, and (as has been suggested above) was sometimes a practical presupposition, even of puritan writers, why did it arouse such controversy? Part of the reason may lie in Hall's somewhat careless phraseology in *The Old Religion*. But a great deal more had to do with the background to the controversy. Burton saw sinister intent in the admission that Rome was a church because a mere three years earlier the same tenet had been advanced in print by Richard Montagu, in the midst of a great many other apparently heterodox positions. Indeed, Montagu's assertion that Rome was a true church had been the particular focus of attacks made on him in the House of Commons, and many of the points raised by Burton and Spencer had been made three years earlier by the anti-Montagu pamphleteers Anthony Wotton and Daniel Featley.[67] The 'Arminian' context of this view thus helped to discredit it in the eyes of moderate puritans. Hall's own espousal of the idea in 1628 might thus appear all the more worrying, especially as he had been raised to the episcopate a year earlier. Hall himself suggested that the opposition mounted against an idea which had aroused no complaint when he had previously expressed it in print could be attributed to anti-episcopal feeling.[68] It seems far more likely that the doubts were caused less by the fact than by the timing of Hall's elevation – after the York House Conference and during the time of the Forced Loan, when 'Arminian' sympathies seemed to be prevailing at court. The year of 1628, in which *The Old Religion* appeared, was a time of important bridge-building between parliamentary moderates and the Privy Council, in which Richard Montagu was rumoured to have been persuaded to retract his views. Hall was clearly a supporter of such parliamentary developments, urging the Commons not to proceed too rigidly for fear of driving the king from his new moderate counsels.[69] Bridge-building with the Arminian camp was something which more hardline divines such as Henry Burton, and MPs such as John Pym and Sir James Perrott, could only view with extreme anxiety, and it is the fear of an atmosphere of

[66] *Ibid.*, pp.105–8, 108–12; Spencer, *Maschil Unmasked*, pp.77, 85, 91.

[67] Featley, *Second Parallel*, ii. pp.76–94; Wotton, *Dangerous Plot*, i. pp.32–47; *Debates in the House of Commons in 1625*, ed. S.R. Gardiner (Camden Society, n.s. 6, 1873), p.180.

[68] Hall, *Works*, VIII: 735.

[69] *Court and Times of Charles I*, I: 449, 451, II: 3, 5; for the context, see R. Cust, *The Forced Loan and English Politics 1626–1628* (Oxford, 1987), pp.72–87.

compromise and retraction which may have generated some of the inflated fears of the implications of Hall's work.

But did Montagu and later writers merely tarnish (in puritan eyes) the argument that Rome was in a sense a true church by associating it with Arminian doctrines? Or were they actually propounding the idea in a new and distinctive way?

DEFENCES OF ROME: HOOKER AND HIS HEIRS

It must be emphasized that the position that Rome was a true church had been causing increasing concern before the 1620s. Once again, Hooker and his successors had been starting to break new ground. Richard Hooker had excited fears as early as the 1580s that he was placing in a far more positive light the admission that Rome was *secundum quid* a church. His *Discourse of Justification*, while seeking to argue that Rome did not deny the foundation directly, had asserted that Rome did deserve the name of a church of Christ, and quoted the foreign divines Mornay and Zanchius to this effect. However, Hooker reversed the order of argument in both of the passages which he cited. Whereas the two foreign authors had first admitted that Rome was a church *secundum quid*, but ended with the damning observation that Rome was destroying its foundation of faith, Hooker reversed the order of these points with the latter remark appearing first, so that the quotations were made to end affirmatively.[70] Combined as this was with apparent assertions that Rome's condition was better than that of the Galatians (who were yet regarded as a church of Christ), and that members of the Church of Rome might well be saved, Hooker's views provoked the condemnation of the puritans Walter Travers and Laurence Thomson. Whitgift's own comment on the controversy, that 'The Church of Rome is not as the Assemblies of Turks, Jews, and Painims', showed that he did not regard Rome's identity as a church as a positive admission in the way that Hooker had implied.[71]

In this early *Discourse*, Hooker had still been careful to emphasize that Rome's errors overthrew the foundation of faith by their consequences, and he did not dissent from the claim that Rome was the Babylon foretold in Revelation.[72] In his later *Laws*, however, he felt less need to hedge around with qualifications his suggestion that Rome was essentially an individual church on a par with other churches in God's family, and wrote loosely of Rome's being 'of the familie of Jesus Christ' and 'a part of the house of God, and a limme of the visible church of Christ'. This time there

[70] Hooker, *Works*, V: 148. [71] *Ibid.*, V: 200–2, 289, 291, 288.
[72] *Ibid.*, V: 118–21, 124–5, 127, 147.

was no nod towards the doctrine of the 'Two Churches' by referring to Rome as Babylon, or by implying the existence of a 'true church' of the orthodox from which Rome was excluded. Willet and the *Christian Letter* reacted with grave anxiety, and retreated back into the 'true church' mode of ecclesiological discourse, suggesting that Rome's 'apostasy' and her identity as Babylon necessarily excluded her from the visible church.[73]

Other avant-garde conformist divines pursued Hooker's positive tone still further. William Covell argued, in his defence of Hooker's *Laws*, that those who denied Rome to be a true church were the same people who denied that the Church of England was a true Christian church.[74] Most worryingly for men such as Willet, Covell chose to conduct his debate on this point in the framework of an irenically minded discussion of the possibilities of reunion with Rome. Here we can observe a sharp discontinuity with previous discussions of this issue. The admission that Rome was a church was, as we have seen, principally generated by polemical requirements: as Bunny argued, the whole point of admitting Rome to be of the church of Christ was not so much to keep her in the church, as to stop her excluding others from it, and to win recusants from her. Covell's implication that this was a positive, irenical gesture was an extension which must have confirmed many puritan fears that the admission was fraught with peril.[75]

Fears were expressed intermittently throughout James' reign, by men such as Willet, Sheldon and even Matthew Sutcliffe, that certain writers in the Church of England were implying that Rome was still a true church of Christ, in which salvation might be possible.[76] Whatever their views concerning salvation in Rome's communion, we can certainly find later members of the Laudian camp adopting a far more combatively positive

[73] Hooker, *Laws*, III, ch.i, 10, V, ch.xxviii, 1; *idem*, *Works*, IV: 29–31; Willet, *Antilogie*, sig.A3v.

[74] Covell, *Just and Temperate Defence*, pp.68, 74. Covell's doctrine of the church is somewhat confused, however. He is keen to defend Hooker's position, and his discussion of the different possible definitions of the church carefully follows Hooker in avoiding 'true church' modes of analysis and emphasizing that all heretics are still part of the 'visible church' through baptism (*ibid.*, p.69). However, his subsequent discussion reveals Covell to be still trapped within 'true church' notions, as seen in his admission that heretics and schismatics have forsaken 'the true church of God', defined as 'the church which is sound and sincere'. There is nothing in Covell's earlier discussion of definitions of the church to prepare the reader for his later distinction of 'this verie true church of Christ' from 'simply the Church' (pp.74–5). Covell thus appears as a transitional figure in the development of English Protestant ecclesiology, although his confusion serves also to demonstrate further the complications that 'true church' notions introduced into Protestant theology.

[75] *Ibid.*, pp.64–7, 77; Bunny, *Treatise*, p.123.

[76] PRO, PROB 11/156/94 (Matthew Sutcliffe's will); Willet, *Antilogie*, sig.A3v; Sheldon, *Sermon at Paules Crosse*, p.45.

approach to the issue of Rome's identity as a church during the Jacobean period. While a Calvinist conformist such as Joseph Hall sought merely to reinterpret previous Elizabethan and Jacobean writers according to a qualified sense of this doctrine,[77] Laudian divines such as John Pocklington by contrast made no attempt to effect such a reconciliation. When Pocklington defended his thesis in Pembroke College Chapel in 1616 that Rome was a true visible church of Christ, it was reported that 'before he propounded his Argumentes [he] did with vehemency of speech inveigh against all those that held the negative in these words saying whosoever held the negative were impii Scelerati perniciosi blasphemi in Christum ipsum.' On being told that he thereby openly accused many famous divines of the Church of England, such as William Fulke, William Whitaker, George Abbot, George Downame and William Perkins, 'he did repeate the former wordes saying they were impii scelerati &c'.[78] In the 1630s, the thesis that Rome was a true church became more important and inflexible as a sign of orthodoxy. A list of 'Certain articles propounded to ministers and lecturers in and about London to be consented unto' in the State Papers for 1635 includes the item 'That the Church of Rome is a true church, and truly so called', with no qualifying phrases or further exposition.[79]

William Laud himself made no attempt to explain away those who had maintained that Rome was no true church. He admitted to having called Rome a true church in his conference with Fisher, but argued, in the manner of Hall's *Reconciler*, that he thereby meant only that she was true in her substance.[80] This substance consisted of her retention of baptism and her profession of Christ's faith: 'a Church that is exceeding corrupt, both in manners and doctrine, and so a dishonour to the name, is yet a true Church in the verity of essence; as a Church is a company of men which

[77] Hall, *Works*, VIII: 730–4.

[78] CUL, VC Ct I.8 fol.258r (Walter Balcanquahall's deposition). Cf. *ibid.*, fols.255r, 255v–256r; *The Petition ... against Pocklington*, p.30.

[79] PRO, SP 16/308/43. Thomas Mason notes that this document is in the hand of Edward Nicholas, clerk of the Privy Council, and that there is no other evidence (save in the document's title) to suggest that Bishop Juxon of London required his clergy to subscribe to its articles: T.A. Mason, *Serving God and Mammon: William Juxon, 1582–1663* (Toronto, 1985), p.62. However, these are almost certainly the 'certaine Articles 11. in number urged upon some Ministers before their admission into Benefices' that were sent to the Oxford fellow Thomas Crosfield in 1636 by John Vicars, schoolmaster of Christ's Hospital in London: *The Diary of Thomas Crosfield*, ed. F.S. Boas (Oxford, 1935), p.89. This would suggest that Juxon's articles were indeed imposed, but only on newly beneficed clergy, which would account for the paucity of references to them in surviving records. In the longer term, however, they would have served to create an entirely Laudian body of clergy in London. I am very grateful to Dr Fincham for alerting me to the significance of the Crosfield passage.

[80] Laud, *Works*, II: 143.

professe the faith of Christ, and are baptized into His name'. He denied, however, having ever called Rome a 'right' church in the sense of an orthodox one. A church thus true in its essence, Laud observed, might still only accept the Scriptures as an imperfect rule of faith, and misuse the sacraments and add more to them.[81] Nevertheless, he would not go so far as Hall or Davenant as to say that, with respect to her doctrine, Rome was 'no church' or 'a false church',[82] although Laud did admit that some of her abuses and corruptions 'work toward the dissolution of a Church'.[83] There is no sense in Laud's writings that Rome's status as a church was simply dependent on which aspect of Rome was being considered, no distinction between a Christian face and an antichristian heart, no sense that Rome is only to be considered a church *secundum quid*.

Richard Montagu similarly offered the conventional and minimal position that Rome is a true church, though not a sound church, in fundamentals. That the Roman Church was not a sound member of the Catholic Church was one of the three propositions with which Montagu confronted his opponent in the *New Gagg*.[84] But this unsoundness did not make her in any sense a false church. Montagu clearly envisaged this as meaning simply that she was not a perfectly orthodox church.[85] The novelty of Montagu's (and Laud's) position can best be illustrated by studying the defence of Montagu's work drawn up by his licenser Francis White, who had shifted allegiance to the 'Arminian' party in the Church of England but only freed himself by degrees from his earlier more Calvinist ecclesiology. In defending Montagu, White glossed his position as saying that Rome was both 'a true and False church at the same instant', and stated frankly that the bare assertion that Rome is a true though not a sound church 'seemeth to yeld more to the Roman Church, then is just'.[86] In order to defend Montagu's position, White thus found that he had to deny what Montagu himself had written, and had to claim that Montagu had maintained what he had in fact signally failed to mention.

One of the crucial things missing in the Laudian view of Rome as simply an erring, corrupt, particular church was the apocalyptic dimension. Previous writers who had made the clearest declarations of Rome's status as a church – men such as Robert Some, Edmund Bunny and Joseph Hall – had all clearly identified Rome as Babylon and the pope as Antichrist. This is true even of the tracts composed in support of Hall by Cholmley and Butterfield.[87] It is difficult to exaggerate the significance of the rejection of

[81] *Ibid.*, II: 144. [82] Hall, *Works*, VIII: 719, 721, 729, 742.
[83] Laud, *Works*, II: 213.
[84] Montagu, *New Gagg*, 'To the Reader'. [85] Montagu, *Appello*, p.139.
[86] Bodl., MS Rawlinson C.573 fol.57v.
[87] Cholmley, *The State*, pp.19–20; Butterfield, *Maschil*, p.1.

the identification of the pope as Antichrist, and of Rome as Babylon, by conformist writers under Laud. A crucial qualification of Rome's status as a true church was thereby removed, and an important overlap with more radical rejections of Rome's status as a church disappeared. It meant that Rome's errors were no longer seen in prophetic terms, as necessary heresies in a coherent programme which worked inevitably towards ever greater corruption. Those truths which she retained were now no longer purely accidental to her nature and purpose. Where Jacobean writers had argued that the pope's status as Antichrist required that Rome be in some sense a true church, under the Laudians writers may be found arguing that, since Rome was a true church in professing the truths of Christianity, it followed that she could not be Babylon and the pope could not be Antichrist. Thus Heylyn and Shelford argued that the pope could not be Antichrist because the pope confessed that Christ had come in the flesh.[88]

CATHOLICITY

This perception of Rome as simply an erring, corrupt, particular church was supplemented by the increasing emphasis that Hooker's heirs placed on another aspect of Rome's status which had tended to place her in a more positive light in the Jacobean Church: the extent to which she was a member of the Catholic Church, and thus on an equal par with other particular churches. As we have seen, Elizabethan and Jacobean writers were capable at times of presenting Rome as a particular church within the universal Catholic Church. However, it was often unclear what membership of the Catholic Church really implied in positive terms for the Church of Rome.

This lack of clarity arose in part because the term 'Catholic Church' was bedevilled by the same sort of semantic confusion that accompanied all Protestant discussions of the church during this period. The '*Holy* Catholic Church', it was generally agreed, denoted the church of the elect.[89] The 'Catholic Church' was sometimes understood as signifying the universal aggregate of Christian churches, as we have seen, with no apparent requirement that its members should uphold a purified faith free from Roman errors. But this definition was constantly confused by the fact that 'catholic' as an adjective was usually understood as referring to purity and

[88] Heylyn, *Briefe Answer*, pp.128–9; Shelford, *Discourses*, p.296.

[89] Davenant, *Determinationes*, pp.214–18; *idem*, *Expositio*, p.93. Cf. Rainolds, *Summe of the Conference*, pp.641, 645.

apostolicity of doctrine, and the 'Catholic Church' was therefore most regularly defined as the aggregate of *orthodox* believers.[90] Richard Field specifically excluded schismatics and heretics from the 'Catholic Church', which he defined as 'that more special number of them which communicate in all things wherein Christians should'. He continued: 'this more special number of right-believing Christians is, for distinction sake, rightly named the Catholic Church; because it consisteth of them only, that without addition, diminution, alteration, or innovation, in matter of doctrine, hold the common faith once delivered to the saints; and without all particular or private division or faction, retain the unity of the spirit in the bond of peace'.[91] Within the unity of the Catholic Church of orthodox believers, many local, particular or national churches existed.[92] However, as defined by Field, heretics and schismatics could not be part of this 'special number of those that in unity hold the entire profession of divine truth'; indeed Field defined the Catholic Church explicitly in opposition to them.[93] The Church of Rome could not therefore be accounted a part of the Catholic Church. The Latin Church had continued still a part of the Catholic Church before the Reformation, but it no longer did so.[94]

English Calvinist divines therefore strongly denied that Rome herself could be regarded as 'Catholic', and attempted to appropriate the term solely to Protestants, who alone embraced the faith of the Catholic universal church of all ages.[95] While this was a conventional point in Protestant apologetic, it could still cause some confusion. As Robert Abbot noted, Rome's use of the term had led 'Catholic' to become a name of curse and shame, and this would lead even educated lay members of the Short Parliament to suspect the term as implying popery. So habitually was the

90 While it was generally *assumed* that 'catholicity' implied purity of doctrine, this was a complicated polemical position. Robert Abbot's *The True Ancient Roman Catholike* is a perfect example of Protestant inconsistencies on this point. Essentially, Abbot always attempts to argue that 'Catholic' denotes universality (and therefore cannot apply to Rome as a particular church) and does not denote purity of doctrine (thereby avoiding the charge of Donatism). Nevertheless, Abbot's 'universal' application of catholicity only really applies to the early church, while in practice he takes the term 'Catholic' in contemporary circumstances to denote doctrinal orthodoxy. All treatments of 'catholicity' theoretically followed the definition of Vincent of Lérins: 'quod ubique, quod semper, quod ab omnibus creditum est'.

91 Field, *Of the Church*, I: 44.

92 H.F. Woodhouse, *The Doctrine of the Church in Anglican Theology 1547–1603* (1954), pp.70–1.

93 Field, *Of the Church*, I: 44, 65. Note also King James' insistence that the Catholic Church broke off all communion with heretics: *The Answere of Master Isaac Casaubon to the Epistle of ... Cardinall Peron* (1612), p.8. On King James' authorship of this tract, see Sommerville, 'Jacobean political thought', p.86 n.90.

94 Field, *Of the Church*, I: 165–7.

95 Abbot, *Defence*, p.17; Sutcliffe, *Briefe Examination*, pp.60, 75.

name applied to Romanists, however, that even Abbot himself may be found having to correct the printer's copy of his works to erase the unintentional slip.[96]

References to Rome being a member of the Catholic Church were therefore highly ambiguous. King James, arguing through Casaubon, granted from Augustine that no salvation was possible outside the faith and communion of the Catholic Church, but also argued that heretics departed from the faith of the Catholic Church, thereby implying that they could not be saved.[97] Clearly, assertions that the Roman Church was merely a member, a branch of the Catholic Church were not intended to suggest that she really shared the same identity as other churches. As an heretical church, salvation was only possible for that minority which God fostered within her. The argument that Rome was part of the Catholic Church was only clear in its implication in the negative sense in which it was generally employed, that is, that Rome was not herself the Catholic Church.

However, whenever Rome was discussed in these terms she was granted a potentially very positive sense in which she shared the same identity as other churches, and was still united with them. After all, the Catholic Church was always spoken of in terms of the unity of its members. It was the point of Rome's being a part of the Catholic Church, a branch of the main root, that was most prominent when Hooker, Covell, Laud and others assessed Rome's status. This was not accompanied, however, by the same sense of that more exclusive unity enjoyed by those special members of the Catholic Church who shared true and orthodox Catholic doctrine – 'the true church'. The ideas of communion and equality which were central to the concept of the Catholic Church were thus unqualified, and were applied more directly to the particular Church of Rome.

Richard Montagu thus stressed that the Catholic Church must be enlarged to every particular member of it, 'the whole aggregation of All Christian professors make and compose this Church'.[98] Rome was thus not the Catholic Church but only a small part of it, a member of it but 'sanum

[96] Abbot, *Defence*, p.17; *idem*, *True Ancient*, pp.103–4, 108; E.S. Cope and W.H. Coates (eds.), *Proceedings of the Short Parliament of 1640* (Camden Society 4th ser. 19, 1977), p.62; BL, Sloane MS 537 fol.34r. Featley's claim that Protestants only called Romanists 'Catholics' 'but by a Sarcasme, or Ironie' (*Clavis*, p.483) was wishful thinking (cf. Downe, *Certaine Treatises*, xii. pp.58, 60–1). See also Brereley, *Protestants Apologie*, p.242.

[97] Casaubon, *Answere*, pp.9, 6–7. Note Crakanthorp's argument that, while heretical churches were still churches, they were not truly connected with Christ by Faith and Charity: Crakanthorp, *Defensio*, p.78.

[98] Montagu, *Appello*, p.121.

membrum ... non est'.[99] Montagu's basic concern was not, like Rainolds and others, to stress Rome's unsoundness, but simply to frustrate her claims to the prerogatives of the whole church. All the individual, particular churches, he explained, are in communion with the one Catholic Church over all the world, out of which there is no salvation. Out of Rome, however, salvation is clearly possible.[100] There is no room in Montagu's analysis for Field's special church of orthodox believers, or for antichristian or idolatrous churches. Montagu is simply concerned with the respective rights of individual churches of varying degrees of orthodoxy.

Like Montagu, Laud explained away passages from St Cyprian's *De Unitate Ecclesiae* which related to the common root of the church (which according to Romanist writers referred to the papal church) and stressed that the Catholic Church must have a Catholic root, and not any particular or local root such as Rome.[101] He explained that 'the Catholic Church and her unity is the "head, root, or matrix" of Rome, and all other particular churches'.[102] Laud and Montagu's vision of the Church of Rome, and of its relation to other churches, mirrored that of Hooker and Covell, and could be incorporated wholly into St Cyprian's picture of individual churches as branches from a single root, many streams from a single source.[103] For most English Protestants before them this was only half the story. Notions of Rome's heresy and consequent defection from Christ, and especially of her identity as Babylon, could not easily be integrated into Cyprian's *schema*. Nor could arguments of Rome's only being a church *secundum quid*. It was only when these notions were removed from writings on Rome, as was happening by the 1630s, that Cyprian's ideas of the essential equality and unity of all particular churches, including Rome, could be fully accepted in their own terms.[104]

Laud did not limit himself to describing Rome as a branch of the Catholic Church. He also explained Rome's relation to the Catholic Church in terms of the way in which universals give essence to their particulars, and have existence through them. This meant that all churches were essentially the same: 'the Church of Rome, and every other particular Church in the world, receive their very essence and being of a church from

[99] Richard Montagu, *ΘΕΑΝΘΡΩΠΙΚΟΝ Seu de Vita Jesu Christi ... Originum Ecclesiasticarum Libri Duo* (1640), ii. p.408.
[100] *Ibid.*, ii. pp.408, 409.
[101] Laud, *Works*, II: 405–10; Richard Montagu, *Antidiatribae ad Priorem Partem Diatribarum J. Caesaris Bulengeri* (1625), p.49. Cf. Andrewes, *Responsio*, p.300.
[102] Laud, *Works*, II: 410.
[103] *The Treatises of S. Caecilius Cyprian* (Oxford, 1839), pp.134–5.
[104] See also below, pp.224–5, 360–1.

the definition of the Catholic Universal Church of Christ; but this universal nature and being of the Church hath no actual existence but in Rome and all other particular churches, *and equal existence in all her particulars*'.[105] This was a crucial point. All the particular churches were thus equally daughters of the Catholic Church:

> the Roman Church and the church of England are but two distinct members of that catholic church which is spread over the face of the earth. Therefore Rome is not the house where the church dwells, but Rome itself, as well as other particular churches, dwells in this great universal house ... Rome and other national churches are in this universal catholic house as so many daughters, to whom (under Christ) the care of the household is committed by God the Father, and the catholic church the mother of all Christians.[106]

Rome thus enjoyed an essential equality with the Protestant Churches. Not only that, but by Laud's arguments the Catholic Church relied upon Rome and other churches for its existence. Rome was thus a manifestation of the Church, and not merely an institution through which the Church's grace functioned in opposition to the institution's own efforts, as Davenant had represented it.[107]

The essence of the Catholic Church for Laud was not true doctrine, but only 'trueness' in the sense of those essential conditions which gave the church its being, namely baptism, faith in Christ, the Scriptures and the sacraments.[108] However, Laud did note that 'catholicity' could refer to soundness in doctrine. Discussing 'Catholic' as an adjective, he noted that Rome was not Catholic 'in any sense of the word'. She was not the universal church, and therefore not catholic in extent, but also she was not 'sound in doctrine, and in things which come near unto upon the foundation too; so not catholic in belief'.[109] He explained in a further footnote that 'every particular church is or may be called catholic, and that truly, so long as it teaches catholic doctrine. In which sense the particular Roman Church was called catholic, so long as it taught all and only those things to be de fide, which the catholic church itself maintained. But now Rome doth not so.'[110] But Laud retained none of Field's sense that churches which were 'catholic' constituted a separate church, or that Rome was in an important sense separated from the church of the orthodox, and thus from Christ.

Other Laudian writers displayed a greater readiness than Laud to bestow

105 Laud, *Works*, II: 410 (my italics). 106 *Ibid*., II: 346. 107 See above, pp.134–5.

108 Laud, *Works*, II: 144.

109 *Ibid*., II: 403. On the adjectival sense of 'Catholic', see also Abbot, *True Ancient*, p.13, and Richard Montagu's remarks in the Short Parliament: Cope and Coates, *Proceedings*, p.62.

110 Laud, *Works*, II: 404 note p.

the adjective 'catholic' upon the Roman Church. James Wedderburn, the Laudian bishop of Dunblane,[111] was prepared to admit Field's point that Augustine and other church Fathers occasionally restrained the name of 'Church' and 'Catholic Church' to only *orthodox* believers, but Wedderburn claimed that 'the same Fathers, when they speake exactly, doe not exclude from the Visible Church Catholike either schismaticks or hereticks, if directly they held the foundation, though denying it indirectly and by consequent'.[112] Wedderburn went much further than Laud by effectively arguing that all particular churches must be catholic churches, regardless of their corruptions. In the past, he affirmed, Rome was called Ecclesia Catholica 'in that sense that other particulare Churches were a Catholique, not the Catholique Church'. Wedderburn declared quite unequivocally that Rome was still a Catholic Church: 'A Catholique Church it was of old, and wee graunt it, to be so still, but the Catholique Church it was never held to be.'[113] According to Wedderburn, her status was that of 'a Catholique Church corrupted'; a phrase which earlier English Protestants would have taken to be a contradiction in terms.[114]

Christopher Potter – one of Laud's vice-chancellors in Oxford in the 1630s – allowed the Church of Rome to be 'catholic' because of her membership of the Catholic Church. Protestants, he said, granted Rome to be a member of the Catholic Church 'for those Catholique verities which she retaines', while at the same time complaining that she was 'one of the most unsound and corrupt members'. But purity of doctrine has lost any ecclesiological meaning in Potter's work, even more so than in Laud's. By allowing Rome to be catholic simply for holding the fundamental truths, which he defined as 'Catholique verities', the only catholicity which Potter denied Rome was 'that the Roman Church and the Catholique are all one'.[115] He admitted that the Fathers had spoken of the Catholic Church in another sense, but not in Field's sense of a church of orthodox belief. The only other sense which Potter conceded was that of the 'fellowship of the Saints', containing only those 'that have spirituall union and communion

111 There are reasonable grounds for treating Wedderburn as one of Laud and Neile's circle: see BL, Burney MS 369 fols.199r, 204r; Laud, *Works*, III: 372. Wedderburn's own ordination was English, all of his livings before he was promoted to the bishopric of Dunblane were in England, and he played an important role in the drafting of the Scottish Prayer Book. On Wedderburn's career, see *DNB*, s.n. 'James Wedderburn'; Milton, 'Laudians', pp.57–8 n.79.

112 BL, Harleian MS 750 fol.68r; cf. fol.67v.

113 *Ibid.*, fol.67r. This also seems to be implied by Richard Corbet, who remarks that 'wee ... accknowledge one universall Catholick church spread over the face of the Whole Earth and many particular Catholick Churches which are partes similares of that one body or Church': Bodl., Rawlinson MS D.853 fol.174Bv.

114 BL, Harleian MS 750 fol.62v.

115 Potter, *Want of Charitie*, i. p.11; cf. p.19.

with Christ as their Saviour', that is, the church of the elect, or what Davenant and others referred to as 'the holy Catholic Church'.[116]

This perspective was all one with the way that these divines treated the concept of church visibility. As we shall see in a later chapter, the Laudians abandoned earlier traditions by limiting notions of church 'invisibility' merely to the church of the elect, and passed over the notion of the relative 'invisibility' of the true church of orthodox believers.[117] These changing styles of definition were indications of a general shift away from Protestant notions of the church as definable primarily in terms of true doctrine, and towards an emphasis on the sacraments as the primary concern in ecclesiology. Unlike doctrine, the sacraments did not permit easy distinctions according to the degree of purity with which they were held, but instead entailed an essential equality among the churches which left no room for any meaningful notion of a church composed solely of orthodox Christians.[118]

Potter's unqualified account of Rome's catholicity implied a significant form of communion. The Protestants (as all writers agreed) always communicated with the Catholic Church, wherever it was.[119] As Potter interpreted the 'Catholic Church', however, this meant that the Protestants were therefore in no degree 'dislinked ... from the Church of Rome itselfe ... so farre as they communicate with the Catholique'.[120] If this was the only sense in which the 'Catholic Church' was conceived, then it demanded the type of communion in spirit which Field had attributed to the Catholic Church of the orthodox. Thus Potter had to claim that the Church of England still had 'a true and reall Union' with the Church of Rome and all other members of 'the Church Universal' 'in Faith and Charity'.[121] Most English Protestant writers would probably have agreed that there might be a notional overlap of Rome with the other churches in those few fundamentals of doctrine and sacraments which constituted the basic requirements for a church. But if Rome was a schismatical church it was difficult to see how a 'true and reall Union in charity' could actually be possible.[122]

116 *Ibid.*, i. pp.54–5. 117 See below, ch.6 pp.298–300.

118 Note William Page's stress on the brotherhood of *all* churches, and his explicit denial that ideas of churches' communion should be narrowly defined according to 1 Peter 2.17: Page, *Imitation*, 'To the Christian Reader' (unpaginated). See also Walter Curll's denial that 2 Timothy 2.22 should be interpreted as enjoining peace *only* with those of a pure heart, but rather that there should be peace *especially* with them: Curll, *Sermon*, p.28.

119 Potter, *Want of Charitie*, i. p.33. 120 *Ibid.*, i. p.56. 121 *Ibid.*, i. p.67.

122 Potter argued that a diversity of opinions among churches did not hinder the unity of the Catholic Church 'so long as ... the bond of Charity is conserved among them' (Potter, *Want of Charitie*, i. p.43). In schism, however, this bond was obviously ruptured. Potter himself complained that Rome denied other particular churches 'the acts and union of Charity' (*ibid.*, i. pp.52–3).

Strikingly, Potter even admitted that, as there can be no just cause to depart from the church of Christ, so whosoever forsook any one member of the body of Christ must confess consequently to forsake the whole.[123] It therefore followed that the Church of England could not actually have left the communion of the Church of Rome: 'her communion we forsake not, no more then the Body of Christ, whereof we acknowledge the Church of Rome to be a member, though corrupted'.[124]

This perception of Rome as a fellow-member of the community of churches was perhaps most vividly captured, not in anything that Laud and other writers directly said, but in what they failed to say. It is the absence of traditional definitions of 'the true church' of orthodox believers which is most striking if their ecclesiology is viewed in context.

SALVATION

As we have seen, ecclesiological developments under Laud increasingly tended to undermine the central role previously granted to *purity* of doctrine, both in assessing the status of individual churches and in the implication of the existence of a wider 'church' of orthodox believers from which heretics were excluded. Instead, it was the simple outward profession of Christianity, and the administration of the sacraments – the fundamental concerns of any visible church – which were taken to constitute the essential basis of a church. This line of argument allowed all churches, pure and corrupt, Protestant and Romanist, to share in the same essence, by which they were able to bring forth God's children. That membership of a visible church should play a more central role in salvation was entirely congruent with developments which historians have noted in the religious thought of many of these churchmen. These same divines were moving inexorably towards a more positive evaluation of the role of the sacraments and public worship in salvation, and consequently allocated a greatly diminished role to the dissemination of pure doctrine.[125]

A tendency to equate membership of a visible church with soteriological assurance was being complained of in James' reign by a variety of divines. Willet expressed alarm as early as 1603, while William Sclater complained in 1619 of the strange kind of charity of some men who were persuaded 'that though Pagans and Infidels shall be damned, yet not any Child of the visible Church shall perish: a strange rule for Charitie to walke by, in

123 *Ibid.*, i. p.74.
124 *Ibid.*, i. pp.74–5.
125 Fincham, *Prelate*, pp.276–88; Tyacke, *Anti-Calvinists*, pp.71, 116–18, 186, 194, 198–216, 221–2, 246–7; Lake, *Anglicans and Puritans*, pp.160–82, 228–30.

iudgement of Election, to bee borne in the Church is now become a marke Infallible of Election to life'.[126]

While this sort of equation could easily be taken to be implied by Laudian writings, it should be emphasized that divines such as Laud did not necessarily reject the axiom that the visible church on earth consisted of both the elect and the reprobate. Nevertheless, in the hands of these divines the invisible church of the elect all but disappeared from discourse about the church. The basic principle that the church could be invisible was not explicitly denied. Richard Montagu admitted in his *Appello Caesarem* that 'The Church is Invisible in her more noble parts; the saints both regnant in heaven, and militant in earth; such as bee secret and occulte intus ... the secret, hidden, the reserved ones of God.'[127] He was careful, however, to maintain that the 'Ecclesia universalis, hoc est Coetus Evocatorum' is and always will be visible and discernible, and that the elect must of necessity exist within a visible church. Even if the real benefit of Christ's incarnation is confined in its application to a few elect out of the multitude, its effects can only be gained through participation in a visible church: it 'is a benefit only imparted in the Church, which was ever subsisting publiquely, visibly, in some place or other, and so shall continue statu quo; that recourse may be had unto it, which without knowledge of the ubi could not be'.[128] Generally, Laudian writers tended to follow Hooker by hardly ever linking the division between the visible and invisible church directly and explicitly to the doctrine of predestination. Those at the centre of the disputes over predestination of the 1620s on the Arminian side, such as White, Montagu and Jackson, preferred to avoid references to 'the elect' when talking of the invisible church. While Montagu referred to the invisible church of 'the Elect according to grace' in his *New Gagg*, his *Appello* was less explicit by referring to 'the secret,

126 Willet, *Thesaurus Ecclesiae*, p.93; William Sclater, *An Exposition with Notes upon the First Epistle of the Thessalonians* (1619), p.35. I owe the latter reference to Julia Merritt. Cf. Preston, *Sermons*, i. p.29.

127 Montagu, *Appello*, p.135; cf. p.134. See also *New Gagg*, pp.49–50. In his *Apparatus ad Origines Ecclesiasticarum* of 1635, when tackling Baronius, Montagu stressed, like Davenant and other mainstream English Protestant writers, the mixed nature of the church on earth, in terms of those who were and were not combined with Christ's body eternally by God's predestination: 'Duplex est ergo ordo in Ecclesia eorum qui pertinent ad Ecclesiam; sunt qui, sic sunt in Ecclesia, ut ipsi sint Ecclesia Dei. Sunt alii qui sic in domo sunt, ut vasa comparata in contumeliam. Illi separatiores, non magis in Domo, quam ex domo. Primi sunt, Primogeniti: & in coelis, hoc est aeterna, & ineffabili Divina praescientia, & praedestinatione, descripti, Hortus revera sunt Conclusus, Intrinsecus, & in occulto Intus. Deo utique; & non hominibus cogniti atque; ideo Invisibiles in hoc mundo. Quorum respectu, Invisibilem Ecclesiam usurpamus ... illam partem humanis oculis non posse ordinarie conspici vel distingui': Montagu, *Apparatus*, pp.3–4.

128 Montagu, *Acts and Monuments*, p.71.

hidden, the reserved ones of God'.[129] Francis White, Montagu's defender at the York House Conference, preferred to write two years earlier in terms of 'the universal number of holy believers of all ages', which was only invisible because its principal part was already in heaven. Thomas Jackson, who with Montagu aroused the ire of the Commons, managed like White to avoid the terms 'invisible church' and 'the elect', and preferred to talk of 'live members of the one holy and catholic church.'[130]

The concept of the invisible church of the elect occurs only once in the whole corpus of Laud's writings – in a footnote in his *Relation of a Conference with Fisher the Jesuit.* Here his whole purpose was to stress that the invisible church of the elect can only exist through the visible, institutional church, and hence to invest the visible church with the promises against universal error that have been granted to its invisible members: 'For the Church of the elect is in the Church of them that are called, and the invisible Church in the visible. Therefore, if the whole Church of the elect cannot err in fundamentals, the whole visible Church in which the same elect are, cannot err.'[131] It was essential, Laud insisted, to locate the invisible church wholly within and with relation to the visible church, 'for else the elect or invisible church is tied to no duty of Christianity. For all such duties are required of the Church as it is visible, and performed in the Church, as it is visible.' Laud cited Hooker and Field in support of this statement, but where Field and other Jacobean writers had placed this positive reflection alongside a formal orthodox definition of the church in terms of the elect (against Romanist arguments), in Laudian times it was only its relation to the visible church which remained.[132]

Laudian writers seldom wrote expressly about the nature of the church in general, but preferred to treat of individual, particular churches. When they did discuss the church in more general terms, it was the visible church which stood at the centre of their concerns. Thus when Francis White discussed the different significations of the word 'Ecclesia' in the context of arguments over church visibility in his 1624 *Replie to Jesuit Fishers Answere*, he managed to avoid any reference to a church of the elect which might exist within the visible church.[133] His discussion of church visibility

[129] Montagu, *Appello*, p.135; *idem*, *New Gagg*, p.49.

[130] Francis White, *A Replie to Jesuit Fishers Answere* (1624), pp.49–50; Jackson, *Works*, XII: 45.

[131] Laud, *Works*, II: 155 note n. [132] *Ibid.*, II: 156 note n.

[133] The nearest White came to this was when he briefly defined the church in one sense as the universal number of holy believers of all ages, which was invisible only because its principal part was in heaven. Some of the church's attributes, he claimed, were to be understood only of 'the better and sounder part thereof': White, *Replie*, pp.49–50, 52. However, his talk of the external visible church as being 'an intermixed or compounded societie, bodie, and state of Christian people' is mostly in terms of the different types of

in his earlier *The Orthodox Faith and Way to the Church* of 1617 was conducted wholly in terms of the external visible church, and omitted any reference at all to the invisible church of the elect. Similarly, Thomas Choun, in his *Collectiones Theologicarum* of 1635, which were dedicated to Laud and licensed by Laud's chaplain William Heywood, was also able to discuss the issue of church invisibility without once alluding to the principle of the invisible church of the elect, following instead Laud's emphasis that the church's ministry and the duties of her members must of necessity be visible.[134]

If the doctrine of the invisible church of the elect was generally side-stepped rather than openly challenged in this period, it was on at least one occasion directly censored. Dr Thomas Weekes, chaplain to Bishop Juxon, saw fit to expunge several passages defending this position from the manuscript of Richard Ward's *Commentary on Matthew* before he was prepared to license it for publication. These included passages expounding in a moderate manner some of what had hitherto been the basic tenets of English Protestant ecclesiology. They included the belief that the church of Christ was not always visible, but could be partly invisible 'quatenus est Catholica'; that the 'Catholic Church' was the church of the elect; that Matthew 16.18–19 spoke of the church as the universal and mystical body of Christ rather than the church as a visible society; that the inward church of Christ should not be called visible; that 'there shall be alwayes a true church, &c. not externall and corporall'; and that wicked men were not true members of the Catholic Church.[135] Weekes' actions suggest that, while Laud and others might have silently accepted such doctrines but judged it undesirable to air them publicly, some of their associates may have been prepared to doubt their orthodoxy.

But how far did this emphasis on the ease of salvation within a visible church serve to modify assessments of the possibilities of salvation within the corrupt Church of Rome? Arguments concerning Rome's status as a true church constantly returned to the question of whether this admission necessarily entailed that members of the Roman Church were saved. While the denial of this conclusion was something of an axiom in Protestant thought, the precise reply could vary according to differing polemical contexts. As we have seen, English Protestants generally argued that salvation was impossible for those who adhered to all of Rome's Tridentine

orthodoxy of divers particular institutional churches, rather than in terms of elect and non-elect individuals (*ibid.*, pp.51–6).

[134] White, *Orthodox Faith*, pp.93–6; Thomas Choun, *Collectiones Theologicarum* (1635), pp.31–4.

[135] Prynne, *Canterburies Doome*, pp.255, 296–9. For orthodox expositions of these doctrines, see Davenant, *Determinationes*, pp.156–7, 214–18; Carleton, *Consensus*, pp.155–7, 166–84.

doctrines, and was only possible for the invincibly ignorant who were fully repentant. Yet from the outset many Protestants, and puritans among them, were willing (when it suited their purpose) to argue that an errant doctrine, which might condemn men by its logical consequences, might yet be held without threatening salvation. This argument served several useful purposes. First, such reasoning helped to explain how the Protestants' natural forefathers might have been saved before the enlightenment of the Reformation had revealed the folly of Rome's errors.[136] Secondly, the argument that people who adhered to doctrinal errors did not necessarily embrace the damnable logical consequences of those errors had become vital for those divines who were seeking to secure the unification of the different Protestant Churches, and most especially unity with the Lutherans. In this context, even a hard-bitten puritan such as Anthony Wotton could emphasize that 'not right beleeving is never able to deprive a man of salvation, but when that we beleeve amisse, is a maine point of salvation'. It was only an obstinate error in a point fundamental to salvation that could prevent salvation: 'obstinately not beleeving, onely then shuts up heaven against us, when either the points we will not beleeve are fundamentall, or our refusing to beleeve, is against our owne iudgement and conscience'.[137]

Salvation inside the Roman Church was generally not discussed in these terms. A judgement of charity might be made for those who were invincibly ignorant of Rome's errors, but emphasis was often placed on the practical impossibility of the mechanics of salvation in the Roman Church. Roman Catholics were simply disabled from hearing the truth, or from realizing the spiritual potential of true doctrine.[138] Nevertheless, in certain contexts even puritan writers admitted that there were reforming elements within the Roman Church (not merely the invincibly ignorant) who believed that Protestantism was true, but dare not confess it for fear of losing their places.[139]

It was unusual, but certainly not unparalleled, to allow explicitly for the salvation of reforming elements within the Roman Church, who must by definition be conscious of her errors. In practice it might commonly be assumed that God would exercise mercy on those more moderate elements within the Roman Church, but this assumption was hardly ever expressed in unequivocal, theoretical terms. Two moderate Jacobean Calvinist writers who did adopt this position, however, were William Bedell and Humphrey Lynde. They were both impelled by a sympathetic recognition of the difficulties faced by those who shared Protestant doctrines yet lacked

136 See below, ch.6.
137 Anthony Wotton, *A Trial of the Romish Clergies Title to the Church* (1608), pp.40–1.
138 Abbot, *Second Part*, p.445.
139 E.g. Bernard, *A Key*, p.77.

the courage to communicate openly with Protestants for fear of the Inquisition. Whatever their personal sympathies, however, both writers emphasized that on the theoretical level men in this position were obliged to flee Babylon by Christ's direct command (Revelation 18.4).[140] Neither divine contradicted the fundamental Protestant orthodoxy that Roman Catholics could only really be saved by making themselves wholly dependent on Christ's merits – that is, as Lynde put it, by 'living Papists, and dying Protestants in the principall foundations of our faith'. If any man died a professed Romanist in the knowledge and belief of the present Roman faith he could not be saved. Lynde quoted in support of this position the redoubtable William Whitaker, who had argued the impossibility of Jesuits or Romanists entering heaven on the grounds of Revelation 14.1, which allowed none belonging to Antichrist to stand in Mount Sion with the Lamb.[141]

Nevertheless, as some divines rejected the doctrine of the Two Churches, and undermined the pride of place given to doctrinal orthodoxy in definitions of the church, so the suggestion that Rome's formal heresies necessarily led to damnation were increasingly qualified. In the 1580s, Richard Hooker had spoken out strongly against the argument that all members of the Roman Church were necessarily damned. Instead, he argued that 'many are partakers of the errour which are not in the heresie of the churche of Rome'. He maintained that it was impossible to specify exactly how far an individual member of the Roman Church absorbed Roman heresies to the extent that these errors subverted the true gospel message, to which the individual still had access. Hooker concluded this point with a passionate vehemence unparalleled in the rest of his writings, which bears witness to the importance which he attached to this principle:

> Let me die, if ever it be proved, that simply an error doth exclude a pope or a cardinal, in such a case, utterly from hope of life. Surely, I must confess unto you, if it be an error to think, that God may be merciful to save men even when they err, my greatest comfort is my error; were it not for the love I bear unto this error, I would neither wish to speak nor live.[142]

If Hooker did not explicitly state that a man living and dying a Romanist in all the points of his faith would be saved, his defender William Covell, as in so many other issues, went further. Covell felt that the polemical context impelled him to maintain unequivocally that a man living and dying in allegiance to the Church of Rome could be saved. Covell's admission was made under polemical pressure, however, and was un-

[140] Bedell, *Two Biographies*, p.257; Bernard, *Judgement*, ii. pp.83–5, 88–90, 92–3, 95–8, 103–4; Bedell, *Certaine Letters*, pp.88–9; Humphrey Lynde, *Via tuta* (4th edn, 1630), pp.30–1, 318–19, 322; Milton, 'Laudians', pp.62–4.

[141] Lynde, *Via Tuta*, pp.320–1, 324.

[142] Hooker, *Works*, V: 120, 164.

paralleled in the Jacobean period.[143] Laud himself did not greatly diverge from the traditional orthodoxy that Romanists could only be saved if they were invincibly ignorant.[144] Confronted by the Jesuit Fisher, who attempted to exploit Laud's admission that salvation was possible within the Church of Rome, Laud very carefully qualified his position along the lines of Jacobean orthodoxy. Salvation was allowed in general terms to 'the ignorant, that could not discern the errors of the Church, so they held the foundation, and conformed themselves to a religious life'.[145] It was only thus allowed to 'silly Christians', to 'some ignorant silly souls, whose humble peaceable obedience makes them safe among any part of men that profess the foundation, Christ'.[146] He quoted Augustine to the effect that, where the foundation is held, for ordinary men it was the simplicity of believing, not the acuteness of understanding, that made them safe.[147] Salvation was thus possible for those 'living and dying in the Roman Church' who 'believe and repent of whatsoever is error or sin in them, be it sin known to them or be it not'.[148]

Laud was adamant, however, that there was a very real threat of damnation in the Roman Church: 'he that confesses a possibility of salvation, does not thereby confess no peril of damnation in the same way'. No Protestants had ever denied the great peril of damnation for any man who lived or died in the Roman persuasion. In fact, in the case of a member of the Church of England who purposely defected to Rome, Laud insisted that 'there is peril, great peril, of damnable both schism and heresy and other sin, by living and dying, in the Roman faith, tainted with so many superstitions, as at this day it is, and their tyranny to boot'. Salvation for the invincibly ignorant could only ever be a possibility, and was not a secure way to salvation. If salvation was a possibility, it was yet 'very probable' that damnation could occur 'if he look not well to the foundation'. The errors of Rome were so many 'that it is very hard to go that way to heaven, especially to them that have had the truth manifested'.[149]

Salvation might be very hard for those in the Roman Church who had seen the truth, but was it impossible? Laud clearly had more than 'silly Christians' and simpletons in mind when he allowed the possibility of salvation in Rome. He was prepared to allow it to those who were intelligent and sincere but misled, and who wished to see a reform of the church's errors:

143 Covell, *Just and Temperate Defence*, p.77. Romanist authors made effective use of this passage, provoking moderate Calvinists such as John Downe to renounce Covell altogether: Downe, *Certaine Treatises*, xii. p.42. I owe the latter reference to Peter Lake.

144 See above, p.136.

145 Laud, *Works*, II: 314.

146 *Ibid.*, II: 319.

147 *Ibid.*, II: 349–50.

148 *Ibid.*, II: 334.

149 *Ibid.*, II: 336, 337, 332, 316, 319.

I am willing to hope there are many among them, which keep within that Church, and yet wish the superstitions abolished which they know, and which pray God to forgive their errors in what they know not; and which hold the foundation firm, and live accordingly, and which would have all things amended that are amiss were it in their power.[150]

Laud warned, however, that such people 'hazard themselves extremely by keeping so close to that which is superstition, and in the case of images comes too near idolatry'.[151]

Nevertheless, the basic principle that Roman Catholics could only really be saved by being Protestants was becoming increasingly blurred by the 1620s. Following Hooker, Laudian divines were less keen to stress adherence to doctrine as a direct cause of damnation, and were more eager to reassert the importance of the role of the will in heresy.[152] Laud made use of Augustine's distinction between a heretic and a plain man who is misled and believes a heretic. Church leaders were only lost if they refused to hear the church's instruction or to use all possible means to come to a knowledge of the truth. But what if, having all access to the truth, they were not convinced by it? Here the damnable error lay only in those who first established the error, and hence misled others who grew up with it, and not with

they which are misled, and swayed with the current of the time, hold the same errors with their leaders, yet not supinely, but with all sober diligence to find out the truth; not pertinaciously, but with all readiness to submit to truth as soon as it shall be found; not uncharitably, but retaining an internal communion with the whole visible church of Christ in the fundamental points of faith.

These people, however misled, were not heretics in the sight of God, and were therefore in a state of salvation.[153]

Increasingly, however, this line of argument led away from the nature of Rome's heretical errors towards the more general question of sincerity in religious belief. The Jesuit Fisher claimed that Francis White, at his conference with him, had maintained that none of Rome's errors were damnable as long as they were not held against the conscience.[154] This was to reverse the direction of White's argument but did no real injustice to his position.

150 *Ibid.*, II: 334. 151 *Ibid.*

152 All English Protestant divines accepted the general principle of the importance of the will in heresy. Heresy was usually defined as the voluntary choosing of an article of faith, and the obstinate maintaining of it against the lawful determinations of the true church (e.g. John Prideaux, 'Heresies Progresse', p.4 in *Certaine Sermons*). In this way it was to be distinguished from simple error and the sin of schism. Apostasy was the highest form of heresy, which blasphemed and persecuted the church (*ibid.*, p.5; Field, *Of the Church*, I: 154–8). However, this distinction of the role of the will was not usually applied directly to those in the post-Reformation Church of Rome. See also below, ch.4.

153 Laud, *Works*, II: 351. 154 *Ibid.*, II: 351–2.

In self-defence, White explained that he had observed the important distinction that Rome's errors were fundamental *reductive*, if those embracing them were to err obstinately, having been better informed. The errors were leaven and stubble, such that God would offer mercy to those 'misled by education, or long custom, or overvaluing the sovereignty of the Roman Church'. Yet White would not presume to judge of Fisher or his salvation, remarking 'for your conscience, you are the happier in your error in that you hold nothing against it while you say so. But this no man can know but yourself.'[155]

What had been an admission to allow for the salvation of the simply ignorant increasingly came to be asserted as a general principle that men had no right to judge of another's salvation. Laud insisted several times in his *Conference* that 'there is a latitude in the faith, especially in reference to different men's salvation'. He would not strictly define salvation for particular men.[156] Whatever was said about doctrinal error, it was in fact impossible to know exactly what prevented or secured an individual's salvation. Whatever was added to the foundation 'may be damnable to some and not to others, according to the knowledge, wisdom, means of information, which some have and others want', and according to negligence, contempt, wilfulness or malice against truth. All or some of these were present in different degrees in every particular man, 'and that in the whole latitude of mankind, from the most wise and learned in the school of Christ, to the simplest idiot, that hath been . . . initiated into the faith by baptism'. It was therefore simply not possible for the church to talk in precise terms of individual salvation: 'the church hath not this knowledge of all particulars, men, and conditions; nor can she apply the conditions to the men, and therefore cannot teach just how far every man must believe, as it relates to the possibility or impossibility of his salvation in every particular'.[157] However unyielding he might be on issues of church authority, there was a side of Laud which was firmly opposed to all attempts to overdogmatize in points of faith, or presumptuously to define on issues of predestination and the like, or to lay down the limits within which salvation might occur. In the 1630s he gave his support to writers whose arguments on such issues tended to undermine the notion that doctrinal error might impede salvation.[158]

155 *Ibid.*, II: 352–3. 156 *Ibid.*, II: 362–3, 402–3, 412.

157 *Ibid.*, II: 412. See also William Fuller, *A Sermon Preached before His Maiestie at Dover Castle* (1625), sig.D3r.

158 See, for example, Laud's dealings with Christopher Potter, William Chillingworth and John Hales. Laud read and suggested revisions to Potter's *Want of Charitie* (Laud, *Works*, VI: 326), and later made him his vice-chancellor at Oxford. Chillingworth was Laud's godson, and Laud had shown a keen interest in securing his reconversion (Orr, *Reason and Authority*, pp.26–32), and in the publication (after acquiring Prideaux's

The emphasis on degrees of sincerity and conscience, rather than on doctrinal error, is noteworthy in the works of Christopher Potter and William Chillingworth against the Jesuit polemicist Edward Knott. Potter's standpoint in his *Want of Charitie* on the issue of salvation in the Church of Rome was problematical. He stated in orthodox fashion that 'our Charity reaches . . . to all those at this day, who in simplicity of heart beleeve the Roman Religion and professe it', but only to those lacking the means or understanding to discover their error.[159] However, Potter failed to introduce the customary reservation that such salvation was only *possible* rather than probable. He also omitted to reiterate the traditional argument that it was not a true belief in the Roman religion, but that it was their Protestantism that ensured the salvation of guileless Romanists. Rather, Potter's implication was that a general repentance was enough to ensure salvation. Potter claimed that charity was not extended to those having understanding, much less to those who professed the Roman religion but did not believe it. But it was clearly the latter category that concerned him. Potter implied elsewhere that sincere Romanists who *did* have understanding might still be saved. While Rome's errors forced the Protestants to leave out of fear of hypocrisy, Potter stated quite plainly that the same errors 'in themselves . . . be not damnable, to those which beleeve as they professe'.[160] It was thus fear of hypocrisy, rather than fear of heresy or idolatry, that had caused the Protestants to leave Rome.

In his *Religion of Protestants*, Laud's free-thinking godson William Chillingworth at first gave an orthodox rendering of this argument, informing his Romanist opponent that 'I know no Protestant that hath any other hope of your salvation but upon these grounds, that unaffected ignorance may excuse you, or true repentance obtain pardon for you.'[161]

endorsement) of Chillingworth's *Religion of Protestants* (Laud, *Works*, V: 165). The archbishop also seems to have been sympathetic towards the anti-dogmatic approach of John Hales (for which, see J.H. Elson, *John Hales of Eton* (New York, 1948), pp.89–93). While Laud reacted strongly against passages in Hales' manuscript *Tract Concerning Schism and Schismatics* which seemed to undermine respect for antiquity and ecclesiastical authority, he obviously approved of Hales' moderation on issues of doctrine which Laud himself shared against the overdefinitions of Calvinists and Romanists, and the archbishop later secured Hales a canonry of Windsor (*ibid.*, pp.24–5). Whatever their sympathies in doctrinal agnosticism, however, Hales' arguments clearly clashed with Laudian views of the rights of ecclesiastical authorities to impose religious ceremonies (*ibid.*, pp.95–102). Peter Heylyn twice refers to 'my dear Friend Mr. Hales' in his *Historia Quinqu-Articularis* (1660), i. pp.56, 66, although it is difficult to believe that the two men would have had much in common besides a shared aversion to Calvinist predestinarianism.

159 Potter, *Want of Charitie*, i. p.77.

160 *Ibid.*, i. p.76; and *ibid.* (2nd edn, Oxford, 1634), p.262. On this passage and later attempts to alter its wording, see William Twisse, *Of the Morality of the Fourth Commandement* (1641), p.3.

161 Chillingworth, *Religion of Protestants* (1845), p.67.

'Invincible ignorance' was the only possible saviour for a Romanist.[162] However, later in the same work Chillingworth suggested that a general repentance would also suffice for those who actually had access to the means to find out the truth, but simply would not make use of them: 'for those that have means to find out the truth, and will not use them, they [Protestants] conceive, though their case be dangerous, yet if they die with a general repentance for all their sins, known and unknown, their salvation is not desperate'.[163] A mere general repentance, however, was binding upon any Christian who hoped for salvation, as was a sincere belief in the religion which he professed. The means of salvation which the Church of Rome offered were thus being defined, at least by some writers under Laud, in ways which were essentially the same as those which operated in the Protestant Churches. In yet another crucial respect, Rome was being perceived in the same terms as other churches, albeit as a gravely erring church.

Shifting Protestant opinions on the possibility of salvation within Rome gave rise to the arguments of the Jesuits Knott and Fisher that salvation was more likely in the Church of Rome, because Rome denied salvation to be possible in the Protestant Church whereas Protestants allowed it to be possible in the Roman Church.[164] This argument could be answered on the traditional grounds that salvation in Rome was only possible for the invincibly ignorant. But Laudian writers such as William Page and Richard Corbet argued far more defensively, by appealing to the need for *sincerity* of belief. Page offered a more general condemnation of the principle of denying salvation to one's enemies. Mainstream Jacobean divines might well have attacked extreme Protestants who denied salvation to *any* within the Roman fold (and thereby undermined the salvation of the Protestants' forefathers) but Page and others tended rather to reject *any* attempt to deny salvation to a professed Christian when the sincerity of his beliefs could not be assessed. Page gloried in the Church of England's charity and defended the general principle that good intentions should be sought out and hoped for, even as Salvian had found them among the Arians.[165] The reasons for charity were 'in that I hope our intentions are good, and that none maintaines a false opinion perversely against his conscience, and this last is, that for some opinions that are not so orthodoxe yet there may be

162 *Ibid.*, p.68. 163 *Ibid.*, p.198.

164 E.g., John Fisher, *True Relations of Sundry Conferences* (1626), iii. pp.63–9.

165 Page, *Imitation*, 'To the Christian Reader' (unpaginated). Page considered Salvian's approach 'a good lesson for the hotspurres of these times, with whom it is a very easy matter to pronounce damnation upon the very least disagreement in Religion'. Page clearly admitted several times in this introduction that there were some among the Protestants who were as liable to fall into this error as were the Romanists.

hopes of salvation, although it be not without smart and punishment'.[166] Robert Shelford was convinced that a Christian error must of its very nature be one of ignorance, and could not be 'of intention or affected malice'.[167]

The main response of Corbet and Page to Fisher's argument was to suggest that Romanists were in danger of damnation, not because of their errors, but because of their lack of reciprocal charity. Corbet merely argued that this point 'argues our Christian charity . . . notwithstanding the superstitions and Idolatryes objected against them by other Reformed Churches, who deny that they can bee saved', and suggested that the Romanists' denial of salvation to the Protestants because they refused Rome's superstitions 'is a ver[y] heigh degree of uncharitableness and ma[y] seeme, without repentance, to expell them heaven'.[168] Page made the point that opinions did not determine salvation: while the English Church's charity did not bring the Romanists any closer to heaven, Romanists' damning of the Church of England brought them nearer to hell.[169]

At the heart of these shifts of opinion on the possibility of salvation within Rome lay more fundamental differences among English Protestants regarding the process of salvation itself. For puritans, and for many Calvinist conformists, salvation was founded on the transforming effect of the Word on the individual believer. 'Invincible ignorance' could therefore never be enough to ensure salvation unless it was combined with a full reliance on Christ's merits, as only this could begin the process of true sanctification. Their insistence on the importance of the availability of true doctrine was not prompted by any belief that direct intellectual acceptance of a catalogue of dry theological definitions was required for eternal life. Rather, this emphasis was prompted by a conviction that acceptance of justification by faith alone was a vital stage in fostering the correct response in the individual, in enabling the mechanics of personal salvation to begin. Hence Robert Abbot's insistence that Roman doctrine was not so much simply invalid, as *disabling* of saving faith. When some Laudians professed their readiness to allow for the salvation of the invincibly ignorant, and even of the learned within Rome, as long as they were sincere in their errors and made merely a *general* repentance, this manifested not only a more optimistic view of Rome's errors, but also a different sense of what people had to *do* to earn salvation. A sincere acceptance of the funda-

166 *Ibid.*, sig.***4r–v. For an example of more popular preaching of the point that Romanists could be saved, see the accusations against Robert Guyon, curate of White Colne, Devon: Matthews, *Walker Revised*, p.227.

167 Shelford, *Discourses*, p.297.

168 Bodl., Rawlinson MS D.853 fol.194v.

169 Page, *Imitation*, sig.***4r.

mentals of Christian religion was itself deemed sufficient. Thus Henry Burton's complaints against Laud's *Conference with Fisher* were prompted, not merely by Laud's inconsistency over the possibility of salvation within Rome's communion, but also by the fact that Laud seemed to grant salvation to the 'invincibly ignorant' without insisting that this sincerity must needs be combined with assurance and the direct embracing of Christ, so that such people did not effectively die as members of the Roman Church.[170] By contrast, the Laudians' diminishing of the importance of true doctrine in the church, and thus of its role in the salvation of individuals, elevated the principle of *sincerity* of belief to be a guiding factor in individual salvation. For the individual, membership of a visible church which professed Christianity provided him with all that was required.

To permit Rome to be a true church of God, and to allow for the salvation of sincere Romanists, may have been as far as most Laudians were prepared to go. But for some churchmen, the acceptance of these principles logically entailed the acceptance of salvation as normative within the Roman just as much as the Protestant Churches, and made reconciliation between the two a distinct possibility. One prelate in the 1630s who believed that to accept Rome as a part of the Catholic Church automatically required one to accept that salvation must be open to all who lived and died as Romanists in all points was the singular Godfrey Goodman, bishop of Gloucester. He can hardly be taken as a representative divine, or even indeed as a Laudian, as Laud and his associates seem to have shared a cold contempt for Goodman as a man.[171] However, Goodman does illustrate in a striking manner how tactically moderate trends in anti-papal polemic might develop, and the startling implications which they might engender, if they were not carefully checked.

In 1637 Goodman suspended one Ridler, minister of Little Dean, for refusing to read a public recantation (drawn up by Goodman himself) of errors which Ridler had allegedly made in a sermon concerning salvation

170 Burton, *A Replie*, pp.346–7, 350, 377–8.

171 See, for example, Goodman's complaints to Laud of the archbishop's treatment of him in a letter of August 1642, in which he also accuses Bishops Howson, Montagu, Curll and Mainwaring of Socinianism (PRO, SP 16/491/137). Laud's distaste for Goodman probably stemmed from Goodman's attempt to obtain the bishopric of Hereford to be used as a place of repose rather than of dynamic episcopal administration (G. Soden, *Godfrey Goodman, Bishop of Gloucester 1583–1656* (1953), pp.211–23). Laud was also particularly incensed by Goodman's desire to resign his bishopric, which Laud saw would bring scorn upon Goodman himself and his calling (*ibid.*, pp.221–2). The archbishop would have been further angered by Goodman's persistent pleas to be allowed to go abroad, which Goodman only later reluctantly admitted was partly in order to view the Roman Church (*ibid.*, pp.273–81).

among Romanists. Ridler had allegedly maintained in a sermon 'That if we are saved the Papists are damned.' A Calvinist bishop such as Hall would probably have instructed Ridler to deliver an explanatory gloss along the lines of the conventional argument that a Romanist who lived and died a Romanist in all points would be damned.[172] Goodman, however, chose to argue that proclaiming Romanists to be damned overthrew the nature of the Church of England's own Reformation, 'for in the eye of the law we are still one with the same Catholike Church'. The Reformation statutes declared that no separation was thereby intended from God's Catholic Church, 'so that to make such a difference between these two Churches, as is between damnation and salvation, certainly is against the Common Lawes, and the Statute Law of this Kingdome'. Moreover, as the Church of England shared with Rome the same Holy Orders, church service, ceremonies, festivals and canon laws, Goodman claimed that Ridler's arguments must undermine the Church of England too, 'and therefore through sides of the Church of Rome they do but give deadly and mortal wounds to the Church of England who affirme, that Papists are damned'. Goodman asserted Laud's own general point that men had no right to intrude upon Christ's judicial power in proclaiming who was damned: 'there is no militant Church without blemishes and imperfections, but as long as the foundation is sound, that we believe in Christ crucified, and that we believe the three Creeds, so long there is hope of Salvation; Severall churches, though differing in many things, yet may be contained in the bounds of the Catholique church'. Goodman concluded with an argument against zealots such as Ridler which English Protestants were more accustomed to directing against Rome, namely that 'there cannot be a greater want of charity, then to exclude men from salvation'.[173]

Despite his relative extremism on this issue, Goodman was making a valid point. If Rome was truly accepted as part of the Catholic Church, could Protestants really make such a distinction between her and the Protestant Churches 'as is between damnation and salvation'? By the 1630s some divines, at least, were not prepared to do so. These doubtless included Richard Montagu, who was later to approve of the idea of intercommunion between Protestants and Romanists. Although he did not tackle the issue of salvation in Rome's communion in print, his unqualified treatment of Rome as part of the Catholic Church clearly implied this.

172 Prynne claims (*Canterburies Doome*, p.241), without citing any evidence, that Ridler actually made his original argument in these terms.

173 Prynne, *Canterburies Doome*, pp.241–2. Goodman here echoed the title of Christopher Potter's treatise, which was an attempt to prove against the Jesuit Knott that the charge of 'want of charity' was justly brought against the Church of Rome for excluding from salvation all those who did not communicate with the Roman Church.

Injudicious expressions of Rome's nature as a true church, and of the possibility of salvation within her, were noted and scathingly attacked, not just by marginal figures such as Henry Burton and Thomas Spencer, but also by established veterans of official anti-Roman polemic such as the dean of Exeter, Matthew Sutcliffe. In his will of November 1628, Sutcliffe wrote that there were those 'amonge us that palliate Popish heresies and ... seek to bring in Poperie' by 'holding the modern synagogue of Rome to be the true Church and that salvation may there be had, where the doctrine of Trent is punctually professed and maintained'. These men, Sutcliffe affirmed in his final testimony, 'I hate as apostate from the faith and traitors to God's true church.'[174] It was clearly Richard Montagu and his associates whom Sutcliffe had in mind here, for he claimed in his will that these apostates functioned 'under the name of Arminius', and he had written a reply to Montagu in these terms which had been stopped at the press.[175]

Nathaniel Bernard, an anti-Laudian preacher in Cambridge, was also convinced that the complex qualifications that were customarily built into discussions of the question of salvation in the Church of Rome were being disregarded, thus paving the way for reconciliation. Preaching in Cambridge in 1632, Bernard allowed that Rome was a particular visible church of Christ, though idolatrous and apostatical, and argued the conventional point that salvation without repentance was impossible in the idolatrous worship decreed by the Council of Trent. He claimed, however, that now 'some of ours (at least in outward profession) teach, that it is possible to be saved in the Romish Religion & Church'. According to Bernard, 'an unsettled judgement' could conclude from this that reconciliation was necessary on earth: 'if we may agree in Heaven, why do we not agree and meet each other halfe way on earth? And hence we have many Cassanders among us, who mediate and wish a reconciliation between the Church of Rome and ours.'[176]

This was a logic that had made sense to the convert Benjamin Carier.[177] Writing before he converted to Rome, and when he considered that some

174 PRO, PROB 11/156/94; Burton, *Seven Vials*, pp.46–52; *idem*, *Babel*, *passim*; Spencer, *Maschil Unmasked*, *passim*.

175 Prynne, *Canterburies Doome*, p.159; *The Diary of John Rous*, ed. M.A.E. Green (Camden Society 66, 1856), p.5.

176 Prynne, *Canterburies Doome*, pp.364–5.

177 On Carier's links with members of the Durham House circle, see above ch.1. Given the Laudians' emphasis on the integrity and importance of the Church of England's episcopal succession, it is noteworthy that Carier was said to have petitioned the pope after his conversion that he be allowed to exercise his orders without further ordination (E.C. Messenger, *The Reformation, the Mass and the Priesthood* (2 vols., 1936–7), II: 456). Bedell (*Certaine Letters*, p.148) cites Carier as a papist who allowed that the Church of England retained the perpetual succession of episcopacy. On Carier's career, see *DNB*, s.n. 'Benjamin Carier'; Tyacke, *Anti-Calvinists*, pp.5–7.

form of reunion was still possible between the Roman and English Churches, Carier had protested that he could not really accept that all the polemical writings against Rome expressed the real cause of opposition to her, because some divines were prepared to allow salvation to sincere Romanists. He observed: 'I have oftentimes heard good Protestants in cold blood confesse that they thought an honest Papist might be saved ... Whereupon I begin to thinke with my selfe; may a papist be saved? surely then we are not devided in God ... wherein then is the cause of this great division?'[178]

Sutcliffe may have been wrong to detect a campaign to reintroduce popery as emphases shifted in relation to Rome's status as a church, and the possibility of salvation within her. He was correct, however, to identify such shifts, and also to suspect that, as Bernard suggested, such arguments theoretically left the door open for reunion schemes.

[178] BCO, MS 270 p.154. The attribution of this MS to Carier is made by the copyist, who has a contemporary hand. Internal evidence also strongly hints at Carier being the author. Many of the points made are identical to those later made in Carier's *Treatise* (1614). Compare, for example, MS 270 (p.154) and *Treatise*, p.41 on the point of contrasting the prefaces of the Reformation statutes of Henry VIII with their results; and MS 270 (p.157) and *Treatise*, p.39, for the argument that King James, as the first monarch of England since Henry VIII who was not the fruit of the Divorce which separated the English Church from Rome, might reunite with Rome.

4

The errors of the Church of Rome

AN 'ANTI-RELIGION'?

The Roman Church was not alone in being judged doctrinally erroneous. In an especially contentious age most forms of Christianity accused each other of heresy. What was unique about the Church of Rome was the nature of the errors that Protestants imputed to her. Protestants generally believed Rome's errors to have a decreed purpose and significance that transcended the ways in which Rome might choose to maintain or defend them. Quite often, doctrines were damned because of their connection with her, rather than Rome being damned for espousing them. The background of the apocalyptic tradition was of fundamental importance here, as it lent a sense of inevitability to Rome's errors, which were preordained and of eschatological significance. Thus George Downame explained that because the pope was Antichrist, he was incapable of doing anything save what was papism and mere antichristianism.[1] Errors which appeared to be fulfilments of scriptural prophecy were thus granted a significance well beyond their apparent doctrinal heterodoxy.

In works of apocalyptic exegesis, and also in many popular works of anti-papal polemic, Rome's errors were therefore depicted, not as a mere hybrid of false and erroneous doctrines and practices, but as the direct embodiment of a false religion. Popery was often presented, especially in the works of converts from Roman Catholicism, as a coherent system of false divinity. It was, as Dr Lake has noted, depicted as 'an anti-religion' – a separate religion which worked by essentially inverting the values and norms of Protestant Christianity.[2]

Crucial here was the theme of deception, whose prominence we have noted in expositions of the Romish Antichrist. Rome was not seen as a Christian church which possessed some errors, but rather as the creator of a type of religion that deliberately falsified and debased Christianity. Rome was guilty, not merely of heresy, but of blasphemy, of a form of counterfeit

[1] Downame, *Papa Antichristus*, p.2. [2] Lake, 'Anti-popery', pp.74–7.

Christianity.[3] This was depicted as a deliberate falsification – in part to serve the purposes of Antichrist. It was also claimed that the same doctrines had been used merely as self-serving ploys by unscrupulous churchmen to increase their wealth and authority, and also deliberately to appeal to man's lower, natural instincts. As Thomas Taylor exclaimed, 'How can a carnall doctrine but prevaile among carnall men?' It was claimed even by moderate-minded authors such as John Dove that Roman priests deliberately kept the people in ignorance in order to preserve their own authority.[4] This was a useful polemical ploy: accusations of insincerity and cynicism did not necessarily undermine the priests' (possibly unconscious) participation in satanic purposes.

Rome's errors might sometimes also be attacked, not just as satanic, but also as senseless, inconsistent and absurd,[5] although controversialists noted that, despite the absurdities of some heresies, other Roman errors were often fairly varnished with colours of piety and holiness.[6] Initially, the convert would be presented with pious and plausible doctrines; only later would they be introduced to the grossest errors. An appearance of moderation and plausibility was thus the most insidious tactic of all.[7] This line of reasoning had important implications for the way in which the writings of more moderate Romanists were read and presented, as we shall see.

These presuppositions could lead to extremely strong condemnations of the religion of the Church of Rome – as heathenism, or even as a form of atheism, and not really a religion at all. Those writers most dedicated to exporting the doctrine of the 'Two Churches' into other debates could be led to associate the Roman religion with satanism.[8] Just as it was sometimes claimed that there was only one true church, and that Rome was not part of it, so arguments that Rome was a separate religion were informed by the conviction, as expressed by Matthew Sutcliffe, that 'there is but one true religion', from which Rome was excluded.[9]

Arguments that Rome promoted a separate religion were not limited to puritan writers, but rather may be found expressed by a whole range of divines, who found this rigid form of anti-popery to be of value in a number of polemical contexts. First, the argument that Romanism was essentially an alien religion was encouraged by the fact that Roman writers

[3] *Ibid.*, pp.73–6; Clifton, 'Fear of popery', pp.146–7.
[4] Taylor, *Christs Victorie*, p.416; Dove, *Perswasion*, p.6; *idem*, *An Advertisement to the English Seminaries and Iesuites* (1610), pp.1–2; Clifton, 'Fear of popery', pp.147–8.
[5] Willet, *Synopsis* (1613), pp.1265–352; Abbot, *Second Part*, pp.762–3.
[6] Abbot, *Second Part*, pp.844–5; White, *The Way*, preface, sigs.**2r–3r.
[7] Burton, *Baiting*, pp.34–5.
[8] Bernard, *A Key*, ep. ded.; Wadkins, 'Theological polemic', pp.125–33.
[9] Sutcliffe, *A Briefe Examination*, p.13.

made similar allegations against the Protestants. As the Jesuit Edward Knott explained, 'any the least difference in faith, cannot stand with salvation on both sides', and Protestantism therefore constituted a separate religion, or no religion at all.[10] But this was not merely a case of polemical tit-for-tat; after all, there was always certain polemical mileage to be gained from appearing more moderate than one's opponent. In fact, it was important to maintain that Rome was a separate religion in order to refute occasional attempts made by moderate Romanists to plead for toleration. In these cases, conformist divines such as Sutcliffe, Powel and Hakewill argued as strongly as puritans that Romanism was a contrary religion, akin to heathenism, and one to which the draconian punishments accorded to pagan religions in the Old Testament Books of Judges and Deuteronomy should be applied.[11] In these cases, Sutcliffe and others explicitly vouchsafed their agreement with the arguments and practice of more hardline Romanists who condemned all forms of religious toleration.[12] The same insistence that popery was a contrary religion was employed to counsel against royal marriages to Roman Catholics, as this enabled pamphleteers to invoke suitable Old Testament texts forbidding marriage to pagan idolaters. The opposition to the Spanish Match should thus have caused James no surprise: he had had ample opportunity to hear such warnings from conformist clerics throughout his reign.[13] Old Testament severities could similarly be invoked against native Roman recusants by branding them as Amalekites. While this identification often merely complemented in rhetorical terms the analogy of Israel for the forces of orthodox Protestantism, it could also sometimes be used to demand the literal implementation of appropriate penalties on the Old Testament model. This line of argument often tended towards the sort of pathological anti-popery which we have described earlier.[14] By such means, anti-papal tracts could imply that Rome's errors were *themselves* her religion, and *were* the Roman Church.

[10] Edward Knott, *Charity Maintained* (1638), preface – cited in C. Russell, *Unrevolutionary England 1603–1642* (1990), p.189; Hakewill, *Answere*, ii. p.175; A. Pritchard, *Catholic Loyalism in Elizabethan England* (1979), p.25 (quoting Parsons); Bunny, *Treatise*, pp.79–80; Milward, *Elizabethan Controversies*, pp.145–7. In answer to William Covell's claim that the Church of England did not condemn all Rome's doctrines, since they taught some good things (though others were contrary to Scripture), the Roman convert Walsingham insisted that any group that held positions against Scripture could not be the true church: Walsingham, *A Search*, p.40.

[11] Sutcliffe, *Briefe Examination*, pp.5–8, 23–30; Hakewill, *Answere*, ii. pp.294–5; Powel, *Consideration of the Papists*, pp.21, 31–2; cf. Russell, *Unrevolutionary England*, p.194.

[12] Hakewill, *Answere*, ii. pp.294–5; Sutcliffe, *Briefe Examination*, pp.14–15, 54–5; Covell, *Modest Examination*, p.201; Powel, *The Catholikes Supplication*, pp.37–8; Abbot, *Defence*, pp.205, 211–12, 231–4.

[13] See above, ch.1 n.86. [14] See above, ch.1.

But this was not the end of the matter. Analyses, even puritan ones, were more subtle than this, and had to be flexible when forced to confront the basic fact that most orthodox Christian doctrines were retained by Rome. Many anti-papal tracts contained lurid depictions of the false religion imposed by the Church of Rome – but the fact remained that the elements of true doctrine and worship remained within her communion. The rationale of popery might be devil-worship, yet the Church of Rome still retained what might appear to be the essentials of true Christian belief. Thus Matthew Sutcliffe commenced his *Abridgement or Survey of Poperie* by admitting that 'the Papistes doe hold and professe the articles of the Creed, and divers other points deduced of them, or consonant unto them, which both the Apostles and ancient fathers, and wee also beleeve and professe'. Therefore, Sutcliffe explained, by the term 'popery'

> wee understand not any point of Christian doctrine generally holden of all Christians, or the doctrine of the prophets or holy Apostles professed generally by the ancient fathers, and truly termed Catholike (for that we hold and professe as well as the Papistes, and farre more syncerely than they, albeit we detest and renounce all Popery) but all those errors and corruptions in doctrine both concerning faith and manners, which the synagogue of Rome and her lovers ... have received, professed and taught, either contrary to the doctrine & institution of Christ and his Apostles, or else above the same, and above the faith of the ancient primitive church.

Popery was thus the sum of Rome's errors – not the sum of their insidious combination with doctrinal truths. In this sense, it could be compared with any of the ancient Christian heresies, such as Arianism. Indeed, popery might appear purer than Arianism since, although papists varied from all the doctrines of the ancient church, they still retained an orthodox doctrine of the Trinity.[15]

FUNDAMENTALS AND ADDITIONS

While it might seem disadvantageous for Protestant controversialists to recognize that Rome retained some orthodox doctrines, at times it could in fact prove an effective polemical ploy. This was especially true when English Protestants wished to claim the high ground of moderation by pointing out how far the Church of England shared many of Rome's doctrines, and concluded that Rome thereby granted the truth of Protestant doctrines. This style of argument proved increasingly fashionable during the late Elizabethan and especially the Jacobean period, as English Protestant controversial writing developed increasingly subtle and flexible forms. It was initially introduced in the works of Edmund Bunny with the

[15] Sutcliffe, *An Abridgement*, pp.1, 2, 5.

intention of appealing to English recusants – and Robert Parsons was quick to identify this moderate line as a new development.[16] The classic example of this approach, and of its purely polemical intent, was William Perkins' *A Reformed Catholike*. In this work Perkins studied the various controversies with the Roman Church, but under each disputed point he described the common ground which both Romanists and Protestants shared before going on to explain those additional points on which the Church of Rome insisted and the Protestants departed from her. A 'Reformed Catholike', Perkins explained, was 'any one that holds the same necessary heads of religion with the Romane Church: yet so, as he pares off and rejects all errours in doctrine whereby the said religion is corrupted.' One of the purposes of Perkins' work was to persuade Roman Catholics to a better opinion of the Protestant religion 'when they shall see how neere we come unto them in sundry points'.[17]

Yet it was quite explicitly *not* Perkins' intent to demonstrate that both churches shared the same foundation. Perkins consciously wrote to refute the opinion 'that our religion and the religion of the present Church of Rome are all one for substance'.[18] In fact, he was adamant that 'they of the Romane Church have razed the foundation'.[19] 'We are to make a separation from the present Church of Rome', he continued, 'in respect of the foundation and substance of true religion.'[20] He began the book with an exposition of Revelation 18.3, and firmly maintained that Rome was not a church of Christ at all.[21] There was some truth in the complaint of the Romanist William Bishop that by such remarks Perkins effectively contradicted his earlier claim that the Roman Church held the necessary foundation of faith with the Church of England.[22] Whether or not it was a complete contradiction, Perkins' 'unchurching' of Rome undoubtedly served a deliberate purpose in helping to divest his earlier admission of any positive, irenical value.

Perkins' approach became a popular one in the Jacobean period. Thus

16 Windsor, 'The controversy', pp.157–8, 160–1. This line of argument was also prefigured by Andrew Perne in the 1560s, though perhaps with more irenical implications in mind: P. Collinson, 'Andrew Perne and his times', in P. Collinson, D. McKitterick and E. Leedham-Green (eds.), *Andrew Perne. Quatercentenary Studies* (Cambridge Bibliographical Society Monograph 11, 1991), p.8.

17 Perkins, *Reformed Catholike*, sigs.A3v–A4r.

18 *Ibid.*, sig.A2r; cf. sig.A3v (*pace* Aveling, 'The English clergy', p.93). Cf. Bunny, *Briefe Answer*, p.111. This is not to deny that some readers could choose to interpret Perkins' strategy in an irenical fashion, if it suited their interests: see F.G.M. Broeyer, 'De Irenische Perkins – Vertaling van de Arminian Everard Booth (1577–1610)', *NAvK* 71–2 (1991); and Hotman's *Syllabus* – discussed below, ch.5 n.94.

19 Perkins, *Reformed Catholike*, sig.A2r. 20 *Ibid.*, pp.290–1.

21 *Ibid.*, pp.1–9, 293–4.

22 Bishop's argument is quoted (and unconvincingly opposed) in Anthony Wotton, *A Defence of M. Perkins Booke* (1606), p.29.

Humphrey Lynde, while attempting to defend the Church of England's continuity, argued that the Church of England accepted three of Rome's four Creeds (the other being the new 'Creed' of Pius IV), two of her seven sacraments, the canon of holy Scripture and the first four General Councils. Rome could thus be said to accept and defend all the points of the religion of the Church of England – a point argued with equal emphasis by the puritans Thomas Beard, Richard Sibbes and Anthony Wotton, as well as by establishment divines such as Robert Abbot and George Hakewill.[23] The points in controversy were thus mostly 'additionals', while the positive doctrine of the Church of England was contained in the few points which were universal and had the consent of the Church of Rome.[24] William Bedell similarly accepted that Rome and the Church of England agreed in all the essential points. What divided them were the 'Trent-additions'.[25]

However, this was a line of argument which was easily open to misunderstanding, as Bedell himself was frequently to discover. His former friend turned Roman convert James Wadsworth attempted in his dispute with Bedell to make use of 'their opinion, who would make the Church of England and the Church of Rome to be still all one in essentiall points, and the differences to be accidentall; confessing the Church of Rome to be a true Church, though sicke, or corrupted, and the Protestants to be derived from it, and reformed'.[26] Wadsworth argued from this that, by her own admission, the Church of England had departed from the Church of Rome for frivolous reasons. In response, Bedell was driven to qualify carefully the word 'accidental', 'which doth not import that our differences are but sleight and of small consideration, but that all those opinions and abuses which we reforme and cut off, are not of the Faith, but superfluous and foraine, yea hurtfull and noisome to it, as the weedes are to the corne, which over-grow and choake it'.[27] As Ussher observed, Antichrist did not just place hay and stubble on the foundation of faith, but far more vile and pernicious matter which wrenched and disturbed the foundation itself.[28]

Essentially, then, the suggestion that Rome erred in 'additionals' was simply a tactically different expression of the fundamental argument that the Romanists held all the essential points of faith but overthrew their foundation by consequent.[29] In this sense Rome did indeed err in the foundation of faith, and her errors were fundamental because they touched

[23] Lynde, *Via Tuta*, pp.72–3; Beard, *Antichrist*, p.247; Sibbes, *Works*, V: 477; IV: 116–17; Anthony Wotton, *Runne from Rome* (1624), p.70; Abbot, *True Ancient*, pp.81–2; Hakewill, *Answere*, ii. p.17; Dove, *Perswasion*, pp.11, 13, 15; Bunny, *Treatise*, pp.91–4.

[24] Lynde, *Via Tuta*, p.76; Abbot, *True Ancient*, pp.111–13.

[25] Bedell, *Certaine Letters*, pp.75, 121. Cf. Hall, *Works*, VIII: 643.

[26] Bedell, *Certaine Letters*, p.75. [27] *Ibid.*, p.76. [28] Ussher, *Works*, II: 490.

[29] For this argument, see Hall, *Works*, VI: 288–90, VIII: 721, 726, 729; Hooker, *Works*, V: 153–5; Hakewill, *Answere*, pp.33–4.

on the most basic tenets of salvation in Christ, the true Word of God, and the right administration of the sacraments.[30] However, the argument that Rome's errors were additions to the foundation of the faith required very careful phrasing and choice of context. As they responded to Roman accusations of disunity, or pursued concrete schemes for Protestant unity, Protestant divines (including puritans such as Wotton) sought to base their irenical arguments around the distinction between 'fundamentals' and 'non-fundamentals', arguing that unnecessary additions to the faith should be disregarded in the interests of Protestant unity in those fundamental articles of faith upon which all agreed.[31] Incautious use of the same distinction of 'fundamentals' and 'non-fundamentals' *vis-à-vis* the Roman Church could therefore easily lead to charges of irenical intent towards her, and it is not surprising to discover that Bedell found himself in trouble again with this reading of the issue in 1630.[32]

Even if talk of Rome's errors being 'additionals' was therefore merely a tactical shift, more moderate Calvinist divines were becoming increasingly unwilling to contradict themselves quite as blatantly as Perkins had done on this issue. A greater uneasiness is perceptible among some episcopalian Calvinists during James' reign when faced with the popular claims that the Roman religion was a false religion, or a form of atheism. This discomfort

30 Field, *Of the Church* , IV: 519.

31 E.g. Wotton, *Trial*, pp.373–4; John Davenant, *An Exhortation to Brotherly Communion betwixt the Protestant Churches* (1641), pp.6–19; *idem*, 'The opinion of bishop Davenant', *passim*, in *Good Counsells for the Peace of Reformed Churches. By Some Reverend and Learned Bishops and Other Divines* (Oxford, 1641); see below, ch.8. The distinction of fundamentals and non-fundamental additions was also important to English Protestants' identification of Protestant witnesses in the medieval church – see below, ch.6. Writers using this fundamental/non-fundamental distinction might at other times seem to deny it: e.g. Wotton, *Trial*, pp.20–1; *idem, Dangerous Plot*, i. p.13 (cf. Russell, *Unrevolutionary England*, p.190). It is worth pointing out the fact that *most* divines (and many of a decidedly anti-ecumenical temperament) could embrace this distinction occasionally, as it is still sometimes implied that the distinction is itself an infallible and distinctive note of a moderate ecumenical theologian: e.g. J. Platt, 'Eirenical Anglicans at the Synod of Dort', in D. Baker (ed.), *Reform and Reformation: England and the Continent c.1500–c.1750* (Studies in Church History Subsidia 2, Oxford, 1979), pp.226–9. For examples of more strongly Calvinist conformists and puritans making this distinction, see Wotton, *Trial*, pp.20–1; John White, *A Defence of the Way to the True Church* (1614), pp.143–9; Richard Bernard, *Rhemes against Rome* (1626), p.29; George Abbot, *A Treatise of the Perpetual Visibilitie, and Succession of the True Church in All Ages* (1624), pp.74–5 – cited in Wadkins, 'Theological polemic', p.142.

32 Bedell's opponent this time was the Divinity Professor at Trinity College, Dublin, Dr Joshua Hoyle, who was to prove a bitter enemy of Bedell throughout the 1630s. Hoyle accused Bedell of having maintained that the difference between the Protestants and the Church of Rome was only in ceremonial matters. Bedell again had to explain himself, this time to Ussher, that he had always professed that 'the differences between us and the Church (or Court rather) of Rome, were not in Fayth (which we had in common) but in certaine additions forreine to it, which by corrupt custome were crept in': Bedell, *Two Biographies*, pp.324, 321; see also his letter to Laud: *ibid.*, p.326.

was significant, and demonstrated how far some moderate Calvinist episcopalians had travelled under the pressure of the tactical debate with Rome. These divines voiced an increasing concern that the argument that all principles of reason and religion were extinguished in Rome might imply that Rome did not still retain fundamental orthodox doctrines. Bishop Lake condemned such arguments as 'too much precisenesse' at Paul's Cross in 1623. Robert Abbot similarly expressed reservations over Perkins' claims that the religion of the Church of Rome was atheism, taking care to emphasize that atheism was only a *sequel* to the errors of popery, and freely confessing to Perkins' Roman opponent that the Cambridge divine's imputation was 'conceived and drawen from forced and impertinent grounds, and therefore breedeth rather cavillation against him, than accusation against them'.[33]

This unease among moderate Calvinists would become further apparent in the exchanges of the *Old Religion* controversy, but also arose in part because divines such as Bedell and Dove, appealing directly to English recusants, were at pains to deny that popery constituted a separate religion. Bedell in his *Motives* insisted that the Reformed Churches' religion was not a contrary religion to that of Rome, but merely a different one – a pure religion compared with one corrupted, a reformed placed against a deformed. Popery, he insisted, was not a false religion.[34] When avant-garde conformists such as William Covell and Meric Casaubon strongly condemned arguments which equated Rome's errors with paganism or Judaism, they were arguing from a position more removed from puritan sensibilities than that of moderate Calvinists such as Arthur Lake and William Bedell, but their unease with such arguments was clearly something which these moderate conforming Calvinists shared.[35]

Nevertheless, while points relating to the question of the precise nature of Rome's religion were beginning to cause some unease on the Calvinist side, Calvinist divines still remained committed to an interpretation which, while it allowed that Rome only erred or differed from Protestants in additionals, still insisted on adding the crucial rider that Rome's additions touched upon fundamental points and threatened to overthrow the foundation. She was still guilty of the severest forms of heresy and idolatry and, in a sense, of apostasy.[36] Her errors, most especially those which related to

33 Fincham, *Prelate*, p.261; Abbot, *Third Part*, pp.4–6.

34 Bedell, *Examination of Motives*, pp.1–2.

35 Covell, *Modest Examination*, pp.201–3; Casaubon, *Vindication*, p.42.

36 Davenant, *Determinationes*, pp.102–4; Abbot, *Defence*, pp.110, 218; Bedell, *Certaine Letters*, pp.40–1. Rome was not literally guilty of apostasy. Francis Mason stressed that heretics such as the Roman Church were distinguished from apostates in that the former still followed Christ's institution in the administration of baptism: Mason, *Vindiciae*, pp.171–2. On Rome's apostasy, see Beard, *Antichrist*, pp.245–8, 259; Downame, *Treatise*,

the doctrine of justification, were seen as razing the foundation of faith. As Thomas Taylor explained, the Roman Church held the Creed and Commandments in outward profession, yet reversed and renounced them all by direct logical consequences. Henry Burton, in answer to the suggestion that Rome did not deny the true faith, emphasized that 'Romes dead faith is indeed for the kind of it, a true dead faith, or a true faith of devils, as one may be said to be a true lyar. But ... this faith of Rome is ... different in kind from the true saving faith of Christ.'[37] To omit such qualifications was to hint at a radical reappraisal of the nature of Rome, and of the Church of England's separation from her.

As Daniel Featley explained it, he could accept that Rome held 'most of the fundamentall and positive articles with us', and that 'most of their errours are by way of addition', but the basic point was that 'a foundation may be as well overthrowne by laying on it more then it will beare, as by taking away that which is necessary to support the building'.[38] It was precisely this point which Featley felt that Richard Montagu was disregarding in his *Appello Caesarem* when Montagu wrote that the Churches of Rome and England agreed 'in Essentials and Fundamentals'. It was here that Featley suspected (perhaps correctly) the influence of the ideas of Montagu's late dean at Windsor, Marc'Antonio de Dominis, the archbishop of Spalato, who had fled to England in 1616 only to return once more to the Roman Church in 1622.[39] Featley had in mind Book 7 of de Dominis' *De Republica Ecclesiastica*, where the archbishop had attempted to clear the Roman Church of the charge of heresy by claiming that the more learned members of the Church of England held that Rome did not

sig.A3r; Abbot, *Defence*, pp.110, 218; Humphrey Lynde, *A Case for the Spectacles* (1638), p.199. One means of avoiding the positive implications of Rome's retention of right doctrine was to maintain that all these orthodox doctrines were held on a different foundation. This was a line of argument popular with a range of Jacobean writers, including Crakanthorp, Abbot, Sutcliffe and Jackson, as well as Perkins and Bernard. This was in theory a more powerful and consistent line of argument, as it maintained that any orthodox doctrine held by the Church of Rome was entirely irrelevant, as this was maintained on a separate foundation, and therefore for the wrong reasons: see Abbot, *Third Part*, p.207; Crakanthorp, *Vigilius Dormitans*, pp.186, 189, 190–1, 193; Sutcliffe, *An Abridgement*, pp.11–18; Carleton, *Directions*, p.64; Jackson, *Works*, II: 95, 125, 160; Bernard, *A Key*, pp.242–4. As Abbot explained, the religion of God effectively remained only at the discretion of the pope. While this argument seemed to work theoretically and was understandably popular with puritan writers, it was a proposition with which many divines seem to have been uncomfortable, as it implied too great a division between the churches and appeared to render the power of doctrine *per se* less important. See above ch.3, and also below, p.220.

37 Wotton, *Trial*, p.375; Abbot, *Second Part*, pp.13–37; Taylor, *Christs Victorie*, p.700; Burton, *Baiting*, pp.90–1.

38 Featley, *Second Parallel*, ii. pp.84–5.

39 *Ibid.*, ii. pp.80–1. For the same parallel, see Matthew Sutcliffe, *A Briefe Censure upon an Appeale to Caesar* (1626), p.4; Yates, *Ibis*, iii. pp.37–8.

err in any fundamental points of faith. De Dominis had argued that heresy consisted in a defect, and not in an excess of belief, so that Rome's errors in additionals could not imply heresy.[40] It was a consistent theme in de Dominis' writings composed while in England that the religion of the Roman and Reformed Churches was 'in the maine essentials and fundamentals the very same.'[41] Clearly this had meant something rather different to de Dominis than it did to other Jacobean polemicists. This provides evidence, however, that far more conciliatory attitudes towards Rome could lurk within the increasingly fashionable rhetoric of moderation. On the claim that additions to the faith could not be heresy, Featley remarked with some alarm that he had been informed that 'this errour ... spreads farre like a Gangreene'.[42] A conflict was clearly emerging in understandings of the meaning of Rome's errors in 'additionals'. By 1629, Robert Butterfield was using the common argument that Rome's errors were additions to the faith in order to argue for a more positive view of the Church of Rome.[43]

The argument that Rome's errors were only additions to the foundation therefore continued to be urged, and continued to cause confusion and misinterpretation. As we have seen with the example of de Dominis, irenical perspectives could be harboured within this argument, especially among those who renounced the apocalyptical vision of Rome's errors. This was manifested in running complaints, well before Montagu took up his pen, that some divines had claimed that the two religions were all one for substance. As originally complained of by Perkins, this attack was mostly directed at the French *politique* divines, but also against the *Catholike Moderator* of Henry Constable. Often the focus for such complaints appears to have been so-called 'church papists', aristocrats appealing for a

[40] De Dominis, *Second Manifesto*, sig.C4v; Featley, *Second Parallel*, ii. p.81. Hall attacked the same work for so slighting Rome's errors 'as if they were not worth our contention; as if our martyrs had been rash, and our quarrels trifling': Hall, *Works*, VIII: 638. For de Dominis' irenical treatment of the controversies between Roman Catholics and Protestants, see his *De Republica Ecclesiastica* (Hanover, 1622), lib.7, cap.10 pp.194–7, and cap.12 *passim* (especially pp.281–322).

[41] *A Sermon Preached in Italian by the Most Reverend Father, Marc'Antony de Dominis, Archb. of Spalato ... Anno 1617* (1617), p.31. De Dominis does, however, make a detailed critique of papal doctrinal errors: *ibid.*, pp.41–55.

[42] Featley, *Second Parallel*, ii. pp.81–2. Featley's fears were well grounded: de Dominis' arguments in his Seventh Book, which were an attempt to reconcile moderate Protestant and Romanist doctrines, profoundly influenced the irenicist Laudian bishop of Edinburgh, William Forbes, in his own attempts to promote such a reconciliation in the doctrinal controversies. See Forbes, *Considerationes*, I: 31, 201–3, 267, 291–3, 373–7; II: 39, 57, 135–7, 285, 301–3, 383–5, 499, 553–5, 595. On Forbes' links with English divines and the Caroline regime, see *DNB*, s.n. 'William Forbes'; Forbes, *Considerationes*, II: 'Preface', p.5; Baillie, *Ladensium* (3rd edn, 1641), 'A Large Supplement', sig.C1r.

[43] Butterfield, *Maschil*, pp.37–40.

practical toleration for the Roman faith.[44] John White in 1608 complained of a generation of 'Politick Romanists' and of the ignorant who thought that there was no difference between the two religions. Nevertheless, there were also clearly some denunciations levelled at Church of England divines who were, in the wake of Hooker, adopting a more moderate line towards the Roman Church. An early Jacobean puritan petition accused Peter Baro of having laboured 'to make men beleeve that the reformed Churches doctrine is not soe differinge from popish doctrine, but that by distinctions they may be reconciled'. By the early 1620s, in the wake of the *de facto* toleration of the Roman religion prompted by the planned Spanish Match, Richard Sheldon was complaining at Paul's Cross of 'Neutralizers' who claimed 'that there is no fundamentall difference, betwixt the Roman and the Reformed Churches'.[45]

By the 1620s, it is possible to find divines among the Durham House Group who were chiefly concerned on this matter to argue that Rome still retained the fundamentals of the true faith. Significantly, they were not concerned to make the crucial qualification that this foundation of true faith was overthrown as a consequence of Rome's errors, which they presumably considered to be an unnecessary reservation which might undermine the former point. At the York House Conference Thomas Morton objected against Richard Montagu that he had infringed Article 19 of the Thirty-Nine Articles by quoting with approval the affirmation of the Roman Catholic ecumenist George Cassander that Rome had remained firm in points of faith.[46] This was an argument which Cosin and Buckeridge were easily able to overthrow by showing that Cassander referred to the *fundamentals* of faith, whereas Article 19 only referred to Rome erring 'in matters of Faith', which need not be fundamentals; a point which Morton accepted.[47] This appears to have been a clumsy mistake on Morton's part, and a surprising one coming from such a skilled and experienced controversial theologian. Morton's instinct was correct, however, in thinking that Montagu's use of Cassander overturned previous ideas about the nature of Rome's errors, even if these could not be shown to be explicitly present in the Article. As an irenical writer, Cassander's claim that Rome remained firm in fundamentals was not intended to be

44 Perkins, *Reformed Catholike*, sigs.A2r, A3v; Henry Constable, *The Catholike Moderator* (1623); D. Rogers, 'The Catholic moderator: a French reply to Bellarmine and its English author, Henry Constable', *Recusant History* 5 (1959–60); D. Wootton, *Paolo Sarpi* (Cambridge, 1983), pp.50–8, 72–3; C. Vivanti, *Lotta politica e pace religiosa in Francia fra Cinque e Seicento* (Turin, 1963); Pritchard, *Loyalism*, p.60 (Sir Thomas Copley). See also below, ch.5.

45 Bodl., Bodley MS 124 p.59; White, *The Way*, ep. ded., and preface, sig.**1r; Sheldon, *Sermon at Paules Crosse*, p.46. Cf. Taylor, *Christs Victorie*, p.686.

46 Cosin, *Works*, II: 33.

47 *Ibid.*, II: 34.

qualified by the recognition that she threatened those fundamentals by her errors, and neither Montagu, nor his defenders at York House, advanced this qualification. In his *Appello* Montagu's main complaint with Rome on the issue of 'fundamentals' was the fact that Rome had promiscuously communicated their status to inferior scholastic points.[48] Rome's error was thus depicted as standing more in overdefinition, in unnecessary superstructures, rather than in heresies which threatened to overthrow the foundation. It is important to note that Montagu's arguments were opposed here not just by pamphleteers such as Featley, but also by a bishop such as Morton, who could generally accept the need for a tactically moderate line of argument against Rome.

The problematic issue of Rome and 'fundamentals' came to the fore again in the 1630s. Thomas Choun, in a work dedicated to Laud and licensed by Laud's chaplain, argued that Rome still remained firm 'in primariis, & fundamentalibus religionis capitibus'.[49] Choun's arguments were discussed at the Court of High Commission at the censuring of John Bastwick, when Laud allegedly declared in Choun's defence that the Church of England and Rome differed 'about' rather than 'in' fundamentals.[50] This incident was raised against Laud at his trial, where the archbishop offered a gloss on his speech which conformed to conventional arguments on this issue. Laud objected to the suggestion that he had maintained that the Church of England differed from Rome 'not in fundamentals, but in circumstantials', whereas 'these are not membra opposita, but fundamentals and superstructures, which may sway quite beside the foundation'.[51] While he stressed that Rome did not differ 'in the prime foundations', Laud claimed that 'they in many things grate close upon them, and in some things fall beside them, to no small hazard of their own souls'.[52] Laud thus accepted the important principle that some of Rome's errors might endanger the foundation, although his more detailed treatment of this principle at his trial was idiosyncratic.[53]

48 Montagu, *Appello*, p.117. 49 Choun, *Collectiones*, pp.45–6.

50 Burton, *For God and the King*, pp.121–2.

51 Laud, *Works*, IV: 336.

52 *Ibid.*, IV: 336–7. Laud made the same point even more plainly in his *Conference with Fisher*, where he explained that a church might hold a fundamental point literally 'and yet err grossly, dangerously, nay damnably, in the exposition of it'. This was Rome's position, as it had gradually changed in its exposition of the Creeds and Councils, and 'lost the sense and meaning of some of them' (*ibid.*, II: 355). An error in a non-fundamental point might thus still grate upon the foundation (*ibid.*, II: 356).

53 At his trial, Laud gave examples of how 'many times "circumstantials" in religion do quite destroy the foundation', but these were all concerned with the reflection in circumstantials of a direct rejection of the Incarnation: Laud, *Works*, IV: 337. Laud is clearly not concerned here with the notion that heretical doctrines might overthrow the foundation of faith by consequent. Laud's prosecutor rightly complained that the archbishop had identified no point of popery which overthrew the foundation. In reply, Laud cited the

However, those who defended Laud against Burton's accusations in 1637 were less careful to acknowledge this principle, and regarded the argument as being concerned simply with Rome's maintenance of the fundamentals of Christian belief. Thus Heylyn, in reply to Burton's arguments against Laud, quoted Article 19 (very much as Cosin had done at York House) and claimed from this that the English Church had not said that it differed from Rome in 'fundamentals'. Heylyn then distorted quotations from the staunch Calvinists Franciscus Junius and William Whitaker, who admitted that Rome retained many things properly pertaining to a true church (such as the ministry and sacraments), in order to claim that 'neither of them thought that Church had erred in Fundamentals' – a conclusion which Whitaker for one would have most vehemently denied. Heylyn went still further, however, by defending Rome's uprightness in maintaining these fundamentals. Heylyn emphasized, as he had already done in a 1627 university disputation, that Rome had been an admirable defender of orthodoxy against heretics such as the Anabaptists – more so, in fact, than clerics such as Burton: 'the Church of Rome doth hold as fast on that foundation, as you, or any Zealot of your acquaintance; and hath done more against the Hereticks of this Age, in maintenance of the Divinitie of our Lord and Saviour, then you, or any one of your Divines, be hee who he will'.[54]

In his own defence of Laud, Christopher Dow similarly pointed to Article 19 as consciously referring to matters distinct from 'fundamentals'. He argued that 'fundamentals' were those points of faith which were absolutely necessary to salvation, and were not lacking in the present Church of Rome.[55] Dow admitted that popery contained 'grosse and palpable errors', and allowed that Rome and the Protestants differed on 'many intercurrent questions concerning points fundamentall disputed among us', but stressed that in these points 'the fundamentalls themselves [are] confessed by both sides', and did not imply that these disputes in any way threatened such fundamentals.[56] A similarly careless treatment of the issue of the Church of Rome and 'fundamentals' may lie behind the

doctrine of transubstantiation, but he did not try to demonstrate how this doctrine endangered the foundation, but instead merely argued that this was an example of a question of mere circumstance (the means of Christ's presence in the sacrament) which both Protestants and Roman Catholics had accounted a point fundamental by both inflicting death and in dying for it (*ibid.*, IV: 337–8). The singularity of Laud's arguments here seems to be due to the fact that he felt called upon to defend the argument that Rome only differed from Protestants in 'circumstantials' (rather than 'about fundamentals'), which was not really consistent with his own views.

54 Heylyn, *Briefe Answer*, p.125; *idem*, *Examen Historicum* (1659), pp.214ff. For an accurate analysis of Montagu's similar distortion of the same passage from Junius, see Featley, *Second Parallel*, ii. pp.76–9. On Heylyn's 1627 disputation see below, ch.6.

55 Dow, *Innovations*, p.47. 56 *Ibid.*, p.48.

allegations made against William Fuller, the dean of Ely. It was claimed against Fuller in 1641 that he had preached 'that there is no difference betweene our church of England, and the church of Rome, in matter of substance, but in circumstance onely which might easily bee reconciled'.[57] This may represent a misinterpretation by his audience (perhaps wilful, perhaps not) of the argument that Rome and the Church of England agreed in fundamentals – a confusion which may have been caused by Fuller's failure carefully to qualify his argument by an emphasis on Rome's errors. It is possible, however, that Fuller's words may have been as reported.

If the fundamentals of faith were unreservedly shared by both churches, it was difficult to see why there should be such intense conflict with Rome. Robert Shelford demanded to know why Protestants quarrelled with Roman Catholics when they believed in the same Baptism and Trinity. Making no reference to Rome's errors, Shelford argued that the Protestants were the pope's 'brethren, who dissent not from him in the main'.[58]

These changed understandings of the nature of Rome's heterodoxy were also reflected in differences which appeared in English Protestant perceptions of Rome's specific errors in doctrine and worship. Anti-papal writers seldom arrived at the same figure when calculating the number of Rome's errors. As one historian has noted, calculations of the number of issues in dispute could vary greatly in number, depending upon whether items such as the worship of images or Mariolatry were accorded a separate heading or were treated as a subset of the sin of idolatry. Generally, however, most anti-papal divines addressed themselves to the major errors concerning good works and justification, the worship of images, papal primacy and infallibility, the eucharistic presence, prayer for the dead, the invocation of saints, clerical marriage and communion in one kind.[59] Willet's *Synopsis* gave an account of twenty-two 'generall Controversies', divided into almost 150 'Questions', but the main errors upon which he focused were entirely conventional.

Although many works attempted to discuss all these errors, scholars more often chose to concentrate upon one or two in particular, which were seen as manifesting Rome's heterodoxy most clearly. Some errors received progressively less attention during the Jacobean period, while others assumed a growing importance, or were subject to increasingly careful

[57] *The Petition and Articles Exhibited in Parliament against Dr. Fuller* (1641), sig.A3r. For the charges against Fuller, see also PRO, MS 30/53/9/11 fols.123v–124r. I owe this last reference to Professor Russell. Cf. the case of Richard Carrier: Gardiner, *Reports*, pp.92, 98.

[58] Shelford, *Discourses*, pp.238, 288.

[59] Cragg, *Freedom and Authority*, pp.172–3, 185–90.

qualification and elaboration. This was in part a reflection of the fact that the Roman side was increasingly dictating the areas of debate. Nevertheless, by the 1630s the importance attached to Rome's different errors by English Protestant writers had clearly shifted. While most divines might still agree on a formal list of Rome's errors, under Laud clear differences emerged as clerics objected to Rome's errors with varying degrees of intensity, and disagreed over the scale of Rome's perceived fault.

ROMAN IDOLATRY

In the eyes of most divines, one religious error loomed larger than all the others – an error which made Rome's guilt almost uniquely despicable. She was not merely guilty of false and heretical opinions, but also maintained other positions which tended towards the sin of idolatry.[60] This charge did not relate simply to the worship of images, or to the invocation of saints, but also to the 'Idol of the Mass' in which, by the doctrine of transubstantiation, the priest was held to recreate God Himself, and the host was presented to the people for adoration. The charge of idolatry also related to the general Protestant conviction that the Romanists advanced the pope above God in their doctrines of ecclesiastical authority. The importance of the imputation of this error to Rome lay in the unequivocal denunciations of idolatry in the Old Testament, and the violence with which idolaters were instructed to be treated in the Book of Deuteronomy.[61] It was the charge of idolatry which sustained the most vehement rejections of the idea of toleration, or of a royal marriage with a Roman Catholic.[62]

John Davenant, bishop of Salisbury, noted that communication of any kind with idolaters was strictly forbidden by Scripture. He stressed the severity which the ancient church had displayed towards men who incurred the least suspicion of committing idolatry.[63] This was a crucial quali-

60 Sutcliffe, *A Briefe Examination*, p.5. On the importance of this error in contemporary anti-popery, see Lake, 'Anti-popery', p.74.

61 E.g. Exodus 32.27–35 (the massacre inflicted on the Israelites for worshipping the Golden Calf) and Deuteronomy 17 (the injunction to stone idolaters to death). These passages and others are collected in John Prideaux, 'Idolatrous Feasting', p.10 (*Certaine Sermons*); Lynde, *Via Tuta*, pp.197–8; Ames, *Fresh Suit*, ii. p.384. On the texts from Deuteronomy, see M. Aston, *England's Iconoclasts I* (Oxford, 1988), pp.363, 472. The striking text of Deuteronomy 27 was repeated every Ash Wednesday in the commination service: *ibid.*, p.360.

62 Powel, *Consideration of the Papists*, pp.21, 31–2; Russell, *Unrevolutionary England*, p.194. Even William Covell, warning against too much familiarity with idolaters, remarked that 'some think' that marriage is not permitted with them, and made no attempt to refute such views: Covell, *Modest Examination*, pp.200–1.

63 Davenant, *Expositio*, pp.385–6. While Davenant urged the intercommunion of all Christian churches, he insisted that this was unlawful with a church such as Rome which was

fication, de Dominis noted, to all the Church of England's pretended moderation towards Rome. If the papists really were idolaters, as was claimed, then they were worse than heretics and should be cast out from society. Matthew Sutcliffe emphasized that, even if no other charge could be made against Rome's religion, the error of idolatry would be sufficient to exclude her members from all Christian churches and commonwealths.[64] The charge of idolatry was also crucial to the identification of Antichrist and Babylon.[65] Joseph Mede emphasized that 'Idolatry is the only Character and Note whereby the great Apostasie of the visible Church is discovered and distinguished from all other Blasphemies, Seditions, and Heresies of what age or time soever.'[66]

The levelling of this charge against Rome was the one point on which all pre-Laudian Church of England writers could agree,[67] and was an accusation which Romanists could not cast back at Protestants.[68] While it allowed puritan divines to revel in Old Testament legalism, it also permitted more moderate Calvinist divines such as Davenant and Morton to construct more pacific justifications of the Church of England's rejection of Rome on *other* issues whenever this was required. Such strategic moderation was possible because the charge of idolatry erected a fundamental bulwark against Rome: it was sufficient cause to make permanent separation from her. However, while moderate Calvinists and puritans could unite behind the accusation of idolatry, the degree of iconophobia involved could be very different. Puritan writings were fuelled by a more fundamental opposition to all forms of belief which posited God's 'immanence' in the world, and moderate puritans such as Perkins, and even conforming Calvinists such as Daniel Featley, maintained an opposition to images of any kind in churches. Radical puritans such as William Ames suggested that this was essential to the refutation of the Roman position, declaring in the 1630s that 'except those which write against the Papists, doe refute all Images instituted for religious signification, they doe not make any difference betwixt us, and a great part of Popish Doctors'. More moderate Calvinist conformists were less iconophobic in their approach, but it

guilty of idolatry: Bodl., MS Rawlinson lett. 76(c) fol.72r: Davenant to Johannes Polyander, 13 April 1635.

64 De Dominis, *Second Manifesto*, sig. D2r; Sutcliffe, *Briefe Examination*, p.23.

65 Perkins, *Reformed Catholike*, pp.302–3; Thomas Gainsford, *The Glory of England* (1618), p.281; Mede, *Works*, pp.318–24.

66 Mede, *Works*, p.324.

67 E.g. Jackson, *Works*, II: 137; Gainsford, *Glory*, pp.270–81; Morton, *Catholike Appeale*, pp.29, 120–1, 238–42, 555–9, 585–7; Lynde, *Via Tuta*, pp.9–10; Davenant, *Expositio*, pp.78, 385–6 and *passim*; Prideaux, 'Idolatrous Feasting', *passim* (*Certaine Sermons*); John Rainolds, *De Romana Ecclesia Idololatria* (1596), *passim*.

68 Lynde, *Via Tuta*, p.83.

would take the ceremonialist excesses of the 1630s for these differences to be fully manifested.[69]

De Dominis undoubtedly exaggerated when he claimed that English Protestants 'principally defend the equity of their separation' from Rome simply by the charge of idolatry.[70] It is clear, however, that this particular imputation had an important role to play in the Church of England's case against Rome, and that for some writers (such as Davenant) it seems to have featured as the most important single grievance against that church. For men such as Prideaux, Rome's idolatry had directly caused the calamities which had afflicted all Christendom by bringing forth God's punishment upon the world.[71]

Image-worship

It was usually argued that Rome's formal doctrine of image-worship was guilty of idolatry, and that Romanist writers actively sponsored such tenets.[72] The crucial passages for illustrating that Rome not only practised but also taught image-worship occurred in the writings of Bellarmine and Vasquez, and most of all Aquinas. Aquinas was seen as the originator of image-worship, whose arguments later Romanist writers were unable to avoid.[73] Bellarmine, claimed Prideaux, went further than the Israelites who worshipped the Calf when he held that any divine worship was terminated in an image, because of its reference to the deity or saint which the object represented.[74] Vasquez went further still. King James cited his *De Cultu*

69 Featley, *Second Parallel*, ii. p.24; Ames, *Fresh Suit*, ii. p.290. For Perkins, see Aston, *Iconoclasts*, pp.442–5, 446 n.85, 450; Ames, *Fresh Suit*, ii. p.143. Contrast Francis White in his defence of Montagu: Bodl., Rawlinson MS C.573 fols.81–2.

70 De Dominis, *Second Manifesto*, sigs.D1v–D2r, E1v. But see George Hakewill's claim in his manuscript tract 'The Wedding Ring' against the Spanish Match that the idolatry of all members of the Roman Church was 'presupposed as a chiefe motive of our separation from their Church': Bodl., Rawlinson MS D.853 fol.113r. See also his confidence in Rainolds' *De Romana Ecclesia Idololatria*: Hakewill, *Answere*, ii. p.257. Cf. Bernard, *Looke beyond Luther*, p.46 (citing 1 Cor. 5.11); William Covell, *A Briefe Answer unto Certaine Reasons* (1606), p.53.

71 Prideaux, 'Idolatrous Feasting', p.10 (*Certaine Sermons*).

72 Prideaux complained that Romanist Schoolmen tried to define idolatry as narrowly as possible. Gregory of Valentia was particularly guilty of narrowing so much the extent of this superstition 'that none of their palpable will-worship shall come within compasse of it': *ibid.*, p.4; cf. Lynde, *Via Tuta*, p.254; Abbot, *Defence*, p.210; *idem*, *Second Part*, p.1185. Prideaux also noted that one Philip Monceus had recently defended Aaron's making of the Golden Calf, and declared Jeroboam's calves to be schismatical rather than idolatrous, in a book which was dedicated to Pope Paul V 'and allowed by the chiefest Doctors of Paris': Prideaux, 'Idolatrous Feasting', pp.6–7 (*Certaine Sermons*). The conflation of the prohibition of images with the first Commandment of the Decalogue was seen as part of this policy: see Aston, *Iconoclasts*, pp.383–6, 388–9.

73 White, *Replie*, pp.241–2; Lynde, *Via Tuta*, p.252; Abbot, *Second Part*, pp.1181, 1194–7.

74 Prideaux, 'Idolatrous Feasting', pp.8–9 (*Certaine Sermons*).

Adoratio as evidence of the worship of devils within the Roman Church.[75] Thomas Jackson admitted the novelty of Vasquez' position, but noted that it had not been officially condemned by Rome, and suspected that the pope himself approved of it.[76]

Protestant writers also maintained that image-worship was imposed in Pope Pius' new Creed of 1564.[77] Davenant complained that no man could now be admitted into the Roman communion unless he were to become a 'down-right Idolater'. It was generally unlawful to have any communion with a church which required idolatrous worship, or at least which demanded that its members believe and profess that such practice was not unlawful.[78]

King James argued that the idol-worship prophesied in Revelation 9.20 was manifested in Rome, as it was 'the maine doctrine of the Roman Church'. The Schoolmen's attempts to justify their forms of image-worship were based on 'nice Philosophicall distinctions' with which they attempted to gloss over Scripture's firm condemnations, but which would not save them on the Day of Judgement.[79] This argument clearly endangered the view that salvation might still be possible within the Roman Church, especially as it was the ignorant who were most likely to be guilty of the sin of idolatry. However, it is noteworthy that no Jacobean divines attempted to find a way around this problem – idolatry could not be justified by casuistry, and idolaters could not be excused on the grounds of ignorance.[80] Even Richard Montagu argued that idolaters could not truly be accounted members of the church.[81]

This absolute condemnation of Rome's doctrine on images was sometimes, however, supplemented by a distinction between Rome's doctrine and her practice on this issue. On some occasions, it might be granted that many Roman controversialists were trying to refine and amend Aquinas' doctrine. Passages of the Council of Trent seemed clearly to condemn it, writers such as Bellarmine and Bishop 'wavered' and 'simpered somewhat', distinguishing carefully between *latria* (the fullness of divine worship given

75 King James, *Political Works*, p.142. James also cited Vasquez against the Jesuit Fisher: LPL, Lambeth MS 1372 fol.59v.

76 Jackson, *Works*, II: 137.

77 See e.g. Overall's list of the points added by Pius to the Nicene Creed in Jewel, *Works*, IV: 1311.

78 'The Opinion of Bishop Davenant', p.12 in *Good Counsells*. On avoiding idolaters, see Davenant, *Determinationes*, pp.39, 41. Cf. Lynde, *Via Tuta*, pp.52–3, 197.

79 King James, *Political Works*, pp.142, 125.

80 Only William Bedell attempted to allow for salvation within Rome by arguing that idolatry was commended there, rather than imposed as absolutely necessary: Bernard, *Judgement*, ii. p.82.

81 Montagu, *Apparatus*, p.3.

to God alone) and *dulia* (the more qualified reverence given to saints).[82] Nevertheless, if Jacobean Protestants admitted the existence of such Roman equivocation, they usually accompanied this admission with a firm condemnation of such shiftings, mental reservations and 'nice Philosophicall distinctions', both as insufficient in themselves, but also as irrelevant in practice, since gross idolatry was committed by the common people in Rome's communion who could not understand such distinctions.[83] King James maintained this position strongly in conference with the Jesuit Fisher, when he supplied '2 or 3 straunge stories' to show that idolatry was indeed committed at a popular level. The purpose of this line of argument was thus not to justify Romanists' doctrinal distinctions, but to show that, even if they were in some sense valid, they were irrelevant and did nothing to curb popular idolatry. As King James put it (in his own inimitable style) Romanist divines were 'like to bawdes, whoe thoughe theye doe not sinne in their owne bodies, yet they are guiltie by inducinge others'.[84]

Nevertheless, this distinction made between Rome's doctrine and practice clearly had a more irenical potential: if the doctrinal distinction of *latria* and *dulia* could be accepted as valid, then popular idolatry could be represented as a problem caused merely by pastoral neglect. For most Jacobean writers, such 'neglect' reflected a conscious unwillingness to reform idolatry which had malicious and prophetic intent. After all, idolatry was, as we have seen, of fundamental importance as a mark of Antichrist, and as such it was unlikely to be a purely accidental result of pastoral carelessness. From this perspective, the sophistication of the Schoolmen's arguments in defence of image-worship simply demonstrated the 'mystery of iniquity'. Robert Abbot scorned 'their absurditie and the vanitie of their distinction' which 'is used but onely for a shew to blind the unadvised and ignorant Reader, but cannot with any intelligent minde acquit them of that idolatrie which we impute unto them'.[85] But the same argument could be used to minimize the Church of Rome's errors on this point. This was precisely the way in which de Dominis employed it. While admitting that *in practice* the vulgar and meaner sort were 'formalissime Idololatras', he stressed that Romanist doctrine might admit a better interpretation. He complained that, when among the Romanists, he had always carefully instructed his own people otherwise, as did some other Romanist divines.[86] If many Romanist pastors could be found, like de Dominis, to be warning their flocks in practice against idolatry then the

[82] Abbot, *Second Part*, pp.1148–9, 1181–2, 1194, 1196, 1221; Sandys, *Europae Speculum*, p.3.
[83] E.g. Lynde, *Via Tuta*, pp.40–1, 212–17; Abbot, *Second Part*, pp.1111, 1187–8; *idem*, *Third Part*, p.33; Morton, *Catholike Appeale*, p.29.
[84] LPL, Lambeth MS 1372 fol.59v.
[85] Abbot, *Second Part*, p.1183.
[86] Neile, *Shiftings*, pp.27–8.

charge could not be used directly against the Roman Church as a whole. This was what Benjamin Carier discovered.[87]

A more moderate assessment of Rome's supposed idolatry which ran along these lines was hinted at earlier – as we would expect – in the irenically minded tracts addressed to English recusants by John Dove, Edmund Bunny and William Bedell. Nevertheless, Dove was firmer in his condemnation of this error in his later *Advertisement*, which was directed against Jesuit attempts to exploit his earlier moderation.[88] Indeed, many divines who might be tempted towards a more moderate line were implacable when in direct controversy with Jesuits. Both Francis White and William Laud, in their conferences with Fisher, were firmly opposed to Rome as both idolatrous in practice, and as capable of causing such idolatry by her dangerous confusion in doctrine. White did not deny that there were many moderating distinctions and qualifications employed by Romanist writers on this issue. But this was not a matter of oversubtle but ultimately valid arguments. White denied Vasquez' distinctions: the worship of images, 'either primarie or secondarie', absolute or respective, was 'a palliate Idolatrie, a reminder of Paganisme'.[89] The very variety of discordant opinions within Rome on this issue was a clear sign of 'corrupt and unsound Doctrine'.[90] Aquinas' gross error had not been condemned at Trent, and 'many late Pontificians' such as Suarez and Vasquez had propounded it as agreeable to Trent's definition, albeit with some incoherent qualifications.[91] Therefore doctrinal error on this point lay at the centre of the Church of Rome.

Laud placed greater emphasis than White did on the *practice* of idolatry, amassing the testimonies of eye-witnesses to its existence in Rome both before and since the Council of Trent.[92] He depicted the doctrines of Vasquez and others more as irresponsible logic-chopping which failed to tackle the practical problem of popular idolatry.[93] Laud implied that Rome's formal position might be blameless by taking the Council of Trent at its word in its declaration against the notion that there was any divinity in images, and its religious care 'that all occasion of dangerous error be prevented'. Laud's main grievance was that there had been very little amendment of popular idolatry since Trent, despite its declared intentions.[94] It was more usual among Jacobean writers to denounce Trent's

[87] Carier, *A Treatise*, p.15. [88] Dove, *Advertisement*, pp.13–16.
[89] White, *Replie*, p.209.
[90] *Ibid.*, p.211.
[91] *Ibid.*, pp.241–2. It was generally agreed that Aquinas was the founder of image-worship: see Lynde, *Via Tuta*, p.252.
[92] Laud, *Works*, II: 310, 311. [93] *Ibid.*, II: 309. [94] *Ibid.*, II: 310–11.

treatment of image-worship as a deliberately ambiguous fraud, as White did.[95]

Laud did not, however, simply reduce idolatry to an issue of pastoral neglect. The Schoolmen's distinctions were 'dangerous' and 'superstitious vanities', and Trent's religious care could not be effectual in the face of the dangers of the present doctrine of the adoration of images. In fact, Laud declared, 'the doctrine itself is so full of danger, that it works strongly, both upon the learned and unlearned, to the scandal of religion, and the perverting of truth'.[96] Both Laud and White thus stood by the charge of idolatry against Rome. Indeed, it was reported in November 1623 that they had refused the king's requests that the word 'idolatry' should be removed from the text of White's *Replie to Fisher*.[97] However, both divines gave their support to Richard Montagu, whose works did much to undermine this charge against Rome.

King James' desire that the word 'idolatry' be removed from White's *Replie* was only part of his wider attempt to discourage more absolute attacks upon the Church of Rome at the time of the Spanish Match. He was only too well aware of the implications of the argument that Charles would be marrying an 'idolatress'. After all, it was precisely this argument that the royal chaplain George Hakewill had employed in his manuscript tract against the Spanish Match, which had actually been sent on to James. The mainstream position under James had been that *every* Romanist was guilty of idolatry. This was a point which Robert Abbot was happy to repeat and stand by, despite his occasional reservations concerning Perkins' vehemence on other issues.[98] Nevertheless, Lancelot Andrewes showed an ability to shift with court politics on this point in the years of the Spanish Match negotiations, when he denied that all Romanists were idolaters.[99] Andrewes may not have been alone. By 1624, Thomas Taylor was complaining that 'I know not by what windlace the Iesuits (as nimble as mischiefe it selfe) have brought it about, to a demurre among Divines; whether these Babylonians be Idolaters or no?'[100]

95 Thus White complained that Trent on this point 'is like Apollo his riddles and responsalls, a nose of waxe, and so ambiguous, that . . . veterane Papists themselves are perplexed in resolving the mysteries thereof'. The main point was that Trent had not denied Aquinas' error, and was sufficiently vague to allow modern Jesuits to claim that Aquinas' arguments were consistent with its teaching: White, *Replie*, p.241.

96 Laud, *Works*, II: 312, 311.

97 *The Court and Times of James I*, ed. T. Birch (2 vols., 1848), II: 435.

98 Abbot, *Defence*, p.210; PRO, SP 14/122/40.

99 PRO, SP 14/122 fol.60v: John Chamberlain to Dudley Carleton, 28 July 1622. Andrewes was here responding to Hakewill's arguments in the latter's 'Wedding Ring' (see above n.70). Joseph Mede reports that Andrewes was present at James' interview with White and Laud, but he would seem to have characteristically remained silent.

100 Taylor, *Two Sermons*, i. p.23. Taylor goes on to provide eight arguments to prove 'That Romanists are formall Idolaters' (*ibid.*, pp.23–4).

It was the works of Richard Montagu, however, that introduced the most significant reservations into accusations of Roman idolatry. Montagu employed the distinction between Rome's doctrine and practice in very much the same way that de Dominis had done. In his *Immediate Addresse* of 1624, Montagu showed himself to be quite prepared to accept Rome's doctrine on images, and the validity of the distinctions employed by her writers. He remarked that 'in their Doctrine of Images they disclayme Idolatry indeed: and take the imputation with great offence, and as the most part of them doe teach in their Booke the use of Images, I see no cause to stile them Idolaters'.[101] He was frank, however, that 'the Peoples practice is ... next doore unto it: very like it, if not the same', and that the vulgar people did not understand the distinction between *latria* and *dulia*. In his *New Gagg*, Montagu repeated that there was little doctrinal difference between the Churches of England and Rome: 'In tearmes there is not much difference: you say they must not have Latria: so wee. You give them Dulia. I quarrell not the terme, though I could: there is a respect due unto, and honour given relatively unto the picture, signe, resemblance, monument of great men ... Saints, Christ. If you call this Dulia, we give it too.'[102] In practice, however, he was sure that *latria* was given.[103] It was up to the Church of Rome to 'change the state' and prove that only *dulia* was offered: 'let practice and doctrine goe together, wee agree'.[104] Montagu did note that the 'new Schooles', with writers such as Vasquez, upheld such idolatry,[105] but he did not take them to be representative of Rome's general doctrine.

It was therefore with some justice that Daniel Featley complained that Montagu, in his *Gagg*, 'seemeth to reconcile us and the Romanists in this poynte'. Montagu, Featley claimed, had divided Rome's doctrine from her practice in such a way 'as though there were noe difference betweene our doctrine and theirs touching this pointe'.[106] This was to place Montagu effectively among the ranks of those moderate Romanist writers who were prepared to disclaim their church's practice. After all, it was precisely these writers (such as Polydore Vergil) whose complaints were the principal sources for Protestant attacks on Rome's idolatry.[107] Montagu's readiness to accept the Romanists' distinction between *latria* and *dulia* was unparalleled in English Protestantism; even Andrewes had rejected the distinction outright. In response, the puritan John Yates felt it necessary to abandon the distinction between doctrine and practice altogether, declaring un-

101 Montagu, *Immediate Addresse*, p.67. 102 Montagu, *New Gagg*, p.318.
103 *Ibid.*, pp.299–300, 309, 318.
104 *Ibid.*, p.319. 105 *Ibid.*, pp.306, 319. 106 Bodl., Rawlinson MS D.831 fol.97v.
107 E.g. Featley, *Second Parallel*, ii. p.24; James, *A Manuduction*, p.81; Abbot, *Second Part*, p.1188.

ambiguously 'let practice go, the Church of Rome teacheth Idolatrie both in *latria* and *dulia*'.[108]

In his *Appello* Montagu was more circumspect on the issue. While still maintaining that Rome's *dulia*, if it intended civil respect, was acceptable, he did not suggest that Rome did indeed teach such *dulia*. Instead, he switched his attention to the idolatry of Aquinas and Vasquez which, he suggested, 'is now an Article of Faith in the Romane Church, and the opposite Doctrine flat Heresie'.[109] In his later writings, however, Montagu seems to return to the moderate position expounded in the *New Gagg*.[110] He still used strong language against Rome's practical idolatry, performed by the vulgar unlearned multitude who could not grasp the curious scholastic distinctions of 'relative' and 'absolute' worship, of *latria* and *dulia* and so on.[111] He admitted that even some learned Romanists were guilty of venerating statues. Images of Christ should indeed be honoured,[112] but the main problem was that the Roman 'magistri' were silent on the issue, and the subject was not clearly and thoroughly taught in sermons. There were some Romanists, Montagu maintained, who propounded the subject acceptably. There were others, however, who urged it beyond all piety and common reason.[113] One of Montagu's main concerns, however, was to warn his Romanist opponent Bulenger against speaking foolishly on such a delicate subject, and thereby leaving himself open to attack from 'nostros Novatores' – the present-day puritan iconomachs.[114] In them the Churches of England and Rome had a common enemy. While approving the removal of images which had been abused to idolatry, Montagu condemned contemporary Calvinist iconoclasts, and even expressed doubts about the motivations of the Greek iconoclast Emperor Leo Isauricus (normally a Protestant hero), suspecting that he may have declared war on images 'ex animo perverso'.[115]

During the 1630s the drive to reintroduce images into churches made assaults on Rome's idolatry all the more suspect. Such attacks are rare

108 Lancelot Andrewes, *A Pattern of Catechistical Doctrine* (Oxford, 1846), pp.128, 131–2 (cf. also Abbot, *Second Part*, p.1181); Yates, *Ibis*, iii. p.17.

109 Montagu, *Appello*, pp.249, 256, 257.

110 Montagu, *Apparatus*, pp.79, 309; *idem*, *ΘΕΑΝΘΡΩΠΙΚΟΝ*, i. p.40; *idem*, *Antidiatribae*, pp.16, 24, 27.

111 Montagu, *ΘΕΑΝΘΡΩΠΙΚΟΝ*, ii. p.82; cf. ii. pp.88–91, 96.

112 *Ibid.*, ii. pp.91–2.

113 *Ibid.*, ii. p.92; cf. p.96.

114 *Ibid.*, ii. pp.95–6.

115 *Ibid.*, ii. pp.92, 101, 102. John Buckeridge also seemed uncomfortable with Leo's actions, although his main concern was to emphasize that the emperor was not a heretic, 'licet forte erraverit', and that he was therefore unjustly excommunicated by Pope Gregory: John Buckeridge, *De Potestate Papae in Rebus Temporalibus* (1614), p.951. King James, by contrast, noted Leo's prosecution of image-worshippers without any criticism: King James, *Political Works*, p.186.

indeed in Laudian literature.[116] Robert Shelford placed Rome's error in an unusually positive light by arguing that, rather than idolatry being the mark of Antichrist, the pope's maintenance of images in fact showed him not to be Antichrist, since Antichrist will have no other idols but himself.[117] It was more common in the Laudian decade for writers to criticize the ignorant iconoclasm which would not allow images in churches, rather than the idolatry which adored them when they were there.[118]

There were few divines, though, who sought openly to exculpate the Roman Church from the doctrine of image-worship.[119] What is more significant in Laudian literature is the general de-emphasis on the issue of idolatry as such, and its replacement at the centre of religious concerns by the problem of profanity and sacrilege.

The mass and transubstantiation

Rome's alleged idolatry was not limited to image-worship, but reached its height in the mass itself. Davenant agreed with Bellarmine that, even if all other controversies between Protestants and Romanists could be composed, peace between them would still be impossible, since Protestants judged the Roman mass to be a horrendous idolatry.[120] The centre-piece of the mass – the re-creation of God – was an idolatrous act, if not in word, then in deed. Intercommunion was thus impossible. The pious must flee from the idolaters and heretics who congregated in the Romish mass; to remain was to be a servant of Antichrist.[121]

It was the doctrine of transubstantiation which lay at the root of this idolatry. As Morton claimed, this doctrine brought direct and necessary idolatry in the worship of the host as the true body of Christ.[122] Transub-

116 For an example of how attacks upon Romanist idolatry could indeed undermine liturgical reform, see Ames' attempt to use the Old Testament texts against Church of England ceremonies: Ames, *Fresh Suit*, ii. pp.384–7. Nevertheless, some strong supporters of Laud still condemned Rome as guilty of worshipping images in the 1630s: e.g. Bodl., MS Eng.th.e.14 p.177 (Richard Steward); BL, Add. MS 20065 fol.21v (Robert Skinner).

117 Shelford, *Discourses*, p.300. This argument had been regularly employed in the past by Jesuit writers. For the conventional English Protestant response, see Willet, *Synopsis* (1600), p.206.

118 E.g. Peter Hausted's sermon in BL, Harleian MS 7019 fol.54.

119 It was objected against one Michael Barnes, a Kentish vicar, that he 'did speak to the justifyinge of the Papists havinge of Images, and sayd they worshipped not the Images, but had them in remembrance of Saints, sayinge, they were in a righter way then wee': Larking, *Proceedings in Kent*, p.191. Barnes is a rare example, and his remarks were made in private.

120 Davenant, *Determinationes*, p.39. 121 *Ibid.*, p.41.

122 Morton, *Catholike Appeale*, pp.120–1. Thomas Jackson ranked the 'heresy' of Christ's real presence by transubstantiation along with that of papal infallibility as being Rome's two chief heresies, which were 'sottishly improbable, and yet apparently most damnably

stantiation therefore came in for severe attack.[123] Thomas Jackson went so far as to suggest that it was more likely that it was Satan's substance that was annexed to the host, rather than Christ's. In transubstantiation, Jackson declared, Satan 'quite inverts all use of these men's sense, faith and reason'. It was therefore 'much to be dreaded, lest the Devil persuade the blind besotted papist, that Christ is present where he himself lies hid'.[124]

However, such irreverent language on sacramental issues was becoming somewhat unfashionable in the Jacobean period. Church of England polemicists such as Crakanthorp and Field became increasingly aware of the need to maintain the doctrine of Christ's presence in the eucharist against Romanists' attempts to identify English Protestant doctrine with the Zwinglian view of the eucharist as purely a memorial.[125] Where earlier Protestant authors had made painstaking distinctions between the 'true' and 'real' presence in the eucharist, Jacobean authors of even a moderate puritan stamp such as Richard Sheldon were happy to employ the term 'real presence' which had earlier been a Romanist monopoly.[126]

Opposition to transubstantiation could also be couched in the more reserved terms which the rhetoric of moderation might require. This was the 'mysterium tremendum' argument, which affirmed the reality of the sacramental presence while maintaining a type of agnosticism concerning the precise nature of the presence.[127] In this way, transubstantiation might be represented simply as an unnecessary attempt to define a mode of presence where this was beyond human capacities. Thus William Perkins was able to argue in his *Reformed Catholike* that the Church of England

idolatrous in their consequences, if erroneous': Jackson, *Works*, II: 166. He also noted that under Mary subscription had been urged upon nothing so much as the real presence; this could only be explained by the working of Satan (*ibid.*, II: 166–7).

123 Jackson launched a bitter assault on the worship of Christ through transubstantiation. It was 'a senseless, blind belief' to think Christ's body present where it could not be perceived: 'to worship that as God, which to our unerring senses is a creature, upon such blind proposals, that Christ's body, by one miracle, may be there – by another unseen – is worse than idolatry committed upon delusion of sense': Jackson, *Works*, II: 207, 208.

124 *Ibid.*, II: 208, 209.

125 C.W. Dugmore, *Eucharistic Doctrine in England from Hooker to Waterland* (1942), pp.53–9. Dugmore is here careful to distinguish 'Central Churchmen' – among whom he numbers Field, Hall, Ussher and Morton – from 'High Churchmen' such as Laud and Andrewes. It is notable that Thomas Jackson is seen to have had a more 'Low-Church' view of the sacrament of the eucharist (*ibid.*, pp.51–3). Whatever his personal links with the Durham House Group, and his agreement with them over the doctrine of predestination, Jackson's ecclesiological views would seem to have remained in earlier Elizabethan traditions: see also pp.139, 220.

126 Sheldon, *Christ on His Throne*, p.44. But note Robert Abbot's antipathy towards the term: Abbot, *True Ancient*, pp.366–7.

127 Dugmore, *Eucharistic Doctrine*, p.61 n.3. There was a certain tension, however: some divines still insisted that it was religious to enquire after the manner of receiving Christ's body in the eucharist, and to know it: Manningham, *Diary*, p.35.

agreed with Rome on Christ's presence in the sacrament, but only differed from her concerning the *manner* of this presence.[128] He was still outspoken, however, on the evils of transubstantiation and its consequence: the idolatrous worship of 'a Breadengod'.[129] This was, after all, rather more than a mere matter of unnecessary definition: it was a point for which the Marian martyrs had given their lives. The doctrine and its practical consequences were inextricably intertwined in fulfilment of apocalyptic prophecy. Thomas Morton declared categorically that the difference between the customs of the Church of England and of Rome in relation to the eucharist was that between Christ and Antichrist.[130] Similarly, on the issue of the eucharistic sacrifice, Morton emphasized that Rome's position should not be dignified with the suggestion that Protestants merely expounded this point in a better way than did Rome. Rome's great sacrilege should not be presented in terms of degrees of error, but should be condemned absolutely.[131]

Morton declared in his 1631 tract on this issue that no sound Protestant could ever rightly think that it was possible to tolerate or reconcile Romanists on the pretence that their eucharistic error only concerned the mode of presence. Although Morton might appear to have constructed a straw man here for rhetorical purposes, in fact he had someone more specific in mind. It is more than likely that Morton was here referring to the work of Richard Montagu, who had quoted from Morton's *Catholike Appeale* a few years earlier while seeking to maintain the precise position that Morton so decried.[132] This provides a clear example of how a tactically moderate expression of a point disputed with Rome could be taken up and used to present an irenical perspective on the issue as a whole, to the consternation of the original author. It was a concern that this might happen which had excited repeated concern throughout James' reign at the newly fashionable 'mysterium tremendum' approach.

Late Elizabethan writers had first expressed concern at Hooker's treatment of the issue in his *Laws*, where he had preferred to emphasize the soteriological aspects of the eucharist, and had devoted little attention to opposing transubstantiation. The authors of the *Christian Letter* were unhappy at what might lurk beneath the positively phrased agnosticism which Hooker and his defender Covell chose to adopt towards the problem of the eucharistic presence. Such concerns were only heightened by the

128 Perkins, *Reformed Catholike*, p.169. 129 *Ibid.*, p.303.

130 Thomas Morton, *Of the Institution of the Sacrament of the Blessed Bodie and Blood of Christ* (1631), i. p.65.

131 J.E.B. Mayor, 'Materials for the life of Thomas Morton, bishop of Durham', *Cambridge Antiquarian Society Communications* 3 (1865), pp.35–6.

132 Morton, *Of the Institution*, i. pp.147–8; *idem*, *Catholike Appeale*, p.93; Montagu, *Appello*, p.290.

increasingly loose talk of a 'real presence' in the sacrament without the necessary caveats against popish errors. The manuscript defence of the Millenary Petition expressed grave concern at how 'in chief places of the lande the doctrine of a reall presence in the Lords Supper hath bin soe taught by some others as the people that hearde yt were infinitely scandalized, and complayned that either transubstantiation or Consubstantiation was publikely preached'.[133]

The vivid language employed by the singular Edward Maie caused even greater concern to Daniel Featley and Richard Sheldon in 1621. As Archbishop Abbot's licenser, Featley attempted in vain to ensure that Maie inserted a passage condemning the doctrine of transubstantiation in order to balance the incautious references to ministers as the 'makers of Christ his body' in Maie's sermon *The Communion of Saints*.[134] In 1626, eucharistic doctrine again gave cause for concern, as the crypto-popish Bishop Goodman delivered a court sermon which was suspected of unorthodoxy on the issue of transubstantiation.[135]

Those more mainstream writers associated with the Durham House Group were unanimous in their rejection of transubstantiation as an explanation of the eucharistic conversion and presence.[136] However, the theme of the inscrutability of the eucharistic presence became far more prominent in their writings. Andrewes had offered something of a model here in his *Responsio*. He argued that both the Church of England and Rome accepted Christ's true presence but stressed that the Church of England did not define the matter too rashly. The question of the mode of presence should not be made *de fide*. He noted that the early Fathers had not taught a change of substance, and that the medieval Schoolmen had admitted that transubstantiation was not a necessary explanation of the eucharistic presence.[137] While he objected to transubstantiation being placed among the articles of faith, Andrewes seemed prepared to allow the doctrine to be listed among opinions that might be debated in the Schools ('Scita Scholae') – an admission that more rigid anti-papists such as Thomas Morton had great problems in trying to explain away.[138]

133 Hooker, *Works*, IV: 45–8; Covell, *Just and Temperate Defence*, pp.113–21; Bodl., Bodley MS 124 p.61.

134 Sheldon, *Christ on His Throne*, sigs.A3v–A4r; Edward Maie, *A Sermon of the Communion of Saints* (1621), p.7.

135 *Court and Times of Charles I*, I: 95; Heylyn, *Cyprianus*, p.153; Laud, *Works*, III: 186–7.

136 Andrewes, *Responsio*, pp.12, 15, 262; Montagu, *New Gagg*, sig.D2v, pp.253–6; Forbes, *Considerationes*, II: 447–65; Laud, *Works*, II: 306, 321, 377; John Buckeridge, *A Sermon ... Touching Prostration and Kneeling in the Worship of God. To which is Added a Discourse concerning Kneeling at the Communion* (1618), pp.100–1.

137 Andrewes, *Responsio*, pp.13, 12, 15, 262.

138 *Ibid.*, p.13; Thomas Morton, *Totius Doctrinalis Controversiae De Eucharistia Decisio* (Cambridge, 1640), p.9. Cf. Francis White in Bodl., MS Rawlinson C.573 fols.87v–88r.

Laud strongly rejected Bellarmine's arguments for conversion 'adductive' and the mistaken notion of Christ's presence as a bodily substance,[139] but he also argued that transubstantiation was chiefly a matter of Rome's having added a 'manner of this His presence'.[140] He demonstrated how Bellarmine's position could, with a careful rephrasing, be made acceptable.[141] Laud was clearly happiest when presenting transubstantiation as an unfortunate and unnecessary, rather than an evil and idolatrous, doctrine, although he also pointed out that the doctrine 'taken properly cannot stand with the grounds of Christian religion'.[142]

Richard Montagu, in his *New Gagg* and *Appello*, offered a similarly moderate assessment of Rome's position on transubstantiation and the eucharist. Against his Romanist opponents' claims that the churches were fundamentally opposed on this point, Montagu asserted that the two churches did not differ on the point of the eucharistic presence, and that it was the *modus* of the sacrament which should not be pried into.[143] He reiterated in his *Appello* that the difference was only concerning the *modus*, and that agreement would be possible if factious spirits on both sides could be removed.[144] Montagu insisted that 'there need be no difference ... The disagreement is only in de modo presentiae: the thing is yeelded to on either side, that there is in the Holy eucharist a Reall presence.' On this point he employed against the opponents of his *New Gagg* the charge which he had originally made against the Jesuits: that they were 'a Faction bred by the Devil', otherwise they would acknowledge that there was no cause why in the point of the sacrament the Church of England and the papists should be so opposed.[145] Montagu claimed the support of Hooker and Andrewes for this view, although in their respective works these writers had placed more emphasis on constructing arguments against Roman attempts to impose such a doctrine as a matter of faith.[146]

To argue in these terms was to suggest that the doctrinal difference between Rome and the Church of England was insignificant, and this threatened to undermine the special place which transubstantiation held in the imputation of Romish heresy and idolatry. This was particularly dangerous as the same distinction of the insignificance of debates over the *modus* was central to Reformed attempts to negotiate with the Lutherans on the question of the eucharist. Featley focused on precisely this point in his critique of Montagu. Featley argued that, on the point of transubstantiation, Montagu made 'the difference betweene us & our Adversaries the

139 Laud, *Works*, II: 322, 364–5. 140 *Ibid.*, II: 320–1. 141 *Ibid.*, II: 322–3.
142 *Ibid.*, II: 306.
143 Montagu, *New Gagg*, preface, pp.251–3, 255; CUL, MS Gg/1/29 fol.98r (from back).
144 Montagu, *Appello*, pp.288–9, 291. 145 *Ibid.*, p.291.
146 *Ibid.*, pp.290–1; cf. Andrewes, *Responsio*, pp.12, 13, 15; Hooker, *Works*, IV: 46–8.

Papistes, very little or nothing at all, soe that we might well be reconciled together'. He objected that, if Montagu was right that 'there is, there need bee, no difference in the point of reall presence', then the Marian martyrs who laid down their lives in this point had been 'grossely & foulely deceived'.[147]

In fact, Montagu did make clear his opposition to the doctrine of transubstantiation, quoting Article 28 to this effect in his *Appello*.[148] His rejection of the doctrine was still clearer in his more detailed discussion of the sacrament in his later *ΘΕΑΝΘΡΩΠΙΚΟΝ*.[149] His emphasis throughout was that the eucharistic presence, its change and its reception, must be understood in mystical rather than corporal terms.[150] He regularly attacked transubstantiation as 'transubstantiationis monstrum',[151] a late innovation of which the Fathers knew nothing,[152] and as the root of other errors.[153] Montagu still attached great importance to the error of transubstantiation in his debates over reunion with Rome in the 1630s.[154] But he clearly did consider that reconciliation on this issue was possible. De Dominis had also shown a particular hostility to the doctrine, but saw reconciliation as still feasible on the grounds that it was an error in philosophy rather than theology.[155] The potential for de Dominis' view clearly existed within the 'mysterium tremendum' principle.

As Montagu only attacked extreme ideas of a 'corporal' presence, he

147 Featley, *Second Parallel*, ii. p.19; Bodl., Rawlinson MS D.831 fol.99r. Cf. Montagu, *New Gagg*, p.253.

148 Montagu, *Appello*, p.297.

149 A more thorough immersion in patristic theology, of the kind embarked upon by Montagu in this work, could easily prompt a strong leaning towards aspects of transubstantiation doctrine, as being nearer to the language of patristic sacramental theology than was Protestantism. This certainly occurred in the thought of Isaac Casaubon: Pattison, *Isaac Casaubon*, pp.221, 224, 226, 401. Montagu, however, still seemed determined to pursue an independent course, and to show that patristic language did not imply the doctrine of transubstantiation.

150 Montagu, *ΘΕΑΝΘΡΩΠΙΚΟΝ*, ii. pp.248, 249, 250–1, 262, 297.

151 *Ibid.*, ii. pp.264, 304, 324.

152 *Ibid.*, ii. pp.264, 320.

153 'Transubstantiatio est illa Helena, quae tot ubique turbus dedit': *ibid.*, ii. p.362. For detailed refutations of transubstantiation, see *ibid.*, ii. pp.251–3, 256, 264–5, 320, 324, 362–6.

154 PRO, MS 31/9/17B: Panzani to Barberini, 4/14 November 1635.

155 When Bishops Neile and Montaigne and Dean Young of Winchester attempted to dissuade the archbishop from defecting to Rome it was the point of transubstantiation upon which they chose to concentrate. Neile reminded de Dominis that he had told the king that he never did nor ever would believe in transubstantiation. De Dominis in reply claimed that he still thought this way, but believed the doctrine to be only an error in philosophy, not in theology. While ubiquity could still be held according to theological principles, which permitted miracles, this was contrary to philosophical principles: Neile, *Shiftings*, pp.13, 23. De Dominis argues that transubstantiation, though an error, is not heretical in his *De Republica Ecclesiastica* (Hanover, 1622), lib.7 p.200. It was later reported that de Dominis had died still renouncing transubstantiation.

was able to pursue doctrines of the real presence which might be more amenable to more moderate Romanist divines, although he made no attempt to investigate this possibility. The young John Cosin's view of the sacrament seems to have edged closer to moderate Romanist perceptions of transubstantiation precisely because he opposed only an extreme, crude formulation of the Roman doctrine.[156] The irenicist Sancta Clara in the 1630s had attempted to argue for the reconcilability of the Thirty-Nine Articles and the Council of Trent by claiming that the Articles only opposed the carnal presence of Christ, 'as though Christ was present in the Sacrament in a carnal or sensible manner, not sacramentally'.[157] Cosin's first collection of Prayer Book notes (written in a 1619 Book of Common Prayer at some time between 1620 and 1638)[158] made extensive use of the writings of the moderate Jesuit Maldonatus, with whose sacramental doctrines Cosin would seem to have had no complaint. He quoted with complete approval Maldonatus' exposition of the meaning of the eucharistic sacrifice, and also argued from the Mass Book itself that Rome denied that the bread and wine underwent a substantial change at the communion, in contrast to 'that doctrine, which private men, the late doctors and schoolmen, have brought up and propagated'.[159] Given Maldonatus' exposition and the words of the Roman liturgy, Rome essentially agreed with the Church of England's own liturgy, and there was no reason for further dispute between the two churches on this issue.[160]

Cosin found in Maldonatus a Romanist divine prepared to deny that extreme 'corporal' view of the sacrament which Montagu so derided. Maldonatus argued that Romanists never said that the sacrament and the thing signified were the same thing. Cosin interpreted this stance as favouring the Church of England's doctrine, and condemning 'that gross conceit of the ignorant papists, that think they see, and taste, and chew the very Body of Christ, corporally, which every man abhors to conceive, even the best learned among the papists as well as we'. By labelling this extreme view and detaching Rome, her liturgy, and her best divines from it, Cosin was able to declare that he could not see 'where any real difference is betwixt us about this real presence, if we would give over the study of contradiction, and understand one another aright.'[161] It was the Genevans whom Cosin generally saw as the Church of England's

156 The danger that attacks on unrepresentative extremes of Roman Catholicism, while outwardly displaying anti-papal zeal, might in fact allow Laudians to draw closer to *moderate* Roman doctrines had been noted already by puritan critics on the issue of image-worship: see Burton, *Tryall*, sigs.F2v–F3r.

157 Cited in N. Sykes, *Old Priest and New Presbyter* (Cambridge, 1956), p.190.

158 Cosin, *Works*, V: xviii.

159 *Ibid.*, V: 115–18, 108, 109.

160 *Ibid.*, V: 120.

161 *Ibid.*, V: 155.

opponents on sacramental issues (at least in the years before his exile in Paris).[162]

William Forbes, the Laudian bishop of Edinburgh, went even further than Cosin and set out to provide a programme for reconciliation with Rome on the issue of the eucharist. He did not deny that transubstantiation was repugnant to the Scriptures and the Fathers.[163] He was adamant, however, that transubstantiation (and consubstantiation too) was not a heresy.[164] Forbes dictated moderation on this issue by asserting that the Greeks agreed with the Romanists on the matter of eucharistic adoration, which was the basis of the Protestants' charge of idolatry in the mass.[165] Transubstantiation, Forbes insisted, was essentially a superfluous opinion; an error and falsehood, but one which was not contrary to real articles of faith.[166] Protestants' claims that transubstantiation was repugnant to the articles of faith, and therefore heretical, impious and blasphemous, had been abundantly refuted by Romanist polemicists. Forbes was shocked by Morton's claim that reconciliation with Rome on this issue could never be possible.[167]

Forbes also offered a defence of the Romanists' adoration of the host.[168] He rejected the attempt to call Romanists bread-worshippers and idolaters (although the accusation of bread-worship had been levelled by King James, among others).[169] Rather than being a malicious doctrine which provoked blatant idolatry, Forbes averred, this was merely a mistaken assumption, and the adoration which it provoked was an understandable consequence of it. Forbes maintained that the Romanists adored the body of Christ on a supposition that was false, but that was not heretical, impious or directly repugnant to the faith.[170] He noted that Buckeridge admitted that the Romanists denied adoring the elements or species.[171] As in the matter of image-worship, the basic problem was that modern Romanists employed valid distinctions which their parishioners did not

162 E.g. *ibid.*, V: 110, 144–5, 164 and *passim*.

163 Forbes, *Considerationes*, II: 447, 451.

164 *Ibid.*, II: 483–503. 165 *Ibid.*, II: 487–91.

166 *Ibid.*, II: 497, 499. Contrast Ussher's observation that it threatened the foundation of the Catholic belief in the Incarnation: Ussher, *Works*, II: 491.

167 Forbes, *Considerationes*, II: 507.

168 Buckeridge was less accommodating. In his defence of the ceremony of bowing to receive the sacrament, he attacked the idolatry involved in the Romanist worship of the bread and wine after consecration, and stressed that Roman Catholics adored the sacrament itself, although he noted that even Suarez disclaimed the worship of the elements: Buckeridge, *Sermon*, pp.33, 37.

169 King James, *Political Works*, p.239, talks of 'the monstrous birth of the breaden-God'. See also Hall, *Works*, V: 348–9; R. Abbot, *Defence*, pp.208–9. Even the Laudian bishop John Towers adopted this tone: Towers, *Four Sermons* (1660), p.39.

170 Forbes, *Considerationes*, II: 547–9. 171 *Ibid.*, II: 551–3.

understand.[172] Rome's failure was thus essentially a pastoral one. Again, Forbes claimed that the Greeks followed the Romanists in adoring Christ in the eucharist.[173] He was thus able to shift polemical ground: rather than an attack on the abuses of the Romish Antichrist, accusations of idolatry could now be condemned as a presumptuous judgement on the worship of a number of different Christian churches.

Like Cosin, Forbes was deeply concerned with the dangers of Protestant over-reaction to transubstantiation, in the shape of Zwinglian memorialism.[174] During the 1630s outspoken attacks upon the popish mass, transubstantiation and the adoration of the host were expunged by the licensers William Heywood, Samuel Baker and Thomas Weekes. Passages were removed from the works of Richard Clerke, Richard Ward and William Jones which attacked the mass as a Baalitish abomination, Romish ideas of sacrifice as blasphemy, and their effective worship of the bread as God.[175] Such censorship manifested a distaste for the irreverent satirical scorn that was customarily heaped on the practical consequences of Rome's errors.[176] But Thomas Weekes also removed Jones' more conventional argument against transubstantiation from the example of the resistance of the Marian martyrs.

The early years of the Long Parliament witnessed many accusations made against ministers that they had upheld the doctrine of transubstantiation. It is highly unlikely that any of these churchmen had directly expounded the doctrine in these terms. The charge seems generally to have been prompted by excessive reverence towards the altar and the sacramental elements, a tendency to affirm spatial connections between the eucharistic presence and its earthly signs, and particularly strong affirmations of Christ's presence in the sacrament, which may have been made without the usual qualifications which attacked papal abuses.[177]

172 *Ibid.*, II: 555. Cf. Carier's claim that learned Romanists argued that in the sacrament 'they doe not worship the Accidents which they see, but the substance which they believe'. However, Carier went beyond Forbes when he concluded that, because the Church of England and King James accepted Christ's real presence, they must therefore accept the Romanist view of the mode of this presence: Carier, *A Treatise*, p.15.

173 Forbes, *Considerationes*, II: 555.

174 *Ibid.*, II: 381, 435.

175 Prynne, *Canterburies Doome*, pp.322–3.

176 E.g. Jones' remark that 'we may scoffe at the Idolatry of the papists; a woman said unto a Priest in Queen Maries dayes, that came to buy a Capon; man canst thou make God Almighty and canst not make a Capon?': *ibid.*, p.322.

177 E.g. Laud, *Works*, VI: 57; cf. IV: 284. See also Dr Clarke of Northampton who, while being questioned in parliament in November 1640 'called the wine sacred wine after the communion was ended': D'Ewes, *Journal*, p.82. Robert Sibthorpe was accused of holding popish doctrines of corporal presence by implication from his argument 'that if the Mayor of Northamptons seate stood above the Communion table, hee would sitt above God Almightie' (*ibid.*). Francis Wright was accused of bowing to, and elevating, the consecrated elements, and saying 'that hee did conceive that ther was moore then a

Part of the misinterpretation was doubtless due to the fact that ceremonial reverence, and the greater emphasis on Christ's presence, as well as the use of language and imagery which could imply a spatial presence in the elements outside the action of communion, were adopted at the same time that the use of the vague 'mysterium tremendum' argument left the means of the eucharistic presence unclear, and transubstantiation effectively unchallenged. Thus Charles Chancy, a vigorous opponent of the new Laudian altar and altar rails in the parish of Ware in Hertfordshire, complained that local clerics bowed before the altar and referred to the sacraments as 'sacrifices', and yet 'they will not indure any man to enquire after what manner Christ is in the Sacrament, whether by way of consubstantiation, or transubstantiation, or in a spirituall manner'.[178] It is certainly possible that doctrines of transubstantiation may have lurked behind the views of those who proposed the 'mysterium tremendum' argument, which placed so much emphasis on Christ's presence in the sacrament. One Hugh Reeve, a clerk of Ampthill in Bedfordshire, was found guilty by the Lords' Committee for Imprisonments in February 1641 of 'maintaining that the Bread and Wine delivered in the Sacrament after Consecration is turned into the very Body and Blood of Christ, by way of Transubstantiation'.[179]

Thus in the 1630s yet another source of the charge of idolatry changed significantly, while the new emphases in the Laudian treatment of the eucharist may have allowed crypto-popish doctrines of the sacrament to exist within the Church of England. By the late 1630s the eucharistic doctrine of the Church of England itself was becoming a matter of dispute, as the increasing ambiguities built into Jacobean conformist expositions of the sacrament facilitated increasingly divergent views of its very nature. The Roman priest Richard Lassels was able to observe this for himself in Paris in the late 1630s when two English ministers, chaplains to either Viscount Scudamore or the earl of Leicester (or conceivably the chaplains of the two different English ambassadors who were there concurrently), fell into dispute concerning the meaning of the Church of England on this point while in conference with a Roman Catholic.[180]

sacramentall presence of Christs bodie ther': *ibid.*, p.261; John White, *The First Century of Scandalous, Malignant Priests* (1643), p.26. One Gawin Nash was also accused of bowing towards the consecrated elements, and of preaching 'that Christ was corporally present in the sacrament; that hee was soe humble as to dwell under a crumme of bread': D'Ewes, *Journal*, p.248.

178 *The Retractation of Mr. Charles Chancy* (1641), p.6.

179 *Lords' Journals*, IV: 170. I am grateful to Professor Russell for this reference. It is difficult to know how far Reeve may simply have explained the eucharistic presence and change in ways which might have implied transubstantiation; it seems unlikely that he would have directly used such a sensitive term. However, it was also claimed in the same charge that Reeve 'hath been confessed by a Popish Priest, and reconciled to the Church of Rome', so that his direct use of the term may not be impossible.

180 Chaney, *The Grand Tour*, p.98.

The invocation of saints

Protestants generally held Rome to be guilty of idolatry in her doctrine and practice of the invocation of the angels and saints, and especially of the Virgin Mary. John Davenant offered proof in his *Expositio* that the Roman Catholics ascribed and displayed supreme religious worship (*latria*) to angels and saints.[181] Thomas Morton insisted that such invocation showed 'Manifold Idolatry'.[182] Here was another area in which moderate puritans and Calvinist conformists were in full agreement.

Nevertheless, this was another subject on which greater reservations were beginning to be expressed by avant-garde conformists, either by pamphleteers anxious to emphasize the common ground with Rome for polemical reasons, or by those divines who were keen to safeguard a due respect towards saints. William Barlow and Anthony Stafford, for example, displayed an anxiety to honour saints and angels which seems to have lacked the necessary anti-papal caveats.[183]

This was not true of the more prominent of Hooker's successors. Laud himself avoided using the term 'idolatry', but strongly opposed the invocation of saints. He was not prepared to accept Rome's claims that she only made the saints 'mediators of intercession', noting that the present Roman Missal included prayers that God should act 'by the merits' of saints. This, wrote Laud, gave 'great scandal to Christ and Christianity'.[184] Richard Montagu, however, showed himself more disposed to accept Rome's defence of the invocation of saints within her communion. He was prepared to assess Rome's error as being simply a mistaken opinion rather than an idolatrous conceit. In his *New Gagg* he objected to prayer to the saints solely on the grounds that the saints themselves were unable to hear such prayers. People may not pray to the saints, he explained, 'not for the unlawfulnesse of the act so much, as for the unaptnes of the Agent'.[185] He declared that he too would pray to saints if the Gagger could prove their knowledge of anything ordinarily.[186]

The same emphasis is clear in Montagu's tract of a few years earlier, *Immediate Addresse unto God Alone*. Here Montagu defended Rome's doctrine from the false imputation that saints were called upon in the same

181 Davenant, *Expositio*, pp.238–40.

182 Morton, *Catholike Appeale*, pp.238–42; cf. Ussher, *Works*, III: 465–6.

183 Stafford, *Life of the Blessed Virgin*, *passim*; P. Croft, 'The religion of Robert Cecil', *HJ* 34 (1991), p.792. It is simply implausible that Barlow would have defended the invocation of saints, as was reported, but we may surmise that this misinterpretation arose from a determined defence of the saints' dignity and of the honour due to their memory.

184 Laud, *Works*, II: 307–8.

185 Montagu, *New Gagg*, p.229.

186 'Proove but onely this, Their knowledge of anything ordinarily, I promise you straight, I will say, Holy Saint Mary, pray for me': *ibid.*, p.229; cf. p.225.

terms as God, although he stressed that this was far otherwise in practice.[187] Unlike Laud, Montagu was prepared to accept Rome's doctrinal claim that the saints were only called upon as mediators; anything which they obtained for us from God was still by and through Christ.[188] Montagu argued that appealing thus to the saints 'is not unlawfull in it selfe' – the only mistake was that Romanists were using such mediators as were not fitting, and were incapable of the office. If they were indeed as Romanists took them to be, then they might be so used.[189] Montagu depicted this opinion as a folly, resting on 'meere coniectures, and uncertainties', rather than an idolatrous heresy.[190] He would not even brand it as impious: 'I will not, I dare not be so harsh and rigorous, as to condemne them of Impietie for so Calling unto them.' Although more was done to saints than was fit or convenient, 'yet nothing is detracted there from the Creator, in giving them that they are not capable of'.[191]

As on the issue of image-worship, Montagu asserted a general distinction between Rome's doctrine and practice. There was no impiety in Rome 'if we take them in the lumpe, at whole sale in their Doctrine, as it were'. However, he admitted that 'I cannot say it doth so for their Practice, as if that also weere so gently to be handled.' Blasphemy was undoubtedly committed by Roman Catholics in practice in calling *upon* saints, which implied them to be the principal donors of the benefits to be received.[192] Once again, however, this was basically a pastoral problem. Daniel Featley was perfectly justified in his complaint that Montagu 'maketh Popish Invocation idle and foolish, but not impious, blasphemous, iniurious to God, and our Saviour'. Featley would therefore hardly have been surprised by the later charges made against a number of minor Laudian clergy that they had defended praying to priests and angels.[193]

Montagu's position may usefully be compared and contrasted with that of the early Jacobean moderate divine John Dove. Anxious as usual to play down conflict (even if this required tenuous reasoning), Dove had suggested that Romanists did not believe that saints could hear them, 'because it cannot be sufficiently prooved'. Like Montagu, Dove remarked that, if

[187] Montagu, *Immediate Addresse*, pp.58–9, 62.
[188] *Ibid.*, pp.60, 62.
[189] *Ibid.*, p.63.
[190] *Ibid.*, p.65.
[191] *Ibid.*, p.66. However, if this was not impiety, it was 'plaine downe right Folly' (*ibid.*, pp.68, 118–19). Contrast Willet's attack on the 'blasphemie' of invocation: Willet, *Synopsis* (1634), p.443.
[192] Montagu, *Immediate Addresse*, pp.66, 68.
[193] Featley, *Second Parallel*, ii. p.30. Thomas Thexton (rector of Gimingham in Norfolk) supposedly prayed for the saints departed and Thomas Tyllot (rector of Depden) was accused of preaching that people should pray mediately by saints and angels to Christ, and so to God: Matthews, *Walker Revised*, pp.274, 346; *The Suffolk Committees for Scandalous Ministers 1644–1646*, ed. C. Holmes (Suffolk Records Society 13, 1970), p.37.

the saints did not hear them, then papists' prayers were merely idle words. However, Dove was more careful to provide a sting in the tail with the reflection that Roman Catholics would answer at the Day of Judgement for every idle word thus spoken.[194]

While Laudian writers undoubtedly differed in their assessments of the gravity of Rome's errors concerning images, the mass and the invocation of saints, none of them seemed prepared to charge Rome's doctrine directly and unreservedly with idolatry, and several were prepared to exculpate it from any impiety. It was the problems of profanity and sacrilege which were more central to the Laudians' concerns. Lancelot Andrewes had led the way in this shift of priorities by explicitly maintaining that the sin of sacrilege was worse than that of idolatry, 'for what idolatry but pollutes, sacrilege pulls quite down'.[195] The term 'idolatry' was also diluted by being given a broader application to refer to more general forms of worldly behaviour,[196] and especially by being applied against puritan opponents. Andrewes had again led the way on this point by attacking a form of spiritual 'idolatry' in the importance which presbyterians attached to their discipline, which had taken the place of the earlier idolatry of image-worship.[197] John Cosin listed among offenders against the second commandment those who carelessly neglected 'to kneele, bow, and prostrate themselves, to uncover their heads; or to stand with seemely awe and reverence before the presence of his Majestie' during divine service.[198] Finally, the sin of idolatry was also downgraded by the Laudians' increasing emphasis on the issue of schism. Divines such as Morton and Davenant had argued that the sin of idolatry justified separation from a particular

194 Dove, *Perswasion*, p.21 (citing Matthew 12.36). Note also William Forbes' moderation on this issue: Forbes, *Considerationes*, II: 177, 185, 187–93, 205–7 (although he severely reprimands some abuses: *ibid.*, II: 289, 291, 305–9, 311).

195 Andrewes, *Sermons*, II: 351.

196 Thus, while Montagu spoke of gross idolaters as being pagans, Turks and Jews, who did not call upon Christ, he also referred to 'Refined Idolaters', whom he described as 'the most part of men in every county and corner of the Christian world, who ensue the pleasures and pomps of the world, against that profession made in Baptisme, the vanities and delights of sin, pride of life, the lusts of the flesh, covetousness, and such like, which is Idololatry, Ephes.5.5': Montagu, *Acts and Monuments*, p.25.

197 Andrewes attacks this tendency as 'the disease of our age, and the just complaint we make of it: that there hath been good riddance made of images, but for imaginations they be daily stamped in great number and instead of the old images set up and deified and worshipped carrying the names and credit of "the Apostles' doctrine", government, etc.': Andrewes, *Sermons*, V: 55 (cf. pp.55–66).

198 Cosin, *Collection of Private Devotions*, p.44.

church, but now some Laudian writers claimed that the sin of schism was worse than that of idolatry.[199]

If Henry Burton was incorrect when he accused Archbishop Laud of only ever talking of Rome's errors and superstitions, and *never* of her idolatry, his observation would have been correct if levelled at many of the churchmen who rose to power under Laud's archiepiscopate.[200] An important barrier which prevented Rome being judged in the same terms as other churches was thereby removed.

ROMAN HERESY

If the charge of idolatry was beginning to be qualified, even greater difficulties and disagreements were emerging between English Protestants over the question of whether Rome was guilty of heresy. This was an entirely commonplace accusation which had been made by English Protestants ever since the Reformation. Nevertheless, as controversialists adopted more subtle and flexible modes of argumentation, and saw the value of placing a greater emphasis on the bonds linking Rome and Protestants, the issue of heresy became more problematical. John Dove had found himself in trouble over his use of the term when he insisted that it be used according to its technical definition. His aim was to deny that Romanists could use this charge against the Church of England, and Dove hence insisted that a heresy could only be a major error which was 'stifly and obstinately defended and maintained, not by a consequent, but directly impugning some Article of faith'. Moreover, he emphasized that a church could not be condemned or judged heretical by private censure, but must be done so publicly by a General Council.[201] Neither of these definitions was strictly in accord with the ways in which heresy was generally imputed to the Roman Church. The impugning of an article of faith by consequent was usually deemed sufficient for this charge to stick, while the need of a General Council's censure for Rome's errors was circumvented by the association of Rome's errors with most of the heresies condemned in the General Councils of the primitive church.

Nevertheless, Dove found that he had painted himself into a corner when Romanist opponents employed his distinctions in defence of the Roman Church. When challenged for not having charged Rome with heresy, Dove merely attempted to dodge the issue altogether by asserting

[199] Davenant, 'Opinion', p.12; Morton, *Catholike Appeale*, p.445; *idem*, *Grand Imposture*, p.371; Oliver Whitbie, *Londons Returne* (1637/8), p.14; BL, Harleian MS 750 fol.70r (James Wedderburn).

[200] Burton, *Replie*, p.237.

[201] Dove, *Perswasion*, pp.13–14.

that he had thereby shown the Church of England to be more charitable than its opponent.[202] Anti-papal controversialists would seem to have paid little attention to Dove's problems, but by the 1620s anxieties over definitions were again becoming noticeable. These may well have had their source in de Dominis' claims that a mere addition to an orthodox body of faith could not be considered a heresy – an opinion which Featley could see spreading in the Church of England.[203] Anthony Wotton plainly felt this too. His *Runne from Rome* of 1624 included a section in which he explained how he felt himself obliged to use the term 'erroneous faith' rather than 'heretical' in order to avoid needless wrangling over the word, 'for it seemes to many somewhat doubtfull what is properly to be called heresy'. Nevertheless, he added the frustrated comment that 'For my part I can not see that any false proposition delivered for an Article of faith, can be lesse then heresie.'[204]

This creeping sense of uncertainty in the use of the term was exacerbated by the Laudian hegemony in the 1630s. By 1640 Robert Baillie was complaining with some justice that neither Laud nor 'any of his favourits in their writtes these twelve yeares bygone hath layed to the charge of Rome in earnest, either idolatrie, heresie or schisme, but by the contrary hath absolved them clearly in formall termes of al those three crimes'.[205] This change of emphasis under Laud was not simply due to an aversion to the term. The fact was that a number of Rome's errors to which the charge of heresy had in the past been applied were in this period undergoing significant reassessment by some divines among Laud's circle.

Predestination, justification and free will

Somewhat surprisingly, the doctrine of predestination, which created so many divisions within Protestantism, was not seen by most English Protestant divines as a doctrine in which Rome was guilty of a fundamental error. Where anti-Calvinist divines were directly accused of Pelagianism, the Roman Church was distinguished from them, and seen instead as inclining more towards semi-Pelagianism. As Willet explained the matter, while Pelagians said that God ordained grace and mercy for all, and was not in any way a cause of reprobation, Romanists 'deny not but that reprobation doth proceed in some respect from the will and decree of God, but that it is not so properly God's act as election is'. Of course, this more restrained assessment of Rome's error was partly a function of the momentum of inter-Protestant disputes, since this angle allowed Arminians to be

202 Dove, *Advertisement*, p.56. 203 See above, p.182. 204 Wotton, *Runne*, p.14.
205 Baillie, *Ladensium*, pp.44–5.

depicted as even worse than Romanists. Thus Anthony Wotton argued against Montagu that the predestinarian opinions branded by the latter as belonging to 'Novellizing Puritanes' were in fact the most common opinion in the Roman schools and were defended by Cardinal Bellarmine, as well as being a general Protestant orthodoxy.[206] Some divines in the Roman Church espoused doctrines of predestination which were as high as anything that hardline Calvinists could muster, so that Romanist attacks upon Calvin which charged him with implying that God was the author of sin could be refuted by maintaining that Calvin said no more than did many Dominican authors.[207] It was only anti-Calvinist divines such as Montagu who chose to avoid this resource and to concentrate on detaching the Church of England from any association with Calvin or his doctrines.

This is not to say that Rome was exculpated from any crimes on related doctrines. Gabriel Powel and Robert Abbot argued strongly that assurance of salvation was vital to the Christian life and message, and claimed that Rome's undermining of this point destroyed the foundation of Christian religion.[208] Romanists were held to err grievously in the associated doctrines of justification, free will and the related point of merits. It was here that Roman Catholics were more regularly associated with the Pelagian heresy, even if they escaped it on the specific doctrine of predestination itself.

The doctrine of justification had traditionally been a central issue in the Church of England's case against Rome. By trusting in their own merits for justification, and making it dependent upon foreseen good works, Romanists were charged with extinguishing the grace of the Gospel and of Christ's merits.[209] Even to Richard Hooker writing in the 1580s, Rome's errors in the point of justification were 'the mystery of the man of sin'.[210] While granting that Christ alone had sufficiently performed the work of redemption, the Romanists allegedly overthrew this point in their exposition of the means whereby this redemption was effectively applied. By attributing to works a virtue which could merit glory in heaven, they plainly overthrew the foundation of faith and extinguished the effect of Christ's merits.[211] Hooker noted that Rome directly granted salvation to be only through Christ, but he still judged that, since she made good works the means by

[206] Willet, *Synopsis* (1600), p.781; Wotton, *Dangerous Plot*, ii. pp.127, 156–60, 167. Note also the use of Bellarmine and Suarez to refute Montagu's arguments in *ibid.*, ii. pp.163–5.

[207] For an example of this technique, see White, *The Way*, pp.264–72.

[208] Powel, *Disputationum*, pp.454–5; Abbot, *Second Part*, p.372. See also Willet, *Synopsis* (1634), pp.1005–8.

[209] Davenant, *Expositio*, p.115.

[210] Hooker, *Works*, V: 110–12.

[211] *Ibid.*, V: 124–5, 153–4.

which this salvation was effected, Rome was still an adversary to Christ's merits and overthrew the foundation of faith.[212]

This position continued to be strongly maintained by Jacobean Calvinist conformists. Robert Abbot insisted that, in her doctrine of justification, Rome erased the foundation of salvation in Christ. To men such as Wotton and Burton, justification was the central issue – and Romanists' rejection of solifidian justification meant that they were all damned.[213] Jacobean writers such as Field therefore still emphasized that there was a 'very main difference' between Protestants and Romanists concerning justification.[214] For polemical purposes, however, they sometimes noted, as Hooker had done, that points of true doctrine pertaining to justification and merits remained within Rome's liturgy and devotional literature. Humphrey Lynde suggested that, when they neared death, many Romanists overthrew their own doctrines by relying wholly on Christ's merits, as indeed Bellarmine was held to have done.[215] To allow for the possibility of salvation within Rome, Morton noted that Romanists might have access to the Protestant doctrine of justification through one point of the Tridentine Creed which emphasized justification by Christ's satisfactory righteousness rather than by inherent merit.[216] But this was not to deny that Rome's treatment of this issue elsewhere overturned the foundation and impeded salvation.

Nevertheless, enough moderate justifications of Rome's orthodoxy on these points remained for some writers to maintain that divisions on these issues were not fundamental. William Covell, writing in defence of Hooker's later, more guarded remarks on this point, went so far as to suggest that the division between Rome and Protestants on the point of justification was simply due to a misunderstanding, and that reconciliation should be sought. Both sides ultimately argued that a justifying faith would be manifested by the production of good works. Covell saw the greater danger as lying in the extreme reaction to this assertion made by the puritan authors of the *Christian Letter*. The puritan response was guilty, Covell maintained, of defending precisely the notion that Roman writers had falsely fathered on Protestantism – namely, that a justifying faith could be barren of good works. Covell was also confident that the Roman defence of good works was more careful and restrained than puritan writers alleged. He asserted that many of the best Roman divines, whatever their notions of free will and good works, would admit that

212 *Ibid.*, V: 156–9.
213 Abbot, *Second Part*, p.445; Wotton, *Trial*, pp.375, 416–19; Burton, *Baiting*, pp.90–1.
214 Field, *Of the Church*, IV: 390–2.
215 Lynde, *Via Tuta*, pp.32–4.
216 Morton, *Grand Imposture*, p.412.

even man's best actions were still stained by having something of the flesh about them.[217]

A number of English divines besides Covell were beginning to display a similar anxiety to avoid the Roman charge that Protestants expounded a justifying faith without good works. The result could easily be that they seemed to swing towards a Roman position. William Sclater complained in 1610 of how, while English Protestants had traditionally maintained that justification was by faith only, some now wished to have works enter justification.[218] John Dove, writing at the same time as Covell, argued in similar fashion that the differences between Protestants and Rome over the issue of faith and good works were not unbridgeable, as both believed that works were necessary. His conclusion, however, that 'our difference is not concerning the worke it selfe, but only concerning the opinion which we ought to conceive of the worke' is awkward and unconvincing.[219]

Writers associated with Laud were more prepared to accept in good faith Rome's occasional admissions that salvation was through Christ's merits alone. The issue of justification does not loom large in Laudian perceptions of Rome's errors.[220] Laud never mentioned it in his lists of Rome's doctrinal errors in his *Conference*.[221] When he briefly touched upon the issue of merits, this was only to show that Rome did not really accept the implications of her own doctrines.[222] Francis White seems to have toyed with a moderate stance on this point. Henry Burton reported that he had asked White around the time of his conference with Fisher to declare fully the difference between the Protestants and Romanists on the doctrine of justification according to the Council of Trent, only to be met by White's reply 'that the difference was but small between us'.[223] In his *Replie to Fisher* White provided a list of more moderate Romanist writers' treatment

217 Covell, *Just and Temperate Defence*, pp.39–40, 42, 46; Hooker, *Works*, IV: 21–3.

218 Sclater, *Threefold Preservative*, sig.D4v.

219 Dove, *Perswasion*, pp.19–20.

220 Shelford considered Whitaker's argument that the pope acknowledged other means of salvation besides Christ's merits 'not worth the answering': Shelford, *Discourses*, pp.295–6. An exception here is John Bramhall, who defended the position 'Onely Faith Justifieth' in a public disputation with the Romanist secular priest Houghton at North Allerton in 1623, to whom he also wished to put arguments 'touching the meritt of Good Works': Bodl., Rawlinson MS D.320 fols.40v–42v, 44r. On this disputation, see also *The Works of . . . John Bramhall* (5 vols., Oxford, 1842–5), I: iv, xvi–xvii. Andrewes also briefly attacked the Tridentine doctrine that inherent righteousness was the formal cause of justification: Andrewes, *Sermons*, V: 166.

221 Laud, *Works*, II: 306, 337–42, 364, 376–7, 417.

222 Like Lynde, Laud quoted Bellarmine's conclusion of his *De Iustificatione* that it was better to trust wholly in Christ's mercy. While Romanists wrote and 'boisterously' preached the point of condignity of merit, Laud commented, 'yet you are content to die, renouncing the condignity of all your own merits, and trust to Christ's': *ibid.*, II: 316–17.

223 Henry Burton, *A Plea to an Appeale* (1626), sig.a4. For Burton's exposition of Trent's errors on man's free will, see *ibid.*, pp.69–73.

of the issue of justification and good works which might indeed be reconciled with Protestant doctrine. However, in the *Replie* at least, this list was compiled for purely polemical reasons. Further on in the same book, White adopted a more traditional anti-papal tone, arguing firmly that the Romanists 'make such a Faith, the foundation of true Iustification, as is common with Devils, James 2.19 and which, according to their owne Doctrine, is no true Vertue'.[224]

Montagu and Forbes argued from the Council of Trent's declaration on justification in Session six (that first justification is *gratuita*) that there was no essential difference between Romanists and Protestants on the doctrine of justification.[225] On the question of good works and merits, Montagu similarly suggested in his *New Gagg* that the two sides were reconcilable. The Protestants did not deny the merit of condignity to good works which were the fruit of faith, thereby going along with 'your owne Doctrine in the Romane Schooles'. All Romanists accepted that men's works only had any merit while in the state of grace, so that all their merit must thus be from grace.[226] The two sides were in essential agreement: 'Reward in Heaven, no man denyeth: Reward appointed for our good workes, all confesse: If this be your merit, we contradict it not. And this is your merit that you plead for.'[227]

As on the question of image-worship, Montagu was more careful in his *Appello* to describe and renounce some of the more exorbitant errors of Jesuit theologians on this point, attacking the presumptuous advancement of the merit of condignity in the works of Bellarmine and Vasquez, and the enormous errors of which the Schools had been guilty since the coming of the Jesuits.[228] This was necessary in order to refute the claim of the Informers against Montagu's *Gagg* that 'hee so extends Meritum ex condigno, that hee would make men beleeve, there is no materiall difference betwixt us and the Papists in this point'.[229] Nevertheless, Montagu still maintained that these errors were contrary to 'the opinion of moderate men in the very Church of Rome'.[230] Forbes argued that to such moderate

224 White, *Replie*, pp.168, 172ff. But note Sancta Clara's use of the more moderate passages from White in order to claim that the Church of England and Rome agreed on justification: Sancta Clara, *Deus, Natura, Gratia*, p.181.

225 Montagu, *New Gagg*, p.145, cf. pp.146–51; Forbes, *Considerationes*, I: 29, cf. I: 75–7, 93–5.

226 Montagu, *New Gagg*, pp.153–4; *Appello*, pp.200–1.

227 Montagu, *New Gagg*, p.154.

228 Montagu, *Appello*, pp.201–3. Cf. Forbes' condemnation of the extreme opinions of some Romanists on the intrinsic worth of good works: *Considerationes*, I: 497.

229 Montagu, *Appello*, p.200.

230 *Ibid.*, p.204. To support this claim, Montagu cited the list compiled in White, *Replie*, p.172. Forbes made a similar use of White's list: Forbes, *Considerationes*, I: 151, 317.

divines on both sides, the dispute regarding the issue of merits was merely a matter of words.[231]

Once again, it was in the traditional Protestant perspective on this issue that the real danger seemed to lie. William Forbes complained that 'rigid Protestants' opposed truth and Christian charity by claiming that the point that faith alone justified was a cause for separation from the Church of Rome. Many Protestants' writings on this issue were crude and indefensible, and Forbes declared firmly that whereas many divines tried to excuse such errors, he would not.[232] Forbes had a strong distaste for the use of the word 'alone' in the traditional Protestant maxim 'faith alone justifies', and recommended that the phrase should be dropped in order to facilitate reunion with Rome.[233] Forbes' emphasis that good works were efficiently necessary for salvation found an echo in Laudian Cambridge.[234] John Prideaux had good reason to warn in a court sermon in the 1630s that 'our doctrine of Justification by faith alone, which our Church Articles terme a wholesome doctrine, and very full of comfort, together with that of Gods preventing and working grace, hath beene of late ... dangerously impugned, by some of our owne side'.[235] Yet another point of heresy traditionally ascribed to Rome had thus been weighed in the balance and found wanting. It was with some justice that Stephen Marshall demanded of the House of Commons in November 1640: 'what one article of faith controverted betwixt us and the Church of Rome is there that our pulpits and presses, and university acts, have not been bold withall [?]'.[236]

Other doctrinal errors

Other errors traditionally ascribed to Rome were subjected to similar reassessment during the years of Laudian ascendancy. William Forbes depicted the modern Romanists' view of purgatory as not only having no foundation in Scripture, but as being plainly repugnant to it, although he emphasized that it was not a heresy. It was an error, but was not against the faith; an error of excess rather than of defect.[237] The best way to remove the controversy was for the Romanists not to hold as an article of faith their opinion of a 'punitive purgatory', and for the Protestants not to

[231] Forbes, *Considerationes*, I: 495. For a discussion of Forbes' views on justification, see C.F. Allison, *The Rise of Moralism* (1966), pp.31–48.

[232] Forbes, *Considerationes*, I: 87–9, 99, 103–7.

[233] *Ibid*., I: 63, 87–9.

[234] See above, pp.75–6.

[235] John Prideaux, 'The Christians expectation', p.11 (*Certaine Sermons*).

[236] Stephen Marshall, *A Sermon Preached before the Honourable House of Commons ... November 17, 1640* (1641), p.32.

[237] Forbes, *Considerationes*, II: 21, 135–7. Forbes here quotes de Dominis.

condemn it as an open heresy, or even as an impiety.[238] Richard Montagu, while rejecting the doctrine of purgatory, did not argue that it was simply impious, but rather anticipated Forbes by emphasizing that Romanist writers were uncertain and contradicted themselves in every point of detail of the doctrine. He therefore complained chiefly that the Romanists were unjustifiably converting an uncertain, disputed point of theology into an article of faith.[239] As on the issue of transubstantiation, the roots of this moderate position may be traced back to Lancelot Andrewes. In dispute with Bellarmine, Andrewes had been most concerned to show that the doctrine of purgatory did not pertain to the true 'catholic' faith, or even to formal ecclesiastical doctrine. In doing so, he admitted that it might have a place among the opinions of the Schools.[240]

This reflects a more general shift among Hooker's disciples in their treatment of Rome's errors. Rather than condemning the heresy, impiety or idolatry of the errors in themselves, these divines tended to place more emphasis on the fact that Rome imposed these errors as fundamental points of faith. This was a position which had been adopted by Andrewes in his dispute with Bellarmine. In his *Tortura Torti* Andrewes had based his opposition to the papal primacy on the fact that the lack of certainty regarding its doctrinal status meant that it could not be *de fide*, so that even if the Oath of Allegiance did undermine it, the Oath could not be incompatible with the Catholic faith.[241] Andrewes' *Responsio ad Apologiam Cardinalis Bellarmini* was basically directed against Bellarmine's claim that King James could not be considered a Catholic because he rejected transubstantiation, the invocation of saints, and the papacy's claims to temporal jurisdiction. Once again, Andrewes concentrated his attention on the defensive posture that these points could not be shown to be required *de fide*, but should remain disputable School points.[242] As we have seen, Andrewes combined this stance with a clear defence of the identification of the pope as Antichrist.[243] Later Laudians, however, rejected this assertion, while still following Andrewes in emphasizing that the problem lay in the actual imposition of Rome's errors rather than in their heretical nature.

Accusations of Roman heresy and idolatry are rare indeed in Laudian writings. Laud himself had complained in his *Conference* that 'it ought to be no easy thing to condemn a man of heresy in foundation of faith; much

[238] *Ibid.*, II: 139. [239] Montagu, *New Gagg*, pp.284–98.
[240] Andrewes, *Responsio*, pp.286–7. This passage is quoted approvingly in Forbes, *Considerationes*, II: 137–9.
[241] Andrewes, *Tortura Torti*, pp.278–332. [242] Andrewes, *Responsio*, *passim*.
[243] See above, p.109.

less a Church'.[244] When Sancta Clara argued in the 1630s that the Church of England's doctrine in her Thirty-Nine Articles could be reconciled with the Church of Rome and the conclusions of the Council of Trent, his work received the active support of some Laudians, and relied on their expositions of Church of England doctrine to enable him to claim that such a reconciliation was possible.[245]

The Roman errors upon which Laudian writers now tended to focus were the traditional ones of communion in one kind, transubstantiation, clerical marriage and the non-vernacular liturgy.[246] None of these were presented with the same 'absolute' flavour that typified their discussion by Elizabethan and Jacobean Calvinist divines. For example, Laudian reservations about Romanist doctrines on clerical marriage were not of the same order as traditional English Protestant complaints. Joseph Hall and Andrew Willet had emphasized that this error was an important manifestation of Rome's antichristianity.[247] Richard Montagu, however, simply claimed that both sides agreed that the imposition of clerical celibacy was an ecclesiastical sanction, and not indispensable. The question at issue, he argued, was not whether priests might marry, but whether it was convenient for them to do so. This was essentially the same exposition as that of the Roman irenicist Sancta Clara.[248]

The rest of these errors did not lend themselves easily to apocalyptic phraseology or anti-ceremonial styles of argument.[249] The question of a

244 Laud, *Works*, II: 29. See also Montagu's emphasis on how difficult it is to define what a heretic is: Montagu, *ΘΕΑΝΘΡΩΠΙΚΟΝ*, ii. p. 409.

245 On justification, Sancta Clara cited Montagu, Duncon and Choun (*Deus, Natura, Gratia* (1634 edn), pp.158, 159; *ibid.* (1635 edn), p.189). See his references to Montagu's *New Gagg* and *Appello Caesarem* in the 1634 edition, pp.7, 55, 68, 133, 158, 181, 211, 245, 260, 276. Among Sancta Clara's English sources are Overall and Andrewes, although he also uses Perkins and Whitaker where it suits him (e.g., *ibid.*, p.69 (Whitaker)). Sancta Clara also described having discussed some of the points with learned English Protestants: Sancta Clara, *Paraphrastica Expositio Articulorum Confessionis Anglicanae*, ed. and tr. F.G. Lee (1865), p.105.

246 The errors of transubstantiation and communion in one kind are those which appear most regularly in Laud's lists of Rome's abuses (Laud, *Works*, II: 306, 337–42, 364, 376–7, 417), although he also raises the abuses of the invocation of saints, image-worship, purgatory and the lack of a vernacular liturgy. Montagu's *New Gagg* only allowed eight of the Gagger's points to be the Church of England's doctrine against the Romanists: that vernacular Scriptures are necessary; that pardons and indulgences are not apostolic; that works of supererogation are impossible; that only faith justifies and good works are not absolutely necessary for salvation; that we may not pray to saints; that the sacrament should be received in both kinds; that there is no purgatory; and that God's image cannot be made: Montagu, *New Gagg*, 'To the Reader'.

247 Hall, *Works*, VI: 162, cf. pp.168–9; Willet, *Synopsis* (1634), p.297.

248 Montagu, *New Gagg*, p.271; Sancta Clara, *Paraphrastica*, p.80.

249 See Willet's comparatively low-key discussions of the issues of vernacular Scriptures (*Synopsis* (1634), pp.27–35) and communion in one kind (*ibid.*, pp.640–7), although he

vernacular liturgy was one in which an attack on Rome could run no risk of affronting Laudian ceremonial susceptibilities. Similarly, the emphasis on the error of communion in one kind allowed the Laudians to attack a Romanist crime of sacrilege rather than of idolatry, and thereby ran no risk of impugning the dignity of the sacrament.[250] Moreover, there were clergy in the provinces who were later even accused of introducing these popish practices,[251] which were also those upon which concessions were more likely from Rome.[252]

It had been de Dominis' complaint that the Church of England had deserted the original terms of her separation from Rome by justifying her departure on the grounds of Rome's alleged heresy and idolatry, thereby following the lead of 'the common schisme' of the heretical Lutherans and Calvinists.[253] It was these charges which to de Dominis made any reconciliation between the Churches of England and Rome impossible. He himself was convinced that the controversies over Rome's errors were not sufficient to obstruct reunion.[254] De Dominis also believed there to be 'good and wise men' in the Church of England who knew that the Church of Rome was not heretical, and who granted that Roman doctrine and worship could be tolerated, if rightly understood. In the early 1620s, however, de Dominis claimed that these moderates did not dare to lift up their heads because the 'puritans' were predominant.[255] With charges of heresy and idolatry gradually being removed from the arena of Protestant/

does in one place attack the latter point as 'an Antichristian practice of the Church of Rome' (p.644).

250 Note Montagu's remark in his 1638 Visitation Articles that 'the popish half-communion is sacrilege': Montagu, *Articles*, tit.III n.16. Montagu often used severe language against Rome on this issue: he threatened that the blood of Romanists perishing in their sins would be required at the hands of 'your ignorant or rather deceitfull guides, that thus mis-leade you from Christs Institution' (Montagu, *New Gagg*, p.265).

251 Edward Shephard (vicar of Great Maplestead) allegedly 'taught the doctrine of purgatory' and Samuel Sowthen (vicar of Manuden, Essex) was accused of administering the sacrament in only one kind: Matthews, *Walker Revised*, pp.162, 163. See also the charges against Richard Carrier: Gardiner, *Reports*, pp.91, 98.

252 See below, p.363.

253 De Dominis, *Second Manifesto*, sig.F2r, cf. G1r.

254 De Dominis, *De Republica Ecclesiastica* (1622), lib.7 cap.11: 'Controversias nostrorum temporum ecclesiasticas dogmatum non posse ulli parti dare iustam causam schismatis.' De Dominis here regarded transubstantiation, with all the controversies regarding papal power, the judgement of controversies, and all disputes regarding the sacraments, purgatory and indulgences, as unnecessary quarrels (*ibid.*, pp.198–201). Even the great controversies concerning grace, free will, predestination and justification were 'indefinibiles, & libertati opinandi relictae' (*ibid.*, pp.201–2; cf. pp.202–78). External rites were no legitimate cause of schism (*ibid.*, cap.12). See his discussion of the invocation of saints (*ibid.*, pp.281–9), images (pp.289–306), the sign of the cross (pp.307–8) and confession and absolution (pp.314–15).

255 Marc'Antonio de Dominis, *De Pace Religionis ... Epistola ad Venerabilem Virum Iosephum Hallum* (Besançon, 1666), pp.7–8 – translated in N. Malcolm, *De Dominis (1560–1624): Venetian, Anglican, Ecumenist, and Relapsed Heretic* (1984), p.63.

Romanist controversy under the Laudians, some form of reconciliation became at least conceivable, and would be actively pursued by one of de Dominis' own disciples among the Laudian episcopate – Bishop Richard Montagu.

Papal authority

As the emphasis placed on Rome's doctrinal errors diminished, churchmen consequently attached greater importance to the pope's usurping claims to universal jurisdiction as Rome's chief error. Opposition to the pope's claim to supreme authority in doctrinal issues was sufficiently important to many Jacobean writers to lead them to overthrow by implication Rome's status as a church. The doctrine of papal infallibility, it was alleged, had replaced the Scriptures in the Roman Church as the basis of Christian belief. George Carleton explained that Rome had, at the Council of Trent, overthrown the foundation of religion by changing the rule of faith in giving traditions the same honour as the Scriptures, so that Rome could no longer be a true church of Christ.[256] These traditions were dependent upon the judgement of the pope, so that the papists had effectively set up in the church another God. At Trent 'they have changed all and made a new Church'.[257] William Fulke similarly complained that by these means the pope had usurped Christ's place *totally*.[258]

Richard Crakanthorp located the introduction of the doctrine of papal infallibility somewhat earlier than did Carleton, at the Lateran Council of Leo X, whose decrees the Council of Trent had then confirmed. This Council had not changed the true and false doctrines taught in the Roman Church, but had caused them to be held on another foundation, 'the pope's word, instead of God's, and Antichrists instead of Christs'. Crakanthorp explained that 'here was now quite a new face of the Romane Church, yea, it was now made a new Church of it selfe, in the very essence thereof distinct from the other part of the Church, and from that which it was before. For although most of the Materialls ... were the same, yet the Formalitie and foundation of their faith and Church were quite altered.'[259]

Since the foundation of the faith had been altered, the scraps of true doctrine which Rome still retained, such as the belief in the Trinity and the Incarnation, were essentially irrelevant, and indeed were not truly believed

256 George Carleton, *Jurisdiction Regall, Episcopall, Papall* (1610), pp.105–6; *idem*, *Directions*, pp.32–5.

257 Carleton, *Directions*, pp.50, 60.

258 R.J. Bauckham, 'The career and theology of Dr. William Fulke, 1537–89' (Cambridge University PhD, 1973), pp.296–8. On Fulke's importance as the official defender of the Church of England, inheriting Jewel's mantle, see *ibid.*, pp.150, 168–71.

259 Crakanthorp, *Vigilius Dormitans*, p.186. See also below, pp.229, 291.

by any members of the Roman Church. The antichristian foundation, Crakanthorp explained, nullified all other points of faith: 'none who hold the popes infallibility in causes of faith for their foundation, either doth, or can beleeve any one doctrine of faith, which they professe'.[260] Crakanthorp did not deny that Rome maintained many truths, but argued that it was impossible for Roman Catholics to believe them.[261] The antichristian foundation poisoned all that was built upon it, rendering even the most certain and orthodox doctrines essentially heretical. The Romanist was thus a heretic in every doctrine which he held, 'and so hereticall therein, that the very holding of Catholike truths becomes unto him hereticall'.[262]

Thomas Jackson similarly argued that this change in the foundation of faith was an open renunciation by Romanists of their allegiance to God and His Word, so that they truly believed no article of the Creed. Carleton stressed that, as Trent had changed the rule of faith, 'all things were then changed, whereby the Church is knowen to be a Church'. The Roman Church was thus, William Perkins observed, not a dying man in whom life still remained, but 'it is rather like a dead carkasse, and is voyd of all spirituall life; as the Popish errours in the foundation doe manifest'.[263]

Emphasis on the error of papal infallibility did not necessarily wholly unchurch Rome. While Perkins and Carleton believed that the doctrine overthrew Rome's nature as a church,[264] Crakanthorp and Jackson argued elsewhere that Rome, according to the means of regeneration which distinguished her from the Jews or Turks, might still be called a true church.[265] Nevertheless, it was clearly a heresy of the greatest possible importance which heavily qualified Rome's claims to be a church at all.

Laudian writers, however, were less concerned with the question of the pope's doctrinal infallibility than with that of his claims to ecclesiastical and secular jurisdiction. The issue of infallibility was scarcely touched upon, and where it did appear it was treated as a self-evidently ridiculous folly which few Romanists truly believed. Montagu referred in passing in his *Appello* to 'this Catholick Roman fancy and infallible madnes' which

260 *Ibid.*, p.189.

261 'Whatsoever truths they maintaine (and no doubt they doe many) those they thinke they doe, and they might doe, but indeed they doe not beleeve, because they hold them for that reason, and upon that foundation which is contrary to faith, and which overthroweth the faith: For to hold or professe that Christ is God, or that there is a God, eo nomine, because the Devill, or Antichrist, or a fallible man testifieth it unto us, is not truly to beleeve, but to overthrow the faith': *ibid.*, p.189.

262 *Ibid.*, pp.190–1, 193.

263 Jackson, *Works*, II: 95, 125, 160; Carleton, *Directions*, p.64; Perkins, *Reformed Catholike*, p.299.

264 Perkins, *Reformed Catholike*, pp.292–5; Carleton, *Consensus*, pp.234–42; *idem*, *Directions*, pp.34, 65, 79, 82–3.

265 Jackson, *Works*, XII: 145; Crakanthorp, *Defensio*, p.78.

attributed to the pope all the assurance of infallibility of a General Council, and which he saw as being the work of the Jesuits, but he made no attempt to follow through the doctrine's implications, or even to treat it as a true part of Rome's faith.[266] Laud similarly ridiculed the opinion that all the infallibility of a General Council derived only from the presence of the infallible pope as 'the most groundless and worthless that ever offered to take possession of the Christian Church'. He was convinced that many learned Romanists scorned this idea 'at the heart', and believed that even the Jesuits laughed at the idea that all Christianity was confined within the doctrine of the Roman Church governed by the pope's infallibility.[267] To Laud, to make a mere man a principle or author of faith brought shame on the Roman Church, rather than antichristian blasphemy.[268] According to Rome's own principles it was vain and useless to urge that the pope should be infallible.[269] Buckeridge, Montagu, Howson and others were more keen to overthrow the pope's general claims to a spiritual supremacy above a General Council on jurisdictional grounds; they sought to establish instead the essential equality of all bishops, and the authority of a General Council as the only body in which a spiritual supremacy could be invested.[270]

A concern with the purely jurisdictional aspects of Rome's errors had characterized some aspects of mainstream anti-papal writing under James. The cause of this lay in the very claims being made by Jesuit theologians. King James wrote in 1612 that, even if agreement could be reached on the controversial points described by the Cardinal du Perron, reconciliation would be impossible because of the importance currently attached to the pope's jurisdictional claims, 'for now adaies, there is as eager contention about the Empire of the Bishop of Rome, as for these or any other points of Christian religion. This alone is now made the article of faith whereon all the rest doe depend.'[271] James Ussher similarly noted that it was upon the point of the pope's supremacy and the subjection of all other churches to her jurisdiction that 'the Romanists do hazard their whole cause, acknowledging the standing or falling of their Church absolutely to depend thereupon', and quoted Bellarmine to this effect.[272] Thomas Morton's *Grand Imposture of the (now) Church of Rome* was directed in part against

[266] Montagu, *Appello*, pp.121–2.

[267] Laud, *Works*, II: 292–4, 299. This was not an observation that was necessarily confined to Laudians: see e.g. Wotton, *Trial*, p.323.

[268] Laud, *Works*, II: 297–8. [269] *Ibid*., II: 301–2.

[270] See Buckeridge, *De Potestate Papae*, pp.199, 208; Montagu, *Antidiatribae*, pp.49–64, 79–82, 115, 117–19; *idem*, *ΘΕΑΝΘΡΩΠΙΚΟΝ*, ii. 158–64, 180–6; Howson, *Certaine Sermons*, pp.102–4, 131–2, 155–6, and *passim*.

[271] Casaubon, *Answere*, p.28. Cf. King James, *Political Works*, p.126.

[272] Ussher, *Works*, IV: 380.

Rome's 'Article of Necessary Subjection to the Romane See', which Morton depicted as 'the onely Hinderance of a free Generall Councell'.[273]

Ussher and Morton's other writings show that they perceived Rome's errors to be far more than purely those of jurisdictional usurpation. Similarly, while King James claimed that all other controversies rested on that of jurisdiction, he still dealt in detail with Rome's other errors in the same tract. His *Monitory Preface* combined a more moderate assessment of political differences with non-Jesuitical Romanists with an exposition of Rome's errors as justifying the identification of the pope as Antichrist and Rome as Babylon.[274] In the list of 'Some of the principall points which with-hold my ioyning unto the Church of Rome' which James presented to the Jesuit Fisher, the point of image-worship appears first, followed by such matters as invocation, hyperdulia and transubstantiation, with 'the opinion of deposing Kings, and giving away their kingdomes by Papall power' appearing last on the list.[275]

Nevertheless, it was this last point that was one of James' major pre-occupations throughout his reign, and which led in the Oath of Allegiance controversy to an emphasis being placed in English Protestant tracts on the purely political side of the controversy with Rome. It was central to James' defence of the Oath that it left people to believe what they wanted outside their civil duty, so that those taking it did not have to reject any particular part of the Roman faith, not even the article of the pope's spiritual authority.

This was a point which was carefully followed by Andrewes and Buckeridge in their defence of the Oath. Thus Andrewes scrupulously insisted that the Oath only denied the pope's temporal power, and did not touch upon his spiritual authority.[276] The Oath, Andrewes explained, had been instituted in order to reveal those Romanists who imbibed specific doctrines relating to political affairs. It did not attack the imbibing of popery as such, but only those who drank so deeply of it as to raise their arms against and depose their king.[277] The Oath did not question or mention the pope's

[273] Morton, *Grand Imposture*, epistle dedicatory.

[274] King James, *Political Works*, pp.129–50.

[275] Milward, *Jacobean Controversies*, p.226. On the origins of this list in the Second Conference with Fisher, see LPL, Lambeth MS 1372 fol.61r.

[276] Andrewes emphasized that there was in the Oath 'nihil contra Catholicam fidem, nihil contra Primatum, vel Apostolicum, vel sedis Apostolicae, nec vel ipsius Pontificis spiritualem, nihil etiam contra potestatem vel Apostolicam, vel Pontificiam in spiritualibus': Andrewes, *Tortura Torti*, p.83; cf. pp.86, 89, 106, 377–8.

[277] *Ibid.*, p.88. Nevertheless, in his later *Responsio*, Andrewes did deal in passing with Rome's corruptions, such as communion in one kind (pp.251–61), the baptism of bells (pp.268–70), the worship of relics (pp.61–9, 274), indulgences (p.395), the invocation of saints (pp.45–61), transubstantiation (pp.261–6), image worship (pp.274–82), and purgatory (pp.285–9).

spiritual power, but (Andrewes was careful to add) this was put to one side, rather than conceded.[278] Buckeridge concentrated his attention almost exclusively on the pope's claims to temporal jurisdiction, and especially on the deposition of kings, in his only major anti-papal work, *De Potestate Papae in Rebus Temporalibus*.[279] The Act theses of the later Laudian bishop John Bancroft, and the 1620 Convocation address of John Bramhall, reveal a similar preoccupation with issues of jurisdiction.[280] Concentration on the purely political aspects of the controversy with Rome had obvious attractions for those who felt uncomfortable with imputing antichristian heresy and idolatry to Rome. Other English Protestants were acutely aware of the danger that the emphasis on political rather than religious considerations in the Oath of Allegiance controversy might overshadow the critique of Rome's other doctrinal errors. Robert Abbot complained in 1615 of men within the Church of England who would only oppose the Romanists on issues such as the pope's temporal sovereignty, which caused sufficient debate among Romanists themselves. A puritan poet of the early 1620s expressed the same fear of the half-hearted English Protestant who

> ... no other fault can spy
> In all Rome's beadroll of iniquity,
> But that, of late, they do profess King-killing;
> Which Catholic point, to credit he's unwilling ...
> And therefore leaving this out of their creed;
> He in the rest, with them is soon agreed.[281]

When debates on the Oath touched upon the pope's spiritual supremacy, it was polemically desirable to represent the Church of England's position on this point as being more moderate than her absolute rejection of the pope's power in temporal matters. James' preoccupation with the issue of temporal authority was so great that he seemed willing at times to grant the

[278] 'Ponimus eam, non concedimus: Ideo autem ponimus, quia non negatur in Juramento': Andrewes, *Tortura Torti*, p.107. Andrewes does, in fact, provide all the arguments which could be raised against the pope's spiritual supremacy: that Peter was only given the keys in the person of the church (*ibid*., pp.51–2, 76–9), and that all the Apostles were equally made pastors (*ibid*., p.62), etc.

[279] It is true that Buckeridge was also following here the agenda laid out by his Romanist opponent. In his introduction, Buckeridge noted that all Bellarmine's arguments concerned the pope's temporal authority, although he also alluded to errors such as the invocation of saints and the sacrifice of the mass: Buckeridge, *De Potestate Papae*, sig.a2r-v.

[280] Clark, *Register*, i. p.207. Bramhall's sermon at the 1620 'Northern Synod' was on the subject of 'the pope's unlawful usurpation of jurisdiction over the Britannic Churches': Bramhall, *Works*, III: 540.

[281] Prynne, *Canterburies Doome*, p.155; C.H. Firth (ed.), *Stuart Tracts 1603–1693* (1903), p.243 ('The Interpreter').

pope a certain form of spiritual primacy,[282] albeit one subject to canonical restrictions. He seems to have envisaged this chiefly in terms of a primacy of honour among fellow-bishops of equal stature. Noting the contentions for primacy of place among the patriarchs in the primitive church, James declared that, if this was the only issue in question, 'I would with all my heart give my consent that the Bishop of Rome should have the first Seate: I being a westerne King would goe with the Patriarch of the West . . . let him in God his Name be Primus Episcopus inter omnes Episcopos, and Princeps Episcoporum; so it be not otherwise but as Peter was Princeps Apostolorum.'[283] In conference with Fisher over ten years later, James repeated that he would be content for the pope to be 'chiefe patriarcke of the West'.[284] James only saw this as a primacy of honour *iure humano*, for order's sake; he explicitly renounced the idea that the hierarchy of the church had an earthly, infallible monarch.[285] Moreover, he was clear in his own mind that the Church of England granted the pope no spiritual primacy. His claim that the Oath would not touch upon this issue rested in part on the fact that it was unnecessary to do so, 'since we have an expresse Oath elsewhere against the popes Primacie in matters Spirituall'.[286]

Laudian writers were equally clear in their rejection of the pope's spiritual supremacy and their condemnation of Rome's erroneous ideas of spiritual monarchy, while they asserted the fundamental equality of all bishops. But they were equally willing to grant to the pope the honour of a patriarchate. Thus Buckeridge maintained that the powers of 'binding and loosing' had been given to Peter on behalf of the whole church, and quoted Cyprian's *De Unitate Ecclesiae* (as did Andrewes and Howson) for the point that all bishops had the power of the Apostles, and therefore of Peter.[287] Among the bishops the pope might enjoy a certain primacy. Buckeridge stressed that the Church of England did not contend about 'primatu ordinis', and was quite prepared to allow Peter to be of a more exalted state among the Apostles, and Rome to be 'Metropolis & Domina

282 This was a point upon which Benjamin Carier was eager to build irenical arguments. As the issue of spiritual supremacy was generally avoided, Carier was able to argue that, in King James' works on the Oath of Allegiance, 'there is nothing . . . why your Majestie, may not when you please admitt the popes supreamacie in spiritualls': Carier, *Treatise*, p.42. However, Carier was not aiming at any corporate system of independent bishoprics: he insisted that the pope 'ought to have some spirituall Jurisdiction in England', and urged that James admit 'the Ancient subordinacion of the church of Canterbury' to Rome, by whose authority all the other English churches were subject to Canterbury (*ibid*., pp.18, 51).

283 King James, *Political Works*, p.127.

284 LPL, Lambeth MS 1372 fol.60r.

285 King James, *Political Works*, p.127.

286 *Ibid*., p.162.

287 Buckeridge, *De Potestate Papae*, pp.199–201. Cf. Howson, *Certaine Sermons*, pp.131–2, 155–6; Andrewes, *Tortura Torti*, p.62.

Orbis'. Nor did they contend about 'primatu executionis' in the Western Patriarchate, since by granting the pope the status of a patriarch they ensured that his authority was effectively controlled within canonical bounds. If the Roman Patriarch were to be granted the power to depose kings, then the same power would be granted to the bishops of Constantinople, Antioch, Alexandria, Jerusalem, in their own patriarchates. It was the pope's claims to an absolute 'primatu iurisdictionis' – a 'potestatem amplissimam' to create laws, such that the will of the pope was taken for a law in itself – which Buckeridge opposed. He located this power only in General Councils.[288]

Richard Montagu's *Antidiatribae* against the Roman polemicist J.C. Bulenger were primarily concerned to deny that the pope had either temporal sovereignty or supremacy in spiritual matters. It was the equality of bishops which Montagu was most keen to assert, against the principle of ecclesiastical monarchy.[289] Rome's primacy had been 'in ordine ecclesiastico, secundum Canones: non Monarchiali, secundum propriam voluntatem', and did not extend beyond the power and prerogative of a patriarch.[290] John Howson's only anti-papal work, his collection of sermons made in Oxford in 1616, was principally concerned to refute the pope's claims to monarchical power over other bishops. He similarly expounded Cyprian's *De Unitate Ecclesiae* in terms of the unity and equality of all bishops, depicting the church as one Universal Bishopric which, like the Trinity , existed in a multiplicity of persons.[291]

This Laudian concentration on the purely jurisdictional aspects of Rome's errors was significant because, unlike the imputation of other doctrinal errors, it tended to dignify the status of the pope as an overreaching bishop rather than Antichrist, whereas previous writers such as Matthew Sutcliffe had been prepared to deny that the pope was a lawful bishop, or that he had any power to ordain.[292] As the refutation of Rome's errors on this point was built upon a defence of the power and equality of all bishops, this meant that the pope himself had a right to his share in this honour and authority. It granted, in fact, that the pope was an indispensable member of a General Council, and principally attempted merely to contain him within the jurisdictional power of a patriarch. Thus Laud

288 Buckeridge, *De Potestate Papae*, p.208.

289 Montagu, *Antidiatribae*, pp. 46–58, 74, 76, 79–81; cf. *idem*, *ΘΕΑΝΘΡΩΠΙΚΟΝ*, ii. pp.176–8.

290 Montagu, *Antidiatribae*, pp.63–4.

291 Howson, *Certaine Sermons*, pp.102–4 and *passim*.

292 Sutcliffe, *An Abridgement*, ch.41. See Francis Mason's uneasy attempt to explain away Sutcliffe's argument in Mason, *Vindiciae*, pp.398–9. Even Willet did not go quite so far, and allowed that the pope had a bishop's powers within his own diocese: *Synopsis* (1600), p.224.

argued that the pope might be president of a General Council 'as well as any other patriarch' although he should not be president (as he was at Trent) at the trial of his own cause.[293] Montagu wrote that the church's ultimate authority was vested in General Councils 'without the pope as Head, or exceeding the bounds and limits of a Patriarchall Bishop'. Montagu's later remarks to the papal agent Panzani that he and others confessed that it would be impossible to convene a General Council without the pope, or determine what would be binding on the whole church in his absence, do not mark any significant departure from these earlier ideas.[294] Indeed, Montagu had hinted in his *New Gagg* that the pope might hold a primacy of honour in such Councils.[295] The development of a defence of the Church of England's own independent rights as a patriarchate meant that this recognition of the pope's patriarchal status could be made with increasing confidence that no threat would thereby be posed to the Church of England's own independence from Rome.[296]

An assault on Rome's jurisdictional errors that emphasized the rights and dignities of bishops could in fact offer a major criticism of the Reformation. This was not simply because the Reformed Churches had rejected episcopacy, but also because of the undignified treatment to which the pope had been subjected. The scorn and indignities suffered by the pope during the Reformation jarred uncomfortably with notions of episcopal dignity, and Montagu was quite prepared to complain that the Reformers had spoiled the pope, not just of the powers which he had unlawfully usurped, but also of many other privileges that were his by right.[297] While the pope did not exercise a universal temporal monarchy,

293 Laud, *Works*, II: 237 note p.

294 PRO, MS 31/9/17B: Panzani to Barberini, 4/14 November 1635. See also Montagu, *ΘΕΑΝΘΡΩΠΙΚΟΝ*, ii. pp.157–8.

295 Montagu, *New Gagg*, p.29.

296 For the defence of the Church of England's separation from Rome on the basis of a claim to her 'Cyprian Privilege' to be governed by her own independent patriarch, see below, pp.337–8.

297 'Gens avium unaquasque; tandem, suas sibi plumas repetendo, furtivis coloribus denudatum, propriis etiam, quod non oportuit improbantque; vehementer επιεικεστεροι, circumcisam aut spoliatam, nudam; ridendam, exibilandam corniculam exposuerunt': Montagu, *Antidiatribae*, p.41. Cf. Howson's warning that some had fallen into the 'malediction' of derogating from Peter's honour 'while in opposition to the over-large and enforced prerogatives, which the Papists ascribe to Saint Peter', an error which he saw as the quality of the Beast, citing Revelation 13.6: Howson, *Certaine Sermons*, pp.110–12, 114. See also the accusation against Richard Nicholls of Peterhouse, 8 January 1640, that in conversation with fellow-commoners he denied the pope to be Antichrist and maintained instead that 'hee was a Great Bishoppe & Prince whome we ought not to abuse': CUL, VC Ct I.57 fols.207r, 208r, 210v. Also note Burton's claim that the English prelates were sensitive to Bastwick's attacks upon the Romish hierarchy through 'consanguinity': Burton, *For God and the King*, p.67, cf. p.108. However, it should be stressed that Montagu and others were still capable of using very severe

Montagu still emphasized that his temporal principalities in Italy and elsewhere were his just possessions.[298]

This growing emphasis on the political and jurisdictional aspects of Rome's errors had further consequences.[299] In particular, it increased the common ground which the Laudians might share with those within the communion of the Church of Rome who raised similar objections to papal authority, such as the Gallican Church. Robert Abbot, as we have seen, complained of this very point. In his commentary upon the Fisher controversy, the only Romanist error which Richard Corbet touched upon was the pope's usurping of a monarchical power above and beyond that of a patriarch who is 'primus in Aristocratia non [so]lus in Monarchia', which was more acceptable. Corbet noted that this more limited patriarchal authority, given by the church, was in fact 'as much as many Thowsand of papists allow the pope; especially in France'.[300] As we shall see, Richard Montagu clearly conceived of the Gallican Church as providing a model for the Church of England's reunion with Rome.[301]

The Benedictine irenicist Leander Jones reported in the 1630s (possibly after conversations with Montagu) that the most learned English Protestants would recognize the pope as Head of the First See and Patriarch of the West, if some controversies over the extent of the pope's jurisdiction could be settled, although he warned that there might be difficulties on the point of transubstantiation.[302] He suggested what Montagu may have had partly in mind, that the Church of England might be united with Rome in the same way that the Greek Church had been at the Council of Florence, with such differences as did exist being tolerated by Rome.[303]

The basic source of Montagu's hopes for reunion may be found in his more general attitudes towards the Church of Rome and her errors, which were expressed in works that had the support of the Durham House Group and later of the Laudian establishment. Shifting views of the nature of the Church of Rome and her errors permitted Montagu to entertain hopes for

language against medieval popes' temporal ambitions, especially their actions against emperors: Buckeridge, *De Potestate Papae*, pp.205–6, 251–2; Montagu, *Antidiatribae*, pp.64, 67–8, 70–3, 93–5; Andrewes, *Tortura Torti*, pp.284–5; *idem*, *Responsio*, pp.90, 154, 159, 175, 299, 386, 465.

298 Montagu, *Antidiatribae*, p.95.

299 See Cosin's remark at Francis White's consecration that the pope's claims to universal jurisdiction were 'the main quarrel . . . betwixt him and us at this day': Cosin, *Works*, I: 93–4. Cf. Laud, *Works*, I: 78, 165.

300 Bodl., Rawlinson MS D.853 fol.174Br-v.

301 See below, pp.266, 344.

302 G. Sitwell, 'Leander Jones' mission to England, 1634–5', *Recusant History* 5 (1959–60), pp.152–3. Compare these points with those made by Montagu to Panzani: PRO, MS 31/9/17B: Panzani to Barberini, 4/14 November 1635.

303 Sitwell, 'Leander Jones', p.140.

reunion with Rome while still employing, on the surface, the same rhetoric of moderation which was used by mainstream anti-papist Jacobean writers. Montagu still maintained, in conversation with Panzani, that there were errors in the Church of Rome which remained to be negotiated away, such as transubstantiation and communion in one kind.[304]

It is most doubtful that Montagu's schemes for reunion with the Church of Rome enjoyed the support of many of the Laudian episcopate, despite Montagu's claims.[305] Nevertheless, the changes in perspective regarding Rome and her errors which prompted Montagu's plans seem to have represented a more general trend in Laudian thinking.

304 PRO, MS 31/9/17B: Panzani to Barberini, 4/14 November 1635.

305 PRO, MS 31/9/17B: Panzani to Barberini, 4/14 November 1635; 27 April/7 May 1636. See below, pp.364–6.

5

Unity and diversity in the Roman communion: inconsistency or opportunity?

THE MEANING OF ROMAN HETEROGENEITY

It was standard practice for Elizabethan and Jacobean Protestants to depict the Roman communion as a unified, centralized and autocratically governed community, in which all papists were simply mindless cogs in a great machine.[1] This was not just a paranoid overestimation of the unity and coherence of papal forces ranged against Protestant England, as some historians have tended to suggest. It was also a view which served a number of important polemical purposes. A central plank of English Protestants' defence of the separation from Rome was the assertion that other churches had been forced to depart from Rome's communion because she now prescribed and imposed satanic doctrines, making dissent or tacit amendment impossible.[2] The arguments which defended the Protestants' pre-Reformation forefathers, as expounded by Field and others, rested on the assumption that Rome had so decayed since Trent that dissent was no longer possible within her communion. The corrupt doctrines of a faction had now been established as necessary to be believed as articles of faith, whereas in the medieval church dissent had still been possible.[3] The Court of Rome had now become the Church of Rome.

When Protestants studied how the Church of Rome perceived herself and defined her own membership, after establishing her doctrine of infallibility, they generally judged her to be no true church at all. Thus Crakanthorp stressed that Rome's only true members, since the Lateran decree had transferred supremacy and infallibility to the pope, were those people who accepted this doctrine: 'he who gainsayeth the popes sentence, in a cause of faith, is none of their Church'.[4] Given the definitions of church membership supplied by Bellarmine and Cusanus, anyone dissenting in any way from the pope could not be accounted a member of that church. The only

1 Weiner, 'Beleaguered isle', pp.30–6; E. Rose, *Cases of Conscience* (1975), p.239.

2 E.g. Morton, *Catholike Appeale*, pp.445–6; *idem*, *Grand Imposture*, pp.387–405; Jackson, *Works*, II: 87–8. See below, ch.7.

3 See below, ch.7.

4 Crakanthorp, *Vigilius Dormitans*, pp.156–7.

people who could truly be considered members of the present Roman Church were those who placed 'their essentiall dependence on the pope, or Antichrist, as on the foundation of their faith'.[5] The more that Rome was assessed in such 'absolute' terms – as if all her members accepted every official doctrine, and all its logical consequences, in all areas of life – the nearer English Protestants came to denying Rome to be a church at all, as her antichristian errors became fundamental to her very nature. Thus Henry Burton argued from these grounds that it was impossible to be saved by normal means in the Roman Church, since papists were taught to hate and abhor the preaching of the Word of God.[6] He claimed that justification by faith, the foundation of Christian religion, had been expressly denied in the Council of Trent.[7]

The essential difference between arguments that declared Rome to be no true church of Christ and those which granted her this status lay in the latter's moderating of this 'absolute' view of Rome. The fragments of true doctrine that remained in Rome were by 'absolute' arguments physically actualized in the form of a hidden congregation within Rome of pure, true worshippers, opposing a hierarchy which in its basic principles obeyed no rules of religion at all. Thus, although William Perkins admitted that the Church of Rome still possessed the Scriptures and the sacraments, he argued that these existed, not for the use of that church, but in order to provide the means of salvation for the true church of God, which existed as a congregation of pure worshippers within the Roman Church.[8] All the redeeming features of the Church of Rome were thus located objectively in the hidden elite of God's true elect who were within the external Roman congregation.[9] Against the argument that Antichrist must sit in the Temple of God, and therefore Rome must be a church of God, Perkins argued more in terms of the Church of God existing within the Church of Rome as wheat among chaff.

The more positive interpretation of Rome's status tended to place more emphasis on the mingling of the true worshippers and the Roman hierarchy, and envisaged popery more as an evil faction, or as a disease, which had taken up residence within an institutional church. Elements of the truth were spread throughout the Roman Church, and were not necessarily concentrated in a tiny elite of true believers. The true church and the false,

[5] *Ibid.*, pp.187, 188–9. [6] Burton, *Seven Vials*, p.31. See also Abbot, *Third Part*, p.5.

[7] Burton, *Seven Vials*, pp.50–1; *idem*, *Truths Triumph over Trent* (1629), *passim*.

[8] Perkins, *Reformed Catholike*, pp.292, 294. Perkins stressed that, if by the Roman Church was understood 'a state or regiment of the people, whereof the pope is head: and the members are all such as doe acknowledge him to be their head and doe beleeve the doctrine established in the Councell of Trent, we take it to bee no Church of God' (*ibid.*, p.293).

[9] Cf. Carleton, *Consensus*, pp.229, 232–3; Bedell, *Examination of Motives*, pp.14–17.

Antichrist and the church in which Antichrist was present, could still be distinguished, but only in a theoretical sense. Ussher wrote that 'we must distinguish the papacy from the Church wherein it is; as the Apostle doth Antichrist from the temple of God, wherein he sitteth'.[10] 'Popery', he commented, 'is nothing else but the botch or plague of that Church; which hazardeth the souls of those it seizeth upon, as much as any infection can do the body.'[11] Francis Mason similarly spoke of popery as 'an ulcer spreading upon the Church'*; antichristianism was built upon the foundation of a true church.[12] But the general point of this view was that the church and its disease were inextricably combined. As Cholmley explained, 'in the Church of Rome there is an inseparable conjunction of Babylon and the people of God'.[13] Rome was at the same time both Babel and Bethel.

Nevertheless, these two interpretations of Rome are best regarded as polarities between which English Protestant writers oscillated, with the 'absolute' view being embraced on certain issues by writers such as Jackson and Crakanthorp who could elsewhere adopt more moderate assessments of Rome's nature.[14] While Ussher, as we have seen, could represent truth and popery as co-existent in the Roman Church, at other times – most notably in his *De Successione* – when he spoke of the same distinction in personal terms, he referred to the minority of Christ's people under Antichrist's priests as a hidden congregation of true believers, very much in Perkins' sense.[15] Field's and Carleton's defence of the separation from Rome rested on such an absolute perspective, which thus remained at the centre of English Protestant thought. It was Rome's inflexibility and her tyrannous imposition of idolatrous doctrines which had impelled the Protestants to leave her in order to escape their forced partaking of her plagues.[16] It was only with the controversy over Joseph Hall's *The Old Religion* that these two polarities were forced into conflict.

In fact, however, important aspects of Protestants' defence against Rome rested upon the claim that there was a chronic diversity of beliefs within even the post-Reformation Roman Church, on which the pope could not impose any sort of doctrinal unity. One of the most frequent charges of Romanists against the Protestants was that, lacking any central authority, they differed among themselves on many fundamental issues, as the divisions between Calvinists and Lutherans demonstrated. This lack of unity, Romanists claimed, meant that the Protestants could not constitute the true

10 Ussher, *Works*, II: 490. 11 *Ibid.*, II: 493.
12 Mason, *Vindiciae*, p.198 ('ecclesiae adnatum ulcus').
13 Cholmley, *The State*, p.20. 14 See above, pp.138, 181n, 220.
15 Ussher, *Works*, II: 1–413 *passim*.
16 See below, ch.7.

church, which was indivisible. English Protestant authors traditionally refuted this argument in part by denying that the Protestants were divided among themselves on fundamental points, explaining away the Lutheran/Calvinist divisions and stressing that Protestants were of 'one religion, one foundation, one heart'.[17] Any divisions which might exist among Protestants were in minor matters, and were besides to be blamed wholly on Rome's obstruction of the calling of a general council for reformation, which had forced each group of Protestants to reform themselves in an uncoordinated manner.[18]

But English Protestant polemicists also turned the Romanists' arguments back upon their authors. Unwilling to allow Rome any higher claims to peace and unity, they claimed that Rome was beset by greater divisions among her writers and churches than were the Protestants.[19] Joseph Hall's 1609 work, entitled ironically *The Peace of Rome*, devoted itself entirely to proving this point.[20] This argument was not just maintained by Calvinist episcopalians – it was a polemical device embraced by Andrew Willet in his *Tetrastylon Papisticum* of 1593, which included a study of 'the repugnant opinions of New Papisters With the old; of the newe one with another; of the same writers with themselves: yea of Popish religion with and in it selfe'. Hall's work was heartily approved by puritans such as Thomas Taylor. Elsewhere, Hall claimed that Bellarmine acknowledged no less than 237 contrarieties of doctrine among Romish divines in fundamental points of faith.[21] Contrasting Protestant and Romanist divisions, Hall maintained that 'Our strife is in ceremonies, theirs in substance; ours in one or two points, theirs in all . . . there is not one point in all divinity, except those wherein we accord with them, wherein they all speak the same.'[22] Disputes within Protestantism over predestination also led to a greater recognition of the divisions within the Roman Church between the Dominicans and Jesuits on this issue.[23] Rome's apparent unity was due to

[17] Field, *Of the Church*, IV: 402–10, 498–515; Bedell, *Certaine Letters*, pp.45–7; Hall, *Works*, VI: 202; White, *Orthodox Faith*, p.284; Andrewes, *Responsio*, pp.416–17, 447–8.

[18] Field, *Of the Church*, I: 341–2.

[19] E.g. Crakanthorp, *Defensio*, pp.182–9; Andrewes, *Responsio*, pp.447–50; George Abbot, *The Reasons which Doctour Hill hath Brought, for the Upholding of Papistry* (Oxford, 1604), p.102; Abbot, *Second Part*, pp.8–10, 339–40, 958–9; Wotton, *A Defence*, p.28.

[20] William Bedell (*Certaine Letters*, p.159) cites Hall's work for evidence of this point.

[21] Willet, *Synopsis* (1613), pp.1325–52; Hall, *Works*, VI: 202. See also Bedell, *Certaine Letters*, pp.44–5, 58, 159; Abbot, *The Reasons*, pp.90–2, 108–10; Taylor, *Christs Victorie*, p.808; Willet, *Antilogie*, pp.47–50; Bernard, *Rhemes against Rome*, pp.127–30; White, *Defence*, pp.208–20.

[22] Hall, *Works*, VI: 203; cf. Powel, *Consideration of the Papists*, pp.63–4.

[23] George Carleton, *An Examination* (2nd edn, 1626), pp.96, 126–7; John Davenant, *Animadversions upon a Treatise Intitled Gods Love to Mankind* (Cambridge, 1641), pp.148, 160, 204, 252; John Plaifere, *Appello Evangelium* (1651), p.432; Downe, *Certaine Treatises*, xii. p.38. Note also Samuel Ward's interest in Jansen's *Augustinus*: SSC, Ward

the fact that her members were more subtle in hiding their disagreements than were the Protestants. Hall observed that Roman dissensions were smothered, or were fought within doors, rather than out in the open, as inter-Protestant disputes tended to be.[24] Such temperate forms of disagreement were actually cited approvingly by Davenant when he wrote urging reunion between the Calvinists and Lutherans. Rome's example showed that it was possible for several churches to live peaceably together using the same service and sacraments, though differing on some issues, as the Thomists and Scotists, and the Dominicans and Jesuits, did.[25]

A particular genre of anti-papal polemic thus developed in which Romanist writers were manipulated in order to act as testimonies of Protestant doctrine and to attack each other. Thomas Bell claimed to have invented this style of controversy, but it was Thomas Morton who made the most systematic use of it in his *Apologia Catholica* (1605) and *Catholike Appeale for Protestants* (1610) in answer to the employment of the same technique by Romanist writers.[26]

Nevertheless, like many new anti-papal polemical strategies devised in the early Jacobean period, this required careful exposition. While hardline Calvinists could revel in the chaos of conflicting opinions which appeared to afflict the Roman Church, more moderate spirits might be tempted to read such arguments as implying that the Roman Church was sufficiently inclusive as to tolerate a wider variety of opinions on doctrinal points than did the Protestant Churches. While a point in the Protestants' favour against Rome's claims to uniformity in belief, this inclusivity could in an irenical context imply that Rome was more tolerant on non-fundamentals than was Calvinism, and was thus a more desirable church for those opposed to unnecessary dogmatism in matters of faith. For those who were repelled by the inflexibility of the decrees of the Synod of Dort, Rome could appear to offer a more tolerable alternative, not least on the issues of free will and predestination, than did current Protestantism. It was Rome's

MS O/7. See also King Charles I, *A Large Declaration concerning the Late Tumults in Scotland* (1639), p.320.

24 Hall, *Works*, VI: 202–3. Cf. Christopher Potter's Protestation of 1631: Bodl., Sancroft MS 21 pp.59–60.

25 Davenant, 'Opinion', pp.22–4 in *Good Counsells*.

26 John Strype, *Annals of the Reformation* (4 vols., Oxford, 1824), IV: 208–11. The *Catholike Appeale* amounted to virtually an official corporate publication of the Church of England. Archbishop Bancroft commanded 'a certaine number of Divines, then at hand' to work upon the treatise. Although it eventually fell to Morton to compose it, John Cosin later claimed that Overall 'revised & amended' the work, and 'in truth was the chief Author of it' (DUL, shelfmark P.IV.40, p.132). I am grateful to Mr A.I. Doyle for drawing this annotation to my attention. On this general strategy, see also Milward, *Jacobean Controversies*, pp.151–6; Cragg, *Freedom and Authority*, pp.167–8; PRO, SP 99/9 fol.61r–v: Dudley Carleton to Archbishop Abbot, 7 Feb. 1612.

supposedly inclusive, undogmatic nature which seems to have inspired the conversions of the young William Chillingworth and of Sir Kenelm Digby.[27]

Chillingworth and Digby provide interesting examples of the potential perils of acknowledging the diversity of views within Rome's communion. These dangers were all the greater as this particular line of argument in Protestant polemic was not usually intended to serve a simply destructive purpose, as illustrating the irredeemable chaos within Rome. By emphasizing the plurality of views within the Roman Church, Protestant writers were also intent upon demonstrating how certain Roman authors actually (and however unwillingly) supported the Protestants' position against Rome.

Moreover, even professional clergy of a Calvinist hue were used to modifying their generally papophobic position, and to recognizing that there were certain Romanists with whom they could do business and from whose writings they could profit. For example, James Ussher, archbishop of Armagh, exchanged scholarly assistance with David Rothe, the Romanist bishop of Ossory, and the Franciscan historian Luke Wadding.[28] Andrew Willet and William Perkins were not alone among puritan authors in making extensive use of Romanist biblical commentators such as Arias Montanus and Aretius. Richard Bernard admitted freely that learned Roman Catholics were impressive scholars on matters concerning the grammar, logic and rhetoric of the bible, and could speak on moral precepts 'very excellently'.[29] English Protestants were also making increasing use of contemporary Roman devotional writers, including the German Jesuit Drexelius.[30] In 1584, Edmund Bunny had gone so far as to publish a

[27] The young Chillingworth believed the Church of England's Articles to be too restrictive a foundation for a comprehensive church, and Protestantism generally to have been guilty of introducing new creeds and definitions, whereas Rome was prepared to tolerate intellectual speculation and to leave her members free to subscribe to the substance of the Thirty-Nine Articles. He even claimed that those with Protestant opinions could live within Rome's communion, although he was soon to be disillusioned: Orr, *Reason and Authority*, pp.14–19. On Digby's conversion and Laud's response see Laud, *Works*, VI: 449–55; Milton, 'Laudians', pp.163–4.

[28] N. Vance, *Irish Literature: A Social History* (Oxford, 1990), pp.47–8. The Dominican Augustine Baker also managed to make use of Robert Cotton's library for his history of medieval English monasticism: Birrell, 'The reconstruction', p.61.

[29] See Willet's apologia in his *Hexapla in Exodum*, sig.A6r; Aveling, 'The English clergy', pp.94, 123; Bernard, *A Key*, pp.100–1.

[30] T. Birrell, 'English Catholic mystics in non-Catholic circles', *The Downside Review* 94 (1976), pp.60–81, 99–117, 213–28. See also J.M. Blom, 'A German Jesuit and his Anglican readers. The case of Jeremias Drexelius (1581–1632)', and A.F. Allison, 'The "Mysticism" of Manchester Al Mondo. Some Catholic borrowings in a seventeenth-century Anglican work of devotion', in G.A.M. Janssens and F.G.A.M. Aarts (eds.), *Studies in Seventeenth Century English Literature, History and Bibliography* (Amsterdam, 1984).

revised version of the popular devotional *Book of the Christian Exercise* composed by the notorious Jesuit controversialist Robert Parsons.[31]

It is important to remember that the constant anxiety of puritan writers concerning the availability of popish books should not be taken as evidence that their own libraries were free of such works – indeed, the opposite was usually the case. Even Romanist polemical writings against Protestantism were greatly sought after by puritan divines, and London booksellers could command a high price for them. Puritan anxieties were prompted, not by the mere availability of such books, but rather because they mistrusted their possible effect on the ungodly reader.[32] Friendly relations with individual papists, or the possession of popish books, were therefore things which many English Protestant divines might share. Yet these were also points which were regularly used as evidence of crypto-popery against those who had aroused more general suspicions of treachery by their failure to endorse rigorously Protestant doctrines.[33] The anxiety generated by these practical compromises with Roman Catholicism may in itself have generated more 'absolute' polemical attacks upon Rome as a response.

Whatever the use that might be made of Roman works of devotion or scholarship, English Protestants did not generally allow this to alter their negative perceptions of the authors themselves, or of the church which claimed their allegiance. As Robert Abbot pungently put it: 'we forbeare not to turne & wind al Popish authors, either of former or latter time, that what gold we can find in their dunghils, we may apply it to the furnishing of the temple of the Lord'. Bunny's *Briefe Answer* of 1589, which replied to Parsons' complaints that Bunny had excised various passages in his own edition of Parsons' devotional work, went on the offensive by typifying Parsons' book as essentially deceitful. Parsons only dealt with matters of godliness, Bunny claimed, as an elaborate pretence, in order to insinuate popish errors the more plausibly. This was therefore an object lesson to

31 R. McNulty, 'A Protestant version of Robert Parsons' first book of the Christian exercise', *Huntington Library Quarterly* 23 (1959–60).

32 For a typical example of a puritan library well stocked with Romanist authors, see J. Blatchly, *The Town Library of Ipswich* (Woodbridge, 1989). Archbishop Abbot's chaplain Thomas Goad wrote in alarm in 1621 that the granting of a monopoly on the import of all foreign books written by popish authors would lead to the increase of prices 'under colour of hinderinge poysonouse bookes', and hence all divines would feel the pinch when they tried to purchase works by Roman worthies such as Bellarmine and Maldonatus: Bodl., Tanner MS 290 fol.46r (Goad to Samuel Ward, 9 January 1621). On the availability of Romanist books in the English market, and the very high prices that they could command, see T. Watt, *Cheap Print and Popular Piety* (Cambridge, 1991), pp.51–2; SUL, Hartlib MS 29/3 fols.20r, 32v.

33 E.g. Lake, *Moderate Puritans*, pp.175, 177; *idem*, 'Significance', pp.174–5; Russell, *Fall*, pp.228–9, 421–2.

beware of popery 'not only in such bookes of theirs, as wherein they professe to treat of these matters: but in the residue to[o], wherein they would in no wise seeme to medle with them, but for to treat of godlines only'.[34]

Whatever polemical use might be made of more moderate Roman authors, they were generally not appreciated in their own terms, or applauded as evidence of more moderate trends within the Roman Church. For example, while John White noted that, on matters of free will, 'the warier sort' of Romanists (including Bellarmine) seemed to agree with the Protestants, he insisted that this was in fact merely 'a dram of their wit to make their Pelagianisme go downe the easlier'. Robert Abbot was similarly sceptical of Romanist claims to trust in Christ's merits, remarking that 'for the cuppe of poison of the whore of Babylon they must use a cover of such good words, least they make men loath to drinke thereof'.[35]

Even when they were not interpreted as being simply deceitful, moderate Romanists were generally played off against more extreme Romanist writers in order to illustrate Rome's disunity and incoherence. The moderate writers were not taken to indicate a significant softening of opinion in the Roman Church; it was the extreme writers who were always perceived as the norm. It was the pronouncements of the latter which Prideaux and Robert Abbot carefully collected to show where Rome's doctrine was really leading.[36] This view was partly dictated by polemical tactics. But it also sprang from a deep-seated conviction of the unreformable nature of the papacy, and also from fundamental notions, which apocalyptic ideas nourished, of the inevitable further decay and corruption of the church under Antichrist. The Roman Church was *destined* to fall increasingly under the sway of antichristian heresies which would more fully express the desires and designs of Antichrist its Head. Each new, extreme doctrinal departure by an individual popish writer therefore indicated the path down which the official church would irresistibly follow.

Thus, when Lancelot Andrewes noted that his opponent du Perron had in one treatise adopted an unusually restrained stance on the invocation of saints, and elsewhere in conversation had allegedly expressed a lack of enthusiasm for the practice, Andrewes found himself unable to respond positively to such moderation. Instead, he strongly denied du Perron's claim that 'oblique, relative Prayer' was all that was sought in the Roman Church, and feared that du Perron would be censured for his moderate doctrine. When Robert Abbot was confronted by his opponent William

[34] Abbot, *Second Part*, p.982; Bunny, *Briefe Answer*, praeface [unfoliated].
[35] White, *The Way*, pp.277–8; Abbot, *Second Part*, p.631 (cf. pp.736, 748).
[36] E.g. Prideaux, 'A Plot for Preferment', p.8, and 'Idolatrous Feasting', pp.6–7 (*Certaine Sermons*); Abbot, *Second Part*, p.631.

Bishop's claim that God alone was the foundation of merits and good works, he complained angrily that Bishop was 'saying that which he thinketh not'. After citing the Rhemist New Testament annotations and the works of Bellarmine against Bishop's argument, Abbot concluded that his opponent must therefore be writing 'very untruly and against his owne knowledge'.[37]

It was to hardline Jesuit writers that English Protestants turned when they wished to uncover Rome's fundamental position. It is true that they would occasionally choose to show how Jesuit doctrines opposed the Roman Church's official formulations, in order to demonstrate their extremism, and the Church of Rome's confusion on such matters. Thus Thomas Morton, in his *Institution*, drew attention to the fact that Bellarmine's arguments for transubstantiation by adduction were 'flat contrary to the faith of the Councell of Trent'.[38] But it was generally assumed that the Jesuits' arguments were simply a clearer manifestation of the degeneracy towards which the Church of Rome was inevitably progressing. In this way, they represented merely a fuller working-out of the heresies which the Council of Trent had enshrined in the church.

Given these attitudes, Roman irenical writers were generally read with little sympathy for their motives. Their role in Jacobean thought was essentially to throw into greater relief the extremism of the Jesuits and the Roman Court. In Thomas James' works, for example, writers such as de Dominis, Sarpi and Ferus were thoroughly exploited, the better to attack the Roman Church. Similarly, James revived the works of the irenicist George Wicelius so that he might serve as part of the Protestants' ancestry,[39] rather than as representing a moderate aspect of the Roman Church, which James still affirmed to be Babylon and the pope Antichrist.[40] In this way, mediatory, irenic Romanists such as Cassander were among the most

37 Andrewes, *Two Answers*, p.76; Abbot, *Second Part*, pp.665–6, 695.

38 Morton, *Of the Institution*, i. p.110. Ussher noted that the Tridentine order of baptism in the Roman Sacerdotal had retained important interrogatories concerning the doctrine of salvation through Christ's merits alone, although these passages had now been removed, presumably through Jesuit influence: Ussher, *Works*, III: 567–8.

39 James edited and published *Notae ad Georgium Wicelium, de Methodo Concordiae Ecclesiasticae* in 1625. James' apparent interest in Wicelius' irenicism in a paper addressed to Richard Montagu (Cosin, *Correspondence*, I: 62) is belied by his remarks in *A Manuduction* (pp.119–22) and in his manuscript 'An Anticoccius' of 1629 in which he uses Wicelius in a separate section with Cajetan, Erasmus and Cassander for a table of 'foure late renowned Papists that lived and died in the Bosome of the Church of Rome agreeing with us in the most substantiall points': QCO, MS 249 pp.40–3. See also James, *A Manuduction*, pp.123–4; Featley, *Clavis*, p.489. Compare also James' use of de Dominis principally as a source for material against Rome in his *A Manuduction* (esp. pp.72, 99–100, 123). Note also the use of Ferus by Robert Abbot: *Defence*, p.128; *Second Part*, pp.295, 392, 610, 1148.

40 QCO, MS 249 pp.303–19.

profitable Romanist writers for Jacobean anti-papal polemicists, as they were prepared to offer a strong critique of some Roman practices and a positive assessment of Protestantism in the interests of reunion. There was always the fear, however, that the use of such writers might encourage English Protestants to consider that some form of accommodation with Rome might be possible, as the irenicists' arguments claimed.

Some irenical writings grew naturally out of the Gallican thought which proved so fruitful a source for English anti-papal polemicists. After all, there was a whole range of Gallican *politique* writings which were directed towards attempting to unite the French nation regardless of its religious differences. In writers such as Pierre de Belloy and Jacques Faye d'Espesses this could take the form of a willingness to question the theological doctrines which separated the Protestants and Romanists. David Wootton has noted, however, that these theorists were in no way inspired to more general irenical ideas. De Belloy's *Apologie Catholique* was written in order to condemn the pope's excommunication of the future Henry IV, and it was for this particular polemical reason that he denied that the Protestants had ever been satisfactorily convicted of heresy. Nevertheless, de Belloy's work did find an English audience, being published in English translation as *A Catholic Apology against the Libels of the League*.[41] Henry Constable's *Examen Pacifique de la Doctrine des Huguenots*, while born of the same crisis, was a more genuine and influential attempt to reconcile Protestants and Romanists which gained a wide readership in Jacobean and Caroline England. Ostensibly the work of a French Catholic, it refuted the argument that the Huguenots should be labelled as heretics.[42] Indeed, it was the work's dangerously irenical perspective against which Constable's anonymous 1623 English translator was most careful to caution his readers. The translator warned in a preface that 'nothing was here written with any intention to urge us Protestants, any whit to depart from our Right in yeelding to a Reconciliation'. The purpose of the book, and of its translator, was rather to persuade Romanists 'to esteeme better of us: and to demonstrate withall, that if they will iudge right, they must needs thinke well'.[43] The work would be seized upon for a different

41 Wootton, *Paolo Sarpi*, p.50. For a discussion of de Belloy's work, see *ibid.*, pp.55–8, 72–3. J.H.M. Salmon agrees with Wootton in seeing de Belloy more as a *politique* than as a Gallican theorist: J.H.M. Salmon, *Renaissance and Revolt* (Cambridge, 1987), p.168.

42 This work, licensed under Archbishop Whitgift's own hand in 1589, was in fact first printed in England by an English author, Henry Constable, probably before his conversion to Romanism. For the background to this work, see Rogers, 'The Catholic moderator', pp.224–35.

43 *The Catholike Moderator* (1623), preface. This translation proved quite popular, going through three impressions in 1623 and one in 1624.

purpose, however, by the irenicist William Forbes.[44]

The reaction of Constable's translator is typical of the general way in which Roman irenicists were approached by Jacobean Calvinist writers. When genuinely moderate, irenical writers such as Sancta Clara emerged, they met with a chorus of disapproval from the traditional Calvinist divines. Thomas Morton was reported to have written a passage against the irenical Romanist Sancta Clara which was stopped at the press by Laud's chaplain, William Bray.[45] Joseph Hall did not join the attacks upon the Franciscan. He did not, however, accept Sancta Clara's writings on the Franciscan's own terms, but instead regarded them as effective propaganda material with which to justify the Church of England against Rome.[46]

Nevertheless, even in the Jacobean period this recognition and manipulation of more moderate Romanist writers was beginning to cause confusion and dispute. Writers such as William Covell and John Dove displayed a readiness even then to appreciate moderate Romanists on their own terms. Dove's remarks on this issue are especially remarkable. Dove particularly concerned himself with the works of Rome's foremost controversial champion, Cardinal Bellarmine. Bellarmine's careful reading of Protestant authors, and his subtly argued and moderate opinions on a number of significant doctrinal points, made him a favourite source for anti-papal writers, who cited him against more extreme Romanists, or accused him of contradicting himself. Dove, however, convinced himself that Bellarmine's writings represented a significant and welcome change in the doctrinal complexion of the Roman Church itself. Bellarmine brought in what might be argued for the Romanist side, Dove claimed, 'for fashion sake', to avoid suspicion of crypto-Protestantism. Despite such cosmetic gestures, however, Dove maintained that in fact

[44] Forbes, *Considerationes*, II: 133, 287, 595. James Wedderburn also noted several passages from the same work in his commonplace book, possibly with a similar intent to Forbes: BL, Harleian MS 749 fols.24r, 46v, 55r, 63v. Cf. Gardiner, *Reports*, p.101.

[45] Larking, *Proceedings in Kent*, p.95. This account (by Daniel Featley) is confirmed by Panzani's independent report that Morton had written against Sancta Clara's book, in a diary entry for 14/24 February 1635: Panzani, *Diary*, p.86 [original, fol.77], and Samuel Hartlib's report of the same rumour in his Ephemerides for 1635: SUL, Hartlib MS 29/3 fol.26r (cf. fol.11r on another planned refutation of *Deus, Natura, Gratia*). Bishop Williams' committee dealing with religious innovations under Laud listed 'The reconciliation of Sancta Clara to knit the Romish and Protestant in one' among 'some dangerous and most reproveable Bookes': *A Copie of the Proceedings of Some Worthy and Learned Divines ...* (1641), p.3.

[46] Hall lists Sancta Clara among 'temperate adversaries' (including others such as Ferus, Cassander, Cusanus, Contarini and Cajetan) whose suffrages might be accepted and made advantage of where they gave a favourable view of the Church of England's controversies and charitable testimonies of the Protestants' personal innocencies: Hall, *Works*, VI: 438. Even this purely pragmatic treatment of Sancta Clara earned Hall some severe criticism: see Bodl., Rawlinson MS D.831 fol.113r.

he [Bellarmine] handleth his matters so cunningly, and so doubtfully, that in his conclusions he agreeth with us in many things, although in divers termes, wherein his predecessors utterly dissented from us. And in many things he sheweth himselfe to be; so far as he dareth, a Protestant, or at the least not a Papist: if we take papistrie to be that which before it was. And whosoever doth observe him well, shal finde how he discourseth of many things superfluous, like one which is more desirous to deceive the time, to fill up the page with varietie of reading multitudes of Fathers, and citations of places, then to refute us. Yet his Volumes are allowed by the Inquisition, and he is rewarded for his learned workes. Therefore I say, papistrie is newely corrected and refined, they hold the same conclusions in generall termes which they did, but they hold them not as they did: they seeke out new defences, as if they could not stand to the olde, and come neerer to us in iudgement every day. For so it hath pleased God in this latter end of the world to lighten their darknesse, and to quicken the dulnesse of their understanding.

Bellarmine, Dove insisted, 'in many points ... is a Protestant, or at the least, not a Papist', and therefore the inescapable conclusion was 'that the Roman religion is refined'.[47]

Clearly, Dove's arguments here were greatly at variance with established English Protestant practice and assumptions. They do not, however, seem to have drawn any direct comment from Protestant authors. This may be explained in part by the fact that they appeared in his brief tract addressed specifically to English recusants, and were thereby tempered by the particular polemical requirements of this field of controversy.

Yet Dove was not entirely alone. William Covell was even more ready to take Roman irenicists seriously. His defence of Hooker included a lengthy section in which Covell wrote with great sympathy of the dilemma of the moderate divine, standing between Rome and the Protestants, who strives for unity but thereby earns the opprobrium of both sides. Covell's discussion of Roman and Protestant irenicists was even-handed, and his praise of Cassander unqualified. Indeed, he complained strongly of Calvin's attack on the Roman irenicist.[48]

The temptation to draw positive conclusions from examples of moderation and dissent within Rome's communion was also evident in the controversy over Hall's *The Old Religion*. Anxious to find arguments to

[47] Dove, *Perswasion*, pp.12, 33. Dove claimed to have demonstrated these points in his volumes composed in answer to Bellarmine's treatises *De Verbo Dei* and *De Christo* 'now beyond the Seas to be printed' (*Perswasion*, p.33). His reasons for publishing overseas were ostensibly because of 'the great difficultie of printing Latine bookes here in London' (*ibid.*), rather than because of any reservations caused by his novel interpretation of Bellarmine's works. However, I have been unable to trace these volumes, if they were ever printed, or any of Dove's replies to the other volumes of Bellarmine's *Disputationes*, which he promised to his readers. For a more typical treatment of Bellarmine, accusing him of being inconsistent and dishonestly adept in argument, see Whitaker, *Praelectiones*, pp.64, 86.

[48] Covell, *Just and Temperate Defence*, pp.64–7, 77.

support the bishop's contention that Rome was in essence a true church, Hall's defender Butterfield fell upon evidence of diversity within Rome's communion as a positive sign of her good standing. Thus Butterfield maintained that the Gallican Church had not received the decrees of the Council of Trent, and hence argued that not all papists held the damnable doctrines of that Council, and that it should not therefore be assumed that all papists were heretics and damned. In response, Burton insisted (more in line with conventional English Protestant readings of the issue) that France only stood out against Trent because of issues of political prerogative, and correctly noted that the Sorbonists had now yielded their unanimous assent to Trent's doctrines and decrees.[49]

As the gulf widened between moderate and radical perceptions of Rome's nature as a church, the wealth of moderate and dissident Romanist opinion which Jacobean Calvinist writers had amassed thus presented an ambiguous legacy which could be used to provide a far more positive evaluation of the Roman Church and its doctrine than had previously been embraced by English Protestantism. It was not until the advent of Montagu and Laud, however, that this potential was fully exploited.

Ironically, part of the positive value which Laudian writers attached to moderate Romanist writers derived from the vehemence of the same Laudians' attack upon those Romanists traditionally regarded as the most extreme and disreputable of the pope's factors, the Jesuits. English Protestants had generally recognized the degree of hostility which the Jesuits and their doctrines aroused even in the Roman Church. Indeed, it was other Romanists' hostility towards the Jesuits that allowed William Prynne to argue that Laud was a crypto-papist despite the fact that the Jesuits had been behind the alleged Habernfeld Plot to kill the archbishop.[50] In Montagu's hands, it was the very extremism of the Jesuits which allowed him to portray the more moderate Roman doctrines as being in opposition to them, and to instil hope for the reunion of the churches.

Lacking the Jacobean Calvinist's absolute and apocalyptic view of Rome and her errors, Laudians in general, and Montagu and Forbes in particular, were able to employ the distinction between moderate and radical Romanist doctrines (which was a constant feature of their works) in a way which allowed more moderate defences of Rome's doctrines to

[49] Butterfield, *Maschil*, pp.107–8; Burton, *Babel*, p.113.

[50] Prynne argued that Laud's opposition to Jesuits did not show him not to be a Romanist; it could merely be the reaction of a pragmatical Romanist bishop opposing the order because they were against all other orders: Laud, *Works*, IV: 494. Prynne noted that the Jesuits had often been banished out of France and other countries, and that the English priests and Jesuits had recently persecuted each other violently, 'no Protestants writing so bitterly against these Popish orders as themselves do one against the other'. On the Habernfeld Plot, see Hibbard, *Popish Plot*, pp.157–62.

have a place of equal importance with Jesuit extremism as representative of Rome's position. When he described Rome's errors and excesses, Montagu's attention was always focused on the doctrines of recent Jesuit Schoolmen. The doctrines of papal infallibility were a recent 'madnes': 'such is their Doctrine since the Jesuites have domineered in their Schooles'. Doctrines of the merit of condignity represented the 'enormous exorbitancie' to which the Schools had grown 'since the Jesuites have swaggered and domineered in them'.[51] On images, Montagu contrasted the idolatry of the 'new Schooles' with the more moderate and acceptable defence of image-worship of other Romanist divines.[52] His appeal throughout his *New Gagg* and *Appello* was to moderate Romanist writers, not simply as useful weapons against more truly Romanist extremists, but as representatives of Rome's true doctrine. Montagu appealed to 'moderate and discreet Pontificians', although he admitted that there were erroneous, factious ones.[53] He did not merely cite these 'moderate and discreet' Romanists against their more radical colleagues, but also often demonstrated how they shared the same views as the Church of England. Thus, on the question of free will, Montagu maintained that there were no material differences between 'the Pontificians, at least of better temper' and the Church of England. He noted that the disputed points on this doctrine were of no great moment. In his *Appello* he more carefully qualified this point by arguing that he meant 'betwixt that Church and ours, for any materiality in this point, betwixt moderate and temperate men on either side', citing the examples of Cassander on Rome's side, and Fricius and Melanchthon on the Protestant side.[54]

Laudian writers were more commonly prepared to argue that Rome's established formal doctrine might still be sound. As we have seen, Montagu and others had already drawn the distinction between Roman doctrine and actual practice when discussing the use of images and the invocation of saints. This meant that they conceded that the heresies and idolatries were not present in the doctrines themselves.[55] John Cosin's detailed study of the Roman liturgy led him to conclude that it contained ammunition against current errors in popular Roman doctrines and prac-

[51] Montagu, *Appello*, pp.122, 203. On the general point of the Jesuits' dominance in the Schools, and their consequent remoulding of traditional doctrine, see Montagu, *ΘΕΑΝΘΡΩΠΙΚΟΝ*, i. p.412. For examples of Montagu's severe language against Jesuits, see Montagu, *Acts and Monuments*, pp.44–5, 414, 423; *idem*, *Appello*, pp.159, 203; *idem*, *New Gagg*, p.65. It is noteworthy that the two Romanist abettors of Montagu's reunion plans – Panzani and Dom Leander – were both strongly anti-Jesuit (Hibbard, *Popish Plot*, pp.65, 263 n.120). Macauley ('Richard Montague', pp.64–5 and n.1, 436 n.2) suggests that Montagu's opposition to Jesuits may also have been rooted in resentment of scholarly malpractice.

[52] See above, pp.194–5. [53] Montagu, *Appello*, p.90. [54] *Ibid.*, pp.95, 83.

[55] See above, pp.191–2, 194–5, 207.

tice. It opposed the Roman practice of private masses, for example, because it assumed the presence of communicants.[56] Similarly, words in the Mass Book argued against the doctrine that the substance of the bread and wine was changed after consecration.[57] Cosin also believed that the form of absolution in the Roman Church's liturgy sufficiently guarded against the error of some ignorant papists who held that absolution could be obtained without contrition.[58] Cosin saw the common principles contained in the liturgies of the Churches of Rome and England as offering a strong base for reconciliation. As long as Rome's public religion (which was the chief concern of Cosin and his associates) persisted in its established form, then the more recent controversial scholastic doctrines were irrelevant. Thus, on the issue of the eucharistic sacrifice, Cosin exclaimed

> Why should we make any controversy about this? They love not the truth of Christ, nor the peace of the Church, that make those disputes between the Church of Rome and us, when we agree, as Christian Churches should, in our Liturgies: what private men's conceits are, what is that to the public approved religion of either Church, which is to be seen in their Liturgies best of all? For, let the schools have what opinions and doctrines they will, and let our new masters frame themselves what divinity they list, as long as neither the one nor the other can get their fancies brought into the service of the Church, honest men may serve God with one heart and one soul, and never trouble themselves with the opinions of them both.[59]

Rome's liturgy, then, might preserve true doctrine, and make more extreme Romanist doctrines irrelevant. But what of the Council of Trent, upon which the modern Church of Rome based herself? Jacobean writers might identify the worst excesses of popery within the Jesuit order, but they held that the Council of Trent had already changed things irreversibly for the worse, and had formally established heretical doctrines as points of Rome's faith. It had been the first task of Trent, noted Prideaux, to secure the survival of the pope's 'Antichristian hierarchy and superstition' by destroying the principle of *sola scriptura*.[60] A new faith was created out of traditions, and a new religion and new foundation thus established.

56 Cosin, *Works*, V: 98. 57 *Ibid.*, V: 108, 109.

58 *Ibid.*, V: 164. Cosin's belief on this point is based on his misunderstanding of a passage from Maldonatus, which does *not* mean that the qualifying phrase to which Cosin refers ('Quantum in me est, et de iure possum, ego te absolvo') was added to Rome's form of absolution; see *ibid.*, V: 164 note b.

59 *Ibid.*, V: 120.

60 John Prideaux, 'Reverence to rulers. A sermon preached at the court', pp.20–1 (*Certaine Sermons*). Prideaux notes that Bellarmine's arguments in his *De Verbo Dei Scripto, et Non Scripto* were 'contrived of purpose to justifie that Councell' (*ibid.*, p.21). Cf. Henry Rogers, *The Protestant Church Existent* (1638), p.111, where he stresses that it was the first decree of Trent, in Session 4, which enthroned unwritten traditions. To dissent from this point was 'to be a Protestant in the maine point', since all errors of faith followed from this.

Trent's doctrines were simply damnable.[61] Morton claimed that 'the three principal points' relating to justification, which had still been preserved inviolate in the works of medieval theologians such as St Bernard, 'seeme to have been anathematized in their last Councell of Trent'.[62] Doctrinal errors had certainly deteriorated further since Trent, but it was at that Council that the fatal die had been cast, and many of Rome's worst heresies had been formally instituted.[63]

Ironically, when Henry Burton seized upon these condemnations of Trent in order to oppose Hall's defence of Rome's status as a church, he drove Hall's defender Cholmley into an outspoken and unparalleled defence of that Council. Cholmley maintained that Trent had reformed some of Rome's doctrines, and he applauded the doctrine contained in the Tridentine Catechism. Cholmley was careful to emphasize that he was making these remarks only in order to display Burton's errors, and not to justify Trent or its Catechism, but there clearly existed sufficient material to justify more moderate assessments of Trent's doctrines, once 'absolute' denials of Rome's heterogeneity were repudiated.[64]

Moreover, general Protestant arguments which invested the Council of Trent with all Rome's greatest heresies ran the risk of being undermined by the widespread rejection of the Council by national churches within Rome's own communion. Jacobean Calvinist authors were happy to describe Roman Catholics' rejection of Trent when they were seeking to oppose Rome's claims to unity and catholicity, but these same writers were less prepared to accept the implications of such diversity for their characterization of the Roman Church. As regards the Gallican Church, the rejection of Trent had effectively been reversed by the acceptance of the decrees of the Tridentine Council by the Assembly of the French Clergy in 1615, as Burton noted.[65] But the rejection of the decrees of Trent elsewhere could still be used as an argument for Rome's moderation, and was thus

[61] Prideaux, *Viginti-duae Lectiones*, i. p.128; Carleton, *Consensus*, p.18; Field, *Of the Church*, IV: 562; Sutcliffe, *An Abridgement*, pp.4–5; Wotton, *Trial*, p.377; Burton, *Baiting*, p.38.

[62] Morton, *Catholike Appeale*, p.460.

[63] This is not to deny that these writers were also capable of noting the sincere reformers among the delegates at Trent, although lamenting that they had been overwhelmed by the papal faction: e.g. Lynde, *Via Tuta*, pp.20–6; Field, *Of the Church*, IV: 562.

[64] Cholmley, *The State*, pp.8–9. For a more negative view of the Tridentine Catechism, see Abbot, *Third Part*, p.195.

[65] Burton, *Babel*, p.113; Wootton, *Paolo Sarpi*, p.87. For observations that the Gallican Church had not received the decrees of the Council of Trent, see Willet, *Antilogie*, pp.15–17; Carleton, *Jurisdiction*, p.110; Downe, *Certaine Treatises*, xii. p.36; Buckeridge, *De Potestate Papae*, p.229; Raleigh, *Certain Queries*, pp.37, 51 and appendix.

employed by de Dominis, when discussing with Thomas Morton his imminent return to Rome.[66]

Laud and his associates were also strongly opposed to Trent, but their opposition tended to focus on the uncanonical nature of its calling and proceedings,[67] and on its lack of authority in adding twelve new articles to the Creed and imposing them as points of faith.[68] Even on this point, however, Buckeridge was happy to point out at the York House Conference that Trent, according to its own terms, could not establish any new articles of faith as necessary to salvation, and concluded that 'as evil as things were carried in the Trident Council, it is hard to demonstrate that the Trident Council hath erred in any article of faith which is directly fundamental'.[69]

Laudian authors generally showed fewer reservations in suggesting that Trent's formally expounded position was more moderate and equivocal than the later formulations of Romanist Schoolmen. On some points of doctrine it met with their clear approval. Montagu could cite Trent's decrees approvingly on the role of man's free will in conversion, and on justification.[70] Andrewes could quote Trent quite happily against indulgences, whose abuse the Council had strongly condemned.[71] Laud, as we have seen, noted the Council's careful warnings against image-worship, which Roman clergy had since failed to enforce.[72] Sancta Clara's later attempts to reconcile the doctrines of Trent and the Thirty-Nine Articles did not meet with disapproval in Laudian circles.

Laudian writers generally placed greater emphasis on Trent's studied ambiguity on many doctrinal points, although they insisted that such

66 When Morton urged the Tridentine canons, de Dominis claimed that there were 'Millies mille . . . in Italia, qui fidem nullam huic Concilio adhibent': Richard Baddeley, *The Life of Dr. Thomas Morton* (York, 1669), p.68. By the 1630s, the non-reception of Trent had in fact become one of the accepted arguments to be used in support of Rome's moderation. William Middleton, when serving as chaplain to Lord Fielding, the English ambassador in Venice, was approached in 1635 by a Franciscan friar asking for his assistance to get him to England. In order to test the sincerity of the Franciscan's intentions, Middleton pretended to plead for Rome, and did so by arguing that she had reformed many things, and 'that all had not received the Councell of Trent; that of those who had, some did mitigate harsher expressions, and were upon courses of Conciliation of both parts, as appeared by a Booke of Franc. a Sancta Clara' (i.e. Sancta Clara's *Deus, Natura, Gratia*). Middleton reported this incident in a letter to Laud in September 1635, printed in Prynne, *Canterburies Doome*, p.429.

67 Laud, *Works*, II: 236–9, 242, 243; Buckeridge, *De Potestate Papae*, pp.69, 70.

68 Laud, *Works*, II: 44, 57, 170, 378 and note l, 379 and note o.

69 Cosin, *Works*, II: 26. This defence of Trent by Buckeridge was quite unnecessary in the context of the Conference, when it would have sufficed simply to have attacked the Council as factious and uncanonical, like the Second Council of Ephesus (*ibid.*, II: 25).

70 Montagu, *Appello*, pp.88–9; *idem*, *New Gagg*, p.145.

71 Andrewes, *Responsio*, p.383.

72 See above, p.192.

doctrinal obscurity was not in itself to be applauded, since its lack of clear definitions had enabled later heresies to flourish.[73] Laud made eager use of Sarpi's observation that Dominicus Soto and Andreas Vega were of opposite views on the issue of assurance, and yet had both written books claiming Tridentine support for their respective opinions, which had been published by authority.[74] Montagu argued that Trent's liberty of belief allowed 'moderate opinions either way' on issues such as the salvation of pagans before the coming of Christ.[75] While Francis White had spoken in frustration of Trent's 'nose of waxe' which could be twisted to suit Vasquez' heresies, William Forbes presented Trent's ambiguities in a more positive light, as giving room for manoeuvre in the search for reconciliation with Rome.[76]

This is not to deny that Laudians could on occasion speak out against the Council of Trent in the most forthright terms.[77] When dealing with those points on which Trent had over-rigidly pronounced anathema, Montagu condemned Trent as 'that Popish Cynosura', and attacked the spirit in which it had been conducted.[78] But his chief complaint was that it had behaved as a faction, and had then laid claim to the authority of a General Council. In this sense, the Council of Trent was rejected, along with the Florentine and Lateran Councils, 'as factious, as bastards, as partiaries, as nothing but the names of Councels'.[79] They were essentially local councils, and their authority was therefore not to be urged upon the Church of England. But while Trent was factiously disposed, Montagu made plain that he did not deny the learning of its members.[80]

[73] Thus Forbes noted that, while the true doctrine of justification could be found in Trent's decrees, her inconsistency had also allowed in dangerously ambiguous scholastic disputations and definitions: Forbes, *Considerationes*, I: 143–7.

[74] Laud, *Works*, II: 57–8.

[75] Montagu, *Acts and Monuments*, pp.49–56.

[76] Thus, on the issue of the merits of congruity and condignity, Forbes noted that the Trent Fathers had avoided mention of either, but knowing of the scholastic quarrels on these issues, had 'according to their custom' judged it best to speak 'only in general and ambiguous terms' on this subject, 'as about very many others': Forbes, *Considerationes*, I: 483–5. He noted that Catharinus and Dominicus Soto had clashed, but both had appealed to the carefully ambiguously worded decree of Trent, which had intentionally been expressed so as to be acceptable to both parties (*ibid.*, I: 243–7; cf. Montagu, *New Gagg*, pp.185–8). He also believed that the ambiguity of the Tridentine Fathers on the issue of invocation might be charitably interpreted as not to be taking it as absolutely necessary: Forbes, *Considerationes*, II: 187.

[77] Thus the papal agent George Con complained that, when discoursing with Laud on the subject of reunion in 1637, the archbishop would stress his desire to adhere to the doctrines of the first 400 years, but would then complain against the Council of Trent: Albion, *Court of Rome*, pp.188–9. Note also the very strong language used against Trent by Cosin in his later *History of Papal Transubstantiation*: *Works*, IV: 264.

[78] Montagu, *Appello*, pp.185, 300.

[79] Montagu, *New Gagg*, preface. Cf. *idem*, *Antidiatribae*, pp.6, 109.

[80] Montagu, *Antidiatribae*, p.6; *idem*, *ΘΕΑΝΘΡΩΠΙΚΟΝ*, ii. p.157.

If Trent had not therefore committed the Church of Rome to fundamental errors from which she was unable to free herself, how far could the errors of her more extreme Jesuit supporters rightly be imputed to her? Richard Montagu emphasized in the 'Address to the Reader' of his *New Gagg* the crucial distinction which he made throughout his work between the public resolutions of the Church of England and the private opinions of its Calvinist members. This argument was not applied solely to the English Church. Montagu established it as a general principle relating to all churches, including the Church of Geneva, and maintained that it held true even in the present Church of Rome, 'notwithstanding the conclusions of the Councell of Trent'.[81] In fact, it emerged in the treatise that Montagu was just as keen to free the institutional Church of Rome from the similar indignity of having Jesuits' errors imputed to her official doctrine.[82]

This meant that the Jesuits' doctrinal errors were not of the same importance in assessing the doctrine of the Roman Church. Accordingly, the opinions of moderate Roman writers might be read in a more positive light, not merely as providing ammunition to oppose Rome's claims to catholicity, but also as expressive of more moderate currents of thought within Roman Catholicism, which might facilitate eventual reconciliation with Rome. Montagu was convinced of the existence within Rome of important moderate divines, 'men of later standing, greater learning, and more ingenuity amongst Roman Confessionists, in that Church, then Baronius, or some other of that rigid stampe'.[83] He was even ready to take seriously the moderation implicit in the doctrine of the pope's indirect deposing power.[84] William Forbes was able to present a platform for reconciliation with Rome on many articles of faith in his *Considerationes Modestae et Pacificae* because, while still offering a very firm critique of Rome's doctrinal irregularities, he was prepared to accept more moderate

[81] Montagu, *New Gagg*, 'To the Reader'; pp.170–1. Cf. *idem*, *Diatribae*, p.156.

[82] E.g. Montagu noted in the *New Gagg*'s preface that the Jesuits had swerved from the Council of Trent by granting a far greater prerogative to the Tridentine Latin edition of the bible than the Council itself had ever intended. See also Montagu, *Diatribae*, p.161. Cf. Maie, *Communion of Saints* (2nd impression), sig.B1v.

[83] Montagu, *Acts and Monuments*, p.463.

[84] While Montagu did not doubt that it was 'the profession generally of the Canonists, Congregatio Oratorii, and many others in the Church of Rome . . . that the pope directly, without any reflecting upon the spirituall ends, hath fulnesse of power and authority over all the world, as well in temporall as spirituall things', he noted, however, that Bellarmine had offered careful qualifications of this doctrine, arguing that as Christ as man on earth had no temporal dominion, therefore the pope, who represented Christ on earth, also had no temporal dominion. While Sixtus V had denounced this qualification, Montagu felt sure that 'doubtlesse, such moderate men as Urban the eighth will never trouble the world therewithall' (Montagu, *Acts and Monuments*, p.494). By contrast, other writers had firmly and comprehensively rejected Bellarmine's arguments on this issue: Field, *Of the Church*, III: 497–518; Abbot, *Third Part*, p.25.

defences of Rome's doctrines as occupying an important and representative position on the spectrum of religious views available in contemporary Roman Catholicism.

The more that moderate Romanists were regarded as representing an important stream in Romanist thought, the more likely it was that the pacificatory, irenical writers such as George Cassander might begin to be appreciated in their own terms. For some, Cassander was not simply a source of useful ammunition against Rome, but rather represented an authoritative voice on the nature of the break with Rome, and thus a possible source of inspiration for irenical ideas. When the young Ralph Brownrigg asked him for an author 'that did fully determine howe farre fourth we ought to depart from the Church of Roome', the later Laudian John Pocklington allegedly directed him to Cassander's *Consultations*, 'as to the best Author for satisfaction of that question'.[85] The young William Chillingworth was inspired to convert to Rome by the conciliatory writings of Cassander, with their emphasis on remaining silent on official articles of belief in the interests of maintaining Christian unity.[86] William Forbes' pacificatory schemes relied upon treating various moderate, irenical Romanist writers as representative of their church's teaching. While he drew heavily on the irenical writings of de Dominis and Cassander, Forbes also made occasional practical use of Constable's *Examen Pacifique*,[87] and of ecumenically minded Romanist writers such as Wicelius and John Barnes.[88] It was the irenical Roman divines who were the especial heroes of Montagu's works. In his *Apparatus*, Montagu argued earnestly for peace with Rome in all the unnecessary controversies which currently plagued theological writings, and he lauded the irenicist George Cassander ('vir usque ad miraculum eruditus ipsissima modestia & probatis anima') and his 'aureum libellum de officio viri pii', and Andreas Fricius, who had suffered unjust condemnation, not just from Jesuits, but also from Calvin.[89]

As we have seen, Cassander had in the past simply been seen as a source of anti-papal material. Thomas Morton had noted with concern in his

[85] CUL, MS VC Ct I.8 fol.255v, MS Mm/1/46 p.387; *The Petition ... against John Pocklington*, p.29.

[86] Orr, *Reason and Authority*, pp.18–19.

[87] E.g. Forbes, *Considerationes*, II: 133, 287, 595.

[88] For Wicelius, see, for example, *ibid.*, I: 87, II: 121–3, 179, 285, 303, 589. For Barnes, see *ibid.*, I: 247–51, II: 67, 133–5, 181, 287, 593–5, 601. It may well have been a fragment of Wicelius' *Methodus concordiae ecclesiasticae* which Montagu reported having come across in a letter to Cosin of 27 May (1626?): BL, Add. MS 4274 fol.97. Montagu could not discover the author's identity, but thought the work 'worth the having'. Cosin also possessed and annotated a copy of Wicelius' *Exercitamena* (1555): DUL, Cosin Library D.IV.38/1.

[89] Montagu, *Apparatus*, p.45.

Catholike Appeale that recent Romanist polemicists had attempted to use Cassander and Wicelius as Protestant witnesses against the Protestants, whereas the Protestants used them against Rome. In order to prove Cassander's status as a *bona fide* Romanist, Morton quoted Beza and Osiander attacking him.[90] For Morton, Calvinist attacks on Cassander strengthened his argument, as they proved Cassander not to be a Protestant. To Richard Montagu however, as to William Covell, Cassander was a far-sighted irenical writer, and the Protestants undermined their claim to moderation and catholicity by opposing him. Calvin's attack upon Cassander, like those of Beza and Osiander, was thus to be deplored.[91]

The Laudian divine Christopher Potter also displayed a notable interest in irenical Romanist writers. He stressed that not all Roman Catholics were 'fully Jesuited', claiming that the possibility of salvation for Protestants was maintained by 'many learned and moderate men living in the outward Communion of that Church (among the French, Venetians, and elsewhere)'.[92] It was Potter's main anxiety to prove from Romanist evidence that the Protestants joined with the Romanists in the fundamental truths which gave her the essence of a church. To this end, Potter cited with approval the *Examen Pacifique*, as well as a remarkable and little-known book, the *Syllabus aliquot Synodorum Colloquiorum Doctorum pro Pace Ecclesiae* of 1628.[93] This work, published under the pseudonym of 'Theodosius Irenaeus', was a large catalogue of learned Romanist and Protesant irenical authors and works (including Richard Montagu's *Appello Caesarem*) which had been compiled explicitly in order to promote reunion between Protestants and Romanists.[94] Potter used the work simply in order

[90] Morton, *Catholike Appeale*, sig.B3r. Note also Robert Abbot's firm denial that Erasmus was a Protestant: R. Abbot, *Third Part*, pp.48–9.

[91] Montagu, *Apparatus*, p.45. See also Covell's remark above p.240.

[92] Potter, *Want of Charitie*, i. p.4.

[93] *Ibid.*, i. p.82.

[94] On the background to this work, see G.H.M. Posthumus Meyjes, 'Jean Hotman's *Syllabus* of eirenical literature', in Baker, *Reform*, pp.175–93. Meyjes points out that this catalogue was purposely disseminated among political and church leaders in the hope that it might form the basis for a form of Christian reunion (*ibid.*, pp.192–3), although the passages which he cites from *Briefe G.M. Lingelsheims, M. Berneggers und Ihrer Freunde*, ed. A. Reifferscheid (Heilbronn, 1889), do not mention any British divines by name (I am very grateful to Dr Ronald Asch for photocopying the relevant sections for me from a copy of Reifferscheid's work in Münster). It would be interesting to know precisely how the work came into Potter's hands. It is tempting to suggest that the work may have been passed on to him by Richard Montagu, who had appointed Potter to the precentorship of Chichester Cathedral in 1631 (Macauley, 'Richard Montague', p.404). Montagu's own *Appello Caesarem* appears in the catalogue, with a note by Hotman that in this work 'la reformation de l'Eglise Anglicane est maintenue; tant contre les Puritains que contre les catholiques Romains; est monstre neantmoins que nous accordons tous les poincts essentiels & fondamentaux de la religion Chrestienne': *Syllabus aliquot synodorum et colloquiorum* (Strasbourg, 1628), sig.D2v. Other English works cited in the catalogue

to support his argument that Romanists allowed salvation among the Protestants, and to this extent he was merely following the polemical practice which Hall explained in his own use of Sancta Clara. However, Potter's *Want of Charitie* constantly invoked the diversity within Rome's communion, not simply in order to undermine the arguments of more implacable Romanist opponents, but to make an important general point concerning church unity. Potter's entire work was argued around notions of church unity in fundamentals which clearly owed their inspiration to the irenicist Acontius, whose *Stratagemata Satanae* he had directed to be printed in Oxford two years earlier.[95]

Sancta Clara's irenical schemes found support among at least some of the Laudians. The Franciscan was well aware of Montagu's reunion plans, and the two may have been in close contact.[96] Augustine Lindsell, a close friend of Montagu and Laud, was responsible for presenting Sancta Clara to Laud when the irenicist was at work on his *Deus, Natura, Gratia*. Laud later claimed at his trial that he had warned that he did not believe that the Franciscan would expound the Thirty-Nine Articles in a way that would help the Church of England, and there seems no reason to doubt the archbishop's word.[97] Nevertheless, Sancta Clara's general aims won some

include the Preface to the Prayer Book, the 1604 Canons, Thomas Morton's *Apologia Catholica*, Thomas Bilson's *Perpetual Government*, Hooker's *Laws of Ecclesiastical Polity*, Sandys' *Relation of the State of Religion* and (rather bizarrely) Perkins' *Reformed Catholike* (*ibid.*, sigs.D1v–D2v).

95 Crosfield, *Diary*, p.50. Acontius' work is cited in the *Syllabus*, sig.C3r. However, Dr Windsor has forcefully argued that the Roman Church could not have been drawn into any of the irenical models proposed by Acontius, which were drawn up more with the Protestants in mind: Windsor, 'The controversy', p.481 n.1.

96 See PRO, MS 31/9/17B: Panzani to Barberini, 10/20 February 1636. Sancta Clara cites Montagu's arguments (chiefly from his *Appello*) in *Deus, Natura, Gratia* (1634 edn), pp.7, 55, 68, 133, 158, 181, 211, 245, 260, 276; see also *idem*, *Paraphrastica*, pp.11, 13, 41, 60, 76, 105. Sancta Clara certainly consulted some more moderate English divines on some of the issues dealt with in this work; see *Paraphrastica*, p.105. The second edition of this work, published in 1635, is greatly expanded in several areas (F.G. Lee's 1865 edition of the *Paraphrastica* – the appendix to Sancta Clara's *Deus, Natura, Gratia* – only uses the text of the shorter 1634 edition). He inserts a number of references to Choun's recently published *Collectiones* (2nd edn, pp.189, 356, 398, 416, 434), and the *Paraphrastica* includes many new references to Saxon material, which may conceivably have been passed on to him by Montagu and Spelman (e.g., 2nd edn, pp.370, 387, 390). It also includes an 'Epistolium Apologeticum', in which he cites Carier's *Treatise* for the congruity of the Church of England's Confession in most points with the Church of Rome, and for the argument that only reasons of political corruption and self-interest separated the Church of England from Rome, between whom a unity might be effected if the puritans could be removed (sig.B4r–v). The later edition also makes many further attacks upon 'Puritans', rather than simply Calvinists (e.g., 2nd edn, pp.165, 218, 364, 382, 389), and its *Paraphrastica* dwells more upon the crime and terror of schism (2nd edn, pp.415–16).

97 Prynne, *Canterburies Doome*, p.427; Laud, *Works*, IV: 326. Laud did, however, keep a bound copy of the work in his study with the king's arms on the cover. A copy of the

support among Laudian writers. Christopher Dow wrote approvingly of the Franciscan's attempts to moderate the differences with Rome, which extremists such as Henry Burton only tried to increase.[98] Peter Heylyn was most concerned in his 1637 *Briefe and Moderate Answer* to deny the direct involvement of the bishops in the publication of Sancta Clara's book, but in his later work he defended the integrity of the treatise, and its possible use in the composition of the controversies with Rome.[99]

A general awareness of the Church of Rome's heterogeneity made Laudians potentially more receptive to the writings of moderate and irenical Romanist divines. This was not a receptivity which was always apparent; Laud himself would seem to have remained singularly unimpressed by the relevance of irenical Romanist ideas or the influence which they might command. Moreover, the roots of this positive perception of Roman diversity may be found among many mainstream writers of the Jacobean period, including King James himself. Nevertheless, liberated from the 'absolute' views of a uniformly antichristian Rome which had neutralized this positive assessment, Laudian writers were at least potentially free to re-examine the significance of the doctrines of more moderate Romanists, and to pursue with more than academic interest the question of the reunion of the churches.

THE POLITICS OF ROMAN HETEROGENEITY

The question of whether Rome's communion was monolithic or heterogeneous was not simply a pedantic theological nicety. It was an issue which was raised in a particularly acute form for all Englishmen since King James himself was dedicated to carrying out a domestic policy which presupposed that, at least on political issues, the Roman communion was divided in a significant and practical way. It was here that the tension between Protestants' theoretical vision of a monolithic papacy and their practical presupposition of Roman heterogeneity was exacerbated, and forced to confront direct political implications.

As a governor rather than a mere theologian, James was more pre-

work was also given to his old college of St John's in 1636 by Arthur and John Amherst: J.F. Fuggles, 'A history of the library of St John's College, Oxford' (Oxford University BLitt, 1975), p.152.

98 Dow, *Innovations*, pp.44–5.

99 Heylyn, *Briefe Answer*, p.123; *idem*, *Cyprianus*, pp.414, 416. See also Bramhall, *Works*, III: 524. On Sancta Clara, see J.B. Dockery, *Christopher Davenport* (1960), and discussions of his work in M. Nedoncelle, *Trois aspects du problème anglo-catholique au XVIIe siècle* (Paris, 1951), pp.88–96; G.H. Tavard, *The Seventeenth Century Tradition* (Leiden, 1978), pp.133–57; R.I. Bradley, 'Christopher Davenport and the Thirty-Nine Articles', *AfR* 52 (1961).

occupied than most English Protestant authors with testing the validity of distinctions between moderate and radical Romanists, at least with respect to their political behaviour. He was committed to weeding out those of his Romanist subjects whose political loyalty he doubted, among whom he included many of the Romanist clergy and lay apostates from Protestantism. On the other hand, he was eager to offer tolerance to those more moderate Romanists who, whatever their other doctrinal errors, were prepared to reject the papal power to depose kings and hence posed him no direct political threat. The Oath of Allegiance would appear to have been merely one aspect of this general policy. It could be construed (and was by some Romanist contemporaries) as a means of enabling moderate Romanists to demonstrate their political obedience to the king and win effective tolerance by repudiating the pope's deposing power without necessarily denying their faith as such. James' words and actions after the Gunpowder Plot would certainly appear to confirm this. He argued publicly after the Plot that Romanists exceeded even devil-worshippers in their capacity to preach the overthrow of governments, but emphasized at the same time that 'many catholics were good men and loyal subjects'. Even the Oath itself was only intermittently imposed on Romanists: James' instructions to the judges in 1608 stipulated that the Oath was only to be tendered to 'apostates and practizers', while judges should show a 'mild inclination' to the rest. Even when James approved a stricter enforcement of the Oath in 1610, he still defended his policy of making a consistent practical distinction between the two different types of Romanists, explaining that 'I have noted two kinds of papists in this kingdom, the one ancient the other apostates, who shall never have my favour or good looks ... For the ancient papists there is divers of them so honest and fair-conditioned men as if I were a subject I could be content to live and spend my time with them.'[100]

James' policy thus rested on accepting the good faith and sincerity of moderate Romanists. At first glance, this would not seem to be a principle that was alien to the thinking of his Protestant subjects. In order to prove the existence and importance of Romanists who opposed the pope's deposing power, English Protestant writers under James made regular polemical use of the political conflicts within Roman Catholicism over the papal supremacy. The French and Venetian Churches here offered plentiful material for Protestant polemicists to employ against Rome's assertions on these points. This was a fundamental division within Rome, as Andrewes, Archbishop Abbot and Bedell pointed out. It particularly attracted the

[100] Fincham and Lake, 'Ecclesiastical policy', pp.184–6; Dures, *English Catholicism*, pp.46–8. Cf. King James, *Political Works*, pp.323, 341.

attention of English Protestant divines during the Oath of Allegiance controversy, when the defence of their temporal liberties by the French Church and crown provided English polemicists, and indeed King James himself, with useful examples with which to justify the Oath's rejection of the pope's usurping claims to universal jurisdiction.[101] For their part, the Gallicans regularly condemned Jesuit contributions to the oath of allegiance controversy.[102] The Oath of Allegiance which the Gallican Third Estate proposed to impose upon the realm at the 1614 Estates General was actually modelled on the Oath enforced by King James.[103]

The divisions among England's own Roman Catholics on issues of ecclesiastical government had attracted much government interest from the last years of Elizabeth onwards following the outbreak of the Archpriest controversy. During this dispute, a minority of seculars (the Appellants) clashed with the Jesuits over the imposition of an Archpriest, and sought toleration from the Protestant government by avowing a greater political loyalty than the Jesuits.[104] The bitter exchanges of the Appellant controversy proved a bonanza for anti-papal polemicists such as Thomas Bell, and the violently anti-Jesuit diatribes of Watson and others were quoted with monotonous regularity in popular anti-papal works.[105] The books of the Appellant priests had all been published in London with the connivance of the authorities, and Bancroft received regular correspondence from Appellant authors.[106] Matthew Sutcliffe intruded into the Appellant controversy itself, and under Archbishop Bancroft the Church of England's propaganda machine was careful to nourish dissenting Romanist works against papal and Jesuit authority in the context of the Oath of Allegiance controversy, when Romanist opinion divided again. Thus the anti-papal *De Potestate Papae* composed by the Scots Roman Catholic William Barclay was posthumously published in London in 1609 after being revised and edited by Archbishop Bancroft. The ensuing controversy over the pope's temporal power between Bellarmine and his colleagues and the

101 Andrewes, *Responsio*, pp.449–50; Bedell, *Certaine Letters*, pp.44–5, 58; Abbot, *The Reasons*, pp.124–5, cf. p.220; King James, *Political Works*, pp.119, 264–5.

102 Milward, *Jacobean Controversies*, pp. 97, 99, 102.

103 W.J. Bouwsma, 'Gallicanism and the nature of Christendom', in A. Molho and J. Tedeschi (eds.), *Renaissance Studies in Honor of Hans Baron* (Dekalb, Ill., 1971), p.827.

104 On the Archpriest controversy see Milward, *Elizabethan Controversies*, pp.116–24; Pritchard, *Loyalism*, ch.7; T.G. Law (ed.), *The Archpriest Controversy* (2 vols., Camden Society n.s. 56 and 58, 1896 and 1898).

105 E.g. Willet, *Antilogie*, pp.14, 30, 32, 35, 56–7, 61, 77, 85, 135–6; Abbot, *Defence*, p.153; *idem*, *Second Part*, pp.729–30; Gifford, 'The controversy', p.29. On Appellant anti-Jesuit writings, see Pritchard, *Loyalism*, pp.175–91. For an example of enthusiastic lay Protestant reading of Appellant works, see Manningham, *Diary*, p.51.

106 Pritchard, *Loyalism*, pp.68, 125–6, 170, 226–7 n.90; Milward, *Elizabethan Controversies*, p.118.

English seculars Thomas Preston and John Barclay attracted the Church of England's closest attention, leading eventually to the intervention of Bishops Buckeridge and Morton, and of Richard Crakanthorp.[107] The government also sponsored other Roman Catholic writings in defence of the Oath of Allegiance.[108]

While these Roman political divisions were noted, it is not clear that English Protestants had much respect for the integrity of the anti-Jesuit participants. There is still less evidence that the recognition of such Roman divisions had any effect on those more 'absolute' views of the monolithic nature of Rome's power which we have seen to be so prominent in Jacobean Calvinist doctrinal analyses. Despite their use of Appellant writings, Calvinist conformist divines did not believe in the good faith of Appellants who claimed to defend King James' cause. Bancroft, who promoted their works against the Jesuits, was reported to have 'termed both sides knaves, but the Appellants good instruments to serve the state'. Robert Abbot claimed that the seculars and Jesuits were as bad as each other, and that the English crown had profited from their conflict 'according to the proverbe, that when theeves fall out, true men come by their goods'. Thomas Bell was happy to exploit Appellant writings, but reflected that their only real motive was 'to save their owne neckes from the halter'. Andrew Willet emphasized that, whatever their supposed differences on the issue of political loyalty, all Romanists were essentially birds of one feather and owed allegiance to the pope.[109]

Some puritans felt an even deeper unease over the Appellant writings, and saw the whole conflict as a sinister, contrived popish plot to obtain toleration. They therefore concentrated on refuting the self-justifications of Appellant writers, rather than exploiting the apparent divisions within Roman Catholicism.[110] Indeed, so great was the distrust of Appellant writers, and so monolithic the English Protestants' image of Rome, that some puritans became increasingly anxious at the government's patronage of these publications. The defence of the Millenary Petition complained of

107 Salmon, *Renaissance*, p.181; Milward, *Jacobean Controversies*, pp.101–9. See also *CSPD 1611–18*, p.22.

108 See T.H. Clancy, *Papist Pamphleteers* (Chicago, 1964); L. Rostenberg, *The Minority Press and the English Crown: A Study in Repression 1558–1625* (Nieuwkoop, 1971); D. Lunn, *The English Benedictines 1540–1688* (1980), chs.2 and 4; Sommerville, 'Jacobean political thought', ch.1. See also Gaffney, 'Religious controversy in Dublin', pp.150–1.

109 Foley, *Records*, I: 42; Abbot, *Defence*, p.8, cf. sigs.A2v–A3r, pp.5–12, 211; Thomas Bell, *The Anatomie of Popish Tyrannie* (1603), pp.145–6; Andrew Willet, *A Catholicon* (1602), sig.A7 (Bell and Willet passages quoted in Weiner, 'Beleaguered isle', p.38). Cf. Thomas James, *The Iesuits Downefall* (Oxford, 1612), sigs.*3v-*4r.

110 Milward, *Elizabethan Controversies*, pp.124–6. The pamphlets in question are *An Antiquodlibet, or An Advertisement to beware of Secular Priests* (1602) and *Let Quilibet Beware Quodlibet* (1602). See also Digges, *Humble Motives*, pp.29–39.

Bancroft's involvement in the publication of Appellant works 'under pretence of pollicy and state wisdome', and James was forced to defend him when the issue was raised at Hampton Court.[111] However much Roman writers acknowledged the damage done to their cause by Appellant writings, and later by those composed by Benedictines in favour of the Oath of Allegiance, more extreme puritans found it impossible to conquer their anxieties over the complicity of the government with Romanist writers. Archbishop Abbot was forced to defend in parliament the comfortable state enjoyed in prison by Thomas Preston – the principal Romanist defender of the Oath and therefore an invaluable weapon for the government – against accusations of favouring popery.[112] In point of fact, Abbot was himself uneasy when offering patronage to Roman ministers. In the same letter in which he informed William Trumbull that he was aiding Preston's work, Abbot complained of the recent defection of the 'Oath' pamphleteer John Barclay to Rome with the rueful comment: 'I trust it will teache us heere how wee putt any confidence in any of the popes brood, howsoever out of politicke reasons they seeme to mince their Popery.'[113]

There was a sense, of course, in which English Protestants were right to doubt Appellant assertions of loyalty to the king. Despite the Appellant Protestation of Allegiance in 1603, one of its signatories led the opposition to the Oath of Allegiance, while two others were executed after refusing to take the Oath.[114] Nevertheless, if James was hoping to assure himself of the validity of his Romanist subjects' avowals of loyalty, his churchmen were unlikely to support him. This became most evident in divines' response to the Oath itself, where the aims of James and his Protestant subjects seemed at times to be completely at variance.

THE OATH OF ALLEGIANCE: A HETEROGENEITY OF MOTIVES

The simple recognition that there were moderate and extreme Romanists was a commonplace of Elizabethan and Jacobean thought. There was an extent to which most English Protestant laymen worked on the practical assumption that there were both good and bad papists, and that these two types might easily be distinguished. This assumption had no clear rationale

111 Bodl., Bodley MS 124 p.63; *CSPD 1603–10*, p.109; Barlow, *Summe*, pp.50–1; cf. Strype, *Whitgift*, III: 409. For an example of the mistakes which might be made by incautious government connivance in Appellant publications, see the case of Robert Southwell's *An Humble Supplication to Her Majesty*, discussed in Pritchard, *Loyalism*, p.68.

112 M.J. Havran, *The Catholics in Caroline England* (1962), pp.63–4. Modern historians have not proved immune to such misinterpretations: e.g. Lambert, 'Committees', p.87.

113 *HMC Downshire* V (1988), p.422.

114 J. Bossy, 'The English catholic community 1603–1625', in A.G.R. Smith (ed.), *The Reign of James VI and I* (1973), pp.93–5.

within the formal English Protestant position against Rome, but worked perfectly well in practice. In part, this is an example of the type of anomalies which occur whenever a severely 'absolute' form of confessional argument meets the realities and practical demands of social and political life, and the compromises which this inevitably entails. Only theorists and extremists have the luxury of organizing their lives around unyielding orthodoxies. For example, even puritanically minded laymen apparently had no qualms in trading directly with the Spanish enemy even at the height of war.[115]

Moreover, James' distinction between moderate and radical Romanists built to some extent on received government wisdom. Although recusancy legislation and Privy Council directives under Elizabeth had often seemed to assume a direct and inescapable correlation between an individual's religious and political loyalties, they did also sometimes distinguish between different types of Romanist. The Royal Proclamation of 1602 had recognized that Romanists could, in a sense, be loyal subjects, and tended to be more anti-Jesuit than anti-Appellant.[116] Practical distinctions between different types of Romanist recusants, and resulting compromises, were typical aspects of the lives of the English Protestant laity, and when the 1604 Canons instructed ministers to distinguish 'Popish recusants' from those 'popishly given' they built on received practical distinctions. When it came to the implementation of penalties against recusants, members of the gentry and nobility often intervened to protect their recusant neighbours to whom they felt bound by ties of kinship, and economic and political interest.[117] The widespread phenomenon of 'church papistry' also helped to complicate confessional boundaries. Even in the Long Parliament, and at the height of fears of a popish plot, godly MPs attempted to ensure that their own recusant friends would be exempted from the further anti-recusant legislation under discussion. Moreover, when it came to international affairs, even dedicated puritans could see the value of supporting

[115] P. Croft, 'Trading with the enemy, 1585–1604', *HJ* 32 (1989), pp.281–302.

[116] Pritchard, *Loyalism*, pp.128–9, 146; Dures, *English Catholicism*, pp.29–34; Havran, *Catholics*, p.30; D. Loades, 'Relations between the Anglican and Roman Catholic Churches in the sixteenth and seventeenth centuries', in Aveling *et al.*, *Rome and the Anglicans*, p.32.

[117] Pritchard, *Loyalism*, p.40; J.C.H. Aveling, *Northern Catholics* (1966), pp.115–18; Dures, *English Catholicism*, pp.31–3, 81–2; Havran, *Catholics*, pp.99–104; D. MacCulloch, 'Catholic and puritan in Elizabethan Suffolk: a county community polarises', *AfR* 72 (1981), pp.257–61; J.T. Cliffe, *The Yorkshire Gentry from the Reformation to the Civil War* (1969), pp.203, 214; F. Heal, *Hospitality in Early Modern England* (Oxford, 1990), pp.169–73; J.C.H. Aveling, *The Handle and the Axe* (1976), pp.158–60; E. Cardwell, *Synodalia. A Collection of Articles of Religion, Canons and Proceedings of Convocation in the Province of Canterbury* (2 vols., Oxford, 1842), I: 309. See also Whitgift's complaint in Strype, *Whitgift*, III: 108; Featley, *Clavis*, p.495.

Catholic France against the Catholic Habsburgs, as the lesser of two evils.[118] Outside the specific confines of polemical debate, authors of works of political geography such as Edwin Sandys also felt free to make more perceptive and value-free analyses of the various divisions within Roman Catholicism.[119]

Nevertheless, James was attempting to push far further than the practical *modus vivendi* outlined above. His hopes that he might secure a certain *de facto* toleration of Romanists, and that Romanist loyalty to himself and the Oath might be seen in positive terms, ran up against a rigidly monolithic theoretical view of the nature of Rome propounded by English Protestants in both doctrinal and political spheres. Whatever the king's plans might have been, the same reluctance to take moderate Romanists seriously which we have noted in general Jacobean anti-popery was manifest in the political situation.

In part, the fortunes of the Oath were hampered by the fact that it followed hard on the heels of the earlier Appellant controversy and the Romanist appeals for toleration which had accompanied James' accession to the throne. These disputes had prompted even conformist writers such as Powel and Robert Abbot to insist that papal moderation or loyalty was essentially impossible, and had led to an emphasis in Protestant writing on the evils of toleration and the need to uphold true religion in unadulterated form for the safety of the State.[120] The Gunpowder Plot had merely acted to heighten the conviction that political loyalty and Roman Catholicism were incompatible. In the wake of the Plot, authors such as Oliver Ormerod insisted that all Romanists without exception were necessarily treacherous: their religion bound them all 'to play the traytours, and to take uppe armes against your countrey'. Another pamphleteer announced in 1606 that 'this will alwayes be the keeping of the dirige, a Papist, a catholick, a traytor, a traytor'. These were not just the arguments of minor pamphleteers: Thomas Morton declared frankly in his *Exact Discoverie of Romish Doctrine* of 1605 that 'now we may aswell expect grapes from thornes, or a white Aethiopian, as loyall subiection from this Religion'.[121]

The Oath of Allegiance emerged in the midst of a collection of severe anti-recusant legislation in the aftermath of the Gunpowder Plot. As J.V. Gifford has pointed out, the king and parliament probably held starkly different views of what the Oath was meant to achieve. Parliament may

118 Russell, *Fall*, pp.234 n.109, 421–2; M.A. Breslow, *A Mirror of England* (Cambridge, Mass., 1970), pp.103–4, 112, 114, 115, 147.

119 Sandys, *Europae Speculum*, *passim*.

120 See above chs.1 and 4; also Russell, *Unrevolutionary England*, pp.189–204.

121 Ormerod, *Picture of a Papist*, p.180; P.S., *Feareful Newes of Thunder and Lightning* (1606); Thomas Morton, *An Exact Discoverie of Romish Doctrine* (1605), pp.51–2; Gifford, 'The controversy', pp.26–8.

well have wanted to pass an Oath which would be unacceptable to pure Romanists, and which would therefore incriminate anyone who refused to take it, thereby unveiling treacherous intent. It would thus simply be another weapon in the drive to flush out recusancy. However, it was apparently the king's hope that he might split the Romanist camp, and marginalize the more extreme Jesuits, by appealing directly to moderate Romanists. This led him to intervene in order to remove from the Oath the denial that the pope could excommunicate the king, thereby making the Oath itself less objectionable to Romanists, and raising the possibility that moderate Romanists might actually take it.[122]

For those Protestants anxious to prosecute Roman Catholicism in all its forms, the possibility that Romanists would actually take the Oath, while still remaining in some sense Romanists, rendered it of little value, and indeed perhaps served to make it dangerous. It was this fear that was strongly expressed by one Jacobean preacher before his sermon at Paul's Cross, who declared simply that 'Conformity to the Oath of Allegiance, and other outward formall satisfactions of the State, concurring with a resolution to continue in Poperie, is farre more pernicious to the State, then open and professed Recusancie.' It was conforming papists, this preacher averred, who posed the greatest danger to the state, especially as their taking of the Oath incurred the displeasure of their priests, who would require them to atone for their misdeed with some heinous offence. Scattered examples of Romanist Oath-takers promising priests that they would find means to atone for their misdeed would suggest that this fear was not quite as unrealistic as it might seem.[123]

It was this conflicting view of the purpose of the Oath which set the tone for debates over recusancy legislation during the rest of James' reign. Parliament constantly presented bills which were directed at the general recusant community, while James consistently altered them so that they only applied to priests and Jesuits.[124] The subsequent administration of the Oath was fitful, to say the least, especially during the time of the Spanish Match, and James continued to be criticized for his lenient treatment of recusants.[125]

What is clear, however, is that most English Protestant writing in the

122 Gifford, 'The controversy', pp.54–6; Questier, 'Phenomenon', pp.183, 213–18.

123 Bernard, *A Key*, sigs.B2v–C2r. Bernard here quotes the words of his friend 'Mr Ro. B.' (perhaps Robert Bolton). For an example of why these fears were raised, see the example of a Romanist who travelled over the Channel with beads and popish books, and yet was willing to take the Oath and conform to the Church of England when requested to do so: *CSPD 1611–18*, p.405. See also Walsham, *Church Papists*.

124 S. Lambert, 'Richard Montagu, Arminianism and censorship', *P&P* 124 (1989), pp.52–3; *idem*, 'Committees', pp.81–3.

125 Gifford, 'Controversy', pp.36, 68–79.

wake of the Oath of Allegiance paid scant attention to the sort of distinction which James seems to have been attempting. After the Gunpowder Plot, most writers (and many officials) were keener to incriminate as many Romanists as possible. Roman Catholicism was represented as essentially a seditious religion, whose practitioners could all be assumed to be traitors, regardless of whether they were secular or Jesuit.[126] Robert Abbot thus insisted against his Romanist opponent that 'in making men Papists you make them eyther actually traitours, or if not actually because they knowe not yet the secret of your occupation, yet in Potentia proxima to bee wrought upon for any traiterous executions. For the fundamentall points of your religion are meerely treason'; although he admitted that there were some orderly, good subjects who were Romanists 'fitter for us then therefore for you', but who 'by their owne wilfulnesse' bore a 'needles disgrace'. Whatever conceptual distinctions might be afforded between 'moderate' and 'radical' papists, Church and Court of Rome, Prideaux argued the basically treasonous nature of all papists, who could not be bound by vows.[127] The 'absolute' faith of Roman Catholics did indeed make rebellion possible: 'none can bee an absolute Papist, but (if hee thoroughly understand himselfe, and live under a Christian Prince that hath renounced the popes authority) must needs, being put unto it, bee an absolute traytour'.[128] This absolute view of Rome was enshrined in the highly emotive prayer for the 5 November in the Prayer Book, which condemned those 'whose Religion is Rebellion, whose Faith is Faction'.

Thomas Jackson, in a sermon delivered on that day, thoroughly endorsed the prayer's argument. The source of the Gunpowder Plotters' action must be sought in the very nature of Rome's religion, which could easily prompt such an attempt again.[129] It was foolish to suggest that all Romish priests and Jesuits would consider themselves obliged in conscience to obey their native king or country in any degree more than Turks or heathens might feel bound by Christian laws when dealing with their religious enemies. Any man who could suggest such a thing, Jackson commented, 'is either a novice, altogether unacquainted with the fundamental points of Romish religion, as it is now taught, or an ambidexter betwixt us and them'.[130] As for those claiming to be Roman Catholics who

126 Sommerville, 'Jacobean political thought', pp.13–14.

127 Abbot, *Defence*, pp.214–15; John Prideaux, 'Gowries conspiracy', pp.11–13 and *passim* (*Certaine Sermons*).

128 John Prideaux, 'Higgaion and Selah: for the discovery of the Powder Plot', p.17 and *passim* (*Certaine Sermons).*

129 Jackson wrote that their act was 'but such a descant upon the grounds of Rome's religion (as it is now taught), as most men of their disposition for religion ... will be ready to make, whensoever opportunity ... shall be offered': Jackson, *Works*, XII: 331–2.

130 *Ibid.*, XII: 341.

were not 'of this temper and resolution', Jackson argued that they could not really be held to be 'true Roman Catholics'.[131]

However, such arguments seemed to undermine King James' claim that the Oath was not designed to prosecute or indeed to touch upon Romanists' religion, but only on certain unnecessary doctrines concerning temporal matters which had been falsely derived from it. It was just this point which was raised by Thomas Morton's Romanist opponent in the early 1630s (possibly Lord Arundel) who had complained of being condemned, not for having a disloyal heart, but simply for being of the Romish religion. In reply, Morton acknowledged that not all lay Romanists accepted the subjection taught by Rome. But while some Romanists might not follow the priests in such seditious doctrines, Morton did not doubt that the doctrine taught by the Jesuits was essentially rebellious.[132] Despite allowing this heterogeneity, Morton accepted the sentiments of the Prayer Book as expounded by Prideaux and Jackson, that the absolute religion of Rome was indeed rebellion and its faith faction. If some members of the Church of Rome did not adhere to such ideas, then they were the less true members of the Romish religion. King James himself had often argued in these terms.[133] The puzzle remained as to how 'moderate papists' on this issue could really be satisfactorily defined. This was a point which English Protestant writers ignored principally because, as has been emphasized, although the issue of papal jurisdiction was a fundamental point of the Roman religion according to Rome's own terms, it was a relatively minor Roman error in the eyes of English Calvinist conformists, who were more preoccupied with delineating Rome's heretical, idolatrous and antichristian doctrines.

These anomalies attest to the problems that English Protestants faced in maintaining a coherent position *vis-à-vis* 'moderate' papists. Practical and polemical requirements generated distinctions over Rome's unity which their theoretical view of Rome could not easily accommodate. Nevertheless, as we have seen, avant-garde conformist divines had an anti-papal ideology of greater flexibility. This was more in keeping with the requirements of James' domestic (as well as his foreign) policy, since it respected the good intentions and honesty of moderate Romanists. For example, as early as 1595, Covell was insisting that only a tiny minority of English recusants would ever support a Spanish invasion, and he later insisted

131 *Ibid.*, XII: 342, 343.

132 Morton, *Discharge*, pp.261–4. Cf. Hakewill, *Answere*, ii. p.301.

133 Speaking to parliament in 1605, while allowing that 'many honest men, seduced with some errors of Popery, may yet remaine good and faithfull Subiects', James declared unequivocally that 'none of those that trewly know and beleeve the whole grounds and Schoole conclusions of their doctrine, can ever prove either good Christians, or faithfull Subiects': King James, *Political Works*, p.285.

against puritan doubters that the Archpriest controversy did represent a genuine division in Romanists' ranks.[134] Lancelot Andrewes composed a typically subtle contribution to the Oath of Allegiance controversy in which he was careful to emphasize that the Oath did not attack all forms of popery as such, and did not question or mention the pope's spiritual power.[135] In the 1621 parliament Richard Neile argued for the better treatment of non-Jesuit priests in prison by adopting James' distinction between those who took the Oath and those who did not. This was necessary, Neile claimed, in order to provide an incentive for loyal Romanists. The Commons promptly denounced Neile as a friend of the papists – a clear indication of how difficult it was for English Protestants to accept the positive implications of divisions within Rome's communion.[136]

The Laudians, as we have seen, attached primary importance to points of ecclesiastical jurisdiction among Rome's errors. As a consequence, the dissension of Appellants and Gallicans on these issues represented a far more significant departure from the Roman Church, and Laudian divines would therefore seem to have shown fewer scruples in accepting fully the implications of James' distinction between moderate and radical papists. This emerged clearly in their defence of the removal (by the authority of the new King Charles) from the prayer for 5 November of the anti-popish passages which Jackson, Prideaux and Morton had so clearly supported. Peter Heylyn stressed that the religion of the Church of Rome was not in itself rebellion, 'though somewhat which hath there beene taught may possibly have beene applyed to rebellious purposes'. He firmly rejected absolute notions of the Roman Church, emphasizing that not all seminary priests and lay papists had written against the Oath of Allegiance, and that 'some have written very learnedly in defence thereof'. A mere collection of popish authors defending the deposition of kings could not be taken to indicate that the Roman religion itself supported such a position.[137] Christopher Dow similarly stressed that the rejection of the Oath was only the practice of a minority: 'the Practise of some of that Religion, and some positions of a Faction, rather than the generally received Faith among them'.[138] Dow cited the classic examples of the French and Venetian states, which were in communion with the Church of Rome, and yet did not acknowledge the pope's power over kings. Dow also noted that some English Roman Catholics and seminary priests liked and approved of the Oath, or left it to the people's conscience. While admitting that some popish authors exalted the pope's power to depose kings, Dow stressed

134 William Covell, *Polimanteia* (Cambridge, 1595), sig.X4r–v; *idem*, *Modest Examination*, p.27.

135 Andrewes, *Tortura Torti*, pp.83, 86–9, 106–7, 377–8.

136 *Notes*, ed. Relf, p.4.

137 Heylyn, *Briefe Answer*, pp.156–7. See above, p.259.

138 Dow, *Innovations*, p.138.

that this could not stain the whole religion: 'all that can be rightly hence inferred, will not reach the Religion or Faith it selfe, which (admit that these were parts of it) is of farre larger extent and different nature, than to receive its Denomination from these few principles, or some mens', or Popes' practises'.[139]

Laud himself shrewdly pointed out that the prayer's identification of Rome's religion with rebellion was contrary to the State's own claim that it only put Jesuits to death for rebellion and treason. He emphasized that 'there was never any law made against the life of a Papist, *quatenus* a Papist only', and quoted James' claim in his *Monitory Preface* that no English papist ever died for his conscience.[140] Laud was quite correct to argue that the retention of this clause ran counter to the logic of James' position on the Oath of Allegiance. Nevertheless, it was expressive of the 'absolute', monolithic view of the nature of Rome and her errors which could not easily accommodate the heterogeneous view of Rome which the Oath required. Laud suggested that the survival of this clause in the Prayer Book was simply 'through inadvertancy'.[141] It seems more likely that its survival bore witness to the inability of the English Church to accept the view of moderation within Rome which the Oath espoused.

Laud and Potter made polemical use of those Romanists who dissented from the papal supremacy much as Jacobean writers had done, albeit without the same accompanying theme of the 'absolute' nature of Rome's errors. Thus Laud expressed the conviction that 'many learned men' in the Roman Church scorned the point that the infallibility of a General Council derived from the pope, and claimed that he himself had heard 'some learned and judicious Roman catholics utterly condemn it'. He also claimed to have been told by 'a great Roman Catholic' that 'the wild extent of the pope's infallibility and jurisdiction, is a mistake'.[142] Laud, in fact, had plentiful contact with such dissenting members of the Roman Church. He paid close attention to the internal divisions within English Catholicism, befriending and supporting those who supported the Oath, endorsing Sir William Howard as a candidate for secretary to the queen, and encouraging these moderate Roman Catholics to have no trust in the papal agent George Con and the Jesuits. In order to undermine Con's plans he worked hard in cultivating the Jesuits' enemies in the Benedictine order, especially the Benedictine superior, William Price.[143] Laud's concern with such matters was doubtless purely pragmatic, and firmly within the Jacobean tradition of manipulating dissensions within the Roman Church. Never-

[139] *Ibid.*, pp.138–41. Cf. Peter Heylyn, *Certamen Epistolare or the Letter-Combate* (1659), pp.66–78.

[140] Laud, *Works*, VI: 53–4. [141] *Ibid.*, VI: 64. [142] *Ibid.*, II: 293, 299 note g.

[143] Hibbard, *Popish Plot*, p.63.

theless, Laud's readiness to follow through the logic of James' distinction between moderate and radical papists left open the possibility that these moderate Romanists might be assessed in much more positive terms.

Christopher Potter made frequent reference in his *Want of Charitie* to the dissensions within the present Church of Rome, noting the rejection of the pope's authority in General Councils 'at this day by the best learned in the Gallicane Church', and the banishing of the Jesuits and the burning of their books in Paris and Venice.[144] Regarding the liberty enjoyed by those churches within Rome's communion, Laud followed King James in emphasizing that the king of Spain and the Spanish were scornful of the very idea of the pope's power over the king's crown, and would soon shrug off their allegiance if the pope were ever so unwise as to attempt to assert it.[145] Nevertheless, the use of arguments based around the independence enjoyed by such churches, especially the Gallican Church, could have wide implications for Protestants who did not recognize the importance of the other issues on which Protestants and Romanists differed.[146]

THE 'CHURCH OF ROME' AND THE 'COURT OF ROME'

Divisions within Rome's communion often defied the definitions of English anti-papal polemicists. However, some significant terms began to enter general circulation, as the problem of how to define Romanists who seemed to be opposing the temporal authority of the pope deepened under James. An increasing distinction came to be made on this issue in terms of the difference between the 'Church of Rome' and the 'Court of Rome', although this distinction was probably made more frequently in popular discourse than in formal polemic.[147] Thomas Morton, writing in 1633, agreed that not all lay Romanists accepted the doctrines of political

144 Potter, *Want of Charitie*, i. pp.8–9, 72.

145 King James, *Political Works*, p.237; Laud, *Works*, II: 223–4; Heylyn, *ΜΙΚΡΟΚΟΣΜΟΣ* (1636 edn), p.34.

146 When Gerard Langbaine republished in English translation the *Review of the Council of Trent* of the Gallican writer du Ranchin in 1638, arguing that du Ranchin justified the rejection by the French of the Tridentine Council 'for matter of Discipline, (and why not ours for matter of Doctrine?)', he expressed the fear that some readers might misconstrue some passages in the work which were excusable rather than commendable. He had a greater fear, however, that 'there will not want some among them that will receive those things with applause which I desire may passe with pardon': [Guillaume du Ranchin], *A Review of the Councell of Trent*, tr. Gerard Langbaine (Oxford, 1638), 'To the Reader'. Extracts made from chapter 10 'Of the unjust Power of the popes' of Langbaine's translation may be found in the State Papers for 1638 (PRO, SP 16/388 fols.249–51).

147 E.g., Sir George Goring, writing to Sir Dudley Carleton in September 1625, reported how the new French queen was strongly urged to protect English recusants by 'her ecclesiastics, who seemed temperate Catholics, but now run the old course, participating more in the Court than the Church of Rome': PRO, SP 16/6/35.

subjection taught by Rome, and expressed the distinction in terms of the difference between the Church and Court of Rome. In order to persuade his recusant opponent to accept the point, Morton cited the example of the Gallican theorists of the Sorbonne: 'those Parisian Doctors would have taught you to distinguish even of Romish Religion: discerning *Romish*, in respect of the Romish Court, from Romish, in respect of the Romish Church in generall. The first, they know, hath often harboured seditious documents, which they have alwayes impugned, for the defence and preservation of the Gallicane Regalities and Liberties.'[148]

This was not to suggest, however, that this was a distinction which might have general importance in perceptions of Rome's nature, or that there might be a significant common ground held by both Protestants and those churches which rejected the 'Romish Court'. Nevertheless, the use of this distinction intruded a dangerous incoherence into contemporary descriptions of the separation from Rome, which explained that the Protestants had departed because the 'Court of Rome' had in fact become wholly predominant over the 'Church of Rome'. This was an incoherence which remained unexplored principally because divisions on the issue of papal jurisdiction, while important polemically because of the claims made by writers such as Bellarmine, remained of only minor significance among the doctrinal errors with which the Roman Church was impugned. Moreover, Protestant writers in the Oath controversy were unconvinced that the seemingly more moderate Romanist theory of the indirect deposing power was really any different from the direct power in substance.[149] While the English and Gallican Churches might find themselves on the same side on this issue, Jacobean Calvinist writers made no attempt to suggest that the situation of the two churches was fundamentally the same.[150] Some moderate writers such as Grotius, committed to a wide

148 Morton, *Discharge*, pp.262–3.

149 Sommerville, 'Jacobean political thought', pp.267–8. See Sommerville on the theory of the indirect deposing power (pp.258–62) and on Romanist disputes regarding the direct power (pp.251–2).

150 The only clear attempt to compare the Gallican Church's situation and doctrine explicitly with that of the Church of England in the Jacobean period was made by the English translator of Edmond Richer's *De Ecclesiastica et Politica Potestate*, the English edition of which appeared in 1612. The anonymous translator directly compared the two churches, arguing that national churches could differ in things which were not necessary to salvation, and noting that King James had acknowledged the Church of Rome to be 'our mother church'. The translator's aims, however, were limited to the intention that the work might act as 'a further warrant and encouragement to the Romish Catholikes of England, for theyr taking of the Oath of Allegiance; seeing so many others of their owne profession in other Countries doe deny the popes infalibility in iudgement and temporal power over Princes, directly against the doctrine of Iesuits': Edmond Richer, *A Treatise of Ecclesiasticall & Politike Power* (1612); Salmon, *Renaissance*, p.187. J.P. Sommerville notes that the author of the introduction to this work was the Frenchman who earlier

latitude on issues of theological doctrine, might cherish hopes of detaching the Gallican Church from Rome and uniting her in a Protestant alliance.[151] However, Grotius' plans won little support among English Protestants, for whom the French Church's commitment to the Church of Rome's doctrinal errors was ultimately of greater significance than her disputing of the pope's claims to universal jurisdiction.

Outside the use that could be made of it in Protestant polemic, the Gallican Church was too close to Rome to be viewed in positive terms by English Protestants. For example, when John Preston rejected the duke of Buckingham's arguments in favour of the French Match over the Spanish Match, 'that the French would not be so rigid in religious observations', the famous court puritan 'only acknowledged this difference, that Spanish Popery was an absolute ingredient to their intended Western Monarchy, but French was not so, & in so much, was less evil'.[152]

For divines who placed greater emphasis on Rome's jurisdictional errors, the Gallican Church represented more than just profitable polemical material for use against Rome. There was much in Gallicanism to attract those Laudians who were more generally concerned with issues of episcopal equality and the supreme authority of General Councils. Gallicanism was essentially a mixture of political and ecclesiastical concerns which, while principally directed against the pope's claims to temporal jurisdiction, also often embraced an advanced conciliarist position along the lines of the Councils of Basle and Constance, emphasizing the liberties enjoyed by the ancient Gallican Church upon which the papacy had impinged in succeeding centuries, and also defending the divine right of bishops, depicting Peter merely as *primus inter pares* in relation to the other Apostles.[153]

wrote *The French Herald* against the papists, which exhorted James to take up arms against them (Sommerville, 'Jacobean political thought', p.76 n.66).

151 Grotius wrote to Casaubon in 1612 with plans for a public confession of all those churches who rejected the Council of Trent and the pope's universal monarchy, to include the moderate Catholics (H.R. Trevor-Roper, *Catholics, Anglicans, and Puritans* (1987), p.54). In the 1630s he was still entertaining hopes, which he communicated to Laud through the English ambassador Viscount Scudamore, that the Gallicans might be detached from Rome in order to enter a northern Protestant alliance (BL, Add. MS 11044 fol.92).

152 Thomas Ball, *The Life of the Renowned Dr. Preston*, ed. E.W. Harcourt (1885), p.108. When Robert Butterfield in his *Maschil* supported his argument that some of the Roman Church conceived better of Tridentine doctrine than was generally held with the marginal comment that 'the French receive not the Council of Trent to this day', Henry Burton was swift to correct him. The kingdom of France, he claimed, had only stood out against the Council of Trent for matters of prerogative. Moreover, as he correctly observed, the Sorbonists had now yielded unanimous assent to Tridentine doctrines and decrees: Butterfield, *Maschil*, pp.107–8; Burton, *Babel*, p.113.

153 Salmon, *Renaissance*, pp.156–62, 167–73; Bouwsma, 'Gallicanism and Christendom', pp.815–26; A.F. Allison, 'Richard Smith's Gallican backers and Jesuit opponents',

In the hands of Richard Montagu, the Gallican Church became, not simply the possible ally of a moderate Protestant alliance as Grotius had envisaged, but the model for a reconciliation of the Church of England with Rome which would allow her to retain her independent rights of jurisdiction. Montagu assured the papal agent Panzani that he and all the clergy of the Church of England believed as much as the Gallican Church did.[154] It was in France that Montagu recommended that a conference should be held of moderate divines to discuss reunion because, as he explained, he considered the opinions of the French to be closest to those of the English Church.[155] In a manuscript tract written about this time he had explicitly compared the English Church's separation from the Church of Rome with that of the French Church.[156]

This represented the ultimate working out of the distinction increasingly being made between the Church of Rome and Court of Rome. As used by Morton, this was a distinction which related purely to political matters. Writers such as Potter, as we have noted, placed a new positive emphasis on the extent to which Protestants could be said to have retained communion with the Church of Rome, which they had never in fact left.[157] It was left to Montagu to make the further step of locating this Church of Rome in real, political terms in those churches which enjoyed a similar independence from the Court of Rome while remaining within Rome's outward general communion. Montagu's position essentially represented the other extreme of the position towards the true church remaining within Rome which had been adopted by Perkins. Where Perkins had actualized Rome's redeeming features objectively in a hidden elite of true worshippers, and other Jacobeans had attempted to combine these elements in a more intangible way with the same church's errors, Montagu actualized the same true church with which the Church of England held communion in the institutional Gallican Church.

It is difficult to discover precisely where Montagu had acquired this conviction that reunion with Rome might be possible along the lines of the independence enjoyed by the Gallican Church. Writing in the early 1620s in his *Antidiatribae*, while he referred regularly to the liberties anciently enjoyed by the French Church, Montagu remarked that the present French

Recusant History 18 (1986–7), pp.329–36. On Gallicanism in general, see V.Martin, *Le Gallicanisme et la réforme catholique* (Paris, 1919), *passim*; A.-G. Martimort, *Le Gallicanisme de Bossuet* (Paris, 1953), pp.17–125.

154 PRO, MS 31/9/17B: Panzani to Barberini, 11/21 May 1636.

155 PRO, MS 31/9/17B: Panzani to Barberini, 23 March/ 2 April 1636.

156 CUL, MS Gg/1/29 fol.101v (from back). For a more detailed discussion of this tract, see above, pp.81 n. 173.

157 See above, pp.156–7, and also below, pp.342–3.

Church had been deprived of all these ancient liberties in more recent times by the papacy.[158]

In 1625, however, the French bishops in the General Assembly, as well as printing a Declaration which asserted their rights to reform monasteries and preachers without papal exemption, had sentenced a dean for his exercise of a papal commission. The papal legate had reacted with fury, claiming that the Assembly had no power to condemn the actions of a papal subdelegate and intending to declare all the Assembly's acts null and void.[159] Sir Dudley Carleton reported with delight the legate's further discomfort over the Assembly's approval of a 'printed peece' which strongly defended 'the absolutnes of Kings, & theyr independency on the pope', prompting him to the reflection 'that yf all Churches in Christendome had maintayned the liberty of this of France very few had bene reformed'.[160] The papal delegate was none other than Cardinal Barberini, and it is therefore not surprising that he reacted very sharply when Panzani reported to him Montagu's appeal to the example of the Gallican Church. Barberini firmly denied that the French Church was an autonomous branch of the Catholic Church, as Montagu seemed to be suggesting.[161]

The French bishops were tenacious defenders of their liberties throughout the 1620s and 1630s.[162] By 1638 rumours had reached the English court that the French were threatening to set up their own patriarchate, while

158 Montagu, *Antidiatribae*, pp.1–2. For examples of Montagu's stress on the independence enjoyed by the French Church and monarchy, see *ibid.*, pp.79, 86, 108–9. For a similarly low estimate of the state of Gallicanism at the turn of the century, see Sandys, *Europae Speculum*, pp.55–6.

159 M.K. Becker, 'Episcopal unrest: Gallicanism in the 1625 Assembly of the Clergy', *Church History* 43 (1974), pp.73–6.

160 PRO, SP 16/19/32.

161 Barberini certainly noted Montagu's Gallican emphasis, and the assumption behind it that the French Church was an autonomous branch of the Catholic Church, as Montagu and other Laudians claimed the Church of England to be. In reply, Barberini stressed that there was no essential difference from Rome in the Gallican Church. The only difference among the so-called national churches in communion with Rome lay in their names, as they were still under the Roman Patriarch. He firmly rejected the view which presented the Gallican Church 'come distinta con pretensione di autorita dalla Chiesa Romana'. The English clergy and Charles liked to talk of the Gallican Church, he continued, because of certain tendencies at the Sorbonne to regard the deposition of kings as heretical, but the French Church did not differ from Rome on the articles necessary for salvation: PRO, MS 31/10/10: Barberini to Panzani, 23 June/3 July 1636 (fols.338–40); Albion, *Court of Rome*, p.185.

162 Allison, 'Richard Smith's Gallican backers', pp.335–6. For an enthusiastic account (composed *c.*1625 after a trip to France) of the full authority retained by French bishops, and of the freedom from papal control more generally enjoyed by the French Church and State, with the clergy subject to the king, see Peter Heylyn, *A Survey of the Estate of France* (1656), pp.109, 219–25.

fresh attempts to draft the Oath of Allegiance in a way which would assuage the pope again focused attention on the relative political liberty enjoyed by the Gallican Church.[163] The Benedictine irenicist Leander Jones, and the king himself, defended the Oath by citing the example of the Gallican Church.[164] There were thus plenty of reasons why Montagu's faith in the Gallican Church's liberties might have been restored. It is also possible that he may have had some communication with the Gallican Dupuy brothers.[165]

Not all Laudian writers expressed such an optimistic assessment of the Gallican Church's position, although Ephraim Pagitt emphasized that church's liberties as 'the best Priviledged of the Churches in Christendome under the pope' and believed it to have declined sufficiently from the pope for some form of reconciliation to be possible between it and the Church of England.[166] It seems highly unlikely that Laud would have been impressed by plans which revolved around the liberties enjoyed by the Gallican Church. He does not seem to have responded positively to Grotius' suggestions in October 1637 that the Gallican French might join a moderate Protestant union if a Spanish pope were to be elected.[167] Laud did, it is true, have a clear interest in the historic liberties of the French Church, and in those Gallican tracts which defended them. In 1639 Laud presented both the Bodleian Library and his own college of St John's with copies of the Gallican Pierre Dupuy's recently published *Traitez des Droits et Libertez de l'Eglise Gallicane* and *Preuves des Libertez de l'Eglise Gallicane*.[168] He does not, however, seem to have regarded these as expressive of the opinions of the contemporary French clergy, and thus as the foundation for a possible reconciliation.[169] Nevertheless, Laudians' increased willingness

163 Albion, *Court of Rome*, pp.242, 249–87. For a more cynical reading of Richelieu's motives, see Robert Baillie, *A Parallel or Briefe Comparison of the Liturgie with the Masse-Book* (1641), ep. ded.

164 Albion, *Court of Rome*, pp.259, 262, 265; Sitwell, 'Leander Jones', p.155. Note also Sancta Clara's citation of the current practice of the French and the *parlement* of Paris concerning the power of kings in order to justify the treatment of this issue in the Thirty-Nine Articles: Sancta Clara, *Paraphrastica*, p.106.

165 See Peiresc's letter of December 1635 to the Dupuy brothers reporting the publication of Richard Montagu's *Apparatus*: *Lettres de Peiresc aux frères Dupuy*, ed. P.T. de Larroque (3 vols., Paris, 1892), III: 418–19. It is also noteworthy that the testimonials of approval prefixed to the *Deus, Natura, Gratia* of the Franciscan irenicist Sancta Clara, with whom Montagu had some contact, include that of Jacques Dreux, a doctor of the Sorbonne.

166 Ephraim Pagitt, *Christianography* (3rd edn, 1640), pp.15, 207. On Pagitt's work, and his links with Laud, see below, ch.6.

167 BL, Add. MS 11044 fols.92r, 94v.

168 Trevor-Roper, *Catholics*, pp.100–1.

169 In his letter to the Oxford University Convocation, which accompanied the volumes, Laud noted that the book had been banned by the French bishops. However, he wrote, it was most fit to be preserved in the libraries of the Reformed Churches, where Protestants might read 'quid de universali regimine ecclesiae Romanae sentiat ecclesia Gallica, etiamsi libere ita loqui aut nolit, aut non audeat': Laud, *Works*, V: 226.

to embrace a certain practical distinction between moderate and radical papists without the usual careful theoretical qualifications prepared the ground for the reunion hopes on Gallican lines which Montagu entertained.

6

Visibility, succession and the church before Luther

THE PROTESTANT CHURCH BEFORE LUTHER

I began with this consideration that there were two sortes of questions betweene the Catholiques and Protestants the one of right or Doctrine the other of Fact or Story. As this, Whether Luther were the new preacher of the protestant fayth. Whether it hadd a visable apparanc of pastors and teachers before this tyme. I resolved to begin my inquiry with the questions of fact ... because they were so few and so comprehensable by all capacytyes and the controversyes of doctrine so many and so Intricate as they required much tyme and Learning for theyr disquisition.[1]

When he set out in this way to resolve his conscience on the issues separating the Roman and Protestant Churches, Walter Montague, son of the earl of Manchester, doubtless followed the instincts of many lay readers of the Roman/Protestant controversy. Rather than the complex and seemingly endless points of doctrinal conflict, it was the more tangible and straightforward questions of historical fact surrounding the separation of the Protestants from the Church of Rome which seemed to offer the clearest guide to the troubled layman. It was here, however, that Montague claimed to have found the weakest point in the Protestant armoury against Rome, and he converted to Rome as a consequence. But how incoherent really was the Church of England's perception of its own past? And how far did this perception complicate English Protestants' understanding of their present relationship with the Roman Church?

Debates between English Protestants and Romanists during the Jacobean and Caroline period revolved around the perennial Romanist demand: 'Where was your church before Luther?' This was a question which was asked with increasing frequency and insistence in Romanist polemic during this period. Not only was it the subject of polemical tracts, but short conversion manuals specifically instructed Romanist priests to

[1] LPL, Lambeth MS 943 p.383. Montague's letter to his father survives here among Laud's papers with a number of crosses made in the margin at various points in his argument, possibly by the archbishop.

raise this issue in debate with lay Protestants,[2] and a number of Protestant divines complained of the consequent problems that this tactic posed for members of their congregations.[3] Writing in 1625, as he contemplated researching 'the Visibility and perpetual succession of the Church', Thomas James complained to Ussher that the issue had been 'set afoot politically by our adversaries the papists, by especial advice from Rome: for it is plausible amongst the people and vulgar sort, and impossible to be answered by every one'.[4]

Why did Romanists choose increasingly to focus upon the issue of the Protestants' ancestry? The answer lies in part in the fact that, in Roman Catholic theology, membership of the visible church and recourse to its services and its doctrinal authority had a more direct soteriological role to play – therefore the visible continuity of an institutional church became the more necessary if men's salvation and their access to a properly validated divine authority were to be assured. The issue of institutional 'visibility' also served to focus the debate, less on the endless disputes over the orthodoxy or otherwise of specific doctrines, but more on the central question of the identity of the true church which confirmed these doctrines.[5]

But the presence of the 'visibility' issue in more popular Romanist pamphlets and disputes is also explicable in part by the fact that Romanists found Protestants to be divided in their replies to this question – and these disagreements reflected some of the ambiguities in Protestant ecclesiology that earlier chapters have revealed.[6] The question of the Protestants' ancestry raised many basic problems concerning the nature of the church, and most especially regarding the church's succession and durability. As it focused tensions in Protestant ecclesiology, so this question also had wider implications for the way in which relations between the contemporary Protestant and Roman Churches were understood.

Faced with the recurring Romanist demand that they demonstrate the location of their church before the Reformation, English Protestants were tempted to reject the challenge as a trick question. As they wished to stress continuity, they sought to answer the demand simply by denying that the Protestants had created a new church, asserting instead that they had

2 Bodl., Rawlinson MS D.853 fols.20–3; Questier, 'Phenomenon', pp.299–301.

3 E.g. Hoby, *Letter to T.H.*, sig.A3v; Gifford, *Sermons*, p.168 – cited in Bauckham, *Tudor Apocalypse*, p.118.

4 Ussher, *Works*, XV: 264. For examples of attempts to respond in more popular vein to Romanist popularizations of the 'visibility' argument, see Samuel Hieron's *An Answer to a Popish Rime* (1604), reprinted in Samuel Hieron, *Workes* (1619), esp. pp.558–63. I owe this reference to Julia Merritt. See also George Jenney, *A Catholike Conference* (1626).

5 Gifford, 'The controversy', pp.94–6; Questier, 'Phenomenon', pp.57–9, 68.

6 See above, especially ch.3.

merely reformed an older one.[7] However, this solution was complicated by the fact that, in other contexts, the Protestants emphasized the degradation of the present Church of Rome and the magnitude of the Protestants' separation from her. Even in the 1580s, Edmund Bunny had recognized that, by agreeing with Romanists' insistence that they constituted an entirely separate church and religion from Rome, English Protestants were leaving themselves open to the demand that they reveal as their forebear a distinct church separate from Rome in the past.[8]

If they had to identify a specific institutional predecessor, mainstream Jacobean divines pointed variously to the primitive church, to orthodox Christians who had remained in communion with the medieval Roman Church, to medieval heretics such as the Waldensians who separated from the Latin communion and were persecuted by Rome, and also to national churches of faithful Christians who had rejected the pope's claims to universal jurisdiction, such as the Greek, Russian and Ethiopian Churches. Jacobean conformists appealed to all these different ancestors simultaneously, with no sense of contradiction, or fear that the different groups might be incompatible.[9] It was left to the Laudians, as always, to distinguish and define potential dichotomies.

The primitive church

It was to the primitive church that Protestants turned first. When Thomas Morton addressed himself to the recurrent question of the origins of the Protestant Church, he emphasized (before going on to deal with Protestants' medieval forebears) that Protestants appealed to the purity of the early beginnings of the Christian church. This was what Luther had claimed, 'and the same is the defence of Protestants, in their whole Profession at this day'.[10] The appeal to the authority of the primitive church was, of course, the basic argument of Jewel's *Apology* of the Church of England and the 'Challenge' debate which it provoked, in which the Church of England laid claim to the writers of the first six centuries of the church. Later divines continued to urge that the Church of England essentially preserved entire the true doctrine of the early church. If Roman-

7 E.g. Hall, *Works*, X: 41; Covell, *Just and Temperate Defence*, pp.73–4.

8 See above pp.133–4; also Bunny, *Treatise*, pp.82–3.

9 E.g. Morton, *Grand Imposture*, p.398; Abbot, *Treatise*, pp.93–7; Prideaux, *Viginti-duae Lectiones*, i. pp.136–43; Simon Birckbek, *The Protestants Evidence* (1635), ii. pp.150–1; Anthony Cade, *A Justification of the Church of England* (1630), pp.138–204; Lynde, *A Case*, pp.267–73.

10 Morton, *Grand Imposture*, p.398. On the use of patristic writings, see S.L. Greenslade, 'The Faculty of Theology', in J.K. McConica (ed.), *The History of the University of Oxford*, vol. III: *The Collegiate University* (Oxford, 1986), pp.321–3.

ists claimed that the doctrines and practices which Protestants had rejected had been observed for many hundreds of years, this was irrelevant beside the Protestants' claim to deduce their doctrines from the earliest years of Christianity. As John White explained the matter, 'Our Adversaries ... may, in some points possible, pretend antiquitie, but *Prioritie*, which is the first and best antiquitie, they cannot in any one thing wherein they refuse us.'[11]

In the Jacobean period, the appeal to the Fathers of the early church became increasingly widespread and intensive among divines of varied doctrinal hue. William Perkins' *Problema de Romanae Fidei Ementito Catholicismo* (1604) was, as one scholar has noted, 'the first English monograph on the Fathers', and as such constituted 'a real ice-breaker in English theology', but one which other puritan writers were happy to defend and follow.[12] Thomas James' plans for new editions of patristic writings and for the systematic analysis of papal corruptions of patristic texts were a rallying point for anti-papal Calvinist divines, whether conformist or puritan, although part of the attraction of these schemes may have lain in the hope that it would be the patristic passages least amenable to their own style of divinity which would be shown to be popish forgeries.[13] By the Jacobean period English Protestant polemic contained few of the sort of anti-patristic remarks in which divines such as Fulke had occasionally indulged, and which Roman Catholic authors had exploited when challenging Protestant claims to 'antiquity'.[14] The Centurists' condemnations of patristic authors was forcing even Calvinist conformists to distance themselves from the Magdeburg writers.[15] Everywhere, the congruence of the modern Church of England and the primitive patristic church was emphasized. The puritan Thomas Taylor thus saw fit to complain of what he regarded as Roman slanders against Protestantism when they suggested that Protestants condemned the Fathers and antiquity.[16]

The early church Fathers were thus fundamental to the Protestant appeal to the past. Nevertheless, discussions of the opinions of the Fathers were undertaken with a certain caution. It was insisted that they should not be understood as sharing in the absolute authority of Scripture; their writings were fallible, often rhetorical, regularly prone to overemphasize certain

11 White, *Defence*, sig.**4v.

12 Windsor, 'Controversy', p.226; Taylor, *Christs Victorie*, p.100.

13 See above, ch.1.

14 E.g. Walsingham, *A Search*, pp.8, 19–22; Brereley, *Protestants Apologie*, pp.74–5, 136.

15 White, *Orthodox Faith*, p.328; Bedell, *Certaine Letters*, p.110; Ussher, *Works*, V: 206. Laudian writers were characteristically more scathing, however: see Pocklington, *Altare Christianum*, p.37; *idem*, *Sunday no Sabbath*, pp.9–10.

16 Taylor, *Christs Victorie*, pp.797–8.

doctrines at the expense of others as the polemical context required. They should only be treated as authoritative on matters where they spoke with one voice, and when they wrote consciously in absolute doctrinal terms.[17] Moreover, there were fears that many surviving patristic texts had been corrupted, and included much spurious material.[18]

As a result, the testimonies of the Fathers were alleged with varying degrees of enthusiasm by different churchmen, and amid this common *polemical* commitment to patristic authorities, divisions started to emerge in the ways that English Protestants treated them. For more firmly Calvinist commentators in particular this appeal to the Fathers was combined with a certain distrust. Gabriel Powel thus complained that St John Chrysostom had been infected with Pelagianism, and expressed more general doubts about the reliability of the Fathers.[19] William Whitaker and Bishop Robert Abbot, for all their patristic learning, felt it necessary to emphasize that, while the Fathers could be shown to support Protestant doctrines, the Protestants themselves dealt with them merely because Romanists insisted on appealing to them. Whitaker emphasized that, even if the Fathers were against Protestant doctrines, this could not harm the Protestants' cause, as the Protestants rested ultimately on true doctrine revealed in the Scriptures.[20] Abbot stressed that the Protestants relied wholly on the authority of Scripture: he only appealed to the ancient church 'against the importunity of the adversarie', although he confessed that 'by the Fathers and Bishops of those times, many things were conceived and delivered amisse'.[21] Thus it was that Calvinist conformists such as George Downame and Robert Abbot, for all their emphasis on the purity of the primitive church, did not flinch from asserting that Antichrist laid his foundations even in the time of the Apostles.[22]

By contrast, divines such as Andrewes, Overall and Montagu were moving beyond invoking patristic authorities simply as a polemical strategy or 'containing tactic' (in Windsor's words), and were more em-

[17] See e.g. Jewel's *Treatise of the Holy Scriptures* (Jewel, *Works*, IV: 1173). For general guides to the interpretation of patristic texts, see also Sutcliffe, *De Turcopapismo*, pp.226–42; Daniel Featley, *Cygnea Cantio* (1629), (esp. pp.30–2); William Perkins, *Problema de Romanae Fidei Ementito Catholicismo* (Cambridge, 1604), pp.2–7; Barlow, *Defence*, pp.56–68; Abbot, *Demonstratio*, p.12; Sebastian Benefield, *Doctrinae Christianae sex capita* (Oxford, 1610), sig.**3r–v; Yates, *Ibis*, ii. pp.87–90; Wotton, *Defence*, pp.461–2; White, *Defence*, pp.430–2; Brereley, *Protestants Apologie*, pp.116–17.

[18] For lists of spurious patristic works, see Perkins, *Problema*, pp.7–44. Cf. Windsor, 'Controversy', p.267.

[19] Powel, *Consideration of the Papists*, pp.93, 86.

[20] Whitaker, *Disputation*, p.669 – quoted in P. Hughes, *Theology of the English Reformers* (1965), p.33; Windsor, 'Controversy', pp.235–6; Questier, 'Phenomenon', pp.46–7.

[21] Abbot, *Third Part*, 'To the Christian Reader' (unfol.).

[22] Abbot, *Defence*, pp.112–13; Brereley, *Protestants Apologie*, pp.113, 129–30.

phatically promoting the strict imitation of patristic doctrine and practice as normative for the present Church of England. In their eyes, the early Fathers of the church should play a far more significant role in guiding scriptural interpretation than the works of more recent Protestant divines.[23] But this more dogmatic form of patristics was emerging at the same time that Calvinist conformists such as Powel were voicing their conviction that Scripture was essentially self-interpreting, and 'that the Fathers indeed did not understande the scriptures, as well as the learned of our times do'.[24] Tensions inevitably resulted. In 1610, Roman Catholics reported that two ministers of the Church of England had preached furiously against each other concerning whether the Fathers should be quoted in sermons.[25] In 1625, John Prideaux warned the congregation at the Oxford Act against reading the Fathers before they had been well grounded in some systematical catechisms.[26] Certainly, a diligent reading of patristic writings could lead to wavering and conversions to Rome. In 1624, the Jesuit Annual Letter claimed that debates on the Fathers divided Protestant opinion at Cambridge and induced conversions to Roman Catholicism. The incompatibility of Calvinist and patristic doctrines of the eucharist induced profound doubts in Isaac Casaubon, for example.[27]

In the Laudian period, the liturgical practice of early Christians – and most especially of the Greek Fathers – became a regularly cited authority for the new ceremonialism.[28] But if scholars such as Montagu were more

23 Windsor, 'Controversy', pp.227–35, 282–4; Davies, *Caroline Captivity*, pp.51–3. Windsor emphasizes the important role played by Overall, rather than Andrewes, in making the appeal to the Fathers central to Church of England apologetics (*ibid.*, pp.237–8). The increase in patristic learning in Jacobean England was noted admiringly even by foreign Romanists: see J.H. Hessels (ed.), *Ecclesiae Londino-Batavae Archivum* (3 vols. in 4, Cambridge, 1887–97), I: 861–2. Contrast the more lukewarm attitude of the early Jacobean avant-garde conformist Covell: Walsingham, *A Search*, p.41.

24 Powel, *Consideration of the Papists*, p.86 note d. Cf. White, *The Way*, p.324.

25 Foley, *Records*, VII: 1013.

26 Cosin, *Correspondence*, I: 77n. See also William Pemble's complaints in his *A Plea for Grace* (1629), p.25 – cited in J. Morgan, *Godly Learning* (Cambridge, 1986), p.103.

27 Foley, *Records*, VII: 1113–14; Questier, 'Phenomenon', pp.47–8; Pattison, *Isaac Casaubon*, pp.221, 224, 226, 401.

28 See especially the invocation of the early Christians' division of their churches, and exclusion of the laity from the area within the rails: Pocklington, *Altare Christianum*, p.62; T. Lawrence, *A Sermon Preached before the Kings Majesty* (1637), pp.9–10; Reeve, *Communion Booke*, p.137; Swan, *Profanomastix*, p.37. For citations of the Greek Father St John Chrysostom, see e.g. William Hardwick, *Conformity with Piety, Requisite in Gods Service* (1638), p.13; Jones, *Londons Looking Backe*, p.24. Heylyn sought to use the so-called 'Liturgy of St John Chrysostom' in defence of the altar policy, although (as John Hacket pointed out) the recent edition of Chrysostom's works (published under the patronage of Sir Henry Savile) had questioned the attribution of this text: Bodl., Cherry MS 2 fol.136r. See also Abbot, *Third Part*, p.349. This is not to deny that, on other matters, Chrysostom could be an attractive source for puritan authors – see Thomas

extreme than earlier divines in their determination to follow patristic example, Laudian pamphleteers such as William Page showed that they were no more consistent than earlier divines when they sought to pick and choose at which times patristic practice should be considered to be prescriptive.[29]

Patristics represented one answer to the question of the Protestants' origins in the early church. A related dispute between Romanists and Protestants arose around the question of the jurisdictional independence of the early church in England. English Protestant authors generally sought to downplay the role of the papally appointed missionary Augustine, and maintained instead that Christianity had first come to England with Joseph of Arimathea, and that the nation had been converted under the apocryphal Christian King Lucius several centuries before Augustine appeared.[30] While English Protestants generally agreed in making this defence, opinion was divided over the question of whether or not the Roman Church should be held to be the 'mother church' on account of the later conversions by the monk Augustine. The position that Rome was indeed the Church of England's 'mother church' had first been broached on the Protestant side by the inconstant Protestant Andrew Perne, but by the 1590s it was being invoked by Saravia, and was then taken up, most notably, by King James himself. This did not necessarily make it an acceptable position for many conformist writers, however. Richard Parkes had sought to embarrass Andrew Willet by contrasting Willet's denial of the position that Rome was 'the mother church' with the king's own defence of the same point. Willet sought to evade the king's remarks, but he was in good company: Matthew Sutcliffe and Richard Crakanthorp were similarly emphatic in rejecting the position.[31] The general acceptance of the legend of Joseph of

Cartwright's recommendation cited in Morgan, *Godly Learning*, p.115. On the use of the Greek Fathers more generally, see Davies, *Caroline Captivity*, pp.52–3.

[29] Windsor, 'Controversy', pp.283–4; Page, *Treatise*, pp.136–9.

[30] Francis Mason, *Of the Consecration of the Bishops of the Church of England* (1613), pp.44–61; Featley, *Clavis*, p.15; Francis Godwin, *A Catalogue of the Bishops of England* (1601), pp.1–3.

[31] Collinson, 'Andrew Perne', p.9; Hadrian Saravia, *De diversis gradibus* (1594), p.57; King James, *Political Works*, p.274; Willet, *Loidoromastix*, pp.17–18; Parkes, *An Apologie*, p.28; Sutcliffe, *A Briefe Examination*, p.100; Crakanthorp, *Defensio*, pp.21–3; White, *Replie*, pp.126–7. See also Brereley, *Protestants Apologie*, p.467; Broughton, *Protestants Demonstrations*, pp.14–15. For puritan complaints against the 'mother church' argument (usually in the work of Saravia) see Hooker, *Works*, IV: 77 (*A Christian Letter*); *An Abridgement of that Booke*, pp.25–6; Willet, *Ecclesia Triumphans*, p.41. On the conversion by the monk Augustine, see White, *The Way*, sect.49; Godwin, *A Catalogue*, pp.3–6; Mason, *Of the Consecration*, pp.56ff. Responding to Romanist citations of King James, Richard Field admitted that Rome was the 'mother church': Field, *Of the Church*, IV: 556.

Arimathea may have helped to keep this particular disagreement muted during this period. Most Laudians manifested little desire to pursue the 'mother church' argument, being more concerned to defend the jurisdictional integrity of the early British Church.[32]

While the ancient church prompted plentiful debate and dispute in the early Stuart period, in the last analysis it was not a central concern in Romanist/Protestant controversy. At the heart of the dispute over the location of the church before Luther lay, not the question of antiquity, but that of succession, of the durability of the true church *after* the first five centuries of Christianity and before the Reformation.

Succession and the 'true church'

The first response of mainstream English Protestant divines to the question of succession was to deny that they needed to provide historical proof for an external visible succession of Protestant professors through the ages. Conformity with Scripture was the only real test of a church's legitimacy, and it was in the Scriptures that the Protestants' religion ultimately lay.[33] Richard Sibbes explained that 'Our present church holds the same positive truths with the apostles before us. Therefore we say, "Our church was before Luther, because our doctrine is apostolical; as also is our church that is continued thereby, because it is built upon apostolical doctrine." Put the case we cannot shew the men, as they ridiculously urge; what is that to the purpose?'[34] Moreover, since the Scriptures held that the catholic faith would remain throughout all ages, it followed that, if the Protestants held the catholic faith, then they must necessarily have existed throughout the medieval period, even if patchy historical records did not reveal them. This was the position that Archbishop Abbot's chaplain Daniel Featley chose to adopt in his public disputation with the Jesuit Fisher in June 1623.[35] Even those writers most diligent in compiling chronological succes-

32 See below, ch.7. Nevertheless, the legend of King Lucius might still accommodate the claim that Rome was the 'mother church', as the conversion of England during his reign was generally said to have been carried out by two preachers sent by Pope Eleutherius: see e.g. Godwin, *A Catalogue*, p.2.

33 R. Fritze, 'Root or link? Luther's position in the historical debate over the legitimacy of the Church of England, 1558–1625', *JEH* (1986), pp.299–300; LPL, Lambeth MS 772 p.16.

34 Sibbes, *Works*, IV: 116.

35 Featley's basic argument at this disputation reduced the whole dispute to a straightforward syllogism: 'That Church whose faith is the Catholike and primitive faith once given to the Saints, without which none can be saved, is so visible, that the names of the professors in all ages may be shewed and proved out of good authors. But the Protestant Church is that Church, whose faith is the catholike and primitive faith once given to the Saints, without which none can be saved. Ergo.', Daniel Featley, *The Fisher Catched in His Owne Net* (1623), p.21. Featley did, however, eventually provide the list of visible Protestant professors of all ages which Fisher demanded – see Featley, *Romish Fisher*,

sions of Protestant believers argued in similar terms that such lists were ultimately unnecessary.[36]

However, the Romanists' gauntlet was defiantly picked up. Edward Chaloner, one of King James' chaplains, stressed the pre-eminency of knowing the church to be catholic and universal *a priori*, from the promises made in Scripture. But he also insisted forcefully that this did not mean that the Protestants suspected their proofs *a posteriori*, from professors of their religion in all ages, to be weak.[37] Humphrey Lynde proudly declared that 'I rather condescend to meete the Adversarie upon his owne ground, and to deale with him at the same weapon which himself hath chosen.'[38]

Faced with the problem of the Church of Rome's predominance during the medieval centuries, Protestants had developed notions of a relative church 'invisibility' in order to locate evidence of both an outward and an inward 'proto-Protestant' separation from the medieval Roman Church. The term 'invisibility' caused widespread misunderstanding then, as now, and requires careful explanation. As we have seen, all English Protestants accepted the general principle that there was an 'invisible' church of the elect, and that the visible institutional church on earth consisted of both the elect and the reprobate. There were important differences regarding how this division was treated, with Laudians tending to avoid discussion of the invisible church of the elect wherever possible, whereas Calvinists tended more easily to conflate understandings of the invisible church of the elect with the congregations of orthodox believers on earth (i.e. the established Protestant Churches).[39]

But this was not the only meaning of the term 'invisibility'. As well as the church of the elect, John Davenant explained that the term could also refer to the diminution of the 'true church' of orthodox believers (not all of whom were necessarily elect) in a time of corruption and oppression. At such a time, this 'true church' could be reduced to so sorry a state in its membership and outward dignity that it might be said for that time to be *in a relative sense* 'invisible', while yet remaining on earth.[40] It was in this

sigs.O2**-R*. For the claim that chronology and historical records were irrelevant for discerning the true church, see also John Prideaux's sermon before King James in the following year: 'Perez-Uzzah, Or The Breach of Uzzah', p.12 (*Certaine Sermons*).

36 E.g. Birckbek, *Protestants Evidence*, pp.19–20; Rogers, *Protestant Church*, pp.42, 114–15.

37 Edward Chaloner, *Credo Ecclesiam Sanctam Catholicam* (1625), p.83.

38 Lynde, *Via Tuta*, sig.A3v.

39 See above, pp.128–30, 158–60.

40 Davenant, *Determinationes*, pp.156–8. Richard Field argued much the same, and stressed: 'In this sense then the Church is said to be sometimes invisible, not because there are none seen, known or found that possess the truth of God; but because even in that company which is the true Church of God, many, and those the greatest are carried into error, so that but some few, and they such, as (if we should judge by outward appearance) are most

relative sense that the term 'invisible church' might be applied to the 'true church' of orthodox believers as the Protestants' ancestry before the Reformation.

This argument thus offered a fundamental solution for early Protestant Reformers and later Protestant polemicists to the problem of Rome's predominance in medieval church history. It warned against identifying the visible church of Christian history with the true church of the Creed, and stressed the theme of persecution, and the perpetual visibility of the church through the succession of right doctrine, upheld by a suffering remnant of true believers.[41]

This theme of an 'invisible' 'saving remnant' gained greater importance and prophetic meaning by its integral role in Protestant apocalyptic expositions of the history of the medieval church and of the Reformation. The texts of 2 Thessalonians 2.3 and of Revelation 12.6 were central to this tradition: the former predicting the universal religious apostasy of the Middle Ages, and the latter – 'the woman fled into the desert' – the flight of the true church from persecution during this period.[42] Thus George Abbot argued that, by the example of Revelation 12.6, 'it cannot bee the true Church, unlesse it should be hidden in the wildernesse'.[43] In fact, just as Romanists claimed that a glorious outward 'visibility' was a mark of the true church, Abbot seems to argue that a relative 'invisibility' was a mark of the same. Romish writers, by saying that the Church of Rome was always in sight and glorious to the eye, 'doe by a consequent proclaime, that they are not the pure and undefiled flying woman, but another painted harlot and strumpet. The true Church is for a time out of sight in the wildernes; but so say they, was their Church never: and therefore will they, nill they, their Church is not the true Church.'[44]

Similarly, Joseph Mede explained to a Cambridge audience in the mid-1620s that the Scriptures predicted that 'the Society of true Believers' could lose both its visibility and its glory, as it had under the 'Idolatrous Antichristianism' of the Middle Ages.[45] It was only at the Reformation that 'after a long day of darkness, and a black night, it pleased God, even of late, somewhat to dispel the cloud, whereby the Society of true Believers became again outwardly visible and conspicuous unto the world'. Mede

unlike to uphold and maintain the truth, are left to defend the same; multitude, authority, reputation and opinion of greatness in others, obscuring them in such sort that they which measure things by outward appearance, can possibly take no notice of them': Field, *Of the Church*, I: 33. See also Abbot, *Third Part*, pp.137–49.

41 Bauckham, *Tudor Apocalypse*, pp.118–22.

42 *Ibid.*, pp.119–21.

43 Abbot, *Treatise*, p.28.

44 *Ibid.*, p.29. Abbot here echoes the argument of William Fulke in his 1577 *Answer of a True Christian* – see Bauckham, *Tudor Apocalypse* , p.122.

45 Mede, *Works*, pp.182–4.

emphasized, however, that this did not mean that in previous ages this 'Society of true Believers' had been physically separate from the rest of the Christian church. Rather, 'for the most part', they continued as members of the same external institutional church as false believers, sharing the same visible sacraments, Word and pastors, 'and submitting to the same Jurisdiction and Regiment, so farre forth as these or any of these had yet some soundness remaining in them'.[46]

The tradition of the relative 'invisibility' of the true church thus never implied that the succession of the Word and ministry were necessarily impaired, or that the true church had existed without them – although the Romanist case against Protestants was based on this misinterpretation. Rather, Protestant notions of relative church 'invisibility' denoted only that the church of true believers had not all been formally, visibly distinguished from the rest of the visible church.

It was not quite that simple, of course. In certain cases English Calvinist divines such as Willet, Benefield, Perkins, Whitaker and John White were prepared to specify that a doctrinal succession alone – without an accompanying institutional succession – was ultimately sufficient for the continuance of the true church.[47] These remarks do have a certain rhetorical significance, but were not consciously intended to imply that the relative invisibility of the true church necessarily involved an interruption in the sacramental and institutional life of the church. However, they do help to demonstrate how the apocalyptic tradition's emphasis on the eternal opposition of the true and false churches, and on the importance of active persecution in identifying them, tended to emphasize the alienation of the 'true church' of orthodox believers from the medieval institutional church.[48] Roman Catholic polemicists delighted in trying to embarrass their English Protestant opponents by quoting the extreme apocalyptic formulations of scholars such as Napier, Fulke and Brocardo. These writers had claimed that the true church had been completely (rather than relatively) invisible during the Middle Ages under the universal apostasy caused by the papal Antichrist. The Romanist pamphleteers sought to use such arguments to undermine English Protestants' claims of the uninterrupted succession of their church, and especially of their episcopate. It is striking that, in reply, English Protestant apologists such as Francis White and Thomas Morton, and even William Chillingworth, refused to repudiate these earlier Protestant writers or their arguments. Instead, they attempted to integrate them within defences of ministerial succession and the perpetual visibility of the church's external forms, by explaining their

[46] *Ibid.*, p.184. [47] See Willet, *Synopsis* (1600), p.69; and below, ch.9.
[48] Bauckham, *Tudor Apocalypse*, pp.118–22.

arguments as intending merely a relative 'invisibility', a relative decline in outward splendour, rather than a total absence of external sacraments and ministry.[49]

The 'heretical' succession

In their search for medieval predecessors, English Protestants' eyes inevitably came to rest on the medieval heretical sects: the Waldensians, Albigensians, Lollards, Hussites and others. Here were manifest examples of unequivocal opposition to Roman doctrines and jurisdiction among groups who had been driven into separation by popish abuses and persecution in the same way that the Protestants had been. The attraction of tracing the Protestant Church before Luther through these small persecuted sects derived in part from the ease with which they fitted into the Protestant apocalyptic tradition of church history, with its stress on the persecution of the tiny spurned church of God's elect by the false church of Antichrist.[50] They also clearly manifested a direct separation from a church to which Elizabethan and Jacobean Protestants also claimed to be irreconcilably opposed.

However, part of the problem of deriving a Protestant succession through groups such as the Waldensians and Albigensians lay in the various heresies which were historically ascribed to them. Foxe's highly eschatological view of history tended to brush aside these problems by stressing these sects' defiance of, and persecution by, the Roman Church. It was the fact of their persecution by Rome – and, indeed, the very accusations of heresy levelled against them – which was (in Foxe's eyes) sufficient in itself to identify a sect as part of the true church, and an ancestor of the Protestants.[51] By contrast, the Jacobean period witnessed more determined efforts by conformist divines to vindicate and dignify sects such as the Waldensians. They renounced the heresies ascribed to such groups as the hostile misreporting of their Romish enemies, and increasingly focused on the 'visibility' of the Waldensians and others by their preservation of an outward and lawful ministry of the Word and sacraments.

[49] Brereley, *Protestants Apologie*, pp.66–8, 222–6; Morton, *Catholike Appeale*, pp.70, 72–3; White, *Orthodox Faith*, p.324; Chillingworth, *Religion of Protestants* (1638 edn), pp.238, 259.

[50] The sects' appearance also played an important role in apocalyptic chronology. Mede, for example, identified this with the first blast of the angelic trumpet: Trevor-Roper, *Catholics*, p.156.

[51] J. Facey, 'John Foxe and the defence of the English Church', in P. Lake and M. Dowling (eds.), *Protestantism and the National Church in Sixteenth Century England* (1987), pp.169–70.

James Ussher's *De Christianarum Ecclesiarum successione et statu Historica Explicatio* of 1613 – an account of the Roman corruption of true doctrine and of the sects' opposition to this change, delivered in a rigidly apocalyptic chronological framework – became the standard work defending the doctrines of the medieval 'heretics' and displaying their congruity with Protestant beliefs.[52] The malicious slandering of these sects in Romanist reports was compared with the Romanists' present attacks upon, and misrepresentation of, Protestants.[53] Their various minor errors were seen as being only in petty matters, and were mostly due to the veiling of the truth at that time by popish iniquities – they would certainly have seen the light at the Reformation and have joined the Protestants.[54] As Prideaux put it: 'It sufficeth us they were ours in the maine, and tended to that perfection which we (by God's mercy) have now in better measure attained.'[55]

Moreover, perhaps in reaction to Romanists' jeers at the Protestants' talk of an 'invisible' church, and their allegations that the English Protestants undermined their ministerial (and especially episcopal) succession by associating themselves with such heretical congregations, Jacobean writers found themselves placing increasing stress on the 'visibility' and multitude of these sects, the high social class of their followers, and the legitimacy of their ministry and succession.[56] Their various confessions

[52] Reprinted in Ussher, *Works*, II: 1–413. For his defence of Waldensian doctrines, see pp.169–91, and for the other sects, pp.231–80, 316–413. Other writers usually refer their readers to Ussher's work for proof that 'These Waldenses and Albigenses are ours': see Bernard, *Looke beyond Luther*, p.23; Bernard, *Judgement*, ii. p.125; Morton, *Grand Imposture*, p.398; Birckbek, *Protestants Evidence*, ii. pp.8–9. On this general point see also Abbot, *Demonstratio*, pp.89–90. Ussher's work supplemented the recent editions of their Apologies, Confessions and Catechisms edited by Lydius and Perin, which one had only to read, Prideaux argued, to see that the Hussites, Wiclifists and Waldensians agreed with the Protestants in all important points of doctrine: Prideaux, 'Perez-Uzzah', p.17 (*Certaine Sermons*); *idem*, *Viginti-duae Lectiones*, i. p.139.

[53] Abbot, *Treatise*, pp.84–6, 100–10; Abbot, *Third Part*, p.146; Prideaux, 'Perez-Uzzah', p.17 (*Certaine Sermons*); *idem*, *Viginti-duae Lectiones*, i. pp.138–9. Cf. Henry Jackson (ed.), *Wickliffes Wicket* (Oxford, 1612), 'To the Christian Reader'.

[54] Abbot, *Treatise*, pp.111–13; Bernard, *Looke beyond Luther*, p.23; Prideaux, *Viginti-duae Lectiones*, i. p.138.

[55] Prideaux, 'Perez-Uzzah', p.17 (*Certaine Sermons*).

[56] Thus Prideaux demanded how the Hussites could ever have been invisible when 40,000 of them assembled under Zizka, while the huge scale of the crusades against the Waldensians and Albigensians showed how multitudinous they were: Prideaux: 'Perez-Uzzah', p.16 (*Certaine Sermons*). Ussher and Robert Abbot noted the vast numbers of Waldensians, Albigensians and Hussites dispersed all over Europe, even in Britain, including the 100,000 Albigensians mustered under the count of Toulouse: Ussher, *Works*, II: 168–9, 351–2, 359–61, 366–8, 413; Abbot, *Second Part*, p.55; *idem*, *Third Part*, pp.145–6. However, both writers still employed the scriptural language of the tiny, suffering remnant, and the historical example of the world over-run by the Arian heresy: Ussher, *Works*, II: 162–5; Abbot, *Third Part*, pp.139–47 esp. p.147. For all George Abbot's talk of

and disputations proved that there was no lack of pastors, and even bishops, among the Hussites, Lollards and Waldensians,[57] and Prideaux argued that visible congregations had separated themselves from Rome during the medieval period and yet remained 'sub legitima Episcoporum & pastorum disciplina'.[58] Chaloner noted that even Bellarmine admitted that the Hussites 'received none into the Office of Pastors, but such as were ordayned by Bishops'.[59] Ussher observed that many bishops were drawn into the ranks of the Albigensians, who practised episcopal ordination.[60] Robert Abbot sought to downplay any schismatic tendencies further by emphasizing that, although these heretical groups severed themselves from the Roman Church, they did not constitute a separate church, but were still members of the same universal church as their persecutors.[61]

The Church of England was a national church which claimed an apostolical succession for its episcopal government, and as such the listing of groups of heretical separatist congregations among its predecessors may still have posed a latent threat to its ecclesiastical polity. Nevertheless, Jacobean writers had done their best to defuse the danger by stressing the 'visibility' and institutional and doctrinal respectability of these various pre-Reformation sects. In the Laudian era, however, all their painstaking efforts were disregarded.

Succession within Rome

Jacobean Calvinist divines never limited their ancestors simply to those in formal separation from the Church of Rome. Edward Chaloner explained that, in the years after the millennium, 'our Church had in those dayes a twofold subsistencie, the one separate from the Church of Rome, the other mixt and conioyned with it'.[62] The latter category 'consisted of those, who making no visible separation from the Roman profession, as not perceiving the mysterie of iniquitie which wrought in it, did yet mislike the grosser errors, which at this day shee maintaineth, and desired a reformation'.[63] This group was often spoken of in terms of an invisible elite, especially among the early Reformers and those whose work particularly emphasized

a necessarily hidden church, he was at the same time eager to stress the large numbers of Hussites and their support among the local nobility: Abbot, *Treatise*, *passim*.

57 Prideaux, *Viginti-duae Lectiones*, i. p.142; Hall, *Works*, IX: 249–51.

58 Prideaux, *Viginti-duae Lectiones*, i. p.140. Cf. Prideaux, 'Perez-Uzzah', p.16 (*Certaine Sermons*): 'It is senselesse that our adversaries contend for in this behalfe; had the Bishops, Priests, and Deacons among them a due forme of Church-government?'

59 Chaloner, *Credo Ecclesiam*, p.94.

60 Ussher, *Works*, II: 387–8.

61 Abbot, *Third Part*, pp.146–7.

62 Chaloner, *Credo Ecclesiam*, p.91. This passage is quoted at length in Birckbek, *Protestants Evidence*, ii. p.150.

63 Chaloner, *Credo Ecclesiam*, p.94.

apocalyptic models. However, later writers such as Prideaux chose to stress the visibility and distinctiveness of those before Luther who had opposed papal corruptions yet remained in communion with the Church of Rome.[64]

The histories of Foxe and the Magdeburg Centurists, and the *Catalogus testium veritatis* of Illyricus certainly provided a cloud of witnesses in this category, as well as the separatist groups described above. In Foxe's history few of these witnesses were members of the established church hierarchy. In fact, the real heroes were the lowly laity, and the clergy were usually depicted as the agents of Antichrist, the clerical power which they defended being seen as almost synonymous with popery.[65] Among Jacobean writers this anti-clerical emphasis was mostly absent. Francis Godwin's *Catalogue of the Bishops of England*, which went through several editions in the Jacobean period, was written partly in order to defuse the anti-clerical potential which the Foxeian tradition had shown itself capable of unleashing. Godwin offered well-balanced biographies of medieval English bishops explicitly to redress the balance and safeguard the episcopal succession.[66]

Catalogues of past witnesses to Protestant doctrine commonly included many important clerics – Schoolmen, abbots, bishops and even popes, such as Adrian VI. Any single exposition of orthodox doctrine, or opposition to papal power or corruptions, could enlist an author or churchman among the Protestant witnesses in an effort to swell their ranks. This could result in strange anomalies. Thus Daniel Featley's protégé Simon Birckbek could describe Gratian's work on canon law as being one of the pillars of popery, while at the same time citing its author as a witness against transubstantiation and the intercession of saints, and in favour of communion in both kinds.[67] Similarly, Jean Gerson, St Bernard and the Englishmen Thomas

[64] Prideaux, *Viginti-duae Lectiones*, i. p.137, cf. p.130.

[65] Facey, 'John Foxe', pp.175–7. For stern attacks on the record of popish archbishops of Canterbury, see also Willet, *Antilogie*, pp.199–200, 253–4.

[66] Godwin makes his intention quite plain in his 'Address to the Reader' where he warns that 'it is not to be denied, that the most part of the Chroniclers and historiographers of our age have borne a hand hard ynough at least upon the Prelates and Clergy of former times . . . For in the vulgar sort . . . is bred a conceit, not onely that the men were wicked, and so their doctrine corrupt . . . but also their functions and callings to be utterly unlawful and Antichristian': Godwin, *A Catalogue*, 'Address to the Reader' (unpaginated). See also M. McKisack, *Medieval History in the Tudor Age* (Oxford, 1971), p.115. Godwin's *Catalogue*, originally published in 1601, was republished in a second edition in 1615 to support Francis Mason's *Of the Consecration of the Bishops in the Church of England* (1613), which itself derived its material mostly from Godwin. Its increasing emphasis on the apostolic succession of the Church of England's episcopate led to its third edition of 1625 being entitled *The Succession of the Bishops of England* – see Milward, *Jacobean Controversies*, p.173.

[67] Birckbek, *Protestants Evidence*, ii. pp.4, 35, 36, 38–9. Cf. Thomas James' remark to Ussher in a letter of 1626 that, while 'doubtless Gratian was one of the first compilers of the popish religion', 'yet he is not so bad as he is made', as many of his worst passages

Gascoin and Thomas Netter were vehement opponents of the Hussites, Waldensians and Lollards respectively, but were all important Protestant witnesses in opposing popish abuses.[68] While these professors certainly had their faults, due to the veiling of the truth under the Roman tyranny, it was argued that these errors were not fundamental and might be pardoned following a general repentance for all errors known and unknown. Moreover, in the crucial matter of justification by faith in Christ alone they were true Protestants.[69]

This question of general repentance and solifidian doctrine touched upon a constant problem for Protestant apologists against Rome: that of the fate of their natural forefathers (as opposed to their *doctrinal* forebears) who had died before the Reformation. Archbishop Tobie Matthew declared in 1616 that 'in the controversy de Ecclesia, our adversaries do not demur themselves, nor entangle others (though needlessly, yet sophistically) in any one quiddity, or cavil, more than in that particular'.[70] The

were later corruptions: Ussher, *Works*, XV: 327. Birckbek's preface 'To the Reader' describes Featley's friendship and encouragement with his work, and his learned counsel during the composition of the book: 'hee (I thanke him) was readie to resolve me when I was in doubt, and to direct mee, (yea and correct mee also) when I was at default'.

68 In defence of Gerson, and especially of his condemnation of the Hussites, see Field, *Of the Church*, IV: 286–7, 304–5, 354–82. Davenant uses Gerson extensively when tackling the issues of ceremonial obligations in his *Expositio*, while Joseph Hall used his rules of meditation as being those of an early Protestant – J. Hall, *Arte of Divine Meditation* (1605), p.46. For the defence of St Bernard as a Protestant forebear who agreed in substance with Wyclif, see the regularly cited John Panke, *Collectanea. Out of St Gregory and St Bernard against the Papists* (Oxford, 1618). See also Abbot, *Treatise*, pp.91–3; Birckbek, *Protestants Evidence*, ii. pp.6, 28–32; Carleton, *Consensus*, pp.224–6; Field, *Of the Church*, IV: 374–6; Morton, *Catholike Appeale*, pp.458–60; White, *Orthodox Faith*, pp.313–15. John Prideaux cites Thomas Gascoin as an early Protestant witness in desiring reformation – see 'Perez-Uzzah', p.14 (*Certaine Sermons*); *idem*, *Viginti-duae Lectiones*, i. p.137. All English Protestant writers make much use of Thomas Netter's theological writings while generally ignoring his major role in the refutation of Wyclif's doctrines. For other examples of inconsistency in the citation of Protestant witnesses, see Brereley, *Protestants Apologie*, pp.111–12.

69 Morton, *Catholike Appeale*, pp.458–60. Archbishop Abbot explained that 'this is our judgement touching many other both before and after the time of Saint Bernard; that, holding Christ the Foundation aright, and groning under the heavy burden of humane traditions, satisfaction and other popish trash, they, by a generall repentance from their errors and lapses knowne and unknowne, and by an assured faith in their Saviour, did finde favour with the Lord ... And in this respect our settled and resolved iudgement is, that when it is asked, Where our Church in former Ages was; we may, besides that which we have formerly answered [regarding the Waldensians etc.], truly say, that it was in England, in France, in Spain, in Italy, yea in Rome it selfe: Spiritus ubi vult spirat': Abbot, *Treatise*, pp.93–4.

70 Ussher, *Works*, XV: 91–2. Matthew urged Ussher to insert a discussion of this point in the projected (but never published) third part of the *De successione*. Thomas Morton similarly remarked twelve years later that he found, in his own experience with papists, that this particular point was 'the greatest barre and hinderance unto us, for their conversion': Morton, *Grand Imposture*, p.414. Cf. Abbot, *Defence*, pp.211–13, 235–8; *idem*, *True Ancient*, pp.201–11.

basic response of Elizabethan and Jacobean divines was that those dying in times of ignorance might be pardoned by a judgement of charity for having sinned ignorantly in minor popish errors as long as they held on to the foundation of belief – salvation by faith in Christ's merits alone – and made a general repentance for sins known and unknown.[71] However, Foxe and others had maintained that justification by faith alone – the central Protestant doctrine – had only been restored by Luther.[72] The problem thus remained of *how* those who were ignorant of this fundamental doctrine before the Reformation could have been able to trust in Christ alone for their salvation.[73] Richard Hooker ran into problems in his sermons at the Temple in 1586 when he attempted to answer this question. Hooker drew a distinction between overthrowing the foundation of faith 'directly' and 'by consequent', and maintained that the Roman Church's doctrine of justification by inherent faith only did the latter. Thus, people might hold a popish doctrine of merit without drawing the logical consequence which overthrew salvation by Christ's merits alone.[74] The problem was that such a distinction might easily imply the salvation of post-Reformation papists, and it was this which caused Walter Travers to denounce Hooker, and Archbishop Whitgift to recommend careful qualifications to Hooker's arguments.[75]

The problem thus remained of how to allow for the salvation of people in the pre-Reformation Roman Church while at the same time denying it to her present members. This conundrum was effectively solved by Richard Field, and his solution rapidly gained acceptance in the Jacobean Church. Field's answer was to give a new positive emphasis to perceptions of the medieval Latin Church. Field claimed that the doctrine of justification by faith alone, and indeed the Protestant position on all those points currently disputed with the Church of Rome, were openly taught in all the Western Churches that were under the Romish tyranny, throughout the medieval period.[76] Field presented a vision of the medieval Latin Church as an arena of far-reaching dispute between a corrupt 'papalist faction' – the Court of Rome – and the rest of the church.[77] Earlier writers had emphasized the orthodoxy of the Anglo-Saxon Church, thereby extending well beyond the traditional Protestant limit of the first five centuries of the church, but had depicted the visible institutional church as being in irreversible decline

[71] R. Bauckham, 'Hooker, Travers and the Church of Rome in the 1580s', *JEH* 29 (1978), pp.45–7.

[72] Facey, 'John Foxe', pp.170–1.

[73] Bauckham, 'Hooker, Travers', pp.46–7.

[74] *Ibid.*, pp.43, 48.

[75] *Ibid.*, pp.47–50. Hooker himself denied that such a consequence should be drawn, and stressed that the Roman doctrine of justification by inherent grace was 'the mystery of the Man of Sin'.

[76] Field, *Of the Church*, II: 1–387.

[77] *Ibid.*, IV: 522–6.

after the millennium, and sinking fast by the thirteenth century. By contrast, Field sought to vindicate the Latin Church throughout the entire pre-Reformation period. In fact, he stressed that 'the Latin Church ... continued the true Church of God even till our time'.[78]

The arguments for the salvation of Protestants' natural forefathers, and for the succession of the 'true church', were essentially combined, as Field answered the customary question of the location of the church before Luther with the reply that 'it was where now it is. If they ask us, which? we answer, it was the known and apparent Church in the world, wherein all our fathers lived and died.'[79] Field did not hesitate to claim that 'all those Christian Catholic Churches in the West part of the world, where the pope formerly tyrannized, and where our fathers lived and died, were the true Protestant Churches of God'.[80] This was because Romish points of false doctrine and error had not been constantly delivered nor generally received in the Latin Church, but only 'doubtfully broached and devised without all certain resolution, or factiously defended by some certain only ... as a dangerous faction'. None of the errors which Luther opposed 'ever found general, uniform, and full approbation'.[81]

Field was very careful, however, to make the crucial reservation that 'the Roman Church is not the same now that it was when Luther began'.[82] The Latin Church before Luther could be magnified only because Field stressed that since the departure of Luther it had been fundamentally altered: 'Formerly, the Church of Rome was the true Church, but had in it a heretical faction: now the Church itself is heretical.'[83] Popish errors had now become the formal doctrine of the present Church of Rome as the Council of Trent, convened after Luther's appearance, had imposed them *de fide*, and thus made the general doctrine of the church damnable:

> In former times, a man might hold the general doctrine of those Churches wherein our fathers lived, and be saved, though the assertions of some men were damnable: now it is clean contrary, touching the present state of the Romish Church: for the general and main doctrine, agreed upon in the council of Trent, in sort as it is most commonly conceived, is damnable.[84]

Thus, if the Latin Church before Luther was a true Protestant Church, Field could still argue with complete consistency that the present Church of Rome 'is an erring, heretical, and apostatical Church ... we may justly

[78] *Ibid.*, I: 165. On the orthodoxy of the Anglo-Saxon Church, see e.g. William Fulke, *A Defence of the Sincere and True Translations of the Holy Scriptures* (Cambridge, 1843), pp.20–7; BL, Add. MS 34601 fols.8r, 129r (Abraham Wheelock); Downe, *Certaine Treatises*, xii. p.14; Montagu, *Diatribae*, p.75. See also V. Sanders, 'The household of Archbishop Parker and the influencing of public opinion', *JEH* 34 (1983), pp.538–9.

[79] Field, *Of the Church*, I: 165. Cf. pp.167, 171.

[80] *Ibid.*, II: 9.

[81] *Ibid.*, I: 166, 171.

[82] *Ibid.*, IV: 522.

[83] *Ibid.*, I: 359–60.

[84] *Ibid.*, IV: 525; I: 359.

account her to be the synagogue of Satan, the faction of antichrist, and that Babylon out of which we must fly, unless we will be partakers of her plagues'.[85]

The novelty of Field's argument was protested by Romanist divines, who claimed that the suggestion that all churches had been Protestant before Luther appeared was 'most directly against that which so many learned Protestantes have as from common knowledge most playnly, & fully confessed to the contrary'.[86] Nevertheless, other Protestant divines were not blind to the efficacy of Field's solution. His arguments were further developed by George Carleton, particularly in his *Consensus Ecclesiae Catholicae contra Tridentinos* (1613), whose conclusions were summarized in his 1615 pamphlet *Directions to Know the True Church*. Carleton argued that the fundamentals of true doctrine had remained in the church until Luther's time.[87] The forefathers had all the necessary means of salvation because they still possessed the basic rule of faith, which was the foundation of the Scriptures rather than the will of the pope.[88] It was at Trent that the Court of Rome had finally prevailed by fraud against the Church of Rome.[89] Before then, the Western church was still in agreement in all fundamental points of doctrine, and its understanding of the pope's supremacy was not a fundamental error.[90] But now the Church of Rome had altered the rule of faith, so that the Roman Church was now established on a foundation other than the Scriptures.[91]

Jacobean Calvinist writers generally followed Carleton's argument that the papal religion only really began at the Council of Trent.[92] John and Francis White, Thomas Morton, Joseph Hall, James Ussher and others all agreed that the Tridentine Council had marked and compelled as *de fide* points of doctrine that had previously only been received as probable, and

[85] *Ibid.*, IV: 572. [86] Brereley, *Protestants Apologie*, p.139.

[87] Carleton, *Consensus*, p.18.

[88] Carleton, *Directions*, p.83.

[89] *Ibid.*, pp.67–8, 82–3. The suggestion that Trent marked an important change in Rome's errors had been argued by earlier writers (e.g. Perkins, *Problema*, p.244) but it is only with the writings of Carleton and Field that this point was used to justify the separation from Rome and to grant a more positive status to the pre-Reformation Latin Church.

[90] Carleton, *Directions*, pp.79, 81; cf. *idem*, *Consensus*, pp.226–7.

[91] Carleton, *Directions*, pp. 32–5, 50–2, 57, 60–5; *idem*, *Consensus*, p.18.

[92] Wotton, *Trial*, pp.356, 377; Burton, *Baiting*, pp.38, 89–90; White, *The Way*, pp.262–3; White, *Orthodox Faith*, p.324; Cade, *Justification*, p.204; Scot, *A Tongue-Combat*, p.86 (*Workes*); Birckbek, *Protestants Evidence*, ii. p.10; Raleigh, *Certain Queries*, p.51. The circle of divines around Paolo Sarpi, whose *History of the Council of Trent* would be published some years after Carleton's *Consensus*, felt that Carleton rather oversimplified the distinction in Rome's condition before and after Trent, and had too positive a view of Rome's errors and corruptions before the Council, affirming 'that the acts of the Counsell of Trent were but the varnish or luster whereby they were more apparent to the world': PRO, SP 14/77 fol.2 – published in G. Cozzi, 'Fra Paolo Sarpi, l'anglicanesimo, e la "Historia del Concilio Tridentino"', *Rivista storica italiana* 63 (1956), p.599.

which people had not before been tied by necessity to believe.[93] Carleton even argued that before the Council of Trent the Church of Rome was still sufficiently uncommitted in the chief points of religion that, if they had not been misled by the intrigues of the pope, its churchmen would have assented to the doctrines of Luther and Calvin more readily than to the Tridentine decrees.[94] This emphasis on the change wrought by the Council of Trent allowed English Protestants to defend more unequivocally the notion that all the necessary means of salvation had been available to the Protestants' natural forefathers under Roman rule, thereby freeing them from the need to rely simply on the principle of God's charity towards their forefathers' invincible ignorance.[95]

A defence of the doctrinal orthodoxy of the pre-Reformation liturgy was vital to the vindication of the Latin Church before Luther. Richard Field's lengthy appendix to the third book of his voluminous *Of the Church* therefore included a detailed defence of 'the mass publicly used in all churches at Luther's appearing', in which he claimed that it was 'clear and evident that both the Liturgy itself, and the profession of such as used it, shows plainly that the Church that then was, never allowed any Romish error, howsoever some did in the midst of her'. In fact, Field asserted, 'the canon of the mass rightly understood, is found to contain nothing in it contrary to the rule of faith, and the profession of the protestant Churches' – it was only the later abuses (against the intent of the canon of the mass) which were opposed.[96] This expanded appendix was not published until 1628, long after Field's death, which led the Scots Covenanter Robert Baillie to suspect that the text might have been interfered with by Laud, who became bishop of London in that year.[97] There is no evidence to support such an allegation, and indeed Field's arguments in this section are entirely consistent with the overall thesis of his book, which never received any criticism from the Protestant side after its publication. By 1640, however, such views could seem dangerously crypto-papist, as in the

93 White, *Replie*, pp.168–9; Morton, *Grand Imposture*, p.418; Cade, *Justification*, pp.202–3 (quoting Carleton and Hall); Burton, *Babel*, p.5; Ussher, *Works*, II: 167; III: 90, 118, 176; Sutcliffe, *An Abridgement*, pp.4–5.

94 Carleton, *Jurisdiction*, p.108.

95 This is not to say that the same writers did not also pursue different sophistical arguments concerning the nature of the forefathers' faith. See, for example, Ussher's argument in his *De successione* (*Works*, II: 167; cf. p.496) that those who were simple in faith were not to be tainted with the major defects in faith taught them by the prelates, as they only intended to believe their teachers as far as they adhered to right doctrine. Richard Crakanthorp similarly argued that, whatever errors against Scripture were accepted by the unlearned at that time, if the Scriptures were accepted as the foundation of faith (which they were) then all these errors were *implicitly* rejected by them: Crakanthorp, *Vigilius Dormitans*, pp.183–4.

96 Field, *Of the Church*, II: 104, 97.

97 Baillie, *Ladensium*, p.101.

intervening period a whole generation of Laudian writers had enthusiastically taken up Field's vindication of the medieval church while at the same time omitting his consistent and careful insistence that, in the Church of Rome, 'the face of religion was not the same, before, and at Luther's appearing, that now it is'.[98]

Before the Laudians, however, even Ussher wrote persuasively of the true doctrine that had been retained in the liturgy of the medieval church. The principles of the catholic faith had still been preserved among the common people, he wrote, in the church's solemnities which commemorated the Trinity, and Christ's Nativity, Passion, Resurrection and Ascension.[99] Moreover, 'the principal point of all', the crucial doctrine of salvation through Christ's merits alone, was still preserved and taught throughout 'those middle times', 'as appeareth most evidently by those instructions and consolations, which were prescribed to be used, unto such as were ready to depart out of this life'.[100] The vehement anti-Romanist William Crashaw published a medieval *Manuale Catholicorum* in 1611 to prove that Protestant doctrine still flourished in popular medieval prayers and meditations.[101]

It was also claimed that a significant section of the medieval ecclesiastical establishment had continued to disseminate true doctrine. The crucial doctrine of salvation through Christ's merits could still be traced in the writings of the medieval Schoolmen.[102] Ussher noted that the Norman Church opposed the worship of images, and that Berengar of Tours had gained wide support in France, England and Italy, which had included many cardinals and synods.[103] Humphrey Lynde emphasized that in England, at any rate, the most substantial points of faith were visibly known and generally published openly, in public libraries and general congregations. Simon Birckbek observed that Wyclif was supported by the nobility and by many in Oxford University (including the chancellor) in opposition to the papal bulls issued against him.[104] Carleton and Ussher were able to vindicate the reputations of the medieval regular clergy by emphasizing instead the role played by the friars as the chief promoters of

[98] Field, *Of the Church*, II: 94. [99] Ussher, *Works*, II: 492.

[100] *Ibid.*, III: 567 – see the examples given pp.567–9; cf. II: 492. See also Field, *Of the Church*, II: 308.

[101] William Crashaw (ed.), *Manuale Catholicorum* (1611). See also P.J. Wallis, 'The library of William Crashaw', *TCBS* 2 (1956), pp.213–28.

[102] Ussher, *Works*, II: 213–14, III: 572–9; Birckbek, *Protestants Evidence*, ii. pp.51–2, 93.

[103] Ussher, *Works*, II: 209–10, 210–11, 214–30; cf. Birckbek, *Protestants Evidence*, i. p.243.

[104] Lynde, *Via Tuta*, p.97; Birckbek, *Protestants Evidence*, ii. pp.72–3.

papal jurisdiction and of the errors associated with it, against the opposition of the priests.[105] In fact, Carleton claimed, truth in matters of doctrine might have prevailed among the clergy at the Council of Trent if it had not been for the presence of the friars.[106]

Medieval general and provincial church councils were increasingly applauded as defenders of true doctrine. Plaudits were not simply directed towards the popular 'conciliarist' Councils of Basle and Constance, but towards all General Councils before the cataclysmic one of Trent. Richard Crakanthorp composed a voluminous vindication of the Fifth General Council, and also planned a vast general history of the medieval Councils to show 'That all the lawful generall Councels which hitherto have beene held, consent with ours, and oppugne the doctrines of the present Church of Rome.'[107] Crakanthorp maintained that, of the councils held from the Second Nicene Council onwards, 'in those ages of the mingled and confessed Church, none of them are either wholly ours or wholly theirs', but that the last two councils – the Fifth Lateran Council and the Council of Trent – completely overthrew the foundation of faith, and therefore 'they and they onely are wholly theirs'. This was a thesis that was enthusiastically endorsed by Archbishop Abbot's chaplain, Daniel Featley.[108]

Even the medieval Schoolmen could be shown to have preserved the elements of right doctrine.[109] Ussher cited many of them against the current Romanist doctrine of merit, and quoted Peter Lombard approvingly on the eucharist as being fundamentally on the side of Berengar of Tours.[110] Indeed, the Master of the Sentences was now emerging as a Protestant hero. It is in this role that he appears in the vast Foxeian church history

105 Ussher, *Works*, III: 50–1; Carleton, *Jurisdiction*, pp.114–23. See also Carleton, *Consensus*, sigs.B2v–B3r, p.198. It was the friars who fulfilled a prophetic function in apocalyptic chronology as the special agents of the Antichrist after the unbinding of Satan in the eleventh century: Ussher, *Works*, II: 291–6; Carleton, *Consensus*, pp.289–319. Wyclif's writings against the friars were an important source for this approach. Carleton employed them to present Wyclif as a defender of the secular priests against the friars, and also in order to use his testimony that one third of the English clergy defended the truth against the friars: Carleton, *Jurisdiction*, pp.114–15, 116–19, 216–17. Ussher quotes lengthily from Wyclif in *Works*, II: 294–6, and cites Carleton's use of similar passages in his *Jurisdiction* (Ussher, *Works*, II: 294, note e).

106 Carleton, *Jurisdiction*, p.108.

107 Crakanthorp, *Vigilius Dormitans*, Epistle Dedicatorie, sig.4r.

108 *Ibid.*, p.1; for Featley's agreement, see *ibid.*, sigs.A2v–A3r. Crakanthorp tended to see the Fifth Lateran Council under Leo X as the point at which the foundation of faith was fundamentally altered by the erection of papal infallibility (*ibid.*, pp.185–7, 198) – an alteration which the Council of Trent then confirmed. Similarly, Henry Rogers was able to supplement the Catalogue of Protestant Professors which he compiled in his 1623 *Answer to Mr. Fisher the Jesuite* with 'a Catalogue of Counsels in all Ages, who professed the same' in his later *Protestant Church*.

109 See above, p.284.

110 Ussher, *Works*, III: 572–8; II: 212.

which Thomas Harding composed in the 1630s.[111] Harding included a substantial section illustrating Lombard's full accord with the Waldensians in over fifty points of doctrine.[112]

In the Universities, not only were the medieval Schoolmen's reputations being revived in the academic sciences, but they were also regaining a certain theological respectability. So much so, in fact, that when King James wrote to the Universities on 24 April 1622, urging them to ensure the inculcation of correct doctrine after John Knight's misreading of the works of Paraeus, he recommended that divinity students 'should apply themselves in the first place to the reading of the Scriptures, next the Councells and the ancient Fathers, *and then the Schoolmen*, excluding those neotericks, both Jesuits and Puritans, who are knowne to be medlers in matters of State and monarchy'.[113] Not all men were happy at the Schoolmen being dignified quite so far.[114] Complaints were regularly made that medieval Schoolmen were being granted too much attention: William Sclater complained of the current citation of friars (rather than the Fathers of the church) in sermons – a practice which he believed would lead people into popery.[115] This was not merely a puritan complaint. John Prideaux, preaching at the Oxford Act in July 1614 (a year before he was awarded the Regius Professorship) deplored the increasing recourse to the Schoolmen's doctrines as a backward trend,[116] although elsewhere he still strongly affirmed that 'the soundest Schoolemen successively have ever defended in substance, concerning Gods purpose, and mans will, his grace, and our abilities, that which our Church of England at this day maintaineth'.[117]

111 BL, Stowe MS 107 fol.3v. Harding's *Annals* were in fact never published: see below p.321.

112 *Ibid.*, fols. 44r–61v.

113 PRO, SP 14/129/58 (my emphasis). However, James' positive remarks here in defence of the Schoolmen should be read in the context of his earlier comment in his *Defence* against Vorstius that, while the Schoolmen were commendable in the main grounds of Christian religion, they were not as reliable in matters of theological controversy: *Workes*, p.371.

114 E.g., John Favour, *Antiquitie Triumphing over Noveltie* (1619), pp.31–3, 50–1. It is noteworthy that the official letter which the Privy Council sent to the vice-chancellor and Heads of Colleges one month later, which is basically a paraphrase of the king's previous letter, quietly drops this reference to the Schoolmen in the appropriate sentence: CUL, MS Mm/1/38 fol.267; C.H. Cooper, *Annals of Cambridge* (5 vols., Cambridge, 1842–1908), III: 143–4; *Acts of the Privy Council, 1621–3*, p.237. It is possible that the amendment was the work of Archbishop Abbot, who was one of the signatories of the Council's letter.

115 Sclater, *Threefold Preservative*, sigs.E3v–E4r. Cf. Morgan, *Godly Learning*, p.103.

116 'Must wee now fall backe to bee catechized by Lumbard, and Aquinas; as though our owne mens doctrine, so evidently grounded in Scripture, not refusing to touch of pure antiquity or any true schoole-learning, were not conclusive, and acute inough, for our abstractive capacities?': Prideaux, *Ephesus Backsliding*, pp.36–7. Cf. Abbot, *Second Part*, p.1132.

117 Prideaux, 'Hezechiah's sicknesse and recovery', p.20 (*Certaine Sermons*). In his own sermons Prideaux habitually studied and quoted the Schoolmen's readings when initially

Here, clearly, were all the necessary ingredients for an alternative and self-sufficient answer to the question of the Protestants' ancestry that was based on the general medieval Christian community, and that could easily jettison any need to appeal to Waldensians or to any notions of a godly elite of true worshippers within or outside the communion of the Church of Rome. Yet this stream of thought was not necessarily developed in opposition to the proto-Protestant line of descent.[118] Field's main concern was to stress that the 'true church' before Luther should not be located *wholly* among men such as Wyclif and Hus, to the exclusion of others.[119]

Moreover, Field balanced his vindication of the medieval church with more traditional emphases. He still occasionally employed the language of the 'saving remnant' when talking of the anti-papal faction in the medieval church (he had, after all, given a detailed definition of the church's occasional relative 'invisibility' earlier in the same work). Field still insisted that those erring in the medieval church were 'the prevailing faction', 'they carrying the greatest shew of the Church'.[120] He explained the Reformation as the removal from the Latin Church of those Christians who wished to shake off the papal yoke, leaving only the papal faction behind.[121] The only redeeming feature of the pre-Reformation Church was that it had within it those who wished the removal of abuses and innovations.[122] The medieval Roman Church had consisted of two sorts of men: 'true living members', and that dangerous faction that only pertained to it in outward profession. Here Field's depiction of the 'saving remnant' of true believers in the corrupt medieval church seems to overlap with his earlier definition of the church of the elect, in typical Calvinist fashion. Thus, the anti-papists before the Reformation are presented as the only ones who were 'principally and in special sort' the church, who held a saving profession of truth in Christ, and to whom alone scriptural references to the church as a fair, undefiled paradise and holy nation pertained.[123] This blurring of language and definitions, along with Field's unequivocal denunciation of

dealing with the text – see *Certaine Sermons*, *passim*. See also his later *Scholasticae Theologiae Syntagma Mnemonicum* (Oxford, 1651), esp. pp.1, 5.

118 It is certainly true that the Waldensians and Albigensians are entirely absent from Field's work, except for a careful dodging of them when his Romanist opponent cites them against him: Field, *Of the Church*, IV: 298. However, Field is careful to defend or explain away the doctrines of Wyclif and Hus: *ibid.*, I: 27, 369; II: 131; IV: 227.

119 'And therefore though we acknowledge Wickliffe, Huss, Jerome of Prague, and the like, who with great magnanimity opposed themselves against the tyranny of the see of Rome ... to have been the worthy servants of God, and holy martyrs and confessors, suffering in the cause of Christ against antichrist; yet do we not think that the Church of God was found only in them, or that there was no other appearance of succession of Church and ministry, as Stapleton, and others of that faction, falsely impute unto us': *ibid.*, I: 171.

120 *Ibid.*, I: 171, 172 ; IV: 535.

121 *Ibid.*, IV: 522–3.

122 *Ibid.*, IV: 523–4.

123 *Ibid.*, IV: 524–5.

Rome as 'the synagogue of Satan, the faction of antichrist, and that Babylon out of which we must fly', kept him within earlier apocalyptical traditions.[124]

Similarly, among other evangelical divines, the positive assessment of institutional churches in the time before Trent was usually tempered by a strong emphasis on verses 1–3 and 7 of the twentieth chapter of the Book of Revelation – the binding of Satan for a thousand years and his subsequent unleashing – as holding the key to medieval chronology. For all their positive remarks on aspects of the pre-Reformation Church, both Ussher's *De successione* and Carleton's *Consensus* commenced with a commentary on these verses of Scripture.[125] The unbinding of Satan in the eleventh century justified the search for, and vindication of, proto-Protestant groups which separated from Rome soon after that date. Although Antichrist triumphed completely only at the Council of Trent, those with the insight to flee Babylon far earlier were still not to be criticized, even if Roman errors were not then so transcendent. Moreover, all writers agreed that Pelagianism was a prominent heresy of the medieval church from which few churchmen were free.[126]

Certainly, the English Protestant vision of the pre-Reformation Church that emerged from all these qualifications and contortions was often far from coherent. In the works of Field and Ussher it is sometimes very difficult to know exactly to which pre-Reformation 'Church' they are referring – whether to the elect, or a saving remnant of true believers, or the general Christian community. At other times, their discussion of the Protestant *Church* before Luther seems to be concerned instead with Protestant *doctrine*, or the two are treated interchangeably. This incoherence in the Protestants' response seems to have been responsible for several conversions to Rome, most notably that of Wat Montague.[127] But it was precisely this incoherence which made the multi-faceted Jacobean approach to the Protestants' past possible, and allowed it to absorb many different arguments while disavowing none.

124 *Ibid.*, IV: 572.

125 Ussher, *Works*, II: 1–21 – cf. 74–98, 158–64 and *passim*; Carleton, *Consensus*, pp.1–4.

126 E.g. Field, *Of the Church*, II: 225, 260; Ussher, *Works*, III: 543–4. Cf. Ussher on the ubiquitous Mariolatry in the medieval centuries: *ibid.*, III: 476–96.

127 For Montague's account of the enquiries which led to his conversion, see LPL, Lambeth MS 943 pp.383–8. The original of the earl of Manchester's reply to his son is in Kent Archives Office, MS U.1475 C.108/1 (I am grateful to Professor Russell for this reference, and for giving me a copy of his transcript of this letter). These two letters were published in abridged form in 1641. A copy in Archbishop Sancroft's hand of Montague's reply to his father's letter survives in Bodl., Rawlinson MS D.853 fols.166v–169r. Archbishop Sancroft believed Manchester's reply to have been composed in his name by Richard Holdsworth: *ibid.*, fol.166r. For Holdsworth's perspective on church history, see Richard Holdsworth, *Praelectiones theologicae* (1661), pp.307–9.

This is not to deny that different Jacobean writers might have a preference for one line of argument rather than another, and that tensions could result. In his own conferences with Fisher, Daniel Featley rejected other conformists' suggestions that he 'prove the visibility of the Protestant Church by having recourse meerely to the corrupt Popish Church'. He felt this to be 'a slipperie & dirtie way', though 'perhaps beaten by some'. Featley protested that he saw no need 'to seek the golden purity of faith, amids the dung, and drosse of Romish superstitions, and depravations in later ages'. In choosing the succession of proto-Protestant witnesses instead, he cited the writings of Abbot, Ussher, Foxe and Illyricus for this 'more excellent way'.[128]

By contrast, other Calvinist conformists were, like Field, especially keen to avoid the suggestion that the Protestants' succession was limited to this proto-Protestant descent, and preferred to emphasize the succession within the pre-Reformation institutional church. Featley's frustration was mirrored by that of Bishop Davenant a mere five years later at the height of the *Old Religion* controversy. With apparent reference to the debate over visibility (and, conceivably, Featley's own contribution to it), Davenant complained that some English Protestants failed to recognize how important it was to grant that Rome was a church, if the perpetuity of the Christian church were to be preserved. Indeed, Joseph Hall argued in later years that the dispute over the *Old Religion*, and the question of Rome's nature as a church, had essentially been prompted by the 'visibility' debate.[129]

These potential clashes represented more general confusions and inconsistencies in the Protestant doctrine of the church, and the constant difficulties experienced by Protestant divines when they tried to establish the precise relationship between the church of the elect and the general Christian community. The underground proto-Protestant descent was a clear manifestation of the 'true church' of orthodox believers; while on the other hand the emphasis on the general pre-Reformation Christian community mirrored those understandings of the church which emphasized its institutional features and identified its members as the whole body of professing Christians. It is therefore not surprising that Laudian writers who approached this issue preferred a systematic and unambiguous rendering of the Protestants' origins which was strongly rooted in an enduring institutional integrity.

128 Featley, *Romish Fisher*, sig.K3*r–v.

129 Lewis, *Joseph Hall*, pp.283, 411.

THE REJECTION OF THE 'INVISIBLE' SUCCESSION

Laudian writers continued the increasing trend towards tracing the pre-Reformation Protestant Church within Rome's own communion. However, they differed from writers such as Field and Carleton because they repudiated all other forms of Protestant descent that related to notions of a relative church 'invisibility'. In rejecting notions of the occasional relative 'invisibility' of the true church, they also repudiated the proto-Protestant descent and apocalyptical framework which accompanied it. Instead, most Laudian authors restricted themselves to developing Field's more positive view of the medieval church, of which the Church of England could be presented as simply a reformed continuation.

The rejection of earlier traditions of church 'invisibility' was not immediate. Hooker's failure to talk in terms of the 'true church' when he discussed the pre-Reformation church had at least implied a rejection of the Foxeian tradition, but had not directly overturned traditional Protestant arguments.[130] Early avant-garde conformists such as William Barlow and William Covell still spoke of the occasional desolation of the visible institutional church, while a writer like Buckeridge might still on occasion allude to an apocalyptic view of church history in his references to the unbinding of Satan after 1000 AD.[131]

In this respect it was Laud and his followers who made the crucial break in the 1620s. The suddenness of the break may be exemplified in the different conferences with the Jesuit Fisher conducted in 1623 by Laud himself and by his colleague Francis White. White was a man moving towards the Durham House Group, but still in the process of detaching himself from more determinedly Calvinist colleagues and habits of

[130] Hooker, *Laws*, III, ch.i, 8. Peter Lake (*Anglicans and Puritans*, p.156) suggests that, when Hooker wrote in this context that God also had his church among those who bowed their knees to Baal, he was effectively making Rome, rather than the Foxeian succession, part of the true church. I would tend to favour a slightly different emphasis in interpreting the passage. Here, at any rate, Hooker's exposition of Elijah's meaning would *seem* to accept that, according to all the usual definitions, Elijah alone was the *true* church. Hooker had made a clear distinction in the same chapter between Christ's mystical body and the visible church, which he had insisted must include the wicked, so that allowing the papists to have remained members of the visible church was not saying much. In defending the salvation of Protestants' natural forefathers and upholding the basic necessity of the preservation of the outward signs of the church's visibility in all ages, Hooker was saying nothing new. Rather, it was Hooker's ignoring of the whole concept of 'the true church' that was most significant, and which both overthrew the Foxeian tradition and dignified the Roman Church as a consequence. I am grateful to Professor Lake for many useful discussions of this point.

[131] Barlow, *Defence*, pp.18–30, esp. pp.18–19; Covell, *Modest Examination*, p.22; Buckeridge, *De Potestate Papae*, 'Conclusio'.

thought,[132] and this is illustrated by the fact that he adopted a different stance to Laud on the 'visibility' issue in the conference.

White's account of church visibility remained within earlier traditions. In his reply to the Jesuit Fisher's emphasis on the need for external pomp and visibility of outward succession in the church, White reiterated the classic Elizabethan and Jacobean Protestant view of the occasional relative 'invisibility' of the visible true church. He offered two alternative definitions of the 'true church': it could refer either to (i) the universal multitude of believers, either all, or their governors, 'free from errour in publicke doctrine', or to (ii) 'a choise and select number of Believers, living either in the common fellowship of the generall visible Church, or united in particular Congregations, by themselves, teaching and professing right Faith in all capitall points, and readie to embrace all divine Truth, when the same is manifested to them'.[133] Only according to the second definition could there be said to be always a true church in the world, either in separate congregations or in the external fellowship of corrupt believers. In this way, 'the true Church [may] be granted at sometimes to be hidden and invisible'.[134]

White emphasized the weighty arguments

> against the glorious and perpetuall Visibilitie of the true Church (according to our adversaries Tenet) ... The prime Rulers and Commanders of the visible Church doe at some times by Ambition, and other enormous Vices, become enemies unto Truth ... and in such times the true Church, under the notion of a true Church, cannot be generally and gloriously visible.[135]

Against 'the Popish Tenet', White presented the Church of England's doctrine to be

> First, that the true Church abideth oftentimes in persecution either of Infidels and externall enemies, or of domesticall foes. And in time of persecution, by either of these enemies, it may be reputed a false Church, or impious Sect by the multitude, and consequently be unknown to the wicked world, under the Notion of holy and true: and in such persecutions the love of many may wane cold ... and iniquitie and infidelitie so abound ... that the number of right beleevers shall be few, and the same may bee compelled to exercise their religion in private.[136]

White even quoted the classic texts from Ockham which claimed that the true church may consist of only a few lay people, and that if all prelates in the world became heretical, God might raise up pastors extraordinarily. White emphasized that 'there may bee an Orthodoxall Apostolicall Church, consisting of a small number of inferiour Pastors, and right beleeving Christians, opposed and persecuted by the Hierarchicall part of

132 On White's shifting allegiance, see e.g. Cosin, *Correspondence*, I: 51, 56 and above, ch.3.
133 White, *Replie*, pp.56–7. 134 *Ibid.*, pp.57, 7. 135 *Ibid.*, p.62.
136 *Ibid.*, pp. 60, 61.

the visible Church'.[137] These were obviously ideas which would appeal to separatist and anti-episcopalian groups within the Church of England, but White, unlike the Laudians who were to follow him, was happy to employ such arguments alongside a defence of the Church of England's episcopal succession. Clearly in White's eyes the doctrinal importance of these ideas in the polemical battle against Rome over-rode any misgivings that he might have had over their possible abuse by separatist groups, who might use them to devalue and oppose the church's hierarchy. Indeed, this anti-hierarchical potential in White's work was heightened by his traditional emphasis on the importance of the experience of persecution in proving the credentials of the true church, and as 'farre more agreeable to the Divine Goodnesse' than a glorious institutional visibility.[138]

In Laud's dispute with the same Jesuit many of White's arguments were conspicuously absent. There was no trace whatsoever of White's central, second definition of the true church as 'a choise and select number of Beleevers', prepared to set up separate congregations. Nor was there any mention of the notion of a relative 'invisibility' of the church, nor any stress on the role of persecution, or the corruption of the church's hierarchy, or indeed of any idea of the succession of true doctrine and of the true church through a minority of despised, possibly exclusively lay, true believers. Instead, Laud's account, on this issue, concerned itself wholly with national, particular churches, and with their use of the right to reform themselves.[139] When faced with the familiar problem for Protestant controversialists of explaining away Luther and Calvin's references to the church's 'invisibility', Laud never attempted to explain such remarks with reference to the relative 'invisibility' of the true church. Instead, he claimed that all such passages referred merely to the invisibility of the church of the elect, which Laud had already effectively deprived of any practical importance outside the particular visible church.[140] When Laud did deal with the

137 *Ibid.*, pp. 67, 104. On 'extraordinary vocation', see also below, ch.9.

138 Replying to Fisher's complaint that, according to Christ's promises, the church should be teaching and baptizing all nations, rather than 'sitting in corners, or hidden underground', White replied that 'of the two, it is farre more agreeable to the Divine Goodnesse (who is a Father of the poore and oppressed) to be present to his little flocke in persecution, and when it flyeth as a Lambe from the Wolfe, and hideth it selfe from the Oppressor, Apoc. 12.14. then that hee hath entayled his perpetuall presence upon ambitious and oppressing Tyrants, which, stiled themselves Pastors, and were ravening Wolves, Scribes, and Pharisees': *ibid.*, pp.96–7. For the same emphasis on the validating significance of persecution, see Abbot, *Demonstratio*, pp.90–2; Downe, *Certaine Treatises*, xii. p.15.

139 Laud, *Works*, II: 170–8, 191–5, 213ff and *passim*.

140 This is clearly illustrated in the passage of Laud's work dealing with the issue of church visibility which has been described earlier. Laud here attempted to deal with objections raised by Bellarmine in his *De Ecclesia militante* (for examples of the constant recurrence of this passage from Bellarmine in Protestant/Catholic debate on ecclesiology, and of the

question of the corruption of the visible church, his main concern was only to reject the idea that any one particular church (Rome) was free from the threat of corruption and therefore able to claim infallibility.[141] If White's argument remained in the classical Protestant tradition of relative church 'invisibility', Laud, his co-defendant at the conference with Fisher, had managed to ignore a very basic element in this tradition, and in the following years several of the divines associated with him were to do the same.

Although Richard Montagu was entirely orthodox in his definition of the invisible church of the elect, he had no time at all for the idea of the relative 'invisibility' of the true church. In his *New Gagg* he simply denied the existence of the concept when his Romanist opponent tried to use it against him. Having described the invisibility of the church of the elect, he abruptly concluded: 'Otherwise then so, wee doe not speak of invisibility.'[142] In his *Appello* Montagu dealt summarily and contemptuously with such ideas. He admitted that 'some men, singular from the doctrine of the Church, in their owne private opinions, had fallen upon, and supported an Invisibility ... I doe call those Some mens doctrines in this point, Private opinions: and so well may I doe, in respect of the disinvalidity and disproportion of them.'[143] Montagu was forced to admit the popularity of such ideas, though. If they were 'private opinions' this did not mean that they had a 'paucity of proposers: for they may bee many, a strong, potent, prevailing party that thus opine, and runne a course to themselves in their owne Tenents, against or beside publick, enacted, and authorized doctrine'.[144] Montagu attempted to link this doctrine to 'Libertines and Brownists' by quite falsely claiming that it was repugnant to the basic point of the necessary visibility of the church on earth 'with visible cognisances, markes and signes to be discerned by', such as the Word of God, the sacraments and the priesthood.[145]

usual method adopted by English Protestant divines to deal with it, see White, *Replie*, pp.58–9; Morton, *Catholike Appeale*, pp.624–5, 661; Field, *Of the Church*, II: 396–7). Laud claimed that Calvin referred solely to the invisible church of the elect, which Laud argued implicitly meant the general visible church, and he quoted Richard Field dealing with this passage and affirming that 'the visible Church never falleth into heresy' (Laud, *Works*, II: 155–6). Laud, however, carefully ignored the following sentence in which Field went on to explain that, in the passages which Bellarmine urged, Calvin and others 'mean not that it [the true Church] is wholly invisible at any time, but that it is not always to be esteemed by outward appearance: that sometimes the state of things is such, that the greatest, in place of ministry, in the Church, pervert all things; and that they that defend the truth make themselves a reproach': Field, *Of the Church*, II: 397. Field makes the inevitable citations from Ockham and the Arian dispute. Laud quotes Field's closing remarks on p.396.

141 Laud, *Works*, II: 141–8, 156–8, 167–9, 178–87.

142 Montagu, *New Gagg*, pp.49–50.

143 Montagu, *Appello*, pp. 133, 136.

144 *Ibid.*, p.136.

145 *Ibid.*, pp.134, 135.

In fact, as we have seen, no English Protestant adhering to this doctrine of relative church 'invisibility' would have denied the necessary visibility of the church on earth – their use of the term was related entirely to degrees of the 'glorious visibility' of the true church. Montagu indeed had recourse to writers such as Morton, Jewel and White in support of the necessary visibility of the church on earth, but ignored the fact that they all also asserted the *relative* invisibility of the *true* church.[146] Francis White had maintained that the true church had been in a sense invisible since Pope Boniface III, but at the same time had stressed that the perpetual visibility of the church lay in her religious exercises and the outward worship of Christ, according to the Word, exercised by legitimate pastors.[147] Thus, when Montagu demanded how the Word could be preached and sacraments administered in an invisible church, he entirely missed the point. Thomas Choun similarly constructed a straw man of the arguments for church invisibility.[148] In point of fact, Montagu's and Choun's misconstrued argument precisely replicated that used by the preceding generation of Romanist pamphleteers against the Church of England.[149]

THE PROTESTANTS' FORERUNNERS REVISED

The changing vision of the 'invisibility' of the church outlined above was reflected in a newly exclusive view of the Protestants' forerunners, and a rejection of the earlier proto-Protestant descent. This resultant change of perspective was a gradual one, however. Some of Laud's associates, such as Francis White and Thomas Jackson, remained within earlier traditions of thought on this issue. White, as we would expect, was happy to cite the Waldensians, the Taborites of Bohemia and 'the Scholers of Wicliffe' along

146 *Ibid.*, pp.138–9. Montagu's citation of Morton was especially fraudulent, as in asserting that Protestants and Romanists differ only in the application, and not in the sense, of church invisibility, Morton was talking wholly in terms of the *relative* invisibility of the *true* church: Morton, *Catholike Appeale*, pp.659–71. Morton quoted Suarez, Sererius and Acosta to demonstrate that the Jesuits admitted the church to be hardly discernible under the Arians (p.660) and liable almost wholly to cease in the time of Antichrist (p.661). This was in reply to his Romanist opponent's quoting of Napier and Brocardo's remarks that the Antichristian pope had possessed the outward visible church for 1,260 years (pp.659–60), which Morton makes no attempt to dismiss as speculative 'private opinions'. Morton had earlier made the customary exposition of Calvin's distinction of the visible and invisible church in reply to Bellarmine's accusation (pp. 624–5).

147 White, *Orthodox Faith*, pp.324, 93–4.

148 Discussing the visibility of the church, Choun ridiculed those whom (he claimed) tried to prove the invisibility of the church itself from the invisibility of faith and holiness: Choun, *Collectiones*, pp.31–2. Like Montagu, he believed himself to have a powerful argument against notions of church invisibility by affirming the obvious visibility of the ministry of the Word and sacraments: *ibid.*, pp.32–4.

149 E.g. Brereley, *Protestants Apologie*, pp.298–326, 631 and *passim*; Norris, *Antidote*, pp.26–49. Countless other examples could be given here.

with the Greek Church as proof that 'the principall articles of the Protestants faith have continued in all ages'.[150] He championed Wyclif and Hus as 'blessed instruments of Christ, vindicating and defending Gods Truth, withheld in Iniquitie'.[151] In fact, White's *Replie to Fisher* seems to treat such sects as the only documentary evidence for the preservation of the true religion in the West before Luther.[152] This was consistent with White's adherence to ideas of relative church invisibility. Thomas Jackson, in his 1613 tract *The Eternal Truth of Scripture and Christian Belief*, described the Albigensians as Christ's 'little flock' who suffered persecution 'for professing most points of our religion'.[153] His later *Treatise of the Holy Catholic Faith and Church*, however, was a little more uneasy on this point, although his misgivings seem to have been prompted more by the sparseness and unreliability of the surviving evidence relating to the medieval sects. Jackson was not apparently motivated by any concern that tracing a pedigree through such small congregations might endanger the episcopal succession, or encourage separatist groups.[154]

Other Laudian writers were more outspoken in their rejection of such proto-Protestant congregations, and of the dangerous principle of tracing a descent through them. Laud himself had stirred up controversy at an Oxford lecture as early as 1603 when, according to his biographer Heylyn, 'he maintained the constant and perpetual visibility of the Church of Christ, derived from the Apostles to the Church of Rome, continued in that Church (as in others of the East and South) till the Reformation'.[155] Heylyn

150 White, *Orthodox Faith*, pp.265–6; *idem*, *Replie*, pp.104–5. White averred that most Roman doctrines were not begun until a thousand years after Christ, and were always opposed by groups such as the Waldensians, 'many in number, and largely diffused through divers Countries . . . whose Doctrine, in the most points, was consonant to that which reformed Churches doe now professe': *ibid.*, p.130.

151 White, *Replie*, p.139.

152 *Ibid.*, p.104. White supplements this with the traditional argument that, if no historical evidence could be shown for any visible church besides the Greek and Roman in this period, yet God's promises guaranteed that 'right Faith may be preserved in persons living in a corrupt visible Church', and according to God's promises, the Protestants could prove themselves to be the perpetual true church simply by holding the apostolic doctrine: *ibid.*, p.105.

153 Jackson, *Works*, II: 23–4, 26–7.

154 Tackling the question 'Where was your Church before Luther?', Jackson admitted the difficulty of citing a visible church in the West altogether distinct from the visible Roman Church, 'unless we will derive our pedigree from the Albigenses, the Picardi, or the poor men of Lyons, which to do I know not how safe it is, unless we had better records of their tenets than I have seen, or than the visible Roman Church, that de facto condemns them for heretics, was willing to propagate to posterity': *ibid.*, XII: 127.

155 Heylyn, *Cyprianus*, p.53. Heylyn was unsure whether this dispute took place at Laud's reading of the theological lecture founded by Mrs. May, 'or some other Chapell-Exercise'. Heylyn is the only authority that we have for this incident, but would appear to have picked up the details of the event from Laud himself during his interview with him which he reports in *Cyprianus*, p.166. The fact that Heylyn's account of Laud's

reports that this aroused the ire of the vice-chancellor George Abbot, who conceived a lifetime's grudge against Laud because these arguments ran counter to his own ideas, and therefore discredited him in public. This was because Abbot, according to Heylyn, 'could not finde any such visibility of the Christian Church, but by tracing it as well as he could from the Berengarians to the Albigenses, from the Albigenses to the Wickliffists, from the Wickliffists unto the Hussites, and from the Hussites unto Luther and Calvin'.[156] This is a blatant misrepresentation of Abbot's position. The *Treatise of the Perpetuall Visibilitie and Succession of the True Church*, which Heylyn cites for these remarks, certainly concentrated on vindicating the 'Waldensian' line of succession, but towards the end of the treatise Abbot made it perfectly clear that this was only one of several possible lines of succession of the 'true church'. Abbot explicitly argued for the visibility of the true church within Rome, and in the other churches of the East and South mentioned by Laud in his lecture.[157] Contrary to Heylyn's account, it seems that it was Laud's position that was exclusive, and that what Abbot presumably objected to was Laud's explicit rejection of the proto-Protestant line of descent, and his exclusive concentration on hierarchical churches.[158]

This interpretation is supported by Laud's hostile response to the publication of Abbot's *Treatise* in 1624. He was careful to show the book to Buckingham and to warn direfully of 'what was like to ensue upon it'.[159] Laud's anxieties may have been aroused in part by Abbot's list of extreme Taborite and Waldensian doctrines, which Abbot claimed the Church of England shared.[160] All Jacobean defences of the Waldensians had acknowledged that these doctrines had been maintained by the sect, but had always stressed that the Protestants only followed such groups in the vital points of faith, while dissenting from them in some other tenets. To Laud, however, such doctrines were obviously all too reminiscent of those

views on this issue is consistent with Laud's own position expressed elsewhere lends it additional credibility.

156 *Ibid.*, pp.53–4. 157 Abbot, *Treatise*, pp.94–7.

158 My reading here differs somewhat from the account in Davies, *Caroline Captivity*, p.58. Far from being a 'sectarian notion of visibility', Abbot's views were quite conventional.

159 Laud, *Works*, III: 145 (Laud's diary entry for 10 January 1624). Laud's representation of the book's dangers clearly had the desired effect, as the king discussed the book with Laud the very next day, and allegedly could hardly believe that Abbot could be the author of so dangerous a tract (*ibid.*). However, Abbot's *Treatise* was merely a reprinting of a lengthy section from Abbot's *The Reasons* (pp.25–71), which had not aroused any controversy when first published in 1604.

160 These included opposition to the rites and administration of most sacraments, hostility to prayers for the dead, disallowing the holy days of almost all saints, and disallowing the consecration of visible things: Abbot, *Treatise*, p.51. Abbot also listed among Waldensian doctrines the belief that holy images should be defaced and auricular confession disregarded: *ibid.*, pp.82–3.

contemporary 'puritan' positions of which he was so keenly aware, and this was enough to tar the whole principle of the proto-Protestant descent in his eyes with dangerous, subversive intent. Certainly, there is no trace of the proto-Protestant line of descent in Laud's *Conference with Fisher*. Where Laud found cause to refer to Hus and Jerome of Prague, he was careful to distance the modern Church of England from them. Instead, Laud seemed to be concerned exclusively with the fortunes of national, hierarchical churches.[161]

A similarly exclusive stance, and misrepresentation of the emphases of the inclusive Jacobean position, is evident in Heylyn's account of an occasion when these two visions of the medieval church clashed head-on in the Oxford Divinity Schools. This occurred on 24 April 1627 when, with the Regius Professor John Prideaux acting as moderator, the respondent Peter Heylyn himself determined in the negative the question 'An Ecclesia unquam fuerit invisibilis.' According to Heylyn's account,[162] in his exposition of this question

> I fell upon a different way from that of D. Prideaux in his Lecture 'de visibilitate Ecclesiae', and other Tractates of and about that time, in which the visibility of the Protestant Church (and consequently of the renowned Church of England), was no otherwise proved, then by looking for it into the scattered conventicles of the Berengarians in Italy, the Waldenses in France, the Wicklifists in England, & the Hussites in Bohemia.

161 Laud managed to make no reference to Wyclif at all. The only time that he cited Hus and Jerome of Prague was when he used the example of the Council of Constance's treachery towards them in order to excuse the Protestants' absence at the Council of Trent, despite the promises of safe conduct that they had been given. Even here, Laud was hasty to emphasize that he was not thereby necessarily siding with Hus and Jerome, but was merely pointing out Rome's violation of public faith: *Works*, II: 160 note u. This may be contrasted with Lancelot Andrewes' discussion of the same point in his *Responsio*, where Andrewes made use of the example of Hus without feeling any need to insert Laud's reservations: Andrewes, *Responsio*, pp.146–7.

162 Heylyn's account in his *Examen Historicum*, pp.214–15, is the only detailed source which we have for this dispute, on which university records seem to be silent. Anthony Wood (*Athenae Oxonienses*, III: 553) seems to rely on Heylyn's account for details of the clash, although he does also refer (as Heylyn does not) to a sermon which Edward Reynolds gave in the chapel of Merton College on 5 August following, in which he 'touched upon the passages which had happened between Prideaux and Heylyn ... to expose Heylyn to disgrace and censure'. Further evidence for the dispute taking place is in the biography of Heylyn written by his son-in-law Dr John Barnard, who describes Heylyn having shown him his thesis from the 1627 disputation, 'which I read over in his house at Lacye's Court; but I had not then either the leisure or good luck to transcribe a copy of it', and presumes that it has now been lost (Peter Heylyn, *Ecclesia Restaurata*, ed. J.C. Robertson (2 vols., Cambridge 1849), I: liv). It was presumably this dispute which Heylyn discussed with Laud when they met in February 1628 (Heylyn, *Cyprianus*, p.166), although there is no evidence to suggest that this was the reason that Laud interviewed him in the first place.

Heylyn reports that he disliked this trend, as undermining the episcopal succession, and therefore 'rather chose to look for a continued visible Church in Asia, Aethiopia, Greece, Italy, yea, and in Rome itself, as also in all the Western Provinces then subject to the power of the popes thereof'.[163]

A reading of Prideaux's 1624 Act lecture 'De Visibilitate Ecclesiae' shows this to be a comprehensive misrepresentation of Prideaux's position. Far from only proving the Protestant Church's visibility in various 'scattered conventicles', Prideaux had offered no less than five alternative arguments to support his affirmative reply to the question of whether a Protestant Church distinct from the papal church had been visible before the Reformation. Among other points, Prideaux argued from the nature of the Reformation itself, that it did not erect a new church, but purified a corrupted old one. Popery was only a disease, from which the church had now been purified by Luther's Reformation, while the essence of the Protestant Church had existed in the Western church before Luther.[164] In his 1637 *Briefe and Moderate Answer* Heylyn would attempt to monopolize this argument (that the Reformation had merely reformed the old church) by presenting it as starkly contrary to the pedigree which he claimed Burton and others traced 'from Wicliffe, Hus, the Albigenses, and the rest which you use to boast of'.[165]

The argument from separate proto-Protestant congregations had only been one argument among many used by Calvinist writers and, contrary to Heylyn's claims, Prideaux had been careful to stress that these separate assemblies were under legitimate bishops and pastors.[166] It was thus Heylyn's view that was the exclusive one, in its rejection of the proto-Protestant descent. Heylyn also claimed that the Church of England

[163] Heylyn, *Examen Historicum*, p.214.

[164] 'Ecclesia Papismo infecta, distincta tamen a morbo inficiente, erat ante Lutheri Reformationem: Sed eadem est hodie quoad essentiam Ecclesiae Protestantium: Ergo Ecclesia Protestantium quoad essentiam praecessit Lutherum': Prideaux, *Viginti-duae Lectiones*, i. p.136. Prideaux's second argument was drawn from those who had opposed papal corruptions before Luther and had agitated for reformation, though remaining within the community of the Church of Rome. Here he cited the catalogues of the Centurists, Illyricus, Foxe, Mornay and Wolfius, and even included sixteenth-century reforming papists such as Wicelius, Cassander and Adrian VI (*ibid.*, i. p.137). Further arguments were based on the congruity of Protestantism with the primitive church, which had unquestionably been visible, and also on a series of logical arguments 'ab absurdo' based on the familiar arguments for relative church invisibility: that if there was no Protestant Church unless 'superiori seculo', then it followed that there was no church extant in the desolation of the tenth century (which Baronius and Bellarmine attested to), and would not be in the future under Antichrist, when the Romanist divines expected the church to lie completely hidden: *ibid.*, i. p.140. Cf. Morton, *Catholike Appeale*, pp.660–1; Davenant, *Determinationes*, pp.158–9.

[165] Heylyn, *Briefe Answer*, pp.71–2.

[166] Prideaux, *Viginti-duae Lectiones*, i. pp.130, 137–9, 140, 142.

received no succession of doctrine or government from any of 'the scattered conventicles', disregarding all the efforts of Ussher and others to prove the contrary to their Romanist opponents. Heylyn contradicted every major English Protestant apologist since the Reformation by claiming that 'the Wicklifists (together with the rest before remembered) held many Heterodoxes in Religion, as different from the established doctrine of the Church of England, as any point which was maintained at that time in the Church of Rome'.[167]

Montagu's position on the proto-Protestant descent was equally unequivocal: in a letter to Cosin in 1625, he firmly opposed himself to 'any lineall deduction from, and extraction out of, Wiclef, Huss, Albigenses, Pauperes de Lugduno, of a visible Church, though never so reverently preached or authoritatively printed'.[168] When called upon to defend Montagu's writings, Francis White (who had, as we have seen, maintained the opposite position) sought an ingenious compromise by effectively separating the issue of church visibility from that of the location of the church before Luther. White applauded Montagu's vindication of the medieval Roman Church as an ancestor for contemporary Protestants, and claimed that this resolved the question 'where was your church before Luther?' However, White took this to refer merely to the question of the Protestants' *natural* forefathers who had erred in the pre-Reformation church. At the same time, White defended the notion of a relative 'invisibility' of the true church, quoting Whitaker in support of the same, and claimed (quite incorrectly) that Montagu had accepted this position.[169] If White was seeking to defend both Montagu's position and the integrity of his own earlier views, it was an unconvincing performance.

It was undoubtedly the need to preserve the Church of England's episcopal succession, and the Laudians' conviction that those promoting this form of relative church 'invisibility' were deliberately undermining that succession, which lay at the heart of Laudians' misgivings with the Foxeian tradition. Montagu emphasized that the question of institutional visibility was especially important to the Church of England because she claimed and proved a succession 'and therefore needes a visibilitie from the time of the Apostles'. 'If any doe thinke otherwise, or cannot doe this', Montagu declared, 'we undertake no patronage at all of them.'[170] Heylyn similarly argued that the Waldensian line of descent 'utterly discontinueth that succession in the Ecclesiasticall Hierarchy, which the Church of England claims from the very Apostles'.[171]

Laud certainly insisted in his *Conference with Fisher* that the true

167 Heylyn, *Examen Historicum*, p.214. 168 Cosin, *Correspondence*, I: 45–6.
169 Bodl., Rawlinson MS C.573 fols.60r, 64v.
170 Montagu, *New Gagg*, p.49. 171 Heylyn, *Examen Historicum*, p.214.

apostolic succession did not lie simply in a personal lineal succession, but in truth of doctrine too. However, if he thereby carefully limited the value of the institutional succession without a succession in doctrine, Laud nowhere hinted that the latter might be traced without the former. The episcopal succession must have true doctrine too, but Laud left no leeway for a succession of true doctrine outside an episcopal succession.[172]

For Montagu, episcopacy itself was the key to the Protestants' succession, and not simply something that needed to be provided for within the terms of a succession of true doctrine. When he rejected the notion that ministers could (in case of necessity) be made without an episcopal ordination based upon the direct, personal succession, Montagu applied to the preservation of a local episcopal succession Christ's promise to St Peter: 'The gates of Hell shall not prevail. Behold I am with you to the end of the world.' This was a promise which Protestant writers had traditionally understood to guarantee the preservation of an elite of true believers rather than a specific institutional foundation.[173]

We have seen that Calvinist episcopalian divines – who were committed to identifying with the proto-Protestant sects by their adherence to the apocalyptic tradition – had been able to derive even an episcopal succession through them. Even the later Laudian Peter Gunning was able to find Waldensian bishops without too much difficulty.[174] By contrast, Heylyn, in his *Briefe and Moderate Answer* argued that a descent through such groups was actually demeaning to an established church. People like Henry Burton might claim a pedigree 'from Wickliffe, Hus, the Albigenses, and the rest which you use to boast of' but, Heylyn sneered, 'the Church of England hath no neede of so poore a shift'.[175] By 1637 a royal chaplain, in an official work commanded by authority and intended to vindicate the government's religious policies, thus felt able publicly to spurn a historical descent which had been a central element in the polemical and historical works of Church of England divines since the Reformation, and to associate that tradition with a minority of anti-episcopalian sectaries.

[172] Laud, *Works*, II: 422–6. On this point see also below, ch.9.

[173] Translation of Montagu, *ΘΕΑΝΘΡΩΠΙΚΟΝ*, ii. p.464, in *Doctor Martin, Late Dean of Ely, His Opinion*, ed. Richard Watson (1662), pp.113–14. See also below, ch.9.

[174] BL, Add. MS 4274 fols.160–3. Writing *c.*1659–60, Gunning claimed against his Romanist opponent that the Waldensians professed the same doctrine as the Church of England (fol.160r) and concluded 'You may easily perceive by these testimonies that the Waldenses were so far From the anarchicall government . . . of Sectarian Conventicles that they did both own & enjoy Episcopal ordinations & government constantly asserting Deacons, Presbyters, Bishops, or three distinct and lawful orders of Clergy' (fol.163r). The Waldensians' recognition of bishops was even attested by the Franciscan irenicist Franciscus a Sancta Clara – see his *Apologia Episcoporum, Seu, Sacri Magistratus Propugnatio* (Cologne, 1640), p.53.

[175] Heylyn, *Briefe Answer*, p.72.

Traducing the proto-Protestant sects became a common pastime in the later years of the Laudian ascendancy. John Pocklington explicitly sided with the medieval Latin Church against such groups, and scathingly attacked Illyricus' classic defence of them as 'that list of persons censured by holy Church, called with some reproach of truth, and Christian Religion, "Catalogus Testium Veritatis"'.[176] Far from being the ancestors of true Protestantism, they were instead the forerunners of contemporary puritan iconoclasts. For some they seemed a by-word for unruly lay religion. Alexander Huish, the incumbent at Beckington during the altar controversy there, was alleged to have complained 'that this riot was like a Waldensian or Swisserland commotion'.[177] 'Waldensian' had become a term of abuse.

A clearer Protestant succession thus emerged, which could be restricted wholly to independent, national episcopal churches. This tended to put a significant new emphasis upon the Church of England's continuity with the pre-Reformation Latin Church and its hierarchy. Jacobean writers had replied to Romanist questions by stating that the Protestant Church before Luther was 'where it is now' – an ambiguous wording which could theoretically encompass notions of a congregation of doctrinally pure believers. Laud's reply to the same question more clearly restricted the Protestants' descent to the established Latin Church. In a subtle change of wording, he answered that: 'it was just there, where *theirs* is now. One and the same Church still, no doubt of that; one in substance, but not one in condition of state and purity: their part of the same Church remaining in corruption, and our part of the same Church under reformation'.[178]

Similarly, Montagu was not concerned to search for the succession of a pure church, or for an orthodoxy which might be in any sense 'invisible'. He declared in an unequivocal syllogism that 'the Church of Rome hath ever been visible. The Church of Rome is and ever was a true Church since it was a Church; therefore the true Church hath been visible.' Montagu did not hereby intend to equate the Church of Rome with *the* true church; he went on to specify that he only meant that she was 'a True Church ratione essentiae, and Being of a Church, not a Sound Church every way in their Doctrine'.[179] His essential point was that there was no room in his vision for 'the true church': any institutional church which retained the funda-

[176] Pocklington, *Altare Christianum*, p.92. This remark was later cited as an article against him in parliament – see *The Petition ... against John Pocklington*. See also Montagu's attack on the works of John Bale: Montagu, *Diatribae*, pp.114–15.

[177] Laud, *Works*, IV: 121. [178] *Ibid.*, II: xiii (my emphasis).

[179] Montagu, *Appello*, pp.139–40. See also Yates, *Ibis*, iii. p.14.

mentals of belief provided a sufficient descent for Protestants, regardless of its errors.

Ignoring traditional arguments of the occasional relative 'invisibility' of the true church, Laud was content to restrict his attention to the point that no single particular national Church (Rome) had the promise of indefectibility, and that it was not necessary to find in any particular church a continual manifestation of the visibility of the whole church.[180] The implication of Laud's words was that the true church must always exist in an orthodox national church, although not always the same one. Laud had no time for any search for catalogues of a minority of pure medieval believers: the traditional argument that 'the reformation of an old corrupted Church' was not 'the building of a new' was for him, and for other Laudian writers, the full and complete answer to the question of the Protestants' origins, rendering all other arguments irrelevant.[181] If the church could be shown to have existed in the institutional Roman Church before Luther, then this was all that needed to be said. Isolated from other arguments, this could imply a far greater continuity with the medieval church than most Jacobean Calvinist writers had assumed. This was especially the case as Laud did not stress the distinction between Rome's position before and after the Council of Trent. Instead, Laud followed the example of Romanist pamphleteers by citing the arguments of Field, Prideaux, Abbot and others for the preservation of true doctrine and the possibility of salvation in the pre-Reformation church, and then applying them to the *present* Church of Rome.[182] By avoiding any reference to the unbinding of Satan in the Middle Ages, and by representing the Reformation, not as the flight from Babylon, but as the exercise by particular national churches of the right of self-reformation,[183] Laud had rendered unnecessary all the potentially dangerous appeals to medieval separatist groups.

The Eastern episcopal churches also acquired a new significance in the 1630s. Heylyn's alternative pedigree of a continued visible church traced through them was just one form of argument which Jacobean Calvinist writers had developed, without any sense that it might cancel out the proto-Protestant descent. It was true that Prideaux had only made a brief

[180] Laud, *Works*, II: 3–23, 421–2 and *passim*.

[181] *Ibid.*, II: xiii. Richard Corbet's contemporaneous notes on this subject, which he forwarded to Buckingham, similarly ignore such groups and restrict themselves entirely to proving the uninterrupted institutional succession of the Church of England: Bodl., Rawlinson MS D.853 fols.174r–175v. William Fuller's discussion of the location of the church before Luther limits itself solely to the salvation of the Protestants' natural forefathers by a general repentance: Fuller, *A Sermon*, sigs.D1v–D2v.

[182] Laud, *Works*, II: xiii–xiv note q (quoting Field), 314–15 and note f (quoting Prideaux and Abbot). Cf. Downe, *Certaine Treatises*, xii. pp.40–1.

[183] Laud, *Works*, II: 167–8, 170–4, 184, 186–94.

passing reference to the Eastern churches in his lecture on the visibility of the church, but most writers accepted their validity as a line of descent for the Protestant Church.[184] The Eastern churches, with their clear separation from Rome, their vernacular liturgies and their relative doctrinal purity, were obviously of immense interest to Church of England apologists. If they had not loomed larger in Protestant accounts of the church before Luther this was mainly, as Archbishop Abbot explained, because of the apocalyptical dimension. Abbot insisted that, if neither the Protestants nor the Church of Rome had existed, then the church would have continued regardless in the medieval period in the Greek and other Eastern Churches. He chose to concentrate on the struggles of the Latin Church, however, because 'in as much as it cannot be denied, but that the prophecies concerning Antichrist, doe most touch the Westerne world, Rome beeing by the holy Ghost evidently designed to bee the seat of the Whore of Babylon, as also because our Romish Standard-bearers are more willing to talke of those parts then of any other'.[185] The most comprehensive treatment of the Eastern and African Churches to be composed before 1640 was at first consciously written within traditional, inclusive Jacobean discussions of the location of the church before Luther.[186] By its third edition, however, and possibly under Laud's influence, Ephraim Pagitt's *Christianographie* had begun to follow Heylyn in seeking to use the Eastern churches' preservation of episcopacy against the anti-episcopalianism of the Reformed Churches.[187]

[184] E.g. Morton, *Grand Imposture*, p.398; Cade, *Justification*, pp.152–5, 203; Abbot, *Treatise*, pp.96–7. James Ussher had expressed a particular interest in studying the professions of the Egyptians and Ethiopians in the south, and of the Greeks and other Christians in the east, as being examples of the location of the Protestant Church before Luther, in the form of the common principles of faith, on the profession of which men were admitted by baptism into the church: Ussher, *Works*, II: 494–5.

[185] Abbot, *Treatise*, pp.96, 97.

[186] Ephraim Pagitt, *Christianographie, or The Description of the Multitude and Sundry Sorts of Christians in the World, not Subject to the Pope. With their Unity, and how they Agree with the Protestants in the Principall Poynts of Difference betweene Them and the Church of Rome* (1635). In his dedication of this work to Francis White, Pagitt refers to Featley's and White's writings against Fisher, acknowledges their help and assistance in his own work and cites with approval the catalogues of Protestant witnesses assembled by Jewel, Ussher, Abbot and Birckbek. He presents his own 'catalogue of Churches' simply as a supplement to their own works on the church before Luther: Pagitt, *Christianographie* (3rd edn, 1640), sigs.a1–a2v.

[187] The 1640 edition is significantly different from the earlier editions of Pagitt's work, most especially in the insertion of a lengthy treatise 'Of the honour and reverence given by the Christians in the World to their Bishops, and Pastors': Pagitt, *Christianographie* (1640 edn), pp.177–222. This edition seems to be a product of the government's anxieties in the wake of the anti-episcopalian agitation in Scotland. It is hardly a coincidence that the work now bears a new dedication to King Charles, and it is possible that the episcopalian emphasis of the new edition was recommended to Pagitt by Laud, who took a close interest in Pagitt's work and whom Pagitt describes as 'my honourable patron'.

Heylyn's use of the Greek Church in direct competition with the proto-Protestant descent was a significant new departure. In the 1630s the Laudians displayed an increasing interest in the Eastern churches, no longer simply in the polemical debate with Rome as preservers of Protestant doctrine, but as orthodox sources which could offer important correctives to contemporary Protestant doctrines and behaviour.[188] If the Laudians' use of the Eastern churches was significantly different from that of previous writers, they were by no means the first to treat them as a line of descent of the true church. The exclusively separatist descent which Heylyn claimed to oppose did not really exist in the Jacobean Church.[189] But Heylyn highlighted the fact that it was now possible to develop a consistent line of argument on the origins of the Protestant Church which could safeguard the episcopal succession and ignore altogether the medieval sects and the apocalyptical dimension.

REASSESSING THE MEDIEVAL CHURCH

It was in this context that Laudian writers further developed the more moderate, positive view of the medieval church which they had inherited from their Jacobean predecessors. The Laudians advanced an increasingly forceful defence of all aspects of the medieval church, encompassing not just those medieval writers who had preserved doctrinal orthodoxy, but also the whole structure of the ecclesiastical establishment and the patterns of piety which it promoted.[190]

Where Prideaux had given a balanced and guardedly positive assessment

[188] See below, ch.8.

[189] Ironically, probably the only clear example among the 'Tractates of and about that time' of the position which Heylyn claims to be opposing occurs in his own *ΜΙΚΡΟΚΟΣΜΟΣ*, in the expanded edition published just two years earlier (1625). Here, in a very sympathetic description of the Albigensians, Heylyn quite clearly states: 'If now the Papists aske mee, where was our Church before the time of Luther, I answer that here it was; that here God was worshipped according to the manner by himselfe prescribed, & by the reformed Churches followed' (p.113). As in his views regarding Antichrist, Heylyn seems to have undergone a rapid alteration of his opinions. The reasons for this change are far from clear. It may be that the life-long grudge which he bore against Prideaux, which was to flare up again at his DD Act in 1633, led him to attempt to undermine Prideaux's reputation by suggesting that his views of church visibility threatened the episcopal succession. Heylyn would have been fully aware that Prideaux was the implacable enemy of the Durham House faction, and may have attempted to use his determination to curry favour with the newly ascendant group. Once again, it may be argued that the shifting views of the unscrupulous Heylyn may serve to illustrate trends in religious thought among the clerical elite and government.

[190] This is not to deny that they still believed the medieval church to have declined from the purity of the primitive church, and to have brought in many corruptions and superstitions which had correctly been removed at the Reformation: e.g. Cosin, *Works*, V: 400, 440.

of the medieval Schoolmen, in Laudian Cambridge the defence of them became more enthusiastic and outspoken. John Normanton, a fellow of Caius, gave 'a very offensive sermon' in Great St Mary's in January 1636 in which he praised Aquinas as 'never enough to be admired St. Thomas'. At the Consistory Court, far from reproving him on this charge, John Cosin, the master of Peterhouse, strongly defended Normanton's praise of 'St. Thomas', telling the other College Heads 'that he did well to call him soe, and that when ever he himselfe should preach in St Maryes he would call him St. Thomas Aquinas'.[191] It was criticism of scholastic authors which was more likely to bring reproof. In 1631, the young Peter Gunning (later to be Regius Professor after the Restoration) had his graces for BA refused by Matthew Wren 'for rayling in his Clerum against Schoole divinity, wheras King James & King Charles commanded young students here in divinity to begin with Lumbard and Thomas'. Gunning protested that 'he had noe ill meaninge against Schoole divinity, but against too much use of it in Sermons', and added, quite understandably, that 'he never heard of those Orders'.[192] King James' recommendations to that effect had been carefully altered in the Privy Council's letter to the University, and King Charles had not specifically re-issued them.[193] It was, of course, quite untrue that James had directed that divinity students *begin* with Lombard and Aquinas.[194] Under Wren's interpretation of the royal injunctions, it is doubtful whether Prideaux would have escaped with his equivocal remarks about the Schoolmen. If the Schoolmen were ever condemned by Laudian writers, it was because of their systematic 'Sabbatarianism' – precisely what English Protestants had hitherto regarded as one of their saving graces.[195]

Generally, the Laudian establishment showed itself to be increasingly sensitive to any attack on members of the medieval church hierarchy, however notorious. Passages in works by Richard Clerke and Richard Ward which roundly condemned Thomas Becket were removed by the Laudian licensers William Heywood and Thomas Weekes respectively. Indeed, there seems to have been a revival of interest in Becket, and perhaps a reassessment of the controversial medieval archbishop, in

[191] BL, Harleian MS 7019 fol.56. Robert Shelford also habitually refers to 'Saint' Thomas Aquinas in his *Discourses*, pp.24, 160, 187, 197, 212. Contrast Wotton, *Defence*, p.576.

[192] PRO, SP 16/193 fol.157. This event is reported by Eleazar Duncon, an associate of Cosin and Bishop Neile, who would doubtless have approved of Wren's behaviour.

[193] See above, n.114. However, they were legally comprehended in his 1629 injunction to the University 'that all those Directions and Orders of our Father of blessed memorie which att any tyme were sent to our said Universitie be dulie observed and put in execution': CUL, MS Collect. Admin. 8 p.703.

[194] See above, p.292.

[195] Peter Heylyn, *The History of the Sabbath* (1636), ii. pp.162, 169–72.

Laudian circles during this period, with both Augustine Lindsell and Richard Montagu studying his letters, and John Cosin adding him to the Prayer Book calendar in his second series of annotations, mostly written prior to 1640.[196] Similarly, if Jacobean writers had defended the reputations of the medieval councils because of their preservation of the essence of right doctrine, Laudian writers were more prone to cite them as authorities against trends in Protestant worship. Thus John Pocklington defended 'the learned Bishops in the Councell of Rhemes' for having adjudged the reading of homilies to be a form of preaching.[197]

The contemporary problems of upholding the honour, dignity, authority, ceremonies and patrimony of the church against the profane encroachments of the laity were leading the Laudians to look upon the medieval centuries in a new light. Traditionally, Protestant heroes had been those kings and lay people who struggled against the church's overweening power, wealth and influence, and who were violent in their opposition to popish superstitions and addiction to ceremony. Laudians, however, were increasingly tempted to identify themselves with the medieval church establishment against such erstwhile anti-clerical heroes, whose affinities with their puritan enemies in the present Church of England seemed all too clear. Richard Montagu wrote of a succession of medieval opponents of sacrilege in the same way that Foxe and the Centurists had depicted a succession of true Protestants opposing the doctrinal errors of the medieval Roman Church.[198] When searching for 'factors of Satan' in the medieval church, John Pocklington did not look to traditional targets such as the friars, the popes and increasing lay superstition and idolatry. Instead, he identified those groups condemned in the ninth-century Council of Aquisgrave for opposing priests, altars and consecrated things, and for forming themselves into common conventicles. Pocklington drew the inevitable comparison between these groups and his contemporary 'puritan' opponents.[199] John Howson similarly attacked the Petrobrusians of St Bernard's time (traditionally depicted as proto-Protestants) for their profanity in abrogating feast-days.[200]

As Laudians sought to defend the church's patrimony, it was these

196 Prynne, *Canterburies Doome*, p.293; BL, Harleian MS 6018 fol.148v; BL, Add. MS 34600 fol.37: Henry Spelman to Bishop Montagu, 17 July 1635; Cosin, *Works*, V: 225. Note also the remarkably sympathetic portrait of Becket in Godwin's *Catalogue*, pp.42–50. By contrast see Richard James' work against Becket composed during this period (Bodl., James MS 1), and the routine attacks on Becket as a 'traitor' in Abbot, *Defence*, p.236; *idem*, *True Ancient*, p.163; Willet, *Antilogie*, p.238; James, *A Manuduction*, p.31.

197 Pocklington, *Sunday no Sabbath*, p.33.

198 Montagu, *Diatribae*, p.73.

199 Pocklington, *Altare Christianum*, pp.122–3.

200 Howson, *A Sermon Preached at S. Maries*, pp.14–15. Thomas Harding treats the Petrobrusians as an important link in the proto-Protestant descent: BL, Stowe MS 107 fol.61v.

separatist, anti-ceremonial sects, and especially the figure of John Wyclif, who began to be presented as having constituted the major threat to the church and true religion. Previous writers such as Field, Carleton, Joseph Hall and Thomas James had carefully explained away Wyclif's opposition to tithes.[201] Richard Montagu displayed less restraint. He deplored Wyclif's attack on tithes and the clergy, and was ready to accept as 'not improbable' the claims of medieval and contemporary Romanist polemicists that Wyclif's conduct was prompted by his failure to gain ecclesiastical preferment. Lay support for Wyclif could be dismissed as the anti-clericalism of noblemen anxious to get their hands on the church's patrimony. 'Let Wickliffe alone: leave him to himselfe,' Montagu concluded, 'for what have ... we to do with him?'[202] Nevertheless, barring Heylyn's scornful remarks in his 1627 disputation and his *Briefe and Moderate Answer*,[203] Laudians generally preferred to ignore Wyclif rather than to risk an outright attack on so powerful a Protestant symbol. However, Sir Edward Dering later reported that Laud's chaplain William Heywood had denied publication to Simon Birckbek's *Protestants Evidence* because its author took occasion to commend Wyclif.[204] In private,

201 Field, *Of the Church*, IV: 227; Carleton, *Jurisdiction*, p.116; Hall, *Works*, V: 122; Thomas James, *An Apologie for John Wickliffe* (Oxford, 1608), *passim*.

202 Montagu, *Diatribae*, pp.97–9. James Wedderburn noted a passage from *ibid*., p.97, in his commonplace book: BL, Harleian MS 749 fol.152v. Jeremy Taylor justified speaking against Wyclif 'because he fell in indignacion because he lost the bishopricke of worcester': BL, Harleian MS 541 fol.110v. This jibe was also directed against Wyclif at the Council of Trent: A. Kenny, 'The accursed memory: the Counter-Reformation reputation of John Wyclif', in Kenny (ed.), *Wyclif in his Times* (Oxford, 1986), p.161.

203 Heylyn, *Examen Historicum*, p. 214; *idem*, *Briefe Answer*, p.72. See also in Heylyn's later works: *Certamen Epistolare* (1659), pp.150–1; *The Way of the Reformation of the Church of England*, p.41 (published in *Ecclesia Vindicata* (1657)). It is interesting to speculate whether Heylyn, and possibly other church historians such as Montagu, were influenced in their rejection of Wyclif by reading the Romanist Nicholas Harpsfield's 'Historia Wicleffiana', which was appended to his *Historia Anglicana Ecclesiastica* (Douai, 1622), pp.661–732. This is severely critical of Wyclif and stresses the similarity of 'Wiclevite' doctrines with those of the contemporary sect of puritans in their *Admonition to Parliament*, on the issues of infant baptism, usury and the use of the sword against the civil magistrate (p.681). Heylyn uses Harpsfield's 'Historia' as his source for the list of Wyclif's errors (compiled originally by Thomas Netter) which he prints in his later *Historia Quinqu-Articularis* (1660), ii. p.8, where he exclaims: 'What Anabaptists, Brownists, Ranters, Quakers, may not as well pretend that our first Reformers were of their Religion, as the Calvinists can, if Wicklifs Doctrine be the rule of our Reformation [?]' (*ibid*., ii. pp.8–9). On Counter-Reformation attacks on Wyclif see also Kenny, 'Accursed Memory', pp.161–7.

204 Edward Dering, *A Discourse of Proper Sacrifice* (1644), 'Preface' sig.d2r. The fact that Birckbek's work was later licensed by one of Bishop *Juxon*'s chaplains (Thomas Weekes) rather than by one of Laud's might give some substance to this allegation, which Dering would have investigated as chairman of the Commons' committee for scandalous publications. Dering is the only source for this episode, however, and it is surprising that Prynne makes no use of it in his charges against Laud's chaplains' activities as licensers (Prynne, *Canterburies Doome*, pp.178–85). It is also noteworthy that no reference to it

Laudian writers were more forward in denying the doctrinal orthodoxy of some of the Protestants' traditional medieval heroes. Thus Cosin in his private annotations to the Prayer Book castigated the 'profane ... harsh and unsavoury questions ... about the eating of Christs Body' that had been raised by 'Berengarius and his followers'. Similarly, Matthew Wren, in the privacy of an interleaved copy of Samuel Ward's *Gratia Discriminans*, described Thomas Bradwardine as an 'enemy of God'.[205] John Pocklington was characteristically more forthright, choosing to lambast in print an almanac published in 1631 by one William Beale, in which the author had inserted the names of some of Foxe's Lollard Martyrs, Wyclif, Jerome of Prague, Hus and Savonarola, in place of some of the medieval saints in the Prayer Book Calendar. Pocklington condemned the compilation as 'a Calendar ... wherein the Holy Martyrs, and Confessors of Jesus Christ ... are rased out, and Traitors, Murderers, Rebels and Hereticks set in their roome'.[206] It would be difficult to find a greater contrast with the works of Andrew Willet, where the testimonies of early Protestant martyrs were consistently accorded a doctrinal significance in their own right, almost on a par with the Fathers.[207]

Praise of the medieval church was shifting increasingly from a defence of the kernel of true doctrine which it had retained in the midst of popish superstitions, towards a celebration of the high standards of piety and the elaborate patterns of public worship which it had sustained. When Laud wrote to Bishop Curll, begging him to exhort others to help pay for the repair of St Paul's Cathedral, the archbishop urged the example of medieval piety with starry-eyed nostalgia: 'Remember former times when Religion was in life, the world in love with it, with what alacritie works of this kind were performed, noe cost spared, nothing too good, noe thing too much for God and his Church, every man being glad of the occasion to poure out a parte of his substance to soe blessed a purpose.'[208] There was certainly nothing new in using medieval generosity as a stick with which to beat contemporary Protestant parsimony. But in the past, this argument had usually been employed in a manner which underlined the fundamental

occurs in Dering's notes as chairman of the sub-committee of religion collected in Larking, *Proceedings in Kent*, pp.80–100, although this collection is far from complete.

205 Cosin, *Works*, V: 105; Tyacke, *Anti-Calvinists*, pp.47–8, 56–7.

206 *An Almanacke for 1631*, ed. William Beale (1631); Pocklington, *Altare Christianum*, p.92. The almanac also included Latimer, Ridley and Cranmer as 'Bishop Martyrs', as well as Luther, Peter Martyr, Melanchthon and Picus Mirandula as 'Confessors', and thus cannot be construed merely as an extreme puritan tract. See also Prynne, *Canterburies Doome*, p.182.

207 See Willet, *Synopsis*, *passim*.

208 Young, *Diary*, p.98 n.4. Similarly, Montagu glorified the piety of the Saxons, and commented that 'the world may take notice how farre these times have degenerated from the religious piety of Predecessors': Montagu, *Diatribae*, p.75.

division between the two different types of religion, in the same way that Moslem piety was occasionally praised in order to criticize Christian profanity.[209]

In Laudian times, however, medieval forms of piety were more likely to be held up for unqualified emulation. This was no time for warnings or restraint. Laud approved the removal of a passage from one of Featley's sermons which warned against 'too much embellishing and beautifying the church', reflecting that there was 'little necessity, God knows, to preach or print against too much adorning of churches among us, where yet so many churches lie very nastily in many places of the kingdom, and no one too much adorned to be found'.[210] Similarly, Walter Balcanquahall, in a sermon preached before King Charles which was published 'by his Majesties speciall commandement', stressed the honouring of churches in previous ages: 'witnesse the infinite cost bestowed by our fore-fathers in fabricke and maintenance of them, the infinite priviledges granted by Christian Princes unto them; although the beginning of our age did scatter as fast as the former age did gather; and the later lawes of taking no more from the Church, were farre more necessary than those former laws, for giving no more to it'.[211] Richard Tedder, preaching at the primary visitation of Bishop Wren in 1636, similarly remarked that 'God cannot complaine for want of an house, but he may thanke the devotion of former times for it; for we are more forward to pull downe, then to set up.'[212]

To compare medieval with contemporary religion was to lament the passing of the 'beauty of holiness'. John Swan clearly had the pre-

209 Thus Joseph Hall, in a sermon at St Paul's Cross in 1608, condemned sacrilegious lay patrons who collected tithes rather than paid them: 'our blind forefathers clothed the Church, you despoil it: their ignorant devotion shall rise in judgment against your reverencing covetousness': Hall, *Works*, V: 12. See also Henry Airay, *Lectures on the Whole Epistle of Saint Paul to the Philippians* (1618), pp.509–10 (cited in Dent, *Reformers*, p.157); Matthew Brookes, *A Sermon Preached at Pauls-Crosse* (1626), pp.27–8. On Brookes as a Calvinist conformist, see Cust, 'Anti-puritanism', p.17; Tyacke, *Anti-Calvinists*, p.262.

210 Laud, *Works*, IV: 282.

211 Walter Balcanquahall, *The Honour of Christian Churches; And the Necessitie of Frequenting of Divine Service and Publike Prayers in Them* (1633), p.11. This sermon may be compared and contrasted with John Howson's second sermon at Paul's Cross in 1597, which argues most of the same points, but is more careful to criticize 'the time of Popery' as being a time when the building, furnishing and maintenance of God's house rose 'to more than was necessarie ... nay to more then was profitable: For many abused the riches of the Church to worldly pompe and the enriching of their friends and kindred'. Howson also criticized how such investment in the church led the clergy to 'inordinate desire of their owne greatnes, and inordinate affection to their friends and kindred' (Howson, *A Second Sermon*, p.30). For similar criticisms of excessive donations to the late medieval church, see also Abbot, *Defence*, pp.200–1; *idem*, *Second Part*, pp.812–13.

212 Richard Tedder, *A Sermon Preached at Wimondham in Norfolke, at the Primary Visitation of ... Matthew, Lord Bishop of Norwich* (1637), p.5.

Reformation period in mind when he lamented that 'Religion hath (now adayes) lost much of that bright beautie, which in Ages heretofore shee was known to have'.[213] John Pocklington similarly noted uncritically how, after the Apostles, 'the piety of Princes, and devotion of God's people in after times gave beauty and wealth to Churches'. He then launched into a lengthy hymn of praise extolling the church fabric and furnishings for which contemporary churches were indebted to the pious zeal of their medieval forebears: glass windows, porches, bells, pinnacles, belfries, pews, font, vestry and so on.[214]

This reverence for church fabric and furniture, and lament for the decay of the medieval 'beauty of holiness', may be contrasted with the mainstream Jacobean Calvinist treatment of this matter, which was exemplified by Joseph Hall in 1623, when he preached on 'the glory of the latter house' at the restoring of the private chapel of the earl of Exeter. Hall placed all his emphasis on the church's *spiritual* glory under the Reformation rather than its past *physical* splendour, preferring true doctrine to the chapel's rich medieval adornments and 'all the treasures, ornaments, privileges, of this transitory world'.[215]

In the 1630s, medieval examples were also cited in support of the various non-canonical forms of reverence which were being promoted. Laud, Wren, Duncon and Pocklington all seized on the fifteenth-century precedent of the statute of the Order of the Garter to justify bowing towards the altar, even though Laud anticipated the natural objection that 'it was the superstition of that age so to do.'[216] William Page, fellow of All Souls, argued in 1635 that the warden and fellows should strictly observe the founder's statutes in praying for the souls of Henry V and all those departed in the faith.[217] In a sermon preached to the University in 1637 in defence of standing at the *Gloria Patri*, John Potinger, a fellow of New College, narrated medieval stories of the miraculous powers of this particular prayer when recited, and while he added apologetically at the end that he did not believe in such tales, he still applauded their message.[218]

[213] Swan, *Profanomastix*, sig.A4r. Robert Hegge, in his *Legend of St Cuthbert*, written in 1626, wrote of Durham Cathedral having grown to the 'hight of her glorie' in the eleventh century: Tyacke, *Anti-Calvinists*, pp.119–20.

[214] Pocklington, *Altare Christianum*, pp.11–12.

[215] Hall, *Works*, V: 191.

[216] Laud, *Works*, VI: 57–8; Christopher Wren, *Parentalia, Or Memoirs of the Family of the Wrens* (1750), p.81; Duncon, *Of Worshipping God*, p.36; Pocklington, *Altare Christianum*, p.133. Pocklington prints out in full the Statutes and Decrees of the Order of the Garter on bowing towards the altar in the second edition of the *Altare Christianum* (2nd edn, 1637), pp.159–60.

[217] Bodl., Barlow MS 54 fols.34v–35v.

[218] Bodl., Rawlinson MS E.21 fols.208v–209r. Note also the accusations against Beaumont of Peterhouse of often 'comending Legendary Stories & fabulous tales of the vertue of the Crosse to fellow Commoners & others of the Colledge': BL, Harleian MS 7019 fol.73.

Distinctively medieval devotional forms such as bodily mortification and contemplative monasticism began for the first time to command uncritical admiration, whereas before they had been satirized, or castigated as 'penal will-worship'.[219] William Watts, describing the precise and severe observance of the Lenten Fast in the primitive church, noted that this admirable asceticism had continued 'in the middle Ages of the Church, too: when a man might have expected, Devotion should have beene cooled'.[220] The monastic life had rarely been unreservedly denigrated in English Protestant thought – after all, it had patristic warrant.[221] Richard Montagu was unusual, however, in saying outright that the 'Monasticall Profession ... might be employed to the great advancement of christian Piety, were it used as it might and ought, *even in these dayes*.'[222]

In Laudian Cambridge, even medieval contemplative monasticism (usually the object of sharp criticism)[223] was beginning to find its supporters. Peter Hausted, chaplain to Edward Martin (the president of Queens' and former chaplain of Laud), preached that 'We have an olde saying, and it is a true one, "Exeat Aula qui vult esse pius." He who desires to lead a devout and godly life, let him remove himselfe as farre as he can possibly from the noyse and tumult of the people.' Noting how, 'in all Ages', godly men had fled into monasteries, Hausted remarked that 'God hath made some for a contemplative life (who indeed of all men are the most happy

219 E.g. Hall, *Works*, V: 385–6, 430–1, VI: 390–4; Davenant, *Expositio*, p.250; Cade, *Justification*, pp.118–20; Sandys, *Europae Speculum*, pp.57–9, 60–72; Robert Burhill's theses at the 1632 Oxford Act (PRO, SP 16/220/35). Note also the scepticism of an older generation of avant-garde conformist: Samuel Harsnet, *A Discovery of the Fraudulent Practises of J. Darrel* (1599), sig.A3r.

220 William Watts, *Mortification Apostolicall* (1637), p.42. Cf. Pocklington, *Altare Christianum*, p.43.

221 Ussher, for example, stressed the importance of early Irish monasticism in retaining and propagating the faith, and praised their strict discipline, sincerity and rejection of mendicancy, although he was careful to contrast this with the rabble of begging friars who had perverted the ideals of early monasticism: Ussher, *Works*, IV: 297–308. This passage occurs in his *Discourse of the Religion Anciently Professed by the Irish and British* (1631). Cf. White, *Orthodox Faith* (2nd edn, 1624), pp.30–4; *idem*, *Replie*, p.84.

222 Montagu, *Acts and Monuments*, p.445 (my italics). See also his arguments that the monasteries should have been reformed at the Reformation, and not profaned: Montagu, *ΘΕΑΝΘΡΩΠΙΚΟΝ*, i. p.384. A similar point was made by King James, who declared that he would not have dissolved all the monasteries 'if he had found them uncorrupted, and observing the canons of their first institution': Casaubon, *Answere*, p.22. Montagu does, however, follow Carleton and Ussher in attacking the friars as 'the principall Proctors and upholders of the Papacy, the Iesuits except, that ever were in the world': Montagu, *Diatribae*, pp.100, 103.

223 Even Thomas Turner, a former chaplain of Laud's, in a sermon before the king in 1635, was highly critical of contemplative monasticism, although Turner could not resist comparing this neglectful, passive piety with that of contemporary sermon addicts: Thomas Turner, *A Sermon Preached before the King at White-Hall* (1635), pp.29–31. This sermon, preached in Turner's capacity as royal chaplain, was published 'by His Majesties command'.

... and hath no imployment, but onely to pray and send up praises unto his gracious Creator and Redeemer).' These men were praised by Hausted as a godly elite, with no hint that their passive life might in any way impede salvation. Hausted's only expressed reservation was that such men did not have an *exclusive* claim to salvation, and that his audience should not 'shut off the unlimited goodnesse of God onely in a Cloyster'.[224]

John Normanton in 1636 similarly praised the monastic estate without qualification, singling out for especial praise the diligent fasting and penance of the Carthusians, and the wisdom of the Emperor Charles V for having given up his riches for a monastic cell at the end of his life.[225] While Normanton received the support of the Laudian Heads Cosin, Martin, Benjamin Laney and William Beale for his sermon, those who chose to attack medieval monasticism could find themselves censored. William Heywood deleted passages from Richard Clerke's book which ridiculed flagellant friars and levelled charges of 'Popish Monkery, Vows, Stews and Incontinency' against the monks and clergy.[226]

Attention was also focused on medieval traditions of piety by John Cosin in his *Collection of Private Devotions*, which provided a series of private devotions linked to the medieval offices. By borrowing and adapting from Sarum liturgical texts, Cosin emphasized those features of Christian spirituality most reminiscent of the medieval church, although he preferred to stress their patristic origins, and presented them as an integral and homogeneous complement to the Book of Common Prayer, rather than an alternative based on different sources.

The medieval church in Laudian eyes was beginning to appear as an oasis of calm, with a wealthy and powerful church able to command the support and devotion of the populace, before the storms of a Reformation which unleashed iconoclasm, rebellion, profanity, anti-clericalism, and constant confessional warfare.[227] At his trial, Laud approved the sentiment of a remark which he was charged to have made that 'the Church had been low these hundred years [i.e. since the Reformation]; but I hoped it would

224 Peter Hausted, *Ten Sermons* (1636), pp.176, 177–8.

225 BL, Harleian MS 7019 fols.55–6. Contrast Favour, *Antiquitie*, p.104, who recounts that Charles 'through heartbreake turned foole, and was shut up in a Monastery'. Cf. Willet, *Antilogie*, p.178.

226 Prynne, *Canterburies Doome*, pp.309, 325.

227 See, for example, Laud's authorization of the MS collection 'Iura et Privilegia Clero Anglicano Adiudicata Ex Parliamentorum Rotulis deprompta' from anno 20.Edw.I to anno 14.Edw.IV, completed by William Ryley in June 1637: LPL, Lambeth MS 323; Laud, *Works*, III: 255. This is not to deny that Laudians could acknowledge the medieval clergy to have enjoyed too much unjustified authority over the laity: e.g. Montagu, *Diatribae*, p.46. For a strikingly negative view of the medieval clergy, see also Andrewes, *Sermons*, V: 167.

flourish again in another hundred'.[228] It was even charged against John Pocklington in 1616 by the fellows of Pembroke College, Cambridge that 'He affirmed it to be an evident signe how acceptable the Romish Religion was to God in former Ages, because there were not then in the times of Popery, so many murthers, adulteries, robberies, &c. as since have beene in the time of Protestancy.' It was also claimed that he 'did then accompte that it did proceede from a greater measure of Gods grace, & assistance of his spirit then nowe commonly he granteth'.[229] These remarks were commonplace – but in Romanist polemic against the Church of England.[230]

When they contemplated the medieval church, the Laudians did not look back to a hidden succession of true believers, who had preserved the essence of right doctrine despite the persecution of a church hierarchy which reviled them as heretics. Their concentration was focused instead entirely upon the general Christian community in which their forefathers had participated, and upon the piety, devotion and reverence which the church, for all its faults, had been able to instil. This should hardly surprise us. Laudian churchmanship was typified by a piety more centred on the sacraments and public worship than on the word, stressing the positive religious value of the rites and ceremonies of the Church of England and rejecting as 'puritan' the word-based piety of the Elizabethan and Jacobean

228 Laud, *Works*, IV: 162. At his trial, seeing the devastation of the established church, Laud withdrew this hope.

229 *The Petition ... against John Pocklington*, p.29; CUL, MS VC Ct I.8 fol.255r; CUL, MS Mm/I/46 p.387. It should be noted, however, that it was Matthew Wren who informed against Pocklington on this charge, which clearly seemed extreme, even to someone of Wren's beliefs. Wren's actions may, however, have been prompted simply by personal antagonism – see the additional complaints made before Bishop Neile in 1614 (which were not repeated when the case was brought before the Consistory Court in 1616) about Pocklington's having broken college customs by seating himself above the senior fellows in chapel (CUL, MS Mm/I/46 p.388). Moreover, the attack on Pocklington cannot be studied apart from the fellows' contemporaneous accusations against his patron Bishop Harsnett, then the master of Pembroke, which included charges of popery among the fifty-seven articles of the 'Querela Pembrochiana' drawn up by the fellows against his mastership of the college. Already Harsnett's chaplain, Pocklington had acted as one of the master's deputies in running the college, along with Thomas Muriell, as Harsnett was regularly away from college on episcopal affairs (he was then bishop of Chichester). As a junior fellow acting in the master's stead, and presumably relishing his sudden authority over his elders, it is hardly surprising that Pocklington had his opponents. He seems, however, to have overturned the accusations of popery made against him. Harsnett reported to the earl of Arundel a year after the case was heard in the Consistory Court that Pocklington had cleared himself of the accusations 'before all the heads of the universitye, and especiallye unto his Matie, as that his Matie was pleased to expresse him selfe with some admiration of the man'. Harsnett also noted that Pocklington was shortly to preach before the king at court, although there is no evidence that the king was sufficiently impressed as to make him one of his chaplains (BL, Add. MS 39948 fol.184).

230 See Willet, *A Retection*, p.31; Brereley, *Protestants Apologie*, pp.589–97.

Church. This de-emphasis on doctrine meant that the medieval sects had precious little left to recommend them as possible ancestors of the present Church of England. Rather, it was clear that the church from which groups such as the Waldensians had separated had been more faithful in preserving those elements which most appealed to Laudian styles of worship – more faithful, in fact, than Protestantism had been since the Reformation. Whatever gains in doctrinal purity the Reformation had afforded (and this was becoming an issue for debate), the Laudians felt keenly that the church itself had been a loser. Jeremy Taylor was accused by his parishioners of preaching 'that the cleargy of the Church of England have mourned in blacke fourescore yeares'.[231]

The medieval church was a place of ceremonial splendour whose loss the Laudians felt very keenly. When the papal agent Panzani visited Cambridge in 1635, he was shown around by Edward Martin, the president of Queens'. Panzani reported that Martin showed him a picture in Jesus College of an early saint 'in abito Pontificale', at which point the Laudian cleric gave a sigh and exclaimed to his guest, 'When will such splendour be restored to our Church!'†[232] Such was the shadow which the splendour of the medieval past cast upon the parsimonious post-Reformation church in Laudian eyes. From such a perspective, the Reformation itself seemed to require a new defence, if indeed such a defence could be found.

This was not everyone's view, of course, even in the 1630s. It has recently been suggested that a commitment to the earlier Foxeian view of church history, with its vision of an 'invisible succession' of true believers, was the 'obsolescent philosophy' of a 'wasting generation', with Ussher a lone and increasingly anachronistic figure amidst the liberated Erasmianism of the 1630s.[233] Nevertheless if, like the debates over apocalypticism more generally, the allied scholarship was becoming increasingly rarefied and suffocatingly dense, the issue of church visibility itself remained a live one in the debate with Rome, and a succession of lesser writers such as Birckbek and Rogers continued to deal with it in the 1630s. Moreover, it was in these years that two of the most ambitious chronologies of all were being composed. Thomas James had died before he had been able to publish his own contribution to the visibility debate – a 1,010-page manuscript, dedicated to Archbishop Abbot, entitled 'An Anticoccius or A Preamble to a greater worke which shall . . . shew the Generall Historie of the Protestant Churches more or lesse visible in all times and in all places.' After James' death, however, his desire to compose a fully updated version of Foxe's

231 BL, Harleian MS 541 fol.111r. I am very grateful to Professor Russell for this reference.
232 PRO, MS 31/9/17B: Panzani to Barberini, 15/25 July 1635.
233 Trevor-Roper, *Catholics*, pp.164–5.

epic was inherited by two men. One of them was Michael Dalton of Lincoln's Inn – author of *The Countrey Justice* – who completed in 1634 his 400-folio tract *The Christian Catholick: Or a Chronographie of the Estate of the Church and Religion (especially in these Western Parts) from the Tyme of our Lord and Saviour Jesus Christ till Martin Luther: Shewinge the Antiquitye of the Religion of Protestants and the Beginning and Novelty of the Papists.*[234] Dalton's work, however, paled before the colossus which was being constructed at the same time in the small village of Souldern in Oxfordshire, where the rector Thomas Harding was labouring to complete his enormous 5,400-folio *Annals of Church Affaires.*[235] Harding saw himself as the new Foxe, although the manuscript's alternative title – 'The image of both churches' – echoed the work of John Bale and indicated Harding's starkly polarized vision of church history.[236]

It is highly significant that, with the opening of the Long Parliament and MPs searching once more to rediscover the lost certainties of the Elizabethan Protestant tradition, their eyes alighted on Dalton and Harding's manuscripts. Dalton prepared a new copy dedicated to the Long Parliament in 1641, but it was Harding's sprawling epic which was ordered to be published by Edward Dering's committee in May 1641.[237] Events soon overcame this attempt to reassert Elizabethan Protestant values, as they did the schemes for limited episcopacy and the reform of the Prayer Book. Both Dalton and Harding eventually died in 1648, with neither of their works having found their way into print. But by then the present condition of the English Church was giving more than sufficient cause for concern.

234 QCO, MS 249; Gonville and Caius College, Cambridge, MS 587; *DNB* s.n. 'Michael Dalton'. An extensive summary of Dalton's work also survives in BL, Sloane MS 4359.

235 SUL, Hartlib MS 29/3 fol.36r–v (where it is implied that Laud intervened in 1635 to prevent Harding writing any more). *DNB* (s.n. 'Thomas Harding') describes Harding's work as 'undiscoverable'. Dr John Adamson, however, has discovered the greater part of Harding's *Annals of Church Affaires* in CUL, Add. MSS 2608–9. I am very grateful to Dr Adamson for sharing his discovery with me. Another smaller portion of Harding's manuscript survives in BL, Stowe MS 107. Almost the entire work can now be reconstructed, although the sections covering the late medieval period onward (the work apparently extended up until the end of James' reign) have not yet come to light. I hope to deal with Harding's work in greater detail elsewhere.

236 CUL, Add. MS 2609 (1) pp.5, 9. Another alternative title of the work ('Looke once more, beyond Luther') echoed the title of a shorter work by Richard Bernard.

237 See the inscriptions in each volume (e.g. CUL, Add. MS 2609 (1) p.568; BL, Stowe MS 107 fol.3v). The cost of such a work must have seemed prohibitive, however (it was estimated at £2,000 in the 1650s) and the committee would appear to have settled for a new edition of Foxe's *Acts and Monuments* instead. A further effort was made to publish Harding's work in the early 1650s, when Ussher and Gataker sought to publish it by subscription. A licence for publication was acquired in 1653, but again with no result. It was later advertised for sale: LPL, Lambeth MS 941 fol.104; *DNB*, s.n. 'Thomas Harding'. Dalton's 1641 copy of his *Chronographie* with its new dedication survives as Gonville and Caius College, Cambridge, MS 496.

7

Separation and reunion

'NON FUGIMUS SED FUGAMUR': CHANGING VIEWS OF THE FLIGHT FROM ROME

As we have seen, Jacobean writers across the whole doctrinal spectrum agreed on the importance of Revelation 18.4 (the flight from Babylon). Not only was it seen as a text which justified separation from the Church of Rome, but it was also interpreted as a divine command which could not be ignored. This was a point argued, not just by moderate puritans such as Willet and Bernard, but also by Calvinist conformists such as Powel, Hakewill and Bedell. Even an avant-garde conformist such as Andrewes argued that the Roman Church was Babylon.[1] It did not exhaust the possible lines of defence, however. When William Bedell confronted the issue of what authority the Protestants had for leaving Rome, he resorted first to the familiar passage from Revelation. This was a justification which was sufficient in itself.[2] But this did not mean that other arguments could not be made, and Bedell chose to buttress his position further by deciding to settle the argument 'at the Bar of Reason out of the common Principles of Christian Doctrine'. Romanists could always quibble about whether the papal monarchy was Babylon and therefore, said Bedell, 'let us for the present set aside the Mystical Arguments from this place, and all other Prophetical Circumstances'.[3] Similarly, Anthony Wotton's popular *Runne from Rome*, which dealt specifically with the separation from Rome, bore the text of Revelation 18.4 on its title-page, but avoided discussing the issue of Antichrist because (as Wotton explained) it was a long controversy which had already been sufficiently disputed elsewhere. He only mentioned Antichrist at the tail-end of his tract 'rather because I thought it would bee

[1] Powel, *Consideration of the Papists*, pp.36–8; Hakewill, *Answere*, ii. p.83; Crakanthorp, *Defensio*, pp.246–51; Bernard, *Judgement*, ii. pp.62–4, 88; Bernard, *Looke beyond Luther*, pp.45–6; Willet, *Synopsis* (1600), p.616; Andrewes, *Tortura*; *idem*, *Responsio*; Windsor, 'The controversy', pp.160–1. Converts from the Roman Church used the scriptural passage in a similar manner when explaining their motives: Questier, 'Phenomenon', p.188.

[2] Bernard, *Judgment*, ii. p.88. [3] *Ibid.*, ii. pp.88–9.

looked for, then that I found it greatly necessarie', since the main body of his treatise had provided arguments which were in themselves sufficient to justify the separation.[4]

It was usually argued that the cause of separation from Babylon lay in the 'plagues' which threatened to infect those who remained within her. It was these doctrinal errors which formed the basis of the justification of the past Reformation and the continuing division of Christendom. When John Rainolds defended the thesis that 'the Reformed Churches . . . have severed themselves lawfully from the Church of Rome', he concentrated entirely on Rome's corruptions in doctrine and manners. The Reformed Churches were not schismatic for separating from Rome; 'they were sacrilegious unless they had done so'. Andrew Willet similarly defended Protestants against the Roman charge of schism by citing the novel doctrines introduced by the antichristian Church of Rome.[5]

In the Jacobean period, however, conformist divines not only wrote of Rome's fundamental doctrinal errors, but also increasingly emphasized that Rome had tyrannically imposed these errors as being necessary to salvation. When Thomas Morton discussed the general question of which corruptions might merit departure from a particular church, he stressed that 'it is not . . . the corruption of a Doctrine, which can alwaies drive a man out of the Church, except other properties of necessary Remooving doe concurre'. He listed these four properties, with relation to Luther's separation from Rome, as follows: the Roman hierarchy's general obstinacy and refusal to reform; the open blaspheming of the way of Truth; the violent enforcement of subscription to new articles of faith; and the compelling of Luther himself to subscribe to satanic doctrines, such as idolatry and Indulgences.[6] Any one of these might give sufficient cause to Luther to depart 'out of Romish Babylon'; indeed, idolatrous customs in the public worship of God justified a separation in themselves.[7] Nevertheless, it was the matter of the imposition of new articles of faith which increasingly interested Jacobean writers. Here, attention was concentrated on the Council of Trent and the new Creed of Pope Pius IV, which had made new articles of belief out of disputable, scholastic points and imposed them as necessary for salvation.[8]

However, this argument was never allowed to stand on its own. While it might justify the continued separation from Rome, there were clear difficulties in a line of argument that concentrated wholly on the new impo-

[4] Wotton, *Runne*, pp.78–9.

[5] Rainolds, *Summe of the Conference*, pp.666–8 (Rainolds ends this section with the inevitable appeal to Revelation 18.4); Willet, *Hexapla on Romans*, p.741.

[6] Morton, *Grand Imposture*, p.387, cf. p.372. [7] *Ibid.*, pp.387, 371–2.

[8] See above, pp.243–4.

sitions of the Tridentine Creed. Not the least of the problems thereby incurred was the simple matter of chronology. This was pointed out by the Roman apostate de Dominis. Noting how 'the milder sort of English Protestants ... complaine that the Catholicks thrust upon them new articles in so many definitions made in the councell of Trent about Iustification, workes, merits, purgatory, Indulgences, &c.' de Dominis observed that these new impositions had been made *after* the Protestants' original separation:

> they had made a most foule, and grosse schisme before any thing was spoken of concerning these articles which they call new; Therefore it is great folly in them to alleage these new articles, as a cloake for their schisme: for the effect cannot goe before his cause ... How can they cast the causes of schisme upon the curses of Rome and Councell of Trident when before the said curses they had devided themselves by schisme, from the Catholick Church?[9]

De Dominis' point was a fair one, which some conformist authors found it difficult to dispute. The Laudian James Wedderburn thus chose to concentrate his attention wholly on the innovations which the Church of Rome had introduced *since* the Reformation when he wished to dissuade people from converting to Rome. He confessed that the initial separation from Rome could not be defended, and might in fact have been schismatical.[10]

As we have seen, a number of divines associated with Laud avoided the previous emphasis on Rome's fundamental doctrinal errors. Instead their attention was concentrated more on the tyrannical way in which the errors had been imposed, and less on the nature of the errors as in themselves damnable.[11] It is true that Laud himself still followed the traditional path of accounting for the separation from Rome by attacking Rome's doctrinal errors. In his *Conference*, while stressing the importance of compulsion,

[9] De Dominis, *Second Manifesto*, sigs.D1v–D2r, E4r, F1v–F2r. This argument had been anticipated by Carleton, but his explanation amounted to a redefinition of the chronology of the Reformation, since it argued that Luther effectively lived and died a member of the medieval church. When preaching against Indulgences, Carleton argued, Luther did not think of revolting from the pope, because he preached doctrines which he was sure the church had held before him, and which were agreeable to the rule of faith which at that time stood unchanged in the church. Luther's appeal was to a General Council. It was only at the Council of Trent that this ultimate recourse was effectively removed, with the rule of faith being changed, and the pope being raised above a General Council as the judge of controversies: Carleton, *Directions*, pp.69–73.

[10] BL, Harleian MS 750 fols.62r–73r.

[11] See above, p.216. William Forbes, in fact, saw this as the major problem. He devoted his *Considerationes Modestae et Pacificae* to demonstrating that Rome's errors were not in themselves heretical or idolatrous. Preaching before the king in June 1633, it was the pope's claims to infallibility and his imposition of new articles of faith which he highlighted as the main bar to religious peace, while noting that the imposition of non-fundamental articles was an error of which Protestants themselves were regularly guilty: John Forbes, *Opera Omnia* (Amsterdam, 1703), I/i. pp.292–3.

Laud emphasized the role played by the Church of Rome's superstitions in themselves as well. While he found it 'most difficult' to specify them, and refused to set down which particular errors of doctrine might give just cause for a separation, Laud stressed in the next sentence that there were indeed 'errors in doctrine, and some of them such as most manifestly endanger salvation' in the Church of Rome. He emphasized that Rome 'hath erred in the doctrine of faith, and dangerously too'. Rome's corruptions 'in the doctrine of faith' were the cause of both the first separation from Rome, and of its continuation.[12] Nevertheless, Laud's refusal to detail precisely which errors of faith might justify departures from a church marked an important step on the road to the reasoning of writers such as Forbes, who argued that such errors in themselves could not provide the justification for such a separation.

In the Jacobean period, conforming divines of varied doctrinal hue stressed the role played by Romish tyranny as part of a more general attempt to readjust the relative importance allotted to matters of doctrine, conscience and God's truth in the break with Rome. All conformists sought instead to employ a rhetoric of moderation, representing the Protestants' flight from Rome in a more qualified and restrained light. There are several possible reasons for this change of emphasis, which can be observed in the writings of a range of Calvinist, as well as avant-garde conformist, divines. It was partly a shift made under polemical pressure from Roman controversialists, who during this period increasingly focused their attack on the issues of visible church continuity and the Protestant crime of schism. This charge could be responded to in a variety of ways. Where the puritan Thomas Beard claimed that the apocalyptic dimension was crucial in order to justify 'our so peremptory and exact a separation', another alternative, as Edmund Bunny and many conformist authors after him recognized, was to deny that so 'peremptory' a separation had in fact taken place.[13] These considerations gave rise to a clutch of metaphors which could be used to describe the process of the Reformation without implying the notions of separation and schism. Images such as the weeding of a field, or a doctor's curing of a malady, had the advantage of suggesting institutional continuity without obliging the author to explain this process in theological or practical terms. This doubtless explains the popularity of these metaphors with a variety of writers, including Ussher, Bedell and Francis White.[14] Nevertheless, the very flexibility and imprecision of such images allowed the almost imperceptible spread of new, more irenically

[12] Laud, *Works*, II: 332, 165–6, 213, cf. pp.378–9.
[13] Beard, *Antichrist*, sig.A3r; Bunny, *Treatise*, pp.79–83.
[14] Ussher, *Works*, XII: 497; Bedell, *Certaine Letters*, p.76; White, *Replie*, p.6.

minded concepts of a 'limited communion' which might still be enjoyed with the Roman Church, as we shall see.

This polemical move by English Protestants was also undoubtedly prompted by the increasing need to counter the arguments of separatists from the English Church. These radical puritans attempted to justify their separation from what they considered to be an unreformed Church of England in terms of the same absolute scripturally based imperatives that were usually invoked to explain the Protestants' flight from Rome.[15] The impact of these groups on conformist thinking about the Reformation emerges clearly in John Prideaux's 1614 sermon *Ephesus Backsliding*. Here, in order to parry separatist arguments against the Church of England, Prideaux was driven to oppose private schisms and to emphasize the orderly and restrained nature of the Church of England's separation from Rome. The departure of Revelation 18.4 had indeed been made, but 'not so much by a locall separation, as a necessary renuntiation'.[16] The Church of England, Prideaux explained, had left, not the good which Rome had, but the poison which she had added. She had also, unlike the separatists, proceeded in a legal and orderly fashion in her Reformation: 'our reformation was orderly by the Magistrates authorized by God in that behalfe: theirs tumultuous, as neere to rebellion, as without warrant'.[17] In this context Prideaux also emphasized the charge of the tyrannical compulsion of her members' consciences, of which the Church of Rome had been guilty, and the Church of England was innocent.

The rhetoric of moderation and peace so strongly advocated by King James himself from the beginning of his reign in England was another key factor in encouraging conformist authors to assess the separation from Rome in more restrained terms. Although this rhetoric doubtless reflected the king's own personality, James was also clearly aware of the polemical advantage to be gained in the more learned forms of Protestant/Romanist debate by claiming the high ground, not simply of spiritual purity, but of moderation and injured innocence. James gave his blessing to more passive interpretations of the Reformation by emphasizing that Rome was guilty of *making* the separation by forcing the Protestants out, as well as having effectively impelled their conscientious withdrawal by maintaining errors which provoked their departure. It was James who first coined the phrase 'Non fugimus, sed fugamur' to describe the Church of England's reluctant departure from Rome, a maxim which was eagerly adopted by Joseph Hall, among others.[18] It was upon Rome that the blame for the schism rested, not simply for her errors which forced others to separate from her,

[15] B.R. White, *The English Separatist Tradition* (Oxford, 1971), *passim*.
[16] Prideaux, *Ephesus Backsliding*, p.12.
[17] *Ibid*., p.13; cf. pp.15–17.
[18] Casaubon, *Answere*, p.14; Hall, *Works*, V: 360.

but also because she had maintained them more and more rigidly without any will to correct them, and had actively driven out those who had tried to reform her abuses. It now became fashionable to stress Luther's early quiescence and obedience. William Bedell, in Luther's defence, noted that Luther for a time showed all good obedience and humble reverence to the pope, and had pronounced rebellion against the emperor to be unlawful. Bedell thus freed Luther from the charge of fomenting rebellion against the emperor, and represented the wars of the Schmalkaldic League as merely a Protestant act of self-defence.[19]

The emphasis on Rome's hardening position and refusal to reform (rather than the Protestants' active repudiation of her communion) was not necessarily out of step with general apocalyptic views of the Protestants' departure from Rome. After all, the theme of persecution was fundamental to English apocalyptic thought. Thomas Jackson compared God's hardening of the pope's heart with his hardening of Pharaoh's heart against the Israelites. It was all part of God's plan to stiffen the pope's resolve, as such rigidity would ensure that there was a more widespread, and more clearly justified departure from her: 'Unless it had been for such a notorious and palpable blindness of heart, in retaining that more than heathenish and idolatrous abomination; the just causes of Luther's revolt had not been so manifest to the world, nor others' departure from the Romish church so general.'[20]

Nevertheless, the argument that the departure from Rome had not been voluntary, whatever its polemical advantages, undoubtedly had the potential to undermine the positive spiritual dynamic within anti-popery. For those who wanted to see the Reformation in wholly positive terms as the rediscovery of the Gospel, and the emergence from the darkness of popery into the light of God's truth, the rejection of popery was an important religious act which gave positive testimony of true faith. The theme of persecution by Antichrist did lend an air of passive suffering to this ideology, but nevertheless the active and willing rejection of the errors of popery was of vital importance in what remained an essentially activist vision of the flight from Rome's corruptions. The emphasis on passivity, and on the legal and orderly fashion of the Reformation, therefore remained for many Calvinist conformists simply an additional rhetorical ploy against Rome, and one which they combined with more radical and dynamic elements. Thus Prideaux emphasized that in refining the language of separation, he had no intention of diminishing the importance of the role played by heresy and idolatry in provoking the separation from Rome. While Prideaux talked of 'our refraining, rather than separation, from

[19] Bedell, *Certaine Letters*, pp.122–4. [20] Jackson, *Works*, I: 297.

Rome's community', he emphasized that it 'was for knowne and convinced abominations': the Reformers had followed the Holy Ghost's command to depart from manifest heresy and open idolatry.[21]

However, the adoption of more pacific justifications of the Reformation undoubtedly generated a certain tension and ambiguity in English Protestant defences of the break with Rome. It was not until the Laudian period, however, that puritan writers explicitly rejected some of the moderated language of separation which Calvinist conformists had been adopting. It was only in Henry Burton's *Replie* to Laud's *Relation of a Conference* that puritan frustration eventually spoke out, and the active and passive visions of the Reformation were presented in stark antithesis. Where Laud denied that the Protestants were guilty of making the miserable rent in Christendom, Burton stoutly affirmed the same with reference to Revelation 18.4, and denied that the division could be accounted miserable 'when Christ Commands it'. The 'best men' did not bemoan the rent in Christendom, Burton declared, but on the contrary 'they rejoyce in it (the cause considered) as in their glory and safety'.[22]

This ultimate division between different assessments of the separation from Rome arose in part because, for Hooker's disciples, pacific justifications of Rome served a more important function. For men such as Overall, Laud and Montagu, a line of argument which stressed the orderly nature of the separation from Rome and denied any active hostility on the Protestants' part was not merely a tactically advantageous polemical ploy against Rome and the separatists, but was also more congenial to their own preoccupation with defending the integrity and continuity of the institutional church. This was an important theme in John Overall's defence of the break with Rome, which ignored the issue of Antichrist and Revelation altogether. Preaching to Convocation in 1605, just after the Gunpowder Plot, Overall charted the framework for a polemical response to Rome which would emphasize the moderation and historicity of the Church of England and her doctrine.[23] Overall's tone was essentially defensive. English writers against Rome should strive to demonstrate that the Church of England had not changed or departed in her doctrine, religion, church, ministry, ecclesiastical order or sacraments from the form of doctrine and religion received in the primitive church. It had only purged out 'superstitiones et abusus, supervacanta et non necessaria', the tares which had been sown over the course of a long time. Most importantly of all, Overall insisted that it should be pointed out that this purgation had been made 'non inordinate, turbulenter, temere, ad

[21] Prideaux, *Ephesus Backsliding*, pp.12, 13.
[22] Burton, *Replie*, pp.238, 225, 237.
[23] CUL, MS Gg/1/29 fols.84–86.

hominum privatorum placita ac decreta; sed publica et synodica Authoritate, justa consultatione et maturo judicio legitime praecedente, iuxta Verbum Dei, consensum Patrum, usum Veterum Synodorum, ac praxim antiquioris et purioris Ecclesiae'.[24]

Here, and in a similar address on the eve of the Cambridge Divinity Act the following year, Overall constantly avoided the language of separation, talking only of a 'purgatio' or 'exterminatio', his emphasis being wholly on the exercising by an independent church of its right of self-reformation. Overall's favourite word, which he constantly invoked with reference to the English Reformation, was 'stability'. This was all a far cry from John Jewel's *complaints* in the early days of the Elizabethan Reformation that 'we manage every thing with so much deliberation, and prudence, and wariness, and circumspection, as if God himself could scarce retain his authority without our ordinances and precautions'.[25]

This emphasis on orderliness and passivity was very important to Laud. He explained that the Roman Catholics were the active agents in the schism, 'for you thrust us from you, because we called for truth and redress of abuses'.[26] The Protestants could not be said to have 'departed', because they did not go voluntarily. Christopher Potter similarly argued that Rome's neglecting of complaints 'forced Luther and his associates to cry out more vehemently; not against the Church but her corruptions. Yet calmely, and without any thought or design of separation at the first.' The pope in reply had beaten them out of doors, excommunicated them and driven them out of Rome's communion, for trying to correct her disorders. Potter's constant argument was that 'Rome cast us out before we left her', for which he happily cited King James' epigrammatic Latin observation.[27]

The emphasis on legality, canonicity and restraint in the Reformation found its clearest expression in the Church of England's defence of her episcopal succession. This was a line of defence which had the approval of even the rigidly anti-papist Archbishop Abbot. It was he who instructed his

[24] *Ibid.*, fol.84v. See also Overall's address on the eve of the Cambridge Divinity Act the following year, where he stressed that the break with Rome had been made 'non turbulenter et incomposite, et populari tumulta, ad Novellorum Doctorum placita, sed iusto ordine in Nationali Synodo, legitima consultatione, ac maturo iudicio adhibito, omnibus dubiis propositis, iuxta Regulam verbi divini, per consensum Patrum et Antiquorum Conciliorum definitiones, ac Primitivae Ecclesiae praxim expositam et applicatam, consideratis, examinatis et conclusis, supremaque in terris Authoritate ratis et confirmatis' (*ibid.*, fol.89r).

[25] *The Zurich Letters 1558–1579*, ed. H. Robinson (2 vols., Cambridge 1842–5), I: 17. This is not to suggest that elsewhere, in formal disputation with a Roman controversialist, Jewel did not recognize the polemical value of arguing that English Protestants had left the Roman Church with the greatest reluctance, and without rancour: Jewel, *Works*, III: 77, 79, 92.

[26] Laud, *Works*, II: 150. Cf. *ibid.*, II: 147, 151; White, *Replie*, p.107.

[27] Potter, *Want of Charitie*, i. p.64, 65; cf. Casaubon, *Answere*, p.14.

chaplain Francis Mason to compose his treatise *Of the Consecration of the Bishops of the Church of England* in 1613. This included a detailed description and defence of the canonicity of the consecration of the Elizabethan bishops, including a full account of the consecration of Matthew Parker, with excerpts from the 'Authenticall records', which were also displayed to imprisoned Romanist priests.[28]

The Church of England's retention of the episcopal succession provided effective ammunition for English Protestants who wished to emphasize the restraint and orderliness of the Church of England's Reformation. However, this was a defence which clearly could not be extended to the continental Reformation, where Protestants had either rejected episcopacy or, where they had chosen to retain the episcopal form of government, the apostolic succession had deliberately been broken.[29] This deficiency among foreign Protestants was all the more significant as, in Laudian hands, episcopacy began to loom larger in the Church of England's defence of the break with Rome. Richard Corbet advanced as his first argument in refutation of the charge of schism the fact that the English Church retained the order of bishops and their direct line of personal succession. He emphasized that the Church of England did not subscribe to any church 'which refuseth the Heirarchy ... The refusall whereof is the espetiall cause why so ma[ny] errors and heresyes have risen amongst men.'[30]

This emphasis on the canonical succession of episcopal orders represented at least one area where English Protestant writers justified their separation from Rome with arguments that were invalid for many continental Reformations. But the whole argument of the legal and restrained nature of the Protestants' break with Rome created constant problems, as it clearly flew in the face of much historical evidence. Laud himself certainly recognized this. When discussing the Protestants' involuntary separation from Rome, the archbishop stressed that he was speaking of the Protestants in general terms, 'taking their whole body and cause together'. He did not doubt that some had been 'peevish' or 'ignorantly zealous' in

[28] See Mason, *Of the Consecration*, ep. ded. When challenged by the Romanist polemicist Thomas Fitzherbert, Abbot invited four imprisoned Romanist priests to Lambeth Palace in May 1614 in order to inspect the Register relating to Parker's consecration and thus demonstrate the validity of the Church of England's succession against Romanists' regular invocation of the Nag's Head myth: Mason, *Vindiciae*, pp.187–8, 404–5, 415–17. Mason's posthumous *Vindiciae* was edited and published by Nathaniel Brent, also on Abbot's advice and recommendation. Note also Prideaux's praise of Mason's efforts: Prideaux, *Viginti-duae Lectiones*, ii. pp.76–7.

[29] See A.J. Mason, *The Church of England and Episcopacy* (Cambridge, 1914), pp.512–27. See also below, ch.9.

[30] Bodl., Rawlinson MS D.853 fols.174Br, 174r. See also below, ch.9.

their separation from Rome.[31] As we shall see, reservations over the sacrilegious excesses of the continental Reformation were increasingly being expressed even by moderate Calvinist authors. Arthur Lake warned in a sermon at Paul's Cross during the first session of James' first parliament that 'our Neighbour-Countreyes may teach us, how little good new-found courses have or will performe, promise they never so much good unto us: Varietie of Heresies, and inconvenient Policies doe now afflict them, and I pray God they may be farre from us'.[32]

However, in its initial separation from Rome, the English Reformation itself might not have completely conformed to the increasingly voiced ideal of moderation and legality. Puritans and Calvinist episcopalians often lamented that there had been a regrettable decline in zeal and Protestant commitment since the courageous days of the early Reformation, which now needed revival.[33] This is a note which is strikingly absent from the writings of Hooker, Andrewes, Howson, Laud and others. As we have seen, the increasing moderation of their own perceptions of the Roman Church, and of the value of those elements of ceremonial worship which she had superstitiously abused, made them increasingly averse to the elements of 'peevish' or 'ignorantly zealous' behaviour evident in the Church of England's own Reformation.[34] The papal agent Panzani reported that a sermon was preached in the Chapel Royal in early 1635 by one of Laud's closest friends in which the authors of England's schism were vehemently attacked. The preacher supposedly compared the separation to the action of a tailor who cut out a number of garments and then found himself unable to piece them together. So much had been cut about and torn apart that now they were hard put to it to rejoin the bits.[35]

Other Laudians noted further examples of destructive frenzy in the Reformation. William Forbes noted that, by abolishing prayers for the dead, the ignorant zeal of the original English Reformers had removed an important element of religious worship which had patristic warrant, 'to the

[31] Laud, *Works*, II: 151, 173–4, 176. Cf. Richard Corbet's rejection of any identification with the continental Reformation, in answer to the question of the location of the church before Luther: 'But why before Luther? We have not subscribed to Luthers writings nor to the Augustan Confession, nor to any other Church which refuseth the Heirarchy': Bodl., Rawlinson MS D.853 fol.174r. On this point, see also Dow, *Innovations*, p.180; Laud, *Works*, III: 351–2, II: 170–3.

[32] Lake, *Ten Sermons*, p.9; see also below, ch.9.

[33] Taylor, *Christs Victorie*, p.714; Caleb Dalechampius, *Christian Hospitalitie* (Cambridge, 1632), p.31.

[34] See above, pp.66, 318–19.

[35] Albion, *Court of Rome*, p.172. This passage does not occur in the PRO Roman transcripts, which Albion cites, although it does occur in the original letter whose date Albion indicates (Panzani to Barberini, 6/16 February 1635) – see Vatican Library, Codices Barberini Latini 8633 fol.146r. I am grateful to Professor Hibbard for sending me her transcript of the original letter.

great scandal of almost all other Christians'.[36] James Wedderburn admitted that 'Our Forefathers purged out some errours and abuses, and as it falls out in all manner of purgations, some good things went with the bad.' In fact, he candidly admitted that 'as for things expedient, wee acknowledge with greife, that some wee want'.[37] Making the usual comparison of the Reformation with the weeding of a field, Wedderburn pushed this metaphor rather further than English Protestants were accustomed by suggesting that the first Reformers 'not sufficiently discerning the good from the bad, doe withall pull up some wholesome grasse too'.[38]

While some of these writers praised the perfection of the Book of Common Prayer,[39] Laud, Bramhall, Cosin and Andrewes clearly felt that it could be improved, and Wren thought that the Interregnum presented a perfect opportunity for it to be surreptitiously amended.[40] Laudian criticisms were increasingly levelled at the Book of Homilies and the anti-popery of the early years of the Reformation which produced them, as Laudian clerics found the Homilies cited with increasing frequency against their reintroduction of images and anti-Sabbatarian policies.[41]

Under the Laudians, attention was increasingly focused on the Henrician Reformation, with no less than four English scholars at work on histories

[36] Forbes, *Considerationes*, II: 97. Cf. *ibid.*, II: 139.

[37] BL, Harleian MS 750 fols.71v, 72v.

[38] *Ibid.*, fol.72r. [39] Hausted, *Sermons*, p.214.

[40] Laud, *Works*, IV: 29; Bramhall, *Works*, I: lxxxvi; Cosin, *Works*, V: 453, 502, 505–7, 512–14, 517, 520; R.L. Ottley, *Lancelot Andrewes* (1894), pp.174–5; G.J. Cuming, *A History of Anglican Liturgy* (1969), p.149. I owe the last reference to Fred Trott.

[41] See the remarks of Bishop Neile at the trial of Henry Sherfield: *A Complete Collection of State Trials*, ed. T.B. and T.J. Howell (33 vols., 1809–26), III: cols.557–8; Laud, *Works*, IV: 200–1; Overall's attack on Wotton in BL, Harleian MS 750 fol.92r; Montagu, *Appello*, pp.260, 262, 263–4. But note also Edmund Reeve's high praise of the Homilies in his *Communion Booke*, introduction, pp.115–16, and appendix; and the fact that Francis White's defence of Montagu avoids commenting on Montagu's attack on the composition of the Homily: Bodl., Rawlinson MS C.573 fols.81–2. Bishop Williams' 1641 Committee on religious innovations noted (in an almost direct quotation from Montagu, *Appello*, p.262) that 'Some have put scorne upon the two books of Homilies, calling them either popular discourses, or a Doctrine usefull for those times wherein they were set forth': *A Copie of the Proceedings*, p.2 (see also the Northamptonshire petition against the 1640 Oath: PRO, SP 16/461 fols.132v–133r, and Bodl., Rawlinson MS D.831 fol.113v). Also note Sancta Clara, *Paraphrastica*, p.84. The Homilies were explicitly recommended 'for a pattern and a boundary, as it were, for the preaching ministers' in King James' 1622 'Directions concerning preachers' (Cardwell, *Documentary Annals*, II: 201–3, as noted by Featley against Montagu: Bodl., Rawlinson MS D.831 fol.97r), and were commended as such by Archbishop Abbot and Bishop Lake in their implementation of the Directions (Cardwell, *Documentary Annals*, II: 205; Fincham, 'Pastoral roles' p.364). For the citing of the Homily of the time and place of prayer against the Book of Sports, see PRO, SP 16/267 fol.24v; Burton, *For God and the King*, p.57, and K.L. Parker, *The English Sabbath* (Cambridge, 1988), pp.175, 201, 202. For the use of the Homily against the Peril of Idolatry against visual display and images, see Burton, *For God and the King*, p.34; William Prynne, *Lame Giles his Haultings* (1630), p.35; Cosin, *Correspondence*, I: 186, 188.

of the period.[42] This was a trend that was heartily applauded by Cardinal Barberini, who instructed the papal agent Panzani to encourage irenical Protestants to study historical issues rather than matters of doctrine, and the enormities involved in Henry's separation in particular, as a way of encouraging them towards reunion.[43] After all, such considerations had helped to drive Benjamin Carier to Rome.[44] The sacrilege involved in Henry VIII's assault upon the church's patrimony was also coming in for increasingly violent attack in public sermons and treatises. In a sermon before the king, Peter Heylyn launched a strong attack upon the violent destruction of consecrated items during the Reformation under Henry and Edward. Under Edward, he declared, the foundations of the state had been almost utterly subverted, and the whole fabric of government dissolved by potent factions.[45] Condemnations of the Reformation's assault upon the goods of the church were often combined with dire warnings of God's impending judgement on those who still retained impropriated tithes.[46]

42 Lord Herbert of Cherbury wrote his life of Henry VIII during this period. Sir Henry Bourgchier, writing to Ussher in April 1629, reported himself to be 'gathering matter for the story of Henry VIII which in time ... I intend to publish': Ussher, *Works*, XV: 436–7. Richard Montagu reported to Bishop Wren in the later 1630s that he had earlier been involved himself in collecting material for a history of the Henrician Reformation: Bodl., Smith MS 21 p.47: Montagu to Wren, 22 February (1637?). Bishop Goodman was also working on a similar history during this period: Soden, *Godfrey Goodman*, pp.102–3. See also SUL, Hartlib MS 29/2 fol.33r.

43 For Barberini's recommendations to Panzani, see Albion, *Court of Rome*, pp.154, 180.

44 Carier, *Treatise*, pp.18, 34, 38, 41. For vindications of Henry's divorce, see Hakewill, *Answere*, ii. pp.9–11; Mason, *Vindiciae*, pp.145–52.

45 Heylyn, *Parable*, p.388 (sermon preached before the king at Windsor, 25 Jan. 1642).

46 Montagu, *Diatribae*, pp.98, 106–10, 226, 523 (against the seizure of church lands), 326 (against Henry VIII's usurping of the pope's rights to first fruits and tenths), 312, 389, 578–9 (warning of God's judgement against sacrilegious impropriators). Montagu was at work on a further defence of the divine right of tithes – 'Decateuticon, or argument of tithes' – in the late 1630s: Bodl., Smith MS 21 p.47: Montagu to Bishop Wren, 22 Feb. (1637?); Bodl., Rawlinson MS D.692 fol.249: Spelman to Montagu, 11 July 1634; Panzani, *Diary*, 14/24 Feb. 1635 p.86 [original: fol.77]. See also Montagu's remarks to Laud: LPL, Lambeth MS 943 fol.619 (printed in Prynne, *Canterburies Doome*, p.555). 'A very learned and pious man' told Jeremy Stephens in the 1650s that Montagu 'would often say, that our kingdome had not yet paid for their sacrilege': BL, Add. MS 11044 fol.233v: Stephens to Viscount Scudamore, 25 July 1653 (I owe this reference to Ian Atherton). Thomas Bayly (an amanuensis to Bishop Lindsell: Matthews, *Walker Revised*, p.211) in a sermon before Sussex assize judges in summer 1640 attacked Henry VIII for destroying abbeys and monasteries and converting land to lay use which had been consecrated for divine use, and warned that all those who took, and who still held, such lands were guilty of sacrilege and would never prosper (PRO, SP 16/461 fol.66r). George Garrard reported attending a sermon in Oxford on 28 August 1636 (the day before the king's visit) at which the preacher railed against Henry VIII and Selden's *History of Tithes*: PRO, SP 16/331/14: Garrard to Viscount Conway, 4 Sept. 1636. Laudians may have had some cause to worry over the potential use of Henry VIII's example against the church. Sir John Wray, arguing in the Commons for the receiving of the London petition against episcopacy in February 1641, 'moved that hee conceived wee might as well meddle with Bishopps now as Henry

Montagu stated unequivocally that the architect of England's break with Rome 'seised on, chopped and changed Church and Religion as he pleased, and turned all things upside downe', conferring lands on laymen who could never have any right to them 'by any authority under heaven'.[47] Cosin and Lindsell were accused in 1630 of having 'tearmed the Reformers of our Church ignorant and unlearned Calvinisticall bishopps', who 'when they tooke away the mass, they tooke away all religion, and the whole service of God, they called it a Reformation, but it was indeed a Deformation'.[48]

Attacks upon the conduct of Henry VIII, and particularly on the alienation of church lands into lay hands during the Reformation, were not an exclusively Laudian phenomenon, however, even if the Laudians' emphasis upon the perils of sacrilege was shriller than most. A commitment to defending clerical property was, perhaps not surprisingly, something which both Laudians and even their most vigorous clerical critics shared. Brian Walton's scheme to improve London ministers' stipends in the 1630s commanded the support of London puritan ministers, as well as dedicated Laudians.[49] In Jacobean times Andrew Willet and Gabriel Powel strongly opposed impropriations, and were especially damning when they considered the use to which monastic lands had been put during the Henrician Reformation.[50]

Nevertheless, by the 1630s some divines regarded these shortcomings in

VIII did with Abbeies in his time': D'Ewes, *Journal*, p.336. By contrast, note the earlier defence of the dissolution of the monasteries in Andrewes, *Responsio*, pp.180–1, 232–3.

47 Montagu, *Diatribae*, p.76.

48 Cosin, *Correspondence*, I: 163, 164; cf. p.178. See also Pagitt's remark, directed at the Scottish Covenanters, that 'to overthrow the policie and government of the ancient Church [i.e. episcopacy] is not a Reformation of the Church, but a Deformation': Pagitt, *Christianographie* (1640 edn), p.222. Probably the first Protestant use of the term 'deformation', at least with regard to the Henrician Reformation, was in fact made by a radical Protestant, Anthony Gilby: see King James, *Political Works*, pp.xviii–xix.

49 Mason, *Serving God*, pp.69–74. Walton's treatise is in LPL, Lambeth MS 273. It was also an issue upon which Ussher and Laud could agree: Bodl., Sancroft MS 18 pp.10–13. For attacks on impropriations, see Willet, *Synopsis* (1613), sig.A5r–v; William Crashaw, *The Sermon Preached at the Crosse* (1608) – quoted in Babbage, *Puritanism*, pp.295–6; Manningham, *Diary*, pp.108–9 (John King); Covell, *Modest Examination*, pp.157–8.

50 Willet, *Antilogie*, pp.113, 235; Powel, *Consideration of the Papists*, pp.127–8. For earlier attacks on Henry VIII, see Anthony Gilby's *Admonition to England and Scotland to Call Them to Reformation* (quoted in King James, *Political Works*, pp.xviii–xix) and Robert Cecil's remarks in *Proceedings in Parliament, 1610*, ed. E.R. Foster (2 vols., 1966), II: 231–2 (I owe this reference to Professor Russell). Panzani was amazed by the strong language used against Henry in Camden's *Life of Queen Elizabeth*: PRO, MS 31/9/17B: Panzani to Barberini, 17/27 April 1635. Nevertheless, in the context of anti-papal controversy, more typical examples of Jacobean divines' attitude are William Bedell's balanced, positive assessment, and Thomas Morton's defence of Henry's Protestant credentials: Bedell, *Certaine Letters*, pp.124, 129–32; Morton, *Catholike Appeale*, pp.456–7. See also Sutcliffe, *De Turcopapismo*, p.482; Willet, *Antilogie*, pp.159, 273.

the early conduct of the Reformation not simply as cause for justified complaint and regret, but rather as facts which called into question the legitimacy of the Reformation itself. In his manuscript tract composed to dissuade potential converts to Rome, James Wedderburn addressed himself more to the issue of how salvation might still be possible in a schismatical church rather than to freeing the Church of England's original reformation from this charge.[51] It was common for English Protestants to argue that members of a schismatical church might be saved as long as they themselves did not begin the schism, and provided that they retained a sincere desire to know the truth, and remained in charity with all other Christians. This argument regularly appeared when Protestants discussed the possible salvation of the invincibly ignorant within Rome's communion. Wedderburn, however, chose to employ this argument in relation to those living within the present *Protestant* Churches.[52] Wedderburn maintained that if the first authors of a separation had left the unity of the church then they should be accounted schismatics and heretics, but insisted that the same charge should not necessarily be levelled at their descendants:

> such of their posteritie as doe not pertenaceously hold theire error, but labour to find out the truth, & are ready to yield unto it being found out, & withal reteyning an internal communion with the whole visible church in the fundamental points of faith, & in Christian charitie, earnestly desire and syncerely endeavour (as theire place and calling will permitt) a perfect union and communion with all Christians, are neither schismaticks nor haeretiques, in the sight of God, & so may be saved.[53]

Thus, Wedderburn concluded, 'the authors of a Schisme may be damned, and yet many of them that (especially in after ages) are involved in it, be saved, if they retain charity to them from whom the Schisme was made'.[54]

Wedderburn rehearsed the traditional argument that the popes themselves had given reasonable cause for the Protestants' separation from them. But this was not an argument which Wedderburn himself found wholly satisfying. In fact, he confessed quite explicitly that the Reformers

51 'Some things to be considered of any one who, living in the Communion of the Church of England, where he was borne & bred, and discerning the grosse Errors and superstitions that be in the Moderne Romane Church, is notwithstanding strongly mooved to leave the one and betake himself to the other, as the only Catholique, without which there can be no salvation': BL, Harleian MS 750 fols.62r–73r. On this work, see also Baillie, *Ladensium* (3rd edn, 1641), 'A Large Supplement', sigs.C1r–v, pp.17–19.

52 BL, Harleian MS 750 fol.62r.

53 *Ibid.*, fol.63v.

54 *Ibid.*, fol.71v. This was an argument which had deeply exercised the mind of Benjamin Carier in the years immediately preceding his conversion to Rome. He reflected in his commonplace book that one born in schism might still be in union with the Catholic Church because 'potest habere animam perfecte unitam': Hakewill, *Answere*, i. p.24. It had been de Dominis' complaint that many in the Church of England were schismatic because in their accusations of heresy and idolatry they showed themselves not to have retained charity towards the Church of Rome (see above, p.218).

should not have left the communion of the Church of Rome, but should have continued in her communion, even at the cost of their lives:

Notwithstanding of all this, it had been better, (in my poore opinion, salvo meliore iudicio) if our Reformers had not so left the Church of Rome, & their obedience to the pope, as they did; but had still communicated with that Church in all things, except those which in their Conscience they held to be altogether unlawfull, and still yeelded Canonicall obedience to the pope salvo iure principum suorum, and prayed for him, as their highest pastor & patriarch; yet professing withall their dislike of such things as were amisse, reprooving them, as their calling and place would have permitted, and using all moderate, peaceable courses to have obtained reformation thereof. But yow may say: So it might have cost them their lives. I answere: so did it the prophets of God whom Jezabell slew, who notwithstanding the Idolls sett up by Jereboam, and the grosser Idolatrie erected by Ahab, left not the Church of Israel, but reprooved their Idolatrie, and in things lawfull communicated with them.[55]

This extraordinary disavowal, by a Protestant bishop, of the act of separation from Rome at the Reformation was the logical end to which the obsessive conformist concern with moderation, legality and passivity in separation were leading. The reduced role of pre-Reformation doctrinal errors left English Protestant divines with a major problem in trying to justify the Reformation itself.

To avoid the dilemma in which Wedderburn found himself, increasing emphasis was placed by Laudian divines on a vision of the Reformation which presented it essentially as the rediscovery by independent churches of their rights to self-reformation. As Robert Skinner explained the Reformation in a sermon before the king at Whitehall in 1634, all that had happened was that 'some particular Churches ... began to reforme and correct them without anie longer expecting with tyred patience the popes good pleasure'.[56] The theme of the reformation of independent churches was especially prominent in Laud's *Conference*. He stressed that particular churches had a right to reform themselves if the general church would not, and defended in detail the right of provincial synods and particular churches to issue decrees in causes of faith, and cases of reformation, if the universal church could not, or would not, obtain a free General Council to reform current abuses.[57] Laud saw the model for the Reformation in the 'formal separation' for more than a hundred years of the African Church from the Roman Church in patristic times.[58]

55 BL, Harleian MS 750 fol.74v.

56 BL, Add. MS 20065 fol.79r.

57 Laud, *Works*, II: 167, 170–84.

58 *Ibid.*, II: 191–4. According to Wood (*Athenae Oxonienses* III: 567) this passage drew upon a manuscript tract 'A Discourse of the African Schism' by Heylyn, which has not survived. One manuscript tract which Laud himself admitted using for his material on patriarchal government was Edward Brerewood's 'A Declaration of the Patriarchall Government of the ancient Church', first published in *Certain Briefe Treatises Written by Diverse*

Richard Montagu provided more specific support for the English Church's jurisdictional independence. In his manuscript tract on recusancy, Montagu based his defence of the Church of England's separation from Rome on her 'Cyprian Privilege' to be governed by her own patriarch:

Our Iland hath ever enjoyed auncientIy the Cyprian Privilege, that is, to be Subject to no Patriarch, but to have a Patriarch of our owne; which that Pope had reference unto, who sayd the Archbishop was Alterius orbis Patriarcha. And though the Patriarch of the West, the Bishop of Rome, had intruded upon it yet the Church and State resuming their owne auncient right, might lawfully doe it, and are not to be accompted schismatiques for so doing.[59]

The idea of an English patriarchate also emerged at Laud's trial, when his prosecutors seized on a passage in Laud's *Conference* concerning Canterbury's patriarchal authority in order to claim that Laud had assumed papal power over England, and 'took on me to be Patriarch of this other world'.[60]

The separation from Rome was thus increasingly being represented in

Learned Men, concerning the Ancient and Moderne Government of the Church (Oxford, 1641) – see Laud, *Works*, II: 203 note x. Laud's passages in his *Conference* against the pope's ecclesiastical supremacy are also said to have used a tract entitled 'The Judgment of Writers on those Texts of Scripture on which the Jesuits found the popedom and the Authority of the Roman Church', which Heylyn composed in 1637 at the archbishop's request (Wood, *Athenae Oxonienses*, III: 567).

59 CUL, MS Gg/1/29 (from back) fol.101r. Montagu here refers to the famous remarks of Pope Urban II to Anselm when the latter was archbishop of Canterbury, as reported by William of Malmesbury. This example is also cited by Laud (*Works*, II: 190). The 'Cyprian Privilege', deriving from the eighth canon of the first Council of Ephesus (451), is also briefly referred to and applied to England in Mason, *Vindiciae*, pp.83, 527–8. The same privilege is recognized as belonging to the Church of England by the Benedictine irenicist John Barnes, whose *Catholico Romanus Pacificus*, in which this argument is developed, was circulating among Scottish Laudians in the 1630s (Baillie, *Ladensium* (3rd edn, 1641), 'A Large Supplement', sig.C2v, pp.19–20). Barnes' arguments regarding the 'Cyprian Privilege' were incorporated as a major theme in Isaac Basire's later *De Antiqua Ecclesiae Britannicae Libertate* (Bruges, 1656). For the archbishop of Canterbury's patriarchal authority according to common law, see Andrewes, *Responsio*, p.474. Defences of the archbishop of Canterbury's jurisdictional privileges were not limited to the later Jacobean and Caroline period: Matthew Parker had earlier sponsored the *De Antiquitate Britannicae Ecclesiae et Privilegiis Ecclesiae Cantuariensis, cum Archiepiscopus eiusdem 70* (1572), but this was privately printed in an edition of only about fifty copies: McKisack, *Medieval History*, p.44.

60 In his defence, Laud denied having pursued this point, and claimed that 'I made use of that passage only to prove that the pope could not be appealed unto out of England, according to their own doctrine': Laud, *Works*, IV: 160. Against his opponents' accusations of Laud's usurpation of monarchical ecclesiastical power, it was clearly in Laud's interest to deny any interest in the general issue of the Church of England's claim to independent patriarchal authority, although it was clearly a line of argument against Rome which would have greatly appealed to him. Nevertheless, it is true that this point remains undeveloped in his published works.

jurisdictional terms,[61] as concerning ecclesiastical relations between independent churches, rather than as a conflict over the purity of doctrine. Of course, there was an extent to which some Protestant Englishmen had always presupposed the especial importance of jurisdictional issues in the Reformation. For instance, civil lawyers, constantly making use of canon law, tended to regard the legal aspects of the Reformation as equal to the spiritual, and still expressed a strong reverence for precedent.[62] Nevertheless, by the 1630s jurisdictional issues were acquiring a relative significance in the defence of the separation from Rome which was undeniably novel. Laud insisted that all the erroneous doctrines prevalent among churches within Rome's communion derived from the fact that these churches had forgotten their own jurisdictional liberties, and had therefore been forced to embrace all the corruptions of the particular Roman Church. By being unable to free themselves from Roman jurisdiction, they were forced to continue in Rome's corrupted religion.[63] For Montagu too, the jurisdictional claims made by Rome provided the central legitimation of the Reformation. It is true that Montagu did not merely present the argument from the 'Cyprian Privilege' to justify England's separation from Rome, although this was the first argument that he advanced. Montagu also argued that the separation would be justifiable even if the Church of England had no such privilege 'but were immediately subject as Suffragans may be according to Canons and Ecclesiasticall Sanctions, unto the Generall Patriarch of the West, the Bishop of Rome' (as Wedderburn had argued), if the pope could be styled a heretic according to the decree of a General Council. But the heresy which Montagu imputed to Rome was concerned not with doctrine at all, but with jurisdiction. The pope's heresy had been committed 'before Luthers tyme' by his 'clayming absolute Monarchisme in the Church and State; which in Hildebrands case was styled Heresie, preferring himselfe above Generall Councills, which by the decrees of the Councills of Constance and Basill is censured for Heresie'.[64]

Some divines under Laud were thus participating in a gradual shift towards a purely political view of the Reformation. This is not to suggest, however, that the question of the independent jurisdictional rights of individual churches was an issue that was neglected by non-Laudian authors. On the contrary, it featured in the works of Calvinist divines such as Prideaux and Ussher, who were careful to respond to Romanist and separatist polemical pressure on this point. Prideaux, in his anxiety to distinguish the Church of England's separation from Rome from the behaviour of those separating from her own communion, was careful to

[61] See above, pp.220–27, 336–7.
[62] B.P. Levack, *The Civil Lawyers in England 1603–1641* (Oxford, 1973), pp.182–6.
[63] Laud, *Works*, II: 213.
[64] CUL, MS Gg/1/29 fol.101r (from back).

justify the Church of England's separation in political terms. In contrast to Wedderburn's arguments, Prideaux stressed that, while their forefathers had 'acknowledged a certain pre-eminence of that See [of Rome]; but it was but a matter of courtesie, at most of humane constitution, not of necessity, or obligation by the Word of God'. Also, the papacy had encroached 'as much upon the Prerogatives of Commonwealths, as the Liberties of the Church'.[65] Ussher made the independent jurisdictional rights exercised by particular churches in the early medieval period the subject of his research throughout the 1620s and 1630s.[66] In particular, he championed the great power which early Irish Metropolitans had exercised, erecting new bishoprics and even archbishoprics.[67] He gave even more detailed attention to issues of ecclesiastical independence in the early church in his voluminous *Britannicarum Ecclesiarum Antiquitates* of 1639.[68] However, Ussher made it clear that he had only studied the question of jurisdictional independence among the early churches because the Romanists – especially Bellarmine – insisted that their whole cause stood or fell upon this point.[69] Moreover, Ussher only studied the independence of particular churches before the unleashing of Satan in the eleventh century.[70] Elsewhere in his *Discourse*, Ussher's attention wandered away from the jurisdictional independence of institutional churches and towards the doctrinal purity of a 'saving remnant' of elect believers, and associated notions of the relative 'invisibility' of the true church under the persecutions of Antichrist.[71] For the later Middle Ages, and the origins of the Reformation itself, Ussher looked to such hidden persecuted groups, rather than to the independent rights of particular churches.

65 Prideaux, *Ephesus Backsliding*, pp.13–14. See also Dove, *Perswasion*, pp.29–31.

66 In his *Discourse* of 1631, Ussher spent three chapters investigating the ancient independence of the Irish Church: Ussher, *Works*, IV: 319–59.

67 Ussher, *Works*, IV: 319–22. See also *ibid.*, IV: 336–57.

68 Ussher was also consulted on this subject by Henry Spelman in 1639, specifically regarding the requests made by the Huguenot canonist Conrad Justellus for information which could assist the Frenchman's polemical writings against Rome on the subject of the ancient patriarchates, in which he accounted the Britannic Churches to be a patriarchate in themselves: BL, Add. MS 34600 fol.172 (Spelman to Ussher). Ussher strongly disputed Spelman's argument that Scotland and Ireland were anciently subject to the Church of England; an indication, perhaps, that his defence of the jurisdictional independence of the Irish Church may have also been aimed at the contemporary intrusions being made into his jurisdiction by Laud, as well as opposing papal usurpations: BL, Add. MS 34600 fols.173 (Spelman to Ussher, 8 June 1639), 179–80 (Ussher to Spelman, 14 August 1639), 186 (Spelman to Ussher, 5 November 1639), 187 (Spelman to Justellus, 13 November 1639). See also Milton, 'Laudians', p.259 n.71.

69 Ussher, *Works*, IV: 380.

70 *Ibid.*, IV: 269. See also Ussher's treatment of the independence and lack of corruption in particular churches before the year 1000 AD in his *De successione*: *ibid.*, II: 39–50, 63, 104–5, 209–10, 220.

71 *Ibid.*, IV: 311.

For these Calvinist writers a concentration on the issue of jurisdiction, like the more general use of a rhetoric of moderation over the separation from Rome, was ultimately simply a tactical ploy in their anti-papal polemic, and did not supersede an emphasis on the purely *doctrinal* reasons for the break with Rome. For example, in the epistle dedicating his anti-papal treatise *The Grand Imposture* to King Charles, Thomas Morton might appear to display an unexpectedly irenical side to his character when he maintained that the only bar to reconciliation with Rome was her insistence that salvation was impossible without belief in the Tridentine Creed, and specifically the article in that Creed which declared the necessity of subjection to the Roman See. However, these remarks need to be read alongside his emphasis in the body of his treatise on the fact that Luther had not contended with Rome merely on matters of ceremony or jurisdiction, but rather on issues that concerned the soul's life, justification and the spiritual worship due to God. William Bedell similarly denied that separation had been made from Rome only in 'ceremonies and matters of order', insisting rather that 'the controversies betweene the Romanists and us, are most about doctrine'.[72]

Writing just prior to his conversion, Benjamin Carier had been convinced that it was only matters of jurisdiction which really separated Rome and the Church of England. The only doctrinal division between the formal doctrine of the Church of England (which Carier located in the Prayer Book and Articles) and that of Rome lay in 'the head of the Church, & the power of the Keyes, & certaine questions belonging thereunto'. By the 1630s a number of divines would seem to have thought along the same lines. Bishop Goodman, in the recantation which he prepared for the puritan Ridler, claimed that the original separation had only been made from Rome for political respects. This was also the view of the irenical Benedictine Dom Leander Jones, and it was upon this assessment that he based his plans for reunion.[73]

LIMITED COMMUNION

As we have seen, many Calvinist controversialists under James, following the king's own lead, found it increasingly convenient to employ a rhetoric of moderation when dealing with the Protestants' separation from Rome.

[72] Morton, *Grand Imposture*, p.418, ep. ded.; Bedell, *Certaine Letters*, p.75.

[73] BCO, MS 270 [p.162]; Prynne, *Canterburies Doome*, pp.241–2; Sitwell, 'Leander Jones', p.139. The Benedictine supporter of the Oath of Allegiance, Thomas Preston, also believed that the pope's claim to deposing power was 'a chiefe occasion why this Kingdom is departed from the obedience to the See Apostolike': Thomas Preston, *A Cleare, Sincere and Modest Confutation* (1616), p.10 – cited in Sommerville, 'Jacobean political thought', p.279 n.102.

This was not really necessary in their own terms, as they still accepted the categorical command of Revelation 18.4. However, they placed increasing emphasis on the notion of a limited and conditional separation from Rome.

It has already been demonstrated that the argument that the Protestants had left, not the truth, but merely the errors of the Church of Rome, restoring the old church rather than creating a new, was fairly conventional in mainstream Jacobean writings. Although this point first emerged as a clear argument in the writings of authors such as Edmund Bunny and Richard Hooker, by the Jacobean period this position may be found in the writings of formidable anti-Romanists such as Prideaux and Richard Bernard.[74] When used by such writers this qualification meant very little since, as has been shown, Roman errors were seen as being now wedded inextricably to the very nature of the present Roman Church. The argument was thus little more than a polemical ploy: if the objected errors were seen as being inseparable from the church's doctrine, then the assertion that the Protestants had separated from the errors but not from the truth within Rome was a mere semantic quibble. Even as such, however, it was open to misinterpretation. King James' declaration that the Church of England did not separate further from the Church of Rome than Rome herself did from her earlier purity was eagerly seized upon by Roman controversialists, and Robert Abbot found himself having to insist that his opponent William Bishop had omitted James' crucial addition that Rome had also departed 'from Christ her Lord and head'.[75]

However unobjectionable to puritan sensibilities this theme of limited separation might be in the hands of a writer such as Richard Bernard, it clearly could present a potentially more moderate assessment of the Roman Church. When employed by writers whose Protestant credentials were in question, for example, such an argument might be taken to have crypto-popish overtones, especially when it was being combined with arguments that seemed to reject the normal rider that Rome's errors were inextricably linked with the Roman Church. This was especially the case as during this period the argument that Protestants separated only from

[74] Windsor, 'The controversy', pp.160–1, 166, 233; Prideaux, *Viginti-duae Lectiones*, i. p.136; Cade, *Justification*, pp.5–6. Bernard claimed that 'wee doe not breake off from her [Rome] simply, but in some respects, that is, as farre forth as she hath forsaken her former selfe; so that if shee would returne to the Catholike Faith and Religion, and forsake her Trentisme, Jesuitisme and Popery ... wee want not charitie towards her, to unite our selves unto her againe': Bernard, *Looke beyond Luther*, p.44. See also Abbot, *True Ancient*, pp.80–1, 111–14; Some, *Godly Treatise*, p.151.

[75] Abbot, *Defence*, p.23; *idem*, *True Ancient*, p.233. King James' suggestion that Rome was 'the mother church' (a point also made by Saravia) created even greater problems for Protestant writers when faced with Roman controversialists anxious to exploit its positive potential: see above, ch.6.

Rome's errors, and not from her *true doctrine*, became subtly modified to read that the separation had been made from Rome's errors, and not from *the Church of Rome herself*. This was a typical example of how an emphasis upon the visible, institutional church, rather than abstract notions of doctrinal purity, gradually slipped into patterns of thought on a whole range of issues under the early Stuarts. As a result of such ambiguities, puritan writers became more doubtful of 'limited separation' arguments. Thus Henry Burton firmly rejected Laud's outwardly conventional claim that the Protestants did not protest against the Church of Rome, but only against her errors. Instead, Burton maintained that Rome's errors had become 'the very body and soule of the Religion faith and practice of that Church'.[76] If Burton was wrong to depict Laud's position as novel, he may well have been accurate in his implication that in Laud's mind at least (though not in the thinking of earlier moderate Calvinist episcopalians) the archbishop's own propositions and those of Burton were essentially antithetical.

Among divines such as Laud, arguments of 'limited separation' acquired a greater urgency and significance. As we have shown, the depiction of Rome as simply an erring fellow member of the Catholic Church required that other churches must still in some sense remain in communion with her.[77] To Jacobean notions of 'limited separation' was added a new meaning, and the further concept of 'limited communion'. If the Church of England had only left Rome's errors, then it followed that she was still united with Rome in those truths which Rome maintained, and since those truths were the essence of the church, it could be argued that the two churches still preserved a meaningful form of unity.

Writings on this matter in the 1630s display the problems created for Laudian authors by the fact that they upheld the idea of Rome's participation in the Catholic Church, while at the same time they failed to undercut the accompanying theme of charitable intercommunion by making any use of 'true church' arguments which maintained that communion was impossible with heretics.[78] This problem is prominent in the work of Christopher Potter. In Potter's earlier sermon at the consecration of Barnaby Potter his position against Rome was implacable, despite the fact that he advocated a more moderate stance on the divisions between Calvinists and Arminians. Potter here emphasized 'our necessary separation from the abominations, idolatry, and tyranny of the Papacy, with which no good Christian can hold any union in faith, any communion in charitie'.[79] In his later work,

[76] Burton, *Replie*, pp.238–9. [77] Potter, *Want of Charitie*, i. p.74. See above, pp.156–7.
[78] On these points, see above ch.3.
[79] Christopher Potter, *A Sermon Preached at the Consecration of ... Barnaby Potter* (1629), pp.64–5.

however, undertaken at the king's special command, Potter adopted a careful qualification of this language. He allowed Rome to be a member of the Catholic Church, and accepted that in a sense the Romanists might be called Catholics. He made it clear in his *Want of Charitie* that 'For the Church of Rome, in those Catholique truths which shee maintaines, we are not at oddes with her, nor need any reconciling.'[80] Potter, however, took this conventional point a little further. He was adamant that a very real form of limited communion still bound the Protestants and Romanists together. Protestants were in no way dislinked from the Church of Rome as far as she communicated with the Catholic Church. Even if the Protestants had departed from Rome, they had not separated from her in any of those things that made her a church, or that she held from Christ or apostolic tradition.[81] Potter expressed this limited communion in clear terms: 'we still have a true and real Union with that and all other members of the Church Universall, in Faith and Charity'.

Part of the reason for Potter's strong advocacy of the notion of limited communion sprang from simple polemical requirements. His opponent Edward Knott rightly noted that, if Rome were now adjudged by Protestants to lack nothing essential to a church, then separation from her could not easily be justified. This was a point which Daniel Featley had already made against Richard Montagu a few years earlier. Potter admitted the principle that whoever forsakes the communion of any one member of the body of Christ must confess consequently to forsake the whole, and therefore insisted that 'her [Rome's] communion we forsake not, no more then the Body of Christ, whereof we acknowledge the Church of Rome a member, though corrupted'.[82] De Dominis had earlier pointed out that, if it was admitted that Rome did not err in fundamentals, then English Protestants' confession that they were wholly divided and separated from the Church of Rome meant that they were guilty of schism from the true Catholic Church and body of Christ.[83]

This was a point that was further developed by the Laudian pamphleteer Christopher Dow. Like other writers he chose to emphasize that the Church of England was still linked to Rome in many ways: 'though we have separated from them in those things which they hold, not as the Church of Christ, but as the Romane and Pontifician; yet we remaine still united in those Articles of faith which that Church yet hath from Apostolicall tradition'. He added, as Potter did, that they were also united 'in the bond of charity', but also mentioned their liturgical unity 'in those acts of Gods worship which they yet practise according to Divine prescript'.[84]

80 Potter, *Want of Charitie*, i. p.19.

81 *Ibid.*, i. pp.56, 66.

82 *Ibid.*, i. pp.74–5; Featley, *Second Parallel*, ii. pp.51–2.

83 De Dominis, *Second Manifesto*, sigs.C3r, C4v, E4r.

84 Dow, *Innovations*, pp.50–1.

Dow emphasized too a continued fellow-feeling with the Romanists.[85] One further important bond of unity which the Church of England shared with Rome was, of course, her retention of the episcopal succession. This was a form of communion which to Ephraim Pagitt made reunion with, for example, the Gallican Church, seem more likely than with any Protestant non-episcopal church.[86]

'Limited communion' was essentially an abstract, theoretical condition. Nevertheless, the increasingly positive appreciation of the degree of diversity within Rome's communion (which we have noted in an earlier chapter) allowed this notion, in the mind of Richard Montagu at least, to acquire a practical relevance. If the Church of England had not separated from the Roman Church, he reasoned, then it must have been merely the Roman Court from which she had departed. This was an argument that even the puritan Thomas Beard could readily accept when it proved polemically advantageous.[87] Nevertheless, Montagu's conviction that divisions within Rome's communion were meaningful led him to believe that the distinction between the Court and Church of Rome could yet be observed within Rome's own communion in the form of the conflict between the papal curia and the independently minded Gallican Church. In fact, Montagu argued, the Church of England's separation from the Court of Rome was exactly the same as that which had been made by the Gallican Church. In a manuscript tract written sometime after 1628 he explicitly compared the English Church's separation from the Church of Rome with that of the French Church:

> The Church of Fraunce, not admitting the Councill of Trent, nor admitting the Superioritie of Popes above Generall Councills, but holding the doctrine of Gerson, Almaine, and the Schoole of Sorbon, depart from the Communion of the pope, but not from the Communion of the Church of Rome. King Henry the .8. of England, departed from the Communion of the pope and Court of Rome, as appeareth in the Article of Supremacie, but not from Communion with the Church of Rome, as appeareth by the Act of the 6. Articles.[88]

The same attempt to use this distinction (between union with the Church of Rome and union with the Court of Rome) as the basis for a reconciliation with Roman Catholicism emerged during Panzani's reunion negotiations in the 1630s.[89]

[85] 'We study to reduce them from their errors, and pray for their salvation, accounting them not quite cut off, but to continue still members (though corrupt ones) of the same Catholike Church' (*ibid.*).

[86] See above, p.268.

[87] Beard, *Antichrist*, p.247.

[88] CUL, MS Gg/1/29 fol.101v (from back). Macauley misreads 'Alcuine' for 'Almaine': Macauley, 'Richard Montague', p.452.

[89] See the Venetian ambassador's report: *CSPVen 1636–9*, p.303 (composed 24 October 1637).

The more that the separation from Rome came to be viewed simply as a matter of jurisdictional independence, the less possible it became to distinguish the Church of England's position from that of the Gallican Church. If the Church of England's separation from Rome was simply a matter of church politics, as it was increasingly being depicted, then, if Rome was prepared to grant to the Church of England her jurisdictional independence, some form of reconciliation might be judged possible, if somewhat unlikely.

REUNION

It was a standard polemical ploy of English Protestants writing against Roman Catholicism to claim that the Church of England was anxious to secure peace and reunion with the Church of Rome. This was argued so that the Church of England could claim the high ground of moderation, and the whole blame for the divisions of Christendom could fall squarely upon the Church of Rome. Protestants were eager to unite with Rome, the argument ran; it was Rome who factiously excommunicated them and upheld the errors which forced the Protestants to leave her communion. However much they might claim a moderate desire for reunion (a tactical ploy which even a puritan such as Richard Bernard was happy to embrace), and pay lip-service to the idea that a General Council might be called to re-establish the unity of the church, mainstream Jacobean Protestants could never seriously entertain the idea that the Church of Rome would yield herself to be fully reformed.[90]

Joseph Hall, in his *Roma Irreconciliabilis*, expressed the fervent wish that the Romanists might be 'drawn back to the sound and pure judgment of the primitive antiquity', but stressed that this was simply impossible, given Rome's very nature, and only attainable by divine intervention: 'Some fools may hope for this ... But for us, unlesse He that doth wonders, by his stretched-out arm from heaven, should mightily, beyond all hope, effect this, we know too well that it cannot be done.' George Hakewill repeated the usual vague platitudes of the need for Christian unity but, confronted with the schemes of Benjamin Carier, he agreed with Hall that reconciliation with Rome was a foolish and impossible dream. Rome's 'stiffe aversenesse', the controversies 'of the highest nature' and Rome's infallibility, which 'we may bee sure they will ever while they are able, without yeelding an inch, as stiffely maintaine, as wee iustly oppugne', together with the impossibility of agreeing on the calling and procedure of a General Council, made any talk of reconciliation idle and foolish.[91]

90 Bernard, *Looke beyond Luther*, p.44.
91 Hall, *Works*, X: 394, 395–6, 396–7; Hakewill, *Answere*, i. p.14; ii. pp.124–5.

As we have seen, hardline views of Rome's nature depicted her errors as being an integral part of her religion. John Preston, preaching against 'those Cassanders that thinke by wit and policie to reconcile us . . . a thing impossible', noted that if Romanists were to abandon any tenet of their church in reunion negotiations it would mean that they accepted the principle of papal fallibility. If they were to accept this, then the foundation of many of Rome's errors would be thereby overthrown, and their church with it, to which they would obviously never consent. It therefore followed that Rome could never change: 'we may goe to them, they cannot come to us'. William Bedell noted that the pope and the Court of Rome, out of fear of their own ruin, detested all reformation just as much as the Protestants hated Rome's tyranny. Reconciliation was quite impossible.[92]

Furthermore, the indivisibility of the one true religion – a concept inherent in the doctrine of the 'Two Churches' and also common to most Calvinist writers – meant that Protestants could not be in a position to compromise on any points. As John Preston explained, reconciliation would be impossible 'for of what materials shall any middle course bee framed, when neyther side can spare the smallest piece of timber in their building? they cannot, because thereby they should bee argued of erring formerly; we cannot, for true Religion is of a brittle nature, breake it you may, bend it you cannot, no not in the least degree.' Any reconciliation would mean reconciling truth and falsehood: nothing could be pared away from, or added to, true religion without earning God's severe punishment.[93]

Moreover, the pope's identity as Antichrist and Rome's as Babylon meant that there could never be any hope that she would reform her errors, since these errors had prophetic importance as the badges by which her antichristian identity might be known. If the pope really was Antichrist, and Rome Babylon, then, as Joseph Hall noted, the only thing which could be truly hoped of Rome was her apocalyptic destruction:

Only this one thing, which God hath promised, we do verily expect; to see the day when the Lord Jesus shall with the breath of his mouth, destroy this lawless man, 2.Thess.ii.8, long since revealed to his Church; and, by the brightness of his glorious coming, fully discover and despatch him. Not only in the means and way, but in the end also, is Rome opposite to heaven. The heaven shall pass away by a change of quality, not an utter destruction of substance; Rome, by destruction, not by change. Of us therefore and them shall that old bucolic verse be verified:

Out of each others' breast their swords they drew,
Nor would they rest till one the other slew.[94]

[92] Preston, *Sermons*, i. pp.15–16; Bedell, *Certaine Letters*, pp.76–7.

[93] Preston, *Sermons*, i. pp.15–16.

[94] Hall, *Works*, X: 394, 395–6, 396–7. John White similarly employed 2 Thessalonians 2 to support his argument that reunion with Rome was impossible: White, *The Way*, preface,

It was this combination of the rhetoric of peaceful moderation with an irreconcilable opposition to Rome which initially misled and then later frustrated Archbishop de Dominis, when he attempted to convert such rhetoric into action by investigating the means by which the desired goal of reunion might be effected. He later complained that the English Protestants had deceived him by claiming that the schism was not their fault, and that they wished for reunion, but were rejected by the pope. When de Dominis took such declarations at their word, 'after I began out of this ground in my private arguments, and publike Sermons to urge an union, which upon their words seemed to me somewhat easily to be concluded; and so thrust my finger further into the wound', he found that in fact Englishmen felt very differently.[95] Instead, he found men who commended and maintained the separation from Rome, and thus made a mockery of all their talk of moderation and reconciliation. 'How can they, which professe themselves mortall Enemyes to the Church of Rome', he complained, 'be thought to desire an union with the Church of Rome?'[96]

In practice, English Protestant ecumenism ignored the Church of Rome altogether, and was directed instead towards the need to rally Protestant forces to oppose the sweeping conquests of the armies of Roman Catholicism in the Thirty Years War. John Dury, for example, deliberately played up the anti-papal potential of his schemes for Protestant reunion, attacking papists who laboured to subvert the foundation of Christian religion.[97] John Davenant built his appeal for Protestant reunion on the fact that the obstacles to union which made reconciliation with Rome impossible did not exist between the Protestant Churches. Rome's usurping of tyrannical authority, her demands for a blind obedience and her insistence that communion could be had only on an obligation to practise (or at least to accept the legitimacy of) idolatrous worship, made such a communion or peace with her unlawful. To come to terms with heretical bodies such as the Roman Church which tried to undermine the foundation of the Christian faith, was to revolt against Christ Himself.[98]

As we have seen, however, many of the foregoing axioms which were so

sig.**1v. On the impossibility of reconciliation with Rome, see also Hall, *Works*, VIII: 351, 394; Bedell, *Certaine Letters*, p.81; Edward Chaloner, 'No peace with Rome' in *Six Sermons* (1629); Jackson, *Works*, XII: 284; Burton, *Babel*, pp.76–7; Burton, *Replie*, pp.237–9; Thomas Clerke, *The Popes Deadly Wound* (1621), pp.1–2, cited in Sommerville, 'Jacobean political thought', p.23; Ussher, *Works*, II: 456ff.; Clark, *Register*, i. pp.208, 215 (Oxford Act theses 1611 (in Comitiis), 1619).

95 De Dominis, *Second Manifesto*, sig.F1v; Chamberlain, *Letters*, II: 379.

96 De Dominis, *Second Manifesto*, sigs.F1v, F2r.

97 A. Milton, '*The Unchanged Peacemaker*? John Dury and the politics of irenicism in England 1630–1643', in M. Greengrass, M. Leslie and T. Raylor (eds.), *Samuel Hartlib and Universal Reformation: Studies in Intellectual Communication* (forthcoming).

98 Davenant, 'Opinion', pp.8–13.

often mustered to demonstrate why any thought of reconciliation with Rome was impossible were being neglected or downgraded by Laud and his followers. The rejection of the pope's identity as Antichrist, the emphasis on issues of ecclesiastical privilege rather than of doctrine, the avoidance of the accusations of heresy or of idolatry against Rome, and the increasing readiness to appreciate the heterogeneous nature of Rome's communion; all these tendencies removed important obstacles to the conceptualization of reunion with Rome, even if most divines remained pessimistic about the chances of such a peace being negotiated.

The net result of the shifts in Laudian ecclesiology which have been described in earlier chapters was to grant Rome an equal status along with other particular churches. She was an erroneous church, but one which was an equal member of the Catholic Church. Christopher Potter had emphasized that other churches could not therefore be separated from her, but must remain in a true and real unity with the Church of Rome. If Rome was simply defined as a true church, then reconciliation with her was a goal which should actively be pursued.[99] In fact, if Rome was to be perceived in these terms, and if the hope could be entertained that the pope might be sufficiently moderate to drop what had now become the major issue dividing the churches – the pope's claims to universal jurisdiction – then reunion with her, as a true though erring church, might legitimately be pursued.

In fact, if the foregoing points were granted, then reunion with Rome could be justified according to the principles of the Protestant union which was being urged by the Calvinist bishops Morton, Hall and Davenant in the 1630s. Indeed, by their arguments, such a reunion was not only justifiable, but it was actually necessary to pursue it to avoid the charge of schism. Morton, Hall and Davenant's views on church unity were most clearly expressed in the letters solicited from them by John Dury in support of his union efforts among the Lutherans and Calvinists in Germany and Sweden in the 1630s. Having first firmly renounced the Church of Rome and explained why reunion was impossible with her, all three writers went on to lay down plans for church union which were strikingly moderate and tolerant on many major doctrinal controversies in the interests of reunion. Given the hostility with which the different Protestant groups regarded each other, these writers had to allow for union between churches which believed each other to undermine important aspects of the Faith.

A form of communion, they reasoned, was possible with a church whose

[99] Thus the Restoration historian Sir George Radcliffe said that, if Laud had intended a policy of gradual reconciliation with Rome, he could not condemn it, because Rome was 'a member of the true Catholic Church of Christ notwithstanding all new opinions or abuses crept in': Hibbard, *Popish Plot*, p.7.

doctrines appeared (to the outside observer) to undermine fundamental points of Faith by logical consequence, as long as that church expressly upheld the same fundamental truths.[100] This, of course, was precisely the way in which Rome herself was commonly said to have erred. Davenant and the others were careful to exclude Rome here, stressing that such a peace and union was unlawful with those who do not exactly disbelieve some fundamental point of Faith, yet 'maintaine some such Heresy as strikes at the heart of Religion, and cuts off the Abettors of it from having any communion with Christ'.[101] Davenant believed that the Church of Rome was guilty of precisely this fault in the case of image-worship. For those who did not accept that Rome was guilty of such an error – and we have seen that some writers indeed disputed it – peace and union in matters of doctrine were therefore justifiable with Rome under the Calvinist bishops' own arguments.

Davenant's affirmation of the principle that 'brotherly communion' was possible 'betwixt a sound and a diseased church' was directed at the Lutherans, but might as appropriately have been applied to Rome, which was frequently distinguished from the Reformed Churches in these terms. Laud and Montagu, as we have noted, described Rome in these terms without further elaboration.[102] Christopher Potter, indeed, had spoken of the existence of a true and real union with Rome in faith and charity. Davenant, however, clearly felt that his reunion principles could coax the different churches even closer together. He wanted, and considered possible, a 'fraternall and spirituall union' between sound and diseased churches, not simply as friends, but as brethren, 'not onely . . . an outward and generall friendship, but . . . a more intimate & spirituall amity and communion'.[103]

There is little indication that principles raised in debates on Protestant union found a conscious echo in the attitudes of Laud and his associates towards the Church of Rome. Nevertheless, it remains true that writings on Protestant church unity expressly encouraged reconciliation on terms which could easily make reunion with Rome appear a logical possibility to those divines who had significantly moderated their views of Rome. This possibility was manifested in Richard Montagu's energetic pursual of reunion with Rome in the 1630s, which he planned in conversation with the papal agent Panzani.

Genuine hopes for reunion, beyond the simple rhetoric of anti-papal polemic, had occasionally surfaced in the Church of England before this time. King James, in his first year on the English throne, had cherished

[100] Davenant, 'Opinion', pp.17–18. [101] *Ibid.*, p.19. [102] See above, pp.148–9.
[103] Davenant, 'Opinion', pp.3–4.

plans for reconciliation with the Church of Rome through the assembly of a free General Council of all Christendom to discuss the basis of religion and the question of papal authority. There is little indication that English Protestant divines shared his optimism and enthusiasm, and the cynical, dismissive response of Pope Clement VIII was a severe set-back for the king, and instilled in him a deep and lasting resentment.[104] James' ecumenical hopes found a variety of expressions during the remainder of his reign but were generally limited to the pan-Protestant ideals which were the theoretical limit to the irenicism of most of his clerical advisers.[105] There were exceptions. In the context of the Oath of Allegiance controversy some appeals were made to Roman princes to force the pope to agree to a General Council, and it was doubtless with the king's advice and support that John Buckeridge closed his treatise *De Potestate Papae in Rebus Temporalibus* with a similar appeal to the Romanist princes.[106] These were not principally intended as schemes for church reunion, however, but instead represented James' attempts to unite with fellow-monarchs in order to crush the doctrine of the pope's authority over princes in temporal matters. Other vague hopes for church union surfaced in the first two decades of the seventeenth century around members of the post-Reformation secular republic of letters, such as Hugo Grotius, although his reunion scheme basically aimed at uniting moderate Protestants and detaching the Gallican Church from the papacy. Moreover, the ideas of Grotius, Sandys, Hotman and others were essentially 'politique' in their inspiration, and often anti-clerical in their sentiments.[107] The retrenchment of the Church of Rome and the polarization of the Protestant and Romanist camps in the wake of the Thirty Years War had deprived hopes of a General Council of Christendom of any sense of reality by the

[104] W.B. Patterson, 'King James I's call for an ecumenical council', in G.J. Cuming and D. Baker (eds.), *Councils and Assemblies* (Studies in Church History 7, Cambridge, 1971), pp.267–75. King Charles certainly remembered the failure of his father's reunion scheme, but in conversation in early 1636 he seems to have considered it to have failed due to disputes over points of precedence: BL, Add. MS 15389 fol.127v: Panzani to Barberini, 23 Jan. 1636.

[105] W.B. Patterson, 'James I and the Huguenot Synod of Tonneins of 1614', *Harvard Theological Review* 65 (1972). Much new light will be shed on James' continuing ecumenical interests in a major study being completed by Professor Patterson.

[106] King James, *Political Works*, p.151; Buckeridge, *De Potestate Papae*, 'Conclusio'.

[107] Posthumus Meyjes, 'Jean Hotman's *Syllabus*', pp.179–80; Trevor-Roper, *Catholics*, pp.52–4, 194–7; *idem*, 'The Church of England and the Greek Church in the time of Charles I', in D. Baker (ed.), *Religious Motivation* (Studies in Church History 15, Oxford, 1978), pp.218–19. Moreover, Edwin Sandys' *Europae Speculum* w seen by Bedell in 1609, not as the blueprint for a general church union, but as an ideal means of persuading the Venetians of the political prudence of breaking with the papacy, 'as if God had directed the pen of the author to that speciall end, to doe him service in this place': Bedell, *Two Biographies*, p.247.

time of the Laudian ascendancy, although at the time of the Spanish Match there were some isolated calls among conformist lay writers for a reunion of Christendom against the common threat of the Turk.[108]

There may, however, have been some members of the Church of England who continued to cherish the hopes for reconciliation with Rome that James had entertained at the beginning of his reign. Henry Constable reported somewhat optimistically to the papal nuncio in 1604 that

> the most learned amongst those who bear the title of Prelate in this kingdom, speak willingly and show themselves desirous of some move towards the reunion of England with the Apostolic See. Many of them have spoken about it with great emotion ... *although the details that they have proposed are not such that they may be approved by a Catholic.*[109]

The last remark, of course, is crucial, and suggests that Constable was being misled by English Protestants' rhetoric of moderation and union in the same way that de Dominis would be later in the same reign. Nevertheless, one or two clerics at court may have had more than a tactical interest in the issue of reunion with Rome. Benjamin Carier, a royal chaplain, wrote a few years later that he had been prompted 'to spend my selfe in the study of spirituall unitie' with the Church of Rome after James had manifested a disposition 'towards peace and union ... at his first entrance upon this kingdome'. William Forbes later complained of the frustration of James' hopes for reunion, which had floundered unnecessarily due to 'the morose and quarrelsome dispositions of a number of would-be theologians'.[110]

Other stray hints of ecumenical aspirations may occasionally be unearthed among Jacobean avant-garde conformist writers. William Covell contributed a remarkably even-handed discussion of the divisions between Rome and the Protestants to his defence of Hooker, in which he lamented the persecution encountered by heroic mediators such as Cassander who strove for unity between the two sides. Both sides were in the wrong in falsely trying to accuse the other of heresy, and Covell expressed the pious hope that reconciliation might be pursued.[111] The second edition of Edward Maie's idiosyncratic sermon *The Communion of Saints* in 1621 promised a much larger work which would assess dispassionately how far the decrees of the Council of Trent would admit of reunion with the Protestants, and Maie assured his readers that 'if I cannot perfect an

[108] T. Cogswell, 'England and the Spanish Match', in Cust and Hughes, *Conflict*, pp.120–1, citing works by Francis Bacon, John Stradling and Sir Henry Goodere. Cf. Covell, *Polimanteia*, sig.Z4r–v.

[109] Patterson, 'King James I's call', p.273 (my italics).

[110] BCO, MS 270 p.153 (cf. Carier, *Treatise*, p.17); Forbes, *Considerationes*, II: 95–7.

[111] Covell, *Just and Temperate Defence*, pp.64–7, 77.

absolute peece . . . yet in a great matter, to make an offer, is a matter great enough'. This promised work was never forthcoming, however, and Maie, like Covell and Carier, was a minor and unrepresentative figure.[112]

After de Dominis returned to Rome (a year after the publication of Maie's sermon), he complained that he had found little open support for his reunion schemes in England when he began to broach them. Nevertheless, he was convinced that there was a sizeable number of men in England whose view of Rome was such as to make them amenable to his reunion plans, even if they were not actively pursuing reunion with Rome themselves. De Dominis made this claim in a letter to Joseph Hall which he wrote shortly before he left England. He claimed that, despite the anti-popery which he so detested, there remained in the Church of England many good and wise men who yearned for church unity, and who did not hold that the Church of Rome was guilty of heresy in doctrine or worship, if these terms were taken in their proper sense. De Dominis claimed (echoing a scriptural passage that was normally reserved for application to the Protestants' forebears within the Roman Church) that there were 7,000 men in the English Church who did not embrace the schismatical anti-papal doctrines of Luther and Calvin. However, de Dominis admitted that 'they dare not lift up their heads, because the puritans have such a predominance both in numbers and in positions of power in church and state'.[113]

De Dominis undoubtedly discussed with English divines in private the irenical ideas which he eventually incorporated into the seventh book of his *De Republica Ecclesiastica*.[114] At least one of those men with whom he discussed these issues would later become a bishop under Laud who pursued reunion with Rome. If the other 6,999 whom de Dominis claimed to know of did not openly reveal themselves, it may still be the case that there existed in England, at least by the 1630s, a number of divines whose perception of Rome made reunion with her at least conceivable. The one divine who was determined to investigate the possibilities of some form of reconciliation with Rome was Richard Montagu.

112 Maie, *Communion of Saints* (second impression, 1621), sigs.B1v–B2r. Carier certainly considered himself out of step with the rest of the clergy: his plans for the reconciliation of England with Rome placed all hope in the initiative of the king and the nobility, and not in the clergy, whom he regarded as generally Calvinists who profited by the division: BCO, MS 270 pp.160–1.

113 Malcolm, *De Dominis*, p.63 (Malcolm's translation of de Dominis, *De Pace Religionis*, pp.7–8). See 1 Kings 19.18.

114 Neile, *Shiftings*, p.18.

RICHARD MONTAGU AND REUNION WITH ROME

Montagu's general interest in the issue of church unity, and of the possibility of the reunion of the Church of England with Rome, may be traced back to his intimacy with de Dominis while the latter was dean of Windsor from 1618 until his return to Rome in 1622. As a prebendary of Windsor, Montagu would seem to have had lengthy discussions with the archbishop on these matters. In his *Immediate Addresse unto God Alone* of 1624, Montagu admitted that he and de Dominis had in private discussed the issue of the invocation of saints, as well as 'many other particulars, disputed of betwixt the sides of Protestants and Romane Catholikes.'[115]

De Dominis' flight to Rome and subsequent fate at the hands of the Inquisition must have quashed Montagu's earlier hopes of reconciliation. On hearing of de Dominis' fate, and of the report that he had steadfastly upheld that the Church of England was a true church, Montagu reflected that de Dominis had proved himself to be 'an honester man then he was taken for, as good as his word unto myself and others'. Rome's treatment of de Dominis demonstrated to Montagu 'upon what desperate terms of separation we stand. No yielding or moderation any way to be hoped for in point of opposition from that Church, so long as Puritan Jesuits beare the sway.'[116]

Apart from the Jesuits, however, Montagu manifested little hostility towards the Church of Rome as such. There are occasional hints in Montagu's correspondence with Cosin in the 1620s that he may have continued secretly to harbour carefully guarded hopes of reunion with moderate Romanists.[117] For all his occasionally vitriolic language, a spirit of reconciliation is often visible in the *New Gagg* and *Appello Caesarem*. In the latter Montagu affirmed in general terms, 'I am for peace and reconciliation, and say still "Beati Pacifici".' In his *Apparatus* of 1635, and his posthumously published *Acts and Monuments*, there is evident an even greater readiness to deplore in an even-handed way the energy wasted in confessional controversies, with the guilt seen as lying on the Protestant side just as much as the Roman. Montagu manifested a clear desire to

115 Montagu, *Immediate Addresse*, p.97. Macauley notes further evidence of Montagu and de Dominis' intimacy in the fact that de Dominis consistently appointed Montagu *locum tenens* during the dean's absences: Macauley, 'Richard Montague', p.143. Their later personal differences (e.g. Montagu, *Immediate Addresse*, ep. ded.; *idem*, *Acts and Monuments*, p.511) mask a similarity of ideas. On this point see Milton, 'Laudians', p.273 n.25.

116 Cosin, *Correspondence*, I: 64.

117 Reporting to Cosin in 1626 how the queen was attended by three priests, Montagu added 'all honest men as they say. I have much to say, but *coram*': Cosin, *Correspondence*, I: 102.

pursue a policy of even-handed pacification and reconciliation which would ignore the unnecessary disputes and dishonest subterfuges of those two exemplars of self-regarding extremism, the puritans and the Jesuits.[118]

Moreover, Montagu had always retained closer links with the world of Roman rather than of Protestant scholarship. He had trampled over the Protestant world's foremost scholars, Casaubon and Scaliger,[119] and was warily shunned by Calvinist divines such as Daniel Heinsius.[120] By contrast, Montagu's *Diatribae* against John Selden had spoken of 'my good friends Andreas Schottus, and Fronto Ducaeus', the famous Jesuit scholars.[121] He sent his own edition of the five books of Eusebius' *Adversus Marcellum Ancyram* to Paris, where they were included in the 1628 edition of the *Bibliotheca Patrum*.[122] He also had close links with important

118 See above, pp.195, 353; Montagu, *Appello*, pp.113, 292; *idem*, *Acts and Monuments*, pp.67, 383, 471; *idem*, *Apparatus*, p.282. Although published after his death, Montagu's *Acts and Monuments* was entered in the Stationers' Company Register on 24 December 1638: Arber, *Registers*, IV: 423.

119 For Montagu's attacks on Casaubon, see his *Apparatus*, 'Praefatio' para.65, and p.136 (described in Pattison, *Isaac Casaubon*, p.338); Montagu, *Acts and Monuments*, p.517; *idem*, *ΘΕΑΝΘΡΩΠΙΚΟΝ*, ii. pp.56–7. Montagu's scathing attack upon the anonymous 'Censurer' in *Acts and Monuments*, p.213, is directed against Casaubon: all the Latin quotations which he makes are from Casaubon's *De Rebus Sacris et Ecclesiasticis Exercitationes XVI. ad Cardinalis Baroni* (1614), p.73. For Montagu's savage attacks on Scaliger, see Montagu's *Diatribae*, pp.316, 321–2, 330, 341, 352–3, 383, 412 (though contrast this with the tone of his earlier letter to Scaliger: Leiden, Bibliotheek der Rijksuniversiteit, MS BPG 77). See other attacks on Scaliger and Casaubon in *Acts and Monuments*, pp.211–14, 237, 240, 364. By contrast, note his high praise for Baronius, and complaints that many 'frivolous exceptions' had been made against his *Annales*: *Acts and Monuments*, pp.211, 314–15, 393. Contrast the very strong language used against Baronius by Isaac Casaubon (Pattison, *Isaac Casaubon*, p.337), George Carleton (*Jurisdiction*, pp.143, 153) and Francis Mason (*Vindiciae*, pp.468–9).

120 P.R. Sellin, *Daniel Heinsius and Stuart England* (Leiden, 1968), pp.91–2.

121 Montagu cited these two scholars as examples of the 'more ingenious' Jesuits who broke their order's general rule that they should only refer derogatively to Protestants (Montagu, *Diatribae*, p.74), although it was only Schottus whom he was prepared to applaud as 'a right honest man indeed' as well as a learned philologer (*ibid.*, p.127). Montagu presumably became acquainted with the two Jesuits while working with Sir Henry Savile in the preparation of the latter's edition of the works of St John Chrysostom (Macauley, 'Richard Montague', ch.3). The Jesuits may also be found extending their regards to Montagu: J. Kemke, *Patricius Junius Bibliothekar der Könige Jacob I. und Carl I. von England. Mitteilungen aus Seinem Briefwechsel* ... (Leipzig, 1898), pp.37–8; Hessels, *Ecclesiae Londino-Batavae Archivum*, I: 862.

122 See Cosin, *Correspondence*, I: 47, 52, 53, 57–8, 61, 64; BL, Add. MS 4274 fol.102; *Lucae Holstenii Epistolae ad Diversos*, ed. J.F. Boissonade (Paris, 1817), p.28 (Holstenius to Meursius, 13 May 1624); Kemke, *Patricius Junius*, pp.52–3 (Holstenius to Young, 2 Nov. 1624); Bodl., Smith MS 76 pp.107 (P. Young to Holstenius, April 1625), 133 (P. Young to Peter Goldman, n.d.); Ussher, *Works*, XV: 233. It was not unusual, of course, for scholarly contacts to cross confessional boundaries. Nevertheless, it is striking that Montagu's scholarly contacts seem to have been almost exclusively Romanist (although see Patrick Young's letter to Johannes Meursius of 31 October 1624 in which Montagu sends his regards to the Dutch scholar, which Meursius returns: Kemke, *Patricius Junius*,

members of the recusant community.[123] Montagu's negotiations with Panzani for a reconciliation with Rome did not therefore come out of a clear sky.[124]

Montagu's meetings with Panzani have already been described in detail elsewhere, and it will not be necessary to give an exhaustive account.[125] Panzani was informed on 28 October 1635 that Montagu wished to speak with him, and the two divines met on 3 November at Montagu's residence in London. They met for a second conversation on 22 March 1636, and had two further meetings on 22 April and 7 May of that year.[126] When Montagu first met Panzani he immediately expressed his desire to negotiate with him for reunion, confessing ingenuously that after having reflected deeply on the matter he could not understand why union had not already been achieved. Montagu suggested that the best way to accomplish the reunion of the churches would be to send moderate-minded representatives from both sides to meet together to discuss reunion, and added that such an assembly (if it could be made with the consent of the pope) would most

pp.51–2, 55). During the 1630s, judging by their correspondence, the European Protestant scholarly community would appear to have been almost wholly ignorant of the publication of Montagu's works on church history. For a rare citation, see *Claude Saumaise & André Rivet. Correspondance échangée entre 1632 et 1648*, ed. J.A.H.G.M. Bots and P.E.-R. Leroy (Amsterdam & Maarssen, 1987), p.126.

123 See Macauley, 'Richard Montague', pp.427–30.

124 Some historians have questioned the value of Panzani's reports of these conversations. George Ornsby, the editor of Cosin's correspondence, simply denied that they were true: Cosin, *Correspondence*, I: 80n. More recently, T.A. Birrell has denied that there was any positive intent behind Charles and Windebank's discussions with Panzani: 'The English government was in fact completely opportunistic on the Catholic question. Discussions of union, toleration, and bishops were encouraged with the sole object of dividing and weakening the Catholic body as a whole' (*The Memoirs of Gregorio Panzani*, ed. J. Berington (Birmingham, 1793; facsimile edn, Farnborough, 1970), Introduction (unpaginated)). It is far from clear that Charles and Windebank were concerned *solely* to create internal dissension among the king's Roman Catholic subjects. They were keen first and foremost to secure the acceptance of the Oath of Allegiance by the Roman Catholic population of Britain – a goal which internal Romanist dissension might in the short term have rendered more, rather than less, difficult. Moreover, Birrell's argument cannot explain the compulsive banter on the subject of reunion in which the king clearly liked to indulge with his friend the papal agent George Con; still less can it explain the detailed discussions of the possibilities of reunion which were actively sought by Windebank (who, after all, was later to convert to Roman Catholicism) and Bishop Montagu. It is perfectly possible to argue for the presence of political motives in the behaviour of the government without discounting that for these two men, if for no one else, the negotiations also offered a chance to discuss more general ecumenical issues.

125 Macauley, 'Richard Montague', pp.445–56.

126 These meetings may be dated more precisely by the entries in Panzani's diary, which was not available to Macauley (although this does not provide any further detail of the discussions themselves). For the dating of the last three meetings, see Panzani, *Diary*, pp.168 [fol.131 of original], 175 [fol.135], 178 [fol.138]. The details of their ensuing conversations are reported in Panzani's letters to Cardinal Barberini, PRO, MS 31/9/17B: 4/14 Nov. 1635, 23 March/2 April 1636; 27 April/ 7 May 1636 and 11/21 May 1636.

fittingly meet in France. This would be appropriate because the English were closest to the French in opinion, as well as in geographical location, and also on account of the kinship links between the two crowns. This assembly could meet in a few months' time, given that the present English ambassador in Paris, Viscount Scudamore, was a good friend of Laud's and of moderate religious persuasions.[127] These plans seem to have gone awry, or so Panzani deduced when Windebank told him in December that Montagu, 'if he could, would quickly take some decision because he is not so timid'.[128] The two seem to have failed to meet in February 1636, although when they met again in March, Montagu greeted Panzani 'con gran festa'.[129]

At their third meeting, Montagu welcomed Panzani and entertained him for an hour. He remarked that if the king resolved publicly to have an ambassador at Rome, he would be happy to be that ambassador. When Panzani remarked that in that case he would be rumoured to be a papist, Montagu replied unflappably that there was no harm in that.[130] The two churchmen had a further meeting in May at which Panzani brought to Montagu a letter directed to Barberini recommending Montagu's son, who wished to visit Rome.[131]

There is nothing in Panzani's account of Montagu's conversations with him that seriously conflicts either with Montagu's stance elsewhere in his published works, or with the basic assumptions behind many Laudians' opposition to Rome. On the crucial issue of papal authority Panzani reported that, when Montagu discussed the pope's supremacy, the English bishop said that he was willing to kiss the pope's feet and acknowledge himself one of the pope's children, and the pope as the head of the church.[132] These reported remarks are reminiscent of Gondomar's reports of King James' occasional fulsome declarations of affection for, and submission to, the pope, and should probably be treated with the same degree of scepticism as to their practical implications.[133] Montagu made his remarks directly after having received from Panzani the sly assurance that Montagu's courage was greatly admired in Rome – a compliment which highly pleased the aged bishop. A certain amount of rhetorical excess is therefore to be expected, and the suggestion that the pope was head of the

[127] PRO, MS 31/9/17B: Panzani to Barberini, 4/14 Nov. 1635.

[128] Macauley, 'Richard Montague', p.447.

[129] PRO, MS 31/9/17B: Panzani to Barberini, 3/13 February 1636; 23 March/2 April 1636.

[130] PRO, MS 31/9/17B: *idem* to *idem*, 27 April/7 May 1636.

[131] PRO, MS 31/9/17B: *idem* to *idem*, 11/21 May 1636.

[132] '... di riconoscere il Papa capo della Chiesa, della quale esso era humil Figlio, e che volontieri baciarebbe li piedi' a S. Sta.': PRO, MS 31/9/17B: *idem* to *idem*, 23 March/2 April 1636.

[133] Cf. Carter, *Secret Diplomacy*, pp.243–4.

church need not be taken literally to imply the abandonment of the Protestant orthodoxy that Christ alone was the head of the church, and that the visible church on earth did not require a single monarchical head.

More significant are Montagu's remarks at his first meeting with Panzani that he and others confessed the pope to be Christ's vicar and the successor of St Peter, without whom it would be impossible to convene a General Council, or determine what would be binding upon the whole church.[134] These remarks are essentially consistent with Montagu's published views, and with Laudian preoccupations, which tended towards according the pope his full status as an important bishop, and indeed a primacy of honour, and therefore an indispensability, in any General Council.[135] Montagu's works, along with those of most Laudian writers (as we have seen), were concerned primarily to deny that the pope had exercised either temporal sovereignty or supremacy in spirituals in the primitive church.[136] It was the point of ecclesiastical monarchy which Montagu was most keen to overthrow, while not denying the significant authority which the pope had exercised in the early church. Thus Montagu emphasized in print the great esteem in which the pope was held in the early church, and the frequent recourse that had been made to the pontiff to judge controversies, although Montagu was careful to insist that such judicial requests were voluntary, and were not inspired by any belief that the pope held any necessary authority as supreme judge.[137] The pope had wide authority in the church, but he exercised it *iure humano*, not *iure divino*; not by necessity, 'sed convenientiae temporalis'.[138]

Given these restrictions, Montagu had been happy to record in detail the celebrations of the pope's dignity and honour in early councils, and the ancient popes' 'privilegia loci et dignitatis'.[139] In his *Antidiatribae* of 1625, Montagu had firmly maintained that the pope no longer had any claim to a primacy of honour; the corruption of medieval popes was contrasted with the purity of the ancient bishops of Rome.[140] By the 1630s, however, Montagu was optimistic that many of the corruptions of the medieval popes were being renounced, especially by the current Pope Urban VIII. In his *ΘΕΑΝΘΡΩΠΙΚΟΝ*, Montagu noted that the medieval popes' claims to spiritual and temporal supremacy had been renounced by some latter-day popes – not just by Adrian VI (whom Protestants regularly cited against the Romanists), but also by Marcellus II, Pius IV, Clement VIII and by the

134 PRO, MS 31/9/17B: Panzani to Barberini, 4/14 November 1635.

135 See above, pp.225–6. See Montagu, *ΘΕΑΝΘΡΩΠΙΚΟΝ*, ii. pp.124–6, 157–8. Montagu's recognition of the pope as Christ's vicar may well have been intended in the same terms in which de Dominis expressed it, in the sense that the same title applied to all bishops: *De Republica Ecclesiastica* (Hanover, 1622), lib.7 cap.10 p.194r.

136 See above, pp.222–7.

137 Montagu, *Antidiatribae*, pp.57–8.

138 *Ibid.*, p.81.

139 *Ibid.*, pp.83–4, 92.

140 E.g. *ibid.*, pp.93–4.

present Pope Urban VIII, 'illa morum & eruditionis celebritate'.[141] If the pope would disengage himself from his claims of monarchical power over the independent rights of other churches, he could inherit the privilege of place and honour which the early popes had enjoyed. Such privileges might already be accorded him. Montagu declared explicitly in a manuscript tract composed some time between 1628 and 1638 that the Church of England *still* gave Rome the same honour which the early church had accorded her: 'for wee give *yet* all reverent regard unto it [the Church of Rome], which Antiquitie gave unto that Sea [*sic*], and Church, and Bishop'.[142]

The honouring of the pope was an important principle for Montagu. This was partly because such respect for the pope had been a constant feature of the primitive church, whose history Montagu had devoted his life to studying, and which he felt should be a guide for all aspects of post-Reformation ecclesiastical life.[143] This 'reverent regard' for the pope also sprang from Montagu's deep preoccupation with the dignity of the episcopal office. This was a theme that was constantly reiterated in all his works, and especially those of the 1630s, which placed a crucial emphasis on the sacramental nature of episcopal orders, and the necessity of their preservation for the very survival of the church and its sacraments.[144] Montagu therefore felt affronted by the scorn and indignities suffered by the Roman bishop, and complained that the Reformers had spoiled the pope of many privileges which were his by right.[145]

Most followers of Laud, as we have seen, were concerned to overturn arguments for the pope's monarchical sovereignty over other churches, and therefore by implication recognized his status as an independent patriarch.[146] To Montagu, this status, far from being an incidental point, was vital to his view of episcopacy and of the church. If the Church of England did indeed, as Montagu claimed, grant to the pope the same reverent regard which antiquity had granted him, then not only was it true, as he told Panzani, that no General Council could be convoked without the pope, but also the pope's judgement might also be accorded the primary honour

141 Montagu, *ΘΕΑΝΘΡΩΠΙΚΟΝ*, pp.175–6. Montagu also believed that Urban VIII accepted Bellarmine's theoretical restrictions on the pope's temporal authority: Montagu, *Acts and Monuments*, p.494. See above, p.247 n. 84. Contrast this positive assessment of Urban with the uncomplimentary picture painted by Joseph Hall in his *Answer to Pope Urbans Inurbanity* (1629) – see Hall, *Works*, X: 227–34.

142 CUL, MS Gg/1/29 fol.98v (from back) (my italics). The general offer to yield to Rome all the honour which she had been given in the early church *if* she would keep the Apostles' doctrine and traditions was a more conventional polemical ploy: see Field, *Of the Church*, III: 264.

143 See above pp.274–5.

144 E.g. Montagu, *Apparatus*, p.56; *idem*, *Antidiatribae*, pp.40, 158, 161, 166; *idem*, *ΘΕΑΝΘΡΩΠΙΚΟΝ*, ii. pp.463–72.

145 Montagu, *Antidiatribae*, pp.41, 95. See above, pp.266–7.

146 See above, pp.224–7.

(though not that of a supreme judge) within that council, and be deferred to on certain controverted issues.[147] This admission seems to be implied (albeit somewhat obliquely) in a curious passage in Montagu's *New Gagg* which touches on this issue.[148]

Montagu's negotiations with Panzani do not reveal a man poised to convert to Rome, but rather one who was convinced that independent churches could exist within Rome's communion. He never implied in his conversations with Panzani that he considered the English Church to be in any way subject to Rome. In a manuscript tract written about this time he had explicitly compared the English Church's separation from the Church of Rome with that of the French Church, and his negotiations would seem to have been inspired by his belief in the autonomy enjoyed by the Gallican Church while remaining within Rome's communion.[149]

Montagu's readiness to grant the pope a formal ecclesiastical primacy such as he had enjoyed in the primitive church, although not one which would serve to place him above his fellow-patriarchs and allow him to intrude into their independent jurisdictions, is strikingly similar to the reunion schemes propounded by de Dominis in his *De Republica Ecclesiastica.* While de Dominis maintained that 'Romanus Pontifex nullum privilegium potest habere iure divino supra alios Episcopos, nec in potestate ordinaria Episcopali', he still admitted that the pope might have some such privilege 'iure tantum Ecclesiastico in certis causis',[150] and strongly denied that the pope was Antichrist.[151] He stressed the equality of all bishops, and

147 Montagu, *Antidiatribae*, pp.57–8. On the general point of the need for an ecclesiastical primacy (though not a monarchy) to manifest unity, see *ibid.*, pp.51, 116, 158; *idem*, *ΘΕΑΝΘΡΩΠΙΚΟΝ*, ii. pp.124–6.

148 Discussing a quotation from Anselm to the effect that the pope was the most fitting person to be referred to for corrections to anything arising in the church against the Catholic faith, Montagu explained that this passage could be interpreted 'well enough' as meaning that if a controversy or heresy which touched upon the Catholic Church were to be referred to a General Council, 'it could not be put over more fitly to any one man by the Church representative in a Councel, then unto the pope, first Bishop of Christendome: of greatest, not absolute power amongst Bishops' (*New Gagg*, p.29). Montagu, however, was certain that this was not Anselm's meaning: the archbishop was simply 'a factionist for Pope Urban, his good Lord and Master'. Montagu's moderate interpretation of this passage was thus unnecessary, and added nothing to his argument. His employment of it might be regarded as a piece of purely academic pedantry, but given his stance in the 1630s it might equally be taken to show a willingness to defend a principle of moderation regarding the pope's continued importance in General Councils. Yates and Featley may therefore have been quite correct to draw attention to this passage in Montagu's book: Yates, *Ibis*, iii. p.11; Featley, *Second Parallel*, ii. pp.35–7.

149 See above, pp.266, 344.

150 De Dominis, *De Republica Ecclesiastica* (1617), lib.4 p.677. De Dominis goes on to show how all the privileges which the pope maintains over other patriarchs *iure divino* belong equally to all bishops (*ibid.*, pp.677–86). See also *De Republica Ecclesiastica* (Hanover, 1622), lib.7 cap.7.

151 De Dominis, *De Republica Ecclesiastica* (Hanover, 1622), p.194.

the *iure divino* nature of their spiritual authority.[152] Like the Laudians, de Dominis also especially emphasized the importance of the derivation of episcopacy from the apostolical succession as a criterion of a true church and therefore an indispensable element in any reunion scheme, while explicitly doubting whether the ministers of the non-episcopal Reformed Churches had the power to ordain.[153] De Dominis had also been persuaded that the pope would yield on the question of his authority over princes, and would approve the Book of Common Prayer, grant communion in both kinds and suffer the disputed points of faith to be handled by Councils. These concessions (if they could be believed) would have met the remaining areas of concern of Montagu and other Laudian divines.[154]

De Dominis' vision of a unified church based around an association of independent and equal *iure divino* bishops, meeting in councils to resolve disputes, clearly had much in common with the ecclesiological preoccupations of most Laudian divines. He was certainly a figure with whom several of them may have had dealings (most notably Montagu and Overall), and one whom they generally mention favourably in later accounts.[155] Like him, they derived from Cyprian a view of the church which was increasingly happy to assert that episcopacy formed a unity in the church, and provided the basis of the unity of the church as a whole.[156] The universal church was depicted by Howson and others as 'this one and undevided Bishopricke', in which each bishop had equal power:

for as there is but una Ecclesia, one universall Church, so there is but Episcopatus unus, onely one Bishopricke in that one universall Church; and that indivisus ... and yet there is a multiplicity of persons, that is, of Bishops, all of one equall power,

152 Malcolm, *De Dominis*, pp.31–2. For de Dominis' general discussion of the issue of schism, see *De Republica Ecclesiastica* (Hanover, 1622), lib.7 pp.132–97 (esp. pp.194–7). Note his emphasis on the visibility of the true church (*ibid.*, pp.142–55). Of all the pope's usurpations, the worst was in asserting universal judgement in matters of faith, which was the main cause of schism (pp.78–9). The recognition and damnation of heresies should be by bishops and councils, and not just by the pope (cap.7).

153 See below, p.466.

154 Neile, *Shiftings*, p.47.

155 King James recommended that whatever de Dominis wrote 'he should first communicate it in Sheets and Chapters one after another to the Bishop [Overall]: whose approbation his Majestie would trust before all others'. This is attested by Cosin (BL, Add. MS 4236 fol.337r), who also records having made a public speech to the archbishop, and subsequently receiving 'a great deale of favour and kindness from him' when relaying messages to de Dominis from Overall. Cosin also gives a notably sympathetic account of de Dominis' actions (*ibid.*, fols.337v-338r; Cosin, *Works*, IV: 160). See also Laud, *Works*, II: 394; Heylyn, *Cyprianus*, pp.107–8. Such encomiums were doubtless written in part as offering a way of criticizing the puritan anti-papal extremism, or radical Calvinism, which supposedly forced de Dominis out.

156 There was, however, some dispute, then and since, concerning the precise content and meaning of the passages in question from Cyprian's *De Unitate*. On papal corruptions of these passages, see Howson, *Certaine Sermons*, pp.155–6; Potter, *Want of Charitie*, i. pp.28–9. On the continuing debate, see *Treatises of Cyprian*, pp.150–2; *St. Cyprian, Treatises*, tr. and ed. R.J. Deferrari (New York, 1958), pp.92–3.

and authority, and dignitie in the particular Churches of that same one Bishopricke; as a Trinitie of persons is found in heaven in one Dietie [*sic*].[157]

While each bishop seemed limited to a particular bishopric, 'yet (as Saint Cyprian saith) a singulis in solidum pars tenetur; every Bishop so holds a part, as that he hath interest and full power in that whole Bishopricke, which spreads over the whole world'.[158] Thus, Howson concluded, 'in the Church there is unus Episcopatus, one onely Bishopricke, and yet many Apostles, and many Bishops of equall power and authoritie', and 'all joyntly make one Monarch, in respect of their inferiours the Priests, and people'.[159] This aristocratic vision of the church could also encompass the need for a certain primacy *inter pares* – 'among them one must hath Primatum ordinis, because Exordium, and ordo must be ab unitate'[160] – as long as this primacy was never exercised as a monarchy.

This view of episcopal authority as a universal, unifying bond could not easily be reconciled with the existence of non-episcopal Protestant Churches. Like de Dominis, the Laudians were becoming increasingly equivocal in their defence of the legitimacy of presbyterian orders.[161] In a sense, unity might indeed more easily and effectively be sought with the Church of Rome than with the non-episcopal Reformed Churches. These visions of church unity based upon a sacerdotal view of the ministry and episcopacy may be contrasted with the more political vision of Grotius or Sarpi.[162]

Nevertheless, divines of a Laudian persuasion could have plenty of

157 Howson, *Certaine Sermons*, pp.102–3; quoting Cyprian, *De Unitate Ecclesiae*, cap.4. Note also the passages from Cyprian's *De Unitate* noted in James Wedderburn's commonplace book under the heading 'Episcopatus quomodo unus': BL, Harleian MS 749 fol.77r.

158 Howson, *Certaine Sermons*, p.103, citing the famous passage from chapter 4 of Cyprian's *De Unitate Ecclesiae*: 'Episcopatus unus est, cuius a singulis in solidum pars tenetur.' This interpretation of the passage has more recently been challenged by M. Bevenot, who has denied that it suggests common ownership of the part or whole. Instead, 'episcopatus' is said to refer to the episcopal power as used through the whole church and 'pars' to that power exercised by the bishop in his local church, as 'in solidum' need not necessarily refer to several bishops. The passage is therefore merely a defence of the authority of local bishops against rivals in their own dioceses: M. Bevenot, '"In Solidum" and St Cyprian: a correction', *Journal of Theological Studies* 6 (1955), pp.244–8.

159 Howson, *Certaine Sermons*, pp.131–2 (citing Cyprian, *De Unitate*).

160 *Ibid*., p.131. Cf. Montagu, *ΘΕΑΝΘΡΩΠΙΚΟΝ*, ii. pp.124–6.

161 See below ch.9, pp.485–93.

162 For the contrast between de Dominis' views and those of Sarpi, see Malcolm, *De Dominis*, p.36. On the divergence of Grotius' views, see the letter from his friend, Bishop Overall, in 1617, explaining that Andrewes and others would object to Grotius' giving to lay powers a definitive judgement in matters of faith, denying the true power and authority of church pastors and ranking episcopacy as unnecessary: Mason, *Church of England*, p.80.

reasons for disliking prevalent Romanist perceptions of the nature of episcopacy. The activities of the pope and his undermining of the principle of episcopal equality by claiming a monarchical authority over other bishops, combined with the Council of Trent's apparent equivocation over the *iure divino* nature of episcopacy, could give just as much ground for concern as the presbyterian doctrine of parity of ministers. Laud objected to Sancta Clara's proposal that the Franciscan write a book in defence of episcopacy against the Scottish Covenanters because 'I did not like the way which the Church of Rome went in the case of episcopacy.'[163] It may have been Laud himself who instilled in Charles his justifiable doubts over Rome's readiness to grant that episcopacy was *iure divino*.[164] However similar their notions of the church might be to those of de Dominis, Laudian divines might just as consistently refrain from entertaining any buoyant hopes for reunion with Rome. Instead, irenical aspirations might be directed more towards union with those Lutheran Churches which had retained episcopacy,[165] or towards other non-Roman episcopalian churches, or even reform-minded Romanist princes.[166]

Nevertheless, on many other issues, Montagu was being fed information by Sancta Clara, Panzani and others which would have satisfied other Laudians' misgivings, had they been prepared to believe that the Roman irenicists were reliable guides to what might be acceptable to the papacy (which, of course, they were not). Sancta Clara, for example, guaranteed the ecclesiastical dignity and authority of the married clergy, and suggested that Charles might retain his current right to appoint bishops, in the same

163 Laud, *Works*, IV: 326–7. Cf. Cosin, *Works*, I: 93–4.

164 For Charles' opinion, see Albion, *Court of Rome*, pp.402–5. Albion also notes (*ibid.*, p.405) the anonymous *A Modest Advertisement concerning the Present Controversie about Church Governement* (1641), which claimed that 'the abusing of episcopacie had beene a great and constant designe of the Papacie; and that it was so in the Trent Councell: no one thing having more exalted that Mother of Abominations, the See of Rome, than the exempting of Presbyters, as Jesuits and others, from the power and government of Bishops'. This is clearly an attempt to deflect extreme presbyterian criticisms of episcopacy by introducing an anti-papal element to the defence of episcopacy, which was certainly not attempted by any Laudian writers during the 1630s.

165 W.J. Tighe, 'William Laud and the reunion of the churches: some evidence from 1637 and 1638', *HJ* 30 (1987). See also below, ch.8.

166 See Ephraim Pagitt's appeal in the epistle dedicatory to the 1640 edition of *Christianographie* to King Charles to work for church unity. Observing that 'for their Discipline, all the Christian Churches in this world, have and do keep, the ancient Ecclesiasticke policy, order and government of Bishops, instituted by our Lord himselfe' (sig.A3r), he argued that it belonged to the king 'being one of the great Monarchs of Christendome, to joyne hand in hand with the other Potentates thereof, to make up the breaches of Zion, and to build up the Walls of Jerusalem'. He should therefore see whether 'Romish Princes' could be persuaded to have communion in both kinds restored, abrogate image-worship and institute the vernacular liturgy and clerical marriage, 'and for some other [i.e. Protestant] Princes and States, who abhorre Idolls, not to permit sacriledge, with some other like things fit to be reformed' (sigs.A3v–A4r).

manner as the king of France. There would be no impairment of the king's privileges as long as they did not cross the Catholic faith.[167] Panzani similarly promised Windebank that, if there was a reunion, the king would be allowed the right of nomination to bishoprics, and a concordat such as that which had been granted in France and Germany, adding the further reassurance that no fuss would be made over the restitution of the loot of the monasteries, given that Cardinal Pole had cancelled the official censures of these actions in Queen Mary's reign. Cardinal Barberini instructed Panzani to emphasize to Montagu that Rome was above all earthly interests, and was motivated only by the desire to heal schism among Christians, thereby hinting to the king that Rome would be liberal in matters of purely temporal interest.[168]

Panzani also assured Windebank that the pope might sacrifice the Jesuits' interest if there was the prospect of reunion, and that he also hoped that the obstacles of Rome's insistence on communion in one kind and the celibacy of the clergy, and her objections to the vernacular liturgy, might be removed.[169] He was also prepared to suggest that the pope might approve of Montagu's scheme for a congress to debate reunion in France. By contrast, more intractable points of controversy were unlikely to be raised in the conversations with Montagu and Windebank because Panzani was given explicit instructions by Barberini that discussions of the veracity of dogmas established by the Church of Rome were to be avoided.[170] On one of the potentially divisive issues – that of the validity of Church of England ordinations – Panzani pointedly would not give his opinion, but passed to another matter when Montagu made it clear that he considered his own episcopal character and priesthood to be unquestionable.[171]

There were also rumours of Pope Urban's readiness to make concessions. Father Philip thought that the vernacular liturgy and communion in both kinds might be granted, and that compromise was possible on the issue of married clergy.[172] Dom Leander in his report compared the Church of England to the Greek Church at the time of the Council of Florence: the Uniate Church offered the possibility of a church administered by a native cardinal, under the pope's ultimate direction. The Benedictine irenicist John Barnes had also expressed hopes that the pope might be per-

167 J.B. Dockery, *Christopher Davenport* (1960), p.153.

168 Albion, *Court of Rome*, pp.176–7, 179.

169 Panzani, *Memoirs*, pp.163, 164.

170 Albion, *Court of Rome*, p.180.

171 PRO, MS 31/9/17B: Panzani to Barberini, April 27/May 7 1636.

172 Albion, *Court of Rome*, p.175. It remains highly unlikely that married clergy would have agreed to having their sacred functions taken over by a celibate priest, as Father Philip hoped!

suaded to dispense with the king of England's feudal subjection, and to grant the English clergy the use of the 'Cyprian Privilege'.[173]

The impracticalities of these schemes need hardly be emphasized, and even the most zealous advocates on both sides clearly differed on the sensitive subject of the reordination of Church of England ministers,[174] although one of the English bishops had earlier suggested to Dom Leander that he would consider it wrong not to yield to reordination in the interests of the peace of the church.[175]

It is difficult to assess just how much support Montagu's reunion schemes might have enjoyed among the Caroline episcopate. Montagu constantly assured Panzani that the other bishops shared his views.[176] In February 1636 Sancta Clara and Father Philip were advising Panzani that Montagu was expected at court that Easter, and that it was hoped that all the moderate bishops would be gathered together 'per trattare in ordine all' Unione'.[177] Montagu did indeed preach at court on 20 March that year as

[173] Trevor-Roper, *Catholics*, pp.111–13; Baillie, *Ladensium* (3rd edn, 1641), 'A Large Supplement', pp.19–20 – quoting from John Barnes' *Catholico Romanus Pacificus*.

[174] Panzani hoped that many of the English bishops would accept reordination in the event of reunion (Albion, *Court of Rome*, p.184). Even Dom Leander probably did not accept the validity of Anglican orders (see Messenger, *The Reformation*, II: 451), and Sancta Clara, while dodging the issue in *Deus, Natura, Gratia* (Sancta Clara, *Paraphrastica*, pp.85–95, esp. p.90), later explicitly concluded that Anglican orders were null (Dockery, *Christopher Davenport*, pp.87–8). See also the report on the more candid expressions by Sancta Clara and Dom Leander of their own views of the Church of England's succession (or lack of it) in Panzani's letter to Barberini: PRO, MS 31/9/17B: 17/27 June 1636. It is clear from Montagu's reported conversations that he held the succession of the bishops of the Church of England to be indisputable and that he would never have submitted to reordination: PRO, MS 31/9/17B: Panzani to Barberini, 23 March/2 April; 27 April/7 May 1636.

[175] PRO, MS 31/9/17B: Panzani to Barberini, 17/27 June 1636. See also Vatican Library, Codices Barberini Latini 8637, fol.163 – again, I am very grateful to Professor Hibbard for providing me with a transcript of this letter. Professor Hibbard has reasonably suggested to me that if the bishop concerned had been Montagu Panzani would undoubtedly have named him, given his earlier disagreements with Montagu on precisely this issue. The most obvious candidate for this remark would be Bishop Goodman. This passage in Panzani's letter occurs in the context of a discussion of a book dealing with the episcopal succession in England, which is sent on to Barberini with the wish that the cardinal read it 'e considerar detto libro solamente quanto alla historia della successione'. This is presumably the book which was earlier given to Panzani by Windebank (see PRO, MS 31/9/17B: Panzani to Barberini, 23 March/2 April 1636), which was very likely Mason's *Vindiciae*.

[176] At their first meeting, Montagu assured Panzani that both archbishops (Laud and Neile), Juxon and some of the other bishops, as well as many of the most learned ministers, held all the opinions of Rome 'circa li Dogmi'. While promising to arrange an interview with Laud, however, he warned Panzani that the archbishop was very fearful and circumspect (PRO, MS 31/9/17B: Panzani to Barberini, 4/14 November 1635). Meeting Panzani again the next year, Montagu again assured him of 'il buon'animo dell' Arcivescovo di Cantuaria', but stressed that it was combined 'con molto timore' (*ibid.*, *idem* to *idem*, 23 March/2 April 1636).

[177] PRO, MS 31/9/17B: Panzani to Barberini, 10/20 February 1636.

part of the series of Lenten court sermons, to which Bishops Juxon, Dee, Piers, Laud, Wren, Towers, Curll and White also contributed.[178] If Montagu did raise the issue of reunion with these his fellow-bishops at court at this time, it seems unlikely that he received any encouragement beyond vague expressions of approval of the general principle of reunion if it might be achieved on favourable terms. When he met Panzani in April, Montagu made no reference to any discussions or further plans, but assured him that only three of the bishops were strongly anti-papist – Morton, Hall and Davenant – and that all the others were 'moderatissimi'.[179]

In the same letter in which he reported Montagu's remarks, Panzani sent to Barberini an assessment of the attitudes of the Church of England's bishops towards Rome. This was almost certainly based upon information supplied by Montagu.[180] While Morton, Hall, Davenant and John Bowle were accounted 'Puritanissimo' and 'nemicissimo nostro', the other bishops were described as being moderately disposed in varying degrees towards the Church of Rome. Bishops Curll, Thornborough and Bridgeman were 'moderato'. Some were more carefully qualified: Richard Corbet was 'non male affetto alla nostra religione'; Barnaby Potter was 'non e cattivo'; Francis Dee was 'non cattivo'; William Piers 'non molto cattivo'; and Francis White, having been 'molto nemico', was now only 'aliquanto moderato'. Others sounded more promising. Neile was 'assai moderato', while Wren, Juxon, William Murray and the unscrupulous careerist Theophilus Field were described as 'molto moderato'. Montagu and Goodman, of course, were lauded for their moderation. Bishops John Bancroft and Robert Wright also seem to have encouraged high hopes. Bancroft was described as experienced in ecclesiastical politics and 'molto nostro amico', while Wright was even 'quasi Cattolico'. However, it is impossible to assess how far these men might have gone along with Montagu's ideas. No other evidence of their beliefs on this matter survives, although this is much as we would expect on such a sensitive issue. The most that can be said is that none of the other Laudian bishops seem to have approached Panzani to discuss the proposals for reunion.[181]

As for Laud himself, as we have seen, he displayed little interest in plans

[178] PRO, LC 5/134 p.2. His sermon is described by Panzani in PRO, MS 31/9/17B: Panzani to Barberini, 23 March/2 April 1636, who writes that Montagu preached (among other things) that altars should be made of stone. Word of this soon came to the ears of William Prynne, who refers to it in his *A Quench-Coale* (1637), pp.44, 51.

[179] PRO, MS 31/9/17B: Panzani to Barberini, 27 April/ 7 May 1636.

[180] Panzani's description is printed in Albion, *Court of Rome*, Appendix V pp.412–14.

[181] The Venetian ambassador reported the following year that eleven bishops had been indicated to Panzani who, along with some of the Lords, the Court and the Universities, and other Protestants who were not squeamish, were to carry through the reconciliation with Rome if terms could be agreed: *CSPVen 1636–9*, p.303. However, this is most probably simply a garbled version of Panzani's own report.

for a church reunion based upon the model of the Gallican Church.[182] It is hard to believe that Laud would have favoured other details of Montagu's plans, either. Certainly the notion of intercommunion was one to which Laud was most firmly opposed: elsewhere he described the argument that convinced papists might still attend Church of England services as 'very base and unworthy'.[183] At his trial, Laud was careful to dissociate himself completely from Montagu's dealings with Panzani, declaring that if Montagu had held intelligence 'with the popes Nuncio, it is nothing to me, being without my privity, knowledge or approbation'.[184] It seems more likely that Laud simply turned a blind eye to Montagu's intrigues. Montagu promised at his first interview with Panzani that he would arrange an interview between the papal agent and the archbishop, but had warned of Laud's circumspection,[185] and obviously nothing came of any overtures which Montagu might have made to Laud. Laud might have trusted Montagu to be discreet. Certainly it is true that no word of Montagu's schemes for reunion and discussions with Panzani spread beyond the court. It was only the reports of Panzani's friend the Venetian ambassador, and of the aggrieved Bishop Goodman who was involved in similar irenical conversations himself, which provided Prynne with any information of Montagu's intimacy with the papal agent.[186]

Other senior associates of Laud expressed their lack of hope in the chances of reconciliation with Rome at various times. Richard Neile was among de Dominis' official inquisitors after the archbishop had requested leave to return to Rome, and shared the committee's scepticism towards de Dominis' claims that Rome was likely to reform.[187] Although White, Laud and Andrewes occasionally lamented Christendom's divisions in general terms and expressed a desire for a General Council, these pious and fairly conventional exhalations should not be treated in themselves as evidence of

182 See above, p.268. Moreover, the thesis 'An religio protestantium sit reconciliabilis cum praesenti Romana?' was determined negatively at the 1634 Oxford Act, presumably with the approval of Laud himself: PRO, SP 16/271/69. As chancellor of the University, Laud had required that all proposed Act theses be sent to him in advance for his approval. Of course, his acceptance of the submission of this thesis might in part have been prompted by the scandal and misinterpretations which would have followed if he had refused it.

183 Laud, *Works*, IV: 319; cf. II: 415–16 (each time opposing the arguments of Azorius); also Potter, *Want of Charitie*, i. pp.66–7. Richard Corbet, however, was happy to cite Azorius' work without reservations: Bodl., Rawlinson MS D.853 fol.175v.

184 Prynne, *Canterburies Doome*, p.554.

185 PRO, MS 31/9/17B: Panzani to Barberini, 4/14 November 1635.

186 Montagu's discretion would seem to have faded towards the end of Panzani's stay, however, when the ageing bishop was foolhardy enough to invite Panzani to Chichester 'con grandissima instanza': BL, Add. MS 15389 fols.366v–367r: Panzani to Barberini, 27 November 1636. Panzani declined the invitation.

187 Neile, *Shiftings*, pp.10–11, 17–18, 21–3. Cf. Gardiner, *Reports*, p.104.

any genuine conviction on their parts that such a council could ever be a serious possibility.[188] Christopher Potter stressed that the continuing separation of the churches was necessary. Buckeridge claimed that transubstantiation and 'the maintenance of the popes vast and unlimited power' 'made the rent and division of the Church uncureable and past all hope'. He averred that the popes would never renounce and disclaim their ambition, or the Schools renounce transubstantiation, although wiser Romanists wished in their hearts that it had never been decreed.[189]

Laudian concerns for general Christian unity are more evident than specific hopes for reunion with Rome. As we have seen, some Laudian divines were capable of adopting an even-handed assessment of the divisions within Christendom,[190] and the 1630s witnessed the return of calls for a general crusade against the Turk, and appeals to Romanist princes to reform the churches within their territories.[191] William Page proclaimed that Protestants and Romanists should set aside their private interests 'and take upon us that generall livery of Christianity' in a crusade against the Turk: 'What a glorious sight would it be to see the red Crosse once againe advanced as it was in the daies of Constantine?' But Page and his patron Bishop Curll both emphasized that they were not aiming at union with Rome. Page complained specifically of how both Romanists and the Laudians' Protestant opponents had misunderstood the intentions behind the Laudians' moderation towards Rome. To make matters clear, Page instructed the Roman Catholics firmly that

> because I say that we are brethren I would not have you think we like not the cause we have in hand, or that we are ready to yeeld unto you, and presently joyne hands with you, as some of you imagine, and many of our side causelesly suspect, but this is all, we would have the breach no greater then it is, and would not have the world believe, because we differ in some things, that wee agree in nothing ... wee will not winke at your faults, or joyne with you in them, but this doth put us in mind to admonish you more gently of them as brethren ... God he knows we are farre enough from yeelding to you as Romanists, yet should we not be charitable to you as Christians, we were much to blame.[192]

Walter Curll similarly disclaimed any intention of pursuing reunion with Rome. 'We must use all means', he remarked, 'to have peace with all

[188] White, *Replie*, p.157; Laud, *Works*, I: 165; II: 141, 150, 245–6, 285–6; Andrewes, *Responsio*, pp.450–1.

[189] Buckeridge, *Sermon*, pp.172–3.

[190] See above, ch.3. Note the impartiality in Laud, *Works*, II: 417; Raleigh, *Certain Queries*, p.18; CUL, MS Gg/1/29 fol.100r (from back); Reeve, *Communion Booke*, pp.90–111; Heylyn, *Cyprianus*, p.39.

[191] Page, *Imitation*, 'To the Christian Reader' [first half unpaginated]; Pagitt, *Christianographie* (1640 edn), sigs.A3v–A4r. On the general unity of the church, see also Choun, *Collectiones*, ch.12 – quoted in Sancta Clara, *Deus, Natura, Gratia* (1635 edn), p.416.

[192] Page, *Imitation*, sig.***3r–v.

men; in Religion, so farre as may stand with the trueth of God, and of a good conscience'. He undoubtedly had Rome in mind when he added that some men were so contentious that peace was impossible with them, 'and therefore in this case, it is enough for us, to seeke peace with them, to speake peace to them; and if they will not have peace with us, our peace will return into our bosomes: that is, wee shall have the comfort of it in our selves, and the reward of it with God, though wee have not the fruit and effect of it with men'.[193]

Nevertheless, there was doubtless some truth in Father Philip's claim that those Englishmen who most desired union with Rome were afraid of confessing it openly, and that, with rumours of foreign wars and therefore the threat of a puritanically minded parliament, even the moderate bishops and clergy tended to be more severe against Romanists through fear.[194] There were other voices at court which might have given Montagu encouragement to think that his hopes for reunion might be shared, and which prompted his remarks to Panzani that every day saw them nearer to reunion 'quasi insensibilimente' with the promotion of moderate men.[195] When Panzani expressed doubts at Montagu's hopes that reunion should proceed swiftly, suggesting that such speed was to be desired and not hoped for, Montagu assured the papal agent that men's language and inclinations towards Rome had been transformed during the last ten years, and that his hopes were not therefore unrealistic.[196] Talk of reunion was certainly in the air at court at this time. Panzani reported that 'many, in common conversation, wished for a reunion',[197] and Secretary Windebank assured him in conversation that all moderate men in church and state thirsted after it.[198] The king himself bantered with the queen, Father Philip, and the papal agent George Con about the relative advantages and disadvantages of reunion with Rome.[199] When Brian Duppa, a close associate of Laud, preached before the king on his appointment as tutor to the Prince of Wales in 1634, he was reported to have described the breach with Rome as

[193] Curll, *Sermon*, pp.30–1. That Curll had the Roman Catholics in mind here is implied by his quotation on the previous page from Gaspari Scioppius' *Classicum belli sacri* (1618), which insisted that all Romanist princes should make war on Protestants (*ibid.*, p.29).

[194] Albion, *Court of Rome*, p.176.

[195] PRO, MS 31/9/17B: Panzani to Barberini, 27 April/7 May 1636.

[196] PRO, MS 31/9/17B: *idem* to *idem*, 11/21 May 1636.

[197] Panzani, *Memoirs*, p.139. See also the report by Father Cyprien de Gamache (a Capuchin of the queen's household) of 'the secret conferences' which the Capuchin Father Vincent 'had with the principal ministers, particular friends of the Archbishop of Canterbury, who wished with him to bring the Protestant religion so near to the Roman Church, that a union should ensue almost imperceptibly': *Court and Times of Charles I*, II: 317. Father Cyprien also refers to the Capuchins having received regular visits from Protestant ministers who enquired into their ceremonies, and believed themselves to hold 'the same fundamental points as the Church of Rome' (*ibid.*, II: 332–3).

[198] Panzani, *Memoirs*, p.164.

[199] Hibbard, *Popish Plot*, p.49.

'unfortunate' and to have advised the king to consider reunion.[200] The same note was sounded beyond court circles. William Fuller was later accused of having preached that the differences between the Church of Rome and the Church of England were only in circumstances, and that reconciliation would be easy.[201] Josiah Tomlinson and Thomas Gibson provide other examples of clerics who were later accused of having been prepared to countenance a reconciliation with Rome, although it would be unwise to take these accusations at face value.[202] While Montagu's claims of substantial support for his reunion plans were undoubtedly exaggerated, they may nevertheless testify to a growing interest among divines in the issue of reunion and a new recognition of the potential for an agreement with Rome on reasonable terms.

Montagu was a central figure in the Laudian movement, and it was around his works that the Durham House Group chose to gather in the 1620s.[203] His reunion efforts should prompt a reassessment of some of the accusations of crypto-popery and reunion aspirations directed against avant-garde conformists in the Jacobean and Caroline periods. Despite the frequent charges, there is little evidence that Laudianism or its earlier manifestations led quite so directly to Rome, or that there was any widespread disposition among Laudians towards conversion to Rome. It is true that there were some conversions during the Interregnum among some younger divines who had been associated with some of Laud's followers.[204] The most notable examples here were Richard Mileson, Thomas Gawen

200 PRO, MS 31/9/17B: Panzani to Barberini, 17/27 February 1636; Hibbard, *Popish Plot*, p.51.

201 *The Petition against Dr. Fuller*, sig.A3r. It is possible that this is the sermon which Panzani mistakenly refers to in a letter to Barberini as being made by an Oxford preacher who claimed that reunion with Rome was an easy matter but for the hostility of the puritans (Albion, *Court of Rome*, p.181).

202 Tomlinson, the rector of High Ongar, was accused by his parishioners before the Commons in 1640 of having 'affirmed the Roman a true church to which Archbishop Laud, a good statesman, would have reconciled the English Church': Matthews, *Walker Revised*, p.165. Gibson, the vicar of Horncastle in Kent, was accused of saying 'that if the pope were received into England by the publique authority hee would not be against itt': J.W.F. Hill, 'The royalist clergy of Lincolnshire', *Reports and Papers of the Lincolnshire Architectural and Archaeological Society* 2 (1938), p.59.

203 Montagu was still sending Laud drafts of his work (in this case the second part of his *ΘΕΑΝΘΡΩΠΙΚΟΝ*) for the archbishop's approval in the late 1630s, giving him 'Power to dispose of what I write, as will fit the Church and State'. He makes the telling comment to Laud in his accompanying letter of March 1639 that 'we are, I know, of the same Religion, drive to the same end, though not the same way': Prynne, *Canterburies Doome*, p.351. Note also the importance attached to Montagu's writings in the 1630s by the Laudian establishment. The first book of his *ΘΕΑΝΘΡΩΠΙΚΟΝ* (1636 – republished with the 'Pars Posterior' of the same work in 1640) was dedicated to King Charles and licensed by Bishop Juxon in person: Arber, *Registers*, IV: 324.

204 See the list of twelve university fellows and/or Anglican clergymen who converted to Rome while in exile, assembled in Chaney, *Grand Tour*, p. 382. To this list may be

and Richard Crashaw. Richard Mileson was Montagu's domestic chaplain and amanuensis and his wife's confessor, and a regular recipient of Montagu's patronage throughout the 1630s.[205] Thomas Gawen was chaplain to Bishop Curll, who appointed him as tutor to his son.[206] Richard Crashaw had John Tournay and Benjamin Laney among his tutors at Pembroke College, Cambridge, and dedicated his *Epigrammatum Sacrorum Liber* to Laney.[207] But such defections were mainly due to the pressures of the Interregnum, and only occurred among the 'weak fringe' of the Laudians.[208] The only accusation against a noteworthy Laudian of having defected to Rome before the civil war was directed at Theodore Price, although this accusation, which was made by Bishop Williams, may have been more a manifestation of personal antipathy.[209] Trevor-Roper is doubtless correct to note that (some improbable and unsubstantiated Roman Catholic reports apart)[210] none of the major Laudian figures were

added three fellows from Cosin's Peterhouse: Francis Blakiston, Christopher Bankes and Richard Nicholls (*ibid*., pp.384, 387; P.G. Stanwood, 'Crashaw at Rome', *Notes and Queries* 211 (1966)). A possible further addition is Richard Hall, rector of St Mary Steps, Exeter, who (according to one of Walker's later correspondents) went abroad, converted, and then returned after 1660, preaching a sermon of recantation in Exeter Cathedral (Matthews, *Walker Revised*, p.114). Isaac Tinkler, a scholar of Caius who matriculated at Peterhouse in 1637, was reported in 1641 as having allegedly left Protestantism and gone abroad: BL, Harleian MS 7019 fol.79 (see also Venn *et al*, *Biographical History*, I: 325, and J. Venn and J.A. Venn (eds.), *Alumni Cantabrigiensis ... Pt 1* (4 vols., 1922–7), s.n. 'Isaac Tinkler'). See also the list of converts in 'D.Y.', *Legenda Lignea with an Answer to Mr Birchleys Moderator* (1653), p.109. On the conversion of Cosin's own son in 1651, see Chaney, *Grand Tour*, pp.97, 384, 385, 390–1, and his *responsa* on entering the English College at Rome in *The Responsa Scholarum*, pp.536–7.

205 On Mileson's links with Montagu, see Macauley, 'Richard Montague', pp.406–7. Mileson joined the Jesuits in 1643, and returned as a Jesuit missioner for the eastern counties, 1651–63. See also Venn *et al*., *Biographical History*, I: 267.

206 On Gawen's career, see Chaney, *Grand Tour*, pp.389–92; *DNB*, s.n. 'Thomas Gawen'.

207 See *DNB*, s.n. 'Richard Crashaw'; Healy, *Richard Crashaw*, *passim*.

208 Trevor-Roper, *Catholics*, pp.109, 113.

209 There has been some confusion in accounts of Price's conversion. Heylyn gives a later account of Bishop Williams' report of Theodore Price's deathbed reconciliation with Rome in his *Examen Historicum*, p.74. This account of Williams' actions is confirmed by the contemporary reference made to this event just three days afterwards (18 Dec. 1631) by William Murray in a letter to Sir Henry Vane (PRO, SP 16/204/72). Montagu and Laney hoped that Price would be elevated to a bishopric – see Cosin, *Correspondence*, I: 24; *Court and Times of Charles I*, II: 21. Against Prynne's later accusation that Laud had been intimate with Price and had especially recommended him to the king for a Welsh bishopric, Laud protested that Price 'was more inward with another Bishop, and who laboured his preferment more than I', but made no attempt to deny Prynne's claim that Price had died reconciled to the Church of Rome (Laud, *Works*, IV: 495). See also Prynne, *Canterburies Doome*, p.355. For Price's long friendship with Laud, see his will: Westminster Public Library, Will Register 1622–35 fol.174v. I owe this reference to Julia Merritt.

210 For example, it was claimed by the Romanist John Sergeant that John Cosin 'had resolved to become a Catholick here in Paris, but that he was put off it by a pretension

ever likely to convert to Rome during the Interregnum. Their interest, and indeed Montagu's too, was in defending the independence and catholic status of the Church of England, and while the episcopal succession survived, and ordained ministers continued to use the Book of Common Prayer, there was no reason why they should ever have contemplated converting to a church which they still considered to be inferior and unreformed.

Clearly, claims that any group of English Protestant divines were contemplating a form of reunion with Rome during this period had little positive evidence on which to base their accusations. The Venetian ambassador's account of some of the soundings at court regarding reunion was not published until 1643, when it appeared in a brief pamphlet entitled *The Pope's Nuntioes*. Even then, William Prynne was cautious about fully accepting the pamphlet's authenticity and made little use of it in his revelations of 'popery' among the Laudians.[211] The details of Montagu's conversations with Panzani remained secret. The accusations were prompted in part by simple rumour. But they also represented a recognition that the ecclesiology of an increasingly predominant faction in the English Church embodied a view of the Church of Rome which could not easily assimilate the stern and unyielding perspective of traditional Elizabethan or Jacobean anti-popery.

As has been described above, perceptions of the Church of Rome among the disciples of Hooker and Andrewes, and the associates of Laud undoubtedly differed from those ideas which had been prevalent in the Jacobean period, although in many cases this was a matter of the refashioning of inherited ideas and the omission of qualifying arguments and reservations, the remoulding of previous arguments, rather than the intrusion of entirely new ideas. But this remoulding in itself had radical potential. This was not a potential which was realized in many cases. Laudian emphases did not create a whole new ecclesiology, even if they made more internally consistent a Jacobean position which was becoming

which (he being a man of high spirits) exasperated him' (Chaney, *Grand Tour*, p.385). While Cosin's view of the relative amenability of Rome and Geneva doubtless changed over the course of his residence in Paris, and his close relations with the Huguenots of Charenton only really developed from the late 1640s, there is no real evidence to support this claim that he was contemplating conversion in the early part of his residence. See also the bizarre reports by Giles Chaissy and the papal agent Rossetti of meetings with Laud and Ussher in the autumn of 1640, at which Ussher's conversion, and Laud's possible conversion and flight to Rome, were supposedly discussed: Hibbard, *Popish Plot*, p.172. On the famous incident of the offer of a cardinal's cap to Laud, see Laud, *Works*, III: 219; IV: 56, 331–2; Albion, *Court of Rome*, pp.148–9; Hibbard, *Popish Plot*, p.44.

211 Prynne, *Canterburies Doome*, p.352, cites the pamphlet with the comment 'if we beleeve it'.

increasingly incoherent. By freeing more moderate perceptions of Rome from their context amid views of Rome's apocalyptic, homogeneous nature as an idolatrous, heretical church, the Laudians had effectively widened the ecclesiological options available. The removal of the identification of the pope as Antichrist, along with the more inflexible visions of the nature of the Church of Rome and of her errors which accompanied it, allowed Laudians to accept Rome as an erring but basically equal institutional church, and therefore one towards which a more moderate, irenic posture was required. This more moderate perception of Rome did not necessarily lead to the reunion schemes which the Laudians' opponents claimed to identify. Many Laudian divines were more concerned to dismantle sections of the edifice of anti-popery which inhibited the promotion of more elaborate forms of ritual and the 'beauty of holiness', rather than to respond to Rome in a wholly positive way. Nevertheless, Montagu's claims of support from the Caroline episcopate may still be noteworthy. We should not presume that such bishops were necessarily interested in the Gallican-inspired reunion schemes of Montagu. It is more likely that most of them shared Laud's hard-headed realism when it came to assessing any hopes of Roman compromise. Few of them, indeed, may have been interested in the general question of relations with the Church of Rome. Nevertheless, that they were 'moderato' in their attitude towards Rome, as Panzani claimed in his report, seems more than likely. Their rejection of the anti-popery of Hall, Morton and Davenant need not have been prompted by any contemplated schemes of reunion with Rome, but it was part of a general shift in their preoccupations and their ecclesiology which automatically entailed a relatively more moderate perception of Rome, which Montagu could clearly recognize. This established a climate of opinion in which Montagu's plans could develop, and a latitude of belief regarding relations between the churches which could comprehend reunion schemes with little sense of strain. De Dominis' 7,000 men could at last lift up their heads. If the Laudian establishment would have rejected Montagu's reunion schemes, they would have rejected them for reasons significantly different from those which the Jacobean Calvinist episcopate would have mustered.

The fact that Richard Montagu could contemplate and pursue reunion with Rome from a standpoint essentially similar to that of many members of the Laudian movement need not therefore hint at a stampede towards Rome on their part. What it surely displays is the simple fact which a century of confessional polemic had done its best to disguise: the Roman and Protestant Churches were a good deal closer to each other in their doctrine than the polarized forms of religious controversy would suggest. The doctrine of the Two Churches, the papal Antichrist, the depiction of popery as a false religion – all these arguments sought to create an absolute doctrinal division which would correspond to the physical and political separation of the churches. By rejecting these polemical forms, the Laudians could not help but bring the Roman and English Churches closer together. Montagu had merely to reject the polemical lenses through which Rome was perceived, he need only restrain himself from following Robert Abbot in spurning Roman orthodoxies with the reflection that they were 'saying that which they think not', to find himself already close to Rome's doorstep, yet with his Protestant principles still intact.

Shifts taking place in perceptions of the Church of Rome were inevitably accompanied by a change in attitude towards the powers of Reformed Protestantism. As the opponents of Carier and Montagu were swift to complain, their irenical and peaceful posture towards Rome only served to destroy the internal unity of the Church of England, and to draw it further away from the continental Reformed Churches.[212] As several historians have noted, much of the force of the 'Protestant Cause' rested upon a polarized view of the nature of church relations, with an 'absolute' view of Rome and the pope as Antichrist juxtaposed with a vision of the essential unity of all the true Protestant churches, distinguished by their pure doctrinal credentials, waging perpetual war against her. As Rome acquired a truer equality with the Protestant Churches, a certain realignment of the Church of England *vis-à-vis* the other Protestant Churches was inevitable.

212 Hakewill, *Answere*, ii. p.19; Sutcliffe, *Briefe Censure*, pp.18–19.

Part II

THE REFORMED CHURCHES

8

Doctrinal links: a harmony of confessions?

'SISTERS OF THE REFORMATION'

Writing in 1645, Joseph Hall provided what may be taken as a definitive account of the way in which the Elizabethan and Jacobean Church of England had viewed her Reformed neighbours:

> Blessed be God, there is no difference in any essential matter betwixt the Church of England and her Sisters of the Reformation. We accord in every point of Christian doctrine without the least variation; their public Confessions and ours are sufficient conviction to the world of our full and absolute agreement. The only difference is in the form of outward administration; wherein also we are so far agreed that we all profess this form not to be essential to the being of a church, though much importing the well or better being of it, according to our several apprehensions thereof; and that we do all retain a reverent and loving opinion of each other in our own several ways, not seeing any reason why so poor a diversity should work any alienation of affection in us, one towards another.[1]

This form of argument may be found in almost every work of anti-papal polemic of the Elizabethan and Jacobean period whenever the writer addressed Roman charges of Protestant disunity. The authors emphasized that all Protestants were in complete agreement over the fundamentals of true doctrine – they merely agreed to differ on minor issues relating to ecclesiastical discipline. The Church of England's basic identification with the forces of Protestantism was unquestioned.

Although this argument became the standard reply to Roman charges of Protestant disunity, there was an extent to which it also served a polemical purpose in controversies among Protestants themselves. For example, English presbyterian groups urged the Church of England's doctrinal affinity with foreign Reformed Churches in order to press for unity in forms of Reformed church discipline. In reply, conformist authors emphasized international Protestant unity the better to defend the Protestant credentials of the current church settlement, which allowed them to conclude that there was no need for further reform. Affirmations of *doctrinal*

[1] Hall, *Works*, VI: 610. See also Scot, *The High-Waies of God and the King*, p.20 (*Workes*).

unity were thus to some extent a function of the genuine discord among Protestants over issues of *discipline*. Joseph Hall's own declaration was made in this specific context.

Nevertheless, the fact that all English Protestants found it advantageous to emphasize the Church of England's doctrinal unity with the Protestant Churches of the continent is a testimony to the basic fact that all sides agreed on this point, even if they chose to draw different conclusions from it. The basis of the identity of the Church of England, and of Reformed Protestantism, thus formed an essential unifying bond between English Protestants, at least until the early seventeenth century. Changing understandings of the nature of ecclesiastical discipline, and of the extent to which it could be separated from doctrinal matters, would gradually but significantly alter how a portion of the members of the Church of England came to view her identity, as we shall see. At the dawn of James' reign, however, a general consensus still seemed to prevail over views of the English Church's identity *vis-à-vis* the Reformed Churches of the continent.

THE UNITY OF THE TRUE CHURCH

Although Protestant unity was a basic tenet of English Protestant thought, it is important to note that, in formal terms, the 'true church' to which English Protestants believed themselves to belong, in opposition to Rome, was not understood as simply comprising the Western Protestant Churches. On the contrary, while the simple union of Protestant Churches was assumed, divines were usually anxious to stress the universality of the true church, against Rome's attempts to define the church in terms of her own communion. Instead, English Protestant divines across the doctrinal spectrum attempted to present themselves as members of the universal church, as 'Catholic Christians', while firmly rejecting divisive terms such as 'Lutheran' and 'Calvinist'.

Robert Abbot insisted that 'our Gospell' is taught 'in Greece, in Africa, in Asia ... we communicate with the Church of the whole world; wheresoever this Gospell is free, there our religion is not bound'. As he explained,

> we apply the name Catholike no more to the congregations of the Protestants, then we doe to all that professe in truth the communion of the universall Church. The name of Protestants being casuall, and arising by occasion in these Northern parts, may haply be inclosed and confined within the bounds of Europe, but the Church of Christ cannot be so inclosed.

Therefore, in certain polemical contexts, even strongly Calvinist writers may be found rejecting the label of 'Protestant' as negative and divisive. Gabriel Powel spurned the term as 'a name given to certaine Germaines, that protested against ... matters certes, that touch us nothing, which never joined with them in protestation'. Similarly, George Abbot utterly disclaimed the names of Lutheran and Calvinist, but was also not that happy with the term 'Protestant' either. Matthew Sutcliffe, determined to find ammunition to use against Richard Montagu, accused the latter of having bestowed upon his faith and friends 'the ignominious name of Protestant put upon Catholicke Christians by Antichrists abetters, and to make them no better then Papists'. The appeal of talking of the church only in general, inclusive terms, against Roman charges of Donatism, may also be noted in a revealing section of the puritan Anthony Wotton's *Trial of the Romish Clergies Title to the Church* in which he presented a very guarded discussion of the sense in which there could be said to be 'one Church of Protestants'.[2]

In a similar way, the Jacobean period witnessed a concerted effort by many divines to claim fellowship with the Eastern churches which had never fallen under the direct control of the Latin Church. This enabled Protestants to present themselves, not as a group dividing from the Roman Church, but as part of the universal church, from which Rome had divided herself. As we have seen, it also served to demonstrate an unromanized medieval succession.[3] In effect, the more that the position of the Roman Church was downgraded, the easier it became for Protestants to reject any 'Protestant' identity and to present themselves merely as 'Catholic'. The Greek, Ethiopian and Russian Churches were therefore increasingly cited against Rome for polemical purposes. The fourth edition of Willet's *Synopsis* (published in 1613) for the first time inserted testimonies of the agreement of these 'east and south Churches' with 'the reformed Churches

2 Abbot, *True Ancient*, pp.97 ('197'), 113–14; Gabriel Powel, *The Supplication* (1604) – quoted in *DNB*, s.n. 'Gabriel Powel'; Abbot, *The Reasons*, pp.77, 80–1; Sutcliffe, *Briefe Censure*, p.4; Wotton, *Trial*, p.309. For opposition to the terms 'Lutheran' and 'Calvinist' see also Abbot, *True Ancient*, p.76; *idem*, *Second Part*, p.339; Davenant, 'Opinion', pp.52–3; and below, pp.407–8. A minor Romanist pamphlet also denied the English Church the name of 'Protestant' as rightly applying only to the Lutherans, although, as his intention was to emphasize Protestant division, the author instead dubbed the Church of England's religion 'Anglianisme', 'because it among the rest hath no one especiall Authour, but is sette forth by the Prince, and Parliament': Thomas Harrab, *Tesseradelphus* (n.p., 1616), sigs.E[iv]r; Aiir. Note also Andrewes' response when Bellarmine complained of the novelty of the term 'Protestant', where Andrewes defended the term on the grounds of temporary convenience, as denoting a certain temporary attitude rather than a positive creed. It was thus a term intended to last only as long as Roman abuses were unreformed: Andrewes, *Responsio*, pp.25–6.

3 Windsor ('The controversy', p.149) notes that there was only scanty information available and little interest in the Eastern churches in the Elizabethan Church, although a controversialist such as Fulke was well aware of their polemical value (see Brereley, *Protestants Apologie*, p.612). For the Greek succession, see above ch.6; also White, *Orthodox Faith*, p.265; *idem*, *Replie*, p.104; Rogers, *Protestant Church*, pp.115–17, 123–7; Downe, *Certaine Treatises*, xii. p.5.

in the west' in their opposition to Rome, and cited their views in every section of the work.[4] Richard Field devoted a large section of Book 3 of his treatise *Of the Church* to demonstrating that the Eastern churches 'agree in one substance of faith, and are so far forth orthodox, that they retain a saving profession of all divine verities absolutely necessary to salvation, and are all members of the true Catholic Church of Christ'. Needless to say, Field believed them to be in agreement with the Protestants in all the principal controversies between the Reformed Churches and Rome. Pagitt's later *Christianographie* was located firmly within this established tradition, and his approach had been anticipated in the works of Brerewood and Purchas, among others. Historians of the early church also began to exploit the idea that Christianity had reached Britain via the Greeks, rather than the Roman Church, thereby avoiding the confusion surrounding references to Rome as the 'mother church'.[5] Archbishop Abbot was similarly alive to the polemical value of Protestant dealings with the Greek Patriarch Cyril Lukaris. Links with the Greek Church developed swiftly during this period as Lukaris' 'Calvinist' confession of faith raised the hopes of Thomas Morton and others that a union with the Greeks might ultimately follow a unification of the Protestant Churches.[6]

Yet much of this ecumenical activity was directed towards the needs of anti-papal polemic, and in more candid moments most English divines expressed a strong distrust of the Greek and Russian Churches. Even Robert Abbot was forced to admit to his Romanist opponent that the Eastern churches did not agree with the Protestants' judgement in all points

[4] Willet, *Synopsis* (1613), sig.B4r and *passim*. Cf. White, *The Way*, pp.406, 409–10; Wotton, *Trial*, p.377; LPL, Lambeth MS 772 p.31; Irenaeus Rodoginus, *Differences in Matters of Religion between Eastern and Western Churches* (1624); Hall, *Works*, VIII: 661, IX: 332–3, 339–40, 359–60, 380; Morton, *Of the Institution*, i. 144; *idem*, *Grand Imposture*, pp.330, 333–4; Favour, *Antiquitie*, pp.464–8; Ussher, *Works*, III: 135–6, 195–7; Downe, *Certaine Treatises*, xii. pp.23–4, 30 ('33'); Scot, *High-Waies*, p.21 (*Workes*). As evidence of general interest, see also Sir Thomas Roe's letter to Bishop Morton describing the present Greek Church in PRO, SP 16/382/31 (*CSPD 1637–8*, pp.263–4). See also Edward Brerewood's *Enquiries Touching the Diversity of Languages and Religions through the Chiefe Parts of the World* (1614), which was incorporated by Samuel Purchas into the first book of his *Pilgrimes*, along with some of the text of Christopher Angelos' *Enchiridion de Institutia Graecorum* (Cambridge, 1619).

[5] Field, *Of the Church*, I: 97–152 (esp. pp.151–2), II: 436. On the Greek origins of the English Church, see Nathaniel Brent's comments in Young, *Diary*, p.107; BL, Harleian MS 374 fol.129r: Abraham Wheelock to Simonds D'Ewes, 26 January 1640. However, the Laudian Pocklington denied that the English Church was descended from the Greeks: *Altare Christianum* (2nd edn, 1637), p.110.

[6] Trevor-Roper, 'Church of England', pp.213–40; Fincham, 'Prelacy and politics', pp.50–1; Windsor, 'The controversy', pp.284–5; W.B. Patterson, 'Educating the Greeks: Anglican scholarships for Greek orthodox students in the early seventeenth century', in K. Robbins (ed.), *Religion and Humanism* (Studies in Church History 17, Oxford, 1981); Morton, 'Opinion', p.18.

of faith, confessing that 'they may erre and we may erre'. In a different polemical context Crakanthorp described the Greeks as heretical. Field followed many Protestant authors in describing the Eastern church as the source of many heresies, and most writers condemned it as the originator of the erroneous doctrines of the corporal presence in the eucharist and image-worship. Abbot saw the present miserable plight of the Greek Churches as God's just revenge upon them for their idolatry. Hall, Thomas Rogers and Thomas Gainsford attacked the many corruptions and superstitions of the present-day Greek and Russian Churches. Gainsford concluded that 'although they are some way more tolerable then the Romish abuses, yet are their best garments ... plighted with errours, and layd up unhandsomely with wrinckles'.[7]

Laudian writers were able to exploit this inconsistency in their opponents' writings, with William Page leaping to the defence of 'those poore Greeks' against Prynne's assault on them as heretics who denied the deity of the Holy Ghost.[8] More generally, the newly favoured Greek Church was exploited by many divines writing in defence of the church policies of the 1630s. It frequently appeared as a source of legitimation for the liturgical and ceremonial innovations of the period, in defence of altars and elaborate church ritual, against the absolute decree of predestination and Sabbatarianism.[9] If the Laudians' appeal to the contemporary Greek Church in the 1630s was not new or distinctive (and neither were the sources – Sandys and Brerewood being those most regularly employed), the features which were appealed to undoubtedly were.

[7] Abbot, *True Ancient*, p.97 ('197'); *idem*, *Second Part*, p.1224; Crakanthorp, *Defensio*, p.103; Heylyn, *ΜΙΚΡΟΚΟΣΜΟΣ* (1625), p.374; Ussher, *Works*, III: 79; Francis Mason, 'The Validity of the Ordination of the Ministers of the Reformed Churches beyond the Seas', in *Certain Briefe Treatises*, p.172; Gainsford, *Glory*, pp.287–8; Scot, *High-Waies*, pp.40–1 (*Workes*). Against the Russian Church see Thomas Rogers, *The Catholic Doctrine of the Church of England* (Cambridge, 1854), pp.74, 79, 114, 153, 169, 206, 240, 243, 278, 285, 296; Hall, *Works*, VI: 173–5, 194–5; PRO, SP 14/66 fol.89: G. Carleton to D. Carleton, 30 September 1611.

[8] Page, *Treatise*, pp.105–6 (although Heylyn follows Prynne's line in his *ΜΙΚΡΟΚΟΣΜΟΣ* (1625), p.339). This is not to deny that Page had a more general concern to vindicate the Greek Church: see Page, *Imitation*, 'introduction'.

[9] Heylyn, *History of the Sabbath*, i. p.190; Hooker, *Laws*, IV, ch.x, 3; Laud, *Works*, II: 24–30; Potter, *Want of Charitie*, i. 37; Samuel Hoard, *Gods Love to Mankind* (1633), p.10; Lawrence, *A Sermon* (1637), p.10; John Browning, *Concerning Publike-Prayer, and the Fasts of the Church. Six Sermons, or Tractates* (1636), p.27; Duncon, *Of Worshipping God*, p.31. On the Greeks, see also Andrewes, *Responsio*, pp.35, 215. Andrewes showed a more independent interest in the Eastern churches, including the Russian Church – for example, he bequeathed an Ostrog bible to his old college of Pembroke: E.P. Tyrrell and J.S.G. Simmons, 'Slavonic books before 1700 in Cambridge libraries', *TCBS* 3 (1959–63). Laud was more interested in earlier manuscripts: on this point, see also G.J. Cuming, 'Eastern liturgies and Anglican divines 1510–1662', in D. Baker (ed.), *The Orthodox Churches and the West* (Studies in Church History 13, Oxford, 1976); Trevor-Roper, 'Church of England', pp.230–8; Fuggles, 'St. John's library', p.127.

Nevertheless, despite these occasional appeals to the authority of various far-flung non-Roman Churches, Protestants generally discussed the 'true church' with relation to divisions within the Western Latin Church, and thus took the term to pertain especially to themselves. Even Archbishop Laud and King Charles were happy to describe themselves as dying in the 'Protestant religion'.[10] Given English Protestants' reservations over aspects of the Eastern churches, this emphasis was also more amenable to more rigidly Reformed ecclesiology, which had tended to place prime importance on the role of doctrine in uniting God's true church on earth.[11] It was this which rendered all divisions over discipline ultimately irrelevant. Although they might formally accept that they were simply members of a vaguely defined universal visible church, Protestants in practice tended to subsume the visible institutional church within notions of the 'true church', which embodied assumptions of a doctrinal unity which was most easily found (and perhaps could *only* be found) among Protestants.

One of the hallmarks of Protestant doctrinal unity was the *Harmonia confessionum fidei*, published in Geneva and sponsored by Theodore Beza,[12] an English edition of which was published in 1586. The 1586 edition caused some controversy in England as it appeared at the height of presbyterian unrest and was published by an avid supporter of the classical movement, whom Whitgift had prevented from publishing a presbyterian work by Walter Travers two years previously. Suspicions that the *Harmony*'s publication in these circumstances was a deliberate presbyterian ploy would have been intensified by the fact that the edition included annotations imposing a distinctly presbyterian gloss on the treatment of the administration of the keys in Jewel's *Apology*, as Richard Bancroft later noted. It was these sort of concerns, rather than any misgivings over affirmations of purely *doctrinal* unity with the foreign Calvinist Churches, which were doubtless the 'speciall causes' behind Archbishop Whitgift's refusal to allow printing of the translation in London, although he failed to prevent the publication of a Cambridge edition, which he later tried to call in.[13]

[10] T.H. Clancy, 'Papist–Protestant–Puritan: English religious taxonomy 1565–1665', *Recusant History* 13 (1975–6), pp.234–5.

[11] Adams, 'Protestant cause', pp.1–3. On the 'true church', see also above, ch.3.

[12] On the background to the *Harmonia*, see C. Bangs, *Arminius: A Study in the Dutch Reformation* (Nashville, 1971), p.298; and below n.15.

[13] Richard Bancroft, *A Survay of the Pretended Holy Discipline* (1593), pp.195–6; J. Morris, 'Restrictive practices in the Elizabethan book trade: the Stationers' Company v. Thomas Thomas 1583–88', *TCBS* 4 (1964–8), pp.283–4, 287. Attempts to read this incident as implying Whitgift's opposition to those seeking more generally to impose 'dogmatic Calvinism' (e.g. White, *Predestination*, p.152 and n.58) seem unwarranted, and ignore the specifically presbyterian context of this incident. Heylyn and Prideaux would later clash

With the demise of the presbyterian upheavals, the *Harmony of Confessions* regained its stature as a fundamental expression of Protestant accord. Thus George Carleton, Robert Abbot, John White and George Hakewill – the first two bishops and the others royal chaplains under James – applauded the work as an invaluable manifestation of Protestant doctrinal unity, 'to be bought in every shop'. It featured fully in Thomas Rogers' semi-official defence of the Thirty-Nine Articles, and Ephraim Pagitt, despite his strong defence of episcopacy in the 1640 edition of his *Christianographie*, clearly felt that there was no longer any danger in citing the *Harmony* as evidence of Protestant agreement.[14]

Despite all the formal assertions of Protestant unity, however, Protestants were undeniably split, and in the division of the Protestant world the Church of England during this period was indisputably ranged on the Calvinist side.[15] This point was argued with particular clarity in 1616 by George Hakewill in the Church of England's official reply 'cum privilegio' to the writings of the apostate Benjamin Carier, who had alleged a Calvinist takeover of an unaligned English Church. Hakewill, appointed personal chaplain to Prince Charles on James' instructions, cited two different types of evidence in support of the argument that the religion of the Church of England and of Calvin should be judged to be the same. First, there was the testimony of Romish and Lutheran writers, who defined themselves in opposition to the Church of England's supposedly 'Calvinist' identity. This was demonstrated through the text of *Regnans in excelsis*, the papal bull against Queen Elizabeth, which had referred to Calvin. Hakewill also cited

over the *Harmonia*'s omission of a clause from Article 20 of the Thirty-Nine Articles relating to the church's authority in ceremonies: Laud, *Works*, V: 89 note c.

14 Abbot, *Second Part*, p.8; White, *The Way*, p.138; Hakewill, *Answere*, ii. p.137; Pagitt, *Christianographie* (3rd edn, 1640), p.109; Rogers, *Catholic Doctrine*, *passim*; Carleton, *Examination*, p.78; White, *Predestination*, p.265. Hakewill also cites 'that other [book] termed *The bodie of Confessions*', but I have not yet been able to identify the work intended. For an example of the puritan invocation of the *Harmony* in defence of their doctrinal position, see Bodl., Bodley MS 124 p.128. However, Arminius appealed to the *Harmonia* against supralapsarian doctrine: Bangs, *Arminius*, p.309 (see also Potter in Plaifere, *Appello Evangelium*, p.417).

15 E.g. G. Westin, *Negotiations about Church Unity 1628–1634* (Uppsala Universitets Årsskrift, 1932), pp.35 n.14 (quoting Paraeus' *Irenicum*), 48 n.10. Throughout John Dury's negotiations in the 1630s, the Church of England was presupposed as being on the Calvinist side, albeit more moderate towards the Lutherans than some. For an interesting exception, however, see J. Whaley, *Religious Toleration and Social Change in Hamburg 1529–1819* (Cambridge, 1985), p.118. It should be remembered that the *Harmonia*, although it included the earlier Lutheran confessions, was intended as a Calvinist response to the Lutheran Formula of Concord: see W.R. Godfrey, 'The Dutch Reformed response', and J. Raitt, 'The French Reformed theological response', in L.W. Spitz and W. Lohff (eds.), *Discord, Dialogue and Concord. Studies in the Lutheran Reformation's Formula of Concord* (Philadelphia, 1977), pp.170–2, 180; J.N. Bakhuizen van den Brink, 'Het Convent te Franeker 27–28 September 1577 en de Harmonia Confessionum', *NAvK* n.s. 32 (1941), pp.235–80.

Lutheran writers, 'who ever range us among the Calvinists'.[16] Secondly, there were those witnesses who declared in positive terms the Church of England's identity with the other Reformed Churches, including 'our owne writers', and 'those of forraine Churches by you [Carier] termed Calvinistical, because with him [Calvin] they ioyne in profession of the same trueth'. In support of this point, Hakewill cited a number of continental Calvinist authors, along with an exchange of letters between Beza and Archbishop Whitgift in the 1590s, 'wherein they both acknowledge that we agree in the substance of true religion'.[17] It is these two types of evidence, from opponents and supporters of the Church of England, that we shall now examine.

CALVINISTS BY DEFAULT: THE CHURCH OF ENGLAND AND THE LUTHERANS

Part of the reason why the Church of England was branded as Calvinist by Romanist and Lutheran writers was the fact that it was both Protestant and strongly anti-Lutheran. From the 1560s onwards, English churchmen had joined ranks with Swiss divines in opposing the increasingly belligerent forces of Lutheranism. Elizabeth had sought in vain to prevent the implementation of the Lutherans' determinedly anti-Calvinist Formula of Concord (1577), depicting it as an implicit separation of the Lutherans from the Church of England, along with the other Reformed Churches.[18] More generally, the Lutheran Church was spoken of as lying apart from the unity of the other Reformed Churches. John Rainolds was frank that, while churches could be distinguished as 'sound' or 'unsound', with the Roman Church in the latter category, there were yet degrees of sincerity and soundness, and the Lutherans were distempered by 'a litle ague'.[19] Rainolds was speaking in 1579, and the following years only served to

[16] Bullinger's official reply to the bull had complained that the label 'Calvinist' was being used to discredit the English Church, but this remark needs to be viewed in the context of the general Protestant rejection of names of division, made with similar spirit by men such as Cartwright. The argument cannot be taken in itself as a 'balanced and eirenic view' (*pace* White, *Predestination*, p.80). For other examples of Romanist authors assuming the Church of England's religion to be Calvinist, see Clancy, 'Papist–Protestant–Puritan', p.234. On charges of 'Calvinism' and 'Calvino-popery' by Gretser and others, see W. Nijenhuis, *Adrianus Saravia* (Leiden, 1980), pp.170–2; B. Hall, 'Puritanism: the problem of definition', in G.J. Cuming (ed.), *Studies in Church History* 2 (1965), p.291.

[17] Hakewill, *Answere*, ii. p.136.

[18] W.B. Patterson, 'The Anglican reaction', in Spitz and Lohff, *Discord*, pp.150–65.

[19] Rainolds, *Summe of the Conference*, p.650. Thomas Scot represents 'Lutherans' as one extreme (and 'Puritans' the other) between which the 'Protestant' walks: Scot, *High-Waies*, p.21 (in *Workes*).

intensify perceptions of Lutheran errors. Even Richard Hooker could take it as read by his audience and opponents that the Lutheran Churches maintained errors greatly repugnant to the truth which might in their consequences overthrow the very foundation of faith.[20] It has justly been observed that it is 'difficult to find an Elizabethan writer approving of Lutheran teachings and methods of worship and advocating them apart from those subjects which had become common to protestantism, including justification by faith'.[21] This view of the Lutherans as partly reformed, and in some way separate from the unity of Protestant Churches, also found expression in certain apocalyptic commentaries, as Brightman and others identified Lutherans with the church of Sardis, as incompletely reformed and soon to suffer defeat.[22]

The chief point at issue here was the eucharist, and the associated doctrines of consubstantiation and ubiquity. For Romanists and Lutherans, and indeed for some irenical writers, the Church of England was understood to be Calvinist principally because of her doctrine of the eucharist, which disowned Lutheran consubstantiation – one of the fundamental divisions between the Lutheran and Calvinist worlds. Certainly, this consideration seems to have lain behind Paraeus' identification of the Church of England as Calvinist in his *Irenicum*.[23] Of equal concern was the related doctrine of ubiquitarianism, that is that Christ is present in the eucharist in body as well as in spirit, and that his body is not therefore confined to one place, but can be everywhere (*ubique*).[24] Even moderate and irenically minded English Calvinists such as Davenant wrote fiercely against the ubiquitarians Jacobus Andreae and Martin Chemnitz as 'adversarii nostri'.[25] John Richardson blanched at the Lutherans' heinous offences regarding the eucharist. Thomas Morton insisted bluntly, in a

20 Hooker, *Works*, V: 125. It is noteworthy that Hooker here cites Beza for this estimation of the Lutheran Churches.

21 B. Hall, 'The early rise and gradual decline of Lutheranism in England (1520–1600)' in Baker, *Reform*, p.106.

22 Brightman cited in Christianson, *Reformers*, p.101; Bernard, *A Key*, sig.D3r–v (note the significance attached in Bernard's apocalyptic schema to the publication of the *Harmonia*).

23 Westin, *Negotiations*, pp.35 n.14, 48 n.10.

24 Ubiquitarianism was of especial concern to English Protestant divines in the 1560s and 1570s – see Patterson, 'The Anglican reaction', p.152.

25 Davenant, *Expositio*, pp.164–7. For other strongly worded attacks on Lutheran ubiquitarians see Prideaux, *Ephesus Backsliding*, p.17; *idem*, *Viginti-duae Lectiones*, i. p.135; Rogers, *Catholic Doctrine*, pp.65, 289, 293. Against hypostatical union, see Prideaux, 'Christians Free-Will Offering', p.11 (in *Certaine Sermons*). Against consubstantiation, see e.g. Thomas Rogers, *Two Dialogues* (1608), sig.O3v; John Michaelson, *The Lawfulnes of Kneeling* (St Andrews, 1620), pp.72, 125–6.

tract supposedly written to encourage union with the Lutherans, that the doctrine of ubiquity inevitably brought in bread-worship.[26]

After the Colloquy of Montbéliard, it was issues relating to free will and predestination that provoked especial hostility in Calvinist/Lutheran relations. Puritan authors in particular were repelled by Lutheran errors relating to the doctrine of predestination, and by the 1590s the Lutherans were the bugbear of much Reformed thinking.[27] Thus the English anti-Calvinists of the 1590s were dubbed 'Lutherans' by men such as William Whitaker, Samuel Ward and John Dove.[28] It was generally argued that Luther himself had not been at fault in such matters, but that it was the later, 'more rigid' Lutherans who were guilty of abandoning the orthodox teaching of their forebear on this point and of bringing in 'a conditionate Predestination'.[29] It was not just puritans who complained. Morton argued that predestination upon foresight of faith and works was pure Pelagianism, and that the Lutheran errors were even worse than those of Roman authors in this regard. Nevertheless, episcopalian Calvinists tended more generally to attach less importance to Lutheran errors on these points. John Richardson (bishop of Ardagh) commented that the Lutheran errors were 'heavy & haynous thinges', but among these grievous errors he rated 'their praevision of Faith' to be 'last & least'.[30]

Lutherans were berated for their errors in public worship too. Whitgift

[26] Morton, 'Opinion', p.13; SUL, Hartlib MS 5/16 fol.1: Richardson to Hartlib, 5 May 1634. See also John Hales, *The Works of John Hales*, ed. D. Dalrymple (3 vols., Glasgow, 1765), II: 110.

[27] On the Colloquy of Montbéliard, see Raitt, 'French Reformed theological response', pp.180–90. On the shift in later Lutheranism, see also R.D. Preus, 'The influence of the Formula of Concord on the later Lutheran orthodoxy', in Spitz and Lohff, *Discord*, pp.98–9. Divisions between Calvinists and Lutherans on this issue can also be dated back to the disputes between Zanchius and Marbach in Strasburg in the 1550s: see D.D. Wallace, *Puritans and Predestination: Grace in English Protestant Theology 1525–1695* (Chapel Hill, 1982), p.34; White, *Predestination*, pp.77–8.

[28] John Dove, *A Sermon Preached at Paules Crosse* (1597), sig.A; Tyacke, *Anti-Calvinists*, pp.33–4, 252; *Two Puritan Diaries*, ed. Knappen, pp.125, 126; Lake, *Moderate Puritans*, p.241. Against universal atonement as held by some Lutherans, see Willet, *Thesaurus Ecclesiae*, pp.37, 88–9. Willet's discussion of universal grace in *Synopsis* (2nd edn, pp.839–94; 3rd edn, pp.783–819) does not discuss papists at all (despite the title of the work), but instead is a general refutation of the arguments of Huberus, Hemmingsen, Snecanus and Puccius for universal grace, stressing instead that Christ died only for the elect.

[29] Morton, 'Opinion', p.20; Davenant, *Animadversions*, p.60; Carleton, *Examination*, p.108; Daniel Featley, 'An examination of certaine pointes delivered in Mr Mountagu his Booke': Bodl., Rawlinson MS D.831 fols.93r, 94r; *Zurich Letters*, II: 73.

[30] Morton, 'Opinion', p.21; SUL, Hartlib MS 5/16 fol.1: Richardson to Hartlib, 5 May 1634. Richardson's mind was chiefly occupied with the errors of consubstantiation or oral manducation, and the communion of idioms. Ussher and Hall also argued that the controverted issues regarding election were best not discussed: 'The Opinion of Archbishop Ussher', p.4 in *Good Counsells*; Hall, 'The Opinion of Bishop Hall', pp.2, 5–7, 21 in *Good Counsells*.

made no attempt to defend the Lutherans against Peter Martyr's criticisms (repeated by Cartwright) that they retained the real presence, images and popish apparel. The archbishop emphasized that, by contrast, the Church of England had rejected these errors and that 'God be thanked, religion is wholly reformed, even to the quick, in this church.'[31] Here Whitgift echoed William Fulke who, while refusing to accuse the Lutherans directly of idolatry, yet would not excuse them from continuing to permit images in churches, with the attendant danger of idolatry. The Lutherans thereby 'in some part' went against the stipulations of the Decalogue, 'deceived in their judgement, and of us not to be defended in their error'. John Dove, too, attacked the Lutheran retention of images in churches, noting with relief that the Church of England could not be accused on this score.[32]

Beyond specific doctrinal errors, English Protestants also distrusted Lutherans because of the determination of many Lutherans to attack the Church of England, along with the other Calvinist Churches, as proponents of a range of different heresies. Most English Protestant divines appear to have been ignorant of many of the writings of later Lutheran theologians: even John Davenant, erstwhile Lady Margaret professor in Cambridge, admitted to his friend Samuel Ward that he could not comment on the relationship of Lutheran to Arminian doctrines 'because I never troubled my selfe much with ye reading of our late Lutheran writers'.[33] Nevertheless, such English Protestants were made aware of the

[31] John Whitgift, *The Works of John Whitgift*, ed. J. Ayre (3 vols., Cambridge, 1851–3), III: 549–50.

[32] Fulke, *A Defence*, p.205; John Dove, *A Defence of Church Government* (1606), p.64. See also Dury's tract seeking to acquit Lutherans from the charge of idolatry: SUL, Hartlib MS 68/6.

[33] Bodl., Tanner MS 71 fol.153: Davenant to Ward, 15 Jan. 1633. Compare also the remarks of Dury's friend William Speed, who had engaged two or three 'holy and able divines' to study for peace with the Lutherans in the 1630s, but reported that they lacked the Lutheran works which would give them an account of the Lutherans' doctrinal position *vis-à-vis* the Calvinists plainly and completely. They only knew the Confession of Augsburg and Chemnitz's *Examination of the Council of Trent* (G. Turnbull, *Hartlib, Dury, and Comenius: Gleanings from Hartlib's Papers* (Liverpool, 1947), p.140). In this respect, Speed's friends were not unrepresentative of English divines in this period. These were the only two Lutheran works regularly cited in English theological writings, and it was unlikely that many second-generation Lutheran works would find their way into libraries. An exception here was the popular run of translations of devotional works by the great Lutheran Schoolman Gerhard: see *STC* nos.11764–82. Gerhard's more substantial *Loci Communes* also found their way into several puritan libraries during this period, e.g. Blatchly, *Ipswich*; F.J. Powicke, 'New light on an old English presbyterian and bookman', *Bulletin of the John Rylands Library* 8 (1924). Not all university divines were as uninformed as Davenant. His friend Samuel Ward seems to have been more familiar with later Lutheran works – see e.g. the citations in SSC, Ward MS L5 fol.42r; Samuel Ward, *Opera Nonnulla* (1658), ii. pp.41, 108. For citations of modern Lutheran divines, see also Richard Parre, *Concio ad clerum ... 1625* (Oxford, 1628); Prideaux, *Viginti-duae Lectiones*, i. p.277. Morton's use of the works of the moderate Gerhard in his

remarks of the more implacably anti-Calvinist Lutheran writers by the fact that these were regularly quoted *in extenso*, and with considerable relish, by English Roman Catholic polemicists in pamphlet controversies. Even the renownedly dispassionate and moderate-minded John Hales found the idea of any form of unity with the Lutherans unthinkable after he had read extracts from their anti-Calvinist diatribes in the works of the Jesuit Robert Parsons.[34] The irenically disposed Joseph Hall also stood aghast at the 'terms and imputations [which] some rigid followers of Luther have . . . cast upon their opposers, [which] I do purposely forbear to specify, as willing rather to lay my hand upon these scars, than to blazen the shame of brethren'.[35]

Political developments also played a role in English Protestants' aversion to Lutheranism. Most of the English political nation shared a deep-seated distrust of the Lutherans for their apparent readiness to side with the forces of the empire against the Calvinists. After the outbreak of the Thirty Years War such resentment became especially acute, as Lutheran Saxony aided the Roman Catholics in their drive against the forces of German Calvinism.[36]

However, there were many inconsistencies and unresolved tensions in English Calvinists' attitudes towards the Lutheran Churches. While they vehemently opposed a number of Lutheran doctrines, Calvinists' fundamentally polarized view of the church and world meant that the Lutherans must be positioned on the Protestant side because of their opposition to Rome. But this was not simply a matter of preserving a consistent polemical case against Rome. Political considerations also necessitated a flexible, and often irenical, response towards the Lutheran brethren. If Lutheran Saxony had seemed to betray the international Protestant cause at the outbreak of the Thirty Years War, it was Lutheran Sweden who by the early 1630s was acting as its champion.[37] The need to marshal Protestant sentiments behind the Swedish king was only one manifestation of a still

Totius Doctrinalis (pp.11–12, 215) was probably the result of reading prompted by the irenicist Dury in the 1630s.

34 E.g. Brereley, *Protestants Apologie*, pp.310, 569–89, 679–711; Hales, *Works*, III ii. pp.110–11.

35 Joseph Hall, *Christian Moderation* (1639) in *Works*, VI: 464.

36 Westin, *Negotiations*, pp.34, 39; Patterson, 'Anglican reaction', pp.164–5; *The Autobiography and Correspondence of Sir Simonds D'Ewes*, ed. J.O. Halliwell (2 vols., 1845), I: 259. On the Elector of Saxony's betrayal of the Palatine cause in the 1630s, see PRO, SP 16/293/14, 16/300/22. It is to Lutherans' political behaviour, as much as to (in puritan eyes) their doctrinal equivocation, that Bernard may allude in his exhortation to 'be no neuterall Lutheran': Richard Bernard, *Christian Advertisements and Counsels of Peace* (1608) – quoted in Collinson, *Religion of Protestants*, p.xiv.

37 For the general admiration for the Swedish king in England in the early 1630s, see Breslow, *Mirror*, pp.128–33.

more fundamental political agenda for European Calvinists. The legal settlement of the empire after the Peace of Augsburg had granted only Lutheranism official legal recognition within the Holy Roman Empire, which made some form of official doctrinal association of Calvinists with the Lutheran Church all the more essential for their survival.

As a result, relations between European Calvinists and Lutherans were marked by a constant tension, oscillating between on the one hand the condemnation of Lutheran doctrinal errors, and on the other, spasmodic irenical drives, which were apparently bent on establishing a doctrinal union, and emphasized the bonds uniting the two churches. This irenical emphasis was not merely for Roman Catholic digestion, but for Lutheran observers too, and was impelled by tangible political concerns and (conceivably) by authentically ecumenical ones. It has sometimes been suggested that, in Europe as a whole, Calvinists' irenical theology was merely 'a concealed form of agitation for itself' and 'by no means a waiving of its confessional position.'[38] Its essential duplicity seems to be exemplified in the suppression of Lutheranism in Calvinist states, and the assumption of even a Calvinist irenicist like Paraeus that Lutherans should eventually become Calvinists.[39] These are natural arguments for Lutheran historians to adopt, but even if we suggest that Calvinist perceptions of the Lutherans were not simply duplicitous, we may grant that they were at least highly problematical, and thus potentially divisive.

Strong promotion of the ideal of Calvino-Lutheran unity may therefore be found among puritan as well as conformist English Calvinists during this period. In works against Rome, and in an irenical context, Calvinist divines (including English ones) were anxious to affirm their unity with Lutheran authors. There were, of course, a great many doctrines upon which both churches could agree – Lutheran divines were generally regarded as being irreproachable on the doctrine of justification (indeed, on the particular point of solifidianism they could be more hardline than many Calvinist authors).[40] Moreover, all English Calvinists recognized the value of many Lutheran writings, which under Elizabeth had still occupied a significant portion of shelf-space in college libraries, although they were gradually being overwhelmed by Reformed works.[41] Certain Lutheran

[38] See W. Elert, *The Structure of Lutheranism* (St Louis, 1962), p.282, and Westin, *Negotiations*, p.33 – both citing H. Leube, *Kalvinismus und Luthertum in Zeitalte der Orthodoxie*, vol.I (Leipzig, 1928).

[39] See Westin, *Negotiations*, pp.37, 58 n.25.

[40] E.g. Thomas Goodwin's remarks in SUL, Hartlib MS 29/2 fol.54r.

[41] For example, at least 60% of the divinity books in Emmanuel College library in 1597 were by Lutherans, although the percentage of Reformed works increases after this date: S. Bush and C.J. Rasmussen, *The Library of Emmanuel College, Cambridge, 1584–1637*

authors continued to enjoy a high reputation, including the Danish Lutheran Neils Hemmingsen for his homiletic works,[42] while Martin Chemnitz's *Examination of the Council of Trent* provided an invaluable fund of anti-papal material which found its way into the libraries and writings of divines across the whole spectrum of English Protestantism.[43] Johannes Gerhard – the greatest Lutheran divine after Chemnitz – was popular in England by the 1630s through translations of his various meditational and catechetical works, which went through several editions.[44]

Both sides in the arguments over ceremonial conformity found it convenient to cite Lutheran authors. Conformists urged their example for kneeling at communion, and John Burgess cited them as accepting the religious use of images, demanding of his puritan opponent William Ames whether the Lutherans were not to be considered 'our divines'. Ames' reply encapsulated the ambiguities in the Reformed attitude to the Lutherans: 'they are in most maine poyntes our Divines: but about this businesse they are no more ours, then about Ubiquitie, Consubstantiation, &c. for whiche they disclaime us, even the wholle Churche of England, as no part of the Catholicke Churche, but Sectaries and Sacramentarians'. But even puritan nonconformists were prepared to hunt among Lutheran authors to boost their arguments, sometimes using the most vehemently anti-Calvinist divines.[45]

(Cambridge, 1986), pp.19, 20. It should be borne in mind, however, that most donors of books to the college before 1600 had no formal affiliation with the college (*ibid.*, p.23).

42 Hemmingsen was all the more agreeable to Calvinists in the first place as he was himself a so-called 'crypto-Calvinist', whose views on the eucharist were therefore less objectionable to Calvinist divines (T.R. Skarsten, 'The reaction of Scandinavia', in Spitz and Lohff, *Discord*, pp.137–40). For a Lutheran attack on Hemmingsen's work, see Conrad Schlüsselburg, *Theologiae Calvinistarum* (Frankfurt, 1592), which discusses Hemmingsen throughout as a Calvinist (e.g. lib.1 fol.69v). Hemmingsen is praised in Hall, *Works*, IX: 476. Hemmingsen's works were published in Elizabethan England and found their way into many college libraries: White, *Predestination*, pp.89–90. Thomas Jackson remembered how Hemmingsen and Melanchthon, as well as Bullinger, were those most in esteem among preachers in the Elizabethan period: *Works*, X: 550–1. On William Perkins' use of Hemmingsen and other Lutheran divines, see D.K. McKim, *Ramism in William Perkins' Theology* (New York, 1986), p.11; Breward, *Perkins*, pp.328–9. However, Hemmingsen's views on predestinarian issues were less popular: see e.g. Willet's attacks in *Synopsis* (1600), pp.784–819 *passim*.

43 In March 1582, the bishop of London granted a licence to print Chemnitz's work, to be translated 'by grave and learned men & so being perused to be printed', although the translation would not seem to have been accomplished: Arber, *Registers*, II: 188r. The *Examen* was among the Protestant books passed on to Sarpi and Fulgentio by William Bedell in Venice in 1608 to encourage their conversion: Bedell, *Two Biographies*, p.244. John Cotton gave Emmanuel College a copy of the book in 1612: Bush and Rasmussen, *The Library*, p.23. Richard Montagu offers Chemnitz high praise in his *Acts and Monuments*, p.520.

44 See above n.33.

45 Rogers, *Two Dialogues*, sig.I2r; Ames, *Fresh Suit*, ii. p.284. The apology of the nonconforming Lincoln ministers – *An Abridgment of that Booke* – even manages to quote

Nevertheless, the tensions remained. While even hardline Calvinists were anxious to promote some form of reunion with the Lutherans, the better to defend the Protestant confessional cause against the onslaughts of the papal Antichrist, their reservations over Lutheran doctrines persisted. Ironically, those most anxious to promote reunion (because of their consciousness of the plight of continental Reformed Protestants and their general desire to take an activist line towards events on the continent) were usually those puritans who were least likely to be able to adopt the flexible and irenical line on doctrines such as predestination that would be essential to ensure an effective reconciliation.[46] If puritans could see the rationale of unity with Lutherans from the international Calvinist perspective, they still found it difficult to overcome their suspicions of Lutheran heterodoxy. This was a problem which the irenicist John Dury was forced constantly to confront in his reunion efforts during the 1630s. Puritan divines were among his most enthusiastic early supporters, but their help swiftly waned when Dury moved beyond the enunciation of pacificatory platitudes and started to pursue more tangible doctrinal compromise.[47]

Puritans displayed an instinctively cautious response to Dury's irenical plans. Walter Welles confessed to Dury in 1630 that 'I had great feare of the Lutheran side.' Part of the problem lay in the similarities between Lutheran errors concerning predestination and the Arminian notions currently shattering internal Calvinist unity. The fear was constantly voiced to Dury that a reconciliation with Lutheranism implied a similar truce with the Arminians. Joseph Mede reported in February 1636 how strong Calvinists in Cambridge, including 'one D[octo]r a great Calvinist for the points of Predestination', and another 'otherwise a wise, discreet, understanding man', rejected Dury's proposed Heads for Pacification with the Lutherans, presumably (Mede thought) for tending to Arminianism.[48] Such fears were in part well grounded: Arminians were certainly aware of the advantage to be gained from an appeal to the Lutheran example, and such considerations may well have lain behind Hugo Grotius' desires for a Protestant

the *Liber Concordiae* and Conrad Schlüsselburg's *Haereticorum Catalogus* (13 vols., Frankfurt, 1597–9), in support of their opposition to 'unlawful' ceremonies: *Abridgement*, pp.45–7.

46 This is a point developed in more detail in my '*The Unchanged Peacemaker*?'.

47 See e.g. Turnbull, *Gleanings*, p.138; SUL, Hartlib MS 9/1 fol.45r–v (Dury to Anon., 21/31 October 1636) and 9/1 fol.49v (Dury to Anon., 3 December 1636); LPL, Lambeth MS 2686 fols.39–42 (Dury to Thomas Ball, 25 June 1639). For a full study of this, see Milton, '*The Unchanged Peacemaker*?'.

48 Turnbull, *Gleanings*, p.168; SUL, Hartlib MS 29/3 fols.8v, 15v–16r; Mede, *Works*, p.1065. On the similarities of Lutheran and Arminian doctrines, see also Bodl., Rawlinson MS D.831 fol.94r.

General Council to solve the Arminian disputes.[49] Concern that Arminians could thus make political capital out of their doctrinal links with the Lutherans could at other times lead English Calvinists to seek to downplay the extent of Lutheran similarity with Arminianism.[50]

The tensions within the Calvinist position in general, and the puritan position in particular, revealed themselves in the attacks made upon Laud in connection with Dury's reunion efforts. Laud found himself accused of lacking Protestant credentials in both directions, being blamed both for supporting Dury in his efforts to reconcile the Lutherans (thereby endangering Reformed orthodoxy), and also for not having sufficiently supported the same negotiations (thereby failing to promote Protestant unity).[51]

It was the moderate episcopalian Calvinists who generally proved more flexible and effective patrons of Protestant ecumenism. Dury found during the 1630s that his most consistent and useful support came from these more moderate Calvinist episcopalians – men such as Bedell, Morton, Hall and Davenant – whose doctrinal perspective was less rigid than that of the outwardly enthusiastic puritans. These moderate Calvinists provided him with discourses on Protestant unity which he published and translated, with letters of recommendation to continental Calvinist divines, with financial support and with written solutions to particular problems which were noteworthy for their success when employed. It was they alone who were likely to be able to make the compromises necessary to tempt the Lutheran Churches, and Dury used the writings of Bedell and Davenant to good effect when dealing with the divines of Sweden and Brunswick.[52] Some, indeed, pursued irenical compromise still more avidly – an example being Richard Field, who went further than most in portraying Calvinists and Lutherans as united together when writing against Rome. That this was not merely an anti-papal polemical strategy is suggested by later reports that King James had toyed with the idea of sending Field into Germany to help reconcile the differences between the two religions.[53]

[49] P. Borschberg, 'State and church in the early politico-religious works of Hugo Grotius' (Cambridge University PhD, 1990).

[50] PRO, SP 105/95 fols.48v–49r: Abbot to Carleton, 29 Dec. 1618. Davenant claimed that Chemnitz's treatment of free will in his *Examen* plainly differed from Arminius, Corvinus and Grevinchovius: Bodl., Tanner MS 71 fol.153: Davenant to Ward, 15 Jan.1633.

[51] Baillie, *Ladensium*, pp.31–2; Prynne, *Canterburies Doome*, p.541. Note Baillie's tortuous attempts at a retraction of his earlier attack on Dury in *Ladensium* (3rd edn, 1641), pp.32–4. Laud himself cited his intermittent patronage of Dury at his trial as evidence of his own Protestant credentials: Prynne, *Canterburies Doome*, p.539.

[52] G. Westin, 'Brev från John Durie åren 1636–1638', *Kyrkohistorisk Årsskrift: Skrifter Utgivna Av Kyrkohistoriska Foreningen* 1/33 (Uppsala, 1934) p.235; SUL, Hartlib MS 5/12 fol.10 (Dury to Bedell, 1 May 1640). Among the published writings see *Good Counsells*; Davenant, *Exhortation*. See also Milton, '*The Unchanged Peacemaker*?'.

[53] Nathaniel Field, *Some Short Memorials concerning the Life of . . . R. Field*, ed. J. Le Neve (1717), p.15; SUL, Hartlib MS 29/2 fol.41r.

Nevertheless, even these divines promoted union with Lutherans by adopting a minimalist position on the necessary prerequisites for Protestant unity. By adopting a 'lowest common denominator' approach, divines could encourage reunion with the Lutherans while reserving the right to condemn much of their established doctrine. Thus Davenant urged the need for unity between all those churches who shared a saving conjunction with the church's personal foundation (Christ), even though some of them (the Calvinists) were much closer to the foundation of true faith and laid better hold upon it. He professed that there were 'severall degrees of Knowledge and Grace' observable among Protestant Churches. Thomas Morton was even more grudging, and Hartlib was 'much grieved' in 1640 to hear that Morton's impending work on the eucharist slipped into 'a very invective and bitter writing against the Lutheran tenets' on ubiquity.[54]

Direct plans for reconciliation were seldom whole-hearted, and were usually shelved whenever they inhibited other proceedings. At the Synod of Dort, George Carleton thought it best to ignore Pierre du Moulin's recommendation of a project of mutual toleration between Calvinists and Lutherans. It would be best not to mention it at the synod, he explained, because it 'doth ill suite with our present business of suppressing the Arminians'. John Hales, as we have seen, made a similarly negative response.[55] This is not to say that the delegates were above invoking the need to pacify the Lutherans. Carleton and his colleagues were seeking to soften some of the rigidities of Calvinist predestinarianism, and the invocation of likely Lutheran opposition to Calvinist extremism was a useful means of justifying such a proceeding, as well as matching the king's own

[54] Davenant, 'Opinion', pp.13, 23–4; PRO, SP 16/463/67 (and see above, ch.7). Brownrigg had reportedly written to Morton on this point 'to put all into a milder strain' but it is not clear how far Morton altered the text (if at all): while scathing in its attack on ubiquitarianism, Morton's work attempts to avoid attacking the Lutherans by arguing that in fact they do not hold such doctrines, appealing to the works of 'noster D. Gherhardus': Morton, *Totius Doctrinalis*, pp.11–12, 215.

[55] Hales, *Works*, III ii. pp.110–11; *Letters from and to Sir Dudley Carleton during his Embassy in Holland (1616–1620)* (1757), pp.331–2. White (*Predestination*, p.183) here seems to misread Carleton's letter, which is concerned with an attempt to close Calvinist ranks by endorsing the existing confessions, and quite explicitly *not* an ecumenical effort inspired by du Moulin's plans for reconciliation with the Lutherans. This is further confirmed by Carleton's letter composed one month later (16 Feb. 1619), in which the mutual recognition of Reformed confessions is envisaged as a way of ensuring 'that none may depart from the received doctrines without the consent of the rest' (Carleton, *Letters*, p.340). This reinforcing of the Calvinist status quo in order to stifle incipient Arminianism was fundamental to du Moulin's plans which were presented to the synod (*ibid.*, pp.325–6) as well as being an important feature of his Tonneins proposals of 1614. It was precisely the additional irenical intention to cultivate the Lutherans which prompted opposition to du Moulin's plans among the British as well as the other delegates.

desire that the synod should not impede future hopes of reunion.[56] Similarly, at the end of the same synod the British divines objected to the phrase in the canons which stated that the Canons of Dort were agreeable to the confessions of 'the Reformed Churches'. Instead, they urged that this should be changed to 'our Reformed Churches' as they (unlike the other delegates) numbered the Lutherans among the Reformed Churches. Some historians have attached great importance to this stipulation as marking a distinctively 'Anglican' irenical agenda, but it may be less significant than it appears. In fact, it was an irenical gesture that cost the delegates little, and it did not necessarily mark an important dividing line between moderate and hardline Calvinists.[57] After all, the presbyterians' appeal to the example of 'the *best* Reformed Churches' (i.e. the Calvinists) implied that the Lutherans still constituted a Reformed Church, albeit a less purified one. Moreover, off guard (or at least off the official record), the British delegates themselves used the term 'Reformed Churches' in a manner exclusive of the Lutherans, while by contrast a puritan like Andrew Willet could on occasion use the term to denote Lutheran scholars.[58] The public invocation of this distinction by the British delegates at Dort therefore appears more as a gesture – made specifically because it cost so little. In fact, the condemnation and persecution of the Remonstrants after Dort cut

56 White, *Predestination*, p.198; Fuller, *Church History*, V: 462–3. Dean John Young (as instructed by Samuel Ward) later urged this point to the king, stressing the danger of alienating the Lutherans by 'to[o] particulare and curious a restraint' of the grace of redemption when making the Dort Canons: Tyacke, *Anti-Calvinists*, pp.97–8. Citing the Lutherans for a disputed doctrine or ceremony was always an effective way of calling the Calvinists' irenical bluff, as the Laudians were to prove.

57 Hales, *Golden Remains*, p.538 (*pace* White, *Predestination*, pp.200–1). The British delegates also wished thereby to distance the Church of England from a direct endorsement of the canons, which they had no authority to give. Again, citing the Lutherans on this point may have helped to distract attention away from the more uncomfortable (and potentially divisive) motive. Although the synod agreed to the change proposed by the British delegates, the word 'our' was not substituted when the canons were published, possibly by Bogerman's means: G. Brandt, *The History of the Reformation ... in ... the Low Countries* (4 vols., 1720–3), III: 282. For a self-consciously irenical reference to 'the Reformed churches on both sides', see Davenant, *Exhortation*, pp.3–4.

58 Even while emphasizing the need not to give offence to the Lutheran Churches in their paper concerning the fifth head of doctrine at Dort, the British delegates distinguished the Calvinist Churches from the Lutherans as 'the Reformed Churches' (see White, *Predestination*, p.198, quoting SSC, Ward MS L2). Willet talks of 'Our Reformed Churches' followed by quotations from Chemnitz or from the Augustan or Saxon confessions in his *Synopsis* (1852 edn, III: 247, 263; V: 262) as does Thomas Rogers in his *Catholic Doctrine*, *passim*. In his role as conformist apologist, Rogers could at times exploit this inconsistency: he opposed puritan complaints that the Church of England separated from 'the Reformed churches' in requiring kneeling at communion by citing the examples of the Lutheran Churches, challenging his opponent as to whether they were to be accounted 'reformed': Rogers, *Two Dialogues*, sigs.I1v–I2r. Similarly, Bancroft cited the Lutheran example of ministerial inequality, but did not refer to them as 'Lutherans', instead using the term 'the reformed Churches in Germany' (e.g. Bancroft, *Survay*, p.121).

off all hopes of union with the Lutherans, whose response was predictably negative.[59]

English Calvinists' perceptions of the Lutheran Church were thus complex and varied. Generally, they shared the aversion to Lutherans expressed by foreign Calvinists, although they were not always quite as scathing in their criticism, perhaps because they were not confronted directly by Lutheran writings or behaviour.

A CALVINIST IDENTITY: UNIFYING ELEMENTS

The basis of the Church of England's 'Calvinist' identity lay in much more than her opposition to Lutheranism. English Protestant writers like Hakewill clearly took it as given that the English Church was bound to the Reformed Churches by more than simply its respective doctrine of the eucharist. As we have seen, among the evidence that he marshalled against Carier, Hakewill cited the correspondence of Whitgift with Beza in the 1590s, which seemed to affirm a far more extensive sense of ecclesiological identity and doctrinal unity. The Jacobean period witnessed countless similar affirmations by conformist divines. John Prideaux, preaching before the king at Woodstock, accused foreign Arminians and Lutherans of slandering 'our Church' by their attacks on Calvinist doctrines regarding the nature of God's will.[60] Those English bishops whom Dury was able to coax into writing in support of his schemes in the 1630s instinctively assumed that they were taking the Calvinist side on a whole range of issues – they spoke of 'our men' Calvin and Zanchius, and described Dury's projects abroad as being to secure union 'betwixt Us & those of Germany who hold the Augustane Confession'.[61]

These remarks typified the more fundamental fact that, whatever its formal doctrines, the *received* doctrine of the English Church tended to be firmly on the Reformed side. This point requires careful exposition, however. As Patrick Collinson has noted, 'The English church settlement rested primarily on the principles of autonomy from Rome and royal supremacy, not in the reception of true doctrine and conformity with the community of Reformed churches. Consequently, relations between England and the centres of continental Reform were never secure and

59 Brandt, *History*, III: 312; IV: 330–1.

60 Strype, *Whitgift*, II: 169–72; Prideaux, 'Hezechiah's sicknesse and recovery', p.19 (*Certaine Sermons*). Prideaux cited the Bremen divine Crocius' response to the work of the Arminian Bertius for the defence of 'our Church' against these attacks.

61 E.g. Morton, 'Opinion', pp.1, 4–5, 10–11, 12. Cf. Jewel's assertion that 'we' executed Servetus: Jewel, *Works*, III: 188 – cited in P. Collinson, 'Calvinism with an Anglican face: the stranger churches in early Elizabethan London and their superintendent', in Baker, *Reform*, p.72.

always subject to political arbitrariness.'[62] As another scholar has observed, Calvinism effectively appeared too late to have any major effect on the foundation documents of the Edwardian, and later Elizabethan Settlement.[63] Nevertheless, the Thirty-Nine Articles were certainly broadly consistent with the Reformed consensus in doctrinal matters, and the generally received interpretation of the doctrine of the church was more directly in line with the tenets of continental Calvinist doctrine. By 1600 there had been ninety editions of Calvin's works published in English, and fifty-six editions of works composed by his successor at Geneva, Theodore Beza, and Calvinist doctrine would appear to have been supreme in the universities where the nation's ministry was educated.[64] When the apostate Benjamin Carier complained that Calvin's *Institutes* had been dispersed throughout the country and were 'cried upp by voices to be the only Current divinitie in Court, and Countrie', the official response composed by Hakewill merely confirmed Carier's observation, emphasizing as it did that 'if it be "cried up by voyces", it is by the voyces of the gravest Bishops, and learnedest divines of our land'.[65]

It must be emphasized that this was no mere Genevan hegemony. On the contrary, in Oxford University at least, towns such as Zurich and Heidelberg exerted at least as important an influence, if not a greater one.[66] But although Dr Dent has perceived in the Elizabethan University of Oxford 'a hybrid and broadly based theological tradition', he has nevertheless conceded that Swiss Reformed theology was the predominant strain in the religion of the Church of England, and that Calvinism was gaining an ever greater hold in the universities towards the end of the century.[67] Official theological scholarship of the later Elizabethan and early Jacobean Church displayed a more evidently Reformed component, whether in the Lambeth

[62] P. Collinson, 'England and international Calvinism 1558–1640', in M. Prestwich (ed.), *International Calvinism 1541–1715* (Oxford, 1985), p.198.

[63] D. MacCulloch, *The Later Reformation in England 1547–1603* (Basingstoke, 1990), pp.70–1.

[64] Collinson, 'England and international Calvinism', p.213; MacCulloch, *Later Reformation*, p.72; C.D. Cremeans, *The Reception of Calvinist Thought in England* (Urbana, 1949), p.65; Dent, *Reformers*, pp.87–102; Collinson, *Religion of Protestants*, pp.81–3; Tyacke, *Anti-Calvinists*, pp.2–5, 29–40, 58–62; R.T. Kendall, *Calvin and English Calvinism* (Oxford, 1979), pp.52–3. On the care taken to draw up the Thirty-Nine Articles in accordance with the Confession of Zurich, see Jewel's letters in *Zurich Letters*, I: 21, 100. Thomas Rogers' exposition of the Thirty-Nine Articles stresses their agreement with the Calvinist Churches. *A Letter of Dr Reinolds to his Friend, concerning his Advice for the Studie of Divinitie* (1613), composed in 1577, especially recommended Calvin's *Institutes* as a guide on points of doctrine.

[65] Hakewill, *Answere*, ii. pp.167–8; Carier, *Treatise*, p.37.

[66] Dent, *Reformers*, pp.1–2, 74–8, 88, 91–3, 96, 238; Collinson, 'England and international Calvinism', pp.214–16.

[67] Dent, *Reformers*, pp.88–9, 97–102.

Articles or in Thomas Rogers' semi-official commentary on the Thirty-Nine Articles. Moreover, it is Theodore Beza who emerges as the most crucial influence on the New Testament of the Authorized Version of the bible, while Calvin's *Institutes* was one of the volumes officially dispatched to Paolo Sarpi to secure his conversion.[68] This sense of a common Calvinist identity is neatly illustrated in a sermon preached before King James in the aftermath of the Gunpowder Plot by Bishop Anthony Rudd, in which the preacher visualized the Plotters declaring 'Come let us cutte them of[f] from beeing a Nation, and let the name of Calvinists bee noe more in remembraunce.'[69]

This community of faith with the Reformed Churches of the continent expressed itself in a variety of ways – through scholarly exchanges, the regular charitable collections for the relief of foreign Protestants and by the existence of the stranger churches in London and elsewhere in the country.

Dr Dent has demonstrated how personal contacts between English exiles and Swiss Reformers were sustained long after Elizabeth's accession by the regular exchange of students and correspondence.[70] Such links continued in the seventeenth century. John Prideaux's Exeter College in Oxford, and Samuel Ward's Sidney Sussex in Cambridge drew a considerable number of students from abroad, as well as providing a port of call for travelling Calvinist scholars, and acting as treasurer for university collections for distressed foreign Calvinist ministers.[71] Even a conformist pamphleteer such as George Hakewill had studied for a time in Heidelberg.[72] At the puritan end of the spectrum, some English divines chose to study at foreign Calvinist centres of learning, especially the University of Leiden, while Dutch trainee ministers not only attended Oxford and Cambridge, but may also be found at the informal household academies run by puritan lumi-

68 I.D. Backus, *The Reformed Roots of the English New Testament* (Pittsburgh, 1980), *passim* (note also the phrasing of the letter of thanks to Beza from the University of Cambridge for the gift of the Codex Bezae in 1581, cited by Basil Hall in *ibid.*, p.xvi); Bedell, *Two Biographies*, p.245.

69 Anthony Rudd, *A Sermon Preached before the Kings Maiestie ... 1605* (1606), sig.D2r. Note also how in Francis Mason's *Vindiciae* the Protestant protagonist 'Orthodox' does not challenge the Romanist 'Philodox''s claim that 'Calvinism' had entered the Church of England: Mason, *Vindiciae*, p.8.

70 Dent, *Reformers*, pp.74–87.

71 Samuel Ward correspondence in Bodl., Tanner MSS vols. 70–6; K. Sharpe, *Sir Robert Cotton 1568–1631. History and Politics in Early Modern England* (Oxford, 1979), p.108; Sellin, *Heinsius*, pp.85–7; J.E. Platt, 'Sixtinus Amama (1593–1629): Franeker professor and citizen of the Republic of Letters', in G.Th. Jensma, F.R.H. Smit and F. Westra (eds.), *Universiteit te Franeker 1585–1811* (Leeuwarden, 1985), pp.240–3; H.J. Honders, *Andreas Rivetus als Invloedrijk Gereformeerd Theoloog in Holland's Bloeitijd* (The Hague, 1930), p.24.

72 Hakewill, *Answere*, i. p.29.

naries such as Thomas Gataker. Dr Grell has drawn attention to the way in which the same network of puritans – men such as Richard Sibbes, Thomas Taylor, John Davenport, William Gouge, Thomas Gataker, John Stoughton and Josias Shute – were involved in the collections for the Palatinate and the initial organization of support for the Protestant ecumenist John Dury, as well as the Feoffees for Impropriations.[73]

Calvinist scholars kept in contact throughout Europe through their participation in that famous and undefinable community, 'the republic of letters'. At its broadest, this international community of scholars was non-denominational, and we should never lose a sense of how shared academic concerns could bridge (in a personal sense) yawning confessional chasms. Scholars of doubtful Calvinist allegiance, such as Johannes Drusius, Gerard Vossius and Isaac Casaubon, could still command a general respect among their Calvinist colleagues for their outstanding academic abilities and personal affability. But the means of communication by which this international 'republic of letters' operated – both by correspondence and by study-tours undertaken by young scholars bearing letters of recommendation from their own masters – also served to coordinate international Calvinist action whenever orthodoxy seemed to be threatened.[74]

Those established English Calvinist scholars in touch with their coreligionists abroad included figures such as James Ussher, John Davenant, Samuel Ward, Arthur Lake, Thomas Morton, Archbishop Abbot, Joseph Hall, Thomas Holland and John Prideaux. They enjoyed links with Dutch Calvinists such as Johannes Polyander, Festus Hommius and Sibrandus Lubbertus; Palatine divines such as Abraham Scultetus and Hendrik Alting; French Calvinists such as Louis Cappel and André Rivet; and divines from Bremen such as Matthias Martinius and Ludovicus Crocius. Bodley's librarian Thomas James, and those internationally minded scholars Cesar Calandrini and John Dury, helped to keep these networks active.[75]

73 O.P. Grell, *Dutch Calvinists in Early Stuart London* (Leiden, 1989), pp.58–9, 180–3; Morgan, *Godly Learning*, pp.245–6, 294–300.

74 *Isaaci Casauboni Epistolae*, ed. T.J. ab Almeloveen (Rotterdam, 1709); *G.J. Vossii et Clarorum Virorum ad Eum Epistolae*, ed. P. Colmesius (1690). On the 'republic of letters' see e.g. Platt, 'Sixtinus Amama'; J.A. Bots, 'André Rivet en zijn positie in de Republiek der Letteren', *Tijdschrift voor Geschiedenis* 84 (1971); Ch. Nisard, *Les Gladiateurs de la république des lettres aux XV, XVI, XVIIe siècles* (Paris, 1860). At the Synod of Dort, the Zeeland delegates emphasized the value of visits to foreign churches and universities for the education of ministers: Hales, *Works*, III ii.p.28.

75 For examples, see the MS correspondence of Sibrandus Lubbertus (BL, Add. MSS 22960–2), Johannes Polyander (Bodl., Rawlinson lett. 76a–c), Thomas James (Bodl., Ballard MS 44) and the correspondence list of Cesar Calandrini (Guildhall Library, MS 7424 fol.49 – I am grateful to Dr Grell for providing me with a copy of his transcription of

The field of anti-papal controversy often witnessed the most effective interaction of these scholars. As the Roman Catholic military threat rallied Protestant forces, so the polemical conflict prompted international Protestant co-operation. In the 1590s, this took the form of the international Calvinist response to the controversial works of the Jesuit Robert Bellarmine. The main Calvinist controversialists – Sibrandus Lubbertus, Franciscus Junius, Daniel Chamier and Lambert Daneau – were in close contact with English divines engaged in the same task of refutation, at first chiefly John Rainolds and William Whitaker. When the voluminous contribution of that implacably presbyterian Calvinist Daneau was posthumously published, his Genevan editor dedicated it to (of all people) Archbishop Whitgift.[76] The Dutch Calvinist Sibrandus Lubbertus anxiously tried to track down the anti-Bellarmine lecture notes of Rainolds and Whitaker after their deaths, and made use of works by Robert Abbot, Gabriel Powel and Thomas Morton. In the early Jacobean period, Lubbertus exchanged notes on anti-papal strategy with Thomas Morton, later bishop of Durham, and dedicated his defence of his refutation of Bellarmine to him. Morton praised Lubbertus' *Replicatio de Principiis* highly, and it was Morton himself who suggested to a friend that Lubbertus' dedication of his next work (*Replicatio de Papa Romano*) to Morton may have tipped the balance in favour of King James granting the deanery of Winchester to him, rather than to a client of the earl of Dunbar. The two divines clearly held each other in very high regard, Morton writing to Lubbertus in 1611 that 'I think it is impossible for anything to escape from your pen which is not most worthy of the approval and applause of all the orthodox Protestants.'*[77] The dawning of the Oath of Allegiance controversy offered foreign Calvinists new ways to endear themselves to the English crown and foster links with their English co-religionists. The French Huguenot leader Pierre du Moulin swiftly discovered this, as his defences of royal absolutism against the works of Bellarmine and du Perron netted him a prebendal stall at Canterbury. Whenever there were jobs for anti-papal polemicists, links with more hardline Calvinists abroad might continue. It was only in the 1630s that patronage dried up – and the largest foreign contributions of all to the defence of James' works, by du Moulin himself and by David

this document). See also the published letter collections such as S.A. Gabbema (ed.), *Illustrium & Clarorum Virorum Epistolae ... distributae in centurias tres* (Leeuwarden, 1669); Ussher *Works*, XV and XVI.

76 Lambert Daneau, *Ad Roberti Bellarmini Disputationes Theologicas ... Responsio* (Geneva, 1596), 'Epistola'.

77 C. van der Woude, *Sibrandus Lubbertus leven en werken* (Kampen, 1963), pp.111, 117–18, 121, 122, 130 n.27; LPL, Lambeth MS 2872 fol.17: Morton to Lubbertus, 26 Dec. 1607; BL, Add. MS 22961 fols.84, 96, 160, 203.

Blondel, found no reward from James' son when they belatedly appeared in the 1630s.[78]

Various English works of anti-papal polemic found their way into Dutch translation, with books on Antichrist being especially popular. Translated authors included Alexander Cooke, William Perkins (especially his ever-popular *Reformed Catholike*), Thomas Morton and Gabriel Powel (whose answer to *A Catholic Supplication* went into three Dutch editions). William Whitaker's complete works were published at Frankfurt and exercised considerable influence on foreign Calvinist scholars, while Bishop Robert Abbot's treatise on Antichrist was a popular source for French Protestant writers. Andrew Willet's voluminous *Synopsis Papismi* was also an important work of reference for foreign Calvinists, with different sections being published in Latin translation until a complete edition appeared in 1614.[79]

Amid all these scholarly links, moderate Calvinist episcopalians regularly corresponded with the same foreign divines who wrote to puritans such as Ames, Gataker and others. This element of overlap between Calvinist conformists and puritans also displayed itself in those other clear manifestations of fellow-feeling with the foreign Calvinist Churches: the charitable collections for the relief of foreign Protestants, organized fasts and the agitation for a confessional foreign policy.

In the Elizabethan period, the destination of contributions for the welfare of oppressed Protestants abroad was Geneva, menaced by Catholic armies.[80] By the end of the century it was the turn of the Huguenots. After 1618, the dispossessed Protestants of the Palatinate were the main recipients of English Calvinist charity. The funds were usually channelled abroad through the Dutch Church at Austin Friars in London.[81] These

[78] Rimbault, *Pierre du Moulin*, pp.61–71, 77–9, 108–14, 210–13; Pierre du Moulin, *Nouveauté du Papisme* (3rd edn, Geneva, 1633); David Blondel, *De La Primauté en l'Eglise* (Geneva, 1641) (see especially 'Préface au Lecteur Chrestien' fol.3r for Blondel's inability to contact Charles or his bishops directly). Note also the suggestion that Richer recanted his treatise on ecclesiastical power because he no longer had a safeguard after James' death: Bodl., Tanner MS 71 fol.25: Isaac Dorislaus to Samuel Ward [December 1629?].

[79] M. A. Shaaber, *Check-list of Works of British Authors Printed Abroad, in Languages Other than English, to 1641* (New York, 1975); C.W. Schoeneveld, *Intertraffic of the Mind* (1983); J. Solé, *Le Débat entre protestants et catholiques français de 1598 à 1685* (4 vols., Université de Lille, 1985), p.89. On the popularity of English puritan writings in the Netherlands, see W.J. op 't Hof, *Engelse pietistische geschriften in het Nederlands, 1598–1622* (Rotterdam, 1987).

[80] Collinson, 'England and international Calvinism', pp.203–7. Collinson points out that the collection of 1582–3 owed much to the support of a number of prominent Protestant councillors. On the 1590 collection for Geneva, see Dent, *Reformers*, pp.79–80.

[81] On the 1620s collections, see Collinson, 'England and international Calvinism', pp.208–10; Grell, *Dutch Calvinists*, ch. 5; D. Underdown, *Fire from Heaven* (1992), p.170.

collections were always opportunities to affirm the cords of common religion which bound the English Church to its Reformed neighbours, and ecclesiastical and political leaders were as happy to endorse this general point as were puritan preachers. A classic example of this phenomenon may be found at the beginning of James' reign, and its timing may not have been entirely coincidental. In a letter to the bishops encouraging contributions to be made for the city of Geneva in 1603, James himself wrote that Geneva had always been famous for her zeal in religion, had harboured Protestants fleeing persecution in the past (including those from England) and now needed help from her friends 'who for community of religion ought to hold the dangers threatening of people so well affected to be their own cause'. The king directed that preachers should excite people's devotion 'to extend it self toward a city deserving so well of the common cause of religion'. Whitgift added a further comment when passing on the letter to his fellow-bishops, applauding the worthy cause of helping to relieve a city 'which maintains the gospel, and for professing thereof endureth these troubles'.[82]

Other divines found in these collections the opportunity to make far more militant affirmations of the unity of the Reformed Calvinist Churches. Appeals to come to the aid of foreign Protestants, whether in financial or military terms, were often couched in the most vivid declarations of the unity of the one true church which transcended national boundaries. Co-religionists abroad were depicted as part of one body, with the natural implication that a threat to one part affected (and endangered) the whole. John Preston, in particular, declared the Protestant Cause to be unified and universal, and spoke of churches or peoples rather than of separate states. Thomas Gataker appealed for the defence of 'our brethren in foraine parts', knit to Englishmen by civil and sacred bonds: 'Neither let any man say; What is their affliction to us? What are those parts to these? What is France or Germanie to England? For What was Jerusalem to Antioch? What was Judah to Joseph?'[83] Failure to respond to the needs of foreign brethren would bring the curse of Meroz (Judges 5.23).[84] Indeed, a number of divines were prepared to designate a concern for the fortunes of

Dr Grell is completing a definitive study of charitable collections for the international Calvinist cause.

[82] Cardwell, *Documentary Annals*, II: 67–9. See also Thomas Morton's appeal for a contribution to the Huguenots in 1622: Bodl., Rawlinson MS B.151 fol.97r.

[83] Thomas Gataker, *A Sparke toward the Kindling of Sorrow for Sion* (1621), pp.32–3, 36–7; Breslow, *Mirror*, p.15.

[84] For all this see Breslow, *Mirror*, pp.14–16; Adams, 'Protestant cause', p.11; Sibbes, *Works*, VI: 66; Gataker, *A Sparke*, pp.37–8; Jackson, *Judah Must*, pp.60–1. See also 'The New Life' (pp.49–53) and 'A sensible Demonstration of the Deity' (p.84) in Preston, *Sermons*; I. Morgan, *Prince Charles' Puritan Chaplain* (1957), pp.188–9.

the church abroad as being in itself a sign of election, and a touchstone of saving faith. John Preston declared in 1625 that if one could hear of the desolation of churches and increase of popery without grieving, then 'it is a sign that you want love to the Lord'. Robert Bolton saw a failure to help continental Protestants as 'an evident touchstone, to try whether our profession be vital or formal'.[85] We can see here a tendency to equate a fellow-feeling with the foreign Reformed Churches with the 'communion of saints', the 'true church' of orthodox Protestant national churches being represented merely as an extension of the community of the godly.

The internationalist tone of these writings was epitomized by William Bradshaw, for whom the term 'foreign' had no meaning in this context:

> Touching the word forreyne, though indeed the things desired by us are in all churches of other countreys fully reformed in doctrine with ours, yet these churches being all the same household of faith that we are, they are not aptly called forreyne ... All Churches and all members of the Church, in what country soever they be, are not to be accounted forreyners one to another, because they are all citizens of heaven, and we all make one family or body.[86]

If puritan voices such as Bradshaw's were rather extreme in this regard, evangelical Calvinist conformists were also prepared to urge the duty to go to the aid of the foreign Reformed Churches, couched in the language of membership of the one true church, and could adopt the rhetoric of holy war with the same conviction as their puritan acquaintances.[87]

While applauded even by Bancroft as symbols of Protestant accord, in practice these charitable collections were generally organized by only a small minority of activists who had been most inspired by the vision of Bradshaw and other puritans.[88] The crucial point is that they invoked a sense of shared Protestant identity which the ecclesiastical establishment clearly felt it necessary publicly to endorse, however far this internationalist flavour might in practice be qualified by practical considerations, and often by more nationalistic, if not positively xenophobic, attitudes. However, by the 1620s, as we shall see, support for foreign Protestants appeared as far more of a direct challenge to the government, and such official support could no longer be presupposed. Moreover, men such as

[85] John Preston, *Breast-Plate of Faith and Love* (1631), pt 2, pp.88–90, 91–2; Robert Bolton, *Works* (4 vols., 1641), III: 345–6 – both cited in J.S. McGee, *The Godly Man in Stuart England* (New Haven, 1976), pp.75, 76.

[86] Bradshaw, *Myld and Just Defence*, p.5: also quoted in Adams, 'Protestant cause', p.23.

[87] Cogswell, *Blessed Revolution*, pp.296–8; Gataker, *A Sparke*, pp.27–9, 32, 37–8; Jackson, *Judah Must*, p.41; Featley, *Clavis*, pp.231–9, 306; Collinson, *Religion of Protestants*, p.88 (Bishop Lake's 1625 fast sermon approving war preparation); Lewis, *Joseph Hall*, p.297.

[88] E.g. Bancroft, *Survay*, p.48. While Bancroft may have paid tribute to the rationale of these collections, this is not to suggest that he did not have his suspicions about this corporate puritan activity: *Tracts Ascribed to Richard Bancroft*, ed. A. Peel (Cambridge, 1953), p.12; P. Collinson, *Godly People* (1982), p.271.

Laud were more than happy directly to intervene, not simply with the organization of the collection, but also with the ideology in which the appeal for funds was couched.[89]

Another oft-cited manifestation of the English Church's sense of identity with the Calvinist Churches of the continent was the existence of the so-called 'stranger churches' of foreign Protestants living in England. Initially established in Edward's reign, the stranger churches had at first been exempt from episcopal jurisdiction, and were intended by some to serve as a model for a Reformed Church to the English Reformers still in the process of building Jerusalem. By the Elizabethan and Jacobean periods, however, their presence was more problematic. The bishop of the diocese was made their superintendent *ex officio*, and the churches were required to use no religious form 'contrary to our law'. They were no longer seen as a model for reform within the English Church, and were more often the focus of conformist anxieties and xenophobic bitterness, as we shall see in the following chapter. Nevertheless, their symbolic meaning remained unquestioned in the Jacobean period, however far this might be compromised in practical terms. In 1625 Richard Crakanthorp, replying on the Church of England's behalf to the jibes of the apostate de Dominis, emphasized how happy the English Church was to be able to provide shelter to foreign Protestants, just as English Protestants had been aided by foreign Protestants at the time of their exile during the Marian reaction. The Jacobean Church of England gloried in her hospitality, rather than seeing in it any diminishing of the integrity of her own forms of church government.[90]

The bonds linking foreign Calvinist Churches to the Church of England found possibly their most striking affirmation in the marriage of King James' daughter Elizabeth to the Elector Palatine in 1613. The marriage itself emerged more from short-term political requirements rather than Protestant convictions, especially since it was planned (abortively) to be paralleled by the marriage of James' male heir to a Roman Catholic princess. Nevertheless, the celebration of the nuptials provided the focus for officially approved paeans of praise for Protestant internationalism from a whole range of court divines, including Willet, John King and even Lancelot Andrewes.[91] Again, changing foreign policy would make invocations of the Palatine cause, and of the Calvinist internationalism which it

[89] See below, p.434.

[90] Collinson, *Godly People*, pp.218, 247–8, 253–4, 256; Crakanthorp, *Defensio*, p.237.

[91] Willet, *Treatise of Salomons Marriage*; John King, *Vitis Palatina* (1614); Andrewes, *Opuscula*, pp.77–93. On translations of Palatine religious works, inspired by the marriage, see Adams, 'Protestant cause', pp.219–20.

exemplified, more problematic, although it would not be until the 1630s that the ideology behind it would be systematically attacked.

A whole range of episodes and institutions thus served to testify to the Church of England's unity with the Reformed Churches of the continent. But English Calvinist internationalists also found themselves forced to intervene more directly in the affairs of their sister-churches in order to demonstrate their loyalties, as continental Calvinism increasingly found itself divided in the early seventeenth century by Arminianism and its forebears. English Calvinists generally supported the more rigorous defenders of Calvinist orthodoxy. Thus Willet devoted a large section of the second edition of his *Synopsis* to the refutation of new strains of heterodoxy appearing among the continental churches – especially in the form of the Bernese pastor Samuel Huberus, along with Gellius Snecanus, Puccius and the Lutheran divines Jacobus Andreae and Neils Hemmingsen.[92] Willet depicted their arguments concerning universal grace as being worse than the errors of the Romanists on this point, and equated them directly with the Pelagian heresy.[93] John Dove launched a similar assault upon Huberus at Paul's Cross in 1597, while attacks upon the Dutch Arminians became the staple fare of Oxford divinity disputations.[94]

In James' reign, divines found active encouragement to involve themselves in overseas Protestant squabbles from the actions of James himself. The king chose to intervene directly over the appointment of the allegedly heterodox German divine Conrad Vorstius to the chair of divinity at Leiden, and was also active in striving to bring about a reconciliation between the Huguenot divines Daniel Tilenus and Pierre du Moulin, who had clashed over the question of the two identities of Christ.[95] The resolution of the latter controversy fed into more general attempts, centred on the 1614 Huguenot National Synod at Tonneins, to draw up a plan for a Protestant General Council, sponsored by King James.[96] At the heart of these activities was not so much an attempt to secure peace between Calvinists and other Protestants, but rather a recognition of the need to bind Calvinist Churches together more tightly and to promote among them

92 Willet, *Synopsis* (1600), pp.784–819; *idem*, *Hexapla on Romans*, pp.280–1, 437–8; N. Tyacke, 'The rise of Arminianism reconsidered', *P&P* 115 (1987), pp.205–6.

93 Willet, *Synopsis* (1600), pp.808, 809–10, 814.

94 Dove, *A Sermon Preached at Paules Crosse* (1597), pp.31, 42, 64–5, 71, 74; Tyacke, *Anti-Calvinists*, pp.72–5.

95 F. Shriver, 'Orthodoxy and diplomacy: James I and the Vorstius affair', *EHR* 336 (1970), pp.449–74. For the du Moulin/Tilenus dispute, see Rimbault, *Pierre du Moulin*, pp.57–60; Patterson, 'James I and the Huguenot Synod', pp.249–51; PRO, SP 14/67/100 and 103, SP 14/70/33 and 37.

96 Patterson, 'James I and the Huguenot Synod', pp.241–70.

a corporate responsibility to defend the tenets of orthodoxy against the new heresies of divines such as Vorstius. Thus James had argued in his 1612 *Declaration* against Vorstius that, were Leiden to become contaminated with Vorstius' heresies, then England would soon be infected too. The king had therefore threatened to 'exhort all other reformed Churches to ioyne with us in a common Councel, how to extinguish and remand to hell these abominable Heresies', arguing that he was merely trying to secure in the United Provinces the establishment 'of that Religion onely . . . which the Reformed Churches of Great Britaine, France and Germanie, by a mutuall consent, have generally embraced'.[97] Similarly, the ecumenical proposals presented at Tonneins in 1614, apparently with James' approval, had envisaged a permanent association of Reformed Churches which would act to safeguard the doctrinal status quo, 'that if some controversy arose afterward whether in England, in France, or in Germany, whether in the Low Countries, or in Switzerland, nothing would be concluded or decided (or even less innovated) concerning the question in controversy, without the General Consent and Approbation of the Provinces which would have signed the said Accord'.[98]

This commitment to defending international Calvinist orthodoxy was still more evident in the Dutch Arminian controversy. The strength of Anglo-Dutch political and economic ties made it inevitable that England would become more closely involved in the developing controversies in the Low Countries over predestination once these conflicts acquired political overtones. Not only were there large Dutch congregations resident in England, but the Dutch cities were also full of English, Scots and other nationalities, who fought in their armies, manned their ships and served the East and West India Companies.[99] Moreover, English religious involvement became inevitable as the pamphlet literature of the Dutch Arminian controversy became saturated with references to the English Church and English authors. From the earliest stages of their conflicts with Arminius, the more rigid Dutch Calvinists (Contra-Remonstrants) such as Sibrandus Lubbertus and Festus Hommius had been anxious to expand the range of the conflict, and to bring in outside support from foreign Reformed Churches to define Calvinist orthodoxy in their favour against Vorstius.[100]

When King James' *Declaration* against Vorstius was published in 1612 it included in its violent assault on the ideas of Vorstius some side-swipes at

97 King James, *Workes*, pp.366, 356, 358 (*A Declaration concerning the Proceedings with the States Generall of the United Provinces of the Low Countreys, in the Cause of D. Conradus Vorstius*). James claimed in similar terms that the acceptance of Vorstius at Leiden stained the honour of 'the reformed Churches' (*ibid.*, p.363).

98 Patterson, 'James I and the Huguenot Synod', p.256.

99 K.L. Sprunger, *Dutch Puritanism* (Leiden, 1982), pp.3–12.

100 Shriver, 'Orthodoxy and diplomacy', pp.452, 468.

his Remonstrant supporters, including the deceased Arminius and Petrus Bertius, who had been foolish enough to send his tract on the apostasy of the saints to Archbishop Abbot when the affair was at its height. Once Abbot's attention had been engaged he played a central role, and it can hardly be a coincidence that the two major English works explicitly directed against Arminians to be published in the period before Dort were composed by Abbot's brother Robert, and by his ex-chaplain Sebastian Benefield, both divinity professors in Oxford. Some Calvinists needed little explicit prompting. George Carleton wrote his own short tract against Arminianism in 1617 because (he admitted)

> I think that there is nothing don in gods churche, but it concerneth me whether on this side, or on that side of the sea. When I heare of the stirres which the sect of Arminians have raised in ... [the Netherlands] ... I take a kind of part. For in suche causes wherin Christs truthe is questioned, who is not of the one part or the other.[101]

The same sense of direct involvement in the clashes over Calvinist orthodoxy is evident in Prideaux's remarks in his sermon *Ephesus Backsliding*, in which he declared that 'Socinus blasphemies, Arminius subtilties, Vorstius novelties, Bertius quiddities, shall rather bee an occasion of further clearing, then shaking the setled truth amongst us.'[102]

This 'further clearing' need not necessarily be limited to continental Calvinism, and zeal to defend the Calvinist cause could easily undermine the unity of English Protestantism. English Calvinists might thereby easily be led into carrying the search for heretics into their own church, turning their attention on native anti-Calvinists, or even on puritans.[103] It was particularly tempting for English Calvinists to employ the accusation 'Arminian' in a native context, because (unlike 'papist') it was a charge

101 Tyacke, *Anti-Calvinists*, pp.72, 88–9; PRO, SP 14/93 fol.135v: George Carleton to Dudley Carleton, 22 October 1617.

102 Prideaux, *Ephesus Backsliding*, p.17.

103 For a puritan example, see George Walker's accusations of Socinianism against the puritan Anthony Wotton. While personal issues (perhaps complicated by Wotton's apparent attempts to endear himself to the establishment in his anti-papal works) were undoubtedly prominent, Walker admitted that he identified Wotton's works as Socinian after having read the recent Arminian controversies in the Netherlands: George Walker, *A True Relation of the Chiefe Passages* (1642), p.6. Nevertheless, it was not just puritans who saw English opponents as Arminians. Davenant seems at times to distinguish between the views of Montagu and those of the Dutch Remonstrants (see his seven-folio treatise on perseverance, which he sent to Ward, in SSC Ward Correspondence), but in the 1630s he assumed that many Laudian doctrinal innovations were inspired by foreign Protestant heterodoxies. See his complaint in a letter to Ward (Bodl., Tanner MS 71 fol.164) of 'so much bouldnes in those that fancy ye Errors and Novelties of forreign D[ivines]' – referring to Cambridge developments and the Commencement theses of Duncon, among others – and his further expressions of concern in the Short Parliament at the spread of Arminian heresies in England: Cope and Coates, *Proceedings*, p.111.

which could be consistently levelled against a professed Protestant, and also avoided the problems created for Protestant irenicists by the use of the term 'Lutheran' as a sign of opprobrium. Thus Wotton presented Richard Montagu's doctrines concerning predestination as being necessarily 'Arminian' because they were not Romanist nor even Lutheran, as the Lutherans did not urge this doctrine 'very strictly nor as a matter undoubtedly revealed: nor doe they presse it in all the particulars brought by M. Mountague'.[104]

A CALVINIST IDENTITY: THE POINTS OF TENSION

No matter how far English Protestants accepted the idea of unity with overseas co-religionists, their identification with them in practice was not always as close as might have been assumed. A number of qualifications were often made. Some were merely technical, such as a formal reluctance to accept the term 'Calvinist', or a concurrent nationalist emphasis on the particular providential role granted to the English. Other restraints on Calvinist internationalism were more serious, reflecting divisions over ecclesiastical discipline, but also over a number of specific doctrinal issues.

First, the formal universalism of Protestant ecclesiology must be remembered, especially in the light of attempts by historians past and present to uncover distinctively 'Anglican' streams of thought during this period. While they assumed that their church was ranged on the side of the other West European Reformed Churches, English Protestants formally resisted the label 'Calvinist'. This did not reflect an 'Anglican' desire to be depicted as independent of the religious divisions of the continent, although some recent historians have been prone to represent it as such. Rather, a figure such as Prideaux was reluctant to allow the term 'Calvinist' to be employed even towards the foreign Reformed Churches themselves.[105] Those who distanced themselves from the term in England included the most dedicated supporters of Calvin's doctrines, and indeed of the Genevan form of church discipline. The formal position that the English Church was merely part of the 'universal church' was adhered to by all types of divines. When Roman Catholics referred to them as 'Calvinists', even presbyterians such as Walter Travers and Thomas Cartwright disclaimed any such term of division, and claimed merely the name of

[104] Wotton, *Dangerous Plot*, ii. pp.167–8.

[105] See above, p.395; and also Prideaux, *Viginti-duae Lectiones*, i. p.277, where he applies to foreign divines such as Lubbertus the epithet 'Calvinists' with the qualification 'ut vulgo audiunt'. For a similar example, see Matthew Sutcliffe's demand that Montagu or his followers provide a definition of 'the doctrine that is called Calvinisme': Sutcliffe, *Briefe Censure*, pp.8–9.

'Catholic Christians', echoing the words of Pacianus, the fourth-century bishop of Barcelona.[106] Even in the 1620s, when the jibe of 'Calvinist' was no longer simply coming from Romanists, but was also being employed by Richard Montagu, puritans such as John Yates still rejected the term as 'factious and schismaticall' and rested happy with Pacianus' definition.[107] In fact, both sides in the 'Arminian' dispute were happy to invoke Pacianus rather than Calvin. There was nothing distinctively 'Laudian', therefore, about the rejection of the label 'Calvinist', or, indeed, the insistence that the Church of England was 'Catholic and Reformed'. The Laudians' most vehement opponents, including those most determined to overturn the Elizabethan Settlement, insisted on the same point. What was far more significant, as we shall see, was what was precisely understood by the terms 'Catholic' and 'Reformed', and how far the Church of England was perceived to be linked to the continent. For Richard Montagu, the term 'Christian Catholic' necessarily implied a lack of interest in the affairs of the continent – for him the two things were mutually exclusive.

The Calvinophilia against which the Laudians defined themselves was to a significant extent a caricature. Their opponents steadfastly denied that they were slavish adherents of Calvin's opinions. Thus Robert Abbot, for all his venemous attacks upon English and Dutch Arminians, constantly emphasized that

> we honour Calvin indeede as a singular instrument of God, for the restoring of the light of his truth, and overthrowing of the throne of the purple whoore of Rome, but we make him no patriarch, wee follow him no further then he approoveth unto us, that he is a follower of Christ: we tie not our selves to him, but use our liberty to dissent from him, and to censure him where hee hath gone awry.

George Hakewill fiercely attacked the apostate Carier's attempt to distinguish 'Calvinisme' from 'the doctrine of England', complaining that this was designed 'to put us off from all fellowship and communion with those Churches, who acknowledge Calvin to have beene an excellent instrument of God, in the abolishing and suppressing of Poperie, and the cleansing and spreading of his trueth'. Nevertheless, he emphasized that Calvin was not accepted uncritically: 'we esteeme [him] as a worthy man, but a man, and consequently subiect to humane error, and frailtie. We maintaine nothing with him because he affirmes it, but because from infallible grounds he proves it.'[108]

106 Lake, *Moderate Puritans*, p.68. See also Abbot, *True Ancient*, p.45; Clancy, 'Papist–Protestant–Puritan', p.234. Pacianus had declared in a famous phrase that 'My name is Christian; my surname is Catholic.'

107 Yates, *Ibis*, ii. pp.1–4, 8.

108 Abbot, *Second Part*, p.220; Hakewill, *Answere*, ii. pp.134, 135. See also Abbot, *True Ancient*, p.96.

It must still be emphasized, however, that, if they rejected the term 'Calvinist', there were yet plenty of English Protestant divines who were happy to acknowledge the influence of Calvin on their church. Indeed, even those late Elizabethan writers who were more tactically moderate towards Rome, such as Edmund Bunny, were unapologetic of the strong influence of Calvin's ideas in the English Church. Bunny made no attempt to deny the Romanist Parsons' allegation that 'a good Minister of England' would speak as one 'trained up in Iohn Calvines schoole'.[109]

A second potential restraint on internationalist emphases lay in contemporary depictions of England as an elect nation with a special role to play in the working out of God's plans. Recent historians have downplayed the significance of incipient nationalism in the apocalyptical histories charted by Foxe and others, rightly pointing out that apocalyptic schema tended to be focused on church rather than nation, and in fact served more to reinforce supranationalist tendencies by their treatment of the true church in opposition to Rome as a mystic, supranational entity.[110] Nevertheless, as Professor Collinson has rightly observed, this was not necessarily the impression gained by all readers, and by the early seventeenth century elect nationhood could certainly be implied from some apocalyptic commentaries. Of course, this was not necessarily triumphalist: these apocalyptic histories, and more especially the torrent of prophetic preaching, which applied the rhetoric of the covenanted nation and the paradigm of Israel to England, were regularly the means used to criticize the nation's shortcomings. The image of England as the nation which had in the past redeemed the suffering Protestants of the continent was also one that could be critical in tone, serving to emphasize the country's neglected duty towards co-religionists in the present.

Nationalism and internationalism could thus co-exist in such schema, and indeed might be mutually dependent. As Peter Lake has noted, 'the assumption that England had a special role to play in the unfolding of God's will relative to Antichrist' was not necessarily precluded by Protestant internationalism, but rather 'tended to come to the fore in moments of national crisis', although England's leading role was generally expounded in combination with a view of the conflict with Rome which 'transcended national boundaries'.[111] However, while this Protestant religiosity inhibited and confused the sense of England as 'special and divinely elect',

[109] Bunny, *Briefe Answer*, pp.52–5.

[110] Bauckham, *Tudor Apocalypse*, pp.86–7; Firth, *Apocalyptic Tradition*, pp.106–8; V.N. Olsen, *John Foxe and the Elizabethan Church* (Berkeley, 1973), pp.36–47.

[111] Collinson, *Birthpangs*, ch.1; M. McGiffert, 'God's controversy with Jacobean England', *American Historical Review* 88 (1983), pp.1151–74; Lake, 'Significance', p.164 n.15. For a later antidote to the 'Hoseads' described by McGiffert, see John Seller, *Five Sermons* (1636), pp.80–94.

it must still be remembered that religiously inspired nationalism, and ethnocentric enthusiasm, were never entirely absent when English Calvinists contemplated their Reformed neighbours, even if such sentiments were not necessarily directly in conflict with Calvinist internationalism.

Calvinists' apparent internationalism was thus never quite straightforward. Moreover, a whole host of practical political and economic considerations often threatened to modify, or even to subvert, the polarized confessionalism which Calvinist ideology aspired to impose on the world. These political ramifications will be discussed in the next chapter. But it is important here to recognize that, regardless of political considerations, there were also significant theological concerns at work that qualified English Calvinists' sense of doctrinal community with the Reformed Churches of the continent. To begin with, there was the problem of presbyterianism, which divines such as Beza had already elevated to the level of true doctrine, including it as one of the notes whereby the 'true church' should be known. This conflict embodied wider disagreements regarding the nature of the ministry and the purpose and function of the church, as we shall see. It also clearly introduced dangerous complications into the effective unity of Protestants, and could make the international Protestant Cause a sensitive and politically charged issue in internal politics. In the 1590s and beyond it also prompted severe attacks upon the wisdom and integrity of Geneva's most famous sons.

But there were other specific doctrinal issues on which English and foreign Calvinists found that their paths were beginning to diverge. One example is Sabbatarianism. A recent scholar has rightly remarked that 'sabbatarianism was to a large extent an English phenomenon, which only affected continental Calvinism sporadically'. Differing views of the requirements of sabbath observance could sometimes act as a focus for disagreement between English and foreign Calvinists. In more candid moments, Dutch divines referred scoffingly to the 'figmentum Anglicanum', but the Dutch stranger church in London had to tread carefully when dealing with puritan complaints over the Dutchmen's practice of banqueting or conducting business on the sabbath.[112] William Ames provoked open conflict at the University of Franeker when he attempted to introduce English-style Sabbatarianism. Dutch anti-Sabbatarianism was also criticized by even the zealous presbyterian Alexander Leighton.[113]

[112] Grell, *Dutch Calvinists*, pp.76–7; R. Bauckham, 'Sabbath and Sunday in the Protestant tradition', in D.A. Carson (ed.), *From Sabbath to Lord's Day* (Grand Rapids, 1982), p.321. Samuel Hartlib recognized that Sabbatarianism was distinctive of English Protestantism, and would need explaining and justifying to foreign Protestants if Protestant unity was to be effected: SUL, Hartlib MS 29/3 fol.8v.

[113] K.L. Sprunger, *The Learned Doctor William Ames* (Urbana, 1972), pp.86–7; Alexander Leighton, *Speculum belli sacri* (Amsterdam, 1624), pp.267–8, 279 – quoted in Breslow,

This was not just a puritan concern: the British delegates at Dort made a formal protest to the synod concerning the profanation of the sabbath in the town.[114]

The problem was not merely one of discipline: much foreign Calvinist theology concerning the sabbath lagged well behind English developments, especially on the question of the divine institution of the Lord's Day. Calvin's *Institutes* contained little that would support Sabbatarian thinking, and indeed argued that the church was not bound to the pattern of one-day-in-seven.[115] While some writers such as John Prideaux argued that it was the Arminians in Holland who were anti-Sabbatarians,[116] it was more often noted that this was a more general problem with Dutch, and also Genevan theologians. After all, the most comprehensive critique of arguments for the morally binding nature of the fourth commandment was written by Franciscus Gomarus, Arminianism's most zealous opponent in the Netherlands.[117] The Church of England itself was experiencing greater tensions around the doctrine of the sabbath, and it was here that Laudian authors found themselves in the novel position of being able to appeal to foreign Calvinist authorities in support of their position.[118] Although they

Mirror, p.93. Zeeland would later become famous for its strict Sabbatarianism, but this is the exception that proves the rule, as Zeeland divines were confessedly inspired by the English example: Grell, *Dutch Calvinists*, p.61. Ames' impact in the Netherlands is noted by Heylyn: *History of the Sabbath*, i. p.8, ii. pp.185–6.

114 Hales, *Golden Remains*, p.545. When discussing the issue more generally, delegations tried to outdo each other in their declarations of native zeal in Sabbatarian discipline: Hales, *Works*, III ii. pp.8–10 (cf. Henry Burton, *The Lords Day, the Sabbath Day* (2nd edn, 1636), p.47). For the Synod of Dort's definitions and regulations of the sabbath (as partly moral and partly ceremonial), see Brandt, *History*, III: 320, cf. pp.326–7. For contemporary observations of lax Sabbatarian practice among foreign Calvinists, see Heylyn, *History of the Sabbath*, preface, i. p.10, ii. pp.180, 184; Theophilus Brabourne, A *Defence of … the Sabbath Day* (2nd edn, 1632), p.398; Thomas Scot, *The Belgicke Pismire*, sig.aa2 (*Workes*).

115 For Calvin's sabbath doctrine, see J.H. Primus, *Holy Time* (Macon, Ga., 1989), pp.120–34. However, Primus does note the more Sabbatarian theology of Junius and Zanchius, with the latter a prominently cited authority in the 1606 edition of Nicholas Bound's *Sabbathum Veteris* (*ibid*., pp.120, 138–44).

116 John Prideaux, *The Doctrine of the Sabbath* (3rd edn, 1635), pp.20–1, 25, 33. For other examples of contributors to the English sabbath controversy associating anti-Sabbatarianism with Remonstrants and Socinians, see Nicholas Byfield, *The Doctrine of the Sabbath Vindicated* (1631), p.128; Twisse, *Of the Morality*, p.94.

117 G.P. van Itterzon, *Franciscus Gomarus* (The Hague, 1929), pp.301–9. During the Sabbatarian controversy in the 1630s, English divines became aware of Gomarus' writings against the sabbath, and the fact that they had not yet been satisfactorily answered: SUL, Hartlib MS 29/2 fols.18v, 19v; Byfield, *Doctrine*, p.140; Heylyn, 'preface' to Prideaux, *Doctrine*, p.6; Brabourne, *A Defence*, p.277; White, *Treatise*, pp.45–6. A substantial section of Twisse's Sabbatarian tract is devoted to the refutation of the arguments of the unimpeachably orthodox French Calvinist divine André Rivet: Twisse, *Of the Morality*, pp.66–106. On this point more generally see my unpublished paper 'Divisions over sabbath doctrine in early Stuart England'.

118 E.g. Francis White, *An Examination and Confutation of a Lawlesse Pamphlet* (1637), pp.135, 141–3; *idem*, *Treatise*, pp.271–4; Christopher Dow, *A Discourse of the Sabbath*

charged their Laudian opponents with cynical hypocrisy for exploiting foreign Calvinist sources, English Calvinists were distinctly uneasy at having to deal with the foreign testimonies marshalled against them.[119]

The Synod of Dort provided an unwelcome shock for the British delegates in a number of other ways, as they found that on several issues their positions conflicted with those of their foreign co-religionists. Before the Arminians arrived at the synod, the English delegates were amazed that some Dutch divines denied baptism to the children of non-Christian parents, even if they had been adopted by Christians.[120] On the point of Christ's descent into hell, English Protestants had moved further from Calvin's position in the years since Willet's exchange with Richard Parkes, and the British delegates registered their disagreement with the Heidelberg Catechism on this point at the synod.[121] Even Archbishop Abbot was aghast at the synod's resolution for removing the apocryphal Scriptures, exclaiming that 'it so savoureth of innovation that I am persuaded it will be distastefull to his Majesty and other Reformed Churches and will give advantage of reioceing to the Church of Rome'.[122]

Most famously, however, the synod's delegates found themselves in difficulties when dealing with the fundamental doctrinal issues at stake at the synod, which pertained to that crucial doctrine of second generation Calvinism, predestination. The 1590s had marked the apex of an English high Calvinism which was personified in the hardline position adopted in the Cambridge disputes by William Whitaker. After that peak, there was an increasing process of elaboration and diversification in English Calvin-

and the Lords Day (2nd edn, 1636), pp.23–4 (cf. *idem*, *Innovations*, pp.89–90); Heylyn, *History of the Sabbath*, preface, ii. pp.172–3, 181; Gilbert Ironside, *Seven Questions of the Sabbath Briefly Disputed* (Oxford, 1637), pp.69, 168–9; David Primerose, *A Treatise of the Sabbath and the Lords-Day* (1636), pp.236, 311–38.

119 E.g. the complaints in Burton, *Lords Day*, p.46; Twisse, *Of the Morality*, pp.42, 147. However, it should be emphasized that, when it came to recommended sabbath *practice*, rather than the theology of the sabbath (and most specifically the question of the institution of the Lord's Day), Reformed authorities were in plentiful supply for English Sabbatarians, and included Calvin himself: e.g. Burton, *Lords Day*, pp.46, 48–62; Primus, *Holy Time*, p.134.

120 Hales, *Works*, III ii. pp.30–1, 33–4, 42–3.

121 Hales, *Golden Remains*, p.545. This shift in English Protestant understandings of the doctrine may be traced through the different editions of Thomas Rogers' *Catholic Doctrine*, the second edition of which distances itself from Calvin's position (Rogers, *Catholic Doctrine*, pp.xii–xiii). Note, however, how Rogers condemns Piscator's doctrine without drawing attention to the Reformed divine's identity: *ibid*., p.61.

122 PRO, SP 105/95 fol.47v: Archbishop Abbot to Dudley Carleton, 27 November 1618. Hall reported to Samuel Ward that King James was indeed 'much disturbed' by this very point, but 'it did a little pacify him to learn that we had publicly required it should be inserted in the Act, that this sentence was without rather than against the allowance of the foreign divines; which you must care may be considerably done when the Act shall be intended to light': Hall, *Works*, X: 505.

ists' treatment of predestinarian issues, and fewer translations were published of foreign Calvinist works on grace. In puritan divinity there arose an increasingly delicate balance between on the one hand a rigid predestinarianism, and on the other the importance allotted to human efforts and good works – the whole voluntaristic conditionality of covenant theology – in practical, pastoral divinity. Voluntaristic emphases were usually combined with a rigid defence of the basic corpus of Calvinist predestinarian doctrine, accepting the severest formulations of the doctrines of the total depravity of man, unconditional election, limited atonement, irresistible grace and the perseverance of the saints. It was these rigid points which were invoked when combating anti-Calvinists and papists.[123] The tensions within this puritan position when it came to the pastoral implications of predestinarian doctrine were already evident. They were becoming more prominent under James and Charles, when puritans increasingly came into conflict with each other over related points concerning justification. This occurred most famously in the clash between John Cotton and William Twisse, but the same problems were also evident in the conflicts between George Walker and Anthony Wotton, between Ezechiel Culverwell and his opponents, and in a number of other cases which only emerged later in print along with other internal puritan debates in the early 1640s.[124]

Other English Calvinists, however, may be seen in the Jacobean period to have been involved in gradually trying to dissociate themselves from the more rigid high Calvinism of the continent, most especially the supralapsarianism of Theodore Beza and his followers, who defended an absolute and irrespective decree of reprobation which was applied to man before the Fall. Throughout Europe, more rigid forms of predestinarian doctrine had provoked controversy in Reformed circles. In England, moderate forms of Calvinism were more resilient – at least in part because they were more clearly endorsed by the Book of Common Prayer. They were also assisted by the fact that the more radical exponents of extreme Calvinism had been disgraced in the presbyterian and separatist movements. Clashes between English Calvinists had already been evident in the formulation of the Lambeth Articles – with Archbishops Hutton and Whitgift seeking to moderate the rigidity of William Whitaker's position.[125]

[123] Lake, 'Calvinism', p.41 n.21; *idem*, *Moderate Puritans*, ch.7.

[124] J.S. Coolidge, *The Pauline Renaissance in England* (Oxford, 1970), pp.91–2, 111–22; SUL, Hartlib MS 29/3 fol.17r; Walker, *True Relation*; Ezechiel Culverwell, *A Briefe Answere to Certaine Objections against the Treatise of Faith* (1626); Bodl., Tanner MS 71 fol.35r: Gataker to Ward, 11 Feb. [1630]; Bodl., Tanner MS 285 fol.64v; Wallace, *Puritans*, pp.85, 108, 147, 225–6 (n.149). Cf. White, *Predestination*, p.309 n.156.

[125] Lake, *Moderate Puritans*, pp.201–26.

Under James, other divines continued gradually to disentangle themselves from the style of high Calvinism which was becoming more prominent on the continent. The writings of Andrew Willet provide a striking example of this process of disengagement, and his own change of view is all the more interesting because it is to some extent datable. As we have seen, Willet's *Synopsis Papismi* of 1600 had contained a firm defence of Calvinist orthodoxy against the heresies of Huberus, Snecanus and Hemmingsen. Willet had himself noted the drift from a more rigid position even among confirmed Calvinists on the issue of universal grace, complaining 'that some heretofore thoroughly perswaded of the trueth, should now begin to stagger in opinion'.[126] In his *Hexapla on Romans* of 1611, however, Willet sought to qualify aspects of his own exposition of predestinarian doctrine. He explicitly retracted the supralapsarian position which he had maintained in his earlier work, and now expounded a sublapsarian position, emphasizing that the object of reprobation was man *after* the Fall, and that the decree itself thus proceeded from prescience of original and actual sin, and was *not* an absolute act of God's will and purpose. He concluded 'and in this resolution of this question (whatsoever I have before thought and written otherwise) I set up my rest, as the safest from any inconvenience, and the fittest to give satisfaction to the contrarie obiections'.[127] In the process, Willet explicitly disagreed with Calvin, Zanchius and Paraeus who had implied that God exercised His absolute power in the decree of reprobation to condemn people irrespective of their sins. Willet believed that it was safer to say that God *might* have done so if He had wished, 'but he dealeth otherwise in this mysterie of reprobation, refusing none but iustly for their sinne'. Willet still claimed, however, that divines such as Amandus Polanus and Paraeus in a sense agreed with him, since they maintained that the reprobate were left in their sins.[128] Willet explicitly disagreed with Calvin, Beza and Martyr 'with other of our

126 Willet, *Synopsis* (1600), p.819. As if to illustrate this point, the copy of Willet's work in Cambridge University Library bears annotations (possibly by the moderate Calvinist John Hacket) which seek to emphasize the more universalist aspects of Willet's position: CUL, shelfmark 4.3.38, pp.821–6, 831.

127 Willet, *Hexapla on Romans*, pp.438–43. Willet was distancing himself from his own earlier position in *Synopsis* (1600), p.820, in which he had followed Junius' distinction of two degrees of reprobation, of which only one was absolute (*Hexapla on Romans*, p.441). Willet's rethinking on this and related points was enshrined in additions to the fourth edition of the *Synopsis* (1613), where he inserted two new paragraphs (p.921) emphasizing the sublapsarian position, which replaced his earlier defence of irrespective reprobation which had made use of the example of Jacob and Esau (1600, p.822). Indeed, Willet directly refutes precisely this earlier argument and example later on the same page: cf. 1600, p.823; 1613, pp.921–2.

128 Willet, *Hexapla on Romans*, p.443. Willet also presents a modification of the doctrine of limited atonement, suggesting that God 'would have all men to be saved' and 'offreth outward meanes unto all of their calling' (*ibid.*, p.451).

learned new writers' who, while distinguishing between election and reprobation in the *execution* of the decrees, still held the decrees themselves to be absolute. Willet rather believed that 'it is the safer way from the beginning of the decree, to the execution, to hold a perpetuall difference betweene election and reprobation'.

Willet's rethinking was clearly prompted by problems which had arisen since 1600 in defending the more rigid position. As he explained, those who expounded an absolute decree of reprobation without relation to sin could not remove the doubt as to how God's mercy was therefore magnified above His justice, if the number of the reprobate far exceeded the number of the elect.[129] It seems more than likely that Willet was prompted here in part by the objections raised on this point by the Dutch Remonstrants, and the difficulties encountered in trying to refute them. It was this conviction that the Arminian controversies displayed the need to amend certain aspects of Calvinist orthodoxy, and to avoid some of the extremes being advocated by the Contra-Remonstrants, which was to become a notable trend in English moderate Calvinist thought, reaching its clearest expression at the Synod of Dort itself.

Willet was not alone in modifying some of the elements of contemporary Calvinist predestinarianism. It has recently been noted that a number of moderate episcopalian Calvinists – such as George Hakewill, Richard Field, John White and Robert Abbot – were also involved in a retreat from Bezan supralapsarianism during the first two decades of James' reign. All were prompted by Roman Catholic accusations that Calvin and Beza taught that God was the author of sin. In order to exculpate them from this charge, these English moderate Calvinists presented a 'minimizing interpretation' of Calvinist doctrine, emphasizing a basically sublapsarian framework and the distinction between positive and negative reprobation.[130] Later refutations of Richard Montagu's works by Matthew

[129] *Ibid.*, pp.443, 447.

[130] White, *Predestination*, pp.153–9, citing Hakewill, *Answere*, White, *The Way*, Field, *Of the Church*, and Abbot, *Third Part*. For another example of creeping sublapsarianism, see Thomas Paske's Commencement thesis in Cambridge in 1613 that 'Subjectum divinae praedestinationis est homo lapsus': BL, Harleian MS 7038 p.89. Peter White may attach rather too much significance to Hakewill and White's insistence on Roman orthodoxy on the point of predestination as typifying their moderate stance (*Predestination*, pp.154–5). Rather, this admission was a commonplace in anti-papal polemic which served a specific controversial purpose, and was repeated by Montagu's opponents in the 1620s (see above, pp.210–11). Dominican authors such as Banez were capable of absolute predestinarian arguments as extreme as anything that the Contra-Remonstrants could come up with, but were cited against Molinists in order to demonstrate Roman disunity. If this line suggested that the Roman doctrine of *predestination* was not Pelagian (*Predestination*, p.157), her doctrines on free will and justification were nevertheless consistently branded with this heresy by the same English controversialists (e.g. White, *The Way*, pp.278, 281).

Sutcliffe and George Carleton similarly claimed that Calvin's views were being misrepresented, and that he was being wrongly accused of arguing that men were damned without respect to sin.[131] All these arguments represented a departure from some aspects of the high Calvinism being defended by the Contra-Remonstrants in the Netherlands.

The crucial point to note, however, is that these writers sought to *defend* Calvin and Beza against accusations, rather than depicting themselves as explicitly dissenting from the Calvinist tradition, or denying the Church of England's place within it. Moreover, freeing Calvin from these imputations generally made it unnecessary for writers to deal specifically with those foreign Calvinists who embraced more rigid doctrines. Supralapsarian authors were rarely (if ever) referred to by name. In his *Synopsis* (at least) Willet did not specify who held these beliefs, while George Carleton managed to make the vaguest of allusions to those whose zeal against the Arminians pushed them too far in the other direction.[132] When seeking to convince his readers that Protestant doctrinal reconciliation was possible, Joseph Hall would later urge as an example the fact that supralapsarian doctrines, which 'upon some straining may . . . yield harsh and unpleasing consequences' were yet 'let go without the mischief of a public division [among Calvinists]'.[133]

Robert Abbot was the only one of these authors who explicitly rejected Beza's supralapsarian doctrine by name. Nevertheless, he did this with care. Even when Abbot repudiated Beza's views and defended his own sublapsarian position as having the warrant of the primitive church and being most agreeable to Scripture, he did not accept the criticisms made of the potential consequences of supralapsarianism, allowing that 'Beza . . . and his followers may have their reasons for that they say, and yet so as to leave the iustice of God without impeachment or challenge.'[134] Although differing from Beza's supralapsarian doctrine, Abbot thus strongly denied that it impeached God's justice, and rejected the charge that Beza had taught predestination to damnation without respect of sin.[135] He also defended Calvin against the charge that he made God the author of sin, and defended Calvin and Beza's teaching on Christ's death and on the question of whether Christ despaired, against the charges made in the *Calvinoturcismus* of the Romanist pamphleteer Gifford. Thomas Rogers contrived to be even more tactful: when he condemned divines who

131 Carleton, *Examination*, p.9; Sutcliffe, *Briefe Censure*, pp.21–2, 29. Sutcliffe almost precisely mirrors Abbot's complaint that his opponent is confusing reprobation and damnation (*ibid*., p.24).

132 Willet, *Synopsis* (1613), pp.921–2; Carleton, *Examination*, p.10.

133 Hall, *Works*, IX: 503.

134 Abbot, *Third Part*, p.58. For Abbot's sublapsarianism, see *ibid*., pp.58–9.

135 *Ibid*., pp.54–5, 57.

enquired into which individuals and what proportion of people were saved or damned, the example that Rogers gave of this error was not an over-zealous Calvinist, but instead was those Romanist authors who declared that Calvin and Beza were reprobate.[136]

Disentangling oneself from continental Calvinist doctrine thus required considerable care, and was usually accompanied by certain rhetorical ploys which assured a Protestant audience of the writer's adherence to the Reformed tradition in general terms. Thus, in the works of Robert Abbot and George Hakewill, qualifications of Calvinist doctrine are buttressed by a careful defence of the personal reputations of Calvin and Beza against Romanist attacks.[137]

Dominant trends in English Calvinism undoubtedly differed from the regnant high Calvinism of the continent, and men such as Willet were not alone in their concern at the rigours of 'hyper-Calvinism' and its capacity to alienate fellow-Protestants. It is not surprising, then, that some English Calvinists displayed an initial reluctance to condemn the Dutch Remonstrants. Committed to securing Calvinist unity, and perhaps aware of the excesses of much Dutch Calvinism, Arthur Lake thus expressed hopes that the Remonstrants might be brought round at Dort if some of the more excessive elements of continental Calvinism were withdrawn from the propositions offered for their assent at the synod.[138] An irenical posture towards the Remonstrants was perfectly compatible with a Calvinist internationalism which, after all, sought to preserve the unity of Protestantism the better to defend it against the forces of Roman Catholicism. Yet even moderate Calvinists such as Ward and Davenant ultimately assured themselves that the Dutch Arminians were guilty of the Pelagian heresy. Carleton emphasized in his *Examination* of Montagu that the Remonstrants' doctrines were the same as the Pelagians, even if they pretended otherwise.[139] Even after their experiences of hyper-Calvinism at Dort, Davenant and Ward remained convinced of the Remonstrants' heresy and their lack of good faith. Davenant emphasized to Ward in a letter of February 1631 that, however much Arminians might *claim* to hold that God's grace was

136 *Ibid.*, pp.72–84, 96–106, 114–20, 124–8; Rogers, *Catholic Doctrine*, p.148.

137 Abbot, *Second Part*, pp.11–12; Hakewill, *Answere*, ii. pp.166–7, iii. p.19. Abbot also defended Calvin against Romanist criticisms of his doctrine of the godhead of Christ: *idem*, *Third Part*, pp.35–41. Hakewill's work is notable as a general defence of Calvin's teaching and reputation on a number of issues (see also ii. pp.137–72) and was published 'cum privilegio'.

138 Lake, 'Calvinism', p.60.

139 Carleton, *Examination*, pp.13, 14, 18, 30, 34–6, 43, 47, 64, 70, 79, 80, 106. Carleton specifically rejected the argument that the Arminians were not quite Pelagian, emphasizing that Pelagius himself had been inconsistent (pp.31–3). Instead, Carleton insisted that the 'Arminian heresie' went further than Pelagius (p.38). Note also Carleton's unpublished tract composed in 1617: Platt, 'Eirenical Anglicans', p.234.

absolute, yet 'when their woords are duly sifted' they could be shown to hold no such thing, but rather to maintain that a man's good will was contingent on man's free will, and preceded the purpose of God to give such a good will.[140]

CALVINIST UNITY UNDER PRESSURE: THE SYNOD OF DORT AND AFTER

Even if they identified the Dutch Arminians directly with the Pelagian heresy, English moderate Calvinists were still not obliged to give a blanket endorsement of Contra-Remonstrant theology. The extent of English episcopalian Calvinists' disaffection from the predestinarian theology of continental Calvinists was vividly demonstrated at the Synod of Dort. At Dort, as several recent historians have shown, the English delegates were committed by both the king's instructions and their own instincts to ensure that the Remonstrants were condemned, but that the emphasis of the canons should be pastoral and edificational. This would ensure that they could disarm potential opponents of orthodox Calvinism while ensuring Calvinist unity and keeping the door open to the more long-term goal of reconciliation with the Lutherans.[141] To this end, the delegates set out to make

[140] SSC, Ward Correspondence, Davenant to Ward, 1 Feb. 1630/1; Samuel Ward, *Gratia Discriminans* (1626); Bodl., Tanner MS 71 fol.10: Ward to Jerome Beale, 28 May 1629. A lone example of a sustainedly indulgent attitude adopted by an English Calvinist towards the Arminians' self-representation is provided by Joseph Hall. Hall's *Via Media* (written *c.*1624) was constructed around the assumption that the Arminians meant what they said when they declared election to be unconditional and God's grace to be absolute (Hall, *Works*, IX: 500–2, 512–13, 515–16). Hall allowed that the Arminians' claims might not necessarily be sincere, but was convinced that peace could only be built around being prepared to assume that they were. See especially Hall's exposition of the Arminians' defence of faith as so far being the gift of God that He works belief in man: 'which how fitly it holds suit with their other tenets, let it be their care to approve unto the church of God. I am sure an ingenuous constancy to this position might be a fair advantage taken for peace' (*ibid.*, p.502). Hall's intent was thus 'to make ... [the] best use of those savoury and wholesome sentences which fall from the better mood of an adversary' (p.518). His irenical reading was essentially political in inspiration: his ambition was 'the public tranquillity' (p.518). His own purely *doctrinal* stance was more unyielding: he publicly defended the Synod of Dort in 1629, declaring himself ready to 'live and die in the suffrage of that reverend synod, and do confidently avow that those other opposed opinions cannot stand with the doctrine of the Church of England' (*Works* VIII: 740). Moreover, he confessed that in his *Via Media* 'I have carried myself so indifferently, that as I have hid my own judgment, so I have rather seemed partial against my own resolutions' (*ibid.*, IX: 518). Hall does, however, consistently present the Church of England's position (and by implication his own) as a middle way between the doctrines of the Remonstrants and Contra-Remonstrants (IX: 506, 511, 514–15, 516).

[141] Lake, 'Calvinism', pp.53–5; see also Platt, 'Eirenical Anglicans'. It is important to grasp that Ward and the others were not simply describing a pre-existing 'Anglican' position, but were in fact in the very process of disentangling themselves from an earlier rigid

sure that the synod also acted to condemn the potentially antinomian excesses of the extreme Calvinism prominent among the Dutch Contra-Remonstrants – men such as Rippertus Sixtus, who taught that a faithful man could commit murder and adultery yet God could not damn him for it. The definitive Contra-Remonstrant statement at the Hague Colloquy was thus the subject of John Davenant's explicit condemnation.[142]

This determination to distance themselves explicitly from the excesses of the Contra-Remonstrants expressed itself in a variety of ways. The British delegates urged that their written determination of the articles in question should be read out aloud, so that their condemnations of Contra-Remonstrant doctrines should be recognized.[143] They also spent four sessions of the synod arguing for the explicit repudiation of a long list of Contra-Remonstrant passages. At the 130th Session Thomas Goad recited a catalogue of extreme Calvinist passages which the English delegates desired might be rejected by the synod, because both Remonstrants and Romanists made use of them to slander Reformed doctrine. They stuck particularly at the phrases 'that God moves the tongues of men to blaspheme' and 'that men are not able to do more good than they actually perform'. Despite their continued insistence that the passages be condemned, and the support of the delegates from Hesse and Bremen for this proposal, the president Johannes Bogerman and the Dutch delegates resolutely refused to comply. They argued at first that the synod should not presume to censure foreign divines. This was an argument which Sibrandus Lubbertus fatally undermined by claiming with some pride that some of the Dutch divines had taught even harsher doctrines than those which the British delegates wished to censure. Nevertheless, the British finally had to be satisfied with the inclusion of the phrase 'and many other such errors' in the canons, so that (as they explained) if they were reprimanded for not having rejected certain extreme predestinarian doctrines, members of the synod might justify themselves by referring to these words.[144]

Such proceedings inevitably caused friction. Nevertheless, the basic sublapsarian position, which helped to avoid some of the more extreme Contra-Remonstrant conclusions, and had been the focus of the delicate manoeuvring of Willet and others, was accepted by all the synod with the sole exception of Franciscus Gomarus. More dispute, however, was caused

Calvinism – a point which is illustrated by Dudley Carleton's complaints of 'the conceits which Dr Ward hath baptised with new words': PRO, SP 105/95 fol.51v.

142 Hales, *Golden Remains*, p.587; White, *Predestination*, p.189. For the quotation from Sixtus, and others from extreme Dutch and German Calvinists, see the hostile contemporary collection in Bodl., Rawlinson MS C.106 fols.8r–11r.

143 Hales, *Golden Remains*, pp.495–6.

144 *Ibid.*, pp.531–7; Brandt, *History*, III: 278–81. See also Hall's regretful remarks in a later letter to Crocius, one of the Bremen delegates: Hall, *Works*, X: 242–3.

by the fact that the English delegation proposed major alterations on the issue of the atonement. Here two of the delegates – Samuel Ward and John Davenant – chose to ally themselves with the moderate divines from Bremen in promoting the doctrine which has become known as hypothetical universalism, arguing that in a sense Christ died for all particular men, and not just for the elect. After Ward and Davenant had talked the other delegates round – helped by Davenant's insistence that the Church of England's confessional articles and liturgy supported his position (as well as by his declaration that he would rather have his right hand cut off than retract his views) – the British delegation defended this point at the synod.[145]

Not surprisingly, much conflict ensued. The ghost of English Calvinism past took the form of Gomarus, Arminius' doughtiest opponent. Gomarus had studied at Cambridge when William Perkins and William Whitaker were at the height of their fame, and he now cited both these writers against what he saw as an unrepresentative British position.[146] Other clashes also took place. Samuel Ward was involved in a disputatious correspondence which Ward himself described as a 'skirmishing' (*velitatio*) with the president of the synod, Bogerman, on the atonement. Ward also came in for harsh criticism on this subject from the Palatine delegates, especially Abraham Scultetus, chaplain to the Elector Palatine. Ward later complained of the jibe of 'more than half Remonstrant' which he had had to suffer at Dort.[147] Some of their continental colleagues' views on the atonement caused especial concern. Balcanquahall considered certain of the Dutch delegates' views on the Second Article to be not simply rigid, but clearly false, and (in a rhetorical style which was clearly becoming standardized among the British delegates) he declared himself prepared to lose his hand rather than subscribe to some of their arguments.[148] The extent of the division was demonstrated when Sibrandus Lubbertus angrily attacked the British delegates for not understanding the state of the Dutch Churches.[149] On the articles concerning free will and conversion the British delegates also strongly condemned Contra-Remonstrant positions,

145 Hales, *Golden Remains*, pp.470–3, 476–7, 577–91; White, *Predestination*, pp.187–92; Lake, 'Calvinism', pp.56–9; Tyacke, *Anti-Calvinists*, pp.96–8; John Platt, 'The British Delegation and the Framing of the Second Head of Doctrine at the Synod of Dort' (I am very grateful to Dr Platt for giving me a copy of this important unpublished paper).

146 Hales, *Golden Remains*, pp.512, 521.

147 Ward's account of his *velitatio* is SSC, Ward MS L4. Its contents are summarized in Lake, 'Calvinism', pp.57, 59. For the Palatine delegates' attacks on Ward, see Hales, *Golden Remains*, pp.512, 521; Ussher, *Works*, XV: 144–5.

148 Hales, *Golden Remains*, pp.509, 512.

149 *Ibid.*, pp.520, 527–8.

although they followed their general policy of not referring to specific authors.[150]

As the first prolonged confrontation of English Calvinists with their continental co-religionists, the synod provided other examples of English alarm at the doctrine of their foreign colleagues.[151] Nevertheless, the synod generally acted as a confirmation of the English Church's links with continental Calvinism. Although the British delegates would not agree to calling the synod's canons the doctrine of the Reformed Churches, and insisted that they were merely not repugnant to the articles of the Church of England, they did still ultimately subscribe to them.[152] Although they insisted on the removal from discussion of certain articles of the Belgic Confession relating to church government, the British delegates delivered a generally positive assessment of the doctrine of that Confession.[153] Similarly, while they disagreed with the Heidelberg Catechism on the interpretation of Christ's descent into hell, and vindicated the English Church's doctrine on this point from the Confessions of other churches, they generally gave the Catechism their approval.[154]

Despite all the conflicts at Dort, then, the synod still gave clear expression to the harmony of the Confessions of the different Reformed Churches, just as Carleton had urged in his first oration to the synod.[155] Whatever the reservations expressed over individual writers, the confessional statements of the Calvinist Churches themselves all went unquestioned. Although the final sessions of the synod were marred by Bogerman's tampering with the canons and the insertion of a personal censure of the Remonstrants (to which the British delegates were vehemently opposed), Walter Balcanquahall affirmed that, in the different delegations' doctrinal treatments of the five articles in dispute, 'praised be God for it, there was seen an incredible Harmony, far greater than almost could be hoped for in so great an Assembly of so many learned men'.[156]

The Dort canons were never ratified in England, although Festus Hommius was received with great courtesy when he formally presented copies of the *Acta* of the synod to James, Prince Charles and Archbishop Abbot, and he received a gift from the king on his departure from England, as well as an honorary doctorate from Oxford University.[157] Nevertheless, the support offered for the synod's canons by a range of opinion stretching from Joseph Hall to the separatist John Robinson was testimony to the

150 White, *Predestination*, pp.192–4. 151 See above p.412.
152 Hales, *Golden Remains*, pp.534–5, 537.
153 *Ibid.*, pp.543–4. 154 *Ibid.*, p.545. 155 White, *Predestination*, p.180.
156 Hales, *Golden Remains*, p.518.
157 P.J. Wijminga, *Festus Hommius* (Leiden, 1899), pp.310–12; *CSPD 1619–23*, pp.240–1.

bonds which still united English Calvinism.[158] Moreover, relations between the delegates after Dort remained at least formally amicable. Festus Hommius corresponded with Ward and Davenant and reminisced about the good old days at Dort; the Palatine divine Abraham Scultetus dedicated a theological work to Bishop Lake in 1620; and Joseph Hall reminisced with Bogerman in the 1630s about their time as students together in Cambridge.[159] The English Calvinist divines, whatever problems they had encountered at Dort, defended the synod's conclusions staunchly at home. The articles themselves were published at Oxford in 1623, and were reprinted in 1624. In the latter year, Bishop Carleton asked Abbot that the articles might be approved by Convocation. In 1629 John Prideaux insisted (incorrectly) at the Oxford Act that 'wee are concluded under an anathema to stand to the Synod of Dort against the Arminians'.[160] Carleton admitted that some divines, 'in zeale to correct this errour' of the Arminians 'have gone somewhat too farre on the right hand'. But nevertheless, when Richard Montagu attacked the Dutch Contra-Remonstrants, Carleton, for all his misgivings and conflicts with them, leapt to their defence, emphasizing that between the Dutch ministers and the Church of England 'in the matter of doctrine there hath beene a care of mutuall consent sought, and by his late Maiestie graciously entertained; and for the publicke good the desire thereof may be continued, though this man should be offended'.[161]

After Dort, the delegates' particular brand of moderate English Calvinism continued its uncertain and sometimes incoherent progress. The correspondence of Ward and Davenant, and of their friends William Bedell, James Ussher and George Downame in the years after Dort displays increasing disagreements and confusion as Ward and Bedell in particular attempted to confront the inter-relationships of grace, free will, predestination and the sacraments.[162] Davenant and Hall were also required to

158 See W.B. Patterson, 'The Synod of Dort and the early Stuart Church', in D.S. Armentrout (ed.), *This Sacred History* (Cambridge, Mass., 1990), p.207.

159 Abraham Scultetus, *Delitiae Evangelicae Pragenses* (Hanover, 1620), ep. ded.; Provinciale Bibliotheek van Friesland, Cod. II No.V fol.8, Cod. F G No.XIII fol.12r (Hall to Bogerman), Cod. F G No.XI fols.10v–11v (Carleton to Bogerman). I am very grateful to Dr Platt for kindly providing me with xeroxes of the Dutch manuscripts. Note also Hall's reference to 'my ancient and truly reverend friend, Mr. Bogermannus' in his *Defence of the Humble Remonstrance*: *Works*, IX: 359. Hommius' letters to Ward are printed in Wijminga, *Festus Hommius*, bijlage L, pp.xix–xxi.

160 Also note a bill in the 1625 parliament wishing to enact that the Synod of Dort's determinations might be received and established as part of the Church of England's doctrine, against which it would be unlawful to write anything: Tyacke, *Anti-Calvinists*, p.152.

161 Carleton, *Examination*, pp.10, 110.

162 Bedell, *Two Biographies*, pp.275–7, 279–80, 281–3, 284–6, 288–91, 298, 301–2, 303–10, 317–23, 335–6, 338–9, 362, 364–5, 371–96.

repeat their Dort experience in 1640 when they were called upon to mediate in the continuing struggles between one of the Bremen delegates at Dort – Ludovicus Crocius – and the accusations of Arminianism directed at him and his associates by another Dort veteran, Hendrik Alting. The peaceable agnosticism which they successfully enjoined on this occasion, as also in their contributions to John Dury's schemes for reunion with the Lutherans, might suggest a more fundamental disengagement from orthodox Calvinism.[163] Certainly Ward and Davenant's correspondence with their puritan friends William Twisse and Robert Jenison reveals a sense of strain as the puritans became aware that their conformist friends were not necessarily prepared to endorse their high Calvinist doctrine of limited atonement.[164]

But a full break between moderate and radical English Calvinism did not occur. It may well have been the case that it was the threat from Arminianism within the Church of England which effectively helped to keep English Calvinism together.[165] Certainly, Ward and Davenant spent much of the 1620s and 1630s refuting Arminian authors, and Davenant urged his friend to suppress his misgivings on the point of baptismal grace, explaining that 'at this time when the Arminians cleave so close to one another it is not convenient to be at such open controversies among ourselves'.[166] Their readiness to attack Arminianism also served to vindicate their own position in the eyes of their puritan supporters. When all was said and done, the English delegates at Dort had signed the synod's canons and were ready to stand by them. For all their reverent agnosticism on predestinarian issues and talk of the need to distinguish 'fundamentals' from 'non-fundamentals', they were prepared to condemn the Arminians

163 Hall, *Works*, X: 235–52; SUL, Hartlib MS 2/2 fols.3r, 8r, 11v, 26r, 5/2 fols.14–19 (cf. the comments of Morton, Bedell and Richardson on the doctrines of the Bremen divines: SUL, Hartlib MS 5/11 fols.1v–2r, 9/1 fol.34v, 5/21 fols.3r–v).

164 Bodl., Tanner MS 71 fol.143 (Jenison to Ward, 12 July 1632) (cf. fols.68, 102); SSC, Ward Correspondence: Twisse to Bishop Davenant, 18 April 1632. The moderate Calvinist Richard Holdsworth was also reported as opposing the hardline Calvinist Twisse on predestination in 1635: SUL, Hartlib MS 29/3 fol.39r. This is not to suggest that the more moderate Calvinists were advocating the abandonment of the significance of the doctrine of predestination in daily life. Davenant insisted 'they are in no wise to be hearkned unto who conceive that this doctrine of Election and Reprobation ought therefore to be quite buried in silence, because profane and wayward men do abuse it either to presumption and licentiousnesse or to despair and rechlesnesse': Davenant, *Animadversions*, p.516. See also the examples of 'excellent uses' following from the doctrine of predestination in *ibid.*, pp.516–35. Cf. Willet, *Thesaurus Ecclesiae*, pp.113–14.

165 I am grateful to Peter Lake for many discussions of this point.

166 Bodl., Tanner MS 71 fol.26r: Davenant to Ward, 15 Dec. 1629 (quoted in Lake, 'Calvinism', p.66); Davenant, *Animadversions*, *passim*; Ward, *Opera Nonnulla*, i. pp.40, 120, 128. Ward explicitly defended the Contra-Remonstrants' arguments made at the Hague Colloquy concerning the grace of conversion: Ussher, *Works*, XV: 404.

as heretics who adhered to orthodox doctrines merely for form's sake, and who refused to recognize that their other positions overturned such doctrines as a consequence. Ward and Davenant saw their own position in stark contrast to the creeping Pelagianism inherent in the Remonstrants' position. Calvinist divisions were played out behind a solid wall erected against Arminian heterodoxy, and in this respect Ward and Davenant's style of Calvinism resembled the rejection of Bezan extremism on the issue of the atonement which emerged in the Amyraldian movement in France.[167] Whatever the differences, a general sense of the unity of Reformed Protestantism was retained – and it was here that the Laudians' break with the past was most evident.

What was crucial in the disengagement from rigorous Calvinism on which English Calvinists embarked was the fact that they continued to appeal to, and to defer to, the authority of Calvin as a symbol of Reformed identity. Their rejection of the doctrine of Calvin's successors was encoded within, and legitimated by, a strong endorsement of the reputations of the foreign Reformed Churches. And it was the anti-Arminianism of these same moderate Calvinists which ensured that their 'minimalized interpretation' of Calvin's doctrines was not attacked by their puritan friends. If the deployment of these symbols of a common Reformed heritage was an effective means of legitimating an English Protestantism which was sometimes moving away from continental tenets, however, a number of divines were clearly beginning to find this required deference and lip-service rather stifling, especially when they found such labelling being used against them. This was partly because, in puritan hands, generally accepted symbols of Protestant orthodoxy were being used in order to root out all ideas of a less than Calvinist hue. Thus in 1582 Richard Swale had found himself identified as a papist in Caius College on the grounds that he had been reluctant to buy Calvin's catechism or Beza's confession. Everard Digby was similarly attacked as a crypto-papist in 1587, with part of the evidence against him being that 'he hath inveighed against Calvinians as schismatic and enemies of the church'. When Daniel Featley declared that anyone who condemned Calvin and Beza symbolized with papists, he thereby stated a simple fact (that Roman Catholics also attacked Calvin), but also identified this activity as the indelible mark of a crypto-popery which might not otherwise be easily detectable.[168]

[167] On Amyraldianism, see B.G. Armstrong, *Calvinism and the Amyraut Heresy* (Madison, 1969). See also Lake, 'Calvinism', p.61 n.74. It should be noted, however, that Davenant protested at the Amyraldians' attempts to claim the support of the British delegates for their views on the atonement: see M. Fuller, *The Life, Letters and Writings of John Davenant, D.D., 1572–1641* (1897), pp.192–200.

[168] C.N.L. Brooke, *A History of Gonville and Caius College* (Woodbridge, 1985), p.92; Lake, *Moderate Puritans*, p.172; Featley, *Clavis*, pp.604–5. The implication that anti-

In dogmatically Calvinist hands, this manipulation of the symbols of Reformed identity was being used in a rigid fashion as a means of denigrating recourse to patristic and medieval writings. In response, the more combative strain of anti-puritanism in the 1590s was already beginning to look askance at the adulation that was heaped on the Genevan divines. Richard Bancroft complained that

> I have heard it credibly reported that in a certaine Colledge in Cambridge, when it happeneth that in there disputations, the authority of Saint Augustine, or of St Ambrose, or of Saint Jerome, or of any other of the ancient Fathers: nay the whole consent of them alltogether is alledged: it is reiected with very greate disdaine: as: what tell you me of Saint Augustine, Saint Ambrose, or of the rest? I regard them not a rush: were they not men? Whereas at other time, when it happeneth that a man of another humor doth aunswere, if it fall out that he beinge pressed with the authority either of Calvin or Beza, shall chance to deny it: you shall see some beginne to smile, in commiseration of such the poore mans simplicity: some grow to be angry in regard of such presumption.

Such complaints should not be taken to brand Bancroft as an anti-Calvinist, however. The convert Humfrey Leech was crestfallen to discover how Bancroft's apparent aversion to Calvinism seemed to vanish when Leech attempted to attack Calvinist doctrines directly.[169]

Bancroft was not the only English Calvinist to protest against the constraints of the Calvinophilic straitjacket. John Dove had strongly endorsed Calvinism in a Paul's Cross sermon in 1596, but found himself severely criticized for irreverence when he ventured to disagree with Beza's views on the subject of divorce without craving pardon in a sermon at the same venue in 1601. In the preface to the printed version of this latter sermon, Dove complained of how Beza's authority 'is with some, more canonicall then the canonicall scriptures'. Much of his audience, he asserted, knew to cheer for Beza but were unacquainted with his writings: they 'have onely heard of his name, but knowe not how to spell it (for they call him Bezer, as also Bellarmine they call Bellamye) . . . it is [not] very likely they have read his workes, and are able to iudge of his doctrine'.[170]

Discontent with puritans' intimidatory manipulation of Calvinist

Calvinist sympathies had Romanist roots was not inherently improbable, however. Attacks on Calvin's doctrines and person were standard in Roman polemics, and are a more obvious source of anti-Calvinist ideas in England than imported Lutheran or Arminian writings, at least in the late Elizabethan and early Jacobean period: see Chaderton's cross-examination of Barrett (LPL, Lambeth MS 2550 fol.164v); Carier's interest in Rainolds' *Calvino-Turcismus* (Pattison, *Isaac Casaubon*, p.277); and the *Christian Letter*'s hints that Hooker's anti-Calvinism had been prompted by Romanist attacks on the Genevan reformer (Hooker, *Works*, IV: 57).

169 Bancroft, *Survay*, p.64; Humfrey Leech, *A Triumph of Truth* (Douai, 1609), p.116 – cited in Dent, *Reformers*, p.421.

170 John Dove, *Of Divorcement. A Sermon Preached at Pauls Crosse* (1601), sigs.A3r, A4r.

shibboleths was thus emerging, but initially this displeasure was not necessarily united with doctrinal dissension. While Bancroft and Dove's complaints would seem to chime in with Hooker's lament that it was 'safer to discuss all the saincts in heaven then M. Calvin', they did not necessarily see events with his eyes.[171] It would be wrong to conflate their frustrated resentment of unthinking partisanship simply with later 'anti-Calvinist' Laudianism. After all, the logic of the conformist position throughout the Elizabethan period (even as expounded by the most rigidly Calvinist divines) had involved an opposition to those who sought too enthusiastically to follow Geneva in matters of discipline as well as doctrine. Clearly there were some differences in conformist and puritan perceptions here. As we have noted, the axiom of Protestant doctrinal unity, and the Reformed heritage which accompanied it, was acknowledged by conformists and puritans alike in the Elizabethan and Jacobean Church, but was put to very different uses. Many puritans employed the point of the unity with foreign churches as a way of campaigning for changes in the discipline of the English Church. Conformist divines, by contrast, emphasized doctrinal unity with the foreign Protestant Churches in order to defend the essential orthodoxy of the English Church. The fact that all Calvinists appealed to Reformed doctrinal unity did not mean that they did not differ profoundly in their interpretation of it.

Nevertheless, the appeal to the foreign Reformed Churches carried potentially subversive undertones, while the uncritical and fiercely loyal defence of the Reformed tradition was becoming theologically stifling. These tendencies were breeding a more determined rejection of the Reformed inheritance, and of the symbolic value attached to it. Such developments were already gathering steam in the last decade of Elizabeth's reign. It is to this new breed of anti-Calvinism that we will now turn.

THE RISE OF ANTI-CALVINISM

As we have seen, most English Protestants would have argued that they were not slavish adherents of individual continental divines. Yet among some divines we can detect an increasing readiness to go further, to be less than courteous in detaching themselves from the ideas of foreign Reformed divines, and to ride roughshod over their symbolic value. These English divines used the charge of Calvinophilia in order to undermine the Reformed heritage more generally, rather than merely to correct the emphases of those puritans determined to use a strict adherence to Reformed authors as a shibboleth.

171 Hooker, *Works*, IV: 57–8.

The 1590s had seen strong conformist attacks upon the discipline of the foreign Calvinist Churches, although most divines attempted to restrict themselves to issues of polity, irrelevant to the essentially doctrinal unity of Reformed Protestantism. But it was comparatively easy for those of a non-Calvinist cast of mind to extend these criticisms into a more general condemnation of foreign Protestantism. William Bedell complained that his Roman convert friend James Wadsworth had mistakenly acquired anti-Calvinist notions in his youth by misreading the works of Hooker, Bancroft and Saravia, falsely construing them as opposing the *doctrine* of Calvin, as well as his discipline.[172] It is quite possible that Wadsworth was not alone. Certainly Hooker was not as careful as other writers to emphasize his doctrinal agreement with Calvin, and the authors of *A Christian Letter* feared the intent which might lie behind Hooker's assault on Calvin's reputation.[173]

Beyond Hooker's restrained attack on Geneva, it is possible to detect a more rigorous strain of thought among English divines who were anxious to dissociate the Church of England from the doctrinal stances of continental Protestantism. What served to make this current of conformist thought distinctive was the fact that many of these divines chose to make their dissension from the doctrine of the Reformed Churches explicit rather than implicit, and to place it within a more general condemnation of the prominence of Calvinist ideas in the Church of England. Moreover, they delighted in side-swipes at the paragons of Reformed orthodoxy. Rather than simply disagreeing with Calvin, they were anxious to denigrate him.

Inevitably, it was the doctrine of predestination, which had caused even moderate Calvinist divines such heartsearching, that was the focus of this more aggressive anti-Calvinism. An early example of this tendency was the sermon delivered by Samuel Harsnett at Paul's Cross in 1585. Harsnett's fierce attack on double predestination was striking in itself, but the sermon was all the more remarkable for the fact that it explicitly attacked Calvinist predestinarianism as a *Genevan* error, prompting Archbishop Whitgift to reprimand the future bishop never to speak on the subject of reprobation again. The explicit targeting of the foreign Reformed tradition was evident again, and met a similarly severe response from Whitgift, in William Barrett's troubles in Cambridge in the 1590s. Barrett combined an assault on more extreme predestinarian doctrines (which would not have been wholly objectionable to moderate Calvinist divines) with direct abuse levelled against some of the traditional paragons of Calvinist divinity, including Beza, Junius, Peter Martyr and Calvin himself.[174] This assault on

172 Bedell, *Certaine Letters*, p.127. 173 Hooker, *Works*, IV: 55–64.

174 While Barrett accused Calvin directly of blasphemy on one point, even he was, however, aware of the political dangers of explicitly damning all the Reformed Churches. He

men who had come to symbolize Reformed orthodoxy, with the corresponding implication that the Church of England did not identify with them, was condemned, not just by the rigidly Calvinist College Heads, but also by Archbishop Whitgift, and even by Adrianus Saravia.[175] The case of Saravia clearly shows that theorists of *iure divino* episcopacy were not yet prepared to be associated with explicit attacks upon the doctrine of the foreign Reformed Churches (for all that they might condemn the polity of these same churches in the most violent terms). Matthew Sutcliffe, one of presbyterianism's most implacable foes and the most fervent early proponent of *iure divino* episcopacy, was later to be a vigorous opponent of Richard Montagu's attempts to elide a condemnation of the Reformed Churches' discipline with an attack upon their doctrine.[176]

It was Calvinist doctrines of predestination that continued to come in for especial attack from anti-Calvinist divines in the early Stuart Church. The criticism was generally aimed at extreme Bezan-style predestinarianism, and was therefore in a sense not that far removed from the reservations that had been expressed by Davenant, Ward, Willet and others. The crucial difference, however, was that these were *public* attacks, and ones which sought to incriminate the traditional heroes of Reformed Protestantism, and the churches which followed them. Thus divines such as Montagu and Francis White launched direct attacks upon Calvin, Beza, the Church of Geneva and the Synod of Dort. Not surprisingly, they were attacked in turn for Arminian or crypto-popish tendencies. By contrast, it is notable that when the puritan Ezechiel Culverwell found himself attacked in the same year as Richard Montagu for maintaining a similarly inclusive doctrine of the atonement, Culverwell vindicated himself (as Montagu did not) by firmly condemning Arminius and defending the Synod of Dort.[177]

The face-saving fiction that Beza had departed from Calvin on the issue of predestination (so that an attack on Bezan doctrines need not incriminate Calvin himself) was also increasingly abandoned among the new breed of anti-Calvinists. Overall had not adopted this notion, and Montagu certainly made no attempt to use the ploy, as he credited Calvin with extreme opinions that implicitly contradicted the doctrine of the Church of England. Francis White's defence of Montagu was even more explicit in associating Calvin with the most extreme exponents of absolute reprobation – divines such as Beza, Trigland and Donteclock. White spelt

therefore utterly denied the charge that he had said that Calvin, Beza, Luther, Martyr and Junius were 'false guides' and 'such young teachers', offering to 'submit my self willingly to any punishment that your Grace [Whitgift] shal think meet to inflict upon me' if he had said any such thing: Strype, *Whitgift*, III: 320.

175 Nijenhuis, *Saravia*, p.133; Strype, *Whitgift*, III: 337.

176 Sutcliffe, *Briefe Censure*, p.36.

177 Culverwell, *Briefe Answere*, sigs.A4r–A5r, A8v, A10r.

out the implications of this doctrine in tones of horror not necessarily far removed from those of Davenant and others. By including Calvin himself among its supporters, however, White implied a far more damning indictment of the doctrine of the foreign Reformed Churches. If White's ecclesiology has at times seemed closer to more traditional lines of thought than that of his Laudian colleagues, his attack on Calvin and Calvinist doctrine here is by contrast as scathing as any attempted by the most audacious Laudian preacher. The distance between the Laudian and moderate Calvinist positions on this issue is exemplified by the way in which Francis White was forced to distort moderate Calvinist writings before he could make them seem to support the Laudian stance. White thus misquoted Robert Abbot's own attack on doctrines of absolute reprobation by inserting into the text the name 'Calvinus', thus transforming an attack on extreme Calvinists into a general assault on the Calvinist tradition, and the teaching of Calvin himself.[178] Thus, as Peter Lake has emphasized, English anti-Calvinism made no attempt to represent itself as the Amyraldian movement did in France, as a return to 'true' Calvinism in reaction to the extremes of Bezan doctrine. As such, it marked a far more self-conscious break with the Reformed tradition.[179]

Anti-Calvinists described the Synod of Dort in similarly dismissive terms. Laud and his colleagues used allegations of closet presbyterianism to discredit the synod *in toto*, as well as condemning the predestinarian doctrines expounded there.[180] An additional ploy was adopted by Francis White. Although the British delegates had ultimately joined ranks in defence of the synod and its decrees, White instead chose to emphasize the stark difference between the written determinations of the British dele-

178 Bodl., Rawlinson MS C.573 fols.32r–33v. Compare the citation of Abbot (fol.33v) with Robert Abbot, *De Gratia et Perseverentia Sanctorum* (1618), praefatio ad lectorem, sig.C2r. White's adroitness here has misled at least one more recent commentator: see Sharpe, *Personal Rule*, p.293. Abbot's rejection of absolute reprobation here was also noted by Dr Walter Raleigh in a court sermon probably delivered in the 1630s: Walter Raleigh, *Reliquiae Raleighanae* (1679), pp.181–2. White also omitted Abbot's attack on Bertius (which balances Abbot's rejection of Perkins in the first half of the sentence) and his description of Perkins as 'noster'. White's position represents a certain hardening of his earlier stance in his *Orthodox Faith* of 1617, where he defended Calvin and Beza by emphasizing that they denied God to be the author of sin, and cited Robert Abbot, Morton, Field and Hakewill's vindications of Calvin's position on this point (pp.227–8). Even here, however, there were hints of White's later sense of detachment in his anxiety to emphasize that 'we of the Church of England are no Calvinists' (by the testimony of Bellarmine, no less), and that therefore 'it is uniust to blame us for their doctrine if it be faultie' (*ibid.*, p.227).

179 White, *Predestination*, p.165; Bodl., Rawlinson MS C.573 fols.34r–35v; Lake, 'Calvinism', p.61 n.74.

180 Laud, *Works*, VI: 246; Bodl., Rawlinson MS C.573 fol.56r; Montagu, *Appello*, p.108. For the delegates' response to the accusations of having supported foreign presbyterianism, see below ch.9.

gation and those of all the other delegates.[181] Even more insultingly, however, the synod might be treated as an irrelevance. Montagu's apathy is as striking as his denunciations of the synod: 'What Ends men had in that synod I know not, nor am curious to enquire how things were carried, I as little understand or care.'[182]

The anti-Calvinist divines' repudiations of the Contra-Remonstrant position were merely one aspect of their taste for conscious assaults on the Reformed tradition in general. Montagu insisted that he could not see why Calvinists should be preferred before Lutherans: 'John Calvin came after in time, and was but a secondary unto Martin Luther; entring in upon his Labours and Reversions: and why should he challenge any priviledge of preferment above Martin Luther?' Montagu complained of his opponents that 'you would make the World beleeve that Ecclesia Anglicana Calvinistat; as if he were the father & founder of our Faith; as if our beleefe were to be pinned unto his sleeve, and absolutely to be taught after his Institutions'. When defending Montagu against the inevitable charges of anti-Calvinism which ensued, White constructed the same straw man as Montagu had done, implying that Montagu's opponents held that Calvin's doctrine was binding upon members of the Church of England. Like Montagu, however, White was concerned not simply to assert that the Church of England was not bound by Calvin's theology, but also made a strong attack on Calvin and his ideas. He then instructed those adhering to Calvin's *doctrine* to read Hooker's preface to the *Laws*, thereby taking this to impugn Calvin's *doctrinal* authority too (just as the Roman convert Wadsworth had done). White then quoted Robert Abbot's praise of Hooker as a scourge of Catharists in order to imply that Abbot approved of Hooker's attack on Calvin.[183]

It was not simply a rejection of Calvinist doctrine that lay at the roots of this disaffection. While most Laudians undoubtedly feared the antinomian consequences (as they saw them) of some Calvinist doctrines, there were few who saw them as fundamental errors and heresies in themselves. William Laud was able to declare in his *Conference with Fisher* that all Protestants agreed with the Church of England 'in the chiefest doctrines, and in the main exceptions which they jointly take against the Roman

181 Bodl., Rawlinson MS C.573 fol.36r. Cf. fol.33v, where the British delegates' suffrage is depicted as refuting 'Calvinian' (as opposed to Contra-Remonstrant) tenets concerning reprobation.

182 Montagu, *Appello*, pp.70–1. Cf. pp.107–8. This apathy is all the more striking as Montagu elsewhere saw the polemical value in expressing his esteem for the British delegates at Dort, and observed that the synod's declarations were in some cases more moderate than those of his current opponents (*ibid.*, pp.69, 108).

183 Bodl., Rawlinson MS C.573 fols.32r–33v; Montagu, *Appello*, 46–7, 58–9.

Church'.[184] While he counselled against their being taught to students too early in their university careers, Laud still granted that Calvin's *Institutes* 'may profitably be read, and as one of their first books for divinity, when they are well-grounded in other learning'. Essentially, Laudians felt a particular animus against Calvin and Calvinist doctrine because of the *de facto* authority that they had established in the Elizabethan and Jacobean Church. Richard Montagu's *New Gagg* was composed explicitly in order to achieve what Carier and Archbishop de Dominis had earlier craved: the removal of Calvinist doctrines from the Church of England's formal polemic by means of a rigid distinction between the church's public resolutions and the private opinions (no matter how widespread) of her members. The Church of England, Montagu claimed, was at a great disadvantage with her adversaries because she had tenets pressed upon her as her established doctrine, which were in fact only the 'Problematical Opinions of private Doctors, or fancies of Factious men.' 'Such disadvantages hath this Church too long endured', he warned.[185] Under Laud, it would endure them no longer.

Given these convictions, assaults upon the integrity of the paragons of Reformed Protestantism served a useful purpose in undermining alternative (and in Laudian eyes potentially subversive) sources of authority. They were thus not isolated or unintentional skirmishes. There were increasing complaints from the 1590s onwards that attacks on Calvin were getting out of hand. In Oxford, William Twisse later reported having heard how in one of the colleges, 'questions were set up to be disputed "Contra Johannem Calvinum"; and that disputations of that nature were sometimes concluded in this manner, "Relinquamus Calvinum in hisce faecibus"'.[186] Andrew Willet inserted into the 1613 edition of his *Synopsis* a complaint of how 'some among us indeed ascribe too little to Luther, Calvin, Beza, and such other worthy instruments', claiming that those that did so were men 'besotted with' Roman scholastic divinity. A puritan petition at the beginning of James' reign forwarded a similar complaint.[187]

It was not simply puritans who were alarmed. Conforming Calvinists, and even bishops, made eloquent complaint in the 1610s and 1620s of the attacks being made upon the persons and doctrines of the leading lights of the Reformed Church. Robert Abbot lamented how 'every ignorant brablet' attacked Calvin, but claimed that, despite these attacks, Calvin

184 The crucial word here may be 'jointly' – allowing the Church of England to distance herself from any anti-papal doctrine which she did not herself explicitly hold.

185 Laud, *Works*, V: 117; Montagu, *New Gagg*, pp.323–4; *idem*, *Appello*, ep. ded.

186 Twisse, *Of the Morality*, p.42 ('38'). Twisse claimed to have heard this report while at Oxford, where he studied 1596–1612.

187 Willet, *Synopsis* (1613), p.85; Bodl., Bodley MS 124 p.170.

went on his stately way. John Prideaux raised similar warnings in a sermon in Oxford in 1614, contrasting 'Luther's zeal' and 'Calvins judicious painfulness' with the 'mongrell temporizers, that are so forward to censure them'. Matthew Sutcliffe and George Carleton protested at Montagu's too ready abuse of Calvin. Sutcliffe was particularly enraged by Montagu's treatment of the Genevan Reformer. He condemned Montagu's failure to preface Calvin's name with 'Master', and compained that Montagu talked as if Bellarmine were to be prized equally with Calvin or Luther. Calvin and Luther were lauded by Sutcliffe as 'great discoverers of the popes Antichristian heresie and policy'. Carleton too demanded to know why Calvin's name and doctrine should be made odious – if the Genevan Reformer had written anything amiss, this was a common human failing. John Yates depicted 'uniust slanders' against Calvin as being 'a thing too usuall', and voiced his own suspicion that such attacks were deliberately made in order 'to derogate from that truth, whose strength was not built upon mans weaknesse'.[188]

The most intemperate attacks upon Calvin were made by men who were clearly fringe figures, tapping into the enormous stocks of Romanist anti-Calvin material. None of these crypto-papists was more vehement than Benjamin Carier, who condemned Calvin as a 'factious fugitive', and his *Institutes* as a 'packet of Schism & atheism'. Carier, however, was a royal chaplain and friend of Casaubon, and cannot entirely be disregarded as an obscure extremist. Others were still more prominent. John Overall, Whitaker's successor as Regius Professor of Divinity in Cambridge, was reproved by the provost for speaking ill of another Reformed divine, Amandus Polanus, and responded by denigrating him further.[189] For all his much vaunted moderation, Overall could clearly be an outspoken critic of foreign Reformed divines. He was reported as saying, when Calvin's *Institutes* were cited in disputation, 'why cite you Calvin? I have studied divinity more yeares than he was yeares of age when he wrote his *Institutions*.'[190]

Richard Montagu had certainly been the most comprehensive in his critique of the foreign Calvinists, but it was not until the 1630s that the open abuse of established Reformed divines became a popular sport. It was then reported of John Normanton of Caius College that 'he usually carried about with him an extract of Calvins errors (as he called them) which in all

188 Abbot, *Second Part*, p.148; Prideaux, *Ephesus Backsliding*; Sutcliffe, *Briefe Censure*, p.20; Carleton, *Examination*, p.61; Yates, *Ibis*, ii. pp.3–4.

189 BCO, MS 270 pp.155, 156; CUL, MS Gg/1/29 fol.104r. Overall also claimed that a work by Polanus had been refused a licence by Bishop Bancroft's examiners in London (presumably because of presbyterian passages), although no other evidence survives to substantiate this.

190 Tyacke, *Anti-Calvinists*, p.142.

companyes he read to ye disgrace of him'.[191] William Twisse made complaint of having heard, at the Oxford Act in 1634, 'Calvinists reckoned up amongst Papists, Pelagians, Arminians, Puritans, as sectaries at least, if not as Heretiques'. Bastwick claimed that at his sentencing in the High Commission Court some of the bishops there present spoke 'very revilingly & basely of Mr. Calvin'. John Howson aimed, not at an individual writer, but at the Geneva Bible itself when he attacked its marginal notes as supposedly agreeing with Arians and Jews, through their failure to gloss certain particular passages as relating to the Trinity or anticipating Christ.[192] Samuel Harsnett, as archbishop of York, was reported in 1630 to have banned the sale within his province of the works of William Perkins and Zacharius Ursinus. Finally, Richard Baylie in 1630, acting as archdeacon of Nottingham, warned ministers not to 'dispute of modern divines among the reformed churches'.[193]

Laudians combined these attacks with demands that rules and canons be produced to oblige them to that deference which had previously been yielded as a natural expression of pan-Protestant identity. 'I [do not] finde it in the Articles of the Church of England that Calvin or Beza are to bee preferred before Saint Austin or Aquinas', Peter Heylyn observed. Similarly, Montagu pointed out matter of factly that the Church of England did not command him to follow Calvin rather than Luther by 'any Rule, Canon, Law or Authority'.[194]

It is important to emphasize, however, that Laudians' distaste for the Calvinist tradition was not pathological. Laudian pamphleteers were not above citing foreign Calvinist divines in support of anti-Sabbatarian arguments in the 1630s, obviously relishing the discomfort of their more self-consciously Calvinist opponents.[195] Writers such as Heylyn and Dow did this with a conscious and heavy-handed irony which partly justified Burton's complaints of cynicism and hypocrisy: 'a bad cause is glad of any Patron, or advocate to plead for it, though the Client have openly stigmatised him for a rascall'. Nevertheless, Francis White was offended at the suggestion that he had appealed to Reformed divines while habitually scorning them elsewhere. White emphasized instead that 'we reverence and much respect all learned and godly Divines, in what Church so ever they live, or teach; yea, although in some Theologicall Questions wee take liberty (upon just reason) to dissent from them'.[196] Moreover, divines such

[191] BL, Harleian MS 7019 fol.66. See also the attack on Calvin's doctrine of election by Thomas Gibson, vicar of Horncastle: Hill, 'Royalist clergy', p.59.

[192] D'Ewes, *Journal*, p.241; Bodl., Rawlinson MS D.320 fols.47r–65v.

[193] Bodl., Rawlinson MS C.421 fol.27; Tyacke, *Anti-Calvinists*, p.183.

[194] Heylyn, *Briefe Answer*, p.119; Montagu, *Appello*, pp.46–7.

[195] See above n.118.

[196] Heylyn, *History of the Sabbath*, preface; Dow, *Discourse*, p.2; Twisse, *Of the Morality*, p.42 ('38'); Burton, *Lords Day*, p.46; White, *Examination*, p.141. However, for a more

as Montagu and Laud were quite capable of praising even Beza on particular points of interpretation, and Laud would appear to have been prepared to defend Beza against Romanist accusations of predestinarian extremism.[197] The crucial point, however, is that Laud's defence of Beza was made in private annotations, rather than in public. His outward position was determined by the need publicly to dissociate the Church of England from the foreign Reformed Churches of the continent.[198]

This desire was also evident in the way that Laud dealt with collections for the Palatinate. As we have seen, these had usually provided an opportunity for the reaffirmation of English Protestant unity with the continent. However, Laud insisted on purging a passage in the proposed brief which described the Palatine ministers as suffering 'for their sincerity and constancy in the true Religion, which we, together with them do professe, and which we are all bound in conscience to maintaine to the utmost of our powers'. In lieu of this passage, Laud inserted the non-committal phrase that the ministers 'suffered for their Religion'.[199]

The most significant development, however, was that Carier, Barrett, Montagu and others followed Roman writers in their explicit use of the word 'Calvinist' as a term of abuse against their opponents. Barrett had been accused in his first retraction of having berated Peter Martyr, Beza, Zanchius, Junius and others as 'Calvinists'.[200] Carier went substantially further in identifying a 'Calvinist' takeover of the English Church in tracts composed before, as well as after, his conversion to Rome.[201] Montagu used the term as a way of disparaging a whole range of doctrines to which he was opposed, including the belief that the pope was Antichrist.[202] These were all doctrines which had their fair share of English Protestant supporters. Small wonder, then, that the leading lights of English Calvinism, who

opportunistic use by White of Calvin and Beza's position on the sabbath as a way of attacking puritan inconsistency in urging their authority on other doctrinal matters, see Bodl., Rawlinson MS C.573 fol.32v.

197 E.g. Montagu, *ΘΕΑΝΘΡΩΠΙΚΟΝ*, i. pp.7–8; Laud, *Works*, VI: 696, 698, 703, 704 (discussed in White, *Predestination*, pp.278–80). Even Montagu suggested that the title of 'Calvinist' was 'more honourable than Gomarian or Arminian' (*Appello*, p.10).

198 Nevertheless, when he was under political pressure in December 1632, Laud would make a point in a Christmas sermon at court of quoting Calvin 'divers times with a great deal of respect', 'which was much marvelled at by the auditory': *Court and Times of Charles I*, II: 214.

199 Prynne, *Canterburies Doome*, p.392. Prynne neatly contrasts this action with the terms used by Archbishop Abbot to promote the collection for relief for the inhabitants of Wesel in 1618 (*ibid.*, pp.392–3). For Laud's reply to this charge, in which he denied having intended to suggest that the religion of the Reformed Churches and of the Church of England was not the same, see *ibid.*, p.540.

200 Strype, *Whitgift*, III: 318–19.

201 Carier, *Treatise*, p.37; BCO, MS 270 p.156; Hakewill, *Answere*, ii. pp.167–8.

202 Montagu, *Appello*, pp.50–1, 158–9 (cf. *ibid.*, pp.114–15; *New Gagg*, p.214); Cosin, *Correspondence*, I: 85, 95.

had most commanded the respect of Calvinist scholars abroad, were also increasingly the subject of Laudian disdain. At the Synod of Dort the British divines had shifted in discomfort as Gomarus propounded supralapsarian doctrines against them with the authority of Perkins and Whitaker. By the early 1630s, William Twisse was complaining to Bishop Davenant that 'some in noe meane place . . . professe it had bene better for the Church of England if Mr. Perkins had never bene borne'.[203]

LAUDIANS AND CONTINENTAL ANTI-CALVINISM

Most avant-garde conformists, and later Laudians, would thus seem to have been engaged in a process of disengagement from the orthodoxies and symbols of the continental Calvinist Churches. But if they emphatically did not share the sense of identity with the Calvinist Churches of the continent which other English churchmen held with varying degrees of intensity, what was the Laudians' attitude towards the continental anti-Calvinists? Did they constitute for these divines an alternative 'Protestant Cause'?

It is certainly true that Laudians did not choose to denounce the Dutch Arminians in the sort of language adopted by even moderate Calvinists such as Davenant. Indeed, they rarely discussed them in public. Their renunciation of the extreme Calvinist doctrines of the Contra-Remonstrants was thus not combined with anti-Arminianism in the manner of a Culverwell or Hall. Christopher Potter, for example, refused to become an Arminian or to 'take part with them in any Faction',[204] but chose to emphasize the Arminians' accuracy in identifying faults in the hyper-Calvinist case which required amendment, and did not specify any Arminian errors.[205] Moreover, Potter explicitly distanced himself from prevalent forms of anti-Arminianism, depicting them as a folly of his youth, when he too had attacked Arminians from the pulpit as the new heretics, 'yet all the while I tooke all this that I talkt, upon trust, and knew not what they said, or thought, but by relation from others; and from their enemies'. After reading Arminian writings he had been cured of this ignorant zeal, and now firmly denied that the Arminians should be labelled as heretics.[206]

This attempt to downplay anti-Arminianism illustrates in itself a move away from continental Calvinism. While not all divines involved in the

203 Tyacke, *Anti-Calvinists*, pp.182–3; SSC, Ward Correspondence (unfoliated bundle): William Twisse to Bishop Davenant, 18 April 1632.

204 Bodl., Sancroft MS 21 p.61 ('The Protestation of Dr Potter, 1631'); Plaifere, *Appello Evangelium*, pp.412, 413, 433 ('Dr Potter His own Vindication of Himselfe'). Note also Montagu, *Appello Caesarem*, pp.10, 42–3, 54

205 Bodl., Sancroft MS 21 p.61; Plaifere, *Appello Evangelium*, pp.417, 419–21.

206 Plaifere, *Appello Evangelium*, pp.414–15, 427–8.

Durham House circle, or later supporters of Laud, manifested clear opinions on predestinarian issues, they generally refrained from condemning the Dutch Arminians, whose opinions were naturally conducive to their own more sacramental soteriology.

This is not to say that such clerics identified closely with the Dutch Arminian movement. There undoubtedly were *some* personal contacts, though. Richard Thomson, a fellow of Clare College, had known Hugo Grotius and kept up a correspondence with friends in Holland – in 1608 he wrote to Dominic Baudius of Arminius' growing reputation in Cambridge.[207] Grotius visited Andrewes and Overall during his sojourn in England in 1613, and Samuel Harsnett had contacts with the Netherlands by the early 1620s. Dutch Arminian writings were also cited and defended by a number of other authors, such as Samuel Brooke, Jerome Beale and Matthew Wren, while Richard Montagu would seem to have exploited Petrus Bertius' *De Apostasia Sanctorum*, and certainly admired and profited from Arminius when he finally borrowed the Dutchman's writings from his friend John Cosin.[208] Nevertheless, the impetus behind direct contacts seems generally to have come from the Dutch side. Petrus Bertius wrote to William Barlow imploring his support merely on the basis of having read his account of the Hampton Court Conference. Grotius' cultivation of Andrewes was to the latter's extreme embarrassment, and it was the Remonstrants who suggested Buckeridge and Neile as more favourable British delegates for the Synod of Dort. Similarly, Laud's contact with Grotius in the 1620s was only reluctant and via a third party.[209]

John Overall was probably the only major English divine who corresponded directly with the continental Arminians. He was a regular and enthusiastic correspondent of Hugo Grotius in the 1610s, and promised in August 1617 to promote 'causam vestram', which he constantly commended to God in his prayers, whenever he had the opportunity.[210] Certainly

207 Dominicus Baudius (ed.), *Epistolarum Centuriae Tres* (Leiden, 1620), iii. pp.730–1 – cited in White, *Predestination*, p.169; Tyacke, *Anti-Calvinists*, p.36.

208 Tyacke, *Anti-Calvinists*, pp.36, 40, 48, 50–1, 164. Note also the contemporary annotations in the copies of Daniel Featley's *Pelagius Redivivus* and *A Second Parallel* in CUL, shelfmark Peterborough K.2.22, which cite and defend Dutch Arminian authors.

209 Bodl., Rawlinson MS E.186 fol.161r: Bertius to Bishop William Barlow, 20 September 1611; Tyacke, *Anti-Calvinists*, pp.20, 70, 120; White, *Predestination*, pp.167–8, 205.

210 White, *Predestination*, pp.165–6, 176; C. Hartsoeker and P. Limborch (eds.), *Praestantium ac Eruditorum Virorum Epistolae Ecclesiasticae et Theologicae* (Amsterdam, 1684), p.485. See also Tyacke, *Anti-Calvinists*, pp.89, 127. It is debatable how far contacts between Remonstrants and English churchmen 'operated towards compromise', as Peter White suggests (p.166). The Remonstrants were clearly anxious to gain direct support from England through men such as Overall, in order to frustrate the designs of the Contra-Remonstrants. That the English churchmen were not prepared to let themselves

Archbishop Abbot and his associates were fully aware of these links. Nevertheless, Grotius would appear to have recognized that neither Overall nor Andrewes would risk directly identifying their own position with that of the Remonstrants.[211] After Dort Andrewes praised Grotius in private, but does not seem to have responded to the Dutchman's letters, following Laud's example in keeping the Dutchman at arm's length.[212] There is less evidence for direct links or substantial reading of Arminian treatises among avant-garde conformists after the mid-1620s. The exchange of respectful correspondence between Vossius and Laud hardly constitutes a rival of the Calvinist 'republic of letters' which we have seen at work.

There are a number of possible reasons for this absence of direct links, and relative lack of interest among avant-garde conformists. Part of the answer is clearly strategic: if Dutch Arminians had become archetypes of crypto-popery, it did the avant-garde conformists' cause no good to be associated with them, especially as after Dort they were a broken reed unable to offer any favours in return. Moreover, the Durham House Group had bought their freedom in the Church of England essentially through the king's Declaration, which had prohibited all discussions of predestinarian issues. Infringement of this directive would needlessly provoke their opponents, as well as enabling critics to charge them with having opposed the king's will. More generally, however, this low profile suited the Durham House divines and their followers as they seem on a more fundamental level to have been less concerned with issues specifically relating to the doctrine of predestination than were their Dutch counterparts.

The Laudians' relative lack of interest in pursuing predestinarian issues was partly a function of the fact that extreme Calvinist doctrines were less established in England than in the Netherlands, and hence prompted less direct a response by posing less of an immediate threat. But, as several historians have noted, this restrained handling of predestinarian issues after the upheavals of the 1610s and early 1620s was more rooted in the fact that these divines were less concerned to construct an alternative doctrine of predestination in the first place. Rather, their interests were far removed from Calvinism, or even anti-Calvinism. The writings of Laud and his associates make it clear that their main preoccupation was with developing

be drawn into the conflict was not necessarily a manifestation of general irenical principles.

211 White, *Predestination*, p.166.

212 *Ibid.*, p.205 (Vossius, *Epistolae*, ii. p.29). A closer contact was G.J. Vossius (White, *Predestination*, pp.206–7). Vossius' connections with the Remonstrants were always more tenuous (he kept up a correspondence with Gomarus until the latter's death). While his English friends were not exclusively of Durham House, it is nevertheless true that his *History of Pelagianism* led to some muted criticism from English Calvinists.

a style of piety more closely oriented around the sacraments and the liturgy, and towards redefining the status of the clergy in relation to them. Their main interest was therefore in ritual and the condition of the visible institutional church; they could generally live with a certain ambiguity on predestinarian points. Such divines would only need to resort to direct anti-Calvinism on predestinarian issues at those times when Calvinist doctrines were clearly being used as barriers to the realization of the sacramental and sacerdotal implications of Prayer Book ritual.[213]

This is not to suggest, however, that Arminian doctrines were not potentially more amenable to such a style of divinity. Their universalist elements, their flight from more rigid forms of Calvinist determinism and their accompanied desire to reassert the need for men to strive to attain their own salvation, were all amenable to the pastoral emphases central to the Book of Common Prayer. Nevertheless, the Laudians' sacramental and sacerdotal preoccupations were not necessarily prominent in the writings of the Dutch Arminians, and there were thus severe limits to the amount of common ground which Laudians and Remonstrants shared, outside their joint concern to oppose the rigours of Bezan predestinarianism. John Overall, for example, was fully aware of the fact that Grotius' ideas of the nature of episcopacy were far distant from his own.[214]

Moreover, as the Arminians became the party of opposition and separation in the Netherlands, and as they became the spokesmen of 'libertas prophetandi', so they doubtless offended the more typically Laudian commitment to the defence of the institutional church. They were certainly unwelcome to Richard Montagu by the 1630s. While he praised their rejection of Calvin and Beza, Montagu complained of the Remonstrants' support for 'licentious liberty of Prophecying', and also their drift towards Socinian and even Gnostic heresies in their interpretation of Old Testament prophecies of Christ's coming.[215]

Laudian identification with the Remonstrants was thus not greatly in evidence. However, the Laudians viewed the conflict in the Netherlands from a fundamentally different set of priorities than those of moderate or radical Calvinists. To the Laudians, the Remonstrants were not in any sense heretics. Indeed, of the two extremes, the Arminians were seen at worst as tolerably overzealous, whereas extreme Calvinists were considered to be actively dangerous. Among the British delegates at Dort, precisely the opposite view obtained: it was the Contra-Remonstrants who

213 Raymer, 'Durham House', pp.97–109.

214 Mason, *Church of England*, p.80. The British delegates at Dort were also anxious to emphasize that the Remonstrants were as strongly in favour of a ministerial parity as their Contra-Remonstrant opponents: Fuller, *John Davenant*, p.100.

215 Montagu, *Acts and Monuments*, pp.47–9.

were seen as being merely overzealous (though requiring fraternal admonition so as not to offend weaker brethren), whereas the Remonstrants were the actively dangerous and potentially (if not actually) heretical party. Other Laudian divines merely adopted an even-handed assessment of the continental divisions. Using the same sort of language as the Protestant irenicists, writers such as Christopher Potter at the same time effectively distanced themselves from the exponents of continental Calvinist orthodoxy. This constituted a serious re-evaluation of relationships between the Reformed Churches.

If the Remonstrants were not ultimately seen as the Laudians' partners, did the burgeoning anti-Calvinism of Laud and his followers lead them to assess more positively those most dedicated anti-Calvinists, the Lutherans? The question of a potential Lutheran influence on Laudian attitudes has been raised by Basil Hall, and the combination would appear natural.[216] Certainly, there was much in the Lutheran Churches that would appeal to Laudian divines. Although practice undoubtedly varied, many Lutheran Churches at this time retained a high ceremonialism which would have made Lancelot Andrewes' mouth water. Seventeenth-century Lutherans generally retained the altar with ornaments against the east wall of the chancel, along with the sign of the cross over the elements, and the sacring bell at the elevation of the host. They usually knelt at the words of institution and received the sacrament in this posture. Images were also retained. When Bulstrode Whitelocke visited Skara Cathedral in Sweden in 1654 he described how

> in the Choir are many pictures of saints and other images; and att the east end of it a high altar, with a rich carpet of velvet embroidered with gold, and a stately crucifix upon it: there are also divers other and lesser crucifixes in several places of the church and Choir. In the vestry ... chalices and pyxes, with pieces of wafer in them; and none could see a difference between this and the Papists' Churches.[217]

Similarly, Lutheran doctrines of adiaphorism, and their anti-Calvinist predestinarian theology were well known and would obviously be welcome to Laudian ears. The early seventeenth century also witnessed an

[216] Hall, 'The early rise', pp.127–8. See also Collinson, *Birthpangs*, p.148.

[217] M. Roberts, 'The Swedish Church' in *idem* (ed.), *Sweden's Age of Greatness 1632–1718* (1973), p.137 – quoting B. Whitelock, *A Journal of Swedish Ambassy* (1855), i. pp.187–8; G.L.C. Frank,'The theology of eucharistic presence in the early Caroline divines, examined in its European theological setting' (University of St Andrews PhD, 1985), pp.195, 371–2. See also the earl of Leicester's description of Danish Lutheran churches in 1632: *HMC De l'Isle* VI: 34; cf. Harrab, *Tesseradelphus*, sig.Biiir. Lutheran churches in Calvinist countries could be much more austere though: see the description in Sir William Brereton, *Travels in Holland the United Provinces, England, Scotland and Ireland*, ed. E. Hawkins (Chetham Society 1, 1844), pp.63–4.

increasing emphasis on the Fathers, and the claim to catholicity, among Lutheran divines.[218]

There is little evidence to suggest that English anti-Calvinism in the 1590s drew directly upon Lutheran writings – some of the early barbed comments about Calvin made by English Protestants may well have been inspired by Romanist authors, and many of the later condemnations of Calvinist predestinarianism echo Romanist accusations just as clearly as they mirror Lutheran attacks on Genevan doctrine.[219] Examples of divines finding inspiration in Lutheranism, or promoting a greater appreciation of those churches, are occasionally found among the English anti-Calvinists, although they are something of a rarity. Richard Hooker had expressed little interest in the Lutherans. Indeed, he had emphasized their desperate errors (and consequent division from the Church of England) in order to promote his argument that the Church of Rome, with her own doctrinal errors, should not be regarded as an altogether alien church.[220] Other authors wrote more charitably, although their comments rarely stretched beyond the sort of irenically minded remarks which we have seen on occasion in the writings of even the most implacable extreme Calvinists.

Some divines, it is true, occasionally found inspiration in Lutheran ceremonies. Thomas Muriell, for example, when he was called upon to explain before Whitgift his defence of auricular confession in 1599, cited the Church of Denmark for the practice.[221] However, examples such as Muriell's may well illustrate an informed arguing position rather than a shift towards a greater interest in, and appreciation of, the Lutheran Churches themselves. The same would seem to hold true for the Laudian period. It is certainly not difficult to find examples of Lutherans being cited by writers such as Montagu, Heylyn, Samuel Hoard, William Page or William Watts in the 1620s and 30s for their opposition to the absolute decree of predestination, or for their support for kneeling at communion, possessing altars or bowing at the name of Jesus.[222] Such appeals were in

[218] For the emphasis on catholicity and the Fathers in the work of Mentzer, Calixtus and Gerhard, see Elert, *Structure of Lutheranism*, pp.274–91; R.D. Preus, *The Theology of Post-Reformation Lutheranism* (2 vols., St Louis, 1970–2), I: 36. Calixtus supposedly drew part of the inspiration for his patristic studies from his observations on a visit to England in 1611–12: W.C. Dowding, *The Life and Correspondence of George Calixtus* (1863), p.59.

[219] See above, n.168.

[220] Hooker, *Works*, V: 125. Hooker's disciple Covell described Lutherans along with 'Zwinglians' as members of a different religion, who should yet be distinguished from heretics and idolators, and whose errors did not actually take away the foundation: Covell, *Modest Examination*, pp.200–1.

[221] LPL, Lambeth MS 3470 fol.210.

[222] Page, *Treatise*, p.19; Hoard, *Gods Love*, p.10; Plaifere, *Appello Evangelium*, pp.418, 428–9; Alexander Read, *A Sermon Preached ... at the Visitation of Brentwood in Essex* (1636), p.9; Humphrey Sydenham, *Five Sermons upon Severall Occasions* (1626–7), p.66;

themselves novel: as we have seen, the Lutheran use of images and their elaborate liturgy had in the past been condemned by puritan and even conformist writers.[223] Nevertheless, Laudian citations of Lutheran behaviour were purely tactical – to divert a charge of popery or Arminianism in relation to a particular ceremony or doctrine. When Laud invoked the example of the Lutherans' pattern of church government at his trial, he would appear to have merely been attempting to display the Protestant credentials of the episcopalian church polity.[224]

This is not to deny that this was a potentially powerful defence. As we have seen, all Calvinists were obliged to maintain the thesis that the Lutherans did not differ from Calvinists in essential matters of faith, and when Laudians called their irenical bluff they scored a palpable hit. Their Calvinist opponents were thus regularly wrong-footed. Simonds D'Ewes found himself embarrassed by his friend Sir Martin Stuteville when the latter drew attention to the incompatibility of D'Ewes' concurrent praise of the Lutheran hero Gustavus Adolphus and vilification of the Arminians, whose predestinarian views the Lutheran king presumably shared. The Laudian Christopher Dow reported with some glee a story that Henry Burton had been embarrassed in public in a similar way. Burton had shown himself ignorant of the fact that all the tenets concerning predestination, free will and falling from grace which he had been in the process of condemning in 'Arminians' were in fact held by Lutherans too. Richard Montagu mocked his opponents for their discomfort in seeking to avoid charging him with Lutheranism for his predestinarian errors, and for having concentrated instead merely on the charge of Arminianism.[225]

Nevertheless, if an appeal to the Lutherans could be polemically effective, it does not seem to have prompted any further curiosity among Laudians into the current state of the Lutheran Churches.[226] The sources for the Laudians' polemical quips were generally limited and predictable,

Heylyn, *Antidotum Lincolniense* (1637), i. p.131; *idem*, *A Coale from the Altar* (1636), p.28; Montagu, *New Gagg*, p.179; Bodl., Rawlinson MS C.573 fol.89r. Heylyn also found Lutheran sources useful for his purposes in his *History of the Sabbath*, ii. pp.180, 184. For the earlier use of Lutheran Churches in defence of kneeling at communion, see Michaelson, *Lawfulnes*, p.125; T. Rogers, *Two Dialogues*, sig.I2r.

223 See above pp.386–7. 224 Laud, *Works*, III: 386.

225 BL, Harleian MS 374 fol.89r–v; Dow, *Innovations*, p.36; Montagu, *Appello*, p.40.

226 At times, moreover, the polemical advantage could consist in depicting the Lutheran Churches in as scathing a manner as possible. Thus Christopher Potter emphasized the 'notable dreames and Dotages' and 'foule corruptions' in Lutheran ceremonies and doctrines, including 'their absurd ubiquity and transubstantiation', the better to exculpate the Arminians, whose errors were fewer, and who should therefore be invited to communion in the same way that the Lutherans were (Plaifere, *Appello Evangelium*, pp.428–9). Potter here mirrors Hooker's tactic (see above), although in the 1630s he espoused a more irenical position in accordance with the schemes of Dury (see his *Want of Charitie*, i. pp.85–91).

being either Edwin Sandys' *Relation of the State of Religion*, or the Confession of Augsburg. The major Lutheran divines of this period – Gerhard, Brochmand, Meisner, Mentzer, Hunnius – were all practically unknown in England. There is little indication that Laudian divines were any better read than other Englishmen of their time in contemporary (or even past) Lutheran literature, although they did make use of the works of Hemmingsen.[227] John Howson would seem to be something of an exception: he exploited the anti-Calvinist works of Hunnius and Schlüsselburg for his attacks on the Geneva Bible.[228] Certainly, no writers in the 1630s displayed any of the diligence shown in the 1590s by Bilson in his mapping out of the arguments of contemporary Lutheran authors for his literal and triumphalist reading of Christ's local descent into hell, or by Bancroft in providing his account of Lutheran doctrines of the imparity of ministers.[229]

Moreover, when discussing the eucharist, Laudian divines followed the standard procedure of condemning the Lutheran doctrine of consubstantiation, along with Roman transubstantiation, and they were also careful to warn against the Lutheran error of ubiquity,[230] although their own doctrine of the eucharistic presence had much more in common with contemporary Lutheranism than they were aware.[231] Further Lutheran emphases on relics and personal guardian angels may have caused some concern, too, although divines such as Montagu, who might have responded positively to these points, would appear to have been unaware of the Lutherans' defence of them.[232] In fact, Laudians were even more critical of Lutherans than were their Calvinist opponents on the issue

227 Tyacke, *Anti-Calvinists*, p.20; White, *Predestination*, p.270; BL, Harleian MS 750 fols.106v–107v.

228 Bodl., Rawlinson MS D.320 fols.60r, 61r. Howson's chaplain Edward Boughen also makes use of Schlüsselburg, though not for a directly anti-Calvinist purpose, in his *A Sermon of Confirmation* (1620), p.60.

229 Wallace, 'Puritan and Anglican', esp. pp.271–7; Bancroft, *Survay*, pp.117–22. Heylyn is clearly struggling to find Lutheran sources in his *History of the Sabbath*, ii. pp.180, 184.

230 Against consubstantiation: e.g. Montagu, *New Gagg*, p.252; White, *Replie*, p.185; Plaifere, *Appello Evangelium*, p.428 (Potter). Laud rejected the doctrine of ubiquity (in the Lutheran polemicist Schlüsselburg) in his 1622 notes on a Capuchin tract: Laud, *Works*, VII: 619 (cited in Frank, 'Eucharistic presence', p.338). While Jeremy Taylor recommended Gerhard's *Loci Communes* for a library, he warned of the author's errors of consubstantiation and ubiquitarianism: J. Taylor, *Works* 1: lxxxix.

231 Frank emphasizes that, despite their rejection of extreme consubstantiation and ubiquitarian positions, the eucharistic theology of many Caroline divines concerning the relationship of the bread to the presence of Christ's body, and on the point of eucharistic adoration, was in fact closer to the Gnesio-Lutheran tradition than to the sixteenth-century English 'true presence' Reformed tradition: Frank, 'Eucharistic presence', chs.4 and 8. However, beyond certain similarities he finds it difficult to find a direct indebtedness (*ibid.*, pp.468–9). For Gerhard's 'mysterium tremendum' emphasis, see his *The Soules Watch* (3rd edn, 1621), p.268.

232 Gerhard complained that Calvinists did not honour saints' relics: F. Kalb, *The Theology of Worship in Seventeenth-Century Lutheranism* (St Louis, 1965), p.47 nn.42–3.

which had most reassured earlier writers of the Lutherans' good faith – that of justification. The rigorous solifidianism of the 'more rigid' Lutheran divines was condemned systematically by William Forbes, who also chided Davenant for following them.[233]

Furthermore, no matter how strong their own distaste for Calvinism, the Laudians generally found the spiteful blend of anti-Calvinism in which Lutheran divines indulged to be rather more than they could stomach. On reading a particularly violent anti-Calvinist tract by the Elector of Saxony's chaplain von Hoenegg, Laud commented that 'I have in my time read much bitterness, but hardly have I seen more gall drop from any man's pen.' Montagu, while employing Lutheran writers to overturn charges of Arminianism, commented 'I wish they were men of more allayed spirits and calmer temper than they are, or do show themselves in opposition.' Potter, similarly, complained of 'the virulent Pamphlets and Prescriptions' of some of Luther's disciples, 'who in a preposterous imitation of his zeale are little lesse than furious'. 'Those virulent fiery Adders of Saxony . . . professe to this day, a perpetuall foehood, and immortall Hostility against us.'[234] It is perhaps worth observing that even divines such as Andrewes could find themselves being attacked as 'Calvinists' in eucharistic matters by even moderate Lutheran writers such as Gerhard – a practice which particularly enraged Montagu.[235]

Things were different in Scotland. A Lutheran influence does appear to have been prominent among Scottish Arminians in the 1630s. Robert Baillie complained of 'their earnest recommendation, to the reading of younger Students the late Lutheran Divines, such as Hutter, Meisner, Gerhard'. It is clear from James Wedderburn's commonplace book that he had read Gerhard and Hunnius. Bishop William Forbes' irenical *Considerationes Modestae* reveal an extensive reading of later Lutheran writers, including Mentzer, Gerhard, Hemmingsen and Chytraeus. Although he included some Gnesio-Lutherans among the 'more rigid Protestants' whom he opposed on the issues of justification and good works, on other doctrines Forbes displayed a concern to defend the Lutherans against the attacks of Calvinist divines, whose views he frequently overturned. Baillie later recollected that when the Scottish Arminian clergy combined a recommendation of Lutheran divines with the new emphasis on Christ's eucharistic presence and the revival of eucharistic ceremonial, along with 'their crying downe, both in private and publick of Calvin, Beza, Martyr, Bucer and the rest of the famous writers, both ancient and late of the

233 Forbes, *Considerationes*, I: 23, 33, 99, 301–3, 387.

234 Laud, *Works*, VII: 87; Montagu, *Appello*, pp.46, 54; Potter, *Want of Charitie*, i. pp.85–6; John Plaifere, *Appello Evangelium*, p.429 (cf. Potter, *Sermon*, p.69).

235 Frank, 'Eucharistic presence', p.93; Montagu, *ΘΕΑΝΘΡΩΠΙΚΟΝ*, ii. p.288.

French and Belgic Churches', Baillie and others were led to suspect that the introduction of Lutheranism was at hand.[236]

During the Interregnum, the perspective of certain English Laudians moved more towards the Scottish interest in Lutheranism, as some pamphleteers such as Thomas Pierce and Peter Heylyn associated the Church of England more directly and systematically with Melanchthonian Lutheranism's moderate views of predestination, and claimed the existence of a Melanchthonian stream of thought running through Reformation history, of which Arminianism constituted merely a stage. Although he emphasized the lack of foreign influence in the English Reformation, Peter Heylyn argued that, if anything, the early English Reformers had looked with special favour on the Lutherans' doctrine, government and form of worship, and he placed the Church of England's doctrine on many issues alongside 'the Moderate or Melancthonian Lutherans'.[237] For Heylyn, 'Melancthonian Lutheranism' provided him with the non-Calvinist Reformation which he so urgently sought. During the same period, John Cosin became increasingly preoccupied with the works of the Heidelberg syncretist George Calixtus, whose works he systematically annotated, and whose portrait he commissioned (along with those of Melanchthon and Gerhard) when he was later bishop of Durham.[238]

However, these developments lay in the future. In the 1630s the English Laudians had yet to develop a coherent or informed attitude towards the Lutheran Churches. Even so, it was at this time that closer relations with one of them – the Church of Sweden – seem to have been contemplated, albeit briefly. When the irenicist John Dury was in Sweden in the years 1636–7 he sent Laud regular reports of the progress of his pacificatory schemes. It rapidly emerged that, while merely polite towards Dury's general irenical ideas, the Swedish divines were far more willing to treat with the Church of England itself in the hope of securing a form of church

[236] Baillie, *Ladensium*, pp.31–2; Forbes, *Considerationes*, I: 33, 301, II: 91–3, 145, 211, 275–7, 353–5, 491–3, 505; BL, Harleian MS 749 fols.73r, 94r, 98r–v (note also the extracts from Camerarius' life of Melanchthon in Harleian MS 750 fols.76v–77r).

[237] Heylyn, *Cyprianus*, pp.3–4, 14, 30, 36; *idem*, *Certamen Epistolare*, pp.154–5; D.D. Wallace, 'The Anglican appeal to Lutheran sources: Philipp Melanchthon's reputation in seventeenth-century England', *Historical Magazine of the Protestant Episcopalian Church* 52 (1983), pp.361–7.

[238] Most of the evidence for Cosin's interest in Calixtus dates from after the outbreak of the civil war: e.g. Cosin, *Works*, V: 299–302. Cosin carefully copied out a tract relating to Calixtus' funeral (see DUL, shelfmark K.4.22 pp.3–21), while Cosin's library at Durham contains fifteen of Calixtus' works, of which eight are annotated by him. Cosin also annotated a work of Gerhard during this period: DUL, shelfmark I.V.16. He also left three works of Gerhard – including the nine-volume *Loci Communes* – to Peterhouse on his escape in 1643–4. Cosin's library at Durham contains volumes by Gerhard from before and after his exile. I owe the information regarding the Gerhard volumes to the kindness of Mr A.I. Doyle.

union. At this time, a radical reformation of the ecclesiastical structure of the Church of Sweden was being contemplated, which would include the erection of a new Ecclesiastical Court, which the Swedes were eager should follow the plan of the Church of England's own Court of High Commission. Laud was most interested in this, and promised to help in building up the government and discipline of the Swedish Church by sending them a pattern of the Church of England's constitution. Several times, Swedish divines professed to Dury their willingness to frame a fundamental Confession of Faith with the British Churches, which the episcopal Church of Denmark might then also join. If a public declaration could be made expressing the Swedish Church's readiness to treat further in doctrinal issues with the British Churches, then Dury intended to act as their agent in informing Laud and the universities of their resolution. Laud seems to have made no attempt to dissuade Dury from such plans. However, Dury proved unable to persuade the Swedish Church to make an overture to Laud before Dury himself had a full commission from Laud and the king, which was not forthcoming. Eventually Dury's plans came to nothing, along with the hopes for English involvement with Sweden in a north Protestant alliance against the empire, with which plans for ecclesiastical union became inextricably linked. Nevertheless, the ecclesiastical union of the Churches of Sweden and England was still a theoretical possibility towards the close of 1637. At that time, as has recently been shown, Grotius communicated to Laud through Viscount Scudamore his hopes that such a union might form the basis of a more general union of the British and Scandinavian Lutheran Churches, excluding the Calvinist Churches. Laud addressed a careful reply to Grotius' suggestions through Scudamore, in which he would seem to have expressed strong doubts over the possibility that the other Reformed Churches would follow the ecclesiastical union of England and Sweden, with those in the Low Countries the least likely of all to comply. Laud would also seem to have objected to the rigidity with which the Lutherans upheld certain doctrines, including (inevitably) consubstantiation, which in Laud's opinion made reconciliation unlikely.[239] It was also true that, like the Remonstrants, Lutheran Churches would not necessarily have provided much joy when it came to some of the Laudians' most cherished notions of *iure divino* episcopacy, and the apostolic, personal succession of bishops, although Laud's

[239] Westin, 'Brev', pp.199, 208, 216–17, 223, 225, 234, 237, 242, 245, 249, 251, 266, 325; Tighe, 'William Laud'. One consequence of all this may have been the inspiration which the Swedish Lutheran Johannes Matthias Gothus continued to derive from the Book of Common Prayer in his own liturgical projects in the 1640s: see T. Harjunpaa, 'Liturgical developments in Sweden and Finland in the era of Lutheran orthodoxy (1593–1700)', *Church History* 37 (1968), pp.14–35 (at pp.28–31).

behaviour towards Sweden would suggest that he, at least, would have tolerated a ministerial imparity that had not preserved a personal succession of bishops.[240]

Nothing, of course, was to come of these vague plans. We should not really be surprised. There could be no 'alternative' Protestant Cause. One of the most vital forces binding the Calvinist community together had been the conviction that the pope was Antichrist, and that there was a 'true church' of orthodox believers engaged in constant warfare with her.[241] But in Laudian ecclesiology, as we have seen, there was no room for a separate 'true church' of the orthodox, from which heretics and schismatics such as Rome would be excluded forever. Nor was it accepted that the pope was Antichrist, or Rome Babylon.

What is even more striking among Laudian thinkers in this period is the clear sense of detachment from the religious divisions of the continent which some divines began to express. Thus Christopher Potter maintained that the divisions between the Lutherans and Calvinists, while they were easily reconcilable and consisted 'rather in formes and phrases of speech, than in substance of doctrine', were in fact irrelevant to the Church of England: 'the jarres and divisions betweene the Lutherans and Calvinists doe little concerne the Church of England, which followeth none but Christ'.[242] In this context, Potter's exposition of Pacianus, renouncing the factious names of Lutherans or Calvinists,[243] was not necessarily new, but was potentially more divisive, implying a divorce from the churches them-

240 Even when hinting at Lutheran influence in the English Reformation, Heylyn emphasized that the English Church was different from other Protestant countries, and that episcopal government had been 'much impaired in power and jurisdiction' by the Lutherans: Heylyn, 'The Way and Manner of the Reformation of the Church of England Declared and Justified', p.69 in *idem*, *Ecclesia Vindicata*. On the German Reformation and superintendents, see Heylyn, *Survey of France*, p.218; *idem*, *Parable*, p.332. On episcopacy, see Gerhard, *Locorum Theologicorum*, tom.2 lib.5 pp.357–73, who justifies extraordinary vocation and the interruption of the personal succession. See also B. Lohse, 'The development of the offices of leadership in the German Lutheran Churches: 1517–1918', and S. Borregaard, 'The post-Reformation developments of the episcopacy in Denmark, Norway and Iceland', in I. Asheim and V. R. Gould (eds.), *Episcopacy in the Lutheran Church?* (Philadelphia, 1970).

241 For the invocation of the threat from Rome as a means to encourage Protestant union, see Morton, 'Opinion', p.17; Davenant, *Exhortation*, p.2. The point of the pope's being Antichrist was one which was avidly shared by Lutheran divines: see R.B. Barnes, *Prophecy and Gnosis. Apocalypticism in the Wake of the Lutheran Reformation* (Stanford, 1988), and e.g. Gerhard, *Locorum Theologicorum*, tom.2 lib.5, pp.365–7; Schlüsselburg, *Haereticorum Catalogus*, VIII: sigs.a2v–a3r, c4v–d2; XIII: 26–30, 63, 66; Dowding, *Calixtus*, pp.165–6.

242 Potter, *Want of Charitie*, i. pp.85–6. For Potter's description of himself as 'neither Arminian, nor Calvinist', see Bodl., Sancroft MS 21 p.61.

243 Potter, *Want of Charitie*, i. pp.82–3.

selves rather than merely from the practice of adopting the names of individuals. Similarly, Richard Montagu's determination not to pin his belief on any man's sleeve was a commonplace, but the whole tenor of his work was not commonplace at all. All English Protestant divines would pride themselves on having studied antiquity, but Montagu's insistence that he had studied it *instead of* following 'the ordinarie and accustomed by-paths' of Reformed writers such as Polanus infused a new combative exclusivity into understandings of the two. Moreover, Montagu insisted that he could not see why Calvinists should be preferred before Lutherans, while at the same time he sought to distance himself from the Lutherans and Arminians. As with Potter, Montagu's rejection of 'names of division' represented not just a standard distaste for exclusive terminology, but a more radical detachment from the churches to which this terminology was generally applied.[244]

Doctrinal issues undoubtedly played their part in alienating Laudian sentiments from the foreign Reformed Churches. However, the crucially distinctive feature of Laudian writing on relations with continental churches was their determination to allot equal if not greater significance to divisions on issues of discipline. This was partly a matter of polemical tactics. Yet this was also prompted by the increasingly problematical nature of church discipline in the Reformed Churches, and especially of understandings of the nature of episcopacy and of the ministry in the Church of England. These issues themselves reflected the concern which lay at the heart of the Laudian programme: the desire to transform English Protestants' perception of the relative importance of discipline *vis-à-vis* doctrine, and of the sacraments *vis-à-vis* preaching. This was combined with a firm belief that the arenas of doctrine and discipline could not be separated with the sort of ease that Hall and others imagined. The Laudians' rejection of the model of church relations expounded by Joseph Hall at the beginning of this chapter was prompted less by their sense of alienation in the crucial unifying area of doctrine (although this was undoubtedly present), but rather by their elevated view of the importance of issues of ecclesiastical discipline, which made impossible the sort of relative agnosticism that Hall favoured. It is the impact of these views on perceptions of the Reformed Churches which we will now examine.

[244] Montagu, *Appello*, pp.11–12, 46–7, 57. Montagu's arguments could sometimes be tortuous in his determination to retain a position of independence from the continent: e.g. his insistence that he had not maintained that the Church of England agreed with Lutherans against the doctrine of absolute election, but merely that the Lutherans *detested* it, and the Church of England *did not teach* it (*Appello*, p.57). While stressing that he does not attack the defects of Calvinist predestinarian doctrine as the Romanists and Lutherans do, Montagu then argues in precisely these terms, and repeats at length the Lutheran argument that Calvinists make God the author of sin (*ibid.*, pp.54–5).

9

'The best Reformed Church': church government and politics

The problem of Reformed church government

Joseph Hall acted as the mouthpiece of English Calvinists when he explained that issues of discipline were of minor importance for relations between the different Reformed Churches. The varying forms of Protestant church government were, he explained, 'not ... essential to the being of a church, though much importing the well or better being of it, according to our several apprehensions thereof', and the different Protestant Churches therefore retained 'a reverent and loving opinion of each other'. While this explanation may have seemed straightforward, it was still problematic in its treatment of an area where Protestants were openly at variance. Most Reformed Churches considered themselves to be 'the best reformed church', and even if few considered their form of church government to be vital to the *esse* (being) of a church, their conviction that it might well 'import the well or better being of it' naturally tended to undermine any suggestion that all forms of church government and ceremony were essentially things indifferent, to be varied at will in each individual church. Even Joseph Hall himself did not always sustain the relativistic tone adopted above. In a different context, Hall could be found urging the Church of England's own form of episcopal church government as 'universal and unalterable' and 'appointed by the Holy Ghost', and maintaining that 'to depart from the judgment and practice of the universal church of Christ ever since the apostles' times, and to betake ourselves to a new invention, cannot but be, besides the danger, vehemently scandalous'.[1] As in matters of doctrine, a sustained tension often existed between the principle of confessional unity and the fact of the Church of England's increasing divergence from continental norms.

[1] Hall, *Works*, VI: 610. Contrast the quotations from Hall in Sykes, *Old Priest*, pp.85, 66–7. Cf. also W. Nijenhuis, 'The controversy between presbyterianism and episcopalianism surrounding and during the Synod of Dort 1618–1619', in *idem*, *Ecclesia Restaurata* (Leiden, 1972), pp.216–17.

Moreover, points of church government were not matters which favoured an agnostic relativism. They inevitably held implications for issues of civil polity. How easily, then, were English Protestants able to seal off the tensions aroused by differences over discipline from the theory of Protestant unity? And how far were English Protestants themselves prepared to treat the areas of doctrine and discipline as entirely dissimilar? As we shall see, Hall's formulation of Protestant relations was very much wishful thinking. New trends in sacramental theology, and the new emphasis attached to the role of the visible, institutional church in the attainment of salvation, meant that differences over external ecclesiastical polity were more likely to become the main focus of inter-Protestant relations, rather than a peripheral area of disagreement.

As in matters of doctrine, there was a sense in which both conformists and puritans could make use of the forms of discipline found within the foreign Reformed Churches to further their own cause. Presbyterians appealed to the example of the 'best reformed churches' for their model of church discipline, while conformist divines could riposte by noting that the same Reformed Churches required subscription and obedience to their own specified liturgy.[2] In practice, of course, the presbyterians stood to gain far more from the example of the Reformed Churches' discipline. It should also be borne in mind that much of the English discussion of the polities of the foreign Reformed Churches took place against the background of puritan attempts to import foreign modes of church government into England. In this context, it is the restraint of English conformist divines towards their co-religionists abroad that is arguably as significant as their hostility towards the presbyterian model of church government.

The argument that both episcopalian and presbyterian forms of church government were equally valid was clearly one that would undergo severe strain during the conflicts over church government in the 1580s. In practice, presbyterianism was not generally tolerant of episcopacy. English presbyterian pamphleteers had urged their form of government as the only legitimate one, and were able to cite foreign Reformed divines who were prepared to make the presbyterian discipline a mark of the true church. William Covell quite rightly warned in 1606 of the 'tyranny of example' at

2 *Puritan Manifestoes*, eds. W.H. Frere and C.E. Douglas (1907), pp.6, 19, 27, 28, 32, 34 and *passim*; Ormerod, *Picture of a Puritane*, i. pp.26–7. For examples of the use of such arguments by King James, Bancroft and other early Jacobean conformists, see Babbage, *Puritanism*, pp.248, 256–7; Oxford University, *Answere*, p.18. For a later Laudian example, see Hoard, *Churches Authority*, pp.3, 12–13. See also Henry Leslie, *A Treatise of the Authority of the Church* (Dublin, 1637), pp.77, 103, 142.

work in the Reformed Churches through the active sponsorship of the presbyterian polity of Geneva.[3] It was also true, as Whitgift did not fail to point out, that foreign presbyterians were prepared to countenance, and the French Reformed indeed insisted upon, the reordination of those who had received their orders in the episcopal Church of England.[4]

In response to such moves, conformist divines in the 1590s adopted a distinctly more aggressive and assertive tone when discussing the state of the foreign Reformed Churches in matters of church polity.[5] The scathing tones employed by Richard Bancroft and Matthew Sutcliffe towards the foreign churches, and indeed even against the figures of Calvin and Beza, surpassed anything that even Hooker could muster. Thus Bancroft's *Survay* launched some savage attacks upon 'their disciplinary Babel'. The presbyterian platform was attacked as a complete novelty unheard of before Calvin, on the details of which the presbyterians themselves were hopelessly confused. Calvin and Beza were condemned as cynical manipulators who curried favour with the multitude and seized autocratic power by underhand methods, after which they behaved as patriarchs, ordering other churches how to arrange their own church government, and stirring up the puritans against the Church of England's own episcopal governors. Sutcliffe's *Treatise of Ecclesiasticall Discipline* was less detailed in its treatment of political events in Geneva, but mounted some severe attacks on the French and Genevan Churches. Sutcliffe also directed some dismissive remarks at the supposed theological acumen of Calvin, Beza and Daneau, condemning them as partial and often confused sources for issues of ecclesiastical government.[6]

The main target of these conformist attacks, however, was English presbyterianism, which had been the most explicit in its critique of the English church polity. Broadsides against the foreign churches were in part simply a means to this end. Bancroft explained frankly that he included his narrative of the misdeeds at Geneva solely

> because certaine persons of the consistoriall humour, doe daily upon every occasion, still dash us in the teeth, with the orders of Geneva: the discipline at Geneva: and the Consistorie in Geneva: as though that forme of discipline had come lately from heaven: with an embassage from God, that all the Churches in the worlde must frame and conforme themselves, to the fashion of Geneva.[7]

[3] Avis, *The Church*, pp.48–51, 123–4; Collinson, *Puritan Movement*, pp.109–15; Sykes, *Old Priest*, pp.54–5; Covell, *Briefe Answer*, p.62; Strype, *Whitgift*, II: 161–7.

[4] Strype, *Whitgift*, III: 183.

[5] See above, introduction.

[6] Bancroft, *Survay*, pp.24–38, 42, 44–8, 50–9, 64; Matthew Sutcliffe, *A Treatise of Ecclesiasticall Discipline* (1590), pp. 1–4, 16, 19–20, 28–9, 76, 94 and *passim*.

[7] Bancroft, *Survay*, p.38.

Calvin and Beza could in a sense be excused for using whatever means were available to spread their discipline: it was the English presbyterians who were principally at fault for simply accepting everything on their authority.[8] Nevertheless, this choice of presbyterian targets was a delicate business, and conformist attacks might easily be taken to be assaults on the reputations of the Genevan divines. After all, Bancroft and others clearly aimed in the process to diminish the esteem in which Calvin and Beza were held in some puritan circles.[9]

Bancroft and his allies did not seek simply to denigrate Calvin's opinions on matters of church polity, however. On the contrary, one line of argument favoured by Bancroft, Sutcliffe and others was to quote Calvin himself *against* the rigid presbyterian attitudes of Beza and the later Calvinists.[10] Even Beza, the scion of international presbyterianism, was often quoted from his letters of 1589 and 1591 to Whitgift in which he denied any intent to compel other churches to submit to the Genevan discipline. Beza's tracts against Saravia, in which he praised godly bishops and moderated his views on the desirability of prelacy, were also frequently cited. By suggesting that even Beza approved of episcopacy in England, conformists hoped to show that the English presbyterians had actually departed from the position of their foreign mentors.[11] However, it was also made clear that if the English presbyterians insisted on invoking the foreign churches and divines as models for reforming the English Church, they would ultimately force English conformist writers to abandon their usual restraint when dealing with their foreign Calvinist brethren. Sutcliffe offered the chilling warning that 'For maintenance of common peace, they have bene hitherto forborne: but if they cease not to practise and to raile, there shall such a wracke be made of their French

[8] *Ibid.*, pp.63–4.

[9] Richard Hooker certainly made fewer concessions to Calvin's reputation, and did not follow Whitgift and Bancroft in depicting him as more positively inclined towards episcopacy than Beza and the puritans: R. Bauckham, 'Richard Hooker and John Calvin: a comment', *JEH* 32 (1981), pp.29–33 at p.32.

[10] Bancroft, *Survay*, pp.112–14, 125–7, 402–5 and *passim*; Sutcliffe, *Treatise*, pp.124–6, 169; William Barlow, *One of the Foure Sermons Preached ... at Hampton Court* (1606), sigs.C4v–D1r, F2r; John King, *The Fourth Sermon Preached at Hampton Court* (Oxford, 1607), pp.35–6; George Downame, *Two Sermons* (1608) ii. pp.26–9, 38, 39; Nijenhuis, *Saravia*, pp.170–1; Covell, *Modest Examination*, p.99; Hall, *Works*, IX: 151–2.

[11] Bancroft, *Survay*, pp.131–41; Sutcliffe, *Treatise*, p.82; Downame, *Two Sermons*, ii. p.29; Ormerod, *Picture of a Puritane*, i. p.48; Mason, 'Validity', pp.137–8; Hall, *Works*, IX: 61 (as well as citing Beza, Hall here repeats his general formula, viz: 'these sisters have learned to differ; and yet to love and reverence each other; and in these cases to enjoy their own forms without prescription of necessity or censure'), 154, 159. Another way in which English Calvinist conformists dealt with Beza's attacks upon bishops was by simply editing such passages out of his works: see John Harmar's translation of *Master Bezaes Sermons upon the three first chapters of the Canticle of Canticles* (Oxford, 1587), discussed in Backus, *Roots*, pp.93–5.

articles of discipline, and Genevian ordinances, that they shall repent that ever they began this quarrell against our church.' His own attack on the tyranny of consistorial government in Geneva indicated what might be in hand.[12]

To be sure, these attacks were framed with careful pacifying reassurances. Against Beza's complaints, Saravia insisted that Sutcliffe, while condemning the presbyterian form of church government and Beza's arguments, had done so with no intent to quarrel with Beza, but only to defend the Church of England against some who cited Beza's name for their actions. Whitgift similarly reassured Beza that Sutcliffe had nowhere mentioned him without honour, and that in another work recently published against the papists Sutcliffe had strongly praised and defended Beza against Romanist slanders.[13] Similarly, when the Calvinist conformist John King discussed the failings of foreign presbyterian governments, he explained how 'with a tender and trembling hand, I confesse do I touch the sores of friends'.[14] It was emphasized that these attacks were not to be construed as assaults upon Beza and Calvin's credentials as exponents of true Reformed *doctrine*.[15] The severe language permitted in matters of church polity would be frowned upon were it to intrude into doctrinal matters. Whitgift encapsulated this distinction in the 1580s and 1590s, when he attacked those who sought 'to traduce' Calvin more generally (in matters of doctrine), but approved those trying 'to control' Calvin in matters of discipline.[16] It was the latter function that he presumably understood Bancroft and Sutcliffe to be performing.

Nevertheless, not all onlookers appreciated this distinction. Beza for one, perceived a more general hostility behind these attacks, as did the French Reformed Churches.[17] Those of a more anti-Calvinist inclination might also miss the significance of the mitigating palliatives that usually prefaced attacks on the Genevan discipline. Thus the wavering deacon Francis Walsingham reported having been especially moved by Bolsec's vitriolic character assassinations of Calvin and Beza because he had previously read Bancroft's *Dangerous Positions* and 'another by D. Sutcliffe' where the lives, counsels and actions of Calvin and Beza were 'so dis-

[12] Sutcliffe, *Treatise*, pp.72, 182–4. [13] Strype, *Whitgift*, II: 174, 168.

[14] King, *Fourth Sermon*, p.21.

[15] Thus Downame emphasized that, while he had been misled in his earlier days by Calvin and Beza on issues of church government, this had been partly due to 'the reverent opinion, which I had *worthily* conceived of them', and affirmed that they could be found to be 'so admirably sound & orthodoxal in the substantiall points of religion': Downame, *Two Sermons*, ii. sigs.¶4r, A4r (my italics).

[16] Trinity College, Cambridge, MS B/14/9 pp.3–4 – quoted in Lake, *Moderate Puritans*, p.211.

[17] Nijenhuis, *Saravia*, pp.124–5, 143.

gracefullie set forth' so that the Genevan worthies were shown to be 'scarse common honest men'. Moreover, the crucial distinction between spheres of discipline and doctrine might easily be disregarded, as we have seen in the case of the Roman convert James Wadsworth.[18]

After the flurry of anti-presbyterian writings of the 1590s, direct attacks upon the government of the foreign Reformed Churches subsided. By the 1620s and 1630s, however, White, Dow, Montagu and other Laudian writers were rehearsing again the attacks made upon Geneva by Bancroft in the 1590s. This time, however, Calvinists objected that Richard Montagu had stepped beyond the extenuating conventions that had previously been observed in complaints against the foreign Reformed Churches. It was objected that, in Laudian hands, the boundary between 'controlling' and 'traducing' Calvin was too readily breached. The Laudians' opponents also alleged that another distinction – that between doctrine and discipline – was being disregarded, with Laudians intent on undermining Calvinist *doctrine* under the guise of attacking the foreign churches' *discipline*. Matthew Sutcliffe, the surviving veteran of Elizabethan anti-presbyterianism, could see the difference, and complained that Montagu was essentially falling into the same trap that had earlier caught Wadsworth:

> He [Montagu] inveigheth against our brethren of France, and the Low Countries, as not conformable to us in their discipline: But his hatred is more to their doctrine of faith then of discipline. This is only to make a division, and to stirre up mens hatred against them, that in the end they and we may have our throats cut for our doctrine of faith.[19]

Sutcliffe's voice was merely one among a host of conformist writers who considered Montagu and his supporters to have overstepped the bounds of what was admissible when treating of foreign Reformed discipline. But how far removed was the Laudian critique of the polity of the foreign churches from that of earlier writers? Did they simply draw attention to a broadening chasm that separated English Protestants' practical assumptions from their theoretical views of the non-episcopalian church polities? As we have seen, even in pre-Laudian times the churches could not always be relied upon to display a mutual respect, as each found their own form of government under attack. But how significant were the supposed deficiencies of the foreign churches taken to be? Behind the simple exchange of abusive rhetoric, more fundamental changes and developments were taking place in the way in which English Protestant divines viewed the

[18] Walsingham, *A Search*, p.17; Bedell, *Certaine Letters*, p.127. Note especially Hakewill's reply to these arguments: Hakewill, *Answere*, ii. pp.166–7, iii. p.19. On Wadsworth, see above, ch.8.

[19] Sutcliffe, *Briefe Censure*, p.36.

different forms of church government. These shifts occurred among Calvinist conformist divines and avant-garde conformists alike throughout the early Stuart period, as each group debated the nature and function of episcopacy.

CHANGING VIEWS OF EPISCOPACY

The argument from divine right

In the Elizabethan Church, early defences of episcopacy had centred on the need to oppose presbyterian *iure divino* claims. In the hands of John Whitgift, episcopacy had initially been defended as a type of church government which was suitable for the Church of England because it was the most appropriate form of government for a monarchical polity. It was emphasized that Scripture laid down no immutable form of church government, so that such matters were essentially 'things indifferent'.[20] Episcopacy's virtue lay in its proven value throughout history in preventing schism. There was no suggestion, at least at first, that episcopacy could in any way be central to the very being and purpose of the church. Here was a line of argument that did not threaten the integrity of other forms of church government, which might be more appropriate for republican polities. Such arguments underpinned Joseph Hall's classic affirmation of the indifferency of issues of church government in inter-Protestant relations.

Nevertheless, the whole rationale of Hall's position seemed under threat with the emergence of the argument that the institution of episcopacy was *iure divino*. The initial impetus for this came from presbyterian claims, which urged further institutional reform of the English Church in order to bring her into line with the foreign Reformed Churches, as well as attacking English episcopacy as unscriptural and unnecessary. In response, some conformist divines forwarded more exalted claims for episcopacy as the form of government appointed by God for His Church. This argument had first been broached by John Bridges, and was taken up with relish by other conformists such as Bilson, Sutcliffe and Bancroft. In their writings episcopacy was taken to be of dominical institution, although it was not always clear whether this conclusion derived from its long historical continuance, or from its apostolical provenance.[21] The implication, however, was clear: only bishops could validly ordain, and the foreign Reformed Churches, even if their orders were not esteemed to be invalid, lacked something necessary to the perfection of the church, and could no longer be regarded

[20] Lake, *Anglicans and Puritans*, pp.88–90. [21] *Ibid.*, pp.90–7.

as being on equal terms with the Church of England in their ecclesiastical government.

Arguments in favour of *iure divino* episcopacy aroused great opposition among English Protestants at first, most notably from John Rainolds and Sir Francis Knollys.[22] However, this attack was not sustained. There are a number of possible reasons for this declining opposition, some of which are directly political. The doctrine emerged at a time when puritanism had lost its main supporters at court, and was being put to flight by a government determined to crush the classical movement. Moderate puritan divines were anxious to cut their losses and turn their attention to practical divinity, and therefore wished to assure the government that they posed no political threat. Few were therefore minded to persist in direct opposition to a theory of episcopal government which the government clearly supported. It may also have been the case that, because of the unbending Calvinism of most of its exponents, the *iure divino* doctrine did not appear to be inextricably linked with the emerging phenomenon of a consistently anti-Reformed temperament among avant-garde conformists, or the growth of new apparently semi-popish ideas on other matters.

It is particularly striking that, among conformist clergy, it was precisely the more rigid Calvinists, the most dedicated anti-papal writers, who were the strongest and most consistent early supporters of *iure divino* episcopacy. Matthew Sutcliffe, John Bridges, George Downame, and later Richard Crakanthorp and George Carleton, all specifically maintained that bishops were *iure divino* – not merely an ancient order, but also apostolic and of divine institution. By contrast, those avant-garde conformist divines who wished to emphasize the sacramental life of the church advanced *iure divino* arguments in a fashion that was far more qualified at first. Hooker is noticeable for his decidedly muted treatment of the *iure divino* case for episcopacy. In line with his more general arguments, he sought to avoid treating episcopacy as an immutable system of government. Hooker's defender Covell made no explicit mention of *iure divino* (as opposed to merely apostolical) claims when he defended episcopacy against the arguments of the moderate puritan John Burgess. *Iure divino* arguments might conceivably have had a greater initial appeal for Calvinist writers with their predilection for more absolute, polarized conceptions of the nature of the church, their vigorous scripturalism and their unwillingness to embrace the colder Whitgiftian, adiaphoristic view of the nature of the visible church. The unbending Calvinism of these early exponents of *iure divino* episcopacy may have helped to secure at least the tacit acceptance of the doctrine among puritan groups, although in the longer term *iure divino*

22 W.D.J. Cargill Thompson, *Studies in the Reformation* (1980), pp.94–130.

views would also become more acceptable to those committed to a more sacerdotal and sacrament-centred view of the visible church, and puritan reservations naturally increased.[23]

By the reign of James I, the doctrine that bishops were *iure divino* had become an established orthodoxy. King James himself gave the argument his full support, and it was also endorsed by the whole of Convocation in the 1606 Canons concerning ecclesiastical government, although these were never confirmed by the king. The doctrine also appeared in the University of Oxford as a formally approved Act thesis in 1602. John Burgess found himself rebuked by Covell in 1606 when he maintained the previously acceptable adiaphoristic position that neither rule by bishops nor by elders was prescribed by the Apostles, but that neither was repugnant to the Word of God. Direct opposition to *iure divino* arguments now came only from Scotland rather than England, in the form of a range of anonymous works against George Downame's exposition of the doctrine, but they would seem to have had little impact in England.[24]

Nevertheless, the position was still confused. Some English Protestants, such as Willet, clearly disagreed with the *iure divino* doctrine, although they did not dare to voice their misgivings in direct conflict with their fellow English Protestants. Instead, their critical remarks were made in works written against Cardinal Bellarmine's use of the doctrine. Many theological works printed in England continued to be at least potentially in opposition to the *iure divino* position, and indeed to bishops more generally. For example, William Perkins scrupulously avoided dealing with issues of ecclesiastical polity directly, but still managed to discuss the platform of church government laid down in Acts without referring to bishops at all. William Bedell, later to be a bishop himself, specifically rejected the *iure divino* position in 1605, but this was in an anti-papal tract that remained in manuscript, although it was widely circulated.[25] The

23 John Bridges, *A Defence of the Government Established* (1587), pp.337–9; Sutcliffe, *Treatise*, pp.67–8; H.C. Porter, *The Inconstant Savage* (1979), p.349; Carleton, *Jurisdiction*; Downame, *Two Sermons*; John Prideaux, *De Episcopatu Epistola* (1660) (and *idem*, *Manuductio* (1657), p.87; *Fasciculus* (1647), pp.204–17); Laud, *Works*, V: 90; Lake, *Anglicans and Puritans*, pp.90–7. For Hooker, see Lake, *Anglicans and Puritans*, pp.220–3; for Covell, see his *Briefe Answer*, pp.32–4; *idem*, *Modest Examination*, pp.101, 104–5.

24 For King James' endorsement, see his *Premonition* (1609), p.44 ('That bishops ought to be in the Church, I ever maintained it, as an Apostolike institution, and so the ordinance of God') – quoted in J.P. Sommerville, 'The royal supremacy and episcopacy "jure divino", 1603–1640', *JEH* 34 (1983), p.552 n.19; Featley, *Cygnea*, pp.12–13; Barlow, *Summe*, p.36; Clark, *Register*, p.203; Covell, *Briefe Answer*, pp.31–4 (although Covell here emphasizes the apostolic succession rather than an explicit *iure divino* position against Burgess); Collinson, *Religion of Protestants*, pp.11–12.

25 Breward, *Perkins*, p.116 n.21; LPL, Lambeth MS 772 pp.145, 151; for Willet, see introduction, p.16. Copies of Bedell's 'Defence of the Answer to Mr. Alabaster's Four

conflict over *iure divino* episcopacy remained latent, at least in England, until the 1630s. It took a Dutch Calvinist minister, Gerson Bucerus, in his *Dissertatio* of 1618, to point out the theoretical conflict between the views expressed against Rome by Willet, Whitaker and other moderate puritans, and the *iure divino* arguments of a Calvinist conformist such as Downame.[26]

The initial reaction of many English Protestants to the arguments over church government may have been similar to that of the young George Downame, who decided to avoid looking into the theological issues out of fear that he might be converted to either episcopalian or presbyterian views, and would then have to follow through their implications. Constant Jessop's father forbade discussion even in private of issues relating to church government, or any mention of them in public, in order to ensure that he would be free to fulfil his ministry. As episcopacy became more entrenched, the dilemma of such ministers became less problematical, but they did not necessarily accept the theological underpinning of the episcopalian position. Older notions more akin to those of Rainolds were still visible even in the universities. For example, there is little sign of a special role for episcopacy in the lectures of the Jacobean Lady Margaret Professor at Oxford Sebastian Benefield, who was happy to resort to foreign Calvinist divines such as Sibrandus Lubbertus for much of his discussion of church government. Even among the arguments of those who defended episcopacy, very different emphases might be observed. The puritan William Ames remarked in the early 1630s that there were still different opinions even among Church of England bishops regarding whether bishops were *iure divino*. Some held that they were, and would give up

Demands' also survive in BL, Add. MS 10055; Bodl., Rawlinson MS C.922; Bodl., MS Eng. th. c.65; Emmanuel College, Cambridge, MS III.1.13. Sommerville ('Royal supremacy', p.556) may thus be optimistic concerning the degree of acceptance of the doctrine of *iure divino* episcopacy in this period.

26 Bucerus, *Dissertatio de Gubernatione Ecclesiae*, pp.294–5, 567–8, 573–88 and *passim*. Bucerus was far from being an obscure, uninformed observer. He had notable links with England: his father had been minister for a time to the Dutch Church at Sandwich, a position which Bucerus held in his turn for a couple of years in the late 1580s, after which he studied briefly in Cambridge before being called back to the Low Countries. He maintained close links with England, especially as a friend and correspondent of Simeon Ruytinck, the pastor of the Dutch Church in London, and was clearly proficient in the English language. His *Dissertatio* – composed as a refutation of Downame's *Sermon Defending the Honourable Function of Bishops* – may have been timed deliberately to coincide with the ratification of the Articles of Perth: as a minister of Veere, where the Scottish staple was based, Bucerus would doubtless have had contacts with the Scots presbyterian church based there. In this context, King James' outraged response to the *Dissertatio* was understandable: C.A. Tukker, 'Gerson Bucerus – Jakobus I – De Statenvertaling', *NAvK* 50 (1969–70); Nijenhuis, 'The controversy', pp.207–20.

their bishoprics if this could not be proved; 'others holding them onely of humane Institution, and yet lawfull'.[27]

Even among those who upheld episcopacy as *iure divino*, there were implicit disagreements about what the term actually signified, although this may have served to encourage the doctrine's passive acceptance rather than to reduce it. It was with some justice that the Calvinist conformist Robert Sanderson observed that 'the truth is, all this ado about Ius Divinum is in the last result no more than a verbal nicety: that term being not always taken in the one and the same latitude of signification.'[28]

One important point that remained undecided in conformist writings was the question of whether episcopacy's dominical institution entailed that it was a perpetual and immutable ordinance of God – how far, that is, it overthrew earlier adiaphoristic notions of church government. For the first *iure divino* writers, *iure divino* and adiaphoristic notions did not seem irreconcilable. On the contrary, writers such as Hooker, Bancroft and Bridges specifically argued that there was no immutable and necessary form of government *prescribed* in Scripture, even though episcopacy might have scriptural warrant and recommendation.[29] This position was similarly maintained by conformist writers in the early part of James' reign, although they avoided Hooker and Whitgift's direct suggestions that bishops might be abolished if their continued existence was deemed inappropriate. Thus the Calvinist episcopalian John King, after expounding the *iure divino* position, raised the point that, even if the presbyterian form of church government could be found in the early church (which he denied), 'one and the selfe-same forme of Church-policie befitteth not all times, and al places, but according to the variety therof ... receiveth, nay requireth variation of orders'.[30]

All writers recognized that the phrase 'iure divino' could sometimes be

[27] Downame, *Two Sermons*, ii, sig.¶4r–v; Constant Jessop, *The Angel of the Church of Ephesus no Bishop of Ephesus* (1644), sig.A2v; Benefield, *Doctrinae Christianae*, pp.23–5; Ames, *Fresh Suit*, i. p.104. Benefield answered Bellarmine's objections concerning Protestants' lack of episcopal succession and ordination with citations of the replies of Whitaker, and of the foreign presbyterians Junius, Daneau and Lubbertus. He also cited Junius for the defence of ordination by presbyters and even deacons, as well as bishops. Similarly, Benefield denied that the use of three bishops for ordination was apostolic – it was sanctioned as pious, but not as necessary.

[28] *The Works of Robert Sanderson, D.D.*, ed. W. Jacobson (6 vols., Oxford, 1854), V: 151 – cited in J. Spurr, *The Restoration Church of England, 1646–1689* (New Haven, 1991), p.134.

[29] M.R. Sommerville, 'Richard Hooker and his contemporaries on episcopacy: an Elizabethan consensus', *JEH* 35 (1984). It should be stressed (*pace* Sykes) that episcopacy was not seen as being dominical simply because of its historical continuance – it was also alleged to be of divine *institution*.

[30] King, *Fourth Sermon*, p.28 (cf. pp.29–30). Cf. Bancroft, *Tracts*, pp.88, 108 (cited in Sommerville, 'Richard Hooker', pp.185–6).

taken to imply an immutable command. Nevertheless, the term was generally interpreted in a mutable sense when debating other issues – most clearly during the Sabbatarian controversy in the 1630s. In their contributions to this debate, divines such as Twisse, Prideaux and Robert Sanderson distinguished two different senses of *iure divino*, and applied a mutable one to both the establishment of the Lord's Day, and to episcopacy. Sanderson rejected a distinction of matters into the categories of simply *iure ecclesiastico* and *iure divino*, but instead distinguished two senses of *iure divino*. The first consisted of those things which are 'primarily, properly, and directly' of divine right as being enjoined by God's express ordinance or command in Scripture, or deducible therefrom 'by necessary, evident, and demonstrative illation'. The second 'larger signification' comprehended those things which could probably be deduced from Scripture by human reason, 'as a thing most convenient to be observed by all such as desire unfeignedly to order their ways according to God's Holy Will'. While things which were *iure divino* in the first sense must be observed inviolably, things *iure divino* in the second sense were such as 'every Particular Church, but much more the Universal, hath a power to alter in a case of necessity'. 'But', Sanderson continued, 'the exercise of that power is so limited to extraordinary cases, that it may not be safe for her at all to exercise it; unless it be for the avoiding of mighty inconveniencies, not otherwise to be avoided.'[31]

These distinctions between the different senses of the term 'iure divino' were rarely explained in the debates on episcopacy. One attempt was made by George Downame in his 1608 sermon defending episcopacy, where he explained the *iure divino* nature of episcopacy in terms of Sanderson's second, 'larger signification' of divine right, though with reference to the distinction between mutable and immutable apostolic institutions:

> Though in respect of the first institution, there is small difference between an apostolical & divine ordinance, because what was ordained by the Apostles, proceeded from God, (in which sense & no other, I doe hold the episcopall function to bee a divine ordinance): yet in respect of perpetuity, difference by some is made betwixt those things which be *divini*, and those which be *apostolici iuris*: the former in their understanding beeing generally, perpetually and immutably necessary; the latter, not so.[32]

Downame's careful distinction was rarely specified elsewhere, as divines often took 'iure apostolico' to mean 'iure divino' and vice versa, so that the potential for an immutable reading of the *iure divino* position clearly

[31] Sanderson, *Works* V: 11–14 (*A Sovereign Antidote against Sabbatarian Errours* (1636)); Twisse, *Of the Morality*, p.42 ('38'); Prideaux, *Doctrine*, p.32.

[32] Downame, *Two Sermons*, ii. p.92 n.2.

persisted.[33] Immutability as such was not generally emphasized, although Saravia had provided an uncompromising reading on this point. However, the Canons of 1606 (supposedly approved by the assembled Convocations of both provinces) had explicitly maintained that the apostolical form of church government should be continued forever, and claimed that it was wrong to suggest that one form of church government would be unfit for other times.[34] The resulting position was confused, to say the least, as Convocation would have been required to question the orthodoxy of Bishop King, who had maintained precisely the position which the Canons condemned in his sermon before the Scots presbyterians in the same year, in the king's presence and with his approbation.[35]

By the Caroline period, however, there was an effort to iron out some of these inconsistencies. To begin with, the dominical institution of episcopacy was now asserted even more directly and inflexibly as an orthodox doctrine of the English Church. A list of 'Certaine articles' to be imposed in London diocese in 1635 included the specification 'That the order of bishops is by the law of God.' Peter Heylyn accused Bishop Williams of having had a mind to 'betray the cause' because he had referred at one point to the *apostolic* institution of episcopacy. Instead, Heylyn insisted that episcopacy must be *iure divino* in an immutable sense or nothing: 'let the Bishop stand alone on Apostolicall right, and no more than so, and doubt it not but some will take it on your word, and then pleade accordingly; that things of Apostolicall institution, may be laid aside'. To assert that episcopacy was *iure apostolico* was thus in Heylyn's eyes a sure sign of disaffection: out of fear of offending the foreign Protestant Churches, Heylyn claimed, Williams had waived 'the maine groundworke and foundation on which ... [we] stand'.[36]

Similarly, Laud insisted that Joseph Hall should alter a defence of episcopacy as apostolic into one which emphasized that it had been instituted by Christ. A bare assertion of apostolical institution, he warned, could risk episcopacy being treated as simply another mutable apostolic tradition. Laud's argument thus reversed the position maintained by earlier conformists such as Downame. Laud was determined to remove the flexibility and ambiguity that loose defences of episcopacy as *iure divino* had been able to incorporate. Indeed, he was especially keen to guard against,

33 For examples of this treatment of apostolic and divine authority as synonymous, see Featley, *Cygnea*, p.13.

34 John Overall, *The Convocation Book of MDCVI. Commonly Called Bishop Overall's Convocation Book* (Oxford, 1844), pp.132, 133–6, 147–50, 155ff.

35 See above. Other *iure divino* theorists who still maintained that the form of government of the church might vary according to the times include John Bridges: Lake, *Anglicans and Puritans*, p.91.

36 PRO, SP 16/308/43; Heylyn, *Antidotum*, ii. pp.7–8. See also D'Ewes, *Journal*, p.241.

not dogmatic presbyterians, but 'some of a milder and subtler alloy ... in the Genevan ... faction' who would be prepared to accept a qualified reading of episcopacy as *iure divino*. It was the very fact that so many divines seemed able to maintain the *iure divino* position without holding it to imply the perpetual necessity of episcopal government as the ordained means of salvation that caused Laud's dissatisfaction. Laud's determination to see the debate merely in terms of the division between the categories of *iure ecclesiastico* (and therefore mutable) and *iure divino* (and therefore immutable) was the same as that adopted by Laudian pamphleteers in the Sabbatarian controversy. In both cases, by ironing out ambiguities embedded in contemporary phraseology, the Laudian divines forced a polarization of opinion and allegiance.[37]

While the *iure divino* status of episcopacy was not therefore necessarily an issue that divided conformist writers, it was in the interpretation of this term (did it denote an apostolical recommendation or a divine prescription?) that a larger split was potentially visible. This could also hold important implications for the way that English divines understood foreign ministerial orders. Moreover, these conflicting interpretations of the *iure divino* position themselves reflected a number of new advances in the way in which episcopacy was perceived, which will now be explored.

Episcopal succession

One notable change occurred in the treatment of the episcopal succession during the Jacobean period. It tended to shift away from mere assertions of the endurance and historical continuance of episcopacy, and towards an emphasis on the linear, personal succession of bishops. This transition was by no means simply an innovation of Laudians or of avant-garde conformists. Rather, many churchmen were happy to emphasize this point as an effective polemical strategy against Rome, although even here there were concerns raised over its possible implications for the integrity of the foreign Reformed Churches. The importance of a linear apostolic succession was initially emphasized by Roman controversialists such as Bellarmine, who made it a mark of the true church, exploiting the arguments of the patristic authors Tertullian and Irenaeus. The initial response of Protestants was to argue that there could be no rightful apostolic succession if the personal succession were not accompanied by a succession in apostolic truth.[38] Without true doctrine, the personal succession was worthless. This mode of thought was the counterpart of the Protestant view of church history, which traced the survival of the church in the medieval centuries by the

[37] Laud, *Works*, VI: 573–5. [38] E.g. Lynde, *Case*, pp.4–6.

succession of true doctrine, rather than through an institutional continuity. Nonetheless, there was a certain ambiguity in the argument here. A succession of doctrine need not simply negate the importance of an institutional succession: the general Protestant argument was merely directed against the importance that Romanists attached to the latter to the exclusion of the former. This imprecision would allow some Protestants to draw the implication that the succession of true doctrine, while undoubtedly more significant than a local institutional succession, still should not exist without it.[39]

During the Jacobean period, divines increasingly emphasized and exploited the Church of England's local episcopal succession. This line of argument was initially developed, not for use against presbyterians, but merely as another weapon against Rome, and was often tacked on to defences of a purely doctrinal succession.[40] As such, it was a card which even puritans were happy to play. Thus Willet invoked the familiar passages of Tertullian and Irenaeus to affirm that a succession of godly bishops was indeed a blessing, even though he still insisted that the mere local succession of bishops could be no sure mark of the church of Christ. William Sclater declared in 1609 (in a sermon otherwise sharply critical of recent trends in avant-garde conformity) that the Church of England's bishops 'have more then probably derived their succession' from the Apostles.[41] Other puritans were less happy to invoke this point, but still contrived to avoid any direct attack upon the notion of an episcopal succession.[42] Puritans might have been reassured by the fact that, as a result of the origins of this argument in anti-papal polemic, it was often combined with a denial that Rome had herself retained an uninterrupted episcopal succession, thereby avoiding the hazard of seeming to place the

39 A.L. Peck, *Anglicanism and Episcopacy* (1958), p.15; Sykes, *Old Priest*, p.16. This was an ambiguity that was more evident in some divines' treatment of the issue than in others'. More emphatically Reformed divines such as Andrew Willet, John White, Anthony Wotton and Sebastian Benefield provide clear arguments for a succession of true doctrine despite an interruption in the personal succession of ministers: Willet, *Synopsis* (1600), p.69; White, *The Way*, pp.402–5, 411; Wotton, *Trial*, pp.396–7; Benefield, *Doctrinae Christianae*, pp.27–8. See also above pp.279–80.

40 See, for example, its treatment in early Jacobean anti-papal tracts by William Bedell and John White. Bedell notes it briefly before proceeding to deal with the defence of extraordinary vocations, while White, having rejected an outward and visible succession, then mentions the Church of England's own episcopal succession almost as an afterthought: LPL, Lambeth MS 772 pp.122–43; White, *The Way*, p.412.

41 Willet, *Hexapla on Romans*, p.433; Sclater, *Threefold Preservative*, sig.E4v. Sclater, however, seems to endorse an apostolic rather than a specifically *iure divino* position (*pace* Fincham, *Prelate*, p.10).

42 E.g. Taylor, *Christs Victorie*, pp.102–4, where Taylor discusses Bellarmine's use of episcopal succession as a note of the church, but manages to avoid the issue of bishops altogether.

Church of England on the side of Rome and against the non-episcopal Reformed Churches on this issue.[43]

While the Church of England's linear episcopal succession had already been polemically employed in a manuscript treatise composed by William Bedell as early as 1605, the most important work to expound it was commissioned by Archbishop Abbot. Abbot encouraged his chaplain Francis Mason to compose his *Of the Consecration of Bishops* (published in 1613) as an exhaustive apologia for the English ministry, in which the official registers of consecration were cited at length to prove the episcopal succession under Edward and Elizabeth.[44] Samuel Ward immediately spied the danger of such an exclusive defence of Anglican orders, and anxiously enquired of Ussher how Mason had defended the vocation and ordination of the ministers of the foreign Reformed Churches. He need not have worried. In fact, Mason would later compose a tract to defend the validity of the ordination of such ministers. Even in his earlier treatise, Mason was careful to ensure in the dialogue format of *Of the Consecration* that it was the Romanist 'Philodox' (and hence the mouthpiece of error) who proposed the argument that, even if the existence of a successive local ordination was insufficient to conclude *positively* that the true church resided there, it could yet be determined *negatively* that there was no church where this successive ordination did not exist.[45] In the future, however, Philodox's argument would find its Laudian supporters.

For all its apparent acceptance by English Protestants, the episcopal succession was clearly an issue that was potentially divisive. An example of how far it might be taken had already been provided by William Covell, writing at the beginning of James' reign. Pressurized by his puritan opponent, Covell had emphasized that bishops acted as spiritual fathers to the laity, and carried a continual succession from the Apostles' hands. Remarkably, Covell did not emphasize a *iure divino* position. Nevertheless, discussion of the issue of personal succession allowed him to adopt an

43 See examples above p.137 n. 33; Chillingworth, *Religion of Protestants* (1845 edn), pp.123–5; Benefield, *Doctrinae Christianae*, pp.26–7; Willet, *Synopsis* (1600), pp.68–9.

44 Bedell's 'Defence of the Answer to Mr. Alabaster's Four Demands' (completed in 1605 but never published) defends the continual succession of bishops in the Church of England, and includes a detailed treatment of the consecration of Archbishop Parker: LPL, MS 772 pp.122–43 (cf. *idem*, *Certaine Letters*, pp.141–4). See also the expanded second edition of Francis Godwin's *Catalogue*, published in 1615. Mason's posthumous *Vindiciae* – an expansion of his earlier *Of the Consecration* – was edited and published by Nathaniel Brent, also on Abbot's advice and recommendation. It is thus important to stress that Mason was writing from within the Calvinist tradition, as chaplain to Abbot, although a later puritan writer would describe him peremptorily as 'Mr Mason, the Bishop of Londons Chaplaine, an Arminian': Walker, *True Relation*, p.19. See also above, pp.329–30.

45 Mason, *Of the Consecration*, p.43; Ussher, *Works*, XV: 85. Peck (*Anglicanism*, p.15) tends rather too easily to assume Philodox's reading of the issue.

especially combative tone. He thus emphasized that the chair of succession of bishops continued even in the present day 'where abomination or desolation (that is heresie or violence) have not broake it off'. Covell argued in a similar tone two years later, this time opposing the more moderate John Burgess. Rejecting Burgess' adiaphoristic arguments, Covell again made little play of an explicit *iure divino* position, but rested his case on a succession of bishops.[46] The crucial difference here lay in the identity of the person addressed. Against a Romanist, the episcopal succession was an effective weapon, although Francis Mason had preferred to interpret the absence of episcopacy and of the personal succession in some Protestant countries as being a 'desolation' brought about by the Roman bishops' refusal to support the Reformation. The non-episcopal Protestant Churches therefore required sympathy rather than chastisement.[47] When the succession was turned against a Protestant opponent, however, it naturally acquired altogether more damaging implications for the integrity of the non-episcopal churches.

Further potential complications arose when clerics tried to define the precise nature of the episcopal succession. Writers such as Fulke, Willet, Sclater and others were happy to maintain that it consisted merely of the authority to ordain which was passed on from minister to minister in unbroken succession. Beginning with Thomas Bilson in the 1590s, however, some English divines began to suggest that it was the grace given in ordination that was transmitted by the apostolical succession. These were not clearly defined, alternative positions, and the arguments of Francis Mason and others seem to oscillate between them.[48] However, in the hands of divines more dedicated to a theology which emphasized the means of grace bestowed in episcopal ordination and consecration, the personal line of succession was potentially of far greater significance.[49] It then became not merely a catalogue of orthodoxy, but a lifeline which had preserved apostolic grace.

Not surprisingly, it was the latter line of argument, with its emphasis on the transmission of apostolic grace, that emerged far more strongly during the 1630s. Laudian pamphleteers such as John Pocklington made enthusiastic use of the passages from Irenaeus and Augustine which had long been popular with Roman polemicists – passages which emphasized the importance that the primitive church had attached to the local succession

[46] Covell, *Modest Examination*, pp.104–5, 115 (for the defence of episcopacy as apostolical, see *ibid.*, p.101); *idem*, *Briefe Answer*, pp.33–4.
[47] Mason, *Of the Consecration*, sig.A3v.
[48] P.F. Bradshaw, *The Angican Ordinal* (1971), pp.45–6.
[49] E.g. Andrewes, *Two Answers*, p.29; Bramhall, *Works*, II: 591 – quoted in G.H. Tavard, *The Quest for Catholicity* (1963), p.61.

of bishops as the very mark that distinguished Catholic Christians from heretics. However, these Laudian authors were happy now to retain the exclusive emphases that Romanists had used in expounding these passages. They avoided earlier Protestant interpretations which had emphasized the qualifying role of true doctrine.[50] They also invoked these passages outside the specifically anti-papal polemical context, using them instead as a way of justifying episcopacy to fellow-Protestants. Pocklington stressed the comfort that English Protestants could gain from knowing their archbishop to be the successor of an apostle, and implied that the personal succession could be a guarantor of true doctrine. Similarly, Christopher Dow underlined 'the necessity of an uninterrupted succession in the Church of those that who shall lawfully be invested with this [episcopal] power, which can at no time be wanting in the Church, without the ruin of that building'.[51]

One of the most extreme defences of the importance of the personal succession was supplied by one John Yates in his *Treatise of the Honour of God's House*, dedicated to Wren's commissary Clere Talbot, and licensed by one of Laud's chaplains. Yates warned that ordination was not justifiable without a bishop 'who is able to derive his succession in that respect from the Apostles', and directly quoted Bellarmine with approval who 'saith truely' (according to Yates) that 'there can be no visible Church where there is no visible succession from the chairs of the Apostles'. Moreover, Yates, along with Richard Montagu, directly associated the personal, episcopal succession with Christ's promise to his Apostles to be with them until the end of the world. In this case, the personal succession directly overthrew Protestants' previous emphasis upon the succession of true doctrine, and would seem to leave the foreign non-episcopal churches with no escape.[52] That the foreign churches were threatened had already

50 E.g. White, *The Way*, pp.402–8; Wotton, *Trial*, pp.299, 393–7, 408; Abbot, *Second Part*, pp.876–7.

51 Pocklington, *Sunday no Sabbath*, p.47; Dow, *Innovations*, p.175. For an example of an unqualified invocation of the passages of Irenaeus and Tertullian by an early Jacobean avant-garde conformist, see Barlow, *One of the Foure Sermons*, sig.E1r–v.

52 John Yates, *A Treatise of the Honour of Gods House* (1637), pp.21–2, 35 and ch.7; Montagu, *ΘΕΑΝΘΡΩΠΙΚΟΝ*, II: 463–4. The precise identity of the author of the former treatise is unclear. It is certainly possible that this John Yates is the same divine whose earlier *Ibis ad Caesarem* had been directed against Richard Montagu (as *STC* seems to suggest). If so, then Yates would appear to be merely one of many divines who trimmed to the Laudian wind in the 1630s. Nevertheless, the extremism of the defence of episcopacy and of the visible church in this treatise is in striking disparity with the tone of the *Ibis*. There are several other ministers of this name active in the 1630s who may be more likely authors of the *Treatise* (see Venn and Venn (eds.), *Alumni Cantabrigiensis*). Sutcliffe had arguably foreshadowed Yates' use of Matthew 28.20 in his *Treatise* (pp.62, 70), but in this tract the force of this point was greatly diminished by the fact that, later in the same work

been implied by de Dominis in the seventh book of his *De Republica Ecclesiastica*, which he completed during the final period of his residence in England, when he was in contact with Montagu, Goodman and others. The archbishop of Spalato had argued that an episcopal succession was a necessary mark of a true church, and remarked that those Protestant Churches where only presbyters ordained might not possess a true ministry.[53]

Order and degree

Much of the disagreement concerning the nature of episcopacy turned largely on the question of whether episcopacy was understood to be a degree of the priesthood, or a separate order altogether. In the Elizabethan period, conformists had been most anxious to emphasize that bishops represented a greater degree of the ministry than ordinary ministers. Most Jacobean and Caroline conformist divines continued to maintain that bishops did not differ from presbyters as a separate order – rather, they were of the same order, but not of the same dignity within that order. While stressing the basic point of the imparity of clerical dignity, they did not accept that this might imply any spiritual difference.[54] There were, admittedly, varying priorities at work among the different authors. To John Davenant, the question of 'order' or 'degree' was a needless quibble which he did not wish to debate. Saravia contrived not to discuss the issue at all. However, to William Bedell and Francis Mason, who sought to justify the validity of the orders of the foreign Reformed Churches, the rejection of the Romanist claim that episcopacy was a separate order rather than merely a degree of the priesthood was the most important point of all. It enabled them to claim that those churches 'which embrace the discipline of Geneva ... also have Bishops in effect' as long as they preserved an element of imparity. As Bedell put it, 'Presbyters might ordaine them a Bishop now, as well as they did in the Primitive Church ... because a Bishop & a Presbyter are not divers orders but degrees in the same.'[55]

(pp.213–21), Sutcliffe maintained that a single form of church government need not always be maintained in the church.

53 Malcolm, *De Dominis*, p.64. Malcolm notes that de Dominis' discussion of the point is very different from that which he had employed some years earlier in volume one of the same work, where the archbishop had carefully refrained from referring to other Protestant Churches.

54 E.g. Prideaux, *De Episcopatu*, p.4; Mede, *Works*, p.34; Tavard, *Quest*, pp.37–8. It is noteworthy that Mede's passages which emphasized that episcopacy constituted merely a degree of the priesthood rather than a separate order were not printed in the 1642 edition of his *Diatribae*, but only appeared in the post-Restoration editions of Mede's complete works: compare Joseph Mede, *Diatribae* (1642), pp.109, 110.

55 Mason, *Church of England*, pp.91–3, 110; Mason, 'Validity', pp.132, 142–62, 173–5; LPL, Lambeth MS 772 pp.132, 144, 146. Ussher also implied that it was this point which

Nevertheless, there were anomalies enshrined in many aspects of the Elizabethan settlement that suggested that bishops might constitute a separate order. This appears most clearly in relation to the ceremony of confirmation.[56] At least one of the puritan petitions at the beginning of James' reign had complained that the rite of confirmation was performed only by bishops. It was objected that this fact might give rise to the error that a bishop is superior to other ministers, not only in jurisdiction, but even in his order and ministerial function. Indeed, John Rainolds argued at the Hampton Court Conference that every minister should be able to confirm his own parishioners.[57] Conformist defenders of the ceremony had therefore generally tended to downplay confirmation's sacramental aspects, and to emphasize that a bishop was only preferred for reasons purely of civil precedence (echoing the arguments of Jerome). For example, John Prideaux and Francis Mason defended confirmation, but insisted that the minister should be a bishop, not by the necessity of the law, but as a recognition of his special honour, while in more extraordinary circumstances the same ceremony could be administered by a presbyter. When defending confirmation at Hampton Court, King James emphasized simply its purely practical value in providing religious instruction for children, and suggested that it should be termed the examination (rather than confirmation) of the said children. Similarly, George Hakewill's account of the benefits of the rite, dedicated (as chaplain) to his patron Prince Charles on the occasion of the prince's own confirmation in 1613, concentrated almost entirely on its value as a confession of faith.[58]

By contrast, when six years later Edward Boughen, chaplain to the avant-garde conformist Bishop Howson, gave a visitation sermon on the subject of confirmation at the request of the bishop, his list of the benefits accorded by the rite concentrated almost exclusively on the soul's reception of the Holy Ghost.[59] Throughout his defence of the ceremony, Boughen emphasized the internal graces and miraculous gifts bestowed thereby. Confirmation was 'the ordinarie meanes whereby we receive the holy Ghost ... to the enc[r]ease & strength of faith', and Boughen followed Optatus' suggestion that its institution by Christ predated, not only His preaching to the Gentiles, but even His preaching to the Jews.[60] Moreover,

allowed him to defend the validity of foreign presbyterian orders: Mason, *Church of England*, p.122.

56 On the practice of confirmation during this period, see Collinson, *Religion of Protestants*, pp.51–2; Fincham, *Prelate*, pp.123–9.

57 Bodl., Bodley MS 124 p.11; Barlow, *Summe*, pp.33–4.

58 Prideaux, *Manuductio*, p.157; Mason, 'Validity', pp.164–5; Barlow, *Summe*, p.7; Babbage, *Puritanism*, p.67; George Hakewill, *The Auncient Ecclesiasticall Practise of Confirmation* (1613), pp.2–3.

59 Boughen, *A Sermon*, p.69.

60 *Ibid*., pp.6, 31, 40, 65–6.

for Boughen the presence of bishops was crucial. He maintained precisely the opposite position to Prideaux and Mason, stating explicitly that those who admitted no hierarchy in their church government, and denied the order of bishops, of necessity must not administer confirmation, as it was only to be performed by bishops.[61] The Laudian Edmund Reeve spelled out this exalted position even more clearly in the 1630s, by insisting that mere priests were simply incapable of administering confirmation ('the giving of the holy Ghost') because it was a distinctive feature of a bishop's ministerial power. Just as a lay person does not have enough 'spirituall power' to absolve a penitent sinner, similarly, Reeve maintained, 'to Confirme, to cause such a measure of the Holy Ghost to descend upon a baptized partie, *a Priest hath not enough spirituall power*, but a Bishop onely'.[62]

The more sacerdotal view of ordination that was becoming current at this time similarly added an exalted, spiritual component to a power exercised only by bishops. Implicit in such arguments was the notion that episcopacy indeed constituted a separate ministerial order, and by the late Jacobean and Caroline period some clerics were beginning to spell this out explicitly. Lancelot Andrewes had been one of the first divines to argue this point directly. In his letters to the Huguenot minister Pierre du Moulin in 1618–19, Andrewes unequivocally denied that presbyters and bishops were all of one order, despite du Moulin's complaints. Against the argument used by Field and Mason (as well as du Moulin) that the fact that bishops were 'consecrated' rather than 'ordained' showed that a separate order was not intended, Andrewes demonstrated that the word 'ordain' was frequently employed by patristic authors to describe the making of bishops.[63] Most strikingly, Andrewes insisted that this position was held by all the members of the Church of England.

The claim that episcopacy was a distinct order rather than a degree of presbytery was also a point of vital importance for William Laud. He defended it as a DD thesis in 1608, and also forced Joseph Hall to adopt the same point in the latter's *Episcopacy by Divine Right Asserted*. He insisted to Hall that this was 'the very main of the cause'. If episcopacy was only different by degree and circumstantially, he argued, then it could only be a

[61] *Ibid.*, p.21 (cf. p.60). [62] Reeve, *Communion Booke*, p.205 (my emphasis).

[63] Andrewes, *Opuscula*, pp.181–3; Mason, 'Validity', pp.142, 158; Field, *Of the Church*, I: 63, 318–23, 324, III: 215–18, IV: 148–51 – cited in Mason, *Church of England*, pp.61–4. Both Francis Mason and Field, in denying episcopacy to be a separate order, represented consecration as an act which simply legitimated and freed for use powers which were inherent in the priesthood. Mason thus insisted that 'that which is added in Episcopall Consecration, whereby a Bishop is distinguished from a Presbyter, is neither Sacrament of order, nor imprinteth a Character': Mason, 'Validity', p.142.

point of positive law, and as such could easily be changed.[64] Insistence on this point, however, ultimately undermined many of the arguments fashioned to excuse the orders of the Reformed Churches. If episcopacy and its power of ordination did indeed constitute a separate order, then ordination by presbyters could only happen outside the church's normal means of salvation.

Classifying episcopacy as a separate order, rather than a degree of the priesthood, represented the ultimate logic of many of the trends in Laudian clericalism. By the 1630s, Laudian authors may be found declaring that the bishops enjoyed, not merely a superiority in temporal jurisdiction, but also inherently greater spiritual knowledge and grace, all apparently as a function of their consecration. Edmund Reeve maintained 'that the Fathers of the Church now and alwaies doe in the great mystery of godlinesse comprehend many things which the common people ... yea also Ministers of the inferiour order ... doe not apprehend'. The bishops, he explained, were 'the holy Fatherhood', or 'Fathers in God', among whom the archbishop was 'the eldest in grace'. Bishops came to be spoken of as the sole guides of the conscience: 'The people must live after Gods minde, and the Bishop must be their guide therin.' Bishops were thus not merely necessary for order's sake, but were supernaturally imbued with a greater learning in divinity. No simile was too great for them. The conformist John Yates exclaimed that 'As in all the world there is none greater then God, so in the Church and Order Ecclesiasticall, there is none greater then the Bishop.'[65]

However, the opinion that episcopacy was a separate order did not command the adherence of all conformists during the 1630s. Even some preachers favourable to Laudianism during this decade, such as George Wall, still maintained the view that episcopacy represented a separate degree of the priesthood rather than a separate order. Writing to John Dury in November 1640, the Irish bishops Richardson and Bedell reported that the current episcopate was not united on the question of the nature of the imparity of bishops and presbyters. While some bishops held that episcopacy constituted a separate order, there were others (including themselves) who held otherwise. On this matter, at least, Bishop Bedell would appear to have had a less exalted doctrine of episcopacy than his friend Archdeacon Samuel Ward![66]

[64] Clark, *Register*, p.206; Laud, *Works*, VI: 575–8; Hall, *Works*, IX: 196–7. Heylyn, in his later *Respondet Petrus*, would condemn Ussher in similar fashion for having maintained that episcopacy constituted merely a degree of the ministry: Mason, *Church of England*, pp.122–3.

[65] Reeve, *Communion Booke*, pp.20, 131, 206; Yates, *Treatise*, p.34.

[66] George Wall, *A Sermon at the Lord Archbishop of Canterbury his Visitation Metropoliticall* (1635), p.7; SUL, Hartlib MS 5/21–2; SSC, Ward MS O/3 fol.1r. The addressee in the latter draft letter of Ward's is here identified as Bedell on the strength of the

As episcopacy came to be depicted as a separate order, it was regarded as occupying a central role in the constitution and nature of the church. As we have seen, Laudian writers derived from Cyprian an aristocratic vision of the universal church as 'this one and undevided Bishopricke' – an association of independent and equal *iure divino* bishops, with episcopal government both forming a unity within the church, and also providing the basis of the unity of the church as a whole.[67] The greater the ontological role granted to bishops in the universal church, the more difficult it became to find a place for the non-episcopal churches within it.

Sacerdotalism and the ministry

The changing emphasis on the *iure divino* status of episcopacy, its nature as a separate order, and the importance of the apostolical succession, were in themselves merely aspects of a far more fundamental shift taking place in English Protestant understandings of the nature of ecclesiastical discipline, of the ministry, and of the visible church itself. Whether or not it was depicted directly in opposition to a puritan emphasis on preaching, the Laudian period witnessed a more general concern among ministers to emphasize that justification was incomplete without the sacramental life of the church. The minister was believed to possess an ontological status in the church, rather than merely a preaching function. Andrew Willet had already sounded warning bells in the 1590s after reading the works of Richard Hooker, whose emphasis on a sacrament-centred style of worship, and stress on the grace bestowed through the ceremonies and rites of the church, Willet had associated with crypto-popery. Avant-garde conformity under James, and Laudianism under Charles, were notable for the emphasis which their protagonists placed upon the importance of liturgical ceremonies and the sacraments as fountains of grace. The efforts expended in beautifying churches and instilling more reverential forms of public devotion reflected this set of priorities.[68]

Hooker and his avant-garde conformist disciples displayed an enhanced concern for the 'beauty of holiness' and the dignity of the clerical order, but were able to do this without necessarily having to appeal to new authorities or to distance themselves wholly from other conformist

references to his reply to the letters of Wadsworth – presumably those published by Bedell as *Certaine Letters*.

67 See above, pp.224–5, 360–1. Such emphases were not unparalleled: see, for example, Crakanthorp, *Defensio*, p.158 – cited in Tavard, *Quest*, p.58. However, the Laudians were arguably more consistent in their implementation of this perspective.

68 Lake, 'Lancelot Andrewes'; Fincham, *Prelate*, pp.231–40, 276–82; Tyacke, *Anti-Calvinists*, ch.8; Andrew Foster, 'Church policies of the 1630s', in Cust and Hughes, *Conflict*.

authors. After all, as we have seen, there was a broader shift even among many anti-Laudian conformists towards a more committed defence of the visible institutional church and of her ceremonies during this period. Andrewes, Laud and their disciples did not always need to import new theological insights in order to justify their view of an enhanced role for the ceremonies and sacraments of the church. They capitalized on more fundamental ambiguities and inconsistencies in the ways that the sacraments and ceremonies of the church were described by English Protestants. Figurative and rhetorical language in prayers and liturgy had often embodied potentially mechanistic views of the workings of grace in the institutional church. The rites of the Book of Common Prayer contained incautious sacramental language which could invite literal as well as figurative readings. Edward Boughen spoke for many Laudians in the 1630s when he attacked what he saw as the 'far-fetched glosses and figurative interpretations' that had been imposed on passages from the Articles, the Ordinal and the Prayer Book, 'and the doctrine of the Sacraments therein delivered'. Instead, he insisted that men should 'take the words as they lye, take them according to the plaine and common sense and understanding of the same words'.[69]

If the avant-garde conformists' new sacramentalism cannot always be identified with direct theological innovations, it was still distinctive in its emphases, and most especially in its rendering of the priorities of the ministry. The resulting sacerdotalism boosted a tendency towards 'negative popery' (the avoidance of anti-papal caveats) and anti-puritanism when promoting ceremonies. One recent scholar has emphasized how the Jacobean Church, and most particularly its episcopate, was split between those who placed preaching at the centre of the minister's duties, and those for whom the sacraments formed the essential ministerial function. Attacks on contemporaries' overvaluing of preaching to the neglect of public prayer and the sacraments were a standard feature of avant-garde conformist writing from the 1590s onwards in the work of Hooker, Howson, Andrewes, Buckeridge and others. As we have seen, it caused great consternation in the circles of moderate puritans such as Willet.[70] But in the 1620s this churchmanship was to acquire an especially assertive tone. In his 1626 consecration sermon at Durham House, Cosin emphasized that clergymen constituted a holy priesthood and were not merely ministers of the Word.[71] In the 1630s, Laudian and non-Laudian divines clashed directly in Cam-

[69] Edward Boughen, *Two Sermons* (1635), i. p.18. Cf. Reeve, *Communion Booke*, *passim*.
[70] Dent, *Reformers*, pp.210–12; Fincham, *Prelate*, pp.231–93; see also above, introduction, p.17.
[71] Cosin, *Works*, I: 95–6; Fincham, *Prelate*, p.277.

bridge as they debated whether preaching was more important than the duties of reading prayers, administering the sacraments and absolution.[72]

At the heart of much of this new churchmanship was a more exalted form of clericalism than had been evident in Elizabethan Protestantism. An enhanced view of the role of the clergy was to some extent a general phenomenon. In puritan evangelical circles just as much as Laudian ones, increasing emphasis was placed on the role of the minister in providing the key to salvation for the congregation. Moreover, all divines (as we have seen) were happy to unite in attempts to boost the stipends of ministers and to defend the *iure divino* nature of tithes.[73] Nevertheless, in avant-garde conformist circles it was the sacerdotal role of the minister, as a channel of God's grace through the sacraments and rites of the church, which was uppermost in men's minds. Laudian sermons were drenched in vivid images celebrating the ministry as a sacrificing priesthood.

Other clerical functions gradually acquired a more clearly sacerdotal gloss. This is particularly noticeable in the case of confession and absolution. A range of conformist divines had increasingly encouraged confession to a minister, along with private confession to God and public confession in the church. Generally, they defended confession to a minister on the grounds of his ability to administer comfort and quieten the layman's conscience. In these defences, the transmission of grace was carefully played down. But some avant-garde conformist divines were keen to emphasize the sacramental aspects of the rite. The treatment of auricular confession in the court sermons of avant-garde conformists such as Barlow, Andrewes and Carier was already causing concern in James' reign.[74] By the 1630s some Laudian divines were moving several stages further, and causing offence among fellow-conformists. Several started to imply that confession was a sacrament (though not operating *ex opere operato*) that was necessary as an ordinary means toward salvation, to the outrage of even moderate Calvinist divines such as Ward and Davenant.[75] Laudian writers also maintained that priests had an authoritative and judicial, as well as a ministerial, power to remit confessed sins, and therefore urged lay

[72] CUL, MS Com Ct I.18 fol.110.

[73] See above p.334. On 'puritan clericalism', see Collinson, *Religion of Protestants*, ch.3; Lake, *Moderate Puritans*, pp.130–3; *idem*, *Anglicans and Puritans*, pp.27–8, 109–10, 112, 114. See also R. O'Day, *The English Clergy* (Leicester, 1979).

[74] Croft, 'Religion of Robert Cecil', p.792; Andrewes, *Two Answers*, p.62; A.J. Loomie, *Spain and the Jacobean Catholics* (2 vols., Catholic Record Society 64 and 68, 1973 and 1979), II: 14.

[75] See especially the Sylvester Adams case in Cambridge: above, ch.1 pp.72–5. Contrast Adams' thesis with that advanced by Richard Hall at the Oxford Act in 1621, which explicitly denied that 'confessio auricularis sit necessaria ad remissionem peccatorum': Clark, *Register*, p.216. In similar tone, Hall's other thesis denied that 'confirmatio sit sacramentum ex instituto divino Ecclesiae absolute necessarium'.

people to confess frequently to a priest.[76] The traditional Protestant doctrine that a priest's absolution was merely declarative was specifically refuted at the Oxford Act in 1632, and in the 1635 articles prepared for London diocese.[77] But lines of demarcation between Laudians and other types of conformist should not be drawn too rigidly here. For example, Joseph Hall had also emphasized that absolution declared by an authorized person 'must needs be of greater force and efficacy than of any private man', however holy. Hall justified this assertion on the grounds that priestly absolution was founded on Christ's commission 'from which all power and virtue is derived in all His ordinances, and we may well say that whatsoever in this case done by God's minister (the key not erring) is ratified in heaven'.[78] It is evident, therefore, that even though Calvinist conformists and moderate puritans alike condemned the extremes of Laudian ceremonialism, they were themselves at least potentially divided in their interpretations of the sacraments.

As a greater emphasis came to be placed on the spiritual, sacramental powers of ministers, the process of their ordination came to attract increasing attention and significance, and thus (by implication) the specific nature of the role played by the bishop in this rite came to be seen as more and more important. From the Elizabethan period onwards, English churchmen had denied that ordination was a sacrament, and even Laudian writers did not seek to maintain this. Nevertheless, they did employ an increasing sacramental and sacerdotal emphasis in describing the minister's ordination and functions.

It should be emphasized from the outset that, even in the pre-Laudian church, a degree of ambiguity bedevilled accounts of ordination just as it did other aspects of the sacramental life of the church. There were occasional allusions made to sacraments being 'channels of grace' without any clear explanation of what this term really meant. Potential divisions between Calvinist conformist and puritan divines were to some extent disguised by the ambiguity and rhetorical nature of the language employed

[76] Montagu, *New Gagg*, pp.79, 83, 84; *idem*, *Appello*, pp.299, 312, 315–16; *idem*, *ΘΕΑΝΘΡΩΠΙΚΟΝ*, ii. pp.464–70; Anthony Sparrow, *A Sermon Concerning Confession of Sinnes, and the Power of Absolution* (1637), pp.10, 14–16; Pocklington, *Altare Christianum*, pp.24, 143; Shelford, *Discourses*, pp.71, 119; Dow, *Innovations*, p.55. See also above, ch.1.

[77] PRO, SP 16/220/35 (the act thesis of William Paul, a royal chaplain); 16/308/43. Passages emphasizing that a priest's absolution is only declarative, and carefully qualified defences of auricular confession, were also purged at the press: Prynne, *Canterburies Doome*, pp.270, 288–9. The retraction prepared for Sylvester Adams, which explicitly allowed of auricular confession and the grace received therefrom, but sought to bring in some Protestant qualifications, was similarly rejected.

[78] Lewis, *Joseph Hall*, p.270. Contrast Andrew Willet, *Hexapla in Leviticum* (Cambridge, 1631), p.70.

when discussing sacraments. Most writers referred to the bestowing of the Holy Ghost in ordination, but the character of the grace given was rarely defined with any precision. The only clear point to emerge was usually negative: that ordination was not a sacrament.

Even so, a change of rhetoric and emphasis is visible among Jacobean conformist authors, even if they did not disagree with their Elizabethan forebears in essential theological terms. All were agreed that a sacrament strictly defined can only refer to a rite which pertains to justification and remission of sins. Nevertheless, while authors such as Robert Abbot and Andrew Willet were most anxious to stress the temporary nature of the grace imparted, and the fact that no indelible character was bestowed through ordination, other conformist divines such as Bilson and Francis Mason sought to emphasize the sense in which ordination could be considered a sacrament, and the extent to which it could be said to bestow a character that might indeed be considered indelible. There was no clear doctrinal difference between these positions. Abbot insisted that ordination involved 'a grace or gift of calling and office, not any sacramentall or iustifying grace'. If a minister did not preach thereafter, he thereby neglected the grace imparted to him. Andrew Willet similarly maintained that Holy Orders did not bestow an indelible character on their recipient, and delivered a decidedly more low-key exposition of the nature of consecration and ordination in the Church of England. Mason's suggestion that ordination *did* bestow an indelible character was not directly opposed to the other divines' reading, since he explained this only in terms of the fact that the act was not repeated, and *not* in the sense that pastoral gifts were necessarily given and retained.[79]

If there was no doctrinal divergence, however, there was clearly an important difference, even among non-Laudians, between those divines who were happy to emphasize the grace given in ordination and to promote positive sacramental language, and others who were more keen to downplay this aspect of the rite. The Laudians were, in a sense, simply building on a trend among some conformists towards a greater sacramental emphasis in their treatment of ordination. Bilson and Hooker had already anticipated much of this development.[80] The crucial difference, however, lay in the Laudians' readiness to apply this logic to the nature of non-episcopalian ministerial orders.

[79] Mason, *Of the Consecration*, p.34; Willet, *Antilogie*, p.64; Abbot, *True Ancient*, pp.399–400.

[80] As on other issues, the response to Montagu sometimes served to open up implicit disagreements among Calvinist conformists. See, for example, Daniel Featley's opposition to Montagu's emphasis on the grace of ordination as implying a sacramental nature: Bodl., Rawlinson MS D.831 fol.100r–v.

All these developments served to complicate the relativistic approach towards matters of church discipline on which Protestant internationalism depended. Moreover, the facile distinction between matters of doctrine and of discipline was fundamentally eroded. Heylyn and Montagu consistently argued the close connection between Calvinist predestinarian doctrine and the presbyterian discipline. When the Laudian Edward Boughen made the implacable declaration in 1635 that 'he that is out at Doctrine, cannot be in at Discipline; he that is out at Discipline, cannot be in at Doctrine' he testified (among other things) to the newly important soteriological role that issues of ecclesiastical discipline and liturgy were seen as playing.[81] Boughen also demonstrated the even starker dichotomy that was emerging between Laudian ecclesiological perceptions and the Church of England's vindication of the foreign Reformed Churches.

PRESBYTERIAN ORDERS AND THE 'UNCHURCHING' OF NON-EPISCOPAL CONGREGATIONS

Recognition of the validity of the foreign Reformed ministry was a *sine qua non* for effective interaction between the Church of England and her sisters of the Reformation. But changing conformist views of episcopacy and of the ministry generated increasing fears in some quarters that the integrity of foreign presbyterian orders was under threat. One of the main objections expressed against the doctrine of *iure divino* episcopacy was that it arguably served to unchurch the foreign Reformed Churches. This was certainly Willet's complaint, and the same conclusion was assumed by foreign Protestants, including Pierre du Moulin. Du Moulin complained to Lancelot Andrewes that if he were to maintain that the French Reformed Church was in error on a point of divine right (as episcopacy was now adjudged to be), this would effectively accuse that church of heresy. If he were to teach that the primacy of bishops was a point of divine right, this would imply that without it there could be no salvation and the church could not stand.[82]

In practice, of course, most English divines did not accept this logic. The phrase 'iure divino' was interpreted in a far more flexible fashion than du Moulin and Willet seemed to fear. All conformist divines were prepared to recognize that the foreign churches existed, and that salvation was possible

[81] Boughen, *Two Sermons*, i. p.4; Montagu, *Appello*, pp.43–4, 72–3; Heylyn, *Historia Quinqu-Articularis*, i. p.37. See also the arguments of Carier in BCO, MS 270 p.162, who represents the development of Calvinist predestinarianism as having been motivated by the need to provide new avenues of grace for the people after their having broken with the bishop and clergy of Geneva.

[82] Andrewes, *Opuscula*, pp.176–7, 189, 198; Willet, *Synopsis* (1600), pp.235–7, 240.

within them. Nevertheless, conformists varied widely in their capacity to integrate this politically necessary admission within their doctrine of episcopacy. This was not easily achieved, and a discontinuity with general perceptions and defences of episcopacy was therefore to be expected. These discontinuities and tensions have tended to be downplayed by some historians, who have leapt perhaps too quickly to the conclusion that, because presbyterian orders were not *explicitly* denied, episcopal government was therefore seen as a thing indifferent. But to focus on the question of whether non-episcopal churches were specifically 'unchurched' is arguably to study the issues from an anachronistic Tractarian perspective, and to pursue what is in effect a red herring.

Although acceptance of presbyterian orders was an accepted principle in the religious thought of at least the Jacobean period, divines did vary in their precise justification for this toleration of presbyterian orders, and in the extent to which they attempted to marry it with their defence of episcopal ordination. At stake was the degree of condescension with which the foreign churches would be treated, and the extent to which a defence of their church government would be allowed to undermine the normative role of episcopacy as the divinely approved form of church government.

Orders in the non-episcopal churches were usually defended according to the so-called 'necessity' argument. This held that in a case of unavoidable necessity, such as that which pertained at the time of the Reformation, when it was not possible to procure bishops to ordain, ordination by a presbyter might be permissible. As Francis Mason expressed it to Archbishop Abbot, 'other Reformed Churches were constrained by necessity to admit extraordinary fathers, That is to receive Ordination from Presbyters, which are but inferior Ministers, rather then to suffer the Fabrick of the Lord Jesus to be dissolved'.[83] Mason explained that orders that were bestowed in a manner that deliberately flouted ecclesiastical law should be esteemed to be no true orders (although even these were not simply null and void, and were true orders 'in the nature of the thing'). However, Mason made it clear that the orders of the foreign Reformed Churches were not to be seen in these terms – as illegal but not entirely null. Rather, the defect in them did not spring from deliberate schism, 'but onely from urgent necessitie, there being no voluntary violation', and therefore in their case they should not be seen as illegal: 'necessitie it selfe is a sufficient dispensation'.[84]

[83] Mason, *Of the Consecration*, sig.A3v. While his argument remains the same, Mason's tone does become slightly less indulgent in his later *Vindiciae*: e.g. the reflection in *Of the Consecration* (p.25) that posterity may lack the means to imitate the established pattern, is supplemented in the *Vindiciae* (p.36) with the phrase 'vel si maxime vellent'.

[84] Mason, *Of the Consecration*, p.26. See also Cade, *Justification*, pp.310–11; Crakanthorp, *Defensio*, pp.230ff; Hooker, *Laws*, VII, ch.xiv, 11; Mason, *Church of England*, pp.34–5,

It is important to remember that affirmations of this 'necessity' were in part *polemical* statements, rather than thoroughly historical ones, and often required a willing suspension of disbelief. Nevertheless, even granted this view of the history of the Reformation, precise understandings of 'necessity' might still vary in the latitude that was granted to non-episcopal churches, and the gravity with which their present state was regarded.

One favourable explanation of 'necessity' focused on the principle of 'extraordinary vocation'. This explained that, presented with no reform-minded bishops in the early continental Reformation, God had called upon different reforming agents. These agents were independent of the established church, but their divine mission was identifiable by clear signs and tokens. It was not just moderate puritans such as Perkins and Fulke who advanced this argument. The vehement anti-presbyterian pamphleteer Matthew Sutcliffe explicitly and aggressively defended extraordinary ordinations, affirming that 'the defection of ordinary priests in the Romish Church being extraordinary, we may not imagine that all ordinary rites and forms were to be observed in the vocation of such, as by the instinct of God's holy spirit were stirred up extraordinarily'. William Bedell, soon to be a bishop himself, was even more positive in asserting the validity of extraordinary vocations, thereby justifying the orders of Luther, Zwingli and Calvin.[85] Romanists generally complained that such an extraordinary vocation could only be proved by the performance of miracles. This requirement was generally disputed by English Protestant divines, although William Bedell for one was prepared to vindicate the Reformers even in these terms on account of the miraculous nature of their success, and even cited puritan exorcisms as proof of the gifts of the spirit at work in the Protestant ministry.[86]

Talk of 'extraordinary vocation' could prompt unease, however. For those anxious to preserve the integrity of the established church against radical puritan appeals to the freedom of the spirit working in the godly, this form of defence seemed unnecessarily dangerous. Saravia, for one, had been scathing in his criticism of Beza's use of the concept of extraordinary vocations.[87] Richard Field clearly felt the need to bring greater order into

63; N. Sykes, *The Church of England and Non-Episcopal Churches in the Sixteenth & Seventeenth Centuries* (1949), *passim*.

85 LPL, Lambeth MS 772 pp.139–40, 183–5; Mason, *Church of England*, p.93. See also Willet, *Hexapla on Romans*, p.482; *idem*, *Synopsis* (1600), pp.724–5.

86 LPL, Lambeth MS 772 pp.249–56. Bedell was writing at the beginning of James' reign, but after the controversies over puritan exorcisms in the 1590s they were generally discredited in the early Stuart Church: see K.V. Thomas, *Religion and the Decline of Magic* (1971), pp.481–6; Harsnett, *A Discovery*, *passim*; D.P. Walker, *Unclean Spirits* (1981), ch.4.

87 Nijenhuis, *Saravia*, pp.111–15, 153. It is notable that Hooker, while acknowledging the possibility of this type of extraordinary vocation, gave no examples, and swiftly passed on to vocations that were extraordinary only in the sense that they departed from the

this line of argument, but he did so, characteristically, by simply imposing a more legalistic gloss upon an essentially Calvinist position. Instead of arguing that ordination by presbyters happened outside the church's permitted discipline but was defensible as an act of necessity, Field suggested that the law itself had always provided canonically for presbyterian ordination in cases of necessity.[88] This was a line followed by most other Jacobean Calvinist conformist divines when they sought directly to exculpate presbyterian orders. They also generally favoured the argument that episcopacy did not constitute a separate order from the normal ministry, so that by extension the power of bestowing orders was inherent in the priesthood itself, with the episcopate merely being granted the right to exercise this inherent power.[89] From this perspective Anthony Cade, for example, was able to claim that a lapse of episcopal ordination represented merely a 'breach of decency and honourable conveniency'.[90]

In these terms, it was easy to claim that episcopacy in a sense existed even in the presbyterian churches wherever a certain degree of ministerial imparity was observed. However, this line of argument was potentially undermined by those divines more wedded to a sacramental view of the episcopal office, or more committed to the necessity of a linear personal succession in apostolic grace. Richard Field's position might be the most coherent one on the question of non-episcopal orders, but it is significant that many divines were not prepared for that amount of consistency, especially when it seemed to make episcopal ordination optional. Instead, they were content to live with a lack of clarity on the question of presbyters' right to ordain, as long as non-episcopalian orders were still vindicated. Certainly, undeniable tensions may be observed in the views of more dedicated conformists, and their position became increasingly incoherent. Richard Hooker did not affirm the immutability of the episcopal form of church government, yet clearly differed from Field in his unwillingness specifically to grant presbyters the right to ordain.[91] Other *iure divino* apologists were also less ready to acknowledge any canonical right of ordination by presbyters. Instead they tended more to see non-episcopal orders as an example of God's free grace being able to flow even in unordained means, in a fashion similar to arguments which explained the salvation of unbaptized infants. This was a tendency rather than a fully

ordained means of *episcopal* ordination and institution: Mason, *Church of England*, pp.59–60. The Romanist Brereley highlighted the differing views of English Protestants on this issue to good effect: *Protestant Apologie*, pp.492, 494–5.

88 Field, *Of the Church*, lib.3 c.39; Downame, *Two Sermons*, ii. p.43; Mason, 'Validity', pp.166–8.

89 See above p.466.

90 Cade, *Justification*, p.311.

91 Hooker, *Laws*, VII, ch.vi, 3–5; Mason, *Church of England*, pp.57–60.

enunciated position, but was implied in some of the less enthusiastic defences of presbyterian orders during the Jacobean period.

The loose use of the term 'necessity' could thus disguise significant differences in the amount of indulgence being granted to the foreign Reformed Churches. These could range from the recognition that their presbyters had a canonical right to ordain, through to suggestions that God might still save them by extraordinary means despite their having gone outside the ordained means for salvation. These differences were rarely spelled out, but if all divines recognized the validity of the non-episcopal churches, there is no doubt that some of them did so with Olympian condescension, seeing presbyterians as being saved by God's special grace rather than through a legitimate contingency.[92]

Another problem with most arguments from 'necessity' was that they tended to limit the defence of foreign churches to the plea of past necessity, passing over in silence the present necessity (if any) for the presbyterian forms. Richard Hooker had been unusually forthright (presumably for political reasons) in suggesting that it was simply no longer possible to restore episcopacy in Scotland.[93] More generally, the failure of presbyterian churches to reintroduce episcopacy was seen as being more problematic. James Ussher at one point looked beyond the immediate polemical value of the argument, and confessed that the French Protestants (living in a state of persecution) had more excuse than the Dutch Church in their abandonment of episcopacy, although he still maintained that he would be happy to embrace intercommunion with either.[94] Nearer home, the bluff of 'present necessity' was already being called in the case of the presbyterian government in the Channel Islands, where Jersey was now forced to accept both the Church of England's liturgy, and the jurisdiction of the bishop of Winchester. In the 1620s Peter Heylyn similarly drew Laud's attention to the island of Guernsey where, he noted, traditional arguments of 'necessity' in the introduction of non-episcopal orders could not be sustained.[95]

92 Lake, *Anglicans and Puritans*, p.97.

93 Hooker, *Laws*, III, ch.xi, 16. Hooker was presumably seeking to avoid (on the advice of his patron Whitgift) incurring the displeasure already visited upon Richard Bancroft for his comments on James' possible plans to reintroduce episcopacy in Scotland (for which, see G. Donaldson, 'Attitude of Whitgift and Bancroft to the Scottish Church', *TRHS* 24 (1942), pp.106–15).

94 Mason, *Church of England*, pp.121–2. Hooker similarly accepted that a restoration of episcopacy was impossible for the French Protestants: *Laws*, III, ch.xi, 16. Francis Mason was unusual in tackling this point directly, and in the candour of his reply that, as episcopacy was not a separate order and it was merely the principle of imparity which required preservation, the presbyterian churches in effect already had bishops, and therefore had no need to seek to receive orders from Protestant bishops now that the original 'necessity' had passed: Mason, 'Validity', pp.173–4.

95 A.J. Eagleston, *Channel Islands under Tudor Government* (Cambridge, 1949), pp.128–42; Russell, *Causes*, p.51; A.F. Scott Pearson, *Thomas Cartwright and Elizabethan Puri-*

The usual solution to the problem of 'present necessity' was to maintain that foreign Calvinists were not opposed to episcopal government as such, but still urgently wished to see it restored in their own countries, even though they were frustrated in these hopes for the time being.[96] This argument was obviously inconsistent with the claims of Bancroft and Sutcliffe in the 1590s that the presbyterian churches had deliberately been established (and were presumably maintained) in a form opposed to episcopacy. However, if the 'necessity' argument were to continue to hold water, especially given the added importance now being granted to episcopacy, it was essential to preserve the belief that foreign Calvinists still maintained a positive view of episcopal government.

Potential divisions were also limited, even when English Calvinist divines came into direct contact with foreign presbyterians, by the fact that divines on both sides of the Channel generally conspired to avoid the logic of the *iure divino* status accorded to episcopacy in the English Church. Instead, foreign divines chose to assume that in England forms of church government were still held to be things indifferent, which were adopted according to whether or not they suited different forms of polity.[97] English divines in their turn chose to focus attention on the purely practical benefits which episcopacy could bring, in solving disputes and avoiding schism, when they urged it on their co-religionists, avoiding direct *iure divino* arguments wherever possible. Indeed, George Downame, with tortuous reasoning, argued that *iure divino* episcopacy should be construed as exclusive and immutable only by those who chose to promote the presbyterian church polity in a similarly exclusive manner. However, for those who commended presbyterian government in a less exclusive manner,

tanism 1535–1603 (Cambridge, 1925), pp.157–66, 373–87; Heylyn, *Survey*, pp.412–22, esp. p.416.

96 E.g. Prideaux, *De Episcopatu*, p.3; Hall, *Works*, IX: 60–1; Mason, 'Validity', pp.137–8.

97 E.g. Sibrandus Lubbertus, *Responsio* (1614), pp.139–40, 186–7 (ignoring Bogerman's earlier warning to him that Englishmen no longer held episcopacy to be adiaphorous, but rather *iure divino*: BL, Add. MS 22962 fol.76v). An especially vivid example is du Moulin's *Defence de la foi catholique contenue au livre de Jacques Ier* in which he was called upon, in his defence of King James' work on the Oath of Allegiance against Coëffeteau, to defend a section in which James gave a trenchant affirmation of *iure divino* episcopacy and reproached the puritans as 'puritano-papists'. Du Moulin switched hastily from quoting directly from the king to some highly idiosyncratic paraphrasing. He defended the insistence on hierarchy in the church with reference to the presbyterian synodical structure, denied that the king had any desire to constrain other churches to use the form of ecclesiastical polity practised in his country, and claimed that James only attacked those of his subjects who complained for the sake of complaining, and not those who differed from him in good conscience (see Rimbault, *Pierre du Moulin*, pp.66–7). Du Moulin presumably got away with this (although his book was translated into English at James' command) because of the value of his firm defence of royal authority in the same work.

as that they doe not condemne all others, neither seeke to force other Churches in their imitation; they are to expect the like moderation from us. For although wee bee well assured that the forme of government by Bishoppes, is the best, as having not onely the warrant of Scripture from the first institution, but also the perpetuall practice of the Church from the Apostles time to our age, for the continuance of it: notwithstandinge, wee doubt not, but where this may not bee had, others may bee admitted; neither doe we denie, but that silver is good, though gould be better.[98]

To Downame, then, the point was not just that continental Calvinists' restraint from anti-episcopalianism enabled English Calvinists to excuse their foreign co-religionists by using arguments based on unwilling 'necessity'. Such restraint by foreign presbyterians also required English divines in their turn to refrain from anti-presbyterianism. Downame still recognized that the *iure divino* argument could undermine presbyterian orders, but would only allow it to do so against *iure divino* presbyterians. Few other divines were happy with quite so blatant an equivocation, which may reflect something of Downame's puritan past, when he had been a close colleague of Willet's at Christ's College.

The only time when English Calvinists were forced to confront the issue of presbyterian orders directly was on those rare occasions when a minister with presbyterian orders sought a cure of souls in the English Church. Thankfully for all concerned, these incidents were few and far between. In Whitgift's time, problems had arisen surrounding the orders of William Whittingham and Walter Travers, both ordained abroad. These examples have received a great deal of attention, but the objections in both cases were somewhat peripheral to the question of the legitimacy of non-episcopal orders. The charge against Whittingham was that he was not properly ordained at all during the Marian exile, even according to the Genevan rite, while Travers was correctly charged with having deliberately sought ordination abroad rather than in England, thereby rendering null the argument from 'necessity' for non-episcopal ordination.[99]

Clearer cases are those of foreigners requesting a cure of souls in England. At least two examples seem unequivocal – those of Cesar Calandrini and Peter de Laune. Cesar Calandrini had received presbyterian orders abroad before graduating BD in Oxford. He was instituted to the rectory of Stapleford Abbots in Essex in 1620, for which he took out letters dimissory from Archbishop Abbot to receive the orders of deacon and priest from any bishop. Resisting suggestions that Calandrini be reordained,

98 Downame, *Two Sermons*, ii. p.95.

99 Bradshaw, *Ordinal*, pp.44–5; Strype, *Whitgift*, III: 115ff.; Mason, *Church of England*, pp.493–6, 498–502. However, Whitgift's recommendation that Travers should be ordained *again* would suggest a more ambiguous stance than that described by Bradshaw (who prefers not to mention this point directly), even if this was not consciously intended to deny the presbyterian ministers' intrinsic ability to ordain.

Bishop Thomas Morton emphasized that foreign pastors' power of ordination should not be denied, and could not be 'without great and intolerable offence to all the foreign Churches'. If English ordination were to be imposed on foreign ministers at all, it should be done with a cautionary note that this was performed 'since it does not appear to us sufficiently clear from the public documents that he was admitted to Holy Orders'.[100]

When Peter de Laune (who translated the Book of Common Prayer into French) was presented to an English benefice, he informed his bishop (John Overall) that he had been ordained by a presbytery at Leiden. Overall displayed a certain reluctance to institute him, urging de Laune 'to advise with good counsell whether by the Laws of the kingdom, he were capable of a Benefice or no among us, unlesse he had been Ordained by a Bishop'. When the matter was put to him, however, Overall agreed that reordination should not be contemplated, stating that he was happy to institute de Laune to the benefice, as long as the Frenchman had no doubts 'whither you be a Priest capable to receive a benefice among Us or no'. While Overall displayed more reluctance than Morton (which we might expect, given their theological differences), their perspective would appear to have been basically the same.[101]

However, if the cases of Calandrini and de Laune demonstrate that it was possible for a man with presbyterian orders to receive a cure of souls in the English Church without reordination, they also show that by the Jacobean period there was no longer a consensus on this point. In the case of Calandrini, Thomas Morton had to over-rule the objections expressed by Archbishop de Dominis. As usual, de Dominis spoke the same language as Richard Montagu, who reported to his friend John Cosin his hopes that Calandrini might be ejected for lacking episcopal ordination, thereby helping 'to vindicate us from those ministers not priests'.[102]

Similar tensions emerged during the Scottish episcopal consecrations of

100 Sykes, *Old Priest*, pp.91–3.

101 BL, Add. MS 4236 fol.338r–v. On the de Laune case, see especially Sykes, *Old Priest*, pp.89–91. Sykes may be overly sanguine in his reading of the event. Overall (on Cosin's account) was clearly opposed to reordination, but *was* in favour of ordaining de Laune on the grounds that the Frenchman might doubt whether his ordination really made him capable of receiving a benefice without episcopal ordination. Another possible example of the toleration of foreign orders in the English Church (although the argument is mostly from silence) may be that of Adrianus Saravia, who almost certainly did *not* receive reordination: Nijenhuis, *Saravia*, pp.111–15. Cosin and Hall's claims of many similar examples (as quoted in Sykes, *Old Priest*, pp.87–8) are difficult to substantiate. See also Willet, *Antilogie*, p.223.

102 Cosin, *Correspondence*, I: 30. Montagu and de Dominis implied that there were other English ministers prepared to use his lack of episcopal ordination against Calandrini: Sykes, *Old Priest*, pp.92–3.

1610. Here the archbishop of Glasgow and the bishops of Brechin and Galloway were summoned to London to receive consecration to the episcopate by a number of English bishops. These included Lancelot Andrewes, who objected that the Scots ministers should first be ordained as presbyters, given that they had not received their ordination from a bishop. At Archbishop Bancroft's urging, however, they were consecrated without this ceremony. This decision was reinforced by the fact that, although these same Scots bishops went on to consecrate other presbyters as bishops, they would not appear to have reordained Scots parochial presbyters.[103] While these events might appear to have been a definitive vindication of non-episcopal orders, there would clearly be problems if Andrewes and his friends were to acquire the authority to judge such issues.

It was at the Synod of Dort that conflicting views of the validity of episcopal and non-episcopal orders threatened to break into the open, as episcopally and non-episcopally ordained ministers met together in conference. These dangers were minimized by the absence of avant-garde conformists from the British delegation. Even without men such as Andrewes, however, the potentially divisive issue of episcopacy lurked constantly in the background. King James had made threatening noises before the opening of the synod in the wake of the Bucerus affair, where the Dutchman Gerson Bucerus' refutation of George Downame's defence of *iure divino* episcopacy had so affronted the king that it had threatened to provoke an international incident. After this initial shock the synod itself trod warily on the subject of episcopacy.[104] As a bishop, the British delegate George Carleton was accorded special honour. He was sometimes addressed as an equal of the president of the synod, with whom he walked at the head of the procession of divines when the synod ended. Some prints of the synod in progress show that Carleton alone had a special canopy over his chair. But such gestures did not in themselves dissolve the tension – indeed, they may have exacerbated it. The prominent Contra-Remonstrant Franciscus Gomarus, for one, appears to have been rankled by the special honour accorded the bishop. When Carleton intervened in one debate, Gomarus angrily snapped that the delegates were to proceed

[103] Sykes, *Old Priest*, pp.101–2. There has been some dispute among historians over the question of whether Bancroft argued that ordination by presbyters was lawful where bishops were unavailable, or whether he defended consecration *per saltum* without the need for ordination to the priesthood, although the former seems by far the most likely: see Bradshaw, *Ordinal*, p.62 and n.2.

[104] On James' response to Bucerus, see Nijenhuis, 'The controversy', pp.210–13; Carleton, *Letters*, pp.278, 282, 285, 293, 301, 308–9, 314. On the Bucerus affair, see also above, pp.25, 457. It proved virtually impossible to avoid the issue of episcopacy during the synod: e.g. Carleton's anger when Ames passed on to him during the synod the Arminian Grevinchovius' book, 'in the preface of which there are cited, out of a writing of Mr. Amyes, certain words very reproachful unto Bishops': Hales, *Works*, III ii. 81.

according to reason, and not according to authority. The English delegates clearly felt uncomfortable that Carleton, despite his higher clerical status, was forced to debate and subscribe to the synodical articles on equal terms with the other delegates.[105]

Moreover, the issue of episcopacy itself arose in the later stages of the synod, when the delegates were asked to pass judgement upon the Belgic Confession. The three articles that concerned church discipline and defended the parity of ministers were sensibly suppressed at the reading of the Confession at the synod. However, while they could have left it at that, the English delegates still insisted on passing exception against the suppressed articles in the synod. In the 145th Session Bishop Carleton, followed by the other delegates, argued that Christ had left behind an imparity of ministers, and that episcopacy had been maintained in the church from the time of the Apostles. Nevertheless, episcopacy was not urged by them as something immutable, or as in any way a separate order. The principal matter raised in private conversations with other delegates was that of the utility of episcopacy in enforcing discipline, George Carleton here following Archbishop Abbot's own emphasis in his correspondence with Carleton's kinsman the ambassador.[106] After all the British delegates had spoken formally in defence of episcopacy during the open session at the synod, there was no reply made by the members of the synod, 'whereupon', Carleton optimistically reported, 'we conceived that they yeelded to the truth of the protestation'.[107]

For some divines, the experience of Dort provided further evidence to support the 'necessity' argument, or so Carleton wished to represent it when Richard Montagu raised the subject in hostile tones. Carleton observed that the continental delegates were weary of presbyterianism, 'and would gladly be freed if they could'.[108] He reported that, in private conference, 'the best learned in that Synode' had told Carleton that they honoured and reverenced the good order and discipline of the Church of England, and wished that it was established among them with all their hearts, but that this could not be hoped for in their state. In fact, these foreign divines gave a classic account of the 'necessity' argument that had so often been rehearsed in their defence:

> their hope was, that seing they could not doe what they desired; God would be mercifull to them, if they did what they could. This was their answere; which I

[105] G.J. Hoenderdaal, 'The debate about Arminius outside the Netherlands', in T.H. Lunsingh Scheurleer and G.H.M. Posthumus Meyjes (eds.), *Leiden University in the Seventeenth Century* (Leiden, 1975), p.153; Hales, *Golden Remains*, pp.485, 487, 519, 549.

[106] Carleton, *Examination*, pp.111–12; PRO SP 105/95 fols.4v–5r: Archbishop Abbot to Dudley Carleton, 22 March 1618–19.

[107] Carleton, *Examination*, pp.111–12.

[108] *Ibid.*, p.111.

thinke is enough to excuse them; that they doe not openly ayme at anarchy and popular confusion. The truth is, they groane under that burthen and would be eased, if they could.[109]

Whatever its veracity, this account was essential to the Calvinist episcopalian world-view and to the justification of the British presence at Dort, and was enthusiastically repeated by the puritan Thomas Scot.[110] To the Laudians, however, the synod represented all that they most disliked, and its failure to condemn non-episcopal church polities was seen by them as a betrayal of episcopacy. Andrewes referred mockingly to the lack of an episcopal presence at the synod.[111] When later defending themselves against the charges of Montagu and others that they had sold out to presbyterianism at the synod, the British delegates ridiculed such 'hot spirits' who would have insisted on making a formal recorded protestation against presbyterianism. Carleton complained that men like Montagu would 'have charged the Churches to blot those articles out of their Confession, and forthwith to reform their government: otherwise not to have yielded approbation to any article of doctrine, as there comprised: but renounced the Synod, and shaken off from his feet the dust of Dort'.[112]

As an image of Richard Montagu or William Laud at the Synod of Dort this could hardly be bettered. Carleton's accusation is significant in that, for the first time, English Calvinist *iure divino* episcopalians consciously identified (and renounced) a more extreme conformist attitude towards the foreign Reformed orders. By the 1630s the Laudians were happy to adhere to their rigid definitions of episcopacy as a separate order regardless of the cost in relations with the foreign Reformed Churches. As in issues of doctrine, they consistently refused to don the mask of international Protestant solidarity which had previously been worn to disguise clear divisions in the Protestant camp. Instead, they defined episcopacy in terms that threatened to overturn the claims of foreign, non-episcopal Reformed Churches to possess a valid ministry and effectual sacraments. Nevertheless, the traditional argument from 'necessity' was not explicitly overthrown; it was simply ignored, and the foreign Reformed Churches left to fend for themselves.

109 *Ibid.*, p.112. Joseph Hall's later account erroneously claims that these remarks were made in open session at the synod (Hall, *Works*, IX: 155). Hall had returned home well before the incident he describes. For another description of the British delegates' opposition to the articles in question from the Belgic Confession, see Francis Godwin, *De Praesulibus Angliae Commentarius* (1616), appendix, pp.13–14.

110 Scot, *A Tongue-Combate*, pp.87–8 (*Workes*).

111 See above, ch.8 p.429. For Andrewes' remark, see P. Welsby, *Lancelot Andrewes 1555–1626* (1964), p.170; Chamberlain, *Letters*, II: 186. This was hardly flattering to George Carleton, who was bishop of Llandaff at the time.

112 Fuller, *John Davenant*, p.103. See also Sutcliffe, *Briefe Censure*, pp.33–4.

Before the 1650s it is very rare to find avant-garde conformist or Laudian writers directly confronting the argument from necessity, or the implications for presbyterian churches of exalted claims for episcopacy as a separate order. The Laudians differed from earlier writers in that they were no longer prepared to weaken arguments for episcopacy by undertaking the mental gymnastics involved in defending presbyterian orders. This did not necessarily mean that they denied the validity of such orders – merely that they no longer felt any compulsion to defend them.

A more critical reading of foreign orders had been evident among avant-garde conformists throughout James' reign. We have already seen how Lancelot Andrewes had seen fit to question their validity. Moreover, for all his legendary timidity, he chose in his sermon at the Palatine Marriage in 1613 to make remarks about presbyterianism and episcopacy which, by implication, severely criticized the Reformed non-episcopal ministry in the Palatinate. In particular, Andrewes' sermon at this most public of celebrations of Reformed unity emphasized the importance of the Church of England's retention of the apostolical church order and condemned the institution of lay elders.[113] His exchange of correspondence with the Huguenot leader Pierre du Moulin in 1618–19 might seem to indicate a certain amount of back-tracking on Andrewes' part, as in this context he granted the historical necessity for non-episcopal ordination and refused to unchurch the foreign Reformed Churches. Nevertheless, Andrewes' *theological* position was as inflexible as ever. He chose in this correspondence to defend episcopacy on the high ground of its necessity as a separate order, and condemned those who maintained that it was merely a degree of the priesthood, or who abandoned altogether an institution that was *iure divino*. Andrewes did not explicitly recognize presbyters' right to ordain in cases of necessity. Rather, he simply denied that he intended to unchurch the non-episcopal churches, on the grounds that one could clearly *see* churches existing without episcopacy, and he did not wish to deny that salvation was possible in such churches. Andrewes accepted the political need to grant that the foreign Reformed Churches had the 'thing' without the 'name' of episcopacy, but he had no longer left any coherent room for this admission within his own doctrine of episcopacy. As in the incident of the consecration of the Scots bishops, Andrewes ultimately climbed down, although not before having claimed his own more rigid doctrine of episcopacy to be that of the Church of England. In his very manner of refusing to unchurch the foreign Reformed Churches,

113 Andrewes, *Opuscula*, pp.91–3. In the course of his sermon Andrewes had to include some politic praise of the Palatine Church, but his insistence on episcopal matters was strikingly indiscreet, and may be contrasted with other sermons celebrating the event, such as Bishop John King's *Vitis Palatina*.

Andrewes had managed to emphasize the disharmony between this more inclusive, politically necessary position, and the exclusive theological logic of the *iure divino* episcopal position. It is therefore not surprising that some divines sought to prevent the publication of Andrewes' letters to du Moulin in the edition of Andrewes' collected works printed in the late 1620s, fearing that the foreign Reformed Churches would be offended.[114]

In a way, Andrewes' correspondence with du Moulin on the king's behalf represented the avant-garde conformists' seizure of the chance to associate the Church of England with their own more rigid position on episcopacy, at precisely the same time that the British delegates at Dort were presenting a more flexible reading of episcopacy. It is hardly surprising, therefore, that both sides clashed so directly a few years later on the matter of how episcopacy had been defended at the synod. The divines of Durham House had clearly harboured their resentment for a long time.

During the 1620s and 1630s, there were constant rumours and complaints that Laudian bishops were denying the orders of non-episcopal churches and unchurching them for their failure to uphold episcopacy. Thomas Taylor complained in the late 1620s and early 1630s of a new breed of anti-Sabbatarians who sowed popery and wished to cast out all the Reformed Churches and to deny them the status of true churches.[115] In his *The Lords Day, the Sabbath Day*, Henry Burton criticized those who 'make no bones even in open Court, to vilify the prime pillars of those Churches themselves, as having no lawfull Ministers, because no Prelates to put them in order', and aimed this charge directly at Laud in his *Replie* to Laud's *Conference with Fisher* in 1640. Gilbert Primerose similarly believed that Laud thought that the French presbyterians had no vocation.[116] Finally, the Benedictine irenicist Dom Leander explained in his 1634 report to Rome how English Protestants with whom he was in contact believed that without their hierarchical form of church government, the very nature and substance of the church was taken away, and therefore held the continental Protestants to be schismatical without it.[117]

There were certainly occasions upon which Archbishop Laud and his followers would appear to have doubted the legitimacy of presbyterian

114 Andrewes, *Opuscula*, pp.178–88, 190–2, 202–16; Heylyn, *Antidotum*, ii. pp.7–8. That it was du Moulin who was subjected to such brow-beatings was especially ironic, as the Frenchman's own position on episcopacy was far more favourable than that of other Huguenot divines, and he apparently asked James for the bishopric of Gloucester in 1624: B.G. Armstrong, 'The changing face of French Protestantism: the influence of Pierre Du Moulin', in R.V. Schnucker (ed.), *Calviniana* (Kirksville, 1988), pp.131–49 – esp. pp.140–1.

115 Taylor, *Christs Victorie*, p.401.

116 Burton, *Lords Day*, p.46; *idem*, *Replie*, p.236; J. Pannier, 'Quelques lettres inédites de pasteurs écossais', *Société de l'Histoire du Protestantisme Français* 60 (1911), p.418.

117 Soden, *Godfrey Goodman*, p.97.

orders. One possible example might be Laud's alleged insistence that the irenicist John Dury should receive Church of England ordination before he could be accepted as an accredited representative of the English Church, although accounts of this incident are not clear and Dury himself would seem to have doubted the regularity of his earlier ordination.[118] Other Laudian divines occasionally seemed to doubt the intrinsic validity of presbyterian orders. John Cosin had emphasized in 1626 that presbyters could not ordain (without leaving any room for the claims of historical 'necessity') and in the privacy of his Prayer Book had queried whether the Genevan sacrament of the eucharist was really a sacrament of religion at all.[119] Cosin's doubts concerning the foreign eucharist had been raised because of the omission of what he believed to be vital words from the French Calvinists' formula of consecration. The same tendency to tie the efficacy of a ceremony or sacrament to the use of specific formulae is also evident in James Wedderburn's remarks to Laud in 1636, when he pointed out that the current Scottish Book of Ordination, though drawn up by Scots bishops, was deficient in 'the very essential words of conferring orders'.[120]

The evidence for unchurching is rarely unambiguous. Nevertheless, it is significant that Laudians during this period do not seem to have inserted any qualifying arguments from necessity when they condemned the non-episcopalian churches, or rejected the validity of ordinations by a presbyter. Moreover, standard arguments that justified the foreign churches by appealing to notions of extraordinary vocation, thereby vindicating Luther, Calvin and Beza, were now being actively purged at the press.[121] The necessary fiction that episcopal government had only been rejected abroad by reluctant necessity was now also being rejected.[122]

118 See J.M. Batten, *John Dury, Advocate of Christian Reunion* (1944), pp.46–7; John Dury, *The Unchanged ... Peacemaker* (1650); William Prynne, *The Time-Serving Proteus and Ambidexter Divine, Uncased to the World* (1650). Dury had supposedly already received presbyterian ordination in the Netherlands, but Laud was reportedly ready to use this as a test of Dury's orthodoxy, and this apparently *before* Dury had acquainted him with his own doubts about his earlier ordination. The matter is not clear, however, as Dury later claimed that in 1626 he had told Bishop Hall of his scruple of conscience concerning this ordination and that, while not renouncing it, he had lost the comfort and assurance of its lawfulness. Dury was ordained in Exeter cathedral by Bishop Hall on 24 February 1634. Hall's involvement in the ceremony would tend to lend support to Dury's account, although it is at least conceivable that the event was intended by Laud as a test of Hall's loyalty just as much as Dury's. However, the absence of references to the issue of ordination (or to Laud's insistence upon it) in his contemporary correspondence might well suggest that Dury later sought to excuse his reordination by claiming Laudian pressure when little direct pressure had in fact been applied.

119 Cosin, *Works*, V: 110, 176. Cf. Andrewes, *Sermons*, III: 263.

120 Sykes, *New Priest*, p.105.

121 Prynne, *Canterburies Doome*, p.260.

122 Heylyn, *Survey*, p.243; *idem*, *ΜΙΚΡΟΚΟΣΜΟΣ* (1625 edn), p.129.

When authors writing on church discipline refused to incorporate escape clauses for the foreign churches, they effectively rejected the argument from necessity. That Burton and others were right to entertain such fears emerges clearly from Laud's correspondence with Joseph Hall during the composition of the latter's *Episcopacy by Divine Right Asserted.* Hall planned to assert that episcopacy should always be retained, but proposed also to make the traditional aside that the presbyterian government might be of some use where episcopacy could not be had. Laud pounced, and urged Hall to reconsider 'whether this concession be not needless here, and in itself of a dangerous consequence'. Since the Scots rebels claimed presbyterianism to be Christ's kingdom and ordinance, and episcopacy to be the opposite, he continued, 'we must not use any mincing terms, but unmask them plainly; nor shall I ever give way to hamper ourselves, for speaking plain truth, though it be against Amsterdam or Geneva'.[123]

Hall in reply admitted to employing 'some mitigations in stating the case' on purpose, 'out of a desire to hold as good terms with our neighbour churches abroad as I safely might'. He emphasized 'how tenderly' Field and George Downame had treated this point, and explained that 'if we may make the case sure for us, with the least aspersion cast upon them who honour our government and cannot obtain it, I conceived it better, especially as the Scottish case so palpably differs, yet I would so determine it as that nothing but necessity can either excuse them or hold up the truth of their being'.[124]

Laud, however, was still unconvinced, and complained again that Hall favoured the foreign churches and authors more 'than our case will now bear'. Hall could only repeat that 'those authors whom I mention with so fair respect are, in those things for which I cite them, our friends'.[125] A sizeable contingent of Laudian divines during the Interregnum were far less convinced that foreign presbyterians were so far their friends, while writers such as Heylyn set out to prove that the rebel Scots and continental presbyterians formed part of a single plot against episcopal church government.[126]

Laud himself clearly came to the very brink of denying the 'necessity' argument and unchurching the foreign non-episcopal churches. One of his Oxford DD theses in 1608 had maintained that a bishop alone could confer orders: we can only speculate about whether or not he chose to insert an escape clause for non-episcopal churches, or whether he refused to 'hamper himself' with 'mincing terms'. Another of his theses at the same Act asserted that episcopacy was an order distinct from the presbyterate, which

123 Laud, *Works*, VI: 573. 124 Hall, *Works*, X: 540–1.
125 Laud, *Works*, VI: 575–8; Hall, *Works*, X: 543.
126 Peter Heylyn, *Aerius Redivivus* (1670), *passim.*

strongly suggests that his thesis on episcopal ordination did not adopt a Fieldian perspective, which would have emphasized canonical orthodoxy and authority rather than inherent sacramental power. William Prynne and Henry Hickman later claimed that Laud had been publicly reproved in the Divinity Schools on this occasion by the Regius Professor Thomas Holland, for attempting to unchurch the continental Protestant Churches, and sowing division between them by a novel popish position. Laud vehemently denied this story, and his accusers never provided the names of those who had supposedly witnessed the event. Nevertheless, it is perhaps worth noting that the two DD theses mentioned above were the principal weapons of the Roman Catholic protagonist 'Philodox', who in Francis Mason's treatise attempted to unchurch the foreign, non-episcopal congregations.[127]

Such an unchurching was clearly implied in a footnote added by Laud to the 1639 edition of his *Conference with Fisher*, where he quoted St Jerome affirming plainly that 'Ecclesia autem non est, quae non habet sacerdotes.' In his gloss on this quotation, Laud claimed that 'in that place most manifest it is that S. Jerome by sacerdos means a bishop only . . . So even with him, no bishop, and no Church.' When this passage was brought against him at his trial, Laud gave the breathtakingly disingenuous explanation that this was 'St. Jerome's opinion[;] no declaration of my own.' But they were certainly not words from which he openly dissented. While Laud mentioned at this point in the trial that the view 'that none but a Bishop can ordain, but *in casu necessitatis*' was 'the opinion of many learned and moderate divines', he quite clearly did not identify the qualification '*in casu necessitatis*' as his own view. Instead, he offered the damning observation that 'this is very considerable in the business, whether an inevitable necessity be cast upon them, or they pluck a kind of necessity upon themselves'. In one of his letters to Hall Laud had expressed himself even more firmly, declaring 'I conceive there is no place where episcopacy may not be had, if there be a Church more than in title only.'[128]

By now, the 'necessity' argument had clearly been exploded for Laud, although his reticence makes it impossible to know exactly how he regarded presbyterian orders.[129] Nevertheless, Laud's close acquaintances

127 Clark, *Register*, I: 206; Heylyn, *Certamen Epistolare*, pp.121–8, 139–44; Laud, *Works*, III: 262; Dent, *Reformers*, pp.233–4; Mason, 'Validity', pp.128–76 (esp. pp.131–2, 141–2, 159–63).

128 Laud, *Works*, II: 194–5 note u, IV: 307 (my emphasis). Even the Romanist 'Philodox' in Francis Mason's dialogue interpreted Jerome's passage as referring to 'priests': Mason, *Of the Consecration*, p.7.

129 An apparent sign of flexibility may have been Laud's preparedness to speak of Lutherans as having retained 'the thing', even if German Lutherans had rejected 'the name' (preferring the term 'superintendents') which might suggest that he did not regard the

would seem to have been prepared to deny their validity, presumably with his approval. When his protégé Viscount Scudamore served as English ambassador to Paris in the 1630s, there was apparently no shortage of English divines around the viscount who were prepared to justify the ambassador's abstention from the Huguenots' communion by unchurching the French Protestant congregations altogether. Reminiscing some years later, John Blondel recalled that 'many priests and divers English divines' attended Scudamore and the earl of Leicester when they were serving as ambassadors at Paris about the year 1640, and that the earl's secretary 'was much troubled to hear them say daily that the Protestants in France had no true ministers or sacraments &c. because they had no true bishops'.[130]

Back in England, the year 1640 saw the publication of the second part of Richard Montagu's *De Originibus Ecclesiasticis*. In a lengthy passage emphasizing the sacerdotal nature of the priesthood, Montagu plainly overthrew the argument from necessity. He echoed Romanist arguments by claiming that ministers who were not ordained by bishops were required to justify their extraordinary vocation by working miracles, since the argument from necessity was 'absurd': it rested on an impossibility since it contradicted Christ's promise of a perpetual institutional succession.[131]

It was only in 1642, when Laud's protégé Jeremy Taylor published his *Episcopacy Asserted*, that these new trends in episcopalian thought were brought together and finally applied in a systematic way to the problem of the foreign non-episcopal churches. Taylor argued that episcopacy was the only order which was derived immediately from Christ, and emphasized that it was to be perpetual and successive. Indeed, in contrast to Andrewes' assurances to du Moulin, Taylor maintained that episcopacy should be ranked among the *credenda* of Christianity. He argued that the episcopate

apostolical succession as necessary: Laud, *Works*, III: 386. It seems likely, however, that here Laud was merely ill-informed of the nature of Lutheran bishops, and misunderstood both the powers wielded by German bishops and their lack of the apostolical succession. This would appear to have been a widespread ignorance. For example, King Charles and Richard Field were under the misapprehension that the Lutherans had preserved the apostolic succession: Field, *Of the Church*, I: 318; J. Bruce (ed.), *Charles I in 1646* (Camden Society 63, 1856), p.26. In fact, the Danish Lutherans had deliberately interrupted it, a point which Sir John Wray correctly noted in a Commons speech in 1641: W.M. Abbott, 'The issue of episcopacy in the Long Parliament, 1640–1648: the reasons for abolition', Oxford University DPhil, 1981, p.99. See also Mason, *Church of England*, pp.520–1; E.H. Dunkley, *The Reformation in Denmark* (1948), pp.70–80; Tighe, 'William Laud', pp.719–20.

130 *HMC Fourteenth Report* Appendix pt2 Portland MSS vol.2 (1894), p.584. I owe this reference to Ian Atherton. See also I. Atherton, 'Viscount Scudamore's "Laudianism": the religious practices of the first Viscount Scudamore', *HJ* 34 (1991), pp.587–8.

131 Montagu, *ΘΕΑΝΘΡΩΠΙΚΟΝ*, ii. pp.463–4. This volume had first been entered in the Stationer's Register as early as 5 May 1638: Arber, *Registers*, IV: 392. The passage cited here from Montagu's work was noted by Dering's parliamentary sub-committee on religion in February 1641: D'Ewes, *Journal*, p.355.

was an order distinct from the presbyterate, rather than simply a degree, and (following Pocklington and others) he noted how the primitive churches had used the succession of their bishops to prove their churches 'Catholic' and their adversaries' heretical, although he now maintained that this was the *only* argument that the Fathers had employed to prove their orthodoxy.[132] Taylor also insisted that confirmation, performed only by bishops, was 'a fundamental point of christianity, an essential ingredient to its composition'.[133]

As for the non-episcopal churches, Taylor echoed Laud's concern that 'we are so bound by public interest to approve all that they do, that we have disabled ourselves to justify our own'. On the point of 'necessity', Taylor first adopted a critical, historical approach and called a time-honoured bluff: at the time of the Reformation there were many reforming bishops who might have been employed in the foreign Reformed Churches' ordinations, but were not. The Reformed Churches might easily have received ordination from the English bishops or the Lutheran Churches. Secondly, Taylor followed Montagu's argument that the very idea that 'necessity' might overturn an essential and perpetual divine ordinance was impossible, as it made a nonsense of God's intentions and promises:

> If God means to build a church in any place, he will do it by means proportionable to that end; that is, by putting them into a possibility of doing and acquiring those things which Himself hath required of necessity to the constitution of a church. So that supposing that ordination by a bishop is necessary for the vocation of priests and deacons (as I have proved it is), and therefore for the founding and perpetuating of a church, either God hath given to all churches opportunity and possibility of such ordinations, and then necessity of the contrary is but pretence and mockery, or if he hath not given such possibility, then there is no church there to be either built or continued, but the candlestick is presently removed.[134]

An 'ordinary necessity' could not therefore excuse the presbyterian churches, and Taylor followed Richard Montagu in pointing out that an extraordinary calling must needs be validated by miracles.[135] For members of Reformed Churches, therefore, the accepted forms of external communion necessary for salvation had been removed. Without 'the sacred order and offices of episcopacy', Taylor commented, 'no priest, no ordination, no consecration of the sacrament, no absolution, no rite or sacrament, legitimately can be performed in order to eternity'. For salvation, these people were forced to rely upon God's special mercy, assessing their 'good life and catholic belief' without the use of sacraments as the normal route

132 Taylor, *Works*, V: 67–8, 105–7, 100 and *passim*.
133 *Ibid.*, V: 29–30.
134 *Ibid.*, V: 119–20.
135 *Ibid.*, V: 121.

to it.[136] Taylor thus placed members of the foreign Reformed Churches in the same effective state as that of Christians living under the Turks.

Speaking disapprovingly from the 1650s (when he was promoting intercommunion with the Huguenots at Charenton), John Cosin argued that Jeremy Taylor had been the first to question the validity of the Huguenot ministry. In a sense he was correct: Taylor was indeed the first to overthrow presbyterian orders explicitly and systematically, although Montagu and perhaps Laud had effectively rejected the argument from necessity and had not shown themselves able or willing to put anything in its place. During the Interregnum there were more Laudian divines – most notably Laud's ex-chaplain Edward Martin – who rejected Huguenot orders, and also several English ministers – such as George Morley and Richard Steward – who declined intercommunion with the Protestants at Charenton (although this might not necessarily represent a denial of presbyterian orders as such).[137] The outright denial of presbyterian orders probably remained a minority position even among Laudian divines. Nevertheless, it was a minority position whose roots lay in a far broader change in Jacobean and Caroline understandings of episcopacy, which is evident in the writings of a great many conformists of the period. It was also a position which had at least one very important lay supporter. That man was none other than King Charles himself. For Charles, like Jeremy Taylor and Archbishop de Dominis, it was the issue of the succession in apostolic grace that was crucial to the nature of the church, so that without bishops 'we should have neither lawful priests, nor sacraments duly administered'. The king thereby deduced that the presbyterian government was 'absolutely unlawful' and 'more erronious than the church of Rome'.[138]

If Charles' views were extreme, they were so only in the sense that he accepted the logical conclusion to which Laudian arguments were leading him. Bereft of saving arguments from 'necessity' to account for their failure to preserve an essential source of saving grace, the Reformed Churches in Laudian eyes relied simply on a readiness to disregard conclusions that the dictates of logic required. This was an indulgence which could no longer be expected.

If the rejection of intercommunion with French Protestants in the 1650s represented a crucial change in English conformist thinking, it had been

[136] *Ibid.*, V: 121–2.

[137] Martin, *His Opinion*, p.102. Laudian divines who refused intercommunion with the Huguenots during the Interregnum included Bishops Bramhall and Sydserf, and Dr Richard Steward: Sykes, *Old Priest*, p.152.

[138] Bruce, *Charles I in 1646*, pp.26–7; *State Papers Collected by Edward, Earl of Clarendon*, ed. R. Scrope and T. Monkhouse (3 vols., Oxford, 1767–86), II: 243, 247, 270. I owe these references to the kindness of Professor Russell. Contrast *ibid.*, II: 263, 359. See also Russell, *Causes*, pp.197–8.

foreshadowed in conformists' differing responses to the threat from the Scots Covenanters in the late 1630s and early 1640s. For all its inconsistencies, the argument from 'necessity' here had the potential to come into its own. In the face of the Scots, Calvinists such as Hall and others concentrated their efforts on vindicating the argument from necessity in the case of foreign Reformed Churches, in order to deny it to the Scots. They were most keen to place the foreign Reformed Churches on the side of the Church of England, to emphasize the fact that they were not opposed to bishops in any way, but rather that they were simply not in a practical position to enjoy them. To Morton, Prideaux, Peter du Moulin the younger, Hall and others, this was an absolutely crucial polemical point.[139] To Laud, however, the threat from Scots presbyterianism required that a still more entrenched and exclusive doctrine of episcopacy should be upheld. In his eyes, the 'necessity' argument, and the vindication of foreign Reformed orders, seemed merely to complicate and undermine the case for episcopacy. With the removal of Laud, however, the question of the Reformed Churches' attitude to episcopacy (did they yearn for it, or had they removed it on principle?) became one of the chief battle-grounds on which the respective claims of episcopacy and presbyterianism were fought before the outbreak of the civil war.[140]

LITURGY AND LIVINGS

It was not just in their lack of episcopacy that conformists considered the foreign Reformed Churches to be deficient in matters of church discipline.

[139] Thomas Morton, A *Sermon Preached before the Kings Most Excellent Maiestie, in the Cathedrall Church of Durham* (Newcastle, 1639), p.41; Prideaux, *De Episcopatu*, p.3; Hall, *Works*, IX: 60–1, 151–2, 154, 155, 159; Peter du Moulin, *A Letter of a French Protestant to A Scotishman of the Covenant* (1640), pp.5–8. See also Joseph Hall, *Humble Remonstrance* (1640); James Ussher, *Iudgement of Doctor Rainoldes* (1641); George Morley, *A Modest Advertisement* (1641); Thomas Aston, *Remonstrance* (1641). For earlier examples, see Crakanthorp, *Defensio*, pp.227–8; Willet, *Synopsis* (1600), pp.726–7.

[140] See, for example, the arguments between Hall and the Smectymnuans over the attitudes of contemporary foreign Calvinist worthies such as André Rivet, Pierre du Moulin, Gislebert Voetius and Abraham Scultetus: Hall, *Works*, IX: 155, 212–13, 280, 292, 371, 372–84, 390, 442–3 (cf. pp.291, 357–8). For examples of the regular invocation of the example of the foreign Reformed Churches by anti-episcopalians, to vindicate presbyterianism's claims and to refute charges that it inevitably caused disorder, see Abbott, 'Issue of episcopacy', pp.64–7, 98–101, 109, 178. John Dury's 'A briefe Declaration of the severall formes of Government, received in the Reformed Churches beyond the Seas' in his collection of *Certain Briefe Treatises* is perhaps the clearest example of the enlisting of foreign Calvinism in support of proposals for a reduced form of episcopacy. Gisbert Voetius was at least one foreign Calvinist divine who looked askance at the views thus attributed to foreign Calvinist Churches: see Dury's anxious letter to him in SUL, Hartlib MS 5/17 fols.1–2. See also *The Petition for the Prelates Briefly Examined* (1641), pp.27–8.

In their liturgies, and in their provision for ministers, the foreign churches were also seen as being inferior to the Church of England, 'the best reformed church'. Once again, there was a tension here between the minimum position (expounded by Hall) that church ceremonies were 'things indifferent', and the maximum position that the Church of England's liturgy and ecclesiastical discipline had preserved ordained forms of worship and channels of sacramental grace compared with which the foreign churches were hampered by a gravely deficient outward discipline.

Throughout this period, conformists still endorsed a formally adiaphorous, minimum position, which sought to vindicate the Church of England's ceremonies in terms of the rights of each particular church to determine its own rites and ceremonies. Most divines would have heartily seconded Archbishop Whitgift's profession to Beza in 1594 that 'there is no mortal man ... who, from his soul, more truly wisheth that every particular Church would mind its own business, and not prescribe the laws of rites and the manner of government to others'.[141]

This perspective was maintained most consistently by early Jacobean Calvinist conformists such as Francis Mason, who insisted in 1605 that the rejection or retention of different ceremonies by the various Reformed Churches was quite acceptable and in no way impaired their union: 'diversity of rites in divers churches independent doth no harm where there is an unity of faith'.[142] Thomas Rogers similarly sought to emphasize the positive side of Calvin's dismissal of the Book of Common Prayer as containing 'tolerabiles ineptiae' – shortcomings in the liturgy were still 'tolerable', because they were ultimately 'things indifferent'.[143] These Calvinist conformists also emphasized foreign Protestants' occasional expressions of approval of the English liturgy, seeing such remarks as the most effective means of justifying the Book of Common Prayer to their puritan opponents.

From the 1590s, however, avant-garde conformists adopted a more combative tone. The Book of Common Prayer was seen not merely as an effective implementation of the Church of England's right to choose her own form of worship, but was also lauded as a flawless work of liturgical scholarship. Hooker had been the first to expound a massively uncritical defence of the positive, edifying value of the ceremonies contained therein. His defender William Covell also applauded the Prayer Book as the most perfect of all the liturgies used in the Reformed Churches, especially as it

141 Strype, *Whitgift*, II: 172.
142 Mason, *Vindication*, p.615 – quoted in Mason, *Church of England*, p.86.
143 Rogers, *Two Dialogues*, sig.E2r–v.

had retained a true reverence in divine service, and had only sparingly dissented from the Roman Church in its public worship.[144]

From such a perspective, it was difficult for Covell to concede the adiaphorous nature of church ceremonies. He admitted reluctantly that it was not 'altogether unfit' if the Reformed Churches were to use different ceremonies, but crossed a minor rubicon when he declared that it would be convenient if possible to have a unity of ceremonies for the whole church.[145] The Book of Common Prayer would obviously be the preferred model for such a uniformity. Few conformists would initially have gone as far as that. Nevertheless, Jacobean conformists (and not just avant-garde ones) were becoming increasingly assertive in their defence of the Book of Common Prayer, and of the wisdom of the Church of England in retaining ancient ceremonies which had been abrogated too hastily abroad. The suggestion that the English liturgy should provide a model for other Reformed Churches, rather than simply being an adiaphoristic alternative, was thus a natural, if significant, progression. Peter Heylyn later claimed that King James had hoped ultimately to establish a single order and discipline in all the Reformed Churches, along with his schemes for unity of doctrine and uniformity of devotion, and to this end had commanded the translation of the Book of Common Prayer into various languages. Heylyn may well have been reporting a passing fancy rather than a determined project on James' part, but it nevertheless provided the pretext for Heylyn to urge Laud in 1629 to reduce the discipline and liturgy of the island of Guernsey to conformity with the Church of England. He hoped that this would be just one stage in the new king's forwarding of his father's project to reduce all the Protestant Churches to a single discipline and liturgy.[146] This tone was also sounded in the Scottish Prayer Book of 1636. While its authors admitted that it would be impossible to impose a uniform liturgy on all churches, they nevertheless gave voice to the wish 'that the whole church of Christ were one, as well in form of public worship as in doctrine, and that as it hath but one Lord and one faith, so it had but one heart and one mouth'.[147]

Laudian addiction to the notion of a single, universal liturgical uniformity was merely one aspect of the more exalted role that ceremonies and the 'beauty of holiness' played in their notions of true religion. For the Laudians, ceremonies were not simply a necessary way of ordering the external life of the church, but were a vital means of expressing the beauty of holiness, which placed them at the centre of the spiritual life of the Christian. Moreover, where Hooker had been content to rest the *legal*

[144] Covell, *Modest Examination*, p.179. [145] *Ibid.*, p.62.
[146] Heylyn, *Survey*, pp.379, 415. Heylyn's account was originally composed in April 1629.
[147] Tyacke, *Anti-Calvinists*, p.253 – cited in Russell, *Fall*, p.39.

defence of church ceremonies on the rights of duly established ecclesiastical authorities over things indifferent, various Laudian preachers and pamphleteers, in their search to vindicate their more elaborate forms of church ritual, were prepared at times to aim much higher. They now invoked direct divine authority for specific ceremonies, in the shape of scriptural injunctions or the hallowed forms of ecclesiastical tradition. For the physical structure of the church, and the ceremonies conducted therein, Laudians invoked Old Testament models and texts, while the altar policy and the practice of bowing at the name of Jesus were justified by direct scriptural mandate.[148] As a result, national churches were theoretically granted far less liberty when determining their liturgies and ceremonies, and the foreign Reformed Churches thus lay open to even greater censure.

For some Laudians, the sanctity of ecclesiastical custom left even the existing Book of Common Prayer open to criticism as being deficient in some ceremonies. Even here, however, this did not lead these divines as a consequence to rank the English Church with all the foreign Reformed Churches, as sharing in their culpability. Instead the foreign churches were blamed for interfering in the Church of England's own reformation. Calvin and Bucer were condemned as being the inspiration behind the abandonment of the much-lamented (by Laudians) First Edwardian Prayer Book in favour of the more uncompromisingly Protestant Second Prayer Book.[149] In their own reformations the foreign churches had done even worse. The preacher John Browning delivered an especially damning indictment. Proclaiming the English Church to be 'the best Reformed for pure Doctrine and perfect Discipline' and 'a pattern and president [*sic*] to al Reformed Churches whatsoever', he scornfully spurned 'some late forraine reformations, who may seeme either not at all to have received, or scarce to have established any set or common prayer'.[150]

In reaction to Laudian attacks on foreign liturgies, some Calvinist conformists in the late 1630s sought to reaffirm the traditions of earlier conformist apologetic. Joseph Hall articulated the Calvinist conformist rejection of Laudian priorities when he emphasized that there was no great difference between the Book of Common Prayer and other Reformed liturgies. While maintaining, in typical conformist fashion, that the Church of England was more fit to lead than to follow in such matters, Hall yet insisted that there was no need for churches to adopt the same liturgy. He also denied that the Greek liturgies favoured by Laudians in the 1630s were

[148] See P. Lake, 'The Laudians and the argument from authority', in B.Y. Kunze and D.D. Brautigam (eds.), *Court, Country, and Culture* (Rochester, 1992).

[149] See above, ch.7 n.40.

[150] Browning, *Concerning Publike-Prayer*, pp.96, 135, 184–5.

any better than the liturgies of the Reformed Churches.[151] Anthony Cade and Henry King also sounded a more traditional note in emphasizing foreign divines' acceptance of the lawfulness of the Book of Common Prayer. The latter followed Francis Mason in emphasizing the involvement of Bucer, Calvin and Martyr in the drawing up of the Second Edwardian Prayer Book as a positive vindication of the Reformed credentials of that book, rather than as a reason for resentment at foreign Protestant pollution.[152]

As popular criticism of the Book of Common Prayer mounted in the late 1630s, King's approach made perfect sense in the battle to regain puritan hearts. Similarly, when Hall reiterated the traditional point that the Reformed Churches had a freedom of choice in enforcing indifferent ceremonies, he was responding to the argument of the puritan Smectymnuans that the Book of Common Prayer's singularity (compared with the liturgies of the other Reformed Churches) effectively divided it from its Reformed brethren and therefore meant that it must constitute a religion separate from that of continental Protestantism. The Smectymnuans' line of argument was not new – it may be found in the writings of earlier nonconformists such as William Bradshaw – but by the 1630s there were some Laudians who would have found the puritans' logic hard to resist, even though they would have regarded their conclusion as a positive endorsement of the Book of Common Prayer, rather than as a criticism of its unreformed character.[153]

Many aspects of foreign liturgies gave grounds for concern to conformists of varied doctrinal hue, but it was the celebration of the eucharist in foreign churches which gave most offence. This was especially alarming to Laudians such as Cosin, who was thereby driven to doubt whether the Huguenots still retained a true sacrament at all. Time and again, it was the question of posture at communion which arose whenever Laudian bishops blurted out their distaste for the practices of the stranger churches.[154] By contrast, a Calvinist conformist such as Thomas Rogers insisted that, while they might not kneel to receive, the foreign Reformed Churches did

151 Hall, *Works*, IX: 310–11, 428.

152 Anthony Cade, *A Sermon Necessary for these Times* (Cambridge, 1639) i. p.30, ii. pp.5–7; Henry King, *A Sermon Preached at St Pauls* (1640), pp.45–6; Francis Mason, *The Authority of the Church in Making Canons and Constitutions concerning Things Indifferent* (2nd edn, Oxford, 1634), pp.21–2. Cf. Hall, *Works*, IX: 284–5.

153 Hall, *Works*, IX: 427. See Bradshaw's assertion that 'the more one church differeth from another in rites and ceremonies the more it useth to differ in substance of doctrine', quoted in Lake, *Moderate Puritans*, p.265.

154 Cosin, *Works*, V: 110; Heylyn, *Survey*, p.341 (cf. p.242). For the stranger churches, see below, pp.511–15.

not *oppose* kneeling as such. He similarly insisted that the Church of England did not condemn the foreign Reformed for not kneeling, but still enjoyed fellowship with them. Other Calvinist conformists contented themselves instead with pointing out the use of unleavened wafers for communion in Geneva, the better to embarrass their puritan critics.[155]

Another favourite gambit of conformists, when puritans urged the example of the foreign Reformed Churches' discipline, was to note the profanation of the sabbath in Calvinist countries.[156] In the 1580s, John Rainolds had compared the state of Oxford unfavourably with Geneva when it came to the reformation of society. By the early Stuart period, however, such favourable comparisons were rarely made, and even a violent presbyterian like Leighton was outspoken in his criticism of the profanation of the sabbath in the Netherlands. Laudians made similar observations, but were more approving of the foreigners' lack of Sabbatarian rigour.[157]

Above and beyond the liturgy of the Church of England, the quality of its ministry gave cause for especial satisfaction to English Protestants of all doctrinal predilections when compared with co-religionists abroad. Joseph Hall adopted a strikingly triumphalist vein when invoking the superior knowledge and skills of British divines over those of other Reformed Churches. His applause of 'Stupor mundi clerus Britannicus' made in a Convocation sermon of 1624 is well known, but it was also a refrain in his Hospital sermon of Easter 1618, when he declared that 'it is no brag to say, that no nation under heaven, since the gospel looked forth into the world, ever had so many, so learned teachers, as this island hath at this day'.[158] Even Willet emphasized that no church in the world could be compared with the Church of England for the quality of its ministers, although when appealing to James at his accession he had clearly felt that matters could be considerably improved and preaching further encouraged.[159]

If such encomiums represented a new self-confidence in the Church of England's position, they also bore witness to an increasing recognition by

155 Rogers, *Two Dialogues*, sigs.F3r, I2r, R3v; Hall, *Works*, IX: 97, 303; Ames, *Fresh Suit*, ii. pp.527–8; Daniel Tilenus, *De Disciplina Ecclesiastica* (Aberdeen, 1622), p.31. Avant-garde conformists, of course, would not have considered the use of unleavened bread to be an error.

156 E.g. Hall, *Works*, IX: 303.

157 Dent, *Reformers*, p.182; Breslow, *Mirror*, pp.92–3; Sprunger, *Ames*, p.167; *idem*, *Dutch Puritanism*, pp.354, 358. Writers such as Heylyn effectively agreed with Rainolds that foreign Calvinists were more strict in opposing dancing, but criticized this as effectively alienating potential converts to Protestantism: Heylyn, *History of the Sabbath*, ii. p.188; *idem*, *ΜΙΚΡΟΚΟΣΜΟΣ* (Oxford, 1636), p.78; Prideaux, *Doctrine*, translator's preface, p.10. See also above, ch.8.

158 Hall, *Works*, X: 29, V: 120 (cf. pp.121–2); Collinson, *Religion of Protestants*, pp.92–3.

159 Willet, *Thesaurus Ecclesiae*, pp.140, 182. Contrast *idem*, *Ecclesia Triumphans*, p.66.

all English Protestant clerics of the deficiencies in the economic and social strength of the church abroad, and concomitant weaknesses in the quality of its personnel and the discipline that it was able to impose. Matthew Sutcliffe had sounded a warning bell in 1590, when his anti-presbyterian arguments had included passages deploring the decay of the ministry and of its learning in those areas where presbyterian government had taken hold.[160] Adrianus Saravia had spoken from experience when he cited the scandalously low clerical incomes of ministers in the Netherlands in his *De Gradibus* printed in the same year. Oxford University's *Answere* to the Millenary Petition's appeal to the example of 'the best reformed churches' was similarly forthright, declaring 'not ... with a detracting spirit, but with griefe of heart: to see the ruines of the Ministery in particular, & generally of al profound learning in other reformed Churches'. Against puritan complaints of the dumb and idle ministry in the present Church of England, it was affirmed that 'there are at this day, more learned men in this land, in this one Kingdome; then are to be found among al the Ministers of the Religion, in France, Flaunders, Germany, Poleland, Denmarke, Geneva, Scotland; or (to speake in a word) in al Europe besides'.[161] Later writers such as Heylyn merely added their voices to a general consensus that the British clergy were 'the richest of any Ministers of the Reformed Churches'.[162]

The undermining of clerical income abroad appeared to many divines to be a significant restriction upon the efficacy of the ministry. Indeed, while puritan writers continued to praise the Dutch Church as a model church the better to criticize English ceremonies by comparison, even writers such as Thomas Scot and Alexander Leighton expressed the same concern as conformists at the undermining of clerical maintenance abroad, and the lack of proper discipline exerted over the various sects that infested Dutch cities.[163]

To other conformist divines, however, the diminution of clerical income appeared as merely one aspect of a more general sacrilegious attack that had been made upon the church and its goods in the foreign reformations. By the 1630s, Joseph Mede was writing in a concerned vein of the sacrilege which had been permitted on the continent. In private correspondence and public disputations, he complained of how 'the Reformed Churches, out of

160 Sutcliffe, *Treatise*, p.185 (cf. p.103 regarding the impoverished Scots ministry); Nijenhuis, *Saravia*, p.123.
161 Oxford University, *Answere*, pp.29–31.
162 Heylyn, *ΜΙΚΡΟΚΟΣΜΟΣ* (Oxford, 1636), p.465.
163 Breslow, *Mirror*, p.93. English separatists abroad often ended up in conflict with the established Dutch Church just as much as they had been with the Church of England.

extreme abomination of Idolatry, have, according to the nature of men, incurred some guilt before God ... by taking away the distinction almost generally between things Sacred and Prophane, and ... they shall one day smart for it'.[164] Indeed, Mede suggested that the time of divine judgement for their sacrilege had probably already come in the shape of the Protestants' reverses in the Thirty Years War: 'If the passages and ground of the continuance of this German War be well considered, would not a man think they spake that of the Apostle, "Thou that hatest idols, dost thou commit Sacrilege?"'[165]

When Mede wrote in 1636 of 'the alienation which appears in our Church of late from the rest of the Reformed' he may well have been describing more than a mere Laudian-centred development.[166] Certainly, he may have been explaining a sense which he himself shared (for all his commitment to the schemes of the Protestant irenicist John Dury) that

> our Church ... goes upon differing Principles from the rest of the Reformed, and so steers her course by another rule then they do. We look after the Form, Rites and Discipline of Antiquity, and endeavour to bring our own as near as we can to that Pattern. We suppose the Reformed Churches have departed farther there-from then needed, and so we are not very solicitous to comply with them; yea we are jealous of such of our own as we see over-zealously addicted to them, lest it be a sign they prefer them before their Mother.

Mede could see, and assumed that his correspondent Hartlib had noted too, 'that this disposition in our Church is of late very much increased'.[167]

Ephraim Pagitt manifested 'this disposition' in his *Christianographie* of 1640. He deplored the sacrilegious violation of bishops' lands in some countries 'for lucres sake', especially attacking the appropriation of church livings in the Dutch Church.[168] In deliberately keeping the ministers in penury and depriving them of all honours, the laity in the foreign Reformed Churches had shown themselves to be 'without any feare of God at all, and more impious then the Gothes, and Vandals, and other barbarous nations; yea then the Turks themselves in their Conquests, who left

164 Mede, *Works*, pp.1017, 1022.

165 *Ibid.*, p.1017 (Romans 2.22); cf. p.23. William Twisse in reply confessed himself melancholic at these remarks, but noted that the Palatinate had suffered more than other countries, even though it was the most free from sacrilege, as bishoprics and monasteries still continued there (*ibid.*, p.1020).

166 *Ibid.*, p.1067. For another example of concern at sacrilege in foreign reformations, contrasting their popular disorder with the monarchical reformation in England, see Hall, *Works*, IX: 158.

167 Mede, *Works*, p.1061.

168 Pagitt, *Christianographie* (1640 edn), sig.A3r, pp.11, 177–222. He does, however, vindicate Calvin and Beza from responsibility for the sacrilegious seizure of church lands in the Genevan Reformation (p.184).

the Christian Clergie their honours'. To Pagitt, the abolition of bishops and spoliation of church livings was responsible for hindering the spread of the Reformation, and ultimately made any unification of Christ's church impossible: 'for this wrong done to Bishops, and seizing upon Church-livings, and all this under colour of reformation, the name of Almighty God is blasphemed, Religion scandalized among them, who are without, and by these their doings, the schisme and breach of the Church is in a manner impossible to be repaired'.[169] It would be impossible for other Protestant Churches, which had so ruined the livings of their churches, to be reconciled with moderate Romanists such as the Gallican Church. The Gallicans could only unite with the Church of England, which had retained the episcopal polity and was the richest and most honourable of all the Reformed Churches.[170]

Such concern at sacrilege had been voiced earlier even by those anxious to retain close relations with the foreign Reformed communities. John King had compared the destruction of the church's patrimony with sowing the land of the church with salt.[171] The Scots Reformation was heartily condemned by a broad cross-section of conformist opinion.[172] While such concerns were therefore not an exclusively Laudian phenomenon, conservatively minded Calvinist conformists did not necessarily carry their moderate puritan brethren with them in these convictions. Mede admitted that, however much he might complain to others in Cambridge of the profanity of foreign reformations, 'the prejudices hereabout are so great, that I have little hope to persuade others to my opinion'.[173] But this sense of foreign Reformers' sacrilege was still most acute among the Laudians, who were certainly more aggressive in drawing attention to it. It was left to King Charles himself, however, to draw the starkest conclusion that 'the reformation of the Church of England hath no relation to the reformation of any other church'.[174]

169 *Ibid.*, pp.191, 206–7 (Pagitt here follows Mede in quoting Romans 2.22). For his attacks on the 'hainousnesse of their rapacity', Pagitt was often indebted to the works of Saravia: e.g. *ibid.*, pp.189–90, 216.

170 *Ibid.*, pp.207, 217.

171 King, *Fourth Sermon*, p.13 (cf. p.47). Even Calvinist conformists such as Hakewill found themselves called upon to condemn the Huguenots' pulling down of churches: Hakewill, *Answere*, ii. pp.253–4.

172 E.g. Leslie, *Treatise*, pp.154, 158; King James, *Political Works*, p.23. But see the discussion of the Scots Reformation in Andrewes, *Responsio*, pp.161–2; Bedell, *Certaine Letters*, pp.128–9; Lake, *Ten Sermons*, p.9.

173 Mede, *Works*, p.1017.

174 Bruce, *Charles I in 1646*, p.26; Russell, *Causes*, p.197.

The Reformed Churches in national and international politics

THE PROTESTANT CAUSE

The question of how the Church of England related to the foreign Reformed Churches, beyond the simple matter of doctrinal unity, was sufficiently complicated in matters of ecclesiastical discipline. In the arena of national and international politics, however, the picture was more complex still, as religious imperatives sought to make their impression felt in areas dominated by more pragmatic considerations. The simple Protestant internationalism expounded in sermon literature was heavily qualified in practice, as other motives came to the fore. Nonetheless, if religious considerations could never manage to dictate practical social or economic policies, politicians could rarely afford to ignore the importance of religious ideology when seeking to explain and justify their actions.

The classic political expression of Reformed unity in foreign affairs was the so-called 'Protestant Cause' – the agitation for a foreign policy based on confessional alliance with the West European Reformed Churches. But not everyone in early Stuart England felt the same degree of commitment to the cause of their co-religionists, and their varying commitments were not necessarily expressed in the same way. In 1632, for example, George Hakewill preached of the duty to defend 'the members of the same Church (though farre distant in place yet linked together by the same faith)' who were suffering under the persecution of God's enemies. It was men's duty to 'assist such an one with their persons or purses, or both (if they be able), or if with neither, yet at leastwise with their prayers'.[175] The sliding scale of commitment to their foreign Protestant brethren that Hakewill outlined is probably a reasonably accurate reflection of the way that English Protestants did respond, with increasing numbers involved as the degree of active commitment decreased.[176]

[175] George Hakewill, *A Sermon Preached at Bar[n]staple: Upon Occasion of the Late Happy Success of Gods Church in Forraine Parts* (1632), p.32. However, Hakewill was clearly aiming higher, and barely disguised his appeal to Charles to intervene militarily in the Thirty Years War: 'the third and last and highest pitch of love of Gods Church is, when a man, but specially a Prince, a King adventures and indangers his crown, his kingdom, his life, and all to deliver the Church from oppression and persecution; and surely greater love than this hath no man, than to hazard all he hath for the good of the Church, whereof he professeth himselfe a member' (*ibid.*).

[176] The activities of the groups involved in public fasts and collections for distressed foreign Protestants have been typified by one commentator as 'a partisan cause and a coterie somewhat out of the main stream of English society' (Collinson, 'England and international Calvinism', p.213). However, the ideological dedication of this minority would seem to have overlapped with the more fitful and equivocal Protestant jingoism of the wider political nation, or at least to have been an application of a more generally accepted ideology.

Thomas Gataker's sermon – *A Sparke toward the Kindling of Sorrow for Sion* – is often quoted as an example of a popular commitment to the cause of the continental Reformed Churches. It is worth emphasizing, however, that (as the title implies) Gataker's sermon was prompted by a perceived *lack* of commitment to the international Calvinist cause, and this among the 'godly' populace just as much as in government circles. Gataker complained that most of the population took no notice of the suffering of the Palatinate 'save as matter of newes and novelty, to furnish discourse, or to feed their itching Athenian-like humours withall ... Yea even among those few, to speake of, that seeme to take these things to heart, hard it is to finde a fellow-feeling affection any thing proportionable to the occasion given of it.'[177]

The Protestant Cause was constantly complicated by trade rivalries or xenophobia, and striking inconsistencies in the ideology and behaviour of individuals inevitably resulted. That there was a large gap between the Protestant Cause in theory and in practice should hardly surprise us – when ideals encroach into the realm of practical politics they generally fall prey to conflicting influences. The link between ideology and politics was never necessarily a clear one. Economic and political concerns might often dictate lines of behaviour seemingly at odds with wider ideological commitments.[178] Moreover, even when MPs and the wider public *did* agitate for a more aggressively Protestant foreign policy, this was not necessarily accompanied by a consistently positive attitude towards their Protestant neighbours. For most of the population, envy and xenophobia were rarely entirely absent when they contemplated the foreigners with whom they supposedly shared confessional bonds. A commitment to a supranational 'true church' did not necessarily manifest itself in an indulgent attitude towards other nations and cultures.

English relations with the Dutch provide a telling example here. English economic relations with the Dutch were tense throughout the entire early Stuart period. Even puritans admitted the shortcomings of the Dutch character, admiration of their defiance of Spain often tending to mingle with criticisms of their arrogance and avarice.[179] The 'blessed revolution' of 1623–4 was motivated more by anti-papal, and specifically by anti-

[177] Gataker, *A Sparke*, sig.A3v.

[178] On the potential conflict between economic and religious motivation, see the discussions of the planned move of the Merchant Adventurers from Middelburg to the Remonstrant stronghold of Amsterdam: J.C. Grayson, 'From protectorate to partnership: Anglo-Dutch relations 1598–1625' (University of London DPhil, 1978), pp.188–9, 203, 204.

[179] On Anglo-Dutch economic relations, see G. Edmundson, *Anglo-Dutch Rivalry during the First Half of the Seventeenth Century* (Oxford, 1910); J.F. Bense, *Anglo-Dutch Relations* (The Hague, 1925), pp.96–111; Grayson, 'Protectorate', chs.7 and 9; Breslow, *Mirror*, pp.94–5.

Spanish, emotions, rather than by an upsurge of pro-Dutch sentiment, a fact which became clear when the Amboyna massacre unleashed a torrent of anti-Dutch feeling at precisely the time when closer links with the Dutch ally were crucial for a war against the Habsburgs.[180] As a result, the puritan geographer Samuel Purchas found himself having to pick his way carefully between ideological and national sentiments when describing events in the Moluccas in his 1625 *Pilgrimes*. He anticipated some blame for relating the deeds of some Dutch against the English, 'as if I sought like an unseasonable and uncharitable Tale-bearer to raise discord betwixt Neighbours', and declared passionately his freedom from anti-Dutch prejudice. Nevertheless, Protestant sympathies could not dictate Purchas' whole treatment, and he felt bound to include passages relating to the Amboyna massacre, fearing that otherwise 'I might ... have beene accounted partiall against mine owne Nation.' The puritan Thomas Scot struggled to excuse the massacre and reaffirm Anglo-Dutch unity, but his was a rare voice.[181]

Nevertheless, there was an important sense in which the conflicting forces of nationalist pragmatism and of supranational confessionalism were able to co-exist in men's minds. A typical example is an anonymous tract addressed to King James in 1615. In this work, the author explained to the king how the British could easily crush their Dutch trading rival by an economic blockade, while yet correcting himself at the end of his tract with the pious reflection that such a conflict should never of course take place because both countries were united by bonds of religion.[182] This inconsistency reflected in part the inevitable disjunctions between ideals and political realities. Nevertheless, it may also be the case that the confessional ideal fed on such a disjunction. That is, the more that political imperatives dictated an aggressive approach towards the Dutch, the more it was deemed important to reiterate one's adherence to the ideal of confessional fraternity. Disregarding the minority of genuine Dutchophiles in

180 On the Amboyna massacre, see the articles by F.W. Stapel and W.Ph. Coolhaas in M.A.P. Meilink-Roelofsz, M.E. van Opstall and G.J. Schutte (eds.), *Dutch Authors on Asian History* (Leiden, 1988). See also the references to the incident in *Sir Dudley Carleton's State Letters, during his Embassy at the Hague, A.D. 1627*, ed. 'T.P.' (1841), pp.7, 21–2, 37, 38, 48–9. On earlier Anglo-Dutch clashes in the Moluccas, see e.g. *Matthew Slade, 1569–1628: Letters to the English Ambassador*, ed. W. Nijenhuis (Leiden, 1986), pp.83, 87. On the response in England to the massacre, see Grell, *Dutch Calvinists*, pp.151–2; Breslow, *Mirror*, pp.85–8; Cogswell, *Blessed Revolution*, pp.274–5.

181 Samuel Purchas, *Hakluytus Posthumus or Purchas His Pilgrimes* (20 vols., Glasgow, 1905–7), I: pp.xlix–xl; Breslow, *Mirror*, pp.88–90. For contrasting views of the significance of Scot's tract, and of long-term anti-Dutch feeling, see Cogswell, *Blessed Revolution*, p.275; Grayson, 'Protectorate', p.288. See also the identification of anti-Dutch feeling with mere 'formalism' and crypto-popery in the puritan verse-tract 'The Interpreter': Firth, *Stuart Tracts*, p.240.

182 LPL, Lambeth MS 513; Grayson, 'Protectorate', p.172.

England, it seems most accurate to depict this Protestant internationalism more as a generally accepted ideology rather than a political straitjacket. It might be used as a means of legitimating apparently divergent behaviour just as often as it might be urged as dictating a particular policy. It could thus provide the crucial encoding with which to legitimate apparently conflicting behaviour. In political and economic terms, the English and the Dutch were moving inexorably away from co-operation towards competition. Few upheld a completely consistent attitude towards foreign Protestants, but most Englishmen accepted the idea that such a consistency was desirable, and in times of crisis the ideal of Protestant internationalism could become a potent symbol, by which political loyalty and orthodoxy could be judged.

Hopes for a consistently confessional foreign policy were doomed to disappointment throughout the period 1559–1640, as Elizabeth, James and Charles consistently refused to endorse one. Under James, it is true, a fortuitous succession of incidents – his alliance with the Protestant League in the face of the apparent revival of the Catholic League and the Cleves–Jülich crisis, the marriage of his daughter Elizabeth to the Elector Palatine, his intervention against Vorstius, the dispatching of the British delegation to Dort – helped to create the illusion that the king was happy to pursue a consciously Protestant foreign policy.[183] Nevertheless, political concerns ultimately directed him away from this straitjacket – indeed, after 1614 James followed a policy of disillusioned withdrawal from European affairs.

The king's equivocal support for international Protestantism ultimately exacerbated English Protestant divisions over foreign policy. Just as the Spanish Match had polarized English Protestant views of the Roman Church, so the outbreak of the Thirty Years War in 1618 vividly demonstrated English Protestants' differing views of the English Church's links with foreign Reformed Protestantism. These tensions were all the more acute because the focus of the continental war was the Rhenish Palatinate, whose queen was James' daughter, and whose children were potential successors to the English throne. The question of England's duty to protect her Reformed sister was thus raised in an especially intense and urgent form. King James, however, was determined to resolve the German situation within the context of a rapprochement with Catholic Spain. To facilitate such a general peace, it was vital that the issue of religious conflict

[183] On the Cleves–Jülich crisis, see G. Parker, *Europe in Crisis 1598–1648* (1981), pp.85, 125–7, 152–3; Grayson, 'Protectorate', ch.6; Adams, 'Protestant cause', chs.5 and 8 (esp. pp.191–2, 199, 216, 219–20, 255, 261).

should be avoided at all costs.[184] As a result, James consistently refused to see the crisis as a war of religion and censured those who represented it as such. He vetoed Archbishop Abbot's proposal that the Elector Frederick's acceptance of the crown of Bohemia should be celebrated publicly in London, he prohibited public prayer for Frederick and Elizabeth as king and queen of Bohemia and forbade his ultimately exiled daughter Elizabeth to enter the country out of fear that she might act as a focus for bellicose Protestant unrest. James' adamant refusal to allow the Palatine cause to be invoked at home provoked widespread unrest and the censuring of a number of prominent preachers, including Joseph Hall and Lewis Bayly. Simon Adams has described how the Bohemian party engaged a number of the most prominent London preachers, including Gouge, Sibbes, Gataker and Taylor, along with the Calvinist wing of the church hierarchy – men such as Davenant, Bedell and Ussher.[185]

This official downplaying of Protestant internationalism was temporarily reversed in the 'blessed revolution' of 1623–4, and in Charles' subsequent policy towards Spain and France, in which his determination to preserve his honour by protecting the Huguenots and coming to the aid of his dispossessed sister placed him on the Protestant side again, and encouraged a revival of governmental invocations of the Protestant Cause.[186] By the late 1620s, however, the government was seeking peace, and the rhetoric of Protestant internationalism was frowned upon once more. But it should be stressed that talk of rallying to the cause of true religion was never entirely absent during the 1630s. In the years 1631–2 Charles certainly contemplated intervention in support of the victorious armies of Gustavus Adolphus, and in the years 1636–8 proposals for a military alliance with Sweden against the empire were again revived, with Charles permitting levies for the Swedish army on British soil.[187] This was simply one aspect of a fleeting attempt to muster anti-Habsburg forces through an alliance with France that was eventually abandoned in the wake of the

184 Adams, 'Protestant cause', p.309. For a sympathetic account of James' policy towards the Thirty Years War, see R. Zaller, '"Interest of state": James I and the Palatinate', *Albion* 6 (1974).

185 Adams, 'Protestant cause', chs.8 and 9 (esp. pp.279, 288, 290–300, 308–18).

186 T. Cogswell, 'Foreign policy and parliament: the case of La Rochelle, 1625–1626', *EHR* 99 (1984), 241–67; *idem*, 'Prelude to Ré: the Anglo-French struggle over La Rochelle, 1624–1627', *History* 71 (1986), 1–21 (esp. pp.18–19). Contrast S. Adams, 'The road to La Rochelle', *Proceedings of the Huguenot Society* 22/5 (1975), p.427. Laud was instructed by Conway in August 1628 to draw up a form of public prayer for the success of the Ile de Rhé expedition which would support the profession of true religion: PRO, SP 16/113/52.

187 L.J. Reeve, *Charles I and the Road to Personal Rule* (Cambridge, 1989), pp.261–91; *HMC De L'Isle* VI: 108–9; PRO, SP 95/4 fols.128, 135v, 140v, 164–6. Reference was made as a matter of course in the diplomatic correspondence of 1637–8 to 'Communem Evangelicorum caussam' and 'communem Causam' (*ibid.*, fols.222v, 238).

Scottish troubles.[188] While hopes for the 'Protestant Cause' might thus be raised spasmodically, the practical policy of the English sovereigns throughout this period failed to match the hopes of the ideologically committed clerics of the kingdom.

Divines responded in various ways to such disappointments. As professional ideologues, the clergy might be assumed to have been willing to follow through the logic of their confessional imperatives in a manner that was impossible for members of the laity whose actions were circumscribed by social and political necessities. This may have been true, but conformist divines were also committed to the defence of the government and of the status quo, and many were happy to deny that confessional issues should dictate government policy. In the 1580s, Archbishop Whitgift had clashed with puritans who campaigned for a more vigorously Protestant foreign policy. In the Jacobean period there was never any shortage of divines who like Whitgift were happy to preserve close ties with their Protestant brethren abroad, but were unprepared to allow Protestant internationalist notions to dictate government policy.[189] The advent of the Spanish Match and Thirty Years War, however, forced a polarization of conformist opinion, as government policy could appear positively hostile, rather than simply indifferent, to Protestant religious imperatives. These developments were co-terminous with the rise to power in the ecclesiastical establishment of divines such as Laud, who possessed the ideological flexibility to be able to embrace the government's pacificatory foreign policy and to adopt a detached (if not positively hostile) attitude towards the more Reformed brethren of the continent. Not only were these divines prepared to make the sort of distinctions between confessional identity and foreign policy which earlier conformists such as Whitgift had tolerated, but a 'hands-off' approach to confessional conflict was also very much in keeping with their ideological preferences. In the 1630s these divines were in the ascendant as the government sought to maintain a jealously guarded neutrality, and the protagonists of Protestant internationalism were placed under especial pressure not to deal too closely with their co-religionists abroad.

Divines soon got the message during the Personal Rule that all dealings with the continent would be seen as potentially treasonous. The Dutch Church in London did not dare to help the burghers of Hanau with money to maintain the city's garrison, reflecting that 'collecting and transmitting money for such political objects would not be without danger to our Community, as it is to be feared that it might be misinterpreted in this

[188] See Hibbard, *Popish Plot*, pp.72–83; Sharpe, *Personal Rule*, pp.509–41.

[189] Lake, 'Significance', pp.163–4, 176.

country, where great attention is paid to Collections, which sometimes cause difficulties.' Laud and others now lectured that the king's foreign policy should determine all forms of contact with the continent. Even irenical activity was carefully overseen. A cowed Joseph Mede feared that the 'inquisition' in Cambridge would brand him indelibly as 'Factious and a Busie-body' if he dared to become involved in John Dury's reunion schemes and thereby be seen 'to meddle in ought that concerns the publick, before the State and those in place declare themselves'. Despite enjoying the status of Regius Professor of Divinity at Oxford, John Prideaux felt that it would be unsafe for him to write in support of Dury's projects. This was not merely an excuse: Prideaux was a man who had enjoyed close links with continental divines, but in the 1630s he was decidedly out of favour and had constantly to watch his back. One man who met him in Oxford in 1640 found Prideaux full of 'restlesse feare' and afraid of doing anything that might anger Laud, 'as walking now under the cloud, & having many spyes set about him for to prie into all his Actions'.[190]

By the 1630s, it was not simply the case that religious considerations were not permitted to dictate foreign policy. Rather, political considerations appear to have been allowed increasingly to intrude into purely religious issues. Previously the battle had been over the question of whether or not English confessional bonds with foreign Protestantism should dictate foreign policy; now Laud and Charles believed that foreign policy considerations should dictate whether these confessional bonds themselves should be sustained. Moreover, Laudian preachers were prepared, not just to clamp down on individuals' contact with Protestant brethren abroad, but even to complain of those who took an interest in continental affairs.[191]

Given this ultimate antipathy, the fact that Laud (and indeed Charles) were on occasion prepared to support Elizabeth of Bohemia should not be overemphasized. Not merely were they as prey as James had been to the influence of purely political considerations, but they lacked any sustaining commitment to the Protestant Cause as a whole. To Charles, it was his honour, rather than his religion, that was at stake in the fate of the Palatinate. Laud's own preparedness at times to deal gallantly with the queen of Bohemia may represent a careful attempt to build up alternative sources of support among his potential enemies. Such courtesies cost Laud little, given the Winter Queen's isolation at that point, and could have been

190 Grell, *Dutch Calvinists*, p.208; Mede, *Works*, p.1062; SUL, Hartlib MS 15/8 fol.3r: Constantine Adams to Hartlib, 5 August 1640.

191 Farmer, *A Sermon*, p.11; [Thomas Lushington], *The Resurrection Rescued* (1659).

to his benefit if politics had not become quite so bitterly polarized at the end of the 1630s.[192]

This shift in degrees of confessional commitment among conformists in the later Jacobean and Caroline period may be observed in two related areas where notions of Protestant internationalism might be expected to have found their practical political expression. These are the charitable collections for foreign churches, and the treatment of the 'stranger churches'.

Charitable collections for foreign Protestant congregations were at the mercy of changing political and ecclesiological perspectives. As we have seen, everyone before Laud felt it necessary to endorse the corporate religious assumptions that lay behind the charitable collections for foreign Protestants. Nevertheless, degrees of enthusiasm undoubtedly varied. Moreover, as James' foreign policy diverged increasingly far from a straightforwardly confessional one, especially after the outbreak of the Thirty Years War, invocations of Protestant unity and appeals for the defence of suffering European Protestants inevitably risked appearing critical and potentially subversive of government policy. James was anxious to keep them under a tight rein, and therefore made sure that collections in the 1620s were overseen by men whom he could trust to take a purely detached view of the suffering of their co-religionists abroad. Charles displayed similar suspicions when four prominent London puritan ministers attempted to promote a circular letter urging contributions for distressed Palatinate ministers in 1628, for which they were charged before High Commission. The first royal collection of the same year was closely supervised by Laud.[193] By contrast, a second royal collection, begun in 1630, was under the control of the more positively inclined Archbishop Abbot (but with Archbishop Harsnett also appointed to keep an eye on things), and was conducted in a more effective fashion and with more impressive results. The 1635 collection, however, hit more fundamental problems as Laud (as we have seen) interfered significantly with the phrasing of the brief for the collection. By this stage, Laud was no longer simply casting a distrustful eye over the collections, but was also insisting on altering the basic ideology within which the appeal for financial support was couched. Laud was not simply introducing a face-saver for the king to avoid committing him to a confessional conflict. He was also exploiting the

192 E.g. PRO, SP 81/37/45, 96; 81/44/1, 3, 28, 53, 126, 201, 253; Laud, *Works*, VII: 40–1, 126, 151–3, 167–8, 185–8, 227–9, 244–5, 252–4, 259–61, 269–71, 289–91, 302–3, 312–13, 321–3, 344–5, 353–4, 358–61.

193 Grell, *Dutch Calvinists*, pp.179–81, 184–92; Prynne, *Canterburies Doome*, p.362; H.R. Trevor-Roper, *Archbishop Laud 1573–1645* (3rd edn, 1988), p.263.

opportunity to make a few points of his own concerning the Church of England's independence from the continental churches.[194]

In the collections themselves, we can see evidence among certain divines of an increasing alienation from the fortunes of continental Protestantism. The distinguished professor of Greek Matthias Pasor was involved in 1627 in raising funds for the relief of the Palatinate, and of ministers from Heidelberg, in the Universities of Oxford and Cambridge. He voiced the fear that Cambridge people seemed to be favouring Arminianism too much, and that they would therefore show less concern for the sufferings of the Calvinist professors of Heidelberg – a suspicion that would seem to be borne out by the relative sums which Pasor eventually collected from each university.[195] Pasor's more general complaint that the collection was a pious and noble cause, but largely unpopular (at least in the Universities) is a useful reminder that the active supporters of the Palatine cause always ultimately represented a minority even of the educated population.[196] Certainly, no Laudian divines were prominently involved in such collections.[197]

The stranger churches also encountered increasing difficulties in these years. These communities provide a prime example of the shifting, fitful and often problematical confessional internationalism of English Protestants at this time. As we have seen, the entertainment of the stranger churches had immense symbolic importance for the Church of England's internationalist Protestant identity, as well as for the church's implicit recognition of the validity of non-episcopalian orders. We can find a minority of individuals keen to develop close links with the stranger communities – most often those puritans for whom foreign Reformed styles of worship and doctrine would have had most appeal. For some, in the Elizabethan period at least, there was the hope that the stranger churches might act, in the words of one distinguished historian, as 'a means of correcting any errant tendency on the part of the English state'. Yet non-puritan clerics too – even those dedicated to building up episcopal authority – maintained strong links with the immigrant churches. It is noteworthy that the Dutchman Adrianus Saravia, who became a natural-

194 On the brief for the relief of the Palatinate, see Laud, *Works*, IV: 312–13, 333, 406, VI: 417, 418; Grell, *Dutch Calvinists*, pp.206–8.

195 Bodl., Tanner MS 72 fols.228, 308. Pasor gives the total sums collected for the relief of the Heidelberg professors in Oxford and Cambridge Universities in Tanner MS 71 fol.32 (cf. MS 71 fol.18; MS 72 fol.264).

196 Bodl., Tanner MS 72 fol.247.

197 One surprising example of apparent Laudian involvement is a letter in 1631 from the exiled clergy of the Upper Palatinate to the bishop of Chichester (then Richard Montagu), although this would appear to have been a case of mistaken identity, the Palatinate divines apparently being under the impression that they were writing to the previous bishop, George Carleton: PRO, SP 81/36 fol.85.

ized Englishman and was the herald of 'divine right' doctrines of episcopacy, had been particularly attracted to the Church of England because he had observed that her bishops were prepared to allow foreigners in their dioceses to maintain different rites and ceremonies from their own, and indeed 'kindly welcomed and aided them'.[198]

In practice, however, the existence of an immigrant community posed a number of social and economic problems. Like any body of immigrants, the foreign Protestant groups inevitably aroused native hostility. This was true among the broader urban populace, but especially among the various city guilds and artisans whose petitions to the Privy Council consistently accused the foreigners of unfair trading practices, or of stealing jobs and accommodation.[199] Moreover, the English Protestant elite (King James included) displayed a readiness to tolerate or encourage such complaints in the interest of short-term financial or political gain. Nevertheless, the growth of exploitative or apparently xenophobic attitudes towards the foreign communities cannot always be treated as a barometer of a changing religious ideology. Such attitudes could still exist simultaneously with a broader commitment to a supranational Reformed identity. When pragmatic attacks were made upon the stranger community's economic power and social autonomy, such assaults were often followed by assurances that the government was still determined to uphold the foreigners' liberties for the sake of the wider Protestant Cause.

The stranger churches were seldom free from worries, however. In 1619, the king, facing increasing financial difficulties, spearheaded the travesty of a Star Chamber case in which almost the whole stranger merchant community in London was accused of illegal export of bullion.[200] But it was not just economic rivalries and nationalist xenophobia which posed a threat to the stranger communities. The continued independence of their churches occasionally seemed in danger too, and they were certainly conscious from the 1590s of the threat posed to them by the new breed of vigorously conformist bishops who seemed to attach special and exclusive importance to the Church of England's own form of liturgy and worship. Fears were expressed in the immigrant communities in the 1590s that the anti-presbyterian Dutchman Saravia might be imposed as superintendent of the Dutch Church as a means of bringing it into the episcopal fold. The more rigorous Canons of 1604 also prompted anxieties that bishops might be tempted to infringe upon the stranger churches' privileges. By 1615, in the midst of a severe economic crisis, the stranger churches had to face complaints that they constituted a state within a state, and proposals that

198 Collinson, 'England and international Calvinism', p.200; Nijenhuis, *Saravia*, p.122.
199 Grell, *Dutch Calvinists*, pp.16–26. 200 *Ibid.*, ch.4.

the size of the communities should be reduced by transferring second-generation immigrants to their local parish churches.[201]

It was not until the 1630s, however, that the stranger churches suffered the first concerted assault upon their jurisdictional independence. The famous drive against the stranger churches by Laud and his allies in the 1630s might seem at first glance to be merely a further example of the inevitable subjugation of confessional identities to political and social imperatives. Certainly, there was an extent to which the policy merely represented the archbishop's determination to exercise his jurisdictional rights. While Laud's attentions were focused on ensuring that the second-generation immigrants attended their parish churches and followed the Book of Common Prayer, there was little explicit discussion of the nature of the stranger churches' polity, and much of the debate provoked by Laud's policies centred on economic issues. It might thus appear that the Laudians' sense of corporate identity with the foreign churches had simply proved insufficiently strong to restrain objectives that were basically political and financial.[202]

Nevertheless, there was clearly more at stake here, and religious considerations were not entirely absent from the Laudians' thinking. It should be noted from the outset that, while King Charles may on occasion have played a significant role in the formulation of 'Laudian' ecclesiastical policies, the attack on the stranger churches was unquestionably Laud's own inspiration.[203] Moreover, the preoccupation with political and economic issues in the exchanges between Laud and the immigrant churches' representatives can be misleading. As a recent historian has noted, these matters were prominent because the stranger communities themselves, in contrast to an earlier self-defence, deliberately chose not to pursue the theme of Protestant unity in negotiations with Laud. This would seem to reflect their awareness that this was a notion that would not carry much weight with the archbishop: it is significant that the theme of international Protestant solidarity *was* invoked by the same congregations when they addressed the king.[204] But if the stranger communities were prepared not to raise religious issues with the archbishop, Laud had no such qualms. In an interview with a deputation from the stranger churches of Kent in early 1635, Laud allegedly 'spake very basely of their communion, said, that

201 Nijenhuis, *Saravia*, p.124; W.J.C. Moens, *The Walloons and their Church at Norwich* (Lymington, 1887–8), pp.61, 86–7; Grell, *Dutch Calvinists*, p.224.

202 On Laud and the stranger churches, see Grell, *Dutch Calvinists*, ch.6; Trevor-Roper, *Laud*, pp.197–204.

203 Davies, *Caroline Captivity*, p.80.

204 Grell, *Dutch Calvinists*, pp.224–5, 230–2; John Bulteel, *A Relation of the Troubles of the Three Forraign Churches in Kent Caused by the Injunctions of W. Laud* (1645), pp.14–15, 20–1.

their Churches used irreverence at their communion, sate altogether as if it were in a Tavern or Alehouse ... that their Ministry and Discipline was not secundum Evangelium, the English was, [and] ... that their Churches were nests and occasions of scisme'.[205]

Other Laudian bishops such as Neile, Wren and Montagu displayed similar religiously inspired hostility, or clearly felt little need to defer to earlier notions of Protestant internationalism. John Overall had intervened in the Norwich Walloon churches' eucharistic practice as early as 1619, when he had sought to prohibit their habit of sitting to receive the sacrament. He was met by the determined resistance of the stranger churches, who invoked the principle of the indifferency of all rites and ceremonies, and the right of different churches to embrace whichever they preferred.[206] Nevertheless, the hostility of these bishops pales before the cheerful contempt expressed towards the Norwich Walloon congregation by Bishop Richard Corbet. When Corbet attempted in 1634 to recover the episcopal chapel which the stranger congregation had been allowed to use since 1619, he wrote that 'Your discipline, I know, cares not much for a consecrated place, & any other roome in Norwiche that hath but breadth and length may serve your turne as well as a chapell. Wherefore I say unto you, without a miracle, Lazare, prodi foras! Depart, and hire some other place for your irregular meetings.' Whatever the jurisdictional or economic issues at stake, for Laudian divines at least they offered a perfect opportunity and created a hostile atmosphere within which they could act upon a more purely religious distaste for the style of worship adopted in the foreign Reformed Churches. It is certainly true that foreign Protestants did not see the matter as a purely jurisdictional one: John Dury complained that the treatment of the stranger churches in England greatly handicapped his irenical efforts in the Netherlands.[207]

Of course, it was not just Laudians who recognized the ecclesiological disharmony that the immigrant presbyterian churches represented in a country whose national church was governed by an episcopal polity, and Laud was not the only divine to make the suggestion that the churches' existence might have implications for the ecclesiological integrity of the English episcopal system. Puritan groups could see this logic, and had been happy to urge the strangers' example upon the national church in the 1580s, and were to do so again in the early 1640s. King James himself was alive to the symbolic implications if the presbyterian stranger churches

[205] Bulteel, *A Relation*, pp.7, 9; Grell, *Dutch Calvinists*, p.229.

[206] Moens, *Walloons*, p.66; Bulteel, *A Relation*, 'To the Reader', sigs.A3v–A4r; A.W. Foster, 'A biography of Archbishop Richard Neile, 1562–1640' (Oxford University DPhil, 1978), pp.271–2; PRO, SP 16/400/45: Bishop Wren to Bishop Montagu.

[207] PRO, SP 16/311/ 77, 343/66.

were to send delegates from his country to the Synod of Dort. The king therefore insisted that the immigrant churches should not be invited to the synod, and complained that the invitation would undermine by implication the Church of England's established form of church government. Moreover, the Laudians were not alone in their desire to dictate to the stranger churches in ceremonial matters. James had already implicitly undermined the principle of their autonomy in ceremonies and church government when he had recommended in 1615 that sermons should be preached and the sacrament administered in stranger churches on Good Friday.[208] Nevertheless, the difference in tone and in churchmanship between James and the later Laudian bishops was real and profound.

The most immediate stimulus for Laud's assault on the stranger churches, however, was his sensitivity to the churches' possible role as an inspiration for native puritans. Not only did they constitute 'a Church within a Church', but Laud argued in a 1632 report that the stranger churches' example encouraged puritans' disobedience to church government. In 1634 he endorsed a further report which made the still more damaging allegation that the immigrants allowed English puritans to become members of their churches, 'and thereby breed a nursery of ill-minded persons to the Church'.[209]

Laud's policy was not merely intended to defend the principle that national churches had the right to enforce their ceremonies on foreigners living within their territories. This became clear when Laud reversed this principle when dealing with English Protestants living abroad. These, he insisted, should conform themselves to their mother church at home, and should not allow themselves to become absorbed into the ecclesiastical habits surrounding them. Again, this was a notably more rigid approach than had been adopted previously. If Laud was seeking to extend his powers of jurisdiction, he was also manifesting a determination to root out alien and (as he saw them) poisonous influences issuing forth from foreign Reformed bodies.[210]

PRESBYTERIANISM AND REBELLION

As we have seen, underlying the Laudian assault on the stranger churches was a conviction that they constituted a subversive political influence. This

208 Grell, *Dutch Calvinists*, pp.32–3; Moens, *Walloons*, pp.64–5.

209 Grell, *Dutch Calvinists*, pp.225–6, 227.

210 W. Nijenhuis, 'Resolutions of Dutch church assemblies concerning English ministers in the Hague, 1633–1651', *NAvK* 62 (1982); Adams, 'Protestant cause', pp.443–7; R.P. Stearns, *Congregationalism in the Dutch Netherlands* (1940); Sprunger, *Dutch Puritanism*, pp.144–52, 236–7, 241–5, 256–9, 264–5, 288–9, 295–306.

derived from the fact that they represented a jurisdictional plurality, but it also expressed a belief that Reformed presbyterianism was inherently revolutionary.

Of course, there was a sense in which this assessment of foreign Protestant 'subversion' had been a conformist commonplace from Elizabethan times. Conformist thought from Whitgift onwards had sought to emphasize the essential incompatibility of presbyterianism and the royal supremacy. James' epigrammatic declaration 'no Bishop no King' encapsulated the conformist position that episcopacy was better suited than was presbyterianism to a monarchical polity. English presbyterians were accused by Covell, Bancroft and others of having promoted popular sedition in their organization of the classical movement, as well as having upheld the incipient democratic principles allegedly present in their platform of church government. Richard Bancroft had described in lurid detail the development of seditious Calvinist resistance theories, with their accompanying threat to all public authority, from Geneva and Scotland to the English puritans.[211] Even evangelical Calvinists such as John King emphasized that presbyterianism was anti-monarchical.[212]

Nevertheless, in other contexts (most specifically an anti-papal context) English Protestants were usually anxious to deny that Protestants could be less loyal members of a polity than Roman Catholics, seeking instead to maintain that it was popery that was a religion of rebellion, rather than Protestantism. For all his penchant for equating puritan and Jesuit styles of disobedience, King James went out of his way to affirm that, unlike the papists' religion, the religion of Protestants did not give any grounds for rebellion. He explained away the two most notorious Protestant justifications of resistance to tyrants, describing Stephanus Junius Brutus' *Vindiciae contra tyrannos* as a papist forgery, and George Buchanan (author of the notorious *De iure regni apud Scotos*) as a poet rather than a divine. This was James' preferred line, and in his defence of the king's work even Lancelot Andrewes insisted that presbyterianism need not be anti-monarchical: although the puritans wanted parity in the church, this did not mean that they wanted uniformity in the state, and they were faithful upholders of the king's supremacy.[213]

Moreover, even where foreign Protestants could be seen to have opposed

211 Covell, *Modest Examination*, pp.35–8 ; Bancroft, *Survay*, pp.14–26, 34–8; Lake, *Anglicans and Puritans*, pp.130–2, 112–13. See also Oxford University, *Answere*, pp.28–9.

212 King, *Fourth Sermon*, pp.21–5.

213 King James, *Political Works*, p.264; Andrewes, *Responsio*, pp.38–9, 473–4. Cf. White, *Replie*, p.577; Willet, *Antilogie*, pp.201–6. On Romanist attempts to use writers such as Buchanan to show that puritanism was more likely to lead to rebellion than was Roman doctrine, see Sommerville, 'Jacobean political thought', pp.262–3; Brereley, *Protestants Apologie*, pp.647–59. See also above, ch.1.

their lawful sovereign, English Protestants sought not simply to deny this, but also defended their co-religionists' actions and denied that they constituted rebellion. This was evident even in the work of Jewel, who defended the actions of the French and Scots in the 1550s, and Jewel's approach was echoed in the defence of the later Dutch Revolt by William Bedell and others.[214] Bedell based his defence of the Protestants' wars in France, the Netherlands and Germany on their customary legal right to self-defence, and denied the impact of religious factors, even in the Scottish Reformation.[215] It was therefore wrong of Roman Catholic opponents to accuse Knox, Calvin or the Huguenots of raising rebellion.[216] Thomas Bilson similarly argued that religion could provide no ground for rebellion, and therefore sought to exculpate the political activities of foreign Protestants against their rulers by claiming that they occurred in types of polity in which resistance might be legitimate. Thus Bilson was able to explain away the resistance theories of Zwingli, Goodman and Knox as having been merely concerned to describe the constitutional or legal systems of particular societies in which resistance was valid according to secular law.[217]

Nevertheless, as more absolutist styles of political thought developed, and more importance was attached to the divine right of kings, the tensions between these principles, and the need to excuse the popular resistance both displayed and vindicated in Calvinist reformations abroad, became more evident. A number of divines from Saravia onwards were beginning to assert that monarchy was part of the necessary structure of all political systems, ordained by God in the Old Testament. These theorists hence added a religious imperative, not only to the political authority wielded by kings, but to the institution of divine right monarchy itself. This rendered all more limited forms of monarchy essentially heretical. In theory, at least, this left the political resistance of foreign Protestants open to the charge of religious heterodoxy, even if the foreign Protestants had asserted no *religious* right to resist. This was an anomaly which could be circumvented, though not without provoking further problems. While James was keen to promote a vindication of Elizabeth's support of the Dutch resistance to Spain in the Convocation of 1606, he swiftly became anxious at the positions that were formulated in order to justify it. By following Saravia in not upholding legal and constitutional rights of resistance, Convocation was forced to defend the validity of all new forms of

214 Jewel, *Works*, I: 73–6; Bedell, *Certaine Letters*, pp.126–34; Laud, *Works*, III: 367; Lake, *Moderate Puritans*, p.319 n.108; Abbot, *Reasons*, pp.164–5.

215 Bedell, *Certaine Letters*, pp. 123–4, 128–9, 132–4.

216 *Ibid.*, pp.135–6.

217 Lake, *Anglicans and Puritans*, pp.132–3; Sommerville, *Politics*, p.11.

government after they had settled – a conclusion that was not at all to King James' taste.[218]

An easier way out of this quandary was to condemn Protestant resistance theories as embodying a religious right to resist. Puritans might occasionally be condemned in this way, but foreign Protestants were only systematically condemned by a small minority of avant-garde conformists. The more vehemently anti-puritan avant-garde conformists were ready to target foreign churches and congregations when they emphasized the political threat from forms of Reformed Protestantism. David Owen, in his *Herod and Pilate Reconciled*, followed contemporary practice in comparing puritan and Jesuit doctrines of rebellion, but went significantly further. While he mostly cited the usual authors such as Junius, Daneau, François Hotman and George Buchanan, he widened their applicability by emphasizing that the works of Buchanan and Goodman were published with the full approval of Beza and the chief ministers of Geneva. Moreover, while he generally vindicated Calvin, Owen noted a single passage in Book 4 of Calvin's *Institutes* which he considered to be 'harsh and dangerous'. Foreign divines were not unaware of the implications of Owen's arguments: the Dutch Reformed congregation in Austin Friars complained that they had been bracketed along with the 'moderne Puritans' as advocates of armed resistance, and as constituting a danger to both church and crown.[219]

Jacobean Calvinist conformists such as Sutcliffe and Hakewill continued to deny that Calvin's *Institutes*, or even the works of Goodman and Knox, contained material against the government of lawful magistrates. Nevertheless, the fact that foreign Calvinists nursed a potentially revolutionary theory of the right to resist, while it was increasingly less true on the continent, continued to cause problems among English Calvinists.[220] The Dutch Arminian controversy raised further embarrassing questions concerning the relation of English and Dutch Calvinist notions of the power of

218 Overall, *Convocation Book*, pp.7–8 (King James to Archbishop Abbot). On the development of absolutist thought in England see Sommerville, *Politics*, ch.1; Lake, *Anglicans and Puritans*, pp.131–9. More recently, it has been argued that divine right theory was not necessarily wedded to any particular concept of monarchical absolutism, and was not in direct conflict with notions that the king was bound by customary laws: see Russell, *Causes*, ch.6; G. Burgess, 'The divine right of kings reconsidered', *EHR* 425 (1992). However, the rhetorical flourishes of divine right theorists could clearly generate *fears* of such a connection, while more Laudian writers showed little desire to deny it. See also below, Conclusion.

219 Owen, *Herod and Pilate*, pp.6, 13, 17, 40–2, 46, 47, 50–1, 53–4; Grell, *Dutch Calvinists*, p.5 and n.11. Owen cites Calvin's *Institutes*, lib.4 cap.20 sect.31 – the same section noted in Q. Skinner, *The Foundations of Modern Political Thought* (2 vols., Cambridge, 1978), II: 232–3.

220 Hakewill, *Answere*, ii. pp.170, 160; Sutcliffe, *Briefe Examination*, p.102.

lay authorities in matters of ecclesiastical government. Saravia was not the only divine in England to realize that the arguments of Remonstrants such as Uytenbogaert and Grotius concerning the rights of lay authorities in ecclesiastical affairs bore more resemblance to the status quo in the English Church than did those of their Dutch Contra-Remonstrant opponents.[221]

The disjunction of the political thought of foreign Reformed divines with that of the Church of England became an even more controversial issue in 1622 when, as we have seen, John Knight cited the arguments of the distinguished Palatine divine Paraeus in support of his defence of the right to resist. Writing earlier in James' reign, Andrew Willet had sought to hedge Paraeus' arguments around with sufficient qualifications as to make his opinions seem orthodox and unremarkable. After Knight's exposition, however, Paraeus' commentary, along with Bucanus' *Loci Communes* and the *Vindiciae contra tyrannos*, was publicly burnt in London and at the Universities of Oxford and Cambridge.[222] The disgrace thus visited upon one of the most distinguished living Calvinist divines, whose judgement had been heard with reverence at the Synod of Dort, caused a good deal of heart-searching among some English divines, but the more rigid conformists of Laud's school responded with alacrity. George Montaigne, bishop of London, delivered a vehement and unqualified assault upon Paraeus to accompany the burning at Paul's Cross. Oxford University published a decree condemning certain positions as false and erroneous, and directed that Paraeus' *Commentary on Romans* be burnt publicly. At Cambridge, the reaction was even stronger. David Owen's 1619 disputation – which was a systematic and scathing critique of Paraeus' political maxims – was published, and moves were afoot among some divines to ensure that the University branded the authors of the burned books with perpetual infamy. The avant-garde conformist faction was clearly at work here, trying to exploit the opportunity to deliver a stinging attack upon the foreign Reformed tradition in general. It was reported that the 'Arminian' faction in the University was seeking to ensure that a Cambridge decree against

221 Nijenhuis, *Saravia*, pp.154–5, 355–8. However, even James felt that Grotius went too far in the authority which he gave the sovereign in ecclesiastical affairs. The precise authority wielded by King James at the Hampton Court Conference became a major point of disagreement between Remonstrants and Contra-Remonstrants, so that James was ultimately forced to instruct his bishops to draw up an account of the Royal Supremacy and the events at Hampton Court for Dutch digestion: see Carleton, *Letters*, pp.208, 223, 229, 239, 243; PRO, SP 105/95 fol.28r–v (Archbishop Abbot to Carleton, 8 Jan. 1619); Borschberg, 'State and church', pp.222–4; D. Nobbs, *Theocracy and Toleration. A Study of the Disputes in Dutch Calvinism from 1600 to 1650* (Cambridge, 1938).

222 Willet, *Hexapla on Romans*, pp.592–4; Chamberlain, *Letters*, II: 443; G.W. Whiting, 'Paraeus, the Stuarts, Laud and Milton', *Studies in Philology* 1 (1953), esp. pp.219–22; J.B. Mullinger, *The University of Cambridge from ... 1535 to the Accession of Charles I* (Cambridge, 1854), p.567; Adams, 'Protestant cause', p.329.

Paraeus couched in 'considerably more bitter language' would be published.[223] Their efforts would seem to have failed,[224] but several years later William Prynne was still complaining of the ignominy and disgrace caused by the burning of the work of Paraeus. Concern at the Laudian manipulation of the incident was merely confirmed at Laud's trial, when the archbishop invoked the burning of Paraeus' works as justifying the argument that the Palatine religion was not the same as that of the Church of England.[225]

Similar tensions emerged in 1627 when the Dutch civil lawyer, Isaac Dorislaus, lecturer in history at Cambridge University, defended subjects' right in certain circumstances to resist their sovereign with reference to the Dutch Revolt against Spain. It was the Laudian Matthew Wren, acting in his capacity as vice-chancellor, who drew the government's attention to the incident, following the general Laudian principle of refusing to tolerate a theoretical inconsistency for the sake of vindicating the actions of foreign Reformed brethren.[226]

The 1620s marked a resurgence among conformist divines of fears of a native presbyterian plot, inspired by Geneva. Andrewes, Howson and Laud voiced fears of an underground presbyterian conspiracy lurking within contemporary nonconformity. But these were fears that were rehearsed with still more conviction by Laudian divines in the 1630s. Historical narratives of the growth of presbyterianism in England, which emphasized the role of Geneva and the seditious political implications, were provided in pamphlets composed by a number of Laudian authors in the 1630s, including Francis White and Christopher Dow. The preface to

223 *Decretum universitatis Oxoniensis damnans propositiones neotericorum infrascriptas* (Oxford, 1622), sig.B2r; David Owen, *Anti-Paraeus: Sive Determinatio de Iure Regio habita Cantabrigiae in Scholis Theologicis, 19 April 1619 contra Davidem Paraeum* (Cambridge, 1622), p.27 and *passim*; Vossius, *Epistolae*, ii. pp.30–1 (partially translated in White, *Predestination*, pp.207–9). On the search for copies of Paraeus in Cambridge, see D.M. Hoyle, 'Near popery yet no popery. Theological debate in Cambridge 1590–1644' (Cambridge University PhD, 1991), p.132. On the respect accorded Paraeus at the Synod of Dort, see Hales, *Golden Remains*, pp.482–3, 493–5.

224 The condemnation, if it was ever agreed to by the Cambridge Convocation, would not appear to have been published, and no copy of it survives in the University Archives (I am grateful to Dr Elizabeth Leedham-Green for advice on this point). The author of the proposed condemnation had expressed his doubts to Doublet that it would ever be published in the provocative language in which it had been drafted: Vossius, *Epistolae*, ii. p.31.

225 William Prynne, *A Briefe Survay and Censure of Mr. Cozens His Couzening Devotions* (1628), pp.98–9; *idem*, *Canterburies Doome*, p.540.

226 P.A. Maccioni and M. Mostert, 'Isaac Dorislaus (1595–1649): the career of a Dutch scholar in England', *TCBS* 8 (1984), 419–70, esp. pp.423–7; Sommerville, *Politics*, pp.72–3; Levack, *Civil Lawyers*, pp.91–5, 224; K. Sharpe, 'The foundation of the Chairs of History at Oxford and Cambridge: an episode in Jacobean politics', *History of Universities* 2 (1982), pp.139–40.

White's anti-Sabbatarian *Treatise* (dedicated to Laud) displayed an obsessive fascination in particular with the singular Alexander Leighton's violently anti-episcopal tract *Sions Plea against the Prelacie*, although this work was hardly representative of puritan opinion when it was published in 1628.[227]

Historians have noted that, in contrast to the anti-presbyterian activities of Bancroft and others in the 1590s, these later fears bore little relation to the size of the radical English presbyterian fringe by Charles' reign, however much they might seek to replicate Bancroft's scare stories. Rather, these passages represented the extent to which Laudian ideology fed upon a negative image of their own version of true religion. As one scholar has recently noted, Laudians presented a vision of a 'populist Puritan conspiracy against all constituted authority', in which ceremonial nonconformity and divisive forms of godly piety were simply aspects of the populist sedition which found its fullest expression in the presbyterian platform.

As anxieties over potential puritan sedition inevitably generated fears of a presbyterian plot, and with divines no longer prepared to pay lip-service to the orthodoxy of their co-religionists abroad, foreign Protestantism inevitably formed part of this paradigm of political sedition, bestowing patriotic credentials on those who upheld episcopacy and monarchical absolutism. The incrimination of foreign Protestants was also prompted by the Laudians' eagerness to include Calvinist theology within this nexus of populist sedition, most importantly in the applied Calvinist doctrine of predestination. Rigid Calvinist predestinarianism was seen as inherently divisive in its separation of the godly and ungodly, and was accused of undermining the corporate, sacramental life of the church by its emphasis on preaching to the detriment of ceremonies.[228]

It is hardly surprising, then, that in the 1630s a Laudian pamphleteer like Peter Heylyn followed Owen's example in not merely paralleling puritan and Jesuit doctrines of rebellion, but in attributing heterodoxy on such issues to prominent Reformed theologians. Heylyn suggested that, if his puritan opponent was right to brand the Roman religion with rebellion, then the application of the same logic to the course of the Calvinist reformations in Geneva and Emden, and the doctrines of Calvin, Paraeus and Buchanan, meant that 'the Puritan religion is rebellion'. When the puritan Henry Burton demanded to know the name of any Protestant who

[227] White, *Treatise*, ep. ded.; Dow, *Innovations*, pp.141, 180, 193–214; Giles Widdowes, *The Schismatical Puritan* (Oxford, 1630), sigs.C2r–v, F3r; Sydenham, *Sermons upon Solemne Occasions*, pp.15, 271; Hoard, *Churches Authority*, pp.37–8; Fincham, *Prelate*, pp.284–6.

[228] S. Foster, *Notes from the Caroline Underground* (Hamden, Conn., 1978); Lake, 'Anti-popery', pp.84–6. See also Carier, *Treatise*, p.27; Prynne, *Canterburies Doome*, p.167.

had ever committed treason against a king, Heylyn was swifter than any Roman Catholic in reply. He could think of many, he declared, thereby overthrowing a fundamental plank of anti-papal polemic at one blow.[229] To the Laudian Christopher Dow 'Genevians' were even worse than Jesuits in allowing the deposition of tyrants, as the Jesuits at least claimed to be obeying a higher authority (the pope), whereas Genevan Protestants held sovereignty to lie with the people.[230] If theological differences implied political ones, the reverse was also taken to be true. The axiom 'no Bishop, no King' thus acquired an even more exclusivist tone, as divines such as Sydenham concluded 'and if neither Bishop nor King, how a God?'[231]

In the hands of Laudian writers, foreign churches were increasingly being depicted, along with the puritanism and Calvinism with which they insisted on associating them, as being fundamentally alien to the principles of proper Christian society and civil government. Seen in these terms, no foreign dignitaries were to be spared, not even the Prince Palatine. In December 1635, the papal agent Panzani reported with glee that Calvin and Geneva had been accused of being the cause of much harm in England in a court sermon delivered before King Charles and the Palatine Prince.[232]

Laudian views of the political heterodoxy of foreign Reformed Churches were not shared by other conformists, however. This division in conformist thought emerged more clearly during the Bishops' Wars. Calvinist conformists such as Thomas Morton and Peter du Moulin (son of the famous Huguenot divine, but a member of the Church of England) were anxious to affirm that the foreign Calvinist Churches were not anti-monarchical or justifiers of rebellion. They thereby sought to undo the damage perpetrated by Heylyn and other Laudian pamphleteers, who had effectively granted the justice of the Covenanters' appeals to Calvin and others as providing them with a religious right of resistance.[233] But the damage had already been done, and King Charles for one had become convinced of Calvin's perfidy. When Morton denied the Scots rebels the support of the foreign Reformed tradition in a sermon before the king, Charles insisted on altering Morton's argument prior to the sermon's publication. The king cited his own reading of the fourth book of Calvin's *Institutes* to justify his rejection of Morton's claim that Calvin did not propound a right of resistance.[234] Charles explained elsewhere his own

229 Heylyn, *Briefe Answer*, pp.156–7; cf. Nicholls, *Supplement*, p.19.

230 Dow, *Innovations*, p.141.

231 Sydenham, *Sermons upon Solemne Occasions*, p.299.

232 Albion, *Court of Rome*, p.179.

233 Morton, *A Sermon*, pp.20–2, 38–9; Du Moulin, *A Letter*, *passim*.

234 PRO, SP 16/437/56. Charles presumably had in mind the same passage cited by Owen – see above n.219. The king's *Large Declaration* does emphasize the discontinuity between the Covenanters' arguments and the doctrines of the Reformed Confessions, and stresses

reading that all forms of presbyterianism were inherently subversive. In rejecting presbyterian government as 'absolutely unlawful', the king listed as one chief argument among many the fact that it had never become established in any country save by rebellion, echoing the arguments of Heylyn (and also, incidentally, generations of Romanist pamphleteers).[235]

Charles' amendment of Morton's sermon may be taken to be as significant an indication as any of the new breed of scepticism among conformist circles as to the political loyalty of Reformed Protestantism. As foreign Protestantism itself became absorbed within an anti-type of true religion, notions of Protestant internationalism were well and truly dead. If Laudian divines believed that Calvin promoted revolution, then they could hardly be expected to pay even lip-service to notions of international Protestant unity.

CATHOLIC OR REFORMED?

The Long Parliament charged Laud at his trial with having 'traitorously endeavoured to cause division and discord between the Church of England and other Reformed Churches'. He was held to have 'expressed his malice and disaffection' to the French and Dutch Churches in particular in a variety of ways, most specifically in abrogating the privileges of the stranger churches, and in allegedly unchurching them through his doctrine of episcopacy.[236]

This charge was part of a broader complaint that the English government had progressively broken off its support for the Huguenots, the Dutch and other continental Protestant powers, most clearly in its retreat from involvement in their military alliance against the Habsburgs.[237] It was the Laudian faction that was consistently blamed for this alienation and withdrawal.[238] In December 1639, the earl of Northumberland complained to the earl of Leicester that 'to think well of [the Reformed Religion] is Cause enough to make [Archbishop Laud] their Enimie; and though he cannot for Shame, avow it in publike; yet in private, he will do [you] all the

the firm opposition to the Covenant among French and Genevan Reformed divines (pp.4, 75). This disagreement with the king's remarks on Morton's sermon might be explained by the fact that Walter Balcanquahall was the ghost writer of the *Large Declaration* (Russell, *Fall*, p.44 n.56), but Charles must have been in sympathy with Balcanquahall's general argument. The absence of specific quotations from Calvin may be significant here.

235 Bruce, *Charles I in 1646*, p.27; Russell, *Causes*, p.197; *Clarendon State Papers*, II: 247, 270.

236 Laud, *Works*, III: 421.

237 Adams, 'Protestant cause', pp.346, 400–13, 420–23.

238 *Ibid.*, pp.21–3, 420–4.

mischiefe he can'.[239] In 1641 Sir John Coke referred to how 'the late aversion of our prelates' from the Huguenots and other Protestant Churches had deprived the English of the means of countering the power of the French crown.[240]

From the perspective of the Interregnum, Laudians would have been justified in viewing such charges with a cynical eye, in the wake of the First Anglo-Dutch War and the sighs of the afflicted stranger churches for the days when bishops ruled the English Church.[241] As we have seen, the confessional identity of English Protestants was constantly modified and qualified in practice throughout the early Stuart period. Political compromise was a temptation to which Laud's opponents were a prey just as much as his supporters. Nevertheless, the early Stuart Church was an arena in which pragmatism and ideology co-existed, and it was often the emphasis on confessional ideology which became more important the more that pragmatism threatened to undermine confessional credentials. The Laudians effectively refused to endorse the ideology of Protestant internationalism. Where previously English Protestants had agreed on the Church of England's confessional identity, but had disagreed in their understandings of its practical implications, now Laudians rejected the ideology itself, and stressed that practical considerations should dictate whether it continued to exist. At the root of this change was not simply a sense that political considerations should over-ride religious concerns. Rather, political considerations were acknowledged because the heterodoxies implicit in the doctrine and discipline of the foreign Protestant Churches were ultimately seen as having directly political implications.

Moreover, if English Calvinists were already drawing apart from their foreign co-religionists in matters of doctrine, then in matters of discipline the Church of England was far more obviously divorced from the continent well before Laud's rise to power. As we have seen, even non-Laudian conformists were increasingly giving expression to the conviction that the Church of England represented the 'best reformed church'. No early Stuart conformist divine doubted that the Church of England's discipline was superior to that of her continental brethren. The ideological disharmony and problems were clear for all to see. As in issues of doctrine, however, it

239 *Sidney Papers*, ed. R.W. Blencowe (1825), p.623. The cipher '542' – usually taken here to refer to 'the Reformed Religion' – may, however, possibly refer more specifically to the Huguenots.

240 *HMC Cowper* II: 296; Abbott, 'Issue of episcopacy', pp.107–8.

241 O.P. Grell, 'From uniformity to tolerance: the effects on the Dutch Church in London of reverse patterns in English church policy from 1634 to 1647', *NAvK* 66 (1986); *idem*, 'A friendship turned sour: puritans and Dutch Calvinists in East Anglia, 1603–1660', in E.S. Leedham-Green (ed.), *Religious Dissent in East Anglia* (Cambridge Antiquarian Society, 1991).

was the way in which this discontinuity was managed that was ultimately vital. The increased importance which they attached to matters of discipline, and the sacerdotal nature of the ministry, gave Laudian thinkers the crucial impulse necessary to break through the careful and creative suspensions of disbelief that had allowed English and continental Calvinists to persist in the conviction that their disagreements over discipline were ultimately unimportant.

If they were not novel in their readiness to allow confessional identities to be compromised, the Laudians did still break new ground in their eagerness to recognize and endorse the intellectual implications of this compromise. If there was an increasing discontinuity between the arguments which English Protestants marshalled in defence of their own church on the one hand, and the ones which they used to vindicate their foreign Reformed brethren on the other, it was Laudian divines who were increasingly prepared to accept this division, and to portray the two in conscious opposition. In their determination to force a polarity, the Laudians, as in so many other issues, provide a mirror image of their puritan opponents.

The Laudians' precise view of the foreign Reformed Churches, and of the Church of England's relation to them, is difficult to pin down directly. They were certainly not the first divines to describe the Church of England as 'the best reformed church' – a remark which even a puritan like Stephen Dennison could easily incorporate within his world-view. But they applied the remark in a newly exclusive fashion.[242] This was noted by George Carleton in 1626, who complained that Montagu's praise of the Church of England and dismissal of Leiden and Geneva was more negative and inflammatory than anything which had previously been urged, and chided him accordingly: 'For though the Church of England be the best Reformed Church, yet it is not the onely Reformed Church. And it might seeme no good providence in us, to stand so by our selves, as to reiect and disdaine the consent of other Churches, though they doe not agree with us in the discipline.'[243] Carleton had here put his finger on a significant point. Whatever they might assert, Laudian divines worked on the practical assumption that the Church of England was the *only* properly Reformed Church. It was this notion that naturally engendered the assumption that the English Church occupied a unique position *between* the forces of Rome and Protestantism.

The Laudians' repudiation of their Reformed sisters emerged most

[242] E.g. Page, *Treatise*, p.19; Hoard, *Churches Authority*, p.39; Browning, *Concerning Publike-Prayer*, pp.96, 184–5. For the information on Stephen Dennison I am indebted to an unpublished article by Peter Lake. I am grateful to Professor Lake for allowing me to read this article in advance of publication.

[243] Carleton, *Examination*, p.110.

clearly, not in any changes of ecclesiological definition, but in their active refusal to accept intercommunion. It was the rejection of intercommunion which had been regarded in the early church as the crucial manifestation of schism. It was this that displayed most clearly the discord between Lutherans and Calvinists, and it was the rejection of intercommunion that marked a significant escalation of the conflict between Remonstrants and Contra-Remonstrants in the Netherlands. By contrast, the earl of Leicester had reasoned in 1632 that it was important for him to attend Dutch services when passing through the Netherlands, the better to affirm their unity in religion. Similarly, Pierre du Moulin had clung to the fact that English Protestants were ready to take communion with the Huguenots when he sought to confute his Romanist opponent's claim that the two Protestant communities differed in religion.[244]

When Laud's protégé Viscount Scudamore refused (presumably with Laud's approval) to receive communion with the French Protestants at Charenton in the 1630s, he broke with all precedent in a fashion which encapsulated the Laudian rejection of the continental Reformed Churches.[245] Given the viscount's impressionable character, and his constant recourse to Laud for advice, it is difficult to believe that he would have embraced such a bold and meaningful initiative in church matters without Laud's knowledge and approval. Moreover, King Charles himself voiced his own conviction that, given their rejection of episcopacy, no one could 'with a safe conscience so far communicate with any of the Calvinists as to receive the sacrament of the Eucharist with them'.[246] In the 1650s, more Laudians refused to attend Huguenot services, leading Edward Hyde to lament that 'some of our Clergymen (whose indiscretions are of a public ill consequence) are too much inclined to publish such a separation'.[247]

The Laudians' concern was not entirely new. A similar anxiety had been expressed in the early 1620s that intercommunion with the foreign Reformed Churches might seem to undermine the Church of England's claims to catholicity. This time, however, the author had been the Romanist apostate Archbishop de Dominis. He had sought to convict the Church of England of schism on a succession of grounds, one of the most promi-

244 *HMC De l'Isle* VI: 37; Pierre du Moulin, *The Buckler of the Faith* (1620), p.345 – quoted in Goode, *Doctrine*, p.95.

245 Atherton, 'Scudamore', p.588.

246 Bruce, *Charles I in 1646*, p.26; Russell, *Causes*, p.197; *Clarendon State Papers*, II: 243.

247 *Clarendon State Papers*, II: 317. Hyde was here seeking to resolve Edward Nicholas' 'scruples' concerning communion with the Huguenots, assuring him that 'our religion is too much one, to be divided in Communion'. He explicitly regretted Scudamore's 'too imperious a dislike' towards the Huguenot Churches during the 1630s. John Cosin was the most notable Laudian who endorsed intercommunion with the French Protestants of Charenton during the Interregnum, although there is no evidence that he personally attended French Protestant services: Cosin, *Works*, IV: 400–9.

nent of which was the allegation that they still enjoyed communion with the foreign Calvinist Churches, who had been guilty of a factious separation from Rome. De Dominis' treatise was responded to in 1625 on behalf of the Church of England by Richard Crakanthorp, who refused to be drawn into disowning the foreign churches, but instead affirmed that the Church of England publicly and 'aperte' professed communion with Geneva and the other overseas churches. Indeed, he held (echoing Richard Field, among others) that it would be a blessed work to draw the foreign churches into closer union with the Church of England.[248] On this point, as on so many others, the Laudians preferred to side with de Dominis rather than their Calvinist conformist brethren.

But if the Church of England was not intimately linked with the Protestant Churches of the continent, where did it belong? Did it simply form part of the wider Catholic Church? It has often been suggested by historians that the descriptions by Andrewes, Laud and others of their church as being essentially 'Catholic and Reformed', rather than merely Protestant, marked a distinctive strain of 'Anglican' thought within the Church of England.[249] As we have seen, such remarks were in fact the common currency of the period, embraced by conforming and nonconforming puritans alike, as well as by Calvinist episcopalians who saw Laud and his allies as crypto-popish in their ecclesiology. The terms themselves, then, are not indicative of any distinctive theological position. It was the significance attached to them, however, that was changing during this period. A common polemical strategy – claiming to be both 'Catholic' and 'Reformed' – acquired a potentially radical twist when combined with a determination to divorce the Church of England from its continental links, and to deny that there was any ontological difference between the Roman and Reformed Churches. It was this development that distinguished avant-garde conformists and the later Laudians from other English Protestants. As on so many other issues, it was the Laudians' perception of a dichotomy between the adjectives 'Catholic' and 'Reformed' that converted the assertion of a 'Catholic and Reformed' position from a general description of orthodox Protestantism into a declaration of an independent middle way peculiar to the Church of England.

The vision of the Church of England as occupying a median position

[248] Crakanthorp, *Defensio*, pp.237, 239.

[249] For the latest and most impressive rehearsal of this position see P. White, 'The *via media* of the early Stuart Church', in K. Fincham (ed.), *The Early Stuart Church* (1993). By contrast, G.H. Tavard has coined the term 'twofold Catholicity' to describe the position of pre-Laudians such as Jewel, who demonstrated the Church of England's 'catholicity' by referring both to the early church Fathers and also to the consensus of the Reformed Churches on the continent: Tavard, *Quest*, pp.29–30.

between the contending continental churches began to be enunciated for the first time during the Laudian period. Moreover, this distinctive 'middle way' was presented by the new breed of conformists, not as the chance product of pragmatic Tudor policies, but rather as a miracle by which God equipped the English Church to fulfil a special divine purpose as the 'honest broker' of Christendom. In former times, the Church of England's peace and prosperity would have been interpreted as the result of God's decision to place her in an optimum position from which to lead the Protestant forces against the Roman Antichrist. But now her providential peace was relished for the distance which it placed between England and the confessional discords of the continent. Heylyn preached before the king that God had so disposed it that the Church of England 'depending on neither party, might in succeeding times be a judge between them, as more inclinable to compose, then expose their quarrels'. But it was left to George Herbert to proclaim the new Anglo-centric orthodoxy, and the death of the Protestant Cause, as he addressed his 'dear mother' the Church of England in simple but definitive terms:

> The mean thy praise and glorie is,
> And long may be.
> Blessed be God, whose love it was
> To double-moat thee with his grace,
> *And none but thee.*[250]

For all the later connotations of moderation which the Anglican 'via media' acquired, its genesis thus lay in a determined exclusivity, and the rejection of an earlier 'Reformed' identity.

[250] Heylyn, *Parable*, p.129; *The English Poems of George Herbert*, ed. C.A. Patrides (1974), p.123 (my emphasis).

Conclusion

Writing in 1641, the parliamentarian pamphleteer Henry Parker believed that he had uncovered in the recent Laudian policies an intention 'to new reforme that Reformation ... which was begunne by Edw[ard] 6. and further matured by Queene Eliz[abeth] ... The pretence was, that our Ancestors in the Reformation did depart too farre from Popery, out of favour to Puritanicall Calvin.' This was, of course, a partisan interpretation – in their own terms, Laud and his followers were simply seeking to return the Church of England 'to the rules of her first reformation'.[1] Nevertheless, Parker's observation that the terms on which the Church of England had separated from Rome, and the relation of the English Church to the Churches of Calvin, had been under review, and that opinions differed in the present church, was true enough.

This book has argued that the religious developments and conflicts which took place during the early Stuart period were prompted in part by a gradual movement by Laudian divines away from an earlier, and perhaps more coherent, view of the Church of England and of its relations with the Churches of Rome and continental Protestantism. Previous divines had located the Church of England on the Protestant side of a polarized Christendom. The Laudians changed all this. Where previous writers had seen anti-popery as a positive form of religious expression, and as a crucial means of vindicating the Protestant credentials of the church's hierarchy, Laudians considered anti-popery to be a destabilizing force, which prompted a false set of religious priorities and encouraged the growth of a puritan-style word-based piety.

On a whole range of issues, this new breed of rigid conformist divine refused to treat Roman doctrines as binary opposites of the values of true religion. Where earlier writers had represented Rome's errors as a coherent system of idolatry and heresy which served to overthrow the basic tenets of Christianity, Laudian-style conformists saw a more mixed bag of errors and pastoral negligence, and considered the jurisdictional claims of the

[1] Henry Parker, *The Altar Dispute* (1641), p.1; Laud, *Works*, VI: 42.

pope to be Rome's greatest crime. But even if they regarded the pope's claims as erroneous, even heretical, they were not prepared to identify the pope himself as the Antichrist, or to embrace the polarized view of church history and contemporary confessional relations which usually accompanied this identification. Similarly, Laudian divines were more comfortable and less equivocal in responding to the suggestion that Rome was in a sense a true church of Christ. They also responded more sympathetically to the writings of moderate Roman Catholic divines, and appreciated the range of beliefs and liberties which remained within Rome's communion.

More broadly, the Laudians rejected views of confessional conflict which had emphasized the Church of England's membership of 'the true church' of orthodox believers mustered against the 'false church' of Rome. Instead, they preferred to view the church on earth as comprehending all Christians who outwardly professed the bare essentials of Christian belief. They viewed the past history of the church in similar terms, and thereby abandoned the need to trace a pre-Reformation ancestry of orthodox believers. As a consequence, union could in theory be sought with the Church of Rome just as legitimately as it might be with other Protestant Churches. Indeed, by abandoning the notion of the unity of 'the true church', Laudians had already undermined the sense of a special corporate identity that the English Church might share with the Reformed Churches of the continent. Denying this identity enabled these same divines to treat the shortcomings of foreign Reformed polities in a more hostile light. Significantly, it also allowed them to adopt a more distant and neutral attitude towards the confessional conflicts of the continent.

This novel perspective on relations between the churches did not develop independently of other religious doctrines or ecclesiastical policies. Rather, it expressed the distinctive views of the nature of the church, of true doctrine and of the sacraments which lay at the heart of the religious innovations of the Personal Rule. The Laudian attachment to 'the beauty of holiness', the importance that they attached to corporate public worship, and their determination to exalt the power of the church and her ministers, were all aspects of the sacrament-centred piety which inevitably challenged previous assumptions of the Church of England's identity *vis-à-vis* Rome and continental Protestants. Moreover, it should also be emphasized that the universalist and inclusive tones which Laudians adopted in viewing the totality of Christian churches on earth was a macrocosm of the universalism that informed their treatment of the local parish. On the parochial level they refused to privilege the 'godly' parishioners over the rest of the congregation, and instead emphasized the common standing of all the laity through the corporate worship of the entire community. Debates on the Church of England's relations with the

Church of Rome and the Reformed Churches of the continent served to focus more clearly the divisions of opinion that were thus developing among English Protestants, as well as to highlight the unresolved problem of the Church of England's self-identity.

We should not suppose, however, that these Laudian ideas came out of nowhere, and that Laudianism was a *diabolus ex machina* of extreme new ecclesiological notions that destroyed a uniformly Calvinist Church of England. Certainly, there is nothing in these developments that would have surprised Andrew Willet. He had clearly perceived the seeds of these attitudes in the writings of Richard Hooker and others at the dawn of the seventeenth century. If he had not died in 1621, but had lived on into the 1630s, Willet would doubtless have felt that his fears of 'semi-popery' had been justified. He would then have seen his own refutations of Bellarmine's defence of altars being employed by Prynne and Hakewill to attack Laudian authors who used precisely the same arguments that the Roman cardinal had employed.[2]

Earlier chapters have repeatedly drawn attention to the potentially divisive trends within Jacobean Protestantism. Many accounts of the Jacobean Church have arguably been too eager to emphasize the degree of unanimity in the church, or its success in incorporating the evangelical impulse within established church structures. This has led one recent study of the period to coin the term 'Jacobean Anglicanism' to describe an apparently unified pre-Laudian church. But this is to ignore the strong reaction taking place against the accommodation of evangelical Calvinist views during the same period.[3] It is vital that accounts of the Jacobean period allow for the existence of anti-puritan controversialists such as Parkes, Owen and Covell, for the anxieties of apparently 'establishment' puritans such as Willet, and for the dramatic conflict between George Abbot and John Howson in the king's presence.

Other recent historians have suggested that the issues separating avant-garde conformists from the rest of English Protestant opinion arose simply by accident, due to Charles I's support for the movement. Had it not been for the political backing of Charles, it has been argued, Laudianism would have remained an essentially pacific movement, 'enriching the sacramental

[2] Prynne, *Quench-Coale*, pp.36–8; George Hakewill, *A Dissertation with Dr. Heylyn: Touching the Pretended Sacrifice in the Eucharist* (1641), pp.54–5. For the citation of Willet (or at least of his recommendation of Nicholas Bownde's work) against Laudian pamphleteers during the Sabbatarian controversy, see Byfield, *Doctrine*, pp.127, 132, 144–5, 181, 207; Twisse, *Of the Morality*, pp.164–5, 239.

[3] Davies, *Caroline Captivity*, pp.6–7, 289–90, 295. See especially the reviews of Patrick Collinson's *Religion of Protestants* and *Birthpangs of Protestant England* by Peter Lake in *JEH* 34 (1983), pp.627–9, and 41 (1990), pp.688–92. See also Fincham and Lake, 'Ecclesiastical policy'.

life of the church' as it had supposedly done in the time of Lancelot Andrewes.[4] But this is to ignore the strongly anti-puritan and politically activist elements within avant-garde conformity. These divines were anxious to use whatever means lay at their disposal to curb the profanity and sectarian excesses that appeared (in their eyes) to besmirch the outward holiness and uniformity of the national church. Here was an aggressive strain of anti-puritanism that was constantly bubbling under the surface of the apparently evangelically minded Jacobean Church. It never died away, but sprang spasmodically into life in the violent polemic of authors such as Parkes or Ormerod, and was ready to be activated once more in the vitriolic writings of Richard Montagu, or the drive of Bishop Neile against lecturers in the diocese of Lincoln.

Moreover, it was not merely the case that there were reactionary conformists to be found among the clergy. There was also a potentially broad anti-puritan body of opinion among the nation at large, whose mobilization could bring avant-garde conformists much-needed public support. Richard Montagu was clearly aware of this. For all his attacks on puritan populism, and his neurotic self-representation as a lone persecuted man, Montagu was aware of the need to write for 'the people'. He commented enthusiastically after the public burning of the writings of the puritan Edward Elton at Paul's Cross that, if matters were organized carefully, the common people could easily be as vehement in their *opposition* to puritanical opinions as they sometimes seemed to be in their support.[5]

But if we grant that there were anti-evangelical elements within the Jacobean Church, we should not necessarily be led into accepting views of the period 1600–40 which see the church as split between two simple factions. That is certainly how Andrew Willet chose to present matters, but different interpretative models are possible.

For a start, it is important to recognize that the views of Hooker and his colleagues were only *potentially* in conflict with the polarized Elizabethan Protestant world-view, and in fact only gradually dissociated themselves from the presuppositions of established thought. Willet and the authors of the *Christian Letter* had to draw forth Hooker's conclusions with little help from their opponent, and often found themselves objecting to his *style* of discussion, rather than to his specific rejection of established doctrines.[6] William Barlow, who clearly was perceived by Willet (and considered

[4] Davies, *Caroline Captivity*, p.302. See also Trevor-Roper, *Catholics*, ch.2, for a similar perspective.

[5] Cosin, *Correspondence*, I: 57, 63. These were prophetic words: for later examples of the anti-puritan crowd in action see T. Harris, *London Crowds in the Reign of Charles II* (Cambridge, 1987).

[6] Hooker, *Works*, IV: 36–7, 71–6.

himself) to belong to a different faction within the church, was yet closer to Willet than to the later Laudians in his doctrine of the church, which had not yet caught up with his Arminian inclinations in doctrines of grace.[7] Andrewes and others were still capable of making the necessary gestures towards more entrenched Elizabethan Protestant notions according to the polemical context, even if a sense of strain is clear. Moreover, few establishment Calvinists showed themselves ready to indulge in the witch-hunt of avant-garde conformists that Willet had urged. Richard Hooker was treated with general respect in Calvinist circles throughout the Jacobean period, although the ceremonialist thrust of his writings was little appreciated before the 1630s. Calvinist writers granted Hooker's stature as an apologist of the Church of England, even though they generally cited his authority only on obscure issues, and preferred to use the more emphatically Reformed writings of Richard Field when discussing the nature of the church.[8] More generally, many of the religious disputes of the 1630s revolved around competing readings of earlier avant-garde conformist authors. Many anti-Laudians reacted in shocked disbelief when Laudians cited the writings of Andrewes or Hooker in support of their position.[9]

It should be emphasized that not all of the components of the unitary 'Laudian' position outlined above were yet in place among the avant-garde conformists. Even some ardent members of the Laudian party in the 1630s, such as Francis White and Thomas Jackson, had still not entirely detached themselves from earlier Elizabethan notions, as we have seen. Indeed, even Archbishop Laud managed to be more traditional in his perspective than some of his colleagues, such as Montagu and Heylyn.[10]

But there is a more fundamental reason why a dualistic model of the Church of England divided theologically between Hooker and his succes-

[7] See above pp.23, 296.

[8] E.g. Benefield, *Doctrinae Christianae*, p.42; Holdsworth, *Praelectiones*, p.108; see above, p.430 (Robert Abbot).

[9] On the Sabbatarian issue, see Byfield, *Doctrine*, pp.31–2, 153; George Abbot, *Vindiciae Sabbathi* (1641), i. pp.20, 120; Richard Bernard, *A Threefold Treatise of the Sabbath* (1641), pp.71, 73, 117, 174; Burton, *Lords Day*, pp.15–16; Twisse, *Of the Morality*, pp.154, 210; Dow, *Discourse*, pp.20, 22–3, 28, 45, 51; White, *Examination*, pp.80–4. Samuel Ward could not believe Sylvester Adams' claim that Andrewes' writings supported Adams' doctrine of absolution (Bodl., Cherry MS 23 p.183), while John Hacket opposed Heylyn's citations from Andrewes' *Opuscula* in support of material altars (Bodl., Cherry MS 2 fol.135v). Francis Tayler complained in his *The Faith of the Church of England concerning Gods Work on Mans Will* (1641) (ep. ded.) that Laudians had disregarded the writings, not just of Whitaker, Perkins and Calvin, but also of Bilson and Andrewes.

[10] Laud's writings here mirror his conduct: in the 1620s he was not an unequivocal defender of Montagu, while his conduct of policy in the 1630s often displayed a greater sensitivity to the needs of diplomacy than did that of his more adventurous colleagues. In these matters, I am in broad agreement with the work of Dr Davies, which has emphasized that Laud was one of the more *tactically* moderate and pragmatic architects of 1630s policies: Davies, *Caroline Captivity*, *passim*, esp. pp.302–3.

sors on the one hand, and a broad swathe of evangelical Calvinism uniting those of a conformist and puritan hue on the other, is unacceptable. It is vital to recognize that many of the charges levelled against Laudian thinking and behaviour, and many of the specific doctrines that provoked most opposition in the 1620s and 1630s, could also have been found in the writings of evangelical episcopalian Calvinist authors too. The *Old Religion* controversy constitutes a notable example here. The Laudians' writings on Rome or Reformed Protestantism were not composed in opposition to a unified and internally coherent Jacobean Calvinist position. It is the internal contradictions within the Calvinist position, and the transformation of Calvinist conformist thought under James, which have a crucial role to play in explaining just why the advent of the Laudians was so problematic for English Protestantism, and why the removal of Laudianism brought a more general assault on the fabric of the Jacobean compromise.

It is therefore crucial that we do not simply juxtapose avant-garde conformist or Laudian positions with a rigid and unified anti-papal position. Historians have often displayed a tendency to treat the Calvinist position in inflexible terms – as an implacable and unflinching anti-popery and anti-Laudianism, consistently committed to an international view of Protestant England's religious obligations. We are often thus presented with a forbidding ideological straitjacket, which impelled its adherents down a single, clearly defined road. This is certainly how a divine such as Willet liked to present the Church of England's position, the better to contrast it with the apparent back-sliding of Hooker and his associates. But things were far less straightforward in practice.

The most obvious point to make about the non-Laudian position is its flexibility. Calvinist, anti-papal divines were quite capable of disagreeing with Calvin's doctrines, of making tactically positive admissions regarding the nature of the Roman Church, and of making practical distinctions between confessional allegiance and the conduct of foreign policy. Even more important than the flexibility of the non-Laudian position, however, is the fact that it was in a process of change. Many recent analyses of the religious developments of this period have tended to present Laudianism alone as being a novel development within English Protestantism.[11] What is less often realized, and what this book has documented, is that all patterns of thought, all groupings within the English Church, were undergoing change and development during this period. If the Jacobean Church was in a sense founded on the alliance between conforming episcopalian Calvinists and moderate puritans, it is nevertheless the case that these two

[11] This is arguably a weakness of the otherwise splendid account of religious developments in Russell, *Causes*, ch.4.

sides were moving further apart during James' reign. Attempts to represent the Jacobean Church as simply the working out of Archbishop Grindal's intentions run the risk of underestimating the dynamic character of the religious politics of the period.

The Calvinist conformist position itself was becoming progressively more complicated in its response to the increasing needs to defend the visible, institutional church. A number of factors pushed Jacobean thinkers towards placing a greater emphasis on the importance of the church as an earthly institution, and therefore towards attaching greater importance to the ceremonial and sacramental life of the visible church. These forces were many, and varied according to the divine concerned. They included the desire to please the pacific instincts of King James, and the need to defend the visible church against the extreme doctrines of the separatists. One especially prominent force for change emerged from the changing nature of the polemical debate with Rome. Roman controversialists increasingly set the terms of a debate in which English Protestants were forced to defend the conservative claims of the Church of England in a more complicated and ambiguous manner than foreign Protestants were obliged to adopt.[12] This shift in Jacobean conformist preoccupations also reflected a more general interest in the church and its succession, and a recognition of the value of the wealth and status which the church had still managed to retain as a result of the English Reformation. This process itself mirrored a substantial revival of church building and renewal of church fabric at the parish level.

These trends are all visible in the Jacobean period, and were not necessarily antipathetical to the norms of Reformed doctrine. On the parochial level the repair of church fabric should certainly not be confused with the more extreme and coerced 'beauty of holiness' that was to invade English parish churches in the 1630s.[13] Rather, these trends towards a greater concern with the needs of the visible church were grafted on to an existing Reformed tradition in England. In doctrinal terms, this was manifested in the habitual qualification of previously cut-and-dried theological definitions. The term *secundum quid* (in a certain sense) appeared with increasing frequency in theological discourse. It was thus argued even

[12] A number of foreign divines considered that the defences of the Reformation made by Jacobean Calvinist conformists such as Field and Carleton were essentially different from those used on the continent. See the remarks of Hendrik Alting and Caspar Streso reported in Mede, *Works*, pp.1057–8, and the reported comments of the Venetian divines: PRO, SP 14/77 fol.2.

[13] For the distinction between the revival of church building in the 1610s and 1620s, and the beautification of churches in the 1630s, see the example of the parish of St Martin-in-the-Fields in Dr Julia Merritt's forthcoming work on early modern Westminster.

by self-consciously Calvinist divines that *in a sense* Christ died for all, and *in a sense* Rome was a true church.[14]

This phenomenon of a general Jacobean 'conformist drift' – a growing preoccupation with the visible church and its concerns, and a tendency to qualify some of the doctrinal rigidities of the previous high Elizabethan Protestant tradition – can help to explain why so many Calvinist conformists, who in some cases had shown themselves directly hostile towards the doctrines (and in some cases the persons) of the 'Arminians' of the 1620s, were prepared to acquiesce to many of the Laudian reforms of the 1630s.[15] This is a phenomenon which has surprised many historians of the period, and has led at least some scholars to question whether there was anything novel at all in the Laudian position, or indeed whether a Laudian 'faction' as such can be held to have existed. But it is not difficult to distinguish Calvinist conformists from Laudians even in the 1630s. Joseph Mede may have been happy to write in support of altars and the integrity of church fabric during the Personal Rule, and was certainly aware of the benefits that would accrue to him for so doing, but he also distinguished his own writings from the extremes of Laudian polemicists such as Heylyn. In his own terms, Mede was provoked into writing moderate 'Jacobean' defences of the new ceremonies so that the gullible young would not be misled into idolatry by the more incautious defences of them being written by divines such as Heylyn.[16] The writings of Shelford, Heylyn, Montagu and others may have been repellent to many Calvinist conformists, and the abrasive ceremonialist drive of the 1630s may have been little to their taste, but the increasing reverence being displayed towards church fabric, sacraments and the clergy need not have been inimical to their views.

A Calvinist conformist drift, retreating from the extremes of Calvinist predestinarianism and some of the rigidities of traditional anti-papal polemic, did not only have the effect of making the Laudian reforms less disagreeable to non-Laudian divines. It also served to render increasingly distinctive the puritans who still remained wedded to the more unyielding, word-centred sentiments of the Elizabethan Protestant tradition.[17] But the puritan world-view itself had not remained static either. Puritans' own patterns of doctrine and behaviour were in a continual process of evolution and adaptation. As we have seen, some moderate puritans such as Willet

14 E.g. Willet, *Hexapla on Romans*, p.451 and above, ch.3.

15 E.g. Davies, *Caroline Captivity*, p.299.

16 Mede, *Works*, p.1041 (cf. pp.1036, 1056). See also P. Lake, 'Serving God and the times: the Calvinist conformity of Robert Sanderson', *Journal of British Studies* 27 (1988); Cust, 'Anti-Puritanism', p.17.

17 This point is made in P. Lake, 'Defining puritanism – again?' (forthcoming from the Massachusetts Historical Society). I am grateful to Professor Lake for allowing me to read a draft of this article in advance of publication.

seemed to qualify aspects of their earlier Calvinism; other puritans were engaged in fierce controversies among themselves over the implications of the developing covenant theology for established predestinarian doctrines. Radical millenarian trends were already becoming apparent in the writings of a number of authors.

Each of these changes served to reinforce the other. Moderate Calvinists were alarmed by the radicalization of the puritan position, while puritans became increasingly concerned by the apparent equivocation of evangelical Calvinist conformists. A growing sense of alienation from puritan extremists was a significant development among conforming Calvinists during this period. In particular, it often reflected the failure of the younger generation of puritan divines to build bridges with Calvinist episcopalians within the church establishment. During the 1630s, many of the leading lights of the newer generation of moderate puritans – such as John Davenport, Philip Nye, John Goodwin, Thomas Hooker, John Cotton and others – were pushed towards extremes that established Calvinist divines saw as unacceptable, and gravely compromising. The crucial bonds linking moderate puritans and episcopalian Calvinists were therefore under threat.

However, this remained for much of this period a *potential* conflict, as the moderate Calvinist position was not consciously developed in opposition to the earlier high Elizabethan Protestant tradition. It was only coherently and aggressively defined on those few occasions when it came into direct conflict with the high Elizabethan puritan position, most notably when moderate Calvinists confronted extreme Calvinist formulations at the Synod of Dort, and in the *Old Religion* controversy. These events threw into sharper focus the constant process of the compromising of ideological imperatives by mainstream Calvinist divines, and the refining (on the part of many of them) of the earlier Elizabethan Protestant synthesis. This created widespread tensions, and Calvinist divines might often shy away from amending their theological position out of a fear of how this might be interpreted. It was thus complained in the 1630s that John Prideaux and William Twisse had engaged themselves so far on the Calvinist side on the doctrine of predestination that they were unable publicly to retract their position, even though their own views might have shifted.[18] The struggles of the Calvinists Joseph Hall, William Bedell and Paul Micklethwaite in negotiating their departure from a rigid high Calvinism in the 1620s and 1630s are particularly instructive, as these individuals soon found themselves accused by puritans of espousing Arminian and popish heterodoxies.[19]

18 Crosfield, *Diary*, p.51.

19 Hall, *Works*, VIII: 719, 740–1; Bedell, *Two Biographies*, pp.317–18, 326; Bodl., Tanner MS 71 fols.68, 72.

The retreat from the norms of the Elizabethan tradition thus required tact and care if it were not to be interpreted as a decline from the principles of confessional orthodoxy. In this context, the manner in which authors wielded confessional symbols was vital, as Hall, Davenant and others recognized. It was here that the issues of 'Catholic and Reformed', of the representation of foreign churches, became crucial in enabling divines to retain the trappings of an uncomplicated confessional identity. What continued to hold together the conformist Calvinist and puritan positions was not so much their acceptance of a defined body of doctrine, but rather their agreement in the *symbolic* use of anti-Romanist and pro-Calvinist sentiments. The new 'Jacobean' emphases of the Calvinist conformist position were upheld alongside a continuing stress on the more rigid aspects of the Elizabethan position. Calvin was applauded even as his doctrine was highly qualified; the pope was condemned as the Antichrist even as pamphleteers insisted on how close the doctrines of Rome and England might be. This was not incidental packaging – it was crucial to the vindication of the sort of compromises that Calvinist conformists were making. These conscious compromises therefore did not necessarily oblige men to abandon their absolute confessionalist positions, even if these might be combined sometimes with incompatible assertions and argumentative moves. Indeed, deference to a more polarized absolute position was all the more important as a way of legitimating the compromises which were made in its logic, whether it be English Calvinists praising Calvin the better to detach themselves from his opinions, or John Dove explaining that the pope was Antichrist in order to vindicate his irenical appeal to recusant Roman Catholics.

The Laudians, then, were not the first to postpone the absolute agenda of confessional allegiance. They were not the first to stress the continuity of the visible church, or to grant that Rome was a true church. They were not the first to applaud England as 'the best reformed church' or to show distaste for foreign Protestants living in England, and for the high Calvinist doctrines of the continent. In this sense, they merely constituted a more radical fall-out from a unified Elizabethan tradition that was breaking up of its own accord. The distinctiveness of the Laudians lay in the way that they presented and understood these moves – and most of all, in what they chose *not* to say. Fundamentally, the Laudians rejected the composite Reformed position developed by the moderate episcopalian Calvinists. Rather than seeking to marry conformist emphases with rigid Reformed confessionalism, they consciously rejected the latter. They were specifically concerned to work a doctrinal polarization – to prise apart the doctrinal bonds which still linked the conforming Calvinist and moderate puritan positions, and to rid conformist views of the more confessionally abrasive and conceptually restrictive theoretical baggage which they still carried from earlier traditions. More than anything, they rejected the past *symbols* of orthodoxy – they refused to pay lip-service to the axioms of the orthodoxy of Calvin, or of the antichristianity of Rome.

In their refusal to vindicate their Protestant credentials along accepted lines, the Laudians brought potential conflicts out into the open. This was not a mere coincidence, or a lapse of care and attention on the Laudians' part. Their rejection of these symbolic statements and allusions was deliberate, because they held that the continued existence of these symbols simply served to undermine the principles of the defence of the visible church, and left a ready door open to sectaries and schismatics. The very fact that such points might retain the allegiance of radical puritans served to demonstrate precisely why they should not be retained. Just as Calvinists feared the insidious influence of the 'conforming papist' more than that of the recusant, so the 'conforming puritan' to many Laudians was the most dangerous of all. The only good puritan was a nonconforming (and preferably exiled) one.

The Laudians' ultimate goal was thus to force open the cracks that were already developing in English Calvinism, to impel a division of moderate from radical opinion in order to secure full-hearted acceptance of their reforms and thus to remake the English Church in their image. In this process, they were especially keen to secure the allegiance of Calvinist conformists, but only if they could effectively work a definitive division between them and the puritan principles which still wedded their ideas to those of nonconformists. Thus Laud and his followers displayed a constant anxiety to cite and reinterpret the writings and actions of Calvinist conformists such as Morton, Davenant, Hall or Prideaux in order to present them as supporters of Laudian ideas and policies, and as opponents of puritanism.[20]

It is hardly surprising, then, that Laudians made a point of denigrating and distancing themselves from the Elizabethan moderate puritan tradition of English Protestantism, represented by figures such as John Foxe, Laurence Humphrey, John Rainolds, William Whitaker, William Fulke, William Perkins and indeed Andrew Willet. Where previous conformists such as Bancroft had sought to appropriate these men for the Elizabethan establishment by seeking to detach them from hardline presbyterians, the Laudians generally sought to repudiate this tradition altogether by associating it directly with presbyterianism. By this means they sought to refashion the Church of England's past identity to favour their own views.

20 See above, *passim*; and for particular examples, see e.g. Wotton, *Dangerous Plot*, ii. p.10; Cosin, *Correspondence*, I: 29, 51, 54, 80, 85–6. For a general discussion of this phenomenon see Milton, 'Censorship' (forthcoming).

This was a striking development. In the early Jacobean period a figure such as John Burgess – a moderate puritan newly won over to the defence of the established church – had still sought to preserve the reputations of luminaries such as Rainolds, Fulke, Whitaker, Perkins and others as loyal members of the Church of England. He did this against the arguments of a radical puritan such as William Ames, who was determined to claim them for a tradition of ceremonial nonconformity which (Ames claimed) had included even the upper echelons of the Elizabethan religious establishment.[21] Calvinist conformists such as Joseph Hall and Anthony Cade had continued to propound a decidedly inclusive, indeed catholic, view of the Church of England's hall of fame, listing Willet along with his *bête noire* Richard Hooker, as well as puritans such as Greenham and evangelical bishops such as the Abbots.[22] By contrast, many of the conformists of the 1630s showed themselves more prepared to allow Ames his tradition, and to abandon the succession of Elizabethan puritan divines who had at times expressed misgivings over certain Church of England ceremonies. Fulke, Humphrey, Rainolds, Foxe, Perkins – all were happily rejected.[23] In a sense, Ames and the Laudians fed off each other: each sought to emphasize the nonconformity of the moderate puritans, and both were happy with the outcome.

It is important to remember that the Laudians were not the only ones who sought to emphasize the dichotomy between moderate puritanism and the conformist position. It had always been part of the Roman Catholic line of attack to try to prise apart these different positions, and to present divines such as Hooker, Field, Mason and others in direct opposition to moderate puritans such as Willet and Fulke. For a long time, the English Protestant response had been to close ranks. It was this, in part, which had enabled Richard Hooker to claim such an authoritative voice as the mouthpiece of the Church of England, even if (as we have seen) Calvinist divines were sparing and very selective in their appeals to his writings.[24]

21 Ames, *Fresh Suit*, ii. pp.33–4, 143, 279–81, 285–6, 368, 472–4. Note also Henry Burton's attempt to claim the tradition of Whitaker, Perkins and Rainolds in his *Replie*, p.134.

22 Lewis, *Joseph Hall*, p.365–6; Collinson, *Religion of Protestants*, p.92 n.1; Cade, *Justification*, *passim*. Even William Covell applauded the anti-papal writings of Fulke, Whitaker, Humphrey and Rainolds: Covell, *Polimanteia*, sig.P4r.

23 E.g. Heylyn, *Coale*, p.21; *idem*, *Antidotum*, p.93; *idem*, *Certamen Epistolare*, p.152; *idem*, *Historia Quinqu-Articularis*, iii. pp.49–60, 62–4; *idem*, *Cyprianus*, pp.50–1; Tyacke, *Anti-Calvinists*, pp.182–3; Bauckham, 'William Fulke', p.406; SSC, Ward Correspondence: William Twisse to Bishop Davenant, 18 April 1632. Contrast Richard Bancroft's attempts to tie these same figures to the establishment by working a division between them and the presbyterians: Lake, *Moderate Puritans*, pp.73, 76, 306 n.60.

24 See above, p.533. Conal Condren has argued in similar terms that it was Jesuits' determination to cite Hooker as normative of English Protestant theology which forced English polemicists to grant him this misleading role as spokesman of the Church of England: Conal Condren, 'The creation of Richard Hooker's public authority: rhetoric,

But for divines such as Richard Montagu, confronted by a Roman opponent who sought to discredit the conformist position by juxtaposing it with moderate puritan ideas, the easiest solution seemed to be to reject the doctrines of Fulke, Whitaker, Willet and others altogether. Moreover, it is highly significant as a manifestation of the breakdown of earlier Reformed consensus, and of the tensions which inter-Protestant debate could generate, that Joseph Hall, under attack for his *Old Religion*, was reduced to consulting the writings of the Roman controversialist Brereley for his list of English Protestant writers who had maintained that Rome was a true church. Brereley had drawn up his list in order to suggest that the specified authors were in fundamental disagreement with the writings of moderate puritans such as Whitaker and Willet. Hall's resort to the Roman writer was thus a tacit admission that the inconsistencies and divisions among English Protestants which Roman Catholic controversialists had claimed to discern were indeed present.[25] Again and again, Laudian arguments were anticipated in Roman Catholic authors – at least in their perception of a division, even if not necessarily in the Roman position itself. This was all rather embarrassing. The Laudians now promoted a division which Romanist pamphleteers had been expounding for years. It should therefore come as no surprise that avant-garde conformist and early Laudian divines often found their strongest early lay patrons among recusants or church papists.[26]

Popish arguments, popish patronage and popish forms of worship – it was only to be expected that Laudian reforms would ultimately generate fears of a popish plot. Nevertheless, it could be argued that it was their changing use of the symbols of confessional orthodoxy that can do most to explain the shape of the conflicts that avant-garde conformist and Laudian divines provoked in the early Stuart Church.

This manipulation of the symbols of orthodoxy arguably lies at the heart of the 'Arminian' dispute. Doubtless clerics differed significantly over issues related to the doctrine of predestination during this period. But it is not always easy to relate these theological differences to the shape of the conflict that emerged. Not all Laudians were conspicuously 'Arminian' in

reputation and reassessment' (I am grateful to Professor Condren for allowing me to read a copy of this important unpublished article). A radical puritan such as William Ames was able to capitalize on the moderate Calvinists' dilemma : see Ames, *Fresh Suit*, ii. p.180 (cf. ii. pp.2, 3, 50, 178–180).

25 See above, pp.143, 478. More traditionally, English Protestants protested at Romanist attempts to portray them as being at variance with one another: e.g. Covell, *Briefe Answer*, p.132; Willet, *Loidoromastix*, 'Further Advertisements'; Dove, *Advertisement*, pp.52–64. Note also how Downe was anxious to explain away the opposition of Willet and Parkes to his Roman Catholic opponent: *Certaine Treatises*, xii. p.34.

26 See above, ch.1 n.70.

their beliefs, and there were serious divisions between Calvinist thinkers on precisely these issues. The disputes that emerged did not necessarily represent the conflict between two different understandings of the nature of the grace of predestination. English Protestant doctrine itself was shifting and pluralistic, varying in tone and content within different polemical contexts. What prompted conflict was the unwillingness of certain divines to pay due deference to the accepted principles of Reformed unity when they discussed these matters, and their refusal to buttress their position by employing the accredited symbols of confessional orthodoxy. This was especially crucial as these theological conflicts occurred at the time of the Spanish Match and the Thirty Years War, when political compromises were apparently being made with confessional allegiances. It is unlikely to be coincidental that the Arminian dispute in the Netherlands first gathered pace at a time of similar confessional tensions over the Twelve Years Truce with Catholic Spain, and reached its head as the time approached for the Truce's renewal.

Whatever the ultimate and sometimes abstruse doctrinal point that was being argued over, the charge of heterodoxy was essentially prompted by a failure to encode a theological discussion within attacks on Rome and a theoretical endorsement of Reformed unity – that is, a perceived refusal to pay lip-service to accepted notions of the Church of England's identity *vis-à-vis* the Roman and Reformed Churches. It was here that the rarefied atmosphere of university debate overlapped directly with the perceptions of the broader mass of the English population. It has been common for the opponents of Dr Tyacke's 'Arminian' thesis to allege that laypeople simply did not understand Calvinist doctrine. It is argued that the refinements of the theological debate were beyond them, and that Christopher Potter's observation that not one in a thousand laymen understood the controversy should warn us against attaching any importance to what was a purely academic dispute.[27] However, the more that the *polemical* nature of theological discourse is grasped, the more its relationship with more popular and political perceptions of religion becomes clear. Even if degrees of theological sophistication undoubtedly varied, university disputations, religious pamphlets, parliamentary debates and popular lay opinion all shared a common manipulation of the symbols of orthodoxy and heterodoxy. Seen in this light, Potter's remark would appear to be almost wholly irrelevant: the fact that the layman was not versed in the arts of controversial theology hardly matters if we are discussing the impact and dynamic of religious conflict.

The *arcana* of theological disputation could often find a ready echo in popular perceptions and demonstrations. John Dove's audience at Paul's

[27] E.g. Green, 'England's wars', pp.104–5.

Cross in 1601 might not have grasped the subtleties of his exposition, but they knew to cheer for 'Bezer' and boo for 'Bellamye', and if Dove sided with the wrong figure, even on a minor point, he found them ready to accuse him of heterodoxy. The Commons debates over religion in the 1620s may not display a profound understanding of the theological points at issue, but they manifest an acute awareness of how Protestant credentials should be displayed or might be undermined, and how the parameters of true and false doctrine should be sign-posted, which was essentially the same as that which was evident in the theological disputations among divines in the universities.[28] If an individual was ready to denigrate Calvin, this would inevitably prompt charges of Arminianism or popery in the House of Commons, but the same deed would provoke similar charges in the universities, or at least prompt a more critical examination of the suspect's words in other contexts. This would happen even if, in its own terms, or in the mouth of a dedicated extoller of the virtues of Geneva, the suspect's precise doctrinal position would have appeared unobjectionable.

The 'Calvinist consensus' of non-Laudian English Protestants did not therefore constitute a single undifferentiated system of thought. Rather, Laud's opponents – evangelical episcopalians and moderate puritans – were held together by a common style of discourse, an agreed use of the *symbols* of orthodoxy and an agreement over the manner in which compromises with confessional imperatives were to be mediated. The Laudians were different specifically in their departure from this style of discourse. The engine behind religious conflict was not their introduction of any specific doctrinal innovations – indeed, many of the ideas which provoked most complaint may be found expressed, in different polemical contexts, among their opponents. Rather, what triggered conflict was the manner in which these ideas were presented, the specific polemical context in which an idea was expressed and the presence or absence of caveats which were standard in a particular polemical genre. It was not therefore the Laudians' rejection of confessional absolutism as such which was most important in generating conflict, but rather their rejection of the standardized ways in which departures from it were negotiated.[29]

[28] Dove, *Of Divorcement*, sigs.A3r, A4r; Lake, 'Significance', p.178 n.53. I am grateful to Professor Lake for many discussions of this issue.

[29] This analysis bears obvious resemblances to that adopted by Glenn Burgess in his study of the political thought of this period in his *The Politics of the Ancient Constitution* (1992). Dr Burgess has identified the existence of 'defined rules for, and boundaries between, a variety of ... [political] languages' in the political culture of the early Stuart period. Ideological or constitutional conflict only occurred where one argument moved outside 'tacitly-recognised boundaries' and intruded into other matters (Burgess, *Politics*, *passim*; *idem*, 'Divine Right', pp.861, 857). King Charles thus provoked conflict only because he was guilty of 'an unidiomatic deployment of the conventions of political discourse' (*Politics*, p.213 – cf. pp.181, 200–1). However, an overly functionalist view of the

This is not to suggest that Laudians simply did not follow confessional models, or were unaware of the need to defend and legitimate their actions. Instead, they made striking and constant use of the symbols and rhetoric of anti-puritanism. They sought to represent the encounter with their opponents as a simple conflict between a traditional conformist establishment and the seditious forces of puritan populism. Of course, anti-puritanism was not a rhetorical form that was limited to Laudians – indeed, some of the Laudians' opponents sought to use this jibe against the Laudians themselves, and even the notorious puritan nonconformist Samuel Hieron staked his claim to the mainstream of the English Church when he declared that

> We doe not hang on Calvins sleeve
> Nor yet on Zuinglius we beleeve:
> And Puritans we doe defie,
> If right the name you doe apply.[30]

The key to the distinctiveness of Laudianism lies, not in any single feature of their arguments, but in their sense of *incompatibility*, their conviction that the refined Jacobean forms of Reformed confessionalism were still unacceptable. For them, notions of church 'invisibility' or the view that the pope was Antichrist *necessarily* overthrew the episcopal succession, deference to foreign Calvinist Churches *inevitably* destroyed the Church of England's 'catholicity', and Calvinist predestinarianism *could not fail* to undermine the sacraments.[31] In assaulting the Jacobean

workings of 'modes of discourse' can run the risk of neglecting the constant tensions that were created by moving between different political languages. It is crucial to recognize the parallel existence of an all-pervading 'language of contrarieties' in the intellectual climate of this age, which could readily be deployed to both explain and generate conflict (see e.g. S. Clark, 'Inversion, misrule and the meaning of witchcraft', *P&P* 87 (1980), pp.104–10; R. Cust, 'News and politics in early seventeenth century England', *P&P* 112 (1986)). Even if contemporaries were capable of upholding both ascending and descending theories of political power simultaneously, and did not necessarily perceive the principles of divine right monarchy and common law to be inherently incompatible, it is also true that they spent much of their time juxtaposing different principles in starkly antagonistic ways (particularly at the popular level). In religious matters, as we have seen, effective controversial theology may have necessitated apparent compromises with absolute confessional imperatives, but the fact that such compromises were achieved by accepted rhetorical conventions did not make them trouble-free and unproblematical. Similarly, more attention may need to be paid to *why* Charles and his allies chose to ignore established rhetorical conventions. Laudian divines generally avoided anti-popery for the very specific reason that they distrusted its puritan potential. Similarly, Charles' failure to encode his wishes in accepted 'common law' forms is unlikely to have been an unintentional slip. Opposition to the *style* of Charles' rule may thus have represented a clear and accurate assessment of the different ideology that lay behind the king's deliberate neglect of rhetorical conventions.

30 Yates, *Ibis*, iii. pp.33–4, 37; Bodl., Cherry MS 2 fols.115r, 135r; Hieron, *Workes*, p.553.

31 For the last point, see the arguments advanced at the York House Conference in Cosin, *Works*, II: 37, 61–3.

Reformed consensus, they sought to retain the 'catholic' qualifications that Jacobean Calvinist episcopalians had adopted, but endeavoured at the same time to remove the Reformed confessionalist core which helped to assure men such as Willet that their church was still orthodox.

Oliver Ormerod had complained in the early years of James' reign that puritans were prone to reason 'from that which is in a certain sense [*secundum quid*] to that which simply is'*. But this was precisely what the Laudians were guilty of: where earlier Calvinist authors had argued that Rome was a true church *secundum quid*, or that Christ died for all men *secundum quid*, the Laudians sought to remove the term *secundum quid* altogether. Edward Boughen's fervent appeal for a return to 'the plaine and common sense and understanding' of the scriptures and liturgy when dealing with the sacraments had a ready audience in the 1630s.[32] At the core of Laudianism lay a literalness and biblical fundamentalism that was as unyielding and exclusive as that of their puritan opponents.

As a result, the Laudians exhibited throughout the 1630s an increasing propensity to resign the monopoly of important elements of the English Protestant tradition to their radical interpreters, and to treat their more moderate expositors in the hierarchy of the established church as either wilfully misled, or as dangerously tolerant towards such extremists. Such important aspects of English Protestantism could only be so confidently jettisoned because the threat from extreme Protestant elements was perceived as being greater (at least for the time being) than that of the traditional Roman Catholic opponents. Once these elements had been removed, however, this polemical readjustment left the way open for a realignment of the Church of England *vis-à-vis* the religious divisions of the continent. For those divines who wished to take it, the path was clear to follow through the logic of the defence of the Church of England's polity and her *iure divino* episcopal succession towards the 'via media' of later Anglicanism.

Laudianism was a novel and distinctive development, but not one that could simply be removed to leave behind a united church. On the contrary, it threw into sharper relief fundamental tensions and ambiguities which had arisen in a church that was progressively moving away from a unified high Elizabethan Protestant synthesis. The failure to secure a religious settlement in the years 1640–2, even after the removal of Laudianism, can be explained with reference to a whole range of political developments and structural problems that beset the 'multiple kingdoms'. But the failure of the religious centre to hold – the failure of Calvinist conformists and moderate puritans to secure the return of the hallowed Elizabethan or

[32] Ormerod, *Picture of a Puritane*, i. p.36. For Boughen, see above p.471.

Jacobean compromise – can be explained in part by the success of the Laudians' determined attempts to force these groups apart, and to destroy the ideological cement of the English Church. In the process, the Laudians helped to tarnish the established Church of England, while their rewriting of the Reformation settlement helped to prompt a more urgent and sceptical review of the legislative basis on which the English Church rested. Nevertheless, if the Laudians ultimately achieved some success in forcing moderate puritans and conforming Calvinists apart, it was because this was a division that was already well underway. If the religious centre fell apart in the early 1640s, the reason lay partly in its own loss of coherence over the previous decades. With another ten years' peace, the Laudians might well have succeeded in their efforts to marginalize puritans and to force Calvinist conformists into acceptance of their priorities, and thus to reshape the English Church in their own image. Their increasing influence in the universities was already producing a new cohort of divines committed to a Laudian church and untroubled by any lingering evangelical sympathies. But this was not to be. The collapse of Caroline government left a church that was still only half-Laudianized, a radicalized puritanism which had still not been effectively marginalized and a seriously divided church.

The removal of the Laudians in 1640 thus left a religious culture that was still divided in its understanding of its own identity, and dangerously ambiguous in its treatment of many polemically central issues. None of this in itself caused civil war – the reasons for that lie in a host of cumulative political forces. Nevertheless, the rise of the Laudians, and the eroded consensus of high Elizabethan Protestantism which their policies highlighted in the country at large, left a nation fatally divided in its religion, at a time when a power vacuum at the centre led men increasingly to have recourse to religion to explain the political deadlock. Religion, however, was no longer in a position to unite the forces of the realm – now it could only further divide them. This was a truth that would haunt not just the following decade, but the rest of the century.

SELECT BIBLIOGRAPHY

MANUSCRIPT SOURCES

ARCHIVES OF THE ENGLISH PROVINCE OF THE SOCIETY OF JESUS (MOUNT STREET, LONDON)

Transcript of Archivio Segreto Vaticano Nunziatura Inghilterra, tom.3A (Diary of Gregorio Panzani).

BALLIOL COLLEGE, OXFORD

MS 270	Miscellaneous seventeenth-century tracts (including pre-conversion tract by Benjamin Carier).

BODLEIAN LIBRARY, OXFORD

Ballard 44	Correspondence of Thomas James.
Barlow 54	Miscellaneous papers of Bishop Thomas Barlow.
Bodley 124	Defence of the Millenary Petition.
Cherry 2	Copies of papers relating to Bishop John Williams.
Cherry 23	Copies of seventeenth-century correspondence.
Clarendon 7	Papers of Secretary Windebank.
Eng.th. e.14	Notebook containing thirty-six Oxford sermons, 1620–33.
Rawlinson C.573	Miscellaneous seventeenth-century religious tracts. (including Francis White's defence of Montagu's *Appello Caesarem*).
Rawlinson D.47	Letter book of Daniel Featley.
Rawlinson D.320	Miscellaneous seventeenth-century religious tracts.
Rawlinson D.692	Miscellaneous seventeenth-century papers.
Rawlinson D.831	Miscellaneous sixteenth- and seventeenth-century theological treatises.
Rawlinson D.853	Miscellaneous papers and tracts relating to English Roman Catholics.
Rawlinson D.912	Miscellaneous papers relating to the University of Oxford from the sixteenth to eighteenth centuries.
Rawlinson D.1331	Theological commonplace book of William Sancroft the elder.

Rawlinson E.21	Miscellaneous seventeenth-century sermons.
Rawlinson lett. 76 a–c	Correspondence of Johannes Polyander.
Sancroft 18, 21	Papers of William Sancroft.
Smith 21	Transcripts of correspondence of John Selden.
Smith 76	Copies of Latin letters of Patrick Young.
Tanner 70–6	Correspondence of Samuel Ward.

BRITISH LIBRARY, LONDON

Additional 4236	Tillotson Papers.
Additional 4274	Letters of archbishops and bishops, *c.*1551–1721 (Thoresby Papers).
Additional 11044	Papers of John, Viscount Scudamore.
Additional 15389	Transcripts of letters of Gregorio Panzani to Cardinal Barberini from the Vatican Archives, Rome.
Additional 20065	Court sermons of Robert Skinner, 1631–41.
Additional 22960–2	Correspondence of Sibrandus Lubbertus.
Additional 34600–1	Correspondence of Sir Henry Spelman.
Additional 35331	Diary of Walter Yonge, 1627–42.
Additional 39948	Huskisson Papers, with copies of Harsnett correspondence.
Burney 369	Correspondence of Meric Casaubon.
Harleian 374	Miscellaneous correspondence, chiefly of Sir Simonds D'Ewes.
Harleian 541	Miscellaneous sixteenth- and seventeenth-century tracts, including Long Parliament diary.
Harleian 749, 750	Commonplace books of James Wedderburn.
Harleian 6018	Loan list of Sir Robert Cotton's library.
Harleian 7019	Miscellaneous seventeenth-century papers, including report on 'innovations' in Laudian Cambridge.
Harleian 7038	Miscellaneous papers relating to Cambridge University in the seventeenth and eighteenth centuries.
Loan 29/50/Bundle 74	Herefordshire petitions to Long Parliament.
Royal MS 10.B.xiii	Tract by David Owen.
Sloane 654	Papers relating to John Dury.
Stowe 107	Volume of Thomas Harding's 'Annals' of church history, covering the period of Henry II's reign.
Stowe 743	Miscellaneous letters, 1570–1640.

CAMBRIDGE UNIVERSITY LIBRARY

Additional 2608–9	Thomas Harding's 'Annals of Church Affairs'.
Additional 3320	'Quaestiones Theologicae' at the University, 1614–33.
Collect. Admin. 8	'Tabor's Book': copies of University jurisdictional documents, 1629–80.
Comm Ct I.18	Act Book of Vice-Chancellor's monday courts, 1626–37.
Gg/1/29	Collection of theological and historical documents, chiefly relating to Bishop Overall.
Mm/1/38	Miscellaneous seventeenth-century documents relating to Cambridge.

Mm/1/46	Miscellaneous seventeenth-century documents.
Mm/4/24	Miscellaneous seventeenth-century documents.
VC Ct I.8	Act Book of Vice-Chancellor's Court, 1612–17.
VC Ct I.57	Act Book of Vice-Chancellor's Court, 1636–9.

DURHAM DEAN AND CHAPTER LIBRARY

Hunter 67	Miscellaneous ecclesiastical papers, 1559–1641.

DURHAM UNIVERSITY LIBRARY

Bishop Cosin Library	Miscellaneous annotated books.

EXETER COLLEGE, OXFORD

MS 48	Diary of Edward Davenant.

GUILDHALL LIBRARY, LONDON

MS 7424	Correspondence list of Cesar Calandrini.

LAMBETH PALACE LIBRARY, LONDON

Lambeth 323	'Jura et Privilegia Clero Anglicano adjudicata, ex Parliamentorum Rotulis ... deprompta, 1637'.
Lambeth 731	Interleaved 1638 Book of Common Prayer of Archbishop Laud.
Lambeth 772	Copy of William Bedell's 'Defence'.
Lambeth 941	Miscellaneous papers, including advertisement for Harding's *Annals*.
Lambeth 943	Papers of Archbishop Laud.
Lambeth 1372	Historical and devotional collections, including account of Fisher Conference.
Lambeth 2550	Papers of Laurence Chaderton.

LEIDEN, BIBLIOTHEEK DER RIJKSUNIVERSITEIT

MS BPG 77	Sixteenth- and seventeenth-century scholarly correspondence.

PROVINCIALE BIBLIOTHEEK VAN FRIESLAND, LEEUWARDEN

Gabbema MSS

PUBLIC RECORD OFFICE, LONDON

LC 5/132	Entry book of warrants to the lord chamberlain of the household, 1628–34.
LC 5/134	Entry book of warrants to the lord chamberlain of the household, 1634–41.

LC 5/135 Entry book of warrants for swearing servants to the king, 1641–2.
PRO 30/53/9 'Diurnall Occurrences'.
PRO 31/9/17B Transcript of Gregorio Panzani's letters from England 1634–7 from the Vatican Archives, Rome.
PRO 31/10/10 Transcripts of letters of Cardinal Barberini to Gregorio Panzani and others, from the Vatican Archives, Rome.
PROB 11 Prerogative Court of Canterbury wills.
SP 14 State Papers Domestic, James I.
SP 16 State Papers Domestic, Charles I.
SP 81 State Papers relating to the German states.
SP 95 State Papers relating to Sweden.
SP 99 State Papers relating to Venice.
SP 105/95 Letterbook of Sir Dudley Carleton, 1616–18.

QUEEN'S COLLEGE, OXFORD

MS 249 'An Anticoccius' – church history tract by Thomas James, 1629.

SHEFFIELD CENTRAL LIBRARY

Wentworth Woodhouse Muniments, Strafford Papers 15

SHEFFIELD UNIVERSITY LIBRARY

Hartlib MSS bundles 2, 5, 9, 15, 33 Miscellaneous correspondence of Samuel Hartlib.
Hartlib 29/2 Hartlib's *Ephemerides*, 1634.
Hartlib 29/3 Hartlib's *Ephemerides*, 1635.

SIDNEY SUSSEX COLLEGE, CAMBRIDGE

Samuel Ward Papers
Samuel Ward Correspondence

VATICAN LIBRARY, ROME

Barberini Latini 8633 (Transcript of part of volume supplied by Professor C. Hibbard).

WESTMINSTER ABBEY, LONDON

Muniment Book 15

WESTMINSTER PUBLIC LIBRARY, LONDON

Will Register 1622–35

PRINTED PRIMARY SOURCES

The place of publication is London unless otherwise stated.

Abbot, George, *The Reasons which Doctour Hill hath Brought, for the Upholding of Papistry* (Oxford, 1604).

A Treatise of the Perpetuall Visibilitie, and Succession of the True Church in All Ages (1624).

Abbot, George, *Vindicae Sabbathi* (1641).

Abbot, Robert, *Antichristi Demonstratio* (1603).

Antilogia adversus Apologiam Andreae Eudaemon-Ioannis (1613).

A Defence of the Reformed Catholicke (1611).

De Gratia et Perseverentia Sanctorum. Exercitationes aliquot habitae in Academia Oxoniensi (1618).

The Second Part of the Defence of the Reformed Catholicke (1611).

The Third Part of the Defence of the Reformed Catholicke (1609).

The True Ancient Roman Catholike (1611).

An Abridgment of that Booke which the Ministers of Lincoln Diocess Delivered to his Maiestie (1605).

Acts of the Privy Council.

Airay, Henry, *Lectures on the Whole Epistle of Saint Paul to the Philippians* (1618).

An Almanacke for 1631, ed. William Beale (1631).

Ames, William, *A Fresh Suit against Human Ceremonies in Gods Worship* (Amsterdam, 1633).

Andrewes, Lancelot, *Opuscula Quaedam Posthuma* (Oxford, 1852).

A Pattern of Catechistical Doctrine (Oxford, 1846).

Responsio ad Apologiam Cardinalis Bellarmini (Oxford, 1851).

Sermons (5 vols., Oxford, 1841–53).

Tortura Torti (Oxford, 1851).

Two Answers to Cardinal Perron and Other Miscellaneous Works (Oxford, 1854).

Anti-Montacutum: An Appeale or Remonstrance of the Orthodox Ministers of the Church of England against Richard Mountagu (1629).

Arber, E. (ed.), *A Transcript of the Registers of the Company of Stationers, 1554–1640* (5 vols., 1875–94).

B., T., *A Preservative to Keep a Protestant from Becoming a Papist* (Oxford, 1629).

Baddeley, Richard, *The Life of Dr Thomas Morton, Late Bishop of Duresme* (York, 1669).

Baillie, Robert, *Ladensium ΑΥΤΟΚΑΤΑΚΡΙΣΙΣ. The Canterburian's Self-Conviction* (Edinburgh, 1640; 3rd edn, 1641).

A Parallel or Briefe Comparison of the Liturgie with the Masse-Book (1641).

Balcanquahall, Walter, *The Honour of Christian Churches; And the Necessitie of Frequenting of Divine Service and Publike Prayers in Them. Delivered in a Sermon at White-Hall before the Kings Most Excellent Majestie* (1633).

Ball, Thomas, *The Life of the Renowned Dr. Preston*, ed. E.W. Harcourt (1885).

Bancroft, Richard, *A Survay of the Pretended Holy Discipline* (1593).

Tracts Ascribed to Richard Bancroft, ed. A. Peel (Cambridge, 1953).

Bargrave, Isaac, *A Sermon Preached before the Honorable Assembly* (1624).

Barlow, Thomas, *Genuine Remains* (1693).

Barlow, William, *An Answer to a Catholicke English-man* (1609).

A Defence of the Articles of the Protestants Religion (1601).
One of the foure Sermons preached ... at Hampton Court (1606).
The Summe and Substance of the Conference ... att Hampton Court (1604).
Basire, Isaac, *De Antiqua Ecclesiae Britannicae Libertate* (Bruges, 1656).
Baudius, Dominicus, *Epistolarum Centuriae Tres* (Leiden, 1620).
Beard, Thomas, *Antichrist the Pope of Rome* (1625).
Bedell, William, *The Copies of Certaine Letters which have Passed betweene Spaine and England in Matter of Religion* (1624).
An Examination of Certaine Motives to Recusansie (Cambridge, 1628).
Two Biographies of William Bedell Bishop of Kilmore. With a Selection of his Letters and an Unpublished Treatise, ed. E.S. Shuckburgh (Cambridge, 1902).
Bedford, Thomas, *Luthers Predecessours* (1624).
Bell, Thomas, *The Anatomie of Popish Tyrannie* (1603).
Benefield, Sebastian, *Doctrinae Christianae sex capita* (Oxford, 1610).
Bernard, Nicholas, *The Judgement of the Late Arch-Bishop of Armagh, and Primate of Ireland. Of Babylon (Rev.18.4) being the Present See of Rome (With a Sermon of Bishop Bedels upon the Same Words.)* (1659).
Bernard, Richard, *The Bible-battells. Or the Sacred Art Military* (1629).
Christian Advertisements and Counsels of Peace (1608).
A Key of Knowledge for the Opening of the Secret Mysteries of St Iohns Mysticall Revelation (1617).
Looke beyond Luther (1623).
Rhemes against Rome (1626).
A Threefold Treatise of the Sabbath (1641).
A Bibliography of Royal Proclamations 1485–1714, ed. R. Steele (2 vols., Oxford, 1910).
Bilson, Thomas, *The True Difference between Christian Subjection and Unchristian Rebellion* (1585).
Birckbek, Simon, *The Protestants Evidence* (1635).
Blondel, David, *De La Primauté en l'Eglise* (Geneva, 1641).
Boughen, Edward, *A Sermon of Confirmation* (1620).
Two Sermons (1635).
Brabourne, Theophilus, *A Defence of ... the Sabbath Day* (2nd edn, 1632).
Bradshaw, William, *A Myld and Iust Defence of Certeyne Arguments* (n.p., 1606).
Bramhall, John, *The Works of ... John Bramhall* (5 vols., Oxford, 1842–5).
Brandt, G., *The History of the Reformation ... in ... the Low Countries* (4 vols., 1720–3).
Brereley, John, *The Protestants Apologie for the Roman Church* (St Omer, 1608).
Brereton, William, *Travels in Holland, the United Provinces, England, Scotland and Ireland*, ed. E. Hawkins (Chetham Society 1, 1844).
Bridges, John, *A Defence of the Government Established* (1587).
Brightman, Thomas, *Works* (1644).
Brinsley, John, *The Glorie of the Latter Temple* (1631).
Brookes, Matthew, *A Sermon Preached at Pauls-Crosse* (1626).
Broughton, Richard, *Protestants Demonstrations, for Catholiks Recusance* (Douai, 1615).
Browning, John, *Concerning Publike-Prayer, and the Fasts of the Church. Six Sermons, or Tractates* (1636).
Bruce, J. (ed.), *Charles I in 1646* (Camden Society 63, 1856).
Bucerus, Gerson, *Dissertatio de Gubernatione Ecclesiae* (Middleburg, 1618).

Buckeridge, John, *De Potestate Papae in Rebus Temporalibus* (1614).
A Sermon ... Touching Prostration and Kneeling in the Worship of God ... To which is Added a Discourse concerning Kneeling at the Communion (1618).
Bulteel, John, *A Relation of the Troubles of the Three forraign Churches in Kent Caused by the Injunctions of W. Laud* (1645).
Bunny, Edmund, *A Briefe Answer* (1589).
A Treatise Tending to Pacification (1586).
Burton, Henry, *Babel no Bethel. That is, the Church of Rome no True Visible Church of Christ. In Answer to Hugh Cholmley's Challenge, and Rob. Butterfield's Maschil, Two Masculine Champions for the Synagogue of Rome* (1629).
The Baiting of the Popes Bull (1627).
For God and the King. The Summe of Two Sermons Preached on the Fifth of November Last in St Matthews Friday-Streete (1636).
Israels Fast (1628).
The Lords Day, the Sabbath Day (2nd edn, 1636).
A Plea to an Appeale (1626).
A Replie to a Relation of the Conference between William Laude and Mr. Fisher the Jesuite (1640).
The Seven Vials or A Briefe and Plaine Exposition upon the 15: and 16: Chapters of the Revelation (1628).
Truths Triumph over Trent (1629).
A Tryall of Private Devotions. Or A Diall for the Houres of Prayer (1628).
Butterfield, Robert, *Maschil. Or a Treatise to Give Instruction, Touching the State of the Church of Rome since the Councell of Trent* (1629).
Byfield, Nicholas, *The Doctrine of the Sabbath Vindicated* (1631).
Cade, Anthony, *A Justification of the Church of England* (1630).
A Sermon Necessary for these Times (Cambridge, 1639).
Calendar of State Papers, Domestic, 1603–1714, ed. M.A.E. Green, J. Bruce *et al.* (27 vols., 1857–97).
Calendar of State Papers, Venetian.
Cardwell, E. (ed.), *Documentary Annals of the Reformed Church of England* (2 vols., 1844).
Carier, Benjamin, *A Treatise Written by Mr. Doctour Carier* (Liège, 1614).
Carleton, Dudley, *Letters from and to Sir Dudley Carleton during his Embassy in Holland (1616–1620)* (1757).
Sir Dudley Carleton's State Letters, during his Embassy at the Hague, A.D. 1627, ed. 'T.P.' (1841).
Carleton, George, *Consensus Ecclesiae Catholicae contra Tridentinos* (1613).
Directions to Know the True Church (1615).
An Examination of those Things wherein the Author of the Late Appeale Holdeth the Doctrines of the Pelagians and Arminians to be the Doctrines of the Church of England (1626; 2nd edn, 1626).
Jurisdiction Regall, Episcopall, Papall. Wherein is Declared how the Pope Hath Intruded upon the Jurisdiction of Temporall Princes, and of the Church (1610).
A Thankfull Remembrance of God's Mercy (1624).
Casaubon, Isaac, *The Answere of Master Isaac Casaubon to the Epistle of ... Cardinall Peron* (1612).

De Rebus Sacris et Ecclesiasticis Exercitationes XVI. ad Cardinalis Baroni (1614).
Isaaci Casauboni Epistolae, ed. T.J. ab Almeloveen (Rotterdam, 1709).
(attrib.), *The Originall of Idolatries*, trans. Abraham Darcie (1624).
Casaubon, Meric, *The Vindication or Defence of Isaac Casaubon* (1624).
Certain Briefe Treatises Written by Divers Learned Men, concerning the Ancient and Moderne Government of the Church (Oxford, 1641).
Chaloner, Edward, *Credo Ecclesiam Sanctam Catholicam ... The Authoritie, Universalitie, and Visibilitie of the Church, Handled and Discussed* (1625).
Six Sermons (1629).
Chamberlain, John, *The Letters of John Chamberlain*, ed. N.E. McClure (2 vols., Philadelphia, 1939).
Champney, Anthony, *A Treatise of the Vocation of Bishops* (1616).
Chancy, Charles, *The Retractation of Mr. Charles Chancy* (1641).
Charles I, King, *A Large Declaration concerning the Late Tumults in Scotland* (1639).
Cheynell, Francis, *Chillingworthi novissima* (1644).
Chillingworth, William, *The Religion of Protestants* (edns 1638, 1845).
Cholmley, Hugh, *The State of the Now-Romane Church. Discussed by Way of Vindication of the Right Reverend Father in God, the Lord Bishop of Exceter, from the Weake Cavills of Henry Burton* (1629).
Choun, Thomas, *Collectiones Theologicarum Quarundam Conclusionum ex diversis Authorum sententiis, perquam breves sparsim exceptae* (1635).
Clarendon, Edward, earl of, *History of the Rebellion and Civil Wars in England*, ed. W.D. Macray (6 vols., Oxford, 1888).
State Papers Collected by Edward, Earl of Clarendon, ed. R. Scrope and T. Monkhouse (3 vols., Oxford, 1767–86).
Clark, A. (ed.), *The Register of the University of Oxford* (Oxford Hist. Society 10, 1887–9), pt i.
Clerke, Thomas, *The Popes Deadly Wound* (1621).
Coke, Sir Edward, *The Lord Coke his Speech and Charge* (1607).
Commons Debates for 1629, ed. W. Notestein and F.H. Relf (Minneapolis, 1921).
A Complete Collection of State Trials, ed. T.B. and T.J. Howell (33 vols., 1809–26).
Constable, Henry, *The Catholike Moderator: Or A Moderate Examination of the Doctrine of the Protestants ... First Written in French by a Catholike Gentleman, and now Faithfully Translated* (second impression, 1623).
Cooke, Alexander, *Pope Joane* (1610).
Cope, E.S., and Coates, W.H. (eds.), *Proceedings of the Short Parliament of 1640* (Camden Society 4th series 19, 1977).
A Copie of the Proceedings of Some Worthy and Learned Divines, Appointed by the Lords to Meet at the Bishop of Lincolnes in Westminster: Touching Innovation in the Doctrine and Discipline of the Church of England (1641).
Cosin, John, *A Collection of Private Devotions*, ed. P.G. Stanwood (Oxford, 1967).
The Correspondence of John Cosin, ed. G. Ornsby (Surtees Society 52, 55, 1868–72).
The Works of ... John Cosin, ed. J. Sansom (5 vols., Oxford, 1843–55).
The Court and Times of Charles I, ed. R.F. Williams (2 vols., 1848).
The Court and Times of James I, ed. T. Birch (2 vols., 1848).

Covell, William, *A Briefe Answer unto Certaine Reasons* (1606).
A Iust and Temperate Defence of the Five Books of Ecclesiastical Policy by R. Hooker (1603).
A Modest and Reasonable Examination (1604).
Polimanteia (Cambridge, 1595).
Crakanthorp, Richard, *Defensio Ecclesiae Anglicanae contra M. Antonii de Dominis* (Oxford, 1847).
Vigilius Dormitans ... Or A Treatise of the Fifth Generall Councell Held at Constantinople, Anno 553 (1631).
Crashaw, Richard, *The Complete Poetry of Richard Crashaw*, ed. G.W. Williams (New York, 1974).
Crashaw, William, *Falsificationum Romanorum* (1606).
Mittimus to the Iubile at Rome (1625).
The Sermon Preached at the Crosse (1608).
(ed.), *Manuale Catholicorum* (1611).
Crosfield, Thomas, *The Diary of Thomas Crosfield*, ed. F.S. Boas (Oxford, 1935).
Culverwell, Ezechiel, *A Briefe Answere to Certaine Objections against the Treatise of Faith* (1626).
Curll, Walter, *A Sermon Preached at White-Hall on the 28. of April* (1622).
Cyprian, St Caecilius, bishop of Carthage, *The Treatises of S. Caecilius Cyprian* (Oxford, 1839).
St. Cyprian, Treatises, tr. and ed. R.J. Deferrari (New York, 1958).
Dalechampius, Caleb, *Christian Hospitalitie* (Cambridge, 1632).
Daneau, Lambert, *Ad Roberti Bellarmini Disputationes Theologicas ... Responsio* (Geneva, 1596).
Davenant, John, *Animadversions upon a Treatise Intitled Gods Love to Mankind* (Cambridge, 1641).
Determinationes Quaestionum Quarundam Theologicarum ... publice disputatarum (2nd edn, Cambridge, 1639).
An Exhortation to Brotherly Communion betwixt the Protestant Churches (1641).
Expositio Epistolae D. Pauli ad Colossenses (3rd edn, Cambridge, 1639).
'The Opinion of Bishop Davenant', in *Good Counsells*.
Debates in the House of Commons in 1625, ed. S.R. Gardiner (Camden Society, n.s. 6, 1873).
Dekker, Thomas, *The Double PP* (1606).
Dent, Arthur, *The Ruine of Rome: Or An Exposition upon the Whole Revelation* (1603).
Dering, Edward, *A Discourse of Proper Sacrifice* (1644).
D'Ewes, Sir Simonds, *The Autobiography and Correspondence of Sir Simonds D'Ewes*, ed. J.O. Halliwell (2 vols., 1845).
The Diary of Sir Simonds D'Ewes 1622–1624, ed. E. Bourcier (Paris, 1974).
The Journal of Sir Simonds D'Ewes from the Beginning of the Long Parliament, ed. W. Notestein (New Haven, 1923).
Digges, Thomas, *Humble Motives* (1601).
Dillingham, Francis, *A Disswasive from Popery* (1599).
Dominis, Marc'Antonio de, *De Pace Religionis ... Epistola ad Venerabilem Virum Iosephum Hallum* (Besançon, 1666).
De Republica Ecclesiastica (vol.1, 1617; vol.3, Hanover, 1622).

The Second Manifesto of Marcus Antonius De Dominis, Archbishop of Spalato ... tr. 'M.G.K.' (Liège, 1623).
A Sermon Preached in Italian, by the Most Reverend Father Marc' Antony de Dominis, Archb. of Spalato ... 1617 (1617).
Donne, John, *The Sermons of John Donne*, ed. G.R. Potter and E.M. Simpson (10 vols., Berkeley, Calif., 1953–62).
Dove, John, *An Advertisement to the English Seminaries and Iesuites* (1610).
A Defence of Church Government (1606).
Of Divorcement. A Sermon Preached at Pauls Crosse (1601).
A Perswasion to the English Recusants (1603).
A Sermon Preached at Pauls Crosse ... Intreating of the Second Comming of Christ (1594).
A Sermon Preached at Paules Crosse (1597).
Dow, Christopher, *A Discourse of the Sabbath and the Lords Day* (2nd edn, 1636).
Innovations Unjustly Charged upon the Present Church and State. Or an Answere to the Most Materiall Passages of a Libellous Pamphlet Made by ... H. Burton (1637).
Downame, George, *Papa Antichristus* (1620).
A Treatise concerning Antichrist (1603).
Two Sermons (1608).
Downame, John, *A Guide to Godlynesse* (1622).
Downe, John, *Certaine Treatises* (Oxford, 1633).
Du Moulin, Peter, *A Letter of a French Protestant to a Scotishman of the Covenant* (1640).
Du Moulin, Pierre, *Nouveauté du Papisme* (3rd edn, Geneva, 1633).
Duncon, Eleazar, *Of Worshipping God towards the Altar ... Being the Substance of a Divinity Lecture Made some Years since at Cambridge*, ed. and tr. 'J.D.' (1660).
Dyke, Jeremiah, *A Sermon Dedicatory. Preached at the Consecration of the Chappell of Epping in Essex. October 28. 1622* (1623).
Eliot, John, *De Jure Majestatis ... and the Letter-Book of Sir John Eliot*, ed. A.B. Grosart (2 vols., 1882).
Falkland, Lucius Cary, Lord, *A Speech to the House of Commons concerning Episcopacy* (1641).
Farmer, Richard, *A Sermon Preached at Pauls Crosse* (1629).
Favour, John, *Antiquitie Triumphing over Noveltie* (1619).
Featley, Daniel, *Ancilla Pietatis* (1625–6).
Clavis Mystica (1636).
Cygnea Cantio (1629).
The Fisher Catched in his Owne Net (1623).
The Practice of Extraordinary Devotion (1630).
The Romish Fisher Caught and Held in his Owne Net (1624).
A Second Parallel together with a Writ of Error Sued against the Appealer (1626).
Field, John, *A Caveat for Parsons Howlet* (1581).
Field, Nathaniel, *Some Short Memorials concerning the Life of ... R. Field*, ed. J. Le Neve (1717).
Field, Richard, *Of the Church* (4 vols., Cambridge, 1847–52).
Firth, C.H. (ed.), *Stuart Tracts 1603–1693* (1903).
Fisher, John, *True Relations of Sundry Conferences* (1626).

Fleming, Gyles, *Magnificence Exemplified: And the Repaire of Saint Pauls Exhorted unto* (1634).
Foley, H. (ed.), *Records of the English Province of the Society of Jesus* (7 vols., 1877–83).
Forbes, John, *Opera Omnia* (Amsterdam, 1703).
Forbes, William, *Considerationes Modestae et Pacificae*, ed. and tr. G. Forbes (2 vols., Oxford, 1850–6).
Fulke, William, *A Defence of the Sincere and True Translations of the Holy Scriptures* (Cambridge, 1843).
A Retentive to Stay Good Christians, against the Motives of R. Bristow (1580).
A Sermon Preached at Hampton Court (1570).
Two Treatises Written against the Papistes (1577).
Fuller, Thomas, *The Church History of Britain*, ed. J.S. Brewer (6 vols., Oxford, 1845).
Fuller, William, *A Sermon Preached before His Maiestie at Dover Castle* (1625).
Gabbema, S.A. (ed.), *Illustrium & Clarorum Virorum Epistolae ... distributae in centurias tres* (Leeuwarden, 1669).
Gainsford, Thomas, *The Glory of England* (1618).
Gardiner, S.R. (ed.), *Reports of Cases in the Courts of Star Chamber and High Commission* (Camden Society n.s. 39, 1886).
Gataker, Thomas, *An Anniversarie Memoriall of Englands Delivery from the Spanish Invasion* (1626).
A Sparke toward the Kindling of Sorrow for Sion (1621).
Gee, John, *The Foot out of the Snare* (1624).
Gerhard, Johann, *Locorum Theologicorum* (9 vols. in 4, Geneva, 1639).
Gifford, George, *Sermons upon the Whole Booke of Revelation* (1596).
A Short Treatise against the Donatists of England (1589).
Godwin, Francis, *A Catalogue of the Bishops of England* (1601).
De Praesulibus Angliae Commentarius (1616).
Good Counsells for the Peace of Reformed Churches. By Some Reverend and Learned Bishops and Other Divines. Translated out of Latine (Oxford, 1641).
Gore, John, *The Way to Well-Doing* (1635).
Gouge, William, *Gods Three Arrows* (1631).
Hakewill, George, *An Answere to a Treatise Written by Dr. Carier* (1616).
An Apologie of the Power and Providence of God (Oxford, 1627).
The Auncient Ecclesiasticall Practise of Confirmation (1613).
A Dissertation with Dr. Heylyn: Touching the Pretended Sacrifice in the Eucharist (1641).
A Sermon Preached at Bar[n]staple: Upon Occasion of the Late Happy Success of Gods Church in Forraine Parts (1632)
Hales, John, *Golden Remains* (1688).
The Works of John Hales, ed. D. Dalrymple (3 vols., Glasgow, 1765).
Hall, Joseph, *The Works of ... Joseph Hall*, ed. P. Wynter (10 vols., Oxford, 1863).
Hardwick, William, *Conformity with Piety, Requisite in Gods Service* (1638).
Harpsfield, Nicholas, *Historia Anglicana Ecclesiastica* (Douai, 1622).
Harrab, Thomas, *Tesseradelphus* (n.p., 1616).
Harsnett, Samuel, *A Discovery of the Fraudulent Practises of J. Darrel* (1599).
Hartsoeker, C., and Limborch, P. (eds.), *Praestantium ac Eruditorum Virorum Epistolae Ecclesiasticae et Theologicae* (Amsterdam, 1684).

Hausted, Peter, *Ten Sermons Preached upon Severall Sundayes and Saints Dayes* (1636).
Herbert, George, *The English Poems of George Herbert*, ed. C.A. Patrides (1974).
Hessels, J.H. (ed.), *Ecclesiae Londino-Batavae Archivum* (3 vols. in 4, Cambridge, 1887–97).
Heylyn, Peter, *Aerius Redivivus* (1670).
Antidotum Lincolniense (1637).
A Briefe and Moderate Answer (1637).
Certamen Epistolare or the Letter-Combate (1659).
A Coale from the Altar (1636).
Cyprianus Anglicus or the History of the Life and Death of . . . William [Laud] (1668).
Ecclesia Restaurata, ed. J.C. Robertson (2 vols., Cambridge, 1849).
Ecclesia Vindicata (1657).
Examen Historicum (1659).
Historia Quinqu-Articularis or A Declaration of the Judgement of the Western Churches . . . in the Five Controverted Points, Reproched in these Last Times by the Name of Arminianism (1660).
The History of the Sabbath (1636).
ΜΙΚΡΟΚΟΣΜΟΣ: A Little Description of the Great World (Oxford, 1621; 2nd edn, Oxford, 1625; 7th edn, Oxford, 1636).
The Parable of the Tares Expounded & Applyed, In Ten Sermons Preached before his Late Majesty King Charles (1659).
A Survey of the Estate of France, and of Some of the Adjoining Ilands (1656).
Heywood, J., and Wright, T. (eds.), *Cambridge University Transactions during the Puritan Controversies* (2 vols., 1854).
Hieron, Samuel, *Workes* (1619).
HMC Cowper II.
HMC De l'Isle VI.
HMC Downshire II, III, IV, V.
HMC Fourteenth Report
HMC Portland III.
HMC Salisbury XIX, XX, XXII.
Hoard, Samuel, *The Churches Authority Asserted* (1637).
Hoard, Samuel, and Mason, Henry, *Gods Love to Mankind, Manifested by Disprooving his Absolute Decree for their Damnation* (1633).
Hoby, Sir Edward, *A Letter to T.H.* (1609).
Holdsworth, Richard, *Praelectiones theologicae* (1661).
Holstenius, Lucas, *Lucae Holstenii Epistolae ad Diversos*, ed. J.F. Boissonade (Paris, 1817).
Hooker, Richard, *The Folger Library Edition of the Works of Richard Hooker*, ed. W.S. Hill (5 vols., Cambridge, Mass., 1977–91).
Howson, John, *Certaine Sermons Made in Oxford, Anno Dom. 1616. wherein, is Proved, that Saint Peter had no Monarchicall Power over the Rest of the Apostles, against Bellarmine, Sanders, Stapleton, and the Rest of that Companie* (1622).
A Second Sermon, Preached at Paules Crosse, the 21. of May 1598 (1598).
A Sermon Preached at Paules Crosse the 4. of December 1597. Wherein is Discoursed, that all Buying and Selling of Spirituall Promotion is Unlawfull (1597).

A Sermon Preached at S. Maries in Oxford, the 17. Day of November, 1602. in Defence of the Festivities of the Church of England, and Namely that of her Maiesties Coronation (2nd impression, Oxford, 1603).
Ironside, Gilbert, *Seven Questions of the Sabbath Briefly Disputed* (Oxford, 1637).
Jackson, Henry (ed.), *Wickliffes Wicket* (Oxford, 1612).
Jackson, Thomas, *The Works of Thomas Jackson* (12 vols., Oxford, 1844).
Jackson, Thomas (of Canterbury), *Judah Must into Captivitie* (1622).
James I, King, *The Political Works of James I*, ed. C.H. McIlwain (Cambridge, Mass., 1918).
The Workes of the Most High and Mighty Prince Iames (1616).
James, Thomas, *An Apologie for John Wickliffe* (Oxford, 1608).
Bellum Gregorianum (Oxford, 1610).
An Explanation or Enlarging of the Ten Articles (Oxford, 1625).
The Humble and Earnest Request of Thomas James (n.d.).
The Humble Supplication of Thomas James (n.d.).
The Iesuits Downefall (Oxford, 1612).
Letters Addressed to Thomas James, ed. G.W. Wheeler (1933).
A Manuduction or Introduction unto Divinitie: Containing a Confutation of Papists by Papists (Oxford, 1625).
A Treatise of the Corruption of Scripture, Councils and Holy Fathers (1611).
Jenney, George, *A Catholike Conference* (1626).
Jessop, Constant, *The Angel of the Church of Ephesus no Bishop of Ephesus* (1644).
Jewel, John, *Works*, ed. J. Ayre (4 vols., Cambridge, 1845–50).
Jones, John, *Londons Looking Backe to Jerusalem* (1630).
Journals of the House of Lords.
Kellison, Matthew, *Examen Reformationis Novae Praesertim Calvinianae* (1616).
King, Henry, *A Sermon Preached at St Pauls* (1640).
King, John, *The Fourth Sermon Preached at Hampton Court* (Oxford, 1607).
Vitis Palatina (1614).
[Knott, Edward], *A Direction to be Observed by N.N.* (1636).
Lake, Arthur, *Ten Sermons* (1640).
Larking, L.B. (ed.), *Proceedings in Kent* (Camden Society 80, 1862).
Laud, William, *The Works of William Laud*, ed. W. Scott and J. Bliss (7 vols., Oxford, 1847–60).
Lawrence, Thomas, *A Sermon Preached before the King's Majesty, at White-hall* (1637).
Two Sermons. The First Preached at St Maries in Oxford July 13. 1634 ... The Second in the Cathedrall Church of Sarum, at the Visitation of ... William Arch-Bp. of Cant. May 23. 1634 (Oxford, 1635).
Leech, Humfrey, *A Triumph of Truth* (Douai, 1609).
Leighton, Alexander, *Speculum belli sacri* (Amsterdam, 1624).
Leslie, Henry, *A Treatise of the Authority of the Church* (Dublin, 1637).
Lingelsheims, George-Michael, *Briefe G.M. Lingelsheims, M. Berneggers und Ihrer Freunde*, ed. A. Reifferscheid (Heilbronn, 1889).
Lubbertus, Sibrandus, *Responsio ad Pietatem Hugonis Grotii* (Franeker, 1614).
[Lushington, Thomas], *The Resurrection Rescued* (1659).
Lynde, Humphrey, *A Case for the Spectacles* (1638).
Via Tuta: The Safe Way: Leading All Christians, by the Testimonies, and

Confessions of our Best Learned Adversaries, to the True, Ancient, and Catholike Faith, now Professed in the Church of England (4th edn, 1630).
M., R., *An Answer to a Lawless Pamphlet Entituled, The Petition and Articles Exhibited in Parliament against Doctor Heywood* (1641).
Maie, Edward, *A Sermon of the Communion of Saints* (1st and 2nd impressions, 1621).
Manningham, John, *The Diary of John Manningham*, ed. R.P. Sorlien (Hanover, N.H., 1976).
Marshall, Stephen, *A Sermon Preached before the Honourable House of Commons ... November 17, 1640* (1641).
Martin, Edward, *Doctor Martin, Late Dean of Ely, his Opinion ... Communicated by Five Pious and Learned Letters in the Time of his Exile*, ed. Richard Watson (1662).
Mason, Francis, *The Authority of the Church in Making Canons and Constitutions concerning Things Indifferent* (2nd edn, Oxford, 1634).
Of the Consecration of the Bishops of the Church of England (1613).
'The Validity of the Ordination of the Ministers of the Reformed Churches beyond the Seas', in *Certain Briefe Treatises.*
Vindiciae Ecclesiae Anglicanae (1625).
Mayer, John, *Ecclesiastica interpretatio* (1627).
Mede, Joseph, *The Apostasy of the Latter Times* (1641).
Diatribae (1642).
The Works of ... Joseph Mede, ed. J. Worthington (1664).
Michaelson, John, *The Lawfulnes of Kneeling* (St Andrews, 1620).
Montagu, Richard, *The Acts and Monuments of the Church before Christ Incarnate* (1642).
Analecta Ecclesiasticarum Exercitationum (1622).
Antidiatribae ad Priorem Partem Diatribarum J. Caesaris Bulengeri Adversus Exercitationes Eruditus Is. Casauboni (1625).
Apparatus ad Origines Ecclesiasticarum (Oxford, 1635).
Appello Caesarem. A Just Appeal from Two Unjust Informers (1625).
Articles of Inquiry Put Forth at the Primary Visitation of R. Montague ... Bishop of Norwich (Cambridge, 1841).
Diatribae upon the First Part of the Late History of Tithes (1621).
A Gagg for the New Gospel? No. A New Gagg for an Old Goose (1624).
Immediate Addresse unto God Alone. First Delivered in a Sermon before his Maiestie at Windsore. Since Revised and Inlarged to a Just Treatise of Invocation of Saints. Occasioned by a False Imputation of M. Antonius De Dominis upon the Authour (1624).
ΘΕΑΝΘΡΩΠΙΚΟΝ Seu de Vita Jesu Christi Domini Nostri Originum Ecclesiasticarum Libri Duo (1640).
Morley, George, *A Modest Advertisement* (1641).
Mornay, Philippe De Plessis, *A Treatise of the Church* (1579).
Morton, Thomas, *Apologia Catholica* (1605).
A Catholike Appeale for Protestants, out of the Confessions of the Romane Doctors, Particularly Answering the Mis-named Catholike Apologie for the Romane Faith, out of the Protestants (1610).
A Defence of the Innocencie of the Three Ceremonies of the Church of England (1618).
A Discharge of Five Imputations of Mis-Allegations, Falsly Charged upon the (now) Bishop of Duresme, by an English Baron (1633).

An Exact Discoverie of Romish Doctrine (1605).
The Grand Imposture of the (now) Church of Rome (2nd edn, 1628).
Of the Institution of the Sacrament of the Blessed Bodie and Blood of Christ (1631).
'The Opinion of Bishop Morton', in *Good Counsells.*
A Sermon Preached before the Kings Most Excellent Maiestie, in the Cathedrall Church of Durham (Newcastle, 1639).
Totius Doctrinalis Controversiae De Eucharistia Decisio (Cambridge, 1640).
[Neile, Richard], *M. Ant. de Dominis Arch-Bishop of Spalato his Shiftings in Religion* (1624).
Nicholls, William, *A Supplement to the Commentary on the Book of Common Prayer ... To which is Added an Introduction to the Liturgy of the Church of England* (1711).
Norris, Silvester, *An Antidote or Soveraigne Remedie* (1615).
Notes of the Debates in the House of Lords ... 1621–28, ed. F.H. Relf (Camden Society 3rd ser. 42, 1929).
Ormerod, Oliver, *The Picture of a Papist* (1606).
The Picture of a Puritane (1605).
Overall, John, *The Convocation Book of MDCVI, Commonly Called Bishop Overall's Convocation Book* (Oxford, 1844).
Owen, David, *Anti-Paraeus: Sive Determinatio de Iure Regio habita Cantabrigiae in Scholis Theologicis, 19 April 1619 contra Davidem Paraeum* (Cambridge, 1622).
Herod and Pilate Reconciled: Or, the Concord of Papist and Puritan ... for the Coercion, Deposition, and Killing of Kings (Cambridge, 1610).
Oxford University, *The Answere of the Vicechancelour* (Oxford, 1603).
Decretum universitatis Oxoniensis damnans propositiones neotericorum infrascriptas (Oxford, 1622).
Page, William (tr. and ed.), *The Imitation of Christ* (Oxford, 1639).
A Treatise or Justification of Bowing at the Name of Jesus. By Way of Answere to an Appendix against it (Oxford, 1631).
Pagitt, Ephraim, *Christianographie, or The Description of the Multitude and Sundry Sorts of Christians in the World, not Subject to the Pope* (1st edn, 1635; 2nd edn, 1636; 3rd edn, 1640).
Panke, John, *Collectanea. Out of St Gregory and St Bernard against the Papists* (Oxford, 1618).
Panzani, Gregorio, *The Memoirs of Gregorio Panzani*, ed. J. Berington (Birmingham, 1793; facsimile edn, Farnborough, 1970).
Parker, Henry, *The Altar Dispute* (1641).
Parker, Robert, *A Scholasticall Discourse against Symbolizing with Antichrist* (?Amsterdam, 1607).
Parkes, Richard, *An Apologie of Three Testimonies* (1607).
A Briefe Answere unto Certaine Obiections (Oxford, 1604).
Parre, Richard, *Concio ad clerum habita Oxoniae ... 1625* (Oxford, 1628).
Peiresc, Nicolas Claude Fabri de, *Lettres de Peiresc aux frères Dupuy*, ed. P.T. de Larroque (Paris, 1892).
Perkins, William, *Problema de Romanae Fidei Ementito Catholicismo* (Cambridge, 1604).
A Reformed Catholike (1634).
The Petition and Articles Exhibited in Parliament against Dr. Fuller (1641).
The Petition and Articles Exhibited in Parliament against Doctor Heywood (1641).

The Petition and Articles or Severall Charge Exhibited in Parliament against John Pocklington (1641).
The Petition for the Prelates Briefly Examined (1641).
Piers, William, *Two Sermons Preached in the Tower* (1642).
Plaifere, John, *Appello Evangelium* (1651).
Pocklington, John, *Altare Christianum* (1637; 2nd edn, 1637).
Sunday no Sabbath (1636).
Potter, Christopher, *A Sermon Preached at the Consecration of . . . Barnaby Potter* (1629).
Want of Charitie Justly Charged, on all such Romanists, as Dare . . . Affirme, that Protestancie Destroyeth Salvation. Or An Answer to a Late Popish Pamphlet Intituled 'Charity Mistaken' (Oxford, 1633; 2nd edn, Oxford, 1634).
Powel, Gabriel, *The Catholikes Supplication unto the Kings Maiestie; for Toleration of Catholike Religion in England* (1603).
A Consideration of the Deprived and Silenced Ministers Arguments (1606).
A Consideration of the Papists Reasons of State and Religion (1604).
Disputationum Theologicarum & Scholasticarum de Antichristo & eius Ecclesiae (1605).
A Refutation of an Epistle Apologeticall (1605).
A Reioynder unto the Mild Defence (1607).
Preston, John, *Sermons Preached before his Maiestie* (1630).
Preston, Thomas, *A Cleare, Sincere and Modest Confutation* (1616).
Prideaux, John, *Castigatio cuiusdam circulatoris, qui R.P. Andream Eudaemon-Johannem Cydonium seipsum nuncupat* (Oxford, 1614).
Certaine Sermons (Oxford, 1637).
De Episcopatu Epistola (1660).
The Doctrine of the Sabbath (3rd edn, 1635).
Ephesus Backsliding Considered and Applyed to these Times (1614).
Fasciculus (1647).
Manuductio (1657).
Scholasticae Theologiae Syntagma Mnemonicum (Oxford, 1651).
Viginti-duae Lectiones de Totidem Religionis Capitibus, praecipue hoc tempore controversis, prout publice habebantur Oxoniae in Vesperiis (3rd edn, Oxford, 1648).
Primerose, David, *A Treatise of the Sabbath and the Lords-Day* (1636).
Proceedings in Parliament, 1610, ed. E.R. Foster (2 vols., 1966).
Prynne, William, *A Briefe Survay and Censure of Mr. Cozens His Couzening Devotions* (1628).
Canterburies Doome or the First Part of a Compleat History of the . . . Tryall . . . of William Laud (1646).
Lame Giles his Haultings (1630).
A Quench-Coale (1637).
The Time-Serving Proteus and Ambidexter Divine, Uncased to the World (1650).
Purchas, Samuel, *Hakluytus Posthumus or Purchas his Pilgrimes* (20 vols., Glasgow, 1905–7).
Puritan Manifestoes, ed. W.H. Frere and C.E. Douglas (1907).
Quelch, William, *Church-Customes Vindicated: In Two Sermons Preached at Kingstone upon Thames* (1636).

Rainolds, John, *De Romana Ecclesia Idololatria* (1596).
A Letter of Dr Reinolds to his Friend, concerning his Advice for the Studie of Divinitie (1613).
The Summe of the Conference betweene John Rainoldes and John Hart (1609).
Raleigh, Walter, *Certain Queries Proposed by Roman Catholicks, and Answered by Dr. Walter Raleigh*, ed. Laurence Howel (1719).
Reliquiae Raleighanae (1679).
[Ranchin, Guillaume du], *A Review of the Councell of Trent*, tr. Gerard Langbaine (Oxford,1638).
Read, Alexander, *A Sermon Preached April 8, 1635 at the Visitation of Brentwood in Essex* (1636).
The Records of the Honourable Society of Lincoln's Inn. The Black Books, ed. W.P. Blaidon and R.F. Roxburgh (3 vols., 1897–1969).
Records of the Kirk of Scotland, ed. A. Peterkin (Edinburgh, 1838).
Reeve, Edmund, *The Communion Booke Catechisme Expounded* (1636).
The Responsa Scholarum of the English College, Rome, Part Two: 1622–1685, ed. A. Kenny (Catholic Record Society 55, 1963).
Richer, Edmond, *A Treatise of Ecclesiasticall & Politike Power* (1612).
Robarts, Foulke, *God's Holy House and Service, According to the Primitive and Most Christian Forme thereof* (1639).
Rodoginus, Irenaeus, *Differences in Matters of Religion between Eastern and Western Churches* (1624).
Rogers, Henry, *An Answer to Mr. Fisher the Jesuite, His Five Propositions concerning Luther* (1623).
The Protestant Church Existent, and Their Faith Professed in all Ages, and by Whom: With a Catalogue of Councels in all Ages, who Professed the Same (1638).
Rogers, Thomas, *The Catholic Doctrine of the Church of England* (Cambridge, 1854).
An Historical Dialogue Touching Antichrist and Poperie (1589).
Two Dialogues (1608).
Rous, John, *The Diary of John Rous*, ed. M.A.E. Green (Camden Society 66, 1856).
Rudd, Anthony, *A Sermon Preached before the Kings Maiestie ... 1605* (1606).
Sancta Clara, Franciscus a, *Apologia Episcoporum, Seu, Sacri Magistratus Propugnatio* (Cologne, 1640).
Deus, Natura, Gratia, sive Tractatus de Praedestinatione (1st edn, Lyons, 1634; 2nd edn, Lyons, 1635).
Paraphrastica Expositio Articulorum Confessionis Anglicanae, ed. and tr. F.G. Lee (1865).
Sanderson, Robert, *The Works of Robert Sanderson, D.D.*, ed. W. Jacobson (6 vols., Oxford, 1854).
Sandys, Sir Edward, *Europae Speculum. Or, A View or Survey of the State of Religion in the Westerne Parts of the World* (The Hague, 1629).
Saravia, Hadrian, *De diversis gradibus* (1594).
Saumaise, Claude, *Claude Saumaise & André Rivet. Correspondance échangée entre 1632 et 1648*, ed. J.A.H.G.M. Bots and P.E.-R. Leroy (Amsterdam and Maarssen, 1987).
Schlüsselburg, Conrad, *Haereticorum Catalogus* (13 vols., Frankfurt, 1597–9).
Theologiae Calvinistarum (Frankfurt, 1592).

Sclater, William, *An Exposition with Notes upon the First Epistle of the Thessalonians* (1619).
A Threefold Preservative (1610).
Scot, Thomas, *The Workes of ... Mr. Thomas Scot* (Utrecht, 1624).
Scultetus, Abraham, *Delitiae Evangelicae Pragenses* (Hanover, 1620).
Seller, John, *Five Sermons* (1636).
Sheldon, Richard, *Christ on His Throne; not in Popish Secrets* (1622).
The First Sermon ... after his Conversion from the Romish Church (1612).
A Sermon Preached at Paules Crosse (1625).
Shelford, Robert, *Five Pious and Learned Discourses* (Cambridge, 1635).
Sibbes, Richard, *The Works of Richard Sibbes*, ed. A.B. Grosart (7 vols., 1862–4).
Sibthorpe, Robert, *Apostolike Obedience* (1627).
Skinner, Robert, *A Sermon Preached before the King at White-Hall* (1634).
Slade, Matthew, *Matthew Slade 1569–1628: Letters to the English Ambassador*, ed. W. Nijenhuis (Leiden, 1986).
Some, Robert, *A Godly Treatise ... Touching the Ministerie, Sacraments, and the Church* (1588).
Sparrow, Anthony, *A Sermon concerning Confession of Sinnes, and the Power of Absolution* (1637).
Spencer, Thomas, *Maschil Unmasked. In a Treatise Defending this Sentence of our Church: Viz. The Present Romish Church hath not the Nature of the True Church. Against the Public Opposition of Mr. Cholmley, and Mr. Butterfield* (1629).
Stafford, Anthony, *The Life of the Blessed Virgin; Together with the Apology of the Author* (1860).
Strype, John, *Annals of the Reformation* (4 vols., Oxford, 1824).
The Life and Acts of John Aylmer (Oxford, 1821).
The Life and Acts of John Whitgift (3 vols., Oxford, 1822).
The Suffolk Committees for Scandalous Ministers 1644–1646, ed. C. Holmes (Suffolk Records Society 13, 1970).
Sutcliffe, Matthew, *An Abridgement or Survey of Poperie* (1606).
A Briefe Examination of a ... Petition (1606).
A Briefe Censure upon an Appeale to Caesar (1626).
De Pontifico Romano (1599).
De Turcopapismo (1599).
De Vera Christi Ecclesia (1600).
The Supplication of Certaine Masse-Priests (1604).
A Treatise of Ecclesiasticall Discipline (1590).
Swan, John, *Profanomastix. Or, A Briefe and Necessarie Direction concerning the Respects which wee Owe to God, and His House, even in Outward Worship, and Reverent Using of Holy Places* (1639).
A Sermon, Pointing out the Chiefe Causes, and Cures, of such Unruly Stirres, as are not Seldome found in the Church of God (1639).
Speculum Mundi (Cambridge, 1635).
Sydenham, Humphrey, *Five Sermons upon Severall Occasions* (1626–7).
Sermons upon Solemne Occasions (1637).
Sydney Papers, ed. R.W. Blencowe (1825).
Syllabus aliquot synodorum et colloquiorum (Strasbourg, 1628).
Tayler, Francis, *The Faith of the Church of England concerning Gods Work on Mans Will* (1641).

Taylor, Jeremy, *Works*, ed. R.G. Heber and C.P. Eden (10 vols., 1847–54).
Taylor, Thomas, *Christs Victorie over the Dragon* (1633).
The Principles of Christian Practice (1635).
Two Sermons (1624).
Tedder, Richard, *A Sermon Preached at Wimondham in Norfolke, at the Primary Visitation of . . . Matthew, Lord Bishop of Norwich* (1637).
Thomson, Richard, *Elenchus Refutationis Torturae Torti* (1611).
Tilenus, Daniel, *De Disciplina Ecclesiastica* (Aberdeen, 1622).
Towers, John, *Four Sermons* (1660).
Turner, Thomas, *A Sermon Preached before the King at White-Hall* (1635).
Twisse, William, *Of the Morality of the Fourth Commandement* (1641).
Two Elizabethan Puritan Diaries, ed. M.M. Knappen (Chicago, 1933).
Ussher, James, 'The Opinion of the Archbishop of Armagh', in *Good Counsells*.
The Whole Works of . . . James Ussher, ed. C.R. Elrington (17 vols., Dublin, 1847–64).
Vossius, Gerardus J., *G.J. Vossii et Clarorum Virorum ad Eum Epistolae*, ed. P. Colmesius (1690).
Walker, George, *Fishers Folly Unfolded* (1624).
A True Relation of the Chiefe Passages (1642).
Wall, George, *A Sermon at the Lord Archbishop of Canterbury his Visitation Metropoliticall* (1635).
Walsingham, Francis, *A Search Made into Matters of Religion* (St Omer, 1609).
Ward, Samuel, *Gratia Discriminans* (1626).
Opera Nonnulla (1658).
Warre, James, *The Touch-stone of Truth* (1634).
Watts, William, *Mortification Apostolicall* (1637).
Whitaker, William, *A Disputation on Holy Scripture, against the Papists*, tr. and ed. W. Fitzgerald (Cambridge, 1849).
Praelectiones . . . de Ecclesia (Cambridge, 1599).
Whitbie, Oliver, *Londons Returne, after the Decrease of the Sicknes* (1637/8).
White, Francis, *An Examination and Confutation of a Lawlesse Pamphlet* (1637).
The Orthodox Faith and Way to the Church Explaned and Justified (1617; 2nd edn, 1624).
A Replie to Jesuit Fishers Answere (1624).
A Treatise of the Sabbath-Day (3rd edn, 1636).
White, John, *A Defence of the Way to the True Church* (1614).
The Way to the True Church (1608).
White, John, *The First Century of Scandalous, Malignant Priests* (1643).
Whitgift, John, *The Works of John Whitgift*, ed. J. Ayre (3 vols., Cambridge, 1851–3).
Widdowes, Giles, *The Schismatical Puritan* (Oxford, 1630).
Willet, Andrew, *An Antilogie* (1603).
Ecclesia Triumphans (1603).
Hexapla in Danielem (Cambridge, 1610).
Hexapla in Exodum (1608).
Hexapla in Genesin (Cambridge, 1605).
Hexapla in Leviticum (Cambridge, 1631).
Hexapla . . . upon the . . . Epistle of . . . Paul to the Romans (Cambridge, 1611).
Limbo-Mastix (1604).
Loidoromastix (1607).

A Retection (1603).
Sacrorum Emblematum Centuria Una (Cambridge, 1588).
Synopsis Papismi (1st edn, 1592; 2nd edn, 1594; 3rd edn, 1600; 4th edn, 1613; 5th edn, 1634; ed. J. Cumming, 10 vols., 1852).
Thesaurus Ecclesiae (Cambridge, 1604).
A Treatise of Salomons Mariage (1612/13).
Wood, Anthony, *Athenae Oxonienses*, ed. P. Bliss (4 vols., 1813–20).
The History and Antiquities of the University of Oxford, ed. J. Gutch (2 vols., Oxford, 1792–6).
Wotton, Anthony, *A Dangerous Plot Discovered ... wherin is Proved that R. Mountague ... Laboureth to Bring in the Faith of Rome and Arminius* (1626).
A Defence of M. Perkins Booke (1606).
Runne from Rome (1624).
A Trial of the Romish Clergies Title to the Church (1608).
Wren, Christopher, *Parentalia, or Memoirs of the Family of the Wrens* (1750).
Wren, Matthew, *A Sermon Preached before the kings Maiestie* (Cambridge, 1627).
Y., D., *Legenda Lignea, with an Answer to Mr Birchleys Moderator* (1653).
Yates, John, *Ibis ad Caesarem or a Submissive Appearance before Caesar, in Answer to Mr. Montague's Appeal, in the Points of Arminianisme and Popery, Maintained and Defended by him, against the Doctrine of the Church of England* (1626).
Yates, John, *A Treatise of the Honour of God's House ... With A Discovery of the True Cause and Cure of our Present Contentions* (1637).
Young, John, *The Diary of John Young*, ed. F.R. Goodman (1928).
The Zurich Letters 1558–1579, ed. H. Robinson (2 vols., Cambridge, 1842–5).

SECONDARY SOURCES

Adams, S., 'Foreign policy and the parliaments of 1621 and 1624', in K. Sharpe (ed.), *Faction and Parliament* (1978).
'The road to La Rochelle', *Proceedings of the Huguenot Society* 22/5 (1975).
Albion, G., *Charles I and the Court of Rome* (Louvain, 1935).
Allison, A.F., 'The "Mysticism" of Manchester Al Mondo. Some Catholic borrowings in a seventeenth-century Anglican work of devotion', in G.A.M. Janssens and F.G.A.M. Aarts (eds.), *Studies in Seventeenth Century English Literature, History and Bibliography* (Amsterdam, 1984).
'Richard Smith's Gallican backers and Jesuit opponents', *Recusant History* 18 (1986–7).
Allison, C.F., *The Rise of Moralism: The Proclamation of the Gospel from Hooker to Baxter* (1966).
Archer, I.W., *The Pursuit of Stability. Social Relations in Elizabethan London* (Cambridge, 1991).
Armstrong, B.G., *Calvinism and the Amyraut Heresy* (Madison, 1969).
'The changing face of French Protestantism: the influence of Pierre Du Moulin', in R.V. Schnucker (ed.), *Calviniana* (Kirksville, 1988).
Asheim, I., and Gould, V.R. (eds.), *Episcopacy in the Lutheran Church?* (Philadelphia, 1970).
Aston, M., *England's Iconoclasts I* (Oxford, 1988).

Atherton, I., 'Viscount Scudamore's "Laudianism": the religious practices of the first Viscount Scudamore', *HJ* 34 (1991).

Atkins, J.M., 'Calvinist bishops, church unity, and the rise of Arminianism', *Albion* 18 (1986).

Aveling, J.C.H., 'The English clergy, Catholic and Protestant, in the 16th and 17th centuries', in J.C.H. Aveling, D.M. Loades and H.R. McAdoo, *Rome and the Anglicans* (Berlin, 1982).

The Handle and the Axe. The Catholic Recusants in England from Reformation to Emancipation (1976).

Northern Catholics. The Catholic Recusants of the North Riding of Yorkshire 1558–1790 (1966).

Avis, P.D.L., *The Church in the Theology of the Reformers* (1981).

Babbage, S.B., *Puritanism and Richard Bancroft* (1962).

Backus, I.D., *The Reformed Roots of the English New Testament* (Pittsburgh, 1980).

Baker, D. (ed.), *Reform and Reformation: England and the Continent c.1500–c.1750* (Studies in Church History Subsidia 2, Oxford, 1979).

Religious Motivation: Biographical and Sociological Problems for the Church Historian (Studies in Church History 15, Oxford, 1978).

Bakhuizen van den Brink, J.N., 'Het Convent te Franeker 27–28 September 1577 en de Harmonia Confessionum', *NAvK* n.s. 32 (1941).

Ball, B.W., *A Great Expectation. Eschatological Thought in English Protestantism to 1660* (Leiden, 1975).

Bangs, C., *Arminius: A Study in the Dutch Reformation* (Nashville, 1971).

Barnes, R.B., *Prophecy and Gnosis. Apocalypticism in the Wake of the Lutheran Reformation* (Stanford, 1988).

Batten, J.M., *John Dury, Advocate of Christian Reunion* (1944).

Bauckham, R., 'Hooker, Travers and the Church of Rome in the 1580s', *JEH* 29 (1978).

'Richard Hooker and John Calvin: a comment', *JEH* 32 (1981).

'Sabbath and Sunday in the Protestant tradition', in D.A. Carson (ed.), *From Sabbath to Lord's Day* (Grand Rapids, 1982).

Tudor Apocalypse (Abingdon, 1978).

Beales, A.C.F., *Education under Penalty* (1963).

Becker, M.K., 'Episcopal unrest: Gallicanism in the 1625 Assembly of the Clergy', *Church History* 43 (1974).

Bense, J.F., *Anglo-Dutch Relations* (The Hague, 1925).

Bernard, G.W., 'The Church of England, c.1559–1642', *History* 75 (1990).

Bevenot, M., '"In Solidum" and St Cyprian: a correction', *Journal of Theological Studies* 6 (1955).

Birrell, T.A., 'English Catholic mystics in non-Catholic circles', *The Downside Review* 94 (1976).

'Introduction' to *The Memoirs of Gregorio Panzani*, ed. J. Berington (facsimile edn, Farnborough, 1970).

'The reconstruction of the library of Isaac Casaubon', in *Hellinga: Festschrift* (Amsterdam, 1980).

Blatchly, J., *The Town Library of Ipswich* (Woodbridge, 1989).

Blom, J.M., 'A German Jesuit and his Anglican readers. The case of Jeremias Drexelius (1581–1632)', in G.A.M. Janssens and F.G.A.M. Aarts (eds.),

Studies in Seventeenth Century English Literature, History and Bibliography (Amsterdam, 1984).
Blunt, R., *The Wonderful Village* (1918).
Borregaard, S., 'The post-Reformation developments of the episcopacy in Denmark, Norway and Iceland', in Asheim and Gould, *Episcopacy*.
Bossy, J., 'The English Catholic community 1603–1625', in A.G.R. Smith (ed.), *The Reign of James VI and I* (1973).
Bots, J.A., 'André Rivet en zijn positie in de Republiek der Letteren', *Tijdschrift voor Geschiedenis* 84 (1971).
Bouwsma, W.J., 'Gallicanism and the nature of Christendom', in A. Molho and J. Tedeschi (eds.), *Renaissance Studies in Honor of Hans Baron* (Dekalb, Ill., 1971).
Brachlow, S., *The Communion of Saints* (Oxford, 1988).
Bradley, R.I., 'Christopher Davenport and the Thirty-Nine Articles', *AfR* 52 (1961).
Bradshaw, P.F., *The Anglican Ordinal* (1971).
Brady, D., *The Contribution of British Writers between 1560 and 1830 to the Interpretation of Revelation 13.16–18* (Tübingen, 1983).
Breslow, M.A., *A Mirror of England* (Cambridge, Mass., 1970).
Breward, I. (ed.), *The Work of William Perkins* (Appleford, 1970).
Broeyer, F.G.M., 'De Irenische Perkins – Vertaling van de Arminian Everard Booth (1577–1610)', *NAvK* 71–2 (1991).
William Whitaker: leven en werk van een Anglocalvinistisch theoloog (Utrecht, 1982).
Brooke, C.N.L., *A History of Gonville and Caius College* (Woodbridge, 1985).
Burgess, G., 'The divine right of kings reconsidered', *EHR* 425 (1992).
The Politics of the Ancient Constitution (1992).
Bush, S., and Rasmussen, C.J., *The Library of Emmanuel College, Cambridge, 1584–1637* (Cambridge, 1986).
Capp, B.S., *The Fifth Monarchy Men* (1972).
'The political dimension of apocalyptical thought', in C.A. Patrides and J. Wittreich (eds.), *The Apocalypse in English Renaissance Thought and Literature* (Manchester, 1984).
Cargill Thompson, W.D.J., *Studies in the Reformation* (1980).
Carter, C.H., *The Secret Diplomacy of the Habsburgs* (New York, 1964).
Chaney, E., *The Grand Tour and the Great Rebellion* (Geneva, 1985).
Christianson, P., *Reformers and Babylon* (Toronto, 1978).
Clancy, T.H., *Papist Pamphleteers* (Chicago, 1964).
'Papist–Protestant–Puritan: English religious taxonomy 1565–1665', *Recusant History* 13 (1975–6).
Clark, S., 'Inversion, misrule and the meaning of witchcraft', *P&P* 87 (1980).
Cliffe, J.T., *The Yorkshire Gentry from the Reformation to the Civil War* (1969).
Clifton, R., 'Fear of popery' in Russell, *Origins*.
'The popular fear of Catholics during the English Revolution', *P&P* 52 (1971).
Cogswell, T., *The Blessed Revolution* (Cambridge, 1989).
'England and the Spanish Match', in Cust and Hughes, *Conflict*.
'Foreign policy and parliament: the case of La Rochelle, 1625–1626', *EHR* 99 (1984).
'Prelude to Ré: the Anglo-French struggle over La Rochelle, 1624–1627', *History* 71 (1986).

Collinson, P., 'Andrew Perne and his times', in P. Collinson, D. McKitterick and E. Leedham-Green (eds.), *Andrew Perne. Quatercentenary Studies* (Cambridge Bibliographical Society Monograph 11, 1991).
The Birthpangs of Protestant England (1988).
'Calvinism with an Anglican face: the stranger churches in early Elizabethan London and their superintendent', in Baker, *Reform.*
'A comment: concerning the name puritan', *JEH* 31 (1980).
The Elizabethan Puritan Movement (1967).
'England and international Calvinism 1558–1640', in M. Prestwich (ed.), *International Calvinism 1541–1715* (Oxford, 1985).
Godly People (1982).
'The Jacobean religious settlement: the Hampton Court Conference', in H. Tomlinson (ed.), *Before the English Civil War* (1983).
The Religion of Protestants (Oxford, 1982).
Coolidge, J.S., *The Pauline Renaissance in England* (Oxford, 1970).
Cooper, C.H., *Annals of Cambridge* (5 vols., Cambridge, 1842–1908).
Costello, W.T., *The Scholastic Curriculum at Early Seventeenth Century Cambridge* (Cambridge, Mass., 1958).
Cozzi, G., 'Fra Paolo Sarpi, l'anglicanesimo e la "Historia del Concilio Tridentino"', *Rivista storica italiana* 63 (1956).
Cragg, G.R., *Freedom and Authority* (Philadelphia, 1975).
Cranfield, N., and Fincham, K. (eds.), 'John Howson's answers to Archbishop Abbot's accusations at his "trial" before James I at Greenwich, 10 June 1615', *Camden Miscellany XXIX* (Camden Society 4th ser. 34, 1987).
Cremeans, C.D., *The Reception of Calvinist Thought in England* (Urbana, 1949).
Cressy, D., *Bonfires and Bells* (1989).
Croft, P., 'The religion of Robert Cecil', *HJ* 34 (1991).
'Trading with the enemy, 1585–1604', *HJ* 32 (1989).
Cuming, G.J., 'Eastern liturgies and Anglican divines 1510–1662', in D. Baker (ed.), *The Orthodox Churches and the West* (Studies in Church History 13, Oxford, 1976).
A History of Anglican Liturgy (1969).
Cust, R., 'Anti-puritanism and urban politics: Charles I and Great Yarmouth', *HJ* 35 (1992).
The Forced Loan and English Politics 1626–1628 (Oxford, 1987).
'News and politics in early seventeenth century England', *P&P* 112 (1986).
Cust, R., and Hughes, A. (eds.), *Conflict in Early Stuart England* (1989).
Davidson, A., 'The conversion of Bishop King: a question of evidence', *Recusant History* 9 (1967–8).
Davies, J., *The Caroline Captivity of the Church* (Oxford, 1992).
Dent, C.M., *Protestant Reformers in Elizabethan Oxford* (Oxford, 1983).
Dickens, A.G., *The English Reformation* (1964).
Dictionary of National Biography (63 vols., 1885–1900).
Dockery, J.B., *Christopher Davenport* (1960).
Donaldson, G., 'The attitude of Whitgift and Bancroft to the Scottish Church', *TRHS* 24 (1942).
Doran, S., 'Religion and politics at the court of Elizabeth I: the Habsburg marriage negotiations of 1559–1567', *EHR* 413 (1989).
Dowding, W.C., *The Life and Correspondence of George Calixtus* (1863).
Doyle, A.I., 'A new Cosin letter', *Durham Philobiblon* 1 (1954).

Dugmore, C.W., *Eucharistic Doctrine in England from Hooker to Waterland* (1942).
Dunkley, E.H., *The Reformation in Denmark* (1948).
Dures, A., *English Catholicism 1558–1642* (1983).
Eagleston, A.J., *Channel Islands under Tudor Government* (Cambridge, 1949).
Edmundson, G., *Anglo-Dutch Rivalry during the First Half of the Seventeenth Century* (Oxford, 1910).
Elert, W., *The Structure of Lutheranism* (St Louis, 1962).
Elliott, E.B., *Horae Apocalypticae* (4 vols., 5th edn, 1862).
Elson, J.H., *John Hales of Eton* (New York, 1948).
Facey, J., 'John Foxe and the defence of the English Church', in Lake and Dowling, *Protestantism.*
Faulkner, T., *An Historical and Topographical Description of Chelsea and its Environs* (2 vols., 1829).
Fielding, J., 'Opposition to the personal rule of Charles I: the diary of Robert Woodford, 1637–41', *HJ* 31 (1988).
Fincham, K., 'Prelacy and politics: Archbishop Abbot's defence of Protestant orthodoxy', *Historical Research* 61 (1988).
Prelate as Pastor (Oxford, 1990).
Fincham, K., and Lake, P., 'The ecclesiastical policy of King James I', *Journal of British Studies* 24 (1985).
Finlayson, M.G., *Historians, Puritanism, and the English Revolution* (Toronto, 1983).
Firth, K., *The Apocalyptic Tradition in Reformation Britain 1530–1645* (Oxford, 1979).
Fletcher, A.J., *The Outbreak of the English Civil War* (1981).
Ford, A., *The Protestant Reformation in Ireland, 1590–1641* (Frankfurt am Main, 1985).
Foster, A., 'Church policies in the 1630s', in Cust and Hughes, *Conflict.*
'The function of a bishop: the career of Richard Neile 1562–1640', in R. O'Day and F. Heal (eds.), *Continuity and Change* (Leicester, 1976).
Foster, S., *Notes from the Caroline Underground* (Hamden, Conn., 1978).
Fritze, R., 'Root or link? Luther's position in the historical debate over the legitimacy of the Church of England, 1558–1625', *JEH* 37 (1986).
Fuller, M., *The Life, Letters and Writings of John Davenant, D.D., 1572–1641* (1897).
Gaffney, D., 'The practice of religious controversy in Dublin, 1600–1641', in W.J. Sheils and D. Wood (eds.), *The Churches, Ireland and the Irish* (Studies in Church History 25, Oxford, 1989).
George, C.H., and K., *The Protestant Mind of the English Reformation 1570–1640* (Princeton, 1961).
Godfrey, W.R., 'The Dutch Reformed response', in Spitz and Lohff, *Discord.*
Goode, W., *The Doctrine of the Church of England as to the Effects of Baptism in the Case of Infants* (1850).
Green, I.M., '"England's wars of religion"? Religious conflict and the English civil wars', in J. van den Berg and P.G. Hoftijzer (eds.), *Church, Change and Revolution* (Leiden, 1991).
'"For children in yeeres and children in understanding": the emergence of the English catechism under Elizabeth and the early Stuarts', *JEH* 37 (1986).
Grell, O.P., *Dutch Calvinists in Early Stuart London* (Leiden, 1989).

'A friendship turned sour: puritans and Dutch Calvinists in East Anglia, 1603–1660', in E.S. Leedham-Green (ed.), *Religious Dissent in East Anglia* (Cambridge Antiquarian Society, 1991).
'From uniformity to tolerance; the effects on the Dutch Church in London of reverse patterns in English church policy from 1634 to 1647', *NAvK* 66 (1986).
Hall, B., 'The early rise and gradual decline of Lutheranism in England (1520–1600)', in Baker, *Reform.*
'Puritanism: the problem of definition', in G.J. Cuming (ed.), *Studies in Church History* 2 (1965).
Harjunpaa, T., 'Liturgical developments in Sweden and Finland in the era of Lutheran orthodoxy (1593–1700)', *Church History* 37 (1968).
Havran, M.J., *The Catholics in Caroline England* (1962).
'The character and principles of an English king: the case of Charles I', *Catholic Historical Review* (1983).
Heal, F., *Hospitality in Early Modern England* (Oxford, 1990).
Healy, T.F., *Richard Crashaw* (Leiden, 1986).
Henderson, G., 'Bible illustrations in the age of Laud', *TCBS* 8 (1982).
Hibbard, C., *Charles I and the Popish Plot* (Chapel Hill, 1983).
Higham, F.M.G., *Catholic and Reformed. A Study of the Anglican Church, 1559–1662* (1962).
Hill, C., *Antichrist in Seventeenth-Century England* (Oxford, 1971).
Puritanism and Revolution (1958).
Hill, J.W.F., 'The royalist clergy in Lincolnshire', *Reports and Papers of the Lincolnshire Architectural and Archaeological Society* 2 (1938).
Hoenderdaal, G.J., 'The debate about Arminius outside the Netherlands', in T.H. Lunsingh Scheurleer and G.H.M. Posthumus Meyjes (eds.), *Leiden University in the Seventeenth Century* (Leiden, 1975).
Hof, W.J. op 't, *Engelse pietistische geschriften in het Nederlands, 1598–1622* (Rotterdam, 1987).
Honders, H.J., *Andreas Rivetus als Invloedrijk Gereformeerd Theoloog in Holland's Bloeitijd* (The Hague, 1930).
Hoyle, D., 'A Commons investigation of Arminianism and popery in Cambridge on the eve of the civil war', *HJ* 29 (1986).
Hughes, P., *Theology of the English Reformers* (1965).
Itterzon, G.P. van, *Franciscus Gomarus* (The Hague, 1929).
Kalb, F., *The Theology of Worship in Seventeenth-Century Lutheranism* (St Louis, 1965).
Kearney, H., *Scholars and Gentlemen: Universities and Society in Pre-Industrial Britain, 1500–1700* (1970).
Kemke, J., *Patricius Junius Bibliothekar der Könige Jacob I. und Carl 1. von England. Mitteilungen aus Seinem Briefwechsel . . .* (Leipzig, 1898).
Kendall, R.T., *Calvin and English Calvinism* (Oxford, 1979).
Kennedy, D.E., 'King James I's College of Controversial Divinity at Chelsea', in *idem* (ed.), *Grounds of Controversy. Three Studies of Late 16th and Early 17th Century English Polemics* (Melbourne, 1989).
Kenny, A., 'The accursed memory: the Counter-Reformation reputation of John Wyclif', in *idem* (ed.), *Wyclif in his Times* (Oxford, 1986).
Lake, P., *Anglicans and Puritans? Presbyterianism and English Conformist Thought from Whitgift to Hooker* (1988).

'Anti-popery: the structure of a prejudice', in Cust and Hughes, *Conflict*.
'Calvinism and the English Church 1570–1635', *P&P* 114 (1987).
'Constitutional consensus and puritan opposition in the 1620s: Thomas Scott and the Spanish Match', *HJ* 25 (1982).
'Defining puritanism – again?' (forthcoming from the Massachusetts Historical Society).
'Lancelot Andrewes, John Buckeridge and avant-garde conformity at the court of James I', in L. Levy Peck (ed.), *The Mental World of the Jacobean Court* (Cambridge, 1991).
'The Laudians and the argument from authority', in B.Y. Kunze and D.D. Brautigam (eds.), *Court, Country and Culture* (Rochester, 1992).
'Matthew Hutton – a puritan bishop?', *History* 64 (1979).
Moderate Puritans and the Elizabethan Church (Cambridge, 1982).
'Presbyterianism, the idea of a national church and the argument from divine right', in Lake and Dowling, *Protestantism*.
'Puritan identities', *JEH* 35 (1984).
'Robert Some and the ambiguities of moderation', *AfR* 71 (1980).
'The significance of the Elizabethan identification of the pope as Antichrist', *JEH* 31 (1980).
'William Bradshaw, Antichrist and the community of the Godly', *JEH* 36 (1985).
Lake, P., and Dowling, M. (eds.), *Protestantism and the National Church in Sixteenth Century England* (1987).
Lambert, S. 'Committees, religion, and parliamentary encroachment on royal authority in early Stuart England', *EHR* 105 (1990).
'Richard Montagu, Arminianism and censorship', *P&P* 124 (1989).
Lamont, W., 'Comment: the rise of Arminianism reconsidered', *P&P* 107 (1985).
Godly Rule: Politics and Religion 1603–1660 (1969).
'Richard Baxter, the Apocalypse and the mad major', *P&P* 55 (1972).
Laplanche, F., *L'Ecriture, le sacre et l'histoire. Erudits et politiques protestants devant la bible en France au XVIIe siècle* (Amsterdam and Maarssen, 1986).
Law, T.G. (ed.), *The Archpriest Controversy* (2 vols., Camden Society n.s. 56 and 58, 1896 and 1898).
Lawson, S., 'From Latin pun . . . ', *Sixteenth-Century Journal* 9 (1978).
Lecler, J., *Toleration and the Reformation* (2 vols., 1960).
Lees, J.C., *The Abbey of Paisley* (Paisley, 1878).
Levack, B.P., *The Civil Lawyers in England 1603–1641* (Oxford, 1973).
Lewis, G., *A Life of Joseph Hall* (1886).
Lindley, K.J., 'The lay Catholics in England in the reign of Charles I', *JEH* 22 (1971).
Loades, D., 'Relations between the Anglican and Roman Catholic Churches in the Sixteenth and seventeenth centuries', in Aveling, Loades and McAdoo, *Rome and the Anglicans*.
Lohse, B., 'The development of the offices of leadership in the German Lutheran Churches: 1517–1918', in Asheim and Gould, *Episcopacy*.
Loomie, A.J., *Spain and the Jacobean Catholics* (2 vols., Catholic Record Society 64 and 68, 1973 and 1979).
Lunn, D., *The English Benedictines 1540–1688* (1980).
Maccioni, P.A., and Mostert, M., 'Isaac Dorislaus (1595–1649): the career of a Dutch scholar in England', *TCBS* 8 (1984).

MacCulloch, D., 'Catholic and puritan in Elizabethan Suffolk: a county community polarises', *AfR* 72 (1981).
The Later Reformation in England, 1547–1603 (Basingstoke, 1990).
Suffolk and the Tudors (Oxford, 1986).
McGee, J.S., *The Godly Man in Stuart England* (New Haven, 1976).
McGiffert, M., 'God's controversy with Jacobean England', *American Historical Review* 88 (1983).
McKim, D.K., *Ramism in William Perkins' Theology* (New York, 1986).
McKisack, M., *Medieval History in the Tudor Age* (Oxford, 1971).
McNeill, J.T., *Unitive Protestantism* (1964).
McNulty, R., 'A Protestant version of Robert Parsons' first book of Christian exercise', *Huntington Library Quarterly* 23 (1959–60).
Malcolm, N., *De Dominis (1560–1624): Venetian, Anglican, Ecumenist, and Relapsed Heretic* (1984).
Martimort, A.-G., *Le Gallicanisme de Bossuet* (Paris, 1953).
Martin, V., *Le Gallicanisme et la réforme catholique* (Paris, 1919).
Mason, A.J., *The Church of England and Episcopacy* (Cambridge, 1914).
Mason, T.A., *Serving God and Mammon: William Juxon, 1582–1663* (Toronto, 1985).
Matthews, A.G., *Walker Revised, being a Revision of John Walker's Sufferings of the Clergy during the Grand Rebellion 1642–60* (Oxford, 1948).
Mayor, J.E.B., 'Materials for the life of Thomas Morton, bishop of Durham', *Cambridge Antiquarian Society Communications* 3 (1865).
Meilink-Roelofsz, M.A.P., van Opstall, M.E., and Schutte, G.J. (eds.), *Dutch Authors on Asian History* (Leiden, 1988).
Messenger, E.C., *The Reformation, the Mass and the Priesthood* (2 vols., 1936–7).
Meyer, A.O., 'Charles I and Rome', *American Historical Review* 19 (1913).
Milner, B.C., *Calvin's Doctrine of the Church* (Leiden, 1970).
Milton, A., '*The Unchanged Peacemaker*? John Dury and the politics of irenicism in England 1630–1643', in M. Greengrass, M. Leslie and T. Raylor (eds.), *Samuel Hartlib and Universal Reformation: Studies in Intellectual Communication* (forthcoming).
Milward, P., *Religious Controversies of the Elizabethan Age* (1977).
Religious Controversies of the Jacobean Age (1978).
Moens, W.J.C., *The Walloons and their Church at Norwich* (Lymington, 1887–8).
Morgan, I., *Prince Charles' Puritan Chaplain* (1957).
Morgan, J., *Godly Learning* (Cambridge, 1986).
Morrill, J.S., 'The attack on the Church of England in the Long Parliament, 1640–42', in D. Beales and G. Best (eds.), *History, Society and the Churches* (1985).
'The religious context of the English civil war', *TRHS* 5th ser. 34 (1984).
Morris, J., 'Restrictive practices in the Elizabethan book trade: the Stationers' Company v. Thomas Thomas 1583–88', *TCBS* 4 (1964–8).
Mullinger, J.B., *The University of Cambridge from ... 1535 to the Accession of Charles I* (Cambridge, 1854).
Nedoncelle, M., *Trois aspects du problème anglo-catholique au XVIIe siècle* (Paris, 1951).
New, J.F.H., *Anglican and Puritan* (Stanford, 1964).
Nijenhuis, W., *Adrianus Saravia* (Leiden, 1980).
'The controversy between presbyterianism and episcopalianism surrounding

and during the Synod of Dordrecht 1618–1619', in *idem*, *Ecclesia Restaurata* (Leiden, 1972).

'Resolutions of Dutch church assemblies concerning English ministers in the Hague, 1633–1651', *NAvK* 62 (1982).

Nisard, Ch., *Les Gladiateurs de la république des lettres aux XV, XVI, XVIIe siècles* (Paris, 1860).

Nobbs, D., *Theocracy and Toleration. A Study of the Disputes in Dutch Calvinism from 1600 to 1650* (Cambridge, 1938).

O'Day, R., *The English Clergy. The Emergence and Consolidation of a Profession 1558–1642* (Leicester, 1979).

Olsen, V.N., *John Foxe and the Elizabethan Church* (Berkeley, 1973).

Orr, R., *Reason and Authority. The Thought of William Chillingworth* (Oxford, 1967).

Ottley, R.L., *Lancelot Andrewes* (1894).

Pannier, J., 'Quelques lettres inédités de pasteurs écossais', *Société de l'Histoire du Protestantisme Français* 60 (1911).

Parker, G., *Europe in Crisis 1598–1648* (1981).

Parker, K.L., *The English Sabbath* (Cambridge, 1988).

Parry, G.J.R., *A Protestant Vision* (Cambridge, 1987).

Patrides, C.A., *Premises and Motifs in Renaissance Thought and Literature* (Princeton, 1982).

Patterson, W.B., 'The Anglican reaction', in Spitz and Lohff, *Discord.*

'Educating the Greeks: Anglican scholarships for Greek orthodox students in the early seventeenth century', in K. Robbins (ed.), *Religion and Humanism* (Studies in Church History 17, Oxford, 1981).

'James I and the Huguenot Synod of Tonneins of 1614', *Harvard Theological Review* 65 (1972).

'King James I's call for an ecumenical council', in G.J. Cuming and D. Baker (eds.), *Councils and Assemblies* (Studies in Church History 7, Cambridge, 1971).

'The peregrinations of Marco Antonio de Dominis 1616–24', in Baker, *Religious Motivation.*

'The Synod of Dort and the early Stuart Church', in D.S. Armentrout (ed.), *This Sacred History* (Cambridge, Mass., 1990).

Pattison, M., *Isaac Casaubon 1559–1614* (2nd edn, Oxford, 1892).

Pearson, A.F. Scott, *Thomas Cartwright and Elizabethan Puritanism 1535–1603* (Cambridge, 1925).

Peck, A.L., *Anglicanism and Episcopacy* (1958).

Platt, J.E., 'Eirenical Anglicans at the Synod of Dort', in Baker, *Reform.*

'Sixtinus Amama (1593–1629): Franeker professor and citizen of the Republic of Letters', in G.Th. Jensma, F.R.H. Smit and F. Westra (eds.), *Universiteit te Franeker 1585–1811* (Leeuwarden, 1985).

Porter, H.C., *The Inconstant Savage* (1979).

Reformation and Reaction in Tudor Cambridge (Cambridge, 1958).

Posthumus Meyjes, G.H.M., 'Jean Hotman's *Syllabus* of eirenical literature', in Baker, *Reform.*

'Protestant irenicism in the sixteenth and seventeenth centuries', in D. Loades (ed.), *The End of Strife* (Edinburgh, 1984).

Powicke, F.J., 'New light on an old English presbyterian and bookman: the Reverend Thomas Hall, B.D.', *Bulletin of the John Rylands Library* 8 (1924).

Preus, R.D., 'The influence of the formula of concord on the later Lutheran orthodoxy', in Spitz and Lohff, *Discord.*

The Theology of Post-Reformation Lutheranism (2 vols., St Louis, 1970–2).

Primus, J.H., *Holy Time* (Macon, Ga., 1989).

Pritchard, A., *Catholic Loyalism in Elizabethan England* (1979).

Quintrell, B.W., 'Lancashire's ills, the king's will and the troubling of Bishop Bridgeman', *Transactions of the Historic Society of Lancashire and Cheshire* 132 (1983 for 1982).

Raitt, J., 'The French Reformed theological response', in Spitz and Lohff, *Discord.*

Read, C., *Mr Secretary Walsingham and the Policy of Queen Elizabeth* (3 vols., Oxford, 1925).

Reeve, L.J., *Charles I and the Road to Personal Rule* (Cambridge, 1989).

Rimbault, L., *Pierre du Moulin* (Paris, 1966).

Roberts, M., 'The Swedish Church', in *idem* (ed.), *Sweden's Age of Greatness 1632–1718* (1973).

Rogers, D., 'The Catholic moderator: a French reply to Bellarmine and its English author, Henry Constable', *Recusant History* 5 (1959–60).

Rose, E., *Cases of Conscience* (1975).

Rostenberg, L., *The Minority Press and the English Crown: A Study in Repression 1558–1625* (Nieuwkoop, 1971).

Russell, C., *The Causes of the English Civil War* (Oxford, 1990).

The Fall of the British Monarchies 1637–1642 (Oxford, 1991).

Parliaments and English Politics 1621–1629 (Oxford, 1979).

Unrevolutionary England 1603–1642 (1990).

(ed.), *The Origins of the English Civil War* (1973).

Salmon, J.H.M., *Renaissance and Revolt* (Cambridge, 1987).

Sanders, V., 'The household of Archbishop Parker and the influencing of public opinion', *JEH* 34 (1983).

Schoeneveld, C.W., *Intertraffic of the Mind* (1983).

Sellin, P.R., *Daniel Heinsius and Stuart England* (Leiden, 1968).

Shaaber, M. A., *Check-list of Works of British Authors Printed Abroad, in Languages other than English, to 1641* (New York, 1975).

Sharpe, K., 'Archbishop Laud', *History Today* 33 (1983).

'Archbishop Laud and the University of Oxford', in H. Lloyd-Jones *et al.* (eds.), *History and Imagination* (1981).

'The foundation of the Chairs of History at Oxford and Cambridge: an episode in Jacobean politics', *History of Universities* 2 (1982).

The Personal Rule of Charles I (Yale, 1992).

Politics and Ideas in Early Stuart England (1989).

Sir Robert Cotton, 1568–1631. History and Politics in Early Modern England (Oxford, 1979).

Shriver, F., 'Hampton Court revisited: James I and the puritans', *JEH* 33 (1982).

'Orthodoxy and diplomacy: James I and the Vorstius affair', *EHR* 336 (1970).

Sitwell, G., 'Leander Jones' mission to England, 1634–5', *Recusant History* 5 (1959–60).

Skarsten, T.R., 'The reaction of Scandinavia', in Spitz and Lohff, *Discord.*

Skinner, Q., *The Foundations of Modern Political Thought* (2 vols., Cambridge, 1978).

Soden, G., *Godfrey Goodman, Bishop of Gloucester 1583–1656* (1953).

Solé, J., *Le Débat entre protestants et catholiques français de 1598 à 1685* (4 vols., Université de Lille, 1985).

Sommerville, J.P., *Politics and Ideology in England, 1603–1640* (1986).
'The royal supremacy and episcopacy "jure divino", 1603–1640', *JEH* 34 (1983).
Sommerville, M.R., 'Richard Hooker and his contemporaries on episcopacy: an Elizabethan consensus', *JEH* 35 (1984).
Spitz, L.W., and Lohff, W. (eds.), *Discord, Dialogue and Concord. Studies in the Lutheran Reformation's Formula of Concord* (Philadelphia, 1977).
Sprunger, K.L., *Dutch Puritanism. A History of English and Scottish Churches of the Netherlands in the Sixteenth and Seventeenth Centuries* (Leiden, 1982).
The Learned Doctor William Ames (Urbana, 1972).
Spurr, J., *The Restoration Church of England, 1646–1689* (New Haven, 1991).
Stanwood, P.G., 'Crashaw at Rome', *Notes and Queries* 211 (1966).
Stearns, R.P., *Congregationalism in the Dutch Netherlands* (1940).
Sykes, N., *The Church of England and Non-Episcopal Churches in the Sixteenth & Seventeenth Centuries* (1949).
Old Priest and New Presbyter (Cambridge, 1956).
Tavard, G.H., *The Quest for Catholicity* (1963).
The Seventeenth Century Tradition (Leiden, 1978).
Thomas, K.V., *Religion and the Decline of Magic* (1971).
Tighe, W.J., 'William Laud and the reunion of the churches: some evidence from 1637 and 1638', *HJ* 30 (1987).
Todd, M., '"An act of discretion": evangelical conformity and the puritan dons', *Albion* 18 (1986).
Toon, P. (ed.), *Puritans, the Millennium and the Future of Israel* (1970).
Trevor-Roper, H.R., *Archbishop Laud 1573–1645* (3rd edn, 1988).
Catholics, Anglicans and Puritans (1987).
'The Church of England and the Greek Church in the time of Charles I', in Baker, *Religious Motivation*.
Tukker, C.A., 'Gerson Bucerus – Jakobus I – De Statenvertaling', *NAvK* 50 (1969–70).
Turnbull, G., *Hartlib, Dury, and Comenius: Gleanings from Hartlib's Papers* (Liverpool, 1947).
Tyacke, N., *Anti-Calvinists. The Rise of English Arminianism c.1590–1640* (Oxford, 1987).
The Fortunes of English Puritanism, 1603–1640 (1990).
'Puritanism, Arminianism and Counter-Revolution', in Russell, *Origins*.
'The rise of Arminianism reconsidered', *P&P* 115 (1987).
Tyrrell, E.P., and Simmons, J.S.G., 'Slavonic books before 1700 in Cambridge libraries', *TCBS* 3 (1959–63).
Underdown, D., *Fire from Heaven* (1992).
Vance, N., *Irish Literature: A Social History* (Oxford, 1990).
Venn, J., and Venn, J.A. (eds.), *Alumni Cantabrigiensis . . . Pt 1* (4 vols., 1922–7).
Venn, J., *et al.*, *Biographical History of Gonville and Caius College* (7 vols., Cambridge, 1897–1978).
Vivanti, C., *Lotta politica e pace religiosa in Francia fra Cinque e Seicento* (Turin, 1963).
Wadkins, T.H., 'King James I meets John Percy, S.J. (26 May, 1622)', *Recusant History* 19 (1988–9).
Walker, D.P., *Unclean Spirits* (1981).
Wallace, D.D., 'The Anglican appeal to Lutheran sources: Philip Melanchthon's

reputation in seventeenth-century England', *Historical Magazine of the Protestant Episcopalian Church* 52 (1983).
'Puritan and Anglican: the interpretation of Christ's descent into hell in Elizabethan theology', *AfR* 69 (1978).
Puritans and Predestination: Grace in English Protestant Theology 1525–1695 (Chapel Hill, 1982).
Wallis, P.J., 'The library of William Crashaw', *TCBS* 2 (1956).
Watt, T., *Cheap Print and Popular Piety* (Cambridge, 1991).
Weiner, C.Z., 'The beleaguered isle. A study of Elizabethan and early Jacobean anticatholicism', *P&P* 51 (1971).
Welsby, P., *Lancelot Andrewes 1555–1626* (1964).
Westin, G., 'Brev från John Durie åren 1636–1638', *Kyrkohistorisk Årsskrift: Skrifter Utgivna Av Kyrkohistorika Foreningen* 1/33 (Uppsala, 1934).
Negotiations about Church Unity 1628–1634 (Uppsala Universitets Årsskrift, 1932).
Whaley, J., *Religious Toleration and Social Change in Hamburg 1529–1819* (Cambridge, 1985).
White, B.R., *The English Separatist Tradition* (Oxford, 1971).
White, P., *Predestination, Policy and Polemic* (Cambridge, 1992).
'A rejoinder', *P&P* 115 (1987).
'The rise of Arminianism reconsidered', *P&P* 101 (1983).
'The *via media* of the early Stuart Church', in K. Fincham (ed.), *The Early Stuart Church* (1993).
Whiting, G.W., 'Paraeus, the Stuarts, Laud and Milton', *Studies in Philology* 1 (1953).
Wijminga, P.J., *Festus Hommius* (Leiden, 1899).
Willson, D.H., 'James I and his literary assistants', *Huntington Library Quarterly* 8 (1944–5).
Woodhouse, H.F., *The Doctrine of the Church in Anglican Theology 1547–1603* (1954).
Wootton, D., *Paolo Sarpi* (Cambridge, 1983).
Woude, C. van der, *Sibrandus Lubbertus leven en werken* (Kampen, 1963).
Zaller, R., '"Interest of state": James I and the Palatinate', *Albion* 6 (1974).

THESES

Abbott, W.M., 'The issue of episcopacy in the Long Parliament, 1640–1648: the reasons for abolition', Oxford University DPhil, 1981.
Adams, S., 'The Protestant cause: religious alliance with the West European Calvinist communities as a political issue in England, 1585–1630', Oxford University DPhil, 1973.
Bauckham, R.J., 'The career and theology of Dr. William Fulke, 1537–89', Cambridge University PhD, 1973.
Borschberg, P., 'State and church in the early politico-religious works of Hugo Grotius', Cambridge University PhD, 1990.
Fincham, K.C., 'Pastoral roles of the Jacobean episcopate in Canterbury province', London University PhD, 1985.
Foster, A.W., 'A biography of Archbishop Richard Neile, 1562–1640', Oxford University DPhil, 1978.
Frank, G.L.C., 'The theology of eucharistic presence in the early Caroline divines,

examined in its European theological setting', University of St Andrews PhD, 1985.

Fuggles, J.F., 'A history of the library of St. John's College, Oxford', Oxford University BLitt, 1975.

Gifford, J.V., 'The controversy over the Oath of Allegiance', Oxford University DPhil, 1971.

Grayson, J.C., 'From protectorate to partnership: Anglo-Dutch relations 1598–1625', London University DPhil, 1978.

Hoyle, D.M., 'Near popery yet no popery. Theological debate in Cambridge 1590–1644', Cambridge University PhD, 1991.

Macauley, J.S., 'Richard Montague Caroline bishop, 1575–1641', Cambridge University PhD, 1965.

Milton, A., 'The Laudians and the Church of Rome, c.1625–1640', Cambridge University PhD, 1989.

Questier, M.C., 'The phenomenon of conversion: change of religion to and from Catholicism in England, 1580–1625', University of Sussex DPhil, 1991.

Raymer, V.E., 'Durham House and the emergence of Laudian piety', Harvard University PhD, 1983.

Sommerville, J.P., 'Jacobean political thought and the controversy over the Oath of Allegiance', Cambridge University PhD, 1981.

Wadkins, T.H., 'Theological polemic and religious culture in early Stuart England', Graduate Theological Union, Berkeley, Calif., PhD, 1988.

Windsor, G., 'The controversy between Roman Catholics and Anglicans from Elizabeth to the Revolution', Cambridge University PhD, 1967.

INDEX

Cambridge Studies in Early Modern British History

Titles in the series

*The Common Peace: Participation and the Criminal Law in Seventeenth-Century England**
CYNTHIA B. HERRUP

Politics, Society and Civil War in Warwickshire, 1620–1660
ANN HUGHES

*London Crowds in the Reign of Charles II: Propaganda and Politics from the Restoration to the Exclusion Crisis**
TIM HARRIS

*Criticism and Compliment: The Politics of Literature in the England of Charles I**
KEVIN SHARPE

Central Government and the Localities: Hampshire, 1649–1689
ANDREW COLEBY

John Skelton and the Politics of the 1520s
GREG WALKER

Algernon Sidney and the English Republic, 1623–1677
JONATHAN SCOTT

Thomas Starkey and the Commonwealth: Humanist Politics and Religion in the Reign of Henry VIII
THOMAS F. MAYER

*The Blind Devotion of the People: Popular Religion and the English Reformation**
ROBERT WHITING

The Cavalier Parliament and the Reconstruction of the Old Regime, 1661–1667
PAUL SEAWARD

The Blessed Revolution: English Politics and the Coming of War, 1621–1624
THOMAS COGSWELL

Charles I and the Road to Personal Rule
L. J. REEVE

George Lawson's 'Politica' and the English Revolution
CONAL CONDREN

Puritans and Roundheads: The Harleys of Brampton Bryan and the Outbreak of the English Civil War
JACQUELINE EALES

An Uncounselled King: Charles I and the Scottish Troubles, 1637–1641
PETER DONALD

*Cheap Print and Popular Piety, 1550–1640**
TESSA WATT

The Pursuit of Stability: Social Relations in Elizabethan London
IAN W. ARCHER

Prosecution and Punishment: Petty Crime and the Law in London and Rural Middlesex, c. 1660–1725
ROBERT B. SHOEMAKER

Algernon Sidney and the Restoration Crisis, 1677–1683
JONATHAN SCOTT

Exile and Kingdom: History and Apocalypse in the Puritan Migration to America
AVIHU ZAKAI

The Pillars of Priestcraft Shaken: The Church of England and its Enemies, 1660–1730
J. A. I. CHAMPION

Stewards, Lords and People: The Estate Steward and his World in Later Stuart England
D. R. HAINSWORTH

Civil War and Restoration in the Three Stuart Kingdoms: The Career of Randal MacDonnell, Marquis of Antrim, 1609–1683
JANE H. OHLMEYER

The Family of Love in English Society, 1550–1630
CHRISTOPHER W. MARSH

*The Bishops' Wars: Charles I's Campaigns against Scotland, 1638–1640**
MARK FISSEL

*John Locke: Resistance, Religion and Responsibility**
JOHN MARSHALL

Constitutional Royalism and the Search for Settlement, c. 1640–1649
DAVID L. SMITH

Intelligence and Espionage in the Reign of Charles II, 1660–1685
ALAN MARSHALL

The Chief Governors: The Rise and Fall of Reform Government in Tudor Ireland, 1536–1588
CIARAN BRADY

Politics and Opinion in Crisis, 1678–1681
MARK KNIGHTS

Catholic and Reformed: The Roman and Protestant Churches in English Protestant Thought, 1604–1640
ANTHONY MILTON

Sir Matthew Hale, 1609–1676: Law, Religion and Natural Philosophy
ALAN CROMARTIE

* *Also published as a paperback*

CYBERLAW

NEWSWORTHY

SEE THE INSIDE BACK COVER FOR MORE EXAMPLES OF EXCITING FEATURES.

Legal Environment

For A New Century

Jeffrey F. Beatty
Boston University

Susan S. Samuelson
Boston University

Australia · Canada · Mexico · Singapore · Spain · United Kingdom · United States

THOMSON
SOUTH-WESTERN
WEST

Legal Environment for a New Century
Jeffrey F. Beatty and Susan S. Samuelson

Editor-in-Chief:
Jack W. Calhoun

Team Leader:
Michael P. Roche

Sr. Acquisitions Editor:
Rob Dewey

Developmental Editor:
Bob Sandman

Marketing Manager:
Nicole C. Moore

Production Editor:
Starratt E. Alexander

Manufacturing Coordinator:
Rhonda Utley

Compositor & Production House:
Navta Associates, Inc.

Printer:
R.R. Donnelley & Sons Company
Willard Manufacturing Division

Permissions Editor:
Lorretta Palagi
Quantum Publishing Services, Inc.

Design Project Manager:
Michelle Kunkler

Internal Design:
Imbue Design/Kim Torbeck, Cincinnati

Cover Designer:
Paul Neff Design

Cover Photo:
Don Wong

Printed in the United States of America
2 3 4 5 04 03 02

For more information contact West Legal Studies in Business, 5191 Natorp Boulevard, Mason, Ohio 45040.
Or you can visit our Internet site at: http://www.westbuslaw.com

Library of Congress Cataloging-in-Publication Data

Beatty, Jeffrey F.
The legal environment for a new century / Jeffrey F. Beatty, Susan S. Samuelson.
p. cm.
Rev. ed. of: Business law for a new century. 2nd ed. c2001.
Includes bibliographical references and index.
ISBN 0-324-01657-3 (alk. paper)
1. Commercial law--United States. 2. Law--United States. I. Samuelson, Susan S. II. Beatty, Jeffrey F. Business law for a new century. III. Title.
KF888 .B37 2002
346.7307--dc21
2001055144

ISBN: 0-324-01657-3

Absolutely Authoritative …

UNDENIABLY ENGAGING

BEATTY
SAMUELSON

LEGAL ENVIRONMENT

Beatty and Samuelson's *Legal Environment for a New Century* brings you:

- **Dynamic writing** that clarifies concepts
- **Outstanding examples** that bring the law to life
- **Practical applications** that encourage independent thinking.

Dear Colleague:

We wrote *Legal Environment for A New Century* as if we were speaking directly to our students. As authors and educators, we have learned over the years that we can teach at our best when our students are intrigued. *Legal Environment for a New Century* provides this intrigue while also imparting the fine details of the law.

In our text, the book's accessible presentation goes hand in hand with legal precision. When students are captivated by the true drama of the law – the conflicts between people, organizations, and even government – they're more eager and willing to read on and learn more.

On the following pages you'll come to see how *Legal Environment* offers you authoritative coverage that is indisputably accurate and an engaging narrative that excites students and shares the drama of the law.

Our standard: Every professor who adopts our text must have a superior teaching experience. We believe we have crafted just the right text to meet this goal. We look forward to teaching with you in the coming terms.

Sincerely,

Jeffrey F. Beatty
Boston University

Susan S. Samuelson
Boston University

Dynamic Writing

While its authoritative coverage gains the respect of professors, *Legal Environment for a New Century's* strong narrative will undoubtedly win over the students. The authors' straight-forward and engaging style provides a rich context for the remarkable quantity of legal material presented.

Chapter-opening vignettes immediately draw students into the chapter's material by illustrating the issues and providing context. For example, Chapter 11 on sales and product liability opens with entrepreneurs Harold and Maude, each of whom has made what they believed was an enforceable agreement, Harold for the sale of his land and Maude for the purchase of toy robots. But only one of them stands to gain money based on the Uniform Commercial Code (UCC). Students are naturally drawn in and are encouraged to learn more about sales and product liability.

Sales, Product Liability, and Negotiable Instruments

11

CHAPTER

He Sued, She Sued. Harold and Maude made a great couple because both were compulsive entrepreneurs. One evening they sat on their penthouse roof deck, overlooking the twinkling Chicago skyline. Harold sipped a decaf coffee while negotiating, over the phone, with a real estate developer in San Antonio. Maude puffed a cigar as she bargained on a different line with a toy manufacturer in Cleveland. They hung up at the same time. "I did it!" shrieked Maude, "I made an incredible deal for the robots—five bucks each!" "No, I did it!" triumphed Harold, "I sold the 50 acres in Texas for $300,000 more than it's worth." They dashed indoors.

Maude quickly scrawled a handwritten memo, which read, "Confirming our deal—100,000 Psychopath Robots—you deliver Chicago—end of summer." She didn't mention a price, or an exact delivery date, or when payment would be made. She signed her memo and faxed it to the toy manufacturer. Harold took more time. He typed a thorough contract, describing precisely the land he was selling, the $2.3 million price, how and when each payment would be made, and the deed conveyed. He signed the contract and faxed it, along with a plot plan showing the surveyed land. Then the happy couple grabbed a bottle of champagne, returned to the deck—and placed a side bet on whose contract would prove more profitable. The loser would have to cook and serve dinner for six months.

Law is notoriously complex, but with trademark style, Beatty and Samuelson are able to make even the most difficult concepts easy to understand. For example, through their dynamic writing, the authors are able to bring students to an understanding of the Uniform Commercial Code (UCC)—something that's ancient in origin, contemporary in usage, admirable in purpose, and flawed in application.

HAROLD AND MAUDE, REVISITED

Harold and Maude each negotiated what they believed was an enforceable agreement, and both filed suit: Harold for the sale of his land, Maude for the purchase of toy robots. Only one prevailed. The difference in outcome demonstrates why everyone in business needs a working knowledge of the Code. As we revisit the happy couple, Harold is clearing the dinner dishes. Maude sits back in her chair, lights a cigar, and compliments her husband on the apple tart.

Harold's contract was for the sale of land and was governed by the common law of contracts, which requires any agreement for the sale of land to be in writing and *signed by the defendant,* in this case the buyer in Texas. Harold signed it, but the buyer never did, so Harold's meticulously detailed document was worth less than a five-cent cigar.

Maude's quickly scribbled memorandum, concerning robot toys, was for the sale of goods and was governed by Article 2 of the UCC. The Code requires less detail and formality in a writing. Because Maude and the seller were both merchants, the document she scribbled could be enforced *even against the defendant,* who had never signed anything. The fact that Maude left out the price and other significant terms was not fatal to a contract under the UCC, though under the common law such omissions would have made the bargain unenforceable.

SCOPE OF ARTICLE 2

Because the UCC changes the common law, it is essential to know whether the Code applies in a given case. Negotiations may lead to an enforceable agreement when the UCC applies, even though the same bargaining would create no contract under the common law.

UCC §2-102: Article 2 applies to the sale of goods.[1] **Goods are things that are movable, other than money and investment securities.** Hats are goods, and so are railroad cars, lumber, books, and bottles of wine. Land is not a good, nor is a house. Article 2 regulates sales, which means that one party transfers title to the other in exchange for money. If you sell your motorcycle to a friend, that is a sale of goods.[2]

MERCHANTS

The UCC evolved to provide merchants with rules that would meet their unique business needs. However, while the UCC offers a contract law that is more flexible than the common law, it also requires a higher level of responsibility from the merchants it serves. Those who make a living by crafting agreements are expected to understand the legal consequences of their words and deeds. Thus

[1] Officially, Article 2 tells us that it applies to *transactions* in goods, which is a slightly broader category than sale of goods. But most sections of Article 2, and most court decisions, focus exclusively on sales, and so shall we.

[2] Because leasing is so important, the drafters of the Code added Article 2A to cover the subject. Article 2A is similar to Article 2, but there are important differences, and anyone engaging in a significant amount of commercial leasing must become familiar with Article 2A. For our purposes, leasing law is a variation on the theme of Article 2, and we will concentrate on the principal melody of sales.

OUTSTANDING EXAMPLES

BEATTY AND SAMUELSON ILLUSTRATE THE POWER AND EXCITEMENT OF THE LAW THROUGH A VARIETY OF INTRIGUING EXAMPLES. WHETHER THEY'RE TRUE-TO-LIFE OR SLIGHTLY EMBELLISHED, THESE EXAMPLES AND STORIES KEEP STUDENTS INTERESTED AND ENCOURAGE THEM TO ARRIVE IN CLASS EAGER TO QUESTION, DISCUSS, AND LEARN.

The authors bring the law to life through numerous excerpted cases in the language of the court. Each case begins with the facts followed by a statement of both the issue and the decision. This presentation makes the judges' reasoning accessible to all readers, while retaining the court's focus and the decision's impact.

CHAPTER 11 • SALES, PRODUCT LIABILITY, AND NEGOTIABLE INSTRUMENTS

Code Provisions Discussed in This Case

Issue	Relevant Code Selection
1. Was this farmer a a "merchant"?	UCC §2-104: A merchant is anyone who routinely deals in the goods involved (or has special knowledge or an agent with such knowledge).
2. Did the memo satisfy the status of frauds?	UCC §2-201(2), the "merchant exception": When two merchants make an oral contract, and one sends a confirming memo to the other within a reasonable time, and the memo is sufficiently definite that it could be enforced against the sender herself, then the memo is also valid against the merchant who receives it, unless he objects within ten days.

COLORADO-KANSAS GRAIN CO. V. REIFSCHNEIDER
817 P.2d 637, 1991 Colo. App. LEXIS 259
Colorado Court of Appeals, 1991

Facts: Albert Reifschneider had been a farmer for 30 years. He owned and operated a 160-acre farm in Colorado. The Colorado-Kansas Grain Co. (CKG) bought and sold agricultural commodities, such as grain. CKG negotiated with Reifschneider to buy corn from him. The parties agreed that CKG would buy 12,500 bushels of corn at a market price of $2.25 per bushel, but Reifschneider told CKG that the deal would have to be approved by the First National Bank, which had loaned him money to grow the crop.

The parties talked with the First National, which approved the sale at the agreed-upon price. Reifschneider told CKG to draw up a contract reflecting the agreement. CKG prepared a written confirmation of the oral agreement, signed it, and mailed it to Reifschneider with instructions to sign it and return the original. Two months later, after Reifschneider had several more conversations with CKG, the farmer informed the company that he would not sign the agreement and believed that they did not have a deal.

CKG purchased 12,500 bushels elsewhere at a higher cost and filed suit. The trial court gave judgment for CKG, concluding that Reifschneider was a merchant and that therefore CKG's memo was binding against him. Reifschneider appealed.

Issues: Was Reifschneider a "merchant"? Did the memo satisfy the statute of frauds?

Excerpts from Judge Jones's Decision: Defendant next contends that the trial court erred in its conclusion that he was a merchant under the UCC. He argues that, for purposes of contract formation regarding the statute of frauds, he is not a merchant and that, therefore, any contract between him and plaintiff cannot be enforced because it was not in writing. We perceive no error.

The question of whether a farmer is or can be a merchant for purposes of this UCC provision has not been addressed in Colorado. The courts among those states which have dealt with this issue are almost evenly split on whether a farmer can be a merchant.

We note that the cases which hold that farmers may be merchants reflect on the fact that today's farmer is involved in far more than simply planting and harvesting crops. Indeed, many farmers possess an extensive knowledge and sophistication regarding the purchase and sale of crops on the various agricultural markets. Often, they are more aptly described as agri-businessmen. Thus, we conclude that, for purposes of [2-201(2)] a farmer may be a merchant.

Beatty and Samuelson use humor judiciously to lighten and enlighten. While taking the law seriously, the authors also employ a certain amount of levity to help students better retain the material. Here, the authors use humor to illustrate important legal points of product liability.

in holding the goods and reselling them, costs such as storage, shipping, and advertising for resale. The seller must deduct expenses saved by the breach. For example, if the contract required the seller to ship heavy machinery from Detroit to San Diego, and the buyer's breach enables the seller to market its goods profitably in Detroit, the seller must deduct from its claimed losses the transportation costs that it saved.

Finally, the seller may simply **sue for the contract price**, if the buyer has accepted the goods *or if* the goods are conforming and resale is impossible.[11] If the goods were manufactured to the buyer's unique specifications, there might be no other market for them, and the seller should receive the contract price.

WARRANTIES AND PRODUCT LIABILITY

You are sitting in a fast-food restaurant in Washington, D.C. Your friend Ben, who works for a congressman, is eating with one hand and gesturing with the other. "We want product liability reform and we want it now," he proclaims, stabbing the air with his free hand. "It's absurd, these multimillion dollar verdicts, just because something has a *slight defect*." He waves angrily at the absurdity, takes a ferocious bite from his burger—and with a loud CRACK breaks a tooth. Ben howls in pain and throws down the bun, revealing a large piece of bone in the meat. As he tips back in misery, his defectively manufactured chair collapses, and Ben slams into the tile, knocking himself unconscious. Hours later, when he revives in the hospital, he refuses to speak to you until he talks with his lawyer. They will discuss **product liability**, which refers to goods that have caused an injury. The harm may be physical, as it was in Ben's case. Or it can be purely economic, as when a corporation buys a computer so defective it must be replaced, costing the buyer lost time and profits. The injured party may have a choice of possible remedies, including:

- *Warranty*, which is an assurance provided in a sales contract
- *Negligence*, which refers to unreasonable conduct by the defendant; and
- *Strict liability*, which prohibits defective products whether the defendant acted reasonably or not.

We discuss each of these remedies in this chapter. What all product liability cases have in common is that a person or business has been hurt by goods. We begin with warranties.

EXPRESS WARRANTIES

A warranty is a contractual assurance that goods will meet certain standards. It is normally a manufacturer or a seller who gives a warranty, and a buyer who relies on it. A warranty might be explicit and written: "The manufacturer

[11] UCC §2-709.

PRACTICAL APPLICATIONS

STUDENTS DEVELOP INDEPENDENT THINKING SKILLS THROUGH *LEGAL ENVIRONMENT FOR A NEW CENTURY'S* STRONG FOCUS ON APPLICATIONS. BECAUSE STUDENTS LEARN BY DOING, BEATTY AND SAMUELSON OFFER A DIVERSE RANGE OF FEATURES THAT HELP THEM UNDERSTAND THE LAW FROM THE INSIDE OUT.

Students are encouraged to think independently with *You Be the Judge*.
This feature provides the facts of a case and the conflicting appellate arguments. The court's decision, however, appears only in the Instructor's Manual. For example, *You Be the Judge* in Chapter 5 (Constitutional Law) takes on Barnes v. Glen Theatre, Inc. Exotic dancers in Indiana feel they have a right to perform nude, despite the state's public indecency statute that prohibits any person from appearing nude in a public place. Does Indiana's statute violate the First Amendment? Students hear both sides, they must then reach their own decision, building on their critical thinking skills.

If the trial court finds that the answer to all three of those questions is "yes," it may judge the material obscene; the state may then prohibit the work. If the state fails to prove any one of the three criteria, though, the work is not obscene. A United States District Court ruled that "As Nasty As They Wanna Be," recorded by 2 Live Crew, was obscene. The appeals court, however, reversed, finding that the state had failed to prove lack of artistic merit.[19]

What if sexual conduct is not obscene? Let's go back to the chapter's starting point, nude dancing.

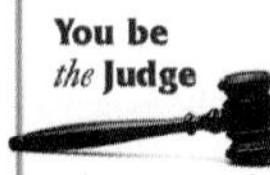

BARNES V. GLEN THEATRE, INC.
501 U.S. 560, 111 S. Ct. 2456, 1991 U.S. LEXIS 3633
United States Supreme Court, 1991

Facts: Indiana's public indecency statute prohibits any person from appearing nude in a public place. State courts have interpreted this to mean that a dancer in a theater or bar must wear pasties and a G-string. A nightclub called the Kitty Kat Lounge and several dancers who wished to perform nude filed suit, seeking an order that the statute was unconstitutional. The United States District Court ruled that the dancing was not expressive conduct and therefore was not entitled to First Amendment protection. The Court of Appeals reversed, declaring that it was nonobscene expressive conduct and thus protected by the First Amendment.

Indiana did not argue that the dancing was obscene. (If that were the issue, the *Miller* test would have determined the outcome.) Instead, Indiana claimed that its general police powers, including the power to protect social order, allowed it to enforce such a statute.

You Be the Judge: Does Indiana's public indecency statute violate the First Amendment?

Argument for Indiana: Your honors, the State of Indiana has no wish to suppress ideas or censor speech. We are not trying to outlaw eroticism or any other legitimate form of expression. We are simply prohibiting nudity in public. We have outlawed all public nudity, not just nightclub performances. Nudity on the beach, in the park, or anywhere in public is prohibited.

We do this to protect societal order, to foster a stable morality. It is well established that the police power of the state includes the right to regulate the public health, safety, and morals. Our citizens disapprove of people appearing in the nude in public places. The citizens of virtually all states feel the same. Decent dress has been a part of good society since time immemorial. Our voting public is entitled to have that standard upheld.

We also enforce this statute because experience has shown that nightclubs such as these are often associated with criminal behavior. Prostitution, illegal drugs, and violence appear too frequently in the vicinity. It is a reasonable step for the State to maintain control over the performances and the people they will attract.

Argument for Kitty Kat: It is apparent beyond debate that dance is expressive conduct. As an art form it has existed for at least several thousand years. Eroticism, also, is not exactly news. Erotic dance is clearly expressive conduct. Indeed, the present dancing derives its strength from its eroticism. If the State did not consider it erotic, doubtless it would have left the dancers alone. This dancing is expressive conduct and deserves the full protection of the First Amendment.

Indiana is choosing a certain type of expression and outlawing it. The state has not outlawed all nudity, since quite obviously nudity in private is beyond the State's reach. Nor has it prohibited all nude performances. Testimony of police at

[19] *Luke Records, Inc. v. Navarro*, 960 F.2d 134, 1992 U.S. App. LEXIS 9592 (11th Cir. 1992).

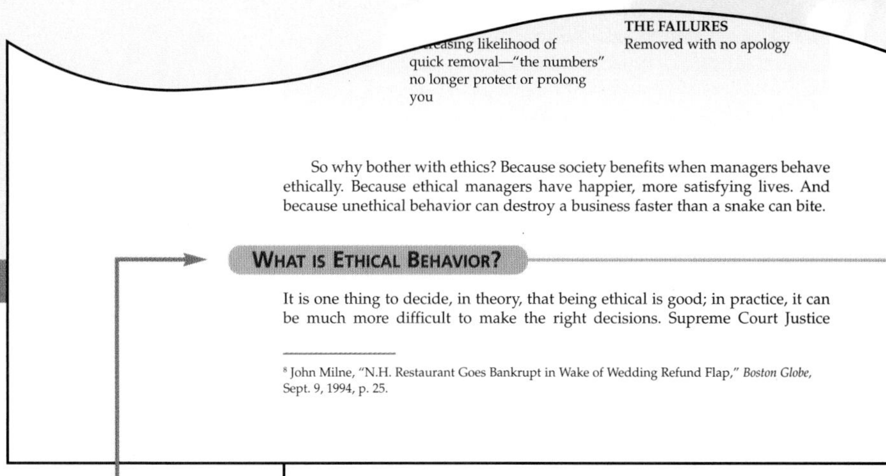

	THE FAILURES
...easing likelihood of quick removal—"the numbers" no longer protect or prolong you	Removed with no apology

So why bother with ethics? Because society benefits when managers behave ethically. Because ethical managers have happier, more satisfying lives. And because unethical behavior can destroy a business faster than a snake can bite.

What is Ethical Behavior?

It is one thing to decide, in theory, that being ethical is good; in practice, it can be much more difficult to make the right decisions. Supreme Court Justice

[8] John Milne, "N.H. Restaurant Goes Bankrupt in Wake of Wedding Refund Flap," *Boston Globe*, Sept. 9, 1994, p. 25.

Beatty and Samuelson move students beyond the theory of ethics to the practical application of ethical behavior. The authors provide students with an ethics checklist that will aid them in making tough decisions. Students are then asked to apply what they've learned to a number of situations. In addition, *Right and Wrong* features, throughout the text, ask ethical questions about cases, legal issues, and commercial practices.

Potter Stewart once said that he could not define pornography, but he knew it when he saw it. Many people feel the same way about ethics—that somehow, instinctively, they know what is right and wrong. In real life, however, ethical dilemmas are often not black and white, but many shades of gray. The purpose of this section is to analyze the following ethics checklist as an aid to managers in making tough decisions:

- What are the facts?
- What are the critical issues?
- Who are the stakeholders?
- What are the alternatives?
- What are the ethical implications of each alternative?
  - Is it legal?
  - How would it look in the light of day?
  - What are the consequences?
  - Does it violate important values?
  - Does it violate the Golden Rule?
  - Is it just?
  - Has the process been fair?
- Is more than one alternative right?
  - Which values are in conflict?
  - Which of these values are most important?
  - Can you find an alternative that is consistent with your values?

Analyzing the Ethics Checklist

What Are the Facts?

Although this question seems obvious, people often forget in the heat of battle to listen to (and, more importantly, to *hear*) all the different viewpoints. Instead of relying on hearsay and rumor, it is crucial to discover the facts, firsthand, from the people involved. It may be easy to condemn a bank robber, until learning the money was needed to buy medicine.

What Are the Critical Issues?

In analyzing ethical dilemmas, expand your thinking to include *all* the important issues. Avoid a narrow focus that encompasses only one or two aspects. In the case of the New Hampshire restaurant that refused to refund a deposit, the owner focused on the narrow legal issue. His interpretation of the *contract* was correct. But if the owner had expanded his thinking to include consideration for his customers, he might have reached a different decision.

CONTENTS: OVERVIEW

CONTENTS

CHAPTER 8

CHAPTER 9

CHAPTER 10

CONCLUSION TO CONTRACTS 261

CHAPTER 11

SALES, PRODUCT LIABILITY, AND NEGOTIABLE INSTRUMENTS 293

BUSINESS ORGANIZATIONS 455

CHAPTER 18

SECURITIES REGULATION 515

GOVERNMENT REGULATION AND PROPERTY 547

CHAPTER 19

ANTITRUST 548

CHAPTER 20

CYBERLAW 573

CHAPTER 21

INTELLECTUAL PROPERTY WITH CYBERLAW 599

CHAPTER 22

PROPERTY 624

PREFACE

We wrote this book to convey our passion for an exciting and profoundly important discipline. The law is notoriously complex, and as authors we are obsessed with accuracy. Yet this intriguing subject also abounds with human conflict and hard-earned wisdom, forces that can make a law book sparkle. We are grateful to the faculty who tell us that this legal environment textbook is precise and authoritative *yet a pleasure to read.* Here are some of the book's key features:

Authoritative. We insist, as you do, on a lawbook that is indisputably accurate. A professor must teach with assurance, confident that every paragraph is the result of exhaustive research and meticulous presentation. Dozens of tough-minded people spent thousands of hours reviewing this book, and we are delighted with the stamp of approval we have received from trial and appellate judges, working attorneys, scholars and teachers.

We reject the cloudy definitions and fuzzy explanations that can invade judicial opinions and legal scholarship. To highlight the most important rules, we use bold print, and then follow with vivacious examples written in clear, forceful English. (See, for example, the description of assault, on page 146.) We cheerfully venture into contentious areas, relying on very recent appellate decisions. (Can computer software be patented? See page 602.) Where there is doubt about the current (or future) status of a doctrine, we say so. In areas of particularly heated debate, we footnote our work: we want you to have absolute trust in this book.

Strong Narrative. The law is full of great stories, and we use them. Your students and ours should come to class excited. In Chapter 3, on dispute resolution (page 49), we explain litigation by tracking a double-indemnity lawsuit. An executive is dead. Did he drown accidentally, obligating the insurance company to pay? Or did the businessman commit suicide, voiding the policy? The student follows the action from the discovery of the body, through each step of the lawsuit, to the final appeal. The chapter offers a detailed discussion of dispute resolution, but it does so by exploiting the human drama that underlies litigation.

Students read stories and remember them. Strong narratives provide a rich context for the remarkable quantity of legal material presented. When students care about the material they are reading, they persevere. We have been delighted to find that they also arrive in class eager to question, discuss and learn.

Precise. The great joy of using English accurately is the power it gives us to attack and dissect difficult issues, rendering them comprehensible to any lay reader. This text takes on the most complex legal topics of the day, yet it is appropriate for *all college and graduate level students*. Accessible prose goes hand in hand with legal precision. We take great pride in walking our readers through the most serpentine mazes this tough subject can offer. UCC section 2-207, on "battle of forms" conflicts, is hardly sexy material, but it is important. We spotlight the real-world need for section 2-207, and then use pin-point directions to guide our readers through its many switchbacks, arriving at a full understanding with sanity and good humor intact. (See page 243.)

As we explore this extraordinary discipline, we lure readers along with quirky anecdotes and colorful diagrams. (Notice that the color display on page 499 clarifies the complex rules of the duty of care in the business judgment rule.) However, before the trip is over we insist that students:

- gauge policy and political considerations,
- grapple with legal and social history,
- spot the nexus between disparate doctrines, and
- confront tough moral choices.

Beyond that, we demand that students incorporate all of these ideas in preventive law analyses, figuring out how to avoid the very problems that have generated our law.

Comprehensive. Staying comprehensive means staying current. Look, for example, at the important field of corporate governance. All texts cover par value, and so do we. Yet a future executive is far likelier to face conflicts over board composition, executive compensation, and shareholder proposals. We present a clear path through this thicket of new issues. We want tomorrow's business leaders to anticipate the challenges that await them and then use their knowledge to avert problems.

This book also provides full coverage of rapidly evolving issues such as cyberlaw, international law, UCC revisions, and countless other topics. For example, the book contains a full chapter on cyberlaw. A second chapter, on intellectual property, includes cyberlaw issues unique to that discipline. Finally, throughout the text we discuss still more cyberlaw issues as they relate to the particular topic; icons highlight those sections. However, this comprehensive coverage does not impede the strong narrative flow. Like you, we are here to teach. We do not use boxes because, in our experience, they disrupt the flow of the text. Students inform us that a box indicates peripheral material, that is, material they routinely skip; we prefer to give them an uncluttered whole. Each chapter also contains several Internet addresses, offering students a quick link to additional knowledge. These addresses, however, are woven into the body of the text, to reinforce the point that new technology and research methods are an integral part of a lively discipline. For example, on page 347, in the chapter on bankruptcy, we provide a Web site that enables students to read about up-to-the minute developments in bankruptcy law. Or in the chapter on starting a business (Chapter 16), students can go to a Web site that offers a sample operating agreement for a limited liability company. We believe that a well-written chapter is seamless and cohesive.

A Book for Students. We have written this book as if we were speaking directly to our students. We provide black letter law, but we also explain concepts in terms that hook students. Over the years, we have learned how much more successfully we can teach when our students are intrigued. No matter what kind of a show we put on in class, *they are only learning when they want to learn.*

Every chapter begins with a story, either fictional or real, to illustrate the issues in the chapter and provide context. Chapter 20 on Cyberlaw begins with the true story of a college student who discovers nude pictures of himself online. These photos had been taken in the locker room without his knowledge. What privacy rights do any of us have? Does the Internet jeopardize them? Students want to know—right away.

Most of today's students were not yet born when Gerald Ford was president. They come to college with varying levels of preparation; many now arrive from other countries. We have found that to teach business law most effectively we must provide its context. Chapter 18 on securities regulation begins with a brief but graphic description of the 1929 stock market crash and the Great Depression (page 515). Only with this background do students grasp the importance and impact of our securities laws.

At the same time, we enjoy offering "nuts and bolts" information that grabs students: how much money corporate directors earn; how scam artists create car accidents in order to file fraudulent insurance claim; how to register an Internet domain name. In Chapter 23, on consumer law, we bring home the issue of credit history by providing phone numbers and Web sites that students can use to check their own credit reports (page 671).

Students respond enthusiastically to this approach. Along with other professors, we have used this text in courses for undergraduates, MBAs and executive MBAs, the students ranging in age from 18 to 55. The book works, as some unsolicited comments indicate:

- An undergraduate wrote, "This is the best textbook I have had in college, on any subject."
- A business law professor stated that the "clarity of presentation is superlative. I have never seen the complexity of contract law made this readable."
- An MBA student commented, "I think the textbook is great. The book is relevant, easy to understand and interesting."

- A state supreme court justice wrote that the book is "a valuable blend of rich scholarship and easy readability. Students and professors should rejoice with this publication."
- A Fortune 500 vice-president, enrolled in an Executive MBA program, commented, "I really liked the chapters. They were crisp, organized and current. The information was easy to understand and enjoyable."
- An undergraduate wrote, "The textbook is awesome. A lot of the time I read more than what is assigned—I just don't want to stop."

Humor. Throughout the text we use humor—judiciously—to lighten and enlighten. Not surprisingly, students have applauded—but is wit appropriate? How dare we employ levity in this venerable discipline? We offer humor because we take law seriously. We revere the law for its ancient traditions, its dazzling intricacy, its relentless though imperfect attempt to give order and decency to our world. Because we are confident of our respect for the law, we are not afraid to employ some levity. Leaden prose masquerading as legal scholarship does no honor to the field.

Humor also helps retention. We have found that students remember a contract problem described in a fanciful setting, and from that setting recall the underlying principle. By contrast, one widget is hard to distinguish from another.

FEATURES

We chose the features for our book with great care. As mentioned above, all features are considered an essential part of the text, and are woven into its body. Also, each feature responds to an essential pedagogical goal. Here are some of those goals and the matching feature.

YOU BE THE JUDGE

GOAL: Get them thinking independently. When reading case opinions, students tend to accept the court's "answer." Judges, of course, try to reach decisions that appear indisputable, when in reality they may be controversial—or wrong. From time to time we want students to think through the problem and reach their own answer. Virtually every chapter contains a *You Be The Judge* feature, providing the facts of the case and conflicting appellate arguments. The court's decision, however, appears only in the Instructor's Manual.

Since students do not know the result, discussions tend to be more free-flowing. For instance, many commentators feel that *Smith v. Van Gorkom*, the landmark case on the business judgment rule, was wrongly decided. However, when students read the court's opinion, they rarely consider the opposing side. Now, with the case presented as *You Be the Judge* in Chapter 17 (page 499), the students disagree with the court at least half the time. They are thinking.

NEWSWORTHY

GOAL: Prove that the law touches each of us every day. Students are intrigued to see the relevancy of what they are learning. Each chapter contains at least one Newsworthy feature—a newspaper or magazine article illustrating the legal issue under discussion. Thus, in Chapter 13 on agency law (page 364), an article about an American diplomat killed by terrorists demonstrates that an agency relationship exists only when the principal has control over its agent.

CYBERLAW

GOAL: Master the present and anticipate the future. The computer has changed all of our lives forever, and the courts and statute books are full of fascinating cyberlaw issues. Do employers have the right to read workers' e-mail? When does an electronic signature satisfy the statute of frauds? May the government halt the export of encryption technology? Cyberlaw is fully discussed in Chapter 20: Cyberlaw and Chapter 21: Intellectual Property with Cyberlaw. Finally, throughout the text we discuss still more cyberlaw issues as they relate to the particular topic; icons highlight those sections.

PREVENTIVE LAW

GOAL: Help managers stay out of court. As every lawyer knows, the best lawsuit is the one that never happens. Some of our students are already in the workforce, and the rest soon will be, so we offer ideas on avoiding legal disputes. Sometimes we provide detailed methods to avoid the particular problem; other times we challenge the students to formulate their own approach to dispute prevention. (See, for example, page 180.)

RIGHT & WRONG

GOAL: Make ethics real. We ask ethical questions about cases, legal issues, and commercial practices. Is it fair for one party to void a contract by arguing, months after the fact, that there was no consideration? Do managers have ethical obligations to older workers for whom employment opportunities may be limited? What is wrong with bribery? What should an executive do if her company sells goods manufactured by underpaid foreign workers? We do not have definitive answers but believe that asking the questions and encouraging discussion reminds students that ethics is an essential element of justice, and of a satisfying life.

WORLD VIEW

GOAL: Bring the world into the classroom. Business is now global. We offer illustrations of how other countries and cultures treat legal issues. For example, the securities regulation chapter, on page 527, discusses the development of a securities market in modern Russia. Students can glimpse the vital role that securities regulation plays in the economic life of a nation and have a chance to explore alternatives to our system.

CASES

GOAL: Let the judges speak. Each case begins with a summary of the facts and a statement of the issue. Next comes a tightly edited version of the decision, in the court's own language, so that students "hear" the law developing in the diverse voices of our many judges. We cite cases using a modified bluebook form. In the principal cases in each chapter, we provide the state or federal citation, the regional citation, and the LEXIS citation. We also give students a brief description of the court. Because many of our cases are so recent, some will have only a regional reporter and a LEXIS citation.

PRACTICE TESTS

GOAL: Encourage students to practice! At the end of the chapters we challenge the students with ten or more problems, including the following:

- *Internet Research Problem.* This question sends students to an Internet address where they can explore issues from the chapter.
- *You Be The Judge Writing Problem.* The students are given appellate arguments on both sides of the question and must prepare a written opinion.
- *Right and Wrong.* This question highlights the ethical issues of a dispute and calls upon the student to formulate a specific, reasoned response.
- *CPA Questions.* For topics covered by the CPA exam, administered by the American Institute of Certified Public Accountants, the practice tests include questions from previous CPA exams.

Answers to the odd-numbered questions are available on the Beatty *Legal Environment for a New Century Web* site at http://beatty.westbuslaw.com/. Here is why. Students often ask us how to study for exams. Reviewing the problems in the end-of-chapter practice tests is helpful, but without the answers students have no way of being sure they are on the right track. The answers to the even-numbered questions appear only in the Instructor's Manual so that faculty can assign them for written or oral presentation.

TEACHING MATERIALS

For more information about any of these ancillaries, contact your Thomson Learning/West Legal Studies in Business Sales Representative for more details, or visit the Beatty *Legal Environment for a New Century* Web site at http://beatty.westbuslaw.com/.

Student Study Guide. (ISBN: 0-324-15796-7) Students may purchase a study guide that includes a chapter outline, chapter objectives, and practice questions. Students can find further practice problems in the Online Quiz at http://beatty.westbuslaw.com/.

Instructor's Manual. (ISBN: 0-324-15797-5) We care about teaching, and wrote this manual ourselves. We have included special features to enhance class discussion and student progress:

- Dialogues. These are a series of questions-and-answers on pivotal cases and topics. The questions provide enough material to teach a full session. In a pinch, you could walk into class with nothing but the manual and use the Dialogues to conduct an exciting class.
- Action learning ideas: interviews, quick research projects, drafting exercises, classroom activities, commercial analyses, and other suggested assignments that get students out of their chairs and into the diverse settings of business law.
- Skits. Various chapters have lively skits that students can perform in class, with no rehearsal, to put legal doctrine in a real-life context.
- A chapter theme and a quote of the day.
- Updates of text material.
- New cases and examples.
- Answers to You Be the Judge cases from the text and to the Practice Test questions found at the end of each chapter.

Test Bank. (ISBN: 0-324-15798-3) The test bank offers hundreds of essay, short answer and multiple choice problems, and may be obtained in hard copy or electronic format.

ExamView Testing Software—Computerized Testing Software. (ISBN: 0-324-16471-8) This testing software contains all of the questions in the printed test bank. This program is an easy-to-use test creation software compatible with Microsoft Windows. Instructors can add or edit questions, instructions, and answers; and select questions by previewing them on the screen, selecting them randomly, or selecting them by number. Instructors can also create and administer quizzes online, whether over the Internet, a local area network (LAN), or a wide area network (WAN).

Microsoft PowerPoint Lecture Review Slides. PowerPoint slides are available for use by students as an aid to note-taking and by instructors for enhancing their lectures. Download these slides at http://beatty.westbuslaw.com/.

InfoTrac College Edition is an online library that contains hundreds of scholarly and popular periodicals, including *American Business Law Journal, Journal of International Business Studies, Environmental Law,* and *Ethics*. You can create a package that provides students access to InfoTrac College Edition when they purchase this textbook. Contact your local Thomson Learning/West Legal Studies Sales Representative to learn more.

Videos are available to qualified adopters using this text. You may be eligible to access the entire library of West videos, a vast selection covering most business law issues. There are some restrictions, and if you have questions, please contact your local Thomson Learning/West Legal Studies Sales Representative or visit http://www.westbuslaw.com/video_library.html.

Interaction with the Authors. This is our standard: Every professor who adopts this book must have a superior experience. We are available to help in any way we can. Adopters of this text often call us or E-mail us to ask questions, obtain a syllabus, offer suggestions, share pedagogical concerns, or inquire about ancillaries. One of the pleasures of working on this project has been our discovery that the text provides a link to so many colleagues around the country. We value those connections, are eager to respond, and would be happy to hear from you.

To the Student

One other tip: Each chapter contains several Internet addresses, offering a resource for further learning. The Practice Test at the end of each chapter also includes an Internet research problem. Sometimes your web browser might not be able to find the entire address, but can find part of it. For example, if you receive an error message when you look for http://www.tannedfeet.com/legal_forms.htm, you might try looking first at http://www.tannedfeet.com and then adding the other parts of the address.

Acknowledgments

We are grateful to the following reviewers who gave such helpful comments on the manuscript of this book:

Gail S. M. Evans
University of Houston—Downtown

Paul Fiorelli
Xavier University

Marsha E. Hass
College of Charleston

Ursula I. Spilger
University of Houston—Downtown

Kurt Stanberry
University of Houston—Downtown

Jeffrey F. Beatty
Phone: (617) 353-6397
E-mail: jfbeatty@bu.edu

Susan S. Samuelson
Phone: (617) 353-2033
E-mail: ssamuels@bu.edu

Boston, Massachusetts
December, 2001

UNIT

1

THE LEGAL ENVIRONMENT

INTRODUCTION TO LAW

1

CHAPTER

Law is powerful. Law is essential. And law is fascinating. We hope this book will persuade you of all three ideas.

THREE IMPORTANT IDEAS ABOUT LAW

POWER

The law displays its muscle every day, to corporate executives, homeless people—and presidents. A driver dies in an automobile accident and the jury concludes that the car had a design defect. The jurors award $8 million to the victim's family. A senior vice-president congratulates himself on a cagey stock purchase but is horrified to receive not profits, but a prison sentence. A homeless person, ordered by local police to stop panhandling, ambles into court and walks out with an order permitting him to beg on the city's streets. A criminal inquiry spreads until a grand jury hears testimony from an unprecedented source—a sitting president of the United States. The strong reach of the law touches us all. To understand something that is powerful is itself power.

Suppose, some years after graduation, you are a mid-level manager at Sublime Corp., which manufactures and distributes video games and related hardware and software. You are delighted with this important position in an excellent company—and especially glad you bring legal knowledge to the job. Sarah, an expert at computer-generated imagery, complains that Rob, her boss, is constantly touching her and making lewd comments. That is sexual harassment and your knowledge of *employment law* helps you respond promptly and carefully. You have dinner with Jake, who has his own software company. Jake wants to manufacture an exciting new video game in cooperation with Sublime, but you are careful not to create a binding deal. (*Contract law.*) Jake mentions that a similar game is already on the market. Do you have the right to market one like it? That answer you already know. (*Intellectual property law.*)

The next day a letter from the Environmental Protection Agency asks how your company disposes of toxic chemicals used to manufacture computer drives. You can discuss it efficiently with in-house counsel, because you have a working knowledge of *environmental law* and *administrative law.* You may think your corporation is about to surge ahead in its field, and you would like to invest in its stock. But wait! Are you engaging in "insider trading"? Your training in *securities law* will distinguish the intelligent investment from the felony. LuYu, your personnel manager, reports that a silicon chip worker often seems drowsy; she suspects drug use. Does she have the right to test him? (*Constitutional law* and *employment law.*) On the other hand, if she fails to test him, could Sublime Corp. be liable for any harm the worker does? (*Tort law* and *agency law.*)

In a mere week you might use your legal training a dozen times, helping Sublime to steer clear of countless dangers. During the coming year you encounter many other legal issues, and you and your corporation benefit from your skills.

It is not only as a corporate manager that you will confront the law. As a voter, investor, juror, entrepreneur, and community member, you will influence and be affected by the law. Whenever you take a stance about a legal issue, whether in the corporate office, the voting booth, or as part of local community groups, you help to create the social fabric of our nation. Your views are vital. This book will offer you knowledge and ideas from which to form and continually reassess your legal opinions and values.

IMPORTANCE

Law is also essential. Every society for which we have any historical record has had some system of laws. Naturally, the systems have varied enormously.

An extraordinary example of a detailed written law comes from the Visigoths, a nomadic European people who overran much of present-day France and Spain during the fifth and sixth centuries A.D. Their code admirably required judges to be "quick of perception, clear in judgment, and lenient in the infliction of penalties." It detailed dozens of crimes. For example, a freeman who kidnapped the slave of another had to repay the owner with four slaves and suffer 100 lashes. If he did not have four slaves to give, the kidnapper was himself reduced to slavery. Sadly, the code explicitly permitted torture of slaves and lower-class freemen, while prohibiting it for nobles.[1]

The Iroquois Native Americans, disregarded by many historians, in fact played a role in the creation of our own government. Five major nations made up the Iroquois group: the Mohawk, Cayuga, Oneida, Onondaga, and Seneca. Each nation governed itself as to domestic issues. But each nation also elected "sachems" to a League of the Iroquois. The league had authority over any matters that were common to all, such as relations with outsiders. Thus, by the fifteenth century, the Iroquois had solved the problem of *federalism:* how to have two levels of government, each with specified powers. Their system impressed Benjamin Franklin and others and influenced the drafting of our Constitution, with its powers divided between state and federal governments.[2] As European nations today seek to create a more united Europe, they struggle with the same problem.

The greatest of all Chinese lawgivers disliked written law altogether. Confucius, who lived from 551 to 479 B.C., understood law within a broader social perspective. He considered good rulers, strong family ties, and an enlightened nobility to be the surest methods to a good society. "As a judge, I decide disputes, for that is my duty; but the best thing that could happen would be to eliminate the causes for litigation!" Although he spoke 2,500 years ago, the distinction Confucius described is still critically important in our society: Which do we trust more—a written law or the people who enforce it?

FASCINATION

Law is intriguing. When the jury awarded $8 million against an auto manufacturer for a defective car design, it certainly demonstrated the law's power. But was the jury's decision right? Should a company have to pay that much for one car accident? Maybe the jury was reacting emotionally. Or perhaps the anger caused by terrible trauma *should* be part of a court case. What about the government's role in auto safety? Would we prefer that a federal agency or a jury make decisions about car design? These are not abstract speculations for philosophers. Verdicts such as this may cause each of us to pay more for our next automobile. Then again, we may be driving safer cars. Legal issues can be complex, but they are never *theoretical.* The law affects us and we know it.

---

[1] S. P. Scott, *Visigothic Code (Forum Judicum)* (Littleton, CO: Fred B. Rothman & Co., 1982), pp. 3, 45.

[2] Jack Weatherford, *Indian Givers* (New York: Fawcett Columbine, 1988), pp. 133–150.

In 1835, the young French aristocrat Alexis de Tocqueville traveled through the United States, observing the newly democratic people and the qualities that made them unique. One of the things that struck de Tocqueville most forcefully was the American tendency to file suit: "Scarcely any political question arises in the United States that is not resolved, sooner or later, into a judicial question."[3] De Tocqueville got it right: for better or worse, we do expect courts to solve many problems. If you wonder about the accuracy of the Frenchman's comment, ask former U.S. president Bill Clinton, who developed a rich understanding of the relationship between public affairs and judicial matters.

Not only do Americans litigate, but they watch one another do it. Almost all of the states permit live television coverage of trials, although federal courts do not. The most heavily viewed event in the history of television was the O. J. Simpson murder trial. Commentators from other countries, including Britain, harshly criticize live trial coverage. Nevertheless, when English nanny Louise Woodward went on trial in Massachusetts for the homicide of an infant, the British were glued to their television sets.

(From time to time we will present issues and views from other countries to give a broader perspective on legal affairs.) Although most nations bar television cameras from the courtroom, a small but growing list of countries permits limited coverage: Australia, Canada, France, Israel, Italy, the Netherlands, Norway, and Spain. British lawyers periodically—and hotly—debate the issue. Proponents of live coverage argue that some famous miscarriages of justice would never have occurred if the public had realized what was happening in the courtroom. For example, prosecutorial deceit led British courts to convict innocent people of terrorism in Northern Ireland. Advocates believe that television cameras would prevent a recurrence. The theory is that a witness would not lie under oath if millions of people were watching.

Opponents contend that television cameras unfairly subject the defendants to a second trial—by popular opinion. The evidence may taint a defendant forever, even one who is ultimately acquitted. Others point to American televised trials and argue that cameras transform what should be a dignified proceeding into frenzied entertainment, causing lawyers and even judges to play roles that are unbecoming and unethical. British barristers—lawyers who are specially trained to appear in court—enjoy wide respect, and many turn up their noses at what they see as American showboating. Thus far, the British have rejected live coverage.

Regardless of where we allow cameras, it is an undeniable benefit of the electronic age that we can obtain information so quickly. From time to time we will mention Web sites of interest. Some of these are for nonprofit groups while others are commercial sites. We do not endorse or advocate on behalf of any group or company, but simply wish to alert you to what is out there. The commercial site of a cable television company devoted to trial broadcasts, http://www.courttv.com/, includes up-to-the-minute information on current cases, often including trial testimony, appeal briefs, and other timely data.

---

[3] Alexis de Tocqueville, *Democracy in America* (1835), Vol. 1, Ch. 16.

The law is a big part of our lives, and it is wise to know something about it. Within a few weeks, you will probably find yourself following legal events in the news with keener interest and deeper understanding. In this chapter, we develop the background for our study. We look at where law comes from: its history and its present-day institutions. In the section on jurisprudence, we examine different theories about what "law" really means. And finally we see how courts—and students—analyze a case.

ORIGINS OF OUR LAW

It would be nice if we could look up "the law" in one book, memorize it, and then apply it. But the law is not that simple, and *cannot* be that simple, because it reflects the complexity of contemporary life. In truth, there is no such thing as "the law." Principles and rules of law actually come from many different sources. Why is this so? In part because we inherited a complex structure of laws from England. We will see that by the time of the American Revolution, English law was already an intricate system.

Additionally, ours is a nation born in revolution and created, in large part, to protect the rights of its people from the government. The Founding Fathers created a national government but insisted that the individual states maintain control in many areas. As a result, each state has its own government with exclusive power over many important areas of our lives. To top it off, the Founders guaranteed many rights to the people alone, ordering national *and* state governments to keep clear. This has worked, but it has caused a multilayered system, with 50 state governments and one federal government all creating and enforcing law.

A summary of English legal history will show the origin of our legal institutions. This brisk summary will also demonstrate that certain problems never go away. Anglo-Saxon England, about 1,000 years ago, was a world utterly different from our own. Yet we can see uncanny foreshadowings of our own unfinished efforts to create a peaceful world.

ENGLISH ROOTS

England in the tenth century was a rustic agricultural community with a tiny population and very little law or order. Danes and Swedes invaded repeatedly, terrorizing the Anglo-Saxon peoples. Criminals were hard to catch in the heavily forested, sparsely settled nation. The king used a primitive legal system to maintain a tenuous control over his people.

England was divided into shires, and daily administration was carried out by a "shire reeve," later called a sheriff. The shire reeve collected taxes and did what he could to keep peace, apprehending criminals and acting as mediator between feuding families. Two or three times a year, a shire court met; lower courts met more frequently.

Contemporary law: Mediation lives on. As we discuss in Chapter 3, on dispute resolution, lawsuits have grown ever more costly. Increasingly, companies are turning to mediation to settle disputes. The humble shire reeve's work is back in vogue.

Because there were so few officers to keep the peace, Anglo-Saxon society created an interesting method of ensuring public order. Every freeman (non-slave) belonged to a group of 10 freemen known as a "tithing," headed by a "tithingman." If anyone injured a person outside his tithing or interfered with the king's property, all 10 men of the tithing could be forced to pay.

Contemporary law: Today, we still use this idea of collective responsibility. In a business partnership, all partners are personally responsible for the debts of the partnership. They could potentially lose their homes and all assets because of the irresponsible conduct of one partner.

When cases did come before an Anglo-Saxon court, the parties would often be represented either by a clergyman, by a nobleman, or by themselves. There were few professional lawyers. Each party produced "oath helpers," usually 12, who would swear that one version of events was correct. The court explicitly gave greater credence to oath helpers from the nobility.

Contemporary law: The Anglo-Saxon oath helpers are probably forerunners of our modern jury of 12 persons. But as to who is telling the truth, that is a question that will never disappear. We deny giving a witness greater credence because of his or her status. But is that accurate? Some commentators believe that jurors are overly impressed with "expert witnesses," such as doctors or engineers, and ignore their own common sense when faced with such "pedigreed" people.

In 1066, the Normans conquered England. William the Conqueror made a claim never before made in England: that he owned all of the land. The king then granted sections of his lands to his favorite noblemen, as his tenants in chief, creating the system of feudalism. These tenants in chief then granted parts of their land to *tenants in demesne,* who actually occupied a particular estate. Each tenant in demesne owed fidelity to his lord (hence "landlord"). So what? Just this: land became the most valuable commodity in all of England, and our law still reflects that.

Contemporary law: Nine hundred years later, American law still regards land as special. The statute of frauds, which we study in the section on contracts, demands that contracts for the sale or lease of property be in writing. And landlord-tenant law, vital to students and many others, still reflects its ancient roots. Some of a landlord's rights are based on the 1,000-year-old tradition that land is uniquely valuable.

In 1250, Henry de Bracton (d. 1268) wrote a legal treatise that still influences us. *De Legibus et Consuetudinibus Angliae (On the Laws and Customs of England),* written in Latin, summarized many of the legal rulings in cases since the Norman Conquest. De Bracton was teaching judges to rule based on previous cases. He was helping to establish the idea of *precedent.* **The doctrine of precedent, which developed gradually over centuries, requires that judges decide current cases based on previous rulings.**

Contemporary law: This vital principle is the heart of American common law. Precedent ensures predictability. Suppose a 17-year-old student promises to lease an apartment from a landlord, but then changes her mind. The landlord sues to enforce the lease. The student claims that she cannot be held to the agreement because she is a minor. The judge will look for precedent, i.e., older cases dealing with the same issue, and he will find many holding that a contract generally may not be enforced against a minor. That precedent is binding on this case, and the student wins. The accumulation of precedent, based on case after case, makes up the **common law.**

During the next few centuries, judges and lawyers acquired special training and skills. Some lawyers began to plead cases full-time and gained unique skill—and power. They represented only those who could pay well.

Parliament passed an ever greater number of laws, generally called **statutes,** the word we still use to mean a law passed by a legislative body. Parliament's statutes swelled in number and complexity until they were unfathomable to anyone but a lawyer.

Contemporary law: Our society still struggles with unequal access to legal talent. Rich people often fare better in court than poor. And many Americans regard law as Byzantine and incomprehensible. A primary purpose of this text is to remove the mystique from the law and to empower you to participate in legal matters.

As lawyers became more highly skilled, they searched ever wider for ways to defeat the other side. One method was by attacking the particular writ in the case. The party bringing the case was called the plaintiff. His first task was to obtain a **writ,** which was a letter from the central government ordering a court to hear the case. Each type of lawsuit required a different writ. For example, a landlord's lawsuit against a tenant required one kind of writ, while a claim of assault needed a different one. If a court decided that the plaintiff's lawyer had used the wrong writ, it would dismiss the lawsuit. This encouraged lawyers for the defendant to attack the writ itself, claiming it was inappropriate. By doing that, they could perhaps defeat the case without ever answering who did what to whom.

Contemporary law: This is the difference between procedure and substance, which will become clear during the course. **Substantive** rules of law state the rights of the parties. For example, it is substantive law that if you have paid the purchase price of land and accepted the deed, you are entitled to occupy the property. **Procedural** rules tell how a court should go about settling disputes. For example, what evidence can be used to establish that you *did* pay for the property? How much evidence is necessary? Who may testify about whether you paid? Those are all issues of procedural law. To this day, lawyers attack procedural aspects of an opponent's case before dealing with the substantive rights.

Here is an actual case from more than six centuries ago, in the court's own language. The dispute illustrates that some things have changed but others never do. The plaintiff claims that he asked the defendant to heal his eye with "herbs and other medicines." He says the defendant did it so badly that he blinded the plaintiff in that eye.

THE OCULIST'S CASE (1329)

LI MS. Hale 137 (1), fo. 150, Nottingham[4]

Attorney Launde [for defendant]: Sir, you plainly see how [the plaintiff claims] that he had submitted himself to [the defendant's] medicines and his care; and after that he can assign no trespass in his person, inasmuch as he submitted himself to his care: but this action, if he has any, sounds naturally in breach of covenant. We demand [that the case be dismissed].

[4] J. Baker and S. Milsom, *Sources of English Legal History* (London: Butterworth & Co., 1986).

Excerpts from Judge Denum's Decision: I saw a Newcastle man arraigned before my fellow justice and me for the death of a man. I asked the reason for the indictment, and it was said that he had slain a man under his care, who died within four days afterwards. And because I saw that he was a [doctor] and that he had not done the thing feloniously but [accidentally] I ordered him to be discharged. And suppose a blacksmith, who is a man of skill, injures your horse with a nail, whereby you lose your horse: you shall never have recovery against him. No more shall you here.

Afterwards the plaintiff did not wish to pursue his case any more.

This case from 1329 is an ancient medical malpractice case. Defendant's lawyer makes a procedural argument. Attorney Launde does not deny that his client blinded the plaintiff. He claims that the plaintiff has brought the wrong kind of lawsuit. Launde argues that the plaintiff should have brought a case of "covenant," i.e., a lawsuit about a contract.

Judge Denum decides the case on a different principle. He gives judgment to the defendant because the plaintiff voluntarily sought medical care. He implies that the defendant would lose only if he had attacked the plaintiff. As we will see when we study negligence law, this case might have a different outcome today. Note also the informality of the judge's ruling. He rather casually mentions that he came across a related case once before and that he would stand by that outcome. The idea of precedent is just beginning to take hold.

Sometimes a judge refused to hear a case, ruling that no such claims were legal. The injured party might then take his case to the Chancellor, in London, whose status in the king's council gave him unique, flexible powers. This *Court of Chancery* had no jury. The court's duty was to accomplish what "good conscience" required, that is, an *equitable* result, and so this more creative use of a court's power became known as **equity.**

Contemporary law: In present-day America, judges still exercise equity powers, based on those cases the Chancery court accepted. For example, a court today might issue an injunction requiring a factory owner to stop polluting the air. The injunction (order to stop) is an equitable remedy. Only a judge can exercise equitable powers because, historically, Chancery had no jury. If a judge grants an injunction, she is said to be exercising equitable powers.

Parliament added statutes on more and more matters, at times conflicting with common law rulings of the various judges. What should a court do when faced with a statute that contradicts well-established precedent? In the seventeenth century, one of England's greatest judges, Lord Coke, addressed the problem. In *Dr. Bonham's Case,*[5] Lord Coke ruled that "when an Act of Parliament is against Common right and reason, or repugnant, or impossible to be performed, the Common Law will control it and adjudge such Act to be void."

Audacious man! In a decision of breathtaking strength, Lord Coke declared that a single judge could overrule the entire Parliament, based on what the judge might consider "common right and reason." This same tension carries on today between elected officials, such as state legislators, and courts, which sometimes declare acts of the legislatures void.

[5] Eng. Rep. 638 (C.P. 1610).

Of course, by the time Lord Coke was on the bench, in the seventeenth century, English common law had also spread across the ocean to the newly created colonies. We will pick up the story in America.

LAW IN THE UNITED STATES

The colonists brought with them a basic knowledge of English law, some of which they were content to adopt as their own. Other parts, such as religious restrictions, were abhorrent to them. Many had made the dangerous trip to America precisely to escape persecution, and they were not interested in re-creating their difficulties in a new land. Finally, some laws were simply irrelevant or unworkable in a world that was socially and geographically so different. American law ever since has been a whitewater river created from two strong currents: one carries the ancient principles of English common law, the other, a zeal and determination for change.

During the nineteenth century, the United States changed from a weak, rural nation into one of vast size and potential power. Cities grew, factories appeared, and sweeping movements of social migration changed the population. Changing conditions raised new legal questions. Did workers have a right to form industrial unions? To what extent should a manufacturer be liable if its product injured someone? Could a state government invalidate an employment contract that required 16-hour workdays? Should one company be permitted to dominate an entire industry?

In the twentieth century, the rate of social and technological change increased, creating new legal puzzles. Were some products, such as automobiles, so inherently dangerous that the seller should be responsible for injuries even if no mistakes were made in manufacturing? Who should clean up toxic waste if the company that had caused the pollution no longer existed? If a consumer signed a contract with a billion dollar corporation, should the agreement be enforced even if the consumer never understood it? Before we can begin to examine the answers to these questions, we need to understand the sources of contemporary law.

SOURCES OF CONTEMPORARY LAW

During the colonial period there were few trained lawyers and fewer lawbooks in America. After the Revolution that changed, and law became a serious, professional career. The first great legal achievement was the adoption of the United States Constitution.

CONSTITUTIONS

UNITED STATES CONSTITUTION

The United States Constitution, adopted in 1789 by the original 13 colonies, is the supreme law of the land.[6] Any law that conflicts with it is void. This Federal

[6] The complete text of the Constitution appears in Appendix A.

Constitution, as it is also known, does three basic things. First, it establishes the national government of the United States, with its three branches. The Constitution creates the Congress, with a Senate and a House of Representatives, and prescribes what laws Congress may pass. The same document establishes the office of the president and the duties that go with it. And it creates the third branch of government, the federal courts, describing what cases they may hear.

Second, the Constitution ensures that the states retain all power not given to the national government. This simple idea has meant that state governments play an important role in all of our lives. Major issues of family law, criminal law, property law, and many other areas are regulated predominantly by the various states.

Third, the Constitution guarantees many basic rights to the American people. Most of these rights are found in the amendments to the Constitution. The First Amendment guarantees the rights of free speech, free press, and the free exercise of religion. The Fourth, Fifth, and Sixth Amendments protect the rights of any person accused of a crime. Other amendments ensure that the government treats all people equally and that it pays for any property it takes from a citizen. Merely by creating a limited government of three branches and guaranteeing basic liberties to all citizens, the Constitution became one of the most important documents ever written.

STATE CONSTITUTIONS

In addition to the Federal Constitution, each state has a constitution that establishes its own government. All states have an executive (the governor), a legislature, and a court system. Thus there are two entire systems of government affecting each of us: a federal government, with power over the entire country, and a state government, exercising those powers that the United States Constitution did not grant to the federal government. This is federalism at work.

STATUTES

The second important source of law is statutory law. The Constitution gave to the United States Congress the power to pass laws on various subjects. These laws are statutes, like those passed by the English Parliament. For example, the Constitution allows Congress to pass statutes about the military: to appropriate money, reorganize divisions, and close bases. You can find any federal statute, on any subject, at the Web site of the United States House of Representatives, which is http://www.house.gov/.

State legislatures also pass statutes. Each state constitution allows the legislature to pass laws on a wide variety of subjects. All state legislatures, for example, may pass statutes about family law issues such as divorce and child custody.

COMMON LAW

As we have seen, the common law originated in England as lawyers began to record decisions and urge judges to follow earlier cases. As judges started to do that, the earlier cases, called **precedent**, took on steadily greater importance. Eventually, judges were *obligated* to follow precedent. **The principle that precedent is binding on later cases is *stare decisis,* which means "let the decision stand."** *Stare decisis* makes the law predictable, and this in turn enables businesses and private citizens to plan intelligently.

EQUITY

Principles of equity, created by the Chancellor in England, traveled to the colonies along with the common law rules. All states permit courts to use equitable powers. An example of a contemporary equitable power is an **injunction**, a court order that someone stop doing something. Suppose a music company is about to issue a new compact disc by a well-known singer, but a composer claims that the recording artist has stolen his song. The composer, claiming copyright violation, could seek an injunction to prevent the company from issuing the compact disc. Every state has a trial court that can issue injunctions and carry out other equitable relief. As was true in medieval England, there is no jury in an equity case.

ADMINISTRATIVE LAW

In a society as large and diverse as ours, the executive and legislative branches of government cannot oversee all aspects of commerce. Congress passes statutes about air safety, but U.S. senators do not stand around air traffic towers, serving coffee to keep everyone awake. The executive branch establishes rules concerning how foreign nationals enter the United States, but presidents are reluctant to sit on the dock of the bay, watching the ships come in. **Administrative agencies** do this day-to-day work.

Most administrative agencies are created by Congress or by a state legislature. Familiar examples at the federal level are the Federal Communications Commission (FCC), which regulates most telecommunications; the Federal Trade Commission (FTC), which oversees interstate trade; and the Immigration and Naturalization Service (INS), which controls our nation's borders. At the state level, regulators set insurance rates for all companies in the state, control property development and land use, and regulate many other issues.

OTHER SOURCES OF LAW

TREATIES

The Constitution authorizes the president to make treaties with foreign nations. These must then be ratified by the United States Senate. When they are ratified, they are as binding upon all citizens as any federal statute. In 1994, the Senate ratified the North American Free Trade Agreement (NAFTA) with Mexico and Canada. NAFTA was controversial then and is perhaps more so today—but it is now the law of the land.

EXECUTIVE ORDERS

In theory all statutes must originate in Congress or a state legislature. But in fact executives also legislate by issuing executive orders. For example, in 1970,

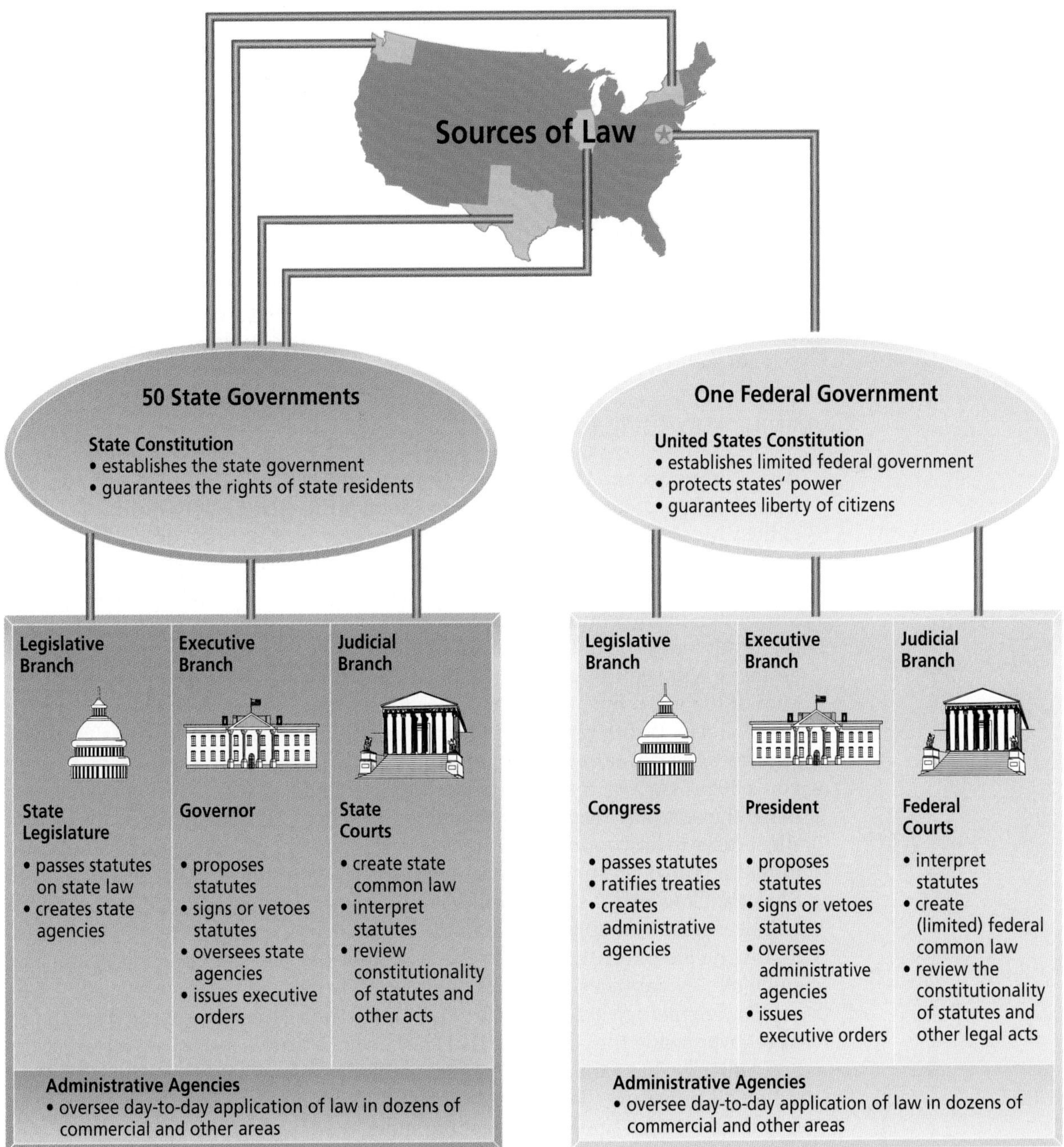

Federal Form of Government. Principles and rules of law come from many sources. The government in Washington creates and enforces law throughout the nation. But 50 state governments exercise great power in local affairs. And citizens enjoy constitutional protection from both state and federal government. The Founding Fathers wanted this balance of power and rights, but the overlapping authority creates legal complexity.

Congress authorized President Nixon to issue wage-price controls in an effort to stabilize the economy. This was a colossal grant of power, allowing the president personally to regulate the nation's economy. Critics charge that Congress should not give away the powers that the people have granted to it, and such delegations of authority have led to extensive lawsuits.

CLASSIFICATIONS OF LAW

We have seen where law comes from. Now we need to classify the law into different types. There are three main classifications that we use throughout this book: criminal and civil law, substantive and procedural law, and public and private law.

CRIMINAL AND CIVIL LAW

It is a crime to embezzle money from a bank, to steal a car, to sell cocaine. **Criminal law concerns behavior so threatening that society outlaws it altogether.** Most criminal laws are statutes, passed by Congress or a state legislature. The government itself prosecutes the wrongdoer, regardless of what the bank president or car owner wants. A district attorney, paid by the government, brings the case to court. The injured party, for example the owner of the stolen car, is not in charge of the case, although she may appear as a witness. The government will seek to punish the defendant with a prison sentence, a fine, or both. If there is a fine, the money goes to the state, not to the injured party.

Civil law is different, and most of this book is about civil law. **The civil law regulates the rights and duties between parties.** Tracy agrees in writing to lease you a 30,000-square-foot store in her shopping mall. She now has a *legal duty* to make the space available. But then another tenant offers her more money, and she refuses to let you move in. Tracy has violated her duty, but she has not committed a crime. The government will not prosecute the case. It is up to you to file a civil lawsuit. Your case will be based on the common law of contract. You will also seek equitable relief, namely an injunction ordering Tracy not to lease to anyone else. You should win the suit, and you will get your injunction and some money damages. But Tracy will not go to jail.

Some conduct involves both civil and criminal law. Suppose Tracy is so upset over losing the court case that she becomes drunk and causes a serious car accident. She has committed the crime of driving while intoxicated, and the state will prosecute. She has also committed negligence, and the injured party will file a lawsuit against her, seeking money.

SUBSTANTIVE AND PROCEDURAL LAW

We saw this distinction in *The Oculist's Case,* and it remains important today. **Substantive law defines the rights of people.** Substantive law requires that a landlord who has signed a lease must deliver the store to her tenant. Most of this book concerns substantive law. **Procedural law establishes the processes for settling disputes.** Procedural law requires that, to get an injunction against Tracy, you must first notify her in writing of your claims and the time and place of the hearing on the injunction.

PUBLIC AND PRIVATE LAW

Public law refers to the rights and obligations of governments as they deal with the nation's citizens. For example, when the Federal Trade Commission prohibits deceptive advertising, that is public law. **Private law** regulates the duties between individuals. Landlord-tenant law is private law.

JURISPRUDENCE

We have had a glimpse of legal history and a summary of the present-day sources of American law. But what *is* law? That question is the basis of a field known as **jurisprudence.** How do we distinguish a moral rule from a legal rule? What is the real nature of law? Can there be such a thing as an "illegal" law?

LAW AND MORALITY

Law is different from morality, yet the two are obviously linked. There are many instances when the law duplicates what all of us would regard as a moral position. It is negligence to drive too fast in a school district, and few would dispute the moral value of that law. And similarly with contract law: if the owner of land agrees in writing to sell property to a buyer at a stated price, the seller must go through with the deal, and the legal outcome matches our moral expectations.

On the other hand, we have had laws that we now clearly regard as immoral. At the turn of the century, a factory owner could typically fire a worker for any reason at all—including, for example, his religious or political views. Today, we would say it is immoral to fire a worker because she is Jewish—and the law invariably prohibits it.

Finally, there are legal issues where the morality is not so clear. You are walking down a country lane and notice a three-year-old child playing with matches near a barn filled with hay. Are you obligated to intervene? No, says the law, though many think that is preposterous. (See Chapter 4, on common law, for details.) A company buys property and then discovers, buried under the ground, toxic waste that will cost $300,000 to clean up. The original owner has gone bankrupt. Should the new owner be forced to pay for the cleanup? If the new owner fails to pay for the job, who will? (See Chapter 24, on environmental law.)

LEGAL POSITIVISM

This philosophy can be simply stated: law is what the sovereign says it is. The **sovereign** is the recognized political power whom citizens obey, so in the United States, both state and federal governments are sovereign. A legal positivist holds that whatever the sovereign declares to be the law *is* the law, whether it is right or wrong.

The primary criticism of legal positivism is that it seems to leave no room for questions of morality. A law permitting a factory owner to fire a worker because she is Catholic is surely different from a law prohibiting arson. Do citizens in a democracy have a duty to consider such differences?

NEWSworthy

Most states allow citizens to pass laws directly at the ballot box, a process called voter referendum. California voters often do this, and during the 1990s, they passed one of the state's most controversial laws. Proposition 187 was designed to curb illegal immigration into the state by eliminating social spending for undocumented aliens. Citizens debated the measure fiercely but passed it by a large margin. One section of the new law forbade public schools from educating illegal immigrants. The law obligated a principal to inquire into the immigration status of all children enrolled in the school and to report undocumented students to immigration authorities. Several San Diego school principals rejected the new rules, stating that they would neither inquire into immigration status nor report undocumented aliens. Their statements produced a heated response. Some San Diego residents castigated the school officials as lawbreakers, claiming that:

- A school officer who knowingly disobeyed a law was setting a terrible example for students, who would assume they were free to do the same
- The principals were advocating permanent residence and a free education for anyone able to evade our immigration laws; and
- The officials were scorning grass-roots democracy by disregarding a law passed by popular referendum.

Others applauded the principals' position, asserting that:

- The referendum's rules would transform school officials from educators into border police, forcing them to cross-examine young children and parents
- The new law was foolish because it punished innocent children for violations committed by their parents; and
- Our nation has long respected civil disobedience based on humanitarian ideals, and these officials were providing moral leadership to the whole community.

Ultimately, no one had to decide whether to obey Proposition 187. A federal judge ruled that only Congress had the power to regulate immigration and that California's attempt was unconstitutional and void. The debate over immigration reform—and ethics—did not end, however. California's governor announced that he would appeal the court's decision, and Congress considered various proposals for cutting off social benefits to illegal immigrants.

NATURAL LAW

St. Thomas Aquinas (1225–1274) answered the legal positivists even before they had spoken. In his *Summa Theologica,* he argued that an unjust law is no law at all and need not be obeyed. It is not enough that a sovereign makes a command. The law must have a moral basis.

Where do we find the moral basis that would justify a law? Aquinas says that "good is that which all things seek after." Therefore, the fundamental rule of all laws is that "good is to be done and promoted, and evil is to be avoided."

This sounds appealing, but also vague. Exactly which laws promote good and which do not? Is it better to have a huge corporation dominate a market or many smaller companies competing? Did the huge company get that way by being better than its competitors? If Wal-Mart moves into a rural area, establishes a mammoth store, and sells inexpensive products, is that "good"? Yes, if you are a consumer who cares only about prices. No, if you are the owner of a Main Street store driven into bankruptcy. Maybe, if you are a resident who values small-town life but wants lower prices.

Natural law is often in the news. Look at one of the most violently contested issues in the history of American law: abortion. In the landmark case of *Roe v. Wade*,[7] the United States Supreme Court ruled that the Constitution protects the right to an abortion, though with some important limitations. The Supreme Court hoped this ruling would settle the issue. It did not. Abortion has reappeared many times before the Supreme Court and dozens of times before lower courts. Does the idea of "natural law" help to settle the debate?

When President Bush nominated Judge Clarence Thomas for a seat on the United States Supreme Court in 1991, one of the first controversies to arise concerned writings and conversations in which it appeared that Judge Thomas had strongly supported natural law. In particular, his statements indicated that he viewed natural law as a reason for outlawing abortion. During his confirmation hearings before the Senate Judiciary Committee, Judge Thomas said that his earlier statements were insignificant and that natural law would not influence his thinking about abortion or other issues.

What does natural law tell us about abortion? Abortion supporters, or those advocating free choice, will say that natural law protects a woman's reproductive rights and that it is violent and unnatural for any government to tell a woman what to do with her body. Opponents of abortion reach the opposite conclusion, arguing that no good can come from terminating the life of a fetus and that a law permitting abortion is no law at all. What do you think?

LEGAL REALISM

Legal realists take a very different tack. They claim it does not matter what is written as law. What counts is who enforces that law and by what process. All of us are biased by issues such as income, education, family background, race, religion, and many other factors. These personal characteristics, they say, determine which contracts will be enforced and which ignored, why some criminals receive harsh sentences while others get off lightly, and so on.

Judge Jones hears a multimillion dollar lawsuit involving an airplane crash. Was the airline negligent? The law is the same everywhere, but legal realists say that Jones's background will determine the outcome. If she spent 20 years representing insurance companies, she will tend to favor the airline. If her law practice consisted of helping the "little guy," she will favor the plaintiff.

Other legal realists argue, more aggressively, that those in power use the machinery of the law to perpetuate their control. The outcome of a given case will be determined by the needs of those with money and political clout. A court puts "window dressing" on a decision, they say, so that society thinks there are

[7] 410 U.S. 113, 93 S. Ct. 705, 1973 U.S. LEXIS 159 (1973).

principles behind the law. A problem with legal realism, however, is its denial that any lawmaker can overcome personal bias. Yet clearly some do act unselfishly.

Summary of Jurisprudence	
Legal Positivism	Law is what the sovereign says.
Natural Law	An unjust law is no law at all.
Legal Realism	*Who* enforces the law counts more than *what* is in writing.

No one school of jurisprudence is likely to seem perfect. We urge you to keep the different schools of thought in mind as you read cases in the book. Ask yourself which school of thought is the best fit for you.

ANALYZING A CASE

Cases are the heart of the law and an important part of this book. Reading them effectively takes practice. The following case is a good place to start. This lawsuit begins, as a certain number do, with a tragedy: the death of a 12-year-old child. Not all lawsuits in the book will be so unhappy, but we offer a fair number of dramatic cases for one reason: when the stakes are high, people care.

Gayle Quigley, the boy's mother, sued a church that relied on prayer rather than traditional medical assistance. Notice the narrow legal issue that the court had to decide: whether the church had a legal duty to summon medical help. To rephrase the point, this case was *not* about whether the death was a tragic loss (it was), or whether it was avoidable (it probably was), or whether church members grieved over the death (they did), or whether the father and nurses *morally* ought to have sought help (you decide).

QUIGLEY v. FIRST CHURCH OF CHRIST, SCIENTIST

65 Cal. App. 4th 1027, 76 Cal. Rptr. 2d 792, 1998 Cal. App. LEXIS 677
California Court of Appeal, 1998

Facts: Gayle Quigley and James Wantland had divorced. They had joint custody of their 12-year-old son, Andrew, who lived with his father. James was a member of the Christian Science church, a religion that regards disease as an "error of the mind" and discourages the use of traditional medicine. Members of the faith rely on Christian Science practitioners, who offer prayer for patients, and nurses, who are trained to provide only practical care, such as bathing and feeding.

On December 16, Andrew complained of feeling ill. James telephoned a Christian Science practitioner, who provided prayer and counseling over the telephone. Andrew's health declined. On December 20, Laura Armstrong, a Christian Science nurse, visited the Wantlands, having been told there was a "very sick" boy there. When Armstrong arrived, she asked James to sign a form stating that the parents agreed to rely on Christian Science treatment. The document provided a space for both parents to sign, but no one telephoned Gayle Quigley or informed her of her son's illness. Armstrong observed that Andrew was not talking or responding to people and that his breathing was quick and abnormal. The nurse was concerned that she could not help Andrew and called a second nurse, who arrived later in the afternoon. Later that day, James telephoned "911" and summoned an ambulance. On arrival at the hospital, Andrew was pronounced dead of what later turned out to be juvenile diabetes.

Gayle Quigley sued the Christian Science church, the practitioner, and the nurses who had participated in Andrew's treatment. She also sued her ex-husband, but this case does not concern him. Quigley alleged that the defendants' refusal to call medical help was *negligence,* meaning a failure to behave the way a reasonable person would. To win a negligence case, a plaintiff must first show that the defendant had a *duty* to the injured person. The defendants asked the court to dismiss the case without a trial, arguing that they had no duty to summon help. The trial court dismissed the case, and Quigley appealed.

Issue: Did the defendants have a duty to summon medical help for Andrew?

Excerpts from Judge Bedsworth's Decision: [The judge began by mentioning an earlier California case, in which the state's highest court ruled that one person generally has no duty to protect another from harm, unless there is a special relationship between the two, such as custody or control. That case also warned that obligating religious counselors to summon outside help might discourage such workers from offering their services at all.]

Quigley [argues] that imposing a duty on Christian Science healers to refer patients to medical care would not have a chilling effect on religious freedom. We disagree. Quigley's own complaint alleges that medical treatment is inconsistent with the tenets of the Christian Science faith, and it is considered "unethical" to provide Christian Science treatment to any patient receiving medical care. Under those circumstances, imposing any duty upon Christian Science healers which required them to encourage patients to seek medical care would directly interfere with their own religious practices. We can hardly conceive of a more chilling effect.

Finally, Quigley [claims that the] defendants voluntarily assumed a duty of due care regarding Andrew's illness, because "Andrew's physical well-being was entrusted to defendants' nationally coordinated system for treating seriously ill children." That contention, however, reveals the most fundamental flaw in Quigley's analysis. As Quigley expressly acknowledges in her complaint, Christian Science treatment is intended to address only a spiritual problem, not a physical one, since Christian Science perceives disease to be an "error of the mind." Indeed, Quigley specifically alleges that Christian Science healers are trained "to not see the reality of the physical symptoms and to see the patient as healed." In this case, the fact that Andrew's problem turned out not to be spiritual, but was instead physical in nature, i.e., juvenile diabetes, does not change the fact that the defendants undertook no responsibility to evaluate the severity of, or otherwise address, Andrew's physical condition or medical needs. Indeed, given their particular beliefs, Christian Science healers are perhaps the group least qualified to carry out such a duty and least likely to assume it.

[Affirmed.]

ANALYSIS

Let's take it from the top. The case is called *Quigley v. First Church of Christ, Scientist.* Gayle Quigley is the plaintiff, the person who is suing. The church, the practitioner, and the nurses are all defendants, the ones being sued. A case generally names only the first plaintiff and the first defendant. In this example, the plaintiff's name happens to appear first but that is not always true. When a defendant loses a trial and files an appeal, *some* courts reverse the names of the parties.

The next lines give the legal citation, which indicates where to find the case in a law library. We explain in the footnote how to locate a book if you plan to do research.[8] The last line informs us that the California Court of Appeal decided the case in 1998.

The *Facts* section provides a background to the lawsuit, written by the authors of this text. The court's own explanation of the facts is often many pages long and may involve complex matters irrelevant to the subject covered in this book, so we relate only what is necessary.

The *Issue* section is very important. It tells you what the court had to decide—and also why you are reading the case. In giving its decision, a court may digress. If you keep in mind the issue and relate the court's discussion to it, you will not get lost.

Excerpts from Judge Bedsworth's Decision is where the court's decision begins. This is called the *holding,* meaning a statement of who wins and who loses. The holding also includes the court's *rationale,* which is the reasoning behind the decision.

The holding that we provide is an edited version of the court's own language. Some judges write clear, forceful prose, others do not. Either way, their words give you an authentic feel of how judges think and rule, so we bring the decision to you in the original. We occasionally use brackets [] to substitute our language for that of the court, either to condense or to clarify. Notice the brackets at the beginning of the *Quigley* decision, in which we summarize the court's discussion of an earlier case. We also leave out a great deal. A court's opinion may be three pages or it may be 75. We want to keep the reading manageable. We do not use ellipsis dots (. . .) to indicate these deletions because more is taken out than is kept in, and we want the text to be clean. If you are curious about the full holding, you can always look it up.

Let us look at a few of Judge Bedsworth's points. The holding begins with mention of an earlier case from the California Supreme Court. The earlier decision is *precedent,* and this court is bound to follow it. The previous suit dealt with religious counselors. That holding included a general rule, that one person owes no duty to protect another, and a more specific one, that religious counselors probably need special protection from legal burdens. Right away, we can sense

---

[8] Because the Quigley case is so recent, its citation is unusually short. We will explain how to read and use a more typical citation. Consider this one:

Academy Chicago Publishers v. Cheever
144 Ill. 2d 24, 578 N.E.2d 981, 1991 Ill. LEXIS 47

This citation provides three different places to find the full text of this case. The first citation is to "Ill. 2d," which means the official court reporter of the state of Illinois, second set. Illinois, like most states, reports its law cases in a series of numbered volumes. After the volumes reach number 999, most reporters start over with a second set of volumes. So this case appears in volume 144 of the second set of Illinois reporters. If you went to a law library and found that volume, you could then turn to page 24 and find the case. The same case is reported in another set of volumes, called the regional reporters. This group of law reports is grouped by geographic region. Illinois is included in the northeast region, so this case appears in volume 578 of the second set of the northeast regional reports, at page 981. Finally, most cases are now also available online through computer law libraries. The third citation is to the online law library operated by LEXIS. Typing "1991 Ill. LEXIS 47" would bring up the same case on the computer.

that Gayle Quigley is going to lose unless this court concludes that her case is different from the earlier one.

The next topic is religious freedom, one of the founding principles of this nation. The plaintiff has urged this court to impose on Christian Science nurses the duty to summon traditional medical care, but the court declares that such an obligation would infringe on the church's basic beliefs. The court is considering *public policy*, that is, the long-term interests of society generally. Judges understand that they not only follow precedent, they help to make it. This court is determined not to interfere with religious freedom—a second reason to dismiss the case. Judges try hard to make their decisions persuasive, and you will often find a court offering two or more reasons to support a ruling.

Finally, the court responds to Quigley's argument that the church here was not a casual stranger to Andrew's suffering. The mother argues that the Christian Science practitioners had voluntarily undertaken Andrew's care and thereby *assumed a duty to provide reasonable care.* In other words, the plaintiff is arguing that even if most people owe no duty to each other, *these defendants* owed a duty because they chose to get involved. The court rejects the argument, ruling that the healers undertook to care only for Andrew's spiritual needs and lacked any training or inclination to administer to physical ailments.

For those three reasons, the court *affirms* the trial court's decision, meaning that it approves the decision and upholds the outcome. If the court had disagreed with the trial court, it might have *reversed* the decision, meaning to undo the result. Judge Bedsworth would then have *remanded* the case, that is, sent it back down to a lower court. The plaintiff would then have received her trial.

Finally, notice what this case was *not* about: whether the defendants did the "right" thing. Judge Bedsworth does not applaud the nurses' conduct. Elsewhere in the decision he suggests that the first nurse should have called an ambulance immediately—but had no *legal duty* to do so.

One of the best reasons to read about legal disputes is so you can avoid them. In *Preventive Law,* we focus on how to anticipate problems and steer clear of them. The *Quigley* case raises unusual issues that will not personally affect many people. Yet it is worth asking ourselves how Gayle Quigley might have prevented this tragedy. How could she have done that?

"YOU BE THE JUDGE"

Many cases involve difficult decisions for juries and judges. Often both parties have legitimate, opposing arguments. Most chapters in this book will have a feature called "You be the Judge," in which we present the facts of a case but not the court's holding. We offer you two opposing arguments based on the kinds of claims the lawyers would have made in court. We leave it up to you to debate and decide which position is stronger or to add your own arguments to those given. The following case is another negligence lawsuit, though with a different issue than in *Quigley.* A suicide caused a distraught family to sue a rock singer and music producer. Once again the defendants asked the judge to dismiss the case. They pointed out, correctly, that a negligence case requires a plaintiff to prove not only duty (as in *Quigley*), but also *foreseeability.* The plaintiff must show that the defendant *could have foreseen the type of harm that occurred.* Could Ozzy Osbourne have foreseen this sad outcome to one of his songs? You be the judge.

MCCOLLUM v. CBS, INC.

202 Cal. App. 3d 989, 249 Cal. Rptr. 187, 1988 Cal. App. LEXIS 909
California Court of Appeal, 1988

Facts: John McCollum, 19 years old, was an alcoholic with serious emotional problems. He listened over and over to music recorded by Ozzy Osbourne on CBS records, particularly two albums called *Blizzard of Oz* and *Diary of a Madman*. He usually listened to the music on the family stereo in the living room because the sound was most intense there. One Friday evening, though, he went to his bedroom and lay on his bed, listening to more Osbourne music. He placed a loaded .22-caliber handgun to his right temple and pulled the trigger.

McCollum's parents sued Osbourne and CBS records, claiming that they negligently aided and encouraged John to commit suicide. The parents' argument was that Osbourne's songs were designed to appeal to unstable youths and that the message of some of his music explicitly urged death. One of the songs John had listened to before his death was "Suicide Solution," which included these lyrics:

Wine is fine but whiskey's quicker
Suicide is slow with liquor
Take a bottle drown your sorrows
Then it floods away tomorrows

Now you live inside a bottle
The reaper's travelling at full throttle
It's catching you but you don't see
The reaper is you and the reaper is me

Breaking law, knocking doors
But there's no one at home
Made your bed, rest your head
But you lie there and moan
Where to hide, Suicide is the only way out
Don't you know what it's really about.[9]

The trial court dismissed the lawsuit, ruling that the plaintiff had not made out a valid negligence claim. The court ruled that the First Amendment's free speech provision protected the rights of Osbourne and CBS to publish any music they wanted. In addition, the court found that the defendants could not have foreseen that anyone would respond to the lyrics by taking his own life. With no foreseeability, the court ruled, the plaintiffs' case must fail. The parents appealed, arguing, among other things, that their son's suicide was foreseeable.

You be the Judge: Was McCollum's suicide foreseeable?

Argument for the Parents: Your honors, for years Ozzy Osbourne has been well-known as the "madman" of rock and roll. The words and music of his songs revolve around bizarre, anti-social beliefs, emphasizing death and satanic worship. Many of his songs suggest that life is hopeless and that suicide is not only acceptable but desirable. Now one of his devoted fans has acted on Osbourne's advice and killed himself. The defendants share responsibility for this tragic death.

Osbourne and CBS knew that many of Osbourne's fans struggled with self-identity, alienation, and substance abuse. Both defendants aggressively targeted this market and reaped enormous profits. They knew that Osbourne was a cult figure to his young fans and had great influence in their lives. They realized that the confused youths who adored Osbourne were precisely those most vulnerable to vicious advice. Yet in spite of their knowledge, both defendants churned out songs such as "Suicide Solution," urging troubled, chemically addicted young people to kill themselves. Not only was it *foreseeable* that one of Osbourne's fans would sooner or later take his life, it was *inevitable*. It is sheer hypocrisy for the defendants, their pockets filled with money taken from McCollum and countless others like him, to pretend surprise. The surprise is that this didn't happen earlier. The only way to ensure that this doesn't occur

[9] Words and music by John Osbourne, Robert Daisley and Randy Rhoads. TRO © Copyright 1981 Essex Music International, Inc., New York, New York and Kord Music Publishers, London, England. Used by permission.

again is to permit a jury to hear the parents' case and, if it is persuaded by the evidence, to award the grieving parents damages.

Argument for Osbourne and CBS: Your honors, we all agree that this death was tragic and unnecessary. But the plaintiffs delude themselves if they think that Mr. Osbourne and CBS bear any responsibility. The fact is that John McCollum was deeply troubled and alcoholic. He was responsible for his life—and for his own death. Next to the young man himself, of course, those who bear the greatest responsibility for his sad life and gruesome end are his parents, the plaintiffs in this case. Mr. Osbourne and CBS sympathize with the parents' bereavement, but not with their attempt to foist responsibility onto others.

If the plaintiffs' far-fetched foreseeability argument were the law—which it is not—every singer, writer, film and television producer would be at risk of several thousand lawsuits every year. Under their theory, a producer who made a bank robbery movie would be liable for every robbery that took place afterward, as would every author or singer who ever mentioned the subject. And, of course, there would be no more movies with bank robberies—or murders, assaults, or even fistfights. There would be no more books or articles on such subjects either. The First Amendment was written to ensure that we *do* have access to arts and entertainment, and to prohibit efforts at silencing artists with outlandish lawsuits. This death was never foreseeable and no jury should ever hear the case.

Foreseeability arises in countless cases, as we will see in the chapter on negligence. Suppose a clerk in a store is assaulted by a criminal. The clerk may sue not only the criminal (who will not have any money) but also the owner of the store. Whether the owner is found liable or not will depend upon whether the owner should have foreseen the assault. Similarly, if a tenant is harmed by defective property, the landlord's liability will be determined in part by foreseeability.

CHAPTER CONCLUSION

We depend upon the law to give us a stable nation and economy, a fair society, a safe place to live and work. These worthy goals have occupied Anglo-Saxon kings and twenty-first-century lawmakers alike. But while law is a vital tool for crafting the society we want, there are no easy answers about how to create it. In a democracy, we all participate in the crafting. Legal rules control us, yet we create them. A working knowledge of the law can help build a successful career—and a solid democracy.

CHAPTER REVIEW

1. There is no one source of the law. Our federal system of government means that law comes from a national government in Washington, D.C., and from 50 state governments.
2. The history of law foreshadows many current legal issues, including mediation, partnership liability, the jury system, the role of witnesses, the special value placed on land, the idea of precedent, and the difference between substantive and procedural law.

3. The primary sources of contemporary law are:
   - United States Constitution and state constitutions
   - Statutes, which are drafted by legislatures
   - Common law, which is the body of cases decided by judges, as they follow earlier cases, known as precedent; and
   - Administrative law, the rules and decisions made by federal and state administrative agencies.
4. Other sources of contemporary law include:
   - Treaties
   - Executive orders
5. Criminal law concerns behavior so threatening to society that it is outlawed altogether. Civil law deals with duties and disputes between parties, not outlawed behavior.
6. Substantive law defines the rights of people. Procedural law describes the processes for settling disputes.
7. Jurisprudence is concerned with the basic nature of law. Three theories of jurisprudence are:
   - Legal positivism: The law is what the sovereign says it is.
   - Natural law: An unjust law is no law at all.
   - Legal realism: Who enforces the law is more important than what the law says.

PRACTICE TEST

1. Can one person really understand all of the legal issues mentioned at the beginning of this chapter? For example, can a business executive know about insider trading and employment law and environmental law and tort law and all of the others? Will a court really hold one person to such knowledge?
2. Why does our law come from so many different sources?
3. The stock market crash of 1929 and the Great Depression that followed were caused in part because so many investors blindly put their money into stocks they knew nothing about. During the 1920s, it was often impossible for an investor to find out what a corporation was planning to do with its money, who was running the corporation, and many other vital things. Congress responded by passing the Securities Act of 1933, which required a corporation to divulge more information about itself before it could seek money for a new stock issue. What *kind* of law did the Congress create? Explain the relationship between voters, Congress, and the law.
4. Union organizers at a hospital wanted to distribute leaflets to potential union members, but hospital rules prohibited leafletting in areas of patient care, hallways, cafeterias, and any areas open to the public. The National Labor Relations Board (NLRB) ruled that these restrictions violated the law and ordered the hospital to permit the activities in the cafeteria and coffee shop. The NLRB may not create common law or statutory law. What kind of law was it creating?
5. Leslie Bergh and his two brothers, Milton and Raymond, formed a partnership to help build a fancy saloon and dance hall in Evanston, Wyoming. Later, Leslie met with his friend and drinking buddy, John Mills, and tricked Mills into investing in the saloon. Leslie did not tell Mills that no one else was investing cash or that the entire enterprise was already insolvent. Mills mortgaged his home, invested $150,000 in the saloon—and lost every penny of it. Mills sued all three partners for fraud. Milton and Raymond defended on the ground that they didn't commit the fraud, only Leslie did. The defendants lost. Was that fair? By holding them liable, what general idea did the court rely on? What Anglo-Saxon legal custom did the ruling resemble?
6. **RIGHT & WRONG** Confucius did not esteem written laws, believing instead that good

rulers were the best guarantee of justice. Does our legal system rely primarily on the rule of law or the rule of people? Which do you instinctively trust more? Legal realists argue that the "rule of law" is a misleading term. What point are they making, and how does it relate to Confucius's principles? Confucius himself was an extraordinarily wise man, full of wisdom about life and compassion for his fellow citizens. Since he was extraordinary, what does that tell us about other rulers by contrast? How does that affect Confucius's own views?

7. Tommy Parker may have been involved in some unsavory activities as an officer in a failed savings and loan institution. A federal agency, the Office of Thrift Supervision (OTS), ordered Tommy not to spend or waste any of his own assets while it was investigating him. Later, Tommy and his wife, Billie, got divorced and divided their property. On February 18, the OTS filed papers in court asking for an order that Billie not spend any of her assets. Billie received a copy of the papers on February 20, and the hearing took place on February 24, without Billie in attendance. The court ordered Billie not to spend any assets except for essential living expenses. Billie appealed, claiming that under court rules she was entitled to five days' notice before the hearing took place and that weekend days are not counted. She had had only two business days' notice. Assume that her counting of the days was correct (which it was). Explain the difference between procedural law and substantive law. Which type of law was Billie relying on? Should her appeal be granted?

8. Plaintiff Miss Universe, Inc. owns the trademark *"Miss U.S.A."* For decades, the company has produced the Miss U.S.A. beauty pageant, seen by many millions of people in the United States. William Flesher and Treehouse Fun Ranch began to hold a nude beauty pageant in California. They called this the "Miss Nude U.S.A." pageant. Most of the contestants were from California; the majority of states were not represented in the contest. Miss Universe sued Flesher and Treehouse, claiming that the public would be confused and misled by the similar names. The company sought an *equitable remedy* in this lawsuit. What does "equitable" mean? What equitable remedy did Miss Universe seek? Should it win?

9. Jack and Jill go up a hill to fetch a pail of water. Jill heads back down with the water. Jack meets a stranger, who introduces herself as Katrina. Jack sells a kilo of cocaine to Katrina, who then mentions that she enjoys her job at the Drug Enforcement Agency. Jill, halfway down the hill, meets Freddy, a motorist whose car has overheated. Freddy is late for a meeting where he expects to make a $3 million profit; he's desperate for water for his car. He promises to pay Jill $500 tomorrow if she will give him the pail of water, which she does. The next day, Jack is in jail and Freddy refuses to pay for Jill's water. Explain the criminal law/civil law distinction and what it means to Jack and Jill. Who will do what to whom, with what results?

10. **YOU BE THE JUDGE WRITING PROBLEM** Should trials be televised? Here are a few arguments to add to those in the chapter. You be the judge. **Argument against Live Television Coverage:** We have tried this experiment and it has failed. Trials fall into two categories: those that create great public interest and those that do not. No one watches dull trials, so we do not need to broadcast them. The few that are interesting have all become circuses. Judges and lawyers have shown that they cannot resist the temptation to play to the camera. Trials are supposed to be about justice, not entertainment. If a citizen seriously wants to follow a case, she can do it by reading the daily newspaper. **Argument for Live Television Coverage:** It is true that some televised trials have been unseemly affairs, but that is the fault of the presiding judges, not the media. Indeed, one of the virtues of television coverage is that millions of people now understand that we

have a lot of incompetent people running our courtrooms. The proper response is to train judges to run a tight trial by prohibiting the grandstanding in which some lawyers may engage. Access to accurate information is the foundation on which a democracy is built and we must not eliminate a source of valuable data just because some judges are ill-trained.

11. In his most famous novel, *The Red and the Black,* the French author Stendhal (1783–1842) wrote: "There is no such thing as 'natural law': this expression is nothing but old nonsense. Prior to laws, what is natural is only the strength of the lion, or the need of the creature suffering from hunger or cold, in short, need." What do you think?

INTERNET RESEARCH PROBLEM

Take a look at http://www.courttv.com. Find two current cases that interest you: one civil, one criminal. Explain the different roles played by each type of law, and summarize the issues in the respective cases.

You can find further practice problems in the Online Quiz at http://beatty.westbuslaw.com or in the Study Guide that accompanies this text.

Business Ethics and Social Responsibility

2

CHAPTER

Under the direction of CEO Robert Mahoney, Diebold, Inc. is now the nation's leading manufacturer of automated teller machines, posting record sales for six consecutive years. The company has also been a cash machine for shareholders, as dividends have increased during each of the past 43 years. For all this, Mr. Mahoney has been rewarded handsomely. His annual compensation—salary, bonuses, and stock—has increased nearly fivefold in the past five years, from $464,250 to $2.37 million.

But Diebold's unionized factory workers have not been so fortunate. Under Mahoney's leadership, the company has shifted work to outside contractors and moved production from Ohio to lower-paying, nonunion plants in the South. Today, unionized workers in Ohio make less than they did a decade ago. Then, Jim Ramey, an assembler at the Ohio plant, earned $11.83 an hour, $24,596 a year. Now he makes $9.93 an hour, $20,654 a year. Then, Diebold employed 800 union workers in Ohio; today it has 58.

Donald Eagon, Diebold's vice-president for communications, says market forces dictate company salaries. Diebold has had to reduce factory workers' pay and cut costs to stay competitive in a global market where competitors look to places like Southeast Asia for cheap labor. And Diebold has had to raise executives' salaries so that they will not be hired away by competitors.[1]

Business is an enormously powerful tool that corporate managers can use to accomplish many goals. They may wish to earn a good living, even to become wealthy, but they can also use their business skills to cure the ill, feed the hungry, entertain the bored, and in many other ways affect their community, their country, and their world.

This book is primarily about the impact of law on business. But law is only one set of rules that governs business; ethics is another. **Ethics is the study of how people ought to act.** Law and ethics are often in harmony. Most reasonable people agree that murder should be prohibited. But law and ethics are not always compatible. In some cases, it might be *ethical* to commit an illegal act; in others, it might be *unethical* to be legal. Here are two examples in which law and ethics might conflict:

> George Hart, a 75-year-old man confined to a wheelchair, robbed a bank in San Diego of $70 so that he could buy heart medicine. He entered a branch of the HomeFed Bank, where he had $4 in his account, and apologized while demanding $70 from a teller, threatening to blow up the bank if she did not comply. Mr. Hart was arrested minutes later when he tried to buy a $69 bottle of heart medicine at a nearby drugstore. Mr. Hart said he "hated to have to go to this extreme," but insisted he had tried every other way to find money to buy the medicine.[2]

In 1963, Martin Luther King, Jr., was arrested in Birmingham, Alabama, for leading illegal sit-ins and marches to protest laws that discriminated against African Americans. When eight local clergymen criticized his activities, King offered this defense:

> We know through painful experience that freedom is never voluntarily given by the oppressor; it must be demanded by the oppressed. . . . Perhaps it is easy for those who have never felt the stinging darts of segregation to say "Wait." . . . [W]hen you see the vast majority of your 20 million Negro brothers smothering in an air-tight cage of poverty in the midst of an affluent society; when you suddenly find your tongue twisted as you seek to explain to your six-year-old daughter why she can't go to the public amusement park that has just been advertised on television, and see tears welling up when she is told that Funtown is closed to colored children. . . . [W]hen you take a cross-country drive and find it necessary to sleep night after night in the uncomfortable corners of your automobile because no motel will accept you. . . . How can [we] advocate breaking some laws and obeying others? The answer lies in the fact that there are two types of laws: just and unjust. I agree with St. Augustine that "an unjust law is not law at all."[3]

---

[1] Michael Winerip, "Canton's Economic Seesaw: Managers' Fortunes Rise as Workers Get Bumpy Ride," *The New York Times,* July 7, 1996, p. 10.

[2] "Bank Robber in Wheelchair Has an Alibi: His Medicine," *The New York Times,* Jan. 18, 1991, p. A16.

[3] Martin Luther King, Jr., "Letter from Birmingham Jail," *The Christian Century,* June 12, 1963.

Could one argue in the case of the bank robber that his actions, while illegal, were ethical? Would the argument be stronger if he had been stealing the money to help someone else? In the case of Martin Luther King, Jr., would it be reasonable to conclude not only that breaking the law was ethical, but also that *obeying* the law would have been *unethical?* Were the eight clergymen who criticized King behaving unethically by upholding these odious laws?

The other chapters of this book focus on legal issues, but this chapter concentrates on ethics. In all of the examples in this chapter, the activities are *legal*, but are they *ethical*?

Why Bother with Ethics?

Business schools teach students how to maximize the profitability of an enterprise, large or small. Does ethical behavior maximize profitability? Some people argue that, in the *long run*, ethical behavior does indeed pay. But they must mean the very long run, because to date there is little evidence that ethical behavior necessarily pays, either in the short or the long run. For example, some companies that began by emphasizing ethical behavior have found this approach more difficult to maintain as they have grown.

Ben & Jerry's Homemade, Inc., an ice cream company, limited the salaries of its top managers to no more than seven times the pay of its lowliest worker. But when the original founders stepped down, they found that they had to pay more to hire their replacements. Typically, mutual funds that specialize in "socially responsible" companies—those with, say, strong environmental or equal-employment records—have performed worse than their ethics-neutral competitors.

Unethical companies may perform well financially. The Morgan Fun Shares fund purchases stock in tobacco, alcohol, and gambling companies on the theory that money can be made from vices, particularly if other investors shun the companies. Even for individuals, unethical behavior is no bar to financial success. The first antitrust laws in America were designed, at least in part, to restrain John D. Rockefeller's unethical activities. Yet, four generations later, his name is still synonymous with wealth and his numerous heirs can live comfortably on their inheritance from him.[4]

Some commentators have even argued that the ethical standards governing individuals do not apply to business. They contend that business is a *game*, with different rules. If insurance companies keep outdated actuarial tables that result in unfairly high premiums or use ingenious devices to discriminate against minorities, they are just playing the game particularly well. If you do not like it, get the law changed. Given these arguments, perhaps it is not surprising that half of the workers in a recent survey admitted that they had committed an illegal or unethical act in the prior year. They blamed the pressures of the workplace, such as difficulty balancing work and family or coping with a demanding boss.

If ethical behavior does not necessarily pay and unethical behavior sometimes does, why bother with ethics?

---

[4] Chapter 19, on antitrust, discusses Rockefeller's career at greater length.

SOCIETY AS A WHOLE BENEFITS FROM ETHICAL BEHAVIOR

John Akers, the former chairman of IBM, argues that, without ethical behavior, a society cannot be economically competitive. He puts it this way:

> Ethics and competitiveness are inseparable. We compete as a society. No society anywhere will compete very long or successfully with people stabbing each other in the back; with people trying to steal from each other; with everything requiring notarized confirmation because you can't trust the other fellow; with every little squabble ending in litigation; and with government writing reams of regulatory legislation, tying business hand and foot to keep it honest. That is a recipe not only for headaches in running a company, it is a recipe for a nation to become wasteful, inefficient, and noncompetitive. There is no escaping this fact: the greater the measure of mutual trust and confidence in the ethics of a society, the greater its economic strength.[5]

PEOPLE FEEL BETTER WHEN THEY BEHAVE ETHICALLY

Every business person has many opportunities to be dishonest. Consider how one person felt when he resisted temptation:

> Occasionally a customer forgot to send a bill for materials shipped to us for processing. . . . It would have been so easy to rationalize remaining silent. After all, didn't they deserve to lose because of their inefficiency? However, upon instructing our staff to inform the parties of their errors, I found them eager to do so. They were actually bursting with pride. . . . Our honesty was beneficial in subtle ways. The "inefficient" customer remained loyal for years. . . . [O]ur highly moral policy had a marvelously beneficial effect on our employees. Through the years, many an employee visited my office to let me know that they liked working for a "straight" company. [6]

Profitability is generally not what motivates managers to care about ethics. Managers want to feel good about themselves and the decisions they have made; they want to sleep at night. Their decisions—to lay off employees, install safety devices in cars, burn a cleaner fuel—affect peoples' lives. When two researchers asked businesspeople why they cared about ethics, the answers had little to do with the profitability:

> The businesspeople we interviewed set great store on the regard of their family, friends, and the community at large. They valued their reputations, not for some nebulous financial gain but because they took pride in their good names.[7]

UNETHICAL BEHAVIOR CAN BE VERY COSTLY

Unethical behavior is a risky business strategy—it may lead to disaster. An engaged couple made a reservation, and put down a $1,500 deposit, to hold their wedding reception at a New Hampshire restaurant. Tragically, the bride

---

[5] David Grier, "Confronting Ethical Dilemmas," unpublished manuscript of remarks at the Royal Bank of Canada, Sept. 19, 1989.

[6] Hugh Aaron, "Doing the Right Thing in Business," *The Wall Street Journal,* June 21, 1993, p. A10. Republished with permission of *The Wall Street Journal;* permission conveyed through the Copyright Clearance Center, Inc.

[7] Amar Bhide and Howard H. Stevenson, "Why Be Honest if Honesty Doesn't Pay?" *Harvard Business Review,* Sept.–Oct. 1990, pp. 121–129, at 127.

died of asthma four months before the wedding. Invoking the terms of the contract, the restaurant owner refused to return the couple's deposit. In a letter to the groom, he admitted, "Morally, I would of course agree that the deposit should be returned." When newspapers reported this story, customers deserted the restaurant and it was forced into bankruptcy—over a $1,500 disagreement.[8] Unethical behavior does not always damage a business, but it certainly has the potential of destroying a company overnight. So why take the risk?

Even if unethical behavior does not devastate a business, it can cause other, subtler damage. In one survey, a majority of those questioned said that they had witnessed unethical behavior in their workplace and that this behavior had reduced productivity, job stability, and profits. Unethical behavior in an organization creates a cynical, resentful, and unproductive workforce.

For these reasons, many of America's major corporations actively encourage ethical behavior in their organizations. More than 500 companies have an ethics officer. These guardians of morality serve two purposes: they act as a sounding board for employees with ethical dilemmas, and they also enforce ethical standards within the company. If your co-worker is stealing office supplies, or you suspect a supervisor of having an affair with a subordinate, call the ethics officer to turn in the thief or to obtain advice on handling the sticky romance.

General Electric uses an illustration like the one below to demonstrate its approach to ethics. The company will not tolerate unethical managers, no matter how good their financial results, but it is willing to support employees who have the right values, whatever their results.

	High Performance	Low Performance
Ethical Values	THE SUPERSTARS: Bound for key leadership roles	THE SECOND-CHANCERS: Given more time or different roles
Unethical Values	? Increasing likelihood of quick removal—"the numbers" no longer protect or prolong you	THE FAILURES Removed with no apology

So why bother with ethics? Because society benefits when managers behave ethically. Because ethical managers have happier, more satisfying lives. And because unethical behavior can destroy a business faster than a snake can bite.

WHAT IS ETHICAL BEHAVIOR?

It is one thing to decide, in theory, that being ethical is good; in practice, it can be much more difficult to make the right decisions. Supreme Court Justice

[8] John Milne, "N.H. Restaurant Goes Bankrupt in Wake of Wedding Refund Flap," *Boston Globe*, Sept. 9, 1994, p. 25.

Potter Stewart once said that he could not define pornography, but he knew it when he saw it. Many people feel the same way about ethics—that somehow, instinctively, they know what is right and wrong. In real life, however, ethical dilemmas are often not black and white, but many shades of gray. The purpose of this section is to analyze the following ethics checklist as an aid to managers in making tough decisions:

- What are the facts?
- What are the critical issues?
- Who are the stakeholders?
- What are the alternatives?
- What are the ethical implications of each alternative?
    - Is it legal?
    - How would it look in the light of day?
    - What are the consequences?
    - Does it violate important values?
    - Does it violate the Golden Rule?
    - Is it just?
    - Has the process been fair?
- Is more than one alternative right?
    - Which values are in conflict?
    - Which of these values are most important?
    - Can you find an alternative that is consistent with your values?

ANALYZING THE ETHICS CHECKLIST

WHAT ARE THE FACTS?

Although this question seems obvious, people often forget in the heat of battle to listen to (and, more importantly, to *hear*) all the different viewpoints. Instead of relying on hearsay and rumor, it is crucial to discover the facts, firsthand, from the people involved. It may be easy to condemn a bank robber, until learning the money was needed to buy medicine.

WHAT ARE THE CRITICAL ISSUES?

In analyzing ethical dilemmas, expand your thinking to include *all* the important issues. Avoid a narrow focus that encompasses only one or two aspects. In the case of the New Hampshire restaurant that refused to refund a deposit, the owner focused on the narrow legal issue. His interpretation of the *contract* was correct. But if the owner had expanded his thinking to include consideration for his customers, he might have reached a different decision.

WHO ARE THE STAKEHOLDERS?

Stakeholders are all the people potentially affected by the decision. That list might include subordinates, bosses, shareholders, suppliers, customers, members of the community in which the business operates, society as a whole, or even more remote stakeholders, such as future generations. The interests of these stakeholders often conflict. Current shareholders may benefit from a company's decision to manufacture a product that contributes to global warming, while future generations are left to contend with a potential environmental nightmare.

WHAT ARE THE ALTERNATIVES?

The next step is to list the reasonable alternatives. A creative manager may find a clever solution that is a winner for everyone. As Rebecca Jewett indicates in her interview later in this chapter, her aim is to find a solution that is "win-win" for all the stakeholders.

WHAT ARE THE ETHICAL IMPLICATIONS OF EACH ALTERNATIVE?

Is the Alternative Legal? Illegal may not always be synonymous with unethical, but, as a general rule, you need to think long and hard about the ethics of any illegal activities.

How Would the Alternative Look in the Light of Day? If your activities were reported on the evening news, how would you feel? Proud? Embarrassed? Horrified? Undoubtedly, sexual harassment would be virtually eliminated if people thought that their parents, spouse, or partner would shortly see a video replay of the offending behavior.

What Are the Consequences of this Alternative? Ask yourself: Am I hurting anyone by this decision? Which alternative will cause the greatest good (or the least harm) to the most people? For example, you would like to fire an incompetent employee. That decision will clearly have adverse consequences for him. But the other employees in your division will benefit and so will the shareholders of your company. Overall, your decision will cause more good than harm.

You should look with a particularly critical eye if an alternative benefits you while harming others. Suppose that you become CEO of a company whose headquarters are located in a distant suburb. You would like to move the headquarters closer to your home to cut your commuting time. Of course, such a decision would be expensive for shareholders and inconvenient for other employees. Do you simply impose your will on the company or consider the consequences for everyone?

This approach to decision making was first developed by two nineteenth-century English philosophers, Jeremy Bentham and John Stuart Mill. It is called *utilitarianism* because Bentham and Mill argued that all decisions should be evaluated according to how much *utility* they create. Some commentators have criticized this approach on practical grounds—benefit and harm are difficult to measure. Others also argue that not all utility is equal. A band of robbers may receive more benefit from stealing money than the victim suffers harm, but most people would nonetheless argue that the decision to steal is wrong. Despite these criticisms, it is wise at least to consider the costs and benefits of a decision.

Does the Alternative Violate Important Values? In addition to consequences, consider fundamental values. It is possible to commit an act that does not harm anyone else, but is still the wrong thing to do. Suppose, for instance, that you are away from home and have the opportunity to engage in a temporary sexual liaison. You are absolutely certain that your spouse will never find out and your partner for the night will have no regrets or guilt. There would be no negative consequences, but you believe that infidelity is wrong, *regardless of the consequences*, so you resist temptation.

Some people question whether, as a diverse, heterogeneous society (not to mention, world), we have common values. But throughout history, and across many different cultures, common values do appear. The following values are almost universal:

- *Consideration* means being aware of and concerned about other people's feelings, desires, and needs. The considerate person is able to imagine how he would feel in someone else's place.
- *Courage* is the strength to act in the face of fear and danger. Courage can require dramatic action (saving a buddy on a battlefield) or quiet strength (doing what you think is right, despite opposition from your boss).
- *Integrity* means being sincere, honest, reliable, and loyal. If you have integrity, you do not criticize others behind their back or take credit for their ideas and efforts.
- *Self-control* is the ability to resist temptation. The person with self-control does not drink or eat too much, party too hard, watch too much television, or spend too much money.

Although reasonable people may disagree about a precise list of important values, most would agree that values matter. Try compiling your own list of values and then check it periodically to see if you are living up to it in your business and personal life.

Does the Alternative Violate the Golden Rule? We all know the Golden Rule: do unto others as you would have them do unto you. If one of the alternatives you are considering would be particularly unpleasant when done to you, reconsider.

Immanuel Kant, an eighteenth-century German philosopher, took the Golden Rule one step further with a concept he called the *categorical imperative*. According to Kant, you should not do something unless you would be willing for everyone else to do it, too (and not just to you). Imagine that you could cheat on an exam without getting caught. You might gain some short-term benefit—a higher grade. But what would happen if everyone cheated? The professor would have to make the exams harder or curve everyone's grade down. If your school developed a reputation for cheating, you might not be able to find a job after graduation. Cheating works only if most people are honest. To take advantage of everyone else's honesty is contemptible.

Is the Alternative Just? Are you respecting individual rights such as liberty (privacy, free speech, and religious freedom), welfare (employment, housing, food, education), and equality? Is it right to read an employee's e-mail or would that violate her right to privacy?

Has the Process Been Fair? Unequal outcomes are acceptable, provided they are the result of a fair process. At the end of a poker game, some players have won and others lost, but no one can complain that the result was unfair, unless players cheated. In a business context, a fair process means applying the same set of rules to everyone. If three of your subordinates are vying for the same promotion, it would be unfair to let one state her case to you but not the others.

Is More than One Alternative Right?

Thus far, the ethics checklist has served two purposes. It helps to clarify the issues at stake. It also filters out decisions that are downright wrong. Have you considered lying to a customer about product specifications? For a start, such an action violates principles of integrity, not to mention the Golden Rule. Nor would you want your activity to be revealed on the front page of the local newspaper.

Oftentimes, however, the most difficult decisions arise not in cases of right versus wrong but in situations of right versus right.[9] President Harry Truman's decision to drop atomic bombs on two Japanese cities is a classic example of right versus right. He argued that if he had not ended the war by using nuclear weapons, more Americans and Japanese would have died during a land invasion. Looking simply at the consequences, he concluded that the terrible suffering by the Japanese people was justified because, ultimately, fewer people died overall. At the same time, Truman's decision violated the Golden Rule and Kant's categorical imperative. Indeed, since the end of World War II, the United States has worked hard to ensure that no one else ever deploys nuclear weapons. The ethics checklist presents no clear-cut answer. In the end, Truman decided that the most right (or least wrong) choice was to end the war quickly.

Nuclear weapons make a dramatic example, but what about a more typical business decision? AT&T adopted a policy of cutting costs to maximize its stock price. To implement this policy, the company laid off 40,000 people, despite record profits. Even as workers suffered, shareholders benefited because the company's stock price rose in response to the layoff announcement. But is stock price the only issue? Does the company have an obligation to protect employee jobs? Is one right more important than another?

Which Values Are in Conflict? There are many ways to justify a decision to lay off workers, even 40,000 of them. If managers avoid layoffs, profits suffer, stock prices fall, companies merge, and executives lose their own jobs. In business school and on the job, managers learn how to analyze, compete, and win. Competing—and winning—are important. But what about other values, such as compassion and caring? Do the individual people affected by this decision matter, too?

Which of these Values Are Most Important? Suppose that, growing up, you had seen family members or neighbors suffering through bouts of unemployment. That experience might have taught you that compassion is a high priority. Managers must determine which values are important in their own lives.

---

[9] For a thoughtful discussion of right versus right, see Joseph L. Badaracco, Jr., *Defining Moments: When Managers Must Choose between Right and Right* (Boston: Harvard Business School Press, 1997).

Can You Find an Alternative that Is Consistent with Your Values? The decision you make not only determines the kind of person you are now, but also sets your course for the future. Can you reach a decision that is consistent with the kind of person you are or want to be? Instead of announcing massive layoffs, some companies offer generous severance packages, retraining programs, and other voluntary methods of reducing the workforce. Shareholders may receive less benefit, but employees suffer less harm.

APPLYING THE ETHICS CHECKLIST: MAKING DECISIONS

An organization has responsibilities to customers, employees, shareholders, and society generally, both here and overseas. Employees also have responsibilities to their organizations. The purpose of this section is to apply the ethics checklist to actual business dilemmas. The checklist does not lead to one particular solution; rather it is a method to use in thinking through ethics problems. The goal is for you to reach a decision that satisfies you. For other examples of ethical dilemmas and suggestions for resolving them, go to http://www.mapnp.org/library/ethics/ethxgde.htm.

ORGANIZATION'S RESPONSIBILITY TO SOCIETY

ETHICS OF ADVERTISING

Facts. In the United States, teenagers routinely list alcohol commercials among their favorite advertisements. Adolescents who frequently see ads for alcohol are more likely to believe that drinkers are attractive, athletic, and successful. They are also more likely to drink, drink excessively, and drink in hazardous situations such as driving a car.

While Secretary of Health and Human Services, Louis W. Sullivan publicly denounced the test marketing of Uptown, a high-tar cigarette targeted at African Americans. He called it "contemptible that the tobacco industry has sought to increase their market" among minorities because this population was "already bearing more than its fair share of smoking-related illness and mortality." More pointed was comedian Jay Leno's jest that R. J. Reynolds named the cigarette Uptown "because the word 'Genocide' was already taken."[10]

A promotion for Request Jeans shows a man pinning a naked woman against a shower wall. In Canada, an advertisement features childlike model Kate Moss lying naked on a couch. Above the couch is a picture of the product being promoted—Calvin Klein's Obsession for Men. In England, an ad for a stereo shows a picture of a woman with these words, "She's terrific in bed, she's witty and intelligent, but she didn't have a Linn hi-fi. Her sister did and I married her sister."

In Peru, a television commercial features Africans who are ready to devour white tourists until diverted by the offer of Nabisco pudding. In another Latin American ad, a man compares the thickness of Goodyear tires to the lips of his black partner.

---

[10] Richard W. Pollay, Jung S. Lee, and David Carter-Whitney, "Separate, but Not Equal: Racial Segmentation in Cigarette Advertising," *Journal of Advertising*, Mar. 1992, vol. 21, no. 1, p. 45.

Critical Issues. What are the obligations of advertising executives and marketing managers to those who see their ads? Is it ethical to sell jeans by glorifying rape? Are men more likely to commit rape as a result of seeing one of these advertisements? Is it ethical to entice teenagers into drinking or African Americans into smoking? An advertising executive asserts that Latin American audiences find racial stereotypes amusing. Does that justify racist ads?

Stakeholders. Ad designers are primarily responsible to their firms and the firms' clients. After all, designers are paid to sell product, not to make the world a better place. But what about the people who see the advertisements? Do the designers have any responsibility to them? Or to society as a whole?

Alternatives. Firms have at least four alternatives in dealing with issues of ethics in advertising. They can:

- Ignore ethics and simply strive to create promotions that sell the most product, whatever the underlying message
- Try, in a general way, to minimize racism, sexism, and other exploitation
- Include, as part of the development process, a systematic, focused review of the underlying messages contained in their advertisements; or
- Refuse to create any ads that are potentially demeaning, insensitive, or dangerous, recognizing that such a stand may lead to a loss of clients.

Ethical Implications. All of these alternatives are perfectly legal. And, far from the ad executives being embarrassed if the ads see the light of day, the whole purpose of ads is to be seen. As for the consequences, the ads may help clients sell their products. But the ads may also harm those who see them by encouraging, among other things, drinking, smoking, sexual assault, racism, and promiscuity. A manager might question whether these ads violate fundamental values. Are they showing consideration for others? Do they encourage self-control? As for the Golden Rule, how would an advertising executive feel about an ad in which he was being sexually assaulted? Or a promotion in which he was assumed to be less valuable than a stereo system? Are these ads just? Do they violate principles of equality? Is the process by which they have been created fair? Have those who may be adversely affected by them had an opportunity to be heard?

Right versus Right. Most people using an ethics checklist would agree that an advertisement making fun of a black man's thick lips is offensive and wrong. But what about subtler issues? In a country with rampant anorexia among teenage girls, is it ethical to run ads with emaciated girls as role models? What about ads for lottery tickets? These tickets are largely purchased by those who can least afford to gamble. If you worked in an advertising agency or marketing department, you might feel a strong sense of loyalty to your company. But what about consideration for those who could be harmed by your ads? You must decide which values are important to you and look for solutions that enable you to live by these values.

Some of the ads described in this section appear stunningly tasteless. They could have been worse, however. The Ad Graveyard (http://zeldman.com/ad.html) offers examples of proposed ads that never saw the light of day, for very obvious reasons.

GANGSTA RAP

Rap artist Ice-T and his band, Body Count, recorded a song called *Cop Killer* in which the singer gleefully anticipates slitting a policeman's throat. (The lyrics to this song are available at http://www.cleat.org/remember/TimeWarner/lyrics.html.

Time Warner, Inc. produced this song and other gangsta rap recordings with violent and sexually degrading lyrics. Recorded music is an important source of profits for the company, which is struggling with a $15 billion debt and a depressed stock price. If Time Warner renounces rap albums, its reputation in the music business—and future profits—might suffer. This damage could spill over into the multimedia market, which is crucial to Time Warner's future.

Although Gerald M. Levin, the company chairman, tried to lead an industry-wide effort to label provocative lyrics, other recording studios refused to cooperate. The companies could not agree on a definition of unacceptable language. Meanwhile, William J. Bennett, who directs a conservative research center, and C. Delores Tucker, the chairwoman of the National Political Congress of Black Women, sent letters to Time Warner board members protesting the company's support of gangsta rap. "I'm sure they've all given little commencement speeches at their prep schools where they deplore violence in society," Mr. Bennett said. "Where do they think violence comes from?"[11] At Time Warner's annual meeting, Ms. Tucker attacked the board of directors for distributing gangsta rap. She accused the company of contributing to the moral corruption of African American men and women. "Shame on our family, Time Warner, for producing this filth," she said.[12] Mr. Levin responded that the company had to balance its commitment to freedom of expression against the music's potential harm. Some Time Warner albums carry a sticker warning parents. Is that enough?

What would you do if you were the chairman of Time Warner? He is concerned about several important stakeholders—shareholders, consumers, suppliers (rap musicians). Which decision would be best for him? For society? For Time Warner shareholders? How would he justify this decision? Even if Time Warner was not ashamed of *Cop Killer*, Ice-T apparently was. The original draft of this chapter included a sample of the lyrics, but Ice-T would not give permission for their use. His lawyer said that Ice-T was so embarrassed by the public's outraged response to the song that he now refuses all requests for permission, in the hope that the lyrics will be forgotten. Which items on the ethics checklist should Ice-T have considered before recording this song? (Ice-T is not the first artist accused of corrupting morals. For a history of controversial music over the last 50 years, tune in to http://ericnuzum.com/banned/index.html.)

ORGANIZATION'S RESPONSIBILITY TO ITS CUSTOMERS

When buying a product, customers often provide more than just money—they reveal personal information, such as their name, address, and credit card

---

[11] Mark Landler, "Time Warner Seeks a Delicate Balance in Rap Music Furor," *The New York Times,* June 5, 1995, p. A1.

[12] Mark Landler, "Time Warner Is Again Criticized for Distributing 'Gangsta' Rap," *The New York Times,* May 16, 1997, p. D5.

number. When surfing the Internet, customers may provide even more intimate information—such as their telephone number, e-mail address, Social Security number, medical history, or sexual preference. Under federal law, Internet operators cannot collect information from children under 13 without parental permission, but adults are fair game.[13] Do Web site operators have an ethical obligation to their adult customers?

Looking for a new car, Dan Gillmor logged on to Autobytel.com. He gave his phone number so that dealers could call him with car prices. Having decided not to buy a car, he forgot all about his online search until several weeks later when he received a phone call at work offering him a new credit card. Without his knowledge, Autobytel had given his telephone number to the credit card company. No wonder that he refused when AT&T demanded his Social Security number before signing him up for cheap long-distance telephone rates over the Internet. To protect his privacy, he ultimately had to select another long-distance carrier.

This invasion of his Internet privacy caused Gillmor some inconvenience. The cost was higher for Naval Petty Officer Timothy McVeigh (who is no relation to the Oklahoma City bomber). When McVeigh filled out a user profile for America Online (AOL), he identified his marital status as "gay." In the midst of a Navy investigation into his sexual preference, a paralegal called AOL's toll-free number and simply asked the identity of the user who had filled out that profile. AOL told all and the Navy ordered McVeigh's dismissal.

Sitting in the privacy of your own home or office, typing into your computer, the Internet *feels* anonymous. It is anything but. E-commerce is booming and thousands of Web sites sell all sorts of stuff. Others give it away, in return for just a little data. You may not even be aware that you have supplied information. Suppose you send a blank e-mail to obtain a password. That e-mail may contain your name and the name of your employer. Or suppose you use your company e-mail account to log on to a pornographic Web site or a support group for victims of breast cancer. The name of your employer and your Internet Protocol address (which can be used to trace you) are available to the Web site operator.

Do companies have an ethical obligation to keep all this personal information confidential? In a survey of the 100 most frequented Web sites, only about half had any privacy policy at all. When policies do exist, they range from sturdy to anemic. *Wired* magazine's Web site states categorically that it "will not release your personal data to anyone else without your consent—period." Amazon.com "does not sell, trade, or rent your personal information to others. We may choose to do so in the future with trustworthy third parties, but you can tell us not to by sending a blank e-mail message to never@amazon.com." This interesting information is not displayed on the opening Web page, however, and is not easy to find. A Federal Trade Commission (FTC) study found that 92 percent of commercial Web sites collect personal information, but only 14 percent disclose their privacy policies. No surprise that only 61 percent of online users have ever seen a privacy notice when surfing the Web.

---

[13] Children's On-Line Privacy Protection Act of 1998.

Ironically, Web site operators have an incentive *not* to disclose their privacy policies. Federal law does not require a policy, but if a Web site posts a policy and then violates it, the FTC will intervene because that constitutes an illegal, deceptive practice. Easier, and safer, then to have no policy at all. In response, a number of nonprofit organizations, such as TRUSTe (http://truste.org), now offer a seal of approval to companies that comply with their privacy standards. So far, however, only a few hundred Web sites have logged on to the TRUSTe plan.

The Electronic Privacy Information Center (http://www.epic.org) reveals the latest on Web privacy issues. For more about ethics on the Web, check in at http://www.netcheck.com. Visitors to this site can post complaints about and praise for Internet businesses. The site's philosophy is that "public pressure is the only real deterrent in this new frontier." Evidently, once posted, many complaints are resolved quickly. Which item on the ethics checklist does that recall?

ORGANIZATION'S RESPONSIBILITY TO ITS EMPLOYEES

EMPLOYEE SAFETY

The following article gives a father's view on ethics in his daughter's workplace.

Early Saturday morning, my daughter Christian was robbed at knife-point. She was working the graveyard shift—alone—at a convenience store near her apartment. When Chrissie got this job, I was appalled. I told her she was crazy. But she is 19. She thinks she's invincible. She figured she could earn money and study during the quiet hours. Instead, she cleaned the storeroom and priced the Pop Tarts because that's what the late shift is supposed to do. With the store's lights ablaze, Chrissie strolled up and down the aisles with her pricing stamp; she was a kind of human guard dog, protecting the place against vandalism. She sold a couple of bucks worth of beer and gasoline and milk and cigarettes. And she listened to how quiet it can get in a darkened neighborhood in the middle of the night.

Then Saturday at about 3 A.M., some idiot high on drugs or wired with fear slipped into the store. He had wrapped his T-shirt around his face as a mask. He showed a knife and told Chrissie if she didn't open the cash register he would stab her or cut her face. She emptied the register. He told her to open the second register. She said it was empty. He got angry. He thought she was lying. He bounced on his toes and barked at her to open the second register. Just then, a customer drove up. The man with the knife grabbed the store money and fled.

I am so relieved she is alive, unhurt. At the same time, I am so angry with managers who hire people too young to know how vulnerable they are, and who put them, alone, in isolated, dangerous posts. I am so angry with the kind of corporate thinking that risks human life for clean floors and soup cans with price stickers. Those stores aren't open at 3 A.M. to sell cereal. They're open because the owners would have to pay someone to clean and stock anyway and you can't clean and stock when the aisles are filled with customers. So you might as well do it during the night. And you might as well keep the doors open, so you can pick up a buck or two from people who can't sleep or don't own beds. The "convenience" isn't the customer's; it's the owner's.

An executive at a convenience store chain (who wished to remain anonymous) responded this way:

> Look, this father has obviously been through a tough time and I don't blame him for being upset. But his allegations are absurd. First of all, convenience stores are called *convenience* stores because they're in busy locations and they're open all the time. That's our market niche. For many people who don't have cars, convenience stores are the only place they have to shop. We're a lifeline for them.
>
> In every store, we do a sales analysis for different time periods during the day. Believe me, we wouldn't be open at night if we weren't making money. As for cleaning and stocking—we can do that anytime. Heck, you see them cleaning and stocking in grocery stores during the day, don't you? As for marking goods, we don't even do that anymore. With all the automated technology, our cash registers read the little stripes on the can and that's all there is to it.
>
> Robberies do happen, but they are relatively rare, and we do everything we can to insure the safety of our employees and the security of our stores. You know, it costs us a lot of money if one of our employees is harmed. In the case of a death, we typically settle for about $1 million, but some people have won jury verdicts of over $8 million. Even when we have insurance, our premiums go sky high if we lose an employee. We try to keep our employees as secure as possible. We hire our own police to visit stores. We install "drop" safes into which employees can put money, but not get it out. We've added items like security cameras and panic buttons. We train our clerks to keep only $30 or $40 in the registers. That's why convenience store robberies have declined two percent over the last four years, while robberies in fast-food chains are way up, doubling in some cities.
>
> One last point. You know, we're human. We hate it when our employees are hurt. And we'll do whatever we can to keep them safe—short of inconveniencing our customers.[14]

What ethical obligations do managers of convenience stores owe their employees? Their customers?

THIRD SHIFT WORKERS

To find out about other ethical dilemmas, we spoke with Rebecca Jewett about some of the issues she faced as president of Chadwick's of Boston. Chadwick's is a catalog company specializing in discount clothes. The company employs 2,000 people and has annual sales of nearly $300 million. Jewett is a graduate of Wellesley College and Harvard Business School.

QUESTION: What ethical dilemmas have you faced in dealing with your employees?

JEWETT: Let me give you one example. We used to run a third shift, from 11 P.M. to 7 A.M., that packed orders. It's a tough shift to run. There's a lot of very poor productivity. It's a shift where people do things like write graffiti on bathroom doors. It makes it very, very difficult to keep the building clean, which is important for everybody else. There's also less management on the third shift. The results just weren't worth the amount we were having to spend. So we decided to close down that shift.

---

[14] "Convenience Store Victimizes," Collin Conner writing in the *St. Petersburg Times*, June 7, 1989, p. 2. Reprinted by permission. *St. Petersburg Times*. Copyright 1989.

QUESTION: One could argue that you had no special obligation to these employees. After all, they had been disruptive and destructive. What did you do?

JEWETT: We could have just laid them off, that's true. Our other choice was to offer them jobs on the first or second shift. We didn't really need them there. It wouldn't have created a financial crisis, but it would have put us in an awkward position. We also had to decide how much advance notice to give them. We could have waited until the last day if we wanted to.

QUESTION: What did you do?

JEWETT: In the end, we offered all of the associates jobs on the first or second shift. We also gave them one month's notice so they would have plenty of time to think things through and make arrangements. There were one or two women who had child care problems during the day, so we let them switch to answering the phones because that department still had a third shift.

QUESTION: How did this decision affect your stakeholders?

JEWETT: It may have hurt financial results, and therefore shareholders, in the short run. But it was nonetheless a good decision for the company because we'll get known as an employer who cares about its associates. What you want to do is to treat people fairly and openly. I try to understand the needs of the associates and our needs as a company and then find the common ground. I always believe that there is a win-win situation for us both.

Did Jewett make the best decision? How do her actions fit into the ethics checklist?

ORGANIZATION'S RESPONSIBILITY TO ITS SHAREHOLDERS

In Japan, a CEO makes 20 to 25 times the pay of an average worker, compared with 30 to 35 times in Germany and 40 times in England. As we saw at the beginning of the chapter, the CEO of Diebold earns $2.37 million a year, while a factory worker receives only $20,654. The executive's salary is 115 times that of the worker. By international standards, the Diebold CEO is overpaid, but his salary looks more modest in comparison with other American companies. The nation's top CEOs average $8.6 million annually, plus perks. This salary is 209 times the pay of the typical worker. American executives also have a lower tax rate than their overseas counterparts, so they take home an even larger share of their pay.

CEO salaries are generally set by a subcommittee of the board of directors. In theory, the subcommittee's goal should be to pay the minimum necessary to attract competent executives. In reality, however, most members of compensation committees are executives from other companies. Their real incentive may be to bid up the "going rate" for executive jobs. Evidence seems to suggest that executive pay has only a tenuous relationship to company performance. When 3M's shares declined 1 percent in value (during a year in which the stock market roared up 33 percent), CEO Livio DeSimone received a 40 percent pay increase to $6 million. Eastman Kodak also had a difficult year as it lost market share, laid off 19,000 workers, earned lower profits, and saw its stock price lag. CEO George Fisher fared better. The board of directors forgave him $1.82 million in interest on loans and granted him stock options worth $57 million.

Even salary plans that base compensation on performance do not always work as shareholders might wish. Under the typical performance plan, executives start with a large base salary that is unrelated to performance. This generous base may encourage them to take undue risks with the company. If the risk pays off, they will make a fortune; if not, they still pocket their large base salary, and shareholders bear the brunt of any disaster. Moreover, there is no obvious best method for evaluating performance. Should pay be based on profits? Stock prices? The overall economy may have as much impact on the company's results as the CEO's performance does. In a booming market, all stock prices tend to rise regardless of the CEO's efforts.

Graef Crystal, a leading authority on executive compensation, has this to say: "If you already have your foot to the floor, if I put any more gas in the tank, I can't go any faster. The only person who benefits from paying a CEO $20 million is his broker."[15]

According to Crystal, there is a relationship between pay and performance for CEOs with less than 10 years of tenure, but not for those who have been at the helm longer. "My theory is that if you've been a CEO for more than ten years, that you have personally appointed virtually every member of the board of directors," he said. "They're your creatures. They're the people you go golfing with, the people who thank you for putting them on the board, so whether or not you play the game fairly is up to what's inside you."[16] For more on executive compensation, pay attention to Graef Crystal's column at http://www.bloomberg.com.

Is there a solution to this problem? What are a CEO's ethical obligations when it comes to pay?

ORGANIZATION'S RESPONSIBILITY OVERSEAS

An American company's ethical obligations do not end at the border. What ethical duties does an American manager owe to stakeholders in countries where the culture and economic circumstances are very different?

Here is a typical story from Guatemala:

> My father left home a long time ago. My mother supported me and my five brothers and sisters by selling tortillas and corn. Our house was a tin shack on the side of the road. We were crowded with all of us in one room, especially when it rained and the roof and sides leaked. There were hundreds of squatters in the neighborhood, but one day the police came and cleared us all out. The owners of the land said we couldn't come back unless we paid rent. How could we afford that? I was 12 and my mother said it was time for me to work. But most people won't hire children. Lots of other kids shine shoes or beg, but I heard that the maquila [clothing factory] was willing to hire children if we would work as hard as older people.
>
> I can keep up with the grown-ups. We work from 6:00 in the morning to 6:30 at night, with half an hour break at noon. We have no other breaks the whole rest of the day. If I don't work fast enough, they hit me, not too hard, and threaten to fire me. Sometimes, if there is too much work to do, they'll lock the doors and not let us out until everything is finished.

---

[15] Sean Keeler, "CEOs Earn Bigger Bucks in U.S. than in Japan, Germany, U.K.," *Montreal Gazette*, Oct. 4, 1994, p. D8.

[16] *Ibid.*

> I'm always really tired at the end of the day and in the morning, too. But I earn $30 a week and without that money, we would not have enough to eat. My mother hopes all of my brothers and sisters can get jobs in the factory, too.
>
> Of course, I'd rather be in school where I could wear a uniform and have friends. Then I could get a job as a clerk at the medical clinic. I would find people's files and tell them how long before the doctor could see them.

American companies have invested more than $56 billion in developing countries. This sum has more than tripled in the last 15 years. Government officials and company executives alike assert that commerce with developing countries is crucial to U.S. prosperity. And the benefit is not one-sided: economists argue that low-wage plants are an essential first step in the modernization of developing countries. Industrialization in Indonesia has meant that only one-third of the children are malnourished, down from one-half. In response to international complaints about working conditions, textile firms in Bangladesh fired 30,000 young workers. Many of these children turned to prostitution or other industries like welding, where conditions are far more dangerous. Jeffrey Sachs, a leading economist and adviser to developing nations, says, "My concern is not that there are too many sweatshops but that there are too few. Those are precisely the jobs that were the steppingstone for Singapore and Hong Kong and those are the jobs that have to come to Africa to get them out of their back-breaking rural poverty."[17]

Many American companies, including such well-known names as Nike, Wal-Mart, Sears, Reebok, The Gap, Liz Claiborne, and Eddie Bauer, have been under attack for making goods in overseas sweatshops. Nike was particularly criticized for giving multimillion dollar endorsement contracts to stars such as Tiger Woods even as it pays its workers in China and Vietnam less than $2 a day and those in Indonesia less than $1 a day. Critics argue that workers in these countries need $3 a day to cover basic food, shelter, and clothing. Nike's chairman, Philip Knight, admitted, "The Nike product has become synonymous with slave wages, forced overtime and arbitrary abuse."[18] In response, Nike has agreed to increase the minimum age for new workers to 18, raise air-quality controls and safety rules to U.S. levels, and allow independent monitoring groups into Nike factories. It has made no promise, however, to raise wages.

What ethical obligations do U.S. companies have to overseas workers? What decisions would you make if you were Philip Knight?

EMPLOYEES' RESPONSIBILITY TO THEIR ORGANIZATION

Joya is the head of the personal insurance division of a large insurance company. She is one of the few women in her industry to reach such a high level. Six months before, she was almost promoted to vice-president, but she lost out to Bill. He is now her boss, and she is determined to make the best of it. She and other department heads have an annual meeting with Bill to award raises and bonuses to all the mid-level managers in their departments. At this year's meeting, they will also discuss who should be promoted to head the marine insurance

---

[17] Allen R. Meyerson, "In Principle, a Case for More 'Sweatshops,'" *The New York Times*, June 22, 1997, p. E5.

[18] Bob Herbert, "Nike Blinks," *The New York Times*, May 21, 1998, p. A37.

division. This decision is important to the firm because the marine division is large and profitable. The decision is also important to other department heads because they all work closely together. One difficult person can make everyone's life miserable. The promotion will mean a substantial raise to the person chosen.

In Joya's opinion, Ichiro is the most qualified person for this position. However, she knows that Bill will not support him. In Bill's view, Ichiro has two strikes against him: he is Japanese and a relatively recent immigrant to the United States. The CEO of the company has taken Ichiro with him several times on trips to Japan to explore the possibility of entering the Japanese market. Bill resents what he perceives as special treatment for Ichiro.

Although Joya is well aware of Bill's biases, she is nonetheless astonished by his behavior at the meeting. When Ichiro's name comes up as a potential candidate for promotion, Bill announces that the middle managers in the marine insurance division strongly object to Ichiro because of his drinking problem. Joya knows that this is all nonsense—Ichiro does not have a drinking problem and the mid-managers in his department think he would be a terrific choice. In her view, Bill is outright lying.

Based on Bill's false information, the other department heads agree that the promotion should go to Jim, who happens to be a friend of Bill's. Joya knows that Jim is unpopular in his division because of his harsh, demanding style. She thinks that his appointment as department head will be disastrous. At the end of the meeting, a satisfied Bill says that he will report the sense of the meeting to the CEO. He is confident that Jim will get the job.

Joya knows the CEO (they exchange pleasantries when passing in the hallways), but they have no regularly scheduled meetings. Nor is Joya likely to have the opportunity to mention Bill's behavior in a casual way. She is concerned that if she reports Bill is lying, the CEO will think she is causing trouble out of jealousy that Bill got the job she wanted.

What should Joya do?

CHAPTER CONCLUSION

Even employees who are ethical in their personal lives may find it difficult to uphold their standards at work if those around them behave differently. Managers wonder what they can do to create an ethical environment in their companies. To help foster a sense of ethics within their organizations, 90 percent of Fortune 500 companies and almost half of all other U.S. companies have developed their own formal ethics codes. For instance, Johnson & Johnson's corporate credo states that managers must make "just and ethical decisions" and all employees must be "good citizens." Many companies have instituted formal ethics training programs for their employees.

In the end, however, the surest way to infuse ethics throughout an organization is for top executives to behave ethically themselves. Few employees will bother to "do the right thing" unless they observe that their bosses value and support such behavior. To ensure a more ethical world, managers must be an example for others, both within and outside their organizations.

For further discussion and updates on ethical issues, check in at http://ethics.acusd.edu/index.html.

CHAPTER REVIEW

1. There are at least three reasons to be concerned about ethics in a business environment:
   - Society as a whole benefits from ethical behavior.
   - People feel better when they behave ethically.
   - Unethical behavior can be very costly.
2. The ethics checklist:
   - What are the facts?
   - What are the critical issues?
   - Who are the stakeholders?
   - What are the alternatives?
   - What are the ethical implications of each alternative?
     - Is it legal?
     - How would it look in the light of day?
     - What are the consequences?
     - Does it violate important values?
     - Does it violate the Golden Rule?
     - Is it just?
     - Has the process been fair?
   - Is more than one alternative right?
     - Which values are in conflict?
     - Which of these values are most important?
     - Can you find an alternative that is consistent with your values?

PRACTICE TEST

1. Interview subject Rebecca Jewett told this story of her life as an MBA student 15 years ago:

   During the spring of my first year, I took a Business Policy class. One of the young men in the class hung a bigger than life-size poster in the back of the room. It was a naked woman chained to a tree next to a Paul Bunyan-type man, fully-clothed in a flannel jacket, with a chain saw. He was starting to de-limb her. The class broke up. The professor was standing there doubled over in laughter. There were 85 men guffawing away as if it were the funniest thing they'd ever seen. The women just sat there with their mouths open.

   Did this professor and these students behave ethically? What would you consider to be ethical behavior in this circumstance for the men, the women, and the professor?

2. An executive gave this account of the dilemma he faced in hiring undocumented workers:

   We have a big temporary workforce. At a time when the labor market was very tight, a guy came to us who runs a temporary agency for Vietnamese workers. He told us he could supply 40 Vietnamese any time. We hired them and, in fact, they were fabulous employees, they had twice the productivity of our best workers. We loved them. But when we asked him if every one of them was legally able to work here, he couldn't produce green cards.

   At that time, it was legal to hire workers without green cards. Would it have been ethical?

3. Executives were considering the possibility of moving their company to a different state. They wanted to determine if employees would be willing to relocate, but they did not want the employees to know the company was contemplating a move because the final decision had not yet been made. Instead of asking the employees directly, the company hired a firm to carry out a telephone survey. When calling the employees, these

"pollsters" pretended to be conducting a public opinion poll and identified themselves as working for the new state's Chamber of Commerce. Has this company behaved in an ethical manner? Would there have been a better way to obtain this information?

4. Mark is an executive for a multinational office equipment company that would like to enter the potentially vast Chinese market. However, the official tariffs on office equipment imported into China are so high that these goods are uncompetitive in the local market. Mark discovers, however, that many companies sell their goods to importers offshore (typically in Hong Kong). These importers then negotiate "special" tariff rates with Chinese officials. Because these custom officials are under pressure to meet revenue targets, sometimes they are willing to negotiate lower, unofficial rates. What would you do if you were Mark?

5. Professor Milton Friedman, a Nobel laureate in economics, has said: "The one and only social responsibility of business is to increase its profits." Dayton Hudson, a department store chain, says in its corporate constitution, "The business of business is serving society, not just making money." Which is it?

6. H. B. Fuller Co. of St. Paul is a leading manufacturer of industrial glues. Its mission statement says the company "will conduct business legally and ethically." It has endowed a university chair in Business Ethics and donates 5 percent of its profits to charity. But now it is under attack for selling its shoemakers' glue, Resistol, in Central America. Many homeless children in these countries have become addicted to Resistol's fumes. So widespread is the problem that glue-sniffers in Central America are called "resistoleros." Glue manufacturers in Europe have added a foul-smelling oil to their glue that discourages abusers. Fuller fears that the smell may also discourage legitimate users. What should Fuller do?

7. According to the Electronic Industries Association, questionable returns have become the toughest problem plaguing the consumer electronics industry. Some consumers purchase electronic equipment to use once or twice for a special occasion and then return it—a radar detector for a weekend getaway or a camcorder to videotape a wedding. Or a customer might return a cordless telephone because he cannot figure out how it works. The retailer's staff lacks the expertise to help, so they refund the customer's money and ship the phone back to the manufacturer labeled as defective. Excessive and unwarranted returns force manufacturers to repackage and reship perfectly good products, imposing extra costs that squeeze their profits and raise prices to consumers. One retailer returned a cordless telephone that was two years old and had been chewed up by a dog. What ethical obligations do consumers and retailers have in these circumstances?

8. Consider this complaint from an ethics professor:

   > I make my living teaching and writing about ethics. . . . But in our own world—in our departments of philosophy and religious studies and medical humanities and ethics institutes—what happens?
   >
   > - Job openings [for instructors] are announced for positions that are already earmarked for specific persons. . . . [O]ver half the positions announced in the official employment newsletter for the American Academy of Religion were not "real."
   > - It is extremely common for letters of application, even those responding to announced openings, to go without acknowledgment.
   > - There are numerous instances of candidates who are brought to campus for interviews and who wait in vain to hear anything from their prospective employers. When the candidates finally call, embarrassed but desperate, they are told, "Oh, that position has been filled."

   Do recruiters have any ethical obligations to job candidates?

9. Six months ago, Todd, David, and Stacey joined a large, prestigious accounting firm in Houston. On paper, these three novices look similar and each graduated from a top MBA program. All three were assigned to work for the same client, a national restaurant chain. They quickly became friends and often lunched together. One day, a senior manager in the firm stopped by the conference room where Todd and David were working to ask if they would like to join him for lunch at the posh Hunter Club nearby. David said, "Thanks, that'd be great, but we usually eat lunch with Stacey. Could she come, too?" The manager hemmed and hawed for a minute, shifted his weight from one foot to the other, and finally said, "The Hunter Club doesn't allow women at lunch." What should Todd and David do?

10. Genentech, Inc. manufactures Protropin, a genetically engineered version of the human growth hormone. This drug's purpose is to enhance the growth of short children. Protropin is an important product for Genentech, accounting for more than one-third of the company's total revenue of $217 million. Although the drug is approved for the treatment of children whose bodies make inadequate quantities of growth hormone, many doctors prescribe it for children with normal amounts of growth hormone who simply happen to be short. There is no firm evidence that the drug actually increases growth for short children with normal growth hormone. Moreover, many people question whether it is appropriate to prescribe such a powerful drug for cosmetic reasons, especially when the drug may not work. Nor is there proof that it is safe over the long term. Is Genentech behaving ethically? Should it discourage doctors from prescribing the drug to normal, short children?

INTERNET RESEARCH PROBLEM

Go to http://www.mapnp.org/library/ethics/ethxgde.htm and click on *Ethics Tools: Resolving Ethical Dilemmas (with Real-to-Life Examples)*. Outline the steps you would take to resolve one of these dilemmas. Use the ethics checklist in this chapter to guide you.

You can find further practice problems in the Online Quiz at http://beatty.westbuslaw.com or in the Study Guide that accompanies this text.

3 CHAPTER

DISPUTE RESOLUTION

Tony Caruso hadn't returned for dinner. His wife, Karen, was nervous. She put on some sandals and hurried across the dunes, a half mile to the ocean shore. She soon came upon Tony's dog, Blue, tied to an old picket fence. Tony's shoes and clothing were piled neatly nearby. Karen and friends searched frantically throughout the evening. A little past midnight, Tony's body washed ashore, his lungs filled with water. A local doctor concluded he had accidentally drowned.

Karen and her friends were not the only ones distraught. Tony had been partners with Beth Smiles in an environmental consulting business, Enviro-Vision. They were good friends, and Beth was emotionally devastated. When she was able to focus on business issues, Beth filed an insurance claim with the Coastal Insurance Group. Beth hated to think about Tony's death in financial terms, but she was relieved that the struggling business would receive $2 million on the life insurance policy.

Several months after filing the claim, Beth received this reply from Coastal: "Under the policy issued to Enviro-Vision, we are conditionally liable in the amount of $1 million in the event of Mr. Caruso's death. If his death is accidental, we are conditionally liable to pay double indemnity of $2 million. But pursuant to section H(5) death by suicide is not covered. After a thorough investigation, we have concluded that Anthony Caruso's death was an act of suicide, as defined in section B(11) of the policy. Your claim is denied in its entirety." Beth was furious. She was convinced Tony was incapable of suicide. And her company could not afford the $2 million loss. She decides to consult her lawyer, Chris Pruitt.

THREE FUNDAMENTAL AREAS OF LAW

This case is a fictionalized version of several real cases based on double indemnity insurance policies. In this chapter we follow Beth's dispute with Coastal from initial interview through appeal, using it to examine three fundamental areas of law: alternative dispute resolution, the structure of our court systems, and civil lawsuits. But first we need to look at the one good kind of dispute—the one that is prevented.

DISPUTE PREVENTION

Over the years, one of the important services attorney Chris Pruitt has done for Enviro-Vision is *prevent disputes.* It is vital to understand and apply this concept in business and professional work and in everyday life. There is an old saying that you have a chance to go broke twice in your life: once when you lose a lawsuit, the other time when you win. The financial and emotional costs of litigation are extraordinarily high.

You can avoid disputes in many different ways. Throughout the text we specify an array of preventive steps as they relate to the different legal problems posed. Here we can mention a few of the potential disputes Enviro-Vision avoided by thinking ahead.

When Beth and Tony started Enviro-Vision, Chris pointed out that, as business partners, the best way to protect both their friendship and their business was with a detailed partnership agreement. Although Beth and Tony found it tedious to create, the agreement helped them avoid problems such as those concerning capital contributions to the partnership, about who owns what, and about hiring and firing employees. Further, Enviro-Vision avoids unjustified firings by giving all employees written job descriptions. It educates employees about sexual harassment. When drafting a contract, Beth has learned to be sure that the client knows exactly what it is getting, when the work is due, what the risks are, and how much it will cost. Each of these practices has prevented potential lawsuits.

When Beth Smiles meets with her lawyer, Chris Pruitt brings a second attorney from his firm, Janet Booker, who is an experienced litigator. If they file a lawsuit, Janet will be in charge, so Chris wants her there for the first meeting. Janet probes about Tony's home life, the status of the business, his personal finances, everything. Beth becomes upset that Janet doesn't seem sympathetic, but Chris explains that Janet is doing her job: she needs all the information, good and bad.

Litigation versus Alternative Dispute Resolution

Janet starts thinking about the two methods of dispute resolution: litigation and alternative dispute resolution. **Litigation** refers to lawsuits, the process of filing claims in court, and ultimately going to trial. **Alternative dispute resolution** is any other formal or informal process used to settle disputes without resorting to a trial. It is increasingly popular with corporations and individuals alike because it is generally cheaper and faster than litigation.

Alternative Dispute Resolution

Janet Booker knows that even after expert legal help, vast expense, and years of work, litigation may leave clients unsatisfied. If she can use alternative dispute resolution (ADR) to create a mutually satisfactory solution in a few months, for a fraction of the cost, she is glad to do it. We will look at different types of ADR and analyze their strengths and weaknesses.

Negotiation

In most cases the parties negotiate, whether personally or through lawyers. Fortunately, the great majority of disputes are resolved this way. Negotiation often begins as soon as a dispute arises and may last a few days or several years.

Mediation

Mediation is the fastest growing method of dispute resolution in the United States. Here, a neutral person, called a mediator, attempts to coax the two disputing parties toward a voluntary settlement. (In some cases, there may be two or more mediators, but we will use the singular.) Generally, the two disputants voluntarily enter mediation, although some judges order the parties to try this form of ADR before allowing a case to go to trial.

A mediator does not render a decision in the dispute, but uses a variety of skills to prod the parties toward agreement. Often a mediator will shuttle between the antagonists, hearing their arguments, sorting out the serious issues from the less important, prompting the parties and lawyers alike to consider new perspectives, and looking for areas of agreement. Mediators must earn the trust of both parties, listen closely, try to diffuse anger and fear, and build the will to settle. Good mediators do not need a law degree, but they must have a sense of humor and low blood pressure.

Mediation has several major advantages. Because the parties maintain control of the process, the two antagonists can speak freely. They need not fear conceding too much, because no settlement takes effect until both parties sign. All discussions are confidential, further encouraging candid talk. This is particularly helpful in cases involving proprietary information that might be revealed during a trial.

Of all forms of dispute resolution, mediation probably offers the strongest "win-win" potential. Since the goal is voluntary settlement, neither party needs to fear that it will end up the loser. This is in sharp contrast to litigation, where one party is very likely to lose. Removing the fear of defeat often encourages thinking and talking that are more open and realistic than negotiations held in the midst of a lawsuit. Studies show that over 75 percent of mediated cases do reach a voluntary settlement. Such an agreement is particularly valuable to parties that wish to preserve a long-term relationship. Consider two companies that have done business successfully for 10 years but now are in the midst of a million dollar trade dispute. A lawsuit could last three or more years and destroy any chance of future trade. However, if the parties mediate the disagreement, they might reach an amicable settlement within a month or two and could quickly resume their mutually profitable business.

This form of ADR works for disputes both big and small. Two college roommates who cannot get along may find that a three-hour mediation session restores tranquillity in the apartment. On a larger scale, consider the work of former United States Senator George Mitchell, who mediated the Anglo-Irish peace agreement, setting Northern Ireland on the path to peace for the first time in three centuries. Like most good mediators, Mitchell was remarkably patient. In an early session, Mitchell permitted the head of one militant party to speak without interruption—for seven straight hours. The diatribe yielded no quick results, but Mitchell believed that after Northern Ireland's tortured history, any nonviolent discussions represented progress.

ARBITRATION

In this form of ADR, the parties agree to bring in a neutral third party, but with a major difference: the arbitrator has the power to impose an award. The arbitrator allows each side equal time to present its case and, after deliberation, issues a binding decision, generally without giving reasons. Unlike mediation, arbitration ensures that there will be a final result, although the parties lose control of the outcome. Arbitration is always faster and cheaper than litigation.

Parties in arbitration give up many rights that litigants retain, including discovery and class action. *Discovery,* as we see below, allows the two sides in a lawsuit to obtain, before trial, documentary and other evidence from the opponent. Arbitration permits both sides to keep secret many files that would have to be divulged in a court case, potentially depriving a party of valuable evidence. A party may have a stronger case than it realizes, and the absence of discovery may permanently deny it that knowledge. A *class action* is a suit in which one injured party represents a large group of people who have suffered similar harm. For example, in an employment discrimination case, a large group of employees who claim similar injury might band together to bring the case, giving themselves much greater clout. Arbitration eliminates this possibility, since injured employees face the employer one at a time. Finally, the fact that an arbitrator may not provide a written, public decision bars other plaintiffs, and society generally, from learning what happened.

MANDATORY ARBITRATION

This variation contains one big difference: the parties agree *in advance* to arbitrate any disputes that may arise. For example, a consumer who purchases a computer or hires a real estate agent may sign an agreement requiring arbitration of any disputes; a customer opening an account with a stockbroker or bank—or health plan—may sign a similar form, often without realizing it. The good news is fewer lawsuits; the bad news is you might be the person kept out of court.

Assume that you live in Miami. Using the Internet, you order a $2,000 ThinkLite laptop computer, which arrives in a carton, loaded with six fat instructional manuals and many small leaflets. You read some of the documents and ignore others. For four weeks you struggle to make your computer work, to no avail. Finally, you telephone ThinkLite and demand a refund, but the company refuses. You file suit in your local court, at which time the company points out that buried among the hundreds of pages it mailed you was a *mandatory arbitration form.* This document prohibits you from filing suit against the company and states that, if you have any complaint with the company, you must fly to Chicago; pay a $2,000 arbitrator's fee; plead your case before an arbitrator selected by the Laptop Trade Association of America; and, in the event you lose, pay ThinkLite's attorney's fees, which could be several thousand dollars. Is that mandatory arbitration provision valid? It is too early to say with finality, but thus far the courts that have faced such clauses have ruled them valid.[1]

OTHER FORMS OF ADR

Several hybrid forms of ADR offer advantages in particular kinds of disputes. In a **minitrial**, the parties agree to stage a short trial before a panel of three "judges." Two of the "judges" are actually executives of the corporate parties; the third is a neutral adviser. Lawyers present shortened versions of their cases. The "judges" then discuss settlement, with the corporate officers relying on the neutral party to act as mediator. This method is useful in commercial disputes where the respective executives interpret the facts very differently.

A **summary jury trial** is initiated and supervised by a court. When a case between two corporations is nearly ready for trial, the judge chooses a mock jury of perhaps six people. With the judge presiding, each lawyer summarizes what the witnesses would say in a real trial. A trial that might take two months can be summarized in a day or two. The "jury" then deliberates. They are asked to reach a consensus if possible, but they may make individual decisions if unavoidable. Each juror fills out a form explaining his impression of the case. The assumption is that once all parties and lawyers learn how jurors might react, their views of the lawsuit should converge, leading to settlement. If this doesn't happen, the parties proceed to a real trial.

Critics argue that summary jury trials can be misleading because juries do not see real witnesses. A lawyer's *summary* of a corporate officer's testimony might sound convincing, but the executive himself might be unpersuasive on the witness stand.

Alternative dispute resolution is controversial, but its surging popularity demonstrates great dissatisfaction with ordinary litigation. A corporate executive faced with a serious legal issue must at least consider the options available. Whatever route she chooses, she should be able to justify the choice in terms of time, cost, and likely satisfaction. Information about ADR is readily available on

---

[1] 1 See, e.g., *Hill v. Gateway 2000*, 105 F.3d 1147, 1997 U.S. App. LEXIS 1877 (7th Cir. 1997), upholding a similar clause.

the Internet; a good place to begin a search is http://www.findlaw.com/01topics/11disputeres/.

To return to our hypothetical case, Janet Booker proposes to Coastal Insurance that they use ADR to expedite a decision in their dispute. Coastal rejects the offer. Coastal's lawyer, Rich Stewart, says that suicide is apparent. He does not want a neutral party to split the difference and award $1 million to Enviro-Vision. Janet reports this explanation to Beth, but adds that she does not believe it. She thinks that Coastal wants the case to drag on as long as possible in the hopes that Enviro-Vision will ultimately settle cheap.

It is a long way to go before trial, but Janet has to prepare her case. The first thing she thinks about is where to file the lawsuit.

COURT SYSTEMS

The United States has two complete systems of courts, state and federal. They are in different buildings, have different judges, and hear different kinds of cases. Each has special powers and certain limitations.

STATE COURTS

The typical state court system forms a pyramid, as Exhibit 3.1 shows.

TRIAL COURTS

Almost all cases start in trial courts, the ones endlessly portrayed on television and film. There is one judge and there will often (but not always) be a jury. This is the only court to hear testimony from witnesses and receive evidence. **Trial courts determine the facts of a particular dispute and apply to those facts the law given by earlier appellate court decisions.**

In the Enviro-Vision dispute, the trial court will decide all important facts that are in dispute. Did Tony Caruso die? Did he drown? Assuming he drowned, was his death accidental or suicide? Once the jury has decided the facts, it will apply the law to those facts. If Tony Caruso died accidentally, contract law provides that Beth Smiles is entitled to double indemnity benefits. If the jury decides he killed himself, the law provides that Beth gets nothing.

Facts are critical. That may sound obvious, but in a course devoted to legal principles, it is easy to lose track of the key role that factual determinations play in the resolution of any dispute. In the Enviro-Vision case, we will see that one bit of factual evidence goes undetected, with costly consequences.

Jurisdiction refers to a court's power to hear a case. In state or federal court, a plaintiff may start a lawsuit only in a court that has jurisdiction over that kind of case. Some courts have very limited jurisdiction, while others have the power to hear almost any case.

Trial Courts of Limited Jurisdiction. These courts may hear only certain types of cases. Small Claims Court has jurisdiction only over civil lawsuits involving a maximum of, say, $2,500 (the amount varies from state to state). Municipal Court has jurisdiction over traffic citations and minor criminal matters. A Juvenile Court hears only cases involving minors. Probate Court is devoted to settling the estates of deceased persons, though in some states it will hear

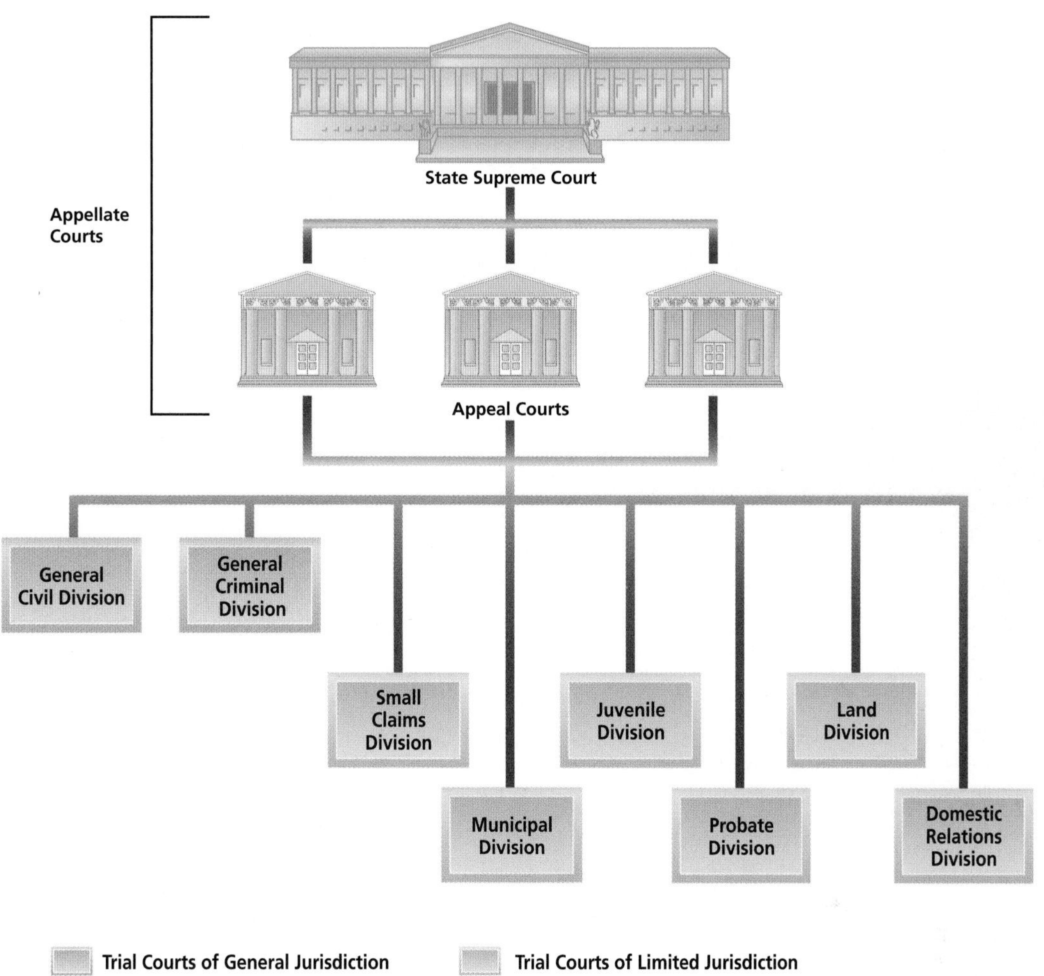

Exhibit 3.1

certain other cases as well. Land Court focuses on disputes about title to land and other real property issues. Domestic Relations Court resolves marital disputes and child custody issues.

Trial Courts of General Jurisdiction. Trial courts of general jurisdiction, however, can hear a very broad range of cases. The most important court, for our purposes, is the General Civil Division. This court may hear virtually any civil lawsuit. In one day it might hear a $450 million shareholders' derivative lawsuit, an employment issue involving freedom of religion, and a foreclosure on a mortgage. Most of the cases we study start in this court.[2] If Enviro-Vision's case against Coastal goes to trial in a state court, it will begin in the trial court of general jurisdiction.

[2] Note that the actual name of the court will vary from state to state. In many states, it is called Superior Court, because it has power superior to the courts of limited jurisdiction. In New York, it is called Supreme Court (anything to confuse the layperson); in some states, it is called Court of Common Pleas; in Oregon and other states it is a Circuit Court. They are all civil trial courts of general jurisdiction.

APPELLATE COURTS

Appellate courts are entirely different from trial courts. Three or more judges hear the case. There are no juries, ever. These courts do not hear witnesses or take new evidence. They hear appeals of cases already tried below. **Appeal courts generally accept the facts given to them by trial courts and review the trial record to see if the court made errors of law.**

Generally, an appeal court will accept a factual finding unless there was *no evidence at all* to support it. If the jury decides that Tony Caruso committed suicide, the appeal court will normally accept that fact, even though the appeal judges consider the jury's conclusion dubious. On the other hand, if a jury concluded that Tony had been murdered, an appeal court would overturn that finding if neither side had introduced any evidence of murder during the trial.

An appeal court reviews the trial record to make sure that the lower court correctly applied the law to the facts. If the trial court made an **error of law,** the appeal court may require a new trial. Suppose the jury concludes that Tony Caruso committed suicide, but votes to award Enviro-Vision $1 million because it feels sorry for Beth Smiles. That is an error of law: if Tony committed suicide, Beth is entitled to nothing. An appellate court will reverse the decision. Or suppose that the trial judge permitted a friend of Tony's to state that he was certain Tony would never commit suicide. Normally, such opinions are not permissible in trial, and it was a legal error for the judge to allow the jury to hear it.

Court of Appeals. The party that loses at the trial court may appeal to the intermediate court of appeals. The party filing the appeal is the **appellant**. The party opposing the appeal (because it won at trial) is the **appellee**.

This court allows both sides to submit written arguments on the case, called **briefs**. Each side then appears for oral argument, usually before a panel of three judges. The appellant's lawyer has about 15 minutes to convince the judges that the trial court made serious errors of law, and that the decision should be **reversed**, that is, nullified. The appellee's lawyer has the same time to persuade the court that the trial court acted correctly, and that the result should be **affirmed**, that is, permitted to stand.

State Supreme Court. This is the highest court in the state, and it accepts some appeals from the court of appeals. In most states, there is no absolute right to appeal to the Supreme Court. If the high court regards a legal issue as important, it accepts the case. It then takes briefs and hears oral argument just as the appeal court did. If it considers the matter unimportant, it refuses to hear the case, meaning that the court of appeals's ruling is the final word on the case.[3]

In most states seven judges, or justices, sit on the Supreme Court. They have the final word on state law.

FEDERAL COURTS

As discussed in Chapter 1, federal courts are established by the United States Constitution, which limits what kinds of cases can be brought in any federal

---

[3] In some states with smaller populations, there is no intermediate appeals court. All appeals from trial courts go directly to the State Supreme Court.

court. See Exhibit 3.2. For our purposes, there are two kinds of civil lawsuits permitted in federal court: federal question cases and diversity cases.

FEDERAL QUESTION CASES

A claim based on the United States Constitution, a federal statute, or a federal treaty is called a federal question case. Federal courts have jurisdiction over these cases. If the Environmental Protection Agency orders Logging Company not to cut in a particular forest, and Logging Company claims that the agency has wrongly deprived it of its property, that suit is based on a federal statute and is thus a federal question. If Little Retailer sues Mega Retailer, claiming that Mega has established a monopoly, that claim is also based on a statute—the Sherman Antitrust Act—and creates **federal question jurisdiction**. Enviro-Vision's potential suit merely concerns an insurance contract. The federal district court has no federal question jurisdiction over the case.

Exhibit 3.2

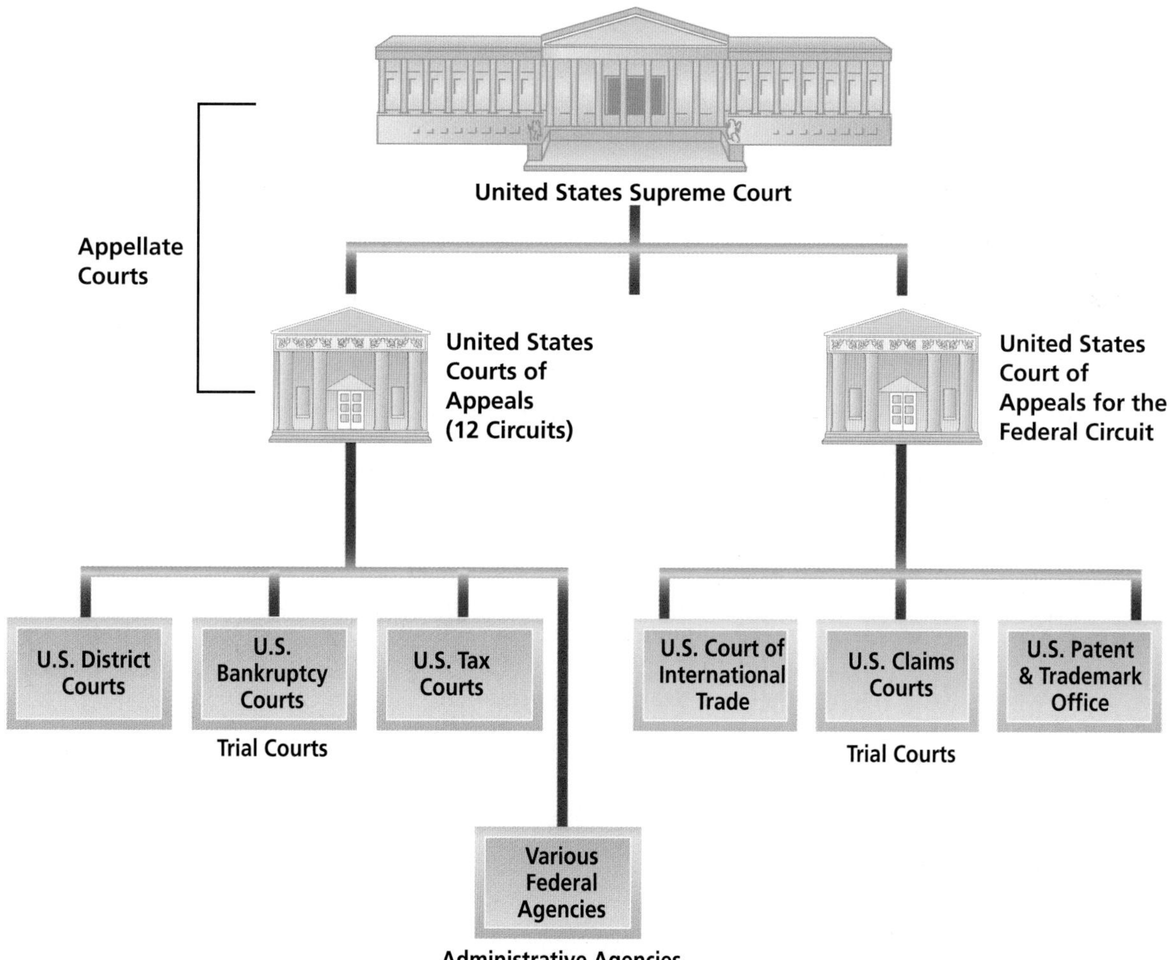

DIVERSITY CASES

Even if no federal law is at issue, federal courts have jurisdiction when (1) the plaintiff and defendant are citizens of different states *and* (2) the amount in dispute exceeds $75,000. The theory behind diversity jurisdiction is that courts of one state might be biased against citizens of another state. To ensure fairness, the parties have the option of federal court.

Enviro-Vision is located in Oregon, and Coastal Insurance is incorporated in Georgia.[4] They are citizens of different states and the amount in dispute far exceeds $75,000. Janet could file this case in United States District Court based on diversity jurisdiction.

TRIAL COURTS

United States District Court. This is the primary trial court in the federal system. The nation is divided into about 96 districts, and each has a district court. States with smaller populations have one district. States with larger populations have several districts; Texas is divided geographically into four districts.

Other Trial Courts. There are other, specialized trial courts in the federal system. Bankruptcy Court, Tax Court, and the United States Court of International Trade all handle name-appropriate cases. The United States Claims Court hears cases brought against the United States, typically on contract disputes.

Judges. The president of the United States nominates all federal court judges, from district court to Supreme Court. The nominees must be confirmed by the Senate.

APPELLATE COURTS

United States Courts of Appeals. These are the intermediate Courts of Appeals. As the map on the next page shows, they are divided into "circuits," which are geographical areas. There are 11 numbered circuits, hearing appeals from district courts. For example, an appeal from the Northern District of Illinois would go to the Court of Appeals for the Seventh Circuit.

A twelfth court, the Court of Appeals for the District of Columbia, hears appeals only from the district court of Washington, D.C. This is a particularly powerful court because so many suits about federal statutes begin in the district court for the District of Columbia. Also in Washington is the thirteenth Court of Appeals, known as the Federal Circuit. It hears appeals from specialized trial courts, as shown in Exhibit 3.2.

Within one circuit there are many circuit judges, up to about 30 judges in the largest circuit, the Ninth. When a case is appealed, three judges hear the appeal, taking briefs and hearing oral argument.

United States Supreme Court. This is the highest court in the country. There are nine justices on the Court. One justice is the Chief Justice, and the other eight are Associate Justices. When they decide a case, each justice casts an equal vote.

---

[4] For diversity purposes, a corporation is a citizen of the state in which it is incorporated and the state in which it has its principal place of business.

The Chief Justice's special power comes from his authority to assign opinions to a given justice. The justice assigned to write an opinion has an opportunity to control the precise language and thus to influence the voting by other justices. For a face-to-face meeting with Supreme Court justices, past and present, introduce yourself to http://oyez.nwu.edu/justices/justices.cgi.

The Supreme Court has the power to hear appeals in any federal case and in certain cases that began in state courts. Generally, it is up to the Court whether or not it will accept a case. A party that wants the Supreme Court to review a lower court ruling must file a **writ of certiorari**, asking the Court to hear the case. The Court receives about 7,500 of these writs every year but currently accepts fewer than 100. Most cases accepted involve either an important issue of constitutional law or an interpretation of a major federal statute.

LITIGATION

Janet Booker decides to file the Enviro-Vision suit in the Oregon trial court. She thinks that a state court judge may take the issue more seriously than a federal district court judge.

PLEADINGS

The documents that begin a lawsuit are called the **pleadings**. These consist of the complaint, the answer, and sometimes a reply.

COMPLAINT

The plaintiff files in court a **complaint**, which is a short, plain statement of the facts she is alleging and the legal claims being made. The purpose of the complaint is to inform the defendant of the general nature of the claims and the need to come into court and protect his interests.

Janet Booker files the complaint, as shown below. Since Enviro-Vision is a partnership, she files the suit on behalf of Beth, personally.

STATE OF OREGON
CIRCUIT COURT

Multnomah County Civil Action No. __________

Elizabeth Smiles,
Plaintiff

JURY TRIAL DEMANDED

v.
Coastal Insurance Company, Inc.,
Defendant

COMPLAINT

Plaintiff Elizabeth Smiles states that:

1. She is a citizen of Multnomah County, Oregon.
2. Defendant Coastal Insurance Company, Inc. is incorporated under the laws of Georgia and has as its usual place of business 148 Thrift Street, Savannah, Georgia.
3. On or about July 5, 2000, plaintiff Smiles ("Smiles"), Defendant Coastal Insurance Co, Inc. ("Coastal") and Anthony Caruso entered into an insurance contract ("the contract"), a copy of which is annexed hereto as Exhibit "A." This contract was signed by all parties or their authorized agents, in Multnomah County, Oregon.
4. The contract obligates Coastal to pay to Smiles the sum of two million dollars ($2 million) if Anthony Caruso should die accidentally.
5. On or about September 18, 2000, Anthony Caruso accidentally drowned and died while swimming.
6. Coastal has refused to pay any sum pursuant to the contract.
7. Coastal has knowingly, willingly and unreasonably refused to honor its obligations under the contract.

WHEREFORE, plaintiff Elizabeth Smiles demands judgment against defendant Coastal for all monies due under the contract; demands triple damages for Coastal's knowing, willing, and unreasonable refusal to honor its obligations; and demands all costs and attorney's fees, with interest.

ELIZABETH SMILES,
By her attorney,
[Signed]
Janet Booker
Pruitt, Booker & Bother
983 Joy Avenue
Portland, OR
October 18, 2000

SERVICE

When she files the complaint in court, Janet gets a summons, which is a paper ordering the defendant to answer the complaint within 20 days. A sheriff or constable then serves the two papers by delivering them to the defendant. Coastal's headquarters are in Georgia, so the state of Oregon has required Coastal to specify someone as its agent for receipt of service in Oregon.

ANSWER

Once the complaint and summons are served, Coastal has 20 days in which to file an answer. Coastal's answer, shown below, is a brief reply to each of the allegations in the complaint. The answer tells the court and the plaintiff exactly what issues are in dispute. Since Coastal admits that the parties entered into the contract that Beth claims they did, there is no need for her to prove that in court. The court can focus its attention on the disputed issue: whether Tony Caruso died accidentally.

STATE OF OREGON
CIRCUIT COURT

Multnomah County — Civil Action No. 00-5626

Elizabeth Smiles,
Plaintiff
v.
Coastal Insurance Company, Inc.,
Defendant

ANSWER

Defendant Coastal Insurance Company, Inc. answers the complaint as follows:

1. Admit.
2. Admit.
3. Admit.
4. Admit.
5. Deny.
6. Admit.
7. Deny.

COASTAL INSURANCE COMPANY, INC.,
By its attorney,
[Signed]
Richard B. Stewart
Kiley, Robbins, Stewart & Glote
333 Victory Boulevard
Portland, OR
October 30, 2000

If the defendant fails to answer in time, the plaintiff will ask for a **default judgment,** which a court will issue if one party fails to appear in court or to answer a pleading.

COUNTER-CLAIM

Sometimes a defendant does more than merely answer a complaint, and files a **counter-claim,** meaning a second lawsuit by the defendant against the plaintiff. Suppose that after her complaint was filed in court, Beth had written a letter to the newspaper, calling Coastal a bunch of "thieves and scoundrels who spend their days mired in fraud and larceny." Coastal would not have found that amusing. The company's answer would have included a counter-claim against Beth for libel, claiming that she falsely accused the insurer of serious criminal acts. Coastal would have demanded money damages.

If Coastal counter-claimed, Beth would have to file a **reply**, which is simply an answer to a counter-claim. Beth's reply would be similar to Coastal's answer, admitting or denying the various allegations.

CLASS ACTIONS

Suppose Janet uncovers evidence that Coastal denies 80 percent of all life insurance claims, calling them suicide. She could ask the court to permit a **class action.** If the court granted her request, she would represent the entire group of plaintiffs, including those who are unaware of the lawsuit or even unaware they were harmed. Class actions can give the plaintiffs much greater leverage, since the defendant's potential liability is vastly increased. In the back of her mind, Janet has thoughts of a class action, *if* she can uncover evidence that Coastal has used a claim of suicide to deny coverage to a large number of claimants.

JUDGMENT ON THE PLEADINGS

A party can ask the court for a judgment based simply on the pleadings themselves, by filing a motion to dismiss. A **motion is a formal request to the court** that the court take some step or issue some order. During a lawsuit the parties file many motions. A **motion to dismiss** is a request that the court terminate a case without permitting it to go further. Suppose that a state law requires claims on life insurance contracts to be filed within three years, and Beth files her claim four years after Tony's death. Coastal would move to dismiss based on this late filing. The court might well agree, and Beth would never get into court.

DISCOVERY

Few cases are dismissed on the pleadings. Most proceed quickly to the next step. **Discovery is the critical, pre-trial opportunity for both parties to learn the strengths and weaknesses of the opponent's case.**

The theory behind civil litigation is that the best outcome is a negotiated settlement and that parties will move toward agreement if they understand the opponent's case. That is likeliest to occur if both sides have an opportunity to examine most of the evidence the other side will bring to trial. Further, if a case does go all the way to trial, efficient and fair litigation cannot take place in a courtroom filled, like a piñata, with surprises. On television dramas, witnesses say astonishing things that amaze the courtroom (and keep viewers hooked through the next commercial). In real trials the lawyers know in advance the answers to practically all the questions asked because discovery has allowed them to see the opponent's documents and question its witnesses. The following are the most important forms of discovery.

Interrogatories. These are written questions that the opposing party must answer, in writing, under oath.

Depositions. These provide a chance for one party's lawyer to question the other party, or a potential witness, under oath. The person being questioned is the **deponent**. Lawyers for both parties are present. During depositions, and in trial, good lawyers choose words carefully and ask questions calculated to advance their cause. A fine line separates ethical, probing questions from those that are tricky, and a similar line divides zealous advocacy from intolerable aggressiveness. For a look at unacceptable behavior during deposition, visit http://nybsa.org/opinions/uncivilerport.html—but make sure your lawyer is with you.

Production of Documents and Things. Each side may ask the other side to produce relevant documents for inspection and copying; to produce physical objects, such as part of a car alleged to be defective; and for permission to enter on land to make an inspection, for example, at the scene of an accident.

Physical and Mental Examination. A party may ask the court to order an examination of the other party, if his physical or mental condition is relevant, for example, in a case of medical malpractice.

Requests for Admission. Either party can insist that the opposing party admit or deny certain facts, to avoid wasting time on points not in dispute. In a medical malpractice case, the plaintiff would request that the doctor admit he performed the surgery and admit what would be the normal level of care a surgeon would provide for such a case (while not expecting the surgeon to admit that he erred).

Janet Booker begins her discovery with interrogatories. Her goal is to learn Coastal's basic position and factual evidence and then follow up with more detailed questioning during depositions. Her interrogatories ask for every fact Coastal relied on in denying the claim. She asks for the names of all witnesses, the identity of all documents, the description of all things or objects that they considered. She requests the names of all corporate officers who played any role in the decision and of any expert witnesses Coastal plans to call. Interrogatory No. 18 demands extensive information on all *other* claims in the past three years that Coastal has denied based on alleged suicide. Janet is looking for evidence that would support a class action.

Beth remarks on how thorough the interrogatories are. "This will tell us what their case is." Janet frowns and looks less optimistic: she's done this before.

Coastal has 30 days to answer Janet's interrogatories. Before it responds, Coastal mails to Janet a notice of deposition, stating its intention to depose Beth Smiles. Beth and Janet will go to the office of Coastal's lawyer, and Beth will answer questions under oath. But at the same time Coastal sends this notice, it sends *25 other notices of deposition.* It will depose Karen Caruso as soon as Beth's deposition is over. Coastal also plans to depose all seven employees of EnviroVision; three neighbors who lived near Tony and Karen's beach house; two policemen who participated in the search; the doctor and two nurses involved in the case; Tony's physician; Jerry Johnson, Tony's tennis partner; Craig Bergson, a college roommate; a couple who had dinner with Tony and Karen a week before his death; and several other people.

Beth is appalled. Janet explains that some of these people might have relevant information. But there may be another reason that Coastal is doing this: the company wants to make this litigation hurt. Janet will have to attend every one of these depositions. Costs will skyrocket.

Janet files a **motion for a protective order**. This is a request that the court limit Coastal's discovery by decreasing the number of depositions. Janet also calls Rich Stewart and suggests that they discuss what depositions are really necessary. Rich insists that all of the depositions are important. This is a $2 million case and Coastal is entitled to protect itself.

Before Beth's deposition date arrives, Rich sends Coastal's answers to Enviro-Vision's interrogatories. The answers contain no useful information whatsoever. For example, Interrogatory No. 10 asked, "If you claim that Anthony Caruso committed suicide, describe every fact upon which you rely in reaching that conclusion." Coastal's answer simply says, "His state of mind, his poor business affairs, and the circumstances of his death all indicate suicide."

Janet calls Rich and complains that the interrogatory answers are a bad joke. Rich disagrees, saying that it is the best information they have so early in the case. After they debate it for 20 minutes, Rich offers to settle the case for $100,000. Janet refuses and makes no counteroffer.

Janet files a **motion to compel answers to interrogatories**, in other words, a formal request that the court order Coastal to supply more complete answers. Janet submits a **memorandum** with the motion, which is a supporting argument. Although it is only a few pages long, the memorandum takes several hours of library research and writing to prepare—more costs. Janet also informs Rich Stewart that Beth will not appear for the deposition, since Coastal's interrogatory answers are inadequate.

Rich now files *his* motion to compel, asking the court to order Beth Smiles to appear for her deposition. The court hears all of the motions together. Janet argues that Coastal's interrogatory answers are hopelessly uninformative and defeat the whole purpose of discovery. She claims that Coastal's large number of depositions creates a huge and unfair expense for a small firm.

Rich claims that the interrogatory answers are the best that Coastal can do thus far and that Coastal will supplement the answers when more information becomes available. He argues against Interrogatory No. 18, the one in which Janet asked for the names of other policyholders whom Coastal considered suicides. He claims that Janet is engaging in a fishing expedition that would violate the privacy of Coastal's insurance customers and provide no information relevant to this case. He demands that Janet make Beth available for a deposition.

These discovery rulings are critical because they will color the entire lawsuit. A trial judge has to make many discovery decisions before a case reaches trial. At times the judge must weigh the need of one party to see documents against the other side's need for privacy. One device a judge can use in reaching a discovery ruling is an ***in camera*** **inspection**, meaning that the judge views the requested documents alone, with no lawyers present, and decides whether the other side is entitled to view them. The following case illustrates how the cost of discovery can easily surpass the value of the lawsuit, particularly when the plaintiff claims that the defendant has similarly injured many other people.

EX PARTE AMERICAN CARPET SALES, INC.

703 So. 2d 950, 1997 Ala. LEXIS 490
Supreme Court of Alabama, 1997

Facts: Kerry and Angela Platt bought flooring for their home from American Carpet. When they got the company's bill, they filed suit, claiming that American Carpet had fraudulently increased the invoice price from the original price of $2,165 to $2,408. The couple also alleged that American Carpet had similarly cheated many other customers. The Platts served discovery requests on American Carpet. The company objected, claiming that the discovery requests were too broad; the trial judge ordered the defendant to furnish the information; and American Carpet appealed.

Issue: Must American Carpet furnish the requested information?

Excerpts from Justice Maddox's Decision: American Carpet objected to production of the following items:

> A copy of all buyer's orders and/or purchase agreements between [American Carpet] and any purchaser in the state of Alabama entered into over the past five years where [American Carpet] charged additional monies to the purchaser after the agreement had been entered into.

American Carpet states that it does not keep a separate list of purchase orders that have been adjusted within the past five years; that its invoices for each year are filed alphabetically by purchaser in individual file folders, with no notation on the folders to indicate which invoices have been adjusted; that within the past five years it has generated approximately 6,000 to 9,000 invoices each year for purchases of carpeting and flooring; and that to provide the information requested, it would have to review manually each one of those files. American Carpet says that in order for it to comply with the request, at a minimum someone would have to review approximately 30,000 invoices and that to do so would require approximately 1,500 man-hours, or 37.5 weeks, for one of its employees. American Carpet also says that the production of those invoices would invade the privacy of its customers by revealing their names and addresses and purchases, and it says that producing those invoices would mean releasing business secrets (specifically its customers' identities).

It is well established that the rules regarding discovery are to be broadly and liberally construed, to ensure that the spirit of the rules is carried out. This Court has held that if there is any likelihood that the information sought by a party will aid that party in pursuing a claim or in defending a claim, then discovery should be allowed. The Court has also said that the particular details of the discovery process must necessarily be left to the sound discretion of the trial court.

Considering the evidence before us, we hold that the trial judge did abuse his discretion in compelling the discovery for a period of five years; consequently, we issue a writ directing the trial court to limit its order compelling discovery, so as to require production only as to a two-year period. ●

The judge rules that Coastal must furnish more complete answers to the interrogatories, especially as to the factual basis of its denial. However, he rules against Interrogatory No. 18, the one concerning other claims Coastal has denied. This simple ruling kills Janet's hope of making a class action of the case. He orders Beth to appear for the deposition. As to future depositions, Coastal may take any 10, but then may take additional depositions only by demonstrating to the court that the deponents have useful information.

Rich proceeds to take Beth's deposition. It takes two full days. He asks about Enviro-Vision's past and present. He learns that Tony appeared to have won their biggest contract ever from Rapid City, Oregon, but that he then lost it when he had a fight with Rapid City's mayor. He inquires into Tony's mood, learns that he was depressed, and probes in every direction he can to find evidence of suicidal motivation. Janet and Rich argue frequently over questions and whether Beth should have to answer them. At times Janet is persuaded and permits Beth to answer; other times she instructs Beth not to answer. For example, toward the end of the second day, Rich asks Beth whether she and Tony had been sexually involved. Janet instructs Beth not to answer. This fight necessitates another trip into court to determine whether Beth must answer. The judge rules that Beth must discuss Tony's romantic life only if Coastal has some evidence that he was involved with someone outside his marriage. It does not have such evidence.

Crucial Clue. Now limited to 10 depositions, Rich selects his nine other deponents carefully. For example, he decides to depose only one of the two nurses; he chooses to question Jerry Johnson, the tennis partner, but not Craig Bergson, the former roommate; and so forth. When we look at the many legal issues this case raises, his choices seem minor. In fact, unbeknownst to Rich or anyone else, his choices may determine the outcome of the case. As we will see later, Craig Bergson has evidence that is possibly crucial to the lawsuit. If Rich decides not to depose him, neither side will ever learn the evidence and the jury will never hear it. A jury can only decide a case based on the evidence presented to it. *Facts are elusive—and often controlling.*

In each deposition, Rich carefully probes with his questions, sometimes trying to learn what he actually does not know, sometimes trying to pin down the witness to a specific version of facts so that Rich knows how the witness will testify at trial. Neighbors at the beach testify that Tony seemed tense; one testifies about seeing Tony, unhappy, on the beach with his dog. Another testifies he had never before seen Blue tied up on the beach. Karen Caruso admits that Tony had been somewhat tense and unhappy the last couple of months. She reluctantly discusses their marriage, admitting there were problems.

Other Discovery. Rich sends Requests to Produce Documents, seeking medical records about Tony. Once again, the parties fight over which records are relevant, but Rich gets most of what he wants. Rich sends Requests for Admission, forcing Beth to commit herself to certain positions, for example, that Tony had lost the Rapid City contract and had been depressed about it.

Plaintiff's Discovery. Janet does less discovery than Rich because most of the witnesses she will call are friendly witnesses. She can interview them privately without giving any information to Coastal. With the help of Beth and Karen, Janet builds her case just as carefully as Rich, choosing the witnesses who will bolster the view that Tony was in good spirits and died accidentally.

She deposes all of the officers of Coastal who participated in the decision to deny insurance coverage, pinning them down as to the limited information they had when they denied Beth's claim.

SUMMARY JUDGMENT

When discovery is completed, both sides may consider seeking summary judgment. **Summary judgment is a ruling by the court that no trial is necessary because there are no *essential* facts in dispute.** The purpose of a trial is to determine the facts of the case, that is, to decide who did what to whom, why, when, and with what consequences. If there are no relevant facts in dispute, then there is no need for a trial.

Suppose Joe sues EZBuck Films, claiming that the company's new movie, *Lover Boy,* violates the copyright of a screenplay that he wrote, called *Love Man.* Discovery establishes that the two stories are suspiciously similar. But EZBuck's lawyer also learns that Joe sold the copyright for *Love Man* to HotShot Pix. EZBuck may or may not have violated a copyright, but there is no need for a trial because Joe *cannot win* even if there is a copyright violation. He does not own the copyright. The court will grant summary judgment for EZBuck.

In the following case, the defendant won summary judgment, meaning that the case never went to trial. And yet, this was only the beginning of trouble for that defendant, William Jefferson Clinton.

JONES v. CLINTON

990 F. Supp. 657, 1998 U.S. Dist. LEXIS 3902
United States District Court for the Eastern District of Arkansas, 1998

Facts: In 1991, Bill Clinton was Governor of Arkansas. Paula Jones worked for a state agency, the Arkansas Industrial Development Commission (AIDC). When Clinton became President, Jones sued him, claiming that he had sexually harassed her. She alleged that, in May 1991, the Governor arranged for her to meet him in a hotel room in Little Rock, Arkansas. When they were alone, he put his hand on her leg and slid it toward her pelvis. She escaped from his grasp, exclaimed, "What are you doing?" and said she was "not that kind of girl." She was upset and confused, and sat on a sofa near the door. She claimed that Clinton approached her, "lowered his trousers and underwear, exposed his penis and told her to kiss it." Jones was horrified, jumped up and said she had to leave. Clinton responded by saying, "Well, I don't want to make you do anything you don't want to do," and pulled his pants up. He added that if she got in trouble for leaving work, Jones should "have Dave call me immediately and I'll take care of it." He also said, "You are smart. Let's keep this between ourselves." Jones remained at AIDC until February 1993, when she moved to California because of her husband's job transfer.

President Clinton denied all of the allegations. He also filed for summary judgment, claiming that Jones had not alleged facts that justified a trial. Jones opposed the motion for summary judgment.

Issue: Was Clinton entitled to summary judgment or was Jones entitled to a trial?

Excerpts from Judge Wright's Decision: [To establish this type of a sexual harassment case, a plaintiff must show that her refusal to submit to unwelcome sexual advances resulted in a tangible job detriment, meaning that she suffered a specific loss. Jones claims that she was denied promotions, given a job with fewer responsibilities, isolated physically, required to sit at a workstation with no work to do, and singled out as the only female employee not to be given flowers on Secretary's Day.]

There is no record of plaintiff ever applying for another job within AIDC, however, and the record shows that not only was plaintiff never downgraded, her position was reclassified upward from a Grade 9 classification to a Grade 11 classification, thereby increasing her annual salary. Indeed, it is undisputed that plaintiff received every merit increase and cost-of-living allowance for which she was eligible during her nearly two-year tenure with the AIDC and consistently received satisfactory job evaluations.

It is plaintiff's burden to come forward with specific facts showing that there is a genuine issue for trial, and the Court finds that her testimony on this point, being of a most general and non-specific nature (and in some cases contradictory to the record), simply does not suffice to create a genuine issue of fact regarding any tangible job detriment as a result of her having allegedly been discouraged from seeking more attractive jobs and reclassification.

Although plaintiff states that her job title upon returning from maternity leave was no longer that of purchasing assistant and that this change in title impaired her potential for promotion, her job duties prior to taking maternity leave and her job duties upon returning to work both involved data input; the difference being that instead of responsibility for data entry of AIDC purchase orders and driving records, she was assigned data entry responsibilities for employment applications. That being so, plaintiff cannot establish a tangible job detriment. A transfer that does not involve a demotion in form or substance and involves only minor changes in working conditions, with no reduction in pay or benefits, will not constitute an adverse employment action, otherwise every trivial personnel action that an irritable employee did not like would form the basis of a discrimination suit.

Finally, the Court rejects plaintiff's claim that she was subjected to hostile treatment having tangible effects when she was isolated physically, made to sit in a location from which she was constantly watched, made to sit at her workstation with no work to do, and singled out as the only female employee not to be given flowers on Secretary's Day. Plaintiff may well have perceived hostility and animus on the part of her supervisors, but these perceptions are merely conclusory in nature and do not, without more, constitute a tangible job detriment.

Similarly, plaintiff's allegations regarding her workstation being moved so that she had to sit directly outside Pennington's office and, at times, not having work to do, describe nothing more than minor or de minimis personnel matters which, again without more, are insufficient to constitute a tangible job detriment or adverse employment action.

Although it is not clear why plaintiff failed to receive flowers on Secretary's Day in 1992, such an omission does not give rise to a federal cause of action in the absence of evidence of some more tangible change in duties or working conditions that constitute a material employment disadvantage.

In sum, the Court finds that a showing of a tangible job detriment or adverse employment action is an essential element of plaintiff's § 1983 quid pro quo sexual harassment claim and that plaintiff has not demonstrated any tangible job detriment or adverse employment action for her refusal to submit to the Governor's alleged advances. The President is therefore entitled to summary judgment [on this claim].

In other words, the court acknowledged that there were factual disputes, but concluded that even if Jones proved each of her allegations, she would still lose the case, because her allegations fell short of a legitimate case of sexual harassment. Jones appealed the case. Later the same year, as the appeal was pending and the House of Representatives was considering whether to impeach President Clinton, the parties settled the dispute. Clinton, without acknowledging any of the allegations, agreed to pay Jones $850,000 to drop the suit.

Janet and Rich each consider moving for summary judgment, but both correctly decide that they would lose. There is one major fact in dispute: Did Tony Caruso commit suicide? Only a jury may decide that issue. As long as there is *some evidence* supporting each side of a key factual dispute, the court may not grant summary judgment.

FINAL PREPARATION

The vast majority of litigation never proceeds to this stage. Well over 90 percent of all lawsuits are settled before trial. But the parties in the Enviro-Vision dispute cannot seem to compromise, so each side gears up for trial. The attorneys make lists of all witnesses they will call. They then prepare each witness very carefully, rehearsing the questions they will ask. It is considered ethical and proper to rehearse the questions, provided the answers are honest and come from the witness. It is unethical and illegal for a lawyer to tell a witness what to say. The lawyers also have colleagues cross-examine each witness, so that the witnesses are ready for the questions the other side's lawyer will ask.

This preparation takes hours and hours, for many days. Beth is frustrated that she cannot do the work she needs to for Enviro-Vision, because she is spending so much time preparing the case. Other employees have to prepare as well, especially for cross-examination by Rich Stewart, and it is a terrible drain on the small firm. More than a year after Janet filed her complaint, they are ready to begin trial.

TRIAL

ADVERSARY SYSTEM

Our system of justice assumes that the best way to bring out the truth is for the two contesting sides to present the strongest case possible to a neutral factfinder. Each side presents its witnesses and then the opponent has a chance to cross-examine. The adversary system presumes that by putting a witness on the stand and letting both lawyers "go at" her, the truth will emerge.

The judge runs the trial. Each lawyer sits at a large table near the front. Beth, looking tense and unhappy, sits with Janet. Rich Stewart sits with a Coastal executive. In the back of the courtroom are benches for the public. On one bench sits Craig Bergson. He will watch the entire proceeding with intense interest and a strange feeling of unease. He is convinced he knows what really happened.

Janet has demanded a jury trial for Beth's case, and Judge Rowland announces that they will now impanel the jury.

RIGHT TO JURY TRIAL

Not all cases are tried to a jury. As a general rule, both plaintiff and defendant have a right to demand a jury trial when the lawsuit is one for money damages. For example, in a typical contract lawsuit, such as Beth's insurance claim, both plaintiff and defendant have a jury trial right whether they are in state or federal court. Even in such a case, though, the parties may waive the jury right, meaning they agree to try the case to a judge.

If the plaintiff is seeking an equitable remedy, such as an injunction, there is no jury right for either party. Equitable rights come from the old Court of Chancery in England, where there was never a jury. Even today, only a judge may give an equitable remedy.

VOIR DIRE

The process of selecting a jury is called *voir dire,* which means "to speak the truth."[5] The court's goal is to select an impartial jury; the lawyers will each try to get a jury as favorable to their side as possible.

---

[5] Students of French note that *voir* means "to see" and assume that *voir dire* should translate, "to see, to speak." However, the legal term is centuries old and derives not from modern French but from Old French, in which *voir* meant "truth."

Potential jurors are questioned individually, sometimes by the judge, and sometimes by the two lawyers as each side tries to ferret out potential bias. Each lawyer may make any number of **challenges for cause**, claiming that a juror has demonstrated probable bias. For example, if a prospective juror in the Enviro-Vision case works for an insurance company, the judge will excuse her on the assumption that she would be biased in favor of Coastal. If the judge perceives no bias, the lawyer may still make a limited number of **peremptory challenges**, entitling him to excuse that juror for virtually any reason, which need not be stated in court. For example, if Rich Stewart believes that a juror seems hostile to him personally, he will use a peremptory challenge to excuse that juror, even if the judge sensed no animosity. The process continues until 14 jurors are seated. Twelve will comprise the jury; the other two are alternates who hear the case and remain available in the event one of the impaneled jurors is taken ill. For a discussion of the jury's responsibility, see http://www.placer.ca.gov/courts/ and click on *Jury Duty: An American Responsibility.*

Although jury selection for a case can sometimes take many days, in the Enviro-Vision case the first day of the hearing ends with the jury selected. In the hallway outside the court, Rich offers Janet $200,000 to settle. Janet reports the offer to Beth and they agree to reject it. Craig Bergson drives home, emotionally confused. Only three weeks before his death, Tony had accidentally met his old roommate and they had had several drinks. Craig believes that what Tony told him answers the riddle of this case.

OPENING STATEMENTS

The next day, each attorney makes an opening statement to the jury, summarizing the proof he or she expects to offer, with the plaintiff going first. Janet focuses on Tony's successful life, his business and strong marriage, and the tragedy of his accidental death.[6]

Rich works hard to establish a friendly rapport with the jury. He expresses regret about the death. Nonetheless, suicide is a clear exclusion from the policy. If insurance companies are forced to pay claims they didn't bargain for, everyone's insurance rates will go up.

BURDEN OF PROOF

In civil cases, the plaintiff has the burden of proof. That means that the plaintiff must convince the jury that its version of the case is correct; the defendant is not obligated to disprove the allegations.

The plaintiff's burden in a civil lawsuit is to prove its case by a **preponderance of the evidence**. It must convince the jury that its version of the facts is at least *slightly more likely* than the defendant's version. Some courts describe this as a "51–49" persuasion, that is, that plaintiff's proof must "just tip" credibility in its favor. By contrast, in a criminal case, the prosecution must demonstrate **beyond a reasonable doubt** that the defendant is guilty. The

---

[6] Janet Booker has dropped her claim for triple damages against Coastal. To have any hope of such a verdict, she would have to show that Coastal had no legitimate reason at all for denying the claim. Discovery has convinced her that Coastal will demonstrate some rational reasons for what it did.

burden of proof in a criminal case is much tougher because the likely consequences are, too. See Exhibit 3.3.

PLAINTIFF'S CASE

Since the plaintiff has the burden of proof, Janet puts in her case first. She wants to prove two things. First, that Tony died. That is easy, since the death certificate clearly demonstrates it and since Coastal does not seriously contest it. Second, in order to win double indemnity damages, she must show that the death was accidental. She will do this with the testimony of the witnesses she calls, one after the other. Her first witness is Beth. When a lawyer asks questions of her own witness, it is **direct examination**. Janet brings out all the evidence she wants the jury to hear: that the business was basically sound, though temporarily troubled, that Tony was a hard worker, why the company took out life insurance policies, and so forth.

Then Rich has a chance to **cross-examine** Beth, which means to ask questions of an opposing witness. He will try to create doubt in the jury's mind. He asks Beth only questions for which he is certain of the answers, based on discovery. Rich gets Beth to admit that the firm was not doing well the year of Tony's death; that Tony had lost the best client the firm ever had; that Beth had reduced salaries; and that Tony had been depressed about business.

RULES OF EVIDENCE

The lawyers are not free simply to ask any question they want. The law of **evidence** determines what questions a lawyer may ask and how the questions are to be phrased, what answers a witness may give, and what documents may be introduced. The goal is to get the best evidence possible before the jurors so they can decide what really happened. In general, witnesses may only testify about things they saw or heard.

These rules are complex, and a thorough explication of them is beyond the scope of this chapter; however, they can be just as important in resolving a dispute as the underlying substantive law. Suppose a plaintiff's case depends upon the jury hearing about a certain conversation, but the rules of evidence prevent the lawyer from asking about it. That conversation might just as well never have occurred.

Janet calls an expert witness, a marine geologist, who testifies about the tides and currents in the area where Tony's body was found. The expert testifies

Exhibit 3.3
Burden of Proof. In a civil lawsuit, a plaintiff wins with a mere preponderance of the evidence. But the prosecution must persuade a jury beyond a reasonable doubt in order to win a criminal conviction.

that even experienced swimmers can be overwhelmed by a sudden shift in currents. Rich objects strenuously that this is irrelevant, because there is no testimony that there *was* such a current at the time of Tony's death. The judge permits the testimony.

Karen Caruso testifies that Tony was in "reasonably good" spirits the day of his death, and that he often took Blue for walks along the beach. Karen testifies that Blue was part Newfoundland. Rich objects that testimony about Blue's pedigree is irrelevant, but Janet insists it will show why Blue was tied up. The judge allows the testimony. Karen says that whenever Blue saw them swim he would instinctively go into the water and pull them to shore. Does that explain why Blue was tied up? Only the jury can answer.

Cross-examination is grim for Karen. Rich slowly but methodically questions her about Tony's state of mind and brings out the problems with the company, his depression, and tension within the marriage. Janet's other witnesses testify essentially as they did during their depositions.

MOTION FOR DIRECTED VERDICT

At the close of the plaintiff's case, Rich moves for a **directed verdict**, that is, a ruling that the plaintiff has entirely failed to prove some aspect of her case. Rich is seeking to win without even putting in his own case. He argues that it was Beth's burden to prove that Tony died accidentally and that she has entirely failed to do that.

A directed verdict is permissible only if the evidence so clearly favors the defendant that reasonable minds could not disagree on it. If reasonable minds could disagree, the motion must be denied. Here, Judge Rowland rules that the plaintiff has put in enough evidence of accidental death that a reasonable person could find in Beth's favor. The motion is denied.

DEFENDANT'S CASE

Rich now puts in his case, exactly as Janet did, except that he happens to have fewer witnesses. He calls the examining doctor, who admits that Tony could have committed suicide by swimming out too far. On cross-examination, Janet gets the doctor to acknowledge that he has no idea whether Tony intentionally drowned. Rich also questions several neighbors as to how depressed Tony had seemed and how unusual it was that Blue was tied up. Some of the witnesses Rich deposed, such as the tennis partner Jerry Johnson, have nothing helpful to Coastal's case, so he does not call them.

Craig Bergson, sitting in the back of the courtroom, thinks how different the trial would have been had he been called as a witness. When he and Tony had the fateful drink, Tony had been distraught: business was terrible, he was involved in an extramarital affair that he could not end, and he saw no way out of his problems. He had no one to talk to and had been hugely relieved to speak with Craig. Several times Tony had said, "I just can't go on like this. I don't want to, anymore." Craig thought Tony seemed suicidal and urged him to see a therapist Craig knew and trusted. Tony had said that it was good advice, but Craig is unsure whether Tony sought any help.

This evidence would have affected the case. Had Rich Stewart known of the conversation, he would have deposed Craig and the therapist. Coastal's case would have been far stronger, perhaps overwhelming. But Craig's evidence will never be heard. Facts are critical. Rich's decision to depose other witnesses and omit Craig may influence the verdict more than any rule of law.

CLOSING ARGUMENT

Both lawyers sum up their case to the jury, explaining how they hope the jury will interpret what they have heard. Janet summarizes the plaintiff's version of the facts, claiming that Blue was tied up so that Tony could swim without worrying about him. Rich claims that business and personal pressures had overwhelmed Tony. He tied up his dog, neatly folded his clothes, and took his own life.

JURY INSTRUCTIONS

Judge Rowland instructs the jury as to its duty. He tells them that they are to evaluate the case based only on the evidence they heard at trial, relying on their own experience and common sense.

He explains the law and the burden of proof, telling the jury that it is Beth's obligation to prove that Tony died. If Beth has proven that Tony died, she is entitled to $1 million; if she has proven that his death was accidental, she is entitled to $2 million. However, if Coastal has proven suicide, Beth receives nothing. Finally, he states that if they are unable to decide between accidental death and suicide, there is a legal presumption that it was accidental. Rich asks Judge Rowland to rephrase the "legal presumption" part, but the judge declines.

VERDICT

The jury deliberates informally, with all jurors entitled to voice their opinion. Some deliberations take two hours; some take two weeks. Many states require a unanimous verdict; others require only, for example, a 10–2 vote in civil cases.

This case presents a close call. No one saw Tony die. Yet even though they cannot know with certainty, the jury's decision will probably be the final word on whether he took his own life. After a day and a half of deliberating, the jury notifies the judge that it has reached a verdict. Rich Stewart quickly makes a new offer: $350,000. Beth hesitates but turns it down.

The judge summons the lawyers to court, and Beth goes as well. The judge asks the foreman if the jury has reached a decision. He states that it has: the jury finds that Tony Caruso drowned accidentally and awards Beth Smiles $2 million.

MOTIONS AFTER THE VERDICT

Rich immediately moves for a **judgment *non obstante veredicto*** (judgment n.o.v.), meaning a judgment notwithstanding the jury's verdict. He is asking the judge to overturn the jury's verdict. Rich argues that the jury's decision went against all of the evidence. He also claims that the judge's instructions were wrong and misled the jury.

Judge Rowland denies the judgment n.o.v. Rich immediately moves for a new trial, making the same claim, and the judge denies the motion. Beth is elated that the case is finally over—until Janet says she expects an appeal. Craig

Bergson, leaving the courtroom, wonders if he did the right thing. He felt sympathy for Beth and none for Coastal. Yet now he is neither happy nor proud.

APPEALS

Two days later, Rich files an appeal to the court of appeal. The same day, he phones Janet and increases his settlement offer to $425,000. Beth is tempted but wants Janet's advice. Janet says the risks of an appeal are that the court will order a new trial, and they would start all over. But to accept this offer is to forfeit over $1.5 million. Beth is unsure what to do. The firm desperately needs cash now. Janet suggests they wait until oral argument, another eight months.

Rich files a brief arguing that there were two basic errors at the trial: first, that the jury's verdict is clearly contrary to the evidence; and second, that the judge gave the wrong instructions to the jury. Janet files a reply brief, opposing Rich on both issues. In her brief, Janet cites many cases that she claims are precedent: earlier decisions by the state supreme court on similar or identical issues. Although the following case is from a different jurisdiction, it is an example of the kind of case that she will rely on.

DAKA, INC. v. BREINER

711 A. 2d 86, 1998 D.C. App. LEXIS 86
District of Columbia Court of Appeals, 1998

Facts: Daka was a contract food service provider for various famous museums in Washington. Daka hired James Breiner, aged fifty-four, to supervise service at the Museum of Natural History and five months later transferred him to the Museum of American History, a more demanding position for which he received a raise. A little more than a year later, Daka fired Breiner, claiming that his job performance had rapidly deteriorated after the transfer. Breiner filed suit, seeking damages for age discrimination. He alleged that his supervisors and co-workers made frequent, crude comments about his age, calling him "over the hill," an "old fogey," an "old fart," and someone who "could not get it up any more."

The jury awarded Breiner $10,000 in compensatory damages and $390,000 in punitive damages. Daka moved for a judgment notwithstanding the verdict (n.o.v.), which the trial court denied. Daka appealed.

Issue: Should the trial court have granted Daka a judgment n.o.v.?

Excerpts from Judge Terry's Decision: Daka contends that its motion for judgment n.o.v. should have been granted. Because a judgment notwithstanding the verdict is proper only in extreme cases, we review the denial of such a motion deferentially. Reversal is warranted only if no reasonable person, viewing the evidence in the light most favorable to the prevailing party, could reach a verdict in favor of that party. In this case Breiner had to prove that he was subjected to unwelcome harassment based on his age, and that this harassment was so severe or pervasive as to alter the conditions of his employment by creating a hostile or abusive working environment. We hold that the evidence was sufficient to meet this burden of proof.

Daka's strongest argument is that the evidence at trial showed that Breiner welcomed comments about his age. "Unwelcome" conduct is conduct which the employee did not solicit or invite and which the employee regarded as undesirable or offensive. It is true, as Daka says, that much of the evidence on this issue was controverted. The record reveals that Breiner sometimes referred to himself in relatively mild age-related terms such as "old man" or "old school," but it is less clear who initiated these remarks. What is obvious, however, is that even if Breiner did invite innocuous epithets such as "old man" or "old school," the subsequent ridicule he received was much more egregious and offensive. It is also evident that Breiner sought to discourage this behavior by making it well known, especially to Mr. Sakell, that he found these insults inappropriate. On three separate occasions Breiner approached Sakell and told him his comments were "against the law" or "illegal." But Sakell was undeterred by these complaints and, if anything, became more abusive toward Breiner. Not only did he insult Breiner in front of, and directly to, Breiner's subordinates, but he also condoned Reeves' improper conduct. Viewing the evidence in the light most favorable to Breiner, as we must, we conclude that there was sufficient evidence that the age-related comments were unwelcome, notwithstanding Daka's evidence to the contrary. On this point there was clearly an issue for the jury to resolve.

Affirmed.

Eight months later, the lawyers representing Coastal and Enviro-Vision appear in the court of appeal to argue their case. Rich, the appellant, goes first. The judges frequently interrupt his argument with questions. Relying on decisions like *Daka,* they show little sympathy for his claim that the verdict was against the facts. They seem more sympathetic with his second point, that the instructions were wrong.

When Janet argues, all of their questions concern the judge's instructions. It appears they believe the instructions were in error. The judges take the case under advisement, meaning they will decide some time in the future—maybe in two weeks, maybe in five months.

Appeal Court Options

The court of appeal can **affirm** the trial court, allowing the decision to stand. The court may **modify** the decision, for example, by affirming that the plaintiff wins but decreasing the size of the award. (That is unlikely here; Beth is entitled to $2 million or nothing.) The court might **reverse and remand**, nullifying the lower court's decision and returning the case to the trial court. Or it could simply **reverse**, turning the loser (Coastal) into the winner, with no new trial.

What will it do here? On the factual issue, it will probably rule in Beth's favor. There *was* evidence from which a jury could conclude that Tony died accidentally. It is true that there was also considerable evidence to support Coastal's position, but that is probably not enough to overturn the verdict. As we saw in the *Daka* case, if reasonable people could disagree on what the evidence proves, an appellate court generally refuses to change the jury's factual findings. The court of appeal is likely to rule that a reasonable jury *could* have found accidental death, even if the appellate judges personally suspect that Tony may have killed himself.

The judge's instructions raise a more difficult problem. Some states would require a more complex statement about "presumptions."[7]

---

[7] Judge Rowland probably should have said, "The law presumes that death is accidental, not suicide. So if there were no evidence either way, the plaintiff would win because we presume accident. But if there is competing evidence, the presumption becomes irrelevant. If you think that Coastal Insurance has introduced some evidence of suicide, then forget the legal presumption. You must then decide what happened based on what you have seen and heard in court, and on any inferences you choose to draw." Note that the judge's instructions were different, though similar.

What does a court of appeal do if it decides the trial court's instructions were wrong? If it believes the error rendered the trial and verdict unfair, it will remand the case, that is, send it back to the lower court for a new trial. However, the court may conclude that the mistake was **harmless error.** A trial judge cannot do a perfect job, and not every error is fatal. The court may decide the verdict was fair in spite of the mistake.

Janet and Beth talk. Beth is very anxious and wants to settle. She does not want to wait four or five months, only to learn that they must start all over. Janet urges that they wait a few weeks to hear from Rich: they don't want to seem too eager.

A week later, Rich telephones and offers $500,000. Janet turns it down, but says she will ask Beth if she wants to make a counter-offer. She and Beth talk. They agree that they will settle for $1 million. Janet then calls Rich and offers to settle for $1.7 million. Rich and Janet debate the merits of the case. Rich later calls back and offers $750,000, saying he doubts that he can go any higher. Janet counters with $1.4 million, saying she doubts she can go any lower. They argue, both predicting that they will win on appeal.

Rich calls, offers $900,000 and says, "That's it. No more." Janet argues for $1.2 million, expecting to nudge Rich up to $1 million. He doesn't nudge, instead saying, "Take it or leave it." Janet and Beth talk it over. Janet telephones Rich and accepts $900,000 to settle the case.

If they had waited for the court of appeal decision, would Beth have won? It is impossible to know. It is certain, though, that whoever lost would have appealed. Months would have passed waiting to learn if the state supreme court would accept the case. If that court had agreed to hear the appeal, Beth would have endured another year of waiting, brief-writing, oral argument, and tense hoping. The high court has all of the options discussed: to affirm, modify, reverse and remand, or simply reverse.

CHAPTER CONCLUSION

No one will ever know for sure whether Tony took his own life. Craig Bergson's evidence might have tipped the scales in favor of Coastal. But even that is uncertain, since the jury could have found him unpersuasive. After two years, the case ends with a settlement and uncertainty—both typical lawsuit results. The missing witness is less common but not extraordinary. The vaguely unsatisfying feeling about it all is only too common and indicates why litigation is best avoided—by dispute prevention.

CHAPTER REVIEW

1. Alternative dispute resolution (ADR) is any formal or informal process to settle disputes without a trial. Mediation, arbitration, and other forms of ADR are growing in popularity.

2. There are two *systems* of courts, one federal and one in each state. A federal court will hear a case only if it involves a federal question or diversity jurisdiction.

3. Trial courts determine facts and apply the law to the facts; appeal courts generally accept the facts found by the trial court and review the trial record for errors of law.

4. A complaint and an answer are the two most important pleadings, that is, documents that start a lawsuit.

5. Discovery is the critical pre-trial opportunity for both parties to learn the strengths and weaknesses of the opponent's case. Important forms of discovery include interrogatories, depositions, production of documents and objects, physical and mental examinations, and requests for admission.

6. A motion is a formal request to the court.

7. Summary judgment is a ruling by the court that no trial is necessary because there are no essential facts in dispute.

8. Generally, both plaintiff and defendant may demand a jury in any lawsuit for money damages.

9. *Voir dire* is the process of selecting jurors in order to obtain an impartial panel.

10. The plaintiff's burden of proof in a civil lawsuit is preponderance of the evidence, meaning that its version of the facts must be at least slightly more persuasive than the defendant's. In a criminal prosecution, the government must offer proof beyond a reasonable doubt in order to win a conviction.

11. The rules of evidence determine what questions may be asked during trial, what testimony may be given, and what documents may be introduced.

12. The verdict is the jury's decision in a case. The losing party may ask the trial judge to overturn the verdict, seeking a judgment *non obstante veredicto* or a new trial. Judges seldom grant either.

13. An appeal court has many options. The court may affirm, upholding the lower court's decision; modify, changing the verdict but leaving the same party victorious; reverse, transforming the loser into the winner; and/or remand, sending the case back to the lower court.

PRACTICE TEST

1. You plan to open a store in Chicago, specializing in beautiful rugs imported from Turkey. You will work with a native Turk who will purchase and ship the rugs to your store. You are wise enough to insist on a contract establishing the rights and obligations of both parties and would prefer an ADR clause. But you want to be sensitive to different cultures and do not want a clause that will magnify a problem or alienate the parties. Is there some way you can accomplish all of this?

2. Solo Serve Corp. signed a lease for space in a shopping center. The lease contained this clause: "Neither Landlord nor tenant shall engage in or permit any activity at or around the Demised Premises which violates any applicable law, constitutes a nuisance, or is likely to bring discredit upon the Shopping Center, or discourage customers from patronizing other occupants of the Shopping Center by other than activities customarily engaged in by reputable businesses." Westowne Associates, the landlord, later leased other space in the center to The Finish Line, an off-track betting business that also had a license to sell food and liquor. Solo Serve sued, claiming that Westowne had breached the lease. Solo Serve requested either a permanent injunction barring The Finish Line from using the center or that The Finish Line pay the cost of relocating its own business.

   The case raises two questions. The minor one is, did Westowne violate the lease? The major one is, how could this dispute have been prevented? It ultimately went to the United States Court of Appeals, costing both sides much time and money.

3. State which court(s) have jurisdiction as to each of these lawsuits:

   (a) Pat wants to sue his next-door neighbor Dorothy, claiming that Dorothy promised to sell him the house next door.

   (b) Paula, who lives in New York City, wants to sue Dizzy Movie Theatres, whose principal place of business is Dallas. She claims that while she was in Texas on holiday, she was injured by their negligent maintenance of a stairway. She claims damages of $30,000.

(c) Phil lives in Tennessee. He wants to sue Dick, who lives in Ohio. Phil claims that Dick agreed to sell him 3,000 acres of farmland in Ohio, worth over $2 million.

(d) Pete, incarcerated in a federal prison in Kansas, wants to sue the United States government. He claims that his treatment by prison authorities violates three federal statutes.

4. Probationary schoolteachers sued the New Madrid, Missouri, school district, claiming that the school district refused to give them permanent jobs because of their union organizing activity. The defendant school district claimed that each plaintiff was refused a permanent job because of inferior teaching. During discovery, the plaintiffs asked for the personnel files of probationary teachers who *had* been offered permanent jobs. The school district refused to provide them, arguing that the personnel files did not indicate the union status of the teachers and therefore would not help the plaintiffs. The trial court ruled that the school district need not release the files. On appeal, the plaintiffs argue that this hindered their ability to prove the real reasons they had been fired. How should the appeal court rule?

5. Students are now suing schools for sexual harassment. The cases raise important issues about the limits of discovery. In a case in Petaluma, California, a girl claimed that she was harassed for years and that the school knew about it and failed to act. According to press reports, she alleges that a boy stood up in class and asked, "I have a question. I want to know if [Jane Doe] has sex with hot dogs." In discovery, the school district sought the parents' therapy records, the girl's diary, and a psychological evaluation of the girl. Should they get those things?

6. British discovery practice differs from that in the United States. Most discovery in Britain concerns documents. The lawyers for the two sides, called solicitors, must deliver to the opposing side a list of all relevant documents in their possession. Each side may then request to look at and copy those it wishes. Depositions are rare. What advantages and disadvantages are there to the British practice?

7. RIGHT & WRONG Trial practice also is dramatically different in Britain. The parties' solicitors do not go into court. Courtroom work is done by different lawyers, called barristers. The barristers are not permitted to interview any witnesses before trial. They know the substance of what each witness intends to say, but do not rehearse questions and answers, as in the United States. Which approach do you consider more effective? More ethical? What is the purpose of a trial? Of pre-trial preparation?

8. Claus Scherer worked for Rockwell International and was paid over $300,000 per year. Rockwell fired Scherer for alleged sexual harassment of several workers, including his secretary, Terry Pendy. Scherer sued in United States District Court, alleging that Rockwell's real motive in firing him was his high salary.

Rockwell moved for summary judgment, offering deposition transcripts of various employees. Pendy's deposition detailed instances of harassment, including comments about her body, instances of unwelcome touching, and discussions of extramarital affairs. Another deposition, from a Rockwell employee who investigated the allegations, included complaints by other employees as to Scherer's harassment. In his own deposition, which he offered to oppose summary judgment, Scherer testified that he could not recall the incidents alleged by Pendy and others. He denied generally that he had sexually harassed anyone. The district court granted summary judgment for Rockwell. Was its ruling correct?

9. Lloyd Dace worked for ACF Industries as a supervisor in the punchpress department of a carburetor factory. ACF demoted Dace to an hourly job on the assembly line, and Dace sued, claiming that ACF discriminated on the basis of age. At trial, Dace showed that he had been 53 years old when demoted and had been replaced by a man aged 40. He offered evidence that ACF's benefits supervisor had attended the meeting at which his demotion was decided, and that the benefits supervisor was aware of the cost savings of replacing Dace with a younger man.

At the end of Dace's case, ACF moved for a directed verdict and the trial court granted it. The judge reasoned that Dace's entire case was based on circumstantial evidence. He held that it was too speculative for the jury to infer age discrimination from the few facts that Dace had offered. Was the trial court correct?

10. **YOU BE THE JUDGE WRITING PROBLEM** Apache Corp. and El Paso Exploration Co. operated a Texas gas well that exploded, burning out of control for over a year. More than 100 plaintiffs sued the two owners, claiming damage to adjoining gas fields. The plaintiffs also sued Axelson, Inc., which manufactured a valve whose failure may have contributed to the explosion. Axelson, in turn, sued Apache and El Paso. Axelson sought discovery from both companies about an internal investigation they had conducted, before the blowout, concerning kickbacks (illegal payments) at the gas field. Axelson claimed that the investigation could shed light on what caused the explosion, but the trial court ruled that the material was irrelevant, and denied discovery. Axelson appealed. Is the investigation discoverable? **Argument for Axelson:** If the companies investigated kickbacks, they were concerned about corruption and mismanagement—both of which can cause employees to cut corners, ignore safety concerns, fabricate reports, and so forth. All of those activities have the potential to cause a serious accident. All parties are entitled to discover material that may lead to relevant evidence, and that could easily happen here. **Argument for Apache and El Paso:** This is a fishing expedition. The investigation was completed before the explosion and is completely unrelated. Any internal investigation has the potential (a) to reveal valuable business or trade secrets and (b) to prove embarrassing to the companies investigated. Axelson's motive is to force the two owners to settle in order to avoid such revelations. Discovery is not supposed to be a weapon.

11. Imogene Williams sued the U.S. Elevator Corp. She claimed that when she entered one of the company's elevators, it went up three floors but failed to open, fell several floors, stopped, and then continued to erratically rise and fall for about 40 minutes. She claimed physical injuries and emotional distress. At trial, U.S. Elevator disputed every allegation. When the judge instructed the jury, he asked them to decide whether the company had been negligent. If it had, the jury was to decide what physical injuries Williams had suffered. The judge also instructed them that she could receive money for emotional damages only if the emotional damages resulted from her physical injury. The jury found for U.S. Elevator, deciding that it had not been negligent.

    On appeal, Williams argues that the judge was wrong in stating that the emotional injuries had to result from the physical injuries. The court of appeal agreed that the instruction was incorrect. There could be emotional damages even if there were no physical injuries. What appellate remedy is appropriate?

INTERNET RESEARCH PROBLEM

You may be called for jury duty before long. Read the summary of the juror's responsibilities at http://www.placer.ca.gov/courts/jury.htm. Some people try hard to get out of jury duty. Why is that a problem in a democratic society?

You can find further practice problems in the Online Quiz at http://beatty.westbuslaw.com or in the Study Guide that accompanies this text.

Common Law, Statutory Law, and Administrative Law

4

Chapter

Jason observes a toddler wander onto the railroad tracks and hears a train approaching. He has plenty of time to pull the child from the tracks with no risk to himself, but chooses to do nothing. The youngster is killed. The child's family sues Jason for his callous behavior, and a court determines that Jason owes—nothing.

"Why can't they just fix the law?" students and professionals often ask, in response to Jason's impunity and countless other legal oddities. Their exasperation is understandable. This chapter cannot guarantee intellectual tranquillity, but it should diminish the sense of bizarreness that law can instill. We will look at three sources of law: common law, statutory law, and administrative law. Most of the law you learn in the course comes from one of these sources. The substantive law will make more sense when you have a solid feel for *how* it was created.

COMMON LAW

Jason and the toddler present a classic legal puzzle: What, if anything, must a bystander do when he sees someone in danger? We will examine this issue to see how the common law works.

The common law is judge-made law. It is the sum total of all the cases decided by appellate courts. The common law of Pennsylvania consists of all cases decided by appellate courts in that state. The Illinois common law of bystander liability is all of the cases on that subject decided by Illinois appellate courts. Two hundred years ago, almost all of the law was common law. Today, most new law is statutory. But common law still predominates in tort, contract, and agency law, and it is very important in property, employment, and some other areas.

We focus on appellate courts because they are the only ones to make rulings of *law,* as discussed in Chapter 3. In a bystander case, it is the job of the state's highest court to say what legal obligations, if any, a bystander has. The trial court, on the other hand, must decide *facts:* Was this defendant able to see what was happening? Was the plaintiff really in trouble? Could the defendant have assisted without peril to himself?

STARE DECISIS

Nothing perks up a course like Latin. ***Stare decisis*** means "let the decision stand." It is the essence of the common law. The phrase indicates that once a court has decided a particular issue, it will generally apply the same rule in future cases. Suppose the highest court of Arizona must decide whether a contract for a new car, signed by a 16-year-old, can be enforced against him. The court will look to see if there is **precedent**, that is, whether the high court of Arizona has already decided a similar case. The Arizona court looks and finds several earlier cases, all holding that such contracts may not be enforced against a minor. The court will apply that precedent and refuse to enforce the contract in this case. Courts do not always follow precedent, but they generally do: *stare decisis.*

Two words explain why the common law is never as easy as we might like: *predictability* and *flexibility.* The law is trying to accommodate both goals. The need for predictability is apparent: people must know what the law is. If contract law changed daily, an entrepreneur who leased factory space and then started buying machinery would be uncertain if the factory would actually be available when she was ready to move in. Will the landlord slip out of the lease? Will the machinery be ready on time? The need for predictability created the doctrine of *stare decisis.*

Yet there must also be flexibility in the law, some means to respond to new problems and changing social mores. As we enter a new millennium, we cannot be encumbered by ironclad rules established before electricity was discovered. These two ideas may be obvious, but they also conflict: the more flexibility we permit, the less predictability we enjoy. We will watch the conflict play out in the bystander cases.

BYSTANDER CASES

This country inherited from England a simple rule about a bystander's obligations: you have no duty to assist someone in peril unless you created the danger.

In *Union Pacific Railway Co. v. Cappier,*[1] through no fault of the railroad, a train struck a man, severing an arm and a leg. Railroad employees saw the incident happen but did nothing to assist him. By the time help arrived, the victim had died. In this 1903 case the court held that the railroad had no duty to help the injured man:

> With the humane side of the question courts are not concerned. It is the omission or negligent discharge of legal duties only which come within the sphere of judicial cognizance. For withholding relief from the suffering, for failure to respond to the calls of worthy charity, or for faltering in the bestowment of brotherly love on the unfortunate, penalties are found not in the laws of men but in [the laws of God].

As harsh as this judgment might seem, it was an accurate statement of the law at that time in both England and the United States: bystanders need do nothing. Contemporary writers found the rule inhumane and cruel, and even judges criticized it. But—*stare decisis*—they followed it. With a rule this old and well established, no court was willing simply to scuttle it. What courts did do was seek openings for small changes.

Eighteen years after the Kansas case of *Cappier,* the court in nearby Iowa found the basis for one exception. Ed Carey was a farm laborer, working for Frank Davis. While in the fields, Carey fainted from sunstroke and remained unconscious. Davis simply hauled him to a nearby wagon and left him in the sun for an additional four hours, causing serious permanent injury. The court's response:

> It is unquestionably the well-settled rule that the master is under no legal duty to care for a sick or injured servant for whose illness or injury he is not at fault. Though not unjust in principle, this rule, if carried unflinchingly and without exception to its logical extreme, is sometimes productive of shocking results. To avoid this criticism [we hold that where] a servant suffers serious injury, or is suddenly stricken down in a manner indicating the immediate and emergent need of aid to save him from death or serious harm, the master, if present is in duty bound to take such reasonable measures as may be practicable to relieve him, even though such master be not chargeable with fault in bringing about the emergency.[2]

And this is how the common law changes: bit by tiny bit. In Iowa, a bystander could now be liable *if* he was the employer and *if* the worker was suddenly stricken and *if* it was an emergency and *if* the employer was present. That is a small change but an important one.

For the next 50 years, changes in bystander law came very slowly. Consider *Osterlind v. Hill,* a case from 1928.[3] Osterlind rented a canoe from Hill's boatyard, paddled into the lake, and promptly fell into the water. For *30 minutes* he clung to the side of the canoe and shouted for help. Hill heard the cries but did nothing; Osterlind drowned. Was Hill liable? No, said the court: a bystander has no liability. Not until half a century later did that same state supreme court reverse its position and begin to require assistance in extreme cases—a long time for Osterlind to hold on.[4]

In the 1970s, changes came more quickly.

---

[1] 66 Kan. 649, 72 P. 281 (1903).

[2] *Carey v. Davis,* 190 Iowa 720, 180 N.W. 889 (1921).

[3] 263 Mass. 73, 160 N.E. 301 (1928).

[4] *Pridgen v. Boston Housing Authority,* 364 Mass. 696, 308 N.E.2d 467 (1974).

TARASOFF v. REGENTS OF THE UNIVERSITY OF CALIFORNIA

17 Cal. 3d 425, 551 P.2d 334, 131 Cal. Rptr. 14

Facts: On October 27, 1969, Prosenjit Poddar killed Tatiana Tarasoff. Tatiana's parents claimed that two months earlier Poddar had confided his intention to kill Tatiana to Dr. Lawrence Moore, a psychologist employed by the University of California at Berkeley. They sued the University, claiming that Dr. Moore should have warned Tatiana and/or should have arranged for Poddar's confinement.

Issue: Did Dr. Moore have a duty to Tatiana Tarasoff, and did he breach that duty?

Excerpts from Justice Tobriner's Decision: Although under the common law, as a general rule, one person owed no duty to control the conduct of another, nor to warn those endangered by such conduct, the courts have carved out an exception to this rule in cases in which the defendant stands in some special relationship to either the person whose conduct needs to be controlled or in a relationship to the foreseeable victim of that conduct. Applying this exception to the present case, we note that a relationship of defendant therapists to either Tatiana or Poddar will suffice to establish a duty of care.

We recognize the difficulty that a therapist encounters in attempting to forecast whether a patient presents a serious danger of violence. Obviously we do not require that the therapist, in making that determination, render a perfect performance; the therapist need only exercise that reasonable degree of skill, knowledge, and care ordinarily possessed and exercised by members of [the field] under similar circumstances.

In the instant case, however, the pleadings do not raise any question as to failure of defendant therapists to predict that Poddar presented a serious danger of violence. On the contrary, the present complaints allege that defendant therapists did in fact predict that Poddar would kill, but were negligent in failing to warn.

In our view, once a therapist does in fact determine, or under applicable professional standards reasonably should have determined, that a patient poses a serious danger of violence to others, he bears a duty to exercise reasonable care to protect the foreseeable victim of that danger.

[The Tarasoffs have stated a legitimate claim against Dr. Moore.]

The *Tarasoff* exception applies when there is some special relationship, such as therapist-patient. What if there is no such relationship? The 1983 case of *Soldano v. O'Daniels*[5] arose when a patron in Happy Jack's bar saw Villanueva threaten Soldano with a gun. The patron dashed next door, into the Circle Inn bar, told the bartender what was happening, and urged him to call the police. The bartender refused. The witness then asked to use the phone to call the police himself, but the bartender again refused. Tragically, the delay permitted Villanueva to kill Soldano.

As in the earlier cases we have seen, this case presented an emergency. But the exception created in *Carey v. Davis* applied only if the bystander was an employer, and that in *Tarasoff* only for a doctor. In *Soldano* the bystander was neither. Should the law require him to act, that is, should it carve a new exception? Here is what the California court decided:

> Many citizens simply "don't want to get involved." No rule should be adopted [requiring] a citizen to open up his or her house to a stranger so that the latter may use the telephone to call for emergency assistance. As Mrs. Alexander in Anthony

---

[5] 141 Cal. App. 3d 443, 190 Cal. Rptr. 310, 1983 Cal. App. LEXIS 1539 (1983).

> Burgess' *A Clockwork Orange* learned to her horror, such an action may be fraught with danger. It does not follow, however, that use of a telephone in a public portion of a business should be refused for a legitimate emergency call.
>
> We conclude that the bartender owed a duty to [Soldano] to permit the patron from Happy Jack's to place a call to the police or to place the call himself. It bears emphasizing that the duty in this case does not require that one must go to the aid of another. That is not the issue here. The employee was not the good samaritan intent on aiding another. The patron was.

Do these exceptions mean that the bystander rule is gone? *Parra v. Tarasco*[6] provides a partial answer. Ernesto Parra was a customer at the Jiminez Restaurant when food became lodged in his throat. The employees did not use the Heimlich maneuver or any other method to try to save him. Parra choked to death. Was the restaurant liable? No, said the Illinois Appeals Court. The restaurant had no obligation to do anything.

The bystander rule, that hardy oak, is alive and well. Various initials have been carved into its bark—the exceptions we have seen and a variety of others—but the trunk is strong and the leaves green. Perhaps someday the proliferating exceptions will topple it, but the process of the common law is slow and that day is nowhere in sight. Indeed, the following article demonstrates that new forces make bystanders even less likely to get involved.

In the past, emergency medical technician Angela Favors often asked bystanders to step aside at accident scenes so she could take over life-saving procedures they had initiated. But in the last year or so, the Grady Memorial Hospital emergency worker has rarely had that problem.

"Now we don't have to worry about telling anyone to move back," said Ms. Favors, a five-year employee. "I've seen times lately when the person has bled out and is by themselves. Everybody standing around can tell you what happened, but nobody has helped." Fewer good samaritans are stepping forward to assist at accidents or other emergencies—apparently because of a growing fear of AIDS and Hepatitis B, metro Atlanta emergency medical personnel say.

The HIV virus, which causes AIDS, and Hepatitis B are blood-borne diseases that are contracted through intimate contact, primarily sexual. Both viruses have been found in saliva, although there are no documented cases of anyone contracting AIDS through saliva. One can contract Hepatitis B through saliva, however, health officials say.

During one recent accident in Doraville, bystanders discouraged others from helping a bloodied, dying victim until paramedics arrived, because of the fear of AIDS, according to one witness.[7]

Yes, apathy and anxiety abound—but so does courage.

---

[6] 9230 Ill. App. 3d 819, 595 N.E.2d 1186, 1992 Ill. App. LEXIS 935 (1992).

[7] Susan Laccetti, "AIDS Awareness," *Atlanta Journal and Constitution*, Nov. 12, 1991, §C, p. 4. Reprinted with permission from The Atlanta Journal and The Atlanta Constitution.

As the freight train rumbled through rural Indiana, conductor Robert Mohr looked ahead and saw what seemed to be a puppy. Then the "puppy" sat up straight and shook her blond curls. Nineteen-month-old Emily Marshall had wandered away from her mother and was playing on the tracks, dead ahead. Engineer Rodney Lindley jammed on the brakes, but could not possibly stop the 96-car, 6,000-ton train. There was no time to jump off and sprint ahead to the girl. Mohr, aged 49, hustled onto the engine's catwalk and clambered forward, as Lindley slowed the train to 10 miles per hour. Gripping a guard rail, Mohr leaned perilously far forward, waited until the engine loomed directly above the child—and deftly booted her to safety. Emily bounced up with nothing worse than a chipped tooth and forehead cuts, and Mohr, the merrier, was a Hoosier hero.

STATUTORY LAW

Most new law is statutory law. Statutes affect each of us every day, in our business, professional, and personal lives. When the system works correctly, this is the one part of the law over which we the people have control. We elect the local legislators who pass state statutes; we vote for the senators and representatives who create federal statutes. If we understand the system, we can affect the largest source of contemporary law. If we live in ignorance of its strengths and pitfalls, we delude ourselves that we participate in a democracy.

As we saw in Chapter 1, there are two systems of government operating in the United States: a national government and 50 state governments. Each level of government has a legislative body. In Washington, D.C., Congress is our national legislature. Congress passes the statutes that govern the nation. In addition, each state has a legislature, which passes statutes for that state only. In this section, we look at how Congress does its work creating statutes. State legislatures operate similarly, but the work of Congress is better documented and obviously of national importance.[8]

BILLS

Congress is organized into two houses, the House of Representatives and the Senate. Either house may originate a proposed statute, which is called a **bill**. The bill must be voted on and approved by both houses. Once both houses pass it, they will send it to the president. If the president signs the bill, it becomes law

---

[8] See the chart of state and federal governments in Chapter 1. A vast amount of information about Congress is available on the Internet. The House of Representatives has a Web page at http://www.house.gov/. The Senate's site appears at http://www.senate.gov. Each page provides links to current law, pending legislation, votes, committees, and more. If you do not know the name of your representative or senator (shame!), the Web page will provide that information. Most state legislatures have Web sites, which you can reach from links found at http://www.ncsl.org/public/sitesleg.htm. These sites typically permit you to read statutes, research legislative history, examine the current calendar, and note upcoming events. For example, the Web site http://housegop.state.il.us/ brings you to the Republican caucus in the Illinois House of Representatives, while the site http://www.housedem.state.il.us/ will take you to the same body's Democratic caucus. Many of these Web sites enable you to e-mail your local representatives.

and is then a statute. If the president opposes the bill, he will veto it, in which case it is not law.[9]

COMMITTEE WORK

If you visit either house of Congress, you will probably find half a dozen legislators on the floor, with one person talking and no one listening. This is because most of the work is done in committees. Both houses are organized into dozens of committees, each with special functions. The House currently has about 27 committees (further divided into about 150 subcommittees) and the Senate has approximately 20 committees (with about 86 subcommittees). For example, the armed services committee of each house oversees the huge defense budget and the workings of the armed forces. Labor committees handle legislation concerning organized labor and working conditions. Banking committees develop expertise on financial institutions. Judiciary committees review nominees to the federal courts. There are dozens of other committees, some very powerful, because they control vast amounts of money, and some relatively weak.

When a bill is proposed in either house, it is referred to the committee that specializes in that subject. Why are bills proposed in the first place? For any of several reasons:

- *New Issue, New Worry.* If society begins to focus on a new issue, Congress may respond with legislation. We consider below, for example, the congressional response to employment discrimination.
- *Unpopular Judicial Ruling.* If a court makes a ruling that Congress disagrees with, the legislators may pass a statute "undoing" the court decision.
- *Criminal Law.* Statutory law, unlike common law, is prospective. Legislators are hoping to control the future. And that is why almost all criminal law is statutory. A court cannot retroactively announce that it *has been* a crime for a retailer to accept kickbacks from a wholesaler. Everyone must know the rules in advance because the consequences—prison, a felony record—are so harsh.

DISCRIMINATION: CONGRESS AND THE COURTS

The civil rights movement of the 1950s and 1960s convinced most Americans that African Americans continued to suffer relentless discrimination in jobs, housing, voting, schools, and other basic areas of life. Demonstrations and boycotts, marches and counter-marches, church bombings and killings persuaded the nation that the problem was vast and urgent.

In 1963, President Kennedy proposed legislation to guarantee equal rights to African Americans in these areas. The bill went to the House Judiciary Committee, which heard testimony for weeks. Witnesses testified that blacks were often unable to vote because of their race, that landlords and home sellers adamantly refused to sell or rent to blacks, that education was still grossly

[9] Congress may, however, attempt to override the veto.

unequal, and that blacks were routinely denied good jobs in many industries. Eventually, the Judiciary Committee approved the bill and sent it to the full House.

The bill was dozens of pages long and divided into "titles," with each title covering a major issue. Title VII concerned employment. We will consider the progress of Title VII in Congress and in the courts. Here is one section of Title VII, as reported to the House floor:[10]

> Sec. 703(a). It shall be an unlawful employment practice for an employer—
>
> (1) to fail or refuse to hire or to discharge any individual, or otherwise to discriminate against any individual with respect to his compensation, terms, conditions, or privileges of employment, because of such individual's race, color, religion, or national origin; or
>
> (2) to limit, segregate, or classify his employees in any way which would deprive or tend to deprive any individual of employment opportunities or otherwise adversely affect his status as an employee, because of such individual's race, color, religion, or national origin.

Debate

The proposed bill was intensely controversial and sparked angry argument throughout Congress. Here are some excerpts from one day's debate on the House floor, on February 8, 1964:[11]

Mr. Waggonner: I speak to you in all sincerity and ask for the right to discriminate if I so choose because I think it is my right. I think it is my right to choose my social companions. I think it is my right if I am a businessman to run it as I please, to do with my own as I will. I think that is a right the Constitution gives to every man. I want the continued right to discriminate and I want the other man to have the right to continue to discriminate against me, because I am discriminated against every day. I do not feel inferior about it.

I ask you to forget about politics, forget about everything except the integrity of the individual, leaving to the people of this country the right to live their lives in the manner they choose to live. Do not destroy this democracy for a Socialist government. A vote for this bill is no less.

Mr. Conte: If the serious cleavage which pitted brother against brother and citizen against citizen during the tragedy of the Civil War is ever to be justified, it can be justified in this House and then in the other body with the passage of this legislation which can and must reaffirm the rights to all individuals which are inherent in our Constitution.

The distinguished poet Mark Van Doren has said that "equality is absolute or no, nothing between can stand," and nothing should now stand between us and the passage of strong and effective civil rights legislation. It is to this that we are united in a strong bipartisan coalition today, and when

---

[10] The section number in the House bill was actually 704(a); we use 703 here because that is the number of the section when the bill became law and the number to which the Supreme Court refers in later litigation.

[11] The order of speakers is rearranged, and the remarks are edited.

the laws of the land proclaim that the 88th Congress acted effectively, judiciously, and wisely, we can take pride in our accomplishments as free men.

Other debate was less rhetorical and aimed more at getting information. The following exchange anticipates a 30-year controversy on quotas:

MR. JOHANSEN: I have asked for this time to raise a question and I would ask particularly for the attention of the gentleman from New York [Mr. Goodell] because of a remark he made—and I am not quarreling with it. I understood him to say there is no plan for balanced employment or for quotas in this legislation. . . . I am raising a question as to whether in the effort to eliminate discrimination—and incidentally that is an undefined term in the bill—we may get to a situation in which employers and conceivably union leaders, will insist on legislation providing for a quota system as a matter of self-protection.

Now let us suppose this hypothetical situation exists with 100 jobs to be filled. Let us say 150 persons apply and suppose 75 of them are Negro and 75 of them are white. Supposing the employer . . . hires 75 white men and 25 Negroes. Do the other 50 Negroes or anyone of them severally have a right to claim they have been discriminated against on the basis of color?

MR. GOODELL: It is the intention of the legislation that if applicants are equal in all other respects there will be no restriction. One may choose from among equals. So long as there is no distinction on the basis of race, creed, or color it will not violate the act.

The debate on racial issues carried on. Later in the day, Congressman Smith of Virginia offered an amendment that could scarcely have been smaller—or more important:

> Amendment offered by Mr. Smith of Virginia: On page 68, line 23, after the word "religion," insert the word "sex."

In other words, Smith was asking that discrimination on the basis of sex also be outlawed, along with the existing grounds of race, color, national origin, and religion. Congressman Smith's proposal produced the following comments:

MR. CELLER: You know, the French have a phrase for it when they speak of women and men. They say "vive la difference." I think the French are right. Imagine the upheaval that would result from adoption of blanket language requiring total equality. Would male citizens be justified in insisting that women share with them the burdens of compulsory military service? What would become of traditional family relationships? What about alimony? What would become of the crimes of rape and statutory rape? I think the amendment seems illogical, ill timed, ill placed, and improper.

MRS. ST. GEORGE: Mr. Chairman, I was somewhat amazed when I came on the floor this afternoon to hear the very distinguished chairman of the Committee on the Judiciary [Mr. Celler] make the remark that he considered the amendment at this point illogical. I can think of nothing more logical than this amendment at this point.

There are still many States where women cannot serve on juries. There are still many States where women do not have equal educational opportunities. In most States and, in fact, I figure it would be safe to say, in all

States—women do not get equal pay for equal work. That is a very well known fact. And to say that this is illogical. What is illogical about it? All you are doing is simply correcting something that goes back, frankly to the Dark Ages.

The debate continued. Some supported the "sex" amendment because they were determined to end sexual bias. But politics are complex. Some *opponents* of civil rights supported the amendment because they believed that it would make the legislation less popular and cause Congress to defeat the entire Civil Rights bill.

That strategy did not work. The amendment passed, and sex was added as a protected trait. And, after more debate and several votes, the entire bill passed the House. It went to the Senate, where it followed a similar route from Judiciary Committee to full Senate. Much of the Senate debate was similar to what we have seen. But some senators raised a new issue, concerning §703(2), which prohibited *segregating or classifying* employees based on any of the protected categories (race, color, national origin, religion, or sex). Senator Tower was concerned that §703(2) meant that an employee in a protected category could never be given any sort of job test. So the Senate amended §703 to include a new subsection:

> Sec. 703(h). Notwithstanding any other provision of this title, it shall not be an unlawful employment practice for an employer . . . to give and to act upon the results of any professionally developed ability test provided that such test . . . is not designed, intended or used to discriminate because of race, color, religion, sex or national origin.

With that amendment, and many others, the bill passed the Senate.

CONFERENCE COMMITTEE

Civil Rights legislation had now passed both houses, but the bills were no longer the same due to the many amendments. This is true with most legislation. The next step is for the two houses to send representatives to a House-Senate Conference Committee. This committee examines all of the differences between the two bills and tries to reach a compromise. With the Civil Rights bill, Senator Tower's amendment was left in; other Senate amendments were taken out. When the Conference Committee had settled every difference between the two versions, the new, modified bill was sent back to each house for a new vote.

The House of Representatives and the Senate again angrily debated the compromise language reported from the Conference Committee. Finally, after years of violent public demonstrations and months of debate, each house passed the same bill. President Johnson promptly signed it. The Civil Rights Act of 1964 was law. See Exhibit 4.1.

Title VII of the Civil Rights Act obviously prohibited an employer from saying to a job applicant, "We don't hire blacks." In some parts of the country, that had been common practice; after the Civil Rights Act passed, it became rare. Employers who routinely hired whites only, or promoted only whites, found themselves losing lawsuits.

A new group of cases arose, those in which some job standard was set that appeared to be racially neutral, yet had a discriminatory effect. In North Carolina, the Duke Power Co. required that applicants for higher paying,

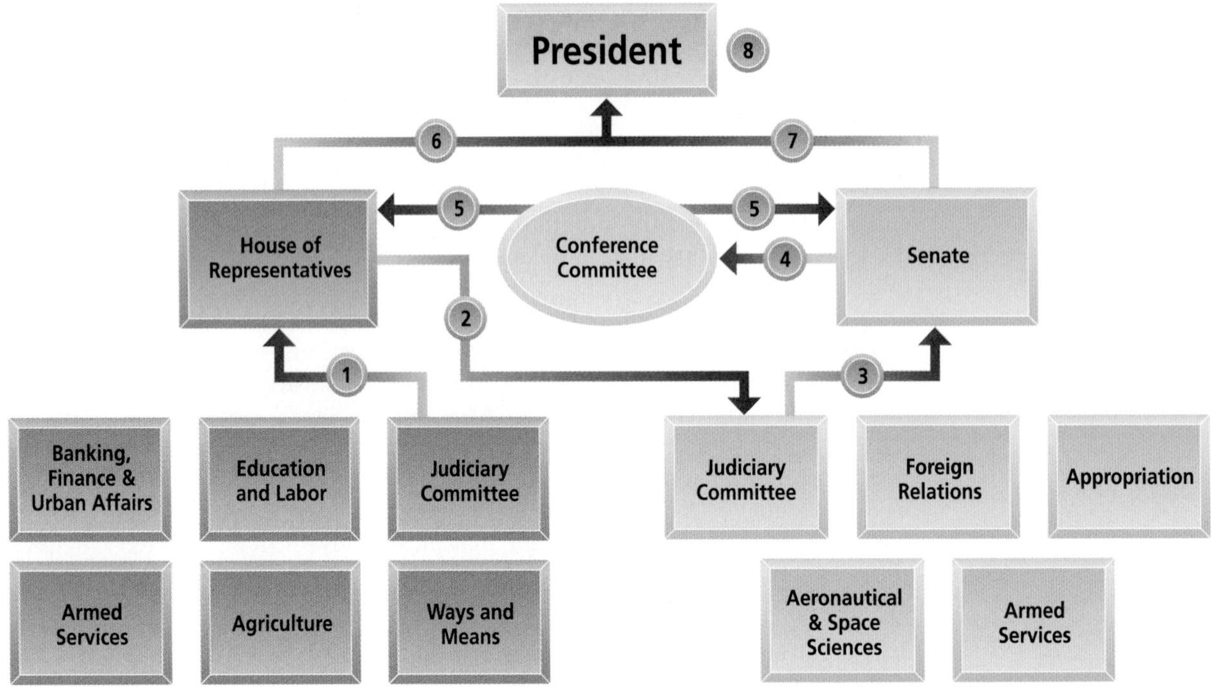

Exhibit 4.1
The two houses of Congress are organized into dozens of committees, a few of which are shown here. The path of the 1964 Civil Rights Act (somewhat simplified) was as follows: (1) The House Judiciary Committee approved the bill and sent it to the full House; (2) the full House passed the bill and sent it to the Senate, where it was assigned to the Senate Judiciary Committee; (3) the Senate Judiciary Committee passed an amended version of the bill and sent it to the full Senate; (4) the full Senate passed the bill with additional amendments. Since the Senate version was now different from the bill the House passed, the bill went to a Conference Committee. The Conference Committee (5) reached a compromise and sent the new version of the bill back to both houses. Each house passed the compromise bill (6 and 7) and sent it to the president, who signed it into law (8).

promotional positions meet two requirements: they must have a high school diploma, and they must pass a standardized written test. There was no evidence that either requirement related to successful job performance. Blacks met the requirements in lower percentages than whites, and consequently whites obtained a disproportionate share of the good jobs.

Title VII did not precisely address this kind of case. It clearly outlawed overt discrimination. Was Duke Power's policy overt discrimination, or was it protected by Senator Tower's amendment, §703(h)? The case went all the way to the Supreme Court, where the Court had to interpret the new law.

STATUTORY INTERPRETATION

Courts are often called upon to interpret a statute, that is, to explain precisely what the language means and how it applies in a given case. There are three primary steps in a court's statutory interpretation:

- *Plain Meaning Rule.* When a statute's words have ordinary, everyday significance, the court will simply apply those words. Section 703(a)(1) of the Civil Rights Act prohibits firing someone because of her religion. Could an employer who had fired a Catholic because of her religion argue that Catholicism is not really a religion, but more of a social group? No. The word "religion" has a plain meaning and courts apply its commonsense definition.
- *Legislative History and Intent.* If the language is unclear, the court must look deeper. Section 703(a)(2) prohibits classifying employees in ways that are discriminatory. Does that section prevent an employer from requiring high school diplomas, as Duke Power did? The explicit language of the statute does not answer the question. The court will look at the law's history to determine the *intent* of the legislature. The court will examine committee hearings, reports, and the floor debates that we have seen.
- *Public Policy.* If the legislative history is unclear, courts will rely on general public policies, such as reducing crime, creating equal opportunity, and so forth. They may include in this examination some of their own prior decisions. Courts assume that the legislature is aware of prior judicial decisions, and if the legislature did not change those decisions, the statute will be interpreted to incorporate them.

Here is how the Supreme Court interpreted the 1964 Civil Rights Act.

GRIGGS v. DUKE POWER CO.

401 U.S. 424, 91 S. Ct. 849, 1971
U.S. LEXIS 134
United States Supreme Court, 1971

Excerpts from Mr. Chief Justice Burger's Decision: The objective of Congress in the enactment of Title VII is plain from the language of the statute. It was to achieve equality of employment opportunities and remove barriers that have operated in the past to favor an identifiable group of white employees over other employees. Under the Act, practices, procedures, or tests neutral on their face, and even neutral in terms of intent, cannot be maintained if they operate to "freeze" the status quo of prior discriminatory employment practices.

The Act proscribes not only overt discrimination but also practices that are fair in form, but discriminatory in operation. The touchstone is business necessity. If an employment practice which operates to exclude Negroes cannot be shown to be related to job performance, the practice is prohibited.

On the record before us, neither the high school completion requirement nor the general intelligence test is shown to bear a demonstrable relationship to successful performance of the jobs for which it was used.

Senator Tower offered an amendment which was adopted verbatim and is now the testing provision of section 703(h). Speaking for the supporters of Title VII, Senator Humphrey endorsed the amendment, stating: "Senators on both sides of the aisle who were deeply interested in Title VII have examined the text of this amendment and have found it to be in accord with the intent and purpose of that title." The amendment was then adopted. From the sum of the legislative history relevant in this case, the conclusion is inescapable that the . . . requirement that employment tests be job related comports with congressional intent.

And so the highest Court ruled that if a job requirement had a discriminatory impact, the employer could use that requirement only if it was related to job performance. Many more cases arose. For almost two decades courts held that, once workers showed that a job requirement had a discriminatory effect, the employer had the burden to prove that the requirement was necessary for the business. The requirement had to be essential to achieve an important goal. If there was any way to achieve that goal without discriminatory impact, the employer had to use it.

CHANGING TIMES

But things changed. In 1989, a more conservative Supreme Court decided *Wards Cove Packing Co. v. Atonio.*[12] The plaintiffs were nonwhite workers in salmon canneries in Alaska. The canneries had two types of jobs, skilled and unskilled. Nonwhites (Filipinos and native Alaskans) invariably worked as low-paid, unskilled workers, canning the fish. The higher paid, skilled positions were filled almost entirely with white workers, who were hired during the off-season in Washington and Oregon.

There was no overt discrimination. But plaintiffs claimed that various practices led to the racial imbalances. The practices included failing to promote from within the company, hiring through separate channels (cannery jobs were done through a union hall, skilled positions were filled out of state), nepotism, and an English language requirement. Once again the case reached the Supreme Court, where Justice White wrote the Court's opinion.

If the plaintiffs succeeded in showing that the job requirements led to racial imbalance, said the Court, the employer now only had to demonstrate that the requirement or practice "serves, in a significant way, the legitimate employment goals of the employer. . . . [T]here is no requirement that the challenged practice be 'essential' or 'indispensable' to the employer's business." In other words, the Court removed the "business necessity" requirement of Griggs and replaced it with "legitimate employment goals."

VOTERS' ROLE

The response to *Wards Cove* was quick. Liberals decried it; conservatives hailed it. Everyone agreed that it was a major change that would make it substantially harder for plaintiffs to bring successful discrimination cases. Why had the Court changed its interpretation? Because the *Court* was different. The Court of the 1980s was more conservative, with a majority of justices appointed by Presidents Nixon and Reagan. And so, the voters' political preference had affected the high Court, which in turn changed the interpretation of a statute passed in response to voter concerns of the 1960s. See Exhibit 4.2.

Democrats introduced bills to reverse the interpretation of *Wards Cove.* President Bush strongly opposed any new bill. He said it would lead to "quotas," that is, that employers would feel obligated to hire a certain percentage of workers from all racial categories to protect themselves from suits. This was the issue that Congressman Johansen had raised in the original House debate in 1964, but it had not been mentioned since.

---

[12] 490 U.S. 642, 109 S. Ct. 2115, 1989 U.S. LEXIS 2794 (1989).

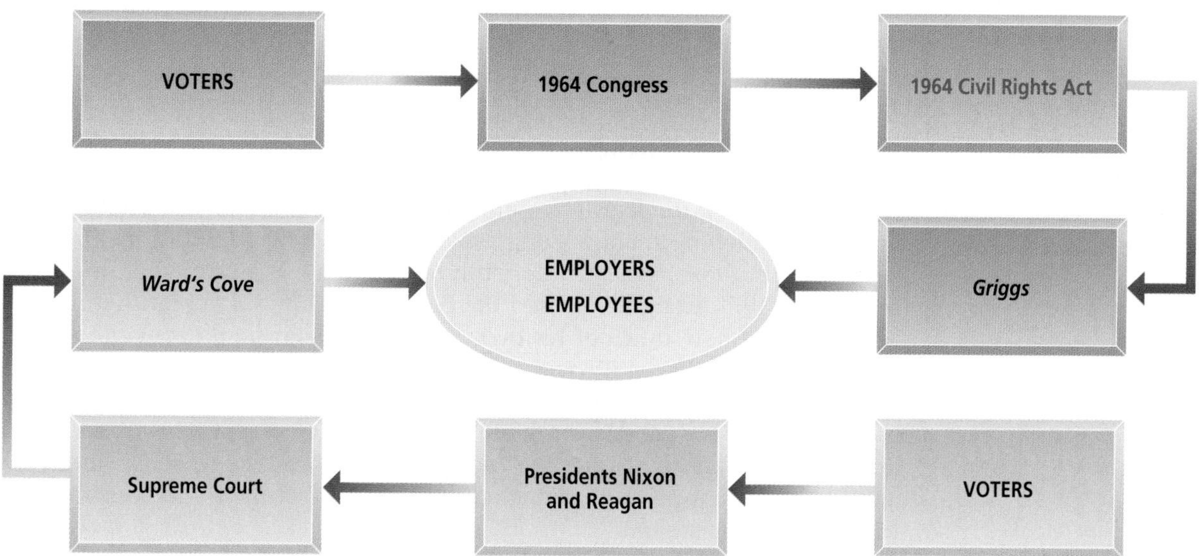

Exhibit 4.2
Statutory interpretation can be just as volatile as the common law, because voters, politicians, and courts all change over time.

Both houses passed bills restoring the "business necessity" holding of *Griggs*. Again there were differences, and a Conference Committee resolved them. After acrimonious debate, both houses passed the compromise bill in October 1990. Was it therefore law? No. President Bush immediately vetoed the bill. He said it would compel employers to adopt quotas.

Congressional Override

When the president vetoes a bill, Congress has one last chance to make it law: an override. If both houses repass the bill, each by a two-thirds margin, it becomes law over the president's veto. Congress attempted to pass the 1990 Civil Rights bill over the Bush veto, but it fell short in the Senate by one vote.

Civil rights advocates tried again, in January 1991, introducing a new bill to reverse the *Wards Cove* rule. Again both houses debated and bargained. The new bill stated that, once an employee proves that a particular employment practice causes a discriminatory impact, the employer must "demonstrate that the challenged practice is job related for the position in question and consistent with business necessity."

Now the two sides fought over the exact meanings of two terms: "job related" and "business necessity." Each side offered definitions, but they could not reach agreement. It appeared that the entire bill would founder over those terms. So Congress did what it often does when faced with a problem of definition: it dropped the issue. Liberals and conservatives agreed not to define the troublesome terms. They would leave that task to courts to perform through statutory interpretation.

With the definitions left out, the new bill passed both houses. In November 1991, President Bush signed the bill into law. The president stated that the new bill had been improved and no longer threatened to create racial quotas. His opponents charged he had reversed course for political reasons, anticipating the 1992 presidential election.

And so, Congress restored the "business necessity" interpretation to its own 1964 Civil Rights Act. No one would say, however, that it had been a simple process.

THE OTHER PLAYER: MONEY

No description of the legislative process would be complete, or even realistic, without mentioning money. Congress has made a few attempts to limit campaign contributions and spending, but to date the efforts are a failure—and a scandal. In 1971, Congress passed the Federal Election Campaign Act (FECA), which limited how much of his own money a federal candidate could spend. Three years later, the statute was amended to place two more limitations on federal campaigns: how much a campaign as a whole could spend, and how much anyone *else* could spend to promote a candidate. One goal was to reduce the power and influence of donors, who gave money expecting favors in return; another purpose was to permit candidates of modest means to compete with millionaire office seekers.

In 1976, the Supreme Court unsettled things in *Buckley v. Valeo,*[13] by ruling that mandatory *spending limits* violate the First Amendment. The Court permitted Congress to limit campaign *contributions,* from individuals and groups, but not to cap the amount that a candidate could spend. This decision was a windfall for wealthy candidates, who could now spend as much of their own money as they chose. It is no coincidence that most members of Congress are very rich.

In 1979, Congress amended the FECA to permit unlimited donations to *political parties* for use in "party building." Initially, party building meant only minor activities like get-out-the-vote drives and distribution of bumper stickers and buttons. Both parties, however, eventually discovered that it was easy to use party-building money in ways that would directly benefit candidates. These funds came to be known as *soft money.* Since the law placed no limit on soft money, the parties went after it feverishly, raising and spending hundreds of millions of dollars every election, effectively destroying any distinction between party building and campaigning. No one writes a $1 million check just to buy bumper stickers, and the influence of donors has grown apace with their contributions. Before the parties can spend the money, they must raise it, and all politicians, both incumbents and outsiders alike, now devote a high percentage of their time to fund-raising.

What do donors expect for their contributions? Access. Corporations, unions, advocacy groups, and rich individuals make large political donations on the assumption that they will later be able to speak directly with powerful politicians about issues that interest them. A corporation seeking to build an oil pipeline in Central Asia might give heavily to a senator with influence in foreign affairs, counting on the contribution to smooth international negotiations. A labor union trying to protect American manufacturing jobs could write a large check, expecting to earn opportunities to speak personally with powerful members of Congress.

A newer route for money to enter politics is through *issue ads.* Increasingly, businesses, labor unions, and advocacy groups run their own political campaigns,

---

[13] 424 U.S. 1, 96 S. Ct. 612, 1976 U.S. LEXIS 16 (1976).

creating television and radio ads designed to support or oppose a given position. As long as the ads do not specifically endorse the election or defeat of a candidate, they are arguably outside the statutory limits on contributions.

Between the candidate's own assets, soft money, and issue ads, it is safe to say that giving and spending on many elections are largely uncontrolled. Some states have passed reform legislation, designed to limit contributions and spending by candidates for statewide office, but Congress has refused to reform federal elections. Various nonprofit, nonpartisan groups vigorously oppose the corrosive effect of campaign money. The nonprofit Center for Public Integrity has brought to light many money scandals in Washington. To see what a sharp spotlight will reveal, glance at the Center's Web page http://www.publicintegrity.org/main.html. Common Cause, which you can visit at http://www.commoncause.org, works hard for campaign finance reform. The Center for Responsive Politics, at http://www.crp.org/, includes in its Web site a dollar-by-dollar description of recent elections, demonstrating which candidates took how much from whom.

As described above, campaign law currently permits wealthy individuals, unions, corporations, and interest groups to funnel large sums of money to political campaigns. Are the contributions ethical? Suppose that you work for a corporation, union, or interest group that contributes heavily. Would you participate in that effort? Would you expect greater access to a politician because of campaign donations? What is the dividing line between legitimate contributions and bribes?

ADMINISTRATIVE LAW

Before beginning this section, please return your seat to its upright position. Stow the tray firmly in the seatback in front of you. Turn off any radios, CD players, or other electronic equipment. Sound familiar? Administrative agencies affect each of us every day in hundreds of ways. They have become the fourth branch of government. Supporters believe that they provide unique expertise in complex areas; detractors regard them as unelected government run amok.

Many administrative agencies are familiar. The Federal Aviation Agency, which requires all airlines to ensure that your seats are upright before takeoff and landing, is an administrative agency. The Internal Revenue Service haunts us every April 15. The Environmental Protection Agency regulates the water quality of the river in your town. The Federal Trade Commission oversees the commercials that shout at you from your television set.

Other agencies are less familiar. You may never have heard of the Bureau of Land Management, but if you go into the oil and gas industry, you will learn that this powerful agency has more control over your land than you do. If you develop real estate in Palos Hills, Illinois, you will tremble every time the Appearance Commission of the City of Palos Hills speaks, since you cannot construct a new building without its approval. If your software corporation wants to hire an Argentine expert on databases, you will get to know the complex workings of the Immigration and Naturalization Service: no one lawfully enters this country without its nod of approval.

BACKGROUND

By the 1880s, the amazing iron horse crisscrossed America. But this technological miracle became an economic headache. Congress worried that the railroads' economic muscle enabled a few powerful corporations to reap unfair profits. The railroad industry needed closer regulation. Who would do it? Courts decide individual cases; they do not regulate industries. Congress itself passes statutes, but it has no personnel to oversee the day-to-day working of a huge industry. For example, Congress lacks the expertise to establish rates for freight passing from Kansas City to Chicago, and it has no personnel to enforce rates once they are set.

A new entity was needed. Congress passed the Interstate Commerce Act, creating the Interstate Commerce Commission (ICC), the first administrative agency. The ICC began regulating freight and passenger transportation over the growing rail system and continued to do so for over 100 years. Congress gave the ICC power to regulate rates and investigate harmful practices, to hold hearings, issue orders, and punish railroads that did not comply.

The ICC was able to hire and develop a staff that was expert in the issues that Congress wanted controlled. The agency had enough flexibility to deal with the problems in a variety of ways: by regulating, investigating, and punishing. And that is what has made administrative agencies an attractive solution for Congress: one entity, focusing on one industry, can combine expertise and flexibility. However, the ICC also developed great power, which voters could not reach, and thereby started the great and lasting conflict over the role of agencies.

During the Great Depression of the 1930s, the Roosevelt administration and Congress created dozens of new agencies. Many were based on social demands, such as the need of the elderly population for a secure income. Political and social conditions dominated again in the 1960s, as Congress created agencies, such as the Equal Employment Opportunity Commission, to combat discrimination.

Then during the 1980s, the Reagan administration made an effort to decrease the number and strength of the agencies. For several years some agencies declined in influence, though others did not. As we begin a new century, there is still controversy about how much power agencies should have, but there is no doubt that administrative agencies are a permanent part of our society.

CLASSIFICATION OF AGENCIES

Agencies exist at the federal, state, and local level. We will focus on federal agencies because they have national impact and great power. Most of the principles discussed apply to state and local agencies as well. Virtually any business or profession you choose to work in will be regulated by at least one administrative agency, and it may be regulated by several.

EXECUTIVE-INDEPENDENT

Some federal agencies are part of the executive branch while others are independent agencies. This is a major distinction. The president has much greater control of executive agencies for the simple reason that he can fire the agency head at any time. An executive agency will seldom diverge far from the president's preferred policies. Some familiar executive agencies are the Internal Revenue Service (part of the Treasury Department); the Federal Bureau of Investigation (Department of Justice); the Food and Drug Administration (Department of Health and Human Services); and the Nuclear Regulatory Commission (Department of Energy).

The president has no such removal power over independent agencies. The Federal Communications Commission (FCC) is an independent agency. For many corporations involved in broadcasting, the FCC has more day-to-day influence on their business than Congress, the courts, and the president combined. Other powerful independent agencies are the Federal Trade Commission, the Securities and Exchange Commission, the National Labor Relations Board, and the Environmental Protection Agency.

ENABLING LEGISLATION

Congress creates a federal agency by passing **enabling legislation**. The Interstate Commerce Act was the enabling legislation that established the ICC. Typically, the enabling legislation describes the problems that Congress believes need regulation, establishes an agency to do it, and defines the agency's powers.

Critics argue that Congress is delegating to another body the powers that only the legislature or courts are supposed to exercise. This puts administrative agencies above the voters. But legal attacks on administrative agencies invariably fail. Courts acknowledge that agencies have become an integral part of a complex economy. As long as there are some limits on an agency's discretion, a court will uphold its powers.

THE ADMINISTRATIVE PROCEDURE ACT

This Act is a major limitation on how agencies do their work. Congress passed the Administrative Procedure Act (APA) in 1946 in an effort to bring uniformity and control to the many federal agencies. The APA regulates how federal agencies make rules, conduct investigations, hold meetings and hearings, reach decisions, and obtain and release information. How much power should agencies have? How much control should we impose on them? These are two of the major questions that businesses and courts face as we enter a new century.

POWER OF AGENCIES

Administrative agencies use three kinds of power to do the work assigned to them: they make rules, they investigate, and they adjudicate.

RULEMAKING

One of the most important functions of an administrative agency is to make rules. In doing this, the agency attempts, prospectively, to establish fair and uniform behavior for all businesses in the affected area. **To create a new rule is to promulgate it.** Agencies promulgate two types of rules: legislative and interpretive.

Legislative Rules. These are the most important agency rules, and they are much like statutes. Here, an agency is changing the law by requiring businesses or private citizens to act in a certain way. For example, the Federal Communications Commission promulgated a rule requiring all cable television systems with more than 3,500 subscribers to develop the capacity to carry at least 20 channels and to make some of those channels available to local community stations. This legislative rule has a heavy financial impact on many cable systems. As far as a cable company is concerned, it is more important than most statutes passed by Congress. Legislative rules have the full effect of a statute.

Interpretive Rules. These rules do not change the law. They are the agency's interpretation of what the law already requires. But they can still affect all of us.

In 1977, Congress passed the Clean Air Act in an attempt to reduce pollution from factories. The Act required the Environmental Protection Agency (EPA) to impose emission standards on certain "stationary sources" of pollution. The definition of "stationary source" became critical. This is about as technical and unsexy as law can get, yet the outcome is critical: it will determine what air goes into our lungs every time we breathe. Environmentalists wanted the term defined to include every smokestack in a factory so that the EPA could regulate each one. The EPA, however, developed the "bubble concept," ruling that "stationary source" meant an entire factory, but not the individual smokestacks. As a result, polluters could shift emission among smokestacks in a single factory to avoid EPA regulation. Environmentalists howled that this gutted the purpose of the statute, but to no avail. The agency had spoken, merely by interpreting a statute.[14]

How Rules Are Made. Corporations fight many a court battle over whether an agency has the right to issue a particular rule and whether it was promulgated properly. The critical issue is this: How much participation is the public entitled to before an agency issues a rule? There are two basic methods of rulemaking.[15]

Informal Rulemaking. On many issues, agencies may use a simple "notice and comment" method of rulemaking. The agency must publish a proposed rule in advance and permit the public a comment period. During this period, the public may submit any objections and arguments, with supporting data. The agency will make its decision and publish the final rule.

For example, the Department of Transportation may use the informal rulemaking procedure to require safety features for all new automobiles. The agency must listen to objections from interested parties, notably car manufacturers, and it must give a written response to the objections. The agency is required to have rational reasons for the final choices it makes. However, it is not obligated to satisfy all parties or do their bidding.

Formal Rulemaking. In the enabling legislation, Congress may require that an agency hold a hearing before promulgating rules. Congress does this to make the agency more accountable to the public. After the agency publishes its proposed rule, it must hold a public hearing. Opponents of the rule, typically

---

[14] An agency's interpretation can be challenged in court, and this one was.

[15] Certain rules may be made with no public participation at all. For example, an agency's internal business affairs and procedures can be regulated without public comment, as can its general policy statements. None of these directly affect the public, and the public has no right to participate.

affected businesses, may cross-examine the agency experts about the need for the rule and may testify against it. When the agency makes its final decision about the rule, it must prepare a formal, written response to everything that occurred at the hearing.

When used responsibly, these hearings give the public access to the agency and can help formulate sound policy. When used irresponsibly, hearings can be manipulated to stymie needed regulation. The most famous example concerns peanut butter. The Food and Drug Administration (FDA) began investigating peanut butter content in 1958. It found, for example, that Jif peanut butter, made by Procter & Gamble, had only 75 percent peanuts and 20 percent of a Crisco-type of base. P&G fought the investigation, and any changes, for years. Finally, in 1965, the FDA proposed a minimum of 90 percent peanuts in peanut butter; P&G wanted 87 percent. The FDA wanted no more than 3 percent hydrogenated vegetable oil; P&G wanted no limit.

The hearings dragged on for months. One day, the P&G lawyer objected to the hearing going forward because he needed to vote that day. Another time, when an FDA official testified that consumer letters indicated the public wanted to know what was really in peanut butter, the P&G attorney demanded that the official bring in and identify the letters—all 20,000 of them. Finally, in 1968, a decade after beginning its investigation, the FDA promulgated final rules requiring 90 percent peanuts but eliminating the 3 percent cap on vegetable oil.[16]

Hybrid Rulemaking. In an effort to avoid the agency paralysis made famous in the peanut butter case, some agencies use hybrid rulemaking, following the informal model but adding a few elements of the formal. The agency may give notice and a comment period, deny the right to a full hearing, but allow limited cross-examination on one or two key issues.

INVESTIGATION

Agencies do an infinite variety of work, but they all need broad factual knowledge of the field they govern. Some companies cooperate with an agency, furnishing information and even voluntarily accepting agency recommendations. For example, the United States Product Safety Commission investigates hundreds of consumer products every year and frequently urges companies to recall goods that the agency considers defective. Many firms comply. (For an up-to-the-minute report on dangerous products and company compliance, proceed carefully to http://www.cpsc.gov/index.html.)

Other companies, however, jealously guard information, often because corporate officers believe that disclosure would lead to adverse rules. To obtain this information, agencies use *subpoenas* and *searches.*

Subpoenas. A **subpoena** is an order to appear at a particular time and place to provide evidence. A **subpoena *duces tecum*** requires the person to appear and bring specified documents. Businesses and other organizations intensely dislike subpoenas and resent government agents plowing through records and questioning employees. What are the limits on an agency's investigation? The information sought:

---

[16] For an excellent account of this high-fat hearing, see Mark J. Green, *The Other Government* (New York: W. W. Norton & Co., 1978), pp. 136–150.

- Must be *relevant* to a lawful agency investigation. The FCC is clearly empowered to investigate the safety of broadcasting towers, and any documents about tower construction are obviously relevant. Documents about employee racial statistics might indicate discrimination, but the FCC lacks jurisdiction on that issue and thus may not obtain such documents.
- Must not be *unreasonably burdensome.* A court will compare the agency's need for the information with the intrusion on the corporation.
- Must not be *privileged.* The Fifth Amendment privilege against self-incrimination means that a corporate officer accused of criminal securities violations may not be compelled to testify about his behavior.

In the following case, a federal agency investigating a married couple demands thousands of documents from their children and over a million documents from hospitals where the couple work. Is the agency entitled to the information?

FEDERAL DEPOSIT INSURANCE CORPORATION v. GARNER

126 F.3d 1138, 1997 U.S. App. LEXIS 25268
Ninth Circuit Court of Appeals, 1997

Facts: The American Commerce National Bank was dangerously close to default, prompting the Federal Deposit Insurance Corporation to investigate. The FDIC concluded that bank directors might have made illegal loans to friends and relatives, causing millions of dollars in losses. The FDIC issued broad subpoenas *duces tecum* to Gerald Garner and his wife, Joan, both of whom were bank directors, seeking personal financial information. The FDIC also subpoenaed the Garners' children, whose trust funds had allegedly benefited from illegal bank practices, and several hospitals where the Garners were corporate officers. To support its subpoenas, the FDIC submitted a declaration from its senior attorney, Playdon, explaining the evidence accumulated thus far. The Playdon Declaration stated that the subpoenas were intended to discover whether the Garners or others had made illegal loans or fraudulent transfers, and whether the Garners had sufficient assets to make litigation cost effective.

The Garners and the hospitals refused to furnish much of the information requested, claiming that the subpoenas were overbroad, and that they invaded the privacy of family members who were not targets of the investigation. The FDIC petitioned the United States District Court, which issued an order enforcing the subpoenas. The Garners appealed.

Issue: Were the FDIC's subpoenas valid?

Excerpts from Judge Brunetti's Decision: Appellants contend that the document requests are overbroad and unduly burdensome. They complain that the subpoenas require the individuals to provide thousands of financial documents and demand over one million documents from Coast Plaza Doctors Hospital. We have held that once an agency establishes that it has properly issued a subpoena, it "should be enforced unless the party being investigated proves the inquiry is unreasonable because it is overbroad or unduly burdensome." Appellants also cite to Federal Rule of Civil Procedure 45(c)(1), which prohibits a party from "imposing undue burden or expense on a person subject" to a subpoena.

Appellants fail to demonstrate that the subpoenas are overbroad or unduly burdensome. They cite to numerous cases which reject burdensome subpoenas. An administrative subpoena may not be so broad so as to be in the nature of a "fishing expedition." What Appellants fail to do is to enunciate how these subpoenas constitute a "fishing expedition," in light of the FDIC's specific and serious allegations of misconduct. Although the FDIC's requests are extensive, we cannot hold that the subpoenas are overbroad or unduly burdensome absent a showing by Appellants of additional support for this position.

We affirm the district court's decision to enforce the *subpoenas duces tecum* against all parties.

Search and Seizure. At times an agency will want to conduct a surprise **search** of an enterprise and **seize** any evidence of wrongdoing. May an agency do that? Yes, although there are limitations. When a particular industry is *comprehensively regulated,* courts will assume that companies know they are subject to periodic, unannounced inspections. In those industries, an administrative agency may conduct a search without a warrant and seize evidence of violations. For example, the mining industry is minutely regulated, with strict rules covering equipment, mining depths, transport and safety structures, air quality, and countless other things. Mining executives know that they are closely watched, and for good reason: mine safety is a matter of life and death, and surprise is an essential element of effective inspection. Accordingly, the Bureau of Mines may make unannounced, warrantless searches to ensure safety.[17] Today, it is a rare case that finds a warrantless search by an administrative agency to have been illegal.

ADJUDICATION

To **adjudicate** a case is to hold a hearing about an issue and then decide it. Agencies adjudicate countless cases. The FCC adjudicates which applicant for a new television license is best qualified. The Occupational Safety and Health Administration (OSHA) holds adversarial hearings to determine whether a manufacturing plant is dangerous.

Most adjudications begin with a hearing before an **administrative law judge** (ALJ). There is no jury. An ALJ is an employee of the agency but is expected to be impartial in her rulings. All parties are represented by counsel. The rules of evidence are informal, and an ALJ may receive any testimony or documents that will help resolve the dispute.

After all evidence is taken, the ALJ makes a decision. The losing party has a right to appeal to an appellate board within the agency. The appellate board has the power to make a ***de novo* decision**, meaning it may ignore the ALJ's decision. A party unhappy with that decision may appeal to federal court.

LIMITS ON AGENCY POWER

There are four primary methods of reining in these powerful creatures: statutory, political, judicial, and informational.

STATUTORY CONTROL

As discussed, the enabling legislation of an agency provides some limits. It may require that the agency use formal rulemaking or investigate only certain issues.

[17] *Donovan v. Dewey,* 452 U.S. 594, 101 S. Ct. 2534, 1980 U.S. LEXIS 58 (1981).

The APA imposes additional controls by requiring basic fairness in areas not regulated by the enabling legislation.

POLITICAL CONTROL

The president's influence is greatest with executive agencies. Congress, though, controls the purse. No agency, executive or independent, can spend money it does not have. An agency that angers Congress risks having a particular program defunded or its entire budget cut. Further, Congress may decide to defund an agency as a cost-cutting measure. In its effort to balance the budget, Congress abolished the Interstate Commerce Commission, transferring its functions to the Transportation Department.

Congress has additional control because it must approve presidential nominees to head agencies. Before approving a nominee, Congress will attempt to determine her intentions. And, finally, Congress may amend an agency's enabling legislation, limiting its power.

JUDICIAL REVIEW

An individual or a corporation directly harmed by an administrative rule, investigation, or adjudication may generally have that action reviewed in federal court.[18] The party seeking review, for example, a corporation, must have suffered direct harm; the courts will not listen to theoretical complaints about an agency action.[19] And that party must first have taken all possible appeals within the agency itself.[20]

Standard on Review. Suppose OSHA promulgates a new rule limiting the noise level within steel mills. Certain mill operators are furious because they will have to retool their mills in order to comply. After exhausting their administrative appeals, they file suit seeking to force OSHA to withdraw the new rule. How does a court decide the case? Or, in legal terms, what standard does a court use in reviewing the case? Does it simply substitute its own opinion for that of the agency? No, it does not. The standard a court uses must take into account:

- *Facts.* Courts generally defer to an agency's factfinding. If OSHA finds that human hearing starts to suffer when decibels reach a particular level, a

---

[18] In two narrow groups of cases, a court may *not* review an agency action. In a few cases, courts hold that a decision is "committed to agency discretion," a formal way of saying that courts will keep hands off. This happens only with politically sensitive issues, such as international air routes. In some cases, the enabling legislation makes it absolutely clear that Congress wanted no court to review certain decisions. Courts will honor that.

[19] The law describes this requirement by saying that a party must have *standing* to bring a case. A college student who has a theoretical belief that the EPA should not interfere with the timber industry has no standing to challenge an EPA rule that prohibits logging in a national forest. A lumber company that was ready to log that area has suffered a direct economic injury: it has standing to sue.

[20] This is the doctrine of **exhaustion of remedies**. A lumber company may not go into court the day after the EPA publishes a proposed ban on logging. It must first *exhaust* its administrative remedies by participating in the administrative hearing and then pursuing appeals within the agency before venturing into court.

court will probably accept that as final. The agency is presumed to have expertise on such subjects. As long as there is *substantial evidence* to support the fact decision, it will be respected.

- *Law.* Courts often—but not always—defer to an agency's interpretation of the law, as the following case illustrates.

HOLLY FARMS CORP. v. NATIONAL LABOR RELATIONS BOARD

517 U.S. 392, 116 S. Ct. 1396, 1996 U.S. LEXIS 2801
United States Supreme Court, 1996

Facts: Holly Farms was a vertically integrated poultry producer, meaning that the company performed many different operations to produce commercial chicken. The company hatched broiler chicks and delivered them to independent farms, where they were raised. When the broilers were seven weeks old, the company sent its live-haul crews to reclaim the birds. The crew included chicken catchers, forklift operators, and "live-haul" drivers. At the farms, the chicken catchers entered the coops, manually captured the broilers, and loaded them into cages. The forklift operator lifted the caged chickens onto the bed of the truck, and the live-haul driver returned the truck, with the loaded cases and the crew, to Holly Farms' processing plant. After that, the chickens . . . well, never mind.

A group of Holly Farms workers organized a union, and the National Labor Relations Board permitted the union to include the company's "live-haul" employees. Holly Farms objected to the new union, claiming that these laborers were actually agricultural workers, who by law were outside the Board's authority.

Labor law defines agriculture this way:

> Agriculture includes . . . the raising of livestock, bees, fur-bearing animals, or poultry, and any practices performed by a farmer or on a farm as an incident to or in conjunction with such farming operations, including preparation for market, delivery to storage or to market or to carriers for transportation to market.

Several United States Courts of Appeals had split over the issue of whether the NLRB's jurisdiction reached live-haul workers, and the dispute reached the United States Supreme Court.

Issue: Did the NLRB accurately interpret labor law by ruling that live-haul workers were employees rather than agricultural workers?

Excerpts from Justice Ginsburg's Decision: Holly Farms argues that under the plain language of the statute, the catching and loading of broilers qualifies as work performed "on a farm as an incident to" the raising of poultry. The corporation emphasizes that [the definition] enumerates "preparation for market" and "delivery to storage or to market" among activities that count as "agriculture." The live-haul employees' work, Holly Farms concludes, enjoys no NLRA protection.

We find Holly Farms' position to be a plausible, but not an inevitable, construction of [this definition]. Hence, we turn to the Board's position, examining only its reasonableness as an interpretation of the governing legislation.

While agreeing that the chicken catchers and forklift operators work "on a farm," the Board contends that their catch and cage work is not incidental to farming operations. Rather, the work is tied to Holly Farms' slaughtering and processing operations, activities that do not constitute "farming" under the statute. We conclude, as we next explain, that the Board's position is based on a reasonable interpretation of the statute, is consistent with the Board's prior holdings, and is supported by the Secretary of Labor's construction of [the definition].

We find the Board's answer reasonable. Once the broilers have grown on the farm for seven weeks, the growers' contractual obligation to raise the birds ends, and the work of the live-haul crew begins. The record reflects minimal overlap between the work of the live-haul crew and the independent growers' raising activities. The growers do not assist the live-haul crews in catching or loading the chickens; their only responsibilities are to move certain equipment from the chicken coops prior to the crews' arrival, and to be present when the crews are on the farms.

In sum, we find persuasive the Board's conclusion that the collection of broilers for slaughter was an activity serving Holly Farms' processing operations, and not Holly Farms' own or the independent growers' farming operations. Again, we stress that the reviewing court's function is limited. For the Board to prevail, it need not show that its construction is the best way to read the statute; rather, courts must respect the Board's judgment so long as its reading is a reasonable one. Regardless of how we might have resolved the question as an initial matter, the Board's decision here reflects a reasonable interpretation of the law and, therefore, merits our approbation. The judgment of the Court of Appeals is accordingly

Affirmed.

Excerpts from Justice O'Connor's Dissenting Opinion: As we said in *Chevron U.S.A. Inc. v. Natural Resources Defense Council, Inc.* [a 1984 case], "First, always, is the question whether Congress has directly spoken to the precise question at issue. If the intent of Congress is clear, that is the end of the matter; for the court, as well as the agency, must give effect to the unambiguously expressed intent of Congress." None of our precedents sanction blind adherence to the Board's position when it is directly contrary to the plain language of the relevant statute.

[Labor law] defines agriculture as "farming in all its branches," including "the raising of . . . poultry," as well as "any practices . . . performed by a farmer or on a farm as an incident to or in conjunction with such farming operations." The coverage intended by Congress is best determined by consulting the language of the statute at issue. Because the relevant portions are perfectly plain and directly speak to the precise question at issue, I would hold that the chicken catchers and forklift operators are agricultural laborers and that the Board's contrary conclusion does not deserve deference.

INFORMATIONAL CONTROL AND THE PUBLIC

We started this section describing the pervasiveness of administrative agencies. We should end it by noting one way in which all of us have some direct control over these ubiquitous authorities: information.

> A popular government, without popular information, or the means of acquiring it, is but a Prologue to a Farce or a Tragedy—or perhaps both. Knowledge will forever govern ignorance, and a people who mean to be their own Governors must arm themselves with the power which knowledge gives.
>
> *James Madison,* President, 1809–1817

Two federal statutes arm us with the power of knowledge.

FREEDOM OF INFORMATION ACT

Congress passed this landmark statute (known as "FOIA") in 1966. It is designed to give all of us, citizens, businesses, and organizations alike, access to the information that federal agencies are using. The idea is to avoid government by secrecy.

Any citizen or executive may make a "FOIA request" to any federal government agency. It is simply a written request that the agency furnish whatever information it has on the subject specified. Two types of data are available under FOIA. Anyone is entitled to information about how the agency operates, how it spends its money, and what statistics and other information it has collected on a given subject. People routinely obtain records about agency policies, environmental hazards, consumer product safety, taxes and spending, purchasing decisions, and agency forays into foreign affairs. A corporation that believes that OSHA is making more inspections of its textile mills than it makes of the competition could demand all relevant information, including OSHA's documents on the mill itself, comparative statistics on different inspections, OSHA's policies on choosing inspection sites, and so forth.

Second, all citizens are entitled to any records the government has *about them.* You are entitled to information that the Internal Revenue Service, or the Federal Bureau of Investigation, has collected about you.

FOIA does not apply to Congress, the federal courts, or the executive staff at the White House. Note also that, since FOIA applies to federal government agencies, you may not use it to obtain information from state or local governments or private businesses. For a step-by-step guide explaining how to make a FOIA request, see http://www.aclu.org/library/foia.html. For dramatic proof of FOIA's power, see http://www.gwu.edu/~nsarchiv, a Web site devoted to government documents that have been declassified as a result of FOIA requests.

Exemptions. An agency officially has 10 days to respond to the request. In reality, most agencies are unable to meet the deadline but are obligated to make good faith efforts. FOIA exempts altogether nine categories from disclosure. The most important exemptions permit an agency to keep confidential information that relates to national security, criminal investigations, internal agency matters such as personnel or policy discussions, trade secrets or financial institutions, or an individual's private life.

Privacy Act

This 1974 statute prohibits federal agencies from giving information about an individual to other agencies or organizations without written consent. There are exceptions, but overall this Act has reduced the government's exchange of information about us "behind our back."

CHAPTER CONCLUSION

"Why can't they just fix the law?" They can, and sometimes they do—but it is a difficult and complex task. "They" includes a great many people and forces, from common law courts to members of Congress to campaign donors to administrative agencies. The courts have made the bystander rule slightly more humane, but it has been a long and bumpy road. Congress managed to restore the legal interpretation of its own 1964 Civil Rights Act, but it took months of debate and compromising. The FDA squeezed more peanuts into a jar of Jif, but it took nearly a decade to get the lid on.

A study of law is certain to create some frustrations. This chapter cannot prevent them all. However, an understanding of how law is made is the first step toward controlling that law.

CHAPTER REVIEW

1. *Stare decisis* means "let the decision stand," and indicates that once a court has decided a particular issue, it will generally apply the same rule in future cases.
2. The common law evolves in awkward fits and starts because courts attempt to achieve two contradictory purposes: predictability and flexibility.
3. The common law bystander rule holds that, generally, no one has a duty to assist someone in peril unless the bystander himself created the danger. Courts have carved some exceptions during the last 100 years, but the basic rule still stands.
4. Bills originate in congressional committees and go from there to the full House of Representatives or Senate. If both houses pass the bill, the legislation normally must go to a Conference Committee to resolve differences between the two versions. The compromise version then goes from the Conference Committee back to both houses, and if passed by both, to the president. If the president signs the bill, it becomes a statute; if he vetoes it, Congress can pass it over his veto with a two-thirds majority in each house.
5. Courts interpret a statute by using the plain meaning rule; then, if necessary, legislative history and intent; and finally, if necessary, public policy.
6. Campaign contributions and spending are largely uncontrolled.
7. Congress creates federal administrative agencies with enabling legislation. The Administrative Procedure Act controls how agencies do their work.
8. Agencies may promulgate legislative rules, which generally have the effect of statutes, or interpretive rules, which merely interpret existing statutes.
9. Agencies have broad investigatory powers and may use subpoenas and, in some cases, warrantless searches to obtain information.
10. Agencies adjudicate cases, meaning that they hold hearings and decide issues. Adjudication generally begins with a hearing before an administrative law judge and may involve an appeal to the full agency or ultimately to federal court.
11. The four most important limitations on the power of federal agencies are statutory control in the enabling legislation and the APA; political control by Congress and the president; judicial review; and the informational control created by the Freedom of Information Act and the Privacy Act.

PRACTICE TEST

1. **RIGHT & WRONG** Suppose you were on a state supreme court and faced with a restaurant-choking case. Should you require restaurant employees to know and employ the Heimlich maneuver to assist a choking victim? If they do a bad job, they could cause additional injury. Should you permit them to do nothing at all? Is there a compromise position? What social policies are most important?
2. **YOU BE THE JUDGE WRITING PROBLEM** An off-duty, out-of-uniform police officer and his son purchased some food from a 7-11 store and were still in the parking lot when a carload of teenagers became rowdy. The officer went to speak to them, and the teenagers assaulted him. The officer shouted to his son to get the 7-11 clerk to call for help. The son entered the store, told the clerk that a police officer needed help, and told the clerk to call the police. He returned 30 seconds later and repeated the request, urging the clerk to say it was a Code 13. The son claimed that the clerk laughed at him and refused to do it. The policeman sued the store. **Argument for the Store:** We sympathize with the police officer and his family, but the store has no liability. A bystander is not obligated to come to the aid of anyone in distress unless the bystander created the peril, and obviously the store did not do so. The policeman should prosecute and sue those who attacked him. **Argument**

for the Policeman: We agree that in general a bystander has no obligation to come to the aid of one in distress. However, when a business that is open to the public receives an urgent request to call the police, the business should either make the call or permit someone else to do it.

3. You sign a two-year lease with a landlord for an apartment. The rent will be $1,000 per month. A clause in the lease requires payment on the first of every month. The clause states that the landlord has the right to evict you if you are even one day late with the payment. You forget to pay on time and deliver your check to the landlord on the third day of the month. He starts an eviction case against you. Who should win? If we enforce the contract, what social result does that have? If we ignore the clause, what effect does that have on contract law?

4. Federal antitrust statutes are complex, but the basic goal is straightforward: to prevent a major industry from being so dominated by a small group of corporations that they destroy competition and injure consumers. Does major league baseball violate the antitrust laws? Many observers say that it does. A small group of owners not only dominate the industry, but actually *own* it, controlling the entry of new owners into the game. This issue went to the United States Supreme Court in 1922. Justice Holmes ruled, perhaps surprisingly, that baseball is exempt from the antitrust laws, holding that baseball is not "trade or commerce." Suppose that a congressman dislikes this ruling and dislikes the current condition of baseball. What could he do?

5. Until recently, every state had a statute outlawing the burning of American flags. But in *Texas v. Johnson*,[21] the Supreme Court declared such statutes unconstitutional, saying that flag burning is symbolic speech, protected by the First Amendment. Does Congress have the power to overrule the Court's ruling?

6. Whitfield, who was black, worked for Ohio Edison. Edison fired him, but then later offered to rehire him. At about that time, another employee, representing Whitfield, argued that Edison's original termination of Whitfield had been race discrimination. Edison rescinded its offer to rehire Whitfield. Whitfield sued Edison, claiming that the rescission of the offer to rehire was in retaliation for the other employee's opposition to discrimination. Edison defended by saying that Title VII of the 1964 Civil Rights Act did not protect in such cases. Title VII prohibits, among other things, an employer from retaliating against *an employee who has opposed* illegal discrimination. But it does not explicitly prohibit an employer from retaliating against one employee based on *another employee's* opposition to discrimination. Edison argued that the statute did not protect Whitfield. Outcome?

Background for Questions 7 through 9. The following three questions all relate to the same disaster. In 1988, terrorists bombed Pan Am flight 103 over Lockerbie, Scotland, killing all passengers. Congress sought to remedy security shortcomings by passing the Aviation Security Improvement Act of 1990, which, among other things, ordered the Federal Aviation Authority (FAA) to prescribe minimum training requirements and minimum staffing levels for airport security. The FAA promulgated rules according to the informal rulemaking process. However, the FAA refused to disclose certain rules, concerning training at specific airports. *Public Citizen, Inc. v. FAA*.[22] Tragically, the issue of airport security would return to haunt the government and the nation.

7. Explain what "promulgated rules according to the informal rulemaking process" means.

8. A public interest group called Public Citizen, Inc., along with family members of those

[21] 491 U.S. 397, 109 S. Ct. 2533, 1989 U.S. LEXIS 3115 (1989).

[22] 988 F.2d 186, 1993 U.S. App. LEXIS 6024 (D.C. Cir. 1993).

who had died at Lockerbie, wanted to know the details of airport security. What steps should they take to obtain the information? Are they entitled to obtain it? How do the attacks of September 11, 2001, affect your answer? In some cases, there may be a tension between public access to information and our national security. How should a court resolve a conflict—or a perceived conflict—between these two important policies?

9. The Aviation Security Improvement Act (ASIA) states that the FAA can refuse to divulge information about airport security. The FAA interprets this to mean that it can withhold the data in spite of FOIA. Public Citizen and the Lockerbie family members interpret FOIA as being the controlling statute, requiring disclosure. Is the FAA interpretation binding?

10. Hiller Systems, Inc. was performing a safety inspection on board the M/V *Cape Diamond,* an oceangoing vessel, when an accident occurred involving the fire extinguishing equipment. Two men were killed. The Occupational Safety and Health Administration (OSHA), a federal agency, attempted to investigate, but Hiller refused to permit any of its employees to speak to OSHA investigators. What could OSHA do to pursue the investigation? What limits were there on what OSHA could do?

INTERNET RESEARCH PROBLEM

Research some pending legislation in Congress. Go to http://www.senate.gov, and click on *bills.* Choose some key words that interest you, and see what your government is doing. Read the summary of the bill, if one is provided, or go to the text of the bill, and scan the introduction. What do the sponsors of this bill hope to accomplish? Do you agree or disagree with their goals?

You can find further practice problems in the Online Quiz at http://beatty.westbuslaw.com or in the Study Guide that accompanies this text.

CONSTITUTIONAL LAW

5

CHAPTER

Suppose you want to dance naked in front of 75 strangers. Do you have the *right* to do it? May the police interrupt your show and insist that you don a few garments? You may consider these odd questions, as relatively few business law students contemplate a career as a nude dancer. Yet the answers to these questions will affect you every day of your life, even if you choose a more prosaic line such as investments or retailing (it is good to have a backup plan).

Consider a very different—yet related—question. A state government wants to reduce the consumption of alcohol by making it expensive. On the theory that competitive ads drive prices down and make drinking more affordable, the legislators pass a statute prohibiting liquor stores from publishing their prices. The new law might have the desired effect—but is it fair? May a state forbid any conduct that it regards as harmful to its citizens? What if the same state passes a law preventing new construction along the coastline? This measure will protect the environment, but in the process it may render some very expensive beachfront property worthless. Whose interest is more important, that of the public or the property owners? Finally, suppose the state chooses to give certain summer camps a tax break because all of their campers come from within the state. May the state do that?

These seemingly unrelated questions all involve the same critical issue: power. Does your state have the *power* to prohibit nude dancing? If so, does that mean it could outlaw a campaign poster on your front lawn? Prohibit political protest? Is the state entitled to abolish liquor ads, for a well-intended purpose? Outlaw beachfront development? May it give tax breaks to organizations that benefit in-state residents?

Questions about regulating nude dancing affect all of us because the answers reveal how much control the government may exercise. Constitutional law is a series of variations on one vital theme: government power.

GOVERNMENT POWER

ONE IN A MILLION

The Constitution of the United States is the greatest legal document ever written. No other written constitution has lasted so long, governed so many, or withstood such challenge. This amazing work was drafted in 1787, when two weeks were needed to make the horseback ride from Boston to Philadelphia, a pair of young cities in a weak and disorganized nation. Yet today, when that trip requires less than two hours by jet, the same Constitution successfully governs the most powerful country on earth. This longevity is a tribute to the wisdom and idealism of the Founding Fathers.

The Constitution is not perfect. The original document contained provisions that were racist.[1] Other sections were unclear, and some needed early amendment. Overall, however, the Constitution has worked astonishingly well and has become the model for many constitutions around the world.

The Constitution is short and relatively easy to read. This brevity is potent. The Founding Fathers, also called the Framers, wanted it to last for centuries, and they understood that would happen only if the document permitted interpretation and "fleshing out" by later generations. The Constitution's versatility is striking, as we can see from the fact that the document can be used to resolve the crazy quilt of questions posed above. The *First Amendment* governs the two issues of nude dancing and liquor advertising. The *Commerce Clause* will resolve whether a state may give tax breaks to summer camps that benefit local residents. Courts will use the *Takings Clause* to decide when a state's efforts to protect the environment have unfairly injured property owners.

When the House of Representatives debated whether to impeach President Clinton for perjury and obstruction of justice, some Republicans and Democrats alike predicted that hearings based on a tawdry sex scandal would undermine the very structure of the federal government. They underestimated the Constitution. A stormy, intensely political inquiry in the House gave way to a

[1] Two provisions explicitly endorsed slavery, belying the proposition that all people are created equal. The "Three-Fifths Clause," in Article I, section 2, required that for purposes of taxation and representation, a slave must be counted as three-fifths of a person. Article I, section 9 ensured that southern states would be permitted to continue importing slaves into the country at least until 1808.

comparatively decorous trial in the Senate. The evidence shamed the president yet also secured his acquittal—precisely the result most citizens wanted. The Framers could scarcely have envisioned a "special prosecutor" reporting graphic sexual evidence, or media that, with frenzied glee, broadcast to the entire world every salacious word of accusation and denial. Yet the document that the Founding Fathers created reaffirmed their genius: both sides got their day in "court," and a Republican-controlled Senate voted not to oust a Democratic president.

This chapter is organized around the issue of power. The first part provides an overview of the Constitution, discussing how it came to be and how it is organized. The second part describes the power given to the three branches of government. The third part is the flip side of power, explaining what individual rights the Constitution guarantees to citizens.

OVERVIEW

Thirteen American colonies gained independence from Great Britain in 1783. The new status was exhilarating. This was the first nation in modern history founded on the idea that the people could govern themselves, democratically. The idea was daring, brilliant, and fraught with difficulties. The states were governing themselves under the Articles of Confederation, but these Articles gave the central government no real power. The government could not tax any state or its citizens and had no way to raise money. A government without the ability to raise money does not govern, it panhandles. The national government also lacked the power to regulate commerce between the states or between foreign nations and any state. This was disastrous. States began to impose taxes on goods entering from other states. The young "nation" was a collection of poor relations, threatening to squabble themselves to death.

By 1787, the Articles were largely deemed a failure, and the states sent a group of 55 delegates to Philadelphia to amend them. These delegates—the Framers of our Constitution—were not a true cross section of the populace. There were no women or blacks, artisans or small farmers. Most were wealthy; all were powerful within their states.

Rather than amend the old document, the Framers set out to draft a new one, to create a government that had never existed before. It was hard going. What structure should the government have? How much power? Representatives like Alexander Hamilton urged a strong central government. They were the *federalists.* The new government must be able to tax and spend, regulate commerce, control the borders, and do all things that national governments routinely do. But Patrick Henry and other *anti-federalists* feared a powerful central government. They had fought a bitter war precisely to get rid of autocratic rulers; they had seen the evil that a distant government could inflict. The anti-federalists insisted that the states retain maximum authority, keeping political control closer to home.

Another critical question was how much power the *people* should have. Most of the aristocratic delegates had little love for the common people and feared that extending this idea of democracy too far would lead to mob rule. Anti-federalists again disagreed. The British had been thrown out, they insisted, to guarantee individual liberty and a chance to participate in the government. Power corrupted. It must be dispersed amongst the people to avoid its abuse.

How to settle these basic differences? By compromise, of course. *The Constitution is a series of compromises about power.* We will see many provisions granting power to one branch of the government while at the same time limiting the power given.

Separation of Powers

One method of limiting power was to create a national government divided into three branches, each independent and equal. Each branch would act as a check on the power of the other two, avoiding the despotic rule that had come from London. Article I of the Constitution created a Congress, which was to have legislative power. Article II created the office of president, defining the scope of executive power. Article III established judicial power by creating the Supreme Court and permitting additional federal courts.

Consider how the three separate powers balance one another: Congress was given the power to pass statutes, a major grant of power. But the president was permitted to veto legislation, a nearly equal grant. Congress, in turn, had the right to override the veto, ensuring that the president would not become a dictator. The president was allowed to appoint federal judges and members of his cabinet, but only with a consenting vote from the Senate.

Federalism

The national government was indeed to have considerable power, but it would still be *limited power.* Article I, section 8 enumerates those issues on which Congress may pass statutes. If an issue is not on the list, Congress has no power to legislate. Thus Congress may create and regulate a post office because postal service is on the list. But Congress may not pass statutes regulating child custody in a divorce: that issue is not on the list. Only the states may legislate child custody issues.

Individual Rights

The original Constitution was silent about the rights of citizens. This alarmed many citizens, who feared that the new federal government would have unlimited power over their lives. So in 1791 the first 10 amendments, known as the Bill of Rights, were added to the Constitution, guaranteeing many liberties directly to individual citizens.

In the next two sections, we look in more detail at the two sides of the great series of compromises: power granted and rights protected.

Power Granted

Congressional Power

Article I of the Constitution creates the Congress with its two houses. Representation in the House of Representatives is proportionate with a state's population, but each state elects two senators. The article establishes who is qualified to serve in Congress, setting only three requirements: age, citizenship, and residence. This obscure provision controls a major contemporary debate.

TERM LIMITS

Toward the end of the twentieth century, many states passed laws limiting the number of terms elected officials could serve, both in state governments and in Congress. Citizens who favored limiting federal terms believed that, over the years, their representatives became ideologically remote from them, members of a Washington power culture rather than servants of the people. We will never know the wisdom of this view because the United States Supreme Court nullified federal term limits. The Framers envisioned a uniform national legislature, ruled the Court, with the people free to choose any representatives who met the minimum qualifications specified in the Constitution. No state government had the power to rewrite those qualifications. The states could limit the years someone might serve in the *state* government, but any attempt to put such a limit on federal officeholders was null and void.[2]

LEGISLATION

One of the most important functions that Article I gives Congress is the power to pass legislation. (For a description of how Congress goes about creating new law, see Chapter 4.) The president has the right to propose a new law and to veto a bill, but only Congress may *enact* one. When legislators have attempted to yield some of this power, they have failed. Congress passed the "line-item veto" bill, granting the president the right to eliminate sections of a spending law that he disliked. This permitted the president, for example, to sign a health care bill into law, providing funds for cancer research and medical training, while striking out money intended for new hospital construction. The goal—and the effect—was to reduce federal spending. The Supreme Court invalidated the law. To eliminate some sections of a bill, said the Court, was essentially to draft new legislation—a power that Article I gave only to Congress.[3]

INTERSTATE COMMERCE

"The Congress shall have power to regulate commerce with foreign nations, and among the several states." This is the **Commerce Clause**, and it is one of the most important powers granted to Congress. With it, the Framers were accomplishing several things in response to the commercial chaos that existed under the Articles of Confederation:

1. *International Commerce—Exclusive Power.* As to international commerce, the Commerce Clause is clear: only the federal government may regulate it. The federal government must speak with one voice when regulating commercial relations with foreign governments.[4]

---

[2] *U.S. Term Limits, Inc. v. Thornton*, 514 U.S. 779, 115 S. Ct. 1842, 1995 U.S. LEXIS 3487 (1995).

[3] *Clinton v. City of New York*, 524 U.S. 417, 118 S. Ct. 2091, 1998 U.S. LEXIS 4215 (1998).

[4] *Michelin Tire Corp. v. Wages, Tax Commissioner*, 423 U.S. 276, 96 S. Ct. 535, 1976 U.S. LEXIS 120 (1976).

2. *Domestic Commerce—Concurrent Power.* As to domestic commerce, the clause gives *concurrent power,* meaning that both Congress and the states may regulate it. Congress is authorized to regulate trade between states; each state regulates business within its own borders. Conflicts are inevitable, and they are important to all of us: *how* business is regulated depends upon *who* does it.

   - **Positive Aspect: Congressional Power.** The Framers wanted to give power to Congress to bring coordination and fairness to trade between the states. This is the positive aspect of the Commerce Clause: **Congress is authorized to regulate interstate commerce.**
   - **Negative or Dormant Aspect: A Limit on the States.** The Framers also wanted to stop the states from imposing the taxes and regulations that were wrecking the nation's domestic trade. This is the negative, or dormant, aspect of the Commerce Clause: **The power of the states to regulate interstate commerce is severely restricted.**

SUBSTANTIAL EFFECT RULE

An early test of the Commerce Clause's positive aspect came in the depression years of the 1930s, in *Wickard v. Filburn.*[5] The price of wheat and other grains had fluctuated wildly, severely harming farmers and the national food market. Congress sought to stabilize prices by limiting the bushels per acre that a farmer could grow. Filburn grew more wheat than federal law allowed and was fined. In defense, he claimed that Congress had no right to regulate him. None of his wheat went into interstate commerce. He sold some locally and used the rest on his own farm as food for livestock and as seed. The Commerce Clause, Filburn claimed, gave Congress no authority to limit what he could do.

The Supreme Court disagreed and held that **Congress may regulate any activity that has a substantial economic effect on interstate commerce**. Filburn's wheat affected interstate commerce because the more he grew for use on his own farm, the less he would need to buy in the open market of interstate commerce. Congress could regulate his farm. Since this ruling, most federal statutes based on the Commerce Clause have been upheld. Congress has used the Commerce Clause to regulate such diverse issues as the working conditions in a factory, discrimination in a motel, and the environmental aspects of coal mining.[6] Each of these has substantial effect on interstate commerce.

In *United States v. Lopez,*[7] however, the Supreme Court ruled that Congress had exceeded its power under the Commerce Clause. Congress had passed a criminal statute called the "Gun-Free School Zones Act," which forbade any individual from possessing a firearm in a school zone. The goal of the statute was obvious: to keep schools safe. Lopez was convicted of violating the Act and appealed his conviction all the way to the high Court, claiming that Congress had

---

[5] 317 U.S. 111, 63 S. Ct. 82, 1942 U.S. LEXIS 1046 (1942).

[6] *Maryland v. Wirts,* 392 U.S. 183, 88 S. Ct. 2017, 1968 U.S. LEXIS 2981 (1968); *Heart of Atlanta Motel v. United States,* 379 U.S. 241, 85 S. Ct. 348, 1964 U.S. LEXIS 2187 (1964); *Hodel v. Indiana,* 452 U.S. 314, 101 S. Ct. 2376, 1981 U.S. LEXIS 34 (1981).

[7] 514 U.S. 549, 115 S. Ct. 1624, 1995 U.S. LEXIS 3039 (1995).

no power to pass such a law. The government argued that the Commerce Clause gave it the power to pass the law, but the Supreme Court was unpersuaded.

> The possession of a gun in a local school zone is in no sense an economic activity that might, through repetition elsewhere, substantially affect any sort of interstate commerce. [Lopez] was a local student at a local school; there is no indication that he had recently moved in interstate commerce, and there is no requirement that his possession of the firearm have any concrete tie to interstate commerce. To uphold the Government's contentions here, we would have to pile inference upon inference in a manner that would bid fair to convert congressional authority under the Commerce Clause to a general police power of the sort retained by the States. [The statute was unconstitutional and void.]

Congress's power is great—but still limited.

STATE LEGISLATIVE POWER

The "dormant" or "negative" aspect of the Commerce Clause governs state efforts to regulate interstate commerce. **The dormant aspect holds that a state statute that discriminates against interstate commerce is invariably unconstitutional.** The following case illustrates the dormant aspect at work.

CAMPS NEWFOUND/ OWATONNA, INC. v. TOWN OF HARRISON, MAINE

520 U.S. 564, 117 S. Ct. 1590, 1997 U.S. LEXIS 3227
United States Supreme Court, 1997

Facts: Under a Maine statute, charitable institutions incorporated in that state were potentially exempt from real estate taxes. However, if the charitable organization operated principally for the benefit of nonresidents of the state, it only qualified for a limited tax break; further, if the organization charged more than $30 per week for its services, it had to pay full real estate taxes. Camps Newfound and Owatonna were Christian Science organizations that operated summer camps in Maine for children of that faith. The campers paid fees of $400 per week, and about 95 percent of them came from out of state. As a result, Maine law required Newfound and Owatonna to pay full real estate taxes.

The camps filed suit, claiming that Maine's tax laws violated the dormant aspect of the Commerce Clause by favoring intrastate institutions over those that engaged in interstate commerce. The Maine trial court agreed with the camps but the Maine Supreme Court reversed, noting that the statute treated all Maine nonprofit companies alike, and that all had an opportunity to qualify for a tax exemption by dispensing their charities instate. The camps appealed to the United States Supreme Court.

Issue: Did the Maine statute violate the dormant aspect of the Commerce Clause?

Excerpts from Justice Stevens's Decision: During the first years of our history as an independent confederation, the National Government lacked the power to regulate commerce among the States. Because each State was free to adopt measures fostering its own local interests without regard to possible prejudice to nonresidents, what Justice Johnson [in an 1824 case] characterized as a "conflict of commercial regulations, destructive to the harmony of the States" ensued. In his view, this "was the immediate cause that led to the forming of a [constitutional] convention."

It is not necessary to look beyond the text of this statute to determine that it discriminates against interstate commerce. The Maine law expressly distinguishes between entities that serve a principally interstate clientele and those that primarily serve an intrastate market, singling out camps that serve mostly in-staters for beneficial tax treatment, and penalizing those camps that do a principally interstate business. As a practical matter, the statute encourages affected entities to limit their out-of-state clientele, and penalizes the principally nonresident customers of businesses catering to a primarily interstate market.

If such a policy were implemented by a statutory prohibition against providing camp services to nonresidents, the statute would almost certainly be invalid. We have consistently held that the Commerce Clause precludes a state from mandating that its residents be given a preferred right of access, over out-of-state consumers, to natural resources located within its borders or to the products derived therefrom.

Avoiding this sort of "economic Balkanization," and the retaliatory acts of other States that may follow, is one of the central purposes of our negative Commerce Clause jurisprudence. And, as we noted in [an earlier case]: "Economic protectionism is not limited to attempts to convey advantages on local merchants; it may include attempts to give local consumers an advantage over consumers in other States." By encouraging economic isolationism, prohibitions on out-of-state access to in-state resources serve the very evil that the dormant Commerce Clause was designed to prevent.

The judgment of the Maine Supreme Judicial Court is reversed.

SUPREMACY CLAUSE

What happens when both the federal and state governments pass regulations that are permissible, but conflicting? For example, Congress passed the Federal Occupational Safety and Health Act (OSHA) establishing many job safety standards, including those for training workers who handle hazardous waste. Congress had the power to do so under the Commerce Clause. Later, Illinois passed its own hazardous waste statutes, seeking to protect both the general public and workers. The state statute did not violate the Commerce Clause because it imposed no restriction on interstate commerce.

Each statute specified worker training and employer licensing. But the requirements differed. Which statute did Illinois corporations have to obey? Article VI of the Constitution contains the answer. **The Supremacy Clause states that the Constitution, and federal statutes and treaties, shall be the supreme law of the land.**

- If there is a conflict between federal and state statutes, the federal law **preempts** the field, meaning it controls the issue. The state law is void.
- Even in cases where there is no conflict, if Congress demonstrates that it intends to exercise exclusive control over an issue, federal law preempts.

Thus state law controls only when there is no conflicting federal law and Congress has not intended to dominate the issue. In the Illinois case, the Supreme Court concluded that Congress intended to regulate the issue exclusively. Federal law therefore preempted the field, and local employers were obligated to obey only the federal regulations.

EXECUTIVE POWER

Article II of the Constitution defines the executive power. Once again the Constitution gives powers in general terms. The basic job of the president is to enforce the nation's laws. Three of his key powers concern appointment, legislation, and foreign policy.

APPOINTMENT

Administrative agencies play a powerful role in business regulation, and the president nominates the heads of most of them. These choices dramatically influence what issues the agencies choose to pursue and how aggressively they do it.[8]

LEGISLATION

The president and his advisers propose bills to Congress. During the last 50 years, a vast number of newly proposed bills have come from the executive branch. Some argue that *too many* proposals come from the president and that Congress has become overly passive. The president, of course, also has the power to veto bills.[9]

FOREIGN POLICY

The president conducts the nation's foreign affairs, coordinating international efforts, negotiating treaties, and so forth. The president is also the commander in chief of the armed forces, meaning that he heads the military. But Article II does not give him the right to declare war—only the Senate may do that. Thus a continuing tension between president and Congress has resulted from the president's use of troops overseas *without* a formal declaration of war. Once again, the Founding Fathers' desire to create a balanced government leads to uncertain application of the law.

JUDICIAL POWER

Article III of the Constitution creates the Supreme Court and permits Congress to establish lower courts within the federal court system.[10] Federal courts have two key functions: adjudication and judicial review.

ADJUDICATING CASES

The federal court system hears criminal and civil cases. All prosecutions of federal crimes begin in United States District Court. That same court has limited jurisdiction to hear civil lawsuits, a subject discussed in Chapter 3, on dispute resolution.

JUDICIAL REVIEW

One of the greatest "constitutional" powers appears nowhere in the Constitution. In 1803 the Supreme Court decided *Marbury v. Madison*.[11] Congress had passed a relatively minor statute that gave certain powers to the Supreme Court, and Marbury wanted the Court to use those powers. The Court

---

[8] For a discussion of administrative agency power, see Chapter 4, on administrative law.

[9] For a discussion of the president's veto power and Congress's power to override a veto, see Chapter 4, on statutory law.

[10] For a discussion of the federal court system, see Chapter 3, on dispute resolution.

[11] 5 U.S. (1 Cranch) 137 (1803).

refused. In an opinion written by Chief Justice John Marshall, the Court held that the statute violated the Constitution because Article III of the Constitution did not grant the Court those powers. The details of the case were insignificant, but the ruling was profound: because the statute violated the Constitution, said the Court, it was void. **Judicial review refers to the power of federal courts to declare a statute or governmental action unconstitutional and void.**

This formidable grab of power has produced two centuries of controversy. The Court was declaring that it alone had the right to evaluate acts of the other two branches of government—the Congress and the executive—and to decide which were valid and which void. The Constitution nowhere grants this power. Undaunted, Marshall declared that "[I]t is emphatically the province and duty of the judicial department to say what the law is." In later cases, the Supreme Court expanded on the idea, holding that it could also nullify state statutes, rulings by state courts, and actions by federal and state officials. In this chapter we have already encountered examples of judicial review, for example, in the *Camps Newfound/Owatonna* case, in which the Supreme Court prohibited the state of Maine from giving preferential tax treatment to summer camps that benefited local residents, and in the *Lopez* case, where the justices declared that Congress lacked the power to pass local gun regulations.

Is judicial review good for the nation? Those who oppose it argue that federal court judges are all appointed, not elected, and that we should not permit judges to nullify a statute passed by elected officials because that diminishes the people's role in their government. Those who favor judicial review insist that there must be one cohesive interpretation of the Constitution and the judicial branch is the logical one to provide it. This dispute about power simmers continuously beneath the surface and occasionally comes to the boil.

YOUNGSTOWN SHEET & TUBE CO. v. SAWYER

343 U.S. 579, 72 S. Ct. 863, 1952 U.S. LEXIS 2625
United States Supreme Court, 1952

Facts: During the Korean War, steel companies and the unions were unable to reach a contract. The union notified the companies that they would strike, beginning April 9, 1952. President Truman declared steel essential to the war effort and ordered his Secretary of Commerce, Sawyer, to take control of the steel mills and keep them running. Sawyer immediately ordered the presidents of the various companies to serve as operating managers for the United States.

On April 30, the federal district court issued an injunction to stop Sawyer from running the mills. That same day the United States Court of Appeals "stayed" the injunction, i.e., it permitted Sawyer to keep operating the mills. The Supreme Court quickly granted *certiorari,* heard argument May 12, and issued its decision June 2 (at least five years faster than most cases reach final decision).

Issue: Did President Truman have the constitutional power to seize the steel mills?

Excerpts from Justice Black's Decision: It is clear that if the President had authority to issue the order he did, it must be found in some provision of the Constitution. And it is not claimed that express constitutional language grants this power to the President. The contention is that presidential power should be implied from the aggregate of his powers under the Constitution [including the clauses stating that "the executive power shall be vested in a President," that "he shall take care that the laws be faithfully executed," and that he "shall be Commander in Chief"].

The order cannot properly be sustained as an exercise of the President's military power as

Commander in Chief. We cannot with faithfulness to our constitutional system hold that the Commander in Chief has the ultimate power as such to take possession of private property in order to keep labor disputes from stopping production. This is a job for the Nation's lawmakers, not for its military authorities.

Nor can the seizure order be sustained because of the several constitutional provisions that grant executive power to the President. In the framework of our Constitution, the President's power to see that the laws are faithfully executed refutes the idea that he is to be a lawmaker. The Constitution limits his functions in the lawmaking process to the recommending of laws he thinks wise and the vetoing of laws he thinks bad. And the Constitution is neither silent nor equivocal about who shall make laws which the President is to execute. The first section of the first article says that "All legislative powers herein granted shall be vested in a Congress of the United States." The Constitution did not subject this lawmaking power of Congress to presidential or military supervision or control.

The Founders of this Nation entrusted the lawmaking power to the Congress alone in both good and bad times. It would do no good to recall the historical events, the fears of power and the hopes for freedom that lay behind their choice. Such a review would but confirm our holding that this seizure order cannot stand.

[The district court's injunction is *affirmed*.]

President Truman disliked anyone telling him what to do, and he disliked even more having the Supreme Court limit his powers during wartime. But he obeyed the Court's order.

Judicial Activism/Judicial Restraint. The power of judicial review is potentially dictatorial. The Supreme Court nullifies statutes passed by Congress (*Marbury v. Madison, United States v. Lopez*) and executive actions (*Youngstown Sheet & Tube*). May it strike down any law it dislikes? In theory, no. The Court should nullify only laws that violate the Constitution. But of course that is circular, since it is the Court that will tell us which laws are violative.

Judicial activism refers to a court's willingness, or even eagerness, to become involved in major issues and to decide cases on constitutional grounds. **Judicial restraint** is the opposite, an attitude that courts should leave lawmaking to legislators and nullify a law only when it unquestionably violates the Constitution.

From the 1950s through the 1970s, the Supreme Court took an active role, deciding many major social issues on constitutional grounds. The landmark 1954 decision in *Brown v. Board of Education*[12] ordered an end to racial segregation in public schools, not only changing the nation's educational systems but altering forever its expectations about race. The Court also struck down many state laws that denied minorities the right to vote. Beginning with *Miranda v. Arizona,*[13] the Court began a sweeping reappraisal of the police power of the state and the rights of criminal suspects during searches, interrogations, trials, and appeals. And in *Roe v. Wade*[14] the Supreme Court established certain rights to abortion, most of which remain after 30 years of continuous litigation and violence.

Beginning in the late 1970s, and lasting to the present, the Court has pulled back from its activism. Some justices believe that the Founding Fathers never intended the judicial branch to take so prominent a role in sculpting the nation's

[12] 347 U.S. 483, 74 S. Ct. 686, 1954 U.S. LEXIS 2094 (1954).

[13] 384 U.S. 436, 86 S. Ct. 1602, 1966 U.S. LEXIS 2817 (1966).

[14] 410 U.S. 113, 93 S. Ct. 705, 1973 U.S. LEXIS 159 (1973).

laws and its social vision. Simple numbers tell part of the story of a changing Court. Every year roughly 7,500 requests for review are made to the Court. In the early 1970s, the Supreme Court accepted almost 200 of these cases, but by the new century, it was taking fewer than 100. The Court's practice of judicial restraint means that major social issues will increasingly be left to state legislatures and Congress. The Court is diminishing its own power. Interestingly, while the Court has reduced its own volume of work, it has emphatically denied to other branches of government the power to interpret the Constitution. When Congress attempted to limit the ability of the states to restrict religious practices, the Court ruled that the legislators had no such power. Congress may *enforce* constitutional rights, but only the courts may define them.[15] For a look at the current justices, the full text of famous cases, and a calendar of pending cases, see http://supct.law.cornell.edu/supct/. You can tour the Court itself and even hear some of the justices read their opinions at http://court.it-services.nwu.edu/oyez/.

Exhibit 5.1 illustrates the balance among Congress, the president, and the Court.

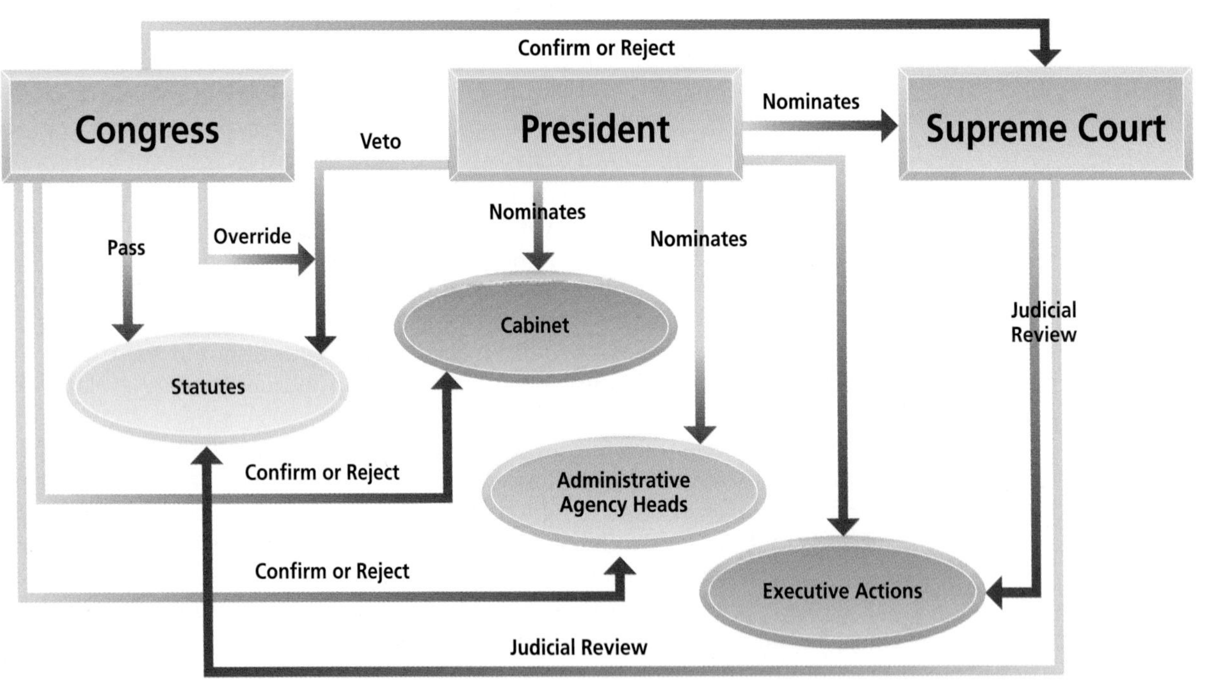

Exhibit 5.1
The Constitution established a federal government of checks and balances. Congress may pass statutes; the president may veto them; and Congress may override the veto. The president nominates cabinet officers, administrative heads, and Supreme Court justices, but the Senate must confirm his nominees. Finally, the Supreme Court (and lower federal courts) exercise judicial review over statutes and executive actions. Unlike the other checks and balances, judicial review is not provided for in the Constitution, but is a creation of the Court itself in *Marbury v. Madison*.

[15] *City of Boerne v. Flores,* 521 U.S. 507, 117 S. Ct. 2157, 1997 U.S. LEXIS 4035 (1997).

PROTECTED RIGHTS

The amendments to the Constitution protect the people of this nation from the power of state and federal government. The First Amendment guarantees rights of free speech, free press, and religion; the Fourth Amendment protects against illegal searches; the Fifth Amendment ensures due process; the Sixth Amendment demands fair treatment for defendants in criminal prosecutions; and the Fourteenth Amendment guarantees equal protection of the law. We consider the First, Fifth, and Fourteenth Amendments in this chapter and the Fourth, Fifth, and Sixth Amendments in Chapter 7, on crime.

The "people" who are protected include citizens and, for most purposes, corporations. Corporations are considered persons and receive most of the same protections. The great majority of these rights also extend to citizens of other countries who are in the United States.

Constitutional rights generally protect only against governmental acts. The Constitution generally does not protect us from the conduct of private parties, such as corporations or other citizens.

INCORPORATION

Constitutional protections apply to federal, state, and local governments. Yet that is not what the Bill of Rights explicitly states. The First Amendment declares that Congress shall not abridge the right of free speech. The Fourteenth Amendment explicitly limits the power only of *state* governments. But a series of Supreme Court cases has extended virtually all of the important constitutional protections to all levels of national, state, and local government. This process is called **incorporation** because rights explicitly guaranteed at one level are incorporated into rights that apply at other levels.

FIRST AMENDMENT: FREE SPEECH

The First Amendment states that "Congress shall make no law . . . abridging the freedom of speech. . . ." In general, we expect our government to let people speak and hear whatever they choose. The Founding Fathers believed democracy would only work if the members of the electorate were free to talk, argue, listen, and exchange viewpoints in any way they wanted. The people could only cast informed ballots if they were informed. "Speech" also includes symbolic conduct, as the following case flamingly illustrates.

TEXAS v. JOHNSON

491 U.S. 397, 109 S. Ct. 2533, 1989
U.S. LEXIS 3115
United States Supreme Court, 1989

Facts: Outside the Republican National Convention in Dallas, Gregory Johnson participated in a protest against policies of the Reagan administration. Participants gave speeches and handed out leaflets. Johnson burned an American flag. He was arrested and convicted under a Texas statute that prohibited desecrating the flag, but the Texas Court of Criminal Appeals reversed on the grounds that the conviction violated the First Amendment. Texas appealed to the United States Supreme Court.

Issue: Does the First Amendment protect flag burning?

Excerpts from Justice Brennan's Decision: The First Amendment literally forbids the abridgment only of "speech," but we have long recognized that its protection does not end at the spoken or written word. While we have rejected the view that an apparently limitless variety of conduct can be labeled "speech," we have acknowledged that conduct may be sufficiently imbued with elements of communication to fall within the scope of the First and Fourteenth Amendments.

In deciding whether particular conduct possesses sufficient communicative elements to bring the First Amendment into play, we have asked whether an intent to convey a particularized message was present, and [whether] the likelihood was great that the message would be understood by those who viewed it. Hence, we have recognized the expressive nature of students' wearing of black armbands to protest American military involvement in Vietnam; of a sit-in by blacks in a "whites only" area to protest segregation; of the wearing of American military uniforms in a dramatic presentation criticizing American involvement in Vietnam; and of picketing about a wide variety of causes.

[The Court concluded that burning the flag was in fact symbolic speech.]

It remains to consider whether the State's interest in reserving the flag as a symbol of nationhood and national unity justifies Johnson's conviction. Johnson was prosecuted because he knew that his politically charged expression would cause "serious offense."

If there is a bedrock principle underlying the First Amendment, it is that the Government may not prohibit the expression of an idea simply because society finds the idea itself offensive or disagreeable. Nothing in our precedents suggests that a State may foster its own view of the flag by prohibiting expressive conduct relating to it.

Could the Government, on this theory, prohibit the burning of state flags? Of copies of the Presidential seal? Of the Constitution? In evaluating these choices under the First Amendment, how would we decide which symbols were sufficiently special to warrant this unique status? To do so, we would be forced to consult our own political preferences, and impose them on the citizenry, in the very way that the First Amendment forbids us to do.

The way to preserve the flag's special role is not to punish those who feel differently about these matters. It is to persuade them that they are wrong. We can imagine no more appropriate response to burning a flag than waving one's own, no better way to counter a flagburner's message than by saluting the flag that burns, no surer means of preserving the dignity even of the flag that burned than by—as one witness here did—according its remains a respectful burial. We do not consecrate the flag by punishing its desecration, for in doing so we dilute the freedom that this cherished emblem represents.

The judgment of the Texas Court of Criminal Appeals is therefore *affirmed.*

Flag burning is an issue that will not go away. For additional thoughts on the subject, ignite either http://www.esquilax.com/flag/, an irreverent page that strongly supports the rights of free speech, or http://www.cfa-inc.org, a site that decries flag burning.

POLITICAL SPEECH

Because the Framers were primarily concerned with enabling democracy to function, political speech has been given an especially high degree of protection. Such speech may not be barred even when it is offensive or outrageous. A speaker, for example, could accuse a U.S. senator of being insane and could use crude, violent language to describe him. The speech is still protected. The speech lacks protection only if it is *intended and likely to create imminent lawless action.*[16] For example, suppose the speaker said, "The senator is inside that restaurant. Let's get some matches and burn the place down." Speech of this sort is not protected. The speaker could be arrested for attempted arson or attempted murder.

TIME, PLACE, AND MANNER

Even when speech is protected, the government may regulate the *time, place,* and *manner* of such speech. A town may require a group to apply for a permit before using a public park for a political demonstration. The town may insist that the demonstration take place during daylight hours and that there be adequate police supervision and sanitation provided. However, the town may not prohibit such demonstrations outright.

The Supreme Court is frequently called upon to balance the rights of the general public with the rights of those seeking to publicize their causes. In *Madsen v. Women's Health Center, Inc.,*[17] the Court ruled that a local judge could limit protesters' access to a family planning clinic. The protesters, opposed to abortion, had repeatedly blocked access to the clinic, harassed patients and doctors at the clinic and at their homes, and paraded with graphic signs and bullhorns. The Court upheld the order prohibiting the protesters from coming within 36 feet of the clinic and also the order that prohibited excessive noise. But the Court overturned a part of the order that had forbidden protesters from displaying graphic images that could be seen inside the clinic. The Court said that the proper remedy was for the clinic to close its curtains.

MORALITY AND OBSCENITY

The regulation of morality and obscenity presents additional problems. Obscenity has never received constitutional protection. The Supreme Court has consistently held that it does not play a valued role in our society and has refused to give protection to obscene works. That is well and good, but it merely forces the question: What is obscene? (For a list of books that have been—and in some cases still are—banned by local, state, or foreign governments, see **http://onlinebooks.library.upenn.edu/banned-books.html**.)

In *Miller v. California,*[18] the Court created a three-part test to determine if a creative work is obscene. The basic guidelines for the factfinder are:

- Whether the average person, applying contemporary community standards, would find that the work, taken as a whole, appeals to the prurient interest
- Whether the work depicts or describes, in a patently offensive way, sexual conduct specifically defined by the applicable state law; and
- Whether the work, taken as a whole, lacks serious literary, artistic, political, or scientific value.

---

[16] *Brandenburg v. Ohio,* 395 U.S. 444, 89 S. Ct. 1827, 1969 U.S. LEXIS 1367 (1969).

[17] 511 U.S. 1016, 114 S. Ct. 1395, 1994 U.S. LEXIS 2671 (1994).

[18] 413 U.S. 15, 93 S. Ct. 2607, 1973 U.S. LEXIS 149 (1973).

If the trial court finds that the answer to all three of those questions is "yes," it may judge the material obscene; the state may then prohibit the work. If the state fails to prove any one of the three criteria, though, the work is not obscene. A United States District Court ruled that "As Nasty As They Wanna Be," recorded by 2 Live Crew, was obscene. The appeals court, however, reversed, finding that the state had failed to prove lack of artistic merit.[19]

What if sexual conduct is not obscene? Let's go back to the chapter's starting point, nude dancing.

BARNES v. GLEN THEATRE, INC.
501 U.S. 560, 111 S. Ct. 2456, 1991 U.S. LEXIS 3633
United States Supreme Court, 1991

Facts: Indiana's public indecency statute prohibits any person from appearing nude in a public place. State courts have interpreted this to mean that a dancer in a theater or bar must wear pasties and a G-string. A nightclub called the Kitty Kat Lounge and several dancers who wished to perform nude filed suit, seeking an order that the statute was unconstitutional. The United States District Court ruled that the dancing was not expressive conduct and therefore was not entitled to First Amendment protection. The Court of Appeals reversed, declaring that it was nonobscene expressive conduct and thus protected by the First Amendment.

Indiana did not argue that the dancing was obscene. (If that were the issue, the *Miller* test would have determined the outcome.) Instead, Indiana claimed that its general police powers, including the power to protect social order, allowed it to enforce such a statute.

You be the Judge: Does Indiana's public indecency statute violate the First Amendment?

Argument for Indiana: Your honors, the State of Indiana has no wish to suppress ideas or censor speech. We are not trying to outlaw eroticism or any other legitimate form of expression. We are simply prohibiting nudity in public. We have outlawed all public nudity, not just nightclub performances. Nudity on the beach, in the park, or anywhere in public is prohibited.

We do this to protect societal order, to foster a stable morality. It is well established that the police power of the state includes the right to regulate the public health, safety, and morals. Our citizens disapprove of people appearing in the nude in public places. The citizens of virtually all states feel the same. Decent dress has been a part of good society since time immemorial. Our voting public is entitled to have that standard upheld.

We also enforce this statute because experience has shown that nightclubs such as these are often associated with criminal behavior. Prostitution, illegal drugs, and violence appear too frequently in the vicinity. It is a reasonable step for the State to maintain control over the performances and the people they will attract.

Argument for Kitty Kat: It is apparent beyond debate that dance is expressive conduct. As an art form it has existed for at least several thousand years. Eroticism, also, is not exactly news. Erotic dance is clearly expressive conduct. Indeed, the present dancing derives its strength from its eroticism. If the State did not consider it erotic, doubtless it would have left the dancers alone. This dancing is expressive conduct and deserves the full protection of the First Amendment.

Indiana is choosing a certain type of expression and outlawing it. The state has not outlawed all nudity, since quite obviously nudity in private is beyond the State's reach. Nor has it prohibited all nude performances. Testimony of police at

---

[19] *Luke Records, Inc. v. Navarro*, 960 F.2d 134, 1992 U.S. App. LEXIS 9592 (11th Cir. 1992).

trial indicated that no arrests have ever been made for nudity as part of a play or ballet. Nudity is no longer anything novel in musicals, ballets, stage plays, or film. Indiana permits nudity in all of them and enforces its moralizing law only against nightclubs.

This is an obvious value judgment on the part of the State. The State is saying that if you can afford to pay for a Broadway show that happens to have nudity, you are free to enjoy it; if your taste or pocketbook leads you to the Kitty Kat Lounge, we deny your right to witness nudity. If the State is allowed to make that appraisal, then it is free to censor any expression—artistic, political, or any other—that it finds inferior. It was precisely to prevent states from outlawing unpopular expression that the Founding Fathers added the First Amendment.

CYBER*LAW*

Concerned that pornography on the Internet was easily available to minors, Congress passed the Communications Decency Act (CDA), making it illegal for any person or company to send "obscene or indecent" communications to anyone under 18. Various plaintiffs, including library associations, booksellers, Internet service providers, and others, filed suit, claiming that the law would diminish the extraordinary opportunities for research and education that the Internet provides. The Supreme Court agreed, striking down the law as a violation of the First Amendment. The justices declared that the law failed to define "indecent." The CDA ignored the obscenity standard provided in *Miller v. California* and outlawed material that *did* have socially redeeming value. The Court noted that the law would deny adults access to a vast amount of material that they were legally entitled to obtain. Finally, the Court pointed out that concerned parents could purchase software to screen out objectionable items, avoiding the need for such far-reaching censorship.[20]

COMMERCIAL SPEECH

This refers to speech that has a **dominant theme to propose a commercial transaction**. For example, most advertisements on television and in the newspapers are commercial speech. This sort of speech is protected by the First Amendment, but the government is permitted to regulate it more closely than other forms of speech. **Commercial speech that is false or misleading may be outlawed altogether.** However, regulations on commercial speech must be reasonable and directed to a legitimate goal, as the following case shows.

44 LIQUORMART, INC. v. RHODE ISLAND

517 U.S. 484, 116 S. Ct. 1495, 1996 U.S. LEXIS 3020
United States Supreme Court, 1996

Facts: Rhode Island passed a statute that prohibited liquor stores from advertising prices, and a second law that barred the media from publicizing such ads. The legislature's goal was to reduce drinking by eliminating the competitive advertising that decreased prices and made alcohol more easily available. Liquor stores filed suit, claiming that the prohibition violated the First Amendment. The United States District Court declared that the laws violated the First Amendment, but the Court of Appeals reversed, holding that the state's theory was logical. The case reached the highest court.

[20] *Reno v. American Civil Liberties Union*, 521 U.S. 844, 117 S. Ct. 2329, 1997 U.S. LEXIS 4037 (1997).

Issue: Did Rhode Island violate the First Amendment by banning advertisements containing liquor prices?

Excerpts from Justice Stevens's Decision: It is the State's interest in protecting consumers from commercial harms that provides the typical reason why commercial speech can be subject to greater governmental regulation than noncommercial speech. Yet bans that target truthful, nonmisleading commercial messages rarely protect consumers from such harms. Instead, such bans often serve only to obscure an underlying governmental policy that could be implemented without regulating speech. In this way, these commercial speech bans not only hinder consumer choice, but also impede debate over central issues of public policy.

Precisely because bans against truthful, nonmisleading commercial speech rarely seek to protect consumers from either deception or overreaching, they usually rest solely on the offensive assumption that the public will respond "irrationally" to the truth. The First Amendment directs us to be especially skeptical of regulations that seek to keep people in the dark for what the government perceives to be their own good.

In evaluating the ban's effectiveness in advancing the State's interest, we note that a commercial speech regulation "may not be sustained if it provides only ineffective or remote support for the government's purpose." For that reason, the State bears the burden of showing not merely that its regulation will advance its interest, but also that it will do so "to a material degree."

Without any findings of fact, or indeed any evidentiary support whatsoever, we cannot agree with the assertion that the price advertising ban will significantly advance the State's interest in promoting temperance.

The State also cannot satisfy the requirement that its restriction on speech be no more extensive than necessary. It is perfectly obvious that alternative forms of regulation that would not involve any restriction on speech would be more likely to achieve the State's goal of promoting temperance. As the State's own expert conceded, higher prices can be maintained either by direct regulation or by increased taxation. Per capita purchases could be limited as is the case with prescription drugs. Even educational campaigns focused on the problems of excessive, or even moderate, drinking might prove to be more effective.

As a result, even under the less than strict standard that generally applies in commercial speech cases, the State has failed to establish a "reasonable fit" between its abridgment of speech and its temperance goal.

The judgment of the Court of Appeals is therefore reversed.

FIFTH AMENDMENT: DUE PROCESS AND THE TAKINGS CLAUSE

You are a third-year student in a combined business/law program at a major state university. You feel great about a difficult securities exam you took in Professor Watson's class. The Dean's Office sends for you, and you enter curiously, wondering if your exam was so good that the Dean is awarding you a prize. Not quite. The exam proctor has accused you of cheating. Based on the accusation, Watson has flunked you. You protest that you are innocent and demand to know what the accusation is. The Dean says that you will learn the details at a hearing, if you wish to have one. She reminds you that if you lose the hearing you will be expelled from the university. Three years of work and your entire career are suddenly on the line.

The hearing is run by Professor Holmes, who will make the final decision. Holmes is a junior faculty member in Watson's department. (Next year, Watson will decide Holmes's tenure application.) At the hearing the proctor accuses you of copying from a student sitting in front of you. Both Watson and Holmes have already compared the two papers and concluded that they are strongly similar. Holmes tells you that you must convince him the charge is wrong. You examine the papers, acknowledge that there are similarities, but plead as best you can that you never copied. Holmes doesn't buy it. The university expels you, placing on your transcript a notation of cheating.

Have you received fair treatment? To answer that, we must look to the Fifth Amendment, which provides several vital protections. We here consider two related provisions, the Due Process Clause and the Takings Clause. Together, they state: "No person shall be . . . deprived of life, liberty, or property without due process of law; nor shall private property be taken for public use, without just compensation." These clauses prevent the government from arbitrarily taking the most valuable possessions of a citizen or corporation. Here we discuss the civil law aspects of these clauses, but due process also applies to criminal law. The reference to "life" refers to capital punishment. The criminal law issues of this subject are discussed in Chapter 7, on crime.

In civil law proceedings, the government does have the right to take a person's liberty or property. But there are three important limitations:

- *Procedural Due Process.* Before depriving anyone of liberty or property, the government must go through certain procedures to ensure that the result is fair.
- *The Takings Clause.* When the government takes property for public use, such as to build a new highway, it has to pay a fair price.
- *Substantive Due Process.* Some rights are so fundamental that the government may not take them from us at all.

Procedural Due Process

The government deprives citizens or corporations of their property in a variety of ways. The Internal Revenue Service may fine a corporation for late payment of taxes. The Customs Service may seize goods at the border. As to liberty, the government may take it by confining someone in a mental institution or by taking a child out of the home because of parental neglect. **The purpose of procedural due process is to ensure that before the government takes liberty or property, the affected person has a fair chance to oppose the action.**

There are two steps in analyzing a procedural due process case:

- Is the government attempting to take liberty or property?
- If so, how much process is due? (If the government is *not* attempting to take liberty or property, there is no due process issue.)

Is the Government Attempting to Take Liberty or Property? Liberty interests are generally easy to spot: confining someone in a mental institution and taking a child from her home are both deprivations of liberty. A property interest may be obvious. Suppose that, during a civil lawsuit, the court **attaches** a defendant's house, meaning it bars the defendant from selling the property at least until the case is decided. This way, if the plaintiff wins, the defendant will have assets to pay the judgment. The court has clearly deprived the defendant of an important interest in his house, and the defendant is entitled to due process. However, a property interest may be subtler than that. A woman holding a job with a government agency has a "property interest" in that job, because her employer has agreed not to fire her without cause, and she can rely on it for income. If the government does fire her, it is taking away that property interest, and she is entitled to due process. A student attending any public school has a property interest in that education. If a public university suspends a law/business student, as described above, it is taking her property, and she, too, should receive due process.

How Much Process Is Due? Assuming that a liberty or property interest is affected, a court must decide how much process is due. Does the person get a formal trial, or an informal hearing, or merely a chance to reply in writing to the charges against her? If she gets a hearing, must it be held before the government deprives her of her property, or is it enough that she can be heard shortly thereafter? **What sort of hearing the government must offer depends upon how important the property or liberty interest is and on whether the government has a competing need for efficiency.** The more important the interest, the more formal the procedures must be.

Neutral Factfinder. Regardless of how formal the hearing, one requirement is constant: the factfinder must be neutral. Whether it is a superior court judge deciding a multimillion dollar contract suit or an employment supervisor deciding the fate of a government employee, the factfinder must have no personal interest in the outcome. In *Ward v. Monroeville,*[21] the plaintiff was a motorist who had been stopped for traffic offenses in a small town. He protested his innocence and received a judicial hearing. But the "judge" at the hearing was the town mayor. Traffic fines were a significant part of the town's budget. The motorist argued that the town was depriving him of procedural due process because the mayor had a financial interest in the outcome of the case. The United States Supreme Court agreed and reversed his conviction.

Attachment of Property. As described above, a plaintiff in a civil lawsuit often seeks to *attach* the defendant's property. This protects the plaintiff, but it may also harm the defendant if, for example, he is about to close a profitable real estate deal. Attachments used to be routine. In *Connecticut v. Doehr,* the Supreme Court required more caution.[22] Based on Doehr, when a plaintiff seeks to attach at the beginning of the trial, a court must look at the plaintiff's likelihood of winning. Generally, the court must grant the defendant a hearing *before* attaching the property. The defendant, represented by a lawyer, may offer evidence as to how attachment would harm him and why it should be denied.

Government Employment. A government employee must receive due process before being fired. Generally, this means some kind of hearing, but not necessarily a formal court hearing. The employee is entitled to know the charges against him, to hear the employer's evidence, and to have an opportunity to tell his side of the story. He is not entitled to have a lawyer present. The hearing "officer" need only be a neutral employee. Further, in an emergency, where the employee is a danger to the public or the organization, the government may suspend with pay, before holding a hearing. It then must provide a hearing before the decision becomes final.

---

[21] 409 U.S. 57, 93 S. Ct. 80, 1972 U.S. LEXIS 11 (1972).

[22] 501 U.S. 1, 111 S. Ct. 2105, 1991 U.S. LEXIS 3317 (1991).

Academic Suspension. There is still a property interest here, but it is the least important of those discussed. When a public school concludes that a student has failed to meet its normal academic standards, such as by failing too many courses, it may dismiss him without a hearing. Due process is served if the student receives notice of the reason and has some opportunity to respond, such as by writing a letter contradicting the school's claims.

In cases of disciplinary suspension or expulsion, courts generally require schools to provide a higher level of due process. In the scenario at the beginning of this section, the university has failed to provide adequate due process.[23] The school has accused the student of a serious infraction. The school must promptly provide details of the charge and cannot wait until the hearing to do so. The student should see the two papers and have a chance to rebut the charge. Moreover, Professor Holmes has demonstrated bias. He appears to have made up his mind in advance. He has placed the burden on the student to disprove the charges. And he probably feels obligated to support Watson's original conclusion, since Watson will be deciding his tenure case next year.

THE TAKINGS CLAUSE

Florence Dolan ran a plumbing store in Tigard, Oregon. She and her husband wanted to enlarge it on land they already owned. But the city government said that they could expand only if they dedicated some of their own land for use as a public bicycle path and for other public use. Does the city have the right to make them do that? For an answer we must look to a different part of the Fifth Amendment.

The Takings Clause is closely related to the Due Process Clause. **The Takings Clause prohibits a state from taking private property for public use without just compensation.** A town wishing to build a new football field may boot you out of your house. But the town must compensate you. The government takes your land through the power of **eminent domain**. Officials must notify you of their intentions and give you an opportunity to oppose the project and to challenge the amount the town offers to pay. But when the hearings are done, the town may write you a check and grind your house into goalposts, whether you like it or not.

More controversial issues arise when a local government does not physically take the property but requires an owner to dedicate some part of the land to public use. Tigard is a city of 30,000 in Oregon. The city developed a comprehensive land use plan for its downtown area in order to preserve green space, to encourage transportation other than autos, and to reduce its flooding problems. Under the plan, when a property owner sought permission to build in the downtown section, the city could require some of her land to be used for public purposes. This has become a standard method of land use planning throughout the nation. States have used it to preserve coastline, urban green belts, and many environmental features.

When Florence Dolan applied for permission to expand, the city required that she dedicate a 15-foot strip of her property to the city as a bicycle pathway and that she preserve, as greenway, a portion of her land within a floodplain.

---

[23] See, e.g., *University of Texas Medical School at Houston v. Than,* 901 S.W.2d 926, 1995 Tex. LEXIS 105 (Tex. 1995).

She sued, and though she lost in the Oregon courts, she won in the United States Supreme Court. The Court held that Tigard City's method of routinely forcing all owners to dedicate land to public use violated the Takings Clause. The city was taking the land, even though title never changed hands.[24]

The Court did not outlaw all such requirements. What it required was that, **before a government may require an owner to dedicate land to a public use, it must show that this owner's proposed building requires this dedication of land**. In other words, it is not enough for Tigard to have a general plan, such as a bicycle pathway, and to make all owners participate in it. Tigard must show that it needs *Dolan's* land *specifically for a bike path and greenway.* This will be much harder for local governments to demonstrate than merely showing a citywide plan. Some observers consider the decision a major advance for the interests of private property. They say that now the government cannot so easily demand that you give up land for public use. Property you have purchased with hard-earned money should truly be yours. Others decry the Court's ruling. In their view, it harms our nation's effort to preserve the environment and gives a freer hand to those who value short-term profit over long-term planning.

SUBSTANTIVE DUE PROCESS

This doctrine is part of the Due Process Clause, but it is entirely different from procedural due process and from government taking. During the first third of the twentieth century, the Supreme Court frequently nullified state and federal laws, asserting that they interfered with basic rights. For example, in a famous 1905 case, *Lochner v. New York,*[25] the Supreme Court invalidated a New York statute that had limited the number of hours that bakers could work in a week. New York had passed the law to protect employee health. But the Court declared that private parties had a basic constitutional right to contract. In this case, the statute interfered with the rights of the employer and the baker to make any bargain they wished. Over the next three decades, the Court struck down dozens of state and federal laws that were aimed at working conditions, union rights, and social welfare generally. This was called **substantive due process** because the Court was looking at the substantive rights being affected, such as the right to contract, not at any procedures.

Critics complained that the Court was interfering with the desires of the voting public by nullifying laws that the justices personally disliked (judicial activism). During the Great Depression, however, things changed. Beginning in 1934, the Court completely reversed itself and began to uphold the types of laws it earlier had struck down. How does the Court now regard substantive due process issues? It treats economic and social regulations differently from cases involving fundamental rights.

Economic and Social Regulations. Generally speaking, the Court will now *presume valid* any statute that regulates economic or social conditions. If the *Lochner* case were heard today, the legislation would be upheld. State or federal laws regulating wages, working conditions, discrimination, union rights, and any similar topics are presumed valid. The Court will invalidate such a law only

---

[24] *Dolan v. City of Tigard,* 512 U.S. 374, 114 S. Ct. 2309, 1994 U.S. LEXIS 4826 (1994).

[25] 198 U.S. 45, 25 S. Ct. 539, 1905 U.S. LEXIS 1153 (1905).

if it is *arbitrary or irrational.* Almost all statutes have some minimal rationality, and most are now upheld.

Fundamental Rights. The standard of review is different for laws that affect **fundamental rights**. The Constitution expressly provides some of these rights, such as the right of free speech, the right to vote, and the right to travel. Other rights do not explicitly appear in the Constitution, but the Supreme Court has determined that they are implied. One of the most important of these is the right to privacy. The Court has decided that the Bill of Rights, taken together, implies a right of privacy for all persons. This includes the right to contraception, to marriage, and, most controversially, to abortion.

Any law that infringes upon a fundamental right is presumed invalid and will be struck down unless it is necessary to a compelling government interest. For example, because it is a fundamental right, no state may outlaw abortion altogether. But the state may require a minor to obtain the consent of a parent or a judge. Although this infringes upon a fundamental right, the government has a compelling interest in regulating the welfare of minors, and this regulation is necessary to achieve that goal.

FOURTEENTH AMENDMENT: EQUAL PROTECTION CLAUSE

Shannon Faulkner wanted to attend The Citadel, a state-supported military college in South Carolina. She was a fine student who met every admission requirement that The Citadel set except one: she was not a male. The Citadel argued that its long and distinguished history demanded that it remain all male. The state government claimed that Ms. Faulkner had no need to attend this particular school. Faulkner responded that she was a citizen of the state and ought to receive the benefits that others got, including the right to a military education. Could the school exclude her on the basis of gender?

The Fourteenth Amendment provides that "No State shall . . . deny to any person within its jurisdiction the equal protection of the laws." This is the **Equal Protection Clause,** and it means that, generally speaking, **governments must treat people equally.** Unfair classifications among people or corporations will not be permitted. A notorious example of unfair classification would be race discrimination: permitting only white children to attend a public school violates the Equal Protection Clause.

Yet clearly, governments do make classifications every day. Rich people pay a higher tax rate than poor people; some corporations are permitted to deal in securities, others are not. To determine which classifications are constitutionally permissible, we need to know what is being classified. There are three major groups of classifications. The outcome of a case can generally be predicted by knowing which group it is in.

- *Minimal Scrutiny: Economic and Social Relations.* Government actions that classify people or corporations on these bases are almost always upheld.
- *Intermediate Scrutiny: Gender.* Government classifications are sometimes upheld.
- *Strict Scrutiny: Race, Ethnicity, and Fundamental Rights.* Classifications based on any of these are almost never upheld.

MINIMAL SCRUTINY: ECONOMIC AND SOCIAL REGULATION

Just as with the Due Process Clause, laws that regulate economic or social issues are presumed valid. They will be upheld if they are *rationally related to a legitimate goal.* This means a statute may classify corporations and/or people and the classifications will be upheld if they make any sense at all. The New York City Transit Authority excluded all methadone users from any employment. The United States District Court concluded that this violated the Equal Protection Clause by unfairly excluding all those who were on methadone. The court noted that even those who tested free of any illegal drugs and were seeking non-safety-sensitive jobs, such as clerks, were turned away. That, said the district court, was irrational.

Not so, said the United States Supreme Court. The Court admitted that the policy might not be the wisest. It would probably make more sense to test individually for illegal drugs rather than automatically exclude methadone users. But, said the Court, it was not up to the justices to choose the best policy. They were only to decide if the policy was rational. Excluding methadone users related rationally to the safety of public transport and therefore did not violate the Equal Protection Clause.[26]

INTERMEDIATE SCRUTINY: GENDER

Classifications based on sex must meet a tougher test than those resulting from economic or social regulation. Such laws must *substantially relate to important government objectives.* Courts have increasingly nullified government sex classifications as societal concern with gender equality has grown.

At about the same time Shannon Faulkner began her campaign to enter The Citadel, another woman sought admission to the Virginia Military Institute, an all-male state school. The Supreme Court held that Virginia had violated the Equal Protection Clause by excluding women from VMI. The Court ruled that gender-based government discrimination requires an "exceedingly persuasive justification," and that Virginia had failed that standard of proof. The Citadel promptly opened its doors to women, while VMI alumni contemplated purchasing the school, to escape altogether the reaches of the Equal Protection Clause.[27]

Today over 800 high school girls wrestle competitively. Some join female clubs but others have no such opportunity and compete with boys—or seek to. Some schools allow girls to join the boys' wrestling team, but others refuse, citing moral reasons, concern for the girls' safety, and the possibility of sexual harassment. If a particular school has no female team, should girls be permitted to wrestle boys? Do they have an equal protection right to do so?

STRICT SCRUTINY: RACE, ETHNICITY, AND FUNDAMENTAL RIGHTS

Any government action that intentionally discriminates against racial or ethnic minorities, or interferes with a fundamental right, is presumed invalid. In

---

[26] *New York City Transit Authority v. Beazer,* 440 U.S. 568, 99 S. Ct. 1355, 1979 U.S. LEXIS 77 (1979).

[27] *United States v. Virginia,* 518 U.S. 515, 116 S. Ct. 2264, 1996 U.S. LEXIS 4259 (1996).

such cases, courts will look at the statute or policy with *strict scrutiny;* that is, courts will examine it very closely to determine whether there is compelling justification for it. The law will be upheld only if it is *necessary to promote a compelling state interest.* Very few meet that test.

- *Racial and Ethnic Minorities.* Any government action that intentionally discriminates on the basis of race or ethnicity is presumed invalid. For example, in *Palmore v. Sidoti,*[28] the state had refused to give child custody to a mother because her new spouse was racially different from the child. The practice was declared unconstitutional. The state had made a racial classification, it was presumed invalid, and the government had no *compelling need* to make such a ruling.
- *Fundamental Rights.* A government action interfering with a fundamental right also receives strict scrutiny and will likely be declared void. For example, New York State gave an employment preference to any veteran who had been a state resident when he entered the military. Newcomers who were veterans were less likely to get jobs, and therefore this statute interfered with the right to travel, a fundamental right. The Supreme Court declared the law invalid.[29]

INDIVIDUAL RIGHTS AND STATE ACTION

All of the rights discussed thus far offer protection only from government action, not from the conduct of private citizens or corporations. Suppose it is Sunday morning. You are happily reading the newspaper, sipping coffee, while your nine-year-old niece, visiting for the weekend, plays hopscotch on your front walk. There is a knock at the front door. The Neighborhood Association has arrived with a stern message: "Get the kid out of the neighborhood; she's not allowed." Astonished and enraged, you call your lawyer. But her answer leaves you dazed: You may not have children in your house. "But this is America!" you shout. "The Constitution," she replies, "does not apply."

Like 50 million other Americans, you live in a *common interest development* (CID). Yours happens to be a gated community of single family homes, all of which were built by a developer. When you bought the house, you automatically joined the Neighborhood Association. Other CIDs take different forms: condominiums, co-ops, or retirement or vacation communities. They are increasingly common, and some observers predict that, soon, about 25 percent of all Americans will live in one.

Some CIDs ban children from living in the development or even visiting. Some prohibit signs on the lawns or windows; others outlaw pets, certain flowers, laundry drying in the sun, day-care centers, or pickup trucks. But various features make CIDs attractive to prospective residents. CIDs are often gated or locked in other ways, so they may be safer than surrounding neighborhoods. The community collects its own fees and operates many services, such as water and sewer, road maintenance, garbage collection, and other work traditionally

---

[28] 466 U.S. 429, 104 S. Ct. 1879, 1984 U.S. LEXIS 69 (1984).

[29] *Attorney General of New York v. Soto-Lopez,* 476 U.S. 898, 106 S. Ct. 2317, 1986 U.S. LEXIS 59 (1986).

done by towns and cities. Because they are privately managed by boards elected by the residents, CIDs often do this work more promptly and efficiently than public agencies.

Towns or cities also find CIDs desirable since the CID does much of the municipal work itself, using fees collected from residents. While costing a local political unit no extra money, the CID offers an expanded tax base—a happy combination for local governments chronically short of revenue.

However, the price residents pay is more than cash: they do indeed forfeit constitutional rights. The Constitution protects citizens from government action, and the local CID is not a government. As the law currently stands, you are probably giving up constitutional protections when you enter a CID. If the Neighborhood Association demands that your niece leave, you will probably have to drive her home. Suppose the nasty Neighborhood Association official also notices that your cat looks heavy. "No cats over 20 pounds," he snarls. "Read the rules." The pet-weight rule is also probably enforceable: get that cat off the sofa and onto a treadmill, fast.

STATE ACTION

In some cases, the Supreme Court has found that a private organization has taken on all the characteristics of a government and thus should be treated as such for constitutional purposes. In *Marsh v. Alabama*,[30] a private company owned an entire town, where its employees lived and worked. The company brought a trespass case against someone distributing religious literature. However, since the company property had "all the characteristics of any other American town," the Supreme Court ruled that it must be *treated* as a town, meaning that constitutional protections must apply. The First Amendment protected the right to distribute religious material. This is the **state action doctrine**. But there are limits. In 1976 the Court ruled that the state action doctrine does not apply to shopping centers because they do not possess all of the attributes of a town.

Before too long the Court will probably have to decide whether a CID is free to make unlimited rules or is subject to the state action doctrine. Like the town in *Marsh*, many CIDs look and act like towns. But in *Marsh* the company owned the town; a CID is a group of owners banding together by agreement. The Court will have to decide whether that agreement can nullify constitutional rights.

---

[30] 326 U.S. 501, 66 S. Ct. 276, 1946 U.S. LEXIS 3097 (1946).

CHAPTER CONCLUSION

The legal battle over power never stops. The obligation of a state to provide equal educational opportunity for both genders relates to whether Tigard, Oregon, may demand some of Ms. Dolan's store lot for public use. Both issues are governed by one amazing document. That same Constitution determines what tax preferences are permissible, and even whether a state may require you to wear clothing. As social mores change in step with broad cultural developments, as the membership of the Supreme Court changes, the balance of power between federal government, state government, and citizens will continue to evolve. There are no easy answers to these constitutional questions because there has never been a democracy so large, so diverse, or so powerful.

CHAPTER REVIEW

1. The Constitution is a series of compromises about power.
2. Article I of the Constitution creates the Congress and grants all legislative power to it. Article II establishes the office of president and defines executive powers. Article III creates the Supreme Court and permits lower federal courts; the article also outlines the powers of the federal judiciary.
3. Under the Commerce Clause, Congress may regulate any activity that has a substantial effect on interstate commerce.
4. A state may not regulate commerce in any way that will interfere with interstate commerce.
5. Under the Supremacy Clause, if there is a conflict between federal and state statutes, the federal law preempts the field. Even without a conflict, federal law preempts if Congress intended to exercise exclusive control.
6. The president's key powers include making agency appointments, proposing legislation, conducting foreign policy, and acting as commander in chief of the armed forces.
7. The federal courts adjudicate cases and also exercise judicial review, which is the right to declare a statute or governmental action unconstitutional and void.
8. Freedom of speech includes symbolic acts. Political speech is protected unless it is intended and likely to create imminent lawless action.
9. The government may regulate the time, place, and manner of speech.
10. Obscene speech is not protected.
11. Commercial speech that is false or misleading may be outlawed; otherwise, regulations on this speech must be reasonable and directed to a legitimate goal.
12. Procedural due process is required whenever the government attempts to take liberty or property. The amount of process that is due depends upon the importance of the liberty or property threatened. (Due process issues involving life are discussed in Chapter 7, on crime.)
13. The Takings Clause prohibits a state from taking private property for public use without just compensation.
14. A substantive due process analysis presumes that any economic or social regulation is valid, and presumes invalid any law that infringes upon a fundamental right.
15. The Equal Protection Clause generally requires the government to treat people equally. Courts apply strict scrutiny in any equal protection case involving race, ethnicity,

or fundamental rights; intermediate scrutiny to any case involving gender; and minimal scrutiny to an economic or social regulation.

16. Generally, constitutional rights protect citizens only from the action of the government, although under the state action doctrine, a private organization may be treated like the government if it has all the characteristics of one.

PRACTICE TEST

1. Michigan's Solid Waste Management Act (SWMA) generally prohibited Michigan counties from accepting for disposal solid waste that had been generated outside that county. Fort Gratiot operated a sanitary landfill in St. Clair County, Michigan. The county denied Fort Gratiot permission to bring in solid waste from out of state, and Fort Gratiot sued. This case involves the negative, or dormant, aspect of the Commerce Clause. What is the difference between that aspect and the positive aspect? What is the evil that the dormant aspect is designed to avoid? How would you rule in this case?

2. **YOU BE THE JUDGE WRITING PROBLEM** Scott Fane was a CPA licensed to practice in New Jersey and Florida. He built his New Jersey practice by making unsolicited phone calls to executives. When he moved to Florida, the Board of Accountancy there prohibited him (and all CPAs) from personally soliciting new business. Fane sued. Does the First Amendment force Florida to forgo foreclosing Fane's phoning? **Argument for Fane:** The Florida regulation violates the First Amendment, which protects commercial speech. Fane was not saying anything false or misleading, but was just trying to secure business. This is an unreasonable regulation, designed to keep newcomers out of the marketplace and maintain steady business and high prices for established CPAs. **Argument for the Florida Board of Accountancy:** Commercial speech deserves—and gets—a lower level of protection than other speech. This regulation is a reasonable method of ensuring that the level of CPA work in our state remains high. CPAs who personally solicit clients are obviously in need of business. They are more likely to bend legal and ethical rules to obtain clients and keep them happy, and will lower the standards throughout the state.

3. Dairy farming in Massachusetts became more expensive than in other states. In order to help its dairy farmers, the state began taxing all milk sales in the state, whether the milk was produced in state or out of state. The money went into a fund that was then distributed among Massachusetts milk producers as a subsidy for their milk. Discuss.

4. President Bush insisted that he had the power to send American troops into combat in the Middle East, without congressional assent. Yet before authorizing force in Operation Desert Storm, he secured congressional authorization. President Clinton stated that he was prepared to invade Haiti without a congressional vote. Yet he bargained hard to avoid an invasion, and ultimately American troops entered without the use of force. Why the seeming double-talk by both presidents?

5. In the early 1970s, President Nixon became embroiled in the Watergate dispute. He was accused of covering up a criminal break-in at the national headquarters of the Democratic Party. Nixon denied any wrongdoing. A United States District Court judge ordered the president to produce tapes of conversations held in his office. Nixon knew that complying with the order would produce damaging evidence, probably destroying his presidency. He refused, claiming executive privilege. The case went to the Supreme Court. Nixon strongly implied that even if the Supreme Court ordered him to produce the tapes, he would refuse. What major constitutional issue did this raise?

6. **RIGHT & WRONG** In the landmark 1965 case of *Griswold v. Connecticut,* the Supreme Court examined a Connecticut statute that

made it a crime for any person to use contraception. The majority declared the law an unconstitutional violation of the right of privacy. Justice Black dissented, saying, "I do not to any extent whatever base my view that this Connecticut law is constitutional on a belief that the law is wise or that its policy is a good one. [It] is every bit as offensive to me as it is to the majority. [There is no criticism by the majority of this law] to which I cannot subscribe—except their conclusion that the evil qualities they see in the law make it unconstitutional." What legal doctrines are involved here? Why did Justice Black distinguish between his personal views on the statute and the power of the Court to overturn it? Should a federal court act as a "superlegislature," nullifying statutes with which it disagrees? If a court aggressively takes on social issues, what dangers—and what advantages—does that present to society?

7. You begin work at Everhappy Corp. at the beginning of November. On your second day at work, you wear a political button on your overcoat, supporting your choice for governor in the upcoming election. Your boss glances at it and says, "Get that stupid thing out of this office or you're history, chump." You protest that his statement (a) violates your constitutional rights and (b) uses a boring cliché. Are you right?

8. Gilleo opposed American participation in the war in the Persian Gulf. She displayed a large sign on her front lawn that read, "Say No to War in the Persian Gulf, Call Congress Now." The city of Ladue prohibited signs on front lawns and Gilleo sued. The city claimed that it was regulating "time, place, and manner." Explain that statement, and decide who should win.

9. A federal statute prohibits the broadcasting of lottery advertisements, except by stations that broadcast in states permitting lotteries. The purpose of the statute is to support efforts of states that outlaw lotteries. Edge Broadcasting operated a radio station in North Carolina (a nonlottery state) but broadcast primarily in Virginia (a lottery state). Edge wanted to advertise Virginia's lottery but was barred by the statute. Did the federal statute violate Edge's constitutional rights?

10. Fox's Fine Furs claims that Ermine owes $68,000 for a mink coat on which she has stopped making payments. Fox goes to court, files a complaint, and also asks the clerk to *garnish* Ermine's wages. A garnishment is a court order to an employer to hold an employee's wages, or a portion of them, and pay the money into court so that there will be money for the plaintiff, if she wins. What constitutional issue does Fox's request for garnishment raise?

11. David Lucas paid $975,000 for two residential lots on the Isle of Palms near Charleston, South Carolina. He intended to build houses on them. Two years later the South Carolina legislature passed a statute that prohibited building seaward of a certain line, and Lucas's property fell in the prohibited zone. Lucas claimed that his land was now useless and that South Carolina owed him its value. Explain his claim. Should he win?

12. This case concerns unequal taxes on property. In Pennsylvania, a county tax commissioner appraises land, meaning that he sets a value for the land, and the owner then pays real estate taxes based on that value. A commissioner valued land at its sales price, whenever it was sold. If land did not sell for many years, he made little or no adjustment in its appraised value. As a result, some property was assessed at 35 times as much as neighboring land. A corporate landowner sued. What constitutional issue is raised? What should the outcome be?

INTERNET RESEARCH PROBLEM

Visit http://onlinebooks.library.upenn.edu/banned-books.html. Find a book that was formerly censored. Find another volume that is currently banned, either in the United States or elsewhere. How have changing mores affected censorship? Will the book that is currently outlawed someday be legal?

You can find further practice problems in the Online Quiz at http://beatty.westbuslaw.com or in the Study Guide that accompanies this text.

TORTS

6

CHAPTER

In a small Louisiana town, Don Mashburn ran a restaurant called Maison de Mashburn. The *New Orleans States-Item* newspaper reviewed his eatery, and here is what the article said:

"'Tain't Creole, 'tain't Cajun, 'tain't French, 'tain't country American, 'tain't good. I don't know how much real talent in cooking is hidden under the mélange of hideous sauces which make this food and the menu a travesty of pretentious amateurism but I find it all quite depressing. Put a yellow flour sauce on top of the duck, flame it for drama and serve it with some horrible multi-flavored rice in hollowed-out fruit and what have you got? A well-cooked duck with an ugly sauce that tastes too sweet and thick and makes you want to scrape off the glop to eat the plain duck. [The stuffed eggplant was prepared by emptying] a shaker full (more or less) of paprika on top of it. [One sauce created] trout à la green plague [while another should have been called] yellow death on duck."

Mashburn sued, claiming that the newspaper had committed libel, damaging his reputation and hurting his business.[1] Trout à la green plague will be the first course on our menu of tort law. Mashburn learned, as you will, why filing such a lawsuit is easier than winning it.

---

[1] *Mashburn v. Collin,* 355 So. 2d 879 (La. 1977).

This odd word "tort" is borrowed from the French, meaning "wrong." And that is what it means in law: a tort is a wrong. More precisely, **a tort is a violation of a duty imposed by the civil law.** When a person breaks one of those duties and injures another, it is a tort. The injury could be to a person or her property. Libel is one example of a tort where, for example, a newspaper columnist falsely accuses someone of being an alcoholic. A surgeon who removes the wrong kidney from a patient commits a different kind of tort, called negligence. A business executive who deliberately steals a client away from a competitor, interfering with a valid contract, commits a tort called interference with a contract. A con artist who tricks money out of you with a phony offer to sell you a boat commits fraud, yet another tort.

Because tort law is so broad, it takes a while to understand its boundaries. To start with, we must distinguish torts from two other areas of law: criminal law and contract law.

It is a crime to steal a car, to embezzle money from a bank, to sell cocaine. As discussed in Chapter 1, society considers such behavior so threatening that the government itself will prosecute the wrongdoer, whether or not the car owner or bank president wants the case to go forward.

In a tort case, it is up to the injured party, the plaintiff, to seek compensation. She must hire her own lawyer, who will file a lawsuit. Her lawyer must convince the court that the defendant breached some legal duty and ought to pay money damages to the plaintiff. The plaintiff has no power to send the defendant to jail. Bear in mind that a defendant's action might be both a crime *and* a tort. The con artist who tricks money out of you with a fake offer to sell you a boat has

Differences between Contract, Tort, and Criminal Law

Type of Obligation	Contract	Tort	Criminal Law
How the obligation is created	The parties agree on a contract, which creates duties for both.	The civil law imposes duties of conduct on all persons.	The criminal law prohibits certain conduct.
How the obligation is enforced	Suit by plaintiff.	Suit by plaintiff.	Prosecution by government.
Possible result	Money damages for plaintiff.	Money damages for plaintiff.	Punishment for defendant, including prison and/or fine.
Example	Raul contracts to sell Deirdre 5,000 pairs of sneakers at $50 per pair, but fails to deliver them. Deirdre buys the sneakers elsewhere for $60 per pair and receives $50,000, her extra expense.	A newspaper falsely accuses a private citizen of being an alcoholic. The plaintiff sues and wins money damages to compensate for her injured reputation.	Leo steals Kelly's car. The government prosecutes Leo for grand theft, and the judge sentences him to two years in prison. Kelly gets nothing.

committed the tort of fraud. You may file a civil suit against him and will collect money damages if you can prove your case. The con artist has also committed the crime of fraud. The state will prosecute, seeking to imprison and fine him.

A tort is also different from a contract dispute. A contract case is based on an agreement two people have already made. For example, Deirdre claims that Raul promised to sell her 10,000 pairs of sneakers at a good price but has failed to deliver them. She files a contract lawsuit. In a tort case, there is usually no "deal" between the parties. Don Mashburn had never met the restaurant critic who attacked his restaurant and obviously had never made any kind of contract. The plaintiff in a tort case claims that *the law itself* creates obligations that the defendant has breached.

Tort law itself is divided into categories. We begin by considering **intentional torts**, that is, harm caused by a deliberate action. Then we will examine **negligence** and **strict liability**, which are injuries caused by neglect.

INTENTIONAL TORTS

DEFAMATION

Defamation refers to false statements that harm someone's reputation. Defamatory statements can be written or spoken. Written defamation is **libel**. Suppose a newspaper accuses a local retail store of programming its cash registers to overcharge customers, when the store has never done so. That is libel. Oral defamation is **slander**. If Professor Wisdom, in class, refers to Sally Student as a drug dealer, and Sally has never sold anything stronger than Arm & Hammer, he has slandered her.

There are four elements to a defamation case. **An element is a fact that a plaintiff must prove to win a lawsuit.** In *any* kind of lawsuit, the plaintiff must prove *all* of the elements to prevail. The elements in a defamation case are:

- *Defamatory Statement.* These are words likely to harm another person's reputation. When Professor Wisdom accuses Sally of dealing drugs, that will clearly harm her reputation.
- *Falseness.* The statement must be false. If Sally Student actually sold marijuana to a classmate, then Professor Wisdom has a defense to slander.
- *Communicated.* The statement must be communicated to at least one person other than the plaintiff. If Wisdom speaks only to Sally and accuses her of dealing drugs, there is no slander.
- *Injury.* In slander cases, the plaintiff generally must show some injury. Sally's injury would be lower reputation in the school, embarrassment, and humiliation. But in libel cases, the law is willing to assume injury. Since libel is written, and more permanent, courts award damages even without proof of injury.[2]

---

[2] When defamation by radio and television became possible, the courts chose to consider it libel, analogizing it to newspapers because of the vast audience. This means that in broadcasting cases, a plaintiff generally does not have to prove damages.

OPINION

Opinion is generally a valid defense in a defamation suit because it cannot be proven true or false. Suppose that a television commentator says, "Frank Landlord certainly does less than many rich people do for our community." Is that defamation? Probably not. Who are the "rich people"? How much do they do? How do we define "does less"? These vague assertions indicate the statement is one of opinion. Even if Frank works hard feeding homeless families, he will probably lose a defamation case. The Internet, of course, permits worldwide dissemination of facts *and* opinion. The Web site http://www.otap.com/angry/ is devoted to *angry comments* aimed at a variety of organizations. Are any of the posted statements defamatory, or are they all opinions?

A related defense involves cases where a supposed statement of fact should not be taken literally. "Reverend Wilson's sermons go on so long, many parishioners suffer brain death before receiving communion." Brain death is a tragic fact of medical science, but this author obviously exaggerates to express her opinion. No defamation.

Mr. Mashburn, who opened the chapter suing over his restaurant review, lost his case. The court held that a reasonable reader would have understood the statements to be opinion only. "A shaker full of paprika" and "yellow death on duck" were not to be taken literally but were merely the author's expression of his personal dislike.

What about a crude description of a college official, appearing in the school's newspaper? You be the judge.

YEAGLE v. COLLEGIATE TIMES

255 Va. 293, 497 S.E.2d 136, 1998 Va. LEXIS 32
Virginia Supreme Court, 1998

Facts: Sharon Yeagle was assistant to the Vice President of Student Affairs at the Virginia Polytechnic Institute and State University. The state had an academic honors program called the Governor's Fellows Program, and one of Yeagle's duties was to help students apply. The school newspaper, the *Collegiate Times*, published an article describing the university's success at placing students in the Fellows Program. The article included a block quotation in larger print, attributed to Yeagle. Underneath Yeagle's name was the phrase, "Director of Butt Licking."

Yeagle sued the *Collegiate Times*, alleging that the vulgar phrase defamed her. The trial court dismissed the case, ruling that no reasonable person would take the words literally, and that the phrase conveyed no factual information. Yeagle appealed to the Virginia Supreme Court.

You be the Judge: Was the phrase defamatory, or was it deliberate exaggeration that no reasonable person would take literally?

Argument for Yeagle: The disgusting phrase that the *Collegiate Times* used to describe Ms. Yeagle is defamatory for several reasons. The conduct described by the words happens to be a crime in Virginia, a violation of the state sodomy statute. Thus the paper is accusing her of criminal offenses that she has never committed.

If, however, defendants argue that the phrase must be interpreted figuratively, then the newspaper has accused Ms. Yeagle of currying favor, or directing others to do so, in a uniquely degrading fashion. The *Collegiate Times* is informing its readers that she performs her job in a sleazy, unprofessional manner evidently because she cannot succeed by merit.

Finally, the *Collegiate Times* is holding Ms. Yeagle up to ridicule and scorn, for no legitimate reason, and with the sole purpose of harming her reputation. The student editors may find it amusing to damage someone's career for their own idle purposes, but hardworking adults will not share the laughter.

Argument for Collegiate Times: Statements are only defamatory if a reasonable reader would understand them as asserting facts that can be proven true or false. There is no such statement in this case, and no defamation. No reasonable reader, after finishing an article about the Fellows Program, would believe that Ms. Yeagle was actually the director as described, or even that there is such a job. From the bluntness of the phrase, it is obvious that the words are hyperbole and have no meaning that can be proven true or false.

The paper chose to inject humor into its coverage of a mundane issue, for the entertainment of its readers. What Ms. Yeagle really objects to is the vulgarity of the phrase, and to that claim the paper pleads guilty. There are two responses. First, the great majority of the paper's readers appreciate lively language that is at times irreverent. Second, vulgarity is not defamation. Freedom of speech is more important than the hurt feelings of an overly sensitive reader. For any reader who is quick to take offense, the proper recourse is not to file suit, but to put down the paper.

PUBLIC PERSONALITIES

The rules of the game change for those who play in public. Public officials and public figures receive less protection from defamation. An example of a **public official** is a police chief. A **public figure** is a movie star, for example, or a multimillionaire playboy constantly in the news. In the landmark case *New York Times Co. v. Sullivan,*[3] the Supreme Court ruled that the free exchange of information is vital in a democracy and is protected by the First Amendment to the Constitution. A public official or public figure can win a defamation case only by proving actual malice by the defendant. **Actual malice means that the defendant knew the statement was false or acted with reckless disregard of the truth.** If the plaintiff merely shows that the defendant newspaper printed incorrect statements, even very damaging ones, he loses. In the *New York Times* case, the police chief of Birmingham, Alabama, claimed that the *Times* falsely accused him of racial violence in his job. He lost the suit because he could not prove that the *Times* had acted with actual malice. If he had demonstrated that the *Times* knew its accusation was false, he would have won.

PRIVILEGE

Defendants receive additional protection from defamation cases when it is important for them to speak freely. **Absolute privilege** exists in courtrooms and legislative hearings. Anyone speaking there, such as a witness in a trial, can say anything at all and never be sued for defamation. Courts extend an absolute privilege in those few instances when candor is essential to a functioning democracy.[4]

Qualified privilege exists when two people have a legitimate need to exchange information. Suppose Trisha Tenant lives in a housing project. She honestly believes that her neighbor is selling guns illegally. She reports this to the manager of the project, who investigates and discovers the guns were toys, being sold legally. Trisha is not liable for slander because she had a good faith

---

[3] 376 U.S. 254, 84 S. Ct. 710, 1964 U.S. LEXIS 1655 (1964).

[4] A witness who lies is guilty of perjury but not liable for slander.

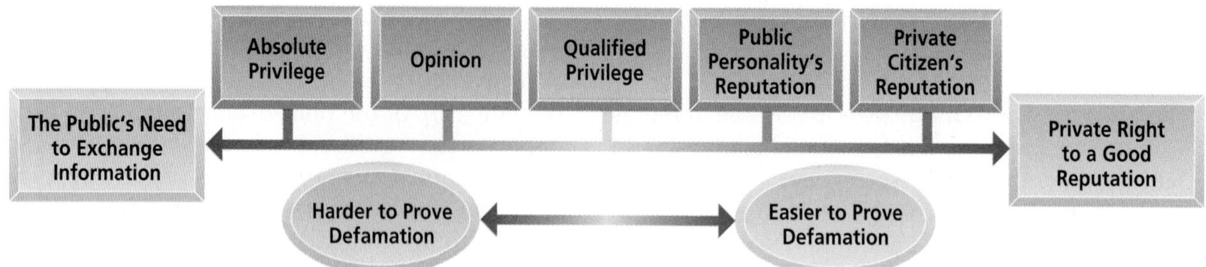

Defamation cases show a tension between the public's need for information and a citizen's right to protect his reputation.

reason to report this, and the manager needed to hear it. As long as Trisha acts in good faith and talks only to someone who ought to know about the activity, she is protected by qualified privilege.

FALSE IMPRISONMENT

False imprisonment is the intentional restraint of another person without reasonable cause and without consent. A bank teller became seriously ill and wanted to go to the doctor, but the bank forbade her to leave until she made a final tally of her accounts. Officials barred her from leaving the bank. That was false imprisonment. The restraint was unreasonable because her accounts could have been verified later.[5]

False imprisonment cases most commonly arise in retail stores, which sometimes detain employees or customers for suspected theft. Most states now have statutes governing the detention of suspected shoplifters. **Generally, a store may detain a customer or worker for alleged shoplifting provided there is a reasonable basis for the suspicion and the detention is done reasonably.** To detain a customer in the manager's office for 20 minutes and question him about where he got an item is lawful. To chain that customer to a display counter for three hours and humiliate him in front of other customers is unreasonable, and false imprisonment.

Assume that you are a junior vice president of a chain of 15 retail clothing stores, all located in your state. The president has asked you to outline a sensible plan, to be given to all employees, for dealing with suspected shoplifters. Here are some ideas to consider:

- Shoplifting is very costly to our society, causing businesses to lose anywhere from $5 billion to $25 billion annually. On the other hand, no one wants to shop in a "police state" environment.
- What is a "reasonable" suspicion of shoplifting? Suppose a clerk sees a customer hurry out, wearing a sweater identical to those on display. Must the clerk have seen the customer put on the sweater?
- What is "reasonable" detention? Can you tackle someone running through the parking lot? Can you shoot him?

[5] Kanner v. First National Bank of South Miami, 287 So. 2d 715, 1974 Fla. App. LEXIS 8989 (Fla. Dist. Ct. App. 1974).

- How much questioning do you want to do, and how much would you prefer to leave to police?
- Some people in our society are biased against others, based on race or gender, while others are entirely free of such prejudices. How do you take that into account?

INTENTIONAL INFLICTION OF EMOTIONAL DISTRESS

What should happen when a defendant's conduct hurts a plaintiff emotionally but not physically? Most courts allow a plaintiff to recover for emotional injury that a defendant intentionally caused.

The intentional infliction of emotional distress results from extreme and outrageous conduct that causes serious emotional harm. A credit officer was struggling vainly to locate Sheehan, who owed money on his car. The officer phoned Sheehan's mother, falsely identified herself as a hospital employee, and said she needed to find Sheehan because his children had been in a serious auto accident. The mother provided Sheehan's whereabouts, which enabled the company to seize his car. But Sheehan spent seven hours frantically trying to locate his supposedly injured children, who in fact were fine. The credit company was liable for the intentional infliction of emotional distress.[6]

By contrast, a muffler shop, trying to collect a debt from a customer, made six phone calls over three months, using abusive language. The customer testified that this caused her to be upset, to cry, and to have difficulty sleeping. The court ruled that the muffler shop's conduct was neither extreme nor outrageous and sent the customer home for another sleepless night.[7]

The following case arose in a setting that guarantees controversy: an abortion clinic.

JANE DOE AND NANCY ROE v. LYNN MILLS

212 Mich. App. 73, 536 N.W. 2d 824, 1995 Mich. App. LEXIS 313
Michigan Court of Appeals, 1995

Facts: Late one night, an anti-abortion protestor named Robert Thomas climbed into a dumpster located behind an abortion clinic. He found documents indicating that Doe and Roe (not their real names) were soon to have abortions at the clinic. Thomas gave the information to Lynn Mills. She and another woman created signs, using the women's names, indicating that they were about to undergo abortions, and urging them not to "kill their babies." Doe and Roe sued, claiming intentional infliction of emotional distress. The trial court gave summary judgment for the defendants, stating that they had a right to express their views on abortion. The plaintiffs appealed.

Issue: Have the plaintiffs made a valid claim of intentional infliction of emotional distress?

---

[6] *Ford Motor Credit Co. v. Sheehan*, 373 So. 2d 956, 1979 Fla. App. LEXIS 15416 (Fla. Dist. Ct. App. 1979).

[7] *Midas Muffler Shop v. Ellison*, 133 Ariz. 194, 650 P.2d 496, 1982 Ariz. App. LEXIS 488 (Ariz. Ct. App. 1982).

Excerpts from the Court's Per Curiam[8] Decision: Liability for the intentional infliction of emotional distress has been found only where the conduct complained of has been so outrageous in character, and so extreme in degree, as to go beyond all possible bounds of decency. Liability does not extend to mere insults, indignities, threats, annoyances, petty oppressions, or other trivialities, [but to cases where] an average member of the community would exclaim "Outrageous!"

The trial court observed that defendants have a constitutional right to "protest peaceably against abortion." However, the objectionable aspect of defendants' conduct does not relate to their views on abortion but, rather, to the fact that defendants gave unreasonable or unnecessary publicity to purely private matters involving plaintiffs.

We believe this is the type of case that might cause an average member of the community, upon learning of defendants' conduct, to exclaim, "Outrageous!" Because reasonable men may differ with regard to whether defendants' conduct may be considered sufficiently outrageous and extreme so as to subject them to liability for intentional infliction of emotional distress, this matter should be determined by the trier of fact.

[Summary judgment for the defendants is reversed, and the case is remanded for trial.]

ADDITIONAL INTENTIONAL TORTS

Battery is an intentional touching of another person in a way that is unwanted or offensive. There need be no intention to *hurt* the plaintiff. If the defendant intended to do the physical act, and a reasonable plaintiff would be offended by it, battery has occurred.

Suppose an irate parent throws a chair at a referee during his daughter's basketball game, breaking the man's jaw. It is irrelevant that the father did not intend to injure the referee. But a parent who cheerfully slaps the winning coach on the back has not committed battery, because a reasonable coach would not be offended.

Assault occurs when a defendant does some act that makes a plaintiff fear an imminent battery. It is assault even though the battery never occurs. Suppose Ms. Wilson shouts "Think fast!" at her husband and hurls a toaster at him. He turns and sees it flying at him. His fear of being struck is enough to win a case of assault, even if the toaster misses.

Fraud is injuring another person by deliberate deception. It is fraud to sell real estate knowing that there is a large toxic waste deposit underground of which the buyer is ignorant. Fraud is a tort that typically occurs during contract negotiation, and it is discussed in detail in Chapter 9, on contracts.

DAMAGES

Mitchel Bien, who is deaf, enters the George Grubbs Nissan dealership, where folks sell cars aggressively—*very* aggressively. Maturelli, a salesman, and Bien communicate by writing messages back and forth. Maturelli takes Bien's own car keys, and the two then test drive a 300ZX. Bien says he does not want the car, but Maturelli escorts him back inside and fills out a sales sheet. Bien repeatedly asks for his keys, but Maturelli only laughs, pressuring him to buy the new car. Minutes pass. Hours pass. Bien becomes frantic, writing a dozen notes, beg-

[8] A per curiam decision is one made by the entire court but not attributed to a specific justice.

ging to leave, threatening to call the police. Maturelli mocks Bien and his physical disabilities. Finally, after four hours, the customer escapes.

Bien sues for the intentional infliction of emotional distress. Two former salesmen from Grubbs testify they have witnessed customers cry, yell, and curse as a result of the aggressive tactics. Doctors state that the incident has traumatized Bien, dramatically reducing his confidence and self-esteem and preventing his return to work even three years later.

The jury awards Bien damages. But how does a jury calculate the money? For that matter, why should a jury even try? Money can never erase pain or undo a permanent injury. The answer is simple: money, however inexact and ineffective, is the only thing a court has to give. Here is how damages are figured.

First, a plaintiff receives money for medical expenses that he has proven by producing bills from doctors, hospitals, physical therapists, and psychotherapists. Bien receives all the money he has paid. If a doctor testifies that he needs future treatment, Bien will offer evidence of how much that will cost. **The single recovery principle requires a court to settle the matter once and for all, by awarding a lump sum for past and future expenses.** A plaintiff may not return in a year and say, "Oh, by the way, there are some new bills."

Second, the defendants are liable for lost wages. The court takes the number of days or months that Bien missed work and multiplies that times his salary. If Bien is currently unable to work, a doctor estimates how many more months he will miss work, and the court adds that to his damages.

Third, a plaintiff is paid for pain and suffering. Bien testifies about how traumatic the four hours were and how the experience has affected his life. He may state that he now fears shopping, suffers nightmares, and seldom socializes. To bolster the case, a plaintiff uses expert testimony, such as the psychiatrists who testified for Bien. Awards for pain and suffering vary enormously, from a few dollars to many millions, depending on the injury and depending on the jury. In some lawsuits, physical and psychological pain are momentary and insignificant; in other cases, the pain is the biggest part of the verdict. In Bien's case, the jury returns with its verdict: $573,815, calculated as in the table on the next page.[9]

PUNITIVE DAMAGES

Here we look at a different kind of award, one that is more controversial and potentially more powerful: punitive damages. The purpose is not to compensate the plaintiff for harm, because compensatory damages will have done that. **Punitive damages are intended to punish the defendant for conduct that is extreme and outrageous.** Courts award these damages in relatively few cases. When an award of punitive damages is made, it is generally in a case of intentional tort, although they occasionally appear in negligence suits.

---

[9] The compensatory damages are described in *George Grubbs Enterprises v. Bien,* 881 S.W.2d 843, 1994 Tex. App. LEXIS 1870 (Tex. Ct. App. 1994). In addition to the compensatory damages described, the jury awarded $5 million in punitive damages. The Texas Supreme Court reversed the award of punitive damages, but not the compensatory. *Id.*, 900 S.W.2d 337, 1995 Tex. LEXIS 91 (Tex. 1995). The high court did not dispute the appropriateness of punitive damages, but reversed because the trial court failed to instruct the jury properly as to how it should determine the assets actually under the defendants' control, an issue essential to punitive damages but not compensatory.

Past medical	$ 70.00
Future medical	6,000.00
Past rehabilitation	3,205.00
Past lost earning capacity	112,910.00
Future lost earning capacity	34,650.00
Past physical symptoms and discomfort	50,000.00
Future physical symptoms and discomfort	50,000.00
Past emotional injury and mental anguish	101,980.00
Future emotional injury and mental anguish	200,000.00
Past loss of society and reduced ability to socially interact with family, former fiancee, and friends, and hearing (i.e., nondeaf) people in general	10,000.00
Future loss of society and reduced ability to socially interact with family, former fiancee, and friends, and hearing people	5,000.00
TOTAL	$573,815.00

The idea behind punitive damages is that certain behavior is so unacceptable that society must make an example of it. A large award of money should deter the defendant from repeating the mistake and others from ever making it. This is social engineering in an extreme form. Predictably, some believe punitive damages represent the law at its most avaricious while others attribute to them great social benefit.

The United States Supreme Court has declared that in awarding punitive damages, a court must consider three "guideposts":

- The reprehensibility of the defendant's conduct;
- The ratio between the harm suffered and the award; and
- The difference between the punitive award and any civil penalties used in similar cases.[10]

Studies indicate that punitive damages are rare and generally modest. Courts award them in about 6 percent of those cases that plaintiffs win. But occasionally punitive awards are huge and generate tremendous publicity. When the *Exxon Valdez* ran aground, it dumped 11 million gallons of oil into the sea; the oil eventually spread 470 miles along the Alaskan coast. Exxon spent over $2 billion cleaning up the spill and paid an additional $1.3 billion in civil and criminal penalties and settlements. A jury found Exxon liable to Alaskan

[10] *BMW of North America, Inc. v. Gore,* 517 U.S. 559, 116 S. Ct. 1589, 1996 U.S. LEXIS 3390 (1996).

fishermen and awarded $286 million in compensatory damages. Two months later, that same jury came back with its award of punitive damages: an even *$5 billion.* To walk through a gallery of photographs devoted to the *Exxon Valdez* and other oil spills, visit http://response.restoration.noaa.gov/photos/gallery.html.

Do punitive damages present the revolting specter of money-grubbing lawyers convincing gullible juries to award preposterous verdicts to avaricious clients? Or do they demonstrate that idealistic lawyers, working with no guarantee of a payday,[11] can use the humane instincts of a jury to force callous corporations to consider something other than the fabled bottom line?

James Walston bought health insurance policies from Monumental Life Insurance, for himself and his wife. One month later, his wife was diagnosed with lung cancer, from which she ultimately died. Walston was entitled to $3,800 for his wife's unsuccessful treatments, but Monumental refused to pay that sum, claiming that the wife's previous, unrelated cancer indicated that Walston had lied on his application. Walston sued.

An insurance industry official testified that the ad that had attracted Walston was deliberately deceptive, proclaiming a $250,000 "high-limit" policy when in reality the plan's design guaranteed that customers would only receive much lower amounts. He also stated that Monumental used a tortured interpretation of the contract language to conclude that the treatment for unrelated cancer indicated fraud. The evidence at trial suggested that both the misleading advertising and the improper denial of benefits were routine practices at Monumental. The jury awarded $3,800 for breach of contract; $120,000 for bad faith denial of benefits; and $10 million in punitive damages. The trial judge reduced the punitive award to $3.2 million and Monumental appealed.

Was the punitive damage award excessive?

BUSINESS TORTS

In this section, we look at four intentional torts that occur almost exclusively in a commercial setting: interference with a contract, interference with a prospective advantage, and the rights to privacy and publicity. Patents, copyrights, and trademarks are discussed in Chapter 21, on intellectual property, as are Lanham Act violations.

TORTIOUS INTERFERENCE WITH BUSINESS RELATIONS

Competition is the essence of business. Successful corporations compete aggressively, and the law permits and expects them to. But there are times when healthy competition becomes illegal interference. This is called tortious interference with business relations. It can take one of two closely related forms—interference with a contract or interference with a prospective advantage.

---

[11] Lawyers normally take personal injury cases on a contingency basis, meaning that they receive no money up-front from their client. Their fee will be a percentage of the plaintiff's judgment *if* she wins. Lawyers often take about one-third of the award. But if the defendant wins, the plaintiff's lawyer will have worked several years for no pay.

TORTIOUS INTERFERENCE WITH A CONTRACT

Tortious interference with a contract exists only if the plaintiff can establish the following four elements:

- There was a contract between the plaintiff and a third party
- The defendant knew of the contract
- The defendant improperly induced the third party to breach the contract or made performance of the contract impossible; and
- There was injury to the plaintiff.

There is nothing wrong with two companies bidding against each other to buy a parcel of land, and nothing wrong with one corporation doing everything possible to convince the seller to ignore all competitors. But once a company has signed a contract to buy the land, it is improper to induce the seller to break the deal. The most commonly disputed issues in these cases concern elements one and three: Was there a contract between the plaintiff and another party? Did the defendant *improperly* induce a party to breach it?

A defendant may also rely on the defense of **justification**, that is, a claim that special circumstances made its conduct fair. To establish justification, a defendant must show that:

- it was acting to protect an *existing economic interest*, such as its own contract with the third party,
- it was acting in the *public interest*, for example, by reporting to a government agency that a corporation was overbilling for government services; or
- the existing contract could be *terminated at will* by either party, meaning that although the plaintiff had a contract, the plaintiff had no long-term assurances, because the other side could end it an any time.

Texaco v. Pennzoil. One of the largest verdicts in the history of American law came in a case of contract interference. Pennzoil made an unsolicited bid to buy 20 percent of Getty Oil at $112.50 per share, and the Getty board approved the agreement. Before the lawyers for both sides could complete the paperwork for the deal, Texaco appeared and offered Getty stockholders $128 per share for the entire company. Getty officers turned their attention to Texaco, but Pennzoil sued, claiming tortious interference. Texaco replied that it had not interfered because there was no binding contract.

The jury bought Pennzoil's argument, and they bought it big: $7.53 billion in actual damages, and $3 billion more in punitive damages. After appeals and frantic negotiations, the two parties reached a settlement. Texaco agreed to pay Pennzoil $3 billion as settlement for having wrongfully interfered with Pennzoil's agreement to buy Getty.

TORTIOUS INTERFERENCE WITH A PROSPECTIVE ADVANTAGE

"Interference with a prospective advantage" is an awkward name for a tort that is simply a variation on interference with a contract. The difference is that, for this tort, there need be no contract; the plaintiff is claiming outside interference with an expected economic relationship. Obviously, the plaintiff must show more than just the hope of a profit. **A plaintiff who has a definite and reasonable expectation of obtaining an economic advantage may sue a corporation that maliciously interferes and prevents the relationship from developing.**

The defense of justification, discussed above, applies here as well. A typical example of justification is that the defendant is simply competing for the same business that the plaintiff seeks. There is nothing wrong with that. It becomes a tort when the defendant sets out to hurt the plaintiff by blocking some advantage from developing.

A group of investors, calling themselves the "IBI" group, signed a contract to buy the Chicago Bulls basketball team. However, the National Basketball Association rejected the deal, informing IBI that it could only purchase the team if it first obtained a suitable stadium. Arthur Wirtz controlled the only acceptable stadium, and he refused to lease the property to IBI. Instead, Wirtz formed a different company and made a competing bid to buy the Bulls franchise. IBI sued, claiming that Wirtz had interfered with its contractual relations and prospective advantage.

The court found that Wirtz had not interfered with IBI's *contract*, because the NBA itself had nullified the deal. However, Wirtz *had* interfered with IBI's prospective advantage. His refusal to lease the stadium was an unfair and anticompetitive act intended to keep IBI from obtaining the team. Wirtz paid millions of dollars for interfering with a prospective advantage.[12]

PRIVACY AND PUBLICITY

We live in a world of dazzling technology, and it is easier than ever—and more profitable—to spy on someone. For example, the Web page http://www.thesmokinggun.com specializes in publishing revealing data about celebrities. Does the law protect us? What power do we have to limit the intrusion of others into our lives and to prohibit them from commercially exploiting information about us? Privacy and publicity law involves four main issues: intrusion, disclosure, false information, and commercial exploitation.

INTRUSION

Intrusion into someone's private life is a tort if a reasonable person would find it offensive. Peeping through someone's windows or wiretapping his telephone are obvious examples of intrusion. In a famous case involving a "paparazzo" photographer and Jacqueline Kennedy Onassis, the court found that the photographer had invaded her privacy by making a career out of photographing her. He had bribed doormen to gain access to hotels and restaurants she visited, had jumped out of bushes to photograph her young children, and had driven power boats dangerously close to her. The court ordered him to stop.[13] Nine years later the paparazzo was found in contempt of court for again taking photographs too close to Ms. Onassis. He agreed to stop once and for all—in exchange for a suspended contempt sentence.

---

[12] *Fishman v. Estate of Wirtz*, 807 F.2d 520, 1986 U.S.App. LEXIS 34177 (7th Cir. 1986).

[13] *Galella v. Onassis*, 487 F.2d 986, 1973 U.S. App. LEXIS 7901 (2d Cir. 1973).

CYBER*LAW*

"Hi, Bob," says the friendly voice on the phone. "Listen, I know you're coming to Happy City this week. We've got a great band playing at Pinky, our club. We're only a block from your hotel."

"Who is this?" Bob demands. "How on earth did you know I am going to Happy City?" The friendly caller laughs and mentions that Pinky features performers dressed only in flamingo feathers, dancing to the beat of Palestrina, a composer who died in 1594. "I know you love feathers and Palestrina," chuckles the caller, "and this is the only place you can get them both." Bob slams the phone down, angry, embarrassed—and astonished.

How does the caller know so much? A month ago, when Bob booked a flight to Happy City, the airline sold his name to Gotcha!, a company that collects and sells information. Gotcha! also purchased data from Fluffy, a Web site about bars. Bob had once clicked onto the site, and while he viewed the page, Fluffy wrote a "cookie" onto Bob's hard drive. The cookie enabled Fluffy to track each visit Bob made to its site and other linked sites. Fluffy learned that Bob visited a site about bars with feather-dancers. When Gotcha! obtained Bob's name from Fluffy, it cross-checked its other databases and discovered Bob was headed for Happy City. Gotcha! had already purchased the names of all guests staying in the five best hotels at Happy City, so it was easy to learn Bob's address. Palestrina? Simple: Three years ago, Bob used his credit card to pay for tickets to a classical concert in Sioux City, Iowa, where he heard two Palestrina pieces. Having discovered Bob's entertainment tastes, Gotcha! was able to make the perfect match with Pinky, to which it sold all the data for a handsome profit.

Is all of this legal? *Any* of it? Is it ethical? There are no final legal answers, because courts are only beginning to rule. For more details, see Chapter 20 on cyberlaw. (Did Bob go to Pinky? Give him a call and find out. His phone number is on the Internet—as is yours—and Bob would be amazed to hear from you.)

DISCLOSURE OF EMBARRASSING PRIVATE FACTS

A defendant (such as a media organization) is liable if it discloses to the public facts that a reasonable person would consider very embarrassing, and in which the public has no legitimate interest. Suppose a local newspaper reports that a particular high school student had a baby out of wedlock. The public has no need of that information, and the paper has committed a tort. By contrast, consider the case of a most unusual body surfer. He agreed to an interview with *Sports Illustrated* but then sued when the magazine divulged odd personal facts, including that he put out cigarettes in his mouth, dove off stairs to impress women, hurt himself so he could collect unemployment, and ate insects. *Sports Illustrated* won. The court held that, bizarre as these revelations were, they were not sensationally embarrassing. Further, they were a legitimate part of a news story about an eccentric and daring body surfer.[14]

FALSE LIGHT

Like defamation, this tort involves false information about the plaintiff. Unlike defamation, this tort can arise without harm to a plaintiff's reputation. **If false**

---

[14] *Virgil v. Sports Illustrated*, 424 F. Supp. 1286, 1976 U.S. Dist. LEXIS 11779 (S.D. Cal. 1976).

information portrays the plaintiff in a way that most people would find offensive, it is "false light." A model named Robyn Douglass posed nude for a photographer and authorized him to publish the photos in *Playboy Magazine.* The photographer sold some to *Playboy* but later sold other photographs to *Hustler Magazine.* The court agreed with Douglass that this placed her in a false light by making her seem to be the sort of person who would pose for *Hustler.* A reasonable person might find that while *Playboy* is mildly erotic, *Hustler* concentrates on sex in ways that are crude and degrading. Douglass won $600,000.[15]

COMMERCIAL EXPLOITATION

This right prohibits the use of someone's likeness or voice for commercial purposes. This business tort is the flip side of privacy and covers the right to make money from publicity. For example, it would be illegal to run a magazine ad showing actress Sharon Stone holding a can of soda, without her permission. The ad would imply that she endorses the product. Someone's identity is her own, and it cannot be exploited unless she permits it.

The cyberlaw example above, about Bob and the feather-dancers, also raises issues of commercial exploitation. When do operators of a Web site have the right to use information about users? Do they need your permission to sell your name and address? Chapter 20 on cyberlaw discusses the issue.

NEGLIGENCE

Party time! A fraternity at the University of Arizona welcomed new members, and the alcohol flowed freely. Several hundred people danced and shrieked and drank, and no one checked for proof of age. A common occurrence—but one that ended tragically. A minor student drove away, intoxicated, and slammed into another car. The other driver, utterly innocent of wrongdoing, was gravely injured.

The drunken student was obviously liable, but his insurance did not cover the huge medical bills. The injured man also sued the fraternity. Should that organization be legally responsible? The question leads to other, similar issues. Should a restaurant that serves an intoxicated adult be liable for resulting harm? If *you* give a party, should you be responsible for any damage caused by your guests?

These are moral questions—but very practical ones, as well. They are typical issues of negligence law. In this contentious area, courts continually face one question: *When someone is injured, how far should responsibility extend?*

We might call negligence the "unintentional" tort because it concerns harm that arises by accident. A person, or perhaps an organization, does some act, neither intending nor expecting to hurt anyone, yet someone is harmed. Should a court impose liability? The fraternity members who gave the party never wanted—or thought—that an innocent man would suffer terrible damage. But he did. Is it in society's interest to hold the fraternity responsible?

---

[15] *Douglass v. Hustler Magazine, Inc.*, 769 F.2d 1128, 1985 U.S. App. LEXIS 19980 (7th Cir. 1985).

Before we can answer this question, we need some background knowledge. Things go wrong all the time, and society needs a means of analyzing negligence cases consistently and fairly. One of America's greatest judges, Benjamin Cardozo, offered such an analysis more than 70 years ago. His decision still dominates negligence thinking today, so we will let him introduce us to Helen Palsgraf.

PALSGRAF v. LONG ISLAND RAILROAD CO.

248 N.Y. 339, 162 N.E.99, 1928 N.Y. LEXIS 1269
New York Court of Appeals, 1928

Facts: Ms. Palsgraf was waiting on a railroad platform. As a train began to leave the station, a man carrying a package ran to catch it. He jumped aboard but looked unsteady, so a guard on the car reached out to help him as another guard, on the platform, pushed from behind. The man dropped the package, which struck the tracks and exploded—since it was packed with fireworks. The shock knocked over some heavy scales at the far end of the platform, and one of them struck Palsgraf. She sued the railroad.

The jury found that the guards had acted negligently, and held the railroad liable. The company appealed.

Issue: Assuming the guards did a bad job assisting the passenger, was the railroad liable for the injuries to Ms. Palsgraf?

Excerpts from Judge Cardozo's Decision: The conduct of the defendant's guard, if a wrong in its relation to the holder of the package, was not a wrong in its relation to the plaintiff, standing far away. Relatively to her it was not negligence at all. Nothing in the situation gave notice that the falling package had in it the potency of peril to persons thus removed. Negligence is not actionable unless it involves the invasion of a legally protected interest, the violation of a right. Proof of negligence in the air, so to speak, will not do.

In every instance, before negligence can be predicated of a given act, back of the act must be sought and found a duty to the individual complaining, the observance of which would have averted or avoided the injury. What the plaintiff must show is "a wrong" to herself; i.e., a violation of her own right, and not merely a wrong to someone else, nor conduct "wrongful" because unsocial.

There was nothing in the situation to suggest to the most cautious mind that the parcel wrapped in newspaper would spread wreckage through the station. If the guard had thrown it down knowingly and willfully, he would not have threatened the plaintiff's safety, so far as appearances could warn him. Liability can be no greater where the act is inadvertent. [Reversed.]

To win a negligence case, the plaintiff must prove five elements:

- Duty of Due Care. The defendant had a duty of due care to this plaintiff.
- Breach. The defendant breached her duty.
- Factual Cause. The defendant's conduct actually caused the injury.
- Foreseeable Harm. It was foreseeable that conduct like the defendant's might cause this type of harm.
- Injury. The plaintiff has actually been hurt.

DUTY OF DUE CARE

The first issue may be the most difficult in all of tort law: Did the defendant have a duty of due care *to the injured person?* The test is generally "foreseeability." **If**

the defendant could have foreseen injury to a particular person, she has a duty to him. If she could not have foreseen the harm, there is usually no duty. Let us apply this principle to the fraternity case.

HERNANDEZ v. ARIZONA BOARD OF REGENTS

177 Ariz. 244, 866 P.2d 1330, 1994 Ariz. LEXIS 6
Arizona Supreme Court, 1994

Facts: At the University of Arizona, the Epsilon Epsilon chapter of Delta Tau Delta fraternity gave a welcoming party for new members. The fraternity's officers knew that the majority of its members were under the legal drinking age, but permitted everyone to consume alcohol. John Rayner, who was under 21 years of age, left the party. He drove negligently and caused a collision with an auto driven by Ruben Hernandez. At the time of the accident, Rayner's blood alcohol level was .15, exceeding the legal limit. The crash left Hernandez blind, severely brain damaged and quadriplegic.

Hernandez sued Rayner, who settled the case, based on the amount of his insurance coverage. The victim also sued the fraternity, its officers and national organization, all fraternity members who contributed money to buy alcohol, the university, and others. The trial court granted summary judgment for all defendants and the court of appeals affirmed. Hernandez appealed to the Arizona Supreme Court.

Issue: Did the fraternity and the other defendants have a duty of due care to Hernandez?

Excerpts from Judge Feldman's Decision: Before 1983, this court arguably recognized the common-law rule of non-liability for tavern owners and, presumably, for social hosts. Traditional authority held that when "an able-bodied man" caused harm because of his intoxication, the act from which liability arose was the consuming not the furnishing of alcohol. However, the common law also provides that:

> One who supplies [a thing] for the use of another whom the supplier knows or has reason to know to be likely because of his youth, inexperience, or otherwise to use it in a manner involving unreasonable risk of physical harm to himself and others is subject to liability for physical harm resulting to them.

We perceive little difference in principle between liability for giving a car to an intoxicated youth and liability for giving drinks to a youth with a car. A growing number of cases have recognized that one of the very hazards that makes it negligent to furnish liquor to a minor is the foreseeable prospect that the [youthful] patron will become drunk and injure himself or others. Accordingly, modern authority has increasingly recognized that one who furnishes liquor to a minor breaches a common law duty owed to innocent third parties who may be injured.

Furnishing alcohol to underaged drinkers violates numerous statutes. The conduct in question violates well-established common-law principles that recognize a duty to avoid furnishing dangerous items to those known to have diminished capacity to use them safely. We join the majority of other states and conclude that as to Plaintiffs and the public in general, Defendants had a duty of care to avoid furnishing alcohol to underage consumers.

Arizona courts, therefore, will entertain an action for damages against [one] who negligently furnishes alcohol to those under the legal drinking age when that act is a cause of injury to a third person. [Reversed and remanded.]

Let us move the liability question away from the fraternity house. Should a *social* host (home owner) be liable for serving alcohol to a guest who then causes an accident? Many states do hold a social host liable for serving a *minor*. New Jersey is one of the few states to go further, and hold a home owner liable even for serving an *adult*. Finally, many states now have some type of **dram act**, making liquor stores, bars, and restaurants liable for serving drinks to intoxicated customers who later cause harm. Which of these rules do you find persuasive?

BREACH OF DUTY

The second element of a plaintiff's negligence case is **breach of duty**. Courts apply the reasonable person standard: **a defendant breaches his duty of due care by failing to behave the way a reasonable person would under similar circumstances**. Reasonable "person" means someone of the defendant's occupation. A taxi driver must drive as a reasonable taxi driver would. A heart surgeon must perform bypass surgery with the care of a trained specialist in that field.

Two medical cases from Texas will illustrate the reasonable person standard. In *Gooden v. Tips*, the plaintiff, Gooden, was struck by an automobile driven by Dr. Tips's patient, who was under the influence of prescription Quaaludes at the time of the accident. The court ruled that the doctor had breached his duty of due care by failing to warn his patient not to drive while taking the drug.[16]

In *Casarez v. NME Hospitals, Inc.*,[17] Dr. Vasquez admitted to a hospital a patient who was terminally ill with acquired immune deficiency syndrome (AIDS). In his admission instruction, the doctor stated that the patient was HIV positive; he also told the nurses of the patient's condition. Dr. Vasquez did not, however, instruct anyone on the procedures to use with the patient. Casarez, a certified nursing assistant, was caring for the patient when he involuntarily spewed blood on Casarez's mouth, eyes, and arm. The patient died the next day. Casarez tested HIV positive.

Casarez sued Dr. Vasquez (among others), claiming that the doctor negligently failed to instruct him how to handle an AIDS patient. The court was unpersuaded. Vasquez was indeed obligated to take precautions with an AIDS patient, but he did everything reasonably required by ensuring that the staff knew of the patient's illness. He had no obligation to instruct staff in special procedures for such a patient because all hospital staff were already trained. Casarez and all others knew precisely what precautions to take, and Vasquez was not liable.

CRIME AND TORT: NEGLIGENT HIRING

In a recent one-year period, more than 1,000 homicides and 2 million attacks occurred in the workplace. Companies must beware because they can be liable for hiring or retaining violent employees. A mailroom clerk with a previous rape and robbery conviction followed a secretary home after work and fatally assaulted her. Even though the murder took place off the company premises, the court held that the defendant would be liable if it knew or should have known of the mail clerk's criminal history.[18] In other cases, companies have been found

[16] 651 S.W.2d 364, 1983 Tex. App. LEXIS 4388 (Tex. Ct. App. 1983).

[17] 883 S.W.2d 360, 1994 Tex. App. LEXIS 2091 (Tex. Ct. App. 1994).

[18] *Gaines v. Monsanto*, 655 S.W.2d 568, 1983 Mo. LEXIS 3439 (Mo. Ct. App. 1983).

liable for failing to check an applicant's driving record, to contact personal references, and to search criminal records.

PREVENTIVE Law

What can an employer do to diminish the likelihood of workplace violence? Many things.

- Make workplace safety a priority. Many employers still do not believe that violence can occur in their company. They are seriously mistaken.
- Evaluate the workplace for unsafe physical features. Install adequate lighting in parking lots and common areas, hire security guards if necessary, and use closed-circuit television and identification cards.
- Ensure that the company uses thorough pre-hire screening, contacts all former employers, and checks all references and criminal records. Nursing homes have paid huge sums for negligently hiring convicted assailants who later attack elderly residents.
- Respond quickly to dangerous behavior. In many cases of workplace violence, the perpetrator had demonstrated repeated bizarre, threatening, or obsessive behavior on the job, but his supervisors had not taken it seriously.

NEGLIGENCE PER SE

In certain areas of life, courts are not free to decide what a "reasonable" person would have done, because the state legislature has made the decision for them. **When a legislature sets a minimum standard of care for a particular activity, in order to protect a certain group of people, and a violation of the statute injures a member of that group, the defendant has committed negligence per se.** A plaintiff who can show negligence per se need not prove breach of duty.

In Minnesota, the state legislature became alarmed about children sniffing glue, and passed a statute prohibiting the sale to a minor of any glue containing toluene. About one month later, 14-year-old Steven Zerby purchased glue containing toluene from a store in his hometown. Steven inhaled the glue and died from injury to his central nervous system. A reasonable person might have made the same error, but that is irrelevant: the clerk violated the statute and the store was liable.[19]

FACTUAL CAUSE AND FORESEEABLE HARM

A plaintiff must also show that the defendant's breach of duty caused the plaintiff's harm. Courts look at two issues to settle causation: Was the defendant's behavior the *factual cause* of the harm? Was *this type of harm foreseeable?*[20]

---

[19] *Zerby v. Warren,* 297 Minn. 134, 210 N.W.2d 58 (1973).

[20] Courts often refer to these two elements, grouped together, as *proximate cause* or *legal cause.* But, as many judges acknowledge, those terms have created confusion, so we use *factual cause* and *foreseeable type of harm,* the issues on which most decisions ultimately focus.

FACTUAL CAUSE

Nothing mysterious here. **If the defendant's breach physically led to the ultimate harm, it is the factual cause.** Suppose that Dom's Brake Shop tells Customer his brakes are now working fine, even though Dom knows that is false. Customer drives out of the shop, cannot stop at a red light, and hits Bicyclist crossing at the intersection. Dom is liable to Bicyclist. Dom's unreasonable behavior was the factual cause of the harm. Think of it as a row of dominoes. The first domino (Dom's behavior) knocked over the next one (failing brakes), which toppled the last one (the cyclist's injury).

Suppose, alternatively, that just as Customer is exiting the repair shop, Bicyclist hits a pothole and tumbles off her cycle, avoiding Customer's auto. Bicyclist's injuries stem from her fall, not from the auto. Customer's brakes still fail, and Dom has breached his duty to Customer, but Dom is not liable to Bicyclist. She would have been hurt anyway. This is a row of dominoes that veers off to the side, leaving the last domino (cyclist's injury) untouched. No factual causation.

FORESEEABLE TYPE OF HARM

For the defendant to be liable, the *type of harm* must have been reasonably foreseeable. In the case above, Dom could easily foresee that bad brakes would cause an automobile accident. He need not have foreseen exactly what happened. He did not know there would be a cyclist nearby. What he could foresee was this general type of harm involving defective brakes.

By contrast, assume the collision of car and bicycle produces a loud crash. Two blocks away, a pet pig, asleep on the window ledge of a twelfth-story apartment, is startled by the noise, awakens with a start, and plunges to the sidewalk, killing a veterinarian who was making a house call. If the vet's family sues Dom, should it win? Dom's negligence was the factual cause: it led to the collision, which startled the pig, which flattened the vet. Most courts would rule, though, that Dom is not liable. The type of harm is too bizarre. Dom could not reasonably foresee such an extraordinary chain of events, and it would be unfair to make him pay for it. See Exhibit 6.1.

Another way of stating that Dom is not liable to the vet's family is by calling the falling pig a *superseding cause.* When one of the "dominoes" in the row is entirely unforeseeable, courts will considert it a superseding cause, letting the defendant off the hook. Negligence cases often revolve around whether the chain of events leading from the defendant's conduct to the injury was broken by a superseding cause.

In *Kowkabany v. The Home Depot, Inc.,*[21] Mr. and Ms. Remseyer bought four 8-foot landscape timbers at a Home Depot store. Mr. Remseyer and a Home Depot employee loaded the timbers into the back seat of his car, leaving them protruding about three feet out the front passenger window. After 20 minutes of driving, Remseyer approached Eva Kowkabany and another girl, both on bicycles. Remseyer thought he could pass the girls safely, but an approaching car

---

[21] 606 So. 2d 716, 1992 Fla. App. LEXIS 10835 (Fla. Dist. Ct. App. 1992).

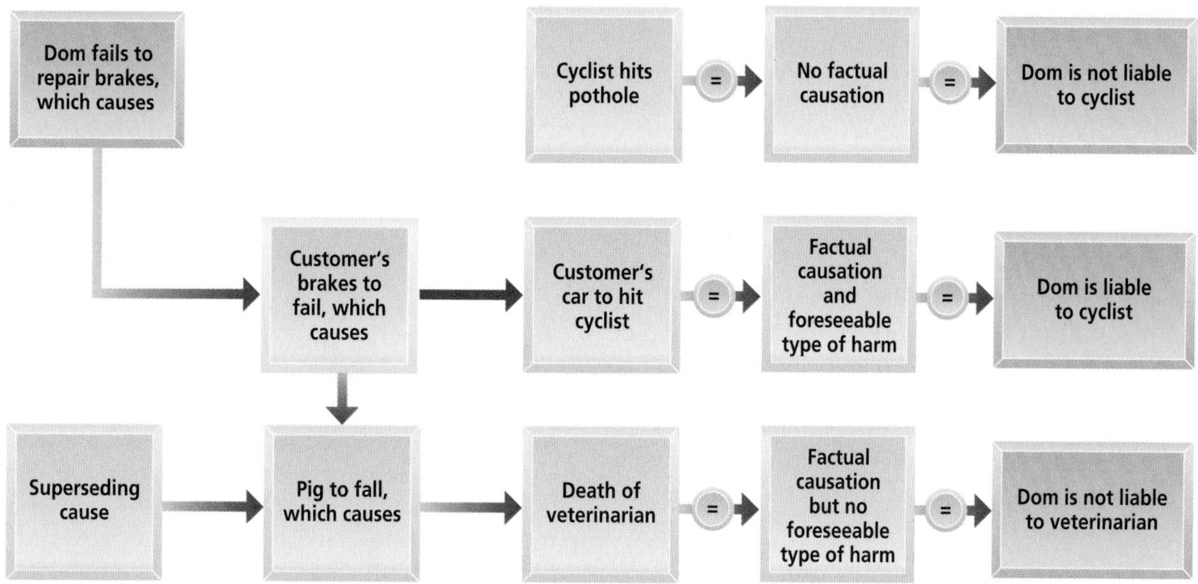

Exhibit 6.1

"squeezed him" and the timber struck Eva Kowkabany, severely injuring her. Kowkabany sued the Home Depot.

The Home Depot defended by saying that Remseyer's negligent driving caused the accident. Remseyer had indeed been negligent. Was his negligence a "superseding cause?" No, held the court, stating that a superseding cause should only be found where the circumstances are highly unusual, extraordinary or bizarre. Remseyer's poor judgment in driving was foreseeable.

Res Ipsa Loquitur

Normally, a plaintiff must prove factual cause and foreseeable type of harm in order to establish negligence. But in a few cases, a court may *infer* that the defendant caused the harm, under the doctrine of ***res ipsa loquitur*** ("the thing speaks for itself"). Suppose a pedestrian is walking along a sidewalk when an air-conditioning unit falls on his head from a third-story window. The defendant, who owns the third-story apartment, denies any wrongdoing, and it may be difficult or impossible for the plaintiff to prove why the air conditioner fell. In such cases, many courts will apply *res ipsa loquitur* and declare that **the facts imply that the defendant's negligence caused the accident**. If a court uses this doctrine, then the defendant must come forward with evidence establishing that it did not cause the harm.

Because *res ipsa loquitur* dramatically shifts the burden of proof from plaintiff to defendant, it applies only when (1) the defendant had exclusive control of the thing that caused the harm, (2) the harm normally would not have occurred without negligence, and (3) the plaintiff had no role in causing the harm. In the air conditioner example, most states would apply the doctrine and force the defendant to prove she did nothing wrong.

GRIFFITH v. VALLEY OF SUN RECOVERY, INC.
126 Ariz. 227, 613 P.2d 1283
Arizona Court of Appeals, 1980

Facts: Don Gorney was a repossession agent, authorized to take cars from owners who are behind on payments. A repossessor is allowed to drive away in such a car, provided he can do it peacefully. Gorney worked for Valley of Sun Recovery. He sought a car belonging to Linda Marsalek and Bob Williams. Gorney knew that there had been other, failed efforts to repossess the car, including a violent confrontation involving attack dogs. He thought he could do better.

Gorney went to the car at 4:00 in the morning. He unscrewed the bulb in an overhead street lamp. He unlocked the car, setting off its alarm, and quickly hid. The alarm aroused the neighborhood. Williams and a neighbor, Griffith, investigated and concluded it was an attempted theft. They called the police. Gorney watched all of this from his hiding place. When everyone had gone, Gorney entered the car, again setting off the alarm and arousing the neighborhood. Williams and Griffith again emerged, as did another neighbor, dressed in his underwear and carrying a shotgun. They all believed they had caught a thief. Williams shouted for the gun and the neighbor passed it to him, but it went off accidentally and severely injured Griffith.

Griffith sued Valley of Sun. The trial court granted summary judgment for Valley of Sun, and Griffith appealed.

You be the Judge:

- Did Valley of Sun have a *duty* to Griffith?
- If so, did the company *breach* its duty?
- If so, was the breach the *factual cause* of the injury?
- If so, was *this type of injury foreseeable?*

Argument for Griffith: Your honors, Mr. Griffith should be allowed to make his case to a jury and let it decide whether Valley of Sun's repossession led to his injury. Valley of Sun had a duty to everyone in the area, because repossessions always involve antagonism and a chance of injury. Gorney breached his duty by acting as though he were Harrison Ford in an adventure film. Had it not been for his preposterous game playing, no neighbors would have been outside, no guns present—and no accidental shooting. This harm was easily foreseeable.

Argument for Valley of Sun Recovery: Your honors, there was no duty, no breach and no causation. Surely Valley of Sun does not have a legal duty to the whole neighborhood. Is a repossession company to become an insurer of the entire city? Even if there had been a duty, there was no breach. Mr. Gorney attempted to repossess when it was least likely anyone would see him. Causation? The car owner created this situation by failing to pay, and the neighbor added a superseding cause by recklessly using a firearm. There is no case for a jury to hear.

INJURY

Finally, a plaintiff must prove that he has been injured. In some cases, injury is obvious. For example, Ruben Hernandez, struck by the intoxicated fraternity member, obviously suffered grievous harm. In other cases, though, injury is unclear. **The plaintiff must persuade the court that he has suffered a harm that is genuine, not speculative.**

Among the most vexing are suits involving future harm. Exposure to toxins or trauma may lead to serious medical problems down the road—or it may not. A woman's knee is damaged in an auto accident, causing severe pain for two years. She is clearly entitled to compensation for her suffering. After two years, all of her troubles may cease. Yet there is a chance that in 15 years the trauma will lead to painful arthritis. A court must decide today the full extent of present *and future* damages.

The following lawsuit concerns a woman's fear of developing AIDS. This worry can be overwhelming. See the online mental health dictionary found at http://www.thebody.com/mental.html. A court must still decide, however, whether the cause of the unhappiness is genuine injury or speculation.

REYNOLDS v. HIGHLAND MANOR, INC.

24 Kan. App. 2d 859, 954 P.2d 11, 1998 Kan. App. LEXIS 20
Kansas Court of Appeals, 1998

Facts: Angelina Reynolds and her family checked into a Holiday Inn, but since the air conditioner did not work they requested a room change. As they were repacking their luggage, Reynolds felt for items left under the bed, and picked up what she thought was a candy wrapper. Reynolds felt a "gush" as she retrieved the item, which unfortunately turned out to be a wet condom. She screamed and quickly washed her hands. There was a second condom under the bed. Reynolds and her husband rushed to an emergency room, taking the condoms with them. Hospital staff said that they were unable to test the contents of the condoms. A doctor examined Reynolds's hand, which had a burn on the middle finger and bloody cuticles, but told her that there was nothing he could do if she had been exposed to infectious diseases.

The condom never was tested. Reynolds sued the motel, claiming among other things that she feared she would die of AIDS. The trial court dismissed the case, ruling that there was no showing of injury. Reynolds appealed.

Issue: Has Reynolds demonstrated injury?

Excerpts from Judge Penland's Decision: Plaintiff testified that after the incident, she feared she would die from AIDS. As a result of this anxiety, she claimed to have suffered headaches, diarrhea, and nausea. She could not say that she ever vomited and conceded that one type of medication she took caused her digestive problems. Plaintiff also testified to crying and shaking, and feeling overwhelmed with stress. Dr. Elias Chediak, the psychiatrist who treated plaintiff following the incident, testified that most of the time he saw her, "she was feeling pretty anxious, crying, feeling distressed," and she reported headaches and tense muscles. Dr. Chediak stated plaintiff had seen a neurologist who performed tests that turned out negative. According to Dr. Chediak, the neurologist concluded that any problems plaintiff had experienced were due to stress. Plaintiff also testified that because of her mental state, her sexual relations with her husband had decreased, but they continued to have unprotected sex after the incident, despite her purported fear she might have HIV.

[In an earlier case,] our Supreme Court held that a plaintiff may recover for anxiety based on reasonable fear that an existing injury will lead to the occurrence of a disease or condition in the future. For the fear to be reasonable, the court held the plaintiff must show that a substantial probability exists that such condition or disease will occur. Anxiety about a disease or condition developing from a physical injury is not recoverable as an element of mental distress where the medical evidence indicates the chance of such occurring is slight.

The uncontroverted evidence established that plaintiff took an HIV test four times following the incident, the last occurring more than 1 year after the incident. When an individual tests negative for HIV more than 1 year after exposure, a greater than 99% probability exists that HIV will not appear. Plaintiff has failed to establish even a minimal possibility, much less a substantial or even significant probability, that she will contract AIDS due to her contact with the condom in the motel. Because her fear of contracting the disease is unreasonable as a matter of law, she may not recover damages.

Affirmed.

DAMAGES

The plaintiff's damages in a negligence case are generally **compensatory damages**, meaning an amount of money that the court believes will restore him to the position he was in before the defendant's conduct caused an injury. In unusual cases, a court may award punitive damages, that is, money intended not to compensate the plaintiff but to punish the defendant. We discussed both forms of damages earlier in this chapter.

CONTRIBUTORY AND COMPARATIVE NEGLIGENCE

Joe is a mental patient in a hospital. The hospital knows he is dangerous to himself and others, but it permits him to wander around unattended. Joe leaves the hospital and steals a gun. Shawn drives by Joe, and Joe waves the gun at him. Shawn notices a police officer a block away. But instead of informing the cop, Shawn leans out his window and shouts, "Hey, knucklehead, what are you doing pointing guns at people?" Joe shoots and kills Shawn.

Shawn's widow sues the hospital for negligently permitting Joe to leave. But the hospital, in defense, claims that Shawn's foolishness got him killed. Who wins? It depends on whether the state in which the suit is heard uses a legal theory called **contributory negligence**. This used to be the law throughout the nation, but it remains in effect in only a few states. It means that, even assuming the defendant is negligent, **if the plaintiff is even *slightly* negligent himself, he recovers nothing**. So if Shawn's homicide occurs in a contributory negligence state, the hospital is not liable regardless of how negligent it was.

Critics attacked the rule as unreasonable. A plaintiff who was 1 percent negligent could not recover from a defendant who was 99 percent negligent. So most states threw out the contributory negligence rule, replacing it with comparative negligence. **In a comparative negligence state, a plaintiff may generally recover even if she is partially negligent.** A jury will be asked to assess the relative negligence of plaintiff and defendant.

Suppose we are in a comparative negligence state, and the jury believes the hospital was 80 percent responsible for Shawn's death, and Shawn himself was 20 percent responsible. It might conclude that the total damages for Shawn's widow are $2 million, based on Shawn's pain in dying and the widow's loss of his income. If so, the hospital would owe $1.6 million, or 80 percent of the damages. See Exhibit 6.2.

Today, most but not all states have adopted some form of comparative negligence. Critics of comparative negligence claim that it rewards a plaintiff for being careless. Suppose, they say, a driver speeds to beat an approaching train, and the railroad's mechanical arm fails to operate. Why should we reward the driver for his foolishness? In response to this complaint, some comparative negligence states do not permit a plaintiff to recover anything if he was more than 50 percent responsible for his injury.

STRICT LIABILITY

Some activities are so naturally dangerous that the law places an especially high burden on anyone who engages in them. A corporation that produces toxic

Exhibit 6.2
Defendant's negligence injures plaintiff, who suffers $2 million in damages.

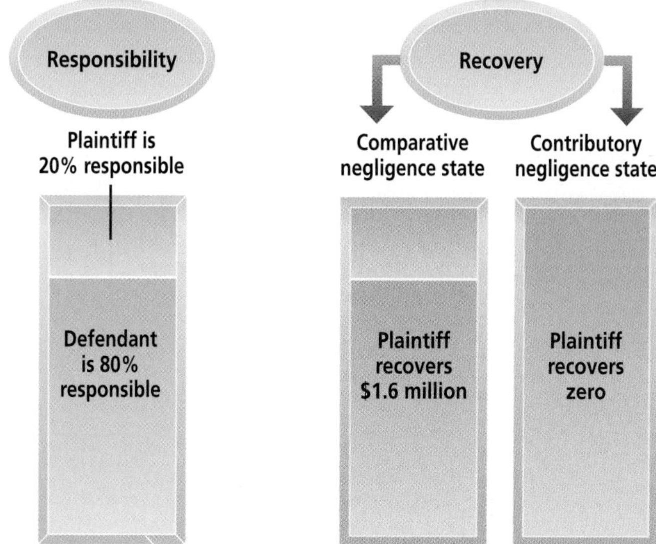

waste can foresee dire consequences from its business that a stationery store cannot. This higher burden is **strict liability**. There are two main areas of business that incur strict liability: *ultrahazardous activity* and *defective products*. Defective products are discussed in Chapter 11, on products liability.

ULTRAHAZARDOUS ACTIVITY

Ultrahazardous activities include using harmful chemicals, operating explosives, keeping wild animals, bringing dangerous substances onto property, and a few similar activities where the danger to the general public is especially great. **A defendant engaging in an ultrahazardous activity is virtually always liable for any harm that results.** Plaintiffs do not have to prove duty or breach or foreseeable harm. Recall the deliberately bizarre case we posed earlier of the pig falling from a window ledge and killing a veterinarian. Dom, the mechanic whose negligence caused the car crash, could not be liable for the veterinarian's death because the plunging pig was a superseding cause. But if the pig was jolted off the window ledge by Sam's Blasting Co., which was doing perfectly lawful blasting for a new building down the street, Sam is liable. Even if Sam took extraordinary care, it will do him no good at trial. The "reasonable person" rule is irrelevant in a strict liability case.

CHAPTER CONCLUSION

This chapter has been a potpourri of sin, a bubbling cauldron of conduct best avoided. Although tortious acts and their consequences are diverse, two generalities apply. First, the boundaries of torts are imprecise, the outcome of a particular case depending to a considerable extent upon the factfinder who analyzes it. Second, the thoughtful executive and the careful citizen, aware of the shifting standards and potentially vast liability, will strive to ensure that his or her conduct never provides that factfinder an opportunity to give judgment.

CHAPTER REVIEW

1. A tort is a violation of a duty imposed by the civil law.
2. Defamation involves a false statement, likely to harm another's reputation, which is uttered to a third person, and causes an injury. Opinion and privilege are valid defenses. Public personalities can win a defamation suit only by proving actual malice.
3. False imprisonment is the intentional restraint of another person without reasonable cause and without consent.
4. The intentional infliction of emotional distress involves extreme and outrageous conduct that causes serious emotional harm.
5. Battery is an intentional touching of another person in a way that is offensive. Assault involves an act that makes the plaintiff fear an imminent battery.
6. Compensatory damages are the normal remedy in a tort case. In unusual cases, the court may award punitive damages, to punish the defendant.
7. Tortious interference with business relations involves the defendant harming an existing contract or a prospective relationship that has a definite expectation of success.
8. The related torts of privacy and publicity involve unreasonable intrusion into someone's private life, disclosure of embarrassing private facts in which the public has no legitimate interest, placing the plaintiff in a false light, or unfair commercial exploitation by using someone's name, likeness, or voice without permission.
9. The five elements of negligence are duty of due care, breach, factual causation, foreseeable type of harm, and injury.
10. If the defendant could foresee that misconduct would injure a particular person, he probably has a duty to her.
11. A defendant breaches his duty of due care by failing to behave the way a reasonable person would under similar conditions.
12. Employers may be liable for neligent hiring.
13. If a legislature sets a minimum standard of care for a particular activity in order to protect a certain group of people, and a violation of the statute injures a member of that group, the defendant has committed *negligence per se.*
14. If an event physically leads to the ultimate harm, it is the factual cause.
15. For the defendant to be liable, the type of harm must have been reasonably foreseeable.
16. The plaintiff must persuade the court that he has suffered a harm that is genuine, not speculative.
17. In a contributory negligence state, a plaintiff who is even slightly responsible for his own injury recovers nothing; in a comparative negligence state, the jury may apportion liability between plaintiff and defendant.
18. A defendant is strictly liable for harm caused by an ultrahazardous activity or a defective product. Strict liability means that if the

defendant's conduct led to the harm, the defendant is liable, even if she exercised extraordinary care.

PRACTICE TEST

1. Benzaquin had a radio talk show in Boston. On the program, he complained about an incident earlier in the day, in which state trooper Fleming had stopped his car, apparently for lack of a proper license plate and safety sticker. Even though Benzaquin explained that the license plate had been stolen and the sticker had fallen onto the dashboard, Fleming refused to let him drive the car away, and Benzaquin and his daughter and two young grandsons had to find other transportation. On the show, Benzaquin angrily recounted the incident, then made the following statements about Fleming and troopers generally: "arrogants wearing troopers' uniforms like tights"; "little monkey, you wind him up and he does his thing"; "we're not paying them to be dictators and Nazis"; "this man is an absolute barbarian, a lunkhead, a meathead." Fleming sued Benzaquin for defamation. Comment.

2. Caldwell, carrying a large purse, was shopping in a K-Mart store. A security guard observed her look at various small items such as stain, hinges, and antenna wire. On occasion she bent down out of sight of the guard. The guard thought he saw Caldwell put something in her purse. Caldwell removed her glasses from her purse and returned them a few times. After she left, the guard approached her in the parking lot and said that he believed she had store merchandise in her pocketbook but was unable to say what he thought was put there. Caldwell opened the purse, and the guard testified he saw no K-Mart merchandise in it. The guard then told Caldwell to return to the store with him. They walked around the store for approximately 15 minutes, while the guard said six or seven times that he saw her put something in her purse. Caldwell left the store after another store employee indicated she could go. Caldwell sued. What kind of suit did she file, and what should the outcome be?

3. Fifteen-year-old Terri Stubblefield was riding in the back seat of a Ford Mustang II when the car was hit from behind. The Mustang was engulfed in a ball of fire, and Terri was severely burned. She died. Terri's family sued Ford, alleging that the car was badly designed—and that Ford knew it. At trial, Terri's family introduced evidence that Ford knew the fuel tank was dangerous and that it could have taken measures to make the tank safe. There was evidence that Ford consciously decided not to remedy the fuel tanks in order to save money. The family sought two different kinds of damages from Ford. What were they?

4. **RIGHT & WRONG** In the *Stubblefield* case in Question 3, the jury awarded $8 million in punitive damages to the family. Ford appealed. Should the punitive damages be affirmed? What are the obligations of a corporation when it knows one of its products may be dangerous? Is an automobile company ethically obligated to make a *totally safe* car? Should we require a manufacturer to improve the safety of its cars if doing so will make them too expensive for many drivers? What would you do if you were a mid-level executive and saw evidence that your company was endangering the lives of consumers to save money? What would you do if you were on a *jury* and saw such evidence?

5. Caudle worked at Betts Lincoln-Mercury dealer. During an office party, many of the employees, including president Betts, were playing with an electric auto condenser, which gave a slight electric shock when touched. Some employees played catch with the condenser. Betts shocked Caudle on the back of his neck and then chased him around, holding the condenser. The shock later caused Caudle to suffer headaches, to pass out, and eventually to require surgery on a nerve in his neck. Even after surgery, Caudle

had a slight numbness on one side of his head. He sued Betts for battery. Betts defended by saying that it was all horseplay and that he had intended no injury. Please rule.

6. **YOU BE THE JUDGE WRITING PROBLEM** Johnny Carson was for many years the star of a well-known television program, *The Tonight Show*. For about 20 years, he was introduced nightly on the show with the phrase, "Here's Johnny!" A large segment of the television watching public associated the phrase with Carson. A Michigan corporation was in the business of renting and selling portable toilets. The company chose the name "Here's Johnny Portable Toilets," and coupled the company name with the marketing phrase, "The World's Foremost Commodian." Carson sued, claiming that the company's name and slogan violated his right to commercial exploitation. **Argument for Carson:** The toilet company is deliberately taking advantage of Johnny Carson's good name. He worked hard for decades to build a brilliant career and earn a reputation as a creative, funny, likable performer. No company has the right to use his name, his picture, or anything else closely identified with him, such as the phrase "Here's Johnny." The pun is personally offensive and commercially unfair. **Argument for Here's Johnny Portable Toilets:** Johnny Carson doesn't own his first name. It is available for anyone to use for any purpose. Further, the popular term "john," meaning toilet, has been around much longer than Carson or even television. We are entitled to make any use of it we want. Our corporate name is amusing to customers who have never heard of Carson, and we are entitled to profit from our brand recognition.

7. Jason Jacque was riding as a passenger in a car driven by his sister, who was drunk and driving 19 mph over the speed limit. She failed to negotiate a curve, skidded off the road, and collided with a wooden utility pole erected by the Public Service Company of Colorado (PSC). Jacque suffered severe brain injury. He sued PSC for negligently installing the pole too close to the highway at a dangerous curve where an accident was likely to happen. The trial court gave summary judgment for PSC, ruling that PSC owed no duty to Jacque. He appealed. Please rule.

8. Ryder leased a truck to Florida Food Service; Powers, an employee, drove it to make deliveries. He noticed that the door strap used to close the rear door was frayed, and he asked Ryder to fix it. Ryder failed to do so in spite of numerous requests. The strap broke, and Powers replaced it with a nylon rope. Later, when Powers was attempting to close the rear door, the nylon rope broke and he fell, sustaining severe injuries to his neck and back. He sued Ryder. The trial court found that Powers's attachment of the replacement rope was a superseding cause, relieving Ryder of any liability, and granted summary judgment for Ryder. Powers appealed. How should the appellate court rule?

9. A new truck, manufactured by General Motors Corp., stalled in rush hour traffic on a busy interstate highway because of a defective alternator, which caused a complete failure of the truck's electrical system. The driver stood nearby and waved traffic around his stalled truck. A panel truck approached the GMC truck, and immediately behind the panel truck, Davis was driving a Volkswagen fastback. Because of the panel truck, Davis was unable to see the stalled GMC truck. The panel truck swerved out of the way of the GMC truck, and Davis drove straight into it. The accident killed him. Davis's widow sued GMC. GMC moved for summary judgment, alleging (1) no duty to Davis, (2) no factual causation, and (3) no foreseeable harm. Comment.

10. A prison inmate bit a hospital employee. The employee sued the state for negligence and lack of supervision, claiming a fear of AIDS. The plaintiff had tested negative for the AIDS virus three times, and there was no proof that

the inmate had the virus. Comment on the probable outcome.

11. **RIGHT & WRONG** Swimming pools in private homes often have diving boards, but those in public parks, hotels, and clubs rarely do. Why is that? Is it good or bad?

12. There is a collision between cars driven by Candy and Zeke, and both drivers are partly at fault. The evidence is that Candy is about 25 percent responsible, for failing to stop quickly enough, and Zeke about 75 percent responsible, for making a dangerous turn. Candy is most likely to win:

    (a) A lawsuit for battery

    (b) A lawsuit for negligence, in a comparative negligence state

    (c) A lawsuit for negligence, in a contributory negligence state

    (d) A lawsuit for strict liability; or

    (e) A lawsuit for assault.

13. Van Houten owned a cat and allowed it to roam freely outside. In the three years he had owned it, it had never bitten anyone. The cat entered Pritchard's garage. Pritchard attempted to move it outside his garage, and the cat bit him. As a direct result of the bite, Pritchard underwent four surgeries, was fitted with a plastic finger joint, and spent more than $39,000 in medical bills. He sued Van Houten, claiming both strict liability and ordinary negligence. Please evaluate his claims.

INTERNET RESEARCH PROBLEM

Take a look at http://response.restoration.noaa.gov/index.html. What are some of the long-term problems associated with oil spills? View some of the photos in the "gallery." Are punitive damages for oil spills appropriate or excessive?

You can find further practice problems in the Online Quiz at http://beatty.westbuslaw.com or in the Study Guide that accompanies this text.

CRIME

7

CHAPTER

Crime can take us by surprise. Stacey tucks her nine-year-old daughter, Beth, into bed. Promising her husband, Mark, that she will be home by 11:00 P.M., she jumps into her car and heads back to Be Patient, Inc. She puts a CD in the player of her $55,000 sedan and tries to relax. Be Patient is a health care organization that owns five geriatric hospitals. Most of its patients use Medicare, and Stacey supervises all billing to their largest client, the federal government.

She parks in a well-lighted spot on the street and walks to her building, failing to notice two men, collars turned up, watching from a parked truck. Once in her office she goes straight to her computer and works on billing issues. Tonight's work goes more quickly than she expected, thanks to new software she helped develop. At 10:30, she emerges from the building with a quick step and a light heart, walks to her car—and finds it missing.

A major crime has occurred during the 90 minutes Stacey was at her desk, but she will never report it to the police. It is a crime that costs Americans countless dollars each year, yet Stacey will not even mention it to friends or family. Stacey is the one who committed it.

When we think of criminals, we imagine the drug dealers and bank robbers endlessly portrayed on television. We do not picture corporate executives sitting at polished desks. "Street crimes" are indeed serious threats to our security and happiness. They deservedly receive the attention of the public and the law. (For a look at the FBI's 10 most wanted list, see http://www.fbi.gov.) But when measured only in dollars, street crime takes second place to white-collar crime, which costs society *tens of billions* of dollars annually.

The hypothetical about Stacey is based on many real cases and is used to illustrate that crime does not always dress the way we expect. Her car was never stolen; it was simply towed. Two parking bureau employees, watching from their truck, saw Stacey park illegally and did their job. Stacey is the criminal. She committed Medicare fraud. Stacey has learned the simple but useful lesson that company profits rise when she charges the government for work Be Patient has never done. For months, she billed the government for imaginary patients. Then she hired a computer hacker to worm into the Medicare computer system and plant a "Trojan horse," a program that seemed useful to Medicare employees but actually contained a series of codes opening the computer to Stacey. Stacey simply entered the Medicare system and altered the calculations for payments owed to Be Patient. Every month, the government paid Be Patient about $10 million for imaginary work. Stacey's scheme was quick and profitable—and a distressingly common crime.

What do we do about cases like these? What *should* we do? These questions involve multifarious fact issues and important philosophical values. In this chapter, we look first at the big picture of criminal law and then focus on that part of it that most affects business—white-collar crime. We examine four major issues:

- *Crime, Society, and Law.* What makes conduct criminal? We enumerate the basic elements that the prosecution must establish to prove that a crime has been committed, and also some of the most common defenses.
- *Crimes that Harm Business.* We look at specific crimes, such as fraud and embezzlement, that cost businesses enormous sums every year.
- *Crimes Committed by Business.* We analyze "white-collar crimes," which are generally committed by employees of corporations or partnerships and may be directed at consumers, other businesses, or the government.
- *Criminal Process and Constitutional Protections.* We examine how the Bill of Rights protects citizens subjected to search, interrogation, and trial. And we pay a final visit to Stacey.

CRIME, SOCIETY, AND LAW

CIVIL LAW/CRIMINAL LAW

Most of this book concerns the civil law—the rights and liabilities that exist between private parties. As we have seen, if one person claims that another has caused her a civil injury, she must file a lawsuit and convince a court of her damages.

The criminal law is different. Conduct is **criminal** when society outlaws it. When a state legislature or Congress concludes that certain behavior threatens the population generally, it passes a statute forbidding that behavior, in other words, declaring it criminal. Medicare fraud, which Stacey committed, is a crime because Congress has outlawed it. Money laundering is a crime because Congress concluded it was a fundamental part of the drug trade and prohibited it.

PROSECUTION

Suppose the police arrest Roger and accuse him of breaking into a video store and stealing 25 cameras, videos, and other equipment. **The owner of the video store is the one harmed, but it is the government that prosecutes crimes.** The local prosecutor will decide whether or not to charge Roger and bring him to trial.

JURY RIGHT

The facts of the case will be decided by a judge or jury. A criminal defendant has a right to a trial by jury for any charge that could result in a sentence of six months or longer. The defendant may demand a jury trial or may waive that right, in which case the judge will be the factfinder.

PUNISHMENT

In a civil lawsuit, the plaintiff seeks a verdict that the defendant is liable for harm caused to her. But in a criminal case, the government asks the court to find the defendant **guilty** of the crime. The government wants the court to **punish** the defendant. If the judge or jury finds the defendant guilty, the court will punish him with a fine and/or a prison sentence. The fine is paid to the government, not to the injured person (although the court will sometimes order **restitution**, meaning that the defendant must reimburse the victim for harm suffered). It is almost always the judge who imposes the sentence. If the jury is not persuaded of the defendant's guilt, it will **acquit** him, that is, find him not guilty.

FELONY/MISDEMEANOR

A **felony** is a serious crime, for which a defendant can be sentenced to one year or more in prison. Murder, robbery, rape, drug dealing, money laundering, wire fraud, and embezzlement are felonies. A **misdemeanor** is a less serious crime, often punishable by a year or less in a county jail. Public drunkenness, driving without a license, and simple possession of one marijuana cigarette are considered misdemeanors in most states.

PUNISHMENT

Why punish a defendant? Sometimes the answer is obvious. If a defendant has committed armed robbery, we want that person locked up. Other cases are not so apparent.

You are the judge in charge of sentencing Jason. He is a 61-year-old minister who has devoted 40 years to serving his community, leading his church, and helping to rehabilitate schools. Fifteen years ago he founded a children's hospital and has raised enormous sums to maintain it. He has labored with local government to rebuild abandoned housing and established a center for battered women. Jason suffers from a terminal illness and will die in three to four years. But the jury has just found that in his zeal to get housing built, Jason took kickbacks from construction firms run by gangsters. The construction companies padded their bills, some of which were paid with state and city money. They kicked back a small amount of this illegal profit to Jason, who gave the money to his charities. Jason thought of himself as Robin Hood, but the law regards him as a felon. You can fine Jason and/or sentence him to prison for a maximum of five years.

A flood of letters urges you to allow Jason to continue raising money and helping others. You need to understand the rationale of punishment. Over the past several centuries, philosophers in many countries—and judges in this country—have proposed various reasons for punishing the guilty.

RESTRAINT

A violent criminal who appears likely to commit more crimes must be physically restrained. Here there is no pretense of prison being anything but a cage to protect the rest of society. (An online group that sees little good and much evil in our system of incarceration gives examples of perceived abuses at http://www.prisonactivist.org/news/.) In Jason's case, there is clearly no reason to restrain him.

DETERRENCE

Imprisonment may deter future crimes in two ways. **Specific deterrence** is intended to teach *this defendant* that crime carries a heavy price tag, in the hope that he will never do it again. **General deterrence** is the goal of demonstrating to *society generally* that crime must be shunned. Notice that both ideas of deterrence are utilitarian; that is, they are *means to an end.* Specific and general deterrence both assume that by imprisoning someone, the law achieves a greater good for everyone. Jason almost certainly requires no specific deterrence. Is general deterrence a reason to imprison him?

RETRIBUTION

The German philosopher Immanuel Kant (1724–1804) rejected the idea of deterrence. He argued that human beings were supremely important and as a result must always be treated as ends in themselves, *never as a means to an end*. Kant would argue that, if deterrence were legitimate, then it would be all right to torture prisoners—even innocent prisoners—if this deterred massive amounts of crime.

For Kant, there is only one valid reason to punish: the prisoner deserves it. This is the idea of **retribution**—giving back to the criminal precisely what she deserves. A moral world, said Kant, requires that the government administer to all prisoners a punishment exactly equal to the crime they committed. A murderer must be put to death (even if he is dying from an illness and would live only a few days); an executive who bribes a government official must suffer a punishment equal to the harm she caused. To Kant, all of Jason's good deeds would be irrelevant, as would his terminal illness. If three years is the appropriate imprisonment for the crime of fraud, then he must serve three years, even if he dies in prison, even if it stops him from raising $10 million for charity.

Related to the idea of retribution is **vengeance**. When a serious crime has occurred, society wants the perpetrator to suffer. If we punish no one, people lose faith in the power and effectiveness of government and may take the law into their own hands.

REHABILITATION

To rehabilitate someone is to provide training so that he may return to a normal life. Most criminal justice experts believe that little or no rehabilitation occurs in a prison, though other forms of punishment may achieve this worthy goal.

Jason's Case. What is your decision? Restraint and specific deterrence are unnecessary. You may imprison him for general deterrence or for retribution. Should you let him go free so that he can raise more money for good causes? In a similar case, a federal court judge decided that general deterrence was essential. To allow someone to go free, he said, would be to send a message that certain people can get away with crime. The judge sentenced the defendant to a prison term, though he shortened the sentence based on the defendant's age and ill health.[1]

THE PROSECUTION'S CASE

In all criminal cases, the prosecution faces several basic issues.

CONDUCT OUTLAWED

Virtually all crimes are created by statute. The prosecution must demonstrate to the court that the defendant's alleged conduct is indeed outlawed by a statute. Returning to Roger, the alleged video thief, the state charges that he stole video cameras from a store, a crime clearly defined by statute as burglary.

BURDEN OF PROOF

In a civil case, the plaintiff must prove her case by a preponderance of the evidence.[2] But in a criminal case, the government must prove its case **beyond a reasonable doubt**. This is because the potential harm to a criminal defendant is far greater. Roger, the video thief, can be fined and/or sent to prison. The stigma of a criminal conviction will stay with him, making it more difficult to obtain work and housing. Therefore, in all criminal cases, if the jury has any significant doubt at all that Roger stole the video cameras, it *must* acquit him. This high standard of proof in a criminal case reflects a very old belief, inherited from English law, that it is better to set 10 guilty people free than to convict a single innocent one. We will see that our law offers many protections for the accused.

---

[1] *United States v. Bergman*, 416 F. Supp. 496, 1976 U.S. Dist. LEXIS 14577 (S.D.N.Y. 1976).

[2] See the earlier discussion in Chapter 3, on dispute resolution.

ACTUS REUS

Actus reus means the "guilty act." **The prosecution must prove that the defendant voluntarily committed a prohibited act.** Suppose Mary Jo files an insurance claim for a stolen car, knowing that her car was not stolen. That is insurance fraud. Filing the claim is the *actus reus:* Mary Jo voluntarily filled out the insurance claim and mailed it. At a bar, Mary Jo describes the claim to her friend, Chi Ling, who laughs and replies, "That's great. It'll serve the company right." Has Chi Ling committed a crime? No. There is no *actus reus,* because Chi Ling has done nothing illegal. Her cynical attitude may contribute to higher premiums for all of us, but criminal law punishes acts, not thoughts or omissions.

MENS REA

The prosecution must also show ***mens rea*****, a "guilty state of mind,"** on the defendant's part. This is harder to prove than *actus reus*—it requires convincing evidence about something that is essentially psychological. Precisely what "state of mind" the prosecution must prove varies, depending on the crime. We will discuss the exact *mens rea* requirement for various crimes later in the chapter. In general, however, there are four mental states that a prosecutor may be required to prove, depending on the crime:

General Intent. Most crimes require a showing of general intent, meaning that the defendant intended to do the prohibited physical action (the *actus reus*). Suppose Miller, a customer in a bar, picks up a bottle and smashes it over the head of Bud. In a trial for criminal assault, the *mens rea* would simply be the intention to hit Bud. The prosecution need not show that Miller intended serious harm, only that he intended the blow.

How will a prosecutor prove what was in Miller's mind? By circumstantial evidence: a witness will describe how Miller picked up the bottle and what he did with it. A jury is free to conclude that Miller intended physical contact since there would be no other reason for his action.

Specific Intent. Some crimes require the prosecution to prove that the defendant willfully intended to do something beyond the physical act. For example, burglary requires proof that the defendant entered a building at night and intended to commit a felony inside, such as stealing property.

Reckless or Negligent Conduct. For a few crimes, the prosecution is concerned more with the defendant's irresponsible conduct than with what the defendant was thinking. **Criminal recklessness** means consciously disregarding a substantial risk of injury. One pedestrian who jokingly points a gun at another commits criminal recklessness. The danger of the gun going off is obvious, and the defendant is guilty even if no shot is fired. A slightly lesser crime, **criminal negligence**, refers to gross deviations from reasonable conduct. A hunter who sees movement and shoots at it, without bothering to determine whether the target is a turkey or a professor, commits criminal negligence.

Strict Liability. In strict liability cases, the prosecution must only prove *actus reus.* If the defendant committed the act, he is guilty, regardless of mental state or irresponsibility. For example, in an effort to improve the environment, many states now hold corporate defendants strictly liable for discharging certain pollutants into the air. If an oil refinery discharges toxic fumes, it is strictly liable, regardless of what efforts it may have taken to control emissions. Thus strict liability crimes are the easiest for a prosecutor to prove and potentially the most dangerous to corporations.

DEFENSES

A criminal defendant will frequently dispute the facts that link her to the crime. For example, she might claim mistaken identity (that she merely resembles the real criminal) or offer an alibi (that she can prove she was elsewhere when the crime was committed). In addition, a defendant may offer **legal defenses**. Many of these are controversial, as we will see.

INSANITY

A defendant who can prove that he was **insane** at the time of the criminal act will be declared not guilty. This reflects the moral basis of our criminal law. Insane people, though capable of great harm, historically have not been considered responsible for their acts. A defendant found to be insane will generally be committed to a mental institution. If and when that hospital determines he is no longer a danger to society, he will, in theory, be released. Some people applaud this as deeply humane, while others see it as muddled thinking that allows guilty people to walk free.

Two basic tests determine whether a defendant is insane. Some states recognize just one; others allow both.

M'Naghten Rule. The defendant must show (1) that he suffered a serious, identifiable mental disease and that because of it (2) he did not understand the nature of his act or did not know that it was wrong. Suppose Jerry, a homeless man, stabs Phil. At trial, a psychiatrist testifies that Jerry suffers from chronic schizophrenia, that he does not know where he is or what he is doing, and that when he stabbed Phil he believed he was sponging down his pet giraffe. If the jury believes the psychiatrist, it may find Jerry not guilty by reason of insanity.

"Irresistible Impulse." Under this test, the defendant must convince a jury that a mental defect left him unable to control his behavior. Jerry testifies that when he stabbed Phil he knew it was wrong but he could not stop himself. His psychiatrist asserts that Jerry's chronic dementia leaves him physically unable to repress violent impulses. If the jury believes the testimony, it may find Jerry not guilty.

What if the alleged mental defect is a result of the defendant's own behavior? You be the judge.

BIEBER v. PEOPLE
856 P.2d 811, 1993 Colo. LEXIS 630
Supreme Court of Colorado, 1993

Facts: Donald Bieber walked up to a truck in which William Ellis was sitting and shot Ellis, whom he did not know, in the back of his head. He threw Ellis's body from the truck and drove away. Shortly before and after the killing, Bieber encountered various people in different places. He sang "God Bless America" and the "Marine Hymn" to them and told them he was a prisoner of war and was being followed by communists. He fired shots at some people, without injuring them, and aimed his gun at others. After the homicide, he told people he had killed a communist on "War Memorial Highway." The police arrested him.

Bieber had a long history of drug abuse. As a teenager, he began using drugs, including amphetamines. As an adult, he continued his heavy drug use, while making money selling drugs. Several years before the homicide, Bieber voluntarily sought treatment for mental impairment, entering a hospital and saying he thought he was going to hurt someone. He was later released into a long-term drug program.

Bieber was charged with first degree murder. He pleaded not guilty by reason of insanity. An expert witness testified that he was insane, suffering from "amphetamine delusional disorder" (ADD), a recognized psychiatric illness resulting from long-term use of amphetamines and characterized by delusions. At trial, Bieber's attorney argued that he was not intoxicated at the time of the crime but that he was insane due to ADD. The trial court refused to instruct that Bieber could be legally insane due to ADD, and the jury found Bieber guilty of first degree murder. He appealed.

You be the Judge: May a jury find that a defendant with ADD is legally insane?

Argument for Bieber: Your honors, Mr. Bieber acknowledges the rule that someone who becomes voluntarily intoxicated and commits an offense is liable for the crime. That rule is irrelevant here, since Mr. Bieber was not intoxicated at the time of this homicide. He was insane.

The state of Colorado has long held that insanity is a valid defense to a criminal charge. It is morally and legally proper to distinguish between people who commit a crime out of viciousness and those who suffer serious mental illness. Mr. Bieber suffered from amphetamine delusional disorder, a serious psychotic illness recognized by the American Psychiatric Association. There was overwhelming evidence that he was out of control and did not know what he was doing at the time of the homicide.

The fact that ADD is brought about by years of amphetamine use should make no difference in an insanity case. This man's reason was destroyed by a serious illness. He should not be treated the same as a cold-blooded killer who carries out a vicious killing for reasons of hatred or personal gain. Mr. Bieber had no motive to injure the victim, and a jury should have been allowed to consider his mental illness.

Argument for the State: Your honors, there is no qualitative difference between a person who drinks or takes drugs knowing that he or she will be momentarily "mentally defective" as an immediate result and one who drinks or takes drugs knowing that he or she may be "mentally defective" as an eventual, long-term result. In both cases, the person is aware of the possible consequences of his or her actions. We do not believe that in the latter case, such knowledge should be excused simply because the resulting affliction is more severe.

It is a matter of common knowledge that the excessive use of liquor or drugs impairs the perceptual, judgmental, and volitional faculties of the user. Also, because the intoxication must be "self-induced," the defendant necessarily must have had the conscious ability to prevent this temporary incapacity from coming into being at all. Self-induced intoxication by its very nature involves culpability. The moral blameworthiness lies in the voluntary impairment of one's mental faculties with knowledge that the resulting condition is a source of potential danger to others.

As a matter of public policy, therefore, we must not excuse a defendant's actions, which endanger others, based upon a mental disturbance or illness that he or she actively and voluntarily contracted. There is no principled basis to distinguish between the short-term and long-term effects of voluntary intoxication by punishing the first and excusing the second. If anything, the moral blameworthiness would seem to be even greater with respect to the long-term effects of many, repeated instances of voluntary intoxication occurring over an extended period of time. We ask that you affirm.

Jury Role. The insanity defense creates fear and confusion in the public, but most experts believe the concern is unwarranted. A Connecticut study showed that the defense was invoked in only one-tenth of 1 percent of criminal prosecutions in that state, and that in over 90 percent of *those* cases it still failed. Juries are reluctant to acquit based on insanity, probably fearing that the defendant will soon be back on the streets. But just the opposite is true. Most defendants acquitted by reason of insanity spend more time in a mental hospital than convicts spend in prison for the same act.

ENTRAPMENT

You go to a fraternity party where you meet a friendly new frat member, Joey. After a drink or two, Joey asks if you can get him some marijuana. You tell him you never use drugs. A week later you accidentally meet Joey in the cafeteria and he repeats the question, promising a very large profit if you will supply him with an ounce. You again say "no thanks." About once a week Joey bumps into you, in the school hallways, in the bookstore, at parties. He continues to ask you to "get him some stuff," and his offers grow more lucrative. Finally, after six requests, you speak to someone who is reputed to deal in drugs. You buy an ounce, then offer it to Joey at a large markup. Joey gratefully hands over the money, takes your package—and flashes his badge in your face, identifying himself as an undercover agent of the State Police. You are speechless, which is fine, since Joey informs you that you have the right to remain silent.

Drugs are a deadly serious problem in our society, involved directly or indirectly in more than half of all street crime. We need creative police efforts. Has this one gone too far? The issue is **entrapment. When the government induces the defendant to break the law, the prosecution must prove beyond a reasonable doubt that the defendant was predisposed to commit the crime.**

If the government cannot prove predisposition, the defendant is not guilty. In other words, the goal is to separate the cases where the defendant was innocent before the government tempted him from those where the defendant was only too eager to break the law.

JACOBSON v. UNITED STATES

503 U.S. 540, 112 S. Ct. 1535, 1992 U.S. LEXIS 2117
United States Supreme Court, 1992

Facts: In 1984, Keith Jacobson, a 56-year-old Nebraska farmer, ordered two magazines from a California adult bookstore: *Bare Boys I* and *Bare Boys II*. The magazines showed photos of nude preteen and teenage boys. At that time, the magazines were legal. The pictures startled Jacobson, who had expected pictures of young men 18 and over. Later, federal law changed, making it illegal to receive through the mail any sexual pictures of children.

Postal inspectors found Jacobson's name on the customer list of the California bookstore and began a two and one-half year campaign to entice him into ordering material that had become illegal. A postal inspector sent him a letter from the "American Hedonist Society," a fictitious organization, urging that members had the right to "read what we desire." Jacobson joined, and answered a questionnaire about his sexual preferences.

Two more fictitious organizations, both the creation of the Postal Service, began mailing him information and questionnaires. Jacobson responded, saying that he liked "good looking young guys (in their late teens and early 20's) doing their thing together," and that he was opposed to pedophilia. After 26 months of periodic contacts, a third fictitious agency began to solicit Jacobson. Finally, Jacobson ordered some sexual material, which depicted young boys engaged in sexual activities. He was arrested and convicted of violating federal law.

Issue: Did the government entrap Jacobson?

Excerpts from Justice White's Decision: By the time petitioner finally placed his order, he had already been the target of 26 months of repeated mailings and communications from Government agents and fictitious organizations.

The sole piece of preinvestigation evidence is petitioner's order and receipt of the *Bare Boys* magazines. But this is scant if any proof of petitioner's predisposition to commit an illegal act, the criminal character of which a defendant is presumed to know. It may indicate a predisposition to view sexually-oriented photographs that are responsive to his sexual tastes; but evidence that merely indicates a generic inclination to act within a broad range, not all of which is criminal, is of little probative value in establishing predisposition. Furthermore, petitioner was acting within the law at the time he received these magazines.

Law enforcement officials go too far when they implant in the mind of an innocent person the disposition to commit the alleged offense and induce its commission in order that they may prosecute. When the Government's quest for convictions leads to the apprehension of an otherwise law-abiding citizen who, if left to his own devices, likely would have never run afoul of the law, the courts should intervene.

We *reverse* the Court of Appeals' judgment affirming the conviction of Keith Jacobson.

Excerpts from Justice O'Connor's Dissenting Opinon: Keith Jacobson was offered only two opportunities to buy child pornography through the mail. Both times, he ordered. Both times, he asked for opportunities to buy more.

The first time the Government sent Mr. Jacobson a catalog of illegal materials, he ordered a set of photographs advertised as picturing "young boys in sex action fun." He enclosed the following note with his order: "I received your brochure and decided to place an order. If I like your product, I will order more later." The second time the Government sent a catalog of illegal materials, Mr. Jacobson ordered a magazine called "Boys Who Love Boys," described as: "11 year old and 14 year old boys get it on in every way possible. Oral, anal sex and heavy masturbation. If you love boys, you will be delighted with this."

It was the jury's task, as the conscience of the community, to decide whether or not Mr. Jacobson was a willing participant in the criminal activity here or an innocent dupe. The jury is the traditional "defense against arbitrary law enforcement." There is no dispute that the jury in this case was fully and accurately instructed on the law of entrapment, and nonetheless found Mr. Jacobson guilty. Because I believe there was sufficient evidence to uphold the jury's verdict, I respectfully *dissent*.

Final Note on Entrapment. In the hypothetical on the fraternity undercover agent buying marijuana from a reluctant seller, most courts would agree that this was entrapment. The seller said "no" five times. Unless the government has other evidence that the defendant was involved in dealing drugs, there appears to be no predisposition, and the entrapment defense is valid.

JUSTIFICATION

A defendant may plead justification where he committed a criminal act in order to avoid a greater harm. The harm being avoided must be greater than the harm caused by the criminal act, it must be imminent, and there must be no other alternative course of action. This rarely successful defense works only when the facts are compelling.

Suppose Roger, the video thief, admits breaking into the store but denies stealing anything. He claims that earlier in the day he had accidentally left in the store newly purchased medicine for his seriously ill son. The son needed his nighttime dosage and no pharmacy would refill Roger's prescription. He either had to break into the store or see his son suffer a potentially fatal seizure. If that is true, it is justification.

DURESS

A defendant may plead duress if she can show that a threat by a third person caused her fear of imminent serious physical harm. The threatened harm must be physical. If Roger, the video thief, could show that a drug addict threatened to kill him if he did not steal the videos, he would have a valid duress defense.

By contrast, assume that Roger, a former accountant, stole the videos because he had been out of work for 14 months. A bank foreclosed his suburban home, and he had exhausted his savings during his job search. He and his two children were subsisting in an abandoned station wagon as his wife lay in a sanitorium, weak with tuberculosis. Roger was desperate for money to make a deposit on an apartment. His claim—and all claims—of *economic* duress will fail because there is no imminent physical harm.

CRIMES THAT HARM BUSINESS

Three major crimes involve taking money from businesses: larceny, fraud, and embezzlement. In each case, the criminal ends up with money or property that belongs to someone else.

LARCENY

It is holiday season at the mall, the period of greatest profits—and the most crime. At the Foot Forum, a teenager limps in wearing ragged sneakers and sneaks out wearing Super Rags, valued at $145. Down the aisle at a home furnishing store, a man is so taken by a $375 power saw that he takes it. Sweethearts swipe sweaters, pensioners pocket produce. All are committing larceny.

Larceny is the trespassory taking of personal property with the intent to steal it. "Trespassory taking" means that someone else originally has the property. The Super Rags are personal property (not real estate), they were in the possession of the Foot Forum, and the teenager deliberately left without paying, intending never to return the goods. That is larceny. By contrast, suppose Fast Eddie leaves Bloomingdale's in New York, descends to the subway system, and jumps over a turnstile without paying. Larceny? No. He has "taken" a service—the train ride—but not personal property.

Every day in the United States, over $25 million in merchandise is stolen from retail stores. Economists estimate that *12 cents out of every dollar* spent in retail stores covers the cost of shoplifting. Some criminal experts believe that drug addicts commit over half of all shoplifting to support their habits. Stores have added electronic surveillance, security patrols, and magnetic antitheft devices, but the problem will not disappear.

FRAUD

Robert Dorsey owned Bob's Highland Chrysler in Highland, Illinois. To finance his purchases, Dorsey had a "floor-plan" loan from the First National Bank of

Highland. Dorsey would order cars from Chrysler, and First National would pay Chrysler for them. In theory, Dorsey would sell the cars and repay First National.

Dorsey began to suffer money problems. Business at the dealership declined, and he was unable to support his extravagant lifestyle. In the spring of 1989, First National found evidence that Dorsey might have sold cars without paying off the loan. The bank contacted a state investigator who, in June 1990, notified Dorsey that he planned to review all dealership records. One week later, a fire engulfed Bob's Highland Chrysler.

Larry Gilbert, a fire investigator, discovered that an electric iron had been connected to a timer, plugged into an electrical outlet, and placed over a pile of papers and files concerning the dealership's financing. The files and the iron had been doused with an accelerant. Two weeks later, there was a second fire at the dealership, and this time investigators found the dealership sales records doused with gasoline.

The saddest part of this true story is that it is only too common. Some experts suggest that 1 percent of corporate revenues are wasted on fraud alone. Dorsey was convicted and imprisoned for committing two crimes that cost business billions of dollars annually—fraud and arson.[3]

Fraud refers to various crimes, all of which have a common element: **the deception of another person for the purpose of obtaining money or property from him.** Robert Dorsey's precise violation was bank fraud, a federal crime. It is **bank fraud** to use deceit to obtain money, assets, securities, or other property under the control of any financial institution. The maximum penalty is a fine of $1 million and/or a prison term of 30 years.[4]

Wire fraud and **mail fraud** are additional federal crimes, involving the use of interstate mail, telegram, telephone, radio, or television to obtain property by deceit.[5] For example, if Marsha makes an interstate phone call to sell land that she does not own, that is wire fraud.

Insurance fraud is another common crime. A Ford suddenly swerves in front of a Toyota, causing it to brake hard. A Mercedes, unable to stop, slams into the Toyota, as the Ford races away. Regrettable accident? No: a "swoop and squat" fraud scheme. The Ford and Toyota drivers were working together, hoping for an accident. The "injured" Toyota driver now goes to a third member of the fraud team—a dishonest doctor—who diagnoses serious back and neck injuries and predicts long-term pain and disability. The driver files a claim against the Mercedes's driver, whose insurer may be forced to pay tens or even hundreds of thousands of dollars for an accident that was no accident. Insurance companies investigate countless cases like this each year, trying to distinguish the honest victim from the criminal.

Finally, Stacey, the hospital executive described in the chapter's introduction, committed a fourth type of fraud. **Medicare fraud** includes using false statements, bribes, or kickbacks to obtain Medicare payments from the federal or state government.[6]

---

[3] *United States v. Dorsey*, 27 F.3d 285, 1994 U.S. App. LEXIS 15010 (7th Cir. 1994).

[4] 18 U.S.C. §1344.

[5] 18 U.S.C. §§1341–1346.

[6] 18 U.S.C. §§1320 et seq. (1994).

ARSON

Robert Dorsey, the Chrysler dealer, committed a second serious crime. **Arson** is the malicious use of fire or explosives to damage or destroy any real estate or personal property. It is both a federal and a state crime. Dorsey used arson to conceal his bank fraud. Most arsonists hope to collect on insurance policies. Every year thousands of buildings burn, particularly in economically depressed neighborhoods, as owners try to make a quick kill or extricate themselves from financial difficulties. We involuntarily subsidize their immorality by paying higher insurance premiums.

EMBEZZLEMENT

This crime also involves illegally obtaining property, but with one big difference: the culprit begins with legal possession. **Embezzlement is the fraudulent conversion of property already in the defendant's possession.**

Professor Beach, in North Dakota, asks his work-study student, Sandy, to drive his car to the repair shop. Sandy drives halfway and then hears on the car radio a forecast of snow. "I don't like snow," she thinks. Sandy turns south and never stops until she reaches Key West, Florida. "This is nicer," she murmurs. Sandy is innocent of larceny because she took the car keys with Beach's permission, but guilty of embezzlement because she converted the auto to her own use.

Wherever money abounds, embezzlement tempts. Banks are prime targets. A loan officer embezzled money simply by creating false loans and taking the money for himself. He paid off earlier loans by taking out new ones and managed to stay ahead of the game until he had embezzled over $5 million. He was eventually caught by a suspicious teller.[7]

Experts point out that much fraud and embezzlement are readily apparent and can be avoided, if corporate leaders will only open their eyes. Here are a few warning signs:

- An employee with extremely high expense accounts.
- Purchase orders for sums much higher than those of other departments or previous job holders.
- Dramatic changes in an employee's lifestyle.

Here are several commonsense steps to avoid embezzlement:

- Require counter-signing for all large purchases.
- Use independent auditors.
- Investigate promptly any employee whose lifestyle suddenly changes.
- Immediately review expense accounts that are significantly above average.

[7] *Peoples State Bank v. American Casualty Co. of Reading, Mich.*, No. Ed-8425-11, *Lawyers Weekly*, May 17, 1993, p. 6A.

COMPUTER CRIME

A 29-year-old computer whiz stole a car—using his keyboard. The man infiltrated a telephone company network and rigged a radio station's call-in promotion, winning himself a splendid new Porsche. He also damaged court-ordered wiretaps of alleged gangsters and may even have jammed the phones on an *Unsolved Mysteries* television episode in which *he was the featured fugitive!* A teenage boy crippled the airport control tower in Worcester, Massachusetts, by breaking into a Bell Atlantic network and causing a computer crash that eliminated all power at the airport. A Russian software expert wormed his way into the account database at one of the world's largest banks, jeopardizing millions of dollars in customer money until he was arrested. Computer crime is on the rise.

Experts estimate that electronic attacks by hackers and organized criminals cause billions of dollars in annual losses to American corporations. (See the statistics at http://www.web-police.org/.) The perpetrators may be teenagers out for a lark, gangsters intent on theft, angry ex-employees seeking revenge, or terrorists. (See the various scams and cons described at http://www.digitalcentury.com/encyclo/update/crime.html.) In all likelihood, less than 10 percent of computer crime is actually reported because large companies are embarrassed to acknowledge their vulnerability.

Three principal **federal statutes outlaw most unauthorized access to a computer.**[8] These laws prohibit unauthorized access to (1) any computer of the federal government, (2) any computer of a financial institution involved with the federal government, and (3) any computer by means of an internet that crosses state lines. The penalties include a maximum sentence of 20 years in prison. Someone who deliberately enters a computer without permission can be found guilty and ordered to pay restitution for all damages, even if he never intended to cause harm.[9] Most states have similar criminal statutes, outlawing electronic intrusion and theft of services or information. Stacey, the hospital executive who opened this chapter by sneaking into government computers, has clearly violated federal law and faces years of incarceration.

Here are a few steps that executives can take to prevent or respond to computer crime:

- Acknowledge vulnerability. Most, if not all, Fortune 500 companies have suffered unauthorized electronic intrusion, and your company probably will, too. The goal is to decrease the frequency and severity of wrongdoing.
- Recognize the likeliest computer criminal: your own employee. Insiders know the system and may abuse it. Provide written security regulations for all employees, and emphasize their importance. Permit computer access only to essential employees, and establish varying levels of security, when appropriate. Boot-level passwords must be mandatory for all employees, and computer users should be required to log file-level passwords onto highly sensitive documents. Maintain computer logs and audit records; in a

[8] 18 U.S.C. §§1030 (computers), 1029 (access devices), and 2511 (wiretaps).

[9] United States v. Sablan, 92 F.3d 865, 1996 U.S. App. LEXIS 19799 (9th Cir. 1996).

large company, hire monitors to search for unusual activity. Make sure that all laptops, desktops, and peripherals are physically secure after business hours.

- Beware of temporary employees, who may have no sense of loyalty to the firm and could be more likely than others to abuse access to a computer system. Employees facing termination must be monitored very closely.
- When you detect possible crimes, take the step that most companies reject: contact law enforcement officials. Temporary embarrassment is better than sustained losses. The FBI has a National Computer Crime Squad, whose agents are trained to deal with crime in private companies as well as incursions into government systems. A criminal who goes unpunished is certain to repeat her profitable crime.

CRIMES COMMITTED BY BUSINESS

A corporation can be found guilty of a crime based on the conduct of any of its **agents**, who include anyone undertaking work on behalf of the corporation. An agent can be a corporate officer, an accountant hired to audit a statement, a salesclerk, or almost any other person performing a job at the company's request.

If an agent commits a criminal act within the scope of his employment and with the intent to benefit the corporation, the company is liable.[10] This means that the agent himself must first be guilty. The normal requirements of *actus reus* and *mens rea* apply. If the agent is guilty, the corporation is, too.

Critics believe that the criminal law has gone too far. It is unfair, they argue, to impose *criminal* liability on a corporation, and thus penalize the shareholders, unless high-ranking officers were directly involved in the illegal conduct. The following case concerns a corporation's responsibility for an employee's death.

WISCONSIN v. KNUTSON, INC.

196 Wis. 2d 86, 537 N.W.2d 420,
1995 Wis. App. LEXIS 1223
Wisconsin Court of Appeals, 1995

Facts: Richard Knutson, Inc. (RKI) was constructing a sanitary sewer line for the city of Oconomowoc. An RKI crew attempted to place a section of corrugated metal pipe in a trench in order to remove groundwater. The backhoe operator misjudged the distance from the backhoe's boom to the overhead power lines and failed to realize he had placed the stick of the boom in contact with the wires. A crew member attempted to attach a chain to the backhoe's bucket and was instantly electrocuted.

The state charged RKI with negligent vehicular homicide under a statute that says: "Whoever causes the death of another human being by the negligent operation or handling of a vehicle is guilty of a Class E felony." The jury convicted, and RKI appealed, claiming that a corporation could not be held guilty under the statute.

---

[10] *New York Central & Hudson River R.R. Co. v. United States*, 212 U.S. 481, 29 S. Ct. 304, 1909 U.S. LEXIS 1832 (1909). And note that what counts is the intention to benefit, not actual benefit. A corporation will not escape liability by showing that the scheme failed.

Issue: May a corporation be guilty of vehicular homicide under the statute?

Excerpts from Judge Anderson's Decision: Here, the statute does not provide a definition of "whoever." We will thus employ extrinsic aids to uncover the legislature's intent.

LaFave and Scott [authors of a leading treatise] summarize the persuasive policy considerations supporting corporate criminal liability. Among those considerations is the factor that the corporate business entity has become a way of life in this country and the imposition of criminal liability is an essential part of the regulatory process. Another consideration centers on the premise that it would be unjust to single out one or more persons for criminal punishment when it is the corporate culture that is the origin of the criminal behavior. Also, the size of many corporations makes it impossible to adequately allocate responsibility to individuals.

An additional consideration is the indirect economic benefits that may accrue to the corporation through crimes against the person. To get these economic benefits, corporate management may shortcut expensive safety precautions, respond forcibly to strikes, or engage in criminal anticompetitive behavior. It has also been suggested that the free market system cannot be depended upon to guide corporate decisions in socially acceptable ways, and the threat of imposition of criminal liability is needed to deter inappropriate (criminal) corporate behavior. We agree that if a penal statute is intended to inhibit an act, a corporation is included within the class of perpetrators if to do so is within the spirit and purpose of the act. [The court concluded that a corporation may be guilty of vehicular homicide.]

Sufficiency of the Evidence: Homicide by negligent use of a vehicle has three elements: (1) that the defendant cause death (2) by criminal negligence (3) in the operation of a vehicle. Criminal negligence differs from ordinary negligence in two respects. First, the risk is more serious—death or great bodily harm as opposed to simple harm. Second, the risk must be more than an unreasonable risk—it must also be substantial.

RKI's management took no action to have the power lines de-energized or barriers erected; rather, management elected to merely warn employees about the overhead lines.

The evidence supports the conclusion that if RKI had enforced the written safety regulations of OSHA, had abided by its own written safety program and had complied with the contract requirements for construction on Wisconsin Electric's property, the electrocution death would likely not have happened. The finder of fact was justified in concluding that RKI operated vehicles in close proximity to the overhead power lines without recognizing the potential hazard to its employees in the vicinity of the vehicles. The jury could reasonably find that RKI's failure to take elementary precautions for the safety of its employees was a substantial cause of the electrocution death.

Judgment *affirmed*.

PUNISHING A CORPORATION

FINES

The most common punishment for a corporation is a fine. This makes sense in that the purpose of a business is to earn a profit, and a fine, theoretically, hurts. But most fines are modest by the present standards of corporate wealth.

Odwalla, Inc. sold fruit juices and nutritional shakes throughout much of the United States. A batch of its apple juice, which contained the highly toxic *E. coli* bacteria, killed a 16-month-old girl and seriously harmed 70 other people. Federal officials prosecuted, charging the company with violating food safety laws. Eventually, the company pleaded guilty, agreed to pay a $1.5 million fine, and submitted to a court-supervised probation for five years. Some public interest law groups applauded the punishment. Critics, though, complained that a million dollar fine is petty change for a large corporation and may have no deterrent effect on other companies. Odwalla has also paid millions of dollars to settle civil lawsuits brought by the injured consumers.

IMPRISONMENT

The corporation itself cannot, of course, be imprisoned—or can it? Federal Judge Doumar found the Allegheny Bottling Co. guilty of price-fixing.[11] Allegheny, a Pepsi distributor, had agreed with a Coca-Cola distributor to fix an artificially high price for both drinks, earning an illegal profit of at least $10 million. Judge Doumar fined the company $1 million and *sentenced the corporation to three years in prison*. He threatened to lock Allegheny's doors and bar the employees from entering for that period. Ultimately, he suspended the sentence, meaning that he would not carry it out provided that Allegheny obeyed the law. His creative approach to sentencing may influence future corporate punishments.

COMPLIANCE PROGRAMS

The **Federal Sentencing Guidelines** are the detailed rules that judges must follow when sentencing defendants convicted of crimes in federal court. The guidelines instruct judges to determine whether, at the time of the crime, the corporation had in place a serious **compliance program**, that is, a plan to prevent and detect criminal conduct at all levels of the company. A company that can point to a detailed, functioning compliance program may benefit from a dramatic reduction in the fine or other punishment meted out. Indeed, a tough compliance program may even convince federal investigators to curtail an investigation and to limit any prosecution to those directly involved, rather than attempting to get a conviction against high-ranking officers or the company itself.

To persuade prosecutors or judges that it seriously intended to follow the law, a company must demonstrate a thorough and effective compliance plan:

- The program must be reasonably capable of reducing the prospect of criminal conduct.
- Specific, high-level officers must be responsible for overseeing the program.
- The company must not place in charge any officers it knows or should have known, from past experience, that are likely to engage in illegal conduct.
- The company must effectively communicate the program to all employees and agents.
- The company must ensure compliance by monitoring employees in a position to cheat and by promptly disciplining any who break the law.

[11] *United States v. Allegheny Bottling Co.*, 695 F. Supp. 856, 1988 U.S. Dist. LEXIS 10693 (E.D. Va. 1988).

SELECTED CRIMES COMMITTED BY BUSINESS

WORKPLACE CRIMES

The workplace can be dangerous. Working on an assembly line exposes factory employees to fast-moving machinery. For a roofer, the first slip may be the last. The invisible radiation in a nuclear power plant can be deadlier than a bullet. The most important statute regulating the workplace is the federal **Occupational Safety and Health Act of 1970 (OSHA)**,[12] which sets safety standards for many industries.[13] May a state government go beyond standards set by OSHA and use the criminal law to punish dangerous conditions? In *People v. O'Neill*,[14] the courts of Illinois answered that question with a potent "yes," permitting a *murder prosecution* against corporate executives. Notice that whereas Wisconsin prosecuted RKI *Corporation* for vehicular homicide, Illinois brought this case against the corporate executives themselves.

Film Recovery Systems was an Illinois corporation in business to extract silver from used X-ray film and then resell it. Steven O'Neill was president of Film Recovery, Charles Kirschbaum was its plant manager, and Daniel Rodriguez the foreman. To extract the silver, workers at Film Recovery soaked the X-ray film in large, open, bubbling vats that contained sodium cyanide.

A worker named Stefan Golab became faint. He left the production area and walked to the lunchroom, where workers found him trembling and foaming at the mouth. He lost consciousness. Paramedics were unable to revive him. They rushed him to a hospital where he was pronounced dead on arrival. The Cook County medical examiner determined that Golab died from acute cyanide poisoning caused by inhalation of cyanide fumes in the plant.

Illinois indicted Film Recovery and several of its managers for murder. The indictment charged that O'Neill and Kirschbaum committed murder by failing to disclose to Golab that he was working with cyanide and other potentially lethal substances and by failing to provide him with appropriate and necessary safety equipment.

The case was tried to a judge without a jury. Workers testified that O'Neill, Kirschbaum, and other managers never told them they were using cyanide or that the fumes they inhaled could be harmful; that management made no effort to ventilate the factory; that Film Recovery gave the workers no goggles or protective clothing; that the chemicals they worked with burned their skin; that breathing was difficult in the plant because of strong, foul orders; and that workers suffered frequent dizziness, nausea, and vomiting.

The trial judge found O'Neill, Kirschbaum, and others guilty of murder. Illinois defines murder as performing an act that the defendant *knows will create a strong probability of death* in the victim, and the judge found they had done that. He found Film Recovery guilty of involuntary manslaughter. Involuntary manslaughter is *recklessly* performing an act that causes death. He sentenced O'Neill, Kirschbaum, and Rodriguez to 25 years in prison.

---

[12] 29 U.S.C. §§651 et seq. (1982).

[13] See Chapter 14, on employment law.

[14] 194 Ill. App. 3d 79, 550 N.E.2d 1090, 1990 Ill. App. LEXIS 65 (Ill. App. Ct. 1990).

The defendants appealed, contending that the verdicts were inconsistent. They argued, and the Illinois Court of Appeals agreed, that the judge had made contradictory findings. Murder required the specific intent of *knowing there was a strong probability of death,* whereas the manslaughter conviction required *reckless* conduct. The appeals court reversed the convictions and remanded for a new trial.

Moments before the new trial was to start, O'Neill, Kirschbaum, and Rodriguez all pleaded guilty to involuntary manslaughter. They received sentences of three years, two years, and four months, respectively.

MONEY LAUNDERING

Money laundering consists of taking the profits of criminal acts and either (1) using the money to promote crime or (2) attempting to conceal the source of the money.[15]

Money laundering is an essential part of the corrosive traffic in drugs. Profits, all in cash, mount so swiftly that the most difficult step for a successful dealer is to use the money without alerting the government. The *Hurley* case, which appears in the following section, details the intricate steps taken by one group of money launderers to make drug money look legitimate. Their profits were extraordinary—and their punishment fitting.

RICO

The **Racketeer Influenced and Corrupt Organizations Act (RICO)**[16] is one of the most powerful and controversial statutes ever written. Congress passed the law primarily to prevent gangsters from taking money they earned illegally and investing it in legitimate businesses. But RICO has expanded far beyond the original intentions of Congress and is now used more often against ordinary businesses than against organized criminals. Some regard this wide application as a tremendous advance in law enforcement, but others view it as an oppressive weapon used to club ethical companies into settlements they should never have to make.

RICO creates both criminal and civil law liabilities. The government may prosecute both individuals and organizations for violating RICO. For example, the government may prosecute a mobster, claiming that he has run a heroin ring for years. It may also prosecute an accounting firm, claiming that it lied about corporate assets in a stock sale, to make the shares appear more valuable than they really were. If the government proves its case, the defendant can be hit with large fines and a prison sentence of up to 20 years. RICO also permits the government to seek forfeiture of the defendant's property. A court may order a convicted defendant to hand over any property or money used in the criminal acts or derived from them. Forfeiture sums can be huge, as the *Hurley* case on the following page indicates.

RICO creates civil liability as well. The government, organizations, and individuals all have the right to file civil lawsuits, seeking damages and, if necessary, injunctions. For example, shareholders claiming that they were harmed by the accounting firm's lies could sue the firm for money lost in buying and

---

[15] 18 U.S.C. §§1956 et seq.

[16] 18 U.S.C. §§1961–1968.

selling the stock. RICO is powerful (and for defendants, frightening) in part because a civil plaintiff can recover **treble damages**, that is, a judgment for three times the harm actually suffered, and can also recover attorney's fees.

What is a violation of RICO? **RICO prohibits using two or more racketeering acts to accomplish any of these goals: (1) investing in or acquiring legitimate businesses with criminal money; (2) maintaining or acquiring businesses through criminal activity; or (3) operating businesses through criminal activity.**

What does that mean in English? It is a two-step process to prove that a person or an organization has violated RICO. We will assume that this is a criminal prosecution, though the steps are similar in a civil lawsuit.

- The prosecutor must show that the defendant committed two or more **racketeering acts**, which are any of a long list of specified crimes: embezzlement, arson, mail fraud, wire fraud, and so forth. Thus, if a gangster ordered a building torched in January and then burned a second building in October, that would be two racketeering acts. If a stockbroker told two customers that Bronx Gold Mines was a promising stock, when she knew that it was worthless, that would be two racketeering acts.
- The prosecutor must show that the defendant used these racketeering acts to accomplish one of the three *purposes* listed above. If the gangster committed two arsons and then used the insurance payments to buy a dry cleaning business, that would violate RICO. If the stockbroker gave fraudulent advice and used the commissions to buy advertising for her firm, that would violate RICO.

The following case involved money laundering and RICO violations.

UNITED STATES v. HURLEY

63 F.3d 1, 1995 U.S. App. LEXIS 19318
United States Court of Appeals for the First Circuit, 1995

Facts: Stephen Saccoccia owned several precious metals companies, including Saccoccia Coin Co. in Rhode Island; Trend Precious Metals in New York City; and two Los Angeles companies, International Metal Marketing and Clinton Import/Export. The federal government used RICO to prosecute Saccoccia and his wife, Donna, along with six others. The government claimed that the defendants engaged in dozens of *racketeering acts* by laundering money, and then used the profits to *invest in and maintain* the precious metals businesses. A jury convicted all eight. The trial court sentenced them to prison and ordered them to forfeit their criminal profits. Here are four of the dispositions, demonstrating that this was no mom-and-pop enterprise:

Defendant	Sentence	Forfeiture
Stephen Saccoccia	8.5 years; 3 years supervised release	$ 37,456,100.79
Joseph Saccoccia	10 years; 3 years supervised release	$ 37,456,100.79
Donna Saccoccia	14 years; 2 years supervised release	$136,344,231.86
Vincent Hurley	18 years; 3 years supervised release	$136,344,231.86

All of the defendants appealed, claiming that there was insufficient evidence of money laundering and, even if money laundering had occurred, of each defendant's involvement in it.

Issue: Was there sufficient evidence of money laundering, and of each defendant's involvement?

Excerpts from Judge Boudin's Decision: The laundering operation took several forms but each began with Stephen Saccoccia receiving large amounts of cash in New York, generated from the sale of cocaine. Often, Saccoccia would send one of his employees, usually unindicted co-conspirator Richard Gizzarelli, to a prearranged location, such as a street corner, to meet a customer's courier. Gizzarelli would bring the cash to the Trend office or Saccoccia's apartment in New York to count it.

The money then followed two different routes. Some of the cash would be used to purchase money orders or gold; the gold and some of the remaining cash would then be shipped to International Metal in Los Angeles. Much of the rest of the cash—up to $200,000 per day—would be sent to Trend and Saccoccia Coin in Rhode Island, either through armored car service or in the car of a Saccoccia employee.

Once the cash reached Rhode Island, it was counted by Saccoccia employees and divided into a number of packets in amounts either greater than or less than $10,000. Most of the cash went to the Trend office in Cranston. Saccoccia employees then drove to local banks where they purchased cashier's checks in amounts less than $10,000 payable to Trend, or cashier's checks in amounts greater than $10,000 payable to companies nominally owned by Hurley. The purpose of these maneuvers—called "smurfing" in law enforcement parlance—was to avoid or minimize the filing of accurate currency transaction reports, which are required by federal law for cash deposits in amounts of $10,000 or more.

Ultimately the local Rhode Island checks would be deposited in, and money from the Hurley accounts wired to, the Trend account at Citizens Bank in Rhode Island. A smaller portion of the cash sent to Rhode Island went to Saccoccia Coin. That cash was used to buy gold without documentation; the gold was then resold to legitimate companies in exchange for checks recorded as payments for gold sales. Some of the cash was also used in the ordinary operations of the Saccoccia Coin Shop, a heavily cash-based enterprise.

A staggering amount of money moved through this laundering operation. [During one 18 month period,] Stephen or Donna Saccoccia wired over $136 million to foreign bank accounts primarily in Colombia; more than $97 million of this amount was wired from the Trend account in Citizens Bank jointly controlled by Donna and Stephen. Apart from the $136 million, substantial sums were retained by the Saccoccias and their employees as compensation.

A rational jury could convict each appellant. Affirmed.

OTHER CRIMES

Additional crimes that affect business appear elsewhere in this text. An increasing number of federal and state statutes are designed to punish those who harm the environment. (See Chapter 24, on environmental law.) Antitrust violations, in which a corporation establishes a monopoly, can lead to criminal prosecutions. The *Allegheny Bottling* case, earlier in the chapter, in which the judge threatened to lock up the company, was an antitrust case based on price-fixing. (See Chapter 19, on antitrust law.) Finally, securities fraud is a crime and can lead to severe prison sentences. (See Chapter 18, on securities law.)

CONSTITUTIONAL PROTECTIONS

The police arrest Jake and charge him with armed robbery and rape. They claim that he entered a convenience store, took all the money from the cash register, robbed the clerk of her wristwatch, and then raped her. Jake refuses to talk, but the police are absolutely certain he is guilty. The community is outraged and wants a conviction. Should the police be allowed to question Jake for hours without stopping? May they lock him in a walk-in freezer? Beat him? After five hours of interrogation, followed by 10 hours in a freezer and a severe beating, Jake confesses. He tells the police where to find the money and the clerk's watch. Does his guilt render the police conduct acceptable?

These are issues of **criminal procedure**. We are no longer looking at the elements of particular crimes, as we have thus far, but at the *process of investigating, interrogating, and trying* a criminal defendant. The first 10 amendments to the United States Constitution, known as the Bill of Rights, control the behavior of all law enforcement officers.[17] In this section, we look at some of the protections these amendments offer.

THE CRIMINAL PROCESS

In order to understand constitutional safeguards, we need to know how the police do their work. The exact steps will vary from case to case, but the summary in Exhibit 7.1 highlights the important steps.

Exhibit 7.1

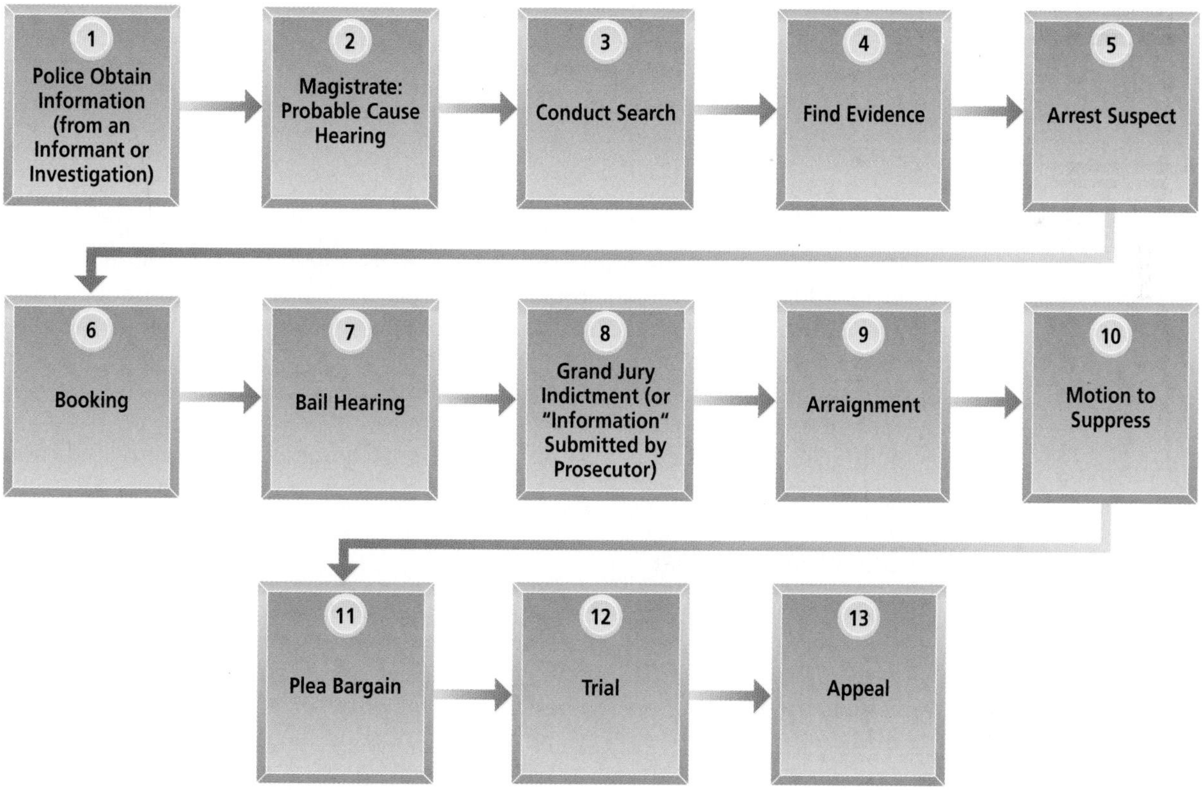

1. Police Obtain Information (from an Informant or Investigation)
2. Magistrate: Probable Cause Hearing
3. Conduct Search
4. Find Evidence
5. Arrest Suspect
6. Booking
7. Bail Hearing
8. Grand Jury Indictment (or "Information" Submitted by Prosecutor)
9. Arraignment
10. Motion to Suppress
11. Plea Bargain
12. Trial
13. Appeal

[17] As discussed in Chapter 5, on constitutional law, most of the protections as written apply only to state government or the federal government. But through the process of **incorporation**, almost all important criminal procedure rights have been expanded to apply to federal, state, and local governments.

INFORMANT

Yasmin is a secretary to Stacey, the Be Patient executive who opened this chapter. On her lunch break, Yasmin gets up the courage to telephone an FBI office and speaks to Moe, an agent. She reports that Stacey routinely charges the government for patients who do not exist. Moe arranges to interview Yasmin at her apartment that evening. He tape-records everything she says, including her own job history, her duties at Be Patient, and how she knows about the fraud. Yasmin has not only seen the false bills, she has entered some of them on computers. The next day, Moe prepares an affidavit for Yasmin to sign, detailing everything she told him. An **affidavit** is simply a written statement signed under oath.

WARRANT

Moe takes Yasmin's affidavit to a United States magistrate, an employee of the federal courts who is similar to a judge. Moe asks the magistrate to issue search warrants for Be Patient's patient records. A **search warrant** is written permission from a neutral official, such as the magistrate, to conduct a search. **A warrant must specify with reasonable certainty the place to be searched and the items to be seized.** This warrant application names all five of Be Patient's hospitals and asks to look through their admission notes, surgery notes, doctors' reports, and discharge data. It states that the records will be copied so that they can be compared with the bills the government has received.

PROBABLE CAUSE

The magistrate will issue a warrant only if there is probable cause. **Probable cause** means that based on all of the information presented **it is likely that evidence of crime will be found in the place mentioned**. The magistrate will look at Yasmin's affidavit to determine (1) whether the informant (Yasmin) is reliable and (2) whether she has a sound basis for the information. If Yasmin is a five-time drug offender whose information has proven wrong in the past, the warrant should not issue. Here, Yasmin's career record is good, she has no apparent motive to lie, and she is in an excellent position to know what she is talking about. The magistrate issues the warrant, specifying exactly what records may be examined.

SEARCH AND SEIZURE

Armed with the warrants, Moe and other agents arrive at the various hospitals, show the warrants, and take away the appropriate records. The **search** may not exceed what is described in the warrant. Even if Moe suspects that Dr. Narkem is illegally drugging certain patients, he may not seize test tube samples from the lab. He may take only the records described in the warrant.

The agents cart the records back to headquarters and enter the data on a computer. The computer compares the records of actual patients with the bills submitted to the government and indicates that 10 percent of all bills are for fictional patients. Moe summarizes the new data on additional affidavits and presents the affidavits to the magistrate, who issues **arrest warrants**, authorizing the FBI to arrest Stacey and others involved in the overbilling.

ARREST

Moe arrives at Be Patient and informs Stacey that she is under arrest. He reads her the *Miranda* warnings, discussed below. He drives Stacey to FBI headquarters where she is **booked**; that is, her name, photograph, and fingerprints are entered in a log, along with the charges. She is entitled to a prompt **bail hearing**. A judge or magistrate will set an amount of bail that she must pay in order to go free pending the trial. The purpose of bail is to ensure that Stacey will appear for all future court hearings.

INDICTMENT

Moe turns all of his evidence over to Larry, the local prosecutor for the United States. Larry presents the evidence to a **grand jury**, which is a group of ordinary citizens, like a trial jury. But the grand jury holds hearings for several weeks at a time, on many different cases. It is the grand jury's job to determine whether there is probable cause that this defendant committed the crime with which she is charged. Larry shows the computer comparison of the bills with the actual patient lists, and the grand jury votes to indict Stacey. An **indictment** is the government's formal charge that the defendant has committed a crime and must stand trial. The grand jury is persuaded that there is probable cause that Stacey billed for 1,550 nonexistent patients, charging the government for $290 million worth of services that were never performed. The grand jury indicts her for (1) Medicare fraud, (2) mail fraud, (3) computer crimes, and (4) RICO violations.[18] It also indicts Be Patient, Inc. and other employees.

ARRAIGNMENT

Stacey is ordered back to court. A clerk reads her the formal charges of the indictment. The judge asks whether Stacey has a lawyer, and of course she does. If she did not, the judge would urge her to get one quickly. If a defendant cannot afford a lawyer, the court will appoint one to represent her free of charge. The judge now asks the lawyer how Stacey pleads to the charges. Her lawyer answers that she pleads not guilty to all charges.

DISCOVERY

During the months before trial, both prosecution and defense will prepare the most effective case possible. There is less formal discovery than in civil trials. The prosecution is obligated to hand over any evidence favorable to the defense that the defense attorney requests. The defense has a more limited obligation to inform the prosecution. In most states, for example, if the defense will be based on an alibi, counsel must explain the alibi to the government before trial. In Stacey's case, most of the evidence is data that both sides already possess.

---

[18] In federal court, when the defendant is charged with a felony, formal charges may be made only by indictment. In many state court cases, the prosecutor is not required to seek an indictment. Instead, she may file an **information**, which is simply a formal written accusation. In state courts, most cases now begin by information.

MOTION TO SUPPRESS

If the defense claims that the prosecution obtained evidence illegally, it will move to suppress it. A **motion to suppress** is a request that the court exclude certain evidence because it was obtained in violation of the Constitution. We look at those violations later.

PLEA BARGAINING

Sometime before trial the two attorneys will meet to consider a **plea bargain**. A plea bargain is an agreement between prosecution and defense that the defendant will plead guilty to a reduced charge, and the prosecution will recommend to the judge a relatively lenient sentence. Based on the RICO violations alone, Stacey faces a possible 20-year prison sentence, along with a large fine and a devastating forfeiture order. The government makes this offer: Stacey will plead guilty to 100 counts of mail fraud; Be Patient will repay all $290 million and an additional $150 million in fines; the government will drop the RICO and computer crime charges and recommend to the judge that Stacey be fined only $1 million and sentenced to three years in prison. In the federal court system, about 75 percent of all prosecutions end in a plea bargain. In state court systems, the number is often higher.

Stacey agrees to the government's offer. The judge accepts the plea, and Stacey is fined and sentenced accordingly. A judge need not accept the bargain, but usually does.

TRIAL AND APPEAL

When there is no plea bargain, the case must go to trial. The mechanics of a criminal trial are similar to those for a civil trial, described in Chapter 3, on dispute resolution. It is the prosecution's job to convince the jury beyond a reasonable doubt that the defendant committed every element of the crime charged. The defense counsel will do everything possible to win an acquittal. In federal courts, prosecutors obtain a conviction in about 80 percent of cases; in state courts, the percentage is slightly lower. Convicted defendants have a right to appeal, and again, the appellate process is similar to that described in Chapter 3.

THE FOURTH AMENDMENT

The Fourth Amendment prohibits the government from making illegal searches and seizures. This amendment protects individuals, corporations, partnerships, and other organizations.

In general, the police must obtain a warrant before conducting a search. There are six exceptions to this rule, in which the police **may search without a warrant**:

- *Plain View.* Police may search if they see a machine gun, for example, sticking out from under the front seat of a parked car.
- *Stop and Frisk.* If police have an articulable reason for suspecting that someone may be armed and dangerous, they may pat him down.
- *Emergencies.* If police pursue a store robber and catch him, they may search.

- *Automobiles.* If police have lawfully stopped a car and observe evidence of other crimes in the car, such as burglary tools, they may search.
- *Lawful Arrest.* Police may always search a suspect they have arrested.
- *Consent.* If someone in lawful occupancy of a home gives consent to a search, the police may do so.

Apart from those six cases, a warrant is required. If the police search without one, they have violated the Fourth Amendment. Even a search conducted with a warrant can violate the amendment. **A search with a warrant violates the Fourth Amendment if:**

- There was no probable cause to issue the warrant
- The warrant does not specify the place to be searched and the things sought; or
- The search extends beyond what is specified in the warrant.

EXCLUSIONARY RULE

Under the exclusionary rule, evidence obtained illegally may not be used at trial against the victim of the search. If the police conduct a warrantless search that is not one of the six exceptions, any evidence they find will be excluded from the trial.

Suppose when Yasmin called the FBI, Moe simply drove straight to one of Be Patient's hospitals and grabbed patient records. Moe lacked a warrant, and his search would be illegal. Stacey's lawyer would file a **motion to suppress** the evidence. Before the trial starts, the judge would hold a hearing. If he agreed that the search was illegal, he would **exclude** the evidence, that is, refuse to allow it in trial. The government could go forward with the prosecution only if it had other evidence.[19]

Is the exclusionary rule a good idea? The Supreme Court created the exclusionary rule to ensure that police conduct legal searches. The theory is simple: if police know in advance that illegally obtained evidence cannot be used in court, they will not be tempted to make improper searches.

Opponents of the rule argue that a guilty person may go free because one police officer bungled. They are outraged by cases like *Coolidge v. New*

---

[19] There are two important exceptions to the exclusionary rule:
Inevitable Discovery Exception. Suppose that Moe's search of Be Patient is declared illegal. But then officials in the Medicare office testify that they were already aware of Be Patient's fraud, had already obtained some proof, and were about to seek a search warrant for the same records that Moe took. If the court believes the testimony, it will allow the evidence to be used. The inevitable discovery exception permits the use of evidence that would inevitably have been discovered even without the illegal search.
Good Faith Exception. Suppose the police use a search warrant believing it to be proper, but it later proves to have been defective. Is the search therefore illegal? No, said the Supreme Court in **United States v. Leon**, 468 U.S. 897, 104 S. Ct. 3405, 1984 U.S. LEXIS 153 (1984). As long as the police reasonably believed the warrant was valid, the search is legal. It would violate the Fourth Amendment if, for example, it was later shown that the police knew the affidavit used to obtain the warrant was filled with lies. In such a case, the search would be illegal and the evidence obtained would be excluded.

Hampshire.[20] Pamela Mason, a 14-year-old babysitter, was brutally murdered. Citizens of New Hampshire were furious, and the state's Attorney General personally led the investigation. Police found strong evidence that Edward Coolidge had done it. They took the evidence to the Attorney General who personally issued a search warrant. The search of Coolidge's car uncovered incriminating evidence, and he was found guilty of murder and sentenced to life in prison. But the United States Supreme Court reversed the conviction. The warrant had not been issued by a neutral magistrate. A law officer may not lead an investigation and simultaneously decide what searches are permissible.

After the Supreme Court reversed Coolidge's conviction, New Hampshire scheduled a new trial, attempting to convict him with evidence lawfully obtained. Before the trial began, Coolidge pleaded guilty to second degree murder. He was sentenced and remained in prison until his release in 1991, 27 years after his arrest.

In fact, very few people do go free because of the exclusionary rule. For example, a study by the General Accounting Office showed that suppression motions were filed in 10.5 percent of all federal prosecutions. But in 80 to 90 percent of those motions, the judge declared that the search was legal. Evidence was actually excluded in only 1.3 percent of all prosecutions. And in about one-half of *those* cases, the court convicted the defendant on other evidence. Only in 0.7 percent of all prosecutions did the defendant go free after the evidence was suppressed. Other studies reveal similar results.[21]

THE FIFTH AMENDMENT

The Fifth Amendment includes three important protections for criminal defendants: due process, double jeopardy, and self-incrimination.

DUE PROCESS

Due process requires fundamental fairness at all stages of the case. The basic elements of due process are discussed in Chapter 5, on constitutional law. In the context of criminal law, due process sets additional limits. The requirement that the prosecution disclose evidence favorable to the defendant is a due process rule. Similarly, if a witness says that a tall white male robbed the liquor store, it would violate due process for the police to place the male suspect in a lineup with four short women and two rabbits.

DOUBLE JEOPARDY

The prohibition against **double jeopardy** means that a criminal defendant may be prosecuted only once for a particular criminal offense. The purpose is to guarantee that the government may not destroy the lives of innocent citizens with repetitive prosecutions. Assume that Roger, the video thief, goes to trial. But the police officer cannot remember what the suspect looked like, and the jury acquits. Later, the prosecutor learns that a second witness actually

---

[20] 403 U.S. 443, 91 S. Ct. 2022, 1971 U.S. LEXIS 25 (1971).

[21] See the discussion in *United States v. Leon* (Justice Brennan, dissenting), cited at footnote 19.

videotaped Roger hauling cameras from the store. Too late. The Double Jeopardy Clause prohibits the state from retrying Roger for the same offense.

SELF-INCRIMINATION

The Fifth Amendment bars the government from forcing any person to testify against himself. In other words, the police may not use mental or physical coercion to force a confession out of someone. (This clause applies only to people; corporations and other organizations are not protected.) Society does not want a government that engages in torture. Such abuse might occasionally catch a criminal, but it would grievously injure innocent people and make all citizens fearful of the government that is supposed to represent them. Also, confessions that are forced out of someone are inherently unreliable. The defendant may confess simply to end the torture. So Jake, the rape-robbery suspect who confessed at the beginning of this section, will never hear his confession used against him in court. Unless the police have other evidence, he will walk free.

When the FBI arrests Stacey for Medicare fraud, she may refuse to answer any questions. The privilege against self-incrimination covers any statement that might help to prosecute her. So, if the FBI agent asks Stacey, "Did you commit Medicare fraud?" she will refuse to answer. If the agent asks, "What are your duties here?" she will also remain silent.

MIRANDA

In *Miranda v. Arizona*,[22] the Supreme Court ruled that a confession obtained from a custodial interrogation may not be used against a defendant unless he was first warned of his Fifth Amendment rights. A "custodial interrogation" means that the police have prevented the defendant from leaving (usually by arresting him) and are asking him questions. If they do that, and obtain a confession from the defendant, they may use that confession in court only if they first warned him of his Fifth Amendment rights. He must be told that:

- He has the right to remain silent
- Anything he says can be used against him at trial
- He has the right to a lawyer; and
- If he cannot afford a lawyer, the court will appoint one for him.

Exclusionary Rule (Again). If the police fail to give these warnings before interrogating a defendant, the exclusionary rule prohibits the prosecution from using any confession. The rationale is the same as for Fourth Amendment searches: suppressing the evidence means that the police will not attempt to get it illegally. But remember that the confession is void only if it results from custodial questioning. Suppose a police officer, investigating a bank robbery, asks a pedestrian if he noticed anything peculiar. The pedestrian says, "You mean after I robbed the bank?" Result? No custodial questioning, and the confession *may* be used against him.

---

[22] 384 U.S. 436, 86 S. Ct. 1602, 1966 U.S. LEXIS 2817 (1966).

THE SIXTH AMENDMENT

The Sixth Amendment guarantees the **right to a lawyer** at all important stages of the criminal process. Stacey, the hospital administrator, is entitled to have her lawyer present during custodial questioning and all court hearings. Because of this right, the government must **appoint a lawyer** to represent, free of charge, any defendant who cannot afford one.

THE EIGHTH AMENDMENT

The Eighth Amendment prohibits cruel and unusual punishment. The most frequently litigated issue under this clause has been capital punishment. In 1972, the United States Supreme Court ruled that Georgia had violated the Eighth Amendment by unfairly enforcing the death penalty, often penalizing African Americans and poor people more harshly than others. In response to the ruling, all states that allowed capital punishment revised their death penalty statutes. In 1976, in *Gregg v. Georgia*,[23] the Court upheld the revised Georgia statute. A state may execute a convicted criminal, provided its procedures guarantee basic fairness.

The Eighth Amendment also outlaws excessive fines. Forfeiture is the most controversial topic under this clause. **Forfeiture** is a *civil* law proceeding that is permitted by many different *criminal* statutes. Once a court has convicted a defendant under certain criminal statutes—such as RICO or a controlled substance law—the government may seek forfeiture of property associated with the criminal act. This can mean forfeiture of cash illegally earned from crime, or forfeiture of real estate where a drug sale took place. Edward Levin twice sold cocaine, with a total value of $250, at his own condominium, in which he had equity of about $68,000. After Levin was convicted of the cocaine sales, the court approved forfeiture of his condominium, finding that the difference between the crime and the penalty was not great enough to violate the Eighth Amendment.[24] The Supreme Court has ruled that the Eighth Amendment does govern forfeiture, but it has not specified when forfeiture becomes excessive.

CHAPTER CONCLUSION

Business crime appears in unexpected places, with surprising suspects. A corporate executive aware of its protean nature is in the best position to prevent it. Classic fraud and embezzlement schemes are often foiled with commonsense preventive measures. Federal Sentencing Guidelines make it eminently worthwhile for corporations to establish aggressive compliance programs. Sophisticated computer and money laundering crimes can be thwarted only with determination and the cooperation of citizens and police agencies. We can defeat business crime if we have the knowledge and the will.

---

[23] 428 U.S. 153, 96 S. Ct. 2909, 1976 U.S. LEXIS 82 (1976).

[24] *United States v. 38 Whalers Cove Drive*, 954 F.2d 29, 1991 U.S. App. LEXIS 26900 (2d Cir. 1991).

CHAPTER REVIEW

1. The rationales for punishment include restraint, deterrence, retribution, and rehabilitation.
2. In all prosecutions, the government must establish that the defendant's conduct was outlawed, that the defendant committed the *actus reus*, and that he had the necessary *mens rea*.
3. In addition to factual defenses, such as mistaken identity or alibi, a defendant may offer various legal defenses, including insanity, entrapment, justification, and duress.
4. Larceny is the trespassory taking of personal property with the intent to steal.
5. Fraud refers to a variety of crimes, all of which involve the deception of another person for the purpose of obtaining money or property.
6. Arson is the malicious use of fire or explosives to damage or destroy real estate or personal property.
7. Embezzlement is the fraudulent conversion of property already in the defendant's possession.
8. Computer crimes include unauthorized access to any government computers or to a computer by means of an interstate line.
9. If a company's agent commits a criminal act within the scope of her employment and with the intent to benefit the corporation, the company is liable.
10. Money laundering consists of taking profits from a criminal act and either using them to promote crime or attempting to conceal their source.
11. RICO prohibits using two or more racketeering acts to invest in legitimate business or carry on certain other criminal acts. RICO permits civil lawsuits as well as criminal prosecutions.
12. The Fourth Amendment prohibits the government from making illegal searches and seizures.
13. The Fifth Amendment requires due process in all criminal procedures and prohibits double jeopardy and self-incrimination.
14. The Sixth Amendment guarantees criminal defendants the right to a lawyer.
15. Information obtained in violation of the Fourth, Fifth, or Sixth Amendment is generally excluded from trial.
16. The Eighth Amendment prohibits excessive fines and cruel and unusual punishments.

PRACTICE TEST

1. Arnie owns a two-family house in a poor section of the city. A fire breaks out, destroying the building and causing $150,000 damage to an adjacent store. The state charges Arnie with arson. Simultaneously, Vickie, the store owner, sues Arnie for the damage to her property. Both cases are tried to juries, and the two juries hear identical evidence of Arnie's actions. But the criminal jury acquits Arnie, while the civil jury awards Vickie $150,000. How did that happen?
2. **YOU BE THE JUDGE WRITING PROBLEM** An undercover drug informant learned from a mutual friend that Philip Friedman "knew where to get marijuana." The informant asked Friedman three times to get him some marijuana, and Friedman agreed after the third request. Shortly thereafter, Friedman sold the informant a small amount of the drug. The informant later offered to sell Friedman three pounds of marijuana. They negotiated the price and then made the sale. Friedman was tried for trafficking in drugs. He argued entrapment. Was Friedman entrapped? **Argument for Friedman:** The undercover agent had to ask three times before Friedman sold him a small amount of drugs. A real drug dealer, predisposed to commit the crime, leaps at an opportunity to

sell. If the government spends time and money luring innocent people into the commission of crimes, all of us are the losers. **Argument for the Government:** Government officials suspected Friedman of being a sophisticated drug dealer, and they were right. When he had a chance to buy three pounds, a quantity only a dealer would purchase, he not only did so, but bargained with skill, showing a working knowledge of the business. Friedman was not entrapped—he was caught.

3. **RIGHT & WRONG** Nineteen-year-old David Lee Nagel viciously murdered his grandparents, stabbing them repeatedly and slitting their throats, all because they denied him use of the family car. He was tried for murder and found not guilty by reason of insanity. He has lived ever since in mental hospitals. In 1994, he applied for release. The two psychiatrists who examined him stated that he was no longer mentally ill and was a danger neither to society nor to himself. Yet the Georgia Supreme Court refused to release him, seemingly because of the brutality of the killings. Comment on the court's ruling. What is the rationale for treating an insane defendant differently from others? Do you find the theory persuasive? If you do, what result must logically follow when psychiatrists testify that the defendant is no longer a danger? Should the brutality of the crime be a factor in deciding whether to prolong the detention? If you do not accept the rationale for treating such defendants differently, explain why not.

4. National Medical Enterprises (NME) is a large for-profit hospital and health corporation. One of its hospitals, Los Altos Hospital, in Long Beach, California, paid one doctor $219,275, allegedly for consulting work. In fact, the government claimed, the payment was in exchange for the doctor's referring to the hospital a large number of Medicare patients. Other NME hospitals engaged in similar practices, said the government. What crime is the government accusing NME of committing?

5. Kathy Hathcoat was a teller at a Pendleton, Indiana, bank. In 1990, she began taking home money that belonged in her cash drawer. Her branch manager, Mary Jane Cooper, caught her. But rather than reporting Hathcoat, Cooper joined in. The two helped cover for each other by verifying that their cash drawers were in balance. They took nearly $200,000 before bank officials found them out. What criminal charge did the government bring against Hathcoat?

6. Federal law requires that all banks file reports with the IRS any time a customer engages in a cash transaction in an amount over $10,000. It is a crime for a bank to "structure" a cash transaction, that is, to break up a single transaction of more than $10,000 into two or more smaller transactions (and thus avoid the filing requirement). In *Ratzlaf v. United States*,[25] the Supreme Court held that in order to find a defendant guilty of structuring, the government must prove that he specifically intended to break the law, that is, that he knew what he was doing was a crime and meant to commit it. Congress promptly passed a law "undoing" *Ratzlaf*. A bank official can now be convicted on evidence that he structured a payment, even with no evidence that he knew it was a crime. The penalties are harsh. (1) Why is structuring so serious? (2) Why did Congress change the law about the defendant's intent?

7. Conley owned video poker machines. They are outlawed in Pennsylvania, but he placed them in bars and clubs. He used profits from the machines to buy more machines. Is he guilty of money laundering?

8. Northwest Telco Corp. (Telco) provides long-distance telephone service. Customers dial a

[25] 510 U.S. 135, 114 S. Ct. 655, 1994 U.S. LEXIS 936 (1994).

general access number, then enter a six-digit access code and then the phone number they want to call. A computer places the call and charges the account. On January 10, 1990, Cal Edwards, a Telco engineer, noticed that Telco's general access number was being dialed exactly every 40 seconds. After each dialing, a different six-digit number was entered, followed by a particular long-distance number. This continued from 10 P.M. to 6 A.M. Why was Edwards concerned?

9. Under a new British law, a police officer must now say the following to a suspect placed under arrest: "You do not have to say anything. But if you do not mention now something which you later use in your defense, the court may decide that your failure to mention it now strengthens the case against you. A record will be made of anything you say and it may be given in evidence if you are brought to trial." What does a police officer in the United States have to say, and what difference does it make at the time of an arrest?

10. After graduating from college, you work hard for 15 years, saving money to buy your dream property. Finally, you spend all your savings to buy a 300-acre farm with a splendid house and pool. Happy, an old college friend, stops by. She is saving her money to make a down payment on a coffee shop in town. You let her have a nice room in your big house for a few months, until she has the funds to make her down payment. But odd acquaintances stop by almost daily for short visits, and you realize that Happy is saving money from marijuana sales. You are unhappy with this, but out of loyalty you permit it to go on for a month. Why is that a big mistake?

INTERNET RESEARCH PROBLEM

A Web site devoted to scams is http://www.digitalcentury.com/encyclo/update/crime.html. Find a current con game that might victimize you. What steps should you take to avoid harm?

You can find further practice problems in the Online Quiz at http://beatty.westbuslaw.com or in the Study Guide that accompanies this text.

International Law

8

CHAPTER

The day after Anfernee graduates from business school, he opens a shop specializing in sports caps and funky hats. Sales are brisk, but Anfernee is making little profit because his American-made caps are expensive. Then an Asian company offers to sell him identical merchandise for 45 percent less than the American suppliers charge. Anfernee is elated, but quickly begins to wonder. Why is the new price so low? Are the foreign workers paid a living wage? Could the Asian company be using child labor? The sales representative expects Anfernee to sell no caps except his. Is that legal? He also requests a $50,000 cash "commission" to smooth the export process in his country. That sounds suspicious. The questions multiply without end. Will the contract be written in English or a foreign language? Must Anfernee pay in dollars or some other currency? The foreign company wants a letter of credit. What does that mean? What law will govern the agreement? If the caps are defective, how will disputes be resolved—and where?

Anfernee should put this lesson under his cap: the world is now one vast economy, and negotiations quickly cross borders. Transnational business grows with breathtaking speed. In 1992, the United States exported $448 billion worth of goods and services; by 2000, that figure had swelled to nearly $1.1 trillion—a 145 percent increase in eight years. Leading exports include industrial machinery, computers, aircraft and other transportation equipment, electronic equipment, and chemicals. Before long, the value of *services* sold internationally may surpass that of goods.

Here are the leading trading partners of the United States:

Rank	Country	Total Trade (Exports plus Imports), 2000 in billions of U.S. dollars[1]
1	Canada	$406
2	Mexico	248
3	Japan	212
4	China	116
5	Germany	87
6	United Kingdom	85
7	Korea	68
8	Taiwan	65
9	France	50
10	Singapore	37

The end is nowhere in sight. By 2010, a dozen developing countries with a total population 10 times that of the United States will account for 40 percent of all export opportunities. In China alone, roughly 300 million people are on the brink of joining the economic middle class—and the rank of potential consumers.

Who are the people who do all of this trading? Anfernee's modest sports cap concern is at one end of the spectrum. At the other are **multinational enterprises (MNEs)**, that is, companies doing business in several countries simultaneously.

MNEs and Power

An MNE can take various forms. It may be an Italian corporation with a wholly owned American subsidiary that manufactures electrical components in Alabama and sells them in Brazil. Or it could be a Japanese company that licenses a software company in India to manufacture computer programs for

[1] Source: United States Census Bureau, http://www.census.gov/foreign-trade/top/dst/2000

sale throughout Europe. One thing is constant: the power of these huge enterprises. Each of the top 10 MNEs earns annual revenue greater than the gross domestic product of *two-thirds of the world's nations*. Over 200 MNEs have annual sales exceeding $1 billion and more cash available at any one time than the majority of countries do. Money means power. This corporate might can be used to create jobs, train workers, and build life-saving medical equipment. Such power can also be used to corrupt government officials, rip up the environment, and exploit already impoverished workers. International law is vital.

TRADE REGULATION

Nations regulate international trade in many ways. In this section, we look at export and import controls that affect trade out of and into the United States. **Exporting** is shipping goods or services out of a country. The United States, with its huge farms, is the world's largest exporter of agricultural products. **Importing** is shipping goods and services into a country. The United States suffers trade deficits every year because the value of its imports exceeds that of its exports, as the chart above indicates.

EXPORT CONTROLS

You and a friend open an electronics business, intending to purchase goods in this country for sale abroad. A representative of TaiLectron stops in to see you. TaiLectron is a Taiwanese electronics company, and the firm wants you to obtain for it a certain kind of infrared dome. The representative explains that this electronic miracle helps helicopters identify nearby aircraft. You find a Pennsylvania company that manufactures the domes, and you realize that you can buy and sell them to TaiLectron for a handsome profit. Any reason not to? As a matter of fact, there is.

All nations limit what may be exported. In the United States, several statutes do this. The **Export Administration Act of 1985**[2] is one. This statute balances the need for free trade, which is essential in a capitalist society, with important requirements of national security. The statute permits the federal government to restrict exports if they endanger national security, harm foreign policy goals, or drain scarce materials.

The Secretary of Commerce makes a **Controlled Commodities List** of those items that meet any of these criteria. No one may export any commodity on the list without a license, and the license may well be denied. A second major limitation comes from the **Arms Export Control Act**.[3] This statute permits the president to create a second list of controlled goods, all related to military weaponry. Again, no person may export any listed item without a license.

The Arms Export Control Act will prohibit you from exporting the infrared domes to the Taiwan company. They are used in the guidance system of 9-M Sidewinder air-to-air missiles, one of the most sophisticated weapons in the American defense arsenal. The Taiwanese government has attempted to obtain

---

[2] 50 U.S.C. §2402 (1994).

[3] 22 U.S.C. §2778 (1994).

the equipment through official channels, but the American government has placed the domes on the list of restricted military items. When a U.S. citizen did send such goods to Taiwan, he was convicted and imprisoned.[4]

CYBERLAW

For national security reasons, the government clearly has the power to prohibit the export of military weaponry. But does that same rationale allow the government to halt the export of encryption technology over the Internet?

Encryption is the process of using a computer program to ensure secrecy. Ordinary text is run through the encryption program, which uses a mathematical formula to transform the information into ciphertext. The ciphertext is unreadable except by those possessing the program. When the encrypted message arrives at another computer, an appropriate *de*cryption program transforms the message back into ordinary text. Scientists and programmers use encryption to protect everything from e-mail to bank ATM transactions to military intelligence.

Using its power under the Arms Export Control Act, the federal government passed regulations that prohibit anyone from posting an encryption program on the Internet without first obtaining a license. Since the World Wide Web is exactly that—worldwide—placing such information on the Web effectively exports it. The government insisted it had the right to ensure that an encryption program could not harm the country's foreign policy or national security.

A graduate student, Daniel Bernstein, developed an encryption program he called "Snuffle." He wanted to place his program on the Web so that he could discuss it with other scientists, but was required to obtain permission first. Instead of filing for a license, he filed suit, claiming that the government's regulation violated his First Amendment right to free speech.

The United States District Court ruled that the licensing regulations did violate the First Amendment and that Bernstein was free to post his program on the Internet. The court explained that the government was engaging in *prior restraint*, that is, barring certain speech before it is uttered, which is almost always illegal. Simply claiming national security was not sufficient grounds for the government to impose this restraint. This is only the beginning of the battle over export control of that most precious commodity of all—information.[5]

IMPORT CONTROLS

TARIFFS

Tariffs are the most widespread method of limiting what may be imported into a nation. **A tariff is a duty (a tax) imposed on goods when they enter a country.** Nations use tariffs primarily to protect their domestic industries. Because the company importing the goods must pay this duty, the importer's costs increase, making the merchandise more expensive for consumers. This renders domestic products more attractive. High tariffs unquestionably help local industry, but

---

[4] *United States v. Tsai*, 954 F.2d 155, 1992 U.S. App. LEXIS 601 (3d Cir. 1992).

[5] Bernstein's court papers and related documents are—fittingly—available on the Web: http://www.eff.org/bernstein/Legal. The government's export regulations appear at http://www.eff.org/pub/Privacy/.

they proportionately harm local buyers. Consumers benefit from zero tariffs, because the unfettered competition drives down prices.

Tariffs change frequently. In 1997, the average duty on goods entering the United States was between 3 and 4 percent. But averages can be misleading. Mexican and Canadian companies send most of their products into the United States duty-free. Vietnam has a less favorable trade status, and tariffs on its goods average between 30 and 40 percent. Tariffs also vary widely from one product to another. Duties on textiles entering the United States are over 10 percent, but some other goods enter duty-free. Other nations also have uneven tariffs. Most goods enter Hong Kong duty-free, and Singapore's tariffs average only 0.3 percent. But duties average 30 percent in Angola and about 50 percent in Bangladesh. As we enter a new century, tariffs in most nations will decrease because of the General Agreement on Tariffs and Trade (GATT), discussed later in this chapter.

Classification. The U.S. Customs Service imposes tariffs at the point of entry into the United States. A customs official inspects the merchandise as it arrives and **classifies** it, in other words, decides precisely what the goods are. This decision is critical because the tariff will vary depending on the classification, as Nissan's recent experience demonstrates.

MARUBENI AMERICA CORP. v. UNITED STATES

35 F.3d 530, 1994 U.S. App. LEXIS 24288
United States Court of Appeals for the Federal Circuit, 1994

Facts: One of Japan's major auto manufacturers, Nissan, found itself in the late 1980s behind the competition in the market for four-wheel drive sport utility vehicles. In order to catch up quickly, Nissan used its "Hardbody" truck line as the basis for designing and building its "Pathfinder" sport utility vehicle. The Pathfinder incorporated the Hardbody's frame side rails, front cab, and front suspension.

When the 1989 models arrived in the United States, the Customs Service had to classify them. The Service uses a **tariff schedule** to do this, which is a long list of goods, carefully described, with each type of good assigned a particular duty. The tariff schedule gave the Customs Service two possible classifications:

> Section 8704.31.00: Motor vehicle for the transport of goods.
>
> Section 8703.23.00: Motor cars and other motor vehicles principally designed for the transport of persons, including stations wagons and racing cars.

The "transport of persons" tariff was 2.5 percent, but the "transport of goods" duty was exactly *10 times higher.* The Customs Service concluded that the Pathfinder was similar to a pickup truck, declared it a "transport of goods" vehicle, and imposed the 25 percent duty, ruining Nissan's hope for profits. The company appealed. Customs appeals go first to the **Court of International Trade (CIT)** in Washington, D.C. The CIT trial included test drives of the Pathfinder and comparison vehicles (including the Hardbody), as well as videotapes of competing vehicles and expert testimony about engineering, design, and marketing. (Indeed, the court's work was so thorough, the next time your car needs servicing you might ask the CIT to take a look at it.) The CIT reversed the Customs Service, declaring the Pathfinder a passenger car. The Service appealed to the federal court of appeals.

Issue: Is the Pathfinder a vehicle for passengers or for the transport of goods?

Excerpts from Judge Rich's Decision: The CIT recognized that the Pathfinder was basically derived from Nissan's Hardbody truck line yet the Pathfinder was based upon totally different design concepts than a truck. The CIT correctly pointed out these differences and more importantly, the reasons behind the design decisions, including the need for speed and economy in manufacturing to capture the changing market, a market into which Nissan was a late entrant. The fact that a vehicle is derived in part from a truck or from a sedan is not, without more, determinative of its intended principal design objectives which were passenger transport and off-road capability.

Substantial structural changes were necessary to meet the design criterion of transporting passengers. The addition of the rear passenger seat required that the gas tank be moved to the rear and the spare tire relocated. This effectively reduces the cargo carrying capacity. Of particular importance was the design of a new rear suspension that was developed specifically to provide a smooth ride for passengers. New and different cross beams, not present on the Hardbody frame, were added to the Pathfinder's frame to accommodate the above changes.

Other design aspects that point to a principal design for passengers include: the spare tire and the rear seat when folded down intrude upon the cargo space; the cargo area is carpeted; a separate window opening in the pop-up tailgate accommodates passengers loading and unloading small packages without having to lower the tailgate. In contrast, the Hardbody truck bed can accommodate loading with a fork lift, clearly a design feature for cargo.

We hold that the court applied the correct legal standards, and that the evidence of record supports the CIT's decision that the Pathfinder is principally designed for the transport of persons.

Valuation. After classifying the imported goods, customs officials impose the appropriate duty *ad valorem*, meaning "according to the value of the goods." In other words, the Service must determine the value of the merchandise before it can tax a percentage of that value. This step can be equally contentious, since goods will have different prices at each stage of manufacturing and delivery. The question is supposed to be settled by the **transaction value** of the goods, meaning the price actually paid for the merchandise when sold for export to the United States (plus shipping and other minor costs). But there is often room for debate, so importers use customs agents to help negotiate the most favorable valuation.

Duties for Dumping and Subsidizing

Dumping means selling merchandise at one price in the domestic market and at a cheaper, unfair price in an international market. Suppose a Singapore company, CelMaker, makes cellular telephones for $20 per unit and sells them in the United States for $12 each, vastly undercutting domestic American competitors. CelMaker may be willing to suffer short-term losses in order to drive out competitors for the American market. Once it has gained control of that market, it will raise its prices, more than compensating for its initial losses. And CelMaker may get help from its home government. Suppose the Singapore government prohibits foreign cellular phones from entering Singapore. CelMaker may sell its phones for $75 at home, earning such high profits that it can afford the temporary losses in America.

In the United States, the Commerce Department investigates suspected dumping. If the Department concludes that the foreign company is selling items at **less than fair value**, and that this harms an American industry, it will impose a **dumping duty** sufficiently high to put the foreign goods back on fair footing with domestic products.

Subsidized goods are also unfair. Suppose the Singapore government permits CelMaker to pay no taxes for 10 years. This enormous benefit will enable the company to produce cheap phones and undersell competitors. Again, the United States imposes a tariff on subsidized goods, called **countervailing duties**. If CelMaker sells phones for $15 that would cost an unsubsidized competitor $21 to make, it will pay a $6 countervailing duty on every phone entering the United States.

NONTARIFF BARRIERS

All countries use additional methods to limit imports. A **quota** is a limit on the quantity of a particular good that may enter a nation. For example, the United States, like most importing nations, has agreements with many developing nations, placing a quota on imported textiles. In some cases, textile imports from a particular country may grow by only a small percentage each year. Without such a limit, textile imports from the developing world would increase explosively because costs are so much lower there. As part of the GATT treaty (discussed below), the wealthier nations pledged to increase textile imports from the developing countries, but whether that has occurred is open to dispute.

An **import ban** means that particular goods are flatly prohibited. Some nations prohibit alcohol imports for religious reasons. The United States bars the importation of narcotic drugs. Virtually all countries from time to time halt certain goods for political purposes, for example, to protest the behavior of the exporting country. The United States has increasingly used economic sanctions in an effort to advance its foreign policy goals. During one 3-year period, it threatened or imposed sanctions 60 times, against 35 nations. Sanctions were aimed at Colombia for permitting drug trafficking; the Netherlands, Switzerland, and other European nations for trading with Cuba; and Taiwan for environmental violations. Proponents of such sanctions consider them essential components of an ethical foreign policy. Opponents regard them as hypocritical efforts to feel morally superior.

Import bans illustrate another aspect of international trade: commerce can be lucrative, but it is also inherently risky, as the following merchants learned.

B-WEST IMPORTS, INC. v. UNITED STATES

75 F.3d 633, 1996 U.S. App. LEXIS 915
United States Court of Appeals for the Federal Circuit, 1996
United States Court of Appeals for the Tenth Circuit, 1992

Facts: In May 1994, President Clinton announced that human rights abuses were continuing in China, and that the United States would respond with limited trade sanctions. The Arms Export Control Act (AECA), discussed earlier in this chapter, also permits the president to "control" arms imports. Based on that power, the president banned munitions from China. B-West Imports was in the business of importing arms from China. B-West and other companies filed suit, claiming that, while the president had the power to regulate arms trading, he had no authority to halt it altogether. The Court of International Trade ruled for the government, holding that the statutory power to "control" included the right to stop such importing altogether. B-West appealed.

Issue: Does the Arms Export Control Act authorize the president to ban arms from China?

Excerpts from Judge Bryson's Decision: Although [the AECA] grants the President the authority to "control" arms imports, the appellants argue that the term "control" limits the President to creating and operating a licensing system for arms importation, and does not allow the President to ban the importation of arms for which import permits have been granted. The appellants' statutory argument is unconvincing.

In the external sector of the national life, Congress does not ordinarily bind the President's hands so tightly that he cannot respond promptly to changing conditions or the fluctuating demands of foreign policy. Accordingly, when Congress uses far-reaching words in delegating authority to the President in the area of foreign relations, courts must assume, unless there is a specific contrary showing elsewhere in the statute or in the legislative history, that the legislators contemplate that the President may and will make full use of that power in any manner not inconsistent with the provisions or purposes of the Act. In a statute dealing with foreign affairs, a grant to the President which is expansive to the reader's eye should not be hemmed in or "cabined, cribbed, confined" by anxious judicial blinders.

As the court noted in [an earlier case] Presidents acting under broad statutory grants of authority have "imposed and lifted embargoes, prohibited and allowed exports, suspended and resumed commercial intercourse with foreign countries." Thus, the broad statutory delegation in the AECA incorporates "the historical authority of the President in the fields of foreign commerce and of importation into the country." We therefore agree with the Court of International Trade that the AECA authorizes the President not only to regulate arms importation through a licensing system, but also to prohibit particular importations altogether when the circumstances warrant.

Affirmed.

Money and politics are a volatile mix, as demonstrated by all recorded history from 3000 B.C. to the present. As long as nations have existed, they have engaged in disputes about quotas and import bans. And that is why more than 100 countries negotiated and signed the GATT treaty, the subject of the next section.

General Agreement on Tariffs and Trade (GATT)

What is GATT? The greatest boon to American commerce in a century. The worst assault on the American economy in 200 years. It depends on whom you ask. Let's start where everyone agrees.

GATT is the General Agreement on Tariffs and Trade. This massive international treaty has been negotiated on and off since the 1940s to eliminate trade barriers and bolster commerce. GATT has already had considerable effect. In 1947, the worldwide average tariff on industrial goods was about 40 percent. By 1994, it had fallen to an average of 5 percent. The world's economies have exploded over that half-century. Proponents of GATT applaud the agreement. Opponents scoff that both lower duties and higher trade would have arrived without GATT.

The most recent round of bargaining took seven hard years. Finally, in 1994, the United States and 125 other countries signed the treaty. A **signatory**, that is, a nation that signs a treaty, is still not bound by the agreement until it is **ratified**, that is, until the nation's legislature votes to honor it. In the United States, Congress voted to ratify GATT in December 1994. If the latest round of cuts is fully implemented, average duties in all signatories should drop to about 3.7 percent. Further, nearly half of all trade in industrial goods will be duty-free, at least in developed countries. That must be good—or is it?

TRADE

Leading supporters of GATT suggest that its lower tariffs will increase world trade by $500 billion by 2005. The U.S. economy alone should grow by $122 billion. But opponents argue that $500 billion is small potatoes when you realize that five years into the new century the total world trade will be about $30 *trillion*.

The United States should be one of the biggest beneficiaries of lower tariffs because for decades this country has imposed lower duties than most other nations. American companies will for once compete on equal footing. A typical American family's annual income should increase by about $1,700 due to the more vigorous domestic economy.

But opponents claim that the United States will be facing nations with unlimited pools of exploited labor. These countries will dominate labor-intensive merchandise such as textiles, eliminating millions of American jobs. It is not fair for U.S. companies to struggle against companies from countries that have no labor standards and dirt cheap pay. This country will lose millions of jobs. And because the job losses will come in low-end employment, those put out of work will be precisely the ones least able to find a new job. The chasm between rich and poor will widen, and we will all be the losers.

WORLD TRADE ORGANIZATION AND THE ENVIRONMENT

GATT created the **World Trade Organization (WTO)** to resolve trade disputes. The WTO is empowered to hear arguments from any signatory nation about tariff violations or nontariff barriers. This international "court" may order compliance from any nation violating GATT and may penalize countries by imposing trade sanctions. Proponents say that it is high time to have one international body to resolve complex issues impartially and create an international body of trade law that corporations can rely on when planning business.

Opponents fear the WTO. GATT generally prohibits nontariff barriers, and the WTO may well rule that some American economic sanctions, discussed above, violate the treaty.

In response, when Congress approved GATT, it passed a second law, nicknamed "Three strikes and *we're* out." Under the law, a group of American judges will review WTO decisions. If the panel concludes that there are three unprincipled rulings against the United States during any five-year period, it may recommend to Congress a vote to withdraw from the WTO. (The official Web site of the WTO, http://www.wto.org/, includes libraries on all sorts of international trade topics, from goods and services to dispute settlement and legal texts.)

Opponents of the new agreement argue that GATT may exacerbate environmental problems. Developing nations will be hard-pressed to pay for newly available goods. To bankroll the new expenses, these nations will sell off natural resources, eviscerating their future for short-term gains. Some statistics substantiate this argument. For example, the Costa Rican government decided to export more beef to the United States. To increase grazing land, the government has permitted over 80 percent of all Costa Rican rain forests to be leveled in just 20 years. The Philippines, in order to increase breeding areas for shrimp, has nearly destroyed its vast supply of mangrove swamps, which are essential spawning grounds for many species of ocean fish. But GATT supporters respond that such ecological damage has gone on independently of GATT and must be controlled accordingly.

Child labor is an even more wrenching issue. The practice exists to some degree in all countries and is common throughout the developing world. The International Labor Organization, an affiliate of the United Nations, estimates that 120 million children between the ages of 5 and 14 work full-time, and 130 million more labor part-time. As the world generally becomes more prosperous, this ugly problem has actually increased. Children in developing countries typically work in agriculture and domestic work, but many toil in mines and others in factories, making rugs, glass, clothing, and other goods.

The rug industry illustrates the international nature of this tragedy. In the 1970s, the Shah of Iran banned child labor in rug factories, but many manufacturers simply packed up and moved to southern Asia. Today, in India and Pakistan, tens of millions of children, some as young as four, toil in rug workrooms, seven days a week, 12 hours a day. Many, shackled to the looms they operate, are essentially slaves, working for pennies a day or, in some cases, for no money at all.

Child labor raises compelling moral questions—and economic ones as well. No American company can compete with an industry that uses slave labor. As discussed above, the United States is relatively quick to impose trade sanctions in response to moral issues. In 1997, Congress passed a statute prohibiting the import of goods created by forced or indentured child labor. The first suit under the new law targeted the carpet factories of southern Asia and sought an outright ban on most rugs from that area. Is this statute humane legislation or cultural imperialism dressed as a nontariff barrier? Should the voters of this country or the WTO decide the issue? In answering such difficult questions, we must bear in mind that child labor is truly universal. The United Farm Workers union estimates that 800,000 underage children help their migrant parents harvest U.S. crops—work that few Americans are willing to do.

Our response to such a troubling moral issue need not take the form of a statute or lawsuit. Duke University is one of the most popular names in sports apparel, and the school sells about $20 million worth of T-shirts, sweatshirts, jackets, caps, and other sportswear bearing its logo. To produce its clothing, the university licenses about 700 companies in the United States and 10 foreign countries. In response to the troubling issue of child labor, Duke adopted a code of conduct that prohibits its manufacturers from using forced or child labor and requires all of the firms to pay a minimum wage, permit union organizing, and maintain a safe workplace. The university plans to monitor the companies producing its apparel and terminate the contract for any firm that violates its rules.

INTELLECTUAL PROPERTY

Some foreign countries, particularly developing nations, have long ignored U.S. copyrights and patents. GATT changes things. It allows this country to halt duty-free imports from, and assess tariffs against, a nation that refuses to honor American copyrights or patents.

In addition, GATT creates certain new types of intellectual property. Rock bands and many performing artists have long complained of "bootlegging." When someone attending a concert makes an unauthorized recording or videotape and then sells it, that is a bootlegged version. Bootlegging is a common practice, earning millions of dollars for people who have contributed nothing to the performance. Under GATT, bootlegging is, for the first time, clearly outlawed in all signatory countries.

GATT SUMMARY

The WTO has already enjoyed some important successes. Under the agency's supervision, 68 of the leading economic powers negotiated a new telecommunications treaty, opening a $600 billion industry to international competition for the first time. And the WTO has resolved many trade disputes that would otherwise have led to bitter tariff wars. The United States has brought over two dozen cases to the agency in its early years, winning some and losing others.

The first major loss concerned film. Eastman Kodak had long complained that the Japanese government, though never prohibiting imports of foreign film, had worked closely with Fuji and other Japanese film manufacturers to make it nearly impossible for American companies to compete. The WTO shocked U.S. officials when it ruled in favor of Fuji, declaring that there were no barriers to American competition. But even that "loss" may have promoted international trade, as the Japanese government guaranteed open markets, and U.S. officials asserted they would monitor implementation of the promises. Other countries have settled claims to avoid a fight in the WTO: Turkey eliminated discriminatory taxes on box office receipts for American films, and Portugal began protecting patents on U.S. pharmaceuticals.

It will be many years before we can fairly evaluate this enormous new treaty. In all likelihood, some of the most extreme claims will prove false, and the agreement's effects will evolve somewhere in the middle. Unquestionably, some industries will suffer, forcing workers into unemployment. Others will discover and exploit lucrative opportunities. Certainly, the environment must be guarded far more carefully than it currently is, whether GATT survives a decade or a century. Perhaps the final cost/benefit analysis of GATT will be decided not by the letter of its voluminous pages but by the spirit and goodwill of those who implement it.

REGIONAL AGREEMENTS

Many regional agreements also regulate international trade. We will briefly describe some that affect the United States.

THE EUROPEAN UNION

The European Union (EU) used to be known as the Common Market. The original six members—Belgium, France, Luxembourg, the Netherlands, West Germany, and Italy—have been joined by Ireland, Denmark, the United Kingdom, Greece, Portugal, Spain, Austria, Finland, and Sweden.

The EU is one of the world's most powerful associations, with a prosperous population of over 300 million. Its sophisticated legal system sets Union-wide standards for tariffs, dumping, subsidies, antitrust, transportation, and many other issues. The first goals of the EU were to eliminate trade barriers between member nations, establish common tariffs with respect to external countries, permit the free movement of citizens across its borders, and coordinate its agricultural and fishing policies for the collective good. After achieving most of

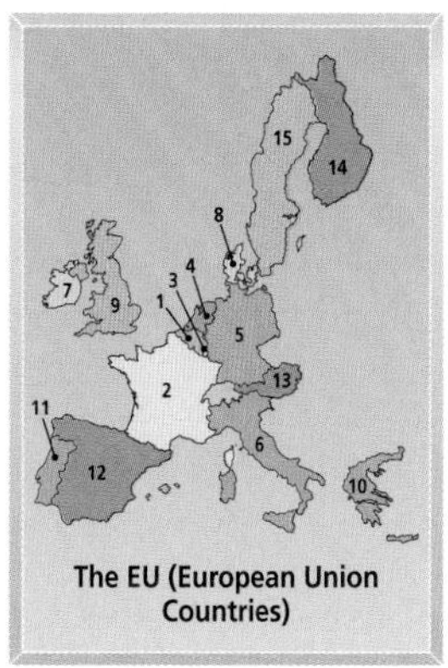
The EU (European Union Countries)

1 Belgium
2 France
3 Luxembourg
4 The Netherlands
5 Germany
6 Italy
7 Ireland
8 Denmark
9 The United Kingdom
10 Greece
11 Portugal
12 Spain
13 Austria
14 Finland
15 Sweden

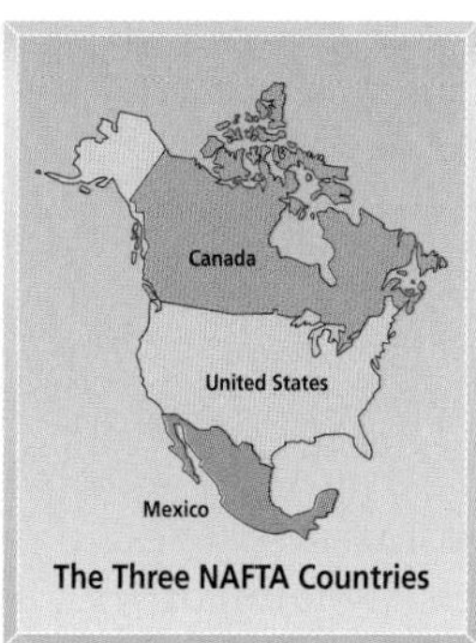

The Three NAFTA Countries

those goals, the EU successfully introduced a common currency, the euro, in all but a few of its member countries.

NAFTA

In 1993, the United States, Canada, and Mexico signed the **North American Free Trade Agreement (NAFTA)**. The principal goal was to eliminate almost all trade barriers, tariff and nontariff, between the three nations. Like GATT, this trilateral (three-nation) compact has been controversial. It is similarly too early to know its overall effects, and there will probably never be agreement on NAFTA's value because the treaty has enriched some while impoverishing others. Unquestionably, trade between the three nations has increased enormously. Mexico now sells more to the United States than do Germany and the United Kingdom combined. The balance of trade between Mexico and the United States has changed dramatically, from a $5.4 billion American surplus in 1992 to an $18 billion deficit in 1996.

Opponents of the treaty argue that NAFTA costs the United States jobs and lowers the living standards of American workers by forcing them to compete with low-paid labor. For example, Swingline Staplers closed a factory in Queens, New York, after 75 years of operation and moved to Mexico. Instead of paying its American workers $11.58 per hour, Swingline pays Mexican workers 50 cents an hour to do the same job. Proponents contend that although some jobs are lost, many others are gained, especially in fields with a future, such as high technology. They claim that as new jobs invigorate the Mexican economy, consumers there will be able to afford American goods for the first time, providing an enormous new market. Both Canadian and Mexican law are available online at http://www.lawsource.com/also/.

ASEAN

The Association of South-East Asian Nations (ASEAN) consists of nine countries: Brunei, Indonesia, Laos, Malaysia, Myanmar, the Philippines, Singapore, Thailand, and Vietnam. The group has negotiated for several years to reduce tariffs and aims to eliminate all duties between its members by 2003.

MERCOSUR

Brazil, Argentina, Uruguay, and Paraguay formed Mercosur to improve commerce among the four South American nations. Trade has in fact increased between Latin America's powerhouse economy, Brazil, and the three other countries. The group is currently considering the creation of a common currency, similar to the euro.

INTERNATIONAL SALES AGREEMENTS

Cowboy boots are hot in France. Actually, they can be uncomfortable no matter where you walk, but the point is they are selling fast in the land of Monet and Debussy. Big Heel, Inc., your small company in Tucson, Arizona, makes superb boots with exquisite detailing, and you realize that France could be a bonanza.

Your first decision is how to produce and sell the boots in France. For our purposes, Big Heel has three choices:

- **Direct Sales.** You can continue to manufacture the boots in Tucson and sell them directly to French retailers.
- **Indirect Sales.** You can manufacture the boots in Tucson and use a French distributor to wholesale them to French stores.
- **Licensing.** You can license a French manufacturer to make Big Heel boots in France and wholesale them.

Each method presents advantages and difficulties. Doing business effectively in a foreign country also requires an understanding of that nation's personal customs and business practices. For a useful discussion of how human interactions affect commerce in Mexico, see http://www.cs.unb.ca/~alopez-o/busfaq.html.

DIRECT SALES

You decide to sell the boots directly. Le Pied D'Or, a new, fast-growing French chain of shoe stores, is interested in buying 10,000 pairs of your boots, at about $300 per pair. You must focus on two principal issues: the sales contract and letters of credit. You are wise enough to know that you must have a written contract—$3 million is a lot of money for Big Heel.

This is a contract for the sale of goods. **Goods** are things that can be moved, such as boots, airplanes, pencils, and computers. A sale of goods is governed by different law than the sale of real estate (e.g., a house) or securities (e.g., a share of stock) or services (e.g., accounting).

WHAT LAW GOVERNS THE SALE OF GOODS?

Potentially, three conflicting laws could govern your boot contract: Arizona law, French law, and an international treaty. Each is different, and it is therefore essential to negotiate which law will control.

Because this contract is for the sale of goods, Arizona law is its **Uniform Commercial Code (UCC)**. The UCC is discussed in the chapters on commercial transactions. It is a statute that has taken the common law principles of contract and modified them to meet the needs of contemporary business. Article 2 of the UCC governs the sale of goods. American business lawyers are familiar with the UCC and will generally prefer that it govern. French law is based on **Roman law** and the **Napoleonic Code** and is obviously different. French lawyers and business executives are naturally partial to it. How to compromise? Perhaps by using a neutral law.

The **United Nations Convention on Contracts for the International Sale of Goods (CISG)** is the result of 50 years of work by various international groups, all seeking to create a uniform, international law on this important subject. Finally, in 1980, a United Nations conference adopted the CISG, though it became the law in individual nations only if and when they adopted it. The United States adopted the CISG in 1988. As of 1996, 46 countries had joined, including most of the principal trading partners of the United States.

The CISG applies automatically to any contract for the sale of goods between two parties, from different countries, each of which is a signatory. France and the United States have both signed. Thus the CISG automatically applies to the Big Heel–Pied D'Or deal unless the parties *specifically opt out*. If the parties want to be governed by other law, they must state very clearly that they exclude the CISG and elect, for example, the UCC.

PREVENTIVE Law

Should the parties allow the CISG to govern? They can make an intelligent choice by first understanding how the CISG differs from other law. Here are a few key differences between the CISG and the UCC:

- *Must the contract be written?* Under the UCC, a contract for the sale of goods valued at over $500 generally must be written to be enforceable. But the CISG does not require a writing for any contract. Be advised that discussions you consider informal or preliminary might create a contract under the CISG.
- *When is an offer irrevocable?* The UCC declares that an offer is irrevocable only if it is in writing and states that it will be held open for a fixed period. But the CISG makes some offers irrevocable even if unwritten.
- *What if an acceptance includes new terms?* Under the UCC, an acceptance generally creates a contract, even if it uses new terms. But the CISG insists on an acceptance that is a "mirror image" of the offer. Almost anything else constitutes a rejection.
- *What remedies are available?* The UCC entitles a plaintiff only to money damages for breach of a sales contract. But the CISG permits many plaintiffs to seek specific performance of the contract, that is, to force the other party to perform the contract.

CHOICE OF FORUM

The parties must decide not only what law governs, but where disagreements will be resolved. The French and American legal systems are dramatically different. In a French civil lawsuit, generally neither side is entitled to depose the other or to obtain interrogatories or even documents, in sharp contrast to the American system where such discovery methods dominate litigation. American lawyers, accustomed to discovery to prepare a case and advance settlement talks, are unnerved by the French system. Similarly, French lawyers are dismayed at the idea of spending two years taking depositions, exchanging paper, and arguing motions, all at great expense. At trial, the contrasts grow. In a French civil trial, there is generally no right to a jury. The rules of evidence are more flexible (and unpredictable), neither side employs its own expert witnesses, and the parties themselves never appear as witnesses.

CHOICE OF LANGUAGE AND CURRENCY

The parties must select a language for the contract and a currency for payment. Language counts because legal terms seldom translate literally. Currency is vital because the exchange rate may alter between the signing and payment. When the Indonesian rupiah plummeted at the end of 1997, an Indonesian company that had contracted in 1997 to buy U.S. computer hardware with dollars found itself paying 85 percent more than expected in March 1998. To avoid such calamities, companies engaged in international commerce often purchase from currency dealers a guarantee to obtain the needed currency at a future date for a guaranteed price. Assuming that Big Heel insists on being paid in U.S. dollars, Pied D'Or could obtain a quote from a currency dealer as to the present cost of obtaining $3 million at the time the boots are to be delivered. Pied D'Or might pay a 5 percent premium for this guarantee, but it will have insured itself against disastrous currency changes. (For up-to-the-minute conversion rates between virtually any two currencies, travel no further than http://www.oanda.com/cgi-bin/ncc.)

Choices Made. The parties agree that the contract price will be paid in U.S. dollars. Pied D'Or is unfamiliar with the UCC and absolutely refuses to make a deal unless either French law or the CISG governs. Your lawyer, Susan Fisher, recommends accepting the CISG, provided that the contract is written in English and that any disputes will be resolved in Arizona courts. Pied D'Or balks at this, but Fisher presses hard, and ultimately those are the terms agreed upon. Fisher is delighted with the arrangement, pointing out that the CISG provisions can all be taken into account as the contract is written, and that by using Arizona courts to settle any dispute, Big Heel has an advantage in terms of familiarity and location.

LETTER OF CREDIT

Because Pied D'Or is new and fast growing, you are not sure it will be able to foot the bill. Pied D'Or provides a letter of reference from its bank, La Banque Bouffon, but this is a small bank in Pleasanterie, France, unfamiliar to you. You need greater assurance of payment, and Fisher recommends that payment be made by **letter of credit**. Here is how the letter will work.

Big Heel demands that the contract include a provision requiring payment by confirmed, irrevocable letter of credit. Le Pied D'Or agrees. The French company now contacts its bank, La Banque Bouffon, and instructs Bouffon to issue a letter of credit to Big Heel. The letter of credit is a promise *by the bank itself* to pay Big Heel, if Big Heel presents certain documents. Banque Bouffon, of course, expects to be repaid by Pied D'Or. The bank is in a good position to assess Pied D'Or's creditworthiness, since it is local and can do any investigating it wants before issuing the credit. It may also insist that Pied D'Or give Bouffon a mortgage on property, or that Pied D'Or deposit money in a separate Bouffon account. Pied D'Or is the **account party** on the letter of credit, and Big Heel is the **beneficiary**.

But at Big Heel you are still not entirely satisfied about getting paid because you don't know anything about Bouffon. That is why you have required a *confirmed* letter of credit. Bouffon will forward its letter of credit to Big Heel's own bank, the Bandito Trust Company of Tucson. Bandito examines the letter and then *confirms* the letter. This is *Bandito's own guarantee* that it will pay Big Heel. Bandito will do this only if it knows, through international banking contacts, that Bouffon is a sound bank. The risk has now been spread to two banks, and at Big Heel you are confident of payment.

You get busy, make excellent boots, and pack them. When they are ready, you truck them to Galveston, where they are taken alongside a ship, *Le Fond de la Mer*. Your agent presents the goods to the ship's officials, along with customs documents that describe the goods. *Le Fond de la Mer*'s officer in turn issues your agent a **negotiable bill of lading**. This document describes exactly the goods received—their quantity, color, quality, and anything else important.

You now take the negotiable bill of lading to Bandito Trust. You also present to Bandito a **draft**, which is simply a formal order to Bandito to pay, based on the letter of credit. Bandito will look closely at the bill of lading, which must specify *precisely* the goods described in the letter of credit. Why so nitpicky? Because the bank is dealing only in paper. It never sees the boots. It is exchanging $3 million of its own money based on instructions in the letter of credit. It should pay only if the bill of lading indicates that *Le Fond de la Mer* received exactly what is described in the letter of credit. Bandito will decide whether the bill of lading is *conforming* or *nonconforming*. If the terms of both documents are identical, the bill of lading is conforming and Bandito must pay. If the terms vary, the bill of lading is nonconforming and Bandito will deny payment. Thus, if the bill of lading indicated 9,000 pairs of boots and 1,000 pairs of sneakers, it is nonconforming and Big Heel would get no money.

Bandito concludes that the documents are conforming, so it issues a check to Big Heel for $3 million. In return, you endorse the bill of lading and other documents over to the Bandito Bank, which endorses the same documents and sends them to Banque Bouffon. Bouffon makes the same minute inspection and then writes a check to Bandito. Bouffon then demands payment from Le Pied D'Or. Pied D'Or pays its bank, receiving in exchange the bill of lading and customs documents. Note that payment in all stages is now complete, though the boots are still rolling on the high seas. Finally, when the boots arrive in Le Havre, Pied D'Or trucks roll up to the wharf and, using the bill of lading and customs documents, collect the boots. See Exhibit 8.1.

Exhibit 8.1

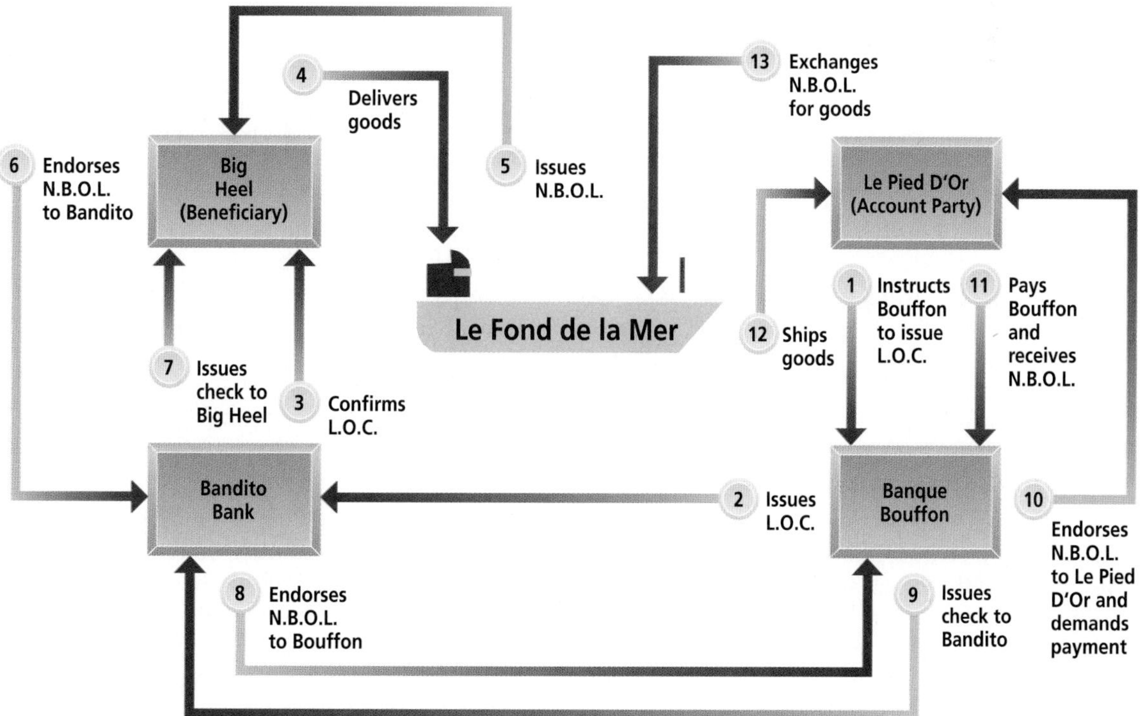

Good news: They fit! Not all customers walk away in such comfort, as the following case indicates.

CENTRIFUGAL CASTING MACHINE CO., INC. v. AMERICAN BANK & TRUST CO.

966 F.2d 1348, 1992 U.S. App. LEXIS 13089
United States Court of Appeals for the Tenth Circuit, 1992

Facts: Centrifugal Casting Machine Co. (CCM) entered into a contract with the State Machinery Trading Co. (SMTC), an agency of the Iraqi government. CCM agreed to manufacture cast iron pipe plant equipment for a total price of $27 million. The contract specified payment of the full amount by confirmed irrevocable letter of credit. The Central Bank of Iraq then issued the letter, on behalf of SMTC (the "account party") to be paid to CCM (the "beneficiary"). The Banca Nazionale del Lavorov (BNL) confirmed the letter.

Following Iraq's invasion of Kuwait on August 2, 1990, President Bush issued two executive orders blocking the transfer of property in the United States in which Iraq held any interest. In other words, no one could use, buy, or sell any Iraqi property or cash. When CCM attempted to draw upon the letter of credit, the United States government intervened. The government claimed that like all Iraqi money in the United States, this money was frozen by the executive order. The United States District Court rejected the government's claim, and the government appealed.

Issue: Is CCM entitled to be paid pursuant to the letter of credit?

Excerpts from Judge Sentelle's Decision: The United States contends on appeal that the freeze of Iraq's assets furthers national policy to punish Iraq by preventing it from obtaining economic benefits from transactions with American citizens, and by preserving such assets both for use as a bargaining chip in resolving this country's differences with Iraq and as a source of compensation for claims Americans may have against Iraq. We agree that these policy considerations are compelling and that we are therefore required to construe Iraqi property interests broadly. However, we are not persuaded these policies would be furthered by [creating] a property interest on behalf of Iraq that would not otherwise be cognizable under governing legal principles.

Two interrelated features of the letter of credit provide it with its unique value in the marketplace and are of critical importance in our consideration of the United States's claim here. First, the simple result [of a letter of credit] is that the issuer [i.e., the bank] substitutes its credit, preferred by the beneficiary, for that of the account party. Second, the issuer's obligation to pay on a letter of credit is completely independent from the underlying commercial transaction between the beneficiary and the account party. Significantly, the issuer must honor a proper demand even though the beneficiary has breached the underlying contract; even though the insolvency of the account party renders reimbursement impossible; and notwithstanding supervening illegality, impossibility, war or insurrection. This principle of independence is universally viewed as essential to the proper functioning of a letter of credit and to its particular value, i.e., its certainty of payment.

This assurance of payment gives letters of credit a central role in commercial dealings, and gives them a particular value in international transactions, in which sophisticated investors knowingly undertake such risks as political upheaval or contractual breach in return for the benefits to be reaped from international trade. Law affecting such an essential instrument of the economy must be shaped with sensitivity to its special characteristics. Accordingly, courts have concluded that the whole purpose of a letter of credit would be defeated by examining the merits of the underlying contract dispute to determine whether the letter should be paid.

Because of the nature of a letter of credit, we conclude that Iraq does not have a property interest in the money CCM received under the letter. The United States contends in essence that Iraq has a property interest in this money because it was allegedly a contract payment made by Iraq, which Iraq should recover because CCM breached the contract. In so arguing, the United States makes a breach of contract claim on behalf of Iraq that Iraq has never made, creates a remedy for the contracting parties in derogation of the remedy they themselves provided and, most importantly, disregards the controlling legal principles with respect to letters of credit.

Affirmed.

Indirect Sales through a Distributor

You might also have decided that Big Heel would be better off doing business through a French shoe distributor, on the theory that the local company would have superior market knowledge and easier access to valuable retailers. The questions you face regarding choice of law, forum, and method of payment are identical to those you face in direct sales; they must be worked out in advance. But there is one additional problem that deserves close attention.

Suppose you choose Voleurs Freres, a French fashion distributor, to do all of Big Heel's work in France. Voleurs Freres will be an **exclusive dealer**, meaning that it will take on no other accounts of cowboy boots. In return, you will give it an **exclusive distributorship**, indicating that no other French distributors will get a chance at Big Heel boots. This is a common method of working. Voleurs Freres benefits because no one else in France may distribute the valuable boots. Big Heel in turn need not worry that Voleurs Freres will devote more energy to a competing boot. It is a tidy relationship, but does it violate antitrust laws?

Antitrust laws make it illegal to destroy competition and capture an entire market. The United States and the EU both have strong antitrust laws that can potentially be applied domestically and in foreign countries.

EU Antitrust Law

The European Union law is found in Articles 85 and 86 of the Treaty of Rome. From the American point of view, the former is more important. **Article 85 outlaws any agreement, contract, or discussion that distorts competition within EU countries.** In other words, any attempt to gain a market edge by *avoiding* competition is going to be suspect. Suppose three Italian cosmetic firms agree to act in unison to increase earnings. They set common prices for makeup and agree that none will undersell the others. This greatly reduces competition, leaving the consumer with fewer options and more expensive products. Their deal violates Article 85.

Will Big Heel's contract with Voleurs Freres violate Article 85? There is no quick answer. You will need to do a careful market analysis and consult with French lawyers, who undoubtedly will have many questions. How popular are Big Heel boots in Europe? How many competitors would like to distribute them? How many other boot companies want Voleurs Freres to sell *their* products? Does the exclusive arrangement between Big Heel and Voleurs Freres diminish competition? Will consumers pay more because of the contract? These questions are a nuisance and an expense, but it is easier and cheaper to make the inquiry now than to face years of antitrust litigation.

AMERICAN ANTITRUST LAW

In the United States, the primary antitrust law is the **Sherman Act.**[6] This statute controls anticompetitive conduct that harms the American market. It will probably not affect the Big Heel–Voleurs Freres contract, since that deal is likely to have consequences only in Europe. But it is important to understand the Sherman Act when facing foreign competition. In effect, this statute is the American counterpart to Article 85. Any conduct that eliminates competition in the United States and enables one company, or group of companies, to control a market probably violates this law. And "any conduct" means that anticompetitive acts taking place in a foreign country may still violate the Sherman Act. A company doing business in the United States **may sue a competitor based on its conduct in a foreign country**, provided the local firm can show (1) that the foreign competitor *intends* to affect the U.S. market, and (2) that the foreign conduct has a *direct and substantial effect* on the U.S. market.

Let's look again at the Italian cosmetics makers. Suppose they decide to act in unison in the United States. They set common prices and agree not to compete with each other. That agreement is illegal. It violates the Sherman Act *even if all arrangements were made in Milan*. The companies intend to affect the U.S. market. When an American cosmetics firm demonstrates that the agreement caused it direct and substantial harm, the company may file suit in the United States against all three Italian corporations and expect to recover large damages.

INTERNATIONAL COMITY

But what if the foreign corporation is doing business in a way that is entirely legal in its native country? May U.S. antitrust law still penalize the company's conduct if it harms American business? That was the question presented in the following case, which raises the issue of **international comity**. The word "comity" in this context means "concomitant jurisdiction," meaning that two courts have the right to hear a particular case. When those two courts are in different nations, the laws of the two countries may conflict. **In the event of a conflict, international comity requires one court to respect the other legal system and decline to hear a suit if it would more logically be resolved in the foreign country.** Does that principle govern the following case? The plaintiffs wanted the case heard in the United States under the Sherman Act, while the defendants

HARTFORD FIRE INSURANCE CO. v. CALIFORNIA

509 U.S. 764, 113 S. Ct. 2891, 1993 U.S. LEXIS 4404
United States Supreme Court, 1993

Facts: Nineteen states and many private plaintiffs filed 36 separate lawsuits against various insurance companies, alleging several conspiracies to violate the Sherman Act. The conspiracies related to commercial general liability (CGL) insurance. CGL insurance covers the insured against accident and damage claims by customers, other companies, or the general public. The defendants were "reinsurance" companies. When a primary insurer issues a CGL policy to a corporation, it usually obtains for itself insurance to cover at least a portion of the risk it is assuming. The availability of reinsurance strongly affects the ability of primary insurers to provide coverage to customers. A primary

[6] See Chapter 19, on antitrust law.

insurer unable to obtain reinsurance will seldom issue coverage.

Lloyd's of London is a major reinsurance center. Various English syndicates, working through Lloyd's, provide reinsurance for companies throughout the world. The plaintiffs alleged that during the 1980s, reinsurers at Lloyd's forced American primary insurers to change the terms of their standard CGL insurance. These changes shortened the time during which a customer could file a claim under its policy, and eliminated certain claims altogether. These changes made CGL less valuable to the insured and more profitable to the reinsurers. The reinsurers were able to impose these changes because (1) there are only a few reinsurers worldwide and (2) all of the reinsurers worked in collusion to limit the coverage. They thus behaved in a monopolistic fashion, controlling the market and reducing customers' insurance coverage.

The United States District Court concluded that since the reinsurers' conduct was legal in Britain, international comity prevented an American court from hearing claims against the London defendants. The court dismissed the case against them. The United States Court of Appeals reversed, holding that the case should go forward in this country. The London reinsurers appealed to the United States Supreme Court.

You be the Judge: Does the principle of international comity prevent an American court from hearing these antitrust claims against London reinsurers?

Argument for the London Reinsurers: Your honors, for several reasons we urge American courts not to hear these antitrust claims against any London reinsurer. Lloyd's of London has been one of the world's most respected insurance organizations since 1688. Beginning in 1879, Parliament has directly regulated Lloyd's, and continues to control it today, pursuant to the Insurance Companies Act of 1982 and appropriate regulations. Under British law, insurance companies and reinsurance companies are expressly exempt from antitrust regulation. Everything that the defendants are alleged to have done in this case is entirely legal in Britain. It is an extraordinarily dangerous idea to permit the courts of one nation to subject foreign nationals to phenomenally expensive litigation for alleged conduct that was absolutely legal and proper where it was done.

Further, even though plaintiffs allege that the defendants' conduct technically violated American laws, there can be no suggestion that any of the reinsurers intended to harm any American corporation or citizen. This is not some shady conspiracy forged on a foggy night in an abandoned shack. The London reinsurers simply attempted to limit their own liability. They chose a lawful means to do it. They were doing, in other words, precisely what the plaintiffs in this case do when they buy insurance!

As this Court well knows, British courts have repeatedly expressed hostility to the extraterritorial application of American antitrust laws. So strong is the antagonism from earlier cases that English law now prohibits companies from supplying evidence and documents for use in antitrust proceedings in the United States. Even if this Court were to permit the suit to go forward, it would be nearly impossible for the plaintiffs to obtain documentary evidence to support their case from the only place from which it can come, England.

For all of these reasons, we urge the Court to rely on international comity and dismiss the case.

Argument for the Plaintiffs: Your honors, the defendants all engaged in conduct that they knew violated American antitrust laws. They did it for one reason: to increase their profits. That, of course, is why any corporation attempts to control a market. Here, by fixing deals with other major reinsurers, the Lloyd's syndicates were able to dictate the terms of American primary insurance and reduce coverage to the plaintiffs.

The defendants argue that they have obeyed British law, and that a so-called conflict in the laws requires American courts to stay away. But there is in fact no conflict between American and British law. It may be true that the reinsurers' monopolistic practices do not violate British law. But that does not mean that British law requires them to behave this way. It is black letter law that American antitrust laws may be applied against conduct that is lawful in a foreign nation. There would be a conflict only if British insurance law required Lloyd's firms to act collusively and attempt to control the American market. Obviously, it does not. The Lloyd's reinsurers are free to obey American law and British law, and that is what they ought to have done. They didn't, and we ask a chance to prove that in court.

These reinsurers are some of the most sophisticated business people in the world. They entered the American insurance market to make a profit and have stayed here many decades because they are earning money. But the profits were not vast enough, so they engaged in monopolistic, collusive practices to cut back the customer's ability to make a claim. And now, in dominating the American market, they claim they should not be governed by American law. Not fair, your honors. They can't have it both ways. If they enter this market, they must be governed by its laws the same as anyone else.

wanted any dispute settled in Britain, where they believed British law would find them innocent of any wrongdoing.

International claims of monopolization will increase as multinational enterprises, already powerful, merge with one another. Boeing Corp., the largest American manufacturer of aircraft, announced its plans to merge with McDonnell-Douglas, its largest American competitor. Federal antitrust regulators examined the deal and approved it, potentially creating the world's largest aerospace company. But the European Union intervened. EU regulators asserted that the new company would have enough clout to subdue competition in Europe and unfairly dominate its aerospace industry. American observers contended that the EU was interfering with an American merger simply to gain market share for the largest European aircraft maker, Airbus Industrie. After seven months of intense EU investigation of the merger and round-the-clock negotiations, Boeing agreed to certain changes. The company gave up its position as exclusive supplier of planes to American, Delta, and Continental Airlines, thus allowing Airbus to bid for those jobs. Boeing also agreed to license certain patents to Airbus and to run McDonnell-Douglas as a separate entity. With those concessions, the EU agreed to Boeing's takeover, and the company acquired McDonnell-Douglas.

LICENSING A FOREIGN MANUFACTURER

Big Heel has a third option when selling abroad, which is to license a French manufacturer to produce Big Heel boots. It should do this only if it is convinced the manufacturer will maintain sufficiently high standards. Even so, there are two major issues.

First, Big Heel must ensure that all of its patents and trademarks are protected. In fact, France will honor both forms of American intellectual property, and there should be no problems. But some nations may ignore American intellectual property rights, and no company should establish a licensing arrangement without investigating. As mentioned above, the GATT should increase respect worldwide for the intellectual property rights created by all nations.

Second, if Big Heel grants an exclusive license to any French manufacturer, it could encounter exactly the same antitrust problems as those discussed above. It must analyze both EU and American antitrust law before taking the risk.

INVESTING ABROAD

Foreign investment is another major source of international commerce. Assume that Ambux is an American communications corporation that decides to invest in a growing overseas market. The president of Ambux is particularly interested in building telephone systems in the former republics of the Soviet Union, reasoning that these economies offer great opportunity for growth. She wants you to report to her on the most important issues concerning possible investment in Uzbekistan and other former Soviet republics. You quickly realize that such an investment presents several related issues:

- Repatriation of profits
- Expropriation
- Sovereign immunity
- Act of State doctrine
- Foreign corrupt practices

REPATRIATION OF PROFITS

Repatriation of profits occurs when an investing company pulls its earnings out of a foreign country and takes them back home. If Ambux builds a telephone system in Uzbekistan, it will plan to make money and then repatriate the profit to its headquarters in the United States. But Ambux must not assume an automatic right to do so. Many countries impose a much higher tax on repatriated profits than on normal income in order to keep the money in domestic commerce. Others bar repatriation altogether. Developing countries in particular want the money for further growth, and they tend to regard repatriation of rapidly earned profit as a close relative of exploitation. Thus, before Ambux invests anywhere, it must ensure that it can repatriate profits or be prepared to live with any limitations the foreign country might impose.

Fortunately, investing in Uzbekistan became more secure in 1994. The Uzbekistan parliament passed a new foreign investment law guaranteeing repatriation of profits without limit. Uzbekistan and the United States then signed a trade treaty guaranteeing unlimited repatriation for American investors. This treaty should suffice. But Ambux might still feel cautious. Uzbekistan is a new nation, and the mechanisms for actually getting the money out of Uzbekistan banks may be slow or faulty. The solution is to get a written agreement from the Minister of Commerce explicitly permitting Ambux to repatriate all profits and providing a clear mechanism to do it through the local banks.

EXPROPRIATION

Many nations, both developed and developing, **nationalize** property, meaning that they declare the national government to be the new owner. For example, during the 1940s and 1950s, Great Britain nationalized its coal, steel, and other heavy industries. The state assumed ownership and paid compensation to the previous owners. In the United States, nationalization is rare, but local governments often take land by eminent domain, to be used for roads or other public works. The United States Constitution requires that the owners be fairly compensated.

When a government takes property owned by foreign investors, it is called **expropriation**. Again, this practice is common and legal, provided there is adequate compensation. The U.S. government historically has acknowledged that the expropriation of American interests is legal, provided the host government pays the owners **promptly and fully, in dollars**. But if compensation is inadequate or long delayed, or made in a local currency that is hard to exchange, the taking is **confiscation**.

The courts of almost all nations concede that confiscation is illegal. But it can be difficult or impossible to prevent because courts of the host country may be partial to their own government. And any attempt to obtain compensation in an American court will encounter two separate problems: sovereign immunity and the Act of State doctrine.

SOVEREIGN IMMUNITY

Sovereign immunity holds that the courts of one nation lack the jurisdiction (power) to hear suits against foreign governments. Most nations respect this principle. In the United States, the **Foreign Sovereign Immunities Act (FSIA)** states that American courts generally cannot entertain suits against foreign governments. This is a difficult hurdle for a company to overcome when seeking compensation for foreign expropriation. There are three exceptions.

Waiver. A lawsuit is permitted against a foreign country that waives its immunity, that is, voluntarily gives up this protection. Suppose the Czech government wishes to buy fighter planes from an American manufacturer. The manufacturer might insist on a waiver in the sales contract, and the Czech Republic might be willing to grant one to get the weapons it desires. If the planes land safely but the checks bounce, the manufacturer may sue.

Commercial Activity. A plaintiff in the United States can sue a foreign country engaged in commercial activity, as opposed to political. Suppose the government of Iceland hires an American ecology-consulting firm to help its fishermen replenish depleted fishing grounds. Since fishing is a for-profit activity, the contract is commercial, and if Iceland refuses to pay, the company may sue in American courts.

Violation of International Law. A plaintiff in this country may sue a foreign government that has confiscated property in violation of international law, provided that the property either ends up in the United States or is involved in commercial activity that affects someone in the United States. Suppose a foreign government confiscates a visiting American ship, with no claim of right, and begins to use it for shipping goods for profit. Later, the ship carries some American produce. The taking was illegal, and it now affects American commerce. The original owner may sue.

ACT OF STATE DOCTRINE

A second doctrine, annoyingly similar to sovereign immunity, could also affect Ambux or any company whose property is confiscated. **The Act of State doctrine requires an American court to abstain from any case in which a court order would interfere with the ability of the president or Congress to conduct foreign affairs.**

In the 1960s, Cuba expropriated American sugar interests, providing little or no compensation to the previous owners. The American owners sued, but in

Banco Nacional de Cuba v. Sabbatino,[7] the United States Supreme Court refused to permit such suits in American courts. The Court ruled that even where there was strong evidence that the expropriation was illegal, American courts should not be involved because the executive and legislative branches must be free to conduct our foreign policy.

INVESTMENT INSURANCE

Companies eager to do business abroad but anxious about expropriation should consider publicly funded insurance. In 1971, Congress established the **Overseas Private Investment Corporation (OPIC)** to insure U.S. investors against overseas losses due to political violence and expropriation. OPIC insurance is available to investors at relatively low rates for investment in almost any country. The agency has had remarkable success at no cost to the U.S. government. Every year, OPIC participates in overseas ventures worth many billions of dollars, earning insurance fees that have paid the agency's entire budget and left a substantial surplus.

Should Ambux investigate OPIC insurance before investing in Uzbekistan? Absolutely. While the Uzbekistan government has the best of intentions with respect to foreign investment, the nation is young and the government has no track record. A government can change course as quickly as a gnat, and often with less planning. Why take unnecessary risks?

FOREIGN CORRUPT PRACTICES ACT

Suppose that while you are investigating Uzbekistan, an official from a nearby country contacts you. This official, Dr. "J.," says that Ambux is the perfect company to install a new, nationwide telephone system for his young republic. You are delighted with his enthusiasm. Over lunch, Dr. J. tells you that he can obtain an exclusive contract for Ambux to do the work, but you will have to pay him a commission of $750,000. Such a deal would be worth millions of dollars for Ambux, and a commission of $750,000 is economically sensible. Should you pay it?

The Foreign Corrupt Practices Act (FCPA)[8] makes it illegal for an American businessperson to give "anything of value" to any foreign official in order to influence an official decision. The classic example of an FCPA violation is bribing a foreign official to obtain a government contract. You must find out exactly why Dr. J. needs so much money, what he plans to do with it, and how he will obtain the contract.

You ask these questions, and Dr. J. responds, "I am a close personal friend of the Minister of the Interior. In my country, you must know people to make things happen. The minister respects my judgment, and some of my fee will find its way to him. Do not trouble yourself with details."

Bad advice. A prison sentence is not a detail. The FCPA permits fines of $100,000 for individuals and $1 million for corporations, as well as prison sentences of up to five years. If you pay money that "finds its way to the minister," you have violated the act.

---

[7] 376 U.S. 398, 84 S. Ct. 923, 1964 U.S. LEXIS 2252 (1964).

[8] 15 U.S.C. §78 et seq.

It is sad but true that in many countries bribery is routine and widely accepted. When Congress investigated foreign bribes to see how common they were, more than 300 U.S. companies admitted paying hundreds of millions of dollars in bribes to foreign officials. Legislators concluded that such massive payments distorted competition between American companies for foreign contracts, interfered with the free market system, and undermined confidence everywhere in our way of doing business. The statutory response was simple: foreign bribery is illegal, plain and simple. The FCPA has two principal requirements:

- *Bribes.* The statute makes it illegal for U.S. companies and citizens to bribe foreign officials to influence a governmental decision. The statute prohibits giving anything of value and also bars using third parties as a conduit for such payments.
- *Record Keeping.* All publicly traded companies—whether they engage in international trade or not—must keep detailed records that prevent hiding or disguising bribes. These records must be available for U.S. government officials to inspect.

Lockheed Corp. secured a $79 million contract to sell C-130 Hercules transport aircraft to Egypt, anticipating a $12 million profit. One expense of obtaining the contract was a $1 million payment, made to a Swiss bank account, for the benefit of a former Lockheed consultant who had since become a member of the Egyptian parliament. Big mistake. In federal court, Lockheed later pleaded guilty to violating the FCPA, acknowledging that it had falsified records to cover up the bribe. The company paid a $24.8 million fine—double its profit. The Lockheed executive directly involved in the bribe, Suleiman Nassar, vice-president of international marketing, received a fine of $125,000 and an 18-month prison sentence.

Not all payments violate the FCPA. **A grease or facilitating payment is legal**, provided the company is paying a foreign official only to expedite performance of a routine function. Grease payments are common in many foreign countries to obtain a permit, process governmental papers, or obtain utility service. For example, the cost of a permit to occupy an office building might be $100, but the government clerk suggests that you will receive the permit faster (within this lifetime) if you pay $150, one-third of which he will pocket. Such small payments are legal. Further, a payment **does not violate the FCPA if it was legal under the written laws** of the country in which it was made. Since few countries establish written codes *permitting* officials to receive bribes, this defense is unlikely to help many Americans who hand out gifts.

Some illegal bribes are blatant. A suitcase full of cash is a ticket to jail. But some payments are subtler. Your company is bidding for the right to build a power station in rural Mexico, and an Italian company is your primary competitor. The Italian company offers to fly all of the relevant Mexican officials and their families to Venice for an all-expenses-paid holiday. Should you match the offer? Such a gift, clearly made to obtain an important contract, would only be lawful if *written* Mexican law permitted it. It is unlikely there is such a law. Never give any gift without checking with a lawyer to assure that local *written* law permits the payment.

Transparency International, an international nonprofit agency based in Germany, publishes a "Corruption Perception Index," gauging how much dishonesty businesspeople and scholars encounter in different nations. In 2000, the agency listed 91 nations on its index. The ten highest ranking countries (perceived *least* corrupt) were Finland, Denmark, New Zealand, Iceland, Singapore, Sweden, Canada, Netherlands and Luxembourg. The agency listed the United States as the sixteenth least corrupt nation. The ten countries ranking lowest (perceived *most* corrupt) were Bangladesh, Nigeria, Uganda, Indonesia, Kenya, Cameroon, Bolivia, Azerbaijan, Ukraine, and Tanzania. The full index is available from Transparency International at http://www.transparency.org.

But corruption is a two-sided coin. Of the roughly 200 nations in the world, only Sweden and the United States prohibit their nationals from bribing foreign officials. Further, in many countries, a bribe paid to a foreign official may be deducted for tax purposes!

American executives have long complained that the FCPA puts their companies at a competitive disadvantage, and political leaders have lobbied for an international agreement. Finally, the efforts are reaching fruition. In December 1997, the Organization for Economic Cooperation and Development (OECD) produced a "Convention of Combatting Bribery of Foreign Public Officials in International Business Transactions." The 29 nations of the OECD include most of the world's economic powers. Five nonmembers of the OECD also signed. The Convention requires signatories to enact criminal penalties for offering or giving bribes to foreign officials. The Convention also compels signatories to enact record-keeping laws that will prevent companies from disguising bribes.

The Convention has various weaknesses, and it remains to be seen whether signatories will implement it aggressively. But the Convention is long overdue. The collapse of several Southeast Asian economies during 1997 and 1998 clearly demonstrated the destructive effects of corruption. Many of the nations that suffered most were considered rife with dishonest officials.

The best way for a company to avoid liability under the FCPA is to hire a compliance officer. This employee should conduct background checks on foreign agents and consultants to ensure that they are not making secret payments to obtain business. The compliance officer should insist on internal company auditing designed to deter and detect illicit payments. She must train all employees in the nuances of the law and create a system for reporting and investigating suspected breaches of the law.

CHAPTER CONCLUSION

Overseas investment, like sales abroad, offers potentially great rewards but significant pitfalls. A working knowledge of international law is essential to any entrepreneur or executive seriously considering foreign commerce. Issues such as choice of law, currency protection, antitrust statutes, and expropriation can mean the difference between profit and loss. As GATT and other treaties lower barriers, international trade will increase, and your awareness of these principles will grow still more valuable.

CHAPTER REVIEW

1. Several statutes restrict exports from the United States that would harm national security, foreign policy, or certain other goals.

2. A tariff is a duty (tax) imposed on goods when they enter a country. The U.S. Customs Service classifies goods when they enter the United States and imposes appropriate tariffs.

3. Most countries, including the United States, impose duties for goods that have been dumped (sold at an unfairly low price in the international market) and for subsidized goods (those benefiting from government financial assistance in the country of origin).

4. The General Agreement on Tariffs and Trade (GATT), ratified by Congress in 1994, is lowering the average duties worldwide. Proponents see it as a boon to trade; opponents see it as a threat to American workers.

5. GATT created the World Trade Organization (WTO), which resolves disputes between signatories to the treaty.

6. A sales agreement between an American company and a foreign company may be governed by the UCC, by the law of the foreign country, or by the United Nations Convention On Contracts For The International Sale Of Goods (CISG). The CISG differs from the UCC in several important respects.

7. A confirmed, irrevocable letter of credit is an important means of facilitating international sales contracts, because the seller is assured of payment by a local bank as long as it delivers the specified goods.

8. Antitrust laws exist in the United States, the European Union (EU), and other countries. International merchants must be careful not to make agreements that would distort competition.

9. International comity requires a local court to respect the legal system of a foreign country and dismiss a lawsuit if the dispute would more logically be resolved in the other nation.

10. A foreign government may restrict repatriation of profits.

11. Expropriation refers to a government taking property owned by foreign investors. U.S. courts regard this as lawful, provided the country pays the American owner promptly and fully, in dollars.

12. Sovereign immunity means that, in general, American courts lack jurisdiction to hear suits against foreign governments, unless the foreign nation has waived immunity, is engaging in commercial activity, or has violated international law.

13. The Act of State doctrine requires an American court to abstain from any case in which a court order would interfere with the ability of the president or Congress to conduct foreign affairs.

14. The Foreign Corrupt Practices Act (FCPA) makes it illegal for an American businessperson to bribe foreign officials.

PRACTICE TEST

1. Arnold Mandel exported certain high-technology electronic equipment. Later, he was in court arguing that the equipment he shipped should not have been on the Department of Commerce's Commodity Control List. What items may be on that list, and why does Mandel care?

2. Sports Graphics, Inc. imports consumer goods, including "Chill" brand coolers, which come from Taiwan. Chill coolers have an outer shell of vinyl, with handles and pockets, and an inner layer of insulation. In a recent federal lawsuit, the issue was whether Chill coolers were technically "luggage" or "articles used for preparing, serving or storing food or beverages." Who were the parties to this dispute likely to be, and why did they care about such a technical description of these coolers?

3. **RIGHT & WRONG** Hector works in Zoey's importing firm. Zoey overhears Hector on the phone say, "O.K., 30,000 ski parkas at $80 per parka. You've got yourself a deal. Thanks a lot." When Hector hangs up, Zoey is furious, yelling, "I told you not to make a deal on those Italian ski parkas without my permission! I think I can get a better price elsewhere." "Relax, Zoey," replies Hector. "I wanted to lock them in, to be sure we had some in case your deal fell through. It's just an oral contract, so we can always back out if we need to." Is that ethical? How far can a company go to protect its interests? Does it matter that another business might make serious financial plans based on the discussion? Apart from the ethics, is Hector's idea smart?

4. **YOU BE THE JUDGE WRITING PROBLEM** Continental Illinois National Bank issued an irrevocable letter of credit on behalf of Bill's Coal Co. for $805,000, with the Allied Fidelity Insurance Co. as beneficiary. Bill's Coal Co. then went bankrupt. Allied then presented to Continental documents that were complete and conformed to the letter of credit. Continental refused to pay. Since Bill's Coal was bankrupt, there was no way Continental would collect once it had paid on the letter. Allied filed suit. Who should win? **Argument for Allied Fidelity:** An irrevocable letter of credit serves one purpose: to assure the seller that it will be paid if it performs the contract. Allied has met its obligation. The company furnished documents demonstrating compliance with the agreement. Continental *must* pay. Continental's duty to pay is an independent obligation, unrelated to the status of Bill's Coal. The bank issued this letter knowing the rules of the game and expecting to make a profit. It is time for Continental to honor its word. **Argument for Continental Bank:** In this transaction, the bank was merely a middleman, helping to facilitate payment of a contract. Allied has fulfilled its obligations under the contract, and we understand the company's desire to be paid. Regrettably, Bill's Coal is bankrupt. No one is going to be paid on this deal. Allied should have researched Bill's financial status more thoroughly before entering into the agreement. While we sympathize with Allied's dilemma, it has only itself to blame and cannot expect the bank to act as some sort of insurance company for a deal gone awry.

5. Jean-François, a French wine exporter, sues Bob Joe, a Texas importer, claiming that Bob Joe owes him $2 million for wine. Jean-François takes the witness stand to describe how the contract was created. Where is the trial taking place?

6. Zenith and other American manufacturers of television sets sued Matsushita and 20 other Japanese competitors, claiming that the Japanese companies had conspired to drive Zenith and the Americans out of the American market. Supposedly, the Japanese companies agreed to maintain artificially high prices in Japan and artificially low prices in the United States. The goal of the low prices in the United States was to destroy American competition, and the goal of the high prices in Japan was to earn sufficient profits at home so that the companies could tolerate the temporary losses in the United States. Is the conduct of Matsushita in Japan subject to the Sherman Act?

7. The Kyrgyz Republic is another of the new nations that broke away from the old Soviet Union. In September 1994, the government of Kyrgyzstan made two independent announcements: (1) it was abolishing all taxes on repatriation; (2) the government was resigning and would shortly be replaced. Explain the significance of these announcements for an American company considering a major investment in Kyrgyzstan.

8. The Instituto de Auxilios y Viviendas is a government agency of the Dominican Republic. Dr. Marion Fernandez, the general administrator of the Instituto and Secretary of the Republic, sought a loan for the Instituto. She requested that Charles

Meadows, an American citizen, secure the Instituto a bank loan of $12 million. If he obtained a loan on favorable terms, he would receive a fee of $240,000. Meadows secured a loan on satisfactory terms, which the Instituto accepted. He then sought his fee, but the Instituto and the Dominican government refused to pay. He sued the government in United States District Court. The Dominican government claimed immunity. Comment.

9. Environmental Tectonics Corp. and W. S. Kirkpatrick & Co. were both competing for a valuable contract with the Nigerian government. Kirkpatrick got it. Tectonics then sued Kirkpatrick in the United States, claiming that Kirkpatrick got the contract only because it bribed Nigerian officials. Kirkpatrick acknowledged that the district court had jurisdiction but argued that it should abstain from hearing the case. What doctrine does Kirkpatrick rely on, and what should the trial court do?

10. Blondek and Tull were two employees of an American company called Eagle Bus. They hoped that the Saskatchewan provincial government would award Eagle a contract for buses. To bolster their chances, they went to Saskatchewan and paid $50,000 to two government employees. Back in the United States, they were arrested and charged with a crime. Suppose they argue that even if they did something illegal, it occurred in Canada, and that is the only nation that can prosecute them. Comment on the defense.

11. Richard Johnson, an American citizen, was a highly trained electrical engineer who had worked for Hughes Aircraft and Norcroft Corp. He strongly believed in the cause of the Provisional Irish Republican Army (PIRA), which at the time was attacking British civilian and military targets in Northern Ireland and England. Johnson researched and developed explosives to be exported to Ireland and used by the PIRA. Christina Reid, an electrical engineer, worked with Johnson on IRA projects. She served as a courier of electronic components for remote-control bombs that the two sent to Northern Ireland. What legal problems did they risk by engaging in these transactions?

INTERNET RESEARCH PROBLEM

At http://www.sweatshops.org/, read about the worldwide problem of sweatshops. Is this a serious problem? If so, what role should the law play in its resolution? What can one student do about it?

You can find further practice problems in the Online Quiz at http://beatty.westbuslaw.com or in the Study Guide that accompanies this text.

UNIT

2

CONTRACTS & THE UCC

Introduction to Contracts

9

CHAPTER

Have a seat. Great to see you. Here, grab a menu. Yes, you're right: the tables at this café are jammed together. In fact, *that's why I chose* the spot. Listen to the conversations around us. Oh, go on, don't worry—eavesdropping is acceptable for academic purposes. To our right, a famous director is chatting with Katrina, the glamorous actress. He is trying to sign her up for a new film, *Body Work*, but she seems hesitant.

Katrina (doubtful): I'm intrigued with the character, Bob, and I'd love to work with you. I *am* concerned about the nude scenes. The one on the tobaggan run was OK. But that scene in the poultry factory—very explicit. I don't work fully nude.

Bob: We'll solve it—what am I, a sleaze? This is fine art, don't give it another thought. We're talking $2.5 million, Katrina. $600,000 up front, the rest deferred, the usual percentages.

Katrina: As you know, my fee is $3 million. I should talk with my agent. I'd need something in writing about the nudity, the percentages, all of it.

Bob: I have to settle this fast. Julia is seriously considering the role.

Katrina (worried): *Julia!* Are you kidding? Bob, I said I'm interested.

Oh, my look at that. Katrina hesitates, Bob nods encouragingly, then sticks out his hand and . . . Katrina shakes! It's a wrap—I guess. Now bend your ear toward the table on our left. The man wants to quit his job and accept a position with a competing company, but the woman, his boss, is insisting he stay.

Emily: I taught you everything you know about computer encryption, Jake, and you're not taking that sophisticated training to my number one competitor.
Jake: Emily, their offer is just too good to turn down. I deserve a chance to expand my horizons. Come on, be human!
Emily (waving a document): Look here, my friend. Page four of your employment contract: "I agree that if I leave the company for any reason, I will not work for a competing firm anywhere in the United States for a period of three years." And here is your lovely, rounded signature. You work for me, Jake, or you go flip burgers.

Gee, that Emily is tough. I guess poor Jake is stuck in his present job. We need something cheerier. Listen to the two women behind you. While I was waiting, they have been bargaining over a vacation condo.

Li-Li: I don't think I can go lower than 485.
Maria: Well . . . $450,000. I guess.
Li-Li: Maria, it has the best ocean view in the whole complex. And you would be on the top floor!
Maria: 460.
Li-Li: 475. My final offer. Do you happen to have the time?
Maria: The time? What's the hurry? Oh . . . OK 475. Shake, partner.
Li-Li: It's a deal. That's great. I'm so happy for you. You're going to love it. Do we need to put this in writing?
Maria: Are you kidding? How long have we known each other, since we were 6?
Li-Li: Five and a half! You're right, why spend the money on lawyers and boring documents? Let's spend it on champagne. Waiter!

The café is a hot bed of contract negotiations—but then, so is our society. These three conversations demonstrate why it is important to understand contract law. Bob and Katrina think they have an agreement, but in fact *they do not*, because the parties have not achieved a meeting of the minds. Jake, if he reads this chapter, will be delighted to learn that *he is free to change jobs*: a court will not enforce Emily's noncompetition agreement. Finally, Li-Li should skip the champagne and instead scratch a simple contract onto a napkin. Without Maria's signature, Li-Li *cannot enforce her friend's promise* to pay.

INTRODUCTION TO CONTRACTS

THE PURPOSE OF A CONTRACT

Parties enter into contracts attempting to control their future. **Contracts exist to make business matters more predictable.** Most contracts work out precisely as the parties intended because the parties fulfill their obligations. Most—but not all. We will study contracts that have gone wrong. We look at these errant deals to learn how to avoid the problems they manifest.

JUDICIAL ACTIVISM VERSUS JUDICIAL RESTRAINT

In most contract cases judges do their best simply to enforce whatever terms the parties agreed to. Even if the contract results in serious harm to one party, a court will generally enforce it. This is **judicial restraint**. On the other hand, some courts practice **judicial activism**. In contract law, this means that a court will ignore certain provisions of a contract, or an entire agreement, if the judge believes that enforcing the deal would be unjust. A court may even be willing to create a contract where none existed, if it appears necessary to avoid injustice. Judicial activism makes the law **more flexible but less predictable**.

ISSUES (AND ANSWERS)

The three contract negotiations above illustrate several basic principles, and we will consider each. **A contract has four elements:**

1. **Agreement.** One party must make a valid offer, and the other party must accept it. (Bob failed to make a clear offer to Katrina.)
2. **Consideration.** There has to be bargaining that leads to an exchange between the parties.
3. **Legality.** The contract must be for a lawful purpose. (Emily's noncompetition agreement is probably illegal.)
4. **Capacity.** The parties must be adults of sound mind.

Contract cases often raise several other important issues, which we examine throughout the next two chapters:

- **Consent.** Neither party may trick or force the other into the agreement.
- **Written Contracts.** Some contracts must be in writing to be enforceable. (Neither Li-Li nor Maria may enforce the condo contract unless there is a signed agreement.)
- **Third Party Interests.** Some contracts affect people other than the parties themselves.
- **Performance and Discharge.** If a party fully accomplishes what the contract requires, his duties are discharged.

- **Remedies.** A court will award money or other relief to a party injured by a breach of contract.

CONTRACTS DEFINED

A contract is a promise that the law will enforce. As we look more closely at the elements of contract law, we will encounter some intricate issues, but remember that we are usually interested in answering three basic questions of common sense, all relating to promises:

- Is it certain that the defendant promised to do something?
- If she did promise, is it fair to make her honor her word?
- If she did *not* promise, are there unusual reasons to hold her liable anyway?

TYPES OF CONTRACTS

BILATERAL AND UNILATERAL CONTRACTS

In a bilateral contract, both parties make a promise. Suppose a producer says to Gloria, "I'll pay you $2 million to star in my new romantic comedy, *A Promise for a Promise*, which we are shooting three months from now in Santa Fe." Gloria says, "It's a deal." That is a bilateral contract. Each party has made a promise to do something. The producer is now bound to pay Gloria $2 million, and Gloria is obligated to show up on time and act in the movie. The vast majority of contracts are bilateral contracts.

In a unilateral contract, one party makes a promise that the other party can accept only *by doing* something. These contracts are less common. Suppose the movie producer says to Leo, "I'll give you a hundred bucks if you mow my lawn this weekend." Leo is not promising to do it. If he mows the lawn, he has accepted the offer and is entitled to his hundred dollars. If he spends the weekend at the beach, neither he nor the producer owes anything.

EXPRESS AND IMPLIED CONTRACTS

In an express contract, the two parties explicitly state all important terms of their agreement. *The great majority* of binding agreements are express contracts. The contract between the producer and Gloria is an express contract, because the parties explicitly state what Gloria will do, where and when she will do it, and how much she will be paid. Some express contracts are oral, as that one was, and some are written.

In an implied contract, the words and conduct of the parties indicate that they intended an agreement. Suppose every Friday, for two months, the producer asks Leo to mow his lawn, and loyal Leo does so each weekend. Then for three more weekends, Leo simply shows up without the producer asking, and the producer continues to pay for the work done. But on the twelfth weekend, when Leo rings the doorbell to collect, the producer suddenly says, "I never asked you to mow it. Scram." The producer is correct that there was no express contract, because the parties had not spoken for several weeks. But a court will probably rule that the conduct of the parties has *implied* a contract. Not only did Leo mow the lawn every weekend, but the producer even paid on three weekends when they had not spoken. It was reasonable for Leo to assume that he had a weekly deal to mow and be paid. Naturally, there is no implied contract thereafter.

Today, the hottest disputes about implied contracts continue to arise in the employment setting. Many employees have "at-will" agreements. This means that the employees are free to quit at any time and the company has the right to fire them at any time, for virtually any reason. Courts routinely enforce at-will contracts. But often a company provides its workers with personnel manuals that guarantee certain rights. The company may assure all workers that they will have a hearing and a chance to present evidence on their behalf before being fired. The legal issue then becomes whether the handbook implies a contract guaranteeing a right to a hearing or whether the company is still at liberty to fire any worker at will.

FEDERAL EXPRESS CORP. v. DUTSCHMANN
846 S.W.2d 282, 1993 Tex. LEXIS 9
Supreme Court of Texas, 1993

Facts: When Marcie Dutschmann began working as a courier at Federal Express, she received an Employment Handbook and Personnel Manual stating that her employment was at-will and "would continue as long as it was mutually satisfactory to both parties." The manual specified that it created no contractual rights. But it also described a "Guaranteed Fair Treatment Policy" (GFTP). According to the GFTP, any employee who was terminated would have a hearing at a Board of Review, at which he could appear and present evidence.

Federal Express fired Dutschmann in October 1987, claiming that she had falsified delivery records. She responded that her termination was in retaliation for her complaints of sexual harassment. She attempted to appeal her termination through the GFTP, but Federal Express did not allow her the kind of hearing that the handbook described. Dutschmann was not allowed to present the documents that she offered, call her own witnesses, cross-examine the company witnesses, or discuss her claims of harassment.

Dutschmann sued. At trial, Federal Express argued that Dutschmann was an employee at-will and that the company was free to fire her at any time without a hearing. Dutschmann contended that the employee handbook and manual created an implied contract that she was entitled to a full, fair hearing. The jury found that the handbooks did create an implied contract and that Federal Express had not given her a fair hearing. The court of appeals affirmed. Federal Express appealed to the Texas Supreme Court.

You be the Judge: Did the employee handbook and manual create an implied contract guaranteeing a fair hearing?

Argument for Federal Express: Your honors, when Federal Express created its employee manuals, it was well aware that some state courts have ruled that these handbooks *may* create an implied contract. And that is why Federal Express wrote employee manuals including the following statements: "The employee's employment is at-will and will continue as long as it is mutually satisfactory to both parties." "This manual does not create any contractual rights. Its use is intended only as a reference." That manual states that it is intended "solely as a guide for management and employees and is not a contract of employment and that no such contract may be implied from its provisions." We think that language is about as clear as it is possible to be, but we didn't stop there. At the inception of Ms. Dutschmann's employment, she signed an agreement stating that she understood the employee manuals *did not constitute a contract*. Freedom to contract means freedom, among other things, to create at-will employment. That is what both parties here voluntarily chose to do.

Argument for Ms. Dutschmann: Your honors, the manuals do state that the employment is at-will. But those manuals then go on to say that *all employees are guaranteed* certain rights, including the rights to a fair, thorough termination hearing. The company refused to hear her evidence and refused to see her documents, because they knew she could prove sexual harassment. So they just fired her, pretending that there was no booklet and no guarantee of a hearing.

Federal Express is trying to have it both ways. The company creates these handsome, glossy booklets, filled with assurances of fair dealing. But then Federal Express comes into court and argues that those words don't really mean anything.

Federal Express knew that guaranteeing fair treatment was a proven way to attract and retain good employees. Would Ms. Dutschmann have gone to work for Federal Express if she had been told she might be sexually harassed and then fired without a fair hearing? Of course not. When a company hands out a booklet and tells employees to rely on it, the company must also keep its part of the bargain.

EXECUTORY AND EXECUTED CONTRACTS

A contract is **executory** when one or more parties has not fulfilled its obligations. Recall Gloria, who agrees to act in the producer's film beginning in three months. The moment Gloria and the producer strike their bargain, they have an executory bilateral express contract. A contract is **executed** when all parties have fulfilled their obligations. When Gloria finishes acting in the movie and the producer pays her final fee, their contract will be fully executed.

VALID, UNENFORCEABLE, VOIDABLE, AND VOID AGREEMENTS

A **valid contract** is one that satisfies all of the law's requirements. A court will therefore enforce it. The contract between Gloria and the producer is a valid contract, and if the producer fails to pay Gloria, she will win a lawsuit to collect the unpaid fee.

An **unenforceable agreement** occurs when the parties intend to form a valid bargain but a court declares that some rule of law prevents enforcing it. Suppose Gloria and the producer orally agree that she will star in his movie, which he will start filming in 18 months. The statute of frauds requires that this contract be in writing, because it cannot be completed within one year. If the producer signs up another actress two months later, Gloria has no claim against him.

A **voidable contract** occurs when the law permits one party to terminate the agreement. This happens, for example, when the other party has committed fraud or misrepresentation. Suppose that Klene Corp. induces Smart to purchase 1,000 acres of Klene land by telling Smart that there is no underground toxic waste, even though Klene knows that just under the topsoil lies an ocean of bubbling purple sludge. Klene is committing fraud. Smart may void the contract, that is, terminate it and owe nothing.

A **void agreement** is one that neither party can enforce, usually because the purpose of the deal is illegal or because one of the parties had no legal authority to make a contract.

REMEDIES CREATED BY JUDICIAL ACTIVISM

Now we turn away from true contracts and consider two remedies created by judicial activism: promissory estoppel and quasi-contract. Each of these remedies has grown in importance over the last 100 years. In each case, a sympathetic plaintiff can demonstrate an injury. But the crux of the matter is this: There is no contract. The plaintiff must hope for more "creative" relief. The two remedies can be confusingly similar. The best way to distinguish them is this:

- In **promissory estoppel** cases, the defendant made a promise that the plaintiff relied on.
- In **quasi-contract** cases, the defendant did not make any promise, but did receive a benefit from the plaintiff.

PROMISSORY ESTOPPEL

A fierce fire swept through Dana and Derek Andreason's house in Utah, seriously damaging it. The good news was that agents for Aetna Casualty promptly visited the Andreasons and helped them through the crisis. The agents reassured the couple that all of the damage was covered by their insurance, instructed them on which things to throw out, and helped them choose materials for repairing other items. The bad news was that the agents were wrong: the Andreasons' policy had expired six weeks before the fire. When Derek Andreason presented a bill for $41,957 worth of meticulously itemized work that he had done under the agents' supervision, Aetna refused to pay.

The Andreasons sued—but not for breach of contract, since the insurance agreement had expired. They sued Aetna under the legal theory of promissory estoppel: **Even when there is no contract, a plaintiff may use promissory estoppel to enforce the defendant's promise if he can show that:**

- The defendant made a promise knowing that the plaintiff would likely rely on it
- The plaintiff did rely on the promise; and
- The only way to avoid injustice is to enforce the promise.

Aetna made a promise to the Andreasons, namely, its assurance that all of the damage was covered by insurance. The company knew that the Andreasons would rely on that promise, which they did by ripping up a floor that might have been salvaged, throwing out some furniture, and buying materials to repair the house. Is enforcing the promise the only way to avoid injustice? Yes, ruled the Utah Court of Appeals.[1] The Andreasons' conduct was reasonable, based on what the Aetna agent said. Under promissory estoppel, the Andreasons received virtually the same amount they would have obtained had the insurance contract been valid.

---

[1] *Andreason v. Aetna Casualty & Surety Co.*, 848 P.2d 171, 1993 Utah App. LEXIS 26 (Utah App. 1993).

QUASI-CONTRACT

Don Easterwood leased over 5,000 acres of farmland in Jackson County, Texas, from PIC Realty for one year. The next year he obtained a second one-year lease. During each year, Easterwood farmed the land, harvested the crops, and prepared the land for the following year's planting. Toward the end of the second lease, after Easterwood had harvested his crop, he and PIC began discussing the terms of another lease. As they negotiated, Easterwood prepared the land for the following year, cutting, plowing, and disking the soil. But the negotiations for a new lease failed, and Easterwood moved off the land. He sued PIC Realty for the value of his work preparing the soil.

Did Easterwood have an express contract? Clearly not. The lease had expired. Did he have an implied contract? No. The parties were actively trying to create a new express contract, so their conduct would not create any kind of an implied agreement. How could he make any legal claim? By relying on the theory of a quasi-contract: **Even when there is no contract, a court may use quasi-contract to compensate a plaintiff who can show that:**

- The plaintiff gave some benefit to the defendant
- The plaintiff reasonably expected to be paid for the benefit and the defendant knew this; and
- The defendant would be unjustly enriched if he did not pay.

If a court finds all of these elements present, it will generally award the value of the goods or services that the plaintiff has conferred. The damages awarded are called ***quantum meruit***, meaning that the plaintiff gets "as much as he deserved." The court is awarding money that it believes the plaintiff *morally ought to have*, even though there was no valid contract entitling her to it. This is judicial activism. The purpose is justice; the term is contradictory.

Don Easterwood testified that in Jackson County, it was common for a tenant farmer to prepare the soil for the following year but then move. In those cases, he claimed, the landowner compensated the farmer for the work done. Other witnesses agreed. The court ruled that indeed there was no contract, but that all elements of quasi-contract had been satisfied. Easterwood gave a benefit to PIC because the land was ready for planting. Easterwood reasonably assumed he would be paid, and PIC Realty knew it. Finally, said the court, it would be unjust to let PIC benefit without paying anything. The court ordered PIC to pay the fair market value of Easterwood's labors.

SOURCES OF CONTRACT LAW

COMMON LAW

Express and implied contracts, promissory estoppel, and quasi-contract were all crafted, over centuries, by appellate courts deciding one contract lawsuit at a time. In this country, the basic principles are similar from one state to another, but there have been significant differences concerning most important contract doctrines. In part because of these differences, the twentieth century saw the rise of two major new sources of contract law: the **Uniform Commercial Code** and the **Restatement of Contracts**.

UNIFORM COMMERCIAL CODE

Business methods changed quickly during the first half of the twentieth century. Executives used new forms of communication, such as telephone and wire, to make deals. Transportation speeded up. Corporations routinely conducted business across state borders and around the world. Executives, lawyers, and judges wanted a body of law for commercial transactions that reflected modern business methods and provided uniformity throughout the United States. That desire gave birth to the Uniform Commercial Code (UCC), created in 1952. The drafters intended the UCC to facilitate the easy formation and enforcement of contracts in a fast-paced world. The Code governs many aspects of commerce, including the sale and leasing of goods, negotiable instruments, bank deposits, letters of credit, investment securities, secured transactions, and other commercial matters. Every state has adopted at least part of the UCC to govern commercial transactions within that state. For our purposes in studying contract, the most important part of the Code is Article 2. The entire UCC is available online at http://www.law.cornell.edu/ucc/ucc.table.html.

UCC Article 2 governs the sale of goods. "Goods" means anything movable, except for money, securities, and certain legal rights. Goods include pencils, commercial aircraft, books, and Christmas trees. Goods do not include land or a house, because neither is movable, nor do they include a stock certificate. A contract for the sale of 10,000 sneakers is governed by the UCC; a contract for the sale of a condominium in Los Angeles is governed by the California common law and its statute of frauds. Thus, when analyzing any contract problem as a student or business executive, you must note whether the agreement concerns the sale of goods.

RESTATEMENT (SECOND) OF CONTRACTS

In 1932, the American Law Institute (ALI), a group of lawyers, scholars, and judges, drafted the Restatement of Contracts, attempting to codify what its members regarded as the best rulings of contract law. In 1979, the ALI issued a new version, the Restatement (Second) of Contracts. Like its predecessor, the Restatement (Second) is not the law anywhere, and in this respect it differs from the common law and the UCC. However, judges often refer to the Restatement (Second) when they decide cases so we, too, will seek its counsel from time to time.

AGREEMENT

MEETING OF THE MINDS

Two parties can form a contract only if they have had a meeting of the minds. This requires that they (1) understood each other and (2) intended to reach an agreement. Recall the café conversation between Katrina and Bob, concerning the new film. Was there a meeting of the minds? Judges make an *objective* assessment of each party's intent. A court will not try to get inside Katrina's head and decide what she was thinking as she shook hands. It will look at the handshake *objectively*, deciding how a reasonable person would interpret the words and conduct. Katrina may honestly have meant to conclude a deal for $3 million with no nude scenes, while Bob might in good faith have believed he was committing himself to $2.5 million and absolute control of the script. Neither belief will control the outcome. A reasonable person observing their discussion would not have known what terms they agreed to, and hence there is no agreement.

OFFER

Bargaining begins with an offer. An offer is a serious matter because it permits the other party to create a contract by accepting. **An offer is an act or a statement that proposes definite terms and permits the other party to create a contract by accepting those terms.**

The person who makes an offer is the **offeror**. The person to whom he makes that offer is the **offeree**. The terms are annoying but inescapable because, like handcuffs, all courts use them. In most contract negotiations, two parties bargain back and forth, maybe for minutes, perhaps for months. Each may make several offers, revoke some proposals, suggest counteroffers, and so forth. For our purposes, the offeror remains the one who made the first offer.

Two questions determine whether a statement is an offer:

- Did the offeror *intend* to make a bargain?
- Are the terms of the offer definite?

PROBLEMS WITH INTENT

Zachary says to Sharon, "Come work in my English language center as a teacher. I'll pay you $500 per week for a 35-hour week, for six months starting Monday." This is a valid offer. Zachary intends to make a bargain and his offer is definite. If Sharon accepts, the parties have a contract that either one can enforce. By contrast, we will consider several categories of statements that are *generally not* valid offers.

INVITATIONS TO BARGAIN

An invitation to bargain is not an offer. Suppose Martha telephones Joe and leaves a message on his answering machine, asking if Joe would consider selling his vacation condo on Lake Michigan. Joe faxes a signed letter to Martha saying, "There is no way I could sell the condo for less than $150,000." Martha promptly sends Joe a cashier's check for that amount. Does she own the condo? No. Joe's fax is not an offer. It is merely an invitation to bargain. Joe is indicating that he would be happy to receive an offer from Martha. He is not promising to sell the condo for $150,000 or for any amount.

PRICE QUOTES

A price quote is generally not an offer. If Imperial Textile sends a list of fabric prices for the new year to its regular customers, the list is not an offer. Once again, the law regards the quote merely as a solicitation of offers.

LETTERS OF INTENT

In complex business negotiations, the parties may spend months bargaining over dozens of interrelated issues. Because each party wants to protect itself during the discussions, ensuring that the other side is serious without binding itself to premature commitments, it *may* make sense during the negotiations to draft a **letter of intent**. The letter can help summarize the progress made thus far, and assist the parties in securing necessary financing. But a letter of intent contains a built-in danger: one party may regard it as less than binding. Yet if it is not binding, what is it?

PREVENTIVE Law

Jones Brothers Construction was the general contractor on a job to expand American Airlines' facilities at O'Hare International Airport. The company invited bids from subcontractors. Quake Construction bid on part of the project, and Jones Brothers orally informed the company that it had won the bid and would soon receive a contract. Jones Brothers wanted the license numbers of the subcontractors that Quake would be using, but Quake could not furnish those numbers until it had assured its subcontractors that they had the job. Quake did not want to give that assurance until it was certain of obtaining the work. So Jones Brothers sent a letter of intent stating that:

- Jones was awarding the contract to Quake
- Quake would begin the specified work immediately
- Jones would pay a lump sum price of $1,060,568
- A contract agreement with detailed terms would be prepared shortly; and
- Jones reserved the right to cancel the letter of intent if the parties could not reach a final agreement.

The parties never signed the full contract, and ultimately Jones Brothers hired another company. Quake sued, seeking to recover the money it had spent in preparation and its loss of anticipated profit. The legal issue: was the letter of intent a valid offer?

The Illinois Supreme Court declared that the letter was ambiguous and sent the case back to the trial court. The document contained many phrases that made it seem like a firm contract. The letter awarded the work to Quake, and authorized the work to begin quickly. On the other hand, the document referred to a future, formal contract, indicating that the parties did not yet consider themselves bound, and it permitted Jones to cancel the letter of intent.[2]

---

[2] *Quake Construction v. American Airlines*, 141 Ill. 2d 281, 565 N.E.2d 990, 1990 Ill. LEXIS 151 (Ill. 1990).

So after several years of litigation, Jones Brothers and Quake had to go *back* to the trial court to establish whether they intended the letter to be binding. Every year there are countless cases just like *Quake*. The problem is that both sides permit ambiguity and vagueness to enter their negotiations. Sometimes parties do this accidentally, by paying too little attention to what they are saying. The solution is simple: think carefully before offering or responding.

At other times, with sophisticated businesspeople, ambiguity may not be so accidental, as one party is trying to get a commitment from the other side without obligating itself. A party may feel *almost* ready to commit, yet still have reservations. It wants the other party to make a commitment, so that planning can go forward. This is understandable, but dangerous.

If you were negotiating for Jones Brothers and wanted to clarify negotiations without committing your company, how could you do it? From Quake's point of view, how should you proceed?

ADVERTISEMENTS

An advertisement is generally not an offer. An advertisement is merely a request for offers. The consumer makes the offer, by selecting merchandise in a store and taking it to the cashier. The seller is free to reject the offer. However, while the common law regards advertisements as mere solicitations, consumers do have protection from those shopkeepers intent upon deceit. Every state has some form of **consumer protection statute**. These statutes outlaw false advertising. For example, an automobile dealer who advertises a remarkably low price but then has only one automobile at that price has probably violated a consumer protection statute because the ad was published in bad faith, to trick consumers into coming to the dealership.

PROBLEMS WITH DEFINITENESS

It is not enough that the offeror intends to enter into an agreement. **The terms of the offer must be definite.** If they are vague, then even if the offeree "accepts" the deal, a court does not have enough information to enforce it and there is no contract.

You want a friend to work in your store for the holiday season. This is a definite offer: "I offer you a job as a salesclerk in the store from November 1 through December 29, 40 hours per week at $10 per hour." But suppose, by contrast, you say: "I offer you a job as a salesclerk in the store from November 1 through December 29, 40 hours per week. We will work out a fair wage once we see how busy things get." Your friend replies, "That's fine with me." This offer is indefinite. What is a fair wage? $5 per hour? $15 per hour? How will the determination be made? There is no binding agreement.

TERMINATION OF OFFERS

As we have seen, the great power that an offeree has is to form a contract by accepting an offer. But this power is lost when the offer is terminated, which can happen in four ways:

Revocation. In general, the offeror may revoke the offer any time before it has been accepted. Revocation is effective as soon as the offeree receives it.

Rejection. If an offeree rejects an offer, the rejection immediately terminates the offer. Suppose a major accounting firm telephones you and offers a job, starting at $80,000. You respond, "Nah. I'm gonna work on my surfing for a year or two." The next day you come to your senses and write the firm, accepting its offer. No contract. Your rejection terminated the offer and ended your power to accept.

Counteroffer. Frederick faxes Kim, offering to sell a 50 percent interest in the Fab Hotel in New York for only $135 million. Kim faxes back, offering to pay $115 million. Moments later, Kim's business partner convinces her that Frederick's offer was a bargain, and she faxes an acceptance of his $135 million offer. Does Kim have a binding deal? No. A counteroffer is a rejection. The parties have no contract at any price.

Expiration. When an offer specifies a time limit for acceptance, that period is binding. If the offer specifies no time limit, the offeree has a reasonable period in which to accept.

Destruction of the subject matter. A used car dealer offers to sell you a rare 1938 Bugatti for $75,000 if you bring cash the next day. You arrive, suitcase stuffed with century notes, just in time to see the dealer fall out of a blimp, dropping 3,000 feet through the air and crushing the Bugatti. The dealer's offer terminated.

ACCEPTANCE

As we have seen, when there is a valid offer outstanding, the offeree can create a contract by accepting. **The offeree must say or do something to accept.** Silence, though golden, is not acceptance. Marge telephones Vick and leaves a message on his answering machine: "I'll pay $75 for your law textbook from last semester. I'm desperate to get a copy, so I will assume you agree unless I hear from you by 6:00 tonight." Marge hears nothing by the deadline and assumes she has a deal. She is mistaken. Vick neither said nor did anything to indicate that he accepted.

When the offer is for a bilateral contract, the offeree generally must accept by making a promise. An employer calls you and says, "If you're able to start work two weeks from today, we can pay you $5,000 per month. Can you do it?" That is an offer for a bilateral contract. You must accept by promising to start in two weeks.

When the offer is for a unilateral contract, the offeree must accept by performing. A newspaper telephones you: "If you write us a 5,000-word article on iguanas that can play bridge, and get it to us by Friday at noon, we'll pay you $750." The newspaper does not want a promise, it wants the article. If—and only if—your work is ready on time, you get paid.

MIRROR IMAGE RULE

If only he had known! A splendid university, an excellent position as department chair—gone. And all because of the mirror image rule. The Ohio State University wrote to Philip Foster offering him an appointment as a professor and chair of the art history department. His position was to begin July 1, and he had until June 2 to accept the job. On June 2, Foster telephoned the Dean and left a message accepting the position, **effective July 15**. Later, Foster thought better of it and wrote the university, accepting the school's starting date of July 1. Too late! Professor Foster never did occupy that chair at Ohio State. The court held that since his acceptance varied the starting date, it was a counteroffer. And a counteroffer, as we know, is a rejection.[3]

The common law mirror image rule requires that acceptance be on precisely the same terms as the offer. If the acceptance contains terms that add to or contradict the offer, even in minor ways, courts generally consider it a counteroffer. The rule worked reasonably well in the nineteenth century, when parties would write an original contract and exchange it, penciling in any changes. But now that businesses use standardized forms to purchase most goods and services, the rule creates enormous difficulties. Sellers use forms they have prepared, with all conditions stated to their advantage, and buyers employ their own forms, with terms they prefer. The forms are exchanged in the mail (or electronically), with neither side clearly agreeing to the other party's terms.

The problem is known as the "battle of forms." Once again, the UCC has entered the fray, attempting to provide flexibility and common sense for those contracts involving the sale of goods. But for contracts governed by the common law, such as Professor Foster's, the mirror image rule is still the law.

UCC AND THE BATTLE OF FORMS

UCC §2-207 dramatically modifies the mirror image rule for the sale of goods. Under this provision, an acceptance that adds additional or different terms *will often create a contract*. The rule is intricate, but may be summarized this way:

> For the sale of goods, the most important factor is whether the parties believe they have a binding agreement. If their conduct indicates that they have a deal, they probably do.
>
> If the offeree *adds new* terms to the offer, acceptance by the offeror generally creates a binding agreement.
>
> If the offeree *changes* the terms of the offer, a court will probably rely on general principles of the UCC to create a fair contract.
>
> If a party wants a contract on its terms only, with no changes, it must clearly indicate that.

Suppose Wholesaler writes to Manufacturer, offering to buy "10,000 wheelbarrows at $50 per unit. Payable on delivery, 30 days from today's date." Manufacturer writes back, "We accept your offer of 10,000 wheelbarrows at $50 per unit, payable on delivery. Interest at normal trade rates for unpaid balances." Manufacturer clearly intends to form a contract. The company has added a new term, but there is still a valid agreement.

[3] *Foster v. Ohio State University*, 41 Ohio App. 3d 86, 534 N.E.2d 1220, 1987 Ohio App. LEXIS 10761 (Ohio Ct. App. 1987).

CONSIDERATION

We have all made promises that we soon regretted. Mercifully, the law does not hold us accountable for everything we say. Yet some promises must be enforced. Which ones? The doctrine of consideration exists for one purpose: to distinguish promises that are binding from those that are not.

Consideration is a required element of any contract. **Consideration means that there must be bargaining that leads to an exchange between the parties.** *Bargaining* indicates that each side is obligating itself in some way *to induce the other side to agree.* Generally, a court will enforce one party's promise only if the other party did something or promised something in exchange.

If one party makes a promise without some kind of bargaining, there is generally no contract. Carol Kelsoe had worked at International Wood Products for many years. One day, her supervisor surprised her by promising her 5 percent of the company's stock. Unfortunately, he never gave her those shares. Heartbroken, Kelsoe sued—and lost.[4] Kelsoe had given nothing in exchange for her supervisor's words. There was no consideration on her part, and she could not enforce his promise. If Kelsoe had assured him that she would remain at International Wood for three extra years (or three extra days) in exchange for the stock, that would have been consideration, and she would have collected her shares.

The thing bargained for can be another promise or action. Usually one party bargains for another promise. Gwynneth says to Ben, "I'm supposed to fly to Chicago in a week, to give a speech. Will you do it for me? I'll give you $15,000." "Sure," Ben responds, "I'll do that for $15,000." The very next day Gwynneth changes her mind. Too late. Ben's *promise* to go to Chicago was consideration. The parties have a deal that either one can enforce.

The thing bargained for can be action, rather than a promise. Manny tells Sandra, "I need someone to hook up my cable T.V. by tonight at 8:00. If you get it done, I'll give you $200." Manny seeks action, not a promise. If Sandra connects the television on time, her work is consideration and the parties have a binding deal.

The thing bargained for can be a promise to do something or a promise to refrain from doing something. Megan promises *to deliver* 1,000 canoes in two months if Casey agrees to pay $300 per canoe. Megan's promise to act is consideration. The most famous of all consideration lawsuits involved a promise to refrain. The case began in 1869, when a well-meaning uncle made a promise to his nephew. Ever since the nephew responded, generations of American law students have dutifully inhaled the facts and sworn by its wisdom; now you, too, may drink it in.

ILLUSORY PROMISE

Annabel calls Jim and says, "I'll sell you my bicycle for 325 bucks. Interested?" Jim says, "I'll look at it tonight in the bike rack. If I like what I see, I'll pay you

---

[4] *Kelsoe v. International Wood Products, Inc.*, 588 So. 2d 877, 1991 Ala. LEXIS 1014 (Supreme Court of Alabama, 1991).

HAMER v. SIDWAY

124 N.Y.538, 27 N.E.256, 1891 N.Y. LEXIS 1396
New York Court of Appeals, 1891

Facts: This is a story with two Storys. William Story wanted his nephew to grow up healthy and prosperous. He promised the 15-year-old boy (also William Story) $5,000 if the lad would refrain from drinking liquor, using tobacco, swearing, and playing cards or billiards for money until his twenty-first birthday. (In that wild era—can you believe it?—the nephew had a legal right to do all those things.) The nephew agreed and, what is more, he kept his word. When he reached his twenty-first birthday, the nephew notified his uncle that he had honored the agreement. The uncle congratulated the young man and promised to give him the money, but said he would wait a few more years before handing over the cash, until the nephew was mature enough to handle such a large sum. The uncle died in 1887 without having paid, and his estate refused to honor the promise. Because the nephew had transferred his rights in the money, it was a man named Hamer who eventually sought to collect from the uncle's estate. The estate argued that since the nephew had given no consideration for the uncle's promise, there was no enforceable contract. The trial court found for the plaintiff, and the uncle's estate appealed.

Issue: Did the nephew give consideration for the uncle's promise?

Excerpts from Justice Parker's Decision: The defendant contends that the contract was without consideration to support it, and therefore invalid. He asserts that the promisee, by refraining from the use of liquor and tobacco, was not harmed, but benefited; that that which he did was best for him to do, independently of his uncle's promise,—and insists that it follows that, unless the promisor was benefited, the contract was without consideration,—a contention which, if well founded, would seem to leave open for controversy in many cases whether that which the promisee did or omitted to do was in fact of such benefit to him as to leave no consideration to support the enforcement of the promisor's agreement. Such a rule could not be tolerated, and is without foundation in the law. Courts will not ask whether the thing which forms the consideration does in fact benefit the promisee or a third party, or is of any substantial value to any one. It is enough that something is promised, done, forborne, or suffered by the party to whom the promise is made as consideration for the promise made to him.

Now applying this rule to the facts before us, the promisee used tobacco, occasionally drank liquor, and he had a legal right to do so. That right he abandoned for a period of years upon the strength of the promise of the testator [that is, the uncle] that for such forbearance he would give him $5,000. We need not speculate on the effort which may have been required to give up the use of those stimulants. It is sufficient that he restricted his lawful freedom of action within certain prescribed limits upon the faith of his uncle's agreement, and now, having fully performed the conditions imposed, it is of no moment whether such performance actually proved a benefit to the promisor, and the court will not inquire into it. ■

three and a quarter in the morning." At sunrise, Jim shows up with the $325 but Annabel refuses to sell. Can Jim enforce their deal? No. He said he would buy the bicycle *if he liked it*, keeping for himself the power to get out of the agreement for any reason at all. He is not committing himself to do anything, and the law considers his promise illusory, that is, not really a promise at all. **An illusory promise is not consideration.** Because he has given no consideration, there is no contract and *neither party* can enforce the deal.

LEGALITY

Soheil Sadri, a California resident, did some serious gambling at Caesar's Tahoe casino in Nevada. And lost. To keep gambling, he wrote checks to Caesar's and then signed two memoranda pledging to repay money advanced. After two days, with his losses totaling more than $22,000, he went home. Back in California, Sadri stopped payment on the checks and refused to pay any of the money he owed Caesar's. The casino sued, and recovered . . . nothing. Sadri relied on an important legal principle to defeat the suit: **a contract that is illegal is void and unenforceable**. We will examine a variety of contracts that may be void.

Gambling is one of America's fastest growing businesses, but a controversial one. Because our citizens—and our states—are divided over the ethics of wagering, conflicts such as the dispute between Sadri and Caesar's are inevitable. The basic rule, however, is clear: **a gambling contract is illegal unless it is specifically authorized by state statute**. In California, as in many states, gambling on credit is not allowed. In other words, it is illegal to lend money to help someone wager. A contract based on a gambling debt is unenforceable. However, in Nevada, gambling on credit is legal, and debt memoranda such as Sadri's are enforceable contracts. Caesar's sued Sadri in California (where he lived). The court admitted that California's attitude toward gambling had changed, and that bingo, poker clubs, and lotteries were common. Nonetheless, the court denied that the new tolerance extended to wagering on credit, stating: "The judiciary cannot protect pathological gamblers from themselves, but we can refuse to participate in their financial ruin."[5]

Caesar's lost and Sadri kept his money. The dispute is a useful starting place from which to examine contract legality because it illustrates two important themes. First, morality is a significant part of contract legality. In refusing to enforce an obligation that Sadri undeniably had made, the California court relied on the human and social consequences of gambling and on the ethics of judicial enforcement of gambling debts. Second, "void" really means just that: **a court will not assist either party to an illegal agreement**, even if its refusal leaves one party obviously shortchanged.

RESTRAINT OF TRADE

Free trade is the basis of the American economy, and any bargain that restricts it is suspect. Most restraint of free trade is barred by antitrust law. But it is the common law that still regulates one restriction on trade: agreements to refrain from competition. Some of these agreements are legal, some are void. They are *very* common: Many readers of this book will read such a clause in their own employment contract.

To be valid, an agreement not to compete must be ancillary to a legitimate bargain. "Ancillary" means that the noncompetition agreement must be part of a larger agreement. Suppose Cliff sells his gasoline station to Mina and the two agree that Cliff will not open a competing gas station within five miles anytime

---

[5] *Metropolitan Creditors Service of Sacramento v. Sadri*, 15 Cal. App. 4th 1821, 1993 Cal. App. LEXIS 559, 19 Cal. Rptr. 2d 646 (Cal. Ct. App. 1993).

during the next two years. Cliff's agreement not to compete is ancillary to the sale of his service station. His noncompetition promise is enforceable. But suppose that Cliff and Mina already had the only two gas stations within 35 miles. They agree between themselves not to hire each other's workers. Their agreement might be profitable to them, because each could now keep wages artificially low. But their deal is ancillary to no legitimate bargain, and it is therefore void.

The two most common settings for legitimate noncompetition agreements are the *sale of a business* and an *employment relationship.*

SALE OF A BUSINESS

Kory has operated a real estate office, Hearth Attack, in a small city for 35 years, building an excellent reputation and many ties with the community. She offers to sell you the business and its goodwill for $300,000. But you need assurance that Kory will not take your money and promptly open a competing office across the street. With her reputation and connections, she would ruin your chances of success. You insist on a noncompete clause in the sale contract. In this clause, Kory promises that for one year she will not open a new real estate office or go to work for a competing company within a 10-mile radius of Hearth Attack. Suppose, six months after selling you the business, Kory goes to work for a competing realtor, two blocks away. You seek an injunction to prevent her from working. Who wins?

When a noncompete agreement is ancillary to the sale of a business, it is enforceable if reasonable in time, geographic area, and scope of activity. In other words, a court will not enforce a noncompete agreement that lasts an unreasonably long time, covers an unfairly large area, or prohibits the seller of the business from doing a type of work that she never had done before. Measured by this test, Kory is almost certainly bound by her agreement. One year is a reasonable time to allow you to get your new business started. A 10-mile radius is probably about the area that Hearth Attack covers, and realty is obviously a fair business from which to prohibit Kory. A court will grant the injunction, barring Kory from her new job.

If, on the other hand, the noncompetition agreement had prevented Kory from working anywhere within 200 miles of Hearth Attack, and she started working 50 miles away, a court would refuse to enforce the contract.

EMPLOYMENT

When you sign an employment contract, the document may well contain a noncompete clause. Employers have legitimate worries that employees might go to a competitor and take with them trade secrets or other proprietary information. Some employers, though, attempt to place harsh restrictions on their employees, perhaps demanding a blanket agreement that the employee will never go to work for a competitor. Once again, courts look at the reasonableness of restrictions placed on an employee's future work. Because the agreement now involves the very livelihood of the worker, a court scrutinizes the agreement more closely.

A noncompete clause in an employment contract is generally reasonable—and enforceable—only to the extent necessary to protect (1) trade secrets, (2) confidential information, or (3) customer lists developed over an

extended period. In general, other restrictions on future employment are unenforceable.[6] Suppose that Gina, an engineer, goes to work for Fission Chips, a silicon chip manufacturer that specializes in defense work. She signs a noncompete agreement promising never to work for a competitor. Over a period of three years, Gina learns some of Fission's proprietary methods of etching information onto the chips. She acquires a great deal of new expertise about chips generally. And she periodically deals with Fission Chips' customers, all of whom are well-known software and hardware manufacturers. Gina accepts an offer from WriteSmall, a competitor. Fission Chips races into court, seeking an injunction to block Gina from working for WriteSmall.

This injunction threatens Gina's career. If she cannot work for a competitor, or use her general engineering skills, what *will* she do? And for exactly that reason, no court will grant such a broad order. The court will allow Gina to work for competitors, including WriteSmall. It will order her not to use or reveal any trade secrets belonging to Fission. She will, however, be permitted to use the general expertise she has acquired, and she may contact former customers since anyone could get their names from the yellow pages.

Back with more law in a minute, but first a check on rush hour traffic.

METRO TRAFFIC CONTROL, INC. v. SHADOW TRAFFIC NETWORK

22 Cal. App. 4th 853, 27 Cal. Rptr. 2d 573, 1994 Cal. App. LEXIS 137
California Court of Appeal, 1994

Facts: Metro Traffic Control contracted with Los Angeles radio stations to gather and broadcast local traffic information. Jeff Baugh and Robin Johnson worked for Metro as air traffic reporters, and Tommy Grskovich worked for Metro as a managing producer. All three had written employment at will contracts, meaning that either party could end the agreement at any time. Each contract contained a noncompete clause that prohibited the employee from working for a competitor for one year after leaving Metro.

One of Metro's customers was radio station KFWB in Los Angeles. Baugh, Johnson, and Grskovich all worked on broadcasts for KFWB. But KFWB did not renew its contract with Metro. Instead, the station gave its business to Metro's competitor, Shadow Traffic. Metro assured Baugh, Johnson, and Grskovich that they would have jobs at Metro, but the three employees left and began working for Shadow, on the KFWB job. Metro sued, seeking an injunction to bar their employment, based on the noncompete clauses. The trial court denied the injunction and Metro appealed.

Issue: Is Metro entitled to an injunction prohibiting its former employees from working for Shadow?

Excerpts from Judge Vogel's Decision: Metro argues that it has protectible trade secrets developed in the course of serving as KFWB's traffic reporter. It describes the trade secrets as information it has about the peculiar requirements imposed by KFWB on Metro's traffic reporting services during the term of their contract relationship. Metro delineates its alleged trade secrets in very general terms. William Gaines, the regional director of Metro, describes the trade secrets as KFWB's "very strict and particular requirements regarding the quality, sound and personality of the anchors reporting over its airways [and] KFWB hand-picks each of its anchors."

[6] If the agreement restricts the employee from *starting a new business*, a court may apply the more lenient standard used for the sale of a business; the noncompete clause will be enforced if reasonable in time, geography, and scope of activity.

It appears that Metro's battery of radio announcers had the "quality, sound and personality" required by KFWB. These are subjective dimensions of the employees who were found acceptable to and approved by KFWB and not part of an informational base belonging to Metro. No doubt Metro conveyed to its employees KFWB's preferences and requirements regarding word choice and factual reporting but that does not amount to the compilation of an intangible personal property right owned by the employer. Actors, musicians, athletes, and others are frequently trained, tutored, and coached to satisfy the requirements of their sponsors and audiences, but their talents belong to them to contract away as they please. Simply hiring personnel who possess the requirements specified by a customer does not convert the employee into a "trade secret."

In summary, Metro has not demonstrated that it possesses any trade secret, and the trial court could rationally conclude that it is unlikely Metro will prevail on the merits. We hold the trial court did not abuse its discretion in denying the preliminary injunction.

Exculpatory Clauses

You decide to capitalize on your expert ability as a skier and open a ski school in Colorado, "Pike's Pique." But you realize that skiing sometimes causes injuries, so you require anyone signing up for lessons to sign this form:

> I agree to hold Pike's Pique and its employees entirely harmless in the event that I am injured in any way or for any reason or cause, including but not limited to any acts, whether negligent or otherwise, of Pike's Pique or any employee or agent thereof.

The day your school opens, Sara Beth, an instructor, deliberately pushes Toby over a cliff because Toby criticized her color combinations. Eddie, a beginning student, "blows out" his knee attempting an advanced racing turn. And Maureen, another student, reaches the bottom of a steep run and slams into a snowmobile that Sara Beth parked there. Maureen, Eddie, and Toby's family all sue Pike's Pique. You defend based on the form you had them sign. Does it save the day?

The form on which you are relying is an **exculpatory clause**, that is, one that attempts to release you from liability in the event of injury to another party. Exculpatory clauses are common. Ski schools use them and so do parking lots, landlords, warehouses, and day-care centers. All manner of businesses hope to avoid large tort judgments by requiring their customers to give up any right to recover. Is such a clause valid? Sometimes. Courts frequently—but not always—ignore exculpatory clauses, finding that one party was forcing the other party to give up legal rights that no one should be forced to surrender.

An exculpatory clause is generally unenforceable when it attempts to exclude an intentional tort or gross negligence. When Sara Beth pushes Toby over a cliff, that is the intentional tort of battery. A court will not enforce the exculpatory clause. Sara Beth is clearly liable.[7] As to the snowmobile at the bottom of the run, if a court determines that was gross negligence (carelessness far greater than ordinary negligence), then the exculpatory clause will again be ignored. If, however, it was ordinary negligence, then we must continue the analysis.

---

[7] Note that Pike's Pique is probably not liable under agency law principles that preclude an employer's liability for an employee's intentional tort.

An exculpatory clause is generally unenforceable when the affected activity is in the public interest, such as medical care, public transportation, or some essential service. What about Eddie's suit against Pike's Pique? Eddie claims that he should never have been allowed to attempt an advanced maneuver. His suit is for ordinary negligence, and the exculpatory clause probably does bar him from recovery. Skiing is a recreational activity. No one is obligated to do it, and there is no strong public interest in ensuring that we have access to ski slopes.

An exculpatory clause is generally unenforceable when the parties have greatly unequal bargaining power. When Maureen flies to Colorado, suppose that the airline requires her to sign a form contract with an exculpatory clause. Because the airline almost certainly has much greater bargaining power, it can afford to offer a "take it or leave it" contract. But because the bargaining power is so unequal, the clause is probably unenforceable.

An exculpatory clause is generally unenforceable unless the clause is clearly written and readily visible. Thus, if Pike's Pique gave all ski students an eight-page contract, and the exculpatory clause was at the bottom of page seven in small print, the average customer would never notice it. The clause would be void.

UNCONSCIONABLE CONTRACTS

Gail Waters was young, naive, and insecure. A serious injury when she was 12 years old left her with an annuity, that is, a guaranteed annual payment for many years. When Gail was 21, she became involved with Thomas Beauchemin, an ex-convict, who introduced her to drugs. Beauchemin suggested that Gail sell her annuity to some friends of his, and she agreed. Beauchemin arranged for a lawyer to draw up a contract, and Gail signed it. She received one $50,000 payment for her annuity, which at that time had a cash value of $189,000 and was worth, over its remaining 25 years, $694,000. Gail later decided this was not an excellent bargain. Was the contract enforceable? That depends on the law of unconscionability.

An unconscionable contract is one that a court refuses to enforce because of fundamental unfairness. Historically, a contract was considered unconscionable if it was "such as no man in his senses and not under delusion would make on the one hand, and as no honest and fair man would accept on the other."[8] The two factors that most often lead a court to find unconscionability are (1) **oppression**, meaning that one party used its superior power to force a contract on the weaker party, and (2) **surprise**, meaning that the weaker party did not fully understand the consequences of its agreement.

Gail Waters won her case. The Massachusetts high court ruled:

> Beauchemin introduced the plaintiff to drugs, exhausted her credit card accounts to the sum of $6,000, unduly influenced her, suggested that the plaintiff sell her annuity contract, initiated the contract negotiations, was the agent of the defendants, and benefited from the contract between the plaintiff and the defendants. The defendants were represented by legal counsel; the plaintiff was not. The cash value of the

---

[8] *Hume v. United States*, 132 U.S. 406, 411, 10 S. Ct. 134, 1889 U.S. LEXIS 1888 (1889), quoting *Earl of Chesterfield v. Janssen*, 38 Eng. Rep. 82, 100 (Ch. 1750).

annuity policy at the time the contract was executed was approximately four times greater than the price to be paid by the defendants. For payment of not more than $50,000 the defendants were to receive an asset that could be immediately exchanged for $189,000, or they could elect to hold it for its guaranteed term and receive $694,000.

The defendants assumed no risk and the plaintiff gained no advantage. We are satisfied that the disparity of interests in this contract is so gross that the court cannot resist the inference that it was improperly obtained and is unconscionable.[9]

CAPACITY AND CONSENT

For Kevin Green, it was love at first sight. She was sleek, as quick as a cat, and a beautiful deep blue. He paid $4,600 cash for the used Camaro. The car soon blew a gasket, and Kevin demanded his money back. But the Camaro came with no guarantee, and Star Chevrolet, the dealer, refused. Kevin repaired the car himself. Next, some unpleasantness on the highway left the car a worthless wreck. Kevin received the full value of the car from his insurance company. Then he sued the dealer, seeking a refund of his purchase price. The dealer pointed out that it was not responsible for the accident, and that the car had no warranty of any kind. Yet the court awarded Kevin the full value of his car. How can this be?

The automobile dealer ignored *legal capacity*. Kevin Green was only 16 years old when he bought the car, and a minor, said the court, has the right to cancel any agreement he made anytime he wants to, for any reason.

Capacity concerns the legal ability of a party to enter a contract. Someone may lack capacity because of his young age or mental infirmity. Consent refers to whether a contracting party truly understood what he was getting into and whether he made the agreement voluntarily. Consent issues arise most often in cases of fraud and mistake.

CAPACITY

Capacity is the legal ability to enter into a contract. An adult of sound mind has the legal capacity to contract. Generally, any deal she enters into will be enforced if all elements we have seen—agreement, consideration, and so forth—are present. But two groups of people usually lack legal capacity: minors and those with a mental impairment.

MINORS

A minor is someone under the age of 18. Because a minor lacks legal capacity, she normally can create only a voidable contract. **A voidable contract may be canceled by the party who lacks capacity.** Notice that *only the party lacking capacity* may cancel the agreement. So a minor who enters into a contract generally may choose between enforcing the agreement or negating it. The other party, however, has no such right.

---

[9] *Waters v. Min Ltd.*, 412 Mass. 64, 587 N.E.2d 231, 1992 Mass. LEXIS 66 (1992).

DISAFFIRMANCE

A minor who wishes to escape from a contract generally may **disaffirm** it; that is, he may notify the other party that he refuses to be bound by the agreement. Because Kevin was 16 when he signed, the deal was voidable. When the Camaro blew a gasket and the lad informed Star Chevrolet that he wanted his money back, he was disaffirming the contract, which he could do for any reason at all. Kevin was entitled to his money back. If Star Chevrolet had understood the law of capacity, it would have towed the Camaro away and returned the young man's $4,600. At least the dealership would have had a repairable automobile.

RESTITUTION

A minor who disaffirms a contract must return the consideration he has received, to the extent he is able. Restoring the other party to its original position is called **restitution**. The consideration that Kevin Green received in the contract was, of course, the Camaro. If Star Chevrolet had delivered a check for $4,600, Kevin would have been obligated to return the car.

What happens if the minor is not able to return the consideration because he no longer has it or it has been destroyed? Most (but not all) states hold that the minor is still entitled to his money back. Kevin Green got his money and Star Chevrolet received a fine lesson.

MENTALLY IMPAIRED PERSONS

A person suffers from a mental impairment if by reason of mental illness or defect he is unable to understand the nature and consequences of the transaction.[10] The mental impairment can be insanity that has been formally declared by a court or mental illness that has never been ruled on but is now evident. The impairment may also be due to some other mental illness, such as schizophrenia, or to mental retardation, brain injury, senility, or any other cause that renders the person unable to understand the nature and consequences of the contract.

A party suffering a mental impairment generally creates only a voidable contract. The impaired person has the right to disaffirm the contract just as a minor does. But again, the contract is voidable, not void. The mentally impaired party generally has the right to full performance if she wishes. Similar rules apply in cases of drug or alcohol **intoxication**. When one party is so intoxicated that he cannot understand the nature and consequences of the transaction, the contract is voidable.

REALITY OF CONSENT

Smiley offers to sell you his house for $300,000, and you agree in writing to buy. After you move in, you discover that the house is sinking into the earth at the rate of six inches per week. In 12 months, your only access to the house will be through the chimney. You sue, asking to **rescind, which means to cancel the agreement**. You argue that when you signed the contract you did not truly

---

[10] Restatement (Second) of Contracts §15.

consent because you lacked essential information. In this section, we look at issues of misrepresentation, fraud, and mistake.

MISREPRESENTATION AND FRAUD

Misrepresentation occurs when a party to a contract says something that is factually wrong. "This house has no termites," says a homeowner to a prospective buyer. If the house is swarming with the nasty pests, the statement is a misrepresentation. The misrepresentation might be innocent or fraudulent. If the owner believes the statement to be true and has a good reason for that belief, he has made an **innocent misrepresentation**. If the owner knows that it is false, the statement is **fraudulent misrepresentation**. To explain these concepts, we will assume that two people are discussing a possible deal. One is the "maker," that is, the person who makes the statement that is later disputed. The other is the "injured person," the one who eventually claims to have been injured by the statement. In order to rescind the contract, the injured person must show that the maker's statement was either fraudulent or a material misrepresentation. She does not have to show both. Innocent misrepresentation and fraud each make a contract voidable. **To rescind a contract based on misrepresentation or fraud, a party must show three things: (1) there was a false statement of fact; (2) the statement was fraudulent or material; and (3) the injured person justifiably relied on the statement.**

ELEMENT ONE: FALSE STATEMENT OF FACT

The injured party must show a false statement of fact. Notice that this does not mean the statement was a lie. If a homeowner says that the famous architect Stanford White designed his house, but Bozo Loco actually did the work, it is a false statement. The owner might have a good reason for the error. Perhaps a local history book identifies the house as a Stanford White. Or his words might be an intentional lie. In either case, it is a false statement of fact.

An **opinion**, though, is not a statement of fact. A realtor says, "I think land values around here will be going up 20 or 30 percent for the foreseeable future." That statement is pretty enticing to a buyer, but it is not a false statement of fact. The maker is clearly stating her own opinion, and the buyer who relies on it does so at his peril. A close relative of opinion is something called puffery. A statement is **puffery** when a reasonable person would realize that it is a sales pitch, representing the exaggerated opinion of the seller. Puffery is not a statement of fact and is never a basis for rescission.

ELEMENT TWO: FRAUD OR MATERIALITY

This is the heart of the case. The injured party must demonstrate that the statement was fraudulent or material:

- The statement was *fraudulent* if the maker intended to induce the other party to contract, either knowing that her words were false or uncertain that they were true.
- The statement was *material* if the maker expected the other party to rely on her words in reaching an agreement.

So the injured party can win by showing either of two very different things. Fraud indicates a bad faith statement, whereas material misrepresentation signifies that the words were inaccurate—and effective.

Consider the examples in the following chart.

The Difference between Fraud and Misrepresentation

Statement. In each case, the words are false.	Owner's Belief	Legal Result	Explanation
1. "The heating system is perfect."	Owner knows this is false.	Fraud.	Owner knew the statement was false and intended to induce the buyer to enter into a contract.
2. "The house is built on solid bedrock."	Owner has no idea what is under the surface.	Fraud.	Owner was not certain the statement was true and intended to induce the buyer to enter into a contract.
3. "The roof is only six years old."	Owner believes the statement is accurate, because when he bought the house six years ago, he was told the roof was new.	Material misrepresentation.	Owner acted in good faith, but the statement is material because owner expects the buyer to rely on it.
4. "The pool is 30 feet long."	Owner believes the statement is accurate because he measured the pool himself, though in fact it is only 29 feet long.	Not a material misrepresentation.	Although this is a misrepresentation, it is not material, since a reasonable buyer would not make a decision based on a one-foot error in the pool length.

ELEMENT THREE: JUSTIFIABLE RELIANCE

The injured party must also show that she actually did rely on the false statement and that her reliance was reasonable. Suppose the seller of a gas station lies through his teeth about the structural soundness of the building. The buyer believes what he hears but does not much care, because he plans to demolish the building and construct a day-care center. There was fraud but no reliance, and the buyer may not rescind.

PLAINTIFF'S REMEDY FOR MISREPRESENTATION OR FRAUD

Both innocent and fraudulent misrepresentation permit the injured party to rescind the contract. In other words, the injured party who proves all three elements will get her money back. She will, of course, have to make restitution to the other party. If she bought land and now wants to rescind, she must return the property to the seller.

But the injured party is not forced to rescind the deal if it makes financial sense to go forward with it. After signing a contract to buy a new house, Nancy learns that the building has a terrible heating system. A new one will cost $12,000. If the seller told her the system was "like new," Nancy may rescind the deal. But it may be economically harmful for her to do so. She might have sold her old house, hired a mover, taken a new job, and so forth. She has the option of fully performing the contract and moving into the new house. What are her other remedies? That will depend on whether the misstatement ("the system is like new") was fraudulent or simply a material misrepresentation.

If the maker's statement is fraudulent, the injured party generally has a choice of rescinding the contract or suing for damages. If the seller's mistake was fraudulent, Nancy will generally be allowed to carry out the contract and sue for damages. She could move into the new house and sue for the difference between what she got and what was promised, which is probably about $12,000, the cost of replacing the heating system. But if the seller's mistake was innocent, and Nancy can prove only material misrepresentation, she has no remedy other than rescission. If she goes forward with the contract, she must accept the house as she finds it.

SPECIAL PROBLEM: SILENCE

We know that a party negotiating a contract may not misrepresent a material fact. But what about silence? Suppose the seller knows the roof is in dreadful condition (since she sleeps under an umbrella) but the buyer never asks. Must the seller disclose what she knows?

This is perhaps the hottest topic today in the law of misrepresentation. A seller who knows something that the buyer does not know is often required to divulge it. The Restatement (Second) of Contracts offers guidance:

Nondisclosure of a fact amounts to misrepresentation only in these four cases:

Where disclosure is necessary *to correct a previous assertion*. During the course of negotiations, one party's perception of the facts may change. When an earlier statement later appears inaccurate, the change generally must be reported.

Where disclosure would correct *a basic mistaken assumption* that the other party is relying on. When one party knows that the other is negotiating with a mistaken assumption about an important fact, the party who knows of the error must correct it.

Where disclosure would correct the other party's mistaken understanding about *a writing* (such as a deed or map).

Where there is *a relationship of trust* between the two parties, for example when a parent is selling to a child.[11]

A seller must report any latent defect he knows about, if a reasonable buyer would not discover it on his own. For example, a property owner who realizes that there is toxic waste underground must reveal that fact. Must she also disclose that those substances are under *adjoining* property?

---

[11] Restatement (Second) of Contracts §162.

STRAWN v. CANUSO

140 N.J. 43, 657 A.2d 420, 1995 N.J. LEXIS 54
Supreme Court of New Jersey, 1995

Facts: Between 1966 and 1978, huge quantities of hazardous chemicals were illegally dumped in the Buzby Landfill in Voorhees Township, New Jersey. Toxic materials escaped, poisoning the groundwater and air. John Canuso, a builder-developer, decided to create a new housing development near Buzby Landfill. Canuso knew about the dangerous chemicals but decided to build anyway. He hired a marketing firm, Fox & Lazo, to sell the houses. Fox also knew about the toxic waste. Canuso and Fox both failed to say anything to buyers about the landfill, even after some homeowners complained about smells. When buyers independently learned what was in Buzby Landfill, they filed suit, and the case reached the New Jersey Supreme Court.

Issue: Does a builder-seller have a duty to disclose toxic waste that is on adjoining land?

Excerpts from Justice O'Hern's Decision: The principal factors shaping the duty to disclose have been the difference in bargaining power between the professional seller of residential real estate and the purchaser of such housing, and the difference in access to information between the seller and the buyer. Those principles guide our decision in this case.

The first factor causes us to limit our holding to professional sellers of residential housing (persons engaged in the business of building or developing residential housing) and the brokers representing them. Neither the reseller of residential real estate nor the seller of commercial property has that same advantage in the bargaining process.

The silence of the Fox & Lazo representatives and the Canuso Management Corporation's principals and employees "created a mistaken impression on the part of the purchaser." Defendants used sales-promotion brochures, newspaper advertisements, and a fact sheet to sell the homes in the development. That material portrayed the development as located in a peaceful, bucolic setting with an abundance of fresh air and clean lake waters. Although the literature mentioned how far the property was from malls, country clubs, and train stations, "neither the brochures, the newspaper advertisements nor any sales personnel mentioned that a landfill [was] located within half a mile of some of the homes."

We hold that a builder-developer of residential real estate or a broker representing it is not only liable to a purchaser for affirmative and intentional misrepresentation, but is also liable for nondisclosure of off-site physical conditions known to it and unknown and not readily observable by the buyer if the existence of those conditions is of sufficient materiality to affect the habitability, use, or enjoyment of the property and, therefore, render the property substantially less desirable or valuable to the objectively reasonable buyer. Whether a matter not disclosed by such a builder or broker is of such materiality, and unknown and unobservable by the buyer, will depend on the facts of each case.

[Remanded to the trial court for determination of damages.]

And so New Jersey has expanded the duty to disclose about as far as any state in the country. A builder-seller there must now take into account not only what the buyer knows about the property that is being sold, but also what the buyer knows about adjoining land. Other states have not ruled on this issue. What would you do if you were selling land in Arizona and knew that there was toxic waste buried under adjoining property? Assume that the Arizona court has not yet ruled on whether there is a legal duty to notify. Would you disclose anyway? What is the right thing to do? What policy makes the most business sense? Would it matter who the buyers were? Suppose your parents were the buyers?

MISTAKE

Most contract principles come from appellate courts, but in the area of "legal mistake" a cow wrote much of the law. The cow was Rose 2d of Aberlone, a gentle animal that lived in Michigan in 1886. Rose's owner, Hiram Walker & Sons, had bought her for $850. After a few years, the company concluded that Rose could have no calves. As a barren cow she was worth much less, so Walker contracted to sell her to T. C. Sherwood for $80. But when Sherwood came to collect Rose, the parties realized she was pregnant. Walker refused to part with the happy mother, and Sherwood sued. Walker defended, claiming that both parties had made a mistake and that the contract was voidable.

BILATERAL MISTAKE

A **bilateral mistake** occurs when both parties negotiate based on the same factual error. Sherwood and Walker both thought Rose was barren, both negotiated accordingly, and both were wrong. The Michigan Supreme Court gave judgment for Walker, the seller, permitting him to rescind the contract because the parties were both wrong about the essence of what they were bargaining for.

If the parties contract based on an important factual error, the contract is voidable by the injured party. Sherwood and Walker were both wrong about Rose's reproductive ability, and the error was basic enough to cause a tenfold difference in price. Walker, the injured party, was entitled to rescind the contract. Note that the error must be *factual*. Suppose Walker sold Rose thinking that the price of beef was going to drop, when in fact the price rose 60 percent in five months. He made a mistake, but it was simply a business prediction that proved wrong. Walker would have no right to rescind.

Conscious Uncertainty. No rescission is permitted where one of the parties knows he is taking on a risk, that is, he realizes there is uncertainty about the quality of the thing being exchanged. Rufus offers 10 acres of mountainous land to Priscilla. "I can't promise you anything about this land," he says, "but they've found gold on every adjoining parcel." Priscilla, panting with gold lust, buys the land, digs long and hard, and discovers—mud. She may not rescind the contract. She understood her risk, and there was no mutual mistake.

UNILATERAL MISTAKE

Sometimes only one party enters a contract under a mistaken assumption, a situation called **unilateral mistake**. In these cases, it is more difficult for the injured party to rescind a contract. To rescind for unilateral mistake, a party must demonstrate that she entered the contract because of a basic factual error and that either (1) enforcing the contract would be unconscionable or (2) the nonmistaken party knew of the error.

CHAPTER CONCLUSION

Contracts govern countless areas of our lives, from intimate family issues to multibillion dollar corporate deals. Understanding contract principles is essential for a successful business or professional career and is invaluable in private life. As we enter a new century, this knowledge is especially important because courts no longer rubber-stamp any agreement that two parties have made. If we know the issues that courts scrutinize, the agreement we draft is likelier to be enforced. We thus achieve greater control over our affairs—the very purpose of a contract.

CHAPTER REVIEW

1. A contract is a promise that the law will enforce. Contracts are intended to make business matters more predictable.
2. The common law governs contracts for services, employment, and real estate. The UCC, Article 2, governs contracts for the sale of goods.
3. In an express contract, the two parties explicitly state all important terms of their agreement. In an implied contract, the words and conduct of the parties indicate that they intended an agreement.
4. A claim of promissory estoppel requires that the defendant made a promise knowing that the plaintiff would likely rely, the plaintiff did rely, and it would be wrong to deny recovery.
5. A claim of quasi-contract requires that the defendant received a benefit, knowing that the plaintiff would expect compensation, and it would be unjust not to grant it.
6. The parties can form a contract only if they have a meeting of the minds.
7. An offer is an act or a statement that proposes definite terms and permits the other party to create a contract by accepting. The terms of the offer must be definite.
8. The offeree must say or do something to accept. The common law mirror image rule requires acceptance on precisely the same terms as the offer.
9. A promise is normally binding only if it is supported by consideration, which requires a bargaining and exchange between the parties.
10. Illegal contracts are void and unenforceable. Claims of illegality often arise concerning noncompete clauses, exculpatory clauses, and unconscionable clauses.
11. Minors and mentally impaired persons generally may disaffirm contracts.
12. Fraud and material misrepresentation are grounds for disaffirming a contract. The injured party must prove a false statement of fact, fraud or materiality, and justifiable reliance.
13. In a bilateral mistake, either party may rescind the contract. In a case of unilateral mistake, the injured party may rescind only in limited circumstances.

PRACTICE TEST

1. Interactive Data Corp. hired Daniel Foley as an assistant product manager at a starting salary of $18,500. Over the next six years, Interactive steadily promoted Foley until he became Los Angeles branch manager at a salary of $56,116. Interactive's officers repeatedly told Foley that he would have his job as long as his performance was adequate. In addition, Interactive distributed an employee handbook that specified "termination guidelines," including a mandatory seven-step pre-termination procedure. Two years later, Foley learned that his recently hired supervisor, Robert Kuhne, was under investigation by the FBI for embezzlement at his previous job. Foley reported this to Interactive officers. Shortly thereafter, Interactive fired Foley. He

sued, claiming that Interactive could only fire him for good cause, after the seven-step procedure. What kind of a claim is he making? Should he succeed?

2. The Hoffmans owned and operated a successful small bakery and grocery store. They spoke with Lukowitz, an agent of Red Owl Stores, who told them that for $18,000 Red Owl would build a store and fully stock it for them. The Hoffmans sold their bakery and grocery store and purchased a lot on which Red Owl was to build the store. Lukowitz then told Hoffman that the price had gone up to $26,000. The Hoffmans borrowed the extra money from relatives, but then Lukowitz informed them that the cost would be $34,000. Negotiations broke off and the Hoffmans sued. The court determined that there was no contract because too many details had not been worked out—the size of the store, its design, and the cost of constructing it. Can the Hoffmans recover any money?

3. Academy Chicago Publishers (Academy) approached the widow of author John Cheever about printing some of his unpublished stories. She signed a contract, which stated:

> The Author will deliver to the Publisher on a mutually agreeable date one copy of the manuscript of the Work as finally arranged by the editor and satisfactory to the Publisher in form and content. . . .
>
> Within a reasonable time and a mutually agreeable date after delivery of the final revised manuscript, the Publisher will publish the Work at its own expense, in such style and manner and at such price as it deems best, and will keep the Work in print as long as it deems it expedient.

Within a year, Academy located and delivered to Mrs. Cheever more than 60 unpublished stories. She refused to go ahead with the project. Academy sued for the right to publish. The trial court ruled that the agreement was valid; the appeals court affirmed; and the case went to the Illinois Supreme Court. Was the contract enforceable?

4. Rebecca, in Honolulu, faxes a job offer to Spike, in Pittsburgh, saying, "We can pay you $55,000 per year, starting June 1." Spike faxes a reply, saying, "Thank you! I accept your generous offer, though I will also need $3,000 in relocation money. See you June 1. Can't wait!" On June 1, Spike arrives, to find that his position is filled by Gus. He sues Rebecca.

   (a) Spike wins $55,000.

   (b) Spike wins $58,000.

   (c) Spike wins $3,000.

   (d) Spike wins restitution.

   (e) Spike wins nothing.

5. An aunt saw her eight-year-old nephew enter the room, remarked what a nice boy he was, and said, "I would like to take care of him now." She promptly wrote a note, promising to pay the boy $3,000 upon her death. Her estate refused to pay. Is it obligated to do so?

6. Brockwell left his boat to be repaired at Lake Gaston Sales. The boat contained electronic equipment and other personal items. Brockwell signed a form stating that Lake Gaston had no responsibility for any loss to any property in or on the boat. Brockwell's electronic equipment was stolen and other personal items were damaged, and he sued. Is the exculpatory clause enforceable?

7. Guyan Machinery, a West Virginia manufacturing corporation, hired Albert Voorhees as a salesman and required him to sign a contract stating that if he left Guyan he would not work for a competing corporation anywhere within 250 miles of West Virginia for a two-year period. Later, Voorhees left Guyan and began working at Polydeck Corp., another West Virginia manufacturer. The only product Polydeck made was urethane screens, which comprised half of 1 percent of Guyan's business. Is Guyan entitled to enforce its noncompete clause?

8. **RIGHT & WRONG** Richard and Michelle Kommit traveled to New Jersey to have fun

in the casinos. While in Atlantic City, they used their MasterCard to withdraw cash from an ATM conveniently located in the "pit," which is the gambling area of a casino. They ran up debts of $5,500 on the credit card and did not pay. The Connecticut National Bank sued for the money. What argument should the Kommits make? Which party, if any, has the moral high ground here? Should a casino offer ATM services in the gambling pit? If a credit card company allows customers to withdraw cash in a casino, is it encouraging them to lose money? Do the Kommits have any ethical right to use the ATM, attempt to win money by gambling, and then seek to avoid liability?

9. The McAllisters had several serious problems with their house, including leaks in the ceiling, a buckling wall, and dampness throughout. They repaired the buckling wall by installing I-beams to support it. They never resolved the leaks and the dampness. When they decided to sell the house, they said nothing to prospective buyers about the problems. They stated that the I-beams had been added for reinforcement. The Silvas bought the house for $60,000. Soon afterwards, they began to have problems with leaks, mildew, and dampness. Are the Silvas entitled to any money damages? Why or why not?

10. **YOU BE THE JUDGE WRITING PROBLEM** Susan Gould was appointed to a three-year probationary position as a teacher at Sewanhaka High School. Normally, after three years, the school board either grants tenure or dismisses the teacher. The Sewanhaka school board notified Gould she would not be rehired. To keep the termination out of her file, Gould agreed to resign. In fact, because Gould had previously taught at a different New York school, state law required that she be given a tenure decision after only two years. If the board failed to do that, the teacher was automatically tenured. When she learned this, Gould sued to rescind her agreement to resign. Is Gould entitled to rescind the contract (i.e., her agreement to resign)? **Argument for Gould:** Both parties assumed that Gould was on probation and could be dismissed after three years. Neither party understood that after three years, Gould actually *had* tenure under New York State law. Gould would never have resigned had she understood she was entitled to tenure. The misunderstanding goes to the essence of the resignation agreement, and she should be permitted to rescind. **Argument for the School Board:** The school board has done nothing wrong here. It is unfair to penalize the school system for an honest mistake. If Gould is serious about her career, she should understand the tenure process and should take the trouble to inform the board about unusual rules that pertain to her case. She failed to do that, causing both parties to negotiate under a misperception, and she must bear the loss.

INTERNET RESEARCH PROBLEM

Visit http://www.law.cornell.edu/states/listing.html. Select a state. Then click on *judicial opinions*. Search for a case concerning "quasi-contract." What are the details of the quasi-contract dispute? Who won and why?

You can find further practice problems in the Online Quiz at http://beatty.westbuslaw.com or in the Study Guide that accompanies this text.

Conclusion to Contracts

10

CHAPTER

Oliver and Perry were college roommates, two sophomores with contrasting personalities. They were sitting in the cafeteria with some friends, Oliver chatting away, Perry slumped on a plastic bench. Oliver suggested that they buy a lottery ticket, as the prize for that week's drawing was $3 million. Perry muttered, "Nah. You never win if you buy just one ticket." Oliver bubbled up, "OK, we'll buy a ticket every week. We'll keep buying them from now until we graduate. Come on, it'll be fun. This month, I'll buy the tickets. Next month, you will, and so on." Other students urged Perry to do it and, finally, grudgingly, he agreed. The two friends carefully reviewed their deal. Each party was providing consideration, namely, the responsibility for purchasing tickets during his month. The amount of each purchase was clearly defined at one dollar. They would start that week and continue until graduation day, two and a half years down the road. Finally, they would share equally any money won. As three witnesses looked on, they shook hands on the bargain. That month, Oliver bought a ticket every week, randomly choosing numbers, and won nothing. The next month, Perry bought a ticket with equally random numbers—and won $52 million. Perry moved out of their dorm room into a suite at the Ritz and refused to give Oliver one red cent. Oliver sued, seeking $26 million, and the return of an Eric Clapton CD that he had loaned to Perry.

If the former friends had read this chapter, they would never have slid into such a mess. In the last chapter, we covered the basics of contract law, and now we put the icing on the cake. We will examine which contracts must be in writing, when third parties have rights or obligations under an agreement, what problems arise in the performance of contracts, and the remedies available when a deal goes awry. Oliver and Perry's case involves the statute of frauds, which tells us which contracts must be written.

WRITTEN CONTRACTS

The rule we examine in this chapter is not exactly news. Parliament passed the original statute of frauds in 1677. The purpose was to prevent lying (fraud) in civil lawsuits. The statute required that in several types of cases, a contract would be enforced only if it were in writing. Almost all states of this country later passed their own statutes making the same requirements. It is important to remember, as we examine the rules and exceptions, that Parliament and the state legislatures all had a commendable, straightforward purpose in passing their respective statutes of fraud: *to provide a court with the best possible evidence of whether the parties intended to make a contract.*

The statute of frauds: A plaintiff may not enforce any of the following agreements, unless the agreement, or some memorandum of it, is in writing and signed by the defendant. The agreements that must be in writing are those:

- For any interest in **land**
- That **cannot be performed within one year**
- To pay the **debt of another**
- Made by an **executor of an estate**
- Made **in consideration of marriage**; and
- For the **sale of goods worth $500 or more**.

UNENFORCEABLE (SORRY, OLIVER)

In other words, when two parties make an agreement covered by any one of these six topics, it must be in writing to be enforceable. Oliver and Perry made a definite agreement to purchase lottery tickets during alternate months and share the proceeds of any winning ticket. But their agreement was to last two and one-half years. As the second item on the list indicates, a contract must be in writing if it cannot be performed within one year. The good news is, Oliver gets back his Eric Clapton CD. The bad news is he gets none of the lottery money. Even though three witnesses saw the deal made, it is unlikely to be enforced in any state. Perry the pessimist will probably walk away with all $52 million.[1]

CONTRACTS THAT MUST BE IN WRITING

AGREEMENTS FOR AN INTEREST IN LAND

A contract for the sale of any interest in land must be in writing to be enforceable. Notice the phrase "interest in land." This means *any legal right* regarding land. A house on a lot is an interest in land. A mortgage, an easement, and a leased apartment are all interests in land. As a general rule, leases must therefore be in writing, although many states have created an exception for short-term leases of a year or less.

EXCEPTION: FULL PERFORMANCE BY THE SELLER

If the seller completely performs her side of a contract for an interest in land, a court is likely to enforce the agreement even if it was oral. Adam orally agrees to sell his condominium to Maggie for $150,000. Adam delivers the deed to Maggie and expects his money a week later, but Maggie fails to pay. Most courts will allow Adam to enforce the oral contract and collect the full purchase price from Maggie.

EXCEPTION: PART PERFORMANCE BY THE BUYER

The buyer of land may be able to enforce an oral contract if she paid part of the purchase price *and either* entered upon the land or made improvements to it. Suppose that Eloise sues Grover to enforce an alleged oral contract to sell a lot in Happydale. She claims they struck a bargain in January. Grover defends based on the statute of frauds, saying that even if the two did reach an oral agreement, it is unenforceable. Eloise proves that she paid 10 percent of the purchase price and that in February she began excavating on the lot, to build a house, and that Grover knew of the work. Eloise has established part performance and will be allowed to enforce her contract.

EXCEPTION: PROMISSORY ESTOPPEL

The other exception to the writing requirement is our old friend promissory estoppel. **If a promisor makes an oral promise that reasonably causes the promisee to rely on it, the promisee *may* be able to enforce the promise, despite the statute of frauds, if that is the only way to avoid injustice.** This

---

[1] Perry might also raise *illegality* as a defense, claiming that a contract for gambling is illegal. That defense is likely to fail. Courts appear to distinguish between the simple purchase of a legal lottery ticket, which friends often share, and the more traditional—and socially dangerous—gambling contracts involving horse racing or casino betting. See, e.g., *Pando v. Fernandez*, 118 A.D.2d 474, 499 N.Y.S.2d 950, 1986 N.Y. App. Div. LEXIS 54345 (N.Y. App. Div. 1986), finding no illegality in an agreement to purchase a lottery ticket, even where the purchaser was a minor! Since an illegality defense would probably fail Perry, it is all the more unfortunate that Oliver did not jot down their agreement in writing.

exception potentially applies to any contract that must be written, such as those for land, those that cannot be performed within one year, and so forth. Suppose an unmarried couple buy a house together. They put the deed in the man's name alone so that he can obtain a certain type of financing. He repeatedly promises to add the woman's name later, but never does so. Both parties contribute to the purchase price and maintenance. If they split up, the woman is probably entitled to one-half the value of the house, based on her reasonable reliance on his promise.[2]

In the following case, the plaintiffs make three valiant efforts to evade the piercing grasp of the statute of frauds. They argue that their contract is not really for the sale of land, that they partly performed, and that they relied on the seller's promise.

HERSHON v. CANNON

1993 U.S. Dist. LEXIS 689
United States District Court,
District of Maryland, 1993

Facts: Mary Drysdale and her husband, Simon Hershon, lived in Washington, D.C. They wanted to buy Tulip Hill, an eighteenth-century mansion located on 54 acres in Anne Arundel County, Maryland, property that was owned by an estate and managed by Jonathan Cannon. Drysdale and Hershon orally agreed with Cannon on a purchase price of $1.2 million. Cannon promised that while the lawyers were drafting the written purchase agreement, he would not seek offers from anyone else. Also, if he received an unsolicited offer, he agreed to give Drysdale and Hershon the opportunity to match it.

Drysdale and Hershon applied for a mortgage to buy Tulip Hill. They also met with the Maryland Historical Commission to discuss improvements to the property. Meanwhile, Cannon sold Tulip Hill to someone else. Drysdale and Hershon sued.

Issue: Did Drysdale and Hershon have an enforceable contract for Tulip Hill?

Excerpts from Judge Hargrove's Decision: Plaintiffs make no allegation that they entered into a written contract regarding Tulip Hill, nor do they allege or present a writing of any sort. Plaintiffs contend that their claim is not barred by the statute of frauds for two reasons. First, the plaintiffs argue that they do not seek to enforce an oral purchase agreement. To the contrary, they seek to enforce Cannon's agreement not to solicit other offers for the property and Cannon's agreement that if another offer arose, the plaintiffs would have the right of first refusal. The court finds this argument unpersuasive and believes that the promise the plaintiffs seek to enforce is indeed unenforceable under the statute of frauds, absent a sufficient "writing" or "memorandum."

Second, the plaintiffs contend that Maryland law recognizes exceptions to the statute of frauds where necessary to avoid injustice, including the doctrines of part-performance and estoppel. Part performance of oral agreements can remove the bar of the statute of frauds if the part performance consists of acts that would not have been done but for the existence of the contract. Even if the plaintiffs' allegations are taken as true, their activities are insufficient to create an issue of material fact as to part performance. While the plaintiffs' actions in meeting with officials from the Maryland Historical Trust, preparing design alternatives for Tulip Hill, applying for mortgages to finance the purchase, and liquidating assets, were consistent with the existence of the alleged agreements, they were also consistent with the absence of the alleged agreements.

[2] *Sullivan v. Rooney*, 404 Mass. 160, 533 N.E.2d 1372, 1989 Mass. LEXIS 49 (1989).

Plaintiffs' activities could have been undertaken in anticipation of a contract for the sale of Tulip Hill.

[As to promissory estoppel] a court must determine if the plaintiff's action or forbearance is definite and substantial in comparison to the remedy sought. [Drysdale and Hershon's reliance was very slight. If the statute of frauds is enforced, and they are unable to buy Tulip Hill, they will not suffer any great injustice.] The court agrees and finds that the plaintiffs' claim based on promissory estoppel fails as a matter of law. [The case is dismissed.]

AGREEMENTS THAT CANNOT BE PERFORMED WITHIN ONE YEAR

Contracts that cannot be performed within one year are unenforceable unless they are in writing. This one-year period begins on the date the parties make the agreement. The critical phrase here is "*cannot be performed* within one year." If a contract *could* be completed within one year, it need not be in writing. Betty gets a job at Burger Brain, throwing fries in oil. Her boss tells her she can have Fridays off for as long as she works there. That oral contract *is* enforceable, whether Betty stays one week or five years. It *could* have been performed within one year if, say, Betty quit the job after six months. Therefore it does not need to be in writing.[3]

If the agreement will *necessarily* take longer than one year to finish, it must be in writing to be enforceable. If Betty is hired for three years as manager of Burger Brain, the agreement is unenforceable unless put in writing. She cannot perform three years of work in one year.

Type of Agreement	Enforceability
Cannot be performed within one year. *Example:* An offer of employment for three years.	Must be in writing to be enforceable.
Might be performed within one year, although could take many years to perform, *Example:* "As long as you work here at Burger Brain you may have Fridays off."	Enforceable whether it is oral or written, since the employee might quit working a month later.

PROMISE TO PAY THE DEBT OF ANOTHER

When one person agrees to pay the debt of another as a favor to that debtor, it is called a **collateral promise**, and it must be in writing to be enforceable. A student applies for a $10,000 loan to help pay for college, and her father agrees to

[3] This is the majority rule. In most states, if a company hires an employee "for life," the contract need not be in writing because the employee could die within one year. "Contracts of uncertain duration are simply excluded [from the statute of frauds]; the provision covers only those contracts whose performance cannot possibly be completed within a year." Restatement (Second) of Contracts §130, Comment a, at 328 (1981). However, a few states disagree. The Illinois Supreme Court ruled that a contract for lifetime employment is enforceable only if written. *McInerney v. Charter Golf, Inc.*, 176 Ill. 2d 482, 680 N.E.2d 1347, 1997 Ill. LEXIS 56 (Ill. 1997).

repay the bank if the student defaults. The bank will insist that the father's promise be in writing, since his oral promise alone is unenforceable.

PROMISE MADE BY AN EXECUTOR OF AN ESTATE

An executor is the person who is in charge of an estate after someone dies. The executor's job is to pay debts of the deceased, obtain money owed to him, and disburse the assets according to the will. In most cases, the executor will use only the estate's assets to pay those debts, but occasionally might offer her own money. **An executor's promise to use her own funds to pay a debt of the deceased must be in writing to be enforceable.**

PROMISE MADE IN CONSIDERATION OF MARRIAGE

Barney is a multimillionaire with the integrity of a gangster and the charm of a tax collector. He proposes to Li-Tsing, who promptly rejects him. Barney then pleads that if Li-Tsing will be his bride, he will give her an island he owns off the coast of California. Li-Tsing begins to see his good qualities and accepts. After they are married, Barney refuses to deliver the deed. Li-Tsing will get nothing from a court either, since **a promise made in consideration of marriage must be in writing to be enforceable.**

WHAT THE WRITING MUST CONTAIN

Each of the five types of contract described above must be in writing in order to be enforceable. What must the writing contain? It may be a carefully typed contract, using precise legal terminology, or an informal memorandum scrawled on the back of a paper napkin at a business lunch. The writing may consist of more than one document, written at different times, with each document making a piece of the puzzle. However, there are some general requirements. **The contract or memorandum:**

- **Must be signed by the defendant, and**
- **Must state with reasonable certainty the name of each party, the subject matter of the agreement, and all of the essential terms and promises.**[4]

SIGNATURE

A statute of frauds typically states that the writing must be "signed by the party to be charged therewith," in other words, the defendant. Judges define "signature" very broadly. Using a pen to write one's name, though sufficient, is not required. A secretary who stamps an executive's signature on a letter fulfills this requirement. Any other mark or logo placed on a document to indicate acceptance, even an "X," will likely satisfy the statute of frauds. Electronic commerce creates new methods of signing—and new controversies, discussed in the Cyberlaw feature later in this chapter.

---

[4] Restatement (Second) of Contracts §131.

REASONABLE CERTAINTY

Suppose Garfield and Hayes are having lunch, discussing the sale of Garfield's vacation condominium. They agree on a price and want to make some notation of the agreement even before their lawyers work out a detailed purchase and sales agreement. A perfectly adequate memorandum might say, "Garfield agrees to sell Hayes his condominium at 234 Baron Boulevard, apartment 18, for $350,000 cash, payable on June 18, 2004, and Hayes promises to pay the sum on that day." They should make two copies of their agreement and sign both. By doing that, they will avoid the problem that Drysdale and Hershon encountered when trying to purchase Tulip Hill, described above. Notice that although Garfield's memo is short, it states all essential terms.

SALE OF GOODS

The UCC requires a writing for the sale of goods worth $500 or more. This is the sixth and final contract that must be written, although the Code's requirements are easier to meet than those of the common law. (In some cases, the Code dispenses altogether with the writing requirement. To read the UCC online, go to http://www.law.cornell.edu/ucc/ucc.table.html. The basic statute of frauds rule is Section 2-201(1). Important exceptions are found at 2-201 (2) and (3).)

The basic UCC rule: **A contract for the sale of goods worth $500 or more is not enforceable unless there is some writing, signed by the defendant, indicating that the parties reached an agreement.** The key difference between the common law rule and the UCC rule is that the Code does not require all of the terms of the agreement to be in writing. The Code demands only an *indication that the parties reached an agreement*. The two things that *are* essential are the signature of the defendant and the quantity of goods being sold. The quantity of goods is required because this is the one term for which there will be no objective evidence. Suppose a short memorandum between textile dealers indicates that Seller will sell to Buyer "grade AA 100% cotton, white athletic socks." If the writing does not state the price, the parties can testify at court about what the market price was at the time of the deal. But how many socks were to be delivered? 100 pairs or 100,000? The quantity must be written. (A basic sale of goods contract appears at http://www.lectlaw.com/forms/f124.txt.)

Today, many contracts are created without paper. An "electronic signature" could mean any of the following: a name typed at the bottom of an e-mail message; a retinal or vocal scan; a name signed by electronic pen on a writing tablet; a magnetic card using a personal identification number; or a public-key digital signature. Are electronic signatures valid? Yes, generally. State legislatures, and Congress, are struggling to create clear rules, and the job is incomplete, but here are the rules so far:

The Uniform Electronic Transaction Act (UETA). This *proposed* legislation was drafted by the National Conference of Commissioners on Uniform State Laws, who also draft the UCC. UETA does not become law until a state adopts it, and thus far fewer than 20 legislatures have done so. UETA declares that a contract or signature may not be denied enforceability simply because it is in electronic form. In other words, the normal rules of contract law apply, but one party may not avoid such a deal simply because it originated in cyberspace.

The Electronic Signatures in Global and National Commerce Act, often called the E-Signature Act. This federal *statute* (not just a proposal) took effect on October 1, 2000. Like UETA, this law states that contracts will not be denied enforcement simply because they are in electronic form, or signed electronically. There are a few exceptions for documents that specific state laws require to be in tangible form, such as wills, divorce agreements, eviction notices, utility shut-off notices, and so on. Under this statute, an electronic signature is any "electronic sound, symbol or process, attached to or logically associated with a contract or other record." This statute applies in any state that has *not* adopted UETA; it indicates Congressional impatience with the slow pace at which the states have reacted to the digital age.

The Uniform Computer Information Transactions Act (UCITA) is another proposal created by the drafters of the UCC. This proposed law covers such issues as shrink-wrap and click-wrap contracts and software licensing agreements. Thus far, only a few states have adopted UCITA, and its future is not yet clear.

The United Nations Commission on International Trade Law (UNCITRAL) has published a Model Law for consideration by countries throughout the world.

With cyberlaw in its early stages, what should an executive do who wants to take advantage *now* of the Internet's commercial opportunities? Be cautious about "electronic signatures." Assume that any commitments you make electronically *could* be enforced against you. Paradoxically, if the amount of the contract is substantial, do *not* assume that the other party's promises, if made electronically, will be enforced unless your lawyer has given you assurance. If in doubt, get a hard copy, signed in ink.

PAROL EVIDENCE

Tyrone agrees to buy Martha's house for $800,000. The contract obligates Tyrone to make a 10 percent down payment immediately and pay the remaining $720,000 in 45 days. As the two parties sign the deal, Tyrone discusses his need for financing. Unfortunately, at the end of 45 days, he has been unable to get a mortgage for the full amount. He claims that the parties orally agreed that he would get his deposit back if he could not obtain financing. But the written agreement says no such thing, and Martha disputes the claim. Who will win? Probably Martha, because of the parol evidence rule. To understand this rule, you need to know two terms. **Parol evidence** refers to anything (apart from the written contract itself) that was said, done, or written before the parties signed the agreement or as they signed it. Martha's conversation with Tyrone about financing the house was parol evidence because it occurred as they were signing the contract. The other important term is **integrated contract**, which means a writing that the parties intend as the final, complete expression of their agreement. Now for the rule.

The parol evidence rule: When two parties make an integrated contract, neither one may use parol evidence to contradict, vary, or add to its terms. Negotiations may last for hours, weeks, or even months. Almost no contract includes everything that the parties said. When parties consider their agreement integrated, any statements they made before or while signing are irrelevant. If a court determines that Martha and Tyrone intended their agreement to be integrated, it will prohibit testimony about Martha's oral promises.

Third Parties

A contract may affect a third party who had no role in forming it. Sometimes the two contracting parties *intend* to benefit a third person. Those are cases of third party beneficiary. In other cases, one of the contracting parties may actually *transfer his rights or responsibilities* to a third party, raising issues of assignment or delegation. We consider these issues one at a time.

Third Party Beneficiary

The two parties who make a contract always intend to benefit themselves. Oftentimes their bargain will also benefit someone else. **A third party beneficiary is someone who was not a party to the contract but stands to benefit from it.** Many contracts create third party beneficiaries. Problems arise when one of the parties fails to perform the contract as expected. The issue is this: *May the third party beneficiary enforce the contract?*

The outcome depends upon the intentions of the two contracting parties. If they intended to benefit the third party, she will probably be permitted to enforce their contract. If they did not intend to benefit her, she probably has no power to enforce the agreement. The Restatement uses a bit more detail to analyze these cases. We must first recall the terms "promisor" and "promisee." The **promisor** is the one who makes the promise that the third party beneficiary is seeking to enforce. The **promisee** is the other party to the contract.

According to the **Restatement (Second) of Contracts §302: A beneficiary of a promise is an intended beneficiary and may enforce a contract if the parties** ***intended*** **her to benefit** ***and if either*** (a) enforcing the promise will satisfy a duty of the promisee to the beneficiary, or (b) the promisee intended to make a gift to the beneficiary.

Any beneficiary who is not an intended beneficiary is an **incidental beneficiary**, and may not enforce the contract. In other words, a third party beneficiary must show two things in order to enforce a contract that two other people created. First, she must show that the two contracting parties were aware of her situation and knew that she would receive something of value from their deal. Second, she must show that the promisee wanted to benefit her for one of two reasons: either to satisfy some duty owed or to make her a gift. Contrasting examples should clarify.

Robert Starrett borrowed money from the Commercial Bank of Georgia, using as security a house that he and his wife, Jerry, owned. Several years later, the couple divorced. They amicably divided their assets in a "settlement agreement," which a court approved. The parties agreed to sell the house and disburse the proceeds in this order: first, to pay taxes and costs of the sale; second, to pay in full Robert Starrett's loan from Commercial; and third, to divide the remaining money, 65 percent to Jerry and 35 percent to Robert. The couple never did sell the property, and Robert Starrett died two years later. Robert's estate gave his 50 percent interest in the house to Commercial, but the bank could make no use of it as long as Jerry was half owner. Commercial filed suit, seeking full title. The estate argued that the bank was only an incidental beneficiary. Who wins? The bank. In their settlement agreement, Robert and Jerry clearly *intended* to benefit the bank, since they stated the bank would be paid before any money was divided between them. Did Robert have a *duty* to the bank? Of course: to repay the loan. Both parts of the test are satisfied, and the bank is an intended beneficiary, entitled to its money.[5]

Now suppose a city contracts to purchase from Seller 20 acres of an abandoned industrial site in a rundown neighborhood for a new domed stadium. The owner of a pizza parlor on the edge of Seller's land might benefit enormously. A once marginal operation could become a gold mine of cheese and pepperoni. However, if the city breaks its agreement to buy the land, will the frustrated pizza owner recover lost profits? No. A stadium is a multimillion dollar investment, and it is most unlikely that the city and the seller of the land were even aware of the owner's existence, let alone that they intended to benefit him. He probably cannot prove either the first element or the second element, and certainly not both.

ASSIGNMENT AND DELEGATION

A contracting party may transfer his rights under the contract, which is called an **assignment of rights**. Or a contracting party may transfer her duties pursuant to the contract, which is a **delegation of duties**. Frequently, a party will do both simultaneously.

For our purposes, the Restatement serves as a good summary of common law provisions. The UCC rules are generally similar. Our first example is a sale of goods case, governed by the UCC, but the outcome would be the same under the Restatement.

Lydia needs 500 bottles of champagne. Bruno agrees to sell them to her for $10,000, payable 30 days after delivery. He transports the wine to her. Bruno happens to owe Doug $8,000 from a previous deal, so he says to Doug, "I don't have the money, but I'll give you my claim to Lydia's $10,000." Doug agrees. Bruno then *assigns* to Doug *his rights* to Lydia's money, and in exchange Doug gives up his claim for $8,000. Bruno is the **assignor, the one making an assignment, and Doug is the assignee, the one receiving an assignment**.

Why would Bruno offer $10,000 when he owed Doug only $8,000? Because all he has is a *claim* to Lydia's money. Cash in hand is often more valuable. Doug, however, is willing to assume some risk for a potential $2,000 gain.

Bruno notifies Lydia of the assignment. Lydia, who owes the money, is called the **obligor**, that is, the one obligated to do something. At the end of 30

---

[5] *Starrett v. Commercial Bank of Georgia*, 226 Ga. App. 598, 486 S.E.2d 923, 1997 Ga. App. LEXIS 708 (Ga Ct. App. 1997).

days, Doug arrives at Lydia's doorstep, asks for his money, and gets it, since Lydia is obligated to him.

Lydia bought the champagne because she knew she could sell it at a profit. She promptly agrees to sell and deliver the 500 bottles to Coretta, at a mountaintop wilderness camp. Lydia has no four-wheel drive cars, so she finds Keith, who is willing to deliver the bottles for $1,000. Lydia *delegates her duty* to Keith to deliver the bottles to Coretta. Keith is now obligated to deliver the bottles to Coretta, the **obligee**, that is, the one who has the obligation coming to her. Lydia also remains obligated to Coretta, the obligee, to ensure that the bottles are delivered.

Assignment and delegation can each create problems. We will examine the most common ones.

Assignment

What Rights Are Assignable?

Any contractual right may be assigned unless assignment

(a) would substantially change the obligor's rights or duties under the contract; or

(b) is forbidden by law or public policy; or

(c) is validly precluded by the contract itself.[6]

Substantial Change. Assignment is prohibited if it would substantially change the obligor's situation. For example, Bruno may assign to Doug the payment from Lydia because it makes no difference to Lydia whether she writes a check to one or the other. But suppose Erica, who lives on a one-quarter acre lot in Hardscrabble, hires Keith to mow her lawn once per week for the summer, for a total fee of $700. Erica pays up front, before she leaves for the summer. May she assign her right to weekly lawn care to Lloyd, who enjoys a three-acre estate in Halcyon, 60 miles distant? No. The extra travel and far larger yard would dramatically change Keith's obligations.

Public Policy. Some assignments are prohibited by public policy. For example, someone who has suffered a personal injury in an automobile accident may not assign her claim to a third person.

Contract Prohibition. Finally, one of the contracting parties may try to prohibit assignment in the agreement itself. Most landlords include in the written lease a clause prohibiting the tenant from assigning the tenancy without the landlord's written permission. Such clauses are generally, but not always, enforced by a court.

How Rights Are Assigned

An assignment may be written or oral, and no particular formalities are required. However, when someone wants to assign rights governed by the

[6] Restatement (Second) of Contracts §317(2). And note that UCC §2-210(2) is, for our purposes, nearly identical.

statute of frauds, she must do it in writing. Suppose City contracts with Seller to buy Seller's land for a domed stadium and then brings in Investor to complete the project. If City wants to assign to Investor its rights to the land, it must do so in writing.

RIGHTS OF THE PARTIES AFTER ASSIGNMENT

Once the assignment is made and the obligor notified, the assignee may enforce her contractual rights against the obligor. If Lydia fails to pay Doug for the champagne she gets from Bruno, Doug may sue to enforce the agreement. The law will treat Doug as though he had entered into the contract with Lydia.

But the reverse is also true. **The obligor may generally raise all defenses against the assignee that she could have raised against the assignor.** Suppose Lydia opens the first bottle of champagne—silently. "Where's the pop?" she wonders. All 500 bottles have gone flat. Bruno has failed to perform his part of the contract, and Lydia may use Bruno's nonperformance as a defense against Doug. If the champagne was indeed worthless, Lydia owes Doug nothing.

DELEGATION OF DUTIES

Garret has always dreamed of racing stock cars. He borrows $250,000 from his sister, Maybelle, in order to buy a car and begin racing. He signs a promissory note in that amount, guaranteeing that he will repay Maybelle the full amount, plus interest, on a monthly basis over 10 years. Regrettably, during his first race, on a Saturday night, Garret discovers that he has a speed phobia. He finally finishes the race at noon on Sunday and quits the business. Garret transfers the car and equipment to Brady, who agrees in writing to pay all money owed to Maybelle. For a few months Brady sends a check, but he is killed while watching bumper cars at a local carnival. Maybelle sues Garret, who defends based on the transfer to Brady. Will his defense work?

Most duties are delegable. But delegation does not by itself relieve the delegator of his own liability to perform the contract.

Garret was the **delegator** and Brady was the **delegatee**. Garret has legally delegated to Brady his duty to repay Maybelle. However, Garret remains personally obligated. When Maybelle sues, she will win. Garret, like many debtors, would have preferred to wash his hands of his debt, but the law is not so obliging.

Garret's delegation to Brady was typical in that it included an assignment at the same time. If he had merely transferred ownership, that would have been only an assignment. If he had convinced Brady to pay off the loan without getting the car, that would have been merely a delegation. He did both at once.

WHAT DUTIES ARE DELEGABLE

The rules concerning what duties may be delegated mirror those about the assignment of rights.

An obligor may delegate his duties unless

(1) delegation would violate public policy, or

(2) the contract prohibits delegation, or

(3) the obligee has a substantial interest in personal performance by the obligor.[7]

Public Policy. Delegation may violate public policy, for example, in a public works contract. If City hires Builder to construct a subway system, state law may prohibit Builder from delegating his duties to Beginner. A public agency should not have to work with parties that it never agreed to hire.

Contract Prohibition. The parties may forbid almost any delegation, and the courts will enforce the agreement. Hammer, a contractor, is building a house and hires Spot as his painter, including in his contract a clause prohibiting delegation. Just before the house is ready for painting, Spot gets a better job elsewhere and wants to delegate his duties to Brush. Hammer may refuse the delegation even if Brush is equally qualified.

Substantial Interest in Personal Performance. Suppose Hammer had omitted the "nondelegation" clause from his contract with Spot. Could Hammer still refuse the delegation on the grounds that he has a substantial interest in having Spot do the work? No. Most duties are delegable. There is nothing so special about painting a house that one particular painter is required to do it. But some kinds of work do require personal performance, and obligors may not delegate these tasks. The services of lawyers, doctors, dentists, artists, and performers are considered too personal to be delegated. There is no single test that will perfectly define this group, but generally when the work will test *the character, skill, discretion, and good faith* of the obligor, she *may not* delegate her job.

NOVATION

As we have seen, a delegator does not get rid of his duties merely by delegating them. But there is one way a delegator can do so. **A novation is a three-way agreement in which the obligor delegates all duties to the delegatee and the obligee agrees to look only to the delegatee for performance. The obligee releases the obligor from all liability.**

Recall Garret, the forlorn race car driver. When he wanted to get out of his obligations to Maybelle, he should have proposed a novation. He would assign all rights and delegate all duties to Brady, and Maybelle would agree that only Brady was obligated by the promissory note, releasing Garret from his responsibility to repay. Why would Maybelle do this? She might conclude that Brady was a financially better bet than Garret who, in turn, might refuse to bring Brady into the deal until Maybelle permits a novation. In the example given, Garret failed to obtain a novation, and hence he and Brady (or Brady's estate) were both liable on the promissory note.

Since a novation has the critical effect of releasing the obligor from liability, you will not be surprised to learn that two parties to a contract sometimes fight over whether some event was a simple delegation of duties or a novation. Here is one such contest. Would you like it in a cone or cup?

---

[7] Restatement (Second) of Contracts §318. And see UCC §2-210, establishing similar limits.

ROSENBERG v. SON, INC.
491 N.W.2d 71, 1992 N.D. LEXIS 202
Supreme Court of North Dakota, 1992

Facts: The Rosenbergs owned a Dairy Queen in Grand Forks, North Dakota. They agreed in writing to sell the Dairy Queen to Mary Pratt. The contract required her to pay $10,000 down and $52,000 over 15 years, at 10 percent interest. Two years later, Pratt assigned her rights and delegated her duties under the sales contract to Son, Inc. The agreement between Pratt and Son contained a "Consent to Assignment" clause that the Rosenbergs signed. Pratt then moved to Arizona and had nothing further to do with the Dairy Queen. The Rosenbergs never received full payment for the Dairy Queen. They sued Mary Pratt.

The trial court gave summary judgment for Pratt, finding that she was no longer obligated on the original contract. The Rosenbergs appealed.

You be the Judge: Did Pratt obtain a novation relieving her of her duties under the original sales contract?

Argument for the Rosenbergs: Your honors, a party cannot escape contract liability merely by assigning its rights and delegating its duties to a third party. It is evident from the express language of the agreement between Pratt and Son, Inc. that the parties only intended an assignment, not a novation. The agreement made no mention of discharging Pratt from liability. It would be odd to write a novation and make no mention of discharge, which happens to be the primary point of a true novation. It is true that the Rosenbergs signed a consent to the assignment, but merely by permitting Son, Inc. to become involved they did not discharge their principal obligor—Pratt.

Argument for Ms. Pratt: Your honors, it is obvious from the contract that Ms. Pratt intended to rid herself entirely of this business. She planned to move out of state, and wanted to terminate all rights and responsibilities in the business. Why would she go to the trouble of assigning rights *and* delegating duties if she still expected to be involved in the business? If that weren't enough, she went one step further, by asking the Rosenbergs to acknowledge the new arrangement—which the Rosenbergs did. If Son, Inc. failed to keep its end of the bargain, then the Rosenbergs should sue that company—not an innocent woman who is long out of the business.

PERFORMANCE AND DISCHARGE

A party is discharged when she has no more duties under a contract. Most contracts are discharged by full performance. In other words, the parties generally do what they promise. Sally agrees to sell Arthur 300 tulip-shaped wine glasses for his new restaurant. Right on schedule, Sally delivers the correct glasses and Arthur pays in full. Contract, full performance, discharge, end of case.

Sometimes the parties discharge a contract by agreement. For example, the parties may agree to **rescind** their contract, meaning that they terminate it by mutual agreement. At times, a court may discharge a party who has not performed. When things have gone amiss, a judge must interpret the contract and issues of public policy to determine who in fairness should suffer the loss. We will analyze the most common issues of performance and discharge, beginning with a look at conditions.

CONDITIONS

Parties often put conditions in a contract. A **condition** is an event that must occur before a party becomes obligated under a contract.[8] Alex would like to buy Kevin's empty lot and build a movie theater on it, but the city's zoning law will not permit such a business in that location. Alex signs a contract to buy Kevin's empty lot in 120 days, provided that within 100 days the city re-zones the area to permit a movie theater. If the city fails to re-zone the area by day 100, Alex is discharged and need not complete the deal. As another example, Friendly Insurance issues a policy covering Vivian's house, promising to pay for any loss due to fire, but only if Vivian furnishes proof of her damages within 60 days of the damage. If the house burns down, Friendly becomes liable to pay. But if Vivian arrives with the proof 70 days after the fire, she collects nothing. Friendly, though it briefly had a duty to pay, was discharged when Vivian failed to furnish the necessary information on time. For an example of a common conditional clause, see http://www.hud.gov/local/lub/lublbp1.html. The clause is designed to protect a purchaser of property who is concerned that the real estate may be contaminated with lead paint.

No special language is necessary to create the condition. Phrases such as "provided that" frequently indicate a condition, but neither those nor any other words are essential. As long as the parties intended to create a condition, a court will enforce it.

Conditions in the Outfield. Professional sports contracts are often full of conditions. Assume that the San Francisco Giants want to sign Tony Fleet to play center field, a key position. The club considers him a fine defensive player but a dubious offensive performer. The many conditional clauses in his contract reflect hard bargaining over a questionable athlete. The Giants might guarantee Fleet $500,000, a modest salary by today's standards. If the speedy outfielder appears in 110 games (out of 162 total), his pay increases to $900,000, and if he plays in 120 games, he earns $1 million. If he receives even one vote for a "Gold Glove" award, which coaches and managers throughout the league award annually to top defensive performers, he earns an extra $100,000, with an additional $200,000 if he wins the award. Need more? The Giants insist on an option to re-sign Fleet for the following season for $800,000 (he has no say in the matter), but if the center-fielder plays in 100 games, the team loses that right, leaving Fleet free to negotiate for higher pay with other teams.

PERFORMANCE

Caitlin has an architect draw up plans for a monumental new house, and Daniel agrees to build it by September 1. Caitlin promises to pay $900,000 on that date.

---

[8] Some courts continue to distinguish between a *condition precedent*, in which the event must occur before any duty arises, and a *condition subsequent*, in which a duty that has arisen is discharged if an event occurs later. Alex's contract involves a condition precedent, while the Friendly Insurance hypothetical employs a condition subsequent. The Restatement (Second), §§224 et seq., has officially abandoned the distinction, however, which is why we do not emphasize it.

The house is ready on time but Caitlin has some complaints. The living room ceiling was supposed to be 18 feet high but it is only 17 feet; the pool was to be azure yet it is aquamarine; the maid's room was not supposed to be wired for cable television but it is. Caitlin refuses to pay anything for the house. Is she justified? Of course not; it would be absurd to give her a magnificent house for free when it has only tiny defects. And that is how a court would decide the case. But in this easy answer lurks a danger. How much leeway will a court permit? Suppose the living room is only 14 feet high, or 12 feet, or 5 feet? What if Daniel finishes the house a month late? Six months late? Three years late? At some point, a court will conclude that Daniel has so thoroughly botched the job that he deserves little or no money. Where is that point? That is a question that businesses—and judges—face everyday.

STRICT PERFORMANCE AND SUBSTANTIAL PERFORMANCE

STRICT PERFORMANCE

Courts dislike strict performance because it enables one party to benefit without paying, and sends the other one home empty-handed. **A party is generally not required to render strict performance unless the contract expressly demands it and such a demand is reasonable.** Caitlin's contract never suggested that Daniel would forfeit all payment if there were minor problems. Even if Caitlin had insisted on such a clause, a court would be unlikely to enforce it, because the requirement is unreasonable.

In some cases, strict performance does make sense. Marshall agrees to deliver 500 sweaters to Leo's store, and Leo promises to pay $20,000 cash on delivery. If Leo has only $19,000 cash and a promissory note for $1,000, he has failed to perform, and Marshall need not give him the sweaters. Leo's payment represents 95 percent of what he promised, but there is a big difference between cash and a promissory note.

SUBSTANTIAL PERFORMANCE

Daniel, the house builder, won his case against Caitlin because he fulfilled most of his obligations, even though he did an imperfect job. Courts often rely on the substantial performance doctrine, especially in cases involving services as opposed to those concerning the sale of goods or land. **In a contract for services, a party that substantially performs its obligations will receive the full contract price, minus the value of any defects.** Daniel receives $900,000, the contract price, minus the value of a ceiling that is one foot too low, a pool the wrong color, and so forth. It will be for the trial court to decide how much those defects are worth. If the court decides the low ceiling is a $10,000 damage, the pool color worth $5,000 and the cable television worth $500, then Daniel receives $884,500.

On the other hand, a party that fails to perform substantially receives nothing on the contract itself and will only recover the value of the work, if any. If the foundation cracks in Caitlin's house and the walls collapse, Daniel will not receive his $900,000. In such a case, he collects only the market value of the work he has done, which is probably zero.

When is performance substantial? There is no perfect test, but courts look at these issues:

- How much benefit has the promisee received?
- If it is a construction contract, can the owner use the thing for its intended purpose?
- Can the promisee be compensated with money damages for any defects?
- Did the promisor act in good faith?

The following case deals with the first three of these issues.

FOLK v. CENTRAL NATIONAL BANK & TRUST CO.

210 Ill. App. 3d 43, 1991 Ill. App. LEXIS 308
Illinois Court of Appeals, 1991

Facts: Byron Dragway, a dragstrip located in Byron, Illinois, needed work. Byron's insurance company insisted that the dragstrip be equipped with concrete retaining walls. Ronald Leek, Byron's president, decided to use the occasion to make other repairs, including resurfacing the 25-year-old surface. The dragstrip's starting area (the "starting pads") had a concrete surface, while the remainder of the track was asphalt. Leek hired Randy Folk to do all of the work. When Folk finished, Leek refused to pay, claiming that the work was shabby and would need to be entirely redone. Folk sued. The trial court gave judgment for Folk in the amount of $140,000, finding that, although there were problems, he had substantially performed. Byron Dragway appealed.

Issue: Did Folk substantially perform?

Excerpts from Justice Woodward's Decision: A contractor is not required to perform perfectly, but rather is held only to the duty of substantial performance in a workmanlike manner. Whether substantial performance has been given will depend upon the relevant facts of each case. However, the burden is on the contractor to prove the elements of substantial performance.

Duane Nichols, president of the United Drug Racers Association (UDRA), testified that the association is the largest owners and drivers association in the nation. It sponsors racing events throughout the country, featuring pro stock cars, super-charged funny cars, dragsters, and exhibition cars, which travel between 180 and 260 miles per hour. Inspecting the new track, Nichols observed that the new concrete [starting] pads were extremely smooth, plus there were significant dips in the concrete surface. Nichols particularly noted a dip where the concrete met the asphalt, an imperfection which would cause cars' tires to spin sideways. He observed several puddles in both asphalt lanes, where the surface dipped. Also, in fall 1987, Nichols attended a local meet held at Byron. Cars were having problems getting down the track, and several of them lost control, with one crashing. Nichols stated that no future UDRA events should be held at the track until the surface was repaired.

As to plaintiff's workmanship, the evidence points convincingly to its poor quality. [One expert] stated the defects of both the concrete starting pads and the asphalt surface were so severe that the total replacement of both was necessary. John Berg of Rockford Blacktop thought that the new asphalt surface would have to be ground off prior to the installation of a new surface.

[Folk did not substantially perform. Judgment reversed, in favor of Byron Dragway.]

PERSONAL SATISFACTION CONTRACTS

Sujata, president of a public relations firm, hires Ben to design a huge multimedia project for her company, involving computer software, music, and live actors, all designed to sell frozen bologna sandwiches to supermarkets. His contract guarantees him two years' employment, provided all of his work "is acceptable in the sole judgment of Sujata." Ben's immediate supervisor is delighted with his work and his colleagues are impressed—all but Sujata. Three months later she fires him, claiming that his work is "uninspired." Does she have the right to do that?

This is a **personal satisfaction contract, in which the promisee makes a personal, subjective evaluation of the promisor's performance.** In resolving disputes like Ben and Sujata's, judges must decide: When is it fair for the promisee to claim that she is not satisfied? May she make that decision for any reason at all, even on a whim?

A court applies a subjective standard only if assessing the work involves personal feelings, taste, or judgment *and* the contract explicitly demands personal satisfaction. A "subjective standard" means that the promisee's personal views will greatly influence her judgment, even if her decision is foolish and unfair. Artistic or creative work, or highly specialized tasks designed for a particular employer, may involve subtle issues of quality and personal preference. Ben's work combines several media and revolves around his judgment. Accordingly, the law applies a subjective standard to Sujata's decision. Since she concludes that his work is uninspired, she may legally fire him, even if her decision is irrational.

In all other cases, a court applies an objective standard to the promisee's decision. An objective standard means that the promisee's judgment of the work must be reasonable.

GOOD FAITH

The parties to a contract must carry out their obligations in good faith. The Restatement (Second) of Contracts §205 states: **"Every contract imposes upon each party a duty of good faith and fair dealing in its performance and its enforcement."** The UCC establishes a similar requirement for all contracts governed by the Code.[9] How far must one side go to meet its good faith burden? The Restatement emphasizes that the parties must remain faithful to the "agreed common purpose and justified expectations of the other party."

Barbara Thomas's employer had a group life insurance policy with Principal Mutual. The policy covered all employees and their dependents, and defined "dependents" to include an unmarried child between 19 and 25 "provided he is attending school on a full-time basis and is dependent upon the [insured parent] for his principal support and maintenance."

Ms. Thomas's 21-year-old daughter, Melinda Warren, enrolled as a cosmetology student. She paid full tuition and attended full-time for more than a year, when tragically she became disabled by ovarian cancer, which left her bedridden. She died of the disease 18 months later, at age 24. Thomas filed a $1,000 life insurance claim with Principal Mutual, but the insurer refused to pay. The company claimed that Warren was not a dependent at the time of her death, since she was not in school. Barbara Thomas sued, claiming not only benefits under the policy but additional damages for bad faith denial of the claim.

---

[9] UCC §1-203.

At trial, the company's officers were unable to provide a sensible explanation for the denial, or even any standards used in making the decision. The jury found that the company had rejected the claim for irrational, grossly unfair reasons. The state supreme court affirmed the verdict of $1,000 on the initial claim—and $750,000 for the company's bad faith denial.[10]

TIME OF THE ESSENCE CLAUSES

> Go, sir, gallop, and don't forget that the world was made in six days. You can ask me for anything you like, except time.
>
> *Napoleon*, to an aide, 1803

A time of the essence clause will generally make contract dates strictly enforceable. Jackie owns the Starburst Hotel. She agrees in writing to sell it to Eduardo, provided that he demonstrates to her by July 2 that he has obtained all financing. Jackie includes a clause stating that "Owner considers that time is of the essence in the performance of this contract." On July 1, Eduardo asks for a one month extension to obtain financing, and Jackie promptly sells the hotel elsewhere. Eduardo is out of luck. The time of the essence clause notified him that he must be prompt, and such a clause is reasonable in a real estate agreement. Notice that without the clause, Jackie would be legally obligated to allow Eduardo a reasonable extension.

BREACH

When one party *materially* breaches a contract, the other party is discharged. A material breach is one that substantially harms the innocent party. The discharged party has no obligation to perform and may sue for damages. Edwin promises that on July 1 he will deliver 20 tuxedos, tailored to fit male chimpanzees, to Bubba's circus for $300 per suit. After weeks of delay, Edwin concedes he hasn't a cummerbund to his name. This is a material breach and Bubba is discharged. Notice that a trivial breach, such as a one day delay in delivering the tuxedos, would not have discharged Bubba.

ANTICIPATORY BREACH

Sally will receive her bachelor's degree in May and already has a job lined up for September—a two-year contract as window display designer for Surebet Department Store. The morning of graduation she reads in the paper that Surebet is going out of business that very day. Sally need not wait until September to learn her fate. Surebet has committed an anticipatory breach by making it unmistakably clear that it will not honor the contract. Sally is discharged and may immediately seek other work. She is also entitled to file suit for breach of contract.

---

[10] *Thomas v. Principal Financial Group*, 566 So. 2d 735, 1990 Ala. LEXIS 614 (Ala. Sup. Ct, 1990).

STATUTE OF LIMITATIONS

A party injured by a breach of contract should act promptly. **A statute of limitations begins to run at the time of injury and will limit the time within which the injured party may file suit.** Statutes of limitation vary widely. In some states, for example, an injured party must sue on oral contracts within three years, on a sale of goods contract within four years, and on some written contracts within five years. Failure to file suit within the time-limits discharges the breaching party.

IMPOSSIBILITY

"Your honor, my client wanted to honor the contract. He just couldn't. Honest." Does the argument work? It depends. A court will discharge an agreement if performing a contract was truly impossible, but not if honoring the deal merely imposed a financial burden.

TRUE IMPOSSIBILITY

These cases are easy—and rare. **True impossibility means that something has happened making it utterly impossible to do what the promisor said he would do.** Francoise owns a vineyard that produces Beaujolais Nouveau wine. She agrees to ship 1,000 cases of *her wine* to Tyrone, a New York importer, as soon as this year's vintage is ready. Tyrone will pay $50 per case. But a fungus wipes out her entire vineyard. Francoise is discharged. It is theoretically impossible for Francoise to deliver wine from her vineyard, and she owes Tyrone nothing.

True impossibility is generally limited to these three causes:

- *Destruction of the Subject Matter*, as happened with Francoise's vineyard.
- *Death of the Promisor in a Personal Services Contract.* When the promisor agrees personally to render a service that cannot be transferred to someone else, her death discharges the contract.
- *Illegality.* If the purpose of a contract becomes illegal, that change discharges the contract.

COMMERCIAL IMPRACTICABILITY AND FRUSTRATION OF PURPOSE

It is rare for contract performance to be truly impossible, but common for it to become a financial burden to one party. Suppose Bradshaw Steel in Pittsburgh agrees to deliver 1,000 tons of steel beams to Rice Construction in Saudi Arabia at a given price, but a week later the cost of raw ore increases 30 percent. A contract once lucrative to the manufacturer is suddenly a major liability. Does that change discharge Bradshaw? Absolutely not. Rice signed the deal *precisely to protect itself against price increases*. The whole purpose of contracts is to enable the parties to control their future.

Yet there may be times when a change in circumstances is so extreme that it would be unfair to enforce a deal. What if a strike made it impossible for

Bradshaw to ship the steel to Saudi Arabia, and the only way to deliver would be by air, at five times the sea cost? Must Bradshaw fulfill its deal? What if war in the Middle East meant that any ships or planes delivering the goods might be fired upon? Other changes could make the contract undesirable for Rice. Suppose the builder wanted steel for a major public building in Riyadh, but the Saudi government decided not to go forward with the construction. The steel would then be worthless to Rice. Must the company still accept it?

None of these hypothetical situations involves true impossibility. It is physically possible for Bradshaw to deliver the goods and for Rice to receive. But in some cases it may be so dangerous or costly to enforce a bargain that a court will discharge it instead. Courts use the related doctrines of commercial impracticability and frustration of purpose to decide when a change in circumstances should permit one side to escape its duties.

Commercial impracticability means some event has occurred that neither party anticipated and *fulfilling the contract would now be extraordinarily difficult and unfair to one party.* If a shipping strike forces Bradshaw to ship by air, the company will argue that neither side expected the strike and that Bradshaw should not suffer a fivefold increase in shipping cost. Bradshaw will probably win the argument.

Frustration of purpose means some event has occurred that neither party anticipated and *the contract now has no value for one party.* If Rice's building project is canceled, Rice will argue that the steel now is useless to the company. Frustration cases are hard to predict. Some states would agree with Rice, but others would hold that it was Rice's obligation to protect itself with a government guarantee that the project would be completed. Courts consider the following factors in deciding impracticability and frustration claims:

- Mere financial difficulties will never suffice to discharge a contract.
- The event must have been truly unexpected.
- If the promisor must use a different means to accomplish her task, at a greatly increased cost, she probably does have a valid claim of impracticability.
- The UCC, like the common law, permits discharge only for major, unforeseen disruptions.

REMEDIES

A remedy is the method a court uses to compensate an injured party. The most common remedy, used in the great majority of lawsuits, is money damages.

The first step that a court takes in choosing a remedy is to decide what interest it is trying to protect. An **interest** is a legal right in something. Someone can have an interest in property, for example, by owning it, or renting it to a tenant, or lending money to buy it. He can have an interest in a *contract* if the agreement gives him some benefit. There are four principal contract interests that a court may seek to protect:

- *Expectation Interest.* This refers to what the injured party reasonably thought she would get from the contract.
- *Reliance Interest.* The injured party may be unable to demonstrate expectation damages, but may still prove that he expended money in reliance on the agreement.
- *Restitution Interest.* An injured party may only be able to demonstrate that she has conferred a benefit on the other party. Here, the objective is to restore to the injured party the benefit she has provided.
- *Equitable Interest.* In some cases, something more than money is needed, such as an order to transfer property to the injured party (specific performance) or an order forcing one party to stop doing something (an injunction).

We will look at all four interests. The first two, expectation and reliance, create what are known as *legal* remedies, because they developed in English courts of *law.* The other interests lead to what are termed *equitable* remedies. Historically, when law courts were unable to help a plaintiff, the injured party would sometimes appeal to the Chancellor in London, who had more flexible authority. The Chancellor's powers became known as equitable remedies, a term still used today.

EXPECTATION INTEREST

This is the most common remedy. **The expectation interest is designed to put the injured party in the position she would have been in had both sides fully performed their obligations.** A court tries to give the injured party the money she would have made from the contract. If accurately computed, this should take into account all the gains she reasonably expected and all the expenses and losses she would have incurred. The injured party should not end up better off than she would have been under the agreement, nor should she suffer serious loss.

William Colby was a former director of the CIA. He wanted to write a book about his 15 years of experiences in Vietnam. He paid James McCarger $5,000 for help in writing an early draft and promised McCarger another $5,000 if the book was published. Then he hired Alexander Burnham to co-write the book. Colby's agent secured a contract with Contemporary Books, which included a $100,000 advance. But Burnham was hopelessly late with the manuscript, and Colby missed his publication date. Colby fired Burnham and finished the book without him. Contemporary published *Lost Victory* several years late, and the book flopped, earning no significant revenue. Because the book was so late, Contemporary paid Colby a total of only $17,000. Colby sued Burnham for his lost expectation interest. The court awarded him $23,000, calculated as follows:

	$100,000	advance, the only money Colby was promised
	– 10,000	agent's fee
	= 90,000	fee for the two authors, combined
divided by 2	= 45,000	Colby's fee
	– 5,000	owed to McCarger under the earlier agreement
	= 40,000	Colby's expectation interest

− 17,000	fee Colby received from Contemporary
= 23,000	Colby's expectation damages, that is, the amount he would have received had Burnham finished on time[11]

The *Colby* case presented an easy calculation of damages. Other contracts are complex. Courts typically divide the expectation damages into three parts: (1) compensatory (or "direct") damages, which represent harm that flowed directly from the contract's breach; (2) consequential (or "special") damages, which represent harm caused by the injured party's unique situation; and (3) incidental damages, which are minor costs such as storing or returning defective goods, advertising for alternative goods, and so forth. The first two—compensatory and consequential—are the important ones.

COMPENSATORY DAMAGES

Compensatory damages are the most common monetary awards for the expectation interest. Courts also refer to these as "direct damages." **Compensatory damages are those that flow directly from the contract.** In other words, these are the damages that inevitably result from the breach. Suppose Ace Productions hires Reina to star in its new movie, *Inside Straight*. Ace promises Reina $3 million, providing she shows up June 1 and works until the film is finished. But in late May, Joker Entertainment offers Reina $6 million to star in its new feature, and on June 1 Reina informs Ace that she will not appear. Reina has breached her contract, and Ace should recover compensatory damages.

What are the damages that flow directly from the contract? Ace obviously has to replace Reina. If Ace hires Kween as its star and pays her a fee of $4 million, Ace is entitled to the difference between what it expected to pay ($3 million) and what the breach forced it to pay ($4 million), or $1 million in compensatory damages. Suppose the rest of the cast and crew are idle for two weeks because of the delay in hiring a substitute, and the lost time costs the producers an extra $2.5 million. Reina is also liable for those expenses. Both the new actress and the delay are inevitable.

REASONABLE CERTAINTY

The injured party must prove the breach of contract caused damages that can be quantified with reasonable certainty. What if *Inside Straight*, now starring Kween, bombs at the box office. Ace proves that each of Reina's last three movies grossed over $60 million, but *Inside Straight* grossed only $28 million. Is Reina liable for the lost profits? No. Ace cannot prove that it was Reina's absence that caused the film to fare poorly. The script may have been mediocre, or Kween's co-stars dull, or the publicity efforts inadequate. Mere "speculative damages" are worth nothing.

CONSEQUENTIAL DAMAGES

In addition to compensatory damages, the injured party may seek consequential damages or, as they are also known, "special damages." **Consequential**

---

[11] *Colby v. Burnham*, 31 Conn. App. 707, 627 A.2d 457, 1993 Conn. App LEXIS 299 (Conn. App. Ct. 1993).

damages are those resulting from the unique circumstances of *this injured party*. The rule concerning this remedy comes from a famous 1854 case, *Hadley v. Baxendale*, which all American law students read. Now it is your turn.

HADLEY v. BAXENDALE

9 Ex. 341, 156 Eng. Rep. 145
Court of Exchequer, 1854

Facts: The Hadleys operated a flour mill in Gloucester. The crankshaft broke, causing the mill to grind to a halt. The Hadleys employed Baxendale to cart the damaged part to a foundry in Greenwich, where a new one could be manufactured. Baxendale promised to make the delivery in one day, but he was late transporting the shaft, and as a result the Hadleys' mill was shut for five extra days. They sued, and the jury awarded damages based in part on their lost profits. Baxendale appealed.

Issue: Should the defendant be liable for profits lost because of his delay in delivering the shaft?

Excerpts from Judge Alderson's Decision: Where two parties have made a contract which one of them has broken, the damages which the other party ought to receive in respect of such breach of contract should be such as may fairly and reasonably be considered either arising naturally, i.e., according to the usual course of things, from such breach of contract itself, or such as may reasonably be supposed to have been in the contemplation of both parties, at the time they made the contract, as the probable result of the breach of it. Now, if the special circumstances under which the contract was actually made were communicated by the plaintiffs to the defendants, and thus known to both parties, the damages resulting from the breach of such a contract, which they would reasonably contemplate, would be the amount of injury which would ordinarily follow from a breach of contract under these special circumstances so known and communicated. But, on the other hand, if these special circumstances were wholly unknown to the party breaking the contract, he, at the most, could only be supposed to have had in his contemplation the amount of injury which would arise generally, and in the great multitude of cases not affected by any special circumstances, from such a breach of contract.

Now, in the present case, if we are to apply the principles above laid down, we find that the only circumstances here communicated by the plaintiffs to the defendants at the time the contract was made, were, that the article to be carried was the broken shaft of a mill, and that the plaintiffs were the millers of that mill. But how do these circumstances shew [sic] reasonably that the profits of the mill must be stopped by an unreasonable delay in the delivery of the broken shaft by the carrier to the third person? Suppose the plaintiffs had another shaft in their possession put up or putting up at the time, and that they only wished to send back the broken shaft to the engineer who made it; it is clear that this would be quite consistent with the above circumstances, and yet the unreasonable delay in the delivery would have no effect upon the intermediate profits of the mill. It follows, therefore, that the loss of profits here cannot reasonably be considered such a consequence of the breach of contract as could have been fairly and reasonably contemplated by both the parties when they made this contract.

[The court ordered a new trial, in which the jury would not be allowed to consider the plaintiffs' lost profits.]

The rule from *Hadley v. Baxendale* has been unchanged ever since: **the injured party may recover consequential damages only if the breaching party should have foreseen them.**

Let us return briefly to *Inside Straight*. Suppose that, long before shooting began, Ace had sold the film's soundtrack rights to Spinem Sound for $2 million. Spinem believed it would make a profit only if Reina appeared in the film, so it demanded the right to discharge the agreement if Reina dropped out. When Reina quit, Spinem terminated the contract. Now, when Ace sues Reina, it will also seek $2 million in consequential damages for the lost music revenue. If Reina knew about Ace's contract with Spinem when she signed to do the film, she is liable for $2 million. If she never realized she was an essential part of the music contract, she owes nothing for the lost profits. (Because damage calculation can be complex, there are companies that specialize in doing the work on behalf of litigants or other interested parties. One such firm explains its services at http://www.ei.com/concentrations/damages.htm.)

INCIDENTAL DAMAGES

Incidental damages are the relatively minor costs that the injured party suffers when responding to the breach. When Reina, the actress, breaches the film contract, the producers may have to leave the set and fly back to Los Angeles to hire a new actress. The cost of travel, renting a room for auditions, and other related expenses are incidental damages.

RELIANCE INTEREST

George plans to manufacture and sell silk scarves during the holiday season. In the summer, he contracts with Cecily, the owner of a shopping mall, to rent a high-visibility stall for $100 per day. George then buys hundreds of yards of costly silk and gets to work cutting and sewing. Then in September, Cecily refuses to honor the contract. George sues and easily proves Cecily breached a valid contract. But what is his remedy?

George cannot establish an expectation interest in his scarf business. He hoped to sell each scarf for a $40 gross profit, and wanted to make $2,000 per day. But how much would he actually have earned? Enough to retire on—or enough to buy a salami sandwich for lunch? A court cannot give him an expectation interest, so George will ask for *reliance damages*. **The reliance interest is designed to put the injured party in the position he would have been in had the parties never entered into a contract.** This remedy focuses on the time and money the injured party spent performing his part of the agreement.

Assuming he is unable to sell the scarves to a retail store (which is probable because retailers will have made purchases long ago), George should be able to recover the cost of the silk fabric he bought and perhaps something for the hours of labor he spent cutting and sewing. However, reliance damages can be difficult to win because *they are harder to quantify*. Judges dislike vague calculations. How much was George's time worth in making the scarves? How good was his work? How likely were the scarves to sell? If George has a track record in the industry, he will be able to show a market price for his services. Without such a record, his reliance claim becomes a tough battle.

In one type of case, courts use reliance damages exclusively. Recall the doctrine of promissory estoppel, which sometimes permits a plaintiff to recover damages even without a valid contract. The plaintiff must show that the defendant made a promise knowing that the plaintiff would likely rely on it, that the plaintiff did rely, and that the only way to avoid injustice is to enforce the promise. In promissory estoppel cases, a court will generally award *only* reliance damages. It would be unfair to give expectation damages for the full benefit of the bargain when, legally, there has been no bargain. Lou says to Costas, who lives in Philadelphia, "You're a great chef. Come out to Los Angeles. My new restaurant needs you, and I can double your salary, if not more." Costas quits his job and travels west, but Lou has no job for him. There is no binding contract, because the terms were too vague; however, the chef will *probably* obtain some reliance damages based on lost income and moving costs.

PREVENTIVE Law

Costas's reliance damages are uncertain. How should he have protected himself?

RESTITUTION INTEREST

Jim and Bonnie Hyler bought an expensive recreational vehicle (RV) from Autorama. The salesman promised the Hylers that a manufacturer's warranty covered the entire vehicle for a year. The Hylers had a succession of major problems with their RV, including windows that wouldn't shut, a door that fell off, a loose windshield, and defective walls. Then they learned that the manufacturer had gone bankrupt. In fact, the Autorama salesman knew of the bankruptcy when he made the sales pitch.

The Hylers returned the RV to Autorama and demanded their money back. They wanted restitution.

The restitution interest is designed to return to the injured party a benefit that he has conferred on the other party, which it would be unjust to leave with that person. Restitution is a common remedy in contracts involving fraud, misrepresentation, mistake, and duress. In these cases, restitution often goes hand-in-hand with **rescission**, which means to "undo" a contract and put the parties where they were before they made the agreement. The court declared that Autorama had misrepresented the manufacturer's warranty by omitting the small fact that the manufacturer itself no longer existed. Autorama was forced to return to the Hylers the full purchase price plus the value of the automobile they had traded. The dealer, of course, was allowed to keep the defective RV and stare out the ill-fitting windows.[12]

Courts also award restitution in cases of quasi-contract, which we examined in Chapter 9. In quasi-contract cases, the parties never made a contract, but one side did benefit the other. A court may choose to award restitution where one party has conferred a benefit on another and it would be unjust for the other party to retain the benefit. Suppose Owner asks Supplier to install a new furnace in her home. Supplier forgets to ask Owner to sign a contract. If the furnace works properly, it would be unfair to let Owner keep it for free, and a court might order full payment as restitution, even though there was no valid contract.

---

[12] *Hyler v. Garner*, 548 N.W.2d 864, 1996 Iowa Sup. LEXIS 322 (Iowa, 1966).

OTHER EQUITABLE INTERESTS

In addition to restitution, the other three equitable powers that concern us are specific performance, injunction, and reformation.

SPECIFIC PERFORMANCE

Leona Claussen owned Iowa farmland. She sold some of it to her sister-in-law, Evelyn Claussen, and, along with the land, granted Evelyn an option to buy additional property at $800 per acre. Evelyn could exercise her option anytime during Leona's lifetime or within six months of Leona's death. When Leona died, Evelyn informed the estate's executor that she was exercising her option. But other relatives wanted the property and the executor refused to sell. Evelyn sued and asked for *specific performance*. She did not want an award of damages; she wanted the land itself. The remedy of specific performance forces the two parties to perform their contract.

A court will award specific performance, ordering the parties to perform the contract, only in cases involving the sale of land or some other asset that is unique. Courts use this equitable remedy when money damages would be inadequate to compensate the injured party. If the subject is unique and irreplaceable, money damages will not put the injured party in the same position she would have been in had the agreement been kept. So a court will order the seller to convey the rare object and the buyer to pay for it.

Historically, every parcel of land has been regarded as unique, and therefore specific performance is always available in real estate contracts. Evelyn Claussen won specific performance. The Iowa Supreme Court ordered Leona's estate to convey the land to Evelyn, for $800 per acre.[13] Generally speaking, either the seller or the buyer may be granted specific performance.

Other unique items, for which a court will order specific performance, include such things as rare works of art, secret formulas, patents, and shares in a closely held corporation. By contrast, a contract for a new Jeep Cherokee Laredo is not enforceable by specific performance. An injured buyer can use money damages to purchase a virtually identical auto.

INJUNCTION

You move into your new suburban house on two acres of land, and the fresh air is exhilarating. But the wind shifts to the west, and you find yourself thinking of farm animals, especially pigs. Your next-door neighbor just started an organic bacon ranch, and the first 15 porkers have checked in. You check out the town's zoning code, discover that it is illegal to raise livestock in the neighborhood, and sue. Money damages will not suffice, because you want the bouquet to disappear. You seek the equitable remedy of injunction. **An injunction is a court order that requires someone to do something or refrain from doing something.**

The court will order your neighbor immediately to cease and desist raising any pigs or other farm animals on his land. "Cease" means to stop, and "desist"

---

[13] *In re Estate of Claussen*, 482 N.W.2d 381, 1992 Iowa Sup. LEXIS 52 (Iowa 1992).

means to refrain from doing it in the future. The injunction will not get you any money, but it will move the pigs out of town, and that was your goal. (The Web site http://www.kinseylaw.com/ATTY%20SERV/civil/complaints/injunction.html provides a sample complaint requesting an injunction.)

In the increasingly litigious world of professional sports, injunctions are commonplace. Brian Shaw was playing professional basketball in Italy when the Boston Celtics flipped him a contract offer. In January, Shaw inked a five-year deal with the Celtics, to begin playing the following October. The player grabbed a $450,000 bonus and a guaranteed salary of over $1 million per year. In June, Shaw reversed direction, informing the Celtics that he would remain with his Italian team. Boston ran a fast break into federal court, seeking an injunction. Shaw argued that when he signed the Celtics' contract he had been homesick for America, and depressed by criticism in the Italian press. He added that no agent had been available to assist him. The court rejected his claims, noting that Shaw was a college graduate and the contract was a simple, standard-form agreement. The judge granted the injunction, blocking Shaw from playing anywhere except Boston.[14]

REFORMATION

The final remedy, and perhaps the least common, is **reformation**, in which a court will partially "rewrite" a contract. Courts seldom do this, because the whole point of a contract is to enable the parties to control their own futures. However, a court may reform a contract if it believes a written agreement includes a simple mistake. Suppose that Roger orally agrees to sell 35 acres to Hannah for $600,000. The parties then draw up a written agreement, accidentally stating the price as $60,000. Most courts would reform the agreement and enforce it.

SPECIAL ISSUES OF DAMAGES

MITIGATION OF DAMAGES

Note one limitation on *all* contract remedies: **A party injured by a breach of contract may not recover for damages that he could have avoided with reasonable efforts.** In other words, when one party perceives that the other has breached or will breach the contract, the injured party must try to prevent unnecessary loss. A party is expected to **mitigate** his damages, that is, to keep damages as low as he reasonably can.

LIQUIDATED DAMAGES

It can be difficult or even impossible to prove how much damage the injured party has suffered. So lawyers and executives negotiating a deal may include in

---

[14] *Boston Celtics Limited Partnership v. Shaw*, 908 F.2d 1041, 1990 U.S. App. LEXIS 12117 (U.S. C App. 1st Cir. 1990).

the contract a **liquidated damages clause, a provision stating in advance how much a party must pay if it breaches**. Is that fair? The answer depends on two factors: **A court will generally enforce a liquidated damages clause if (1) at the time of creating the contract it was very difficult to estimate actual damages,** ***and*** **(2) the liquidated amount is reasonable.** In any other case, the liquidated damage will be considered a penalty and will prove unenforceable.

CHAPTER CONCLUSION

A moment's caution! Often that is the only thing needed to avoid years of litigation. Yes, the broad powers of a court may enable it to compensate an injured party, but problems of proof demonstrate that the best solution is a carefully drafted contract and socially responsible behavior.

CHAPTER REVIEW

1. Contracts that must be in writing to be enforceable concern:
   - The sale of any interest in land
   - Agreements that cannot be performed within one year
   - Promises to pay the debt of another
   - Promises made by an executor of an estate
   - Promises made in consideration of marriage; and
   - The sale of goods over $500
2. The writing must be signed by the defendant and must state the name of all parties, the subject matter of the agreement, and all essential terms and promises.
3. A third party beneficiary is an intended beneficiary and may enforce a contract *only* if the parties intended her to benefit from the agreement *and* (1) enforcing the promise will satisfy a debt of the promisee to the beneficiary, or (2) the promisee intended to make a gift to the beneficiary.
4. An assignment transfers the assignor's contract rights to the assignee. A delegation transfers the delegator's duties to the delegatee.
5. A party generally may assign contract rights unless doing so would substantially change the obligor's rights or duties; is forbidden by law; or is validly precluded by the contract.
6. Duties are delegable unless delegation would violate public policy; the contract prohibits delegation; or the obligee has a substantial interest in personal performance by the obligor.
7. Unless the obligee agrees otherwise, delegation does not discharge the delegator's duty to perform.
8. A condition is an event that must occur before a party becomes obligated.
9. Strict performance, which requires one party to fulfill its duties perfectly, is unusual. In construction and service contracts, substantial performance is generally sufficient to entitle the promisor to the contract price, minus the cost of defects.
10. Good faith performance is required in all contracts.
11. True impossibility means that some event has made it impossible to perform an agreement. Commercial impracticability means that some unexpected event has made it extraordinarily difficult and unfair for one party to perform its obligations.

12. A remedy is the method a court uses to compensate an injured party.

13. The expectation interest puts the injured party in the position she would have been in had both sides fully performed. It has three components: Compensatory, consequential, and incidental damages.

14. The reliance interest puts the injured party in the position he would have been in had the parties never entered into a contract.

15. The restitution interest returns to the injured party a benefit that she has conferred on the other party, which it would be unjust to leave with that person.

16. Specific performance, ordered only in cases of a unique asset, requires both parties to perform the contract.

17. An injunction is a court order that requires someone to do something or refrain from doing something.

PRACTICE TEST

1. **CPA QUESTION** Able hired Carr to restore Able's antique car for $800. The terms of their oral agreement provided that Carr was to complete the work within 18 months. Actually, the work could be completed within one year. The agreement is:

   (a) unenforceable because it covers services with a value in excess of $500

   (b) unenforceable because it covers a time period in excess of one year

   (c) enforceable because personal service contracts are exempt from the statute of frauds

   (d) enforceable because the work could be completed within one year

2. **RIGHT & WRONG** Jacob Deutsch owned commercial property. He orally agreed to rent it for six years to Budget Rent-A-Car. Budget took possession, began paying monthly rent, and over a period of several months expended about $6,000 in upgrading the property. Deutsch was aware of the repairs. After a year, Deutsch attempted to evict Budget. Budget claimed it had a six-year oral lease, but Deutsch claimed that such a lease was worthless. Please rule. Is it ethical for Deutsch to use the statute of frauds in attempting to defeat the lease? Assume that, as landlord, you had orally agreed to rent premises to a tenant, but then for business reasons preferred not to carry out the deal. Would you evict a tenant if you thought the statute of frauds would enable you to do so? How should you analyze the problem? What values are most important to you?

3. Intercontinental Metals Corp. (IMC) contracted with the accounting firm of Cherry, Bekaert & Holland to perform an audit. Cherry issued its opinion about IMC, giving all copies of its report directly to the company. IMC later permitted Dun & Bradstreet to examine the statements, and Raritan River Steel Company saw a report published by Dun & Bradstreet. Relying on the audit, Raritan sold IMC $2.2 million worth of steel on credit, but IMC promptly went bankrupt. Raritan sued Cherry, claiming that IMC was not as sound as Cherry had reported, and that the accounting firm had breached its contract with IMC. Comment on Raritan's suit.

4. Nationwide Discount Furniture hired Rampart Security to install an alarm in its warehouse. A fire would set off an alarm in Rampart's office, and the security company was then supposed to notify Nationwide immediately. A fire did break out, but Rampart allegedly failed to notify Nationwide, causing the fire to spread next door and damage a building owned by Gasket Materials Corp. Gasket sued Rampart for breach of contract, and Rampart moved for summary judgment. Comment.

5. Pizza of Gaithersburg, Maryland, owned five pizza shops. Pizza arranged with Virginia Coffee Service to install soft drink machines

in each of its stores and maintain them. The contract made no mention of the rights of either party to delegate. Virginia Coffee delegated its duties to the Macke Co., leading to litigation between Pizza and Macke. Pizza claimed that Virginia Coffee was barred from delegating because Pizza had a close working relationship with the president of Virginia Coffee, who personally kept the machines in working order. Was the delegation legal?

6. Evans built a house for Sandra Dyer, but the house had some problems. The garage ceiling was too low. Load-bearing beams in the "great room" cracked and appeared to be steadily weakening. The patio did not drain properly. Pipes froze. Evans wanted the money promised for the job, but Dyer refused to pay. Comment.

7. Omega Concrete had a gravel pit and factory. Access was difficult, so Omega contracted with Union Pacific Railroad (UP) for the right to use a private road that crossed UP property and tracks. The contract stated that use of the road was solely for Omega employees and that Omega would be responsible for closing a gate that UP planned to build where the private road joined a public highway. In fact, UP never constructed the gate. Omega had no authority to construct the gate. Mathew Rogers, an Omega employee, was killed by a train while using the private road to reach Omega. Rogers's family sued Omega, claiming, among other things, that Omega failed to keep the gate closed as the contract required. Is Omega liable based on that failure?

8. **YOU BE THE JUDGE WRITING PROBLEM** Kuhn Farm Machinery, a European company, signed an agreement with Scottsdale Plaza Resort, of Arizona, to rent 190 guestrooms for its North American dealers' convention during March 1991. Kuhn invited its top 200 independent dealers from the United States and Canada and about 25 of its own employees from the United States, Europe, and Australia, although it never mentioned those plans to Scottsdale.

   On August 2, 1990, Iraq invaded Kuwait, and on January 16, 1991, the United States and allied forces were at war with Iraq. Iraqi leaders threatened terrorist acts against the United States and its allies. Kuhn became concerned about the safety of those traveling to Arizona, especially its European employees. By mid-February, 11 of the top 50 dealers with expense-paid trips had either canceled their plans to attend or failed to sign up. Kuhn postponed the convention. The resort sued. The trial court discharged the contract under the doctrines of commercial impracticability and frustration of purpose. The resort appealed. Did commercial impracticability or frustration of purpose discharge the contract? **Argument for Scottsdale Plaza Resort:** The resort had no way of knowing that Kuhn anticipated bringing executives from Europe, and even less reason to expect that if anything interfered with their travel, the entire convention would become pointless. Most of the dealers could have attended the convention. **Argument for Kuhn:** The parties never anticipated the threat of terrorism. Kuhn wanted this convention so that its European executives, among others, could meet top North American dealers. That is now impossible. As a result, the contract has no value at all to Kuhn, and its obligations should be discharged by law.

9. Racicky was in the process of buying 320 acres of ranch land. While that sale was being negotiated, Racicky signed a contract to sell the land to Simon. Simon paid $144,000, the full price of the land. But Racicky then went bankrupt, before he could complete the purchase of the land, let alone its sale. Which of these remedies should Simon seek: expectation, restitution, or specific performance?

10. **RIGHT & WRONG** The National Football League owns the copyright to the broadcasts of its games. It licenses local television stations to telecast certain games and maintains a "blackout rule," which prohibits stations

from broadcasting home games that are not sold out 72 hours before the game starts. Certain home games of the Cleveland team were not sold out, and the NFL blocked local broadcast. But several bars in the Cleveland area were able to pick up the game's signal by using special antennas. The NFL wanted the bars to stop showing the games. What did it do? Was it unethical of the bars to broadcast the games that they were able to pick up? Apart from the NFL's legal rights, do you think it had the moral right to stop the bars from broadcasting the games?

INTERNET RESEARCH PROBLEM

You represent a group of neighborhood residents in a large city who are protesting construction of a skyscraper that will violate building height limitations. Draft a complaint, requesting an appropriate injunction. You may use the sample injunction complaint found at http://www.kinseylaw.com/ATTY%20SERV/civil/complaints/injunction.html.

You can find further practice problems in the Online Quiz at http://beatty.westbuslaw.com or in the Study Guide that accompanies this text.

Sales, Product Liability, and Negotiable Instruments

11

CHAPTER

He Sued, She Sued. Harold and Maude made a great couple because both were compulsive entrepreneurs. One evening they sat on their penthouse roof deck, overlooking the twinkling Chicago skyline. Harold sipped a decaf coffee while negotiating, over the phone, with a real estate developer in San Antonio. Maude puffed a cigar as she bargained on a different line with a toy manufacturer in Cleveland. They hung up at the same time. "I did it!" shrieked Maude, "I made an incredible deal for the robots—five bucks each!" "No, I did it!" triumphed Harold, "I sold the 50 acres in Texas for $300,000 more than it's worth." They dashed indoors.

Maude quickly scrawled a handwritten memo, which read, "Confirming our deal—100,000 Psychopath Robots—you deliver Chicago—end of summer." She didn't mention a price, or an exact delivery date, or when payment would be made. She signed her memo and faxed it to the toy manufacturer. Harold took more time. He typed a thorough contract, describing precisely the land he was selling, the $2.3 million price, how and when each payment would be made, and the deed conveyed. He signed the contract and faxed it, along with a plot plan showing the surveyed land. Then the happy couple grabbed a bottle of champagne, returned to the deck—and placed a side bet on whose contract would prove more profitable. The loser would have to cook and serve dinner for six months.

Neither Harold nor Maude ever heard again from the other parties. The toy manufacturer sold the robots to another retailer at a higher price. Maude was forced to buy comparable toys elsewhere for $9 each. She sued. And the Texas property buyer changed his mind, deciding to develop a Club Med in Greenland and refusing to pay Harold for his land. He sued. Only one of the two plaintiffs succeeded. Which one?

SALES

The adventures of Harold and Maude illustrate the Uniform Commercial Code (UCC) in action. The Code is the single most important source of law for people engaged in commerce and controls the vast majority of contracts made every day in every state. The Code is old in origin, contemporary in usage, admirable in purpose, and flawed in application. "Yeah, yeah, that's fascinating," snaps Harold, "but who wins the bet?" Relax, Harold, we'll tell you in a minute.

DEVELOPMENT OF THE UCC

Throughout the first half of the twentieth century, commercial transactions changed dramatically in this country, as advances in transportation and communication revolutionized negotiation and trade. The nation needed a modernized business law to give nationwide uniformity and predictability in a new and faster world. In 1942, two groups of scholars, the American Law Institute (ALI) and the National Conference of Commissioners on Uniform State Laws (NCCUSL), began the effort to draft a modern, national law of commerce. The scholars debated and formulated for nearly a decade. Finally, in 1952, the lawyers published their work—the Uniform Commercial Code. The entire Code is available online at **http://www.law.cornell.edu/ucc/ucc.table.html**.

The ALI and the NCCUSL have revised the Code several times since then, with the most recent major revisions coming in 2001.

Remember that the UCC in a sense is artificial because it is the creation of scholars, not legislators. No section of the Code, new or old, has any legal effect until a state legislature adopts it. In fact, all 50 states and the District of Columbia have adopted the UCC, but some have adopted the early versions from the 1950s and partially revised them, while other states have adopted more recent texts. Louisiana, with its French law heritage, has not adopted Articles 2, 2A, or 6 in any form. In 2001, the drafters proposed significant revisions to Articles 1 and 2, but as this book goes to press, the suggested changes have not been adopted by any state. The drafters have not achieved nationwide uniformity, but they have brought commercial law much closer to that goal.

This chapter is designed to:

- illustrate key elements of the Code *that have changed the common law rules* of contracts
- survey the leading doctrines of product liability; and

Article 1: ***General Provisions***	The purpose of the code, general guidance in applying it, and definitions.
Article 2: ***Sale of Goods***	The sale of *goods*, such as a new car, 20,000 pairs of gloves, or 101 Dalmations. This article is the heart of the UCC.
Article 2A: ***Leases***	A temporary exchange of goods for money, such as renting a car.
Article 2B: ***Software and Licenses***	Electronic contracts and the software that powers them.
Article 3: ***Negotiable Instruments***	The use of checks, promissory notes, and other negotiable instruments.
Article 4: ***Bank Deposits and Collections***	The rights and obligations of banks and their customers.
Article 4A: ***Funds Transfers***	An instruction, given by a bank customer, to credit a sum of money to another's account.
Article 5: ***Letters of Credit***	The use of credit, extended by two or more banks, to facilitate a contract between two parties who do not know each other and require guarantees by banks they trust.
Article 6: ***Bulk Transfers***	The sale of a major part of a company's inventory or equipment.
Article 7: ***Warehouse Receipts, Bills of Lading, and Other Documents of Title***	Documents proving ownership of goods that are being transported or stored.
Article 8: ***Investment Securities***	Rights and liabilities concerning shares of stock or other ownership of an enterprise.
Article 9: ***Secured Transaction***	A sale of goods in which the seller keeps a financial stake in the goods he has sold, such as a car dealer who may repossess the car if the buyer fails to make payments.

- highlight important features of negotiable instruments.

We focus on *changes* the Code makes because in many areas the UCC virtually duplicates the common law. Our discussion reflects recent Code revisions that states have *actually adopted*. At the beginning of the new millenium, the drafters have made substantial—and controversial—recommendations for revision of many of the Code's core articles. However, those revisions have not yet been widely adopted. They will not be allowed an appearance in this book yet and must hover in the wings, hoping for a role in a few years.

HAROLD AND MAUDE, REVISITED

Harold and Maude each negotiated what they believed was an enforceable agreement, and both filed suit: Harold for the sale of his land, Maude for the purchase of toy robots. Only one prevailed. The difference in outcome demonstrates why everyone in business needs a working knowledge of the Code. As we revisit the happy couple, Harold is clearing the dinner dishes. Maude sits back in her chair, lights a cigar, and compliments her husband on the apple tart.

Harold's contract was for the sale of land and was governed by the common law of contracts, which requires any agreement for the sale of land to be in writing and *signed by the defendant,* in this case the buyer in Texas. Harold signed it, but the buyer never did, so Harold's meticulously detailed document was worth less than a five-cent cigar.

Maude's quickly scribbled memorandum, concerning robot toys, was for the sale of goods and was governed by Article 2 of the UCC. The Code requires less detail and formality in a writing. Because Maude and the seller were both merchants, the document she scribbled could be enforced *even against the defendant,* who had never signed anything. The fact that Maude left out the price and other significant terms was not fatal to a contract under the UCC, though under the common law such omissions would have made the bargain unenforceable.

SCOPE OF ARTICLE 2

Because the UCC changes the common law, it is essential to know whether the Code applies in a given case. Negotiations may lead to an enforceable agreement when the UCC applies, even though the same bargaining would create no contract under the common law.

UCC §2-102: Article 2 applies to the sale of goods.[1] **Goods are things that are movable, other than money and investment securities.** Hats are goods, and so are railroad cars, lumber, books, and bottles of wine. Land is not a good, nor is a house. Article 2 regulates sales, which means that one party transfers title to the other in exchange for money. If you sell your motorcycle to a friend, that is a sale of goods.[2]

MERCHANTS

The UCC evolved to provide merchants with rules that would meet their unique business needs. However, while the UCC offers a contract law that is more flexible than the common law, it also requires a higher level of responsibility from the merchants it serves. Those who make a living by crafting agreements are expected to understand the legal consequences of their words and deeds. Thus

---

[1] Officially, Article 2 tells us that it applies to *transactions* in goods, which is a slightly broader category than sale of goods. But most sections of Article 2, and most court decisions, focus exclusively on sales, and so shall we.

[2] Because leasing is so important, the drafters of the Code added Article 2A to cover the subject. Article 2A is similar to Article 2, but there are important differences, and anyone engaging in a significant amount of commercial leasing must become familiar with Article 2A. For our purposes, leasing law is a variation on the theme of Article 2, and we will concentrate on the principal melody of sales.

many sections of the Code offer two rules: one for "merchants" and one for everybody else.

UCC §2-104: A merchant is someone who routinely deals in the particular goods involved, or who appears to have special knowledge or skill in those goods, or who uses agents with special knowledge or skill in those goods. A used car dealer is a "merchant" when it comes to selling autos, because he routinely deals in them. He is not a merchant when he goes to a furniture store and purchases a new sofa.

The UCC frequently holds a merchant to a higher standard of conduct than a non-merchant. For example, a merchant may be held to an oral contract if she received written confirmation of it, even though the merchant herself never signed the confirmation. That same confirmation memo, arriving at the house of a non-merchant, would *not* create a binding deal.

CONTRACT FORMATION

The common law expected the parties to form a contract in a fairly predictable and traditional way: the offeror made a clear offer that included all important terms, and the offeree agreed to all terms. Nothing was left open. The drafters of the UCC recognized that businesspeople frequently do not think or work that way and that the law should reflect business reality.

FORMATION BASICS: SECTION 2-204

UCC §2-204 provides three important rules that enable parties to make a contract quickly and informally:

1. *Any Manner That Shows Agreement.* The parties may make a contract in any manner sufficient to show that they reached an agreement. They may show the agreement with words, writings, or even their conduct. Lisa negotiates with Ed to buy 300 barbecue grills. The parties agree on a price, but other business prevents them from finishing the deal. Then six months later Lisa writes, "Remember our deal for 300 grills? I still want to do it if you do." Ed doesn't respond, but a week later a truck shows up at Lisa's store with the 300 grills, and Lisa accepts them. The combination of their original discussion, Lisa's subsequent letter, Ed's delivery, and her acceptance all adds up to show that they reached an agreement. The court will enforce their deal, and Lisa must pay the agreed-upon price.

2. *Moment of Making Is Not Critical.* The UCC will enforce a deal even though it is difficult, in common law terms, to say exactly when it was formed. Was Lisa's deal formed when they orally agreed? When he delivered? She accepted? The Code's answer: it doesn't matter. The contract is enforceable.

3. *One or More Terms May Be Left Open.* The common law insisted that the parties clearly agree on all important terms. The Code changes that. **Under the UCC, a court may enforce a bargain even though one or more terms were left open.** Lisa's letter never said when she required delivery of the barbecues or when she would pay. Under the UCC, the omission is not fatal. As

long as there is some certain basis for giving damages to the injured party, the court will do just that. If Lisa refused to pay, a court would rule that the parties assumed she would pay within a commercially reasonable time, such as 30 days.

STATUTE OF FRAUDS

UCC §2-201 requires a writing for any sale of goods worth $500 or more. However, under the UCC, the writing need not completely summarize the agreement. The Code only requires a writing *sufficient to indicate* that the parties made a contract. In other words, the writing need not be a contract. A simple memo, or a letter or informal note, mentioning that the two sides reached an agreement, is enough.

In general, the writing must be signed by the defendant, that is, whichever party is claiming there was no deal. Dick signs and sends to Shirley a letter saying, "This is to acknowledge your agreement to buy all 650 books in my rare book collection for $188,000." Shirley signs nothing. A day later, Louis offers Dick $250,000. Is Dick free to sell? No. He signed the memo, it indicates a contract, and Shirley can enforce it against him.

Now reverse the problem. Suppose that after Shirley receives Dick's letter, she decides against rare books in favor of original scripts from the *South Park* television show. Dick sues. Shirley wins because she signed nothing.

ENFORCEABLE ONLY TO QUANTITY STATED

Since the writing only has to indicate that the parties agreed, it need not state every term of their deal. But one term is essential: quantity. **The Code will enforce the contract only up to the quantity of goods stated in the writing.** This is logical, since a court can surmise other terms, such as price, based on market conditions. Buyer agrees to purchase pencils from Seller. The market value of the pencils is easy to determine, but a court would have no way of knowing whether Buyer meant to purchase 1,000 pencils or 100,000; the quantity must be stated.

MERCHANT EXCEPTION

This is a major change from the common law. **When two merchants make an oral contract, and one sends a confirming memo to the other within a reasonable time, and the memo is sufficiently definite that it could be enforced against the sender herself, then the memo is also valid against the merchant who receives it, unless he objects within 10 days.** Laura, a tire wholesaler, signs and sends a memo to Scott, a retailer, saying, "Confm yr order today—500 tires cat #886—cat price." Scott realizes he can get the tires cheaper elsewhere and ignores the memo. Big mistake. Both parties are merchants, and Laura's memo is sufficient to bind her. So it also satisfies the statute of frauds against Scott, unless he objects within 10 days.

The following case illustrates the merchant exception.

Code Provisions Discussed in this Case

Issue	Relevant Code Selection
1. Was this farmer a a "merchant"?	UCC §2-104: A merchant is anyone who routinely deals in the goods involved (or has special knowledge or an agent with such knowledge).
2. Did the memo satisfy the status of frauds?	UCC §2-201(2), the "merchant exception": When two merchants make an oral contract, and one sends a confirming memo to the other within a reasonable time, and the memo is sufficiently definite that it could be enforced against the sender herself, then the memo is also valid against the merchant who receives it, unless he objects within ten days.

COLORADO-KANSAS GRAIN CO. v. REIFSCHNEIDER

817 P.2d 637, 1991 Colo. App. LEXIS 259
Colorado Court of Appeals, 1991

Facts: Albert Reifschneider had been a farmer for 30 years. He owned and operated a 160-acre farm in Colorado. The Colorado-Kansas Grain Co. (CKG) bought and sold agricultural commodities, such as grain. CKG negotiated with Reifschneider to buy corn from him. The parties agreed that CKG would buy 12,500 bushels of corn at a market price of $2.25 per bushel, but Reifschneider told CKG that the deal would have to be approved by the First National Bank, which had loaned him money to grow the crop.

The parties talked with the First National, which approved the sale at the agreed-upon price. Reifschneider told CKG to draw up a contract reflecting the agreement. CKG prepared a written confirmation of the oral agreement, signed it, and mailed it to Reifschneider with instructions to sign it and return the original. Two months later, after Reifschneider had several more conversations with CKG, the farmer informed the company that he would not sign the agreement and believed that they did not have a deal.

CKG purchased 12,500 bushels elsewhere at a higher cost and filed suit. The trial court gave judgment for CKG, concluding that Reifschneider was a merchant and that therefore CKG's memo was binding against him. Reifschneider appealed.

Issues: Was Reifschneider a "merchant"? Did the memo satisfy the statute of frauds?

Excerpts from Judge Jones's Decision: Defendant next contends that the trial court erred in its conclusion that he was a merchant under the UCC. He argues that, for purposes of contract formation regarding the statute of frauds, he is not a merchant and that, therefore, any contract between him and plaintiff cannot be enforced because it was not in writing. We perceive no error.

The question of whether a farmer is or can be a merchant for purposes of this UCC provision has not been addressed in Colorado. The courts among those states which have dealt with this issue are almost evenly split on whether a farmer can be a merchant.

We note that the cases which hold that farmers may be merchants reflect on the fact that today's farmer is involved in far more than simply planting and harvesting crops. Indeed, many farmers possess an extensive knowledge and sophistication regarding the purchase and sale of crops on the various agricultural markets. Often, they are more aptly described as agribusinessmen. Thus, we conclude that, for purposes of [2-201(2)] a farmer may be a merchant.

Here, the record reflects that defendant had dealt in corn or other agricultural commodities for at least twenty years. Moreover, defendant had served as president of a corporation involved in the purchase and sale of hay under futures contracts. And, defendant also had sold his own hay crops to third parties under futures contracts.

Furthermore, given defendant's level of experience and sophistication in the selling of corn and in futures contracts generally, we are unpersuaded that his lack of experience in corn futures precludes the determination of his status as a merchant. Thus, we conclude that under the circumstances of this case, the trial court did not err in concluding that defendant was a merchant. Accordingly, because the contract at issue here was between merchants and because defendant received a written confirmation and failed to object in writing within ten days of such receipt, a contract was formed under [§2-201(2)].

The judgment is *affirmed*.

ADDED TERMS: SECTION 2-207

Under the common law's mirror image rule, when one party makes an offer, the offeree must accept those exact terms. If the offeree adds or alters any terms, the acceptance is ineffective and the offeree's response becomes a counteroffer. In one of its most significant modifications of contract law, the UCC changes that result. **Under §2-207, an acceptance that adds or alters terms will often create a contract.** The Code has made this change in response to the *battles of the form*. Every day, corporations buy and sell millions of dollars of goods using preprinted forms. The vast majority of all contracts involve such documents. Typically, the buyer places an order using a preprinted form, and the seller acknowledges with its own preprinted acceptance form. Because each form contains language favorable to the party sending it, the two documents rarely agree. The Code's drafters concluded that the law must cope with real practices.

INTENTION

The parties must still *intend* to create a contract. Section 2-207 is full of exceptions, but there is no change in this basic requirement of contract law. If the differing forms indicate that the parties never reached agreement, there is no contract.

ADDITIONAL OR DIFFERENT TERMS

An offeree may include a new term in his acceptance and still create a binding deal. Suppose Breeder writes to Pet Shop, offering to sell 100 guinea pigs at $2 each. Pet Shop faxes a memo saying, "We agree to buy 100 g.p. We receive normal industry credit for any unhealthy pig." Pet Shop has added a new term, concerning unhealthy pigs, but the parties have created a binding contract because the writings show they intended an agreement. Now the court must decide what the terms of the contract are, since there is some discrepancy. The first step is to decide whether the new language is an *additional term* or a *different term*.

Additional terms are those that raise issues not covered in the offer. The "unhealthy pig" issue is an additional term because the offer said nothing about it. **When both parties are *merchants*, additional terms generally become part**

of the bargain.[3] Both Pet Shop and Breeder are merchants, and the additional term about credit for unhealthy animals does become part of their agreement.

Different terms *contradict* those in the offer. Suppose Brilliant Corp. orders 1,500 cellular phones from Makem Co., for use by Brilliant's sales force. Brilliant places the order using a preprinted form stating that the product is fully warranted for normal use and that seller is liable for compensatory *and consequential* damages. This means, for example, that Makem would be liable for lost profits if a salesman's phone fails during a lucrative sales pitch. Makem responds with its own memo stating that in the event of defective phones, Makem is liable only to repair or replace, and *is not liable for consequential damages, lost profits, or any other damages.*

Makem's acceptance has included a different term because its language contradicts the offer. **Different terms cancel each other out. The Code then supplies its own terms, called gap-fillers,** which cover prices, delivery dates and places, warranties, and other subjects. The Code's gap-filler about warranties *does* permit recovery of compensatory and consequential damages. Therefore, Makem *would* be liable for lost profits.

PREVENTIVE Law

Section 2-207 is a noble but imperfect attempt to cope with battles of form. How can you avoid a disastrous surprise?

First, *read all terms on both contracts.* Know everybody's terms, and figure out the important differences. This may sound obvious, but many merchants never read the fine print on *either* form. Second, if some of the terms on your contract are essential, insist that the other party accept them in writing. Third, if the other side refuses to accept terms that you consider vital, *calculate your potential loss.* If your potential liability is more than you consider acceptable, your choices are to terminate the negotiations or to obtain insurance.

PERFORMANCE AND REMEDIES

The Code's practical, flexible approach also shapes its rules about contract performance and remedy. Once again, our goal in this chapter is to highlight doctrines that demonstrate a *change or evolution in common law principles.*

BUYER'S REMEDIES

A seller is expected to deliver what the buyer ordered. **Conforming goods satisfy the contract terms.** Non-conforming goods do not.[4] Frame Shop orders from Wholesaler a large quantity of walnut wood, due on March 15, to be used for picture frames. If Wholesaler delivers, on March 8, high quality *cherry* wood, it has shipped non-conforming goods.

---

[3] There are three circumstances in which additional terms do *not* become part of the agreement: when the original offer *insisted on its own terms;* when the additional term *materially alters* the offer, that is, makes a dramatic change in the proposal; and when the offeror *promptly objects* to the new terms.

[4] UCC §2-106(2)

A buyer has the right to **inspect the goods** before paying or accepting,[5] and may **reject non-conforming goods** by notifying the seller within a reasonable time.[6] Frame Shop may lawfully open Wholesaler's shipping crates before paying, and is entitled to refuse the cherry wood. However, when the buyer rejects non-conforming goods, **the seller has the right to cure**, by delivering conforming goods before the contract deadline.[7] If Wholesaler delivers walnut wood by March 15, Frame Shop must pay in full. The Code even permits the seller to cure *after* the delivery date, if doing so is reasonable. Notice the UCC's eminently pragmatic goal: to make contracts work.

COVER

If the seller breaches, the buyer may *cover* by reasonably obtaining substitute goods; it may then obtain the difference between the contract price and its cover price, plus incidental and consequential damages, minus expenses saved.[8] Retailer orders 10,000 pairs of ballet shoes from Shoemaker, at $55 per pair, to be delivered August 1. When no shoes dance through the door, Shoemaker explains that its workers in Europe are on strike, and no delivery date can be guaranteed. Retailer purchases comparable shoes elsewhere for $70, and files suit. Retailer will win $150,000, representing the increased cost of $15 per pair.

INCIDENTAL AND CONSEQUENTIAL DAMAGES

An injured buyer is generally entitled to incidental and consequential damages. Incidental damages cover such costs as advertising for replacements, sending buyers to obtain new goods, and shipping the replacement goods. Consequential damages are those resulting from the unique circumstances of *this injured party*. They can be much more extensive and may include lost profits. **A buyer expecting to resell goods may obtain the loss of profit caused by the seller's failure to deliver.** In the ballet shoes case, suppose Retailer has contracts to resell the goods to ballet companies at an average profit of $10 per pair. Retailer is also entitled to those lost profits.

SELLER'S REMEDIES

Of course, a seller has rights, too. Sometimes a buyer breaches before the seller has delivered the goods, for example, by failing to make a payment due under the contract. If that happens, **the seller may refuse to deliver the goods.**[9]

If a buyer unjustly refuses to accept or pay for goods, the injured seller may resell them. **If the resale is commercially reasonable, the seller may recover the difference between the resale price and contract price, plus incidental damages, minus expenses saved.**[10] Incidental damages are expenses the seller incurs

---

[5] UCC §2-513.

[6] UCC §§2-601, 602.

[7] UCC §2-508.

[8] UCC §2-712.

[9] UCC §2-705.

[10] UCC §2-706

in holding the goods and reselling them, costs such as storage, shipping, and advertising for resale. The seller must deduct expenses saved by the breach. For example, if the contract required the seller to ship heavy machinery from Detroit to San Diego, and the buyer's breach enables the seller to market its goods profitably in Detroit, the seller must deduct from its claimed losses the transportation costs that it saved.

Finally, the seller may simply **sue for the contract price**, if the buyer has accepted the goods *or if* the goods are conforming and resale is impossible.[11] If the goods were manufactured to the buyer's unique specifications, there might be no other market for them, and the seller should receive the contract price.

WARRANTIES AND PRODUCT LIABILITY

You are sitting in a fast-food restaurant in Washington, D.C. Your friend Ben, who works for a congressman, is eating with one hand and gesturing with the other. "We want product liability reform and we want it now," he proclaims, stabbing the air with his free hand. "It's absurd, these multimillion dollar verdicts, just because something has a *slight defect*." He waves angrily at the absurdity, takes a ferocious bite from his burger—and with a loud CRACK breaks a tooth. Ben howls in pain and throws down the bun, revealing a large piece of bone in the meat. As he tips back in misery, his defectively manufactured chair collapses, and Ben slams into the tile, knocking himself unconscious. Hours later, when he revives in the hospital, he refuses to speak to you until he talks with his lawyer. They will discuss **product liability**, which refers to goods that have caused an injury. The harm may be physical, as it was in Ben's case. Or it can be purely economic, as when a corporation buys a computer so defective it must be replaced, costing the buyer lost time and profits. The injured party may have a choice of possible remedies, including:

- *Warranty*, which is an assurance provided in a sales contract
- *Negligence*, which refers to unreasonable conduct by the defendant; and
- *Strict liability*, which prohibits defective products whether the defendant acted reasonably or not.

We discuss each of these remedies in this chapter. What all product liability cases have in common is that a person or business has been hurt by goods. We begin with warranties.

EXPRESS WARRANTIES

A warranty is a contractual assurance that goods will meet certain standards. It is normally a manufacturer or a seller who gives a warranty, and a buyer who relies on it. A warranty might be explicit and written: "The manufacturer

[11] UCC §2-709.

warrants that the lightbulbs in this package will provide 100 watts of power for 2,000 hours." Or a warranty could be oral: "Don't worry, this machine can harvest any size of wheat crop ever planted in the state."

An express warranty is one that the seller creates with his words or actions.[12] Whenever a seller *clearly indicates* to a buyer that the goods being sold will meet certain standards, she has created an express warranty. For example, if the salesclerk for a paint store tells a professional house painter that "this exterior paint will not fade for three years, even in direct sunlight," that is an express warranty and the store is bound by it. The store is also bound by express warranty if the clerk gives the painter a brochure making the same promise, or a sample that indicates the same thing.

The seller may **disclaim** a warranty. **A disclaimer is a statement that particular warranty *does not* apply.** The seller may disclaim an oral express warranty by including in the sales contract a statement such as "sold as is," or "any oral promises are disclaimed." Written express warranties generally *cannot* be disclaimed.

IMPLIED WARRANTIES

Emily sells Sam a new jukebox for his restaurant, but the machine is so defective it never plays a note. When Sam demands a refund, Emily scoffs that she never made any promises. She is correct that she made no express warranties, but is liable nonetheless. Many sales are covered by implied warranties.

Implied warranties are those created by the Code itself, not by any act or statement of the seller.

IMPLIED WARRANTY OF MERCHANTABILITY

This is the most important warranty in the Code. **Unless excluded or modified, a warranty that the goods shall be merchantable is implied in a contract for their sale, if the seller is a merchant with respect to goods of that kind.** *Merchantable* means that the goods are fit for the ordinary purposes for which they are used.[13] This rule contains several important principles:

- *Unless excluded or modified* means that the seller does have a chance to escape this warranty. A seller may disclaim this warranty provided he actually mentions the word *merchantability*. A seller also has the option to disclaim *all* warranties, by stating that the goods are sold "as is" or "with all faults."
- *Merchantability* requires that goods be fit for their normal purposes. A ladder, to be merchantable, must be able to rest securely against a building and support someone who is climbing it. The ladder need not be serviceable as a boat ramp.
- *Implied* means that the law itself imposes this liability on the seller.

---

[12] UCC §2-313.

[13] UCC §2-314(1).

- *A merchant with respect to goods of that kind* means that the seller is someone who routinely deals in these goods or holds himself out as having special knowledge about these goods.

Dacor Corp. manufactured and sold scuba diving equipment. Dacor ordered air hoses from Sierra Precision, specifying the exact size and couplings so that the hose would fit safely into Dacor's oxygen units. Within a year, customers returned a dozen Dacor units, complaining that the hose connections had cracked and were unusable. Dacor recalled 16,000 units and refit them at a cost of $136,000. Dacor sued Sierra and won its full costs. Sierra was a merchant with respect to scuba hoses, because it routinely manufactured and sold them. The defects were life-threatening to scuba divers, and the hoses could not be used for normal purposes.[14]

The scuba equipment was not merchantable, because a properly made scuba hose should never crack under normal use. But what if the product being sold is food, and the food contains something that is harmful—yet quite normal?

GOODMAN v. WENCO FOODS, INC.

333 N.C. 1, 423 S.E.2d 444, 1992 N.C.LEXIS 671
Supreme Court of North Carolina, 1992

Facts: Fred Goodman and a friend stopped for lunch at a Wendy's restaurant in Hillsborough, North Carolina. Goodman had eaten about half of his double hamburger when he bit down and felt immediate pain in his lower jaw. He took from his mouth a triangular piece of cow bone, about one-sixteenth to one-quarter inch thick and one-half inch long, along with several pieces of his teeth. Goodman's pain was intense and his dental repairs took months.

The restaurant purchased all of its meat from Greensboro Meat Supply Company (GMSC). Wendy's required its meat to be chopped and "free from bone or cartilage in excess of 1/8 inch in any dimension." GMSC beef was inspected continuously by state regulators and was certified by the United States Department of Agriculture (USDA). The USDA considered any bone fragment less than three-quarters of an inch long to be "insignificant."

Goodman sued, claiming a breach of the implied warranty of merchantability. The trial court dismissed the claim, ruling that the bone was natural to the food and that the hamburger was therefore fit for its ordinary purpose. The appeals court reversed this, holding that a hamburger could be unfit even if the bone occurred naturally. Wendy's appealed to the state's highest court.

Issue: Was the hamburger unfit for its ordinary purpose because it contained a harmful but natural bone?

Excerpts from Judge Exum's Decision: We hold that when a substance in food causes injury to a consumer of the food, it is not a bar to recovery against the seller that the substance was "natural" to the food, provided the substance is of such a size, quality or quantity, or the food has been so processed, or both, that the substance's presence should not reasonably have been anticipated by the consumer.

A triangular, one-half-inch, inflexible bone shaving is indubitably "inherent" in or "natural" to a cut of beef, but whether it is so "natural" to hamburger as to put a consumer on his guard—whether it "is to be reasonably expected by the consumer"—is, in most cases, a question for the

[14] *Dacor Corp. v. Sierra Precision*, 1993 U.S. Dist. LEXIS 8009 (N.D. Ill. 1993).

jury. We are not requiring that the respondent's hamburgers be perfect, only that they be fit for their intended purpose. It is difficult to conceive of how a consumer might guard against the type of injury present here, short of removing the hamburger from its bun, breaking it apart and inspecting its small components.

Wendy's argues that the evidence supported its contention that its hamburger complied with [federal and state] standards. Wendy's reasons that [state and federal regulators permit] some bone fragments in meat and that its hamburgers are therefore merchantable as a matter of law. The court of appeals rejected this argument, noting that compliance "with all state and federal regulations is only some evidence which the jury may consider in determining whether the product was merchantable." We agree.

We thus conclude, as did the court of appeals majority, that a jury could reasonably determine the meat to be of such a nature, i.e., hamburger, and the bone in the meat of such a size that a consumer of the meat should not reasonably have anticipated the bone's presence. The court of appeals therefore properly reversed the directed verdict for Wendy's on plaintiff's implied warranty of merchantability claim.

IMPLIED WARRANTY OF FITNESS FOR A PARTICULAR PURPOSE

The other warranty that the law imposes on sellers is the implied warranty of fitness for a particular purpose. This cumbersome name is often shortened to the *warranty of fitness*. **Where the seller at the time of contracting knows about a particular purpose for which the buyer wants the goods, and knows that the buyer is relying on the seller's skill or judgment, there is (unless excluded or modified) an implied warranty that the goods shall be fit for such purpose.**[15]

Notice that the seller must know about some special use the buyer intends, and realize that the buyer is relying on the seller's judgment. Suppose a lumber salesman knows that a buyer is relying on his advice to choose the best wood for a house being built in a swamp. The Code implies a warranty that the wood sold will withstand those special conditions.

Once again, a seller may disclaim this warranty if she clearly states "as is" or "sold with all faults," or some similar language.

NEGLIGENCE

A buyer of goods may have remedies other than warranty claims. One is negligence. Here we focus on how this law applies to the sale of goods. Negligence is notably different from contract law. In a contract case, the two parties have reached an agreement, and the terms of their bargain will usually determine how to settle any dispute. If the parties agreed that the seller disclaimed all warranties, then the buyer may be out of luck. But in a negligence case, there has been no bargaining between the parties, who may never have met. A consumer injured by an exploding cola bottle is unlikely to have bargained for her beverage with the CEO of the cola company. Instead, the law *imposes* a standard of conduct on everyone in society, corporation and individual alike. The two key elements of this standard, for present purposes, are *duty* and *breach*. A plaintiff injured by goods she bought must show that the defendant, usually a manufacturer or seller of a product, had a duty to her and breached that duty. A

---

[15] UCC §2-315.

defendant has a duty of due care to anyone who could foreseeably be injured by its misconduct. Generally, it is the duty to act as *a reasonable person* would in like circumstances; a defendant who acts unreasonably has breached its duty.

In negligence cases concerning the sale of goods, plaintiffs most often raise one or more of these claims:

- *Negligent Design.* The buyer claims that the product injured her because the manufacturer designed it poorly. Negligence law requires a manufacturer to design a product free of *unreasonable* risks. The product does not have to be absolutely safe. An automobile that guaranteed a driver's safety could be made but would be prohibitively expensive. Reasonable safety features must be built-in, if they can be included at a tolerable cost.
- *Negligent Manufacture.* The buyer claims that the design was adequate but that failure to inspect or some other sloppy conduct caused a dangerous product to leave the plant.
- *Failure to Warn.* A manufacturer is liable for failing to warn the purchaser or users about the dangers of normal use and also foreseeable misuse. However, there is no duty to warn about obvious dangers, a point evidently lost on some manufacturers. A Batman costume unnecessarily included this statement: "For play only: Mask and chest plate are not protective; cape does not enable user to fly."

Ibrahim Boumelhem, aged four, began playing with a Bic disposable lighter that his parents had bought. He started a fire that burned his legs and severely burned his six-month-old brother over 85 percent of his body. Ibrahim's father sued Bic, claiming that the lighter was negligently designed because it could have been child-proof. He also claimed failure to warn, because the lighter did not clearly warn of the danger to children.

The *Boumelhem* court considered evidence and analyses from several other cases against Bic. The court noted that consumers use over 500 million disposable lighters annually in the United States. Each lighter provides 1,000 to 2,000 lights. During one three-year period, children playing with disposable lighters started 8,100 fires annually, causing an average of 180 people to die every year, of whom 140 were children under five. Another 990 people were injured. The average annual cost of deaths, injuries, and property damage from child-play fires was estimated at $310 to $375 million, or 60 to 75 cents per lighter sold. Bic had acknowledged in earlier litigation that it was foreseeable lighters would get into children's hands and injure them. Bic had also agreed that it was feasible to make a more child-resistant lighter.

How should the court rule? Does this case present an irresponsible parent launching a frivolous lawsuit, or a callous corporation disregarding children's safety to make a few extra dollars?

STRICT LIABILITY

The other tort claim that an injured person can bring against the manufacturer or seller of a product is strict liability. Like negligence, strict liability is a burden created by the law rather than by the parties. And, as with all torts, strict liability concerns claims of physical harm. But there is a key distinction between negligence and strict liability: in a negligence case, the injured buyer must demonstrate that the seller's conduct was unreasonable. Not so in strict liability.

In strict liability, the injured person need not prove that the defendant's conduct was unreasonable. The injured person must show only that the defendant manufactured or sold a product that was defective and that the defect caused harm. Almost all states permit such lawsuits, and most of them have adopted the summary of strict liability provided by the Restatement (Second) of Torts §402A. (The American Law Institute has voted to revise strict liability law, but its proposed changes have not been widely adopted, so we focus on existing law.) Because §402A is the most frequently cited section in all of tort law, we quote it in full:

(1) One who sells any product in a defective condition unreasonably dangerous to the user or consumer or to his property is subject to liability for physical harm thereby caused to the ultimate user or consumer, or to his property, if

(a) the seller is engaged in the business of selling such a product, and

(b) it is expected to and does reach the user or consumer without substantial change in the condition in which it is sold.

(2) The rule stated in Subsection (1) applies although

(a) the seller has exercised all possible care in the preparation and sale of his product, and

(b) the user or consumer has not bought the product from or entered into any contractual relation with the seller.

These are the key terms in subsection (1):

- *Defective condition unreasonably dangerous to the user.* The defendant is liable only if the product is defective when it leaves his hands. There must be something wrong with the goods. If they are reasonably safe and the buyer's mishandling of the goods causes the harm, there is no strict liability. If you attempt to open a soda bottle by knocking the cap against a counter, and the glass shatters and cuts you, the manufacturer owes nothing.

  The article sold must be *more dangerous* than the ordinary consumer would expect. A carving knife can produce a lethal wound, but everyone knows that, and a sharp knife is not unreasonably dangerous. On the other hand, prescription drugs may harm in ways that neither a layperson nor a doctor would anticipate. The manufacturer *must provide adequate warnings* of any dangers that are not apparent.

- *In the business of selling.* The seller is liable only if she normally sells this kind of product. Suppose your roommate makes you a peanut butter sandwich and, while eating it, you cut your mouth on a sliver of glass that was in the jar. The peanut butter manufacturer faces strict liability as does the grocery store where your roommate bought the goods. But your roommate is not strictly liable because he does not serve sandwiches as a business.

- *Reaches the user without substantial change.* Obviously, if your roommate put the glass in the peanut butter thinking it was funny, neither the manufacturer nor the store is liable.

And here are the important phrases in subsection (2).

- *Has exercised all possible care.* This is the heart of strict liability, which makes it a potent claim for consumers. *It is no defense that the seller used reasonable care.* If the product is dangerously defective and injures the user, the seller is liable even if it took every precaution to design and manufacture the product safely. Suppose the peanut butter jar did in fact contain a glass sliver when it left the factory. The manufacturer proves that it uses extraordinary care in keeping foreign particles out of the jars and thoroughly inspects each container before it is shipped. The evidence is irrelevant. The manufacturer has shown that it was not negligent in packaging the food, but reasonable care is irrelevant in strict liability.
- *No contractual relation.* This means that the injured party need not have bought the goods directly from the party responsible for the defect. Suppose the manufacturer that made the peanut butter sold it to a distributor, which sold it to a wholesaler, which sold it to a grocery store, which sold it to your roommate. You may sue the manufacturer, distributor, wholesaler, and store, even though you never contracted with any of them.

The following case finds §402A poised at the cutting edge of another major tort issue.

AMERICAN TOBACCO CO., INC. v. GRINNELL

951 S.W.2d 420, 1997 Tex. LEXIS 56
Texas Supreme Court, 1997

Facts: In 1952, 19-year-old Wiley Grinnell began smoking Lucky Strikes cigarettes, which the American Tobacco Co. manufactured. He smoked until 1985, when his doctors told him he had lung cancer. Soon afterward, he filed suit against American Tobacco, alleging strict liability and other claims. Tragically, he died within a year, but his family continued the litigation. The trial court dismissed the case, but the appeals court reversed. American Tobacco appealed.

Issue: Have the Grinnells made valid strict liability claims?

Excerpts from Judge Cornyn's Decision: A product may be unreasonably dangerous because of a defect in marketing, design, or manufacturing. The Grinnells allege that the cigarettes sold by American were unreasonably dangerous due to each of the three types of defect.

Marketing Defect: A defendant's failure to warn of a product's potential dangers when warnings are required is a type of marketing defect. [However, under §402A, if the "ordinary consumer with knowledge common to the community" is aware of the danger, there is generally no duty to warn.] Regarding the general health risks associated with smoking, the Tennessee Supreme Court held as early as 1898 that these risks were "generally known." On certiorari, the United States Supreme Court observed:

We should be shutting our eyes to what is constantly passing before them were we to affect an ignorance of the fact that a belief in [cigarettes'] deleterious effects, particularly upon young people, has become very general, and that communications are constantly finding their way into the public press denouncing their use as fraught with great danger. . . .

We conclude that the general health dangers attributable to cigarettes were commonly known as a matter of law by the community when Grinnell began smoking. We cannot conclude, however, that the specific danger of nicotine addiction was common knowledge when Grinnell began smoking. Addiction is a danger apart from the direct physical dangers of smoking because the addictive nature of cigarettes multiplies the likelihood of and contributes to the smoker's ultimate injury, in Grinnell's case, lung cancer. This Court has also recognized the seriousness of addiction and the need for manufacturers to warn of this danger in the context of prescription drugs.

The Surgeon General spoke to the addictive nature of tobacco in [a 1988 report]. In that report, the Surgeon General concluded that: (1) cigarettes and other forms of tobacco are addicting, (2) nicotine is the drug in tobacco that causes addiction, and (3) the pharmacologic and behavioral processes that determine tobacco addiction are similar to those that determine addiction to drugs such as heroin and cocaine.

Because we conclude that American did not conclusively establish that the danger of addiction to nicotine was common knowledge, the Grinnells may maintain their strict liability marketing defect claims to the extent they are based on the addictive qualities of cigarettes, if no other defenses defeat those claims.

Design Defect: The duty to design a safe product is an obligation imposed by law. [In an earlier case, the court held that in evaluating design defects, a jury should consider: the utility of the product to the user and the general public; the availability of a safer design; the ability of the manufacturer to eliminate the unsafe characteristics of the design; and the knowledge and expectations of the ordinary users.]

Ultimately, the Grinnells essentially concede that no reasonably safer alternatives exist, but argue that all cigarettes are defective and unreasonably dangerous nonetheless. Because American conclusively proved that no reasonably safer alternative design exists for its cigarettes, we hold that summary judgment was proper on all of the Grinnells' design defect claims, including those based on the addictive quality of cigarettes.

Manufacturing Defect: [The Grinnells offered evidence that the cigarettes contained pesticide residue.] Under Texas law, a plaintiff has a manufacturing defect claim when a finished product deviates, in terms of its construction or quality, from the specifications or planned output in a manner that renders it unreasonably dangerous. American, conceding that its cigarettes contain pesticide residue, argues that summary judgment was proper because all cigarette manufacturers fumigate their tobacco with some type of pesticide, and residue inevitably remains after fumigation. Simply because certain precautions or improvements in manufacturing technology, which could eliminate pesticide residue from cigarettes, are universally disregarded by an entire industry does not excuse their omission. Although pesticide residue may be found in many if not all cigarettes, it is not an ingredient American intended to incorporate into its cigarettes. Analyzed in this light, the presence of pesticide residue could be a manufacturing defect, not a design defect. Therefore, American did not conclusively negate the existence of a defect in its cigarettes.

[The court permitted the Grinnells' case to go forward on the failure to warn and defective manufacturing claims, as they related to nicotine addiction. The court granted summary judgment for American Tobacco as to almost all of the Grinnells' other claims, including negligence, breach of warranty, fraud, and misrepresentation.]

Tobacco use is more common in almost all other countries than it is in the United States. Tobacco *litigation*, however, is less common—or was. Plaintiffs in other nations are beginning to follow the American lead. In Canada, plaintiffs have brought individual and class action claims similar to those made by the

Grinnells. French antismoking groups have won lawsuits claiming that the tobacco companies made insufficient warnings on cigarette packs. In Brazil, the family of a deceased smoker won damages for his death. Japanese plaintiffs are attempting to block the import of American tobacco products. Meanwhile, in the United States, more than half of the state governments have filed class action suits seeking to recoup the health care costs created by tobacco-related illnesses. The first four states to settle their cases were Florida, Minnesota, Mississippi, and Texas, which agreed to accept a total of *$36 billion* from the tobacco companies to end the litigation. During discovery in these cases, the states uncovered thousands of tobacco company documents demonstrating the industry's awareness of nicotine's addictive power. These papers now circulate among overseas plaintiffs, enhancing their ability to seek compensation.

NEGOTIABLE INSTRUMENTS

The first part of this chapter has covered Articles 2 and 2A of the UCC, dealing with contracts and product liability. Articles 3 and 4 of the Code regulate negotiable instruments and the second half of the chapter focuses on this important topic.

COMMERCIAL PAPER

In early human history, people lived on whatever they could hunt, grow, or make for themselves. Over time, people improved their standard of living by bartering for goods and services they could not make themselves. But traders needed a method for keeping account of who owed how much to whom. The first currencies—gold and silver—had two disadvantages: they were easy to steal and heavy to carry. Paper currency solved the weight problem, but was even easier to filch than gold. As a result, money had to be kept in a safe place, and banks developed to meet that need. However, money in a vault is not very useful unless it can be readily spent. Society needed a system for transferring paper funds easily. Commercial paper is that system. The UCC's goal is to facilitate commerce by transforming these pieces of paper into something almost as easily transferable and reliable as money. (For more on the history of money, see http://www.ex.ac.uk/~RDavies/arian/llyfr.html.

TYPES OF NEGOTIABLE INSTRUMENTS

There are two kinds of commercial paper: negotiable and non-negotiable instruments. Article 3 of the Code covers only negotiable instruments; non-negotiable instruments are governed by ordinary contract law. There are also two categories of negotiable instruments: notes and drafts.

A **note** (also called a **promissory note**) is your promise that you will pay money. A promissory note is used in virtually every loan transaction, whether the borrower is buying a multimillion dollar company or a TV set. For example, when you borrow money from Aunt Leila to buy a car, you will sign a note promising to repay the money. You are the **maker** because you are the one who has made the promise. Aunt Leila is the **payee** because she expects to be paid. (The Web site http://www.legaldocs.com/ provides a sample promissory note with fill-in blanks.)

In this note, Romeo is the maker and Juliet is the payee.

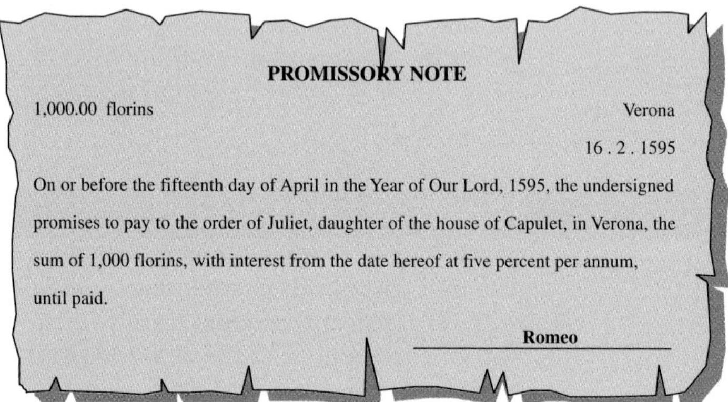
PROMISSORY NOTE

1,000.00 florins Verona

16 . 2 . 1595

On or before the fifteenth day of April in the Year of Our Lord, 1595, the undersigned promises to pay to the order of Juliet, daughter of the house of Capulet, in Verona, the sum of 1,000 florins, with interest from the date hereof at five percent per annum, until paid.

Romeo

A **draft** is an order directing someone else to pay money for you. A **check** is the most common form of a draft—it is an order telling a bank to pay money. In a draft, three people are involved: the **drawer** orders the **drawee** to pay money to the **payee**. Now before you slam the book shut in despair, let us sort out the players. Suppose that Jana Novotna wins the Corel WTA Tour in New York. The WTA writes her a check for $500,000. This check is simply an order by the WTA (the drawer) to its bank (the drawee) to pay money to Novotna (the payee). The terms make sense if you remember that, when you take money out of your account, you *draw* it out. Therefore, when you write a check, you are the draw*er* and the bank is the draw*ee*. The person to whom you make out the check is being paid, so she is called the pay*ee*.

The following table illustrates the difference between notes and drafts. Even courts sometimes confuse the terms *drawer* (the person who signs a check) and *maker* (someone who signs a promissory note). **Issuer** is an all-purpose term that means both maker and drawer.

	Who Pays	**Who Plays**
Note	You make a promise that you will pay.	Two people are involved: maker and payee.
Draft	You order someone else to pay.	Three people are involved: drawer, drawee, and payee.

THE FUNDAMENTAL "RULE" OF COMMERCIAL PAPER

The possessor of a piece of commercial paper has an unconditional right to be paid, as long as (1) the paper is *negotiable*; (2) it has been *negotiated* to the possessor; (3) the possessor is a *holder in due course*; and (4) the issuer cannot claim a valid *defense*.

NEGOTIABILITY

To work as a substitute for money, commercial paper must be freely transferable in the marketplace, just as money is. In other words, it must be *negotiable*.

The possessor of *non*-negotiable commercial paper has the same rights—no more, no less—as the person who made the original contract. With non-negotiable commercial paper, the transferee's rights are *conditional* because they depend upon the rights of the original party to the contract. If, for some reason, the original party loses his right to be paid, so does the transferee. The value of non-negotiable commercial paper is greatly reduced because the transferee cannot be absolutely sure what his rights are or whether he will be paid at all.

Suppose that Krystal buys a used car from the Trustie Car Lot for her business, Krystal Rocks. She cannot afford to pay the full $15,000 right now, but she is willing to sign a note promising to pay later. Trustie is happy to sell a car to Krystal, but he needs the cash *now*. Reggie's Finance Co. offers to buy Krystal's promissory note from Trustie, but the price Reggie is willing to pay depends upon whether her note is negotiable.

If Krystal's promissory note is non-negotiable, Reggie gets exactly the same rights that Trustie had. As the saying goes, he steps into Trustie's shoes. Suppose that Trustie tampered with the odometer and, as a result, Krystal's car is worth only $12,000. If, under contract law, she owes Trustie only $12,000, then that is all she has to pay Reggie, even though the note *says* $15,000.

The possessor of *negotiable* commercial paper has *more* rights than the person who made the original contract. With negotiable commercial paper, the transferee's rights are *unconditional*. He is entitled to be paid the full amount of the note, regardless of the relationship between the original parties. If Krystal's promissory note is a negotiable instrument, she must pay the full amount to whoever has possession of it, no matter what complaints she might have against Trustie.

Exhibit 11.1 illustrates the difference between negotiable and non-negotiable commercial paper.

Because negotiable instruments are more valuable than non-negotiable ones, it is important for buyers and sellers to be able to tell, easily and accurately, if an instrument is indeed negotiable. To be negotiable:

1. **The Instrument Must Be in *Writing*.**
2. **The Instrument Must Be *Signed* By the Maker or Drawer.**
3. **The Instrument Must Contain an *Unconditional Promise* or *Order to Pay*.** If Krystal's promissory note says, "I will pay $15,000 as long as the car is still in working order," it is not negotiable because it is making a conditional promise. The instrument must also contain a promise or order to pay. It is

Exhibit 11.1

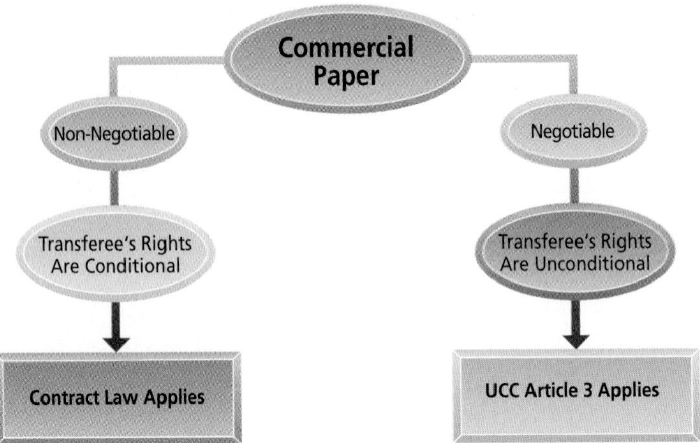

not enough simply to say, "Krystal owes Trustie $15,000." She has to indicate that she owes the money and also that she intends to pay it. "Krystal promises to pay Trustie $15,000," would work.

4. **The Instrument Must State a *Definite Amount* of Money.** "I promise to pay Trustie one-third of my profits this year" would not work, because the amount is unclear. If Krystal's note says, "I promise to pay $15,000 worth of diamonds," it is not negotiable because it does not state a definite amount of *money*.

5. **The Instrument Must Be Payable on *Demand* or at a *Definite Time*.** A demand instrument is one that must be paid whenever the holder requests payment. If an instrument is undated, it is treated as a demand instrument and is negotiable. An instrument can be negotiable even if it will not be paid until some time in the future, provided that the payment date can be determined when the document is made. A graduate of a well-known prep school has written a generous check to his alma mater each year, but for payment date he puts, "The day the headmaster is fired." These checks are not negotiable because they are neither payable on demand nor at a definite time.

6. **The Instrument Must Be Payable to *Order* or to *Bearer*. Order paper** must include the words "Pay to the order of" someone. By including the word "order," the maker is indicating that the instrument is not limited to only one person. "Pay to the order of Trustie Car Lot" means that the money will be paid to Trustie *or to anyone Trustie designates*. If the note is made out "To bearer," it is **bearer paper** and can be redeemed by *any* holder in due course.

The rules for checks are different from other negotiable instruments. All checks are, by definition, negotiable. Most checks are preprinted with the words, "Pay to the order of," but sometimes people inadvertently cross out "order of." Even so, the check is still negotiable. Checks are frequently received by consumers who, sadly, have not completed a course on business law. The drafters of the UCC did not think it fair to penalize them when the drawer of the check was the one who made the mistake.

CYBERLAW

An instrument must be signed by the maker or drawer. This sounds straightforward, but what does it mean to sign a note or draft? Many people, for example, use computer programs that permit them to pay bills online. How do they sign an online check? How does their bank know the signature is valid? The answer is a "digital signature." This computer signature does not look like handwriting; instead, it is a unique series of letters and numbers in code. A digital signature can actually be safer than the traditional signature on paper (called a "wet" signature). If the digital document is dishonestly altered, the sender and recipient can tell.

In the following case, a set of notes deviated slightly from the requirements of the UCC. Are the notes negotiable despite the errors?

IN RE BOARDWALK MARKETPLACE SECURITIES LITIGATION

688 F. Supp. 115, 1987 U.S. Dist. LEXIS 15122
United States District Court, District of Connecticut, 1987

Facts: Investors purchased interests in limited partnerships that were organized to redevelop property in Atlantic City, New Jersey. To finance their purchases, the investors executed promissory notes payable to American Funding Limited. The notes stated, in part:

> I will pay ____ monthly installments of principal and interest, each in the amount of $ ____, commencing on the ____ day of ____ 19 ____ (estimated first payment date). Lender will notify me in writing of the first payment due date, the amount of the first payment, the date of the first payment, the date of the final payment and the amount of the final payment.

In the blanks, someone had handwritten figures representing the number of monthly payments, the amount of each payment, and an estimated date on which the payments were to begin.

American Funding Limited sold these notes to various banks. When the redevelopment plan collapsed, many of the investors ceased making payments on their notes. The investors asserted that the notes were non-negotiable because the payment date was not definite. The banks argued that, whether or not the payment date was definite, equity demanded that the notes be treated as if they were negotiable so that the banks, which were innocent of all wrongdoing, could collect the money owed them. If the notes were non-negotiable, the banks' right to collect might be defeated by claims the investors had against American Funding.

Issues: Did these notes comply with UCC requirements for negotiability? If not, should the notes be treated as if they were negotiable?

Excerpts from Judge Eginton's Decision: The investors pose a narrow challenge to the notes' claimed negotiability, alleging that they are neither payable on demand nor at a definite time. The initial question is whether these notes are payable at a "definite time."

The notes do not satisfy the requirements of definite time. Subsection (a) [of the UCC] reads "on or before a stated date or at a fixed period after a stated date." Logically, a note containing an estimated first payment date and a provision which states that the lender will notify the maker of the actual first payment date does not fall within the confines of this subsection.

The overarching concern of the Code and thereby Article Three is to promote the free flow of commerce. The decision was made that a set of formal requisites which the terms of commercial paper must meet would best serve these purposes. One requisite is that the paper be negotiable. The formalities of negotiability arose in history out of the law merchant. Today, they are codified in Article Three. There is no particular magic to them; the drafters could have chosen other formalities, although some are obvious.

Because the prerequisites to negotiability are formal, it is both simple and necessary to comply with them. To hold that these notes are negotiable would certainly preserve the integrity of these notes and in that limited sense serve the interests of commerce; however, it would reward shoddy drafting and introduce unnecessary doubt into the formalities of negotiability. The reason for employing formalities in legal rules is to preclude the kinds of arguments that the banks offer to circumvent them here. It will not do to argue that the goal of promoting the expansion of commerce with predictably negotiable paper is served by artful reconstruction of the formalities set up initially to serve that same goal.

[The court concluded that the notes were not negotiable.]

Was the result in this case fair? These investors were using a technicality of Article 3 to avoid paying legitimate debt. Why should the banks (and their shareholders or depositors) suffer when they had absolutely no involvement in the investment scheme?

NEGOTIATION

To be negotiated, order paper must first be *indorsed* and then *delivered* to the transferee. Bearer paper must simply be *delivered* to the transferee; no indorsement is required.[16]

An indorsement is the signature of the payee. Tess writes a rent check for $475 to her landlord, Larnell. If Larnell signs the back of the check and delivers it to Patty, he has met the two requirements for negotiating order paper: indorsement and delivery. If Larnell delivers the check to Patty but forgets to sign it, the check has not been indorsed and therefore cannot be negotiated—it has no value to Patty.

HOLDER IN DUE COURSE

A holder in due course has an automatic right to receive payment for a negotiable instrument (unless the issuer can claim a valid defense). If the possessor of an instrument is not a holder in due course, then his right to payment depends upon the relationship between the issuer and payee. He inherits whatever claims and defenses arise out of that contract. Clearly, then, holder in due course status dramatically increases the value of an instrument because it enhances the probability of being paid.

REQUIREMENTS FOR BEING A HOLDER IN DUE COURSE

Under §3-302 of the UCC, a holder in due course is a *holder* who has given *value* for the instrument, in *good faith, without notice* of outstanding claims or other defects.

Holder. A **holder** is someone who has possession of a negotiable instrument that she received through a valid negotiation. Tristesse gives Felix a check

[16] The UCC spells the word "indorsed." Outside the UCC, the word is more commonly spelled "endorsed."

payable to him. Because Felix owes his mother money, he indorses the check and delivers it to her. This is a valid negotiation because Felix has both indorsed the instrument and delivered it. Therefore, Felix's mother is a holder.

Value. A holder in due course must give value for an instrument. **Value** means that the holder has *already* done something in exchange for the instrument. Felix's mother has already loaned him money, so she has given value.

Good Faith. There are two tests to determine if a holder acquired an instrument in good faith. The holder must meet both of these tests:

- **Subjective Test.** Did the holder *believe* the transaction was honest in fact?
- **Objective Test.** Did the transaction *appear* to be commercially reasonable?

Felix persuades his elderly neighbor, Serena, that he has invented a fabulous beauty cream guaranteed to remove wrinkles. She gives him a $10,000 promissory note, payable in 90 days, in return for exclusive sales rights in Pittsburgh. Felix sells the note to his old friend Dick for $2,000. Felix never delivers the sales samples to Serena. When Dick presents the note to Serena, she refuses to pay on the grounds that Dick is not a holder in due course. She contends that he did not buy the note in good faith.

Dick fails both tests. Any friend of Felix knows he is not trustworthy, especially when presenting a promissory note signed by an elderly neighbor. Dick did not believe the transaction was honest in fact. Also, $10,000 notes are not usually discounted to $2,000; $9,000 would be more normal. This transaction is not commercially reasonable, and Dick should have realized immediately that Felix was up to no good.

Notice of Outstanding Claims or Other Defects. In certain circumstances, a holder is on notice that an instrument has an outstanding claim or other defect:

1. **The Instrument Is Overdue.** An instrument is overdue the day after its due date. At that point, the recipient ought to wonder why no one has bothered to collect the money owed. A check is overdue 90 days after its date. Any other *demand* instrument is overdue (1) the day after a request for payment is made or (2) a reasonable time after the instrument was issued.

The holder of this note should realize that there may be a problem.

PROMISSORY NOTE

$500.00 September 5, 1950

On or before 60 days after date, I promise to pay $500 to the order of Soames for value received.

Irene

2. **The Instrument Is Dishonored.** To dishonor an instrument is to refuse to pay it. For example, once a check has been stamped, "Insufficient Funds" by the bank, it has been dishonored, and no one who obtains it afterward can be a holder in due course.

3. **The Instrument Is Altered, Forged, or Incomplete.** Anyone who knows that an instrument has been altered or forged cannot be a holder in due course. Suppose Joe wrote a check to Tony for $200. While showing the check to Liza, Tony cackles to himself and says, "Can you believe what that goof did? Look, he left the line blank after the words 'two hundred.'" Taking his pen out with a flourish, Tony changes the zeroes to nines and adds the words, "ninety-nine." He then indorses the check over to Liza, who is definitely not a holder in due course.

4. **The Holder Has Notice of Certain Claims or Disputes.** No one can qualify as a holder in due course if she is on notice that (1) someone else has a claim to the instrument or (2) there is a dispute between the original parties to the instrument. Matt hires Sheila to put aluminum siding on his house. In payment, he gives her a $15,000 promissory note with the due date left blank. They agree that the note will not be due until 60 days after completion of the work. Despite the agreement, Sheila fills in the date immediately and sells the note to Rupert at American Finance Corp., who has bought many similar notes from Sheila. Rupert knows that the note is not supposed to be due until after the work is finished. Usually, before he buys a note from her, he demands a signed document from the homeowner certifying that the work is complete. Also, he lives near Matt and can see that Matt's house is only half finished. Rupert is not a holder in due course because he has reason to suspect there is a dispute between Sheila and Matt.

DEFENSES AGAINST A HOLDER IN DUE COURSE

Negotiable instruments are meant to be a close substitute for money, and, as a general rule, holders expect to be paid. **However, the issuer of a negotiable instrument is not required to pay if:**

1. His signature on the instrument was forged.
2. After signing the instrument, his debts were discharged in bankruptcy.
3. He was a minor at the time he signed the instrument.
4. The amount of the instrument was altered after he signed it. (Although, if he left the instrument blank, he *is* liable for any amounts later filled in.)
5. He signed the instrument under duress, while mentally incapacitated or as part of an illegal transaction.
6. He was tricked into signing the instrument without knowing what it was and without any reasonable way to find out.

In the following case, a farmer says he is not liable on a note. You be the judge.

FDIC v. CULVER

640 F. Supp. 725, 1986 U.S. Dist. LEXIS 23201
United States District Court, District of Kansas, 1986

Facts: Gary Culver, a farmer in Missouri, was having financial problems. He agreed that Nasib Ed Kalliel would assume financial control of the farm, while Culver managed the farming operation. Culver would receive both a salary and a share of the profits. After a few months, Culver informed Kalliel that he urgently needed money to stave off foreclosure. One week later, the Rexford State Bank in Rexford, Kansas, wire-transferred $30,000 to Culver's bank in King City, Missouri. Culver thought that Kalliel would be responsible for repaying the money.

About one week later, Jerry Gilbert, who worked for Kalliel, approached Culver and told him that "Rexford State Bank wanted to know where the $30,000 went, for their records." Gilbert presented Culver with a document and asked him to sign it. According to Gilbert, the document was merely a receipt for the $30,000 Culver had received. Culver signed the document without intending to commit himself to its repayment.

The document Culver signed was a preprinted promissory note form, payable to the Rexford State Bank. It contained no execution date, maturity date, principal amount, or interest rate. Although Culver assumed that the figure $30,000 would eventually be written on the document, some unknown individual filled in $50,000 instead and also filled in all other blanks. Although Culver received only $30,000, the Rexford State Bank had deposited the full $50,000 in an account controlled by Kalliel.

The Federal Deposit Insurance Corporation (FDIC), representing the Rexford State Bank, sued Culver to enforce the note. Culver acknowledged that the FDIC was a holder in due course, but asserted the defense of fraud, relying on a provision of the UCC stating:

> [A] holder in due course . . . takes the instrument free from . . . (2) all defenses of any party to the instrument with whom the holder has not dealt except . . . (c) such misrepresentation as has induced the party to sign the instrument with neither knowledge nor reasonable opportunity to obtain knowledge of its character or its essential terms.

You be the Judge: Can Culver use the defense of fraud to avoid paying the $50,000 note?

Argument for the FDIC (representing the Rexford Bank): Under the statute, Culver is liable on the note unless, when he signed it, he had "neither knowledge nor *reasonable opportunity* to obtain knowledge of its character or essential terms." Culver had every opportunity to obtain knowledge of the note—all he had to do was read it before he signed it. That's hardly too much to ask. He knows how to read; he simply could not be bothered to take the effort. It is bad luck for Culver, but he could easily have prevented this misfortune if he had been careful and prudent. The Rexford Bank, on the other hand, is completely without fault.

Culver also alleges he is not responsible because the note was blank when he signed it. But the UCC provides that "when an incomplete instrument has been completed, [a holder in due course] may enforce it as completed." Culver in effect signed a blank check, and now he is responsible for whatever amount someone else fills in.

Culver has a valid claim against Gilbert or Kalliel or whoever filled in the note. But neither of those men is before the court today. As between the careless Culver and the innocent Rexford Bank, Culver must pay.

Argument for Culver: The UCC clearly provides that someone who is induced by misrepresentation to sign a note "without knowledge of its character" is not liable on the instrument. Culver had no idea that the "receipt" was really a promissory note. These two types of instruments are totally different in character. Obviously, he would never have signed the document if he had known it was a note, especially since it was blank. All of the important terms on the note were missing: execution date, maturity date, principal amount, and interest rate. He had no way to learn of those terms. He clearly did not know the "character" of the document. This is a classic case of fraud.

The FDIC says that Culver was negligent. Look, this is Missouri, where people trust each other. Culver was crossing the street one day, preoccupied with his farm, when someone he knows well asked him to sign a receipt. Any reasonable person in Missouri would have done precisely as Culver did. Now the FDIC is trying to collect $50,000 from him, when all he ever received was $30,000. What if the note had been for $50 million, would the FDIC want that too?

CONSUMER EXCEPTION

In the eighteenth and nineteenth centuries, negotiable instruments often circulated through several hands. The business community treated them as money. The concept of holder in due course was essential because the instruments had little use if they could not be transferred for value. In the modern banking system, however, instruments are much less likely to circulate. Currently, the most common use for negotiable instruments is in consumer transactions. A consumer pays for a refrigerator by giving the store a promissory note. The store promptly sells the note to a finance company. Even if the refrigerator is defective, under Article 3 the consumer must pay full value on the note because the finance company is a holder in due course. Some commentators have argued that the concept of holder in due course no longer serves a useful purpose and that it should be eliminated once and for all (and with it Article 3 of the UCC).

No state has yet taken such a dramatic step. Instead, some states have forbidden sellers from taking any negotiable instruments, other than a check, as payment for consumer goods or services. Other states require promissory notes given by a consumer to carry the words "consumer paper." Notes with this legend are non-negotiable.

Meanwhile, the Federal Trade Commission (FTC) has special rules for consumer sales. A **consumer sale** is one in which a consumer borrows money from a lender to purchase goods and services from a seller who is affiliated with the lender. If Sears loans money to Gerald to buy a big-screen TV at Sears, that is a consumer sale. It is not a consumer sale if Gerald borrows money from his cousin Vinnie to buy the TV from Sears. The FTC requires all promissory notes in consumer sales to contain the following language:

NOTICE

> ANY HOLDER OF THIS CONSUMER CREDIT CONTRACT IS SUBJECT TO ALL CLAIMS AND DEFENSES WHICH THE DEBTOR COULD ASSERT AGAINST THE SELLER OF GOODS OR SERVICES OBTAINED PURSUANT HERETO OR WITH THE PROCEEDS HEREOF. RECOVERY HEREUNDER BY THE DEBTOR SHALL NOT EXCEED AMOUNTS PAID BY THE DEBTOR HEREUNDER.

Under §3-106(d) of the UCC, no one can be a holder in due course of an instrument with this language. If the language is omitted from a consumer note, it is possible to be a holder in due course, but the seller can be punished by a fine of up to $10,000.

Law

Sometime in your life, you may well sign a promissory note for a consumer loan. Before signing, make sure that the note contains this FTC language.

CHAPTER CONCLUSION

The development of the UCC was an enormous and ambitious undertaking. Its goal was to facilitate the free flow of commerce across this large nation. By any measure, the UCC has been a success. Each and every day, thousands of businesspeople comply with the UCC as they sign contracts, write checks, and deliver promissory notes. It is worth remembering, however, that the terms of the UCC are precise and that failure to comply with these exacting provisions can lead to unfortunate consequences. In some ways, the UCC is like a marine drill instructor: rigid, but predictable if you follow the rules.

CHAPTER REVIEW

1. The Code is designed to modernize commercial law and make it uniform throughout the country. Article 2 applies to the sale of goods.
2. A merchant is someone who routinely deals in the particular goods involved, or who appears to have special knowledge or skill in those goods, or who uses agents with special knowledge or skill.
3. UCC §2-204 permits the parties to form a contract in any manner that shows agreement.
4. For the sale of goods worth $500 or more, UCC §2-201 requires some writing that indicates an agreement.
5. A merchant who receives a signed memo confirming an oral contract may become liable if he fails to object within 10 days.
6. UCC §2-207 governs an acceptance that does not "mirror" the offer. *Additional* terms usually become part of the contract. *Different* terms contradict the offer, and are generally replaced by the Code's own gap-filler terms.
7. An injured seller my resell the goods and obtain the difference between the contract and resale prices. An injured buyer may buy substitute goods and obtain the difference between the contract and cover prices.
8. Product liability may arise in various ways:
   - A party may *create* an express warranty with words or actions. The Code may *imply* a warranty of merchantability or fitness for a particular purpose.
   - A seller will be liable if her conduct is not that of a reasonable person.
   - A seller may be strictly liable for a defective product that reaches the user without substantial change.
9. The possessor of non-negotiable commercial paper has the same rights—no more, no less—as the person who made the original contract. The possessor of negotiable commercial paper has more rights than the person who made the original contract.
10. The possessor of a piece of commercial paper has an unconditional right to be paid, as long as:
    - The paper is negotiable
    - It has been negotiated to the possessor
    - The possessor is a holder in due course; and
    - The issuer cannot claim a valid defense.
11. To be negotiable, an instrument must:
    - Be in writing
    - Be signed by the maker or drawer
    - Contain an unconditional promise or order to pay

- State a definite amount of money
- Be payable on demand or at a definite time; and
- Be payable to order or to bearer.

12. To be negotiated, order paper must first be indorsed and then delivered to the transferee. Bearer paper must simply be delivered to the transferee; no indorsement is required.

13. A holder in due course is a holder who has given value for the instrument, in good faith, without notice of outstanding claims or other defects.

14. The Federal Trade Commission requires all promissory notes in consumer sales to contain language preventing any subsequent holder from being a holder in due course.

PRACTICE TEST

1. Nina owns a used car lot. She signs and sends a fax to Seth, a used car wholesaler who has a huge lot of cars in the same city. The fax says, "Confirming our agrmt—I pick any 15 cars fr yr lot—30% below blue book." Seth reads the fax, laughs, and throws it away. Two weeks later, Nina arrives and demands to purchase 15 of Seth's cars. Is he obligated to sell?

2. **YOU BE THE JUDGE WRITING PROBLEM** United Technologies advertised a used Beechcraft Baron airplane for sale in an aviation journal. Attorney Thompson Comerford spoke with a United agent who described the plane as "excellently maintained" and said it had been operated "under §135 flight regulations," meaning the plane had been subject to airworthiness inspections every 100 hours. Comerford arrived at a Dallas airport to pick up the plane, where he paid $80,000 for it. He signed a sales agreement stating that the plane was sold "as is" and that there were "no representations or warranties, express or implied, including the condition of the aircraft, its merchantability or its fitness for any particular purpose." Comerford attempted to fly the plane home, but immediately experienced problems with its brakes, steering, ability to climb, and performance while cruising. (Otherwise it was fine.) He sued, claiming breach of express and implied warranties. Did United Technologies breach express or implied warranties? **Argument for Comerford:** United described the airplane as "excellently maintained," knowing that Mr. Comerford would rely. The company should not be allowed to say one thing and put the opposite in writing. **Argument for United Technologies:** Comerford is a lawyer, and we assume he can read. The contract clearly stated that the plane was sold as is. There were no warranties.

3. To satisfy the UCC statute of frauds regarding the sale of goods, which of the following must generally be in writing?

   (a) Designation of the parties as buyer and seller

   (b) Delivery terms

   (c) Quantity of the goods

   (d) Warranties to be made

4. **RIGHT & WRONG** Texaco, Inc. and other oil companies sold mineral spirits in bulk to distributors, which then resold to retailers. Mineral spirits are used for cleaning, and are harmful or fatal if swallowed. Texaco allegedly knew that the retailers, such as hardware stores, frequently packaged the mineral spirits (illegally) in used half-gallon milk containers and sold them to consumers, often with no warnings on the packages. David Hunnings, aged 21 months, found a milk container in his home, swallowed the mineral spirits, and died. The Hunningses sued Texaco in negligence. The trial court dismissed the complaint and the Hunningses appealed. What is the legal standard in a negligence case? Have the plaintiffs made out a valid case of negligence? Assume that Texaco knew about the repackaging and the grave risk, but continued to sell in bulk because doing so was profitable. (If the plaintiffs cannot prove those facts, they will lose even if

they *do* get to a jury.) Would that make you angry? Should the case go to a jury? Or did the fault still lie with the retailer and/or the parents?

5. **CPA QUESTION** Which of the following factors is least important in determining whether a manufacturer is strictly liable in tort for a defective product?

   (a) The negligence of the manufacturer

   (b) The contributory negligence of the plaintiff

   (c) Modifications to the product by the wholesaler

   (d) Whether the product caused injuries

6. Lewis River Golf, Inc. grew and sold sod. It bought seed from defendant, O. M. Scott & Sons, under an express warranty. But the sod grown from the Scott seeds developed weeds, a breach of Scott's warranty. Several of Lewis River's customers sued, unhappy with the weeds in their grass. Lewis River lost most of its customers, cut back its production from 275 acres to 45 acres, and destroyed all remaining sod grown from Scott's seeds. Eventually, Lewis River sold its business at a large loss. A jury awarded Lewis River $1,026,800, largely for lost profits and loss of goodwill. Scott appealed, claiming that a plaintiff may not recover for lost profits and goodwill. Comment.

7. George Robinson purchased a certificate of deposit from the West Greeley National Bank in Colorado and directed that the proceeds be paid to his stepdaughter, Loretta Wygant, upon his death. One year later, however, he orally requested the bank to change the beneficiary to his new wife, Hope Robinson. Six months later he died. Both the widow and stepdaughter claimed the proceeds of the certificate. The stepdaughter argued that the certificate of deposit was a negotiable instrument and, therefore, required her indorsement to change the beneficiary. Do you agree?

8. **CPA QUESTION** In order to negotiate bearer paper, one must:

   (a) Indorse the paper

   (b) Indorse and deliver the paper with consideration

   (c) Deliver the paper

   (d) Deliver and indorse the paper

9. Gina and Douglas Felde purchased a Dodge Daytona with a 70,000-mile warranty. They signed a loan contract with the dealer to pay for the car in 48 monthly installments of $250. The dealer sold the contract to the Chrysler Credit Corp. Soon, the Feldes complained that the car had developed a tendency to accelerate abruptly and without warning. Neither of two Dodge dealers was able to correct the problem. The Feldes filed suit against Chrysler Credit Corp., but the company refused to rescind the loan contract. The company argued that, as a holder in due course on the note, it was entitled to be paid regardless of any defects in the car. How would you decide this case if you were the judge?

10. **RIGHT & WRONG** S. J. Littlegreen owned the Lookout Mountain Hotel. In financial trouble, he put the hotel on the market at a price of $850,000. C. Abbott Gardner was his real estate agent. To obtain more time to sell, Littlegreen decided to refinance his debt. Mr. Rupe agreed to lend Littlegreen $300,000. When this loan was ready for closing, Gardner informed Littlegreen that he expected a commission of 5 percent of the amount of the loan, or $15,000. Gardner threatened to block the loan if his demands were not met. Littlegreen needed the proceeds of the loan badly, so he agreed to give Gardner $4,000 in cash and a promissory note for $11,000. On what grounds might Littlegreen claim that the note is invalid? Would this be a valid defense? Even if Gardner was in the right legally, was he in the right ethically? Would he like everyone in

town to know that he had squeezed Littlegreen in this way? How would he have felt if he had been in Littlegreen's position? Does might make right?

11. Catherine Wagner suffered serious physical injuries in an automobile accident and became acutely depressed as a result. One morning, she received a check for $17,400 in settlement of her claims arising out of the accident. She indorsed the check and placed it on the kitchen table. She then called Robert Scherer, her long-time roommate, to tell him the check had arrived. That afternoon, she jumped from the roof of her apartment building, killing herself. The police found the check and a note from her, stating that she was giving it to Scherer. Had Wagner negotiated the check to Scherer?

INTERNET RESEARCH PROBLEMS

Look at http://www.insure.com/auto/. Which cars are safer than average? Less safe? How important is auto safety to you? Are you willing to pay more for a safe car? Who should be the final judge of auto safety: auto companies, insurance companies, juries, government regulators, or consumers?

Go to http://www.legaldocs.com and fill in the blanks of a promissory note. Who is the maker, and who is the payee of your note? Did you create a demand note?

You can find further practice problems in the Online Quiz at http://beatty.westbuslaw.com or in the Study Guide that accompanies this text.

Secured Transactions and Bankruptcy

12

CHAPTER

Dear Help-for-All:

Somebody must be crazy. When I got out of school, I paid $18,000 for a used Lexus. I made every payment for over two years. I shelled out over 9,000 bucks for that car. Then I got laid off through no fault of my own. I missed a few payments and the bank repossessed the car. They auctioned off the Lexus. Now the bank's lawyer phones and says I'm still liable for over $5,000. I owe money for a car I can't drive anymore? If they say I really have to pay all that money, I'm heading straight for Bankruptcy Court.

Signed,

Still Sane, I Hope

Dear Still Sane,

I am sympathetic but unfortunately the bank is entitled to its money. When you bought the car, you signed two documents: a note, in which you promised to pay the full balance owed, and a security agreement, which said that if you stopped making payments, the bank could repossess the vehicle and sell it.

There are two problems. First, even after two years of writing checks you might still have owed about $10,000 (because of interest). Second, cars depreciate quickly. Your $18,000 vehicle probably had a market value of about

$8,000 thirty months later. The security agreement allowed the bank to sell the Lexus at auction, where prices are still lower. Your car evidently fetched about $5,000. That leaves a deficiency of $5,000—for which you are legally responsible, regardless of who is driving the car. Bankruptcy law can indeed provide important relief, though the process is not so easy nor the results so absolute as many people think.

Sorry,

Help-for-Almost-All

SECURED TRANSACTIONS AND BANKRUPTCY: INTRODUCTION[1]

We can sympathize with "Still Sane," but the bank is entitled to its money. The buyer and the bank had entered into a secured transaction, meaning that one party gave credit to another, insisting on full repayment *and* the right to seize certain property if the debt went unpaid.

It is essential to understand the basics of this law because we live and work in a world economy based solidly—or shakily—on credit. An equally important and closely related topic is bankruptcy law. A debtor unable to pay his bills may end up in Bankruptcy Court, along with a host of creditors clamoring to be paid. We will examine major issues of bankruptcy law in the second half of this chapter, but we begin by looking at secured transactions.

Article 9 of the Uniform Commercial Code (UCC) governs secured transactions in personal property. Article 9 employs terms not used elsewhere, so we must lead off with some definitions:

- **Fixtures** are goods that have become attached to real estate. For example, heating ducts are *goods* when a company manufactures them but they become *fixtures* when installed in a house.
- **Security interest** means an interest in personal property or fixtures that secures the performance of some *obligation*. If an automobile dealer sells you a new car on credit and retains a security interest, it means she is keeping legal rights *in your car*, including the right to drive it away if you fall behind in your payments. Usually, the obligation is to pay money, such as the money due on the new car, though occasionally the obligation is to perform some other action.
- **Secured party** is the person or company that holds the security interest. The automobile dealer who sells you a car on credit is the secured party.

---

[1] In this chapter we use more footnotes than usual, for two reasons. First, Article 9 is a challenging series of interlocking provisions, and many readers will want to peruse the actual Code (in the appendix) to reinforce the myriad concepts. Second, the revised Article 9 is substantially rewritten and entirely renumbered; experienced practitioners may appreciate guidelines as they encounter new rules and discover familiar concepts in unexpected places. Without Ariadne's thread, Theseus would still be stumbling through the Cretan labyrinth.

- **Collateral** is the property subject to a security interest. When a dealer sells you a new car and keeps a security interest, the vehicle is the collateral.
- **Debtor and Obligor.** For our purposes, **debtor** refers to a person who has some original ownership interest in the collateral. (Having a security interest in the collateral does not make one a debtor.) If Alice borrows money from a bank and uses her Mercedes as collateral, she is the debtor because she owns the car. **Obligor** means a person who must repay money or perform some other task.

  The obligor and debtor are generally the same person, but not always. When Alice borrows money from a bank and uses her Mercedes as collateral, she is the obligor, because she must repay the loan; as we know, Alice is also the debtor. However, suppose that Toby borrows money from a bank and provides no collateral; Jake co-signs the loan as a favor to Toby, using his Steinway piano as collateral. *Jake* is the only debtor, because he owns the piano. *Both parties* are obligors, because both have agreed to repay the loan.
- **Security agreement** is the contract in which the debtor gives a security interest to the secured party. This agreement protects the secured party's rights in the collateral.
- **Default** occurs when the debtor fails to pay money that is due, for example, on a loan or for a purchase made on credit. Default also includes other failures by the debtor, such as failing to keep the collateral insured.
- **Repossession** occurs when the secured party takes back collateral because the debtor has defaulted.
- **Perfection** is a series of steps the secured party must take to protect its rights in the collateral against people other than the debtor.
- **Financing statement** is a record intended to notify the general public that the secured party has a security interest in the collateral.
- **Record** refers to information written on paper *or* stored in an electronic or other medium.
- **Authenticate** means to sign a document *or* to use any symbol or encryption method that identifies the person and clearly indicates she is adopting the record as her own. You authenticate a security agreement when you sign the papers at an auto dealership. A corporation electronically authenticates a loan agreement by using the Internet to transmit a public-key signature. (See the contract law Chapter 10 on statute of frauds for a discussion of that encryption method.)

Here is an example using the terms just discussed. A medical equipment company manufactures a CAT scan machine and sells it to a clinic for $2 million, taking $500,000 cash and the clinic's promise to pay the rest over five years. The clinic simultaneously authenticates a security agreement, giving the manufacturer a security interest in the CAT scan. The manufacturer then electronically files a financing statement in an appropriate state agency. This perfects the manufacturer's rights, meaning that its security interest in the CAT scan is now valid against all the world. Exhibit 12.1 illustrates this transaction.

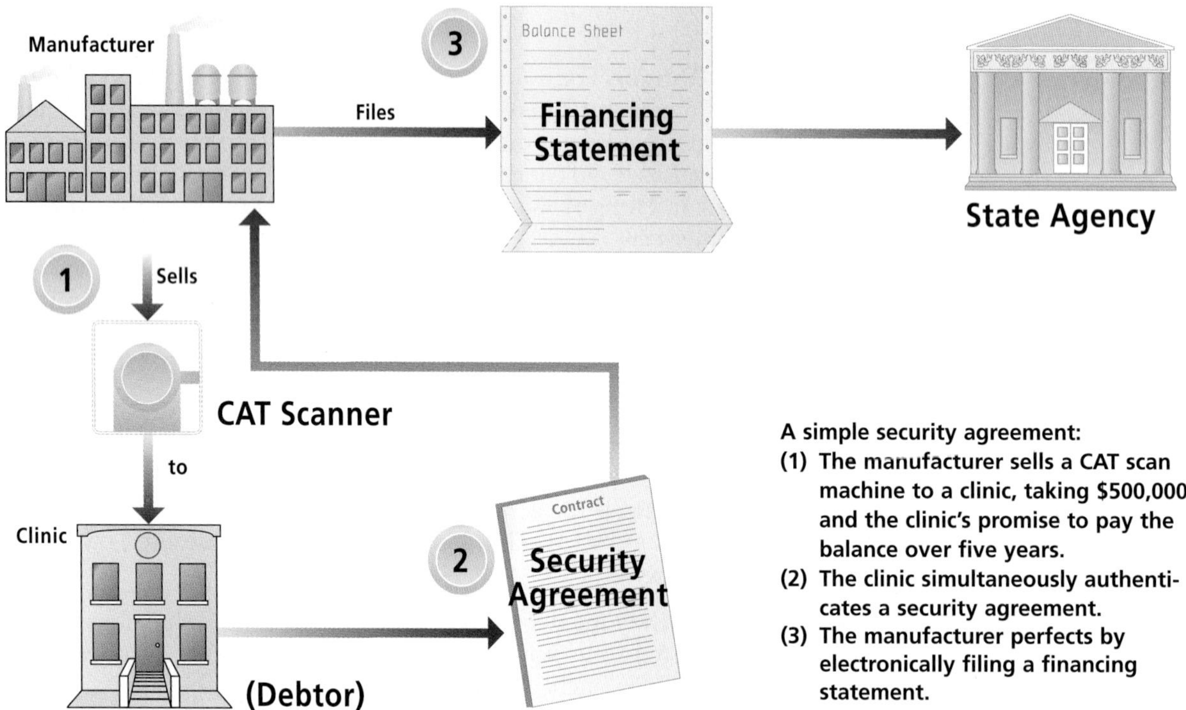

Exhibit 12.1

If the clinic goes bankrupt and many creditors try to seize its assets, the manufacturer has first claim to the CAT scan machine. The clinic's bankruptcy is of great importance. When a debtor has money to pay all of its debts, there are no concerns about security interests. A creditor insists on a security interest to protect itself in the event the debtor *cannot* pay all of its debts. The secured party intends (1) to give itself a legal interest in specific property of the debtor and (2) to establish a priority claim in that property, ahead of other creditors.

ARTICLE 9 REVISIONS

The American Law Institute and the National Conference of Commissioners on Uniform State Laws have rewritten Article 9, and the proposed revisions are now the law in most states. **All citations in this chapter are to the 2000 Revision of Article 9.** The Uniform Commercial Code is available online at http://www.law.cornell.edu/ucc/ucc.table.html.[2] For the actual statutory versions of Article 9 that have been adopted state-by-state, go to http://www.law.cornell.edu/uniform/ucc.html#a9.

[2] When researching any article of the Code online, be certain that you are reading the most recent revision.

SCOPE OF REVISED ARTICLE 9

Article 9 applies to any transaction intended to create a security interest in personal property or fixtures. The personal property that may be used as collateral includes:

- **Goods**, which are things that are movable.
- **Inventory**, meaning goods held by someone for sale or lease, such as all of the beds and chairs in a furniture store.
- **Instruments**, such as drafts, checks, certificates of deposit, and notes.
- **Investment Property**, which refers primarily to securities and related rights.
- **Documents of Title**, which are the proof of ownership retained by someone who ships or stores goods.
- **Accounts**, meaning the right to receive payment for goods sold or leased.
- **Deposit accounts**, which refers to money placed in banks.
- **General intangibles**, a residual category that includes collateral such as copyrights, patents, trademarks, goodwill, and the right to payment of some loans.
- **Chattel Paper**, which is a record that indicates two things: (1) an obligor owes money and (2) a secured party has a security interest in specific goods. Chattel paper most commonly occurs in a consumer sale on credit. If a dealer sells an air conditioner to a customer, who agrees in writing to make monthly payments and also agrees that the dealer has a security interest in the air conditioner, that agreement is chattel paper. The confusing point is that the same chattel paper may be collateral for a second security interest. The dealer who sells the air conditioner could use the chattel paper to obtain a loan. If the dealer gives the chattel paper to a bank as collateral for the loan, the bank has a security interest in the chattel paper, while the dealer continues to have a security interest in the air conditioner. **Electronic chattel paper** is the same thing except that it is an electronic record rather than a writing.

In sum, Article 9 applies anytime the parties intended to create a security interest in any of the items listed above.

ATTACHMENT OF A SECURITY INTEREST

Attachment is a vital step in a secured transaction. This means that the secured party has taken three steps to create an enforceable security interest:

- The two parties made a security agreement *and either* the debtor has *authenticated a security agreement* describing the collateral *or* the secured party has obtained *possession* or *control*.
- The secured party has given value to obtain the security agreement; and
- The debtor has rights in the collateral.[3]

AGREEMENT

Without an agreement, there can be no security interest. Generally the agreement either must be written on paper and signed by the debtor, or electronically recorded and authenticated by the debtor. The agreement must reasonably identify the collateral. For example, a security agreement may properly describe the collateral as "all equipment in the store at 123 Periwinkle Street."[4]

A security agreement at a minimum might:

- State that Happy Homes, Inc. and Martha agree that Martha is buying an Arctic Co. refrigerator, and identify the exact unit by its serial number
- Give the price, the down payment, the monthly payments, and interest rate
- State that because Happy Homes is selling Martha the refrigerator on credit, it has a security interest in the refrigerator; and
- Provide that if Martha defaults on her payments, Happy Homes is entitled to repossess the refrigerator.

An actual security agreement will add many details, such as Martha's obligation to keep the refrigerator in good condition and to deliver it to the store if she defaults; a precise definition of "default"; and how Happy Homes may go about repossessing the goods if Martha defaults.

CONTROL AND POSSESSION

In certain cases, the security agreement need not be in writing if the parties have an oral agreement and the secured party has either **control** or **possession**. For many kinds of collateral it is safer for the secured party actually to take the item than to rely upon a security agreement.

For deposit accounts, electronic chattel paper and certain other collateral, the security interest attaches if the secured party has *control*. Generally speaking, *control means that the secured party has certain exclusive rights to dispose of the collateral*. If Peter deposits $250,000 in Smiley Bank and instructs the bank to dispose of the money as instructed by Wendy, then Wendy has control of the money.

For most other forms of collateral, a security interest attaches if the secured party has *possession*. For example, if you loan your neighbor $175,000 and he gives you a Winslow Homer watercolor as collateral, you have an attached security interest in the painting once it is in your possession.

The court decided the following case based on former Article 9, but the outcome would be the same under the revised Code.

---

[3] UCC §9-203.

[4] A security agreement may not use a **super-generic term** such as "all of Smith's personal property." We will see later that, by contrast, such a super-generic description is legally adequate in a *financing statement*.

IN RE CFLC, INC.

209 B.R. 508, 1997 Bankr. LEXIS 821
United States Bankruptcy Appellate Panel of the Ninth Circuit, 1997

Facts: Expeditors was a freight company that supervised importing and exporting for Everex Systems, Inc. Expeditors negotiated rates and services for its client and frequently had possession of Everex's goods. During a 17-month period, Expeditors sent over 300 invoices to Everex. Each invoice stated that the customer either had to accept all of the invoice's terms or to pay cash, receiving no work on credit. One of those terms gave Expeditors a security interest in all of the customer's property in its possession. In other words, if the customer failed to pay a bill, Expeditors asserted a right to keep the goods.

Everex filed for bankruptcy and Expeditors claimed the right to sell Everex's goods, worth about $81,000. The trial judge rejected the claim, ruling that Expeditors lacked a valid security interest. Expeditors appealed.

Issue: Did Expeditors have a security interest in Everex's goods?

Excerpts from Judge Ollason's Decision: Under the common law, silence in the face of an offer is not an acceptance, unless there is a relationship between the parties or a previous course of dealing pursuant to which silence would be understood as acceptance.

In this case, Expeditors and Everex had been doing business for about one and one-half years. They had never discussed the terms of the invoice nor negotiated for a security interest. Everex had never expressly acknowledged the invoice terms by accepting or objecting to them, nor did it take actions which acknowledged Expeditors' alleged general lien on the goods. Its only pertinent acts were its payment of the invoices and silence as to the added terms.

The evidence consisting of Everex's receipt and payment of invoices containing terms for a general lien in the goods in favor of Expeditors did not amount to an agreement for such a security interest, pursuant to [revised section 9-102]. As a matter of law, the repetitive sending by Expeditors to Everex of terms which Expeditors wished to be made part of the oral contract was not evidence of course of dealing because an agreement did not exist as to the security interest which could be supplemented by such evidence.

Affirmed.

Expeditors thought—or hoped—that it had a security interest, but the invoices failed to achieve that goal, so the company failed to obtain the money it was owed. How should Expeditors have protected itself?

VALUE

For the security interest to attach, the secured party must give value. Usually, the value will be apparent. If a bank loans $400 million to an airline, that money is the value, and the bank may therefore obtain a security interest in the planes that the airline is buying. The parties may also agree that some of the value will be given in the future. For example, a finance company might extend a $5 million line of credit to a retail store even though the store initially takes only $1 million of the money. The Code considers the entire $5 million line of credit to be value.[5]

[5] UCC §9-204(c).

DEBTOR RIGHTS IN THE COLLATERAL

The debtor can only grant a security interest in goods if he has some legal right to those goods himself. Typically, the debtor owns the goods. But a debtor may also give a security interest if he is leasing the goods or even if he is a bailee, meaning that he is lawfully holding them for someone else.

RESULT

Once the security interest has attached to the collateral, the secured party is protected against the debtor. If the debtor fails to pay, the secured party may repossess the collateral.

ATTACHMENT TO FUTURE PROPERTY

The security agreement may specify that the security interest attaches to personal property that the debtor does not yet possess but might obtain in the future.

AFTER-ACQUIRED PROPERTY

After-acquired property refers to items that the debtor obtains after the parties have made their security agreement. **The parties may agree that the security interest attaches to after-acquired property.**[6] Basil is starting a catering business, but owns only a beat-up car. He borrows $55,000 from the Pesto Bank, which takes a security interest in the car. But Pesto also insists on an after-acquired clause. When Basil purchases a commercial stove, cooking equipment, and freezer, Pesto's security interest attaches to each item as Basil acquires it.

PROCEEDS

Proceeds are whatever is obtained by a debtor who sells the collateral or otherwise disposes of it. **The secured party *automatically* obtains a security interest in the proceeds of the collateral.**[7] Suppose the Pesto Bank obtains a security interest in Basil's $4,000 freezer. Basil then decides he needs a larger model and sells the original freezer to his neighbor for $3,000. The $3,000 cash is proceeds, in which Pesto automatically obtains a security interest.

PERFECTION

NOTHING LESS THAN PERFECTION

Once the security interest has attached to the collateral, the secured party is protected *against the debtor*. Pesto Bank loaned money to Basil and has a security interest in all of his property. If Basil defaults on his loan, Pesto may insist he deliver the goods to the bank. If he fails to do that, the bank can seize the

---

[6] UCC §9-204(a).

[7] UCC §9-203(f).

collateral. But Pesto's security interest is valid only against Basil; if a third person claims some interest in the goods, the bank may never get them. For example, Basil might have taken out *another* loan, from his friend Olive, and used the same property as collateral. Olive knew nothing about the bank's original loan. To protect itself against Olive, and all other parties, the bank must *perfect* its interest.

There are several kinds of perfection:

- Perfection by filing
- Perfection by possession or control
- Perfection of consumer goods
- Perfection of movable collateral and fixtures

In some cases, the secured party will have a choice of which method to use; in other cases, only one method works.

Perfection by Filing

The most common way to perfect is by filing a financing statement with the appropriate state agency. A **financing statement** gives the names of all parties, describes the collateral, and outlines the security interest, enabling any interested person to learn about it. Suppose the Pesto Bank obtains a security interest in Basil's catering equipment and then perfects by filing with the Secretary of State in the state capital. When Basil asks his friend Olive for a loan, she will check the records to see if anyone has a security interest in the catering equipment. Olive's search uncovers Basil's previous security agreement, and she realizes it would be unwise to make the loan. If Basil were to default, the collateral would go straight to Pesto Bank, leaving Olive empty-handed. See Exhibit 12.2.

Article 9 prescribes one form, to be used nationwide for financing statements.[8] The financing form is available online at http://www.intercountyclearance.com/ra9/ra9ucc1.pdf. Remember that the filing may be done on paper or electronically.

The most common problems that arise in filing cases are (1) whether the financing statement contained enough information to put other people on notice of the security interest, and (2) whether the secured party filed the papers in the right place.

Contents of the Financing Statement

A financing statement is sufficient if it provides the name of the debtor, the name of the secured party, and an indication of the collateral.[9]

The name of the debtor is critical because that is what an interested person will use to search among the millions of other financing statements on file. If

[8] UCC §9-521.

[9] UCC §9-502(a).

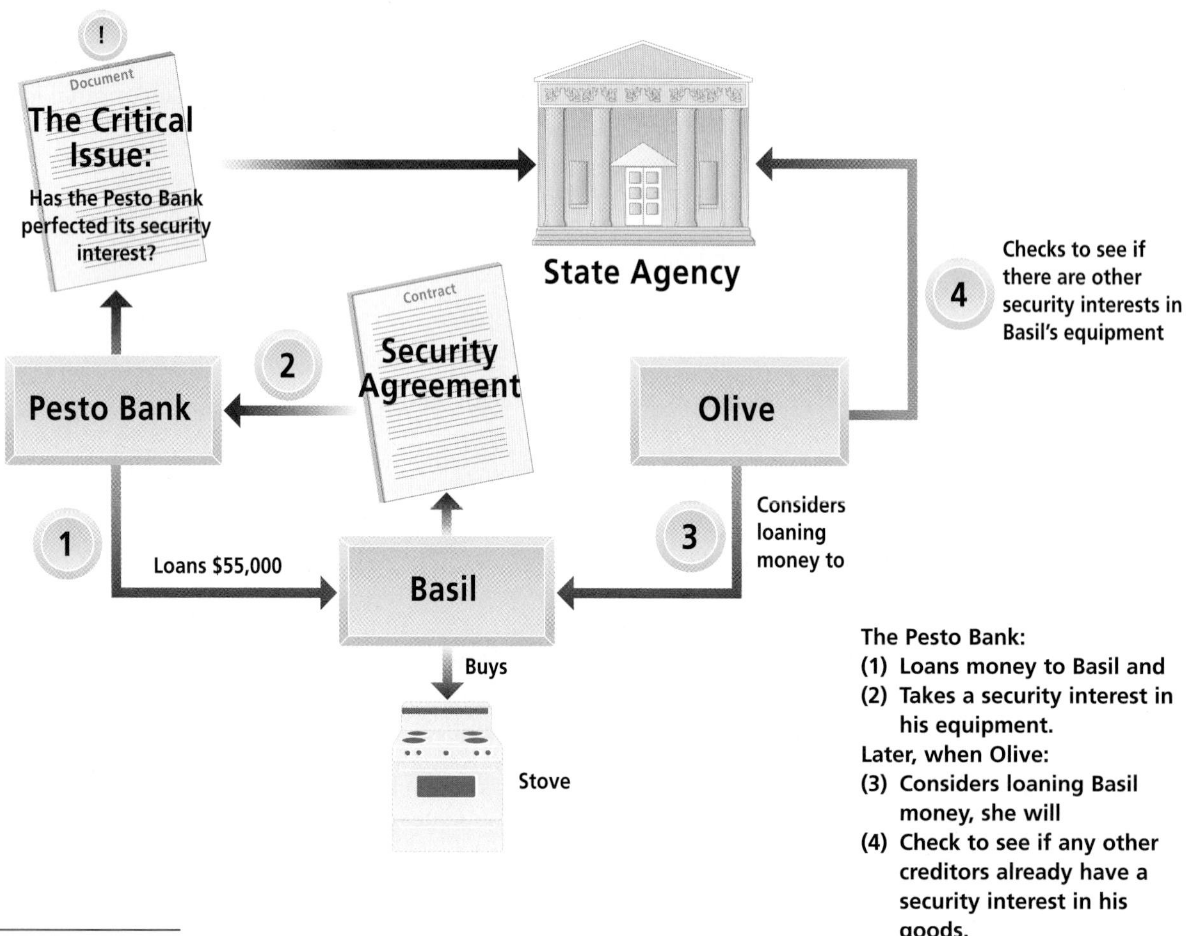

Exhibit 12.2

the debtor is a "registered organization," such as a corporation, limited partnership or limited liability company, the official, registered name of the company is the only one acceptable. If the debtor is a person, or an unregistered organization (such as a club), then the legal name is required. Trade names are not sufficient.

The collateral must be described reasonably so that another party contemplating a loan to the debtor will understand which property is already secured. A financing statement could properly state that it applies to "all inventory in the debtor's Houston warehouse." If the debtor has given a security interest in everything he owns, then it is sufficient to state simply that the financing statement covers "all assets" or "all personal property."

Article 9 devotes considerable space to the "correct name" issue because cases such as the following have been all too familiar. Although the case was decided under former Article 9, the outcome would be the same under the revised Code.

THE FIRST NATIONAL BANK OF LACON v. STRONG
278 Ill. App. 3d 762, 633 N.E.2d 432, 1996 Ill. App. LEXIS 169
Illinois Court of Appeal, 1996

Facts: Elmer and Pam Strong leased and operated service stations. They were incorporated as "E. Strong Oil Co.," although they used "Strong Oil Co." as their trade name. The First National Bank of Lacon loaned the couple $75,000. The promissory note named "Strong Oil Co." as the borrower. Both Elmer and Pam signed the note, along with an agreement that gave the bank a security interest in the company's inventory, equipment, accounts, and other assets. The bank filed a financing statement, listing the debtor as "Strong Oil Co."

The Illinois Department of Revenue seized all of the company's assets, claiming $229,000 in unpaid motor fuel taxes. The bank sued, claiming that it was entitled to all of the property, based on its security interest. The issue was whether the bank had perfected its interest. If the bank had perfected, it was entitled to the property. If the bank had failed to do so, because it filed under the name Strong rather than "E. Strong," the Department could take everything. The trial court found that the bank had validly perfected its interest, and the Department appealed.

You be the Judge: Did the bank have a perfected security interest in the property?

Argument for the Department of Revenue: Financing statements are designed to permit interested parties to search an index and determine quickly if a debtor has other creditors. Accuracy is essential because the statements are indexed alphabetically by debtor. There are millions of secured transactions annually, and many companies and organizations have similar names. A creditor looking under "E. Strong" would be far from "Strong Oil," where the bank chose to file. Must a searcher also look under "Elmer Strong," "E & P Strong," "Strong Oil," "Strong Gasoline," "Strong Service Stations," and a hundred other permutations? Because the bank could not be bothered to verify the name of its debtor, it failed to perfect and must suffer the loss.

Argument for the Bank: The Department's greed exceeds its common sense. The purpose of filing is to give a reasonably prudent creditor the chance to check on the credit of its prospective debtor. The company was most widely known as the Strong Oil Co. Any prudent company that considered extending credit to the Strongs would have looked under Strong Oil—exactly where the bank filed. The Code was never intended to elevate nit-picking to the status of policy.

PLACE AND DURATION OF FILING

Article 9 specifies *where* a secured party must file. These provisions may vary from state to state, so it is essential to check local law: a misfiled record accomplishes nothing. Generally speaking, a party must file in a central filing office located in the state where an individual debtor lives, or where an organization has its executive office.[10]

Once a financing statement has been filed, it is effective for five years (except for a manufactured home, where it lasts 30 years). After five years, the statement will expire and leave the secured party unprotected, unless she files a continuation statement within six months prior to expiration. The continuation statement is valid for an additional five years, and a secured party may file one periodically, forever.[11] You may see a standard amendment form, used for continuations, at http://www.intercountyclearance.com/.

---

[10] UCC §9-307.

[11] UCC §9-515.

PERFECTION BY POSSESSION OR CONTROL

For most types of collateral, in addition to filing, a secured party generally may perfect by possession or control (described above). So if the collateral is a diamond brooch or 1,000 shares of stock, a bank may perfect its security interest by holding the items until the loan is paid off.

Perfection by possession has some advantages. Notice to other parties is very clear, and if the debtor defaults, a secured party obviously has no difficulties repossessing. However, both possession and control impose one important duty: **a secured party must use reasonable care in the custody and preservation of collateral in her possession or control.**[12]

PERFECTION OF CONSUMER GOODS

The Code gives special treatment to security interests in most consumer goods. Merchants cannot file a financing statement for every bed, television, and stereo for which a consumer owes money. To understand the UCC's treatment of these transactions, we need to know two terms. The first is *consumer goods*, which are those used primarily for personal, family, or household purposes. The second term is *purchase money security interest*.

A purchase money security interest (PMSI) is one taken by the person who sells the collateral or by the person who advances money so the debtor can buy the collateral.[13] Assume the Gobroke Home Center sells Marion a $5,000 stereo system. The sales document requires a payment of $500 down and $50 per month for the next 300 years, and gives Gobroke a security interest in the system. Because the security interest was "taken by the seller," the document is a PMSI. It would also be a PMSI if a bank had loaned Marion the money to buy the system and the document gave the bank a security interest. See Exhibit 12.3.

But aren't all security interests PMSIs? No, many are not. Suppose a bank loans a retail company $800,000 and takes a security interest in the store's present inventory. That is not a PMSI since the store did not use the money to purchase the collateral.

What must Gobroke Home Center do to perfect its security interest? Nothing. **A PMSI in consumer goods perfects automatically, without filing.**[14] Marion's new stereo is clearly consumer goods, because she will use it only in her home. Gobroke's security interest is a PMSI, so the interest has perfected automatically.

Note that the Code provisions about perfecting generally do not apply to motor vehicles, trailers, mobile homes, boats or farm tractors.[15] These types of secured interests are governed by state law, which frequently require a security interest to be noted directly on the vehicle's certificate of title.

---

[12] UCC §9-207.

[13] UCC §9-103.

[14] UCC §9-309(1).

[15] UCC §9-311(a)(2).

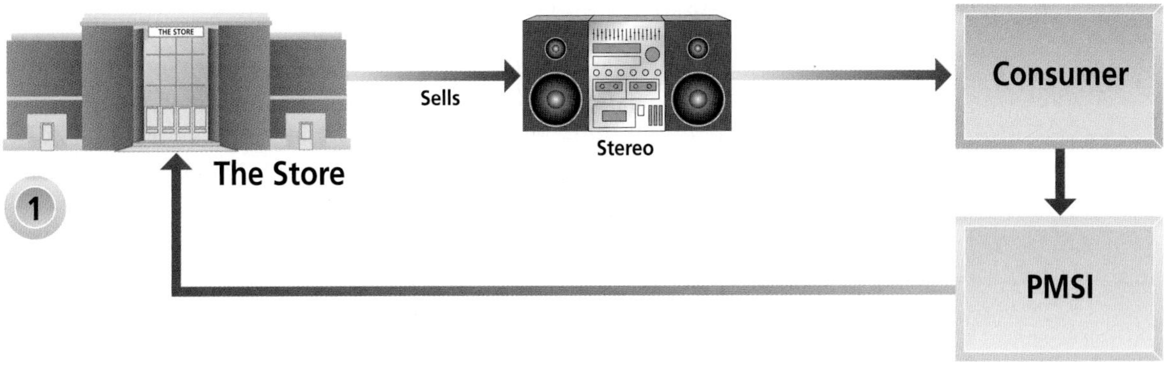

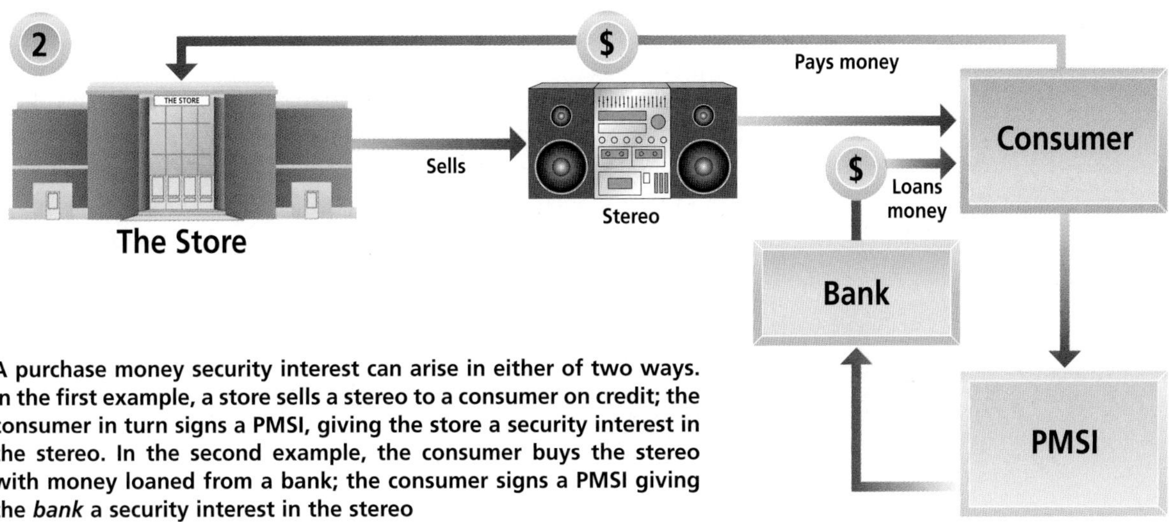

A purchase money security interest can arise in either of two ways. In the first example, a store sells a stereo to a consumer on credit; the consumer in turn signs a PMSI, giving the store a security interest in the stereo. In the second example, the consumer buys the stereo with money loaned from a bank; the consumer signs a PMSI giving the *bank* a security interest in the stereo

Exhibit 12.3

PROTECTION OF BUYERS

Generally, once a security interest is perfected, it remains effective regardless of whether the collateral is sold, exchanged, or transferred in some other way. Bubba's Bus Co. needs money to meet its payroll, so it borrows $150,000 from Francine's Finance Co., which takes a security interest in Bubba's 180 buses and perfects its interest. Bubba, still short of cash, sells 30 of his buses to Antelope Transit. But even that money is not enough to keep Bubba solvent: he defaults on his loan to Francine and goes into bankruptcy. Francine pounces on Bubba's buses. May she repossess the 30 that *Antelope* now operates? Yes. The security interest continued in the buses even after Antelope purchased them, and Francine can whisk them away.

There are some exceptions to this rule. The Code gives a few buyers special protection.

BUYERS IN ORDINARY COURSE OF BUSINESS

A buyer in ordinary course of business (BIOC) is someone who buys goods in good faith from a seller who routinely deals in such goods.[16] For example, Plato's Garden Supply purchases 500 hemlocks from Socrates' Farm, a grower. Plato is a BIOC: he is buying in good faith and Socrates routinely deals in hemlocks. This is an important status, because a BIOC is generally not affected by security interests in the goods. However, if Plato realized that the sale violated another party's rights in the goods, there would be no good faith. If Plato knew that Socrates was bankrupt and had agreed with a creditor not to sell any of his inventory, Plato would not achieve BIOC status.

A buyer in ordinary course of business takes the goods free of a security interest created by his seller even though the security interest is perfected.[17] Suppose that, a month before Plato made his purchase, Socrates borrowed $200,000 from the Athenian Bank. Athenian took a security interest in all of Socrates' trees and perfected by filing. Then Plato purchased his 500 hemlocks. If Socrates defaults on the loan, Athenian will have *no right* to repossess the 500 trees that are now at the Garden Supply. Plato took them free and clear. (Of course, Athenian can still attempt to repossess other trees from Socrates.) The BIOC exception is designed to encourage ordinary commerce. A buyer making routine purchases should not be forced to perform a financing check before buying.

BUYERS OF CHATTEL PAPER, INSTRUMENTS, AND DOCUMENTS

We have seen that debtors often use chattel paper and instruments as collateral. Because each of these is so easily transferred, the Code gives buyers special protection. **A buyer who purchases chattel paper or instruments in good faith in the ordinary course of her business, and then obtains *possession or control*, generally takes free of any security interest.**[18]

PRIORITIES AMONG CREDITORS

What happens when two creditors have a security interest in the same collateral? The party who has **priority** in the collateral gets it. Typically, the debtor lacks assets to pay everyone, so all creditors struggle to be the first in line. After the first creditor has repossessed the collateral, sold it, and taken enough of the proceeds to pay off his debt, there may be nothing left for anyone else. (There may not even be enough to pay the first creditor all that he is due, in which case that creditor will sue for the deficiency.) Who gets priority? There are three principal rules.

---

[16] UCC §1-201(9).

[17] UCC §9-320(a). In fact, the buyer takes free of the security interest *even if the buyer knew of it*. Yet a BIOC, by definition, must be acting in good faith. Is this a contradiction? No. Plato might know that a third party has a security interest in Socrates' crops, yet not realize that his purchase violates the third party's rights. Generally, for example, a security interest will permit a retailer to sell consumer goods, the presumption being that part of the proceeds will go to the secured party. A BIOC cannot be expected to determine what a retailer plans to do with the money he is paid.

[18] UCC §9-330(a)(b)(d).

The first rule is easy: **a party with a perfected security interest takes priority over a party with an unperfected interest.**[19] This is the whole point of perfecting: to ensure that your security interest gets priority over everyone else's. On August 15, Meredith's Market, an antique store, borrows $100,000 from the Happy Bank, which takes a security interest in all of Meredith's inventory. Happy Bank does not perfect. On September 15, Meredith uses the same collateral to borrow $50,000 from the Suspicion Bank, which files a financing statement the same day. On October 15, as if on cue, Meredith files for bankruptcy and stops paying both creditors. Suspicion wins because it holds a perfected interest, whereas the Happy Bank holds merely an unperfected interest.

The second rule: **if neither secured party has perfected, the first interest to attach gets priority.**[20] Suppose that Suspicion Bank and Happy Bank had both failed to perfect. In that case, Happy Bank would have the first claim to Meredith's inventory, since Happy's interest *attached* first.

And the third rule follows logically: **between perfected security interests, the first to file *or* perfect wins.**[21] Diminishing Perspective, a railroad, borrows $75 million from the First Bank, which takes a security interest in Diminishing's rolling stock (railroad cars) and immediately perfects by filing. Two months later, Diminishing borrows $100 million from Second Bank, which takes a security interest in the same collateral and also files. When Diminishing arrives, on schedule, in bankruptcy court, both banks will race to seize the rolling stock. First Bank gets the railcars because it perfected first.

March 1:	April 2:	May 3:	The Winner:
First Bank loans money and perfects its security interest by filing a financing statement.	Second Bank loans money and perfects its security interest by filing a financing statement.	Diminishing goes bankrupt, and both banks attempt to take the rolling stock.	First Bank, because it perfected first.

The general rules of priority are quite straightforward. However, you will not be surprised to learn that there are some exceptions.

Priority Exceptions

You may recall that a purchase money security interest (PMSI) is a security interest taken by the seller of the collateral or by a lender whose loan enables the debtor to buy the collateral. A PMSI can be created only in goods, fixtures, and software. **A PMSI that is promptly perfected generally takes priority over a conflicting perfected security interest (even one perfected earlier).** The holder of the PMSI is sometimes required to notify other secured parties of the new

---

[19] UCC §9-322(a)(2).

[20] UCC §9-322(a)(3).

[21] UCC §9-322(a)(1).

PMSI, and generally must perfect before the goods are sold or shortly thereafter, depending on what type of collateral is involved.

On February 1, Tool Shop borrows $100,000 from the Gargoyle Bank, giving Gargoyle a security interest in after-acquired property. Then on November 1, Manufacturer sells a specially built lathe to Tool Shop for $80,000, taking a PMSI in the machine. When the lathe arrives at the Tool Shop, Gargoyle's earlier security interest attaches to the same collateral. Who wins? Manufacturer, provided it promptly perfects its PMSI.

Another significant exception involves perfection by possession or control. **A party that uses possession or control to perfect its interest in deposit accounts, investment property, letter-of-credit rights, or instruments generally obtains priority over a party that perfected earlier by filing.**

DEFAULT AND TERMINATION

We have reached the end of the line. Either the debtor has defaulted, or it has performed its obligations and may terminate the security agreement.

DEFAULT

The parties define "default" in their security agreement. **Generally, a debtor defaults when he fails to make payments due or enters bankruptcy proceedings.** The parties can agree that other acts will constitute default, such as the debtor's failure to maintain insurance on the collateral. When a debtor defaults, the secured party has two principal options: (1) it may take possession of the collateral, or (2) it may file suit against the debtor for the money owed. The secured party does not have to choose between these two remedies; it may try one after the other, or both simultaneously.[22]

TAKING POSSESSION OF THE COLLATERAL

When the debtor defaults, the secured party may take possession of the collateral.[23] The secured party may act on its own, without any court order, and simply take the collateral, provided this can be done *without a breach of the peace*. Otherwise, the secured party must file suit against the debtor and request that the court *order* the debtor to deliver the collateral.

DISPOSITION OF THE COLLATERAL

Once the secured party has obtained possession of the collateral, it has two choices. The secured party may (1) dispose of the collateral or (2) retain the collateral as full satisfaction of the debt. Notice that until the secured party disposes of the collateral, the debtor has the right to **redeem** it, that is, to pay the full value of the debt and retrieve her property.[24]

---

[22] UCC §9-601(a)(b)(c).

[23] UCC §9-609.

[24] UCC §9-623.

Disposal of the Collateral. **A secured party may sell, lease, or otherwise dispose of the collateral in any commercially reasonable manner.**[25] Typically, the secured party will sell the collateral in either a private or a public sale. First, however, the debtor must receive *reasonable notice* of the time and place of the sale, so that she may bid on the collateral. The higher the price that the secured party gets for the collateral, the lower the balance still owed by the debtor. Giving the debtor notice of the sale, and a chance to bid, ensures that the collateral will not be sold for an unreasonably low price.

Suppose Bank loans $65,000 to Farmer to purchase a tractor. While still owing $40,000, Farmer defaults. Bank takes possession of the tractor and then notifies Farmer that it intends to sell the tractor at an auction. Farmer has the right to attend and bid on the tractor.

When the secured party has sold the collateral, it applies the proceeds of the sale: first, to its expenses in repossessing and selling the collateral, and second, to the debt.[26] Assume Bank sold the tractor for $35,000, and that the process of repossessing and selling the tractor cost $5,000. Bank applies the remaining $30,000 to the debt.

Deficiency or Surplus. The sale of the tractor yielded $30,000 to be applied to the debt, which was $40,000. The disposition has left a **deficiency**, that is, insufficient funds to pay off the debt. **The debtor is liable for any deficiency.** So the bank will sue the farmer for the remaining $10,000. On the other hand, sometimes the sale of the collateral yields a **surplus**, that is, a sum greater than the debt. In that case, the secured party must pay the surplus to the debtor.[27] Finally, when a secured party disposes of collateral in a *commercially unreasonable* manner, it will be liable to the debtor for the shortfall.

Acceptance of Collateral. In many cases, the secured party has the option to satisfy the debt simply by keeping the collateral. **Acceptance refers to a secured party's retention of the collateral as full or partial satisfaction of the debt.** *Partial satisfaction* means that the debtor will still owe some deficiency to the secured party.[28] Generally speaking, a secured party may accept the collateral as full satisfaction unless the debtor objects.

A secured party who wishes to accept the collateral must notify the debtor. If the debtor agrees in an authenticated record, then the secured party may keep the collateral as full *or* partial satisfaction of the debt. If the debtor does not respond within 20 days, the secured party may still accept the collateral as *full* satisfaction but *not* as partial satisfaction. In other words, the debtor's silence does not give the secured party the right to keep the goods and still sue for more money.

Occasionally, the secured party will prefer to ignore its rights in the collateral and simply sue the debtor. **A secured party may sue the debtor for the full debt.**[29]

---

[25] UCC §9-610.

[26] UCC §9-615(a).

[27] UCC §9-615(d)

[28] UCC §9-620.

[29] UCC §9-601(a).

TERMINATION

Finally, we need to look at what happens when a debtor does not default, but pays the full debt. (You are forgiven if you lost track of the fact that things sometimes work out smoothly.) Once that happens, the secured party must complete a **termination statement**, a document indicating that it no longer claims a security interest in the collateral.[30]

OVERVIEW OF BANKRUPTCY

As you may have noticed in the first half of this chapter, many of the cases involving secured transactions are decided in bankruptcy court as part of an overall sorting out of a debtor's financial problems. The U.S. Bankruptcy Code (Code) has three primary goals:

- *To preserve as much of the debtor's property as possible.*
- *To divide the debtor's assets fairly between the debtor and creditors.*
- *To divide the debtor's assets fairly among creditors.*

The following options are available under the Bankruptcy Code:

Number	Topic	Description
Chapter 7	Liquidation	The bankrupt's assets are sold to pay creditors. If the debtor owns a business, it terminates. The creditors have no right to the debtor's future earnings.
Chapter 9	Municipal bankruptcies	This chapter is not covered in this book.
Chapter 11	Reorganization	This chapter is designed for businesses and wealthy individuals. Businesses continue in operation, and creditors receive a portion of both current assets and future earnings.
Chapter 12	Family farmers	This chapter is not covered in this book.
Chapter 13	Consumer reorganizations	Chapter 13 offers reorganizations for the typical consumer. Creditors usually receive a portion of the individual's current assets and future earnings.

All of the Code's chapters have one of two objectives—rehabilitation or liquidation. Chapters 11 and 13, for instance, focus on rehabilitation. Many debtors

[30] UCC §9-513.

can return to financial health provided they have the time and breathing space to work out their problems. These chapters hold creditors at bay while the debtor develops a payment plan. In return for retaining some of their assets, debtors typically promise to pay creditors a portion of their future earnings. However, when debtors are unable to develop a feasible plan for rehabilitation under Chapter 11 or 13, Chapter 7 provides for liquidation (also known as a **straight bankruptcy**). Most of the debtor's assets are distributed to creditors, but the debtor has no obligation to share future earnings.

Debtors are often eligible to file under more than one chapter. No choice is irrevocable because both debtors and creditors have the right to ask the court to convert a case from one chapter to another at any time during the proceedings. (The text of the Bankruptcy Code is available at http://www4.law.cornell.edu/uscode/11/.)

CHAPTER 7 LIQUIDATION

All bankruptcy cases proceed in a roughly similar pattern, regardless of chapter. We use Chapter 7 as a template to illustrate common features of all bankruptcy cases. Later on, the discussions of the other chapters will indicate how they differ from Chapter 7.

FILING A PETITION

Any individual, partnership, corporation, or other business organization that lives, conducts business, or owns property in the United States can file under the Code. (Chapter 13, however, is available only to individuals.) The traditional term for someone who could not pay his debts was "**bankrupt**," but the Code uses the term "**debtor**" instead. We use both terms interchangeably.

A case begins with the filing of a bankruptcy petition in federal district court. Debtors may go willingly into the bankruptcy process by filing a **voluntary petition** or they may be dragged into court by creditors who file an **involuntary petition**. The district court typically refers bankruptcy cases to a specialized bankruptcy judge. Either party can appeal the decision of the bankruptcy judge back to the district court and, from there, to the federal appeals court.

VOLUNTARY PETITION

Any debtor may file for bankruptcy. It is not necessary that the debtor's liabilities exceed assets. Debtors sometimes file a bankruptcy petition because cash flow is so tight they cannot pay their debts, even though they are not technically insolvent. The voluntary petition must include the following documents:

Document	Description
Petition	Begins the case. Easy to fill out, it requires checking a few boxes and typing in little more than name, address, and Social Security number.
List of Creditors	The names and addresses of all creditors.

Document	Description
Schedule of Assets and Liabilities	A list of the debtor's assets and debts.
Claim of Exemptions	A list of all assets that the debtor is entitled to keep.
Schedule of Income and Expenditures	The debtor's job, income, and expenses.
Statement of Financial Affairs	A summary of the debtor's financial history and current financial condition. In particular, the debtor must list any recent payments to creditors and any other property held by someone else for the debtor.

Involuntary Petition

Creditors may force a debtor into bankruptcy by filing an involuntary petition. The creditors' goal is to preserve as much of the debtor's assets as possible and to ensure that all creditors receive a fair share. Naturally, the Code sets strict limits—debtors cannot be forced into bankruptcy every time they miss a credit card payment. **An involuntary petition must meet all of the following requirements:**

- The debtor must owe at least $10,000 in unsecured claims to the creditors who file.
- If the debtor has at least 12 creditors, three or more must sign the petition. If the debtor has fewer than 12 creditors, any one of them can file a petition.
- The creditors must allege either that a custodian for the debtor's property has been appointed in the prior 120 days or that the debtor has generally not been paying debts that are due.

What does "a custodian for the debtor's property" mean? *State* laws sometimes permit the appointment of a custodian to protect a debtor's assets. The Code allows creditors to pull a case out from under state law and into federal bankruptcy court by filing an involuntary petition. Creditors also have the right to file an involuntary petition if they can show that the debtor is not paying debts. In the event that a debtor objects to an involuntary petition, the bankruptcy court must hold a trial to determine whether the creditors have met the Code's requirements.

Once a voluntary petition is filed or an involuntary petition approved, the bankruptcy court issues an **order for relief**. This order is an official acknowledgment that the debtor is under the jurisdiction of the court, and it is, in a sense, the start of the whole bankruptcy process. An involuntary debtor must now make all the filings that accompany a voluntary petition.

Trustee

The trustee is responsible for gathering the bankrupt's assets and dividing them among creditors. Creditors have the right to elect the trustee, but often they do not bother. In this case, the **U.S. Trustee** makes the selection. The U.S. Attorney General appoints a U.S. Trustee for each region of the country to administer the bankruptcy law.

CREDITORS

The U.S. Trustee calls a meeting of creditors sometime within 20 to 40 days after the order for relief. At the meeting, the bankrupt must answer (under oath) any question the creditors pose about his financial situation. If the creditors want to elect a trustee, they do so at this meeting.

Unsecured creditors must submit a *proof of claim* within 90 days after the meeting of creditors. The proof of claim is a simple form stating the name of the creditor and the amount of the claim. **Secured creditors do not file proofs of claim unless the claim exceeds the value of their collateral.** In this case, they are unsecured creditors for the excess amount and must file a proof of claim for it. Suppose that Deborah borrows $750,000 from Morton in return for a mortgage on her house. If she does not repay the debt, he can foreclose. Unfortunately, property values plummet, and by the time Deborah files a voluntary petition in bankruptcy, the house is worth only $500,000. Morton is a secured creditor for $500,000 and need file no proof of claim for that amount. But he is an unsecured creditor for $250,000 and will lose his right to this excess amount unless he files a proof of claim for it.

AUTOMATIC STAY

A fox chased by hounds has no time to make rational long-term decisions. What that fox needs is a safe burrow. Similarly, it is difficult for debtors to make sound financial decisions when hounded night and day by creditors shouting, "Pay me! Pay me!" The Code is designed to give debtors enough breathing space to sort out their affairs sensibly. An automatic stay is a safe burrow for the bankrupt. It goes into effect as soon as the petition is filed. **An automatic stay prohibits creditors from collecting debts that the bankrupt incurred before the petition was filed.** Creditors may not sue a bankrupt to obtain payment nor may they take other steps, outside of court, to pressure the debtor for payment. In the following case, the landlord ate crow instead of Chinese food.

IN RE SECHUAN CITY INC.

96 B.R. 37, 1989 Bankr. LEXIS 103
United States Bankruptcy Court, Eastern District of Pennsylvania, 1989

Facts: The Sechuan Garden restaurant leased space from North American Motor Inns, Inc. (Hotel). The entrance to the restaurant was in the Hotel lobby. The restaurant did not have a liquor license, but the Hotel bar would deliver drinks to restaurant guests at their tables. Sechuan Garden filed a voluntary petition in bankruptcy. Although the Hotel manager, Jose Garcia, knew that the bankruptcy court had entered an automatic stay, he posted the following signs at all Hotel entrances, in the Hotel lobby, and immediately outside the restaurant doors located in the lobby.

The restaurant's revenues dropped $1,000 a week for three weeks until Garcia finally removed the signs. Garcia testified that he had posted the signs to "shame" and "embarrass" the restaurant's owners into paying their bills.

NOTICE
NO ALCOHOLIC BEVERAGES ARE ALLOWED
TO BE CONSUMED IN THE RESTAURANT AREA
UNDER PENALTY OF LAW
THANKS
N.A.M.I. MGMT

THE TENANT HAS DISHONORED ITS
OBLIGATION FOR PAYMENT
TO THE LANDLORD

NOTICE
NO ALCOHOLIC BEVERAGES ARE ALLOWED
TO BE CONSUMED IN THE RESTAURANT AREA
UNDER PENALTY OF LAW
THANKS
N.A.M.I. MGMT

Issue: Did the Hotel violate Sechuan Garden's automatic stay?

Excerpts from Judge Fox's Decision:[31] The automatic stay is one of the fundamental debtor protections provided by the bankruptcy laws. It gives the debtor a breathing spell from his creditors. It stops all collection efforts, all harassment, and all foreclosure actions. It permits the debtor to attempt a repayment or reorganization plan or simply to be relieved of the financial pressures that drove him into bankruptcy.

The automatic stay also provides creditor protection. Without it, certain creditors would be able to pursue their own remedies against the debtor's property. Those who acted first would obtain payment of the claims in preference to and to the detriment of other creditors.

The language of [the Code] is very broad, and is designed to prevent creditor coercion and harassment of the debtor. The conduct prohibited ranges from that of an informal nature, such as by telephone contact or by dunning letters to more formal judicial and administrative proceedings.

Here, I conclude that the Hotel undertook a studied effort to coerce payment of the [restaurant's] prepetition claim. While the lessor did not bring suit against the debtor, its actions were designed to place the debtor in a position of either paying the lessor's prepetition claim or losing business due to defendants' actions. These actions were prohibited by the automatic stay and resulted in clear harm to the debtor.

[The court ordered the hotel to pay the bankruptcy trustee $3,000 in damages and $600 in attorney's fees.]

BANKRUPTCY ESTATE

The filing of the bankruptcy petition creates a new legal entity separate from the debtor—the **bankruptcy estate**. All of the bankrupt's assets pass to the estate, except exempt property and new property that the debtor acquires after the petition is filed.

EXEMPT PROPERTY

The Code permits *individual* debtors (but not organizations) to keep some property for themselves. This exempt property saves the debtor from destitution during the bankruptcy process and provides the foundation for a new life once the process is over.

In this one area of bankruptcy law, the Code defers to state law. Although the Code lists various types of exempt property, it permits states to opt out of

---

[31] It's no surprise that Judge Fox appreciates the importance of an automatic stay.

the federal system and define a different set of exemptions. A majority of states have indeed opted out of the Code, and for their residents the Code exemptions are irrelevant.

Under the *federal* Code, a debtor is allowed to exempt only $15,000 of the value of her home. If the home is worth more than that, the trustee sells it and returns $15,000 of the proceeds to the debtor. Most *states* exempt items such as the debtor's home, household goods, cars, work tools, disability and pension benefits, alimony, and health aids. Indeed, some states set no limit on the value of exempt property. Both Florida and Texas, for example, permit debtors to keep homes of unlimited value and a certain amount of land. Not surprisingly, these generous exemptions sometimes lead to abuses.

Who could argue with the Texas statute that permits debtors to keep their clothing? Even bankrupts have the right to some last shred of dignity. But what if that clothing includes a Rolex watch? In a section of his opinion entitled "Putting the Cartier before the Horse," Judge Leif M. Clark ruled that a debtor needed his Rolex to preserve "a semblance of dignity."[32]

Many debtors are also living a dignified existence in Florida. Former baseball commissioner Bowie Kuhn sold his (nonexempt) home in New Jersey and bought a million dollar (exempt) mansion in Florida immediately before he filed for bankruptcy. Kuhn is in good company. Former bank president Roy Talmo cruised between bankruptcy court and his 7,000-square-foot mansion in a Rolls-Royce. Marvin L. Warner, former ambassador to Switzerland, bought a 160-acre horse farm in Florida on the eve of bankruptcy.

The Florida statute was intended to protect nineteenth-century pioneers who bore the risks of homesteading in wild swampland. Life in Florida may be safer now, but the bankruptcy protection remains. All efforts to change the law have been soundly defeated.

The latest news on bankruptcy is available at http://www.abiworld.org/.

VOIDABLE PREFERENCES

A major goal of the bankruptcy system is to divide the debtor's assets fairly among creditors. It would not be fair, or in keeping with this goal, if debtors were permitted to pay off some of their creditors immediately before filing a bankruptcy petition. Such a payment is called a **preference** because it gives unfair preferential treatment to a creditor. **The trustee can void any transfer to a creditor that took place in the 90-day period before the filing of a petition if the creditor received more from the transfer than she would have received during the bankruptcy process.**

FRAUDULENT TRANSFERS

Suppose that a debtor sees bankruptcy inexorably approaching across the horizon like a tornado. He knows that, once the storm hits and he files a petition, everything he owns except a few items of exempt property will become part of the bankruptcy estate. Before that happens, he may be tempted to give some of

[32] *In re Leva*, 96 B.R. 723, 1989 Bankr. LEXIS 257 (Bankr. W.D. Tex. 1989).

his property to friends or family to shelter it from the tornado. If he succumbs to temptation, however, he is committing a fraudulent transfer.

A transfer is fraudulent if it is made within the year before a petition is filed and its purpose is to hinder, delay, or defraud creditors. The trustee can void any fraudulent transfer. Fraudulent transfers sound similar to voidable preferences, but there is an important distinction: voidable preferences pay legitimate debts, while fraudulent transfers protect the debtor's assets from legitimate creditors. For example, Lawrence Williams and his wife, Diana, enjoyed a luxurious lifestyle while his investment bank flourished. But when the bank failed, Lawrence was faced with debts of $6 million. On the eve of the bankruptcy filing, Diana suddenly announced that she wanted a divorce. In what had to be the most amicable breakup ever, Lawrence willingly transferred all of his assets to her. The court found that the transfer had been fraudulent.[33]

PAYMENT OF CLAIMS

Imagine a crowded delicatessen on Saturday evening. People are pushing and shoving because they know there is not enough food for everyone; some customers will go home hungry. The delicatessen could simply serve whoever pushes to the front of the line, or it could establish a number system to ensure that the most deserving customers are served first. The Code has, in essence, adopted a number system to prevent a free-for-all fight over the bankrupt's assets. Indeed, one of the Code's primary goals is to ensure that creditors are paid in the proper order, not according to who pushes to the front of the line.

All claims are placed in one of three classes: (1) secured claims, (2) priority claims, and (3) unsecured claims. **The trustee pays the bankruptcy estate to the various classes of claims in order of rank.** A higher class is paid in full before the next class receives any payment at all. The debtor is entitled to any funds remaining after all claims have been paid. The payment order is shown in Exhibit 12.4.

SECURED CLAIMS

Creditors whose loans are secured by specific collateral are paid first. Secured claims are fundamentally different from all other claims because they are paid by selling a specific asset, not out of the general funds of the estate.

Exhibit 12.4

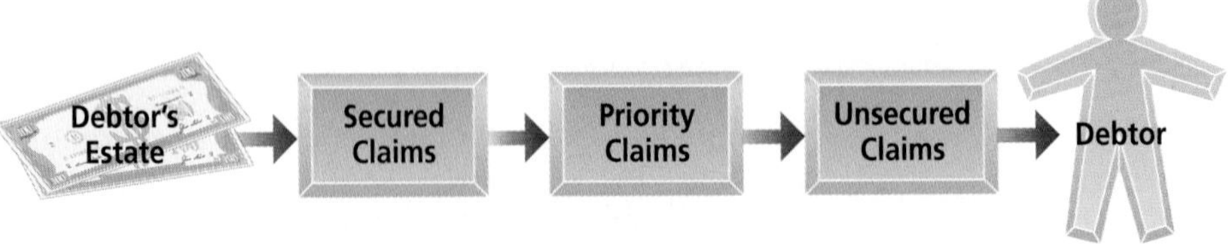

[33] *In re Williams*, 159 B.R. 648, 1993 Bankr. LEXIS 1482 (Bankr. D.R.I. 1993), *remanded*, 190 B.R. 728, 1996 U.S. Dist. LEXIS 539.

PRIORITY CLAIMS

Each category of priority claims is paid in order, with the first group receiving full payment before the next group receives anything. Priority claims include:

- Administrative expenses (such as fees to the trustee, lawyers, and accountants).
- Back wages to the debtor's employees for work performed during the 90 days prior to the date of the petition.
- Alimony and child support.
- Income and property taxes.

UNSECURED CLAIMS

Last, and frequently very much least, unsecured creditors have now reached the delicatessen counter. They can only hope that some food remains.

DISCHARGE

Filing a bankruptcy petition is embarrassing, time-consuming, and disruptive. It can affect the debtor's credit rating for years, making the simplest car loan a challenge. To encourage debtors to file for bankruptcy despite the pain involved, the Code offers a powerful incentive: the **fresh start**. Once a bankruptcy estate has been distributed to creditors, they cannot make a claim against the debtor for money owed before the filing, *whether or not they actually received any payment*. These pre-petition debts are **discharged**. All is forgiven, if not forgotten.

Discharge is an essential part of bankruptcy law. Without it, debtors would have little incentive to take part. To avoid abuses, however, the Code limits both the type of debts that can be discharged and the circumstances under which discharge can take place.

DEBTS THAT CANNOT BE DISCHARGED

The following debts are among those that can never be discharged. The debtor remains liable in full until they are paid:

- Recent income and property taxes.
- Money obtained by fraud.
- Cash advances on a credit card taken out within 60 days before the order of relief.
- Debts omitted from the Schedule of Assets and Liabilities that the debtor filed with the petition, if the creditor did not know about the bankruptcy and therefore did not file a proof of claim.
- Money owed for alimony, maintenance, or child support.
- Debts stemming from intentional and malicious injury.

- Student loans guaranteed by the government cannot be discharged for seven years after the due date. The bankruptcy court may discharge these loans only if the student has acted in good faith and payment of the loans would cause undue hardship.

CIRCUMSTANCES THAT PREVENT DEBTS FROM BEING DISCHARGED

The Code also prohibits the discharge of debts under the following circumstances:

- *Business Organizations.* Under Chapter 7 (but *not* the other chapters), the debts of partnerships and corporations cannot be discharged. Once its assets have been distributed, the organization must cease operation. If the company resumes business again, it becomes responsible for all its pre-filing debts.
- *Repeated Filings for Bankruptcy.* Congress feared that some debtors, attracted by the lure of a fresh start, would make a habit of bankruptcy. Therefore, a debtor who has received a discharge under Chapter 7 or 11 cannot receive another discharge under Chapter 7 for at least six years after the prior filing.
- *Revocation.* A court can revoke a discharge within one year if it discovers the debtor engaged in fraud or concealment.
- *Dishonesty or Bad Faith Behavior.* The court may deny discharge altogether if the debtor has made fraudulent transfers, hidden assets, falsified records, or otherwise acted in bad faith.

REAFFIRMATION

Sometimes debtors are willing to **reaffirm** a debt, meaning they promise to pay even after discharge. They may want to reaffirm a secured debt to avoid losing the collateral. For example, a debtor who has taken out a loan secured by a car may reaffirm that debt so that the finance company will agree not to repossess it. Sometimes debtors reaffirm because they feel guilty, or they want to maintain a good relationship with the creditor. They may have borrowed from a family member or an important supplier. Because discharge is a fundamental pillar of the bankruptcy process, courts look closely at each reaffirmation to ensure that the creditor has not unfairly pressured the bankrupt. To be valid, either the court must determine that the reaffirmation is in the debtor's best interest and does not impose undue hardship, or the attorney representing the debtor must file an affidavit in court stating that the debtor's consent was informed and voluntary and the agreement does not create a hardship.

At some point in your life, you will borrow money. What moral obligation do you have to repay legitimate debts? Should you take the view that, if bankruptcy laws permit you to default on debts, then why not do so? Alternatively, if you get over your head in debt, should you struggle to pay even though you legitimately qualify for bankruptcy protection? Do the laws determine for you what is right and wrong, or should you have your own standard?

CHAPTER 11 REORGANIZATION

For a business, the goal of a Chapter 7 bankruptcy is euthanasia—putting it out of its misery by shutting it down and distributing its assets to creditors. Chapter 11 has a much more complicated and ambitious goal—resuscitating a business so that it can ultimately emerge as a viable economic concern.

Both individuals and businesses can use Chapter 11. Businesses usually prefer Chapter 11 over Chapter 7 because Chapter 11 does not require them to dissolve at the end as Chapter 7 does. The threat of death creates a powerful incentive to try rehabilitation under Chapter 11. Individuals, however, tend to prefer Chapter 13 because it is specifically designed for them.

A Chapter 11 proceeding follows many of the same steps as Chapter 7: a petition (either voluntary or involuntary), order for relief, meeting of creditors, proofs of claim, and an automatic stay. There are, however, some significant differences.

DEBTOR IN POSSESSION

Chapter 11 does not require a trustee. The bankrupt is called the **debtor in possession** and, in essence, serves as trustee. The debtor in possession has two jobs: to operate the business and to develop a plan of reorganization. A trustee is chosen only if the debtor is incompetent or uncooperative. In that case, the creditors can elect the trustee, but if they do not choose to do so, the U.S. Trustee appoints one.

CREDITORS' COMMITTEE

In a Chapter 11 case, the creditors' committee plays a particularly important role because typically there is no neutral trustee to watch over their interests. The committee has the right to help develop the plan of reorganization and to participate in any other way necessary to protect the interests of its constituency. The U.S. Trustee typically appoints the seven largest *un*secured creditors to the committee. Secured creditors do not serve because their interests require less protection. If the debtor is a corporation, the U.S. Trustee may also appoint a committee of **equity security holders** to represent shareholder interests.

PLAN OF REORGANIZATION

Once the bankruptcy petition is filed, an automatic stay goes into effect to provide the debtor with temporary relief from creditors. The next stage is to develop a plan of reorganization that provides for the payment of debts and the continuation of the business. For the first 120 days after the order for relief, the debtor has the exclusive right to propose a plan. If the shareholders and creditors accept it, then the bankruptcy case terminates. If the creditors or shareholders reject the debtor's plan, they may file their own version. The debtor has a strong incentive to develop a fair plan the first time because the creditors' proposals are likely to be less favorable.

Confirmation of the Plan

All the creditors and shareholders have the right to vote on the plan of organization. In preparation for the vote, each creditor and shareholder is assigned to a class. Chapter 11 classifies claims in the same way as Chapter 7: (1) secured claims, (2) priority claims, and (3) unsecured claims. Each secured claim is usually in its own class because each one is secured by different collateral. Shareholders are also divided into classes, depending upon their interests. For example, holders of preferred stock are in a different class from common shareholders.

The bankruptcy court will approve a plan if a majority *of each class* votes in favor of it. Even if some classes vote against the plan, the court can still confirm it under what is called a **cramdown** (as in "the plan is crammed down the creditors' throats"). The court will only impose a cramdown if, in its view, the plan is fair. If the court rejects the plan of reorganization, the creditors must develop a new one.

Discharge

A confirmed plan of reorganization is binding on the debtor, creditors, and shareholders. **The debtor now owns the assets in the bankrupt estate, free of all obligations except those listed in the plan.** Under a typical plan of reorganization, the debtor gives some current assets to creditors and also promises to pay them a portion of future earnings. In contrast, the Chapter 7 debtor typically relinquishes all assets (except exempt property) to creditors but then has no obligation to turn over future income. Exhibit 12.5 illustrates the steps in a Chapter 11 bankruptcy.

In the United States, most financially troubled companies liquidate under Chapter 7 rather than reorganizing under Chapter 11. As the following article explains, the opposite is true in Asia.

Exhibit 12.5

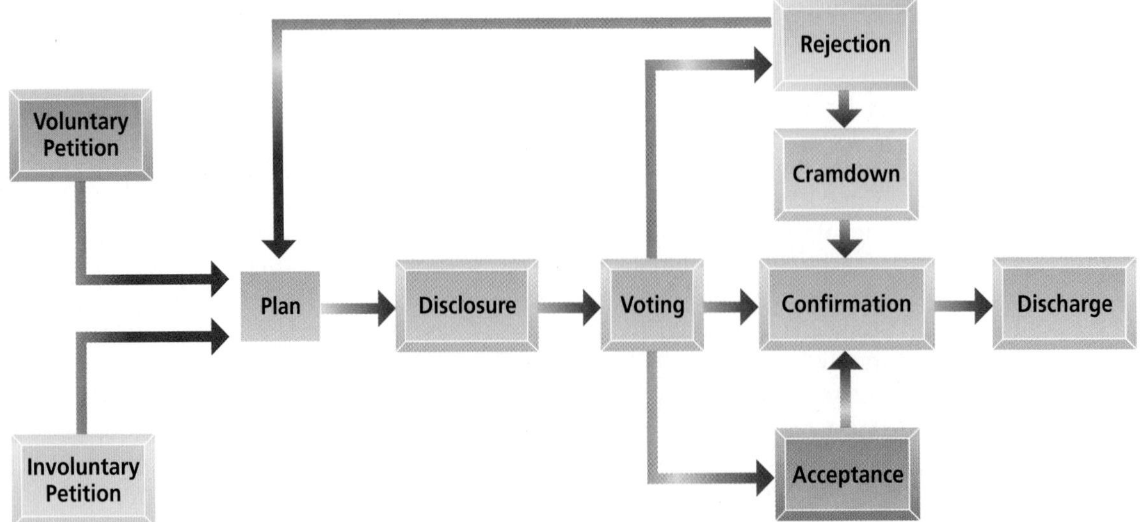

No business failure in Japan has been more traumatic than that of Hokkaido Takushoku Bank, one of the nation's biggest financial institutions. Its collapse sent the entire financial system into a tailspin and set off alarm bells that are still ringing in markets worldwide.

But now, take a walk inside the marble-pillared, wood-paneled halls of the bank's headquarters here on the northern island of Hokkaido. On a recent morning, more than 120 customers bustled about, making deposits and withdrawals. It is not that the bank rose like a phoenix from the ashes. It just never burned up. After announcing that the bank had failed, the government plugged it into a life-support system, and nothing really changed. It will be acquired soon by another institution, but many of its money-losing operations could continue indefinitely under another name.

Something similar is happening throughout Asia: corporations are "failing" in record numbers, but many keep on going anyway. As a result, the feeble are not eliminated, the fat is not trimmed, and the region's long-term prospects suffer. In Asia, big companies often hang on until they simply expire in a cloud of debt, rather than liquidate themselves or file for bankruptcy protection to restructure. In most countries here, the legal framework for bankruptcy is vague and loosely formed, management is given little protection against creditors, and there is rarely any thoroughgoing change. This sets the stage, not for a Darwinian struggle, but for survival of the flimsiest.[34]

CHAPTER 13 CONSUMER REORGANIZATIONS

The purpose of Chapter 13 is to rehabilitate an individual debtor. It is not available at all to businesses or to individuals with more than $250,000 in unsecured debts or $750,000 in secured debts. Under Chapter 13, the bankrupt consumer typically keeps most of her assets in exchange for a promise to repay some of her debts using future income. Therefore, to be eligible, the debtor must have a regular source of income. Individuals usually choose this chapter because it is easier and cheaper than Chapters 7 and 11. Consequently, more money is retained for both creditors and debtor.

A bankruptcy under Chapter 13 generally follows the same course as Chapter 11: the debtor files a petition, creditors submit proofs of claim, the court imposes an automatic stay, the debtor files a plan, and the court confirms the plan. But there are some differences.

BEGINNING A CHAPTER 13 CASE

To initiate a Chapter 13 case, the debtor must file a voluntary petition. **Creditors cannot use an involuntary petition to force a debtor into Chapter 13.** In all Chapter 13 cases, the U.S. Trustee appoints a trustee to supervise the debtor although the debtor remains in possession of the bankruptcy estate. The trustee also serves as a central clearinghouse for the debtor's payments to creditors. The

---

[34] Sheryl WuDunn, "Bankruptcy the Asian Way," *The New York Times*, Sept. 8, 1998, p. C1. Copyright © 1998 by The New York Times Co. Reprinted by permission.

debtor pays the trustee who, in turn, transmits these funds to creditors. For this service, the trustee is allowed to keep 10 percent of the payments.

PLAN OF PAYMENT

The debtor must file a plan of payment within 15 days after filing the voluntary petition. Only the debtor can file a plan; the creditors have no right to file their own version. Under the plan, the debtor must (1) commit some future earnings to pay off debts, (2) promise to pay all secured and priority claims in full, and (3) treat all remaining classes equally.

Within 30 days after filing the plan of payment, the debtor must begin making payments to the trustee under the plan. The trustee holds these payments until the plan is confirmed and then transmits them to creditors. The debtor continues to make payments to the trustee until the plan has been fully implemented. If the plan is rejected, the trustee returns the payments to the debtor.

Only the bankruptcy court has the authority to confirm or reject a plan of payment. Creditors have no right to vote on it. However, to confirm a plan, the court must ensure that:

- All of the unsecured creditors receive at least as much as they would have under Chapter 7
- The plan is feasible and the bankrupt will be able to make the promised payments
- The plan does not extend beyond three years without good reason and in no event lasts longer than five years; and
- The debtor is acting in good faith, making a reasonable effort to pay obligations.

In the following case, a creditor argued that the debtor's plan was not made in good faith.

IN RE LEMAIRE

898 F.2d 1346, 1990 U.S. App. LEXIS 4374
United States Court of Appeals for the Eighth Circuit, 1990

Facts: As Paul Handeen got out of his car one Sunday morning, Gregory LeMaire shot at him nine times with a bolt action rifle. Bullets struck Handeen in the mouth, neck, spine, arm, knee, and ankle. LeMaire pleaded guilty to a charge of aggravated assault and served 27 months in prison. After his release, he earned a doctorate from the University of Minnesota.

Handeen received a judgment of $50,000 against LeMaire. To avoid paying this judgment, LeMaire filed a bankruptcy petition under Chapter 13. He proposed a plan under which he would pay his creditors 42 percent of their claims. The bankruptcy court confirmed the plan over Handeen's objection. Handeen appealed to the district court, arguing that LeMaire had not filed his plan in good faith. The district court affirmed and, upon appeal, the appeals court also affirmed. Handeen then asked for a rehearing. This time, the appeals court granted a rehearing *en banc*. (Usually, only three judges hear an appeal. "*En banc*" means that all the judges on the court hear it.)

Issues: Is a judgment awarded to the victim of an intentional shooting dischargeable under Chapter 13? Did LeMaire file his plan in good faith?

Excerpts from Judge Gibson's Decision: In evaluating LeMaire's motivation and sincerity, the bankruptcy court balanced Handeen's desire to be compensated for his injuries against LeMaire's desire to have a fresh start and found the latter to outweigh the former in importance. The court noted that, while LeMaire had been unable to pay his debt to his victim, he had paid his debt to society by serving a prison sentence and had attempted to reorder his life and make a fresh start. The court found that forcing LeMaire to be burdened the rest of his life with a judgment which would continue to accrue interest, result in endless garnishments, and prevent him from accumulating property would be inimical to such a fresh start. The court concluded that LeMaire had made a wholehearted attempt to pay Handeen as much as possible, and that LeMaire's motivation was proper and his sincerity real.

We do not believe that LeMaire has fulfilled the good faith requirement of Chapter 13. The record here very clearly indicates that LeMaire intended to kill Handeen, and he nearly succeeded in his intention. While pre-filing conduct is not determinative of the good faith issue, it is nevertheless relevant. When we consider the pre-filing conduct here, including the maliciousness of the injury which LeMaire inflicted upon Handeen, in light of the lack of other factors sufficient to establish good faith, we are persuaded that the bankruptcy court clearly erred in finding that LeMaire proposed his plan in good faith.

We remand this case to the district court with instructions to remand, in turn, to the bankruptcy court for further proceedings consistent with this opinion.

DISCHARGE

Once confirmed, a plan is binding on all creditors, whether they like it or not. **The debtor is washed clean of all pre-petition debts except those provided for in the plan, but, unlike under Chapter 7, the debts are not *permanently* discharged.** If the debtor violates the plan, all of the debts are revived, and the creditors have a right to recover them under Chapter 7. The debts become permanently discharged only when the bankrupt fully complies with the plan.

If the debtor's circumstances change, the debtor, the trustee, or unsecured creditors can ask the court to modify the plan. Most such requests come from debtors whose income has declined. However, if the debtor's income rises, the creditors or the trustee can, in theory, ask that payments increase, too.

CHAPTER CONCLUSION

Borrowed money is the lubricant that keeps a modern economy motoring smoothly. Without it, many consumers would never own a home or a car, and many businesses would be unable to grow. But unless these debts are repaid, the economy will falter. Secured transactions are one method for insuring that creditors are paid.

Bankruptcy law is the safety net that catches those who are not able to meet their financial obligations. Bankruptcy laws cannot create assets where there are none (or not enough), but they can ensure that the debtor's assets, however limited, are fairly divided between the debtor and creditors. Any bankruptcy system that accomplishes this goal must be deemed a success.

CHAPTER REVIEW

1. Article 9 applies to any transaction intended to create a security interest in personal property or fixtures.
2. Attachment means that (1) the two parties made a security agreement *and either* the debtor has *authenticated a security agreement* describing the collateral *or* the secured party has obtained *possession or control*; and (2) the secured party gave value in order to get the security agreement; and (3) the debtor has rights in the collateral.
3. Attachment protects against the debtor. Perfection of a security interest protects the secured party against parties other than the debtor.
4. Filing is the most common way to perfect. For many forms of collateral, the secured party may also perfect by obtaining either possession or control.
5. A purchase money security interest (PMSI) is one taken by the person who sells the collateral or advances money so the debtor can buy the collateral.
6. A buyer in ordinary course of business (BIOC) takes the goods free of a security interest created by his seller even though the security interest is perfected.
7. Priority among secured parties is generally as follows:
   - **(a)** A party with a perfected security interest takes priority over a party with an unperfected interest.
   - **(b)** If neither secured party has perfected, the first interest to attach gets priority.
   - **(c)** Between perfected security interests, the first to file or perfect wins.
8. When the debtor defaults, the secured party may take possession of the collateral on its own, without a court order, if it can do so without a breach of the peace.
9. A secured party may sell, lease, or otherwise dispose of the collateral in any commercially reasonable way, or it may ignore the collateral and sue the debtor for the full debt.
10. When the debtor pays the full debt, the secured party must complete a termination statement, notifying the public that it no longer claims a security interest in the collateral.
11. The following chart sets out the important elements of each bankruptcy chapter.

	Chapter 7	Chapter 11	Chapter 13
Objective	Liquidation	Reorganization	Consumer reorganization
Who May Use It	Individual or organization	Individual or organization	Individual
Type of Petition	Voluntary or involuntary	Voluntary or involuntary	Only voluntary
Administration of Bankruptcy Estate	Trustee	Debtor in possession (trustee selected only if debtor is unable to serve)	Trustee
Selection of Trustee	Creditors have right to elect trustee; otherwise, U.S. Trustee makes appointment.	Usually no trustee	Appointed by U.S. Trustee
Participation in Formulation of Plan	No plan is filed.	Both creditors and debtor can propose plans.	Only debtor can propose a plan.
Creditor Approval of Plan	Creditors do not vote.	Creditors vote on plan, but court may approve plan without the creditors' support.	Creditors do not vote on plan.
Impact on Debtor's Post-petition Income	Not affected; debtor keeps all future earnings.	Must contribute toward payment of pre-petition debts	Must contribute toward payment of pre-petition debts

PRACTICE TEST

Note to the student: The following cases and problems were decided under the former Article 9. In each instance, the outcome would be the same under the revised laws.

1. **CPA QUESTION** Under the UCC Secured Transactions Article, perfection of a security interest by a creditor provides added protection against other parties in the event the debtor does not pay its debts. Which of the following parties is **not** affected by perfection of a security interest?

   (a) Other prospective creditors of the debtor

   (b) The trustee in a bankruptcy case

   (c) A buyer in the ordinary course of business

   (d) A subsequent personal injury judgment creditor

2. Eugene Ables ran an excavation company. He borrowed $500,000 from the Highland Park State Bank. Ables signed a note promising to repay the money and an agreement giving Highland a security interest in all of his equipment, including after-acquired equipment. Several years later, Ables agreed with Patricia Myers to purchase a Bantam Backhoe

from her for $16,000, which he would repay at the rate of $100 per month, while he used the machine. Ables later defaulted on his note to Highland, and the bank attempted to take the backhoe. Myers and Ables contended that the bank had no right to take the backhoe. Was the backhoe covered by Highland's security interest? Did Ables have sufficient rights in the backhoe for the bank's security interest to attach?

3. Jerry Payne owed the First State Bank of Pflugerville $342,000. The loan was secured by a 9.25-carat diamond ring. The bank claimed a default on the loan and, without notifying Payne, sold the ring. But the proceeds did not pay off the full debt, and the bank sued Payne for the deficiency. Is Payne liable for the deficiency?

4. John and Clara Lockovich bought a 22-foot Chaparrel Villian II boat from Greene County Yacht Club for $32,500. They paid $6,000 cash and borrowed the rest of the purchase money from Gallatin National Bank, which took a security interest in the boat. Gallatin filed a financing statement in *Greene* County, Pennsylvania, where the bank was located. But Pennsylvania law at that time required financing statements to be filed in the county of the debtor's residence, and the Lockoviches lived in *Allegheny* County. The Lockoviches soon washed up in Bankruptcy Court. Other creditors demanded that the boat be sold, claiming that Gallatin's security interest had been filed in the wrong place. Who wins? (Please be advised: this is a trick question.)

5. McMann Golf Ball Co. manufactured, as you might suppose, golf balls. Barwell, Inc. sold McMann a "preformer," a machine that makes golf balls, for $55,000. Barwell delivered the machine on February 20. McMann paid $3,000 down, the remainder to be paid over several years, and signed an agreement giving Barwell a security interest in the preformer. Barwell did not perfect its interest. On March 1, McMann borrowed $350,000 from First of America Bank, giving the bank a security interest in McMann's present and after-acquired property. First of America perfected by filing on March 2. McMann, of course, became insolvent, and both Barwell and the bank attempted to repossess the preformer. Who gets it?

6. **RIGHT & WRONG** On November 5, The Fred Hawes Organization, Inc., a small subcontractor, opened an account with Basic Distribution Corp., a supplier of construction materials. Hawes promised to pay its bills within 30 days of purchase. Although Hawes purchased a substantial quantity of goods on credit from Basic, it made few payments on the accounts until the following March when it paid Basic over $21,000. On May 14, Hawes filed a voluntary petition under Chapter 7. Does the bankruptcy trustee have a right to recover this payment? Is it fair to Hawes's other creditors if Basic is allowed to keep the $21,000 payment?

7. Mark Milbank built custom furniture in Port Chester, New York. His business was unsuccessful, and he repeatedly borrowed money from his wife and her father. He promised that the loans would enable him to spend more time with his family. Instead, he spent more time in bed with his next-door neighbor. After the divorce, his ex-wife and her father demanded repayment of the loans. When Milbank filed under Chapter 13, his ex-wife and her father asked the court not to discharge Milbank's debts on the grounds that he had acted in bad faith toward them. Should the bankruptcy court discharge Milbank's loans?

8. **CPA QUESTION** Decal Corp. incurred substantial operating losses for the past three years. Unable to meet its current obligations, Decal filed a petition of reorganization under Chapter 11 of the federal Bankruptcy Code. Which of the following statements is correct?

   (a) A creditors' committee, if appointed, will consist of unsecured creditors.

(b) The court must appoint a trustee to manage Decal's affairs.

(c) Decal may continue in business only with the approval of a trustee.

(d) The creditors' committee must select a trustee to manage Decal's affairs.

9. **CPA QUESTION** A voluntary petition filed under the liquidation provisions of Chapter 7 of the federal Bankruptcy Code:

(a) Is **not** available to a corporation unless it has previously filed a petition under the reorganization provisions of Chapter 11 of the Code

(b) Automatically stays collection actions against the debtor **except** by secured creditors

(c) Will be dismissed unless the debtor has 12 or more unsecured creditors whose claims total at least $5,000

(d) Does **not** require the debtor to show that the debtor's liabilities exceed the fair market value of assets

10. **YOU BE THE JUDGE WRITING PROBLEM** Lydia D'Ettore received a degree in computer programming at Devry Institute of Technology, with a grade-point average of 2.51. To finance her education, she borrowed $20,516.52 from a federal student loan program. After graduation, she could not find a job in her field, so she went to work as a clerk at a salary of $12,500. D'Ettore and her daughter lived with her parents free of charge. After setting aside $50 a month in savings and paying bills that included $233 for a new car (a Suzuki Samurai) and $50 for jewelry from Zales, her disposable income was $125 per month. D'Ettore asked the bankruptcy court to discharge the debts she owed Devry. Under the Code, these student loans cannot be discharged unless they impose an "undue hardship" on the debtor. Did the debts to Devry Institute impose an undue hardship on D'Ettore? **Argument for D'Ettore:** Lydia D'Ettore lives at home with her parents. Even so, her disposable income is a meager $125 a month. She would have to spend every single penny of her disposable income for nearly 15 years to pay back her $20,000 debt to Devry. That would be an undue hardship. **Argument for the Creditors:** The U.S. government guaranteed D'Ettore's loan. Therefore, if the court discharges it, the American taxpayer will have to pay the bill. Why should taxpayers subsidize an irresponsible student? D'Ettore must also stop buying new cars and jewelry. And why should the government pay her debts while she saves money every month?

INTERNET RESEARCH PROBLEM

Draft a security agreement in which your friend gives you a security interest in her $20,000 home entertainment system, in exchange for a loan of $12,000. Because the collateral is something that she uses daily, what special concerns do you have? How will you protect yourself? Next, find the UCC1 financing form at http://www.intercountyclearance.com/ra9/ra9ucc1.pdf. Print the form, then complete it. In what office of your state should you file in order to perfect?

You can find further practice problems in the Online Quiz at http://beatty.westbuslaw.com or in the Study Guide that accompanies this text.

UNIT

3

AGENCY & EMPLOYMENT

AGENCY

13

CHAPTER

It was a perfect spring day in Ashland, Ohio. Roger was having a great game as his Ohio State lacrosse team played a close match against Ashland University. Carefully gauging an Ashland pass, Roger stuck his stick out, intercepted the ball, whipped around, and launched a shot on goal. Score! His hands went up in the air. He never saw the Ashland player jump him from behind and knock him to the ground. But he did see the player stand over him, yelling obscenities. He also saw his teammate Brian grab the opponent in a bear hug. And he saw the Ashland player twist violently, throwing Brian to the ground, where he lay motionless. Brian never walked again—the blow to his head as he hit the ground left him a paraplegic. Brian sued Ashland, alleging that the university was responsible for his injury.[1]

Brian's parents hired a real estate broker to find a new house that was handicap accessible. They were so delighted with the one-story bungalow she located that they did not begrudge paying her an $18,000 commission. But after the sale they discovered that the seller of the house had also paid her a commission. They sued for the return of their $18,000.

Nonetheless, the house was perfect for their needs, and they stocked it with all the custom-made items that Brian required. Because these medical devices were so expensive, they asked their insurance agent to increase their

---

[1] Based on *Hanson v. Kynast*, 24 Ohio St. 3d 171, 494 N.E.2d 1091, 1986 Ohio LEXIS 667 (Ohio 1986).

house coverage from $400,000 to $800,000. Brian and his parents suffered a terrible blow a few months later when they returned home from an exhausting visit to the hospital to find their new house burned to the ground. They were even more distressed when they discovered that the insurance agent had misread his notes and only increased their policy to $480,000. They sued him for $320,000.

This example raises several questions of agency law. Thus far, this book has primarily dealt with issues of individual responsibility: What happens if *you* knock someone down or *you* sign an agreement? Agency law, on the other hand, is concerned with your responsibility for the actions of others. What happens if your agent assaults someone or enters into an agreement? Agency law presents a significant trade-off: if you do everything yourself, you have control over the result. But the size and scope of your business (and your life) will be severely limited. Once you hire other people, you can accomplish a great deal more, but your risk of legal liability increases immensely. Though it might be safer to do everything yourself, that is not a practical decision for most business owners (or most people). The alternative is to hire carefully and to limit the risks as much as possible by understanding the law of agency.

Was Ashland University liable for Brian's injuries? It would have been if the Ashland player had been an agent of the university. But, on a similar set of facts, the Ohio Supreme Court held that the Ashland player was not an agent because Ashland had no *control* over him and he was not playing for the school's *benefit*. However, the real estate broker was an agent for Brian's parents. She violated her *duty of loyalty* to them when she acted for both buyer and seller in the same transaction, without disclosing her dual role to both parties. An agent who violates this important duty must forfeit her commission. And the insurance agent violated his *duty of care* when he bought a policy in the wrong amount for Brian's parents. An agent who violates this duty is liable for the harm his carelessness has caused—in this case $320,000.

CREATING AN AGENCY RELATIONSHIP

Principals have substantial liability for the actions of their agents.[2] Therefore, disputes about whether an agency relationship exists are not mere legal quibbles but important issues with potentially profound financial consequences. According to the Restatement of Agency:

> Agency is the fiduciary relation which results from the manifestation of consent by one person to another that the other shall act on his behalf and subject to his control, and consent by the other so to act.[3]

---

[2] The word "principal" is always used when referring to a person. It is not to be confused with the word "principle," which refers to a fundamental idea.

[3] Section 1 of the Restatement (Second) of Agency (1958), prepared by the American Law Institute.

In other words, in an agency relationship, someone (the agent) agrees to perform a task for, and under the control of, someone else (the principal). To create an agency relationship, there must be:

- A **principal** and
- An **agent**
- Who mutually **consent** that the agent will act on behalf of the principal and
- Be subject to the principal's **control**
- Thereby creating a **fiduciary** relationship.

CONSENT

To establish consent, the principal must ask the agent to do something and the agent must agree. In the most straightforward example, Brian's parents asked their insurance agent to buy a policy on their house, and he agreed. Matters were more complicated, however, when David Hudson went drinking at a tavern in Little Compton, Rhode Island. The beer he drank was brewed by Anheuser-Busch and sold to a distributor who sold it to the tavern who hired a bartender who served Hudson—all too many glasses. After leaving the tavern, Hudson crashed into Christopher Lawrence's car, killing the young man. Lawrence's parents sued Anheuser-Busch and the distributor alleging that the companies had an agency relationship with the tavern. The court, however, found that no agency relationship existed because neither the brewer nor the distributor ever agreed that the tavern would act on their behalf. Without consent, there was no agency relationship and, thus, no liability for brewer or distributor.[4]

CONTROL

Principals are liable for the acts of their agents because they exercise control over the agents. If principals direct their agents to commit an act, it seems fair to hold the principal liable when that act causes harm. In the following example, did Northwest Airlines exercise control over Kuwait Air?

The horse-drawn caisson wound slowly through Arlington National Cemetery and stopped in front of lot number 59, the section reserved for victims of terrorist acts. The flag-draped casket of William L. Stanford, one of the two Agency for International Development auditors killed by plane hijackers in Iran, was carried to the gravesite amid full military honors. Three volleys of rifle fire pierced the unusually warm December air as scores of family, friends, and colleagues lowered their heads and wept. Stanford, 52, was killed as he was traveling to join his wife and 13-year-old daughter in Karachi, Pakistan, where he intended to spend the holidays.[5]

---

[4] *Lawrence v. Anheuser-Busch, Inc.*, 523 A.2d 864, 1987 R.I. LEXIS 451 (R.I. 1987).

[5] Mary Jordan, "Terrorists' Victim Is Buried," *The Washington Post*, Dec. 18, 1984, p. A14.

The hijacked plane—with William Stanford aboard—was a Kuwait Airways (KA) flight from Kuwait to Pakistan. Stanford had originally purchased a ticket on Northwest Airlines but had traded in his Northwest ticket for a seat on the KA flight. Stanford's widow sued Northwest on the theory that KA was Northwest's agent. The airlines had an agreement permitting passengers to exchange tickets from one to another. In this case, however, the court found that no agency relationship existed because Northwest had no *control* over KA.[6] Northwest did not tell KA how to fly planes or handle terrorists; therefore it should not be liable when KA made fatal errors. An agent and principal must not only *consent* to an agency relationship, but the principal must also have *control* over the agent.

FIDUCIARY RELATIONSHIP

A fiduciary relationship is a special relationship, with high standards. The beneficiary places special confidence in the fiduciary who, in turn, is obligated to act in good faith and candor, putting his own needs second. The purpose of a fiduciary relationship is for one person to benefit another. **Agents have a fiduciary duty to their principals.** When, in the chapter introduction, Brian's parents hired a real estate broker to find a house for them, she was a fiduciary, obligated to act in their best interest alone. She violated this duty when she also acted for the seller of the house, without telling Brian's parents.

All three elements—consent, control, and a fiduciary duty—are necessary to create an agency relationship. In some relationships, for example, there might be a *fiduciary duty* but no *control*. A trustee of a trust must act for the benefit of the beneficiaries, but the beneficiaries have no right to control the trustee. Therefore, a trustee is not an agent of the beneficiaries. *Consent* is present in every contractual relationship, but that does not necessarily mean that the two parties are agent and principal. If Horace sells his car to Lily, they both expect to benefit under the contract, but neither has a *fiduciary duty* to the other and neither *controls* the other, so there is no agency relationship.

ELEMENTS NOT REQUIRED FOR AN AGENCY RELATIONSHIP

Consent, control, and a fiduciary relationship are necessary to establish an agency relationship. The following elements are **not** required:

- *A Written Agreement.* In most cases, an agency agreement does not have to be in writing. An oral understanding is valid, except in one circumstance—the **equal dignities rule**. According to this rule, if an agent is empowered to enter into a contract that must be in writing, then the appointment of the agent must also be written. For example, under the statute of frauds a contract for the sale of land is unenforceable unless in writing, so the agency agreement to sell land must also be *in writing*.
- *A Formal Agreement.* The principal and agent need not agree formally that they have an agency relationship. They do not even have to think the word

[6] *Stanford v. Kuwait Airways Corp.*, 648 F. Supp. 1158, 1986 U.S. Dist. LEXIS 18880 (S.D.N.Y. 1986).

"agent." As long as they act like an agent and a principal, the law will treat them as such.

- *Consideration.* An agency relationship need not meet all the standards of contract law. For example, a contract is not valid without consideration, but an agency agreement is valid even *if the agent is not paid.*

DUTIES OF AGENTS TO PRINCIPALS

Agents owe a fiduciary duty to their principals. In the following example, these employees of International Creative Management (ICM) were agents—they had agreed to act on behalf of ICM and be subject to its control. Did they violate their duty?

At 11:30 one night, Jeff Berg, the chairman of ICM in Hollywood, received an emergency phone call from a company assistant. Unexpectedly returning to the office, the assistant had come upon several employees hauling boxes of files out to their cars. The culprits were four top employees leaving to start their own creative management firm. "This was an act of trespass," Mr. Berg said. "We have been advised by counsel that this conduct is actionable." Mr. Berg added that the material taken involved documents about clients and the firm's business matters. ICM represented stars such as Mel Gibson, Julia Roberts, Arnold Schwarzenegger, Michelle Pfeiffer, and Jodie Foster. Under pressure from Mr. Berg, the employees returned all the files by dawn.[7]

DUTY OF LOYALTY

The agent must act solely for the benefit of the principal in all matters connected with the agency.[8] The agent has an obligation to put the principal first, to strive to accomplish the principal's goals. By removing files that belonged to ICM, these employees were violating their duty of loyalty to their principal because they were acting in their own interest, not that of their principal. It is not surprising that, once caught, they returned the property immediately.

An agent is bound by the duty of loyalty, *whether or not the agent and principal have consciously agreed to it.* The agent should know his obligations. However, a principal and agent can change this rule by agreement. ICM could, for example, have granted its employees permission to remove the files, in which case, they would not have been liable. The various components of the duty of loyalty follow.

OUTSIDE BENEFITS

An agent may not receive profits unless the principal knows and approves. Suppose that Hope, an employee of ICM, has been representing Arnold Schwarzenegger in his latest movie negotiations.[9] He often drives her to

---

[7] Bernard Weinraub, "After Dark, 4 Agents Light Out," *The New York Times*, Mar. 30, 1995, p. C13.

[8] Restatement (Second) of Agency §387.

meetings in his new Humvee military vehicle. He is so thrilled that she has arranged for him to star in the new movie, *Little Men*, that he buys her a Humvee. Can Hope keep this generous gift? Only with ICM's permission. She must tell ICM about the Humvee; the company may then take the vehicle itself or allow her to keep it.

CONFIDENTIAL INFORMATION

The ability to keep secrets is important in any relationship, but especially a fiduciary relationship. Agents can neither disclose nor use for their own benefit any confidential information they acquire during their agency. As the following case shows, this duty continues even after the agency relationship ends.

ABKCO MUSIC, INC. v. HARRISONGS MUSIC, LTD.

722 F.2d 988, 1983 U.S. App. LEXIS 15562
United States Court of Appeals for the Second Circuit, 1983

Facts: Bright Tunes Music Corp. (Bright Tunes) owned the copyright to the song "He's So Fine." The company sued George Harrison, a Beatle, alleging that the Harrison composition "My Sweet Lord" copied "He's So Fine." At the time the suit was filed, Allen B. Klein handled the business affairs of the Beatles.

Klein (representing Harrison) met with the president of Bright Tunes to discuss possible settlement of the copyright lawsuit. Klein suggested that Harrison might be interested in purchasing the copyright to "He's So Fine." Shortly thereafter, Klein's management contract with the Beatles expired. Without telling Harrison, Klein began negotiating with Bright Tunes to purchase the copyright to "He's So Fine" for himself. To advance these negotiations, Klein gave Bright Tunes information about royalty income for "My Sweet Lord"—information that he had gained as Harrison's agent.

The trial judge in the copyright case ultimately found that Harrison had infringed the copyright on "He's So Fine" and assessed damages of $1,599,987. After the trial, Klein purchased the "He's So Fine" copyright from Bright Tunes and with it, the right to recover from Harrison for the breach of copyright.

Issue: Did Klein violate his fiduciary duty to Harrison by using confidential information after the agency relationship terminated?

Excerpts from Judge Pierce's Decision: There is no doubt that the relationship between Harrison and [Klein] prior to the termination of the management agreement was that of principal and agent, and that the relationship was fiduciary in nature. [A]n agent has a duty not to use confidential knowledge acquired in his employment in competition with his principal. This duty exists as well after the employment is terminated as during its continuance. On the other hand, use of information based on general business knowledge or gleaned from general business experience is not covered by the rule, and the former agent is permitted to compete with his former principal in reliance on such general publicly available information.

The evidence presented herein is not at all convincing that the information imparted to Bright Tunes by Klein was publicly available. Under the circumstances of this case, where there was sufficient evidence to support the district judge's finding that confidential information passed hands, or, at least was utilized in a

[9] Do not be confused by the fact that these ICM employees work as agents for movie stars. As employees of ICM, their duty is to the company. The employees are agents of ICM, and ICM works for the celebrities.

manner inconsistent with the duty of a former fiduciary at a time when litigation was still pending, we conclude that the district judge did not err in holding that [Klein] had breached [his] duty to Harrison.

While the initial attempt to purchase [the copyright to "He's So Fine"] was several years removed from the eventual purchase on [Klein]'s own account, we are not of the view that such a fact rendered [Klein] unfettered in the later negotiations. Taking all of these circumstances together, we agree that [Klein's] conduct did not meet the standard required of him as a former fiduciary.

To listen to the two songs involved in this case, tune in to http://www.benedict.com.

Klein was angry that the Beatles had failed to renew his management contract. Was it reasonable for him to think that he owed no duty to the principal who had fired him? Should his sense of ethics have told him that his behavior was wrong? Would the ethics checklist in Chapter 2 have helped Klein to make a better decision?

COMPETITION WITH THE PRINCIPAL

Agents are not allowed to compete with their principal in any matter within the scope of the agency business. If Allen Klein had purchased the "He's So Fine" copyright while he was George Harrison's agent, he would have committed an additional sin against the agency relationship. Owning song rights was clearly part of the agency business, so Klein could not make such purchases without Harrison's consent. Once the agency relationship ends, however, so does the rule against competition. Klein was entitled to buy the "He's So Fine" copyright after the agency relationship ended (as long as he did not use confidential information).

CONFLICT OF INTEREST BETWEEN TWO PRINCIPALS

Unless otherwise agreed, an agent may not act for two principals whose interests conflict. Suppose Travis represents both director Steven Spielberg and actress Julia Roberts. Spielberg is casting the title role in his new movie, *Nancy Drew: Girl Detective*, a role that Roberts covets. Travis cannot represent these two clients when they are negotiating with each other, unless they both know about the conflict and agree to ignore it. The following article illustrates the dangers of acting for two principals at once.

Faced with growing health care and retirement costs, the Sisters of Charity decided to sell a 207-acre property that they owned in New Jersey. The order of nuns soon found, however, that the world is not always a charitable place. They agreed to sell the land to Linpro for nearly $10 million. But before the deal closed, Linpro signed a contract to resell the property to Sammis for $34 million. So, you say, the sisters made a bad deal. There is no law against that. But it turned out that the nuns' lawyer, Peter Berkley, also represented Sammis. He knew about the deal between Sammis and Linpro, but never told the sisters. Was that the charitable—or legal—thing to do? For ideas on how Berkley should have handled this delicate situation, look at the discussion on dual agency at http://www.royallepage.ca/halifax/agency.htm.

SECRETLY DEALING WITH THE PRINCIPAL

If a principal hires an agent to arrange a transaction, the agent may not become a party to the transaction without the principal's permission. Matt Damon became an overnight sensation after starring in the movie *Good Will Hunting*. Suppose that he hired Trang to read scripts for him. Unbeknownst to Damon, Trang had written her own script, which she thought would be ideal for him. She may not sell it to him without revealing that she wrote it herself. Damon may be perfectly happy to buy Trang's script, but he has the right, as her principal, to know that she is the person selling it.

APPROPRIATE BEHAVIOR

An agent may not engage in inappropriate behavior that reflects badly on the principal. This rule applies even to *off-duty* conduct. For instance, a group of New York City Police officers who were attending a meeting in Washington, D.C. went on a drunken rampage in their hotel. They sprayed fire extinguishers, set off alarms, and slid naked down escalator railings that they had lubricated with beer. Although the officers were off-duty and in a different city, their conduct caused bystanders to lose respect for their principal—the New York City Police Department. Afterwards, many of these officers were dismissed from the force.

OTHER DUTIES OF AN AGENT

In June, Mr. and Mrs. Harding left for a five-week trip to England. Before leaving, they hired Angie to sell or rent their vacation house in Grantham, New Hampshire. The regional "Multiple Listing Service" was the best way to publicize a house for sale. But Angie was busy with one thing or another and never got around to listing the Harding's house. However, at the end of June, Angie was contacted by the Fords, who happened to be friends of friends. They told her that their son was a contractor who would like to build a house for them in Grantham, but they needed to rent a place to live in the meantime. Angie showed them the Hardings' house as a rental. Although it was not quite right for the Fords (too many stairs, no separate apartment for Mrs. Ford's mother), it was the best they had seen, so they offered to rent it for a year at $750 per month, beginning the first of September.

Angie called Mrs. Harding in England and told her that the Fords "were a nice couple who might very well be interested in buying the house after a year's rental." Mrs. Harding responded that $750 was too low, especially over the summer months when the house often rented out for as much as $1,000 per *week*. She proposed a contract from September 1 to June 1 at a rent of $800 per month. Angie indicated that the Fords would probably be willing to make a deal on that basis because they loved the house. Mrs. Harding told Angie to call back if there was any problem, but otherwise she would sign the lease when she returned home. The following week, the Fords told Angie that they would agree to $800 a month, but insisted on being able to stay from September to September so that they would have time to complete construction on their new house.

Angie had a list of the Hardings' phone numbers in England, but she made no further effort to contact them there. Instead, she left a message on their home answering machine. When the Fords pressed her three or four times for a definite answer, she said she could not get in touch with the Hardings and suggested the Fords look for another house. When Mrs. Harding returned home, she called Angie and was told that "the Fords are coming up next week to confirm everything." Mrs. Harding called the Fords herself. She then learned the truth about what had happened and also that the Fords were going to Grantham to look at another house, which they ultimately rented.

Although Angie had not violated her *duty of loyalty* to the Hardings, they were still angry at her. Had she violated any of the other duties that agents owe to their principals?

DUTY TO OBEY INSTRUCTIONS

An agent must obey her principal's instructions, unless the principal directs her to behave illegally or unethically. Mrs. Harding instructed Angie to call her if the Fords rejected the offer. Angie violated her duty to obey instructions when she neglected to call Mrs. Harding back. If, however, the Hardings had asked her to say that the house's basement was dry, when in fact it looked like a rice paddy every spring, Angie would be under no obligation to follow those illegal instructions.

DUTY OF CARE

An agent has a duty to act with reasonable care. In other words, an agent must act as a reasonable person would, under the circumstances. A reasonable person would not have left a message on the Hardings' home answering machine when she knew they were in Europe.

Under some circumstances, an agent is held to a higher—or lower—standard than usual. **An agent with special skills is held to a higher standard because she is expected to use those skills.** A trained real estate agent should know enough to use the "Multiple Listing Service."

But suppose the Hardings had asked their neighbor, Jed, to help them sell their house. Jed is not a trained real estate agent, and he is not being paid, which makes him a *gratuitous agent*. A gratuitous agent is held to a lower standard because he is doing his principal a favor and, as the old saying goes, you get what you pay for—up to a point. **Gratuitous agents are liable if they commit *gross* negligence, but not *ordinary* negligence.** If Jed, as a gratuitous agent, left the Hardings an important message on their answering machine because he forgot they were in England, he would not be liable to them for that ordinary negligence. But if the answering machine had a message that *warned* him the Hardings were away and would not be picking up messages, he would be liable for gross negligence and a violation of his duty.

DUTY TO PROVIDE INFORMATION

An agent has a duty to provide the principal with all information in her possession that she has reason to believe the principal wants to know. She also has a duty to provide accurate information. Did Angie violate this duty? In the following case, the agent violated both its duty of care and its duty to provide information.

GRIGSBY v. O.K. TRAVEL

118 Ohio App. 3d 671, 693 N.E.2d 1142, 1997 Ohio App. LEXIS 875
Court of Appeals of Ohio, 1997

Facts: In the window of O.K. Travel, Oma Grigsby saw an advertisement for a tour of Israel that was organized by Trinity Tours. Grigsby signed up for the tour and paid O.K. About a week before Grigsby was to leave for the tour, O.K discovered that Trinity was out of business. O.K. contacted the American Society of Travel Agents, which notified O.K. that Trinity did not carry the financial bond required by the state of Ohio. Grigsby filed suit against O.K., alleging that it had violated its duty of care and its duty to provide information.

Issue: Did O.K. violate the duties it owed Grigsby?

Excerpts from Judge Painter's Decision: Customers come to travel agents because these agents hold themselves out as having knowledge about how to travel to places "foreign" to the traveler. For this reason, travel agents are the special agents of the traveler for securing a trip. A travel agent is more than a ticket supplier. Travel agents have become a professional segment of today's complex travel world.

When assisting in planning a vacation, a travel agent has a duty to act with the care, skill, and diligence that a fiduciary rendering that kind of service would reasonably be expected to use. The agent must make reasonable inquiries into the current financial stability of the person or entity with whom she recommended her principal do business. The duty, then, is to discover and disclose material information that is reasonably obtainable. If a tour operator or promoter defaults due to discoverable circumstances, the travel agent earning a commission from selling the tours should bear the loss if the agent fails to disclose the relevant risks.

Trinity, as a tour promoter, was required to register with the Secretary of State before commencing business in this state. A tour promoter must also provide a bond ($50,000 for interstate or international travel) in favor of the state before commencing operations. Upon registration, a tour promoter shall use the statement "registered Ohio tour promoter" and its registration number in any and all advertisements in Ohio. The advertisement for the Israel tour from Trinity was devoid of this statement and Trinity's registration number. Trinity could not have even provided a registration number because it was not registered in Ohio and never provided a bond, as statutorily required.

O.K. breached its duty to Grigsby by failing to disclose to Grigsby that Trinity was not registered in Ohio and had no bond posted which could have provided security in case it defaulted. This information was reasonably obtainable, and in fact should have been clear to O.K. (at least O.K. was put on notice), because Trinity's advertisement did not have the statutorily required language and registration number.

The judgment of the trial court in favor of Grigsby is affirmed.

PRINCIPAL'S REMEDIES WHEN THE AGENT BREACHES A DUTY

A principal has three potential remedies when an agent breaches her duty:

- The principal can recover from the agent any **damages** the breach has caused. Thus, if the Hardings can only rent their house for $600 a month instead of the $800 the Fords offered, Angie would be liable for $2,400—$200 a month for one year.

- If an agent breaches the duty of loyalty, he must turn over to the principal any **profits** he has earned as a result of his wrongdoing. Thus, after Klein violated his duty of loyalty to Harrison, he forfeited profits he would have earned from the copyright of "He's So Fine."

- If the agent has violated her duty of loyalty, the principal may **rescind** the transaction. When Trang sold a script to her principal, Matt Damon, without telling him that she was the author, she violated her duty of loyalty. Damon could rescind the contract to buy the script.[10]

DUTIES OF PRINCIPALS TO AGENTS

In a typical agency relationship, the agent agrees to perform tasks for the principal, and the principal agrees to pay the agent. The range of tasks undertaken by an agent is limited only by the imagination of the principal. Because the agent's job can be so varied, the law has needed to define an agent's duties carefully. The role of the principal, on the other hand, is typically less complicated—often little more than writing a check to pay the agent. Thus the law enumerates fewer duties for the principal. Primarily, the principal must reimburse the agent for reasonable expenses and cooperate with the agent in performing agency tasks. The respective duties of agents and principals can be summarized as follows:

Duties of Agents to Principals	Duty of Principals to Agents
Duty of loyalty	Duty to reimburse
Duty to obey instructions	Duty to cooperate
Duty of care	
Duty to provide information	

DUTY TO REIMBURSE THE AGENT

As a general rule, the principal must **indemnify** (that is, reimburse) the agent for any expenses she has reasonably incurred. These reimbursable expenses fall into three categories:

- **A principal must indemnify an agent for any expenses or damages reasonably incurred in carrying out his agency responsibilities.** For example, Peace Baptist Church of Birmingham, Alabama, asked its pastor to buy land for a new church. He paid part of the the purchase price out of his own pocket, but the church refused to reimburse him. Although the pastor lost in church, he won in court.[11]

---

[10] A principal can rescind his contract with an agent who has violated her duty, but, as we shall see later in the chapter, the principal might not be able to rescind a contract with a third party when the agent misbehaves.

[11] *Lauderdale v. Peace Baptist Church of Birmingham*, 246 Ala. 178, 19 So. 2d 538, 1944 Ala. LEXIS 508 (1944).

- **A principal must indemnify an agent for tort claims brought by a third party if the principal authorized the agent's behavior and the agent did not realize he was committing a tort.** Marisa owns all the apartment buildings on Elm Street, except one. She hires Rajiv to manage the units and tells him that, under the terms of the leases, she has the right to ask guests to leave if a party becomes too rowdy. But she forgets to tell Rajiv that she does not own one of the buildings, which happens to house a college sorority. One night, when the sorority is having a rambunctious party, Rajiv hustles over and starts ejecting the noisy guests. The sorority is furious and sues Rajiv for trespass. If the sorority wins its suit against Rajiv, Marisa would have to pay the judgment, plus Rajiv's attorney's fees, because she had told him to quell noisy parties, and he did not realize he was trespassing.
- **The principal must indemnify the agent for any liability she incurs from third parties as a result of entering into a contract on the principal's behalf, including attorney's fees and reasonable settlements.** An agent signed a contract to buy cucumbers for Vlasic Food Products Co. to use in making pickles. When the first shipment of cucumbers arrived, Vlasic inspectors found them unsuitable and directed the agent to refuse the shipment. The agent found himself in a pickle when the cucumber farmer sued. The agent notified Vlasic, but the company refused to defend him. He settled the claim himself for $29,000 and, in turn, sued Vlasic. The court ordered Vlasic to reimburse the agent because he had notified them of the suit and had acted reasonably and in good faith.[12]

Duty to Cooperate

Principals have a duty to cooperate with their agent:

- **The principal must furnish the agent with the opportunity to work.** If Lewis agrees to serve as Ida's real estate agent, Ida must allow Lewis access to the house. It is unlikely that Lewis will be able to sell the house without taking anyone inside.
- **The principal cannot unreasonably interfere with the agent's ability to accomplish his task.** Ida allows Lewis to show the house, but she refuses to clean it and then makes disparaging comments to prospective purchasers. "I really get tired of living in such a dank, dreary house," she says. "And the neighborhood children are vicious juvenile delinquents." This behavior would constitute unreasonable interference with an agent.
- **The principal must perform her part of the contract.** Once the agent has successfully completed the task, the principal must pay him, even if the principal has changed her mind and no longer wants the agent to perform. Ida is a 78-year-old widow who has lived alone for many years in a house that she loves. Her asking price is outrageously high. But, lo and behold, Lewis finds a couple who are happy to pay Ida's price. There is only one problem. Ida does not really want to sell. She put her house on the market because she enjoys showing it to all the folks who move to town. She rejects

---

[12] *Long v. Vlasic Food Products Co.*, 439 F.2d 229, 1971 U.S. App. LEXIS 11455 (4th Cir. 1971).

the offer. Now there is a second problem. The contract provided that Lewis would find a willing buyer at the asking price. Since he has done so, Ida must pay his real estate commission, even if she does not want to sell her house.

TERMINATING AN AGENCY RELATIONSHIP

Either the agent or the principal can terminate the agency relationship at any time. In addition, the relationship terminates automatically if the principal or agent can no longer perform their required duties or a change in circumstances renders the agency relationship pointless.

TERMINATION BY AGENT OR PRINCIPAL

The two parties—principal and agent—have five choices in terminating their relationship:

- *Term Agreement.* The principal and agent can agree in advance how long their relationship will last. Alexandra hires Boris to help her purchase exquisite enameled Easter eggs made for the Russian czars by Fabergé. If they agree that the relationship will last five years, they have a term agreement.
- *Achieving a Purpose.* The principal and agent can agree that the agency relationship will terminate when the principal's goals have been achieved. Alexandra and Boris might agree that their relationship will end when Alexandra has purchased 10 eggs.
- *Mutual Agreement.* No matter what the principal and agent agree at the start, they can always change their minds later on, as long as the change is mutual. If Boris and Alexandra originally agree to a five-year term, but after only three years Boris decides he wants to go back to business school and Alexandra runs out of money, they can decide together to terminate the agency.
- *Agency at Will.* If they make no agreement in advance about the term of the agreement, either principal or agent can terminate at any time.
- *Wrongful Termination.* An agency relationship is a *personal* relationship. Hiring an agent is not like buying a book. You might not care which copy of the book you buy, but you do care which agent you hire. If an agency relationship is not working out, the courts will not force the agent and principal to stay together. **Either party always has the *power* to walk out. They may not, however, have the *right*.** If one party's departure from the agency relationship violates the agreement and causes harm to the other party, the wrongful party must pay damages. He will nonetheless be permitted to leave. If Boris has agreed to work for Alexandra for five years but he wants to leave after three, he can leave, provided he pays Alexandra the cost of hiring and training a replacement.

If the agent is a *gratuitous* agent (i.e., is not being paid), he has both the power and the right to quit any time he wants, regardless of the agency agreement. If Boris is doing this job for Alexandra as a favor, he will not owe her damages when he stops work.

Principal or Agent Can No Longer Perform Required Duties

If the principal or the agent is unable to perform the duties required under the agency agreement, the agreement terminates.

- **If either the agent or the principal fails to obtain (or keep) a license necessary to perform duties under the agency agreement, the agreement ends.** Caleb hires Allegra to represent him in a lawsuit. If she is disbarred, their agency agreement terminates because the agent is no longer allowed in court. Alternatively, if Emil hires Bess to work in his gun shop, their agency relationship terminates when he loses his license to sell firearms.
- **The bankruptcy of the agent or the principal terminates an agency relationship only if it affects their ability to perform.** Bankruptcy rarely interferes with an agent's responsibilities. After all, there is generally no reason why an agent cannot continue to act for the principal whether the agent is rich or poor. If Lewis, the real estate agent, becomes bankrupt he can continue to represent Ida or anyone else who wants to sell a house. The bankruptcy of a principal is different, however, because after filing for bankruptcy, the principal loses control of his assets. A bankrupt principal may be unable to pay the agent or honor contracts that the agent enters into on his behalf. Therefore, the bankruptcy of a principal is more likely to terminate an agency relationship.
- **An agency relationship terminates upon the death or incapacity of either the principal or the agent.** Agency is a personal relationship, and when the principal dies, the agent cannot act on behalf of a nonexistent person.[13] Of course, a nonexistent person cannot act either, so the relationship also terminates when the agent dies. Incapacity has the same legal effect because either the principal or the agent is, at least temporarily, unable to act.
- **If the agent violates her duty of loyalty, the agency agreement automatically terminates.** Agents are appointed to represent the principal's interest; if they fail to do so, there is no point to the relationship. Sam is negotiating a military procurement contract on behalf of his employer, Missiles R Us, Inc. In the midst of these negotiations, he becomes very friendly with Louisa, the government negotiator. One night over drinks, he tells Louisa what Missiles' real costs are on the project and the lowest bid it could possibly make. By passing on this confidential information, Sam has violated his duty of loyalty, and his agency relationship terminates.

---

[13] Restatement (Second) of Agency §120, Comment *a*.

CHANGE IN CIRCUMSTANCES

After the agency agreement is negotiated, circumstances may change. If these changes are significant enough to undermine the purpose of the agreement, then the relationship ends automatically. Andrew hires Melissa to sell his country farm for $100,000. Shortly thereafter, the largest oil reserve in North America is discovered nearby. The farm is now worth 10 times Andrew's asking price. Melissa's authority terminates automatically. Other changes in circumstance that affect an agency agreement are:

- *Loss or Destruction of Subject Matter.* Andrew hired Damian to sell his Palm Beach condominium, but before Damian could even measure the living room, Andrew's creditors attached the condo. Damian is no longer authorized to sell the real estate because Andrew has "lost" the subject matter of his agency agreement with Damian.
- *Change of Law.* If the agent's responsibilities become illegal, the agency agreement terminates. Oscar has hired Marta to ship him succulent avocados from California's Imperial Valley. Before she sends the shipment, Mediterranean fruit flies are discovered, and all fruits and vegetables in California are quarantined. The agency agreement terminates because it is now illegal to ship the California avocados.

EFFECT OF TERMINATION

Once an agency relationship ends, the agent no longer has the authority to act for the principal. If she continues to act, she is liable to the principal for any damages he incurs as a result. The Mediterranean fruit fly quarantine ended Marta's agency. If she sends Oscar the avocados anyway and he is fined for possession of a fruit fly, Marta must pay the fine.

The agent loses her authority to act, but some of the duties of both the principal and agent continue even after the relationship ends:

- *Principal's Duty to Indemnify Agent.* Oscar must reimburse Marta for expenses she incurred before the agency ended. If Marta accumulated mileage on her car during her search for the perfect avocado, Oscar must pay her for gasoline and depreciation. But he owes her nothing for her expenses after the agency relationship ends.
- *Confidential Information.* Remember the "He's So Fine" case earlier in the chapter. George Harrison's agent used confidential information to negotiate, on his own behalf, the purchase of the "He's So Fine" copyright. An agent is not entitled to use confidential information, even after the agency relationship terminates.

LIABILITY

Thus far, this chapter has dealt with the relationship *between* principals and agents. Although an agent can dramatically increase his principal's ability to accomplish her goals, an agency relationship also dramatically increases the risk of legal liability to third parties. A principal may be liable in contract for agreements that the agent signs and also liable in tort for harm the agent causes. Indeed, once a principal hires an agent, she may be liable to third parties for his acts, even if he disobeys instructions. Agents may also find themselves liable to third parties.

PRINCIPAL'S LIABILITY FOR CONTRACTS

Many agents are hired for the primary purpose of entering into contracts on behalf of their principals. Salespeople, for example, may do little other than sign on the dotted line. Most of the time, the principal is delighted to be bound by these contracts. But even if the principal is unhappy (because, say, the agent has disobeyed orders), the principal generally cannot rescind contracts entered into by the agent. After all, if someone is going to be penalized, it should be the principal who hired the disobedient agent, not the innocent third party.

The principal is bound by the acts of an agent if (1) the agent had *authority*, or (2) the principal, for reasons of fairness, is *estopped* from denying that the agent had authority, or (3) the principal *ratifies* the acts of the agent.

To say that the principal is "bound by the acts" of the agent means that the principal is as liable as if he had performed the acts himself. It also means that the principal is liable for statements the agent makes to a third party. In addition, the principal is deemed to know any information that the agent knows or should know.

AUTHORITY

A principal is bound by the acts of an agent if the agent has authority. There are three types of authority: express, implied, and apparent. Express and implied authority are categories of actual authority because the agent *is* truly authorized to act for the principal. In apparent authority, the principal is liable for the agent's actions even though the agent was *not* authorized.

Express Authority. The principal grants **express authority** by words or conduct that, reasonably interpreted, cause the agent to believe the principal desires her to act on the principal's account.[14] In other words, the principal asks the agent to do something and the agent does it. Craig calls his stockbroker, Alice, and asks her to buy 100 shares of Superior Corp. for his account. She has *express authority* to carry out this transaction.

Implied Authority. **Unless otherwise agreed, authority to conduct a transaction includes authority to do acts that are reasonably necessary to accomplish it.**[15] David has recently inherited a house from his grandmother. He hires Nell to auction off the house and its contents. She hires an auctioneer, advertises the event, rents a tent, and generally does everything necessary to conduct a successful auction. After withholding her expenses, she sends the tidy balance to David. Totally outraged, he calls her on the phone, "How dare you hire an auctioneer and rent a tent? I never gave you permission! I absolutely *refuse* to pay these expenses!"

---

[14] Restatement (Second) of Agency §26.

[15] Restatement (Second) of Agency §35.

David is wrong. A principal almost never gives an agent absolutely complete instructions. Unless some authority were implied, David would have had to say, "Open the car door, get in, put the key in the ignition, drive to the store, buy stickers, mark an auction number on each sticker" . . . and so forth. To solve this problem, the law assumes that the agent has authority to do anything that is *reasonably* necessary to accomplish her task.

Apparent Authority. **A principal can be liable for the acts of an agent who is not, in fact, acting with authority if the principal's conduct causes a third party reasonably to believe that the agent is authorized.** In the case of *express* and *implied* authority, the principal has authorized the agent to act. Apparent authority is different: the principal has *not* authorized the agent, but has done something to make an innocent third party *believe* the agent is authorized. As a result, the principal is every bit as liable to the third party as if the agent did have authority.

For example, Zbigniew Lambo and Scott Kennedy were brokers at Paulson Investment Co., a stock brokerage firm in Oregon. The two men violated securities laws by selling unregistered stock, which ultimately proved to be worthless. Kennedy and Lambo were liable, but they were unable to repay the money. Either Paulson or its customers would end up bearing the loss. What is the fair result? The law takes the view that the principal is liable, not the third party, because the principal, by word or deed, allowed the third party to believe that the agent was acting on the principal's behalf. The principal could have prevented the third party from losing money.

Although the two brokers did not have *actual* or *implied* authority to sell the stock (Paulson had not authorized them to break the law), the company was nonetheless liable on the grounds that the brokers had *apparent* authority. Paulson had sent letters to its customers notifying them when it hired Kennedy. The two brokers made sales presentations at Paulson's offices. The company had never told customers that the two men were not authorized to sell this worthless stock.[16] Thus the agents *appeared* to have authority, even though they did not. Of course, Paulson had the right to recover from Kennedy and Lambo, if it could ever persuade them to pay.

Remember that the issue in apparent authority is always what the *principal* has done to make the *third party* believe that the *agent* has authority. Suppose that Kennedy and Lambo never worked for Paulson but, on their own, printed up Paulson stationery. The company would not be liable for the stock the two men sold, because it had never done or said anything that would reasonably make a third party believe that the men were its agents.

ESTOPPEL

No one may claim that a person was *not* his agent, if he knew that others thought the person *was* acting on his behalf, and he failed to correct their belief. He is *estopped* from denying an agency relationship. Paul Murphy approached the Sperry Rand Corp. with a promising idea for marketing Remington shavers. A dermatologist had recently conducted a pilot study indicating that the Remington product was better for the skin than ordinary razors

---

[16] *Badger v. Paulson Investment Co.*, 311 Or. 14, 803 P.2d 1178, 1991 Ore. LEXIS 7 (S.Ct. OR 1991).

and other electric shavers. Murphy proposed hiring a dermatologist to do a more thorough study that could be used as the basis for a national marketing campaign. Sperry Rand agreed to Murphy's plan. Murphy later produced a report from Dr. William Hill, Jr., indicating that Remington was indeed superior. Sperry Rand publicized this report in full-page advertisements in newspapers and magazines. There was only one problem—Hill had not written the report and had not agreed to allow his name to be used in the ad campaign. Murphy had *said* he was Hill's agent and had negotiated on Hill's behalf, but neither statement was true. Murphy did *not* have *apparent authority* because Hill had done nothing to lead Sperry Rand to believe Murphy was his agent.

The court, however, found Sperry Rand not liable on a theory of estoppel. Hill discovered the ad campaign in March but did not complain to Sperry Rand until November. By the simple act of making a prompt phone call, the doctor could have prevented most of the harm the advertisements caused him. Because Hill did not tell Sperry Rand of its error, he lost his right to recover damages from the corporation.[17]

Estoppel is, in a sense, a first cousin to *apparent authority*. In cases of apparent authority, the principal has done something to lead a reasonable person to believe that the person pretending to be an agent really is an agent. In the case of estoppel, the principal has never done anything affirmatively to imply that the person pretending to be an agent really is one, but when he finds out people think he has an agent, he does not tell them otherwise.

RATIFICATION

If a person accepts the benefit of an unauthorized transaction or fails to repudiate it, then he is as bound by the act as if he had originally authorized it. He has *ratified* the act.[18] Many of the cases in agency law involve instances in which one person acts *without* authority for another. To avoid liability, the alleged principal shows that he had not authorized the task at issue. But sometimes, after the fact, the principal decides that he approves of what the agent has done even though it was not authorized at the time. The law would be perverse if it did not permit the principal, under those circumstances, to agree to the deal the agent has made. The law is not perverse, but it is careful. Even if an agent acts without authority, the principal can decide later to be bound by her actions as long as these requirements are met:

- The "agent" indicates to the third party that she is acting for a principal.
- The "principal" knows all the material facts of the transaction.
- The "principal" accepts the benefit of the whole transaction, not just part.
- The third party does not withdraw from the contract before ratification.

A night clerk at the St. Regis Hotel in Detroit, Michigan, was brutally murdered in the course of a robbery. A few days later, the *Detroit News* reported that the St. Regis management had offered a $1,000 reward for any information

---

[17] *Sperry Rand Corp. v. Hill*, 356 F.2d 181, 1966 U.S. App. LEXIS 7491 (1st Cir. 1966).

[18] Restatement (Second) of Agency §82.

leading to the arrest and conviction of the killer. Two days after the article appeared, Robert Jackson turned in the man who was subsequently convicted of the crime. But then it was Jackson's turn to be robbed—the hotel refused to pay the reward on the grounds that the manager who had made the offer had no authority. Jackson still had one weapon left: he convinced the court that the hotel had ratified the offer. One of the hotel's owners admitted he read the *Detroit News*. The court concluded that if someone reads a newspaper, he is sure to read any articles about a business he owns; therefore, the owner must have been aware of the offer. He accepted the benefit of the reward by failing to revoke it publicly. This failure to revoke constituted a ratification and the hotel was liable.[19]

Estoppel and ratification are easy to confuse. *Ratification* applies when the principal accepts the benefit of the contract. The hotel owner benefited from the reward because he wanted the murderer to be caught. *Estoppel* applies when the alleged principal does *not* want the benefit of the contract, but delays in telling the innocent third party of the mistake. The doctor did not want his name tied to a nonexistent research report in a national ad campaign. If the doctor had accepted the benefit of the contract, by receiving payment, for instance, then he would have ratified the contract. As it was, he accepted no benefit, but he waited so long to contact Sperry Rand that he was *estopped* from recovering damages.

SUBAGENTS

Many of the examples in this chapter involve a single agent acting for a principal. Real life is often more complex. Daniel, the owner of a restaurant, hires Michaela to manage it. She in turn hires chefs, waiters, and dishwashers. Daniel has never even met the restaurant help, yet they are also his agents, albeit a special category called **subagent**. Michaela is called an **intermediary agent**—someone who hires subagents for the principal.

As a general rule, an agent has no authority to delegate her tasks to another unless the principal authorizes her to. But when an agent is authorized to hire a subagent, the principal is as liable for the acts of the subagent as he is for the acts of a regular agent. Daniel authorizes Michaela to hire a restaurant staff. She hires Lydia to serve as produce buyer. When Lydia buys food for the restaurant, Daniel must pay the bill.

AGENT'S LIABILITY FOR CONTRACTS

The agent's liability on a contract depends upon how much the third party knows about the principal. Disclosure is the agent's best protection against liability.

FULLY DISCLOSED PRINCIPAL

An agent is not liable for any contracts she makes on behalf of a *fully* disclosed principal. A principal is fully disclosed if the third party knows of his

[19] *Jackson v. Goodman*, 69 Mich. App. 225, 244 N.W.2d 423, 1976 Mich. App. LEXIS 741 (Mich. Ct. App. 1976).

existence and his *identity*. Augusta acts as agent for Parker when he buys Tracey's prize-winning show horse. Augusta and Tracey both grew up in posh Grosse Pointe, Michigan, where they attended the same elite schools. Tracey does not know Parker, but she figures any friend of Augusta's must be okay. She figures wrong—Parker is a charming deadbeat. He injures Tracey's horse, fails to pay the full contract price, and promptly disappears from the face of the earth. Tracey angrily demands that Augusta make good on Parker's debt. Unfortunately for Tracey, Parker was a fully disclosed principal—Tracey knew of his *existence* and his *identity*. Although Tracey partly relied on Augusta's good character when contracting with Parker, Augusta is not liable because Tracey knew who the principal was and could have (should have) investigated him. Augusta did not promise anything herself, and Tracey's only recourse is against the principal, Parker (wherever he may be).

To avoid liability when signing a contract on behalf of a principal, an agent must clearly state that she is an agent and must also identify the principal. Augusta should sign a contract on behalf of her principal, Parker, as follows: "Augusta, as agent for Parker" or "Parker, by Augusta, Agent."

PARTIALLY DISCLOSED PRINCIPAL

In the case of a *partially* disclosed principal, the third party can recover from either the agent or the principal. A principal is partially disclosed if the third party knew of his *existence* but not his *identity*. Suppose that, when approaching Tracey about the horse, Augusta simply says, "I have a friend who is interested in buying your champion." Any friend of Augusta's is a friend of Tracey's—or so Tracey thinks. Parker is a partially disclosed principal because Tracey knows only that he exists, not who he is. She cannot investigate his credit because she does not know his name. Tracey relies solely on what she is able to learn from the agent, Augusta. Of course, the principal, Parker, is also liable because the contract was made on his behalf.

UNDISCLOSED PRINCIPAL

In the case of an *undisclosed* principal, the third party can recover from either the agent or the principal. A principal is undisclosed if the third party did not know of his existence. Suppose that Augusta simply asks to buy the horse herself, without mentioning that she is purchasing it for Parker. In this case, Parker is an undisclosed principal because Tracey does not know that Augusta is acting for someone else. Both Parker and Augusta are liable. As Exhibit 13.1 illustrates, the principal is *always* liable, but the agent is not unless the principal's identity is a mystery.

In some ways, the concept of an undisclosed principal violates principles of contract law. If Tracey does not even know that Parker exists, how can they have an agreement or a meeting of the minds? Is such an arrangement fair to Tracey? No matter, a contract with an undisclosed principal is binding. The following incident illustrates why.

William Zeckendorf was a man with a plan. For years he had been eyeing a six-block tract of land along New York's East River. It was a wasteland of slums and slaughterhouses, but he could see its potential. The meat packers had

Exhibit 13.1

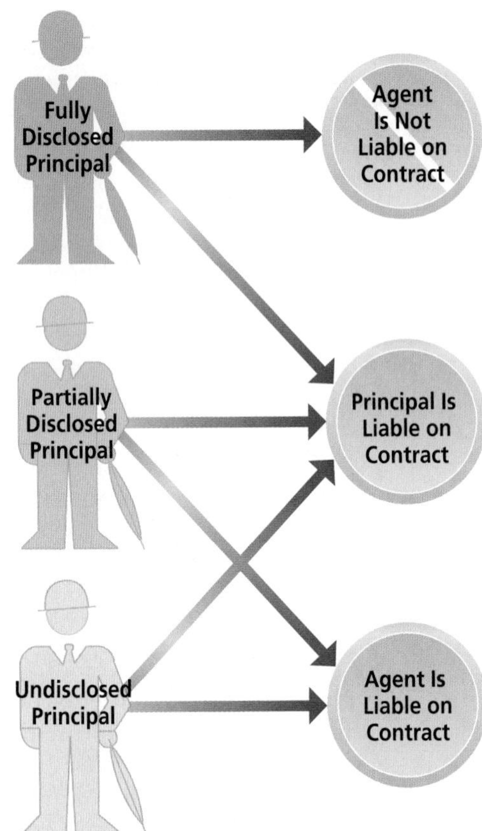

refused to sell to him, however, because they knew they would never be permitted to build slaughterhouses in Manhattan again. Finally, in 1946, he got the phone call he had been waiting for. The companies were willing to sell—at $17 a square foot, when surrounding land cost less than $5. Undeterred, Zeckendorf immediately put down a $1 million deposit. But to make his investment worthwhile, he needed to buy the neighboring property—once the slaughterhouses were gone, this other land would be much more valuable. Zeckendorf was well-known as a wealthy real estate developer; he had begun his business career managing the Astor family's real estate holdings. If he personally tried to negotiate the purchase of the surrounding land, word would soon get out that he was trying to put together a large parcel. Prices would skyrocket and the project would become too costly. So he hired agents to purchase the land for him. To further conceal his involvement, he went to South America for a month. When he returned, his agents had completed 75 different purchases, and he owned 18 acres of land.

Shortly afterwards, the United Nations began seeking a site for its headquarters. President Truman favored Boston, Philadelphia, or a location in the Midwest. The UN committee suggested Greenwich or Stamford, Connecticut. But John D. Rockefeller settled the question once and for all. He purchased Zeckendorf's land for $8.5 million and donated it to the UN (netting Zeckendorf a profit of $2 million). Without the cooperation of agency law, the UN headquarters would not be in New York today.

The law permits the concept of an undisclosed principal out of commercial necessity. The following article suggests that Harvard behaved unethically when it purchased land secretly. Do you agree?

NEWSworthy

Harvard University has bought 52 acres during the past nine years in a secret buying spree that increases the school's land in Allston (across the river from its Cambridge headquarters) by more than a third. Working through the Beal Cos., a prominent real estate development company, Harvard spent $88 million to buy 14 separate parcels. Harvard officials said the university made the purchases without revealing its identity to the sellers, residents, local politicians, or city officials because property owners would have drastically inflated the prices if they knew Harvard was the buyer. "We were really driven by the need to get these properties at fair market value" and avoid "overly inflated acquisition costs," said James H. Rowe, vice-president for public affairs at Harvard. But those who were left in the dark—including Mayor Thomas M. Menino—weren't buying it. "That's absurd," Menino scoffed. "Without informing anyone or telling anybody? That's total arrogance." Menino was so incensed that he adopted a mocking singsong tone to express his view of Harvard's attitude, saying: "We're from Harvard, and we're going to do what we want."

"As far as I'm concerned, they practiced a deception," said Ray Mellone, chairman of a neighborhood task force. "There are a lot of people who are going to say we can't trust them. We have to make the process work, and that means making the neighborhood involved, not having deals made in a back room and then coming to us and saying: 'Take it or leave it.'"[20]

Because of concerns about fair play, there are some exceptions to the rule on undisclosed principals. **A third party is not bound to the contract with an undisclosed principal if (1) the contract specifically provides that the third party is not bound to anyone other than the agent, or (2) the agent lies about the principal because she knows the third party would refuse to contract with him.** A cagey property owner, when approached by one of Harvard's agents, could have asked for a clause in the contract providing that the agent was not representing someone else. If the agent told the truth, the owner could have demanded a higher price. If the agent lied, then the owner could have rescinded the contract when the truth emerged.

UNAUTHORIZED AGENT

Thus far in this section, we have been discussing an agent's liability to a third party for a transaction that was authorized by the principal. Sometimes, however, agents act without the authority of a principal. **If the agent has no authority (express, implied, or apparent), the principal is not liable to the third party and the agent is.** Suppose that Augusta agrees to sell Parker's horse to Tracey. Unfortunately, Parker has never met Augusta and has certainly not authorized this transaction. Augusta is hoping that she can persuade him to sell, but Parker refuses. Augusta, but not Parker, is liable to Tracey for breach of contract.

---

[20] Tina Cassidy and Dan Aucoin, "Harvard Reveals Secret Purchases of 52 Acres Worth $88M in Allston," *The Boston Globe*, June 10, 1997, p. A1. Republished with permission of The Boston Globe; permission conveyed through the Copyright Clearance Center, Inc.

PRINCIPAL'S LIABILITY FOR TORTS

A master is liable for physical harm caused by the negligent conduct of servants within the scope of employment.[21] This principle of liability is called ***respondeat superior***, which is a Latin phrase that means, "let the master answer." Under the theory of *respondeat superior*, the principal is liable for the agent's misbehavior whether or not the principal was at fault. Indeed, the principal is liable even if he forbade or tried to prevent the agent from misbehaving. This sounds like a harsh rule. The logic is that, since the principal controls the agent, he should be able to prevent misbehavior. If he cannot prevent it, at least he can *insure* against the risks. Furthermore, the principal may have deeper pockets than the agent or the injured third party and thus be better able to *afford* the cost of the agent's misbehavior.

To apply the principle of *respondeat superior*, it is important to understand each of the following terms: *master and servant, scope of employment, negligent and intentional torts*, and *physical harm*.

MASTER AND SERVANT

There are two kinds of agents: (1) *servants* and (2) *independent contractors*. **A principal *may be* liable for the torts of a servant but generally is *not* liable for the torts of an independent contractor.** Because of this rule, the distinction between a servant and an independent contractor is important. Employees are always servants. When determining if other agents are servants, courts consider whether:

- The principal controls details of the work.
- The principal supplies the tools and place of work.
- The agents work full-time for the principal.
- The agents are paid by time, not by the job.
- The work is part of the regular business of the principal.
- The principal and agents believe they have an employer-employee relationship.
- The principal is in business.[22]

Do not be misled by the term *servant*. A servant does not mean Jeeves, the butler, or Maisie, the maid. In fact, if Mrs. Dillworth hires Jeeves and Maisie for the evening from a catering firm, they are *not* her servants, they are independent contractors. On the other hand, the president of General Motors is a servant of that corporation.

Principals prefer agents to be considered independent contractors not servants because, as a general rule, principals are not liable for the torts of an independent contractor. There is, however, one exception to this rule: **The principal**

---

[21] Restatement (Second) of Agency §243.

[22] Restatement (Second) of Agency §220(2).

is liable for the physical torts of an independent contractor *only if* the principal has been negligent in hiring or supervising her. Remember that, under *respondeat superior*, the principal is liable *without fault* for the physical torts of servants. The case of independent contractors is different: the principal is liable only if he was *at fault* by being careless in his hiring or supervising. Was the supermarket at fault in the following case?

DURAN v. FURR'S SUPERMARKETS, INC.

921 S.W.2d 778, 1996 Tex. App. LEXIS 1345
Court of Appeals of Texas, 1996

Facts: Steve Romero was an off-duty police officer working as a security guard for Furr's Supermarkets. He approached a car parked in the supermarket's fire lane and began yelling at a passenger to move it. The passenger, Graciela Duran, asked Romero for his name. He opened the car door and tried to pull her out, all the while threatening to arrest her. Duran ultimately required surgery to repair the injury that his tugs and twists caused to her left arm.

Duran filed suit against Furr's. The supermarket filed a motion for summary judgment on the grounds that it was not responsible for Romero's conduct because he was an independent contractor. Duran argued that Furr's had been negligent in hiring Romero. The trial court granted the motion for summary judgment.

Issues: Was Furr's negligent in hiring Romero? Is it liable for Romero's conduct?

Excerpts from Judge McClure's Decision: The basis of responsibility under the doctrine of negligent hiring is the master's own negligence in hiring or retaining in his employ an incompetent servant whom the master knows or by the exercise of reasonable care should have known was incompetent or unfit and thereby creating an unreasonable risk of harm to others. The evidence showed that Furr's did not require Romero to complete a job application and otherwise made no inquiry into his background as a police officer. Furr's never interviewed Romero or spoke with him before he began working at the store. If Furr's had conducted an investigation of Romero's performance as a police officer, it would have learned that Romero had a prior complaint for using vulgar and abusive language towards a member of the public while on duty as a police officer.

Duran argues that this complaint demonstrates Romero's propensity for aggressive behavior so that Furr's could have reasonably anticipated that Romero might verbally and physically abuse a patron of the store. On the other hand, Furr's argues that even if it had discovered the prior complaint, the information would not have caused Furr's to reasonably anticipate his physical assault upon Duran. In attempting to distinguish between the prior verbal abuse complaint and the physical assault upon Duran, Furr's ignores the evidence showing that Romero first verbally abused Duran during this incident. According to Duran, the verbal abuse escalated into the physical assault. We find that a fact question is raised whether knowledge of this abusive language complaint would put a reasonable person on notice that Romero might verbally abuse a store patron, and that such conduct might escalate into a physical assault. Because of the existence of this fact issue, summary judgment on this ground is improper.

SCOPE OF EMPLOYMENT

Principals are only liable for torts that a servant commits within the *scope of employment*. If an employee leaves a pool of water on the floor of a store and a customer slips and falls, the employer is liable. But if the same employee leaves water on his own kitchen floor and a friend falls, the employer is not liable because the employee is not acting within the scope of employment. A servant is acting within the scope of employment if the act:

- Is one that servants are generally responsible for
- Takes place during hours that the servant is generally employed
- Is part of the principal's business
- Is similar to the one the principal authorized
- Is one for which the principal supplied the tools; and
- Is not seriously criminal.

Scope of employment cases raise two major issues: authorization and abandonment.

Authorization. In authorization cases, the agent is clearly working for the principal but commits an act that the principal has not authorized. Although Jane has often told the driver of her delivery van not to speed, Hank ignores her instructions and plows into Bernadette. At the time of the accident, he is working for Jane, delivering flowers for her shop, but his act is not authorized. **An act is within the scope of employment, even if expressly forbidden, if it is of the same general nature as that authorized or if it is incidental to the conduct authorized.**[23] Hank was authorized to drive the van, but not to speed. However, his speeding was of the same general nature as the authorized act, so Jane is liable to Bernadette. In the following case, an employee engaged in unauthorized behavior while on company business. Did his actions fall within the scope of his employment? You be the judge.

You be *the* Judge

CONNER v. MAGIC CITY TRUCKING SERVICE, INC.

592 So. 2d 1048, 1992 Ala. LEXIS 26
Supreme Court of Alabama, 1992

Facts: Sarah Conner worked for A-Pac, which was building a roadway. A-Pac had hired Magic City to supply dirt. Conner was responsible for punching holes in a ticket to tally the amount of dirt each Magic City truck brought in. When a driver was ready to dump the dirt from the truck, Conner would often release the truck's latch as a courtesy to the driver, who would otherwise have to climb out of the truck to release it.

Magic City employee David King drove up wearing a Halloween mask. Conner punched King's load ticket but ignored the mask. King asked, "You're not going to say anything?" Conner did not comment or respond to this question, and King left. He later returned to Conner's post with a second load of dirt, this time without the mask. Conner punched his load ticket, and King told her to release the latch on his truck quickly or else he would "put [his] friend" on her. Conner attempted to release the latch but could not budge it. Conner told King, who had a tool for forcing the release of the latch, to release it himself. King again threatened to "put [his] friend" on her if Conner did not quickly release the latch. King began chasing Conner with a very large snake. King's Magic City supervisor laughed as Conner ran from King. Eventually, King gave up the chase and threw the snake at Conner. She collapsed with severe medical problems.

[23] Restatement (Second) of Agency §229(1).

You be the Judge: Under *respondeat superior*, is Magic City liable for the actions of its employee, King? Was King acting within the scope of his employment?

Argument for Conner: An employee is acting within the scope of his employment if the conduct is of the same general nature as that authorized or incidental to that authorized. Sarah Conner would never have met David King if he had not been working for Magic City. He was angry at her because she did not release the latch on his truck. What could be more incidental to his job than that?

Respondeat superior is based on the concept of control. The principal is able to control the agent to prevent him from misbehaving. While David King was tormenting Sarah Conner, King's supervisor stood and *laughed*. He did not even tell King to stop. Sarah Conner has suffered serious injuries as a result of King's behavior on the job. In all fairness, Magic City should bear liability for the harm caused by its employee.

Argument for Magic City: When King brought in the Halloween mask and snake, he was not acting in furtherance of his employer's goals or business. His employer did not approve of or condone his behavior. Snakes have nothing to do with King's job, and his actions were not within the scope of his employment.

Conner blames Magic City because King's supervisor stood by and laughed. Consciously or not, people often react to bizarre antics with laughter even when they disapprove of the behavior. Magic City is sorry King behaved so badly. But the company did *not* authorize his actions and should not be liable for them.

Abandonment. The second major issue in a *scope of employment* case involves abandonment. **The master is liable for the actions of the servant that occur while the servant is at work, but not for actions that occur after the servant has abandoned the master's business.** Although the rule sounds straightforward, the difficulty lies in determining whether the employee has in fact abandoned the master's business. The employer is liable if the employee is simply on a *detour* from company business, but the employer is not liable if the employee is off on a *frolic of his own*. Suppose that Hank, the delivery van driver, speeds during his afternoon commute home. A servant is generally not acting within the scope of his employment when he commutes to and from work, so his master, Jane, is not liable. Or suppose that, while on the way to a delivery, he stops to see his favorite movie classic, *Dead on Arrival*. Unable to see in the darkened theater, he knocks Anna down, causing grave harm. Jane is not liable because Hank's visit to the movies is outside the scope of his employment. On the other hand, if Hank stops at the Burger King drive-in window en route to making a delivery, Jane is liable when he crashes into Anna on the way out of the parking lot, because this time he is simply making a detour.

NEGLIGENT AND INTENTIONAL TORTS

The master is liable if the servant commits a negligent tort that causes physical harm to a person or property. When Hank crashes into Anna, he is committing a negligent tort, and Jane is liable if all the other requirements for *respondeat superior* are met.

A master is *not* liable for the *intentional* torts of the servant *unless* the servant was motivated, at least in part, by a desire to serve the master, or the conduct was reasonably foreseeable. During an NBA basketball game, Hakeem pushes Alonzo into some chairs under the basket to prevent him from scoring a breakaway lay-up. Hakeem's team is liable for his actions because he was motivated, at least in part, by a desire to help his team. But if Hakeem hits Alonzo in the parking lot after the playoffs are over, Hakeem's team is not liable because he is no longer motivated by a desire to help the team. His motivation now is personal revenge or frustration.

The courts (of law, not basketball) are generally expansive in their definition of behavior that is intended to serve the master. In one case, a police trainee shot a fellow officer while practicing his quick draw technique. In another, a drunken sailor knocked a shipmate out of bed with the admonition, "Get up, you big son of a bitch, and turn to," after which the two men fought. The courts ruled that both the police trainee and the sailor were motivated by a desire to serve their master and, therefore, the master was liable for their intentional torts.[24]

PHYSICAL HARM

In the case of *physical* torts, a master is liable for the negligent conduct of a servant that occurs within the scope of employment. The rule for *nonphysical* torts (that is, torts that harm only reputation, feelings, or wallet) is different. Nonphysical torts are treated more like a contract claim, and the principal is liable only if the servant acted with actual, implied, or apparent authority. For example, the Small Business Administration (SBA) granted Midwest Knitting Mills, Inc. more than $2 million in loans, but the SBA employee in charge of the case never told Midwest. (He was allegedly a drug addict.) The company sued the SBA for the negligence of its employee. Although the conduct had occurred within the scope of employment, it was a nonphysical tort. Since the employee had not acted with actual, implied, or apparent authority, the SBA was not liable.[25]

Misrepresentation and defamation are, however, treated differently from other nonphysical torts.

Misrepresentation.

A principal is liable if:

- The agent makes a misrepresentation
- The agent has express, implied, or apparent authority
- The third party relies on the misrepresentation; and
- The third party suffers harm.

This rule applies to any agent, not just a servant. If the agent is authorized to make a *truthful* statement, the principal is liable for any related *false* statement.

Althea hires Morris, a real estate agent, to sell a piece of land. Morris knows that part of the land floods every spring, but when Helen inquires about flooding, Morris lies. He is not authorized to make the false statement, but he is authorized to make statements about the land. Althea is liable to Helen for any harm caused by Morris's misrepresentation, even though Morris is an independent contractor.

---

[24] *Nelson v. American-West African Line, Inc.*, 86 F.2d 730, 1936 U.S. App. LEXIS 3841 (2d Cir. 1936), and *Thompson v. United States*, 504 F. Supp. 1087, 1980 U.S. Dist. LEXIS 15834 (D.S.D. 1980).

[25] *Midwest Knitting Mills, Inc. v. United States*, 741 F. Supp. 1345, 1990 U.S. Dist. LEXIS 8663 (E.D. Wis. 1990).

Defamation.

A principal is liable if:

- The agent makes a defamatory statement
- The agent has express, implied, or apparent authority; and
- The third party is harmed by the statement.

Again, this rule applies to all agents, not simply to servants. If the agent is authorized to make a *truthful* statement, the principal is liable for any related *defamatory* statements.

A newspaper reporter writes an untrue story alleging that the mayor has been taking kickbacks from contractors who work for the city. The reporter has defamed the mayor, and the newspaper is liable because the reporter is an agent authorized to write the article, even though he is not authorized to write false statements.

Electronic communication has created new risks for employers. They fear that their employees may commit libel by sending flaming e-mails or violate intellectual property laws by downloading copyrighted software from the Internet. Is the company liable in these circumstances? What if an employee posts defamatory information on an Internet newsgroup? Even if the employee is not authorized, she may have *apparent* authority—especially if the posting appears with a company e-mail address. For this reason, companies increasingly monitor their employees' e-mail content and Internet usage. Some companies also require employees, when posting on a newsgroup, to include a disclaimer that they do not speak for their company.

AGENT'S LIABILITY FOR TORTS

The focus of this section has been on the *principal's* liability for the agent's torts. But it is important to remember that **agents are always liable for their own torts**. Agents who commit torts are personally responsible, whether or not their principal is also liable. Even if the tort was committed to benefit the principal, the agent is still liable. So the sailor who got into a fistfight while rousting a shipmate from bed is liable even though he thought he was acting for the benefit of his principal.

This rule makes obvious sense. If the agent were not liable, he would have little incentive to be careful. Imagine Hank driving his delivery van for Jane. If he were not personally liable for his own torts, he might think, "If I drive fast enough, I can make it through that light even though it just turned red. And if I don't, what the heck, it'll be Jane's problem, not mine." Agents, as a rule, may have fewer assets than their principal, but it is important that their personal assets be at risk in the event of their negligent behavior.

If the agent and principal are *both* liable, which does the injured third party sue? The principal and the agent are *jointly and severally* liable, which means that the injured third party can sue either one or both, as she chooses. Of course, she cannot recover twice. If she collects the full amount from the principal, she cannot sue the agent, and vice versa. If she recovers from the principal, he can sue the agent.

CHAPTER CONCLUSION

When students enroll in a business law course, they fully expect to learn about torts and contracts, corporations and partnerships. They probably do not think much about agency law; many of them have not even heard the term before. Yet it is an area of the law that affects us all because each of us has been and will continue to be both an agent and a principal many times in our lives.

CHAPTER REVIEW

1. In an agency relationship, a principal and an agent mutually consent that the agent will act on behalf of the principal and be subject to the principal's control, thereby creating a fiduciary relationship.
2. An agent owes these duties to the principal: duty of loyalty, duty to obey instructions, duty of care, and duty to provide information.
3. The principal has three potential remedies when the agent breaches her duty: recovery of damages the breach has caused, recovery of any profits earned by the agent from the breach, and rescission of any transaction with the agent.
4. The principal has two duties to the agent: to reimburse legitimate expenses, and to cooperate with the agent.
5. Both the agent and the principal have the power to terminate an agency relationship, but they may not have the right. If the termination violates the agency agreement and causes harm to the other party, the wrongful party must pay damages.
6. An agency relationship automatically terminates if the principal or agent can no longer perform the required duties or if a change in circumstances renders the agency relationship pointless.
7. A principal is bound by the contracts of the agent if the agent has express, implied, or apparent authority.
8. The principal grants express authority by words or conduct that, reasonably interpreted, cause the agent to believe that the principal desires her to act on the principal's account.
9. Implied authority includes authority to do acts that are incidental to a transaction, usually accompany it, or are reasonably necessary to accomplish it.
10. Apparent authority means that a principal is liable for the acts of an agent who is not, in fact, acting with authority if the principal's conduct causes a third party reasonably to believe that the agent is authorized.
11. An agent is not liable for any contract she makes on behalf of a fully disclosed principal. In the case of a partially disclosed or undisclosed principal, both the agent and the principal are liable on the contract.
12. Under *respondeat superior*, a master is liable when a servant acting within the scope of employment commits a negligent tort that causes physical harm to a person or property. Under some circumstances, a master is also liable for a servant's intentional torts.
13. The principal is only liable for the physical torts of an independent contractor if the principal has been negligent in hiring or supervising him.
14. A principal is liable for nonphysical torts only if the servant acts with actual, implied, or apparent authority.
15. Agents are always liable for their own torts.

PRACTICE TEST

1. The German-American Vocational League was formed in New York during World War

II to serve as a propaganda agency for the German Reich. Under U.S. law, all foreign agents were required to register. Neither the Vocational League nor its officers registered. When they were charged with violating U.S. law, they argued that they were not agents of the German government because they had no formal agency agreement. Their one written agreement with the German Reich said nothing about being a propaganda agency. Is a formal contract necessary to establish an agency relationship?

2. **RIGHT & WRONG** Radio TV Reports (RTV) was in the business of recording, transcribing, and monitoring radio and video programming for its clients. The Department of Defense (DOD) in Washington was one of RTV's major clients. Paul Ingersoll worked for RTV until August 31. In July, the DOD solicited bids for a new contract for the following year. During this same month, Ingersoll formed his own media monitoring business, Transmedia. RTV and Transmedia were the only two bidders on the DOD contract, which was awarded to Transmedia. Did Ingersoll violate his fiduciary duty to RTV? Aside from his legal obligations, did Ingersoll behave ethically? How does his behavior look in the light of day? Was it right?

3. David and Fiona Rookard purchased tickets for a trip through Mexico from a Mexicoach office in San Diego. Mexicoach told them that the trip would be safe. It did not tell them, however, that their tickets had disclaimers written in Spanish warning that, under Mexican law, a bus company is not liable for any harm that befalls its passengers. The Rookards did not read Spanish. They were injured in a bus accident caused by gross negligence on the part of the driver. Did Mexicoach violate its duty to provide information?

4. Penny Wilson went to Arlington Chrysler-Plymouth-Dodge to buy an automobile. Penny told Arlington that, as a minor, she could not buy the car unless she obtained credit life insurance that would pay the balance of any loan owing if her mother died. She also disclosed that her mother had cancer. Arlington was an agent for Western Pioneer Life Insurance Co. Western Pioneer reported that a credit insurance policy would be valid unless Mrs. Wilson died within six months. In fact, the policy was invalid if Mrs. Wilson died of cancer within *one year*. Seven months later, Mrs. Wilson died and Western Pioneer refused to pay. Penny Wilson sued Western Pioneer and Arlington. The trial court found Western Pioneer liable, but not Arlington. Was Western Pioneer liable for Arlington's legal expenses?

5. One Friday afternoon, a custodian at the Lazear Elementary School in Oakland, California, raped an 11-year-old student in his office on the school premises. The student sued the school district on a theory of *respondeat superior*. Is the school district liable for this intentional tort by its employee?

6. This article appeared in *The New York Times*:

> A week after criminal charges were announced in the death of tennis star Vitas Gerulaitis, his mother filed suit yesterday against eight defendants, including the owner of the Long Island estate where Mr. Gerulaitis died of carbon monoxide poisoning last fall. Prosecutors have charged that a new swimming pool heater, installed at a cost of $8,000, was improperly vented and sent deadly fumes into a pool house where Mr. Gerulaitis was taking a nap. The lawsuit accuses the companies that manufactured, installed and maintained the pool heater, and the mechanic who installed it, with negligence and reckless disregard for human life. It makes similar charges against the owners of the oceanfront estate, Beatrice Raynes and her son Martin, a real-estate executive.[26]

Why would the owners of the estate be liable?

[26] Vivian S. Toy, "Gerulaitis's Mother Files Suit in Son's Carbon Monoxide Death," *The New York Times*, June 1, 1995, p. B5.

7. **CPA QUESTION** A principal will **not** be liable to a third party for a tort committed by an agent:

   (a) Unless the principal instructed the agent to commit the tort

   (b) Unless the tort was committed within the scope of the agency relationship

   (c) If the agency agreement limits the principal's liability for the agent's tort

   (d) If the tort is also regarded as a criminal act

8. A. B. Rains worked as a broker for the Joseph Denunzio Fruit Co. Raymond Crane offered to sell Rains nine carloads of emperor grapes. Rains accepted the offer on behalf of Denunzio. Later, Rains and Denunzio discovered that Crane was an agent for John Kazanjian. Who is liable on this contract?

9. Roy Watson bought vacuum cleaners from T & F Distributing Co. and then resold them door-to-door. He was an independent contractor. Before hiring Watson, the president of T & F checked with two former employers but could not remember if he called Watson's two references. Watson had an extensive criminal record, primarily under the alias Leroy Turner, but he was listed in FBI records under both Leroy Turner and Roy Watson. T & F granted Watson sales territory that included Neptune City, New Jersey. This city required that all "peddlers" such as Watson be licensed. Applicants for this license were routinely fingerprinted. T & F never insisted that Watson apply for such a license. Watson attacked Miriam Bennett after selling a vacuum cleaner to her at her home in Neptune City. Is T & F liable to Bennett?

10. **YOU BE THE JUDGE WRITING PROBLEM** Sara Kearns went to an auction at Christie's to bid on a tapestry for her employer, Nardin Fine Arts Gallery. The good news is that she purchased a Dufy tapestry for $77,000. The bad news is that it was not the one her employer had told her to buy. In the excitement of the auction, she forgot her instructions. Nardin refused to pay and Christie's filed suit. Is Nardin liable for the unauthorized act of its agent? **Argument for Christie's:** Kearns executed a bidder form as agent for Nardin. This is a common practice for many purchasers. Christie's cannot possibly ascertain in each case the exact nature of the bidder's authority. Whether or not Kearns had actual authority, she certainly had apparent authority and Nardin is liable. **Argument for Nardin:** Kearns was not authorized to purchase the Dufy tapestry, and therefore Christie's must recover from her, not us.

INTERNET RESEARCH PROBLEM

Acting as an undisclosed principal, William Zeckendorf employed agents to purchase the land in New York on which the United Nations headquarters was ultimately built. Can you find any other examples on the Internet of business dealings in which agents made purchases for an undisclosed principal? Were these business arrangements ethical? What risks did the agents face?

You can find further practice problems in the Online Quiz at http://beatty.westbuslaw.com or in the Study Guide that accompanies this text.

14 CHAPTER

EMPLOYMENT LAW

"On the killing beds you were apt to be covered with blood, and it would freeze solid; if you leaned against a pillar, you would freeze to that, and if you put your hand upon the blade of your knife, you would run a chance of leaving your skin on it. The men would tie up their feet in newspapers and old sacks, and these would be soaked in blood and frozen, and then soaked again, and so on, until by nighttime a man would be walking on great lumps the size of the feet of an elephant. Now and then, when the bosses were not looking, you would see them plunging their feet and ankles into the steaming hot carcass of the steer. . . . The cruelest thing of all was that nearly all of them—all of those who used knives—were unable to wear gloves, and their arms would be white with frost and their hands would grow numb, and then of course there would be accidents."[1]

[1] From Upton Sinclair, *The Jungle* (New York: Bantam Books, 1981), p. 80, a 1906 novel about the meat-packing industry.

INTRODUCTION

For most of history, the concept of career planning was unknown. By and large, people were born into their jobs. Whatever their parents had been—landowner, soldier, farmer, servant, merchant, or beggar—they became, too. People not only knew their place, they also understood the rights and obligations inherent in each position. The landowner had the right to receive labor from his tenants, but he also cared for them if they fell ill. Certainly, there were abuses, but at a time when people held religious convictions about their position in life and workers had few expectations that their lives would be better than their parents', the role of law was limited. The primary English law of employment simply established that, in the absence of a contract, an employee was hired for a year at a time. This rule was designed to prevent injustice in an agrarian society. If an employee worked through harvest time, the landowner could not fire him in the unproductive winter. Conversely, a worker could not stay the winter and then leave for greener pastures in the spring.

In the eighteenth and nineteenth centuries, the Industrial Revolution profoundly altered the employment relationship. Many workers left the farms and villages for large factories in the city. Bosses no longer knew their workers personally, so they felt little responsibility toward them. The old laws that had suited an agrarian economy with stable relationships did not fit the new employment conditions. Instead of duties and responsibilities, courts emphasized the freedom to contract. Since employees could quit their factory jobs whenever they wanted, it was only fair for employers to have the same freedom to fire a worker. That was indeed the rule adopted by the courts: unless workers had an explicit employment contract, they were employees at will. **An employee at will could be fired for a good reason, a bad reason, or no reason at all.** For nearly a century, this was the basic common law rule of employment. A court explained the rule this way:

> Precisely as may the employee cease labor at his whim or pleasure, and, whatever be his reason, good, bad, or indifferent, leave no one a legal right to complain; so, upon the other hand, may the employer discharge, and, whatever be his reason, good, bad, or indifferent, no one has suffered a legal wrong.[2]

However evenhanded this common law rule of employment may have sounded in theory, in practice it could lead to harsh results. The lives of factory workers were grim. It was not as if they could simply pack up and leave; conditions were no better elsewhere. For the worker, freedom to contract often meant little more than freedom to starve to death. Courts and legislatures gradually began to recognize that individual workers were generally unable to negotiate fair contracts with powerful employers. Over the course of the twentieth century, employment law changed dramatically. Now, the employment relationship is more strictly regulated by statutes and by the common law. No longer can a boss discharge an employee for any reason whatsoever.

Note that many of the statutes discussed in this chapter were passed by Congress and therefore apply nationally. The common law, however, comes

---

[2] *Union Labor Hospital Assn. v. Vance Redwood Lumber Co.*, 112 P.886, 888, 1910 Cal. LEXIS 417 (Cal. 1910).

from state courts and only applies locally. We will look at a sampling of cases that illustrate national trends, even though the law may not be the same in every state.

This chapter covers four topics in employment law: (1) employment security, (2) safety and privacy in the workplace, (3) financial protection, and (4) employment discrimination.

EMPLOYMENT SECURITY

NATIONAL LABOR RELATIONS ACT

Without unions to represent employee interests, employers could simply fire any troublemaking workers who complained about conditions in factories or mines. By joining together, workers could bargain with their employers on more equal terms. Naturally, the owners fought against the unions, firing organizers and even hiring goons to beat them up. Distressed by anti-union violence, Congress passed the **National Labor Relations Act** in 1935. Known as the **NLRA** or the **Wagner Act**, this statute:

- Created the National Labor Relations Board to enforce labor laws
- Prohibits employers from penalizing workers who engage in union activity (for example, joining a preexisting union or forming a new one); and
- Requires employers to "bargain in good faith" with unions.

Labor law is covered at greater length in Chapter 15.

FAMILY AND MEDICAL LEAVE ACT

In 1993, Congress passed the Family and Medical Leave Act (FMLA), which guarantees both men and women up to 12 weeks of *unpaid* leave each year for childbirth, adoption, or medical emergencies for themselves or a family member. An employee who takes a leave must be allowed to return to the same or an equivalent job with the same pay and benefits. The FMLA applies only to companies with at least 50 workers and to employees who have been with the company full-time for at least a year. About 44 percent of women and 50 percent of men in the workforce are covered.

When Randy Seale's wife went into premature labor with triplets, he stayed home from his job as a truck driver with Associated Milk Producers, Inc. in Roswell, New Mexico. However, the milk of human kindness did not flow in this company's veins: it promptly fired the expectant father. Since Seale was an employee at will, the company's action would have been perfectly legal without the FMLA. But after the U.S. Department of Labor filed suit, the company agreed to pay Seale $10,000.

Concerned that the FMLA would impose too heavy a burden on business, Congress appointed a bipartisan commission to study its impact. The commission reported that, because leaves are unpaid, only about 4 percent of eligible workers actually ask for time off. More than three-quarters of the companies surveyed said that the cost of compliance was small. The commission generally found "an overall picture of enhanced employee productivity, good will and willingness 'to go the extra mile.'" The commission's report is available at **http://www.ilr.cornell.edu/library/e_archive/gov_reports/default.html?page=family_medical%2Ffamily_medical**.

WRONGFUL DISCHARGE

Olga Monge was a schoolteacher in her native Costa Rica. After moving to New Hampshire, she attended college in the evenings to earn U.S. teaching credentials. At night, she worked at the Beebe Rubber Co. During the day, she cared for her husband and three children. When she applied for a better job at her plant, the foreman offered to promote her if she would be "nice" and go out on a date with him. When she refused, he assigned her to a lower wage job, took away her overtime, made her clean the washrooms, and generally ridiculed her. Finally, she collapsed at work and he fired her.[3]

Imagine that you are one of the judges who decided this case. Olga Monge has been treated abominably, but she was an employee at will and, as you well know, could be fired for any reason. But how can you let the foreman get away with this despicable behavior? The New Hampshire Supreme Court decided that even an employee at will has rights:

> We hold that a termination by the employer of a contract of employment at will which is motivated by bad faith or malice or based on retaliation is not in the best interest of the economic system or the public good and constitutes a breach of the employment contract.[4]

The employment at will doctrine was created by the courts. Because that rule has sometimes led to absurdly unfair results, the courts have now created a major exception to the rule—**wrongful discharge**. The *Monge* case illustrates this concept. ***Wrongful discharge* prohibits an employer from firing a worker for a *bad reason*.** There are three categories of wrongful discharge claims: public policy, contract law, and tort law.

PUBLIC POLICY

The *Monge* case is an example of the **public policy rule**. Unfortunately, naming the rule is easier than defining it, because its definition and application vary from state to state. **In essence, the public policy rule prohibits an employer from firing a worker for a reason that violates basic social rights, duties, or responsibilities.** Virtually every employee who has ever been fired feels that a horrible injustice has been done. The difficulty, from the courts' perspective, is to distinguish those cases of dismissal that are offensive enough to arouse the community at large from those that outrage only the employee. The courts have primarily applied the public policy rule when an employee refuses to violate the law or insists upon exercising a legal right or performing a legal duty.

Refusing to Violate the Law. Larry Downs went to Duke Hospital for surgery on his cleft palate. When he came out of the operating room, the doctor instructed a nurse, Marie Sides, to give Downs enough anesthetic to immobilize

---

[3] *Monge v. Beebe*, 114 N.H. 130, 316 A.2d 549, 1974 N.H. LEXIS 223 (1974).

[4] Id. at 133.

him. Sides refused because she thought the anesthetic was wrong for this patient. The doctor angrily administered the anesthetic himself. Shortly thereafter, Downs stopped breathing. Before the doctors could resuscitate him, he suffered permanent brain damage. When Downs's family sued the hospital, Sides was called to testify. A number of Duke doctors told her that she would be "in trouble" if she testified. She did testify and, after three months of harassment, was fired. When she sued Duke University, the court held:

> It would be obnoxious to the interests of the state and contrary to public policy and sound morality to allow an employer to discharge any employee, whether the employment be for a designated or unspecified duration, on the ground that the employee declined to commit perjury, an act specifically enjoined by statute. To hold otherwise would be without reason and contrary to the spirit of the law.[5]

As a general rule, employees may not be discharged for refusing to break the law. For example, courts have protected employees who refused to participate in an illegal price-fixing scheme, falsify pollution control records required by state law, pollute navigable waters in violation of federal law, or assist a supervisor in stealing from customers.[6] In the following case, an employee refused to commit a misdemeanor—indecent exposure.

WAGENSELLER v. SCOTTSDALE MEMORIAL HOSPITAL

147 Ariz. 370, 710 P.2d 1025, 1985 Ariz. LEXIS 250
Supreme Court of Arizona, 1985

Facts: Kay Smith was Catherine Wagenseller's supervisor at Scottsdale Memorial Hospital. Together with nurses from other hospitals, the two women went on an eight-day rafting trip down the Colorado River. As the trip progressed, Wagenseller became increasingly offended by Smith's behavior: heavy drinking, and public urination, defecation, and bathing. At the end of the trip, Wagenseller refused to join in a parody of the song "Moon River," which concluded with members of the group "mooning" the audience. After returning from the trip, Smith and others performed the "Moon River" skit twice at the hospital. Again, Wagenseller refused to participate. Smith began harassing Wagenseller, using abusive language and embarrassing her in front of other staff. Before the trip, Wagenseller had received consistently favorable job performance evaluations. Six months after the outing, she was fired. Wagenseller contended she was fired for reasons that contravene public policy.

The trial court dismissed her claims on a motion for summary judgment. The appeals court affirmed this dismissal. Wagenseller appealed.

Issue: Does the public policy doctrine prohibit the hospital from firing Wagenseller?

Excerpts from Judge Feldman's Decision: The Hospital argues that an "at-will" employee may be fired for cause, without cause, or for "bad" cause. In recent years there has been apparent dissatisfaction with the absolutist

[5] *Sides v. Duke University*, 74 N.C. App. 331, 328 S.E.2d 818, 1985 N.C. App. LEXIS 3501 (N.C. Ct. App. 1985).

[6] *Tameny v. Atlantic Richfield Co.*, 27 Cal. 3d 167, 610 P.2d 1330, 1980 Cal. LEXIS 171 (1980); *Trombetta v. Detroit, T. & I. R. R.*, 81 Mich. App. 489, 265 N.W.2d 385, 1978 Mich. App. LEXIS 2153 (Mich. Ct. App. 1978); *Sabine Pilot Service, Inc. v. Hauck*, 28 Tex. Sup. J. 339, 687 S.W.2d 733, 1985 Tex. LEXIS 755 (1985); *Vermillion v. AAA Pro Moving & Storage*, 146 Ariz. 215, 704 P.2d 1360, 1985 Ariz. App. LEXIS 592 (Ariz. Ct. App. 1985).

formulation of the common law at-will rule. With the rise of large corporations conducting specialized operations and employing relatively immobile workers who often have no other place to market their skills, recognition that the employer and employee do not stand on equal footing is realistic. In addition, unchecked employer power, like unchecked employee power, has been seen to present a distinct threat to the public policy carefully considered and adopted by society as a whole. As a result, it is now recognized that a proper balance must be maintained among the employer's interest in operating a business efficiently and profitably, the employee's interest in earning a livelihood, and society's interest in seeing its public policies carried out.

The trend has been to modify the at-will rule by creating exceptions to its operation. The most widely accepted approach is the "public policy" exception, which permits recovery upon a finding that the employer's conduct undermined some important public policy. In general, it can be said that public policy concerns what is right and just and what affects the citizens of the State collectively. It is to be found in the State's constitution and statutes and, when they are silent, in its judicial decisions.

[T]he interests of the economic system will be fully served if employers may fire for good cause or without cause. The interests of society as a whole will be promoted if employers are forbidden to fire for cause which is "morally wrong." We therefore adopt the public policy exception to the at-will termination rule. We hold that an employer may fire for good cause or for no cause. He may not fire for bad cause—that which violates public policy.

[Not all unfair terminations are violations of public policy.] For example the Oregon Supreme Court refused to recognize a cause of action for the discharge of an employee who claimed he was wrongfully terminated for exercising his statutory right as a stockholder to examine the books of his corporate employer. The court based its determination on its finding that the right claimed was "not one of public policy, but the private and proprietary interest of stockholders, as owners of the corporation."

In the case before us, Wagenseller refused to participate in activities which arguably would have violated our indecent exposure statute. [T]his statute was enacted to preserve and protect the commonly recognized sense of privacy and decency. The statute does, therefore, recognize bodily privacy as a "citizen's social right." We are compelled to conclude that termination of employment for refusal to participate in public exposure of one's buttocks is a termination contrary to the policy of this state. [The Arizona Supreme Court overturned the lower court's grant of summary judgment and remanded the case for trial.]

Does an employer ever have the right to require workers to participate in an illegal scheme? Suppose that compliance with state pollution control regulations would force a company out of business. When the life of the company is at stake, does the boss have a right to expect a worker to cooperate by fudging records?

Exercising a Legal Right. As a general rule, an employer may not discharge a worker for exercising a legal right if that right supports public policy. Dorothy Frampton injured her arm while working at the Central Indiana Gas Co. Her employer (and its insurance company) paid her medical expenses and her salary during the four months she was unable to work. When she discovered that she also qualified for benefits under the state's workers' compensation plan, she filed a claim and received payment. One month later, the company fired her without giving a reason. In her suit against the gas company, the court held:

> The [Workers' Compensation] Act creates a duty in the employer to compensate employees for work-related injuries and a right in the employee to receive such

> compensation. If employers are permitted to penalize employees for filing workmen's compensation claims, a most important public policy will be undermined. Employees will not file claims for justly deserved compensation—opting, instead, to continue their employment without incident. The end result, of course, is that the employer is effectively relieved of his obligation.[7]

Performing a Legal Duty. **Courts have consistently held that an employee may not be fired for serving on a jury.** Employers sometimes have difficulty replacing employees who are called up for jury duty and, therefore, prefer that their workers find some excuse for not serving. But jury duty is an important civic duty that employers are not permitted to undermine.

What about an employee who performs a good deed that is not legally required? Kevin Gardner had just parked his armored truck in front of a bank in Spokane, Washington, when he saw a man with a knife chase the manager out of the bank. While running past the truck, the manager looked directly at Gardner and yelled, "Help me, help me." Gardner got out of his truck and locked the door. By then, the suspect had grabbed another woman, put his knife to her throat, and dragged her into the bank. Gardner followed them in, tackled the suspect, and disarmed him. The rescued woman hailed Gardner as a hero, but his employer fired him for violating a "fundamental" company rule that forbade drivers to leave their armored trucks unattended. However, the court held for Gardner on the grounds that, although there is no affirmative legal duty to intervene in such a situation, society values and encourages voluntary rescuers when a life is in danger.[8]

Unlike Kevin Gardner's heroics, which did not injure his employer, whistleblowers do harm their employers (at least in the short run). **Whistleblowers** are employees who disclose illegal behavior on the part of their employer. Here is the story of Henry Boisvert.

FMC Corp. sold 9,000 Bradley Fighting Vehicles to the U.S. Army for as much as $1.5 million each. But the Bradley was controversial from the moment it began rolling off FMC's manufacturing lines. Designed to carry soldiers around battlefields in Eastern Europe, its ability to "swim" across rivers and lakes was an important part of its job description. But Henry Boisvert, a testing supervisor for FMC, charged that the Bradley swam like a rock. Boisvert said he first encountered problems with the Bradley in the early days of the Army procurement process. He had one driven into a test pond and watched it quickly fill with water. FMC welders who worked on Bradleys claimed they weren't given enough time to do their work properly and so would simply fill gaps with putty. FMC quashed Boisvert's report on the Bradley and fired him when he refused to sign a falsified version. FMC disputes his account, but a jury ultimately agreed with him.[9]

---

[7] *Frampton v. Central Indiana Gas Co.*, 260 Ind. 249, 297 N.E.2d 425, 1973 Ind. LEXIS 522 (1973).

[8] *Gardner v. Loomis Armored, Inc.*, 913 P.2d 377, 1996 Wash. LEXIS 109 (1996).

[9] Lee Gomes, "A Whistle-Blower Finds Jackpot at the End of His Quest," *The Wall Street Journal*, April 27, 1998, p. B1. Republished with permission of The Wall Street Journal; permission conveyed through the Copyright Clearance Center, Inc.

The law on whistleblowers varies across the country. Federal statutes protect certain kinds of employee conduct in specific industries. Some states provide broad protection and others offer none at all. As a general rule, however, whistleblowers are protected in the following situations:

- *Wrongdoing by Government Contractors.* Henry Boisvert refused to sign his name to a report he thought was inaccurate. As a result, he may soon be signing a check from FMC for $100 million. Boisvert recovered from FMC under the False Claims Act, a statute Congress amended in 1986 to prevent retaliation against employees who report wrongdoing by government contractors. The Act permits individuals to sue these contractors on behalf of the federal government and to receive between 15 and 30 percent of any damage awards. In the first 10 years of the statute, the government recovered $3.3 billion, with $195 million going to those who blew the whistle. The Act also prohibits employers from firing workers who bring suit under the statute. In 1997, a federal district court in Houston held that the False Claims Act is unconstitutional.[10] This decision has been criticized by other courts, and ultimately the United States Supreme Court may have to decide the fate of the Act.
- *Constitutional Protection for Government Employees.* Employees of federal, state, and local governments have a right to free speech under the United States Constitution. Therefore, the government cannot retaliate against public employees who blow the whistle, as long as the employee is speaking out on a matter of public concern. For example, a New York City child welfare agency received numerous reports that six-year-old Elisa Izquierdo was being abused. After Elisa was beaten to death by her mother, ABC News broadcast an interview with a social worker from the agency. She stated on air that "The workers who are considered the best workers are the ones who seem to be able to move cases out quickly. . . . There are lots of fatalities the press doesn't know anything about." By giving this interview, the social worker violated New York City rules prohibiting employees from disclosing information about families supervised by city agencies. The city suspended the social worker from her job, and she sued. The court acknowledged that the government has the right to prohibit some employee speech. However, if the employee speaks on matters of public concern, the government bears the burden of justifying any retaliation. In this case, the court held for the social worker. The city reinstated her and gave her back pay.[11]
- *Statutory Protection for Federal Employees.* Congress passed the Civil Service Reform Act in 1978 and the Whistleblower Protection Act in 1989. These two statutes prevent retaliation against federal employees who report wrongdoing. They also permit the award of back pay and attorney's fees to the whistleblower. This statute was used to prevent the National Park Service from disciplining two managers who wrote a report expressing concern over development in Yellowstone National Park.

---

[10] *United States v. St. Luke's Episcopal Hospital*, 982 F. Supp. 1261, 1997 U.S. Dist. LEXIS 16954 (S.D. Tex. 1997).

[11] *Harman v. City of New York*, 140 F.3d 111, 1998 U.S. App. LEXIS 5567 (2d Cir. 1998).

- *When an Employee Is Involved in the Illegal Activity.* As we have seen, courts protect employees from retaliation for refusing to commit an illegal act. As a variation on the same theme, most courts will protect employees who report illegal activity out of fear that otherwise they will be implicated. For example, Emart Sheets was quality control director for Teddy's Frosted Foods, Inc., a frozen food producer. The company fired him after he reported to his boss that some of the company's vegetables were substandard and some meat products were underweight. The court held that his discharge was wrongful because, as director of quality control, he might have been prosecuted for violating Connecticut food labeling laws.[12]
- *When an Employee Is Not Involved in Illegal Activity.* The courts in some states will protect employees who disclose illegal activities even if they are not personally involved. An Illinois court held that International Harvester Co. could not fire an employee for telling law enforcement officials about a co-worker's criminal activities.[13] The outcome was different for Donald Smith, however. He had been employed by Calgon Carbon Corp. for his entire adult life, working his way up from floor sweeper to Supervisor of Warehouse and Inventory Control. He discovered that 73,000 pounds of caustic soda had spilled into the river next to the warehouse. His boss told him to ignore the spill, but Smith instead reported it to corporate headquarters. He was fired. The court held that, since Smith had no responsibility for reporting spills, the public's interest "in harmony and productivity in the workplace must prevail over the public's interest in encouraging an employee in Smith's position to express his 'informed view.'"[14]

For more information about the legal rights of whistleblowers, see http://www.whistleblowers.org/. The Web site at http://www.whistleblower.org/www/checklist.htm offers advice to those who are thinking about blowing the whistle.

CONTRACT LAW

Traditionally, many employers (and employees) thought that only a formal, signed document qualified as an employment contract. Increasingly, however, courts have been willing to enforce an employer's more casual promises, whether written or oral. Sometimes courts have also been willing to *imply* contract terms in the absence of an *express* agreement.

Truth in Hiring. **Oral promises made during the hiring process can be enforceable, even if not approved by the company's top executives.** When the Tanana Valley Medical-Surgical Group, Inc. hired James Eales as a physician's assistant, it promised him that as long as he did his job, he could stay there until retirement age. Six years later the company fired him without cause. The Alaska Supreme Court held that the clinic's promise was enforceable.[15]

---

[12] *Sheets v. Teddy's Frosted Foods, Inc.*, 179 Conn. 471, 427 A.2d 385, 1980 Conn. LEXIS 690 (1980).

[13] *Palmateer v. International Harvester Co.*, 85 Ill. 2d 124, 421 N.E.2d 876, 1981 Ill. LEXIS 282 (1981).

[14] *Smith v. Calgon Carbon Corp.*, 917 F.2d 1338, 1990 U.S. App. LEXIS 19193 (3rd Cir. 1990).

[15] *Eales v. Tanana Valley Medical-Surgical Group, Inc.*, 663 P.2d 958, 1983 Alas. LEXIS 430 (Alaska 1983).

When the Automobile Club of Michigan hired William J. Bullock as a salesman, his supervisor promised him lifetime employment as long as he did not steal company funds. Fourteen years later, Bullock was fired when he failed to meet new company sales quotas. He sued the club, alleging that it had breached the supervisor's 14-year-old promise. The auto club argued that the suit should be dismissed because policy statements in subsequent employee handbooks made clear that no employee jobs were guaranteed. The Michigan Supreme Court held that an employer's oral promise is enforceable even if contradicted by later written policies.[16]

In the cases of both Eales and Bullock, the employer could have kept its promise but chose not to. **Courts have also held employers liable when they make promises that they *cannot* keep.** An engineer recovered $160,000 after a defense contractor laid him off. When the firm had hired him, it did not tell him that its work on the B-2 bomber was being scaled back. The firm also had lied about how much of the company's work was defense related. Therefore the contractor was liable even though it had no work for the engineer to do. Victoria Stewart joined the New York law firm, Jackson & Nash, because it promised her a major environmental law client. The client never materialized, and the firm's efforts to obtain new clients failed. A court decided that she had a valid claim.[17]

Employee Handbooks. The employee handbook at Blue Cross & Blue Shield stated that employees could be fired only for just cause and then only after warnings, notice, a hearing, and other procedures. Charles Toussaint was fired summarily five years after he joined the insurance company. Although this decision was ultimately reviewed by the personnel department, company president, and chairman of the board of trustees, Toussaint was not given the benefit of all of the procedures in the handbook. The court held that **an employee handbook creates a contract.**[18]

PREVENTIVE Law

Employers concerned about their potential liability for implied contracts are now taking steps to protect themselves. Some employers require new hires to sign a document acknowledging that (1) they are employees at will, (2) they can be terminated at any time for any reason, and (3) no one at the company has made any oral representations concerning the terms of employment. These employers caution interviewers not to make promises. Their employee handbooks now feature stern legal warnings, rather than friendly welcomes.

Alternatively, some employers establish a "peer review" process to ensure workers are not fired for bad reasons. Ruth Hatton, who had worked for 19 years as a waitress at the Red Lobster chain, was fired for stealing a guest comment card. Within three weeks after she asked for a peer review, the company convened a panel consisting of two managers and three hourly workers to review the case. Hatton had pocketed the guest comment card of a couple after they complained that she was uncooperative and their prime rib was too rare. She testified that she had taken the meat back to the kitchen several times and

---

[16] *Bullock v. Automobile Club of Michigan*, 432 Mich. 472, 444 N.W.2d 114, 1989 Mich. LEXIS 1411 (1989).

[17] *Stewart v. Jackson & Nash*, 976 F.2d 86, 1992 U.S. App. LEXIS 23373 (2d Cir. 1992).

[18] *Toussaint v. Blue Cross & Blue Shield*, 408 Mich. 579, 292 N.W.2d 880, 1980 Mich. LEXIS 227 (1980).

had even offered the couple a free dessert. She also said that she had intended to show the card to her boss, but forgot. Although initially the panelists split by rank, with the hourly employees supporting Hatton, they eventually agreed unanimously to restore her job, but did not give her the three weeks' pay she had missed. Both sides were content with the outcome and avoided protracted litigation. Many companies mandate that, if the internal review process fails, the case must go to binding arbitration, not to court.

DaimlerChrysler instituted such a program of internal review and external arbitration for all nonunion salaried employees, including the chief executive officer. Nationally, more than half of all executive contracts require that disputes go to arbitration, not litigation.

Covenant of Good Faith and Fair Dealing. A covenant of good faith and fair dealing prohibits one party to a contract from interfering with the other's right to benefit under the contract. **In some cases, courts will imply a covenant of good faith and fair dealing in an at-will employment relationship.**

When Forrest Fleming went to work for Parametric Technology Corp., the company promised him valuable stock options if he met his sales goals. He would not be able to *exercise* the options (that is, purchase the stock), however, until several years after they were granted and then only if he was still employed by the company. During his four years with Parametric, Fleming received options to purchase about 18,000 shares for as little as 25 cents each. The shares ultimately traded in the market for as much as $50. Although Fleming exercised some options, the company fired him three months before he became eligible to purchase an additional 1,000 shares. The jury awarded him $1.6 million in damages. Although Parametric had not violated the explicit terms of the option agreement, the jury believed it had violated the covenant of good faith and fair dealing by firing Fleming to prevent him from exercising his remaining options.

TORT LAW

Workers have successfully sued their employers under the following tort theories.

Defamation. **Employers may be liable for defamation when they give false and unfavorable references about a former employee.** John R. Glennon, Jr., was the branch manager of Dean Witter's Nashville office. Dean Witter fired him and filed a termination notice with the National Association of Securities Dealers saying that Glennon "was under internal review for violating investment-related statutes." This statement was untrue, and Witter had to pay $1.5 million in damages for defamation.

More than half of the states, however, recognize a qualified privilege for employers who give references about former employees. A **qualified privilege** means that employers are liable only for false statements that they know to be false or that are primarily motivated by ill will. After Becky Chambers left her job at American Trans Air, Inc., she discovered that her former boss was telling anyone who called for a reference that Chambers "does not work good with other people," is a "troublemaker," and "would not be a good person to rehire." Chambers was unable, however, to present compelling evidence that her boss had been primarily motivated by ill will. Neither Trans Air nor the boss was held liable for these statements because they were protected by the qualified privilege.[19]

Even if the employer wins, a trial is an expensive and time-consuming undertaking. Not surprisingly, companies are leery about offering any references for former employees. The company gains little benefit from giving an honest evaluation and may suffer substantial liability. As a matter of policy, many companies instruct their managers to reveal only a person's salary and dates of employment and not to offer an opinion on job performance. According to one survey, only 55 percent of former employers are totally honest when they give references.

Employers are afraid of liability if they give a negative reference, but are they liable if they tell less than the whole truth? Generally, courts have held that employers do not have a legal obligation to disclose information about former employees. For example, while Jeffrey St. Clair worked at the St. Joseph Nursing Home, he was disciplined 24 times for actions ranging from extreme violence to drug and alcohol use. When he applied for a job with Maintenance Management Corp. (MMC), St. Joseph refused to give any information other than St. Clair's dates of employment. When he savagely murdered a security guard at his new job, the guard's family sued, but the court dismissed the case.[20] In some recent cases, however, courts have held that, when a former worker is potentially dangerous, employers do have an obligation to disclose this information. For example, officials from two junior high schools gave Robert Gadams glowing letters of recommendation without mentioning that he had been fired for inappropriate sexual conduct with students. While an assistant principal at a new school, he molested a 13-year-old. Her parents sued the former employers. The court held that the writer of a letter of recommendation owes to third parties (in this case, the student) "a duty not to misrepresent the facts in describing the qualifications and character of a former employee, if making these misrepresentations would present a substantial, foreseeable risk of physical injury to the third persons."[21] As a result of cases such as this, it makes sense to disclose past violent behavior.

To assist employers who are asked for references, Lehigh economist Robert Thornton has written "The Lexicon of Intentional Ambiguous Recommendations" (LIAR). For a candidate with interpersonal problems, he suggests saying, "I am pleased to say that this person is a former colleague of mine." For the lazy worker, "In my opinion, you will be very fortunate to get this person to work for you." For the criminal, he suggests, "He's a man of many convictions" and "I'm sorry we let her get away." For the untrustworthy candidate, "Her true ability is deceiving."[22]

---

[19] *Chambers v. American Trans Air, Inc.*, 577 N.E.2d 612, 1991 Ind. App. LEXIS 1413 (Ind. Ct. App. 1991).

[20] *Moore v. St. Joseph Nursing Home, Inc.*, 184 Mich. App. 766, 459 N.W.2d 100, 1990 Mich. App. LEXIS 285 (Mich. Ct. App. 1990).

[21] *Randi W. v. Muroc Joint Unified School District*, 14 Cal. 4th 1066, 929 P.2d 582, 1997 Cal. LEXIS 10 (1997), modified, 14 Cal. 4th 1282c, 97 Cal. Daily Op. Service 1439.

[22] *The Wall Street Journal*, Mar. 22, 1994, p. 1.

All joking aside, what if someone calls you to check references on a former employee who had a drinking problem? The job is driving a van for junior high school sports teams. What is the manager's ethical obligation in this situation? Many managers say that, in the case of a serious problem such as alcoholism, sexual harassment, or drug use, they will find a way to communicate that an employee is unsuitable. What if the ex-employee says she is reformed? Aren't people entitled to a second chance? Is it right to risk a defamation suit against your company to protect others from harm?

Intentional Infliction of Emotional Distress. **Employers who condone cruel treatment of their workers face liability under the tort of intentional infliction of emotional distress.** For example:

- When a 57-year-old social-work manager at Yale–New Haven Hospital was fired, she was forced to place her personal belongings in a plastic bag and was escorted out the door by security guards in full view of gaping co-workers. A supervisor told her that she would be arrested for trespassing if she returned. A jury awarded her $105,000.
- An employee swore at a co-worker and threatened her with a knife because she rejected his sexual advances. Her superiors fired her for complaining about the incident. A court held that the employer had inflicted emotional distress.[23]
- On the other hand, another court held that an employee who was fired for dating a co-worker did not have a valid claim for infliction of emotional distress.[24]

SAFETY AND PRIVACY IN THE WORKPLACE

WORKPLACE SAFETY

In 1970, Congress passed the Occupational Safety and Health Act (OSHA) to ensure safe working conditions. Under OSHA:

- Employers must comply with specific health and safety standards. For example, health care personnel who work with blood are not permitted to eat or drink in areas where the blood is kept and must not put their mouths on any instruments used to store blood. Protective clothing—gloves, gowns, and laboratory coats—must be impermeable to blood.
- Employers are under a general obligation to keep their workplace "free from recognized hazards that are causing or are likely to cause death or serious physical harm" to employees.

---

[23] *Hogan v. Forsyth Country Club Co.*, 79 N.C. App. 483, 340 S.E.2d 116, 1986 N.C. App. LEXIS 2098 (N.C. Ct. App. 1986).

[24] *Patton v. J. C. Penney Co.*, 301 Or. 117, 719 P.2d 854, 1986 Ore. LEXIS 1144 (1986).

- Employers must keep records of all workplace injuries and accidents.
- The Occupational Safety and Health Administration (also known as OSHA) may inspect workplaces to ensure that they are safe. OSHA may assess fines for violations and order employers to correct unsafe conditions.

EMPLOYEE PRIVACY

Upon opening the country's first moving assembly line 80 years ago, Henry Ford issued a booklet, "Helpful Hints and Advice to Employees," that warned against drinking, gambling, borrowing money, taking in boarders, and practicing poor hygiene. Ford also created a department of 100 investigators for door-to-door checks on his employees. The right to hire, fire, and make an honest profit is enshrined in American tradition. But so is the right to privacy. Justice Louis D. Brandeis called it the "right to be let alone—the most comprehensive of rights and the right most valued by civilized men."

Employers have a legitimate interest in increasing productivity and profits. With this goal in mind, some companies ban workplace romances for fear that they will upset other employees. Wal-Mart fired two employees for living together because one of them was married to someone else. The court upheld Wal-Mart's right to do so.[25]

In an era of rapidly expanding health care costs, employers are also concerned about the health of their workers. Some companies have banned *off-duty* smoking and have even fired employees who show traces of nicotine in their blood. But health—and privacy concerns—do not end with smoking. Some employers would prefer not to hire gay workers because AIDS treatments are so expensive. What protection do workers have against intrusive employers?

OFF-DUTY CONDUCT

At least 29 jurisdictions have passed laws that protect the right of employees to smoke cigarettes while off-duty. Some of these statutes permit *any* lawful activity when off-duty, including drinking socially, having high cholesterol, being overweight, or engaging in dangerous hobbies—bungee jumping or roller blading, for instance. Whether these statutes also protect extramarital sexual activity is unclear because in many states such behavior is illegal.

ALCOHOL AND DRUG TESTING

Government employees can be tested for drug and alcohol use only if they show signs of use or if they are in a job where this type of abuse endangers the public. Most states permit private employers to administer alcohol and drug tests. According to one survey, more than 80 percent of large firms test employees for drugs.

---

[25] *State of New York v. Wal-Mart Stores, Inc.*, 621 N.Y.S. 2d 158, 1995 N.Y. App. Div. LEXIS 17 (N.Y. App. Div. 1995).

LIE DETECTOR TESTS

Under the Employee Polygraph Protection Act of 1988, employers may not require, or even *suggest*, that an employee or job candidate submit to a lie detector test, except as part of an "on-going investigation" into crimes that have occurred.

ELECTRONIC MONITORING OF THE WORKPLACE

Technological advances in communications have raised a host of new privacy issues.

More than one-third of American companies monitor employee use of electronic equipment in the workplace: telephone calls, voice mail, e-mail, and Internet usage. **The Electronic Communications Privacy Act of 1986 (ECPA) permits employers to monitor workers' telephone calls and e-mail messages if (1) the employee consents, (2) the monitoring occurs in the ordinary course of business, or (3) in the case of e-mail, the employer provides the e-mail system.** However, bosses may not disclose any private information revealed by the monitoring.

About 15 percent of companies monitor their employees' e-mail (as compared with the 40 percent that listen to telephone conversations). Although workers may feel that their e-mail should be private, employers argue that this monitoring improves employee productivity and protects the company from lawsuits. For example, a West Coast company fired a woman "because of a tough economy." When she sued, her attorneys demanded access to the company's e-mail system as part of the discovery process. They found a message from the woman's supervisor saying, "Get that bitch out of here as fast as you can. I don't care what it takes. Just do it." The supervisor had long since erased the message from his computer, but it had remained buried in the system. A few hours after the message was revealed in court, the company settled for $250,000. If the employee had known that his e-mail would be read by others, perhaps he would not have sent such an inflammatory statement.

Many companies also monitor employee use of the Internet. They are concerned not only about lawsuits but also that workers may be wasting time. During one month, employees at IBM, Apple Computer, and AT&T logged on to *Penthouse* magazine's Web site 12,823 times, using the equivalent of more than 347 workdays. One company discovered that some of its employees were using their company computers to buy and sell child pornography. Companies fear that even legal logging on to sexually explicit sites may give rise to sexual harassment claims.

In the following case, two employees used company e-mail to trash talk. Could they be fired for their indiscretion?

MICHAEL A. SMYTH v. THE PILLSBURY CO.
914 F. Supp. 97, 1996 U.S. Dist. LEXIS 776
United States District Court for the Eastern District of Pennsylvania, 1996

Facts: The Pillsbury Co. repeatedly assured its employees that all company e-mail was confidential. The company promised not to intercept e-mail or use it against employees as grounds for reprimand or termination. One evening at home, Michael Smyth and his supervisor engaged in a series of e-mail exchanges that threatened to "kill the backstabbing bastards" (that is, company sales managers) and referred to the planned holiday party as the "Jim Jones Koolaid affair." The company found out about these e-mails and fired both men. Smyth sued, alleging that the company had violated his right to privacy.

You be the Judge: Is company e-mail private?

Argument for Smyth: The public policy doctrine prohibits an employer from firing a worker for a reason that violates basic social rights, duties, or responsibilities. Privacy is a fundamental social right that tort law protects. There are two issues under tort law:

- Did Pillsbury intrude into Smyth's life in a manner that any reasonable person would find offensive?
- Did Smyth have a reasonable expectation of privacy?

The answer to both of these questions is a resounding, "Yes." Today, people use e-mail almost as often as the telephone. They correspond not only with co-workers but also with friends and family members. Sitting in the privacy of their office or home, they do not expect their employer to be reading their e-mail.

Particularly in this case, Smyth had a reasonable expectation of privacy. The company had told him repeatedly that it would not read his e-mail. How could the company make such a promise and then fire him because he believed it?

Argument for Pillsbury: Smyth behaved in an unprofessional and unacceptable manner. The company had no choice but to fire him after he made death threats against other employees. What if the company had done nothing and he had carried out those threats?

Furthermore, Smyth could not have a reasonable expectation of privacy with an e-mail system that the company established and maintained for the use of its employees. Nor would a reasonable person find this intrusion offensive. No one forced Smyth to share his feelings about the company; he wrote and sent those e-mail messages *voluntarily*. This juvenile and inappropriate behavior demonstrated that he is totally unsuited for employment at Pillsbury. He has no one to blame but himself.

FINANCIAL PROTECTION

Congress and the states have enacted laws that provide employees with a measure of financial security. All of the laws in this section were created by statute, not by the courts.

FAIR LABOR STANDARDS ACT

Passed in 1938, the Fair Labor Standards Act (FLSA) regulates wages and limits child labor. The wage provisions do not apply to managerial, administrative, or professional staff, which means that accounting, consulting, and law firms (among others) are free to require as many hours a week as their employees can humanly perform without having to pay overtime or the minimum wage.

MINIMUM WAGE

The current federal minimum wage is $5.15 per hour, although some states have set a higher minimum. Employers can pay students and apprentices under age 20 a training wage of $4.25 per hour.

OVERTIME PAY

The FLSA does not limit the number of hours a week that an employee can work (or a student can study!), but it does specify that workers must be paid time and a half for any hours over 40 in one week.

CHILD LABOR

The FLSA prohibits "oppressive child labor," which means that children under 14 may work only in agriculture and entertainment. Fourteen- and 15-year-olds are permitted to work *limited* hours after school in nonhazardous jobs. Sixteen- and 17-year-olds may work *unlimited* hours in nonhazardous jobs.

WORKERS' COMPENSATION

Workers' compensation statutes ensure that employees receive payment for injuries incurred at work. Before workers' comp, injured employees could recover damages only if they sued their employer. It is the brave (or carefree) worker who is willing to risk a suit against his own boss. Lawsuits poison the atmosphere at work. Moreover, employers frequently won these suits by claiming that (1) the injured worker was contributorily negligent, (2) a fellow employee had caused the accident, or (3) the injured worker had assumed the risk of injury. As a result, seriously injured workers (or their families) often had no recourse against the employer.

Workers' comp statutes provide a fixed, certain recovery to the injured employee, no matter who was at fault for the accident. In return, employees are not permitted to sue their employers for negligence. The amounts allowed (for medical expenses and lost wages) under workers' comp statutes are often less than a worker might recover in court, but the injured employee trades the certainty of some recovery for the higher risk of rolling the dice at trial. Payments are approved by an administrative board that conducts an informal hearing into each claim. These payments are funded either through the purchase of private insurance or by a tax on employers—a tax that is based on how many injuries their employees have suffered. Thus employers have an incentive to maintain a safe working environment.

As the following article indicates, however, employees who suffer particularly egregious injuries may prefer to sue in court rather than accept the relatively small payments available under workers' comp.

A 27-year-old assistant manager at Saks Fifth Avenue, who was raped twice by a security guard, filed a $50 million negligence suit against the swanky retailer. In its background check, the store had failed to discover that the guard had previously been convicted of sexual assault. Despite its apparent negligence, Saks asked to have the case dismissed on the grounds that the attack was covered by workers' comp. Such a ruling would limit damages to lost wages and medical expenses—far less than the $50 million the manager sought.

Saks little imagined the furor its defense would create. A New York congresswoman and a state senator drafted federal and state laws that would prohibit employers from using workers' comp statutes in sex crimes. The National Organization of Women threatened to boycott the store and asked top fashion designers to stop doing business with Saks. In the end, the retailer agreed to give the manager a "substantial cash payment" and to drop the workers' comp defense in any further sexual assault cases. Said Rep. Carolyn Maloney, "Employers have to stop using workers' comp as a shield when negligence in the workplace results in rape. It's a terribly sad day in America when rape is considered all in a day's work."

SOCIAL SECURITY

The federal Social Security system began in 1935, during the depths of the Great Depression, to provide a basic safety net for the elderly, ill, and unemployed. **Currently, the Social Security system pays benefits to workers who are retired, disabled, or temporarily unemployed and to the spouses and children of disabled or deceased workers.** It also provides medical insurance to the retired and disabled.

The Social Security program is financed through a tax on wages that is paid by employers, employees, and the self-employed. Currently, employees pay a tax of 6.2 percent on their first $76,200 of income, and employers must match the employee's contribution. Since the self-employed have no boss to pay half the Social Security tax, they must pay both halves themselves.

Although the Social Security system has done much to reduce poverty among the elderly, many worry that it cannot survive in its current form. When workers pay taxes, the proceeds do not go into a savings account for their retirement, but instead are used to pay benefits to current retirees. In 1940, there were 40 workers for each retiree; currently, there are 3.3. By 2030, when the last baby boomers retire, there will be only 2 workers to support each retiree—a prohibitive burden. No wonder baby boomers are often cautioned not to count on Social Security when making their retirement plans.

The Federal Unemployment Tax Act (FUTA) is the part of the Social Security system that provides support to the unemployed. FUTA establishes some national standards, but states are free to set their own benefit levels and payment schedules. These payments are funded by a tax on employers. A worker who quits voluntarily or is fired for just cause is ineligible for benefits. While receiving payments, she must make a good faith effort to look for other employment.

PENSION BENEFITS

In 1974, Congress passed the Employee Retirement Income Security Act (ERISA) to protect workers covered by private pension plans. Under ERISA, employers are not required to establish pension plans, but if they do, they must follow these federal rules. The law was aimed, in particular, at protecting benefits of retired workers if their companies subsequently go bankrupt. The statute also prohibits risky investments by pension plans. In addition, the statute sets rules on the vesting of benefits. (An employer cannot cancel *vested* benefits; *non-vested* benefits are forfeited when the employee leaves.) Before ERISA, retirement benefits at some companies did not vest until the employee retired—if he quit or was fired before retirement, even after years of service, he lost his pension. Under current law, employee benefits vest after five years of employment.

EMPLOYMENT DISCRIMINATION

In the last four decades, Congress has enacted important legislation to prevent discrimination in the workplace.

EQUAL PAY ACT OF 1963

Under the Equal Pay Act, an employee may not be paid at a lesser rate than employees of the opposite sex for equal work. "Equal work" means tasks that require equal skill, effort, and responsibility under similar working conditions. If the employee proves that she is not being paid equally, the employer will be found liable unless the pay difference is based on merit, productivity, seniority, or some factor other than sex. A "factor other than sex" includes prior wages, training, profitability, performance in an interview, and value to the company. For example, female agents sued Allstate Insurance Co. because its salary for new agents was based, in part, on prior salary. The women argued that this system was unfair because it perpetuated the historic wage differences between men and women. The court, however, held for Allstate.[26]

Some employees have argued that equal pay for equal work is not enough to remedy the effects of past discrimination. They point to examples such as (female) librarians in Virginia who, with 10 years of experience and a master's degree, earn the same salary as (male) maintenance supervisors with a high school diploma. The solution, they argue, is **comparable worth**—equal pay for work of comparable value. Two people should be paid the same if their jobs, however different, require the same level of skill, education, and responsibility.

Supporters of comparable worth argue that traditional female occupations, such as nurse, teacher, waitress, and secretary, pay less than equivalent male jobs because of bias left over from the days of open discrimination against women. For instance, Westinghouse Corp. formerly had separate male and female job categories with corresponding wage rates. After the Equal Pay Act, the company kept female grades 1–5 in place and made the male jobs into grades 6–10, with higher wages. As a general rule, the more a job category is dominated by women, the less it pays.

Opponents of comparable worth argue that it would be a disastrous intrusion into the marketplace and would create economic chaos as courts, consultants, and managers struggled to assess the value of jobs. Only the market can

---

[26] *Kouba v. Allstate Insurance Co.*, 691 F.2d 873, 1982 U.S. App. LEXIS 24479 (9th Cir. 1982).

set wages at an equilibrium between supply and demand. If librarians feel that janitors are overpaid, there is a simple solution—they should become janitors, too. Although some employers have agreed to undertake comparable worth studies to settle litigation, the courts have generally not been receptive to this concept. The Equal Pay Act does not require equal pay for work of comparable worth.

In the absence of overt discrimination, U.S. courts have by and large let market forces set wages. The European Union (EU) has taken a different approach. To reduce the wage disparities between men and women, it requires member countries to adopt comparable worth regulations. To implement a comparable worth pay plan, a company must determine the relative value of its jobs by conducting detailed evaluation studies that consider the skill, level of responsibility, physical and mental effort, and working conditions of each job.

TITLE VII

Title VII of the Civil Rights Act of 1964 prohibits employers from discriminating on the basis of race, color, religion, sex, or national origin. (The text of Title VII is available at http://www.eeoc.gov/laws/vii.html.) Originally, "sex" was not included in the statute, but two days before passage, Rep. Howard Smith of Virginia added this word. His intention was not to promote equal opportunity for women, but rather to scuttle the bill. He figured that nobody—but nobody—would vote for a statute that prohibited discrimination against women. He thought wrong, and the most important piece of antidiscrimination legislation in the United States passed. Title VII prohibits (1) discrimination in the workplace, (2) sexual harassment, and (3) discrimination because of pregnancy. It also permits employers to develop affirmative action plans.

PROOF OF DISCRIMINATION

Discrimination under Title VII means firing, refusing to hire, failing to promote, or otherwise reducing a person's employment opportunities because of race, color, religion, sex, or national origin. This protection applies to every stage of the employment process from job ads to postemployment references and includes placement, wages, benefits, and working conditions.

Plaintiffs in Title VII cases can prove discrimination two different ways: disparate treatment and disparate impact.

Disparate Treatment. To prove a disparate treatment case, the plaintiff must show that she was treated differently because of her sex, race, color, religion, or national origin. The required steps in a disparate treatment case are shown on the following page.

Proving a case of disparate treatment is like a tennis match. Here is how the match goes:

1. The plaintiff serves the ball by making a ***prima facie*** case. That means she presents evidence that an employer has discriminated against her. At this point, she does not have to *prove* discrimination; she must simply produce evidence that could *indicate* discrimination. She does not have to ace the

Step 1.	The plaintiff presents evidence that the defendant has discriminated against her because of a protected trait. This is called a *prima facie* case. The plaintiff is not required to prove discrimination; she need only create a *presumption* that discrimination occurred.
Step 2.	The defendant must present evidence that its decision was based on *legitimate, nondiscriminatory* reasons.
Step 3.	To win, the plaintiff must now prove that the employer discriminated. She may do so by showing that the reasons offered were simply a *pretext.*

defendant at this stage; she simply has to put the ball in play. Suppose that Louisa applies for a job coaching a boys' high school ice hockey team. She was an All-American hockey star in college and made the U.S. National team. Although Louisa is obviously qualified for the job, Harry, the school principal, rejects her and continues to interview other people. This is not *proof* of discrimination, because Harry may have a perfectly good, nondiscriminatory explanation. However, his behavior could have been motivated by discrimination.

2. The ball is now in Harry's court. He must show a legitimate, nondiscriminatory reason for rejecting Louisa. He might say, for example, that he wanted someone with prior coaching experience. Although Louisa is clearly a great player whom he admires immensely, she has never coached before. This is a great return shot, and the ball is back in Louisa's court.

3. Louisa must now prove, by a preponderance of the evidence, that Harry's reason was simply a *pretext* for not hiring her. She might show that he had recently hired a male tennis coach who had no prior coaching experience. Or Harry's assistant might testify that Harry said, "No way I'm going to put a woman on the ice with those guys." If she can present evidence such as this, Louisa wins the point and match.

Disparate Impact. Disparate impact becomes an issue if the employer has a rule that, on its face, is not discriminatory, but in practice excludes too many people in a protected group. The steps in a disparate impact case are:

Step 1.	The plaintiff must present a *prima facie* case. The plaintiff is not required to prove discrimination; he need only show a disparate impact—that the employment practice in question excludes a disproportionate number of people in a protected group (women and minorities, for instance).
Step 2.	The defendant must show that the employment practice was job-related.
Step 3.	To win, the plaintiff must now prove either that the employer's reason is a pretext or that other, less discriminatory, rules would achieve the same results.

Suppose that Harry will only hire teachers who are at least 5 feet 10 inches tall and weigh 170 pounds. He says he is afraid that students will literally push around anyone smaller. When Chou Ping, an Asian male, applies for a job, he cannot meet Harry's physical requirements. Here is what might happen in their legal contest:

1. Chou Ping must show that Harry's rule, in *fact*, eliminates more women or minorities than white males. He might offer evidence that 50 percent of all white males can meet Harry's standard, but only 20 percent of white women and Asian males qualify.
2. Harry must demonstrate that his rule is *job-related*. He might produce evidence, for example, that teachers are regularly expected to wrestle students into their classroom seats. Further, he cites studies showing his standards are essential for this task.
3. Chou Ping will still win if he shows either that Harry's reason is a pretext or that other, less discriminatory rules would achieve the same results. Perhaps all teachers could take a self-defense course or engage in martial arts training.

Is Harry's reason valid? Compare his situation with a case involving firefighters. The city of Columbus, Ohio, required all applicants for firefighting jobs to take a written examination and a physical test. Nine percent of male applicants passed the physical test, compared with 2 percent of women. This evidence established a *prima facie* case. Columbus responded that physical skill was important for firefighters and the test was job-related. However, the city's own consultant had told it that four physical attributes are important for firefighters: strength, endurance, agility, and good health. The city's exam was a poor test of endurance and did not test agility at all. The court ordered the city to prepare a new physical exam that was job-related. The court explicitly stated that the city was not required to hire a quota of women; it was simply obligated to use a selection method that reasonably measured job performance.[27]

RELIGION

Employers must make *reasonable accommodation* for a worker's religious beliefs unless the request would cause *undue hardship* for the business. Scott Hamby told his manager at Wal-Mart that he could never work on Sunday because that was his Sabbath. It also happened to be one of the store's busiest days. When the manager forced Hamby to quit, he promptly sued on the grounds of religious discrimination. Lawsuits such as his are on the rise as more businesses remain open on Sundays. Wal-Mart denied wrongdoing but settled the case with a cash payment of undisclosed amount. It also established a company-wide training program on religious accommodation.

---

[27] *Brunet v. City of Columbus*, 642 F. Supp. 1214, 1986 U.S. Dist. LEXIS 25574 (S.D. Ohio 1986).

DEFENSES TO CHARGES OF DISCRIMINATION

Under Title VII, the defendant has three possible defenses.

Merit. A defendant is not liable if he shows that the person he favored was the most qualified. Test results, education, or productivity can all be used to demonstrate merit, provided they relate to the job in question. Harry can show that he hired Bruce instead of Louisa because Bruce has a master's degree in physical education and seven years of coaching experience. On the other hand, the fact that Bruce scored higher on the National Latin Exam in the eighth grade is not a good reason to hire him over Louisa.

Seniority. A legitimate seniority system is legal, even if it perpetuates past discrimination. Suppose that Harry has always chosen the most senior assistant coach to take over as head coach when a vacancy occurs. Since the majority of the senior assistant coaches are male, most of the head coaches are, too. Such a system does not violate Title VII.

Bona Fide Occupational Qualification. An employer is permitted to establish discriminatory job requirements if they are *essential* to the position in question. Such a requirement is called a **bona fide occupational qualification (BFOQ)**. Catholic schools may, if they choose, refuse to hire non-Catholic teachers; mail order companies may refuse to hire men to model women's clothing. Generally, however, courts are not sympathetic to claims of BFOQ. They have, for example, almost always rejected BFOQ claims that are based on customer preference. Thus airlines could not refuse to hire male flight attendants even though travelers prefer female attendants.[28] The major exception to this customer preference rule is sexual privacy: an employer may refuse to hire women to work in a men's bathroom and vice versa.

The Hooters restaurant chain refused to hire male waiters, arguing that its customers preferred attractive, buxom young women in revealing uniforms. Hooters asserted that it hired only women because the primary function of a Hooters Girl was to "provide vicarious sexual recreation." The Equal Employment Opportunity Commission (EEOC) countered, however, that "no physical trait unique to women is required to serve food and drink to customers in a restaurant." It ordered Hooters to pay $10 million to the men who were denied jobs as waiters.[29] After a public outcry ensued, the EEOC withdrew its order. It stated that, since a group of men had filed a private lawsuit already, the commission would devote its resources to other cases. Hooters settled the private lawsuit for $3.75 million and a promise that it would create a few support jobs, such as bartender and host, that could be filled by men or women. The settlement allows Hooters to continue to hire a female staff of Hooters Girls.

AFFIRMATIVE ACTION

Affirmative action has become a hot political issue: white males protest that such programs are reverse discrimination against them; political candidates campaign on anti-affirmative action platforms.

---

[28] *Diaz v. Pan American World Airways, Inc.*, 442 F.2d 385, 1971 U.S. App. LEXIS 10920 (5th Cir. 1971).

[29] As discussed below, under Title VII the EEOC has the right to file suit on behalf of a plaintiff.

Affirmative action is not required by Title VII, nor is it prohibited. Affirmative action programs have three different sources:

- *Litigation.* Courts have the power under Title VII to order affirmative action to remedy the effects of past discrimination.
- *Voluntary Action.* Employers can voluntarily introduce an affirmative action plan to remedy the effects of past practices or to achieve equitable representation of minorities and women.
- *Government Contracts.* In 1965, President Johnson signed Executive Order 11246, which prohibits discrimination by federal contractors. This order had a profound impact on the American workplace because one-third of all workers are employed by companies that do business with the federal government. If an employer found that women or minorities were underrepresented in its workplace, it was required to establish goals and timetables to correct the deficiency. In 1995, however, the Supreme Court dramatically limited the extent to which the government can require contractors to establish affirmative action programs. The Court ruled that these programs are permissible only if they serve a "compelling national interest" and are "narrowly tailored" so that they minimize the harm to white males. The government must be able to show that (1) the programs are needed to overcome specific past discrimination, (2) they have time limits, and (3) nondiscriminatory alternatives are not available.[30] Vowing to "mend, not end" affirmative action, President Clinton directed administration officials to review all federal programs. As a result of this review, the administration eliminated or altered 17 affirmative action programs, leading to a sharp decrease in the number of federal contracts awarded to companies owned by women and minorities.

Despite concerns about affirmative action, a federal panel set up to study the progress made by women and minorities in American industry found that white males constitute 29 percent of the workforce, but hold 95 percent of senior management positions.

SEXUAL HARASSMENT

When Professor Anita Hill accused Supreme Court nominee Clarence Thomas of sexually harassing her, people across the country were glued to their televisions, watching the Senate hearings on her charges. Thomas was ultimately confirmed to the Supreme Court, but "sexual harassment" became a household phrase. The number of cases—and the size of the damage awards—skyrocketed. In 1997, more than 15,000 sexual harassment charges were filed.

Everyone has heard of sexual harassment, but few people know exactly what it is. Men fear that a casual comment or glance will be met with career-ruining charges; women claim that men "just don't get it." So what is sexual harassment anyway? **Sexual harassment involves unwelcome sexual advances, requests for sexual favors, and other verbal or physical conduct of**

---

30 *Adarand Constructors, Inc. v. Pena*, 515 U.S. 200, 115 S. Ct. 2097, 1995 U.S. LEXIS 4037 (1995).

a sexual nature. There are two major categories of sexual harassment: (1) *quid pro quo* and (2) hostile work environment.

Quid Pro Quo. From a Latin phrase that means "this for that," *quid pro quo* harassment occurs if any aspect of a job is made contingent upon sexual activity. In other words, when a banker says to a secretary, "You can be promoted to teller if you sleep with me," that is *quid pro quo* sexual harassment.

Hostile Work Environment. This is a more subtle claim and the one that managers worry about most. An employee has a valid claim of sexual harassment if sexual talk and innuendo are so pervasive that they interfere with her (or his) ability to work. Courts have found that offensive jokes, comments about clothes or body parts, and public displays of pornographic pictures create a hostile environment. In the following case, the company president repeatedly insulted and demeaned his female employees.

TERESA HARRIS v. FORKLIFT SYSTEMS, INC.

510 U.S. 17, 114 S. Ct. 367, 1993 U.S. LEXIS 7155
United States Supreme Court, 1993

Facts: Teresa Harris was a manager at Forklift Systems; Charles Hardy was its president. Hardy frequently made inappropriate sexual comments to Harris and other women at the company. For example, he said to Harris, in the presence of others, "You're a woman, what do you know?" and "We need a man as the rental manager." He called her "a dumb ass woman" and suggested that the two of them "go to the Holiday Inn to negotiate her raise." He also asked Harris and other female employees to get coins from his front pants pocket. He insisted that Harris and other women pick up objects he had thrown on the ground. When Harris complained to Hardy, he apologized and claimed he was only joking. A month later, while Harris was arranging a deal with one of Forklift's customers, he asked her, in front of other employees, "What did you do, promise the guy some sex Saturday night?"

Harris sued Forklift, claiming that Hardy had created an abusive work environment. The federal trial court ruled against Harris on the grounds that Hardy's comments might offend a reasonable woman, but they were not severe enough to have a serious impact on Harris's psychological well-being. The appeals court confirmed, and the Supreme Court granted certiorari.

Issue: To be a violation of Title VII, must sexual harassment seriously affect the employee's psychological well-being?

Excerpts from Justice O'Connor's Decision: Title VII of the Civil Rights Act of 1964 makes it "an unlawful employment practice for an employer to discriminate against any individual with respect to his compensation, terms, conditions, or privileges of employment, because of such individual's race, color, religion, sex, or national origin." As we made clear in [a prior case] this language "is not limited to 'economic' or 'tangible' discrimination. The phrase 'terms, conditions, or privileges of employment' evinces a congressional intent 'to strike at the entire spectrum of disparate treatment of men and women in employment'," which includes requiring people to work in a discriminatorily hostile or abusive environment. When the workplace is permeated with "discriminatory intimidation, ridicule, and insult," that is "sufficiently severe or pervasive to alter the conditions of the victim's employment and create an abusive working environment," Title VII is violated.

This standard, which we reaffirm today, takes a middle path between making actionable any conduct that is merely offensive and requiring the conduct to cause a tangible psychological injury. As we pointed out in [the prior case], "mere utterance of an epithet which engenders offensive feelings in an employee," does not sufficiently affect the conditions of employment to implicate Title VII. Conduct that is not severe or pervasive enough to create an objectively hostile or abusive work environment—an environment that a reasonable person would find hostile or abusive—is beyond Title VII's purview. Likewise, if the victim does not subjectively perceive the environment to be abusive, the conduct has not actually altered the conditions of the victim's employment, and there is no Title VII violation.

But Title VII comes into play before the harassing conduct leads to a nervous breakdown. A discriminatorily abusive work environment, even one that does not seriously affect employees' psychological well-being, can and often will detract from employees' job performance, discourage employees from remaining on the job, or keep them from advancing in their careers. Moreover, even without regard to these tangible effects, the very fact that the discriminatory conduct was so severe or pervasive that it created a work environment abusive to employees because of their race, gender, religion, or national origin offends Title VII's broad rule of workplace equality.

We therefore believe the [trial court] erred in relying on whether the conduct "seriously affected plaintiff's psychological well-being" or led her to "suffer injury." Certainly Title VII bars conduct that would seriously affect a reasonable person's psychological well-being, but the statute is not limited to such conduct. So long as the environment would reasonably be perceived, and is perceived, as hostile or abusive . . . there is no need for it also to be psychologically injurious.

Employees who commit sexual harassment are liable for their own misdeeds. But is their company also liable? The Supreme Court has held that:

- If the victimized employee has suffered a "tangible employment action" such as firing, demotion, or reassignment, the company is liable to her for sexual harassment by a supervisor.
- If the victimized employee has not suffered a tangible employment action, the company is not liable if it can prove that (1) it used reasonable care to prevent and correct sexually harassing behavior, and (2) the employee unreasonably failed to take advantage of the complaint procedure or other preventive opportunities provided by the company.[31]

Corning Consumer Products Co. asks its employees to apply four tests in determining whether their behavior constitutes sexual harassment:

- Would you say or do this in front of your spouse or parents?
- What about in front of a colleague of the opposite sex?
- Would you like your behavior reported in your local newspaper?
- Does it need to be said or done at all?

PROCEDURES AND REMEDIES

Before a plaintiff in a Title VII case brings suit, she must first file a complaint with a federal agency, the Equal Employment Opportunity Commission (EEOC). (The EEOC's Web site is http://www.eeoc.gov/.) The EEOC then has the

[31] *Burlington Industries, Inc. v. Ellerth*, 524 U.S. 742, 118 S. Ct. 2257, 1998 U.S. LEXIS 4217 (1998); *Faragher v. Boca Raton*, 524 U.S. 775, 118 S. Ct. 2275, 1998 U.S. LEXIS 4216 (1998).

right to sue on behalf of the plaintiff. This is a favorable arrangement for the plaintiff because the government pays the legal bill. If the EEOC decides not to bring the case, or does *not* make a decision within six months, it issues a **right to sue letter**, and the plaintiff may proceed on her own in court. The number of employment discrimination cases more than doubled between 1992 and 1996 (from 10,000 to 23,000). At the same time, the EEOC dramatically decreased the number of lawsuits that it filed—from 322 in 1995 to 161 in 1996. Many states also have their own version of the EEOC, but these state commissions are often understaffed.

Remedies available to the successful plaintiff include hiring, reinstatement, retroactive seniority, back pay, reasonable attorney's fees, and punitive damages of up to $300,000.

PREGNANCY

Under the Pregnancy Discrimination Act of 1978, an employer may not fire or refuse to hire a woman because she is pregnant. An employer must also treat pregnancy as any other temporary disability. If, for example, employees are allowed time off from work for other medical disabilities, women must also be allowed a maternity leave. The United States, Australia, and New Zealand are the only industrialized nations that do not require employers to provide paid maternity leave.

AGE DISCRIMINATION

The Age Discrimination in Employment Act (ADEA) of 1967 prohibits age discrimination against employees or job applicants who are at least 40 years old. An employer may not fire, refuse to hire, fail to promote, or otherwise reduce a person's employment opportunities because he is 40 or older. Under this statute, an employer may not require a worker to retire at any age. Police and top-level corporate executives are exempted from the retirement rules, so they may indeed be forced to retire at a certain age.

The procedure for an age-bias claim is similar to that under Title VII—plaintiffs must first file a charge with the EEOC. If the EEOC does not take action, they can file suit themselves.

In the following case, Sears did not actually *fire* the employees; it simply made work so unpleasant for them that they quit. In the eyes of the law, that is as bad as terminating them.

JAMES v. SEARS, ROEBUCK & CO.

21 F.3d 989, 1994 U.S. App. LEXIS 7073
United States Court of Appeals for the Tenth Circuit, 1994

Facts: Sears offered the employees in its Ogden, Utah retail store and service center a buy-out. Employees who agreed to quit would receive a week of severance pay for each year they had worked at Sears, up to 26 weeks. At the same time, Sears also offered early retirement to employees 50 years of age or older. Employees accepting early retirement *lost* 35 percent of their accrued pension.

Sears made it clear to the plaintiffs, all of whom were over 50, that if they did not accept the offer, a pretext would be found for firing them. Although the plaintiffs were top sellers, their supervisors threatened, pressured, and systematically "wrote them up" for failing to meet sales quotas that other salespeople almost never met. An internal Sears' document showed that the company expected 13 older employees, but no employees under 40, to leave under the retirement/buy-out plan. A jury found that the company had discriminated against the plaintiffs on the basis of age. The company appealed.

Issue: Did Sears discriminate against its employees because of their age?

Excerpts from Judge Brorby's Decision: The facts before the jury presented either an ill-conceived and poorly executed corporate efficiency move or a deliberate corporate attempt to reduce payroll costs by replacing experienced and well-paid workers 40 years of age or older with lesser experienced and lower paid, younger workers.

A perceived demotion or reassignment to a job with lower status or lower pay may, depending upon the individual facts of the case, constitute aggravating factors that would justify a finding of constructive discharge. ["Constructive discharge" means forcing someone to quit. It is the legal equivalent of firing someone.] An offer of early retirement may constitute constructive discharge if the employee demonstrates each choice facing the employee makes him worse off, and if he refuses the offer and decides to stay, his employer will treat him less favorably than other employees because of age. Therefore, the record fully supports the jury's finding of constructive discharge of the retail store Plaintiffs.

Sears told some nontargeted employees they could retain their assignments when they were offered the buy-out. Sears cut only the jobs of the two oldest, full-time clerical employees of the center, while it hired part-time, predominantly younger clerical employees shortly afterwards.

The jury heard sufficient evidence to infer Sears' reasons were pretextual and the real reason for Sears' actions was the Plaintiffs' ages. Accordingly, we affirm its findings of age discrimination and constructive discharge.

During a recession in the early 1990s, companies felt great pressure to lower costs. They were sometimes tempted to replace older, higher paid workers with younger, less expensive employees. Courts traditionally held that replacing expensive, older workers with cheaper, younger ones was illegal discrimination under the ADEA. Indeed, in the *Sears* case above, the court castigated the company for its "deliberate corporate attempt to reduce payroll costs by replacing experienced and well-paid workers 40 years of age or older with lesser experienced and lower paid, younger workers." In some recent cases, however, courts have held that an employer is entitled to prefer *lower paid* workers even if that preference results in the company also choosing *younger* workers. As the court put it in one case, "An action based on price differentials represents the very quintessence of a legitimate business decision."[32] The Supreme Court has not ruled on this issue directly, but it has suggested that the primary goal of the ADEA is to prevent employment decisions based on stereotypes about the productivity and competence of older workers. Policies that have the effect of treating older people more harshly do not violate the law as long as the employer is wholly motivated by factors other than age.[33]

A court summed up the age discrimination dilemma thus:

> We are not unmindful of the pain attendant with the loss of any job, particularly when the loss is sustained by an older worker for whom retraining may be more

[32] *Marks v. Loral Corp.*, 57 Cal. App. 4th 30, 1997 Cal. App. LEXIS 611 (Cal. Ct. App. 1997).

[33] *Hazen Paper Co. v. Biggins*, 507 U.S. 604, 113 S. Ct. 1701, 1993 U.S. LEXIS 2978 (1993).

> difficult. [W]e are [also] not unmindful that the image of some newly minted whippersnapper MBA who tries to increase corporate profits—and his or her own compensation—by across-the-board layoffs is not a pretty one. Even so, [Congress never] intended the age discrimination laws to inhibit the very process by which a free market economy—decision making on the basis of cost—is conducted and by which, ultimately, real jobs and wealth are created.[34]
>
> Apart from legal issues, does a "newly minted whippersnapper MBA" (or any other manager) have an ethical obligation to older employees for whom opportunities may be limited? How would you want to be treated when you are old?

AMERICANS WITH DISABILITIES ACT

Passed in 1990, the Americans with Disabilities Act (ADA) prohibits employers from discriminating on the basis of disability. (The text of the ADA is available at http://www.eeoc.gov/laws/ada.html. The Justice Department's ADA home page is http://www.usdoj.gov/crt/ada/adahom1.htm.) As with Title VII, a plaintiff under the ADA must first file a charge with the EEOC. If the EEOC decides not to file suit, the individual may do so himself.

A disabled person is someone with a physical or mental impairment that substantially limits a major life activity, or someone who is regarded as having such an impairment. This definition includes people with mental illness, visual impairment, epilepsy, dyslexia, and AIDS, or who are *recovered* drug addicts and alcoholics. It does not cover people with sexual disorders, pyromania, exhibitionism, homosexuality, or compulsive gambling.

An employer may not disqualify an employee or job applicant because of disability as long as she can, with *reasonable accommodation*, perform the essential *functions* of the job. An accommodation is not reasonable if it would create *undue hardship* for the employer. In one case, a court held that a welder who could perform 88 percent of a job was doing the essential functions. Reasonable accommodation includes buying necessary equipment, providing readers or interpreters, or permitting a part-time schedule. In determining undue hardship, *relative* cost, not *absolute* cost, is the issue. Even an expensive accommodation—such as hiring a full-time reader—is not considered an undue hardship unless it imposes a significant burden on the overall finances of the company.

An employer may not ask about disabilities before making a job offer. The interviewer may ask only whether an applicant can perform the work. Nor can an employer require applicants to take a medical exam unless the exam is (1) job-related and (2) required of all applicants for similar jobs. However, drug testing is permitted. After a job offer has been made, an employer may require a medical test, but it must be related to the *essential functions* of the job. For example, an employer could not test the cholesterol of someone applying for an accounting job because high cholesterol is no impediment to good accounting.

An employer may not discriminate against someone because of his *relationship* with a disabled person. For example, an employer cannot refuse to hire an applicant because he has a child with Down's syndrome or a spouse with cancer.

---

[34] *Marks, supra*, note 32.

In 1997, the EEOC issued rules on the treatment of mental disabilities. These rules were based on an assumption of parity—that physical and mental disabilities should be treated the same. The difficulty is that physical ailments such as diabetes and deafness may be easy to diagnose, but what does a supervisor do when an employee is chronically late, rude, or impulsive? Does this mean the worker is mentally disabled or just a lazy, irresponsible jerk? Among other accommodations, the EEOC rules indicated that employers should be willing to put up barriers to isolate people who have difficulty concentrating, provide detailed day-to-day feedback to those who need greater structure in performing their jobs, or allow workers on antidepressants to come to work later if they are groggy in the morning.

Although these rules are still new, early signs indicate that the courts are not as accommodating of mental illness as the EEOC. In one case, for example, an engineer had been criticized for his "negative attitude." Later his supervisor warned him that he might be terminated if his behavior did not improve. He then told the company that the warning had caused him to be depressed, which, in turn, affected his ability to interact with other people. He asked, as a special accommodation, that he be assigned to clerical work that did not require him to run meetings. The company fired him. Although EEOC guidelines state that interacting with others is a major life activity, the court held that it is not. Therefore the engineer was not disabled for purposes of the ADA.[35]

While lauding the ADA's objectives, many managers have been apprehensive about its impact on the workplace. On the plus side, they acknowledge that society is clearly better off if every member has the opportunity to work. And as advocates for the disabled point out, we are all, at best, only temporarily able-bodied.

It also turns out that the costs of complying with the ADA have been far less than managers originally feared. One survey found that the median cost per disabled employee is $233. Sears, Roebuck & Co. is committed to employing people with disabilities, and its workforce includes people with a wide range of disabilities. Yet most of the company's accommodations have cost little or nothing. Sears allowed an employee recovering from foot surgery to wear sneakers on the sales floor. The company purchased a $250 ergonomic chair for a worker with a sore back. In contrast, Sears must spend roughly $2,000 to terminate and replace an employee.

When cases go to litigation, employers win about 90 percent of the time. Workers are caught in something of a legal Catch-22: they must prove that they can perform the essential functions of the job, but they must also show that their disability limits a major life activity. Employees have filed tens of thousands of complaints, however, so many legal question marks remain. In the end, the courts must do a sensitive job of balancing the needs of the disabled with the rights of managers to run a profitable business.

PREVENTIVE Law

Every applicant feels slightly apprehensive before a job interview, but now the interviewer may be even more nervous—fearing that every question is a potential land mine of liability. Most interviewers (and students who have read this chapter) would know better than Delta Airlines interviewers who allegedly

[35] *Soileau v. Guildford of Maine*, 105 F.3d 12, 1997 U.S. App. LEXIS 1171 (1st Cir. 1997).

asked applicants about their sexual preference, birth control methods, and abortion history. The most common gaffe on the part of interviewers? Asking women about their child-care arrangements. That question assumes the woman is responsible for child care. The list below provides guidelines for interviewers.

Don't Even Consider Asking	**Go Ahead and Ask**
Can you perform this function with or without reasonable accommodation?	Would you need reasonable accommodation in this job?
How many days were you sick last year?	How many days were you absent from work last year?
What medications are you currently taking?	Are you currently using drugs illegally?
Where were you born?	Are you authorized to work in the United States?
How old are you?	What work experience have you had?
When did you graduate from college?	Where did you go to college?
How did you learn this language?	What languages do you speak and write fluently?
Have you ever been arrested?	Have you ever been convicted?
Do you plan to have children? How old are your children? What method of birth control do you use?	Can you work weekends? Travel extensively?
What is your corrected vision?	Do you have 20/20 corrected vision?
Are you a man or a woman? Are you single or married? What does your spouse do? What will happen if your spouse is transferred? What clubs, societies, or lodges do you belong to?	Leave well enough alone!

CHAPTER CONCLUSION

Although managers sometimes feel overwhelmed by the long list of laws that protect workers, the United States guarantees its workers fewer rights than virtually any other industrialized nation. For instance, Japan, Great Britain, France, Germany, and Canada all require employers to show just cause before terminating workers. Although American employers are no longer insulated from minimum standards of fairness, reasonable behavior, and compliance with important policies, they still have great freedom to manage their employees.

CHAPTER REVIEW

1. The traditional common law rule of employment provided that an employee at will could be fired for a good reason, a bad reason, or no reason at all.
2. The National Labor Relations Act prohibits employers from penalizing workers for union activity.
3. The Family and Medical Leave Act guarantees workers up to 12 weeks of unpaid leave each year for childbirth, adoption, or medical emergencies for themselves or a family member.
4. An employer who fires a worker for a *bad* reason is liable under a theory of wrongful discharge.
5. Oral promises made during the hiring process may be enforceable, even if not approved by the company's top executives. An employee handbook may create a contract.
6. The goal of the Occupational Safety and Health Act is to ensure safe conditions in the workplace.
7. The Fair Labor Standards Act regulates minimum and overtime wages. It also limits child labor.
8. Workers' compensation statutes ensure that employees receive payment for injuries incurred at work.
9. The Social Security system pays benefits to workers who are retired, disabled, or temporarily unemployed and to the spouses and children of disabled or deceased workers.
10. The Employee Retirement Income Security Act regulates private pension plans.
11. The Equal Pay Act prohibits an employer from considering the gender of a worker when setting compensation.
12. Title VII of the Civil Rights Act of 1964 prohibits employers from discriminating on the basis of race, color, religion, sex, or national origin.
13. The Age Discrimination in Employment Act prohibits age discrimination against employees or job applicants who are age 40 or older.
14. The Americans with Disabilities Act prohibits employers from discriminating on the basis of disability.

PRACTICE TEST

1. When Theodore Staats went to his company's "Council of Honor Convention," he was accompanied by a woman who was not his wife although he told everyone she was. The company fired him. Staats alleged that his termination violated public policy because it infringed upon his freedom of association. He also alleged that he had been fired because he was too successful—his commissions were so high, he out-earned even the highest paid officer of the company. Has Staat's employer violated public policy?
2. This article appeared in *The Wall Street Journal*:

   When Michelle Lawrence discovered she was pregnant, she avoided telling Ron Rogers, the owner of the Los Angeles public relations agency where she worked as manager of media relations. "I had heard he wasn't crazy about pregnant women," she says. Instead, she asked her immediate supervisor to pass along the news. Mr. Rogers didn't speak to her for a week. His first comment was, "Congratulations on your pregnancy. My sister vomited for months." A few weeks later, Ms. Lawrence was fired. Mr. Rogers told her the business was shifting away from her area of expertise.[36]

Does Lawrence have a valid claim against Rogers? Under what law?

3. Reginald Delaney managed a Taco Time restaurant in Portland, Oregon. Some of his customers told Mr. Ledbetter, the district manager, that they would not be eating there so often because there were too many black employees. Ledbetter told Delaney to fire Ms. White, who was black. Delaney did as he was told. Ledbetter's report on the incident said: "My notes show that Delaney told me that White asked him to sleep with her and that when he would not that she started causing dissension within the crew. She asked him to come over to her house and that he declined." Delaney refused to sign the report because it was untrue, so Ledbetter fired him. What claim might Delaney make against his former employer?

4. When Walton Weiner interviewed for a job with McGraw-Hill, Inc., he was assured that the company would not terminate an employee without "just cause." Weiner also signed a contract specifying that his employment would be subject to the provisions of McGraw-Hill's handbook. The handbook said, "[The] company will resort to dismissal for just and sufficient cause only, and only after all practical steps toward rehabilitation or salvage of the employee have been taken and failed. However, if the welfare of the company indicates that dismissal is neccessary, then that decision is arrived at and is carried out forthrightly." After eight years, Weiner was fired suddenly for "lack of application." Does Weiner have a valid claim against McGraw-Hill?

5. **RIGHT & WRONG** John Mundorf hired three women to work for Gus Construction Co. as traffic controllers at road construction sites in Iowa. Male members of the construction crew incessantly referred to the women as "f—king flag girls." They repeatedly asked the women if they "wanted to f—k" or engage in oral sex. One crew member held a woman up to the cab window so other men could touch her. Another male employee exposed himself to the women. Male employees also urinated in a woman's water bottle and the gas tank of her car. Mundorf, the supervisor, was present during some of these incidents. He talked to crew members about their conduct, but the abuse soon resumed and continued until the women quit. What claim might the women make against their co-workers? Is Gus Construction Co. liable for the acts of its employees? What procedure must the women follow to pursue their claim? Why do you think these men behaved this way? Why did they want to humiliate their co-workers? What should the supervisor have done when he observed these incidents? What would you have done if you were the supervisor? A fellow employee?

6. **CPA QUESTION** An unemployed CPA generally would receive unemployment compensation benefits if the CPA:

   (a) Was fired as a result of the employer's business reversals

   (b) Refused to accept a job as an accountant while receiving extended benefits

   (c) Was fired for embezzling from a client

   (d) Left work voluntarily without good cause

[36] Sue Shellenbarger, "As More Pregnant Women Work, Bias Complaints Rise," *The Wall Street Journal*, Dec. 6, 1993, p. B1.

7. Debra Agis worked in a Ground Round restaurant. The manager, Roger Dionne, informed the waitresses that "there was some stealing going on." Until he found out who was doing it, he intended to fire all the waitresses in alphabetical order, starting with the letter "A." Dionne then fired Agis. Does she have a valid claim against her employer?

8. The Duke Power Co. refused to transfer any employees at its generating plant to better jobs unless they had a high school diploma or could pass an intelligence test. The company was willing to pay two-thirds of the tuition for an employee's high school training. Neither a high school education nor the intelligence test was significantly related to successful job performance. Both requirements disqualified African Americans at a substantially higher rate than white applicants. Is the company in violation of Title VII?

9. The Lillie Rubin boutique in Phoenix would not permit Dick Kovacic to apply for a job as a salesperson. It only hired women to work in sales because fittings and alterations took place in the dressing room or immediately outside. The customers were buying expensive clothes and demanded a male-free dressing area. Has the Lillie Rubin store violated Title VII? What would its defense be?

10. **YOU BE THE JUDGE WRITING PROBLEM** Nationwide Insurance Co. circulated a memorandum asking all employees to lobby in favor of a bill that had been introduced in the Pennsylvania House of Representatives. By limiting the damages that an injured motorist could recover from a person who caused an accident, this bill would have saved Nationwide significant money. Not only did John Novosel refuse to lobby, but he privately criticized the bill for harming consumers. Nationwide was definitely not on his side—it fired him. Novosel filed suit, alleging that his discharge had violated public policy by infringing his right to free speech. Did Nationwide violate public policy by firing Novosel? **Argument for Novosel:** The United States Constitution and the Pennsylvania Constitution both guarantee the right to free speech. Nationwide has violated an important public policy by firing Novosel for expressing his opinions. **Argument for Nationwide:** For all the high-flown talk about the Constitution, what we have here is an employee who refused to carry out company policy. If the employee prevails in this case, where will it all end? What if an employee for a tobacco company refuses to market cigarettes because he does not approve of smoking? How can businesses operate without loyalty from their employees?

11. When Thomas Lussier filled out a Postal Service employment application, he did not admit that he had twice pleaded guilty to charges of disorderly conduct. Lussier suffered from Post Traumatic Stress Disorder (PTSD) acquired during military service in Vietnam. Because of this disorder, he sometimes had panic attacks that required him to leave meetings. He was also a recovered alcoholic and drug user. During his stint with the Postal Service, he had some personality conflicts with other employees. Once another employee hit him. He also had one episode of "erratic emotional behavior and verbal outburst." In the meantime, a postal employee in Ridgewood, New Jersey, killed four colleagues. The Postmaster General encouraged all supervisors to identify workers who had dangerous propensities. Lussier's boss discovered that he had lied on his employment application about the disorderly conduct charges and fired him. Is the Postal Service in violation of the law?

INTERNET RESEARCH PROBLEM

At http://www.disgruntled.com/dishome.html, employees tell how and why they were fired. If these employees filed a lawsuit, would they win? Under what legal theory?

You can find further practice problems in the Online Quiz at http://beatty.westbuslaw.com or in the Study Guide that accompanies this text.

Labor Law

15

CHAPTER

A strike! For five weeks the union workers have been walking picket lines at JMJ, a manufacturer of small electrical engines. An entire town of 70,000 citizens, most of them blue-collar workers, is sharply divided, right down to the McNally kitchen table. Buddy, age 48, has worked on the assembly lines at JMJ for more than 25 years. Now he's sipping coffee in the house where he grew up. His sister Kristina, age 46, is a vice-president for personnel at JMJ. The two have always been close. In high school, Kristina idolized her older brother, the football and track star. Buddy was immensely proud of his kid sister's academic triumphs, boasting to the world that she would "be the first lady president." Today, though, conversation is halting.

"It's time to get back together, Buddy," Kristina murmurs. "The strike is hurting the whole company—and the town."

"Not the *whole* town, Kristina," he tries to quip lightly. "Your management pals still have fat incomes and nice houses."

"Oh yeah?" she attempts to joke, "you haven't seen our porch lately."

"Go talk to Tony Falcione," Buddy replies. "He can't pay his rent."

"Talk to the Ericksons," Kristina snaps back, "they don't even work for JMJ. Their sandwich shop is going under because none of you guys stop in for lunch. Come back to work."

"Never. Not with that clause on the table."

That clause is management's proposal for the new union contract—one that Kristina helped draft. The company officers want the right to subcontract work, that is, to send it out for other companies to perform.

"Buddy, we need the flexibility. K-Ball is underselling us by 35 percent. If we can't compete, there won't be *any* jobs or *any* contract!"

"The way to save money is not by sending our jobs overseas, where a bunch of foreigners will work for 50 bucks a month."

"OK, fine. Tell me how we *should* save money."

"Kristina, I really do not know how you can sit at this table and say these things—in this household. You never would have got a fancy college degree if Dad hadn't made union wages."

"If we can't sell motors to Latin America, we're out of business. *Then* what's your union going to do for you? All we're asking is the right to subcontract some of the smallest components. Everything else gets built here."

"This is just the start. Next it'll be the wiring, then the batteries, then you'll assemble the whole thing over there—and that'll be it for me. You take that clause off the table, we'll be back in 15 minutes."

"Never."

Buddy stands up. They stare silently, sadly, at each other, and then Kristina says, in a barely audible voice, "I have to tell you this. My boss is starting to talk about hiring replacement workers." Buddy walks out.

Some Americans revere unions, believing that organized labor has pulled the working class up from poverty and shielded it from exploitative management. Others loathe organized labor, convinced that unions foment mindless conflicts, decrease productivity, increase costs, and harm corporations and the economy generally. Why do unions exist?

UNIONS DEVELOP . . . AND THE LAW RESPONDS

During the nineteenth century, as industrialization spread across America, workers found employment conditions increasingly unbearable and wages inadequate. Here is a contemporary account of mining in the American West:

> View their work! Descending from the surface in the shaft-cages, they enter narrow galleries where the air is scarce respirable. By the dim light of their lanterns a dingy rock surface, braced by rotting props, is visible. The stenches of decaying vegetable matter, hot foul water, and human excretions intensify the effects of the heat. The men throw off their clothes at once. Only a light breech-cloth covers their hips, and thick-soled shoes protect their feet from the scorching rocks and steaming rills of water that trickle over the floor. Except for these coverings they toil naked, with heavy drops of sweat starting from every pore.[1]

---

[1] Eliot Lord, *Comstock Mining and Miners* (Washington: G.P.O., 1883), p. 386, *quoted in* Richard E. Lingenfelter, *The Hardrock Miners* (Berkeley: University of California Press, 1974), p. 13.

Temperatures in the mines were well over 100 degrees. Miners drank more than three gallons of water every day. Some suddenly collapsed, with swollen veins, purple faces, and glazed eyes. Within minutes they were dead, but even before they died, their places in the mine were taken by other workers desperate for pay.

Conditions were equally oppressive in the new factories back east. Workers, often women and sometimes children, worked 60 to 70 hours per week and sometimes more, standing at assembly lines in suffocating, dimly lit factories, performing monotonous yet dangerous work with heavy machinery. A visitor to a factory in Lowell, Massachusetts, in 1855 was shocked by the degrading conditions and the exhausting hours required of all workers.

> I inquired of the agent of a principal factory whether it was the custom of the manufacturers to do anything for the physical, intellectual, and moral welfare of their work-people. "We never do," he said. "As for myself, I regard my work-people just as I regard my machinery. So long as they can do my work for what I choose to pay them, I keep them, getting out of them all I can. What they do or how they fare outside my walls I don't know, nor do I consider it my business to know. When my machines get old and useless, I reject them and get new, and these people are part of my machinery."[2]

Because of the intolerable conditions and impoverishing wages, workers began to band together into unions. But early in the nineteenth century, American courts regarded any coordinated effort by workers as a criminal conspiracy. Courts convicted workers merely for the *act of joining together*, even if no strike took place. In 1842, the Massachusetts high court became the first to reject this use of the criminal law. The court ruled that workers could join together for legitimate economic goals; their efforts would become criminal only if the workers used illegal means to achieve them.[3] Other courts came to agree, and so management resorted to the civil law to curtail unions.

In 1890, Congress passed the Sherman Act to outlaw monopolies.[4] For the next 40 years, courts relied on this statute to issue anti-strike injunctions, declaring that strikes illegally restrained trade. A company could usually obtain an immediate injunction merely by alleging that a strike *might* cause harm. Courts were so quick to issue injunctions that most companies became immune to union efforts. But with the economic collapse of 1929 and the vast suffering of the Great Depression, public sympathy shifted to the workers. Congress responded with the first of several landmark statutes.

In 1932, Congress passed the **Norris-LaGuardia Act**, which prohibited federal court injunctions in nonviolent labor disputes. No longer could management obtain an injunction merely by mentioning the word "strike." By taking away the injunction remedy, Congress was declaring that workers should be permitted to organize unions and to use their collective power to achieve legitimate economic ends. The statute led to explosive growth in union membership.

In 1935, Congress passed the Wagner Act, generally known as the **National Labor Relations Act (NLRA)**. This is the most important of all labor laws. A

---

[2] Massachusetts Senate Dock. no. 21, 1868, p. 23, *quoted in* Norman Ware, *The Industrial Worker* (Chicago: Quadrangle Books, 1964), p. 77.

[3] *Commonwealth v. Hunt*, 45 Mass. 111, 4 Met. 111 (1842).

[4] See Chapter 19, on antitrust law.

fundamental aim of the NLRA is the establishment and maintenance of industrial peace, to preserve the flow of commerce. The NLRA ensures the right of workers to form unions and encourages management and unions to bargain collectively and productively. For our purposes, §§7 and 8 of the NLRA are the most important.

Section 7 guarantees employees the right to organize and join unions, bargain collectively through representatives of their own choosing, and engage in other concerted activities. This is the cornerstone of union power. With the enactment of the NLRA, Congress put an end to any notion that unions were criminal or inherently illegal by explicitly recognizing that workers could join together and bargain as a group, using their collective power to seek better conditions. Section 8 reinforces these rights by outlawing *unfair labor practices.*

Section 8(a) makes it an unfair labor practice (ULP) for an employer:

- To interfere with union organizing efforts
- To dominate or interfere with any union
- To discriminate against a union member, or
- To refuse to bargain collectively with a union.

The NLRA also established the **National Labor Relations Board (NLRB)** to administer and interpret the statute and to adjudicate labor cases. For example, when a union charges that an employer has committed an unfair labor practice—say, by refusing to bargain—the ULP charge goes first to the NLRB.

The NLRB has two primary tasks:

- *Representation.* The Board decides whether a particular union is entitled to represent a group of employees.
- *Unfair Labor Practices.* The Board adjudicates claims by either the employer or workers that the other side has committed a ULP.

To accomplish these tasks, the NLRB has several divisions. Although the agency is headquartered in Washington, it performs the greatest volume of its work in local offices. **Regional offices**, each headed by a regional director, are located throughout the country. These local offices handle most ULP claims. The General Counsel, a staff of lawyers, investigates such claims. If the General Counsel's office believes that a party has committed a ULP, it prosecutes the case before an administrative law judge (ALJ).

The **Board** itself, which sits in Washington, has five members, all appointed by the president. The Board makes final agency decisions about representation and ULP cases. But note that the Board has no power to *enforce* its orders. If it is evident that the losing party will not comply, the Board must petition a federal appeals court to enforce the order. Typically, the steps resulting in an appeal follow this pattern: the Board issues a decision, for example, finding that a company has unfairly refused to bargain with a union. The Board orders the company to bargain. The Board then appeals to the United States Court of Appeals to enforce its order, and the company *cross-appeals,* requesting the court *not* to enforce the Board's order. (The NLRB describes its mission and methods at http://www.nlrb.gov/.)

Throughout the 1930s and 1940s, unions grew in size and power. As strikes became more common, employers complained loudly of union abuse. Unions coerced unwilling workers to join and engaged in *secondary boycotts*, picketing an innocent company to stop it from doing business with an employer the union was fighting. In 1947, Congress responded with the Taft-Hartley Act, also known as the **Labor-Management Relations Act**, designed to curb union abuses. The statute amended §8 of the NLRA to outlaw certain unfair labor practices *by unions*.

Section 8(b) makes it an unfair labor practice for a union:

- To interfere with employees who are exercising their labor rights under §7
- To encourage an employer to discriminate against a particular employee because of a union dispute
- To refuse to bargain collectively, or
- To engage in an illegal strike or boycott, particularly secondary boycotts.

Finally, in the 1950s the public became aware that certain labor leaders were corrupt. Some officers stole money from large union treasuries, rigged union elections, and stifled opposition within the organization. In response, in 1959, Congress passed the Landrum-Griffin Act, generally called the **Labor-Management Reporting and Disclosure Act (LMRDA)**. The LMRDA requires union leadership to make certain financial disclosures and guarantees free speech and fair elections within a union.

These landmark federal labor laws are outlined below:

Four Key Labor Statutes

Norris-LaGuardia Act (1932)	Prohibits federal court injunctions in peaceful strikes.
National Labor Relations Act (1935)	Guarantees workers' right to organize unions and bargain collectively. Prohibits an employer from interfering with union organizing or discriminating against union members. Requires an employer to bargain collectively.
Labor-Management Relations Act (1947)	Prohibits union abuses such as coercing employees to join. Outlaws secondary boycotts.
Labor-Management Reporting and Disclosure Act (1959)	Requires financial disclosures by union leadership. Guarantees union members free speech and fair elections.

NEWSworthy

Today, labor abuses are less visible—but as ugly as ever. From New York City to Los Angeles, desperately poor, frightened immigrants cut and sew about half of all the garments this country produces, often working in appalling sweatshops where conditions are little better than in nineteenth-century factories. Frequently, the employees are undocumented immigrants who speak no

English, know nothing of their rights, and fear that any complaints they make will lead to deportation. Exploitative owners force the workers to toil 50 to 60 hours a week with few breaks in cramped rooms with weak lighting, no ventilation, and inadequate sanitation. Pay is below the minimum wage—and vicious bosses often steal the small amounts they promised. For a report on sweatshops in the United States, see http://www.uniteunion.org/sweatshops/sweatshop.html.

STATE LABOR LAW

All states have labor statutes. Some are comprehensive, while others focus on narrow issues. For example, certain states prohibit particular kinds of picketing, while many states outlaw strikes by public employees. A court enforces a state statute when no federal law applies. In general, when a federal law such as the NLRA does apply, it controls the outcome. This is the doctrine of *preemption*, discussed in Chapter 5, on constitutional law. **Preemption: states have no jurisdiction to regulate any labor issue that is governed by federal law.**

In this chapter, we look principally at federal law because it is uniform and because it controls the most fundamental issues of labor policy.

LABOR UNIONS TODAY

Organized labor is shrinking in the United States. In the 1950s, about 25 percent of the workforce belonged to a union. Today, only about 15 percent of all workers are union members. Employers point to this figure with satisfaction and claim that it shows that unions have failed their memberships. In an increasingly high-tech, service-oriented economy, employers argue, there is no place for organized labor. Union supporters respond that although the country has shed many old factories, workers have not benefited. Throughout the 1980s and 1990s, they assert, compensation for executives has soared into the stratosphere, with many CEOs earning several million dollars per year, while wages for the average worker, in real dollars, have fallen for two decades and are now 22 percent below their levels of the 1970s.

Whether organized labor is disappearing from the United States or is only retreating temporarily, labor law still affects many. About 17 million workers are union members. The largest unions are national in scope, with hundreds of affiliated **locals** throughout the country. A local is the regional union, which represents workers at a particular company. For example, over 2.2 million teachers belong to the National Education Association, with thousands of locals spread throughout the nation.

For the first time in U.S. history, a significant number of doctors are joining unions. Most are doing this in response to managed health care. Many physicians complain that health maintenance organizations require them to spend less time with patients, do more paperwork to justify their medical choices, and offer fewer services and medications to deserving patients. To reverse that trend, both doctors and nurses are forming their own labor organizations. (For the most recent union statistics, work your way to the Web site of the Bureau of Labor Statistics, at http://www.bls.gov.)

ORGANIZING A UNION

EXCLUSIVITY

It is difficult to organize a union. When a worker starts to talk about collective action, or when an organizer appears from a national union, many employees are suspicious or fearful; some may be hostile. Management will generally be opposed—sometimes fiercely opposed—to any union organizing effort. The fight can become ugly, and all because of one principle: *exclusivity*.

Under §9 of the NLRA, a validly recognized union is the exclusive representative of the employees. This means that the union will represent all of the designated employees, regardless of whether a particular worker *wants* to be represented. The company may not bargain directly with any employee in the group, nor with any other organization representing the designated employees.

A collective bargaining unit is the precisely defined group of employees who will be represented by a particular union. Suppose a hotel workers' union attempts to organize the Excelsior Hotel. The union will seek to represent some of Excelsior's employees, but not all. The union may represent, for example, all maids, busboys, and bellhops. Those employees are in the collective bargaining unit. Many other people who work for the hotel will *not* be in the collective bargaining unit. Managers who run the hotel, reservation agents who work in other cities, launderers who work in separate facilities for a different employer—all of these people are *outside* the collective bargaining unit and will be unaffected by the union's bargaining.

It is the union's *exclusive* right to bargain for the unit that gives the organization its power. But some employees may be unhappy with the way a union exercises this power. In the following case, workers believed the union was failing to represent them on a vital issue. Should they be allowed to bargain on their own behalf? You be the judge.

You be *the* Judge

EMPORIUM CAPWELL CO. v. WESTERN ADDITIONAL COMMUNITY ORGANIZATION

420 U.S. 50, 95 S. Ct. 977, 1975 U.S. LEXIS 134
United States Supreme Court, 1975

Facts: Emporium Capwell operated a department store in San Francisco. The Department Store Employees Union represented all stock workers. Several black union members complained to the union about racial discrimination in promotions, asserting that highly qualified black workers were routinely passed over in favor of less qualified whites. The union promised to pursue the issue with management, but the black employees were not satisfied with the union's effort. The unhappy workers demanded to speak with top management of the store and then, without the union's permission, picketed the store and handed out leaflets accusing the company of discrimination. Emporium Capwell fired the picketing employees. The resulting case went all the way to the Supreme Court.

In most labor cases, the union is on one side and management is on the other. In this case, the black employees were on one side, with the union on the other. The union argued that exclusivity prohibited any group of workers from demanding to meet separately with management. It claimed that the disgruntled workers violated the NLRA by insisting on separate bargaining, and that it was proper for the company to fire the workers. In other words, the union placed a higher value on exclusivity than on maintaining the jobs of those employees. The black workers, on the other hand, argued that eliminating discrimination was more important than union exclusivity. They insisted that management had no right to fire them and that they were entitled to get their jobs back and to bargain independently.

You be the Judge: **Did the picketing employees violate the NLRA by demanding to bargain directly with management?**

Argument for the Union: Your honors, exclusivity is the core of a union's strength. If management is free to talk with employees individually—or if it can be *compelled* to talk with them—the union has no leverage. An astute manager will quickly use worker conflicts as a tool to divide the union and destroy it. By cutting deals with favored employees, management could demonstrate to all workers that affiliation with the union is a losing tactic, and that the smart worker bargains for himself—and then does what management tells him to do.

Racial discrimination is a terrible evil. It must be eradicated from the workplace. This union is committed to fighting prejudice. But the union must do it *collectively*. If an exception to the principle of exclusivity can be carved out for one important issue, such as race discrimination, then an exception can be carved out for other important issues, such as gender bias, age discrimination, language differences, retirement pay, health benefits . . . and on and on. To allow this group of picketers to pursue a worthy goal with separate bargaining would be to destroy the union—and ensure that no valuable goals are obtained.

Argument for the Picketing Workers: Congress granted employees the right to organize *for their mutual benefit*, not to advance the cause of unions. A labor organization is a means to an end, not an end in itself. When a union fails to support its members on a vital issue, employees must be free to fend for themselves. Race discrimination is not a simple bargaining issue like retirement benefits; it is a vital matter of human dignity. This union failed to act promptly and vigorously to protect its black members and end discrimination. Why should those employees now be shackled to an organization that has failed them?

It makes no difference *why* the union failed to protect its members. Weak-kneed, docile union leadership can be just as devastating to the cause of racial equality as bad faith. We are not asking that union members be free to pursue every petty complaint directly with management. To equate racial justice with retirement benefits is to ignore the singular evil of discrimination. We merely ask that, when a union fails to protect its members concerning a profound issue such as this, the injured employees be allowed to speak for themselves.

ORGANIZING

A union organizing effort generally involves the following pattern.

CAMPAIGN

Union organizers talk with employees—or attempt to talk—and interest them in forming a union. The organizers may be employees of the company, who simply chat with fellow workers about unsatisfactory conditions. Or a union may send nonemployees of the company to hand out union leaflets to workers as they arrive and depart from the factory.

AUTHORIZATION CARDS

Union organizers ask workers to sign authorization cards, which state that the particular worker requests the specified union to act as her sole bargaining representative.

Recognition

If a union obtains authorization cards from a sizable percentage of workers, it seeks **recognition** as the exclusive representative for the bargaining unit. The union may ask the employer to recognize it as the bargaining representative, but most of the time employers refuse to recognize the union voluntarily. The NLRA permits an employer to refuse recognition.

Petition

Assuming that the employer does not voluntarily recognize a union, the union generally petitions the NLRB for an election. It must submit to the NLRB regional office authorization cards signed by at least 30 percent of the workers. The regional office verifies whether there are enough valid cards to warrant an election and looks closely at the proposed bargaining unit to make sure that it is appropriate. If the regional director determines that the union has identified an appropriate bargaining unit and has enough valid cards, it orders an election.

Election

The NLRB closely supervises the election to ensure fairness. All members of the proposed bargaining unit vote on whether they want the union to represent them. If more than 50 percent of the workers vote for the union, the NLRB designates that union as the exclusive representative of all members of the bargaining unit. When unions hold representation elections in private corporations, they win about half the time. Labor organizations claim that management typically uses paid company time to campaign against the union. Employers respond that labor loses elections because workers fear that a union will hurt them, not help. Among public employers, unions generally do much better, winning about 85 percent of representation campaigns. Public employers often do not campaign against the union.

These are some of the issues that most commonly arise during an organizing effort: (1) What may a union do during its organizing campaign? (2) What may the employer do to defeat the campaign? (3) What is an appropriate bargaining unit?

What Workers May Do

The NLRA guarantees employees the right to talk among themselves about forming a union, to hand out literature, and ultimately to join a union.[5] Workers may urge other employees to sign authorization cards and may vigorously push their cause. When employees hand out leaflets, the employer generally may not limit the content. In one case, a union distributed leaflets urging workers to vote against political candidates who opposed minimum wage laws. The employer objected to the union using company property to distribute the information, but the Supreme Court upheld the union's right. Even though the

[5] NLRA §7.

content of the writing was not directly related to the union, the connection was close enough that the NLRA protected the union's activity.[6]

There are, of course, limits to what union organizers may do. The statute permits an employer to restrict organizing discussions if they interfere with discipline or production. A worker on a moving assembly line has no right to walk away from his task to talk with other employees about organizing a union; the employer may insist that the worker stay at his job and leave discussions until lunch or some other break.[7]

WHAT EMPLOYERS MAY DO

As mentioned above, an employer may prohibit employees from organizing if the efforts interfere with the company's work. In a retail store, for example, management may prohibit union discussions in the presence of customers, because the discussions could harm business.

May the employer speak out against a union organizing drive? Yes. Management is entitled to communicate to the employees why it believes a union will be harmful to the company. But the employer's efforts must be limited to explanation and advocacy. **The employer may vigorously present anti-union views to its employees, but may not use either threats or promises of benefits to defeat a union drive.**[8] Notice that the employer is prohibited not only from threatening reprisals, such as firing a worker who favors the union, but also from offering benefits designed to defeat the union. A company that has vigorously rejected employee demands for higher wages may not suddenly grant a 10 percent pay increase in the midst of a union campaign.

It is an unfair labor practice for an employer to interfere with a union organizing effort. Normally, a union claiming such interference will file a ULP charge. If the Board upholds the union's claim, it will order the employer to stop its interference and permit a fair election. In some cases, though, management's interference is so pervasive and intrusive that the Board may conclude an election would be pointless. **When an employer outrageously interferes with a union organizing campaign, the NLRB may forgo the normal election, certify the union as the exclusive representative, and order the company to bargain.** This *bargaining order* is an extreme measure, and the Board uses it only when an employer has shown extreme anti-union animus. In the following case, the union contended that the employer had done just that.

---

[6] *Eastex, Inc. v. NLRB*, 434 U.S. 1045, 98 S. Ct. 888, 1978 U.S. LEXIS 547 (1978).

[7] *NLRB v. Babcock & Wilcox Co.*, 351 U.S. 105, 76 S. Ct. 679, 1956 U.S. LEXIS 1721 (1956).

[8] *NLRB v. Gissel Packing Co.*, 395 U.S. 575, 89 S. Ct. 1918, 1969 U.S. LEXIS 3172 (1969).

NLRB AND UNION OF NEEDLETRADES INDUSTRIAL AND TEXTILE EMPLOYEES, LOCAL 76 v. INTERSWEET, INC.

125 F.3d 1064, 1997 U.S. App. LEXIS 25240
United States Court of Appeals for the Seventh Circuit, 1997

Facts: Intersweet, Inc. manufactured sugar wafers, but conditions in the plant had gone sour. The Needletrades Union conducted three organizational meetings, and 19 of the company's 31 employees signed union representation cards. Later that same month, Intersweet's owner, Julius Meerbaum, suddenly fired all employees. The next day, he recalled 10 of the 31 workers. Eight of the 10 had not signed union cards and the others *claimed* they had not. Meerbaum required the rehired employees to work 50 to 60 hours per week, instead of the normal 40. Workers overheard company supervisors say that no one active in the union would ever be rehired.

An administrative law judge ruled that the company had committed outrageous unfair labor practices, and ordered the company to bargain with the union, without an election. The NLRB petitioned the court of appeals to enforce its order.

Issue: Was the NLRB's order to bargain justified?

Excerpts from Judge Rovner's Decision: Between the time of the mass terminations and the imposition of the [bargaining] order, Julius Meerbaum, who had been responsible for the shutdown of the plant in 1993, passed away. Intersweet argues that Julius' death obviated the need for the bargaining order by removing any lingering impact of the unfair practices for which he was responsible. Although Julius Meerbaum had passed away, three members of Intersweet's previous management staff, John Meerbaum, Jose Diaz and David Sabin, were still running the company. Thus, aside from the fact that Julius was gone, Intersweet's management had not meaningfully changed, and the company was still controlled by the Meerbaum family. In fact, because the individuals that were still present had been responsible for implementing Julius' directive to shut down the plant, the Board found that they may be more closely associated with the terminations than Julius himself, whose involvement was remote and perhaps even unknown to the workers.

The Board did not abuse its discretion in determining that the change in circumstances did not alleviate the need for a bargaining order. Intersweet discharged its entire workforce, rehired only those employees that it believed had not signed union cards, and then openly disclosed to returning employees that the terminations were related to union affiliation. It is difficult to imagine a more egregious attempt to defeat unionization. The management team responsible for these practices remained essentially intact, and there is no reason to believe that the workforce, although expanded, would not continue to be chilled by the earlier actions. The Board considered each of Intersweet's arguments and rejected them in a well-reasoned opinion. We find no abuse of discretion, and the Board's petition for enforcement of its order is GRANTED.

APPROPRIATE BARGAINING UNIT

When a union petitions the NLRB for an election, the Board determines whether the proposed bargaining unit is appropriate. **The Board generally certifies a proposed bargaining unit if and only if the employees share a community of interest.** Employers frequently assert that the bargaining unit is inappropriate. If the Board agrees with the employer and rejects the proposed bargaining unit, it dismisses the union's request for an election. The Board pays particular attention to two kinds of employees: managerial and confidential.

Managerial employees must be excluded from the bargaining unit.[9] An employee is managerial if she is so closely aligned with management that her membership in the bargaining unit would create a conflict of interest between her union membership and her actual work. Courts generally find such a conflict only if *the employee is substantially involved in the employer's labor policy.*

For example, a factory worker who spends one-third of his time performing assembly work but two-thirds of his time supervising a dozen other workers is so closely aligned with management that he could not fairly be part of the bargaining unit. There would be constant tension between his supervisory work and his advocacy on behalf of the union. By contrast, an engineer who analyzes production methods and merely reports her findings to management may not be closely aligned with the employer. Unless the engineer has actual control over personnel decisions, she can probably be included in a bargaining unit of other engineers.[10]

Confidential employees are generally excluded from the bargaining unit.[11] A confidential employee is one who works so closely with executives or other management employees that there would be a conflict of interest if the employee were in the bargaining unit. An executive secretary may be so intimately acquainted with her boss's ideas, plans, and other confidential information that it would be unfair to allow her to join a bargaining unit of other secretaries.

Once the Board has excluded managerial and confidential employees, it looks at various criteria to decide whether the remaining employees should logically be grouped in one bargaining unit, that is, whether they share a **community of interest**. The Board looks for:

- Rough equality of pay and benefits, and methods of computing both
- Similar total hours per week and type of work
- Similar skills and training, and
- Previous bargaining history and the number of authorization cards from any different groups within the unit.

Having applied these criteria to all members of the proposed unit, the Board either certifies the bargaining unit or rejects the unit and dismisses the union's petition. Suppose the employees in a public high school decide to organize. The Board will probably find that an appropriate bargaining unit includes all academic teachers and physical education teachers because they do roughly similar work and are paid similarly. The principal and vice-principal will not be included in the unit because their work is supervisory and administrative and they are paid on a separate scale.

---

[9] *NLRB v. Bell Aerospace Co., Div. of Textron, Inc.*, 416 U.S. 267, 94 S. Ct. 1757, 1974 U.S. LEXIS 35 (1974).

[10] See, e.g., *NLRB v. Case Corp.*, 995 F.2d 700, 1993 U.S. App. LEXIS 13246 (7th Cir. 1993).

[11] *Ibid.*

COLLECTIVE BARGAINING

The goal of bargaining is a contract, which is called a **collective bargaining agreement (CBA)**. As mentioned, Congress passed the NLRA to foster industrial peace, and a CBA is designed to do that. But problems arise as union and employer advocate their respective positions. Three of the most common conflicts are (1) whether an issue is a mandatory subject of bargaining, (2) whether the parties are bargaining in good faith, and (3) how to enforce the agreement. For a Web site devoted to articles and reports on collective bargaining, see http://www.ilr.cornell.edu/depts/ICB/briefing/.

SUBJECTS OF BARGAINING

The NLRA *permits* the parties to bargain almost any subject they wish, but *requires* them to bargain certain issues. **Mandatory subjects include wages, hours, and other terms and conditions of employment.** Either side may propose to bargain *other* subjects, but neither side may insist upon bargaining them.

Management and unions often disagree as to whether a particular topic is mandatory or not. Typically, unions attempt to expand the number of mandatory subjects, seeking more input into a greater number of issues, while the company argues that subjects are not mandatory and are none of the union's business. In general, a court is likely to find a given issue mandatory when it *directly relates* to individual workers; when a subject only indirectly affects employees, it is likely to be found not mandatory. In passing the NLRA, Congress never intended a union negotiator to become an equal partner in running the business.

Courts generally find these subjects to be mandatory: pay, benefits, order of layoffs and recalls, production quotas, work rules (such as safety practices), retirement benefits, and in-plant food service and prices (e.g., cafeteria food). Courts usually consider these subjects to be nonmandatory: product type and design, advertising, sales, financing, corporate organization, and location of plants.

Today, some of the angriest disputes between management and labor arise from a company's desire to subcontract work and/or to move plants to areas with cheaper costs. **Subcontracting** means that a manufacturer, rather than producing all parts of a product and then assembling them, contracts for other companies, frequently overseas, to make some of the parts. Is a business free to subcontract work? That depends on management's motive. **A company that subcontracts in order to maintain its economic viability is probably *not* required to bargain first; however, bargaining *is* mandatory if the subcontracting is designed to replace union workers with cheaper labor.**

Dorsey Trailers manufactured dump trucks. During a period of heavy sales, Dorsey subcontracted some of its production work to Bankhead Enterprises, which agreed to manufacture two trucks per week and split the profits. The union filed a ULP charge, claiming that subcontracting was a mandatory subject of bargaining, and that Dorsey had no right to make the deal before negotiating with the union.

The court noted that Dorsey was losing business because it could not fill orders fast enough. The dump truck industry was cyclical, and in a period of strong demand, the company had to be able to manufacture its goods quickly. Dorsey had been unable to hire enough welders and other skilled workers to keep up with demand. The court stated that Dorsey could not survive without the subcontracting. Further, the company had not reduced union jobs; it had simply failed to add more union workers—through no fault of its own. Dorsey was free to subcontract without bargaining the issue.[12]

Ford and the United Auto Workers (UAW) signed a contract aimed at resolving the subcontracting issue. Ford employs roughly 100,000 UAW workers. The CBA requires the company to maintain UAW jobs at no less than 95 percent of the current number. If Ford begins to manufacture auto parts that it previously subcontracted, the company is permitted to pay dramatically lower wages to all those hired to do the new work. Thus each side gets something: the union obtains additional jobs, while Ford pays less to the new workers.

Plant closings, which can result in hundreds or thousands of lost jobs, are also a volatile issue. Although the job losses are potentially greater than those that result from subcontracting, management is not obligated to bargain such a decision. **An employer is not required to bargain over the closing of a plant, only the *effects* of the closing.**[13]

The reasoning behind this rule is basic: the company that opened a plant ought to be able to close it. The competing interest of the employees—the need for work—is obviously strong but not strong enough to mandate bargaining. Further, having concluded that the employer has the right to shut down a facility, courts also allow the employer to do so fairly quickly. Management may need speed and flexibility in effecting such major business changes. In contrast, the union will want to slow down or prevent the closing. The two sides will have few things to discuss, and mandated bargaining will gain little for employees while potentially costing the company time and money. When a plant closing will cost jobs, management must bargain such things as the order of layoffs, but it need not bargain the closing itself.

EMPLOYER AND UNION SECURITY

Both the employer and the union will seek clauses making their positions more secure. Management, above all, wants to be sure that there will be no strikes during the course of the agreement. For its part, the union tries to ensure that its members cannot be turned away from work during the CBA's term, and that all newly hired workers will affiliate with the union. We look at several union security issues.

No Strike/No Lockout. Most agreements include some form of no-strike clause, meaning that the union promises not to strike during the term of the contract. In turn, unions insist on a no-lockout clause, meaning that in the event of a labor dispute, management will not prevent union members from working. **No-strike and no-lockout clauses are both legal.**

Closed Shop. A closed shop means the employer must hire only union members. Though obviously very attractive to a union, effectively giving it veto

---

[12] *Dorsey Trailers, Inc. Northumberland PA Plant v. NLRB*, 134 F.3d 125, 1998 U.S. App. LEXIS 764 (3rd. Cir. 1998).

[13] *First National Maintenance Corp. v. NLRB*, 452 U.S. 666, 101 S. Ct. 2573, 1981 U.S. LEXIS 117 (1981).

power over new hires, a closed shop is not possible. **A closed shop is illegal.** Indeed, for a union to bargain for a closed shop violates the NLRA.

Union and Agency Shops. In a union shop, membership in the union becomes compulsory *after* the employee has been hired. Thus management retains an unfettered right to hire whom it pleases, but all new employees who fit into the bargaining unit must affiliate with the union. **A union shop is generally legal.** There are two limitations, however. First, new members need not join the union for 30 days. Second, the new members, after joining the union, can only be required to pay initiation fees and union dues. If the new hire decides he does not want to participate in the union, the union may not compel him to do so, and management may not terminate him (pursuant to a CBA) for his refusal. This is a compromise, designed to protect workers from having to play an active role in a union, while ensuring that the union receives normal dues from all employees, whether they participate in union affairs or not. If employees could avoid dues, they would be "free riders," benefiting from the union's bargaining without paying for it.

An **agency shop** is similar to a union shop. Here, the new hire must pay union fees but need not actually join the organization. In both a union shop and an agency shop, the worker may insist on paying only the percentage of dues that is devoted to collective bargaining, contract administration, and grievances. An employee could refuse to pay, for example, the percentage of union dues devoted to organizing other companies.[14]

Some states have passed so-called **right to work** laws, which restrict or even outlaw union shop and agency shop agreements. These statutes typically prohibit a labor organization from demanding that all employees join the union or pay dues. Right to work laws prompt an intense response from both supporters and opponents of organized labor, and the Internet offers plenty of evidence. At http://www.nrtw.org/, the National Right to Work Legal Defense Foundation explains these statutes and counsels employees about their rights to reject union membership and avoid paying dues. The organization also discusses what it considers to be union abuses. Meanwhile, the AFL-CIO, the nation's largest labor organization, offers statistics demonstrating that union workers earn higher pay than their nonunion counterparts in virtually all jobs and professions, and that wages are lower in right to work states than elsewhere in the country. See its Web site at http://www.aflcio.org/.

Hot Cargo Clause. A hot cargo clause would prohibit an employer from doing business with a specified company. A union might like such a clause to put pressure on the *other* company, where the union already has a dispute. But the effort must fail: **hot cargo clauses are illegal**.

DUTY TO BARGAIN

Both the union and the employer must bargain in good faith with an open mind. However, they are *not* obligated to reach an agreement. This means that the two sides must meet and make a reasonable effort to reach a contract. The goal is good faith bargaining, with the hope that it will lead to a contract and

---

[14] *Communications Workers of America v. Beck*, 487 U.S. 735, 108 S. Ct. 2641, 1988 U.S. LEXIS 3030 (1988).

labor peace. Each side must listen to the other's proposals and consider possible compromises. But the NLRA does not require agreement. Suppose a union proposes a 15 percent pay increase, and management offers a 1 percent raise. Each side is required to attend bargaining sessions, listen to the other side's proposal, and consider its supporting argument. But neither side has to agree. Management need not raise its offer to 2 percent, nor must the union drop its demand. However, **if an employer states that it is financially unable to meet the union's demands, the union is entitled to see records that support the claim.** It is an unfair labor practice for an employer to say, "We can't afford a pay raise now," and then refuse to supply its financial data. An employer could easily destroy good faith bargaining if it were allowed to claim financial impossibility without demonstrating it. Similarly, if an employer argues that it must subcontract work to save money, it must furnish the documents it is relying on in making its proposal.

Sometimes an employer will attempt to make changes without bargaining the issues at all. However, **management may not unilaterally change wages, hours, or terms and conditions of employment without bargaining the issues to impasse.** "Bargaining to impasse" means that both parties must continue to meet and bargain in good faith until it is clear that they cannot reach an agreement. The goal in requiring collective bargaining is to bring the parties together, to reach an agreement that brings labor peace. In one case, the union won an election, but before bargaining could begin, management changed the schedule from five 8-hour days to four 10-hour days a week. The company also changed its layoff policy from one of strict seniority to one based on ability and began laying off employees based on alleged poor performance. The court held that each of these acts violated the company's duty to bargain. The employer ultimately might be allowed to make every one of these changes, but first it had to bargain the issues to impasse.[15]

For the same reasons, though the employer may implement new policies after impasse, it may *implement only what it has proposed at the table*. Again, it would defeat the purpose of the NLRA if a company were free to implement a business decision that it had never proposed; the two sides *could not* have discussed plans that were never offered at the table. Exhibit 15.1 outlines the respective bargaining rights and responsibilities between employers and unions.

Illegal implementation put major league baseball players back on the field after the longest strike in sports history. The CBA had expired, and the players' union bargained with team owners throughout the spring and summer. The two sides could not agree, primarily because the owners demanded a salary cap, which would give all teams equal payrolls. In August the players struck, ending the season without a World Series for the first time in more than 100 years. The two sides continued talking until December, when the owners announced they were implementing their salary cap proposal and changing various aspects of "free agency," the policy that allows a player to seek the highest salary from any team. A federal district court judge ruled that the owners had violated the NLRA by unilaterally imposing new rules concerning a mandatory subject (free agency) that they had never bargained. The judge ordered the owners back to the table, and the parties finally agreed to a new CBA.

---

[15] *Adair Standish Corp. v. NLRB*, 912 F.2d 854, 1990 U.S. App. LEXIS 14670 (6th Cir. 1990).

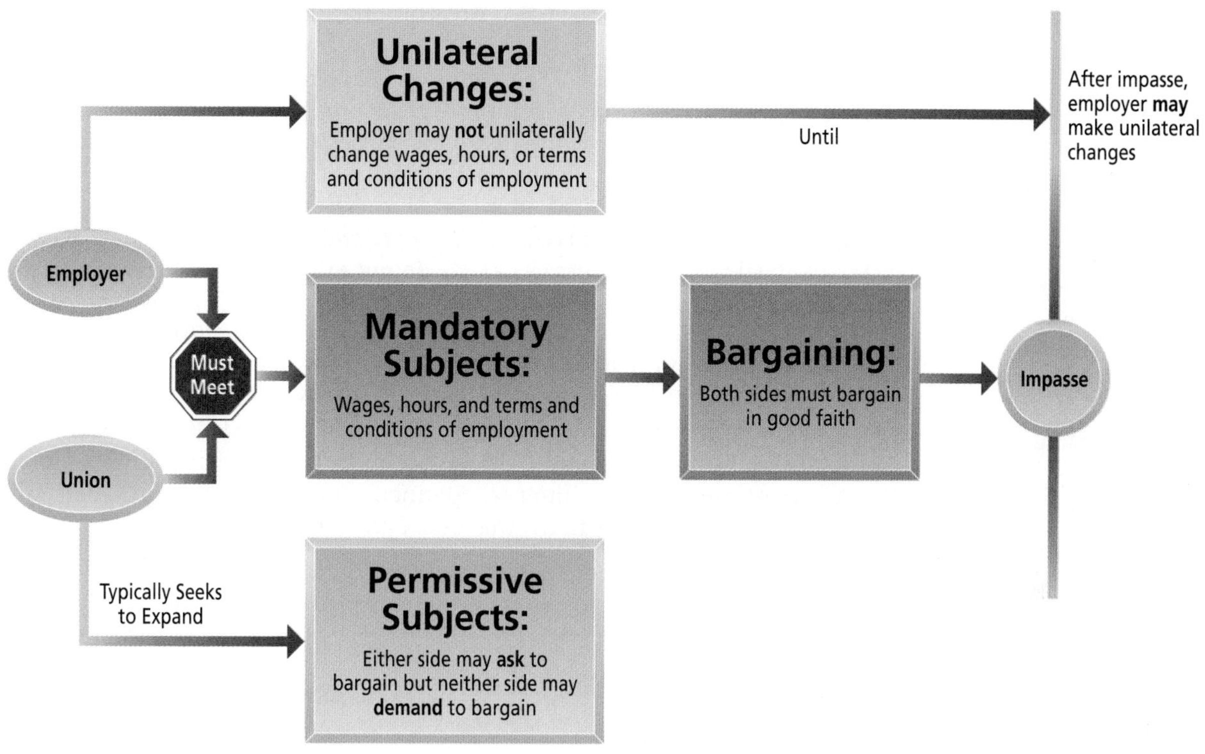

Exhibit 15.1
The NLRA requires that the employer and the union meet. They *must* bargain mandatory subjects and *may* bargain permissive subjects. The employer may not make any unilateral change concerning a mandatory subject until bargaining has reached an impasse.

ENFORCEMENT

Virtually all collective bargaining agreements provide for their own enforcement, typically through **grievance-arbitration**. Suppose a company transfers an employee from the day shift to the night shift, and the worker believes the contract prohibits such a transfer for any employee with her seniority. The employee complains to the union, which files a **grievance**, that is, a formal complaint with the company, notifying management that the union claims a contract violation. Generally, the CBA establishes some kind of informal hearing, usually conducted by a member of management, at which the employee, represented by the union, may state her case and respond to the company's assertions. The manager has a limited time period—say, seven days—to decide the grievance.

If, after the manager's decision, the employee is still dissatisfied, the union normally has the right to appeal to some kind of formal hearing, perhaps before a top company executive or committee. This appeal hearing is slightly more formal. If this hearing still fails to satisfy the employee, the union typically may file for **arbitration**, that is, a formal hearing before a neutral arbitrator. In the arbitration hearing, each side is represented by its lawyer. The arbitrator is required to decide the case based on the CBA. An arbitrator finds either for the employee, and orders the company to take certain corrective action, or for the employer, and dismisses the grievance. (The American Arbitration Association offers its rules, procedures, and forms at http://www.adr.org/.)

A CBA also permits the company to file a grievance. Its complaint normally goes directly to arbitration. In the vast majority of grievances, the arbitrator's decision is final. In a limited number of cases, however, the losing party attempts to convince a federal court that the arbitration award is unjust. Usually, such an appeal is futile. **Courts generally do not examine the merits of an arbitrator's decision.** The idea of all contracts, including CBAs, is to give the parties a chance to control their own destiny. When a CBA states that grievances should be settled by arbitration, courts seldom undercut the contract by reviewing the arbitrator's award. Of course, a rule would hardly be a rule without an exception. **A court may refuse to enforce an arbitrator's award that is contrary to public policy.** So if an arbitrator's decision encourages either party to violate the law or engage in clearly immoral conduct, a court will probably nullify the award. But like most exceptions, this one is very narrowly interpreted, as the following case illustrates.

UNITED PAPERWORKERS INTERNATIONAL UNION v. MISCO, INC.

484 U.S. 29, 108 S. Ct. 364, 1987 U.S. LEXIS 5028
United States Supreme Court, 1987

Facts: Misco, Inc. operated a paper plant in Louisiana. The company had a collective bargaining agreement with the United Paperworkers (the Union), which permitted either side to file grievances and take them to final, binding arbitration. The CBA also permitted the company to post work rules. Rule II.1 notified employees that they could be dismissed for bringing alcohol or drugs onto company premises or arriving for work under the influence of such substances.

Isiah Cooper, an employee covered by the CBA, operated a slitter-rewinder machine, which used sharp blades to cut rolling coils of paper. The machine was hazardous and had caused numerous injuries over the years. Cooper had twice been reprimanded for deficient performance. Two days after the second reprimand, police searched Cooper's house, pursuant to a search warrant, and discovered a large amount of marijuana. Later that day, police apprehended Cooper in the backseat of another worker's car, a white Cutlass, parked in the company lot. There was marijuana smoke in the air and a lighted marijuana cigarette in the ashtray in the front seat. Police arrested Cooper and then searched *his* car, where they found a plastic scales case and some marijuana.

When the Company learned of Cooper's presence in the white Cutlass, it discharged him for having drugs on the premises. He filed a grievance. Eight months later, shortly before the arbitration hearing began, the Company learned that the police had found marijuana in Cooper's own car. The arbitrator found in Cooper's favor, stating that because he was in the backseat of the Cutlass and the marijuana was in the front, the Company had no evidence he had used or possessed an illegal substance on the premises. The arbitrator refused to consider the marijuana found in Cooper's own car because the Company had not known about it when it fired him.

The Company filed suit in United States District Court, which vacated the arbitrator's decision, holding that public policy prohibits the use of marijuana. The court of appeals affirmed the district court, and the union sought review by the Supreme Court.

Issue: Was the district court correct in overruling the arbitrator on public policy grounds?

Excerpts from Justice White's Decision: The Court made clear almost 30 years ago that the courts play only a limited role when asked to review the decision of an arbitrator. The courts are not authorized to reconsider the merits of an award even though the parties may allege that the award rests on errors of fact or on misinterpretation of the contract. The federal policy of settling labor disputes by arbitration would be undermined if courts had the final say on the merits of the awards.

The Company's position, simply put, is that the arbitrator committed grievous error in finding that the evidence was insufficient to prove that Cooper had possessed or used marijuana on company property. But the court of appeals, although it took a distinctly jaundiced view of the arbitrator's decision in this regard, was not free to refuse enforcement because it considered Cooper's presence in the white Cutlass, in the circumstances, to be ample proof that Rule II.1 was violated. No dishonesty [on the arbitrator's part] is alleged; only improvident, even silly, factfinding is claimed.

Nor was it open to the court of appeals to refuse to enforce the award because the arbitrator, in deciding whether there was just cause to discharge, refused to consider evidence unknown to the Company at the time Cooper was fired. The parties bargained for arbitration to settle disputes and were free to set the procedural rules for arbitrators to follow if they chose. Article VI of the agreement, entitled "Arbitration Procedure," did set some ground rules for the arbitration process. It forbade the arbitrator to consider hearsay evidence, for example, but evidentiary matters were otherwise left to the arbitrator. Here the arbitrator ruled that in determining whether Cooper had violated Rule II.1, he should not consider evidence not relied on by the employer in ordering the discharge, particularly in a case like this where there was no notice to the employee or the Union prior to the hearing that the Company would attempt to rely on after-discovered evidence. This, in effect, was a construction of what the contract required when deciding discharge cases: an arbitrator was to look only at the evidence before the employer at the time of discharge.

The parties did not bargain for the facts to be found by a court, but by an arbitrator chosen by them who had more opportunity to observe Cooper and to be familiar with the plant and its problems. Nor does the fact that it is inquiring into a possible violation of public policy excuse a court for doing the arbitrator's task.

The judgment of the court of appeals is *reversed.*

CONCERTED ACTION

Concerted action refers to any tactics union members take in unison to gain some bargaining advantage. It is this power that gives a union strength. **The NLRA guarantees the right of employees to engage in concerted action for mutual aid or protection.**[16] The most common forms of concerted action are strikes and picketing.

STRIKES

The NLRA guarantees employees the right to strike, but with some limitations.[17] A union has a guaranteed right to call a strike if the parties are unable to reach a collective bargaining agreement. A union may call a strike to exert economic pressure on management, to protest an unfair labor practice, or to

[16] NLRA §7.

[17] NLRA §13.

preserve work that the employer is considering sending elsewhere. (For a listing of unions currently on strike, see http://www.igc.org/strike/.) Note that the right to strike can be waived. Management will generally insist that the CBA include a no-strike clause, which prohibits the union from striking while the CBA is in force. A strike is illegal in several other situations as well; here we mention the most important.

COOLING OFF PERIOD

Once the union agrees to a CBA, it may not strike to terminate the agreement, or modify it, without giving management 60 days' notice. Suppose a union contract expires July 1. The two sides attempt to bargain a new contract, but progress is slow. The union may strike as an economic weapon, but must notify management of its intention to do so *and then must wait 60 days*. This cooling off period is designed to give both sides a chance to reassess negotiations and to decide whether some additional compromise would be wiser than enduring a strike.

STATUTORY PROHIBITION

Many states have outlawed strikes by public employees. In some states, the prohibition applies to selected employees, such as firefighters or teachers. In other states, *all* public employees are barred from striking, whether or not they have a contract. The purpose of these statutes is to ensure that unions do not use the public health or welfare as a weapon to secure an unfair bargaining advantage. However, even employees subject to such a rule may find other tactics to press their cause.

Jen has worked hard throughout high school, achieving a 3.8 GPA and high test scores, and now she is ready to apply to some of the best colleges in the country. All of her teachers think she is an extraordinary student—yet no one will write her a letter of recommendation.

The teacher's union has been bargaining a new contract for a year and a half. The teachers seek a 4 percent raise; the school board has offered 1 percent. The struggle has grown increasingly bitter. There will be no strike—state law prohibits that—but the teachers have decided they will "work to rule," meaning that they will do only what their (expired) contract requires: teach classes, issue grades, and so forth. No teacher will write a letter of recommendation, coach a team, supervise detention, or offer extra help to a student.

"This stinks," wails Jen. "I've never asked for extra assistance. I've tried to be helpful in class, and a lot of times, I've tutored other kids. This is the one time in my life I really need my teachers to be there for me, and they're turning their backs."

"My heart goes out to Jen," responds her American history teacher, "but our problem is simple: as long as we quietly ask for decent pay, no one listens. Students and parents notice us only when they suffer inconvenience."

"This is a moral outrage!" shouts Jen's father. "These so-called teachers have no right to hurt my child over their pay disputes. If they were serious about their profession, they would do everything they could to help the children who are entrusted to them. Our high school normally sends 95 percent of its students to good colleges, and now the teachers are sabotaging everything."

"If the parents were serious about education," the history teacher retorts, "or truly concerned about their children's welfare, they would demand that the town pay respectable salaries. They prefer lower taxes so they can spend more on fancy cars."

Who is right?

VIOLENT STRIKES

The NLRA prohibits violent strikes. Violence does sometimes occur on the picket line, when union members attempt to prevent other workers from entering the job site. Or a union may stage a **sit-down strike**, in which members stop working but remain at their job posts, physically blocking replacement workers from taking their places. Any such violence is illegal.

PARTIAL STRIKES

A partial strike occurs when employees stop working temporarily, then resume, then stop again, and so forth. This tactic is particularly disruptive because management cannot bring in replacement workers. A union may either walk off the job or stay on it, but it may not alternate.

REPLACEMENT WORKERS

When employees go on strike, management generally wants to replace them to keep the company operating. When replacement workers begin to cross a union picket line, tempers are certain to explode, and entire communities may feel the repercussions. Are replacement workers legal? Yes. **Management has the right to hire replacement workers during a strike.** May the employer offer the replacement workers *permanent* jobs, or must the company give union members their jobs back when the strike is over? It depends on the type of strike.

After an *economic strike*, an employer may not discriminate against a striker, but the employer is *not* obligated to lay off a replacement worker to give a striker his job back. An economic strike is one intended to gain wages or benefits. When a union bargains for a pay raise but fails to get it and walks off the job, that is an economic strike. During such a strike, an employer may hire permanent replacement workers. When the strike is over, the company has no obligation to lay off the replacement workers to make room for the strikers. However, if the company does hire more workers, it may not discriminate against the strikers.

After a *ULP strike*, a union member is entitled to her job back, even if that means the employer must lay off a replacement worker. Suppose management refuses to bargain in good faith, by claiming poverty without producing records to substantiate its claim. The union strikes. Management's refusal to bargain was an unfair labor practice, and the strike is a ULP strike. When it ends, the striking workers must get their jobs back.

GENERAL INDUSTRIAL EMPLOYEES UNION, LOCAL 42 v. NLRB

951 F.2d 1308, 1991 U.S. App. LEXIS 30086
Court of Appeals for the District of Columbia, 1991

Facts: Mohawk Liqueur Corp.'s collective bargaining agreement with Local 42 (the union) was about to expire, and the parties were negotiating a new contract. Mohawk submitted its final offer, including a statement that it would not pay the last cost of living adjustment (COLA) due under the *old* contract for work already performed. The union declared this an unfair labor practice and struck. Mohawk unilaterally implemented its final offer and refused to pay the COLA. Negotiations resumed, and about two months later Mohawk agreed to make the old COLA payment. The company then warned the workers that they would be permanently replaced if they failed to return by August 4.

On August 3, the union met. The workers agreed that the COLA payment was no longer an issue, but voted to continue the strike. The employees hoped to force Mohawk to divulge the names of certain workers the company planned to discharge; they also wanted the company to offer a general amnesty to all strikers and grant certain financial benefits. Mohawk replaced all striking workers. On August 11, the union voted to return to work. Mohawk reinstated some but not all of the strikers, and five months later the parties reached a new contract.

The Board determined that what had begun as a ULP strike had changed into an economic one, and that Mohawk had lawfully replaced some workers permanently. The union appealed.

Issue: Was Mohawk entitled to replace workers permanently?

Excerpts from Judge Silberman's Decision: Employees who take part in [an economic strike] run the risk of permanent replacement by new hires. But unfair labor practice strikers are entitled to reinstatement if they wish to return to work and, if denied reemployment, are also entitled to back pay from the date of denial.

The causes of a strike can, of course, change over time. Sometimes a strike that starts for economic reasons is prolonged by the employer's subsequent unlawful conduct and is thereby "converted" from an economic to an unfair labor practice strike. Similarly (although there are fewer examples), an unfair labor practice strike can be converted to an economic strike if the illegal acts that originally caused the dispute fade in significance and the employees continue the strike solely to enforce their economic demands on the employer.

The [August 3 union] meeting's avowed purpose was to decide whether to prolong the strike. The minutes of the meeting, the motion by which the strikers decided not to return to work, and the testimony before the ALJ all demonstrate that the reasons for continuing the strike had nothing whatsoever to do with Mohawk's prior violations of the NLRA. Rather, the record indicates that the strikers wished to obtain information on discharges, amnesty for strike misconduct, and COLAs in the new contract. The May 31 COLA came into the deliberations only when the Union negotiator and attorney explained why it was no longer a reason to strike. The evidence relating to both the August 11 negotiating session (such as testimony that the parties agreed the COLA issue had been "settled" and the Union's announcement that it was withdrawing its COLA grievance) and the August 12 Union meeting also supports the Board's conclusion that the strike was prolonged for reasons entirely unrelated to Mohawk's unfair labor practices.

[The Board's order, declaring the permanent replacements lawful, is *affirmed*.]

PICKETING

Picketing the employer's workplace in support of a strike is generally lawful. Striking workers are permitted to establish picket lines at the employer's job site and to urge all others—employees, replacement workers, and customers—not to cross the line. But the picketers are not permitted to use physical force to *prevent* anyone from crossing the line. The NLRA does not authorize or protect violence on the picket line. The company may terminate violent picketers and permanently replace them, regardless of the nature of the strike.

Secondary boycotts are generally illegal. A secondary boycott is a picket line established not at the employer's premises but at the workplace of a *different* company that does business with the union's employer. Such a boycott is designed to put pressure on the union's employer by forcing other companies to stop doing business with it. Suppose Union is on strike against Truck Co. Union is free to picket Truck Co.'s office or terminal. If Truck Co. hires replacement workers, the trucks will be back on the road, making deliveries. Now Union wants to put additional pressure on Truck Co., so it sets up picket lines at a *supermarket* where Truck Co. delivers. Union attempts to persuade customers not to shop at the store and other workers, including delivery drivers, not to enter the premises. If allowed, the picketing might result in the supermarket demanding that Truck Co. compromise with Union. But this is a secondary boycott, so it is illegal. Truck Co. and the supermarket will obtain an injunction, prohibiting the secondary boycott. See Exhibit 15.2.

LOCKOUTS

The workers have bargained with management for weeks, and discussions have turned belligerent. It is 6:00 A.M., the start of another day at the factory. But as 150 employees arrive for work, they are amazed to find the company's gate locked and armed guards standing on the other side. What is this? A lockout.

The power of a union comes ultimately from its potential to strike. But management, too, has weapons. In a lockout, management prohibits workers from entering the premises, denying the employees work and a chance to earn a paycheck. Most, but not all, lockouts are legal.

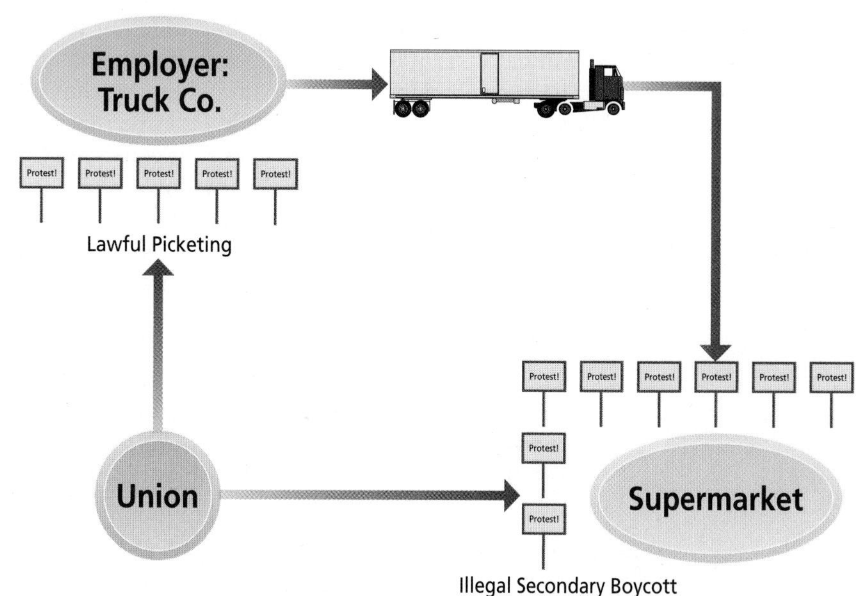

Exhibit 15.2
A union striking against Truck Co. may lawfully picket the employer, using peaceful means to urge all others to stay away. But if the union attempts to put indirect pressure on Truck Co. by picketing one of the company's customers, it is engaging in an illegal secondary boycott.

A defensive lockout is almost always legal. It is one way management can respond to union pressure such as a sit-down strike or a **whipsaw strike**, which may occur when a union is simultaneously bargaining with various employers. Suppose a machinists' union is simultaneously bargaining a contract with three engine manufacturers, attempting to obtain an identical contract from all of the companies. To pressure the companies, the union might choose to strike against only *one* of the manufacturers. This is a whipsaw strike, and it can be very effective because the struck company, losing money while the others profit, will push strongly for a compromise. But management of all three companies may respond by locking out the workers from *all* factories, even those where no strike is under way. That is a defensive lockout, and it is legal.

An offensive lockout is legal if the parties have reached a bargaining impasse. Management, bargaining a new CBA with a union, may wish to use a lockout to advance its position. It is allowed to do so *provided the parties have reached an impasse*. If there is no impasse, a lockout will *probably* be illegal. Most courts consider that a lockout before impasse indicates hostility to the union. That kind of general antagonism to a union is illegal because the NLRA guarantees employees the right to organize. In addition, management usually *must notify the union before locking it out*. Again, the purpose of the NLRA is to bring the parties together through bargaining. A lockout is a legitimate method to pressure a union into compromise, but it can have that effect only if the union is warned and given a chance to bargain.

MULTI-EMPLOYER BARGAINING AND ANTITRUST LAW

Unions often bargain simultaneously with several—or even hundreds—of employers in a particular industry. Multi-employer bargaining can benefit both sides. For the union, it is a way to obtain a contract for employees in many plants, or even nationwide, all at once. For management, it is a way of avoiding costly whipsaw strikes, in which a union closes one employer at a time, achieving maximum leverage in the process.

Does multi-employer bargaining violate antitrust law? The Sherman Act prohibits companies from banding together to fix costs, destroy competition, or dominate a market.[18] Individual workers unhappy with a multi-employer contract have periodically filed suit, claiming that multi-employer bargaining violates the Sherman Act by allowing companies to agree on uniform wages. These lawsuits invariably fail, however. **The Supreme Court has consistently held that multi-employer bargaining does not violate antitrust laws.** Congress passed the NLRA in order to achieve labor peace, and multi-employer bargaining helps accomplish that goal. Employers *do* diminish competition when they bargain together, but strikes pose a greater threat to the economy than employer collusion. Today, more than 40 percent of major collective bargaining agreements involve groups of employers in such diverse industries as construction, transportation, retail trade, clothing manufacture, real estate, and professional sports.

The Supreme Court has gone even further, permitting a group of employers to *implement* a proposal together, once the parties have bargained to impasse. The CBA between the National Football League (NFL) and the football players'

---

[18] See Chapter 19 on antitrust law.

union expired. During negotiations for a new contract, the NFL proposed a plan that would allow each club in the league a "developmental squad" of six players, who would practice with the team but play in games only as substitutes for injured players. The parties negotiated but could not agree on the pay or benefits for these players. The NFL unilaterally implemented a salary of $1,000 per week by sending each of its member clubs a uniform contract for use with developmental squad players. Claiming that the NFL clubs had violated the Sherman Act, 235 of the players filed suit. They lost. The Supreme Court held that the NLRA took precedence over the antitrust laws and affirmed the owners' right to implement.[19]

REGULATING UNION AFFAIRS

Along with a union's exclusive bargaining power goes a duty of fairness to all of its members. Known as the union's *duty of fair representation*, it was created by the NLRA and the Labor-Management Reporting and Disclosure Act. **The duty of fair representation requires that a union represent all members fairly, impartially, and in good faith.** A union is not entitled to favor some members over others. No union may discriminate against a member based on impermissible characteristics such as race or sex. A union is allowed to discipline a member for certain acts, such as engaging in an illegal strike or working for wages below union scale. But the union may *not* discipline a member for criticizing union leadership or attempting to replace the leadership through a proper election.

Unions must make reasonable decisions about whether to pursue an employee's grievance. A member may sue his union, claiming that the organization violated its duty of fair representation by deciding not to pursue a grievance on his behalf. But courts generally allow unions a *wide range of latitude* in deciding whether to pursue a grievance. **A union's decision not to file a grievance is illegal only if it was arbitrary, discriminatory, or in bad faith.**

Most employees fail when claiming that a union violated its duty of fair representation. Ramon Hayes worked at the Peoples Gas, Light and Coke Co. Peoples Gas fired him for theft, and the union filed a grievance. Before the grievance could be arbitrated, Hayes was convicted on drug charges. The union, mistakenly believing Hayes had been convicted on the *theft* accusation, withdrew its grievance. Later, the union learned of its error, but refused to pursue the grievance because Peoples Gas had added the drug charge as a reason for the dismissal. A court ruled that the union had probably been inept and negligent in dismissing the original grievance, but had shown no *bad faith* in its belief that the grievance was futile. The union had not violated its duty of fair representation.[20]

---

[19] *Brown v. Pro Football, Inc.*, 518 U.S. 231, 116 S. Ct. 2116, 1996 U.S. LEXIS 4047 (1996).

[20] *Hayes v. People's Gas, Light and Coke Co.*, 1992 U.S. App. LEXIS 30592 (7th Cir. 1992).

CHAPTER CONCLUSION

Workers first attempted to organize unions in this country about 200 years ago in response to appalling working conditions. These conditions are *generally* better today, and contemporary clashes between union and management are less likely to stem from sweltering temperatures in a mine than from a management decision to subcontract work or from a teacher's refusal to write college recommendations. But although the flash points have changed, labor law is still dominated by issues of organizing, collective bargaining, and concerted action.

CHAPTER REVIEW

1. Section 7 of the National Labor Relations Act (NLRA) guarantees employees the right to organize and join unions, bargain collectively, and engage in other concerted activities.
2. Section 8(a) of the NLRA makes it an unfair labor practice for an employer to interfere with union organizing, discriminate against a union member, or refuse to bargain collectively.
3. Section 8(b) of the NLRA makes it an unfair labor practice for a union to interfere with employees who are exercising their rights under §7, to encourage an employer to discriminate against an employee because of a labor dispute, to refuse to bargain collectively, or to engage in an illegal strike or boycott.
4. Section 9 of the NLRA makes a validly recognized union the *exclusive* representative of the employees.
5. During a union organizing campaign, an employer may vigorously present anti-union views to its employees, but it may not use threats or promises of benefits to defeat the union effort.
6. The National Labor Relations Board (NLRB) will certify a proposed bargaining unit only if the employees share a community of interest.
7. The employer and the union *must* bargain over wages, hours, and other terms and conditions of employment. They *may* bargain other subjects, but neither side may insist on doing so.
8. The union and the employer must bargain in good faith, but they are not obligated to reach an agreement. Management may not unilaterally change wages, hours, or terms and conditions of employment without bargaining to impasse.
9. The NLRA guarantees employees the right to strike, with some limitations.
10. After an *economic* strike, an employer is not obligated to lay off replacement workers to give a striker her job back, but it may not discriminate against a striker. After a *ULP* strike, the striking worker must get her job back.
11. Picketing the employer's workplace in support of a strike is generally lawful; a secondary boycott is generally illegal.
12. An employer may lock out workers, but only after giving them notice.
13. Multi-employer bargaining and implementation do not violate antitrust laws.
14. The duty of fair representation requires that a union represent all members fairly, impartially, and in good faith.

PRACTICE TEST

1. Power, Inc. operated a surface coal mine in central Pennsylvania. Financial losses led it to lay off a number of employees. After that, several employees contacted the United Mine Workers of America (UMWA), which began an organizing drive at the company. Power's general manager and foreman both warned the miners that if the company was unionized, it would be shut down. An office manager told one of the miners that the company would get rid of union supporters. Shortly

before the election was to take place, Power laid off 13 employees, all of whom had signed union cards. One employee, who had not signed a union card, had low seniority but was not laid off. Later, one of Power's lawyers told several miners that anyone caught helping the 13 laid-off workers by contributing to a union hardship fund would "be out there looking for help from somebody else." Comment.

2. Triec, Inc. is a small electrical contracting company in Springfield, Ohio, owned by its executives Yeazell, Jones, and Heaton. Employees contacted the International Brotherhood of Electrical Workers, which began an organizing drive. Six of the 11 employees in the bargaining unit signed authorization cards. The company declined to recognize the union, which petitioned the NLRB to schedule an election. The company then granted several new benefits for all workers, including higher wages, paid vacations, and other measures. When the election was held, only 2 of the 11 bargaining unit members voted for the union. Did the company violate the NLRA?

3. Q-1 Motor Express was an interstate trucking company. When a union attempted to organize Q-1's drivers, it met heavy resistance. A supervisor told one driver that if he knew what was good for him, he would stay away from the union organizer. The company president told another employee that he had the right to fire everybody, close the company, and then rehire new drivers after 72 hours. He made numerous other threats to workers and their families. Based on the extreme nature of the company's opposition, what exceptional remedy did the union seek before the NLRB?

4. Douglas Kuroda worked for the Hertz Corp. He and his supervisor had a heated argument in which Kuroda told his boss, "You may have a master's degree but you don't know shit." The supervisor instructed Kuroda to punch out for the day, but Kuroda refused to leave until security officers escorted him off the premises. Hertz fired him, and Kuroda filed a grievance. The union represented Kuroda at an arbitration hearing. During the hearing, the union made no objection to certain evidence that the company offered to demonstrate why it fired Kuroda. The arbitrator ruled in favor of the company. Kuroda sued his union (and also Hertz). What kind of claim is he making against the union? Is he likely to win his claim?

5. Gibson Greetings, Inc. had a plant in Berea, Kentucky, where the workers belonged to the International Brotherhood of Firemen & Oilers. The old CBA expired, and the parties negotiated a new one, but were unable to reach an agreement on economic issues. The union struck. At the next bargaining session, the company claimed that the strike violated the *old* CBA, which had a no-strike clause and which stated that the terms of the old CBA would continue in force as long as the parties were bargaining a *new* CBA. The company refused to bargain until the union at least agreed that by bargaining, the company was not giving up its claim of an illegal strike. The two sides returned to bargaining, but meanwhile the company hired replacement workers. Eventually, the striking workers offered to return to work, but Gibson refused to rehire many of them. In court, the union claimed that the company had committed a ULP by (1) insisting the strike was illegal and (2) refusing to bargain until the union acknowledged the company's position. Why is it very important to the union to establish the company's act as a ULP? Was it a ULP?

6. **YOU BE THE JUDGE WRITING PROBLEM** Plainville Ready Mix Concrete Co. was bargaining a CBA with the drivers' union. Negotiations went forward, on and off, over many months, with wages the major source of disagreement. Plainville made its final offer of $9.50 per hour, with step increases of $.25 per hour in a year and another $.25 per hour the following year. The plan also included certain incentive pay. The union refused to accept the offer, and the two sides reached an impasse. Plainville then announced it was

implementing its plans. It established a wage rate of $9.50 per hour but eliminated the step increases and incentive pay. Was the company's implementation of the wage increase legal? **Argument for Plainville:** The NLRA only requires the company to bargain in good faith, which we did. The law does not obligate us to agree to anything. Once the parties reached an impasse, Plainville could implement any plan it wanted. **Argument for the Union:** When the parties reach an impasse, the employer is permitted to implement whatever it proposed at the bargaining table. It would defeat the purpose of collective bargaining if a company could implement plans it had never proposed.

7. Eads Transfer, Inc. was a moving and storage company with a small workforce represented by the General Teamsters, Chauffeurs and Helpers Union. When the CBA expired, the parties failed to reach agreement on a new one, and the union struck. As negotiations continued, Eads hired temporary replacement workers. After 10 months of the strike, some union workers offered to return to work, but Eads made no response to the offer. Two months later, more workers offered to return to work, but Eads would not accept any of the offers. Eventually, Eads notified all workers that they would not be allowed back to work until a new CBA had been signed. The union filed ULP claims against the company. Please rule.

8. Olivetti Office U.S.A., Inc. was located in Newington, Connecticut, and its workers were represented by the United Automobile, Aerospace and Agriculture Implement Workers of America. The company's president reported to the union that Olivetti was losing money. He insisted that unless the union renegotiated certain wage increases in the current CBA, Olivetti would subcontract work to cheaper parts of the country to save money. The union requested to bargain over the proposed subcontracting, and Olivetti agreed. But when the sides met, the company would not permit the union to see the financial data that supported its arguments. After several meetings, the company declared an impasse, implemented its subcontracting proposal, and laid off workers in Connecticut. The union claimed this was a ULP. Was it?

9. Fred Schipul taught English at the Thomaston (Connecticut) High School for 18 years. When the position of English Department chairperson became vacant, Schipul applied, but the Board of Education appointed a less senior teacher. Schipul filed a grievance, based on a CBA provision that required the Board to promote the most senior teacher where two or more applicants were equal in qualification. Before the arbitrator ruled on the grievance, the Board eliminated all department chairpersons. The arbitrator ruled in Schipul's favor. The Board then reinstated all department chairs—all but the English Department. Comment.

10. Labor Day is a national holiday originally intended to celebrate the contributions of working men and women. But for most people today it simply means a day off from work—or the day before school begins. What are some reasons that unions have declined in membership and power? Are there are any reasons to think that organized labor may rebound and increase its strength?

11. **RIGHT & WRONG** The chapter refers in several places to the contentious issue of subcontracting. Make an argument for management in favor of a company's ethical right to subcontract, and one for unions in opposition.

INTERNET RESEARCH PROBLEM

Take a look at http://www.uniteunion.org/sweatshops/sweatshop.html. What are sweatshops? Do they exist in the United States? Click on students against sweatshops. Describe a current student campaign about this issue. Do you agree or disagree with what the students are doing? Why?

You can find further practice problems in the Online Quiz at http://beatty.westbuslaw.com or in the Study Guide that accompanies this text.

UNIT

4

BUSINESS ORGANIZATIONS

Starting a Business

16

CHAPTER

At long last, Rachel was in love. For years, she had yearned to start her own business, but the perfect concept always eluded her. Then, surfing the Internet one day, she found the idea she had been searching for: movie theaters that show only classic films. Sure, you can rent *Star Wars* or *Gone with the Wind* anytime, but the little box at home cannot compete with a large screen and digital sound. At home, Atlanta simply does not burn as hot. According to the Internet, these theaters were already a rave success in Paris. Why not in Des Moines?

Rachel began looking for investors. Finally, at her nineteenth lunch meeting, she found Ross, who was as enthusiastic as she. Two days later, they signed a lease on a suitable property. Prospects for the business looked great. Then, while riding his bike on company business, Ross crashed into a pedestrian. Only when Rachel was served with a complaint did she learn that their business was a partnership, which meant that she and Ross were both personally liable for his accident.

In a panic, Rachel resumed surfing the Net, this time looking for legal information. She downloaded a sample corporate charter and formed a corporation, BigScreen, Inc. Now she and Ross enjoyed limited liability and could sell stock to outside investors. Their college friend from Hong Kong, Liang, was the first to buy shares. But other prospective purchasers insisted that BigScreen be organized as an S corporation for tax reasons. Back to the Internet, where

Rachel learned that non-resident aliens could not hold stock in S corps. Liang's participation disqualified BigScreen.

By this time, Rachel was surfing in desperation. At last she found an answer: BigScreen could become a limited liability company. This form of business provided all the advantages of an S corp with none of the disadvantages. She and Ross immediately formed an LLC, transferred BigScreen's assets, and sighed in relief—until tax day. The IRS considered their transfer of assets to be a sale. Suddenly, they faced a huge tax bill, with no way to pay it. Ross announced he was withdrawing from the business.

"You promised to stay five years," Rachel insisted.

"Yeah," Ross agreed, "but I never signed the operating agreement, so tough luck for you."

"Ross, I trusted you," Rachel protested.

"Frankly, my dear, I don't give a damn," replied Ross, slamming the door as he left.

Many people dream of starting their own business. They look for exactly the right idea to power a company to success. Creativity is an important ingredient for any successful start-up. So are hard work and finely honed business skills. And so is the law. Legal issues can have as profound an impact on the success of a company as any business decision.

To begin, entrepreneurs must select a form of organization. The correct choice can reduce taxes, liability, and conflict while facilitating outside investment. If entrepreneurs do not make a choice for themselves, the law will automatically select a (potentially undesirable) default option. (To see if you have the right characteristics to be an entrepreneur, check out "The Entrepreneur Test" at http://www.liraz.com/webquiz.htm.)

SOLE PROPRIETORSHIPS

A sole proprietorship is an unincorporated business owned by a single person. It is the most common form of business organization. For example, 15-year-old Andre Ware sells safety products—reflectors, fire extinguishers, smoke detectors—door-to-door in Plano, Texas. In Cleveland, Linda Brazdil runs ExSciTe (which stands for Excellence in Science Teaching), a company that helps teachers prepare hands-on science experiments in the classroom using such basic items as vinegar, lemon juice, and red cabbage. (Students do *not* have to eat their mistakes.)

Sole proprietorships are easy and inexpensive to create and operate. There is no need to hire a lawyer or register with the government. The company is not even required to file a separate tax return—all profits and losses are reported on the owner's personal return. A very few states, such as California, require sole proprietors to obtain a business license. Some cities and towns also require a business license. And states generally require sole proprietors to register their business name if it is different from their own. Linda Brazdil, for example, would file a "d/b/a" or "doing business as" certificate for "ExSciTe."

Sole proprietorships also have some serious disadvantages. First, the owner of the business is responsible for all of the business's debts. If ExSciTe cannot pay its suppliers or if a student is injured by an exploding cabbage, Linda Brazdil is *personally* liable. She may have to sell her house and car to pay the debt. Second, the owner of a sole proprietorship has limited options for financing her business. Debt is generally her only source of working capital because she has no stock to sell. If someone else brings in capital and helps with the management of the business, then it is a partnership, not a sole proprietorship. For this reason, sole proprietorships work best for small businesses without large capital needs. Go to http://www.ezaccounting.com/previewcal1a.html for help in preparing a sole proprietorship balance sheet and income statement.

GENERAL PARTNERSHIPS

Traditionally, partnerships were regulated by common law, but inconsistency among the states became troublesome as interstate commerce grew. To solve this problem, the National Conference of Commissioners on Uniform State Laws drafted the Uniform Partnership Act in 1914 and then revised it in the 1990s. A majority of states have now passed the Revised Uniform Partnership Act (RUPA), so we use it as the basis for our discussion of partnership law.

Partnerships have two important advantages: they do not pay *taxes* and they are *easy to form*. Partnerships, however, also have some major disadvantages:

- *Liability.* Each partner is personally liable for the debts of the enterprise whether or not she caused them.
- *Funding.* Financing a partnership may be difficult because the firm cannot sell shares as a corporation does. The capital needs of the partnership must be met by contributions from partners or by borrowing.
- *Management.* Managing a partnership can also be difficult because, in the absence of an agreement to the contrary, all partners have an equal say in running the business.
- *Transferability.* A partner only has the right to transfer the *value* of her partnership interest, not the interest itself. Thus a mother who is a partner in a law firm can pass on to her son the value of her partnership interest, not the right to be a partner in the firm (or even the right to work there).

TAXES

A partnership is not a taxable entity, which means it does not pay taxes itself. All income and losses are passed through to the partners and reported on their personal income tax returns. Corporations, by contrast, are taxable entities and pay income tax on their profits. Shareholders must then pay tax on dividends from the corporation. Thus a dollar is taxed only once before it ends up in a partner's bank account, but twice before it is deposited by a shareholder.

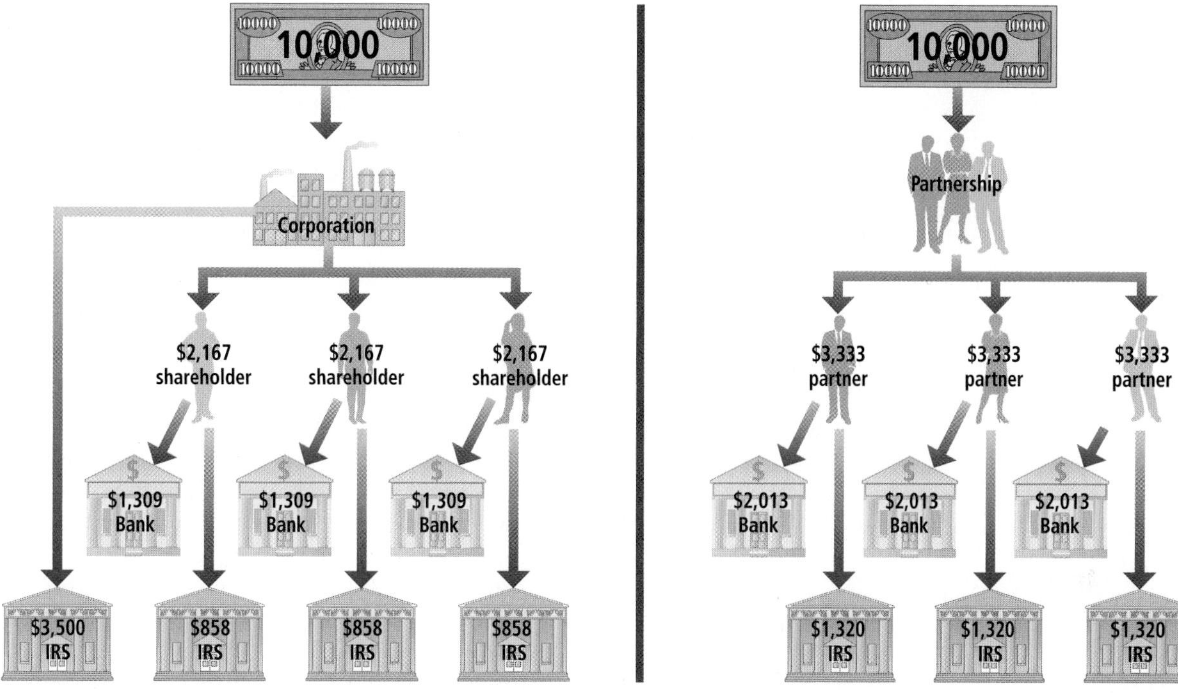

Exhibit 16.1

Exhibit 16.1 compares the single taxation of partnerships with the double taxation of corporations. Suppose, as shown in the exhibit, that a corporation and a partnership each receive $10,000 in additional income. The corporation pays tax at a top rate of 35 percent.[1] Thus the corporation pays $3,500 of the $10,000 in tax. The corporation pays out the remaining $6,500 as a dividend of $2,167 to each of its three shareholders. Then the shareholders are taxed at the top individual rate of 39.6 percent, which means they each pay a tax of $858. They are each left with $1,309. Of the initial $10,000, more than 60 percent ($6,074) has gone to the Internal Revenue Service (IRS).

Compare the corporation to a partnership. The partnership itself pays no taxes, so it can pass on $3,333 to each of its partners. At the 39.6 percent rate, they will each pay an individual income tax of $1,320. As partners, they pocket $2,013, which is $704 more than they could keep as shareholders. Of the partnership's initial $10,000, about 40 percent ($3,960) has gone to the IRS—compared with the corporation's 60 percent.

FORMATION

A partnership is an association of two or more co-owners who carry on a business for profit.[2] Each co-owner is called a *general partner*. Like sole proprietorships, partnerships are easy to form. Although, practically speaking, a partnership *should* have a written agreement, RUPA does not *require* anything in the way of forms or filings or agreements. If people act like partners—by

[1] This is the federal tax rate; most states also levy a corporate tax.

[2] RUPA §101 (6).

sharing management and profits—the law will treat them as such and if they do not act like partners, then nothing they say or write will make them a partnership. (Use the search engine at http://www.toolkit.cch.com/ to find information about partnership agreements and many other partnership issues.)

For example, Kevin and Brenda formed an electrical contracting business. The business did so well that Kevin's first wife, Cynthia, asked the court to increase his child support payments. Kevin argued that, because he and Brenda were partners, he was entitled to only half of the business's profits. Therefore his child support should not be increased.

Cynthia claimed that Kevin and Brenda were *not* partners because Kevin had reported all the income from the business on his personal return while Brenda had reported none. Kevin had even put "sole proprietorship" in bold letters on the top of his tax return. No written partnership agreement existed. Kevin and Brenda never informed their accountant that they were a partnership. When Kevin answered interrogatories for Cynthia's lawsuit, he stated that he was sole owner and that Brenda worked for him. Nonetheless, the court held that Brenda and Kevin were partners because Brenda helped manage the business and shared in its profits.[3]

PARTNERSHIP BY ESTOPPEL

Brenda and Kevin wanted to be partners so that they could share the profits of their business. In *partnership by estoppel*, non-partners are treated as if they were actually partners and are forced to share liability. **Partnership by estoppel applies if:**

- **Participants tell other people that they are partners (even though they are not), or they allow other people to say, without contradiction, that they are partners**
- **A third party relies on this assertion; and**
- **The third party suffers harm.**

Dr. William Martin was held liable under a theory of partnership by estoppel because: he told a patient that he and Dr. John Maceluch were partners (although they were not); the patient relied on this statement and made appointments to see Dr. Maceluch; and she was harmed by Dr. Maceluch's malpractice. He refused to come to the hospital when she was in labor and, as a result, her child was born with brain damage. Although Dr. Martin was out of the country at the time, he was as liable as if he had committed the malpractice himself.[4]

LIABILITY

Under RUPA, **every partner is an agent of the partnership**. Thus the entire partnership is liable for the act of one partner in, say, signing a contract. **A partnership is also liable for any torts that a partner commits in the ordinary**

---

[3] *In Re Marriage of Cynthia Hassiepen*, 269 Ill. App. 3d 559, 646 N.E.2d 1348, 1995 Ill. App. LEXIS 101.

[4] *Haught v. Maceluch*, 681 F.2d 290, 1982 U.S. App. LEXIS 17123 (5th Cir. 1982).

course of the partnership's business. Thus, if one partner wields a careless calculator, the whole partnership is liable.

It gets worse. **If a partnership does not have enough assets to pay its debts, creditors may go after the personal property of individual partners, whether or not they were in any way responsible for the debt.** Because partners have *joint and several liability,* creditors can sue the partners together or in separate lawsuits or in any combination (although creditors cannot recover more than once and they must go after the partnership first). Daniel Matter knows first-hand about the risks of a partnership. A former partner in the accounting firm Pannell Kerr Foster, he thought he had heard the last of the firm when he resigned his partnership. He was wrong. *Seven* years later, he and 260 other former partners of the California firm were served with a 78-page lawsuit seeking $24 million in damages. The lawsuit alleged that Pannell Kerr Foster had been negligent in preparing financial reports for a client. Although Daniel Matter had never worked for that particular client, he had been a partner when the audit was done. At age 53, Matter feared losing everything he owned.

MANAGEMENT

The management of a partnership can be a significant challenge.

MANAGEMENT RIGHTS

Unless the partnership agrees otherwise, partners share both profits and losses equally and each partner has an equal right to manage the business.[5] In a large partnership, with hundreds of partners, too many cooks can definitely spoil the firm's profitability. That is why large partnerships are almost always run by one or a few partners who are designated as **managing partners** or **members of the executive committee**. Some firms are run almost dictatorially by the partner who brings in the most business (called a "rainmaker"). Nonetheless, even in relatively autocratic firms, the atmosphere tends to be less hierarchical than in a corporation, where employees are accustomed to the concept of having a boss. Whatever the reality, partners by and large like to think of themselves as being the equal of every other partner. The following article illustrates how English law firms have dealt with these management issues.

It is still fashionable in legal circles to talk about City of London law firms as being unmanageable and to blame the partnership structure. "It's a bit like trying to run a [publicly traded corporation] with all the shareholders standing in your office," says Geoffrey Howe, managing partner of Clifford Chance, the UK's largest law partnership.

As law firms began to grow dramatically and competition increased, the weaknesses of partnership—conservatism, slowness of response and decision taking—forced them to adopt corporate management systems within the partnership structure. "Management by committee had become unworkable," says Bill Tudor John, senior partner of Allen & Overy.

---

[5] Partnerships have the right to change internal management rules, but they cannot alter the rules governing their relationship with outsiders (such as the rules on liability).

Most firms agree that there is no right or wrong way of managing law firms. But a pattern has emerged. The partnership as a whole remains the supreme decision-taking body, but the issues on which all partners must vote have been substantially reduced. Partnership votes tend to be confined to the election of new partners, profit share, and changes to the partnership agreement. Executive management has devolved to the managing partner assisted by outsiders brought in to perform specific tasks.[6]

MANAGEMENT DUTIES

Partners have a *fiduciary duty* to the partnership. This duty means that:

- *Partners are liable to the partnership for gross negligence or intentional misconduct.*
- *Partners cannot compete with the partnership.* Each partner must turn over to the partnership all earnings from any activity that is related to the partnership's business. Thus law firms would typically expect a partner to turn over any fees he earned as a director of a company, but he could keep royalties from his novel on scuba diving.
- *A partner may not take an opportunity away from the partnership unless the other partners consent.* If the partnership wants to buy a private plane and a partner hears of one for sale, she must give the partnership an opportunity to buy it before she purchases it herself.
- *If a partner engages in a conflict of interest, he must turn over to the partnership any profits he earned from that activity.* In the following case, one partner bought partnership property secretly. Is that a conflict of interest?

MARSH v. GENTRY

642 S.W.2d 574, 1982 Ky. LEXIS 315
Supreme Court of Kentucky, 1982

Facts: Tom Gentry and John Marsh were partners in a business that bought and sold racehorses. The partnership paid $155,000 for *Champagne Woman*, who subsequently had a foal named *Excitable Lady*. The partners decided to sell *Champagne Woman* at the annual Keeneland auction, the world's premier thoroughbred horse auction. On the day of the auction, Gentry decided to bid on the horse personally, without telling Marsh. Gentry bought *Champagne Woman* for $135,000. Later, he told Marsh that someone from California had approached him about buying *Excitable Lady*. Marsh agreed to the sale. Although he repeatedly asked Gentry the name of the purchaser, Gentry refused to tell him. Not until 11 months later, when *Excitable Lady* won a race at Churchill Downs, did Marsh learn that Gentry had been the purchaser. Marsh became the Excitable Man.

Issue: Did Gentry violate his fiduciary duty when he bought partnership property without telling his partner?

Excerpts from Justice O'Hara's Decision: Admittedly, at an auction sale, the specific

[6] "The pitfalls of partnership," *Financial Times*, Feb. 23, 1996, p. 18. Reprinted with permission of the Financial Times.

identity of a purchaser cannot be ascertained before the sale, but [Kentucky partnership law] required a full disclosure by Gentry to Marsh that he would be a prospective purchaser. As to the private sale of *Excitable Lady*, Marsh consented to a sale from the partnership, at a specified price, to the prospective purchaser in California. Even though Marsh obtained the stipulated purchase price, a partner has an absolute right to know when his partner is the purchaser. Partners scrutinize buy-outs by their partners in an entirely different light than an ordinary third party sale. This distinction is vividly made without contradiction when Marsh later indicated that he would not have consented to either sale had he known that Gentry was the purchaser. Under these facts, it is obvious that Gentry failed to disclose all that he knew concerning the sales, including his desire to purchase partnership property.

[P]artners, in their relations with other partners, [must] maintain a higher degree of good faith due to the partnership agreement. The requirement of full disclosure among partners as to partnership business cannot be escaped. Had Gentry made a full disclosure to his partner of his intentions to purchase the partnership property, Marsh would not later be heard to complain of the transaction.

Finally, Gentry maintains that it is an accepted practice at auction sales of thoroughbreds for one partner to secretly bid on partnership stock to accomplish a buy-out. We would emphatically state, however, for the benefit of those engaged in such practices, that where an "accepted business practice" conflicts with existing law, the law whether statutory or court ordered, is controlling. To hold otherwise would be chaotic.

TERMINATING A PARTNERSHIP

A partnership begins with an association of two or more people. Appropriately, the end of a partnership begins with a *dissociation*. **A dissociation occurs when a partner quits.**

DISSOCIATION

A partnership is a personal relationship built on trust. All partners are agents for the partnership, and each partner is personally liable for its debts. Under these circumstances, courts will not force someone to remain in a partnership, no matter what the partnership agreement says. **A partner always has the *power* to leave a partnership but may not have the *right*.** In other words, a partner can always dissociate, but she may have to pay damages for any harm that her departure causes.

A dissociation is a fork in the road: **when one or more partners dissociate, the partnership can either buy out the departing partner(s) and continue in business or wind up the business and terminate the partnership.** Exhibit 16.2 illustrates the dissociation process under RUPA. Most large firms provide in their partnership agreement that, upon dissociation, the business continues. If, however, the partnership chooses to terminate the business, it must follow three steps: dissolution, winding up, and termination.

THREE STEPS TO TERMINATION

Dissolution. The rules on dissolution depend, in part, on the type of partnership. If the partners have agreed in advance how long the partnership will last, it is a **term partnership**. At the end of the specified term, the partnership automatically ends. Otherwise, it is a **partnership at will**, which means that any of the partners can leave at any time, for any reason.

Exhibit 16.2

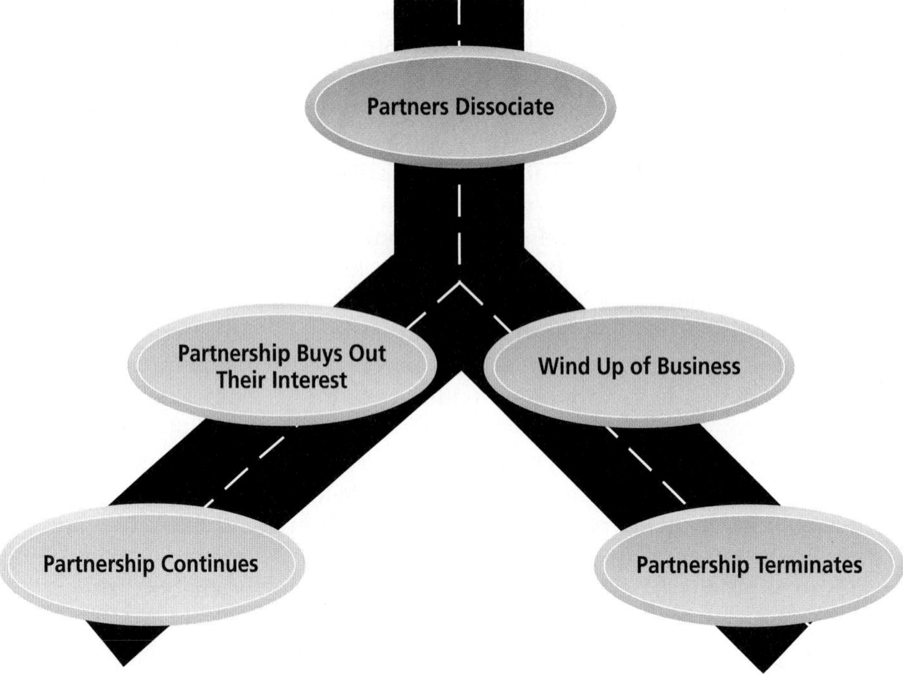

RUPA provides certain circumstances under which a partnership automatically dissolves (although partners can always overrule RUPA and decide by unanimous vote to continue the partnership). According to RUPA, a partnership dissolves:

- In a partnership at will, when a partner withdraws.
- In a term partnership when:
  - A partner is dissociated and half of the remaining partners vote to wind up the partnership business.
  - All the partners agree to dissolve.
  - The term expires or the partnership achieves its goal.
- In any partnership when:
  - An event occurs that the partners had agreed would cause dissolution.
  - The partnership business becomes illegal.
  - A court determines that the partnership is unlikely to succeed. If the partners simply cannot get along or they cannot make a profit, any partner has the right to ask a court to dissolve the partnership. For example, two men formed a partnership to buy The San Juan Star, Puerto Rico's English-language newspaper. They ended up in court, each bitterly accusing the other of having violated the partnership agreement. Their hostility was so great that the judge ultimately decided he could not tell who was at fault and, furthermore, the two men could never run a business together. The court ordered one partner to buy out the other. If the

partners could not agree on a buy-out, the judge was prepared to order a sale of the newspaper to outsiders.[7]

Winding Up. During the winding up process, all debts of the partnership are paid, and the remaining proceeds are distributed to the partners.

Termination. After the sometimes lengthy and complex winding up, the actual termination of a partnership is anticlimactic. Termination happens automatically once the winding up is finished. The partnership is not required to do anything official; it can go out of the world even more quietly and simply than it came in.

PROFESSIONAL CORPORATIONS

Most states now allow professionals to incorporate, but in a special way. These organizations are called "professional corporations" or "PCs." **In many states, PCs provide more liability protection than a partnership.** If a member of a PC commits malpractice, the corporation's assets are at risk, but not the personal assets of the innocent members. If Drs. Sharp, Payne, and Graves form a *partnership*, all the partners will be personally liable when Dr. Payne accidentally leaves her scalpel inside a patient. If the three doctors have formed a *PC* instead, Dr. Payne's Aspen condo and the assets of the PC will be at risk, but not the personal assets of the two other doctors.

Generally, the shareholders of a PC are not personally liable for the contract debts of the organization, such as leases or bank loans. Thus, if Sharp, Payne & Graves, P.C. is unable to pay its rent, the landlord cannot recover from the personal assets of any of the doctors. As partners, the doctors would be personally liable.

PCs have some limitations. First, all shareholders of the corporation must be members of the same profession. For Sharp, Payne & Graves, P.C., that means all shareholders must be licensed physicians. Other valued employees cannot own stock. Second, like other corporations, the required legal technicalities for forming and maintaining a PC are expensive and time-consuming. Third, tax issues can be complicated. A PC is a separate taxable entity, like any other corporation. It must pay tax on its profits, and then its shareholders pay tax on any dividends they receive. *Salaries*, however, are deductible from firm profits. Thus the PC can avoid taxes on its profits by paying out all profits as salary. But any profits remaining in firm coffers *at the end of the year* are taxable. To avoid tax, PCs must be careful to calculate their profits accurately and pay them out before year's end. This chore can be time-consuming, and any error may cause unnecessary tax liability.

LIMITED PARTNERSHIPS

The owners of the Montreal Expos asked investment banker Jacques Menard to find a buyer for the baseball team. Instead, he found 11 other people to help him buy the team. They formed a limited partnership, and each purchaser invested

---

[7] *Nemazee Capital Corp. v. Angulo Capital Corp.*, 1996 U.S. Dist. LEXIS 10750 (S. Dist. NY, 1996).

between $1 million and $7 million. During their first year of ownership, the Expos lost nearly $5 million and their final 14 home games, finishing in the cellar of their division. Given this dismal showing, management had no choice but to fire popular team manager, Buck Rodgers. Then a concrete beam in the team's stadium collapsed.

Fortunately, the owners had formed a *limited* partnership. Limited partnerships and general partnerships have similar names but, like many siblings, they operate very differently. Here are the major differences between these two types of organizations.

STRUCTURE

General partnerships have only *general* partners. Limited partnerships have two types of partners—*limited* partners and *general* partners. A limited partnership must have at least one of each.

LIABILITY

All the partners in a general partnership are *personally* liable for the debts of the partnership. **In a limited partnership, only the general partners are *personally* liable.** As a rule, the limited partners are like corporate shareholders—they risk only their investment in the partnership (which is called their "capital contribution"). No matter how much money the Expos lose, creditors cannot take the personal property of the limited partners. Once the assets of the limited partnership are exhausted, the creditors can go after the personal wealth of the general partners.

One potential pitfall does lurk for limited partners: a limited partner will be treated as a general partner (and therefore be *personally* liable to a third party) if (1) the limited partner helps control the business and (2) the third party reasonably believes that the limited partner is a general partner. Many disputes have arisen over this rule. However, the most recent version of the Revised Uniform Limited Partnership Act has reduced litigation on this issue by listing these specific circumstances under which a limited partner will *not* be considered a general partner:

- Being an agent or employee of the partnership
- Being a consultant to the partnership
- Guaranteeing partnership debt
- Attending a partnership meeting
- Voting on various partnership activities[8]

For example, as a limited partner in a real estate partnership, Cassidy is not personally liable for the partnership's debts even if she goes to work for it as a

[8] The National Conference of Commissioners of Uniform State Laws prepared the original Limited Partnership Act in 1916. Since then, the Act has been amended twice—in 1976 and 1985. Most states have passed some version of the revised Act.

project manager. But if, in dealing with potential customers, she implies that she is a general partner, she becomes as liable as one.

Again, the general partners of a limited partnership are personally liable for all the debts of the partnership. Back in Montreal, that might be of some concern to Claude Brochu, the Expos' general partner. If creditors are unable to collect from the team, they will claim Brochu's house and other personal assets. To avoid this problem, Brochu could have formed a corporation—Brochu, Inc.—to serve as general partner. Then, only the assets of the corporation, not Brochu's personal assets, would have been at risk. This is precisely what most entrepreneurs do when they form limited partnerships. The major disadvantage is simply the effort of forming two entities—the corporate general partner and the limited partnership.

Some states now permit limited liability limited partnerships. **In a *limited liability limited partnership*, the general partner is not personally liable for the debts of the partnership.** These statutes effectively remove the major disadvantage of limited partnerships.

FORMATION

General partnerships can be formed very casually, sometimes without the partners even being aware of it. Not so for limited partnerships: the general partners must file a **certificate of limited partnership** with their Secretary of State. Although most limited partnerships do have a partnership agreement, it is not required. (A sample limited partnership agreement is available at http://www.legaldocs.com/ or http://www.tannedfeet.com/legal_forms.htm.) Failure to comply with the necessary formalities can cause serious problems, as the following case illustrates.

CELLWAVE TELEPHONE SERVICES L.P. v. FCC

30 F.3d 1533, 1994 U.S. App. LEXIS 21834
United States Court of Appeals for the D.C. Circuit, 1994

Facts: Cellwave Telephone Services Limited Partnership applied to the Federal Communications Commission (FCC) for a license to operate and construct cellular telephone systems in two rural areas. The FCC awards these licenses by lottery. Cellwave won the lottery, but upon investigation, the FCC discovered that Cellwave had never filed its limited partnership certificate with the Secretary of State in Delaware although all the limited partners had signed the limited partnership agreement. The FCC dismissed Cellwave's application on the grounds that the partnership did not exist when the application was filed.

You be the Judge: Did the FCC have the right to dismiss Cellwave's application?

Argument for Cellwave: Of all the petty, bureaucratic decisions! The limited partnership was effectively in existence as soon as the limited partners signed the agreement. It is not as if the Secretary of State had to *approve* the certificate in any way. He could not refuse to accept it for filing. The filing simply provides an official record that the partnership exists. But the FCC did not need official notice; it had the original agreement, which is better than a certificate from the Secretary of State.

Argument for the FCC: The number one priority of the FCC is to ensure adequate service for everyone in America. For many people in rural areas, a cellular phone is the most reliable means of communication. When it awards a license, the FCC has to be sure that the licensee will be able to develop a telephone system. Without these strict rules, people would sign up for the lottery and then, once they had won, try to put together a company. The FCC cannot take that chance with rural citizens. If Cellwave cannot manage a simple legal task like organizing a limited partnership, how can it run a telephone system?

Cellwave argues that all the limited partners had signed the limited partnership agreement and that is sufficient. The FCC did not make up the rules; it is simply following Delaware law, which says very precisely, "a limited partnership is formed at the time of the filing of the initial certificate of limited partnership in the Office of the Secretary of State." What could be clearer than that? If Cellwave has a problem with the law, it should talk with its legislators.

MANAGEMENT

General partners have the right to manage a limited partnership. That is only fair, considering they also bear the risk of personal liability. Limited partners are essentially passive investors with few management rights beyond the right to be informed about the partnership business. Exhibit 16.3 illustrates the roles of the partners in a limited partnership. Limited partnership agreements can, however, expand the rights of limited partners. These agreements, for example, often permit a substantial majority (i.e., two-thirds) of the limited partners to remove a general partner. In any event, when *general* partnerships grow large, management becomes difficult. But because *limited* partners are not allowed to manage, a limited partnership can handle a very large number of partners.

TRANSFER OF OWNERSHIP

Limited partners do not have an automatic right to sell their interests in the partnership to a new limited partner; they can generally do so only if the partnership agreement or the other partners permit. However, unless the partnership agreement provides otherwise, limited partners do have the right to withdraw, and the partnership must compensate them for their interest. A general partner in a limited partnership has the right to withdraw at any time. The limited partnership can continue as long as at least one general partner remains and is willing to carry on the business.

Limited partnerships and general partnerships have one crucial attribute in common: neither is a taxable entity. Income is taxed only once before landing in a partner's pocket, and partners can deduct losses against their other income. Tax issues become even more important if the business is sold. When a corporation sells its assets, the corporation pays tax first. Then when it distributes the profits to the shareholders, they pay tax, too. If a limited partnership sells its

Exhibit 16.3

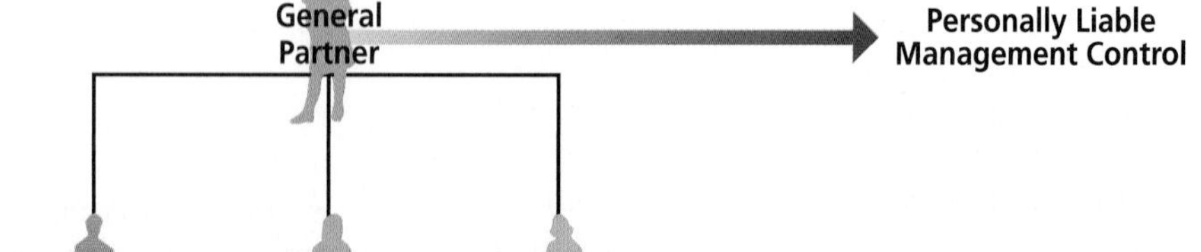

assets, the profits go straight to the partners because the partnership itself pays no taxes. For this reason, business lawyers often advise entrepreneurs to consider a limited partnership instead of a corporation. Nevertheless, clients sometimes resist because they are simply not as familiar with the limited partnership form.

CORPORATIONS

Although the concept of a corporation is very old—it began with the Greeks and spread from them through the Romans into English law—corporations were traditionally viewed with deep suspicion. What were shareholders doing to need limited liability? Why did they have to cower behind a corporate shield? For this reason, shareholders originally needed special permission to form a corporation. In England, corporations could be created only by special charter from the king or, later, from Parliament. But with the advent of the Industrial Revolution, large-scale manufacturing enterprises needed huge amounts of capital from investors who were not involved in management and did not want to be personally liable for the debts of an organization that they were not managing. In 1811, New York became the first jurisdiction in the United States to permit routine incorporation.[9]

State laws regulate corporations, but federal statutes determine their tax status. Many states treat small corporations differently and even give them a different name: close corporations. The federal tax code also provides more favorable tax treatment to some small corporations and calls them S corporations. But the two sets of statutes are completely independent. Thus a close corporation or a regular (nonclose) corporation may or may not be an S corporation. Exhibit 16.4 illustrates the difference between state and IRS regulation of corporations.

CORPORATIONS IN GENERAL

When Judy George was a young child, her parents started a plating business using a process her father had invented. Like many entrepreneurs, her parents devoted so much time and energy to this new project that they were rarely at

Exhibit 16.4
Both a regular and a close corporation can be either a C or an S corporation.

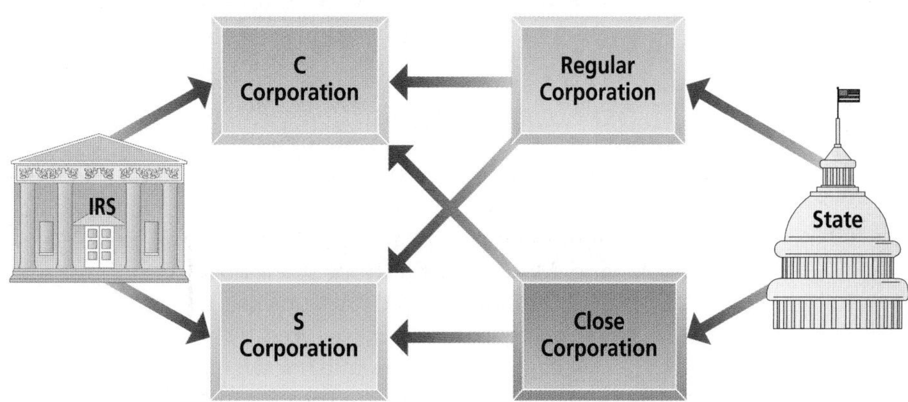

[9] An Act Relative to Incorporation for Manufacturing Purpose, 1811 N.Y. Laws ch. 67, §111.

home. Feeling abandoned by her parents, George became obsessed with her surroundings. If she could make her room just the way she wanted it, she would feel safe. As she put it, "Design was a way of fulfilling my own personal fantasy." She also vowed that one day she would start her own business to make money and create beautiful designs. George realized her dream when she started Domain, an upscale, European-style chain of furniture stores.

George's lawyer suggested that she incorporate Domain. He explained that a corporation would offer the protection of limited liability. If Domain flopped and could not pay its bills, George and her backers would lose their investment in the company, but not their other assets.

He also explained that limited liability does not protect against all debts. Individuals are always responsible for their *own* acts. If a Domain employee was in an accident with a company van, Domain would be liable for any harm to the other driver, but its investors would not be personally liable. If George herself crashed the van, Domain would be liable, and *so would George*. If Domain did not pay the judgment, George would have to, from her personal assets if necessary. A corporation protects managers and investors from personal liability for the debts of the corporation and the actions of others, but not against personal negligence (or other torts and crimes).

Corporations have other advantages besides limited liability. They provide flexibility for enterprises small (with one owner) and large (thousands of shareholders). For example, partnership interests are not transferable without the permission of the other partners, whereas corporate stock can be easily bought and sold. Further, when a sole proprietor dies, legally so does the business. But corporations have perpetual existence: they can continue without their founders.

The major disadvantage of a corporation is simply the expense and effort required to create and operate it. Because corporations are taxable entities, they must pay taxes and file returns. The cost of establishing a corporation may exceed $1,000 in legal and filing fees, not to mention the cost of the annual filings that states require. Corporations must also hold annual meetings for both shareholders and directors. Minutes of these meetings must be kept indefinitely in the company minute book.

Judy George knew that she needed at least $3 million to get Domain up and running. She could not borrow that much money, so she needed to sell stock. She chose the corporate form of organization primarily because it would be the most convenient for raising funds.

CLOSE CORPORATIONS

Reynoldo has always been a fabulous cook. He, his son Juan, and Juan's friend Marta have decided to open a restaurant featuring "cucina nueva"—modern, light Latin American food. Reynoldo will do the cooking in the back, while Juan and Marta run the front operation, everything from maitre d' to accountant. They will finance the start-up costs of *Abogado Verde* by borrowing from the local bank; the loan will be secured by a mortgage on their houses. One of the first questions they face is, What form of organization? A sole proprietorship will not work, because there are three of them. They are concerned about the liability of a partnership. A corporation may be the best option, except it seems like an expensive bother. Who would be on their board of directors? Why do they even need a board? They have no plans to sell shares to the public. They want to act like a partnership, with all decisions made equally, but they need the legal protection of a corporation.

Their lawyer suggests that a close corporation might be the best choice. Originally, the terms "**close corporation**" and "**closely held corporation**" referred simply to a company whose stock was not publicly traded on a stock exchange (in other words, a "privately held" company). Most close corporations are small, although some privately held corporations, such as Hallmark Cards, Inc. and Mars, Inc. (maker of Mars candy bars) are huge. Beginning in New York in 1948, states began to amend their corporation statutes to make special provisions for entrepreneurs such as the *Abogado Verde* team. By now, roughly half the states have made some special accommodation for close corporations. In some states, a corporation must affirmatively elect to be treated as a close corporation; in others, any corporation can take advantage of these special provisions. Now when lawyers refer to close corporations, they usually mean not merely a privately held company, but one that has taken advantage of the close corporation provisions of its state code.

Although the provisions of close corporation statutes vary from state to state, they tend to have certain common themes:

- **Protection of Minority Shareholders.** Marta is concerned that Reynoldo and Juan may form an alliance and vote against her. Close corporations are permitted great leeway to prevent such problems. For example, *Abogado Verde, Inc.* could require a unanimous vote of all shareholders to choose officers, set salaries, or pay dividends. It could grant each shareholder veto power over all important corporate decisions. With provisions such as these, Marta can ensure that she has input into all important decisions.

- **Transfer Restrictions.** What would happen if Reynoldo sold some of his shares to his other (irresponsible) children? Or if Marta and Juan broke up, and Juan sold shares to his new girlfriend? Close corporation statutes often limit a shareholder's ability to sell shares without first offering them to the other owners. Similarly, if Reynoldo died, Juan and Marta would have the first option to buy his stock.

- **Flexibility.** Close corporations can typically operate without a board of directors, a formal set of bylaws, or annual shareholder meetings.

- **Dispute Resolution.** The three shareholders are allowed to agree in advance that any one of them can dissolve the corporation if some particular event occurs or, if they choose, for any reason at all. Marta could, for example, insist on the right to dissolve the corporation herself at any time, or if revenues for a month fall below a certain level. Even without such an agreement, a shareholder can ask a court to dissolve a close corporation if the other owners behave "oppressively" or "unfairly." The mere threat of such an action will be some check on Reynoldo and Juan.

The following case illustrates that, no matter how badly a shareholder behaves, her rights in a close corporation are still protected.

MICHAEL L. RETZER v. NANCY B. RETZER

578 So. 2d 580, 1990 Miss. LEXIS 858
Supreme Court of Mississippi, 1990

Facts: Shortly after Mr. and Mrs. Retzer were married, they moved to Greenville, Mississippi, and opened a McDonald's restaurant. Mr. Retzer managed the restaurant, working 18 hours a day. Mrs. Retzer made little contribution to the business. Mr. Retzer subsequently purchased four additional McDonald's restaurants, transferring ownership of them to Retzer and Retzer, Inc., a Mississippi close corporation. Mr. and Mrs. Retzer each owned 1,600 shares of the corporation.

Mr. Retzer discovered that his wife was having an affair with their attorney. As a condition for salvaging their marriage, Mrs. Retzer agreed to end the affair. She also permitted the corporation to issue 10 additional shares to Mr. Retzer to give him corporate control.

Mrs. Retzer was a profligate spender, often paying more than $3,000 for a dress. When she overdrew her checking account, an officer at the bank would notify Mr. Retzer so that he could replenish her account. Once, when he let her checks bounce, Mrs. Retzer came to his office and began throwing pieces of valuable porcelain. Mr. Retzer called the pastor to calm her down.

Despite the agreement with her husband, Mrs. Retzer continued her affair. The Retzers subsequently divorced on the grounds of Mrs. Retzer's adultery. Their joint net worth was $4 million.

Issue: What are Mr. Retzer's obligations to Mrs. Retzer as a minority shareholder in Retzer and Retzer, Inc.?

Excerpts from Justice Hawkins's Decision: Where divorce has been granted to the husband on the ground of the wife's adultery, this court has consistently denied any alimony, period. Mr. Retzer does have substantial financial obligations to Mrs. Retzer, however, arising from her ownership of almost half of the shares of Retzer and Retzer, Inc.

Courts look quite differently upon the respective duties existing between majority and minority shareholders in publicly held and close corporations. Retzer and Retzer, Inc., is a very close corporation, which has existed solely for the financial benefit of two people, the Retzers. For almost two decades, and through Mr. Retzer's management, the corporation has indeed furnished them both with large incomes. Now, through ownership of ten more shares than she, Mr. Retzer has control of the management of Retzer and Retzer. As such, under well-settled principles he has a fiduciary obligation to Mrs. Retzer in the management of her property. He has a trustee's duty to preserve, protect and produce income from her corporate shares.

He must manage the corporation prudently, and after paying necessary and reasonable expenses, and setting aside whatever is reasonably necessary for corporate reserves and equipment and facilities, pay her 49.8 percent of the net remaining. He will not be acting at arm's length, but as trustee over her shares. He must keep her currently, fully and accurately informed and abreast of his management, and under regular periodic accounting. While their interest as husband and wife was essentially identical, now they are adverse to each other. This will make his conduct as trustee that much more subject to close scrutiny by a chancery court.

With the hostility existing between them, it would no doubt be preferable if somehow the property of Mr. and Mrs. Retzer were entirely separate, with neither depending on the other. The fact remains that at present they are Siamese twins in Retzer and Retzer. If the burden becomes unduly oppressive for either, the chancery court is not without power to give relief, even to appointing a receivership for the corporation or dissolving it.

This case also alludes to the major disadvantage of a close corporation. Because minority shareholders are given such a strong voice, it is easy for stalemates to develop. In such a case, shareholders may ask a court to dissolve the enterprise. Is your relationship ready for entrepreneurship? The Web site http://www.ltbn.com/ offers advice to entrepreneurial couples.

S CORPORATIONS

Although entrepreneurs are often optimistic about the likely success of their new enterprise, in truth, the majority of new businesses lose money in their early years. Only about half of all start-ups *survive* as long as eight years. Congress created S corporations (aka "S corps") to encourage entrepreneurship through tax breaks. The name "S corporation" comes from the provision of the Internal Revenue Code that created this form of organization. **Shareholders of S corps have the best of all worlds: the limited liability of a corporation and the tax status of a partnership.** Like a partnership, an S corp is not a taxable entity—all of the company's profits and losses pass through to the shareholders, who pay tax at their individual rates. It avoids the double taxation of a regular corporation (called a "C corporation"). If, as is often the case, the start-up loses money, investors can deduct these losses against their other income.

When a group of wealthy investors decided to start a magazine called *Living Alternatives*, their lawyer suggested they organize as an S corp. The investors knew that magazines are risky and that most start-ups fail. But successful magazines are very profitable, and these investors believed in the magazine's mission—teaching consumers how to protect the environment. Typical articles covered solar power and compost toilets. The magazine failed after a year, in part, the owners speculated, because the name did not sound like an environmental journal. At least, the investors could deduct these losses against their other (ample) income. Without this incentive, many of them would never have made the initial investment.

If *Living Alternatives* had been profitable, the investors might have decided to continue as an S corporation to avoid the double taxation on dividends. Eventually, however, most companies terminate their S election because of the limitations on this form of organization:

- There can be only one class of stock (although voting rights can vary within the class).
- There can be only 75 shareholders.
- Shareholders must be individuals, estates, charities, pension funds, or trusts, not partnerships or corporations.
- Shareholders must be citizens or residents of the United States, not nonresident aliens.
- All shareholders must agree that the company should be an S corporation.

Although *most* states follow the federal lead on S corporations, a small number treat an S corp like a regular C corporation. In these states, the companies must pay state corporate tax.

LIMITED LIABILITY COMPANIES

You may be thinking that there are already as many different forms of organization as any entrepreneur could possibly need, but, as you have seen, none of them is perfect. In a continuing search for earthly perfection, states recently began to permit limited liability companies (LLCs). **An LLC offers the limited liability of a corporation and the tax status of a partnership, without the disadvantages of an S corporation.**

To organize an LLC, you generally need two documents: a charter and an operating agreement. The charter is short, containing basic information such as name and address. It must be filed with the Secretary of State in your jurisdiction. (A sample charter is available at http://www.lectlaw.com/formb.htm.)

An operating agreement sets out the rights and obligations of the owners, called *members*. Although some states do not require an operating agreement, lawyers recommend them as a way to avoid disputes. A sample is shown at http://www.tannedfeet.com/legal_forms.htm. The following case illustrates the perils of not having an operating agreement.

ZAUGG & ZAUGG ARCHITECTS v. WAGNER

1997 Ohio App. LEXIS 3987
Court of Appeals of Ohio, 1997

Facts: John and Marion Zaugg were partners in Zaugg & Zaugg Architects. They agreed with four other men—Edmonds, Schenk, Siegenthaler, and Wagner—to build a residential golf course. The Zauggs were to furnish architectural services in return for partial payment and part ownership in the project. One year after the Zauggs began working on the venture, the group set up a limited liability company called "Glenleigh Falls Development Co., Ltd." They filed Articles of Organization with the Secretary of State in Ohio and began work on the operating agreement.

Three months after the Articles were filed, the Zauggs billed Glenleigh $108,178.54 for the hundreds of hours they had worked on the project. Shortly thereafter, the group met to sign the operating agreement. Schenk refused to sign and announced he was withdrawing from the venture. Siegenthaler said he would not sign until the agreement had been reviewed by his attorney. The remaining members (including the two Zauggs) did sign. Shortly thereafter, the Zauggs agreed to accept payment of only $58,288.54. When even this amount was not forthcoming, they withdrew from the LLC and filed suit, seeking payment for their architectural services. Wagner and Glenleigh (the LLC) counter-claimed, alleging that the Zauggs had wrongfully withdrawn.

Issue: Did the Zauggs wrongfully withdraw from the limited liability company?

Excerpts from Judge Milligan's Decision: The draft operating agreement provided that no member shall have the right to voluntarily withdraw from the company. [Appellants (Glenleigh and Wagner)] argue that the Zauggs are bound by the withdrawal provision, as they signed the agreement. Appellant ignores the requirement that the agreement be a valid agreement of the members. The agreement was not the agreement of the members, but only the agreement of some of the members. The agreement could not bind several of the members, while the remainder of the members would be governed by a separate inconsistent set of rules, all in governance of the same legal entity.

It is apparent from both the document itself and the evidence concerning the discussions surrounding its drafting that the members had not reached agreement on the provisions in this operating agreement. Because this agreement is not a valid agreement of the members of the company, the Zauggs were permitted to withdraw from the company in accordance with [state statute] and were not bound by the withdrawal provision of the incomplete, proposed agreement.

LLCs have become a popular form of organization. Here are some of the reasons:

- **Limited Liability.** As in a corporation, members are not personally liable for debts of the company. They risk only their investment.
- **Tax Status.** As in a partnership, income flows through the company to the individual members, avoiding the double taxation of a corporation.
- **Duration.** As we will see in the next chapter, a partnership terminates upon the death, withdrawal, or bankruptcy of a partner. In many states, an LLC survives the departure of a member.
- **Management.** LLCs are permitted to have managers, who may or may not be members. Managers of an LLC are not personally liable, in contrast with the general partners of a limited partnership, who are. Unlike corporations, LLCs are not required to hold annual meetings or maintain a minute book.
- **Flexibility.** Unlike S corporations, LLCs can have members that are corporations, partnerships, or non-resident aliens. LLCs can also have different classes of stock.

But this is an imperfect world, and even LLCs have flaws:

- **Legal Uncertainties.** LLCs are a new form of organization. Although Wyoming passed the first LLC statute in 1978, most states did not follow suit until after 1991. This means three things. First, state laws vary widely. This inconsistency can be confusing if you form an LLC in one state, but do business in several others. Second, there are few court decisions interpreting the LLC statutes. These few cases sometimes disagree.[10] Third, some entrepreneurs are reluctant to try the unfamiliar. Said Diane Nelson, co-owner of Diane Nelson Fine Art in Laguna Beach, California, "We were really considering it. We felt insecure; we didn't know enough. We formed an S corporation instead, because we were familiar with it."
- **The IRS versus the States.** Individual states regulate the formation of an LLC, but the IRS determines its tax status. Coordination among these various jurisdictions is not always smooth. The original IRS regulations had strict requirements for LLCs, and states had no choice but to reflect these requirements in their laws. But then, in 1996, the IRS eliminated most of its requirements. Some states have followed the IRS lead, but others have not.

---

[10] For example, a federal court in Michigan held that an LLC is a partnership for purposes of diversity jurisdiction, which means that if any member lives in the same state as the opposing party, the case cannot be heard in federal court. However, an Illinois court held the opposite—that an LLC is a corporation for purposes of jurisdiction, which means that it is treated as a resident only of the state in which it was formed.

California, for one, has announced that it will not. To take one example, the IRS has eliminated its original rule that LLCs have at least two members. Many states, however, still prohibit one-member LLCs.

- **Expenses.** Some states, such as California, charge higher fees for LLCs than for corporations.
- **Transferability of Interests.** In some states, a member must have permission from the other owners to transfer all his ownership rights. Without this approval, the new owner may not, for example, be able to vote.
- **Going Public.** LLCs must be privately held; they cannot sell stock publicly (on an exchange or otherwise). However, it is relatively easy to switch from an LLC to a corporation if the members decide to go public.
- **Changing to an LLC.** Despite these flaws, you are convinced that an LLC is right for you. You are going to switch your corporation to an LLC first thing Monday morning. Hold on for one second. The IRS considers this change to be a sale of the corporate assets, so you would have to pay taxes on their value. For this reason, few corporations have made the change. However, switching from a partnership to an LLC is not considered a sale and does not have the same adverse tax impact.

LIMITED LIABILITY PARTNERSHIPS

Some states will not permit *professionals* to organize as an LLC but instead offer the option of a limited liability partnership (LLP). Traditionally, a member of an LLP was protected from liability for the misconduct of other members or employees, but was still personally responsible for her own malpractice and the contract debts of the partnership (such as bank loans and leases). However, the modern trend is to permit professionals to form LLCs or to provide partners in LLPs with the same liability protection as members of LLCs.

Partners in an LLP are not *personally* liable for debts of the partnership (whether arising from contract or tort). However, partners are always liable for their own misconduct. Suppose that Oliver, Ed, and Jessie, three newly minted CPAs, form an LLP. Jessie has inherited $100 million, but Ed and Oliver's combined net worth will barely buy a ticket to the movies. Flush with optimism, the three partners rent fancy downtown space. Unfortunately, Oliver forgets on which side of the ledger to put the debits and credits, so he botches an annual audit for the firm's major client. Embroiled in malpractice litigation, the firm is unable to pay its rent. The jury in the malpractice case returns a verdict for $5 million. Who is liable for what? Only the LLP is liable for the overdue rent. Only Oliver and the LLP are liable for the malpractice verdict. Ed and Jessie just lose their investment in the LLP. Neither the landlord nor the client has any right to Jessie's personal fortune.

Does this result seem unfair? Some states that permit professionals to limit their liability through LLPs or LLCs also require that they maintain a certain amount of malpractice insurance.

JOINT VENTURES

Dutch entertainment giant PolyGram, which has been steadily muscling into the mainstream movie business, announced a key partnership with longtime Hollywood players Tom Pollock and Ivan Reitman. The five-year deal calls for PolyGram, the world's largest recorded-music company, to set up a joint venture in Santa Barbara that will generate three to five films a year. PolyGram, which scored a major hit with *Bean*, will own a third of the yet-to-be-named production company. Pollock, head of Universal Studios' movie operations for a decade, and Reitman, who directed *Animal House*, *Ghostbusters*, *Twins*, and *Dave*, will own the rest.

PolyGram did not disclose how much it will invest in the joint venture, which will handle Reitman's movies and seek projects from other directors and producers. The company has made similar joint venture deals with director Tony Scott and actress Jodie Foster. "PolyGram is taking a reasonably conservative approach in these joint ventures with pretty professional names," said Harold Vogel, an analyst at Cowen & Co. in New York.[11]

This newspaper article refers to this business arrangement as both a "partnership" and a "joint venture." What is the difference in meaning? **A joint venture is a partnership for a limited purpose.** PolyGram, Pollock, and Reitman do not intend to work together on all their movies. They have joined together for the limited purpose of making three to five films a year. If they had joined in a full-scale partnership, all three parties would be bound by contracts that any one of them signed. In a joint venture, only contracts relating to the limited purpose are binding on all three. If PolyGram signs a music contract with Sheryl Crow, Pollock and Reitman are not liable on that contract. But if the PolyGram/Pollock/Reitman joint venture enters into a contract with Jennifer Aniston to star in a movie, Pollock and Reitman are liable, too. Nonprofit enterprises do not qualify as joint ventures—the purpose, however limited, must include making a profit.

FRANCHISES

This chapter has presented an overview of the various forms of organization. Franchises are not, strictly speaking, a separate form of organization. They are included here because they represent an important option for entrepreneurs. In the United States, 1 in 12 small businesses is a franchise. Franchises generate sales of close to $1 trillion each year and provide jobs for more than eight million people. Well-known franchises include Dunkin' Donuts, Midas Muffler, and McDonald's. Most franchisors and franchisees are corporations, although they could legally choose to be any of the forms discussed in this chapter.

Buying a franchise is a compromise between starting one's own business as an entrepreneur and working for someone else as an employee. Franchisees are free to choose which franchise to buy, where to locate it, and how to staff it. But

[11] Dave McNary, "PolyGram Sets Up Key Joint Venture," *The Daily News of Los Angeles*, Feb. 14, 1998, p. B2. Reprinted with permission.

they are not completely on their own. They are buying an established business with all the kinks worked out. In case the owner has never boiled water before, the McDonald's operations manual explains everything from how to set the temperature controls on the stove, to the number of seconds that fries must cook, to the length of time they can be held in the rack before being discarded. And a well-known name like McDonald's or Mrs. Fields ought, by itself, to bring customers through the door.

There is, however, a fine line between being helpful and being oppressive. Franchisees sometimes complain that franchisor control is too tight—tips on cooking fries might be appreciated, but rules on how often to sweep the floor are not. Sometimes franchisors, in their zeal to maintain standards, prohibit innovation that appeals to regional tastes. Just because spicy biscuits are unpopular in New England does not mean they should be banned in the South.

Franchises can be very costly to acquire, anywhere from several thousand dollars to $1.2 million. That fee is usually payable up front, whether or not a cookie or burger is ever sold. On top of the up-front fee, franchisees also pay an annual fee that is a percentage of *gross sales revenues*, not *profit*. Sometimes the fee seems to eat up all the profits. Franchisees also complain when they are forced to buy supplies from headquarters. In theory, the franchisors can purchase hamburger meat and paper plates more cheaply in bulk. On the other hand, the franchisees are a captive audience, and they allege that headquarters has little incentive to keep prices low. Franchisees also grumble when they are forced to contribute to expensive "co-op advertising" that benefits all the outlets in the region. As the following article illustrates, franchisees can have very different experiences.

For James Hamilton, a franchise was the greatest thing since, well, sliced bread. His first Subway sandwich shop, opened six years ago in the Lemon Grove area of San Diego, was such a success that he has since acquired five other shops.

But Robert Rosinski's three Little Caesar's Pizza Restaurants landed Rosinski in the soup. The parent company allowed other Little Caesar's stores to open nearby and then began running national ads that offered two pizzas for $5.99, $1.26 less than they cost Rosinski to make. Driven to the brink of bankruptcy, he sold his stores back to the franchisor for pennies on the dollar.[12]

Although franchises were once relatively unregulated, the states and the federal government have dramatically increased their supervision and regulation of these businesses. The Federal Trade Commission (FTC) requires that, at least 10 days prior to the sale, franchisors must give prospective franchisees an **offering circular** that reveals, among other interesting facts:

- Any litigation against the company
- Whether it has ever gone through bankruptcy proceedings
- All fees
- Estimates of the required initial investment

---

[12] Frank Green, "Franchise Is a Ticket to Freedom, or Failure," *San-Diego Union-Tribune*, May 31, 1994, p. C-3.

- What goods must be purchased from the franchisor
- The number of franchisees in operation
- How many franchisees have gone out of business in the prior year

The offering circular must also contain audited financial statements and a sample set of the contracts that a franchisee is expected to sign. For more information about FTC rules on offering circulars, see http://www.ftc.gov/.

The purpose of the offering circular is to ensure that the franchisor discloses all relevant facts. It is not a guarantee of quality. Under FTC rules, the following notice must appear in bold on the cover page of the offering circular: **"To protect you, we've required your franchisor to give you this information. We haven't checked it, and don't know if it's correct."**

Suppose you obtain an offering circular for "Shrinking Cats," a franchise that offers psychiatric services for neurotic felines. The company has lost money on all the outlets it operates itself; it has sold only three franchises, two of which have gone out of business; and all the required contracts are ridiculously favorable to the franchisor. Nevertheless, the FTC will still permit sales as long as the franchisor discloses all the information required in the offering circular. Nor will the FTC investigate to make sure that the information is accurate. After the fact, if the FTC discovers the franchisor has violated the rules, it may sue on your behalf. (You also would have the right to bring suit.) But that is cold comfort amidst the devastation of a failed business.

Some states also regulate the sale of franchises. They often require franchisors to register and to provide offering circulars, but the franchisor can use the same circular to meet the requirements of both the state and the FTC. The states that do regulate franchisors are often stricter than the FTC. California, for instance, requires franchisors to file all advertisements ahead of time. Some states will not permit a franchisor to register unless it can meet minimum capital requirements. State laws may also prohibit unfair terms in the franchising contract.

Despite efforts on the part of the federal and state governments to regulate this important area of commerce, many franchisees feel that the playing field is not yet level. However, the following case has helped even the score.

VYLENE ENTERPRISES, INC. v. NAUGLES, INC.

90 F.3d 1472, 1996 U.S. App. LEXIS 24005
United States Court of Appeals for the Ninth Circuit, 1996

Facts: Vylene Enterprises, Inc. bought a restaurant franchise in Long Beach, California, from Naugles, Inc. The franchise agreement did not grant Vylene an exclusive territory. Ten years later, Naugles opened a new restaurant that offered smaller portions at a lower price. It was 1.4 miles from Vylene's location. Vylene had already been struggling financially, and this new restaurant caused a further decline in sales. Vylene sued Naugles.

Issue: Did Naugles have the right to open a new restaurant near an existing franchise?

Excerpts from Judge Nelson's Decision: Vylene did not have any rights to exclusive territory under the terms of the franchise agreement, and we do not impliedly read any such rights into the contract. [Notwithstanding, under California law, all contracts have an implied covenant of good faith and fair dealing.] Naugles' construction of a competing restaurant within a mile and a half of Vylene's restaurant was a breach of the covenant of good faith and fair dealing. The bad faith character of the move becomes clear when one considers that building the competing restaurant had the potential to not only hurt Vylene, but also to reduce Naugles' royalties from Vylene's operations.

In a recent survey of U.S. franchisors, 63 percent said they are currently selling franchises overseas; 83 percent said they would like to. The top five foreign markets are Western Europe, the Pacific Rim, South America, Central Europe, and Southeast Asia. In Japan, a businessman named Kyiochi Yamaguchi already owns six American franchises: Bathtub Doctor, Sparkle Wash, Metal Maintenance, Ceiling Magic, Blind Magic, and NonSlide. He would like to acquire a seventh franchise—his possible choices range from pizza restaurants to sign makers to Internet advertisers. For more information about franchising overseas, browse the International Franchise Association's Web site at http://www.franchise.org.[13]

CHAPTER CONCLUSION

The process of starting a business is immensely time-consuming. Eighteen-hour days are the norm. Not surprisingly, entrepreneurs are sometimes reluctant to spend their valuable time on legal issues that, after all, do not contribute directly to the bottom line. No customer buys more biscuits because the franchise is a limited liability company instead of a corporation. Wise entrepreneurs know, however, that careful attention to legal issues is an essential component of success. The form of organization affects everything from taxes to liability to management control. The idea for the business may come first, but legal considerations occupy a close second place.

CHAPTER REVIEW

	Separate Taxable Entity	Personal Liability for Owners	Ease of Formation	Transferable Interests (Easily Bought and Sold)	Perpetual Existence	Other Features
Sole Proprietorship	No	Yes	Very easy	No, can only sell entire business	No	
General Partnership	No	Yes	Easy	No	No	Management can be difficult.
Professional Corporation	Yes	Yes, for own malpractice, not for malpractice of others or contract debts of organization	Difficult	Shareholders must all be members of same profession.	Yes, as long as it has shareholders	Complex tax issues

[13] Jan Norman, "A World of Franchises," *The Orange County Register*, Sept. 16, 1997, p. CO1.

	Separate Taxable Entity	Personal Liability for Owners	Ease of Formation	Transferable Interests (Easily Bought and Sold)	Perpetual Existence	Other Features
Limited Partnership	No	Yes, for general partner No, for limited partners	Difficult	Yes (for limited) partners), unless partnership agreement provides otherwise	No	
Limited Liability Limited Partnership	No	No	Difficult	Yes (for limited) partners), unless partnership agreement provides otherwise	No	
Corporation	Yes	No	Difficult	Yes	Yes	
Close Corporation	Yes, for C corporation No, for S corporation	No	Difficult	Transfer restrictions	Yes	Protection of minority shareholders No board of directors required Stalemates may develop.
S Corporation	No	No	Difficult	Transfer restrictions	Yes	Only 75 shareholders Only one class of stock Share-holders must be individuals, estates, trusts, charities, or pension funds and be citizens or residents of the United States. All shareholders must agree to S status.
Limited Liability Company	No	No	Difficult	Varies by state	Varies by state	No limit on the number of shareholders, the number of classes of stock, or the type of shareholder
Limited Liability Partnership	No	Varies by state, but generally no	Difficult	No	No	
Joint Venture	No	Yes	Easy	No	No	Partnership for a limited purpose
Franchise	All these issues depend on the form of organization chosen by participants.					Established business Name recognition Management assistance Loss of control Fees may be high.

PRACTICE TEST

1. **RIGHT & WRONG** Lee McNeely told Hardee's officials that he was interested in purchasing multiple restaurants in Arkansas. A Hardee's officer told him that any of the company-owned stores in Arkansas would be available for purchase. However, the company urged him to open a new store in Maumelle and sent him a letter estimating first-year sales at around $800,000. McNeely built the Maumelle restaurant, but gross sales the first year were only $508,000. When McNeely asked to buy an existing restaurant, a Hardee's officer refused, informing him that Hardee's rarely sold company-owned restaurants. The offering circular contained no misstatements, but McNeely brought suit alleging fraud in the sale of the Maumelle franchise. Does McNeely have a valid claim against Hardee's? Apart from the legal issues, did Hardee's officers behave ethically? Would they want their behavior to be publicized? Would they like to be treated this way themselves? Is all fair in love, war, and franchising?

2. **CPA QUESTION** Assuming all other requirements are met, a corporation may elect to be treated as an S corporation under the Internal Revenue Code if it has:

   (a) Both common and preferred stockholders

   (b) A partnership as a stockholder

   (c) Seventy-five or fewer stockholders

   (d) The consent of a majority of the stockholders

3. Under Delaware law, a corporation cannot appear in court without a lawyer, but a partnership can. Fox Hollow Ventures, Ltd. was a limited liability company. One of its employees, who was not a lawyer, appeared in court to represent the company. Does an LLC more closely resemble a partnership, which may represent itself in court, or a corporation, which requires representation by a lawyer?

4. **CPA QUESTION** Which of the following statements is correct concerning the similarities between a limited partnership and a corporation?

   (a) Each is created under a statute and must file a copy of its certificate with the proper state authorities.

   (b) All corporate stockholders and all partners in a limited partnership have limited liability.

   (c) Both are recognized for federal income tax purposes as taxable entities.

   (d) Both are allowed statutorily to have perpetual existence.

5. Alan Dershowitz, a law professor famous for his wealthy clients (O. J. Simpson, Claus von Bulow, Leona Helmsley), joined with other lawyers to open a kosher delicatessen, Maven's Court. Dershowitz met with greater success at the bar than in the kitchen—the deli failed after barely a year in business. One supplier sued for overdue bills. What form of organization would have been the best choice for Maven's Court?

6. **CPA QUESTION** A joint venture is a(n):

   (a) Association limited to no more than two persons in business for profit

   (b) Enterprise of numerous co-owners in a nonprofit undertaking

   (c) Corporate enterprise for a single undertaking of limited duration

   (d) Association of persons engaged as co-owners in a single undertaking for profit

7. Mrs. Meadows opened a biscuit shop called The Biscuit Bakery. The business was not incorporated. Whenever she ordered supplies, she was careful to sign the contract in the name of the business, not personally: The Biscuit Bakery by Daisy Meadows. Unfortunately, she had no money to pay her flour bill. When the vendor threatened to sue

her, Mrs. Meadows told him that he could only sue the business, because all the contracts were in the business's name. Will Mrs. Meadows lose her dough?

8. **YOU BE THE JUDGE WRITING PROBLEM** Heinz Wartski invented a data collector device to analyze fuel consumption and acceleration in automobiles. He and Terence Bedford formed Fleet Tech, Inc., a close corporation, to develop and market the device. When the venture did not succeed as anticipated, Bedford induced the board of directors to fire Wartski. With Fleet Tech's money all but gone and its debts mounting, the directors voted to authorize Bedford either to sell the company or to file for bankruptcy. Bedford offered to buy the shares for $1. The sale took place, over Wartski's objection. Shortly after buying all the stock, Bedford sold the company to Allied Corp. for $890,267 and a promise of future royalty payments totaling at least $1.2 million. Do Wartski or any of the other shareholders have a right to share in these payments?
Argument for Wartski: Shareholders in a close corporation owe each other a fiduciary duty. Bedford should not be allowed to profit at the expense of the other shareholders.
Argument for Bedford: The directors fired Wartski because he ruined the company. They then authorized Bedford to sell what was left. Everything Bedford did was legal.

9. A bulldozer burned to ashes in Arkansas. For Lawrence Nolen, the good news was that the bulldozer was insured. The bad news was that Dennis Burnett claimed half the proceeds as Nolen's partner. Nolen and Burnett had not signed a partnership agreement. This is how Nolen testified at trial:

> Burnett talked of buying a dozer. I told him I could borrow the money and set up payments on it. Later I told him if he'd come up with his $5,000 that half the dozer was his. That was the deal. I bought the dozer, borrowed the money from the bank. The note was in my name. I bought the insurance on the dozer. I had a bank account in my name and it was used only for the dozer business. In the meantime I paid him for his time. I may have opened an account at the store for N&B Dozer just to keep my purchases at the store separate from my personal purchases.

Others testified that the parties had agreed they would divide any and all profits on an equal basis, one-half to each, once the bank loan had been paid in full. Had Nolen and Burnett formed a partnership to own and operate the bulldozer?

10. The Logan Wright Foundation (LWF), an Oklahoma nonprofit corporation, was a partner in a partnership formed to operate two Sonic Drive-In restaurants. LWF asked the court to require the IRS to return taxes that LWF had paid on behalf of Sonic. LWF argued that it was not responsible for Sonic's taxes because LWF was merely a limited partner, with limited liability to the partnership's creditors, including the IRS. The partnership had never filed a certificate of limited partnership with the Secretary of State. Is it a valid limited partnership?

INTERNET RESEARCH PROBLEM

At http://www.ftc.gov, the Federal Trade Commission provides information on enforcement cases it has brought against franchisors who violate FTC rules. Do you see a pattern? Are some violations more common than others? How can you avoid falling prey to an unsuitable franchise offering?

You can find further practice problems in the Online Quiz at http://beatty.westbuslaw.com or in the Study Guide that accompanies this text.

CORPORATIONS

17

CHAPTER

Lindsey and Eben had been good friends since statistics class. Then the dot.com business plan they created for their capstone course won first prize in the school competition. A number of family and friends offered seed funding. Koolsite.com was on its way!

The two entrepreneurs intended to talk with a lawyer, but they were so busy working on their Web site, that they kept postponing this chore. They rented space, hired employees, signed contracts. Finally, their investors insisted that they see a lawyer.

The news she had to deliver was not good. Although Eben had been very careful to sign the lease in the name of koolsite.com, Inc., he was nonetheless personally liable for the rent because the business had not actually been incorporated. That was a shock. The lawyer went on to talk about minute books and shareholder meetings and corporate bank accounts. Lindsey and Eben sat in her office thinking, "Blah, blah, blah." The lawyer, however, would not let them leave until the incorporation forms were complete.

For a year, the duo did nothing but work on their business (and play a few rounds of foosball). Then the economy turned down and suddenly survival became touch and go. Their financial picture became even darker when an irate customer sued koolsite.com for injuries he received from an item he had ordered through the Web site. As Lindsey rummaged in her desk drawers, looking for the lawyer's telephone number, she reassured Eben, "At least we're not personally liable, only the corporation is. He's welcome to one used foosball game."

The lawyer, however, had a different attitude. According to her, the two entrepreneurs might be personally liable. The company did not have enough assets to pay its liabilities, and the two founders had failed to observe the required corporate formalities. They should not have ignored all that "blah, blah" stuff.

Despite these bumps in the road, koolsite.com did survive, and even edged into profitability. Eventually, it was able to go public, selling shares in the open market. At that point, Eben sold some of his stock and took (really) early retirement. He was still a shareholder, though, so he kept his eye on the company. Frankly, he was a little distressed by some of Lindsey's decisions. Did she have to move company headquarters closer to her beach house? That cost the shareholders a pretty penny. And it seemed that no matter how the stock price performed, her compensation always went up . . . a lot.

Eben was getting pretty annoyed. But what could he do? He had the right to go to shareholder meetings and complain, but what would that accomplish? Only the directors could fire Lindsey, and they all seemed to be friends of hers. Eben might try to organize shareholders to vote out the board, but that would be a difficult and expensive undertaking.

As he stewed, Lindsey continued to make bad decision after bad decision. Clearly, her entrepreneurial skills did not suit a large company. At long last, the board took action. The good news was that it fired Lindsey. The bad news was that it gave her a $100 million severance package. Eben was so furious, he filed suit to prevent the payment.

In this chapter, you will learn how to form a corporation. You will also learn about the rights and responsibilities of corporate managers and shareholders. And you will see why Eben's lawsuit was unsuccessful. Corporate managers have great leeway in running a corporation.

INCORPORATION PROCESS

Someone who organizes a corporation is called a **promoter**. **A promoter is personally liable on any contract he signs before the corporation is formed.** In the opening scenario, Eben signs the lease for koolsite.com before the corporation is formed, only to discover that he is personally responsible. After formation, the corporation can **adopt** the contract, in which case, both it and the promoter are liable. The promoter can get off the hook personally only if the landlord agrees to a **novation**, that is, a new contract with the corporation alone.

The mechanics of incorporation are easy: simply fill out the form and mail it (with a check) to the Secretary of State. Nonetheless, this document needs to be completed with some care. The corporate charter defines the corporation, including everything from the company's name to the number of shares it will issue. States use different terms to refer to a charter; some call it the "articles of incorporation," others use "articles of organization," and still others say "certificate" instead of "articles." All of these terms mean the same thing. Similarly, some states use the term "shareholders," and others use "stockholders"; they are both the same.

There is no federal corporation code, which means that a company can incorporate only under state, not federal, law. No matter where a company actually does business, it may incorporate in any state. This decision is important because the organization must live by the laws of whichever state it chooses for incorporation. Like snowflakes, no two state laws are identical, but many have similar features. To encourage even more similarity, the American Bar Association drafted the Revised Model Business Corporation Act (the Model Act) as a guide for states. Many states use the Model Act as a guide, although some of the largest or most commercially important states, such as California, New York, and Delaware, do not. Therefore, in this chapter we will give examples from both the Model Act and specific states, especially Delaware. Why Delaware? Despite its small size, it has a disproportionate influence on corporate law. More than 280,000 corporations are incorporated there, including 60 percent of Fortune 500 companies.

WHERE TO INCORPORATE?

A company is called a **domestic corporation** in the state where it incorporates and a **foreign corporation** everywhere else. Companies generally incorporate either in the state where they do most of their business or in Delaware. They typically must pay filing fees and franchise taxes in their state of incorporation as well as in any state in which they do business. To avoid this double set of fees, a business that will be operating primarily in one state would probably select that state for incorporation rather than Delaware. But if a company is going to do business in several states, it might consider choosing Delaware (or, perhaps, Ohio, Pennsylvania, Nevada or one of the other states with sophisticated corporate laws). More information about Delaware law is available at http://www.state.de.us/corp/. Or browse http://www.findlaw.com/11stategov/indexcorp.html for links to all state corporation Web sites.

Delaware offers corporations several advantages:

- *Laws that Favor Management.* For example, if the shareholders want to take a vote in writing instead of holding a meeting, many other states require the vote to be unanimous; Delaware requires only a majority to agree. The Delaware legislature also tries to keep up-to-date by changing its code to reflect new developments in corporate law.
- *An Efficient Court System.* Delaware has a special court (called "Chancery Court") that hears nothing but business cases and has judges who are experts in corporate law.
- *An Established Body of Precedent.* Because so many businesses incorporate in the state, its courts hear a vast number of corporate cases, creating a large body of precedent. Thus lawyers feel they can more easily predict the

outcome of a case in Delaware than in a state where few corporate disputes are tried each year.

THE CHARTER

Once a company has decided *where* to incorporate, the next step is to prepare and file the charter. The charter must always be filed with the Secretary of State; some jurisdictions also require that it be filed in a county office. A sample article of incorporation is available at http://www.lectlaw.com/forms/f163.txt.

NAME

The Model Act imposes two requirements in selecting a name. First, all corporations must use one of the following words in their name: "corporation," "incorporated," "company," or "limited." Delaware also accepts some additional terms, such as, "association" or "institute." Second, under both the Model Act and Delaware law, a new corporate name must be different from that of any corporation, limited liability company, or limited partnership that already exists *in that state*. If your name is Freddy Dupont, you cannot name your corporation "Freddy Dupont, Inc." because Delaware already has a company named E. I. Dupont de Nemours & Co. It does not matter that Freddy Dupont is your real name or that the existing company is a large chemical business while you want to open a video arcade. The names are too similar.

ADDRESS AND REGISTERED AGENT

A company must have an official address in the state in which it is incorporated so that the Secretary of State knows where to contact it and so that anyone who sues the corporation can serve the complaint in-state. Since most companies incorporated in Delaware do not actually have an office there, they hire a registered agent to serve as their official presence in the state. Agents typically charge about $100 annually for this service.

INCORPORATOR

The incorporator signs the charter and delivers it to the Secretary of State for filing. Incorporators are not required to buy stock nor do they necessarily have any future relationship with the company. Typically, the lawyer who forms the corporation serves as its incorporator.

PURPOSE

The corporation is required to give its purpose for existence. Most companies use a very broad purpose clause such as:

> The nature of the business or purposes to be conducted or promoted is to engage in any lawful act or activity for which corporations may be organized under the General Corporation Law of Delaware.

STOCK

The charter must provide three items of information about the company's stock.

Number of Shares. Before stock can be sold, it must first be authorized in the charter. The corporation can authorize as many shares as the incorporators choose, but the more shares, the higher the filing fee. In Delaware, the price is $.01 per share for the first 20,000 shares (a total of $200); $.005 apiece for up to 2 million shares; and $.004 each for all shares over 2 million. If a company wants more shares after incorporation, it simply amends its charter and pays the additional fee.

Stock that has been authorized but not yet sold is called **authorized and unissued**. Stock that has been sold is termed **authorized and issued** or **outstanding**. Stock that the company has sold but later bought back is **treasury stock**.

Par Value. The concept of par value was designed to protect investors. Originally, par value was supposed to be close to market price. A company could not issue stock at a price less than par, which meant that it could not sell to insiders at a sweetheart price well below market value. (Once the stock was *issued*, it could be *traded* at any price.) In modern times, par value does not relate to market value; it is usually some nominal figure such as 1¢ or $1 per share. Companies may even issue stock with no par value. The Model Act does not use the term "par value" and permits stock to be issued at any price set by the board of directors.

Classes and Series. Different shareholders often make different contributions to a company. Some may be involved in management, while others may simply contribute financially. Early investors may feel that they are entitled to more control than those who come along later (and who perhaps take less risk). Corporate structure can be infinitely flexible in defining the rights of these various shareholders. Stock can be divided into categories called **classes**, and these classes can be further divided into subcategories called **series**. All stock in a series has the same rights, and all series in a class are fundamentally the same, except for minor distinctions. For example, in a class of preferred stock, all shareholders may be entitled to a dividend, but the amount of the dividend may vary by series. Different classes of stock, however, may have very different rights—a class of preferred stock is different from a class of common stock. Exhibit 17.1 illustrates the concept of class and series.

Defining the rights of a class or series of stock is like baking a cake—the stock can contain virtually any combination of the following ingredients (although the result may not be to everyone's taste):

- *Dividend Rights.* The charter establishes whether the shareholder is entitled to dividends and, if so, in what amount.
- *Voting Rights.* Shareholders are usually entitled to elect directors and vote on charter amendments, among other issues, but these rights can vary between different series and classes of stock. When Ford Motor Co. went public in 1956, it issued Class B common stock to members of the Ford family. This class of stock holds 40 percent of the voting power of the company and, thus, can elect 40 percent of the directors. These rights give the Ford

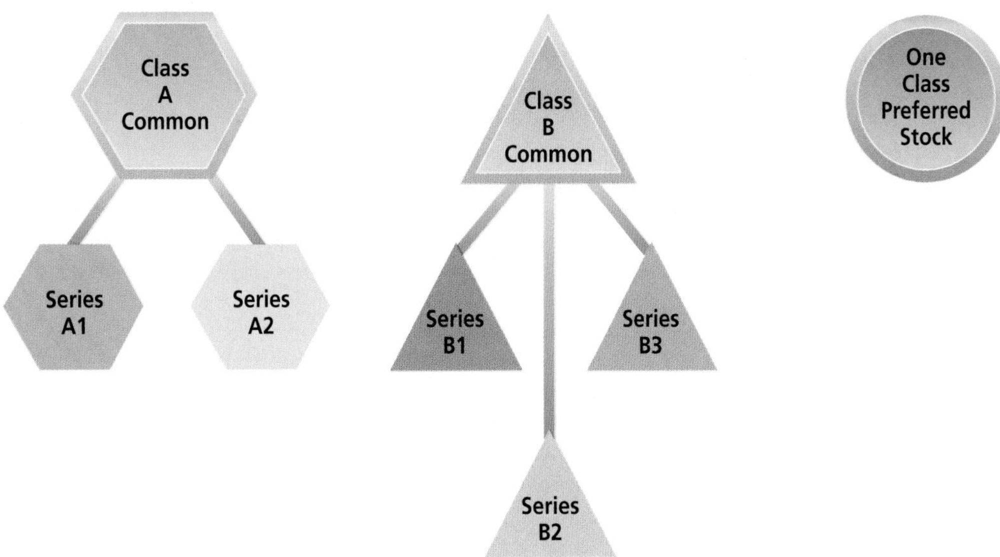

Exhibit 17.1

family effective control over the company. Not surprisingly, the chairman of the company is often named "Ford."

- *Liquidation Rights.* The charter specifies the order in which classes of stockholders will be paid upon dissolution of the company.

These are the ingredients for any class or series of stock. Some stock comes prepackaged like a cake mix. "Preferred" and "common" stock are two classic types. The Model Act does not use these terms, but many states still do.

Owners of *preferred stock* have preference on dividends and liquidation. If a class of preferred stock is entitled to dividends, then it must receive its dividends before common stockholders are paid theirs. If holders of ***cumulative* preferred stock** miss their dividend one year, common shareholders cannot ever be paid until this missing dividend is distributed to the cumulative preferred shareholders, no matter how long that takes. Alternatively, holders of ***non*-cumulative preferred stock** lose an annual dividend for good if the company cannot afford it in the year it is due. When a company dissolves, preferred stockholders have the right to receive their share of corporate assets before common shareholders. Exhibit 17.2 illustrates the order of payment for dividends.

***Common* stock is last in line for any corporate payouts, including dividends and liquidation payments.** If the company is liquidated, creditors of the company and preferred shareholders are paid before common shareholders.

AFTER INCORPORATION

DIRECTORS AND OFFICERS

Once the corporation is organized, shareholders elect directors. Under the Model Act, a corporation is required to have at least one director, unless all the shareholders sign an agreement that eliminates the board. To elect directors,

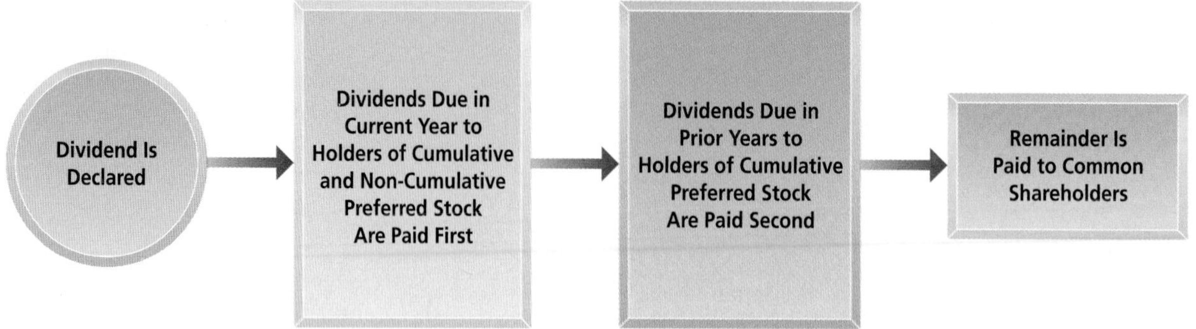

Exhibit 17.2

the shareholders may hold a meeting, or, in the more typical case for a small company, they elect directors by **written consent**. A typical written consent looks like this:

Classic American Novels, Inc.
Written Consent

The undersigned shareholders of Classic American Novels, Inc., a corporation organized and existing under the General Corporation Law of the State of Wherever, hereby agree that the following action shall be taken with full force and effect as if voted at a validly called and held meeting of the shareholders of the corporation:

Agreed: That the following people are elected to serve as directors for one year, or until their successors have been duly elected and qualified:

Herman Melville

Louisa May Alcott

Mark Twain

Dated: ________ Signed: ____________________
Willa Cather

Dated: ________ Signed: ____________________
Nathaniel Hawthorne

Dated: ________ Signed: ____________________
Harriet Beecher Stowe

Once shareholders have chosen the directors, the directors must elect the officers of the corporation. They can use a consent form, if they wish. The Model Act is flexible. It simply requires a corporation to have whatever officers are described in the bylaws. The same person can hold more than one office.

The written consents and any records of actual meetings are kept in a **minute book**, which is the official record of the corporation. Entrepreneurs sometimes feel they are too busy to bother with all these details, but, if a corporation is ever sold, the lawyers for the buyers will *insist* on a well-organized and complete minute book. In one case, a company that was seeking a $100,000 bank loan could not find all of its minutes. Many of its early shareholders and directors were not available to re-authorize prior deeds. In the end, the company had to merge itself into a newly created corporation so it could start fresh with a new set of corporate records. The company spent $10,000 on this task, a large chunk out of the $100,000 loan.

BYLAWS

The **bylaws** list all the "housekeeping" details for the corporation. For example, bylaws set the date of the annual shareholders' meeting, define what a quorum is (i.e., what percentage of stock must be represented for a meeting to count), indicate how many directors there will be, give titles to officers, and establish the fiscal (i.e., tax) year of the corporation. A sample set of bylaws is available at http://www.lectlaw.com/forms/f151.txt and http://www.tannedfeet.com/legal_forms.htm.

ISSUING DEBT

Most start-up companies begin with some combination of equity and debt. Equity (i.e., stock) is described in the charter; debt is not. Authorizing debt is often one of the first steps a new company takes. There are several types of debt:

- **Bonds** are long-term debt secured by company assets. If the company is unable to pay the debt, creditors have a right to specific assets, such as accounts receivable or inventory.
- **Debentures** are long-term *unsecured* debt. If the company cannot meet its obligations, the debenture holders are paid after bondholders, but before stockholders.
- **Notes** are short-term debt, typically payable within five years. They may be either secured or unsecured.

DEATH OF THE CORPORATION

Sometimes, business ideas are not successful and the corporation fails. This death can be voluntary (the shareholders elect to terminate the corporation) or forced (by court order). Sometimes, a court takes a step that is much more damaging to shareholders than simply dissolving the corporation—it removes the shareholders' limited liability.

PIERCING THE CORPORATE VEIL

One of the major purposes of a corporation is to protect its owners—the shareholders—from personal liability for the debts of the organization. Sometimes, however, a court will **pierce the corporate veil**; that is, the court will hold shareholders personally liable for the debts of the corporation. Courts generally pierce a corporate veil in four circumstances:

- *Failure to Observe Formalities.* If an organization does not act like a corporation, it will not be treated like one. It must, for example, hold required shareholders' and directors' meetings (or sign consents), keep a minute book as a record of these meetings, and make all the required state filings. In addition, officers must be careful to sign all corporate documents with a corporate title, not as an individual. An officer should sign like this:

Classic American Novels, Inc.

By: ______________________________

Stephen Crane, President

- *Commingling of Assets.* Nothing makes a court more willing to pierce a corporate veil than evidence that shareholders have mixed their assets with those of the corporation. Sometimes, for example, shareholders may use corporate assets to pay their personal debts. If shareholders commingle assets, it is genuinely difficult for creditors to determine which assets belong to whom. This confusion is generally resolved in favor of the creditors—*all* assets are deemed to belong to the corporation.
- *Inadequate Capitalization.* If the founders of a corporation do not raise enough capital (either through debt or equity) to give the business a fighting chance of paying its debts, courts may require shareholders to pay corporate obligations.
- *Fraud.* If fraud is committed in the name of a corporation, victims can make a claim against the personal assets of the shareholders who profited from the fraud.

Although it is difficult to feel sorry for shareholders who commit intentional wrongdoing such as fraud, some of these corporate sins involve carelessness more than anything else. That was certainly the case for Lindsey and Eben in the opening scenario. What about the following case—was the wrongdoing careless or intentional?

RICE v. ORIENTAL FIREWORKS CO.

75 Or. App. 627, 707 P.2d 1250, 1985 Ore. App. LEXIS 3928
Oregon Court of Appeals, 1985

Facts: J. C. Oriental Fireworks, Inc. was a broker and distributor of professional display fireworks. Gregory Rice filed this claim against Oriental and J. C. Chou for injuries Rice suffered while setting off fireworks. Although Rice bought the fireworks from the corporation, he sought to pierce the corporate veil and obtain a judgment against Chou personally. The trial court, however, granted Chou's motion to be removed from the case as a defendant. Chou then dismissed Oriental's Oregon lawyer and allowed an uncontested judgment to be entered against the company for $432,000 because the corporation had virtually no assets to pay the judgment.

Chou and his wife owned all the stock of the six-year-old company. Chou was president, treasurer, and chairman of the board; his wife was vice-president. The Chous kept no records or minutes of any meetings of the shareholders or directors, except for a signed unanimous consent in lieu of the directors' first meeting. The corporation grossed from $230,000 to $400,000 annually, but its assets never exceeded $13,182. It had never obtained liability insurance, although, as Chou stated, accidents do occur, and lawsuits arise "as a general rule, right after July 4th." Chou also indicated that the lack of liability insurance motivated injured customers to bring actions against other defendants.

Issue: Can the plaintiff pierce the corporate veil and hold Chou personally liable?

Excerpts from Judge Warren's Decision: There are three criteria for imposing liability on a shareholder: (1) The shareholder must have controlled the corporation; (2) the shareholder must have engaged in improper conduct in his exercise of control over the corporation; and (3) the shareholder's improper conduct must have caused plaintiff's inability to obtain an adequate remedy from the corporation.

We conclude that plaintiff has demonstrated a *prima facie* case for disregarding the corporate form of Oriental. Chou had complete control over officer and director decisions and, with his wife, has control over shareholder decisions. Chou engaged in improper conduct in the exercise of control over Oriental in two respects. First, he disregarded corporate roles and formalities which serve to protect the rights and define the responsibilities of owners, directors, officers, employees, creditors, government entities and the public at large. Second, Chou failed adequately to capitalize the corporation. A corporation is inadequately capitalized when its assets are insufficient to cover its potential liabilities, which are reasonably foreseeable from the nature of the corporation's business. Finally, there can be no doubt that Chou's failure adequately to capitalize or obtain insurance coverage for Oriental has caused plaintiff to have an inadequate remedy against the corporation.

Reversed and *remanded*.

TERMINATION

Terminating a corporation is a three-step process:

- *Vote.* The directors recommend to the shareholders that the corporation be dissolved, and a majority of the shareholders agree.
- *Filing.* The corporation files "Articles of Dissolution" with the Secretary of State.
- *Winding Up.* The officers of the corporation pay its debts and distribute the remaining property to shareholders. When the winding up is completed, the corporation ceases to exist.

The Secretary of State may dissolve a corporation that violates state law by, for example, failing to pay the required annual fees. Similarly, a court may dissolve a corporation if it is insolvent or if its directors and shareholders cannot resolve conflict over how the corporation should be managed. The court will then appoint a receiver to oversee the winding up.

THE ROLE OF CORPORATE MANAGEMENT

Now you know how to avoid some of the legal pitfalls that can ensnare the unwary entrepreneur when organizing a corporation. But what happens as the business grows? In the beginning, many entrepreneurs fund their start-up themselves (with the aid of credit cards), but most expect that the business will ultimately attract outside investors. This concept of outside investors is, in historical terms, relatively new. Before the Industrial Revolution in the eighteenth and nineteenth centuries, a business owner typically supplied both capital and management. However, the capital needs of the great manufacturing enterprises spawned by the Industrial Revolution were larger than any small group of individuals could supply. To find capital, firms sought outside investors, who often had neither the knowledge nor the desire to manage the enterprise. Investors without management skills complemented managers without capital. ("Manager" includes both directors and officers.)

Modern businesses still have the same vast need for capital and the same division between managers and investors. As businesses grow, shareholders are too numerous and too uninformed to manage the enterprises they own. Therefore, they elect directors to manage for them. The directors set policy and then appoint officers to implement corporate goals. The Model Act describes the directors' role thus: "All corporate powers shall be exercised by or under the authority of, and the business and affairs of the corporation managed under the direction of, its board of directors. . . ."

Directors have the authority to manage the corporate business, but they also have important responsibilities to shareholders and perhaps to other **stakeholders** who are affected by corporate decisions, such as employees, customers, creditors, suppliers, and neighbors. The interests of these various stakeholders often conflict. What are the rights—and responsibilities—of directors and officers to manage these conflicts?

Managers have a fiduciary duty to act in the best interests of the corporation's shareholders. Since shareholders are primarily concerned about their return on investment, managers must *maximize shareholder value*, which means providing shareholders with the highest possible financial return from dividends and stock price. However, reality is more complicated than this simple rule indicates. It is often difficult to determine which strategy will best maximize shareholder value. And what about *stake*holders? Must managers totally ignore their interests? In the following case, the court explicitly permits the board to consider the interests of stakeholders over those of some shareholders.

UNOCAL CORP. v. MESA PETROLEUM CO.

493 A.2d 946, 1985 Del. LEXIS 482
Supreme Court of Delaware, 1985

Facts: Mesa Petroleum Co. offered to purchase 64 million shares of Unocal's stock at a cash price of $54 per share. Upon merger of the two companies, Mesa planned to exchange the remaining Unocal shares for "junk bonds" that Mesa (but no one else, including the court) valued at $54 per share. Unocal's investment bankers advised the board of directors that the Mesa proposal was wholly inadequate and that an offer of over $60 per share would have been reasonable. The board rejected the Mesa offer and then made its own competing offer of $72 per share to all shareholders except Mesa. (This type of offer is called a "selective exchange offer.") The board's offer effectively preempted Mesa, because no shareholder would accept the $54 Mesa offer when the $72 Unocal offer was also available. The Delaware court issued a preliminary injunction against Unocal's offer unless it included Mesa.

Issues: Could Unocal make an offer to buy stock from all shareholders except Mesa? In making this offer, did Unocal have the right to consider the interests of other stakeholders?

Excerpts from Justice Moore's Decision: In the board's exercise of corporate power to forestall a takeover bid our analysis begins with the basic principle that corporate directors have a fiduciary duty to act in the best interests of the corporation's stockholders. The restriction placed upon a selective stock repurchase is that the directors may not have acted solely or primarily out of a desire to perpetuate themselves in office. This entails an analysis by the directors of the nature of the takeover bid and its effect on the corporate enterprise. Examples of such concerns may include: inadequacy of the price offered, nature and timing of the offer, questions of illegality, the impact on "constituencies" other than shareholders (i.e., creditors, customers, employees, and perhaps even the community generally), the risk of nonconsummation, and the quality of securities being offered in the exchange. While not a controlling factor, it also seems to us that a board may reasonably consider the basic stockholder interests at stake, including those of short-term speculators, whose actions may have fueled the coercive aspect of the offer at the expense of the long-term investor.

In adopting the selective exchange offer, the board stated that its objective was either to defeat the inadequate Mesa offer or, should the offer still succeed, provide its stockholders with $72 a share. We find that both purposes are valid. However, such efforts would have been thwarted by Mesa's participation in the exchange offer. First, if Mesa could tender its shares, Unocal would effectively be subsidizing the former's continuing effort to buy Unocal stock at $54 per share. Second, Mesa could not, by definition, fit within the class of shareholders being protected from its own coercive and inadequate tender offer. Thus, we are satisfied that the selective exchange offer is reasonably related to the threats posed.

The decision of the Court of Chancery is therefore *reversed*, and the preliminary injunction is *vacated*.

This case illustrates the inherent conflicts of interest facing every board. The court suggests that the interests of the directors themselves and of short-term speculators are secondary to those of long-term investors and other stakeholders. The next section looks more closely at directors' responsibilities to their various constituencies.

THE BUSINESS JUDGMENT RULE

Officers and directors have a fiduciary duty to act in the best interests of their stockholders, but under the **business judgment rule** the courts allow managers great leeway in carrying out this responsibility. The business judgment rule is not a statute, but a common law concept that virtually every court in the country recognizes. To be protected by the business judgment rule, managers must act in good faith:

Duty of Loyalty	**1.** Without a conflict of interest
Duty of Care	**2.** With the care that an ordinarily prudent person would take in a similar situation, and
	3. In a manner they reasonably believe to be in the best interests of the corporation.

The business judgment rule is two shields in one: it protects both the manager and her decision. If a manager has complied with the rule, a court will not hold her personally liable for any harm her decision has caused the company, nor will the court rescind her decision. If the manager violates the business judgment rule, then she has the burden of proving that her decision was fair to the shareholders. If it was not fair, she may be held personally liable, and the decision can be rescinded.

The business judgment rule accomplishes three goals:

- *It permits directors to do their job.* If directors were afraid they would be liable for every decision that led to a loss, they would never make a decision, or at least not a risky one.
- *It keeps judges out of corporate management.* Without the business judgment rule, judges would be tempted, if not required, to second-guess managers' decisions.
- *It encourages directors to serve.* No one in his right mind would serve as a director if he knew that every decision was open to attack in the courtroom.

Analysis of the business judgment rule is divided into two parts. The obligation of a manager to act without a conflict of interest is called the **duty of loyalty**. The requirements that a manager act with care and in the best interests of the corporation are referred to as the **duty of care**.

DUTY OF LOYALTY

The duty of loyalty prohibits managers from making a decision that benefits them at the expense of the corporation.

SELF-DEALING

Consider whether the manager in the following article has violated his duty of loyalty to Vie de France:

To its Washington, D.C. customers, the name Vie de France conjures up the tastes and smells of freshly baked croissants or crusty baguettes. But according to Lloyd J. Faul, a fired executive, not all of the smells emanating from the company were pleasant. Grands Moulins de Paris International, France's largest flour miller, bought 26 percent of Vie de France and then dispatched Jean-Paul Vilgrain to serve as Vie's CEO. Vilgrain's family was one of Grand Moulins' largest shareholders. Faul alleges that, once installed, Vilgrain sold a license to a Japanese company to sell products in Japan under the name "Vie de France" in exchange for royalties to be paid to Grands Moulins (not to Vie de France). He refused to approve a sale of Vie de France to Pillsbury unless Pillsbury would purchase flour mixes sold by Grands Moulins. Vilgrain also locked Faul out of Vie's headquarters when Faul refused to falsify an affidavit that would allow Vilgrain's son to renew his American working papers.[1]

Self-dealing is a violation of the duty of loyalty. In **business self-dealing**, the manager makes decisions that benefit other companies with which he has a relationship. In **personal self-dealing**, the manager himself benefits.

Once a manager engages in self-dealing, the business judgment rule no longer applies. This does not mean the manager is automatically liable to the corporation or that his decision is automatically void. All it means is that the court will no longer presume that the transaction was acceptable. Instead,

[1] B. H. Lawrence, "En Garde; the Battle at Vie de France," *The Washington Post*, Apr. 24, 1989, p. F1.

the court will scrutinize the deal more carefully. **A self-dealing transaction is valid if disinterested members of the board of directors or disinterested shareholders approve it or if the transaction was fair to the corporation.** ("Disinterested" means that they do not benefit from the transaction themselves.) Exhibit 17.3 illustrates the rules on self-dealing.

What about the Vie de France transactions? They had not been approved by the disinterested members of the board of directors or the disinterested shareholders. Were they fair to the corporation? If the deals were not fair, the corporation could rescind them and hold Vilgrain personally liable. In the end, however, none of the Vie de France shareholders filed suit against the company or Vilgrain. A few months after Faul left the company, Vilgrain was named president and CEO. Two years later, the company sold its bakery business, keeping only its restaurant and frozen food divisions.

CORPORATE OPPORTUNITY

The self-dealing rules prevent managers from *forcing* their companies into unfair deals. The corporate opportunity doctrine is the reverse—it prohibits managers from *excluding* their company from favorable deals. **Managers are in violation of the corporate opportunity doctrine if they compete against the corporation without its consent.**

Charles Guth was president of Loft, Inc., which operated a chain of candy stores. These stores sold Coca-Cola. Guth purchased the Pepsi-Cola Co. personally, without offering the opportunity to Loft. The Delaware court found that Guth had violated the corporate opportunity doctrine and ordered him to

Exhibit 17.3

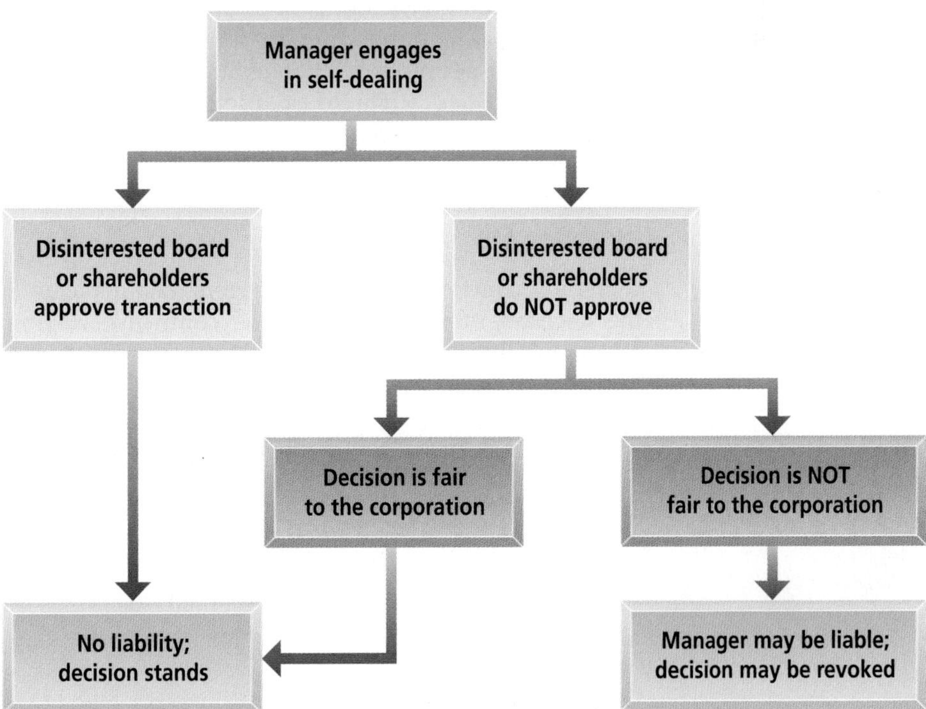

transfer all his shares in Pepsi to Loft.[2] That was in 1939, and Pepsi-Cola was bankrupt; today, PepsiCo, Inc. is worth $53 billion.

DUTY OF CARE

In addition to the *duty of loyalty*, managers also owe a *duty of care*. **The duty of care requires officers and directors to act in the best interests of the corporation and to use the same care that an ordinarily prudent person would in the management of her own assets.**

RATIONAL BUSINESS PURPOSE

Courts generally agree in principle that directors and officers are liable for decisions that have no rational business purpose. In practice, however, these same courts have been extremely supportive of managerial decisions, looking hard to find some justification. For decades, the Chicago Cubs baseball team refused to install lights in Wrigley Field. Cubs' fans could only take themselves out to the ball game during the day. A shareholder sued on the grounds that the Cubs' revenues were peanuts and crackerjack compared with those generated by other teams that played at night. The Cubs defended their decision on the grounds that a large night crowd would cause the neighborhood to deteriorate, depressing the value of Wrigley Field (which was not owned by the Cubs). The court rooted for the home team and found that the Cubs' excuse was a "rational purpose" and a legitimate exercise of the business judgment rule.[3]

LEGALITY

Courts are generally unsympathetic to managers who engage in illegal behavior, even if their goal is to help the company. For example, the managing director of an amusement park in New York State used corporate funds to purchase the silence of people who threatened to complain that the park was illegally operating on Sunday. The court ordered the director to repay the money he had spent on bribes, even though the company had earned large profits on Sundays.[4]

INFORMED DECISION

Generally, courts will protect managers who make an *informed* decision, even if the decision ultimately harms the company. Making an informed decision means carefully investigating the facts. However, even if the decision is uninformed, the directors will not be held liable if the decision was entirely fair to the shareholders.

Exhibit 17.4 provides an overview of the duty of care.

---

[2] *Guth v. Loft*, 5 A.2d 503, 23 Del. Ch. 255, 1939 Del. LEXIS 13 (Del. 1939).

[3] *Shlensky v. Wrigley*, 95 Ill. App. 2d 173, 237 N.E.2d 776, 1968 Ill. App. LEXIS 1107 (Ill. App. Ct. 1968).

[4] *Roth v. Robertson*, 64 Misc. 343, 118 N.Y.S. 351, 1909 N.Y. Misc. LEXIS 279 (N.Y. 1909).

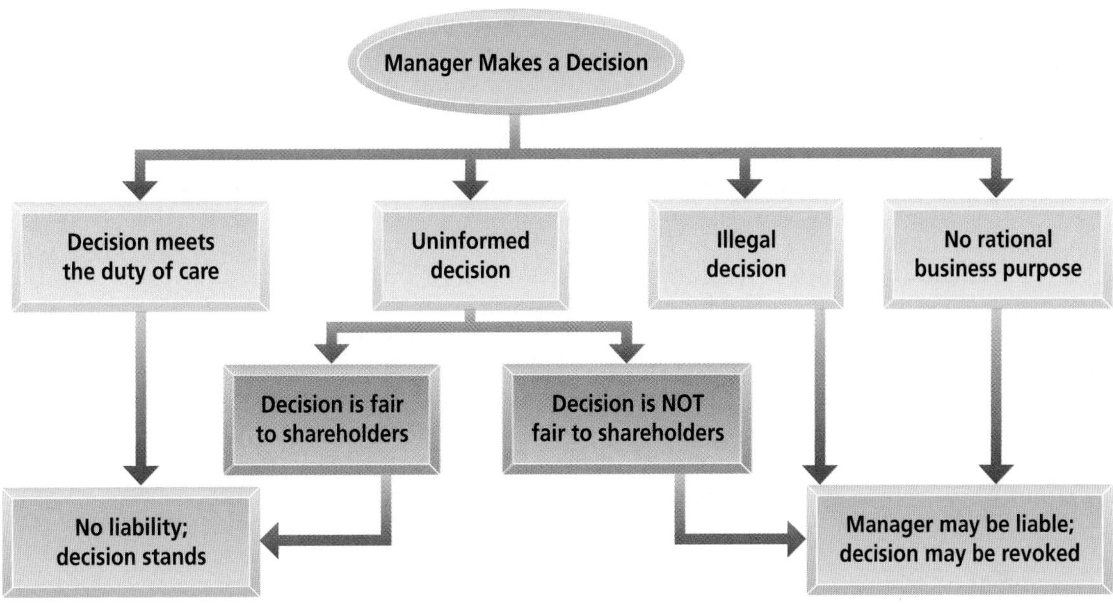

Exhibit 17.4

In the following case, shareholders sued the board of directors for accepting a purchase price that they felt was too low. Did the directors violate their duty of care? You be the judge.

SMITH v. VAN GORKOM

488 A.2d 858, 1985 Del. LEXIS 590
Supreme Court of Delaware, 1985

Facts: Trans Union was a publicly traded company in the railcar leasing business. Jerome Van Gorkom had been its chief executive officer for more than 17 years. He was nearing the mandatory retirement age of 65 and was concerned about maximizing the value of his 75,000 shares of Trans Union stock. In the preceding five years, Trans Union's stock had traded at a high of $39.50 and a low of $24.25 per share. The price was now about $37.

Although Trans Union had hundreds of millions of dollars in annual cash flow, it did not have enough income to take advantage of large investment tax credits (ITCs). Van Gorkom fretted that competitors who could efficiently use their ITCs would be able to cut their lease prices and take business away from Trans Union. He believed that Trans Union would be more profitable if it were bought by a company that could use the credits.

On September 13, Van Gorkom met with Jay Pritzker, a well-known corporate takeover specialist, to discuss the potential market for Trans Union. Van Gorkom suggested to Pritzker that a leveraged buyout (LBO) could be done at $55 per share. (In an LBO, the acquiring company buys the target company's stock using a loan secured by the target's assets.) On Thursday, September 18, Pritzker offered to buy all of Trans Union's stock for $55 per share. The offer expired three days later, on Sunday evening.

On Saturday, Van Gorkom met separately with senior managers and later with the board of directors. Salomon Brothers, the company's investment banker, was not invited to attend. At both meetings, Van Gorkom disclosed the offer and described its terms, but furnished no copies of the proposed agreement. At the first meeting with senior management, the managers' reaction to the Pritzker proposal was completely negative—they feared losing their jobs, they did not like Pritzker, and they thought the price was too low. Nevertheless, Van Gorkom proceeded to the board meeting.

The board was composed of five inside and five outside directors. Of the outside directors, four were corporate CEOs and one was the former Dean of the University of Chicago Business School. None was an investment banker or trained financial analyst. All members of the board were familiar with the company's financial condition and the ITC problem. They had all recently reviewed the company's five-year forecast as well as a comprehensive 18-month study by a well-known consulting firm.

Van Gorkom explained that the issue was not whether $55 per share was the highest price the company could obtain, but whether it was a fair price that the stockholders should be given the opportunity to accept or reject. He also explained that the company had the right to accept a higher offer, if one were made. Van Gorkom did not disclose to the board that he had proposed the $55 price in his negotiations with Pritzker. The company's attorney advised the directors that they might be sued if they failed to accept the offer. The company's chief financial officer said that $55 was "in the range of a fair price" for an LBO, but "at the beginning of the range." The board approved the sale.

Van Gorkom executed the agreement at a formal social event that he hosted for the opening of the Chicago Lyric Opera. Neither he nor any other director read the agreement before signing it. The company issued a press release announcing that Trans Union had entered into a "definitive" agreement with Pritzker. At the same time, it hired Salomon Brothers to solicit other offers. No one else made a firm offer, perhaps because other bidders believed the company was already committed to Pritzker. On February 10, 69 percent of the stockholders of Trans Union voted in favor of the Pritzker proposal.

The plaintiff, Alden Smith, objected to the sale because he did not want to pay tax on the huge profits he realized.

You be the Judge: Did the directors of Trans Union violate their duty of care to the corporation by making an uninformed decision? Did the shareholders consent to the board's decision?

Argument for the Shareholders: The whole procedure for this sale was shockingly casual. Van Gorkom signed the final agreement at a social function. When the directors voted to sell the company, they had not (1) tried to negotiate a higher price with Pritzker, (2) read the agreement, (3) consulted their investment bankers, or (4) determined the intrinsic value of the company. The stock price simply represents the value of a minority stake (one share); a controlling share is worth more, but the board did not know how much more.

The board did not know this important information and neither did the shareholders when they approved the sale. For that reason, the shareholder consent is invalid.

Argument for the Board of Directors: Pritzker paid a fair price for the Trans Union stock. It represented a premium of (1) 62 percent over the average of the high and low price in the prior year, (2) 48 percent over the last closing price, and (3) 39 percent over the highest price at which the stock had *ever* traded. The plaintiffs suggest that the "intrinsic value" of the company was higher. The board hired Salomon Brothers to look for better offers and agreed to pay them a fee equal to three-eighths of 1 percent of any increase over $55 that the company received. Salomon would have earned millions of dollars if it had found a buyer willing to pay more than Pritzker.

Jerome Van Gorkom served the company for 24 years, and he knew $55 was a favorable price. He also had an enormous incentive to obtain the highest price available because he personally owned 75,000 shares. The five inside directors had collectively worked for the company for 116 years. The outside directors knew the company well, and they were experienced business people; four of them were CEOs of their own large companies. The board was forced to make a decision quickly because Pritzker's offer expired in three days. What could an expert have discovered in three days that the board did not already know? The Trans Union lawyer warned the directors that if they refused the offer, they would be sued.

Alden Smith's tax problems are not a legitimate reason to hold the board liable. The business judgment rule is meant to protect a board that makes a good faith decision. This board did what it thought best for all of the company's shareholders, not for Alden Smith alone.

Remember that managers are only liable if they make an uninformed decision *and* the transaction is unfair to the shareholders. If the appeals court in the *Trans Union* case determined that the directors had violated their duty of care, it would remand the case to the lower court to determine if $55 was a fair price.

Recently, some states have modified their business judgment rule to increase protection for directors. These states either limit liability by statute or permit corporations to include charter provisions that shield directors from personal liability.

TAKEOVERS

The business judgment rule is an important guideline for officers and directors in the routine management of corporations. Beginning in the 1980s, however, the business judgment rule also played a crucial role in the merger mania that swept corporate America. In addition, both Congress and many state legislatures passed statutes that defined the roles of the various combatants in hostile takeovers.

There are three ways to acquire control of a company:

- *Buy the company's assets.* Such a sale must be approved by both the shareholders and the board of directors of the acquired company.
- *Merge with the company.* In a merger, one company absorbs another. The acquired company ceases to exist. A merger must also be approved by the shareholders and the board of directors of the target company. If the current directors object, an acquiring company could buy enough stock to replace the board, but these battles are difficult and often end in defeat for the acquirer.
- *Buy stock from the shareholders.* This method is called a **tender offer** because the acquirer asks shareholders to "tender," or offer their stock for sale. Unlike the other methods of obtaining control, approval from the board of directors of the target company is not strictly necessary. As long as shareholders tender enough stock, the acquirer gains control. A tender offer is called a **hostile takeover**, if the board of the target resists.

FEDERAL REGULATION OF TENDER OFFERS: THE WILLIAMS ACT

The Williams Act applies only if the target company's stock is publicly traded. Under the Williams Act:

- Any individual or group who together acquire more than 5 percent of a company's stock must file a public disclosure document (called a "Schedule 13D") with the Securities and Exchange Commission (SEC)
- On the day a tender offer begins, a bidder must file a disclosure statement with the SEC
- A bidder must keep a tender offer open for at least 20 days initially and for at least 10 days after any change in the terms of the offer

- Any shareholder may withdraw acceptance of the tender offer at any time while the offer is still open
- If the bidder raises the price offered, all selling shareholders must be paid the higher price, regardless of when they tendered; and
- If the stockholders tender more shares than the bidder wants to buy, the bidder must purchase shares pro rata (in other words, it must buy the same proportion from everyone, not first come, first served).

STATE REGULATION OF TAKEOVERS

COMMON LAW OF TAKEOVERS

To fend off attack, potential targets often adopt defensive measures known as **antitakeover devices** or **shark repellents**. (Acquiring companies are sometimes called **sharks**.) **Poison pills** are among the most common antitakeover devices. A target company will, for example, amend its charter to provide that it can issue one share of preferred stock to each of its shareholders. If a shark purchases more than 20 percent of the target's stock and subsequently merges with the target, the preferred stock is convertible into a share of the shark. This device makes a takeover much more expensive for the shark.

Antitakeover devices are a mixed blessing—they are beneficial if used to ensure that shareholders receive the highest possible price for their stock in the event of a sale. But they can be harmful to shareholders if used only to protect management from being fired. **When establishing takeover defenses, shareholder welfare must be the board's primary concern.** The directors may institute shark repellents, but they must do so to ensure that bids are high, not to protect their own jobs.

STATE ANTITAKEOVER STATUTES

When fighting takeover battles, companies have also found support in state governments. Legislators may not care if a group of directors is thrown into the unemployment line, but they do fear the impact on the local economy if a major employer leaves. When the Belzberg family threatened a hostile takeover of auto parts manufacturer Arvin Industries, the second largest employer in Columbus, Indiana, the state legislature quickly passed a tough antitakeover bill that had been drafted by Arvin's own lawyers. Arvin and the Belzbergs quickly settled.

Most states have now passed laws to deter hostile takeovers. Among the common varieties:

- *Statutes that Automatically Impede Hostile Takeovers.* These statutes, for instance, might ban hostile (but not friendly) mergers for five years after the acquirer buys 10 percent of a company.
- *Statutes that Authorize Companies to Fight Off Hostile Takeovers.* These statutes typically permit management, when responding to a hostile takeover, to consider the welfare of company *stake*holders, such as the community, customers, suppliers, and employees. Some even go so far as to allow management to consider the regional or national economy.

Most of these statutes do not totally eliminate hostile takeovers. A determined, well-financed bidder can still be successful. About one-third of hostile bidders win their fight. But these state statutes do tip the playing field in favor of management. In the process, they prevent some takeovers that shareholders might want, but they also ensure that shareholders receive a high price in those takeovers that are successful.

Supporters of these state statutes argue that large, publicly traded corporations owe a duty to all of their constituencies. The loss of a large corporate presence can be immensely disruptive to a community. Perhaps a state should have the right to prevent economic upheaval within its borders.

Opponents contend that shareholders own the company and their interests ought to be paramount. Antitakeover legislation entrenches management and prevents shareholders from obtaining the premium that accompanies a takeover. Opponents also argue that, if other stakeholders are so concerned with the well-being of the company, let them put their money where their mouths are and buy stock. And if current managers cannot offer shareholders as high a stock price as an outside raider, they ought to be replaced. What is the ethical choice for directors?

THE ROLE OF SHAREHOLDERS

As we have seen, ***directors*, not *shareholders*, have the right to manage the corporate business**. Although corporate shareholders own $13 trillion in assets worldwide, their power over these enterprises is very limited. At one time, corporate stock was primarily owned by individuals, but now institutional investors—pension plans, mutual funds, insurance companies, banks, foundations, and university endowments—own more than 50 percent of all shares publicly traded in the United States. Traditionally, unhappy shareholders did little more than the "Wall Street walk"—they sold their shares. As the following article illustrates, however, even in the Magic Kingdom shareholders have begun to rebel against what they perceive as high-handed management.

Michael Eisner's ears are ringing these days with other people's theories about management and corporate governance. The chairman and chief executive of Walt Disney Co. isn't impressed. "I don't know whether pension funds and law professors really know how these companies are run," he says. "I didn't go to business school, so I didn't have the benefit of two years of intensive training in this area," he adds facetiously. "But what I read about what is expected I find quite counterintuitive—for me and for this company."

Mr. Eisner's intuition has consistently won big returns for investors during his 12½ years at the helm. But his way of doing things is getting him something much less appealing: shareholder pressure to reform. Some shareholders are upset about two cases of executive pay: the contract the board recently gave Mr. Eisner to stay another 10 years that included eight million stock options, and a multimillion dollar payout the board made to terminate Michael Ovitz's failed 14-month stint as company president. *Executive Compensation Reports*, a newsletter, estimates that Mr. Eisner's package is the largest options grant ever to a sitting chief executive.

While a number of major corporations have felt heat from shareholder activists in recent years, Disney has until now been protected from such critics by its strong returns. As Mr. Eisner likes to point out, Disney's market capitalization has soared to $53 billion from $2 billion under his leadership. Critics acknowledge Disney's impressive track record, but counter that the company's snowballing success has left it dangerously dependent on just one man who, despite a talented team of division heads, has a propensity to micromanage, a history of heart trouble, and no heir apparent. The current flare-up raises a key question: Is success a substitute for strong corporate-governance standards that check a company's management in good times as well as bad?[5]

What control do shareholders have over Michael Eisner at Disney? The next section of this chapter explores the rights of shareholders (and includes the case in which Disney shareholders sued Michael Eisner). Corporate governance is of such interest to investors that many Web sites contain discussions of these issues. Take a look, for example, at http://www.corpgov.net.

RIGHTS OF SHAREHOLDERS

Shareholders have neither the *right* nor the *obligation* to manage the day-to-day business of the enterprise. If you own stock in Starbucks Corp., your share of stock plus $1.50 entitles you to a cup of coffee, the same as everyone else. By the same token, if the pipes freeze and the local Starbucks store floods, the manager has no right to call you, as a shareholder, to help clean up the mess. What rights do shareholders have?

RIGHT TO INFORMATION

Under the Model Act, shareholders with a proper purpose have the right to inspect and copy the corporation's minute book, accounting records, and shareholder lists. A **proper purpose** is one that aids the shareholder in managing and protecting her investment. If, for example, Celeste is convinced that the directors of Devil Desserts, Inc., are mismanaging the company, she might demand a list of other shareholders so that she can ask them to join her in a lawsuit. The company may not *like* this purpose, but it is *proper* and the company is required to give her the list. If, however, Celeste wants to use the shareholder list as a potential source for her new mail-order catalog featuring exercise equipment, the company could legitimately turn her down.

RIGHT TO VOTE

A corporation must have at least one class of stock with voting rights.

---

[5] Bruce Orwall and Joann S. Lublin, "The Plutocracy: If a Company Prospers, Should Its Directors Behave by the Book?" *The Wall Street Journal*, Feb. 2, 1997, p. 1. Republished with permission of The Wall Street Journal; permission conveyed through the Copyright Clearance Center, Inc.

PROXIES

Shareholders who do not wish to attend a shareholders' meeting may appoint someone else to vote for them. Confusingly, both this person and the document the shareholder signs to appoint the substitute voter are called a **proxy**. Under SEC rules, companies are not required to solicit proxies. However, a meeting is invalid without a certain percentage of shareholders in attendance, either in person or by proxy. This attendance requirement is referred to as a **quorum**. As a practical matter, if a public company with thousands of investors does not solicit proxies, it will not obtain a quorum. Therefore, virtually all public companies do solicit proxies. Along with the proxy, the company must also give shareholders a **proxy statement** and an **annual report**. The proxy statement provides information on everything from management compensation to a list of directors who miss too many meetings. The annual report contains detailed financial data.

Under SEC rules, companies can offer (but not require) electronic delivery of proxy statements and annual reports. Intel Corp. was one of the first companies to make its proxy statements and annual reports available on a Web site. The company first sent investors a request for consent to receive the documents electronically. About 10 percent of shareholders returned the consent. The company then sent them notice of the Web site address. Proxy cards (for voting) could not be downloaded, however; each shareholder was sent a hard copy. Read about Intel's policies on corporate governance at http://www.intc.com/intel/finance/corp_gov.htm.

Typically, only the company itself solicits proxies for a shareholder meeting, but sometimes shareholders who disapprove of company policies try to convince other shareholders to appoint them as proxy instead of management. These dissident shareholders must also prepare a proxy statement that discloses, among other information, who they are, how they are financing their opposition, and how many other proxy contests they have participated in. If enough shareholders give their proxies to the dissidents, then the dissidents can elect themselves or their representatives to replace the board of directors.

SHAREHOLDER PROPOSALS

Some shareholders who oppose a company policy may not aspire to a board seat or perhaps cannot afford to send material individually to other investors. Such shareholders may use an alternative method, provided by the SEC, for communicating with fellow shareholders. **Under SEC rules, any shareholder who owns at least 1 percent of the company or $2,000 of stock can require that one proposal be placed in the company's proxy statement to be voted on at the shareholder meeting.** In practice, many of these resolutions have a political agenda: save the environment, withdraw from Myanmar, protect gay and lesbian workers. Others relate to corporate-governance issues: eliminate pensions for directors and permit secret ballots. Each year, public companies vote on about 450 shareholder proposals. Prior to 1985, only *two* proposals had been approved—ever. Currently, about 10 to 20 receive a majority vote each year, a definite improvement (or deterioration, depending on your perspective).

As the following article illustrates, companies generally view shareholder proposals as a nuisance.

At the General Electric shareholder meeting last month, there were several items of business likely to irritate even the most mild-mannered CEO. First, there was a proposal to limit GE's spending on political contributions, which the resolution's sponsor labeled "nothing more than a thinly disguised bribe." Then there was a proposal to cap the chief executive officer's salary, linking it to the pay of the lowliest janitor in the company. And finally there was Sister Patricia Daly.

Sister Pat stood up to advocate a shareholder resolution on GE's pollution of the Hudson River. She called on the company to publicize the danger of eating fish from the river and to stop fostering misleading studies. And she compared the company's claims that PCBs are harmless with claims made by tobacco industry executives about the harmlessness of smoking.

That is when John F. Welch, Jr., GE's chairman and chief executive, blew up. "That's an outrageous comparison," he shouted at the nun. "You owe it to God to be on the side of truth." As Sister Pat, a Dominican nun from Newton, New Jersey, recalled afterwards, "He totally lost it."

In the end, the resolution was backed by 7.6 percent of the shares voted at the meeting, a figure GE characterized as a resounding defeat but which was sufficient to get it on the proxy ballot again next year. Although Sister Pat's resolution failed, it clearly rattled the company.[6]

If a company refuses to include a shareholder proposal in its proxy material, shareholders can appeal to the SEC. These are the major SEC regulations on shareholder resolutions:

- *The proposals are generally not binding on the company.* The SEC recommends that proposals be in the form of a request or recommendation because state laws sometimes prohibit resolutions that are binding on the company.
- *If dissident shareholders are running for director, they must prepare their own proxy statement; they cannot piggyback on the company's.* If shareholders could run for director simply by placing their name in the proxy statement, the result might be hundreds of candidates and thousands of confused shareholders.
- *The proposal cannot relate to the ordinary business operations of the corporation.* Shareholders of Excalibur Technologies, Inc. proposed that the company post its SEC filings on the company Web site. You might think that a "Technologies" company would willingly agree. You might also think that the SEC would favor the widest possible disclosure. You would be wrong. The SEC ruled the proposal out of bounds because it related to ordinary business operations.
- *The proposal cannot interfere with the company's proxy solicitation.* Management can exclude more than one proposal on the same topic and proposals that were voted down decisively in the past.

---

[6] Elizabeth Kolbert, "It's the Nun Vs. the C.E.O," *The New York Times*, May 25, 1998, p. B1.

If you would like to sponsor your own shareholder proposal, http://www.iraa.com offers step-by-step instructions.

SHAREHOLDER MEETINGS

A company must hold an **annual meeting** of shareholders, if for no other reason than to elect directors. Everyone who owns stock on the **record date** must be sent notice of a meeting. As the following article illustrates, shareholders meetings everywhere have become less peaceful.

Managers the world over have at least one attribute in common: they like their annual meetings short and sweet. And generally they used to get exactly that. In the United States, often the larger the company, the fewer the shareholders in attendance. Annual meetings were dull affairs, with droning presentations by management. Japanese companies went even further, stacking their meetings with employees who regularly broke into enthusiastic applause. The typical annual meeting in Japan lasted barely half an hour.

But with the rise of shareholder activism in both countries, annual meetings have become more contentious. To reduce attendance, some U.S. companies have relocated their meetings. Florida Progress, a utility with many elderly investors who lived in Florida, moved its annual meeting to Texas. Only 25 shareholders attended, down from the usual 300.

Japanese companies worry not only about dissident shareholders, but also about **sokaiya**—gangsters who threaten to disrupt an annual meeting unless the company pays them off. To solve these twin problems, 95 percent of the companies traded on the Tokyo Stock Exchange now hold their annual meetings on the same day. This solution not only spreads both shareholders and gangsters thin, but also limits press coverage.

Perhaps Bell & Howell has the most effective solution. It was the first American company to supplement its traditional annual meeting with a "cybercast" online. Internet attendees could ask questions via e-mail. Questions lose some of their sting when zapped via e-mail.

ELECTION AND REMOVAL OF DIRECTORS

Shareholders have the right to elect directors and also to remove them from office. Under the Model Act, shareholders can remove directors at any time for any reason. In theory, shareholders elect directors and directors then appoint officers. Typically, however, the *real* relationship between directors and shareholders in public companies is very different from this formula. Yes, shareholders elect the directors, but the shareholders almost always vote for nominees chosen by the board itself. And the board's nominating committee rarely chooses candidates that the CEO opposes. The *officers* are really choosing the *directors*, not the other way around.

COMPENSATION FOR OFFICERS AND DIRECTORS

For many children, *Pat the Bunny* is their first book. It contains few words but much interaction. "Readers" can pat the bunny, sniff the flowers, and play peekaboo with the blanket. After *Pat the Bunny*, many children graduate to *The Poky Little Puppy*, *Richard Scarry's Busy, Busy Town*, and *Disney's Mulan*, all published by Golden Books Family Entertainment, Inc.

Despite its portfolio of classics, Golden Books was having financial difficulties. The company hired Richard Snyder, an experienced publishing executive, to solve its distribution and sales problems. Such experience does not come cheap. At Golden Books, he was the third highest paid executive in the publishing industry. But an executive does not live by pay alone. Snyder relocated the company to posh new quarters, hired a private chef, and used the corporate jet for vacations. He also hired other executives (including his wife) at salaries two to three times the industry average. In return, investors expected the stock price to zoom. They just did not expect it to zoom *down*. Not only did the stock price plummet 80 percent, but the company was put up for sale. In the midst of this turmoil, the board doubled Snyder's salary and paid him a $500,000 signing bonus for extending his contract two years.

To many investors, sky-high executive compensation has become the symbol of all that is wrong with corporate governance. As the following case demonstrates, however, shareholders' efforts to challenge executive compensation have met with little success. An officer's salary is presumed to be reasonable unless she voted for it as a director of the company. To be successful in challenging an executive's compensation, shareholders must prove that the board was grossly uninformed or that the amount was so high that it had *no relation* to the value of the services performed and was really a gift. The courts tend to be unsympathetic to this line of argument.

BREHM v. EISNER

746 A.2d 244; 2000 Del. LEXIS 51
Supreme Court of Delaware, 2000

Facts: Michael Ovitz was an important talent broker in Hollywood. He was also a long-time friend of Disney Chairman and CEO Michael Eisner. Although Ovitz lacked experience managing a diversified public company, Disney hired him to be its president. Eisner unilaterally negotiated Ovitz's employment agreement and the board approved it.

After 14 months, all parties agreed that the experiment had failed, so Ovitz left Disney—but not empty-handed. Under his contract, he was entitled to $140 million in severance pay. When the board originally approved this agreement, it had known how the severance payment would be calculated but it had not realized how high the total cost could be. Graef Crystal, the compensation expert who had advised the directors, later said that he wished he had done this calculation for them.

Shareholders of Disney sued to prevent payment. After the lower court dismissed their claim, the shareholders appealed to the Supreme Court of Delaware.

Issue: Did the Disney directors have the right to pay $140 million to an employee who had worked at the company unsuccessfully and for only 14 months?

Excerpts from Justice Veasey's Decision: [I]n making business decisions, directors must consider all material information reasonably available, and the directors' process is actionable only if grossly negligent. Merely because Crystal now regrets not having calculated the package is not reason enough to overturn the judgment of the Board then. It is the essence of the business judgment rule that a court will not apply 20/20 hindsight to second guess a board's decision, except in rare cases where a transaction may be so egregious on its face that the board approval cannot meet the test of business judgment. I think it a correct statement of law that the duty of care is still fulfilled even if a Board does not know the exact amount of a severance payout but nonetheless is fully informed about the manner in which such a payout would be calculated. A board is not required to be informed of every fact, but rather is required to be reasonably informed.

Plaintiffs allege that the Board committed a violation constituting waste. Plaintiffs basically quarrel with the Board's judgment in evaluating Ovitz' worth vis a vis the lavish payout to him. [T]he size and structure of executive compensation are inherently matters of judgment. The judicial standard for determination of corporate waste is well developed. Roughly, a waste entails an exchange of corporate assets for consideration so disproportionately small as to lie beyond the range at which any reasonable person might be willing to trade. Such a transfer is in effect a gift. If, however, there is any substantial consideration received by the corporation, and if there is a good faith judgment that in the circumstances the transaction is worthwhile, there should be no finding of waste, even if the fact finder would conclude ex post that the transaction was unreasonably risky. Any other rule would deter corporate boards from the optimal rational acceptance of risk. Courts do not measure, weigh or quantify directors' judgments.

[T]he facts in the Complaint show that Ovitz' performance as president was disappointing at best, that Eisner admitted it had been a mistake to hire him. Plaintiffs may disagree with the Board's judgment as to how this matter should have been handled. But where, as here, there is no reasonable doubt as to the disinterest of or absence of fraud by the Board, mere disagreement cannot serve as grounds for imposing liability based on alleged breaches of fiduciary duty and waste. To rule otherwise would invite courts to become super-directors, measuring matters of degree in business decisionmaking and executive compensation. Such a rule would run counter to the foundation of our jurisprudence. ■

Directors not only set the salaries of company officers, they also determine their own compensation (unless the charter or bylaws provide otherwise). Directors of Fortune 200 companies earn on average $114,000 annually, consisting of $53,000 in cash, $59,000 in stock, and $2,000 in pension benefits. Over a recent four-year period, compensation for directors at Fortune 200 companies has risen 45 percent. Directors of small companies earn much less, about $12,000 annually in cash, but they are often granted substantial stock options, which could, in theory, increase dramatically in value.

For more information about executive compensation, pay attention to http://www.paywatch.org. Run by the AFL-CIO labor union, this Web site has an understandably jaundiced view of lavish paychecks. Wondering about your own current or future salary? Check in at http://www.wageweb.com/ to find compensation data for over 150 different types of jobs.

Fundamental Corporate Changes

A corporation must seek shareholder approval before undergoing any of the following fundamental changes: a merger, a sale of major assets, dissolution of the corporation, or an amendment to the charter or bylaws.

RIGHT TO DISSENT

If a corporation (that is not publicly traded) decides to undertake a fundamental change, the Model Act and many state laws require the company to buy back the stock of any shareholders who object. This process is referred to as **dissenters' rights**, and the company must pay "fair value" for the stock. Fundamental changes include a merger, an exchange of the company's stock for that of another firm, a sale of most of the company's assets, or an amendment to the charter that would adversely affect a shareholder's rights (to vote, for instance).

RIGHT TO PROTECTION FROM OTHER SHAREHOLDERS

Anyone who owns enough stock to control a corporation has a fiduciary duty to minority shareholders. (Minority shareholders are those with less than a controlling interest.) The courts have long recognized that minority shareholders are entitled to extra protection because it is easy (perhaps even natural) for controlling shareholders to take advantage of them. For example:

- The Sinclair Oil Company owned 97 percent of Sinven Co. Sinclair violated its fiduciary duty to Sinven's minority shareholders when it forced Sinven to pay dividends large enough to bankrupt the company.[7]
- A court refused to allow one brother, who was a majority shareholder of the family company, to force the other to sell his shares. According to the court, a minority shareholder can be ejected only for a reason that is fair or has a business purpose.[8]

ENFORCING SHAREHOLDER RIGHTS

Shareholders in serious conflict with management have three different mechanisms for enforcing their rights: a derivative lawsuit, a direct lawsuit, or a class action.

DERIVATIVE LAWSUITS

A derivative lawsuit is brought by *shareholders* to remedy a wrong to the *corporation*. The suit is brought in the name of the corporation, and all proceeds of the litigation go to the corporation. The shareholders of Disney were upset when the board of directors approved a $140 million severance package for Michael Ovitz. Technically, however, the directors had injured the *corporation*, not the *shareholders*. And who would authorize a suit by the corporation against the directors? The directors, of course. Because the directors are unlikely to file

---

[7] *Sinclair Oil Corp. v. Levien*, 280 A.2d 717, 1971 Del. LEXIS 225 (Del. 1971).

[8] *Lerner v. Lerner*, 306 Md. 771, 511 A.2d 501, 1986 Md. LEXIS 264 (Md. 1986).

suit against themselves, shareholders are permitted to bring a *derivative* action, in the name of the corporation, against managers who have violated their duty to the corporation. All damages, however, go *to the corporation*; the individual shareholders benefit only to the extent that the settlement causes their stock to rise in value.

Litigation is tremendously expensive. How can shareholders afford to sue if they are not entitled to damages? A corporation that loses a derivative suit must pay the legal fees of the victorious shareholders. Most derivative lawsuits are brought by lawyers seeking to earn these fees. (Losing shareholders are generally not required to pay the corporation's legal fees.)

There is a complication, however: **Because a derivative lawsuit is brought in the name of the corporation, shareholders must *make demand* on the corporation, unless demand would *clearly be futile*.** That is, before filing a derivative suit, the shareholders must first ask the board to bring the suit itself. Understandably, boards almost always reject this request. Shareholders rarely have luck convincing a court that the board's rejection was a mistake. Therefore, the shareholders' only real hope is to refuse to make demand on the grounds that such demand would clearly be futile either because the directors had a conflict of interest or because the decision violated the business judgment rule. In the *Brehm* case, Disney shareholders argued that demand would be futile both because Michael Eisner controlled the board of directors and because the directors had violated the business judgment rule by making an uninformed decision. However, the court was unconvinced and the derivative action failed, as many do.

Direct Lawsuits

Shareholders are permitted to sue the corporation directly only if their own rights have been harmed. If, for example, the corporation denies shareholders the right to inspect its books and records or to hold a shareholder meeting, they may sue in their own name and keep any damages awarded. The corporation is not required to pay the shareholders' legal fees; winning shareholders can use part of any damage award for this purpose.

Class Action Lawsuits

If a group of shareholders all have the same claim, they can join together and file suit as a class action, rather than suing separately. By joining forces, they can share the expense and effort of litigation. It is also far more efficient for the judicial system for one court to try one case than for tens or hundreds of courts all over the country to try the same issue. For obvious reasons, companies tend to resist class actions. In such suits, management is assailed by many small shareholders who otherwise could not afford to (or would not bother to) sue individually.

CHAPTER CONCLUSION

Corporations first became prominent in the eighteenth and nineteenth centuries as a means for businesses to raise the outside capital needed for large-scale manufacturing. Shareholders without management skills complemented managers without capital. Although this separation between management and owners makes great economic sense and has contributed significantly to the rise of the American economy, it also creates complex legal issues. How can shareholders ensure that the corporation will operate in their best interest? How can managers make tough decisions without second-guessing by shareholders? Balancing the interests of managers and shareholders is a complex problem the law has struggled to resolve, without completely satisfying either side.

CHAPTER REVIEW

1. Promoters are personally liable for contracts they sign before the corporation is formed unless the corporation and the third party agree to a novation.
2. Companies generally incorporate in the state in which they will be doing business. However, if they intend to operate in several states, they may choose to incorporate in a jurisdiction known for its favorable corporate laws, such as Delaware or Nevada.
3. A corporate charter must generally include the company's name, address, registered agent, purpose, and a description of its stock.
4. A court may, under certain circumstances, pierce the corporate veil and hold shareholders personally liable for the debts of the corporation.
5. Termination of a corporation is a three-step process requiring a shareholder vote, the filing of "Articles of Dissolution," and the winding up of the enterprise's business.
6. Officers and directors have a fiduciary duty to act in the best interests of the shareholders of the corporation.
7. The business judgment rule protects managers from liability for their decisions as long as the managers observe the duty of care and the duty of loyalty.
8. Under the duty of loyalty, managers may not take advantage of an opportunity that rightfully belongs to the corporation.
9. If managers enter into an agreement on behalf of their corporation that benefits them personally, then the business judgment rule does not apply. The managers may be liable unless the board of directors or the shareholders have first approved the transaction or it was fair to the corporation.
10. Under the duty of care, managers must make honest, informed decisions that have a rational business purpose.
11. The Williams Act regulates the activities of a bidder in a tender offer for stock in a publicly traded corporation.
12. Virtually all publicly held companies solicit proxies from their shareholders. A proxy authorizes someone else to vote in place of the shareholder.
13. Under certain circumstances, public companies must include shareholder proposals in the proxy statement.
14. A shareholder who objects to a fundamental change in the corporation can insist that her shares be bought out at fair value. This protection is referred to as "dissenters' rights."
15. Controlling shareholders have a fiduciary duty to minority shareholders.

16. A derivative lawsuit is brought by shareholders to remedy a wrong to the corporation. The suit is brought in the name of the corporation, and all proceeds of the litigation go to the corporation.

17. If a group of shareholders all have the same claim against the corporation, they can join together and file a class action, rather than suing separately.

PRACTICE TEST

1. Michael Ferns incorporated Erin Homes, Inc. to manufacture mobile homes. He issued himself a stock certificate for 100 shares for which he made no payment. He and his wife served as officers and directors of the organization, but, during the eight years of its existence, the corporation held only one meeting. Erin always had its own checking account, and all proceeds from the sales of mobile homes were deposited there. It filed federal income tax returns each year, using its own federal identification number. John and Thelma Laya paid $17,500 to purchase a mobile home from Erin, but the company never delivered it to them. The Layas sued Erin Homes and Michael Ferns, individually. Should the court "pierce the corporate veil" and hold Ferns personally liable?

2. **CPA QUESTION** A corporate stockholder is entitled to which of the following rights?

   (a) Elect officers

   (b) Receive annual dividends

   (c) Approve dissolution

   (d) Prevent corporate borrowing

3. An appraiser valued a subsidiary of Signal Co. at between $230 million and $260 million. Six months later, Burmah Oil offered to buy the subsidiary at $480 million, giving Signal only three days to respond. The board of directors accepted the offer, without obtaining an updated evaluation of the subsidiary or determining if other companies would offer a higher price. Members of the board were sophisticated, with a great deal of experience in the oil industry. A Signal Co. shareholder sued to prevent the sale. Is the Signal board protected by the business judgment rule?

4. **YOU BE THE JUDGE WRITING PROBLEM** Asher Hyman and Stephen Stahl formed a corporation named "Ampersand" to produce plays. Both men were employed by the corporation. After producing one play, Stahl decided to write *Philly's Beat*, focusing on the history of rock and roll in Philadelphia. As the play went into production, however, the two men quarreled over Hyman's repeated absences from work and the company's serious financial difficulties. Stahl resigned from Ampersand and formed another corporation to produce the play. Did the opportunity to produce *Philly's Beat* belong to Ampersand? **Argument for Stahl:** Ampersand was formed for the purpose of producing plays, not writing them. When Stahl wrote *Philly's Beat*, he was not competing against Ampersand. Furthermore, Ampersand could not afford to produce the play even if it had had the opportunity. **Argument for Hyman:** Ampersand was in the business of producing plays, and it wanted *Philly's Beat*. Ampersand was perfectly able to afford the cost of production—until Stahl resigned.

5. Shareholders lost their gamble when they bought stock of Jackpot Enterprises, Inc. Fed up with management, a shareholder asked the company to include a proposal in the proxy statement that would require the board of directors to sell or merge the company. Must Jackpot include this proposal in its proxy statement?

6. William H. Sullivan, Jr., purchased all the voting shares of the New England Patriots Football Club, Inc. (the Old Patriots). He organized a new corporation called the New Patriots Football Club, Inc. The boards of directors of the two companies agreed to merge. After the merger, the nonvoting stock

in the Old Patriots was to be exchanged for cash. Do minority shareholders of the Old Patriots have the right to prevent the merger? If so, under what theory?

7. Daniel Cowin was a minority shareholder of Bresler & Reiner, Inc., a public company that developed real estate in Washington, D.C. He alleged numerous instances of corporate mismanagement, fraud, self-dealing, and breach of fiduciary duty by the board of directors. He sought damages for the diminished value of his stock. Could Cowin bring this suit as a direct action, or must it be a derivative suit?

8. The board of directors of Finalco Group, Inc. decided to sell most of the company's assets to Western Savings and Loan Association. Shortly after the proposed sale was announced, Finalco's largest shareholder said he opposed the transaction. Does Finalco need his approval for the sale?

9. Prior to the DuPont Co.'s annual shareholder meeting, Friends of the Earth Oceanic Society submitted a proposal requiring the company to (1) accelerate its phaseout of the production of chlorofluorocarbons and halons, (2) present to shareholders a report detailing research and development efforts to find environmentally sound substitutes, and (3) report to shareholders on marketing plans to sell those substitutes. Must DuPont include this proposal in its proxy material for the annual meeting?

10. **RIGHT & WRONG** Edgar Bronfman, Jr., dropped out of high school to go to Hollywood and write songs and produce movies. Eventually, he left Hollywood to work in the family business—the Bronfmans own 36 percent of Seagram Co., a liquor and beverage conglomerate. Promoted to president of the company at the age of 32, Bronfman seized a second chance to live his dream. Seagram received 70 percent of its earnings from its 24 percent ownership of DuPont Co. Bronfman sold this stock at *less than market value* to purchase (at an inflated price) 80 percent of MCA, a movie and music company that had been a financial disaster for its prior owners. Some observers thought Bronfman had gone Hollywood, others that he had gone crazy. After the deal was announced, the price of Seagram shares fell 18 percent. Was there anything Seagram shareholders could do to prevent what to them was not a dream but a nightmare? Apart from legal issues, was Bronfman's decision ethical? What ethical obligations does he owe Seagram's shareholders?

INTERNET RESEARCH PROBLEMS

Think of an idea for a new company and prepare a corporate charter for your business. You can find a sample Delaware charter at http://www.state.de.us/corp/. For extra credit, find a sample charter for your own state.

Starting at http://www.corporateinformation.com/, find information on a company's shareholder proposals. (Type in a company name, then click on *FreeEdgar Filings*; choose *View Filings* and *Proxy Statement*.) What were these proposals about? What was the outcome of the shareholder vote? Can you find a proposal that shareholders supported?

You can find further practice problems in the Online Quiz at http://beatty.westbuslaw.com or in the Study Guide that accompanies this text.

18 CHAPTER

SECURITIES REGULATION

In 1926, America was gripped by a fever of stock market speculation. "Playing the market" became a national mania. The most engrossing news on any day's front page was the market. Up and up it soared. The cause of this psychological virus is uncertain, but the focus of the infection was the New York Stock Exchange. Between 1926 and 1929, annual volume leaped from 451 million to over 1.1 billion shares. In one year alone, the price of AT&T went from $179.50 to $335.62.

Much of this feverish trading was done on margin. Customers put down only 10 or 20 percent of a stock's purchase price and then borrowed the rest from their broker. This easy-payment plan excited the gambling instinct of unwary amateurs and professional speculators alike. By September 1929, the volume of these margin loans was equal to about half the entire public debt of the United States.

On September 4, 1929, stock prices began to soften, and for the next month they slid gently. Over the weekend of October 19, brokers sent out thousands of margin calls, asking customers to pay down loans that now exceeded the value of their stock. If customers failed to pay, brokers dumped their stock on the market, causing prices to fall further and brokers to make more margin calls. Soon there was a mad scramble of selling as prices plunged in wild disorder. Tens of thousands of investors across the country were wiped out. On Tuesday, October 29, 1929, the speculative boom completely collapsed. That day, 4 million shares were traded, a record that stood for 30 years. From the peak of the bull market in September to the debacle of October 29, over $32 billion of equity value simply vanished from the earth.

The stock market crash spawned the Great Depression—the most pervasive, persistent, and destructive economic crisis the nation has ever faced. Retail trade fell by one-half, automobile production by two-thirds, steel by three-quarters. In 1933, more businesses failed than in any other year in history. Surviving businesses responded to the crisis by cutting dividends, reducing inventories, laying off workers, slashing wages, and canceling capital investments.

Unemployment statistics were the most poignant of all. In 1932, one in every five people in the labor force was out of a job. Million of others were underemployed, working only two or three days a week for wages that could not support a family. Distress cut indiscriminately across all economic and social classes. Bankers, insurance agents, architects, and lawyers joined the throng of unemployed. Articles such as the following were common in newspapers across the land:

> *New York, Jan. 6, 1933 (AP)*—After vainly trying to get a stay of dispossession until Jan. 15 from his apartment in Brooklyn, yesterday, Peter J. Cornell, 48 years old, a former roofing contractor out of work and penniless, fell dead in the arms of his wife. A doctor gave the cause of his death as heart disease, and the police said it had at least partly been caused by the bitter disappointment of a long day's fruitless attempt to prevent himself and his family being put out on the streets.[1]

INTRODUCTION

At the time of the great stock market crash, there was no federal securities law, only state law. Congress recognized that the country needed a national securities system if it was to avoid another such catastrophe. In 1933, Congress passed the Securities Act of 1933 (1933 Act) to regulate the issuance of new securities. The next year, it passed the Securities Exchange Act of 1934 (1934 Act) to regulate companies with publicly traded securities. The 1934 Act also established the Securities and Exchange Commission (SEC), the regulatory agency that oversees the securities industry.

THE SECURITIES AND EXCHANGE COMMISSION

The SEC is generally well regarded by those it regulates and has a reputation for hiring lawyers who are both intelligent and practical. The SEC creates law in three different ways:

[1] The material in this section is adapted from Cabell Phillips, *From the Crash to the Blitz* (Toronto: Macmillan, 1969).

- **Rules.** The securities statutes are often little more than general guides. Through its rules, the SEC fills in the crucial details.
- **Releases.** These are informal pronouncements from the SEC on current issues. Releases often operate as two-way communication. When the SEC issues a release to announce a proposed change in the rules, it also asks for comments on the proposal.
- **No-Action Letters.** Anyone who is in doubt about whether a particular transaction complies with the securities laws can ask the SEC directly. The response is called a no-action letter because it states that "the staff will recommend that the Commission take no action" if the transaction is done in a specified manner.

In addition to creating laws, the SEC has the power to enforce them. It can bring **cease and desist** orders against those who violate the securities laws, and it can also levy fines or confiscate profits from illegal transactions. Those accused of wrongdoing can appeal these sanctions to the courts. The SEC does not have the authority to bring a criminal action; it refers criminal cases to the Justice Department.

WHAT IS A SECURITY?

Both the 1933 and the 1934 Acts regulate securities. The official definition of a security includes a note, stock, treasury stock, bond, debenture, evidence of indebtedness, certificate of interest or participation in any profit-sharing agreement, collateral-trust certificate, preorganization certificate or subscription, and 15 other equivalents. Courts have interpreted this definition to mean that **a security is any transaction in which the buyer (1) invests money in a common enterprise and (2) expects to earn a profit predominantly from the efforts of others.**

This definition covers investments that are not necessarily called *securities.* For example, they may be called orange trees. W. J. Howey Co. owned large citrus groves in Florida. It sold these trees to investors, most of whom were from out of state and knew nothing about farming. Purchasers were expected to hire someone to take care of their trees. Someone like Howey-in-the-Hills, Inc., a related company that just happened to be in the service business. Customers were free to hire any service company, but 85 percent of the acreage was covered by service contracts with Howey-in-the-Hills. The court held that Howey was selling a security (no matter how orange or tart), because the purchaser was investing in a common enterprise (the orange grove) expecting to earn a profit from Howey's farmwork.

Other courts have interpreted the term "security" to include animal breeding arrangements (chinchillas, silver foxes, or beavers, take your pick); condominium purchases in which the developer promises the owner a certain level of income from rentals; and even investments in whiskey. Life Partners was a company that aimed to help AIDS patients. Was it selling a security?

SEC v. LIFE PARTNERS, INC.
87 F.3d 536, 1996 U.S. App. LEXIS 16117
United States Court of Appeals for the District of Columbia Circuit, 1996

Facts: Life Partners, Inc. (LPI) bought life insurance policies from AIDS victims at a discount from face value. It then repackaged these policies and sold them to investors who recovered the full face value of the policy after the patient died. LPI evaluated the patient's medical condition, reviewed his insurance policy, negotiated the purchase price, and prepared the legal documents. Investors could pay as little as $650 and buy as little as 3 percent of the benefits of a policy. Once an investor acquired an interest in a policy, she could avail herself of LPI's ongoing administrative services, which included monitoring the patient's health, assuring that the policy did not lapse, and arranging for resale of the investor's interest if requested.

Although the investment might sound macabre, it offered a valuable benefit to the terminally ill patient who was able to secure much needed income in the final years of life when employment was unlikely and medical bills were overwhelming. This arrangement was known as a "viatical settlement" after the ecclesiastical term "viaticum" (communion given to the dying). The viatical settlement industry emerged during the late 1980s as a result of the AIDS crisis and grew rapidly, from $5 million in life insurance policies in 1989 to roughly $200 million in 1995. LPI was the largest viatical settlement organizer in the country, accounting for approximately one-half of the total settlement volume in 1994. The SEC sued LPI, alleging that it was selling a security without registration.

You be the Judge: Was Life Partners selling a security?

Argument for the SEC: LPI purchases policies from dying patients. The company then pools these policies, sells fractional interests to investors, and pays off investors when the patients die. The investors play no role, other than writing a check. These viatical settlements are clearly a common enterprise in which investors rely completely on the efforts of LPI.

Argument for LPI: The securities laws do not apply to LPI's efforts, which take place *before* the investors make their purchase. At that point, the investors can evaluate LPI for themselves. After the purchase, profitability is determined by the timing of the patient's death, which is outside LPI's control (we hope). After the investment, LPI plays only a clerical role; thus the investors are not earning a profit predominantly from its efforts.

SECURITIES ACT OF 1933

The 1933 Act requires that, before offering or selling securities, the issuer must register the securities with the SEC, unless the securities qualify for an exemption. An issuer is the company that issues the stock. Registering securities with the SEC in a public offering is a major undertaking, but the 1933 Act exempts some securities and also some particular types of transactions from the full-blown registration requirements of a public offering.

It is also important to remember that **when an issuer registers securities, the SEC does not investigate the quality of the offering.** Permission from the SEC to sell securities does not mean that the company has a good product or will be successful. SEC approval simply means that, on the surface, the company has answered all relevant questions about itself and its major products. The guiding principle of the federal securities laws is that investors can make a reasoned decision on whether to buy or sell securities if they have full and accurate information about a company and the security it is selling. For example, the

Green Bay Packers football team sold an offering of stock to finance stadium improvements. The prospectus admitted:

> IT IS VIRTUALLY IMPOSSIBLE that any investor will ever make a profit on the stock purchase. The company will pay no dividends, and the shares cannot be sold.

This does not sound like a stock you want in your children's college fund; on the other hand, the SEC will not prevent Green Bay from selling it, or you from buying it, as long as you understand what the risks are.

One last point: **the 1933 Act prohibits fraud in *any* securities transaction.** Anyone who issues fraudulent securities is in violation of the 1933 Act, whether or not the securities are registered. Both the SEC and any purchasers of the stock can sue the issuer.

Companies must deliver certain documents to investors and also file them with the SEC. Most companies now make their required SEC filings electronically, using the EDGAR (Electronic Data Gathering, Analysis, and Retrieval) system. Once filed with the SEC, this information is available online (at http://www.sec.gov). Each day, Web surfers "hit" EDGAR half a million times and download 2.5 million pages.

Companies can fulfill their SEC filing requirements online with EDGAR, but delivering documents to investors electronically is more difficult because computer literacy and availability among investors vary widely. The SEC does permit issuers to communicate electronically with investors, provided that the following standards are met:

- *Consent.* Although many investors have computers, an issuer cannot assume that all do, or that all want to receive data this way. Therefore, an electronic document is only valid if the investor agrees to receive information in this form.
- *Notice.* A company cannot simply post information on its Internet Web site, because investors will not necessarily know it is there. The issuer must notify investors, via e-mail or snail mail, that information is available.
- *Access.* The recipients must have access to the information for a reasonable period of time and be able to download or print it. The investor can always request the paper version of a document, even after consenting to electronic delivery.

Companies communicate with investors via the Internet, and so does the SEC. Omnigene Diagnostics, Inc. was touted on various online investment bulletin boards, so when the SEC halted trading in this dubious stock, it announced the action on America Online. SEC enforcement officials also regularly surf the Net, looking for illegal activity.

GENERAL EXEMPTION

Before offering securities for sale, the issuer must determine whether they are exempt from registration under the 1933 Act. Typically, exemptions are based on two factors: the type of security and the type of transaction. However, the National Securities Markets Improvement Act of 1996 gave the SEC new authority under both the 1933 and the 1934 Acts to grant exemptions that are "in the public interest" and "consistent with the protection of investors."

EXEMPT SECURITIES

The 1933 Act exempts some types of securities from registration because they (1) are inherently low risk, (2) are regulated by other statutes, or (3) are not really investments. The following securities are exempt from registration:

- **Government securities**, which include any security issued or guaranteed by federal or state government
- **Bank securities**, which include any security issued or guaranteed by a bank
- **Short-term notes**, which are high-quality negotiable notes or drafts that are due within nine months of issuance and are not sold to the general public
- **Nonprofit issues**, which include any security issued by a nonprofit religious, educational, or charitable organization
- **Insurance policies and annuity contracts**, which are governed by insurance regulations[2]

EXEMPT TRANSACTIONS

Section 4(2) of the 1933 Act exempts from registration "transactions by an issuer not involving any public offering." These are simple words to define a complex problem. In effect, the 1933 Act says that an issuer is not required to register securities that are sold in a private offering, that is, an offering with only a few investors or a relatively small amount of money involved. In private offerings, the full-blown disclosure of a public offering is neither necessary nor appropriate. For instance, a group of sophisticated investors who know an industry well do not need full disclosure. If the amount at stake is less than $10 million or $15 million, it would not make economic sense for the issuer to incur the heavy expense of a public offering.

There is an important distinction between exempt *securities* and exempt *transactions*. Exempt *securities* are always exempt, throughout their lives, no matter how many times they are sold. Stock sold in an exempt *transaction* is exempt only that one time, not necessarily in any subsequent sale. Suppose that Country Bank sells stock to the public. Under the 1933 Act, the bank is never required to register these securities, no matter how many times they are sold. On the other hand, suppose that Tumbleweed, Inc., a quilt maker, sells $5 million worth of stock in a private offering that is exempt from registration. Shamika buys 100 shares of this stock. Seven years later, the company decides to sell stock in a public offering that must be registered. As part of this public offering, Shamika sells her 100 shares. This time, the shares must be registered because they are being sold in a *public offering*.

---

[2] Life Partners was selling the rights to already existing policies, not the policies themselves. The insurance companies that issued the policies initially were not required to register them.

Most small companies use private, not public, offerings to raise capital. There are three different types of private offerings—intrastate, Regulation D, and Regulation A—each with its own set of rules.

INTRASTATE OFFERING EXEMPTION

Under SEC Rule 147, an issuer is not required to register securities that are offered and sold only to residents of the state in which the issuer is incorporated and does business. This exemption was designed to provide local financing for local businesses. To qualify under Rule 147, 80 percent of the issuer's revenues and assets must be in-state, and it must also intend to spend 80 percent of the offering's proceeds in-state. Neither the issuer nor any purchaser can sell the securities outside the state for nine months after the offering.

Rule 147 is a **safe harbor**—if an issuer totally complies with it, the offering definitely qualifies as intrastate. But even if the issuer does not comply absolutely with the rule, the SEC or the courts may still consider the offering to be intrastate; however, the issuer cannot be sure in advance how the decision will come out. Sonic was a Utah corporation that sold stock to Utah residents. *Seven* months later, the company sold stock to an Illinois company. Although Sonic violated Rule 147 by making the second sale too early, the court held that the company had nonetheless qualified for an intrastate offering because it had not intended, at the time of the original offering, to sell stock outside Utah.[3] Although Sonic had not totally complied with Rule 147, it had come close enough to avoid liability. A safe harbor is safer, but a voyage outside its boundaries does not necessarily end in disaster.

REGULATION D

Three different types of private offerings can be made under Regulation D (often referred to as Reg D) under Rules 504, 505, and 506.

Rule 504. Under this rule, a company:

- May sell up to $1 million in securities during each 12-month period
- May advertise and sell the stock to an unlimited number of investors, and
- Is not required to register with the SEC.

Furthermore, the stock is not restricted, which means that the purchaser can resell it without registration. Essentially, the SEC does not want to get involved in such small offerings (except in the case of fraud, in which it is always interested). Some observers question the SEC's hands-off approach to these small offerings—$1 million may not be much to a company, but it can mean a great deal to individual investors.

Rule 505. This rule permits a company to sell up to $5 million of stock during each 12-month period, subject to the following restrictions:

---

[3] *Busch v. Carpenter*, 827 F.2d 653, 1987 U.S. App. LEXIS 11034 (10th Cir. 1987).

- The company may not advertise the stock publicly. Therefore, a company generally cannot place offering materials on its Web site, although the SEC has been working with companies to develop Web sites with password protection that enable qualified investors to view offering documents online.
- The issuer can sell to as many *accredited investors* as it wants, but is limited to only 35 *unaccredited investors*. **Accredited investors** are institutions (such as banks and insurance companies) or wealthy individuals (with a net worth of more than $1 million or an annual income of more than $200,000).
- The company need not provide information to accredited investors but must make some disclosure to unaccredited investors. This requirement provides issuers with a serious incentive to avoid unaccredited investors because the disclosure requirements, although less demanding than for a public offering, are nonetheless burdensome.
- Stock purchased under this rule is restricted, which means it must be purchased for investment purposes. As a general rule, the buyer cannot resell the security, either publicly or privately, for one year.

Rule 506. This rule is similar to Rule 505. The differences are that:

- There is no limit on the amount of stock a company can sell.
- If an unaccredited purchaser is unsophisticated, he must have a **purchaser representative** to help him evaluate the investment. Is an *unsophisticated* investor someone who does not care for opera? No, it is someone who is unable to assess the risks of the offering himself.

The following table sets out the menu of choices under Reg D:

	Maximum Value of Securities Sold in a 12-Month Period	Maximum Number of Investors	Is Disclosure Required?	Is Public Advertising Permitted?	Are Securities Restricted?
Rule 504	$1 million	No limit	No	Yes	No
Rule 505	$5 million	No limit on accredited investors; no more than 35 unaccredited investors	Only for unaccredited investors	No	Yes
Rule 506	No limit	No limit on accredited investors; no more than 35 unaccredited investors, who must either be sophisticated or have a purchaser representative	Only for unaccredited investors	No	Yes

REGULATION A

Although an offering under Regulation A is *called* a private offering, it really is a small public offering. **Reg A permits an issuer to sell $5 million of securities publicly in any 12-month period.** The issuer must give each purchaser an offering circular that provides the same disclosure required for unaccredited investors under Reg D. The following table compares a public offering, Reg A, and Reg D:

	Public Offering	Regulation A	Regulation D
Maximum Value of Securities Sold	No limit	$5 million	$1 million, $5 million, or no limit, depending on the rule
Public Solicitation of Purchasers	Permitted	Permitted	Permitted only under Rule 504
Suitability Requirements for Purchasers	No requirements	No requirements	Must determine if investors are accredited or sophisticated (no requirement for Rule 504)
Disclosure Requirements	Elaborate registration statement, audited financials	Offering circular that is less detailed than a registration statement	Rule 504: none Rules 505 and 506: none for accredited investors, the same requirements as Reg A for unaccredited investors
Resale of Securities	Permitted	Permitted	Permitted under Rule 504, otherwise not permitted for one year
Number of Offerings in 1997	5,890	111	2,528

DIRECT PUBLIC OFFERINGS

Traditionally, a small company either sold stock to people it knew or hired an investment banker to place the securities. But now, as many as one-third of the companies trying to raise capital in the United States for the first time do a direct public offering (DPO) instead of going through Wall Street. The catch is that the companies have to sell the stock themselves. They make these offerings under Reg A or Rule 504 because both permit public offerings of stock without registration under the 1933 Act. Here is how some companies do it:

In 1995, Spring Street Brewery, a New York microbrewery, became the first company to conduct an offering on the Internet. It established a home page that allowed potential investors to examine and download its offering documents. In the end, it raised $1.6 million.

Thanksgiving Coffee Co. of Fort Bragg, California, used both cybertechnology and the old-fashioned face-to-face approach. It had originally planned simply to sell to its loyal customer base. "You think that everybody who knows about you will line up around the block to buy stock, but you have to put the offering in front of potential investors' faces seven times to get them to take action," says Thanksgiving general manager Rick Moon. He did just that. He put offering notices on coffee-bean bags; he hung announcements on bean dispensers. Vendors got the advertisements, as did mail-order customers. Information about the stock sale appeared on the company's Web site, in its catalog, and in advertisements in targeted magazines. Anyone who called about the stock got regular updates on the offering. In the end, the huge effort paid off. By the time the offering closed, Thanksgiving Coffee had sold 20 percent of its stock for $1.25 million.[4]

PUBLIC OFFERINGS

When a company wishes to raise significant amounts of capital from a large number of people, it is time for a public offering. A company's first public sale of securities is called an **initial public offering** or an **IPO**. Here is one company's experience with an IPO.

Shortly after graduating from the Massachusetts Institute of Technology, Daniel Schwinn and Frank Slaughter founded Shiva Corp. (pronounced SHE-va) in Burlington, Massachusetts. (Information about the company is available at http://www.Shiva.com.) The company makes hardware and software that allow personal computers to tie directly into a corporate network from outside the office. Although within a decade sales had reached $42 million and net income was $2.7 million, the company was constantly strapped for cash to fund expansion. Its two founders began thinking about a public offering.

UNDERWRITING

As we have seen, companies can sell stock directly to the public, but they primarily do so if the amounts involved are small. Shiva sought to raise more than $20 million, so it decided to hire an investment bank to serve as underwriter. In a **firm commitment** underwriting, the underwriter buys the stock from the issuer and resells it to the public. The underwriter bears the risk that the stock may sell at a lower price than expected. In a **best efforts** underwriting, the underwriter does not buy the stock but instead acts as the company's agent in selling it. If the stock sells at a low price, the company, not the underwriter, is the loser.

In underwriting, as in life, timing is everything. As it happened, just when Shiva hoped to complete its offering, Wall Street's interest in the high-tech sector suddenly cooled. Investment bankers offered the company only $6 a share for its stock. Shiva decided to wait. Within three months, the market in high-tech stocks picked up again. The company's president, Frank Ingari, and its chief financial officer, Cynthia Deysher, went to New York to sign on with the

---

[4] Stephanie Gruner, "When Mom & Pop Go Public," *INC.*, Dec. 1996, p. 66. Republished with permission of INC. Magazine; permission conveyed through the Copyright Clearance Center, Inc.

investment bank Goldman Sachs. Shiva agreed to sell Goldman 2.4 million shares at a tentative price of $12 per share.

REGISTRATION STATEMENT

The **registration statement** has two purposes: to notify the SEC that a sale of securities is pending and to disclose information to prospective purchasers. The registration statement must include detailed information about the issuer and its business, a description of the stock, the proposed use of the proceeds from the offering, audited balance sheets for two years, and audited income statements for the three years before that. Preparing a registration statement is neither quick—it typically takes two to three months—nor inexpensive. Shiva spent $900,000 on audits and other expenses.

Within a month of hiring an investment bank, Shiva filed its *preliminary* draft of the registration statement with the SEC. This preliminary draft is called a **red herring** because it contains a notice in red ink warning that the securities cannot yet be sold.[5] The SEC typically spends between 30 and 100 days reviewing this preliminary draft of the registration statement. Remember that the Commission does not assess the value of the stock or the merit of the investment. Its role is to ensure that the company has disclosed enough to enable investors to make an informed decision.

PROSPECTUS

Typically, buyers never see the registration statement; they are given the **prospectus** instead. In the SEC filing, the prospectus is a pull-out section in the middle of the registration statement. The prospectus includes all of the important disclosures about the company, while the registration statement includes additional information that is of interest to the SEC but not to the typical investor, such as the names and addresses of the lawyers for the issuer and underwriter. All investors must receive a copy of the prospectus before purchasing the stock.

SALES EFFORT

The SEC closely regulates an issuer's sales effort. Its goal is to prevent a company from hyping a stock before the prospectus is available to investors.

Pre-Filing Period. This is the time before the registration statement is filed. It is also known as the **quiet period**. The SEC permits only the merest of sales effort—an announcement that the offering will be made, but no mention of the price or the underwriter. Even a speech by a company officer, press releases, or postings on the company's Web site praising the company can be considered an illegal sales effort during this period.

Waiting Period. This is the time after the registration statement has been filed but before the SEC has approved it. The underwriter can publish a **tombstone**

---

[5] The term "red herring" is a bit of a joke because, outside securities offerings, it means a false clue.

ad, that is, a simple, unadorned announcement of the offering that includes the amount and type of security, the name of the underwriter, and the price of stock. You can see many of these ads in the *The Wall Street Journal* and also on company Web sites. During the waiting period, the underwriter may distribute the preliminary prospectus. It can also solicit offers, but cannot make sales. The underwriter uses this period to estimate market demand for the stock. It **makes book**, meaning that it talks with traders to determine how many shares it can sell and at what price. It also takes **indications of interest** from traders but makes no sales.

During the waiting period, Goldman and Shiva began the **road show**—the cross-country road trip to convince traders that Shiva was a stock their clients should buy. Ingari and Schwinn spent a grueling two weeks visiting 16 cities. At each stop, they made the same impassioned pitch to such influential traders as Fidelity Investments, Wellington Management, Janus, and Alliance Capital. "We felt like door-to-door salesmen," Ingari said. So strong was the response that in the second week of the road show, Goldman suggested raising the price to $15 a share, from $12, and selling an additional 360,000 shares. When the road show ended, orders for the stock exceeded the number of shares by a factor of 30. That the IPO would be hot was certain. But how hot?

GOING EFFECTIVE

Once its review of the preliminary registration statement is complete, the SEC sends the issuer a **comment letter**, listing changes that must be made to the registration statement. An issuer almost always amends the registration statement at least once, and sometimes more than once. After the SEC has approved a final registration statement (which includes, of course, the final prospectus), the issuer then decides on a date to **go effective**, that is, to begin selling the stock. One last step remained: Goldman and Shiva had to agree on an opening price. They decided to raise the price from $12 to $15 per share. Shiva would sell to Goldman at $13.95 per share, and Goldman, in turn, would sell it on the market at $15.

The night before the sale, Shiva executives and the underwriters met for dinner and made bets about the next day's closing price and trading volume. No one guessed nearly high enough. As soon as Goldman sold at $15, the price zoomed to $30.50. The stock closed that day at $31.50 per share. At Goldman, there were hugs, tears of joy, and champagne toasts. But founders Schwinn and Slaughter, with their stock suddenly worth $30 million each, suffered chest pains. And Ingari, the president and chief executive, felt even worse. As the value of his stake in Shiva soared past $14 million, he fled to the men's room. "I was ready to throw up, I was sweating badly, and I could barely stand up. When I looked in the mirror, I had blood coming out of my nose."

In the end, Shiva raised $28 million that day, and its founders and other insiders, who sold about 700,000 shares, took home another $10 million. Goldman earned almost $3 million, or 7 percent of the proceeds. Did Goldman price the offering too low? Pricing an IPO is more art than science. Everyone would like the price to rise gently. At all cost, however, the underwriter wishes to avoid a disaster in which the stock price collapses, leaving it with a large loss. Of course, the underwriter looks bad if the company sells stock for a lot less than it is worth. Shares that Goldman sold in the morning for $15 were trading for twice that amount later in the day. Half of the initial worth of Shiva's stock, or about $43 million, went into the pockets of early buyers who "flipped" the stock, selling it immediately to other investors. Since that opening day, the stock price has climbed as high as $85 per share. In hindsight, Goldman should have priced the stock higher, but it is not clear that it or anyone else could reasonably have predicted the market's reaction.

Frank Slaughter went home after the IPO and spent a day "scrubbing toilets—to retain some humility." He had come through one of the most unnerving, and quintessential, rites of passage of the American capitalist system. The company obtained money to develop new products and build factories. The public got a chance to buy in. And the company's founders, and other key insiders, found a way to cash out.[6]

In its transition to a market economy, Russia is developing a securities market. To date, this market has tended to be underregulated and overhyped. The Russian government began by issuing privatization vouchers to all its citizens. These vouchers could be used to invest in newly privatized companies. Investment options varied widely. At a "privatization festival" in a Moscow exhibition hall, young men and women with neat business suits and alarmingly friendly smiles waved photocopies of their factories' business plans. Shares in these enterprises have since turned out to be worthless.

Because investing in legitimate enterprises proved so difficult, millions of Russians were attracted to the MMM Joint Stock Co. Its shareholders paid with cash instead of vouchers, but they could double their investment in a month. MMM's massive advertising campaign (evidently where most of its investors' money went) worked wonders, too. After *Newsweek* ran a story describing MMM as a "fast-growing" company, TV ads claimed that "according to analysts of the American magazine *Newsweek* MMM Invest is the most promising company in Russia."

Shortly thereafter, Russian authorities called MMM a scam and arrested Sergei Mavrodi, its president. Angry shareholders carried banners reading "Hands Off Mavrodi." Meanwhile, MMM devalued its shares by more than 99 percent in a single day. The Russian government indicated that it did not intend to bail shareholders out. That left Russian investors on their own with MMM, a company that once said it could not turn in its first-quarter balance sheets because the only copy was stolen off a bus on the way to the Finance Ministry.[7]

SALES OF RESTRICTED SECURITIES

After the public offering, Shiva insiders still owned a substantial block of stock. Between them, Schwinn, Slaughter, and Ingari held stock or options for 2.8 million shares. With the stock trading as high as $85 per share, on paper they were

---

[6] The information about Shiva Corp. is from Glenn Rifkin, "Anatomy of a Highflying IPO, Nosebleeds and All," *The New York Times*, Feb. 19, 1995, p. F7.

[7] Carrol Bogert, Betsy McKay, and Dorinda Elliott, "Our Life as Ivan Investor," *Newsweek*, Aug. 15, 1994, p. 61. © 1994 Newsweek, Inc. All rights reserved. Reprinted by permission.

worth $238 million, but they could not actually sell their stock, at least not right away. **Rule 144 limits the resale of two types of securities: control securities and restricted securities.**

A **control security** is stock held by any shareholder who owns more than 10 percent of a class of stock or by any officer or director. In any three-month period, such an insider can sell only an amount of stock equal to the average weekly trading volume for the prior four weeks or 1 percent of the number of shares outstanding, whichever is greater. Shiva had 9,589,000 shares outstanding and an (unusually high) average weekly trading volume of roughly 938,000. A Shiva insider could sell at most 938,000 shares during each three-month period. In a company with a more typical trading volume, the number might be a tenth of that. The purpose of this rule is to protect other investors from precipitous declines in stock price. If company insiders sold all of their stock in one day, the price would plunge, causing losses to the other shareholders.

For owners of restricted securities, the rules are more complex. A *restricted security* is any stock purchased in a private offering (such as Regulation D). These securities may not be sold within one year of the offering. After the first year, restricted securities can be sold as long as the sale does not exceed the limitations that apply to control stock: the greater of the average weekly trading volume for the prior four weeks or 1 percent of the number of shares outstanding. After two years, restricted securities can be sold freely, unless they are also control securities, in which case those restrictions still apply. Exhibit 18.1 illustrates the sale of restricted securities under Rule 144.

LIABILITY

LIABILITY FOR UNREGISTERED SECURITIES

Section 12(a)(1) of the 1933 Act imposes liability on anyone who sells a security that is not registered and not exempt. The purchaser of the security can demand rescission—a return of his money in exchange for the stock—or, if he no longer owns the stock, he can ask for damages.

Exhibit 18.1
The Sale of Restricted Securities under Rule 144

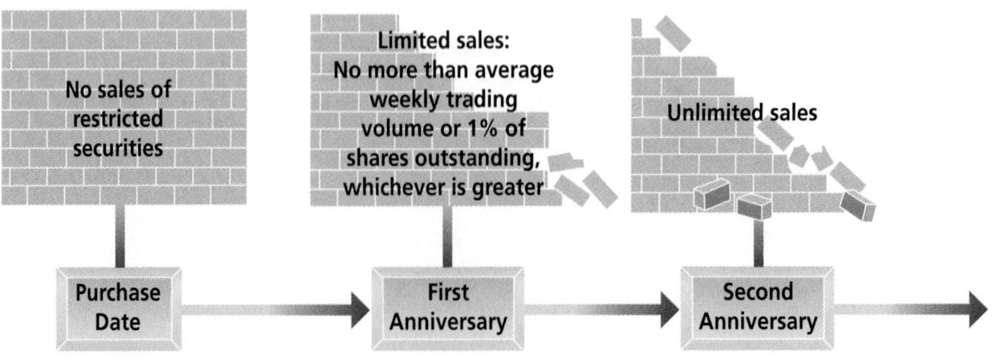

FRAUD

Under §12(a)(2) of the 1933 Act, the seller of a security is liable for making any material misstatement or omission, either oral or written, in connection with the offer or sale of a security. This provision applies to both *public* and *private* offerings if there is some use of interstate commerce, such as the mails, telephone (even for an intrastate call), or check (which clears). It is difficult to imagine a securities transaction that does not involve interstate commerce. The SEC provides information on how to invest wisely and avoid securities fraud at http://www.sec.gov/invkhome.htm. The North American Securities Association also offers advice on "how to spot a con artist" and popular securities scams (http://www/nasaa.org/investoredu). You can obtain disciplinary reports on securities firms or individual brokers at http://www.nasdr.com. To report fraud, contact the SEC at its Complaint Center (http://www.sec.gov/enforce/comctr.htm) or via e-mail at enforcement@sec.gov.

CRIMINAL LIABILITY

Under §24 of the 1933 Act, the Justice Department can prosecute anyone who willfully violates the Act. The maximum penalty is five years' imprisonment and a $10,000 fine.

LIABILITY FOR THE REGISTRATION STATEMENT

Section 11 of the 1933 Act establishes the penalties for any errors in a registration statement. **If a final registration statement contains a material misstatement or omission, the purchaser of the security can recover from everyone who signed the registration statement.** This list of signatories includes the issuer, its directors, and chief officers; experts (such as auditors, engineers, or lawyers); and the underwriters. Everyone who signed the registration statement is jointly and severally liable for any error, except the experts, who are liable only for misstatements in the part of the registration statement for which they were responsible.[8] Thus an auditor is liable for misstatements in the financials but not, say, for omissions about the CEO's criminal past.

To prevail under §11, the plaintiff need only prove that there was a material misstatement or omission and that she lost money. **Material** means important enough to affect an investor's decision. The plaintiff does not have to prove that she relied on (or even *read*) the registration statement, that she bought the stock from the issuer, or that the defendant was negligent. The plaintiff can recover the difference between what she paid for the stock and its value on the date of the lawsuit. Suppose that Pet Detective, Inc. does an IPO. A week later, Ace Investora buys 1,000 shares at $10 a share. He knows nothing about the company, but he likes the name. This stock turns out to be a dog—Pet Detective has only two agencies, not the 200 stated in the registration statement. When the stock falls to 10 cents, Investora can sue under §11 for $9,900.

All is not hopeless, however, for those who have signed the registration statement. If the statement contains a material misstatement or omission, the

[8] Joint and several liability is discussed in Chapter 16.

company is liable and has no defense. But everyone else who signed the registration statement can avoid liability by showing that he investigated the registration statement as thoroughly as a "prudent person in the management of his own property." This investigation is called **due diligence**. Its importance cannot be overstated. The SEC does not conduct its own investigation to ensure that the registration statement is accurate. It can only ensure that, on the surface, the issuer has supplied all relevant information. If an issuer chooses to lie, the SEC has no way of knowing. It is the job of the underwriters to check the accuracy of the filing. Thus underwriters typically spend two or three weeks visiting the company, reading all its corporate documents (including minutes back to the beginning), and calling its bankers, customers, suppliers, and competitors to ensure that the registration statement is accurate and no skeletons have been overlooked.

When §11 was first passed, investment bankers were outraged. Some predicted that this liability provision would cause capital in America to dry up, that grass would grow on Wall Street. In fact, the first case under §11 arose 35 years and 27,000 registration statements later. In this case—*Escott v. Barchris Construction Corp.*—the registration statement was seriously flawed.[9] The underwriter failed to read the minutes of the executive committee meetings that revealed the company to be in serious financial condition. Much of the company's alleged backlog of orders was to nonexistent corporations. Proceeds of the offering were earmarked to pay off debt, not to buy new plant and equipment, as the registration statement had indicated. The company's directors, underwriters, and underwriters' counsel were liable.

Although *Barchris* still strikes fear in the hearts of underwriters, some commentators now argue that underwriters do not take their due diligence obligations seriously enough. Was there adequate disclosure in the following case?

IN RE DONALD J. TRUMP CASINO SECURITIES LITIGATION

7 F.3d 357, 1993 U.S. App. LEXIS 26691
United States Court of Appeals for the Third Circuit, 1993

Facts: Donald J. Trump formed the Taj Mahal Associates Limited Partnership, which sold $675 million in bonds to the public. The partnership used the proceeds to purchase and complete construction on the Taj Mahal, a casino/hotel occupying 17 acres of land on the boardwalk in Atlantic City, New Jersey. The Taj Mahal was widely touted as Atlantic City's largest and most lavish casino resort. After the partnership filed for bankruptcy, the purchasers of the bonds filed suit, alleging that the bond prospectus contained material misstatements and omissions.

Issue: Did the Taj Mahal prospectus contain material omissions or misstatements?

Excerpts from Judge Becker's Decision: The plaintiffs allege that the prospectus contained material misrepresentations. Their principal claim is that the defendants had neither an honest belief in nor a reasonable basis for one statement in the prospectus: "The Partnership believes that funds generated from the operation of the Taj Mahal will be sufficient to cover all of its debt service (interest and principal)."

[9] 283 F. Supp. 643, 1968 U.S. Dist. LEXIS 3853 (S.D.N.Y. 1968).

The prospectus at issue contained an abundance of warnings and cautionary language which bore directly on the prospective financial success of the Taj Mahal and on the Partnership's ability to repay the bonds. [N]o reasonable investor could believe anything but that the Taj Mahal bonds represented a rather risky, speculative investment which might yield a high rate of return, but which alternatively might result in no return or even a loss. For example, [the prospectus] stated:

> The Taj Mahal has not been completed and, accordingly, has no operating history. The Taj Mahal will be the largest casino/hotel complex in Atlantic City, with approximately twice the room capacity and casino space of many of the existing casino/hotels in Atlantic City. [No] other casino/hotel operator has had experience operating a complex the size of the Taj Mahal in Atlantic City. Consequently, no assurance can be given that, once opened, the Taj Mahal will be profitable or that it will generate cash flow sufficient to provide for the payment of the debt service.

The prospectus additionally reported that there were risks of delay in the construction of the Taj Mahal and a risk that the casino might not receive the numerous essential licenses and permits from the state regulatory authorities.

In this case the Partnership did not bury the warnings about risks amidst the bulk of the prospectus. Indeed, it was the allegedly misleading statement which was buried amidst the cautionary language. Moreover, an investor would have read the sentence immediately following the challenged statement, which cautioned: "no assurance can be given, however, that actual operating results will meet the Partnership's expectations."

Within this broad context the statement at issue was, at worst, harmless. In other words, cautionary language, if sufficient, renders the alleged omissions or misrepresentations immaterial as a matter of law. Of course, a vague or blanket (boilerplate) disclaimer which merely warns the reader that the investment has risks will ordinarily be inadequate to prevent misinformation. To suffice, the cautionary statements must be substantive and tailored to the specific future projections, estimates or opinions in the prospectus which the plaintiffs challenge.

[W]e think it clear that the accompanying warnings and cautionary language served to negate any potentially misleading effect that the prospectus' statement about the Partnership's belief in its ability to repay the bonds would have on a reasonable investor.

Stuart Wechsler, a New York lawyer representing the bondholders, bemoaned this decision as "another nail in the coffin of prospectus disclosure. The prospectus is becoming a useless document."[10] Is Mr. Wechsler's interpretation of this case correct?

SECURITIES EXCHANGE ACT OF 1934

Most buyers do not purchase new securities from the issuer in an initial public offering. Rather they buy stock that is publicly traded in the open market. This stock is, in a sense, *secondhand* because others, perhaps many others, have already owned it. The purpose of the 1934 Act is to maintain the integrity of this secondary market.

---

[10] Edward Felsenthal, "Prospectus Liability," *The Wall Street Journal*, Oct. 18, 1993, p. B8.

GENERAL PROVISIONS OF THE 1934 ACT

REGISTRATION REQUIREMENTS

As we have seen, the 1933 Act requires an issuer to register securities before selling them. That is a onetime effort for the company. The 1933 Act does not require the issuer to provide shareholders with any additional information in later years. Suppose that an automobile company registered and sold securities for the first time in 1946. Purchasers of those securities knew a lot about the firm—in 1946. But how can current investors assess the company? The 1934 Act plugs this hole. It requires issuers with publicly traded stock to continue to make information available to the public so that current—and potential—shareholders can evaluate the company. It is often said that the 1933 Act registers securities, and the 1934 Act registers companies.

Under the 1934 Act, an issuer must register with the SEC if (1) it completes a public offering under the 1933 Act, or (2) its securities are traded on a national exchange (such as the New York Stock Exchange), or (3) it has at least 500 shareholders and total assets that exceed $10 million. A company can *de*register if its number of shareholders falls below 300 or if it has fewer than 500 shareholders and assets of less than $10 million.

DISCLOSURE REQUIREMENTS—SECTION 13

Like the 1933 Act, the 1934 Act focuses on disclosure. The difference is that the 1933 Act requires onetime disclosure when a company sells stock to the public. The 1934 Act requires *ongoing*, regular disclosure for any company with a class of stock that is publicly traded. Companies that are required to register under the 1934 Act are called **reporting companies**. There are currently more than 15,000 reporting companies.

Section 13 requires reporting companies to file the following documents:

- An initial, detailed information statement when the company first registers (similar to the filing required under the 1933 Act)
- Annual reports on Form 10-K, containing audited financial statements, a detailed analysis of the company's performance, and information about officers and directors
- Quarterly reports on Form 10-Q, which are less detailed than 10-Ks and contain unaudited financials
- Form 8-Ks to report any significant developments, such as bankruptcy, a change in control, a purchase or sale of significant assets, the resignation of a director as a result of a policy dispute, or a change in auditing firms

Recall that under the 1933 Act a prospectus must be given to investors. Under the 1934 Act, a reporting company is only required to send the annual report to shareholders. It files the other reports with the SEC; these documents are a matter of public record and are available to anyone, shareholder or not, who goes in person to an SEC public reading room or who accesses SEC records through EDGAR, its online system. Also, companies often place these reports on their Internet Web sites.

Proxy Requirements—Section 14

As discussed in Chapter 17, most shareholders of public corporations do not attend annual shareholder meetings. Instead, the company solicits their proxies, permitting them to vote by mail rather than in person. If a company solicits proxies, it is required to supply shareholders with a proxy statement that is intended to give them enough information to make informed decisions about the company. The proxy statement contains detailed information about officers and directors, including their experience, relationship with the company, and compensation. (The annual report provides financial information.) Proxy statements must also be filed with the SEC. Proxy contests and shareholder proposals are discussed in Chapter 17.

Under SEC rules, a company is not *required* to solicit proxies from shareholders, but if it does not, it is unlikely to obtain the quorum needed for the meeting to be held. In any event, a company cannot avoid its responsibility to inform shareholders. Whether or not it solicits proxies, it is still required to furnish shareholders with an information statement that contains essentially the same material as a proxy statement.

Short-Swing Trading—Section 16

During congressional hearings after the 1929 stock market crash, witnesses testified that insiders had manipulated the stock market. For example, insiders would buy a large block of stock, announce a substantial dividend, and then divest before the dividend was reduced. Section 16 was designed to prevent corporate insiders—officers, directors, and shareholders who own more than 10 percent of the company—from taking unfair advantage of privileged information to manipulate the market.

Section 16 takes a two-pronged approach:

- First, insiders must **report** their trades of company stock on Form 4 by the tenth day of the following month.
- Second, insiders must **turn over to the corporation** any profits they make from the purchase and sale or sale and purchase of company securities in a six-month period. Section 16 is a strict liability provision. It applies even if the insider did not actually take advantage of secret information or try to manipulate the market; if she bought and sold or sold and bought stock in a six-month period, she is liable.

Suppose that Manuela buys 20,000 shares of her company's stock in June at $10 a share. In September, her (uninsured) summer house in Florida is destroyed by a hurricane. To raise money for rebuilding, she sells the stock at $12 per share, making a profit of $40,000. Her house will have to remain in ruins because she has violated §16 and must turn over the profit to her company.

As some observers have commented, §16 is both too broad and too narrow: it penalizes innocent trading where there is no insider information and ignores guilty insider trading that has occurred only once in a six-month period. During the stock market mini-crash in 1987, many officers and directors bought stock of their own companies to take advantage of bargain prices. If they had sold stock any time in the previous six months, their subsequent purchase violated §16 because they had *sold and then purchased* stock. But, if an insider sells stock because he knows the company's profit figures are down, he has not violated §16 unless he had also bought stock in the prior six months. (As we will see, he may be in violation of Rule 10b-5.)

LIABILITY

SECTION 18

Under §18, anyone who makes a false or misleading statement in a filing under the 1934 Act is liable to buyers or sellers who (1) acted in reliance on the statement and (2) can prove that the price at which they bought or sold was affected by the false filing. Section 18 applies to all filings under the 1934 Act, including proxy statements and annual reports.

SECTION 10(b)

Section 18 applies only to *filings* under the 1934 Act. What happens if a company executive makes a false public *statement* about the company? Or writes an untrue statement somewhere other than in a filing? In one case, a corporate officer bought up shares of his company's stock even as he made pessimistic public statements about the company. That is the type of behavior that §10(b) is designed to prevent. **Section 10(b) prohibits fraud in connection with the purchase and sale of any security, whether or not the security is registered under the 1934 Act.**

The SEC adopted Rule 10b-5 to clarify §10(b), but the rule is still a relatively vague, catch-all provision designed to fill any holes left by other sections of the securities laws.[11] Interpretation has largely been left to the courts, which generally have interpreted Rule 10b-5 as follows:

- **A Misstatement or Omission of a Material Fact.** Anyone who fails to disclose material information, or makes incomplete or inaccurate disclosure, is liable. **Material** has the same meaning as under the 1933 Act: important enough to affect an investor's decision. For example, a company repeatedly and falsely denied that it was involved in merger negotiations. It was liable even though the negotiations had only been in a preliminary stage.[12]
- ***Scienter.*** This is a legal term meaning *willfully, knowingly, or recklessly*. To be liable under Rule 10b-5, the defendant must have (1) known (or been reckless in not knowing) that the statement was inaccurate and (2) intended for the plaintiff to rely on the statement. Negligence is not enough. A group of

---

[11] Rule 10b-5 prohibits any person, in connection with a purchase or sale of any security, from (1) employing any device, scheme, or artifice to defraud; (2) making any untrue statement of a material fact or omitting to state a material fact necessary in order to make the statements made, in light of the circumstances under which they were made, not misleading; or (3) engaging in any act, practice, or course of business that operates or would operate as a fraud or deceit upon any person.

[12] *Basic Inc. v. Levinson*, 485 U.S. 224, 108 S. Ct. 978, 1988 U.S. LEXIS 1197 (1988).

shareholders sued the accounting firm Ernst & Ernst because it had failed to discover, during the course of an audit, that a company's chief executive was stealing funds. According to the shareholders, the auditors should have discovered that the executive refused to allow anyone else to open his mail and, therefore, should have been suspicious of other wrongdoing. The court found Ernst & Ernst not liable. Although it may have been negligent, it had not *intentionally* or even *recklessly* facilitated fraud.[13]

- **Purchase or Sale.** Rule 10b-5 includes both buyers and sellers. It does not include, however, someone who *failed* to purchase stock because of a material misstatement. In the case of the company executive who spread negative rumors about his company while he bought stock, those who sold because of his false rumors could sue under Rule 10b-5, but not those who simply failed to buy.
- **Reliance.** To bring suit, a plaintiff must show that she relied on the misstatement or omission. In the case of open-market trades, reliance is difficult to prove, so the courts are willing to assume it.

During a recent nine-year period, 25 percent of the corporations in America, including each of the 10 biggest firms in Silicon Valley, were sued by shareholders. Some commentators call these suits "legalized extortion"; others say it is the only way to prevent fraud.[14] Consider these two case histories.

Kenwood and Helena Perkins lived in the upscale San Diego community of Rancho Bernardo and were looking forward to a comfortably secure retirement. That was before they invested in Technical Equities Corp. Its auditors and brokerage firms were well-known, but that did not prevent the company from collapsing in the largest financial scandal in California's history. The Perkinses were devastated. "I had fears of going on welfare," Mrs. Perkins said. Instead, Mr. Perkins went back to work at age 65. The couple sold their home and moved to a trailer park. Then they joined a lawsuit against the company, its bankers, investment bankers, and auditors. After legal fees, they recovered about 60 percent of their losses. "We're still living in the mobile home park," Mr. Perkins said, "but our future is reasonably secure, and it would not have been without that money."

John G. Adler came to the United States from his native Hungary, as a penniless 19-year-old escaping the Russians. After 20 years with IBM, he became president of Adaptec, a computer parts manufacturer in Milpitas, California. The company's revenues exceeded $100 million, but one year, Mr. Adler learned that various sales glitches would cause fourth-quarter revenues to be about 15 percent lower than Wall Street expected. The shortfall seemed minor, but Mr. Adler decided to hold a conference call to alert the handful of analysts who followed his company. When the market opened the next day, Adaptec's stock fell more than 30 percent. Within three days, the first of seven lawsuits had been filed against the company, alleging that it should have made a public announcement, not a private phone call. In the end, the company spent $2 million in legal

[13] *Ernst & Ernst v. Hochfelder*, 425 U.S. 185, 96 S. Ct. 1375, 1976 U.S. LEXIS 2 (1976).

[14] Jim Barlow, "Stock Suit Filings Wear Down Firms," *Houston Chronicle*, May 4, 1995, p. 1.

fees and settled the cases for $4.3 million. Adler objected to the settlement because he felt he had done nothing wrong, but lawyers advised him that a trial would cost far more.[15]

THE PRIVATE SECURITIES LITIGATION REFORM ACT OF 1995

In 1995, Congress passed an amendment to the 1934 Act intended to discourage fraud suits by shareholders. Under this amendment, companies are liable to shareholders for so-called forward-looking statements (that is, financial projections or statements about future plans) *only if* (1) the company fails to include a warning that the predictions may not come to pass, *and* (2) the shareholders can show that company executives knew the predictions were false. Suppose a pharmaceutical company predicts that a new drug will generate billions in sales, but two years later the drug is a total failure. Before 1995, shareholders would have had a strong case against the company, but now the company would not be liable as long as it had disclosed, at the time of making the prediction, reasons why the drug might not be a success. Even if the company failed to mention these reasons, it would be liable only if executives knew the prediction to be false when they made it.

Thus far this statute has not diminished the number of lawsuits filed under §10(b). (Shareholders even sued Shiva, the company discussed earlier in this chapter, when its stock price fell.) However, the nature of the allegations has changed. Now, the majority of these suits allege accounting fraud or insider trading; very few are based solely on claims of misleading predictions.[16] For more information about these lawsuits, browse at **http://securities.stanford.edu**. This site provides over 1,000 securities fraud complaints, as well as court orders and written testimony.

INSIDER TRADING

Insider trading is immensely tempting. Anyone with reliable secret information can earn millions of dollars overnight. Costandi Nasser bought shares of Santa Fe International, Inc. after learning that Kuwait Petroleum Co. was set to acquire the company. His profit? $4.6 million in three weeks. The down-side? Insider trading is a crime punishable by fines of up to $1.1 million and prison sentences of up to 10 years. The guilty party may also be forced to turn over to the SEC three times the profit made. Ivan Boesky paid $100 million and spent two years in prison. Dennis Levine suffered an $11.6 million penalty and three years in prison.

Why is insider trading a crime? Who is harmed? After all, if you buy or sell stock in a company, presumably you are reasonably content with the price or you would not have traded. There are three reasons why insider trading is illegal:

---

[15] Diana B. Henriques, "Investing It; Making It Harder for Investors to Sue," *The New York Times*, Sept. 10, 1995, p. 1.

[16] Some plaintiffs tried to do an end run around this statute by filing suit in a state court (under more favorable state law). Congress passed the Securities Litigation Uniform Standards Act of 1998 to force plaintiffs in certain types of securities cases to file suit in federal court (under federal law).

- It offends our fundamental sense of fairness. No one wants to be in a poker game with marked cards.
- Investors will lose confidence in the market if they feel that insiders have an unfair advantage.
- Investment banks typically "make a market" in stocks, meaning that they hold extra shares so that orders can be filled smoothly. If an insider buys stock because she knows the company is about to sign an important contract, she earns the profit on that information at the expense of the marketmaker who sold her the stock. These marketmakers expect to earn a certain profit. If they do not earn it from normal stock appreciation, they simply raise the commission they charge for being a marketmaker. As a result, everyone who buys and sells stock pays a slightly higher price because insider trading skims off some of the profits.

As noted, Rule 10b-5 is a vaguely worded rule that generally prohibits fraud. The language of the rule never explicitly mentions insider trading, but courts have interpreted it to prohibit this activity. Although the courts are nominally *interpreting* the rule, in fact, they are more or less fashioning this crime out of whole cloth. Insider trading has been described as "the judicial oak that has grown from little more than a legislative acorn." The current rules on insider trading are as follows:

- **Strangers.** The SEC has argued many times that anyone in possession of nonpublic material information must disclose it or refrain from trading. The courts, however, have definitively rejected this approach. The Supreme Court has held that **someone who trades on inside information is liable only if he has a fiduciary duty to the company whose stock he has traded**. Suppose that, while looking in a dumpster, Harry finds correspondence indicating that MediSearch, Inc. will shortly announce a major breakthrough in the treatment of AIDS. Harry buys the stock, which promptly quadruples in value. Harry will be dining at the Ritz, not in the dumpster nor in federal prison, because he has no fiduciary duty to MediSearch.
- **Fiduciaries.** Anyone who works for a company is a fiduciary. **A fiduciary violates Rule 10b-5 if she trades stock of her company while in possession of nonpublic material information.** If the Director of Research for MediSearch learns of the promising new treatment for AIDS and buys stock in the company before the information is public, she has violated Rule 10b-5. This rule applies not only to employees who work for the company, but also to constructive insiders—others who have an indirect employment relationship, such as employees of the company's auditors or law firm. Thus, if a lawyer who works at the firm that is patenting MediSearch's new discovery buys stock before the information is public, she has violated Rule 10b-5.
- **Tippers.** Now things become really complicated. **Insiders who pass on nonpublic, material information are liable under Rule 10b-5, even if they do not trade themselves, as long as (1) they know the information is confidential and (2) they expect some personal gain.** Personal gain is loosely defined. Essentially, any gift to a friend counts as personal gain. W. Paul

Thayer was a corporate director, deputy defense secretary, and former fighter pilot ace who gave stock tips to his girlfriend in lieu of paying her rent. That counted as personal gain, and he spent a year and a half in prison.

- **Tippees. Those who receive tips—tippees—are liable for trading on inside information, even if they do not have a fiduciary relationship to the company, as long as (1) they know the information is confidential, (2) they know it came from an insider who was violating his fiduciary duty, and (3) the insider expected some personal gain.** Barry Switzer, then head football coach at the University of Oklahoma, went to a track meet to see his son compete. While sunbathing on the bleachers, he overheard someone talking about a company that was going to be acquired. Switzer bought the stock but was acquitted of insider trading charges, because the insider had not breached his fiduciary duty. He had not tipped anyone on purpose—he had simply been careless. Also, Switzer did not know that the insider was breaching a fiduciary duty, and the insider expected no personal gain.[17]
- **Takeovers.** Frustrated by its lack of success under Rule 10b-5, the SEC adopted Rule 14e-3. **This rule prohibits trading on inside information during a tender offer if the trader knows the information was obtained from either the bidder or the target company.** The trader or tipper need not have violated a fiduciary duty. (Tender offers are discussed in detail in Chapter 17, on shareholders.)
- **Misappropriation.** In an effort to tighten the insider trading noose further, the SEC developed a new theory—misappropriation. Under this theory, **a person is liable if he trades in securities (1) for personal profit, (2) using confidential information, and (3) in breach of a fiduciary duty to the source of the information**. This theory applies even if that source was not the company whose stock was traded. Foster Winans wrote a column for *The Wall Street Journal* entitled, "Heard on the Street" in which he reported rumors he had heard about companies. Frequently, the stock of these companies would rise or fall in response to his story. He began leaking information about his columns in advance to Peter Brant, a stockbroker at Kidder, Peabody & Co. Brant would trade the stock and split the profits with Winans. After the first episode, the SEC noticed the abnormally large trade. When it called the company to find out who was buying, the officers said they could think of no explanation except that the company had been the subject of a "Heard on the Street" column. It was all over for Winans, though the SEC let him pass on information a few more times, to make sure.

But had Winans and Brant violated Rule 10b-5? Not according to traditional insider trading rules. Neither of them had a fiduciary relationship to the company whose stock was traded. When the case went to the Supreme Court, it split 4–4 on the issue of misappropriation (there were only eight judges because one had resigned and his successor had not yet been appointed). However, the

---

[17] *SEC v. Switzer*, 590 F. Supp. 756, 1984 U.S. Dist. LEXIS 15303 (W.D. Okla. 1984). After this case, some wags joked, "When Barry Switzer listens, people talk."

Court did find 8–0 that Winans was guilty of mail and wire fraud for having violated *The Wall Street Journal*'s rules about confidentiality.[18] Ten years later, the Supreme Court finally resolved the misappropriation issue.

UNITED STATES v. O'HAGAN

521 U.S. 642, 117 S. Ct. 2199, 1997 U.S. LEXIS 4033
United States Supreme Court, 1997

Facts: Grand Metropolitan PLC (Grand Met) hired the law firm of Dorsey & Whitney to represent it in a takeover of Pillsbury Co. James O'Hagan, a partner in Dorsey & Whitney, did not work for Grand Met, but he did purchase significant amounts of Pillsbury stock during this period. After Grand Met publicly announced its takeover attempt, the price of Pillsbury stock rose dramatically. O'Hagan sold his stock at a profit of more than $4.3 million. A jury convicted O'Hagan of misappropriation in violation of §10(b), and he was sentenced to prison.[19] The appeals court reversed, ruling that misappropriation is not a violation of §10(b). The Supreme Court granted *certiorari.*

Issue: Is misappropriation a violation of §10(b)?

Excerpts from Justice Ginsburg's Decision: Under the "traditional" or "classical theory" of insider trading liability, §10(b) and Rule 10b-5 are violated when a corporate insider trades in the securities of his corporation on the basis of material, nonpublic information. The classical theory applies not only to officers, directors, and other permanent insiders of a corporation, but also to attorneys, accountants, consultants, and others who temporarily become fiduciaries of a corporation.

The "misappropriation theory" holds that a person commits fraud "in connection with" a securities transaction, and thereby violates §10(b) and Rule 10b-5, when he misappropriates confidential information for securities trading purposes, in breach of a duty owed to the source of the information. Under this theory, a fiduciary's undisclosed, self-serving use of a principal's information to purchase or sell securities, in breach of a duty of loyalty and confidentiality, defrauds the principal of the exclusive use of that information.

The two theories are complementary, each addressing efforts to capitalize on nonpublic information through the purchase or sale of securities. The classical theory targets a corporate insider's breach of duty to shareholders with whom the insider transacts; the misappropriation theory outlaws trading on the basis of nonpublic information by a corporate "outsider" in breach of a duty owed not to a trading party, but to the source of the information. The misappropriation theory is thus designed to protect the integrity of the securities markets against abuses by "outsiders" to a corporation who have access to confidential information that will affect the corporation's security price when revealed, but who owe no fiduciary or other duty to that corporation's shareholders.

A company's confidential information qualifies as property to which the company has a right of exclusive use. The undisclosed misappropriation of such information, in violation of a fiduciary duty constitutes fraud akin to embezzlement.

The theory is also well-tuned to an animating purpose of the Exchange Act: to insure honest securities markets and thereby promote investor confidence. Although informational disparity is inevitable in the securities markets, investors likely would hesitate to venture their capital in a market where trading based on misappropriated nonpublic information is unchecked by law. An

[18] *Carpenter v. United States*, 484 U.S. 19, 108 S. Ct. 316, 1987 U.S. LEXIS 4815 (1987).

[19] This was not the sum total of O'Hagan's problems. He used the profits he gained through this trading to conceal his previous embezzlement of client funds. There is a moral here.

investor's informational disadvantage vis-à-vis a misappropriator with material, nonpublic information stems from contrivance, not luck; it is a disadvantage that cannot be overcome with research or skill.

It makes scant sense to hold a lawyer like O'Hagan a §10(b) violator if he works for a law firm representing the target of a tender offer, but not if he works for a law firm representing the bidder. The text of the statute requires no such result. The misappropriation at issue here was properly made the subject of a §10(b) charge because it meets the statutory requirement that there be "deceptive" conduct "in connection with" securities transactions.

PREVENTIVE Law

If you learn confidential information about a company, what can you do? Of course, it is always safe not to trade. If you want to trade anyway, you should wait 24 to 48 hours after the information is disseminated through wire services or in the financial press.

FOREIGN CORRUPT PRACTICES ACT

In the 1970s, more than 450 major U.S. corporations paid millions of dollars in foreign bribes. The Japanese premier and the Italian president both resigned after it was revealed that Lockheed had paid them off. In the Netherlands, members of the royal family were implicated in the scandal. Many of these payments had been labeled "commissions" or other legitimate business expenses and then illegally deducted from the company's income tax. In response, Congress passed the Foreign Corrupt Practices Act as an amendment to the 1934 Act.

Under the Foreign Corrupt Practices Act, it is a crime for *any American company* (whether reporting under the 1934 Act or not) to make or promise to make payments or gifts to foreign officials, political candidates, or parties in order to influence a governmental decision, even if the payment is legal under local law. There is one exception: it is legal for a company to make payments to a foreign official to expedite a "routine governmental action." Anyone who violates the law is subject to fines of up to $100,000 and imprisonment for up to five years.

Congress believed that the ready availability of corporate "slush funds" had facilitated the payment of bribes. Therefore, it also tightened accounting standards for companies that report under the 1934 Act. It requires *reporting companies* to (1) keep books that accurately and fairly reflect the transactions of the issuer, and (2) maintain a system of internal controls that ensures transactions are executed only "in accordance with management's authorization."

For years, American companies complained that they were handicapped when competing against rivals who could bribe their way to success overseas. The U.S. government estimated that American companies lost contracts worth more than $15 billion a year to competitors who paid bribes. But in 1997, 34 developed countries signed a treaty in Paris outlawing bribery of foreign officials.

What's wrong with bribery anyway? Many businesspeople think it is relatively harmless, just a cost of doing business, like New York's high taxes or Germany's high labor costs. Corruption is not a victimless crime. Poor people in poor countries are the losers when officials are on the take: corruption means that good projects are squeezed out by bad ones. And corruption can reduce a country's entire administration to a state of decay. Honest officials give up. Bribes grow

RIGHT & WRONG

ever bigger and more ubiquitous. The trough becomes less well stocked; the snouts plunge deeper.[20]

Which countries are most corrupt? Nigeria, Bolivia, Colombia, Russia, and Pakistan lead the list of shame. The most honest? Denmark, Finland, Sweden, New Zealand, and Canada. (The United States is fifteenth on the honest list.)

BLUE SKY LAWS

At the end of the nineteenth century, years before the great stock market crash, states had already begun to regulate the sale of securities. These statutes are called **blue sky laws** (because crooks were willing to sell naive investors a "piece of the great blue sky"). Currently, all states and the District of Columbia have blue sky laws. To sell securities, an issuer must comply with both state and federal securities laws. "Blue skying" a 50-state securities offering is no small feat, because there is little uniformity among the statutes. Although most states have adopted the Uniform Securities Act, they have so customized it that "uniform" is a misnomer. Often, securities approved by the SEC will be offered only in a limited number of states either because state securities commissioners have denied clearance or because the issuer will not make the effort to seek clearance in all jurisdictions.

Although the 1933 Act is primarily concerned with adequate disclosure, many state statutes focus on the quality of the investment and require a so-called **merit review**. In 1981, the Massachusetts securities commissioner refused to allow Apple Computer Co. to sell its initial public offering in Massachusetts because he believed the stock, selling at 92 times earnings, was too risky. He "protected" Massachusetts residents from this investment.

Most states now permit so-called SCORs (small company offering registrations). If a company issues less than $1 million in stock in a 12-month period, it is required to file only a relatively simple form (U-7) in any state in which it wishes to sell the securities. The company is then free to advertise and sell to anyone in these states. There is no limit on the number of investors. Each year, somewhere between 80 and 100 companies file a SCOR. (Such an offering is already exempt from registration with the SEC under Rule 504.)

To make life easier for issuers of stock, Congress also passed the National Securities Markets Improvement Act of 1996. Essentially, states may no longer regulate offerings of securities that are:

- Traded on a national exchange
- Exempt under Rule 506, or
- Sold to "qualified purchasers"

The states may still prosecute those who commit securities fraud. They may also require issuers to file notices and pay fees for all offerings except those involving nationally traded securities.

[20] "Who Will Listen to Mr. Clean?" *The Economist*, Aug. 2, 1997, p. 52. © 1997 The Economist Newspaper Groups, Inc.

CHAPTER CONCLUSION

The 1929 stock market crash and the Great Depression that followed were an economic catastrophe for the United States. The Securities Act of 1933 and the Securities Exchange Act of 1934 were designed to prevent such disasters from ever occurring again. This country has enjoyed more than 70 years of prosperity that is based, at least in part, on a reliable and honest securities market. The securities laws deserve some of the credit for that stability.

CHAPTER REVIEW

1. A security is any transaction in which the buyer invests money in a common enterprise and expects to earn a profit predominantly from the efforts of others.
2. Before any offer or sale, an issuer must register securities with the SEC, unless the securities qualify for an exemption.
3. These securities are exempt from the registration requirement: government securities, bank securities, short-term notes, nonprofit issues, insurance policies, and annuity contracts.
4. The following table compares the different types of securities offerings:

	Public Offering	Intrastate Offering	Regulation A	Regulation D: Rule 504	Regulation D: Rule 505	Regulation D: Rule 506
Maximum Value of Securities Sold	Unlimited	Unlimited	\$5 million	\$1 million	\$5 million	Unlimited
Public Solicitation of Purchasers	Permitted	Permitted	Permitted	Permitted	Not permitted	Not permitted
Suitability Requirements for Purchasers	No requirements	Must reside in issuer's state	No requirements	No requirements	No limit on accredited investors; no more than 35 unaccredited investors	No limit on accredited investors; no more than 35 unaccredited investors who, if unsophisticated, must have a purchaser representative
Disclosure Requirements	Elaborate registration statement; audited financials	None	Offering circular that is less detailed than a registration statement	None	Same requirements as Reg A for unaccredited investors; no disclosure to accredited investors	Same requirements as Reg A for unaccredited investors; no disclosure to accredited investors
Resale of Securities	Permitted	Permitted, but may not be made out of state for nine months	Permitted	Permitted	Not permitted for one year	Not permitted for one year

5. If a final registration statement contains a material misstatement or omission, the purchaser of a security offered under that statement can recover from everyone who signed it.

6. The 1934 Act requires public companies to make regular filings with the SEC.

7. Under §16, insiders who buy and sell or sell and buy company stock within a six-month period must turn over to the corporation any profits from the trades.

8. Section 10(b) prohibits fraud in connection with the purchase and sale of any security, whether or not the issuer is registered under the 1934 Act.

9. Section 10(b) also prohibits insider trading.

10. Under the Foreign Corrupt Practices Act, it is a crime for any U.S. company to make payments to foreign officials to influence a government decision. This statute also requires reporting companies to keep accurate records.

PRACTICE TEST

1. Christopher Stenger bought 12 Impressionist paintings from R. H. Love Galleries for $1.5 million. Love told Stenger that art investment would produce a safe profit. The two men agreed that Stenger could exchange any painting within five years for any one or two other paintings with the same or greater value. When Stenger's paintings did not increase in value, he sued Love, arguing that the right to trade paintings made them securities. Is Stenger correct?

2. **CPA QUESTION** When a common stock offering requires registration under the Securities Act of 1933:

   (a) The registration statement is automatically effective when filed with the SEC

   (b) The issuer would act unlawfully if it were to sell the common stock without providing the investor with a prospectus

   (c) The SEC will determine the investment value of the common stock before approving the offering

   (d) The issuer may make sales 10 days after filing the registration statement

3. Fluor, an engineering and construction company, was awarded a $1 billion project to build a coal gasification plant in South Africa. Fluor signed an agreement with a South African client that prohibited them both from announcing the agreement until March 10. Accordingly, Fluor denied all rumors that a major transaction was pending. Between March 3 and March 6, the State Teachers Retirement Board pension fund sold 288,257 shares of Fluor stock. After the contract was announced, the stock price went up. Did Fluor violate Rule 10b-5?

4. **CPA QUESTION** Hamilton Corp. makes a $4.5 million securities offering under Rule 505 of Regulation D of the Securities Act of 1933. Under this regulation, Hamilton is:

   (a) Required to provide full financial information to accredited investors only

   (b) Allowed to make the offering through a general solicitation

   (c) Limited to selling to no more than 35 nonaccredited investors

   (d) Allowed to sell to an unlimited number of investors both accredited and nonaccredited

5. Does this excerpt from *The Boston Globe* reveal any potential securities law problems?

   Berkshire Ice Cream's down-home investment strategy is paying off for more than 100 people who last year put up $800 to $1,000 to "own" a company cow. Last month, the company sent out about $32,000 to investors who bought a total of 110 cows a year ago, with the expectation of a 20 percent annual return on their money. [I]nitially, there were 63 investors who agreed to finance the purchase of a cow—which the company then cares for—in return for a piece of the company's profits.[21]

6. **RIGHT & WRONG** Ira Waldbaum was president and controlling shareholder of Waldbaum, Inc., a large supermarket chain. After deciding to accept A & P's offer to purchase the chain, he told his sister, Shirley Witkin, about the offer so that she would be ready to sell her shares. He admonished her not to tell anyone, but she told her daughter, Susan Loeb, who passed the word (and the warning) on to her husband, Keith Loeb. The next day, Keith told his broker, Robert Chestman, about the impending sale and ordered some Waldbaum stock. Chestman purchased 11,000 shares of the stock for himself and his clients, at a price of roughly $25 per share. The A&P offer was for $50 per share. Did Chestman violate Rule 10b-5? Whether or not Chestman's trades were legal, did they harm anyone? How do they look in the light of day? Were Loeb's actions right? How might they have affected his wife (and other stakeholders)?

7. **CPA QUESTION** Pace Corp. previously issued 300,000 shares of its common stock. The shares are now actively traded on a national securities exchange. The original offering was exempt from registration under the Securities Act of 1933. Pace has $2.5 million in assets and 425 shareholders. With regard to the Securities Exchange Act of 1934, Pace is:

   (a) Required to file a registration statement because its assets exceed $2 million in value

   (b) Required to file a registration statement even though it has fewer than 500 shareholders

   (c) Not required to file a registration statement because the original offering of its stock was exempt from registration

   (d) Not required to file a registration statement unless insiders own at least 5 percent of its outstanding shares of stock

8. **YOU BE THE JUDGE WRITING PROBLEM** World-Wide Coin Investments, Inc. sold rare coins, precious metals, camera equipment, and Coca-Cola collector items. Its stock was registered with the SEC under the 1934 Act. Joseph Hale was the controlling shareholder, chairman of the board, CEO, and president. World-Wide's independent auditor warned Hale that the company's faulty system of accounting procedures was causing problems with inventory control. Furthermore, the auditor could not document transactions, and it had found that the books and records of the company were inaccurate. Is World-Wide in violation of the Foreign Corrupt Practices Act? **Argument for the SEC:** Without exception, all reporting companies are required to maintain accurate books and records. **Argument for World-Wide:** This is a small company, and the cost of such an elaborate internal control system would bankrupt it.

9. Consider this scenario from the periodical *Investor's Business Daily, Inc.*:

   You're in line at the grocery store when you overhear a stranger say: "That new widget is going to make XYZ Co. a fortune. I can't wait until the product launches tomorrow."

   What do you do? (a) Nothing? (b) Call your broker and buy as much XYZ Co. stock as you possibly can?

10. Malaga Arabian Limited Partnership sold investments in the Spanish Arabian horse industry under Rule 506. James E. Mark, who purchased one of the partnership interests,

---

[21] Ellen Labr, "Investors Milk Profits of Ice Cream Firm," *The Boston Globe*, July 30, 1995, p. 38.

alleged that the partnership violated Rule 506 because it never gave him any disclosure about the risks of the investment. He was not an accredited investor. At trial, the partnership said that it had surveyed investors to ensure that they were either accredited or sophisticated but had not actually read the surveys and did not have them available for the trial court. Is this offering exempt from registration under the 1933 Act?

11. CoolCom, Inc. sends notice to all its shareholders that its annual report and proxy soliciting materials are on its Internet Web site. It provides investors with the Internet location and a telephone number that they may call to request a paper copy. Is CoolCom in compliance with SEC rules?

INTERNET RESEARCH PROBLEM

Choose a company, go to the EDGAR database at the SEC (http://www.sec.gov), and look at all filings this company has made during the last year. What filings has it made and why? Extra credit: search EDGAR for a prospectus for an initial public offering.

You can find further practice problems in the Online Quiz at http://beatty.westbuslaw.com or in the Study Guide that accompanies this text.

UNIT

5

GOVERNMENT REGULATION & PROPERTY

ANTITRUST

19

CHAPTER

Mike Elliott was not looking for trouble when he brought an order form for Girl Scout cookies to work. Mr. Elliott, an employee at DaimlerChrysler's factory in Dearborn, Michigan, started asking co-workers to buy a few boxes on behalf of his girlfriend's eight-year-old daughter. "I worked for four or five hours, and suddenly this lady came up to me and said that a guy who worked 50 feet down the line from me was selling them cheaper," Mr. Elliott says. "The first thing that everyone thinks is, 'You're trying to rip me off.'"

In an increasingly competitive marketplace, price wars are breaking out over Thin Mints and Peanut Butter Patties. The 36,500-member Michigan Metro Council, citing rising costs and the need to subsidize inner city troops, reluctantly raised its price to $3 a box this year. The neighboring—but much smaller—Macomb County Girl Scout Council stayed at $2.50 a box, setting the stage for a marketing battle. However, most of the troops in this skirmish are not Scouts: they are grown-ups who peddle the cookies at work. Such scenarios have been repeated in other parts of the country, as many of the nation's 330 Girl Scout councils go through their annual pricing debate. Why don't the councils simply agree on one national price? Because antitrust laws prohibit price-fixing.[1]

---

[1] Rebecca Blumenstein, "Cookie Price War Sends Adult Troops into Marketing Battle," *The Wall Street Journal*, Mar. 8, 1996, p. A1. Republished with permission of The Wall Street Journal; permission conveyed through the Copyright Clearance Center. Inc.

Competition is an essential element of the American economic system. What are the laws governing competition? Why have they developed this way? How can business executives make the right decisions?

IN THE BEGINNING

Throughout much of the nineteenth century, competition in America was largely a local affair. The country was so big and transportation so poor that companies primarily competed in small local markets. It was too costly to transport goods great distances. State laws rather than national statutes regulated competition.

By the second half of the nineteenth century, four railroad lines crossed the continent from coast to coast. For the first time, national markets were a real possibility. John D. Rockefeller saw the potential. In 1859, Edwin L. Drake, a retired railroad conductor, drilled the first commercially successful oil well in the United States. Three years later, when the 23-year-old Rockefeller entered the scene, the oil industry was full of producers too small to benefit from economies of scale. Production was inefficient, and prices varied dramatically in different parts of the country.

Rockefeller set out to reorganize the industry. He began by buying refineries, first in Cleveland and then in other cities. He and his partners spread into all segments of the oil industry—buying oil fields, building pipelines, and establishing an efficient marketing system. To unify the management of these companies, they transferred their stock to the Standard Oil Trust. By 1870, Rockefeller had achieved his goal—the Standard Oil Trust controlled virtually all the oil in the country, from producer to consumer. Rockefeller was the wealthiest person in the world. Even now, his great-grandchildren can live comfortably on their inheritances.

Some of Rockefeller's tactics were controversial. When a competitor tried to build an oil pipeline, Rockefeller used every weapon short of violence to stop it. He planted stories in the press suggesting the pipes would leak and ruin nearby fields. He flooded local builders with orders for tank cars so no workers would be available to build the pipeline. When the pipeline was finished, he refused to allow his oil to flow through it. These tactics were frightening, especially in an industry as important as oil. What if Rockefeller decided to raise prices unfairly? Or cut off oil altogether? Newspapers began to attack him ferociously.

SHERMAN ACT

With the coming of the railroads, it became clear that large companies might be able to control other industries as well. To prevent extreme concentrations of economic power, Congress passed the **Sherman Act** in 1890. It was one of the first national laws designed to regulate competition. Because this statute was aimed at the Standard Oil Trust and other similar organizations, it was termed **antitrust** legislation. In 1892, the Ohio Supreme Court dissolved the Standard Oil Trust, which was replaced by the Standard Oil Co. But the government was not satisfied until a spring day in 1911, when Supreme Court Chief Justice Edward White quietly read aloud his dramatic 20,000-word opinion ordering the breakup of Standard Oil.[2] The 33 companies that made up Standard Oil were forced to compete as separate businesses. Today, descendants of Standard Oil include Amoco, Atlantic Richfield, Chevron, Exxon Mobil, and Pennzoil. Imagine what kind of giant they would be if still united.

For the first 70 or so years after the passage of the Sherman Act, most scholars and judges took the view that large concentrations of economic power were suspect, even if they had no obvious impact on competition itself. Big was bad. Big meant too much economic and political power. As Senator John Sherman, sponsor of the Sherman Act, put it, a nation that "would not submit to an emperor should not submit to an autocrat of trade." Fragmented, competitive markets were desirable in and of themselves. Standard Oil should not control the oil markets, even if the company was very efficient and had gained control by completely acceptable methods.

CHICAGO SCHOOL

Beginning in the 1960s and 1970s, however, a group of influential economists and lawyers at the University of Chicago began to argue that the goal of antitrust enforcement should be *efficiency*. Let a company grow as large as it likes provided that this growth is based on a superior product or lower costs, not ruthless tactics. Insist on a clean fight, and do not handicap large successful companies to help the slower runners. Some companies will thrive, others will die, but in either case, the consumer will come out ahead. Adherents of the **Chicago School** argued further that the market should decide the most efficient size for each industry. In some cases, such as automobiles or long-distance telephone service, the most efficient size might be very large indeed. Under traditional antitrust analysis, courts often asked, "Has a *competitor* been harmed?" The Chicago School suggests that courts should ask instead, "Has *competition* been harmed?"

At the turn of the twentieth century, President Theodore Roosevelt personally plotted the breakup of Standard Oil. (As one of Rockefeller's compatriots said of Roosevelt, "We bought the son of a bitch, and then he didn't stay bought.") At the turn of the twenty-first century, two descendants of Standard Oil—Exxon and Mobil—announced their intention to merge. This time, not one politician so much as grabbed a microphone to object to the recombination. Where once size alone was cause for concern, now regulators believe that a certain bulk may be necessary if American companies are to compete in the intense global economy.

Antitrust policy, however, continues to evolve. Adherents of the so-called **Post Chicago School** are beginning to recognize that competition alone may not be enough to protect consumers. For example, an industry with a large number of competitors may foster collusion, not competition. Or, activities that appear consumer-friendly, such as giving a product away for free, may in the long run harm consumers. (Take, for example, Microsoft's decision to give away its Internet browser. Although consumers benefit in the short run, the Justice Department has alleged that this give-away will ultimately harm consumers by

---

[2] *Standard Oil Company of New Jersey v. United States*, 221 U.S. 1, 31 S. Ct. 502, 1911 U.S. LEXIS 1725 (1911).

driving competitors out of business.) Now, when deciding whether to take action, federal trustbusters are beginning to focus directly on consumers, asking two questions: Will this action cause consumers to pay higher prices? Are the higher prices sustainable in the face of existing competition? As you read the cases in this chapter, think about which factors the court considered important: size, competition, or the impact on consumers.

OVERVIEW OF ANTITRUST LAWS

The major provisions of the antitrust laws are:

- Section 1 of the Sherman Act prohibits all agreements "in restraint of trade."
- Section 2 of the Sherman Act bans "monopolization"—the wrongful acquisition of a monopoly.
- The Clayton Act prohibits anticompetitive mergers, tying arrangements, and exclusive dealing agreements.
- The Robinson-Patman Act bans price discrimination that reduces competition.

The full text of all the antitrust statutes is available at http://www.ftc.gov/ogc/stat2.htm.

In 1914, Congress passed the **Clayton Act** in part because the courts were not enforcing the Sherman Act as strictly as it had intended. The purpose of the Clayton Act was to clarify the earlier statute. As a result, the two laws overlap significantly. The **Robinson-Patman Act** (passed in 1936) is an amendment to the Clayton Act. Rather than systematically reviewing the terms of each statute in order, this chapter focuses instead on the *kinds of behavior* that the antitrust laws regulate.

Violations of the antitrust laws are divided into two categories: ***per se*** and **rule of reason**. As the name implies, *per se* violations are automatic. Defendants charged with this type of violation cannot defend themselves by saying, "But the impact wasn't so bad," or "No one was hurt." The court will not listen to excuses, and the defendants are subject to both *criminal* and *civil* penalties. Typically, the Justice Department has sought criminal sanctions only against *per se* violators.

Rule of reason violations, on the other hand, are illegal only if they have an anticompetitive impact. To determine if an activity is an unreasonable restraint of trade, the courts consider its circumstances, intent, and impact. For example, if competitors join together and agree that they will not deal with a particular supplier, their action is illegal only if it harms competition. Although rule of reason violators may be subject to civil penalties or private lawsuits, traditionally the Justice Department has not sought criminal penalties against them.

Both the Justice Department and the Federal Trade Commission (FTC) have authority to enforce the antitrust laws. However, only the Justice Department can bring criminal proceedings; the FTC is limited to civil injunctions and other administrative remedies. In addition to the government, anyone injured by an antitrust violation has the right to sue for damages. The United States is unusual in this regard—in most other countries, only the government is able to sue antitrust violators. A successful plaintiff can recover treble damages from the defendant. Nonetheless, many companies prefer to leave antitrust enforcement to the government and avoid burdensome legal fees.

In developing a competitive strategy, managers typically consider two different approaches:

- Cooperative strategies that allow companies to work together to their mutual advantage
- Aggressive strategies, designed to create an advantage over competitors

COOPERATIVE STRATEGIES

Three types of cooperative strategies are potentially illegal:

- **Horizontal agreements** among competitors. An agreement between Levi Strauss and Calvin Klein Jeans—both manufacturers of denim jeans—would be a horizontal agreement.
- **Vertical agreements** among participants at different stages of the production process. An agreement between Levi Strauss and the Limited—one company makes jeans, the other sells them—would be a vertical agreement.
- **Mergers and joint ventures** among competitors. Here, companies go beyond simple agreements to combine forces more permanently.

The following table lists the cooperative strategies that will be discussed in this chapter:

Horizontal Strategies	Vertical Strategies	Mergers
Market division	Reciprocal dealing	Horizontal mergers
Price-fixing	Price discrimination	Vertical mergers
Bid-rigging		Joint ventures
Refusal to deal		

HORIZONTAL COOPERATIVE STRATEGIES

Although the term "cooperative strategies" *sounds* benign, these tactics are often harmful to competition. Many horizontal cooperative strategies are *per se* violations of the law and can lead to prison terms, heavy fines, and expensive lawsuits with customers and competitors.

MARKET DIVISION

Any effort by a group of competitors to divide its market is a *per se* violation of §1 of the Sherman Act. Illegal arrangements include agreements to allocate customers, territory, or products. For example, these business schools would be in violation if:

- Georgetown agreed to accept only men and, in return, George Washington would take only women[3]
- Stanford agreed to accept only students from west of the Mississippi, leaving the east to Yale, or
- Northwestern agreed not to provide courses in entrepreneurship, while the University of Chicago eliminated its international offerings.

PRICE-FIXING AND BID-RIGGING

When competitors agree on the prices at which they will buy or sell products or services, their price-fixing is a *per se* violation of §1 of the Sherman Act. Bid-rigging is also a *per se* violation. In bid-rigging, competitors eliminate price competition by agreeing on who will submit the lowest bid. In an early case, the defendants argued that price-fixing was only wrong if the prices were *unfair*. The Supreme Court disagreed. In its view, prices should be set by markets, not by competitors—or judges. Moreover, "the reasonable price fixed today may become the unreasonable price of tomorrow."[4]

For the better part of a century, price-fixing and bid-rigging have been illegal, yet they never seem to go away. Here are some examples:

- *Dairy Industry.* Using a computer to analyze the bids that schools received on their milk contracts, the Florida Attorney General uncovered a pervasive price-fixing scheme. By some estimates, price-fixing raised milk prices in Florida by 14 percent. Forty-three companies were convicted or pleaded guilty; two dozen individuals went to prison. Companies paid fines in excess of $90 million.
- *College Athletics.* Colleges began to complain about the cost of their athletic programs. In particular, the cost of the coaching staffs seemed out of control. After all, some assistant coaches were being paid as much as $70,000 a year. In response, NCAA schools (that is, members of the National Collegiate Athletic Association) agreed to cap the salaries of assistant coaches at (a very stingy) $12,000. But a court blew the whistle, finding that the NCAA had engaged in illegal price-fixing. A jury awarded the coaches $66 million.
- *Airlines.* The Justice Department accused eight major airlines of negotiating agreements to raise fares and end discounts by sending elaborate signals

---

[3] This, of course, does not mean that all single-sex schools are violating the antitrust laws. They are in violation only if their admissions policy results from an agreement with competitors.

[4] *United States v. Trenton Potteries Co.*, 273 U.S. 392, 47 S. Ct. 377, 1927 U.S. LEXIS 975 (1927).

about planned price changes over their jointly owned computerized ticket information system. Alaska Airlines, American, Continental, Delta, Northwest, TWA, United, and USAir agreed to new rules designed to prevent price-fixing in their industry.

For information about new and interesting price-fixing cases, check out http://www.antitrust.org/.

Antitrust laws in the United States are stricter—and more diligently enforced—than those in most other countries. How far offshore do our laws stretch? American companies that engage in anticompetitive behavior overseas are generally subject to U.S. antitrust laws only if their behavior has an impact on trade in the United States. When are foreign companies subject to U.S. antitrust laws? The following case addresses this issue.

UNITED STATES v. NIPPON PAPER INDUSTRIES CO., LTD.

109 F.3d 1, 1997 U.S. App. LEXIS 4939
United States Court of Appeals for the First Circuit, 1997

Facts: Nippon Paper Industries Co., Ltd. (NPI) was a Japanese company that manufactured fax paper. In a series of meetings held only in Japan, NPI agreed with a group of other companies to fix the price of thermal fax paper throughout North America. NPI subsequently sold $6 million worth of the paper in the United States at inflated prices. The U.S. Justice Department obtained a criminal indictment alleging that NPI had violated §1 of the Sherman Act.

NPI moved to dismiss the indictment on the grounds that the conduct in question, if it occurred at all, had taken place in Japan. The district court agreed with NPI and dismissed the case. The Justice Department appealed.

Issue: Does the Sherman Act apply to conduct that took place entirely overseas?

Excerpts from Judge Selya's Decision: Our law has long presumed that legislation of Congress, unless a contrary intent appears, is meant to apply only within the territorial jurisdiction of the United States. In *American Banana Co.*, the Court considered the application of the Sherman Act in a civil action concerning conduct which occurred entirely in Central America and which had no discernible effect on imports to the United States. The Court held that the defendant's actions abroad were not proscribed by the Sherman Act.

Our jurisprudence is precedent-based, but it is not static. In *Hartford Fire Ins. Co.*, the Justices [permitted] antitrust claims under Section One to go forward despite the fact that the actions which allegedly violated Section One occurred entirely on British soil. While noting *American Banana*'s initial disagreement with this proposition, the *Hartford Fire Court* deemed it "well established by now that the Sherman Act applies to foreign conduct that was meant to produce and did in fact produce some substantial effect in the United States."

To sum up, the case law now conclusively establishes that antitrust actions predicated on wholly foreign conduct which has an intended and substantial effect in the United States come within Section One's jurisdictional reach. We accept the government's cardinal argument, reverse the order of the district court, reinstate the indictment, and remand for further proceedings.

The ethics discussion in Chapter 2 considered the possibility that illegal behavior could sometimes be ethical. Price-fixing is a *per se* violation of the law. Are there times when it might nonetheless be ethical? For example, every year the Council of Fashion Designers of America puts on a major fashion show under tents in New York's Bryant Park. This show offers an opportunity for up-and-coming designers to mix with more established names—and to attract media attention. The newcomers complained, however, that they could not compete with famous designers and attract vital media attention without hiring top models. But the price of these superstar models was too high: upwards of $10,000 for a three-hour show. Sympathetic to the newcomers' plight, the Council capped modeling fees at $750 an hour for supermodels and $500 for rookies. Is this price-fixing illegal? Is it ethical to protect the inexperienced designers?

Refusals to Deal

Every company generally has the right to decide with whom it will or will not do business. **However, a refusal to deal violates the Sherman Act if it harms competition.** In a **refusal to deal**, a group of competitors boycotts a buyer, supplier, or even another competitor. This is a rule of reason violation, illegal only if it harms competition. For example, a group of clothing manufacturers agreed that they would not sell apparel to retailers who also bought from style pirates—companies that copied the manufacturers' designs. The Supreme Court held that this was an illegal refusal to deal because it was harming competition.[5]

Vertical Cooperative Strategies

Vertical cooperative strategies are agreements among participants at different stages of the production process.

Reciprocal Dealing Agreements

Under a reciprocal dealing agreement, a buyer refuses to purchase goods from a supplier unless the supplier also purchases items from the buyer. Imagine that you are in the business of processing beets into sugar. During this process, it is easy to separate the seeds, which can then be used to grow more beets. Why not suggest to your beet suppliers that they buy their seeds from you? Why not further suggest that if *they* are not willing, you will find other suppliers who are?[6]

You are proposing a reciprocal dealing agreement. In the past, such arrangements were common. Many major corporations even kept computer records of purchases, sales, and "balance of trade" with other companies. Although these arrangements might have made *business* sense, the government took the view that they were also *rule of reason* violations of the Sherman Act; that is, they were illegal if they had an anticompetitive effect. The government brought suit against several companies, including a beet processor. It also halted a number of mergers that might have resulted in internal reciprocal arrangements. In recent years, however, the government has brought few of these cases. Reciprocal

---

[5] *Fashion Originators' Guild of America, Inc. v. Federal Trade Commission*, 312 U.S. 457, 61 S. Ct. 703, 1941 U.S. LEXIS 1318 (1941).

[6] See *Betaseed, Inc. v. U & I, Inc.*, 681 F.2d 1203, 1982 U.S. App. LEXIS 17190 (9th Cir. 1982).

dealing agreements are likely to be a problem now only if they foreclose a *significant share* of the market and if the participants *agree* not to buy from others.

PRICE DISCRIMINATION

Under the Robinson-Patman Act, it is illegal to charge different prices to different purchasers if:

- The items are the same, and
- The price discrimination lessens competition.

However, it is legal to charge a lower price to a particular buyer if:

- The costs of serving this buyer are lower, or
- The seller is simply meeting competition.

Congress passed the Robinson-Patman Act (RPA) in 1936 to prevent large chains from driving small, local stores out of business. Owners of these "Ma and Pa stores" complained that the large chains could sell goods cheaper because suppliers charged them lower prices. As a result of the RPA, managers who would otherwise like to develop different pricing strategies for specific customers or regions may hesitate to do so for fear of violating this statute. In reality, however, they have little to fear.

Under the RPA, a plaintiff must prove that price discrimination occurred and that it lessened competition. It is now perfectly permissible, for example, for a supplier to sell at a different price to its Texas and California distributors, or to its health care and educational distributors, as long as the distributors are not in competition with each other.

The RPA also expressly permits price variations that are based on differences in cost. Thus Mattel would be perfectly within its legal rights to sell dolls to Toys "R" Us at a lower price than to the local Toy Shoppe if Mattel's costs are lower. Toys "R" Us often buys shipments the size of railroad containers that cost less to deliver than individual cartons. Toys "R" Us may also be willing to purchase in February—a month when toy demand is low. If it is cheaper to sell to Toys "R" Us, Mattel can legitimately charge lower prices.

Over the last decade, the federal government has virtually abandoned its enforcement of the RPA. Between 1937 and 1971, the FTC brought an average of 40 price discrimination cases each year; recently, it has averaged only one or two. Some federal officials have even urged that the RPA be repealed to prevent it from interfering with the smooth operation of the market. This fade-out of government action has left enforcement in the hands of individual plaintiffs, but these cases are receiving little encouragement from the courts.

The Supreme Court has, for instance, made it much more difficult for plaintiffs to win damages in price discrimination cases. When Chrysler Motors sold cars to dealers in Birmingham, Alabama, it charged the J. Truett Payne dealership more than other dealers in the area. Unable to compete, Payne went out of business. The accepted formula for determining damages in a Robinson-Patman Act case had been the difference between the two prices times the number of units purchased. These numbers were easy to calculate. However, in *Payne*, the Supreme Court held that it is not enough to prove that competitors are able to buy at a lower cost. The plaintiff must also show that these competitors passed their savings on to customers and, as a result, plaintiff lost profits.[7] These are difficult facts to prove. As a result of cases such as this, antitrust lawyers often advise their clients not to worry too much about price discrimination suits because dissatisfied customers will usually not seek damages in court but will instead try to negotiate a better price.

MERGERS AND JOINT VENTURES

The Clayton Act prohibits mergers that are anticompetitive. Companies with substantial assets must notify the FTC *before* consummating a merger.[8] This notification gives the government an opportunity to prevent a merger ahead of time, rather than trying to untangle one after the fact.

Mergers have never been more popular. In one recent year, the U.S. government examined 4,728 proposed mergers, almost double the average of the prior five years. Among the mega-deals the government has recently reviewed are Eon's $80 billion offer for Mobil Corp. and Bell Atlantic's $23 billion purchase of Nynex.

HORIZONTAL MERGERS

A horizontal merger involves companies that compete in the same market. Traditionally, the government has aggressively sought to prevent horizontal mergers that could lead to a monopoly or even a highly concentrated industry. In the *Von's Grocery* case, decided in 1966, the Supreme Court upheld the Justice Department in its suit to prevent the merger of two grocery chains that represented only 7.5 percent of the grocery market in Los Angeles.[9] Compare that decision with the following case, decided almost 20 years later.

UNITED STATES v. WASTE MANAGEMENT, INC.

743 F.2d 976, 1984 U.S. App. LEXIS 18843
United States Court of Appeals for the Second Circuit, 1984

Facts: Waste Management, Inc. (WMI) acquired Texas Industrial Disposal, Inc. (TIDI). Both companies were in the trash collection business. In Dallas, their combined market share was 48.8 percent. The trial court held that the merger was illegal and ordered WMI to divest itself of TIDI.

Issue: Did WMI violate the Clayton Act by acquiring TIDI?

Excerpts from Judge Winter's Decision: A post-merger market share of 48.8 percent is sufficient to establish *prima facie* illegality under *United States v. Philadelphia National Bank* and its progeny. That

[7] *J. Truett Payne Co., Inc. v. Chrysler Motors Corp.*, 451 U.S. 557, 101 S. Ct. 1923, 1981 U.S. LEXIS 49, (1981).

[8] Notification is required if (1) one company has assets of at least $100 million and the other has assets of at least $10 million, and (2) the acquiring company is purchasing stock worth at least $15 million or 15 percent of the voting securities of the acquired company.

[9] *United States v. Von's Grocery Co.*, 384 U.S. 270, 86 S. Ct. 1478, 1966 U.S. LEXIS 2823 (1966).

decision held that large market shares are a convenient proxy for appraising the danger of monopoly power resulting from a horizontal merger. Under its rationale, a merger resulting in a large market share is presumptively illegal, rebuttable only by a demonstration that the merger will not have anticompetitive effects.

[In the present case, the *Philadelphia National Bank*] presumption is rebutted by the fact that competitors can enter the Dallas waste hauling market with such ease. WMI argues that it is unable to raise prices over the competitive level because new firms would quickly enter the market and undercut them. A person wanting to start in the trash collection business can acquire a truck, a few containers, drive the truck himself, and operate out of his home. A great deal depends on the individual's personal initiative, and whether he has the desire and energy to perform a high quality of service. If he measures up well by these standards, he can compete successfully with any other company for a portion of the trade, even though a small portion. Over the last 10 years or so a number of companies have started in the commercial trash collection business.

We conclude that the 48.8 percent market share attributed to WMI does not accurately reflect future market power. Since that power is in fact insubstantial, the merger does not, therefore, substantially lessen competition in the relevant market and does not violate the [Clayton Act].

Traditionally, market share was the most important factor in evaluating mergers. As *Waste Management* indicates, however, market share is no longer the sole issue in merger cases. The government and the courts now also consider how the merger will affect competition and consumers. Thus the government cleared a merger between aircraft giants Boeing and McDonnell Douglas, which together have a virtual monopoly on the American aircraft business. But the aircraft market is global, and American companies face severe competition from Europe's Airbus consortium. Therefore, the government believes that the merger will not harm competition.

Conversely, the FTC blocked the merger of office supply giants, Staples, Inc. and Office Depot. Nationally, these two retailers control only 4 percent of the market for office supplies. Is the FTC harking back to the days of *Von's Grocery*? Not exactly. The office superstores' national market share is relatively low because they have no stores at all in many areas of the country. Rather than national market share, the FTC focused instead on their ability to control prices locally. The agency found that, when both stores operate in the same market, prices are significantly lower than when only one store is present. Thus a box of file folders costs $1.72 in Orlando, Florida (where both stores compete) and $4.17 in nearby Leesburg (where Office Depot has a monopoly). In the FTC's view, if the two stores combined, they would have enough power in local markets to raise prices and harm consumers.

Ralph Nader, a longtime consumer advocate, runs a Web site that assesses potential mergers from the consumer point of view. You can find it at http://www.citizen.org/. Or, for a merger simulation game, play with http://www.antitrust.org/.

Making sense of American antitrust law can be difficult enough, but, as the following article illustrates, antitrust laws around the world vary greatly.

When it comes to competition policy, there may be little common ground across the globe. Roughly half of the World Trade Organization's 132 members do not even have competition laws, and those that do have widely differing views. Some countries, for example, tolerate price-fixing, while others unreservedly condemn it. There are also disagreements on important issues such as the standards by which proposed mergers should be judged.[10] Information on antitrust policy around the world is available at http://www.oecd.org/daf/clp/LINKS.HTM.

VERTICAL MERGERS

A vertical merger involves companies at different stages of the production process—for example, when a producer of a final good acquires a supplier or vice versa. Vertical mergers can also be anticompetitive, especially if they reduce entry into a market by putting a lock on an important supplier or a top distributor. Consider the following example.

International Management Group (IMG) is a management conglomerate that dominates the tennis world. IMG operates tournaments, sets up exhibitions, holds broadcast rights, and manages the careers of more than 100 pros, including top-ranked player Pete Sampras. Recently, IMG acquired the Nick Bolletieri Tennis Academy, training ground for many of the sport's present and future stars. IMG's competitors question whether this acquisition violates the antitrust laws. Says the head coach of another tennis academy, "You name it, IMG owns it, owns tournaments, owns the players, owns the academy. It's impossible to compete at that level, so we don't even bother to try.[11]

IMG's acquisition of the Nick Bolletieri Tennis Academy was a vertical merger—IMG acquired a source of supply for its management group. The Justice Department has not been overly concerned about vertical mergers. The department's guidelines provide that it will challenge vertical mergers only if they are likely to increase entry barriers in a concentrated market. For many years, the Justice Department did not challenge *any* vertical mergers. Recently, however, the FTC forced the restructuring of four vertical mergers. In one case, a leading western utility bought a coal producer. The FTC required the merged company to sell some of the coal mines. These cases may augur a new "get-tough" stance by the government.

JOINT VENTURES

A joint venture is a partnership for a limited purpose—the companies do not combine permanently, they simply work together on a specific project. The government will usually permit a joint venture, even between competitors with significant market power. The FTC approved, over strenuous objections from competitors, a joint venture between General Motors and Toyota to produce cars.

---

[10] "The Borders of Competition," *The Economist*, July 4, 1998, p. 69.

[11] Robin Finn, "Mixed Doubles: Players as Business," *The New York Times*, Mar. 16, 1994, p. B17. Copyright © 1994 by The New York Times Co. Reprinted by permission.

AGGRESSIVE STRATEGIES

The goal of an aggressive strategy is to gain an unfair advantage over competitors.

MONOPOLIZATION

Aggressive competition is beneficial for consumers—up until the moment a company develops enough power to control a market. One purpose of the Sherman Act is to prevent this type of control. **Under §2 of the Act, it is illegal to monopolize or attempt to monopolize a market.** To monopolize means to acquire a monopoly in the wrong way. *Having* a monopoly is legal unless it is *gained* or *maintained* by using wrongful tactics.

To determine if a defendant has illegally monopolized, we must ask three questions:

- **What is the market?** Without knowing the market, it is impossible to determine if someone is controlling it.
- **Does the company control the market?** Without control, there is no monopoly.
- **How did the company acquire or maintain its control?** Monopolization is illegal only if gained or kept in the wrong way.

WHAT IS THE MARKET?

This question is not as easy to answer as it sounds. Some people refer to the antitrust laws as the "Economists' Full-Employment Acts" because antitrust litigation requires testimony from economic experts.

Imagine that your company sells soft drinks with unusual food flavors—steak and cheese, among others. For some reason, you are the only company that sells food-flavored soft drinks so, by definition, you control 100 percent of the market. But is that the *relevant* market? Perhaps the relevant market is flavored drinks or soft drinks or all beverages. The question economists ask is: **How high can your prices rise before your buyers will switch to a different product?** If a price rise from $1.00 to $1.05 a bottle causes many of your customers to desert to Snapple or Coke, it is clear you are part of a larger market. Moreover, if changes in the prices of other drinks affect *your* sales, your products and theirs are probably close competitors. However, if you could raise your price to $5.00 per bottle and still hold on to many of your customers, then you might well be in your own market.

DOES THE COMPANY CONTROL THE MARKET?

You have 100 percent of the food-flavored soft drink market (although only 1 percent of the overall soft drink market and an infinitesimal percentage of the total beverage market). Traditionally, courts considered a share anywhere between 70 and 90 percent to constitute a monopoly. However, in the following case, Judge Kozinski indicates that market share is not important if other competitors can enter the market anytime they want (or anytime you raise your prices or lower your quality). **No matter what your market share, you do not have a monopoly unless you can exclude competitors or control prices.** Judge Kozinski certainly has a sense of humor—his opinion is larded with movie titles. How many can you find?

UNITED STATES v. SYUFY ENTERPRISES

903 F.2d 659, 1990 U.S. App. LEXIS 7396
United States Court of Appeals for the Ninth Circuit, 1990

Facts: Raymond Syufy entered the Las Vegas cinema market with a splash by opening a six-screen theater. His theaters are among the finest built and best run in the nation, making him something of a local hero. Syufy's entry into the Las Vegas market caused a stir, precipitating a titanic bidding war. Soon, theaters in Las Vegas were paying some of the highest license fees in the nation, while distributors sat back and watched the easy money roll in. After a hard-fought battle among several contenders, Syufy gained the upper hand. Three of his rivals saw their future as rocky and decided to sell out to Syufy, leaving a small exhibitor of mostly second-run films as Syufy's only competitor in Las Vegas. The Justice Department brought this antitrust suit to force Syufy to disgorge the theaters he had purchased from his former competitors.

Issue: Did Syufy have an illegal monopoly?

Excerpts from Judge Kozinski's Decision: Monopoly power is the power to exclude competition or control prices. Time after time, we have recognized this basic fact of economic life: A high market share, though it may ordinarily raise an inference of monopoly power, will not do so in a market with low entry barriers or other evidence of a defendant's inability to control prices or exclude competitors.

When Syufy acquired his competitors' theaters he temporarily diminished the number of competitors in the Las Vegas first-run film market. But this does not necessarily indicate foul play; many legitimate market arrangements diminish the number of competitors. It would be odd if they did not, as the nature of competition is to make winners and losers. If there are no significant barriers to entry, however, eliminating competitors will not enable the survivors to reap a monopoly profit; any attempt to raise prices above the competitive level will lure into the market new competitors able and willing to offer their commercial goods or personal services for less.

Syufy was unable to maintain market share. [In one year,] Syufy raked in 93 percent of the gross box office from first-run films in Las Vegas. [Three years later,] that figure had fallen to 75 percent. The government insists that 75 percent is still a large number, and we are hard-pressed to disagree; but that's not the point. The antitrust laws do not require that rivals compete in a dead heat, only that neither is unfairly kept from doing his personal best.

It can't be said often enough that the antitrust laws protect competition, not competitors. The record here conclusively demonstrates that neither acquiring the screens of his competitors nor working hard at better serving the public gave Syufy deliverance from competition.

The Justice Department also alleges that Syufy, top gun in the Las Vegas movie market, had the power to push around Hollywood's biggest players, dictating to them what prices they could charge for their movies. The evidence does not support this view. Syufy has at all times paid license fees far in excess of the national average. While successful, Syufy is in no position to put the squeeze on distributors. It would have been risky business even to try.

By finding that Syufy did not possess the power to set prices or to exclude competition, the district court removed the firing pins from the government's litigation arsenal. Without these essential elements, its lawsuit collapses like a house of cards.

HOW DID THE COMPANY ACQUIRE OR MAINTAIN ITS CONTROL?

***Possessing* a monopoly is not necessarily illegal; using "*bad acts*" to acquire or maintain one is.** If the law prohibited the mere possession of a monopoly, it might discourage companies from producing excellent products or offering low prices. Anyone who can produce a better product cheaper than anyone else is entitled to a monopoly. In your case, you have very cleverly developed a secret method for adding flavors to carbonated water. You also have an efficient factory and highly trained workers, so you can sell your drinks for 5¢ a bottle less than your competitors. If, in fact, you do have a monopoly, it is for all the right reasons. You have demonstrated exactly the kind of innovative, efficient behavior that benefits consumers. If you were sued for a violation of the antitrust laws, you would win.

Some companies use ruthless tactics to acquire or maintain a monopoly. It is these "bad acts" that render a monopoly illegal. In the past, the definition of bad acts was broad, and any company with a monopoly could be in violation unless it showed that, despite its best efforts to duck, a monopoly had been *thrust upon* it. In 1945, a famous judge, with the appropriate name of Learned Hand, found that Alcoa's monopoly in the aluminum industry was illegal because the company had repeatedly expanded capacity to anticipate demand.[12] In his view, the company should have waited to expand until demand actually existed. Alcoa was in violation because it could have easily *avoided* a monopoly—the monopoly had not been thrust upon it.

Everyone makes mistakes. Although Learned Hand is generally considered one of the greatest judges of his era, most commentators now believe that Alcoa was wrongly decided. *Berkey Photo* is a more typical modern case.[13] *Berkey* accused Eastman Kodak Co. of repeatedly and unnecessarily changing the size of its cameras to confound competitors who manufactured film to fit them. Although Learned Hand most likely would have found such actions to be illegal, the *Berkey* court rejected the view that monopolies are acceptable only if *thrust upon* the defendant and instead held that aggressive competitive strategies are legal even if they have the effect of hindering competitors. In finding Kodak not liable, the court reasoned that the company would not have repeatedly changed camera and film specifications if consumers had objected. The success or failure of Kodak's strategy ought to be determined in the market and not by the courts. The following news report details British Airways' aggressive tactics against a competitor. Would the *Berkey* court have considered this strategy acceptable?

---

[12] *United States v. Aluminum Co. of America*, 148 F.2d 416, 1945 U.S. App. LEXIS 4091 (2d Cir. 1945). Judge Hand's parents did not necessarily foresee his illustrious career when naming him. "Learned" was his mother's maiden name, and it was the tradition in his family to give the mother's name to one of the children.

[13] *Berkey Photo, Inc. v. Eastman Kodak Co.*, 603 F.2d 263, 1979 U.S. App. LEXIS 13692 (2d Cir. 1979), cert. denied, 444 U.S. 1093, 100 S. Ct. 1061, 1980 U.S. LEXIS 923 (1980).

Lord King, the chairman of British Airways (BA), apologized to Richard Branson, the head of Virgin Atlantic Airways, for BA's dirty tricks. Among other tactics, BA:

- Approached Virgin's customers to persuade them to switch to BA flights
- Refused to cooperate on maintenance and training
- Obtained customers' files by tapping into Virgin's computer
- Contacted customers and pretended to represent Virgin, and
- Spread untrue, harmful rumors about Mr. Branson.

London's High Court ordered BA to pay Branson $900,000 in libel damages. Shortly thereafter, Lord King lost his job.

Branson recently filed an antitrust suit against BA in the United States, seeking $325 million in damages. Were BA's actions legitimate competitive strategies? Or did the company go too far?

RIGHT & WRONG

Whether or not these activities were *legal*, were they *ethical*? How do you think Lord King felt when these activities were reported in the newspaper? Would he have minded if Branson had used the same tactics against BA? Did BA's strategy pay in the short run? In the long run? If you were running BA, what guidelines would you give your employees?

PREDATORY PRICING

Predatory pricing occurs when a company lowers its prices below cost to drive competitors out of business. Once the predator has the market to itself, it raises prices to make up lost profits—and more besides.

Recall that, under §2 of the Sherman Act, it is illegal "to monopolize" and also to "attempt to monopolize." Typically, the goal of a predatory pricing scheme is either to win control of a market or to maintain it. A ban on these schemes prevents monopolization and attempts to monopolize. To win a predatory pricing case, the plaintiff must prove three elements:

- The defendant is selling its products *below cost*.
- The defendant *intends* that the plaintiff go out of business.
- If the plaintiff does go out of business, the defendant will be able to earn sufficient profits to *recoup* its prior losses.

The classic example of predatory pricing is a large grocery store that comes into a small town offering exceptionally low prices subsidized by profits from its other branches. Once all the "Ma and Pa" corner groceries go out of business, MegaGrocery raises its prices to much higher levels.

Predatory pricing offers a good example of how attitudes toward antitrust laws have changed. Formerly, courts took predatory pricing very seriously. The term certainly *sounds* bad. But despite its name, courts generally are not as concerned about predatory pricing now as they used to be. For one thing, consumers benefit from price wars, at least in the short run. For another, the cases are hard to prove. Here is why:

- **The defendant is selling its products below cost.** This rule sounds sensible, but what does "cost" mean? As you know from your economics courses, there are many different kinds of costs—total, average variable, marginal, to name a few. Under current law, any price below *average variable cost* is generally presumed to be predatory.[14] The rule may be easy to state, but, in real life, average variable cost is difficult to calculate. First, plaintiffs must obtain most of the data from the defendant. Even if a defendant has a good idea of what its average variable costs are, it will not necessarily tell all in court. Moreover, many of the economic decisions about what items fit into which cost category are subjective. It is difficult for the plaintiff to prove that its subjective view is closer to the truth than the defendant's.
- **The defendant intends that the plaintiff go out of business.** Even if Ma and Pa can calculate MegaGrocery's average variable cost to the satisfaction of a court, they will not necessarily win their case. They must prove that MegaGrocery intended to put them out of business. That is a pretty tall order, short of finding some smoking gun like a strategic plan that explicitly says MegaGrocery wants Ma and Pa gone.
- **If the plaintiff does go out of business, the defendant will be able to earn sufficient profits to recoup its prior losses.** Until Ma and Pa go out of business, MegaGrocery will lose money—after all, it is selling food below cost. To win their case, Ma and Pa must show that MegaGrocery will be able to make up all its lost profits once the corner grocery is out of the way. They need to prove, for example, that no other grocery chain will come to town. It is difficult to prove a negative proposition like that, especially in the grocery business where barriers to entry are low.

Recently, plaintiffs simply have not had much success with predatory pricing suits. For example, Liggett began selling generic cigarettes 30 percent below the price of branded cigarettes. Brown & Williamson retaliated by introducing its own generics at an even lower price. Liggett sued, claiming that Brown's prices were below cost. The Supreme Court agreed that Brown was not only selling below cost but also intended to harm Liggett. Brown still won the case, however, because there was no evidence that it would be able to recover its losses from the below-cost pricing. If Brown raised its prices, other competitors would come back into the market.[15]

TYING ARRANGEMENTS

A tying arrangement is an agreement to sell a product on the condition that the buyer also purchases a different (or tied) product. A tying arrangement is illegal under §3 of the Clayton Act and §1 of the Sherman Act if:

---

[14] To calculate average variable cost, add all the firm's costs except its fixed costs and then divide by the total quantity of output.

[15] *Brooke Group Ltd. v. Brown & Williamson Tobacco Corp.*, 509 U.S. 209, 113 S. Ct. 2578, 1993 U.S. LEXIS 4245 (1993).

- Two products are clearly separate
- The seller requires the buyer to purchase the two products together
- The seller has significant power in the market for the tying product, and
- The seller is shutting out a significant part of the market for the tied product.

Six movie distributors refused to sell individual films to television stations. Instead, they insisted that a station buy an entire package of movies. To obtain classics such as *Treasure of the Sierra Madre* and *Casablanca* (the **tying product**), the station also had to purchase such forgettable films as *Nancy Drew Troubleshooter*, *Gorilla Man*, and *Tugboat Annie Sails Again* (the **tied product**).[16] Is this an illegal tying arrangement? These are the questions to ask:

- **Are the two products clearly separate?** A left and right shoe are not separate products, and a seller can legally require that they be purchased together. *Gorilla Man*, on the other hand, is a separate product from *Casablanca*.
- **Is the seller requiring the buyer to purchase the two products together?** Yes, that is the whole point of these "package deals."
- **Does the seller have significant power in the market for the tying product?** In this case, the tying products are the classic movies. Since they are copyrighted, no one else can show them without the distributor's permission. The six distributors controlled a great many classic movies. So, yes, they do have significant market power.
- **Is the seller shutting out a significant part of the market for the tied product?** In this case, the tied products are the undesirable films like *Tugboat Annie Sails Again*. Television stations forced to take the unwanted films did not buy "B" movies from other distributors. These other distributors were effectively foreclosed from a substantial part of the market.

In the following case, Mercedes-Benz decided to include floor mats as standard equipment. Is that illegal tying?

LLOYD DESIGN CORP. v. MERCEDES-BENZ OF NORTH AMERICA, INC.

66 Cal. App. 4th 716, 1998 Cal. App. LEXIS 768
Court of Appeal of California, 1998

Facts: Mercedes-Benz sells less than 1 percent of all automobiles in this country, but among luxury cars, it holds about a 10 percent market share. Floor mats were originally optional accessories in Mercedes cars. Lloyd Design Corp. sold floor mats to some Mercedes dealerships, which, in turn, sold the mats to consumers. Mercedes then decided to make floor mats standard equipment. Dealers reported that luxury car customers expected floor mats, and a growing number of competitors provided them.

Lloyd had been selling some $250,000 in floor mats to Mercedes dealerships in California, but

---

[16] *United States v. Loew's Inc.*, 371 U.S. 38, 83 S. Ct. 97, 1962 U.S. LEXIS 2332 (1962).

lost this entire business after the change in policy. Lloyd filed suit against Mercedes, claiming that the decision to deliver the cars with floor mats constituted an illegal tying arrangement.

You be the Judge: **Did Mercedes engage in illegal tying when it provided floor mats in its automobiles?**

Argument for Lloyd: These two products—cars and floor mats—are clearly separate products. They have traditionally been sold separately. Mercedes is now requiring that they be purchased together. The company has significant power in the market for luxury cars and is forcing customers to buy a product that they may not want. This is a classic case of illegal tying and, like all tying arrangements, it serves no purpose beyond the suppression of competition.

Argument for Mercedes: Floor mats are not a separate product; they are a fundamental part of the car. Does Lloyd believe that Mercedes should sell just the engine and the body, and that everything else—including the mirrors, seats, and steering wheel—is a different product?

Moreover, Mercedes controls only 10 percent of the luxury car market; it cannot force consumers to buy a product they do not want. Nor is Mercedes attempting to control the floor mat market. This market is still highly competitive, but now manufacturers are competing to sell to Mercedes, rather than to dealers. There is no harm to competition and no illegal tying. Nor is there any harm to consumers—they are receiving a floor mat for free.

CONTROLLING DISTRIBUTORS AND RETAILERS

The goal of an aggressive strategy is to force competitors out of a market—by undercutting their prices or tying products together, for example. Controlling distributors and retailers is another method for excluding competitors. It is difficult to compete in a market if you are foreclosed from the best distribution channels.

ALLOCATING CUSTOMERS AND TERRITORY

As you saw earlier in this chapter, a *horizontal* agreement by *competitors* to allocate customers and territories is a *per se* violation of §1 of the Sherman Act. **However, a *vertical* allocation of customers or territory is illegal only if it adversely affects competition in the market as a whole.** It is a rule of reason, not a *per se*, violation.

Suppose that Hi-Fat Favorites, Inc. produces an expensive, rich, creamy ice cream. It grants its distributors the exclusive right to sell in a particular territory or the exclusive right over a particular type of customer (convenience stores, university dining halls, or large grocery chains). In return for these exclusive rights, Hi-Fat requires the distributors to stock a large range of flavors, hire highly trained (expensive) sales help, and advertise widely. Such requirements not only increase sales but also enhance distributor loyalty. The distributors have such a large investment in Hi-Fat's products that they are reluctant to switch to another manufacturer. A change would mean unloading a large inventory, developing new advertisements, and laying off some of the sales force.

Hi-Fat clearly has good business reasons for adopting such a plan. It is reducing **intrabrand** competition (among its *dealers*) but enhancing **inter-brand** competition (between *brands*). With its committed dealer network, Hi-Fat can compete more fiercely against other brands. Vertical allocation is a rule of reason violation, which means that the law will intervene only if Hi-Fat's activities have an anticompetitive impact on the market as a whole. But since Hi-Fat's plan increases inter-brand competition, it is unlikely to have an anticompetitive impact.

EXCLUSIVE DEALING AGREEMENTS

An **exclusive dealing contract** is one in which a distributor or retailer agrees with a supplier not to carry the products of any other supplier. **Under §1 of the Sherman Act and §3 of the Clayton Act, exclusive dealing contracts are subject to a rule of reason and are illegal only if they have an anticompetitive effect.**

Consider the case of Ben & Jerry's. With over $100 million in sales, it was a major player in the ice cream market. And some of its competitors alleged that it was playing hardball. Just ask Amy Miller. She started Amy's Ice Creams in a small storefront in Austin, Texas. Her ice cream was so popular that she decided to begin producing pints for sale in grocery stores. But when she tried to enter the Houston market, Sunbelt, the dominant distributor in the area, refused to carry her desserts. She thinks Sunbelt turned her down because Ben & Jerry's had forbidden it to carry other premium brands.

Ironically, the ice cream was once in the other bowl, so to speak. When Ben and Jerry were the new boys on the block, they discovered that Pillsbury (owner of Häagen-Dazs) included provisions in its contracts that prohibited distributors from carrying Ben & Jerry's brand. When Ben & Jerry's produced written contracts containing these exclusory clauses, Pillsbury backed down immediately. Thereafter, no one in the industry used written distribution contracts.

Amy Miller threatened to sue Ben & Jerry's for violating the antitrust laws with exclusive dealing contracts. In determining if these agreements had an anticompetitive impact on the market, a court would consider the following factors:

- **The number of other distributors available.** Amy said that no one but Sunbelt would do because only the best distributors were able to preserve the ice cream's quality.
- **The portion of the market foreclosed by the exclusive dealing agreements.** Without Sunbelt, Amy's Ice Creams could not penetrate the Houston market, so it had to shut down its pint production line.
- **The ease with which new distributors could enter the market.** Sunbelt had few, if any, competitors. Presumably, the market was a difficult one to enter.
- **The possibility that Amy could distribute the products herself.** Not a chance. Amy could barely manage to *make* the ice cream.
- **The legitimate business reasons that might have led the distributor to accept an exclusive contract.** Here is what Sunbelt's vice-president had to say: "We already had our table full with super premium pints. We felt Amy's was an underfinanced product and we would have had to replace a high-volume product to give it a shot. And we personally did not think the product was very good. We also did not know if the company had the finances to assure continuous production."[17]

---

[17] Rickie Windle, "Ben & Jerry's Creams Amy's," *Austin Business Journal*, Oct. 4, 1993, vol. 13, no. 33, §1, p. 1.

Would an exclusive dealing agreement between Ben & Jerry's and Sunbelt be anticompetitive? If so, would their business reasons justify the contract?

RESALE PRICE MAINTENANCE

Peter Polites (pronounced po-LEE-tus), owner of a Nine West store in New Jersey, slashed the price of a popular, smart-looking women's shoe last winter, knowing he would attract many more customers—and still earn a smooth 60 percent on each pair. But Mr. Polites's sale irritated some managers at large department stores down the hall in the Mall at Short Hills. One Nordstrom manager, he said, walked into Mr. Polites's small store, picked some shoes off the shelf, looked at the prices, slammed them down, and left without a word.

Mr. Polites said the Nordstrom manager later explained that the flats Mr. Polites had reduced to $49.99 from $60 were included on a confidential list of styles—known as the "off-limits list"—whose prices Nine West Group, Inc. rarely, if ever, lets stores mark down. Mr. Polites's low prices also maddened executives at Nine West, the footwear giant that says it sells one out of every five pairs of shoes sold to women in the United States. Vincent Camuto, chief executive of Nine West, called Mr. Polites and demanded that he end his sale. When Mr. Polites refused, Mr. Camuto told him that in that case, "We can't ship you those shoes."[18]

Is it legal for Nine West to cut off a retailer who refuses to raise his prices? This question is at the heart of an important antitrust conundrum—the validity of **resale price maintenance (RPM)**. RPM means the manufacturer sets *minimum* prices that retailers may charge. In other words, it prevents retailers from discounting. Why does the manufacturer care? After all, once the retailer purchases the shoes, the manufacturer has made its profit. The only way the manufacturer makes more money is to raise its *wholesale* price, not the *retail* price. RPM guarantees a profit margin for the *retailer*.

Manufacturers argue that they ought to have the right to decide how and at what price their products are sold. They may, for instance, want to promote an upscale brand image, one that could be destroyed by discount prices. Or the manufacturer may expect its dealers to provide a higher level of service than discounters can afford. Consumer advocates contend, however, that manufacturers such as Nine West are simply protecting dealers from competition. Discounting may or may not harm products, but, they insist, RPM certainly hurts consumers.

Amid this controversy, the Supreme Court agreed to decide a new RPM case. Spray-Rite was an herbicide dealer selling products manufactured by Monsanto. Spray-Rite claimed that Monsanto terminated the dealership contract because other dealers had complained about Spray-Rite's discount prices. Monsanto countered that Spray-Rite had not spent enough money training its salespeople or promoting the products. The jury, however, found for Spray-Rite and awarded $3.5 million in damages, which were trebled to $10.5 million. Monsanto appealed to the Supreme Court.[19]

---

[18] Melody Petersen, "Treading a Contentious Line," *The New York Times*, Jan. 13, 1999, p. C1.

[19] *Monsanto Co. v. Spray-Rite Corp.*, 465 U.S. 752, 104 S. Ct. 1464, 1984 U.S. LEXIS 39 (1984).

Many commentators expected the Supreme Court to decide that RPM was a rule of reason, not a *per se*, violation. The Court ruled unanimously, however, that **RPM is a *per se* violation of the law. A manufacturer may not enter into an agreement with distributors to fix prices.** The Court did create a potential loophole by saying that an agreement cannot be inferred simply because a manufacturer cuts off one distributor after receiving complaints from another. Unilateral action by a manufacturer to set prices is legal; an agreement with distributors about prices is not.[20]

PREVENTIVE Law

RPM is illegal. How can a manager stay out of trouble?

- Never agree with a customer on the price that the customer will charge for a product.
- Never promise a customer that you will terminate a competing retailer for selling at a discount.
- Be aware that any efforts to impose a pricing schedule on a retailer or distributor, whether by using incentives or threats, *may* be a violation of the law.

VERTICAL MAXIMUM PRICE-FIXING

In *Spray-Rite,* the Supreme Court held that resale price maintenance is a *per se* violation of the Sherman Act. In that case, the manufacturer set the *minimum* prices its distributors could charge. **Vertical *maximum* price fixing, (when a manufacturer sets *maximum* prices) however, is a *rule of reason* violation of the Sherman Act.** The defendant is liable only if the price-fixing harms competition. (You remember, from earlier in this chapter, that all *horizontal* price-fixing is a *per se* violation.)

When State Oil Co. leased a gas station to Barkat Khan, it set a maximum price that Khan could charge for gas. Khan sued State Oil, alleging a *per se* violation of the Sherman Act. The Supreme Court ruled in favor of the oil company, on the grounds that cutting prices to increase business is the very essence of competition and, furthermore, low prices benefit consumers.[21]

---

[20] The court decided that Monsanto had engaged in RPM because it had terminated Spray-Rite as part of an agreement with other distributors.

[21] *State Oil Co. v. Khan*, 522 U.S. 3, 118 S. Ct. 275, 1997 U.S. LEXIS 6705 (1997).

CHAPTER CONCLUSION

The purpose of the antitrust laws in the United States is to keep businesses on a narrow road. On the one hand, they may not swerve to one side and work too closely with competitors. Nor may they swerve to the other side and attack competitors too aggressively. Although managers sometimes resent the constraints imposed on them by antitrust laws, it is these laws that ensure the fair and open competition necessary for a healthy economy. In the end, the antitrust laws benefit us all. To learn more about antitrust law, see **http://www.webcounsel.com/**, which has a comprehensive list of antitrust Web sites.

CHAPTER REVIEW

1. There are two categories of antitrust violations: *per se* and rule of reason. *Per se* violations are automatic; courts do not consider mitigating circumstances. Rule of reason violations, on the other hand, are illegal only if they have an anticompetitive impact.

2. Any effort by a group of competitors to divide their market is a *per se* violation of the Sherman Act. Illegal arrangements include agreements to allocate customers, territory, or products.

3. Price-fixing and bid-rigging are *per se* violations of the Sherman Act.

4. Every company generally has the right to decide with whom it will do business. However, the Sherman Act prohibits competitors from joining together in an agreement to exclude a particular supplier, buyer, or even another competitor, if the agreement would hurt competition.

5. Reciprocal dealing agreements violate the Sherman Act if they foreclose competitors from a significant part of the market.

6. The Robinson-Patman Act prohibits companies from selling the same item at different prices if the sale lessens competition. However, a seller may charge different prices if these prices reflect different costs.

7. Under the Clayton Act, the federal government has the authority to prohibit anticompetitive mergers and joint ventures.

8. Possessing a monopoly need not be illegal; acquiring or maintaining it through "bad acts" is.

9. To determine if a company is guilty of monopolization, ask three questions:
   - What is the market?
   - Does the company control the market?
   - How did the company acquire its control?

10. To win a predatory pricing case, a plaintiff must prove three elements:
    - The defendant is selling its products below cost.
    - The defendant intends that the plaintiff go out of business.
    - If the plaintiff does go out of business, the defendant will be able to earn sufficient profit to recoup its prior losses.

11. A tying arrangement is illegal if:
    - The two products are clearly separate
    - The seller requires that the buyer purchase the two products together
    - The seller has significant power in the market for the tying product, and
    - The seller is shutting out a significant part of the market for the tied product.

12. Efforts by a manufacturer to allocate customers or territory among its distributors are subject to a rule of reason. These allocations are illegal only if they adversely affect competition in the market.

13. An exclusive dealing contract is one in which a distributor or retailer agrees with a supplier

not to carry the products of any other supplier. Exclusive dealing contracts are subject to a rule of reason and are prohibited only if they have an anticompetitive effect.

14. When a manufacturer enters into an agreement with distributors or retailers to fix minimum prices, this arrangement is called resale price maintenance. RPM is a *per se* violation of the law.

15. Vertical maximum price-fixing is a rule of reason violation of the Sherman Act. It is illegal only if it has an adverse impact on competition.

PRACTICE TEST

1. Harcourt Brace Jovanovich (HBJ) granted BRG an exclusive license to market HBJ's bar review materials in Georgia and to use HBJ's trade name. HBJ agreed not to compete with BRG in Georgia, and BRG agreed not to compete with HBJ outside the state. HBJ was entitled to receive $100 per student enrolled by BRG and 40 percent of revenues over $350 per student. Did this agreement violate the antitrust laws?

2. Fifty bakeries in New York formed an association. They developed a system of distribution under which stores were only allowed to buy from a single baker. A store that wanted to shift to another baker had to consult the association and pay cash to the former baker. The association also decided to raise the retail price of bread from 75 to 85 cents. All the association's members printed the new price on their bread sleeves. Are the bakeries in violation of the antitrust laws?

3. Fifty restaurants in Boston threatened to stop accepting the American Express card if the company refused to reduce the commission it charged on each purchase. Visa International, one of American Express's rivals, offered to pay the group's legal expenses. American Express then lowered its commission. For restaurants that processed more than $10 million in annual volume, American Express reduced charges from 3.25 percent to 2.75 percent. Rates for restaurants processing less than $10 million but more than $1 million a year fell to 3 percent. The company did not lower rates for restaurants with volume lower than $1 million a year. Have either the restaurants, Visa, or American Express potentially violated the antitrust laws?

4. Reserve Supply Corp., a cooperative of 379 lumber dealers, charged that Owens-Corning Fiberglass Corp. violated the Robinson-Patman Act by selling at lower prices to Reserve's competitors. Owens-Corning claimed that it had granted lower prices to a number of Reserve's competitors in order to meet, but not beat, the prices of other insulation manufacturers. Before lowering prices, Owens-Corning salespeople were required to seek approval from higher level officials in the company who checked that the discount prices were necessary to meet the competition. Is Owens-Corning in violation of the Robinson-Patman Act?

5. BAR/BRI is a company that prepares law students for bar exams. With branches in 45 states, it has the largest share of the bar review market in the country. Barpassers is a much smaller company located only in Arizona and California. BAR/BRI distributed pamphlets on campuses falsely suggesting Barpassers was near bankruptcy. Enrollments in Barpassers' courses dropped, and the company was forced to postpone plans for expansion. Does Barpassers have an antitrust claim against BAR/BRI?

6. **YOU BE THE JUDGE WRITING PROBLEM** American Academic Suppliers (AAS) and Beckley-Cardy (B-C) both sold educational supplies to schools. B-C's sales began to plummet, and it was rapidly losing market share. The company responded by reducing its catalogue prices 5 to 12 percent. It also offered a discount of 25 to 40 percent in states in which AAS was making substantial gains. What claim might AAS make against B-C? Is it likely to prevail in court? **Argument for**

AAS: B-C has committed predatory pricing. The company is selling below cost for the purpose of driving us out of business. **Argument for B-C:** Even if we were to drive AAS out of business, we do not have enough market power to recoup our losses.

7. Two medical supply companies in the San Francisco area provide oxygen to homes of patients. The companies are owned by the doctors who prescribe the oxygen. These doctors make up 60 percent of the lung specialists in the area. Does this arrangement create an antitrust problem?

8. Japanese companies sell more products in the United States than American companies sell in Japan. American business leaders and members of Congress have long been concerned about this imbalance. They suspect that the Japanese system of keiretsu tends to block efforts by U.S. companies to enter Japanese markets. Keiretsu are traditional groups of Japanese companies that tend to deal primarily with one another and are often affiliated by means of minority shareholdings, shared directors, memberships in common organizations, and dealings with the same banks. Could the U.S. Justice Department challenge these keiretsu arrangements under American antitrust law? What provisions of antitrust law might the system of keiretsu violate?

9. Videos of *Jurassic Park* and *Snow White and the Seven Dwarfs* were due in stores the same month. The stores ought to have been delighted at the prospect of having two blockbusters to sell, but instead they were worried—how to price the videos? Both Disney (*Snow White*) and MCA/Universal (*Jurassic Park*) were longtime proponents of MAP—minimum advertised pricing. In other words, if retailers sold the videos at prices below $14.95, the studios would not subsidize their advertising budgets. Many retailers would have *liked* to sell the videos at $14.95, but they were afraid competitors would undercut them. To make matters even more complicated, they had all heard rumors that Disney planned to take other steps against retailers who ignored MAP, such as delaying shipment of the next hit—*The Lion King*. Is MAP legal? What if the studios take "other steps"?

10. **RIGHT & WRONG** A mildly retarded 18-year-old woman and her mother (the Nelsons) brought a malpractice suit against one of the doctors at the Monroe Regional Medical Center. As a result, the Monroe Clinic notified the Nelsons that it would no longer treat them on a nonemergency basis. The patients then went to another local clinic, which was later acquired by Monroe. The merged clinic refused to treat the Nelsons on a nonemergency basis, so the Nelsons were obliged to seek medical treatment in another town 40 miles away. Has Monroe violated the antitrust laws? Whether or not the Monroe clinic has violated the antitrust laws, is it ethical to deny treatment to a patient?

INTERNET RESEARCH PROBLEM

Choose one of the antitrust cases featured at http:///www.antitrust.org/. Prepare a short argument for each side of the case. Did the right side win?

You can find further practice problems in the Online Quiz at http://beatty.westbuslaw.com or in the Study Guide that accompanies this text.

CYBERLAW

20

CHAPTER

Jason always said that his computer was his best friend. He was online all the time, sending instant messages to his friends, listening to music, doing research for his courses, and, OK, maybe playing a few games now and again. Occasionally, the computer could be annoying. It would crash once in awhile, trashing part of a paper he had forgotten to save. And there was the time that a copy of an e-mail he sent Lizzie complaining about Caroline somehow ended up in Caroline's mailbox. He was pretty irritated when the White Sox tickets he bought at an online auction turned out to be for a Little League team. And he was tired of all the spam advertising pornographic Web sites. But these things happen and, despite the petty annoyances, his computer was an important part of his life.

Then one day, Jason received a panicked instant message from a teammate on the college wrestling squad telling him to click on a certain Web site pronto to see someone they knew. When Jason eagerly clicked he discovered, to his total horror, that he was featured—in the nude. The Web site was selling videos showing him and other members of the wrestling team in the locker room in various states of undress. Other videos, from other locker and shower rooms, were for sale, too, showing football players and wrestlers from dozens of universities. The videos had titles like "Straight Off the Mat" and "Voyeur Time." No longer trusting technology, Jason pulled on his running shoes and dashed over to the office of his business law professor.

More than two billion people use the Internet[1] worldwide. Computers and the Internet—cyberspace—together comprise one of the great technological developments of the twentieth century. Inevitably, new technologies create the need for new law. In the thirteenth century, England was one of the first countries to develop passable roads. Like the Internet, these roadways greatly enhanced communication, creating social and business opportunities, but also enabled new crimes. Good roads meant that bad guys could sneak out of town without paying their bills. Parliament responded with laws to facilitate the collection of out-of-town debts. Similarly, while the Internet has opened up enormous opportunities in both our business and personal lives, it has also created the need for new laws, both to pave the way for these opportunities and to limit their dangers.

The process of lawmaking never stops. Judges sit and legislatures meet—all in an effort to create better rules and a better society. However, in an established area of law, such as contracts, the basic structure changes little. Cyberlaw is different, because it is still very much in its infancy. Not only are new laws being created almost daily, but whole areas of regulation are, as yet, unpaved roads. Although the process of rule making has progressed well, much debate still surrounds cyberspace law and much work remains to be done. This chapter focuses on the existing rules and also discusses the areas of regulation that are still incomplete and in debate.

Cyberlaw affects many areas of our lives. You will have noticed that this book contains numerous Cyberlaw features throughout. Chapter 10, for instance, discusses the validity of electronic contracts and signatures, Chapter 18 deals with cyber issues in securities law, and Chapter 21 contains a lengthy discussion of cyberlaw and intellectual property. This chapter, however, deals with issues that are unique to the cyber world, such as online privacy, hacking, and spam. If some of the words confuse you, the Web site at http://www.matisse.net/files/glossary.html provides a glossary of Internet terms.

Before beginning this chapter in earnest, let's return briefly to Jason, the wrestler. What recourse does Jason have for his Internet injuries? The nude video incident actually happened at Illinois State University and seven other colleges. Approximately 30 athletes filed suit against GTE and PSINet for selling the videos online. The outcome of that case is revealed later in this chapter. What about Jason's other computer injuries? Lizzie was not being a good friend, but it was perfectly legal for her to forward Jason's e-mail to Caroline. The seller of the White Sox tickets violated both federal and state fraud statutes. Spam—unsolicited commercial e-mail—is not illegal, but it is certainly annoying. Internet service providers (ISPs), such as America Online (AOL), have a number of legal weapons they can use against it, but a lawsuit is a slow and awkward tool for killing such a flourishing weed.

---

[1] The term "Internet" means "the international computer network of both Federal and non-Federal interoperable packet switched data networks." 47 U.S. §230 (f) (1). It is a giant network that connects smaller groups of linked computer networks. The World Wide Web is a decentralized collection of documents containing text, pictures, and sound that is accessible from Internet sites. It is a subnetwork of the Internet.

PRIVACY

The Internet has vastly increased our ability to communicate quickly and widely. There was a time when intraoffice memos were typed, photocopied, and then hand-delivered by messengers. Catalog orders were sent via regular mail, a comparatively slow, inefficient, and costly method.

As wonderful as computerized communication can be, though, it is not without its dangers. Consumers enter the most personal data—credit card numbers, bank accounts, lists of friends, medical information, product preferences—on the Internet. Who will have access to this data? Who can see it, use it, sell it? Many people fear that the Internet is a very large window through which the government, employers, business, and even criminals can find out more than they should about you and your money, habits, beliefs, and health. Even e-mail has its dangers. Who has not been embarrassed by an e-mail that ended up in the wrong mailbox?

Many commentators argue that, without significant changes in the law, our privacy will be obliterated. At the moment, however, privacy on the Internet is very much like the weather—everyone talks about it, but (so far) no one has done much about it. The three major sources of privacy concerns are Internet tracking, the hard drive, and e-mail.

INTERNET TRACKING

OF COOKIES AND CACHES

After once ordering a book from Amazon.com, the next time you log on, you'll be greeted with the message: "Hello, [Your Name]. We have recommendations for you in Books, Music, and more." Click on the link and you may find that, because you bought a GMAT study guide the first time, Amazon will entice you with other guides for standardized tests. However did Amazon know? Many Web sites automatically place a cookie on the hard drive of your computer when you visit them. **A cookie is a small file that includes an identification number and personal data such as your addresses (both e-mail and regular), phone and credit card numbers, and searches you have made or advertisements you have clicked on.**[2]

Some cookies track activity on a specific Web site, others follow a user from site to site, along the entire Internet trail. Indeed, a whole industry of Internet marketing firms knows how to target Web banners to individual surfers. Thus, if you visit Web sites for hotels in Togo, you might, without your knowledge, be linked invisibly to an Internet marketing company that automatically will record this site visit in a cookie on your hard drive. Then, when you visit a travel site, in less time than it takes you to say "click," the marketing company can automatically retrieve your cookie, realize you are interested in Togo, and show you banner ads for travel there. You, meanwhile, are blissfully unaware that you have a dossier in cyberspace.

---

[2] Legend has it that the term "cookie" refers to the Hansel and Gretel fairy tale. An evil stepmother forced her husband to take his two young children out into the woods and lose them. Anticipating such a plan, the children left a trail of bread crumbs to follow home. Legend does not reveal why these files are called cookies rather than crumbs.

One company now markets a databank with the names of 150 million registered voters. Anyone can buy a list of voters that is sliced and diced however they want, say, Republicans between the ages of 45 and 60 with Hispanic surnames and incomes greater than $50,000. This company can also transmit specially tailored banner ads to voters surfing the Web.[3]

Cookies can be remarkably convenient. Amazon.com has patented its so-called "One-Click" system that permits a shopper to buy an item by clicking once on the button. What could be easier than that? One-click buying would not be possible without cookies. Industry representatives also argue that, without the revenue from cookie-based banner ads, many Internet sites would not be free to consumers.

Even without cookies, your computer creates a dossier about you. When you surf the Web, your computer stores a copy of the Web pages you visit in a cache file on your hard drive. Thus anyone with access to your hard drive could get a good idea of your regular stopping places. Would you be concerned if your boss knew that you were visiting sites that specialized in job searches, politics (either to the right or the left), cancer, sex, or, for that matter, any non-job-related site?

THE STATE OF PRIVACY ON THE INTERNET

Almost since its inception, the Internet has caused persistent worries over privacy. Despite these concerns, Internet users continue to reveal vast quantities of personal data. No other invention has ever created such an incentive to be indiscreet. A recent survey illustrates this point.[4]

Many Internet users feel that their privacy has been violated:	• 28% have received an offensive e-mail from a stranger. • 25% have caught a computer virus, typically from infected e-mail. • 17% know someone who was fired or disciplined because of e-mailing or Web browsing at work. • 4% have been cheated while purchasing online.
Nonetheless, Internet users are still willing to reveal personal data:	• 55% have sought health information. • 48% have used a credit card to purchase an item online. • 43% have looked for financial data, such as stock prices. • 36% have gone to a support-group site that provides information about a specific medical condition or personal situation. • 25% have made friends with someone that they met online.

[3] For example, during the 2000 Republican presidential primaries, time was running short for John McCain to obtain enough voter signatures to get his name on the Virginia ballot. For $5,000, his campaign hired a company to send Internet advertisements to registered Republican voters in Virginia. When people in this database went online, they would see a McCain banner asking them to sign his petition.

[4] Pew Research Center. Available at http://www.pewinternet.org.

SELF-REGULATION OF ONLINE PRIVACY

Who will protect consumers from themselves? Who will determine how this gold mine of information can be used? **Web advertisers currently operate with little regulation governing the collection or use of personal data.** They have adamantly resisted government rules, preferring instead self-regulation under the auspices of an industry group, the Network Advertising Initiative (NAI). In 1999, representatives of the Federal Trade Commission (FTC) and the Department of Commerce met with the NAI to negotiate principles of self-regulation. However, many Internet companies are not members of NAI and, therefore, are not subject to its rules. Moreover, consumer advocates complain that no one from consumer groups was involved in developing the NAI guidelines.

Under NAI principles, Web sites must provide notice, consent, access, and security.

1. *A Web site should provide "clear and conspicuous notice" of its privacy policy.* Many sites do provide this information. In other sites, however, privacy policies are both difficult to locate and hard to understand. Moreover, Web site operators can change their policy without notice or warning.
2. *Consumers should be able to choose whether or not their data will be collected.* This issue has been enormously contentious. The NAI proposed a so-called opt-out policy, meaning that a company would have the right to use whatever information it collected unless a consumer affirmatively filed a notice requesting confidentiality. Most consumer advocates prefer an opt-in policy, meaning that consumer data is private unless a Web site obtains the consumer's permission to disclose it.
3. *A Web site should provide consumers reasonable access to their own data.* This requirement sounds reasonable. Implementation is more complicated. Should consumers be entitled to access all information about themselves? Data collected years ago? Data now sitting on computer tapes stored in a distant off-site facility? Should consumers have the right to insist on changes to inaccurate information? (No, I didn't buy *The Joy of Sex*, it was *The Joy of Cooking*.)
4. *Web sites should provide reasonable security for collected data.* Any organization that collects information should ensure that nothing will be revealed without the consumer's permission. But how will companies ensure that only authorized people gain access? How can they know who the inquirer really is?

Perhaps because the NAI principles are still so open to interpretation and disagreement, they make little provision for enforcement. Watchdog organizations such as the Electronic Frontier Foundation (http://eff.org), Electronic Privacy Information Center (http://www.epic.org), and the Pew Research Center (http://www.pewinternet.org) try to keep an eye on the industry. A number of nonprofit organizations, such as TRUSTe, offer a seal of approval to Web sites that comply with its standards (http://truste.org). (Information about NAI principles is available at http://www.epic.org/privacy/internet/NAI_analysis.html.)

These NAI principles are simply guidelines, not laws. If you ran a Web site, what principles would you follow? What rules would be fair to you and Web users?

THE FAILURE OF SELF-REGULATION

As the new millennium dawned, a series of incidents illustrated the fragility of privacy on the Internet. Newspapers revealed that the federal Office of National Drug Control Policy was using cookies to track requests for drug information on its Web site. The resulting uproar led the government to ban the use of cookies on all federal Web sites.

At the same time, DoubleClick Inc. was in the news. This company was in the business of placing banner advertisements on Web sites. It tracked individual surfers across different sites and used this information to tailor ads to match the user's specific interests. In the process, DoubleClick built an extensive database of who clicks on what ads.

The DoubleClick database gave advertisers general demographic information about the types of consumers who were interested in their products. No one complained much about that. Indeed, some argued that this method benefited Web surfers who now only saw ads for relevant products. Then DoubleClick purchased Abacus Direct, another national database. By matching up the two data sources, DoubleClick could link consumers by name to the sites they had visited, the advertisements they had clicked on, and the items they had purchased. Thus, for instance, DoubleClick would have the ability to provide an insurance company with a list of health sites that a prospective customer had visited.

The FTC announced an investigation and two states filed suit. But before the courts of law had an opportunity to rule, DoubleClick decided it was suffering too much damage in the court of public opinion. After months of uproar, the company admitted that it had made a mistake by trying to combine the two databases. The company, however, continued its practice of maintaining an anonymous database.

GOVERNMENT REGULATION OF ONLINE PRIVACY

Members of Congress have filed more than 300 bills to regulate online privacy. So intense, however, is the debate between industry and consumer advocates that no consensus—and little law—has emerged. Despite the deadlock, Congress has passed one important new statute: The Children's Online Privacy Protection Act of 1998.

CHILDREN'S ONLINE PRIVACY PROTECTION ACT OF 1998

COPPA, as this statute is known, prohibits Internet operators from collecting information from children under 13 without parental permission. It also requires sites to disclose how they will use any information they acquire. The standard for obtaining parental consent is on a sliding scale—a higher standard applies if the information will be disclosed publicly. If the Web site only intends to use information internally, it can obtain parental consent by e-mail. But if the personal data will be disclosed to third parties, parental consent must be obtained by regular mail, fax, e-mail with an official digital signature, a telephone call from the parent, or it must be accompanied by a credit card number. Enforcement is in the hands of the FTC, which has the option of eliminating the sliding scale after two years and applying the tougher standard to all transactions. (An explanation of the statute is available at http://www.ftc.gov/bcp/conline/pubs/buspubs/coppa.htm.) Children's Web sites claim that the cost of complying with COPPA is upwards of $100,000 per site. As a result, some sites now simply turn away children under 13 (which may have the unintended consequence of diverting them to unregulated, more adult Web pages).

Shortly after COPPA became law, the FTC brought an action against Young Investor (http://www.younginvestor.com). This site asked children about their weekly allowance, spending habits, work history, plans for college, and family finances. In addition, it asked for the child's name, address, age, and e-mail address. The site promised that all answers would be anonymous but, in fact, it could match names with surveys. Under a consent decree, Young Investor agreed to post a privacy policy and obtain parental consent before collecting personal information from children.

THE FTC SEEKS HELP FROM CONGRESS

The FTC originally had supported the concept of self-regulation in the online industry. The agency became increasingly convinced, however, that self-regulation was not sufficient and that Congress needed to take action. An FTC survey of online sites revealed, for instance, that while almost all commercial Web sites collected information, only 20 percent abided by all four of the NAI principles: notice, consent, access, and security. Even more discouraging, the seal system proposed by TRUSTe had proven ineffective—only 8 percent of the sites displayed a privacy seal.

The FTC asked Congress to enact online privacy legislation. (A copy of the FTC report is available at http://www.ftc.gov/reports/privacy2000/privacy2000.pdf.) A number of major online companies, such as eBay, the online auctioneer, have joined in the call for federal legislation. They fear that if the federal government fails to act, the states will fill the vacuum. Fifty different state laws would be much more troublesome for them than one federal statute.

THE ROLE OF THE COURTS

Courts are also a possible source of Internet regulation. The case on the following page held that a statute prohibiting the use of customer data was in violation of the First Amendment to the Constitution. Could this analysis apply also to online privacy regulation?

YOUR HARD DRIVE AS WITNESS (AGAINST YOU)

Many people confide their deepest secrets to their computers. Would you want everything you have ever typed into your computer to be revealed publicly? Monica Lewinsky certainly did not. Investigators in the President Clinton impeachment case discovered damaging evidence on the hard drive of Lewinsky's computer—evidence she clearly thought was private, including copies of deleted e-mails and drafts of letters she had never sent. What protection do you have for information stored on your computer?

U.S. WEST, INC. v. FEDERAL COMMUNICATIONS COMMISSION

182 F.3d 1224; 1999 U.S. App. LEXIS 20785
United States Court of Appeals for the Tenth Circuit, 1999

Facts: The Telecommunications Act of 1996 requires a telecommunications carrier to obtain permission from its customers before using or disclosing information about them. (The court refers to customer information as "CPNI."[5]) FCC regulations implementing this statute adopted an opt-in approach, which requires a carrier to obtain prior approval from customers before using their CPNI.

U.S. West sued the FCC alleging that the regulations violated the First Amendment because they prohibited U.S. West from communicating information about its customers. The First Amendment states, "Congress shall make no law . . . abridging the freedom of speech."

Issue: Do the FCC regulations violate the First Amendment?

Excerpts from Judge Tacha's Decision: [T]his case is a harbinger of difficulties encountered in this age of exploding information, when rights bestowed by the United States Constitution must be guarded as vigilantly as in the days of handbills on public sidewalks.

No one disputes that the commercial speech based on CPNI is truthful and nonmisleading. We therefore proceed directly to [the next issue:] Does the government have a substantial state interest in regulating speech involving CPNI? [T]he government must show that the dissemination of the information desired to be kept private would inflict specific and significant harm on individuals, such as undue embarrassment or ridicule, intimidation or harassment, or misappropriation of sensitive personal information for the purposes of assuming another's identity. [W]e live in an open society where information may usually pass freely. A general level of discomfort from knowing that people can readily access information about us does not necessarily rise to the level of a substantial state interest for it is not based on an identified harm.

The government never states it directly, but we infer that disclosure of CPNI information could prove embarrassing to some and that the government seeks to combat this potential harm. We have some doubts about whether this interest, as presented, rises to the level of "substantial." [N]otwithstanding our reservations, we assume for the sake of this appeal that the government has asserted a substantial state interest in protecting people from the disclosure of sensitive and potentially embarrassing personal information.

[N]ext the government must demonstrate that the harms it recites are real and that its restriction will in fact alleviate them to a material degree. While protecting against disclosure of sensitive and potentially embarrassing personal information may be important in the abstract, we have no indication of how it may occur in reality with respect to CPNI. Indeed, we do not even have indication that the disclosure might actually occur. The government presents no evidence regarding how and to whom carriers would disclose CPNI.

Even assuming, arguendo, that the state interests in privacy and competition are substantial and that the regulations directly and materially advance those interests, we do not find, on this record, the FCC rules regarding customer approval properly tailored. The CPNI regulations must be no more extensive than necessary to serve the stated interests. [T]he FCC's failure to adequately consider an obvious and substantially less restrictive alternative, an opt-out strategy, indicates that it did not narrowly tailor the CPNI regulations regarding customer approval.

The [FCC argues] that the record contains adequate support that the CPNI regulations are

[5] The data included the quantity, type, destination, and amount of use of a telecommunications service as well as information contained in telephone bills.

narrowly tailored because a study conducted by U.S. West shows that a majority of individuals, when affirmatively asked for approval to use CPNI, refused to grant it. The U.S. West study shows that 33% of those called refused to grant approval to use their CPNI, 28% granted such approval, and 39% either hung up or asked not to be called again. U.S. West secured a 72% affirmative response rate from customers whom it solicited after they initiated contact with the company for some other reason. This study may simply reflect that a substantial number of individuals are ambivalent or disinterested in the privacy of their CPNI or that consumers are averse to marketing generally.

Even assuming that telecommunications customers value the privacy of CPNI, the FCC record does not adequately show that an opt-out strategy would not sufficiently protect customer privacy. The FCC merely speculates that there are a substantial number of individuals who feel strongly about their privacy, yet would not bother to opt-out if given notice and the opportunity to do so. Such speculation hardly reflects the careful calculation of costs and benefits that our commercial speech jurisprudence requires.

[W]e find that the CPNI regulations violate the First Amendment.

Criminal Law

The Fourth Amendment to the Constitution prohibits unreasonable searches and seizures by the government. In enforcing this provision of the Constitution, the courts ask: Did the person being searched have a legitimate expectation of privacy in the place searched or the item seized? If yes, then the government must obtain a warrant from a court before conducting the search. (For more on this topic, investigate Chapter 7, on crime.) The Fourth Amendment applies to computers.

To give an example, Mark Simons worked for the federal government at the Foreign Bureau of Information Services (FBIS). FBIS notified its employees that they could use their computers only for government business and that, thenceforth, the agency would conduct electronic audits to ensure compliance. While monitoring the system, FBIS discovered that Simons illegally had downloaded child pornography from the Internet onto his government computer. Government investigators, operating without a warrant, reviewed and copied all of the picture files Simons had downloaded. He was convicted of receiving child pornography and sentenced to 18 months in prison. On appeal, he alleged that the search was illegal because it had been conducted without a warrant. The court held that, in light of FBIS's announced policy, Simons did not have a reasonable expectation of privacy in the files downloaded from the Internet. His conviction stood.[6]

Civil Litigation

Increasingly, computers are fair game in civil litigation. Suppose that you have sued your company for wrongful termination. The company counterclaims, alleging that you have cheated on your expense account. During litigation, it might subpoena your computer to find support for its allegations. Or suppose that, during the midst of a bitter divorce, your spouse alleges that you have shown pornography to your children. Your computer—with its Web trail—

---

[6] 206 F.3d 392, 2000 U.S. App. LEXIS 2877 (4th Cir. 2000).

could end up in court. The following article illustrates how fragile privacy is when hard drives become pawns in litigation.

Each day, Ted Reeve pours his life into his home computer. He spends hours reading news online, and dutifully records monthly payments for his Visa card and Toyota Camry, along with ATM withdrawals. He regularly types up notes from talks with his doctor. It never occurred to him that such personal data could be extracted and shared among strangers. But that's what happened when his computer's hard drive was copied by two investigators retained for his employer, Northwest Airlines. Working right in his living room with a program called EnCase, they excavated every last bit and byte from his desktop hard drive.

Northwest suspected that its flight-attendant union had used the Internet to run an illegal call-in-sick campaign to disrupt the airline. So the airline won a court order to search 20 or so hard drives at flight attendants' homes and union offices. As people commit an ever-growing pile of information to computers, their hard drives are becoming a digital mother lode for lawyers. More federal courts are approving searches of home PCs for evidence in civil cases.[7]

The United States has always been particularly protective of a free press. In 1980, Congress passed the Privacy Policy Act (PPA) to enhance press protection. **This statute requires the government to obtain a warrant before searching or seizing the papers of anyone engaged in publishing a newspaper, book, or broadcast.** The PPA also protects anyone who uses the Internet to broadcast messages. The victim of an unlawful search can sue for damages, but any evidence seized is admissible in a criminal trial.

For example, Steve Jackson Games, Inc. (SJG) operated an electronic bulletin board. The government suspected that one of SJG's employees illegally had copied and distributed a computer file belonging to Bell South. Although SJG was not suspected of illegal activity, the government did not notify the company or ask for its help. Instead, government agents obtained a warrant to search SJG's offices and seize computer hardware and software containing the illegal program. The agents who conducted the search admitted afterward that they were (shockingly!) ignorant of the PPA. In the zeal of their search, they seized SJG computers that contained drafts of magazine articles and a book intended for publication, *Gurps Cyberpunk*. Although the agents could have copied all the files and returned the computers within hours, they did not do so for months. This delay cost SJG money. The court held that the agents had violated the PPA and ordered them to pay $51,040 in damages.[8]

E-MAIL

E-mails may feel ephemeral, but they can do lasting damage. They typically stay stored on your own computer and on your provider's system long after you have hit the delete button. For example, when the federal government sued

---

[7] Michael J. McCarthy, "In Airline's Suit, PC Becomes Legal Pawn, Raising Privacy Issues," *The Wall Street Journal*, May 24, 2000, p.1. Republished with permission of The Wall Street Journal; permission conveyed through the Copyright Clearance Center, Inc.

[8] *Steve Jackson Games Incorporated v. U.S. Secret Service*, 816 F. Supp. 432, 1993 U.S. Dist. LEXIS 3378, aff'd, 36 F.3d 457, 1994 U.S. App. LEXIS 30323 (5th Cir.).

Microsoft for antitrust violations, some of the most damaging evidence against the company was extracted from its own e-mail archives. E-mail that had long since been "deleted" rose from the dead to haunt the company. Even online chat rooms store all posted comments for years. The Electronic Communications Privacy Act of 1986 (ECPA) is a federal statute that regulates e-mail.

ELECTRONIC COMMUNICATIONS PRIVACY ACT OF 1986

The ECPA prohibits the unauthorized interception or disclosure of wire and electronic communications by, among others, the government, Internet service providers (ISPs), and employers. The definition of electronic communication includes e-mail and transmissions from pagers and cellular phones. Violators are subject to both criminal and civil penalties. Under this statute:

1. **Any intended recipient of an e-mail has the right to disclose it.** Thus, if you sound off to a friend about your boss, the (erstwhile) friend legally may forward that e-mail to the boss or anyone else.
2. **ISPs generally are prohibited from disclosing electronic messages to anyone other than the addressee**, unless this disclosure is necessary for the performance of their service or for the protection of their own rights or property. Note, however, that an ISP does have the right to disclose the existence of an e-mail and the identity of the parties. Thus, if you e-mailed the Republican National Committee headquarters, your ISP legally could disclose that fact, although it could not reveal the contents of your message.
3. **An employer has the right to monitor workers' e-mail messages if (1) the employee consents, (2) the monitoring occurs in the ordinary course of business, or (3) the employer provides the e-mail system.** Chapter 14, on employment law, contains *Smyth v. Pillsbury*, a case brought under the ECPA by an unhappy employee.
4. **The government has the right to access e-mail messages if it first obtains a search warrant or court order.**

Timothy McVeigh learned about the dangers of e-mail the hard way. A highly decorated, 17-year veteran of the U.S. Navy, he was the senior enlisted man on the nuclear submarine *U.S.S. Chicago*. McVeigh sent an e-mail via AOL to Helen Hajne, a civilian organizer of a toy drive for children of the Chicago crew. McVeigh used the screen name "boysrch," although he signed the e-mail "Tim." Hajne searched AOL's "member profile directory," where she discovered that boysrch's marital status was "gay." This information ultimately landed on the desk of McVeigh's commanding officer. A Navy paralegal telephoned AOL and asked the identity of boysrch. AOL promptly and willingly revealed that this screen name belonged to McVeigh. The Navy then moved to discharge McVeigh for homosexual conduct. He sued under the ECPA, and a federal court issued an injunction prohibiting the Navy from discharging him. The court held that the Navy should not have asked for information from AOL without obtaining a search warrant or court order.[9]

---

[9] The court would not have granted this request, however, because such a search would have violated the "don't ask, don't tell" policy of the U.S. military. *McVeigh v. Cohen*, 983 F. Supp. 215, 1998 U.S. Dist. LEXIS 790, 1998.

COMMON LAW REGULATION OF E-MAIL PRIVACY

In addition to the ECPA, some lawsuits have alleged that employers who read their workers' e-mails are violating the common law right of privacy. **Under the common law, intrusion into someone's private life is a tort if a reasonable person would find it offensive.** (For a review of the tort of invasion of privacy, peek at Chapter 6, on torts.) Did Microsoft violate an employee's privacy? You be the judge.

BILL MCLAREN, JR. v. MICROSOFT CORPORATION

1999 Tex App. LEXIS 4103
Court of Appeals of Texas, 1999

Facts: Microsoft suspended Bill McLaren from his job pending an investigation into allegations of sexual harassment and "inventory questions." In response, he sent a memorandum requesting that no one tamper with his Microsoft office workstation or his e-mail. Ignoring this request, Microsoft accessed e-mail files in the "personal folders" on McLaren's computer. These files were password protected, but the company "decrypted" McLaren's personal password. The company then fired him.

McLaren filed suit against Microsoft for invasion of privacy. He alleged that he had a reasonable expectation of privacy in password-protected personal e-mail files.

You be the Judge: **Would a reasonable person find this intrusion offensive? Does an employee have a reasonable expectation of privacy in his e-mail files?**

Argument for McLaren: A company might have a legitimate right to read employee e-mails in the general course of events, but these e-mails were different. When Microsoft developed a system that permitted employees to store e-mails in personal folders with password protection, the company was creating an expectation of privacy. The whole point of a password is to safeguard privacy. Microsoft lured McLaren into storing personal messages and then betrayed him by breaking into his folders.

Argument for Microsoft: To win this case, McLaren must show that the intrusion on his privacy was unreasonable. These folders were part of an e-mail system owned and administered by Microsoft and made available to McLaren so that he could perform the functions of his job. These files were no more private than a locked file cabinet that Microsoft provided for his office.

McLaren could not have thought that it would take Microsoft more than two seconds to crack his password. Therefore, any expectation of privacy on his part was unreasonable. Moreover, these e-mail messages were transmitted over Microsoft's network and, thus, had already been accessible to third parties at some point.

McLaren was under suspicion of sexual harassment and inventory theft. Even if he had a reasonable expectation of privacy, a company's interest in preventing inappropriate and unprofessional conduct, not to mention illegal activity, outweighed his privacy rights.

ENCRYPTION

Even as some new technology *threatens* privacy in cyberspace, other advances offer *protection*. Encryption software is designed to safeguard the confidentiality of Internet communications. It uses a mathematical algorithm to translate plain text into unreadable ciphertext for transmission, and a key that converts the ciphertext back into plain text upon receipt. Some of these codes are virtually unbreakable. Most retail Web sites, for instance, use encryption software to protect credit card numbers. This software can also protect the anonymity of communications such as e-mail. Although privacy advocates laud the development of secure encryption systems, law enforcement officials fear that criminals will use the software to hide the tracks of their crimes.

Encryption software also has potential military uses—after all, the Allies' victory in World War II was greatly aided by their breaking of the Nazi Enigma code. For this reason, the U.S. government has issued Export Administration Regulations to control the export of encryption software. **Generally, these regulations require a license for the export of encryption software** to any country except the European Union, Australia, Canada, Norway, the Czech Republic, Hungary, Poland, Japan, New Zealand, and Switzerland. The term "export" also includes posting the software on the Internet, unless foreign access to the site is somehow restricted. These regulations apply, however, only to software in electronic form, not in hardcopy.

Some researchers have challenged the encryption regulations as a violation of the First Amendment's right to free speech, but no court has issued a definitive ruling. Peter Junger taught a course on computers and the law at the Case Western University Law School. He sought to post on his Web site encryption code that he had written to demonstrate how computers work. Because this posting would be an export under the regulations, Professor Junger requested an export license from the Department of Commerce. The department granted permission to export a printed book chapter containing encryption code, but not the electronic software.

Junger filed suit, alleging that his software was protected under the First Amendment. A court of appeals held that encryption software is subject to First Amendment protection, but also that the government can regulate this speech to further "an important or substantial governmental interest." The appeals court remanded the case to the trial court to determine if national security interests outweighed the value of free speech.[10] For an update on this and other encryption cases, search http://www.cdt.org/crypto/litigation/.

PREVENTIVE Law

So what can you do to protect your privacy online? Here are some possibilities:

- Some Web surfers are opting for self-help measures:
  - About a quarter of Internet users have given a fake name or false personal information to a Web site.
  - About 20 percent of online users have used secondary e-mail addresses to disguise their identity.
  - Remember, before you click, to look for a Web site's privacy policy. If you cannot find one, or do not like what you find, you have the right to go elsewhere.
- The Electronic Privacy Information Center offers a menu of privacy tools at http://www.epic.org/privacy/tools.html.
- The Privacy Council (http://www.privacycouncil.com/) offers advice about shopping and surfing anonymously on the Web.
- Anonymizer (http://www.anonymizer.com/) provides an anonymous surfing service.

---

[10] *Junger v. Daley*, 209 F.3d 481, 2000 U.S. App. LEXIS 6161 (6th Cir. 2000).

- Privaseek (http://www.privaseek.com/) has developed Persona, software that permits Internet users to control how their personal information is used by sites they visit.

CRIME ON THE INTERNET

Computers and the Internet are responsible for much good—together they have created enormous opportunities for communication, education, and entertainment. They have increased productivity and created astounding business opportunities. However, for the dishonest and unscrupulous, the Internet has also opened new frontiers in crime.

HACKING

Gaining unauthorized access to a computer system is called hacking. The Pentagon reports that hackers make more than 250,000 attempts annually on its computers. The goal of hackers is varied; some do it for little more than the thrill of the challenge. Other hackers' goals may be industrial espionage, extortion, or theft of credit card information. Whatever the motive, hacking is a major crime. A survey of U.S. corporations, government agencies, and colleges revealed that 70 percent had experienced computer security breaches within the year. No surprise then that American companies spend more than $6 billion annually on computer security systems.

Hacking is illegal under the federal Computer Fraud and Abuse Act of 1986 (CFAA).[11] This statute applies to any computer attached to the Internet. **The CFAA prohibits**:

- Computer espionage
- The theft of financial information
- The theft of information from the U.S. government
- Interstate theft from a computer
- Computer trespass
- Computer fraud
- Intentional, reckless, and negligent damage to a computer
- Trafficking in computer passwords for the purpose of affecting interstate commerce
- Computer extortion

Almost half of the states have also adopted statutes prohibiting computer crime. A list of these statutes is available at http://www.cybercrimes.net/State/state_index.html. For advice on how to report a computer crime, visit

[11] 18 U.S.C. §1030.

http://cybercrimes.net/Reporting/reporting.html. The CFAA has been an essential tool in fighting cybercrime. Unfortunately, because the Internet is truly international, cybercriminals do not always fall within the jurisdiction of American laws. For example, a computer virus called ILOVEYOU caused an estimated $7 billion worth of damage worldwide. Although the perpetrator would have been subject to prosecution under the CFAA in the United States, he lived in the Philippines, which did not have laws prohibiting cybercrime. Nor could the suspect be extradited automatically to the United States because the extradition treaty only applied if both nations had the same law. The Philippines ultimately dropped all charges against the suspect.

FRAUD

Fraud is a growth business on the Internet. The Internet's anonymity and speed facilitate fraud, and computers help criminals identify and contact victims. Common scams include the sale of merchandise that is either defective or non-existent, billing for services that are touted as "free," fraudulent stock offers, fake scholarship search services, business opportunity scams (for a small investment, you will get rich), and credit card scams (for a fee, you can get a credit card, even with a poor credit rating).

Fraud is the deception of another person for the purpose of obtaining money or property from him. It can be prosecuted under state law or the Computer Fraud and Abuse Act. In addition, federal mail and wire fraud statutes prohibit the use of mail or wire communication in furtherance of a fraudulent scheme.[12] Civil cases can be brought under Section 5 of the FTC act, which prohibits "unfair and deceptive acts or practices." (Chapter 7, on crime, discusses fraud, while Chapter 23, on consumer law, contains a detailed discussion of the FTC act.)

AUCTIONS

One of the most rapidly growing venues for Internet fraud is online auctions. The FTC reports that Internet auctions are the number one source of consumer complaints about online activities. Wrongdoers either sell goods they do not own, provide defective goods, or offer fakes. eBay says that only one-tenth of one percent of its auctions involves fraud, but with upwards of $9 billion worth of goods being auctioned on the Internet each year, even one-tenth of one percent begins to add up.

Shilling is an increasingly popular online auction fraud. Shilling means that a seller either bids on his own goods or agrees to cross-bid with a group of other sellers. **Shilling is prohibited because the owner drives up the price of his own item by bidding on it.** Thus, for example, Kenneth Walton, a San Francisco lawyer, put up for auction on eBay an abstract painting purportedly by famous artist Richard Diebenkorn. A bidder offered $135,805 before eBay withdrew the item in response to charges that Walton had placed a bid on the painting himself and had also engaged in cross-bidding with a group of other eBay users. Walton claimed that he had placed the bids for friends.

---

[12] 18 U.S.C. §§1341–1346.

To date, eBay generally has responded to shillers by suspending them for 30 days on the first offense and indefinitely on the second. Shillers are also subject to suit under general anti-fraud statutes. In addition, some states explicitly prohibit shilling.[13]

The FTC has initiated Project Safebid, under which it educates law enforcement officials and then maintains a national database of Internet auction fraud complaints so that it can refer cases to the appropriate law enforcement agencies. For fraud prevention tips, sneak over to http://www.consumer.gov/knowfraud/index.html. To file a fraud complaint, click on http://www.ifccfbi.gov.

IDENTITY THEFT

Identity theft is one of the scariest crimes against property. Although it existed before computers, the Internet has made it much easier. As the following article reveals, even the nation's top military officers are not immune.

As chairman of the Joint Chiefs of Staff, General John V. Shalikashvili was responsible for the nation's security. Unfortunately, while he was protecting the country, his identity was stolen and his security jeopardized. When Congress approved his appointment to the Joint Chiefs of Staff, the Congressional Record reported not only his promotion but also his Social Security number. Glen Roberts posted the Social Security numbers of Shalikashvili and 4,000 other military officers on his Web site (http://www.glr.com). His point? As a privacy advocate, he wanted to illustrate that too much private information is available on the Web. At least three different people used the officers' numbers to apply for credit cards, obtain cash, and charge $200,000 worth of goods.

Although the owner of a credit card must generally pay only the first $50 that is stolen (as discussed in Chapter 23 on consumer law), the time and effort required to undo the damage can be substantial. Identity theft may also involve more than a few credit cards. In addition to Social Security numbers, thieves may "steal" other information such as a victim's date of birth or mother's maiden name. Armed with this data, they can take over a person's identity, opening new accounts, obtaining bank loans and telephone line hookups, acquiring a passport and driver's license, or even committing (additional) crimes under their new identity. Meanwhile, the victim may find himself unable to obtain a credit card, loan, or job. One victim spent several nights in jail after he was arrested for a crime that his alter ego had committed.

Responding to these concerns, Congress passed the Identity Theft and Assumption Deterrence Act of 1998.[14] **This statute prohibits the use of false identification to commit fraud or other crime.** It also permits the victim to seek restitution in court. The statute requires the FTC to set up a hotline (at 877-IDTHEFT, 877-438-4338) and Web site (http://www.consumer.gov/idtheft) for those who want to report identity theft or seek help handling it.

---

[13] For example, New Mexico law provides that "It shall be unlawful to employ shills or puffers at any such auction sale or to offer or to make or to procure to be offered or made any false bid or offer any false bid to buy or pretend to buy any article sold or offered for sale." N.M. Stat. §61-16-14.

[14] 18 U.S. 1028.

FIGHTING INTERNET CRIME

Mark Jakob learned that he who commits a crime by the Internet can be caught by the Internet. One morning, as the stock market opened, a news release announced that Emulex Corp. would have to restate its earnings and was being investigated by the Securities and Exchange Commission (SEC). Within minutes, the company's stock plummeted by more than half—from $113 to $43. In an instant, $2.45 billion in market capitalization vanished. Needlessly. It turned out the press release was a phony. In less than a week, the FBI accused Jakob, 23 years old and a recent community college student. He had "sold short" Emulex stock, that is, he had bet the stock would decline. Desperate when the stock went up instead, causing him a $97,000 paper loss, Jakob allegedly issued the phony release. It solved his problems temporarily—his loss turned into a profit of nearly $250,000—but the FBI was able to track the e-mail and the news release and make the arrest.

The good news is: Cyberspace has given the government new and better methods for fighting crime. The bad news is: These crime-fighting tools may threaten our privacy. As Supreme Court Justice Louis Brandeis famously observed in 1928,

> The progress of science in furnishing the Government with the means of espionage is not likely to stop with wire-tapping. Ways may some day develop by which the Government, without removing papers from secret drawers, can reproduce them in court, and by which it will be enabled to expose to a jury the most intimate occurrences of the home. That places the liberty of every man in the hands of every petty officer.[15]

As the Jakob case illustrated, the Internet has been fertile ground for con artists perpetrating securities fraud. Nonetheless, protests greeted the SEC's announcement that it planned to monitor Web sites, bulletin boards, and chat groups for suspicious phrases like "get rich quick." The SEC also intended to track e-mail addresses to discover the identity of anonymous writers.

Then came the news that the FBI was using a computer program called "Carnivore" to intercept e-mail from terrorists, hackers, and other criminals. (Even the FBI acknowledged that the choice of names was unfortunate.) Once installed on an ISP, Carnivore (and other "dragnet" programs) works like a wiretap to track e-mail. Carnivore cannot be employed without a court order. The FBI had reportedly used it to intercept e-mail between terrorist Osama bin Laden in Afghanistan and his network of agents around the world. Privacy advocates worry, though, that Carnivore could also be used to monitor the e-mail of political dissidents or others who espouse unpopular views. (For the FBI's view on Carnivore, investigate http://www.fbi.gov/.)

Reasonable people can disagree about how much privacy Internet users need. While Great Britain enacted an e-mail wiretap law that grants greater powers to the government than the FBI uses with Carnivore, the European Union (EU) proposed a set of privacy guidelines that are stricter than any in the United States. In Great Britain, the new statute permits law enforcement agencies to

[15] *Olmstead v. U.S.*, 277 US 438; 1928 US LEXIS 694 (US Sup. Ct. 1928).

intercept e-mail messages without first obtaining a search warrant. Meanwhile, the EU requires that, before collecting personal data, companies must ask permission, reveal who will be receiving the information, and let the person providing the information review it. (These standards are disclosed at http://www.europa.eu.int/comm/internal_market/en/media/dataprot/index.htm.) The EU also prohibits companies from transmitting personal data to countries without adequate protection—such as the United States. The EU recently proposed a set of rules that U.S. sites must meet to be in compliance with European standards. There are, as yet, however, no penalties for those who violate the rules.

INTERNET SERVICE PROVIDERS AND WEB HOSTS

Internet service providers (ISPs) are companies, such as AOL and CompuServe, that provide connection to the Internet. Web hosts post Web pages on the Internet. Both play important roles in the Internet. As the legal structure that supports the Internet develops, so have legal issues involving these players.

SPAM

Spam is officially known as *unsolicited commercial e-mail* (UCE) or unsolicited bulk e-mail (UBE). Whatever it is called, it can be annoying as millions of these messages clog ISP computers and consumer mailboxes. As much as 30 percent of all e-mail is spam. It is estimated that roughly half of all spam is fraudulent—either in content (promoting a scam) or in packaging (the headers or return address are false). Most fraudulent bulk e-mails promote "get rich quick" schemes, miracle health cures, or sex products.

Some observers have expressed concern that the rise of bulk e-mail could hamper the growth of the Internet. At a minimum, bulk e-mail adds to the cost of connecting to the Internet. Consumers pay for connection time to download unwanted messages, and ISPs have to support the additional traffic. Moreover, both consumers and ISPs must endure the cost of outages caused by an overload of bulk e-mail. ISPs also argue that their reputations as service providers are harmed when consumers blame them for unsolicited advertisements. Because recipients of bulk e-mail often send back angry replies, those who send spam have learned to use fake return addresses, thereby tarnishing the reputation of innocents.

Spam differs fundamentally from another curse of the modern age, junk mail, in that the recipients, not the senders, largely bear the cost. Some observers estimate that spam costs each Internet user about $2 per month. ISPs typically use filters to block this unwanted mail, but these programs are not foolproof nor do they eliminate the cost of dealing with the millions of unwanted e-mails that enter the system.

FRAUDULENT SPAM

The nature of the spam determines its legal treatment. Fraudulent e-mails can be attacked like any other fraud on the Internet—through state fraud statutes, through the CFAA, or by the FTC. Concerned that deceptive bulk e-mail poses a threat to consumer confidence in online commerce, the FTC has advocated legislation to require that commercial messages bear accurate headers and domain names, and include accurate contact information in the text of the message.

The FTC has also brought a substantial number of anti-spam cases. For example, a company based in the Caribbean country of Dominica sent bulk e-mail to consumers informing them that their "orders had been received and processed" and their credit cards charged for amounts up to $899. The spam contained a forged header to hide the identity of the actual sender. If the recipients had any questions about the "order," the e-mail advised them to call a particular telephone number in area code 767 to speak with an operator. The consumers did not know that this area code was in Dominica and that, by making the call, they would incur substantial international long-distance charges (which the wrongdoer shared with the telephone company). After dialing the number, the consumer reached an adult entertainment service. Under the terms of the settlement, the defendants were enjoined permanently from falsifying information in the "from" and "subject" lines of e-mails, as well as in the text of the message.[16]

NON-FRAUDULENT SPAM

Non-fraudulent spam is a more complex issue because there are no ready-made laws to deal with it. Initially, many observers (including the FTC) hoped that self-regulation would work, but volume continues to grow. ISPs have adopted a number of extra-legal strategies to combat this plague. Some ISPs share information about "spammer-friendly" service providers and then join together to block all messages from them. ISPs are also becoming increasingly creative in adapting old laws to fight this new battle.

Applicable Laws. The following case illustrates the wide range of laws that ISPs have used to challenge spam.

AMERICA ONLINE, INC. v. LCGM, INC.

46 F. Supp. 2d 444; 1998 U.S. Dist. LEXIS 20144
United States District Court for the Eastern District of Virginia

Facts: AOL is an Internet service provider that has registered "AOL" as a trademark and "aol.com" as a domain name.[17] LCGM operated pornographic Web sites. Although AOL's Terms of Service contract prohibited the sending of bulk e-mail, LCGM transmitted to AOL members more than 92 *million* spam messages over seven months advertising its adult Web sites. LCGM used a software program that "harvested" e-mail addresses from AOL-sponsored adult chat rooms. To disguise the real origin of these e-mails, LCGM put "aol.com" in the "from" line. Not surprisingly, many AOL members thought AOL had endorsed these sites and, in response, sent more than 450,000 complaints to AOL.

AOL filed a motion for summary judgment, asking the court to enjoin LCGM from sending spam and holding the company liable for damages.

---

[16] *FTC v. Benoit*, No. 3:99 CV 181 (W.D.N.C. filed May 11, 1999).

[17] For more on trademarks, domain names, and the Lanham Act (discussed later in this case), see Chapter 21 on intellectual property.

Issue: Is LCGM liable to AOL for the unsolicited bulk e-mails? Is AOL entitled to summary judgment?

Excerpts from Judge Lee's Decision:

Count I: [T]he Lanham Act

The undisputed facts establish that defendants violated the Lanham Act, which makes it unlawful to use in commerce any false designation of origin which is likely to cause confusion as to the origin of goods. [T]he use of "aol.com" in defendants' e-mails was likely to cause confusion as to the origin of defendants' goods and services. The recipient of such a message would be led to conclude the sender was an AOL member or AOL, the Internet Service Provider. Indeed, plaintiff alleges that this designation did cause such confusion among many AOL members, who believed that AOL sponsored and authorized defendants' bulk e-mailing practices and pornographic web sites.

Count II: [The Federal Trademark and Dilution Act of 1995]

The undisputed facts establish that defendants violated the Federal Trademark Dilution Act of 1995, which provides relief to an owner of a mark whose mark is used by another person in commerce "if such use begins after the mark has become famous and causes dilution of the distinctive quality of the mark." [T]he "AOL" mark is tarnished, and thus diluted, by association with defendants' bulk e-mail practices.

Count III: The Computer Fraud and Abuse Act

The facts before the Court establish that defendants violated the [section of the] Computer Fraud and Abuse Act, which prohibits individuals from "intentionally accessing a computer without authorization or exceeding authorized access, and thereby obtaining information from any protected computer." Defendants have admitted to maintaining an AOL membership and using that membership to harvest the e-mail addresses of AOL members. Defendants' actions violated AOL's Terms of Service, and as such was [sic] unauthorized. As a result of these actions, plaintiff [suffered] damages to its computer network, reputation and goodwill.

Count IV: Trespass to Chattels under the Common Law of Virginia

The undisputed facts establish that defendants' actions constituted a trespass to chattels under Virginia common law. A trespass to chattels occurs when one party intentionally uses or intermeddles with personal property in rightful possession of another without authorization. One who commits a trespass to chattel is liable to the possessor of the chattel if the chattel is impaired as to its "condition, quality, or value." [T]o the extent that defendants' multitudinous electronic mailings demand the disk space and drain the processing power of plaintiff's computer equipment, those resources are not available to serve subscribers. Therefore, the value of that equipment is diminished even though it is not physically damaged by defendants' conduct.

Damages: AOL's claim for damages is unliquidated and therefore the Court must determine the issue at trial. Thus, the Court denies plaintiff's Motion for Summary Judgment on the issue of damages. However, the Court finds that AOL is entitled to injunctive relief preventing defendants from further distributing unsolicited bulk e-mail messages to AOL members. Defendants are further enjoined from using "aol.com" to send and distribute e-mail messages and from using the AOL network for the purpose of harvesting the addresses of AOL members

This case provides a blueprint to ISPs who seek to stop spam. Filing individual lawsuits against each offender, however, is a slow, tedious method for halting an entire industry. Anti-spamming legislation would be more efficient, although as the next section reveals, that is easier said than done.

Constitutional Issues—The First Amendment. As we have seen in our discussion of privacy, commercial speech is protected by the First Amendment, albeit more weakly than other forms of speech, such as political opinions. What about spam—is it protected by the Constitution?

Cyber Promotions, Inc. sued AOL, alleging that its attempts to block Cyber's bulk e-mail violated the First Amendment. The court, however, ruled against Cyber. The First Amendment only protects against government action. Cyber argued that the Internet is a public resource and, therefore, AOL's access to it made the company similar to a government entity. The court rejected this argument, holding that neither the Internet nor AOL's accessway to it are public systems.[18]

Constitutional Issues—The Commerce Clause. Some states have passed anti-spam laws. For example, Washington State prohibits the use of false headings in electronic mail.[19] "Headings" refers to both subject lines and origin information (saying an e-mail is from AOL when it is really from Porn Queen).

A court in Washington held, however, that this statute violates the Commerce Clause of the Constitution. The Commerce Clause severely restricts the states' right to regulate interstate commerce.[20] In the case in question, the state of Washington sued Jason Heckel, based in Oregon, for sending millions of unsolicited e-mails to people both inside and outside of Washington. The court granted summary judgment to Heckel on the grounds that:

- The statute regulated activity that occurred wholly outside of Washington.
- There is no easy way to determine if an e-mail recipient lives in Washington and, therefore, the statute places an impermissible burden on interstate commerce.
- If anti-spam laws were permitted, a spammer could be subject to many inconsistent laws.[21]

In short, the laws on spam are in a state of flux. Stay tuned.

Communications Decency Act of 1996

The Internet is an enormously powerful tool for disseminating information. But what if some of this information happens to be false or in violation of our privacy rights? Is an ISP liable for transmitting it to the world?

In 1995, a trial judge in New York held that an ISP, Prodigy Services Company, was potentially liable for defamatory statements that an unidentified person posted on one of its bulletin boards.[22] The message alleged that the president of an investment bank had committed "criminal and fraudulent acts." It was not only a false statement, it was posted on the most widely read financial computer bulletin board in the country. Although one can only feel sympathy for the target of this slur, the decision nonetheless alarmed many observers who argued that there was no way ISPs could review every piece of information that hurtles through their portals. The next year, Congress overruled the Prodigy case by passing the **Communications Decency Act of 1996** (CDA).[23] **Under this statute, ISPs are not liable for information that is provided by someone else.** The following case, which was featured in the chapter opener, illustrates how broadly this statute has been interpreted.

---

[18] *Cyber Promotions, Inc. v. America Online, Inc.*, 948 F. Supp. 436; 1996 U.S. Dist. LEXIS 19073.

[19] Rev. Code Wash. §19.190.010.

[20] This provision is discussed at greater length in Chapter 5, on constitutional law.

[21] *State of Washington v. Heckel*, No. 98-2-25480-7 SEA (Wash. Super. Ct. 2000).

[22] *Stratton Oakmont, Inc. v. Prodigy Services Company*, 1995 N.Y. Misc. LEXIS 229.

[23] 47 U.S. 230.

JOHN DOES v. FRANCO PRODUCTIONS

2000 U.S. Dist. LEXIS 8645
United States District Court for the Northern District of Illinois

Facts: A group of college athletes was secretly videotaped in various states of undress by hidden cameras in restrooms, locker rooms, and showers. These videotapes were sold on Web sites hosted by GTE and PSINet. The Web sites also showed pictures taken from the videotapes. The athletes had not authorized the videotapes and only learned about their existence from a newspaper article. They brought suit against the producers and distributors of the videotapes, and against the Web hosts, GTE and PSINet. The Court dismissed the plaintiffs' complaint against GTE and PSINet, finding that they were ISPs and therefore immune from suit under the CDA. The plaintiffs amended their complaint, alleging that GTE and PSINet were also liable in their capacity as Web site hosts. GTE and PSINet filed a motion to dismiss.

Issues: Are GTE and PSINet liable for the posting and sale of unauthorized videos? Should their motion to dismiss be granted?

Excerpts from Judge Kocoras's Decision: Section 230(c)(1) [of the CDA] provides, "No provider or user of an interactive computer service shall be treated as the publisher or speaker of any information provided by another information content provider." This creates a federal immunity to any cause of action that would make service providers liable for information originating with a third-party user of the service. Plaintiffs have recast the dismissed claims raised in their previous complaint by alleging that they are bringing the instant suit against GTE and PSINet in their capacity as "web site host[s]" rather than service providers. In this capacity as web hosts, Plaintiffs claim that GTE and PSINet acted as "information content provider[s]" and would, thus, not be immune from suit under the CDA.

Immunity under the CDA is not limited to service providers who contain their activity to editorial exercises or those who do not engage in web hosting, but rather, Congress provided immunity even where the interactive service provider has an active, even aggressive role in making available content prepared by others. The deficiency in Plaintiffs' allegations is the notion that involvement in web hosting activities transforms an entity into an information content provider.

Perhaps the Court is obtuse in its consistent misunderstanding of Plaintiffs' cause of action, but it is still at a loss to understand how GTE's and PSINet's roles in the descriptions or presentation of the images on the Web site impact the creation or development of the images and videotapes themselves. Plaintiffs' explain that "the culpable conduct is not only the taking of the videotapes but also disseminating them on the Internet and offering them for sale and selling them." This makes no clearer Plaintiffs' theory that GTE and PSINet were somehow content providers.

Plaintiffs do not allege that GTE or PSINet themselves sold or offered for sale the videotapes at issue. Plaintiffs simply allege that GTE and PSINet, as web hosts, provided a medium through which others could sell or offer for sale the videotapes at issue. However, by offering web hosting services which enable someone to create a web page, GTE and PSINet are not magically rendered the creators of those web pages. As such, Plaintiffs' new characterization of GTE and PSINet as web hosts neither prevents these defendants from being deemed service providers protected by immunity under the CDA nor makes them content providers unprotected by the CDA's immunity.

For the reasons set forth above, the Court grants Defendants GTE's and PSINet's motion to dismiss.

1. An employee at AnswerThink Consulting group in Miami posted criticism of his boss on a Yahoo bulletin board. Without telling him, Yahoo revealed his identity to his employer and he was fired.
2. Four New Jersey boarding school students bought the drug DMX from eBay. After taking the drug, they began vomiting and became disoriented.

Generally, the law has not held Internet middlemen liable for what happens on their watch (i.e., on their Web site). Courts generally have taken the view that online providers are like the telephone company—simply transmitters of information. But do these companies have a moral obligation? Should eBay review listings before posting them to keep drugs and other illegal items at bay? Should Yahoo at least have notified the employee before revealing his identity? Should GTE and PSINet have asked questions about nude videos of college students?

CHAPTER CONCLUSION

The Internet has changed our lives in ways that were inconceivable a generation ago. Like a racer coming off a delayed start, the law is rushing to catch up. Not only will laws change as legislators and courts learn from experience, but new laws inevitably will be needed. Old laws will also be applied in new ways. For example, the role of antitrust law in cyberspace is, at the moment, uncertain. For example, Microsoft has been charged with illegal monopolization and some commentators have suggested that other major Internet companies may also have violated antitrust laws. Thus far, however, the courts have not ruled definitively.

Inevitably, the law of cyberspace will become increasingly international. What does Europe accomplish by regulating Internet privacy if its citizens spend a good portion of their time on American Web sites? What will the FTC do if scam artists, or spammers, operate offshore? Leaders of e-commerce companies around the world have formed the Global Business Dialogue on Electronic Commerce to develop policies and advise governments on cyberspace issues. (To learn more about this organization, travel to http://www.gbd.org.) Effective regulation of cyberspace will require cooperation among nations and between government and industry.

CHAPTER REVIEW

1. Currently, there is little regulation governing the collection or use of personal data on the Internet. Under principles established by the Network Advertising Initiative, Web sites should provide notice, consent, access, and security for personal data.
2. The Children's Online Privacy Protection Act of 1998 prohibits Internet operators from collecting information from children under 13

without parental permission. It also requires sites to disclose how they will use any information they acquire.

3. The Fourth Amendment to the Constitution prohibits unreasonable searches and seizures by government agents. This provision applies to computers.

4. The Privacy Policy Act requires the government to obtain a warrant before searching or seizing the papers of anyone engaged in publishing a newspaper, book, or broadcast.

5. The Electronic Communications Privacy Act of 1986 prohibits the unauthorized interception or disclosure of wire and electronic communications by, among others, the government, Internet service providers (ISPs), and employers. Under this statute:
   - Any intended recipient of an e-mail has the right to disclose it.
   - ISPs generally are prohibited from disclosing e-mail messages to anyone other than the addressee, unless this disclosure is necessary for the performance of their service or for the protection of their own rights or property.
   - An employer has the right to monitor workers' e-mail messages if (1) the employee consents, (2) the monitoring occurs in the ordinary course of business, or (3) the employer provides the e-mail system.
   - The government has the right to access e-mail messages if it first obtains a search warrant or court order.

6. Under the common law, intrusion into someone's private life is a tort if a reasonable person would find it offensive.

7. Generally, anyone seeking to export (or post on the Internet) encryption software must first obtain a license from the government.

8. Hacking is illegal under the federal Computer Fraud and Abuse Act of 1986. The CFAA prohibits:
   - Computer espionage
   - The theft of financial information
   - The theft of information from the U.S. government
   - Interstate theft from a computer
   - Computer trespass
   - Computer fraud
   - Intentional, reckless, and negligent damage to a computer
   - Trafficking in computer passwords for the purpose of affecting interstate commerce
   - Computer extortion

9. Fraud is the deception of another person for the purpose of obtaining money or property from him.

10. The Identity Theft and Assumption Deterrence Act of 1998 prohibits the use of false identification to commit fraud or other crime.

11. Those who send spam may be in violation of:
   - The Lanham Act, which prohibits the false use of a trademark.
   - The Federal Trademark and Dilution Act of 1995, which prohibits the use of a trademark in a way that dilutes its value.
   - The Computer Fraud and Abuse Act, which prohibits anyone from accessing a computer without authorization.
   - Trespass to chattels provisions of common law.

12. Under the Communications Decency Act of 1996, ISPs and Web hosts are not liable for information that is provided by someone else.

PRACTICE TEST

1. Three travel agents used fictitious accounts to steal 61 million frequent flyer miles from American Airlines. They traded this mileage in for 546 free tickets, with a value of $1.3 million. As evidence in the criminal trial, prosecutors used electronic communications

from the agents on SABRE, American's computerized travel reservations system. The agents alleged that this search was illegal under the Fourth Amendment to the Constitution. Do you agree?

2. Philip Karn, Jr., applied for a license from the Department of State to export a book entitled *Applied Cryptography*, and two diskettes with the electronic version of software code that was contained in print form in the book. The Department of State granted his request for the book, but not the software. He sued, alleging that this decision violated his First Amendment right to free speech. Does Karn have a valid claim?

3. To demonstrate the inadequacies of existing computer security systems, Cornell student Robert Morris created a computer virus. His plan, however, went awry, as plans sometimes do. He thought his virus would be relatively harmless, but it ran amok, crashing scores of computers at universities, military sites, and medical research sites. Under what statute might Morris be charged? Has he committed a crime, or is he liable only for civil penalties? Does it matter that he did not intend to cause damage?

4. **YOU BE THE JUDGE—WRITING PROBLEM** Less than a week after the hideous bombing of the Murrah Federal Building in Oklahoma City, someone posted messages on an AOL bulletin board advertising T-shirts with shockingly tasteless slogans, such as "Putting Kids to Bed—Oklahoma 1995." (Many children were killed in the bombing.) Purchasers were instructed to call "Ken" at the home number of Kenneth Zeran. It was, however, a (hideously unfunny) prank because Zeran knew nothing about the shirts. He did, however, receive scores of angry calls and death threats from people who had been appalled by the violence in Oklahoma. Zeran called AOL, which agreed to remove the posting, but refused to print a retraction. Several more messages were posted before AOL was able to shut down the accounts from which they were sent. Is AOL liable to Zeran? **Argument for AOL:** The Communications Decency Act of 1996 protects the company from liability. **Argument for Zeran:** AOL was slow in shutting down the accounts that generated these messages because it did not have an adequate record-keeping system. The company also should have printed a retraction and kept watch to make sure no more messages got posted. If the CDA gives blanket immunity, ISPs will have no incentive to be helpful to victims of "pranks" such as these.

5. During the course of ten months, Joseph Melle sent more than 60 million unsolicited e-mail advertisements to AOL members. What charges could AOL bring against him? Would the company be successful in its lawsuit?

6. Anthony Davis operated a computer bulletin board system that permitted users to send and receive e-mail, access the Internet, and download software. Davis's system had one attribute that distinguished it from, say, AOL. It specialized in pornography. Alerted by an anonymous tip, the Oklahoma City Police Department obtained a warrant to search his premises for "equipment, order materials, papers, membership lists and other paraphernalia pertaining to the distribution or display of pornographic material." During their raid, the officers seized computer equipment that contained 150,000 e-mails in electronic storage, some of which had not been retrieved by the recipients. Alleging that the e-mails had not been included in the warrant, Davis filed suit against the police officers for violations of the Electronic Communications Privacy Act. Does Davis have a valid claim?

7. Cyber Promotions sent spam to CompuServe subscribers. Many of them complained and even threatened to cancel their CompuServe memberships unless the company stopped the unsolicited e-mail. CompuServe asked the company to stop and also set up filters to intercept the spam, but Cyber managed to evade the filters and the onslaught continued.

Does CompuServe have a valid claim against Cyber Promotions?

8. **RIGHT & WRONG** Matt Drudge published a report on his Web site (http://www.drudgereport.com) that White House aide Sidney Blumenthal "has a spousal abuse past that has been effectively covered up. There are court records of Blumenthal's violence against his wife." The Drudge Report is an electronic publication focusing on Hollywood and Washington gossip. AOL paid Drudge $3,000 a month to make the Drudge Report available to AOL subscribers. Drudge e-mailed his reports to AOL, which then posted them. Before posting, however, AOL had the right to edit content. Drudge ultimately retracted his allegations against Blumenthal, who sued AOL. He alleged that under the Communications Decency Act of 1996, AOL was a "content provider" because it paid Drudge and edited what he wrote. Do you agree? Putting liability aside, what moral obligation did AOL have to its members? To Blumenthal? Should AOL be liable for content it bought and provided to its members?

9. Craig Hare offered computers and related equipment for sale on various Internet auction Web sites. He accepted payment but not responsibility—he never shipped the goods. Both the FTC and the U.S. Attorney General in Florida (that is, the prosecutor for the federal government) brought charges against him. What charges did they bring? Why would these two separate agencies of the federal government both bring suit?

10. What can you do to protect your privacy online? Draw up a concrete list of steps that you might reasonably consider. Are there some actions that you would not be willing to take, either because they are not worth the effort or because they are too sneaky?

Internet Research Problem

At http://www.ftc.gov/bcp/conline/edcams/kidzprivacy/, the FTC offers advice to Web site operators about how to comply with the Children's Online Privacy Protection Act. Find a Web site that does comply and one that does not.

You can find further practice problems in the Online Quiz at http://beatty.westbuslaw.com or in the Study Guide that accompanies this text.

INTELLECTUAL PROPERTY WITH CYBERLAW

21

CHAPTER

It is hard to imagine that a Goliath like the $12 billion American music industry could see a 19-year-old college sophomore as a threat to its long-term financial health. But when Brian Matiash, a computer engineering major, boots up the computer in his dorm room at Syracuse University on a typical evening, several hundred e-mail messages will await him, each a request for digital copies of recorded music. He will fire up his computer, which is equipped with a hard drive that holds copies of literally hundreds of songs and a CD burner, a device that allows him to copy those songs onto blank compact disks.

Mr. Matiash is part of a thriving underground network of digital music scavengers, mostly college students, who copy and trade music files globally over the Internet in violation of copyright laws. To the recording industry, Mr. Matiash's hobby is deeply disturbing. There are suddenly hundreds if not thousands of people around the globe creating vast electronic libraries of copy-protected music and posting it to the Internet in a format that allows for sound of near-CD quality. That means that potential consumers have a free alternative to buying music.

Mr. Matiash said, "I feel bad sometimes because I know I'm making a mess for the music companies. I know it's technically a crime." Last year, Polygram and 11 other record companies joined the Recording Industry Association of America in lawsuits accusing three commercial Web sites of copyright infringement. That suit was settled, but most music distribution is generated not by commercial sites but by hobbyists. The Recording Industry Association of America employs people to surf the Web looking for sites where copy-protected material is posted and is experimenting with software that automatically searches the Internet for such sites. When sites are found, officials usually notify the Internet service provider, often a university, which then typically asks the site's owner to remove the offending material. So far, that effort does not appear to have slowed the pirates. "I pretty much can guarantee everyone that I can find any song I want on the Internet if you give me a day or two," Mr. Matiash said.[1]

INTRODUCTION

For much of history, land was the most valuable form of property. It was the primary source of wealth and social status. Today, intellectual property is a major source of wealth. New ideas—for manufacturing processes, computer programs, medicines, books—bring both affluence and influence.

Although both can be valuable assets, land and intellectual property are fundamentally different. The value of land lies in the owner's right to exclude, to prevent others from entering it. Intellectual property, however, has little economic value unless others use it. This ability to share intellectual property is both good news and bad. On the one hand, the owner can produce and sell unlimited copies of, say, a software program, but, on the other hand, the owner has no easy way to determine if someone is using the program for free. The high cost of developing intellectual property, combined with the low cost of reproducing it, makes it particularly vulnerable to theft. As much as 35 percent of the software in use in America may be bootlegged (that is, copied and sold without permission).

Because intellectual property is nonexclusive, many people see no problem in using it for free. For example, students often argue that it is okay to copy CDs for their friends. How can copying a few CDs hurt a big recording studio? But if record companies earn lower royalties, they will produce fewer songs and music lovers everywhere will suffer. Some commentators suggest that the United States has been a technological leader partly because its laws have always provided strong protection for intellectual property. The Constitution provided for patent protection early in the country's history. In contrast, one of the oldest civilizations in the world, China, has been relatively slow in developing new technology. It did not institute a patent system until 1985.

[1] Jason Chervokas, "Internet CD Copying Tests Music Industry," *The New York Times*, Apr. 6, 1998, p. D3. Copyright © 1998 by The New York Times Co. Reprinted by permission.

PATENTS

A patent is a grant by the government that permits the inventor exclusive use of an invention for 20 years (or 14 years in the case of design patents). During this period, no one may make, use, or sell the invention without permission. In return, the inventor publicly discloses information about the invention that anyone can use upon expiration of the patent.

TYPES OF PATENTS

There are three types of patents: utility patents, design patents, and plant patents.

UTILITY PATENT

Whenever people use the word "patent" by itself, they are referring to a utility patent. This type of patent is available to those who invent (or significantly improve) any of the following:

Type of Invention	Example
Mechanical invention	A hydraulic jack used to elevate heavy aircraft
Electrical invention	A prewired, portable wall panel for use in large, open-plan offices
Chemical invention	The chemical 2-chloroethylphosphonic acid used as a plant growth regulator
Process	A method for applying a chemical compound to an established plant such as rice in order to inhibit the growth of weeds selectively; the application can be patented separately from the actual chemical
Machine	A device that enables a helicopter pilot to control all flight functions (pitch, roll, and heave) with one hand
Composition of matter	A sludge used as an explosive at construction sites; the patent specifies the water content, the density, and the types of solids contained in the mixture

A patent is not available solely for an idea, but only for its tangible application. Thus patents are *not* available for laws of nature, scientific principles, mathematical algorithms, or formulas such as $a^2 + b^2 = c^2$. In recent years, the status of computer software has been controversial: Is it an (unpatentable) mathematical formula or a (patentable) process or machine? The following case answers this question.

STATE STREET BANK & TRUST CO. v. SIGNATURE FINANCIAL GROUP, INC.

149 F.3d 1368, 1998 U.S. App. LEXIS 16869
United States Court of Appeals for the Federal Circuit,[2] 1998

Facts: Signature Financial Group, Inc. owns a patent on a computer software program that aids in the administration of mutual funds. The so-called Hub and Spoke System allows several mutual funds, or "Spokes," to pool their investment funds into a single portfolio, or "Hub." In this way, the funds can share administrative costs. Each Spoke sells shares to the public, and the cost of these shares depends upon the value of the assets pooled in the Hub. Therefore, each day within hours of the close of the stock market, each fund's administrator must know the value to the nearest penny of its pooled shares. The Signature software made this calculation.

State Street Bank and Trust Co. negotiated with Signature for a license to use its software. When negotiations broke down, State Street brought suit alleging that the patent was invalid. The trial court granted State Street's motion for summary judgment.

Issue: Is data processing software patentable?

Excerpts from Judge Rich's Decision: [The Supreme] Court has held that mathematical algorithms are not patentable subject matter to the extent that they are merely abstract ideas. From a practical standpoint, this means that to be patentable an algorithm must be applied in a "useful" way.

Today, we hold that the transformation of data, representing discrete dollar amounts, by a machine through a series of mathematical calculations into a final share price, constitutes a practical application of a mathematical algorithm, formula, or calculation, because it produces "a useful, concrete and tangible result"—a final share price momentarily fixed for recording and reporting purposes.

The question of whether a claim encompasses statutory subject matter should focus on the essential characteristics of the subject matter, in particular, its practical utility. For purpose of our analysis, [this] claim is directed to a machine programmed with the Hub and Spoke software and admittedly produces a "useful, concrete, and tangible result." This renders it statutory subject matter, even if the useful result is expressed in numbers, such as price, profit, percentage, cost, or loss.

Reversed and remanded.

The *State Street* case could have a profound impact on e-commerce as companies rush to patent techniques for doing business over the Internet. For example, Priceline.com recently received a patent for the reverse auction system offered on its Web site (http://www.priceline.com). Customers list the price (backed up by a credit card) that they are willing to pay for an airline ticket, hotel room, car, or other item. Priceline then scours its database to find a seller willing to make a deal at that price.

Proponents of these patents argue that they permit innovators on the Internet to protect their ideas. Otherwise, it is easy for copycats to open a rival Web site overnight. Critics counter that these patents could stifle e-commerce by limiting the use of new ideas. For example, a company called E-Data has sued, claiming that it owns the patent for the idea of selling software over the Internet.

[2] Recall from Chapter 3 that the Court of Appeals for the Federal Circuit is the thirteenth United States Court of Appeals. It hears appeals from specialized trial courts.

DESIGN PATENT

A design patent protects the appearance, not the function, of an item. It is granted to anyone who invents a new, original, and ornamental design for an article. For example, Braun, Inc. patented the look of its handheld electric blenders. Design patents last only 14 years, not 20.

PLANT PATENT

Anyone who creates a new type of plant can patent it, *provided that* the inventor is able to reproduce it asexually—through grafting, for instance, not by planting its seeds. For example, one company patented its unique heather plant.

REQUIREMENTS FOR A PATENT

To obtain a patent, the inventor must show that her invention meets all of the following tests:

- **Novel.** An invention is not patentable if it (1) is known or has already been used in this country, or (2) has been described in a publication here or overseas. For example, an inventor discovered a new use for existing chemical compounds but was not permitted to patent it because the chemicals had already been described in prior publications, though the new uses had not.[3]
- **Nonobvious.** An invention is not patentable if it is obvious to a person with ordinary skill in that particular area. An inventor was not allowed to patent a waterflush system designed to remove cow manure from the floor of a barn because it was obvious.[4]
- **Useful.** To be patented, an invention must be useful. It need not necessarily be commercially valuable, but it must have some current use. Being merely of scientific interest is not enough. Thus a company was denied a patent for a novel process for making steroids because they had no therapeutic value.[5]

A searchable database of all patents issued since 1976 is available at the Patent and Trademark Office's Web site: http://www.uspto.gov/patft/index.html. To find out just how creative inventors can be, check out the Wacky Patent of the Month at http://www.colitz.com/site/wacky.htm.

PATENT APPLICATION AND ISSUANCE

To obtain a patent, the inventor must file a complex application with the federal Patent and Trademark Office (PTO) in Washington, D.C. If a patent examiner determines that the application meets all legal requirements, the PTO will issue the patent. If the examiner denies the patent application, the inventor can appeal that decision to the PTO Board of Appeals and from there to the Court of

---

[3] *In re Schoenwald*, 964 F.2d 1122, 1992 U.S. App. LEXIS 10181 (Fed. Cir. 1992).

[4] *Sakraida v. Ag Pro, Inc.*, 425 U.S. 273, 96 S. Ct. 1532, 1976 U.S. LEXIS 146 (1976).

[5] *Brenner v. Manson*, 383 U.S. 519, 86 S. Ct. 1033, 1966 U.S. LEXIS 2907 (1966).

Appeals for the Federal Circuit in Washington. Alternatively, upon denial of the application, the inventor can file suit against the PTO in the federal district court in Washington.

PRIORITY BETWEEN TWO INVENTORS

When two people invent the same product, who is entitled to a patent—the first to invent or the first to file an application? Generally, the person who invents and *puts the invention into practice* has priority over the first filer. Having the idea is not enough—the inventor must actually use the product.

PRIOR SALE

However, an inventor must apply for a patent within one year of selling the product commercially. The purpose of this rule is to encourage prompt disclosure of inventions. It prevents someone from inventing a product, selling it for years, and then obtaining a 20-year monopoly with a patent.

PROVISIONAL PATENT APPLICATION

Investors who are unable to assess the market value of their ideas sometimes hesitate to file a patent application because the process is expensive and cumbersome. To solve this problem, the PTO now permits inventors to file a **provisional patent application (PPA)**. The PPA is a simpler, shorter, cheaper application that gives inventors the opportunity to show their ideas to potential investors without incurring the full expense of a patent application. PPA protection lasts only one year. To maintain protection after that time, the inventor must file a regular patent application. So far, about 10 percent of all patent applications have been for provisional patents.

DURATION OF A PATENT

After 1861, patents in the United States were valid for 17 years from the date of *issuance*. However, in 1994, Congress ratified an international treaty called the General Agreement on Tariffs and Trade (GATT). One of GATT's provisions required patents in all signatory countries to be valid for 20 years from the date of *filing*. (This change does not apply to design patents, which are still valid for only 14 years.) The average patent in the United States is issued 19 months after filing, so this change is generally favorable to inventors who will, on average, have 18 years and five months of coverage instead of 17 years. Sometimes, however, the PTO takes considerably longer than 19 months to issue a patent. In some cases of delay, the patent may be extended for up to 5 years beyond the typical 20-year term.

INFRINGEMENT

A patent holder has the exclusive right to use the invention during the term of the patent. The holder can bring suit to recover damages and to enjoin the future use of any product that is substantially the same as the patent. A court may award damages to compensate for (1) reasonable royalties, (2) lost profits, and (3) interest since the date of the infringement. In the case of intentional infringement or bad faith, a court may treble the damages and also award attorney's fees.

The PTO issued a patent to Compton's New Media for a technique that allowed computer users to retrieve information from multimedia databases. Compton's had developed this technique for its CD-ROM encyclopedia. After the PTO issued this patent, Compton's announced that it would begin to charge licensing fees to all other software companies that used the same technology—virtually everyone with multimedia CD-ROMs. Many in the computer industry protested to the PTO, claiming that the patented technology was neither new nor nonobvious because it had already been used many times. The PTO reversed itself and rejected Compton's application.

This example illustrates a troublesome problem with software patents. Before 1980, software could not be patented. Therefore, companies protected it by keeping it secret. Even though software can now be patented, many companies have not taken advantage of this change in the law. They have elected to continue keeping their software secret. As a result, the PTO cannot always determine what is novel and what is not because it does not know what is being used secretly.

Submarine patents present a similar problem. These are patent applications that lie submerged in the PTO for years, without anyone knowing they are there. The technology becomes widespread and competitors happily go about using it. Suddenly, the PTO issues a patent, and the new owner has the right to demand licensing fees from current users. For example, Microsoft recently obtained a patent for cascading style sheets. This widely used technology facilitates the design of Web pages. Much to everyone's relief, Microsoft offered to license the technology for free. Nevertheless, technology companies worry that other patent applications may be lurking in the PTO. In the wrong hands, they could threaten the structure of the online world.

COPYRIGHTS

The holder of a copyright owns the *particular tangible expression* of an idea, but not the underlying idea or method of operation. Abner Doubleday could copyright a book setting out his particular version of the rules of baseball, but he could not copyright the rules themselves nor could he require players to pay him a royalty. Similarly, the inventor of double-entry bookkeeping could copyright a pamphlet explaining his system but not the system itself.

Unlike patents, the ideas underlying copyrighted material need not be novel. Two movies that came out at the same time—*Armageddon* and *Deep Impact*—were both based on the idea of meteors destroying the earth. Neither violated the other's copyright because their expressions of the basic idea were different.

The Copyright Act lists nine protected categories: literature, music, drama, choreography, pictures, sculpture, movies, recordings, and architectural works. A copyright is valid until 70 years after the death of the work's only or last living author. In the case of works owned by a corporation—Mickey Mouse, for instance—the copyright lasts 95 years from publication or 120 years from creation. Once the copyright expires, anyone may use the material. Mark Twain died in 1910, so anyone may now publish *Tom Sawyer* without permission and without paying a copyright fee.

A work is automatically copyrighted once it is in tangible form. For example, once a songwriter puts notes on paper, the work is copyrighted without further ado. But if she whistles a happy tune without writing it down, the song is not copyrighted, and anyone else could use it without permission. Registration with the Copyright Office of the Library of Congress is necessary only if the holder wishes to bring suit to enforce the copyright. Although authors still routinely place the copyright symbol (©) on their works, such a precaution is not necessary in the United States. However, some lawyers still recommend using the copyright symbol because other countries recognize it. Also, the penalties for intentional copyright infringement are heavier than for unintentional violations, and the presence of a copyright notice is evidence that the infringer's actions were intentional.

Infringement

Anyone who uses copyrighted material without permission is violating the Copyright Act. **To prove a violation, the plaintiff must present evidence that the work was original** and that either:

- The infringer actually copied the work, or
- The infringer had access to the original and the two works are substantially similar.

A court may (1) prohibit the infringer from committing further violations, (2) order destruction of the infringing material, and (3) require the infringer to pay damages, profits earned, and attorney's fees. The chapter opener illustrates how widespread copyright infringement has become.

Fair Use

The purpose of copyright laws is to encourage creative work. A writer who can control, and profit from, artistic work will be inclined to produce more. If enforced oppressively, however, the copyright laws could stifle creativity by denying access to copyrighted work. **The doctrine of *fair use* permits limited use of copyrighted material without permission of the author for purposes such as criticism, comment, news reporting, scholarship, or research.** Courts generally do not permit a use that will decrease revenues from the original work by, say, competing with it. A reviewer is permitted, for example, to quote from a book without the author's permission, but, as we see below, online music companies cannot download entire versions of copyrighted songs.

Also under the fair use doctrine, faculty members are permitted to photocopy and distribute copyrighted materials to students, as long as the materials are brief and the teacher's action is spontaneous. If, over his breakfast coffee one morning, Professor Learned spots a terrific article in *Mad Magazine* that perfectly illustrates a point he intends to make in class that day, the fair use doctrine permits him to photocopy the page and distribute it to his class. However, under a misinterpretation of the fair use doctrine, some faculty were in the habit of routinely preparing lengthy course packets of copyrighted material without permission of the authors. In *Basic Books, Inc. v. Kinko's Graphic Corp.*,[6] a federal court held that this practice violated the copyright laws because the material was more than one short passage and because it was sold to students. Now, when professors put together course packets, they (or the copy shop) must obtain permission and pay a royalty for the use of copyrighted material.

NEWSworthy

After releasing the third Star Wars movie, *The Return of the Jedi*, Lucasfilm, Ltd. waited 16 years to produce the fourth film in the series, *Episode I—The Phantom Menace*. Many of *Episode I*'s most fervent fans were born after *Jedi* came out. The myth of Star Wars was kept alive by books, fanzines (magazines devoted to Star Wars), fan fiction (unauthorized stories about Star Wars characters), and Internet Web sites such as http://www.theforce.net and http://www.flyingarmadillo.com.

For all those years, Lucasfilm made no protest. Then, several months before *Episode I*'s release, the studio began to crack down on unauthorized use of its copyrighted characters. It even filed suit against Little, Brown & Co. for publishing *The Unauthorized Star Wars Compendium*. Little, Brown claims fair use, that it is simply commenting and reporting on an important cultural phenomenon. Meanwhile, Paramount Pictures has taken action against Star Trek Web sites, and 20th Century Fox is going after sites that feature its hit TV show, *The X-Files*.

ONLINE MUSIC

A fierce war is raging in the entertainment world between traditional music producers and online entrepreneurs (a/k/a "pirates") who have figured out how to turn music from a CD into downloadable files on the Internet. As the chapter opener illustrates, much copyrighted music is now singing in cyberspace.

In one of the first cases to challenge this practice, UMG Recordings, Inc. charged MP3.com, Inc. with copyright infringement. MP3.com had uploaded tens of thousands of CDs onto its Web site. A service called My.MP3.com allowed subscribers to download files for free. The subscriber simply had to "prove" he owned a CD by inserting his copy into his CD-ROM drive for a few seconds. Thereafter, he could access this CD via the Internet from any computer in the world. MP3.com argued that it was doing nothing more than storing subscriber CDs and, anyway, its activities were protected under the fair use doctrine. UMG took a darker view, claiming that MP3.com was, in fact, replaying recordings it had copied without permission.

The court scolded MP3.com, saying "The complex marvels of cyberspatial communication may create difficult legal issues; but not in this case. Defendant's infringement of plaintiff's copyrights is clear." The court dismissed the fair use defense, holding that UMG has the right to decide how its property is used and is entitled to a license fee from MP3.com.[7]

---

[6] 758 F. Supp. 1522, 1991 U.S. Dist. LEXIS 3804 (S.D.N.Y. 1991). A federal appeals court reached the same result in *Princeton University Press v. Michigan Document Services, Inc.*, 99 F.3d 1381, 1996 U.S. App. LEXIS 29132 (6th Cir. 1996).

[7] *UMG Recordings, Inc. v. MP3.com*, 92 F.Supp. 2d 349; 2000 U.S. Dist. LEXIS 5761 (S.D.N.Y. 2000).

PARODY

Parody has a long history in the United States—some of our most cherished songs have been the basis of parodies. Before Francis Scott Key wrote the words to the *Star-Spangled Banner*, other lyrics that mocked colonial governors had been set to the same music. (The tune was well known as a drinking song.) During the Civil War, this parody of the *Battle Hymn of the Republic* expressed anti-war sentiment:

> Tell Abe Lincoln of Antietam's bloody dell
> Tell Abe Lincoln where a thousand heroes fell
> Tell Abe Lincoln and his gang to go to hell
> And we'll go marching home.

The Capitol Steps, a singing group in Washington, wrote this version of Jerome Kern's song *Old Man River* to make fun of the scandals during President Clinton's administration:

> Ol' Man Zipper, that Ol' Man Zipper
> He must know somethin', but don't say nothin'
> He just keeps pollin', his polls keep rollin' along

(For more parodies by the Capitol Steps, dance over to their Web site: http://www.capsteps.com/.) Have the Capitol Steps violated Kern's copyright? After all, they did use his music. What if the words in a parody are in poor taste or express opinions with which the original creator disagrees? The Capitol Steps appear to be on safe ground. The United States has a long history of protecting the expression of unpopular ideas, and the Supreme Court recently extended this protection to parodies. The rap group 2 Live Crew recorded a parody of the song *Oh, Pretty Woman*. The group had asked permission, but the holder of the copyright refused. Justice David Souter wrote, "We are called upon to decide whether 2 Live Crew's commercial parody of Roy Orbison's song, 'Oh, Pretty Woman,' may be a fair use within the meaning of the Copyright Act of 1976." The Court's decision included Appendix A and Appendix B, which incorporated the full lyrics of the songs. The following are excerpts from those appendices in the Court's decision.

Original:	**Parody:**
Pretty Woman, walking down the street,	Big hairy woman you need to shave that stuff
Pretty Woman, the kind I like to meet,	Big hairy woman you know I bet it's tough
Pretty Woman, I don't believe you, you're not the truth,	Big hairy woman all that hair it ain't legit
No one could look as good as you Mercy	'Cause you look like "Cousin It" Big hairy woman

The Court held that parody is a fair use of copyrighted material as long as the use of the original is not excessive. The parody may copy enough to remind the audience of the original work but not so much that the parody harms the market for the original. The Supreme Court remanded the case to the trial court to determine if the 2 Live Crew version had copied too much or harmed the market for a nonparody rap version of *Oh, Pretty Woman*.[8] The two sides ultimately settled with 2 Live Crew agreeing to pay royalties.

COMPUTERS

Computers have created their own unique copyright problems. The Copyright Act includes "computer databases, and computer programs to the extent that they incorporate authorship in the programmer's expression of original ideas, as distinguished from the ideas themselves." However, courts have hundreds of years of experience with ordinary copyrights, whereas computer issues are new.

SOFTWARE

A computer software program has three different parts:

- **Codes.** Both source and object codes can be copyrighted. Computer programmers write programs in source code, which is then translated into object code for the computer to read. The object code is a series of 0s and 1s that flip switches in the computer. Although object codes can be read only by machines, not humans, they are nonetheless copyrightable.[9]
- **Structure.** Two programs that accomplish the same result may have a very different structure. This structure is copyrightable. Rand Jaslow copied the program that Elaine Whelan designed to manage the finances of a dental lab. Although the programs were written in a different computer language, Jaslow had copied Whelan's structure and organization. The court held that Jaslow had violated Whelan's copyright.[10]
- **Look and Feel.** Two computer programs may accomplish the same tasks, but nonetheless look very different on screen. They may, for example, use different icons and different commands. One program may symbolize "delete" by using a trash can while another uses a red circle with a line through it. In the following case, Lotus Development Corp. argued that Borland International, Inc. had violated copyright law by copying the look and feel of Lotus's most popular program. You be the judge.

---

[8] *Campbell v. Acuff-Rose Music, Inc.*, 510 U.S. 569, 114 S. Ct. 1164, 1994 U.S. LEXIS 2052 (1994).

[9] *Apple Computer, Inc. v. Franklin Computer Corp.*, 714 F.2d 1240, 1983 U.S. App. LEXIS 24388 (3rd Cir. 1983).

[10] *Whelan Assoc., Inc. v. Jaslow Dental Laboratory, Inc.*, 797 F.2d 1222, 1986 U.S. App. LEXIS 27796 (3rd Cir. 1986).

LOTUS DEVELOPMENT CORP. v. BORLAND INTERNATIONAL, INC.
516 U.S. 233, 116 S. Ct. 804, 1996 U.S. LEXIS 470
United States Supreme Court, 1996

Facts: Lotus 1–2–3 is a computer spreadsheet program that Lotus designed, copyrighted, and sold. Users manipulate and control the program via a series of menu commands, such as "Copy," "Print," and "Quit." In all, 1–2–3 has 469 commands arranged into more than 50 menus and submenus.

Borland has a spreadsheet program, entitled "Quattro Pro." Borland did not copy any of Lotus's underlying computer code, but, to make the program attractive to 1–2–3 users, Quattro Pro contained a "Lotus Emulation Interface." After activating this Interface, Borland users would see the Lotus menu commands on their screens and could interact with Quattro Pro as if using Lotus 1–2–3, albeit with a slightly different screen and with many Borland options not available in the Lotus program. Borland admits that it copied Lotus's program but argues that the "look and feel" of a program are not copyrightable.

You be the Judge: Can Lotus copyright the look and feel of its computer program?

Argument for Borland: Under the Copyright Act, no one can copyright an idea or a method of operation. A method of operation means the process by which a machine works, whether it be a car, food processor, computer, or VCR. The Lotus menu is like the buttons on a VCR—Record, Play, Stop/Eject. How the buttons are arranged and labeled does not make them an expression of the abstract method of operating a VCR. Instead, the buttons are themselves the method of operation. Highlighting the "Print" command in Lotus 1–2–3, or typing the letter "P," is analogous to pressing a VCR button labeled "Play." Just as one could not operate a buttonless VCR, it would be impossible to operate Lotus 1–2–3 without using its menu.

Under Lotus's theory, every computer program would have different commands. The user might, for example, have to learn many different commands for Print. This is not only absurd, but an unreasonable burden on computer users. At some point, computer programs will have to duplicate each other because there are only so many ways to tell a computer to print.

Argument for Lotus: An author can copyright the expression of an idea, but not the idea itself. Lotus could not copyright the idea of a spreadsheet program, but it can copyright its unique expression of that idea—the types and arrangement of commands, for instance. In developing Quattro Pro, Borland could have constructed a perfectly satisfactory menu using its own commands, not Lotus's. Instead of "Quit," Borland could have said "Exit." Instead of "Copy," Borland could have said "Clone," "Ditto," or "Duplicate." We know that Borland could have constructed an alternate menu because, in fact, it did. Quattro Pro users have a choice between the Lotus or the Quattro Pro menu.

All computer software is nothing more than a method for operating a computer. If the court agrees with Borland, virtually no software would be copyrightable. Borland argues that the Lotus commands are the same as buttons on a VCR. There is one significant difference, however: VCRs are not copyrightable, whereas computer programs are.

Lotus worked for years to develop 1–2–3 and Borland simply stole it. Lotus had a dominant share of the spreadsheet market, and Borland knew its program could not compete unless it attracted 1–2–3 users. It is clear that Borland violated Lotus's copyright.

INTERNET

The good news is that Mary Schmich wrote an influential article in the *Chicago Tribune*. The bad news is that people deleted her name, attributed the article to Kurt Vonnegut, and sent it around the world via e-mail. Tom Tomorrow's cartoon was syndicated to 100 newspapers, but, by the time the last papers received it, the cartoon had already gone zapping around cyberspace. Since his name had been deleted, some editors thought *he* had plagiarized it.

In response to such incidents, Congress recently passed the **Digital Millennium Copyright Act**, which provides that:

- It is illegal to delete copyright information, such as the name of the author or the title of the article. It is also illegal to distribute false copyright information. Thus, anyone who e-mailed Schmich's article without her name on it, or who claimed it was his own work, would be violating the law.
- It is also illegal to circumvent encryption or scrambling devices that protect copyrighted works. For example, some software programs are designed so that they can only be copied once. Anyone who overrides this protective device to make another copy is violating the law. Also, if movies and songs are distributed in a scrambled form over the Internet to people who pay for the descrambler, anyone who unscrambles without paying is in violation. The statute does permit purchasers of copyrighted software to make one backup copy.

TRADEMARKS

A trademark is any combination of words and symbols that a business uses to identify its products or services and distinguish them from others. Trademarks are important to both consumers and businesses. Consumers use trademarks to distinguish between competing products. People who feel that Nike shoes fit their feet best can rely on the Nike trademark to know they are buying the shoe they want. A business with a high-quality product can use a trademark to develop a loyal base of customers who are able to distinguish its product from another.

TYPES OF MARKS

There are four different types of marks:

- **Trademarks** are affixed to goods in interstate commerce.
- **Service marks** are used to identify services, not products. Fitness First, Burger King, and Weight Watchers are service marks. For the remainder of this chapter, the terms "trademark" and "mark" are used to refer to both trademarks and service marks.
- **Certification marks** are words or symbols used by a person or an organization to attest that products and services produced by others meet certain standards. The Good Housekeeping Seal of Approval means that the Good Housekeeping organization has determined that a product meets its standards.
- **Collective marks** are used to identify members of an organization. The Lions Club, the Girls Scouts of America, and the Masons are examples of collective marks.

OWNERSHIP AND REGISTRATION

Under common law, the first person to use a mark in trade owns it. Registration with the federal government is not necessary. However, under the federal Lanham Act, the owner of a mark may register it on the Lanham Act Principal Register. Once the mark is registered, the symbol ® may be placed next to it. Registration has several advantages:

- Even if a mark has been used in only one or two states, registration makes it valid nationally.
- Registration notifies the public that a mark is in use because anyone who applies for registration first searches the Public Register to ensure that no one else has rights to the mark.
- Five years after registration, a mark becomes virtually incontestable because most challenges are barred.
- The damages available under the Lanham Act are higher than under common law.
- The holder of a registered trademark has first option to use it as an Internet domain name.

Under the Lanham Act, the owner files an application with the PTO (Patent and Trademark Office) in Washington, D.C. The PTO will accept an application only if the owner has already used the mark attached to a product in interstate commerce or promises to use the mark within six months after the filing. (The PTO will also grant one six-month extension automatically and has the right to grant extensions for up to three years from filing.) In addition, the applicant must be the first to use the mark in interstate commerce. Initially, the trademark is valid for 10 years, but the owner can renew it for an unlimited number of 10-year terms as long as the mark is still in use. For the first five years after registration, the mark can be challenged by anyone who believes that it is not valid. Trademark searches are free on PTO's Web site: http://www.uspto.gov/tmdb/index.html.

VALID TRADEMARKS

Words (Reebok), symbols (Microsoft's flying window logo), phrases ("Just do it"), shapes (a Coca-Cola bottle), sounds (NBC's three chimes), and even scents (plumeria blossoms on sewing thread) can be trademarked. **To be valid, a trademark must be distinctive**—that is, the mark must clearly distinguish one product from another. There are five basic categories of distinctive marks:

- **Fanciful marks** are made-up words such as Converse or Saucony.
- **Arbitrary marks** use existing words that do *not* describe the product—Prince tennis racquets, for example. No one really thinks that these racquets are designed by or for royalty.
- **Suggestive marks** *indirectly* describe the product's function. Greyhound implies that the bus line is swift, and Coppertone suggests what customers will look like after applying the product.

- Marks with **secondary meaning** cannot, by themselves, be trademarked, unless they have been used so long that they are now associated with the product in the public's mind. When a film company released a movie called *Ape*, it used as an illustration a picture that looked like a scene from *King Kong*—a gigantic gorilla astride the World Trade Center in New York City. The court held that the movie posters of *King Kong* had acquired a secondary meaning in the mind of the public, so the *Ape* producers were forced to change their poster.[11]
- **Trade dress** is the image and overall appearance of a business or product. It may include size, shape, color, or texture. The Supreme Court held that a Mexican restaurant was entitled to protection under the Lanham Act for the shape and general appearance of the exterior of its restaurant as well as the decor, menu, servers' uniforms, and other features reflecting the total image of the restaurant.[12]

The following categories are not distinctive and *cannot* be trademarked:

- **Similar to an Existing Mark.** To avoid confusion, the PTO will not grant a trademark that is similar to one already in existence on a similar product. Once the PTO had granted a trademark for "Pledge" furniture polish, it refused to trademark "Promise" for the same product. "Chat noir" and "black cat" were also too similar because one is simply a translation of the other. Houghton-Mifflin Co. sued to prevent a punk rock band from calling itself Furious George because the name is too similar to Curious George, the star of a series of children's books.
- **Generic Trademarks.** No one is permitted to trademark an item's ordinary name—"shoe" or "book," for example. Sometimes, however, a word begins as a trademark and later becomes a generic name. Zipper, escalator, aspirin, linoleum, thermos, yo-yo, and nylon all started out as trademarks, but became generic. Once a name is generic, the owner loses the trademark because the name can no longer be used to distinguish one product from another—all products are called the same thing. That is why, in advertisements for Sanka, people ask for "a cup of Sanka-brand decaffeinated coffee." And why Xerox Corp. encourages people to say, "I'll photocopy this document," rather than "I'll xerox it." Martini, jeep, and rollerblade are trademarks that seem destined for generic status.
- **Descriptive Marks.** Words cannot be trademarked if they simply describe the product—such as "low-fat," "green," or "crunchy." Descriptive words can, however, be trademarked if they do *not* describe that particular product because they then become distinctive rather than descriptive. "Blue Diamond" is an acceptable trademark for nuts as long as the nuts are neither blue nor diamond-shaped.

---

[11] *Paramount Pictures Corp. v. Worldwide Entertainment Corp.*, 2 Media L. Rep. 1311, 195 U.S.P.Q. (BNA) 536, 1977 U.S. Dist. LEXIS 17931 (S.D.N.Y. 1977).

[12] *Two Pesos, Inc. v. Taco Cabana, Inc.*, 505 U.S. 763, 112 S. Ct. 2753, 1992 U.S. LEXIS 4533 (1992).

Microsoft introduced its Internet Explorer software to great fanfare. There was only one problem: SyNet, Inc. had trademarked the name a year before. What was Microsoft to do? First, it offered $75,000 to buy the rights to the name, but the owner of SyNet refused to sell. Then Microsoft claimed that Internet Explorer could not be trademarked at all because it was a descriptive mark. Microsoft argued that Internet Explorer simply described software for surfing the Net, just as chocolate fudge describes candy. However, a day after trial began in federal court in Chicago, SyNet accepted Microsoft's $5 million settlement offer.

- **Names.** The PTO generally will not grant a trademark in a surname because other people are already using it and have the right to continue. No one could register "Jefferson" as a trademark. However, a surname can be used as part of a longer title—"Jefferson Home Tours," for instance. Similarly, no one can register a geographical name such as "Boston" unless it is also associated with another word, such as "Boston Ale."
- **Deceptive Marks.** The PTO will not register a mark that is deceptive. It refused to register a trademark with the words "National Collection and Credit Control" and an eagle superimposed on a map of the United States because this trademark gave the impression that the organization was an official government agency.
- **Scandalous or Immoral Trademarks.** The PTO refused to register a mark that featured a nude man and woman embracing. In upholding the PTO's decision, the court was unsympathetic to arguments that this was the perfect trademark for a newsletter on sex.[13]

In the following case, the Supreme Court decided whether a color could be trademarked.

QUALITEX & CO. v. JACOBSON PRODUCTS, INC.

514 U.S. 159, 115 S. Ct. 1300, 1995 U.S. LEXIS 2408
United States Supreme Court, 1995

Facts: Since the 1950s, Qualitex has used a special shade of green-gold color on the pads that it makes for dry cleaning presses. After Jacobson Products (a Qualitex rival) began to use a similar shade on its own press pads, Qualitex registered its color as a trademark and filed suit against Jacobson for trademark infringement.

Issue: Does the Lanham Act permit a color to be trademarked?

Excerpts from Justice Breyer's Decision: The language of the Lanham Act describes [trademarks] in the broadest of terms. It says that trademarks "include any word, name, symbol, or device, or any combination thereof." Since human beings might use as a "symbol" or "device" almost anything at all that is capable of carrying meaning, this language, read literally, is not restrictive. If a shape, a sound, and a fragrance can act as symbols why can a color not do the same?

[13] *In re McGinley*, 660 F.2d 481, 211 U.S.P.Q. (BNA) 668, 1981 CCPA LEXIS 177 (C.C.P.A. 1981).

We cannot find in the basic objectives of trademark law any obvious theoretical objection to the use of color alone as a trademark, where that color identifies and distinguishes a particular brand (and thus indicates its "source"). Indeed, the district court, in this case, entered findings that show Qualitex's green-gold press pad color has met these requirements. The green-gold color acts as a symbol. Having developed secondary meaning (for customers identified the green-gold color as Qualitex's), it identifies the press pad's source.

Jacobson says that, if the law permits the use of color as a trademark, it will produce uncertainty and unresolvable court disputes about what shades of a color a competitor may lawfully use. Because lighting (morning sun, twilight mist) will affect perceptions of protected color, competitors and courts will suffer from "shade confusion" as they try to decide whether use of a similar color on a similar product does, or does not, confuse customers and thereby infringe a trademark. We do not believe, however, that color, in this respect, is special. Courts traditionally decide quite difficult questions about whether two words or phrases or symbols are sufficiently similar, in context, to confuse buyers. They have had to compare, for example, such words as "Bonamine" and "Dramamine" (motion-sickness remedies); "Huggies" and "Dougies" (diapers); "Cheracol" and "Syrocol" (cough syrup).

We conclude that the Ninth Circuit erred in barring Qualitex's use of color as a trademark.

INFRINGEMENT

To win an infringement suit, the trademark owner must show that the defendant's trademark is likely to deceive customers about who has made the goods or provided the services. The rightful owner is entitled to (1) an injunction prohibiting further violations, (2) destruction of the infringing material, (3) up to three times actual damages, (4) any profits the infringer earned on the product, and (5) attorney's fees.

Many Web sites give away free information and (try to) make money selling advertisements. To be successful, the sites must attract hordes of visitors. What can they do to lure cybersurfers? Some site operators embed words like "sex" and "nudity" in invisible coding, even if the sites have nothing to do with sex. Although visitors cannot see the words, search engines will still call up the site. Not content with these generic lures, Calvin Designer Label (no relation to Calvin Klein, the clothing designer) embedded the words "Playboy" and "Playmate" in machine-readable code on its Web site. A federal court entered a restraining order preventing Calvin Designer from infringing on Playboy's trademarks.[14]

FEDERAL TRADEMARK DILUTION ACT OF 1995

Before Congress passed the Federal Trademark Dilution Act of 1995, a trademark owner could win an infringement lawsuit only by proving that consumers would be deceived about who had really made the product. **The new statute prevents others from using a trademark in a way that dilutes its value**, even though consumers are not confused about the origin of the product. Thus, for example, Hasbro, Inc. trademarked "Candyland" for use on a children's board

[14] *Playboy Enterprises, Inc. v. Calvin Designer Label*, 985 F. Supp. 1220, 1997 U.S. Dist. LEXIS 14345 (N.D. Cal. 1997).

game. Internet Entertainment Group, Ltd. used the name Candyland to identify a sexually explicit Internet site (http://www.candyland.com). Although consumers were unlikely to think that Hasbro had developed the Candyland site, the court held that Internet Entertainment had diluted the value of the Candyland trademark.[15]

DOMAIN NAMES

Internet addresses, known as domain names, can be immensely valuable. Shopping.com paid $750,000 to acquire its domain name from the previous (lucky) owner. Compaq Computer Corp. purchased altavista.com for its Altavista search engine from (the unrelated) Altavista Technologies, Inc. The price was $3.3 million.

Who has rights to a domain name? The National Science Foundation, which traditionally maintained the Internet, granted Network Solutions, Inc. (NSI), a private company, the right to allocate domain names. In the beginning, NSI charged no fee for domain names and the rule was "first come, first served." Then so-called "cybersquatters" began to register domain names, not to use, but to sell to others. Some cybersquatters specialized in catchy words or phrases (food.com). Others focused on celebrity names—offering "Michael J. Fox" for $10,000 or "Bill Gates" for $1 million. A religious group, called the Friend to Friend Foundation, even financed its operations by registering hundreds of domain names for resale.

What if cybersquatters obtain a domain name that happens to be someone else's trademark—Coca-Cola.com, for example? In response to complaints, NSI began suspending any domain name that was challenged by the holder of a registered trademark. For instance, NSI would not allow Princeton Review to keep kaplan.com, which Princeton had acquired simply to inconvenience its archrival in the test preparation business. Congress then passed the Anticybersquatting Consumer Protection Act, which permits both trademark owners and famous people to sue anyone who registers their name as a domain name in "bad faith." The rightful owner of a trademark is entitled to damages of up to $100,000. Some fear, however, that this statute will become a heavy club in the hands of corporations who may use it to threaten innocent holders of domain names. Critics cite as examples the boy who registered his nickname, Pokey, only to be threatened by the maker of Pokey toys and a girl named Veronica whose domain name was challenged by Archie Comics. To discover if your name has been taken, explore http://www.networksolutions.com/cgi-bin/whois/whois.

Ironically, some of the companies that have complained most loudly about cybersquatters sometimes find the mouse is in the other hand—companies are buying up insulting domain names to prevent critics from acquiring them. To avoid Toys "R" Us's fate (which was lampooned on the site http://www.toysrussucks.com), some companies now routinely acquire the domain name that combines their corporate name with "sucks." Still, critics can be creative. See, for example http://www.untied.com, which offers pages of complaints about United Airlines and includes advice on how to sue the airline in small claims

---

[15] *Hasbro, Inc. v. Internet Entertainment Group*, 1996 U.S. Dist LEXIS 11626 (N.D. Wash. 1996).

court. Some companies have filed suit to prevent this negative use of their names, but the courts have generally been unsympathetic. A federal court in California ruled against Bally Total Fitness Holding Corp. when it sued the owner and operator of http://www.compupix.com/ballysucks.[16] The court held that no reasonable consumer would assume that the Web site was in any way sponsored by or affiliated with Bally.

Sometimes businesses want to trademark a domain name. The PTO will issue such a trademark only for services offered via the Internet. Thus it trademarked "eBay" for "on-line trading services in which seller posts items to be auctioned and bidding is done electronically." The PTO will not trademark a domain name that is merely an address and does not identify the service provided.

As both the value and the number of domain names have soared, the government decided to transfer all management of the Internet, including the allocation of names, to a private, nonprofit, international organization, the Internet Corporation for Assigned Names and Numbers (Icann). The United Nations World Intellectual Property Organization has begun drafting a proposed set of rules for the allocation of domain names.

HARMONIZING INTERNATIONAL LAWS

In a global economy, intellectual property is no longer limited to one country or region. Many American patents, copyrights, and trademarks are valuable overseas just as foreign intellectual property rights have value here—BMW, Beaujolais, and the Beatles are some obvious examples. A number of treaties protect intellectual property worldwide.

The United States and roughly 150 other countries have signed the Paris Convention for the Protection of Industrial Property. The **Paris Convention** requires the patent office in each member country to accept and recognize all patent and trademark applications filed with it by anyone who lives in any member country. For example, the French patent office cannot refuse to accept an application from an American, as long as the American has complied with French law.

It would be convenient if a patent filed in one country were valid in all others, but the Paris Convention stops short of this accommodation. Filing in one country does *not* count as filing in another. Instead, the treaty supplies a grace period. When a patent is registered in one member country, the owner has a one-year grace period in which to file elsewhere. If the owner files in another member country during the grace period, the filing is deemed to have occurred on the date of the original filing. The grace period for trademarks is only six months.

The United States and about 100 other countries have signed the **Patent Cooperation Treaty**. It permits an inventor to file a patent application in a selected country—such as the United States or Japan—or with the international bureau of the United Nations World Intellectual Property Organization (WIPO) in Geneva. The application is then sent to whichever member countries the

---

16 *Bally Total Fitness Holding Corp. v. Faber*, 29 F. Supp. 2d 1161, 1998 U.S. Dist. LEXIS 21459 (C.D. Cal. 1998).

inventor has designated on the form. Each of these countries has the right to decide whether or not to grant the patent.

Roughly 120 countries, including the United States, have signed the **Berne Convention**, requiring signatory countries to provide automatic copyright protection to any works created in another member country. The protection does not expire until 50 years after the death of the author.[17] The **WIPO Copyright Treaty** adds computer programs and databases to the list of copyrightable materials.

Under the **Madrid Agreement**, any trademark registered with the international registry is valid in all signatory countries. Only about 30 countries have signed this treaty. The United States is not among them, largely because it does not want to recognize trademarks that have not been used in this country.

The goal of the **Trademark Law Treaty** is to simplify and harmonize the process of applying for trademarks around the world. So far, however, only eight countries have signed this treaty.

For more information on these treaties, travel to the WIPO Web site at http://www.wipo.org/.

TRADE SECRETS

A trade secret is a formula, device, process, method, or compilation of information that, when used in business, gives the owner an advantage over competitors who do not know it. Although a company can patent some types of trade secrets, it may be reluctant to do so because patent registration requires that the formula be disclosed publicly. In addition, patent protection expires after 20 years. Some types of trade secrets are not patentable—customer lists, business plans, manufacturing processes, marketing strategies. As the following news report indicates, trade secrets can be a company's most valuable asset.

At Slick 50, Inc., sneakiness is company policy. The handful of employees privy to the secret formula for the fancy engine treatment, which has nearly $80 million in annual sales, must swear a notarized oath of silence. Only those few who need to know are in possession of the combination to the fireproof vault with eight-inch-thick walls in which the sole printed copy of the Slick 50 recipe is housed. They alone are entrusted with the multiple passwords to the specially encoded database where the computer version is filed. When the company ships ingredients to hired blenders around the country, it dispatches them in odd allotments of containers identified only by numbered codes and mixing instructions. Masking chemicals are included in every batch so that chemical analysis to determine exactly what it takes to concoct the stuff is virtually impossible.

Despite the company's precautions, an employee at a Slick processing plant in the Cayman Islands was able to figure out the formula. He threatened to disclose it unless the company paid him $2.5 million. Fortunately for the

[17] Under U.S. law, copyrights last 70 years. The United States must grant works created in other signatory countries a copyright that lasts either 50 years or the length of time granted in that country, whichever is longer, but in no case longer than 70 years.

company, when the extortionist faxed his demands, he included a cover page listing his mailbox address. The police arrested him immediately. As criminals go, he was not very slick.[18]

To aid businesses in protecting their trade secrets, the National Conference of Commissioners on Uniform State Laws has approved the Uniform Trade Secrets Act (UTSA). To be protected under the UTSA, the owner of a trade secret must make a reasonable effort to keep the information confidential. For example, a company required employees to sign an agreement promising to keep trade secrets confidential, but the agreement did not list the particular information the firm considered secret. Instead of destroying important diagrams, the company simply put them in the trash. In addition, it had not marked its technical documents "confidential." The court held that the company had *not* met the standards of the UTSA and was therefore not entitled to trade secret protection.[19]

Anyone who misappropriates a trade secret is liable to the owner for (1) actual damages, (2) unjust enrichment, or (3) a reasonable royalty. Misappropriation means acquiring a trade secret wrongfully by, for example, theft, bribery, or espionage. If the misappropriation was willful or malicious, the court may award attorney's fees and double damages. The following case deals with a typical issue: Are customer lists trade secrets?

MORLIFE, INC. v. PERRY

56 Cal. App. 4th 1514, 1997 Cal. App. LEXIS 648
Court of Appeal of California, 1997

Facts: Morlife, Inc. repaired roofs on commercial buildings. Carl Bowersmith was production manager, and Lloyd Perry was a sales representative. Perry signed an agreement not to disclose information about Morlife's customers if he ever left the company. When the two men resigned to start a competing business, Perry took with him the collection of business cards he had accumulated while at Morlife. These cards represented approximately 75 to 80 percent of the company's customers. Perry immediately began soliciting these clients, and 32 switched to him.

Morlife filed suit, claiming that Perry had violated the Uniform Trade Secrets Act. The court found for Morlife, awarded it $39,293.47 in damages, and ordered Perry not to use Morlife's trade secrets.

Issue: Did Perry violate the Uniform Trade Secrets Act?

Excerpts from Judge Ruvolo's Decision: [W]e acknowledge the important legal right of persons to engage in businesses and occupations of their choosing. Some would count this freedom as one of the most cherished commercial rights we possess. Yet also fundamental to the preservation of our free market economic system is the concomitant right to have the ingenuity and industry one invests in the success of the business or occupation protected from the gratuitous use of that "sweat-of-the-brow" by others.

[C]ourts are reluctant to protect customer lists to the extent they embody information which is "readily ascertainable" through public sources, such as business directories. On the other hand,

[18] Anne Reifenberg, "How Secret Formula for Coveted Slick 50 Fell into Bad Hands," *The Wall Street Journal*, Oct. 25, 1995, p. A1. Republished with permission of The Wall Street Journal; permission conveyed through the Copyright Clearance Center, Inc.

[19] *Electro-Craft Corp. v. Controlled Motion, Inc.*, 332 N.W. 2d 890, 1983 Minn. LEXIS 1127 (Minn. 1983).

where the employer has expended time and effort identifying customers with particular needs or characteristics, courts will prohibit former employees from using this information to capture a share of the market. As a general principle, the more difficult information is to obtain, and the more time and resources expended by an employer in gathering it, the more likely a court will find such information constitutes a trade secret.

In the case at bar, Morlife's president testified about the difficulty encountered by sales personnel in getting past the "gatekeepers" and identifying and gaining access to the actual decisionmakers with the authority to purchase roofing services. Morlife developed its customer base by investment in telemarketing, sales visits, mailings, advertising, membership in trade associations, referrals and research. Out of 100 persons contacted by the telemarketing department, only about 10 result in contacts. He estimated an initial visit by a Morlife salesperson costs the company $238.

The record amply supports that reasonable steps were taken by Morlife to protect the information from disclosure. [C]ustomer information was stored on computer with restricted access. Moreover, in its employment contract signed by Perry, Morlife included a confidentiality provision expressly referring to its customer names and telephone numbers. The Morlife employee handbook contained an express statement that employees shall not use or disclose Morlife secrets or confidential information subsequent to their employment including "lists of present and future customers."

The judgment is affirmed.

Morlife brought this case in state court under the Uniform Trade Secrets Act. Until recently, the sole federal law on trade secrets prohibited theft only from the federal government, not from private businesses. When the theft of trade secrets reached $24 billion a year, Congress began to fear that, without a national plan to protect economic information, the country could not maintain its industrial and economic edge or safeguard national security. Congress responded with **the Economic Espionage Act of 1996. This statute prohibits any attempt to steal trade secrets for the benefit of someone other than the owner, including for the benefit of any foreign government.** Thus Kai-Lo Hsu was charged under this statute for his alleged attempt to steal the formula for manufacturing Taxol, an anticancer drug produced by Bristol-Myers. Hsu's employer, Yuen Foong Paper Co. in Taiwan, wanted to diversify into biotechnology and obtain technology from advanced countries.[20]

In formulating a policy on trade secrets, a company should:

- Identify specific information that is a trade secret.
- Set out the company's trade secret policy in writing (including what is secret) and require employees to sign this agreement. The company cannot simply identify everything as secret. Both employees and courts are less likely to treat a policy seriously if the company makes no effort to distinguish the important from the trivial.
- Allow access only to those employees who need the information to perform their jobs.
- Remind employees who leave the firm that they are still bound by the trade secret agreement.

[20] *United States v. Kai-Lo Hsu*, 155 F.3d 189, 1998 U.S. App. LEXIS 20810 (3rd Cir. 1998).

CHAPTER CONCLUSION

Intellectual property takes many different forms. It can be an Internet domain name, a software program, a cartoon character, a formula for motor oil, or a process for making anticancer drugs. Because of its great variety, intellectual property is difficult to protect. Yet, for many individuals and companies, intellectual property is the most valuable asset they will ever own. As its economic value increases, so does the need to understand the rules of intellectual property law.

CHAPTER REVIEW

	Patent	Copyright	Trademark	Trade Secrets
Protects:	Mechanical, electrical, chemical inventions; processes; machines; composition of matter; designs; plants	The tangible expression of an idea, but not the idea itself	Words and symbols that a business uses to identify its products or services	A formula, device, process, method, or compilation of information that, when used in business, gives the owner an advantage over competitors who do not know it
Requirements for Legal Protection:	Application approved by PTO	An item is automatically copyrighted once it is in tangible form.	Use is the only requirement; registration is not necessary but does offer some benefits.	Must be kept confidential
Duration:	20 years after the application is filed (14 years for a design patent)	70 years after the death of the work's only or last living author	Valid for 10 years but the owner can renew for an unlimited number of terms as long as the mark is still being used	As long as it is kept confidential

PRACTICE TEST

1. For many years, the jacket design for Webster's Ninth New Collegiate Dictionary featured a bright red background. The front was dominated by a "bull's eye" logo. The center of the bull's eye was white with the title of the book in blue. Merriam-Webster registered this logo as a trademark. Random House published a dictionary with a red dust jacket, the title in large black and white letters, and Random House's "house" logo—an angular drawing of a house—in white. What claim might Merriam-Webster make against Random House? Would it be successful?

2. "Hey, Paula," a pop hit that spent months on the music charts, was back on the radio 30 years later, but in a form the song's author never intended. Talk-show host Rush Limbaugh played a version with the same music as the original but with lyrics that poked fun at President Bill Clinton's alleged sexual misconduct with Paula Jones. Has Limbaugh violated the author's copyright?

3. From the following description of Jean-Pierre Foissey's activities one evening, can you guess what he is doing and why?

   Mr. Foissey waits until sundown. Then it is time to move. A friend whom he employs drops him off by car near the plum orchard, turning off the headlights as they approach. Mr. Foissey and another operative move quickly through adjacent cornfields and enter the orchard, careful not to leave footprints. Armed with a flashlight, his associate crawls through the orchard reading aloud the numbers on labels attached to the trees by the grower. Mr. Foissey picks leaves off the trees and marks the tree numbers on them. He takes those leaves back to an expert who will examine their size, shape, color, and texture, and also test their DNA.[21]

4. Rebecca Reyher wrote (and copyrighted) a children's book entitled *My Mother Is the Most Beautiful Woman in the World*. The story was based on a Russian folktale told to her by her own mother. Years later, the children's TV show *Sesame Street* televised a skit entitled "The Most Beautiful Woman in the World." The *Sesame Street* version took place in a different locale and had fewer frills, but the sequence of events in both stories was identical. The author of the *Sesame Street* script denied he had ever seen Reyher's book but said his skit was based on a story told to his sister some 20 years before. Has *Sesame Street* infringed Reyher's copyright?

5. Roger Schlafly applied for a patent for two prime numbers. (A prime number cannot be evenly divided by any number other than itself and 1, for example, 3, 7, 11, 13.) Schlafly's numbers are a bit longer—one is 150 digits, the other is 300. His numbers, when used together, can help perform the type of mathematical operation necessary for exchanging coded messages by computer. Should the PTO issue this patent?

6. DatagraphiX manufactured and sold computer graphics equipment that allowed users to transfer large volumes of information directly from computers to microfilm. Customers were required to keep maintenance documentation on-site for the DatagraphiX service personnel. The service manual carried this legend: "No other use, direct or indirect, of this document or of any information derived therefrom is authorized. No copies of any part of this document shall be made without written approval by DatagraphiX." Additionally, on every page of the maintenance manual, the company placed warnings that the information was proprietary and not to be duplicated. Frederick J. Lennen left DatagraphiX to start his own company that serviced DatagraphiX equipment. Can DatagraphiX prevent Lennen from using its manuals?

7. Richard Q. Yardley applied for a design patent on a watch with a caricatured figure on the dial. The character's arms served as the hour and minute hands of the watch. Because Yardley had copyrighted the design on the watch, the PTO rejected his application for a design patent. Should Yardley be permitted to obtain both a copyright and a patent on the same design?

8. Babe Ruth was one of the greatest baseball players of all time. After Ruth's death, his daughters registered the words "Babe Ruth" as a trademark. MacMillan, Inc. published a baseball calendar that contained three Babe Ruth photos. Ruth's daughters did not own

[21] Thomas Kamm, "Patented Plums Give French Fruit Sleuth His Raison D'être," *The Wall Street Journal*, Sept. 18, 1995, p. A1.

the specific photographs, but they objected to the use of Ruth's likeness. As holders of the Babe Ruth trademark, do his daughters have the right to prevent others from publishing pictures of Ruth without their permission?

9. Harper & Row signed a contract with former President Gerald Ford to publish his memoirs. As part of the deal, the two agreed that *Time* magazine could print an excerpt from the memoirs shortly before the book was published. *Time* was to pay $25,000 for this right. Before *Time* published its version, *Nation* magazine published an *unauthorized* excerpt. *Time* canceled its article and refused to pay the $25,000. Harper sued *Nation* for copyright infringement. What was *Nation*'s defense? Was it successful?

10. Frank B. McMahon wrote one of the first psychology textbooks to feature a light and easily readable style. He also included many colloquialisms and examples that appealed to a youthful student market. Charles G. Morris wrote a psychology textbook that copied McMahon's style. Has Morris infringed McMahon's copyright?

11. **RIGHT & WRONG** After Edward Miller left his job as a salesperson at the New England Insurance Agency, Inc., he took some of his New England customers to his new employer. At New England, the customer lists had been kept in file cabinets. Although the company did not restrict access to these files, it claimed there was a "you do not peruse my files and I do not peruse yours" understanding. The lists were not marked "confidential" or "not to be disclosed." Did Miller steal New England's trade secrets? Whether or not he violated the law, was it ethical for him to use this information at his new job?

12. **YOU BE THE JUDGE—WRITING PROBLEM** Three inventors developed a software program that generated a particularly clear screen display on a computer. The PTO refused to issue a patent for this software. Do the inventors have a right to a patent? **Argument for the PTO:** This software is merely a series of mathematical formulas that cannot be patented. **Argument for the inventors:** The program is not merely a mathematical concept or an abstract idea, but rather a specific machine to produce a useful, concrete, and tangible result.

INTERNET RESEARCH PROBLEM

Think of a name for an interesting new product. Click on TESS (Trademark Electronic Search System) at http://www.uspto.gov/ to see if this name is available as a trademark. Also look at http://www.networksolutions.com/cgi-bin/whois/whois to see if it is available as an Internet domain name.

You can find further practice problems in the Online Quiz at http://beatty.westbuslaw.com or in the Study Guide that accompanies this text.

PROPERTY

CHAPTER 22

Charley lives in retirement in his modest bungalow, counting pennies to make his meager savings last. Then everything changes—or does it? He is playing bridge with three friends: a rabbi, a bishop, and a banker. As rain beats against the roof and everyone murmurs about possible flooding, the banker suddenly announces to the astonished group that he is obscenely rich and is going to give $100,000 to everyone at the table. "Meet me at the bank tomorrow at 10:00, and the money is yours." Shouts! Hugs! Tears!

That night, as rain continues to lash the house, Charley smiles in his sleep, dreaming that he is floating in a tropical paradise. He awakens to discover that he *is* floating. His bedroom is filled with water, and Charley's head is now pressing against the ceiling. To avoid a flooding catastrophe, the Power Company has released a nearby dam, inundating 150 acres. The flood level on Charley's property is 16 feet and rising. Charley squirms through a broken window and escapes from his uninsured house just as it disappears beneath roiling black water.

The next morning, Charley, sneezing, arrives at the bank, where the bishop and rabbi grimly announce that the banker died before he could sign the three cashier's checks. There is no money. Charley, dazed and distraught, sues the Power Company for the damage to his house compensation and recovers—nothing. The company was *legally entitled* to destroy his house! Desperate, he seeks his $100,000 from the bank. Read on for the result.

A bewildering two days for Charley, but instructive for us, as we have glimpsed two issues of property law. The Power Company was entitled to destroy his house if it chose, because it owned an *easement*. The banker's promise will be settled according to the law of *gifts*. Our survey will focus on three primary topics: Real Property, Landlord-Tenant Law, and Personal Property.

REAL PROPERTY

NATURE OF REAL PROPERTY

We need to define a few terms. A **grantor** is an owner who conveys his property, or some interest in it, to someone else, called the **grantee**. If you sell your house to Veronica, you are the grantor and she is the grantee. Real property may be any of the following:

- **Land.** Land is the most common and important form of real property. In England, land was historically the greatest source of wealth and social status, far more important than industrial or commercial enterprises. As a result, the law of real property has been of paramount importance for nearly 1,000 years, developing very gradually to reflect changing conditions. Some real property terms sound medieval for the simple reason that they *are* medieval. (For a fascinating look at the English and Roman roots of our property law, dig down to http://www.snowcrest.net/siskfarm/tableoc4.html#TC3a.)
- **Buildings.** Buildings are real property. Houses, office buildings, and factories all fall (or stand) in this category.
- **Subsurface Rights.** In most states, the owner of the land also owns anything under the surface, down to the center of the earth. In some cases the subsurface rights may be worth far more than the surface land, for example if there is oil or gold underfoot. Although the landowner generally owns these rights, she may sell them, while retaining ownership of the surface land.
- **Air Rights.** The owner of land owns the air space above the land. Suppose you own an urban parking lot. The owner of an adjacent office building wishes to build a walkway across your parking lot to join her building with a neighboring skyscraper. The office owner needs your permission to build across the air space and will expect to pay you a handsome fee for the privilege.
- **Plant Life.** Plant life growing on land is real property, whether the plants are naturally occurring, such as trees, or cultivated crops. When a landowner sells his property, plant life is automatically included in the sale, unless the parties agree otherwise.

- **Fixtures.** Fixtures are goods that have become attached to real property. A house (which is real property) contains many fixtures. The furnace and heating ducts were goods when they were manufactured and when they were sold to the builder, because they were movable. But when the builder attached them to the house, the items became fixtures. By contrast, neither the refrigerator nor the grand piano is a fixture.

When an owner sells real property, the buyer normally takes the fixtures, unless the parties specify otherwise. Sometimes it is difficult to determine whether something is a fixture. The general rule is this: **an object is a fixture if a reasonable person would consider the item to be a permanent part of the property**, taking into account attachment, adaptation, and other objective manifestations of permanence:

- *Attachment.* If an object is attached to property in such a way that removing it would damage the property, it is probably a fixture. Heating ducts could be removed from a house, but only by ripping open walls and floors, so they are fixtures.
- *Adaptation.* Something that is made or adapted especially for attachment to the particular property is probably a fixture, such as custom-made bookshelves fitted in a library.
- *Other Manifestations of Permanence.* If the owner of the property clearly intends the item to remain permanently, it is probably a fixture. Suppose a homeowner constructs a large concrete platform in his backyard, then buys a heavy metal shed and puts it on the platform. His preparatory work indicates that he expects the shed to remain permanently, and a court would likely declare it a fixture.

ESTATES IN REAL PROPERTY

Use and ownership of real estate can take many different legal forms. A person may own property outright, having the unrestricted use of the land and an unlimited right to sell it. However, someone may also own a lesser interest in real property. For example, you could inherit the *use* of a parcel of land during your lifetime, but have no power to leave the land to your heirs. Or you could retain ownership and possession of some land yet allow a corporation to explore for oil and drill wells. The different rights that someone can hold in real property are known as **estates** or **interests**. Both terms simply indicate specified rights in property.

FREEHOLD ESTATES

The owner of a freehold estate has the present right to possess the property and to use it in any lawful way she wants. The three most important freehold estates are (1) fee simple absolute, (2) fee simple defeasible, and (3) life estate.

Fee Simple Absolute

A fee simple absolute provides the owner with the greatest possible control of the property. This is the most common form of land ownership. Suppose Cecily inherits a fee simple interest in a 30-acre vineyard. She may use the land for any purpose that the law allows. She may continue to raise grapes, or, if she hates wine, she may rip up the vines and build a condominium complex. Although zoning laws may regulate her use, nothing in Cecily's estate itself limits her use of the land. Cecily may pass on to her heirs her entire estate, that is, her full fee simple absolute.

Fee Simple Defeasible

Other estates contain more limited rights than the fee simple absolute. Wily establishes the Wily Church of Perfection. Upon his death, Wily leaves a 100-acre estate to the church for as long as it keeps the name "Wily Church of Perfection." Wily has included a significant limitation in the church's ownership. The church has a fee simple defeasible.

A fee simple defeasible may terminate upon the occurrence of some limiting event. If the congregation decides to rename itself the Happy Valley Church of Perfection, the church automatically loses its estate in the 100 acres. Ownership of the land then **reverts** to Wily's heirs, meaning title goes back to them. Because the heirs might someday inherit the land, they are said to have a *future interest* in the 100 acres. A landowner may create a fee simple defeasible to ensure that property is used in a particular way, or is *not* used in a specified manner. In the following case, a California city was surprised to learn that this ancient doctrine still has plenty of life.

WALTON v. CITY OF RED BLUFF

2 Cal. App. 4th 117, 3 Cal. Rptr. 2d 275, 1991 Cal. App. LEXIS 1474
California Court of Appeal, 1991

Facts: In 1908 and 1916, Mrs. Elizabeth Kraft and her son, Edward Kraft, granted to the city of Red Bluff two adjoining properties, with buildings, for use as a public library. The grants from the Krafts required continuous use as a public library and stated that the property would return to the Kraft family if the city ever used it for other purposes.

In 1986, Red Bluff decided that the buildings were too small for its needs and moved all of the books to a new building nearby. The city used the Kraft property for other civic purposes such as town meetings, social gatherings, and school tutoring. Herbert Kraft Walton, a descendant and heir, filed suit seeking to have the property reconveyed to him. The trial court found for Red Bluff, and Walton appealed.

Issue: Did Red Bluff violate the terms of the grants, so the property must now revert to Walton?

Excerpts from Judge Carr's Decision: The grants provide in part: "If the property herein conveyed shall at any time be abandoned by the said Town of Red Bluff, . . . or if the said property shall cease to be used, for library purposes, by said Town, . . . or shall be put to [any] use other [than] the uses and purposes herein specifically referred to, . . . then the grant and conveyance herein made shall cease and terminate, and the title to the said property and all the improvements thereon shall at once revert to [the Kraft family].

Red Bluff admits all the books were removed from the library as of September 1986. The trial court framed the issue as one of abandonment. But the grantors specified that "if the said property shall cease to be used, for library purposes" the grants terminate.

Whether Red Bluff intended to "abandon" the use purpose of the property or not, it removed the books and stopped using the premises for library purposes. The grants defined library purposes broadly to include various educational endeavors, but there is no evidence any of these other activities took place. It stopped using the grant for library purposes and the property must go back to the Kraft heir.

At oral argument Red Bluff focussed on the "changed conditions" doctrine. The power of termination expires when it becomes "obsolete." In a leading case involving a covenant restricting the use of lots to residential purposes it was said that "where there has been a change in the uses to which the property in the neighborhood is being put, so that such property is no longer residence property, it would be unjust, oppressive, and inequitable to give effect to the restrictions, if such change has resulted from causes other than their breach." In this case the alleged change in circumstance is that Red Bluff needs a bigger, modern library building, not that the present building cannot be used for the purposes of the grant or that the use of surrounding property makes operation of a library impracticable. In these circumstances there is nothing inequitable about enforcing the restriction in the grant.

The judgment is *reversed* with directions to the trial court to enter a judgment [granting title to] Walton.

LIFE ESTATE

A life estate is exactly what you would think: **an estate for the life of some named person**. For example, Aretha owns Respect Farm, and in her will she leaves it to Max, for his lifetime. Max is the **life tenant**. He is entitled to live on the property and work it as a normal farm during his lifetime, though he is obligated to maintain it properly. The moment Max dies, the farm reverts to Aretha or her heirs.

CONCURRENT ESTATES

When two or more people own real property at the same time, they have concurrent estates. In a **tenancy in common**, the owners have an equal interest in the entire property. Each co-tenant has the right to sell her interest to someone else, or to leave it to her heirs upon her death. A **joint tenancy** is similar, except that upon the death of one joint tenant (owner), his interest passes *to the surviving joint tenants*, not to his heirs.

To provide special rights for married couples, some states have created **tenancy by the entirety** and **community property**. These forms of ownership allow one spouse to protect some property from the other, and from the other's creditors.

Condominiums and **cooperatives** are most common in apartment buildings with multiple units, though they can be used in other settings, such as a cluster of houses on a single parcel of land. In a condominium, the owner of the apartment typically has a fee simple absolute in his particular unit. He is normally entitled to sell or lease the unit, must pay taxes on it, and may receive the normal tax deduction if he is carrying a mortgage. All unit owners belong to a condominium association, which manages the common areas. In a cooperative, the residents generally do not own their particular unit. Instead, they are shareholders in a corporation that owns the building and leases specified units to the shareholders.

NONPOSSESSORY INTERESTS

All of the estates and interests that we have examined thus far focused on one thing: possession of the land. Now we look at interests that *never* involve possession. These interests may be very valuable, even though the holder never lives on the land.

EASEMENTS

The Alabama Power Co. drove a flatbed truck over land owned by Thomas Burgess, damaging the property. The power company did this to reach its power lines and wooden transmission poles. Burgess had never given Alabama Power permission to enter his land, and he sued for the damage that the heavy trucks caused. He recovered—nothing. Alabama Power had an easement to use Burgess's land.

An easement gives one person the right to enter land belonging to another and make a limited use of it, without taking anything away. Burgess had bought his land from a man named Denton, who years earlier had sold an easement to Alabama Power. The easement gave the power company the right to construct several transmission poles on one section of Denton's land and to use reasonable means to reach the poles. Alabama Power owned that easement forever, and when Burgess bought the land, he took it subject to the easement. Alabama Power drove its trucks across a section of land where the power company had never gone before, and the easement did not explicitly give the company this right. But the court found that the company had no other way to reach its poles, and therefore the easement allowed this use. Burgess is stuck with his uninvited guest as long as he owns the land.[1]

Property owners normally create easements in one of two ways. A **grant** occurs when a landowner expressly intends to convey an easement to someone else. This is how Alabama Power acquired its easement. A **reservation** occurs when an owner sells land but keeps some right to enter the property. A farmer might sell 40 acres to a developer but reserve an easement giving him the right to drive his equipment across a specified strip of the land.

In the chapter's opening scenario, the Power Company had a flood easement on Charley's property. If Charley had read the following case, he might not have bought the land.

CARVIN v. ARKANSAS POWER AND LIGHT

14 F.3d 399, 1993 U.S. App. LEXIS 33986
United States Court of Appeals for the Eighth Circuit, 1993

Facts: Between 1923 and 1947, Arkansas Power & Light (AP&L) constructed several dams on two Arkansas lakes, Hamilton and Catherine. The company then obtained "flood easements" on property adjoining the lakes. AP&L obtained some of the easements by grant and others by reservation, selling lakeside property and keeping the easement. These flood easements permitted AP&L to "clear of trees, brush and other obstructions and to submerge by water"

[1] *Burgess v. Alabama Power Co.*, 658 So. 2d 435, 1995 Ala. LEXIS 119 (Ala. 1995).

certain acreage, which was described exactly. AP&L properly recorded the easements, and when the current landowners bought lakeside property, they were aware of the documents.

During one 12-hour period in May 1990, extraordinarily heavy rains fell in the Ouachita River Basin, including both lakes. In some areas, over 10 inches of rain fell, causing the water to reach the highest levels ever recorded, even washing away the equipment designed to measure rainfall. To avoid flooding Lake Hamilton, AP&L opened the gates of a dam called Carpenter. This caused Lake Catherine to flood, with water in some places rising 25 feet. This flood caused massive damage to the plaintiffs' houses, with water in some cases rising to the roof level.

Several dozen landowners sued, claiming that AP&L was negligent in opening one dam without simultaneously opening another and also in failing to warn homeowners of the intended action. The federal district court granted summary judgment for AP&L, based on the flood easements, and the landowners appealed.

Issue: Did the easements relieve AP&L from liability for flooding?

Excerpts from Judge Gibson's Decision: This case involves a variety of easement forms, executed on different dates, but all with the same background. Some expressly reserved the right to "submerge" the land up to 307 feet and to "flood any part" of "said lands." Others conveyed the right to "flood any and all of said lands." Others granted the right to flood to a certain level, varying from 315 feet to 329 feet, elevations clearly much higher than the normal lake level. Two of the three forms used, and the condemnation decree, specifically granted the right to flood the lands "by waters impounded by a dam." The language is plain and specific. The obvious purpose of the flood and flowage rights is to protect AP&L from liability from its management of the lake in circumstances such as occurred in the extremely heavy rainfall in the seven hours on May 19 and 20. When AP&L opened the flood gates during the heaviest rains experienced since the dam was built, with the resultant flooding on the property of the shores in Lake Catherine, it was exercising rights retained by it or granted to it in the documents creating the property interest of the landowners. We can only conclude that protection from liability for flooding of the plaintiffs' land was the very reason the dam owner purchased the easement.

The issues in this case are extremely close. The loss of property is most substantial and the result seems harsh. [However, in view of the property interest created by the documents involving each of the landholders, we cannot place liability on AP&L in such circumstances. [Affirmed.]

PROFIT

A *profit* gives one person the right to enter land belonging to another and take something away. You own 100 acres of vacation property, and suddenly a mining company informs you that the land contains valuable nickel deposits. You may choose to sell a profit to the mining company, allowing it to enter your land and take away the nickel. You receive cash up front, and the company earns money from the sale of the mineral.

LICENSE

A license gives the holder temporary permission to enter upon another's property. Unlike an easement or profit, a license is a *temporary* right. When you attend a basketball game by buying a ticket, the basketball club that sells you the ticket is the licensor and you are the licensee. You are entitled to enter the licensor's premises, namely the basketball arena, and to remain during the game, though the club can revoke the license if you behave unacceptably.

MORTGAGE

Generally, in order to buy a house, a prospective owner must borrow money. The bank or other lender will require security before it hands over its money, and the most common form of security for a real estate loan is a mortgage. **A mortgage is a security interest in real property.** The homeowner who borrows money is the **mortgagor**, because she is *giving* the mortgage to the lender. The lender, in turn, is the **mortgagee**, the party acquiring a security interest. The mortgagee in most cases obtains a **lien** on the house, meaning the right to foreclose on the property if the mortgagor fails to pay back the money borrowed.

SALE OF REAL PROPERTY

For most people, buying or selling a house is the biggest, most important financial transaction they will make. Here we consider several of the key issues that may arise.

SELLER'S OBLIGATIONS CONCERNING THE PROPERTY

Historically, the common law recognized the rule of caveat emptor in the sale of real property—that is, let the buyer beware. If a buyer walked into his new living room and fell through the floor into a lake of toxic waste, it was his tough luck. But the common law changes with the times, and today courts place an increasing burden of fairness on the sellers of real estate. Two of the most significant obligations are the implied warranty of habitability and the duty to disclose defects.

IMPLIED WARRANTY OF HABITABILITY

Most states now impose an implied warranty of habitability on a builder who sells a new home. This means that, whether he wants to or not, the builder is guaranteeing that the new house contains **adequate materials and good workmanship**. The law implies this warranty because of the inherently unequal position of builder and buyer. Some defects might be obvious to a lay observer, such as a room with no roof or a front porch that sways whenever the neighbors sneeze. But only the builder will know if he made the frame with proper wood, if the heating system was second rate, the electrical work shabby, and so forth. Note that in most states the law implies this warranty to protect buyers of residential, but not commercial, property.

DUTY TO DISCLOSE DEFECTS

The seller of a home must disclose facts that a buyer does not know and cannot readily observe, if they materially affect the property's value. Roy and Charlyne Terrell owned a house in the Florida Keys, where zoning codes required all living areas to be 15 feet above sea level. They knew that their house violated the code because a bedroom and bathroom were on the ground floor. They offered to sell the house to Robert Revitz, assuring him that the property complied with all codes and that flood insurance would cost about $350 per year. Revitz bought the house, moved in, and later learned that because of the code violations, flood insurance would be slightly more expensive—costing just over *$36,000 per year*. He sued and won. The court declared that the Terrells had a duty to disclose the code violations; it ordered a rescission of the contract, meaning that Revitz got his money back. The court mentioned that the duty to disclose was wide-ranging and included leaking roofs, insect infestation, cracks in walls and foundations, and any other problems that a buyer might be unable to discern.[2]

SALES CONTRACT AND TITLE EXAMINATION

The statute of frauds requires that an agreement to sell real property must be in writing to be enforceable. A contract for the sale of a house is often several pages of dense legal reading, in which the lawyers for the buyer and seller attempt to allocate risks for every problem that might go wrong. However, the contract *need* not be so thorough. A written contract for the sale of land is generally valid if it includes the names of all parties, a precise description of the property being sold, the price, and signatures.

Once the parties have agreed to the terms and signed a contract, the buyer's lawyer performs a **title examination**, which means that she, or someone she hires, searches through the local land registry for all documents that relate to the property. The purpose is to ensure that the seller actually has valid title to this land, since it is dispiriting to give someone half a million dollars for property and then discover that he never owned it and neither do you. Even if the seller owns the land, his title may be subject to other claims, such as an easement or profit.

CLOSING AND DEEDS

While the buyer is checking the seller's title, she also probably needs to arrange financing, as described above in the section on mortgages. When the title work is complete and the buyer has arranged financing, the parties arrange a **closing**, a meeting at which the property is actually sold. The seller brings to the closing a **deed**, which is the document proving ownership of the land. The seller signs the deed over to the buyer in exchange for the purchase price. The buyer pays the price either with a certified check and/or by having her lender pay. If a lender pays part or all of the price, the buyer executes a mortgage to the lender as part of the closing.

RECORDING

Recording the deed means filing it with the official state registry. The registry clerk places a photocopy of the deed in the agency's bound volumes and indexes the deed by the name of the grantor and the grantee. Recording is a critical step in the sale of land, because it puts all the world on notice that the

---

[2] *Revitz v. Terrell*, 572 So. 2d 996, 1990 Fla. App. LEXIS 9655 (Fla. Dist. Ct. App. 1990).

grantor has sold the land. It has little effect between grantor and grantee: once the deed and money are exchanged, the sale is generally final between those two. But recording is vital to protect the general public.

You have spotted your dream vacation property on a pristine beach in Mexico. The next-door neighbor, a retired U.S. citizen, offers to sell you the property at a fair price. You draw up a contract in English and take the plunge. Mistake! Buying land in any foreign country presents pitfalls that you must consider. You might construct a $700,000 beach house, only to discover that you do not own the sandy soil on which it stands. In Mexico, all land within 66 feet of the high-tide mark is federal property and cannot be sold to anyone. Further, as a foreigner, you have no right to buy Mexican real estate within 31 miles of the ocean. Thousands of innocent U.S. citizens have lost millions of dollars paying for Mexican property they never acquire. Your friendly neighbor may have known of the local law and intended to cheat you, or he may have been equally ignorant and be horrified to learn that his own house stands on slippery ground. Know and respect local laws and customs before you write a check. (And by the way, in Mexico, a contract is binding only if written in Spanish.)

LAND USE REGULATION

ZONING

Zoning statutes are state laws that permit local communities to regulate building and land use. The local communities, whether cities, towns, or counties, then pass zoning ordinances that control many aspects of land development. For example, a town's zoning ordinance may divide the community into an industrial zone where factories may be built, a commercial zone in which stores of a certain size are allowed, and several residential zones in which only houses may be constructed. Within the residential zones, there may be further divisions, for example, permitting two-family houses in certain areas and requiring larger lots in others. For a look at the zoning code of one city—Portland, Oregon—go to http://www.planning.ci.portland.or.US/ed_over.html.

An owner prohibited by an ordinance from erecting a certain kind of building, or adding on to his present building, may seek a **variance** from the zoning board, meaning an exception granted for special reasons unique to the property. Whether a board will grant a variance generally depends upon the type of the proposed building, the nature of the community, the reason the owner claims he is harmed by the ordinance, and the reaction of neighbors.

Many people abhor "adult" businesses, such as strip clubs and pornography shops. Urban experts agree that a large number of these establishments in a neighborhood often causes crime to increase and property values to drop. Nonetheless, many people patronize such businesses, which can earn a good profit. Should a city have the right to restrict adult businesses? New York City officials determined that the number of sex shops had grown steadily for two decades and that their presence harmed various neighborhoods. With the support of community groups, the city passed a zoning ordinance that prohibited adult businesses from all residential neighborhoods, from some commercial districts, *and* from being within 500 feet of schools, houses of worship, day-care centers, or other sex shops (to avoid clustering). Owners and patrons of these shops protested, claiming that the city was unfairly denying the public access to a form of entertainment that it obviously desired. Are such ordinances good? Are they fair? Why or why not?

EMINENT DOMAIN

Eminent domain is the power of the government to take private property for public use. A government may need land to construct a highway, airport, university, or public housing. All levels of government—federal, state, and local—have this power. But the Fifth Amendment to the United States Constitution states: ". . . nor shall private property be taken for public use, without just compensation." The Supreme Court has held that this clause, the Takings Clause, applies not only to the federal government but also to state and local governments. So, although all levels of government have the power to take property, they must pay the owner a fair price.

A "fair price" generally means the reasonable market value of the land. Generally, if the property owner refuses the government's offer, the government will file suit seeking **condemnation** of the land, that is, a court order specifying what compensation is just and awarding title to the government.

LANDLORD-TENANT LAW

On a January morning in Studio City, California, Alpha Donchin took her small Shih Tzu for a walk. Suddenly, less than a block from her house, two large rottweilers attacked Donchin and her pet. The heavy animals mauled the 14-pound Shih Tzu, and when Donchin picked her dog up, the rottweilers knocked her down, breaking her hip and causing other serious injuries.

Ubaldo Guerrero, who lived in a rented house nearby, owned the two rottweilers, and Donchin sued him. But she also sued Guerrero's *landlord*, David Swift, who lived four blocks away from the rental property. Donchin claimed that the landlord was liable for her injuries, because he knew of the dogs' vicious nature and permitted them to escape from the property he rented to Guerrero. Should the landlord be liable for injuries caused by his tenant's dogs?

As is typical of many landlord-tenant issues, the law in this area is in flux. Under the common law, a landlord had no liability for injuries caused by animals belonging to a tenant, and many states adhere to that rule. But some states are expanding the landlord's liability for injuries caused on or near his property. The California court ruled that Donchin could maintain her suit against Swift. If Donchin could prove that Swift knew the dogs were dangerous and allowed them to escape through a defective fence, the landlord would be liable for her injuries.[3]

---

[3] *Donchin v. Guerrero*, 34 Cal. App. 4th 1832, 1995 Cal. App. LEXIS 462 (Cal. Ct. App. 1995).

One reason for the erratic evolution of landlord-tenant law is that it is really a combination of three venerable areas of law: property, contract, and negligence. The confluence of these legal theories produces results that are unpredictable but interesting and important. (To read some articles on the latest issues in this rapidly evolving area, visit http://little.nhlink.net/nhlink/housing/cto/.) We begin our examination of landlord-tenant law with an analysis of the different types of tenancy.

Recall that a freehold estate is the right to possess real property and use it in any lawful manner. **When an owner of a freehold estate allows another person temporary, exclusive possession of the property, the parties have created a landlord-tenant relationship.** The freehold owner is the **landlord**, and the person allowed to possess the property is the **tenant**. The landlord has conveyed a **leasehold** interest to the tenant, meaning the right to temporary possession. Courts also use the word "**tenancy**" to describe the tenant's right to possession. A leasehold may be commercial or residential.

THREE LEGAL AREAS COMBINED

Property law influences landlord-tenant cases because the landlord is conveying rights in real property to the tenant. She is also keeping a **reversionary interest** in the property, meaning the right to possess the property when the lease ends. Contract law plays a role because the basic agreement between the landlord and tenant is a contract. **A lease is a contract that creates a landlord-tenant relationship.** And negligence law increasingly determines the liability of landlord and tenant when there is an injury to a person or property. Many states have combined these three legal issues into landlord-tenant statutes; you can see a typical statute at http://www.rilin.state.ri.us/Statutes/TITLE34/34-18/INDEX.HTM.

LEASE

The statute of frauds generally requires that a lease be in writing. Some states will enforce an oral lease if it is for a short term, such as one year or less, but even when an oral lease is permitted, it is wiser for the parties to put their agreement in writing, because a written lease avoids many misunderstandings. At a minimum, a lease must state the names of the parties, the premises being leased, the duration of the agreement, and the rent. But a well-drafted lease generally includes many provisions, called covenants. A **covenant** is simply a promise by either the landlord or the tenant to do something or refrain from doing something. For example, most leases include a covenant concerning the tenant's payment of a security deposit and the landlord's return of the deposit, a covenant describing how the tenant may use the premises, and several covenants about who must maintain and repair the property, who is liable for damage, and so forth. The parties should also agree about how the lease may be terminated and whether the parties have the right to renew it.

TYPES OF TENANCY

There are four types of tenancy: a tenancy for years, a periodic tenancy, a tenancy at will, and a tenancy at sufferance. The most important feature distinguishing one from the other is how each tenancy terminates. In some cases, a tenancy terminates automatically, while in others, one party must take certain steps to end the agreement.

TENANCY FOR YEARS

Any lease for a stated, fixed period is a tenancy for years. If a landlord rents a summer apartment for the months of June, July, and August of next year, that is a tenancy for years. A company that rents retail space in a mall beginning January 1, 2002, and ending December 31, 2007, also has a tenancy for years. A tenancy for years terminates automatically when the agreed period ends.

PERIODIC TENANCY

A periodic tenancy is created for a fixed period and then automatically continues for additional periods until either party notifies the other of termination. This is probably the most common variety of tenancy, and the parties may create one in either of two ways. Suppose a landlord agrees to rent you an apartment "from month to month, rent payable on the first." That is a periodic tenancy. The tenancy automatically renews itself every month, unless either party gives adequate notice to the other that she wishes to terminate. A periodic tenancy could also be for one-year periods—in which case it automatically renews for an additional year if neither party terminates—or for any other period.

TENANCY AT WILL

A tenancy at will has no fixed duration and may be terminated by either party at any time. Tenancies at will are unusual tenancies.[4] Typically, the agreement is vague, with no specified rental period and with payment, perhaps, to be made in kind. The parties might agree, for example, that a tenant farmer could use a portion of his crop as rent. Since either party can end the agreement at any time, it provides no security for either landlord or tenant.

TENANCY AT SUFFERANCE

A tenancy at sufferance occurs when a tenant remains on the premises, against the wishes of the landlord, after the expiration of a true tenancy. Thus a tenancy at sufferance is not a true tenancy because the tenant is staying without the landlord's agreement. The landlord has the option of seeking to evict the tenant or of forcing the tenant to pay rent for a new rental period.

---

[4] The courts of some states, annoyingly, use the term "tenancy at will" for what are, in reality, periodic tenancies. They do this to bewilder law students and even lawyers, a goal at which they are quite successful. This text uses tenancy at will in its more widely known sense, meaning a tenancy terminable at any time.

LANDLORD'S DUTIES

DUTY TO DELIVER POSSESSION

The landlord's first important duty is to deliver possession of the premises at the beginning of the tenancy, that is, to make the rented space available to the tenant. In most cases, this presents no problems and the new tenant moves in. But what happens if the previous tenant has refused to leave when the new tenancy begins? In most states, the landlord is legally required to remove the previous tenant. In some states, it is up to the new tenant either to evict the existing occupant or begin charging him rent.

QUIET ENJOYMENT

All tenants are entitled to quiet enjoyment of the premises, meaning the right to use the property without the interference of the landlord. Most leases expressly state this covenant of quiet enjoyment. And if a lease includes no such covenant, the law implies the right of quiet enjoyment anyway, so all tenants are protected. If a landlord interferes with the tenant's quiet enjoyment, he has breached the lease, entitling the tenant to damages.

The most common interference with quiet enjoyment is an eviction, meaning some act that forces the tenant to abandon the premises. Of course, some evictions are legal, as when a tenant fails to pay the rent. But some evictions are illegal. There are two types of eviction: actual and constructive.

ACTUAL EVICTION

If a landlord prevents the tenant from possessing the premises, he has actually evicted her. Suppose a landlord decides that a group of students are "troublemakers." Without going through lawful eviction procedures in court, the landlord simply waits until the students are out of the apartment and changes all the locks. By denying the students access to the premises, the landlord has actually evicted them and has breached their right of quiet enjoyment.

CONSTRUCTIVE EVICTION

If a landlord substantially interferes with the tenant's use and enjoyment of the premises, he has constructively evicted her. Courts construe certain behavior as the equivalent of an eviction. In these cases, the landlord has not actually prevented the tenant from possessing the premises, but has instead interfered so greatly with her use and enjoyment that the law regards the landlord's actions as equivalent to an eviction. In the following case, a group of students alleged constructive eviction.

HOME RENTALS CORP v. CURTIS

236 Ill. App. 3d 994, 602 N.E.2d 859, 1992 Ill. App. LEXIS 1745
Illinois Court of Appeals, 1992

Facts: Home Rentals Corp. owned about 300 rental properties, including a single-family house located near Southern Illinois University (SIU). Henry Fisher was a rental agent for Home Rentals. In February, Fisher agreed to rent the house to a group of four SIU students. The house was then in good condition. The parties signed a written lease, for the rental period from August 17 to the following August 13 at a rent of $740 per month. The students paid $1,980, to cover a security deposit and the last two months' rent.

When the students arrived in August, they found the house in dreadful condition, as the court describes. They refused to live in it, and Home Rentals sued for $6,900, the value of the year's lease minus the money paid. The students counter-claimed, arguing constructive eviction. The trial court found for the students and awarded them $1,980. Home Rentals appealed.

Issue: Did Home Rentals constructively evict the students?

Excerpts from Judge Harrison's Decision: The first to reach the scene was Mike Fraser, who arrived in Carbondale on August 15. At that time the electricity had not yet been turned on, and he was not able to view the premises during daylight hours until Wednesday, August 16. What Fraser found then was a house that was not fit for human habitation.

Roaches had overrun the rooms. The kitchen was so filthy and so infested by bugs that food could not be stored there. The living room carpet smelled, and one could actually see outside through holes in the wall around the frame of the front door. The bathrooms were unsanitary, and when the water was turned on the following day, August 17, Fraser discovered that not one of the toilets in the building worked. He also discovered that one of the bathtubs did not drain at all, while another drained only slowly, and that bathroom waste water drained directly onto the floor of the basement. In attempting to explain this open drain at trial, Henry Fisher tried to assert that it was simply part of the washing machine hookup. As evidence that this was laundry-related, he pointed to white matter on the basement floor by the drain which he claimed was spilled laundry detergent. Other evidence indicated, however, that the white matter was, in fact, a mass of roach eggs.

Fraser testified that he spoke with Fisher at Home Rentals on the 16th and told him that the place was uninhabitable because of the filth and the roaches. Fisher's response was to suggest that the students buy roach bombs and cleaning supplies to take care of the problems themselves, although he did offer to reimburse them for those items and represented that he would arrange to have an exterminator spray.

Hopeful that the situation might somehow be salvaged, defendants spent several days attempting on their own to make the house liveable. Although an exterminator finally appeared on Friday, August 18, or Saturday, August 19, the problem of roach infestation continued, and Home Rentals did nothing about the dirt or plumbing problems. On Monday, August 21, defendants finally gave up. They packed up their property and sought housing elsewhere.

A constructive eviction occurs where a landlord has done "something of a grave and permanent character with the intention of depriving the tenant of enjoyment of the premises."

The record is clear that defendants had notified Home Rentals of all their complaints by August 17, when the lease term was scheduled to commence. This was four full days before they finally gave up and moved.

Considering the magnitude of the problems, four days were opportunity enough for Home Rentals to act. We note, moreover, that there is no indication that giving Home Rentals additional time would have made any difference.

Affirmed.

DUTY TO MAINTAIN PREMISES

In most states, a landlord has a duty to deliver the premises in a habitable condition and a continuing duty to maintain the habitable condition. This duty overlaps with the quiet enjoyment obligation, but it is not identical. The tenant's right to quiet enjoyment focuses primarily on the tenant's *ability to use* the rented property. The landlord's duty to maintain the property focuses on whether the property *meets a particular legal standard*. The required standard may be stated in the lease, created by a state statute, or implied by law.

LEASE

The lease itself generally obligates the landlord to maintain the exterior of any buildings and the common areas. If a lease does not do so, state law may imply the obligation.

BUILDING CODES

Many state and local governments have passed building codes, which mandate minimum standards for commercial and/or residential property. The codes are likely to be stricter for residential property and may demand such things as minimum room size, sufficient hot water, secure locks, proper working kitchens and bathrooms, absence of insects and rodents, and other basics of decent housing. Generally, all rental property must comply with the building code, whether the lease mentions the code or not.

IMPLIED WARRANTY OF HABITABILITY

Students Maria Ivanow, Thomas Tecza, and Kenneth Gearin rented a house from Les and Martha Vanlandingham. The monthly rent was $900. But the roommates failed to pay any rent for the final five months of the tenancy. After they moved out, the Vanlandinghams sued. How much did the landlords recover? Nothing. The landlords had breached the implied warranty of habitability.

The implied warranty of habitability requires that a landlord meet all standards set by the local building code, or that the premises be fit for human habitation. Most states, though not all, *imply* this warranty of habitability, meaning that the landlord must meet this standard whether the lease includes it or not.

The Vanlandinghams breached the implied warranty. The students had complained repeatedly about a variety of problems. The washer and dryer, which were included in the lease, frequently failed. A severe roof leak caused water damage in one of the bedrooms. Defective pipes flooded the bathroom. The refrigerator frequently malfunctioned, and the roommates repaired it several times. The basement often flooded, and when it was dry, rats and opossums lived in it. The heat sometimes failed.

In warranty of habitability cases, a court normally considers the severity of the problems and their duration. In the case of Maria Ivanow and friends, the court abated (reduced) the rent 50 percent. The students had already paid more than the abated rent to the landlord, so they owed nothing for the last five months.[5]

---

[5] *Vanlandingham v. Ivanow*, 246 Ill. App. 3d 348, 615 N.E.2d 1361, 1993 Ill. App. LEXIS 985 (Ill. Ct. App. 1993).

TENANT REMEDIES FOR DEFECTIVE CONDITIONS

Different states allow various remedies for defective conditions. For tenant rights in your state, see http://www.tenantsunion.org/tulist.html, which provides links to tenant organizations throughout the nation. For a useful series of form letters concerning defective conditions, problems with neighbors, interference with quiet enjoyment, and other common tenant concerns, see http://little.nhlink.net/nhlink/housing/cto/letters/letrs.htm. Many states allow a tenant to withhold rent, representing the decreased value of the premises. In some states, if a tenant notifies the landlord of a serious defect and the landlord fails to remedy the problem, the tenant may deduct a reasonable amount of money from the rental payment and have the repair made himself. Also, a landlord who refuses to repair significant defects is breaching the lease and/or state law, and the tenant may simply sue for damages.

DUTY TO RETURN SECURITY DEPOSIT

Most landlords require tenants to pay a security deposit, in case the tenant damages the premises. In many states, a landlord must either return the security deposit soon after the tenant has moved out or notify the tenant of the damage and the cost of the repairs. A landlord who fails to do so may owe the tenant damages of two or even three times the deposit.

TENANT'S DUTIES

DUTY TO PAY RENT

> My landlord said he's gonna raise the rent. "Good," I said, " 'cause I can't raise it."
> *Slappy White,* comedian, 1921–1995

Rent is the compensation the tenant pays the landlord for use of the premises, and paying the rent, despite Mr. White's wistful hope, is the tenant's foremost obligation. The lease normally specifies the amount of rent and when it must be paid. Typically, the landlord requires that rent be paid at the beginning of each rental period, whether that is monthly, annually, or otherwise.

If the tenant fails to pay rent on time, the landlord has several remedies. She is entitled to apply the security deposit to the unpaid rent. She may also sue the tenant for nonpayment of rent, demanding the unpaid sums, cost of collection, and interest. Finally, the landlord may evict a tenant who has failed to pay rent.

State statutes prescribe the steps a landlord must take to evict a tenant for nonpayment. Typically, the landlord must serve a termination notice on the tenant and wait for a court hearing. At the hearing, the landlord must prove that the tenant has failed to pay rent on time. If the tenant has no excuse for the nonpayment, the court grants an order evicting him. The order authorizes a sheriff to remove the tenant's goods and place them in storage, at the tenant's expense. However, if the tenant was withholding rent because of unlivable conditions, the court may refuse to evict. The Web site http://www.tiac.net/users/nhpoa/other.htm contains invaluable information about a landlord's rights and remedies in every state in the country.

DUTY TO USE PREMISES PROPERLY

A lease normally lists what a tenant may do in the premises and prohibits other activities. For example, a residential lease allows the tenant to use the property for normal living purposes, but not for any retail, commercial, or industrial purpose.

A tenant is liable to the landlord for any significant damage he causes to the property. The tenant is not liable for normal wear and tear. If, however, he knocks a hole in a wall or damages the plumbing, the landlord may collect the cost of repairs, either by using the security deposit or by suing, if necessary.

INJURIES

TENANT'S LIABILITY

A tenant is generally liable for injuries occurring within the premises she is leasing, whether that is an apartment, a store, or otherwise. If a tenant permits grease to accumulate on a kitchen floor and a guest slips and falls, the tenant is liable. If a merchant negligently installs display shelving that tips onto a customer, the merchant pays for the harm. Generally, a tenant is not liable for injuries occurring in common areas over which she has no control, such as exterior walkways. If a tenant's dinner guest falls because the building's common stairway has loose steps, the landlord is probably liable.

LANDLORD'S LIABILITY

Historically, the common law held a landlord responsible only for injuries that occurred in the common areas, or due to the landlord's negligent maintenance of the property. Increasingly, though, the law holds landlords liable under the normal rules of negligence law. **In many states, a landlord must use reasonable care to maintain safe premises and is liable for foreseeable harm.** For example, most states now have building codes that require a landlord to maintain structural elements in safe condition. States further imply a warranty of habitability, which mandates reasonably safe living conditions.

As always, the common law advances in a disorderly fashion, and state courts disagree about what "reasonable care" requires. The following pair of cases illustrate the diversity of issues—and conflicting arguments—that a landlord must consider before renting units. You make the calls.

MCGUIRE v. K & G MANAGEMENT CO.

1998 Ohio App. LEXIS 4742
Ohio Court of Appeals, 1998

Facts: The McGuire family rented a second-story apartment from K & G Management, which managed a residential complex on behalf of Avant Co. Robin McGuire notified K & G that a window screen in her son's bedroom was loose and had fallen out once. Neighbors had also complained about loose-fitting screens. Five days after Robin reported the loose screen, her son, 26-month-old Devin, was playing in his bedroom with his eight-year-old cousin. Somehow, Devin fell or leaned into the window screen, which gave way. Devin fell to the ground and was seriously hurt.

The McGuires filed suit against K & G and Avant, claiming negligence. In Ohio (and most states), a landlord has a statutory duty to "make all repairs and do whatever is reasonably necessary to put and keep the premises in a fit and habitable condition." The trial court granted summary judgment for both defendants, ruling that the defendants had no duty to install screens strong enough to restrain a child. The McGuires appealed.

You be the Judge: **Are the McGuires entitled to a trial on their claim of negligence?**

Argument for the McGuires: Both defendants have a statutory duty to keep the apartment fit and habitable, and both failed to do that. The screen was loose and they knew it, but failed to fix it. The danger of a child falling was entirely foreseeable, and the defendants are responsible. No parent can watch a child 24 hours a day. Young children climb and play anywhere they can reach. A landlord who makes a profit renting apartments to families should use reasonable care to protect all family members, young and old.

Argument for K & G and Avant: A window screen is not a child restraint. A screen is designed to keep insects and birds out, not to hold children in. A normal window screen, no matter how tightly installed, would not restrain a child. If all landlords throughout the state are suddenly obligated to install child-proof screens, let the legislature announce the new rule and provide time to comply. We do not think that the voters want to pay the additional rent required to cover such a huge expense.

MATTHEWS v. AMBERWOOD ASSOCIATES LIMITED PARTNERSHIP, INC.

351 Md. 544, 719 A.2d 199, 1998 Md. LEXIS 807
Maryland Court of Appeals, 1998

Facts: Shelly Morton leased an apartment owned by Amberwood and operated by Monocle Management. The lease permitted the landlord to evict any tenant who broke the "House Rules," one of which prohibited pets. Morton kept her boyfriend's pit bull, named Rampage, in her apartment. At times, she kept Rampage chained outside the apartment house. When Morton was near the dog, he was not violent, but when she was absent, Rampage would attempt to attack anyone who came near him. Numerous maintenance workers had been unable to perform service work because Rampage barked and lunged at them. The workers reported each of these incidents to Monocle.

Shanita Matthews and her 16-month-old son, Tevin, visited Morton and her child, something they had done many times. As the adults worked on a puzzle in the dining room, the children played in the living room. Morton briefly left the apartment, and suddenly Rampage attacked Tevin. The dog grabbed the boy by the neck and shook him. Matthews was unable to free her son. She yelled for help and called 911. Morton reentered the apartment, could not free the boy, grabbed a knife, and repeatedly stabbed the animal, which finally released Tevin. An ambulance arrived, but an hour after reaching the hospital, Tevin died from his injuries.

Matthews sued Amberwood and Monocle. The jury awarded her $5,018,750 for the wrongful death of her son. The defendants appealed.

You be the Judge: **Does a landlord owe a duty to a social guest of a tenant for an attack within the tenant's apartment?**

Argument for Matthews: The House Rules prohibited pets. Monocle knew that Morton was breaking the rule and keeping an especially dangerous animal. Monocle should have acted to protect the other residents and all guests to the complex. The companies' failure to enforce their own rules led directly to the death of a child.

Argument for the Defendants: Neither the owner nor the management company has control over the apartment or what goes on inside it. The companies could not have foreseen this attack, nor could they have done anything to stop it. Matthews knew the dog's nature. She had no business leaving her son alone with such a vicious beast.

CRIME

Landlords may be liable in negligence to tenants or their guests for criminal attacks that occur on the premises. Courts have struggled with this issue and have reached opposing results in similar cases. The very prevalence of crime sharpens the debate. What must a landlord do to protect a tenant? Courts typically answer the question by looking at four factors.

- *Nature of the Crime.* How did the crime occur? Could the landlord have prevented it?
- *Reasonable Person Standard.* What would a reasonable landlord have done to prevent this type of crime? What did the landlord actually do?
- *Foreseeability.* Was it reasonably foreseeable that such a crime might occur? Were there earlier incidents or warnings?
- *Prevalence of Crime in the Area.* If the general area, or the particular premises, has a high crime rate, courts are more likely to hold that the crime was foreseeable and the landlord responsible.

PERSONAL PROPERTY

Personal property means all property other than real property. Real property, as we know, refers to land and things firmly attached to it. All other property is personal: a bus, a toothbrush, a share of stock. Most personal property is goods, meaning something that can be moved. We have already examined the purchase and sale of goods, which are governed by the Uniform Commercial Code. Now we look at several important aspects of personal property, including gifts, found property and bailments.

GIFTS

A gift is a voluntary transfer of property from one person to another without any consideration. It is the lack of consideration that distinguishes a gift from a contract. Contracts usually consist of mutual promises to do something in the future. Each promise is consideration for the other one, and the mutual consideration makes each promise enforceable. But a gift is a one-way transaction, without consideration. The person who gives property away is the **donor** and the one who receives it is the **donee**.

A gift involves three elements:

- The donor intends to transfer ownership of the property to the donee immediately.
- The donor delivers the property to the donee.
- The donee accepts the property.

INTENTION TO TRANSFER OWNERSHIP

The donor must intend to transfer ownership to the property right away, immediately giving up all control of the item. Notice the two important parts of this element. First, the donor's intention must be to *transfer ownership*, that is, to give title to the donee. Merely proving that the owner handed you property does not guarantee that you have received a gift; if the owner only intended that you use the item, there is no gift and she can demand it back.

Second, the donor must also intend the property to transfer *immediately*. A promise to make a gift in the future is unenforceable. Promises about future behavior are governed by contract law, and a contract is unenforceable without consideration. That is why poor Charley, at the beginning of this chapter, will never collect his $100,000 from the banker. If the banker had handed Charley the cash as he gushed his extravagant words, Charley could keep the money. However, the banker's promise to make the gift the next day is legally worthless. Nor does Charley have an enforceable contract, since there was no consideration for the banker's promise.

A *revocable gift* is a contradiction in terms, because it violates the rule just discussed. It is not a gift and the donee keeps nothing.[6] Suppose Harold tells his daughter Faith, "The mule is yours from now on, but if you start acting stupid again, I'm taking her back." Harold has retained some control over the animal, which means he has not intended to transfer ownership. There is no gift, and Harold still owns the mule.

DELIVERY

PHYSICAL DELIVERY

The donor must deliver the property to the donee. Generally, this involves physical delivery. If Anna hands Eddie a Rembrandt drawing, saying, "I want you to have this forever,"she has satisfied the delivery requirement. This is the element missing from the banker's "gift" to Charley.

CONSTRUCTIVE DELIVERY

Physical delivery is the most common and the surest way to make a gift, but it is not always necessary. **A donor makes constructive delivery by transferring ownership without a physical delivery.** Most courts permit constructive delivery only when physical delivery is impossible or extremely inconvenient. Suppose Anna wants to give her niece Jen a blimp, which is parked in a hangar at the airport. The blimp will not fit through the doorway of Jen's dorm. Instead of flying the aircraft to the university, Anna may simply deliver to Jen the certificate of title and the keys to the blimp. When she has done that, Jen owns the aircraft.

DELIVERY TO AN AGENT

A donor might deliver the property to an agent, either someone working for him or for the donee. If the donor delivers the property to his own agent, there

[6] The only exception to this rule is a gift *causa mortis*, discussed below.

is no gift. By definition, the agent works for the donor, and thus the donor still has control and ownership of the property. But if the donor delivers the property to the donee's agent, the gift is made.

Inter Vivos Gifts and Gifts *Causa Mortis*

A gift can be either *inter vivos* or *causa mortis*. **An *inter vivos* gift means a gift made during life, that is, when the donor is not under any fear of impending death.** The vast majority of gifts are *inter vivos*, involving a healthy donor and donee. Shirley, age 30 and in good health, gives her husband Terry an eraser for his birthday. This is an *inter vivos* gift, which is absolute. The gift becomes final upon delivery, and the donor may not revoke it. If Shirley and Terry have a fight the next day, Shirley has no power to erase her gift.

A gift *causa mortis* is one made in contemplation of approaching death. The gift is valid if the donor dies as expected, but is revoked if he recovers. Suppose Lance's doctors have told him he will probably die of a liver ailment within a month. Lance calls Jane to his bedside and hands her a fistful of emeralds, saying, "I'm dying; these are yours." Jane sheds a tear, then sprints to the bank. If Lance dies of the liver ailment within a few weeks, Jane gets to keep the emeralds. The law permits the gift *causa mortis* to act as a substitute for a will, since the donor's delivery of the property clearly indicates his intentions. But note that this kind of gift is revocable. Since a gift *causa mortis* is conditional (upon the donor's death), the donor has the right to revoke it at any time before he dies. If Lance telephones Jane the next day and says that he has changed his mind, he gets the jewels back. Further, if the donor recovers and does not die as expected, the gift is automatically revoked.

Acceptance

The donee must accept the gift. This rarely leads to disputes, but if a donee should refuse a gift and then change her mind, she is out of luck. Her repudiation of the donor's offer means there is no gift, and she has no rights in the property.

The following case offers neighbors, relatives, failing health, and plenty of money—always a volatile mix.

JAMISON v. ESTATE OF GOODLETT

56 Ark. App. 71, 938 S.W.2d 865, 1997 Ark. App. LEXIS 75
Arkansas Court of Appeals, 1997

Facts: Robert Goodlett, a bachelor, owned a 300-acre farm, a store, and other property in Arkansas. His cousin lived on an adjoining farm; the cousin's daughter, Sara Goodlett Jamison, and her husband, Val, often visited Robert. Goodlett became ill and asked Val Jamison to take him to the hospital. The next day, while hospitalized, Goodlett asked Jamison to help him pay some bills. Jamison arranged for bank officials to visit the hospital, where, with Goodlett's agreement, they empowered Jamison to use Goodlett's checking account.

According to Jamison, when Goodlett learned from his doctor that he must undergo life-threatening surgery, Goodlett said that he wanted to give all of his property and money to Jamison and his wife. There were no other witnesses. Jamison had a lawyer draw up a "power of attorney" form, which Goodlett signed, giving Jamison the right to dispose of Goodlett's property. Goodlett actually lived several more years. During that period, Jamison transferred the farm to his wife and all of Goodlett's cash, about

$185,000, to himself. He continued to pay all of Goodlett's bills; paid taxes in Goodlett's name on the interest earned from the cash; leased the land to another farmer in Goodlett's name; and gave Goodlett periodic reports on the money and the farm. Jamison claimed that Goodlett never objected to the transfer of the money and property and that, if he had, Jamison would have given it back. After Goodlett died, a trial court ordered the Jamisons to return the property and cash (with interest) to the estate. They appealed, claiming an *inter vivos* gift.

You be the Judge: Did Goodlett make an *inter vivos* gift?

Argument for the Jamisons: Your honors, the three elements of a valid gift are intent, delivery, and acceptance, and all three are undeniably present. Robert Goodlett had a long-term friendship with his relative Sara and her husband, Val, which is why he turned to them when he became ill. Goodlett asked bank officers to give Jamison the power to sign checks. Goodlett also signed a power of attorney, understanding that Jamison then had complete control of the property and money. Goodlett lived for several years without once objecting to the arrangement. He intended this transfer as a gift. Delivery occurred when the property changed hands. The Jamisons' acceptance is obvious because they operated the farm and controlled the money for several years. The gift is complete and the estate has no legitimate claim, only a greedy desire for money that Goodlett disposed of long ago.

Argument for the Estate: The Jamisons probably did help Robert Goodlett, and they should be thanked. But there was no gift and they may not keep his property. The element of intent requires that the donor give up ownership immediately and permanently. Yet the Jamisons' conduct indicated that Goodlett never gave up ownership. They paid taxes and leased the property in Goodlett's name, reported the farm's condition to him, and remained willing to return the property if he asked for it. A "revocable" gift is no gift at all. Goodlett never objected to the Jamisons' role as caretaker because it never occurred to him that they would claim ownership rights.

The following table distinguishes between a contract and a gift:

A Contract and a Gift Distinguished

A Contract:

Lou: I will pay you $2,000 to paint the house, if you promise to finish by July 3.	Abby: I agreed to paint the house by July 3, for $2,000.

Lou and Abby have a contract. Each promise is consideration in support of the other promise. Lou and Abby can each enforce the other's promise.

A Gift:

Lou hands Phil two opera tickets, while saying:

Lou: I want you to have these two tickets to *Rigoletto*.	Phil: Hey, thanks.

This is a valid *inter vivos* gift. Lou intended to transfer ownership immediately and deliver the property to Phil, who now owns the tickets.

Neither Contract nor Gift:

Lou: You're a great guy. Next week, I'm going to give you two tickets to *Rigoletto*.	Jason: Hey, thanks.

There is no gift because Lou did not intend to transfer ownership immediately, and he did not deliver the tickets. There is no contract because Jason has given no consideration to support Lou's promise.

BAILMENT

A bailment is the rightful possession of goods by one who is not the owner. The one who delivers the goods is the **bailor** and the one in possession is the **bailee**. Bailments are common. Suppose you are going out of town for the weekend and loan your motorcycle to Stan. You are the bailor and your friend is the bailee. When you check your suitcase with the airline, you are again the bailor and the airline is the bailee. If you rent a car at your destination, you become the bailee while the rental agency is the bailor. In each case, someone other than the true owner has rightful, temporary possession of personal property.

The parties generally—but not always—create a bailment by agreement. In each of the examples, the parties agreed to the bailment. In two cases, the agreement included payment, which is common but not essential. When you buy your airline ticket, you pay for your ticket, and the price includes the airline's agreement, as bailee, to transport your suitcase. When you rent a car, you pay the bailor for the privilege of using it. By loaning your motorcycle, you engage in a bailment without either party paying compensation.

A bailment without any agreement is called a constructive, or involuntary, bailment. Suppose you find a wristwatch in your house that you know belongs to a friend. You are obligated to return the watch to the true owner, and until you do so, you are the bailee, liable for harm to the property. This is called a constructive bailment because, with no agreement between the parties, the law is *construing* a bailment.

Because the bailor is the one who delivers the goods to another, the bailor is typically the owner, but he need not be. Suppose that Stan, who borrowed your motorcycle, allows his girlfriend Sheila to try out the bike, and she takes it to a mall where she jumps over a row of six parked cars. Stan, the bailee from you, has become a bailor, and Sheila is his bailee.

CONTROL

To create a bailment, the bailee must assume physical control with intent to possess. A bailee may be liable for loss or damage to the property. But it is not fair to hold him liable unless he has taken physical control of the goods, intending to possess them.

Disputes about whether someone has taken control often arise in parking lot cases. When a car is damaged or stolen, the lot's owner may try to avoid liability by claiming it lacked control of the parked auto and therefore was not a bailee. If the lot is a "park and lock" facility, where the car's owner retains the key and the lot owner exercises no control at all, then there may be no bailment, and no liability for damage. (For a sample automobile bailment form, see http://www.gate.net/~legalsvc/autobail.html.)

By contrast, when a driver leaves her keys with a parking attendant, the lot clearly is exercising control of the auto, and the parties have created a bailment. The lot is probably liable for loss or damage. What about cases in the middle, where the driver keeps her keys but the lot owner exercises *some other control*? There is no uniform rule, but the trend is probably toward liability for the lot owner.

RIGHTS OF THE BAILEE

The bailee's primary right is possession of the property. Anyone who interferes with the bailee's rightful possession is liable to her. **The bailee is typically, though not always, permitted to use the property.** Obviously, a customer is permitted to drive a car rented from an agency. When a farmer loans his tractor to a neighbor, the bailee is entitled to use the machine for normal farm purposes. But some bailees have no authority to use the goods. If you store your furniture in a warehouse, the storage company is your bailee, but it has no right to curl up in your bed. The bailee may or may not be entitled to compensation, depending on the parties' agreement.

DUTIES OF THE BAILEE

The bailee is strictly liable to redeliver the goods on time to the bailor or to whomever the bailor designates. Strict liability means there are virtually no exceptions. Rudy stores his $6,000 drum set with Melissa's Warehouse while he is on vacation. Blake arrives at the warehouse and shows a forged letter, supposedly from Rudy, granting Blake permission to remove the drums. If Melissa permits Blake to take the drums, she will owe Rudy $6,000, even if the forgery was a high-quality job.

DUE CARE

The bailee is obligated to exercise due care. **The level of care required depends upon who receives the benefit of the bailment.** There are three possibilities.

- *Sole Benefit of Bailee.* If the bailment is for the sole benefit of the bailee, the bailee is required to use **extraordinary care** with the property. Generally, in these cases, the bailor loans something for free to the bailee. Since the bailee is paying nothing for the use of the goods, most courts (though not all) consider her the only one to benefit from the bailment. If your neighbor loans you a power lawn mower, the bailment is probably for your sole benefit. You are liable if you are even slightly inattentive in handling the lawn mower and can expect to pay for virtually any harm done.
- *Mutual Benefit.* When the bailment is for the mutual benefit of bailor and bailee, the bailee must use **ordinary care** with the property. Ordinary care is what a reasonably prudent person would use under the circumstances. When you rent a car, you benefit from the use of the car, and the agency profits from the fee you pay. When the airline hauls your suitcase to your destination, both parties benefit. Most bailments benefit both parties, and courts decide the majority of bailment disputes under this standard.
- *Sole Benefit of Bailor.* When the bailment benefits only the bailor, the bailee must use only **slight care**. This kind of bailment is called a **gratuitous bailment**, and the bailee is liable only for **gross negligence**. Sheila enters a greased-pig contest and asks you to hold her $140,000 diamond engagement ring while she competes. You put the ring in your pocket. Sheila wins the $20 first prize, but the ring has disappeared. This was a gratuitous bailment, and you are not liable to Sheila unless she can prove gross negligence

on your part. If the ring dropped from your pocket or was stolen, you are not liable. If you used the ring to play catch with friends, you are liable.

BURDEN OF PROOF

In an ordinary negligence case, the plaintiff has the burden of proof to demonstrate that the defendant was negligent and caused the harm alleged. In bailment cases, the burden of proof is reversed. **Once the bailor has proven the existence of a bailment and loss or harm to the goods, a presumption of negligence arises, and the burden shifts to the bailee to prove adequate care.** This is a major change from ordinary negligence cases. Georgina's car is struck by another auto. If Georgina sues for negligence, it is her burden to prove that the defendant was driving unreasonably and caused the harm. By comparison, assume that Georgina rents Sam her sailboat for a month. At the end of the month, Sam announces that the boat is at the bottom of Lake Michigan. If Georgina sues Sam, she only needs to demonstrate that the parties had a bailment and that he failed to return the boat. The burden then shifts to Sam to prove that the boat was lost through no fault of his own. If he cannot meet that burden, Georgina recovers the full value of the boat.

In the following case, the court looks at the two principal issues we have examined: whether there was a bailment, and whether the bailee exercised adequate care.

GIN v. WACKENHUT CORP.

741 F. Supp. 1454, 1990 U.S. Dist. LEXIS 8718
United States District Court for the District of Hawaii, 1990

Facts: Max Gin and Johnnie Fong had a partnership specializing in wholesale jewelry. They often traveled to jewelry shows and conventions to display their wares. Max Gin left a jewelry show in Miami and went to the airport, where he intended to catch a flight to New Orleans, for another trade show. Gin checked his suitcases with a curbside skycap and proceeded to the departure gate. He held one carry-on bag, containing $140,000 in jewelry.

Wackenhut operated the security checkpoint at the entrance to the departure gate. Like most, this checkpoint had an X-ray machine for baggage and a magnetometer to detect metal carried by passengers. Gin waited at one side until the line of people waiting for the magnetometer had dwindled. He then placed his bag on the conveyor belt and stepped up to the magnetometer. Just at that moment a woman wearing a heavy coat abruptly cut in front of Gin and passed through the magnetometer. She activated the metal detection alarm. The Wackenhut employee who operated the magnetometer motioned for Gin to wait on the terminal side of the machine, while the woman emptied her pockets onto a tray. She passed through the machine again and once more the alarm sounded. She emptied more items from her pockets, but again set off the alarm. Only on the fourth attempt did she proceed through the magnetometer. Gin walked through the machine, went to pick up his jewelry bag, and found it gone. He dashed through the departure lounge searching for the bag and sought police help, but to no avail.

Gin sued, alleging negligent bailment. Wackenhut defended, claiming that no bailment had arisen and that, even if it had, the company used adequate care.

Issues: Was there a bailment? If so, did Wackenhut use adequate care?

Excerpts from Judge King's Decision: Although the law of bailments is well settled, the brevity of the alleged bailment makes this case somewhat novel.

This court is convinced that in the instant case a bailment was created. In proceeding through the security checkpoint, plaintiff placed his bag upon the X-ray conveyor belt. From the moment the bag entered the machine the plaintiff surrendered control to the defendant. The defendant could stop the bag in the machine for prolonged examination, could run it through the machine a second time, or could order it opened for an examination of its contents. Further, passengers such as the plaintiff have virtually no control over the length of time they will be separated from their bag. This time could vary from a few seconds to several minutes. It is also noteworthy that plaintiff could not retrieve his bag until the Wackenhut employee operating the magnetometer permitted plaintiff to pass into the concourse area. Due to the orientation of the X-ray machine and the magnetometer, it was impossible for a passenger waiting in line for the magnetometer to see his bag after it emerged from the X-ray machine. Although the period of separation might be brief, the plaintiff had surrendered possession and control of his belongings and a bailment was created.

Negligence: Under Florida law, once a plaintiff has proven the existence of a bailment, and demonstrated the failure of the bailee to return the bailed goods, a presumption of negligence on the part of the bailee arises. In order to avoid liability for the lost goods, the defendant has the burden of showing that he exercised the degree of care required by the nature of the bailment.

The court finds that Wackenhut failed to exercise the requisite degree of care in the instant case. Wackenhut knew passengers could not keep a visual watch over their bags throughout the inspection process. In addition, the defendant's own witness testified that carry-on bags had been lost, either through theft or inadvertence, an average of twice each week over the past several years. Despite this knowledge the defendant evidently made no effort either to more closely coordinate the screening of passengers with their baggage, to reorient the X-ray machine and magnetometer so that passengers could watch their bags during the security check, or to simply post a sign alerting passengers that thefts frequently occurred.

[The court awarded the plaintiffs $140,000.]

RIGHTS AND DUTIES OF THE BAILOR

The bailor's rights and duties are the reverse of the bailee's. The bailor is entitled to the return of his property on the agreed-upon date. He is also entitled to receive the property in good condition and to recover damages for harm to the property, if the bailee failed to use adequate care.

LIABILITY FOR DEFECTS

Depending upon the type of bailment, the bailor is potentially liable for known or even unknown defects in the property. **If the bailment is for the sole benefit of the bailee, the bailor must notify the bailee of any known defects.** Suppose Megan lends her stepladder to Dave. The top rung is loose and Megan knows it, but forgets to tell Dave. The top rung crumbles and Dave falls onto his girlfriend's iguana. Megan is liable to Dave and the girlfriend unless the defect in the ladder was obvious. Notice that Megan's liability is not only to the bailee, but also to any others injured by the defects. Megan would not be liable if she had notified Dave of the defective rung.

In a mutual-benefit bailment, the bailor is liable not only for known defects but also for unknown defects that the bailor could have discovered with reasonable diligence. Suppose RentaLot rents a power sander to Dan.

RentaLot does not realize that the sander has faulty wiring, but a reasonable inspection would have revealed the problem. When Dan suffers a serious shock from the defect, RentaLot is liable to him, even though it was unaware of the problem.

CHAPTER CONCLUSION

Real property law is ancient but forceful, as waterfront property owners discovered when a power company flooded their land and an old-fashioned easement deprived them of compensation. Had the families understood nonpossessory interests, they might have declined to buy the property. Landlord-tenant law, by contrast, is new and rapidly changing, especially as to liability for injuries. Personal property law affects most of us every day, as we park a car, leave goods with a repair shop, or put our suitcases through an X-ray machine. Understanding property law can be worth a lot of money—but never carry all of it with you.

CHAPTER REVIEW

1. Real property includes land, buildings, air and subsurface rights, plant life, and fixtures. A fixture is any good that has become attached to other real property.
2. A fee simple absolute provides the owner with the greatest possible control of the property, including the right to make any lawful use of it and to sell it. A fee simple defeasible may terminate upon the occurrence of some limiting event. A life estate permits the owner to possess the property during her life, but not to sell it or leave it to heirs.
3. An easement gives a person the right to enter land belonging to another and make a limited use of it, without taking anything away.
4. The implied warranty of habitability means that a builder selling a new home guarantees the adequacy of materials and workmanship.
5. The seller of a home must disclose facts that a buyer does not know and cannot readily observe, if they materially affect the property's value.
6. When an owner of a freehold estate allows another person temporary, exclusive possession of the property, the parties have created a landlord-tenant relationship.
7. Any lease for a stated, fixed period is a tenancy for years. A periodic tenancy is created for a fixed period and then automatically continues for additional periods until either party notifies the other of termination. A tenancy at will has no fixed duration and may be terminated by either party at any time. A tenancy at sufferance occurs when a tenant remains, against the wishes of the landlord, after the expiration of a true tenancy.
8. A landlord may be liable for constructive eviction if he substantially interferes with the tenant's use and enjoyment of the premises.
9. The implied warranty of habitability requires that a landlord meet all standards set by the local building code and/or that the premises be fit for human habitation.
10. The tenant is obligated to pay the rent, and must pay the landlord for any significant damage he causes to the property.

11. At common law, a landlord had very limited liability for injuries on the premises, but today many courts require a landlord to use reasonable care and hold her liable for foreseeable harm.

12. A gift is a voluntary transfer of property from one person to another without consideration. The elements of a gift are intention to transfer ownership immediately, delivery, and acceptance.

13. A bailment is the rightful possession of goods by one who is not the owner. The one who delivers the goods is the bailor and the one in possession is the bailee. To create a bailment, the bailee must assume physical control with intent to possess.

14. The bailee is obligated to exercise due care. The level of care required depends upon who receives the benefit of the bailment: if the bailee is the sole beneficiary, she must use extraordinary care; if the parties mutually benefit, the bailee must use ordinary care; and if the bailor is the sole beneficiary of the bailment, the bailee must use only slight care.

PRACTICE TEST

1. Paul and Shelly Higgins had two wood stoves in their home. Each rested on, but was not attached to, a built-in brick platform. The downstairs wood stove was connected to the chimney flue and was used as part of the main heating system for the house. The upstairs stove, in the master bedroom, was purely decorative. It had no stovepipe connecting it to the chimney. The Higginses sold their house to Jack Everitt, and neither party said anything about the two stoves. Is Everitt entitled to either stove? Both stoves?

2. In 1944, W. E. Collins conveyed land to the Church of God of Prophecy. The deed said: "This deed is made with the full understanding that should the property fail to be used for the Church of God, it is to be null and void and property to revert to W. E. Collins or heirs." In the late 1980s, the church wished to move to another property and sought a judicial ruling that it had the right to sell the land. The trial court ruled that the church owned a fee simple absolute and had the right to sell the property. Comment.

3. **CPA QUESTION** On July 1, 1992, Quick, Onyx, and Nash were deeded a piece of land as tenants in common. The deed provided that Quick owned one-half the property and Onyx and Nash owned one-quarter each. If Nash dies, the property will be owned as follows:

   (a) Quick ½, Onyx ½.

   (b) Quick ⅝, Onyx ⅜.

   (c) Quick ⅓, Onyx ⅓, Nash's heirs ⅓.

   (d) Quick ½, Onyx ¼, Nash's heirs ¼.

4. Summey Building Systems built a condominium project in Myrtle Beach, South Carolina. The project included an adjacent parking deck. Shortly after Summey relinquished control to the condominium association, the deck began to experience problems. Water and caustic materials leaked through the upper deck and dripped onto cars parked underneath. Cracks appeared, and an expert concluded that the bond between the top deck and the structural supports was insufficient. Repairs would cost about $205,000. Summey had never warranted that the deck would be free of all problems. Is the company liable for the repairs?

5. Kenmart Realty sued to evict Mr. and Ms. Alghalabio for nonpayment of rent and sought the unpaid monies, totaling several thousand dollars. In defense, the Alghalabios claimed that their apartment was infested with rats. They testified that there were numerous rat holes in the walls of the living room, bedroom, and kitchen, that there were rat droppings all over the apartment, and that on one occasion they saw their toddler holding a live rat. They testified that the landlord had refused numerous requests to exterminate. Please rule on the landlord's suit.

6. **YOU BE THE JUDGE WRITING PROBLEM** Dominion Bank owned a large office building in Washington, D.C. Because it planned to sell the building, the bank stopped leasing new space, and 5 of the 13 floors became vacant. Tenants complained to the bank that vagrants were using the empty spaces for drug deals and prostitution. Jane Doe, a secretary who worked in the building, was dragged to an empty, unlocked floor and raped. She sued the bank. A security expert testified that all vacant offices and floors should have been sealed off. Is the bank liable for Doe's injuries? **Argument for Jane Doe:** The bank created a dangerous situation by gradually abandoning a commercial building. The bank should be held to a "reasonable person" standard, one that it clearly failed to meet. **Argument for Dominion Bank:** The bank is not a police force. The bank's obligation was to keep the rented premises in good working order, which it did.

7. While in her second year at the Juilliard School of Music in New York City, Ann Rylands had a chance to borrow for one month a rare Guadagnini violin, made in 1768. She returned the violin to the owner in Philadelphia, but telephoned her father to ask if he would buy it for her. He borrowed money from his pension fund and paid the owner. Ann traveled to Philadelphia to pick up the violin. She had exclusive possession of the violin for the next 20 years, using it in her professional career. Unfortunately, she became an alcoholic, and during one period when she was in a treatment center, she entrusted the violin to her mother for safekeeping. At about that time, her father died. When Ann was released from the center, she requested return of the violin, but her mother refused. Who owns the violin?

8. **RIGHT & WRONG** Jane says to Cody, "If you will agree to work as my yard man, I'll pay you $1,000 per week for a normal work week. You can start on Monday, and I'll guarantee you eight months' work." Cody is elated at his good fortune and agrees to start work on Monday. Later that day, Cody, still rejoicing, says to Beth, his girlfriend, "You know those sapphire earrings in the jewelry store that you're wild about? At the end of next week I'm going to buy them for you." On Monday, Jane realizes what a foolish thing she said, and refuses to hire Cody. Cody, in turn, refuses to buy the earrings for Beth. Cody sues Jane and wins; Beth sues Cody and loses. Why the opposite outcomes? What basic ideas of fairness underlie the two results?

9. Ronald Armstead worked for First American Bank as a courier. His duties included making deliveries between the bank's branches in Washington, D.C. Armstead parked the bank's station wagon near the entrance of one branch in violation of a sign saying: "No Parking Rush Hour Zone." In the rear luggage section of the station wagon were four locked bank dispatch bags, containing checks and other valuable documents. Armstead had received tickets for illegal parking at this spot on five occasions. Shortly after Armstead entered the bank, a tow truck arrived and its operator prepared to tow the station wagon. Transportation Management, Inc. operated the towing service on behalf of the District of Columbia. Armstead ran out to the vehicle and told the tow truck operator that he was prepared to drive the vehicle away immediately. But the operator drove away with the station wagon in tow. One and one-half hours later, a bank employee paid for the car's release, but one dispatch bag, containing documents worth $107,000, was missing. First American sued Transportation Management and the District of Columbia. The defendants sought summary judgment, claiming they could not be liable. Were they correct?

10. **YOU BE THE JUDGE WRITING PROBLEM** Eileen Murphy often cared for her elderly neighbor, Thomas Kenney. He paid her $25 per day for her help and once gave her a bank certificate of deposit worth $25,000. Murphy alleged that shortly before his death, Kenney

gave her a large block of shares in three corporations. He called his broker, to instruct him to transfer the shares to Murphy's name, but the broker was unavailable. So Kenney told Murphy to write her name on the shares and keep them, which she did. Two weeks later Kenney died. When Murphy presented the shares to Kenney's broker to transfer ownership to her, the broker refused because Kenney had never signed them over to Murphy. Was Murphy entitled to the $25,000? To the shares? **Argument for Murphy:** The purpose of the law is to do what a donor intended, and it is obvious that Kenney intended Murphy to have the $25,000 and the shares. **Argument for the Estate:** Murphy is not entitled to the $25,000 because we have no way of knowing what Kenney's intentions were when he gave her the money. She is not entitled to the shares of stock because Kenney's failure to endorse them over to her meant he never delivered them.

INTERNET RESEARCH PROBLEMS

Go to http://www.tenantsunion.org/tulist.html, and search for the law of your state concerning a landlord's obligation to provide a habitable apartment. Now assume that you are living in a rental unit with serious defects. Draft a letter to the landlord asking for prompt repairs. You may use the form letters provided at http://little.nhlink.net/nhlink/housing/cto/letters/letrs.htm as a guide.

You own a helicopter worth $250,000. A business associate wishes to use it for one week to show prospective clients around various islands in the Caribbean. You are willing to let him use it, for a fee of $15,000. Draft a bailment agreement. Use the form supplied at http://www.gate.net/~legalsvc/autobail.html as a model.

You can find further practice problems in the Online Quiz at http://beatty.westbuslaw.com or in the Study Guide that accompanies this text.

CONSUMER LAW

23 CHAPTER

Three women signed up for a lesson at the Arthur Murray dance studio in Washington, D.C. Expecting a session of decorous fun, they instead found themselves in a nightmare of humiliation and coercion:

- "First of all, I did not want the [additional] lesson, and I think it was unpleasant because I had three, maybe four, people, as I say, pressuring me to buy something by a certain time, and I do recall asking that I be let to think, let me think it over, and I was told that the contest would end at 6 o'clock or something to that effect and if I did not sign by a certain time it would be too late. I think we got under the deadline by maybe a minute or two. If I had been given time to think, I would not have signed that contract."

- "I tried to say no and get out of it and I got very, very upset because I got frightened at paying out all that money and having nothing to fall back on. I remember I started crying and couldn't stop crying. All I thought of was getting out of there. So finally after—I don't know how much time, Mr. Mara said, well, I could sign up for 250 hours, which was half the 500 Club, which would amount to $4,300. So I finally signed it. After that, I tried to raise the money from the bank and found I couldn't get a loan for that amount and I didn't have any savings and I had to get a bank loan to pay for it. That was when I went back and asked him to cancel that contract. But Mr. Mara said that he couldn't cancel it."

- "I did not join the carnival. I did not wish to join the carnival, and while it was only an additional $55, I had no desire to join. [My instructor] asked everyone in the room to sit down in a circle around me and he stood me up in that circle, in the middle of the circle, and said, 'Everybody, I want you to look at this woman here who is too cheap to join the carnival. I just want you to look at a woman like that. Isn't it awful?'"

Because of abuses such as these, the Federal Trade Commission ordered the Arthur Murray dance studio to halt its high-pressure sales techniques, limit each contract to no more than $1,500 in dance lessons, and permit all contracts to be canceled within seven days.[1]

INTRODUCTION

Years ago consumers typically dealt with merchants they knew well. A dance instructor in a small town would not stay in business long if he tormented his elderly, vulnerable clients. As the population of this country grew and cities expanded, however, merchants became less and less subject to community pressure. The law has supplemented, if not replaced, these informal policing mechanisms. Both Congress and the states have passed statutes that protect consumers from the unscrupulous. But the legal system in America is generally too slow and expensive to handle small cases. The women who fell into the web of Arthur Murray lost a few thousand dollars and suffered some emotional distress, but they had neither the wealth nor the energy to sue the studio themselves. To aid consumers such as these, Congress empowered federal agencies to enforce consumer laws. The Federal Trade Commission (FTC) is the most important of these agencies.

FEDERAL TRADE COMMISSION

Congress created the FTC in 1915 to regulate business. Although its original focus was on antitrust law, it now regulates a wide range of business activities that affect consumers, everything from advertising to consumer loans to warranties to debt collection practices.[2] It is, if you will, the consumer's best friend in Washington. The FTC has several options for enforcing the law:

- *Voluntary Compliance.* When the FTC determines that a business has violated the law, it first asks the offender to sign a voluntary compliance affidavit promising to stop the prohibited activity.
- *Administrative Hearings and Appeals.* If the company refuses to stop voluntarily, the FTC takes the case to an administrative law judge (ALJ) within the

---

[1] *In re Arthur Murray Studio of Washington, Inc.*, 78 F.T.C. 401, 1971 FTC LEXIS 75 (1971).

[2] Chapter 19 discusses the FTC's role in antitrust enforcement.

agency. The violator may settle the case at this point by signing a **consent order**. If the case proceeds to a hearing, the ALJ has the right to issue a **cease and desist order**, commanding the violator to stop the offending activity. The FTC issued a cease and desist order against the Arthur Murray dance studio. A defendant can appeal such an order to the five Commissioners of the FTC, from there to a federal appeals court, and ultimately to the United States Supreme Court. Both the Commissioners and the Fifth Circuit Court of Appeals confirmed the cease and desist order against Arthur Murray. The case never reached the Supreme Court.

- *Penalties.* The penalty for each violation of a voluntary compliance affidavit, consent order, or cease and desist order is $11,000. The same penalty also applies to each knowing violation of (1) an FTC rule or (2) a cease and desist order issued against *someone else*. For example, the Arthur Murray studio could be liable for violating an FTC cease and desist order prohibiting high-pressure sales by the Fred Astaire studio. In addition, the FTC can file suit in federal court asking for damages on behalf of an injured consumer if (1) the defendant has violated FTC rules and (2) a reasonable person would have known under the circumstances that the conduct was dishonest or fraudulent.

SALES

Section 5 of the Federal Trade Commission Act (FTC Act) prohibits "unfair and deceptive acts or practices." You can report an unfair or deceptive practice to the FTC at its Web site (http://www.ftc.gov).

DECEPTIVE ACTS OR PRACTICES

Many deceptive acts or practices involve advertisements. **Under the FTC Act, an advertisement is deceptive if it contains an important misrepresentation or omission that is likely to mislead a reasonable consumer.** A company advertised that a pain-relief ointment called "Aspercreme" provided "the strong relief of aspirin right where you hurt." From this ad and the name of the product, do you assume that the ointment contains aspirin? Are you a reasonable consumer? Consumers surveyed in a shopping mall believed the product contained aspirin. In fact, it does not. The FTC required the company to disclose that there is no aspirin in Aspercreme.[3] You may have noticed that television advertisements for this product still state, "Aspercreme does not contain aspirin."

Is there anything wrong with the ads on the following page?

Do not believe a word of them, warns the FTC. It takes more than three minutes a day to get a washboard stomach, no matter what equipment you use. As for the #1 Doctor Recommended Ensure, the doctors in the survey were asked which liquid meal they would choose, if they were going to recommend one to a patient. In fact, most doctors would not recommend Ensure to the healthy adults pictured in the advertisements. The half-price cars were for lease, not

[3] *In re Thompson Medical Co., Inc.*, 104 F.T.C. 648, 1984 FTC LEXIS 6 (1984).

sale. By the end of the lease, owners would have paid only half the value of the cars, but they would also have to return the cars to the dealer. Was the company in the following case deceptive about its cure for baldness?

FTC v. PANTRON I CORP.

33 F.3d 1088, 1994 U.S. App. LEXIS 22977
United States Court of Appeals for the Ninth Circuit, 1994

Facts: Pantron I Corp. marketed the Helsinki Formula, a conditioner and shampoo costing $49.95 for a three-month supply. Pantron's advertisements (including late-night infomercials hosted by the "Man from U.N.C.L.E.," Robert Vaughn) claimed scientific studies proved that the Formula promoted growth of new hair on bald men.

At trial, three doctors testified that there was "no reason to believe" from current scientific data that the Helsinki Formula would cure or prevent baldness and that the studies on which Pantron relied did not meet generally accepted scientific standards. Users of the Helsinki Formula (or any other baldness cure) may indeed experience hair regrowth because of the *placebo effect*. Frequently, products with no medicinal value work for psychological reasons. A patient who takes sugar pills believing they are pain relievers may feel better, although the pills themselves are worthless in treating pain. Hair growth products have a particularly strong placebo effect.

Pantron introduced evidence from 18 men who experienced hair regrowth or a reduction in hair loss after using the Formula. It also introduced evidence of a "consumer satisfaction survey" that showed positive results in 70 percent of those who had used the product for six months or more. Over half of Pantron's orders came from repeat purchasers; it received very few written complaints; and fewer than 3 percent of its customers asked for their money back.

The trial court decided that Pantron could state, in its advertisements, that the Helsinki Formula was effective to some extent for some people in treating baldness. However, the ads must disclose that (1) the Formula was more likely to stop hair loss than grow new hair, and (2) the claims were not supported by scientific studies that met U.S. standards.

Issue: Are the advertisements for the Helsinki Formula deceptive?

Excerpts from Judge Reinhardt's Decision: Where, as here, a product's effectiveness arises solely as a result of the placebo effect, a representation that the product is effective constitutes a false advertisement even though some consumers may experience positive results. Under the evidence in the record before us, it appears that massaging vegetable oil on one's head would likely produce the same positive results as using the Helsinki Formula. All that might be required would be for Wesson Oil to remove Florence Henderson as its flack and substitute infomercials with Mr. Vaughn that promote its product as a baldness cure.

As the FTC has explained, "The Commission cannot accept as proof of a product's efficacy a psychological reaction stemming from a belief which, to a substantial degree, was caused by respondent's deceptions." Indeed, were we to hold otherwise, advertisers would be encouraged to foist unsubstantiated claims on an unsuspecting public in the hope that consumers would believe the ads and the claims would be self-fulfilling. Moreover, allowing advertisers to rely on the placebo effect would not only harm those individuals who were deceived; it would create a substantial economic cost as well, by allowing sellers to fleece large numbers of consumers who, unable to evaluate the efficacy of an inherently useless product, make repeat purchases of that product. [W]e conclude that the district court erred in deciding that the FTC had not shown that Pantron's effectiveness claims were false.

UNFAIR PRACTICES

The FTC Act also prohibits unfair acts or practices. **The Commission considers a practice to be *unfair* if it meets all of the following three tests:**

- *It causes a substantial consumer injury.* This can mean physical or financial injury. A furnace repair company that dismantled home furnaces for "inspection" and then refused to reassemble them until the consumers agreed to buy services or replacement parts had caused a substantial consumer injury.
- *The harm of the injury outweighs any countervailing benefit.* A pharmaceutical company sold a sunburn remedy without conducting adequate tests to ensure that it worked. The expense of these tests would have forced the company to raise the product's price. The company had demonstrated that the product was safe, and there was evidence in the medical literature that the ingredients when used in other products were effective. The FTC determined that, although the company was technically in violation of its rules, the benefit to consumers of a cheaper product more than outweighed the risk of injury to them.
- *The consumer could not reasonably avoid the injury.* The FTC is particularly vigilant in protecting susceptible consumers—such as the elderly or the ill—who are less able to avoid injury. For instance, the Commission looks especially carefully at those who offer a cure for cancer.

In addition, the FTC may decide that a practice is unfair simply because it violates public policy even if it does not meet these three tests. The Commission refused to allow a mail-order company to file collection suits in states far from where the defendants lived because the practice was unfair, whether or not it met the three tests.

What is the difference between *deceptive* and *unfair*? Consider this case: Audio Communications, Inc. (ACI) ran a telephone service for children. By dialing a 900 number, children could listen to recorded stories or games featuring characters such as Santa Claus and the Easter Bunny. ACI ran advertisements on children's TV shows and in children's magazines. The FTC held that the ads were *deceptive* because they did not reveal that the phone calls cost money. Moreover, the ads promised a free gift in return for one phone call. In reality, callers (who were, after all, young children) could not obtain a gift without following several complicated steps that were explained very rapidly. Often, more than one call was necessary to obtain the gift. This practice was also *unfair* because children often made the calls without parental permission. Parents (who paid the bill) had little control over children (who made the call). In its consent order, the FTC required ACI to include in all of its advertisements the following statement: "Kids, you must ask your mom or dad and get their permission before you call. This call costs money."[4]

CYBER*LAW*

The Internet opens the way to a brave new world of information. Whatever you want to know, you likely can find it on the Internet: The population of Tanzania? The weather in Beijing? The schedule of performances for the Spanish Riding School in Vienna? But information flows both ways. While you are downloading data from the Web, you may also be uploading all sorts of personal information. Some sites explicitly disclose that the price of admission is data about you. Other sites secretly place a cookie on your hard drive—not a chewy treat, but a file to store the information that you provide. When you revisit the site, it automatically enters your hard drive and opens the cookie file so that it knows who you are. Have you noticed that some Web sites greet you by name when you sign on? This feature can be a real convenience—no need to reenter your credit card number each time you place an order. But do you really want your credit card number—or your taste in music—floating in cyberspace?

Both private industry and the government are beginning to take small steps toward greater privacy protection. Some Web browsers have a feature that automatically notifies you whenever a Web site transmits a cookie to your hard drive. The Center for Democracy and Technology (http://www.cdt.org) filed a complaint with the FTC alleging that Intel, the microchip manufacturer, committed an unfair trade practice when it shipped the Pentium III chip. This chip came embedded with a serial number that could be used to identify the source of any Internet communications such as e-mail or online purchases. Intel thought the serial number would be helpful in controlling hackers and online fraud. When privacy advocates objected, Intel began shipping the chip with the serial number turned off. However, a clever hacker or webmaster might be able to activate the feature secretly. It turned out that Intel was not alone in using serial numbers to identify a source computer. The Windows operating system

---

[4] F.T.C., 56 C.F.R. 22432 (May 15, 1991).

automatically embedded a unique identifying number in every document created by Word or Excel. Microsoft, creator of Windows, agreed to eliminate the identifying number in subsequent software releases. Even video games played over a network automatically generate an ID number that enables the server to verify the authenticity of the software. The moral? Do not expect to be anonymous on the Internet.

The FTC continues to investigate the need for more privacy regulations to protect consumers. Meanwhile, the agency's Web site offers tips for protecting your privacy: *A Consumer's Guide to Travel in Cyberspace* (http://www.ftc.gov/bcp/conline/pubs/online/sitesee/index.html).

The European Union (EU) recently introduced a privacy law that is much tougher than U.S. regulations. Before a company in the EU can sell your personal data to another firm, it must ask your permission, tell you who will be receiving the information, and let you review the material so you can correct any errors.

Ordinarily, when the EU passes a law that is different from U.S. laws, both sides live and let live. That may not be possible in this case because the new statute prohibits companies in the EU from transmitting personal data to countries without adequate protection—such as the United States. This provision could force a change in the way many American companies routinely do business and strain trade relations between the United States and the EU.

OTHER SALES PRACTICES

BAIT AND SWITCH

FTC rules prohibit bait and switch advertisements: a merchant may not advertise a product and then disparage it to consumers in an effort to sell a different item. In addition, merchants must have enough stock on hand to meet reasonable demand for any advertised product. Sears, Roebuck and Co. ran many advertisements like the following:

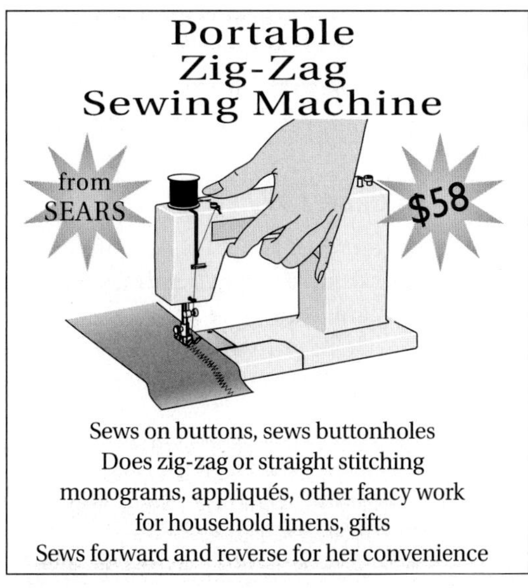

When eager customers went to buy this fabulous item, they were told that the machines were noisy, did not come with Sears's standard sewing machine guarantee, and could neither stitch in reverse nor do buttonholes. Also, the store was out of stock and would not be receiving any new machines for a long time.[5]

This is bait and switch advertising, and it violates FTC rules. The **bait** is an alluring offer that sounds almost too good to be true. Of course, it is. The advertiser does not wish to sell the advertised merchandise; it wants to **switch** consumers to another, higher-priced product. The real purpose of the advertisement is simply to find customers who are interested in buying.

MAIL OR TELEPHONE ORDER MERCHANDISE

Roughly 50 percent of American adults order from a catalogue each year. Before the FTC issued rules, catalogue companies often failed to deliver orders when promised. Now, only 5 percent of orders fail to meet the following **FTC guidelines on mail and telephone order merchandise:**

- Mail-order companies must ship an item within the time stated or, if no time is given, within 30 days after receipt of the order.
- If a company cannot ship the product when promised, it must send the customer a notice with the new shipping date and an opportunity to cancel. If the new shipping date is within 30 days of the original one, and the customer does not cancel, the order is still on.
- If the company cannot ship within 30 days of the original date, it must send the customer another notice. This time, however, the company must cancel the order unless the customer returns the notice, indicating that he still wants the item.

For example, Dell Computer Corp. advertised that its Dimension computer came with the "Dell Software Suite." In fact, for several months the suite was not available. Instead of the software, Dell sent customers a coupon for the suite "when available." The FTC charged Dell with violations of the mail or telephone order rules because the company:

- Knew it could not ship the software within 30 days
- Failed to offer buyers the opportunity to cancel their orders, and
- Did not cancel the orders automatically as it should have under the rules.[6]

UNORDERED MERCHANDISE

Under §5 of the FTC Act, anyone who receives unordered merchandise in the mail can treat it as a gift. She can use it, throw it away, or do whatever else she wants with it.

There you are, watching an infomercial for Anushka products, guaranteed to fight that scourge of modern life—cellulite! Rushing to your phone, you place

---

[5] *In re Sears, Roebuck and Co.*, 89 F.T.C. 229, 1977 FTC LEXIS 225 (1977).

[6] *United States v. Dell Computer Corp.*, 1998 FTC LEXIS 30 (1998).

an order. The Anushka cosmetics arrive, but for some odd reason, the cellulite remains. A month later another bottle arrives, like magic, in the mail. The magic spell is broken, however, when you get your credit card bill and see that, without your authorization, the company has charged you for the new supply of Anushka. Is this a hot new marketing technique? Not exactly. The FTC ordered the company to cease and desist this unfair and deceptive practice. The company improperly billed its customers, said the FTC, and should have notified them that they were free to treat the unauthorized products as a gift, to use or throw out as they wished.[7]

DOOR-TO-DOOR SALES

Consumers at home need special protection from unscrupulous salespeople. In a store, customers can simply walk out, but at home they may feel trapped. Also, it is difficult at home to compare products or prices offered by competitors. Under the FTC door-to-door rules, **a salesperson is required to notify the buyer that she has the right to cancel the transaction prior to midnight of the third business day thereafter.** This notice must be given both orally and in writing; the actual cancellation must be in writing. The seller must return the buyer's money within 10 days. The following news report illustrates an illegal method of selling magazine subscriptions.

A federal judge assessed a $50,000 civil penalty against a door-to-door magazine sales company. Customers who purchased magazine subscriptions from Tork & Associates were given (partial) receipts that misrepresented their right to cancel. The receipt indicated that a customer wishing to cancel was required to submit a copy of the complete receipt, the canceled check, the salesperson's name, the magazine name, the date of the transaction, and the total cost. Since the salesperson never gave the customer the complete receipt, it was difficult to comply. In two years, Tork generated $2 million in revenues.[8]

A vice-president of Grolier, the encyclopedia company, made the following statement:

> The proposition that a buyer should have the right to whimsically change his mind with respect to a transaction which has been formalized by an agreement containing all of the elements of a legally binding contract, is indeed, a revolutionary legal concept. This proposal represents an attack on the basic contractual concepts which are the foundation of the American economic system.[9]

Do you agree with this statement? Why is this executive so concerned about customers having three days to reconsider door-to-door sales?

---

[7] *In the Matter of Synchronal Corp.*, 116 F.T.C. 1190, 1993 FTC LEXIS 280 (1993).

[8] Nancy Stancill, "Door-to-Door Firm Hit with $50,000 Penalty," *Houston Chronicle*, Jan. 28, 1993, p. A17.

[9] Quoted in Douglas Whaley, *Problems and Materials on Consumer Law* (Boston: Little, Brown & Co., 1991), at p. 135.

CONSUMER CREDIT

Historically, the practice of charging interest on loans was banned by most countries and by three of the most prominent religions—Christianity, Islam, and Judaism. As the European economy developed, however, money lending became essential. To compromise, governments began to permit interest charges but limited the maximum rate to 6 percent. European settlers carried this concept to the United States, which soon adopted the 6 percent rule, too.

Even in modern times, most states limit the maximum interest rate a lender may charge. The New York usury statute permits rates as high as 25 percent, while the California limit is 12 percent. The penalty for violating usury statutes varies among the states. Depending upon the jurisdiction, the borrower may be allowed to keep (1) the interest above the usury limit, (2) all of the interest, or (3) all of the loan and the interest.

Before Congress passed the Truth in Lending Act (TILA), lenders found many creative methods to disguise the real interest rate and circumvent the law. For example, they would use a so-called add-on rate. That is, they would charge the permissible interest rate but would insist that the borrower begin to repay the loan in installments immediately. The borrower only had effective use of the money for half the term of the loan. Suppose that a car dealer loaned a customer $3,600 for three years, at 8 percent. The total interest would be $0.08 \times \$3,600 \times 3 =$ $864. If the borrower was required to repay $100 of the principal each month, she would be repaying half the loan within 18 months, but would still pay the full $864 in interest. This customer's real interest rate was 16 percent, not 8 percent.

TRUTH IN LENDING ACT

The problem with add-ons and other such devices designed to hide the real rate of interest from the authorities is that they also hide it from the borrower. Before TILA, many consumers had no idea what interest rate they were really paying. Congress passed the statute to ensure that consumers were adequately informed about credit terms before entering into a loan and could compare the cost of credit. TILA does not regulate interest rates or the terms of a loan; these are still set by state law. It simply requires lenders to *disclose* the terms of a loan in an understandable and complete manner.

TILA applies to a transaction only if all of the following tests are met:

- *It is a consumer loan.* That means a loan to an individual for personal, family, or household purposes but not a loan to a business. For example, TILA does not apply to a loan on a truck used to sell produce.
- *The loan has a finance charge or will be repaid in more than four installments.* Sometimes finance charges masquerade as installment plans. Boris can pay for his big-screen TV in six monthly installments of $200 each, or he can pay $900 cash up front. If he chooses the installment plan, he is effectively paying a finance charge of $300. That is why TILA applies to loans with more than four installments.
- *The loan is for less than $25,000 or secured by a mortgage on real estate.* If Boris borrows money to buy a $1 million house, TILA applies, but not if he buys a $50,000 yacht.

- *The loan is made by someone in the business of offering credit.* If Boris borrows $5,000 from his friend Ludmilla to buy a riding mower, TILA does not apply. If he borrows the money from Friendly Neighborhood Loan Depot, Inc., TILA does apply.

REQUIRED DISCLOSURE

In all loans regulated by TILA:

- *The disclosure must be clear and in meaningful sequence.* A finance company violated TILA when it loaned money to Dorothy Allen. The company made all the required disclosures but scattered them throughout the loan document and intermixed them with confusing terms that were not required by TILA.[10] A TILA disclosure statement should not be a game of *Where's Waldo?*
- *The lender must disclose the finance charge.* The finance charge is the amount, in dollars, the consumer will pay in interest and fees over the life of the loan. It is important for consumers to know this amount because otherwise they may not understand the real cost of the loan. Of course, the longer the loan, the higher the finance charge. Someone who borrows $5 for 10 years at 10 percent annual interest will pay $0.50 each year for 10 years, for a total finance charge of $5—equal to the principal borrowed. In 25-year mortgages, the finance charge will almost always exceed the amount of the principal.
- *The creditor must also disclose the annual percentage rate (APR).* This number is the actual rate of interest the consumer pays on an annual basis. Without this disclosure, it would be easy in a short-term loan to disguise a very high APR because the finance charge is low. Boris borrows $5 for lunch from his employer's credit union. Under the terms of the loan, he must repay $6 the following week. His finance charge is only $1, but his APR is astronomical—20 percent per week for a year.

All TILA loans must meet these three requirements. TILA requires additional disclosure for two types of loans—open-end credit and closed-end credit.

Open-End Credit. This is a credit transaction in which the lender makes a *series* of loans that the consumer can repay at once or in installments. The typical Visa or MasterCard account is open-end credit—the cardholder has a choice of paying his balance in full each month or making only the required minimum payment.[11] The lender must disclose credit terms in any advertisements. In addition, before beginning an open-end credit account, the lender must disclose to the consumer when a finance charge will be imposed and how the finance charge will be calculated (for example, whether it will be based on the account balance at the beginning of the billing cycle, the end, or somewhere in between). **In each statement, the lender must disclose the following:** the amount owed at the beginning of the billing cycle (the previous balance); amounts and dates of all purchases, credits and payments; finance charges; and the date by which

---

[10] *Allen v. Beneficial Fin. Co. of Gary*, 531 F.2d 797, 1976 U.S. App. LEXIS 12935 (7th Cir. 1976).

[11] Open-end credit rules apply to all consumer credit cards.

a bill must be paid to avoid finance charges. The Federal Reserve Board offers advice on choosing a credit card at http://www.federalreserve.gov/pubs/shop/.

Closed-End Credit. In a closed-end transaction, there is only one loan, and the borrower knows the amount and the payment schedule in advance. Boris enters into a closed-end transaction when he buys a $20,000 car and agrees to make specified monthly payments over five years. Before a consumer enters into a closed-end transaction, the lender must disclose the cash price; the total down payment; the amount financed; an itemized list of all other charges; the number, amount, and due dates of payments; the total amount of payments; late payment charges; penalties for prepaying the loan; and the lender's security interest in the item purchased.[12]

OTHER TILA PROVISIONS

Rescission. Under TILA, consumers have the right to rescind a mortgage for up to three business days after the signing. If the lender does not comply with the disclosure provisions of TILA, the consumer can rescind for up to three years from the date of the mortgage. Scam artists sometimes prey upon the elderly who are vulnerable to pressure and upon the poor who may not have access to conventional financing. These swindlers offer home equity loans, secured by a second mortgage, to finance fraudulent repairs. (There are, of course, many legitimate lenders in the home equity business.) The following news report shows scam artists at work.

Mack and Jacqueline Moon of East Baltimore hired a home improvement contractor to install a dropped ceiling, paneling, and cabinets in the unfinished basement of their rowhouse. The couple were determined not to put a second mortgage on their house, anticipating they would need backup money to pay medical expenses for their 10-year-old daughter who had lupus. They signed the contract a few days later after a second salesman assured them, "We were able to work it out, and you don't have to worry about a mortgage." The Moons were never given copies of the loan documents nor told of the 17 percent interest rate. A year later, when they tried to use their home's equity to pay medical bills for their daughter, who had since died, they discovered they had given a second mortgage to the lender without knowing it.[13]

The Moons were able to rescind the loan because the lender had not made adequate disclosure. This right of rescission does *not* apply to a *first* mortgage used to finance a home purchase or to any refinancing with the consumer's existing lender. The table on the following page summarizes the major provisions of TILA.

Advertising. TILA is meant to enable consumers to shop around and compare available financing alternatives. With this goal in mind, the statute requires lenders to advertise their rates accurately. A lender cannot "bait and switch";

---

[12] See Chapter 12, on secured transactions, for a discussion of security interests.

[13] Lorraine Mirabella, "With Hopes of Improving Their Homes, Many Owners Fall Prey to Loan Scams," *Baltimore Sun*, Sep. 4, 1994, p. 1K. Reprinted with permission.

TILA applies to a transaction only if:	• It is a consumer loan • The loan has a finance charge or will be repaid in more than four installments • The loan is for less than $25,000 or to secure a mortgage on real estate, and • The loan is made by someone in the business of offering credit.
In all loans regulated by TILA:	• The disclosure must be clear and in meaningful sequence, and • The lender must disclose the finance charge and the annual percentage rate (APR).
Consumers have the right to rescind a mortgage:	• For up to three business days after the signing, or • For up to three years from the date of the mortgage if the lender does not comply with TILA disclosure provisions. • This provision does not apply if the mortgage is a first mortgage used to finance a house purchase or a refinancing with the consumer's existing lender.

that is, it cannot advertise rates unless they are generally available to anyone who applies. Moreover, if the lender advertises any credit terms, it must tell the whole story. For example, if it advertises "Nothing down, 12 months to pay," it must also disclose the APR and other terms of repayment.

Enforcement. The FTC generally has the right to enforce TILA. In addition, consumers who have been injured by any violation (except for the advertising provisions) have the right to file suit.

Special Credit Card Rules. Your wallet is missing, and with it your cash, your driver's license, a photo of your dog, a coupon for a free video rental and—oh! no!—all your credit cards! It is a disaster, to be sure. But it could have been worse. There was a time when you would have been responsible for every charge the thief rang up. **Now, under TILA, you are liable only for the first $50 in charges the thief makes before you notify the credit card company.** If you call the company before any charges are made, you have no liability at all. But if, by the time you contact the company, the speedy robber has completely furnished her apartment on your card, you are still liable only for $50. Of course, if you carry a wallet full of cards, $50 for each one can add up to a sizable total.

Suppose that a credit card company mails a card to you that you did not order and someone steals it out of your mailbox. You know nothing about the card until the bills arrive. If you did not request the card, and it is not a renewal or substitute for a card you already have, you are not liable, even for the $50.

You use your credit card to buy a new computer at ShadyComputers. When you arrive home and start to load software, you discover the hard disk is only 1 gigabyte, not 20 gigabytes as advertised. The computer crashes six times the first day. In short, you have a major, $2,200 problem. But all is not lost. **In the event of a dispute between a customer and a merchant, the credit card company cannot bill the customer if** (1) she makes a good faith effort to resolve the dispute, (2) the dispute is for more than $50, and (3) the merchant is in the same state where she lives or is within 100 miles of her home.

What happens if the merchant and the consumer cannot resolve their dispute? Or if the merchant is not in the same state as the consumer? Clearly, credit card companies do not want to be caught in the middle between consumer and merchant. In practice, they now require all merchants to sign a contract specifying that, in the event of a dispute between the merchant and a customer, the credit card company has the right to charge back the merchant's account. If a customer seems to have a reasonable claim against a merchant, the credit card company will typically transfer the credit it has given the merchant back to the customer's account. Of course, the merchant can try to sue the customer for any money owed.

If the merchant agrees to provide a refund, it must send a credit notice to the credit card company within seven business days, and the credit card company must credit the customer's account within three business days.

Debit Cards. So your wallet is missing, and with it your debit card. No problem, right, it is just like a credit card? Wrong. Debit cards look and feel like credit cards, but legally they are a different plastic altogether. Debit cards work like checks (which is why they are also called **check cards**). When you use your debit card, the bank deducts money directly from your account, which means there is no bill to pay at the end of the month (and no interest charges on unpaid bills). That is the good news. The bad news is that your liability for a stolen debit card is much greater. If you report the theft within two days of discovering it, the bank will make good on all losses above $50. If you wait until after two days, your bank will only replace stolen funds above $500. After 60 days, all losses are yours: the bank will not repay any stolen funds.

FAIR CREDIT BILLING ACT

The Fair Credit Billing Act (FCBA) provides additional protection for credit card holders. Is there anyone in America who has not sometime or other discovered an error in a credit card bill? Before Congress passed the FCBA in 1975, a dispute with a credit card company often deteriorated into an avalanche of threatening form letters that ignored any response from the hapless cardholder. **Under the FCBA:**

- If, within 60 days of receipt of a bill, a consumer writes to a credit card company to complain about the bill, the company must acknowledge receipt of the complaint within 30 days.
- Within two billing cycles (but no more than 90 days) the credit card company must investigate the complaint and respond:
  - In the case of an error, by correcting the mistake and notifying the consumer
  - If there is no error, by writing to the consumer with an explanation.
- Whether or not there was a mistake, if the consumer requests it, the credit card company must supply documentary evidence to support its position—for example, copies of the bill signed by the consumer or evidence that the package actually arrived.

- The credit card company cannot try to collect the disputed debt or close or suspend the account until it has responded to the consumer complaint.
- The credit card company cannot report to credit agencies that the consumer has an unpaid bill until 10 days after the response. If the consumer still disputes the charge, the credit card company may report the amount to a credit agency but must disclose that it is disputed.

In the following case, American Express made a big mistake picking on a law professor. The court's opinion was written by Abner J. Mikva, a highly regarded judge on the federal appeals court. He was clearly exasperated by American Express's arguments and used strong language to reprimand the company—and the lower court. Since Judge Mikva had served in Congress, he could speak with some authority about Congress's approach to consumer legislation.

GRAY v. AMERICAN EXPRESS CO.

743 F.2d 10, 240 U.S. App. D.C. 10, 1984 U.S. App. LEXIS 19033
United States Court of Appeals for the District of Columbia Circuit, 1984

Facts: In December, Oscar Gray used his American Express credit card to buy airline tickets costing $9,312. American Express agreed that Gray could pay for the tickets in 12 monthly installments. In January, Gray paid $3,500 and then in February an additional $1,156. In March, American Express billed Gray by mistake for the entire remaining balance, which he did not pay. In April, Gray and his wife went out for dinner to celebrate their wedding anniversary. When he tried to pay with his American Express card, the restaurant told him that the credit card company had not only refused to accept the charges for the meal, but had instructed the restaurant to confiscate and destroy the card. While still at the restaurant, Gray spoke to an American Express employee on the telephone who informed him, "Your account is canceled as of now."

Gray wrote to American Express, pointing out the error. For more than a year, the company failed to respond to Gray or to investigate his claim. It then turned the bill over to a collection agency. Gray sued American Express for violating the Fair Credit Billing Act. The trial court granted summary judgment to American Express and dismissed the complaint on the grounds that Gray had waived his rights under the Act.

Issue: Is American Express liable to Gray for violating the Fair Credit Billing Act?

Excerpts from Judge Mikva's Decision: The contract between Gray and American Express provides: "We can revoke your right to use [the card] at any time. We can do this with or without cause and without giving you notice." American Express concludes from this language that the cancellation was not of the kind prohibited by the Act, even though the Act regulates other aspects of the relationship between the cardholder and the card issuer.

[T]he Act states that, during the pendency of a disputed billing, the card issuer shall not cause the cardholder's account to be restricted or closed because of the failure of the obligor to pay the amount in dispute. American Express seems to argue that, despite that provision, it can exercise its right to cancellation for cause unrelated to the disputed amount, or for no cause, thus bringing itself out from under the statute. At the very least, the argument is audacious. American Express would restrict the efficacy of the statute to those situations where the parties had not agreed to a "without cause, without notice" cancellation clause, or to those cases where the cardholder can prove that the sole reason for cancellation was the amount in dispute. We doubt that Congress painted with such a faint brush.

The effect of American Express's argument is to allow the equivalent of a "waiver" of coverage of the Act simply by allowing the parties to contract it away. Congress usually is not so tepid in its approach to consumer problems. The rationale of consumer protection legislation is to even out the inequalities that consumers normally bring to the bargain. To allow such protection to be waived by boiler plate language of the contract puts the legislative process to a foolish and unproductive task. A court ought not impute such nonsense to a Congress intent on correcting abuses in the market place.

The district court's order of summary judgment and dismissal is hereby *vacated*.

FAIR CREDIT REPORTING ACT

Gossip and rumor can cause great harm. Bad enough when whispered behind one's back, worse yet when placed in files and distributed to potential creditors. Most adults rely on credit—to acquire a house, credit cards, or overdraft privileges at the bank. A sullied credit report makes life immensely more difficult. The goal of the Fair Credit Reporting Act (FCRA) is to ensure that consumer credit reports are accurate.

The FCRA regulates **consumer reporting agencies**. These are businesses that supply consumer reports to third parties. If an insurance agency or bank conducts its own investigation to determine whether a consumer is creditworthy, the FCRA does not apply. A **consumer report** is any communication about a consumer's creditworthiness, character, general reputation, or lifestyle that is considered as a factor in establishing credit, obtaining insurance, securing a job, acquiring a government license, or for any other legitimate business need.

Under the FCRA:

- A consumer report can be used only for a legitimate business need, and a consumer reporting agency must be careful not to supply reports that will be used for any other purpose. A nosy neighbor does not have the right to order a report.
- A consumer reporting agency cannot report obsolete information. Ordinary credit information is obsolete after seven years, bankruptcies after 10 years. **Investigative reports** that discuss character, reputation, or lifestyle become obsolete in three *months*. Some commentators argue that the type of information contained in investigative reports is not relevant and should not be used at all. Although the FCRA does not limit the kinds of information that can be collected and reported, it does specify that an investigative report cannot be ordered without first informing the consumer.
- An employer cannot request a consumer report on any current or potential employee without the employee's permission. An employer cannot take action because of information in the consumer report without first giving the current or potential employee a copy of the report and a description of the employee's rights under this statute.
- Anyone who makes an adverse decision against a consumer because of a credit report must reveal the name and address of the reporting agency that supplied the information. An "adverse decision" includes denying credit or charging higher rates.
- Upon request from a consumer, a reporting agency must disclose all information in his file, the source of the information (except for investigative reports), the name of anyone to whom a report has been sent in the prior

year (two years for employment purposes), and the name of anyone who has requested a report in the prior year.

- If a consumer tells an agency that some of the information is incorrect, the agency must investigate and delete data that it finds to be untrue. The consumer also has the right to give the agency a short report telling his side of the story. The agency must then include the consumer's statement with any credit reports it supplies and also, at the consumer's request, send the statement to anyone who has received a report within six months (or two years for employment purposes).

The following article illustrates the usefulness of the FCRA.

Kimberly Dorcik wanted a new job. An assistant manager at a Lechters housewares store, she applied for the manager's position at Ups 'N Downs, a women's clothing store a dozen doors away in Solano Mall, in Fairfield, California. But her hopes for the job, which paid a few thousand dollars more than the $22,000 she was earning, vanished, she said, when the staff member taking her application whispered: "We're not supposed to tell anybody, but we pull credit reports on people. Is that going to be a problem?"

Ms. Dorcik remembers mumbling a noncommittal response, but she knew that it was going to be a problem. Three years earlier, when she was 19, she had had emergency surgery resulting from complications from pregnancy. Because of what she calls a clerical error, $30,000 in medical bills were still unpaid and in dispute, tainting her credit history. Ms. Dorcik did not get the job, and she said she was almost certain that the deciding factor was her credit history. The FCRA now requires employers to tell applicants like Ms. Dorcik if credit histories are being used as part of hiring. Employers will also have to obtain written permission from applicants before even requesting a credit history. If someone is turned down for a job and a credit report was used in the decision, the applicant can presumably weed out wrong information in the report and reapply.[14]

A recent survey revealed that 70 percent of credit reports contain errors. About one-third of the reports contain serious mistakes. Consumer advocates recommend that every year you check your credit reports from each of the three major reporting agencies: Equifax (800-685-1111; http://www.equifax.com), Experian (800-682-7654; http://www.experian.com/), and Trans Union (800-916-8800; http://www.transunion.com/). A report is free if you have been turned down for credit within 60 days; otherwise, it generally costs $8, although, in some states, it is free. If you find any errors, notify the agency in writing and warn it that failing to make corrections is a violation of the law. At http://www.ftc.gov/bcp/conline/pubs/credit/crdtdis.htm, the FTC offers advice on how to dispute credit report errors.

Also, under the Financial Services Modernization Act of 1999, banks must notify consumers before disclosing any personal information to a third party. The bank may not make the disclosure if the consumer objects. Moreover, it is

[14] Anthony Ramirez, "Name, Resumé, References. And How's Your Credit," *The New York Times*, Aug. 31, 1997, p. F8. Copyright © 1997 by The New York Times Co. Reprinted by permission.

illegal to use false pretenses to obtain information about a customer from a bank.

FAIR DEBT COLLECTION PRACTICES ACT

The introduction to the Fair Debt Collection Practices Act (FDCPA) states that "Abusive debt collection practices contribute to the number of personal bankruptcies, to marital instability, to the loss of jobs, and to invasions of individual privacy."[15] Congress did not mention it, but debt collection practices can also disrupt Super Bowl Sunday. Debt collectors want to catch their prey off guard, and what better time than when the entire nation is at home, glued to the television? If the phone rings, sports fans assume it is a friend calling to gab about the game.

Is that legal? It depends. The FDCPA provides that a collector must, within five days of contacting a debtor, send the debtor a written notice containing the amount of the debt, the name of the creditor to whom the debt is owed, and a statement that if the debtor disputes the debt (in writing), the collector will cease all collection efforts until it has sent evidence of the debt. **Also under the FDCPA, collectors may not:**

- Call or write a debtor who has notified the collector in writing that he wishes no further contact
- Call or write a debtor who is represented by an attorney
- Call a debtor before 8:00 a.m. or after 9:00 p.m.
- Threaten a debtor or use obscene or abusive language
- Call or visit the debtor at work if the consumer's employer prohibits such contact
- Imply that they are attorneys when they are not
- Threaten to arrest consumers who do not pay their debts
- Make other false or deceptive threats, that is, threats that would be illegal if carried out or which the collector has no intention of doing—such as suing the debtor or seizing property
- Contact acquaintances of the debtor for any reason other than to locate the debtor (and then only once), or
- Tell acquaintances that the consumer is in debt.

Of course, these rules do not prevent the collector from filing suit against the debtor. In the event of a violation of the FDCPA, the debtor is entitled to damages, court costs, and attorney's fees. The FTC also has authority to enforce the Act.

The following case illustrates the types of abuses that the FDCPA was designed to prevent.

---

[15] 15 U.S.C. §1692(a).

PITTMAN v. J. J. MAC INTYRE CO. OF NEVADA

969 F. Supp. 609, 1997 U.S. Dist. LEXIS 15826
United States District Court for the District of Nevada, 1997

Facts: Marijo Pittman defaulted on a $1,500 loan from the Boulder Dam Credit Union. J. J. Mac Intyre Co. tried to collect the loan for Boulder. Pittman reached a settlement with Boulder and then filed suit against Mac Intyre for violating the FDCPA. Mac Intyre filed a motion to dismiss Pittman's lawsuit. The details of Mac Intyre's activities are set out in the opinion of the court.

Issue: Did Mac Intyre violate the FDCPA?

Excerpts from Judge George's Decision: The FDCPA provides that a debt collector, without prior consent of the consumer, may not communicate with a consumer in connection with the collection of any debt at any unusual time or place or a time or place known or which should be known to be inconvenient to the consumer. Pittman alleges that on January 31, the defendant called her at her place of employment, in [an] effort to collect on the debt. The defendant's own account summary states that Pittman told the defendant that she could not talk at work. Pittman alleges that she had told this to the defendant many times prior. Notwithstanding the warning on January 31 and the alleged warnings on prior occasions, the defendant called the plaintiff again on September 7 at her place of employment to collect on the debt. This court finds that under this set of facts, plaintiff could be entitled to relief for the defendant's alleged violation.

Plaintiff also alleges that the defendant violated [the section] of the FDCPA which prohibits a debt collector from engaging "in any conduct the natural consequence of which is to harass, oppress, or abuse any person in connection with the collection of a debt." Plaintiff alleges that any of the three communications at issue constitutes a violation of this provision. [P]laintiff also could show, given the facts presented, that the defendant's calls on January 31 and September 7 to Pittman's work place were abusive and made for the purpose of harassment.

On August 14, plaintiff satisfied her debt directly with Boulder. Plaintiff alleges that the defendant's phone calls on September 7 and September 25 in which the defendant made further attempts to collect on the fully satisfied debt, violated the FDCPA [which] specifically prohibits "the false representation of the character, amount, or legal status of any debt." The defendant's primary argument is that it cannot be held liable for violation of these sections because the defendant had no knowledge that the plaintiff had satisfied the debt with the original creditor. [T]he defendant's own account summary has multiple entries stating that the plaintiff was making payments directly to Boulder. [U]nder these circumstances, a trier of fact could conclude that the conduct of the defendant was "unfair or unconscionable."

IT IS HEREBY ORDERED that defendant J. J. Mac Intyre Co., Inc.'s motion to dismiss is DENIED.

If a debt collector calls you, what can you do? First of all, be sure to write down his name and the name of the agency for which he works. Tell the caller that you are recording the conversation and then do so. Send a letter to the agency, requesting that it not contact you. Report any violations to the FTC at http://www.ftc.gov/bcp/conline/pubs/credit/fdc.htm.

EQUAL CREDIT OPPORTUNITY ACT

The Equal Credit Opportunity Act (ECOA) prohibits any creditor from discriminating against a borrower because of race, color, religion, national

origin, sex, marital status, age (as long as the borrower is old enough to enter into a legal contract), or because the borrower is receiving welfare. A lender must respond to a credit application within 30 days. If a lender rejects an application, it must either tell the applicant why or notify him that he has the right to a written explanation of the reasons for the rejection. The following news report illustrates the types of abuses that the ECOA is designed to prevent.

NEWSworthy

Florence and Joe made an offer to buy a new home at the Meadowood housing development near Tampa. The developer accepted their offer, contingent upon their obtaining a mortgage. When the couple filed an application with Rancho Mortgage and Investment Corp., they were surprised by the hostility of Rancho's loan processor. She requested information they had already supplied and repeatedly questioned them about whether they intended to occupy the house, which was about 80 miles from their jobs. Florence and Joe insisted they wanted to live near their son and daughter-in-law and escape city crime. Rancho turned down their mortgage, refusing to give either an oral or a written explanation. The house was sold to another buyer.

Joe and Florence didn't get mad, they got even. They sued under the ECOA. Rancho was ordered to pay the African American couple $35,000.[16]

In the following case, the lender asked a spouse to co-sign her husband's loan. Did this request violate the ECOA? You be the judge.

You be *the* Judge

AMERICAN SECURITY BANK, N.A. v. YORK
1992 U.S. Dist. LEXIS 14309
United States District Court for the District of Columbia, 1992

Facts: John York and Michael Lipson borrowed money several times from American Security Bank (ASB) to finance their business deals. When the two men met with their loan officer to request an additional $13.5 million, he told them that their wives would have to sign any additional loan. ASB imposed this requirement before undertaking any study of the two men's creditworthiness. Under the ASB's standards, York and Lipson were entitled to the loan on their own merits, without their wives' signatures. In granting the loan, ASB did not actually consider the wives' personal assets or the assets that each couple held jointly.

The two wives signed the loan, the two husbands defaulted, and ASB sued for payment. The two wives counter-claimed, alleging that ASB had violated the Equal Credit Opportunity Act and that, therefore, neither they nor their husbands were required to repay the loan. They also asked for damages. ASB filed a motion for summary judgment, asking the court to dismiss the counter-claim.

You be the Judge: Did ASB violate the Equal Credit Opportunity Act when it insisted that a wife guarantee her husband's loan? What is the appropriate remedy for a violation?

Argument for ASB: There was a time when banks and other lenders would not give credit to a married woman without her husband's permission. The purpose of the ECOA is to permit married women to obtain credit on their own. In this case, the two women are arguing that ASB violated the law by *giving* them credit. This interpretation stands the law on its head. They are taking a statute designed to prevent the *denial* of credit

[16] Robert J. Bruss, "Home Buyers Sue Mortgage Lender for Racial Discrimination," *Tampa Tribune*, Nov. 5, 1994, p. 3.

and saying it applies to the *granting* of a loan. That is clearly not what Congress had in mind.

Even if ASB did violate the ECOA, the loan is still valid. The two women may be entitled to some damages, but this is a $13.5 million loan. Surely, they are not suggesting that their damages for this technical violation equal $13.5 million. If ASB has violated the Act, the court should enforce the loan and impose modest damages.

Argument for Ms. York and Ms. Lipson: ASB misreads the ECOA. This statute prevents discrimination because of marital status. These two women had no connection to the loan except that they were married to the men who wanted to borrow money. The two women had no ownership interest in the business and played no role in the loan negotiations. If they had not been married, the ASB would never have asked them to sign the note. The bank discriminated on the basis of marital status when it demanded of a married woman what it would not have asked of a single person.

ASB asked the wives to sign before even checking their husbands' credit status. ASB has admitted that the two husbands were creditworthy on their own. If the men had not been married, ASB would have given them the loan. ASB asked the wives to sign, simply because they were there.

As for the damage question, if ASB had not violated the ECOA, the two wives would not have signed the loan and they would not now be liable. If they have to pay the loan, their damages are indeed $13.5 million.

CONSUMER LEASING ACT

If you, like many other consumers, lease a car rather than buy it, you are protected under the Consumer Leasing Act (CLA) as long as your lessor regularly leases items to individuals for personal use and the total payments under the lease do not exceed $25,000. The CLA does not apply to the rental of real property—that is, to house or apartment leases. **Before a lease is signed, a lessor must disclose the following in writing:**

- All required payments, including deposits, down payments, taxes, and license fees
- The number and amount of each monthly payment
- Balloon payments (that is, payments due at the end of the lease)
- Required insurance payments
- Available warranties
- Maintenance requirements
- Penalties for late payments
- The consumer's right to purchase the leased property
- The consumer's right to terminate a lease early
- Any penalties for early termination

MAGNUSON-MOSS WARRANTY ACT

When Senator Frank E. Moss sponsored the Magnuson-Moss Warranty Act, this is how he explained the need for such a statute:

> [W]arranties have for many years confused, misled, and frequently angered American consumers. . . . Consumer anger is expected when purchasers of consumer products discover that their warranty may cover a 25-cent part but not the $100 labor charge or that there is full coverage on a piano so long as it is shipped at the purchaser's expense to the factory. . . . There is a growing need to generate consumer understanding by clearly and conspicuously disclosing the terms and conditions of the warranty and by telling the consumer what to do if his guaranteed product becomes defective or malfunctions.[17]

The Magnuson-Moss Warranty Act does not require manufacturers or sellers to provide a warranty on their products. **The Act does require any supplier that offers a written warranty on a consumer product that costs more than $15 to disclose the terms of the warranty in simple, understandable language *before the sale*.** Required disclosure includes the following:

- The name and address of the warrantor
- The parts that are covered and those that are not
- What services the warrantor will provide, at whose expense, and for what period of time
- A statement of what the consumer must do and what expenses he must pay

Although suppliers are not required to offer a warranty, if they do offer one they must indicate whether it is *full* or *limited*. Under a **full warranty**, the warrantor must promise to fix a defective product for a reasonable time without charge; if, after a reasonable number of efforts to fix the defective product, it still does not work, the consumer must have the right to a refund or a replacement without charge; but the warrantor is not required to cover damage caused by the consumer's unreasonable use.

CONSUMER PRODUCT SAFETY

In 1969, the federal government estimated that consumer products caused 30,000 deaths, 110,000 disabling injuries, and 20 million trips to the doctor. Toys were among the worst offenders, injuring 700,000 children a year. Children were cut by Etch-a-Sketch glass panels, choked by Zulu gun darts, and burned by Little Lady toy ovens. Although injured consumers had the right to seek damages under tort law, Congress passed the Consumer Product Safety Act (CPSA) in 1972 to prevent injuries from occurring in the first place. This Act created the Consumer Product Safety Commission to evaluate consumer products and develop safety standards. The Commission can impose civil and criminal penalties on those who violate its standards. Individuals have the right to sue under the CPSA for damages, including attorney's fees, from anyone who knowingly violates a consumer product safety rule. You can find out about product recalls or file a report on an unsafe product at the Commission's Web site (http://www.cpsc.gov/).

---

[17] Quoted in David G. Epstein and Steve H. Nickles, *Consumer Law* (Eagan, Minn.: West, 1981).

In the following news report, an investigator for the Consumer Product Safety Commission describes his job.

I gather information on accidents through the newspapers, hospitals, and call-in complaints, and then I go out to investigate the people involved. The agency has a database, covering close to 100 hospital emergency rooms, which constantly key in data to determine when, where, and how accidents occur. If that information causes us to have suspicions that a product is dangerous, then we review corporate records to determine whether the company is in compliance with whatever law may apply. If our suspicions remain, then we collect a sample of the suspect product and submit it to our Washington, D.C. laboratory for engineering analysis. If the product is proven to be defective, we ask the company to recall the product, and if it should refuse, we have the authority to take further legal action. However, most companies want to comply. We do not get involved with people being reimbursed for having been ripped off or mistreated in any way. We represent the consumer public as opposed to the individual.[18]

CHAPTER CONCLUSION

Virtually no one will go through life without reading an advertisement, ordering from a catalogue, borrowing money, needing a credit report, or using a consumer product. It is important to know your rights.

CHAPTER REVIEW

1. The Federal Trade Commission (FTC) prohibits "unfair and deceptive acts or practices." A practice is unfair if it meets the following three tests:
   - It causes a substantial consumer injury.
   - The harm of the injury outweighs any countervailing benefit.
   - The consumer could not reasonably avoid the injury.
2. The FTC considers an advertisement to be deceptive if it contains an important misrepresentation or omission that is likely to mislead a reasonable consumer.
3. FTC rules prohibit bait and switch advertisements. A merchant may not advertise a product and then disparage it to consumers in an effort to sell a different item.
4. Consumers may keep as a gift any unordered merchandise that they receive in the mail.
5. Under the FTC door-to-door rules, a salesperson is required to notify the buyer that she has the right to cancel the transaction prior to midnight of the third business day thereafter.
6. In all loans regulated by the Truth in Lending Act (TILA), the disclosure must be clear and

[18] Beatrice Michaels Shapiro, "Product Safety Investigator," *Chicago Tribune*, Aug. 23, 1992, p. 33. Reprinted with permission.

in meaningful sequence. The lender must disclose the finance charge and the annual percentage rate.

7. Under TILA, consumers have the right to rescind a mortgage (other than a first mortgage) for three business days after the signing. If the lender does not comply with the disclosure provisions of TILA, the consumer may rescind for up to three years from the date of the mortgage.

8. Under TILA, a credit card holder is liable only for the first $50 in unauthorized charges made before the credit card company is notified that the card was stolen.

9. In the event of a dispute between a customer and a merchant, the credit card company cannot bill the customer if:
   - She makes a good faith effort to resolve the dispute
   - The dispute is for more than $50, and
   - The merchant is in the same state where she lives or is within 100 miles of her home.

10. Under the Fair Credit Billing Act, a credit card company must promptly investigate and respond to any consumer complaints about a credit card bill.

11. Under the Fair Credit Reporting Act:
    - A consumer report can be used only for a legitimate business need
    - A consumer reporting agency cannot report obsolete information
    - An employer cannot request a consumer report on any current or potential employee without the employee's permission, and
    - Anyone who makes an adverse decision against a consumer because of a credit report must reveal the name and address of the reporting agency that supplied the negative information.

12. Under the Fair Debt Collection Practices Act, a debt collector may not harass or abuse debtors.

13. The Equal Credit Opportunity Act prohibits any creditor from discriminating against a borrower on the basis of race, color, religion, national origin, sex, marital status, age, or because the borrower is receiving welfare.

14. The Magnuson-Moss Warranty Act requires any supplier that offers a written warranty on a consumer product costing more than $15 to disclose the terms of the warranty in simple and readily understandable language before the sale.

15. The Consumer Product Safety Commission evaluates consumer products and develops safety standards.

PRACTICE TEST

1. In August, Dorothy Jenkins went to First American Mortgage and Loan Association of Virginia (the Bank) to sign a second mortgage on her home. Her first mortgage was with a different bank. She left the closing without a copy of the required Truth in Lending Act disclosure forms. Jenkins defaulted on her loan payments, and, the following May, the Bank began foreclosure proceedings on her house. In June, she notified the Bank that she wished to rescind the loan. Does Jenkins have a right to rescind the loan 10 months after it was made?

2. **YOU BE THE JUDGE WRITING PROBLEM** Process cheese food slices must contain at least 51 percent natural cheese. Imitation cheese slices, by contrast, contain little or no natural cheese and consist primarily of water, vegetable oil, flavoring agents, and fortifying agents. Kraft, Inc. makes Kraft Singles, which are individually wrapped process cheese food slices. When Kraft began losing market share to imitation slices that were advertised as both less expensive and equally nutritious as Singles, Kraft responded with a series of advertisements designed to inform consumers that Kraft Singles cost more than imitation slices because they are made from five ounces of milk. Kraft does use five ounces of milk in making each Kraft Single, but 30

percent of the calcium contained in the milk is lost during processing. Imitation slices contain the same amount of calcium as Kraft Singles. Are the Kraft advertisements deceptive? **Argument for Kraft:** This statement is completely true—Kraft does use five ounces of milk in each Kraft Single. The FTC is assuming that the only value of milk is the calcium. In fact, people might prefer having milk rather than vegetable oil and flavoring agents, regardless of the calcium. **Argument for the FTC:** It is deceptive to advertise more milk if the calcium is the same after all the processing.

3. Joel Curtis was two and his brother, Joshua, was three years old when their father left both children asleep in the rear seat of his automobile while visiting a friend. His cigarette lighter was on the dashboard of the car. After awaking, Joshua began playing with the lighter and set fire to Joel's diaper. Do the parents have a claim against the manufacturer of the lighter under the Consumer Product Safety Act?

4. Josephine Rutyna was a 60-year-old widow who suffered from high blood pressure and epilepsy. A bill collector from Collections Accounts Terminal, Inc. called her and demanded that she pay $56 she owed to Cabrini Hospital Medical Group. She told him that Medicare was supposed to pay the bill. Shortly thereafter, Rutyna received a letter from Collections that stated:

   > You have shown that you are unwilling to work out a friendly settlement with us to clear the above debt. Our field investigator has now been instructed to make an investigation in your neighborhood and to personally call on your employer. The immediate payment of the full amount, or a personal visit to this office, will spare you this embarrassment.

   Has Collections violated the law?

5. Thomas Pinner worked at a Sherwin-Williams paint store that was managed by James Schmidt. Pinner and Schmidt had a falling out when, according to Pinner, "a relationship began to bloom between Pinner and one of the young female employees, the one Schmidt was obsessed with." Pinner quit. Schmidt claimed that Pinner owed the company $121.71 for paint he had taken but not paid for. Sherwin-Williams reported this information to Chilton, who ran a credit reporting agency. Pinner's attorney sent a letter to Chilton notifying him that Pinner disputed the accuracy of the Sherwin-Williams charges. Chilton contacted Schmidt who confirmed that Pinner's account remained delinquent. Chilton failed to note in Pinner's file that a dispute was pending. Thereafter, Pinner was denied credit cards at two stores. Have Schmidt and Chilton violated the Fair Credit Reporting Act?

6. Kathleen Carroll, a single woman, applied for an Exxon credit card. Exxon rejected her application without giving any specific reason and without providing the name of the credit bureau it had used. When Carroll asked for a reason for the rejection, she was told that the credit bureau did not have enough information about her to establish creditworthiness. In fact, Exxon had denied her credit application because she did not have a major credit card or a savings account, she had been employed for only one year, and she had no dependents. Did Exxon violate the law?

7. In October, Renie Guimond discovered that her credit report at TransUnion Credit Information Co. incorrectly stated that she was married, used the name "Ruth Guimond," and had a credit card from Saks Fifth Avenue. After she reported the errors, TransUnion wrote her in November to say that it had removed this information. However, in March, TransUnion again published the erroneous information. The following October, TransUnion finally removed the incorrect information from her file. Guimond was never denied credit because of these mistakes. Is TransUnion liable for violating the Fair Credit Reporting Act?

8. The National Coalition for Consumer Education and MasterCard International created the following quiz to help consumers

find out how smart they are about buying on credit:

(a) What's the best way to correct a mistake on your credit card bill?

(i) Call your credit card issuer immediately and explain the mistake.

(ii) Circle the mistake in red and return the bill to your card issuer.

(iii) Immediately write a letter to your credit card issuer and clearly describe the problem.

(b) How should you handle an unauthorized charge (a purchase that you didn't make) if you see one on your credit card statement?

(i) Write a letter to the company that accepted your card for payment to absolve yourself of any liability.

(ii) Call your credit issuer immediately to alert them.

(iii) Note the error on your credit card bill and refuse to pay it.[19]

9. Thomas Waldock purchased a 1983 BMW 320i from Universal Motors, Inc. It was warranted "to be free of defects in materials or workmanship for a period of three years or 36,000 miles, whichever occurs first." Within the warranty period, the car's engine failed and upon examination was found to be extensively damaged. Universal denied warranty coverage because it concluded that Waldock damaged the engine by overrevving it. Waldock vehemently disputed BMW's contention. He claimed that, while being driven at a low speed, the engine emitted a gear-crunching noise, ceased operation, and would not restart. Is Universal in violation of the law?

10.

GET ENOUGH BROADLOOM TO CARPET ANY AREA OF YOUR HOME OR APARTMENT UP TO 150 SQUARE FEET CUT, MEASURED, AND READY FOR INSTALLATION FOR ONLY $77. GET 100% DUPONT CONTINUOUS FILAMENT NYLON PILE BROADLOOM. CALL COLLECT

When customers called this number, New Rapids Carpet Center, Inc. sent salespeople to visit them at home to sell them carpet that was not as advertised—it was not continuous filament nylon pile broadloom, and the price was not $77. Has New Rapids violated a consumer law?

11. RIGHT & WRONG After TNT Motor Express hired Joseph Bruce Drury as a truck driver, it ordered a background check from Robert Arden & Associates. TNT provided Drury's Social Security number and date of birth, but not his middle name. Arden discovered that a Joseph *Thomas* Drury, who coincidentally had the same birth date as Joseph *Bruce* Drury, had served a prison sentence for drunk driving. Not knowing that it had the wrong Drury, Arden reported this information to TNT, which promptly fired Drury. When he asked why, the TNT executive merely stated, "We do not discuss these matters." Did TNT violate the law? Whether or not TNT was in violation, did its executives behave ethically? Who would have been harmed or helped if TNT managers had informed Drury of the Arden report?

INTERNET RESEARCH PROBLEMS

The Consumer Product Safety Commission (http://www.cpsc.gov) lists products that have

---

[19] "Give Yourself Some Credit if You Pass This Quiz," *Times-Picayune*, Apr. 7, 1994, p. E5. Permission granted by the Times-Picayune Publishing Corporation. All rights reserved. Reprinted with permission.

been recalled and provides consumers with a telephone number for contacting the manufacturer. Choose a recalled product and telephone the manufacturer to find out how it is handling the problem. Also see if you can find the manufacturer's Web site to learn if it has disclosed the recall there. What do you think of the manner in which the manufacturer has handled the recall? Is the manufacturer providing adequate protection to consumers?

You can find further practice problems in the Online Quiz at http://beatty.westbuslaw.com or in the Study Guide that accompanies this text.

ENVIRONMENTAL LAW

24

CHAPTER

"When my mother was left a widow almost 50 years ago, she taught school to support her family. A few years after my father's death, she took her savings and bought a small commercial building on a downtown lot in our little town in Oregon. The building, she said, would offer what my father couldn't—a source of support in her old age. In one half of the building was a children's clothing store, in the other a dry cleaners. The two stores served Main Street shoppers for years.

"Now the building that once represented security has produced a menace with the potential to bankrupt my mother. The discovery of contamination in city park well water triggered groundwater tests in the area. Waste products discarded by dry cleaners were identified as a likely source of contamination. Although a dry cleaner hasn't operated for 20 years on my mother's property, chemicals remain in the soil. Mother knew nothing of this hazard until a letter came from the Oregon Department of Environmental Quality. It said she should decide if she would oversee further testing and cleanup herself or if she would let the government handle it. In either case, my mother would pay the costs.

"The building is worth just under $70,000. Cleanup costs will be at least $200,000. At 84, my mother has enough savings to preserve her independence. She does not have enough money to bear the enormous costs of new community standards. The dry cleaner that operated in my mother's building disposed of chemicals the same way other dry cleaners did. None of these businesses was operated in a negligent fashion. They followed standards accepted by the community at the time. Now we are learning that we must live more carefully if we are to survive in a world that is safe and clean. My question is: Who will pay? Who will be responsible for cleaning up environmental messes made before we knew better?"[1]

INTRODUCTION

The environmental movement in the United States began in 1962 with the publication of Rachel Carson's book, *Silent Spring*. She exposed the deadly—and lingering—impact of DDT and other pesticides. These chemicals spread a wide web, poisoning not only the targeted insects, but the entire food chain—fish, birds, and even humans. Since Carson first sounded the alarm, environmental issues have appeared regularly in the news—everything from acute disasters such as the *Exxon Valdez* oil spill in Alaska to chronic concerns over pesticide residues in food. For more about Rachel Carson (and links to other environmental Web sites), visit http://www.rachelcarson.org/.

The environmental movement began with the fervor of a moral crusade. How could anyone be against a clean environment? It has become clear, however, that the issue is more complex. It is not enough simply to say, "We are against pollution." As the opening vignette reveals, the question is: Who will pay? Who will pay for past damage inflicted before anyone understood the harm that pollutants cause? Who will pay for current changes necessary to prevent damage now and in the future? Are car owners willing to spend $100 or $1,000 more per car to prevent air pollution? Are easterners ready to ban oil drilling in the Arctic National Wildlife Refuge in Alaska if that means higher prices for heating oil? Will loggers in the West give up their jobs to protect endangered species? Are all consumers willing to pay more to insulate their homes? George Bush, a Republican president, said, "Beyond all the studies, the figures, and the debates, the environment is a moral issue." But Newt Gingrich, a Republican Speaker of the House of Representatives, called the Environmental Protection Agency "the biggest job-killing agency in inner-city America."[2]

The cost-benefit trade-off is particularly complex in environmental issues because those who pay the cost often do not receive the benefit. If a company dumps toxic wastes into a stream, its shareholders benefit by avoiding the expense of safe disposal. Those who fish or drink the waters pay the real costs without receiving any of the benefit. Economists use the term ***externality*** to describe the situation in which people do not bear the full cost of their decisions. Externalities prevent the market system from achieving a clean environment on its own. Only government involvement can realign costs and benefits.

---

[1] Carolyn Scott Kortge, "Taken to the Cleaners," *Newsweek*, Oct. 23, 1995, p. 16. Reprinted with permission.

[2] Both men are quoted in Robert V. Percival, Alan S. Miller, Christopher H. Schroeder, and James P. Leape, *Environmental Regulation* (Boston: Little, Brown & Co., 1992), p. 1, and 1995 supp. p. 2.

ENVIRONMENTAL PROTECTION AGENCY

Thirty years ago, environmental abuses were (ineffectively) governed by tort law and a smattering of local ordinances. Now, environmental law is a mammoth structure of federal and state regulation. In 1970, Congress created the Environmental Protection Agency (EPA) to consolidate environmental regulation under one roof. Among government agencies, only the military is larger. When Congress passes a new environmental law, the EPA issues regulations to implement it. The agency can bring administrative enforcement action against those who violate its regulations. An administrative law judge (ALJ) within the agency hears these actions. Either party can appeal this decision to a United States Court of Appeals and, from there, to the Supreme Court. Those who violate environmental laws are liable for civil damages. In addition, some statutes, such as the Clean Water Act, the Resource Conservation and Recovery Act, and the Endangered Species Act, provide for *criminal* penalties, including imprisonment. The EPA is not shy about seeking criminal prosecutions of those who knowingly violate these statutes, and of those corporate officers who fail to prevent criminal negligence by their employees.

AIR POLLUTION

On October 26, 1948, almost half of the 10,000 people in Donora, Pennsylvania, fell ill from air pollution. A weather inversion trapped industrial pollutants in the air, creating a lethal smog. Twenty residents ultimately died. Although air pollution rarely causes this type of acute illness, it can cause or increase the severity of diseases that are annoying, chronic, or even fatal—such as pneumonia, bronchitis, emphysema, and cancer. Even apart from the health risks, air pollution can be irritating: it blocks visibility, damages car exteriors, and grimes windowsills.

There are three major sources of air pollution: coal-burning utility plants, factories, and motor vehicles. Residential furnaces, farm operations, forest fires, and dust from mines and construction sites also contribute. Local regulation is ineffective in controlling air pollution. For instance, when cities limited pollution from factory smokestacks, plants simply built taller stacks that sent the pollution hundreds, or even thousands, of miles away. Local governments had little incentive to prevent this long-distance migration. Recognizing the national nature of the problem, Congress passed three air pollution laws during the 1950s and 1960s. With little enforcement bite and no EPA to ensure implementation, these statutes had minimal impact.

CLEAN AIR ACT

Dissatisfied by this lack of progress, Congress passed the Clean Air Act of 1970. **The Clean Air Act has four major provisions:**

- **Primary Standards.** Congress directed the EPA to establish **national ambient air quality standards** (known as NAAQSs) for primary pollution, that is, pollution that harms the public health. The EPA's mandate was to set standards that protected public health and provided an adequate margin of safety *without regard to cost*. Pollution may not exceed these limits anyplace in the country. The EPA must regularly update the rules to reflect the latest scientific evidence.

- **Secondary Standards.** Congress also directed the EPA to establish NAAQSs for pollution that may not be a threat to health but has other unpleasant effects, such as obstructing visibility and harming plants or other materials.

- **State Implementation Plans (SIPs).** The Clean Air Act envisioned a partnership between the EPA and the states. After the EPA set primary and secondary standards, states would produce SIPs to meet the primary standards within three years and the secondary standards within a reasonable time. If a SIP was not acceptable, the EPA would produce its own plan for that state. In formulating their SIPs, states were required to identify the major sources of pollution. Each polluter would then be given a pollution limit to bring the area into compliance with national standards. The worse the pollution in a particular area, the tougher the regulations.

- **Citizen Suits.** The Clean Air Act (and many other environmental statutes) permits anyone to file suit against a polluter or against the EPA for failing to enforce the statute. Citizens have often been more assertive than the EPA in enforcing environmental statutes. For instance, the Arizona Center for Law in the Public Interest has sued the EPA more than a dozen times for failing to impose sufficiently strict air quality standards on Phoenix and Tucson.

Although air quality throughout the country has improved dramatically, a 1990 EPA study revealed that, 20 years after passage of the Clean Air Act, virtually every American was still breathing unsafe levels of some pollutants. In 1990, Congress amended the Act, setting more realistic goals but also higher penalties for failure. For instance, the deadline for Los Angeles was extended to 2010, but the penalty for noncompliance was increased—a cutoff of federal highway funds (a serious blow indeed in Los Angeles) and the threat of even stricter controls. Already, everything in California from lawn mowers to bakeries to barbecue grills is subject to increasingly strict standards. Recently, the city of Los Angeles asked the EPA for permission to weaken some of its antipollution regulations, such as required ride-share programs at shopping centers and sports arenas. The EPA rejected this request, however, and insisted on the tougher standards. Information about violations of the Clean Air Act is available online at http://www.EPA.gov/oeca/sfi.

In the following case, a power plant argued that the EPA had imposed a solution whose cost far outweighed its benefit. There is only one Grand Canyon. Should visibility there be preserved at any cost?

CENTRAL ARIZONA WATER CONSERVATION DISTRICT v. EPA

990 F.2d 1531, 1993 U.S. App. LEXIS 5881
United States Court of Appeals for the Ninth Circuit, 1993

Facts: In the Clean Air Act, Congress directed the EPA to issue regulations that would protect visibility at national landmarks. The Navaho Generating Station (NGS) is a power plant 12 miles from the Grand Canyon. In response to a citizen suit filed by the Environmental Defense Fund under the Clean Air Act, the EPA ordered NGS to reduce its sulfur dioxide emissions by 90 percent. To do so would cost NGS $430 million initially in capital expenditures and then $89.6 million annually. Average winter visibility in the Grand Canyon would be improved by at most 7 percent, but perhaps less. NGS sued to prevent implementation of the EPA's order. A court may nullify an EPA order if it determines that the agency action was arbitrary and capricious.

You be the Judge: **Did the EPA act arbitrarily and capriciously in requiring NGS to spend half a billion dollars to improve winter visibility at the Grand Canyon by at most 7 percent?**

Argument for NGS: This case is a perfect example of environmentalism run amok. Half a billion dollars for the chance of increasing winter visibility at the Grand Canyon by 7 percent? No rational person would choose to spend his own money that way, but the EPA is happy to spend NGS's. Winter visitors to the Grand Canyon would undoubtedly prefer that NGS provide them with a free lunch rather than a 7 percent improvement in visibility. The EPA order is simply a waste of money.

Argument for the EPA: Under the Clean Air Act, Congress instructed the EPA to protect visibility at national landmarks such as the Grand Canyon. How can NGS, or anyone else, measure the benefit of protecting a national treasure like the Grand Canyon? Even people who never have and never will visit it during the winter sleep better at night knowing that the Canyon is protected. NGS has been causing harm to the Grand Canyon, and now it should remedy the damage.

Courts generally defer to federal agencies, whose experts deal with similar problems all the time. The EPA has greater expertise in these matters than either NGS or this court.

Although the Clean Air Act reduced concentrations of some of the most harmful chemicals—carbon monoxide, sulfur dioxide, ground-level ozone—new scientific evidence indicated that the EPA standards were not strict enough. Even lower levels of these chemicals can cause health problems. In response to this new evidence, the EPA tightened its standards, predicting that stricter rules could save 20,000 lives a year and eliminate 250,000 cases of asthma. However, critics argued that the benefits of these regulations were too low to justify the enormous costs. They pointed to a recent study calculating that EPA regulations during the last 10 years cost about $50 million for each year of life saved. (In other words, for each $50 million spent, one person lives one year longer.) In contrast, home smoke alarms cost about $200,000 for each additional year of life, and mammograms for women over 50 cost a mere $17,000 for each year saved. The Clean Air Act directs the EPA to set air quality standards without regard to cost. How much is a year of life worth? What if it is your life?[3]

[3] "Clean Air, Dirty Fight," *The Economist*, Mar. 15, 1997, p. 29.

NEW SOURCES OF POLLUTION

Some states had air so clean that they could have allowed air quality to decline and still have met EPA standards. However, the Clean Air Act declared that one of its purposes was to "protect and enhance" air quality. Using this phrase, the Sierra Club sued the EPA to prevent it from approving any SIPs that met EPA standards but nonetheless permitted a decline in air quality. As a result of this suit, the EPA developed a prevention of significant deterioration (PSD) program. **No one may undertake a building project that will cause a major increase in pollution without first obtaining a permit from the EPA.** The agency will grant permits only if an applicant can demonstrate that (1) its emissions will not cause an overall decline in air quality and (2) it has installed the **best available control technology** for every pollutant.

The PSD program prohibits any deterioration in current air quality, *regardless of health impact*. In essence, national policy values a clean environment for its own sake, apart from any health benefits.

ACID RAIN

In some places, rain is now 10 times more acidic than it would naturally be. The results of acid rain are visible in the eastern United States and Canada—damaged forests, crops, and lakes. Acid is primarily created by sulfur emissions from large coal-burning utility plants in the Midwest. Many of these plants were built before the Clean Air Act, when the easiest way to meet state and local standards (while keeping electricity prices low) was to build tall stacks that would send the sulfur dioxide far away. Terrific for Ohio, not so wonderful for Maine.

The Clean Air Act banned the tall-stack solution, leaving coal plants, in theory, with two choices: install (expensive) scrubbers or buy (cheaper) low-sulfur western coal. Under pressure from members who represented states with high-sulfur coal, Congress compromised and required all power plants to install scrubbers regardless of the coal they burned. In this way, western coal would have no advantage.

In 1990, Congress amended the Clean Air Act to require power plants to cut their sulfur dioxide emissions by half. This time, however, Congress did not specify how the goal should be achieved and instead offered new methods for minimizing costs and maximizing economic efficiency. **Power plants have four options for meeting emissions standards: (1) installing scrubbers, (2) using low-sulfur coal, (3) switching to alternative fuels (such as natural gas), or (4) trading emissions allowances.** This last alternative requires some explanation. Each year, every utility receives an emissions allowance, meaning that it is allowed to emit a certain number of tons of pollutants. If a company does not need its entire allowance, because it uses cleaner fuels or has installed pollution control devices, it can sell the leftover allowance to other companies or stockpile the allowance for future use. Plants with high levels of pollution either buy more allowances or reduce their own emissions, depending on which alternative is cheaper. In effect, the government establishes the maximum amount of pollution, and then the market sets the price for meeting the national standard.

The market for sulfur dioxide emissions has become remarkably efficient and effective. Power plants now have a financial incentive to reduce pollution through innovation. In some years, pollution from sulfur dioxide has declined by as much as 25 percent, at a cost one-tenth the original estimate. For more information on the emissions trading program, click on http://www.epa.gov/acidrain/. This Web site reveals who has bought allowances and at what cost. Note that sometimes the highest bidders are organizations such as the Maryland Environmental Law Society, which buy emissions allowances simply to keep polluters from using them.

AUTOMOBILE POLLUTION

The Clean Air Act of 1970 directed the EPA to reduce automobile pollution levels by 90 percent within six years. Although the technology to achieve this goal did not then exist, Congress believed that the auto industry would, if forced, be able to develop the necessary innovations. This approach has been referred to as **technology forcing**, in the sense that the industry will be forced to develop the technology. Indeed, by 1975, General Motors developed a catalytic converter that not only reduced harmful emissions but improved fuel economy.

Although new cars are 97 percent cleaner than 1970 models, motor vehicles are still a major source of air pollution, releasing more than 50 percent of the hazardous pollutants in the air. Each car may be cleaner, but Americans are driving more—and bigger—cars more miles on more trips. During 1970, Americans traveled one trillion miles, but by 2000 the total had increased to four trillion miles. To counteract this increase, Congress has required oil companies to produce cleaner gasoline. It has also required automakers to build **low-emission vehicles**, such as cars powered by electricity or natural gas. The most polluted cities must also reduce auto use by encouraging car pools.

AIR TOXICS

Some pollutants are so potent that even tiny amounts cause harm. For instance, the EPA has never been able to establish a safe level of exposure to asbestos. Each year, 2.7 billion pounds of toxics spew into the air in the United States, causing an estimated annual increase of 3,000 cancer deaths. Because the Clean Air Act directed the EPA to set safety standards that provided an adequate margin of safety without regard to cost, the agency in theory has no choice except an outright ban on some pollutants. Such a ban would shut down the steel, chemical, and petroleum industries, among others. The EPA does not consider such a strategy to be politically viable.

The Environmental Defense Fund sued the EPA to force compliance with the law. Nevertheless, by 1990, the agency had proposed standards for only seven substances. Although these standards do not eliminate health risks, they are set at the lowest feasible level given existing technology. The courts have upheld these standards.

In 1990 amendments to the Clean Air Act, Congress directed the EPA to set standards for each of 189 specific pollutants and any other toxics the EPA wanted to include. The EPA may base these standards initially on the **maximum achievable control technology (MACT)**. Within eight years of developing MACT rules, the EPA must raise the standards to a level at which the risk of cancer from these substances is no more than one in one million over a lifetime. This two-step process is meant to create an incentive for polluters to continue to develop better technology.

Under the Clean Air Act, the EPA is required to create a Web site showing what would happen if an accident occurred at any of the 66,000 locations around the United States where dangerous chemicals are stored. But the Federal Bureau of Investigation and the Central Intelligence Agency are concerned that this worst-case data would enable a terrorist group to identify the most dangerous industrial sites in the United States with a few clicks on a laptop. The EPA's security consultants estimate that putting this information on a Web site would double the probability of a terrorist attack.

GLOBAL WARMING

Over the last 100 years, the average temperature worldwide has increased between 0.5° and 1.1°F. If current trends continue, the world's average temperature over the next 100 years will rise another 2° to 6°, producing the warmest climate in the history of humankind. (By comparison, the planet is only 5° to 9° warmer than during the last ice age.) The impact of this climate change is potentially catastrophic: a rise in sea level that would engulf coastal areas, a devastating decline in fishing stocks, the death of major forests, and a loss of farmland worldwide.

Global warming is the most complex environmental problem of the new millennium because its cause is uncertain and any solution requires international political cooperation coupled with major lifestyle changes. Very little is known about global warming with scientific certainty; much of the evidence is circumstantial. Most scientists now believe that certain gases—chlorofluorocarbons, carbon dioxide, methane, and nitrous oxide—create a greenhouse effect by trapping heat in the earth's atmosphere. Since the great epoch of industrialization began in the eighteenth century, the amount of these gases released into the atmosphere has increased dramatically, and the earth has also become strikingly warmer.

Skeptics argue, however, that the world naturally goes through cycles of heat and cold and it is simply in a heat cycle now. Moreover, they insist that we should have much clearer proof of the connection between the greenhouse gases and global warming before undertaking the major changes that any reduction would require—such as driving smaller cars on fewer trips or paying higher prices for gas and oil. The Energy Department has estimated that, to fight global warming effectively, U.S. gasoline prices would have to rise by as much as $1.91 a gallon and electricity prices might have to increase by 86 percent. Despite these doubts, a number of major corporations such as British Petroleum and DuPont have voluntarily reduced their emissions, arguing that the scientific evidence of global warming is alarming enough to justify immediate action. To see a skeptical view of global warming, click on http://www.globalwarming.org/index.html. A more balanced view is available at http://www.law.pace.edu/lawschool/env/energy/globalwarming.html.

In 1997, representatives of more than 150 countries met in Kyoto, Japan, to discuss reducing greenhouse gases. Many eyes turned toward the United States, which, with 5 percent of the world's population, consumes 25 percent of its energy—more than twice as much as the next industrial country. The United States ultimately signed the Kyoto Protocol, which requires the country to reduce emissions by 2012 to a level 7 percent below 1990 amounts.

Treaties are not binding in the United States until ratified by the Senate, however, and U.S. negotiators have said that they will not submit the treaty for ratification unless other countries develop a system of trading emissions like the one that has worked so well in the United States (see the discussion above under Acid Rain). Such a system would permit the United States to meet its goals by paying other nations to reduce their pollution to levels lower than the treaty requires. This plan makes economic sense because the cost of reducing pollution overseas, where few controls are in place, is four times cheaper than in the United States, where all the easy, inexpensive options have long since been implemented.

Opponents point out, however, that Ukraine and Russia are the only two countries that have met their Kyoto guidelines, and unfortunately, their success is the result of economic collapse not deliberate policy. Critics argue that the U.S. trading plan is simply a way to permit the United States to continue its polluting ways by paying off desperate Eastern European countries.

Developing countries such as India and China refused to make cuts in emissions or to commit to the trading plan. In their view, global warming has been caused by the excesses of rich countries, and any cure that involved poorer nations would unfairly hinder their economic growth.

WATER POLLUTION

One day, thousands of Milwaukeeans suddenly began to suffer nausea, cramps, and diarrhea. The suspected culprit? *Cryptosporidium*, a tiny protozoan that usually resides in the intestines of cattle and other animals. Ironically, the parasite may have entered Milwaukee's water supply at a purification plant on Lake Michigan. Officials suspect that infected runoff from dairy farms spilled into Lake Michigan near the plant's intake pipe. Doctors advised those with a damaged immune system (such as AIDS patients) to avoid drinking municipal water. Most Milwaukeeans were taking no chances—more than 800,000 switched to boiled or bottled water.

Polluted water can cause a number of loathsome diseases, such as typhus and dysentery. But by 1930, most American cities had dramatically reduced outbreaks of waterborne diseases by chlorinating their water. (The parasite that caused the Milwaukee outbreak is relatively immune to chlorine.) However, industrial discharges into the water supply have increased rapidly, with a visible impact on water quality. These industrial wastes may not induce acute illnesses like typhus, but they can cause serious diseases such as cancer. There is more at stake than health alone; clean water is valued for esthetics, recreation, and fishing.

CLEAN WATER ACT

In 1972, Congress passed a statute that is now called the Clean Water Act (CWA). This statute had two ambitious goals: (1) to make all navigable water suitable for swimming and fishing by 1983, and (2) to eliminate the discharge of pollutants into navigable water by 1985. Like the Clean Air Act, the CWA sets goals without regard to cost; leaves enforcement primarily to the states, with oversight by the EPA; and permits citizen suits. Also, like the Clean Air Act, the CWA's goals have not been met.

INDUSTRIAL DISCHARGES

The CWA prohibits any single producer from discharging pollution into water without a permit from the EPA. Before granting a permit, the EPA must set limits, by industry, on the amount of each type of pollution any single producer (called a **point source**) can discharge. These limits must be based on the **best available technology**. The EPA faces a gargantuan task in determining the best available technology that each industry can use to reduce pollution. Furthermore, standards become obsolete quickly as technology changes.

The CWA also requires the EPA to measure water quality broadly to determine if the permit system is working. Until clean water standards are met, every point source is held to the same standard, whether it is discharging into a clean ocean that can handle more pollution or a stagnant lake that cannot. Since determining the impact of a particular discharge may not be possible, especially when it is mingled with others, it is easier for the EPA to set the same standards for everyone. Easier and fairer—Congress did not want states to lure industry with promises of laxer pollution rules.

WATER QUALITY STANDARDS

The CWA requires states to set EPA-approved water quality standards and develop plans to achieve them. The first step in developing a plan is to determine how each body of water is used. Standards may vary depending upon the designated use—higher for recreational lakes than for a river used to irrigate farmland. No matter what the water's designated use, standards may not be set at a level lower than its current condition. Congress is not in the business of permitting more pollution.

States are supposed to pay special attention to so-called **non-point sources**, that is, pollutants with no single source, such as water runoff from agricultural land or city streets. This runoff may contain gasoline, pesticides, or bacteria. Congress left non-point source pollution to the states because it is so difficult to regulate. This regulation also involves complex issues such as land use planning that are, in theory, better handled at the local level than by national fiat. However optimistic Congress may have been, to date the states have not successfully implemented this section of the CWA. They appear to lack both the political will and the technological know-how, for which they are not totally to blame. Determining the impact of individual pollutants on the overall quality of a body of water used for many different purposes is a complex problem. Land use planning requires a delicate and volatile mix of consensus and control.

As the ambitious goals set by the CWA have not been met, Congress has granted numerous extensions. Evaluating progress under the statute depends upon one's perspective. The EPA, for instance, proudly announces on its Web site that whereas only a third of the nation's waters were safe for fishing and swimming in 1972, today two-thirds are safe (http://www.EPA.gov/owow/CWA/history.htm). Environmental advocates are less impressed. When the agency's own independent auditing branch examined environmental enforcement, it found widespread violations of the law. For instance, 75 percent of the streams in Missouri were not swimmable. Many environmental advocates have filed citizen suits to force the EPA to toughen its enforcement. In response to a suit by the Sierra Club, the federal court in Atlanta ordered the EPA to enforce the CWA more diligently.[4] In the following case, the American Canoe Association challenged the EPA for failing to enforce the CWA.

AMERICAN CANOE ASSOCIATION, INC. v. EPA

30 F. Supp. 2d 908, 1998 U.S. Dist. LEXIS 19785
United States District Court for the Eastern District of Virginia, 1998

Facts: The American Canoe Society sued the EPA for failing to require the state of Virginia to establish total maximum daily loads (TMDLs) for Virginia's waters. A TMDL is a plan assessing the reduction in pollution that is necessary to meet CWA standards. A TMDL also allocates responsibility among polluters for this reduction. The EPA contends that it is not required to take action until a state submits a TMDL, at which point it must approve or disapprove the plan. The EPA filed a motion to dismiss.

Issue: Does the CWA require the EPA to take action against a state that has not submitted a required plan?

Excerpts from Judge Ellis's Decision: Under EPA's reading of the statute, its duty to approve or disapprove TMDLs and promulgate its own lists in the event of disapproval is triggered only by the states' submission of TMDL lists. In EPA's view, inaction by states, for however long a period, imposes no duty on EPA. Plaintiffs respond that Virginia's failure to submit its TMDL lists by the 1979 deadline or in the nearly twenty years following constitutes a constructive submission that no TMDLs are required for the state's water, which the CWA compels EPA to disapprove as inadequate.

Under EPA's theory of the case, a statute creates a[n] enforceable duty only when it provides a date-certain deadline for agency action. Here, EPA alleges, no date-certain deadline exists. [T]he CWA appears to offer such a readily-ascertainable deadline. [It] provides that state TMDL lists must be submitted to the EPA no later than 180 days after EPA's publication of its first water pollutants list (June 26, 1979); that EPA must approve or disapprove the submissions within 30 days after that (July 26, 1979); and that if disapproved, the EPA must promulgate its own TMDL lists within 30 days (August 25, 1979). The deadline for EPA's approval or disapproval of state submissions would appear to be July 26, 1979.

EPA's alternative interpretation of the statute would allow recalcitrant states to short-circuit the Clean Water Act and render it a dead letter. It seems highly likely that Congress intended that EPA should be required to act not only when states promulgate lists that fail to meet the standards, but also when states completely ignore their mandatory statutory responsibilities and fail to promulgate any list at all. Here, the appropriate remedy for the plaintiffs' TMDL complaints would appear to be an order directing EPA to approve or disapprove Virginia's constructive submission within 30 days and, if the submission is disapproved, to proceed to promulgate its own lists.

WETLANDS

Wetlands are the transition areas between land and open water. They may look like swamps, they may even be swamps, but their unattractive appearance should not disguise their vital role in the aquatic world. They are natural

[4] *Sierra Club v. Hankinson*, 939 F. Supp. 872, 1996 U.S. Dist. LEXIS 13853 (N.D. Ga. 1996).

habitats for many fish and wildlife. They also serve as a filter for neighboring bodies of water, trapping chemicals and sediments. Moreover, they are an important aid in flood control because they can absorb a high level of water and then release it slowly after the emergency is past.

The CWA prohibits any discharge of dredge and fill material into wetlands without a permit. Although filling in wetlands requires a permit, many other activities that harm wetlands, such as draining them, do not. (However, many states require permits for draining wetlands.) Between 1975 and 1985, more than three million acres of wetlands were destroyed. In the following decade, only one million acres of wetlands disappeared. Although some people consider that to be good news, others view it as an ecological disaster. The government's official policy is no net loss of wetlands. Some scientists have recommended that the nation actually restore 10 million acres.

SEWAGE

Plumbing drains must be attached to either a septic system or a sewer line. A septic system is, in effect, a freestanding waste treatment plant. A sewer line, on the other hand, feeds into a publicly owned wastewater treatment plant, also known as a municipal sewage plant. Under the CWA, a municipality must obtain a permit for any discharge from a wastewater treatment plant. To obtain a permit, the municipality must first treat the waste to reduce its toxicity. However, taxpayers have stubbornly resisted the large increases in taxes or fees necessary to fund required treatments. Since the fines imposed by the EPA are almost always less than the cost of treatment, some cities have been slow to comply. The following news report illustrates the complex trade-offs between costs and benefits.

In the two years since Tom Cox took over as general manager of Constitution Marina, located in one of the sludgiest pockets of Boston's infamously sludgy Inner Harbor, he has seen an entire ecosystem reborn before his eyes. At the mouth of a now-sealed effluent pipe that once poured sewer waste directly into his anchorage, baby herring and krill shrimp feed. "This spring, for the first time in a decade, we even had porpoises in the Inner Harbor, and seals flopping onto my docks. Boston Harbor," Cox says, "is definitely back."[5]

Back? The Boston Harbor? The harbor that was gruesomely swamped with human waste during the disastrous crash of the old Deer Island treatment plant? The harbor that only a few years ago still reeked of 350 years of ill use?

The harbor has passed a vital milestone on its voyage from toilet bowl for 43 cities and towns to tourist attraction and recharging jobs engine. The new $183 million Deer Island sewage-treatment plant received a formal commission, and its predecessor, an obsolete and overburdened albatross that once channeled raw sewage directly in the bay, was bulldozed into dust.

This transformation has not come cheap. Sewer user charges for residents of the greater Boston area have risen more than 560 percent in the past decade, becoming among the highest in the country. These charges are expected to rise an additional 50 to 75 percent in the next few years. In protest, angry ratepayers dumped tea boxes full of sewer bills into the harbor.

---

[5] Tom Mashberg, "Harbor Cleans Up Its Act," *Boston Herald*, July 30, 1995, p. 1. Reprinted with permission of the Boston Herald.

OTHER WATER POLLUTION STATUTES

The Safe Drinking Water Act of 1974:

- Requires the EPA to set national standards for contaminants potentially harmful to human health that are found in drinking water
- Assigns enforcement responsibility to the states but permits the EPA to take enforcement action against states that do not adhere to the standards
- Prohibits the use of lead in any pipes through which drinking water flows, and
- Requires community water systems to send every customer an annual *consumer confidence report* disclosing the level of contaminants in the drinking water. (One can only hope that consumers will remain confident after receiving the report.) To find out more about your drinking water, turn on **http://www.epa.gov/ogwdw/dwinfo.htm**.

The **Ocean Dumping Act of 1972** prohibits the dumping of wastes in ocean water without a permit from the EPA.

Congress passed the **Oil Pollution Act of 1990** in response to the mammoth 1989 *Exxon Valdez* oil spill in Prince William Sound, Alaska. To prevent defective boats from leaking oil, this statute sets design standards for ships operating in U.S. waters. It also requires shipowners to pay for damage caused by oil discharged from their ships.

Although few would argue with the concept that those who spill ought to pay, there has been great controversy over how to measure damages. The U.S. government proposed that damages should be based on the subjective value that people assign to an injured area. Suppose that an oil spill prevents 1,000 people from using a beach. The government proposal would base the fine on the value that these people report (in a survey) that they place on a day of swimming or walking on the beach. If sea fowl are injured by the spill, nearby residents would be asked what they would be willing to pay to save a bird from death. Oil companies prefer to pay only the cost of fixing the damage. If 1,000 seagulls are killed by a spill, oil companies contend that the proper fine should equal the cost of cleaning up the area and increasing the number of seagulls. That might mean importing seagulls or augmenting their food supply.

WASTE DISPOSAL

The time is 1978. The place is 96th Street in Niagara Falls, New York. Six women are afflicted with breast cancer, one man has bladder cancer, another suffers from throat cancer. A seven-year-old boy suddenly goes into convulsions and dies of kidney failure. Other residents have chromosomal abnormalities, epilepsy, respiratory problems, and skin diseases. This street is three blocks away from Love Canal.

In 1945, Hooker Chemical Co. disposed of 21,800 tons of 82 different chemicals by dumping them into Love Canal or burying them nearby. An internal memorandum warned that this decision would lead to "potential future hazard" and be a "potential source of lawsuits." A year later, the company's lawyer wrote that "children in the neighborhood use portions of the water for swimming and, as a matter of fact, just before we left the site we saw several young children walking down the path with what appeared to be bathing costumes in hand." He suggested that Hooker build a fence around the canal, but the company never did. Instead, it sold the land to the local school board to build an elementary school. When the company's executive vice-president recommended against the sale, the company inserted a clause in the deed to eliminate the company's liability.

Schoolchildren tripped over drums of chemicals that worked their way up to the surface. Some children were burned playing with hot balls of chemical residue—what they called "fire stones"—that popped up through the ground. Homeowners noticed foul odors in their basements after heavy rains. Finally, a national health emergency was declared at Love Canal, and a joint federal-state program relocated 800 families. In 1994, Occidental Chemical Corp. (which had since bought Hooker) agreed to pay the state of New York $98 million to settle a lawsuit over Love Canal.[6] Two years later, the EPA settled its lawsuit with Occidental for $129 million.

In its time, what Hooker did was not unusual. Companies historically dumped waste in waterways, landfills, or open dumps. Out of sight was out of mind. Waste disposal continues to be a major problem in the United States. It has been estimated that the cost of cleaning up existing waste products will exceed $1 *trillion*. At the same time, the country continues to produce more than six billion tons of agricultural, commercial, industrial, and domestic waste each year. Ironically, air and water pollution control devices have added to the problem because the pollutants they remove from the air and water become waste that must be discarded somewhere.

Two major statutes regulate wastes. The Resource Conservation and Recovery Act (RCRA) focuses on *preventing* future Love Canals by regulating the production and disposal of solid wastes, both toxic and otherwise. The Comprehensive Environmental Response, Compensation, and Liability Act (CERCLA), also referred to as **Superfund**, focuses on *cleaning up* existing hazardous waste sites.

Resource Conservation and Recovery Act

The RCRA establishes rules for treating both hazardous wastes and other forms of solid waste (such as ordinary garbage).

Solid Waste

Before 1895, the city of New York did not collect garbage. Residents simply piled it up in the streets, causing the streets to rise five feet in height over the century. At present, each American generates 4.4 pounds of solid waste a day, an increase of 60 percent since 1960.

---

[6] William Glaberson, "Love Canal: Suit Focuses on Records from 1940s," *The New York Times*, Oct. 22, 1990, p. B1. Copyright © 1990 by The New York Times Co. Reprinted by permission.

But most Americans never gave much thought to their garbage until the infamous case of the garbage barge. The trouble arose in 1983 when the New York legislature banned new landfills (garbage dumps) on Long Island. Three years later, the landfill began to fill up in Islip, a bedroom community outside New York City. Lowell Herrelson, an Alabama businessman, offered to put the Islip garbage on a barge and ship it to another state. But once he filled the barge, no other state would take the garbage. Loaded with 3,186 tons of waste, the barge traveled over 6,000 miles in five months and was turned away by six states and three countries before returning to New York and anchoring near the Statue of Liberty. Its movements were reported daily in the newspapers and even became the subject of the *Tonight Show* monologue: "The only town to send its garbage on a 6,000 mile cruise." The garbage was ultimately burned in a Brooklyn incinerator, but not before Herrelson had lost $500,000 in the venture. Islip introduced recycling and built a $38 million garbage incinerator.

The disposal of nonhazardous solid waste has generally been left to the states, but they must follow guidelines set by the RCRA. **The RCRA**:

- Bans new open dumps
- Requires that garbage be sent to sanitary landfills
- Sets minimum standards for landfills
- Requires landfills to monitor nearby groundwater
- Requires states to develop a permit program for landfills; and
- Provides some financial assistance to aid states in waste management.

The federal Office of Management and Budget (OMB) objected to the solid waste regulations that the EPA intended to issue under the RCRA because, according to the OMB's calculations, complying with the proposed regulations would have cost more than $19 billion for every life saved. Not worth it, said the OMB. As a result, the EPA's revised regulations are more flexible than the original version.

The dispute between the EPA and the OMB typifies the ongoing conflict in environmental law. On the one hand, the EPA argues that scientific data are uncertain and the health risks of pollutants may be much worse than we realize. The EPA's goal is to stop pollution virtually without regard to cost. The OMB, on the other hand, prefers to base decisions on a numerical cost-benefit analysis. The OMB believes that a clean-air-and-water-for-its-own-sake approach makes little economic sense. Is a human life worth $19 billion?

UNDERGROUND STORAGE TANKS

Concerned that underground gasoline storage tanks were leaking into water supplies, Congress required the EPA to issue regulations for detecting and correcting leaks in existing tanks and establishing specifications for new receptacles. Anyone who owns property with an underground storage tank must notify the EPA and comply with regulations that require installation of leak detectors, periodic testing, and, in some cases, removal of old tanks.

IDENTIFYING HAZARDOUS WASTES

The EPA must establish criteria for determining what is, and is not, hazardous waste. It must then prepare a list of wastes that qualify as hazardous.

TRACKING HAZARDOUS WASTES

Anyone who creates, transports, stores, treats, or disposes of more than a certain quantity of hazardous wastes must apply for an EPA permit. All hazardous wastes must be tracked from creation to final disposal. They must be disposed of at a certified facility. Any company that generates more than 100 kilograms of hazardous waste in any month (roughly 200,000 firms nationwide) must obtain an identification number for its wastes. When it ships this waste to a disposal facility, it must send along a multicopy manifest that identifies the waste, the transporter, and the destination. The company must notify the EPA if it does not receive a receipt from the disposal site indicating that the waste has been received.

The penalties for violating the RCRA are serious, as the following case illustrates.

UNITED STATES v. KELLY
167 F.3d 1176, 1999 U.S. App. LEXIS 2093
United States Court of Appeals for the Seventh Circuit, 1999

Facts: Leo Kelly owned and operated a business that removed underground storage tanks. In a surprise inspection, the Wisconsin Department of Natural Resources (WDNR) discovered 150 rusted barrels leaking hazardous wastes onto Kelly's land. He refused to remove the barrels until the WDNR obtained a court order.

Later, CCF, Inc. hired Kelly to remove six underground storage tanks from its property. Small amounts of hazardous waste—gasoline, heating oil, diesel fuel, and sludge—remained in the tanks. Although the WDNR told Kelly to take the tanks to a licensed facility, Kelly instead sent them to Winter Auto Salvage, which does not sound like, and in fact was not, a licensed hazardous waste facility. A jury convicted Kelly of violating the RCRA, and the court sentenced him to 41 months in prison. Kelly appealed.

Issue: Did Kelly violate the RCRA?

Excerpts from Judge Coffey's Decision: At trial, Kelly put forth a "mistake of fact" defense and he attempted to establish that in spite of the fact that he had been warned and instructed to deposit the barrels at a site licensed to accept hazardous materials, he somehow mistakenly believed that the substance in the barrels was nothing but gasoline, which he admits is hazardous but, he avers, is not "waste," and thus is not governed by RCRA.

Kelley apparently would have us establish a rule that mandates [jury] instructions be given in a RCRA case which divides the term "hazardous waste" into two separate components, each with its distinct definition. We do not agree that this proposed division is required. What is necessary is that the jury find Kelly knowingly transported "hazardous waste" as defined by RCRA. The jury heard conflicting testimony on the issue of whether Kelly had knowledge of what was inside the barrels, and agreed with the government's position. It was a question of credibility for the jurors to decide, and they simply did not believe Kelly.

[Affirmed.]

SUPERFUND

In the vignette that opened this chapter, an elderly woman faced financial ruin from the cost of cleaning up pollutants that her dry cleaner tenants had left. The RCRA was designed to ensure safe disposal of current hazardous wastes. In contrast, the goal of Superfund (also known as CERCLA) is to clean up hazardous wastes that have been improperly dumped in the past.

Under CERCLA, anyone who has ever owned or operated a site on which hazardous wastes are found, or who has transported wastes to the site, or who has arranged for the disposal of wastes that were released at the site, is liable for (1) the cost of cleaning up the site, (2) any damage done to natural resources, and (3) any required health assessments.

In a "shovels first, lawyers later" approach, Congress established a $15.2 billion revolving trust fund (Superfund) for the EPA to use in cleaning up sites even before obtaining reimbursement from those responsible for the damage. Any reimbursements go into the trust fund to be used to repair other sites. The trust fund was initially financed by a tax on the oil and chemical industries, which produce the bulk of hazardous waste. Recently, however, the taxes expired, and Congress has thus far refused to renew them, thereby threatening the viability of the statute.

Since its creation in 1980, Superfund has been hugely controversial. President Carter signed the statute immediately before he left office, but the Reagan administration that followed largely ignored it. During its first five years, the EPA cleaned up only five sites. Congress then took action to strengthen enforcement. As a result, twice as many cleanups have been completed in the past 5 years as in the preceding 12. However, these cleanups cost more than $30 billion and have typically taken 11 years per site. Meanwhile, one in four Americans, including 10 million children below the age of 12, lives within 4 miles of a Superfund site.

Property owners have complained, and litigated, bitterly because:

- Current and former owners are liable, even though they did nothing illegal at the time, and indeed even if they did nothing more than own property where someone else dumped hazardous wastes. In addition, officers or controlling shareholders in closely held corporations can be personally liable for operations of the company.
- Polluters have joint and several liability—each polluter is responsible for the entire cost of cleaning up a site, even if it contributed only a portion of the pollution. A polluter can reduce its liability only by proving that it caused a smaller percentage of the damage, but that proof is often impossible.
- The expense of a Superfund cleanup can be devastating—higher than $100 million on some sites. Property owners have often viewed litigation as a better investment. More than 50 percent of total Superfund spending has gone to administrative and legal expenses.
- Congress requires that land be returned to pristine condition. Owners point to scientific evidence indicating that this goal is often impossible to achieve, given existing knowledge. Once again, cost-benefit analysis enters the

picture as property owners argue that the cost of perfection is higher than the benefit. To encourage redevelopment of contaminated land, the EPA has implemented a "Brownsfield" program that bases the cleanup levels for some property on potential risk to human health. However, Superfund proponents counter that, to be safe, all hazardous wastes should be removed. They offer as Exhibit A the Forrest Glen real estate development in upstate New York. The developers knew they could buy the land cheap because it had been used as a hazardous waste dump. Instead of cleaning it up, they slapped on a bucolic name. Now chemicals ooze up on lawns.

PREVENTIVE Law

Virtually any commercial real estate is at risk for Superfund liability. Before purchasing land, it is important to investigate whether it has ever been used to dispose of hazardous wastes. Consider testing the soil and groundwater. It might also be a good idea to ask the seller for indemnification against CERCLA liability or to purchase CERCLA insurance.

In the following case, the Supreme Court clarified an important issue of Superfund liability.

UNITED STATES v. BESTFOODS

524 U.S. 51, 118 S. Ct. 1876, 1998 U.S. LEXIS 3733
United States Supreme Court, 1998

Facts: Ott Chemical Co. was a wholly owned subsidiary of CPC International, Inc. Some of Ott's managers also worked directly for CPC. Ott littered the land around its chemical plant with thousands of leaking and exploding drums of hazardous waste, and the soil and water were saturated with noxious chemicals. The EPA estimated that the cost of cleaning up the site would be tens of millions of dollars. It filed suit under CERCLA against CPC. Ott was bankrupt.

The district court concluded that CPC was liable under CERCLA. The court of appeals reversed, holding that CPC was not liable for the actions of its subsidiary. The Supreme Court granted *certiorari*.

Issue: When is a parent liable under CERCLA for the actions of its subsidiary?

Excerpts from Justice Souter's Decision: It is a general principle of corporate law deeply ingrained in our economic and legal systems that a parent corporation is not liable for the acts of its subsidiaries. But there is an equally fundamental principle of corporate law, applicable to the parent-subsidiary relationship as well as generally, that the corporate veil may be pierced and the shareholder held liable for the corporation's conduct when the corporate form would otherwise be misused to accomplish certain wrongful purposes, on the shareholder's behalf. Nothing in CERCLA purports to rewrite this well-settled rule. The Court of Appeals was accordingly correct in holding that when (but only when) the corporate veil may be pierced, may a parent corporation be charged with CERCLA liability for its subsidiary's actions.

[However,] nothing in the statute's terms bars a parent corporation from direct liability for its own actions in operating a facility owned by its subsidiary. The question is not whether the parent operates the subsidiary, but rather whether it operates the facility, and that operation is evidenced by participation in the activities of the facility, not the subsidiary. The District Court emphasized the facts that CPC placed its own high-level officials on Ott's board of directors and in key management positions at Ott, and that those individuals made major policy decisions and conducted day-to-day operations at the facility. In imposing direct liability on these grounds, the District Court failed to recognize that it is entirely appropriate for directors of a parent corporation to serve as directors of its subsidiary, and that fact alone may not serve to expose the parent corporation to liability for its subsidiary's acts. The Government would have to show that, despite the general presumption to the contrary, the officers and directors were acting in their capacities as CPC officers and directors, and not as Ott officers and directors, when they committed those acts.

The District Court found that G.R.D. Williams, CPC's governmental and environmental affairs director, actively participated in and exerted control over a variety of Ott environmental matters. We think that these findings are enough to raise an issue of CPC's operation of the facility through Williams's actions. Prudence thus counsels us to remand for reevaluation of Williams's role, and of the role of any other CPC agent who might be said to have had a part in operating the facility.

It is so ordered.

The following article suggests one innovative solution to Superfund problems.

Wells, Maine—Michael Salmon looks through a high chain-link fence at a hazardous waste dump with a gaze that a cat might give to a caged canary. Mr. Salmon is part of a radical experiment here to end litigation among the parties believed to have sent their used motor oil to this dump. For a fee, his company, TRC Cos., Windsor, Connecticut, will assume the liability burdens of 397 major players in the case. Then TRC will schedule a site cleanup. When the slight, crew-cut 43-year-old vice-president for TRC looks through the fence, he is thinking about how his work crews can make a kind of cement out of the seven-foot thick piles of oil sludge layered under this birdless, weed-filled field and then bury the cement in an underground vault. In two years, he says, it will be a baseball field.

Until now, nobody has figured out how to stop this type of litigation. TRC's solution? Trim the number of liable parties to one. TRC agreed to take on everyone's liability—for a price. And an insurance company agreed to issue TRC a new type of environmental-insurance policy called a "cleanup-cost cap," to protect TRC against higher than expected cleanup costs. Lawyers say the basic cleanup costs are between $10 million and $15 million, with the insurance policy roughly double that. This summer, again assuming the final details are resolved, the lawyers will walk away from this case, leaving Mr. Salmon and his TRC crews to start the cleanup.[7]

CHEMICALS

More than 70,000 chemicals are used in food, drugs, cosmetics, pesticides, and other products. Some of these chemicals are known to accumulate in human tissue and cause, among other harm, cancer, birth defects, and neurological damage. A man born in the 1940s is twice as likely to develop cancer as his grandfather was. Many scientists believe that chemicals are a likely culprit for this increased risk. However, only 2 percent of these 70,000 chemicals have been

[7] John J. Fialka, "Maine Experiment May Point the Way to Ending Tangle of Litigation Around U.S. Superfund Law," *The Wall Street Journal*, Apr. 29, 1998, p. A24. Republished with permission of The Wall Street Journal; permission conveyed through the Copyright Clearance Center, Inc.

adequately tested to determine their total health impact. Almost 70 percent have not been tested at all. Scientists know virtually nothing about their impact on the health of wildlife.

Several federal agencies share responsibility for regulating chemicals. The Food and Drug Administration (FDA) has control over foods, drugs, and cosmetics. The Occupational Safety and Health Administration (OSHA) is responsible for protecting workers from exposure to toxic chemicals. The Nuclear Regulatory Commission (NRC) regulates radioactive substances. The EPA regulates pesticides and other toxic chemicals.

Federal Insecticide, Fungicide, and Rodenticide Act

The Federal Insecticide, Fungicide, and Rodenticide Act (FIFRA) requires manufacturers to register all pesticides with the EPA. Before registering a pesticide, the EPA must ensure that its benefits exceed its (then-known) risks. However, many of the 50,000 pesticides currently registered with the EPA were approved at a time when little was known about their risks. In 1972, Congress directed the EPA to reevaluate all registered pesticides and cancel those whose risks exceed their benefits. This process has been very slow. Before the EPA cancels a registration, the manufacturer is entitled to a formal hearing, which may take several years. In the event of an emergency, the EPA may order an immediate suspension; otherwise the chemical stays on the market until the hearing. If a pesticide is banned, the EPA must reimburse end users of the chemicals for their useless inventory.

Federal Food, Drug, and Cosmetic Act

The Federal Food, Drug, and Cosmetic Act requires the EPA to set maximum levels for pesticide residue in raw or processed food. The Food and Drug Administration can confiscate food with pesticide levels that exceed the EPA standards.

Food Quality Protection Act of 1996

The Food Quality Protection Act requires the EPA to set pesticide standards at levels that are safe for children. If the data for children are unclear, the EPA must reduce levels to one-tenth the amount now permitted in food. The EPA must also consider all sources of exposure. Thus, for example, in setting limits for pesticides on grapes, the EPA must factor in other sources of pesticides, such as drinking water.

This statute is highly controversial. The pesticide industry argues that the EPA could effectively ban many valuable chemicals for years while careful research into their impact on children is conducted. Environmental advocates, on the other hand, are dismayed that the EPA has not demanded more thorough research before setting standards for some pesticides.

Toxic Substances Control Act

The Toxic Substances Control Act (TSCA) regulates chemicals other than pesticides, foods, drugs, and cosmetics. For example, it regulates lead in gasoline and paints. **Before selling a new chemical (or an old chemical being used for a new purpose), the manufacturer must register it with the EPA.** As part of the registration process, the manufacturer must present evidence of the chemical's impact on health and the environment. The EPA may prohibit the manufacture, sale, or a particular use of any chemical that poses an unreasonable risk.

NATURAL RESOURCES

Thus far, this chapter has focused on the regulation of pollution. Congress has also passed statutes whose purpose is to preserve the country's natural resources.

NATIONAL ENVIRONMENTAL POLICY ACT

The National Environmental Policy Act of 1969 (NEPA) requires all *federal agencies* to prepare an *environmental impact statement* (EIS) for every major federal action significantly affecting the quality of the human environment. An EIS is a major undertaking—often hundreds, if not thousands, of pages long. It must discuss (1) environmental consequences of the proposed action, (2) available alternatives, (3) direct and indirect effects, (4) energy requirements, (5) impact on urban quality, historic, and cultural resources, and (6) means to mitigate adverse environmental impacts. Once a draft report is ready, the federal agency must hold a hearing to allow for outside comments.

The EIS requirement applies not only to actions *undertaken* by the federal government, but also to activities *regulated* or *approved* by the government. For instance, the following projects required an EIS:

- Expanding the Snowmass ski area in Aspen, Colorado—because approval was required by the Forest Service
- Adding a runway to the Sky Harbor airport in Tempe, Arizona
- Killing a herd of wild goats that was causing damage at the Olympic National Park (outside Seattle)
- Closing a road to create a beachside pavilion in Redondo Beach, California
- Creating a golf course outside Los Angeles—because the project required a government permit to build in wetlands.

The EIS process is controversial. If a project is likely to have an important impact, environmentalists almost always litigate the adequacy of the EIS. Industry advocates argue that environmentalists are simply using the EIS process to delay—or halt—any projects they oppose. In 1976, seven years after NEPA was passed, a dam on the Teton River in Idaho burst, killing 17 people and causing $1 billion in property damage. The Department of the Interior had built the dam in the face of allegations that its EIS was incomplete; it did not, for example, confirm that a large earth-filled dam resting on a riverbed was safe. To environmentalists, this tragedy graphically illustrated the need for a thorough EIS.

Researchers have found that the EIS process generally has a beneficial impact on the environment. The mere prospect of preparing an EIS tends to eliminate the worst projects. Litigation over the EIS eliminates the next weakest group. If an agency does a good faith EIS, honestly looking at the available alternatives, projects tend to be kinder to the environment, at little extra cost.

ENDANGERED SPECIES ACT

The Endangered Species Act (ESA):

- Requires the Secretary of Commerce or the Secretary of the Interior to prepare a list of species that are in danger of becoming extinct
- Requires the government to develop plans to revive these species
- Requires all federal agencies to ensure that their actions will not jeopardize an endangered species
- Prohibits any sale or transport of these species
- Makes any taking of an endangered animal species unlawful—taking is defined as harassing, harming, killing, or capturing any endangered species or modifying its habitat in such a way that its population is likely to decline—and
- Prohibits the taking of any endangered plant species on federal property.

No environmental statute has been more controversial than the ESA. In theory, everyone is in favor of saving endangered species. There are currently 632 endangered species (306 animals and 326 plants) on the U.S. list, and species are becoming extinct at 50 to 100 times the rate one would expect to occur naturally. To quote the House of Representatives Report on the ESA:

> As we homogenize the habitats in which these plants and animals evolved . . . we threaten their—and our own—genetic heritage . . . . Who knows, or can say, what potential cures for cancer or other scourges, present or future, may lie locked up in the structures of plants which may yet be undiscovered, much less analyzed?

In practice, however, the cost of saving a species can be astronomical. One of the earliest ESA battles involved the snail darter—a three-inch fish that lived in the Little Tennessee River. The Supreme Court upheld a decision under the ESA to halt work on a dam that would have blocked the river, flooding 16,500 acres of farmland and destroying the snail darter's habitat. To the dam's supporters, this decision was ludicrous: stopping a dam (on which $100 million in taxpayer money had already been spent) to save a little fish that no one had ever even thought of before the dam (or damn) controversy. The real agenda, they argued, was simply to halt development. Environmental advocates argued, however, that the wanton destruction of whole species will ultimately and inevitably lead to disaster for humankind. In the end, Congress overruled the Supreme Court and authorized completion of the dam. It turned out that the snail darter has survived in other rivers.

The snail darter was the first in a long line of ESA controversies that have included the spotted owl, the gnatcatcher, and the San Bruno Elfin butterfly, among others. Although the government pays out $227 million a year to enforce the ESA, and private citizens spend millions more, only about 55 species have revived enough to be delisted since 1973 when the statute was passed. Much time and money have been spent on litigation.

Recently, the government introduced the Habitat Conservation Plan (HCP) as a blueprint for compromise. In an HCP, developers agree to conserve some land in return for developing other property as they want. These deals contain a "no surprises" clause, meaning that the government has no right to retrieve land once it has been approved for development, even if scientists later determine that a particular species needs that habitat for survival. Unfortunately, the natural world is full of surprises, and environmentalists worry about the ultimate impact of these HCPs. In the short run, however, the success has been striking. For example, to save the gnatcatcher, a songbird found near San Diego, federal and local governments agreed to set aside 82,000 acres that they owned. They bought an additional 27,000 acres, at a cost of $300 million, and developers donated 63,000 acres more. In return, the developers earned the right to build on their remaining land without limitation. More than 16 million acres, including 10 percent of timberland in the Pacific Northwest, are now designated HCPs.

In the long run, the real issue is not how much land developers will give up, but how each of us will change our lifestyle. The government recently announced that nine wild salmon species in the Pacific Northwest are threatened. The Columbia River used to be home to 16 million salmon, but dozens of dams now block the river, interfering with the fish's annual migration. Fewer than a million salmon remain. The following article discusses some of the remedies that may be necessary to save the salmon.

NEWSworthy

With the salmon crisis, you step out the door and the rain that's running off your front lawn, awash in fertilizer, is a problem. You drive to work (alone) and you are adding to the oil and other chemicals that all eventually drain into the streams. You work for a company that wants to expand its offices into what is a salmon habitat, which describes just about every wetland within a day's drive of Seattle. At home, you turn on a light that is fed cheaply by the very dams that make it nearly impossible for salmon to swim upstream. For us to change this chain of events requires changing our lifestyles, which is something most Northwesterners have always seemed loath to do. We don't want anyone to tell us what to do with our lot size or with that instrument that is most integral to life here: the sport utility vehicle. All of a sudden being for the salmon means being against building a new home wherever you'd like, being for increased taxes, being prepared to change suburban life.

As this new debate begins, the phrase "putting salmon before people" will be heard over and over. Somehow the people need to line up behind the fish, that the fish are like the canary in the coal mine. Now, the salmon are making us look not just at what we can do with the rivers but at what we can do with the way we commute and choose our homes and shop and live. The question is, Will it be too much of a hassle for us to look at ourselves?[8]

---

[8] Robert Sullivan, "And Now, the Salmon War," *The New York Times*, Mar. 20, 1999, p. A15.

CHAPTER CONCLUSION

Environmental laws have a pervasive impact on our lives. The cost has been great—whether it is the higher price for cars with pollution control devices or the time spent filling out environmental impact statements. Some argue that cost is irrelevant, that a clean environment has incalculable value for its own sake. Others insist on a more pragmatic approach and want to know if the benefits outweigh the costs.

What benefits has the country gained from environmental regulation? Since 1970, when Congress created the EPA, the record on common air pollutants, such as lead, has been extraordinarily successful. Total emissions of lead nationwide have declined by 96 percent. Before 1970, emissions of sulfur dioxide had been increasing rapidly. Since then, in spite of strong economic growth and an increase in population, these emissions have dropped. Despite this progress, however, 107 million Americans live in areas that do not meet EPA quality standards.

As for water, wetland acreage continues to decline at a rapid rate. However, the number of Americans whose sewage goes to wastewater treatment facilities has increased from 85 million to 173 million. Two-thirds of the nation's waters are safe for fishing and swimming, up from only one-third when the Clean Water Act was passed.

Despite this progress, as a nation we still face many intractable problems. We have not developed a political consensus on global warming. The health effects of pesticides in our food supply are uncertain. Superfund and the Endangered Species Act are mired in a thornbush of litigation. One government agency concluded:

> Taken as a whole, environmental trends data suggest that over the past two decades the United States has been fairly successful in protecting and improving environmental quality when the existence of a problem has been widely recognized and the sources of the problem well defined. In cases where general recognition of a problem emerged slowly over time, or where the sources of a problem were diverse and widely dispersed, progress has been slow and painful, at best.[9]

If, after reading this chapter, you are concerned about the future of the environment, click on http://www.goldmanprize.org/ to read about people who have made a difference around the world. This Web site highlights winners of the Goldman Environmental Prize, an award that is given each year to six environmental heroes—one from each inhabited continent. The prizes are awarded for sustained and important efforts to preserve the environment.

[9] Council on Environmental Quality, Twentieth Annual Report (1990).

CHAPTER REVIEW

1. The following table provides a list of environmental statutes:

Air Pollution	Water Pollution	Waste Disposal	Chemicals	Natural Resources
Clean Air Act	Clean Water Act	Resource Conservation and Recovery Act	Federal Insecticide, Fungicide, and Rodenticide Act	National Environmental Policy Act
	Safe Drinking Water Act	Comprehensive Environmental Response, Compensation, and Liability Act (Superfund or CERCLA)	Federal Food, Drug, and Cosmetic Act	Endangered Species Act
	Ocean Dumping Act		Food Quality Protection Act	
	Oil Pollution Act		Toxic Substances Control Act	

2. Under the Clean Air Act of 1970, the Environmental Protection Agency must establish national ambient air quality standards for both primary and secondary pollution. States must produce implementation plans to meet the EPA standards.

3. Under the Clean Air Act, power plants may trade emission allowances.

4. The Clean Water Act prohibits the discharge of pollution into water without a permit from the EPA. States must set EPA-approved water quality standards and develop plans to achieve them. The Clean Water Act also prohibits any discharge of dredge and fill material into a wetland without a permit.

5. The Safe Drinking Water Act requires the EPA to set national standards for every contaminant potentially harmful to human health that is found in drinking water.

6. The Ocean Dumping Act prohibits the dumping of wastes in ocean water without a permit from the EPA.

7. The Oil Pollution Act of 1990 sets design standards for ships operating in U.S. waters and requires shipowners to pay for damage caused by oil discharged from their ships.

8. The Resource Conservation and Recovery Act establishes rules for treating hazardous wastes and other forms of solid waste.

9. Under CERCLA, anyone who has ever owned or operated a site on which hazardous wastes are found, or who has transported wastes to the site, or who has arranged for the disposal of wastes that were released at the site, is liable for (1) the cost of cleaning up the site, (2) any damage done to natural resources, and (3) any required health assessments.

10. The Federal Insecticide, Fungicide, and Rodenticide Act requires manufacturers to register all pesticides with the EPA.

11. The Federal Food, Drug, and Cosmetic Act requires the EPA to set maximum levels for pesticide residue in raw or processed food.

The Food Quality Protection Act requires the EPA to set pesticide standards at levels that are safe for children.

12. Under the Toxic Substances Control Act, manufacturers must register new chemicals with the EPA.
13. The National Environmental Policy Act requires all federal agencies to prepare an environmental impact statement for every major federal action significantly affecting the quality of the environment.
14. The Endangered Species Act prohibits activities that cause harm to endangered species.

PRACTICE TEST

1. Astro Circuit Corp. in Lowell, Massachusetts, manufactured printed circuit boards. David Boldt was in charge of the production line. In theory, the company pretreated its industrial waste to remove toxic metals, but, in practice, the factory was producing twice as much wastewater as the treatment facility could handle. The company often bypassed the treatment facility and dumped wastewater directly into the city sewer. Once, when caught by the city, Boldt wrote a letter implying that the violation was a temporary aberration. Boldt felt that he was caught "between the devil and the deep blue sea." It was his job to keep the production line moving, but he had no place to put the waste product. Has Boldt violated the law? What penalties might he face?
2. The U.S. Forest Service planned to build a road in the Nez Perce National Forest in Idaho to provide access to loggers. Is the Forest Service governed by any environmental statutes? Must it seek permission before building the road?
3. In 1963, FMC Corp. purchased a manufacturing plant in Virginia from American Viscose Corp., the owner of the plant since 1937. During World War II, the government's War Production Board had commissioned American Viscose to make rayon for airplanes and truck tires. In 1982, inspections revealed carbon disulfide, a chemical used to manufacture this rayon, in groundwater near the plant. American Viscose was out of business. Who is responsible for cleaning up the carbon disulfide? Under what statute?
4. Tariq Ahmad owned Shankman Laboratories. He decided to dispose of some of the lab's hazardous chemicals by shipping them to his home in Pakistan. He sent the chemicals to Castelazo & Associates (in the United States) to prepare the materials for shipment. Ahmad did not tell the driver who picked up the chemicals that they were hazardous. Nor did he give the driver any written documentation. Ahmad had packed the chemicals hurriedly in flimsy containers that were unsafe for transporting hazardous materials. He also grossly misrepresented to Castelazo the amount and type of hazardous material that he was shipping to Pakistan. Has Ahmad violated U.S. law? What penalties might he face?
5. Lead is a poison that has no known beneficial function in the body but can cause anemia, kidney damage, severe brain damage, and death. The EPA set national ambient air quality standards for lead at a level that would prevent the occurrence of erythrocyte protoprophyrin (EP) elevation in children. Although EP elevation by itself has no known adverse health effects, it is one of the first measurable indicators of exposure to lead. The Lead Industries Association challenged this standard in court, arguing that (1) the EPA did not have authority to set a standard based on EP elevation when there was no evidence that EP elevation caused harm, and (2) the EPA should have considered the devastating economic impact of its decision on industrial sources of lead emissions. How would you decide this case if you were the judge?

6. Why has the United States been more successful in controlling air pollution than water pollution?

7. Suppose that you are the manager of the General Motors HumVee plant in Mishawaka, Indiana. HumVees are the successor to the U.S. Army jeep and have become popular recreational vehicles among the rich and famous. Arnold Schwarzenegger has several. The HumVee requires special protective paint that reacts with other chemicals during the application process to create ozone, a pollutant. You want to increase production of HumVees. Are there any legal requirements you must observe, or can you simply increase production?

8. Alcan Aluminum Corp. manufactures aluminum sheet in Oswego, New York. It hired the Mahler Cos. to dispose of an emulsion used during the manufacturing process. This emulsion contained a variety of hazardous substances. Without Alcan's knowledge, Mahler dumped the emulsion into a borehole that connected to deep underground mines along the Susquehanna River in Pennsylvania. You can guess what happened next. Approximately 100,000 gallons of water contaminated with hazardous substances spilled from the borehole into the river. The EPA paid to clean up the river and then sued Alcan along with others who had hired Mahler for hazardous waste disposal. All other defendants settled. The court entered judgment against Alcan in the amount of $473,790.18, which was the difference between the full response costs the government had incurred in cleaning the river and the amount the government had recovered from the settling defendants. Is Alcan required to pay this amount?

9. In 1991, Illinois passed a statute requiring its four largest generating plants to install scrubbers so that they could continue using high-sulfur Illinois coal. What federal law was this Illinois statute designed to overcome? Extra credit question: On what grounds did a federal appeals court strike down the Illinois statute?

10. The marbled murrelet is a rare seabird that lives only in old-growth forests on the West Coast. Logging has destroyed so much of its habitat that its numbers in California have declined from 60,000 to between 2,000 and 5,000. Pacific Lumber Co. wanted to harvest trees from 137 acres of land it owned in the Owl Creek forest in California. It originally received approval to log, on the condition that it would cooperate with regulators to protect the murrelet. But the company sneaked in one weekend and cut down trees before it met the condition. Caught in the act, it promised no more logging until it had a plan to protect the birds. This time it waited until the long weekend over Thanksgiving to take down some more trees. Finally, a federal court ordered a permanent halt to any further logging. There was no evidence that the company had harmed the murrelet. Had it violated the law?

11. **RIGHT & WRONG** Geronimo Villegas owned a blood-testing lab in Brooklyn, New York. He threw vials of human blood from the lab into the Hudson River. A group of eighth graders on a field trip to Staten Island discovered 70 of these glass vials along the shore. Ten vials contained blood infected with the highly contagious hepatitis-B virus. Did Villegas violate the Clean Water Act? Why had Villegas disposed of the vials in this way? Whether or not he was in violation of the statute, was his behavior ethical? Did he violate any of the ethical tests from Chapter 2?

12. **YOU BE THE JUDGE WRITING PROBLEM** The Lordship Point Gun Club operated a trap and skeet shooting club in Stratford, Connecticut, for 70 years. During this time, customers deposited close to 5 million tons of lead shot and 11 million pounds of clay target fragments on land around the club and in Long Island Sound. Forty-five percent of sediment samples taken from the Sound

exceeded the established limits for lead. Was the Gun Club in violation of the RCRA? **Argument for the Gun Club:** The Gun Club does not *dispose* of hazardous wastes, within the meaning of the RCRA. Congress meant the statute to apply only to companies in the business of manufacturing articles that produce hazardous waste. If the Gun Club happens to produce wastes, that is only *incidental* to the normal use of a product. **Argument for the plaintiff:** Under the RCRA, lead shot is hazardous waste. The law applies to anyone who produces hazardous waste, no matter how.

INTERNET RESEARCH PROBLEMS

1. Using the information provided at http://www.globalwarming.org/index.htm and http://www.law.pace.edu/lawschool/env/energy/globalwarming.html, write an essay summarizing your views on global warming. What should our own government, and other governments, do? What should you do personally?

2. Choose a body of water located near you and look at http://www.EPA.gov/surf/locate/index.html to learn about its environmental health. Is the water more or less polluted than you expected?

You can find further practice problems in the Online Quiz at http://beatty.westbuslaw.com or in the Study Guide that accompanies this text.

APPENDIX A

THE CONSTITUTION OF THE UNITED STATES

Preamble

We the People of the United States, in Order to form a more perfect Union, establish justice, insure domestic Tranquility, provide for the common defence, promote the general Welfare, and secure the Blessings of Liberty to ourselves and our Posterity, do ordain and establish this Constitution for the United States of America.

ARTICLE I LEGISLATIVE DEPARTMENT

Section 1. Two Houses

All legislative Powers herein granted shall be vested in a Congress of the United States, which shall consist of a Senate and House of Representatives.

Section 2. House of Representatives

The House of Representatives shall be composed of Members chosen every second Year by the People of the several States, and the Electors in each State shall have the Qualifications requisite for Electors of the most numerous Branch of the State Legislature.

No Person shall be a Representative who shall not have attained to the Age of twenty five Years, and been seven Years a Citizen of the United States, and who shall not, when elected, be an Inhabitant of that State in which he shall be chosen.

Representatives and direct Taxes shall be apportioned among the several States which may be included within this Union, according to their respective Numbers, which shall be determined by adding to the whole Number of free Persons, including those bound to Service for a Term of Years, and excluding Indians not taxed, three fifths of all other Persons. The actual Enumeration shall be made within three Years after the first Meeting of the Congress of the United States, and within every subsequent Term of ten Years, in such Manner as they shall by Law direct. The number of Representatives shall not exceed one for every thirty Thousand, but each State shall have at Least one Representative; and until such enumeration shall be made, the State of New Hampshire shall be entitled to chuse three, Massachusetts eight, Rhode Island and Providence Plantations one, Connecticut five, New-York six, New Jersey four, Pennsylvania eight, Delaware one, Maryland six, Virginia ten, North Carolina five, South Carolina five, and Georgia three.

When vacancies happen in the Representation from any State, the Executive Authority thereof shall issue Writs of Election to fill such vacancies.

The House of Representatives shall chuse their Speaker and other Officers; and shall have the sole Power of Impeachment.

Section 3. Senate

The Senate of the United States shall be composed of two Senators from each State, chosen by the Legislature thereof, for six Years; and each Senator shall have one Vote.

Immediately after they shall be assembled in Consequence of the first Election, they shall be divided as equally as may be into three Classes. The Seats of the Senators of the first Class shall be vacated at the Expiration of the second Year, of the second Class at the Expiration of the fourth Year, and of the third Class at the Expiration of the sixth Year, so that one third may be chosen every second Year; and if Vacancies happen by Resignation or otherwise, during the Recess of the Legislature of any State, the Executive thereof may make temporary Appointments until the next Meeting of the Legislature, which shall then fill such Vacancies.

No Person shall be a Senator who shall not have attained to the Age of thirty Years, and been nine Years a Citizen of the United States, and who shall not, when elected, be an Inhabitant of that State for which he shall be chosen.

The Vice President of the United States shall be President of the Senate, but shall have no Vote, unless they be equally divided.

The Senate shall chuse their other Officers, and also a President pro tempore, in the Absence of the Vice President, or when he shall exercise the Office of President of the United States.

The Senate shall have the sole power to try all Impeachments. When sitting for that Purpose, they shall be an Oath or Affirmation. When the President of the United States is tried, the Chief Justice shall preside: And no Person shall be convicted without the Concurrence of two thirds of the Members present.

Judgment in Cases of Impeachment shall not extend further than to removal from Office, and disqualification to hold and enjoy any Office of honor, Trust or Profit under the United States: but the Party convicted shall nevertheless be liable and subject to Indictment, Trial, Judgment and Punishment, according to Law.

Section 4. Elections and Meetings of Congress

The Times, Places and Manner of holding Elections for Senators and Representatives, shall be prescribed in each State by the Legislature thereof: but the Congress may at any time by Law make or alter such Regulations, except as to the Places of chusing Senators.

The Congress shall assemble at least once in every Year, and such Meeting shall be on the first Monday in December, unless they shall by Law appoint a different Day.

Section 5. Powers and Duties of the Houses

Each House shall be the Judge of the Elections, Returns and Qualifications of its own Members, and a Majority of each shall constitute a Quorum to do Business; but a smaller Number may adjourn from day to day, and may be authorized to compel the Attendance of absent Members, in such Manner, and under such Penalties as each House may provide.

Each House may determine the Rules of its Proceedings, punish its Members for disorderly Behaviour, and, with the Concurrence of two thirds, expel a Member.

Each House shall keep a Journal of its Proceedings, and from time to time publish the same, excepting such Parts as may in their Judgment require Secrecy; and the Yeas and Nays of the Members of either House on any question shall, at the Desire of one fifth of those Present, be entered on the Journal.

Neither House, during the Session of Congress, shall, without the Consent of the other, adjourn for more than three days, nor to any other Place than that in which the two Houses shall be sitting.

Section 6. Prilileges of and Prohibitions upon Members

The Senators and Representatives shall receive a Compensation for their Services, to be ascertained by Law, and paid out of the Treasury of the United States. They shall in all Cases, except Treason, Felony and Breach of the Peace, be privileged from Arrest during their Attendance at the Session of their respective Houses, and in going to and returning from the same; and for any Speech or Debate in either House, they shall not be questioned in any other Place.

No Senator or Representative shall, during the Time for which he was elected, be appointed to any civil Office under the Authority of the United States, which shall have been created, or the Emoluments whereof shall have been encreased during such time; and no Person holding any Office under the United States, shall be a Member of either House during his Continuance in Office.

Section 7. Revenue Bills, Presdent's Veto

[1] All Bills for raising Revenue shall originate in the House of Representatives; but the Senate may propose or concur with Amendments as on other Bills.

[2] Every Bill which shall have passed the House of Representatives and the Senate, shall, before it becomes a Law- be presented to the President of the United States; If he approve he shall sign it, but if not he shall return t, with his Objections to the House in which it shall have originated, who shall enter the Objections at large on their journal, and proceed to reconsider it. If after such Reconsideration two thirds of that House shall agree to pass the Bill, it shall be sent, together with the Objections, to the other House, by which it shall likewise be reconsidered, and if approved by two thirds of that House, it shall become a Law. But in all such Cases the Votes of both Houses shall be determined by yeas and Nays, and the Names of the Persons voting for and against the Bill shall be entered on the Journal of each House respectively. If any Bill shall not be returned by the President within ten Days (Sundays excepted) after it shall have been present to him, the Same shall be a Law, in like Manner as if he had signed it, unless the Congress by their Adjournment prevents its Return, in which Case it shall not be a Law.

[3] Every Order, Resolution, or Vote to Which the Concurrence of the Senate and House of Representatives may be necessary (except on a question of Adjournment) shall be'presented to the President of the United States; and before the Same shall take Effect, shall be approved by him, or being disapproved by him, shall be repassed by two thirds of the Senate and House of Representatives, according to the Rules and Limitations prescribed in the Case of a Bill.

Section 8. Legislative Powers of Congress

The Congress shall have Power to lay and collect Taxes, Duties, Imposts and Excises, to pay the Debts and provide for the common Defence and general Welfare of the United States; but all Duties, Imposts and Excises shall be uniform throughout the United States;

To borrow Money on the credit of the United States;

To regulate Commerce with foreign Nations, and among the several States, and with the Indian Tribes;

To establish an uniform Rule of Naturalization, and uniform Laws on the subject of Bankruptcies throughout the United States;

To coin Money, regulate the Value thereof, and of foreign Coin, and fix the Standard of Weights and Measures;

To provide for the Punishment of counterfeiting the Securities and current Coin of the United States;

To establish Post Offices and post Roads;

To promote the Progress of Science and useful Arts, by securing for limited Times to Authors and Inventors the exclusive Right to their respective Writings and Discoveries;

To constitute Tribunals inferior to the supreme Court;

To define and punish Piracies and Felonies committed on the high Seas, and Offenses against the Law of Nations;

To declare War, grant Letters of Marque and Reprisal, and make Rules concerning Captures on Land and Water;

To raise and support Armies, but no Appropriation of Money to that Use shall be for a longer Term than two Years;

To provide and maintain a Navy;

To make Rules for the Government and Regulation of the land and naval Forces;

To provide for calling forth the Militia to execute the Laws of the Union, suppress Insurrections and repel Invasions;

To provide for organizing, arming, and disciplining, the Militia, and for governing such Part of them as may be employed in the Service of the United States, reserving to the States respectively, the Appointment of the Officers, and the Authority of training the Militia according to the discipline described by Congress;

To exercise exclusive Legislation in all Cases whatsoever, over such District (not exceeding ten Miles square) as may, by Cession of particular States, and the Acceptance of Congress, become the Seat of the Government of the United States, and to exercise like Authority over all Places purchased by the Consent of the Legislature of the State in which the Same shall be, for the Erection of Forts, Magazines, Arsenals, dock-Yards, and other needful Buildings;—And

To make all Laws which shall be necessary and proper for carrying into Execution the foregoing Powers, and all other Powers vested by this Constitution in the Government of the United States, or in any Department or Officer thereof.

Section 9 Prohibitions upon the United States

The Migration or Importation of such Persons as any of the States now existing shall think proper to admit, shall not be prohibited by the Congress prior to the Year one thousand eight hundred and eight, but a Tax or Duty may be imposed on such Importation, not exceeding ten dollars for each Person.

The Privilege of the Writ of Habeas Corpus shall not be suspended, unless when in Cases of Rebellion or Invasion the public Safety may require it.

No Bill of Attainder or ex post facto Law shall be passed.

No Capitation, or other direct, Tax shall be laid, unless in Proportion to the Census or Enumeration herein before directed to be taken.

No Tax or Duty shall be laid on Articles exported from any State.

No Preference shall be given by any Regulation of Commerce or Revenue to the Ports of one State over those of another; nor shall Vessels bound to, or from, one State, be obliged to enter, clear, or pay Duties in another.

No Money shall be drawn from the Treasury, but in Consequence of Appropriations made by Laws; and a regular Statement and Account of the Receipts and Expenditures of all public Money shall be published from time to time.

No Title of Nobility shall be granted by the United States: And no Person holding any Office of Profit or Trust under them, shall, without the Consent of the Congress, accept of any present, Emolument, Office, or Title, of any kind whatever, from any King, Prince, or foreign State.

Section 10. Prohibitions upon the States

No State shall enter into any Treaty, Alliance, or Confederation; grant Letters of Marque and Reprisal; coin Money; emit Bills of Credit; make any Thing but gold and silver Coin a Tender in Payment of Debts; pass any Bill of Attainder, ex post facto Law, or Law impairing the Obligation of Contracts, or grant any Title of Nobility.

No State shall, without the Consent of the Congress, lay any Imposts or Duties on Imports or Exports, except what may be absolutely necessary for executing its inspection Laws: and the net Produce of all Duties and Imposts, laid by any State on Imports or Exports, shall be for the Use of the Treasury of the United States; and all such Laws shall be subject to the Revision and Controul of the Congress.

No State shall, without the Consent of Congress, lay any Duty of Tonnage, keep Troops, or Ships of War in time of Peace, enter into any Agreement or Compact with another State, or with a foreign Power, or engage in War, unless actually invaded, or in such imminent Danger as will not admit of delay.

ARTICLE II EXECUTIVE DEPARTMENT

Section 1. Terms, Election, Qualifications, Salary, Oath of Office

The executive Power shall be vested in a President of the United States of America. He shall hold his Office during the Term of four Years, and, together with the Vice President, chosen for the same Term, be elected, as follows:

Each State shall appoint, in such Manner as the Legislature thereof may direct, a Number of Electors, equal to the whole Number of Senators and Representatives to which the State may be entitled in the Congress: but no Senator or Representative, or Person holding an Office of Trust or Profit under the United States, shall be appointed an Elector.

The Electors shall meet in their respective States, and vote by Ballot for two Persons, of whom one at least shall not be an Inhabitant of the same State with themselves. And they shall make a list of all the Persons voted for, and of the Number of Votes for each; which List they shall sign and certify, and transmit sealed to the Seat of the Government of the United States, directed to the President of the Senate. The President of the Senate shall, in the presence of the Senate and House of Representatives, open all the Certificates, and the Votes shall be counted. The Person having the greatest Number of Votes shall be the President, if such Number be a Majority of the whole Number of Electors appointed; and if there be more than one who have such Majority, and have an equal Number of Votes, then the House of Representatives shall immediately chuse by Ballot one of them for President; and if no Person have a Majority, then from the five highest on the List the said House shall in like Manner chuse the President. But in chusing the President, the Votes shall be taken by States, the Representation from each State having one Vote; A quorum for this Purpose shall consist of a Member or Members from two thirds of the States, and a Majority of all the States shall be necessary to a Choice. In every Case, after the Choice of the President, the Person having the greatest Number of Votes of the Electors shall be the Vice President. But if there should remain two or more who have equal Votes, the Senate shall chuse from them by Ballot the Vice President.

The Congress may determine the Time of Chusing the Electors, and the Day on which they shall give their Votes; which Day shall be the same throughout the United States.

No Person except a natural born Citizen, or a Citizen of the United States, at the time of the Adoption of this Constitution, shall be eligible to the Office of President; neither shall any Person be eligible to that Office who shall not have attained to the Age of thirty five Years, and been fourteen Years a Resident within the United States.

In Case of the Removal of the President from Office, or of his Death, Resignation, or Inability to discharge the Powers and Duties of the said Office, the Same shall devolve on the Vice President, and the Congress may by Law provide for the Case of Removal, Death, Resignation or Inability, both of the President and Vice President, declaring what Officer shall then act as President, and such Officer shall act accordingly, until the Disability be removed, or a President shall be elected.

The President shall, at stated Times, receive for his Services, a Compensation, which shall neither be encreased nor diminished during the Period for which he shall have been elected, and he shall not receive within that Period any other Emolument from the United States, or any of them.

Before he enter on the Execution of his Office, he shall take the following Oath or Affirmation:—"I do solemnly swear (or affirm) that I will faithfully execute the Office of President of the United States, and will to the best of my Ability, preserve, protect and defend the Constitution of the United States."

Section 2. President's Powers

The President shall be Commander in Chief of the Army and Navy of the United States, and of the Militia of the several States, when called into the actual Service of the United States; he may require the Opinion, in writing, of the principal Officer in each of the executive Departments, upon any Subject relating to the Duties of their respective Offices, and he shall have Power to grant Reprieves and Pardons for Offenses against the United States, except in Cases of Impeachment.

He shall have Power, by and with the Advice and Consent of the Senate, to make Treaties, providing two thirds of the Senators present concur; and he shall nominate, and by and with the Advice and Consent of the Senate, shall appoint Ambassadors, other public Ministers and Consuls, Judges of the supreme Court, and all other Officers of the United States, whose Appointments are not herein otherwise provided for, and which shall be established by Law: but the Congress may by Law vest the Appointment of such inferior Officers, as they think proper, in the President alone, in the Courts of Law, or in the Heads of Departments.

The President shall have Power to fill up all Vacancies that may happen during the Recess of the Senate, by granting Commissions which shall expire at the End of their next Session.

Section 3. President's Duties

He shall from time to time give to the Congress Information of the State of the Union, and recommend to their Consideration such Measures as he shall judge necessary and expedient; he may, on extraordinary Occasions, convene both Houses, or either of them, and in Case of Disagreement between them, with Respect to the Time of Adjournment, he may adjourn them to such Time as he shall think proper, he shall receive Ambassadors and other public Ministers; he shall take Care that the Laws be faithfully executed, and shall Commission all the Offices of the United States.

Section 4. Impeachment

The President, Vice President and all civil Officers of the United States, shall be removed from Office on Impeachment for, and Conviction of, Treason, Bribery, or other high Crimes and Misdemeanors.

ARTICLE III JUDICIAL DEPARTMENT

Section 2. Jurisdiction

The judicial Power of the United States, shall be vested in one supreme Court, and in such inferior Courts as the Congress may from time to time ordain and establish. The Judges, both of the supreme and inferior Courts, shall hold their Offices during good Behaviour, and shall, at Times, receive for their Services, a Compensation, which shall not be diminished during their Continuance in Office.

Section 2. Jurisdiction

The judicial Power shall extend to all Cases, in Law and Equity, arising under this Constitution, the Laws of the United States, and Treaties made, or which shall be made, under their Authority;—to all Cases affecting Ambassadors, other public Ministers and Consuls;—to all Cases of admiralty and maritime Jurisdiction;—to Controversies to which the United States shall be a Party;—to controversies between two or more States;—between a State and Citizens of another State;—between Citizens of different States;—between Citizens of the same State claiming Lands under Grants of different States; and between a State, or the Citizens thereof, and foreign States, Citizens or Subjects.

In all Cases affecting Ambassadors, other public Ministers and Consuls, and those in which a State shall be Party, the supreme Court shall have original Jurisdiction. In all the other Cases before mentioned, the supreme Court shall have appellate Jurisdiction, both as to Law and Fact, with such Exceptions, and under such Regulations as the Congress shall make.

The Trial of all Crimes, except in Cases of Impeachment, shall be by Jury; and such Trial shall be held in the State where the said Crimes shall have been committed; but when not committed within any State, the Trial shall be at such Place or Places as the Congress may by Law have directed.

Section 3. Treason

[1] Treason against the United States, shall consist only in levying War .igainit them, or in adhering to their Enemies, giving them Aid and Comfort. No Person shall be convicted of Treason unless on the Testimony of two Witnesses to the same overt Act, or on Confession in open Court.

[2] Congress shall have Power to declare the Punishment of Treason, but no of Treason shall work Corruption of Blood, or Forfeiture except during f the Person attainted.

ARTICLE IV RELATIONS OF STATES

Section 1. Full Faith and Credit

Full Faith and Credit shall be given in each State to the public Acts, Records, and judicial Proceedings of every other State. And the Congress may by general Laws prescribe the Manner in which such Acts, Records and Proceedings shall be proved, and the Effect thereof.

Section 2. Rights in One State of Citizens of Another

The Citizens of each State shall be entitled to all Privileges and Immunities of Citizens in the several States.

A Person charged in any State with Treason, Felony, or other Crime, who shall flee from Justice, and be found in another State, shall on Demand of the executive Authority of the State from which he fled, be delivered up, to be removed to the State having Jurisdiction of the Crime.

No Person held to Service or Labour in one State, under the Laws thereof, escaping into another, shall, in Consequence of any Law or Regulation therein, be discharged from such Service or Labour, but shall be delivered up on Claim of the Party to whom such Service or Labour may be due.

Section 3. New States, Territories

New States may be admitted by the Congress into this Union; but no new State shall be formed or erected within the Jurisdiction of any other State; nor any State be formed by the Junction of two or more States, or Parts of States, without the Consent of the Legislatures of the States concerned as well as the Congress.

The Congress shall have Power to dispose of and make all needful Rules and Regulations respecting the Territory or other Property belonging to the United States; and nothing in this Constitution shall be so construed as to Prejudice any Claims of the United States, or of any particular State.

Section 4. Protection Afforded to States by the nation

The United States shall guarantee to every State in this Union a Republican Form of Government, and shall protect each of them against Invasion; and on Application of the Legislature, or of the Executive (when the Legislature cannot be convened) against domestic Violence.

ARTICLE V PROISIONS FOR AMENDMENT

The Congress, whenever two thirds of both Houses shall deem it necessary, shall propose Amendments to this Constitution, or, on the Application of the Legislatures of two thirds of the several States, shall call a Convention for proposing Amendments, which, in either Case, shall be valid to all Intents and Purposes, as Part of this Constitution, when ratified by the Legislatures of three fourths of the several States, or by Conventions in three fourths thereof, as the one or the other Mode of Ratification may be proposed by the Congress; Provided that no Amendment which may be made prior to the Year One thousand eight hundred and eight shall in any Manner affect the first and fourth Clauses in the Ninth Section of the first Article; and that no State, without its Consent, shall be deprived of its equal Suffrage in the Senate.

ARTICLE VI NATIONAL DEBTS, SUPREMACY OF NATIONAL LAW, OATH

Section 1. Validity of Debts

[1] All Debts contracted and Engagements entered into, before the Adoption of this Constitution, shall be as valid against the United States under this Constitution, as under the Confederation.

Section 2. Supremacy of National Law

[2] This Constitution, and the Laws of the United States which shall be made in Pursuance thereof; and all Treaties made, or which shall be made, under the Authority of the United States, shall be the supreme Law of the Land; and the Judges in every State shall be bound thereby, any Thing in the Constitution or Laws of any State to the Contrary notwithstanding.

Section 3. Oaths of Office

[3] The Senators and Representatives before mentioned, and the Members of the several State Legislatures, and all executive and judicial Officers, both of the United States and of the Several States, shall be bound by Oath or Affirmation, to support this Constitution; but no religious Test shall ever be required as a Qualification to any Office or public Trust under the United States.

ARTICLE VII ESTABLISHMENT OF CONSTITUTION

The Ratification of the Conventions of nine States, shall be sufficient for the Establishment of this Constitution between the States so ratifying the Same.

Articles in addition to, and amendments of, the Constitution of the United States of America, proposed by Congress, and ratified by the Legislatures of the several states, pusuant to the Fifth Article of the original Constitution.

1ST AMENDMENT [1791] Freedom of Religion, Speech, Press, Assembly, and Petition

Congress shall make no law respecting an establishment of religion, or prohibiting the free exercise thereof; or abridging the freedom of speech, or the press; or the right of the people peaceably to assemble, and to petition the Government for a redress of grievances.

2ND AMENDMENT [1791] Right to Keep and Bear Arms

A well regulated Militia, being necessary to the security for a free State, the right of the people to keep and bear Arms, shall not be infringed.

3RD AMENDMENT [1791] Quartering of Troops

No Soldier shall, in time of peace be quartered in any house, without the consent of the Owner, nor in time of war, but in a manner to be prescribed by law.

4TH AMENDMENT [1791]

Search and Seizures

The right of the people to be secure in their persons, houses, papers, and effects, against unreasonable searches and seizures, shall not be violated, and no Warrants shall issue, but upon probable cause, supported by Oath or Affirmation, and particularly describing the place to be searched, and the persons or things to be seized.

5TH AMENDMENT [1791]

Criminal Proceedings, Eminent Domain

No person shall be held to answer for a capital, or otherwise infamous crime, unless on a presentment or indictment of a Grand Jury, except in cases arising in the land or naval forces, or in the Militia, when in actual service in time of War or public danger; nor shall any person be subject for the same offense to be twice put in jeopardy of life or limb; nor shall be compelled in any criminal case to be a witness against himself, nor be deprived of life, liberty, or property, without due process of law; nor shall private property be taken for public use, without just compensation.

6TH AMENDMENT [1791]

Criminal Proceedings

In all criminal prosecutions, the accused shall enjoy the right to a speedy and public trial, by an impartial jury of the State and district wherein the crime shall have been committed, which district shall have been previously ascertained by law, and to be informed of the nature and cause of the accusation; to be confronted with the Witnesses against him; to have compulsory process for obtaining witnesses in his favor, and to have the Assistance of counsel for his defence.

7TH AMENDMENT [1791]

Jury Trial in Civil Cases

In suits at common law, where the value in controversy shall exceed twenty dollars, the right of trial by jury shall be preserved, and no fact tried by a jury, shall be otherwise re-examined in any Court of the United States, than according to the rules of the common law.

8TH AMENDMENT [1791]

Excessive Punishments

Excessive bail shall not be required, no excessive fines imposed, nor cruel and unusual punishments inflicted.

9TH AMENDMENT [1791]

Unenumerated Rights

The enumeration in the Constitution, of certain rights, shall not be construed to deny or disparage others retained by the people.

10TH AMENDMENT [1791]

Powers Reserved to States

The powers not delegated to the United States by the Constitution, nor prohibited by it to the States, are reserved to the States respectively, or to the people.

11TH AMENDMENT [1791]

Suits against States

The judicial power of the United States shall not be construed to extend to any suit in law or equity, commenced or prosecuted against one of the United States by Citizens of another State, or by Citizens or Subjects of any Foreign State.

12TH AMENDMENT [1804]

Presidential, Vice Presidential Elections

The Electors shall meet in their respective states and vote by ballot for President and Vice-President, one of whom, at least, shall not be an inhabitant of the same state with themselves; they shall name in their ballots the person voted for as President, and in distinct ballots the person voted for as Vice-President, and they shall make distinct lists of all persons voted for as President, and of all persons voted for as Vice-President, and of the number of votes for each, which lists they shall sign and certify, and transmit sealed to the seat of the government of the United States, directed to the President of the Senate;—The President of the Senate shall, in the presence of the Senate and House of Representatives, open all the certificates and the votes shall then be counted;—The person having the greatest number of votes for President, shall be the President, if such number be a majority of the whole number of Electors appointed; and if no person have such majority, then from the persons having the highest numbers not exceeding three on the list of those voted for as President, the House of Representatives shall choose immediately, by ballot, the President. But in choosing the President, the votes shall be taken by states, the representation from each state having one vote; a quorum for this purpose shall consist of a member or members from two-thirds of the states, and a majority of all the states shall be necessary to a choice. And if the House of Representatives shall not choose a President whenever the right of choice shall devolve upon them, before the fourth day of March next following, then the Vice-President shall act as President, as in the case of the death or other constitutional disability of the President. The person having the greatest number of votes as Vice-President, shall be the Vice-President, if such number be a majority of the whole number of Electors appointed, and if no person have a majority, then from the two highest numbers on the list, the Senate shall choose the Vice-President; a quorum for the purpose shall consist of two-thirds of the whole number of Senators, and a majority of the whole number shall be necessary to a choice. But no person constitutionally ineligible to the office of President shall be eligible to that of the Vice-President of the United States.

13TH AMENDMENT [1865]

Slavery, Involuntary Servitude

Section 1. Neither slavery nor involuntary servitude, except as a punishment for crime whereof the party shall have been duly convicted, shall exist within the United States, or any place subject to their jurisdiction.

Section 2. Congress shall have power to enforce this article by appropriate legislation.

14TH AMENDMENT [1868]

Section 1. All persons born or naturalized in the United States, and subject to the jurisdiction thereof, are citizens of the United States and of the State wherein they reside. No State shall make or enforce any law which shall abridge the privileges or immunities of citizens of the United States; nor shall any State deprive any person of life, liberty, or property, without due process of law; nor deny to any person within its jurisdiction the equal protection of the laws.

Section 2. Representatives shall be appointed among the several States according to their respective numbers, counting the whole number of persons in each State, excluding Indians not taxed. But when the right to vote at any election for the choice of electors for President and Vice President of the United States, Representatives in Congress, the Executive and Judicial officers of a State, or the members of the Legislature thereof, is denied to any of the male inhabitants of such State, being twenty-one years of age, and citizens of the United States, or in any way abridged, except for participation in rebellion, or other crime, the basis of representation therein shall be reduced in the proportion which the number of such male citizens shall bear the whole number of male citizens twenty-one years of age in such State.

Section 3. No person shall be a Senator or Representative in Congress, or elector of President and Vice President, or hold any office, civil or military, under the United States, or under any State, who, having previously taken an oath, as a member of Congress, or as an officer of the United States, or as a member of any State legislature, or as an executive or judicial officer of any State, to support the Constitution of the United States, shall have engaged in insurrection or rebellion against the same, or given aid or comfort to the enemies thereof. But Congress may by a vote of two-thirds of each House, remove such disability.

Section 4. The validity of the public debt of the United States, authorized by law, including debts incurred for payment of pensions and bounties for services in suppressing insurrection or rebellion, shall not be questioned. But neither the United States nor any State shall assume or pay any debt or obligation incurred in aid of insurrection of rebellion against the United States, or any claim for the loss or emancipation of any slave; but all such debts, obligations and claims shall be held illegal and void.

Section 5. The Congress shall have power to enforce, by appropriate legislation, the provisions of this article.

15TH AMENDMENT [1870]

Right to Vote

Section 1. The right of citizens of the United States to vote shall not be denied or abridged by the United States or by any State on account of race, color, or previous condition of servitude.

Section 2. The Congress shall have power to enforce this article by appropriate legislation.

16TH AMENDMENT [1913]

Income Tax

The Congress shall have power to lay and collect taxes on incomes, from whatever source derived, without apportionment among the several States, and without regard to any census or enumeration.

17TH AMENDMENT [1913]

Election of Senators

The Senate of the United States shall be composed of two Senators from each State, elected by the people thereof, for six years; and each Senator shall have one vote. The electors in each State shall have the qualifications requisite for electors of the most numerous branch of the State legislatures.

When vacancies happen in the representation of any State in the Senate, the executive authority of each State shall issue writs of election to fill such vacancies; *Provided,* That the legislature of any State may empower the executive thereof to make temporary appointments until the people fill the vacancies by election as the legislature may direct.

This amendment shall not be construed as to affect the election or term of any Senator chosen before it becomes valid as part of the Constitution.

18TH AMENDMENT [1919]

Section 1. After one year from the ratification of this article the manufacture, sale, or transportation of intoxicating liquors within, the importation thereof into, or the exportation thereof from the United States and all territory subject to the jurisdiction thereof for beverage purposes is hereby prohibited.

Section 2. The Congress and the several States shall have concurrent power to enforce this article by appropriate legislation.

Section 3. This article shall be inoperative unless it shall have been ratified as an amendment to the Constitution by the legislatures of the several States, as provided in the Constitution, within seven years from the date of the submission hereof to the States by the Congress.

19TH AMENDMENT [1920]

The right of citizens of the United States to vote shall not be denied or abridged by the United States or by any State on account of sex.

Congress shall have power to enforce this article by appropriate legislation.

20TH AMENDMENT [1933]

Section 1. The terms of the President and Vice President shall end at noon on the 20th day of January, and the terms of Senators and Representatives at noon on the 3d day of January, of the years in which such terms would have ended if this article had not been ratified; and the terms of their successors shall then begin.

Section 2. The Congress shall assemble at least once in every year, and such meeting shall begin at noon on the 3d day of January, unless they shall by law appoint a different day.

Section 3. If, at the time fixed for the beginning of the term of the President, the President elect shall have died, the Vice President elect shall become President. If a President shall not have been chosen before the time fixed for the beginning of his term, or if the President elect shall have failed to qualify, then the Vice

President elect shall act as President until a President shall have qualified; and the Congress may by law provide for the case wherein neither a President elect nor a Vice President elect shall have qualified, declaring who shall then act as President, or the manner in which one who is to act shall be selected, and such person shall act accordingly until a President or Vice President shall have qualified.

Section 4. The Congress may by law provide for the case of the death of any of the persons from whom the House of Representatives may choose a President whenever the right of choice shall have devolved upon them, and for the case of the death of any of the persons from whom the Senate may choose a Vice President whenever the right of choice shall have devolved upon them.

Section 5. Sections 1 and 2 shall take effect on the 15th day of October following the ratification of this article.

Section 6. This article shall be inoperative unless it shall have been ratified as an amendment to the Constitution by the legislatures of three-fourths of the several States within seven years from the date of its submission.

21ST AMENDMENT [1933]

Section 1. No person shall be elected to the office of the President more than twice, and no person who has held the office of President, or acted as President, for more than two years of a term to which some other person was elected President shall be elected to the office of the President more than once. But this Article shall not apply to any person holding the office of President when this Article was proposed by the Congress, and shall not prevent any person who may be holding the office of President, or acting as President, during the term within which this Article becomes operative from holding the office of President, or acting as President during the remainder of such term.

Section 2. This article shall be inoperative unless it shall have been ratified as an amendment to the Constitution by the legislatures of three-fourths of the several States within seven years from the date of its submission to the States by the Congress.

22ND AMENDMENT [1951]

Section 1. No person shall be elected to the office of the President more than twice, and no person who has held the office of President, or acted as President, for more than two years of a term to which some other person was elected President shall be elected to the office of the President more than once. But this Article shall not apply to any person holding the office of President when this Article was proposed by the Congress, and shall not prevent any person who may be holding the office of President, or acting as President, during the term within which this Article becomes operative from holding the office of President, or acting as President during the remainder of such term.

Section 2. This article shall be inoperative unless it shall have been ratified as an amendment to the Constitution by the legislatures of three-fourths of the several States within seven years from the date of its submission to the States by the Congress.

23RD AMENDMENT [1961]

Section 1. The District constituting the seat of Government of the United States shall appoint in such manner as the Congress may direct:

A number of electors of President and Vice President equal to the whole number of Senators and Representatives in Congress to which the District would be entitled if it were a State, but in no event more than the least populous State; they shall be in addition to those appointed by the States, but they shall be considered, for the purposes of the election of President and Vice President, to be electors appointed by a State; and they shall meet in the District and perform such duties as provided by the twelfth article of amendment.

Section 2. The Congress shall have power to enforce this article by appropriate legislation.

24TH AMENDMENT [1964]

Section 1. The right of citizens of the United States to vote in any primary or other election for President or Vice President, for electors for President or Vice President, or for Senator or Representative in Congress, shall not be denied or abridged by the United States or any State by reason of failure to pay any poll tax or other tax.

Section 2. The Congress shall have power to enforce this article by appropriate legislation.

25TH AMENDMENT [1967]

Section 1. In case of the removal of the President from office or of his death or resignation, the Vice President shall become President.

Section 2. Whenever there is a vacancy in the office of the Vice President, the President shall nominate a Vice President who shall take office upon confirmation by a majority vote of both Houses of Congress.

Section 3. Whenever the President transmits to the President pro tempore of the Senate and the Speaker of the House of Representatives his written declaration that he is unable to discharge the powers and duties of his office, and until he transmits to them a written declaration to the contrary, such powers and duties shall be discharged by the Vice President as Acting President.

Section 4. Whenever the Vice President and a majority of either the principal officers of the executive departments or of such other body as Congress may by law provide, transmit to the President pro tempore of the Senate and the Speaker of the House of Representatives their written declaration that the President is unable to discharge the powers and duties of his office, the Vice President shall immediately assume the powers and duties of the office as Acting President.

Thereafter, when the President transmits to the President pro tempore of the Senate and the Speaker of the House of Representatives his written declaration that no inability exists, he shall resume the powers and duties of his office unless the Vice President and a majority of either the principal officers of the executive department or of such other body as Congress may by law provide, transmit within four days to the President pro tempore of the Senate and the Speaker of the House of Representatives their written declaration that the President is unable to discharge the powers and duties of his office. Thereupon Congress shall decide the issue, assembling within forty-eight hours for that purpose if not in session. If the Congress, within twenty-one days after receipt of the latter written declaration, or, if Congress is not in session, within twenty-one days after Congress is required to assemble, determines by two-thirds vote of both Houses that the President shall continue to discharge the same as Acting President; otherwise, the President shall resume the powers and duties of his office.

26TH AMENDMENT [1971]

Section 1. The right of citizens of the United States, who are eighteen years of age or older, to vote shall not be denied or abridged by the United States or by any State on account of age.

Section 2. The Congress shall have power to enforce this article by appropriate legislation.

27TH AMENDMENT [1992]

No law, varying the compensation for the services of the Senators and Representatives, shall take effect, until an election of Representatives shall have intervened.

APPENDIX B

UNIFORM COMMERCIAL CODE

ARTICLE 1

GENERAL PROVISIONS

PART 1 Short Title, Construction, Application and Subject Matter of the Act

§ 1–101. Short Title.

This Act shall be known and may be cited as Uniform Commercial Code.

§ 1–102. Purposes; Rules of Construction; Variation by Agreement.

(1) This Act shall be liberally construed and applied to promote its underlying purposes and policies.

(2) Underlying purposes and policies of this Act are

(a) to simplify, clarify and modernize the law governing commercial transactions;

(b) to permit the continued expansion of commercial practices through custom, usage and agreement of the parties;

(c) to make uniform the law among the various jurisdictions.

(3) The effect of provisions of this Act may be varied by agreement, except as otherwise provided in this Act and except that the obligations of good faith, diligence, reasonableness and care prescribed by this Act may not be disclaimed by agreement but the parties may by agreement determine the standards by which the performance of such obligations is to be measured if such standards are not manifestly unreasonable.

(4) The presence in certain provisions of this Act of the words "unless otherwise agreed" or words of similar import does not imply that the effect of other provisions may not be varied by agreement under subsection (3).

(5) In this Act unless the context otherwise requires

(a) words in the singular number include the plural, and in the plural include the singular;

(b) words of the masculine gender include the feminine and the neuter, and when the sense so indicates words of the neuter gender may refer to any gender.

§ 1–103. Supplementary General Principles of Law Applicable.

Unless displaced by the particular provisions of this Act, the principles of law and equity, including the law merchant and the law relative to capacity to contract, principal and agent, estoppel, fraud, misrepresentation, duress, coercion, mistake, bankruptcy, or other validating or invalidating cause shall supplement its provisions.

§ 1–104. Construction Against Implicit Repeal.

This Act being a general act intended as a unified coverage of its subject matter, no part of it shall be deemed to be impliedly repealed by subsequent legislation if such construction can reasonably be avoided.

§ 1–105. Territorial Application of the Act; Parties' Power to Choose Applicable Law.

(1) Except as provided hereafter in this section, when a transaction bears a reasonable relation to this state and also to another state or nation the parties may agree that the law either of this state or of such other state or nation shall govern their rights and duties. Failing such agreement this Act applies to transactions bearing an appropriate relation to this state.

(2) Where one of the following provisions of this Act specifies the applicable law, that provision governs and a contrary agreement is effective only to the extent permitted by the law (including the conflict of laws rules) so specified:

Rights of creditors against sold goods. Section 2–402.

Applicability of the Article on Leases. Sections 2A–105 and 2A–106.

Applicability of the Article on Bank Deposits and Collections. Section 4–102.

Governing law in the Article on Funds Transfers. Section 4A–507.

[Publisher's Editorial Note: If a state adopts the repealer of Article 6—Bulk Transfers (Alternative A), there should not be any item relating to bulk transfers. If, however, a state adopts Revised Article 6—Bulk Sales (Alternative B), then the item relating to bulk sales should read as follows:]

Bulk sales subject to the Article on Bulk Sales. Section 6–103.

Applicability of the Article on Investment Securities. Section 8–110.

Perfection provisions of the Article on Secured Transactions. Section 9–103.

§ 1–106. Remedies to Be Liberally Administered.

(1) The remedies provided by this Act shall be liberally administered to the end that the aggrieved party may be put in as good a position as if the other party had fully performed but neither consequential or special nor penal damages may be had except as specifically provided in this Act or by other rule of law.

(2) Any right or obligation declared by this Act is enforceable by action unless the provision declaring it specifies a different and limited effect.

§ 1–107. Waiver or Renunciation of Claim or Right After Breach.

Any claim or right arising out of an alleged breach can be discharged in whole or in part without consideration by a written waiver or renunciation signed and delivered by the aggrieved party.

§ 1–108. Severability.

If any provision or clause of this Act or application thereof to any person or circumstances is held invalid, such invalidity shall not affect other provisions or applications of the Act which can be given effect without the invalid provision or application, and to this end the provisions of this Act are declared to be severable.

§ 1–109. Section Captions.

Section captions are parts of this Act.

PART 2 General Definitions and Principles of Interpretation

§ 1–201. General Definitions.

Subject to additional definitions contained in the subsequent Articles of this Act which are applicable to specific Articles or Parts thereof, and unless the context otherwise requires, in this Act:

(1) "Action" in the sense of a judicial proceeding includes recoupment, counterclaim, set-off, suit in equity and any other proceedings in which rights are determined.

(2) "Aggrieved party" means a party entitled to resort to a remedy.

(3) "Agreement" means the bargain of the parties in fact as found in their language or by implication from other circumstances including course of dealing or usage of trade or course of performance as provided in this Act (Sections 1–205, 2–208, and 2A–207). Whether an agreement has legal consequences is determined by the provisions of this Act, if applicable; otherwise by the law of contracts (Section 1–103). (Compare "Contract".)

(4) "Bank" means any person engaged in the business of banking.

(5) "Bearer" means the person in possession of an instrument, document of title, or certificated security payable to bearer or indorsed in blank.

(6) "Bill of lading" means a document evidencing the receipt of goods for shipment issued by a person engaged in the business of transporting or forwarding goods, and includes an airbill. "Airbill" means a document serving for air transportation as a bill of lading does for marine or rail transportation, and includes an air consignment note or air waybill.

(7) "Branch" includes a separately incorporated foreign branch of a bank.

(8) "Burden of establishing" a fact means the burden of persuading the triers of fact that the existence of the fact is more probable than its non-existence.

(9) "Buyer in ordinary course of business" means a person who in good faith and without knowledge that the sale to him is in violation of the ownership rights or security interest of a third party in the goods buys in ordinary course from a person in the business of selling goods of that kind but does not include a pawnbroker. All persons who sell minerals or the like (including oil and gas) at wellhead or minehead shall be deemed to be persons in the business of selling goods of that kind. "Buying" may be for cash or by exchange of other property or on secured or unsecured credit and includes receiving goods or documents of title under a pre-existing contract for sale but does not include a transfer in bulk or as security for or in total or partial satisfaction of a money debt.

(10) "Conspicuous": A term or clause is conspicuous when it is so written that a reasonable person against whom it is to operate ought to have noticed it. A printed heading in capitals (as: NON-NEGOTIABLE BILL OF LADING) is conspicuous. Language in the body of a form is "conspicuous" if it is in larger or other contrasting type or color. But in a telegram any stated term is "conspicuous". Whether a term or clause is "conspicuous" or not is for decision by the court.

(11) "Contract" means the total legal obligation which results from the parties' agreement as affected by this Act and any other applicable rules of law. (Compare "Agreement".)

(12) "Creditor" includes a general creditor, a secured creditor, a lien creditor and any representative of creditors, including an assignee for the benefit of creditors, a trustee in bankruptcy, a receiver in equity and an executor or administrator of an insolvent debtor's or assignor's estate.

(13) "Defendant" includes a person in the position of defendant in a cross-action or counterclaim.

(14) "Delivery" with respect to instruments, documents of title, chattel paper, or certificated securities means voluntary transfer of possession.

(15) "Document of title" includes bill of lading, dock warrant, dock receipt, warehouse receipt or order for the delivery of goods, and also any other document which in the regular course of business or financing is treated as adequately evidencing that the person in possession of it is entitled to receive, hold and dispose of the document and the goods it covers. To be a document of title a document must purport to be issued by or addressed to a bailee and purport to cover goods in the bailee's possession which are either identified or are fungible portions of an identified mass.

(16) "Fault" means wrongful act, omission or breach.

(17) "Fungible" with respect to goods or securities means goods or securities of which any unit is, by nature or usage of trade, the equivalent of any other like unit. Goods which are not fungible shall be deemed fungible for the purposes of this Act to the extent that under a particular agreement or document unlike units are treated as equivalents.

(18) "Genuine" means free of forgery or counterfeiting.

(19) "Good faith" means honesty in fact in the conduct or transaction concerned.

(20) "Holder," with respect to a negotiable instrument, means the person in possession if the instrument is payable to bearer or, in the case of an instrument payable to an identified person, if the identified person is in possession. "Holder" with respect to a document of title means the person in possession if the goods are deliverable to bearer or to the order of the person in pos-session.

(21) To "honor" is to pay or to accept and pay, or where a credit so engages to purchase or discount a draft complying with the terms of the credit.

(22) "Insolvency proceedings" includes any assignment for the benefit of creditors or other proceedings intended to liquidate or rehabilitate the estate of the person involved.

(23) A person is "insolvent" who either has ceased to pay his debts in the ordinary course of business or cannot pay his debts as they become due or is insolvent within the meaning of the federal bankruptcy law.

(24) "Money" means a medium of exchange authorized or adopted by a domestic or foreign government and includes a monetary unit of account established by an intergovernmental organization or by agreement between two or more nations.

(25) A person has "notice" of a fact when

(a) he has actual knowledge of it; or

(b) he has received a notice or notification of it; or

(c) from all the facts and circumstances known to him at the time in question he has reason to know that it exists.

A person "knows" or has "knowledge" of a fact when he has actual knowledge of it. "Discover" or "learn" or a word or phrase of similar import refers to knowledge rather than to reason to know. The time and circumstances under which a notice or notification may cease to be effective are not determined by this Act.

(26) A person "notifies" or "gives" a notice or notification to another by taking such steps as may be reasonably required to inform the other in ordinary course whether or not such other actually comes to know of it. A person "receives" a notice or notification when

(a) it comes to his attention; or

(b) it is duly delivered at the place of business through which the contract was made or at any other place held out by him as the place for receipt of such communications.

(27) Notice, knowledge or a notice or notification received by an organization is effective for a particular transaction from the time when it is brought to the attention of the individual conducting that transaction, and in any event from the time when it would have been brought to his attention if the organization had exercised due diligence. An organization exercises due diligence if it maintains reasonable routines for communicating significant information to the person conducting the transaction and there is reasonable compliance with the routines. Due diligence does not require an individual acting for the organization to communicate information unless such communication is part of his regular duties or unless he has reason to know of the transaction and that the transaction would be materially affected by the information.

(28) "Organization" includes a corporation, government or governmental subdivision or agency, business trust, estate, trust, partnership or association, two or more persons having a joint or common interest, or any other legal or commercial entity.

(29) "Party", as distinct from "third party", means a person who has engaged in a transaction or made an agreement within this Act.

(30) "Person" includes an individual or an organization (See Section 1–102).

(31) "Presumption" or "presumed" means that the trier of fact must find the existence of the fact presumed unless and until evidence is introduced which would support a finding of its non-existence.

(32) "Purchase" includes taking by sale, discount, negotiation, mortgage, pledge, lien, issue or re-issue, gift or any other voluntary transaction creating an interest in property.

(33) "Purchaser" means a person who takes by purchase.

(34) "Remedy" means any remedial right to which an aggrieved party is entitled with or without resort to a tribunal.

(35) "Representative" includes an agent, an officer of a corporation or association, and a trustee, executor or administrator of an estate, or any other person empowered to act for another.

(36) "Rights" includes remedies.

(37) "Security interest" means an interest in personal property or fixtures which secures payment or performance of an obligation. The retention or reservation of title by a seller of goods notwithstanding shipment or delivery to the buyer (Section 2–401) is limited in effect to a reservation of a "security interest". The term also includes any interest of a buyer of accounts or chattel paper which is subject to Article 9. The special property interest of a buyer of goods on identification of those goods to a contract for sale under Section 2–401 is not a "security interest", but a buyer may also acquire a "security interest" by complying with Article 9. Unless a consignment is intended as security, reservation of title thereunder is not a "security interest", but a consignment in any event is subject to the provisions on consignment sales (Section 2–326).

Whether a transaction creates a lease or security interest is determined by the facts of each case; however, a transaction creates a security interest if the consideration the lessee is to pay the lessor for the right to possession and use of the goods is an obligation for the term of the lease not subject to termination by the lessee, and

(a) the original term of the lease is equal to or greater than the remaining economic life of the goods,

(b) the lessee is bound to renew the lease for the remaining economic life of the goods or is bound to become the owner of the goods,

(c) the lessee has an option to renew the lease for the remaining economic life of the goods for no additional consideration or nominal additional consideration upon compliance with the lease agreement, or

(d) the lessee has an option to become the owner of the goods for no additional consideration or nominal additional consideration upon compliance with the lease agreement.

A transaction does not create a security interest merely because it provides that

(a) the present value of the consideration the lessee is obligated to pay the lessor for the right to possession and use of the goods is substantially equal to or is greater than the fair market value of the goods at the time the lease is entered into,

(b) the lessee assumes risk of loss of the goods, or agrees to pay taxes, insurance, filing, recording, or registration fees, or service or maintenance costs with respect to the goods,

(c) the lessee has an option to renew the lease or to become the owner of the goods,

(d) the lessee has an option to renew the lease for a fixed rent that is equal to or greater than the reasonably predictable fair market rent for the use of the goods for the term of the renewal at the time the option is to be performed, or

(e) the lessee has an option to become the owner of the goods for a fixed price that is equal to or greater than the reasonably predictable fair market value of the goods at the time the option is to be performed.

For purposes of this subsection (37):

(x) Additional consideration is not nominal if (i) when the option to renew the lease is granted to the lessee the rent is stated to be the fair market rent for the use of the goods for the term of the renewal determined at the time the option is to be performed, or (ii) when the option to become the owner of the goods is granted to the lessee the price is stated to be the fair market value of the goods determined at the time the option is to be performed. Additional consideration is nominal if it is less than the lessee's reasonably predictable cost of performing under the lease agreement if the option is not exercised;

(y) "Reasonably predictable" and "remaining economic life of the goods" are to be determined with reference to the facts and circumstances at the time the transaction is entered into; and

(z) "Present value" means the amount as of a date certain of one or more sums payable in the future, discounted to the date certain. The discount is determined by the interest rate specified by the parties if the rate is not manifestly unreasonable at the time the transaction is entered into; otherwise, the discount is determined by a commercially reasonable rate that takes into account the facts and circumstances of each case at the time the transaction was entered into.

(38) "Send" in connection with any writing or notice means to deposit in the mail or deliver for transmission by any other usual means of communication with postage or cost of transmission provided for and properly addressed and in the case of an instrument to an address specified thereon or otherwise agreed, or if there be none to any address reasonable under the circumstances. The receipt of any writing or notice within the time at which it would have arrived if properly sent has the effect of a proper sending.

(39) "Signed" includes any symbol executed or adopted by a party with present intention to authenticate a writing.

(40) "Surety" includes guarantor.

(41) "Telegram" includes a message transmitted by radio, teletype, cable, any mechanical method of transmission, or the like.

(42) "Term" means that portion of an agreement which relates to a particular matter.

(43) "Unauthorized" signature means one made without actual, implied, or apparent authority and includes a forgery.

(44) "Value". Except as otherwise provided with respect to negotiable instruments and bank collections (Sections 3–303, 4–210 and 4–211) a person gives "value" for rights if he acquires them

(a) in return for a binding commitment to extend credit or for the extension of immediately available credit whether or not drawn upon and whether or not a chargeback is provided for in the event of difficulties in collection; or

(b) as security for or in total or partial satisfaction of a pre-existing claim; or

(c) by accepting delivery pursuant to a pre-existing contract for purchase; or

(d) generally, in return for any consideration sufficient to support a simple contract.

(45) "Warehouse receipt" means a receipt issued by a person engaged in the business of storing goods for hire.

(46) "Written" or "writing" includes printing, typewriting or any other intentional reduction to tangible form.

§ 1–202. Prima Facie Evidence by Third Party Documents.

A document in due form purporting to be a bill of lading, policy or certificate of insurance, official weigher's or inspector's certificate, consular invoice, or any other document authorized or required by the contract to be issued by a third party shall be prima facie evidence of its own authenticity and genuineness and of the facts stated in the document by the third party.

§ 1–203. Obligation of Good Faith.

Every contract or duty within this Act imposes an obligation of good faith in its performance or enforcement.

§ 1–204. Time; Reasonable Time; "Seasonably".

(1) Whenever this Act requires any action to be taken within a reasonable time, any time which is not manifestly unreasonable may be fixed by agreement.

(2) What is a reasonable time for taking any action depends on the nature, purpose and circumstances of such action.

(3) An action is taken "seasonably" when it is taken at or within the time agreed or if no time is agreed at or within a reasonable time.

§ 1–205. Course of Dealing and Usage of Trade.

(1) A course of dealing is a sequence of previous conduct between the parties to a particular transaction which is fairly to be regarded as establishing a common basis of understanding for interpreting their expressions and other conduct.

(2) A usage of trade is any practice or method of dealing having such regularity of observance in a place, vocation or trade as to justify an expectation that it will be observed with respect to the transaction in question. The existence and scope of such a usage are to be proved as facts. If it is established that such a usage is embodied in a written trade code or similar writing the interpretation of the writing is for the court.

(3) A course of dealing between parties and any usage of trade in the vocation or trade in which they are engaged or of which they are or should be aware give particular meaning to and supplement or qualify terms of an agreement.

(4) The express terms of an agreement and an applicable course of dealing or usage of trade shall be construed wherever reasonable as consistent with each other, but when such construction is unreasonable express terms control both course of dealing and usage of trade and course of dealing controls usage of trade.

(5) An applicable usage of trade in the place where any part of performance is to occur shall be used in interpreting the agreement as to that part of the performance.

(6) Evidence of a relevant usage of trade offered by one party is not admissible unless and until he has given the other party such notice as the court finds sufficient to prevent unfair surprise to the latter.

§ 1–206. Statute of Frauds for Kinds of Personal Property Not Otherwise Covered.

(1) Except in the cases described in subsection (2) of this section a contract for the sale of personal property is not enforceable by way of action or defense beyond five thousand dollars in amount or value of remedy unless there is some writing which indicates that a contract for sale has been made between the parties at a defined or stated price, reasonably identifies the subject matter, and is signed by the party against whom enforcement is sought or by his authorized agent.

(2) Subsection (1) of this section does not apply to contracts for the sale of goods (Section 2–201) nor of securities (Section 8–113) nor to security agreements (Section 9–203).

§ 1–207. Performance or Acceptance Under Reservation of Rights.

A party who with explicit reservation of rights performs or promises performance or assents to performance in a manner demanded or offered by the other party does not thereby prejudice the rights reserved. Such words as "without prejudice", "under protest" or the like are sufficient.

§ 1–208. Option to Accelerate at Will.

A term providing that one party or his successor in interest may accelerate payment or performance or require collateral or additional collateral "at will" or "when he deems himself insecure" or in words of similar import shall be construed to mean that he shall have power to do so only if he in good faith believes that the prospect of payment or performance is impaired. The burden of establishing lack of good faith is on the party against whom the power has been exercised.

§ 1–209. Subordinated Obligations.

An obligation may be issued as subordinated to payment of another obligation of the person obligated, or a creditor may subordinate his right to payment of an obligation by agreement with either the person obligated or another creditor of the person obligated. Such a subordination does not create a security interest as against either the common debtor or a subordinated creditor. This section shall be construed as declaring the law as it existed prior to the enactment of this section and not as modifying it. Added 1966.

Note: This new section is proposed as an optional provision to make it clear that a subordination agreement does not create a security interest unless so intended.

ARTICLE 2

SALES

PART 1 Short Title, Construction and Subject Matter

§ 2–101. Short Title.

This Article shall be known and may be cited as Uniform Commercial Code—Sales.

§ 2–102. Scope; Certain Security and Other Transactions Excluded From This Article.

Unless the context otherwise requires, this Article applies to transactions in goods; it does not apply to any transaction which although in the form of an unconditional contract to sell or present sale is intended to operate only as a security transaction nor does this Article impair or repeal any statute regulating sales to consumers, farmers or other specified classes of buyers.

§ 2–103. Definitions and Index of Definitions.

(1) In this Article unless the context otherwise requires

(a) "Buyer" means a person who buys or contracts to buy goods.

(b) "Good faith" in the case of a merchant means honesty in fact and the observance of reasonable commercial standards of fair dealing in the trade.

(c) "Receipt" of goods means taking physical possession of them.

(d) "Seller" means a person who sells or contracts to sell goods.

(2) Other definitions applying to this Article or to specified Parts thereof, and the sections in which they appear are:

"Acceptance". Section 2–606.
"Banker's credit". Section 2–325.
"Between merchants". Section 2–104.
"Cancellation". Section 2–106(4).
"Commercial unit". Section 2–105.
"Confirmed credit". Section 2–325.
"Conforming to contract". Section 2–106.
"Contract for sale". Section 2–106.
"Cover". Section 2–712.
"Entrusting". Section 2–403.
"Financing agency". Section 2–104.
"Future goods". Section 2–105.
"Goods". Section 2–105.
"Identification". Section 2–501.
"Installment contract". Section 2–612.
"Letter of Credit". Section 2–325.
"Lot". Section 2–105.
"Merchant". Section 2–104.
"Overseas". Section 2–323.
"Person in position of seller". Section 2–707.
"Present sale". Section 2–106.
"Sale". Section 2–106.
"Sale on approval". Section 2–326.
"Sale or return". Section 2–326.
"Termination". Section 2–106.

(3) The following definitions in other Articles apply to this Article:

"Check". Section 3–104.
"Consignee". Section 7–102.
"Consignor". Section 7–102.
"Consumer goods". Section 9–109.
"Dishonor". Section 3–502.
"Draft". Section 3–104.

(4) In addition Article 1 contains general definitions and principles of construction and interpretation applicable throughout this Article.

§ 2–104. Definitions: "Merchant"; "Between Merchants"; "Financing Agency".

(1) "Merchant" means a person who deals in goods of the kind or otherwise by his occupation holds himself out as having knowledge or skill peculiar to the practices or goods involved in the transaction or to whom such knowledge or skill may be attributed by his employment of an agent or broker or other intermediary who by his occupation holds himself out as having such knowledge or skill.

(2) "Financing agency" means a bank, finance company or other person who in the ordinary course of business makes advances against goods or documents of title or who by arrangement with either the seller or the buyer intervenes in ordinary course to make or collect payment due or claimed under the contract for sale, as by purchasing or paying the seller's draft or making advances against it or by merely taking it for collection whether or not documents of title accompany the draft. "Financing agency" includes also a bank or other person who similarly intervenes between persons who are in the position of seller and buyer in respect to the goods (Section 2–707).

(3) "Between merchants" means in any transaction with respect to which both parties are chargeable with the knowledge or skill of merchants.

§ 2–105. Definitions: Transferability; "Goods"; "Future" Goods; "Lot"; "Commercial Unit".

(1) "Goods" means all things (including specially manufactured goods) which are movable at the time of identification to the contract for sale other than the money in which the price is to be paid, investment securities (Article 8) and things in action. "Goods" also includes the unborn young of animals and growing crops and other identified things attached to realty as described in the section on goods to be severed from realty (Section 2–107).

(2) Goods must be both existing and identified before any interest in them can pass. Goods which are not both existing and identified are "future" goods. A purported pres

ent sale of future goods or of any interest therein operates as a contract to sell.

(3) There may be a sale of a part interest in existing identified goods.

(4) An undivided share in an identified bulk of fungible goods is sufficiently identified to be sold although the quantity of the bulk is not determined. Any agreed proportion of such a bulk or any quantity thereof agreed upon by number, weight or other measure may to the extent of the seller's interest in the bulk be sold to the buyer who then becomes an owner in common.

(5) "Lot" means a parcel or a single article which is the subject matter of a separate sale or delivery, whether or not it is sufficient to perform the contract.

(6) "Commercial unit" means such a unit of goods as by commercial usage is a single whole for purposes of sale and division of which materially impairs its character or value on the market or in use. A commercial unit may be a single article (as a machine) or a set of articles (as a suite of furniture or an assortment of sizes) or a quantity (as a bale, gross, or carload) or any other unit treated in use or in the relevant market as a single whole.

§ 2–106. Definitions: "Contract"; "Agreement"; "Contract for Sale"; "Sale"; "Present Sale"; "Conforming" to Contract; "Termination"; "Cancellation".

(1) In this Article unless the context otherwise requires "contract" and "agreement" are limited to those relating to the present or future sale of goods. "Contract for sale" includes both a present sale of goods and a contract to sell goods at a future time. A "sale" consists in the passing of title from the seller to the buyer for a price (Section 2–401). A "present sale" means a sale which is accomplished by the making of the contract.

(2) Goods or conduct including any part of a performance are "conforming" or conform to the contract when they are in accordance with the obligations under the contract.

(3) "Termination" occurs when either party pursuant to a power created by agreement or law puts an end to the contract otherwise than for its breach. On "termination" all obligations which are still executory on both sides are discharged but any right based on prior breach or performance survives.

(4) "Cancellation" occurs when either party puts an end to the contract for breach by the other and its effect is the same as that of "termination" except that the cancelling party also retains any remedy for breach of the whole contract or any unperformed balance.

§ 2–107. Goods to Be Severed From Realty: Recording.

(1) A contract for the sale of minerals or the like (including oil and gas) or a structure or its materials to be removed from realty is a contract for the sale of goods within this Article if they are to be severed by the seller but until severance a purported present sale thereof which is not effective as a transfer of an interest in land is effective only as a contract to sell.

(2) A contract for the sale apart from the land of growing crops or other things attached to realty and capable of severance without material harm thereto but not described in subsection (1) or of timber to be cut is a contract for the sale of goods within this Article whether the subject matter is to be severed by the buyer or by the seller even though it forms part of the realty at the time of contracting, and the parties can by identification effect a present sale before severance.

(3) The provisions of this section are subject to any third party rights provided by the law relating to realty records, and the contract for sale may be executed and recorded as a document transferring an interest in land and shall then constitute notice to third parties of the buyer's rights under the contract for sale.

PART 2 Form, Formation and Readjustment of Contract

§ 2–201. Formal Requirements; Statute of Frauds.

(1) Except as otherwise provided in this section a contract for the sale of goods for the price of $500 or more is not enforceable by way of action or defense unless there is some writing sufficient to indicate that a contract for sale has been made between the parties and signed by the party against whom enforcement is sought or by his authorized agent or broker. A writing is not insufficient because it omits or incorrectly states a term agreed upon but the contract is not enforceable under this paragraph beyond the quantity of goods shown in such writing.

(2) Between merchants if within a reasonable time a writing in confirmation of the contract and sufficient against the sender is received and the party receiving it has reason to know its contents, it satisfies the requirements of subsection (1) against such party unless written notice of objection to its contents is given within ten days after it is received.

(3) A contract which does not satisfy the requirements of subsection (1) but which is valid in other respects is enforceable

(a) if the goods are to be specially manufactured for the buyer and are not suitable for sale to others in the ordinary course of the seller's business and the seller, before notice of repudiation is received and under circumstances which reasonably indicate that the goods are for the buyer, has made either a substantial beginning of their manufacture or commitments for their procurement; or

(b) if the party against whom enforcement is sought admits in his pleading, testimony or otherwise in court that a contract for sale was made, but the contract is not enforceable under this provision beyond the quantity of goods admitted; or

(c) with respect to goods for which payment has been made and accepted or which have been received and accepted (Sec. 2–606).

§ 2–202. Final Written Expression: Parol or Extrinsic Evidence.

Terms with respect to which the confirmatory memoranda of the parties agree or which are otherwise set forth in a writing in-tended by the parties as a final expression of their agreement with respect to such terms as are included therein may not be contradicted by evidence of any prior agreement or of a contemporaneous oral agreement but may be explained or supplemented

(a) by course of dealing or usage of trade (Section 1–205) or by course of performance (Section 2–208); and

(b) by evidence of consistent additional terms unless the court finds the writing to have been intended also as a complete and exclusive statement of the terms of the agreement.

§ 2–203. Seals Inoperative.

The affixing of a seal to a writing evidencing a contract for sale or an offer to buy or sell goods does not constitute the writing a sealed instrument and the law with respect to sealed instruments does not apply to such a contract or offer.

§ 2–204. Formation in General.

(1) A contract for sale of goods may be made in any manner sufficient to show agreement, including conduct by both parties which recognizes the existence of such a contract.

(2) An agreement sufficient to constitute a contract for sale may be found even though the moment of its making is undetermined.

(3) Even though one or more terms are left open a contract for sale does not fail for indefiniteness if the parties have intended to make a contract and there is a reasonably certain basis for giving an appropriate remedy.

§ 2–205. Firm Offers.

An offer by a merchant to buy or sell goods in a signed writing which by its terms gives assurance that it will be held open is not revocable, for lack of consideration, during the time stated or if no time is stated for reasonable time, but in no event may such period of irrevocability exceed three months; but any such term of assurance on a form supplied by the offeree must be separately signed by the offeror.

§ 2–206. Offer and Acceptance in Formation of Contract.

(1) Unless other unambiguously indicated by the language or circumstances

(a) an offer to make a contract shall be construed as inviting acceptance in any manner and by any medium reasonable in the circumstances;

(b) an order or other offer to buy goods for prompt or current shipment shall be construed as inviting acceptance either by a prompt promise to ship or by the prompt or current shipment of conforming or nonconforming goods, but such a shipment of non-conforming goods does not constitute an acceptance if the seller seasonably notifies the buyer that the shipment is offered only as an accommodation to the buyer.

(2) Where the beginning of a requested performance is a reasonable mode of acceptance an offeror who is not notified of acceptance within a reasonable time may treat the offer as having lapsed before acceptance.

§ 2–207. Additional Terms in Acceptance or Confirmation.

(1) A definite and seasonable expression of acceptance or a written confirmation which is sent within a reasonable time operates as an acceptance even though it states terms additional to or different from those offered or agreed upon, unless acceptance is expressly made conditional on assent to the additional or different terms.

(2) The additional terms are to be construed as proposals for addition to the contract. Between merchants such terms become part of the contract unless:

(a) the offer expressly limits acceptance to the terms of the offer;

(b) they materially alter it; or

(c) notification of objection to them has already been given or is given within a reasonable time after notice of them is received.

(3) Conduct by both parties which recognizes the existence of a contract is sufficient to establish a contract for sale although the writings of the parties do not otherwise establish a contract. In such case the terms of the particular contract consist of those terms on which the writings of the parties agree, together with any supplementary terms incorporated under any other provisions of this Act.

§ 2–208. Course of Performance or Practical Construction.

(1) Where the contract for sale involves repeated occasions for performance by either party with knowledge of the nature of the performance and opportunity for objection to it by the other, any course of performance accepted or acquiesced in without objection shall be relevant to determine the meaning of the agreement.

(2) The express terms of the agreement and any such course of performance, as well as any course of dealing and usage of trade, shall be construed whenever reasonable as consistent with each other; but when such construction is unreasonable, express terms shall control course of performance and course of performance shall control both course of dealing and usage of trade (Section 1–205).

(3) Subject to the provisions of the next section on modification and waiver, such course of performance shall be relevant to show a waiver or modification of any term inconsistent with such course of performance.

§ 2–209. Modification, Rescission and Waiver.

(1) An agreement modifying a contract within this Article needs no consideration to be binding.

(2) A signed agreement which excludes modification or rescission except by a signed writing cannot be otherwise modified or rescinded, but except as between merchants such a requirement on a form supplied by the merchant must be separately signed by the other party.

(3) The requirements of the statute of frauds section of this Article (Section 2–201) must be satisfied if the contract as modified is within its provisions.

(4) Although an attempt at modification or rescission does not satisfy the requirements of subsection (2) or (3) it can operate as a waiver.

(5) A party who has made a waiver affecting an executory portion of the contract may retract the waiver by reasonable notification received by the other party that strict performance will be required of any term waived, unless the retraction would be unjust in view of a material change of position in reliance on the waiver.

§ 2–210. Delegation of Performance; Assignment of Rights.

(1) A party may perform his duty through a delegate unless otherwise agreed or unless the other party has a substantial interest in having his original promisor perform or control the acts required by the contract. No delegation of performance relieves the party delegating of any duty to perform or any liability for breach.

(2) Unless otherwise agreed all rights of either seller or buyer can be assigned except where the assignment would materially change the duty of the other party, or increase materially the burden or risk imposed on him by his contract, or impair materially his chance of obtaining return performance. A right to damages for breach of the whole contract or a right arising out of the assignor's due performance of his entire obligation can be assigned despite agreement otherwise.

(3) Unless the circumstances indicate the contrary a prohibition of assignment of "the contract" is to be construed as barring only the delegation to the assignee of the assignor's performance.

(4) An assignment of "the contract" or of "all my rights under the contract" or an assignment in similar general terms is an assignment of rights and unless the language or the circumstances (as in an assignment for security) indicate the contrary, it is a delegation of performance of the duties of the assignor and its acceptance by the assignee constitutes a promise by him to perform those duties. This promise is enforceable by either the assignor or the other party to the original contract.

(5) The other party may treat any assignment which delegates performance as creating reasonable grounds for insecurity and may without prejudice to his rights against the assignor demand assurances from the assignee (Section 2–609).

PART 3 General Obligation and Construction of Contract

§ 2–301. General Obligations of Parties.

The obligation of the seller is to transfer and deliver and that of the buyer is to accept and pay in accordance with the contract.

§ 2–302. Unconscionable Contract or Clause.

(1) If the court as a matter of law finds the contract or any clause of the contract to have been unconscionable at the time it was made the court may refuse to enforce the contract, or it may enforce the remainder of the contract without the unconscionable clause, or it may so limit the application of any unconscionable clause as to avoid any unconscionable result.

(2) When it is claimed or appears to the court that the contract or any clause thereof may be unconscionable the parties shall be afforded a reasonable opportunity to present evidence as to its commercial setting, purpose and effect to aid the court in making the determination.

§ 2–303. Allocation or Division of Risks.

Where this Article allocates a risk or a burden as between the parties "unless otherwise agreed", the agreement may not only shift the allocation, but may also divide the risk or burden.

§ 2–304. Price Payable in Money, Goods, Realty, or Otherwise.

(1) The price can be made payable in money or otherwise. If it is payable in whole or in part in goods each party is a seller of the goods which he is to transfer.

(2) Even though all or part of the price is payable in an interest in realty the transfer of the goods and the seller's obligations with reference to them are subject to this Article, but not the transfer of the interest in realty or the transferor's obligations in connection therewith.

§ 2–305. Open Price Term.

(1) The parties if they so intend can conclude a contract for sale even though the price is not settled. In such a case the price is a reasonable price at the time for delivery if

(a) nothing is said as to price; or

(b) the price is left to be agreed by the parties and they fail to agree; or

(c) the price is to be fixed in terms of some agreed market or other standard as set or recorded by a third person or agency and it is not so set or recorded.

(2) A price to be fixed by the seller or by the buyer means a price for him to fix in good faith.

(3) When a price left to be fixed otherwise than by agreement of the parties fails to be fixed through fault of one party the other may at his option treat the contract as cancelled or himself fix a reasonable price.

(4) Where, however, the parties intend not to be bound unless the price be fixed or agreed and it is not fixed or

agreed there is no contract. In such a case the buyer must return any goods already received or if unable so to do must pay their reasonable value at the time of delivery and the seller must return any portion of the price paid on account.

§ 2–306. Output, Requirements and Exclusive Dealings.

(1) A term which measures the quantity by the output of the seller or the requirements of the buyer means such actual output or requirements as may occur in good faith, except that no quantity unreasonably disproportionate to any stated estimate or in the absence of a stated estimate to any normal or otherwise comparable prior output or requirements may be tendered or demanded.

(2) A lawful agreement by either the seller or the buyer for exclusive dealing in the kind of goods concerned imposes unless otherwise agreed an obligation by the seller to use best efforts to supply the goods and by the buyer to use best efforts to promote their sale.

§ 2–307. Delivery in Single Lot or Several Lots.

Unless otherwise agreed all goods called for by a contract for sale must be tendered in a single delivery and payment is due only on such tender but where the circumstances give either party the right to make or demand delivery in lots the price if it can be apportioned may be demanded for each lot.

§ 2–308. Absence of Specified Place for Delivery.

Unless otherwise agreed

(a) the place for delivery of goods is the seller's place of business or if he has none his residence; but

(b) in a contract for sale of identified goods which to the knowledge of the parties at the time of contracting are in some other place, that place is the place for their delivery; and

(c) documents of title may be delivered through customary banking channels.

§ 2–309. Absence of Specific Time Provisions; Notice of Termination.

(1) The time for shipment or delivery or any other action under a contract if not provided in this Article or agreed upon shall be a reasonable time.

(2) Where the contract provides for successive performances but is indefinite in duration it is valid for a reasonable time but unless otherwise agreed may be terminated at any time by either party.

(3) Termination of a contract by one party except on the happening of an agreed event requires that reasonable notification be received by the other party and an agreement dispensing with notification is invalid if its operation would be unconscionable.

§ 2–310. Open Time for Payment or Running of Credit; Authority to Ship Under Reservation.

Unless otherwise agreed

(a) payment is due at the time and place at which the buyer is to receive the goods even though the place of shipment is the place of delivery; and

(b) if the seller is authorized to send the goods he may ship them under reservation, and may tender the documents of title, but the buyer may inspect the goods after their arrival before payment is due unless such inspection is inconsistent with the terms of the contract (Section 2–513); and

(c) if delivery is authorized and made by way of documents of title otherwise than by subsection (b) then payment is due at the time and place at which the buyer is to receive the documents regardless of where the goods are to be received; and

(d) where the seller is required or authorized to ship the goods on credit the credit period runs from the time of shipment but post-dating the invoice or delaying its dispatch will correspondingly delay the starting of the credit period.

§ 2–311. Options and Cooperation Respecting Performance.

(1) An agreement for sale which is otherwise sufficiently definite (subsection (3) of Section 2–204) to be a contract is not made invalid by the fact that it leaves particulars of performance to be specified by one of the parties. Any such specification must be made in good faith and within limits set by commercial reasonableness.

(2) Unless otherwise agreed specifications relating to assortment of the goods are at the buyer's option and except as otherwise provided in subsections (1)(c) and (3) of Section 2–319 specifications or arrangements relating to shipment are at the seller's option.

(3) Where such specification would materially affect the other party's performance but is not seasonably made or where one party's cooperation is necessary to the agreed performance of the other but is not seasonably forthcoming, the other party in addition to all other remedies

(a) is excused for any resulting delay in his own performance; and

(b) may also either proceed to perform in any reasonable manner or after the time for a material part of his own performance treat the failure to specify or to cooperate as a breach by failure to deliver or accept the goods.

§ 2–312. Warranty of Title and Against Infringement; Buyer's Obligation Against Infringement.

(1) Subject to subsection (2) there is in a contract for sale a warranty by the seller that

(a) the title conveyed shall be good, and its transfer rightful; and

(b) the goods shall be delivered free from any security interest or other lien or encumbrance of which the buyer at the time of contracting has no knowledge.

(2) A warranty under subsection (1) will be excluded or modified only by specific language or by circumstances which give the buyer reason to know that the person selling does not claim title in himself or that he is purporting

to sell only such right or title as he or a third person may have.

(3) Unless otherwise agreed a seller who is a merchant regularly dealing in goods of the kind warrants that the goods shall be delivered free of the rightful claim of any third person by way of infringement or the like but a buyer who furnishes specifications to the seller must hold the seller harmless against any such claim which arises out of compliance with the specifications.

§ 2–313. Express Warranties by Affirmation, Promise, Description, Sample.

(1) Express warranties by the seller are created as follows:

(a) Any affirmation of fact or promise made by the seller to the buyer which relates to the goods and becomes part of the basis of the bargain creates an express warranty that the goods shall conform to the affirmation or promise.

(b) Any description of the goods which is made part of the basis of the bargain creates an express warranty that the goods shall conform to the description.

(c) Any sample or model which is made part of the basis of the bargain creates an express warranty that the whole of the goods shall conform to the sample or model.

(2) It is not necessary to the creation of an express warranty that the seller use formal words such as "warrant" or "guarantee" or that he have a specific intention to make a warranty, but an affirmation merely of the value of the goods or a statement purporting to be merely the seller's opinion or commendation of the goods does not create a warranty.

§ 2–314. Implied Warranty: Merchantability; Usage of Trade.

(1) Unless excluded or modified (Section 2–316), a warranty that the goods shall be merchantable is implied in a contract for their sale if the seller is a merchant with respect to goods of that kind. Under this section the serving for value of food or drink to be consumed either on the premises or elsewhere is a sale.

(2) Goods to be merchantable must be at least such as

(a) pass without objection in the trade under the contract description; and

(b) in the case of fungible goods, are of fair average quality within the description; and

(c) are fit for the ordinary purpose for which such goods are used; and

(d) run, within the variations permitted by the agreement, of even kind, quality and quantity within each unit and among all units involved; and

(e) are adequately contained, packaged, and labeled as the agreement may require; and

(f) conform to the promises or affirmations of fact made on the container or label if any.

(3) Unless excluded or modified (Section 2–316) other implied warranties may arise from course of dealing or usage of trade.

§ 2–315. Implied Warranty: Fitness for Particular Purpose.

Where the seller at the time of contracting has reason to know any particular purpose for which the goods are required and that the buyer is relying on the seller's skill or judgment to select or furnish suitable goods, there is unless excluded or modified under the next section an implied warranty that the goods shall be fit for such purpose.

§ 2–316. Exclusion or Modification of Warranties.

(1) Words or conduct relevant to the creation of an express warranty and words or conduct tending to negate or limit warranty shall be construed wherever reasonable as consistent with each other, but subject to the provisions of this Article on parol or extrinsic evidence (Section 2–202) negation or limitation is inoperative to the extent that such construction is unreasonable.

(2) Subject to subsection (3), to exclude or modify the implied warranty of merchantability or any part of it the language must mention merchantability and in case of a writing must be conspicuous, and to exclude or modify any implied warranty of fitness the exclusion must be by a writing and conspicuous. Language to exclude all implied warranties of fitness is sufficient if it states, for example, that "There are no warranties which extend beyond the description on the face hereof."

(3) Notwithstanding subsection (2)

(a) unless the circumstances indicate otherwise, all implied warranties are excluded by expressions like "as is", "with all faults" or other language which in common understanding calls the buyer's attention to the exclusion of warranties and makes plain that there is no implied warranty; and

(b) when the buyer before entering into the contract has examined the goods or the sample or model as fully as he desired or has refused to examine the goods there is no implied warranty with regard to defects which an examination ought in the circumstances to have revealed to him; and

(c) an implied warranty can also be excluded or modified by course of dealing or course of performance or usage of trade.

(4) Remedies for breach of warranty can be limited in accordance with the provisions of this Article on liquidation or limitation of damages and on contractual modification of remedy (Sections 2–718 and 2–719).

§ 2–317. Cumulation and Conflict of Warranties Express or Implied.

Warranties whether express or implied shall be construed as consistent with each other and as cumulative, but if such construction is unreasonable the intention of the parties shall determine which warranty is dominant. In ascertaining that intention the following rules apply:

(a) Exact or technical specifications displace an inconsistent sample or model or general language of description.

(b) A sample from an existing bulk displaces inconsistent general language of description.

(c) Express warranties displace inconsistent implied warranties other than an implied warranty of fitness for a particular purpose.

§ 2–318. Third Party Beneficiaries of Warranties Express or Implied.

Note: If this Act is introduced in the Congress of the United States this section should be omitted. (States to select one alternative.)

Alternative A A seller's warranty whether express or implied extends to any natural person who is in the family or household of his buyer or who is a guest in his home if it is reasonable to expect that such person may use, consume or be affected by the goods and who is injured in person by breach of the warranty. The seller may not exclude or limit the operation of this section.

Alternative B A seller's warranty whether express or implied extends to any natural person who may reasonably be expected to use, consume or be affected by the goods and who is injured in person by breach of the warranty. A seller may not exclude or limit the operation of this section.

Alternative C A seller's warranty whether express or implied extends to any person who may reasonably be expected to use, consume or be affected by the goods and who is injured by breach of the warranty. A seller may not exclude or limit the operation of this section with respect to injury to the person of an individual to whom the warranty extends. As amended 1966.

§ 2–319. F.O.B. and F.A.S. Terms.

(1) Unless otherwise agreed the term F.O.B. (which means "free on board") at a named place, even though used only in connection with the stated price, is a delivery term under which

(a) when the term is F.O.B. the place of shipment, the seller must at that place ship the goods in the manner provided in this Article (Section 2–504) and bear the expense and risk of putting them into the possession of the carrier; or

(b) when the term is F.O.B. the place of destination, the seller must at his own expense and risk transport the goods to that place and there tender delivery of them in the manner provided in this Article (Section 2–503);

(c) when under either (a) or (b) the term is also F.O.B. vessel, car or other vehicle, the seller must in addition at his own expense and risk load the goods on board. If the term is F.O.B. vessel the buyer must name the vessel and in an appropriate case the seller must comply with the provisions of this Article on the form of bill of lading (Section 2–323).

(2) Unless otherwise agreed the term F.A.S. vessel (which means "free alongside") at a named port, even though used only in connection with the stated price, is a delivery term under which the seller must

(a) at his own expense and risk deliver the goods alongside the vessel in the manner usual in that port or on a dock designated and provided by the buyer; and

(b) obtain and tender a receipt for the goods in exchange for which the carrier is under a duty to issue a bill of lading.

(3) Unless otherwise agreed in any case falling within subsection (1)(a) or (c) or subsection (2) the buyer must seasonably give any needed instructions for making delivery, including when the term is F.A.S. or F.O.B. the loading berth of the vessel and in an appropriate case its name and sailing date. The seller may treat the failure of needed instructions as a failure of cooperation under this Article (Section 2–311). He may also at his option move the goods in any reasonable manner preparatory to delivery or shipment.

(4) Under the term F.O.B. vessel or F.A.S. unless otherwise agreed the buyer must make payment against tender of the required documents and the seller may not tender nor the buyer demand delivery of the goods in substitution for the documents.

§ 2–320. C.I.F. and C. & F. Terms.

(1) The term C.I.F. means that the price includes in a lump sum the cost of the goods and the insurance and freight to the named destination. The term C. & F. or C.F. means that the price so includes cost and freight to the named destination.

(2) Unless otherwise agreed and even though used only in connection with the stated price and destination, the term C.I.F. destination or its equivalent requires the seller at his own expense and risk to

(a) put the goods into the possession of a carrier at the port for shipment and obtain a negotiable bill or bills of lading covering the entire transportation to the named destination; and

(b) load the goods and obtain a receipt from the carrier (which may be contained in the bill of lading) showing that the freight has been paid or provided for; and

(c) obtain a policy or certificate of insurance, including any war risk insurance, of a kind and on terms then current at the port of shipment in the usual amount, in the currency of the contract, shown to cover the same goods covered by the bill of lading and providing for payment of loss to the order of the buyer or for the account of whom it may concern; but the seller may add to the price the amount of premium for any such war risk insurance; and

(d) prepare an invoice of the goods and procure any other documents required to effect shipment or to comply with the contract; and

(e) forward and tender with commercial promptness all the documents in due form and with any indorsement necessary to perfect the buyer's rights.

(3) Unless otherwise agreed the term C. & F. or its equivalent has the same effect and imposes upon the seller the same obligations and risks as a C.I.F. term except the obligation as to insurance.

(4) Under the term C.I.F. or C. & F. unless otherwise agreed the buyer must make payment against tender of

the required documents and the seller may not tender nor the buyer demand delivery of the goods in substitution for the documents.

§ 2–321. C.I.F. or C. & F.: "Net Landed Weights"; "Payment on Arrival"; Warranty of Condition on Arrival.

Under a contract containing a term C.I.F. or C. & F.

(1) Where the price is based on or is to be adjusted according to "net landed weights", "delivered weights", "out turn" quantity or quality or the like, unless otherwise agreed the seller must reasonably estimate the price. The payment due on tender of the documents called for by the contract is the amount so estimated, but after final adjustment of the price a settlement must be made with commercial promptness.

(2) An agreement described in subsection (1) or any warranty of quality or condition of the goods on arrival places upon the seller the risk of ordinary deterioration, shrinkage and the like in transportation but has no effect on the place or time of identification to the contract for sale or delivery or on the passing of the risk of loss.

(3) Unless otherwise agreed where the contract provides for payment on or after arrival of the goods the seller must before payment allow such preliminary inspection as is feasible; but if the goods are lost delivery of the documents and payment are due when the goods should have arrived.

§ 2–322. Delivery "Ex-Ship".

(1) Unless otherwise agreed a term for delivery of goods "ex-ship" (which means from the carrying vessel) or in equivalent language is not restricted to a particular ship and requires delivery from a ship which has reached a place at the named port of destination where goods of the kind are usually discharged.

(2) Under such a term unless otherwise agreed

(a) the seller must discharge all liens arising out of the carriage and furnish the buyer with a direction which puts the carrier under a duty to deliver the goods; and

(b) the risk of loss does not pass to the buyer until the goods leave the ship's tackle or are otherwise properly unloaded.

§ 2–323. Form of Bill of Lading Required in Overseas Shipment; "Overseas".

(1) Where the contract contemplates overseas shipment and contains a term C.I.F. or C. & F. or F.O.B. vessel, the seller unless otherwise agreed must obtain a negotiable bill of lading stating that the goods have been loaded on board or, in the case of a term C.I.F. or C. & F., received for shipment.

(2) Where in a case within subsection (1) a bill of lading has been issued in a set of parts, unless otherwise agreed if the -documents are not to be sent from abroad the buyer may demand tender of the full set; otherwise only one part of the bill of lading need be tendered. Even if the agreement expressly requires a full set

(a) due tender of a single part is acceptable within the provisions of this Article on cure of improper delivery (subsection (1) of Section 2–508); and

(b) even though the full set is demanded, if the documents are sent from abroad the person tendering an incomplete set may nevertheless require payment upon furnishing an indemnity which the buyer in good faith deems adequate.

(3) A shipment by water or by air or a contract contemplating such shipment is "overseas" insofar as by usage of trade or agreement it is subject to the commercial, financing or shipping practices characteristic of international deep water commerce.

§ 2–324. "No Arrival, No Sale" Term.

Under a term "no arrival, no sale" or terms of like meaning, unless otherwise agreed,

(a) the seller must properly ship conforming goods and if they arrive by any means he must tender them on arrival but he assumes no obligation that the goods will arrive unless he has caused the non-arrival; and

(b) where without fault of the seller the goods are in part lost or have so deteriorated as no longer to conform to the contract or arrive after the contract time, the buyer may proceed as if there had been casualty to identified goods (Section 2–613).

§ 2–325. "Letter of Credit" Term; "Confirmed Credit".

(1) Failure of the buyer seasonably to furnish an agreed letter of credit is a breach of the contract for sale.

(2) The delivery to seller of a proper letter of credit suspends the buyer's obligation to pay. If the letter of credit is dishonored, the seller may on seasonable notification to the buyer require payment directly from him.

(3) Unless otherwise agreed the term "letter of credit" or "banker's credit" in a contract for sale means an irrevocable credit issued by a financing agency of good repute and, where the shipment is overseas, of good international repute. The term "confirmed credit" means that the credit must also carry the direct obligation of such an agency which does business in the seller's financial market.

§ 2–326. Sale on Approval and Sale or Return; Consignment Sales and Rights of Creditors.

(1) Unless otherwise agreed, if delivered goods may be returned by the buyer even though they conform to the contract, the transaction is

(a) a "sale on approval" if the goods are delivered primarily for use, and

(b) a "sale or return" if the goods are delivered primarily for resale.

(2) Except as provided in subsection (3), goods held on approval are not subject to the claims of the buyer's creditors until acceptance; goods held on sale or return are subject to such claims while in the buyer's possession.

(3) Where goods are delivered to a person for sale and such person maintains a place of business at which he deals in goods of the kind involved, under a name other

than the name of the person making delivery, then with respect to claims of creditors of the person conducting the business the goods are deemed to be on sale or return. The provisions of this subsection are applicable even though an agreement purports to reserve title to the person making delivery until payment or resale or uses such words as "on consignment" or "on memorandum". However, this subsection is not applicable if the person making delivery

(a) complies with an applicable law providing for a consignor's interest or the like to be evidenced by a sign, or

(b) establishes that the person conducting the business is generally known by his creditors to be substantially engaged in selling the goods of others, or

(c) complies with the filing provisions of the Article on Secured Transactions (Article 9).

(4) Any "or return" term of a contract for sale is to be treated as a separate contract for sale within the statute of frauds section of this Article (Section 2–201) and as contradicting the sale aspect of the contract within the provisions of this Article on parol or extrinsic evidence (Section 2–202).

§ 2–327. Special Incidents of Sale on Approval and Sale or Return.

(1) Under a sale on approval unless otherwise agreed

(a) although the goods are identified to the contract the risk of loss and the title do not pass to the buyer until acceptance; and

(b) use of the goods consistent with the purpose of trial is not acceptance but failure seasonably to notify the seller of election to return the goods is acceptance, and if the goods conform to the contract acceptance of any part is acceptance of the whole; and

(c) after due notification of election to return, the return is at the seller's risk and expense but a merchant buyer must follow any reasonable instructions.

(2) Under a sale or return unless otherwise agreed

(a) the option to return extends to the whole or any commercial unit of the goods while in substantially their original condition, but must be exercised seasonably; and

(b) the return is at the buyer's risk and expense.

§ 2–328. Sale by Auction.

(1) In a sale by auction if goods are put up in lots each lot is the subject of a separate sale.

(2) A sale by auction is complete when the auctioneer so announces by the fall of the hammer or in other customary manner. Where a bid is made while the hammer is falling in acceptance of a prior bid the auctioneer may in his discretion reopen the bidding or declare the goods sold under the bid on which the hammer was falling.

(3) Such a sale is with reserve unless the goods are in explicit terms put up without reserve. In an auction with reserve the auctioneer may withdraw the goods at any time until he announces completion of the sale. In an auction without reserve, after the auctioneer calls for bids on an article or lot, that article or lot cannot be withdrawn unless no bid is made within a reasonable time. In either case a bidder may retract his bid until the auctioneer's announcement of completion of the sale, but a bidder's retraction does not revive any previous bid.

(4) If the auctioneer knowingly receives a bid on the seller's behalf or the seller makes or procures such a bid, and notice has not been given that liberty for such bidding is reserved, the buyer may at his option avoid the sale or take the goods at the price of the last good faith bid prior to the completion of the sale. This subsection shall not apply to any bid at a forced sale.

PART 4 Title Creditors and Good Faith Purchasers

§ 2–401. Passing of Title; Reservation for Security; Limited Application of This Section.

Each provision of this Article with regard to the rights, obligations and remedies of the seller, the buyer, purchasers or other third parties applies irrespective of title to the goods except where the provision refers to such title. Insofar as situations are not covered by the other provisions of this Article and matters concerning title became material the following rules apply:

(1) Title to goods cannot pass under a contract for sale prior to their identification to the contract (Section 2–501), and unless otherwise explicitly agreed the buyer acquires by their identification a special property as limited by this Act.

Any retention or reservation by the seller of the title (property) in goods shipped or delivered to the buyer is limited in effect to a reservation of a security interest. Subject to these provisions and to the provisions of the Article on Secured Transactions (Article 9), title to goods passes from the seller to the buyer in any manner and on any conditions explicitly agreed on by the parties.

(2) Unless otherwise explicitly agreed title passes to the buyer at the time and place at which the seller completes his performance with reference to the physical delivery of the goods, despite any reservation of a security interest and even though a document of title is to be delivered at a different time or place; and in particular and despite any reservation of a security interest by the bill of lading

(a) if the contract requires or authorizes the seller to send the goods to the buyer but does not require him to deliver them at destination, title passes to the buyer at the time and place of shipment; but

(b) if the contract requires delivery at destination, title passes on tender there.

(3) Unless otherwise explicitly agreed where delivery is to be made without moving the goods,

(a) if the seller is to deliver a document of title, title passes at the time when and the place where he delivers such documents; or

(b) if the goods are at the time of contracting already identified and no documents are to be delivered, title passes at the time and place of contracting.

(4) A rejection or other refusal by the buyer to receive or retain the goods, whether or not justified, or a justified revocation of acceptance revests title to the goods in the seller. Such revesting occurs by operation of law and is not a "sale".

§ 2–402. Rights of Seller's Creditors Against Sold Goods.

(1) Except as provided in subsections (2) and (3), rights of unsecured creditors of the seller with respect to goods which have been identified to a contract for sale are subject to the buyer's rights to recover the goods under this Article (Sections 2–502 and 2–716).

(2) A creditor of the seller may treat a sale or an identification of goods to a contract for sale as void if as against him a retention of possession by the seller is fraudulent under any rule of law of the state where the goods are situated, except that retention of possession in good faith and current course of trade by a merchant-seller for a commercially reasonable time after a sale or identification is not fraudulent.

(3) Nothing in this Article shall be deemed to impair the rights of creditors of the seller

(a) under the provisions of the Article on Secured Transactions (Article 9); or

(b) where identification to the contract or delivery is made not in current course of trade but in satisfaction of or as security for a pre-existing claim for money, security or the like and is made under circumstances which under any rule of law of the state where the goods are situated would apart from this Article constitute the transaction a fraudulent transfer or voidable preference.

§ 2–403. Power to Transfer; Good Faith Purchase of Goods; "Entrusting".

(1) A purchaser of goods acquires all title which his transferor had or had power to transfer except that a purchaser of a limited interest acquires rights only to the extent of the interest purchased. A person with voidable title has power to transfer a good title to a good faith purchaser for value. When goods have been delivered under a transaction of purchase the purchaser has such power even though

(a) the transferor was deceived as to the identity of the purchaser, or

(b) the delivery was in exchange for a check which is later dishonored, or

(c) it was agreed that the transaction was to be a "cash sale", or

(d) the delivery was procured through fraud punishable as larcenous under the criminal law.

(2) Any entrusting of possession of goods to a merchant who deals in goods of that kind gives him power to transfer all rights of the entruster to a buyer in ordinary course of business.

(3) "Entrusting" includes any delivery and any acquiescence in retention of possession regardless of any condition expressed between the parties to the delivery or acquiescence and regardless of whether the procurement of the entrusting or the possessor's disposition of the goods have been such as to be larcenous under the criminal law.

(4) The rights of other purchasers of goods and of lien creditors are governed by the Articles on Secured Transactions (Article 9), Bulk Transfers (Article 6) and Documents of Title (Article 7).

PART 5 Performance

§ 2–501. Insurable Interest in Goods; Manner of Identification of Goods.

(1) The buyer obtains a special property and an insurable interest in goods by identification of existing goods as goods to which the contract refers even though the goods so identified are nonconforming and he has an option to return or reject them. Such identification can be made at any time and in any manner explicitly agreed to by the parties. In the absence of explicit agreement identification occurs

(a) when the contract is made if it is for the sale of goods already existing and identified;

(b) if the contract is for the sale of future goods other than those described in paragraph (c), when goods are shipped, marked or otherwise designated by the seller as goods to which the contract refers;

(c) when the crops are planted or otherwise become growing crops or the young are conceived if the contract is for the sale of unborn young to be born within twelve months after contracting or for the sale of crops to be harvested within twelve months or the next normal harvest season after contracting whichever is longer.

(2) The seller retains an insurable interest in goods so long as title to or any security interest in the goods remains in him and where the identification is by the seller alone he may until default or insolvency or notification to the buyer that the identification is final substitute other goods for those identified.

(3) Nothing in this section impairs any insurable interest recognized under any other statute or rule of law.

§ 2–502. Buyer's Right to Goods on Seller's Insolvency.

(1) Subject to subsection (2) and even though the goods have not been shipped a buyer who has paid a part or all of the price of goods in which he has a special property under the provisions of the immediately preceding section may on making and keeping good a tender of any unpaid portion of their price recover them from the seller if the seller becomes insolvent within ten days after receipt of the first installment on their price.

(2) If the identification creating his special property has been made by the buyer he acquires the right to recover the goods only if they conform to the contract for sale.

§ 2–503. Manner of Seller's Tender of Delivery.

(1) Tender of delivery requires that the seller put and hold conforming goods at the buyer's disposition and give the

buyer any notification reasonably necessary to enable him to take delivery. The manner, time and place for tender are determined by the agreement and this Article, and in particular

(a) tender must be at a reasonable hour, and if it is of goods they must be kept available for the period reasonably necessary to enable the buyer to take possession; but

(b) unless otherwise agreed the buyer must furnish facilities reasonably suited to the receipt of the goods.

(2) Where the case is within the next section respecting shipment tender requires that the seller comply with its provisions.

(3) Where the seller is required to deliver at a particular destination tender requires that he comply with subsection (1) and also in any appropriate case tender documents as described in subsections (4) and (5) of this section.

(4) Where goods are in the possession of a bailee and are to be delivered without being moved

(a) tender requires that the seller either tender a negotiable document of title covering such goods or procure acknowledgment by the bailee of the buyer's right to possession of the goods; but

(b) tender to the buyer of a non-negotiable document of title or of a written direction to the bailee to deliver is sufficient tender unless the buyer seasonably objects, and receipt by the bailee of notification of the buyer's rights fixes those rights as against the bailee and all third persons; but risk of loss of the goods and of any failure by the bailee to honor the non-negotiable document of title or to obey the direction remains on the seller until the buyer has had a reasonable time to present the document or direction, and a refusal by the bailee to honor the document or to obey the direction defeats the tender.

(5) Where the contract requires the seller to deliver documents

(a) he must tender all such documents in correct form, except as provided in this Article with respect to bills of lading in a set (subsection (2) of Section 2–323); and

(b) tender through customary banking channels is sufficient and dishonor of a draft accompanying the documents constitutes non-acceptance or rejection.

§ 2–504. Shipment by Seller.

Where the seller is required or authorized to send the goods to the buyer and the contract does not require him to deliver them at a particular destination, then unless otherwise agreed he must

(a) put the goods in the possession of such a carrier and make such a contract for their transportation as may be reasonable having regard to the nature of the goods and other circumstances of the case; and

(b) obtain and promptly deliver or tender in due form any document necessary to enable the buyer to obtain possession of the goods or otherwise required by the agreement or by usage of trade; and

(c) promptly notify the buyer of the shipment.

Failure to notify the buyer under paragraph (c) or to make a proper contract under paragraph (a) is a ground for rejection only if material delay or loss ensues.

§ 2–505. Seller's Shipment Under Reservation.

(1) Where the seller has identified goods to the contract by or before shipment:

(a) his procurement of a negotiable bill of lading to his own order or otherwise reserves in him a security interest in the goods. His procurement of the bill to the order of a financing agency or of the buyer indicates in addition only the seller's expectation of transferring that interest to the person named.

(b) a non-negotiable bill of lading to himself or his nominee reserves possession of the goods as security but except in a case of conditional delivery (subsection (2) of Section 2–507) a non-negotiable bill of lading naming the buyer as consignee reserves no security interest even though the seller retains possession of the bill of lading.

(2) When shipment by the seller with reservation of a security interest is in violation of the contract for sale it constitutes an improper contract for transportation within the preceding section but impairs neither the rights given to the buyer by shipment and identification of the goods to the contract nor the seller's powers as a holder of a negotiable document.

§ 2–506. Rights of Financing Agency.

(1) A financing agency by paying or purchasing for value a draft which relates to a shipment of goods acquires to the extent of the payment or purchase and in addition to its own rights under the draft and any document of title securing it any rights of the shipper in the goods including the right to stop delivery and the shipper's right to have the draft honored by the buyer.

(2) The right to reimbursement of a financing agency which has in good faith honored or purchased the draft under commitment to or authority from the buyer is not impaired by subsequent discovery of defects with reference to any relevant document which was apparently regular on its face.

§ 2–507. Effect of Seller's Tender; Delivery on Condition.

(1) Tender of delivery is a condition to the buyer's duty to accept the goods and, unless otherwise agreed, to his duty to pay for them. Tender entitles the seller to acceptance of the goods and to payment according to the contract.

(2) Where payment is due and demanded on the delivery to the buyer of goods or documents of title, his right as against the seller to retain or dispose of them is conditional upon his making the payment due.

§ 2–508. Cure by Seller of Improper Tender or Delivery; Replacement.

(1) Where any tender or delivery by the seller is rejected because non-conforming and the time for performance has

not yet expired, the seller may seasonably notify the buyer of his intention to cure and may then within the contract time make a conforming delivery.

(2) Where the buyer rejects a non-conforming tender which the seller had reasonable grounds to believe would be acceptable with or without money allowance the seller may if he seasonably notifies the buyer have a further reasonable time to substitute a conforming tender.

§ 2–509. Risk of Loss in the Absence of Breach.

(1) Where the contract requires or authorizes the seller to ship the goods by carrier

(a) if it does not require him to deliver them at a particular destination, the risk of loss passes to the buyer when the goods are duly delivered to the carrier even though the shipment is under reservation (Section 2–505); but

(b) if it does require him to deliver them at a particular destination and the goods are there duly tendered while in the possession of the carrier, the risk of loss passes to the buyer when the goods are there duly so tendered as to enable the buyer to take delivery.

(2) Where the goods are held by a bailee to be delivered without being moved, the risk of loss passes to the buyer

(a) on his receipt of a negotiable document of title covering the goods; or

(b) on acknowledgment by the bailee of the buyer's right to possession of the goods; or

(c) after his receipt of a non-negotiable document of title or other written direction to deliver, as provided in subsection (4)(b) of Section 2–503.

(3) In any case not within subsection (1) or (2), the risk of loss passes to the buyer on his receipt of the goods if the seller is a merchant; otherwise, the risk passes to the buyer on tender of delivery.

(4) The provisions of this section are subject to contrary agreement of the parties and to the provisions of this Article on sale on approval (Section 2–327) and on effect of breach on risk of loss (Section 2–510).

§ 2–510. Effect of Breach on Risk of Loss.

(1) Where a tender or delivery of goods so fails to conform to the contract as to give a right of rejection the risk of their loss remains on the seller until cure or acceptance.

(2) Where the buyer rightfully revokes acceptance he may to the extent of any deficiency in his effective insurance coverage treat the risk of loss as having rested on the seller from the beginning.

(3) Where the buyer as to conforming goods already identified to the contract for sale repudiates or is otherwise in breach before risk of their loss has passed to him, the seller may to the extent of any deficiency in his effective insurance coverage treat the risk of loss as resting on the buyer for a commercially reasonable time.

§ 2–511. Tender of Payment by Buyer; Payment by Check.

(1) Unless otherwise agreed tender of payment is a condition to the seller's duty to tender and complete any delivery.

(2) Tender of payment is sufficient when made by any means or in any manner current in the ordinary course of business unless the seller demands payment in legal tender and gives any extension of time reasonably necessary to procure it.

(3) Subject to the provisions of this Act on the effect of an instrument on an obligation (Section 3–310), payment by check is conditional and is defeated as between the parties by dishonor of the check on due presentment.

§ 2–512. Payment by Buyer Before Inspection.

(1) Where the contract requires payment before inspection non-conformity of the goods does not excuse the buyer from so making payment unless

(a) the non-conformity appears without inspection; or

(b) despite tender of the required documents the circumstances would justify injunction against honor under the provisions of this Act (Section 5–114).

(2) Payment pursuant to subsection (1) does not constitute an acceptance of goods or impair the buyer's right to inspect or any of his remedies.

§ 2–513. Buyer's Right to Inspection of Goods.

(1) Unless otherwise agreed and subject to subsection (3), where goods are tendered or delivered or identified to the contract for sale, the buyer has a right before payment or acceptance to inspect them at any reasonable place and time and in any reasonable manner. When the seller is required or authorized to send the goods to the buyer, the inspection may be after their arrival.

(2) Expenses of inspection must be borne by the buyer but may be recovered from the seller if the goods do not conform and are rejected.

(3) Unless otherwise agreed and subject to the provisions of this Article on C.I.F. contracts (subsection (3) of Section 2–321), the buyer is not entitled to inspect the goods before payment of the price when the contract provides

(a) for delivery "C.O.D." or on other like terms; or

(b) for payment against documents of title, except where such payment is due only after the goods are to become available for inspection.

(4) A place or method of inspection fixed by the parties is presumed to be exclusive but unless otherwise expressly agreed it does not postpone identification or shift the place for delivery or for passing the risk of loss. If compliance becomes impossible, inspection shall be as provided in this section unless the place or method fixed was clearly intended as an indispensable condition failure of which avoids the contract.

§ 2–514. When Documents Deliverable on Acceptance; When on Payment.

Unless otherwise agreed documents against which a draft is drawn are to be delivered to the drawee on acceptance of the draft if it is payable more than three days after presentment; otherwise, only on payment.

§ 2–515. Preserving Evidence of Goods in Dispute.

In furtherance of the adjustment of any claim or dispute

(a) either party on reasonable notification to the other and for the purpose of ascertaining the facts and preserving evidence has the right to inspect, test and sample the goods including such of them as may be in the possession or control of the other; and

(b) the parties may agree to a third party inspection or survey to determine the conformity or condition of the goods and may agree that the findings shall be binding upon them in any subsequent litigation or adjustment.

PART 6 Breach, Repudiation and Excuse

§ 2–601. Buyer's Rights on Improper Delivery.

Subject to the provisions of this Article on breach in installment contracts (Section 2–612) and unless otherwise agreed under the sections on contractual limitations of remedy (Sections 2–718 and 2–719), if the goods or the tender of delivery fail in any respect to conform to the contract, the buyer may

(a) reject the whole; or

(b) accept the whole; or

(c) accept any commercial unit or units and reject the rest.

§ 2–602. Manner and Effect of Rightful Rejection.

(1) Rejection of goods must be within a reasonable time after their delivery or tender. It is ineffective unless the buyer seasonably notifies the seller.

(2) Subject to the provisions of the two following sections on rejected goods (Sections 2–603 and 2–604),

(a) after rejection any exercise of ownership by the buyer with respect to any commercial unit is wrongful as against the seller; and

(b) if the buyer has before rejection taken physical possession of goods in which he does not have a security interest under the provisions of this Article (subsection (3) of Section 2–711), he is under a duty after rejection to hold them with reasonable care at the seller's disposition for a time sufficient to permit the seller to remove them; but

(c) the buyer has no further obligations with regard to goods rightfully rejected.

(3) The seller's rights with respect to goods wrongfully rejected are governed by the provisions of this Article on seller's remedies in general (Section 2–703).

§ 2–603. Merchant Buyer's Duties as to Rightfully Rejected Goods.

(1) Subject to any security interest in the buyer (subsection (3) of Section 2–711), when the seller has no agent or place of business at the market of rejection a merchant buyer is under a duty after rejection of goods in his possession or control to follow any reasonable instructions received from the seller with respect to the goods and in the absence of such instructions to make reasonable efforts to sell them for the seller's account if they are perishable or threaten to decline in value speedily. Instructions are not reasonable if on demand indemnity for expenses is not forthcoming.

(2) When the buyer sells goods under subsection (1), he is entitled to reimbursement from the seller or out of the proceeds for reasonable expenses of caring for and selling them, and if the expenses include no selling commission then to such commission as is usual in the trade or if there is none to a reasonable sum not exceeding ten per cent on the gross proceeds.

(3) In complying with this section the buyer is held only to good faith and good faith conduct hereunder is neither acceptance nor conversion nor the basis of an action for damages.

§ 2–604. Buyer's Options as to Salvage of Rightfully Rejected Goods.

Subject to the provisions of the immediately preceding section on perishables if the seller gives no instructions within a reasonable time after notification of rejection the buyer may store the rejected goods for the seller's account or reship them to him or resell them for the seller's account with reimbursement as provided in the preceding section. Such action is not acceptance or conversion.

§ 2–605. Waiver of Buyer's Objections by Failure to Particularize.

(1) The buyer's failure to state in connection with rejection a particular defect which is ascertainable by reasonable inspection precludes him from relying on the unstated defect to justify rejection or to establish breach

(a) where the seller could have cured it if stated seasonably; or

(b) between merchants when the seller has after rejection made a request in writing for a full and final written statement of all defects on which the buyer proposes to rely.

(2) Payment against documents made without reservation of rights precludes recovery of the payment for defects apparent on the face of the documents.

§ 2–606. What Constitutes Acceptance of Goods.

(1) Acceptance of goods occurs when the buyer

(a) after a reasonable opportunity to inspect the goods signifies to the seller that the goods are conforming or that he will take or retain them in spite of their nonconformity; or

(b) fails to make an effective rejection (subsection (1) of Section 2–602), but such acceptance does not occur until the buyer has had a reasonable opportunity to inspect them; or

(c) does any act inconsistent with the seller's ownership; but if such act is wrongful as against the seller it is an acceptance only if ratified by him.

(2) Acceptance of a part of any commercial unit is acceptance of that entire unit.

§ 2–607. Effect of Acceptance; Notice of Breach; Burden of Establishing Breach After Acceptance; Notice of Claim or Litigation to Person Answerable Over.

(1) The buyer must pay at the contract rate for any goods accepted.

(2) Acceptance of goods by the buyer precludes rejection of the goods accepted and if made with knowledge of a non-conformity cannot be revoked because of it unless the acceptance was on the reasonable assumption that the non-conformity would be seasonably cured but acceptance does not of itself impair any other remedy provided by this Article for non-conformity.

(3) Where a tender has been accepted

(a) the buyer must within a reasonable time after he discovers or should have discovered any breach notify the seller of breach or be barred from any remedy; and

(b) if the claim is one for infringement or the like (subsection (3) of Section 2–312) and the buyer is sued as a result of such a breach he must so notify the seller within a reasonable time after he receives notice of the litigation or be barred from any remedy over for liability established by the litigation.

(4) The burden is on the buyer to establish any breach with respect to the goods accepted.

(5) Where the buyer is sued for breach of a warranty or other obligation for which his seller is answerable over

(a) he may give his seller written notice of the litigation. If the notice states that the seller may come in and defend and that if the seller does not do so he will be bound in any action against him by his buyer by any determination of fact common to the two litigations, then unless the seller after seasonable receipt of the notice does come in and defend he is so bound.

(b) if the claim is one for infringement or the like (subsection (3) of Section 2–312) the original seller may demand in writing that his buyer turn over to him control of the litigation including settlement or else be barred from any remedy over and if he also agrees to bear all expense and to satisfy any adverse judgment, then unless the buyer after seasonable receipt of the demand does turn over control the buyer is so barred.

(6) The provisions of subsections (3), (4) and (5) apply to any obligation of a buyer to hold the seller harmless against infringement or the like (subsection (3) of Section 2–312).

§ 2–608. Revocation of Acceptance in Whole or in Part.

(1) The buyer may revoke his acceptance of a lot or commercial unit whose non-conformity substantially impairs its value to him if he has accepted it

(a) on the reasonable assumption that its non-conformity would be cured and it has not been seasonably cured; or

(b) without discovery of such non-conformity if his acceptance was reasonably induced either by the difficulty of discovery before acceptance or by the seller's assurances.

(2) Revocation of acceptance must occur within a reasonable time after the buyer discovers or should have discovered the ground for it and before any substantial change in condition of the goods which is not caused by their own defects. It is not effective until the buyer notifies the seller of it.

(3) A buyer who so revokes has the same rights and duties with regard to the goods involved as if he had rejected them.

§ 2–609. Right to Adequate Assurance of Performance.

(1) A contract for sale imposes an obligation on each party that the other's expectation of receiving due performance will not be impaired. When reasonable grounds for insecurity arise with respect to the performance of either party the other may in writing demand adequate assurance of due performance and until he receives such assurance may if commercially reasonable suspend any performance for which he has not already received the agreed return.

(2) Between merchants the reasonableness of grounds for insecurity and the adequacy of any assurance offered shall be determined according to commercial standards.

(3) Acceptance of any improper delivery or payment does not prejudice the aggrieved party's right to demand adequate assurance of future performance.

(4) After receipt of a justified demand failure to provide within a reasonable time not exceeding thirty days such assurance of due performance as is adequate under the circumstances of the particular case is a repudiation of the contract.

§ 2–610. Anticipatory Repudiation.

When either party repudiates the contract with respect to a performance not yet due the loss of which will substantially impair the value of the contract to the other, the aggrieved party may

(a) for a commercially reasonable time await performance by the repudiating party; or

(b) resort to any remedy for breach (Section 2–703 or Section 2–711), even though he has notified the repudiating party that he would await the latter's performance and has urged retraction; and

(c) in either case suspend his own performance or proceed in accordance with the provisions of this Article on the seller's right to identify goods to the contract notwithstanding breach or to salvage unfinished goods (Section 2–704).

§ 2–611. Retraction of Anticipatory Repudiation.

(1) Until the repudiating party's next performance is due he can retract his repudiation unless the aggrieved party has since the repudiation cancelled or materially changed his position or otherwise indicated that he considers the repudiation final.

(2) Retraction may be by any method which clearly indicates to the aggrieved party that the repudiating party intends to perform, but must include any assurance justifiably demanded under the provisions of this Article (Section 2–609).

(3) Retraction reinstates the repudiating party's rights under the contract with due excuse and allowance to the aggrieved party for any delay occasioned by the repudiation.

§ 2–612. "Installment Contract"; Breach.

(1) An "installment contract" is one which requires or authorizes the delivery of goods in separate lots to be separately accepted, even though the contract contains a clause "each delivery is a separate contract" or its equivalent.

(2) The buyer may reject any installment which is non-conforming if the non-conformity substantially impairs the value of that installment and cannot be cured or if the non-conformity is a defect in the required documents; but if the non-conformity does not fall within subsection (3) and the seller gives adequate assurance of its cure the buyer must accept that installment.

(3) Whenever non-conformity or default with respect to one or more installments substantially impairs the value of the whole contract there is a breach of the whole. But the aggrieved party reinstates the contract if he accepts a non-conforming installment without seasonably notifying of cancellation or if he brings an action with respect only to past installments or demands performance as to future installments.

§ 2–613. Casualty to Identified Goods.

Where the contract requires for its performance goods identified when the contract is made, and the goods suffer casualty without fault of either party before the risk of loss passes to the buyer, or in a proper case under a "no arrival, no sale" term (Section 2–324) then

(a) if the loss is total the contract is avoided; and

(b) if the loss is partial or the goods have so deteriorated as no longer to conform to the contract the buyer may nevertheless demand inspection and at his option either treat the contract as avoided or accept the goods with due allowance from the contract price for the deterioration or the deficiency in quantity but without further right against the seller.

§ 2–614. Substituted Performance.

(1) Where without fault of either party the agreed berthing, loading, or unloading facilities fail or an agreed type of carrier becomes unavailable or the agreed manner of delivery otherwise becomes commercially impracticable but a commercially reasonable substitute is available, such substitute performance must be tendered and accepted.

(2) If the agreed means or manner of payment fails because of domestic or foreign governmental regulation, the seller may withhold or stop delivery unless the buyer provides a means or manner of payment which is commercially a substantial equivalent. If delivery has already been taken, payment by the means or in the manner provided by the regulation discharges the buyer's obligation unless the regulation is discriminatory, oppressive or predatory.

§ 2–615. Excuse by Failure of Presupposed Conditions.

Except so far as a seller may have assumed a greater obligation and subject to the preceding section on substituted performance:

(a) Delay in delivery or non-delivery in whole or in part by a seller who complies with paragraphs (b) and (c) is not a breach of his duty under a contract for sale if performance as agreed has been made impracticable by the occurrence of a contingency the non-occurrence of which was a basic assumption on which the contract was made or by compliance in good faith with any applicable foreign or domestic governmental regulation or order whether or not it later proves to be invalid.

(b) Where the causes mentioned in paragraph (a) affect only a part of the seller's capacity to perform, he must allocate production and deliveries among his customers but may at his option include regular customers not then under contract as well as his own requirements for further manufacture. He may so allocate in any manner which is fair and reasonable.

(c) The seller must notify the buyer seasonably that there will be delay or non-delivery and, when allocation is required under paragraph (b), of the estimated quota thus made available for the buyer.

§ 2–616. Procedure on Notice Claiming Excuse.

(1) Where the buyer receives notification of a material or indefinite delay or an allocation justified under the preceding section he may by written notification to the seller as to any delivery concerned, and where the prospective deficiency substantially impairs the value of the whole contract under the provisions of this Article relating to breach of installment contracts (Section 2–612), then also as to the whole,

(a) terminate and thereby discharge any unexecuted portion of the contract; or

(b) modify the contract by agreeing to take his available quota in substitution.

(2) If after receipt of such notification from the seller the buyer fails so to modify the contract within a reasonable time not exceeding thirty days the contract lapses with respect to any deliveries affected.

(3) The provisions of this section may not be negated by agreement except in so far as the seller has assumed a greater obligation under the preceding section.

PART 7 Remedies

§ 2–701. Remedies for Breach of Collateral Contracts Not Impaired.

Remedies for breach of any obligation or promise collateral or ancillary to a contract for sale are not impaired by the provisions of this Article.

§ 2–702. Seller's Remedies on Discovery of Buyer's Insolvency.

(1) Where the seller discovers the buyer to be insolvent he may refuse delivery except for cash including payment for all goods theretofore delivered under the contract, and stop delivery under this Article (Section 2–705).

(2) Where the seller discovers that the buyer has received goods on credit while insolvent he may reclaim the goods upon demand made within ten days after the receipt, but if misrepresentation of solvency has been made to the particular seller in writing within three months before delivery the ten day limitation does not apply. Except as provided in this subsection the seller may not base a right to reclaim goods on the buyer's fraudulent or innocent misrepresentation of solvency or of intent to pay.

(3) The seller's right to reclaim under subsection (2) is subject to the rights of a buyer in ordinary course or other good faith purchaser under this Article (Section 2–403). Successful reclamation of goods excludes all other remedies with respect to them.

§ 2–703. Seller's Remedies in General.

Where the buyer wrongfully rejects or revokes acceptance of goods or fails to make a payment due on or before delivery or repudiates with respect to a part or the whole, then with respect to any goods directly affected and, if the breach is of the whole contract (Section 2–612), then also with respect to the whole undelivered balance, the aggrieved seller may

(a) withhold delivery of such goods;

(b) stop delivery by any bailee as hereafter provided (Section 2–705);

(c) proceed under the next section respecting goods still unidentified to the contract;

(d) resell and recover damages as hereafter provided (Section 2–706);

(e) recover damages for non-acceptance (Section 2–708) or in a proper case the price (Section 2–709);

(f) cancel.

§ 2–704. Seller's Right to Identify Goods to the Contract Notwithstanding Breach or to Salvage Unfinished Goods.

(1) An aggrieved seller under the preceding section may

(a) identify to the contract conforming goods not already identified if at the time he learned of the breach they are in his possession or control;

(b) treat as the subject of resale goods which have demonstrably been intended for the particular contract even though those goods are unfinished.

(2) Where the goods are unfinished an aggrieved seller may in the exercise of reasonable commercial judgment for the purposes of avoiding loss and of effective realization either complete the manufacture and wholly identify the goods to the contract or cease manufacture and resell for scrap or salvage value or proceed in any other reasonable manner.

§ 2–705. Seller's Stoppage of Delivery in Transit or Otherwise.

(1) The seller may stop delivery of goods in the possession of a carrier or other bailee when he discovers the buyer to be insolvent (Section 2–702) and may stop delivery of carload, truckload, planeload or larger shipments of express or freight when the buyer repudiates or fails to make a payment due before delivery or if for any other reason the seller has a right to withhold or reclaim the goods.

(2) As against such buyer the seller may stop delivery until

(a) receipt of the goods by the buyer; or

(b) acknowledgment to the buyer by any bailee of the goods except a carrier that the bailee holds the goods for the buyer; or

(c) such acknowledgment to the buyer by a carrier by reshipment or as warehouseman; or

(d) negotiation to the buyer of any negotiable document of title covering the goods.

(3)

(a) To stop delivery the seller must so notify as to enable the bailee by reasonable diligence to prevent delivery of the goods.

(b) After such notification the bailee must hold and deliver the goods according to the directions of the seller but the seller is liable to the bailee for any ensuing charges or damages.

(c) If a negotiable document of title has been issued for goods the bailee is not obliged to obey a notification to stop until surrender of the document.

(d) A carrier who has issued a non-negotiable bill of lading is not obliged to obey a notification to stop received from a person other than the consignor.

§ 2–706. Seller's Resale Including Contract for Resale.

(1) Under the conditions stated in Section 2–703 on seller's remedies, the seller may resell the goods concerned or the undelivered balance thereof. Where the resale is made in good faith and in a commercially reasonable manner the seller may recover the difference between the resale price and the contract price together with any incidental damages allowed under the provisions of this Article (Section 2–710), but less expenses saved in consequence of the buyer's breach.

(2) Except as otherwise provided in subsection (3) or unless otherwise agreed resale may be at public or private sale including sale by way of one or more contracts to sell or of identification to an existing contract of the seller. Sale may be as a unit or in parcels and at any time and place and on any terms but every aspect of the sale including

the method, manner, time, place and terms must be commercially reasonable. The resale must be reasonably identified as referring to the broken contract, but it is not necessary that the goods be in existence or that any or all of them have been identified to the contract before the breach.

(3) Where the resale is at private sale the seller must give the buyer reasonable notification of his intention to resell.

(4) Where the resale is at public sale

(a) only identified goods can be sold except where there is a recognized market for a public sale of futures in goods of the kind; and

(b) it must be made at a usual place or market for public sale if one is reasonably available and except in the case of goods which are perishable or threaten to decline in value speedily the seller must give the buyer reasonable notice of the time and place of the resale; and

(c) if the goods are not to be within the view of those attending the sale the notification of sale must state the place where the goods are located and provide for their reasonable inspection by prospective bidders; and

(d) the seller may buy.

(5) A purchaser who buys in good faith at a resale takes the goods free of any rights of the original buyer even though the seller fails to comply with one or more of the requirements of this section.

(6) The seller is not accountable to the buyer for any profit made on any resale. A person in the position of a seller (Section 2–707) or a buyer who has rightfully rejected or justifiably revoked acceptance must account for any excess over the amount of his security interest, as hereinafter defined (subsection (3) of Section 2–711).

§ 2–707. "Person in the Position of a Seller".

(1) A "person in the position of a seller" includes as against a principal an agent who has paid or become responsible for the price of goods on behalf of his principal or anyone who otherwise holds a security interest or other right in goods similar to that of a seller.

(2) A person in the position of a seller may as provided in this Article withhold or stop delivery (Section 2–705) and resell (Section 2–706) and recover incidental damages (Section 2–710).

§ 2–708. Seller's Damages for Non-Acceptance or Repudiation.

(1) Subject to subsection (2) and to the provisions of this Article with respect to proof of market price (Section 2–723), the measure of damages for non-acceptance or repudiation by the buyer is the difference between the market price at the time and place for tender and the unpaid contract price together with any incidental damages provided in this Article (Section 2–710), but less expenses saved in consequence of the buyer's breach.

(2) If the measure of damages provided in subsection (1) is inadequate to put the seller in as good a position as performance would have done then the measure of damages is the profit (including reasonable overhead) which the seller would have made from full performance by the buyer, together with any incidental damages provided in this Article (Section 2–710), due allowance for costs reasonably incurred and due credit for payments or proceeds of resale.

§ 2–709. Action for the Price.

(1) When the buyer fails to pay the price as it becomes due the seller may recover, together with any incidental damages under the next section, the price

(a) of goods accepted or of conforming goods lost or damaged within a commercially reasonable time after risk of their loss has passed to the buyer; and

(b) of goods identified to the contract if the seller is unable after reasonable effort to resell them at a reasonable price or the circumstances reasonably indicate that such effort will be unavailing.

(2) Where the seller sues for the price he must hold for the buyer any goods which have been identified to the contract and are still in his control except that if resale becomes possible he may resell them at any time prior to the collection of the judgment. The net proceeds of any such resale must be credited to the buyer and payment of the judgment entitles him to any goods not resold.

(3) After the buyer has wrongfully rejected or revoked acceptance of the goods or has failed to make a payment due or has repudiated (Section 2–610), a seller who is held not entitled to the price under this section shall nevertheless be awarded damages for non-acceptance under the preceding section.

§ 2–710. Seller's Incidental Damages.

Incidental damages to an aggrieved seller include any commercially reasonable charges, expenses or commissions incurred in stopping delivery, in the transportation, care and custody of goods after the buyer's breach, in connection with return or resale of the goods or otherwise resulting from the breach.

§ 2–711. Buyer's Remedies in General; Buyer's Security Interest in Rejected Goods.

(1) Where the seller fails to make delivery or repudiates or the buyer rightfully rejects or justifiably revokes acceptance then with respect to any goods involved, and with respect to the whole if the breach goes to the whole contract (Section 2–612), the buyer may cancel and whether or not he has done so may in addition to recovering so much of the price as has been paid

(a) "cover" and have damages under the next section as to all the goods affected whether or not they have been identified to the contract; or

(b) recover damages for non-delivery as provided in this Article (Section 2–713).

(2) Where the seller fails to deliver or repudiates the buyer may also

(a) if the goods have been identified recover them as provided in this Article (Section 2–502); or

(b) in a proper case obtain specific performance or replevy the goods as provided in this Article (Section 2–716).

(3) On rightful rejection or justifiable revocation of acceptance a buyer has a security interest in goods in his possession or control for any payments made on their price and any expenses reasonably incurred in their inspection, receipt, transportation, care and custody and may hold such goods and resell them in like manner as an aggrieved seller (Section 2–706).

§ 2–712. "Cover"; Buyer's Procurement of Substitute Goods.

(1) After a breach within the preceding section the buyer may "cover" by making in good faith and without unreasonable delay any reasonable purchase of or contract to purchase goods in substitution for those due from the seller.

(2) The buyer may recover from the seller as damages the difference between the cost of cover and the contract price together with any incidental or consequential damages as hereinafter defined (Section 2–715), but less expenses saved in consequence of the seller's breach.

(3) Failure of the buyer to effect cover within this section does not bar him from any other remedy.

§ 2–713. Buyer's Damages for Non-Delivery or Repudiation.

(1) Subject to provisions of this Article with respect to the proof of market price (Section 2–723), the measure of damages for non-delivery or repudiation by the seller is the difference between the market price at the time when the buyer learned of the breach and the contract price together with any incidental and consequential damages provided in this Article (Section 2–715), but less expenses saved in consequence of the seller's breach.

(2) Market price is to be determined as of the place for tender or, in cases of rejection after arrival or revocation of acceptance, as of the place of arrival.

§ 2–714. Buyer's Damages for Breach in Regard to Accepted Goods.

(1) Where the buyer has accepted goods and given notification (subsection (3) of Section 2–607) he may recover as damages for any non-conformity of tender the loss resulting in the ordinary course of events from the seller's breach as determined in any manner which is reasonable.

(2) The measure of damages for breach of warranty is the difference at the time and place of acceptance between the value of the goods accepted and the value they would have had if they had been as warranted, unless special circumstances show proximate damages of a different amount.

(3) In a proper case any incidental and consequential damages under the next section may be recovered.

§ 2–715. Buyer's Incidental and Consequential Damages.

(1) Incidental damages resulting from the seller's breach include expenses reasonably incurred in inspection, receipt, transportation and care and custody of goods rightfully rejected, any commercially reasonable charges, expenses or commissions in connection with effecting cover and any other reasonable expense incident to the delay or other breach.

(2) Consequential damages resulting from the seller's breach include

(a) any loss resulting from general or particular requirements and needs of which the seller at the time of contracting had reason to know and which could not reasonably be prevented by cover or otherwise; and

(b) injury to person or property proximately resulting from any breach of warranty.

§ 2–716. Buyer's Right to Specific Performance or Replevin.

(1) Specific performance may be decreed where the goods are unique or in other proper circumstances.

(2) The decree for specific performance may include such terms and conditions as to payment of the price, damages, or other relief as the court may deem just.

(3) The buyer has a right of replevin for goods identified to the contract if after reasonable effort he is unable to effect cover for such goods or the circumstances reasonably indicate that such effort will be unavailing or if the goods have been shipped under reservation and satisfaction of the security interest in them has been made or tendered.

§ 2–717. Deduction of Damages From the Price.

The buyer on notifying the seller of his intention to do so may deduct all or any part of the damages resulting from any breach of the contract from any part of the price still due under the same contract.

§ 2–718. Liquidation or Limitation of Damages; Deposits

(1) Damages for breach by either party may be liquidated in the agreement but only at an amount which is reasonable in the light of the anticipated or actual harm caused by the breach, the difficulties of proof of loss, and the inconvenience or nonfeasibility of otherwise obtaining an adequate remedy. A term fixing unreasonably large liquidated damages is void as a penalty.

(2) Where the seller justifiably withholds delivery of goods because of the buyer's breach, the buyer is entitled to restitution of any amount by which the sum of his payments exceeds

(a) the amount to which the seller is entitled by virtue of terms liquidating the seller's damages in accordance with subsection (1), or

(b) in the absence of such terms, twenty per cent of the value of the total performance for which the buyer is obligated under the contract or $500, whichever is smaller.

(3) The buyer's right to restitution under subsection (2) is subject to offset to the extent that the seller establishes

(a) a right to recover damages under the provisions of this Article other than subsection (1), and

(b) the amount or value of any benefits received by the buyer directly or indirectly by reason of the contract.

(4) Where a seller has received payment in goods their reasonable value or the proceeds of their resale shall be treated as payments for the purposes of subsection (2); but if the seller has notice of the buyer's breach before reselling goods received in part performance, his resale is subject to the conditions laid down in this Article on resale by an aggrieved seller (Section 2–706).

§ 2–719. Contractual Modification or Limitation of Remedy.

(1) Subject to the provisions of subsection (2) and (3) of this section and of the preceding section on liquidation and limitation of damages,

(a) the agreement may provide for remedies in addition to or in substitution for those provided in this Article and may limit or alter the measure of damages recoverable under this Article, as by limiting the buyer's remedies to return of the goods and repayment of the price or to repair and replacement of non-conforming goods or parts; and

(b) resort to a remedy as provided is optional unless the remedy is expressly agreed to be exclusive, in which case it is the sole remedy.

(2) Where circumstances cause an exclusive or limited remedy to fail of its essential purpose, remedy may be had as provided in this Act.

(3) Consequential damages may be limited or excluded unless the limitation or exclusion is unconscionable. Limitation of consequential damages for injury to the person in the case of consumer goods is prima facie unconscionable but limitation of damages where the loss is commercial is not.

§ 2–720. Effect of "Cancellation" or "Rescission" on Claims for Antecedent Breach.

Unless the contrary intention clearly appears, expressions of "cancellation" or "rescission" of the contract or the like shall not be construed as a renunciation or discharge of any claim in damages for an antecedent breach.

§ 2–721. Remedies for Fraud.

Remedies for material misrepresentation or fraud include all remedies available under this Article for non-fraudulent breach. Neither rescission or a claim for rescission of the contract for sale nor rejection or return of the goods shall bar or be deemed inconsistent with a claim for damages or other remedy.

§ 2–722. Who Can Sue Third Parties for Injury to Goods.

Where a third party so deals with goods which have been identified to a contract for sale as to cause actionable injury to a party to that contract

(a) a right of action against the third party is in either party to the contract for sale who has title to or a security interest or a special property or an insurable interest in the goods; and if the goods have been destroyed or converted a right of action is also in the party who either bore the risk of loss under the contract for sale or has since the injury assumed that risk as against the other;

(b) if at the time of the injury the party plaintiff did not bear the risk of loss as against the other party to the contract for sale and there is no arrangement between them for disposition of the recovery, his suit or settlement is subject to his own interest, as a fiduciary for the other party to the contract;

(c) either party may with the consent of the other sue for the benefit of whom it may concern.

§ 2–723. Proof of Market Price: Time and Place.

(1) If an action based on anticipatory repudiation comes to trial before the time for performance with respect to some or all of the goods, any damages based on market price (Section 2–708 or Section 2–713) shall be determined according to the price of such goods prevailing at the time when the aggrieved party learned of the repudiation.

(2) If evidence of a price prevailing at the times or places described in this Article is not readily available the price prevailing within any reasonable time before or after the time described or at any other place which in commercial judgment or under usage of trade would serve as a reasonable substitute for the one described may be used, making any proper allowance for the cost of transporting the goods to or from such other place.

(3) Evidence of a relevant price prevailing at a time or place other than the one described in this Article offered by one party is not admissible unless and until he has given the other party such notice as the court finds sufficient to prevent unfair -surprise.

§ 2–724. Admissibility of Market Quotations.

Whenever the prevailing price or value of any goods regularly bought and sold in any established commodity market is in issue, reports in official publications or trade journals or in newspapers or periodicals of general circulation published as the reports of such market shall be admissible in evidence. The circumstances of the preparation of such a report may be shown to affect its weight but not its admissibility.

§ 2–725. Statute of Limitations in Contracts for Sale.

(1) An action for breach of any contract for sale must be commenced within four years after the cause of action has accrued. By the original agreement the parties may reduce the period of limitation to not less than one year but may not extend it.

(2) A cause of action occurs when the breach occurs, regardless of the aggrieved party's lack of knowledge of the breach. A breach of warranty occurs when tender of delivery is made, except that where a warranty explicitly extends to future performance of the goods and discovery

of the breach must await the time of such performance the cause of action accrues when the breach is or should have been discovered.

(3) Where an action commenced within the time limited by subsection (1) is so terminated as to leave available a remedy by another action for the same breach such other action may be commenced after the expiration of the time limited and within six months after the termination of the first action unless the termination resulted from voluntary discontinuance or from dismissal for failure or neglect to prosecute.

(4) This section does not alter the law on tolling of the statute of limitations nor does it apply to causes of action which have accrued before this Act becomes effective.

ARTICLE 2A LEASES

PART 1 General Provisions

§ 2A–101. Short Title.

This Article shall be known and may be cited as the Uniform Commercial Code—Leases.

§ 2A–102. Scope.

This Article applies to any transaction, regardless of form, that creates a lease.

§ 2A–103. Definitions and Index of Definitions.

(1) In this Article unless the context otherwise requires:

(a) "Buyer in ordinary course of business" means a person who in good faith and without knowledge that the sale to him [or her] is in violation of the ownership rights or security interest or leasehold interest of a third party in the goods buys in ordinary course from a person in the business of selling goods of that kind but does not include a pawnbroker. "Buying" may be for cash or by exchange of other property or on secured or unsecured credit and includes receiving goods or documents of title under a pre-existing contract for sale but does not include a transfer in bulk or as security for or in total or partial satisfaction of a money debt.

(b) "Cancellation" occurs when either party puts an end to the lease contract for default by the other party.

(c) "Commercial unit" means such a unit of goods as by commercial usage is a single whole for purposes of lease and division of which materially impairs its character or value on the market or in use. A commercial unit may be a single article, as a machine, or a set of articles, as a suite of furniture or a line of machinery, or a quantity, as a gross or carload, or any other unit treated in use or in the relevant market as a single whole.

(d) "Conforming" goods or performance under a lease contract means goods or performance that are in accordance with the obligations under the lease contract.

(e) "Consumer lease" means a lease that a lessor regularly engaged in the business of leasing or selling makes to a lessee who is an individual and who takes under the lease primarily for a personal, family, or household purpose [, if the total payments to be made under the lease contract, excluding payments for options to renew or buy, do not exceed $].

(f) "Fault" means wrongful act, omission, breach, or default.

(g) "Finance lease" means a lease with respect to which:

(i) the lessor does not select, manufacture, or supply the goods;

(ii) the lessor acquires the goods or the right to possession and use of the goods in connection with the lease; and

(iii) one of the following occurs:

(A) the lessee receives a copy of the contract by which the lessor acquired the goods or the right to possession and use of the goods before signing the lease contract;

(B) the lessee's approval of the contract by which the lessor acquired the goods or the right to possession and use of the goods is a condition to effectiveness of the lease contract;

(C) the lessee, before signing the lease contract, receives an accurate and complete statement designating the promises and warranties, and any disclaimers of warranties, limitations or modifications of remedies, or liquidated damages, including those of a third party, such as the manufacturer of the goods, provided to the lessor by the person supplying the goods in connection with or as part of the contract by which the lessor acquired the goods or the right to possession and use of the goods; or

(D) if the lease is not a consumer lease, the lessor, before the lessee signs the lease contract, informs the lessee in writing (a) of the identity of the person supplying the goods to the lessor, unless the lessee has selected that person and directed the lessor to acquire the goods or the right to possession and use of the goods from that person, (b) that the lessee is entitled under this Article to the promises and warranties, including those of any third party, provided to the lessor by the person supplying the goods in connection with or as part of the contract by which the lessor acquired the goods or the right to possession and use of the goods, and (c) that the lessee may communicate with the person supplying the goods to the lessor and receive an accurate and complete statement of those promises and warranties, including any disclaimers and limitations of them or of remedies.

(h) "Goods" means all things that are movable at the time of identification to the lease contract, or are fixtures (Section 2A–309), but the term does not include money, documents, instruments, accounts, chattel paper, general intangibles, or minerals or the like, including oil and gas, before extraction. The term also includes the unborn young of animals.

(i) "Installment lease contract" means a lease contract that authorizes or requires the delivery of goods in separate lots to be separately accepted, even though the lease contract contains a clause "each delivery is a separate lease" or its equivalent.

(j) "Lease" means a transfer of the right to possession and use of goods for a term in return for consideration, but a sale, including a sale on approval or a sale or return, or retention or creation of a security interest is not a lease. Unless the context clearly indicates otherwise, the term includes a sublease.

(k) "Lease agreement" means the bargain, with respect to the lease, of the lessor and the lessee in fact as found in their language or by implication from other circumstances including course of dealing or usage of trade or course of performance as provided in this Article. Unless the context clearly indicates otherwise, the term includes a sublease agreement.

(l) "Lease contract" means the total legal obligation that results from the lease agreement as affected by this Article and any other applicable rules of law. Unless the context clearly indicates otherwise, the term includes a sublease contract.

(m) "Leasehold interest" means the interest of the lessor or the lessee under a lease contract.

(n) "Lessee" means a person who acquires the right to possession and use of goods under a lease. Unless the context clearly indicates otherwise, the term includes a sublessee.

(o) "Lessee in ordinary course of business" means a person who in good faith and without knowledge that the lease to him [or her] is in violation of the ownership rights or security interest or leasehold interest of a third party in the goods, leases in ordinary course from a person in the business of selling or leasing goods of that kind but does not include a pawnbroker. "Leas-ing" may be for cash or by exchange of other property or on secured or unsecured credit and includes receiving goods or documents of title under a pre-existing lease contract but does not include a transfer in bulk or as security for or in total or partial satisfaction of a money debt.

(p) "Lessor" means a person who transfers the right to possession and use of goods under a lease. Unless the context clearly indicates otherwise, the term includes a sublessor.

(q) "Lessor's residual interest" means the lessor's interest in the goods after expiration, termination, or cancellation of the lease contract.

(r) "Lien" means a charge against or interest in goods to secure payment of a debt or performance of an obligation, but the term does not include a security interest.

(s) "Lot" means a parcel or a single article that is the subject matter of a separate lease or delivery, whether or not it is sufficient to perform the lease contract.

(t) "Merchant lessee" means a lessee that is a merchant with respect to goods of the kind subject to the lease.

(u) "Present value" means the amount as of a date certain of one or more sums payable in the future, discounted to the date certain. The discount is determined by the interest rate specified by the parties if the rate was not manifestly unreasonable at the time the transaction was entered into; otherwise, the discount is determined by a commercially reasonable rate that takes into account the facts and circumstances of each case at the time the transaction was entered into.

(v) "Purchase" includes taking by sale, lease, mortgage, security interest, pledge, gift, or any other voluntary transaction creating an interest in goods.

(w) "Sublease" means a lease of goods the right to possession and use of which was acquired by the lessor as a lessee under an existing lease.

(x) "Supplier" means a person from whom a lessor buys or leases goods to be leased under a finance lease.

(y) "Supply contract" means a contract under which a lessor buys or leases goods to be leased.

(z) "Termination" occurs when either party pursuant to a power created by agreement or law puts an end to the lease contract otherwise than for default.

(2) Other definitions applying to this Article and the sections in which they appear are:

"Accessions". Section 2A–310(1).
"Construction mortgage". Section 2A–309(1)(d).
"Encumbrance". Section 2A–309(1)(e).
"Fixtures". Section 2A–309(1)(a).
"Fixture filing". Section 2A–309(1)(b).
"Purchase money lease". Section 2A–309(1)(c).

(3) The following definitions in other Articles apply to this Article:

"Account". Section 9–106.
"Between merchants". Section 2–104(3).
"Buyer". Section 2–103(1)(a).
"Chattel paper". Section 9–105(1)(b).
"Consumer goods". Section 9–109(1).
"Document". Section 9–105(1)(f).
"Entrusting". Section 2–403(3).
"General intangibles". Section 9–106.
"Good faith". Section 2–103(1)(b).
"Instrument". Section 9–105(1)(i).
"Merchant". Section 2–104(1).
"Mortgage". Sect 9–105(1)(j).
"Pursuant to commitment". Section 9–105(1)(k).
"Receipt". Section 2–103(1)(c).
"Sale". Section 2–106(1).
"Sale on approval". Section 2–326.
"Sale or return". Section 2–326.
"Seller". Section 2–103(1)(d).

(4) In addition Article 1 contains general definitions and principles of construction and interpretation applicable throughout this Article.

As amended in 1990.

§ 2A–104. Leases Subject to Other Law.

(1) A lease, although subject to this Article, is also subject to any applicable:

(a) certificate of title statute of this State: (list any certificate of title statutes covering automobiles, trailers, mobile homes, boats, farm tractors, and the like);

(b) certificate of title statute of another jurisdiction (Section 2A–105); or

(c) consumer protection statute of this State, or final consumer protection decision of a court of this State existing on the effective date of this Article.

(2) In case of conflict between this Article, other than Sections 2A–105, 2A–304(3), and 2A–305(3), and a statute or decision referred to in subsection (1), the statute or decision controls.

(3) Failure to comply with an applicable law has only the effect specified therein.

As amended in 1990.

§ 2A–105. Territorial Application of Article to Goods Covered by Certificate of Title.

Subject to the provisions of Sections 2A–304(3) and 2A–305(3), with respect to goods covered by a certificate of title issued under a statute of this State or of another jurisdiction, compliance and the effect of compliance or noncompliance with a certificate of title statute are governed by the law (including the conflict of laws rules) of the jurisdiction issuing the certificate until the earlier of (a) surrender of the certificate, or (b) four months after the goods are removed from that jurisdiction and thereafter until a new certificate of title is issued by another jurisdiction.

§ 2A–106. Limitation on Power of Parties to Consumer Lease to Choose Applicable Law and Judicial Forum.

(1) If the law chosen by the parties to a consumer lease is that of a jurisdiction other than a jurisdiction in which the lessee resides at the time the lease agreement becomes enforceable or within 30 days thereafter or in which the goods are to be used, the choice is not enforceable.

(2) If the judicial forum chosen by the parties to a consumer lease is a forum that would not otherwise have jurisdiction over the lessee, the choice is not enforceable.

§ 2A–107. Waiver or Renunciation of Claim or Right After Default.

Any claim or right arising out of an alleged default or breach of warranty may be discharged in whole or in part without consideration by a written waiver or renunciation signed and delivered by the aggrieved party.

§ 2A–108. Unconscionability.

(1) If the court as a matter of law finds a lease contract or any clause of a lease contract to have been unconscionable at the time it was made the court may refuse to enforce the lease contract, or it may enforce the remainder of the lease contract without the unconscionable clause, or it may so limit the application of any unconscionable clause as to avoid any unconscionable result.

(2) With respect to a consumer lease, if the court as a matter of law finds that a lease contract or any clause of a lease contract has been induced by unconscionable conduct or that unconscionable conduct has occurred in the collection of a claim arising from a lease contract, the court may grant appropriate relief.

(3) Before making a finding of unconscionability under subsection (1) or (2), the court, on its own motion or that of a party, shall afford the parties a reasonable opportunity to present evidence as to the setting, purpose, and effect of the lease contract or clause thereof, or of the conduct.

(4) In an action in which the lessee claims unconscionability with respect to a consumer lease:

(a) If the court finds unconscionability under subsection (1) or (2), the court shall award reasonable attorney's fees to the lessee.

(b) If the court does not find unconscionability and the lessee claiming unconscionability has brought or maintained an action he [or she] knew to be groundless, the court shall award reasonable attorney's fees to the party against whom the claim is made.

(c) In determining attorney's fees, the amount of the recovery on behalf of the claimant under subsections (1) and (2) is not controlling.

§ 2A–109. Option to Accelerate at Will.

(1) A term providing that one party or his [or her] successor in interest may accelerate payment or performance or require collateral or additional collateral "at will" or "when he [or she] deems himself [or herself] insecure" or in words of similar import must be construed to mean that he [or she] has power to do so only if he [or she] in good faith believes that the prospect of payment or performance is impaired.

(2) With respect to a consumer lease, the burden of establishing good faith under subsection (1) is on the party who exercised the power; otherwise the burden of establishing lack of good faith is on the party against whom the power has been exercised.

PART 2 Formation and Construction of Lease Contract

§ 2A–201. Statute of Frauds.

(1) A lease contract is not enforceable by way of action or defense unless:

(a) the total payments to be made under the lease contract, excluding payments for options to renew or buy, are less than $1,000; or

(b) there is a writing, signed by the party against whom enforcement is sought or by that party's authorized agent, sufficient to indicate that a lease contract has been made between the parties and to describe the goods leased and the lease term.

(2) Any description of leased goods or of the lease term is sufficient and satisfies subsection (1)(b), whether or not it is specific, if it reasonably identifies what is described.

(3) A writing is not insufficient because it omits or incorrectly states a term agreed upon, but the lease contract is not enforceable under subsection (1)(b) beyond the lease term and the quantity of goods shown in the writing.

(4) A lease contract that does not satisfy the requirements of subsection (1), but which is valid in other respects, is en-forceable:

(a) if the goods are to be specially manufactured or obtained for the lessee and are not suitable for lease or sale to others in the ordinary course of the lessor's business, and the lessor, before notice of repudiation is received and under circumstances that reasonably indicate that the goods are for the lessee, has made either a substantial beginning of their manufacture or commitments for their procurement;

(b) if the party against whom enforcement is sought admits in that party's pleading, testimony or otherwise in court that a lease contract was made, but the lease contract is not enforceable under this provision beyond the quantity of goods admitted; or

(c) with respect to goods that have been received and accepted by the lessee.

(5) The lease term under a lease contract referred to in subsection (4) is:

(a) if there is a writing signed by the party against whom enforcement is sought or by that party's authorized agent specifying the lease term, the term so specified;

(b) if the party against whom enforcement is sought admits in that party's pleading, testimony, or otherwise in court a lease term, the term so admitted; or

(c) a reasonable lease term.

§ 2A–202. Final Written Expression: Parol or Extrinsic Evidence.

Terms with respect to which the confirmatory memoranda of the parties agree or which are otherwise set forth in a writing intended by the parties as a final expression of their agreement with respect to such terms as are included therein may not be contradicted by evidence of any prior agreement or of a contemporaneous oral agreement but may be explained or supplemented:

(a) by course of dealing or usage of trade or by course of performance; and

(b) by evidence of consistent additional terms unless the court finds the writing to have been intended also as a complete and exclusive statement of the terms of the agreement.

§ 2A–203. Seals Inoperative.

The affixing of a seal to a writing evidencing a lease contract or an offer to enter into a lease contract does not render the writing a sealed instrument and the law with respect to sealed instruments does not apply to the lease contract or offer.

§ 2A–204. Formation in General.

(1) A lease contract may be made in any manner sufficient to show agreement, including conduct by both parties which recognizes the existence of a lease contract.

(2) An agreement sufficient to constitute a lease contract may be found although the moment of its making is undetermined.

(3) Although one or more terms are left open, a lease contract does not fail for indefiniteness if the parties have intended to make a lease contract and there is a reasonably certain basis for giving an appropriate remedy.

§ 2A–205. Firm Offers.

An offer by a merchant to lease goods to or from another person in a signed writing that by its terms gives assurance it will be held open is not revocable, for lack of consideration, during the time stated or, if no time is stated, for a reasonable time, but in no event may the period of irrevocability exceed 3 months. Any such term of assurance on a form supplied by the offeree must be separately signed by the offeror.

§ 2A–206. Offer and Acceptance in Formation of Lease Contract.

(1) Unless otherwise unambiguously indicated by the language or circumstances, an offer to make a lease contract must be construed as inviting acceptance in any manner and by any medium reasonable in the circumstances.

(2) If the beginning of a requested performance is a reasonable mode of acceptance, an offeror who is not notified of acceptance within a reasonable time may treat the offer as having lapsed before acceptance.

§ 2A–207. Course of Performance or Practical Construction.

(1) If a lease contract involves repeated occasions for performance by either party with knowledge of the nature of the performance and opportunity for objection to it by the other, any course of performance accepted or acquiesced in without objection is relevant to determine the meaning of the lease agreement.

(2) The express terms of a lease agreement and any course of performance, as well as any course of dealing and usage of trade, must be construed whenever reasonable as consistent with each other; but if that construction is unreasonable, express terms control course of performance, course of performance controls both course of dealing and usage of trade, and course of dealing controls usage of trade.

(3) Subject to the provisions of Section 2A–208 on modification and waiver, course of performance is relevant to show a waiver or modification of any term inconsistent with the course of performance.

§ 2A–208. Modification, Rescission and Waiver.

(1) An agreement modifying a lease contract needs no consideration to be binding.

(2) A signed lease agreement that excludes modification or rescission except by a signed writing may not be otherwise modified or rescinded, but, except as between merchants, such a requirement on a form supplied by a merchant must be separately signed by the other party.

(3) Although an attempt at modification or rescission does not satisfy the requirements of subsection (2), it may operate as a waiver.

(4) A party who has made a waiver affecting an executory portion of a lease contract may retract the waiver by reasonable notification received by the other party that strict

performance will be required of any term waived, unless the retraction would be unjust in view of a material change of position in reliance on the waiver.

§ 2A–209. Lessee Under Finance Lease as Beneficiary of Supply Contract.

(1) The benefit of a supplier's promises to the lessor under the supply contract and of all warranties, whether express or implied, including those of any third party provided in connection with or as part of the supply contract, extends to the lessee to the extent of the lessee's leasehold interest under a finance lease related to the supply contract, but is subject to the terms of the warranty and of the supply contract and all defenses or claims arising therefrom.

(2) The extension of the benefit of a supplier's promises and of warranties to the lessee (Section 2A–209(1)) does not: (i) modify the rights and obligations of the parties to the supply contract, whether arising therefrom or otherwise, or (ii) impose any duty or liability under the supply contract on the lessee.

(3) Any modification or rescission of the supply contract by the supplier and the lessor is effective between the supplier and the lessee unless, before the modification or rescission, the supplier has received notice that the lessee has entered into a finance lease related to the supply contract. If the modification or rescission is effective between the supplier and the lessee, the lessor is deemed to have assumed, in addition to the obligations of the lessor to the lessee under the lease contract, promises of the supplier to the lessor and warranties that were so modified or rescinded as they existed and were available to the lessee before modification or rescission.

(4) In addition to the extension of the benefit of the supplier's promises and of warranties to the lessee under subsection (1), the lessee retains all rights that the lessee may have against the supplier which arise from an agreement between the lessee and the supplier or under other law.

As amended in 1990.

§ 2A–210. Express Warranties.

(1) Express warranties by the lessor are created as follows:

(a) Any affirmation of fact or promise made by the lessor to the lessee which relates to the goods and becomes part of the basis of the bargain creates an express warranty that the goods will conform to the affirmation or promise.

(b) Any description of the goods which is made part of the basis of the bargain creates an express warranty that the goods will conform to the description.

(c) Any sample or model that is made part of the basis of the bargain creates an express warranty that the whole of the goods will conform to the sample or model.

(2) It is not necessary to the creation of an express warranty that the lessor use formal words, such as "warrant" or "guarantee," or that the lessor have a specific intention to make a warranty, but an affirmation merely of the value of the goods or a statement purporting to be merely the lessor's opinion or commendation of the goods does not create a warranty.

§ 2A–211. Warranties Against Interference and Against Infringement; Lessee's Obligation Against Infringement.

(1) There is in a lease contract a warranty that for the lease term no person holds a claim to or interest in the goods that arose from an act or omission of the lessor, other than a claim by way of infringement or the like, which will interfere with the lessee's enjoyment of its leasehold interest.

(2) Except in a finance lease there is in a lease contract by a lessor who is a merchant regularly dealing in goods of the kind a warranty that the goods are delivered free of the rightful claim of any person by way of infringement or the like.

(3) A lessee who furnishes specifications to a lessor or a supplier shall hold the lessor and the supplier harmless against any claim by way of infringement or the like that arises out of compliance with the specifications.

§ 2A–212. Implied Warranty of Merchantability.

(1) Except in a finance lease, a warranty that the goods will be merchantable is implied in a lease contract if the lessor is a merchant with respect to goods of that kind.

(2) Goods to be merchantable must be at least such as

(a) pass without objection in the trade under the description in the lease agreement;

(b) in the case of fungible goods, are of fair average quality within the description;

(c) are fit for the ordinary purposes for which goods of that type are used;

(d) run, within the variation permitted by the lease agreement, of even kind, quality, and quantity within each unit and among all units involved;

(e) are adequately contained, packaged, and labeled as the lease agreement may require; and

(f) conform to any promises or affirmations of fact made on the container or label.

(3) Other implied warranties may arise from course of dealing or usage of trade.

§ 2A–213. Implied Warranty of Fitness for Particular Purpose.

Except in a finance lease, if the lessor at the time the lease contract is made has reason to know of any particular purpose for which the goods are required and that the lessee is relying on the lessor's skill or judgment to select or furnish suitable goods, there is in the lease contract an implied warranty that the goods will be fit for that purpose.

§ 2A–214. Exclusion or Modification of Warranties.

(1) Words or conduct relevant to the creation of an express warranty and words or conduct tending to negate or limit a warranty must be construed wherever reasonable as consistent with each other; but, subject to the provisions of Section 2A–202 on parol or extrinsic evidence, negation or limitation is inoperative to the extent that the construction is unreasonable.

(2) Subject to subsection (3), to exclude or modify the implied warranty of merchantability or any part of it the language must mention "merchantability", be by a writing, and be conspicuous. Subject to subsection (3), to exclude or modify any implied warranty of fitness the exclusion must be by a writing and be conspicuous. Language to exclude all implied warranties of fitness is sufficient if it is in writing, is conspicuous and states, for example, "There is no warranty that the goods will be fit for a particular purpose".

(3) Notwithstanding subsection (2), but subject to subsection (4),

(a) unless the circumstances indicate otherwise, all implied warranties are excluded by expressions like "as is," or "with all faults," or by other language that in common understanding calls the lessee's attention to the exclusion of warranties and makes plain that there is no implied warranty, if in writing and conspicuous;

(b) if the lessee before entering into the lease contract has examined the goods or the sample or model as fully as desired or has refused to examine the goods, there is no implied warranty with regard to defects that an examination ought in the circumstances to have revealed; and

(c) an implied warranty may also be excluded or modified by course of dealing, course of performance, or usage of trade.

(4) To exclude or modify a warranty against interference or against infringement (Section 2A–211) or any part of it, the language must be specific, be by a writing, and be conspicuous, unless the circumstances, including course of performance, course of dealing, or usage of trade, give the lessee reason to know that the goods are being leased subject to a claim or interest of any person.

§ 2A–215. Cumulation and Conflict of Warranties Express or Implied.

Warranties, whether express or implied, must be construed as consistent with each other and as cumulative, but if that construction is unreasonable, the intention of the parties determines which warranty is dominant. In ascertaining that intention the following rules apply:

(a) Exact or technical specifications displace an inconsistent sample or model or general language of description.

(b) A sample from an existing bulk displaces inconsistent general language of description.

(c) Express warranties displace inconsistent implied warranties other than an implied warranty of fitness for a particular purpose.

§ 2A–216. Third-Party Beneficiaries of Express and Implied Warranties.

Alternative A A warranty to or for the benefit of a lessee under this Article, whether express or implied, extends to any natural person who is in the family or household of the lessee or who is a guest in the lessee's home if it is reasonable to expect that such person may use, consume, or be affected by the goods and who is injured in person by breach of the warranty. This section does not displace principles of law and equity that extend a warranty to or for the benefit of a lessee to other persons. The operation of this section may not be excluded, modified, or limited, but an exclusion, modification, or limitation of the warranty, including any with respect to rights and remedies, effective against the lessee is also effective against any beneficiary designated under this section.

Alternative B A warranty to or for the benefit of a lessee under this Article, whether express or implied, extends to any natural person who may reasonably be expected to use, consume, or be affected by the goods and who is injured in person by breach of the warranty. This section does not displace principles of law and equity that extend a warranty to or for the benefit of a lessee to other persons. The operation of this section may not be excluded, modified, or limited, but an exclusion, modification, or limitation of the warranty, including any with respect to rights and remedies, effective against the lessee is also effective against the beneficiary designated under this section.

Alternative C A warranty to or for the benefit of a lessee under this Article, whether express or implied, extends to any person who may reasonably be expected to use, consume, or be affected by the goods and who is injured by breach of the warranty. The operation of this section may not be excluded, modified, or limited with respect to injury to the person of an individual to whom the warranty extends, but an exclusion, modification, or limitation of the warranty, including any with respect to rights and remedies, effective against the lessee is also effective against the beneficiary designated under this section.

§ 2A–217. Identification.

Identification of goods as goods to which a lease contract refers may be made at any time and in any manner explicitly agreed to by the parties. In the absence of explicit agreement, identification occurs:

(a) when the lease contract is made if the lease contract is for a lease of goods that are existing and identified;

(b) when the goods are shipped, marked, or otherwise designated by the lessor as goods to which the lease contract refers, if the lease contract is for a lease of goods that are not existing and identified; or

(c) when the young are conceived, if the lease contract is for a lease of unborn young of animals.

§ 2A–218. Insurance and Proceeds.

(1) A lessee obtains an insurable interest when existing goods are identified to the lease contract even though the goods identified are nonconforming and the lessee has an option to reject them.

(2) If a lessee has an insurable interest only by reason of the lessor's identification of the goods, the lessor, until default or insolvency or notification to the lessee that identification is final, may substitute other goods for those identified.

(3) Notwithstanding a lessee's insurable interest under subsections (1) and (2), the lessor retains an insurable

interest until an option to buy has been exercised by the lessee and risk of loss has passed to the lessee.

(4) Nothing in this section impairs any insurable interest recognized under any other statute or rule of law.

(5) The parties by agreement may determine that one or more parties have an obligation to obtain and pay for insurance covering the goods and by agreement may determine the beneficiary of the proceeds of the insurance.

§ 2A–219. Risk of Loss.

(1) Except in the case of a finance lease, risk of loss is retained by the lessor and does not pass to the lessee. In the case of a finance lease, risk of loss passes to the lessee.

(2) Subject to the provisions of this Article on the effect of default on risk of loss (Section 2A–220), if risk of loss is to pass to the lessee and the time of passage is not stated, the following rules apply:

(a) If the lease contract requires or authorizes the goods to be shipped by carrier

(i) and it does not require delivery at a particular destination, the risk of loss passes to the lessee when the goods are duly delivered to the carrier; but

(ii) if it does require delivery at a particular destination and the goods are there duly tendered while in the possession of the carrier, the risk of loss passes to the lessee when the goods are there duly so tendered as to enable the lessee to take delivery.

(b) If the goods are held by a bailee to be delivered without being moved, the risk of loss passes to the lessee on acknowledgment by the bailee of the lessee's right to possession of the goods.

(c) In any case not within subsection (a) or (b), the risk of loss passes to the lessee on the lessee's receipt of the goods if the lessor, or, in the case of a finance lease, the supplier, is a merchant; otherwise the risk passes to the lessee on tender of delivery.

§ 2A–220. Effect of Default on Risk of Loss.

(1) Where risk of loss is to pass to the lessee and the time of passage is not stated:

(a) If a tender or delivery of goods so fails to conform to the lease contract as to give a right of rejection, the risk of their loss remains with the lessor, or, in the case of a finance lease, the supplier, until cure or acceptance.

(b) If the lessee rightfully revokes acceptance, he [or she], to the extent of any deficiency in his [or her] effective insurance coverage, may treat the risk of loss as having remained with the lessor from the beginning.

(2) Whether or not risk of loss is to pass to the lessee, if the lessee as to conforming goods already identified to a lease contract repudiates or is otherwise in default under the lease contract, the lessor, or, in the case of a finance lease, the supplier, to the extent of any deficiency in his [or her] effective insurance coverage may treat the risk of loss as resting on the lessee for a commercially reasonable time.

§ 2A–221. Casualty to Identified Goods.

If a lease contract requires goods identified when the lease contract is made, and the goods suffer casualty without fault of the lessee, the lessor or the supplier before delivery, or the goods suffer casualty before risk of loss passes to the lessee pursuant to the lease agreement or Section 2A–219, then:

(a) if the loss is total, the lease contract is avoided; and

(b) if the loss is partial or the goods have so deteriorated as to no longer conform to the lease contract, the lessee may nevertheless demand inspection and at his [or her] option either treat the lease contract as avoided or, except in a finance lease that is not a consumer lease, accept the goods with due allowance from the rent payable for the balance of the lease term for the deterioration or the deficiency in quantity but without further right against the lessor.

PART 3 Effect of Lease Contract

§ 2A–301. Enforceability of Lease Contract.

Except as otherwise provided in this Article, a lease contract is effective and enforceable according to its terms between the parties, against purchasers of the goods and against creditors of the parties.

§ 2A–302. Title to and Possession of Goods.

Except as otherwise provided in this Article, each provision of this Article applies whether the lessor or a third party has title to the goods, and whether the lessor, the lessee, or a third party has possession of the goods, notwithstanding any statute or rule of law that possession or the absence of possession is fraudulent.

§ 2A–303. Alienability of Party's Interest Under Lease Contract or of Lessor's Residual Interest in Goods; Delegation of Performance; Transfer of Rights.

(1) As used in this section, "creation of a security interest" includes the sale of a lease contract that is subject to Article 9, Secured Transactions, by reason of Section 9–102(1)(b).

(2) Except as provided in subsections (3) and (4), a provision in a lease agreement which (i) prohibits the voluntary or involuntary transfer, including a transfer by sale, sublease, creation or en-forcement of a security interest, or attachment, levy, or other judicial process, of an interest of a party under the lease contract or of the lessor's residual interest in the goods, or (ii) makes such a transfer an event of default, gives rise to the rights and remedies provided in subsection (5), but a transfer that is prohibited or is an event of default under the lease agreement is otherwise effective.

(3) A provision in a lease agreement which (i) prohibits the creation or enforcement of a security interest in an interest of a party under the lease contract or in the lessor's residual interest in the goods, or (ii) makes such a transfer an event of default, is not enforceable unless, and then only to the extent that, there is an actual transfer by the lessee of the lessee's right of possession or use of the goods in violation of the provision or an actual delegation of a material performance of either party to the lease contract in violation of the provision. Neither the granting nor the

enforcement of a security interest in (i) the lessor's interest under the lease contract or (ii) the lessor's residual interest in the goods is a transfer that materially impairs the prospect of obtaining return performance by, materially changes the duty of, or materially increases the burden or risk imposed on, the lessee within the purview of subsection (5) unless, and then only to the extent that, there is an actual delegation of a material performance of the lessor.

(4) A provision in a lease agreement which (i) prohibits a transfer of a right to damages for default with respect to the whole lease contract or of a right to payment arising out of the transferor's due performance of the transferor's entire obligation, or (ii) makes such a transfer an event of default, is not enforceable, and such a transfer is not a transfer that materially impairs the prospect of obtaining return performance by, materially changes the duty of, or materially increases the burden or risk imposed on, the other party to the lease contract within the purview of subsection (5).

(5) Subject to subsections (3) and (4):

(a) if a transfer is made which is made an event of default under a lease agreement, the party to the lease contract not making the transfer, unless that party waives the default or otherwise agrees, has the rights and remedies described in Section 2A–501(2);

(b) if paragraph (a) is not applicable and if a transfer is made that (i) is prohibited under a lease agreement or (ii) materially impairs the prospect of obtaining return performance by, materially changes the duty of, or materially increases the burden or risk imposed on, the other party to the lease contract, unless the party not making the transfer agrees at any time to the transfer in the lease contract or otherwise, then, except as limited by contract, (i) the transferor is liable to the party not making the transfer for damages caused by the transfer to the extent that the damages could not reasonably be prevented by the party not making the transfer and (ii) a court having jurisdiction may grant other appropriate relief, including cancellation of the lease contract or an injunction against the transfer.

(6) A transfer of "the lease" or of "all my rights under the lease", or a transfer in similar general terms, is a transfer of rights and, unless the language or the circumstances, as in a transfer for security, indicate the contrary, the transfer is a delegation of duties by the transferor to the transferee. Acceptance by the transferee constitutes a promise by the transferee to perform those duties. The promise is enforceable by either the transferor or the other party to the lease contract.

(7) Unless otherwise agreed by the lessor and the lessee, a delegation of performance does not relieve the transferor as against the other party of any duty to perform or of any liability for default.

(8) In a consumer lease, to prohibit the transfer of an interest of a party under the lease contract or to make a transfer an event of de-fault, the language must be specific, by a writing, and conspicuous.

As amended in 1990.

§ 2A–304. Subsequent Lease of Goods by Lessor.

(1) Subject to Section 2A–303, a subsequent lessee from a lessor of goods under an existing lease contract obtains, to the extent of the leasehold interest transferred, the leasehold interest in the goods that the lessor had or had power to transfer, and except as provided in subsection (2) and Section 2A–527(4), takes subject to the existing lease contract. A lessor with voidable title has power to transfer a good leasehold interest to a good faith subsequent lessee for value, but only to the extent set forth in the preceding sentence. If goods have been delivered under a transaction of purchase, the lessor has that power even though:

(a) the lessor's transferor was deceived as to the identity of the lessor;

(b) the delivery was in exchange for a check which is later dishonored;

(c) it was agreed that the transaction was to be a "cash sale"; or

(d) the delivery was procured through fraud punishable as larcenous under the criminal law.

(2) A subsequent lessee in the ordinary course of business from a lessor who is a merchant dealing in goods of that kind to whom the goods were entrusted by the existing lessee of that lessor before the interest of the subsequent lessee became enforceable against that lessor obtains, to the extent of the leasehold interest transferred, all of that lessor's and the existing lessee's rights to the goods, and takes free of the existing lease contract.

(3) A subsequent lessee from the lessor of goods that are subject to an existing lease contract and are covered by a certificate of title issued under a statute of this State or of another jurisdiction takes no greater rights than those provided both by this section and by the certificate of title statute.

As amended in 1990.

§ 2A–305. Sale or Sublease of Goods by Lessee.

(1) Subject to the provisions of Section 2A–303, a buyer or sublessee from the lessee of goods under an existing lease contract obtains, to the extent of the interest transferred, the leasehold interest in the goods that the lessee had or had power to transfer, and except as provided in subsection (2) and Section 2A–511(4), takes subject to the existing lease contract. A lessee with a voidable leasehold interest has power to transfer a good leasehold interest to a good faith buyer for value or a good faith sublessee for value, but only to the extent set forth in the preceding sentence. When goods have been delivered under a transaction of lease the lessee has that power even though:

(a) the lessor was deceived as to the identity of the lessee;

(b) the delivery was in exchange for a check which is later dishonored; or

(c) the delivery was procured through fraud punishable as larcenous under the criminal law.

(2) A buyer in the ordinary course of business or a sublessee in the ordinary course of business from a lessee who is a merchant dealing in goods of that kind to whom the

goods were entrusted by the lessor obtains, to the extent of the interest transferred, all of the lessor's and lessee's rights to the goods, and takes free of the existing lease contract.

(3) A buyer or sublessee from the lessee of goods that are subject to an existing lease contract and are covered by a certificate of title issued under a statute of this State or of another jurisdiction takes no greater rights than those provided both by this section and by the certificate of title statute.

§ 2A–306. Priority of Certain Liens Arising by Operation of Law.

If a person in the ordinary course of his [or her] business furnishes services or materials with respect to goods subject to a lease contract, a lien upon those goods in the possession of that person given by statute or rule of law for those materials or services takes priority over any interest of the lessor or lessee under the lease contract or this Article unless the lien is created by statute and the statute provides otherwise or unless the lien is created by rule of law and the rule of law provides otherwise.

§ 2A–307. Priority of Liens Arising by Attachment or Levy on, Security Interests in, and Other Claims to Goods.

(1) Except as otherwise provided in Section 2A–306, a creditor of a lessee takes subject to the lease contract.

(2) Except as otherwise provided in subsections (3) and (4) and in Sections 2A–306 and 2A–308, a creditor of a lessor takes subject to the lease contract unless:

(a) the creditor holds a lien that attached to the goods before the lease contract became enforceable;

(b) the creditor holds a security interest in the goods and the lessee did not give value and receive delivery of the goods without knowledge of the security interest; or

(c) the creditor holds a security interest in the goods which was perfected (Section 9–303) before the lease contract became enforceable.

(3) A lessee in the ordinary course of business takes the leasehold interest free of a security interest in the goods created by the lessor even though the security interest is perfected (Section 9–303) and the lessee knows of its existence.

(4) A lessee other than a lessee in the ordinary course of business takes the leasehold interest free of a security interest to the extent that it secures future advances made after the secured party acquires knowledge of the lease or more than 45 days after the lease contract becomes enforceable, whichever first occurs, unless the future advances are made pursuant to a commitment entered into without knowledge of the lease and before the expiration of the 45-day period.

As amended in 1990.

§ 2A–308. Special Rights of Creditors.

(1) A creditor of a lessor in possession of goods subject to a lease contract may treat the lease contract as void if as against the creditor retention of possession by the lessor is fraudulent under any statute or rule of law, but retention of possession in good faith and current course of trade by the lessor for a commercially reasonable time after the lease contract becomes enforceable is not fraudulent.

(2) Nothing in this Article impairs the rights of creditors of a lessor if the lease contract (a) becomes enforceable, not in current course of trade but in satisfaction of or as security for a pre-existing claim for money, security, or the like, and (b) is made under circumstances which under any statute or rule of law apart from this Article would constitute the transaction a fraudulent transfer or voidable preference.

(3) A creditor of a seller may treat a sale or an identification of goods to a contract for sale as void if as against the creditor retention of possession by the seller is fraudulent under any statute or rule of law, but retention of possession of the goods pursuant to a lease contract entered into by the seller as lessee and the buyer as lessor in connection with the sale or identification of the goods is not fraudulent if the buyer bought for value and in good faith.

§ 2A–309. Lessor's and Lessee's Rights When Goods Become Fixtures.

(1) In this section:

(a) goods are "fixtures" when they become so related to particular real estate that an interest in them arises under real estate law;

(b) a "fixture filing" is the filing, in the office where a mortgage on the real estate would be filed or recorded, of a financing statement covering goods that are or are to become fixtures and conforming to the requirements of Section 9–402(5);

(c) a lease is a "purchase money lease" unless the lessee has possession or use of the goods or the right to possession or use of the goods before the lease agreement is enforceable;

(d) a mortgage is a "construction mortgage" to the extent it secures an obligation incurred for the construction of an improvement on land including the acquisition cost of the land, if the recorded writing so indicates; and

(e) "encumbrance" includes real estate mortgages and other liens on real estate and all other rights in real estate that are not ownership interests.

(2) Under this Article a lease may be of goods that are fixtures or may continue in goods that become fixtures, but no lease exists under this Article of ordinary building materials incorporated into an improvement on land.

(3) This Article does not prevent creation of a lease of fixtures pursuant to real estate law.

(4) The perfected interest of a lessor of fixtures has priority over a conflicting interest of an encumbrancer or owner of the real estate if:

(a) the lease is a purchase money lease, the conflicting interest of the encumbrancer or owner arises before the goods become fixtures, the interest of the lessor is perfected by a fixture filing before the goods become fixtures or within ten days thereafter, and the lessee has an interest of record in the real estate or is in possession of the real estate; or

(b) the interest of the lessor is perfected by a fixture filing before the interest of the encumbrancer or owner is of record, the lessor's interest has priority over any conflicting interest of a predecessor in title of the encumbrancer or owner, and the lessee has an interest of record in the real estate or is in possession of the real estate.

(5) The interest of a lessor of fixtures, whether or not perfected, has priority over the conflicting interest of an encumbrancer or owner of the real estate if:

(a) the fixtures are readily removable factory or office machines, readily removable equipment that is not primarily used or leased for use in the operation of the real estate, or readily removable replacements of domestic appliances that are goods subject to a consumer lease, and before the goods become fixtures the lease contract is enforceable; or

(b) the conflicting interest is a lien on the real estate obtained by legal or equitable proceedings after the lease contract is enforceable; or

(c) the encumbrancer or owner has consented in writing to the lease or has disclaimed an interest in the goods as fixtures; or

(d) the lessee has a right to remove the goods as against the encumbrancer or owner. If the lessee's right to remove terminates, the priority of the interest of the lessor continues for a reasonable time.

(6) Notwithstanding subsection (4)(a) but otherwise subject to subsections (4) and (5), the interest of a lessor of fixtures, including the lessor's residual interest, is subordinate to the conflicting interest of an encumbrancer of the real estate under a construction mortgage recorded before the goods become fixtures if the goods become fixtures before the completion of the construction. To the extent given to refinance a construction mortgage, the conflicting interest of an encumbrancer of the real estate under a mortgage has this priority to the same extent as the encumbrancer of the real estate under the construction mortgage.

(7) In cases not within the preceding subsections, priority between the interest of a lessor of fixtures, including the lessor's residual interest, and the conflicting interest of an encumbrancer or owner of the real estate who is not the lessee is determined by the priority rules governing conflicting interests in real estate.

(8) If the interest of a lessor of fixtures, including the lessor's residual interest, has priority over all conflicting interests of all owners and encumbrancers of the real estate, the lessor or the lessee may (i) on default, expiration, termination, or cancellation of the lease agreement but subject to the agreement and this Article, or (ii) if necessary to enforce other rights and remedies of the lessor or lessee under this Article, remove the goods from the real estate, free and clear of all conflicting interests of all owners and encumbrancers of the real estate, but the lessor or lessee must reimburse any encumbrancer or owner of the real estate who is not the lessee and who has not otherwise agreed for the cost of repair of any physical injury, but not for any diminution in value of the real estate caused by the absence of the goods removed or by any necessity of replacing them. A person entitled to reimbursement may refuse permission to remove until the party seeking removal gives adequate security for the performance of this obligation.

(9) Even though the lease agreement does not create a security interest, the interest of a lessor of fixtures, including the lessor's residual interest, is perfected by filing a financing statement as a fixture filing for leased goods that are or are to become fixtures in accordance with the relevant provisions of the Article on Secured Transactions (Article 9).

As amended in 1990.

§ 2A–310. Lessor's and Lessee's Rights When Goods Become Accessions.

(1) Goods are "accessions" when they are installed in or affixed to other goods.

(2) The interest of a lessor or a lessee under a lease contract entered into before the goods became accessions is superior to all interests in the whole except as stated in subsection (4).

(3) The interest of a lessor or a lessee under a lease contract entered into at the time or after the goods became accessions is superior to all subsequently acquired interests in the whole except as stated in subsection (4) but is subordinate to interests in the whole existing at the time the lease contract was made unless the holders of such interests in the whole have in writing consented to the lease or disclaimed an interest in the goods as part of the whole.

(4) The interest of a lessor or a lessee under a lease contract described in subsection (2) or (3) is subordinate to the interest of

(a) a buyer in the ordinary course of business or a lessee in the ordinary course of business of any interest in the whole acquired after the goods became accessions; or

(b) a creditor with a security interest in the whole perfected before the lease contract was made to the extent that the creditor makes subsequent advances without knowledge of the lease contract.

(5) When under subsections (2) or (3) and (4) a lessor or a lessee of accessions holds an interest that is superior to all interests in the whole, the lessor or the lessee may (a) on default, expiration, termination, or cancellation of the lease contract by the other party but subject to the provisions of the lease contract and this Article, or (b) if necessary to enforce his [or her] other rights and remedies under this Article, remove the goods from the whole, free and clear of all interests in the whole, but he [or she] must reimburse any holder of an interest in the whole who is not the lessee and who has not otherwise agreed for the cost of repair of any physical injury but not for any diminution in value of the whole caused by the absence of the goods removed or by any necessity for replacing them.

A person entitled to reimbursement may refuse permission to remove until the party seeking removal gives adequate security for the performance of this obligation.

§ 2A–311. Priority Subject to Subordination.

Nothing in this Article prevents subordination by agreement by any person entitled to priority.

As added in 1990.

PART 4 Performance of Lease Contract: Repudiated, Substituted and Excused

§ 2A–401. Insecurity: Adequate Assurance of Performance.

(1) A lease contract imposes an obligation on each party that the other's expectation of receiving due performance will not be impaired.

(2) If reasonable grounds for insecurity arise with respect to the performance of either party, the insecure party may demand in writing adequate assurance of due performance. Until the insecure party receives that assurance, if commercially reasonable the insecure party may suspend any performance for which he [or she] has not already received the agreed return.

(3) A repudiation of the lease contract occurs if assurance of due performance adequate under the circumstances of the particular case is not provided to the insecure party within a reasonable time, not to exceed 30 days after receipt of a demand by the other party.

(4) Between merchants, the reasonableness of grounds for insecurity and the adequacy of any assurance offered must be determined according to commercial standards.

(5) Acceptance of any nonconforming delivery or payment does not prejudice the aggrieved party's right to demand adequate assurance of future performance.

§ 2A–402. Anticipatory Repudiation.

If either party repudiates a lease contract with respect to a performance not yet due under the lease contract, the loss of which performance will substantially impair the value of the lease contract to the other, the aggrieved party may:

(a) for a commercially reasonable time, await retraction of repudiation and performance by the repudiating party;

(b) make demand pursuant to Section 2A–401 and await assurance of future performance adequate under the circumstances of the particular case; or

(c) resort to any right or remedy upon default under the lease contract or this Article, even though the aggrieved party has notified the repudiating party that the aggrieved party would await the repudiating party's performance and assurance and has urged retraction. In addition, whether or not the aggrieved party is pursuing one of the foregoing remedies, the aggrieved party may suspend performance or, if the aggrieved party is the lessor, proceed in accordance with the provisions of this Article on the lessor's right to identify goods to the lease contract notwithstanding default or to salvage unfinished goods (Section 2A–524).

§ 2A–403. Retraction of Anticipatory Repudiation.

(1) Until the repudiating party's next performance is due, the repudiating party can retract the repudiation unless, since the repudiation, the aggrieved party has cancelled the lease contract or materially changed the aggrieved party's position or otherwise indicated that the aggrieved party considers the repudiation final.

(2) Retraction may be by any method that clearly indicates to the aggrieved party that the repudiating party intends to perform under the lease contract and includes any assurance demanded under Section 2A–401.

(3) Retraction reinstates a repudiating party's rights under a lease contract with due excuse and allowance to the aggrieved party for any delay occasioned by the repudiation.

§ 2A–404. Substituted Performance.

(1) If without fault of the lessee, the lessor and the supplier, the agreed berthing, loading, or unloading facilities fail or the agreed type of carrier becomes unavailable or the agreed manner of delivery otherwise becomes commercially impracticable, but a commercially reasonable substitute is available, the substitute performance must be tendered and accepted.

(2) If the agreed means or manner of payment fails because of domestic or foreign governmental regulation:

(a) the lessor may withhold or stop delivery or cause the supplier to withhold or stop delivery unless the lessee provides a means or manner of payment that is commercially a substantial equivalent; and

(b) if delivery has already been taken, payment by the means or in the manner provided by the regulation discharges the lessee's obligation unless the regulation is discriminatory, oppressive, or predatory.

§ 2A–405. Excused Performance.

Subject to Section 2A–404 on substituted performance, the following rules apply:

(a) Delay in delivery or nondelivery in whole or in part by a lessor or a supplier who complies with paragraphs (b) and (c) is not a default under the lease contract if performance as agreed has been made impracticable by the occurrence of a contingency the nonoccurrence of which was a basic assumption on which the lease contract was made or by compliance in good faith with any applicable foreign or domestic governmental regulation or order, whether or not the regulation or order later proves to be invalid.

(b) If the causes mentioned in paragraph (a) affect only part of the lessor's or the supplier's capacity to perform, he [or she] shall allocate production and deliveries among his [or her] customers but at his [or her] option may include regular customers not then under contract for sale or lease as well as his [or her] own requirements for further manufacture. He [or she] may so allocate in any manner that is fair and reasonable.

(c) The lessor seasonably shall notify the lessee and in the case of a finance lease the supplier seasonably shall notify the lessor and the lessee, if known, that there will be delay or nondelivery and, if allocation is required under paragraph (b), of the estimated quota thus made available for the lessee.

§ 2A–406. Procedure on Excused Performance.

(1) If the lessee receives notification of a material or indefinite delay or an allocation justified under Section 2A–405, the lessee may by written notification to the lessor as to any goods involved, and with respect to all of the goods if under an installment lease contract the value of the whole lease contract is substantially impaired (Section 2A–510):

(a) terminate the lease contract (Section 2A–505(2)); or

(b) except in a finance lease that is not a consumer lease, modify the lease contract by accepting the available quota in substitution, with due allowance from the rent payable for the balance of the lease term for the deficiency but without further right against the lessor.

(2) If, after receipt of a notification from the lessor under Section 2A–405, the lessee fails so to modify the lease agreement within a reasonable time not exceeding 30 days, the lease contract lapses with respect to any deliveries affected.

§ 2A–407. Irrevocable Promises: Finance Leases.

(1) In the case of a finance lease that is not a consumer lease the lessee's promises under the lease contract become irrevocable and independent upon the lessee's acceptance of the goods.

(2) A promise that has become irrevocable and independent under subsection (1):

(a) is effective and enforceable between the parties, and by or against third parties including assignees of the parties; and

(b) is not subject to cancellation, termination, modification, repudiation, excuse, or substitution without the consent of the party to whom the promise runs.

(3) This section does not affect the validity under any other law of a covenant in any lease contract making the lessee's promises irrevocable and independent upon the lessee's acceptance of the goods.

As amended in 1990.

PART 5 Default

A. In General

§ 2A–501. Default: Procedure.

(1) Whether the lessor or the lessee is in default under a lease contract is determined by the lease agreement and this Article.

(2) If the lessor or the lessee is in default under the lease contract, the party seeking enforcement has rights and remedies as provided in this Article and, except as limited by this Article, as provided in the lease agreement.

(3) If the lessor or the lessee is in default under the lease contract, the party seeking enforcement may reduce the party's claim to judgment, or otherwise enforce the lease contract by self-help or any available judicial procedure or nonjudicial procedure, including administrative proceeding, arbitration, or the like, in accordance with this Article.

(4) Except as otherwise provided in Section 1–106(1) or this Article or the lease agreement, the rights and remedies referred to in subsections (2) and (3) are cumulative.

(5) If the lease agreement covers both real property and goods, the party seeking enforcement may proceed under this Part as to the goods, or under other applicable law as to both the real property and the goods in accordance with that party's rights and remedies in respect of the real property, in which case this Part does not apply.

As amended in 1990.

§ 2A–502. Notice After Default.

Except as otherwise provided in this Article or the lease agreement, the lessor or lessee in default under the lease contract is not entitled to notice of default or notice of enforcement from the other party to the lease agreement.

§ 2A–503. Modification or Impairment of Rights and Remedies.

(1) Except as otherwise provided in this Article, the lease agreement may include rights and remedies for default in addition to or in substitution for those provided in this Article and may limit or alter the measure of damages recoverable under this Article.

(2) Resort to a remedy provided under this Article or in the lease agreement is optional unless the remedy is expressly agreed to be exclusive. If circumstances cause an exclusive or limited remedy to fail of its essential purpose, or provision for an exclusive remedy is unconscionable, remedy may be had as provided in this Article.

(3) Consequential damages may be liquidated under Section 2A–504, or may otherwise be limited, altered, or excluded unless the limitation, alteration, or exclusion is unconscionable. Limitation, alteration, or exclusion of consequential damages for injury to the person in the case of consumer goods is prima facie unconscionable but limitation, alteration, or exclusion of damages where the loss is commercial is not prima facie unconscionable.

(4) Rights and remedies on default by the lessor or the lessee with respect to any obligation or promise collateral or ancillary to the lease contract are not impaired by this Article.

As amended in 1990.

§ 2A–504. Liquidation of Damages.

(1) Damages payable by either party for default, or any other act or omission, including indemnity for loss or diminution of anticipated tax benefits or loss or damage to lessor's residual interest, may be liquidated in the lease agreement but only at an amount or by a formula that is

reasonable in light of the then anticipated harm caused by the default or other act or omission.

(2) If the lease agreement provides for liquidation of damages, and such provision does not comply with subsection (1), or such provision is an exclusive or limited remedy that circumstances cause to fail of its essential purpose, remedy may be had as provided in this Article.

(3) If the lessor justifiably withholds or stops delivery of goods because of the lessee's default or insolvency (Section 2A–525 or 2A–526), the lessee is entitled to restitution of any amount by which the sum of his [or her] payments exceeds:

(a) the amount to which the lessor is entitled by virtue of terms liquidating the lessor's damages in accordance with subsection (1); or

(b) in the absence of those terms, 20 percent of the then present value of the total rent the lessee was obligated to pay for the balance of the lease term, or, in the case of a consumer lease, the lesser of such amount or $500.

(4) A lessee's right to restitution under subsection (3) is subject to offset to the extent the lessor establishes:

(a) a right to recover damages under the provisions of this Article other than subsection (1); and

(b) the amount or value of any benefits received by the lessee directly or indirectly by reason of the lease contract.

§ 2A–505. Cancellation and Termination and Effect of Cancellation, Termination, Rescission, or Fraud on Rights and Remedies.

(1) On cancellation of the lease contract, all obligations that are still executory on both sides are discharged, but any right based on prior default or performance survives, and the cancelling party also retains any remedy for default of the whole lease contract or any unperformed balance.

(2) On termination of the lease contract, all obligations that are still executory on both sides are discharged but any right based on prior default or performance survives.

(3) Unless the contrary intention clearly appears, expressions of "cancellation," "rescission," or the like of the lease contract may not be construed as a renunciation or discharge of any claim in damages for an antecedent default.

(4) Rights and remedies for material misrepresentation or fraud include all rights and remedies available under this Article for default.

(5) Neither rescission nor a claim for rescission of the lease contract nor rejection or return of the goods may bar or be deemed inconsistent with a claim for damages or other right or remedy.

§ 2A–506. Statute of Limitations.

(1) An action for default under a lease contract, including breach of warranty or indemnity, must be commenced within 4 years after the cause of action accrued. By the original lease contract the parties may reduce the period of limitation to not less than one year.

(2) A cause of action for default accrues when the act or omission on which the default or breach of warranty is based is or should have been discovered by the aggrieved party, or when the default occurs, whichever is later. A cause of action for indemnity accrues when the act or omission on which the claim for indemnity is based is or should have been discovered by the indemnified party, whichever is later.

(3) If an action commenced within the time limited by subsection (1) is so terminated as to leave available a remedy by another action for the same default or breach of warranty or indemnity, the other action may be commenced after the expiration of the time limited and within 6 months after the termination of the first action unless the termination resulted from voluntary discontinuance or from dismissal for failure or neglect to prosecute.

(4) This section does not alter the law on tolling of the statute of limitations nor does it apply to causes of action that have accrued before this Article becomes effective.

§ 2A–507. Proof of Market Rent: Time and Place.

(1) Damages based on market rent (Section 2A–519 or 2A–528) are determined according to the rent for the use of the goods concerned for a lease term identical to the remaining lease term of the original lease agreement and prevailing at the times specified in Sections 2A–519 and 2A–528.

(2) If evidence of rent for the use of the goods concerned for a lease term identical to the remaining lease term of the original lease agreement and prevailing at the times or places described in this Article is not readily available, the rent prevailing within any reasonable time before or after the time described or at any other place or for a different lease term which in commercial judgment or under usage of trade would serve as a reasonable substitute for the one described may be used, making any proper allowance for the difference, including the cost of transporting the goods to or from the other place.

(3) Evidence of a relevant rent prevailing at a time or place or for a lease term other than the one described in this Article offered by one party is not admissible unless and until he [or she] has given the other party notice the court finds sufficient to prevent unfair surprise.

(4) If the prevailing rent or value of any goods regularly leased in any established market is in issue, reports in official publications or trade journals or in newspapers or periodicals of general circulation published as the reports of that market are admissible in evidence. The circumstances of the preparation of the report may be shown to affect its weight but not its admissibility.

As amended in 1990.

B. Default by Lessor

§ 2A–508. Lessee's Remedies.

(1) If a lessor fails to deliver the goods in conformity to the lease contract (Section 2A–509) or repudiates the lease

contract (Section 2A–402), or a lessee rightfully rejects the goods (Section 2A–509) or justifiably revokes acceptance of the goods (Section 2A–517), then with respect to any goods involved, and with respect to all of the goods if under an installment lease contract the value of the whole lease contract is substantially impaired (Section 2A–510), the lessor is in default under the lease contract and the lessee may:

(a) cancel the lease contract (Section 2A–505(1));

(b) recover so much of the rent and security as has been paid and is just under the circumstances;

(c) cover and recover damages as to all goods affected whether or not they have been identified to the lease contract (Sections 2A–518 and 2A–520), or recover damages for nondelivery (Sections 2A–519 and 2A–520);

(d) exercise any other rights or pursue any other remedies provided in the lease contract.

(2) If a lessor fails to deliver the goods in conformity to the lease contract or repudiates the lease contract, the lessee may also:

(a) if the goods have been identified, recover them (Section 2A–522); or

(b) in a proper case, obtain specific performance or replevy the goods (Section 2A–521).

(3) If a lessor is otherwise in default under a lease contract, the lessee may exercise the rights and pursue the remedies provided in the lease contract, which may include a right to cancel the lease, and in Section 2A–519(3).

(4) If a lessor has breached a warranty, whether express or implied, the lessee may recover damages (Section 2A–519(4)).

(5) On rightful rejection or justifiable revocation of acceptance, a lessee has a security interest in goods in the lessee's possession or control for any rent and security that has been paid and any expenses reasonably incurred in their inspection, receipt, transportation, and care and custody and may hold those goods and dispose of them in good faith and in a commercially reasonable manner, subject to Section 2A–527(5).

(6) Subject to the provisions of Section 2A–407, a lessee, on notifying the lessor of the lessee's intention to do so, may deduct all or any part of the damages resulting from any default under the lease contract from any part of the rent still due under the same lease contract.

As amended in 1990.

§ 2A–509. Lessee's Rights on Improper Delivery; Rightful Rejection.

(1) Subject to the provisions of Section 2A–510 on default in installment lease contracts, if the goods or the tender or delivery fail in any respect to conform to the lease contract, the lessee may reject or accept the goods or accept any commercial unit or units and reject the rest of the goods.

(2) Rejection of goods is ineffective unless it is within a reasonable time after tender or delivery of the goods and the lessee seasonably notifies the lessor.

§ 2A–510. Installment Lease Contracts: Rejection and Default.

(1) Under an installment lease contract a lessee may reject any delivery that is nonconforming if the nonconformity substantially impairs the value of that delivery and cannot be cured or the nonconformity is a defect in the required documents; but if the nonconformity does not fall within subsection (2) and the lessor or the supplier gives adequate assurance of its cure, the lessee must accept that delivery.

(2) Whenever nonconformity or default with respect to one or more deliveries substantially impairs the value of the installment lease contract as a whole there is a default with respect to the whole. But, the aggrieved party reinstates the installment lease contract as a whole if the aggrieved party accepts a nonconforming delivery without seasonably notifying of cancellation or brings an action with respect only to past deliveries or demands performance as to future deliveries.

§ 2A–511. Merchant Lessee's Duties as to Rightfully Rejected Goods.

(1) Subject to any security interest of a lessee (Section 2A–508(5)), if a lessor or a supplier has no agent or place of business at the market of rejection, a merchant lessee, after rejection of goods in his [or her] possession or control, shall follow any reasonable instructions received from the lessor or the supplier with respect to the goods. In the absence of those instructions, a merchant lessee shall make reasonable efforts to sell, lease, or otherwise dispose of the goods for the lessor's account if they threaten to decline in value speedily. Instructions are not reasonable if on demand indemnity for expenses is not forthcoming.

(2) If a merchant lessee (subsection (1)) or any other lessee (Section 2A–512) disposes of goods, he [or she] is entitled to reimbursement either from the lessor or the supplier or out of the proceeds for reasonable expenses of caring for and disposing of the goods and, if the expenses include no disposition commission, to such commission as is usual in the trade, or if there is none, to a reasonable sum not exceeding 10 percent of the gross proceeds.

(3) In complying with this section or Section 2A–512, the lessee is held only to good faith. Good faith conduct hereunder is neither acceptance or conversion nor the basis of an action for -damages.

(4) A purchaser who purchases in good faith from a lessee pursuant to this section or Section 2A–512 takes the goods free of any rights of the lessor and the supplier even though the lessee fails to comply with one or more of the requirements of this Article.

§ 2A–512. Lessee's Duties as to Rightfully Rejected Goods.

(1) Except as otherwise provided with respect to goods that threaten to decline in value speedily (Section 2A–511) and subject to any security interest of a lessee (Section 2A–508(5)):

(a) the lessee, after rejection of goods in the lessee's possession, shall hold them with reasonable care at the lessor's or the supplier's disposition for a reasonable time after the lessee's seasonable notification of rejection;

(b) if the lessor or the supplier gives no instructions within a reasonable time after notification of rejection, the lessee may store the rejected goods for the lessor's or the supplier's account or ship them to the lessor or the supplier or dispose of them for the lessor's or the supplier's account with reimbursement in the manner provided in Section 2A–511; but

(c) the lessee has no further obligations with regard to goods rightfully rejected.

(2) Action by the lessee pursuant to subsection (1) is not acceptance or conversion.

§ 2A–513. Cure by Lessor of Improper Tender or Delivery; Replacement.

(1) If any tender or delivery by the lessor or the supplier is rejected because nonconforming and the time for performance has not yet expired, the lessor or the supplier may seasonably notify the lessee of the lessor's or the supplier's intention to cure and may then make a conforming delivery within the time provided in the lease contract.

(2) If the lessee rejects a nonconforming tender that the lessor or the supplier had reasonable grounds to believe would be acceptable with or without money allowance, the lessor or the supplier may have a further reasonable time to substitute a conforming tender if he [or she] seasonably notifies the lessee.

§ 2A–514. Waiver of Lessee's Objections.

(1) In rejecting goods, a lessee's failure to state a particular defect that is ascertainable by reasonable inspection precludes the lessee from relying on the defect to justify rejection or to establish default:

(a) if, stated seasonably, the lessor or the supplier could have cured it (Section 2A–513); or

(b) between merchants if the lessor or the supplier after rejection has made a request in writing for a full and final written statement of all defects on which the lessee proposes to rely.

(2) A lessee's failure to reserve rights when paying rent or other consideration against documents precludes recovery of the payment for defects apparent on the face of the documents.

§ 2A–515. Acceptance of Goods.

(1) Acceptance of goods occurs after the lessee has had a reasonable opportunity to inspect the goods and

(a) the lessee signifies or acts with respect to the goods in a manner that signifies to the lessor or the supplier that the goods are conforming or that the lessee will take or retain them in spite of their nonconformity; or

(b) the lessee fails to make an effective rejection of the goods (Section 2A–509(2)).

(2) Acceptance of a part of any commercial unit is acceptance of that entire unit.

§ 2A–516. Effect of Acceptance of Goods; Notice of Default; Burden of Establishing Default After Acceptance; Notice of Claim or Litigation to Person Answerable Over.

(1) A lessee must pay rent for any goods accepted in accordance with the lease contract, with due allowance for goods rightfully rejected or not delivered.

(2) A lessee's acceptance of goods precludes rejection of the goods accepted. In the case of a finance lease, if made with knowledge of a nonconformity, acceptance cannot be revoked because of it. In any other case, if made with knowledge of a nonconformity, acceptance cannot be revoked because of it unless the acceptance was on the reasonable assumption that the nonconformity would be seasonably cured. Acceptance does not of itself impair any other remedy provided by this Article or the lease agreement for nonconformity.

(3) If a tender has been accepted:

(a) within a reasonable time after the lessee discovers or should have discovered any default, the lessee shall notify the lessor and the supplier, if any, or be barred from any remedy against the party not notified;

(b) except in the case of a consumer lease, within a reasonable time after the lessee receives notice of litigation for infringement or the like (Section 2A–211) the lessee shall notify the lessor or be barred from any remedy over for liability established by the litigation; and

(c) the burden is on the lessee to establish any default.

(4) If a lessee is sued for breach of a warranty or other obligation for which a lessor or a supplier is answerable over the following apply:

(a) The lessee may give the lessor or the supplier, or both, written notice of the litigation. If the notice states that the person notified may come in and defend and that if the person notified does not do so that person will be bound in any action against that person by the lessee by any determination of fact common to the two litigations, then unless the person notified after seasonable receipt of the notice does come in and defend that person is so bound.

(b) The lessor or the supplier may demand in writing that the lessee turn over control of the litigation including settlement if the claim is one for infringement or the like (Section 2A–211) or else be barred from any remedy over. If the demand states that the lessor or the supplier agrees to bear all expense and to satisfy any adverse judgment, then unless the lessee after seasonable receipt of the demand does turn over control the lessee is so barred.

(5) Subsections (3) and (4) apply to any obligation of a lessee to hold the lessor or the supplier harmless against infringement or the like (Section 2A–211).

As amended in 1990.

§ 2A–517. Revocation of Acceptance of Goods.

(1) A lessee may revoke acceptance of a lot or commercial unit whose nonconformity substantially impairs its value to the lessee if the lessee has accepted it:

(a) except in the case of a finance lease, on the reasonable assumption that its nonconformity would be cured and it has not been seasonably cured; or

(b) without discovery of the nonconformity if the lessee's acceptance was reasonably induced either by the lessor's assurances or, except in the case of a finance lease, by the difficulty of discovery before acceptance.

(2) Except in the case of a finance lease that is not a consumer lease, a lessee may revoke acceptance of a lot or commercial unit if the lessor defaults under the lease contract and the default substantially impairs the value of that lot or commercial unit to the lessee.

(3) If the lease agreement so provides, the lessee may revoke acceptance of a lot or commercial unit because of other defaults by the lessor.

(4) Revocation of acceptance must occur within a reasonable time after the lessee discovers or should have discovered the ground for it and before any substantial change in condition of the goods which is not caused by the nonconformity. Revocation is not effective until the lessee notifies the lessor.

(5) A lessee who so revokes has the same rights and duties with regard to the goods involved as if the lessee had rejected them.

As amended in 1990.

§ 2A–518. Cover; Substitute Goods.

(1) After a default by a lessor under the lease contract of the type described in Section 2A–508(1), or, if agreed, after other default by the lessor, the lessee may cover by making any purchase or lease of or contract to purchase or lease goods in substitution for those due from the lessor.

(2) Except as otherwise provided with respect to damages liquidated in the lease agreement (Section 2A–504) or otherwise determined pursuant to agreement of the parties (Sections 1–102(3) and 2A–503), if a lessee's cover is by a lease agreement substantially similar to the original lease agreement and the new lease agreement is made in good faith and in a commercially reasonable manner, the lessee may recover from the lessor as damages (i) the present value, as of the date of the commencement of the term of the new lease agreement, of the rent under the new lease agreement applicable to that period of the new lease term which is comparable to the then remaining term of the original lease agreement minus the present value as of the same date of the total rent for the then remaining lease term of the original lease agreement, and (ii) any incidental or consequential damages, less expenses saved in consequence of the lessor's default.

(3) If a lessee's cover is by lease agreement that for any reason does not qualify for treatment under subsection (2), or is by purchase or otherwise, the lessee may recover from the lessor as if the lessee had elected not to cover and Section 2A–519 governs.

As amended in 1990.

§ 2A–519. Lessee's Damages for Non-delivery, Repudiation, Default, and Breach of Warranty in Regard to Accepted Goods.

(1) Except as otherwise provided with respect to damages liquidated in the lease agreement (Section 2A–504) or otherwise determined pursuant to agreement of the parties (Sections 1–102(3) and 2A–503), if a lessee elects not to cover or a lessee elects to cover and the cover is by lease agreement that for any reason does not qualify for treatment under Section 2A–518(2), or is by purchase or otherwise, the measure of damages for non-delivery or repudiation by the lessor or for rejection or revocation of acceptance by the lessee is the present value, as of the date of the default, of the then market rent minus the present value as of the same date of the original rent, computed for the remaining lease term of the original lease agreement, together with incidental and consequential damages, less expenses saved in consequence of the lessor's default.

(2) Market rent is to be determined as of the place for tender or, in cases of rejection after arrival or revocation of acceptance, as of the place of arrival.

(3) Except as otherwise agreed, if the lessee has accepted goods and given notification (Section 2A–516(3)), the measure of damages for non-conforming tender or delivery or other default by a lessor is the loss resulting in the ordinary course of events from the lessor's default as determined in any manner that is reasonable together with incidental and consequential damages, less expenses saved in consequence of the lessor's default.

(4) Except as otherwise agreed, the measure of damages for breach of warranty is the present value at the time and place of acceptance of the difference between the value of the use of the goods accepted and the value if they had been as warranted for the lease term, unless special circumstances show proximate damages of a different amount, together with incidental and consequential damages, less expenses saved in consequence of the lessor's default or breach of warranty.

As amended in 1990.

§ 2A–520. Lessee's Incidental and Consequential Damages.

(1) Incidental damages resulting from a lessor's default include expenses reasonably incurred in inspection, receipt, transportation, and care and custody of goods rightfully rejected or goods the acceptance of which is justifiably revoked, any commercially reasonable charges, expenses or commissions in connection with effecting cover, and any other reasonable expense incident to the default.

(2) Consequential damages resulting from a lessor's default include:

(a) any loss resulting from general or particular requirements and needs of which the lessor at the time of contracting had reason to know and which could not reasonably be prevented by cover or otherwise; and

(b) injury to person or property proximately resulting from any breach of warranty.

§ 2A–521. Lessee's Right to Specific Performance or Replevin.

(1) Specific performance may be decreed if the goods are unique or in other proper circumstances.

(2) A decree for specific performance may include any terms and conditions as to payment of the rent, damages, or other relief that the court deems just.

(3) A lessee has a right of replevin, detinue, sequestration, claim and delivery, or the like for goods identified to the lease contract if after reasonable effort the lessee is unable to effect cover for those goods or the circumstances reasonably indicate that the effort will be unavailing.

§ 2A–522. Lessee's Right to Goods on Lessor's Insolvency.

(1) Subject to subsection (2) and even though the goods have not been shipped, a lessee who has paid a part or all of the rent and security for goods identified to a lease contract (Section 2A–217) on making and keeping good a tender of any unpaid portion of the rent and security due under the lease contract may recover the goods identified from the lessor if the lessor becomes insolvent within 10 days after receipt of the first installment of rent and security.

(2) A lessee acquires the right to recover goods identified to a lease contract only if they conform to the lease contract.

C. Default by Lessee

§ 2A–523. Lessor's Remedies.

(1) If a lessee wrongfully rejects or revokes acceptance of goods or fails to make a payment when due or repudiates with respect to a part or the whole, then, with respect to any goods involved, and with respect to all of the goods if under an installment lease contract the value of the whole lease contract is substantially impaired (Section 2A–510), the lessee is in default under the lease contract and the lessor may:

(a) cancel the lease contract (Section 2A–505(1));

(b) proceed respecting goods not identified to the lease contract (Section 2A–524);

(c) withhold delivery of the goods and take possession of goods previously delivered (Section 2A–525);

(d) stop delivery of the goods by any bailee (Section 2A–526);

(e) dispose of the goods and recover damages (Section 2A–527), or retain the goods and recover damages (Section 2A–528), or in a proper case recover rent (Section 2A–529);

(f) exercise any other rights or pursue any other remedies provided in the lease contract.

(2) If a lessor does not fully exercise a right or obtain a remedy to which the lessor is entitled under subsection (1), the lessor may recover the loss resulting in the ordinary course of events from the lessee's default as determined in any reasonable manner, together with incidental damages, less expenses saved in consequence of the lessee's default.

(3) If a lessee is otherwise in default under a lease contract, the lessor may exercise the rights and pursue the remedies provided in the lease contract, which may include a right to cancel the lease. In addition, unless otherwise provided in the lease -contract:

(a) if the default substantially impairs the value of the lease contract to the lessor, the lessor may exercise the rights and pursue the remedies provided in subsections (1) or (2); or

(b) if the default does not substantially impair the value of the lease contract to the lessor, the lessor may recover as provided in subsection (2).

As amended in 1990.

§ 2A–524. Lessor's Right to Identify Goods to Lease Contract.

(1) After default by the lessee under the lease contract of the type described in Section 2A–523(1) or 2A–523(3)(a) or, if agreed, after other default by the lessee, the lessor may:

(a) identify to the lease contract conforming goods not already identified if at the time the lessor learned of the default they were in the lessor's or the supplier's possession or control; and

(b) dispose of goods (Section 2A–527(1)) that demonstrably have been intended for the particular lease contract even though those goods are unfinished.

(2) If the goods are unfinished, in the exercise of reasonable commercial judgment for the purposes of avoiding loss and of effective realization, an aggrieved lessor or the supplier may either complete manufacture and wholly identify the goods to the lease contract or cease manufacture and lease, sell, or otherwise dispose of the goods for scrap or salvage value or proceed in any other reasonable manner.

As amended in 1990.

§ 2A–525. Lessor's Right to Possession of Goods.

(1) If a lessor discovers the lessee to be insolvent, the lessor may refuse to deliver the goods.

(2) After a default by the lessee under the lease contract of the type described in Section 2A–523(1) or 2A–523(3)(a) or, if agreed, after other default by the lessee, the lessor has the right to take possession of the goods. If the lease contract so provides, the lessor may require the lessee to assemble the goods and make them available to the lessor at a place to be designated by the lessor which is reasonably convenient to both parties. Without removal, the lessor may render unusable any goods employed in trade or business, and may dispose of goods on the lessee's premises (Section 2A–527).

(3) The lessor may proceed under subsection (2) without judicial process if it can be done without breach of the peace or the lessor may proceed by action.

As amended in 1990.

§ 2A–526. Lessor's Stoppage of Delivery in Transit or Otherwise.

(1) A lessor may stop delivery of goods in the possession of a carrier or other bailee if the lessor discovers the lessee to be insolvent and may stop delivery of carload, truckload, planeload, or larger shipments of express or freight if the lessee repudiates or fails to make a payment due before delivery, whether for rent, security or otherwise under the lease contract, or for any other reason the lessor has a right to withhold or take possession of the goods.

(2) In pursuing its remedies under subsection (1), the lessor may stop delivery until

(a) receipt of the goods by the lessee;

(b) acknowledgment to the lessee by any bailee of the goods, except a carrier, that the bailee holds the goods for the lessee; or

(c) such an acknowledgment to the lessee by a carrier via reshipment or as warehouseman.

(3) (a) To stop delivery, a lessor shall so notify as to enable the bailee by reasonable diligence to prevent delivery of the goods.

(b) After notification, the bailee shall hold and deliver the goods according to the directions of the lessor, but the lessor is liable to the bailee for any ensuing charges or damages.

(c) A carrier who has issued a nonnegotiable bill of lading is not obliged to obey a notification to stop received from a person other than the consignor.

§ 2A–527. Lessor's Rights to Dispose of Goods.

(1) After a default by a lessee under the lease contract of the type described in Section 2A–523(1) or 2A–523(3)(a) or after the lessor refuses to deliver or takes possession of goods (Section 2A–525 or 2A–526), or, if agreed, after other default by a lessee, the lessor may dispose of the goods concerned or the undelivered balance thereof by lease, sale, or otherwise.

(2) Except as otherwise provided with respect to damages liquidated in the lease agreement (Section 2A–504) or otherwise determined pursuant to agreement of the parties (Sections 1–102(3) and 2A–503), if the disposition is by lease agreement substantially similar to the original lease agreement and the new lease agreement is made in good faith and in a commercially reasonable manner, the lessor may recover from the lessee as damages (i) accrued and unpaid rent as of the date of the commencement of the term of the new lease agreement, (ii) the present value, as of the same date, of the total rent for the then remaining lease term of the original lease agreement minus the present value, as of the same date, of the rent under the new lease agreement applicable to that period of the new lease term which is comparable to the then remaining term of the original lease agreement, and (iii) any incidental damages allowed under Section 2A–530, less expenses saved in consequence of the lessee's default.

(3) If the lessor's disposition is by lease agreement that for any reason does not qualify for treatment under subsection (2), or is by sale or otherwise, the lessor may recover from the lessee as if the lessor had elected not to dispose of the goods and Section 2A–528 governs.

(4) A subsequent buyer or lessee who buys or leases from the lessor in good faith for value as a result of a disposition under this section takes the goods free of the original lease contract and any rights of the original lessee even though the lessor fails to comply with one or more of the requirements of this Article.

(5) The lessor is not accountable to the lessee for any profit made on any disposition. A lessee who has rightfully rejected or justifiably revoked acceptance shall account to the lessor for any excess over the amount of the lessee's security interest (Section 2A–508(5)).

As amended in 1990.

§ 2A–528. Lessor's Damages for Non-acceptance, Failure to Pay, Repudiation, or Other Default.

(1) Except as otherwise provided with respect to damages liquidated in the lease agreement (Section 2A–504) or otherwise determined pursuant to agreement of the parties (Sections 1–102(3) and 2A–503), if a lessor elects to retain the goods or a lessor elects to dispose of the goods and the disposition is by lease agreement that for any reason does not qualify for treatment under Section 2A–527(2), or is by sale or otherwise, the lessor may recover from the lessee as damages for a default of the type described in Section 2A–523(1) or 2A–523(3)(a), or, if agreed, for other default of the lessee, (i) accrued and unpaid rent as of the date of default if the lessee has never taken possession of the goods, or, if the lessee has taken possession of the goods, as of the date the lessor repossesses the goods or an earlier date on which the lessee makes a tender of the goods to the lessor, (ii) the present value as of the date determined under clause (i) of the total rent for the then remaining lease term of the original lease agreement minus the present value as of the same date of the market rent at the place where the goods are located computed for the same lease term, and (iii) any incidental damages allowed under Section 2A–530, less expenses saved in consequence of the lessee's default.

(2) If the measure of damages provided in subsection (1) is inadequate to put a lessor in as good a position as performance would have, the measure of damages is the present value of the profit, including reasonable overhead, the lessor would have made from full performance by the lessee, together with any incidental damages allowed under Section 2A–530, due allowance for costs reasonably incurred and due credit for payments or proceeds of disposition.

As amended in 1990.

§ 2A–529. Lessor's Action for the Rent.

(1) After default by the lessee under the lease contract of the type described in Section 2A–523(1) or 2A–523(3)(a) or, if agreed, after other default by the lessee, if the lessor complies with -subsection (2), the lessor may recover from the lessee as -damages:

(a) for goods accepted by the lessee and not repossessed by or tendered to the lessor, and for conforming goods lost or damaged within a commercially reasonable time after risk of loss passes to the lessee (Section 2A–219), (i) accrued and unpaid rent as of the date of entry of judgment in favor of the lessor, (ii) the present value as of the same date of the rent for the then remaining lease term of the lease agreement, and (iii) any incidental damages allowed under Section 2A–530, less expenses saved in consequence of the lessee's default; and

(b) for goods identified to the lease contract if the lessor is unable after reasonable effort to dispose of them at a reasonable price or the circumstances reasonably indicate that effort will be unavailing, (i) accrued and unpaid rent as of the date of entry of judgment in favor of the lessor, (ii) the present value as of the same date of the rent for the then remaining lease term of the lease agreement, and (iii) any incidental damages allowed under Section 2A–530, less expenses saved in consequence of the lessee's default.

(2) Except as provided in subsection (3), the lessor shall hold for the lessee for the remaining lease term of the lease agreement any goods that have been identified to the lease contract and are in the lessor's control.

(3) The lessor may dispose of the goods at any time before collection of the judgment for damages obtained pursuant to subsection (1). If the disposition is before the end of the remaining lease term of the lease agreement, the lessor's recovery against the lessee for damages is governed by Section 2A–527 or Section 2A–528, and the lessor will cause an appropriate credit to be provided against a judgment for damages to the extent that the amount of the judgment exceeds the recovery available pursuant to Section 2A–527 or 2A–528.

(4) Payment of the judgment for damages obtained pursuant to subsection (1) entitles the lessee to the use and possession of the goods not then disposed of for the remaining lease term of and in accordance with the lease agreement.

(5) After default by the lessee under the lease contract of the type described in Section 2A–523(1) or Section 2A–523(3)(a) or, if agreed, after other default by the lessee, a lessor who is held not entitled to rent under this section must nevertheless be awarded damages for non-acceptance under Section 2A–527 or Section 2A–528.

As amended in 1990.

§ 2A–530. Lessor's Incidental Damages.

Incidental damages to an aggrieved lessor include any commercially reasonable charges, expenses, or commissions incurred in stopping delivery, in the transportation, care and custody of goods after the lessee's default, in connection with return or disposition of the goods, or otherwise resulting from the default.

§ 2A–531. Standing to Sue Third Parties for Injury to Goods.

(1) If a third party so deals with goods that have been identified to a lease contract as to cause actionable injury to a party to the lease contract (a) the lessor has a right of action against the third party, and (b) the lessee also has a right of action against the third party if the lessee:

(i) has a security interest in the goods;

(ii) has an insurable interest in the goods; or

(iii) bears the risk of loss under the lease contract or has since the injury assumed that risk as against the lessor and the goods have been converted or destroyed.

(2) If at the time of the injury the party plaintiff did not bear the risk of loss as against the other party to the lease contract and there is no arrangement between them for disposition of the re-covery, his [or her] suit or settlement, subject to his [or her] own interest, is as a fiduciary for the other party to the lease contract.

(3) Either party with the consent of the other may sue for the benefit of whom it may concern.

§ 2A–532. Lessor's Rights to Residual Interest.

In addition to any other recovery permitted by this Article or other law, the lessor may recover from the lessee an amount that will fully compensate the lessor for any loss of or damage to the lessor's residual interest in the goods caused by the default of the lessee.

As added in 1990.

ARTICLE 3

NEGOTIABLE INSTRUMENTS

PART 1 General Provisions and Definitions

§ 3–101. Short Title.

This Article may be cited as Uniform Commercial Code—Negotiable Instruments.

§ 3–102. Subject Matter.

(a) This Article applies to negotiable instruments. It does not apply to money or to payment orders governed by Article 4A. A negotiable instrument that is also a certificated security under Section 8–102(1)(a) is subject to Article 8 and to this Article.

(b) In the event of conflict between the provisions of this Article and those of Article 4, Article 8, or Article 9, the provisions of Article 4, Article 8 and Article 9 prevail over those of this Article.

(c) Regulations of the Board of Governors of the Federal Reserve System and operating circulars of the Federal Reserve Banks supersede any inconsistent provision of this Article to the extent of the inconsistency.

§ 3–103. Definitions.

(a) In this Article:

(1) "Acceptor" means a drawee that has accepted a draft.

(2) "Drawee" means a person ordered in a draft to make payment.

(3) "Drawer" means a person that signs a draft as a person ordering payment.

(4) "Good faith" means honesty in fact and the observance of reasonable commercial standards of fair dealing.

(5) "Maker" means a person that signs a note as promisor of payment.

(6) "Order" means a written instruction to pay money signed by the person giving the instruction. The instruction may be addressed to any person, including the person giving the instruction, or to one or more persons jointly or in the alternative but not in succession. An authorization to pay is not an order unless the person authorized to pay is also instructed to pay.

(7) "Ordinary care" in the case of a person engaged in business means observance of reasonable commercial standards, prevailing in the area in which that person is located, with respect to the business in which that person is engaged. In the case of a bank that takes an instrument for processing for collection or payment by automated means, reasonable commercial standards do not require the bank to examine the instrument if the failure to examine does not violate the bank's prescribed procedures and the bank's procedures do not vary unreasonably from general banking usage not disapproved by this Article or Article 4.

(8) "Party" means party to an instrument.

(9) "Promise" means a written undertaking to pay money signed by the person undertaking to pay. An acknowledgment of an obligation by the obligor is not a promise unless the obligor also undertakes to pay the obligation.

(10) "Prove" with respect to a fact means to meet the burden of establishing the fact (Section 1–201(8)).

(11) "Remitter" means a person that purchases an instrument from its issuer if the instrument is payable to an identified person other than the purchaser.

(b) Other definitions applying to this Article and the sections in which they appear are:

"Acceptance" Section 3–409.
"Accommodated party" Section 3–419.
"Accommodation indorsement" Section 3–205.
"Accommodation party" Section 3–419.
"Alteration" Section 3–407.
"Blank indorsement" Section 3–205.
"Cashier's check" Section 3–104.
"Certificate of deposit" Section 3–104.
"Certified check" Section 3–409.
"Check" Section 3–104.
"Consideration" Section 3–303.
"Draft" Section 3–104.
"Fiduciary" Section 3–307.
"Guarantor" Section 3–417.
"Holder in due course" Section 3–302.
"Incomplete instrument" Section 3–115.
"Indorsement" Section 3–204.
"Indorser" Section 3–204.
"Instrument" Section 3–104.
"Issue" Section 3–105.
"Issuer" Section 3–105.
"Negotiable instrument" Section 3–104.
"Negotiation" Section 3–201.
"Note" Section 3–104.
"Payable at a definite time" Section 3–108.
"Payable on demand" Section 3–108.
"Payable to bearer" Section 3–109.
"Payable to order" Section 3–110.
"Payment" Section 3–603.
"Person entitled to enforce" Section 3–301.
"Presentment" Section 3–501.
"Reacquisition" Section 3–207.
"Represented person" Section 3–307.
"Special indorsement" Section 3–205.
"Teller's check" Section 3–104.
"Traveler's check" Section 3–104.
"Value" Section 3–303.

(c) The following definitions in other Articles apply to this Article:

"Bank" Section 4–105.
"Banking day" Section 4–104.
"Clearing house" Section 4–104.
"Collecting bank" Section 4–105.
"Customer" Section 4–104.
"Depositary bank" Section 4–105.
"Documentary draft" Section 4–104.
"Intermediary bank" Section 4–105.
"Item" Section 4–104.
"Midnight deadline" Section 4–104.
"Payor bank" Section 4–105.
"Suspends payments" Section 4–104.

(d) In addition, Article 1 contains general definitions and principles of construction and interpretation applicable throughout this Article.

§ 3–104. Negotiable Instrument.

(a) "Negotiable instrument" means an unconditional promise or order to pay a fixed amount of money, with or without interest or other charges described in the promise or order, if it:

(1) is payable to bearer or to order at the time it is issued or first comes into possession of a holder;

(2) is payable on demand or at a definite time; and

(3) does not state any other undertaking or instruction by the person promising or ordering payment to do any act in addition to the payment of money except that the promise or order may contain (i) an undertaking or power to give, maintain, or protect collateral to secure payment, (ii) an authorization or power to the holder to confess judgment or realize on or dispose of collateral, or (iii) a waiver of the benefit of any law intended for the advantage or protection of any obligor.

(b) "Instrument" means negotiable instrument.

(c) An order that meets all of the requirements of subsection (a) except subparagraph (1) and otherwise falls within the definition of "check" in subsection (f) is a negotiable instrument and a check.

(d) Notwithstanding subsection (a), a promise or order other than a check is not an instrument if, at the time it is issued or first comes into possession of a holder, it con–

tains a conspicuous statement, however expressed, indicating that the writing is not an instrument governed by this Article.

(e) An instrument is a "note" if it is a promise, and is a "draft" if it is an order. If an instrument falls within the definition of both "note" and "draft," the person entitled to enforce the instrument may treat it as either.

(f) "Check" means (i) a draft, other than a documentary draft, payable on demand and drawn on a bank or (ii) a cashier's check or teller's check. An instrument may be a check even though it is described on its face by another term such as "money order."

(g) "Cashier's check" means a draft with respect to which the drawer and drawee are the same bank or branches of the same bank.

(h) "Teller's check" means a draft drawn by a bank (i) on another bank, or (ii) payable at or through a bank.

(i) "Traveler's check" means an instrument that (i) is payable on demand, (ii) is drawn on or payable at or through a bank, (iii) is designated by the term "traveler's check" or by a substantially similar term, and (iv) requires, as a condition to payment, a countersignature by a person whose specimen signature appears on the instrument.

(j) "Certificate of deposit" means an instrument containing an acknowledgment by a bank that a sum of money has been received by the bank, and a promise by the bank to repay the sum of money. A certificate of deposit is a note of the bank.

§ 3–105. Issue of Instrument.

(a) "Issue" means the first delivery of an instrument by the maker or drawer, whether to a holder or nonholder, for the purpose of giving rights on the instrument to any person.

(b) An unissued instrument, or an unissued incomplete instrument (Section 3–115) that is completed, is binding on the maker or drawer, but nonissuance is a defense. An instrument that is conditionally issued or is issued for a special purpose is binding on the maker or drawer, but failure of the condition or special purpose to be fulfilled is a defense.

(c) "Issuer" applies to issued and unissued instruments and means any person that signs an instrument as maker or drawer.

§ 3–106. Unconditional Promise or Order.

(a) Except as provided in subsections (b) and (c), for the purposes of Section 3–104(a), a promise or order is unconditional unless it states (i) an express condition to payment or (ii) that the promise or order is subject to or governed by another writing, or that rights or obligations with respect to the promise or order are stated in another writing; however, a mere reference to another writing does not make the promise or order conditional.

(b) A promise or order is not made conditional (i) by a reference to another writing for a statement of rights with respect to collateral, prepayment, or acceleration, or (ii) because payment is limited to resort to a particular fund or source.

(c) If a promise or order requires, as a condition to payment, a countersignature by a person whose specimen signature appears on the promise or order, the condition does not make the promise or order conditional for the purposes of Section 3–104(a). If the person whose specimen signature appears on an instrument fails to countersign the instrument, the failure to countersign is a defense to the obligation of the issuer, but the failure does not prevent a transferee of the instrument from becoming a holder of the instrument.

(d) If a promise or order at the time it is issued or first comes into possession of a holder contains a statement, required by applicable statutory or administrative law, to the effect that the rights of a holder or transferee are subject to claims or defenses that the issuer could assert against the original payee, the promise or order is not thereby made conditional for the purposes of Section 3–104(a), but there cannot be a holder in due course of the promise or order.

§ 3–107. Instrument Payable in Foreign Money.

Unless the instrument otherwise provides, an instrument that states the amount payable in foreign money may be paid in the foreign money or in an equivalent amount in dollars calculated by using the current bank-offered spot rate at the place of payment for the purchase of dollars on the day on which the instrument is paid.

§ 3–108. Payable on Demand or at a Definite Time.

(a) A promise or order is "payable on demand" if (i) it states that it is payable on demand or at sight, or otherwise indicates that it is payable at the will of the holder, or (ii) it does not state any time of payment.

(b) A promise or order is "payable at a definite time" if it is payable on elapse of a definite period of time after sight or acceptance or at a fixed date or dates or at a time or times readily ascertainable at the time the promise or order is issued, subject to rights of (i) prepayment, (ii) acceleration, or (iii) extension at the option of the holder or (iv) extension to a further definite time at the option of the maker or acceptor or automatically upon or after a specified act or event.

(c) If an instrument, payable at a fixed date, is also payable upon demand made before the fixed date, the instrument is payable on demand until the fixed date and, if demand for payment is not made before that date, becomes payable at a definite time on the fixed date.

§ 3–109. Payable to Bearer or to Order.

(a) A promise or order is payable to bearer if it:

(1) states that it is payable to bearer or to the order of bearer or otherwise indicates that the person in possession of the promise or order is entitled to payment,

(2) does not state a payee, or

(3) states that it is payable to or to the order of cash or otherwise indicates that it is not payable to an identified person.

(b) A promise or order that is not payable to bearer is payable to order if it is payable (i) to the order of an identified person or (ii) to an identified person or order. A promise or order that is payable to order is payable to the identified person.

(c) An instrument payable to bearer may become payable to an identified person if it is specially indorsed as stated in Section 3–205(a). An instrument payable to an identified person may become payable to bearer if it is indorsed in blank as stated in Section 3–205(b).

§ 3–110. Identification of Person to Whom Instrument Is Payable.

(a) A person to whom an instrument is payable is determined by the intent of the person, whether or not authorized, signing as, or in the name or behalf of, the maker or drawer. The instrument is payable to the person intended by the signer even if that person is identified in the instrument by a name or other identification that is not that of the intended person. If more than one person signs in the name or behalf of the maker or drawer and all the signers do not intend the same person as payee, the instrument is payable to any person intended by one or more of the signers.

(b) If the signature of the maker or drawer of an instrument is made by automated means such as a check-writing machine, the payee of the instrument is determined by the intent of the person who supplied the name or identification of the payee, whether or not authorized to do so.

(c) A person to whom an instrument is payable may be identified in any way including by name, identifying number, office, or account number. For the purpose of determining the holder of an instrument, the following rules apply:

(1) If an instrument is payable to an account and the account is identified only by number, the instrument is payable to the person to whom the account is payable. If an instrument is payable to an account identified by number and by the name of a person, the instrument is payable to the named person, whether or not that person is the owner of the account identified by number.

(2) If an instrument is payable to:

(i) a trust, estate, or a person described as trustee or representative of a trust or estate, the instrument is payable to the trustee, the representative, or a successor of either, whether or not the beneficiary or estate is also named;

(ii) a person described as agent or similar representative of a named or identified person, the instrument is payable either to the represented person, the representative, or a successor of the representative;

(iii) a fund or organization that is not a legal entity, the instrument is payable to a representative of the members of the fund or organization; or

(iv) an office or to a person described as holding an office, the instrument is payable to the named person, the incumbent of the office, or a successor to the incumbent.

(d) If an instrument is payable to two or more persons alternatively, it is payable to any of them and may be negotiated, discharged, or enforced by any of them in possession of the instrument. If an instrument is payable to two or more persons not alternatively, it is payable to all of them and may be negotiated, discharged, or enforced only by all of them. If an instrument payable to two or more persons is ambiguous as to whether it is payable to the persons alternatively, the instrument is payable to the persons alternatively.

§ 3–111. Place of Payment.

Except as otherwise provided for items in Article 4, an instrument is payable at the place of payment stated in the instrument. If no place of payment is stated, an instrument is payable at the address of the drawee or maker stated in the instrument. If no address is stated, the place of payment is the place of business of the drawee or maker. If a drawee or maker has more than one place of business, the place of payment is any place of business of the drawee or maker chosen by the person entitled to enforce the instrument. If the drawee or maker has no place of business, the place of payment is the residence of the drawee or maker.

§ 3–112. Interest.

(a) Unless otherwise provided in the instrument, (i) an instrument is not payable with interest, and (ii) interest on an interest-bearing instrument is payable from the date of the instrument.

(b) Interest may be stated in an instrument as a fixed or variable amount of money or it may be expressed as a fixed or variable rate or rates. The amount or rate of interest may be stated or described in the instrument in any manner and may require reference to information not contained in the instrument. If an instrument provides for interest but the amount of interest payable cannot be ascertained from the description, interest is payable at the judgment rate in effect at the place of payment of the instrument and at the time interest first accrues.

§ 3–113. Date of Instrument.

(a) An instrument may be antedated or postdated. The date stated determines the time of payment if the instrument is payable at a fixed period after date. Except as provided in Section 4–401(3), an instrument payable on demand is not payable before the date of the instrument.

(b) If an instrument is undated, its date is the date of its issue or, in the case of an unissued instrument, the date it first comes into possession of a holder.

§ 3–114. Contradictory Terms of Instrument.

If an instrument contains contradictory terms, typewritten terms prevail over printed terms, handwritten terms prevail over both, and words prevail over numbers.

§ 3–115. Incomplete Instrument.

(a) "Incomplete instrument" means a signed writing, whether or not issued by the signer, the contents of which show at the time of signing that it is incomplete but that the signer intended it to be completed by the addition of words or numbers.

(b) Subject to subsection (c), if an incomplete instrument is an instrument under Section 3–104, it may be enforced (i) according to its terms if it is not completed, or (ii) according to its terms as augmented by completion. If an incomplete instrument is not an instrument under Section 3–104 but, after completion, the requirements of Section 3–104 are met, the instrument may be enforced according to its terms as augmented by completion.

(c) If words or numbers are added to an incomplete instrument without authority of the signer, there is an alteration of the incomplete instrument governed by Section 3–407.

(d) The burden of establishing that words or numbers were added to an incomplete instrument without authority of the signer is on the person asserting the lack of authority.

§ 3–116. Joint and Several Liability; Contribution.

(a) Except as otherwise provided in the instrument, two or more persons who have the same liability on an instrument as makers, drawers, acceptors, indorsers who are indorsing joint payees, or anomalous indorsers, are jointly and severally liable in the capacity in which they sign.

(b) Except as provided in Section 3–417(e) or by agreement of the affected parties, a party with joint and several liability that pays the instrument is entitled to receive from any party with the same joint and several liability contribution in accordance with applicable law.

(c) Discharge of one party with joint and several liability by a person entitled to enforce the instrument does not affect the right under subsection (b) of a party with the same joint and several liability to receive contribution from the party discharged.

§ 3–117. Other Agreements Affecting an Instrument.

Subject to applicable law regarding exclusion of proof of contemporaneous or prior agreements, the obligation of a party to an instrument to pay the instrument may be modified, supplemented, or nullified by a separate agreement of the obligor and a person entitled to enforce the instrument if the instrument is issued or the obligation is incurred in reliance on the agreement or as part of the same transaction giving rise to the agreement. To the extent an obligation is modified, supplemented, or nullified by an agreement under this section, the agreement is a defense to the obligation.

§ 3–118. Statute of Limitations.

(a) Except as provided in subsection (e), an action to enforce the obligation of a party to pay a note payable at a definite time must be commenced within six years after the payment date or dates stated in the note or, if a payment date is accelerated, within six years after the accelerated payment date.

(b) Except as provided in subsection (d) or (e), if demand for payment is made to the maker of a note payable on demand, an action to enforce the obligation of a party to pay the note must be commenced within six years after the demand. If no demand for payment is made to the maker, an action to enforce the note is barred if neither principal nor interest on the note has been paid for a continuous period of 10 years.

(c) Except as provided in subsection (d), an action to enforce the obligation of a party to an unaccepted draft to pay the draft must be commenced within six years after dishonor of the draft or 10 years after the date of the draft, whichever period expires first.

(d) An action to enforce the obligation of the acceptor of a certified check or the issuer of a teller's check, cashier's check, or traveler's check must be commenced within six years after demand for payment is made to the acceptor or issuer, as the case may be.

(e) An action to enforce the obligation of a party to a certificate of deposit to pay the instrument must be commenced within six years after demand for payment is made to the maker, but if the instrument states a maturity date and the maker is not required to pay before that date, the six-year period begins when a demand for payment is in effect and the maturity date has passed.

(f) This subsection applies to an action to enforce the obligation of a party to pay an accepted draft, other than a certified check. If the obligation of the acceptor is payable at a definite time, the action must be commenced within six years after the payment date or dates stated in the draft or acceptance. If the obligation of the acceptor is payable on demand, the action must be commenced within six years after the date of the acceptance.

(g) Unless governed by other law regarding claims for indemnity or contribution, an action (i) for conversion of an instrument, for money had and received, or like action based on conversion, (ii) for breach of warranty, or (iii) to enforce an obligation, duty, or right arising under this Article and not governed by this section must be commenced within three years after the cause of action accrues.

§ 3–119. Notice of Right to Defend Action.

In an action for breach of an obligation for which a third person is answerable over pursuant to this Article or Article 4, the defendant may give the third person written notice of the litigation, and the person notified may then give similar notice to any other person who is answerable over. If the notice states (i) that the person notified may come in and defend and (ii) that failure to do so will bind the person notified in an action later brought by the person giving the notice as to any determination of fact common to the two litigations, the person notified is so bound unless after seasonable receipt of the notice the person notified does come in and defend.

PART 2 Negotiation, Transfer and Indorsement

§ 3–201. Negotiation.

(a) "Negotiation" means a transfer of possession, whether voluntary or involuntary, of an instrument to a person who thereby becomes its holder if possession is obtained from a person other than the issuer of the instrument.

(b) Except for a negotiation by a remitter, if an instrument is payable to an identified person, negotiation requires transfer of possession of the instrument and its indorsement by the holder. If an instrument is payable to bearer, it may be negotiated by transfer of possession alone.

§ 3–202. Negotiation Subject to Rescission.

(a) Negotiation is effective even if obtained (i) from an infant, a corporation exceeding its powers, or a person without capacity, or (ii) by fraud, duress, or mistake, or in breach of duty or as part of an illegal transaction.

(b) To the extent permitted by law, negotiation may be rescinded or may be subject to other remedies, but those remedies may not be asserted against a subsequent holder in due course or a person paying the instrument in good faith and without knowledge of facts that are a basis for rescission or other remedy.

§ 3–203. Rights Acquired by Transfer.

(a) An instrument is transferred when it is delivered by a person other than its issuer for the purpose of giving to the person receiving delivery the right to enforce the instrument.

(b) Transfer of an instrument, regardless of whether the transfer is a negotiation, vests in the transferee any right of the transferor to enforce the instrument, including any right as a holder in due course, but the transferee cannot acquire rights of a holder in due course by a transfer, directly or indirectly, from a holder in due course if the purchaser engaged in fraud or illegality affecting the instrument.

(c) Unless otherwise agreed, if an instrument is transferred for value and the transferee does not become a holder because of lack of indorsement by the transferor, the transferee has a specifically enforceable right to the unqualified indorsement of the transferor, but negotiation of the instrument does not occur until the indorsement is made.

(d) If a transferor purports to transfer less than the entire instrument, negotiation of the instrument does not occur. The transferee obtains no rights under this Article and has only the rights of a partial assignee.

§ 3–204. Indorsement.

(a) "Indorsement" means a signature, other than that of a maker, drawer, or acceptor, that alone or accompanied by other words, is made on an instrument for the purpose of (i) negotiating the instrument, (ii) restricting payment of the instrument, or (iii) incurring indorser's liability on the instrument, but regardless of the intent of the signer, a signature and its accompanying words is an indorsement unless the accompanying words, the terms of the instrument, the place of the signature, or other circumstances unambiguously indicate that the signature was made for a purpose other than indorsement. For the purpose of determining whether a signature is made on an instrument, a paper affixed to the instrument is a part of the instrument.

(b) "Indorser" means a person who makes an indorsement.

(c) For the purpose of determining whether the transferee of an instrument is a holder, an indorsement that transfers a security interest in the instrument is effective as an unqualified indorsement of the instrument.

(d) If an instrument is payable to a holder under a name that is not the name of the holder, indorsement may be made by the holder in the name stated in the instrument or in the holder's name or both, but signature in both names may be required by a person paying or taking the instrument for value or -collection.

§ 3–205. Special Indorsement; Blank Indorsement; Anomalous Indorsement.

(a) If an indorsement is made by the holder of an instrument, whether payable to an identified person or payable to bearer, and the indorsement identifies a person to whom it makes the instrument payable, it is a "special indorsement." When specially indorsed, an instrument becomes payable to the identified person and may be negotiated only by the indorsement of that person. The principles stated in Section 3–110 apply to special indorsements.

(b) If an indorsement is made by the holder of an instrument and it is not a special indorsement, it is a "blank indorsement." When indorsed in blank, an instrument becomes payable to bearer and may be negotiated by transfer of possession alone until specially indorsed.

(c) The holder may convert a blank indorsement that consists only of a signature into a special indorsement by writing, above the signature of the indorser, words identifying the person to whom the instrument is made payable.

(d) "Anomalous indorsement" means an indorsement made by a person that is not the holder of the instrument. An anomalous indorsement does not affect the manner in which the instrument may be negotiated.

§ 3–206. Restrictive Indorsement.

(a) An indorsement limiting payment to a particular person or otherwise prohibiting further transfer or negotiation of the instrument is not effective to prevent further transfer or negotiation of the instrument.

(b) An indorsement stating a condition to the right of the indorsee to receive payment does not affect the right of the indorsee to enforce the instrument. A person paying the instrument or taking it for value or collection may disregard the condition, and the rights and liabilities of that person are not affected by whether the condition has been fulfilled.

(c) The following rules apply to an instrument bearing an indorsement (i) described in Section 4–201(2), or (ii) in blank or to a particular bank using the words "for deposit," "for collection," or other words indicating a purpose of having the instrument collected for the indorser or for a particular account:

(1) A person, other than a bank, that purchases the instrument when so indorsed converts the instrument unless the proceeds of the instrument are received by the indorser or are applied consistently with the indorsement.

(2) A depositary bank that purchases the instrument or takes it for collection when so indorsed converts the instrument unless the proceeds of the instrument are received by the indorser or applied consistently with the indorsement.

(3) A payor bank that is also the depositary bank or that takes the instrument for immediate payment over the counter from a person other than a collecting bank converts the instrument unless the proceeds of the instrument are received by the indorser or applied consistently with the indorsement.

(4) Except as otherwise provided in paragraph (3), a payor bank or intermediary bank may disregard the indorsement and is not liable if the proceeds of the instrument are not received by the indorser or applied consistently with the indorsement.

(d) Except for an indorsement covered by subsection (c), the following rules apply to an instrument bearing an indorsement using words to the effect that payment is to be made to the indorsee as agent, trustee, or other fiduciary for the benefit of the indorser or another person:

(1) Unless there is notice of breach of fiduciary duty as provided in Section 3–307, a person that purchases the instrument from the indorsee or takes the instrument from the indorsee for collection or payment may pay the proceeds of payment or the value given for the instrument to the indorsee without regard to whether the indorsee violates a fiduciary duty to the indorser.

(2) A later transferee of the instrument or person that pays the instrument is neither given notice nor otherwise affected by the restriction in the indorsement unless the transferee or payor knows that the fiduciary dealt with the instrument or its proceeds in breach of fiduciary duty.

(e) Purchase of an instrument bearing an indorsement to which this section applies does not prevent the purchaser from becoming a holder in due course of the instrument unless the purchaser is a converter under subsection (c).

(f) In an action to enforce the obligation of a party to pay the instrument, the obligor has a defense if payment would violate an indorsement to which this section applies and the payment is not permitted by this section.

§ 3–207. Reacquisition.

Reacquisition of an instrument occurs if it is transferred, by negotiation or otherwise, to a former holder. A former holder that reacquires the instrument may cancel indorsements made after the reacquirer first became a holder of the instrument. If the cancellation causes the instrument to be payable to the reacquirer or to bearer, the reacquirer may negotiate the instrument. An indorser whose indorsement is canceled is discharged, and the discharge is effective against any later holder.

PART 3 Enforcement of Instruments

§ 3–301. Person Entitled to Enforce Instrument.

"Person entitled to enforce" an instrument means (i) the holder of the instrument, (ii) a nonholder in possession of the instrument who has the rights of a holder, or (iii) a person not in possession of the instrument who is entitled to enforce the instrument pursuant to Section 3–309. A person may be a person entitled to enforce the instrument even though the person is not the owner of the instrument or is in wrongful possession of the instrument.

§ 3–302. Holder in Due Course.

(a) Subject to subsection (c) and Section 3–106(d), "holder in due course" means the holder of an instrument if:

(1) the instrument when issued or negotiated to the holder does not bear such apparent evidence of forgery or alteration or is not otherwise so irregular or incomplete as to call into question its authenticity, and

(2) the holder took the instrument (i) for value, (ii) in good faith, (iii) without notice that the instrument is overdue or has been dishonored or that there is an uncured default with respect to payment of another instrument issued as part of the same series, (iv) without notice that the instrument contains an unauthorized signature or has been altered, (v) without notice of any claim to the instrument stated in Section 3–306, and (vi) without notice that any party to the instrument has any defense or claim in recoupment stated in Section 3–305(a).

(b) Notice of discharge of a party to the instrument, other than discharge in an insolvency proceeding, is not notice of a defense under subsection (a), but discharge is effective against a person who became a holder in due course with notice of the discharge. Public filing or recording of a document does not of itself constitute notice of a defense, claim in recoupment, or claim to the instrument.

(c) Except to the extent a transferor or predecessor in interest has rights as a holder in due course, a person does not acquire rights of a holder in due course of an instrument taken (i) by legal process or by purchase at an execution, bankruptcy, or creditor's sale or similar proceeding, (ii) by purchase as part of a bulk transaction not in ordinary course of business of the transferor, or (iii) as the successor in interest to an estate or other organization.

(d) If, under Section 3–303(a)(1), the promise of performance that is the consideration for an instrument has been partially performed, the holder may assert rights as a holder in due course of the instrument only to the fraction of the amount payable under the instrument equal to the value of the partial performance divided by the value of the promised performance.

(e) If (i) the person entitled to enforce an instrument has only a security interest in the instrument and (ii) the person obliged to pay the instrument has a defense, claim in recoupment or claim to the instrument that may be asserted against the person who granted the security interest, the person entitled to enforce the instrument may assert rights as a holder in due course only to an amount payable under the instrument which, at the time of enforcement of the instrument, does not exceed the amount of the unpaid obligation secured.

(f) To be effective, notice must be received at such time and in such manner as to give a reasonable opportunity to act on it.

(g) This section is subject to any law limiting status as a holder in due course in particular classes of transactions.

§ 3–303. Value and Consideration.

(a) An instrument is issued or transferred for value if:

(1) the instrument is issued or transferred for a promise of performance, to the extent the promise has been performed;

(2) the transferee acquires a security interest or other lien in the instrument other than a lien obtained by judicial pro-ceedings;

(3) the instrument is issued or transferred as payment of, or as security for, an existing obligation of any person, whether or not the obligation is due;

(4) the instrument is issued or transferred in exchange for a negotiable instrument; or

(5) the instrument is issued or transferred in exchange for the incurring of an irrevocable obligation to a third party by the person taking the instrument.

(b) "Consideration" means any consideration sufficient to support a simple contract. The drawer or maker of an instrument has a defense if the instrument is issued without consideration. If an instrument is issued for a promise of performance, the drawer or maker has a defense to the extent performance of the promise is due and the promise has not been performed. If an instrument is issued for value as stated in subsection (a), the instrument is also issued for consideration.

§ 3–304. Overdue Instrument.

(a) An instrument payable on demand becomes overdue at the earliest of the following times:

(1) on the day after the day demand for payment is duly made;

(2) if the instrument is a check, 90 days after its date; or

(3) if the instrument is not a check, when the instrument has been outstanding for a period of time after its date which is unreasonably long under the circumstances of the particular case in light of the nature of the instrument and trade usage.

(b) With respect to an instrument payable at a definite time the following rules apply: (1) If the principal is payable in installments and a due date has not been accelerated, the instrument becomes overdue upon default under the instrument for nonpayment of an installment, and the instrument remains overdue until the default is cured. (2) If the principal is not payable in installments and the due date has not been accelerated, the instrument becomes overdue on the day after the due date. (3) If a due date with respect to principal has been accelerated, the instrument becomes overdue on the day after the accelerated due date.

(c) Unless the due date of principal has been accelerated, an instrument does not become overdue if there is default in payment of interest but no default in payment of principal.

§ 3–305. Defenses and Claims in Recoupment.

(a) Except as stated in subsection (b), the right to enforce the obligation of a party to pay the instrument is subject to the -following:

(1) A defense of the obligor based on (i) infancy of the obligor to the extent it is a defense to a simple contract, (ii) duress, lack of legal capacity, or illegality of the transaction that nullifies the obligation of the obligor, (iii) fraud that induced the obligor to sign the instrument with neither knowledge nor reasonable opportunity to learn of its character or its essential terms, or (iv) discharge of the obligor in insolvency proceedings.

(2) A defense of the obligor stated in another section of this Article or a defense of the obligor that would be available if the person entitled to enforce the instrument were enforcing a right to payment under a simple contract.

(3) A claim in recoupment of the obligor against the original payee of the instrument if the claim arose from the transaction that gave rise to the instrument. The claim of the obligor may be asserted against a transferee of the instrument only to reduce the amount owing on the instrument at the time the action is brought.

(b) The right of a holder in due course to enforce the obligation of a party to pay the instrument is subject to defenses of the obligor stated in subsection (a)(1), but is not subject to defenses of the obligor stated in subsection (a)(2) or claims in recoupment stated in subsection (a)(3) against a person other than the holder.

(c) Except as stated in subsection (d), in an action to enforce the obligation of a party to pay the instrument, the obligor may not assert against the person entitled to enforce the instrument a defense, claim in recoupment, or claim to the instrument (Section 3–306) of another person, but the other person's claim to the instrument may be asserted by the obligor if the other person is joined in the action and personally asserts the claim against the person entitled to enforce the instrument. An obligor is not obliged to pay the instrument if the person seeking enforcement of the instrument does not have rights of a holder in due course and the obligor proves that the instrument is a lost or stolen instrument.

(d) In an action to enforce the obligation of an accommodation party to pay an instrument, the accommodation party may assert against the person entitled to enforce the instrument any defense or claim in recoupment under subsection (a) that the accommodated party could assert against the person entitled to enforce the instrument, except the defenses of discharge in insolvency proceedings, infancy, or lack of legal capacity.

§ 3–306. Claims to an Instrument.

A person taking an instrument, other than a person having rights of a holder in due course, is subject to a claim of a property or possessory right in the instrument or its proceeds, including a claim to rescind a negotiation and to recover the instrument or its proceeds. A person having rights of a holder in due course takes free of the claim to the instrument.

§ 3–307. Notice of Breach of Fiduciary Duty.

(a) This section applies if (i) an instrument is taken from a fiduciary for payment or collection or for value, (ii) the taker has knowledge of the fiduciary status of the fiduciary, and (iii) the represented person makes a claim to the instrument or its proceeds on the basis that the transaction of the fiduciary is a breach of fiduciary duty. Notice of breach of fiduciary duty by the fiduciary is notice of the claim of the represented person. "Fiduciary" means an agent, trustee, partner, corporation officer or director, or other representative owing a fiduciary duty with respect to the instrument. "Represented person" means the principal, beneficiary, partnership, corporation, or other person to whom the duty is owed.

(b) If the instrument is payable to the fiduciary, as such, or to the represented person, the taker has notice of the breach of fiduciary duty if the instrument is (i) taken in payment of or as security for a debt known by the taker to be the personal debt of the fiduciary, (ii) taken in a transaction known by the taker to be for the personal benefit of the fiduciary, or (iii) deposited to an account other than an account of the fiduciary, as such, or an account of the represented person.

(c) If the instrument is made or drawn by the fiduciary, as such, payable to the fiduciary personally, the taker does not have notice of the breach of fiduciary duty unless the taker knows of the breach of fiduciary duty.

(d) If the instrument is made or drawn by or on behalf of the represented person to the taker as payee, the taker has notice of the breach of fiduciary duty if the instrument is (i) taken in payment of or as security for a debt known by the taker to be the personal debt of the fiduciary, (ii) taken in a transaction known by the taker to be for the personal benefit of the fiduciary, or (iii) deposited to an account other than an account of the fiduciary, as such, or an account of the represented person.

§ 3–308. Proof of Signatures and Status as Holder in Due Course.

(a) In an action with respect to an instrument, the authenticity of, and authority to make, each signature on the instrument is admitted unless specifically denied in the pleadings. If the validity of a signature is denied in the pleadings, the burden of establishing validity is on the person claiming validity, but the signature is presumed to be authentic and authorized unless the action is to enforce the liability of the purported signer and the signer is dead or incompetent at the time of trial of the issue of validity of the signature. If an action to enforce the instrument is brought against a person as the undisclosed principal of a person who signed the instrument as a party to the instrument, the plaintiff has the burden of establishing that the defendant is liable on the instrument as a represented person pursuant to Section 3–402(a).

(b) If the validity of signatures is admitted or proved and there is compliance with subsection (a), a plaintiff producing the instrument is entitled to payment if the plaintiff proves entitlement to enforce the instrument under Section 3–301, unless the defendant proves a defense or claim in recoupment. If a defense or claim in recoupment is proved, the right to payment of the plaintiff is subject to the defense or claim except to the extent the plaintiff proves that the plaintiff has rights of a holder in due course which are not subject to the defense or claim.

§ 3–309. Enforcement of Lost, Destroyed, or Stolen Instrument.

(a) A person not in possession of an instrument is entitled to enforce the instrument if (i) that person was in rightful possession of the instrument and entitled to enforce it when loss of possession occurred, (ii) the loss of possession was not the result of a voluntary transfer by that person or a lawful seizure, and (iii) that person cannot reasonably obtain possession of the instrument because the instrument was destroyed, its whereabouts cannot be determined, or it is in the wrongful possession of an unknown person or a person that cannot be found or is not amenable to service of process.

(b) A person seeking enforcement of an instrument pursuant to subsection (a) must prove the terms of the instrument and the person's right to enforce the instrument. If that proof is made, Section 3–308 applies to the case as though the person seeking enforcement had produced the instrument. The court may not enter judgment in favor of the person seeking enforcement unless it finds that the person required to pay the instrument is adequately protected against loss that might occur by reason of a claim by another person to enforce the instrument. Adequate protection may be provided by any reasonable means.

§ 3–310. Effect of Instrument on Obligation for Which Taken.

(a) Unless otherwise agreed, if a certified check, cashier's check, or teller's check is taken for an obligation, the obligation is discharged to the same extent discharge would result if an amount of money equal to the amount of the instrument were taken in payment of the obligation. Discharge of the obligation does not affect any liability that the obligor may have as an indorser of the instrument.

(b) Unless otherwise agreed and except as provided in subsection (a), if a note or an uncertified check is taken for an obligation, the obligation is suspended to the same extent the obligation would be discharged if an amount of money equal to the amount of the instrument were taken.

(1) In the case of an uncertified check, suspension of the obligation continues until dishonor of the check or

until it is paid or certified. Payment or certification of the check results in discharge of the obligation to the extent of the amount of the check.

(2) In the case of a note, suspension of the obligation continues until dishonor of the note or until it is paid. Payment of the note results in discharge of the obligation to the extent of the payment.

(3) If the check or note is dishonored and the obligee of the obligation for which the instrument was taken has possession of the instrument, the obligee may enforce either the instrument or the obligation. In the case of an instrument of a third person which is negotiated to the obligee by the obligor, discharge of the obligor on the instrument also discharges the obligation.

(4) If the person entitled to enforce the instrument taken for an obligation is a person other than the obligee, the obligee may not enforce the obligation to the extent the obligation is suspended. If the obligee is the person entitled to enforce the instrument but no longer has possession of it because it was lost, stolen, or destroyed, the obligation may not be enforced to the extent of the amount payable on the instrument, and to that extent the obligee's rights against the obligor are limited to enforcement of the instrument.

(c) If an instrument other than one described in subsection (a) or (b) is taken for an obligation, the effect is (i) that stated in subsection (a) if the instrument is one on which a bank is liable as maker or acceptor, or (ii) that stated in subsection (b) in any other case.

§ 3–311. Accord and Satisfaction by Use of Instrument.

(a) This section applies if a person against whom a claim is asserted proves that (i) that person in good faith tendered an instrument to the claimant as full satisfaction of the claim, (ii) the amount of the claim was unliquidated or subject to a bona fide dispute, and (iii) the claimant obtained payment of the instrument.

(b) Unless subsection (c) applies, the claim is discharged if the person against whom the claim is asserted proves that the instrument or an accompanying written communication contained a conspicuous statement to the effect that the instrument was tendered as full satisfaction of the claim.

(c) Subject to subsection (d), a claim is not discharged under subsection (b) if the claimant is an organization and proves that within a reasonable time before the tender, the claimant sent a conspicuous statement to the person against whom the claim is asserted that communications concerning disputed debts, including an instrument tendered as full satisfaction of a debt, are to be sent to a designated person, office or place, and the instrument or accompanying communication was not received by that designated person, office, or place.

(d) Notwithstanding subsection (c), a claim is discharged under subsection (b) if the person against whom the claim is asserted proves that within a reasonable time before collection of the instrument was initiated, an agent of the claimant having direct responsibility with respect to the disputed obligation knew that the instrument was tendered in full satisfaction of the claim, or received the instrument and any accompanying written communication.

PART 4 Liability of Parties

§ 3–401. Signature.

(a) A person is not liable on an instrument unless (i) the person signed the instrument, or (ii) the person is represented by an agent or representative who signed the instrument and the signature is binding on the represented person under Section 3–402.

(b) A signature may be made (i) manually or by means of a device or machine, and (ii) by the use of any name, including any trade or assumed name, or by any word, mark, or symbol executed or adopted by a person with present intention to authenticate a writing.

§ 3–402. Signature by Representative.

(a) If a person acting, or purporting to act, as a representative signs an instrument by signing either the name of the represented person or the name of the signer, the represented person is bound by the signature to the same extent the represented person would be bound if the signature were on a simple contract. If the represented person is bound, the signature of the representative is the "authorized signature of the represented person" and the represented person is liable on the instrument, whether or not identified in the instrument.

(b) If a representative signs the name of the representative to an instrument and that signature is an authorized signature of the represented person, the following rules apply:

(1) If the form of the signature shows unambiguously that the signature is made on behalf of the represented person who is identified in the instrument, the representative is not liable on the instrument.

(2) Subject to subsection (c), if (i) the form of the signature does not show unambiguously that the signature is made in a representative capacity or (ii) the represented person is not identified in the instrument, the representative is liable on the instrument to a holder in due course that took the instrument without notice that the representative was not intended to be liable on the instrument. With respect to any other person, the representative is liable on the instrument unless the representative proves that the original parties to the instrument did not intend the representative to be liable on the instrument.

(c) If a representative signs the name of the representative as drawer of a check without indication of the representative status and the check is payable from an account of the represented person who is identified on the check, the signer is not liable on the check if the signature is an authorized signature of the represented person.

§ 3–403. Unauthorized Signature.

(a) Except as otherwise provided in this Article, an unauthorized signature is ineffective except as the signature of the unauthorized signer in favor of a person who in good faith pays the instrument or takes it for value. An unauthorized signature may be ratified for all purposes of this Article.

(b) If the signature of more than one person is required to constitute the authorized signature of an organization, the signature of the organization is unauthorized if one of the required signatures is missing.

(c) The civil or criminal liability of a person who makes an unauthorized signature is not affected by any provision of this Article that makes the unauthorized signature effective for the purposes of this Article.

§ 3–404. Impostors; Fictitious Payees.

(a) If an impostor by use of the mails or otherwise induces the maker or drawer of an instrument to issue the instrument to the impostor, or to a person acting in concert with the impostor, by impersonating the payee of the instrument or a person authorized to act for the payee, an indorsement of the instrument by any person in the name of the payee is effective as the indorsement of the payee in favor of any person that in good faith pays the instrument or takes it for value or for collection.

(b) If (i) a person whose intent determines to whom an instrument is payable (Section 3–110(a) or (b)) does not intend the person identified as payee to have any interest in the instrument, or (ii) the person identified as payee of the instrument is a fictitious person, the following rules apply until the instrument is negotiated by special indorsement:

(1) Any person in possession of the instrument is its holder.

(2) An indorsement by any person in the name of the payee stated in the instrument is effective as the indorsement of the payee in favor of any person that in good faith pays the instrument or takes it for value or for collection.

(c) Under subsection (a) or (b) an indorsement is made in the name of a payee if (i) it is made in a name substantially similar to that of the payee or (ii) the instrument, whether or not indorsed, is deposited in a depositary bank to an account in a name substantially similar to that of the payee.

(d) With respect to an instrument to which subsection (a) or (b) applies, if a person paying the instrument or taking it for value or for collection fails to exercise ordinary care in paying or taking the instrument and that failure substantially contributes to loss resulting from payment of the instrument, the person bearing the loss may recover from the person failing to exercise ordinary care to the extent the failure to exercise ordinary care contributed to the loss.

§ 3–405. Employer Responsibility for Fraudulent Indorsement by Employee.

(a) This section applies to fraudulent indorsements of instruments with respect to which an employer has entrusted an employee with responsibility as part of the employee's duties. The following definitions apply to this section:

(1) "Employee" includes, in addition to an employee of an employer, an independent contractor and employee of an independent contractor retained by the employer.

(2) "Fraudulent indorsement" means (i) in the case of an instrument payable to the employer, a forged indorsement purporting to be that of the employer, or (ii) in the case of an instrument with respect to which the employer is drawer or maker, a forged indorsement purporting to be that of the person identified as payee.

(3) "Responsibility" with respect to instruments means authority (i) to sign or indorse instruments on behalf of the employer, (ii) to process instruments received by the employer for bookkeeping purposes, for deposit to an account, or for other disposition, (iii) to prepare or process instruments for issue in the name of the employer, (iv) to supply information determining the names or addresses of payees of instruments to be issued in the name of the employer, (v) to control the disposition of instruments to be issued in the name of the employer, or (vi) to otherwise act with respect to instruments in a responsible capacity. "Responsibility" does not include the assignment of duties that merely allow an employee to have access to instruments or blank or incomplete instrument forms that are being stored or transported or are part of incoming or outgoing mail, or similar access.

(b) For the purpose of determining the rights and liabilities of a person who, in good faith, pays an instrument or takes it for value or for collection, if an employee entrusted with responsibility with respect to the instrument or a person acting in concert with the employee makes a fraudulent indorsement to the instrument, the indorsement is effective as the indorsement of the person to whom the instrument is payable if it is made in the name of that person. If the person paying the instrument or taking it for value or for collection fails to exercise ordinary care in paying or taking the instrument and that failure substantially contributes to loss resulting from the fraud, the person bearing the loss may recover from the person failing to exercise ordinary care to the extent the failure to exercise ordinary care contributed to the loss.

(c) Under subsection (b) an indorsement is made in the name of the person to whom an instrument is payable if (i) it is made in a name substantially similar to the name of that person or (ii) the instrument, whether or not indorsed, is deposited in a depositary bank to an account in a name substantially similar to the name of that person.

§ 3–406. Negligence Contributing to Forged Signature or Alteration of Instrument.

(a) A person whose failure to exercise ordinary care substantially contributes to an alteration of an instrument or to the making of a forged signature on an instrument is precluded from asserting the alteration or the forgery against a person that, in good faith, pays the instrument or takes it for value.

(b) If the person asserting the preclusion fails to exercise ordinary care in paying or taking the instrument and that failure substantially contributes to loss, the loss is allocated between the person precluded and the person asserting the preclusion according to the extent to which the failure of each to exercise ordinary care contributed to the loss.

(c) Under subsection (a) the burden of proving failure to exercise ordinary care is on the person asserting the preclusion. Under subsection (b) the burden of proving failure to exercise ordinary care is on the person precluded.

§ 3–407. Alteration.

(a) "Alteration" means (i) an unauthorized change in an instrument that purports to modify in any respect the obligation of a party to the instrument, or (ii) an unauthorized addition of words or numbers or other change to an incomplete instrument relating to the obligation of any party to the instrument.

(b) Except as provided in subsection (c), an alteration fraudulently made by the holder discharges any party to whose obligation the alteration applies unless that party assents or is precluded from asserting the alteration. No other alteration discharges any party, and the instrument may be enforced according to its original terms.

(c) If an instrument that has been fraudulently altered is acquired by a person having rights of a holder in due course, it may be enforced by that person according to its original terms. If an incomplete instrument is completed and is then acquired by a person having rights of a holder in due course, it may be enforced by that person as completed, whether or not the completion is a fraudulent alteration.

§ 3–408. Drawee Not Liable on Unaccepted Draft.

A check or other draft does not of itself operate as an assignment of funds in the hands of the drawee available for its payment, and the drawee is not liable on the instrument until the drawee accepts it.

§ 3–409. Acceptance of Draft; Certified Check.

(a) "Acceptance" means the drawee's signed agreement to pay a draft as presented. It must be written on the draft and may consist of the drawee's signature alone. Acceptance may be made at any time and becomes effective when notification pursuant to instructions is given or the accepted draft is delivered for the purpose of giving rights on the acceptance to any -person.

(b) A draft may be accepted although it has not been signed by the drawer, is otherwise incomplete, is overdue, or has been dishonored.

(c) If a draft is payable at a fixed period after sight and the acceptor fails to date the acceptance, the holder may complete the acceptance by supplying a date in good faith.

(d) "Certified check" means a check accepted by the bank on which it is drawn. Acceptance may be made as stated in subsection (a) or by a writing on the check which indicates that the check is certified. The drawee of a check has no obligation to certify the check, and refusal to certify is not dishonor of the check.

§ 3–410. Acceptance Varying Draft.

(a) If the terms of a drawee's acceptance vary from the terms of the draft as presented, the holder may refuse the acceptance and treat the draft as dishonored. In that case, the drawee may cancel the acceptance.

(b) The terms of a draft are not varied by an acceptance to pay at a particular bank or place in the United States, unless the acceptance states that the draft is to be paid only at that bank or place.

(c) If the holder assents to an acceptance varying the terms of a draft, the obligation of each drawer and indorser that does not expressly assent to the acceptance is discharged.

§ 3–411. Refusal to Pay Cashier's Checks, Teller's Checks, and Certified Checks.

(a) In this section, "obligated bank" means the acceptor of a certified check or the issuer of a cashier's check or teller's check bought from the issuer.

(b) If the obligated bank wrongfully (i) refuses to pay a cashier's check or certified check, (ii) stops payment of a teller's check, or (iii) refuses to pay a dishonored teller's check, the person asserting the right to enforce the check is entitled to compensation for expenses and loss of interest resulting from the nonpayment and may recover consequential damages if the obligated bank refused to pay after receiving notice of particular circumstances giving rise to the damages.

(c) Expenses or consequential damages under subsection (b) are not recoverable if the refusal of the obligated bank to pay occurs because (i) the bank suspends payments, (ii) the obligated bank is asserting a claim or defense of the bank that it has reasonable grounds to believe is available against the person entitled to enforce the instrument, (iii) the obligated bank has a reasonable doubt whether the person demanding payment is the person entitled to enforce the instrument, or (iv) payment is prohibited by law.

§ 3–412. Obligation of Maker.

A maker of a note is obliged to pay the note (i) according to its terms at the time it was issued or, if not issued, at the time it first came into possession of a holder, or (ii) if the maker signed an incomplete instrument, according to its terms when completed as stated in Sections 3–115 and 3–407. The obligation is owed to a person entitled to enforce the note or to an indorser that paid the note pursuant to Section 3–415.

§ 3–413. Obligation of Acceptor.

(a) An acceptor of a draft is obliged to pay the draft (i) according to its terms at the time it was accepted, even though the acceptance states that the draft is payable "as originally drawn" or equivalent terms, (ii) if the acceptance varies the terms of the draft, according to the terms of the draft as varied, or (iii) if the acceptance is of a draft that is an incomplete instrument, according to its terms when completed as stated in Sections 3–115 and 3–407.

The obligation is owed to a person entitled to enforce the draft or to the drawer or an indorser that paid the draft pursuant to Section 3–414 or 3–415.

(b) If the certification of a check or other acceptance of a draft states the amount certified or accepted, the obligation of the acceptor is that amount. If (i) the certification or acceptance does not state an amount, (ii) the instrument is subsequently altered by raising its amount, and (iii) the instrument is then negotiated to a holder in due course, the obligation of the acceptor is the amount of the instrument at the time it was negotiated to the holder in due course.

§ 3–414. Obligation of Drawer.

(a) If an unaccepted draft is dishonored, the drawer is obliged to pay the draft (i) according to its terms at the time it was issued or, if not issued, at the time it first came into possession of a holder, or (ii) if the drawer signed an incomplete instrument, according to its terms when completed as stated in Sections 3–115 and 3–407. The obligation is owed to a person entitled to enforce the draft or to an indorser that paid the draft pursuant to Section 3–415.

(b) If a draft is accepted by a bank and the acceptor dishonors the draft, the drawer has no obligation to pay the draft because of the dishonor, regardless of when or by whom acceptance was obtained.

(c) If a draft is accepted and the acceptor is not a bank, the obligation of the drawer to pay the draft if the draft is dishonored by the acceptor is the same as the obligation of an indorser stated in Section 3–415(a) and (c).

(d) Words in a draft indicating that the draft is drawn without recourse are effective to disclaim all liability of the drawer to pay the draft if the draft is not a check or a teller's check, but they are not effective to disclaim the obligation stated in subsection (a) if the draft is a check or a teller's check.

(e) If (i) a check is not presented for payment or given to a depositary bank for collection within 30 days after its date, (ii) the drawee suspends payments after expiration of the 30-day period without paying the check, and (iii) because of the suspension of payments the drawer is deprived of funds maintained with the drawee to cover payment of the check, the drawer to the extent deprived of funds may discharge its obligation to pay the check by assigning to the person entitled to enforce the check the rights of the drawer against the drawee with respect to the funds.

§ 3–415. Obligation of Indorser.

(a) Subject to subsections (b), (c) and (d) and to Section 3–419(d), if an instrument is dishonored, an indorser is obliged to pay the amount due on the instrument (i) according to the terms of the instrument at the time it was indorsed, or (ii) if the indorser indorsed an incomplete instrument, according to its terms when completed as stated in Sections 3–115 and 3–407. The obligation of the indorser is owed to a person entitled to enforce the instrument or to a subsequent indorser that paid the instrument pursuant to this section.

(b) If an indorsement states that it is made "without recourse" or otherwise disclaims liability of the indorser, the indorser is not liable under subsection (a) to pay the instrument.

(c) If notice of dishonor of an instrument is required by Section 3–503 and notice of dishonor complying with that section is not given to an indorser, the liability of the indorser under subsection (a) is discharged.

(d) If a draft is accepted by a bank after an indorsement was made and the acceptor dishonors the draft, the indorser is not liable under subsection (a) to pay the instrument.

(e) If an indorser of a check is liable under subsection (a) and the check is not presented for payment, or given to a depositary bank for collection, within 30 days after the day the indorsement was made, the liability of the indorser under subsection (a) is discharged.

§ 3–416. Transfer Warranties.

(a) A person that transfers an instrument for consideration warrants to the transferee and, if the transfer is by indorsement, to any subsequent transferee that:

(1) the warrantor is a person entitled to enforce the instrument,

(2) all signatures on the instrument are authentic and authorized,

(3) the instrument has not been altered,

(4) the instrument is not subject to a defense or claim in recoupment stated in Section 3–305(a) of any party that can be asserted against the warrantor, and

(5) the warrantor has no knowledge of any insolvency proceeding commenced with respect to the maker or acceptor or, in the case of an unaccepted draft, the drawer.

(b) A person to whom the warranties under subsection (a) are made and who took the instrument in good faith may recover from the warrantor as damages for breach of warranty an amount equal to the loss suffered as a result of the breach, but not more than the amount of the instrument plus expenses and loss of interest incurred as a result of the breach.

(c) The warranties stated in subsection (a) cannot be disclaimed with respect to checks. Unless notice of a claim for breach of warranty is given to the warrantor within 30 days after the claimant has reason to know of the breach and the identity of the warrantor, the warrantor is discharged to the extent of any loss caused by the delay in giving notice of the claim.

(d) A cause of action for breach of warranty under this section accrues when the claimant has reason to know of the breach.

§ 3–417. Presentment Warranties.

(a) If an unaccepted draft is presented to the drawee for payment or acceptance and the drawee pays or accepts the draft, (i) the person obtaining payment or acceptance, at the time of presentment, and (ii) a previous transferor of the draft, at the time of transfer, warrant to the drawee making payment or accepting the draft in good faith that:

(1) the warrantor is or was, at the time the warrantor transferred the draft, a person entitled to enforce the draft or authorized to obtain payment or acceptance of the draft on behalf of a person entitled to enforce the draft;

(2) the draft has not been altered; and

(3) the warrantor has no knowledge that the signature of the purported drawer of the draft is unauthorized.

(b) A drawee making payment may recover from any warrantor damages for breach of warranty equal to the amount paid by the drawee less the amount the drawee received or is entitled to receive from the drawer because of payment of the draft. In addition the drawee is entitled to compensation for expenses and loss of interest resulting from the breach. The right of the drawee to recover damages under this subsection is not affected by any failure of the drawee to exercise ordinary care in making payment. If the drawee accepts the draft (i) breach of warranty is a defense to the obligation of the acceptor, and (ii) if the acceptor makes payment with respect to the draft, the acceptor is entitled to recover from any warrantor for breach of warranty the amounts stated in the first two sentences of this subsection.

(c) If a drawee asserts a claim for breach of warranty under subsection (a) based on an unauthorized indorsement of the draft or an alteration of the draft, the warrantor may defend by proving that the indorsement is effective under Section 3–404 or 3–405 or the drawer is precluded under Section 3–406 or 4–406 from asserting against the drawee the unauthorized indorsement or alteration.

(d) This subsection applies if (i) a dishonored draft is presented for payment to the drawer or an indorser or (ii) any other instrument is presented for payment to a party obliged to pay the instrument, and payment is received. The person obtaining payment and a prior transferor of the instrument warrant to the person making payment in good faith that the warrantor is or was, at the time the warrantor transferred the instrument, a person entitled to enforce the instrument or authorized to obtain payment on behalf of a person entitled to enforce the instrument. The person making payment may recover from any warrantor for breach of warranty an amount equal to the amount paid plus expenses and loss of interest resulting from the breach.

(e) The warranties stated in subsections (a) and (d) cannot be disclaimed with respect to checks. Unless notice of a claim for breach of warranty is given to the warrantor within 30 days after the claimant has reason to know of the breach and the identity of the warrantor, the warrantor is discharged to the extent of any loss caused by the delay in giving notice of the claim.

(f) A cause of action for breach of warranty under this section accrues when the claimant has reason to know of the breach.

§ 3–418. Payment or Acceptance by Mistake.

(a) Except as provided in subsection (c), if the drawee of a draft pays or accepts the draft and the drawee acted on the mistaken belief that (i) payment of the draft had not been stopped under Section 4–403, (ii) the signature of the purported drawer of the draft was authorized, or (iii) the balance in the drawer's account with the drawee represented available funds, the drawee may recover the amount paid from the person to whom or for whose benefit payment was made or, in the case of acceptance, may revoke the acceptance. Rights of the drawee under this subsection are not affected by failure of the drawee to exercise ordinary care in paying or accepting the draft.

(b) Except as provided in subsection (c), if an instrument has been paid or accepted by mistake and the case is not covered by subsection (a), the person paying or accepting may recover the amount paid or revoke acceptance to the extent allowed by the law governing mistake and restitution.

(c) The remedies provided by subsection (a) or (b) may not be asserted against a person who took the instrument in good faith and for value. This subsection does not limit remedies provided by Section 3–417 for breach of warranty.

§ 3–419. Instruments Signed for Accommodation.

(a) If an instrument is issued for value given for the benefit of a party to the instrument ("accommodated party") and another party to the instrument ("accommodation party") signs the instrument for the purpose of incurring liability on the instrument without being a direct beneficiary of the value given for the instrument, the instrument is signed by the accommodation party "for accommodation."

(b) An accommodation party may sign the instrument as maker, drawer, acceptor, or indorser and, subject to subsection (d), is obliged to pay the instrument in the capacity in which the accommodation party signs. The obligation of an accommodation party may be enforced notwithstanding any statute of frauds and regardless of whether the accommodation party receives consideration for the accommodation.

(c) A person signing an instrument is presumed to be an accommodation party and there is notice that the instrument is signed for accommodation if the signature is an anomalous indorsement or is accompanied by words indicating that the signer is acting as surety or guarantor with respect to the obligation of another party to the instrument. Except as provided in Section 3–606, the obligation of an accommodation party to pay the instrument is not affected by the fact that the person enforcing the obligation had notice when the instrument was taken by that person that the accommodation party signed the instrument for accommodation.

(d) If the signature of a party to an instrument is accompanied by words indicating unambiguously that the party is guaranteeing collection rather than payment of the obligation of another party to the instrument, the signer is obliged to pay the amount due on the instrument to a person entitled to enforce the instrument only if (i) execution of judgment against the other party has been returned unsatisfied, (ii) the other party is insolvent or in an insolvency proceeding, (iii) the other party cannot be served with process, or (iv) it is otherwise apparent that payment cannot be obtained from the party whose obligation is guaranteed.

(e) An accommodation party that pays the instrument is entitled to reimbursement from the accommodated party and is entitled to enforce the instrument against the accommodated party. An accommodated party that pays the instrument has no right of recourse against, and is not entitled to contribution from, an accommodation party.

§ 3–420. Conversion of Instrument.

(a) The law applicable to conversion of personal property applies to instruments. An instrument is also converted if the instrument lacks an indorsement necessary for negotiation and it is purchased or taken for collection or the drawee takes the instrument and makes payment to a person not entitled to receive payment. An action for conversion of an instrument may not be brought by (i) the maker, drawer, or acceptor of the instrument or (ii) a payee or indorsee who did not receive delivery of the instrument either directly or through delivery to an agent or a co-payee.

(b) In an action under subsection (a), the measure of liability is presumed to be the amount payable on the instrument, but recovery may not exceed the amount of the plaintiff's interest in the instrument.

(c) A representative, other than a depositary bank, that has in good faith dealt with an instrument or its proceeds on behalf of one who was not the person entitled to enforce the instrument is not liable in conversion to that person beyond the amount of any proceeds that it has not paid out.

PART 5 Dishonor

§ 3–501. Presentment.

(a) "Presentment" means a demand (i) to pay an instrument made to the maker, drawee, or acceptor or, in the case of a note or accepted draft payable at a bank, to the bank, or (ii) to accept a draft made to the drawee, by a person entitled to enforce the instrument.

(b) Subject to Article 4, agreement of the parties, clearing house rules and the like,

(1) presentment may be made at the place of payment of the instrument and must be made at the place of payment if the instrument is payable at a bank in the United States; may be made by any commercially reasonable means, including an oral, written, or electronic communication; is effective when the demand for payment or acceptance is received by the person to whom presentment is made; is effective if made to any one of two or more makers, acceptors, drawees or other payors; and

(2) without dishonoring the instrument, the party to whom presentment is made may (i) treat presentment as occurring on the next business day after the day of presentment if the party to whom presentment is made has established a cut-off hour not earlier than 2 p.m. for the receipt and processing of instruments presented for payment or acceptance and presentment is made after the cut-off hour, (ii) require exhibition of the instrument, (iii) require reasonable identification of the person making presentment and evidence of authority to make it if made on behalf of another person, (iv) require a signed receipt on the instrument for any payment made or surrender of the instrument if full payment is made, (v) return the instrument for lack of a necessary indorsement, or (vi) refuse payment or acceptance for failure of the presentment to comply with the terms of the instrument, an agreement of the parties, or other law or applicable rule.

§ 3–502. Dishonor.

(a) Dishonor of a note is governed by the following rules:

(1) If the note is payable on demand, the note is dishonored if presentment is duly made and the note is not paid on the day of presentment.

(2) If the note is not payable on demand and is payable at or through a bank or the terms of the note require presentment, the note is dishonored if presentment is duly made and the note is not paid on the day it becomes payable or the day of presentment, whichever is later.

(3) If the note is not payable on demand and subparagraph (2) does not apply, the note is dishonored if it is not paid on the day it becomes payable.

(b) Dishonor of an unaccepted draft other than a documentary draft is governed by the following rules:

(1) If a check is presented for payment otherwise than for immediate payment over the counter, the check is dishonored if the payor bank makes timely return of the check or sends timely notice of dishonor or nonpayment under Section 4–301 or 4–302, or becomes accountable for the amount of the check under Section 4–302.

(2) If the draft is payable on demand and subparagraph (1) does not apply, the draft is dishonored if presentment for payment is duly made and the draft is not paid on the day of presentment.

(3) If the draft is payable on a date stated in the draft, the draft is dishonored if (i) presentment for payment is duly made and payment is not made on the day the draft becomes payable or the day of presentment, whichever is later, or (ii) presentment for acceptance is duly made before the day the draft becomes payable and the draft is not accepted on the day of presentment.

(4) If the draft is payable on elapse of a period of time after sight or acceptance, the draft is dishonored if presentment for acceptance is duly made and the draft is not accepted on the day of presentment.

(c) Dishonor of an unaccepted documentary draft occurs according to the rules stated in subparagraphs (2), (3), and (4) of subsection (b) except that payment or acceptance may be delayed without dishonor until no later than the close of the third business day of the drawee following the day on which payment or acceptance is required by those subparagraphs.

(d) Dishonor of an accepted draft is governed by the following rules:

(1) If the draft is payable on demand, the draft is dishonored if presentment for payment is duly made and the draft is not paid on the day of presentment.

(2) If the draft is not payable on demand, the draft is dishonored if presentment for payment is duly made and payment is not made on the day it becomes payable or the day of presentment, whichever is later.

(e) In any case in which presentment is otherwise required for dishonor under this section and presentment is excused under Section 3–504, dishonor occurs without presentment if the instrument is not duly accepted or paid.

(f) If a draft is dishonored because timely acceptance of the draft was not made and the person entitled to demand acceptance consents to a late acceptance, from the time of acceptance the draft is treated as never having been dishonored.

§ 3–503. Notice of Dishonor.

(a) The obligation of an indorser stated in Section 3–415(a) and the obligation of a drawer stated in Section 3–414(c) may not be enforced unless (i) the indorser or drawer is given notice of dishonor of the instrument complying with this section or (ii) notice of dishonor is excused under Section 3–504(c).

(b) Notice of dishonor may be given by any person; may be given by any commercially reasonable means including an oral, written, or electronic communication; is sufficient if it reasonably identifies the instrument and indicates that the instrument has been dishonored or has not been paid or accepted. Return of an instrument given to a bank for collection is a sufficient notice of dishonor.

(c) Subject to Section 3-504(d), with respect to an instrument taken for collection by a collecting bank, notice of dishonor must be given (i) by the bank before midnight of the next banking day following the banking day on which the bank receives notice of dishonor of the instrument, and (ii) by any other person within 30 days following the day on which the person receives notice of dishonor. With respect to any other instrument, notice of dishonor must be given within 30 days following the day on which dishonor occurs.

§ 3–504. Excused Presentment and Notice of Dishonor.

(a) Presentment for payment or acceptance of an instrument is excused if (i) the person entitled to present the instrument cannot with reasonable diligence make presentment, (ii) the maker or acceptor has repudiated an obligation to pay the instrument or is dead or in insolvency proceedings, (iii) by the terms of the instrument presentment is not necessary to enforce the obligation of indorsers or the drawer, or (iv) the drawer or indorser whose obligation is being enforced waived presentment or otherwise had no reason to expect or right to require that the instrument be paid or accepted.

(b) Presentment for payment or acceptance of a draft is also excused if the drawer instructed the drawee not to pay or accept the draft or the drawee was not obligated to the drawer to pay the draft.

(c) Notice of dishonor is excused if (i) by the terms of the instrument notice of dishonor is not necessary to enforce the obligation of a party to pay the instrument, or (ii) the party whose obligation is being enforced waived notice of dishonor. A waiver of presentment is also a waiver of notice of dishonor.

(d) Delay in giving notice of dishonor is excused if the delay was caused by circumstances beyond the control of the person giving the notice and the person giving the notice exercised reasonable diligence after the cause of the delay ceased to operate.

§ 3–505. Evidence of Dishonor.

(a) The following are admissible as evidence and create a presumption of dishonor and of any notice of dishonor stated:

(1) a document regular in form as provided in subsection (b) which purports to be a protest;

(2) a purported stamp or writing of the drawee, payor bank, or presenting bank on or accompanying the instrument stating that acceptance or payment has been refused unless reasons for the refusal are stated and the reasons are not consistent with dishonor;

(3) a book or record of the drawee, payor bank, or collecting bank, kept in the usual course of business which shows dishonor, even if there is no evidence of who made the entry.

(b) A protest is a certificate of dishonor made by a United States consul or vice consul, or a notary public or other person authorized to administer oaths by the law of the place where dishonor occurs. It may be made upon information satisfactory to that person. The protest must identify the instrument and certify either that presentment has been made or, if not made, the reason why it was not made, and that the instrument has been dishonored by nonacceptance or nonpayment. The protest may also certify that notice of dishonor has been given to some or all parties.

PART 6 Discharge and Payment

§ 3–601. Discharge and Effect of Discharge.

(a) The obligation of a party to pay the instrument is discharged as stated in this Article or by an act or agreement with the party which would discharge an obligation to pay money under a simple contract.

(b) Discharge of the obligation of a party is not effective against a person acquiring rights of a holder in due course of the instrument without notice of the discharge.

§ 3–602. Payment.

(a) Subject to subsection (b), an instrument is paid to the extent payment is made (i) by or on behalf of a party obliged to pay the instrument, and (ii) to a person entitled to enforce the instrument. To the extent of the payment, the obligation of the party obliged to pay the instrument is discharged even though payment is made with knowledge of a claim to the instrument under Section 3–306 by another person.

(b) The obligation of a party to pay the instrument is not discharged under subsection (a) if:

(1) a claim to the instrument under Section 3–306 is enforceable against the party receiving payment and (i) payment is made with knowledge by the payor that payment is prohibited by injunction or similar process of a court of competent jurisdiction, or (ii) in the case of an instrument other than a cashier's check, teller's check, or certified check, the party making payment accepted, from the person having a claim to the instrument, indemnity against loss resulting from refusal to pay the person entitled to enforce the instrument, or

(2) the person making payment knows that the instrument is a stolen instrument and pays a person that it knows is in wrongful possession of the instrument.

§ 3–603. Tender of Payment.

(a) If tender of payment of an obligation of a party to an instrument is made to a person entitled to enforce the obligation, the effect of tender is governed by principles of law applicable to tender of payment of an obligation under a simple contract.

(b) If tender of payment of an obligation to pay the instrument is made to a person entitled to enforce the instrument and the tender is refused, there is discharge, to the extent of the amount of the tender, of the obligation of an indorser or accommodation party having a right of recourse against the obligor making the tender.

(c) If tender of payment of an amount due on an instrument is made by or on behalf of the obligor to the person entitled to enforce the instrument, the obligation of the obligor to pay interest after the due date on the amount tendered is discharged. If presentment is required with respect to an instrument and the obligor is able and ready to pay on the due date at every place of payment stated in the instrument, the obligor is deemed to have made tender of payment on the due date to the person entitled to enforce the instrument.

§ 3–604. Discharge by Cancellation or Renunciation.

(a) A person entitled to enforce an instrument may, with or without consideration, discharge the obligation of a party to pay the instrument (i) by an intentional voluntary act such as surrender of the instrument to the party, destruction, mutilation, or cancellation of the instrument, cancellation or striking out of the party's signature, or the addition of words to the instrument indicating discharge, or (ii) by agreeing not to sue or otherwise renouncing rights against the party by a signed writing.

(b) Cancellation or striking out of an indorsement pursuant to subsection (a) does not affect the status and rights of a party derived from the indorsement.

§ 3–605. Discharge of Indorsers and Accommodation Parties.

(a) For the purposes of this section, the term "indorser" includes a drawer having the obligation stated in Section 3–414(c).

(b) Discharge of the obligation of a party to the instrument under Section 3–605 does not discharge the obligation of an indorser or accommodation party having a right of recourse against the discharged party.

(c) If a person entitled to enforce an instrument agrees, with or without consideration, to a material modification of the obligation of a party to the instrument, including an extension of the due date, there is discharge of the obligation of an indorser or accommodation party having a right of recourse against the person whose obligation is modified to the extent the modification causes loss to the indorser or accommodation party with respect to the right of recourse. The indorser or accommodation party is deemed to have suffered loss as a result of the modification equal to the amount of the right of recourse unless the person enforcing the instrument proves that no loss was caused by the modification or that the loss caused by the modification was less than the amount of the right of recourse.

(d) If the obligation of a party to an instrument is secured by an interest in collateral and impairment of the value of the interest is caused by a person entitled to enforce the instrument, there is discharge of the obligation of an indorser or accommodation party having a right of recourse against the obligor to the extent of the impairment. The value of an interest in collateral is impaired to the extent (i) the value of the interest is reduced to an amount less than the amount of the right of recourse of the party asserting discharge, or (ii) the reduction in value of the interest causes an increase in the amount by which the amount of the right of recourse exceeds the value of the interest. The burden of proving impairment is on the party asserting discharge.

(e) If the obligation of a party to an instrument is secured by an interest in collateral not provided by an accommodation party and the value of the interest is impaired by a person entitled to enforce the instrument, the obligation of any party who is jointly and severally liable with respect to the secured obligation is discharged to the extent the impairment causes the party asserting discharge to pay more than that party would have been obliged to pay, taking into account rights of contribution, if impairment had not occurred. If the party asserting discharge is an accommodation party not entitled to discharge under subsection (d), the party is deemed to have a right to contribution based on joint and several liability rather than a right to reimbursement. The burden of proving impairment is on the party asserting discharge.

(f) Under subsection (d) or (e) causation of impairment includes (i) failure to obtain or maintain perfection or recordation of the interest in collateral, (ii) release of collateral without substitution of collateral of equal value,

(iii) failure to perform a duty to preserve the value of collateral owed, under Article 9 or other law, to a debtor or surety or other person secondarily liable, or (iv) failure to comply with applicable law in disposing of collateral.

(g) An accommodation party is not discharged under subsection (c) or (d) unless the person agreeing to the modification or causing the impairment knows of the accommodation or has notice under Section 3–419(c) that the instrument was signed for accommodation. There is no discharge of any party under subsection (c), (d), or (e) if (i) the party asserting discharge consents to the event or conduct that is the basis of the discharge, or (ii) the instrument or a separate agreement of the party provides for waiver of discharge under this section either specifically or by general language indicating that parties to the instrument waive defenses based on suretyship or impairment of collateral.

ARTICLE 4

BANK DEPOSITS AND COLLECTIONS

PART 1 General Provisions and Definitions

§ 4–101. Short Title.

This Article may be cited as Uniform Commercial Code—Bank Deposits and Collections.

§ 4–102. Applicability.

(a) To the extent that items within this Article are also within Articles 3 and 8, they are subject to those Articles. If there is conflict, this Article governs Article 3, but Article 8 governs this Article.

(b) The liability of a bank for action or non-action with respect to an item handled by it for purposes of presentment, payment, or collection is governed by the law of the place where the bank is located. In the case of action or non-action by or at a branch or separate office of a bank, its liability is governed by the law of the place where the branch or separate office is located.

§ 4–103. Variation by Agreement; Measure of Damages; Action Constituting Ordinary Care.

(a) The effect of the provisions of this Article may be varied by agreement, but the parties to the agreement cannot disclaim a bank's responsibility for its lack of good faith or failure to exercise ordinary care or limit the measure of damages for the lack or failure. However, the parties may determine by agreement the standards by which the bank's responsibility is to be measured if those standards are not manifestly unreasonable.

(b) Federal Reserve regulations and operating circulars, clearing-house rules, and the like have the effect of agreements under subsection (a), whether or not specifically assented to by all parties interested in items handled.

(c) Action or non-action approved by this Article or pursuant to Federal Reserve regulations or operating circulars is the exercise of ordinary care and, in the absence of special instructions, action or non-action consistent with clearing-house rules and the like or with a general banking usage not disapproved by this Article, is prima facie the exercise of ordinary care.

(d) The specification or approval of certain procedures by this Article is not disapproval of other procedures that may be reasonable under the circumstances.

(e) The measure of damages for failure to exercise ordinary care in handling an item is the amount of the item reduced by an amount that could not have been realized by the exercise of ordinary care. If there is also bad faith it includes any other damages the party suffered as a proximate consequence.

§ 4–104. Definitions and Index of Definitions.

(a) In this Article, unless the context otherwise requires:

(1) "Account" means any deposit or credit account with a bank, including a demand, time, savings, passbook, share draft, or like account, other than an account evidenced by a certificate of deposit;

(2) "Afternoon" means the period of a day between noon and midnight;

(3) "Banking day" means the part of a day on which a bank is open to the public for carrying on substantially all of its banking functions;

(4) "Clearing house" means an association of banks or other payors regularly clearing items;

(5) "Customer" means a person having an account with a bank or for whom a bank has agreed to collect items, including a bank that maintains an account at another bank;

(6) "Documentary draft" means a draft to be presented for acceptance or payment if specified documents, certificated securities (Section 8–102) or instructions for uncertificated securities (Section 8–102), or other certificates, statements, or the like are to be received by the drawee or other payor before acceptance or payment of the draft;

(7) "Draft" means a draft as defined in Section 3–104 or an item, other than an instrument, that is an order;

(8) "Drawee" means a person ordered in a draft to make payment;

(9) "Item" means an instrument or a promise or order to pay money handled by a bank for collection or payment. The term does not include a payment order governed by Article 4A or a credit or debit card slip;

(10) "Midnight deadline" with respect to a bank is midnight on its next banking day following the banking day on which it receives the relevant item or notice or from which the time for taking action commences to run, whichever is later;

(11) "Settle" means to pay in cash, by clearing-house settlement, in a charge or credit or by remittance, or otherwise as agreed. A settlement may be either provisional or final;

(12) "Suspends payments" with respect to a bank means that it has been closed by order of the supervisory authorities, that a public officer has been appointed to take it over, or that it ceases or refuses to make payments in the ordinary course of business.

(b) Other definitions applying to this Article and the sections in which they appear are:

"Agreement for electronic presentment" Section 4–110.
"Bank" Section 4–105.
"Collecting bank" Section 4–105.
"Depository bank" Section 4–105.
"Intermediary bank" Section 4–105.
"Payor bank" Section 4–105.
"Presenting bank" Section 4–105.
"Presentment notice" Section 4–110.

(c) The following definitions in other Articles apply to this Article:

"Acceptance" Section 3–409.
"Alteration" Section 3–407.
"Cashier's check" Section 3–104.
"Certificate of deposit" Section 3–104.
"Certified check" Section 3–109.
"Check" Section 3–104.
"Good faith" Section 3–103.
"Holder in due course" Section 3–302.
"Instrument" Section 3–104.
"Notice of dishonor" Section 3–503.
"Order" Section 3–103.
"Ordinary care" Section 3–103.
"Person entitled to enforce" Section 3–301.
"Presentment" Section 3–501.
"Promise" Section 3–103.
"Prove" Section 3–103.
"Teller's check" Section 3–104.
"Unauthorized signature" Section 3–403.

(d) In addition, Article 1 contains general definitions and principles of construction and interpretation applicable throughout this Article.

As amended in 1990 and 1994.

§ 4–105. "Bank"; "Depositary Bank"; "Payor Bank"; "Intermediary Bank"; "Collecting Bank"; "Presenting Bank".

In this Article:

(1) "Bank" means a person engaged in the business of banking, including a savings bank, savings and loan association, credit union, or trust company;

(2) "Depositary bank" means the first bank to take an item even though it is also the payor bank, unless the item is presented for immediate payment over the counter;

(3) "Payor bank" means a bank that is the drawee of a draft;

(4) "Intermediary bank" means a bank to which an item is transferred in course of collection except the depositary or payor bank;

(5) "Collecting bank" means a bank handling an item for collection except the payor bank;

(6) "Presenting bank" means a bank presenting an item except a payor bank.

§ 4–106. Payable Through or Payable at Bank: Collecting Bank.

(a) If an item states that it is "payable through" a bank identified in the item, (i) the item designates the bank as a collecting bank and does not by itself authorize the bank to pay the item, and (ii) the item may be presented for payment only by or through the bank.

Alternative A

(b) If an item states that it is "payable at" a bank identified in the item, the item is equivalent to a draft drawn on the bank.

Alternative B

(b) If an item states that it is "payable at" a bank identified in the item, (i) the item designates the bank as a collecting bank and does not by itself authorize the bank to pay the item, and (ii) the item may be presented for payment only by or through the bank.

(c) If a draft names a nonbank drawee and it is unclear whether a bank named in the draft is a co-drawee or a collecting bank, the bank is a collecting bank.

§ 4–107. Separate Office of Bank.

A branch or separate office of a bank is a separate bank for the purpose of computing the time within which and determining the place at or to which action may be taken or notices or orders shall be given under this Article and under Article 3.

§ 4–108. Time of Receipt of Items.

(a) For the purpose of allowing time to process items, prove balances, and make the necessary entries on its books to determine its position for the day, a bank may fix an afternoon hour of 2 P.M. or later as a cutoff hour for the handling of money and items and the making of entries on its books.

(b) An item or deposit of money received on any day after a cutoff hour so fixed or after the close of the banking day may be treated as being received at the opening of the next banking day.

§ 4–109. Delays.

(a) Unless otherwise instructed, a collecting bank in a good faith effort to secure payment of a specific item drawn on a payor other than a bank, and with or without the approval of any person involved, may waive, modify, or extend time limits imposed or permitted by this [Act] for a period not exceeding two additional banking days without discharge of drawers or indorsers or liability to its transferor or a prior party.

(b) Delay by a collecting bank or payor bank beyond time limits prescribed or permitted by this [Act] or by instructions is excused if (i) the delay is caused by interruption of communication or computer facilities, suspension of payments by another bank, war, emergency conditions, failure of equipment, or other circumstances beyond the control of the bank, and (ii) the bank exercises such diligence as the circumstances require.

§ 4–110. Electronic Presentment.

(a) "Agreement for electronic presentment" means an agreement, clearing-house rule, or Federal Reserve regulation or operating circular, providing that presentment of an item may be made by transmission of an image of an item or information describing the item ("presentment notice") rather than delivery of the item itself. The agreement may provide for procedures governing retention, presentment, payment, dishonor, and other matters concerning items subject to the agreement.

(b) Presentment of an item pursuant to an agreement for presentment is made when the presentment notice is received.

(c) If presentment is made by presentment notice, a reference to "item" or "check" in this Article means the presentment notice unless the context otherwise indicates.

§ 4–111. Statute of Limitations.

An action to enforce an obligation, duty, or right arising under this Article must be commenced within three years after the [cause of action] accrues.

PART 2 Collection of Items: Depositary and Collecting Banks

§ 4–201. Status of Collecting Bank as Agent and Provisional Status of Credits; Applicability of Article; Item Indorsed "Pay Any Bank".

(a) Unless a contrary intent clearly appears and before the time that a settlement given by a collecting bank for an item is or becomes final, the bank, with respect to an item, is an agent or sub-agent of the owner of the item and any settlement given for the item is provisional. This provision applies regardless of the form of indorsement or lack of indorsement and even though credit given for the item is subject to immediate withdrawal as of right or is in fact withdrawn; but the continuance of ownership of an item by its owner and any rights of the owner to proceeds of the item are subject to rights of a collecting bank, such as those resulting from outstanding advances on the item and rights of recoupment or setoff. If an item is handled by banks for purposes of presentment, payment, collection, or return, the relevant provisions of this Article apply even though action of the parties clearly establishes that a particular bank has purchased the item and is the owner of it.

(b) After an item has been indorsed with the words "pay any bank" or the like, only a bank may acquire the rights of a holder until the item has been:

(1) returned to the customer initiating collection; or

(2) specially indorsed by a bank to a person who is not a bank.

§ 4–202. Responsibility for Collection or Return; When Action Timely.

(a) A collecting bank must exercise ordinary care in:

(1) presenting an item or sending it for presentment;

(2) sending notice of dishonor or nonpayment or returning an item other than a documentary draft to the bank's transferor after learning that the item has not been paid or accepted, as the case may be;

(3) settling for an item when the bank receives final settlement; and

(4) notifying its transferor of any loss or delay in transit within a reasonable time after discovery thereof.

(b) A collecting bank exercises ordinary care under subsection (a) by taking proper action before its midnight deadline following receipt of an item, notice, or settlement. Taking proper action within a reasonably longer time may constitute the exercise of ordinary care, but the bank has the burden of establishing timeliness.

(c) Subject to subsection (a)(1), a bank is not liable for the insolvency, neglect, misconduct, mistake, or default of another bank or person or for loss or destruction of an item in the possession of others or in transit.

§ 4–203. Effect of Instructions.

Subject to Article 3 concerning conversion of instruments (Section 3–420) and restrictive indorsements (Section 3–206), only a collecting bank's transferor can give instructions that affect the bank or constitute notice to it, and a collecting bank is not liable to prior parties for any action taken pursuant to the instructions or in accordance with any agreement with its transferor.

§ 4–204. Methods of Sending and Presenting; Sending Directly to Payor Bank.

(a) A collecting bank shall send items by a reasonably prompt method, taking into consideration relevant instructions, the nature of the item, the number of those items on hand, the cost of collection involved, and the method generally used by it or others to present those items.

(b) A collecting bank may send:

(1) an item directly to the payor bank;

(2) an item to a nonbank payor if authorized by its transferor; and

(3) an item other than documentary drafts to a nonbank payor, if authorized by Federal Reserve regulation or operating circular, clearing-house rule, or the like.

(c) Presentment may be made by a presenting bank at a place where the payor bank or other payor has requested that presentment be made.

§ 4–205. Depositary Bank Holder of Unindorsed Item.

If a customer delivers an item to a depositary bank for collection:

(1) the depositary bank becomes a holder of the item at the time it receives the item for collection if the customer at the time of delivery was a holder of the item, whether or not the customer indorses the item, and, if the bank satisfies the other requirements of Section 3–302, it is a holder in due course; and

(2) the depositary bank warrants to collecting banks, the payor bank or other payor, and the drawer that the amount of the item was paid to the customer or deposited to the customer's account.

§ 4–206. Transfer Between Banks.

Any agreed method that identifies the transferor bank is sufficient for the item's further transfer to another bank.

§ 4–207. Transfer Warranties.

(a) A customer or collecting bank that transfers an item and receives a settlement or other consideration warrants to the transferee and to any subsequent collecting bank that:

(1) the warrantor is a person entitled to enforce the item;

(2) all signatures on the item are authentic and authorized;

(3) the item has not been altered;

(4) the item is not subject to a defense or claim in recoupment (Section 3–305(a)) of any party that can be asserted against the warrantor; and

(5) the warrantor has no knowledge of any insolvency proceeding commenced with respect to the maker or acceptor or, in the case of an unaccepted draft, the drawer.

(b) If an item is dishonored, a customer or collecting bank transferring the item and receiving settlement or other consideration is obliged to pay the amount due on the item (i) according to the terms of the item at the time it was transferred, or (ii) if the transfer was of an incomplete item, according to its terms when completed as stated in Sections 3–115 and 3–407. The obligation of a transferor is owed to the transferee and to any subsequent collecting bank that takes the item in good faith. A transferor cannot disclaim its obligation under this subsection by an indorsement stating that it is made "without recourse" or otherwise disclaiming liability.

(c) A person to whom the warranties under subsection (a) are made and who took the item in good faith may recover from the warrantor as damages for breach of warranty an amount equal to the loss suffered as a result of the breach, but not more than the amount of the item plus expenses and loss of interest incurred as a result of the breach.

(d) The warranties stated in subsection (a) cannot be disclaimed with respect to checks. Unless notice of a claim for breach of warranty is given to the warrantor within 30 days after the claimant has reason to know of the breach and the identity of the warrantor, the warrantor is discharged to the extent of any loss caused by the delay in giving notice of the claim.

(e) A cause of action for breach of warranty under this section accrues when the claimant has reason to know of the breach.

§ 4–208. Presentment Warranties.

(a) If an unaccepted draft is presented to the drawee for payment or acceptance and the drawee pays or accepts the draft, (i) the person obtaining payment or acceptance, at the time of presentment, and (ii) a previous transferor of the draft, at the time of transfer, warrant to the drawee that pays or accepts the draft in good faith that:

(1) the warrantor is, or was, at the time the warrantor transferred the draft, a person entitled to enforce the draft or authorized to obtain payment or acceptance of the draft on behalf of a person entitled to enforce the draft;

(2) the draft has not been altered; and

(3) the warrantor has no knowledge that the signature of the purported drawer of the draft is unauthorized.

(b) A drawee making payment may recover from a warrantor damages for breach of warranty equal to the amount paid by the drawee less the amount the drawee received or is entitled to receive from the drawer because of the payment. In addition, the drawee is entitled to compensation for expenses and loss of interest resulting from the breach. The right of the drawee to recover damages under this subsection is not affected by any failure of the drawee to exercise ordinary care in making payment. If the drawee accepts the draft (i) breach of warranty is a defense to the obligation of the acceptor, and (ii) if the acceptor makes payment with respect to the draft, the acceptor is entitled to recover from a warrantor for breach of warranty the amounts stated in this subsection.

(c) If a drawee asserts a claim for breach of warranty under subsection (a) based on an unauthorized indorsement of the draft or an alteration of the draft, the warrantor may defend by proving that the indorsement is effective under Section 3–404 or 3–405 or the drawer is precluded under Section 3–406 or 4–406 from asserting against the drawee the unauthorized indorsement or alteration.

(d) If (i) a dishonored draft is presented for payment to the drawer or an indorser or (ii) any other item is presented for payment to a party obliged to pay the item, and the item is paid, the person obtaining payment and a prior transferor of the item warrant to the person making payment in good faith that the warrantor is, or was, at the time the warrantor transferred the item, a person entitled to enforce the item or authorized to obtain payment on behalf of a person entitled to enforce the item. The person making payment may recover from any warrantor for breach of warranty an amount equal to the amount paid plus expenses and loss of interest resulting from the breach.

(e) The warranties stated in subsections (a) and (d) cannot be disclaimed with respect to checks. Unless notice of a claim for breach of warranty is given to the warrantor within 30 days after the claimant has reason to know of the breach and the identity of the warrantor, the warrantor is discharged to the extent of any loss caused by the delay in giving notice of the claim.

(f) A cause of action for breach of warranty under this section accrues when the claimant has reason to know of the breach.

§ 4–209. Encoding and Retention Warranties.

(a) A person who encodes information on or with respect to an item after issue warrants to any subsequent collecting bank and to the payor bank or other payor that the information is correctly encoded. If the customer of a depositary bank encodes, that bank also makes the warranty.

(b) A person who undertakes to retain an item pursuant to an agreement for electronic presentment warrants to any subsequent collecting bank and to the payor bank or other payor that retention and presentment of the item comply with the agreement. If a customer of a depositary bank undertakes to retain an item, that bank also makes this warranty.

(c) A person to whom warranties are made under this section and who took the item in good faith may recover from the warrantor as damages for breach of warranty an amount equal to the loss suffered as a result of the breach, plus expenses and loss of interest incurred as a result of the breach.

§ 4–210. Security Interest of Collecting Bank in Items, Accompanying Documents and Proceeds.

(a) A collecting bank has a security interest in an item and any accompanying documents or the proceeds of either:

(1) in case of an item deposited in an account, to the extent to which credit given for the item has been withdrawn or applied;

(2) in case of an item for which it has given credit available for withdrawal as of right, to the extent of the credit given, whether or not the credit is drawn upon or there is a right of charge-back; or

(3) if it makes an advance on or against the item.

(b) If credit given for several items received at one time or pursuant to a single agreement is withdrawn or applied in part, the security interest remains upon all the items, any accompanying documents or the proceeds of either. For the purpose of this section, credits first given are first withdrawn.

(c) Receipt by a collecting bank of a final settlement for an item is a realization on its security interest in the item, accompanying documents, and proceeds. So long as the bank does not receive final settlement for the item or give up possession of the item or accompanying documents for purposes other than collection, the security interest continues to that extent and is subject to Article 9, but:

(1) no security agreement is necessary to make the security interest enforceable (Section 9–203 (1)(a));

(2) no filing is required to perfect the security interest; and

(3) the security interest has priority over conflicting perfected security interests in the item, accompanying documents, or proceeds.

§ 4–211. When Bank Gives Value for Purposes of Holder in Due Course.

For purposes of determining its status as a holder in due course, a bank has given value to the extent it has a security interest in an item, if the bank otherwise complies with the requirements of Section 3–302 on what constitutes a holder in due course.

§ 4–212. Presentment by Notice of Item Not Payable by, Through, or at Bank; Liability of Drawer or Indorser.

(a) Unless otherwise instructed, a collecting bank may present an item not payable by, through, or at a bank by sending to the party to accept or pay a written notice that the bank holds the item for acceptance or payment. The notice must be sent in time to be received on or before the day when presentment is due and the bank must meet any requirements of the party to accept or pay under Section 3–501 by the close of the bank's next banking day after it knows of the requirement.

(b) If presentment is made by notice and payment, acceptance, or request for compliance with a requirement under Section 3–501 is not received by the close of business on the day after maturity or, in the case of demand items, by the close of business on the third banking day after notice was sent, the presenting bank may treat the item as dishonored and charge any drawer or indorser by sending it notice of the facts.

§ 4–213. Medium and Time of Settlement by Bank.

(a) With respect to settlement by a bank, the medium and time of settlement may be prescribed by Federal Reserve regulations or circulars, clearing-house rules, and the like, or agreement. In the absence of such prescription:

(1) the medium of settlement is cash or credit to an account in a Federal Reserve bank of or specified by the person to receive settlement; and

(2) the time of settlement, is:

(i) with respect to tender of settlement by cash, a cashier's check, or teller's check, when the cash or check is sent or delivered;

(ii) with respect to tender of settlement by credit in an account in a Federal Reserve Bank, when the credit is made;

(iii) with respect to tender of settlement by a credit or debit to an account in a bank, when the credit or debit is made or, in the case of tender of settlement by authority to charge an account, when the authority is sent or delivered; or

(iv) with respect to tender of settlement by a funds transfer, when payment is made pursuant to Section 4A–406(a) to the person receiving settlement.

(b) If the tender of settlement is not by a medium authorized by subsection (a) or the time of settlement is not fixed by subsection (a), no settlement occurs until the tender of settlement is accepted by the person receiving settlement.

(c) If settlement for an item is made by cashier's check or teller's check and the person receiving settlement, before its midnight deadline:

(1) presents or forwards the check for collection, settlement is final when the check is finally paid; or

(2) fails to present or forward the check for collection, settlement is final at the midnight deadline of the person receiving settlement.

(d) If settlement for an item is made by giving authority to charge the account of the bank giving settlement in the bank receiving settlement, settlement is final when the charge is made by the bank receiving settlement if there are funds available in the account for the amount of the item.

§ 4–214. Right of Charge—Back or Refund; Liability of Collecting Bank: Return of Item.

(a) If a collecting bank has made provisional settlement with its customer for an item and fails by reason of dishonor, suspension of payments by a bank, or otherwise to receive settlement for the item which is or becomes final, the bank may revoke the settlement given by it, charge back the amount of any credit given for the item to its customer's account, or obtain refund from its customer, whether or not it is able to return the item, if by its midnight deadline or within a longer reasonable time after it learns the facts it returns the item or sends notification of the facts. If the return or notice is delayed beyond the bank's midnight deadline or a longer reasonable time after it learns the facts, the bank may revoke the settlement, charge back the credit, or obtain refund from its customer, but it is liable for any loss resulting from the delay. These rights to revoke, charge back, and obtain refund terminate if and when a settlement for the item received by the bank is or becomes final.

(b) A collecting bank returns an item when it is sent or delivered to the bank's customer or transferor or pursuant to its instructions.

(c) A depositary bank that is also the payor may charge back the amount of an item to its customer's account or obtain refund in accordance with the section governing return of an item received by a payor bank for credit on its books (Section 4–301).

(d) The right to charge back is not affected by:

(1) previous use of a credit given for the item; or

(2) failure by any bank to exercise ordinary care with respect to the item, but a bank so failing remains liable.

(e) A failure to charge back or claim refund does not affect other rights of the bank against the customer or any other party.

(f) If credit is given in dollars as the equivalent of the value of an item payable in foreign money, the dollar amount of any charge-back or refund must be calculated on the basis of the bank-offered spot rate for the foreign money prevailing on the day when the person entitled to the charge-back or refund learns that it will not receive payment in ordinary course.

As amended in 1990.

§ 4–215. Final Payment of Item by Payor Bank; When Provisional Debits and Credits Become Final; When Certain Credits Become Available for Withdrawal.

(a) An item is finally paid by a payor bank when the bank has first done any of the following:

(1) paid the item in cash;

(2) settled for the item without having a right to revoke the settlement under statute, clearing-house rule, or agreement; or

(3) made a provisional settlement for the item and failed to revoke the settlement in the time and manner permitted by statute, clearing-house rule, or agreement.

(b) If provisional settlement for an item does not become final, the item is not finally paid.

(c) If provisional settlement for an item between the presenting and payor banks is made through a clearing house or by debits or credits in an account between them, then to the extent that provisional debits or credits for the item are entered in accounts between the presenting and payor banks or between the presenting and successive prior collecting banks seriatim, they become final upon final payment of the item by the payor bank.

(d) If a collecting bank receives a settlement for an item which is or becomes final, the bank is accountable to its customer for the amount of the item and any provisional credit given for the item in an account with its customer becomes final.

(e) Subject to (i) applicable law stating a time for availability of funds and (ii) any right of the bank to apply the credit to an obligation of the customer, credit given by a bank for an item in a customer's account becomes available for withdrawal as of right:

(1) if the bank has received a provisional settlement for the item, when the settlement becomes final and the bank has had a reasonable time to receive return of the item and the item has not been received within that time;

(2) if the bank is both the depositary bank and the payor bank, and the item is finally paid, at the opening of the bank's second banking day following receipt of the item.

(f) Subject to applicable law stating a time for availability of funds and any right of a bank to apply a deposit to an obligation of the depositor, a deposit of money becomes available for withdrawal as of right at the opening of the bank's next banking day after receipt of the deposit.

§ 4–216. Insolvency and Preference.

(a) If an item is in or comes into the possession of a payor or collecting bank that suspends payment and the item has not been finally paid, the item must be returned by the receiver, trustee, or agent in charge of the closed bank to the presenting bank or the closed bank's customer.

(b) If a payor bank finally pays an item and suspends payments without making a settlement for the item with its customer or the presenting bank which settlement is or becomes final, the owner of the item has a preferred claim against the payor bank.

(c) If a payor bank gives or a collecting bank gives or receives a provisional settlement for an item and thereafter suspends payments, the suspension does not prevent or interfere with the settlement's becoming final if the finality occurs automatically upon the lapse of certain time or the happening of certain events.

(d) If a collecting bank receives from subsequent parties settlement for an item, which settlement is or becomes final and the bank suspends payments without making a settlement for the item with its customer which settlement is or becomes final, the owner of the item has a preferred claim against the collecting bank.

PART 3 Collection of Items: Payor Banks

§ 4–301. Deferred Posting; Recovery of Payment by Return of Items; Time of Dishonor; Return of Items by Payor Bank.

(a) If a payor bank settles for a demand item other than a documentary draft presented otherwise than for immediate payment over the counter before midnight of the banking day of receipt, the payor bank may revoke the settlement and recover the settlement if, before it has made final payment and before its midnight deadline, it

(1) returns the item; or

(2) sends written notice of dishonor or nonpayment if the item is unavailable for return.

(b) If a demand item is received by a payor bank for credit on its books, it may return the item or send notice of dishonor and may revoke any credit given or recover the amount thereof withdrawn by its customer, if it acts within the time limit and in the manner specified in subsection (a).

(c) Unless previous notice of dishonor has been sent, an item is dishonored at the time when for purposes of dishonor it is returned or notice sent in accordance with this section.

(d) An item is returned:

(1) as to an item presented through a clearing house, when it is delivered to the presenting or last collecting bank or to the clearing house or is sent or delivered in accordance with clearing-house rules; or

(2) in all other cases, when it is sent or delivered to the bank's customer or transferor or pursuant to instructions.

§ 4–302. Payor Bank's Responsibility for Late Return of Item.

(a) If an item is presented to and received by a payor bank, the bank is accountable for the amount of:

(1) a demand item, other than a documentary draft, whether properly payable or not, if the bank, in any case in which it is not also the depositary bank, retains the item beyond midnight of the banking day of receipt without settling for it or, whether or not it is also the depositary bank, does not pay or return the item or send notice of dishonor until after its midnight deadline; or

(2) any other properly payable item unless, within the time allowed for acceptance or payment of that item, the bank either accepts or pays the item or returns it and accompanying documents.

(b) The liability of a payor bank to pay an item pursuant to subsection (a) is subject to defenses based on breach of a presentment warranty (Section 4–208) or proof that the person seeking enforcement of the liability presented or transferred the item for the purpose of defrauding the payor bank.

§ 4–303. When Items Subject to Notice, Stop-Payment Order, Legal Process, or Setoff; Order in Which Items May Be Charged or Certified.

(a) Any knowledge, notice, or stop-payment order received by, legal process served upon, or setoff exercised by a payor bank comes too late to terminate, suspend, or modify the bank's right or duty to pay an item or to charge its customer's account for the item if the knowledge, notice, stop-payment order, or legal process is received or served and a reasonable time for the bank to act thereon expires or the setoff is exercised after the earliest of the following:

(1) the bank accepts or certifies the item;

(2) the bank pays the item in cash;

(3) the bank settles for the item without having a right to revoke the settlement under statute, clearing-house rule, or agreement;

(4) the bank becomes accountable for the amount of the item under Section 4–302 dealing with the payor bank's responsibility for late return of items; or

(5) with respect to checks, a cutoff hour no earlier than one hour after the opening of the next banking day after the banking day on which the bank received the check and no later than the close of that next banking day or, if no cutoff hour is fixed, the close of the next banking day after the banking day on which the bank received the check.

(b) Subject to subsection (a), items may be accepted, paid, certified, or charged to the indicated account of its customer in any order.

PART 4 Relationship Between Payor Bank and Its Customer

§ 4–401. When Bank May Charge Customer's Account.

(a) A bank may charge against the account of a customer an item that is properly payable from the account even though the charge creates an overdraft. An item is properly payable if it is authorized by the customer and is in accordance with any agreement between the customer and bank.

(b) A customer is not liable for the amount of an overdraft if the customer neither signed the item nor benefited from the proceeds of the item.

(c) A bank may charge against the account of a customer a check that is otherwise properly payable from the account, even though payment was made before the date of the check, unless the customer has given notice to the bank of the postdating describing the check with reasonable certainty. The notice is effective for the period stated in Section 4–403(b) for stop-payment orders, and must be received at such time and in such manner as to afford the bank a reasonable opportunity to act on it before the bank takes any action with respect to the check described in Section 4–303. If a bank charges against the account of a customer a check before the date stated in the notice of postdating, the bank is liable for damages for the loss resulting from its act. The loss may include damages for dishonor of subsequent items under Section 4–402.

(d) A bank that in good faith makes payment to a holder may charge the indicated account of its customer according to:

(1) the original terms of the altered item; or

(2) the terms of the completed item, even though the bank knows the item has been completed unless the bank has notice that the completion was improper.

§4–402. Bank's Liability to Customer for Wrongful Dishonor; Time of Determining Insufficiency of Account.

(a) Except as otherwise provided in this Article, a payor bank wrongfully dishonors an item if it dishonors an item that is properly payable, but a bank may dishonor an item that would create an overdraft unless it has agreed to pay the overdraft.

(b) A payor bank is liable to its customer for damages proximately caused by the wrongful dishonor of an item. Liability is limited to actual damages proved and may include damages for an arrest or prosecution of the customer or other consequential damages. Whether any consequential damages are proximately caused by the wrongful dishonor is a question of fact to be determined in each case.

(c) A payor bank's determination of the customer's account balance on which a decision to dishonor for insufficiency of available funds is based may be made at any time between the time the item is received by the payor bank and the time that the payor bank returns the item or gives notice in lieu of return, and no more than one determination need be made. If, at the election of the payor bank, a subsequent balance determination is made for the purpose of reevaluating the bank's decision to dishonor the item, the account balance at that time is determinative of whether a dishonor for insufficiency of available funds is wrongful.

As amended in 1990.

See Appendix IX for material relating to changes made in text in 1990.

§ 4–403. Customer's Right to Stop Payment; Burden of Proof of Loss.

(a) A customer or any person authorized to draw on the account if there is more than one person may stop payment of any item drawn on the customer's account or close the account by an order to the bank describing the item or account with reasonable certainty received at a time and in a manner that affords the bank a reasonable opportunity to act on it before any action by the bank with respect to the item described in Section 4–303. If the signature of more than one person is required to draw on an account, any of these persons may stop payment or close the account.

(b) A stop-payment order is effective for six months, but it lapses after 14 calendar days if the original order was oral and was not confirmed in writing within that period. A stop-payment order may be renewed for additional six-month periods by a writing given to the bank within a period during which the stop-payment order is effective.

(c) The burden of establishing the fact and amount of loss resulting from the payment of an item contrary to a stop-payment order or order to close an account is on the customer. The loss from payment of an item contrary to a stop-payment order may include damages for dishonor of subsequent items under Section 4–402.

§ 4–404. Bank Not Obliged to Pay Check More Than Six Months Old.

A bank is under no obligation to a customer having a checking account to pay a check, other than a certified check, which is presented more than six months after its date, but it may charge its customer's account for a payment made thereafter in good faith.

§ 4–405. Death or Incompetence of Customer.

(a) A payor or collecting bank's authority to accept, pay, or collect an item or to account for proceeds of its collection, if otherwise effective, is not rendered ineffective by incompetence of a customer of either bank existing at the time the item is issued or its collection is undertaken if the bank does not know of an adjudication of incompetence. Neither death nor incompetence of a customer revokes the authority to accept, pay, collect, or account until the bank knows of the fact of death or of an adjudication of incompetence and has reasonable opportunity to act on it.

(b) Even with knowledge, a bank may for 10 days after the date of death pay or certify checks drawn on or before that date unless ordered to stop payment by a person claiming an interest in the account.

§ 4–406. Customer's Duty to Discover and Report Unauthorized Signature or Alteration.

(a) A bank that sends or makes available to a customer a statement of account showing payment of items for the account shall either return or make available to the customer the items paid or provide information in the statement of account sufficient to allow the customer reasonably to identify the items paid. The statement of account provides sufficient information if the item is described by item number, amount, and date of payment.

(b) If the items are not returned to the customer, the person retaining the items shall either retain the items or, if the items are destroyed, maintain the capacity to furnish legible copies of the items until the expiration of seven years after receipt of the items. A customer may request an item from the bank that paid the item, and that bank must provide in a reasonable time either the item or, if the item has been destroyed or is not otherwise obtainable, a legible copy of the item.

(c) If a bank sends or makes available a statement of account or items pursuant to subsection (a), the customer must exercise reasonable promptness in examining the statement or the items to determine whether any payment was not authorized because of an alteration of an item or because a purported signature by or on behalf of the customer was not authorized. If, based on the statement or items provided, the customer should reasonably have discovered the unauthorized payment, the customer must promptly notify the bank of the relevant facts.

(d) If the bank proves that the customer failed, with respect to an item, to comply with the duties imposed on the customer by subsection (c), the customer is precluded from asserting against the bank:

(1) the customer's unauthorized signature or any alteration on the item, if the bank also proves that it suffered a loss by reason of the failure; and

(2) the customer's unauthorized signature or alteration by the same wrong-doer on any other item paid in good faith by the bank if the payment was made before the bank received notice from the customer of the unauthorized signature or alteration and after the customer had been afforded a reasonable period of time, not exceeding 30 days, in which to examine the item or statement of account and notify the bank.

(e) If subsection (d) applies and the customer proves that the bank failed to exercise ordinary care in paying the item and that the failure substantially contributed to loss, the loss is allocated between the customer precluded and the bank asserting the preclusion according to the extent to which the failure of the customer to comply with subsection (c) and the failure of the bank to exercise ordinary care contributed to the loss. If the customer proves that the bank did not pay the item in good faith, the preclusion under subsection (d) does not apply.

(f) Without regard to care or lack of care of either the customer or the bank, a customer who does not within one year after the statement or items are made available to the customer (subsection (a)) discover and report the customer's unauthorized signature on or any alteration on the item is precluded from asserting against the bank the unauthorized signature or alteration. If there is a preclusion under this subsection, the payor bank may not recover for breach or warranty under Section 4–208 with respect to the unauthorized signature or alteration to which the preclusion applies.

§ 4–407. Payor Bank's Right to Subrogation on Improper Payment.

If a payor bank has paid an item over the order of the drawer or maker to stop payment, or after an account has been closed, or otherwise under circumstances giving a basis for objection by the drawer or maker, to prevent zunjust enrichment and only to the extent necessary to prevent loss to the bank by reason of its payment of the item, the payor bank is subrogated to the rights

(1) of any holder in due course on the item against the drawer or maker;

(2) of the payee or any other holder of the item against the drawer or maker either on the item or under the transaction out of which the item arose; and

(3) of the drawer or maker against the payee or any other holder of the item with respect to the transaction out of which the item arose.

PART 5 Collection of Documentary Drafts

§ 4–501. Handling of Documentary Drafts; Duty to Send for Presentment and to Notify Customer of Dishonor.

A bank that takes a documentary draft for collection shall present or send the draft and accompanying documents for presentment and, upon learning that the draft has not been paid or accepted in due course, shall seasonably notify its customer of the fact even though it may have discounted or bought the draft or extended credit available for withdrawal as of right.

§ 4–502. Presentment of "On Arrival" Drafts.

If a draft or the relevant instructions require presentment "on arrival", "when goods arrive" or the like, the collecting bank need not present until in its judgment a reasonable time for arrival of the goods has expired. Refusal to pay or accept because the goods have not arrived is not dishonor; the bank must notify its transferor of the refusal but need not present the draft again until it is instructed to do so or learns of the arrival of the goods.

§ 4–503. Responsibility of Presenting Bank for Documents and Goods; Report of Reasons for Dishonor; Referee in Case of Need.

Unless otherwise instructed and except as provided in Article 5, a bank presenting a documentary draft:

(1) must deliver the documents to the drawee on acceptance of the draft if it is payable more than three days after presentment; otherwise, only on payment; and

(2) upon dishonor, either in the case of presentment for acceptance or presentment for payment, may seek and follow instructions from any referee in case of need designated in the draft or, if the presenting bank does not choose to utilize the referee's services, it must use diligence and good faith to ascertain the reason for dishonor, must notify its transferor of the dishonor and of the results of its effort to ascertain the reasons therefor, and must request instructions.

However the presenting bank is under no obligation with respect to goods represented by the documents except to follow any reasonable instructions seasonably received; it has a right to reimbursement for any expense incurred in following instructions and to prepayment of or indemnity for those expenses.

§ 4–504. Privilege of Presenting Bank to Deal With Goods; Security Interest for Expenses.

(a) A presenting bank that, following the dishonor of a documentary draft, has seasonably requested instructions but does not receive them within a reasonable time may store, sell, or otherwise deal with the goods in any reasonable manner.

(b) For its reasonable expenses incurred by action under subsection (a) the presenting bank has a lien upon the goods or their proceeds, which may be foreclosed in the same manner as an unpaid seller's lien.

ARTICLE 4A

FUNDS TRANSFERS

PART 1 Subject Matter and Definitions

§ 4A–101. Short Title.

This Article may be cited as Uniform Commercial Code—Funds Transfers.

§ 4A–102. Subject Matter.

Except as otherwise provided in Section 4A–108, this Article applies to funds transfers defined in Section 4A–104.

§ 4A–103. Payment Order—Definitions.

(a) In this Article:

(1) "Payment order" means an instruction of a sender to a receiving bank, transmitted orally, electronically, or in writing, to pay, or to cause another bank to pay, a fixed or determinable amount of money to a beneficiary if:

(i) the instruction does not state a condition to payment to the beneficiary other than time of payment,

(ii) the receiving bank is to be reimbursed by debiting an account of, or otherwise receiving payment from, the sender, and

(iii) the instruction is transmitted by the sender directly to the receiving bank or to an agent, funds-transfer system, or communication system for transmittal to the receiving bank.

(2) "Beneficiary" means the person to be paid by the beneficiary's bank.

(3) "Beneficiary's bank" means the bank identified in a payment order in which an account of the beneficiary is to be credited pursuant to the order or which otherwise is to make payment to the beneficiary if the order does not provide for payment to an account.

(4) "Receiving bank" means the bank to which the sender's instruction is addressed.

(5) "Sender" means the person giving the instruction to the receiving bank.

(b) If an instruction complying with subsection (a)(1) is to make more than one payment to a beneficiary, the instruction is a separate payment order with respect to each payment.

(c) A payment order is issued when it is sent to the receiving bank.

§ 4A–104. Funds Transfer—Definitions.

In this Article:

(a) "Funds transfer" means the series of transactions, beginning with the originator's payment order, made for the purpose of making payment to the beneficiary of the order. The term includes any payment order issued by the originator's bank or an intermediary bank intended to carry out the originator's payment order. A funds transfer is completed by acceptance by the beneficiary's bank of a payment order for the benefit of the beneficiary of the originator's payment order.

(b) "Intermediary bank" means a receiving bank other than the originator's bank or the beneficiary's bank.

(c) "Originator" means the sender of the first payment order in a funds transfer.

(d) "Originator's bank" means (i) the receiving bank to which the payment order of the originator is issued if the originator is not a bank, or (ii) the originator if the originator is a bank.

§ 4A–105. Other Definitions.

(a) In this Article:

(1) "Authorized account" means a deposit account of a customer in a bank designated by the customer as a source of payment orders issued by the customer to the bank. If a customer does not so designate an account, any account of the customer is an authorized account if payment of a payment order from that account is not inconsistent with a restriction on the use of that account.

(2) "Bank" means a person engaged in the business of banking and includes a savings bank, savings and loan association, credit union, and trust company. A branch or separate office of a bank is a separate bank for purposes of this Article.

(3) "Customer" means a person, including a bank, having an account with a bank or from whom a bank has agreed to receive payment orders.

(4) "Funds-transfer business day" of a receiving bank means the part of a day during which the receiving bank is open for the receipt, processing, and transmittal of payment orders and cancellations and amendments of payment orders.

(5) "Funds-transfer system" means a wire transfer network, automated clearing house, or other communication system of a clearing house or other association of banks through which a payment order by a bank may be transmitted to the bank to which the order is addressed.

(6) "Good faith" means honesty in fact and the observance of reasonable commercial standards of fair dealing.

(7) "Prove" with respect to a fact means to meet the burden of establishing the fact (Section 1–201(8)).

(b) Other definitions applying to this Article and the sections in which they appear are:

"Acceptance" Section 4A–209
"Beneficiary" Section 4A–103

"Beneficiary's bank" Section 4A–103
"Executed" Section 4A–301
"Execution date" Section 4A–301
"Funds transfer" Section 4A–104
"Funds-transfer system rule" Section 4A–501
"Intermediary bank" Section 4A–104
"Originator" Section 4A–104
"Originator's bank" Section 4A–104
"Payment by beneficiary's bank to beneficiary" Section 4A–405
"Payment by originator to beneficiary" Section 4A–406
"Payment by sender to receiving bank" Section 4A–403
"Payment date" Section 4A–401
"Payment order" Section 4A–103
"Receiving bank" Section 4A–103
"Security procedure" Section 4A–201
"Sender" Section 4A–103

(c) The following definitions in Article 4 apply to this Article:
"Clearing house" Section 4–104
"Item" Section 4–104
"Suspends payments" Section 4–104

(d) In addition Article 1 contains general definitions and principles of construction and interpretation applicable throughout this Article.

§ 4A–106. Time Payment Order Is Received.

(a) The time of receipt of a payment order or communication cancelling or amending a payment order is determined by the rules applicable to receipt of a notice stated in Section 1–201(27). A receiving bank may fix a cut-off time or times on a funds-transfer business day for the receipt and processing of payment orders and communications cancelling or amending payment orders. Different cut-off times may apply to payment orders, cancellations, or amendments, or to different categories of payment orders, cancellations, or amendments. A cut-off time may apply to senders generally or different cut-off times may apply to different senders or categories of payment orders. If a payment order or communication cancelling or amending a payment order is received after the close of a funds-transfer business day or after the appropriate cut-off time on a funds-transfer business day, the receiving bank may treat the payment order or communication as received at the opening of the next funds-transfer business day.

(b) If this Article refers to an execution date or payment date or states a day on which a receiving bank is required to take action, and the date or day does not fall on a funds-transfer business day, the next day that is a funds-transfer business day is treated as the date or day stated, unless the contrary is stated in this Article.

§ 4A–107. Federal Reserve Regulations and Operating Circulars.

Regulations of the Board of Governors of the Federal Reserve System and operating circulars of the Federal Reserve Banks supersede any inconsistent provision of this Article to the extent of the inconsistency.

§ 4A–108. Exclusion of Consumer Transactions Governed by Federal Law.

This Article does not apply to a funds transfer any part of which is governed by the Electronic Fund Transfer Act of 1978 (Title XX, Public Law 95–630, 92 Stat. 3728, 15 U.S.C. § 1693 et seq.) as amended from time to time.

PART 2 Issue and Acceptance of Payment Order

§ 4A–201. Security Procedure.

"Security procedure" means a procedure established by agreement of a customer and a receiving bank for the purpose of (i) verifying that a payment order or communication amending or cancelling a payment order is that of the customer, or (ii) detecting error in the transmission or the content of the payment order or communication. A security procedure may require the use of algorithms or other codes, identifying words or numbers, encryption, callback procedures, or similar security devices. Comparison of a signature on a payment order or communication with an authorized specimen signature of the customer is not by itself a security procedure.

§ 4A–202. Authorized and Verified Payment Orders.

(a) A payment order received by the receiving bank is the authorized order of the person identified as sender if that person authorized the order or is otherwise bound by it under the law of agency.

(b) If a bank and its customer have agreed that the authenticity of payment orders issued to the bank in the name of the customer as sender will be verified pursuant to a security procedure, a payment order received by the receiving bank is effective as the order of the customer, whether or not authorized, if (i) the security procedure is a commercially reasonable method of providing security against unauthorized payment orders, and (ii) the bank proves that it accepted the payment order in good faith and in compliance with the security procedure and any written agreement or instruction of the customer restricting acceptance of payment orders issued in the name of the customer. The bank is not required to follow an instruction that violates a written agreement with the customer or notice of which is not received at a time and in a manner affording the bank a reasonable opportunity to act on it before the payment order is accepted.

(c) Commercial reasonableness of a security procedure is a question of law to be determined by considering the wishes of the customer expressed to the bank, the circumstances of the customer known to the bank, including the size, type, and -frequency of payment orders normally issued by the customer to the bank, alternative security procedures offered to the customer, and security procedures in general use by customers and receiving banks similarly situated. A security procedure is deemed to be commercially reasonable if (i) the security procedure was chosen by the customer after the bank offered, and the customer refused, a security procedure that was commercially reasonable for that customer, and (ii) the customer expressly agreed in writing to be bound by any payment order, whether or not authorized, issued in its name and accepted by the bank in compliance with the security procedure chosen by the customer.

(d) The term "sender" in this Article includes the customer in whose name a payment order is issued if the order is the authorized order of the customer under subsection (a), or it is effective as the order of the customer under subsection (b).

(e) This section applies to amendments and cancellations of payment orders to the same extent it applies to payment orders.

(f) Except as provided in this section and in Section 4A–203(a)(1), rights and obligations arising under this section or Section 4A–203 may not be varied by agreement.

§ 4A–203. Unenforceability of Certain Verified Payment Orders.

(a) If an accepted payment order is not, under Section 4A–202(a), an authorized order of a customer identified as sender, but is effective as an order of the customer pursuant to Section 4A–202(b), the following rules apply:

(1) By express written agreement, the receiving bank may limit the extent to which it is entitled to enforce or retain payment of the payment order.

(2) The receiving bank is not entitled to enforce or retain payment of the payment order if the customer proves that the order was not caused, directly or indirectly, by a person (i) entrusted at any time with duties to act for the customer with respect to payment orders or the security procedure, or (ii) who obtained access to transmitting facilities of the customer or who obtained, from a source controlled by the customer and without authority of the receiving bank, information facilitating breach of the security procedure, regardless of how the information was obtained or whether the customer was at fault. Information includes any access device, computer software, or the like.

(b) This section applies to amendments of payment orders to the same extent it applies to payment orders.

§ 4A–204. Refund of Payment and Duty of Customer to Report with Respect to Unauthorized Payment Order.

(a) If a receiving bank accepts a payment order issued in the name of its customer as sender which is (i) not authorized and not effective as the order of the customer under Section 4A–202, or (ii) not enforceable, in whole or in part, against the customer under Section 4A–203, the bank shall refund any payment of the payment order received from the customer to the extent the bank is not entitled to enforce payment and shall pay interest on the refundable amount calculated from the date the bank received payment to the date of the refund. However, the customer is not entitled to interest from the bank on the amount to be refunded if the customer fails to exercise ordinary care to determine that the order was not authorized by the customer and to notify the bank of the relevant facts within a reasonable time not exceeding 90 days after the date the customer received notification from the bank that the order was accepted or that the customer's account was debited with respect to the order. The bank is not entitled to any recovery from the customer on account of a failure by the customer to give notification as stated in this section.

(b) Reasonable time under subsection (a) may be fixed by agreement as stated in Section 1–204(1), but the obligation of a receiving bank to refund payment as stated in subsection (a) may not otherwise be varied by agreement.

§ 4A–205. Erroneous Payment Orders.

(a) If an accepted payment order was transmitted pursuant to a security procedure for the detection of error and the payment order (i) erroneously instructed payment to a beneficiary not intended by the sender, (ii) erroneously instructed payment in an amount greater than the amount intended by the sender, or (iii) was an erroneously transmitted duplicate of a payment order previously sent by the sender, the following rules apply:

(1) If the sender proves that the sender or a person acting on behalf of the sender pursuant to Section 4A–206 complied with the security procedure and that the error would have been detected if the receiving bank had also complied, the sender is not obliged to pay the order to the extent stated in paragraphs (2) and (3).

(2) If the funds transfer is completed on the basis of an erroneous payment order described in clause (i) or (iii) of subsection (a), the sender is not obliged to pay the order and the receiving bank is entitled to recover from the beneficiary any amount paid to the beneficiary to the extent allowed by the law governing mistake and restitution.

(3) If the funds transfer is completed on the basis of a payment order described in clause (ii) of subsection (a), the sender is not obliged to pay the order to the extent the amount received by the beneficiary is greater than the amount intended by the sender. In that case, the receiving bank is entitled to recover from the beneficiary the excess amount received to the extent allowed by the law governing mistake and restitution.

(b) If (i) the sender of an erroneous payment order described in subsection (a) is not obliged to pay all or part of the order, and (ii) the sender receives notification from the receiving bank that the order was accepted by the bank or that the sender's account was debited with respect to the order, the sender has a duty to exercise ordinary care, on the basis of information available to the sender, to discover the error with respect to the order and to advise the bank of the relevant facts within a reasonable time, not exceeding 90 days, after the bank's notification was received by the sender. If the bank proves that the sender failed to perform that duty, the sender is liable to the bank for the loss the bank proves it incurred as a result of the failure, but the liability of the sender may not exceed the amount of the sender's order.

(c) This section applies to amendments to payment orders to the same extent it applies to payment orders.

§ 4A–206. Transmission of Payment Order Through Funds-Transfer or Other Communication System.

(a) If a payment order addressed to a receiving bank is transmitted to a funds-transfer system or other third-party communication system for transmittal to the bank, the system is deemed to be an agent of the sender for the purpose of transmitting the payment order to the bank. If there is a discrepancy between the terms of the payment order transmitted to the system and the terms of the payment order transmitted by the system to the bank, the terms of the payment order of the sender are those transmitted by the system. This section does not apply to a funds-transfer system of the Federal Reserve Banks.

(b) This section applies to cancellations and amendments of payment orders to the same extent it applies to payment orders.

§ 4A–207. Misdescription of Beneficiary.

(a) Subject to subsection (b), if, in a payment order received by the beneficiary's bank, the name, bank account number, or other identification of the beneficiary refers to a nonexistent or unidentifiable person or account, no person has rights as a beneficiary of the order and acceptance of the order cannot occur.

(b) If a payment order received by the beneficiary's bank identifies the beneficiary both by name and by an identifying or bank account number and the name and number identify different persons, the following rules apply:

(1) Except as otherwise provided in subsection (c), if the beneficiary's bank does not know that the name and number refer to different persons, it may rely on the number as the proper identification of the beneficiary of the order. The beneficiary's bank need not determine whether the name and number refer to the same person.

(2) If the beneficiary's bank pays the person identified by name or knows that the name and number identify different persons, no person has rights as beneficiary except the person paid by the beneficiary's bank if that person was entitled to receive payment from the originator of the funds transfer. If no person has rights as beneficiary, acceptance of the order cannot occur.

(c) If (i) a payment order described in subsection (b) is accepted, (ii) the originator's payment order described the beneficiary inconsistently by name and number, and (ii) the beneficiary's bank pays the person identified by number as permitted by subsection (b)(1), the following rules apply:

(1) If the originator is a bank, the originator is obliged to pay its order.

(2) If the originator is not a bank and proves that the person identified by number was not entitled to receive payment from the originator, the originator is not obliged to pay its order unless the originator's bank proves that the originator, before acceptance of the originator's order, had notice that payment of a payment order issued by the originator might be made by the beneficiary's bank on the basis of an identifying or bank account number even if it identifies a person different from the named beneficiary. Proof of notice may be made by any admissible evidence. The originator's bank satisfies the burden of proof if it proves that the originator, before the payment order was accepted, signed a writing stating the information to which the notice relates.

(d) In a case governed by subsection (b)(1), if the beneficiary's bank rightfully pays the person identified by number and that person was not entitled to receive payment from the originator, the amount paid may be recovered from that person to the extent allowed by the law governing mistake and restitution as follows:

(1) If the originator is obliged to pay its payment order as stated in subsection (c), the originator has the right to recover.

(2) If the originator is not a bank and is not obliged to pay its payment order, the originator's bank has the right to recover.

§ 4A–208. Misdescription of Intermediary Bank or Beneficiary's Bank.

(a) This subsection applies to a payment order identifying an intermediary bank or the beneficiary's bank only by an identifying number.

(1) The receiving bank may rely on the number as the proper identification of the intermediary or beneficiary's bank and need not determine whether the number identifies a bank.

(2) The sender is obliged to compensate the receiving bank for any loss and expenses incurred by the receiving bank as a result of its reliance on the number in executing or attempting to execute the order.

(b) This subsection applies to a payment order identifying an intermediary bank or the beneficiary's bank both by name and an identifying number if the name and number identify different persons.

(1) If the sender is a bank, the receiving bank may rely on the number as the proper identification of the intermediary or beneficiary's bank if the receiving bank, when it executes the sender's order, does not know that the name and number identify different persons. The receiving bank need not determine whether the name and number refer to the same person or whether the name refers to a bank. The sender is obliged to compensate the receiving bank for any loss and expenses incurred by the receiving bank as a result of its reliance on the number in executing or attempting to execute the order.

(2) If the sender is not a bank and the receiving bank proves that the sender, before the payment order was accepted, had notice that the receiving bank might rely on the number as the proper identification of the intermediary or beneficiary's bank even if it identifies a person different from the bank identified by name, the rights and obligations of the sender and the receiving bank are governed by subsection (b)(1), as though the sender were a bank. Proof of notice may be made by any admissible evidence. The receiving bank satisfies the burden of proof if it proves that the sender, before the payment order was accepted, signed a writing stating the information to which the notice relates.

(3) Regardless of whether the sender is a bank, the receiving bank may rely on the name as the proper identification of the intermediary or beneficiary's bank if the receiving bank, at the time it executes the sender's order, does not know that the name and number identify different persons. The receiving bank need not determine whether the name and number refer to the same person.

(4) If the receiving bank knows that the name and number identify different persons, reliance on either the name or the number in executing the sender's payment order is a breach of the obligation stated in Section 4A–302(a)(1).

§ 4A–209. Acceptance of Payment Order.

(a) Subject to subsection (d), a receiving bank other than the beneficiary's bank accepts a payment order when it executes the order.

(b) Subject to subsections (c) and (d), a beneficiary's bank accepts a payment order at the earliest of the following times:

(1) when the bank (i) pays the beneficiary as stated in Section 4A–405(a) or 4A–405(b), or (ii) notifies the beneficiary of receipt of the order or that the account of the beneficiary has been credited with respect to the order unless the notice indicates that the bank is rejecting the order or that funds with respect to the order may not be withdrawn or used until receipt of payment from the sender of the order;

(2) when the bank receives payment of the entire amount of the sender's order pursuant to Section 4A–403(a)(1) or 4A–403(a)(2); or

(3) the opening of the next funds-transfer business day of the bank following the payment date of the order if, at that time, the amount of the sender's order is fully covered by a withdrawable credit balance in an authorized account of the sender or the bank has otherwise received full payment from the sender, unless the order was rejected before that time or is rejected within (i) one hour after that time, or (ii) one hour after the opening of the next business day of the sender following the payment date if that time is later. If notice of rejection is received by the sender after the payment date and the authorized account of the sender does not bear interest, the bank is obliged to pay interest to the sender on the amount of the order for the number of days elapsing after the payment date to the day the sender receives notice or learns that the order was not accepted, counting that day as an elapsed day. If the withdrawable credit balance during that period falls below the amount of the order, the amount of interest payable is reduced accordingly.

(c) Acceptance of a payment order cannot occur before the order is received by the receiving bank. Acceptance does not occur under subsection (b)(2) or (b)(3) if the beneficiary of the payment order does not have an account with the receiving bank, the account has been closed, or the receiving bank is not permitted by law to receive credits for the beneficiary's account.

(d) A payment order issued to the originator's bank cannot be accepted until the payment date if the bank is the beneficiary's bank, or the execution date if the bank is not the beneficiary's bank. If the originator's bank executes the originator's payment order before the execution date or pays the beneficiary of the originator's payment order before the payment date and the payment order is subsequently canceled pursuant to Section 4A–211(b), the bank may recover from the beneficiary any payment received to the extent allowed by the law governing mistake and restitution.

§ 4A–210. Rejection of Payment Order.

(a) A payment order is rejected by the receiving bank by a notice of rejection transmitted to the sender orally, electronically, or in writing. A notice of rejection need not use any particular words and is sufficient if it indicates that the receiving bank is rejecting the order or will not execute or pay the order. Rejection is effective when the notice is given if transmission is by a means that is reasonable in the circumstances. If notice of rejection is given by a means that is not reasonable, rejection is effective when the notice is received. If an agreement of the sender and receiving bank establishes the means to be used to reject a payment order, (i) any means complying with the agreement is reasonable and (ii) any means not complying is not reasonable unless no significant delay in receipt of the notice resulted from the use of the noncomplying means.

(b) This subsection applies if a receiving bank other than the beneficiary's bank fails to execute a payment order despite the existence on the execution date of a withdrawable credit balance in an authorized account of the sender sufficient to cover the order. If the sender does not receive notice of rejection of the order on the execution date and the authorized account of the sender does not bear interest, the bank is obliged to pay interest to the sender on the amount of the order for the number of days elapsing after the execution date to the earlier of the day the order is canceled pursuant to Section 4A–211(d) or the day the sender receives notice or learns that the order was not executed, counting the final day of the period as an elapsed day. If the withdrawable credit balance during that period falls below the amount of the order, the amount of interest is reduced accordingly.

(c) If a receiving bank suspends payments, all unaccepted payment orders issued to it are deemed rejected at the time the bank suspends payments.

(d) Acceptance of a payment order precludes a later rejection of the order. Rejection of a payment order precludes a later acceptance of the order.

§ 4A–211. Cancellation and Amendment of Payment Order.

(a) A communication of the sender of a payment order cancelling or amending the order may be transmitted to the receiving bank orally, electronically, or in writing. If a security procedure is in effect between the sender and the receiving bank, the communication is not effective to cancel or amend the order unless the communication is verified pursuant to the security procedure or the bank agrees to the cancellation or amendment.

(b) Subject to subsection (a), a communication by the sender cancelling or amending a payment order is effective to cancel or amend the order if notice of the communication is received at a time and in a manner affording the receiving bank a reasonable opportunity to act on the communication before the bank accepts the payment order.

(c) After a payment order has been accepted, cancellation or amendment of the order is not effective unless the receiving bank agrees or a funds-transfer system rule allows cancellation or amendment without agreement of the bank.

(1) With respect to a payment order accepted by a receiving bank other than the beneficiary's bank, cancellation or amendment is not effective unless a conforming cancellation or amendment of the payment order issued by the receiving bank is also made.

(2) With respect to a payment order accepted by the beneficiary's bank, cancellation or amendment is not effective unless the order was issued in execution of an unauthorized payment order, or because of a mistake by a sender in the funds transfer which resulted in the issuance of a payment order (i) that is a duplicate of a payment order previously issued by the sender, (ii) that orders payment to a beneficiary not entitled to receive payment from the originator, or (iii) that orders payment in an amount greater than the amount the beneficiary was entitled to receive from the originator. If the payment order is canceled or amended, the beneficiary's bank is entitled to recover from the beneficiary any amount paid to the beneficiary to the extent allowed by the law governing mistake and restitution.

(d) An unaccepted payment order is canceled by operation of law at the close of the fifth funds-transfer business day of the receiving bank after the execution date or payment date of the order.

(e) A canceled payment order cannot be accepted. If an accepted payment order is canceled, the acceptance is nullified and no person has any right or obligation based on the acceptance. Amendment of a payment order is deemed to be cancellation of the original order at the time of amendment and issue of a new payment order in the amended form at the same time.

(f) Unless otherwise provided in an agreement of the parties or in a funds-transfer system rule, if the receiving bank, after accepting a payment order, agrees to cancellation or amendment of the order by the sender or is bound by a funds-transfer system rule allowing cancellation or amendment without the bank's agreement, the sender, whether or not cancellation or amendment is effective, is liable to the bank for any loss and expenses, including reasonable attorney's fees, incurred by the bank as a result of the cancellation or amendment or attempted cancellation or amendment.

(g) A payment order is not revoked by the death or legal incapacity of the sender unless the receiving bank knows of the death or of an adjudication of incapacity by a court of competent jurisdiction and has reasonable opportunity to act before acceptance of the order.

(h) A funds-transfer system rule is not effective to the extent it conflicts with subsection (c)(2).

§ 4A–212. Liability and Duty of Receiving Bank Regarding Unaccepted Payment Order.

If a receiving bank fails to accept a payment order that it is obliged by express agreement to accept, the bank is liable for breach of the agreement to the extent provided in the agreement or in this Article, but does not otherwise have any duty to accept a payment order or, before acceptance, to take any action, or refrain from taking action, with respect to the order except as provided in this Article or by express agreement. Liability based on acceptance arises only when acceptance occurs as stated in Section 4A–209, and liability is limited to that provided in this Article. A receiving bank is not the agent of the sender or beneficiary of the payment order it accepts, or of any other party to the funds transfer, and the bank owes no duty to any party to the funds transfer except as provided in this Article or by express agreement.

PART 3 Execution of Sender's Payment Order by Receiving Bank

§ 4A–301. Execution and Execution Date.

(a) A payment order is "executed" by the receiving bank when it issues a payment order intended to carry out the payment order received by the bank. A payment order received by the beneficiary's bank can be accepted but cannot be executed.

(b) "Execution date" of a payment order means the day on which the receiving bank may properly issue a payment order in execution of the sender's order. The execution date may be determined by instruction of the sender but cannot be earlier than the day the order is received and, unless otherwise determined, is the day the order is received. If the sender's instruction states a payment date, the execution date is the payment date or an earlier date on which execution is reasonably necessary to allow payment to the beneficiary on the payment date.

§ 4A–302. Obligations of Receiving Bank in Execution of Payment Order.

(a) Except as provided in subsections (b) through (d), if the receiving bank accepts a payment order pursuant to Section 4A–209(a), the bank has the following obligations in executing the order:

(1) The receiving bank is obliged to issue, on the execution date, a payment order complying with the sender's order and to follow the sender's instructions concerning (i) any intermediary bank or funds-transfer system to be used in carrying out the funds transfer, or (ii) the means by which payment orders are to be transmitted in the funds transfer. If the originator's bank issues a payment order to an intermediary bank, the originator's bank is obliged to instruct the intermediary bank according to the instruction of the originator. An intermediary bank in the funds transfer is similarly bound by an instruction given to it by the sender of the payment order it accepts.

(2) If the sender's instruction states that the funds transfer is to be carried out telephonically or by wire transfer or otherwise indicates that the funds transfer is to be carried out by the most expeditious means, the receiving bank is obliged to transmit its payment order by the most expeditious available means, and to instruct any intermediary bank accordingly. If a sender's instruction states a payment date, the receiving bank is obliged to transmit its payment order at a time and by means reasonably necessary to allow payment to the beneficiary on the payment date or as soon thereafter as is feasible.

(b) Unless otherwise instructed, a receiving bank executing a payment order may (i) use any funds-transfer system if use of that system is reasonable in the circumstances, and (ii) issue a payment order to the beneficiary's bank or to an intermediary bank through which a payment order conforming to the sender's order can expeditiously be issued to the beneficiary's bank if the receiving bank exercises ordinary care in the selection of the intermediary bank. A receiving bank is not required to follow an instruction of the sender designating a funds-transfer system to be used in carrying out the funds transfer if the receiving bank, in good faith, determines that it is not feasible to follow the instruction or that following the instruction would unduly delay completion of the funds transfer.

(c) Unless subsection (a)(2) applies or the receiving bank is otherwise instructed, the bank may execute a payment order by transmitting its payment order by first class mail or by any means reasonable in the circumstances. If the receiving bank is instructed to execute the sender's order by transmitting its payment order by a particular means, the receiving bank may issue its payment order by the means stated or by any means as expeditious as the means stated.

(d) Unless instructed by the sender, (i) the receiving bank may not obtain payment of its charges for services and expenses in connection with the execution of the sender's order by issuing a payment order in an amount equal to the amount of the sender's order less the amount of the charges, and (ii) may not instruct a subsequent receiving bank to obtain payment of its charges in the same manner.

§ 4A–303. Erroneous Execution of Payment Order.

(a) A receiving bank that (i) executes the payment order of the sender by issuing a payment order in an amount greater than the amount of the sender's order, or (ii) issues a payment order in execution of the sender's order and then issues a duplicate order, is entitled to payment of the amount of the sender's order under Section 4A–402(c) if that subsection is otherwise satisfied. The bank is entitled to recover from the beneficiary of the erroneous order the excess payment received to the extent allowed by the law governing mistake and restitution.

(b) A receiving bank that executes the payment order of the sender by issuing a payment order in an amount less than the amount of the sender's order is entitled to payment of the amount of the sender's order under Section 4A–402(c) if (i) that subsection is otherwise satisfied and (ii) the bank corrects its mistake by issuing an additional payment order for the benefit of the beneficiary of the sender's order. If the error is not corrected, the issuer of the erroneous order is entitled to receive or retain payment from the sender of the order it accepted only to the extent of the amount of the erroneous order. This subsection does not apply if the receiving bank executes the sender's payment order by issuing a payment order in an amount less than the amount of the sender's order for the purpose of obtaining payment of its charges for services and expenses pursuant to instruction of the sender.

(c) If a receiving bank executes the payment order of the sender by issuing a payment order to a beneficiary different from the beneficiary of the sender's order and the funds transfer is completed on the basis of that error, the sender of the payment order that was erroneously executed and all previous senders in the funds transfer are not obliged to pay the payment orders they issued. The issuer of the erroneous order is entitled to recover from the beneficiary of the order the payment received to the extent allowed by the law governing mistake and restitution.

§ 4A–304. Duty of Sender to Report Erroneously Executed Payment Order.

If the sender of a payment order that is erroneously executed as stated in Section 4A–303 receives notification from the receiving bank that the order was executed or that the sender's account was debited with respect to the order, the sender has a duty to exercise ordinary care to determine, on the basis of information available to the sender, that the order was erroneously executed and to notify the bank of the relevant facts within a reasonable time not exceeding 90 days after the notification from the bank was received by the sender. If the sender fails to perform that duty, the bank is not obliged to pay interest on any amount refundable to the sender under Section 4A–402(d) for the period before the bank learns of the execution error. The bank is not entitled to any recovery from the sender on account of a failure by the sender to perform the duty stated in this section.

§ 4A–305. Liability for Late or Improper Execution or Failure to Execute Payment Order.

(a) If a funds transfer is completed but execution of a payment order by the receiving bank in breach of Section 4A–302 results in delay in payment to the beneficiary, the bank is obliged to pay interest to either the originator or the beneficiary of the funds transfer for the period of delay caused by the improper execution. Except as provided in subsection (c), additional damages are not recoverable.

(b) If execution of a payment order by a receiving bank in breach of Section 4A–302 results in (i) noncompletion of the funds transfer, (ii) failure to use an intermediary bank designated by the originator, or (iii) issuance of a payment order that does not comply with the terms of the payment order of the originator, the bank is liable to the originator for its expenses in the funds transfer and for incidental expenses and interest losses, to the extent not covered by subsection (a), resulting from the improper execution. Except as provided in subsection (c), additional damages are not recoverable.

(c) In addition to the amounts payable under subsections (a) and (b), damages, including consequential damages, are recoverable to the extent provided in an express written agreement of the receiving bank.

(d) If a receiving bank fails to execute a payment order it was obliged by express agreement to execute, the receiving bank is liable to the sender for its expenses in the transaction and for incidental expenses and interest losses resulting from the failure to execute. Additional damages, including consequential damages, are recoverable to the extent provided in an express written agreement of the receiving bank, but are not otherwise recoverable.

(e) Reasonable attorney's fees are recoverable if demand for compensation under subsection (a) or (b) is made and refused before an action is brought on the claim. If a claim is made for breach of an agreement under subsection (d) and the agreement does not provide for damages, reasonable attorney's fees are recoverable if demand for compensation under subsection (d) is made and refused before an action is brought on the claim.

(f) Except as stated in this section, the liability of a receiving bank under subsections (a) and (b) may not be varied by agreement.

PART 4 Payment

§ 4A–401. Payment Date.

"Payment date" of a payment order means the day on which the amount of the order is payable to the beneficiary by the beneficiary's bank. The payment date may be determined by instruction of the sender but cannot be earlier than the day the order is received by the beneficiary's bank and, unless otherwise determined, is the day the order is received by the beneficiary's bank.

§ 4A–402. Obligation of Sender to Pay Receiving Bank.

(a) This section is subject to Sections 4A–205 and 4A–207.

(b) With respect to a payment order issued to the beneficiary's bank, acceptance of the order by the bank obliges the sender to pay the bank the amount of the order, but payment is not due until the payment date of the order.

(c) This subsection is subject to subsection (e) and to Section 4A–303. With respect to a payment order issued to a receiving bank other than the beneficiary's bank, acceptance of the order by the receiving bank obliges the sender to pay the bank the amount of the sender's order. Payment by the sender is not due until the execution date of the sender's order. The obligation of that sender to pay its payment order is excused if the funds transfer is not completed by acceptance by the beneficiary's bank of a payment order instructing payment to the beneficiary of that sender's payment order.

(d) If the sender of a payment order pays the order and was not obliged to pay all or part of the amount paid, the bank receiving payment is obliged to refund payment to the extent the sender was not obliged to pay. Except as provided in Sections 4A–204 and 4A–304, interest is payable on the refundable amount from the date of payment.

(e) If a funds transfer is not completed as stated in subsection (c) and an intermediary bank is obliged to refund payment as stated in subsection (d) but is unable to do so because not permitted by applicable law or because the bank suspends payments, a sender in the funds transfer that executed a payment order in compliance with an instruction, as stated in Section 4A–302(a)(1), to route the funds transfer through that intermediary bank is entitled to receive or retain payment from the sender of the payment order that it accepted. The first sender in the funds transfer that issued an instruction requiring routing through that intermediary bank is subrogated to the right of the bank that paid the intermediary bank to refund as stated in subsection (d).

(f) The right of the sender of a payment order to be excused from the obligation to pay the order as stated in subsection (c) or to receive refund under subsection (d) may not be varied by agreement.

§ 4A–403. Payment by Sender to Receiving Bank.

(a) Payment of the sender's obligation under Section 4A–402 to pay the receiving bank occurs as follows:

(1) If the sender is a bank, payment occurs when the receiving bank receives final settlement of the obligation through a Federal Reserve Bank or through a funds-transfer system.

(2) If the sender is a bank and the sender (i) credited an account of the receiving bank with the sender, or (ii) caused an account of the receiving bank in another bank to be credited, payment occurs when the credit is withdrawn or, if not withdrawn, at midnight of the day on which the credit is withdrawable and the receiving bank learns of that fact.

(3) If the receiving bank debits an account of the sender with the receiving bank, payment occurs when the debit is made to the extent the debit is covered by a withdrawable credit balance in the account.

(b) If the sender and receiving bank are members of a funds-transfer system that nets obligations multilaterally among participants, the receiving bank receives final settlement when settlement is complete in accordance with the rules of the system. The obligation of the sender to pay the amount of a payment order transmitted through the funds-transfer system may be satisfied, to the extent permitted by the rules of the system, by setting off and applying against the sender's obligation the right of the sender to receive payment from the receiving bank of the amount of any other payment order transmitted to the sender by the receiving bank through the funds-transfer system. The aggregate balance of obligations owed by each sender to each receiving bank in the funds-transfer system may be satisfied, to the extent permitted by the rules of the system, by setting off and applying against that balance the aggregate balance of obligations owed to the sender by other members of the system. The aggregate balance is determined after the right of setoff stated in the second sentence of this subsection has been exercised.

(c) If two banks transmit payment orders to each other under an agreement that settlement of the obligations of each bank to the other under Section 4A–402 will be made at the end of the day or other period, the total amount owed with respect to all orders transmitted by one bank shall be set off against the total amount owed with respect to all orders transmitted by the other bank. To the extent of the setoff, each bank has made payment to the other.

(d) In a case not covered by subsection (a), the time when payment of the sender's obligation under Section 4A–402(b) or 4A–402(c) occurs is governed by applicable principles of law that determine when an obligation is satisfied.

§ 4A–404. Obligation of Beneficiary's Bank to Pay and Give Notice to Beneficiary.

(a) Subject to Sections 4A–211(e), 4A–405(d), and 4A–405(e), if a beneficiary's bank accepts a payment order, the bank is obliged to pay the amount of the order to the beneficiary of the order. Payment is due on the payment date of the order, but if acceptance occurs on the payment date after the close of the funds-transfer business day of the bank, payment is due on the next funds-transfer business day. If the bank refuses to pay after demand by the beneficiary and receipt of notice of particular circumstances that will give rise to consequential damages as a result of nonpayment, the beneficiary may recover damages resulting from the refusal to pay to the extent the bank had notice of the damages, unless the bank proves that it did not pay because of a reasonable doubt concerning the right of the beneficiary to payment.

(b) If a payment order accepted by the beneficiary's bank instructs payment to an account of the beneficiary, the bank is obliged to notify the beneficiary of receipt of the order before midnight of the next funds-transfer business day following the payment date. If the payment order does not instruct payment to an account of the beneficiary, the bank is required to notify the beneficiary only if notice is required by the order. Notice may be given by first class mail or any other means reasonable in the circumstances. If the bank fails to give the required notice, the bank is obliged to pay interest to the beneficiary on the amount of the payment order from the day notice should have been given until the day the beneficiary learned of receipt of the payment order by the bank. No other damages are recoverable. Reasonable attorney's fees are also recoverable if demand for interest is made and refused before an action is brought on the claim.

(c) The right of a beneficiary to receive payment and damages as stated in subsection (a) may not be varied by agreement or a funds-transfer system rule. The right of a beneficiary to be -notified as stated in subsection (b) may be varied by agreement of the beneficiary or by a funds-transfer system rule if the -beneficiary is notified of the rule before initiation of the funds transfer.

§ 4A–405. Payment by Beneficiary's Bank to Beneficiary.

(a) If the beneficiary's bank credits an account of the beneficiary of a payment order, payment of the bank's obligation under Section 4A–404(a) occurs when and to the extent (i) the beneficiary is notified of the right to withdraw the credit, (ii) the bank lawfully applies the credit to a debt of the beneficiary, or (iii) funds with respect to the order are otherwise made available to the beneficiary by the bank.

(b) If the beneficiary's bank does not credit an account of the beneficiary of a payment order, the time when payment of the bank's obligation under Section 4A–404(a) occurs is governed by principles of law that determine when an obligation is sat-isfied.

(c) Except as stated in subsections (d) and (e), if the beneficiary's bank pays the beneficiary of a payment order under a condition to payment or agreement of the beneficiary giving the bank the right to recover payment from the beneficiary if the bank does not receive payment of the order, the condition to payment or agreement is not enforceable.

(d) A funds-transfer system rule may provide that payments made to beneficiaries of funds transfers made through the system are provisional until receipt of payment by the beneficiary's bank of the payment order it accepted. A beneficiary's bank that makes a payment that is provisional under the rule is entitled to refund from the beneficiary if (i) the rule requires that both the beneficiary and the originator be given notice of the provisional nature of the payment before the funds transfer is initiated, (ii) the beneficiary, the beneficiary's bank and the originator's bank agreed to be bound by the rule, and (iii) the beneficiary's bank did not receive payment of the payment order that it accepted. If the beneficiary is obliged to refund payment to the beneficiary's bank, acceptance of the payment order by the beneficiary's bank is nullified and no payment by the originator of the funds transfer to the beneficiary occurs under Section 4A–406.

(e) This subsection applies to a funds transfer that includes a payment order transmitted over a funds-transfer system that (i) nets obligations multilaterally among participants, and (ii) has in effect a loss-sharing agreement among participants for the purpose of providing funds necessary to complete settlement of the obligations of one or more participants that do not meet their settlement obligations. If the beneficiary's bank in the funds transfer accepts a payment order and the system fails to complete settlement pursuant to its rules with respect to any payment order in the funds transfer, (i) the acceptance by the beneficiary's bank is nullified and no person has any right or obligation based on the acceptance, (ii) the beneficiary's bank is entitled to recover payment from the beneficiary, (iii) no payment by the originator to the beneficiary occurs under Section 4A–406, and (iv) subject to Section 4A–402(e), each sender in the funds transfer is excused from its obligation to pay its payment order under Section 4A–402(c) because the funds transfer has not been completed.

§ 4A–406. Payment by Originator to Beneficiary; Discharge of Underlying Obligation.

(a) Subject to Sections 4A–211(e), 4A–405(d), and 4A–405(e), the originator of a funds transfer pays the beneficiary of the originator's payment order (i) at the time a payment order for the benefit of the beneficiary is accepted by the beneficiary's bank in the funds transfer and (ii) in an amount equal to the amount of the order accepted by the beneficiary's bank, but not more than the amount of the originator's order.

(b) If payment under subsection (a) is made to satisfy an obligation, the obligation is discharged to the same extent discharge would result from payment to the beneficiary of the same amount in money, unless (i) the payment under subsection (a) was made by a means prohibited by the contract of the beneficiary with respect to the obligation, (ii) the beneficiary, within a reasonable time after receiving notice of receipt of the order by the beneficiary's bank, notified the originator of the beneficiary's refusal of the payment, (iii) funds with respect to the order were not withdrawn by the beneficiary or applied to a debt of the beneficiary, and (iv) the beneficiary would suffer a loss that could reasonably have been avoided if payment had been made by a means complying with the contract. If payment by the originator does not result in discharge under this section, the originator is subrogated to the rights of the beneficiary to receive payment from the beneficiary's bank under Section 4A–404(a).

(c) For the purpose of determining whether discharge of an obligation occurs under subsection (b), if the beneficiary's bank accepts a payment order in an amount equal to the amount of the originator's payment order less charges of one or more receiving banks in the funds transfer, payment to the beneficiary is deemed to be in the amount of the originator's order unless upon demand by the beneficiary the originator does not pay the beneficiary the amount of the deducted charges.

(d) Rights of the originator or of the beneficiary of a funds transfer under this section may be varied only by agreement of the originator and the beneficiary.

PART 5 Miscellaneous Provisions

§ 4A–501. Variation by Agreement and Effect of Funds-Transfer System Rule.

(a) Except as otherwise provided in this Article, the rights and obligations of a party to a funds transfer may be varied by agreement of the affected party.

(b) "Funds-transfer system rule" means a rule of an association of banks (i) governing transmission of payment orders by means of a funds-transfer system of the association or rights and obligations with respect to those orders, or (ii) to the extent the rule governs rights and obligations between banks that are parties to a funds transfer in which a Federal Reserve Bank, acting as an intermediary bank, sends a payment order to the beneficiary's bank. Except as otherwise provided in this Article, a funds-transfer system rule governing rights and obligations between participating banks using the system may be effective even if the rule conflicts with this Article and indirectly affects another party to the funds transfer who does not consent to the rule. A funds-transfer system rule may also govern rights and obligations of parties other than participating banks using the system to the extent stated in Sections 4A–404(c), 4A–405(d), and 4A–507(c).

§ 4A–502. Creditor Process Served on Receiving Bank; Setoff by Beneficiary's Bank.

(a) As used in this section, "creditor process" means levy, attachment, garnishment, notice of lien, sequestration, or similar process issued by or on behalf of a creditor or other claimant with respect to an account.

(b) This subsection applies to creditor process with respect to an authorized account of the sender of a payment order if the creditor process is served on the receiving bank. For the purpose of determining rights with respect to the creditor process, if the receiving bank accepts the payment order the balance in the authorized account is deemed to be reduced by the amount of the payment order to the extent the bank did not otherwise receive payment of the order, unless the creditor process is served at a time and in a manner affording the bank a reasonable opportunity to act on it before the bank accepts the payment order.

(c) If a beneficiary's bank has received a payment order for payment to the beneficiary's account in the bank, the following rules apply:

(1) The bank may credit the beneficiary's account. The amount credited may be set off against an obligation owed by the beneficiary to the bank or may be applied to satisfy creditor process served on the bank with respect to the account.

(2) The bank may credit the beneficiary's account and allow withdrawal of the amount credited unless creditor process with respect to the account is served at a time and in a manner affording the bank a reasonable opportunity to act to prevent withdrawal.

(3) If creditor process with respect to the beneficiary's account has been served and the bank has had a reasonable opportunity to act on it, the bank may not reject the payment order except for a reason unrelated to the service of process.

(d) Creditor process with respect to a payment by the originator to the beneficiary pursuant to a funds transfer may be served only on the beneficiary's bank with respect to the debt owed by that bank to the beneficiary. Any other bank served with the creditor process is not obliged to act with respect to the process.

§ 4A–503. Injunction or Restraining Order With Respect to Funds Transfer.

For proper cause and in compliance with applicable law, a court may restrain (i) a person from issuing a payment order to initiate a funds transfer, (ii) an originator's bank from executing the payment order of the originator, or (iii) the beneficiary's bank from releasing funds to the beneficiary or the beneficiary from withdrawing the funds. A court may not otherwise restrain a person from issuing a payment order, paying or receiving payment of a payment order, or otherwise acting with respect to a funds transfer.

§ 4A–504. Order in Which Items and Payment Orders May Be Charged to Account; Order of Withdrawals From Account.

(a) If a receiving bank has received more than one payment order of the sender or one or more payment orders and other items that are payable from the sender's account, the bank may charge the sender's account with respect to the various orders and items in any sequence.

(b) In determining whether a credit to an account has been withdrawn by the holder of the account or applied to a debt of the holder of the account, credits first made to the account are first withdrawn or applied.

§ 4A–505. Preclusion of Objection to Debit of Customer's Account.

If a receiving bank has received payment from its customer with respect to a payment order issued in the name of the customer as sender and accepted by the bank, and the customer received notification reasonably identifying the order, the customer is precluded from asserting that the bank is not entitled to retain the payment unless the customer notifies the bank of the customer's objection to the payment within one year after the notification was received by the customer.

§ 4A–506. Rate of Interest.

(a) If, under this Article, a receiving bank is obliged to pay interest with respect to a payment order issued to the bank, the amount payable may be determined (i) by agreement of the sender and receiving bank, or (ii) by a funds-transfer system rule if the payment order is transmitted through a funds-transfer system.

(b) If the amount of interest is not determined by an agreement or rule as stated in subsection (a), the amount is calculated by multiplying the applicable Federal Funds rate by the amount on which interest is payable, and then multiplying the product by the number of days for which interest is payable. The applicable Federal Funds rate is the average of the Federal Funds rates published by the Federal Reserve Bank of New York for each of the days for which interest is payable divided by 360. The Federal Funds rate for any day on which a published rate is not available is the same as the published rate for the next preceding day for which there is a published rate. If a receiving bank that accepted a payment order is required to refund payment to the sender of the order because the funds transfer was not completed, but the failure to complete was not due to any fault by the bank, the interest payable is reduced by a percentage equal to the reserve requirement on deposits of the receiving bank.

§ 4A–507. Choice of Law.

(a) The following rules apply unless the affected parties otherwise agree or subsection (c) applies:

(1) The rights and obligations between the sender of a payment order and the receiving bank are governed by the law of the jurisdiction in which the receiving bank is located.

(2) The rights and obligations between the beneficiary's bank and the beneficiary are governed by the law of the jurisdiction in which the beneficiary's bank is located.

(3) The issue of when payment is made pursuant to a funds transfer by the originator to the beneficiary is governed by the law of the jurisdiction in which the beneficiary's bank is located.

(b) If the parties described in each paragraph of subsection (a) have made an agreement selecting the law of a particular jurisdiction to govern rights and obligations between each other, the law of that jurisdiction governs those rights and obligations, whether or not the payment order or the funds transfer bears a reasonable relation to that jurisdiction.

(c) A funds-transfer system rule may select the law of a particular jurisdiction to govern (i) rights and obligations between participating banks with respect to payment orders transmitted or processed through the system, or (ii) the rights and obligations of some or all parties to a funds transfer any part of which is carried out by means of the system. A choice of law made pursuant to clause (i) is binding on participating banks. A choice of law made pursuant to clause (ii) is binding on the originator, other sender, or a receiving bank having notice that the funds-transfer system might be used in the funds transfer and of the choice of law by the system when the originator, other sender, or receiving bank issued or accepted a payment order. The beneficiary of a funds transfer is bound by the choice of law if, when the funds transfer is initiated, the beneficiary has notice that the funds-transfer system might be used in the funds transfer and of the choice of law by the system. The law of a jurisdiction selected pursuant to this subsection may govern, whether or not that law bears a reasonable relation to the matter in issue.

(d) In the event of inconsistency between an agreement under subsection (b) and a choice-of-law rule under subsection (c), the agreement under subsection (b) prevails.

(e) If a funds transfer is made by use of more than one funds-transfer system and there is inconsistency between choice-of-law rules of the systems, the matter in issue is governed by the law of the selected jurisdiction that has the most significant relationship to the matter in issue.

ARTICLE 9

SECURED TRANSACTIONS; SALES OF ACCOUNTS AND CHATTEL PAPER

Note: The adoption of this Article should be accompanied by the repeal of existing statutes dealing with conditional sales, trust receipts, factor's liens where the factor is given a non-possessory lien, chattel mortgages, crop mortgages, mortgages on railroad equipment, assignment of accounts and generally statutes regulating security interests in personal property.

Where the state has a retail installment selling act or small loan act, that legislation should be carefully examined to determine what changes in those acts are needed to conform them to this Article. This Article primarily sets out rules defining rights of a secured party against persons dealing with the debtor; it does not prescribe regulations and controls which may be necessary to curb abuses arising in the small loan business or in the financing of consumer purchases on credit. Accordingly there is no intention to repeal existing regulatory acts in those fields by enactment or re-enactment of Article 9. See Section 9–203(4) and the Note thereto.

PART 1 Short Title, Applicability and Definitions

§ 9–101. Short Title.

This Article shall be known and may be cited as Uniform Commercial Code—Secured Transactions.

§ 9–102. Policy and Subject Matter of Article.

(1) Except as otherwise provided in Section 9–104 on excluded transactions, this Article applies

(a) to any transaction (regardless of its form) which is intended to create a security interest in personal property or fixtures including goods, documents, instruments, general intangibles, chattel paper or accounts; and also

(b) to any sale of accounts or chattel paper.

(2) This Article applies to security interests created by contract including pledge, assignment, chattel mortgage, chattel trust, trust deed, factor's lien, equipment trust, conditional sale, trust receipt, other lien or title retention contract and lease or consignment intended as security. This Article does not apply to statutory liens except as provided in Section 9–310.

(3) The application of this Article to a security interest in a secured obligation is not affected by the fact that the obligation is itself secured by a transaction or interest to which this Article does not apply.

§ 9–103. Perfection of Security Interest in Multiple State Transactions.

(1) Documents, instruments and ordinary goods.

(a) This subsection applies to documents and instruments and to goods other than those covered by a certificate of title described in subsection (2), mobile goods described in subsection (3), and minerals described in subsection (5).

(b) Except as otherwise provided in this subsection, perfection and the effect of perfection or non-perfection of a security interest in collateral are governed by the law of the jurisdiction where the collateral is when the last event occurs on which is based the assertion that the security interest is perfected or unperfected.

(c) If the parties to a transaction creating a purchase money security interest in goods in one jurisdiction understand at the time that the security interest attaches that the goods will be kept in another jurisdiction, then the law of the other jurisdiction governs the perfection and the effect of perfection or non-perfection of the security interest from the time it attaches until thirty days after the debtor receives possession of the goods and thereafter if the goods are taken to the other jurisdiction before the end of the thirty-day period.

(d) When collateral is brought into and kept in this state while subject to a security interest perfected under the law of the jurisdiction from which the collateral was removed, the security interest remains perfected, but if action is required by Part 3 of this Article to perfect the security interest,

(i) if the action is not taken before the expiration of the period of perfection in the other jurisdiction or the end of four months after the collateral is brought into this state, whichever period first expires, the security interest becomes unperfected at the end of that period and is thereafter deemed to have been unperfected as against a person who became a purchaser after removal;

(ii) if the action is taken before the expiration of the period specified in subparagraph (i), the security interest continues perfected thereafter;

(iii) for the purpose of priority over a buyer of consumer goods (subsection (2) of Section 9–307), the period of the effectiveness of a filing in the jurisdiction from which the collateral is removed is governed by the rules with respect to perfection in subparagraphs (i) and (ii).

(2) Certificate of title.

(a) This subsection applies to goods covered by a certificate of title issued under a statute of this state or of another jurisdiction under the law of which indication of a security interest on the certificate is required as a condition of perfection.

(b) Except as otherwise provided in this subsection, perfection and the effect of perfection or non-perfection of the security interest are governed by the law (including the conflict of laws rules) of the jurisdiction issuing the certificate until four months after the goods are removed from that jurisdiction and thereafter until the goods are registered in another jurisdiction, but in any event not beyond surrender of the certificate. After the expiration of that period, the goods are not covered by the certificate of title within the meaning of this section.

(c) Except with respect to the rights of a buyer described in the next paragraph, a security interest, perfected in another jurisdiction otherwise than by notation on a certificate of title, in goods brought into this state and thereafter covered by a certificate of title issued by this state is subject to the rules stated in paragraph (d) of subsection (1).

(d) If goods are brought into this state while a security interest therein is perfected in any manner under the law of the jurisdiction from which the goods are removed and a certificate of title is issued by this state and the certificate does not show that the goods are subject to the security interest or that they may be subject to security interests not shown on the certificate, the security interest is subordinate to the rights of a buyer of the goods who is not in the business of selling goods of that kind to the extent that he gives value and receives delivery of the goods after issuance of the certificate and without knowledge of the security interest.

(3) Accounts, general intangibles and mobile goods.

(a) This subsection applies to accounts (other than an account described in subsection (5) on minerals) and general intangibles (other than uncertificated securities) and to goods which are mobile and which are of a type normally used in more than one jurisdiction, such as motor vehicles, trailers, rolling stock, airplanes, shipping containers, road building and construction machinery and commercial harvesting machinery and the like, if the goods are equipment or are inventory leased or held for lease by the debtor to others, and are not covered by a certificate of title described in subsection (2).

(b) The law (including the conflict of laws rules) of the jurisdiction in which the debtor is located governs the perfection and the effect of perfection or non-perfection of the security interest.

(c) If, however, the debtor is located in a jurisdiction which is not a part of the United States, and which does not provide for perfection of the security interest by filing or recording in that jurisdiction, the law of the jurisdiction in the United States in which the debtor has its major executive office in the United States governs the perfection and the effect of perfection or non-perfection of the security interest through filing. In the alternative, if the debtor is located in a jurisdiction which is not a part of the United States or Canada and the collateral is accounts or general intangibles for money due or to become due, the security interest may be perfected by notification to the account debtor. As used in this paragraph, "United States" includes its territories and possessions and the Commonwealth of Puerto Rico.

(d) A debtor shall be deemed located at his place of business if he has one, at his chief executive office if he has more than one place of business, otherwise at his residence. If, however, the debtor is a foreign air carrier under the Federal Aviation Act of 1958, as amended, it shall be deemed located at the designated office of the agent upon whom service of process may be made on behalf of the foreign air carrier.

(e) A security interest perfected under the law of the jurisdiction of the location of the debtor is perfected until the expiration of four months after a change of the debtor's location to another jurisdiction, or until perfection would have ceased by the law of the first jurisdiction, whichever period first expires. Unless perfected in the new jurisdiction before the end of that period, it becomes unperfected thereafter and is deemed to have been unperfected as against a person who became a purchaser after the change.

(4) Chattel paper.

The rules stated for goods in subsection (1) apply to a possessory security interest in chattel paper. The rules stated for accounts in subsection (3) apply to a non-possessory security interest in chattel paper, but the security interest may not be perfected by notification to the account debtor.

(5) Minerals.

Perfection and the effect of perfection or non-perfection of a security interest which is created by a debtor who has an interest in minerals or the like (including oil and gas) before extraction and which attaches thereto as extracted, or which attaches to an account resulting from the sale thereof at the wellhead or minehead are governed by the law (including the conflict of laws rules) of the jurisdiction wherein the wellhead or minehead is located.

(6) Uncertificated securities.

The law (including the conflict of laws rules) of the jurisdiction of organization of the issuer governs the perfection and the effect of perfection or non-perfection of a security interest in uncertificated securities.

§ 9–104. Transactions Excluded From Article.

This Article does not apply

(a) to a security interest subject to any statute of the United States, to the extent that such statute governs the rights of parties to and third parties affected by transactions in particular types of property; or

(b) to a landlord's lien; or

(c) to a lien given by statute or other rule of law for services or materials except as provided in Section 9–310 on priority of such liens; or

(d) to a transfer of a claim for wages, salary or other compensation of an employee; or

(e) to a transfer by a government or governmental subdivision or agency; or

(f) to a sale of accounts or chattel paper as part of a sale of the business out of which they arose, or an assignment of accounts or chattel paper which is for the purpose of collection only, or a transfer of a right to payment under a contract to an assignee who is also to do the performance under the contract or a transfer of a single account to an assignee in whole or partial satisfaction of a preexisting indebtedness; or

(g) to a transfer of an interest in or claim in or under any policy of insurance, except as provided with respect to proceeds (Section 9–306) and priorities in proceeds (Section 9–312); or

(h) to a right represented by a judgment (other than a judgment taken on a right to payment which was collateral); or

(i) to any right of set-off; or

(j) except to the extent that provision is made for fixtures in Section 9–313, to the creation or transfer of an interest in or lien on real estate, including a lease or rents thereunder; or

(k) to a transfer in whole or in part of any claim arising out of tort; or

(l) to a transfer of an interest in any deposit account (subsection (1) of Section 9–105), except as provided with respect to proceeds (Section 9–306) and priorities in proceeds (Section 9–312).

§ 9–105. Definitions and Index of Definitions.

(1) In this Article unless the context otherwise requires:

(a) "Account debtor" means the person who is obligated on an account, chattel paper or general intangible;

(b) "Chattel paper" means a writing or writings which evidence both a monetary obligation and a security interest in or a lease of specific goods, but a charter or other contract involving the use or hire of a vessel is not chattel paper. When a transaction is evidenced both by such a security agreement or a lease and by an instrument or a series of instruments, the group of writings taken together constitutes chattel paper;

(c) "Collateral" means the property subject to a security interest, and includes accounts and chattel paper which have been sold;

(d) "Debtor" means the person who owes payment or other performance of the obligation secured, whether or not he owns or has rights in the collateral, and includes the seller of accounts or chattel paper. Where the debtor and the owner of the collateral are not the same person, the term "debtor" means the owner of the collateral in any provision of the Article dealing with the collateral, the obligor in any provision dealing with the obligation, and may include both where the context so requires;

(e) "Deposit account" means a demand, time, savings, passbook or like account maintained with a bank, savings and loan association, credit union or like organization, other than an account evidenced by a certificate of deposit;

(f) "Document" means document of title as defined in the general definitions of Article 1 (Section 1–201), and a receipt of the kind described in subsection (2) of Section 7–201;

(g) "Encumbrance" includes real estate mortgages and other liens on real estate and all other rights in real estate that are not ownership interests;

(h) "Goods" includes all things which are movable at the time the security interest attaches or which are fixtures (Section 9–313), but does not include money, documents, instruments, accounts, chattel paper, general intangibles, or minerals or the like (including oil and gas) before extraction. "Goods" also includes standing timber which is to be cut and removed under a conveyance or contract for sale, the unborn young of animals, and growing crops;

(i) "Instrument" means a negotiable instrument (defined in Section 3–104), or a certificated security (defined in Section 8–102) or any other writing which evidences a right to the payment of money and is not itself a security agreement or lease and is of a type which is in ordinary course of business transferred by delivery with any necessary indorsement or assignment;

(j) "Mortgage" means a consensual interest created by a real estate mortgage, a trust deed on real estate, or the like;

(k) An advance is made "pursuant to commitment" if the secured party has bound himself to make it, whether or not a subsequent event of default or other event not within his control has relieved or may relieve him from his obligation;

(l) "Security agreement" means an agreement which creates or provides for a security interest;

(m) "Secured party" means a lender, seller or other person in whose favor there is a security interest, including a person to whom accounts or chattel paper have been sold. When the holders of obligations issued under an indenture of trust, equipment trust agreement or the like are represented by a trustee or other person, the representative is the secured party;

(n) "Transmitting utility" means any person primarily engaged in the railroad, street railway or trolley bus business, the electric or electronics communications transmission business, the transmission of goods by pipeline, or the transmission or the production and transmission of electricity, steam, gas or water, or the provision of sewer service.

(2) Other definitions applying to this Article and the sections in which they appear are:

"Account". Section 9–106.
"Attach". Section 9–203.
"Construction mortgage". Section 9–313(1).
"Consumer goods". Section 9–109(1).
"Equipment". Section 9–109(2).
"Farm products". Section 9–109(3).
"Fixture". Section 9–313(1).
"Fixture filing". Section 9–313(1).
"General intangibles". Section 9–106.
"Inventory". Section 9–109(4).
"Lien creditor". Section 9–301(3).
"Proceeds". Section 9–306(1).
"Purchase money security interest". Section 9–107.
"United States". Section 9–103.

(3) The following definitions in other Articles apply to this Article:

"Check". Section 3–104.
"Contract for sale". Section 2–106.
"Holder in due course". Section 3–302.
"Note". Section 3–104.
"Sale". Section 2–106.

(4) In addition Article 1 contains general definitions and principles of construction and interpretation applicable throughout this Article.

§ 9–106. Definitions: "Account"; "General Intangibles".

"Account" means any right to payment for goods sold or leased or for services rendered which is not evidenced by an instrument or chattel paper, whether or not it has been earned by performance. "General intangibles" means any personal property (including things in action) other than goods, accounts, chattel paper, documents, instruments, and money. All rights to payment earned or unearned under a charter or other contract involving the use or hire of a vessel and all rights incident to the charter or contract are accounts.

§ 9–107. Definitions: "Purchase Money Security Interest".

A security interest is a "purchase money security interest" to the extent that it is

(a) taken or retained by the seller of the collateral to secure all or part of its price; or

(b) taken by a person who by making advances or incurring an obligation gives value to enable the debtor to acquire rights in or the use of collateral if such value is in fact so used.

§ 9–108. When After-Acquired Collateral Not Security for Antecedent Debt.

Where a secured party makes an advance, incurs an obligation, releases a perfected security interest, or otherwise gives new value which is to be secured in whole or in part by after-acquired property his security interest in the after-acquired collateral shall be deemed to be taken for new value and not as security for an antecedent debt if the debtor acquires his rights in such collateral either in the ordinary course of his business or under a contract of purchase made pursuant to the security agreement within a reasonable time after new value is given.

§ 9–109. Classification of Goods; "Consumer Goods"; "Equipment"; "Farm Products"; "Inventory".

Goods are

(1) "consumer goods" if they are used or bought for use primarily for personal, family or household purposes;

(2) "equipment" if they are used or bought for use primarily in business (including farming or a profession) or by a debtor who is a non-profit organization or a governmental subdivision or agency or if the goods are not included in the definitions of inventory, farm products or consumer goods;

(3) "farm products" if they are crops or livestock or supplies used or produced in farming operations or if they are products of crops or livestock in their unmanufactured states (such as ginned cotton, wool-clip, maple syrup, milk and eggs), and if they are in the possession of a debtor engaged in raising, fattening, grazing or other farming operations. If goods are farm products they are neither equipment nor inventory;

(4) "inventory" if they are held by a person who holds them for sale or lease or to be furnished under contracts of service or if he has so furnished them, or if they are raw materials, work in process or materials used or consumed in a business. Inventory of a person is not to be classified as his equipment.

§ 9–110. Sufficiency of Description.

For purposes of this Article any description of personal property or real estate is sufficient whether or not it is specific if it reasonably identifies what is described.

§ 9–111. Applicability of Bulk Transfer Laws.

The creation of a security interest is not a bulk transfer under Article 6 (see Section 6–103).

§ 9–112. Where Collateral Is Not Owned by Debtor.

Unless otherwise agreed, when a secured party knows that collateral is owned by a person who is not the debtor, the owner of the collateral is entitled to receive from the secured party any surplus under Section 9–502(2) or under Section 9–504(1), and is not liable for the debt or for any deficiency after resale, and he has the same right as the debtor.

(a) to receive statements under Section 9–208;

(b) to receive notice of and to object to a secured party's proposal to retain the collateral in satisfaction of the indebtedness under Section 9–505;

(c) to redeem the collateral under Section 9–506;

(d) to obtain injunctive or other relief under Section 9–507(1); and

(e) to recover losses caused to him under Section 9–208(2).

§ 9–113. Security Interests Arising Under Article on Sales.

A security interest arising solely under the Article on Sales (Article 2) is subject to the provisions of this Article except that to the extent that and so long as the debtor does not have or does not lawfully obtain possession of the goods

(a) no security agreement is necessary to make the security interest enforceable; and

(b) no filing is required to perfect the security interest; and

(c) the rights of the secured party on default by the debtor are governed by the Article on Sales (Article 2).

§ 9–114. Consignment.

(1) A person who delivers goods under a consignment which is not a security interest and who would be required to file under this Article by paragraph (3)(c) of Section 2–326 has priority over a secured party who is or becomes a creditor of the consignee and who would have a perfected security interest in the goods if they were the property of the consignee, and also has priority with respect to identifiable cash proceeds received on or before delivery of the goods to a buyer, if

(a) the consignor complies with the filing provision of the Article on Sales with respect to consignments (paragraph (3)(c) of Section 2–326) before the consignee receives possession of the goods; and

(b) the consignor gives notification in writing to the holder of the security interest if the holder has filed a financing statement covering the same types of goods before the date of the filing made by the consignor; and

(c) the holder of the security interest receives the notification within five years before the consignee receives possession of the goods; and

(d) the notification states that the consignor expects to deliver goods on consignment to the consignee, describing the goods by item or type.

(2) In the case of a consignment which is not a security interest and in which the requirements of the preceding subsection have not been met, a person who delivers goods to another is subordinate to a person who would have a perfected security interest in the goods if they were the property of the debtor.

PART 2 Validity of Security Agreement and Rights of Parties Thereto

§ 9–201. General Validity of Security Agreement.

Except as otherwise provided by this Act a security

agreement is effective according to its terms between the parties, against purchasers of the collateral and against creditors. Nothing in this Article validates any charge or practice illegal under any statute or regulation thereunder governing usury, small loans, retail installment sales, or the like, or extends the application of any such statute or regulation to any transaction not otherwise subject thereto.

§ 9–202. Title to Collateral Immaterial.

Each provision of this Article with regard to rights, obligations and remedies applies whether title to collateral is in the secured party or in the debtor.

§ 9–203. Attachment and Enforceability of Security Interest; Proceeds; Formal Requisites.

(1) Subject to the provisions of Section 4–210 on the security interest of a collecting bank, Section 8–321 on security interests in securities and Section 9–113 on a security interest arising under the Articles on Sales and Leases, a security interest is not enforceable against the debtor or third parties with respect to the collateral and does not attach unless:

(a) the collateral is in the possession of the secured party pursuant to agreement, or the debtor has signed a security agreement which contains a description of the collateral and in addition, when the security interest covers crops growing or to be grown or timber to be cut, a description of the land concerned;

(b) value has been given; and

(c) the debtor has rights in the collateral.

(2) A security interest attaches when it becomes enforceable against the debtor with respect to the collateral. Attachment occurs as soon as all of the events specified in subsection (1) have taken place unless explicit agreement postpones the time of attaching.

(3) Unless otherwise agreed a security agreement gives the secured party the rights to proceeds provided by Section 9–306.

(4) A transaction, although subject to this Article, is also subject to . . .*, and in the case of conflict between the provisions of this Article and any such statute, the provisions of such statute control. Failure to comply with any applicable statute has only the effect which is specified therein.

*Note: At * in subsection (4) insert reference to any local statute regulating small loans, retail installment sales and the like.*

The foregoing subsection (4) is designed to make it clear that certain transactions, although subject to this Article, must also comply with other applicable legislation.

This Article is designed to regulate all the "security" aspects of transactions within its scope. There is, however, much regulatory legislation, particularly in the consumer field, which supplements this Article and should not be repealed by its enactment. Examples are small loan acts, retail installment selling acts and the like. Such acts may provide for licensing and rate regulation and may prescribe particular forms of contract. Such provisions should remain in force despite the enactment of this Article. On the other hand if a retail installment selling act contains provisions on filing, rights on default, etc., such provisions should be repealed as inconsistent with this Article except that inconsistent provisions as to deficiencies, penalties, etc., in the Uniform Consumer Credit Code and other recent related legislation should remain because those statutes were drafted after the substantial enactment of the Article and with the intention of modifying certain provisions of this Article as to consumer credit.

§ 9–204. After-Acquired Property; Future Advances.

(1) Except as provided in subsection (2), a security agreement may provide that any or all obligations covered by the security agreement are to be secured by after-acquired collateral.

(2) No security interest attaches under an after-acquired property clause to consumer goods other than accessions (Section 9–314) when given as additional security unless the debtor acquires rights in them within ten days after the secured party gives value.

(3) Obligations covered by a security agreement may include future advances or other value whether or not the advances or value are given pursuant to commitment (subsection (1) of Section 9–105).

§ 9–205. Use or Disposition of Collateral Without Accounting Permissible.

A security interest is not invalid or fraudulent against creditors by reason of liberty in the debtor to use, commingle or dispose of all or part of the collateral (including returned or repossessed goods) or to collect or compromise accounts or chattel paper, or to accept the return of goods or make repossessions, or to use, commingle or dispose of proceeds, or by reason of the failure of the secured party to require the debtor to account for proceeds or replace collateral. This section does not relax the requirements of possession where perfection of a security interest depends upon possession of the collateral by the secured party or by a bailee.

§ 9–206. Agreement Not to Assert Defenses Against Assignee; Modification of Sales Warranties Where Security Agreement Exists.

(1) Subject to any statute or decision which establishes a different rule for buyers or lessees of consumer goods, an agreement by a buyer or lessee that he will not assert against an assignee any claim or defense which he may have against the seller or lessor is enforceable by an assignee who takes his assignment for value, in good faith and without notice of a claim or defense, except as to defenses of a type which may be asserted against a holder in due course of a negotiable instrument under the Article on Negotiable Instruments (Article 3). A buyer who as part of one transaction signs both a negotiable instrument and a security agreement makes such an agreement.

(2) When a seller retains a purchase money security interest in goods the Article on Sales (Article 2) governs the

sale and any disclaimer, limitation or modification of the seller's warranties.

§ 9–207. Rights and Duties When Collateral Is in Secured Party's Possession.

(1) A secured party must use reasonable care in the custody and preservation of collateral in his possession. In the case of an instrument or chattel paper reasonable care includes taking necessary steps to preserve rights against prior parties unless otherwise agreed.

(2) Unless otherwise agreed, when collateral is in the secured party's possession

(a) reasonable expenses (including the cost of any insurance and payment of taxes or other charges) incurred in the custody, preservation, use or operation of the collateral are chargeable to the debtor and are secured by the collateral;

(b) the risk of accidental loss or damage is on the debtor to the extent of any deficiency in any effective insurance coverage;

(c) the secured party may hold as additional security any increase or profits (except money) received from the collateral, but money so received, unless remitted to the debtor, shall be applied in reduction of the secured obligation;

(d) the secured party must keep the collateral identifiable but fungible collateral may be commingled;

(e) the secured party may repledge the collateral upon terms which do not impair the debtor's right to redeem it.

(3) A secured party is liable for any loss caused by his failure to meet any obligation imposed by the preceding subsections but does not lose his security interest.

(4) A secured party may use or operate the collateral for the purpose of preserving the collateral or its value or pursuant to the order of a court of appropriate jurisdiction or, except in the case of consumer goods, in the manner and to the extent provided in the security agreement.

§ 9–208. Request for Statement of Account or List of Collateral.

(1) A debtor may sign a statement indicating what he believes to be the aggregate amount of unpaid indebtedness as of a specified date and may send it to the secured party with a request that the statement be approved or corrected and returned to the debtor. When the security agreement or any other record kept by the secured party identifies the collateral a debtor may similarly request the secured party to approve or correct a list of the collateral.

(2) The secured party must comply with such a request within two weeks after receipt by sending a written correction or approval. If the secured party claims a security interest in all of a particular type of collateral owned by the debtor he may indicate that fact in his reply and need not approve or correct an itemized list of such collateral. If the secured party without reasonable excuse fails to comply he is liable for any loss caused to the debtor thereby; and if the debtor has properly included in his request a good faith statement of the obligation or a list of the collateral or both the secured party may claim a security interest only as shown in the statement against persons misled by his failure to comply. If he no longer has an interest in the obligation or collateral at the time the request is received he must disclose the name and address of any successor in interest known to him and he is liable for any loss caused to the debtor as a result of failure to disclose. A successor in interest is not subject to this section until a request is received by him.

(3) A debtor is entitled to such a statement once every six months without charge. The secured party may require payment of a charge not exceeding $10 for each additional statement furnished.

PART 3 Rights of Third Parties; Perfected and Unperfected Security Interests; Rules of Priority

§ 9–301. Persons Who Take Priority Over Unperfected Security Interests; Rights of "Lien Creditor".

(1) Except as otherwise provided in subsection (2), an unperfected security interest is subordinate to the rights of

(a) persons entitled to priority under Section 9–312;

(b) a person who becomes a lien creditor before the security interest is perfected;

(c) in the case of goods, instruments, documents, and chattel paper, a person who is not a secured party and who is a transferee in bulk or other buyer not in ordinary course of business or is a buyer of farm products in ordinary course of business, to the extent that he gives value and receives delivery of the collateral without knowledge of the security interest and before it is perfected;

(d) in the case of accounts and general intangibles, a person who is not a secured party and who is a transferee to the extent that he gives value without knowledge of the security interest and before it is perfected.

(2) If the secured party files with respect to a purchase money se-curity interest before or within ten days after the debtor receives possession of the collateral, he takes priority over the rights of a transferee in bulk or of a lien creditor which arise be-tween the time the security interest attaches and the time of filing.

(3) A "lien creditor" means a creditor who has acquired a lien on the property involved by attachment, levy or the like and in-cludes an assignee for benefit of creditors from the time of assignment, and a trustee in bankruptcy from the date of the filing of the petition or a receiver in equity from the time of appointment.

(4) A person who becomes a lien creditor while a security interest is perfected takes subject to the security interest only to the extent that it secures advances made before he becomes a lien creditor or within 45 days thereafter or made without knowledge of the lien or pursuant to a commitment entered into without knowledge of the lien.

§ 9–302. When Filing Is Required to Perfect Security Interest; Security Interests to Which Filing Provisions of This Article Do Not Apply.

(1) A financing statement must be filed to perfect all security interests except the following:

(a) a security interest in collateral in possession of the secured party under Section 9–305;

(b) a security interest temporarily perfected in instruments or documents without delivery under Section 9–304 or in proceeds for a 10 day period under Section 9–306;

(c) a security interest created by an assignment of a beneficial interest in a trust or a decedent's estate;

(d) a purchase money security interest in consumer goods; but filing is required for a motor vehicle required to be registered; and fixture filing is required for priority over conflicting interests in fixtures to the extent provided in Section 9–313;

(e) an assignment of accounts which does not alone or in conjunction with other assignments to the same assignee transfer a significant part of the outstanding accounts of the assignor;

(f) a security interest of a collecting bank (Section 4–210) or in securities (Section 8–321) or arising under the Articles on Sales and Leases (see Section 9–113) or covered in subsection (3) of this section;

(g) an assignment for the benefit of all the creditors of the transferor, and subsequent transfers by the assignee thereunder.

(2) If a secured party assigns a perfected security interest, no filing under this Article is required in order to continue the perfected status of the security interest against creditors of and transferees from the original debtor.

(3) The filing of a financing statement otherwise required by this Article is not necessary or effective to perfect a security interest in property subject to

(a) a statute or treaty of the United States which provides for a national or international registration or a national or international certificate of title or which specifies a place of filing different from that specified in this Article for filing of the security interest; or

(b) the following statutes of this state; [list any certificate of title statute covering automobiles, trailers, mobile homes, boats, farm tractors, or the like, and any central filing statute]; but during any period in which collateral is inventory held for sale by a person who is in the business of selling goods of that kind, the filing provisions of this Article (Part 4) apply to a security interest in that collateral created by him as debtor; or

(c) a certificate of title statute of another jurisdiction under the law of which indication of a security interest on the certificate is required as a condition of perfection (subsection (2) of Section 9–103).

(4) Compliance with a statute or treaty described in subsection (3) is equivalent to the filing of a financing statement under this Article, and a security interest in property subject to the statute or treaty can be perfected only by compliance therewith except as provided in Section 9–103 on multiple state transactions. Duration and renewal of perfection of a security interest perfected by compliance with the statute or treaty are governed by the provisions of the statute or treaty; in other respects the security interest is subject to this Article.

Amended in 1972 and 1977.

§ 9–303. When Security Interest Is Perfected; Continuity of Perfection.

(1) A security interest is perfected when it has attached and when all of the applicable steps required for perfection have been taken. Such steps are specified in Sections 9–302, 9–304, 9–305 and 9–306. If such steps are taken before the security interest attaches, it is perfected at the time when it attaches.

(2) If a security interest is originally perfected in any way permitted under this Article and is subsequently perfected in some other way under this Article, without an intermediate period when it was unperfected, the security interest shall be deemed to be perfected continuously for the purposes of this Article.

§ 9–304. Perfection of Security Interest in Instruments, Documents, and Goods Covered by Documents; Perfection by Permissive Filing; Temporary Perfection Without Filing or Transfer of Possession.

(1) A security interest in chattel paper or negotiable documents may be perfected by filing. A security interest in money or instruments (other than certificated securities or instruments which constitute part of chattel paper) can be perfected only by the secured party's taking possession, except as provided in subsections (4) and (5) of this section and subsections (2) and (3) of Section 9–306 on proceeds.

(2) During the period that goods are in the possession of the issuer of a negotiable document therefor, a security interest in the goods is perfected by perfecting a security interest in the document, and any security interest in the goods otherwise perfected during such period is subject thereto.

(3) A security interest in goods in the possession of a bailee other than one who has issued a negotiable document therefor is perfected by issuance of a document in the name of the secured party or by the bailee's receipt of notification of the secured party's interest or by filing as to the goods.

(4) A security interest in instruments (other than certificated securities) or negotiable documents is perfected without filing or the taking of possession for a period of 21 days from the time it attaches to the extent that it arises for new value given under a written security agreement.

(5) A security interest remains perfected for a period of 21 days without filing where a secured party having a perfected security interest in an instrument (other than a certificated security), a negotiable document or goods in possession of a bailee other than one who has issued a negotiable document therefor

(a) makes available to the debtor the goods or documents representing the goods for the purpose of ultimate sale or exchange or for the purpose of loading, unloading, storing, shipping, transshipping, manufacturing, processing or otherwise dealing with them in a manner preliminary to their sale or exchange, but priority between conflicting security interests in the goods is subject to subsection (3) of Section 9–312; or

(b) delivers the instrument to the debtor for the purpose of ultimate sale or exchange or of presentation, collection, renewal or registration of transfer.

(6) After the 21 day period in subsections (4) and (5) perfection depends upon compliance with applicable provisions of this Article.

§ 9–305. When Possession by Secured Party Perfects Security Interest Without Filing.

A security interest in letters of credit and advices of credit (subsection (2)(a) of Section 5–116), goods, instruments (other than certificated securities), money, negotiable documents, or chattel paper may be perfected by the secured party's taking possession of the collateral. If such collateral other than goods covered by a negotiable document is held by a bailee, the secured party is deemed to have possession from the time the bailee receives notification of the secured party's interest. A security interest is perfected by possession from the time possession is taken without a relation back and continues only so long as possession is retained, unless otherwise specified in this Article. The security interest may be otherwise perfected as provided in this Article before or after the period of possession by the secured party.

§ 9–306. "Proceeds"; Secured Party's Rights on Disposition of Collateral.

(1) "Proceeds" includes whatever is received upon the sale, exchange, collection or other disposition of collateral or proceeds. Insurance payable by reason of loss or damage to the collateral is proceeds, except to the extent that it is payable to a person other than a party to the security agreement. Money, checks, deposit accounts, and the like are "cash proceeds". All other proceeds are "non-cash proceeds".

(2) Except where this Article otherwise provides, a security interest continues in collateral notwithstanding sale, exchange or other disposition thereof unless the disposition was authorized by the secured party in the security agreement or otherwise, and also continues in any identifiable proceeds including collections received by the debtor.

(3) The security interest in proceeds is a continuously perfected security interest if the interest in the original collateral was perfected but it ceases to be a perfected security interest and becomes unperfected ten days after receipt of the proceeds by the debtor unless

(a) a filed financing statement covers the original collateral and the proceeds are collateral in which a security interest may be perfected by filing in the office or offices where the financing statement has been filed and, if the proceeds are acquired with cash proceeds, the description of collateral in the financing statement indicates the types of property constituting the proceeds; or

(b) a filed financing statement covers the original collateral and the proceeds are identifiable cash proceeds; or

(c) the security interest in the proceeds is perfected before the expiration of the ten day period.

Except as provided in this section, a security interest in proceeds can be perfected only by the methods or under the circumstances permitted in this Article for original collateral of the same type.

(4) In the event of insolvency proceedings instituted by or against a debtor, a secured party with a perfected security interest in proceeds has a perfected security interest only in the following proceeds:

(a) in identifiable non-cash proceeds and in separate deposit accounts containing only proceeds;

(b) in identifiable cash proceeds in the form of money which is neither commingled with other money nor deposited in a deposit account prior to the insolvency proceedings;

(c) in identifiable cash proceeds in the form of checks and the like which are not deposited in a deposit account prior to the insolvency proceedings; and

(d) in all cash and deposit accounts of the debtor in which proceeds have been commingled with other funds, but the perfected security interest under this paragraph (d) is

(i) subject to any right to set-off; and

(ii) limited to an amount not greater than the amount of any cash proceeds received by the debtor within ten days before the institution of the insolvency proceedings less the sum of (I) the payments to the secured party on account of cash proceeds received by the debtor during such period and (II) the cash proceeds received by the debtor during such period to which the secured party is entitled under paragraphs (a) through (c) of this subsection (4).

(5) If a sale of goods results in an account or chattel paper which is transferred by the seller to a secured party, and if the goods are returned to or are repossessed by the seller or the secured party, the following rules determine priorities:

(a) If the goods were collateral at the time of sale, for an indebtedness of the seller which is still unpaid, the original security interest attaches again to the goods and continues as a perfected security interest if it was perfected at the time when the goods were sold. If the security interest was originally perfected by a filing which is still effective, nothing further is required to continue the perfected status; in any other case, the secured party must take possession of the returned or repossessed goods or must file.

(b) An unpaid transferee of the chattel paper has a security interest in the goods against the transferor. Such security interest is prior to a security interest asserted under paragraph (a) to the extent that the transferee of the chattel paper was entitled to priority under Section 9–308.

(c) An unpaid transferee of the account has a security interest in the goods against the transferor. Such security interest is subordinate to a security interest asserted under paragraph (a).

(d) A security interest of an unpaid transferee asserted under paragraph (b) or (c) must be perfected for protection against creditors of the transferor and purchasers of the returned or repossessed goods.

§ 9–307. Protection of Buyers of Goods.

(1) A buyer in ordinary course of business (subsection (9) of Section 1–201) other than a person buying farm products from a person engaged in farming operations takes free of a security interest created by his seller even though the security interest is perfected and even though the buyer knows of its existence.

(2) In the case of consumer goods, a buyer takes free of a security interest even though perfected if he buys without knowledge of the security interest, for value and for his own personal, family or household purposes unless prior to the purchase the secured party has filed a financing statement covering such goods.

(3) A buyer other than a buyer in ordinary course of business (subsection (1) of this section) takes free of a security interest to the extent that it secures future advances made after the secured party acquires knowledge of the purchase, or more than 45 days after the purchase, whichever first occurs, unless made pursuant to a commitment entered into without knowledge of the purchase and before the expiration of the 45 day period.

§ 9–308. Purchase of Chattel Paper and Instruments.

A purchaser of chattel paper or an instrument who gives new value and takes possession of it in the ordinary course of his business has priority over a security interest in the chattel paper or instrument

(a) which is perfected under Section 9–304 (permissive filing and temporary perfection) or under Section 9–306 (perfection as to proceeds) if he acts without knowledge that the specific paper or instrument is subject to a security interest; or

(b) which is claimed merely as proceeds of inventory subject to a security interest (Section 9–306) even though he knows that the specific paper or instrument is subject to the security interest.

§ 9–309. Protection of Purchasers of Instruments, Documents and Securities.

Nothing in this Article limits the rights of a holder in due course of a negotiable instrument (Section 3–302) or a holder to whom a negotiable document of title has been duly negotiated (Section 7–501) or a bona fide purchaser of a security (Section 8–302) and the holders or purchasers take priority over an earlier security interest even though perfected. Filing under this Article does not constitute notice of the security interest to such holders or purchasers.

§ 9–310. Priority of Certain Liens Arising by Operation of Law.

When a person in the ordinary course of his business furnishes services or materials with respect to goods subject to a security interest, a lien upon goods in the possession of such person given by statute or rule of law for such materials or services takes priority over a perfected security interest unless the lien is statutory and the statute expressly provides otherwise.

§ 9–311. Alienability of Debtor's Rights: Judicial Process.

The debtor's rights in collateral may be voluntarily or involuntarily transferred (by way of sale, creation of a security in-terest, attachment, levy, garnishment or other judicial process) notwithstanding a provision in the security agreement prohibiting any transfer or making the transfer constitute a default.

§ 9–312. Priorities Among Conflicting Security Interests in the Same Collateral.

(1) The rules of priority stated in other sections of this Part and in the following sections shall govern when applicable: Section 4–208 with respect to the security interests of collecting banks in items being collected, accompanying documents and proceeds; Section 9–103 on security interests related to other jurisdictions; Section 9–114 on consignments.

(2) A perfected security interest in crops for new value given to enable the debtor to produce the crops during the production season and given not more than three months before the crops become growing crops by planting or otherwise takes priority over an earlier perfected security interest to the extent that such earlier interest secures obligations due more than six months before the crops become growing crops by planting or otherwise, even though the person giving new value had knowledge of the earlier security interest.

(3) A perfected purchase money security interest in inventory has priority over a conflicting security interest in the same inventory and also has priority in identifiable cash proceeds received on or before the delivery of the inventory to a buyer if

(a) the purchase money security interest is perfected at the time the debtor receives possession of the inventory; and

(b) the purchase money secured party gives notification in writing to the holder of the conflicting security interest if the holder had filed a financing statement covering the same types of inventory (i) before the date of the filing made by the purchase money secured party, or (ii) before the beginning of the 21 day period where the purchase money security interest is temporarily perfected without filing or possession (subsection (5) of Section 9–304); and

(c) the holder of the conflicting security interest receives the notification within five years before the debtor receives possession of the inventory; and

(d) the notification states that the person giving the notice has or expects to acquire a purchase money security interest in inventory of the debtor, describing such inventory by item or type.

(4) A purchase money security interest in collateral other than inventory has priority over a conflicting security interest in the same collateral or its proceeds if the purchase money security interest is perfected at the time the

debtor receives possession of the collateral or within ten days thereafter.

(5) In all cases not governed by other rules stated in this section (including cases of purchase money security interests which do not qualify for the special priorities set forth in subsections (3) and (4) of this section), priority between conflicting security interests in the same collateral shall be determined according to the following rules:

(a) Conflicting security interests rank according to priority in time of filing or perfection. Priority dates from the time a filing is first made covering the collateral or the time the security interest is first perfected, whichever is earlier, provided that there is no period thereafter when there is neither filing nor perfection.

(b) So long as conflicting security interests are unperfected, the first to attach has priority.

(6) For the purposes of subsection (5) a date of filing or perfection as to collateral is also a date of filing or perfection as to proceeds.

(7) If future advances are made while a security interest is perfected by filing, the taking of possession, or under Section 8–321 on securities, the security interest has the same priority for the purposes of subsection (5) with respect to the future advances as it does with respect to the first advance. If a commitment is made before or while the security interest is so perfected, the security interest has the same priority with respect to advances made pursuant thereto. In other cases a perfected security interest has priority from the date the advance is made.

§ 9–313. Priority of Security Interests in Fixtures.

(1) In this section and in the provisions of Part 4 of this Article referring to fixture filing, unless the context otherwise requires

(a) goods are "fixtures" when they become so related to particular real estate that an interest in them arises under real estate law

(b) a "fixture filing" is the filing in the office where a mortgage on the real estate would be filed or recorded of a financing statement covering goods which are or are to become fixtures and conforming to the requirements of subsection (5) of Section 9–402

(c) a mortgage is a "construction mortgage" to the extent that it secures an obligation incurred for the construction of an improvement on land including the acquisition cost of the land, if the recorded writing so indicates.

(2) A security interest under this Article may be created in goods which are fixtures or may continue in goods which become fixtures, but no security interest exists under this Article in ordinary building materials incorporated into an improvement on land.

(3) This Article does not prevent creation of an encumbrance upon fixtures pursuant to real estate law.

(4) A perfected security interest in fixtures has priority over the conflicting interest of an encumbrancer or owner of the real estate where

(a) the security interest is a purchase money security interest, the interest of the encumbrancer or owner arises before the goods become fixtures, the security interest is perfected by a fixture filing before the goods become fixtures or within ten days thereafter, and the debtor has an interest of record in the real estate or is in possession of the real estate; or

(b) the security interest is perfected by a fixture filing before the interest of the encumbrancer or owner is of record, the security interest has priority over any conflicting interest of a predecessor in title of the encumbrancer or owner, and the debtor has an interest of record in the real estate or is in possession of the real estate; or

(c) the fixtures are readily removable factory or office machines or readily removable replacements of domestic appliances which are consumer goods, and before the goods become fixtures the security interest is perfected by any method permitted by this Article; or

(d) the conflicting interest is a lien on the real estate obtained by legal or equitable proceedings after the security interest was perfected by any method permitted by this Article.

(5) A security interest in fixtures, whether or not perfected, has priority over the conflicting interest of an encumbrancer or owner of the real estate where

(a) the encumbrancer or owner has consented in writing to the security interest or has disclaimed an interest in the goods as fixtures; or

(b) the debtor has a right to remove the goods as against the encumbrancer or owner. If the debtor's right terminates, the priority of the security interest continues for a reasonable time.

(6) Notwithstanding paragraph (a) of subsection (4) but otherwise subject to subsections (4) and (5), a security interest in fixtures is subordinate to a construction mortgage recorded before the goods become fixtures if the goods become fixtures before the completion of the construction. To the extent that it is given to refinance a construction mortgage, a mortgage has this priority to the same extent as the construction mortgage.

(7) In cases not within the preceding subsections, a security interest in fixtures is subordinate to the conflicting interest of an encumbrancer or owner of the related real estate who is not the debtor.

(8) When the secured party has priority over all owners and encumbrancers of the real estate, he may, on default, subject to the provisions of Part 5, remove his collateral from the real estate but he must reimburse any encumbrancer or owner of the real estate who is not the debtor and who has not otherwise agreed for the cost of repair of any physical injury, but not for any diminution in value of the real estate caused by the absence of the goods removed or by any necessity of replacing them. A person entitled to reimbursement may refuse permission to remove until the secured party gives adequate security for the performance of this obligation.

§ 9–314. Accessions.

(1) A security interest in goods which attaches before they

are installed in or affixed to other goods takes priority as to the goods installed or affixed (called in this section "accessions") over the claims of all persons to the whole except as stated in subsection (3) and subject to Section 9–315(1).

(2) A security interest which attaches to goods after they become part of a whole is valid against all persons subsequently acquiring interests in the whole except as stated in subsection (3) but is invalid against any person with an interest in the whole at the time the security interest attaches to the goods who has not in writing consented to the security interest or disclaimed an interest in the goods as part of the whole.

(3) The security interests described in subsections (1) and (2) do not take priority over

(a) a subsequent purchaser for value of any interest in the whole; or

(b) a creditor with a lien on the whole subsequently obtained by judicial proceedings; or

(c) a creditor with a prior perfected security interest in the whole to the extent that he makes subsequent advances

if the subsequent purchase is made, the lien by judicial proceedings obtained or the subsequent advance under the prior perfected security interest is made or contracted for without knowledge of the security interest and before it is perfected. A purchaser of the whole at a foreclosure sale other than the holder of a perfected security interest purchasing at his own foreclosure sale is a subsequent purchaser within this section.

(4) When under subsections (1) or (2) and (3) a secured party has an interest in accessions which has priority over the claims of all persons who have interests in the whole, he may on default subject to the provisions of Part 5 remove his collateral from the whole but he must reimburse any encumbrancer or owner of the whole who is not the debtor and who has not otherwise agreed for the cost of repair of any physical injury but not for any diminution in value of the whole caused by the absence of the goods removed or by any necessity for replacing them. A person entitled to reimbursement may refuse permission to remove until the secured party gives adequate security for the performance of this obligation.

§ 9–315. Priority When Goods Are Commingled or Processed.

(1) If a security interest in goods was perfected and subsequently the goods or a part thereof have become part of a product or mass, the security interest continues in the product or mass if

(a) the goods are so manufactured, processed, assembled or commingled that their identity is lost in the product or mass; or

(b) a financing statement covering the original goods also covers the product into which the goods have been manufactured, processed or assembled.

In a case to which paragraph (b) applies, no separate security interest in that part of the original goods which has been manufactured, processed or assembled into the product may be claimed under Section 9–314.

(2) When under subsection (1) more than one security interest attaches to the product or mass, they rank equally according to the ratio that the cost of the goods to which each interest originally attached bears to the cost of the total product or mass.

§ 9–316. Priority Subject to Subordination.

Nothing in this Article prevents subordination by agreement by any person entitled to priority.

§ 9–317. Secured Party Not Obligated on Contract of Debtor.

The mere existence of a security interest or authority given to the debtor to dispose of or use collateral does not impose contract or tort liability upon the secured party for the debtor's acts or omissions.

§ 9–318. Defenses Against Assignee; Modification of Contract After Notification of Assignment; Term Prohibiting Assignment Ineffective; Identification and Proof of Assignment.

(1) Unless an account debtor has made an enforceable agreement not to assert defenses or claims arising out of a sale as provided in Section 9–206 the rights of an assignee are subject to

(a) all the terms of the contract between the account debtor and assignor and any defense or claim arising therefrom; and

(b) any other defense or claim of the account debtor against the assignor which accrues before the account debtor receives notification of the assignment.

(2) So far as the right to payment or a part thereof under an assigned contract has not been fully earned by performance, and notwithstanding notification of the assignment, any modification of or substitution for the contract made in good faith and in accordance with reasonable commercial standards is effective against an assignee unless the account debtor has otherwise agreed but the assignee acquires corresponding rights under the modified or substituted contract. The assignment may provide that such modification or substitution is a breach by the assignor.

(3) The account debtor is authorized to pay the assignor until the account debtor receives notification that the amount due or to become due has been assigned and that payment is to be made to the assignee. A notification which does not reasonably identify the rights assigned is ineffective. If requested by the account debtor, the assignee must seasonably furnish reasonable proof that the assignment has been made and unless he does so the account debtor may pay the assignor.

(4) A term in any contract between an account debtor and an assignor is ineffective if it prohibits assignment of an account or prohibits creation of a security interest in a general intangible for money due or to become due or

requires the account debtor's consent to such assignment or security interest.

PART 4 Filing

§ 9–401. Place of Filing; Erroneous Filing; Removal of Collateral.

First Alternative Subsection (1)

(1) The proper place to file in order to perfect a security interest is as follows:

(a) when the collateral is timber to be cut or is minerals or the like (including oil and gas) or accounts subject to subsection (5) of Section 9–103, or when the financing statement is filed as a fixture filing (Section 9–313) and the collateral is goods which are or are to become fixtures, then in the office where a mortgage on the real estate would be filed or recorded;

(b) in all other cases, in the office of the [Secretary of State].

Second Alternative Subsection (1)

(1) The proper place to file in order to perfect a security interest is as follows:

(a) when the collateral is equipment used in farming operations, or farm products, or accounts or general intangibles arising from or relating to the sale of farm products by a farmer, or consumer goods, then in the office of the ____________ in the county of the debtor's residence or if the debtor is not a resident of this state then in the office of the ____________ in the county where the goods are kept, and in addition when the collateral is crops growing or to be grown in the office of the ____________ in the county where the land is located;

(b) when the collateral is timber to be cut or is minerals or the like (including oil and gas) or accounts subject to subsection (5) of Section 9–103, or when the financing statement is filed as a fixture filing (Section 9–313) and the collateral is goods which are or are to become fixtures, then in the office where a mortgage on the real estate would be filed or recorded;

(c) in all other cases, in the office of the [Secretary of State].

Third Alternative Subsection (1)

(1) The proper place to file in order to perfect a security interest is as follows:

(a) when the collateral is equipment used in farming operations, or farm products, or accounts or general intangibles arising from or relating to the sale of farm products by a farmer, or consumer goods, then in the office of the ____________ in the county of the debtor's residence or if the debtor is not a resident of this state then in the office of the ____________ in the county where the goods are kept, and in addition when the collateral is crops growing or to be grown in the office of the ____________ in the county where the land is located;

(b) when the collateral is timber to be cut or is minerals or the like (including oil and gas) or accounts subject to subsection (5) of Section 9–103, or when the financing statement is filed as a fixture filing (Section 9–313) and the collateral is goods which are or are to become fixtures, then in the office where a mortgage on the real estate would be filed or recorded;

(c) in all other cases, in the office of the [Secretary of State] and in addition, if the debtor has a place of business in only one county of this state, also in the office of ____________ of such county, or, if the debtor has no place of business in this state, but resides in the state, also in the office of ____________ of the county in which he resides.

Note: One of the three alternatives should be selected as subsection (1).

(2) A filing which is made in good faith in an improper place or not in all of the places required by this section is nevertheless effective with regard to any collateral as to which the filing complied with the requirements of this Article and is also effective with regard to collateral covered by the financing statement against any person who has knowledge of the contents of such financing statement.

(3) A filing which is made in the proper place in this state continues effective even though the debtor's residence or place of business or the location of the collateral or its use, whichever controlled the original filing, is thereafter changed.

Alternative Subsection (3)

[(3) A filing which is made in the proper county continues effective for four months after a change to another county of the debtor's residence or place of business or the location of the collateral, whichever controlled the original filing. It becomes ineffective thereafter unless a copy of the financing statement signed by the secured party is filed in the new county within said period. The security interest may also be perfected in the new county after the expiration of the four-month period; in such case perfection dates from the time of perfection in the new county. A change in the use of the collateral does not impair the effectiveness of the original filing.]

(4) The rules stated in Section 9–103 determine whether filing is necessary in this state.

(5) Notwithstanding the preceding subsections, and subject to subsection (3) of Section 9–302, the proper place to file in order to perfect a security interest in collateral, including fixtures, of a transmitting utility is the office of the [Secretary of State]. This filing constitutes a fixture filing (Section 9–313) as to the collateral described therein which is or is to become fixtures.

(6) For the purposes of this section, the residence of an organization is its place of business if it has one or its chief executive office if it has more than one place of business.

Note: *Subsection (6) should be used only if the state chooses the Second or Third Alternative Subsection (1).*

§ 9–402. Formal Requisites of Financing Statement; Amendments; Mortgage as Financing Statement.

(1) A financing statement is sufficient if it gives the names of the debtor and the secured party, is signed by the debtor, gives an address of the secured party from which information concerning the security interest may be obtained, gives a mailing address of the debtor and contains a statement indicating the types, or describing the items, of collateral. A financing statement may be filed before a security agreement is made or a security interest otherwise attaches. When the financing statement covers crops growing or to be grown, the statement must also contain a description of the real estate concerned. When the financing statement covers timber to be cut or covers minerals or the like (including oil and gas) or accounts subject to subsection (5) of Section 9–103, or when the financing statement is filed as a fixture filing (Section 9–313) and the collateral is goods which are or are to become fixtures, the statement must also comply with subsection (5). A copy of the security agreement is sufficient as a financing statement if it contains the above information and is signed by the debtor. A carbon, photographic or other reproduction of a security agreement or a financing statement is sufficient as a financing statement if the security agreement so provides or if the original has been filed in this state.

(2) A financing statement which otherwise complies with subsection (1) is sufficient when it is signed by the secured party instead of the debtor if it is filed to perfect a security interest in

(a) collateral already subject to a security interest in another jurisdiction when it is brought into this state, or when the debtor's location is changed to this state. Such a financing statement must state that the collateral was brought into this state or that the debtor's location was changed to this state under such circumstances; or

(b) proceeds under Section 9–306 if the security interest in the original collateral was perfected. Such a financing statement must describe the original collateral; or

(c) collateral as to which the filing has lapsed; or

(d) collateral acquired after a change of name, identity or corporate structure of the debtor (subsection (7)).

(3) A form substantially as follows is sufficient to comply with subsection (1):

Name of debtor (or assignor) ____________________
Address ____________________
Name of secured party (or assignee) ____________________
Address ____________________
1. This financing statement covers the following types (or items) of property:
(Describe) ____________________
2. (If collateral is crops) The above described crops are growing or are to be grown on:
(Describe Real Estate) ____________________

3. (If applicable) The above goods are to become fixtures on*

*Where appropriate substitute either "The above timber is standing on ____________" or "The above minerals or the like (including oil and gas) or accounts will be financed at the wellhead or minehead of the well or mine located on ____________"

(Describe Real Estate) ____________ and this financing statement is to be filed [for record] in the real estate records. (If the debtor does not have an interest of record) The name of a record owner is____________________

4. (If products of collateral are claimed) Products of the collateral are also covered.

(use	
	____________________
whichever is	Signature of Debtor (or Assignor)
	____________________
applicable)	Signature of Secured Party (or Assignee)

(4) A financing statement may be amended by filing a writing signed by both the debtor and the secured party. An amendment does not extend the period of effectiveness of a financing statement. If any amendment adds collateral, it is effective as to the added collateral only from the filing date of the amendment. In this Article, unless the context otherwise requires, the term "financing statement" means the original financing statement and any amendments.

(5) A financing statement covering timber to be cut or covering minerals or the like (including oil and gas) or accounts subject to subsection (5) of Section 9–103, or a financing statement filed as a fixture filing (Section 9–313) where the debtor is not a transmitting utility, must show that it covers this type of collateral, must recite that it is to be filed [for record] in the real estate records, and the financing statement must contain a description of the real estate [sufficient if it were contained in a mortgage of the real estate to give constructive notice of the mortgage under the law of this state]. If the debtor does not have an interest of record in the real estate, the financing statement must show the name of a record owner.

(6) A mortgage is effective as a financing statement filed as a fixture filing from the date of its recording if

(a) the goods are described in the mortgage by item or type; and

(b) the goods are or are to become fixtures related to the real estate described in the mortgage; and

(c) the mortgage complies with the requirements for a financing statement in this section other than a recital that it is to be filed in the real estate records; and

(d) the mortgage is duly recorded.

No fee with reference to the financing statement is required other than the regular recording and satisfaction fees with respect to the mortgage.

(7) A financing statement sufficiently shows the name of the debtor if it gives the individual, partnership or corporate name of the debtor, whether or not it adds other trade names or names of partners. Where the debtor so changes his name or in the case of an organization its name, identity or corporate structure that a filed financing statement becomes seriously misleading, the filing is not effective to

perfect a security interest in collateral acquired by the debtor more than four months after the change, unless a new appropriate financing statement is filed before the expiration of that time. A filed financing statement remains effective with respect to collateral transferred by the debtor even though the secured party knows of or consents to the transfer.

(8) A financing statement substantially complying with the requirements of this section is effective even though it contains minor errors which are not seriously misleading.

Note: Language in brackets is optional.

Note: Where the state has any special recording system for real estate other than the usual grantor-grantee index (as, for instance, a tract system or a title registration or Torrens system) local adaptations of subsection (5) and Section 9–403(7) may be necessary. See Mass.Gen.Laws Chapter 106, Section 9–409.

§ 9–403. What Constitutes Filing; Duration of Filing; Effect of Lapsed Filing; Duties of Filing Officer.

(1) Presentation for filing of a financing statement and tender of the filing fee or acceptance of the statement by the filing officer constitutes filing under this Article.

(2) Except as provided in subsection (6) a filed financing statement is effective for a period of five years from the date of filing. The effectiveness of a filed financing statement lapses on the expiration of the five year period unless a continuation statement is filed prior to the lapse. If a security interest perfected by filing exists at the time insolvency proceedings are commenced by or against the debtor, the security interest remains perfected until termination of the insolvency proceedings and thereafter for a period of sixty days or until expiration of the five year period, whichever occurs later. Upon lapse the security interest becomes unperfected, unless it is perfected without filing. If the security interest becomes unperfected upon lapse, it is deemed to have been unperfected as against a person who became a purchaser or lien creditor before lapse.

(3) A continuation statement may be filed by the secured party within six months prior to the expiration of the five year period specified in subsection (2). Any such continuation statement must be signed by the secured party, identify the original statement by file number and state that the original statement is still effective. A continuation statement signed by a person other than the secured party of record must be accompanied by a separate written statement of assignment signed by the secured party of record and complying with subsection (2) of Section 9–405, including payment of the required fee. Upon timely filing of the continuation statement, the effectiveness of the original statement is continued for five years after the last date to which the filing was effective whereupon it lapses in the same manner as provided in subsection (2) unless another continuation statement is filed prior to such lapse. Succeeding continuation statements may be filed in the same manner to continue the effectiveness of the original statement. Unless a statute on disposition of public records provides otherwise, the filing officer may remove a lapsed statement from the files and destroy it immediately if he has retained a microfilm or other photographic record, or in other cases after one year after the lapse. The filing officer shall so arrange matters by physical annexation of financing statements to continuation statements or other related filings, or by other means, that if he physically destroys the financing statements of a period more than five years past, those which have been continued by a continuation statement or which are still effective under subsection (6) shall be retained.

(4) Except as provided in subsection (7) a filing officer shall mark each statement with a file number and with the date and hour of filing and shall hold the statement or a microfilm or other photographic copy thereof for public inspection. In addition the filing officer shall index the statement according to the name of the debtor and shall note in the index the file number and the address of the debtor given in the statement.

(5) The uniform fee for filing and indexing and for stamping a copy furnished by the secured party to show the date and place of filing for an original financing statement or for a continuation statement shall be $____________ if the statement is in the standard form prescribed by the [Secretary of State] and otherwise shall be $____________, plus in each case, if the financing statement is subject to subsection (5) of Section 9–402, $____________. The uniform fee for each name more than one required to be indexed shall be $____________. The secured party may at his option show a trade name for any person and an extra uniform indexing fee of $____________; shall be paid with respect thereto.

(6) If the debtor is a transmitting utility (subsection (5) of Section 9–401) and a filed financing statement so states, it is effective until a termination statement is filed. A real estate mortgage which is effective as a fixture filing under subsection (6) of Section 9–402 remains effective as a fixture filing until the mortgage is released or satisfied of record or its effectiveness otherwise terminates as to the real estate.

(7) When a financing statement covers timber to be cut or covers minerals or the like (including oil and gas) or accounts subject to subsection (5) of Section 9–103, or is filed as a fixture filing, [it shall be filed for record and] the filing officer shall index it under the names of the debtor and any owner of record shown on the financing statement in the same fashion as if they were the mortgagors in a mortgage of the real estate described, and, to the extent that the law of this state provides for indexing of mortgages under the name of the mortgagee, under the name of the secured party as if he were the mortgagee thereunder, or where indexing is by description in the same fashion as if the financing statement were a mortgage of the real estate described.

Note: In states in which writings will not appear in the real estate records and indices unless actually recorded the bracketed language in subsection (7) should be used.

§ 9-404. Termination Statement.

(1) If a financing statement covering consumer goods is filed on or after ____________, then within one month or within ten days following written demand by the debtor after there is no outstanding secured obligation and no commitment to make advances, incur obligations or otherwise give value, the secured party must file with each filing officer with whom the financing statement was filed, a termination statement to the effect that he no longer claims a security interest under the financing statement, which shall be identified by file number. In other cases whenever there is no outstanding secured obligation and no commitment to make advances, incur obligations or otherwise give value, the secured party must on written demand by the debtor send the debtor, for each filing officer with whom the financing statement was filed, a termination statement to the effect that he no longer claims a security interest under the financing statement, which shall be identified by file number. A termination statement signed by a person other than the secured party of record must be accompanied by a separate written statement of assignment signed by the secured party of record complying with subsection (2) of Section 9-405, including payment of the required fee. If the affected secured party fails to file such a termination statement as required by this subsection, or to send such a termination statement within ten days after proper demand therefor, he shall be liable to the debtor for one hundred dollars, and in addition for any loss caused to the debtor by such failure.

(2) On presentation to the filing officer of such a termination statement he must note it in the index. If he has received the termination statement in duplicate, he shall return one copy of the termination statement to the secured party stamped to show the time of receipt thereof. If the filing officer has a microfilm or other photographic record of the financing statement, and of any related continuation statement, statement of assignment and statement of release, he may remove the originals from the files at any time after receipt of the termination statement, or if he has no such record, he may remove them from the files at any time after one year after receipt of the termination statement.

(3) If the termination statement is in the standard form prescribed by the [Secretary of State], the uniform fee for filing and indexing the termination statement shall be $____________, and otherwise shall be $____________, plus in each case an additional fee of $____________ for each name more than one against which the termination statement is required to be indexed.

> **Note:** *The date to be inserted should be the effective date of the revised Article 9.*

§ 9-405. Assignment of Security Interest; Duties of Filing Officer; Fees.

(1) A financing statement may disclose an assignment of a security interest in the collateral described in the financing statement by indication in the financing statement of the name and address of the assignee or by an assignment itself or a copy thereof on the face or back of the statement. On presentation to the filing officer of such a financing statement the filing officer shall mark the same as provided in Section 9-403(4). The uniform fee for filing, indexing and furnishing filing data for a financing statement so indicating an assignment shall be $____________ if the statement is in the standard form prescribed by the [Secretary of State] and otherwise shall be $____________, plus in each case an additional fee of $____________ for each name more than one against which the financing statement is required to be indexed.

(2) A secured party may assign of record all or part of his rights under a financing statement by the filing in the place where the original financing statement was filed of a separate written statement of assignment signed by the secured party of record and setting forth the name of the secured party of record and the debtor, the file number and the date of filing of the financing statement and the name and address of the assignee and containing a description of the collateral assigned. A copy of the assignment is sufficient as a separate statement if it complies with the preceding sentence. On presentation to the filing officer of such a separate statement, the filing officer shall mark such separate statement with the date and hour of the filing. He shall note the assignment on the index of the financing statement, or in the case of a fixture filing, or a filing covering timber to be cut, or covering minerals or the like (including oil and gas) or accounts subject to subsection (5) of Section 9-103, he shall index the assignment under the name of the assignor as grantor and, to the extent that the law of this state provides for indexing the assignment of a mortgage under the name of the assignee, he shall index the assignment of the financing statement under the name of the assignee. The uniform fee for filing, indexing and furnishing filing data about such a separate statement of assignment shall be $____________ if the statement is in the standard form prescribed by the [Secretary of State] and otherwise shall be $____________, plus in each case an additional fee of $____________; for each name more than one against which the statement of assignment is required to be indexed. Notwithstanding the provisions of this subsection, an assignment of record of a security interest in a fixture contained in a mortgage effective as a fixture filing (subsection (6) of Section 9-402) may be made only by an assignment of the mortgage in the manner provided by the law of this state other than this Act.

(3) After the disclosure or filing of an assignment under this section, the assignee is the secured party of record.

§ 9-406. Release of Collateral; Duties of Filing Officer; Fees.

A secured party of record may by his signed statement release all or a part of any collateral described in a filed financing statement. The statement of release is sufficient if it contains a description of the collateral being released, the name and address of the debtor, the name and address of the secured party, and the file number of the financing statement. A statement of release signed by a person other than the secured party of record must be accompanied by a separate written statement of assignment signed by the secured party of record and complying with subsection (2) of Section 9–405, including payment of the required fee. Upon presentation of such a statement of release to the filing officer he shall mark the statement with the hour and date of filing and shall note the same upon the margin of the index of the filing of the financing statement. The uniform fee for filing and noting such a statement of release shall be $____________ if the statement is in the standard form prescribed by the [Secretary of State] and otherwise shall be $____________, plus in each case an additional fee of $____________ for each name more than one against which the statement of release is required to be indexed.

[§ 9–407. Information From Filing Officer].

[(1) If the person filing any financing statement, termination state-ment, statement of assignment, or statement of release, furnishes the filing officer a copy thereof, the filing officer shall upon re-quest note upon the copy the file number and date and hour of the filing of the original and deliver or send the copy to such person.]

[(2) Upon request of any person, the filing officer shall issue his certificate showing whether there is on file on the date and hour stated therein, any presently effective financing statement naming a particular debtor and any statement of assignment thereof and if there is, giving the date and hour of filing of each such statement and the names and addresses of each secured party therein. The uniform fee for such a certificate shall be $____________ if the request for the certificate is in the standard form prescribed by the [Secretary of State] and otherwise shall be $____________. Upon request the filing officer shall furnish a copy of any filed financing statement or statement of assignment for a uniform fee of $____________ per page.]

Note: This section is proposed as an optional provision to require filing officers to furnish certificates. Local law and practices should be consulted with regard to the advisability of adoption.

§ 9–408. Financing Statements Covering Consigned or Leased Goods.

A consignor or lessor of goods may file a financing statement using the terms "consignor," "consignee," "lessor," "lessee" or the like instead of the terms specified in Section 9–402. The provisions of this Part shall apply as appropriate to such a financing statement but its filing shall not of itself be a factor in determining whether or not the consignment or lease is intended as security (Section 1–201(37)). However, if it is determined for other reasons that the consignment or lease is so intended, a security interest of the consignor or lessor which attaches to the consigned or leased goods is perfected by such filing.

PART 5 Default

§ 9–501. Default; Procedure When Security Agreement Covers Both Real and Personal Property.

(1) When a debtor is in default under a security agreement, a secured party has the rights and remedies provided in this Part and except as limited by subsection (3) those provided in the security agreement. He may reduce his claim to judgment, foreclose or otherwise enforce the security interest by any available judicial procedure. If the collateral is documents the secured party may proceed either as to the documents or as to the goods covered thereby. A secured party in possession has the rights, remedies and duties provided in Section 9–207. The rights and remedies referred to in this subsection are cumulative.

(2) After default, the debtor has the rights and remedies provided in this Part, those provided in the security agreement and those provided in Section 9–207.

(3) To the extent that they give rights to the debtor and impose duties on the secured party, the rules stated in the subsections referred to below may not be waived or varied except as provided with respect to compulsory disposition of collateral (subsection (3) of Section 9–504 and Section 9–505) and with respect to redemption of collateral (Section 9–506) but the parties may by agreement determine the standards by which the fulfillment of these rights and duties is to be measured if such standards are not manifestly unreasonable:

(a) subsection (2) of Section 9–502 and subsection (2) of Section 9–504 insofar as they require accounting for surplus proceeds of collateral;

(b) subsection (3) of Section 9–504 and subsection (1) of Section 9–505 which deal with disposition of collateral;

(c) subsection (2) of Section 9–505 which deals with acceptance of collateral as discharge of obligation;

(d) Section 9–506 which deals with redemption of collateral; and

(e) subsection (1) of Section 9–507 which deals with the secured party's liability for failure to comply with this Part.

(4) If the security agreement covers both real and personal property, the secured party may proceed under this Part as to the personal property or he may proceed as to both the real and the personal property in accordance with his rights and remedies in respect of the real property in which case the provisions of this Part do not apply.

(5) When a secured party has reduced his claim to judgment the lien of any levy which may be made upon his collateral by virtue of any execution based upon the judgment shall relate back to the date of the perfection of the security interest in such collateral. A judicial sale, pursuant to such execution, is a foreclosure of the security interest by judicial procedure within the meaning of this section, and the secured party may purchase at the sale and thereafter hold the collateral free of any other requirements of this Article.

§ 9–502. Collection Rights of Secured Party.

(1) When so agreed and in any event on default the secured party is entitled to notify an account debtor or the obligor on an instrument to make payment to him whether or not the assignor was theretofore making collections on the collateral, and also to take control of any proceeds to which he is entitled under Section 9–306.

(2) A secured party who by agreement is entitled to charge back uncollected collateral or otherwise to full or limited recourse against the debtor and who undertakes to collect from the account debtors or obligors must proceed in a commercially reasonable manner and may deduct his reasonable expenses of realization from the collections. If the security agreement secures an indebtedness, the secured party must account to the debtor for any surplus, and unless otherwise agreed, the debtor is liable for any deficiency. But, if the underlying transaction was a sale of accounts or chattel paper, the debtor is entitled to any surplus or is liable for any deficiency only if the security agreement so provides.

§ 9–503. Secured Party's Right to Take Possession After Default.

Unless otherwise agreed a secured party has on default the right to take possession of the collateral. In taking possession a secured party may proceed without judicial process if this can be done without breach of the peace or may proceed by action. If the security agreement so provides the secured party may require the debtor to assemble the collateral and make it available to the secured party at a place to be designated by the secured party which is reasonably convenient to both parties. Without removal a secured party may render equipment unusable, and may dispose of collateral on the debtor's premises under Section 9–504.

§ 9–504. Secured Party's Right to Dispose of Collateral After Default; Effect of Disposition.

(1) A secured party after default may sell, lease or otherwise dispose of any or all of the collateral in its then condition or following any commercially reasonable preparation or processing. Any sale of goods is subject to the Article on Sales (Article 2). The proceeds of disposition shall be applied in the order following to

(a) the reasonable expenses of retaking, holding, preparing for sale or lease, selling, leasing and the like and, to the extent provided for in the agreement and not prohibited by law, the reasonable attorneys' fees and legal expenses incurred by the secured party;

(b) the satisfaction of indebtedness secured by the security interest under which the disposition is made;

(c) the satisfaction of indebtedness secured by any subordinate security interest in the collateral if written notification of demand therefor is received before distribution of the proceeds is completed. If requested by the secured party, the holder of a subordinate security interest must seasonably furnish reasonable proof of his interest, and unless he does so, the secured party need not comply with his demand.

(2) If the security interest secures an indebtedness, the secured party must account to the debtor for any surplus, and, unless otherwise agreed, the debtor is liable for any deficiency. But if the underlying transaction was a sale of accounts or chattel paper, the debtor is entitled to any surplus or is liable for any deficiency only if the security agreement so provides.

(3) Disposition of the collateral may be by public or private proceedings and may be made by way of one or more contracts. Sale or other disposition may be as a unit or in parcels and at any time and place and on any terms but every aspect of the disposition including the method, manner, time, place and terms must be commercially reasonable. Unless collateral is perishable or threatens to decline speedily in value or is of a type customarily sold on a recognized market, reasonable notification of the time and place of any public sale or reasonable notification of the time after which any private sale or other intended disposition is to be made shall be sent by the secured party to the debtor, if he has not signed after default a statement renouncing or modifying his right to notification of sale. In the case of consumer goods no other notification need be sent. In other cases notification shall be sent to any other secured party from whom the secured party has received (before sending his notification to the debtor or before the debtor's renunciation of his rights) written notice of a claim of an interest in the collateral. The secured party may buy at any public sale and if the collateral is of a type customarily sold in a recognized market or is of a type which is the subject of widely distributed standard price quotations he may buy at private sale.

(4) When collateral is disposed of by a secured party after default, the disposition transfers to a purchaser for value all of the debtor's rights therein, discharges the security interest under which it is made and any security interest or lien subordinate thereto. The purchaser takes free of all such rights and interests even though the secured party fails to comply with the requirements of this Part or of any judicial proceedings

(a) in the case of a public sale, if the purchaser has no knowledge of any defects in the sale and if he does not buy in collusion with the secured party, other bidders or the person conducting the sale; or

(b) in any other case, if the purchaser acts in good faith.

(5) A person who is liable to a secured party under a guaranty, indorsement, repurchase agreement or the like and who receives a transfer of collateral from the secured party or is subrogated to his rights has thereafter the rights and duties of the secured party. Such a transfer of collateral is not a sale or disposition of the collateral under this Article.

§ 9–505. Compulsory Disposition of Collateral; Acceptance of the Collateral as Discharge of Obligation.

(1) If the debtor has paid sixty per cent of the cash price in the case of a purchase money security interest in consumer goods or sixty per cent of the loan in the case of

another security interest in consumer goods, and has not signed after default a statement renouncing or modifying his rights under this Part a secured party who has taken possession of collateral must dispose of it under Section 9–504 and if he fails to do so within ninety days after he takes possession the debtor at his option may recover in conversion or under Section 9–507(1) on secured party's liability.

(2) In any other case involving consumer goods or any other collateral a secured party in possession may, after default, propose to retain the collateral in satisfaction of the obligation. Written notice of such proposal shall be sent to the debtor if he has not signed after default a statement renouncing or modifying his rights under this subsection. In the case of consumer goods no other notice need be given. In other cases notice shall be sent to any other secured party from whom the secured party has received (before sending his notice to the debtor or before the debtor's renunciation of his rights) written notice of a claim of an interest in the collateral. If the secured party receives objection in writing from a person entitled to receive notification within twenty-one days after the notice was sent, the secured party must dispose of the collateral under Section 9–504. In the absence of such written objection the secured party may retain the collateral in satisfaction of the debtor's obligation.

§ 9–506. Debtor's Right to Redeem Collateral.

At any time before the secured party has disposed of collateral or entered into a contract for its disposition under Section 9–504 or before the obligation has been discharged under Section 9–505(2) the debtor or any other secured party may unless otherwise agreed in writing after default redeem the collateral by tendering fulfillment of all obligations secured by the collateral as well as the expenses reasonably incurred by the secured party in retaking, holding and preparing the collateral for disposition, in arranging for the sale, and to the extent provided in the agreement and not prohibited by law, his reasonable attorneys' fees and legal expenses.

§ 9–507. Secured Party's Liability for Failure to Comply With This Part.

(1) If it is established that the secured party is not proceeding in accordance with the provisions of this Part disposition may be ordered or restrained on appropriate terms and conditions. If the disposition has occurred the debtor or any person entitled to notification or whose security interest has been made known to the secured party prior to the disposition has a right to recover from the secured party any loss caused by a failure to comply with the provisions of this Part. If the collateral is consumer goods, the debtor has a right to recover in any event an amount not less than the credit service charge plus ten per cent of the principal amount of the debt or the time price differential plus 10 per cent of the cash price.

(2) The fact that a better price could have been obtained by a sale at a different time or in a different method from that selected by the secured party is not of itself sufficient to establish that the sale was not made in a commercially reasonable manner. If the secured party either sells the collateral in the usual manner in any recognized market therefor or if he sells at the price current in such market at the time of his sale or if he has otherwise sold in conformity with reasonable commercial practices among dealers in the type of property sold he has sold in a commercially reasonable manner. The principles stated in the two preceding sentences with respect to sales also apply as may be appropriate to other types of disposition. A disposition which has been approved in any judicial proceeding or by any bona fide creditors' committee or representative of creditors shall conclusively be deemed to be commercially reasonable, but this sentence does not indicate that any such approval must be obtained in any case nor does it indicate that any disposition not so approved is not commercially reasonable.

ARTICLE 10

EFFECTIVE DATE AND REPEALER

§ 10–101. Effective Date.

This Act shall become effective at midnight on December 31st following its enactment. It applies to transactions entered into and events occurring after that date.

§ 10–102. Specific Repealer; Provision for Transition.

(1) The following acts and all other acts and parts of acts inconsistent herewith are hereby repealed: (Here should follow the acts to be specifically repealed including the following:

Uniform Negotiable Instruments Act
Uniform Warehouse Receipts Act
Uniform Sales Act
Uniform Bills of Lading Act
Uniform Stock Transfer Act
Uniform Conditional Sales Act
Uniform Trust Receipts Act
Also any acts regulating:
Bank collections
Bulk sales
Chattel mortgages
Conditional sales
Factor's lien acts
Farm storage of grain and similar acts
Assignment of accounts receivable)

(2) Transactions validly entered into before the effective date specified in Section 10–101 and the rights, duties and interests flowing from them remain valid thereafter and may be terminated, completed, consummated or enforced as required or permitted by any statute or other law amended or repealed by this Act as though such repeal or amendment had not occurred.

Note: *Subsection (1) should be separately prepared for each state. The foregoing is a list of statutes to be checked.*

§ 10–103. General Repealer.

Except as provided in the following section, all acts and parts of acts inconsistent with this Act are hereby repealed.

§ 10–104. Laws Not Repealed.

(1) The Article on Documents of Title (Article 7) does not repeal or modify any laws prescribing the form or contents of documents of title or the services or facilities to be afforded by bailees, or otherwise regulating bailees' businesses in respects not specifically dealt with herein; but the fact that such laws are violated does not affect the status of a document of title which otherwise complies with the definition of a document of title (Section 1–201).

[(2) This Act does not repeal ____________ *, cited as the Uniform Act for the Simplification of Fiduciary Security Transfers, and if in any respect there is any inconsistency between that Act and the Article of this Act on investment securities (Article 8) the provisions of the former Act shall control.]

> *Note: At * in subsection (2) insert the statutory reference to the Uniform Act for the Simplification of Fiduciary Security Transfers if such Act has previously been enacted. If it has not been enacted, omit subsection (2).*

ARTICLE 11
(REPORTERS' DRAFT) EFFECTIVE DATE AND TRASITION PROVISIONS

This material has been numbered Article 11 to distinguish it from Article 10, the transition provision of the 1962 Code, which may still remain in effect in some states to cover transition problems from pre-Code law to the original Uniform Commercial Code. Adaptation may be necessary in particular states. The terms "[old Code]" and "[new Code]" and "[old U.C.C.]" and "[new U.C.C.]" are used herein, and should be suitably changed in each state.

> *Note: This draft was prepared by the Reporters and has not been passed upon by the Review Committee, the Permanent Editorial Board, the American Law Institute, or the National Conference of Commissioners on Uniform State Laws. It is submitted as a working draft which may be adapted as appropriate in each state.*

§ 11–101. Effective Date.

This Act shall become effective at 12:01 A.M. on ____________, 19 ____________.

§ 11–102. Preservation of Old Transition Provision.

The provisions of [here insert reference to the original transition provision in the particular state] shall continue to apply to [the new U.C.C.] and for this purpose the [old U.C.C. and new U.C.C.] shall be considered one continuous statute.

§ 11–103. Transition to [New Code]—General Rule.

Transactions validly entered into after [effective date of old U.C.C.] and before [effective date of new U.C.C.], and which were subject to the provisions of [old U.C.C.] and which would be subject to this Act as amended if they had been entered into after the effective date of [new U.C.C.] and the rights, duties and interests flowing from such transactions remain valid after the latter date and may be terminated, completed, consummated or enforced as required or permitted by the [new U.C.C.]. Security interests arising out of such transactions which are perfected when [new U.C.C.] becomes effective shall remain perfected until they lapse as provided in [new U.C.C.], and may be continued as permitted by [new U.C.C.], except as stated in Section 11–105.

§ 11–104. Transition Provision on Change of Requirement of Filing.

A security interest for the perfection of which filing or the taking of possession was required under [old U.C.C.] and which attached prior to the effective date of [new U.C.C.] but was not perfected shall be deemed perfected on the effective date of [new U.C.C.] if [new U.C.C.] permits perfection without filing or authorizes filing in the office or offices where a prior ineffective filing was made.

§ 11–105. Transition Provision on Change of Place of Filing.

(1) A financing statement or continuation statement filed prior to [effective date of new U.C.C.] which shall not have lapsed prior to [the effective date of new U.C.C.] which shall remain effective for the period provided in the [old Code], but not less than five years after the filing.

(2) With respect to any collateral acquired by the debtor subsequent to the effective date of [new U.C.C.], any effective financing statement or continuation statement described in this section shall apply only if the filing or filings are in the office or offices that would be appropriate to perfect the security interests in the new collateral under [new U.C.C.].

(3) The effectiveness of any financing statement or continuation statement filed prior to [effective date of new U.C.C.] may be continued by a continuation statement as permitted by [new U.C.C.], except that if [new U.C.C.] requires a filing in an office where there was no previous financing statement, a new financing statement conforming to Section 11–106 shall be filed in that office.

(4) If the record of a mortgage of real estate would have been effective as a fixture filing of goods described therein if [new U.C.C.] had been in effect on the date of recording the mortgage, the mortgage shall be deemed effective as a fixture filing as to such goods under subsection (6) of Section 9–402 of the [new U.C.C.] on the effective date of [new U.C.C.].

§ 11–106. Required Refilings.

(1) If a security interest is perfected or has priority when this Act takes effect as to all persons or as to certain persons without any filing or recording, and if the filing of a financing statement would be required for the perfection

or priority of the security interest against those persons under [new U.C.C.], the perfection and priority rights of the security interest continue until 3 years after the effective date of [new U.C.C.]. The perfection will then lapse unless a financing statement is filed as provided in subsection (4) or unless the security interest is perfected otherwise than by filing.

(2) If a security interest is perfected when [new U.C.C.] takes effect under a law other than [U.C.C.] which requires no further filing, refiling or recording to continue its perfection, perfection continues until and will lapse 3 years after [new U.C.C.] takes effect, unless a financing statement is filed as provided in subsection (4) or unless the security interest is perfected otherwise than by filing, or unless under subsection (3) of Section 9–302 the other law continues to govern filing.

(3) If a security interest is perfected by a filing, refiling or recording under a law repealed by this Act which required further filing, refiling or recording to continue its perfection, perfection continues and will lapse on the date provided by the law so repealed for such further filing, refiling, or recording unless a financing statement is filed as provided in subsection (4) or unless the security interest is perfected otherwise than by filing.

(4) A financing statement may be filed within six months before the perfection of a security interest would otherwise lapse. Any such financing statement may be signed by either the debtor or the secured party. It must identify the security agreement, statement or notice (however denominated in any statute or other law repealed or modified by this Act), state the office where and the date when the last filing, refiling or recording, if any, was made with respect thereto, and the filing number, if any, or book and page, if any, of recording and further state that the security agreement, statement or notice, however denominated, in another filing office under the [U.C.C.] or under any statute or other law repealed or modified by this Act is still effective. Section 9–401 and Section 9–103 determine the proper place to file such a financing statement. Except as specified in this subsection, the provisions of Section 9–403(3) for continuation statements apply to such a financing statement.

§ 11–107. Transition Provisions as to Priorities.

Except as otherwise provided in [Article 11], [old U.C.C.] shall apply to any questions of priority if the positions of the parties were fixed prior to the effective date of [new U.C.C.]. In other cases questions of priority shall be determined by [new U.C.C.].

§ 11–108. Presumption that Rule of Law Continues Unchanged.

Unless a change in law has clearly been made, the provisions of [new U.C.C.] shall be deemed declaratory of the meaning of the [old U.C.C.].

GLOSSARY

Accounts Any right to receive payment for goods sold or leased, other than rights covered by chattel paper or instruments. (Chapter 12)

Accredited investor Under the Securities Act of 1933, an accredited investor is an institution (such as a bank or insurance company) or any individual with a net worth of more than $1 million or an annual income of more than $200,000. (Chapter 18)

Acquit To find the defendant not guilty of the crime for which he was tried. (Chapter 7)

Act of State doctrine A rule requiring American courts to abstain from cases if a court order would interfere with the ability of the President or Congress to conduct foreign policy. (Chapter 8)

Actus reus The guilty act. The prosecution must show that a criminal defendant committed some proscribed act. In a murder prosecution, taking another person's life is the actus reus. (Chapter 7)

Adjudicate To hold a formal hearing in a disputed matter and issue an official decision. (Chapter 4)

Administrative law Concerns all agencies, boards, commissions, and other entities created by a federal or state legislature and charged with investigating, regulating, and adjudicating a particular industry or issue. (Chapter 1)

Affidavit A written statement signed under oath. (Chapter 7)

Affirm A decision by an appellate court to uphold the judgment of a lower court. (Chapter 3)

After-acquired property Items that a debtor obtains after making a security agreement with the secured party. (Chapter 12)

Agent A person who acts for a principal. (Chapter 7, 13)

Alternative dispute resolution Any method of resolving a legal conflict other than litigation, such as: negotiation, arbitration, mediation, mini-trials, and summary jury trials. (Chapter 3)

Annual report Each year, public companies must send their shareholders an annual report that contains detailed financial data. (Chapter 17)

Appellant The party who appeals a lower court decision to a higher court. (Chapter 3)

Appellate court Any court in a state or federal system that reviews cases that have already been tried. (Chapter 3)

Appellee The party opposing an appeal from a lower court to a higher court. (Chapter 3)

Arbitration A form of alternative dispute resolution in which the parties hire a neutral third party to hear their respective arguments, receive evidence, and then make a binding decision. (Chapter 15)

Arson Malicious use of fire or explosives to damage or destroy real estate or personal property. (Chapter 7)

Assignment The act by which a party transfers contract rights to a third person. (Chapter 10)

Assignor The party who assigns contract rights to a third person. (Chapter 16)

Attachment A court order seizing property of a party to a civil action, so that there will be sufficient assets available to pay the judgment. (Chapter 5, 12)

Authorized and unissued stock Stock that has been approved by the corporation's charter, but has not yet been sold. (Chapter 17)

Authorized and issued stock Stock that has been approved by the corporation's charter and subsequently sold. (Chapter 17)

B

Bailee A person who rightfully possesses goods belonging to another. (Chapter 22)

Bailor One who creates a bailment by delivering goods to another. (Chapter 22)

Bilateral contract A binding agreement in which each party has made a promise to the other. (Chapter 9)

Bill A proposed statute that has been submitted for consideration to Congress or a state legislature. (Chapter 4)

Blue sky laws State securities laws. (Chapter 18)

Bona fide occupational qualification A job requirement that would otherwise be discriminatory is permitted in situations in which it is essential to the position in question. (Chapter 14)

Bonds Long-term debt secured by some of the issuing company's assets. (Chapter 17)

Brief The written legal argument that an attorney files with an appeal court. (Chapter 3)

Business judgment rule A common law rule that protects managers from liability if they are acting without a conflict of interest, and make informed decisions that have a rational business purpose. (Chapter 17)

Bylaws A document that specifies the organizational rules of a corporation or other organization, such as the date of the annual meeting and the required number of directors. (Chapter 17)

C

Challenge for cause An attorney's request, during voir dire, to excuse a prospective juror because of apparent bias. (Chapter 3)

Chattel paper Any writing that indicates two things: (1) a debtor owes money and (2) a secured party has a security interest in specific goods. The most common chattel paper is a document indicating a consumer sale on credit. (Chapter 12)

Check An instrument in which the drawer orders the drawee bank to pay money to the payee. (Chapter 11)

Chicago School A theory of antitrust law first developed at the University of Chicago. Adherents to this theory believe that antitrust enforcement should focus on promoting efficiency and should not generally be concerned about the size or number of competitors in any market. (Chapter 19)

Civil law The large body of law concerning the rights and duties between parties. It is distinguished from criminal law, which concerns behavior outlawed by a government. (Chapter 1)

Class action A method of litigating a civil lawsuit in which one or more plaintiffs (or occasionally defendants) seek to represent an entire group of people with similar claims against a common opponent. (Chapter 3)

Classification The process by which the Customs Service decides what label to attach to imported merchandise, and therefore what level of tariff to impose. (Chapter 8)

Close corporation A corporation with a small number of shareholders. Its stock is not publicly traded. (Chapter 16)

Collateral The property subject to a security interest. (Chapter 12)

Collateral promises A promise to pay the debt of another person, as a favor to the debtor. (Chapter 10)

Collective bargaining Contract negotiations between an employer and a union. (Chapter 15)

Comity A doctrine that requires a court to abstain from hearing a case out of respect for another court that also has jurisdiction. International comity demands that an American court refuse to hear a case in which a foreign court shares jurisdiction if there is a conflict between the laws and if it is more logical for the foreign court to take the case. (Chapter 8)

Commerce clause One of the powers granted by Article I, §8 of the Constitution, it gives Congress exclusive power to regulate international commerce and concurrent power with the states to regulate domestic commerce. (Chapter 5)

Common law Judge-made law, that is, the body of all decisions made by appellate courts over the years. (Chapter 1)

Compensatory damages Those that flow directly from the contract. (Chapter 6, 10)

Complaint A pleading, filed by the plaintiff, providing a short statement of the claim. (Chapter 3)

Concerted action Tactics, such as a strike, used by a union to gain a bargaining advantage. (Chapter 15)

Condition A condition is an event that must occur in order for a party to be obligated under a contract. (Chapter 10)

Confiscation Expropriation without adequate compensation of property owned by foreigners. (Chapter 8)

Consent order An agreement entered into by a wrongdoer and an administrative agency (such as the Securities and Exchange Commission or the Federal Trade Commission) in which the wrongdoer agrees not to violate the law in the future. (Chapter 23)

Consequential damages Those resulting from the unique circumstances of this injured party. (Chapter 10)

Contributory negligence A rule of tort law that permits a negligent defendant to escape liability if she can demonstrate that the plaintiff's own conduct contributed in any way to the plaintiff's harm. (Chapter 6)

Control security Stock owned by any officer or director of the issuer, or by any shareholder who holds more than 10 percent of a class of stock of the issuer. (Chapter 18)

Counter-claim A claim made by the defendant against the plaintiff. (Chapter 3)

Cross-examination During a hearing, for a lawyer to question an opposing witness. (Chapter 3)

Damages (1) The harm that a plaintiff complains of at trial, such as an injury to her person, or money lost because of a contract breach. (2) Money awarded by a trial court for injury suffered. (Chapter 13)

De novo The power of an appellate court or appellate agency to make a new decision in a matter under appeal, entirely ignoring the findings and conclusions of the lower court or agency official. (Chapter 4)

Debentures Long-term, unsecured debt, typically issued by a corporation. (Chapter 17)

Debtor A person who owes money or some other obligation to another party. (Chapter 12)

Default The failure to perform an obligation, such as the failure to pay money when due. (Chapter 12)

Default judgment Court order awarding one party everything it requested because the opposing party failed to respond in time. (Chapter 3)

Delegation The act by which a party to a contract transfers duties to a third person who is not a party to the contract. (Chapter 10)

Deponent The person being questioned in a deposition. (Chapter 3)

Direct examination During a hearing, for a lawyer to question his own witness. (Chapter 3)

Directed verdict The decision by a court to instruct a jury that it must find in favor of a particular party because, in the judge's opinion, no reasonable person could disagree on the outcome. (Chapter 3)

Disaffirmance The act of notifying the other party to a contract that the party giving the notice refuses to be bound by the agreement. (Chapter 9)

Discharge (1) A party to a contract has no more duties. (2) A party to an instrument is released from liability. (Chapter 12)

Disclaimer A statement that a particular warranty does not apply. (Chapter 11)

Domestic corporation A corporation is a domestic corporation in the state in which it was formed. (Chapter 17)

Donee A person who receives a gift. (Chapter 22)

Donor A person who makes a gift to another. (Chapter 22)

Draft The drawer of this instrument orders someone else to pay money. Checks are the most common form of draft. The drawer of a check orders a bank to pay money. (Chapter 8, 11)

Drawee The person who pays a draft. In the case of a check, the bank is the drawee. (Chapter 11)

Drawer The person who issues a draft. (Chapter 11)

Due Process Clause Part of the Fifth Amendment. Procedural due process ensures that before depriving anyone of liberty or property, the government must go through procedures which ensure that the deprivation is fair. Substantive due process holds that certain rights, such as privacy, are so fundamental that the government may not eliminate them. (Chapter 7)

Dumping Selling merchandise at one price in the domestic market and at a cheaper, unfair price in an international market. (Chapter 8)

Eminent domain The power of the government to take private property for public use. (Chapter 5)

Employee at will A worker whose job does not have a specified duration. (Chapter 14)

Enabling legislation A statute authorizing the creation of a new administrative agency and specifying its powers and duties. (Chapter 4)

Equal Protection Clause Part of the Fourteenth Amendment, it generally requires the government to treat equally situated people the same. (Chapter 5)

Equity The broad powers of a court to fashion a remedy where justice demands it and no common law remedy exists. An injunction is an example of an equitable remedy. (Chapter 1)

Error of law A mistake made by a trial judge that concerns a legal issue as opposed to a factual matter. Permitting too many leading questions is a legal error; choosing to believe one witness rather than another is a factual matter. (Chapter 3)

Estate The legal entity that holds title to assets after the owner dies and before the property is distributed. (Chapter 22)

Exclusive dealing agreement A potential violation of §1 of the Sherman Act, in which a distributor or retailer agrees with a supplier not to carry the products of any other supplier. (Chapter 19)

Exculpatory clause A contract provision that attempts to release one party from liability in the event the other party is injured. (Chapter 9)

Executed contract A binding agreement in which all parties have fulfilled all obligations. (Chapter 9)

Executory contract A binding agreement in which one or more of the parties has not fulfilled its obligations. (Chapter 9)

Express authority Conduct of a principal that, reasonably interpreted, causes the agent to believe that the principal desires him to do a specific act. (Chapter 13)

Expropriation A government's seizure of property or companies owned by foreigners. (Chapter 8)

Federal question jurisdiction One of the two main types of civil cases that a United States district court has the power to hear. It involves a federal statute or a constitutional provision. (Chapter 3)

Felony The most serious crimes, typically those for which the defendant could be imprisoned for more than a year. (Chapter 7)

Fiduciary duty An obligation to behave in a trustworthy and confidential fashion toward the object of that duty. (Chapter 13)

Financing statement A document that a secured party files to give the general public notice that the secured party has a secured interest in the collateral. (Chapter 12)

Fixtures Goods that are attached to real estate. (Chapter 12)

Foreign corporation A corporation formed in another state. (Chapter 17)

Foreign Sovereign Immunity Act A federal statute that protects other nations from suit in courts of the United States, except under specified circumstances. (Chapter 8)

Fraud Deception of another person to obtain money or property from her. (Chapter 7)

Fundamental rights In constitutional law, those rights that are so basic that any governmental interference with them is suspect and likely to be unconstitutional. (Chapter 5)

GATT See General Agreement on Tariffs and Trade. (Chapter 8)

General deterrence See Deterrence. (Chapter 7)

General intangibles Potential sources of income such as copyrights, patents, trademarks, goodwill and certain other rights to payment. (Chapter 12)

Gift A voluntary transfer of property from one person to another without consideration. (Chapter 22)

Gift causa mortis A gift made in contemplation of approaching death. (Chapter 22)

Goods Anything movable, except for money, securities, and certain legal rights. (Chapter 8, 12)

Grantee The person who receives property, or some interest in it, from the owner. (Chapter 22)

Grantor (1) An owner who conveys property, or some interest in it. (2) Someone who creates a trust. (Chapter 22)

Harmless error A ruling made by a trial court which an appeals court determines was legally wrong but not fatal to the decision. (Chapter 3)

Holder in due course Someone who has given value for an instrument, in good faith, without notice of outstanding claims or other defenses. (Chapter 11)

Illusory promise An apparent promise that is unenforceable because the promisor makes no firm commitment. (Chapter 9)

Indictment The government's formal charge that a defendant has committed a crime. (Chapter 7)

Injunction A court order that a person either do or stop doing something. (Chapter 1)

Integrated contract A writing that the parties intend as the complete and final expression of their agreement. (Chapter 10)

Intentional tort An act deliberately performed that violates a legally imposed duty and injures someone. (Chapter 6)

Inter vivos gift A gift made "during life," that is, when the donor is not under any fear of impending death. (Chapter 22)

Interest A legal right in something, such as ownership or a mortgage or a tenancy. (Chapter 10)

Inventory Goods that the seller is holding for sale or lease in the ordinary course of its business. (Chapter 12)

Issuer The maker of a promissory note or the drawer of a draft. (Chapter 11)

Judicial activism The willingness shown by certain courts (and not by others) to decide issues of public policy, such as constitutional questions (free speech, equal protection, etc.) and matters of contract fairness (promissory estoppel, unconscionability, etc.). (Chapter 5, 9)

Judicial restraint A court's preference to abstain from adjudicating major social issues and to leave such matters to legislatures. (Chapter 5, 9)

Jurisprudence The study of the purposes and philosophies of the law, as opposed to particular provisions of the law. (Chapter 1)

Justification A criminal defense in which the defendant establishes that he broke the law to avoid a greater harm. (Chapter 6)

Letter of credit A commercial device used to guarantee payment in international trade, usually between parties that have not previously worked together. (Chapter 8)

Libel See Defamation. (Chapter 6)

Lien A security interest created by rule of law, often based on labor that the secured party has expended on the collateral. (Chapter 22)

Litigation The process of resolving disputes through formal court proceedings. (Chapter 3)

Maker The issuer of a promissory note. (Chapter 11)

Material Important or significant. Information that would affect a person's decision if he knew it. (Chapter 18)

Mediation The process of using a neutral person to aid in the settlement of a legal dispute. A mediator's decision is non-binding. (Chapter 3)

Mens rea Guilty state of mind. (Chapter 7)

Mini-trial A form of alternative dispute resolution in which the parties present short versions of their cases to a panel of three "judges." (Chapter 3)

Minute book Records of shareholder meetings and directors's meetings are kept in the corporation's minute book. (Chapter 17)

Misdemeanor A less serious crime, typically one for which the maximum penalty is incarceration for less than a year, often in a jail, as opposed to a prison. (Chapter 7)

Misrepresentation A factually incorrect statement made during contract negotiations. (Chapter 9)

Mitigation One party acts to minimize its losses when the other party breaches a contract. (Chapter 10)

Modify An appellate court order changing a lower court ruling. (Chapter 3)

Mortgagee A creditor who obtains a security interest in real property, typically in exchange for money given to the mortgagor to buy the property. (Chapter 22)

Mortgagor A debtor who gives a mortgage (security interest) in real property to a creditor, typically in exchange for money used to buy the property. (Chapter 22)

Motion to suppress A request that the court exclude evidence because it was obtained in violation of the Constitution. (Chapter 7)

Multinational enterprise A corporation that is doing business in more than one country simultaneously. (Chapter 8)

N

NAFTA See North American Free Trade Agreement. (Chapter 8)

National Labor Relations Board (NLRB) The administrative agency charged with overseeing labor law. (Chapter 15)

Nationalization A government's seizure of property or companies. (Chapter 8)

Negligence per se Violation of a standard of care set by statute. Driving while intoxicated is illegal; thus, if a drunk driver injures a pedestrian, he has committed negligence per se. (Chapter 6)

Note An unconditional, written promise that the maker of the instrument will pay a specific amount of money on demand or at a definite time. When issued by a corporation, a note refers to short-term debt, typically payable within five years. (Chapter 11, 17)

Novation If there is an existing contract between A and B, a novation occurs when A agrees to release B from all liability on the contract in return for C's willingness to accept B's liability. (Chapter 17)

O

Obligee The party to a contract who is entitled to receive performance from the other party. (Chapter 10)

Obligor The party to a contract who is required to do something for the benefit of the other party. (Chapter 10, 12)

Offeree The party in contract negotiations who receives the first offer. (Chapter 9)

Offeror The party in contract negotiations who makes the first offer. (Chapter 9)

P

Parol evidence Written or oral evidence, outside the language of a contract, offered by one party to clarify interpretation of the agreement. (Chapter 10)

Partnership at will A partnership that has no fixed duration. A partner has the right to resign from the partnership at any time. (Chapter 16)

Payee Someone who is owed money under the terms of an instrument. (Chapter 11)

Peremptory challenge During voir dire, a request by one attorney that a prospective juror be excused for an unstated reason. (Chapter 3)

Perfection A series of steps a secured party must take to protect its rights in collateral against people other than the debtor. (Chapter 12)

Pleadings The documents that begin a lawsuit: the complaint, the answer, the counter-claim and reply. (Chapter 3)

Precedent An earlier case that decided the same legal issue as that presently in dispute, and which therefore will control the outcome of the current case. (Chapter 1, 4)

Preemption The doctrine, based on the Supremacy Clause, by which any federal statute takes priority whenever (1) a state statute conflicts or (2) there is no conflict but Congress indicated an intention to control the issue involved. (Chapter 5)

Preferred stock Owners of preferred stock have a right to receive dividends and liquidation proceeds of the company before common shareholders. (Chapter 17)

Preponderance of the evidence The level of proof that a plaintiff must meet to prevail in a civil lawsuit. It means that the plaintiff must offer evidence that, in sum, is slightly more persuasive than the defendant's evidence. (Chapter 3)

Prima facie "At first sight." A fact or conclusion that is presumed to be true unless someone presents evidence to disprove it. (Chapter 14)

Principal In an agency relationship, the principal is the person for whom the agent is acting. (Chapter 13)

Private law Refers to the rights and duties between individuals that they themselves have created, for example, by entering into a contract or employment relationship. (Chapter 1)

Probable cause In a search and seizure case, it means that the information available indicates that it is more likely than not that a search will uncover particular criminal evidence. (Chapter 7)

Procedural law The rules establishing how the legal system itself is to operate in a particular kind of case. (Chapter 1)

Proceeds Anything that a debtor obtains from the sale or disposition of collateral. Normally, proceeds refers to cash obtained from the sale of the secured property. (Chapter 12)

Product liability The potential responsibility that a manufacturer or seller has for injuries caused by defective goods. (Chapter 11)

Promissory estoppel A doctrine in which a court may enforce a promise made by the defendant even when there is no contract, if the defendant knew that the plaintiff was likely to rely on the promise, the plaintiff did in fact rely, and enforcement of it is the only way to avoid injustice. (Chapter 9)

Promissory note The maker of the instrument promises to pay a specific amount of money. (Chapter 11)

Promoter The person who creates a corporation by raising capital and undertaking the legal steps necessary for formation. (Chapter 17)

Prospectus Under the Securities Act of 1933, an issuer must provide this document to anyone who purchases a security in a public transaction. The prospectus contains detailed information about the issuer and its business, a description of the stock, and audited financial statements. (Chapter 18)

Proxy (1) A person whom the shareholder designates to vote in his place. (2) The written form (typically a card) that the shareholder uses to appoint a designated voter. (Chapter 17)

Proxy statement When a public company seeks proxy votes from its shareholders, it must include a proxy statement. This statement contains information about the company, such as a detailed description of management compensation. (Chapter 17)

Public law refers to the rights and obligations of governments as they deal with the nation's citizens, for example, by taxing individuals, zoning neighborhoods, and regulating advertisements. (Chapter 1)

Q

Quantum meruit "As much as she deserves." The damages awarded in a quasi-contract case. (Chapter 9)

Quasi-contract A legal fiction in which, to avoid injustice, the court awards damages as if a contract had existed, although one did not. (Chapter 9)

Quorum The number of voters that must be present for a meeting to count. (Chapter 17)

R

Ratification When someone accepts the benefit of an unauthorized transaction or fails to repudiate it once he has learned of it, he is then bound by it. (Chapter 8)

Record date To vote at a shareholders meeting, a shareholder must own stock on the record date. (Chapter 12, 17)

Red herring A preliminary prospectus. (Chapter 18)

Reformation The process by which a court rewrites a contract to ensure its accuracy or viability. (Chapter 10)

Refusal to deal An agreement among competitors that they will not trade with a particular supplier or buyer. Such an agreement is a rule of reason violation of the Sherman Act. (Chapter 19)

Registration statement A document filed with the Securities and Exchange Commission under the Securities Act of 1933 by an issuer seeking to sell securities in a public transaction. (Chapter 18)

Remand The power of an appellate court to return a case to a lower court for additional action. (Chapter 3)

Repossess A secured party takes collateral because the debtor has defaulted on payments. (Chapter 12)

Res ipsa loquitur A doctrine of tort law holding that the facts may imply negligence when the defendant had exclusive control of the thing that caused the harm, the accident would not normally have occurred without negligence, and the plaintiff played no role in causing the injury. (Chapter 6)

Resale price maintenance A per se violation of the Sherman Act in which a manufacturer enters into an agreement with retailers about the prices they will charge. (Chapter 19)

Rescind To cancel a contract. (Chapter 10, 13)

Restitution Restoring an injured party to its original position. (Chapter 9)

Restricted security Any stock purchased in a private offering (such as one under Regulation D). (Chapter 18)

Retribution Giving a criminal defendant the punishment he deserves. (Chapter 7)

Reverse The power of an appellate court to overrule a lower court and grant judgment for the party that had lost in the lower court. (Chapter 3)

Rule of reason violation An action that breaches the antitrust laws only if it has an anticompetitive impact. (Chapter 18)

S

Security agreement A contract in which the debtor gives a security interest to the secured party. (Chapter 12)

Security interest An interest in personal property or fixtures that secures the performance of some obligation. (Chapter 12)

Signatory A person, company, or nation that has signed a legal document, such as a contract, agreement, or treaty. (Chapter 8)

Slander See Defamation. (Chapter 6)

Sovereign Refers to the recognized political power whom citizens obey. In the United States, the federal and all of the state governments are sovereigns. (Chapter 1)

Specific deterrence See Deterrence. (Chapter 7)

Stare decisis "Let the decision stand." A basic principle of the common law, it means that precedent is usually binding. (Chapter 1)

Statute A law passed by a legislative body, such as Congress. (Chapter 1)

Statute of frauds This law provides that certain contracts are not enforceable unless in writing. (Chapter 10)

Strict liability A tort doctrine holding to a very high standard all those who engage in ultrahazardous activity (e.g., using explosives) or who manufacture certain products. (Chapter 6)

Subpoena An order to appear, issued by a court or government body. (Chapter 4)

Subpoena duces tecum An order to produce certain documents or things before a court or government body. (Chapter 4)

Substantive due process See Due Process Clause. (Chapter 5)

Substantive law Rules that establish the rights of parties. For example, the prohibition against slander is substantive law, as opposed to procedural law. (Chapter 1)

Summary jury trial A form of alternative dispute resolution in which a small panel of jurors hears shortened, summarized versions of the evidence. (Chapter 3)

Tenancy by the entirety A form of joint ownership available only to married couples. If one member of the couple dies, the property goes automatically to the survivor. Creditors cannot attach the property, nor can one owner sell the property without the other's permission. (Chapter 22)

Tender offer A public offer to buy a block of stock directly from shareholders. (Chapter 17)

Term partnership When the partners agree in advance on the duration of a partnership. (Chapter 16)

Treasury stock Stock that has been bought back by its issuing corporation. (Chapter 17)

Unconscionable contract An agreement that a court refuses to enforce because it is fundamentally unfair as a result of unequal bargaining power by one party. (Chapter 9)

Unilateral contract A binding agreement in which one party has made an offer that the other can accept only by action, not words. (Chapter 9)

Void agreement An agreement that neither party may legally enforce, usually because the purpose of the bargain was illegal or because one of the parties lacked capacity to make it. (Chapter 9)

Voidable contract An agreement that, because of some defect, may be terminated by one party, such as a minor, but not by both parties. (Chapter 9)

Whistleblower Someone who discloses wrongful behavior. (Chapter 14)

Writ An order from a government compelling someone to do a particular thing. (Chapter 1)

TABLE OF CASES

<*>Bold pages indicate a discussion of the case.

D

E

F

G

H

K

L

M

N

O

INDEX

A

D

E

T

U

More Features.

World View

Right & Wrong